1994 PRICE GUIDE TO

BASEBALL CARDS

BY DR. JAMES BECKETT

THIRTEENTH EDITION

HOUSE OF COLLECTIBLES • NEW YORK

Sale of this book without a front cover may be unauthorized. If this book is coverless, it may have been reported to the publisher as "unsold or destroyed" and neither the author nor the publisher may have received payment for it.

© 1993 by James Beckett III

All rights reserved under International and Pan-American Copyright Conventions.

℡ This is a registered trademark of Random House, Inc.

Published by: House of Collectibles
201 East 50th Street
New York, New York 10022

Distributed by Ballantine Books, a division of Random House, Inc., New York, and simultaneously in Canada by Random House of Canada Limited, Toronto.

Manufactured in the United States of America

Library of Congress Catalog Card Number: 92-75370

ISBN: 0-876-37906-4

Thirteenth Edition: April 1993

10 9 8 7 6 5 4 3 2 1

Table of Contents

Advertisers

About the Author

Jim Beckett, the leading authority on sport card values in the United States, maintains a wide range of activities in the world of sports. He possesses one of the finest collections of sports cards and autographs in the world, has made numerous appearances on radio and television, and has been frequently cited in many national publications. He was awarded the first "Special Achievement Award" for Contributions to the Hobby by the National Sports Collectors Convention in 1980, the "Jock-Jaspersen Award" for Hobby Dedication in 1983, and the "Buck Barker, Spirit of the Hobby" Award in 1991.

Dr. Beckett is the author of *The Sport Americana Baseball Card Price Guide*, *The Official Price Guide to Baseball Cards*, *The Sport Americana Price Guide to Baseball Collectibles*, *The Sport Americana Baseball Memorabilia and Autograph Price Guide*, *The Sport Americana Football Card Price Guide*, *The Official Price Guide to Football Cards*, *The Sport Americana Hockey Card Price Guide*, *The Official Price Guide to Hockey Cards*, *The Sport Americana Basketball Card Price Guide and Alphabetical Checklist*, *The Official Price Guide to Basketball Cards*, and *The Sport Americana Baseball Card Alphabetical Checklist*. In addition, he is the founder, publisher, and editor of *Beckett Baseball Card Monthly*, *Beckett Basketball Monthly*, *Beckett Football Card Monthly*, *Beckett Hockey Monthly*, and *Beckett Focus on Future Stars*, magazines dedicated to advancing the card collecting hobby.

Jim Beckett received his Ph.D. in Statistics from Southern Methodist University in 1975. Prior to starting Beckett Publications in 1984, Dr. Beckett served as an Associate Professor of Statistics at Bowling Green State University and as a Vice President of a consulting firm in Dallas, Texas. He currently resides in Dallas with his wife, Patti, and their daughters, Christina, Rebecca, and Melissa.

How To Use This Book

Isn't it great? Every year this book gets bigger and bigger with all the new sets coming out. But even more exciting is that every year there are more collectors, more shows, more stores, and more interest in the cards we love so much. This edition has been enhanced and expanded from the previous edition. The cards you collect — who appears on them, what they look like, where they are from, and (most important to most of you) what their current values are — enumerated within. Many of the features contained in the other Beckett Price Guides have been incorporated into this volume since condition grading, nomenclature, and many other aspects of collecting are common to the card hobby in general. We hope you find the book both interesting and useful in your collecting pursuits.

The Beckett Guide has been successful where other attempts have failed because it is complete, current, and valid. This Price Guide contains not just one, but three prices by condition for all the baseball cards listed. These account for most of the baseball cards in existence. The prices were added to the card lists just prior to printing and reflect not the author's opinions or desires but the going retail prices for each card, based on the marketplace (sports memorabilia conventions and shows, sports card shops, hobby papers, current mail-order catalogs, local club meetings, auction results, and other firsthand reportings of actually realized prices).

What is the best price guide available on the market today? Of course card sellers will prefer the price guide with the highest prices, while card buyers will naturally prefer the one with the lowest prices. Accuracy, however, is the true test. Use the price guide used by more collectors and dealers than all the others combined. Look for the Beckett name. I won't put my name on anything I won't stake my reputation on. Not the lowest and not the highest — but the most accurate, with integrity.

To facilitate your use of this book, read the complete introductory section on the following pages before going to the pricing pages. Every collectible field has its own terminology; we've tried to capture most of these terms and definitions in our glossary. Please read carefully the section on grading and the condition of your cards, as you will not be able to determine which price column is appropriate for a given card without first knowing its condition.

The Official

Price Guide

to

Baseball Cards

Introduction

Welcome to the exciting world of baseball card collecting, America's fastest-growing avocation. You have made a good choice in buying this book, since it will open up to you the entire panorama of this field in the simplest, most concise way. It is estimated that a third of a million different baseball cards have been issued during the past century. And the number of total cards put out by all manufacturers last year has been estimated at several billion, with an initial wholesale price of more than $500 million. Sales of older cards by dealers may account for a like amount. With all that cardboard available in the marketplace, it should be no surprise that several million sports fans like you collect baseball cards today, and that number is growing by hundreds of thousands each year.

The growth of *Beckett Baseball Card Monthly* is another indication of this rising crescendo of popularity for baseball cards. Founded in 1984 by Dr. James Beckett, the author of this Price Guide, *Beckett Baseball Card Monthly* has grown to the pinnacle of the baseball card hobby with more than a million readers anxiously awaiting each enjoyable issue.

So collecting baseball cards — while still pursued as a hobby with youthful exuberance by kids in the neighborhood — has also taken on the trappings of an industry, with thousands of full- and part-time card dealers, as well as vendors of supplies, clubs and conventions. In fact, each year since 1980 thousands of hobbyists have assembled for a National Sports Collectors Convention, at which hundreds of dealers have displayed their wares, seminars have been conducted, autographs penned by sports notables, and millions of cards changed hands. These colossal affairs have been staged in Los Angeles, Detroit, St. Louis, Chicago, New York, Anaheim, Arlington (Texas), San Francisco, Atlantic City, and Atlanta. So baseball card collecting really is national in scope!

This increasing interest has been reflected in card values. As more collectors compete for available supplies, card prices (especially for premium-grade cards) rise. A national publication indicated a "very strong advance" in baseball card prices during the past decade, and a quick perusal of prices in this book compared to the figures in earlier editions of this Price Guide will quickly confirm this. Which brings us back around again to the book you have in your hands. It is the best annual guide available to this exciting world of baseball cards. Read it and use it. May your enjoyment and your card collection increase in the coming months and years.

How to Collect

Each collection is personal and reflects the individuality of its owner. There are no set rules on how to collect cards. Since card collecting is a hobby or leisure pastime, what you collect, how much you collect, and how much time and money you spend collecting are entirely up to you. The funds you have available for collecting and your own personal taste should determine how you collect. Information and ideas presented here are intended to help you get the most enjoyment from this hobby.

It is impossible to collect every card ever produced. Therefore, beginners as well as intermediate and advanced collectors usually specialize in some way. One of the reasons this hobby is popular is that individual collectors can define and tailor their collecting methods to match their own tastes. To give you some ideas of the various approaches to collecting, we will list some of the more popular areas of specialization.

Many collectors select complete sets from particular years. For example, they may concentrate on assembling complete sets from all the years since their birth or since they became avid sports fans. They may try to collect a card for every player during that specified period of time. Many others wish to acquire only certain players. Usually such players are the superstars of the sport, but occasionally collectors will specialize in all the cards of players who attended a particular college or came from a certain town. Some collectors are only interested in the first cards or Rookie Cards of certain players. A handy guide for collectors interested in pursuing the hobby this way is the *Sport Americana Baseball Card Alphabetical Checklist No. 5.*

Another fun way to collect cards is by team. Most fans have a favorite team, and it is natural for that loyalty to be translated into a desire for cards of the players on that favorite team. For most of the recent years, team sets (all the cards from a given team for that year) are readily available at a reasonable price. *The Sport Americana Team Baseball Card Checklist* will open up this field to the collector.

Obtaining Cards

Several avenues are open to card collectors. Cards still can be purchased in the traditional way: by the pack at the local candy, grocery, or drug stores. But there are also thousands of card shops across the country that specialize in selling cards individually or by the pack, box, or set. Another alternative is the thousands of card shows held each month around the country, which feature anywhere from five to 800 tables of sports cards and memorabilia for sale. For many years, it has been possible to purchase complete sets of baseball cards through mail-order advertisers found in traditional sports media publications, such as *The Sporting News*, *Baseball Digest*,

Street & Smith yearbooks, and others. These sets also are advertised in the card collecting periodicals. Many collectors will begin by subscribing to at least one of the hobby periodicals, all with good up-to-date information. In fact, subscription offers can be found in the advertising section of this book.

Most serious card collectors obtain old (and new) cards from one or more of several main sources: (1) trading or buying from other collectors or dealers; (2) responding to sale or auction ads in the hobby publications; (3) buying at a local hobby store; and/or (4) attending sports collectibles shows or conventions. We advise that you try all four methods since each has its own distinct advantages: (1) trading is a great way to make new friends; (2) hobby periodicals help you keep up with what's going on in the hobby (including when and where the conventions are happening); (3) stores provide the opportunity to enjoy personalized service and consider a great diversity of material in a relaxed sports-oriented atmosphere; and (4) shows allow you to choose from multiple dealers and thousands of cards under one roof in a competitive situation.

Preserving Your Cards

Cards are fragile. They must be handled properly in order to retain their value. Careless handling can easily result in creased or bent cards. It is, however, not recommended that tweezers or tongs be used to pick up your cards since such utensils might mar or indent card surfaces and thus reduce those cards' conditions and values. In general, your cards should be handled directly as little as possible. This is sometimes easier to say than to do.

Although there are still many who use custom boxes, storage trays, or even shoe boxes, plastic sheets are the preferred method of many collectors for storing cards. A collection stored in plastic pages in a three-ring album allows you to view your collection at any time without the need to touch the card itself. Cards can also be kept in single holders (of various types and thickness) designed for the enjoyment of each card individually. For a large collection, some collectors may use a combination of the above methods. When purchasing plastic sheets for your cards, be sure that you find the pocket size that fits the cards snugly. Don't put your 1951 Bowmans in a sheet designed to fit 1981 Topps. Most hobby and collectibles shops and virtually all collectors' conventions will have these plastic pages available in quantity for the various sizes offered, or you can purchase them directly from the advertisers in this book. Also, remember that pocket size isn't the only factor to consider when looking for plastic sheets. Other factors such as safety, economy, appearance, availability, or personal preference also may indicate which types of sheets a collector may want to buy.

Damp, sunny and/or hot conditions — no, this is not a weather forecast — are three elements to avoid in extremes if you are interested in preserving your collection. Too much (or too little) humidity can cause gradual deterioration of a card. Direct, bright sun (or fluorescent light) over time will bleach out the color of a card. Extreme heat accelerates the decomposition of the card. On the other hand, many cards have lasted more than 50 years without much scientific intervention. So be cautious, even if the above factors typically present a problem only when present in the extreme. It never hurts to be prudent.

Collecting vs. Investing

Collecting individual players and collecting complete sets are both popular vehicles for investment and speculation. Most investors and speculators stock up on complete sets or on quantities of players they think have good investment potential. There is obviously no guarantee in this book, or anywhere else for that matter, that cards will outperform the stock market or other investment alternatives in the future. After all, baseball cards do not pay quarterly dividends and cards cannot be sold at their "current values" as easily as stocks or bonds. Nevertheless, investors have noticed a favorable long-term trend in the past performance of baseball and other sports collectibles, and certain cards and sets have outperformed just about any other investment in some years. Many hobbyists maintain that the best investment is and always will be the building of a collection, which traditionally has held up better than outright speculation.

Some of the obvious questions are: Which cards? When to buy? When to sell? The best investment you can make is in your own education. The more you know about your collection and the hobby, the more informed the decisions you will be able to make. We're not selling investment tips. We're selling information about the current value of baseball cards. It's up to you to use that information to your best advantage.

Terminology

Each hobby has its own language to describe its area of interest. The nomenclature traditionally used for trading cards is derived from the *American Card Catalog*, published in 1960 by Nostalgia Press. That catalog, written by Jefferson Burdick (who is called the "Father of Card Collecting" for his pioneering work), uses letter and number designations for each separate set of cards. The letter used in the ACC designation refers to the generic type of card. While both sport and non-sport issues are classified in the ACC, we shall confine ourselves to the sport issues. The following list defines the letters and their meanings as used by the *American Card Catalog*.

(none) or N - 19th Century U.S. Tobacco
B - Blankets

    D - Bakery Inserts Including Bread
    E - Early Candy and Gum
    F - Food Inserts
    H - Advertising
    M - Periodicals
    PC - Postcards
    R - Candy and Gum since 1930

Following the letter prefix and an optional hyphen are one-, two-, or three-digit numbers, 1-999. These typically represent the company or entity issuing the cards. In several cases, the ACC number is extended by an additional hyphen and another one- or two-digit numerical suffix. For example, the 1957 Topps regular-series baseball card issue carries an ACC designation of R414-11. The "R" indicates a Candy or Gum card produced since 1930. The "414" is the ACC designation for Topps Chewing Gum baseball card issues, and the "11" is the ACC designation for the 1957 regular issue (Topps' eleventh baseball set). Like other traditional methods of identification, this system provides order to the process of cataloging cards; however, most serious collectors learn the ACC designation of the popular sets by repetition and familiarity, rather than by attempting to "figure out" what they might or should be. From 1948 forward, collectors and dealers commonly refer to all sets by their year, maker, type of issue, and any other distinguishing characteristic. For example, such a characteristic could be an unusual issue or one of several regular issues put out by a specific maker in a single year. Regional issues are usually referred to by year, maker, and sometimes by title or theme of the set.

Glossary/Legend

Our glossary defines terms frequently used in the card collecting hobby. Many of these terms are also common to other types of sports memorabilia collecting. Some terms may have several meanings depending on use.

    AAS - Action All-Stars, a postcard-size set issued by Donruss during the mid-1980s.

    ACC - Acronym for American Card Catalog.

    ALP - Alphabetical checklist.

    ANN - Announcer.

    AS - All-Star card. A card portraying an All-Star Player of the previous year that says "All-Star" on its face.

    ATG - All-Time Great card.

    ATL - All-Time Leaders card.

    AU - With autograph.

    BC - Bonus Card

    BL - Blue letters.

BLANKET - A felt square (normally 5 to 6 inches) portraying a baseball player.

BOX - Card issued on a box or a card depicting a Boxer.

BRICK - A group of 50 or more cards having common characteristics that is intended to be bought, sold or traded as a unit.

CABINETS - Popular and highly valuable photographs on thick card stock produced in the 19th and early 20th century.

CH - Community Heroes (Upper Deck).

CHECKLIST - A list of the cards contained in a particular set. The list is always in numerical order if the cards are numbered. Some unnumbered sets are artificially numbered in alphabetical order, by team and alphabetically within the team, or by uniform number for convenience.

CL - Checklist card. A card that lists in order the cards and players in the set or series. Older checklist cards in Mint condition that have not been marked are very desirable and command premiums.

CO - Abbreviation for Coach.

COIN - A small disc of metal or plastic portraying a player in its center.

COLLECTOR - A person who engages in the hobby of collecting cards primarily for his own enjoyment, with any profit motive being secondary.

COLLECTOR ISSUE - A set produced for the sake of the card itself with no product or service sponsor. It derives its name from the fact that most of these sets are produced for sale directly to the hobby market.

COM - Card issued by the Post Cereal Company through their mail-in offer.

COMBINATION CARD - A single card depicting two or more players (but not a team card).

COMM - Commissioner.

COMMON CARD - The typical card of any set; it has no premium value accruing from subject matter, numerical scarcity, popular demand, or anomaly.

CONVENTION - A gathering of dealers and collectors at a single location for the purpose of buying, selling, and trading sports memorabilia items. Conventions are open to the public and sometimes feature autograph guests, door prizes, contests, seminars, etc. They are frequently referred to simply as "shows."

CONVENTION ISSUE - A set produced in conjunction with a sports collectibles convention to commemorate or promote the show.

COR - Corrected card.

COUPON - See Tab.

CREASE - A wrinkle on the card, usually caused by bending the card. Creases are a common (and serious) defect resulting from careless handling.

CY - Cy Young Award.

DC - Draft Choice.

DD - Diamond Debut (Upper Deck).

DEALER - A person who engages in buying, selling, and trading sports collectibles or supplies. A dealer may also be a collector, but as a dealer, his main goal is to earn a profit.

DIE-CUT - A card with part of its stock partially cut, allowing one or more parts to be folded or removed. After removal or appropriate folding, the remaining part of the card can frequently be made to stand up.

DISC - A circular-shaped card.

DISPLAY CARD - A sheet, usually containing three to nine cards, that is printed and used by the manufacturer to advertise and/or display the packages containing his products and cards. The backs of display cards are blank or contain advertisements.

DK - Diamond King (artwork produced by Perez-Steele for Donruss).

DP - Double Print (a card that was printed in double the quantity compared to the other cards in the same series) or a Draft Pick card.

DS - Diamond Skills (Upper Deck).

DT - Dream Team (produced by Score in 1990, 1991 and 1992).

EP - Elite Performer (1991 Ultra).

ERA - Earned Run Average.

ERR - Error card. A card with erroneous information, spelling, or depiction on either side of the card. Most errors are not corrected by the producing card company.

EXHIBIT - The generic name given to thick-stock, postcard-size cards with single color obverse pictures. The name is derived from the Exhibit Supply Co. of Chicago, the principal manufacturer of this type of card. These also are known as Arcade cards since they were found in many arcades.

FDP - First Draft Pick.

FOIL - Foil embossed stamp on card.

FRAN - The Franchise card (1991 Score).

FS - Father/son card.

FULL SHEET - A complete sheet of cards that has not been cut up into individual cards by the manufacturer. Also called an uncut sheet.

GL - Green letters.

HIGH NUMBER - The cards in the last series of numbers in a year in which such higher-numbered cards were printed or distributed in significantly lesser amounts than the lower-numbered cards. The high-number designation refers to a scarcity of the high-numbered cards. Not all years have high numbers in terms of this definition.

HL - Highlight card.

HOF - Hall of Fame, or a card that portrays a Hall of Famer (HOFer).

HOR - Horizontal pose on card as opposed to the standard vertical orientation found on most cards.

I - Idols.

IA - In Action card.

IF - Infielder.

INSERT - A card of a different type or any other sports collectible (typically a poster or sticker) contained and sold in the same package along with a card or cards of a major set. An insert card is either unnumbered or not numbered in the same sequence as the major set. Sometimes the inserts are randomly distributed and are not found in every pack.

ISSUE - Synonymous with set, but usually used in conjunction with a manufacturer, e.g., a Topps issue.

K - Strikeout.

KM - K-Man (1991 Score).

KP - Kid Picture (a subset issued in the Topps Baseball sets of 1972 and 1973).

LAYERING - The separation or peeling of one or more layers of the card stock, usually at the corner of the card.

LEGITIMATE ISSUE - A set produced to promote or boost sales of a product or service, e.g., bubblegum, cereal, cigarettes, etc. Most collector issues are not legitimate issues in this sense.

LHP - Lefthanded pitcher.

LID - A circular-shaped card (possibly with tab) that forms the top of the container for the product being promoted.

LL - League leaders card or large letters on card.

MAJOR SET - A set produced by a national manufacturer of cards containing a large number of cards. Usually 100 or more different cards comprise a major set.

MB - Master Blaster (1991 Score).

MC - Members Choice (Topps Stadium Club).

MEM - Memorial card. For example, the 1990 Donruss and Topps Bart Giamatti cards.

MG - Manager.

MINI - A small card; for example, a 1975 Topps card of identical design but smaller dimensions than the regular Topps issue of 1975.

ML - Major League.

MVP - Most Valuable Player.

NAU - No autograph on card.

NH - No-Hitter card.

NNOF - No Name on Front (1949 Bowman).

NOF - Name on Front (1949 Bowman).

NON-SPORT CARD - A card from a set whose major theme is a subject other than a sports subject. A card of a sports figure or event that is part of a non-sport set is still a non-sport card, e.g., while the "Look 'N' See" non-sport card set contains a card of Babe Ruth, a sports figure, that card is a non-sport card.

NOTCHING - The grooving of the card, usually caused by fingernails, rubber bands, or bumping card edges against other objects.

OBVERSE - The front, face, or pictured side of the card.

OF - Outfield or Outfielder.

OLY - Olympics (see the 1985 Topps and 1988 Topps Traded sets; the members of the U.S. Olympic Baseball teams were featured subsets in both of these sets).

ORG - Organist.

P - Pitcher or Pitching pose.

P1 - First Printing.

P2 - Second Printing.

P3 - Third Printing.

PANEL - An extended card that is composed of two or more individual cards. Often the panel forms the back part of the container for the product being promoted, e.g., a Hostess panel, a Bazooka panel, an Esskay Meat panel.

PCL - Pacific Coast League.

PLASTIC SHEET - A clear, plastic page that is punched for insertion into a binder (with standard three-ring spacing) containing pockets for displaying cards. Many different styles of sheets exist with pockets of varying sizes to hold the many differing card formats. Also called a display sheet or storage sheet.

PREMIUM - A card, sometimes on photographic stock, that is purchased or obtained in conjunction with, or redemption for, another card or product. The premium is not packaged in the same unit as the primary item.

PRES - President.

PUZZLE CARD - A card whose back contains a part of a picture which, when joined correctly with other puzzle cards, forms the completed picture.

PUZZLE PIECE - A die-cut piece designed to interlock with similar pieces.

PVC - Polyvinyl Chloride, a substance used to make many of the popular card display protective sheets. Non-PVC sheets are considered preferable for long-term storage of cards by many.

RARE - A card or series of cards of very limited availability. Unfortunately, "rare" is a subjective term frequently used indiscriminately to hype value. "Rare" cards are harder to obtain than "scarce" cards.

RB - Record Breaker card.

REGIONAL - A card or set of cards issued and distributed only in a limited geographical area of the country.

REVERSE - The back or narrative side of the card.

RHP - Righthanded pitcher.

RIF - Rifleman (1991 Score).

ROY - Rookie of the Year.

RP - Relief pitcher.

RR - Rated Rookies (a subset featured in Donruss sets).

SA - Super Action card.

SASE - Self-Addressed, Stamped Envelope.

SB - Stolen Bases.

SCARCE - A card or series of cards of limited availability. This subjective term is sometimes used indiscriminately to hype value. "Scarce" cards are not as difficult to obtain as "rare" cards.

SCR - Script name on back (1949 Bowman).

SEMI-HIGH - A card from the next to last series of a sequentially issued set. It has more value than an average card and generally less value than a high number. A card is not called a semi-high unless the next to last series in which it exists has an additional premium attached to it.

SERIES - The entire set of cards issued by a particular producer in a particular year; e.g., the 1971 Topps series. Also, within a particular set, series can refer to a group of (consecutively numbered) cards printed at the same time; e.g., the first series of the 1957 Topps issue (#'s1-88).

SET - One each of the entire run of cards of the same type produced by a particular manufacturer during a single year. In other words, if you have a complete set of 1976 Topps then you have every card from #1 up to and including #660, i.e., all of the different cards that were produced.

SH - Shades (Score Pinnacle).

SI - Sidelines.

SKIP-NUMBERED - A set that has many unissued card numbers between the lowest number in the set and the highest number in the set; e.g., the 1948 Leaf baseball set contains 98 cards skip-numbered from #1 to #168. A major set in which a few numbers were not printed is not considered to be skip-numbered.

SLUG - Silver Slugger card (1991 Bowman).

SP - Single or Short Print (a card which was printed in lesser quantity compared to the other cards in the same series; see also DP and TP).

SPECIAL CARD - A card that portrays something other than a single player or team; for example, a card that portrays the previous year's statistical leaders or the results from the previous year's World Series.

SR - Star Rookies (Upper Deck).

SS - Shortstop.

STAMP - Adhesive-backed papers depicting a player. The stamp may be individual or in a sheet of many stamps. Moisture must be applied to the adhesive in order for the stamp to be attached to another surface.

STAR CARD - A card that portrays a player of some repute, usually determined by his ability, however, sometimes referring to sheer popularity.

STICKER - A card with a removable layer that can be affixed to (stuck onto) another surface.

STOCK - The cardboard or paper on which the card is printed.

STRIP CARDS - A sheet or strip of cards, particularly popular in the 1920s and 1930s, with the individual cards usually separated by broken or dotted lines.

SUPERSTAR CARD - A card that portrays a superstar; e.g., a Hall of Famer or player with strong Hall of Fame potential.

SV - Super Veteran (see 1982 Topps).

TAB - A card portion set off from the rest of the card, usually with perforations, that may be removed without damaging the central character or event depicted by the card.

TBC - Turn Back the Clock cards.

TC - Team Checklist cards.

TEAM CARD - A card that depicts an entire team.

TEST SET - A set, usually containing a small number of cards, issued by a national card producer and distributed in a limited section or sections of the country. Presumably, the purpose of a test set is to test market appeal for a particular type of card.

TL - Team Leader card.

TP - Triple Print (a card that was printed in triple the quantity compared to the other cards in the same series).

TRIMMED - A card cut down from its original size. Trimmed cards are undesirable to most collectors.

UER - Uncorrected Error.

UMP - Umpire.

USA - Team USA cards.

VAR - Variation card. One of two or more cards from the same series with the same number (or player with identical pose if the series is unnumbered) differing from one another by some aspect, the different feature stemming from the printing or stock of the card. This can be caused when the manufacturer of the cards notices an error in one or more of the cards, makes the changes, and then resumes the print run. In this case there will be two versions or variations of the same card. Sometimes one of the variations is relatively scarce.

VERT - Vertical pose on card.

WAS - Washington National League (1974 Topps).

WS - World Series card.

YL - Yellow Letters (1958 Topps).

YT - Yellow Team (1958 Topps).

* - to denote multi-sport sets.

Understanding Card Values

Determining Value

Why are some cards more valuable than others? Obviously, the economic laws of supply and demand are applicable to card collecting just as they are to any other field where a commodity is bought, sold or traded in a free, unregulated market.

Supply (the number of cards available on the market) is less than the total number of cards originally produced since attrition diminishes that original quantity. Each year a percentage of cards is typically thrown away, destroyed or otherwise lost to collectors. This percentage is much, much smaller today than it was in the past because more and more people have become increasingly aware of the value of their cards.

For those who collect only Mint condition cards, the supply of older cards can be quite small indeed. Until recently, collectors were not so conscious of the need to preserve the condition of their cards. For this reason, it is difficult to know exactly how many 1953 Topps are currently available, Mint or otherwise. It is generally accepted that there are fewer 1953 Topps available than 1963, 1973 or 1983 Topps cards. If demand were equal for each of these sets, the law of supply and demand would increase the price for the least available sets. Demand, however, is never equal for all sets, so price correlations can be complicated. The demand for a card is influenced by many factors. These include: (1) the age of the card; (2) the number of cards printed; (3) the player(s) portrayed on the card; (4) the attractiveness and popularity of the set; and (5) the physical condition of the card.

In general, (1) the older the card, (2) the fewer the number of the cards printed, (3) the more famous, popular and talented the player, (4) the more attractive and popular the set, and (5) the better the condition of the card, the higher the value of the card will be. There are exceptions to all but one of these factors: the condition of the card. Given two cards similar in all respects except condition, the one in the best condition will always be valued higher.

While those guidelines help to establish the value of a card, the countless exceptions and peculiarities make any simple, direct mathematical formula to determine card values impossible.

Regional Variation

Since the market varies from region to region, card prices of local players may be higher. This is known as a regional premium. How significant the premium is — and if there is any premium at all — depends on the local popularity of the team and the player.

The largest regional premiums usually do not apply to superstars, who often are so well known nationwide that the prices of their key cards are too high for local dealers to realize a premium.

Lesser stars often command the strongest premiums. Their popularity is concentrated in their home region, creating local demand that greatly exceeds overall demand.

Regional premiums can apply to popular retired players and sometimes can be found in the areas where the players grew up or starred in college.

A regional discount is the converse of a regional premium. Regional discounts occur when a player has been so popular in his region for so long that local collectors and dealers have accumulated quantities of his key cards. The abundant supply may make the cards available in that area at the lowest prices anywhere.

Set Prices

A somewhat paradoxical situation exists in the price of a complete set vs. the combined cost of the individual cards in the set. In nearly every case, the sum of the prices for the individual cards is higher than the cost for the complete set. This is prevalent especially in the cards of the past few years. The reasons for this apparent anomaly stem from the habits of collectors and from the carrying costs to dealers. Today, each card in a set normally is produced in the same quantity as all others in its set.

Many collectors pick up only stars, superstars and particular teams. As a result, the dealer is left with a shortage of certain player cards and an abundance of others. He therefore incurs an expense in simply "carrying" these less desirable cards in stock. On the other hand, if he sells a complete set, he gets rid of large numbers of cards at one time. For this reason, he generally is willing to receive less money for a complete set. By doing this, he recovers all of his costs and also makes a profit.

The disparity between the price of the complete set and the sum of the individual cards also has been influenced by the fact that some of the major manufacturers now are pre-collating card sets. Since "pulling" individual cards from the sets of all three manufacturers involves a specific type of labor (and cost), the singles or star card market is not affected significantly by pre-collation.

Set prices also do not include rare card varieties, unless specifically stated. Of course, the prices for sets do include one example of each type for the given set, but this is the least expensive variety.

Scarce Series

Scarce series occur because cards issued before 1974 were made available to the public each year in several series of finite numbers of cards, rather than all cards of the set being available for purchase at one time. At some point during the year, usually toward the end of the baseball season, interest in current year baseball cards waned. Consequently, the manufacturers produced smaller numbers of these later-series cards.

Nearly all nationwide issues from post-World War II manufacturers (1948 to 1973) exhibit these series variations. In the past, Topps, for example, may have issued series consisting of many different numbers of cards, including 55, 66, 80, 88 and others. Recently, Topps has settled on what is now its standard sheet size of 132 cards, six of which comprise its 792-card set.

While the number of cards within a given series is usually the same as the number of cards on one printed sheet, this is not always the case. For example, Bowman used 36 cards on its standard printed sheets, but in 1948 substituted 12 cards during later print runs of that year's baseball cards. Twelve of the cards from the initial sheet of 36 cards were removed and replaced by 12 different cards giving, in effect, a first series of 36 cards and a second series of 12 new cards. This replacement produced a scarcity of 24 cards — the 12 cards removed from the original sheet and the 12 new cards added to the sheet. A full sheet of 1948 Bowman cards (second printing) shows that card numbers 37 through 48 have replaced 12 of the cards on the first printing sheet.

The Topps Company also has created scarcities and/or excesses of certain cards in many of its sets. Topps, however, has most frequently gone the other direction by double printing some of the cards. Double printing causes an abundance of cards of the players who are on the same sheet more than one time. During the years from 1978 to 1981, Topps double printed 66 cards out of their large 726-card set. The Topps practice of double printing cards in earlier years is the most logical explanation for the known scarcities of particular cards in some of these Topps sets.

From 1988 through 1990, Donruss short printed and double printed certain cards in its major sets. Ostensibly this was because of its addition of bonus team MVP cards in its regular-issue wax packs.

We are always looking for information or photographs of printing sheets of cards for research. Each year, we try to update the hobby's knowledge of distribution anomalies. Please let us know at the address in this book if you have first-hand knowledge that would be helpful in this pursuit.

Grading Your Cards

Each hobby has its own grading terminology — stamps, coins, comic books, record collecting, etc. Collectors of sports cards are no exception. The one invariable criterion for determining the value of a card is its condition: the better the condition of the card, the more valuable it is. Condition grading, however, is subjective. Individual card dealers and collectors differ in the strictness of their grading, but the stated condition of a card should be determined without regard to whether it is being bought or sold.

No allowance is made for age. A 1952 card is judged by the same standards as a 1992 card. But there are specific sets and cards that are condition sensitive (marked with "!" in the Price Guide) because of their border color, consistently poor centering, etc. Such cards and sets sometimes command premiums above the listed percentages in Mint condition.

Centering

Current centering terminology uses numbers representing the percentage of border on either side of the main design. Obviously, centering is diminished in importance for borderless cards such as Stadium Club.

Slightly Off-Center (60/40): A slightly off-center card is one that upon close inspection is found to have one border bigger than the opposite border. This degree once was offensive to only purists, but now some hobbyists try to avoid cards that are anything other than perfectly centered.

Off-Center (70/30): An off-center card has one border that is noticeably more than twice as wide as the opposite border.

Badly Off-Center (80/20 or worse): A badly off-center card has virtually no border on one side of the card.

Miscut: A miscut card actually shows part of the adjacent card in its larger border and consequently a corresponding amount of its card is cut off.

Corner Wear

Corner wear is the most scrutinized grading criteria in the hobby. These are the major categories of corner wear:

Corner with a slight touch of wear: The corner still is sharp, but there is a slight touch of wear showing. On a dark-bordered card, this shows as a dot of white.

Fuzzy corner: The corner still comes to a point, but the point has just begun to fray. A slightly "dinged" corner is considered the same as a fuzzy corner.

Slightly rounded corner: The fraying of the corner has increased to where there is only a hint of a point. Mild layering may be evident. A "dinged" corner is considered the same as a slightly rounded corner.

Rounded corner: The point is completely gone. Some layering is noticeable.

Badly rounded corner: The corner is completely round and rough. Severe layering is evident.

Creases

A third common defect is the crease. The degree of creasing in a card is difficult to show in a drawing or picture. On giving the specific condition of an expensive card for sale, the seller should note any creases additionally. Creases can be categorized as to severity according to the following scale.

Light Crease: A light crease is a crease that is barely noticeable upon close inspection. In fact, when cards are in plastic sheets or holders, a light crease may not be seen (until the card is taken out of the holder). A light crease on the front is much more serious than a light crease on the card back only.

Medium Crease: A medium crease is noticeable when held and studied at arm's length by the naked eye, but does not overly detract from the appearance of the card. It is an obvious crease, but not one that breaks the picture surface of the card.

Heavy Crease: A heavy crease is one that has torn or broken through the card's picture surface, e.g., puts a tear in the photo surface.

Alterations

Deceptive Trimming: This occurs when someone alters the card in order (1) to shave off edge wear, (2) to improve the sharpness of the corners, or (3) to improve centering — obviously their objective is to falsely increase the perceived value of the card to an unsuspecting buyer. The shrinkage usually is evident only if the trimmed card is compared to an adjacent full-sized card or if the trimmed card is itself measured.

Obvious Trimming: Obvious trimming is noticeable and unfortunate. It is usually performed by non-collectors who give no thought to the present or future value of their cards.

Deceptively Retouched Borders: This occurs when the borders (especially on those cards with dark borders) are touched up on the edges and corners with magic marker or crayons of appropriate color in order to make the card appear to be Mint.

Categorization of Defects

Miscellaneous Flaws

The following are common minor flaws that, depending on severity, lower a card's condition by one to four grades and often render it no better than Excellent-Mint: bubbles (lumps in surface), gum and wax stains, diamond cutting (slanted borders), notching, off-centered backs, paper wrinkles, scratched-off cartoons or puzzles on back, rubber band marks, scratches, surface impressions and warping.

The following are common serious flaws that, depending on severity,

Centering

Well-centered

Slightly Off-centered

Off-centered

Badly Off-centered

Miscut

Corner Wear

The partial cards shown here have been photographed at 300%. This was done in order to magnify each card's corner wear to such a degree that differences could be shown on a printed page.

The 1962 Topps Mickey Mantle card definitely has a rounded corner. Some may say that this card is badly rounded, but that is a judgment call.

The 1962 Topps Hank Aaron card has a slightly rounded corner. Note that there is definite corner wear evident by the fraying and that there is no longer a sharp point to which the corner converges.

The 1962 Topps Gil Hodges card has corner wear; it is slightly better than the Aaron card above. Nevertheless, some collectors might classify this Hodges corner as slightly rounded.

The 1962 Topps Manager's Dream card showing Mantle and Mays has slight corner wear. This is not a fuzzy corner as very slight wear is noticeable on the card's photo surface.

The 1962 Topps Don Mossi card has very slight corner wear such that it might be called a fuzzy corner. A close look at the original card shows that the corner is not perfect, but almost. However, note that corner wear is somewhat academic on this card. As you can plainly see, the heavy crease going across his name breaks through the photo surface.

lower a card's condition at least four grades and often render it no better than Good: chemical or sun fading, erasure marks, mildew, miscutting (severe off-centering), holes, bleached or retouched borders, tape marks, tears, trimming, water or coffee stains and writing.

Condition Guide
Grades
Mint (Mt) - A card with no flaws or wear. The card has four perfect corners, 60/40 or better centering from top to bottom and from left to right, original gloss, smooth edges and original color borders. A Mint card does not have print spots, color or focus imperfections.

Near Mint-Mint (NrMt-Mt) - A card with one minor flaw. Any one of the following would lower a Mint card to Near Mint-Mint: one corner with a slight touch of wear, barely noticeable print spots, color or focus imperfections. The card must have 60/40 or better centering in both directions, original gloss, smooth edges and original color borders.

Near Mint (NrMt) - A card with one minor flaw. Any one of the following would lower a Mint card to Near Mint: one fuzzy corner or two to four corners with slight touches of wear, 70/30 to 60/40 centering, slightly rough edges, minor print spots, color or focus imperfections. The card must have original gloss and original color borders.

Excellent-Mint (ExMt) - A card with two or three fuzzy, but not rounded, corners and centering no worse than 80/20. The card may have no more than two of the following: slightly rough edges, very slightly discolored borders, minor print spots, color or focus imperfections. The card must have original gloss.

Excellent (Ex) - A card with four fuzzy but definitely not rounded corners and centering no worse than 80/20. The card may have a small amount of original gloss lost, rough edges, slightly discolored borders and minor print spots, color or focus imperfections.

Very Good (Vg) - A card that has been handled but not abused: slightly rounded corners with slight layering, slight notching on edges, a significant amount of gloss lost from the surface but no scuffing and moderate discoloration of borders. The card may have a few light creases.

Good (G), **Fair** (F), **Poor** (P) - A well-worn, mishandled or abused card: badly rounded and layered corners, scuffing, most or all original gloss missing, seriously discolored borders, moderate or heavy creases, and one or more serious flaws. The grade of Good, Fair or Poor depends on the severity of wear and flaws. Good, Fair and Poor cards generally are used only as fillers.

The most widely used grades are defined above. Obviously, many cards will not perfectly fit one of the definitions.

Therefore, categories between the major grades known as in-between grades are used, such as Good to Very Good (G-Vg), Very Good to Excellent (VgEx), and Excellent-Mint to Near Mint (ExMt-NrMt). Such grades indicate a card with all qualities of the lower category but with at least a few qualities of the higher category.

The *Sport Americana Baseball Card Price Guide* lists each card and set in three grades, with the middle grade valued at about 40-45% of the top grade, and the bottom grade valued at about 10-15% of the top grade.

The value of cards that fall between the listed columns can also be calculated using a percentage of the top grade. For example, a card that falls between the top and middle grades (Ex, ExMt or NrMt in most cases) will generally be valued at anywhere from 50% to 90% of the top grade.

Similarly, a card that falls between the middle and bottom grades (G-Vg, Vg or VgEx in most cases) will generally be valued at anywhere from 20% to 40% of the top grade.

There are also cases where cards are in better condition than the top grade or worse than the bottom grade. Cards that grade worse than the lowest grade are generally valued at 5-10% of the top grade.

When a card exceeds the top grade by one — such as NrMt-Mt when the top grade is NrMt, or Mint when the top grade is NrMt-Mt — a premium of up to 50% is possible, with 10-20% the usual norm.

When a card exceeds the top grade by two — such as Mint when the top grade is NrMt, or NrMt-Mt when the top grade is ExMt — a premium of 25-50% is the usual norm. But certain condition sensitive cards or sets, particularly those from the pre-war era, can bring premiums of up to 100% or even more.

Unopened packs, boxes and factory-collated sets are considered Mint in their unknown (and presumed perfect) state. Once opened, however, each card can be graded (and valued) in its own right by taking into account any defects that may be present in spite of the fact that the card has never been handled.

Selling Your Cards

Just about every collector sells cards or will sell cards eventually. Someday you may be interested in selling your duplicates or maybe even your whole collection. You may sell to other collectors, friends or dealers. You may even sell cards you purchased from a certain dealer back to that same dealer. In any event, it helps to know some of the mechanics of the typical transaction between buyer and seller.

Dealers will buy cards in order to resell them to other collectors who are interested in the cards. Dealers will always pay a higher percentage for items that (in their opinion) can be resold quickly, and a much lower percentage for those items that are perceived as having low demand and hence are slow moving. In either case, dealers must buy at a price that allows for the expense of doing business and a margin for profit.

If you have cards for sale, the best advice we can give is that you get several offers for your cards — either from card shops or at a card show — and take the best offer, all things considered. Note, the "best" offer may not be the one for the highest amount. And remember, if a dealer really wants your cards, he won't let you get away without making his best competitive offer. Another alternative is to place your cards in an auction as one or several lots.

Many people think nothing of going into a department store and paying $15 for an item of clothing for which the store paid $5. But if you were selling your $15 card to a dealer and he offered you $5 for it, you might think his mark-up unreasonable. To complete the analogy: most department stores (and card dealers) that consistently pay $10 for $15 items eventually go out of business. An exception is when the dealer has lined up a willing buyer for the item(s) you are attempting to sell, or if the cards are so Hot that it's likely he'll have to hold the cards for only a short period of time.

In those cases, an offer of up to 75 percent of book value still will allow the dealer to make a reasonable profit considering the short time he will need to hold the merchandise. In general, however, most cards and collections will bring offers in the range of 25 to 50 percent of retail price. Also consider that most material from the past five to 10 years is plentiful. If that's what you're selling, don't be surprised if your best offer is well below that range.

Interesting Notes

The first card numerically of an issue is the single card most likely to obtain excessive wear. Consequently, you typically will find the price on the #1 card (in NrMt or Mint condition) somewhat higher than might otherwise be the case. Similarly, but to a lesser extent (because normally the less important, reverse side of the card is the one exposed), the last card numerically in an issue also is prone to abnormal wear. This extra wear and tear occurs because the first and last cards are exposed to the elements (human element included) more than any other cards. They are generally end cards in any brick formations, rubber bandings, stackings on wet surfaces, and like activities.

Sports cards have no intrinsic value. The value of a card, like the value of other collectibles, can be determined only by you and your enjoyment in viewing and possessing these cardboard treasures.

Remember, the buyer ultimately determines the price of each baseball card. You are the determining price factor because you have the ability to say "No" to the price of any card by not exchanging your hard-earned money for a given card. When the cost of a trading card exceeds the enjoyment you will receive from it, your answer should be "No." We assess and report the prices. You set them!

We are always interested in receiving the price input of collectors and dealers from around the country. We happily credit major contributors. We welcome your opinions, since your contributions assist us in ensuring a better guide each year. If you would like to join our survey list for the next editions of this book and others authored by Dr. Beckett, please send your name and address to Dr. James Beckett, 4887 Alpha Road, Suite 200, Dallas, Texas 75244.

Advertising

Within this Price Guide you will find advertisements for sports memorabilia material, mail order, and retail sports collectibles establishments. All advertisements were accepted in good faith based on the reputation of the advertiser; however, neither the author, the publisher, the distributors, nor the other advertisers in this Price Guide accept any responsibility for any particular advertiser not complying with the terms of his or her ad.

Readers also should be aware that prices in advertisements are subject to change over the annual period before a new edition of this volume is issued each spring. When replying to an advertisement late in the baseball year, the reader should take this into account, and contact the dealer by phone or in writing for up-to-date price information. Should you come into contact with any of the advertisers in this guide as a result of their advertisement herein, please mention this source as your contact.

Additional Reading

With the increase in popularity of the hobby in recent years, there has been a corresponding increase in available literature. Below is a list of the books and periodicals that receive our highest recommendation and that we hope will further advance your knowledge and enjoyment of our great hobby.

The Sport Americana Baseball Card Card Price Guide by Dr. James Beckett (Fifteenth Edition, $15.95, released 1993, published by Edgewater Book Company) — the most comprehensive Price Guide and checklist ever issued on baseball cards.

The Official Price Guide to Baseball Cards by Dr. James Beckett (Thirteenth Edition, $5.99, released 1993, published by The House of Collectibles) — an abridgment of the *Sport Americana Price Guide* in a convenient and economical pocket-size format providing Dr. Beckett's pricing of the major baseball sets since 1948.

The Sport Americana Price Guide to Baseball Collectibles by Dr. James Beckett (Second Edition, $12.95, released 1988, published by Edgewater Book Company) — the complete guide and checklist with up-to-date values for box cards, coins, labels, Canadian cards, stamps, stickers, pins, etc.

The Sport Americana Football Card Price Guide by Dr. James Beckett (Ninth Edition, $14.95, released 1992, published by Edgewater Book Company) — the most comprehensive Price Guide and checklist ever issued on football cards. No serious football card hobbyist should be without it.

The Official Price Guide to Football Cards by Dr. James Beckett (Twelfth Edition, $5.99, released 1992, published by The House of Collectibles) — an abridgment of the *Sport Americana Price Guide* listed above in a convenient and economical pocket-size format providing Dr. Beckett's pricing of the major football sets since 1948.

The Sport Americana Hockey Card Price Guide by Dr. James Beckett (Second Edition, $12.95, released 1992, published by Edgewater Book Company) — the most comprehensive Price Guide and checklist ever issued on hockey cards.

The Official Price Guide to Hockey Cards by Dr. James Beckett (Second Edition, $5.99, released 1993, published by The House of Collectibles) — an abridgment of the *Sport Americana Price Guide* listed above in a convenient and economical pocket-size format providing Dr. Beckett's pricing of the major hockey sets since 1951.

The Sport Americana Basketball Card Price Guide and Alphabetical

Checklist by Dr. James Beckett (Second Edition, $12.95, released 1992, published by Edgewater Book Company) — the most comprehensive combination Price Guide and alphabetical checklist ever issued on basketball cards.

The Official Price Guide to Basketball Cards by Dr. James Beckett (Second Edition, $5.99, released 1992, published by The House of Collectibles) — an abridgment of the *Sport Americana Price Guide* listed above in a convenient and economical pocket-size format providing Dr. Beckett's pricing of the major basketball sets since 1948.

The Sport Americana Baseball Card Alphabetical Checklist by Dr. James Beckett (Fifth Edition, $14.95, released 1992, published by Edgewater Book Company) — an alphabetical listing, by the last name of the player portrayed on the card, of virtually all baseball cards (major league and minor league) produced up through the 1992 major sets.

The Sport Americana Price Guide to the Non-Sports Cards 1930-1960 by Christopher Benjamin and Dennis W. Eckes ($14.95, released 1991, published by Edgewater Book Company) — the definitive guide to virtually all popular non-sports American tobacco and bubblegum cards issued between 1930 and 1960. In addition to cards, illustrations and prices for wrappers also are included.

The Sport Americana Price Guide to the Non-Sports Cards by Christopher Benjamin (Fourth Edition, $14.95, released 1992, published by Edgewater Book Company) — the definitive guide to all popular non-sports American cards. In addition to cards, illustrations and prices for wrappers also are included. This volume covers non-sports cards from 1961 to 1992.

The Sport Americana Baseball Address List by Jack Smalling (Seventh Edition, $12.95, released 1992, published by Edgewater Book Company) — the definitive guide for autograph hunters, giving addresses and deceased information for virtually all Major League Baseball players past and present.

The Sport Americana Team Baseball Card Checklist by Jeff Fritsch (Sixth Edition, $12.95, released 1992, published by Edgewater Book Company) — includes all Topps, Bowman, Donruss, Fleer, Score, Play Ball, Goudey, and Upper Deck cards, with the players portrayed on the cards listed with the teams for whom they played. The book is invaluable to the collector who specializes in an individual team because it is the most complete baseball card team checklist available.

The Sport Americana Team Football and Basketball Card Checklist by Jane Fritsch, Jeff Fritsch, and Dennis Eckes (First Edition, $10.95, released 1990, published by Edgewater Book Company) — the book is invaluable to the collector who specializes in an individual team because it is the most complete football and basketball card team checklist available.

The Encyclopedia of Baseball Cards, Volume I: 19th Century Cards by Lew Lipset ($11.95, released 1983, published by the author) — everything you ever wanted to know about 19th century cards.

The Encyclopedia of Baseball Cards, Volume II: Early Gum and Candy Cards by Lew Lipset ($10.95, released 1984, published by the author) — everything you ever wanted to know about early candy and gum cards.

The Encyclopedia of Baseball Cards, Volume III: 20th Century Tobacco Cards, 1909-1932 by Lew Lipset ($12.95, released 1986, published by the author) — everything you ever wanted to know about old tobacco cards.

Beckett Baseball Card Monthly, published and edited by Dr. James Beckett — contains the most extensive and accepted monthly Price Guide, collectible glossy superstar covers, colorful feature articles, "who's Hot and who's Not" section, Convention Calendar, tips for beginners, "Readers Write" letters to and responses from the editor, information on errors and varieties, autograph collecting tips and profiles of the sport's Hottest stars. Published every month, *BBCM* is the hobby's largest paid circulation periodical. *Beckett Football Card Monthly*, *Beckett Basketball Monthly*, *Beckett Hockey Monthly* and *Beckett Focus on Future Stars* were built on the success of *BBCM*.

Prices in this Guide

Prices found in this guide reflect current retail rates just prior to the printing of this book. They do not reflect the FOR SALE prices of the author, the publisher, the distributors, the advertisers, or any card dealers associated with this guide. No one is obligated in any way to buy, sell or trade his or her cards based on these prices. The price listings were compiled by the author from actual buy/sell transactions at sports conventions, sports card shops, buy/sell advertisements in the hobby papers, for sale prices from dealer catalogs and price lists, and discussions with leading hobbyists in the U.S. and Canada. All prices are in U.S. dollars.

Acknowledgments

A great deal of diligence, hard work, and dedicated effort went into this year's volume. The high standards to which we hold ourselves, however, could not have been met without the expert input and generous amount of time contributed by many people. Our sincere thanks are extended to each and every one of you.

A complete list of these invaluable contributors appears after the Price Guide section.

1948 Bowman

The 48-card Bowman set of 1948 was the first major set of the post-war period. Each 2 1/16" by 2 1/2" card had a black and white photo of a current player, with his biographical information printed in black ink on a gray back. Due to the printing process and the 36-card sheet size upon which Bowman was then printing, the 12 cards marked with an SP in the checklist are scarcer numerically, as they were removed from the printing sheet in order to make room for the 12 high numbers (37-48). Many cards are found with over-printed, transposed, or blank backs. The set features the Rookie Cards of Hall of Famers Yogi Berra, Ralph Kiner, Stan Musial, Red Schoendienst, and Warren Spahn. Half of the cards in the set feature New York players (Yankees or Giants).

	NRMT	VG-E	GOOD
COMPLETE SET (48)	3600.	1600.	450.00
COMMON PLAYER (1-36)	20.00	9.00	2.50
COMMON PLAYER (37-48)	30.00	13.50	3.80

		NRMT	VG-E	GOOD
☐ 1	Bob Elliott	100.00	20.00	6.00
☐ 2	Ewell Blackwell	50.00	23.00	6.25
☐ 3	Ralph Kiner	200.00	90.00	25.00
☐ 4	Johnny Mize	110.00	50.00	14.00
☐ 5	Bob Feller	250.00	115.00	31.00
☐ 6	Yogi Berra	575.00	250.00	70.00
☐ 7	Pete Reiser SP	60.00	27.00	7.50
☐ 8	Phil Rizzuto SP	250.00	115.00	31.00
☐ 9	Walker Cooper	20.00	9.00	2.50
☐ 10	Buddy Rosar	20.00	9.00	2.50
☐ 11	Johnny Lindell	23.00	10.50	2.90
☐ 12	Johnny Sain	50.00	23.00	6.25
☐ 13	Willard Marshall SP	38.00	17.00	4.70
☐ 14	Allie Reynolds	50.00	23.00	6.25
☐ 15	Eddie Joost	20.00	9.00	2.50
☐ 16	Jack Lohrke SP	38.00	17.00	4.70
☐ 17	Enos Slaughter	100.00	45.00	12.50
☐ 18	Warren Spahn	325.00	145.00	40.00
☐ 19	Tommy Henrich	30.00	13.50	3.80
☐ 20	Buddy Kerr SP	38.00	17.00	4.70
☐ 21	Ferris Fain	25.00	11.50	3.10
☐ 22	Floyd Bevens SP	40.00	18.00	5.00
☐ 23	Larry Jansen	25.00	11.50	3.10
☐ 24	Dutch Leonard SP	38.00	17.00	4.70
☐ 25	Barney McCosky	20.00	9.00	2.50
☐ 26	Frank Shea SP	38.00	17.00	4.70
☐ 27	Sid Gordon	20.00	9.00	2.50
☐ 28	Emil Verban SP	38.00	17.00	4.70
☐ 29	Joe Page SP	50.00	23.00	6.25
☐ 30	Whitey Lockman SP	45.00	20.00	5.75
☐ 31	Bill McCahan	20.00	9.00	2.50
☐ 32	Bill Rigney	20.00	9.00	2.50
☐ 33	Bill Johnson	23.00	10.50	2.90
☐ 34	Sheldon Jones SP	38.00	17.00	4.70
☐ 35	Snuffy Stirnweiss	25.00	11.50	3.10
☐ 36	Stan Musial	900.00	400.00	115.00
☐ 37	Clint Hartung	35.00	16.00	4.40
☐ 38	Red Schoendienst	175.00	80.00	22.00
☐ 39	Augie Galan	30.00	13.50	3.80
☐ 40	Marty Marion	80.00	36.00	10.00
☐ 41	Rex Barney	35.00	16.00	4.40
☐ 42	Ray Poat	30.00	13.50	3.80
☐ 43	Bruce Edwards	30.00	13.50	3.80
☐ 44	Johnny Wyrostek	30.00	13.50	3.80
☐ 45	Hank Sauer	40.00	18.00	5.00
☐ 46	Herman Wehmeier	30.00	13.50	3.80
☐ 47	Bobby Thomson	80.00	36.00	10.00
☐ 48	Dave Koslo	60.00	27.00	7.50

1949 Bowman

The cards in this 240-card set measure approximately 2 1/16" by 2 1/2". In 1949 Bowman took an intermediate step between black and white and full color with this set of tinted photos on colored backgrounds. Collectors should note the series price variations, which reflect some inconsistencies in the printing process. There are four major varieties in name printing, which are noted in the checklist below: NOF: name on front; NNOF: no name on front; PR: printed name on back; and SCR: script name on back. These variations resulted when Bowman used twelve of the lower numbers to fill out the last press sheet of 36 cards, adding to numbers 217-240. Cards 1-3 and 5-73 can be found with either gray or white backs. The set features the Rookie Cards of Hall of Famers Roy Campanella, Bob Lemon, Robin Roberts, Duke Snider, and Early Wynn as well as Rookie Cards of Richie Ashburn and Gil Hodges.

	NRMT	VG-E	GOOD
COMPLETE SET (240)	16500.	7400.	2100.
COMMON (1-3/5-36/73)	18.00	8.00	2.30
COMMON PLAYER (37-72)	20.00	9.00	2.50
COMMON PLAYER (4/74-108)	17.00	7.75	2.10
COMMON PLAYER (109-144)	15.00	6.75	1.90
COMMON PLAYER (145-180)	90.00	40.00	11.50
COMMON PLAYER (181-240)	80.00	36.00	10.00

		NRMT	VG-E	GOOD
☐	1 Vern Bickford	90.00	18.00	5.50
☐	2 Whitey Lockman	20.00	9.00	2.50
☐	3 Bob Porterfield	20.00	9.00	2.50
☐	4A Jerry Priddy NNOF	42.00	19.00	5.25
☐	4B Jerry Priddy NOF	44.00	20.00	5.50
☐	5 Hank Sauer	22.50	10.00	2.80
☐	6 Phil Cavarretta	22.50	10.00	2.80
☐	7 Joe Dobson	18.00	8.00	2.30
☐	8 Murry Dickson	18.00	8.00	2.30
☐	9 Ferris Fain	20.00	9.00	2.50
☐	10 Ted Gray	18.00	8.00	2.30
☐	11 Lou Boudreau	65.00	29.00	8.25
☐	12 Cass Michaels	18.00	8.00	2.30
☐	13 Bob Chesnes	18.00	8.00	2.30
☐	14 Curt Simmons	35.00	16.00	4.40
☐	15 Ned Garver	18.00	8.00	2.30
☐	16 Al Kozar	18.00	8.00	2.30
☐	17 Earl Torgeson	18.00	8.00	2.30
☐	18 Bobby Thomson	30.00	13.50	3.80
☐	19 Bobby Brown	55.00	25.00	7.00
☐	20 Gene Hermanski	18.00	8.00	2.30
☐	21 Frank Baumholtz	20.00	9.00	2.50
☐	22 Peanuts Lowrey	18.00	8.00	2.30
☐	23 Bobby Doerr	65.00	29.00	8.25
☐	24 Stan Musial	600.00	275.00	75.00
☐	25 Carl Scheib	18.00	8.00	2.30
☐	26 George Kell	50.00	23.00	6.25
☐	27 Bob Feller	175.00	80.00	22.00
☐	28 Don Kolloway	18.00	8.00	2.30
☐	29 Ralph Kiner	100.00	45.00	12.50
☐	30 Andy Seminick	20.00	9.00	2.50
☐	31 Dick Kokos	18.00	8.00	2.30
☐	32 Eddie Yost	25.00	11.50	3.10
☐	33 Warren Spahn	175.00	80.00	22.00
☐	34 Dave Koslo	18.00	8.00	2.30
☐	35 Vic Raschi	50.00	23.00	6.25
☐	36 Pee Wee Reese	210.00	95.00	26.00
☐	37 Johnny Wyrostek	20.00	9.00	2.50
☐	38 Emil Verban	20.00	9.00	2.50
☐	39 Billy Goodman	22.50	10.00	2.80
☐	40 Red Munger	20.00	9.00	2.50
☐	41 Lou Brissie	20.00	9.00	2.50
☐	42 Hoot Evers	20.00	9.00	2.50
☐	43 Dale Mitchell	22.50	10.00	2.80
☐	44 Dave Philley	20.00	9.00	2.50
☐	45 Wally Westlake	20.00	9.00	2.50
☐	46 Robin Roberts	280.00	125.00	35.00
☐	47 Johnny Sain	35.00	16.00	4.40
☐	48 Willard Marshall	20.00	9.00	2.50
☐	49 Frank Shea	22.00	10.00	2.80
☐	50 Jackie Robinson	850.00	375.00	105.00
☐	51 Herman Wehmeier	20.00	9.00	2.50
☐	52 Johnny Schmitz	20.00	9.00	2.50
☐	53 Jack Kramer	20.00	9.00	2.50
☐	54 Marty Marion	30.00	13.50	3.80
☐	55 Eddie Joost	20.00	9.00	2.50
☐	56 Pat Mullin	20.00	9.00	2.50
☐	57 Gene Bearden	22.00	10.00	2.80
☐	58 Bob Elliott	22.00	10.00	2.80
☐	59 Jack Lohrke	20.00	9.00	2.50
☐	60 Yogi Berra	325.00	145.00	40.00
☐	61 Rex Barney	22.00	10.00	2.80
☐	62 Grady Hatton	20.00	9.00	2.50
☐	63 Andy Pafko	22.50	10.00	2.80
☐	64 Dom DiMaggio	30.00	13.50	3.80
☐	65 Enos Slaughter	95.00	42.50	12.00
☐	66 Elmer Valo	22.50	10.00	2.80
☐	67 Alvin Dark	35.00	16.00	4.40
☐	68 Sheldon Jones	20.00	9.00	2.50
☐	69 Tommy Henrich	30.00	13.50	3.80
☐	70 Carl Furillo	75.00	34.00	9.50
☐	71 Vern Stephens	22.50	10.00	2.80
☐	72 Tommy Holmes	22.50	10.00	2.80
☐	73 Billy Cox	30.00	13.50	3.80
☐	74 Tom McBride	17.00	7.75	2.10
☐	75 Eddie Mayo	17.00	7.75	2.10
☐	76 Bill Nicholson	22.50	10.00	2.80
☐	77 Ernie Bonham	17.00	7.75	2.10
☐	78A Sam Zoldak NNOF	42.00	19.00	5.25
☐	78B Sam Zoldak NOF	17.00	7.75	2.10
☐	79 Ron Northey	17.00	7.75	2.10
☐	80 Bill McCahan	17.00	7.75	2.10
☐	81 Virgil Stallcup	17.00	7.75	2.10
☐	82 Joe Page	25.00	11.50	3.10
☐	83A Bob Scheffing NNOF	42.00	19.00	5.25

☐ 83B	Bob Scheffing NOF	17.00	7.75	2.10	☐ 132B	Al Evans PR	15.00	6.75	1.90
☐ 84	Roy Campanella	800.00	350.00	100.00	☐ 133	Aaron Robinson	15.00	6.75	1.90
☐ 85A	Johnny Mize NNOF	90.00	40.00	11.50	☐ 134	Hank Borowy	15.00	6.75	1.90
☐ 85B	Johnny Mize NOF	150.00	70.00	19.00	☐ 135	Stan Rojek	15.00	6.75	1.90
☐ 86	Johnny Pesky	25.00	11.50	3.10	☐ 136	Hank Edwards	15.00	6.75	1.90
☐ 87	Randy Gumpert	17.00	7.75	2.10	☐ 137	Ted Wilks	15.00	6.75	1.90
☐ 88A	Bill Salkeld NNOF	42.00	19.00	5.25	☐ 138	Buddy Rosar	15.00	6.75	1.90
☐ 88B	Bill Salkeld NOF	17.00	7.75	2.10	☐ 139	Hank Arft	15.00	6.75	1.90
☐ 89	Mizell Platt	17.00	7.75	2.10	☐ 140	Ray Scarborough	15.00	6.75	1.90
☐ 90	Gil Coan	17.00	7.75	2.10	☐ 141	Tony Lupien	15.00	6.75	1.90
☐ 91	Dick Wakefield	17.00	7.75	2.10	☐ 142	Eddie Waitkus	20.00	9.00	2.50
☐ 92	Willie Jones	19.00	8.50	2.40	☐ 143A	Bob Dillinger SCR	42.00	19.00	5.25
☐ 93	Ed Stevens	17.00	7.75	2.10	☐ 143B	Bob Dillinger PR	20.00	9.00	2.50
☐ 94	Mickey Vernon	35.00	16.00	4.40	☐ 144	Mickey Haefner	15.00	6.75	1.90
☐ 95	Howie Pollet	20.00	9.00	2.50	☐ 145	Sylvester Donnelly	90.00	40.00	11.50
☐ 96	Taft Wright	17.00	7.75	2.10	☐ 146	Mike McCormick	100.00	45.00	12.50
☐ 97	Danny Litwhiler	17.00	7.75	2.10	☐ 147	Bert Singleton	90.00	40.00	11.50
☐ 98A	Phil Rizzuto NNOF	110.00	50.00	14.00	☐ 148	Bob Swift	90.00	40.00	11.50
☐ 98B	Phil Rizzuto NOF	210.00	95.00	26.00	☐ 149	Roy Partee	90.00	40.00	11.50
☐ 99	Frank Gustine	17.00	7.75	2.10	☐ 150	Allie Clark	90.00	40.00	11.50
☐ 100	Gil Hodges	250.00	115.00	31.00	☐ 151	Mickey Harris	90.00	40.00	11.50
☐ 101	Sid Gordon	17.00	7.75	2.10	☐ 152	Clarence Maddern	90.00	40.00	11.50
☐ 102	Stan Spence	17.00	7.75	2.10	☐ 153	Phil Masi	90.00	40.00	11.50
☐ 103	Joe Tipton	17.00	7.75	2.10	☐ 154	Clint Hartung	100.00	45.00	12.50
☐ 104	Eddie Stanky	30.00	13.50	3.80	☐ 155	Mickey Guerra	90.00	40.00	11.50
☐ 105	Bill Kennedy	17.00	7.75	2.10	☐ 156	Al Zarilla	90.00	40.00	11.50
☐ 106	Jake Early	17.00	7.75	2.10	☐ 157	Walt Masterson	90.00	40.00	11.50
☐ 107	Eddie Lake	17.00	7.75	2.10	☐ 158	Harry Brecheen	105.00	47.50	13.00
☐ 108	Ken Heintzelman	17.00	7.75	2.10	☐ 159	Glen Moulder	90.00	40.00	11.50
☐ 109A	Ed Fitzgerald SCR	40.00	18.00	5.00	☐ 160	Jim Blackburn	90.00	40.00	11.50
☐ 109B	Ed Fitzgerald PR	15.00	6.75	1.90	☐ 161	Jocko Thompson	90.00	40.00	11.50
☐ 110	Early Wynn	130.00	57.50	16.50	☐ 162	Preacher Roe	145.00	65.00	18.00
☐ 111	Red Schoendienst	80.00	36.00	10.00	☐ 163	Clyde McCullough	90.00	40.00	11.50
☐ 112	Sam Chapman	15.00	6.75	1.90	☐ 164	Vic Wertz	110.00	50.00	14.00
☐ 113	Ray LaManno	15.00	6.75	1.90	☐ 165	Snuffy Stirnweiss	100.00	45.00	12.50
☐ 114	Allie Reynolds	35.00	16.00	4.40	☐ 166	Mike Tresh	90.00	40.00	11.50
☐ 115	Dutch Leonard	15.00	6.75	1.90	☐ 167	Babe Martin	90.00	40.00	11.50
☐ 116	Joe Hatton	15.00	6.75	1.90	☐ 168	Doyle Lade	90.00	40.00	11.50
☐ 117	Walker Cooper	15.00	6.75	1.90	☐ 169	Jeff Heath	90.00	40.00	11.50
☐ 118	Sam Mele	15.00	6.75	1.90	☐ 170	Bill Rigney	90.00	40.00	11.50
☐ 119	Floyd Baker	15.00	6.75	1.90	☐ 171	Dick Fowler	90.00	40.00	11.50
☐ 120	Cliff Fannin	15.00	6.75	1.90	☐ 172	Eddie Pellagrini	90.00	40.00	11.50
☐ 121	Mark Christman	15.00	6.75	1.90	☐ 173	Eddie Stewart	90.00	40.00	11.50
☐ 122	George Vico	15.00	6.75	1.90	☐ 174	Terry Moore	125.00	57.50	15.50
☐ 123	Johnny Blatnick	15.00	6.75	1.90	☐ 175	Luke Appling	150.00	70.00	19.00
☐ 124A	D. Murtaugh SCR	45.00	20.00	5.75	☐ 176	Ken Raffensberger	90.00	40.00	11.50
☐ 124B	D. Murtaugh PR	22.00	10.00	2.80	☐ 177	Stan Lopata	90.00	40.00	11.50
☐ 125	Ken Keltner	17.00	7.75	2.10	☐ 178	Tom Brown	90.00	40.00	11.50
☐ 126A	Al Brazle SCR	40.00	18.00	5.00	☐ 179	Hugh Casey	100.00	45.00	12.50
☐ 126B	Al Brazle PR	15.00	6.75	1.90	☐ 180	Connie Berry	90.00	40.00	11.50
☐ 127A	Hank Majeski SCR	40.00	18.00	5.00	☐ 181	Gus Niarhos	80.00	36.00	10.00
☐ 127B	Hank Majeski PR	15.00	6.75	1.90	☐ 182	Hal Peck	80.00	36.00	10.00
☐ 128	Johnny VanderMeer	25.00	11.50	3.10	☐ 183	Lou Stringer	80.00	36.00	10.00
☐ 129	Bill Johnson	17.00	7.75	2.10	☐ 184	Bob Chipman	80.00	36.00	10.00
☐ 130	Harry Walker	15.00	6.75	1.90	☐ 185	Pete Reiser	105.00	47.50	13.00
☐ 131	Paul Lehner	15.00	6.75	1.90	☐ 186	Buddy Kerr	80.00	36.00	10.00
☐ 132A	Al Evans SCR	40.00	18.00	5.00	☐ 187	Phil Marchildon	80.00	36.00	10.00

			NRMT	VG-E	GOOD
☐	188	Karl Drews	80.00	36.00	10.00
☐	189	Earl Wooten	80.00	36.00	10.00
☐	190	Jim Hearn	80.00	36.00	10.00
☐	191	Joe Haynes	80.00	36.00	10.00
☐	192	Harry Gumbert	80.00	36.00	10.00
☐	193	Ken Trinkle	80.00	36.00	10.00
☐	194	Ralph Branca	110.00	50.00	14.00
☐	195	Eddie Bockman	80.00	36.00	10.00
☐	196	Fred Hutchinson	100.00	45.00	12.50
☐	197	Johnny Lindell	90.00	40.00	11.50
☐	198	Steve Gromek	80.00	36.00	10.00
☐	199	Tex Hughson	80.00	36.00	10.00
☐	200	Jess Dobernic	80.00	36.00	10.00
☐	201	Sibby Sisti	80.00	36.00	10.00
☐	202	Larry Jansen	95.00	42.50	12.00
☐	203	Barney McCosky	80.00	36.00	10.00
☐	204	Bob Savage	80.00	36.00	10.00
☐	205	Dick Sisler	90.00	40.00	11.50
☐	206	Bruce Edwards	80.00	36.00	10.00
☐	207	Johnny Hopp	95.00	42.50	12.00
☐	208	Dizzy Trout	95.00	42.50	12.00
☐	209	Charlie Keller	110.00	50.00	14.00
☐	210	Joe Gordon	110.00	50.00	14.00
☐	211	Boo Ferriss	80.00	36.00	10.00
☐	212	Ralph Hamner	80.00	36.00	10.00
☐	213	Red Barrett	80.00	36.00	10.00
☐	214	Richie Ashburn	550.00	250.00	70.00
☐	215	Kirby Higbe	80.00	36.00	10.00
☐	216	Schoolboy Rowe	95.00	42.50	12.00
☐	217	Marino Pieretti	80.00	36.00	10.00
☐	218	Dick Kryhoski	80.00	36.00	10.00
☐	219	Virgil Fire Trucks	95.00	42.50	12.00
☐	220	Johnny McCarthy	80.00	36.00	10.00
☐	221	Bob Muncrief	80.00	36.00	10.00
☐	222	Alex Kellner	80.00	36.00	10.00
☐	223	Bobby Hofman	80.00	36.00	10.00
☐	224	Satchell Paige	1300.00	575.00	160.00
☐	225	Jerry Coleman	115.00	52.50	14.50
☐	226	Duke Snider	1200.00	550.00	150.00
☐	227	Fritz Ostermueller	80.00	36.00	10.00
☐	228	Jackie Mayo	80.00	36.00	10.00
☐	229	Ed Lopat	150.00	70.00	19.00
☐	230	Augie Galan	80.00	36.00	10.00
☐	231	Earl Johnson	80.00	36.00	10.00
☐	232	George McQuinn	80.00	36.00	10.00
☐	233	Larry Doby	175.00	80.00	22.00
☐	234	Rip Sewell	80.00	36.00	10.00
☐	235	Jim Russell	80.00	36.00	10.00
☐	236	Fred Sanford	80.00	36.00	10.00
☐	237	Monte Kennedy	80.00	36.00	10.00
☐	238	Bob Lemon	275.00	125.00	34.00
☐	239	Frank McCormick	80.00	36.00	10.00
☐	240	Babe Young UER (Photo actually Bobby Young)	150.00	45.00	15.00

1950 Bowman

The cards in this 252-card set measure approximately 2 1/16" by 2 1/2". This set, marketed in 1950 by Bowman, represented a major improvement in terms of quality over their previous efforts. Each card was a beautifully colored line drawing developed from a simple photograph. The first 72 cards are the scarcest in the set, while the final 72 cards may be found with or without the copyright line. This was the only Bowman sports set to carry the famous "5-Star" logo. Key rookies in this set are Hank Bauer, Don Newcombe, and Al Rosen.

	NRMT	VG-E	GOOD
COMPLETE SET (252)	10000.	4600.	1250.
COMMON PLAYER (1-36)	55.00	25.00	7.00
COMMON PLAYER (37-72)	55.00	25.00	7.00
COMMON PLAYER (73-108)	18.00	8.00	2.30
COMMON PLAYER (109-144)	18.00	8.00	2.30
COMMON PLAYER (145-180)	18.00	8.00	2.30
COMMON PLAYER (181-216)	18.00	8.00	2.30
COMMON PLAYER (217-252)	20.00	9.00	2.50

			NRMT	VG-E	GOOD
☐	1	Mel Parnell	200.00	40.00	12.00
☐	2	Vern Stephens	60.00	27.00	7.50
☐	3	Dom DiMaggio	70.00	32.00	8.75
☐	4	Gus Zernial	65.00	29.00	8.25
☐	5	Bob Kuzava	55.00	25.00	7.00
☐	6	Bob Feller	200.00	90.00	25.00
☐	7	Jim Hegan	60.00	27.00	7.50
☐	8	George Kell	100.00	45.00	12.50
☐	9	Vic Wertz	60.00	27.00	7.50
☐	10	Tommy Henrich	65.00	29.00	8.25
☐	11	Phil Rizzuto	175.00	80.00	22.00
☐	12	Joe Page	65.00	29.00	8.25
☐	13	Ferris Fain	60.00	27.00	7.50
☐	14	Alex Kellner	55.00	25.00	7.00
☐	15	Al Kozar	55.00	25.00	7.00

☐	16	Roy Sievers	65.00	29.00	8.25
☐	17	Sid Hudson	55.00	25.00	7.00
☐	18	Eddie Robinson	55.00	25.00	7.00
☐	19	Warren Spahn	225.00	100.00	28.00
☐	20	Bob Elliott	60.00	27.00	7.50
☐	21	Pee Wee Reese	225.00	100.00	28.00
☐	22	Jackie Robinson	700.00	325.00	90.00
☐	23	Don Newcombe	150.00	70.00	19.00
☐	24	Johnny Schmitz	55.00	25.00	7.00
☐	25	Hank Sauer	60.00	27.00	7.50
☐	26	Grady Hatton	55.00	25.00	7.00
☐	27	Herman Wehmeier	55.00	25.00	7.00
☐	28	Bobby Thomson	65.00	29.00	8.25
☐	29	Eddie Stanky	60.00	27.00	7.50
☐	30	Eddie Waitkus	55.00	25.00	7.00
☐	31	Del Ennis	70.00	32.00	8.75
☐	32	Robin Roberts	150.00	70.00	19.00
☐	33	Ralph Kiner	125.00	57.50	15.50
☐	34	Murry Dickson	55.00	25.00	7.00
☐	35	Enos Slaughter	125.00	57.50	15.50
☐	36	Eddie Kazak	60.00	27.00	7.50
☐	37	Luke Appling	85.00	38.00	10.50
☐	38	Bill Wight	55.00	25.00	7.00
☐	39	Larry Doby	70.00	32.00	8.75
☐	40	Bob Lemon	110.00	50.00	14.00
☐	41	Hoot Evers	55.00	25.00	7.00
☐	42	Art Houtteman	55.00	25.00	7.00
☐	43	Bobby Doerr	100.00	45.00	12.50
☐	44	Joe Dobson	55.00	25.00	7.00
☐	45	Al Zarilla	55.00	25.00	7.00
☐	46	Yogi Berra	400.00	180.00	50.00
☐	47	Jerry Coleman	65.00	29.00	8.25
☐	48	Lou Brissie	55.00	25.00	7.00
☐	49	Elmer Valo	55.00	25.00	7.00
☐	50	Dick Kokos	55.00	25.00	7.00
☐	51	Ned Garver	55.00	25.00	7.00
☐	52	Sam Mele	55.00	25.00	7.00
☐	53	Clyde Vollmer	55.00	25.00	7.00
☐	54	Gil Coan	55.00	25.00	7.00
☐	55	Buddy Kerr	55.00	25.00	7.00
☐	56	Del Crandall	70.00	32.00	8.75
☐	57	Vern Bickford	55.00	25.00	7.00
☐	58	Carl Furillo	75.00	34.00	9.50
☐	59	Ralph Branca	65.00	29.00	8.25
☐	60	Andy Pafko	60.00	27.00	7.50
☐	61	Bob Rush	55.00	25.00	7.00
☐	62	Ted Kluszewski	90.00	40.00	11.50
☐	63	Ewell Blackwell	60.00	27.00	7.50
☐	64	Alvin Dark	65.00	29.00	8.25
☐	65	Dave Koslo	55.00	25.00	7.00
☐	66	Larry Jansen	60.00	27.00	7.50
☐	67	Willie Jones	55.00	25.00	7.00
☐	68	Curt Simmons	60.00	27.00	7.50
☐	69	Wally Westlake	55.00	25.00	7.00
☐	70	Bob Chesnes	55.00	25.00	7.00
☐	71	Red Schoendienst	110.00	50.00	14.00
☐	72	Howie Pollet	55.00	25.00	7.00
☐	73	Willard Marshall	18.00	8.00	2.30
☐	74	Johnny Antonelli	35.00	16.00	4.40
☐	75	Roy Campanella	300.00	135.00	38.00
☐	76	Rex Barney	20.00	9.00	2.50
☐	77	Duke Snider	300.00	135.00	38.00
☐	78	Mickey Owen	20.00	9.00	2.50
☐	79	Johnny VanderMeer	25.00	11.50	3.10
☐	80	Howard Fox	18.00	8.00	2.30
☐	81	Ron Northey	18.00	8.00	2.30
☐	82	Whitey Lockman	20.00	9.00	2.50
☐	83	Sheldon Jones	18.00	8.00	2.30
☐	84	Richie Ashburn	110.00	50.00	14.00
☐	85	Ken Heintzelman	18.00	8.00	2.30
☐	86	Stan Rojek	18.00	8.00	2.30
☐	87	Bill Werle	18.00	8.00	2.30
☐	88	Marty Marion	25.00	11.50	3.10
☐	89	Red Munger	18.00	8.00	2.30
☐	90	Harry Brecheen	20.00	9.00	2.50
☐	91	Cass Michaels	18.00	8.00	2.30
☐	92	Hank Majeski	18.00	8.00	2.30
☐	93	Gene Bearden	20.00	9.00	2.50
☐	94	Lou Boudreau	50.00	23.00	6.25
☐	95	Aaron Robinson	18.00	8.00	2.30
☐	96	Virgil Trucks	20.00	9.00	2.50
☐	97	Maurice McDermott	18.00	8.00	2.30
☐	98	Ted Williams	800.00	350.00	100.00
☐	99	Billy Goodman	20.00	9.00	2.50
☐	100	Vic Raschi	35.00	16.00	4.40
☐	101	Bobby Brown	35.00	16.00	4.40
☐	102	Billy Johnson	20.00	9.00	2.50
☐	103	Eddie Joost	18.00	8.00	2.30
☐	104	Sam Chapman	18.00	8.00	2.30
☐	105	Bob Dillinger	18.00	8.00	2.30
☐	106	Cliff Fannin	18.00	8.00	2.30
☐	107	Sam Dente	18.00	8.00	2.30
☐	108	Ray Scarborough	18.00	8.00	2.30
☐	109	Sid Gordon	18.00	8.00	2.30
☐	110	Tommy Holmes	20.00	9.00	2.50
☐	111	Walker Cooper	18.00	8.00	2.30
☐	112	Gil Hodges	100.00	45.00	12.50
☐	113	Gene Hermanski	18.00	8.00	2.30
☐	114	Wayne Terwilliger	22.50	10.00	2.80
☐	115	Roy Smalley	18.00	8.00	2.30
☐	116	Virgil Stallcup	18.00	8.00	2.30
☐	117	Bill Rigney	18.00	8.00	2.30
☐	118	Clint Hartung	18.00	8.00	2.30
☐	119	Dick Sisler	20.00	9.00	2.50
☐	120	John Thompson	18.00	8.00	2.30
☐	121	Andy Seminick	18.00	8.00	2.30
☐	122	Johnny Hopp	20.00	9.00	2.50
☐	123	Dino Restelli	18.00	8.00	2.30
☐	124	Clyde McCullough	18.00	8.00	2.30
☐	125	Del Rice	18.00	8.00	2.30
☐	126	Al Brazle	18.00	8.00	2.30
☐	127	Dave Philley	18.00	8.00	2.30
☐	128	Phil Masi	18.00	8.00	2.30
☐	129	Joe Gordon	22.50	10.00	2.80

☐ 130	Dale Mitchell	20.00	9.00	2.50
☐ 131	Steve Gromek	18.00	8.00	2.30
☐ 132	Mickey Vernon	22.50	10.00	2.80
☐ 133	Don Kolloway	18.00	8.00	2.30
☐ 134	Paul Trout	18.00	8.00	2.30
☐ 135	Pat Mullin	18.00	8.00	2.30
☐ 136	Warren Rosar	18.00	8.00	2.30
☐ 137	Johnny Pesky	22.00	10.00	2.80
☐ 138	Allie Reynolds	35.00	16.00	4.40
☐ 139	Johnny Mize	75.00	34.00	9.50
☐ 140	Pete Suder	18.00	8.00	2.30
☐ 141	Joe Coleman	18.00	8.00	2.30
☐ 142	Sherm Lollar	25.00	11.50	3.10
☐ 143	Eddie Stewart	18.00	8.00	2.30
☐ 144	Al Evans	18.00	8.00	2.30
☐ 145	Jack Graham	18.00	8.00	2.30
☐ 146	Floyd Baker	18.00	8.00	2.30
☐ 147	Mike Garcia	25.00	11.50	3.10
☐ 148	Early Wynn	65.00	29.00	8.25
☐ 149	Bob Swift	18.00	8.00	2.30
☐ 150	George Vico	18.00	8.00	2.30
☐ 151	Fred Hutchinson	22.50	10.00	2.80
☐ 152	Ellis Kinder	18.00	8.00	2.30
☐ 153	Walt Masterson	18.00	8.00	2.30
☐ 154	Gus Niarhos	18.00	8.00	2.30
☐ 155	Frank Shea	20.00	9.00	2.50
☐ 156	Fred Sanford	20.00	9.00	2.50
☐ 157	Mike Guerra	18.00	8.00	2.30
☐ 158	Paul Lehner	18.00	8.00	2.30
☐ 159	Joe Tipton	18.00	8.00	2.30
☐ 160	Mickey Harris	18.00	8.00	2.30
☐ 161	Sherry Robertson	18.00	8.00	2.30
☐ 162	Eddie Yost	20.00	9.00	2.50
☐ 163	Earl Turgeson	18.00	8.00	2.30
☐ 164	Sibby Sisti	18.00	8.00	2.30
☐ 165	Bruce Edwards	18.00	8.00	2.30
☐ 166	Joe Hatton	18.00	8.00	2.30
☐ 167	Preacher Roe	35.00	16.00	4.40
☐ 168	Bob Scheffing	18.00	8.00	2.30
☐ 169	Hank Edwards	18.00	8.00	2.30
☐ 170	Dutch Leonard	18.00	8.00	2.30
☐ 171	Harry Gumbert	18.00	8.00	2.30
☐ 172	Peanuts Lowrey	18.00	8.00	2.30
☐ 173	Lloyd Merriman	18.00	8.00	2.30
☐ 174	Hank Thompson	25.00	11.50	3.10
☐ 175	Monte Kennedy	18.00	8.00	2.30
☐ 176	Sylvester Donnelly	18.00	8.00	2.30
☐ 177	Hank Borowy	18.00	8.00	2.30
☐ 178	Ed Fitzgerald	18.00	8.00	2.30
☐ 179	Chuck Diering	18.00	8.00	2.30
☐ 180	Harry Walker	18.00	8.00	2.30
☐ 181	Marino Pieretti	18.00	8.00	2.30
☐ 182	Sam Zoldak	18.00	8.00	2.30
☐ 183	Mickey Haefner	18.00	8.00	2.30
☐ 184	Randy Gumpert	18.00	8.00	2.30
☐ 185	Howie Judson	18.00	8.00	2.30
☐ 186	Ken Keltner	20.00	9.00	2.50
☐ 187	Lou Stringer	18.00	8.00	2.30
☐ 188	Earl Johnson	18.00	8.00	2.30
☐ 189	Owen Friend	18.00	8.00	2.30
☐ 190	Ken Wood	18.00	8.00	2.30
☐ 191	Dick Starr	18.00	8.00	2.30
☐ 192	Bob Chipman	18.00	8.00	2.30
☐ 193	Pete Reiser	22.50	10.00	2.80
☐ 194	Billy Cox	22.50	10.00	2.80
☐ 195	Phil Cavarretta	25.00	11.50	3.10
☐ 196	Doyle Lade	18.00	8.00	2.30
☐ 197	Johnny Wyrostek	18.00	8.00	2.30
☐ 198	Danny Litwhiler	18.00	8.00	2.30
☐ 199	Jack Kramer	18.00	8.00	2.30
☐ 200	Kirby Higbe	18.00	8.00	2.30
☐ 201	Pete Castiglione	18.00	8.00	2.30
☐ 202	Cliff Chambers	18.00	8.00	2.30
☐ 203	Danny Murtaugh	20.00	9.00	2.50
☐ 204	Granny Hamner	25.00	11.50	3.10
☐ 205	Mike Goliat	18.00	8.00	2.30
☐ 206	Stan Lopata	18.00	8.00	2.30
☐ 207	Max Lanier	18.00	8.00	2.30
☐ 208	Jim Hearn	18.00	8.00	2.30
☐ 209	Johnny Lindell	18.00	8.00	2.30
☐ 210	Ted Gray	18.00	8.00	2.30
☐ 211	Charlie Keller	20.00	9.00	2.50
☐ 212	Jerry Priddy	18.00	8.00	2.30
☐ 213	Carl Scheib	18.00	8.00	2.30
☐ 214	Dick Fowler	18.00	8.00	2.30
☐ 215	Ed Lopat	35.00	16.00	4.40
☐ 216	Bob Porterfield	20.00	9.00	2.50
☐ 217	Casey Stengel MG	150.00	70.00	19.00
☐ 218	Cliff Mapes	22.00	10.00	2.80
☐ 219	Hank Bauer	85.00	38.00	10.50
☐ 220	Leo Durocher MG	70.00	32.00	8.75
☐ 221	Don Mueller	35.00	16.00	4.40
☐ 222	Bobby Morgan	20.00	9.00	2.50
☐ 223	Jim Russell	20.00	9.00	2.50
☐ 224	Jack Banta	20.00	9.00	2.50
☐ 225	Eddie Sawyer MG	22.00	10.00	2.80
☐ 226	Jim Konstanty	40.00	18.00	5.00
☐ 227	Bob Miller	20.00	9.00	2.50
☐ 228	Bill Nicholson	22.00	10.00	2.80
☐ 229	Frank Frisch MG	45.00	20.00	5.75
☐ 230	Bill Serena	20.00	9.00	2.50
☐ 231	Preston Ward	20.00	9.00	2.50
☐ 232	Al Rosen	70.00	32.00	8.75
☐ 233	Allie Clark	20.00	9.00	2.50
☐ 234	Bobby Shantz	35.00	16.00	4.40
☐ 235	Harold Gilbert	20.00	9.00	2.50
☐ 236	Bob Cain	20.00	9.00	2.50
☐ 237	Bill Salkeld	20.00	9.00	2.50
☐ 238	Nippy Jones	20.00	9.00	2.50
☐ 239	Bill Howerton	20.00	9.00	2.50
☐ 240	Eddie Lake	20.00	9.00	2.50
☐ 241	Neil Berry	20.00	9.00	2.50
☐ 242	Dick Kryhoski	20.00	9.00	2.50
☐ 243	Johnny Groth	20.00	9.00	2.50

		NRMT	VG-E	GOOD
☐	244 Dale Coogan	20.00	9.00	2.50
☐	245 Al Papai	20.00	9.00	2.50
☐	246 Walt Dropo	30.00	13.50	3.80
☐	247 Irv Noren	22.50	10.00	2.80
☐	248 Sam Jethroe	22.50	10.00	2.80
☐	249 Snuffy Stirnweiss	22.00	10.00	2.80
☐	250 Ray Coleman	20.00	9.00	2.50
☐	251 John Moss	20.00	9.00	2.50
☐	252 Billy DeMars	75.00	23.00	7.50

1951 Bowman

The cards in this 324-card set measure approximately 2 1/16" by 3 1/8". Many of the obverses of the cards appearing in the 1951 Bowman set are enlargements of those appearing in the previous year. The high number series (253-324) is highly valued and contains the true "Rookie" cards of Mickey Mantle and Willie Mays. Card number 195 depicts Paul Richards in caricature. George Kell's card (number 46) incorrectly lists him as being in the "1941" Bowman series. Player names are found printed in a panel on the front of the card. These cards were supposedly also sold in sheets in variety stores in the Philadelphia area.

	NRMT	VG-E	GOOD
COMPLETE SET (324)	21000.	9500.	2600.
COMMON PLAYER (1-36)	20.00	9.00	2.50
COMMON PLAYER (37-72)	18.00	8.00	2.30
COMMON PLAYER (73-108)	15.00	6.75	1.90
COMMON PLAYER (109-144)	15.00	6.75	1.90
COMMON PLAYER (145-180)	15.00	6.75	1.90
COMMON PLAYER (181-216)	15.00	6.75	1.90
COMMON PLAYER (217-252)	15.00	6.75	1.90
COMMON PLAYER (253-324)	60.00	27.00	7.50

		NRMT	VG-E	GOOD
☐	1 Whitey Ford	1325.00	325.00	105.00
☐	2 Yogi Berra	475.00	210.00	60.00
☐	3 Robin Roberts	80.00	36.00	10.00
☐	4 Del Ennis	25.00	11.50	3.10
☐	5 Dale Mitchell	23.00	10.50	2.90
☐	6 Don Newcombe	45.00	20.00	5.75
☐	7 Gil Hodges	90.00	40.00	11.50
☐	8 Paul Lehner	20.00	9.00	2.50
☐	9 Sam Chapman	20.00	9.00	2.50
☐	10 Red Schoendienst	80.00	36.00	10.00
☐	11 Red Munger	20.00	9.00	2.50
☐	12 Hank Majeski	20.00	9.00	2.50
☐	13 Eddie Stanky	25.00	11.50	3.10
☐	14 Alvin Dark	30.00	13.50	3.80
☐	15 Johnny Pesky	25.00	11.50	3.10
☐	16 Maurice McDermott	20.00	9.00	2.50
☐	17 Pete Castiglione	20.00	9.00	2.50
☐	18 Gil Coan	20.00	9.00	2.50
☐	19 Sid Gordon	20.00	9.00	2.50
☐	20 Del Crandall UER	23.00	10.50	2.90
	(Misspelled Crandell on card)			
☐	21 Snuffy Stirnweiss	22.00	10.00	2.80
☐	22 Hank Sauer	25.00	11.50	3.10
☐	23 Hoot Evers	20.00	9.00	2.50
☐	24 Ewell Blackwell	25.00	11.50	3.10
☐	25 Vic Raschi	35.00	16.00	4.40
☐	26 Phil Rizzuto	110.00	50.00	14.00
☐	27 Jim Konstanty	25.00	11.50	3.10
☐	28 Eddie Waitkus	20.00	9.00	2.50
☐	29 Allie Clark	20.00	9.00	2.50
☐	30 Bob Feller	140.00	65.00	17.50
☐	31 Roy Campanella	275.00	125.00	34.00
☐	32 Duke Snider	275.00	125.00	34.00
☐	33 Bob Hooper	20.00	9.00	2.50
☐	34 Marty Marion	27.00	12.00	3.40
☐	35 Al Zarilla	20.00	9.00	2.50
☐	36 Joe Dobson	20.00	9.00	2.50
☐	37 Whitey Lockman	20.00	9.00	2.50
☐	38 Al Evans	18.00	8.00	2.30
☐	39 Ray Scarborough	18.00	8.00	2.30
☐	40 Gus Bell	30.00	13.50	3.80
☐	41 Eddie Yost	20.00	9.00	2.50
☐	42 Vern Bickford	18.00	8.00	2.30
☐	43 Billy DeMars	18.00	8.00	2.30
☐	44 Roy Smalley	18.00	8.00	2.30
☐	45 Art Houtteman	18.00	8.00	2.30
☐	46 George Kell 1941 UER	55.00	25.00	7.00
☐	47 Grady Hatton	18.00	8.00	2.30
☐	48 Ken Raffensberger	18.00	8.00	2.30
☐	49 Jerry Coleman	23.00	10.50	2.90
☐	50 Johnny Mize	60.00	27.00	7.50
☐	51 Andy Seminick	18.00	8.00	2.30
☐	52 Dick Sisler	20.00	9.00	2.50

☐ 53 Bob Lemon	50.00	23.00	6.25
☐ 54 Ray Boone	25.00	11.50	3.10
☐ 55 Gene Hermanski	18.00	8.00	2.30
☐ 56 Ralph Branca	30.00	13.50	3.80
☐ 57 Alex Kellner	18.00	8.00	2.30
☐ 58 Enos Slaughter	60.00	27.00	7.50
☐ 59 Randy Gumpert	18.00	8.00	2.30
☐ 60 Chico Carrasquel	25.00	11.50	3.10
☐ 61 Jim Hearn	18.00	8.00	2.30
☐ 62 Lou Boudreau	50.00	23.00	6.25
☐ 63 Bob Dillinger	18.00	8.00	2.30
☐ 64 Bill Werle	18.00	8.00	2.30
☐ 65 Mickey Vernon	20.00	9.00	2.50
☐ 66 Bob Elliott	20.00	9.00	2.50
☐ 67 Roy Sievers	20.00	9.00	2.50
☐ 68 Dick Kokos	18.00	8.00	2.30
☐ 69 Johnny Schmitz	18.00	8.00	2.30
☐ 70 Ron Northey	18.00	8.00	2.30
☐ 71 Jerry Priddy	18.00	8.00	2.30
☐ 72 Lloyd Merriman	18.00	8.00	2.30
☐ 73 Tommy Byrne	15.00	6.75	1.90
☐ 74 Billy Johnson	17.00	7.75	2.10
☐ 75 Russ Meyer	18.00	8.00	2.30
☐ 76 Stan Lopata	15.00	6.75	1.90
☐ 77 Mike Goliat	15.00	6.75	1.90
☐ 78 Early Wynn	50.00	23.00	6.25
☐ 79 Jim Hegan	17.00	7.75	2.10
☐ 80 Pee Wee Reese	150.00	70.00	19.00
☐ 81 Carl Furillo	40.00	18.00	5.00
☐ 82 Joe Tipton	15.00	6.75	1.90
☐ 83 Carl Scheib	15.00	6.75	1.90
☐ 84 Barney McCosky	15.00	6.75	1.90
☐ 85 Eddie Kazak	15.00	6.75	1.90
☐ 86 Harry Brecheen	17.00	7.75	2.10
☐ 87 Floyd Baker	15.00	6.75	1.90
☐ 88 Eddie Robinson	15.00	6.75	1.90
☐ 89 Hank Thompson	17.00	7.75	2.10
☐ 90 Dave Koslo	15.00	6.75	1.90
☐ 91 Clyde Vollmer	15.00	6.75	1.90
☐ 92 Vern Stephens	17.00	7.75	2.10
☐ 93 Danny O'Connell	15.00	6.75	1.90
☐ 94 Clyde McCullough	15.00	6.75	1.90
☐ 95 Sherry Robertson	15.00	6.75	1.90
☐ 96 Sandy Consuegra	15.00	6.75	1.90
☐ 97 Bob Kuzava	15.00	6.75	1.90
☐ 98 Willard Marshall	15.00	6.75	1.90
☐ 99 Earl Torgeson	15.00	6.75	1.90
☐ 100 Sherm Lollar	17.00	7.75	2.10
☐ 101 Owen Friend	15.00	6.75	1.90
☐ 102 Dutch Leonard	15.00	6.75	1.90
☐ 103 Andy Pafko	17.00	7.75	2.10
☐ 104 Virgil Trucks	17.00	7.75	2.10
☐ 105 Don Kolloway	15.00	6.75	1.90
☐ 106 Pat Mullin	15.00	6.75	1.90
☐ 107 Johnny Wyrostek	15.00	6.75	1.90
☐ 108 Virgil Stallcup	15.00	6.75	1.90
☐ 109 Allie Reynolds	30.00	13.50	3.80
☐ 110 Bobby Brown	35.00	16.00	4.40
☐ 111 Curt Simmons	20.00	9.00	2.50
☐ 112 Willie Jones	15.00	6.75	1.90
☐ 113 Bill Nicholson	17.00	7.75	2.10
☐ 114 Sam Zoldak	15.00	6.75	1.90
☐ 115 Steve Gromek	15.00	6.75	1.90
☐ 116 Bruce Edwards	15.00	6.75	1.90
☐ 117 Eddie Miksis	15.00	6.75	1.90
☐ 118 Preacher Roe	30.00	13.50	3.80
☐ 119 Eddie Joost	15.00	6.75	1.90
☐ 120 Joe Coleman	15.00	6.75	1.90
☐ 121 Jerry Staley	15.00	6.75	1.90
☐ 122 Joe Garagiola	150.00	70.00	19.00
☐ 123 Howie Judson	15.00	6.75	1.90
☐ 124 Gus Niarhos	15.00	6.75	1.90
☐ 125 Bill Rigney	15.00	6.75	1.90
☐ 126 Bobby Thomson	30.00	13.50	3.80
☐ 127 Sal Maglie	50.00	23.00	6.25
☐ 128 Ellis Kinder	15.00	6.75	1.90
☐ 129 Matt Batts	15.00	6.75	1.90
☐ 130 Tom Saffell	15.00	6.75	1.90
☐ 131 Cliff Chambers	15.00	6.75	1.90
☐ 132 Cass Michaels	15.00	6.75	1.90
☐ 133 Sam Dente	15.00	6.75	1.90
☐ 134 Warren Spahn	125.00	57.50	15.50
☐ 135 Walker Cooper	15.00	6.75	1.90
☐ 136 Ray Coleman	15.00	6.75	1.90
☐ 137 Dick Starr	15.00	6.75	1.90
☐ 138 Phil Cavarretta	20.00	9.00	2.50
☐ 139 Doyle Lade	15.00	6.75	1.90
☐ 140 Eddie Lake	15.00	6.75	1.90
☐ 141 Fred Hutchinson	20.00	9.00	2.50
☐ 142 Aaron Robinson	15.00	6.75	1.90
☐ 143 Ted Kluszewski	40.00	18.00	5.00
☐ 144 Herman Wehmeier	15.00	6.75	1.90
☐ 145 Fred Sanford	17.00	7.75	2.10
☐ 146 Johnny Hopp	17.00	7.75	2.10
☐ 147 Ken Heintzelman	15.00	6.75	1.90
☐ 148 Granny Hamner	15.00	6.75	1.90
☐ 149 Bubba Church	15.00	6.75	1.90
☐ 150 Mike Garcia	17.00	7.75	2.10
☐ 151 Larry Doby	35.00	16.00	4.40
☐ 152 Cal Abrams	15.00	6.75	1.90
☐ 153 Rex Barney	17.00	7.75	2.10
☐ 154 Pete Suder	15.00	6.75	1.90
☐ 155 Lou Brissie	15.00	6.75	1.90
☐ 156 Del Rice	15.00	6.75	1.90
☐ 157 Al Brazle	15.00	6.75	1.90
☐ 158 Chuck Diering	15.00	6.75	1.90
☐ 159 Eddie Stewart	15.00	6.75	1.90
☐ 160 Phil Masi	15.00	6.75	1.90
☐ 161 Wes Westrum	20.00	9.00	2.50
☐ 162 Larry Jansen	17.00	7.75	2.10
☐ 163 Monte Kennedy	15.00	6.75	1.90
☐ 164 Bill Wight	15.00	6.75	1.90
☐ 165 Ted Williams	675.00	300.00	85.00
☐ 166 Stan Rojek	15.00	6.75	1.90

☐	167	Murry Dickson	15.00	6.75	1.90
☐	168	Sam Mele	15.00	6.75	1.90
☐	169	Sid Hudson	15.00	6.75	1.90
☐	170	Sibby Sisti	15.00	6.75	1.90
☐	171	Buddy Kerr	15.00	6.75	1.90
☐	172	Ned Garver	15.00	6.75	1.90
☐	173	Hank Arft	15.00	6.75	1.90
☐	174	Mickey Owen	17.00	7.75	2.10
☐	175	Wayne Terwilliger	15.00	6.75	1.90
☐	176	Vic Wertz	17.00	7.75	2.10
☐	177	Charlie Keller	17.00	7.75	2.10
☐	178	Ted Gray	15.00	6.75	1.90
☐	179	Danny Litwhiler	15.00	6.75	1.90
☐	180	Howie Fox	15.00	6.75	1.90
☐	181	Casey Stengel MG	100.00	45.00	12.50
☐	182	Tom Ferrick	15.00	6.75	1.90
☐	183	Hank Bauer	35.00	16.00	4.40
☐	184	Eddie Sawyer MG	17.00	7.75	2.10
☐	185	Jimmy Bloodworth	15.00	6.75	1.90
☐	186	Richie Ashburn	65.00	29.00	8.25
☐	187	Al Rosen	30.00	13.50	3.80
☐	188	Bobby Avila	20.00	9.00	2.50
☐	189	Erv Palica	15.00	6.75	1.90
☐	190	Joe Hatton	15.00	6.75	1.90
☐	191	Billy Hitchcock	15.00	6.75	1.90
☐	192	Hank Wyse	15.00	6.75	1.90
☐	193	Ted Wilks	15.00	6.75	1.90
☐	194	Peanuts Lowrey	15.00	6.75	1.90
☐	195	Paul Richards MG (Caricature)	20.00	9.00	2.50
☐	196	Billy Pierce	30.00	13.50	3.80
☐	197	Bob Cain	15.00	6.75	1.90
☐	198	Monte Irvin	110.00	50.00	14.00
☐	199	Sheldon Jones	15.00	6.75	1.90
☐	200	Jack Kramer	15.00	6.75	1.90
☐	201	Steve O'Neill MG	15.00	6.75	1.90
☐	202	Mike Guerra	15.00	6.75	1.90
☐	203	Vernon Law	30.00	13.50	3.80
☐	204	Vic Lombardi	15.00	6.75	1.90
☐	205	Mickey Grasso	15.00	6.75	1.90
☐	206	Conrado Marrero	15.00	6.75	1.90
☐	207	Billy Southworth MG	15.00	6.75	1.90
☐	208	Blix Donnelly	15.00	6.75	1.90
☐	209	Ken Wood	15.00	6.75	1.90
☐	210	Les Moss	15.00	6.75	1.90
☐	211	Hal Jeffcoat	15.00	6.75	1.90
☐	212	Bob Rush	15.00	6.75	1.90
☐	213	Neil Berry	15.00	6.75	1.90
☐	214	Bob Swift	15.00	6.75	1.90
☐	215	Ken Peterson	15.00	6.75	1.90
☐	216	Connie Ryan	15.00	6.75	1.90
☐	217	Joe Page	20.00	9.00	2.50
☐	218	Ed Lopat	35.00	16.00	4.40
☐	219	Gene Woodling	40.00	18.00	5.00
☐	220	Bob Miller	15.00	6.75	1.90
☐	221	Dick Whitman	15.00	6.75	1.90
☐	222	Thurman Tucker	15.00	6.75	1.90
☐	223	Johnny VanderMeer	25.00	11.50	3.10
☐	224	Billy Cox	20.00	9.00	2.50
☐	225	Dan Bankhead	17.00	7.75	2.10
☐	226	Jimmy Dykes MG	18.00	8.00	2.30
☐	227	Bobby Schantz UER (Sic, Shantz)	20.00	9.00	2.50
☐	228	Cloyd Boyer	17.00	7.75	2.10
☐	229	Bill Howerton	15.00	6.75	1.90
☐	230	Max Lanier	15.00	6.75	1.90
☐	231	Luis Aloma	15.00	6.75	1.90
☐	232	Nelson Fox	150.00	70.00	19.00
☐	233	Leo Durocher MG	55.00	25.00	7.00
☐	234	Clint Hartung	15.00	6.75	1.90
☐	235	Jack Lohrke	15.00	6.75	1.90
☐	236	Warren Rosar	15.00	6.75	1.90
☐	237	Billy Goodman	17.00	7.75	2.10
☐	238	Pete Reiser	20.00	9.00	2.50
☐	239	Bill MacDonald	15.00	6.75	1.90
☐	240	Joe Haynes	15.00	6.75	1.90
☐	241	Irv Noren	17.00	7.75	2.10
☐	242	Sam Jethroe	17.00	7.75	2.10
☐	243	Johnny Antonelli	17.00	7.75	2.10
☐	244	Cliff Fannin	15.00	6.75	1.90
☐	245	John Berardino	25.00	11.50	3.10
☐	246	Bill Serena	15.00	6.75	1.90
☐	247	Bob Ramazzotti	15.00	6.75	1.90
☐	248	Johnny Klippstein	15.00	6.75	1.90
☐	249	Johnny Groth	15.00	6.75	1.90
☐	250	Hank Borowy	15.00	6.75	1.90
☐	251	Willard Ramsdell	15.00	6.75	1.90
☐	252	Dixie Howell	15.00	6.75	1.90
☐	253	Mickey Mantle	8750.	3900.	1100.
☐	254	Jackie Jensen	150.00	70.00	19.00
☐	255	Milo Candini	60.00	27.00	7.50
☐	256	Ken Sylvestri	60.00	27.00	7.50
☐	257	Birdie Tebbetts	70.00	32.00	8.75
☐	258	Luke Easter	70.00	32.00	8.75
☐	259	Chuck Dressen MG	80.00	36.00	10.00
☐	260	Carl Erskine	125.00	57.50	15.50
☐	261	Wally Moses	65.00	29.00	8.25
☐	262	Gus Zernial	70.00	32.00	8.75
☐	263	Howie Pollet	65.00	29.00	8.25
☐	264	Don Richmond	60.00	27.00	7.50
☐	265	Steve Bilko	65.00	29.00	8.25
☐	266	Harry Dorish	60.00	27.00	7.50
☐	267	Ken Holcombe	60.00	27.00	7.50
☐	268	Don Mueller	70.00	32.00	8.75
☐	269	Ray Noble	60.00	27.00	7.50
☐	270	Willard Nixon	60.00	27.00	7.50
☐	271	Tommy Wright	60.00	27.00	7.50
☐	272	Billy Meyer MG	60.00	27.00	7.50
☐	273	Danny Murtaugh	65.00	29.00	8.25
☐	274	George Metkovich	60.00	27.00	7.50
☐	275	Bucky Harris MG	80.00	36.00	10.00
☐	276	Frank Quinn	60.00	27.00	7.50
☐	277	Roy Hartsfield	60.00	27.00	7.50
☐	278	Norman Roy	60.00	27.00	7.50

			NRMT	VG-E	GOOD
☐	279	Jim Delsing.............60.00	27.00	7.50
☐	280	Frank Overmire.........60.00	27.00	7.50
☐	281	Al Widmar.............60.00	27.00	7.50
☐	282	Frank Frisch MG.......100.00	45.00	12.50
☐	283	Walt Dubiel...........60.00	27.00	7.50
☐	284	Gene Bearden..........65.00	29.00	8.25
☐	285	Johnny Lipon..........60.00	27.00	7.50
☐	286	Bob Usher.............60.00	27.00	7.50
☐	287	Jim Blackburn.........60.00	27.00	7.50
☐	288	Bobby Adams...........60.00	27.00	7.50
☐	289	Cliff Mapes...........65.00	29.00	8.25
☐	290	Bill Dickey CO.......175.00	80.00	22.00
☐	291	Tommy Henrich CO......75.00	34.00	9.50
☐	292	Eddie Pellegrini......60.00	27.00	7.50
☐	293	Ken Johnson...........60.00	27.00	7.50
☐	294	Jocko Thompson........60.00	27.00	7.50
☐	295	Al Lopez MG..........125.00	57.50	15.50
☐	296	Bob Kennedy...........65.00	29.00	8.25
☐	297	Dave Philley..........60.00	27.00	7.50
☐	298	Joe Astroth...........60.00	27.00	7.50
☐	299	Clyde King............60.00	27.00	7.50
☐	300	Hal Rice..............60.00	27.00	7.50
☐	301	Tommy Glaviano........60.00	27.00	7.50
☐	302	Jim Busby.............60.00	27.00	7.50
☐	303	Marv Rotblatt.........60.00	27.00	7.50
☐	304	Al Gettell............60.00	27.00	7.50
☐	305	Willie Mays.........3750.	1700.	475.00
☐	306	Jim Piersall.........125.00	57.50	15.50
☐	307	Walt Masterson........60.00	27.00	7.50
☐	308	Ted Beard.............60.00	27.00	7.50
☐	309	Mel Queen.............60.00	27.00	7.50
☐	310	Erv Dusak.............60.00	27.00	7.50
☐	311	Mickey Harris.........60.00	27.00	7.50
☐	312	Gene Mauch............80.00	36.00	10.00
☐	313	Ray Mueller...........60.00	27.00	7.50
☐	314	Johnny Sain...........80.00	36.00	10.00
☐	315	Zack Taylor MG........60.00	27.00	7.50
☐	316	Duane Pillette........60.00	27.00	7.50
☐	317	Smoky Burgess.........90.00	40.00	11.50
☐	318	Warren Hacker.........60.00	27.00	7.50
☐	319	Red Rolfe MG..........70.00	32.00	8.75
☐	320	Hal White.............60.00	27.00	7.50
☐	321	Earl Johnson..........60.00	27.00	7.50
☐	322	Luke Sewell MG........65.00	29.00	8.25
☐	323	Joe Adcock...........100.00	45.00	12.50
☐	324	Johnny Pramesa.......125.00	38.00	12.50

1952 Bowman

The cards in this 252-card set measure approximately 2 1/16" by 3 1/8". While the Bowman set of 1952 retained the card size

introduced in 1951, it employed a modification of color tones from the two preceding years. The cards also appeared with a facsimile autograph on the front and, for the first time since 1949, premium advertising on the back. The 1952 set was apparently sold in sheets as well as in gum packs. Artwork for 15 cards that were never issued was discovered in the early 1980s. Notable Rookie Cards in this set are Lew Burdette, Gil McDougald, and Minnie Minoso.

	NRMT	VG-E	GOOD
COMPLETE SET (252) 9400.00	4200.00	1200.00
COMMON PLAYER (1-36) 20.00	9.00	2.50
COMMON PLAYER (37-72) 18.00	8.00	2.30
COMMON PLAYER (73-108) 15.00	6.75	1.90
COMMON PLAYER (109-144) 15.00	6.75	1.90
COMMON PLAYER (145-180) 15.00	6.75	1.90
COMMON PLAYER (181-216) 14.00	6.25	1.75
COMMON PLAYER (217-252) 33.00	15.00	4.10

			NRMT	VG-E	GOOD
☐	1	Yogi Berra............600.00	180.00	60.00
☐	2	Bobby Thomson.........35.00	16.00	4.40
☐	3	Fred Hutchinson.......25.00	11.50	3.10
☐	4	Robin Roberts.........70.00	32.00	8.75
☐	5	Minnie Minoso........100.00	45.00	12.50
☐	6	Virgil Stallcup.......20.00	9.00	2.50
☐	7	Mike Garcia...........22.00	10.00	2.80
☐	8	Pee Wee Reese........110.00	50.00	14.00
☐	9	Vern Stephens.........22.00	10.00	2.80
☐	10	Bob Hooper............20.00	9.00	2.50
☐	11	Ralph Kiner...........70.00	32.00	8.75
☐	12	Max Surkont...........20.00	9.00	2.50
☐	13	Cliff Mapes...........20.00	9.00	2.50
☐	14	Cliff Chambers........20.00	9.00	2.50
☐	15	Sam Mele..............20.00	9.00	2.50
☐	16	Turk Lown.............20.00	9.00	2.50
☐	17	Ed Lopat..............35.00	16.00	4.40
☐	18	Don Mueller...........22.00	10.00	2.80
☐	19	Bob Cain..............20.00	9.00	2.50

☐	20	Willie Jones	20.00	9.00	2.50	☐	77	Eddie Robinson	15.00	6.75	1.90
☐	21	Nellie Fox	50.00	23.00	6.25	☐	78	Lloyd Merriman	15.00	6.75	1.90
☐	22	Willard Ramsdell	20.00	9.00	2.50	☐	79	Lou Brissie	15.00	6.75	1.90
☐	23	Bob Lemon	60.00	27.00	7.50	☐	80	Gil Hodges	80.00	36.00	10.00
☐	24	Carl Furillo	35.00	16.00	4.40	☐	81	Billy Goodman	16.00	7.25	2.00
☐	25	Mickey McDermott	20.00	9.00	2.50	☐	82	Gus Zernial	16.00	7.25	2.00
☐	26	Eddie Joost	20.00	9.00	2.50	☐	83	Howie Pollet	15.00	6.75	1.90
☐	27	Joe Garagiola	75.00	34.00	9.50	☐	84	Sam Jethroe	16.00	7.25	2.00
☐	28	Roy Hartsfield	20.00	9.00	2.50	☐	85	Marty Marion CO	20.00	9.00	2.50
☐	29	Ned Garver	20.00	9.00	2.50	☐	86	Cal Abrams	15.00	6.75	1.90
☐	30	Red Schoendienst	65.00	29.00	8.25	☐	87	Mickey Vernon	17.00	7.75	2.10
☐	31	Eddie Yost	22.00	10.00	2.80	☐	88	Bruce Edwards	15.00	6.75	1.90
☐	32	Eddie Miksis	20.00	9.00	2.50	☐	89	Billy Hitchcock	15.00	6.75	1.90
☐	33	Gil McDougald	70.00	32.00	8.75	☐	90	Larry Jansen	16.00	7.25	2.00
☐	34	Alvin Dark	25.00	11.50	3.10	☐	91	Don Kolloway	15.00	6.75	1.90
☐	35	Granny Hamner	20.00	9.00	2.50	☐	92	Eddie Waitkus	15.00	6.75	1.90
☐	36	Cass Michaels	20.00	9.00	2.50	☐	93	Paul Richards MG	16.00	7.25	2.00
☐	37	Vic Raschi	25.00	11.50	3.10	☐	94	Luke Sewell MG	16.00	7.25	2.00
☐	38	Whitey Lockman	20.00	9.00	2.50	☐	95	Luke Easter	16.00	7.25	2.00
☐	39	Vic Wertz	20.00	9.00	2.50	☐	96	Ralph Branca	20.00	9.00	2.50
☐	40	Bubba Church	18.00	8.00	2.30	☐	97	Willard Marshall	15.00	6.75	1.90
☐	41	Chico Carrasquel	20.00	9.00	2.50	☐	98	Jimmy Dykes MG	20.00	9.00	2.50
☐	42	Johnny Wyrostek	18.00	8.00	2.30	☐	99	Clyde McCullough	15.00	6.75	1.90
☐	43	Bob Feller	125.00	57.50	15.50	☐	100	Sibby Sisti	15.00	6.75	1.90
☐	44	Roy Campanella	225.00	100.00	28.00	☐	101	Mickey Mantle	2400.	1100.	300.
☐	45	Johnny Pesky	25.00	11.50	3.10	☐	102	Peanuts Lowrey	15.00	6.75	1.90
☐	46	Carl Scheib	18.00	8.00	2.30	☐	103	Joe Haynes	15.00	6.75	1.90
☐	47	Pete Castiglione	18.00	8.00	2.30	☐	104	Hal Jeffcoat	15.00	6.75	1.90
☐	48	Vern Bickford	18.00	8.00	2.30	☐	105	Bobby Brown	25.00	11.50	3.10
☐	49	Jim Hearn	18.00	8.00	2.30	☐	106	Randy Gumpert	15.00	6.75	1.90
☐	50	Jerry Staley	18.00	8.00	2.30	☐	107	Del Rice	15.00	6.75	1.90
☐	51	Gil Coan	18.00	8.00	2.30	☐	108	George Metkovich	16.00	7.25	2.00
☐	52	Phil Rizzuto	90.00	40.00	11.50	☐	109	Tom Morgan	16.00	7.25	2.00
☐	53	Richie Ashburn	60.00	27.00	7.50	☐	110	Max Lanier	15.00	6.75	1.90
☐	54	Billy Pierce	25.00	11.50	3.10	☐	111	Hoot Evers	15.00	6.75	1.90
☐	55	Ken Raffensberger	18.00	8.00	2.30	☐	112	Smoky Burgess	17.00	7.75	2.10
☐	56	Clyde King	18.00	8.00	2.30	☐	113	Al Zarilla	15.00	6.75	1.90
☐	57	Clyde Vollmer	18.00	8.00	2.30	☐	114	Frank Hiller	15.00	6.75	1.90
☐	58	Hank Majeski	18.00	8.00	2.30	☐	115	Larry Doby	25.00	11.50	3.10
☐	59	Murry Dickson	18.00	8.00	2.30	☐	116	Duke Snider	200.00	90.00	25.00
☐	60	Sid Gordon	18.00	8.00	2.30	☐	117	Bill Wight	15.00	6.75	1.90
☐	61	Tommy Byrne	18.00	8.00	2.30	☐	118	Ray Murray	15.00	6.75	1.90
☐	62	Joe Presko	18.00	8.00	2.30	☐	119	Bill Howerton	15.00	6.75	1.90
☐	63	Irv Noren	20.00	9.00	2.50	☐	120	Chet Nichols	15.00	6.75	1.90
☐	64	Roy Smalley	18.00	8.00	2.30	☐	121	Al Corwin	15.00	6.75	1.90
☐	65	Hank Bauer	30.00	13.50	3.80	☐	122	Billy Johnson	15.00	6.75	1.90
☐	66	Sal Maglie	25.00	11.50	3.10	☐	123	Sid Hudson	15.00	6.75	1.90
☐	67	Johnny Groth	18.00	8.00	2.30	☐	124	Birdie Tebbetts	16.00	7.25	2.00
☐	68	Jim Busby	18.00	8.00	2.30	☐	125	Howie Fox	15.00	6.75	1.90
☐	69	Joe Adcock	25.00	11.50	3.10	☐	126	Phil Cavarretta	20.00	9.00	2.50
☐	70	Carl Erskine	30.00	13.50	3.80	☐	127	Dick Sisler	15.00	6.75	1.90
☐	71	Vernon Law	25.00	11.50	3.10	☐	128	Don Newcombe	30.00	13.50	3.80
☐	72	Earl Torgeson	18.00	8.00	2.30	☐	129	Gus Niarhos	15.00	6.75	1.90
☐	73	Jerry Coleman	20.00	9.00	2.50	☐	130	Allie Clark	15.00	6.75	1.90
☐	74	Wes Westrum	16.00	7.25	2.00	☐	131	Bob Swift	15.00	6.75	1.90
☐	75	George Kell	45.00	20.00	5.75	☐	132	Dave Cole	15.00	6.75	1.90
☐	76	Del Ennis	20.00	9.00	2.50	☐	133	Dick Kryhoski	15.00	6.75	1.90

☐	134	Al Brazle	15.00	6.75	1.90			
☐	135	Mickey Harris	15.00	6.75	1.90			
☐	136	Gene Hermanski	15.00	6.75	1.90			
☐	137	Stan Rojek	15.00	6.75	1.90			
☐	138	Ted Wilks	15.00	6.75	1.90			
☐	139	Jerry Priddy	15.00	6.75	1.90			
☐	140	Ray Scarborough	15.00	6.75	1.90			
☐	141	Hank Edwards	15.00	6.75	1.90			
☐	142	Early Wynn	50.00	23.00	6.25			
☐	143	Sandy Consuegra	15.00	6.75	1.90			
☐	144	Joe Hatton	15.00	6.75	1.90			
☐	145	Johnny Mize	60.00	27.00	7.50			
☐	146	Leo Durocher MG	45.00	20.00	5.75			
☐	147	Marlin Stuart	15.00	6.75	1.90			
☐	148	Ken Heintzelman	15.00	6.75	1.90			
☐	149	Howie Judson	15.00	6.75	1.90			
☐	150	Herman Wehmeier	15.00	6.75	1.90			
☐	151	Al Rosen	25.00	11.50	3.10			
☐	152	Billy Cox	18.00	8.00	2.30			
☐	153	Fred Hatfield	15.00	6.75	1.90			
☐	154	Ferris Fain	16.00	7.25	2.00			
☐	155	Billy Meyer MG	15.00	6.75	1.90			
☐	156	Warren Spahn	110.00	50.00	14.00			
☐	157	Jim Delsing	15.00	6.75	1.90			
☐	158	Bucky Harris MG	30.00	13.50	3.80			
☐	159	Dutch Leonard	15.00	6.75	1.90			
☐	160	Eddie Stanky	17.00	7.75	2.10			
☐	161	Jackie Jensen	35.00	16.00	4.40			
☐	162	Monte Irvin	50.00	23.00	6.25			
☐	163	Johnny Lipon	15.00	6.75	1.90			
☐	164	Connie Ryan	15.00	6.75	1.90			
☐	165	Saul Rogovin	15.00	6.75	1.90			
☐	166	Bobby Adams	15.00	6.75	1.90			
☐	167	Bobby Avila	16.00	7.25	2.00			
☐	168	Preacher Roe	28.00	12.50	3.50			
☐	169	Walt Dropo	16.00	7.25	2.00			
☐	170	Joe Astroth	15.00	6.75	1.90			
☐	171	Mel Queen	15.00	6.75	1.90			
☐	172	Ebba St.Claire	15.00	6.75	1.90			
☐	173	Gene Bearden	15.00	6.75	1.90			
☐	174	Mickey Grasso	15.00	6.75	1.90			
☐	175	Randy Jackson	15.00	6.75	1.90			
☐	176	Harry Brecheen	16.00	7.25	2.00			
☐	177	Gene Woodling	20.00	9.00	2.50			
☐	178	Dave Williams	20.00	9.00	2.50			
☐	179	Pete Suder	15.00	6.75	1.90			
☐	180	Ed Fitzgerald	15.00	6.75	1.90			
☐	181	Joe Collins	18.00	8.00	2.30			
☐	182	Dave Koslo	14.00	6.25	1.75			
☐	183	Pat Mullin	14.00	6.25	1.75			
☐	184	Curt Simmons	16.00	7.25	2.00			
☐	185	Eddie Stewart	14.00	6.25	1.75			
☐	186	Frank Smith	14.00	6.25	1.75			
☐	187	Jim Hegan	15.00	6.75	1.90			
☐	188	Charlie Dressen MG	16.00	7.25	2.00			
☐	189	Jim Piersall	20.00	9.00	2.50			
☐	190	Dick Fowler	14.00	6.25	1.75			
☐	191	Bob Friend	25.00	11.50	3.10
☐	192	John Cusick	14.00	6.25	1.75
☐	193	Bobby Young	14.00	6.25	1.75
☐	194	Bob Porterfield	14.00	6.25	1.75
☐	195	Frank Baumholtz	14.00	6.25	1.75
☐	196	Stan Musial	525.00	240.00	65.00
☐	197	Charlie Silvera	18.00	8.00	2.30
☐	198	Chuck Diering	14.00	6.25	1.75
☐	199	Ted Gray	14.00	6.25	1.75
☐	200	Ken Silvestri	14.00	6.25	1.75
☐	201	Ray Coleman	14.00	6.25	1.75
☐	202	Harry Perkowski	14.00	6.25	1.75
☐	203	Steve Gromek	14.00	6.25	1.75
☐	204	Andy Pafko	15.00	6.75	1.90
☐	205	Walt Masterson	14.00	6.25	1.75
☐	206	Elmer Valo	14.00	6.25	1.75
☐	207	George Strickland	14.00	6.25	1.75
☐	208	Walker Cooper	14.00	6.25	1.75
☐	209	Dick Littlefield	14.00	6.25	1.75
☐	210	Archie Wilson	14.00	6.25	1.75
☐	211	Paul Minner	14.00	6.25	1.75
☐	212	Solly Hemus	14.00	6.25	1.75
☐	213	Monte Kennedy	14.00	6.25	1.75
☐	214	Ray Boone	15.00	6.75	1.90
☐	215	Sheldon Jones	14.00	6.25	1.75
☐	216	Matt Batts	14.00	6.25	1.75
☐	217	Casey Stengel MG	175.00	80.00	22.00
☐	218	Willie Mays	1300.00	575.00	160.00
☐	219	Neil Berry	33.00	15.00	4.10
☐	220	Russ Meyer	33.00	15.00	4.10
☐	221	Lou Kretlow	33.00	15.00	4.10
☐	222	Dixie Howell	33.00	15.00	4.10
☐	223	Harry Simpson	33.00	15.00	4.10
☐	224	Johnny Schmitz	33.00	15.00	4.10
☐	225	Del Wilber	33.00	15.00	4.10
☐	226	Alex Kellner	33.00	15.00	4.10
☐	227	Clyde Sukeforth CO	33.00	15.00	4.10
☐	228	Bob Chipman	33.00	15.00	4.10
☐	229	Hank Arft	33.00	15.00	4.10
☐	230	Frank Shea	33.00	15.00	4.10
☐	231	Dee Fondy	33.00	15.00	4.10
☐	232	Enos Slaughter	100.00	45.00	12.50
☐	233	Bob Kuzava	33.00	15.00	4.10
☐	234	Fred Fitzsimmons CO	35.00	16.00	4.40
☐	235	Steve Souchock	33.00	15.00	4.10
☐	236	Tommy Brown	33.00	15.00	4.10
☐	237	Sherm Lollar	35.00	16.00	4.40
☐	238	Roy McMillan	35.00	16.00	4.40
☐	239	Dale Mitchell	35.00	16.00	4.40
☐	240	Billy Loes	40.00	18.00	5.00
☐	241	Mel Parnell	35.00	16.00	4.40
☐	242	Everett Kell	33.00	15.00	4.10
☐	243	Red Munger	33.00	15.00	4.10
☐	244	Lew Burdette	65.00	29.00	8.25
☐	245	George Schmees	33.00	15.00	4.10
☐	246	Jerry Snyder	33.00	15.00	4.10
☐	247	Johnny Pramesa	33.00	15.00	4.10

☐ 248	Bill Werle	33.00	15.00	4.10
☐ 249	Hank Thompson	35.00	16.00	4.40
☐ 250	Ike Delock	33.00	15.00	4.10
☐ 251	Jack Lohrke	33.00	15.00	4.10
☐ 252	Frank Crosetti CO	165.00	42.50	13.00

1953 Bowman Color

The cards in this 160-card set measure approximately 2 1/2" by 3 3/4". The 1953 Bowman Color set, considered by many to be the best looking set of the modern era, contains Kodachrome photographs with no names or facsimile autographs on the face. The backs contain a blank stat line for recording the player's 1953 statistics. Numbers 113 to 160 are somewhat more difficult to obtain, with numbers 113 to 128 being the most difficult. There are two cards of Al Corwin (126 and 149). There are no key Rookie Cards in this set.

	NRMT	VG-E	GOOD
COMPLETE SET (160)	11000.	5000.	1400.
COMMON PLAYER (1-96)	30.00	13.50	3.80
COMMON PLAYER (97-112)	35.00	16.00	4.40
COMMON PLAYER (113-128)	55.00	25.00	7.00
COMMON PLAYER (129-160)	42.00	19.00	5.25

☐ 1	Dave Williams	90.00	18.00	5.50
☐ 2	Vic Wertz	33.00	15.00	4.10
☐ 3	Sam Jethroe	33.00	15.00	4.10
☐ 4	Art Houtteman	30.00	13.50	3.80
☐ 5	Sid Gordon	30.00	13.50	3.80
☐ 6	Joe Ginsberg	30.00	13.50	3.80
☐ 7	Harry Chiti	30.00	13.50	3.80
☐ 8	Al Rosen	50.00	23.00	6.25
☐ 9	Phil Rizzuto	115.00	52.50	14.50

☐ 10	Richie Ashburn	95.00	42.50	12.00
☐ 11	Bobby Shantz	40.00	18.00	5.00
☐ 12	Carl Erskine	40.00	18.00	5.00
☐ 13	Gus Zernial	33.00	15.00	4.10
☐ 14	Billy Loes	35.00	16.00	4.40
☐ 15	Jim Busby	30.00	13.50	3.80
☐ 16	Bob Friend	33.00	15.00	4.10
☐ 17	Gerry Staley	30.00	13.50	3.80
☐ 18	Nellie Fox	70.00	32.00	8.75
☐ 19	Alvin Dark	40.00	18.00	5.00
☐ 20	Don Lenhardt	30.00	13.50	3.80
☐ 21	Joe Garagiola	80.00	36.00	10.00
☐ 22	Bob Porterfield	30.00	13.50	3.80
☐ 23	Herman Wehmeier	30.00	13.50	3.80
☐ 24	Jackie Jensen	40.00	18.00	5.00
☐ 25	Hoot Evers	30.00	13.50	3.80
☐ 26	Roy McMillan	33.00	15.00	4.10
☐ 27	Vic Raschi	40.00	18.00	5.00
☐ 28	Smoky Burgess	33.00	15.00	4.10
☐ 29	Bobby Avila	33.00	15.00	4.10
☐ 30	Phil Cavarretta	33.00	15.00	4.10
☐ 31	Jimmy Dykes MG	33.00	15.00	4.10
☐ 32	Stan Musial	550.00	250.00	70.00
☐ 33	Pee Wee Reese HOR	480.00	220.00	60.00
☐ 34	Gil Coan	30.00	13.50	3.80
☐ 35	Maurice McDermott	30.00	13.50	3.80
☐ 36	Minnie Minoso	60.00	27.00	7.50
☐ 37	Jim Wilson	30.00	13.50	3.80
☐ 38	Harry Byrd	30.00	13.50	3.80
☐ 39	Paul Richards MG	33.00	15.00	4.10
☐ 40	Larry Doby	45.00	20.00	5.75
☐ 41	Sammy White	30.00	13.50	3.80
☐ 42	Tommy Brown	30.00	13.50	3.80
☐ 43	Mike Garcia	33.00	15.00	4.10
☐ 44	Berra/Bauer/Mantle	475.00	210.00	60.00
☐ 45	Walt Dropo	33.00	15.00	4.10
☐ 46	Roy Campanella	265.00	120.00	33.00
☐ 47	Ned Garver	30.00	13.50	3.80
☐ 48	Hank Sauer	33.00	15.00	4.10
☐ 49	Eddie Stanky MG	33.00	15.00	4.10
☐ 50	Lou Kretlow	30.00	13.50	3.80
☐ 51	Monte Irvin	60.00	27.00	7.50
☐ 52	Marty Marion MG	40.00	18.00	5.00
☐ 53	Del Rice	30.00	13.50	3.80
☐ 54	Chico Carrasquel	30.00	13.50	3.80
☐ 55	Leo Durocher MG	60.00	27.00	7.50
☐ 56	Bob Cain	30.00	13.50	3.80
☐ 57	Lou Boudreau MG	50.00	23.00	6.25
☐ 58	Willard Marshall	30.00	13.50	3.80
☐ 59	Mickey Mantle	2500.	1150.	325.00
☐ 60	Granny Hamner	30.00	13.50	3.80
☐ 61	George Kell	65.00	29.00	8.25
☐ 62	Ted Kluszewski	60.00	27.00	7.50
☐ 63	Gil McDougald	60.00	27.00	7.50
☐ 64	Curt Simmons	33.00	15.00	4.10
☐ 65	Robin Roberts	80.00	36.00	10.00
☐ 66	Mel Parnell	33.00	15.00	4.10

☐ 67 Mel Clark	30.00	13.50	3.80
☐ 68 Allie Reynolds	50.00	23.00	6.25
☐ 69 Charlie Grimm MG	33.00	15.00	4.10
☐ 70 Clint Courtney	30.00	13.50	3.80
☐ 71 Paul Minner	30.00	13.50	3.80
☐ 72 Ted Gray	30.00	13.50	3.80
☐ 73 Billy Pierce	40.00	18.00	5.00
☐ 74 Don Mueller	33.00	15.00	4.10
☐ 75 Saul Rogovin	30.00	13.50	3.80
☐ 76 Jim Hearn	30.00	13.50	3.80
☐ 77 Mickey Grasso	30.00	13.50	3.80
☐ 78 Carl Furillo	50.00	23.00	6.25
☐ 79 Ray Boone	33.00	15.00	4.10
☐ 80 Ralph Kiner	85.00	38.00	10.50
☐ 81 Enos Slaughter	85.00	38.00	10.50
☐ 82 Joe Astroth	30.00	13.50	3.80
☐ 83 Jack Daniels	33.00	15.00	4.10
☐ 84 Hank Bauer	50.00	23.00	6.25
☐ 85 Solly Hemus	30.00	13.50	3.80
☐ 86 Harry Simpson	30.00	13.50	3.80
☐ 87 Harry Perkowski	30.00	13.50	3.80
☐ 88 Joe Dobson	30.00	13.50	3.80
☐ 89 Sandy Consuegra	30.00	13.50	3.80
☐ 90 Joe Nuxhall	40.00	18.00	5.00
☐ 91 Steve Souchock	30.00	13.50	3.80
☐ 92 Gil Hodges	125.00	57.50	15.50
☐ 93 Phil Rizzuto and	240.00	110.00	30.00
Billy Martin			
☐ 94 Bob Addis	30.00	13.50	3.80
☐ 95 Wally Moses CO	33.00	15.00	4.10
☐ 96 Sal Maglie	45.00	20.00	5.75
☐ 97 Eddie Mathews	200.00	90.00	25.00
☐ 98 Hector Rodriguez	35.00	16.00	4.40
☐ 99 Warren Spahn	200.00	90.00	25.00
☐ 100 Bill Wight	35.00	16.00	4.40
☐ 101 Red Schoendienst	90.00	40.00	11.50
☐ 102 Jim Hegan	38.00	17.00	4.70
☐ 103 Del Ennis	40.00	18.00	5.00
☐ 104 Luke Easter	38.00	17.00	4.70
☐ 105 Eddie Joost	35.00	16.00	4.40
☐ 106 Ken Raffensberger	35.00	16.00	4.40
☐ 107 Alex Kellner	35.00	16.00	4.40
☐ 108 Bobby Adams	35.00	16.00	4.40
☐ 109 Ken Wood	35.00	16.00	4.40
☐ 110 Bob Rush	35.00	16.00	4.40
☐ 111 Jim Dyck	35.00	16.00	4.40
☐ 112 Toby Atwell	35.00	16.00	4.40
☐ 113 Karl Drews	55.00	25.00	7.00
☐ 114 Bob Feller	325.00	145.00	40.00
☐ 115 Cloyd Boyer	55.00	25.00	7.00
☐ 116 Eddie Yost	60.00	27.00	7.50
☐ 117 Duke Snider	600.00	275.00	75.00
☐ 118 Billy Martin	325.00	145.00	40.00
☐ 119 Dale Mitchell	60.00	27.00	7.50
☐ 120 Marlin Stuart	55.00	25.00	7.00
☐ 121 Yogi Berra	600.00	275.00	75.00
☐ 122 Bill Serena	55.00	25.00	7.00

☐ 123 Johnny Lipon	55.00	25.00	7.00
☐ 124 Charlie Dressen MG	65.00	29.00	8.25
☐ 125 Fred Hatfield	55.00	25.00	7.00
☐ 126 Al Corwin	55.00	25.00	7.00
☐ 127 Dick Kryhoski	55.00	25.00	7.00
☐ 128 Whitey Lockman	60.00	27.00	7.50
☐ 129 Russ Meyer	42.00	19.00	5.25
☐ 130 Cass Michaels	42.00	19.00	5.25
☐ 131 Connie Ryan	42.00	19.00	5.25
☐ 132 Fred Hutchinson	45.00	20.00	5.75
☐ 133 Willie Jones	42.00	19.00	5.25
☐ 134 Johnny Pesky	45.00	20.00	5.75
☐ 135 Bobby Morgan	42.00	19.00	5.25
☐ 136 Jim Brideweser	42.00	19.00	5.25
☐ 137 Sam Dente	42.00	19.00	5.25
☐ 138 Bubba Church	42.00	19.00	5.25
☐ 139 Pete Runnels	45.00	20.00	5.75
☐ 140 Al Brazle	42.00	19.00	5.25
☐ 141 Frank Shea	42.00	19.00	5.25
☐ 142 Larry Miggins	42.00	19.00	5.25
☐ 143 Al Lopez MG	65.00	29.00	8.25
☐ 144 Warren Hacker	42.00	19.00	5.25
☐ 145 George Shuba	45.00	20.00	5.75
☐ 146 Early Wynn	125.00	57.50	15.50
☐ 147 Clem Koshorek	42.00	19.00	5.25
☐ 148 Billy Goodman	45.00	20.00	5.75
☐ 149 Al Corwin	42.00	19.00	5.25
☐ 150 Carl Scheib	42.00	19.00	5.25
☐ 151 Joe Adcock	50.00	23.00	6.25
☐ 152 Clyde Vollmer	42.00	19.00	5.25
☐ 153 Whitey Ford	500.00	230.00	65.00
☐ 154 Turk Lown	42.00	19.00	5.25
☐ 155 Allie Clark	42.00	19.00	5.25
☐ 156 Max Surkont	42.00	19.00	5.25
☐ 157 Sherm Lollar	45.00	20.00	5.75
☐ 158 Howard Fox	42.00	19.00	5.25
☐ 159 Mickey Vernon UER	50.00	23.00	6.25
(Photo actually			
Floyd Baker)			
☐ 160 Cal Abrams	85.00	26.00	8.50

1953 Bowman B/W

The cards in this 64-card set measure approximately 2 1/2" by 3 3/4". Some collectors believe that the high cost of producing the 1953 color series forced Bowman to issue this set in black and white, since the two sets are identical in design except for the element of color. This set was also produced in fewer numbers than its color counterpart, and is popular among

collectors for the challenge involved in completing it. There are no key Rookie Cards in this set. The backs contain a blank stat line for recording the player's 1953 statistics.

	NRMT	VG-E	GOOD
COMPLETE SET (64)	2500.00	1150.00	325.00
COMMON PLAYER (1-64)	35.00	16.00	4.40

		NRMT	VG-E	GOOD
☐	1 Gus Bell	125.00	25.00	10.00
☐	2 Willard Nixon	35.00	16.00	4.40
☐	3 Bill Rigney	35.00	16.00	4.40
☐	4 Pat Mullin	35.00	16.00	4.40
☐	5 Dee Fondy	35.00	16.00	4.40
☐	6 Ray Murray	35.00	16.00	4.40
☐	7 Andy Seminick	35.00	16.00	4.40
☐	8 Pete Suder	35.00	16.00	4.40
☐	9 Walt Masterson	35.00	16.00	4.40
☐	10 Dick Sisler	38.00	17.00	4.70
☐	11 Dick Gernert	35.00	16.00	4.40
☐	12 Randy Jackson	35.00	16.00	4.40
☐	13 Joe Tipton	35.00	16.00	4.40
☐	14 Bill Nicholson	38.00	17.00	4.70
☐	15 Johnny Mize	125.00	57.50	15.50
☐	16 Stu Miller	40.00	18.00	5.00
☐	17 Virgil Trucks	38.00	17.00	4.70
☐	18 Billy Hoeft	40.00	18.00	5.00
☐	19 Paul LaPalme	35.00	16.00	4.40
☐	20 Eddie Robinson	35.00	16.00	4.40
☐	21 Clarence Podbielan	35.00	16.00	4.40
☐	22 Matt Batts	35.00	16.00	4.40
☐	23 Wilmer Mizell	40.00	18.00	5.00
☐	24 Del Wilber	35.00	16.00	4.40
☐	25 Johnny Sain	55.00	25.00	7.00
☐	26 Preacher Roe	55.00	25.00	7.00
☐	27 Bob Lemon	125.00	57.50	15.50
☐	28 Hoyt Wilhelm	125.00	57.50	15.50
☐	29 Sid Hudson	35.00	16.00	4.40
☐	30 Walker Cooper	35.00	16.00	4.40
☐	31 Gene Woodling	50.00	23.00	6.25
☐	32 Rocky Bridges	35.00	16.00	4.40
☐	33 Bob Kuzava	35.00	16.00	4.40
☐	34 Ebba St.Claire	35.00	16.00	4.40
☐	35 Johnny Wyrostek	35.00	16.00	4.40
☐	36 Jim Piersall	50.00	23.00	6.25
☐	37 Hal Jeffcoat	35.00	16.00	4.40
☐	38 Dave Cole	35.00	16.00	4.40
☐	39 Casey Stengel MG	325.00	145.00	40.00
☐	40 Larry Jansen	38.00	17.00	4.70
☐	41 Bob Ramazzotti	35.00	16.00	4.40
☐	42 Howie Judson	35.00	16.00	4.40
☐	43 Hal Bevan	35.00	16.00	4.40
☐	44 Jim Delsing	35.00	16.00	4.40
☐	45 Irv Noren	38.00	17.00	4.70
☐	46 Bucky Harris MG	55.00	25.00	7.00
☐	47 Jack Lohrke	35.00	16.00	4.40
☐	48 Steve Ridzik	35.00	16.00	4.40
☐	49 Floyd Baker	35.00	16.00	4.40
☐	50 Dutch Leonard	35.00	16.00	4.40
☐	51 Lou Burdette	50.00	23.00	6.25
☐	52 Ralph Branca	40.00	18.00	5.00
☐	53 Morrie Martin	35.00	16.00	4.40
☐	54 Bill Miller	35.00	16.00	4.40
☐	55 Don Johnson	35.00	16.00	4.40
☐	56 Roy Smalley	35.00	16.00	4.40
☐	57 Andy Pafko	38.00	17.00	4.70
☐	58 Jim Konstanty	40.00	18.00	5.00
☐	59 Duane Pillette	35.00	16.00	4.40
☐	60 Billy Cox	40.00	18.00	5.00
☐	61 Tom Gorman	35.00	16.00	4.40
☐	62 Keith Thomas	35.00	16.00	4.40
☐	63 Steve Gromek	35.00	16.00	4.40
☐	64 Andy Hansen	45.00	20.00	5.75

1954 Bowman

The cards in this 224-card set measure approximately 2 1/2" by 3 3/4". A contractual problem apparently resulted in the *deletion of the number 66 Ted Williams card from this Bowman set, thereby creating a scarcity that is highly valued among collectors. The set price below does NOT include number 66 Williams but does include number 66 Jim Piersall, the apparent replacement for Williams in spite of the fact that Piersall was already number 210 to appear later in the set. Many errors in players' statistics exist (and some were corrected) while a few players' names were printed on the front, instead of appearing as a facsimile autograph. The notable Rookie Cards in this set are Harvey Kuenn and Don Larsen.*

	NRMT	VG-E	GOOD
COMPLETE SET (224)	4500.00	2000.00	575.00
COMMON PLAYER (1-128)	10.00	4.50	1.25
COMMON PLAYER (129-224)	15.00	6.75	1.90

		NRMT	VG-E	GOOD
☐ 1	Phil Rizzuto	135.00	40.00	13.50
☐ 2	Jackie Jensen	15.00	6.75	1.90
☐ 3	Marion Fricano	10.00	4.50	1.25
☐ 4	Bob Hooper	10.00	4.50	1.25
☐ 5	Billy Hunter	10.00	4.50	1.25
☐ 6	Nellie Fox	25.00	11.50	3.10
☐ 7	Walt Dropo	11.00	4.90	1.40
☐ 8	Jim Busby	10.00	4.50	1.25
☐ 9	Dave Williams	10.00	4.50	1.25
☐ 10	Carl Erskine	15.00	6.75	1.90
☐ 11	Sid Gordon	10.00	4.50	1.25
☐ 12	Roy McMillan	11.00	4.90	1.40
☐ 13	Paul Minner	10.00	4.50	1.25
☐ 14	Jerry Staley	10.00	4.50	1.25
☐ 15	Richie Ashburn	35.00	16.00	4.40
☐ 16	Jim Wilson	10.00	4.50	1.25
☐ 17	Tom Gorman	10.00	4.50	1.25
☐ 18	Hoot Evers	10.00	4.50	1.25
☐ 19	Bobby Shantz	12.50	5.75	1.55
☐ 20	Art Houtteman	10.00	4.50	1.25
☐ 21	Vic Wertz	11.00	4.90	1.40
☐ 22	Sam Mele	10.00	4.50	1.25
☐ 23	Harvey Kuenn	33.00	15.00	4.10
☐ 24	Bob Porterfield	10.00	4.50	1.25
☐ 25	Wes Westrum	11.00	4.90	1.40
☐ 26	Billy Cox	12.50	5.75	1.55
☐ 27	Dick Cole	10.00	4.50	1.25
☐ 28	Jim Greengrass	10.00	4.50	1.25
☐ 29	Johnny Klippstein	10.00	4.50	1.25
☐ 30	Del Rice	10.00	4.50	1.25
☐ 31	Smoky Burgess	11.00	4.90	1.40
☐ 32	Del Crandall	11.00	4.90	1.40
☐ 33A	Vic Raschi	20.00	9.00	2.50
	(No mention of trade on back)			
☐ 33B	Vic Raschi	35.00	16.00	4.40
	(Traded to St.Louis)			
☐ 34	Sammy White	10.00	4.50	1.25
☐ 35	Eddie Joost	10.00	4.50	1.25
☐ 36	George Strickland	10.00	4.50	1.25
☐ 37	Dick Kokos	10.00	4.50	1.25
☐ 38	Minnie Minoso	20.00	9.00	2.50
☐ 39	Ned Garver	10.00	4.50	1.25
☐ 40	Gil Coan	10.00	4.50	1.25
☐ 41	Alvin Dark	13.00	5.75	1.65
☐ 42	Billy Loes	11.00	4.90	1.40
☐ 43	Bob Friend	11.00	4.90	1.40
☐ 44	Harry Perkowski	10.00	4.50	1.25
☐ 45	Ralph Kiner	45.00	20.00	5.75
☐ 46	Rip Repulski	10.00	4.50	1.25
☐ 47	Granny Hamner	10.00	4.50	1.25
☐ 48	Jack Dittmer	10.00	4.50	1.25
☐ 49	Harry Byrd	10.00	4.50	1.25
☐ 50	George Kell	30.00	13.50	3.80
☐ 51	Alex Kellner	10.00	4.50	1.25
☐ 52	Joe Ginsberg	10.00	4.50	1.25
☐ 53	Don Lenhardt	10.00	4.50	1.25
☐ 54	Chico Carrasquel	10.00	4.50	1.25
☐ 55	Jim Delsing	10.00	4.50	1.25
☐ 56	Maurice McDermott	10.00	4.50	1.25
☐ 57	Hoyt Wilhelm	30.00	13.50	3.80
☐ 58	Pee Wee Reese	75.00	34.00	9.50
☐ 59	Bob Schultz	10.00	4.50	1.25
☐ 60	Fred Baczewski	10.00	4.50	1.25
☐ 61	Eddie Miksis	10.00	4.50	1.25
☐ 62	Enos Slaughter	45.00	20.00	5.75
☐ 63	Earl Torgeson	10.00	4.50	1.25
☐ 64	Eddie Mathews	65.00	29.00	8.25
☐ 65	Mickey Mantle	1000.	450.00	125.00
☐ 66A	Ted Williams	5000.	1500.	500.00
☐ 66B	Jim Piersall	100.00	45.00	12.50
☐ 67	Carl Scheib	10.00	4.50	1.25
☐ 68	Bobby Avila	11.00	4.90	1.40
☐ 69	Clint Courtney	10.00	4.50	1.25
☐ 70	Willard Marshall	10.00	4.50	1.25
☐ 71	Ted Gray	10.00	4.50	1.25
☐ 72	Eddie Yost	11.00	4.90	1.40
☐ 73	Don Mueller	11.00	4.90	1.40
☐ 74	Jim Gilliam	22.00	10.00	2.80
☐ 75	Max Surkont	10.00	4.50	1.25
☐ 76	Joe Nuxhall	11.00	4.90	1.40
☐ 77	Bob Rush	10.00	4.50	1.25
☐ 78	Sal Yvars	10.00	4.50	1.25
☐ 79	Curt Simmons	11.00	4.90	1.40
☐ 80	Johnny Logan	15.00	6.75	1.90
☐ 81	Jerry Coleman	11.00	4.90	1.40
☐ 82	Billy Goodman	11.00	4.90	1.40
☐ 83	Ray Murray	10.00	4.50	1.25
☐ 84	Larry Doby	15.00	6.75	1.90
☐ 85	Jim Dyck	10.00	4.50	1.25
☐ 86	Harry Dorish	10.00	4.50	1.25
☐ 87	Don Lund	10.00	4.50	1.25
☐ 88	Tom Umphlett	10.00	4.50	1.25

☐	89 Willie Mays	425.00	190.00	52.50
☐	90 Roy Campanella	150.00	70.00	19.00
☐	91 Cal Abrams	10.00	4.50	1.25
☐	92 Ken Raffensberger	10.00	4.50	1.25
☐	93 Bill Serena	10.00	4.50	1.25
☐	94 Solly Hemus	10.00	4.50	1.25
☐	95 Robin Roberts	40.00	18.00	5.00
☐	96 Joe Adcock	11.00	4.90	1.40
☐	97 Gil McDougald	20.00	9.00	2.50
☐	98 Ellis Kinder	10.00	4.50	1.25
☐	99 Pete Suder	10.00	4.50	1.25
☐	100 Mike Garcia	11.00	4.90	1.40
☐	101 Don Larsen	45.00	20.00	5.75
☐	102 Billy Pierce	12.50	5.75	1.55
☐	103 Steve Souchock	10.00	4.50	1.25
☐	104 Frank Shea	10.00	4.50	1.25
☐	105 Sal Maglie	15.00	6.75	1.90
☐	106 Clem Labine	12.50	5.75	1.55
☐	107 Paul LaPalme	10.00	4.50	1.25
☐	108 Bobby Adams	10.00	4.50	1.25
☐	109 Roy Smalley	10.00	4.50	1.25
☐	110 Red Schoendienst	40.00	18.00	5.00
☐	111 Murry Dickson	10.00	4.50	1.25
☐	112 Andy Pafko	11.00	4.90	1.40
☐	113 Allie Reynolds	20.00	9.00	2.50
☐	114 Willard Nixon	10.00	4.50	1.25
☐	115 Don Bollweg	10.00	4.50	1.25
☐	116 Luke Easter	11.00	4.90	1.40
☐	117 Dick Kryhoski	10.00	4.50	1.25
☐	118 Bob Boyd	10.00	4.50	1.25
☐	119 Fred Hatfield	10.00	4.50	1.25
☐	120 Mel Hoderlein	10.00	4.50	1.25
☐	121 Ray Katt	10.00	4.50	1.25
☐	122 Carl Furillo	20.00	9.00	2.50
☐	123 Toby Atwell	10.00	4.50	1.25
☐	124 Gus Bell	11.00	4.90	1.40
☐	125 Warren Hacker	10.00	4.50	1.25
☐	126 Cliff Chambers	10.00	4.50	1.25
☐	127 Del Ennis	12.50	5.75	1.55
☐	128 Ebba St.Claire	10.00	4.50	1.25
☐	129 Hank Bauer	22.00	10.00	2.80
☐	130 Milt Bolling	15.00	6.75	1.90
☐	131 Joe Astroth	15.00	6.75	1.90
☐	132 Bob Feller	95.00	42.50	12.00
☐	133 Duane Pillette	15.00	6.75	1.90
☐	134 Luis Aloma	15.00	6.75	1.90
☐	135 Johnny Pesky	18.00	8.00	2.30
☐	136 Clyde Vollmer	15.00	6.75	1.90
☐	137 Al Corwin	15.00	6.75	1.90
☐	138 Gil Hodges	70.00	32.00	8.75
☐	139 Preston Ward	15.00	6.75	1.90
☐	140 Saul Rogovin	15.00	6.75	1.90
☐	141 Joe Garagiola	50.00	23.00	6.25
☐	142 Al Brazle	15.00	6.75	1.90
☐	143 Willie Jones	15.00	6.75	1.90
☐	144 Ernie Johnson	20.00	9.00	2.50
☐	145 Billy Martin	70.00	32.00	8.75
☐	146 Dick Gernert	15.00	6.75	1.90
☑	147 Joe DeMaestri	15.00	6.75	1.90
☐	148 Dale Mitchell	17.00	7.75	2.10
☐	149 Bob Young	15.00	6.75	1.90
☐	150 Cass Michaels	15.00	6.75	1.90
☐	151 Pat Mullin	15.00	6.75	1.90
☐	152 Mickey Vernon	17.00	7.75	2.10
☐	153 Whitey Lockman	17.00	7.75	2.10
☐	154 Don Newcombe	25.00	11.50	3.10
☐	155 Frank Thomas	20.00	9.00	2.50
☐	156 Rocky Bridges	15.00	6.75	1.90
☐	157 Turk Lown	15.00	6.75	1.90
☐	158 Stu Miller	17.00	7.75	2.10
☐	159 Johnny Lindell	15.00	6.75	1.90
☐	160 Danny O'Connell	15.00	6.75	1.90
☐	161 Yogi Berra	175.00	80.00	22.00
☐	162 Ted Lepcio	15.00	6.75	1.90
☐	163A Dave Philley	20.00	9.00	2.50
	(No mention of			
	trade on back)			
☐	163B Dave Philley	30.00	13.50	3.80
	(Traded to			
	Cleveland)			
☐	164 Early Wynn	50.00	23.00	6.25
☐	165 Johnny Groth	15.00	6.75	1.90
☐	166 Sandy Consuegra	15.00	6.75	1.90
☐	167 Billy Hoeft	15.00	6.75	1.90
☐	168 Ed Fitzgerald	15.00	6.75	1.90
☐	169 Larry Jansen	17.00	7.75	2.10
☐	170 Duke Snider	175.00	80.00	22.00
☐	171 Carlos Bernier	15.00	6.75	1.90
☐	172 Andy Seminick	15.00	6.75	1.90
☐	173 Dee Fondy	15.00	6.75	1.90
☐	174 Pete Castiglione	15.00	6.75	1.90
☐	175 Mel Clark	15.00	6.75	1.90
☐	176 Vern Bickford	15.00	6.75	1.90
☐	177 Whitey Ford	110.00	50.00	14.00
☐	178 Del Wilber	15.00	6.75	1.90
☐	179 Morrie Martin	15.00	6.75	1.90
☐	180 Joe Tipton	15.00	6.75	1.90
☐	181 Les Moss	15.00	6.75	1.90
☐	182 Sherm Lollar	17.00	7.75	2.10
☐	183 Matt Batts	15.00	6.75	1.90
☐	184 Mickey Grasso	15.00	6.75	1.90
☐	185 Daryl Spencer	15.00	6.75	1.90
☐	186 Russ Meyer	15.00	6.75	1.90
☐	187 Vernon Law	17.00	7.75	2.10
☐	188 Frank Smith	15.00	6.75	1.90
☐	189 Randy Jackson	15.00	6.75	1.90
☐	190 Joe Presko	15.00	6.75	1.90
☐	191 Karl Drews	15.00	6.75	1.90
☐	192 Lou Burdette	20.00	9.00	2.50
☐	193 Eddie Robinson	15.00	6.75	1.90
☐	194 Sid Hudson	15.00	6.75	1.90
☐	195 Bob Cain	15.00	6.75	1.90
☐	196 Bob Lemon	40.00	18.00	5.00
☐	197 Lou Kretlow	15.00	6.75	1.90

☐	198	Virgil Trucks	17.00	7.75	2.10
☐	199	Steve Gromek	15.00	6.75	1.90
☐	200	Conrado Marrero	15.00	6.75	1.90
☐	201	Bobby Thomson	20.00	9.00	2.50
☐	202	George Shuba	17.00	7.75	2.10
☐	203	Vic Janowicz	20.00	9.00	2.50
☐	204	Jack Collum	15.00	6.75	1.90
☐	205	Hal Jeffcoat	15.00	6.75	1.90
☐	206	Steve Bilko	15.00	6.75	1.90
☐	207	Stan Lopata	15.00	6.75	1.90
☐	208	Johnny Antonelli	20.00	9.00	2.50
☐	209	Gene Woodling	20.00	9.00	2.50
☐	210	Jim Piersall	20.00	9.00	2.50
☐	211	Al Robertson	15.00	6.75	1.90
☐	212	Owen Friend	15.00	6.75	1.90
☐	213	Dick Littlefield	15.00	6.75	1.90
☐	214	Ferris Fain	17.00	7.75	2.10
☐	215	Johnny Bucha	15.00	6.75	1.90
☐	216	Jerry Snyder	15.00	6.75	1.90
☐	217	Hank Thompson	17.00	7.75	2.10
☐	218	Preacher Roe	20.00	9.00	2.50
☐	219	Hal Rice	15.00	6.75	1.90
☐	220	Hobie Landrith	15.00	6.75	1.90
☐	221	Frank Baumholtz	15.00	6.75	1.90
☐	222	Memo Luna	15.00	6.75	1.90
☐	223	Steve Ridzik	15.00	6.75	1.90
☐	224	Bill Bruton	45.00	9.00	2.70

1955 Bowman

The cards in this 320-card set measure approximately 2 1/2" by 3 3/4". The Bowman set of 1955 is known as the "TV set" because each player photograph is cleverly shown within a television set design. The set contains umpire cards, some transposed pictures (e.g., Johnsons and Bollings), an incorrect spelling for

Harvey Kuenn, and a traded line for Palica (all of which are noted in the checklist below). Some three-card advertising strips exist, the backs of these panels contain advertising for Bowman products. Advertising panels seen include Nellie Fox/Carl Furillo/Carl Erskine, Hank Aaron/Johnny Logan/Eddie Miksis, and a panel including Early Wynn and Pee Wee Reese. The notable Rookie Cards in this set are Elston Howard and Don Zimmer.

	NRMT	VG-E	GOOD
COMPLETE SET (320)	5300.00	2400.00	650.00
COMMON PLAYER (1-96)	8.00	3.60	1.00
COMMON PLAYER (97-224)	6.50	2.90	.80
COMMON PLAYER (225-320)	15.00	6.75	1.90

☐	1	Hoyt Wilhelm	100.00	20.00	6.00
☐	2	Alvin Dark	12.00	5.50	1.50
☐	3	Joe Coleman	8.00	3.60	1.00
☐	4	Eddie Waitkus	8.00	3.60	1.00
☐	5	Jim Robertson	8.00	3.60	1.00
☐	6	Pete Suder	8.00	3.60	1.00
☐	7	Gene Baker	8.00	3.60	1.00
☐	8	Warren Hacker	8.00	3.60	1.00
☐	9	Gil McDougald	18.00	8.00	2.30
☐	10	Phil Rizzuto	55.00	25.00	7.00
☐	11	Bill Bruton	9.00	4.00	1.15
☐	12	Andy Pafko	9.00	4.00	1.15
☐	13	Clyde Vollmer	8.00	3.60	1.00
☐	14	Gus Keriazakos	8.00	3.60	1.00
☐	15	Frank Sullivan	8.00	3.60	1.00
☐	16	Jim Piersall	11.00	4.90	1.40
☐	17	Del Ennis	9.00	4.00	1.15
☐	18	Stan Lopata	8.00	3.60	1.00
☐	19	Bobby Avila	9.00	4.00	1.15
☐	20	Al Smith	9.00	4.00	1.15
☐	21	Don Hoak	10.00	4.50	1.25
☐	22	Roy Campanella	110.00	50.00	14.00
☐	23	Al Kaline	160.00	70.00	20.00
☐	24	Al Aber	8.00	3.60	1.00
☐	25	Minnie Minoso	18.00	8.00	2.30
☐	26	Virgil Trucks	9.00	4.00	1.15
☐	27	Preston Ward	8.00	3.60	1.00
☐	28	Dick Cole	8.00	3.60	1.00
☐	29	Red Schoendienst	28.00	12.50	3.50
☐	30	Bill Sarni	8.00	3.60	1.00
☐	31	Johnny Temple	12.00	5.50	1.50
☐	32	Wally Post	10.00	4.50	1.25
☐	33	Nellie Fox	22.50	10.00	2.80
☐	34	Clint Courtney	8.00	3.60	1.00
☐	35	Bill Tuttle	8.00	3.60	1.00
☐	36	Wayne Belardi	8.00	3.60	1.00
☐	37	Pee Wee Reese	75.00	34.00	9.50
☐	38	Early Wynn	28.00	12.50	3.50
☐	39	Bob Darnell	8.00	3.60	1.00

☐ 40	Vic Wertz	9.00	4.00	1.15
☐ 41	Mel Clark	8.00	3.60	1.00
☐ 42	Bob Greenwood	8.00	3.60	1.00
☐ 43	Bob Buhl	9.00	4.00	1.15
☐ 44	Danny O'Connell	8.00	3.60	1.00
☐ 45	Tom Umphlett	8.00	3.60	1.00
☐ 46	Mickey Vernon	9.00	4.00	1.15
☐ 47	Sammy White	8.00	3.60	1.00
☐ 48A	Milt Bolling ERR	10.00	4.50	1.25
	(Name on back is			
	Frank Bolling)			
☐ 48B	Milt Bolling COR	30.00	13.50	3.80
☐ 49	Jim Greengrass	8.00	3.60	1.00
☐ 50	Hobie Landrith	8.00	3.60	1.00
☐ 51	Elvin Tappe	8.00	3.60	1.00
☐ 52	Hal Rice	8.00	3.60	1.00
☐ 53	Alex Kellner	8.00	3.60	1.00
☐ 54	Don Bollweg	8.00	3.60	1.00
☐ 55	Cal Abrams	8.00	3.60	1.00
☐ 56	Billy Cox	9.00	4.00	1.15
☐ 57	Bob Friend	9.00	4.00	1.15
☐ 58	Frank Thomas	9.00	4.00	1.15
☐ 59	Whitey Ford	75.00	34.00	9.50
☐ 60	Enos Slaughter	30.00	13.50	3.80
☐ 61	Paul LaPalme	8.00	3.60	1.00
☐ 62	Royce Lint	8.00	3.60	1.00
☐ 63	Irv Noren	9.00	4.00	1.15
☐ 64	Curt Simmons	9.00	4.00	1.15
☐ 65	Don Zimmer	30.00	13.50	3.80
☐ 66	George Shuba	9.00	4.00	1.15
☐ 67	Don Larsen	20.00	9.00	2.50
☐ 68	Elston Howard	70.00	32.00	8.75
☐ 69	Billy Hunter	8.00	3.60	1.00
☐ 70	Lou Burdette	11.00	4.90	1.40
☐ 71	Dave Jolly	8.00	3.60	1.00
☐ 72	Chet Nichols	8.00	3.60	1.00
☐ 73	Eddie Yost	9.00	4.00	1.15
☐ 74	Jerry Snyder	8.00	3.60	1.00
☐ 75	Brooks Lawrence	10.00	4.50	1.25
☐ 76	Tom Poholsky	8.00	3.60	1.00
☐ 77	Jim McDonald	8.00	3.60	1.00
☐ 78	Gil Coan	8.00	3.60	1.00
☐ 79	Willie Miranda	8.00	3.60	1.00
☐ 80	Lou Limmer	8.00	3.60	1.00
☐ 81	Bobby Morgan	8.00	3.60	1.00
☐ 82	Lee Walls	8.00	3.60	1.00
☐ 83	Max Surkont	8.00	3.60	1.00
☐ 84	George Freese	8.00	3.60	1.00
☐ 85	Cass Michaels	8.00	3.60	1.00
☐ 86	Ted Gray	8.00	3.60	1.00
☐ 87	Randy Jackson	8.00	3.60	1.00
☐ 88	Steve Bilko	8.00	3.60	1.00
☐ 89	Lou Boudreau MG	25.00	11.50	3.10
☐ 90	Art Ditmar	8.00	3.60	1.00
☐ 91	Dick Marlowe	8.00	3.60	1.00
☐ 92	George Zuverink	8.00	3.60	1.00
☐ 93	Andy Seminick	8.00	3.60	1.00
☐ 94	Hank Thompson	9.00	4.00	1.15
☐ 95	Sal Maglie	12.00	5.50	1.50
☐ 96	Ray Narleski	11.00	4.90	1.40
☐ 97	Johnny Podres	18.00	8.00	2.30
☐ 98	Jim Gilliam	18.00	8.00	2.30
☐ 99	Jerry Coleman	7.50	3.40	.95
☐ 100	Tom Morgan	6.50	2.90	.80
☐ 101A	Don Johnson ERR	10.00	4.50	1.25
	(Photo actually			
	Ernie Johnson)			
☐ 101B	Don Johnson COR	30.00	13.50	3.80
☐ 102	Bobby Thomson	12.00	5.50	1.50
☐ 103	Eddie Mathews	55.00	25.00	7.00
☐ 104	Bob Porterfield	6.50	2.90	.80
☐ 105	Johnny Schmitz	6.50	2.90	.80
☐ 106	Del Rice	6.50	2.90	.80
☐ 107	Solly Hemus	6.50	2.90	.80
☐ 108	Lou Kretlow	6.50	2.90	.80
☐ 109	Vern Stephens	7.50	3.40	.95
☐ 110	Bob Miller	6.50	2.90	.80
☐ 111	Steve Ridzik	6.50	2.90	.80
☐ 112	Granny Hamner	6.50	2.90	.80
☐ 113	Bob Hall	6.50	2.90	.80
☐ 114	Vic Janowicz	10.00	4.50	1.25
☐ 115	Roger Bowman	6.50	2.90	.80
☐ 116	Sandy Consuegra	6.50	2.90	.80
☐ 117	Johnny Groth	6.50	2.90	.80
☐ 118	Bobby Adams	6.50	2.90	.80
☐ 119	Joe Astroth	6.50	2.90	.80
☐ 120	Ed Burtschy	6.50	2.90	.80
☐ 121	Rufus Crawford	6.50	2.90	.80
☐ 122	Al Corwin	6.50	2.90	.80
☐ 123	Marv Grissom	6.50	2.90	.80
☐ 124	Johnny Antonelli	7.50	3.40	.95
☐ 125	Paul Giel	7.50	3.40	.95
☐ 126	Billy Goodman	7.50	3.40	.95
☐ 127	Hank Majeski	6.50	2.90	.80
☐ 128	Mike Garcia	7.50	3.40	.95
☐ 129	Hal Naragon	6.50	2.90	.80
☐ 130	Richie Ashburn	25.00	11.50	3.10
☐ 131	Willard Marshall	6.50	2.90	.80
☐ 132A	Harvey Kueen ERR	12.50	5.75	1.55
	(Sic, Kuenn)			
☐ 132B	Harvey Kuenn COR	30.00	13.50	3.80
☐ 133	Charles King	6.50	2.90	.80
☐ 134	Bob Feller	65.00	29.00	8.25
☐ 135	Lloyd Merriman	6.50	2.90	.80
☐ 136	Rocky Bridges	6.50	2.90	.80
☐ 137	Bob Talbot	6.50	2.90	.80
☐ 138	Davey Williams	6.50	2.90	.80
☐ 139	Shantz Brothers	10.00	4.50	1.25
	(Wilmer and Bobby)			
☐ 140	Bobby Shantz	7.50	3.40	.95
☐ 141	Wes Westrum	7.50	3.40	.95
☐ 142	Rudy Regalado	6.50	2.90	.80
☐ 143	Don Newcombe	18.00	8.00	2.30
☐ 144	Art Houtteman	6.50	2.90	.80

145 Bob Nieman	6.50	2.90	.80
146 Don Liddle	6.50	2.90	.80
147 Sam Mele	6.50	2.90	.80
148 Bob Chakales	6.50	2.90	.80
149 Cloyd Boyer	6.50	2.90	.80
150 Billy Klaus	6.50	2.90	.80
151 Jim Brideweser	6.50	2.90	.80
152 Johnny Klippstein	6.50	2.90	.80
153 Eddie Robinson	6.50	2.90	.80
154 Frank Lary	12.50	5.75	1.55
155 Gerry Staley	6.50	2.90	.80
156 Jim Hughes	6.50	2.90	.80
157A Ernie Johnson ERR	10.00	4.50	1.25
(Photo actually			
Don Johnson)			
157B Ernie Johnson COR	30.00	13.50	3.80
158 Gil Hodges	40.00	18.00	5.00
159 Harry Byrd	6.50	2.90	.80
160 Bill Skowron	25.00	11.50	3.10
161 Matt Batts	6.50	2.90	.80
162 Charlie Maxwell	7.50	3.40	.95
163 Sid Gordon	6.50	2.90	.80
164 Toby Atwell	6.50	2.90	.80
165 Maurice McDermott	6.50	2.90	.80
166 Jim Busby	6.50	2.90	.80
167 Bob Grim	12.00	5.50	1.50
168 Yogi Berra	110.00	50.00	14.00
169 Carl Furillo	18.00	8.00	2.30
170 Carl Erskine	18.00	8.00	2.30
171 Robin Roberts	30.00	13.50	3.80
172 Willie Jones	6.50	2.90	.80
173 Chico Carrasquel	6.50	2.90	.80
174 Sherm Lollar	7.50	3.40	.95
175 Wilmer Shantz	6.50	2.90	.80
176 Joe DeMaestri	6.50	2.90	.80
177 Willard Nixon	6.50	2.90	.80
178 Tom Brewer	6.50	2.90	.80
179 Hank Aaron	250.00	115.00	31.00
180 Johnny Logan	7.50	3.40	.95
181 Eddie Miksis	6.50	2.90	.80
182 Bob Rush	6.50	2.90	.80
183 Ray Katt	6.50	2.90	.80
184 Willie Mays	250.00	115.00	31.00
185 Vic Raschi	10.00	4.50	1.25
186 Alex Grammas	6.50	2.90	.80
187 Fred Hatfield	6.50	2.90	.80
188 Ned Garver	6.50	2.90	.80
189 Jack Collum	6.50	2.90	.80
190 Fred Baczewski	6.50	2.90	.80
191 Bob Lemon	27.00	12.00	3.40
192 George Strickland	6.50	2.90	.80
193 Howie Judson	6.50	2.90	.80
194 Joe Nuxhall	7.50	3.40	.95
195A Erv Palica	7.50	3.40	.95
(Without trade)			
195B Erv Palica	30.00	13.50	3.80
(With trade)			

196 Russ Meyer	6.50	2.90	.80
197 Ralph Kiner	30.00	13.50	3.80
198 Dave Pope	6.50	2.90	.80
199 Vernon Law	7.50	3.40	.95
200 Dick Littlefield	6.50	2.90	.80
201 Allie Reynolds	17.00	7.75	2.10
202 Mickey Mantle	575.00	250.00	70.00
203 Steve Gromek	6.50	2.90	.80
204A Frank Bolling ERR	10.00	4.50	1.25
(Name on back is			
Milt Bolling)			
204B Frank Bolling COR	30.00	13.50	3.80
205 Rip Repulski	6.50	2.90	.80
206 Ralph Beard	6.50	2.90	.80
207 Frank Shea	6.50	2.90	.80
208 Ed Fitzgerald	6.50	2.90	.80
209 Smoky Burgess	7.50	3.40	.95
210 Earl Torgeson	6.50	2.90	.80
211 Sonny Dixon	6.50	2.90	.80
212 Jack Dittmer	6.50	2.90	.80
213 George Kell	22.00	10.00	2.80
214 Billy Pierce	10.00	4.50	1.25
215 Bob Kuzava	6.50	2.90	.80
216 Preacher Roe	12.00	5.50	1.50
217 Del Crandall	7.50	3.40	.95
218 Joe Adcock	7.50	3.40	.95
219 Whitey Lockman	7.50	3.40	.95
220 Jim Hearn	6.50	2.90	.80
221 Hector Brown	6.50	2.90	.80
222 Russ Kemmerer	6.50	2.90	.80
223 Hal Jeffcoat	6.50	2.90	.80
224 Dee Fondy	6.50	2.90	.80
225 Paul Richards MG	17.50	8.00	2.20
226 Bill McKinley UMP	25.00	11.50	3.10
227 Frank Baumholtz	15.00	6.75	1.90
228 John Phillips	15.00	6.75	1.90
229 Jim Brosnan	20.00	9.00	2.50
230 Al Brazle	15.00	6.75	1.90
231 Jim Konstanty	20.00	9.00	2.50
232 Birdie Tebbetts MG	17.50	8.00	2.20
233 Bill Serena	15.00	6.75	1.90
234 Dick Bartell CO	20.00	9.00	2.50
235 Joe Paparella UMP	25.00	11.50	3.10
236 Murry Dickson	15.00	6.75	1.90
237 Johnny Wyrostek	15.00	6.75	1.90
238 Eddie Stanky MG	20.00	9.00	2.50
239 Edwin Rommel UMP	25.00	11.50	3.10
240 Billy Loes	17.50	8.00	2.20
241 Johnny Pesky CO	20.00	9.00	2.50
242 Ernie Banks	400.00	180.00	50.00
243 Gus Bell	17.50	8.00	2.20
244 Duane Pillette	15.00	6.75	1.90
245 Bill Miller	15.00	6.75	1.90
246 Hank Bauer	40.00	18.00	5.00
247 Dutch Leonard CO	15.00	6.75	1.90
248 Harry Dorish	15.00	6.75	1.90
249 Billy Gardner	17.50	8.00	2.20

☐ 250	Larry Napp UMP	25.00	11.50	3.10
☐ 251	Stan Jok	15.00	6.75	1.90
☐ 252	Roy Smalley	15.00	6.75	1.90
☐ 253	Jim Wilson	15.00	6.75	1.90
☐ 254	Bennett Flowers	15.00	6.75	1.90
☐ 255	Pete Runnels	17.50	8.00	2.20
☐ 256	Owen Friend	15.00	6.75	1.90
☐ 257	Tom Alston	15.00	6.75	1.90
☐ 258	John Stevens UMP	25.00	11.50	3.10
☐ 259	Don Mossi	25.00	11.50	3.10
☐ 260	Edwin Hurley UMP	25.00	11.50	3.10
☐ 261	Walt Moryn	15.00	6.75	1.90
☐ 262	Jim Lemon	20.00	9.00	2.50
☐ 263	Eddie Joost	15.00	6.75	1.90
☐ 264	Bill Henry	15.00	6.75	1.90
☐ 265	Albert Barlick UMP	85.00	38.00	10.50
☐ 266	Mike Fornieles	15.00	6.75	1.90
☐ 267	Jim Honochick UMP	80.00	36.00	10.00
☐ 268	Roy Lee Hawes	15.00	6.75	1.90
☐ 269	Joe Amalfitano	20.00	9.00	2.50
☐ 270	Chico Fernandez	15.00	6.75	1.90
☐ 271	Bob Hooper	15.00	6.75	1.90
☐ 272	John Flaherty UMP	25.00	11.50	3.10
☐ 273	Bubba Church	15.00	6.75	1.90
☐ 274	Jim Delsing	15.00	6.75	1.90
☐ 275	William Grieve UMP	25.00	11.50	3.10
☐ 276	Ike Delock	15.00	6.75	1.90
☐ 277	Ed Runge UMP	30.00	13.50	3.80
☐ 278	Charlie Neal	30.00	13.50	3.80
☐ 279	Hank Soar UMP	25.00	11.50	3.10
☐ 280	Clyde McCullough	15.00	6.75	1.90
☐ 281	Charles Berry UMP	25.00	11.50	3.10
☐ 282	Phil Cavarretta	20.00	9.00	2.50
☐ 283	Nestor Chylak UMP	25.00	11.50	3.10
☐ 284	Bill Jackowski UMP	25.00	11.50	3.10
☐ 285	Walt Dropo	17.50	8.00	2.20
☐ 286	Frank Secory UMP	25.00	11.50	3.10
☐ 287	Ron Mrozinski	15.00	6.75	1.90
☐ 288	Dick Smith	15.00	6.75	1.90
☐ 289	Arthur Gore UMP	25.00	11.50	3.10
☐ 290	Hershell Freeman	15.00	6.75	1.90
☐ 291	Frank Dascoli UMP	25.00	11.50	3.10
☐ 292	Marv Blaylock	15.00	6.75	1.90
☐ 293	Thomas Gorman UMP	30.00	13.50	3.80
☐ 294	Wally Moses CO	17.50	8.00	2.20
☐ 295	Lee Ballanfant UMP	25.00	11.50	3.10
☐ 296	Bill Virdon	35.00	16.00	4.40
☐ 297	Dusty Boggess UMP	25.00	11.50	3.10
☐ 298	Charlie Grimm MG	20.00	9.00	2.50
☐ 299	Lon Warneke UMP	30.00	13.50	3.80
☐ 300	Tommy Byrne	15.00	6.75	1.90
☐ 301	William Engeln UMP	25.00	11.50	3.10
☐ 302	Frank Malzone	30.00	13.50	3.80
☐ 303	Jocko Conlan UMP	100.00	45.00	12.50
☐ 304	Harry Chiti	15.00	6.75	1.90
☐ 305	Frank Umont UMP	25.00	11.50	3.10
☐ 306	Bob Cerv	25.00	11.50	3.10

☐ 307	Babe Pinelli UMP	30.00	13.50	3.80
☐ 308	Al Lopez MG	50.00	23.00	6.25
☐ 309	Hal Dixon UMP	25.00	11.50	3.10
☐ 310	Ken Lehman	15.00	6.75	1.90
☐ 311	Lawrence Goetz UMP	25.00	11.50	3.10
☐ 312	Bill Wight	15.00	6.75	1.90
☐ 313	Augie Donatelli UMP	40.00	18.00	5.00
☐ 314	Dale Mitchell	17.50	8.00	2.20
☐ 315	Cal Hubbard UMP	100.00	45.00	12.50
☐ 316	Marion Fricano	15.00	6.75	1.90
☐ 317	William Summers UMP	30.00	13.50	3.80
☐ 318	Sid Hudson	15.00	6.75	1.90
☐ 319	Al Schroll	15.00	6.75	1.90
☐ 320	George Susce Jr.	50.00	10.00	3.00

1989 Bowman

The 1989 Bowman set, which was actually produced by Topps, contains 484 cards measuring approximately 2 1/2" by 3 3/4". The fronts have white-bordered color photos with facsimile autographs and small Bowman logos. The backs are scarlet and feature charts detailing 1988 player performances vs. each team. The cards are checklisted below alphabetically according to teams in the AL and NL as follows: Baltimore Orioles (1-18), Boston Red Sox (19-36), California Angels (37-54), Chicago White Sox (55-72), Cleveland Indians (73-91), Detroit Tigers (92-109), Kansas City Royals (110-128), Milwaukee Brewers (129-146), Minnesota Twins (147-164), New York Yankees (165-183), Oakland Athletics (184-202), Seattle Mariners (203-220), Texas Rangers (221-238), Toronto Blue Jays (239-257), Atlanta Braves (262-279), Chicago Cubs (280-298), Cincinnati

Reds (299-316), Houston Astros (317-334), Los Angeles Dodgers (335-352), Montreal Expos (353-370), New York Mets (371-389), Philadelphia Phillies (390-408), Pittsburgh Pirates (409-426), St. Louis Cardinals (427-444), San Diego Padres (445-462), and San Francisco Giants (463-480). Cards 258-261 form a father\son subset. The player selection is concentrated on prospects and "name" players. The cards were released in midseason 1989 in wax, rack, and cello pack formats. The key Rookie Cards in this set are Jim Abbott, Steve Avery, Andy Benes, Royce Clayton, Ken Griffey Jr., Tino Martinez, Gary Sheffield, John Smoltz, Robin Ventura, and Jerome Walton. Topps also produced a limited Bowman "Tiffany" set with supposedly only 6,000 sets being produced. This Tiffany version is valued approximately from five to ten times the values listed below.

	MT	EX-MT	VG
COMPLETE SET (484)	15.00	6.75	1.90
COMPLETE FACT.SET (484)	15.00	6.75	1.90
COMMON PLAYER (1-484)	.04	.02	.01

		MT	EX-MT	VG
☐	1 Oswald Peraza	.04	.02	.01
☐	2 Brian Holton	.04	.02	.01
☐	3 Jose Bautista	.04	.02	.01
☐	4 Pete Harnisch	.15	.07	.02
☐	5 Dave Schmidt	.04	.02	.01
☐	6 Gregg Olson	.40	.10	.05
☐	7 Jeff Ballard	.04	.02	.01
☐	8 Bob Melvin	.04	.02	.01
☐	9 Cal Ripken	.50	.23	.06
☐	10 Randy Milligan	.04	.02	.01
☐	11 Juan Bell	.10	.05	.01
☐	12 Billy Ripken	.04	.02	.01
☐	13 Jim Traber	.04	.02	.01
☐	14 Pete Stanicek	.04	.02	.01
☐	15 Steve Finley	.35	.16	.04
☐	16 Larry Sheets	.04	.02	.01
☐	17 Phil Bradley	.04	.02	.01
☐	18 Brady Anderson	.60	.25	.08
☐	19 Lee Smith	.07	.03	.01
☐	20 Tom Fischer	.04	.02	.01
☐	21 Mike Boddicker	.04	.02	.01
☐	22 Rob Murphy	.04	.02	.01
☐	23 Wes Gardner	.04	.02	.01
☐	24 John Dopson	.04	.02	.01
☐	25 Bob Stanley	.04	.02	.01
☐	26 Roger Clemens	.40	.18	.05
☐	27 Rich Gedman	.04	.02	.01
☐	28 Marty Barrett	.04	.02	.01
☐	29 Luis Rivera	.04	.02	.01
☐	30 Jody Reed	.04	.02	.01
☐	31 Nick Esasky	.04	.02	.01
☐	32 Wade Boggs	.25	.11	.03
☐	33 Jim Rice	.07	.03	.01
☐	34 Mike Greenwell	.07	.03	.01
☐	35 Dwight Evans	.07	.03	.01
☐	36 Ellis Burks	.07	.03	.01
☐	37 Chuck Finley	.07	.03	.01
☐	38 Kirk McCaskill	.04	.02	.01
☐	39 Jim Abbott	1.00	.45	.13
☐	40 Bryan Harvey	.25	.11	.03
☐	41 Bert Blyleven	.07	.03	.01
☐	42 Mike Witt	.04	.02	.01
☐	43 Bob McClure	.04	.02	.01
☐	44 Bill Schroeder	.04	.02	.01
☐	45 Lance Parrish	.07	.03	.01
☐	46 Dick Schofield	.04	.02	.01
☐	47 Wally Joyner	.08	.04	.01
☐	48 Jack Howell	.04	.02	.01
☐	49 Johnny Ray	.04	.02	.01
☐	50 Chili Davis	.07	.03	.01
☐	51 Tony Armas	.04	.02	.01
☐	52 Claudell Washington	.04	.02	.01
☐	53 Brian Downing	.04	.02	.01
☐	54 Devon White	.07	.03	.01
☐	55 Bobby Thigpen	.04	.02	.01
☐	56 Bill Long	.04	.02	.01
☐	57 Jerry Reuss	.04	.02	.01
☐	58 Shawn Hillegas	.04	.02	.01
☐	59 Melido Perez	.12	.05	.02
☐	60 Jeff Bittiger	.04	.02	.01
☐	61 Jack McDowell	.25	.11	.03
☐	62 Carlton Fisk	.12	.05	.02
☐	63 Steve Lyons	.04	.02	.01
☐	64 Ozzie Guillen	.04	.02	.01
☐	65 Robin Ventura	1.00	.45	.13
☐	66 Fred Manrique	.04	.02	.01
☐	67 Dan Pasqua	.04	.02	.01
☐	68 Ivan Calderon	.04	.02	.01
☐	69 Ron Kittle	.04	.02	.01
☐	70 Daryl Boston	.04	.02	.01
☐	71 Dave Gallagher	.04	.02	.01
☐	72 Harold Baines	.07	.03	.01
☐	73 Charles Nagy	.60	.25	.08
☐	74 John Farrell	.04	.02	.01
☐	75 Kevin Wickander	.04	.02	.01
☐	76 Greg Swindell	.07	.03	.01
☐	77 Mike Walker	.04	.02	.01
☐	78 Doug Jones	.07	.03	.01
☐	79 Rich Yett	.04	.02	.01
☐	80 Tom Candiotti	.04	.02	.01
☐	81 Jesse Orosco	.04	.02	.01
☐	82 Bud Black	.04	.02	.01
☐	83 Andy Allanson	.04	.02	.01
☐	84 Pete O'Brien	.04	.02	.01
☐	85 Jerry Browne	.04	.02	.01
☐	86 Brook Jacoby	.04	.02	.01

☐ 87	Mark Lewis	.30	.14	.04
☐ 88	Luis Aguayo	.04	.02	.01
☐ 89	Cory Snyder	.04	.02	.01
☐ 90	Oddibe McDowell	.04	.02	.01
☐ 91	Joe Carter	.25	.11	.03
☐ 92	Frank Tanana	.04	.02	.01
☐ 93	Jack Morris	.10	.05	.01
☐ 94	Doyle Alexander	.04	.02	.01
☐ 95	Steve Searcy	.04	.02	.01
☐ 96	Randy Bockus	.04	.02	.01
☐ 97	Jeff M. Robinson	.04	.02	.01
☐ 98	Mike Henneman	.07	.03	.01
☐ 99	Paul Gibson	.04	.02	.01
☐ 100	Frank Williams	.04	.02	.01
☐ 101	Matt Nokes	.07	.03	.01
☐ 102	Rico Brogna UER	.20	.09	.03
	(Misspelled Ricco on card back)			
☐ 103	Lou Whitaker	.07	.03	.01
☐ 104	Al Pedrique	.04	.02	.01
☐ 105	Alan Trammell	.07	.03	.01
☐ 106	Chris Brown	.04	.02	.01
☐ 107	Pat Sheridan	.04	.02	.01
☐ 108	Chet Lemon	.04	.02	.01
☐ 109	Keith Moreland	.04	.02	.01
☐ 110	Mel Stottlemyre Jr.	.07	.03	.01
☐ 111	Bret Saberhagen	.07	.03	.01
☐ 112	Floyd Bannister	.04	.02	.01
☐ 113	Jeff Montgomery	.07	.03	.01
☐ 114	Steve Farr	.04	.02	.01
☐ 115	Tom Gordon UER	.10	.05	.01
	(Front shows autograph of Don Gordon)			
☐ 116	Charlie Leibrandt	.04	.02	.01
☐ 117	Mark Gubicza	.04	.02	.01
☐ 118	Mike Macfarlane	.15	.07	.02
☐ 119	Bob Boone	.07	.03	.01
☐ 120	Kurt Stillwell	.04	.02	.01
☐ 121	George Brett	.20	.09	.03
☐ 122	Frank White	.04	.02	.01
☐ 123	Kevin Seitzer	.07	.03	.01
☐ 124	Willie Wilson	.04	.02	.01
☐ 125	Pat Tabler	.04	.02	.01
☐ 126	Bo Jackson	.20	.09	.03
☐ 127	Hugh Walker	.10	.05	.01
☐ 128	Danny Tartabull	.10	.05	.01
☐ 129	Teddy Higuera	.04	.02	.01
☐ 130	Don August	.04	.02	.01
☐ 131	Juan Nieves	.04	.02	.01
☐ 132	Mike Birkbeck	.04	.02	.01
☐ 133	Dan Plesac	.04	.02	.01
☐ 134	Chris Bosio	.04	.02	.01
☐ 135	Bill Wegman	.04	.02	.01
☐ 136	Chuck Crim	.04	.02	.01
☐ 137	B.J. Surhoff	.04	.02	.01
☐ 138	Joey Meyer	.04	.02	.01
☐ 139	Dale Sveum	.04	.02	.01
☐ 140	Paul Molitor	.10	.05	.01
☐ 141	Jim Gantner	.04	.02	.01
☐ 142	Gary Sheffield	2.00	.90	.25
☐ 143	Greg Brock	.04	.02	.01
☐ 144	Robin Yount	.20	.09	.03
☐ 145	Glenn Braggs	.04	.02	.01
☐ 146	Rob Deer	.07	.03	.01
☐ 147	Fred Toliver	.04	.02	.01
☐ 148	Jeff Reardon	.07	.03	.01
☐ 149	Allan Anderson	.04	.02	.01
☐ 150	Frank Viola	.07	.03	.01
☐ 151	Shane Rawley	.04	.02	.01
☐ 152	Juan Berenguer	.04	.02	.01
☐ 153	Johnny Ard	.10	.05	.01
☐ 154	Tim Laudner	.04	.02	.01
☐ 155	Brian Harper	.07	.03	.01
☐ 156	Al Newman	.04	.02	.01
☐ 157	Kent Hrbek	.07	.03	.01
☐ 158	Gary Gaetti	.04	.02	.01
☐ 159	Wally Backman	.04	.02	.01
☐ 160	Gene Larkin	.04	.02	.01
☐ 161	Greg Gagne	.04	.02	.01
☐ 162	Kirby Puckett	.40	.18	.05
☐ 163	Dan Gladden	.04	.02	.01
☐ 164	Randy Bush	.04	.02	.01
☐ 165	Dave LaPoint	.04	.02	.01
☐ 166	Andy Hawkins	.04	.02	.01
☐ 167	Dave Righetti	.04	.02	.01
☐ 168	Lance McCullers	.04	.02	.01
☐ 169	Jimmy Jones	.04	.02	.01
☐ 170	Al Leiter	.04	.02	.01
☐ 171	John Candelaria	.04	.02	.01
☐ 172	Don Slaught	.04	.02	.01
☐ 173	Jamie Quirk	.04	.02	.01
☐ 174	Rafael Santana	.04	.02	.01
☐ 175	Mike Pagliarulo	.04	.02	.01
☐ 176	Don Mattingly	.25	.11	.03
☐ 177	Ken Phelps	.04	.02	.01
☐ 178	Steve Sax	.07	.03	.01
☐ 179	Dave Winfield	.20	.09	.03
☐ 180	Stan Jefferson	.04	.02	.01
☐ 181	Rickey Henderson	.20	.09	.03
☐ 182	Bob Brower	.04	.02	.01
☐ 183	Roberto Kelly	.15	.07	.02
☐ 184	Curt Young	.04	.02	.01
☐ 185	Gene Nelson	.04	.02	.01
☐ 186	Bob Welch	.07	.03	.01
☐ 187	Rick Honeycutt	.04	.02	.01
☐ 188	Dave Stewart	.07	.03	.01
☐ 189	Mike Moore	.04	.02	.01
☐ 190	Dennis Eckersley	.12	.05	.02
☐ 191	Eric Plunk	.04	.02	.01
☐ 192	Storm Davis	.04	.02	.01
☐ 193	Terry Steinbach	.07	.03	.01
☐ 194	Ron Hassey	.04	.02	.01
☐ 195	Stan Royer	.20	.09	.03
☐ 196	Walt Weiss	.07	.03	.01

☐ 197	Mark McGwire	.35	.16	.04			
☐ 198	Carney Lansford	.07	.03	.01			
☐ 199	Glenn Hubbard	.04	.02	.01			
☐ 200	Dave Henderson	.07	.03	.01			
☐ 201	Jose Canseco	.40	.18	.05			
☐ 202	Dave Parker	.07	.03	.01			
☐ 203	Scott Bankhead	.04	.02	.01			
☐ 204	Tom Niedenfuer	.04	.02	.01			
☐ 205	Mark Langston	.07	.03	.01			
☐ 206	Erik Hanson	.20	.09	.03			
☐ 207	Mike Jackson	.04	.02	.01			
☐ 208	Dave Valle	.04	.02	.01			
☐ 209	Scott Bradley	.04	.02	.01			
☐ 210	Harold Reynolds	.04	.02	.01			
☐ 211	Tino Martinez	.30	.14	.04			
☐ 212	Rich Renteria	.04	.02	.01			
☐ 213	Rey Quinones	.04	.02	.01			
☐ 214	Jim Presley	.04	.02	.01			
☐ 215	Alvin Davis	.04	.02	.01			
☐ 216	Edgar Martinez	.25	.11	.03			
☐ 217	Darnell Coles	.04	.02	.01			
☐ 218	Jeffrey Leonard	.04	.02	.01			
☐ 219	Jay Buhner	.10	.05	.01			
☐ 220	Ken Griffey Jr.	4.50	2.00	.55			
☐ 221	Drew Hall	.04	.02	.01			
☐ 222	Bobby Witt	.07	.03	.01			
☐ 223	Jamie Moyer	.04	.02	.01			
☐ 224	Charlie Hough	.04	.02	.01			
☐ 225	Nolan Ryan	.60	.25	.08			
☐ 226	Jeff Russell	.04	.02	.01			
☐ 227	Jim Sundberg	.04	.02	.01			
☐ 228	Julio Franco	.07	.03	.01			
☐ 229	Buddy Bell	.07	.03	.01			
☐ 230	Scott Fletcher	.04	.02	.01			
☐ 231	Jeff Kunkel	.04	.02	.01			
☐ 232	Steve Buechele	.04	.02	.01			
☐ 233	Monty Fariss	.30	.14	.04			
☐ 234	Rick Leach	.04	.02	.01			
☐ 235	Ruben Sierra	.30	.14	.04			
☐ 236	Cecil Espy	.04	.02	.01			
☐ 237	Rafael Palmeiro	.15	.07	.02			
☐ 238	Pete Incaviglia	.04	.02	.01			
☐ 239	Dave Stieb	.07	.03	.01			
☐ 240	Jeff Musselman	.04	.02	.01			
☐ 241	Mike Flanagan	.04	.02	.01			
☐ 242	Todd Stottlemyre	.10	.05	.01			
☐ 243	Jimmy Key	.07	.03	.01			
☐ 244	Tony Castillo	.04	.02	.01			
☐ 245	Alex Sanchez	.04	.02	.01			
☐ 246	Tom Henke	.07	.03	.01			
☐ 247	John Cerutti	.04	.02	.01			
☐ 248	Ernie Whitt	.04	.02	.01			
☐ 249	Bob Brenly	.04	.02	.01			
☐ 250	Rance Mulliniks	.04	.02	.01			
☐ 251	Kelly Gruber	.07	.03	.01			
☐ 252	Ed Sprague	.30	.14	.04			
☐ 253	Fred McGriff	.20	.09	.03			
☐ 254	Tony Fernandez	.07	.03	.01			
☐ 255	Tom Lawless	.04	.02	.01			
☐ 256	George Bell	.07	.03	.01			
☐ 257	Jesse Barfield	.04	.02	.01			
☐ 258	Roberto Alomar w/Dad	.30	.14	.04			
☐ 259	Ken Griffey Jr./Sr.	1.00	.45	.13			
☐ 260	Cal Ripken Jr./Sr.	.20	.09	.03			
☐ 261	M.Stottlemyre Jr./Sr.	.05	.02	.01			
☐ 262	Zane Smith	.04	.02	.01			
☐ 263	Charlie Puleo	.04	.02	.01			
☐ 264	Derek Lilliquist	.10	.05	.01			
☐ 265	Paul Assenmacher	.04	.02	.01			
☐ 266	John Smoltz	.60	.25	.08			
☐ 267	Tom Glavine	.50	.23	.06			
☐ 268	Steve Avery	1.00	.45	.13			
☐ 269	Pete Smith	.07	.03	.01			
☐ 270	Jody Davis	.04	.02	.01			
☐ 271	Bruce Benedict	.04	.02	.01			
☐ 272	Andres Thomas	.04	.02	.01			
☐ 273	Gerald Perry	.04	.02	.01			
☐ 274	Ron Gant	.40	.18	.05			
☐ 275	Darrell Evans	.07	.03	.01			
☐ 276	Dale Murphy	.10	.05	.01			
☐ 277	Dion James	.04	.02	.01			
☐ 278	Lonnie Smith	.04	.02	.01			
☐ 279	Geronimo Berroa	.04	.02	.01			
☐ 280	Steve Wilson	.04	.02	.01			
☐ 281	Rick Sutcliffe	.07	.03	.01			
☐ 282	Kevin Coffman	.04	.02	.01			
☐ 283	Mitch Williams	.07	.03	.01			
☐ 284	Greg Maddux	.30	.14	.04			
☐ 285	Paul Kilgus	.04	.02	.01			
☐ 286	Mike Harkey	.12	.05	.02			
☐ 287	Lloyd McClendon	.04	.02	.01			
☐ 288	Damon Berryhill	.04	.02	.01			
☐ 289	Ty Griffin	.08	.04	.01			
☐ 290	Ryne Sandberg	.40	.18	.05			
☐ 291	Mark Grace	.30	.14	.04			
☐ 292	Curt Wilkerson	.04	.02	.01			
☐ 293	Vance Law	.04	.02	.01			
☐ 294	Shawon Dunston	.07	.03	.01			
☐ 295	Jerome Walton	.10	.05	.01			
☐ 296	Mitch Webster	.04	.02	.01			
☐ 297	Dwight Smith	.10	.05	.01			
☐ 298	Andre Dawson	.15	.07	.02			
☐ 299	Jeff Sellers	.04	.02	.01			
☐ 300	Jose Rijo	.07	.03	.01			
☐ 301	John Franco	.07	.03	.01			
☐ 302	Rick Mahler	.04	.02	.01			
☐ 303	Ron Robinson	.04	.02	.01			
☐ 304	Danny Jackson	.04	.02	.01			
☐ 305	Rob Dibble	.20	.09	.03			
☐ 306	Tom Browning	.07	.03	.01			
☐ 307	Bo Diaz	.04	.02	.01			
☐ 308	Manny Trillo	.04	.02	.01			
☐ 309	Chris Sabo	.25	.11	.03			
☐ 310	Ron Oester	.04	.02	.01			

☐ 311 Barry Larkin	.15	.07	.02
☐ 312 Todd Benzinger	.04	.02	.01
☐ 313 Paul O'Neill	.07	.03	.01
☐ 314 Kal Daniels	.07	.03	.01
☐ 315 Joel Youngblood	.04	.02	.01
☐ 316 Eric Davis	.10	.05	.01
☐ 317 Dave Smith	.04	.02	.01
☐ 318 Mark Portugal	.04	.02	.01
☐ 319 Brian Meyer	.04	.02	.01
☐ 320 Jim Deshaies	.04	.02	.01
☐ 321 Juan Agosto	.04	.02	.01
☐ 322 Mike Scott	.04	.02	.01
☐ 323 Rick Rhoden	.04	.02	.01
☐ 324 Jim Clancy	.04	.02	.01
☐ 325 Larry Andersen	.04	.02	.01
☐ 326 Alex Trevino	.04	.02	.01
☐ 327 Alan Ashby	.04	.02	.01
☐ 328 Craig Reynolds	.04	.02	.01
☐ 329 Bill Doran	.04	.02	.01
☐ 330 Rafael Ramirez	.04	.02	.01
☐ 331 Glenn Davis	.07	.03	.01
☐ 332 Willie Ansley	.12	.05	.02
☐ 333 Gerald Young	.04	.02	.01
☐ 334 Cameron Drew	.04	.02	.01
☐ 335 Jay Howell	.04	.02	.01
☐ 336 Tim Belcher	.07	.03	.01
☐ 337 Fernando Valenzuela	.07	.03	.01
☐ 338 Ricky Horton	.04	.02	.01
☐ 339 Tim Leary	.04	.02	.01
☐ 340 Bill Bene	.04	.02	.01
☐ 341 Orel Hershiser	.07	.03	.01
☐ 342 Mike Scioscia	.04	.02	.01
☐ 343 Rick Dempsey	.04	.02	.01
☐ 344 Willie Randolph	.07	.03	.01
☐ 345 Alfredo Griffin	.04	.02	.01
☐ 346 Eddie Murray	.12	.05	.02
☐ 347 Mickey Hatcher	.04	.02	.01
☐ 348 Mike Sharperson	.04	.02	.01
☐ 349 John Shelby	.04	.02	.01
☐ 350 Mike Marshall	.04	.02	.01
☐ 351 Kirk Gibson	.07	.03	.01
☐ 352 Mike Davis	.04	.02	.01
☐ 353 Bryn Smith	.04	.02	.01
☐ 354 Pascual Perez	.04	.02	.01
☐ 355 Kevin Gross	.04	.02	.01
☐ 356 Andy McGaffigan	.04	.02	.01
☐ 357 Brian Holman	.10	.05	.01
☐ 358 Dave Wainhouse	.10	.05	.01
☐ 359 Dennis Martinez	.07	.03	.01
☐ 360 Tim Burke	.04	.02	.01
☐ 361 Nelson Santovenia	.04	.02	.01
☐ 362 Tim Wallach	.07	.03	.01
☐ 363 Spike Owen	.04	.02	.01
☐ 364 Rex Hudler	.04	.02	.01
☐ 365 Andres Galarraga	.04	.02	.01
☐ 366 Otis Nixon	.07	.03	.01
☐ 367 Hubie Brooks	.04	.02	.01
☐ 368 Mike Aldrete	.04	.02	.01
☐ 369 Tim Raines	.07	.03	.01
☐ 370 Dave Martinez	.07	.03	.01
☐ 371 Bob Ojeda	.04	.02	.01
☐ 372 Ron Darling	.07	.03	.01
☐ 373 Wally Whitehurst	.10	.05	.01
☐ 374 Randy Myers	.07	.03	.01
☐ 375 David Cone	.15	.07	.02
☐ 376 Dwight Gooden	.12	.05	.02
☐ 377 Sid Fernandez	.07	.03	.01
☐ 378 Dave Proctor	.04	.02	.01
☐ 379 Gary Carter	.07	.03	.01
☐ 380 Keith Miller	.04	.02	.01
☐ 381 Gregg Jefferies	.20	.09	.03
☐ 382 Tim Teufel	.04	.02	.01
☐ 383 Kevin Elster	.04	.02	.01
☐ 384 Dave Magadan	.07	.03	.01
☐ 385 Keith Hernandez	.07	.03	.01
☐ 386 Mookie Wilson	.07	.03	.01
☐ 387 Darryl Strawberry	.25	.11	.03
☐ 388 Kevin McReynolds	.07	.03	.01
☐ 389 Mark Carreon	.04	.02	.01
☐ 390 Jeff Parrett	.04	.02	.01
☐ 391 Mike Maddux	.04	.02	.01
☐ 392 Don Carman	.04	.02	.01
☐ 393 Bruce Ruffin	.04	.02	.01
☐ 394 Ken Howell	.04	.02	.01
☐ 395 Steve Bedrosian	.04	.02	.01
☐ 396 Floyd Youmans	.04	.02	.01
☐ 397 Larry McWilliams	.04	.02	.01
☐ 398 Pat Combs	.10	.05	.01
☐ 399 Steve Lake	.04	.02	.01
☐ 400 Dickie Thon	.04	.02	.01
☐ 401 Ricky Jordan	.10	.05	.01
☐ 402 Mike Schmidt	.35	.16	.04
☐ 403 Tom Herr	.04	.02	.01
☐ 404 Chris James	.04	.02	.01
☐ 405 Juan Samuel	.04	.02	.01
☐ 406 Von Hayes	.04	.02	.01
☐ 407 Ron Jones	.04	.02	.01
☐ 408 Curt Ford	.04	.02	.01
☐ 409 Bob Walk	.04	.02	.01
☐ 410 Jeff D. Robinson	.04	.02	.01
☐ 411 Jim Gott	.04	.02	.01
☐ 412 Scott Medvin	.04	.02	.01
☐ 413 John Smiley	.07	.03	.01
☐ 414 Bob Kipper	.04	.02	.01
☐ 415 Brian Fisher	.04	.02	.01
☐ 416 Doug Drabek	.07	.03	.01
☐ 417 Mike LaValliere	.04	.02	.01
☐ 418 Ken Oberkfell	.04	.02	.01
☐ 419 Sid Bream	.04	.02	.01
☐ 420 Austin Manahan	.10	.05	.01
☐ 421 Jose Lind	.04	.02	.01
☐ 422 Bobby Bonilla	.15	.07	.02
☐ 423 Glenn Wilson	.04	.02	.01
☐ 424 Andy Van Slyke	.10	.05	.01

☐ 425 Gary Redus	.04	.02	.01
☐ 426 Barry Bonds	.40	.18	.05
☐ 427 Don Heinkel	.04	.02	.01
☐ 428 Ken Dayley	.04	.02	.01
☐ 429 Todd Worrell	.07	.03	.01
☐ 430 Brad DuVall	.04	.02	.01
☐ 431 Jose DeLeon	.04	.02	.01
☐ 432 Joe Magrane	.04	.02	.01
☐ 433 John Ericks	.04	.02	.01
☐ 434 Frank DiPino	.04	.02	.01
☐ 435 Tony Pena	.04	.02	.01
☐ 436 Ozzie Smith	.15	.07	.02
☐ 437 Terry Pendleton	.12	.05	.02
☐ 438 Jose Oquendo	.04	.02	.01
☐ 439 Tim Jones	.04	.02	.01
☐ 440 Pedro Guerrero	.07	.03	.01
☐ 441 Milt Thompson	.04	.02	.01
☐ 442 Willie McGee	.07	.03	.01
☐ 443 Vince Coleman	.07	.03	.01
☐ 444 Tom Brunansky	.07	.03	.01
☐ 445 Walt Terrell	.04	.02	.01
☐ 446 Eric Show	.04	.02	.01
☐ 447 Mark Davis	.04	.02	.01
☐ 448 Andy Benes	.50	.23	.06
☐ 449 Ed Whitson	.04	.02	.01
☐ 450 Dennis Rasmussen	.04	.02	.01
☐ 451 Bruce Hurst	.07	.03	.01
☐ 452 Pat Clements	.04	.02	.01
☐ 453 Benito Santiago	.07	.03	.01
☐ 454 Sandy Alomar Jr.	.25	.11	.03
☐ 455 Garry Templeton	.04	.02	.01
☐ 456 Jack Clark	.07	.03	.01
☐ 457 Tim Flannery	.04	.02	.01
☐ 458 Roberto Alomar	.75	.35	.09
☐ 459 Carmelo Martinez	.04	.02	.01
☐ 460 John Kruk	.07	.03	.01
☐ 461 Tony Gwynn	.25	.11	.03
☐ 462 Jerald Clark	.15	.07	.02
☐ 463 Don Robinson	.04	.02	.01
☐ 464 Craig Lefferts	.04	.02	.01
☐ 465 Kelly Downs	.04	.02	.01
☐ 466 Rick Reuschel	.04	.02	.01
☐ 467 Scott Garrelts	.04	.02	.01
☐ 468 Wil Tejada	.04	.02	.01
☐ 469 Kirt Manwaring	.04	.02	.01
☐ 470 Terry Kennedy	.04	.02	.01
☐ 471 Jose Uribe	.04	.02	.01
☐ 472 Royce Clayton	.40	.18	.05
☐ 473 Robby Thompson	.04	.02	.01
☐ 474 Kevin Mitchell	.10	.05	.01
☐ 475 Ernie Riles	.04	.02	.01
☐ 476 Will Clark	.40	.18	.05
☐ 477 Donell Nixon	.04	.02	.01
☐ 478 Candy Maldonado	.04	.02	.01
☐ 479 Tracy Jones	.04	.02	.01
☐ 480 Brett Butler	.07	.03	.01
☐ 481 Checklist Card	.05	.01	.00
☐ 482 Checklist Card	.05	.01	.00
☐ 483 Checklist Card	.05	.01	.00
☐ 484 Checklist Card	.05	.01	.00

1990 Bowman

The 1990 Bowman set was issued in the standard card size of 2 1/2" by 3 1/2". This was the second issue by Topps using the Bowman name. The set consists of 528 cards, increased from 1989's edition of 484 cards. The cards feature a white border with the player's photo inside and the Bowman logo on top. Again, the Bowman cards were issued with the backs featuring team by team statistics. The card numbering is in team order with the teams themselves being ordered alphabetically within each league. The set numbering is as follows: Atlanta Braves (1-20), Chicago Cubs (21-40), Cincinnati Reds (41-60), Houston Astros (61-81), Los Angeles Dodgers (82-101), Montreal Expos (102-121), New York Mets (122-142), Philadelphia Phillies (143-162), Pittsburgh Pirates (163-182), St. Louis Cardinals (183-202), San Diego Padres (203-222), San Francisco Giants (223-242), Baltimore Orioles (243-262), Boston Red Sox (263-282), California Angels (283-302), Chicago White Sox (303-322), Cleveland Indians (323-342), Detroit Tigers (343-362), Kansas City Royals (363-383), Milwaukee Brewers (384-404), Minnesota Twins (405-424), New York Yankees (425-444), Oakland A's (445-464), Seattle Mariners (465-484), Texas Rangers (485-503), and Toronto Blue Jays (504-524). The key Rookie

Cards in this set are Carlos Baerga, Delino DeShields, Cal Eldred, Travis Fryman, Leo Gomez, Juan Gonzalez, Marquis Grissom, Chuck Knoblauch, Ray Lankford, Kevin Maas, Ben McDonald, Jose Offerman, John Olerud, Frank Thomas, Mo Vaughn, and Larry Walker. Topps also produced a Bowman Tiffany glossy set. Production of these Tiffany Bowmans was reported to be approximately 3,000 sets. These Tiffany versions are valued at approximately five to ten times the values listed below.

	MT	EX-MT	VG
COMPLETE SET (528) 15.00		6.75	1.90
COMPLETE FACT.SET (528) ...15.00		6.75	1.90
COMMON PLAYER (1-528) 04		.02	.01
☐ 1 Tommy Greene 12		.05	.02
☐ 2 Tom Glavine 25		.11	.03
☐ 3 Andy Nezelek 04		.02	.01
☐ 4 Mike Stanton 15		.07	.02
☐ 5 Rick Luecken 04		.02	.01
☐ 6 Kent Mercker 12		.05	.02
☐ 7 Derek Lilliquist 04		.02	.01
☐ 8 Charlie Leibrandt 04		.02	.01
☐ 9 Steve Avery 60		.25	.08
☐ 10 John Smoltz 25		.11	.03
☐ 11 Mark Lemke 07		.03	.01
☐ 12 Lonnie Smith 04		.02	.01
☐ 13 Oddibe McDowell 04		.02	.01
☐ 14 Tyler Houston 10		.05	.01
☐ 15 Jeff Blauser 07		.03	.01
☐ 16 Ernie Whitt 04		.02	.01
☐ 17 Alexis Infante 04		.02	.01
☐ 18 Jim Presley 04		.02	.01
☐ 19 Dale Murphy 10		.05	.01
☐ 20 Nick Esasky 04		.02	.01
☐ 21 Rick Sutcliffe 07		.03	.01
☐ 22 Mike Bielecki 04		.02	.01
☐ 23 Steve Wilson 04		.02	.01
☐ 24 Kevin Blankenship 04		.02	.01
☐ 25 Mitch Williams 07		.03	.01
☐ 26 Dean Wilkins 04		.02	.01
☐ 27 Greg Maddux 20		.09	.03
☐ 28 Mike Harkey 07		.03	.01
☐ 29 Mark Grace 20		.09	.03
☐ 30 Ryne Sandberg 35		.16	.04
☐ 31 Greg Smith 10		.05	.01
☐ 32 Dwight Smith 04		.02	.01
☐ 33 Damon Berryhill 04		.02	.01
☐ 34 Earl Cunningham UER 12		.05	.02
(Errant * by the			
word "in")			
☐ 35 Jerome Walton 07		.03	.01
☐ 36 Lloyd McClendon 04		.02	.01
☐ 37 Ty Griffin 04		.02	.01
☐ 38 Shawon Dunston 07		.03	.01
☐ 39 Andre Dawson 12		.05	.02
☐ 40 Luis Salazar 04		.02	.01
☐ 41 Tim Layana 04		.02	.01
☐ 42 Rob Dibble 07		.03	.01
☐ 43 Tom Browning 04		.02	.01
☐ 44 Danny Jackson 04		.02	.01
☐ 45 Jose Rijo 07		.03	.01
☐ 46 Scott Scudder 04		.02	.01
☐ 47 Randy Myers UER 07		.03	.01
(Career ERA .274,			
should be 2.74)			
☐ 48 Brian Lane 10		.05	.01
☐ 49 Paul O'Neill 07		.03	.01
☐ 50 Barry Larkin 12		.05	.02
☐ 51 Reggie Jefferson 25		.11	.03
☐ 52 Jeff Branson 10		.05	.01
☐ 53 Chris Sabo 07		.03	.01
☐ 54 Joe Oliver 10		.05	.01
☐ 55 Todd Benzinger 04		.02	.01
☐ 56 Rolando Roomes 04		.02	.01
☐ 57 Hal Morris 15		.07	.02
☐ 58 Eric Davis 10		.05	.01
☐ 59 Scott Bryant 12		.05	.02
☐ 60 Ken Griffey Sr. 07		.03	.01
☐ 61 Darryl Kile 15		.07	.02
☐ 62 Dave Smith 04		.02	.01
☐ 63 Mark Portugal 04		.02	.01
☐ 64 Jeff Juden 20		.09	.03
☐ 65 Bill Gullickson 04		.02	.01
☐ 66 Danny Darwin 04		.02	.01
☐ 67 Larry Andersen 04		.02	.01
☐ 68 Jose Cano 04		.02	.01
☐ 69 Dan Schatzeder 04		.02	.01
☐ 70 Jim Deshaies 04		.02	.01
☐ 71 Mike Scott 04		.02	.01
☐ 72 Gerald Young 04		.02	.01
☐ 73 Ken Caminiti 07		.03	.01
☐ 74 Ken Oberkfell 04		.02	.01
☐ 75 Dave Rohde 04		.02	.01
☐ 76 Bill Doran 04		.02	.01
☐ 77 Andujar Cedeno 20		.09	.03
☐ 78 Craig Biggio 10		.05	.01
☐ 79 Karl Rhodes 04		.02	.01
☐ 80 Glenn Davis 07		.03	.01
☐ 81 Eric Anthony 30		.14	.04
☐ 82 John Wetteland 15		.07	.02
☐ 83 Jay Howell 04		.02	.01
☐ 84 Orel Hershiser 07		.03	.01
☐ 85 Tim Belcher 07		.03	.01
☐ 86 Kiki Jones 10		.05	.01
☐ 87 Mike Hartley 04		.02	.01
☐ 88 Ramon Martinez 15		.07	.02
☐ 89 Mike Scioscia 04		.02	.01
☐ 90 Willie Randolph 07		.03	.01
☐ 91 Juan Samuel 04		.02	.01
☐ 92 Jose Offerman 20		.09	.03

☐ 93 Dave Hansen	.15	.07	.02
☐ 94 Jeff Hamilton	.04	.02	.01
☐ 95 Alfredo Griffin	.04	.02	.01
☐ 96 Tom Goodwin	.15	.07	.02
☐ 97 Kirk Gibson	.07	.03	.01
☐ 98 Jose Vizcaino	.10	.05	.01
☐ 99 Kal Daniels	.04	.02	.01
☐ 100 Hubie Brooks	.04	.02	.01
☐ 101 Eddie Murray	.10	.05	.01
☐ 102 Dennis Boyd	.04	.02	.01
☐ 103 Tim Burke	.04	.02	.01
☐ 104 Bill Sampen	.04	.02	.01
☐ 105 Brett Gideon	.04	.02	.01
☐ 106 Mark Gardner	.12	.05	.02
☐ 107 Howard Farmer	.04	.02	.01
☐ 108 Mel Rojas	.12	.05	.02
☐ 109 Kevin Gross	.04	.02	.01
☐ 110 Dave Schmidt	.04	.02	.01
☐ 111 Denny Martinez	.07	.03	.01
☐ 112 Jerry Goff	.04	.02	.01
☐ 113 Andres Galarraga	.04	.02	.01
☐ 114 Tim Wallach	.07	.03	.01
☐ 115 Marquis Grissom	.60	.25	.08
☐ 116 Spike Owen	.04	.02	.01
☐ 117 Larry Walker	.90	.40	.11
☐ 118 Tim Raines	.07	.03	.01
☐ 119 Delino DeShields	.60	.25	.08
☐ 120 Tom Foley	.04	.02	.01
☐ 121 Dave Martinez	.07	.03	.01
☐ 122 Frank Viola UER	.07	.03	.01
(Career ERA .384,			
should be 3.84)			
☐ 123 Julio Valera	.15	.07	.02
☐ 124 Alejandro Pena	.04	.02	.01
☐ 125 David Cone	.12	.05	.02
☐ 126 Dwight Gooden	.10	.05	.01
☐ 127 Kevin D. Brown	.04	.02	.01
☐ 128 John Franco	.07	.03	.01
☐ 129 Terry Bross	.07	.03	.01
☐ 130 Blaine Beatty	.04	.02	.01
☐ 131 Sid Fernandez	.07	.03	.01
☐ 132 Mike Marshall	.04	.02	.01
☐ 133 Howard Johnson	.07	.03	.01
☐ 134 Jaime Roseboro	.07	.03	.01
☐ 135 Alan Zinter	.10	.05	.01
☐ 136 Keith Miller	.04	.02	.01
☐ 137 Kevin Elster	.04	.02	.01
☐ 138 Kevin McReynolds	.07	.03	.01
☐ 139 Barry Lyons	.04	.02	.01
☐ 140 Gregg Jefferies	.12	.05	.02
☐ 141 Darryl Strawberry	.20	.09	.03
☐ 142 Todd Hundley	.15	.07	.02
☐ 143 Scott Service	.04	.02	.01
☐ 144 Chuck Malone	.04	.02	.01
☐ 145 Steve Ontiveros	.04	.02	.01
☐ 146 Roger McDowell	.04	.02	.01
☐ 147 Ken Howell	.04	.02	.01

☐ 148 Pat Combs	.07	.03	.01
☐ 149 Jeff Parrett	.04	.02	.01
☐ 150 Chuck McElroy	.12	.05	.02
☐ 151 Jason Grimsley	.10	.05	.01
☐ 152 Len Dykstra	.07	.03	.01
☐ 153 Mickey Morandini	.25	.11	.03
☐ 154 John Kruk	.07	.03	.01
☐ 155 Dickie Thon	.04	.02	.01
☐ 156 Ricky Jordan	.04	.02	.01
☐ 157 Jeff Jackson	.10	.05	.01
☐ 158 Darren Daulton	.07	.03	.01
☐ 159 Tom Herr	.04	.02	.01
☐ 160 Von Hayes	.04	.02	.01
☐ 161 Dave Hollins	.60	.25	.08
☐ 162 Carmelo Martinez	.04	.02	.01
☐ 163 Bob Walk	.04	.02	.01
☐ 164 Doug Drabek	.07	.03	.01
☐ 165 Walt Terrell	.04	.02	.01
☐ 166 Bill Landrum	.04	.02	.01
☐ 167 Scott Ruskin	.04	.02	.01
☐ 168 Bob Patterson	.04	.02	.01
☐ 169 Bobby Bonilla	.12	.05	.02
☐ 170 Jose Lind	.04	.02	.01
☐ 171 Andy Van Slyke	.10	.05	.01
☐ 172 Mike LaValliere	.04	.02	.01
☐ 173 Willie Greene	.50	.23	.06
☐ 174 Jay Bell	.07	.03	.01
☐ 175 Sid Bream	.04	.02	.01
☐ 176 Tom Prince	.04	.02	.01
☐ 177 Wally Backman	.04	.02	.01
☐ 178 Moises Alou	.50	.23	.06
☐ 179 Steve Carter	.04	.02	.01
☐ 180 Gary Redus	.04	.02	.01
☐ 181 Barry Bonds	.30	.14	.04
☐ 182 Don Slaught UER	.04	.02	.01
(Card back shows			
headings for a pitcher)			
☐ 183 Joe Magrane	.04	.02	.01
☐ 184 Bryn Smith	.04	.02	.01
☐ 185 Todd Worrell	.04	.02	.01
☐ 186 Jose DeLeon	.04	.02	.01
☐ 187 Frank DiPino	.04	.02	.01
☐ 188 John Tudor	.04	.02	.01
☐ 189 Howard Hilton	.10	.05	.01
☐ 190 John Ericks	.04	.02	.01
☐ 191 Ken Dayley	.04	.02	.01
☐ 192 Ray Lankford	1.00	.45	.13
☐ 193 Todd Zeile	.15	.07	.02
☐ 194 Willie McGee	.07	.03	.01
☐ 195 Ozzie Smith	.12	.05	.02
☐ 196 Milt Thompson	.04	.02	.01
☐ 197 Terry Pendleton	.10	.05	.01
☐ 198 Vince Coleman	.07	.03	.01
☐ 199 Paul Coleman	.12	.05	.02
☐ 200 Jose Oquendo	.04	.02	.01
☐ 201 Pedro Guerrero	.07	.03	.01
☐ 202 Tom Brunansky	.07	.03	.01

☐ 203 Roger Smithberg 10	.05	.01
☐ 204 Eddie Whitson................04	.02	.01
☐ 205 Dennis Rasmussen 04	.02	.01
☐ 206 Craig Lefferts 04	.02	.01
☐ 207 Andy Benes 15	.07	.02
☐ 208 Bruce Hurst....................07	.03	.01
☐ 209 Eric Show 04	.02	.01
☐ 210 Rafael Valdez 10	.05	.01
☐ 211 Joey Cora 04	.02	.01
☐ 212 Thomas Howard 12	.05	.02
☐ 213 Rob Nelson 04	.02	.01
☐ 214 Jack Clark 07	.03	.01
☐ 215 Garry Templeton 04	.02	.01
☐ 216 Fred Lynn 07	.03	.01
☐ 217 Tony Gwynn 20	.09	.03
☐ 218 Benito Santiago...............07	.03	.01
☐ 219 Mike Pagliarulo 04	.02	.01
☐ 220 Joe Carter 20	.09	.03
☐ 221 Roberto Alomar 40	.18	.05
☐ 222 Bip Roberts 07	.03	.01
☐ 223 Rick Reuschel 04	.02	.01
☐ 224 Russ Swan 10	.05	.01
☐ 225 Eric Gunderson 10	.05	.01
☐ 226 Steve Bedrosian.............04	.02	.01
☐ 227 Mike Remlinger...............10	.05	.01
☐ 228 Scott Garrelts.................04	.02	.01
☐ 229 Ernie Camacho................04	.02	.01
☐ 230 Andres Santana 12	.05	.02
☐ 231 Will Clark 30	.14	.04
☐ 232 Kevin Mitchell.................10	.05	.01
☐ 233 Robby Thompson 04	.02	.01
☐ 234 Bill Bathe........................04	.02	.01
☐ 235 Tony Perezchica 04	.02	.01
☐ 236 Gary Carter 07	.03	.01
☐ 237 Brett Butler.....................07	.03	.01
☐ 238 Matt Williams..................10	.05	.01
☐ 239 Earnie Riles 04	.02	.01
☐ 240 Kevin Bass 04	.02	.01
☐ 241 Terry Kennedy.................04	.02	.01
☐ 242 Steve Hosey 50	.23	.06
☐ 243 Ben McDonald 50	.23	.06
☐ 244 Jeff Ballard......................04	.02	.01
☐ 245 Joe Price.........................04	.02	.01
☐ 246 Curt Schilling 15	.07	.02
☐ 247 Pete Harnisch 07	.03	.01
☐ 248 Mark Williamson..............04	.02	.01
☐ 249 Gregg Olson 10	.05	.01
☐ 250 Chris Myers 10	.05	.01
☐ 251A David Segui ERR 30	.14	.04
(Missing vital stats		
at top of card back		
under name)		
☐ 251B David Segui COR 10	.05	.01
☐ 252 Joe Orsulak 04	.02	.01
☐ 253 Craig Worthington 04	.02	.01
☐ 254 Mickey Tettleton..............07	.03	.01
☐ 255 Cal Ripken 40	.18	.05
☐ 256 Billy Ripken.....................04	.02	.01
☐ 257 Randy Milligan 04	.02	.01
☐ 258 Brady Anderson 10	.05	.01
☐ 259 Chris Hoiles 40	.18	.05
☐ 260 Mike Devereaux..............07	.03	.01
☐ 261 Phil Bradley.....................04	.02	.01
☐ 262 Leo Gomez 50	.23	.06
☐ 263 Lee Smith 07	.03	.01
☐ 264 Mike Rochford 04	.02	.01
☐ 265 Jeff Reardon 07	.03	.01
☐ 266 Wes Gardner 04	.02	.01
☐ 267 Mike Boddicker 04	.02	.01
☐ 268 Roger Clemens 35	.16	.04
☐ 269 Rob Murphy 04	.02	.01
☐ 270 Mickey Pina 07	.03	.01
☐ 271 Tony Pena 04	.02	.01
☐ 272 Jody Reed 04	.02	.01
☐ 273 Kevin Romine 04	.02	.01
☐ 274 Mike Greenwell 07	.03	.01
☐ 275 Maurice Vaughn..............35	.16	.04
☐ 276 Danny Heep 04	.02	.01
☐ 277 Scott Cooper 40	.18	.05
☐ 278 Greg Blosser 20	.09	.03
☐ 279 Dwight Evans UER 07	.03	.01
(* by "1990 Team		
Breakdown")		
☐ 280 Ellis Burks 07	.03	.01
☐ 281 Wade Boggs 20	.09	.03
☐ 282 Marty Barrett...................04	.02	.01
☐ 283 Kirk McCaskill 04	.02	.01
☐ 284 Mark Langston.................07	.03	.01
☐ 285 Bert Blyleven...................07	.03	.01
☐ 286 Mike Fetters 10	.05	.01
☐ 287 Kyle Abbott 20	.09	.03
☐ 288 Jim Abbott 20	.09	.03
☐ 289 Chuck Finley 07	.03	.01
☐ 290 Gary DiSarcina................20	.09	.03
☐ 291 Dick Schofield 04	.02	.01
☐ 292 Devon White 07	.03	.01
☐ 293 Bobby Rose 07	.03	.01
☐ 294 Brian Downing 04	.02	.01
☐ 295 Lance Parrish 07	.03	.01
☐ 296 Jack Howell.....................04	.02	.01
☐ 297 Claudell Washington 04	.02	.01
☐ 298 John Orton 10	.05	.01
☐ 299 Wally Joyner 07	.03	.01
☐ 300 Lee Stevens 10	.05	.01
☐ 301 Chili Davis 07	.03	.01
☐ 302 Johnny Ray 04	.02	.01
☐ 303 Greg Hibbard 20	.09	.03
☐ 304 Eric King 04	.02	.01
☐ 305 Jack McDowell.................20	.09	.03
☐ 306 Bobby Thigpen.................04	.02	.01
☐ 307 Adam Peterson 04	.02	.01
☐ 308 Scott Radinsky 15	.07	.02
☐ 309 Wayne Edwards 04	.02	.01
☐ 310 Melido Perez 04	.02	.01

☐ 311	Robin Ventura	.60	.25	.08
☐ 312	Sammy Sosa	.15	.07	.02
☐ 313	Dan Pasqua	.04	.02	.01
☐ 314	Carlton Fisk	.10	.05	.01
☐ 315	Ozzie Guillen	.04	.02	.01
☐ 316	Ivan Calderon	.04	.02	.01
☐ 317	Daryl Boston	.04	.02	.01
☐ 318	Craig Grebeck	.15	.07	.02
☐ 319	Scott Fletcher	.04	.02	.01
☐ 320	Frank Thomas	4.00	1.80	.50
☐ 321	Steve Lyons	.04	.02	.01
☐ 322	Carlos Martinez	.04	.02	.01
☐ 323	Joe Skalski	.04	.02	.01
☐ 324	Tom Candiotti	.04	.02	.01
☐ 325	Greg Swindell	.07	.03	.01
☐ 326	Steve Olin	.20	.09	.03
☐ 327	Kevin Wickander	.04	.02	.01
☐ 328	Doug Jones	.07	.03	.01
☐ 329	Jeff Shaw	.04	.02	.01
☐ 330	Kevin Bearse	.04	.02	.01
☐ 331	Dion James	.04	.02	.01
☐ 332	Jerry Browne	.04	.02	.01
☐ 333	Joey Belle	.50	.23	.06
☐ 334	Felix Fermin	.04	.02	.01
☐ 335	Candy Maldonado	.04	.02	.01
☐ 336	Cory Snyder	.04	.02	.01
☐ 337	Sandy Alomar Jr.	.10	.05	.01
☐ 338	Mark Lewis	.12	.05	.02
☐ 339	Carlos Baerga	1.25	.55	.16
☐ 340	Chris James	.04	.02	.01
☐ 341	Brook Jacoby	.04	.02	.01
☐ 342	Keith Hernandez	.07	.03	.01
☐ 343	Frank Tanana	.04	.02	.01
☐ 344	Scott Aldred	.20	.09	.03
☐ 345	Mike Henneman	.04	.02	.01
☐ 346	Steve Wapnick	.04	.02	.01
☐ 347	Greg Gohr	.15	.07	.02
☐ 348	Eric Stone	.10	.05	.01
☐ 349	Brian DuBois	.04	.02	.01
☐ 350	Kevin Ritz	.10	.05	.01
☐ 351	Rico Brogna	.04	.02	.01
☐ 352	Mike Heath	.04	.02	.01
☐ 353	Alan Trammell	.07	.03	.01
☐ 354	Chet Lemon	.04	.02	.01
☐ 355	Dave Bergman	.04	.02	.01
☐ 356	Lou Whitaker	.07	.03	.01
☐ 357	Cecil Fielder UER	.20	.09	.03
	(* by "1990 Team Breakdown")			
☐ 358	Milt Cuyler	.20	.09	.03
☐ 359	Tony Phillips	.04	.02	.01
☐ 360	Travis Fryman	1.50	.65	.19
☐ 361	Ed Romero	.04	.02	.01
☐ 362	Lloyd Moseby	.04	.02	.01
☐ 363	Mark Gubicza	.04	.02	.01
☐ 364	Bret Saberhagen	.07	.03	.01
☐ 365	Tom Gordon	.07	.03	.01
☐ 366	Steve Farr	.04	.02	.01
☐ 367	Kevin Appier	.25	.11	.03
☐ 368	Storm Davis	.04	.02	.01
☐ 369	Mark Davis	.04	.02	.01
☐ 370	Jeff Montgomery	.07	.03	.01
☐ 371	Frank White	.04	.02	.01
☐ 372	Brent Mayne	.15	.07	.02
☐ 373	Bob Boone	.07	.03	.01
☐ 374	Jim Eisenreich	.04	.02	.01
☐ 375	Danny Tartabull	.07	.03	.01
☐ 376	Kurt Stillwell	.04	.02	.01
☐ 377	Bill Pecota	.04	.02	.01
☐ 378	Bo Jackson	.15	.07	.02
☐ 379	Bob Hamelin	.12	.05	.02
☐ 380	Kevin Seitzer	.07	.03	.01
☐ 381	Rey Palacios	.04	.02	.01
☐ 382	George Brett	.15	.07	.02
☐ 383	Gerald Perry	.04	.02	.01
☐ 384	Teddy Higuera	.04	.02	.01
☐ 385	Tom Filer	.04	.02	.01
☐ 386	Dan Plesac	.04	.02	.01
☐ 387	Cal Eldred	1.00	.45	.13
☐ 388	Jaime Navarro	.20	.09	.03
☐ 389	Chris Bosio	.04	.02	.01
☐ 390	Randy Veres	.04	.02	.01
☐ 391	Gary Sheffield	.50	.23	.06
☐ 392	George Canale	.04	.02	.01
☐ 393	B.J. Surhoff	.04	.02	.01
☐ 394	Tim McIntosh	.10	.05	.01
☐ 395	Greg Brock	.04	.02	.01
☐ 396	Greg Vaughn	.15	.07	.02
☐ 397	Darryl Hamilton	.12	.05	.02
☐ 398	Dave Parker	.07	.03	.01
☐ 399	Paul Molitor	.10	.05	.01
☐ 400	Jim Gantner	.04	.02	.01
☐ 401	Rob Deer	.07	.03	.01
☐ 402	Billy Spiers	.04	.02	.01
☐ 403	Glenn Braggs	.04	.02	.01
☐ 404	Robin Yount	.15	.07	.02
☐ 405	Rick Aguilera	.07	.03	.01
☐ 406	Johnny Ard	.07	.03	.01
☐ 407	Kevin Tapani	.35	.16	.04
☐ 408	Park Pittman	.04	.02	.01
☐ 409	Allan Anderson	.04	.02	.01
☐ 410	Juan Berenguer	.04	.02	.01
☐ 411	Willie Banks	.25	.11	.03
☐ 412	Rich Yett	.04	.02	.01
☐ 413	Dave West	.04	.02	.01
☐ 414	Greg Gagne	.04	.02	.01
☐ 415	Chuck Knoblauch	1.00	.45	.13
☐ 416	Randy Bush	.04	.02	.01
☐ 417	Gary Gaetti	.04	.02	.01
☐ 418	Kent Hrbek	.07	.03	.01
☐ 419	Al Newman	.04	.02	.01
☐ 420	Danny Gladden	.04	.02	.01
☐ 421	Paul Sorrento	.25	.11	.03
☐ 422	Derek Parks	.10	.05	.01

☐ 423	Scott Leius	.25	.11	.03
☐ 424	Kirby Puckett	.30	.14	.04
☐ 425	Willie Smith	.07	.03	.01
☐ 426	Dave Righetti	.04	.02	.01
☐ 427	Jeff D. Robinson	.04	.02	.01
☐ 428	Alan Mills	.12	.05	.02
☐ 429	Tim Leary	.04	.02	.01
☐ 430	Pascual Perez	.04	.02	.01
☐ 431	Alvaro Espinoza	.04	.02	.01
☐ 432	Dave Winfield	.15	.07	.02
☐ 433	Jesse Barfield	.04	.02	.01
☐ 434	Randy Velarde	.04	.02	.01
☐ 435	Rick Cerone	.04	.02	.01
☐ 436	Steve Balboni	.04	.02	.01
☐ 437	Mel Hall	.04	.02	.01
☐ 438	Bob Geren	.04	.02	.01
☐ 439	Bernie Williams	.30	.14	.04
☐ 440	Kevin Maas	.25	.11	.03
☐ 441	Mike Blowers	.04	.02	.01
☐ 442	Steve Sax	.07	.03	.01
☐ 443	Don Mattingly	.20	.09	.03
☐ 444	Roberto Kelly	.12	.05	.02
☐ 445	Mike Moore	.04	.02	.01
☐ 446	Reggie Harris	.10	.05	.01
☐ 447	Scott Sanderson	.04	.02	.01
☐ 448	Dave Otto	.04	.02	.01
☐ 449	Dave Stewart	.07	.03	.01
☐ 450	Rick Honeycutt	.04	.02	.01
☐ 451	Dennis Eckersley	.12	.05	.02
☐ 452	Carney Lansford	.07	.03	.01
☐ 453	Scott Hemond	.10	.05	.01
☐ 454	Mark McGwire	.30	.14	.04
☐ 455	Felix Jose	.20	.09	.03
☐ 456	Terry Steinbach	.07	.03	.01
☐ 457	Rickey Henderson	.20	.09	.03
☐ 458	Dave Henderson	.04	.02	.01
☐ 459	Mike Gallego	.04	.02	.01
☐ 460	Jose Canseco	.30	.14	.04
☐ 461	Walt Weiss	.04	.02	.01
☐ 462	Ken Phelps	.04	.02	.01
☐ 463	Darren Lewis	.20	.09	.03
☐ 464	Ron Hassey	.04	.02	.01
☐ 465	Roger Salkeld	.20	.09	.03
☐ 466	Scott Bankhead	.04	.02	.01
☐ 467	Keith Comstock	.04	.02	.01
☐ 468	Randy Johnson	.15	.07	.02
☐ 469	Erik Hanson	.07	.03	.01
☐ 470	Mike Schooler	.04	.02	.01
☐ 471	Gary Eave	.04	.02	.01
☐ 472	Jeffrey Leonard	.04	.02	.01
☐ 473	Dave Valle	.04	.02	.01
☐ 474	Omar Vizquel	.07	.03	.01
☐ 475	Pete O'Brien	.04	.02	.01
☐ 476	Henry Cotto	.04	.02	.01
☐ 477	Jay Buhner	.07	.03	.01
☐ 478	Harold Reynolds	.04	.02	.01
☐ 479	Alvin Davis	.04	.02	.01
☐ 480	Darnell Coles	.04	.02	.01
☐ 481	Ken Griffey Jr.	1.25	.55	.16
☐ 482	Greg Briley	.04	.02	.01
☐ 483	Scott Bradley	.04	.02	.01
☐ 484	Tino Martinez	.12	.05	.02
☐ 485	Jeff Russell	.04	.02	.01
☐ 486	Nolan Ryan	.50	.23	.06
☐ 487	Robb Nen	.10	.05	.01
☐ 488	Kevin Brown	.10	.05	.01
☐ 489	Brian Bohanon	.10	.05	.01
☐ 490	Ruben Sierra	.20	.09	.03
☐ 491	Pete Incaviglia	.04	.02	.01
☐ 492	Juan Gonzalez	2.00	.90	.25
☐ 493	Steve Buechele	.04	.02	.01
☐ 494	Scott Coolbaugh	.04	.02	.01
☐ 495	Geno Petralli	.04	.02	.01
☐ 496	Rafael Palmeiro	.12	.05	.02
☐ 497	Julio Franco	.07	.03	.01
☐ 498	Gary Pettis	.04	.02	.01
☐ 499	Donald Harris	.10	.05	.01
☐ 500	Monty Fariss	.07	.03	.01
☐ 501	Harold Baines	.07	.03	.01
☐ 502	Cecil Espy	.04	.02	.01
☐ 503	Jack Daugherty	.04	.02	.01
☐ 504	Willie Blair	.10	.05	.01
☐ 505	Dave Stieb	.07	.03	.01
☐ 506	Tom Henke	.07	.03	.01
☐ 507	John Cerutti	.04	.02	.01
☐ 508	Paul Kilgus	.04	.02	.01
☐ 509	Jimmy Key	.07	.03	.01
☐ 510	John Olerud	.60	.25	.08
☐ 511	Ed Sprague	.07	.03	.01
☐ 512	Manny Lee	.04	.02	.01
☐ 513	Fred McGriff	.20	.09	.03
☐ 514	Glenallen Hill	.07	.03	.01
☐ 515	George Bell	.07	.03	.01
☐ 516	Mookie Wilson	.04	.02	.01
☐ 517	Luis Sojo	.15	.07	.02
☐ 518	Nelson Liriano	.04	.02	.01
☐ 519	Kelly Gruber	.07	.03	.01
☐ 520	Greg Myers	.04	.02	.01
☐ 521	Pat Borders	.07	.03	.01
☐ 522	Junior Felix	.07	.03	.01
☐ 523	Eddie Zosky	.15	.07	.02
☐ 524	Tony Fernandez	.07	.03	.01
☐ 525	Checklist 1-132 UER	.05	.01	.00
	(No copyright mark			
	on the back)			
☐ 526	Checklist 133-264	.05	.01	.00
☐ 527	Checklist 265-396	.05	.01	.00
☐ 528	Checklist 397-528	.05	.01	.00

1991 Bowman

This 704-card standard size (2 1/2" by 3 1/2") set marked the third straight year that Topps issued a set using the Bowman name. The cards are arranged in team order by division as follows: AL East, AL West, NL East, and NL West. Some of the specials in the set include cards made for all the 1990 MVPs in each minor league, the leader sluggers by position (Silver Sluggers), and special cards commemorating long-time baseball figure Jimmie Reese, General Colin Powell, newly inducted Hall of Famer Rod Carew and Rickey Henderson's 938th Stolen Base. The cards themselves are designed just like the 1990 Bowman set while the backs again feature the innovative team by team breakdown of how the player did the previous year against a green background. The set numbering is as follows: Toronto Blue Jays (6-30), Milwaukee Brewers (31-56), Cleveland Indians (57-82), Baltimore Orioles (83-106), Boston Red Sox (107-130), Detroit Tigers (131-154), New York Yankees (155-179), California Angels (187-211), Oakland Athletics (212-238), Seattle Mariners (239-264), Texas Rangers (265-290), Kansas City Royals (291-316), Minnesota Twins (317-341), Chicago White Sox (342-366), St. Louis Cardinals (385-409), Chicago Cubs (411-433), Montreal Expos (434-459), New York Mets (460-484), Philadelphia Phillies (485-508), Pittsburgh Pirates (509-532), Houston Astros (539-565), Atlanta Braves (566-590), Los Angles Dodgers (591-615), San Fransico Giants (616-641), San Diego Padres (642-665), and Cincinnati Reds

(666-691). Special subsets feature AL Silver Sluggers (367-375) and NL Silver Sluggers (376-384). There are two instances of misnumbering in the set; Ken Griffey (should be 255) and Ken Griffey Jr. are both numbered 246 and Donovan Osborne (should be 406) and Thomson/Branca share number 410. The noteworthy Rookie Cards in this set are Jeff Bagwell, Bret Boone, Jeromy Burnitz, Eric Karros, Ryan Klesko, Kenny Lofton, Sam Militello, Mike Mussina, Phil Plantier, Ivan Rodriguez, Tim Salmon, Reggie Sanders, Todd Van Poppel, Bob Wickman.

	MT	EX-MT	VG
COMPLETE SET (704)	15.00	6.75	1.90
COMPLETE FACT.SET (704)	15.00	6.75	1.90
COMMON PLAYER (1-704)	.04	.02	.01
☐ 1 Rod Carew I	.15	.07	.02
☐ 2 Rod Carew II	.15	.07	.02
☐ 3 Rod Carew III	.15	.07	.02
☐ 4 Rod Carew IV	.15	.07	.02
☐ 5 Rod Carew V	.15	.07	.02
☐ 6 Willie Fraser	.04	.02	.01
☐ 7 John Olerud	.15	.07	.02
☐ 8 William Suero	.10	.05	.01
☐ 9 Roberto Alomar	.20	.09	.03
☐ 10 Todd Stottlemyre	.07	.03	.01
☐ 11 Joe Carter	.12	.05	.02
☐ 12 Steve Karsay	.25	.11	.03
☐ 13 Mark Whiten	.12	.05	.02
☐ 14 Pat Borders	.04	.02	.01
☐ 15 Mike Timlin	.10	.05	.01
☐ 16 Tom Henke	.07	.03	.01
☐ 17 Eddie Zosky	.04	.02	.01
☐ 18 Kelly Gruber	.07	.03	.01
☐ 19 Jimmy Key	.04	.02	.01
☐ 20 Jerry Schunk	.10	.05	.01
☐ 21 Manny Lee	.04	.02	.01
☐ 22 Dave Stieb	.04	.02	.01
☐ 23 Pat Hentgen	.15	.07	.02
☐ 24 Glenallen Hill	.04	.02	.01
☐ 25 Rene Gonzales	.04	.02	.01
☐ 26 Ed Sprague	.15	.07	.02
☐ 27 Ken Dayley	.04	.02	.01
☐ 28 Pat Tabler	.04	.02	.01
☐ 29 Denis Boucher	.12	.05	.02
☐ 30 Devon White	.07	.03	.01
☐ 31 Dante Bichette	.04	.02	.01
☐ 32 Paul Molitor	.10	.05	.01
☐ 33 Greg Vaughn	.10	.05	.01
☐ 34 Dan Plesac	.04	.02	.01
☐ 35 Chris George	.10	.05	.01
☐ 36 Tim McIntosh	.04	.02	.01
☐ 37 Franklin Stubbs	.04	.02	.01

☐	38	Bo Dodson	15	.07	.02	☐	95	Arthur Rhodes	35	.16	.04
☐	39	Ron Robinson	04	.02	.01	☐	96	Juan Bell	04	.02	.01
☐	40	Ed Nunez	04	.02	.01	☐	97	Mike Mussina	1.50	.65	.19
☐	41	Greg Brock	04	.02	.01	☐	98	Jeff Ballard	04	.02	.01
☐	42	Jaime Navarro	07	.03	.01	☐	99	Chris Hoiles	10	.05	.01
☐	43	Chris Bosio	04	.02	.01	☐	100	Brady Anderson	07	.03	.01
☐	44	B.J. Surhoff	04	.02	.01	☐	101	Bob Milacki	04	.02	.01
☐	45	Chris Johnson	10	.05	.01	☐	102	David Segui	04	.02	.01
☐	46	Willie Randolph	07	.03	.01	☐	103	Dwight Evans	07	.03	.01
☐	47	Narciso Elvira	10	.05	.01	☐	104	Cal Ripken	30	.14	.04
☐	48	Jim Gantner	04	.02	.01	☐	105	Mike Linskey	12	.05	.02
☐	49	Kevin Brown	04	.02	.01	☐	106	Jeff Tackett	15	.07	.02
☐	50	Julio Machado	04	.02	.01	☐	107	Jeff Reardon	07	.03	.01
☐	51	Chuck Crim	04	.02	.01	☐	108	Dana Kiecker	04	.02	.01
☐	52	Gary Sheffield	25	.11	.03	☐	109	Ellis Burks	07	.03	.01
☐	53	Angel Miranda	12	.05	.02	☐	110	Dave Owen	04	.02	.01
☐	54	Teddy Higuera	04	.02	.01	☐	111	Danny Darwin	04	.02	.01
☐	55	Robin Yount	10	.05	.01	☐	112	Mo Vaughn	10	.05	.01
☐	56	Cal Eldred	35	.16	.04	☐	113	Jeff McNeely	20	.09	.03
☐	57	Sandy Alomar Jr.	07	.03	.01	☐	114	Tom Bolton	04	.02	.01
☐	58	Greg Swindell	07	.03	.01	☐	115	Greg Blosser	10	.05	.01
☐	59	Brook Jacoby	04	.02	.01	☐	116	Mike Greenwell	07	.03	.01
☐	60	Efrain Valdez	04	.02	.01	☐	117	Phil Plantier	50	.23	.06
☐	61	Ever Magallanes	10	.05	.01	☐	118	Roger Clemens	25	.11	.03
☐	62	Tom Candiotti	04	.02	.01	☐	119	John Marzano	04	.02	.01
☐	63	Eric King	04	.02	.01	☐	120	Jody Reed	04	.02	.01
☐	64	Alex Cole	04	.02	.01	☐	121	Scott Taylor	10	.05	.01
☐	65	Charles Nagy	20	.09	.03	☐	122	Jack Clark	07	.03	.01
☐	66	Mitch Webster	04	.02	.01	☐	123	Derek Livernois	10	.05	.01
☐	67	Chris James	04	.02	.01	☐	124	Tony Pena	04	.02	.01
☐	68	Jim Thome	20	.09	.03	☐	125	Tom Brunansky	07	.03	.01
☐	69	Carlos Baerga	20	.09	.03	☐	126	Carlos Quintana	04	.02	.01
☐	70	Mark Lewis	10	.05	.01	☐	127	Tim Naehring	07	.03	.01
☐	71	Jerry Browne	04	.02	.01	☐	128	Matt Young	04	.02	.01
☐	72	Jesse Orosco	04	.02	.01	☐	129	Wade Boggs	12	.05	.02
☐	73	Mike Huff	04	.02	.01	☐	130	Kevin Morton	10	.05	.01
☐	74	Jose Escobar	10	.05	.01	☐	131	Pete Incaviglia	04	.02	.01
☐	75	Jeff Manto	04	.02	.01	☐	132	Rob Deer	07	.03	.01
☐	76	Turner Ward	10	.05	.01	☐	133	Bill Gullickson	04	.02	.01
☐	77	Doug Jones	04	.02	.01	☐	134	Rico Brogna	10	.05	.01
☐	78	Bruce Egloff	10	.05	.01	☐	135	Lloyd Moseby	04	.02	.01
☐	79	Tim Costo	20	.09	.03	☐	136	Cecil Fielder	12	.05	.02
☐	80	Beau Allred	04	.02	.01	☐	137	Tony Phillips	04	.02	.01
☐	81	Albert Belle	12	.05	.02	☐	138	Mark Leiter	10	.05	.01
☐	82	John Farrell	04	.02	.01	☐	139	John Cerutti	04	.02	.01
☐	83	Glenn Davis	07	.03	.01	☐	140	Mickey Tettleton	07	.03	.01
☐	84	Joe Orsulak	04	.02	.01	☐	141	Milt Cuyler	07	.03	.01
☐	85	Mark Williamson	04	.02	.01	☐	142	Greg Gohr	07	.03	.01
☐	86	Ben McDonald	10	.05	.01	☐	143	Tony Bernazard	04	.02	.01
☐	87	Billy Ripken	04	.02	.01	☐	144	Dan Gakeler	04	.02	.01
☐	88	Leo Gomez	15	.07	.02	☐	145	Travis Fryman	40	.18	.05
☐	89	Bob Melvin	04	.02	.01	☐	146	Dan Petry	04	.02	.01
☐	90	Jeff M. Robinson	04	.02	.01	☐	147	Scott Aldred	04	.02	.01
☐	91	Jose Mesa	04	.02	.01	☐	148	John DeSilva	20	.09	.03
☐	92	Gregg Olson	07	.03	.01	☐	149	Rusty Meacham	10	.05	.01
☐	93	Mike Devereaux	07	.03	.01	☐	150	Lou Whitaker	07	.03	.01
☐	94	Luis Mercedes	20	.09	.03	☐	151	Dave Haas	10	.05	.01

☐ 152 Luis de los Santos	.04	.02	.01
☐ 153 Ivan Cruz	.15	.07	.02
☐ 154 Alan Trammell	.07	.03	.01
☐ 155 Pat Kelly	.15	.07	.02
☐ 156 Carl Everett	.25	.11	.03
☐ 157 Greg Cadaret	.04	.02	.01
☐ 158 Kevin Maas	.10	.05	.01
☐ 159 Jeff Johnson	.10	.05	.01
☐ 160 Willie Smith	.04	.02	.01
☐ 161 Gerald Williams	.20	.09	.03
☐ 162 Mike Humphreys	.15	.07	.02
☐ 163 Alvaro Espinoza	.04	.02	.01
☐ 164 Matt Nokes	.04	.02	.01
☐ 165 Wade Taylor	.04	.02	.01
☐ 166 Roberto Kelly	.07	.03	.01
☐ 167 John Habyan	.04	.02	.01
☐ 168 Steve Farr	.04	.02	.01
☐ 169 Jesse Barfield	.04	.02	.01
☐ 170 Steve Sax	.07	.03	.01
☐ 171 Jim Leyritz	.04	.02	.01
☐ 172 Robert Eenhoorn	.12	.05	.02
☐ 173 Bernie Williams	.10	.05	.01
☐ 174 Scott Lusader	.04	.02	.01
☐ 175 Torey Lovullo	.04	.02	.01
☐ 176 Chuck Cary	.04	.02	.01
☐ 177 Scott Sanderson	.04	.02	.01
☐ 178 Don Mattingly	.15	.07	.02
☐ 179 Mel Hall	.04	.02	.01
☐ 180 Juan Gonzalez	.35	.16	.04
Minor League MVP			
☐ 181 Hensley Meulens	.08	.04	.01
Minor League MVP			
☐ 182 Jose Offerman	.10	.05	.01
Minor League MVP			
☐ 183 Jeff Bagwell	1.25	.55	.16
Minor League MVP			
☐ 184 Jeff Conine	.25	.11	.03
Minor League MVP			
☐ 185 Henry Rodriguez	.20	.09	.03
Minor League MVP			
☐ 186 Jimmie Reese CO	.07	.03	.01
☐ 187 Kyle Abbott	.07	.03	.01
☐ 188 Lance Parrish	.07	.03	.01
☐ 189 Rafael Montalvo	.10	.05	.01
☐ 190 Floyd Bannister	.04	.02	.01
☐ 191 Dick Schofield	.04	.02	.01
☐ 192 Scott Lewis	.10	.05	.01
☐ 193 Jeff D. Robinson	.04	.02	.01
☐ 194 Kent Anderson	.04	.02	.01
☐ 195 Wally Joyner	.07	.03	.01
☐ 196 Chuck Finley	.07	.03	.01
☐ 197 Luis Sojo	.04	.02	.01
☐ 198 Jeff Richardson	.10	.05	.01
☐ 199 Dave Parker	.07	.03	.01
☐ 200 Jim Abbott	.12	.05	.02
☐ 201 Junior Felix	.04	.02	.01
☐ 202 Mark Langston	.07	.03	.01
☐ 203 Tim Salmon	1.00	.45	.13
☐ 204 Cliff Young	.04	.02	.01
☐ 205 Scott Bailes	.04	.02	.01
☐ 206 Bobby Rose	.04	.02	.01
☐ 207 Gary Gaetti	.04	.02	.01
☐ 208 Ruben Amaro	.12	.05	.02
☐ 209 Luis Polonia	.07	.03	.01
☐ 210 Dave Winfield	.04	.02	.01
☐ 211 Bryan Harvey	.04	.02	.01
☐ 212 Mike Moore	.04	.02	.01
☐ 213 Rickey Henderson	.12	.05	.02
☐ 214 Steve Chitren	.10	.05	.01
☐ 215 Bob Welch	.04	.02	.01
☐ 216 Terry Steinbach	.07	.03	.01
☐ 217 Earnest Riles	.04	.02	.01
☐ 218 Todd Van Poppel	.50	.23	.06
☐ 219 Mike Gallego	.04	.02	.01
☐ 220 Curt Young	.04	.02	.01
☐ 221 Todd Burns	.04	.02	.01
☐ 222 Vance Law	.04	.02	.01
☐ 223 Eric Show	.04	.02	.01
☐ 224 Don Peters	.10	.05	.01
☐ 225 Dave Stewart	.07	.03	.01
☐ 226 Dave Henderson	.04	.02	.01
☐ 227 Jose Canseco	.20	.09	.03
☐ 228 Walt Weiss	.04	.02	.01
☐ 229 Dann Howitt	.04	.02	.01
☐ 230 Willie Wilson	.04	.02	.01
☐ 231 Harold Baines	.07	.03	.01
☐ 232 Scott Hemond	.04	.02	.01
☐ 233 Joe Slusarski	.10	.05	.01
☐ 234 Mark McGwire	.20	.09	.03
☐ 235 Kirk Dressendorfer	.10	.05	.01
☐ 236 Craig Paquette	.20	.09	.03
☐ 237 Dennis Eckersley	.12	.05	.02
☐ 238 Dana Allison	.10	.05	.01
☐ 239 Scott Bradley	.04	.02	.01
☐ 240 Brian Holman	.04	.02	.01
☐ 241 Mike Schooler	.04	.02	.01
☐ 242 Rich DeLucia	.04	.02	.01
☐ 243 Edgar Martinez	.07	.03	.01
☐ 244 Henry Cotto	.04	.02	.01
☐ 245 Omar Vizquel	.04	.02	.01
☐ 246 Ken Griffey Jr.	.50	.23	.06
(See also 255)			
☐ 247 Jay Buhner	.07	.03	.01
☐ 248 Bill Krueger	.04	.02	.01
☐ 249 Dave Fleming	1.00	.45	.13
☐ 250 Patrick Lennon	.12	.05	.02
☐ 251 Dave Valle	.04	.02	.01
☐ 252 Harold Reynolds	.04	.02	.01
☐ 253 Randy Johnson	.07	.03	.01
☐ 254 Scott Bankhead	.04	.02	.01
☐ 255 Ken Griffey Sr. UER	.07	.03	.01
(Card number is 246)			
☐ 256 Greg Briley	.04	.02	.01
☐ 257 Tino Martinez	.10	.05	.01

☐ 258 Alvin Davis	.04	.02	.01	
☐ 259 Pete O'Brien	.04	.02	.01	
☐ 260 Erik Hanson	.04	.02	.01	
☐ 261 Bret Boone	1.00	.45	.13	
☐ 262 Roger Salkeld	.10	.05	.01	
☐ 263 Dave Burba	.10	.05	.01	
☐ 264 Kerry Woodson	.15	.07	.02	
☐ 265 Julio Franco	.07	.03	.01	
☐ 266 Dan Peltier	.12	.05	.02	
☐ 267 Jeff Russell	.04	.02	.01	
☐ 268 Steve Buechele	.04	.02	.01	
☐ 269 Donald Harris	.04	.02	.01	
☐ 270 Robb Nen	.04	.02	.01	
☐ 271 Rich Gossage	.07	.03	.01	
☐ 272 Ivan Rodriguez	1.25	.55	.16	
☐ 273 Jeff Huson	.04	.02	.01	
☐ 274 Kevin Brown	.07	.03	.01	
☐ 275 Dan Smith	.20	.09	.03	
☐ 276 Gary Pettis	.04	.02	.01	
☐ 277 Jack Daugherty	.04	.02	.01	
☐ 278 Mike Jeffcoat	.04	.02	.01	
☐ 279 Brad Arnsberg	.04	.02	.01	
☐ 280 Nolan Ryan	.40	.18	.05	
☐ 281 Eric McCray	.10	.05	.01	
☐ 282 Scott Chiamparino	.07	.03	.01	
☐ 283 Ruben Sierra	.15	.07	.02	
☐ 284 Geno Petralli	.04	.02	.01	
☐ 285 Monty Fariss	.07	.03	.01	
☐ 286 Rafael Palmeiro	.10	.05	.01	
☐ 287 Bobby Witt	.04	.02	.01	
☐ 288 Dean Palmer UER	.20	.09	.03	
(Photo actually				
Dan Peltier)				
☐ 289 Tony Scruggs	.10	.05	.01	
☐ 290 Kenny Rogers	.04	.02	.01	
☐ 291 Bret Saberhagen	.07	.03	.01	
☐ 292 Brian McRae	.20	.09	.03	
☐ 293 Storm Davis	.04	.02	.01	
☐ 294 Danny Tartabull	.07	.03	.01	
☐ 295 David Howard	.10	.05	.01	
☐ 296 Mike Boddicker	.04	.02	.01	
☐ 297 Joel Johnston	.10	.05	.01	
☐ 298 Tim Spehr	.10	.05	.01	
☐ 299 Hector Wagner	.04	.02	.01	
☐ 300 George Brett	.10	.05	.01	
☐ 301 Mike Macfarlane	.04	.02	.01	
☐ 302 Kirk Gibson	.07	.03	.01	
☐ 303 Harvey Pulliam	.15	.07	.02	
☐ 304 Jim Eisenreich	.04	.02	.01	
☐ 305 Kevin Seitzer	.07	.03	.01	
☐ 306 Mark Davis	.04	.02	.01	
☐ 307 Kurt Stillwell	.04	.02	.01	
☐ 308 Jeff Montgomery	.04	.02	.01	
☐ 309 Kevin Appier	.07	.03	.01	
☐ 310 Bob Hamelin	.07	.03	.01	
☐ 311 Tom Gordon	.07	.03	.01	
☐ 312 Kerwin Moore	.15	.07	.02	
☐ 313 Hugh Walker	.04	.02	.01	
☐ 314 Terry Shumpert	.04	.02	.01	
☐ 315 Warren Cromartie	.04	.02	.01	
☐ 316 Gary Thurman	.04	.02	.01	
☐ 317 Steve Bedrosian	.04	.02	.01	
☐ 318 Danny Gladden	.04	.02	.01	
☐ 319 Jack Morris	.10	.05	.01	
☐ 320 Kirby Puckett	.20	.09	.03	
☐ 321 Kent Hrbek	.07	.03	.01	
☐ 322 Kevin Tapani	.07	.03	.01	
☐ 323 Denny Neagle	.15	.07	.02	
☐ 324 Rich Garces	.10	.05	.01	
☐ 325 Larry Casian	.04	.02	.01	
☐ 326 Shane Mack	.07	.03	.01	
☐ 327 Allan Anderson	.04	.02	.01	
☐ 328 Junior Ortiz	.04	.02	.01	
☐ 329 Paul Abbott	.10	.05	.01	
☐ 330 Chuck Knoblauch	.30	.14	.04	
☐ 331 Chili Davis	.07	.03	.01	
☐ 332 Todd Ritchie	.10	.05	.01	
☐ 333 Brian Harper	.04	.02	.01	
☐ 334 Rick Aguilera	.07	.03	.01	
☐ 335 Scott Erickson	.20	.09	.03	
☐ 336 Pedro Munoz	.25	.11	.03	
☐ 337 Scott Leius	.04	.02	.01	
☐ 338 Greg Gagne	.04	.02	.01	
☐ 339 Mike Pagliarulo	.04	.02	.01	
☐ 340 Terry Leach	.04	.02	.01	
☐ 341 Willie Banks	.10	.05	.01	
☐ 342 Bobby Thigpen	.04	.02	.01	
☐ 343 Roberto Hernandez	.20	.09	.03	
☐ 344 Melido Perez	.07	.03	.01	
☐ 345 Carlton Fisk	.10	.05	.01	
☐ 346 Norberto Martin	.10	.05	.01	
☐ 347 Johnny Ruffin	.15	.07	.02	
☐ 348 Jeff Carter	.10	.05	.01	
☐ 349 Lance Johnson	.04	.02	.01	
☐ 350 Sammy Sosa	.07	.03	.01	
☐ 351 Alex Fernandez	.15	.07	.02	
☐ 352 Jack McDowell	.10	.05	.01	
☐ 353 Bob Wickman	.40	.18	.05	
☐ 354 Wilson Alvarez	.10	.05	.01	
☐ 355 Charlie Hough	.04	.02	.01	
☐ 356 Ozzie Guillen	.04	.02	.01	
☐ 357 Cory Snyder	.04	.02	.01	
☐ 358 Robin Ventura	.20	.09	.03	
☐ 359 Scott Fletcher	.04	.02	.01	
☐ 360 Cesar Bernhardt	.10	.05	.01	
☐ 361 Dan Pasqua	.04	.02	.01	
☐ 362 Tim Raines	.07	.03	.01	
☐ 363 Brian Drahman	.10	.05	.01	
☐ 364 Wayne Edwards	.04	.02	.01	
☐ 365 Scott Radinsky	.04	.02	.01	
☐ 366 Frank Thomas	1.25	.55	.16	
☐ 367 Cecil Fielder SLUG	.10	.05	.01	
☐ 368 Julio Franco SLUG	.05	.02	.01	
☐ 369 Kelly Gruber SLUG	.05	.02	.01	

☐ 370 Alan Trammell SLUG	.05	.02	.01	☐ 423 Jessie Hollins	.12	.05	.02
☐ 371 Rickey Henderson SLUG	.10	.05	.01	☐ 424 Shawon Dunston	.07	.03	.01
☐ 372 Jose Canseco SLUG	.10	.05	.01	☐ 425 Dave Smith	.04	.02	.01
☐ 373 Ellis Burks SLUG	.05	.02	.01	☐ 426 Greg Maddux	.10	.05	.01
☐ 374 Lance Parrish SLUG	.05	.02	.01	☐ 427 Jose Vizcaino	.04	.02	.01
☐ 375 Dave Parker SLUG	.05	.02	.01	☐ 428 Luis Salazar	.04	.02	.01
☐ 376 Eddie Murray SLUG	.10	.05	.01	☐ 429 Andre Dawson	.10	.05	.01
☐ 377 Ryne Sandberg SLUG	.12	.05	.02	☐ 430 Rick Sutcliffe	.07	.03	.01
☐ 378 Matt Williams SLUG	.05	.02	.01	☐ 431 Paul Assenmacher	.04	.02	.01
☐ 379 Barry Larkin SLUG	.05	.02	.01	☐ 432 Erik Pappas	.04	.02	.01
☐ 380 Barry Bonds SLUG	.10	.05	.01	☐ 433 Mark Grace	.10	.05	.01
☐ 381 Bobby Bonilla SLUG	.08	.04	.01	☐ 434 Dennis Martinez	.07	.03	.01
☐ 382 Darryl Strawberry SLUG	.10	.05	.01	☐ 435 Marquis Grissom	.15	.07	.02
☐ 383 Benny Santiago SLUG	.05	.02	.01	☐ 436 Wilfredo Cordero	.50	.23	.06
☐ 384 Don Robinson SLUG	.05	.02	.01	☐ 437 Tim Wallach	.07	.03	.01
☐ 385 Paul Coleman	.04	.02	.01	☐ 438 Brian Barnes	.12	.05	.02
☐ 386 Milt Thompson	.04	.02	.01	☐ 439 Barry Jones	.04	.02	.01
☐ 387 Lee Smith	.07	.03	.01	☐ 440 Ivan Calderon	.04	.02	.01
☐ 388 Ray Lankford	.30	.14	.04	☐ 441 Stan Spencer	.10	.05	.01
☐ 389 Tom Pagnozzi	.04	.02	.01	☐ 442 Larry Walker	.20	.09	.03
☐ 390 Ken Hill	.07	.03	.01	☐ 443 Chris Haney	.10	.05	.01
☐ 391 Jamie Moyer	.04	.02	.01	☐ 444 Hector Rivera	.10	.05	.01
☐ 392 Greg Carmona	.10	.05	.01	☐ 445 Delino DeShields	.15	.07	.02
☐ 393 John Ericks	.04	.02	.01	☐ 446 Andres Galarraga	.04	.02	.01
☐ 394 Bob Tewksbury	.07	.03	.01	☐ 447 Gilberto Reyes	.04	.02	.01
☐ 395 Jose Oquendo	.04	.02	.01	☐ 448 Willie Greene	.20	.09	.03
☐ 396 Rheal Cormier	.15	.07	.02	☐ 449 Greg Colbrunn	.25	.11	.03
☐ 397 Mike Milchin	.12	.05	.02	☐ 450 Rondell White	.50	.23	.06
☐ 398 Ozzie Smith	.10	.05	.01	☐ 451 Steve Frey	.04	.02	.01
☐ 399 Aaron Holbert	.12	.05	.02	☐ 452 Shane Andrews	.20	.09	.03
☐ 400 Jose DeLeon	.04	.02	.01	☐ 453 Mike Fitzgerald	.04	.02	.01
☐ 401 Felix Jose	.07	.03	.01	☐ 454 Spike Owen	.04	.02	.01
☐ 402 Juan Agosto	.04	.02	.01	☐ 455 Dave Martinez	.04	.02	.01
☐ 403 Pedro Guerrero	.07	.03	.01	☐ 456 Dennis Boyd	.04	.02	.01
☐ 404 Todd Zeile	.07	.03	.01	☐ 457 Eric Bullock	.04	.02	.01
☐ 405 Gerald Perry	.04	.02	.01	☐ 458 Reid Cornelius	.12	.05	.02
☐ 406 Donovan Osborne UER	.50	.23	.06	☐ 459 Chris Nabholz	.10	.05	.01
(Card number is 410)				☐ 460 David Cone	.10	.05	.01
☐ 407 Bryn Smith	.04	.02	.01	☐ 461 Hubie Brooks	.04	.02	.01
☐ 408 Bernard Gilkey	.15	.07	.02	☐ 462 Sid Fernandez	.07	.03	.01
☐ 409 Rex Hudler	.04	.02	.01	☐ 463 Doug Simons	.10	.05	.01
☐ 410 Thomson/Branca Shot	.10	.05	.01	☐ 464 Howard Johnson	.07	.03	.01
Bobby Thomson				☐ 465 Chris Donnels	.12	.05	.02
Ralph Branca				☐ 466 Anthony Young	.12	.05	.02
(See also 406)				☐ 467 Todd Hundley	.04	.02	.01
☐ 411 Lance Dickson	.10	.05	.01	☐ 468 Rick Cerone	.04	.02	.01
☐ 412 Danny Jackson	.04	.02	.01	☐ 469 Kevin Elster	.04	.02	.01
☐ 413 Jerome Walton	.04	.02	.01	☐ 470 Wally Whitehurst	.04	.02	.01
☐ 414 Sean Cheetham	.12	.05	.02	☐ 471 Vince Coleman	.07	.03	.01
☐ 415 Joe Girardi	.04	.02	.01	☐ 472 Dwight Gooden	.07	.03	.01
☐ 416 Ryne Sandberg	.25	.11	.03	☐ 473 Charlie O'Brien	.04	.02	.01
☐ 417 Mike Harkey	.07	.03	.01	☐ 474 Jeromy Burnitz	.30	.14	.04
☐ 418 George Bell	.07	.03	.01	☐ 475 John Franco	.07	.03	.01
☐ 419 Rick Wilkins	.10	.05	.01	☐ 476 Daryl Boston	.04	.02	.01
☐ 420 Earl Cunningham	.04	.02	.01	☐ 477 Frank Viola	.07	.03	.01
☐ 421 Heathcliff Slocumb	.04	.02	.01	☐ 478 D.J. Dozier	.10	.05	.01
☐ 422 Mike Bielecki	.04	.02	.01	☐ 479 Kevin McReynolds	.07	.03	.01

☐ 480 Tom Herr	.04	.02	.01
☐ 481 Gregg Jefferies	.07	.03	.01
☐ 482 Pete Schourek	.12	.05	.02
☐ 483 Ron Darling	.07	.03	.01
☐ 484 Dave Magadan	.07	.03	.01
☐ 485 Andy Ashby	.12	.05	.02
☐ 486 Dale Murphy	.07	.03	.01
☐ 487 Von Hayes	.04	.02	.01
☐ 488 Kim Batiste	.20	.09	.03
☐ 489 Tony Longmire	.10	.05	.01
☐ 490 Wally Backman	.04	.02	.01
☐ 491 Jeff Jackson	.04	.02	.01
☐ 492 Mickey Morandini	.10	.05	.01
☐ 493 Darrel Akerfelds	.04	.02	.01
☐ 494 Ricky Jordan	.04	.02	.01
☐ 495 Randy Ready	.04	.02	.01
☐ 496 Darrin Fletcher	.04	.02	.01
☐ 497 Chuck Malone	.04	.02	.01
☐ 498 Pat Combs	.04	.02	.01
☐ 499 Dickie Thon	.04	.02	.01
☐ 500 Roger McDowell	.04	.02	.01
☐ 501 Len Dykstra	.07	.03	.01
☐ 502 Joe Boever	.04	.02	.01
☐ 503 John Kruk	.07	.03	.01
☐ 504 Terry Mulholland	.04	.02	.01
☐ 505 Wes Chamberlain	.20	.09	.03
☐ 506 Mike Lieberthal	.20	.09	.03
☐ 507 Darren Daulton	.07	.03	.01
☐ 508 Charlie Hayes	.04	.02	.01
☐ 509 John Smiley	.07	.03	.01
☐ 510 Gary Varsho	.04	.02	.01
☐ 511 Curt Wilkerson	.04	.02	.01
☐ 512 Orlando Merced	.20	.09	.03
☐ 513 Barry Bonds	.20	.09	.03
☐ 514 Mike LaValliere	.04	.02	.01
☐ 515 Doug Drabek	.07	.03	.01
☐ 516 Gary Redus	.04	.02	.01
☐ 517 William Pennyfeather	.15	.07	.02
☐ 518 Randy Tomlin	.20	.09	.03
☐ 519 Mike Zimmerman	.10	.05	.01
☐ 520 Jeff King	.04	.02	.01
☐ 521 Kurt Miller	.25	.11	.03
☐ 522 Jay Bell	.07	.03	.01
☐ 523 Bill Landrum	.04	.02	.01
☐ 524 Zane Smith	.04	.02	.01
☐ 525 Bobby Bonilla	.10	.05	.01
☐ 526 Bob Walk	.04	.02	.01
☐ 527 Austin Manahan	.04	.02	.01
☐ 528 Joe Ausanio	.10	.05	.01
☐ 529 Andy Van Slyke	.07	.03	.01
☐ 530 Jose Lind	.04	.02	.01
☐ 531 Carlos Garcia	.20	.09	.03
☐ 532 Don Slaught	.04	.02	.01
☐ 533 Gen. Colin Powell	.15	.07	.02
☐ 534 Frank Bolick	.12	.05	.02
☐ 535 Gary Scott	.15	.07	.02
☐ 536 Nikco Riesgo	.12	.05	.02
☐ 537 Reggie Sanders	.75	.35	.09
☐ 538 Tim Howard	.10	.05	.01
☐ 539 Ryan Bowen	.15	.07	.02
☐ 540 Eric Anthony	.07	.03	.01
☐ 541 Jim Deshaies	.04	.02	.01
☐ 542 Tom Nevers	.12	.05	.02
☐ 543 Ken Caminiti	.07	.03	.01
☐ 544 Karl Rhodes	.04	.02	.01
☐ 545 Xavier Hernandez	.04	.02	.01
☐ 546 Mike Scott	.07	.03	.01
☐ 547 Jeff Juden	.07	.03	.01
☐ 548 Darryl Kile	.07	.03	.01
☐ 549 Willie Ansley	.07	.03	.01
☐ 550 Luis Gonzalez	.20	.09	.03
☐ 551 Mike Simms	.10	.05	.01
☐ 552 Mark Portugal	.04	.02	.01
☐ 553 Jimmy Jones	.04	.02	.01
☐ 554 Jim Clancy	.04	.02	.01
☐ 555 Pete Harnisch	.07	.03	.01
☐ 556 Craig Biggio	.07	.03	.01
☐ 557 Eric Yelding	.04	.02	.01
☐ 558 Dave Rohde	.04	.02	.01
☐ 559 Casey Candaele	.04	.02	.01
☐ 560 Curt Schilling	.07	.03	.01
☐ 561 Steve Finley	.07	.03	.01
☐ 562 Javier Ortiz	.04	.02	.01
☐ 563 Andujar Cedeno	.10	.05	.01
☐ 564 Rafael Ramirez	.04	.02	.01
☐ 565 Kenny Lofton	1.00	.45	.13
☐ 566 Steve Avery	.20	.09	.03
☐ 567 Lonnie Smith	.04	.02	.01
☐ 568 Kent Mercker	.07	.03	.01
☐ 569 Chipper Jones	.75	.35	.09
☐ 570 Terry Pendleton	.10	.05	.01
☐ 571 Otis Nixon	.07	.03	.01
☐ 572 Juan Berenguer	.04	.02	.01
☐ 573 Charlie Leibrandt	.04	.02	.01
☐ 574 David Justice	.30	.14	.04
☐ 575 Keith Mitchell	.20	.09	.03
☐ 576 Tom Glavine	.20	.09	.03
☐ 577 Greg Olson	.04	.02	.01
☐ 578 Rafael Belliard	.04	.02	.01
☐ 579 Ben Rivera	.15	.07	.02
☐ 580 John Smoltz	.10	.05	.01
☐ 581 Tyler Houston	.04	.02	.01
☐ 582 Mark Wohlers	.20	.09	.03
☐ 583 Ron Gant	.12	.05	.02
☐ 584 Ramon Caraballo	.12	.05	.02
☐ 585 Sid Bream	.04	.02	.01
☐ 586 Jeff Treadway	.04	.02	.01
☐ 587 Javier Lopez	.60	.25	.08
☐ 588 Deion Sanders	.20	.09	.03
☐ 589 Mike Heath	.04	.02	.01
☐ 590 Ryan Klesko	1.00	.45	.13
☐ 591 Bob Ojeda	.04	.02	.01
☐ 592 Alfredo Griffin	.04	.02	.01
☐ 593 Raul Mondesi	.50	.23	.06

☐	594	Greg Smith	.04	.02	.01	☐	651	Eddie Whitson	.04	.02	.01
☐	595	Orel Hershiser	.07	.03	.01	☐	652	Oscar Azocar	.04	.02	.01
☐	596	Juan Samuel	.04	.02	.01	☐	653	Wes Gardner	.04	.02	.01
☐	597	Brett Butler	.07	.03	.01	☐	654	Bip Roberts	.07	.03	.01
☐	598	Gary Carter	.07	.03	.01	☐	655	Robbie Beckett	.12	.05	.02
☐	599	Stan Javier	.04	.02	.01	☐	656	Benito Santiago	.07	.03	.01
☐	600	Kal Daniels	.04	.02	.01	☐	657	Greg W.Harris	.04	.02	.01
☐	601	Jamie McAndrew	.15	.07	.02	☐	658	Jerald Clark	.04	.02	.01
☐	602	Mike Sharperson	.04	.02	.01	☐	659	Fred McGriff	.12	.05	.02
☐	603	Jay Howell	.04	.02	.01	☐	660	Larry Andersen	.04	.02	.01
☐	604	Eric Karros	1.50	.65	.19	☐	661	Bruce Hurst	.07	.03	.01
☐	605	Tim Belcher	.07	.03	.01	☐	662	Steve Martin	.10	.05	.01
☐	606	Dan Opperman	.10	.05	.01	☐	663	Rafael Valdez	.04	.02	.01
☐	607	Lenny Harris	.04	.02	.01	☐	664	Paul Faries	.10	.05	.01
☐	608	Tom Goodwin	.07	.03	.01	☐	665	Andy Benes	.07	.03	.01
☐	609	Darryl Strawberry	.12	.05	.02	☐	666	Randy Myers	.07	.03	.01
☐	610	Ramon Martinez	.10	.05	.01	☐	667	Rob Dibble	.07	.03	.01
☐	611	Kevin Gross	.04	.02	.01	☐	668	Glenn Sutko	.04	.02	.01
☐	612	Zakary Shinall	.15	.07	.02	☐	669	Glenn Braggs	.04	.02	.01
☐	613	Mike Scioscia	.04	.02	.01	☐	670	Billy Hatcher	.04	.02	.01
☐	614	Eddie Murray	.10	.05	.01	☐	671	Joe Oliver	.04	.02	.01
☐	615	Ronnie Walden	.10	.05	.01	☐	672	Freddy Benavides	.04	.02	.01
☐	616	Will Clark	.20	.09	.03	☐	673	Barry Larkin	.10	.05	.01
☐	617	Adam Hyzdu	.15	.07	.02	☐	674	Chris Sabo	.07	.03	.01
☐	618	Matt Williams	.07	.03	.01	☐	675	Mariano Duncan	.04	.02	.01
☐	619	Don Robinson	.04	.02	.01	☐	676	Chris Jones	.04	.02	.01
☐	620	Jeff Brantley	.04	.02	.01	☐	677	Gino Minutelli	.10	.05	.01
☐	621	Greg Litton	.04	.02	.01	☐	678	Reggie Jefferson	.10	.05	.01
☐	622	Steve Decker	.15	.07	.02	☐	679	Jack Armstrong	.04	.02	.01
☐	623	Robby Thompson	.04	.02	.01	☐	680	Chris Hammond	.10	.05	.01
☐	624	Mark Leonard	.10	.05	.01	☐	681	Jose Rijo	.07	.03	.01
☐	625	Kevin Bass	.04	.02	.01	☐	682	Bill Doran	.04	.02	.01
☐	626	Scott Garrelts	.04	.02	.01	☐	683	Terry Lee	.10	.05	.01
☐	627	Jose Uribe	.04	.02	.01	☐	684	Tom Browning	.04	.02	.01
☐	628	Eric Gunderson	.04	.02	.01	☐	685	Paul O'Neill	.07	.03	.01
☐	629	Steve Hosey	.15	.07	.02	☐	686	Eric Davis	.07	.03	.01
☐	630	Trevor Wilson	.04	.02	.01	☐	687	Dan Wilson	.15	.07	.02
☐	631	Terry Kennedy	.04	.02	.01	☐	688	Ted Power	.04	.02	.01
☐	632	Dave Righetti	.04	.02	.01	☐	689	Tim Layana	.04	.02	.01
☐	633	Kelly Downs	.04	.02	.01	☐	690	Norm Charlton	.07	.03	.01
☐	634	Johnny Ard	.04	.02	.01	☐	691	Hal Morris	.07	.03	.01
☐	635	Eric Christopherson	.15	.07	.02	☐	692	Rickey Henderson	.10	.05	.01
☐	636	Kevin Mitchell	.07	.03	.01	☐	693	Sam Militello	.50	.23	.06
☐	637	John Burkett	.04	.02	.01			Minor League MVP			
☐	638	Kevin Rogers	.15	.07	.02	☐	694	Matt Mieske	.25	.11	.03
☐	639	Bud Black	.04	.02	.01			Minor League MVP			
☐	640	Willie McGee	.07	.03	.01	☐	695	Paul Russo	.20	.09	.03
☐	641	Royce Clayton	.15	.07	.02			Minor League MVP			
☐	642	Tony Fernandez	.07	.03	.01	☐	696	Domingo Mota	.10	.05	.01
☐	643	Ricky Bones	.20	.09	.03			Minor League MVP			
☐	644	Thomas Howard	.04	.02	.01	☐	697	Todd Guggiana	.10	.05	.01
☐	645	Dave Staton	.25	.11	.03			Minor League MVP			
☐	646	Jim Presley	.04	.02	.01	☐	698	Marc Newfield	.40	.18	.05
☐	647	Tony Gwynn	.12	.05	.02			Minor League MVP			
☐	648	Marty Barrett	.04	.02	.01	☐	699	Checklist 1	.05	.02	.01
☐	649	Scott Coolbaugh	.04	.02	.01	☐	700	Checklist 2	.05	.02	.01
☐	650	Craig Lefferts	.04	.02	.01	☐	701	Checklist 3	.05	.02	.01

☐ 702	Checklist 4	.05	.02	.01
☑ 703	Checklist 5	.05	.02	.01
☐ 704	Checklist 6	.05	.02	.01

1992 Bowman

The cards in this 705-card set measure the standard size (2 1/2" by 3 1/2") and feature posed and action color player photos on a UV-coated white card face. A gradated orange bar accented with black diagonal stripes carries the player's name at the bottom right corner. The backs display close-up color photos and biography on a burlap-textured background. Below the photo, statistical information appears in a yellow-and-white grid with the player's name in a red bar at the top of the grid. Interspersed throughout the set are 45 special cards with an identical front design except for a textured gold-foil border. The foil cards were inserted one per wax pack and two per jumbo (23 regular cards) pack. These foil cards feature past and present Team USA players and minor league POY Award winners. Their backs have the same burlap background but display one of three emblems: 1) U.S. Baseball Federation; 2) Topps Team USA 1992; or 3) National Association of Professional Baseball Leagues. The player's name and biography are shown in a blue-and-white box above these emblems. Some of the regular and special cards picture players in civilian clothing who are still in the farm system. The cards are numbered on the back. The key Rookie Cards in this set are

Carlos Delgado, Cliff Floyd, Pat Listach, David Nied, Brien Taylor, and Nigel Wilson.

	MT	EX-MT	VG
COMPLETE SET (705)	100.00	45.00	12.50
COMMON PLAYER (1-705)	.08	.04	.01

☐ 1	Ivan Rodriguez	1.00	.45	.13
☐ 2	Kirk McCaskill	.08	.04	.01
☐ 3	Scott Livingstone	.20	.09	.03
☐ 4	Salomon Torres	.50	.23	.06
☐ 5	Carlos Hernandez	.08	.04	.01
☐ 6	Dave Hollins	.25	.11	.03
☐ 7	Scott Fletcher	.08	.04	.01
☐ 8	Jorge Fabregas	.20	.09	.03
☐ 9	Andujar Cedeno	.12	.05	.02
☐ 10	Howard Johnson	.10	.04	.01
☐ 11	Trevor Hoffman	.25	.11	.03
☐ 12	Roberto Kelly	.12	.05	.02
☐ 13	Gregg Jefferies	.10	.04	.01
☐ 14	Marquis Grissom	.25	.11	.03
☐ 15	Mike Ignasiak	.20	.09	.03
☐ 16	Jack Morris	.15	.07	.02
☐ 17	William Pennyfeather	.15	.07	.02
☐ 18	Todd Stottlemyre	.10	.04	.01
☐ 19	Chito Martinez	.08	.04	.01
☐ 20	Roberto Alomar	.60	.25	.08
☐ 21	Sam Militello	.50	.23	.06
☐ 22	Hector Fajardo	.25	.11	.03
☐ 23	Paul Quantrill	.15	.07	.02
☐ 24	Chuck Knoblauch	.50	.23	.06
☐ 25	Reggie Jefferson	.30	.14	.04
☐ 26	Jeremy McGarity	.15	.07	.02
☐ 27	Jerome Walton	.08	.04	.01
☐ 28	Chipper Jones	1.25	.55	.16
☐ 29	Brian Barber	.40	.18	.05
☐ 30	Ron Darling	.10	.04	.01
☐ 31	Roberto Petagine	.30	.14	.04
☐ 32	Chuck Finley	.08	.04	.01
☐ 33	Edgar Martinez	.10	.04	.01
☐ 34	Napoleon Robinson	.15	.07	.02
☐ 35	Andy Van Slyke	.12	.05	.02
☐ 36	Bobby Thigpen	.08	.04	.01
☐ 37	Travis Fryman	1.00	.45	.13
☐ 38	Eric Christopherson	.10	.05	.01
☐ 39	Terry Mulholland	.08	.04	.01
☐ 40	Darryl Strawberry	.35	.16	.04
☐ 41	Manny Alexander	.30	.14	.04
☐ 42	Tracy Sanders	.35	.16	.04
☐ 43	Pete Incaviglia	.08	.04	.01
☐ 44	Kim Batiste	.15	.07	.02
☐ 45	Frank Rodriguez	.50	.23	.06
☐ 46	Greg Swindell	.10	.04	.01
☐ 47	Delino DeShields	.25	.11	.03
☐ 48	John Ericks	.08	.04	.01
☐ 49	Franklin Stubbs	.08	.04	.01

☐ 50	Tony Gwynn	.35	.16	.04
☐ 51	Clifton Garrett	.15	.07	.02
☐ 52	Mike Gardella	.15	.07	.02
☐ 53	Scott Erickson	.15	.07	.02
☐ 54	Gary Caraballo	.15	.07	.02
☐ 55	Jose Oliva	.35	.16	.04
☐ 56	Brook Fordyce	.10	.05	.01
☐ 57	Mark Whiten	.10	.04	.01
☐ 58	Joe Slusarski	.08	.04	.01
☐ 59	J.R. Phillips	.15	.07	.02
☐ 60	Barry Bonds	.60	.25	.08
☐ 61	Bob Milacki	.08	.04	.01
☐ 62	Keith Mitchell	.15	.07	.02
☐ 63	Angel Miranda	.15	.07	.02
☐ 64	Raul Mondesi	.60	.25	.08
☐ 65	Brian Koelling	.15	.07	.02
☐ 66	Brian McRae	.12	.05	.02
☐ 67	John Patterson	.20	.09	.03
☐ 68	John Wetteland	.08	.04	.01
☐ 69	Wilson Alvarez	.08	.04	.01
☐ 70	Wade Boggs	.30	.14	.04
☐ 71	Darryl Ratliff	.15	.07	.02
☐ 72	Jeff Jackson	.08	.04	.01
☐ 73	Jeremy Hernandez	.15	.07	.02
☐ 74	Darryl Hamilton	.10	.04	.01
☐ 75	Rafael Belliard	.08	.04	.01
☐ 76	Rick Trlicek	.20	.09	.03
☐ 77	Felipe Crespo	.20	.09	.03
☐ 78	Carney Lansford	.10	.04	.01
☐ 79	Ryan Long	.20	.09	.03
☐ 80	Kirby Puckett	.75	.35	.09
☐ 81	Earl Cunningham	.10	.05	.01
☐ 82	Pedro Martinez	.75	.35	.09
☐ 83	Scott Hatteberg	.15	.07	.02
☐ 84	Juan Gonzalez	1.25	.55	.16
☐ 85	Robert Nutting	.15	.07	.02
☐ 86	Calvin Reese	.30	.14	.04
☐ 87	Dave Silvestri	.30	.14	.04
☐ 88	Scott Ruffcorn	.60	.25	.08
☐ 89	Rick Aguilera	.10	.04	.01
☐ 90	Cecil Fielder	.35	.16	.04
☐ 91	Kirk Dressendorfer	.08	.04	.01
☐ 92	Jerry DiPoto	.20	.09	.03
☐ 93	Mike Felder	.08	.04	.01
☐ 94	Craig Paquette	.08	.04	.01
☐ 95	Elvin Paulino	.20	.09	.03
☐ 96	Donovan Osborne	.60	.25	.08
☐ 97	Hubie Brooks	.08	.04	.01
☐ 98	Derek Lowe	.25	.11	.03
☐ 99	David Zancanaro	.20	.09	.03
☐ 100	Ken Griffey Jr.	2.00	.90	.25
☐ 101	Todd Hundley	.08	.04	.01
☐ 102	Mike Trombley	.30	.14	.04
☐ 103	Ricky Gutierrez	.15	.07	.02
☐ 104	Braulio Castillo	.25	.11	.03
☐ 105	Craig Lefferts	.08	.04	.01
☐ 106	Rick Sutcliffe	.10	.04	.01
☐ 107	Dean Palmer	.50	.23	.06
☐ 108	Henry Rodriguez	.20	.09	.03
☐ 109	Mark Clark	.15	.07	.02
☐ 110	Kenny Lofton	1.25	.55	.16
☐ 111	Mark Carreon	.08	.04	.01
☐ 112	J.T. Bruett	.15	.07	.02
☐ 113	Gerald Williams	.20	.09	.03
☐ 114	Frank Thomas	4.00	1.80	.50
☐ 115	Kevin Reimer	.08	.04	.01
☐ 116	Sammy Sosa	.08	.04	.01
☐ 117	Mickey Tettleton	.10	.04	.01
☐ 118	Reggie Sanders	.75	.35	.09
☐ 119	Trevor Wilson	.08	.04	.01
☐ 120	Cliff Brantley	.12	.05	.02
☐ 121	Spike Owen	.08	.04	.01
☐ 122	Jeff Montgomery	.08	.04	.01
☐ 123	Alex Sutherland	.15	.07	.02
☐ 124	Brien Taylor	5.00	2.30	.60
☐ 125	Brian Williams	.50	.23	.06
☐ 126	Kevin Seitzer	.10	.04	.01
☐ 127	Carlos Delgado	3.50	1.55	.45
☐ 128	Gary Scott	.10	.04	.01
☐ 129	Scott Cooper	.25	.11	.03
☐ 130	Domingo Jean	.35	.16	.04
☐ 131	Pat Mahomes	.50	.23	.06
☐ 132	Mike Boddicker	.08	.04	.01
☐ 133	Roberto Hernandez	.20	.09	.03
☐ 134	Dave Valle	.08	.04	.01
☐ 135	Kurt Stillwell	.08	.04	.01
☐ 136	Brad Pennington	.35	.16	.04
☐ 137	Jermaine Swinton	.15	.07	.02
☐ 138	Ryan Hawblitzel	.50	.23	.06
☐ 139	Tito Navarro	.25	.11	.03
☐ 140	Sandy Alomar	.10	.04	.01
☐ 141	Todd Benzinger	.08	.04	.01
☐ 142	Danny Jackson	.08	.04	.01
☐ 143	Melvin Nieves	.75	.35	.09
☐ 144	Jim Campanis	.20	.09	.03
☐ 145	Luis Gonzalez	.12	.05	.02
☐ 146	Dave Doorneweerd	.20	.09	.03
☐ 147	Charlie Hayes	.08	.04	.01
☐ 148	Greg Maddux	.20	.09	.03
☐ 149	Brian Harper	.08	.04	.01
☐ 150	Brent Miller	.15	.07	.02
☐ 151	Shawn Estes	.30	.14	.04
☐ 152	Mike Williams	.30	.14	.04
☐ 153	Charlie Hough	.08	.04	.01
☐ 154	Randy Myers	.10	.04	.01
☐ 155	Kevin Young	.75	.35	.09
☐ 156	Rick Wilkins	.08	.04	.01
☐ 157	Terry Shumpert	.08	.04	.01
☐ 158	Steve Karsay	.25	.11	.03
☐ 159	Gary DiSarcina	.10	.04	.01
☐ 160	Deion Sanders	.40	.18	.05
☐ 161	Tom Browning	.08	.04	.01
☐ 162	Dickie Thon	.08	.04	.01
☐ 163	Luis Mercedes	.25	.11	.03

☐ 164	Riccardo Ingram	.25	.11	.03		
☐ 165	Tavo Alvarez	.40	.18	.05		
☐ 166	Rickey Henderson	.30	.14	.04		
☐ 167	Jaime Navarro	.10	.04	.01		
☐ 168	Billy Ashley	1.00	.45	.13		
☐ 169	Phil Dauphin	.20	.09	.03		
☐ 170	Ivan Cruz	.15	.07	.02		
☐ 171	Harold Baines	.10	.04	.01		
☐ 172	Bryan Harvey	.08	.04	.01		
☐ 173	Alex Cole	.08	.04	.01		
☐ 174	Curtis Shaw	.20	.09	.03		
☐ 175	Matt Williams	.10	.05	.01		
☐ 176	Felix Jose	.10	.04	.01		
☐ 177	Sam Horn	.08	.04	.01		
☐ 178	Randy Johnson	.10	.04	.01		
☐ 179	Ivan Calderon	.08	.04	.01		
☐ 180	Steve Avery	.50	.23	.06		
☐ 181	William Suero	.12	.05	.02		
☐ 182	Bill Swift	.08	.04	.01		
☐ 183	Howard Battle	.35	.16	.04		
☐ 184	Ruben Amaro	.10	.05	.01		
☐ 185	Jim Abbott	.20	.09	.03		
☐ 186	Mike Fitzgerald	.08	.04	.01		
☐ 187	Bruce Hurst	.10	.04	.01		
☐ 188	Jeff Juden	.15	.07	.02		
☐ 189	Jeromy Burnitz	.40	.18	.05		
☐ 190	Dave Burba	.08	.04	.01		
☐ 191	Kevin Brown	.10	.04	.01		
☐ 192	Patrick Lennon	.12	.05	.02		
☐ 193	Jeff McNeely	.20	.09	.03		
☐ 194	Wilfredo Cordero	.50	.23	.06		
☐ 195	Chili Davis	.10	.04	.01		
☐ 196	Milt Cuyler	.08	.04	.01		
☐ 197	Von Hayes	.08	.04	.01		
☐ 198	Todd Revenig	.20	.09	.03		
☐ 199	Joel Johnston	.08	.04	.01		
☐ 200	Jeff Bagwell	.75	.35	.09		
☐ 201	Alex Fernandez	.10	.04	.01		
☐ 202	Todd Jones	.15	.07	.02		
☐ 203	Charles Nagy	.25	.11	.03		
☐ 204	Tim Raines	.12	.05	.02		
☐ 205	Kevin Maas	.12	.05	.02		
☐ 206	Julio Franco	.10	.04	.01		
☐ 207	Randy Velarde	.08	.04	.01		
☐ 208	Lance Johnson	.08	.04	.01		
☐ 209	Scott Leius	.08	.04	.01		
☐ 210	Derek Lee	.15	.07	.02		
☐ 211	Joe Sondrini	.20	.09	.03		
☐ 212	Royce Clayton	.40	.18	.05		
☐ 213	Chris George	.10	.05	.01		
☐ 214	Gary Sheffield	.75	.35	.09		
☐ 215	Mark Gubicza	.08	.04	.01		
☐ 216	Mike Moore	.08	.04	.01		
☐ 217	Rick Huisman	.30	.14	.04		
☐ 218	Jeff Russell	.08	.04	.01		
☐ 219	D.J. Dozier	.10	.04	.01		
☐ 220	Dave Martinez	.08	.04	.01		
☐ 221	Alan Newman	.20	.09	.03		
☐ 222	Nolan Ryan	1.50	.65	.19		
☐ 223	Teddy Higuera	.08	.04	.01		
☐ 224	Damon Buford	.30	.14	.04		
☐ 225	Ruben Sierra	.40	.18	.05		
☐ 226	Tom Nevers	.10	.05	.01		
☐ 227	Tommy Greene	.08	.04	.01		
☐ 228	Nigel Wilson	3.50	1.55	.45		
☐ 229	John DeSilva	.12	.05	.02		
☐ 230	Bobby Witt	.08	.04	.01		
☐ 231	Greg Cadaret	.08	.04	.01		
☐ 232	John Vander Wal	.25	.11	.03		
☐ 233	Jack Clark	.10	.04	.01		
☐ 234	Bill Doran	.08	.04	.01		
☐ 235	Bobby Bonilla	.20	.09	.03		
☐ 236	Steve Olin	.08	.04	.01		
☐ 237	Derek Bell	.35	.16	.04		
☐ 238	David Cone	.10	.05	.01		
☐ 239	Victor Cole	.30	.14	.04		
☐ 240	Rod Bolton	.08	.04	.01		
☐ 241	Tom Pagnozzi	.08	.04	.01		
☐ 242	Rob Dibble	.10	.04	.01		
☐ 243	Michael Carter	.15	.07	.02		
☐ 244	Don Peters	.10	.05	.01		
☐ 245	Mike LaValliere	.08	.04	.01		
☐ 246	Joe Perona	.12	.05	.02		
☐ 247	Mitch Williams	.08	.04	.01		
☐ 248	Jay Buhner	.10	.04	.01		
☐ 249	Andy Benes	.12	.05	.02		
☐ 250	Alex Ochoa	.20	.09	.03		
☐ 251	Greg Blosser	.15	.07	.02		
☐ 252	Jack Armstrong	.08	.04	.01		
☐ 253	Juan Samuel	.08	.04	.01		
☐ 254	Terry Pendleton	.12	.05	.02		
☐ 255	Ramon Martinez	.12	.05	.02		
☐ 256	Rico Brogna	.10	.05	.01		
☐ 257	John Smiley	.10	.04	.01		
☐ 258	Carl Everett	.20	.09	.03		
☐ 259	Tim Salmon	1.25	.55	.16		
☐ 260	Will Clark	.60	.25	.08		
☐ 261	Ugueth Urbina	.25	.11	.03		
☐ 262	Jason Wood	.15	.07	.02		
☐ 263	Dave Magadan	.10	.04	.01		
☐ 264	Dante Bichette	.08	.04	.01		
☐ 265	Jose DeLeon	.08	.04	.01		
☐ 266	Mike Neill	.75	.35	.09		
☐ 267	Paul O'Neill	.10	.04	.01		
☐ 268	Anthony Young	.12	.05	.02		
☐ 269	Greg W. Harris	.08	.04	.01		
☐ 270	Todd Van Poppel	.40	.18	.05		
☐ 271	Pete Castellano	.30	.14	.04		
☐ 272	Tony Phillips	.15	.07	.02		
☐ 273	Mike Gallego	.08	.04	.01		
☐ 274	Steve Cooke	.30	.14	.04		
☐ 275	Robin Ventura	.50	.23	.06		
☐ 276	Kevin Mitchell	.12	.05	.02		
☐ 277	Doug Linton	.12	.05	.02		

☐ 278	Robert Eenhoorn	.12	.05	.02
☐ 279	Gabe White	.25	.11	.03
☐ 280	Dave Stewart	.10	.04	.01
☐ 281	Mo Sanford	.15	.07	.02
☐ 282	Greg Perschke	.15	.07	.02
☐ 283	Kevin Flora	.25	.11	.03
☐ 284	Jeff Williams	.15	.07	.02
☐ 285	Keith Miller	.08	.04	.01
☐ 286	Andy Ashby	.15	.07	.02
☐ 287	Doug Dascenzo	.08	.04	.01
☐ 288	Eric Karros	1.75	.80	.22
☐ 289	Glenn Murray	.20	.09	.03
☐ 290	Troy Percival	.40	.18	.05
☐ 291	Orlando Merced	.12	.05	.02
☐ 292	Peter Hoy	.15	.07	.02
☐ 293	Tony Fernandez	.10	.04	.01
☐ 294	Juan Guzman	2.00	.90	.25
☐ 295	Jesse Barfield	.08	.04	.01
☐ 296	Sid Fernandez	.10	.04	.01
☐ 297	Scott Cepicky	.35	.16	.04
☐ 298	Garret Anderson	.15	.07	.02
☐ 299	Cal Eldred	1.25	.55	.16
☐ 300	Ryne Sandberg	1.00	.45	.13
☐ 301	Jim Gantner	.08	.04	.01
☐ 302	Mariano Rivera	.20	.09	.03
☐ 303	Ron Lockett	.15	.07	.02
☐ 304	Jose Offerman	.10	.04	.01
☐ 305	Denny Martinez	.10	.04	.01
☐ 306	Luis Ortiz	.20	.09	.03
☐ 307	David Howard	.08	.04	.01
☐ 308	Russ Springer	.35	.16	.04
☐ 309	Chris Howard	.15	.07	.02
☐ 310	Kyle Abbott	.15	.07	.02
☐ 311	Aaron Sele	.75	.35	.09
☐ 312	David Justice	.75	.35	.09
☐ 313	Pete O'Brien	.08	.04	.01
☐ 314	Greg Hansell	.35	.16	.04
☐ 315	Dave Winfield	.20	.09	.03
☐ 316	Lance Dickson	.08	.04	.01
☐ 317	Eric King	.08	.04	.01
☐ 318	Vaughn Eshelman	.15	.07	.02
☐ 319	Tim Belcher	.10	.04	.01
☐ 320	Andres Galarraga	.08	.04	.01
☐ 321	Scott Bullett	.20	.09	.03
☐ 322	Doug Strange	.08	.04	.01
☐ 323	Jerald Clark	.08	.04	.01
☐ 324	Dave Righetti	.08	.04	.01
☐ 325	Greg Hibbard	.08	.04	.01
☐ 326	Eric Hillman	.35	.16	.04
☐ 327	Shane Reynolds	.15	.07	.02
☐ 328	Chris Hammond	.10	.04	.01
☐ 329	Albert Belle	.35	.16	.04
☐ 330	Rich Becker	.35	.16	.04
☐ 331	Eddie Williams	.15	.07	.02
☐ 332	Donald Harris	.08	.04	.01
☐ 333	Dave Smith	.08	.04	.01
☐ 334	Steve Fireovid	.08	.04	.01
☐ 335	Steve Buechele	.08	.04	.01
☐ 336	Mike Schooler	.08	.04	.01
☐ 337	Kevin McReynolds	.10	.04	.01
☐ 338	Hensley Meulens	.08	.04	.01
☐ 339	Benji Gil	.40	.18	.05
☐ 340	Don Mattingly	.35	.16	.04
☐ 341	Alvin Davis	.08	.04	.01
☐ 342	Alan Mills	.08	.04	.01
☐ 343	Kelly Downs	.08	.04	.01
☐ 344	Leo Gomez	.20	.09	.03
☐ 345	Tarrik Brock	.15	.07	.02
☐ 346	Ryan Turner	.75	.35	.09
☐ 347	John Smoltz	.20	.09	.03
☐ 348	Bill Sampen	.08	.04	.01
☐ 349	Paul Byrd	.25	.11	.03
☐ 350	Mike Bordick	.15	.07	.02
☐ 351	Jose Lind	.08	.04	.01
☐ 352	David Wells	.08	.04	.01
☐ 353	Barry Larkin	.20	.09	.03
☐ 354	Bruce Ruffin	.08	.04	.01
☐ 355	Luis Rivera	.08	.04	.01
☐ 356	Sid Bream	.08	.04	.01
☐ 357	Julian Vasquez	.15	.07	.02
☐ 358	Jason Bere	.35	.16	.04
☐ 359	Ben McDonald	.15	.07	.02
☐ 360	Scott Stahoviak	.40	.18	.05
☐ 361	Kirt Manwaring	.08	.04	.01
☐ 362	Jeff Johnson	.08	.04	.01
☐ 363	Rob Deer	.10	.04	.01
☐ 364	Tony Pena	.08	.04	.01
☐ 365	Melido Perez	.10	.04	.01
☐ 366	Clay Parker	.08	.04	.01
☐ 367	Dale Sveum	.08	.04	.01
☐ 368	Mike Scioscia	.08	.04	.01
☐ 369	Roger Salkeld	.15	.07	.02
☐ 370	Mike Stanley	.08	.04	.01
☐ 371	Jack McDowell	.12	.05	.02
☐ 372	Tim Wallach	.10	.04	.01
☐ 373	Billy Ripken	.08	.04	.01
☐ 374	Mike Christopher	.15	.07	.02
☐ 375	Paul Molitor	.12	.05	.02
☐ 376	Dave Stieb	.08	.04	.01
☐ 377	Pedro Guerrero	.10	.04	.01
☐ 378	Russ Swan	.08	.04	.01
☐ 379	Bob Ojeda	.08	.04	.01
☐ 380	Donn Pall	.08	.04	.01
☐ 381	Eddie Zosky	.15	.07	.02
☐ 382	Darnell Coles	.08	.04	.01
☐ 383	Tom Smith	.15	.07	.02
☐ 384	Mark McGwire	.50	.23	.06
☐ 385	Gary Carter	.10	.04	.01
☐ 386	Rich Amaral	.12	.05	.02
☐ 387	Alan Embree	.50	.23	.06
☐ 388	Jonathan Hurst	.30	.14	.04
☐ 389	Bobby Jones	1.00	.45	.13
☐ 390	Rico Rossy	.15	.07	.02
☐ 391	Dan Smith	.20	.09	.03

☐	392	Terry Steinbach	.10	.04	.01			
☐	393	Jon Farrell	.20	.09	.03			
☐	394	Dave Anderson	.08	.04	.01			
☐	395	Benny Santiago	.12	.05	.02			
☐	396	Mark Wohlers	.20	.09	.03			
☐	397	Mo Vaughn	.12	.05	.02			
☐	398	Randy Kramer	.08	.04	.01			
☐	399	John Jaha	.60	.25	.08			
☐	400	Cal Ripken	1.00	.45	.13			
☐	401	Ryan Bowen	.15	.07	.02			
☐	402	Tim McIntosh	.08	.04	.01			
☐	403	Bernard Gilkey	.10	.05	.01			
☐	404	Junior Felix	.08	.04	.01			
☐	405	Cris Colon	.20	.09	.03			
☐	406	Marc Newfield	.40	.18	.05			
☐	407	Bernie Williams	.25	.11	.03			
☐	408	Jay Howell	.08	.04	.01			
☐	409	Zane Smith	.08	.04	.01			
☐	410	Jeff Shaw	.08	.04	.01			
☐	411	Kerry Woodson	.20	.09	.03			
☐	412	Wes Chamberlain	.12	.05	.02			
☐	413	Dave Mlicki	.25	.11	.03			
☐	414	Benny Distefano	.08	.04	.01			
☐	415	Kevin Rogers	.08	.04	.01			
☐	416	Tim Naehring	.10	.04	.01			
☐	417	Clemente Nunez	.60	.25	.08			
☐	418	Luis Sojo	.08	.04	.01			
☐	419	Kevin Ritz	.08	.04	.01			
☐	420	Omar Olivares	.08	.04	.01			
☐	421	Manuel Lee	.08	.04	.01			
☐	422	Julio Valera	.15	.07	.02			
☐	423	Omar Vizquel	.08	.04	.01			
☐	424	Darren Burton	.20	.09	.03			
☐	425	Mel Hall	.08	.04	.01			
☐	426	Dennis Powell	.08	.04	.01			
☐	427	Lee Stevens	.08	.04	.01			
☐	428	Glenn Davis	.10	.04	.01			
☐	429	Willie Greene	.50	.23	.06			
☐	430	Kevin Wickander	.08	.04	.01			
☐	431	Dennis Eckersley	.15	.07	.02			
☐	432	Joe Orsulak	.08	.04	.01			
☐	433	Eddie Murray	.20	.09	.03			
☐	434	Matt Stairs	.30	.14	.04			
☐	435	Wally Joyner	.10	.04	.01			
☐	436	Rondell White	.50	.23	.06			
☐	437	Rob Maurer	.20	.09	.03			
☐	438	Joe Redfield	.15	.07	.02			
☐	439	Mark Lewis	.10	.04	.01			
☐	440	Darren Daulton	.10	.04	.01			
☐	441	Mike Henneman	.08	.04	.01			
☐	442	John Cangelosi	.08	.04	.01			
☐	443	Vince Moore	.15	.07	.02			
☐	444	John Wehner	.10	.05	.01			
☐	445	Kent Hrbek	.10	.04	.01			
☐	446	Mark McLemore	.08	.04	.01			
☐	447	Bill Wegman	.08	.04	.01			
☐	448	Robby Thompson	.08	.04	.01			
☐	449	Mark Anthony	.15	.07	.02			
☐	450	Archi Cianfrocco	.20	.09	.03			
☐	451	Johnny Ruffin	.15	.07	.02			
☐	452	Javier Lopez	.75	.35	.09			
☐	453	Greg Gohr	.15	.07	.02			
☐	454	Tim Scott	.15	.07	.02			
☐	455	Stan Belinda	.08	.04	.01			
☐	456	Darrin Jackson	.10	.04	.01			
☐	457	Chris Gardner	.15	.07	.02			
☐	458	Esteban Beltre	.15	.07	.02			
☐	459	Phil Plantier	.30	.14	.04			
☐	460	Jim Thome	.30	.14	.04			
☐	461	Mike Piazza	1.00	.45	.13			
☐	462	Matt Sinatro	.08	.04	.01			
☐	463	Scott Servais	.08	.04	.01			
☐	464	Brian Jordan	.60	.25	.08			
☐	465	Doug Drabek	.10	.04	.01			
☐	466	Carl Willis	.08	.04	.01			
☐	467	Bret Barberie	.12	.05	.02			
☐	468	Hal Morris	.10	.04	.01			
☐	469	Steve Sax	.10	.04	.01			
☐	470	Jerry Willard	.08	.04	.01			
☐	471	Dan Wilson	.15	.07	.02			
☐	472	Chris Hoiles	.12	.05	.02			
☐	473	Rheal Cormier	.15	.07	.02			
☐	474	John Morris	.08	.04	.01			
☐	475	Jeff Reardon	.12	.05	.02			
☐	476	Mark Leiter	.08	.04	.01			
☐	477	Tom Gordon	.08	.04	.01			
☐	478	Kent Bottenfield	.25	.11	.03			
☐	479	Gene Larkin	.08	.04	.01			
☐	480	Dwight Gooden	.12	.05	.02			
☐	481	B.J. Surhoff	.08	.04	.01			
☐	482	Andy Stankiewicz	.25	.11	.03			
☐	483	Tino Martinez	.10	.05	.01			
☐	484	Craig Biggio	.10	.04	.01			
☐	485	Denny Neagle	.12	.05	.02			
☐	486	Rusty Meacham	.08	.04	.01			
☐	487	Kal Daniels	.08	.04	.01			
☐	488	Dave Henderson	.08	.04	.01			
☐	489	Tim Costo	.20	.09	.03			
☐	490	Doug Davis	.15	.07	.02			
☐	491	Frank Viola	.10	.04	.01			
☐	492	Cory Snyder	.08	.04	.01			
☐	493	Chris Martin	.15	.07	.02			
☐	494	Dion James	.08	.04	.01			
☐	495	Randy Tomlin	.08	.04	.01			
☐	496	Greg Vaughn	.10	.04	.01			
☐	497	Dennis Cook	.08	.04	.01			
☐	498	Rosario Rodriguez	.10	.05	.01			
☐	499	Dave Staton	.20	.09	.03			
☐	500	George Brett	.25	.11	.03			
☐	501	Brian Barnes	.08	.04	.01			
☐	502	Butch Henry	.20	.09	.03			
☐	503	Harold Reynolds	.08	.04	.01			
☐	504	David Nied	4.00	1.80	.50			
☐	505	Lee Smith	.10	.04	.01			

☐	506	Steve Chitren	.08	.04	.01	☐	563	Rick Greene FOIL	.40	.18	.05
☐	507	Ken Hill	.08	.04	.01	☐	564	Gary Gaetti	.08	.04	.01
☐	508	Robbie Beckett	.12	.05	.02	☐	565	Ozzie Guillen	.08	.04	.01
☐	509	Troy Afenir	.08	.04	.01	☐	566	Charles Nagy FOIL	.35	.16	.04
☐	510	Kelly Gruber	.10	.04	.01	☐	567	Mike Milchin	.12	.05	.02
☐	511	Bret Boone	1.00	.45	.13	☐	568	Ben Shelton	.30	.14	.04
☐	512	Jeff Branson	.08	.04	.01	☐	569	Chris Roberts FOIL	1.00	.45	.13
☐	513	Mike Jackson	.08	.04	.01	☐	570	Ellis Burks	.10	.04	.01
☐	514	Pete Harnisch	.08	.04	.01	☐	571	Scott Scudder	.08	.04	.01
☐	515	Chad Kreuter	.08	.04	.01	☐	572	Jim Abbott FOIL	.40	.18	.05
☐	516	Joe Vitko	.30	.14	.04	☐	573	Joe Carter	.35	.16	.04
☐	517	Orel Hershiser	.12	.05	.02	☐	574	Steve Finley	.10	.04	.01
☐	518	John Doherty	.20	.09	.03	☐	575	Jim Olander FOIL	.15	.07	.02
☐	519	Jay Bell	.08	.04	.01	☐	576	Carlos Garcia	.20	.09	.03
☐	520	Mark Langston	.10	.04	.01	☐	577	Gregg Olson	.10	.04	.01
☐	521	Dann Howitt	.08	.04	.01	☐	578	Greg Swindell FOIL	.12	.05	.02
☐	522	Bobby Reed	.15	.07	.02	☐	579	Matt Williams FOIL	.15	.07	.02
☐	523	Roberto Munoz	.15	.07	.02	☐	580	Mark Grace	.15	.07	.02
☐	524	Todd Ritchie	.10	.05	.01	☐	581	Howard House FOIL	.30	.14	.04
☐	525	Bip Roberts	.10	.04	.01	☐	582	Luis Polonia	.10	.04	.01
☐	526	Pat Listach	2.50	1.15	.30	☐	583	Erik Hanson	.08	.04	.01
☐	527	Scott Brosius	.15	.07	.02	☐	584	Salomon Torres FOIL	.50	.23	.06
☐	528	John Roper	.40	.18	.05	☐	585	Carlton Fisk	.20	.09	.03
☐	529	Phil Hiatt	.50	.23	.06	☐	586	Bret Saberhagen	.12	.05	.02
☐	530	Denny Walling	.08	.04	.01	☐	587	Chad McConnell FOIL	.75	.35	.09
☐	531	Carlos Baerga	.50	.23	.06	☐	588	Jimmy Key	.08	.04	.01
☐	532	Manny Ramirez	1.25	.55	.16	☐	589	Mike Macfarlane	.08	.04	.01
☐	533	Pat Clements	.08	.04	.01	☐	590	Barry Bonds FOIL	.75	.35	.09
☐	534	Ron Gant	.20	.09	.03	☐	591	Jamie McAndrew	.12	.05	.02
☐	535	Pat Kelly	.10	.05	.01	☐	592	Shane Mack	.10	.04	.01
☐	536	Billy Spiers	.08	.04	.01	☐	593	Kerwin Moore	.12	.05	.02
☐	537	Darren Reed	.08	.04	.01	☐	594	Joe Oliver	.08	.04	.01
☐	538	Ken Caminiti	.10	.04	.01	☐	595	Chris Sabo	.10	.04	.01
☐	539	Butch Huskey	.30	.14	.04	☐	596	Alex Gonzalez	.30	.14	.04
☐	540	Matt Nokes	.08	.04	.01	☐	597	Brett Butler	.10	.04	.01
☐	541	John Kruk	.10	.04	.01	☐	598	Mark Hutton	.40	.18	.05
☐	542	John Jaha FOIL	.60	.25	.08	☐	599	Andy Benes FOIL	.12	.05	.02
☐	543	Justin Thompson	.30	.14	.04	☐	600	Jose Canseco	.60	.25	.08
☐	544	Steve Hosey	.60	.25	.08	☐	601	Darryl Kile	.15	.07	.02
☐	545	Joe Kmak	.15	.07	.02	☐	602	Matt Stairs FOIL	.40	.18	.05
☐	546	John Franco	.10	.04	.01	☐	603	Robert Butler FOIL	.30	.14	.04
☐	547	Devon White	.10	.04	.01	☐	604	Willie McGee	.10	.04	.01
☐	548	Elston Hansen FOIL	.30	.14	.04	☐	605	Jack McDowell FOIL	.20	.09	.03
☐	549	Ryan Klesko	1.00	.45	.13	☐	606	Tom Candiotti	.08	.04	.01
☐	550	Danny Tartabull	.12	.05	.02	☐	607	Ed Martel	.20	.09	.03
☐	551	Frank Thomas FOIL	8.00	3.60	1.00	☐	608	Matt Mieske FOIL	.50	.23	.06
☐	552	Kevin Tapani	.10	.04	.01	☐	609	Darrin Fletcher	.08	.04	.01
☐	553	Willie Banks	.20	.09	.03	☐	610	Rafael Palmeiro	.12	.05	.02
☐	554	B.J. Wallace FOIL	1.25	.55	.16	☐	611	Bill Swift FOIL	.10	.05	.01
☐	555	Orlando Miller	.15	.07	.02	☐	612	Mike Mussina	2.00	.90	.25
☐	556	Mark Smith	.75	.35	.09	☐	613	Vince Coleman	.10	.04	.01
☐	557	Tim Wallach FOIL	.10	.05	.01	☐	614	Scott Cepicky FOIL UER	.50	.23	.06
☐	558	Bill Gullickson	.08	.04	.01			(Bats: LEFLT)			
☐	559	Derek Bell FOIL	.50	.23	.06	☐	615	Mike Greenwell	.12	.05	.02
☐	560	Joe Randa FOIL	.40	.18	.05	☐	616	Kevin McGehee	.15	.07	.02
☐	561	Frank Seminara	.40	.18	.05	☐	617	Jeffrey Hammonds FOIL	3.50	1.55	.45
☐	562	Mark Gardner	.08	.04	.01	☐	618	Scott Taylor	.10	.05	.01

☐ 619	Dave Otto 08	.04	.01
☐ 620	Mark McGwire FOIL ...75	.35	.09
☐ 621	Kevin Tatar 15	.07	.02
☐ 622	Steve Farr 08	.04	.01
☐ 623	Ryan Klesko FOIL ...1.50	.65	.19
☐ 624	Dave Fleming 1.00	.45	.13
☐ 625	Andre Dawson 20	.09	.03
☐ 626	Tino Martinez FOIL....12	.05	.02
☐ 627	Chad Curtis 50	.23	.06
☐ 628	Mickey Morandini 12	.05	.02
☐ 629	Gregg Olson FOIL 10	.05	.01
☐ 630	Lou Whitaker 12	.05	.02
☐ 631	Arthur Rhodes 40	.18	.05
☐ 632	Brandon Wilson 15	.07	.02
☐ 633	Lance Jennings 20	.09	.03
☐ 634	Allen Watson 60	.25	.08
☐ 635	Len Dykstra 10	.04	.01
☐ 636	Joe Girardi 08	.04	.01
☐ 637	Kiki Hernandez FOIL ...40	.18	.05
☐ 638	Mike Hampton 15	.07	.02
☐ 639	Al Osuna 08	.04	.01
☐ 640	Kevin Appier 10	.04	.01
☐ 641	Rick Helling FOIL 40	.18	.05
☐ 642	Jody Reed 08	.04	.01
☐ 643	Ray Lankford 40	.18	.05
☐ 644	John Olerud 25	.11	.03
☐ 645	Paul Molitor FOIL......12	.05	.02
☐ 646	Pat Borders 08	.04	.01
☐ 647	Mike Morgan 08	.04	.01
☐ 648	Larry Walker 40	.18	.05
☐ 649	Pete Castellano FOIL ...40	.18	.05
☐ 650	Fred McGriff 30	.14	.04
☐ 651	Walt Weiss...............08	.04	.01
☐ 652	Calvin Murray FOIL ...1.50	.65	.19
☐ 653	Dave Nilsson 40	.18	.05
☐ 654	Greg Pirkl 40	.18	.05
☐ 655	Robin Ventura FOIL ...1.00	.45	.13
☐ 656	Mark Portugal 08	.04	.01
☐ 657	Roger McDowell 08	.04	.01
☐ 658	Rick Hirtensteiner ......30 FOIL	.14	.04
☐ 659	Glenallen Hill 08	.04	.01
☐ 660	Greg Gagne 08	.04	.01
☐ 661	Charles Johnson FOIL...2.00	.90	.25
☐ 662	Brian Hunter 20	.09	.03
☐ 663	Mark Lemke 08	.04	.01
☐ 664	Tim Belcher FOIL 10	.05	.01
☐ 665	Rich DeLucia 08	.04	.01
☐ 666	Bob Walk 08	.04	.01
☐ 667	Joe Carter FOIL 40	.18	.05
☐ 668	Jose Guzman 08	.04	.01
☐ 669	Otis Nixon 08	.04	.01
☐ 670	Phil Nevin FOIL 4.00	1.80	.50
☐ 671	Eric Davis 12	.05	.02
☐ 672	Damion Easley 75	.35	.09
☐ 673	Will Clark FOIL..........75	.35	.09
☐ 674	Mark Kiefer 15	.07	.02

☐ 675	Ozzie Smith..............20	.09	.03
☐ 676	Manny Ramirez FOIL ...2.00	.90	.25
☐ 677	Gregg Olson 10	.04	.01
☐ 678	Cliff Floyd 1.50	.65	.19
☐ 679	Duane Singleton 15	.07	.02
☐ 680	Jose Rijo 10	.04	.01
☐ 681	Willie Randolph..........10	.04	.01
☐ 682	Michael Tucker FOIL ...2.00	.90	.25
☐ 683	Darren Lewis 10	.04	.01
☐ 684	Dale Murphy 40	.18	.05
☐ 685	Mike Pagliarulo 08	.04	.01
☐ 686	Paul Miller 15	.07	.02
☐ 687	Mike Robertson 25	.11	.03
☐ 688	Mike Devereaux 10	.04	.01
☐ 689	Pedro Astacio 75	.35	.09
☐ 690	Alan Trammell 12	.05	.02
☐ 691	Roger Clemens 75	.35	.09
☐ 692	Bud Black 08	.04	.01
☐ 693	Turk Wendell 25	.11	.03
☐ 694	Barry Larkin FOIL 30	.14	.04
☐ 695	Todd Zeile 08	.04	.01
☐ 696	Pat Hentgen 15	.07	.02
☐ 697	Eddie Taubensee 20	.09	.03
☐ 698	Guillermo Velasquez ...20	.09	.03
☐ 699	Tom Glavine 30	.14	.04
☐ 700	Robin Yount 25	.11	.03
☐ 701	Checklist 1 08	.01	.00
☐ 702	Checklist 2 08	.01	.00
☐ 703	Checklist 3 08	.01	.00
☐ 704	Checklist 4 08	.01	.00
☐ 705	Checklist 5 08	.01	.00

1981 Donruss

*The cards in this 605-card set measure
2 1/2" by 3 1/2". In 1981 Donruss launched
itself into the baseball card market with a
set containing 600 numbered cards and*

five unnumbered checklists. Even though the five checklist cards are unnumbered, they are numbered below (601-605) for convenience in reference. The cards are printed on thin stock and more than one pose exists for several popular players. The numerous errors of the first print run were later corrected by the company. These are marked P1 and P2 in the checklist below. The key Rookie Cards in this set are Tim Raines and Jeff Reardon.

	NRMT-MT	EXC	G-VG
COMPLETE SET (605)	60.00	27.00	7.50
COMMON PLAYER (1-605)	.10	.05	.01
☐ 1 Ozzie Smith	3.50	1.55	.45
☐ 2 Rollie Fingers	1.00	.45	.13
☐ 3 Rick Wise	.10	.05	.01
☐ 4 Gene Richards	.10	.05	.01
☐ 5 Alan Trammell	.90	.40	.11
☐ 6 Tom Brookens	.10	.05	.01
☐ 7A Duffy Dyer P1	.15	.07	.02
(1980 batting average has decimal point)			
☐ 7B Duffy Dyer P2	.10	.05	.01
(1980 batting average has no decimal point)			
☐ 8 Mark Fidrych	.12	.05	.02
☐ 9 Dave Rozema	.10	.05	.01
☐ 10 Ricky Peters	.10	.05	.01
☐ 11 Mike Schmidt	3.00	1.35	.40
☐ 12 Willie Stargell	1.00	.45	.13
☐ 13 Tim Foli	.10	.05	.01
☐ 14 Manny Sanguillen	.12	.05	.02
☐ 15 Grant Jackson	.10	.05	.01
☐ 16 Eddie Solomon	.10	.05	.01
☐ 17 Omar Moreno	.10	.05	.01
☐ 18 Joe Morgan	1.00	.45	.13
☐ 19 Rafael Landestoy	.10	.05	.01
☐ 20 Bruce Bochy	.10	.05	.01
☐ 21 Joe Sambito	.10	.05	.01
☐ 22 Manny Trillo	.10	.05	.01
☐ 23A Dave Smith P1	.25	.11	.03
(Line box around stats is not complete)			
☐ 23B Dave Smith P2	.25	.11	.03
(Box totally encloses stats at top)			
☐ 24 Terry Puhl	.10	.05	.01
☐ 25 Bump Wills	.10	.05	.01
☐ 26A John Ellis P1 ERR	.40	.18	.05
(Photo on front shows Danny Walton)			
☐ 26B John Ellis P2 COR	.15	.07	.02
☐ 27 Jim Kern	.10	.05	.01
☐ 28 Richie Zisk	.10	.05	.01

☐ 29 John Mayberry	.10	.05	.01
☐ 30 Bob Davis	.10	.05	.01
☐ 31 Jackson Todd	.10	.05	.01
☐ 32 Alvis Woods	.10	.05	.01
☐ 33 Steve Carlton	2.00	.90	.25
☐ 34 Lee Mazzilli	.10	.05	.01
☐ 35 John Stearns	.10	.05	.01
☐ 36 Roy Lee Jackson	.10	.05	.01
☐ 37 Mike Scott	.25	.11	.03
☐ 38 Lamar Johnson	.10	.05	.01
☐ 39 Kevin Bell	.10	.05	.01
☐ 40 Ed Farmer	.10	.05	.01
☐ 41 Ross Baumgarten	.10	.05	.01
☐ 42 Leo Sutherland	.10	.05	.01
☐ 43 Dan Meyer	.10	.05	.01
☐ 44 Ron Reed	.10	.05	.01
☐ 45 Mario Mendoza	.10	.05	.01
☐ 46 Rick Honeycutt	.10	.05	.01
☐ 47 Glenn Abbott	.10	.05	.01
☐ 48 Leon Roberts	.10	.05	.01
☐ 49 Rod Carew	2.00	.90	.25
☐ 50 Bert Campaneris	.12	.05	.02
☐ 51A Tom Donahue P1 ERR	.15	.07	.02
(Name on front misspelled Donahue)			
☐ 51B Tom Donohue P2 COR	.10	.05	.01
☐ 52 Dave Frost	.10	.05	.01
☐ 53 Ed Halicki	.10	.05	.01
☐ 54 Dan Ford	.10	.05	.01
☐ 55 Garry Maddox	.10	.05	.01
☐ 56A Steve Garvey P1	1.00	.45	.13
("Surpassed 25 HR")			
☐ 56B Steve Garvey P2	.75	.35	.09
("Surpassed 21 HR")			
☐ 57 Bill Russell	.12	.05	.02
☐ 58 Don Sutton	.60	.25	.08
☐ 59 Reggie Smith	.12	.05	.02
☐ 60 Rick Monday	.12	.05	.02
☐ 61 Ray Knight	.12	.05	.02
☐ 62 Johnny Bench	2.00	.90	.25
☐ 63 Mario Soto	.10	.05	.01
☐ 64 Doug Bair	.10	.05	.01
☐ 65 George Foster	.20	.09	.03
☐ 66 Jeff Burroughs	.10	.05	.01
☐ 67 Keith Hernandez	.30	.14	.04
☐ 68 Tom Herr	.12	.05	.02
☐ 69 Bob Forsch	.10	.05	.01
☐ 70 John Fulgham	.10	.05	.01
☐ 71A Bobby Bonds P1 ERR	.20	.09	.03
(986 lifetime HR)			
☐ 71B Bobby Bonds P2 COR	.12	.05	.02
(326 lifetime HR)			
☐ 72A Rennie Stennett P1	.15	.07	.02
("Breaking broke leg")			
☐ 72B Rennie Stennett P2	.10	.05	.01
(Word "broke" deleted)			

☐ 73	Joe Strain	10	.05	.01
☐ 74	Ed Whitson	10	.05	.01
☐ 75	Tom Griffin	10	.05	.01
☐ 76	Billy North	10	.05	.01
☐ 77	Gene Garber	10	.05	.01
☐ 78	Mike Hargrove	12	.05	.02
☐ 79	Dave Rosello	10	.05	.01
☐ 80	Ron Hassey	10	.05	.01
☐ 81	Sid Monge	10	.05	.01
☐ 82A	Joe Charboneau P1	15	.07	.02
	('78 highlights,			
	"For some reason")			
☐ 82B	Joe Charboneau P2	12	.05	.02
	(Phrase "For some			
	reason" deleted)			
☐ 83	Cecil Cooper	12	.05	.02
☐ 84	Sal Bando	12	.05	.02
☐ 85	Moose Haas	10	.05	.01
☐ 86	Mike Caldwell	10	.05	.01
☐ 87A	Larry Hisle P1	15	.07	.02
	('77 highlights, line			
	ends with "28 RBI")			
☐ 87B	Larry Hisle P2	10	.05	.01
	(Correct line "28 HR")			
☐ 88	Luis Gomez	10	.05	.01
☐ 89	Larry Parrish	10	.05	.01
☐ 90	Gary Carter	1.00	.45	.13
☐ 91	Bill Gullickson	1.00	.45	.13
☐ 92	Fred Norman	10	.05	.01
☐ 93	Tommy Hutton	10	.05	.01
☐ 94	Carl Yastrzemski	2.00	.90	.25
☐ 95	Glenn Hoffman	10	.05	.01
☐ 96	Dennis Eckersley	1.75	.80	.22
☐ 97A	Tom Burgmeier P1	15	.07	.02
	ERR (Throws: Right)			
☐ 97B	Tom Burgmeier P2	10	.05	.01
	COR (Throws: Left)			
☐ 98	Win Remmerswaal	10	.05	.01
☐ 99	Bob Horner	12	.05	.02
☐ 100	George Brett	4.00	1.80	.50
☐ 101	Dave Chalk	10	.05	.01
☐ 102	Dennis Leonard	10	.05	.01
☐ 103	Renie Martin	10	.05	.01
☐ 104	Amos Otis	12	.05	.02
☐ 105	Graig Nettles	12	.05	.02
☐ 106	Eric Soderholm	10	.05	.01
☐ 107	Tommy John	20	.09	.03
☐ 108	Tom Underwood	10	.05	.01
☐ 109	Lou Piniella	12	.05	.02
☐ 110	Mickey Klutts	10	.05	.01
☐ 111	Bobby Murcer	12	.05	.02
☐ 112	Eddie Murray	3.00	1.35	.40
☐ 113	Rick Dempsey	12	.05	.02
☐ 114	Scott McGregor	10	.05	.01
☐ 115	Ken Singleton	12	.05	.02
☐ 116	Gary Roenicke	10	.05	.01
☐ 117	Dave Revering	10	.05	.01
☐ 118	Mike Norris	10	.05	.01
☐ 119	Rickey Henderson	13.00	5.75	1.65
☐ 120	Mike Heath	10	.05	.01
☐ 121	Dave Cash	10	.05	.01
☐ 122	Randy Jones	10	.05	.01
☐ 123	Eric Rasmussen	10	.05	.01
☐ 124	Jerry Mumphrey	10	.05	.01
☐ 125	Richie Hebner	10	.05	.01
☐ 126	Mark Wagner	10	.05	.01
☐ 127	Jack Morris	2.00	.90	.25
☐ 128	Dan Petry	12	.05	.02
☐ 129	Bruce Robbins	10	.05	.01
☐ 130	Champ Summers	10	.05	.01
☐ 131A	Pete Rose P1	2.00	.90	.25
	(Last line ends with			
	"see card 251")			
☐ 131B	Pete Rose P2	2.00	.90	.25
	(Last line corrected			
	"see card 371")			
☐ 132	Willie Stargell	1.00	.45	.13
☐ 133	Ed Ott	10	.05	.01
☐ 134	Jim Bibby	10	.05	.01
☐ 135	Bert Blyleven	40	.18	.05
☐ 136	Dave Parker	40	.18	.05
☐ 137	Bill Robinson	12	.05	.02
☐ 138	Enos Cabell	10	.05	.01
☐ 139	Dave Bergman	10	.05	.01
☐ 140	J.R. Richard	12	.05	.02
☐ 141	Ken Forsch	10	.05	.01
☐ 142	Larry Bowa UER	12	.05	.02
	(Shortshop on front)			
☐ 143	Frank LaCorte UER	10	.05	.01
	(Photo actually			
	Randy Niemann)			
☐ 144	Denny Walling	10	.05	.01
☐ 145	Buddy Bell	12	.05	.02
☐ 146	Ferguson Jenkins	50	.23	.06
☐ 147	Dannny Darwin	10	.05	.01
☐ 148	John Grubb	10	.05	.01
☐ 149	Alfredo Griffin	10	.05	.01
☐ 150	Jerry Garvin	10	.05	.01
☐ 151	Paul Mirabella	10	.05	.01
☐ 152	Rick Bosetti	10	.05	.01
☐ 153	Dick Ruthven	10	.05	.01
☐ 154	Frank Taveras	10	.05	.01
☐ 155	Craig Swan	10	.05	.01
☐ 156	Jeff Reardon	6.00	2.70	.75
☐ 157	Steve Henderson	10	.05	.01
☐ 158	Jim Morrison	10	.05	.01
☐ 159	Glenn Borgmann	10	.05	.01
☐ 160	LaMarr Hoyt	12	.05	.02
☐ 161	Rich Wortham	10	.05	.01
☐ 162	Thad Bosley	10	.05	.01
☐ 163	Julio Cruz	10	.05	.01
☐ 164A	Del Unser P1	15	.07	.02
	(No "3B" heading)			
☐ 164B	Del Unser P2	10	.05	.01

(Batting record on back
corrected ("3B")

☐ 165 Jim Anderson	10	.05	.01
☐ 166 Jim Beattie	10	.05	.01
☐ 167 Shane Rawley	10	.05	.01
☐ 168 Joe Simpson	10	.05	.01
☐ 169 Rod Carew	2.00	.90	.25
☐ 170 Fred Patek	10	.05	.01
☐ 171 Frank Tanana	12	.05	.02
☐ 172 Alfredo Martinez	10	.05	.01
☐ 173 Chris Knapp	10	.05	.01
☐ 174 Joe Rudi	12	.05	.02
☐ 175 Greg Luzinski	12	.05	.02
☐ 176 Steve Garvey	75	.35	.09
☐ 177 Joe Ferguson	10	.05	.01
☐ 178 Bob Welch	40	.18	.05
☐ 179 Dusty Baker	12	.05	.02
☐ 180 Rudy Law	10	.05	.01
☐ 181 Dave Concepcion	15	.07	.02
☐ 182 Johnny Bench	2.00	.90	.25
☐ 183 Mike LaCoss	10	.05	.01
☐ 184 Ken Griffey	35	.16	.04
☐ 185 Dave Collins	10	.05	.01
☐ 186 Brian Asselstine	10	.05	.01
☐ 187 Garry Templeton	12	.05	.02
☐ 188 Mike Phillips	10	.05	.01
☐ 189 Pete Vuckovich	12	.05	.02
☐ 190 John Urrea	10	.05	.01
☐ 191 Tony Scott	10	.05	.01
☐ 192 Darrell Evans	12	.05	.02
☐ 193 Milt May	10	.05	.01
☐ 194 Bob Knepper	10	.05	.01
☐ 195 Randy Moffitt	10	.05	.01
☐ 196 Larry Herndon	10	.05	.01
☐ 197 Rick Camp	10	.05	.01
☐ 198 Andre Thornton	12	.05	.02
☐ 199 Tom Veryzer	10	.05	.01
☐ 200 Gary Alexander	10	.05	.01
☐ 201 Rick Waits	10	.05	.01
☐ 202 Rick Manning	10	.05	.01
☐ 203 Paul Molitor	1.25	.55	.16
☐ 204 Jim Gantner	12	.05	.02
☐ 205 Paul Mitchell	10	.05	.01
☐ 206 Reggie Cleveland	10	.05	.01
☐ 207 Sixto Lezcano	10	.05	.01
☐ 208 Bruce Benedict	10	.05	.01
☐ 209 Rodney Scott	10	.05	.01
☐ 210 John Tamargo	10	.05	.01
☐ 211 Bill Lee	10	.05	.01
☐ 212 Andre Dawson UER	2.00	.90	.25

(Middle name Fernando,
should be Nolan)

☐ 213 Rowland Office	10	.05	.01
☐ 214 Carl Yastrzemski	2.00	.90	.25
☐ 215 Jerry Remy	10	.05	.01
☐ 216 Mike Torrez	10	.05	.01
☐ 217 Skip Lockwood	10	.05	.01

☐ 218 Fred Lynn	12	.05	.02
☐ 219 Chris Chambliss	12	.05	.02
☐ 220 Willie Aikens	10	.05	.01
☐ 221 John Wathan	10	.05	.01
☐ 222 Dan Quisenberry	25	.11	.03
☐ 223 Willie Wilson	20	.09	.03
☐ 224 Clint Hurdle	10	.05	.01
☐ 225 Bob Watson	12	.05	.02
☐ 226 Jim Spencer	10	.05	.01
☐ 227 Ron Guidry	25	.11	.03
☐ 228 Reggie Jackson	2.50	1.15	.30
☐ 229 Oscar Gamble	10	.05	.01
☐ 230 Jeff Cox	10	.05	.01
☐ 231 Luis Tiant	12	.05	.02
☐ 232 Rich Dauer	10	.05	.01
☐ 233 Dan Graham	10	.05	.01
☐ 234 Mike Flanagan	12	.05	.02
☐ 235 John Lowenstein	10	.05	.01
☐ 236 Benny Ayala	10	.05	.01
☐ 237 Wayne Gross	10	.05	.01
☐ 238 Rick Langford	10	.05	.01
☐ 239 Tony Armas	10	.05	.01
☐ 240A Bob Lacy P1 ERR	20	.09	.03

(Name misspelled
Bob "Lacy")

☐ 240B Bob Lacey P2 COR	10	.05	.01
☐ 241 Gene Tenace	10	.05	.01
☐ 242 Bob Shirley	10	.05	.01
☐ 243 Gary Lucas	10	.05	.01
☐ 244 Jerry Turner	10	.05	.01
☐ 245 John Wockenfuss	10	.05	.01
☐ 246 Stan Papi	10	.05	.01
☐ 247 Milt Wilcox	10	.05	.01
☐ 248 Dan Schatzeder	10	.05	.01
☐ 249 Steve Kemp	10	.05	.01
☐ 250 Jim Lentine	10	.05	.01
☐ 251 Pete Rose	2.00	.90	.25
☐ 252 Bill Madlock	12	.05	.02
☐ 253 Dale Berra	10	.05	.01
☐ 254 Kent Tekulve	12	.05	.02
☐ 255 Enrique Romo	10	.05	.01
☐ 256 Mike Easler	10	.05	.01
☐ 257 Chuck Tanner MG	10	.05	.01
☐ 258 Art Howe	12	.05	.02
☐ 259 Alan Ashby	10	.05	.01
☐ 260 Nolan Ryan	8.00	3.60	1.00
☐ 261A Vern Ruhle P1 ERR	40	.18	.05

(Photo on front
actually Ken Forsch)

☐ 261B Vern Ruhle P2 COR	15	.07	.02
☐ 262 Bob Boone	12	.05	.02
☐ 263 Cesar Cedeno	12	.05	.02
☐ 264 Jeff Leonard	12	.05	.02
☐ 265 Pat Putnam	10	.05	.01
☐ 266 Jon Matlack	10	.05	.01
☐ 267 Dave Rajsich	10	.05	.01
☐ 268 Billy Sample	10	.05	.01

☐ 269	Damaso Garcia	12	.05	.02			
☐ 270	Tom Buskey	10	.05	.01			
☐ 271	Joey McLaughlin	10	.05	.01			
☐ 272	Barry Bonnell	10	.05	.01			
☐ 273	Tug McGraw	12	.05	.02			
☐ 274	Mike Jorgensen	10	.05	.01			
☐ 275	Pat Zachry	10	.05	.01			
☐ 276	Neil Allen	10	.05	.01			
☐ 277	Joel Youngblood	10	.05	.01			
☐ 278	Greg Pryor	10	.05	.01			
☐ 279	Britt Burns	12	.05	.02			
☐ 280	Rich Dotson	12	.05	.02			
☐ 281	Chet Lemon	12	.05	.02			
☐ 282	Rusty Kuntz	10	.05	.01			
☐ 283	Ted Cox	10	.05	.01			
☐ 284	Sparky Lyle	12	.05	.02			
☐ 285	Larry Cox	10	.05	.01			
☐ 286	Floyd Bannister	10	.05	.01			
☐ 287	Byron McLaughlin	10	.05	.01			
☐ 288	Rodney Craig	10	.05	.01			
☐ 289	Bobby Grich	12	.05	.02			
☐ 290	Dickie Thon	12	.05	.02			
☐ 291	Mark Clear	10	.05	.01			
☐ 292	Dave Lemanczyk	10	.05	.01			
☐ 293	Jason Thompson	12	.05	.02			
☐ 294	Rick Miller	10	.05	.01			
☐ 295	Lonnie Smith	15	.07	.02			
☐ 296	Ron Cey	12	.05	.02			
☐ 297	Steve Yeager	10	.05	.01			
☐ 298	Bobby Castillo	10	.05	.01			
☐ 299	Manny Mota	12	.05	.02			
☐ 300	Jay Johnstone	12	.05	.02			
☐ 301	Dan Driessen	10	.05	.01			
☐ 302	Joe Nolan	10	.05	.01			
☐ 303	Paul Householder	10	.05	.01			
☐ 304	Harry Spilman	12	.05	.01			
☐ 305	Cesar Geronimo	10	.05	.01			
☐ 306A	Gary Mathews P1 ERR	20	.09	.03			
	(Name misspelled)						
☐ 306B	Gary Matthews P2 COR	12	.05	.02			
☐ 307	Ken Reitz	10	.05	.01			
☐ 308	Ted Simmons	20	.09	.03			
☐ 309	John Littlefield	10	.05	.01			
☐ 310	George Frazier	10	.05	.01			
☐ 311	Dane Iorg	10	.05	.01			
☐ 312	Mike Ivie	10	.05	.01			
☐ 313	Dennis Littlejohn	10	.05	.01			
☐ 314	Gary Lavelle	10	.05	.01			
☐ 315	Jack Clark	25	.11	.03			
☐ 316	Jim Wohlford	10	.05	.01			
☐ 317	Rick Matula	10	.05	.01			
☐ 318	Toby Harrah	12	.05	.02			
☐ 319A	Dwane Kuiper P1 ERR	15	.07	.02			
	(Name misspelled)						
☐ 319B	Duane Kuiper P2 COR	10	.05	.01			
☐ 320	Len Barker	10	.05	.01			
☐ 321	Victor Cruz	10	.05	.01			
☐ 322	Dell Alston	10	.05	.01			
☐ 323	Robin Yount	4.00	1.80	.50			
☐ 324	Charlie Moore	10	.05	.01			
☐ 325	Lary Sorensen	10	.05	.01			
☐ 326A	Gorman Thomas P1	20	.09	.03			
	(2nd line on back: "30 HR mark 4th")						
☐ 326B	Gorman Thomas P2	12	.05	.02			
	("30 HR mark 3rd")						
☐ 327	Bob Rodgers MG	10	.05	.01			
☐ 328	Phil Niekro	60	.25	.08			
☐ 329	Chris Speier	10	.05	.01			
☐ 330A	Steve Rodgers P1	20	.09	.03			
	ERR (Name misspelled)						
☐ 330B	Steve Rogers P2 COR	10	.05	.01			
☐ 331	Woodie Fryman	10	.05	.01			
☐ 332	Warren Cromartie	10	.05	.01			
☐ 333	Jerry White	10	.05	.01			
☐ 334	Tony Perez	40	.18	.05			
☐ 335	Carlton Fisk	2.00	.90	.25			
☐ 336	Dick Drago	10	.05	.01			
☐ 337	Steve Renko	10	.05	.01			
☐ 338	Jim Rice	30	.14	.04			
☐ 339	Jerry Royster	10	.05	.01			
☐ 340	Frank White	12	.05	.02			
☐ 341	Jamie Quirk	10	.05	.01			
☐ 342A	Paul Spittorff P1 ERR	15	.07	.02			
	(Name misspelled)						
☐ 342B	Paul Splittorff P2 COR	10	.05	.01			
☐ 343	Marty Pattin	10	.05	.01			
☐ 344	Pete LaCock	10	.05	.01			
☐ 345	Willie Randolph	12	.05	.02			
☐ 346	Rick Cerone	10	.05	.01			
☐ 347	Rich Gossage	20	.09	.03			
☐ 348	Reggie Jackson	2.50	1.15	.30			
☐ 349	Ruppert Jones	10	.05	.01			
☐ 350	Dave McKay	10	.05	.01			
☐ 351	Yogi Berra CO	40	.18	.05			
☐ 352	Doug DeCinces	12	.05	.02			
☐ 353	Jim Palmer	1.75	.80	.22			
☐ 354	Tippy Martinez	10	.05	.01			
☐ 355	Al Bumbry	10	.05	.01			
☐ 356	Earl Weaver MG	12	.05	.02			
☐ 357A	Bob Picciolo P1 ERR	15	.07	.02			
	(Name misspelled)						
☐ 357B	Rob Picciolo P2 COR	10	.05	.01			
☐ 358	Matt Keough	10	.05	.01			
☐ 359	Dwayne Murphy	10	.05	.01			
☐ 360	Brian Kingman	10	.05	.01			
☐ 361	Bill Fahey	10	.05	.01			
☐ 362	Steve Mura	10	.05	.01			
☐ 363	Dennis Kinney	10	.05	.01			
☐ 364	Dave Winfield	3.00	1.35	.40			
☐ 365	Lou Whitaker	90	.40	.11			
☐ 366	Lance Parrish	25	.11	.03			

☐ 367	Tim Corcoran	.10	.05	.01
☐ 368	Pat Underwood	.10	.05	.01
☐ 369	Al Cowens	.10	.05	.01
☐ 370	Sparky Anderson MG	.12	.05	.02
☐ 371	Pete Rose	2.00	.90	.25
☐ 372	Phil Garner	.12	.05	.02
☐ 373	Steve Nicosia	.10	.05	.01
☐ 374	John Candelaria	.12	.05	.02
☐ 375	Don Robinson	.10	.05	.01
☐ 376	Lee Lacy	.10	.05	.01
☐ 377	John Milner	.10	.05	.01
☐ 378	Craig Reynolds	.10	.05	.01
☐ 379A	Luis Pujols P1 ERR	.15	.07	.02
	(Name misspelled)			
☐ 379B	Luis Pujols P2 COR	.10	.05	.01
☐ 380	Joe Niekro	.12	.05	.02
☐ 381	Joaquin Andujar	.12	.05	.02
☐ 382	Keith Moreland	.12	.05	.02
☐ 383	Jose Cruz	.12	.05	.02
☐ 384	Bill Virdon MG	.10	.05	.01
☐ 385	Jim Sundberg	.10	.05	.01
☐ 386	Doc Medich	.10	.05	.01
☐ 387	Al Oliver	.12	.05	.02
☐ 388	Jim Norris	.10	.05	.01
☐ 389	Bob Bailor	.10	.05	.01
☐ 390	Ernie Whitt	.10	.05	.01
☐ 391	Otto Velez	.10	.05	.01
☐ 392	Roy Howell	.10	.05	.01
☐ 393	Bob Walk	.35	.16	.04
☐ 394	Doug Flynn	.10	.05	.01
☐ 395	Pete Falcone	.10	.05	.01
☐ 396	Tom Hausman	.10	.05	.01
☐ 397	Elliott Maddox	.10	.05	.01
☐ 398	Mike Squires	.10	.05	.01
☐ 399	Marvis Foley	.10	.05	.01
☐ 400	Steve Trout	.10	.05	.01
☐ 401	Wayne Nordhagen	.10	.05	.01
☐ 402	Tony LaRussa MG	.12	.05	.02
☐ 403	Bruce Bochte	.10	.05	.01
☐ 404	Bake McBride	.10	.05	.01
☐ 405	Jerry Narron	.10	.05	.01
☐ 406	Rob Dressler	.10	.05	.01
☐ 407	Dave Heaverlo	.10	.05	.01
☐ 408	Tom Paciorek	.12	.05	.02
☐ 409	Carney Lansford	.30	.14	.04
☐ 410	Brian Downing	.12	.05	.02
☐ 411	Don Aase	.10	.05	.01
☐ 412	Jim Barr	.10	.05	.01
☐ 413	Don Baylor	.12	.05	.02
☐ 414	Jim Fregosi MG	.10	.05	.01
☐ 415	Dallas Green MG	.10	.05	.01
☐ 416	Dave Lopes	.12	.05	.02
☐ 417	Jerry Reuss	.12	.05	.02
☐ 418	Rick Sutcliffe	.35	.16	.04
☐ 419	Derrel Thomas	.10	.05	.01
☐ 420	Tom Lasorda MG	.12	.05	.02
☐ 421	Charlie Leibrandt	.90	.40	.11
☐ 422	Tom Seaver	2.00	.90	.25
☐ 423	Ron Oester	.10	.05	.01
☐ 424	Junior Kennedy	.10	.05	.01
☐ 425	Tom Seaver	2.00	.90	.25
☐ 426	Bobby Cox MG	.10	.05	.01
☐ 427	Leon Durham	.10	.05	.01
☐ 428	Terry Kennedy	.12	.05	.02
☐ 429	Silvio Martinez	.10	.05	.01
☐ 430	George Hendrick	.12	.05	.02
☐ 431	Red Schoendienst MG	.15	.07	.02
☐ 432	Johnnie LeMaster	.10	.05	.01
☐ 433	Vida Blue	.12	.05	.02
☐ 434	John Montefusco	.10	.05	.01
☐ 435	Terry Whitfield	.10	.05	.01
☐ 436	Dave Bristol MG	.10	.05	.01
☐ 437	Dale Murphy	1.00	.45	.13
☐ 438	Jerry Dybzinski	.10	.05	.01
☐ 439	Jorge Orta	.10	.05	.01
☐ 440	Wayne Garland	.10	.05	.01
☐ 441	Miguel Dilone	.10	.05	.01
☐ 442	Dave Garcia MG	.10	.05	.01
☐ 443	Don Money	.10	.05	.01
☐ 444A	Buck Martinez P1 ERR	.15	.07	.02
	(Reverse negative)			
☐ 444B	Buck Martinez	.10	.05	.01
	P2 COR			
☐ 445	Jerry Augustine	.10	.05	.01
☐ 446	Ben Oglivie	.12	.05	.02
☐ 447	Jim Slaton	.10	.05	.01
☐ 448	Doyle Alexander	.10	.05	.01
☐ 449	Tony Bernazard	.10	.05	.01
☐ 450	Scott Sanderson	.12	.05	.02
☐ 451	David Palmer	.10	.05	.01
☐ 452	Stan Bahnsen	.10	.05	.01
☐ 453	Dick Williams MG	.10	.05	.01
☐ 454	Rick Burleson	.10	.05	.01
☐ 455	Gary Allenson	.10	.05	.01
☐ 456	Bob Stanley	.10	.05	.01
☐ 457A	John Tudor P1 ERR	.35	.16	.04
	(Lifetime W-L "9.7")			
☐ 457B	John Tudor P2 COR	.35	.16	.04
	(Corrected "9-7")			
☐ 458	Dwight Evans	.35	.16	.04
☐ 459	Glenn Hubbard	.10	.05	.01
☐ 460	U.L. Washington	.10	.05	.01
☐ 461	Larry Gura	.10	.05	.01
☐ 462	Rich Gale	.10	.05	.01
☐ 463	Hal McRae	.12	.05	.02
☐ 464	Jim Frey MG	.10	.05	.01
☐ 465	Bucky Dent	.12	.05	.02
☐ 466	Dennis Werth	.10	.05	.01
☐ 467	Ron Davis	.10	.05	.01
☐ 468	Reggie Jackson UER	2.50	1.15	.30
	(32 HR in 1970,			
	should be 23)			
☐ 469	Bobby Brown	.10	.05	.01
☐ 470	Mike Davis	.10	.05	.01

☐ 471 Gaylord Perry	60	.25	.08
☐ 472 Mark Belanger	12	.05	.02
☐ 473 Jim Palmer	1.75	.80	.22
☐ 474 Sammy Stewart	10	.05	.01
☐ 475 Tim Stoddard	10	.05	.01
☐ 476 Steve Stone	12	.05	.02
☐ 477 Jeff Newman	10	.05	.01
☐ 478 Steve McCatty	10	.05	.01
☐ 479 Billy Martin MG	25	.11	.03
☐ 480 Mitchell Page	10	.05	.01
☐ 481 Cy Young Winner 1980	1.00	.45	.13
Steve Carlton			
☐ 482 Bill Buckner	12	.05	.02
☐ 483A Ivan DeJesus P1 ERR	15	.07	.02
(Lifetime hits "702")			
☐ 483B Ivan DeJesus P2 COR	10	.05	.01
(Lifetime hits "642")			
☐ 484 Cliff Johnson	10	.05	.01
☐ 485 Lenny Randle	10	.05	.01
☐ 486 Larry Milbourne	10	.05	.01
☐ 487 Roy Smalley	10	.05	.01
☐ 488 John Castino	10	.05	.01
☐ 489 Ron Jackson	10	.05	.01
☐ 490A Dave Roberts P1	15	.07	.02
(Career Highlights: "Showed pop in")			
☐ 490B Dave Roberts P2	10	.05	.01
("Declared himself")			
☐ 491 MVP: George Brett	2.00	.90	.25
☐ 492 Mike Cubbage	10	.05	.01
☐ 493 Rob Wilfong	10	.05	.01
☐ 494 Danny Goodwin	10	.05	.01
☐ 495 Jose Morales	10	.05	.01
☐ 496 Mickey Rivers	12	.05	.02
☐ 497 Mike Edwards	10	.05	.01
☐ 498 Mike Sadek	10	.05	.01
☐ 499 Lenn Sakata	10	.05	.01
☐ 500 Gene Michael MG	10	.05	.01
☐ 501 Dave Roberts	10	.05	.01
☐ 502 Steve Dillard	10	.05	.01
☐ 503 Jim Essian	10	.05	.01
☐ 504 Rance Mulliniks	10	.05	.01
☐ 505 Darrell Porter	10	.05	.01
☐ 506 Joe Torre MG	12	.05	.02
☐ 507 Terry Crowley	10	.05	.01
☐ 508 Bill Travers	10	.05	.01
☐ 509 Nelson Norman	10	.05	.01
☐ 510 Bob McClure	10	.05	.01
☐ 511 Steve Howe	12	.05	.02
☐ 512 Dave Rader	10	.05	.01
☐ 513 Mick Kelleher	10	.05	.01
☐ 514 Kiko Garcia	10	.05	.01
☐ 515 Larry Biittner	10	.05	.01
☐ 516A Willie Norwood P1	15	.07	.02
(Career Highlights "Spent most of")			
☐ 516B Willie Norwood P2	10	.05	.01
("Traded to Seattle")			
☐ 517 Bo Diaz	10	.05	.01
☐ 518 Juan Beniquez	10	.05	.01
☐ 519 Scot Thompson	10	.05	.01
☐ 520 Jim Tracy	10	.05	.01
☐ 521 Carlos Lezcano	10	.05	.01
☐ 522 Joe Amalfitano MG	10	.05	.01
☐ 523 Preston Hanna	10	.05	.01
☐ 524A Ray Burris P1	15	.07	.02
(Career Highlights: "Went on ...")			
☐ 524B Ray Burris P2	10	.05	.01
("Drafted by ...")			
☐ 525 Broderick Perkins	10	.05	.01
☐ 526 Mickey Hatcher	10	.05	.01
☐ 527 John Goryl MG	10	.05	.01
☐ 528 Dick Davis	10	.05	.01
☐ 529 Butch Wynegar	10	.05	.01
☐ 530 Sal Butera	10	.05	.01
☐ 531 Jerry Koosman	12	.05	.02
☐ 532A Geoff Zahn P1	15	.07	.02
(Career Highlights: "Was 2nd in")			
☐ 532B Geoff Zahn P2	10	.05	.01
("Signed a 3 year")			
☐ 533 Dennis Martinez	35	.16	.04
☐ 534 Gary Thomasson	10	.05	.01
☐ 535 Steve Macko	10	.05	.01
☐ 536 Jim Kaat	20	.09	.03
☐ 537 Best Hitters	2.50	1.15	.30
George Brett			
Rod Carew			
☐ 538 Tim Raines	5.00	2.30	.60
☐ 539 Keith Smith	10	.05	.01
☐ 540 Ken Macha	10	.05	.01
☐ 541 Burt Hooton	10	.05	.01
☐ 542 Butch Hobson	12	.05	.02
☐ 543 Bill Stein	10	.05	.01
☐ 544 Dave Stapleton	10	.05	.01
☐ 545 Bob Pate	10	.05	.01
☐ 546 Doug Corbett	10	.05	.01
☐ 547 Darrell Jackson	10	.05	.01
☐ 548 Pete Redfern	10	.05	.01
☐ 549 Roger Erickson	10	.05	.01
☐ 550 Al Hrabosky	10	.05	.01
☐ 551 Dick Tidrow	10	.05	.01
☐ 552 Dave Ford	10	.05	.01
☐ 553 Dave Kingman	12	.05	.02
☐ 554A Mike Vail P1	15	.07	.02
(Career Highlights: "After two ...")			
☐ 554B Mike Vail P2	10	.05	.01
("Traded to ...")			
☐ 555A Jerry Martin P1	15	.07	.02
(Career Highlights: "Overcame a ...")			
☐ 555B Jerry Martin P2	10	.05	.01

("Traded to ...")

☐ 556A	Jesus Figueroa P1	.15	.07	.02
	(Career Highlights: "Had an ...")			
☐ 556B	Jesus Figueroa P2	.10	.05	.01
	("Traded to ...")			
☐ 557	Don Stanhouse	.10	.05	.01
☐ 558	Barry Foote	.10	.05	.01
☐ 559	Tim Blackwell	.10	.05	.01
☐ 560	Bruce Sutter	.20	.09	.03
☐ 561	Rick Reuschel	.12	.05	.02
☐ 562	Lynn McGlothen	.10	.05	.01
☐ 563A	Bob Owchinko P1	.10	.05	.01
	(Career Highlights: "Traded in ...")			
☐ 563B	Bob Owchinko P2	.10	.05	.01
	("Involved in a ...")			
☐ 564	John Verhoeven	.10	.05	.01
☐ 565	Ken Landreaux	.10	.05	.01
☐ 566A	Glen Adams P1 ERR	.15	.07	.02
	(Name misspelled)			
☐ 566B	Glen Adams P2 COR	.10	.05	.01
☐ 567	Hosken Powell	.10	.05	.01
☐ 568	Dick Noles	.10	.05	.01
☐ 569	Danny Ainge	2.00	.90	.25
☐ 570	Bobby Mattick MG	.10	.05	.01
☐ 571	Joe Lefebvre	.10	.05	.01
☐ 572	Bobby Clark	.10	.05	.01
☐ 573	Dennis Lamp	.10	.05	.01
☐ 574	Randy Lerch	.10	.05	.01
☐ 575	Mookie Wilson	.50	.23	.06
☐ 576	Ron LeFlore	.12	.05	.02
☐ 577	Jim Dwyer	.10	.05	.01
☐ 578	Bill Castro	.10	.05	.01
☐ 579	Greg Minton	.10	.05	.01
☐ 580	Mark Littell	.10	.05	.01
☐ 581	Andy Hassler	.10	.05	.01
☐ 582	Dave Stieb	.35	.16	.04
☐ 583	Ken Oberkfell	.10	.05	.01
☐ 584	Larry Bradford	.10	.05	.01
☐ 585	Fred Stanley	.10	.05	.01
☐ 586	Bill Caudill	.10	.05	.01
☐ 587	Doug Capilla	.10	.05	.01
☐ 588	George Riley	.10	.05	.01
☐ 589	Willie Hernandez	.12	.05	.02
☐ 590	MVP: Mike Schmidt	1.50	.65	.19
☐ 591	Cy Young Winner 1980: Steve Stone	.10	.05	.01
☐ 592	Rick Sofield	.10	.05	.01
☐ 593	Bombo Rivera	.10	.05	.01
☐ 594	Gary Ward	.10	.05	.01
☐ 595A	Dave Edwards P1	.15	.07	.02
	(Career Highlights: "Sidelined the")			
☐ 595B	Dave Edwards P2	.10	.05	.01
	("Traded to ...")			
☐ 596	Mike Proly	.10	.05	.01

☐ 597	Tommy Boggs	.10	.05	.01
☐ 598	Greg Gross	.10	.05	.01
☐ 599	Elias Sosa	.10	.05	.01
☐ 600	Pat Kelly	.10	.05	.01
☐ 601A	Checklist 1 P1 ERR Unnumbered (51 Donahue)	.15	.02	.00
☐ 601B	Checklist 1 P2 COR Unnumbered (51 Donohue)	.75	.08	.02
☐ 602	Checklist 2 Unnumbered	.15	.02	.00
☐ 603A	Checklist 3 P1 ERR Unnumbered (306 Mathews)	.15	.02	.00
☐ 603B	Checklist 3 P2 COR Unnumbered (306 Matthews)	.15	.02	.00
☐ 604A	Checklist 4 P1 ERR Unnumbered (379 Pujois)	.15	.02	.00
☐ 604B	Checklist 4 P2 COR Unnumbered (379 Pujols)	.15	.02	.00
☐ 605A	Checklist 5 P1 ERR Unnumbered (566 Glen Adams)	.15	.02	.00
☐ 605B	Checklist 5 P2 COR Unnumbered (566 Glenn Adams)	.15	.02	.00

1982 Donruss

The 1982 Donruss set contains 653 numbered cards and the seven unnumbered checklists; each card measures 2 1/2" by 3 1/2". The first 26 cards of this set are entitled Donruss Diamond Kings (DK) and

feature the artwork of Dick Perez of Perez-Steele Galleries. The set was marketed with puzzle pieces rather than with bubble gum. There are 63 pieces to the puzzle, which, when put together, make a collage of Babe Ruth entitled "Hall of Fame Diamond King." The card stock in this year's Donruss cards is considerably thicker than that of the 1981 cards. The seven unnumbered checklist cards are arbitrarily assigned numbers 654 through 660 and are listed at the end of the list below. The key Rookie Cards in this set are George Bell, Cal Ripken Jr., Steve Sax, Lee Smith, and Dave Stewart.

	NRMT-MT	EXC	G-VG
COMPLETE SET (660)	100.00	45.00	12.50
COMPLETE FACT.SET (660)	100.00	45.00	12.50
COMMON PLAYER (1-660)	.10	.05	.01

☐ 1 Pete Rose DK	1.75	.80	.22
☐ 2 Gary Carter DK	.50	.23	.06
☐ 3 Steve Garvey DK	.30	.14	.04
☐ 4 Vida Blue DK	.15	.07	.02
☐ 5A Alan Trammel DK ERR	1.00	.45	.13
(Name misspelled)			
☐ 5B Alan Trammell DK	.25	.11	.03
COR			
☐ 6 Len Barker DK	.15	.07	.02
☐ 7 Dwight Evans DK	.15	.07	.02
☐ 8 Rod Carew DK	.75	.35	.09
☐ 9 George Hendrick DK	.15	.07	.02
☐ 10 Phil Niekro DK	.25	.11	.03
☐ 11 Richie Zisk DK	.15	.07	.02
☐ 12 Dave Parker DK	.15	.07	.02
☐ 13 Nolan Ryan DK	3.50	1.55	.45
☐ 14 Ivan DeJesus DK	.15	.07	.02
☐ 15 George Brett DK	1.50	.65	.19
☐ 16 Tom Seaver DK	.75	.35	.09
☐ 17 Dave Kingman DK	.15	.07	.02
☐ 18 Dave Winfield DK	1.25	.55	.16
☐ 19 Mike Norris DK	.15	.07	.02
☐ 20 Carlton Fisk DK	.75	.35	.09
☐ 21 Ozzie Smith DK	1.00	.45	.13
☐ 22 Roy Smalley DK	.15	.07	.02
☐ 23 Buddy Bell DK	.15	.07	.02
☐ 24 Ken Singleton DK	.15	.07	.02
☐ 25 John Mayberry DK	.15	.07	.02
☐ 26 Gorman Thomas DK	.15	.07	.02
☐ 27 Earl Weaver MG	.12	.05	.02
☐ 28 Rollie Fingers	.75	.35	.09
☐ 29 Sparky Anderson MG	.12	.05	.02
☐ 30 Dennis Eckersley	1.50	.65	.19
☐ 31 Dave Winfield	2.50	1.15	.30
☐ 32 Burt Hooton	.10	.05	.01
☐ 33 Rick Waits	.10	.05	.01

☐ 34 George Brett	3.00	1.35	.40
☐ 35 Steve McCatty	.10	.05	.01
☐ 36 Steve Rogers	.10	.05	.01
☐ 37 Bill Stein	.10	.05	.01
☐ 38 Steve Renko	.10	.05	.01
☐ 39 Mike Squires	.10	.05	.01
☐ 40 George Hendrick	.12	.05	.02
☐ 41 Bob Knepper	.10	.05	.01
☐ 42 Steve Carlton	1.50	.65	.19
☐ 43 Larry Biittner	.10	.05	.01
☐ 44 Chris Welsh	.10	.05	.01
☐ 45 Steve Nicosia	.10	.05	.01
☐ 46 Jack Clark	.20	.09	.03
☐ 47 Chris Chambliss	.12	.05	.02
☐ 48 Ivan DeJesus	.10	.05	.01
☐ 49 Lee Mazzilli	.10	.05	.01
☐ 50 Julio Cruz	.10	.05	.01
☐ 51 Pete Redfern	.10	.05	.01
☐ 52 Dave Stieb	.20	.09	.03
☐ 53 Doug Corbett	.10	.05	.01
☐ 54 Jorge Bell	6.00	2.70	.75
☐ 55 Joe Simpson	.10	.05	.01
☐ 56 Rusty Staub	.12	.05	.02
☐ 57 Hector Cruz	.10	.05	.01
☐ 58 Claudell Washington	.10	.05	.01
☐ 59 Enrique Romo	.10	.05	.01
☐ 60 Gary Lavelle	.10	.05	.01
☐ 61 Tim Flannery	.10	.05	.01
☐ 62 Joe Nolan	.10	.05	.01
☐ 63 Larry Bowa	.12	.05	.02
☐ 64 Sixto Lezcano	.10	.05	.01
☐ 65 Joe Sambito	.10	.05	.01
☐ 66 Bruce Kison	.10	.05	.01
☐ 67 Wayne Nordhagen	.10	.05	.01
☐ 68 Woodie Fryman	.10	.05	.01
☐ 69 Billy Sample	.10	.05	.01
☐ 70 Amos Otis	.12	.05	.02
☐ 71 Matt Keough	.10	.05	.01
☐ 72 Toby Harrah	.12	.05	.02
☐ 73 Dave Righetti	.50	.23	.06
☐ 74 Carl Yastrzemski	1.50	.65	.19
☐ 75 Bob Welch	.30	.14	.04
☐ 76A Alan Trammel ERR	1.50	.65	.19
(Name misspelled)			
☐ 76B Alan Trammel COR	.60	.25	.08
☐ 77 Rick Dempsey	.12	.05	.02
☐ 78 Paul Molitor	1.00	.45	.13
☐ 79 Dennis Martinez	.25	.11	.03
☐ 80 Jim Slaton	.10	.05	.01
☐ 81 Champ Summers	.10	.05	.01
☐ 82 Carney Lansford	.12	.05	.02
☐ 83 Barry Foote	.10	.05	.01
☐ 84 Steve Garvey	.60	.25	.08
☐ 85 Rick Manning	.10	.05	.01
☐ 86 John Wathan	.10	.05	.01
☐ 87 Brian Kingman	.10	.05	.01
☐ 88 Andre Dawson UER	2.00	.90	.25

(Middle name Fernando,
should be Nolan)

☐	89 Jim Kern	.10	.05	.01
☐	90 Bobby Grich	.12	.05	.02
☐	91 Bob Forsch	.10	.05	.01
☐	92 Art Howe	.10	.05	.01
☐	93 Marty Bystrom	.10	.05	.01
☐	94 Ozzie Smith	2.00	.90	.25
☐	95 Dave Parker	.35	.16	.04
☐	96 Doyle Alexander	.10	.05	.01
☐	97 Al Hrabosky	.10	.05	.01
☐	98 Frank Taveras	.10	.05	.01
☐	99 Tim Blackwell	.10	.05	.01
☐	100 Floyd Bannister	.10	.05	.01
☐	101 Alfredo Griffin	.10	.05	.01
☐	102 Dave Engle	.10	.05	.01
☐	103 Mario Soto	.10	.05	.01
☐	104 Ross Baumgarten	.10	.05	.01
☐	105 Ken Singleton	.12	.05	.02
☐	106 Ted Simmons	.12	.05	.02
☐	107 Jack Morris	1.50	.65	.19
☐	108 Bob Watson	.12	.05	.02
☐	109 Dwight Evans	.25	.11	.03
☐	110 Tom Lasorda MG	.12	.05	.02
☐	111 Bert Blyleven	.35	.16	.04
☐	112 Dan Quisenberry	.12	.05	.02
☐	113 Rickey Henderson	4.50	2.00	.55
☐	114 Gary Carter	.90	.40	.11
☐	115 Brian Downing	.12	.05	.02
☐	116 Al Oliver	.12	.05	.02
☐	117 LaMarr Hoyt	.12	.05	.02
☐	118 Cesar Cedeno	.12	.05	.02
☐	119 Keith Moreland	.10	.05	.01
☐	120 Bob Shirley	.10	.05	.01
☐	121 Terry Kennedy	.10	.05	.01
☐	122 Frank Pastore	.10	.05	.01
☐	123 Gene Garber	.10	.05	.01
☐	124 Tony Pena	.20	.09	.03
☐	125 Allen Ripley	.10	.05	.01
☐	126 Randy Martz	.10	.05	.01
☐	127 Richie Zisk	.10	.05	.01
☐	128 Mike Scott	.12	.05	.02
☐	129 Lloyd Moseby	.10	.05	.01
☐	130 Rob Wilfong	.10	.05	.01
☐	131 Tim Stoddard	.10	.05	.01
☐	132 Gorman Thomas	.12	.05	.02
☐	133 Dan Petry	.10	.05	.01
☐	134 Bob Stanley	.10	.05	.01
☐	135 Lou Piniella	.12	.05	.02
☐	136 Pedro Guerrero	.30	.14	.04
☐	137 Len Barker	.10	.05	.01
☐	138 Rich Gale	.10	.05	.01
☐	139 Wayne Gross	.10	.05	.01
☐	140 Tim Wallach	1.00	.45	.13
☐	141 Gene Mauch MG	.10	.05	.01
☐	142 Doc Medich	.10	.05	.01
☐	143 Tony Bernazard	.10	.05	.01

☐	144 Bill Virdon MG	.10	.05	.01
☐	145 John Littlefield	.10	.05	.01
☐	146 Dave Bergman	.10	.05	.01
☐	147 Dick Davis	.10	.05	.01
☐	148 Tom Seaver	1.50	.65	.19
☐	149 Matt Sinatro	.10	.05	.01
☐	150 Chuck Tanner MG	.10	.05	.01
☐	151 Leon Durham	.10	.05	.01
☐	152 Gene Tenace	.10	.05	.01
☐	153 Al Bumbry	.10	.05	.01
☐	154 Mark Brouhard	.10	.05	.01
☐	155 Rick Peters	.10	.05	.01
☐	156 Jerry Remy	.10	.05	.01
☐	157 Rick Reuschel	.12	.05	.02
☐	158 Steve Howe	.10	.05	.01
☐	159 Alan Bannister	.10	.05	.01
☐	160 U.L. Washington	.10	.05	.01
☐	161 Rick Langford	.10	.05	.01
☐	162 Bill Gullickson	.25	.11	.03
☐	163 Mark Wagner	.10	.05	.01
☐	164 Geoff Zahn	.10	.05	.01
☐	165 Ron LeFlore	.12	.05	.02
☐	166 Dane Iorg	.10	.05	.01
☐	167 Joe Niekro	.12	.05	.02
☐	168 Pete Rose	1.50	.65	.19
☐	169 Dave Collins	.10	.05	.01
☐	170 Rick Wise	.10	.05	.01
☐	171 Jim Bibby	.10	.05	.01
☐	172 Larry Herndon	.10	.05	.01
☐	173 Bob Horner	.12	.05	.02
☐	174 Steve Dillard	.10	.05	.01
☐	175 Mookie Wilson	.12	.05	.02
☐	176 Dan Meyer	.10	.05	.01
☐	177 Fernando Arroyo	.10	.05	.01
☐	178 Jackson Todd	.10	.05	.01
☐	179 Darrell Jackson	.10	.05	.01
☐	180 Alvis Woods	.10	.05	.01
☐	181 Jim Anderson	.10	.05	.01
☐	182 Dave Kingman	.12	.05	.02
☐	183 Steve Henderson	.10	.05	.01
☐	184 Brian Asselstine	.10	.05	.01
☐	185 Rod Scurry	.10	.05	.01
☐	186 Fred Breining	.10	.05	.01
☐	187 Danny Boone	.10	.05	.01
☐	188 Junior Kennedy	.10	.05	.01
☐	189 Sparky Lyle	.12	.05	.02
☐	190 Whitey Herzog MG	.12	.05	.02
☐	191 Dave Smith	.10	.05	.01
☐	192 Ed Ott	.10	.05	.01
☐	193 Greg Luzinski	.12	.05	.02
☐	194 Bill Lee	.10	.05	.01
☐	195 Don Zimmer MG	.10	.05	.01
☐	196 Hal McRae	.12	.05	.02
☐	197 Mike Norris	.10	.05	.01
☐	198 Duane Kuiper	.10	.05	.01
☐	199 Rick Cerone	.10	.05	.01
☐	200 Jim Rice	.25	.11	.03

☐ 201	Steve Yeager	.10	.05	.01	☐ 258 Cecil Cooper	.12	.05	.02
☐ 202	Tom Brookens	.10	.05	.01	☐ 259 Dave Rozema	.10	.05	.01
☐ 203	Jose Morales	.10	.05	.01	☐ 260 John Tudor	.12	.05	.02
☐ 204	Roy Howell	.10	.05	.01	☐ 261 Jerry Mumphrey	.10	.05	.01
☐ 205	Tippy Martinez	.10	.05	.01	☐ 262 Jay Johnstone	.12	.05	.02
☐ 206	Moose Haas	.10	.05	.01	☐ 263 Bo Diaz	.10	.05	.01
☐ 207	Al Cowens	.10	.05	.01	☐ 264 Dennis Leonard	.10	.05	.01
☐ 208	Dave Stapleton	.10	.05	.01	☐ 265 Jim Spencer	.10	.05	.01
☐ 209	Bucky Dent	.12	.05	.02	☐ 266 John Milner	.10	.05	.01
☐ 210	Ron Cey	.12	.05	.02	☐ 267 Don Aase	.10	.05	.01
☐ 211	Jorge Orta	.10	.05	.01	☐ 268 Jim Sundberg	.10	.05	.01
☐ 212	Jamie Quirk	.10	.05	.01	☐ 269 Lamar Johnson	.10	.05	.01
☐ 213	Jeff Jones	.10	.05	.01	☐ 270 Frank LaCorte	.10	.05	.01
☐ 214	Tim Raines	1.25	.55	.16	☐ 271 Barry Evans	.10	.05	.01
☐ 215	Jon Matlack	.10	.05	.01	☐ 272 Enos Cabell	.10	.05	.01
☐ 216	Rod Carew	1.50	.65	.19	☐ 273 Del Unser	.10	.05	.01
☐ 217	Jim Kaat	.15	.07	.02	☐ 274 George Foster	.12	.05	.02
☐ 218	Joe Pittman	.10	.05	.01	☐ 275 Brett Butler	2.50	1.15	.30
☐ 219	Larry Christenson	.10	.05	.01	☐ 276 Lee Lacy	.10	.05	.01
☐ 220	Juan Bonilla	.10	.05	.01	☐ 277 Ken Reitz	.10	.05	.01
☐ 221	Mike Easler	.10	.05	.01	☐ 278 Keith Hernandez	.25	.11	.03
☐ 222	Vida Blue	.12	.05	.02	☐ 279 Doug DeCinces	.12	.05	.02
☐ 223	Rick Camp	.10	.05	.01	☐ 280 Charlie Moore	.10	.05	.01
☐ 224	Mike Jorgensen	.10	.05	.01	☐ 281 Lance Parrish	.25	.11	.03
☐ 225	Jody Davis	.12	.05	.02	☐ 282 Ralph Houk MG	.10	.05	.01
☐ 226	Mike Parrott	.10	.05	.01	☐ 283 Rich Gossage	.20	.09	.03
☐ 227	Jim Clancy	.10	.05	.01	☐ 284 Jerry Reuss	.10	.05	.01
☐ 228	Hosken Powell	.10	.05	.01	☐ 285 Mike Stanton	.10	.05	.01
☐ 229	Tom Hume	.10	.05	.01	☐ 286 Frank White	.12	.05	.02
☐ 230	Britt Burns	.10	.05	.01	☐ 287 Bob Owchinko	.10	.05	.01
☐ 231	Jim Palmer	1.25	.55	.16	☐ 288 Scott Sanderson	.10	.05	.01
☐ 232	Bob Rodgers MG	.10	.05	.01	☐ 289 Bump Wills	.10	.05	.01
☐ 233	Milt Wilcox	.10	.05	.01	☐ 290 Dave Frost	.10	.05	.01
☐ 234	Dave Revering	.10	.05	.01	☐ 291 Chet Lemon	.10	.05	.01
☐ 235	Mike Torrez	.10	.05	.01	☐ 292 Tito Landrum	.10	.05	.01
☐ 236	Robert Castillo	.10	.05	.01	☐ 293 Vern Ruhle	.10	.05	.01
☐ 237	Von Hayes	.30	.14	.04	☐ 294 Mike Schmidt	2.50	1.15	.30
☐ 238	Renie Martin	.10	.05	.01	☐ 295 Sam Mejias	.10	.05	.01
☐ 239	Dwayne Murphy	.10	.05	.01	☐ 296 Gary Lucas	.10	.05	.01
☐ 240	Rodney Scott	.10	.05	.01	☐ 297 John Candelaria	.10	.05	.01
☐ 241	Fred Patek	.10	.05	.01	☐ 298 Jerry Martin	.10	.05	.01
☐ 242	Mickey Rivers	.10	.05	.01	☐ 299 Dale Murphy	1.00	.45	.13
☐ 243	Steve Trout	.10	.05	.01	☐ 300 Mike Lum	.10	.05	.01
☐ 244	Jose Cruz	.12	.05	.02	☐ 301 Tom Hausman	.10	.05	.01
☐ 245	Manny Trillo	.10	.05	.01	☐ 302 Glenn Abbott	.10	.05	.01
☐ 246	Lary Sorensen	.10	.05	.01	☐ 303 Roger Erickson	.10	.05	.01
☐ 247	Dave Edwards	.10	.05	.01	☐ 304 Otto Velez	.10	.05	.01
☐ 248	Dan Driessen	.10	.05	.01	☐ 305 Danny Goodwin	.10	.05	.01
☐ 249	Tommy Boggs	.10	.05	.01	☐ 306 John Mayberry	.10	.05	.01
☐ 250	Dale Berra	.10	.05	.01	☐ 307 Lenny Randle	.10	.05	.01
☐ 251	Ed Whitson	.10	.05	.01	☐ 308 Bob Bailor	.10	.05	.01
☐ 252	Lee Smith	7.00	3.10	.85	☐ 309 Jerry Morales	.10	.05	.01
☐ 253	Tom Paciorek	.12	.05	.02	☐ 310 Rufino Linares	.10	.05	.01
☐ 254	Pat Zachry	.10	.05	.01	☐ 311 Kent Tekulve	.12	.05	.02
☐ 255	Luis Leal	.10	.05	.01	☐ 312 Joe Morgan	.75	.35	.09
☐ 256	John Castino	.10	.05	.01	☐ 313 John Urrea	.10	.05	.01
☐ 257	Rich Dauer	.10	.05	.01	☐ 314 Paul Householder	.10	.05	.01

☐ 315 Garry Maddox........10	.05	.01
☐ 316 Mike Ramsey........10	.05	.01
☐ 317 Alan Ashby........10	.05	.01
☐ 318 Bob Clark........10	.05	.01
☐ 319 Tony LaRussa MG........12	.05	.02
☐ 320 Charlie Lea........10	.05	.01
☐ 321 Danny Darwin........10	.05	.01
☐ 322 Cesar Geronimo........10	.05	.01
☐ 323 Tom Underwood........10	.05	.01
☐ 324 Andre Thornton........10	.05	.01
☐ 325 Rudy May........10	.05	.01
☐ 326 Frank Tanana........12	.05	.02
☐ 327 Dave Lopes........12	.05	.02
☐ 328 Richie Hebner........10	.05	.01
☐ 329 Mike Flanagan........12	.05	.02
☐ 330 Mike Caldwell........10	.05	.01
☐ 331 Scott McGregor........10	.05	.01
☐ 332 Jerry Augustine........10	.05	.01
☐ 333 Stan Papi........10	.05	.01
☐ 334 Rick Miller........10	.05	.01
☐ 335 Graig Nettles........12	.05	.02
☐ 336 Dusty Baker........12	.05	.02
☐ 337 Dave Garcia MG........10	.05	.01
☐ 338 Larry Gura........10	.05	.01
☐ 339 Cliff Johnson........10	.05	.01
☐ 340 Warren Cromartie........10	.05	.01
☐ 341 Steve Comer........10	.05	.01
☐ 342 Rick Burleson........10	.05	.01
☐ 343 John Martin........10	.05	.01
☐ 344 Craig Reynolds........10	.05	.01
☐ 345 Mike Proly........10	.05	.01
☐ 346 Ruppert Jones........10	.05	.01
☐ 347 Omar Moreno........10	.05	.01
☐ 348 Greg Minton........10	.05	.01
☐ 349 Rick Mahler........10	.05	.01
☐ 350 Alex Trevino........10	.05	.01
☐ 351 Mike Krukow........10	.05	.01
☐ 352A Shane Rawley ERR......75	.35	.09
(Photo actually		
Jim Anderson)		
☐ 352B Shane Rawley COR......10	.05	.01
☐ 353 Garth Iorg........10	.05	.01
☐ 354 Pete Mackanin........10	.05	.01
☐ 355 Paul Moskau........10	.05	.01
☐ 356 Richard Dotson........10	.05	.01
☐ 357 Steve Stone........12	.05	.02
☐ 358 Larry Hisle........10	.05	.01
☐ 359 Aurelio Lopez........10	.05	.01
☐ 360 Oscar Gamble........10	.05	.01
☐ 361 Tom Burgmeier........10	.05	.01
☐ 362 Terry Forster........10	.05	.01
☐ 363 Joe Charboneau........10	.05	.01
☐ 364 Ken Brett........10	.05	.01
☐ 365 Tony Armas........10	.05	.01
☐ 366 Chris Speier........10	.05	.01
☐ 367 Fred Lynn........12	.05	.02
☐ 368 Buddy Bell........12	.05	.02

☐ 369 Jim Essian........10	.05	.01
☐ 370 Terry Puhl........10	.05	.01
☐ 371 Greg Gross........10	.05	.01
☐ 372 Bruce Sutter........20	.09	.03
☐ 373 Joe Lefebvre........10	.05	.01
☐ 374 Ray Knight........12	.05	.02
☐ 375 Bruce Benedict........10	.05	.01
☐ 376 Tim Foli........10	.05	.01
☐ 377 Al Holland........10	.05	.01
☐ 378 Ken Kravec........10	.05	.01
☐ 379 Jeff Burroughs........10	.05	.01
☐ 380 Pete Falcone........10	.05	.01
☐ 381 Ernie Whitt........10	.05	.01
☐ 382 Brad Havens........10	.05	.01
☐ 383 Terry Crowley........10	.05	.01
☐ 384 Don Money........10	.05	.01
☐ 385 Dan Schatzeder........10	.05	.01
☐ 386 Gary Allenson........10	.05	.01
☐ 387 Yogi Berra CO........40	.18	.05
☐ 388 Ken Landreaux........10	.05	.01
☐ 389 Mike Hargrove........12	.05	.02
☐ 390 Darryl Motley........10	.05	.01
☐ 391 Dave McKay........10	.05	.01
☐ 392 Stan Bahnsen........10	.05	.01
☐ 393 Ken Forsch........10	.05	.01
☐ 394 Mario Mendoza........10	.05	.01
☐ 395 Jim Morrison........10	.05	.01
☐ 396 Mike Ivie........10	.05	.01
☐ 397 Broderick Perkins........10	.05	.01
☐ 398 Darrell Evans........12	.05	.02
☐ 399 Ron Reed........10	.05	.01
☐ 400 Johnny Bench........1.50	.65	.19
☐ 401 Steve Bedrosian........25	.11	.03
☐ 402 Bill Robinson........12	.05	.02
☐ 403 Bill Buckner........12	.05	.02
☐ 404 Ken Oberkfell........10	.05	.01
☐ 405 Cal Ripken Jr. 50.00	23.00	6.25
☐ 406 Jim Gantner........12	.05	.02
☐ 407 Kirk Gibson........75	.35	.09
☐ 408 Tony Perez........35	.16	.04
☐ 409 Tommy John UER........20	.09	.03
(Text says 52-56 as		
Yankee, should be		
52-26)		
☐ 410 Dave Stewart........3.00	1.35	.40
☐ 411 Dan Spillner........10	.05	.01
☐ 412 Willie Aikens........10	.05	.01
☐ 413 Mike Heath........10	.05	.01
☐ 414 Ray Burris........10	.05	.01
☐ 415 Leon Roberts........10	.05	.01
☐ 416 Mike Witt........15	.07	.02
☐ 417 Bob Molinaro........10	.05	.01
☐ 418 Steve Braun........10	.05	.01
☐ 419 Nolan Ryan UER......8.00	3.60	1.00
(Nisnumbering of		
Nolan's no-hitters		
on card back)		

☐ 420	Tug McGraw	12	.05	.02
☐ 421	Dave Concepcion	12	.05	.02
☐ 422A	Juan Eichelberger	75	.35	.09
	ERR (Photo actually			
	Gary Lucas)			
☐ 422B	Juan Eichelberger	10	.05	.01
	COR			
☐ 423	Rick Rhoden	10	.05	.01
☐ 424	Frank Robinson MG	30	.14	.04
☐ 425	Eddie Miller	10	.05	.01
☐ 426	Bill Caudill	10	.05	.01
☐ 427	Doug Flynn	10	.05	.01
☐ 428	Larry Andersen UER	10	.05	.01
	(Misspelled Anderson			
	on card front)			
☐ 429	Al Williams	10	.05	.01
☐ 430	Jerry Garvin	10	.05	.01
☐ 431	Glenn Adams	10	.05	.01
☐ 432	Barry Bonnell	10	.05	.01
☐ 433	Jerry Narron	10	.05	.01
☐ 434	John Stearns	10	.05	.01
☐ 435	Mike Tyson	10	.05	.01
☐ 436	Glenn Hubbard	10	.05	.01
☐ 437	Eddie Solomon	10	.05	.01
☐ 438	Jeff Leonard	10	.05	.01
☐ 439	Randy Bass	12	.05	.02
☐ 440	Mike LaCoss	10	.05	.01
☐ 441	Gary Matthews	12	.05	.02
☐ 442	Mark Littell	10	.05	.01
☐ 443	Don Sutton	40	.18	.05
☐ 444	John Harris	10	.05	.01
☐ 445	Vada Pinson CO	12	.05	.02
☐ 446	Elias Sosa	10	.05	.01
☐ 447	Charlie Hough	12	.05	.02
☐ 448	Willie Wilson	12	.05	.02
☐ 449	Fred Stanley	10	.05	.01
☐ 450	Tom Veryzer	10	.05	.01
☐ 451	Ron Davis	10	.05	.01
☐ 452	Mark Clear	10	.05	.01
☐ 453	Bill Russell	12	.05	.02
☐ 454	Lou Whitaker	50	.23	.06
☐ 455	Dan Graham	10	.05	.01
☐ 456	Reggie Cleveland	10	.05	.01
☐ 457	Sammy Stewart	10	.05	.01
☐ 458	Pete Vuckovich	12	.05	.02
☐ 459	John Wockenfuss	10	.05	.01
☐ 460	Glenn Hoffman	10	.05	.01
☐ 461	Willie Randolph	12	.05	.02
☐ 462	Fernando Valenzuela	40	.18	.05
☐ 463	Ron Hassey	10	.05	.01
☐ 464	Paul Splittorff	10	.05	.01
☐ 465	Rob Picciolo	10	.05	.01
☐ 466	Larry Parrish	10	.05	.01
☐ 467	Johnny Grubb	10	.05	.01
☐ 468	Dan Ford	10	.05	.01
☐ 469	Silvio Martinez	10	.05	.01
☐ 470	Kiko Garcia	10	.05	.01
☐ 471	Bob Boone	12	.05	.02
☐ 472	Luis Salazar	10	.05	.01
☐ 473	Randy Niemann	10	.05	.01
☐ 474	Tom Griffin	10	.05	.01
☐ 475	Phil Niekro	40	.18	.05
☐ 476	Hubie Brooks	35	.16	.04
☐ 477	Dick Tidrow	10	.05	.01
☐ 478	Jim Beattie	10	.05	.01
☐ 479	Damaso Garcia	10	.05	.01
☐ 480	Mickey Hatcher	10	.05	.01
☐ 481	Joe Price	10	.05	.01
☐ 482	Ed Farmer	10	.05	.01
☐ 483	Eddie Murray	2.00	.90	.25
☐ 484	Ben Oglivie	12	.05	.02
☐ 485	Kevin Saucier	10	.05	.01
☐ 486	Bobby Murcer	12	.05	.02
☐ 487	Bill Campbell	10	.05	.01
☐ 488	Reggie Smith	12	.05	.02
☐ 489	Wayne Garland	10	.05	.01
☐ 490	Jim Wright	10	.05	.01
☐ 491	Billy Martin MG	25	.11	.03
☐ 492	Jim Fanning MG	10	.05	.01
☐ 493	Don Baylor	12	.05	.02
☐ 494	Rick Honeycutt	10	.05	.01
☐ 495	Carlton Fisk	1.50	.65	.19
☐ 496	Denny Walling	10	.05	.01
☐ 497	Bake McBride	10	.05	.01
☐ 498	Darrell Porter	10	.05	.01
☐ 499	Gene Richards	10	.05	.01
☐ 500	Ron Oester	10	.05	.01
☐ 501	Ken Dayley	10	.05	.01
☐ 502	Jason Thompson	10	.05	.01
☐ 503	Milt May	10	.05	.01
☐ 504	Doug Bird	10	.05	.01
☐ 505	Bruce Bochte	10	.05	.01
☐ 506	Neil Allen	10	.05	.01
☐ 507	Joey McLaughlin	10	.05	.01
☐ 508	Butch Wynegar	10	.05	.01
☐ 509	Gary Roenicke	10	.05	.01
☐ 510	Robin Yount	3.00	1.35	.40
☐ 511	Dave Tobik	10	.05	.01
☐ 512	Rich Gedman	15	.07	.02
☐ 513	Gene Nelson	10	.05	.01
☐ 514	Rick Monday	10	.05	.01
☐ 515	Miguel Dilone	10	.05	.01
☐ 516	Clint Hurdle	10	.05	.01
☐ 517	Jeff Newman	10	.05	.01
☐ 518	Grant Jackson	10	.05	.01
☐ 519	Andy Hassler	10	.05	.01
☐ 520	Pat Putnam	10	.05	.01
☐ 521	Greg Pryor	10	.05	.01
☐ 522	Tony Scott	10	.05	.01
☐ 523	Steve Mura	10	.05	.01
☐ 524	Johnnie LeMaster	10	.05	.01
☐ 525	Dick Ruthven	10	.05	.01
☐ 526	John McNamara MG	10	.05	.01
☐ 527	Larry McWilliams	10	.05	.01

☐ 528 Johnny Ray	.15	.07	.02
☐ 529 Pat Tabler	.20	.09	.03
☐ 530 Tom Herr	.12	.05	.02
☐ 531A San Diego Chicken	1.50	.65	.19
COR (With TM)			
☐ 531B San Diego Chicken	1.50	.65	.19
ERR (Without TM)			
☐ 532 Sal Butera	.10	.05	.01
☐ 533 Mike Griffin	.10	.05	.01
☐ 534 Kelvin Moore	.10	.05	.01
☐ 535 Reggie Jackson	2.00	.90	.25
☐ 536 Ed Romero	.10	.05	.01
☐ 537 Derrel Thomas	.10	.05	.01
☐ 538 Mike O'Berry	.10	.05	.01
☐ 539 Jack O'Connor	.10	.05	.01
☐ 540 Bob Ojeda	.40	.18	.05
☐ 541 Roy Lee Jackson	.10	.05	.01
☐ 542 Lynn Jones	.10	.05	.01
☐ 543 Gaylord Perry	.40	.18	.05
☐ 544A Phil Garner ERR	.75	.35	.09
(Reverse negative)			
☐ 544B Phil Garner COR	.12	.05	.02
☐ 545 Garry Templeton	.12	.05	.02
☐ 546 Rafael Ramirez	.10	.05	.01
☐ 547 Jeff Reardon	2.00	.90	.25
☐ 548 Ron Guidry	.25	.11	.03
☐ 549 Tim Laudner	.10	.05	.01
☐ 550 John Henry Johnson	.10	.05	.01
☐ 551 Chris Bando	.10	.05	.01
☐ 552 Bobby Brown	.10	.05	.01
☐ 553 Larry Bradford	.10	.05	.01
☐ 554 Scott Fletcher	.30	.14	.04
☐ 555 Jerry Royster	.10	.05	.01
☐ 556 Shooty Babitt UER	.10	.05	.01
(Spelled Babbitt			
on front)			
☐ 557 Kent Hrbek	2.50	1.15	.30
☐ 558 Yankee Winners	.12	.05	.02
Ron Guidry			
Tommy John			
☐ 559 Mark Bomback	.10	.05	.01
☐ 560 Julio Valdez	.10	.05	.01
☐ 561 Buck Martinez	.10	.05	.01
☐ 562 Mike Marshall	.20	.09	.03
(Dodger hitter)			
☐ 563 Rennie Stennett	.10	.05	.01
☐ 564 Steve Crawford	.10	.05	.01
☐ 565 Bob Babcock	.10	.05	.01
☐ 566 Johnny Podres CO	.12	.05	.02
☐ 567 Paul Serna	.10	.05	.01
☐ 568 Harold Baines	1.00	.45	.13
☐ 569 Dave LaRoche	.10	.05	.01
☐ 570 Lee May	.12	.05	.02
☐ 571 Gary Ward	.10	.05	.01
☐ 572 John Denny	.10	.05	.01
☐ 573 Roy Smalley	.10	.05	.01
☐ 574 Bob Brenly	.10	.05	.01
☐ 575 Bronx Bombers	1.75	.80	.22
Reggie Jackson			
Dave Winfield			
☐ 576 Luis Pujols	.10	.05	.01
☐ 577 Butch Hobson	.12	.05	.02
☐ 578 Harvey Kuenn MG	.12	.05	.02
☐ 579 Cal Ripken Sr. CO	.12	.05	.02
☐ 580 Juan Berenguer	.10	.05	.01
☐ 581 Benny Ayala	.10	.05	.01
☐ 582 Vance Law	.10	.05	.01
☐ 583 Rick Leach	.10	.05	.01
☐ 584 George Frazier	.10	.05	.01
☐ 585 Phillies Finest	1.50	.65	.19
Pete Rose			
Mike Schmidt			
☐ 586 Joe Rudi	.10	.05	.01
☐ 587 Juan Beniquez	.10	.05	.01
☐ 588 Luis DeLeon	.10	.05	.01
☐ 589 Craig Swan	.10	.05	.01
☐ 590 Dave Chalk	.10	.05	.01
☐ 591 Billy Gardner MG	.10	.05	.01
☐ 592 Sal Bando	.12	.05	.02
☐ 593 Bert Campaneris	.12	.05	.02
☐ 594 Steve Kemp	.10	.05	.01
☐ 595A Randy Lerch ERR	.75	.35	.09
(Braves)			
☐ 595B Randy Lerch COR	.10	.05	.01
(Brewers)			
☐ 596 Bryan Clark	.10	.05	.01
☐ 597 Dave Ford	.10	.05	.01
☐ 598 Mike Scioscia	.35	.16	.04
☐ 599 John Lowenstein	.10	.05	.01
☐ 600 Rene Lachemann MG	.10	.05	.01
☐ 601 Mick Kelleher	.10	.05	.01
☐ 602 Ron Jackson	.10	.05	.01
☐ 603 Jerry Koosman	.12	.05	.02
☐ 604 Dave Goltz	.10	.05	.01
☐ 605 Ellis Valentine	.10	.05	.01
☐ 606 Lonnie Smith	.12	.05	.02
☐ 607 Joaquin Andujar	.12	.05	.02
☐ 608 Garry Hancock	.10	.05	.01
☐ 609 Jerry Turner	.10	.05	.01
☐ 610 Bob Bonner	.10	.05	.01
☐ 611 Jim Dwyer	.10	.05	.01
☐ 612 Terry Bulling	.10	.05	.01
☐ 613 Joel Youngblood	.10	.05	.01
☐ 614 Larry Milbourne	.10	.05	.01
☐ 615 Gene Roof UER	.10	.05	.01
(Name on front			
is Phil Roof)			
☐ 616 Keith Drumwright	.10	.05	.01
☐ 617 Dave Rosello	.10	.05	.01
☐ 618 Rickey Keeton	.10	.05	.01
☐ 619 Dennis Lamp	.10	.05	.01
☐ 620 Sid Monge	.10	.05	.01
☐ 621 Jerry White	.10	.05	.01
☐ 622 Luis Aguayo	.10	.05	.01

1983 Donruss

☐	623 Jamie Easterly..............10	.05	.01
☐	624 Steve Sax.................3.00	1.35	.40
☐	625 Dave Roberts..............10	.05	.01
☐	626 Rick Bosetti................10	.05	.01
☐	627 Terry Francona.............10	.05	.01
☐	628 Pride of Reds.............1.50	.65	.19
	Tom Seaver		
	Johnny Bench		
☐	629 Paul Mirabella 10	.05	.01
☐	630 Rance Mulliniks 10	.05	.01
☐	631 Kevin Hickey...............10	.05	.01
☐	632 Reid Nichols 10	.05	.01
☐	633 Dave Geisel................10	.05	.01
☐	634 Ken Griffey.................25	.11	.03
☐	635 Bob Lemon MG............15	.07	.02
☐	636 Orlando Sanchez..........10	.05	.01
☐	637 Bill Almon 10	.05	.01
☐	638 Danny Ainge...............75	.35	.09
☐	639 Willie Stargell.............75	.35	.09
☐	640 Bob Sykes.................10	.05	.01
☐	641 Ed Lynch...................10	.05	.01
☐	642 John Ellis..................10	.05	.01
☐	643 Ferguson Jenkins..........40	.18	.05
☐	644 Lenn Sakata................10	.05	.01
☐	645 Julio Gonzalez.............10	.05	.01
☐	646 Jesse Orosco..............10	.05	.01
☐	647 Jerry Dybzinski............10	.05	.01
☐	648 Tommy Davis CO..........12	.05	.02
☐	649 Ron Gardenhire............10	.05	.01
☐	650 Felipe Alou CO.............12	.05	.02
☐	651 Harvey Haddix CO.........12	.05	.02
☐	652 Willie Upshaw.............10	.05	.01
☐	653 Bill Madlock...............12	.05	.02
☐	654A DK Checklist ERR 50	.05	.02
	(Unnumbered)		
	(With Trammel)		
☐	654B DK Checklist COR 15	.02	.00
	(Unnumbered)		
	(With Trammell)		
☐	655 Checklist 1 15	.02	.00
	(Unnumbered)		
☐	656 Checklist 2................15	.02	.00
	(Unnumbered)		
☐	657 Checklist 3................15	.02	.00
	(Unnumbered)		
☐	658 Checklist 4................15	.02	.00
	(Unnumbered)		
☐	659 Checklist 5................15	.02	.00
	(Unnumbered)		
☐	660 Checklist 6................15	.02	.00
	(Unnumbered)		

The cards in this 660-card set measure 2 1/2" by 3 1/2". The 1983 Donruss base-ball set, issued with a 63-piece Diamond King puzzle, again leads off with a 26-card Diamond Kings (DK) series. Of the remaining 634 cards, two are combination cards, one portrays the San Diego Chicken, one shows the completed Ty Cobb puzzle, and seven are unnumbered checklist cards. The seven unnumbered checklist cards are arbitrarily assigned numbers 654 through 660 and are listed at the end of the list below. The Donruss logo and the year of issue are shown in the upper left corner of the obverse. The card backs have black print on yellow and white and are numbered on a small ball design. The complete set price below includes only the more common of each variation pair. The key Rookie Cards in this set are Wade Boggs, Julio Franco, Tony Gwynn, Howard Johnson, Willie McGee, Ryne Sandberg, and Frank Viola.

	NRMT-MT	EXC	G-VG
COMPLETE SET (660) 130.00		57.50	16.50
COMPLETE FACT.SET (660) ...140.00		65.00	17.50
COMMON PLAYER (1-660) 10		.05	.01

☐	1 Fernando Valenzuela DK ...30	.14	.04
☐	2 Rollie Fingers DK.............30	.14	.04
☐	3 Reggie Jackson DK...........75	.35	.09
☐	4 Jim Palmer DK................50	.23	.06
☐	5 Jack Morris DK................50	.23	.06
☐	6 George Foster DK.............15	.07	.02
☐	7 Jim Sundberg DK.............15	.07	.02
☐	8 Willie Stargell DK.............30	.14	.04
☐	9 Dave Stieb DK.................15	.07	.02

☐ 10 Joe Niekro DK	.15	.07	.02
☐ 11 Rickey Henderson DK	2.00	.90	.25
☐ 12 Dale Murphy DK	.40	.18	.05
☐ 13 Toby Harrah DK	.15	.07	.02
☐ 14 Bill Buckner DK	.15	.07	.02
☐ 15 Willie Wilson DK	.15	.07	.02
☐ 16 Steve Carlton DK	.60	.25	.08
☐ 17 Ron Guidry DK	.15	.07	.02
☐ 18 Steve Rogers DK	.15	.07	.02
☐ 19 Kent Hrbek DK	.25	.11	.03
☐ 20 Keith Hernandez DK	.15	.07	.02
☐ 21 Floyd Bannister DK	.15	.07	.02
☐ 22 Johnny Bench DK	.60	.25	.08
☐ 23 Britt Burns DK	.15	.07	.02
☐ 24 Joe Morgan DK	.30	.14	.04
☐ 25 Carl Yastrzemski DK	.60	.25	.08
☐ 26 Terry Kennedy DK	.15	.07	.02
☐ 27 Gary Roenicke	.10	.05	.01
☐ 28 Dwight Bernard	.10	.05	.01
☐ 29 Pat Underwood	.10	.05	.01
☐ 30 Gary Allenson	.10	.05	.01
☐ 31 Ron Guidry	.20	.09	.03
☐ 32 Burt Hooton	.10	.05	.01
☐ 33 Chris Bando	.10	.05	.01
☐ 34 Vida Blue	.12	.05	.02
☐ 35 Rickey Henderson	3.50	1.55	.45
☐ 36 Ray Burris	.10	.05	.01
☐ 37 John Butcher	.10	.05	.01
☐ 38 Don Aase	.10	.05	.01
☐ 39 Jerry Koosman	.12	.05	.02
☐ 40 Bruce Sutter	.20	.09	.03
☐ 41 Jose Cruz	.12	.05	.02
☐ 42 Pete Rose	1.25	.55	.16
☐ 43 Cesar Cedeno	.12	.05	.02
☐ 44 Floyd Chiffer	.10	.05	.01
☐ 45 Larry McWilliams	.10	.05	.01
☐ 46 Alan Fowlkes	.10	.05	.01
☐ 47 Dale Murphy	.75	.35	.09
☐ 48 Doug Bird	.10	.05	.01
☐ 49 Hubie Brooks	.15	.07	.02
☐ 50 Floyd Bannister	.10	.05	.01
☐ 51 Jack O'Connor	.10	.05	.01
☐ 52 Steve Senteney	.10	.05	.01
☐ 53 Gary Gaetti	.40	.18	.05
☐ 54 Damaso Garcia	.10	.05	.01
☐ 55 Gene Nelson	.10	.05	.01
☐ 56 Mookie Wilson	.12	.05	.02
☐ 57 Allen Ripley	.10	.05	.01
☐ 58 Bob Horner	.12	.05	.02
☐ 59 Tony Pena	.12	.05	.02
☐ 60 Gary Lavelle	.10	.05	.01
☐ 61 Tim Lollar	.10	.05	.01
☐ 62 Frank Pastore	.10	.05	.01
☐ 63 Garry Maddox	.10	.05	.01
☐ 64 Bob Forsch	.10	.05	.01
☐ 65 Harry Spilman	.10	.05	.01
☐ 66 Geoff Zahn	.10	.05	.01
☐ 67 Salome Barojas	.10	.05	.01
☐ 68 David Palmer	.10	.05	.01
☐ 69 Charlie Hough	.12	.05	.02
☐ 70 Dan Quisenberry	.12	.05	.02
☐ 71 Tony Armas	.10	.05	.01
☐ 72 Rick Sutcliffe	.25	.11	.03
☐ 73 Steve Balboni	.10	.05	.01
☐ 74 Jerry Remy	.10	.05	.01
☐ 75 Mike Scioscia	.12	.05	.02
☐ 76 John Wockenfuss	.10	.05	.01
☐ 77 Jim Palmer	1.00	.45	.13
☐ 78 Rollie Fingers	.60	.25	.08
☐ 79 Joe Nolan	.10	.05	.01
☐ 80 Pete Vuckovich	.10	.05	.01
☐ 81 Rick Leach	.10	.05	.01
☐ 82 Rick Miller	.10	.05	.01
☐ 83 Graig Nettles	.15	.05	.02
☐ 84 Ron Cey	.12	.05	.02
☐ 85 Miguel Dilone	.10	.05	.01
☐ 86 John Wathan	.10	.05	.01
☐ 87 Kelvin Moore	.10	.05	.01
☐ 88A Byrn Smith ERR	.15	.07	.02
(Sic, Bryn)			
☐ 88B Bryn Smith COR	.75	.35	.09
☐ 89 Dave Hostetler	.10	.05	.01
☐ 90 Rod Carew	1.25	.55	.16
☐ 91 Lonnie Smith	.12	.05	.02
☐ 92 Bob Knepper	.10	.05	.01
☐ 93 Marty Bystrom	.10	.05	.01
☐ 94 Chris Welsh	.10	.05	.01
☐ 95 Jason Thompson	.10	.05	.01
☐ 96 Tom O'Malley	.10	.05	.01
☐ 97 Phil Niekro	.40	.18	.05
☐ 98 Neil Allen	.10	.05	.01
☐ 99 Bill Buckner	.12	.05	.02
☐ 100 Ed VandeBerg	.10	.05	.01
☐ 101 Jim Clancy	.10	.05	.01
☐ 102 Robert Castillo	.10	.05	.01
☐ 103 Bruce Berenyi	.10	.05	.01
☐ 104 Carlton Fisk	1.25	.55	.16
☐ 105 Mike Flanagan	.12	.05	.02
☐ 106 Cecil Cooper	.12	.05	.02
☐ 107 Jack Morris	1.25	.55	.16
☐ 108 Mike Morgan	.35	.16	.04
☐ 109 Luis Aponte	.10	.05	.01
☐ 110 Pedro Guerrero	.25	.11	.03
☐ 111 Len Barker	.10	.05	.01
☐ 112 Willie Wilson	.12	.05	.02
☐ 113 Dave Beard	.10	.05	.01
☐ 114 Mike Gates	.10	.05	.01
☐ 115 Reggie Jackson	1.50	.65	.19
☐ 116 George Wright	.10	.05	.01
☐ 117 Vance Law	.10	.05	.01
☐ 118 Nolan Ryan	7.00	3.10	.85
☐ 119 Mike Krukow	.10	.05	.01
☐ 120 Ozzie Smith	1.50	.65	.19
☐ 121 Broderick Perkins	.10	.05	.01

☐ 122 Tom Seaver	1.25	.55	.16		
☐ 123 Chris Chambliss	.12	.05	.02		
☐ 124 Chuck Tanner MG	.10	.05	.01		
☐ 125 Johnnie LeMaster	.10	.05	.01		
☐ 126 Mel Hall	1.75	.80	.22		
☐ 127 Bruce Bochte	.10	.05	.01		
☐ 128 Charlie Puleo	.10	.05	.01		
☐ 129 Luis Leal	.10	.05	.01		
☐ 130 John Pacella	.10	.05	.01		
☐ 131 Glenn Gulliver	.10	.05	.01		
☐ 132 Don Money	.10	.05	.01		
☐ 133 Dave Rozema	.10	.05	.01		
☐ 134 Bruce Hurst	.50	.23	.06		
☐ 135 Rudy May	.10	.05	.01		
☐ 136 Tom Lasorda MG	.12	.05	.02		
☐ 137 Dan Spillner UER	.10	.05	.01		
(Photo actually					
Ed Whitson)					
☐ 138 Jerry Martin	.10	.05	.01		
☐ 139 Mike Norris	.10	.05	.01		
☐ 140 Al Oliver	.12	.05	.02		
☐ 141 Daryl Sconiers	.10	.05	.01		
☐ 142 Lamar Johnson	.10	.05	.01		
☐ 143 Harold Baines	.50	.23	.06		
☐ 144 Alan Ashby	.10	.05	.01		
☐ 145 Garry Templeton	.12	.05	.02		
☐ 146 Al Holland	.10	.05	.01		
☐ 147 Bo Diaz	.10	.05	.01		
☐ 148 Dave Concepcion	.12	.05	.02		
☐ 149 Rick Camp	.10	.05	.01		
☐ 150 Jim Morrison	.10	.05	.01		
☐ 151 Randy Martz	.10	.05	.01		
☐ 152 Keith Hernandez	.20	.09	.03		
☐ 153 John Lowenstein	.10	.05	.01		
☐ 154 Mike Caldwell	.10	.05	.01		
☐ 155 Milt Wilcox	.10	.05	.01		
☐ 156 Rich Gedman	.10	.05	.01		
☐ 157 Rich Gossage	.20	.09	.03		
☐ 158 Jerry Reuss	.10	.05	.01		
☐ 159 Ron Hassey	.10	.05	.01		
☐ 160 Larry Gura	.10	.05	.01		
☐ 161 Dwayne Murphy	.10	.05	.01		
☐ 162 Woodie Fryman	.10	.05	.01		
☐ 163 Steve Comer	.10	.05	.01		
☐ 164 Ken Forsch	.10	.05	.01		
☐ 165 Dennis Lamp	.10	.05	.01		
☐ 166 David Green	.10	.05	.01		
☐ 167 Terry Puhl	.10	.05	.01		
☐ 168 Mike Schmidt	2.00	.90	.25		
(Wearing 37					
rather than 20)					
☐ 169 Eddie Milner	.10	.05	.01		
☐ 170 John Curtis	.10	.05	.01		
☐ 171 Don Robinson	.10	.05	.01		
☐ 172 Rich Gale	.10	.05	.01		
☐ 173 Steve Bedrosian	.10	.05	.01		
☐ 174 Willie Hernandez	.12	.05	.02		

☐ 175 Ron Gardenhire	.10	.05	.01
☐ 176 Jim Beattie	.10	.05	.01
☐ 177 Tim Laudner	.10	.05	.01
☐ 178 Buck Martinez	.10	.05	.01
☐ 179 Kent Hrbek	.50	.23	.06
☐ 180 Alfredo Griffin	.10	.05	.01
☐ 181 Larry Andersen	.10	.05	.01
☐ 182 Pete Falcone	.10	.05	.01
☐ 183 Jody Davis	.10	.05	.01
☐ 184 Glenn Hubbard	.10	.05	.01
☐ 185 Dale Berra	.10	.05	.01
☐ 186 Greg Minton	.10	.05	.01
☐ 187 Gary Lucas	.10	.05	.01
☐ 188 Dave Van Gorder	.10	.05	.01
☐ 189 Bob Dernier	.10	.05	.01
☐ 190 Willie McGee	2.50	1.15	.30
☐ 191 Dickie Thon	.10	.05	.01
☐ 192 Bob Boone	.12	.05	.02
☐ 193 Britt Burns	.10	.05	.01
☐ 194 Jeff Reardon	1.25	.55	.16
☐ 195 Jon Matlack	.10	.05	.01
☐ 196 Don Slaught	.50	.23	.06
☐ 197 Fred Stanley	.10	.05	.01
☐ 198 Rick Manning	.10	.05	.01
☐ 199 Dave Righetti	.15	.07	.02
☐ 200 Dave Stapleton	.10	.05	.01
☐ 201 Steve Yeager	.10	.05	.01
☐ 202 Enos Cabell	.10	.05	.01
☐ 203 Sammy Stewart	.10	.05	.01
☐ 204 Moose Haas	.10	.05	.01
☐ 205 Lenn Sakata	.10	.05	.01
☐ 206 Charlie Moore	.10	.05	.01
☐ 207 Alan Trammell	.50	.23	.06
☐ 208 Jim Rice	.20	.09	.03
☐ 209 Roy Smalley	.10	.05	.01
☐ 210 Bill Russell	.12	.05	.02
☐ 211 Andre Thornton	.10	.05	.01
☐ 212 Willie Aikens	.10	.05	.01
☐ 213 Dave McKay	.10	.05	.01
☐ 214 Tim Blackwell	.10	.05	.01
☐ 215 Buddy Bell	.12	.05	.02
☐ 216 Doug DeCinces	.12	.05	.02
☐ 217 Tom Herr	.12	.05	.02
☐ 218 Frank LaCorte	.10	.05	.01
☐ 219 Steve Carlton	1.25	.55	.16
☐ 220 Terry Kennedy	.10	.05	.01
☐ 221 Mike Easler	.10	.05	.01
☐ 222 Jack Clark	.15	.07	.02
☐ 223 Gene Garber	.10	.05	.01
☐ 224 Scott Holman	.10	.05	.01
☐ 225 Mike Proly	.10	.05	.01
☐ 226 Terry Bulling	.10	.05	.01
☐ 227 Jerry Garvin	.10	.05	.01
☐ 228 Ron Davis	.10	.05	.01
☐ 229 Tom Hume	.10	.05	.01
☐ 230 Marc Hill	.10	.05	.01
☐ 231 Dennis Martinez	.12	.05	.02

☐ 232 Jim Gantner	.12	.05	.02
☐ 233 Larry Pashnick	.10	.05	.01
☐ 234 Dave Collins	.10	.05	.01
☐ 235 Tom Burgmeier	.10	.05	.01
☐ 236 Ken Landreaux	.10	.05	.01
☐ 237 John Denny	.10	.05	.01
☐ 238 Hal McRae	.12	.05	.02
☐ 239 Matt Keough	.10	.05	.01
☐ 240 Doug Flynn	.10	.05	.01
☐ 241 Fred Lynn	.12	.05	.01
☐ 242 Billy Sample	.10	.05	.01
☐ 243 Tom Paciorek	.12	.05	.02
☐ 244 Joe Sambito	.10	.05	.01
☐ 245 Sid Monge	.10	.05	.01
☐ 246 Ken Oberkfell	.10	.05	.01
☐ 247 Joe Pittman UER	.10	.05	.01
(Photo actually			
Juan Eichelberger)			
☐ 248 Mario Soto	.10	.05	.01
☐ 249 Claudell Washington	.10	.05	.01
☐ 250 Rick Rhoden	.10	.05	.01
☐ 251 Darrell Evans	.12	.05	.02
☐ 252 Steve Henderson	.10	.05	.01
☐ 253 Manny Castillo	.10	.05	.01
☐ 254 Craig Swan	.10	.05	.01
☐ 255 Joey McLaughlin	.10	.05	.01
☐ 256 Pete Redfern	.10	.05	.01
☐ 257 Ken Singleton	.12	.05	.02
☐ 258 Robin Yount	2.50	1.15	.30
☐ 259 Elias Sosa	.10	.05	.01
☐ 260 Bob Ojeda	.10	.05	.01
☐ 261 Bobby Murcer	.12	.05	.02
☐ 262 Candy Maldonado	1.00	.45	.13
☐ 263 Rick Waits	.10	.05	.01
☐ 264 Greg Pryor	.10	.05	.01
☐ 265 Bob Owchinko	.10	.05	.01
☐ 266 Chris Speier	.10	.05	.01
☐ 267 Bruce Kison	.10	.05	.01
☐ 268 Mark Wagner	.10	.05	.01
☐ 269 Steve Kemp	.10	.05	.01
☐ 270 Phil Garner	.12	.05	.02
☐ 271 Gene Richards	.10	.05	.01
☐ 272 Renie Martin	.10	.05	.01
☐ 273 Dave Roberts	.10	.05	.01
☐ 274 Dan Driessen	.10	.05	.01
☐ 275 Rufino Linares	.10	.05	.01
☐ 276 Lee Lacy	.10	.05	.01
☐ 277 Ryne Sandberg	40.00	18.00	5.00
☐ 278 Darrell Porter	.10	.05	.01
☐ 279 Cal Ripken	18.00	8.00	2.30
☐ 280 Jamie Easterly	.10	.05	.01
☐ 281 Bill Fahey	.10	.05	.01
☐ 282 Glenn Hoffman	.10	.05	.01
☐ 283 Willie Randolph	.12	.05	.01
☐ 284 Fernando Valenzuela	.15	.07	.02
☐ 285 Alan Bannister	.10	.05	.01
☐ 286 Paul Splittorff	.10	.05	.01
☐ 287 Joe Rudi	.10	.05	.01
☐ 288 Bill Gullickson	.20	.09	.03
☐ 289 Danny Darwin	.10	.05	.01
☐ 290 Andy Hassler	.10	.05	.01
☐ 291 Ernesto Escarrega	.10	.05	.01
☐ 292 Steve Mura	.10	.05	.01
☐ 293 Tony Scott	.10	.05	.01
☐ 294 Manny Trillo	.10	.05	.01
☐ 295 Greg Harris	.10	.05	.01
☐ 296 Luis DeLeon	.10	.05	.01
☐ 297 Kent Tekulve	.12	.05	.02
☐ 298 Atlee Hammaker	.10	.05	.01
☐ 299 Bruce Benedict	.10	.05	.01
☐ 300 Fergie Jenkins	.40	.18	.05
☐ 301 Dave Kingman	.12	.05	.02
☐ 302 Bill Caudill	.10	.05	.01
☐ 303 John Castino	.10	.05	.01
☐ 304 Ernie Whitt	.10	.05	.01
☐ 305 Randy Johnson	.10	.05	.01
☐ 306 Garth Iorg	.10	.05	.01
☐ 307 Gaylord Perry	.40	.18	.05
☐ 308 Ed Lynch	.10	.05	.01
☐ 309 Keith Moreland	.10	.05	.01
☐ 310 Rafael Ramirez	.10	.05	.01
☐ 311 Bill Madlock	.12	.05	.02
☐ 312 Milt May	.10	.05	.01
☐ 313 John Montefusco	.10	.05	.01
☐ 314 Wayne Krenchicki	.10	.05	.01
☐ 315 George Vukovich	.10	.05	.01
☐ 316 Joaquin Andujar	.10	.05	.01
☐ 317 Craig Reynolds	.10	.05	.01
☐ 318 Rick Burleson	.10	.05	.01
☐ 319 Richard Dotson	.10	.05	.01
☐ 320 Steve Rogers	.10	.05	.01
☐ 321 Dave Schmidt	.10	.05	.01
☐ 322 Bud Black	.40	.18	.05
☐ 323 Jeff Burroughs	.10	.05	.01
☐ 324 Von Hayes	.12	.05	.02
☐ 325 Butch Wynegar	.10	.05	.01
☐ 326 Carl Yastrzemski	1.25	.55	.16
☐ 327 Ron Roenicke	.10	.05	.01
☐ 328 Howard Johnson	6.00	2.70	.75
☐ 329 Rick Dempsey UER	.12	.05	.02
(Posing as a left-			
handed batter)			
☐ 330A Jim Slaton	.10	.05	.01
(Bio printed			
black on white)			
☐ 330B Jim Slaton	.15	.07	.02
(Bio printed			
black on yellow)			
☐ 331 Benny Ayala	.10	.05	.01
☐ 332 Ted Simmons	.12	.05	.02
☐ 333 Lou Whitaker	.50	.23	.06
☐ 334 Chuck Rainey	.10	.05	.01
☐ 335 Lou Piniella	.12	.05	.02
☐ 336 Steve Sax	.75	.35	.09

□	337	Toby Harrah	10	.05	.01
□	338	George Brett	2.50	1.15	.30
□	339	Dave Lopes	12	.05	.02
□	340	Gary Carter	75	.35	.09
□	341	John Grubb	10	.05	.01
□	342	Tim Foli	10	.05	.01
□	343	Jim Kaat	15	.07	.02
□	344	Mike LaCoss	10	.05	.01
□	345	Larry Christenson	10	.05	.01
□	346	Juan Bonilla	10	.05	.01
□	347	Omar Moreno	10	.05	.01
□	348	Chili Davis	50	.23	.06
□	349	Tommy Boggs	10	.05	.01
□	350	Rusty Staub	12	.05	.02
□	351	Bump Wills	10	.05	.01
□	352	Rick Sweet	10	.05	.01
□	353	Jim Gott	15	.07	.02
□	354	Terry Felton	10	.05	.01
□	355	Jim Kern	10	.05	.01
□	356	Bill Almon UER	10	.05	.01
		(Expos/Mets in 1983,			
		not Padres/Mets)			
□	357	Tippy Martinez	10	.05	.01
□	358	Roy Howell	10	.05	.01
□	359	Dan Petry	10	.05	.01
□	360	Jerry Mumphrey	10	.05	.01
□	361	Mark Clear	10	.05	.01
□	362	Mike Marshall	12	.05	.02
□	363	Lary Sorensen	10	.05	.01
□	364	Amos Otis	12	.05	.02
□	365	Rick Langford	10	.05	.01
□	366	Brad Mills	10	.05	.01
□	367	Brian Downing	12	.05	.02
□	368	Mike Richardt	10	.05	.01
□	369	Aurelio Rodriguez	10	.05	.01
□	370	Dave Smith	10	.05	.01
□	371	Tug McGraw	12	.05	.02
□	372	Doug Bair	10	.05	.01
□	373	Ruppert Jones	10	.05	.01
□	374	Alex Trevino	10	.05	.01
□	375	Ken Dayley	10	.05	.01
□	376	Rod Scurry	10	.05	.01
□	377	Bob Brenly	10	.05	.01
□	378	Scot Thompson	10	.05	.01
□	379	Julio Cruz	10	.05	.01
□	380	John Stearns	10	.05	.01
□	381	Dale Murray	10	.05	.01
□	382	Frank Viola	3.00	1.35	.40
□	383	Al Bumbry	10	.05	.01
□	384	Ben Oglivie	10	.05	.01
□	385	Dave Tobik	10	.05	.01
□	386	Bob Stanley	10	.05	.01
□	387	Andre Robertson	10	.05	.01
□	388	Jorge Orta	10	.05	.01
□	389	Ed Whitson	10	.05	.01
□	390	Don Hood	10	.05	.01
□	391	Tom Underwood	10	.05	.01

□	392	Tim Wallach	20	.09	.03
□	393	Steve Renko	10	.05	.01
□	394	Mickey Rivers	10	.05	.01
□	395	Greg Luzinski	12	.05	.02
□	396	Art Howe	10	.05	.01
□	397	Alan Wiggins	10	.05	.01
□	398	Jim Barr	10	.05	.01
□	399	Ivan DeJesus	10	.05	.01
□	400	Tom Lawless	10	.05	.01
□	401	Bob Walk	10	.05	.01
□	402	Jimmy Smith	10	.05	.01
□	403	Lee Smith	2.25	1.00	.30
□	404	George Hendrick	12	.05	.02
□	405	Eddie Murray	1.75	.80	.22
□	406	Marshall Edwards	10	.05	.01
□	407	Lance Parrish	15	.07	.02
□	408	Carney Lansford	12	.05	.02
□	409	Dave Winfield	2.00	.90	.25
□	410	Bob Welch	25	.11	.03
□	411	Larry Milbourne	10	.05	.01
□	412	Dennis Leonard	10	.05	.01
□	413	Dan Meyer	10	.05	.01
□	414	Charlie Lea	10	.05	.01
□	415	Rick Honeycutt	10	.05	.01
□	416	Mike Witt	10	.05	.01
□	417	Steve Trout	10	.05	.01
□	418	Glenn Brummer	10	.05	.01
□	419	Denny Walling	10	.05	.01
□	420	Gary Matthews	12	.05	.02
□	421	Charlie Leibrandt UER	12	.05	.02
		(Liebrandt on			
		front of card)			
□	422	Juan Eichelberger UER	10	.05	.01
		(Photo actually			
		Joe Pittman)			
□	423	Cecilio Guante UER	12	.05	.02
		(Listed as Matt			
		on card)			
□	424	Bill Laskey	10	.05	.01
□	425	Jerry Royster	10	.05	.01
□	426	Dickie Noles	10	.05	.01
□	427	George Foster	12	.05	.02
□	428	Mike Moore	1.00	.45	.13
□	429	Gary Ward	10	.05	.01
□	430	Barry Bonnell	10	.05	.01
□	431	Ron Washington	10	.05	.01
□	432	Rance Mulliniks	10	.05	.01
□	433	Mike Stanton	10	.05	.01
□	434	Jesse Orosco	10	.05	.01
□	435	Larry Bowa	12	.05	.02
□	436	Biff Pocoroba	10	.05	.01
□	437	Johnny Ray	10	.05	.01
□	438	Joe Morgan	60	.25	.08
□	439	Eric Show	10	.05	.01
□	440	Larry Biittner	10	.05	.01
□	441	Greg Gross	10	.05	.01
□	442	Gene Tenace	10	.05	.01

☐ 443 Danny Heep	10	.05	.01
☐ 444 Bobby Clark	10	.05	.01
☐ 445 Kevin Hickey	10	.05	.01
☐ 446 Scott Sanderson	10	.05	.01
☐ 447 Frank Tanana	12	.05	.02
☐ 448 Cesar Geronimo	10	.05	.01
☐ 449 Jimmy Sexton	10	.05	.01
☐ 450 Mike Hargrove	12	.05	.02
☐ 451 Doyle Alexander	10	.05	.01
☐ 452 Dwight Evans	25	.11	.03
☐ 453 Terry Forster	10	.05	.01
☐ 454 Tom Brookens	10	.05	.01
☐ 455 Rich Dauer	10	.05	.01
☐ 456 Rob Picciolo	10	.05	.01
☐ 457 Terry Crowley	10	.05	.01
☐ 458 Ned Yost	10	.05	.01
☐ 459 Kirk Gibson	35	.16	.04
☐ 460 Reid Nichols	10	.05	.01
☐ 461 Oscar Gamble	10	.05	.01
☐ 462 Dusty Baker	12	.05	.02
☐ 463 Jack Perconte	10	.05	.01
☐ 464 Frank White	12	.05	.02
☐ 465 Mickey Klutts	10	.05	.01
☐ 466 Warren Cromartie	10	.05	.01
☐ 467 Larry Parrish	10	.05	.01
☐ 468 Bobby Grich	12	.05	.02
☐ 469 Dane Iorg	10	.05	.01
☐ 470 Joe Niekro	12	.05	.02
☐ 471 Ed Farmer	10	.05	.01
☐ 472 Tim Flannery	10	.05	.01
☐ 473 Dave Parker	35	.16	.04
☐ 474 Jeff Leonard	10	.05	.01
☐ 475 Al Hrabosky	10	.05	.01
☐ 476 Ron Hodges	10	.05	.01
☐ 477 Leon Durham	10	.05	.01
☐ 478 Jim Essian	10	.05	.01
☐ 479 Roy Lee Jackson	10	.05	.01
☐ 480 Brad Havens	10	.05	.01
☐ 481 Joe Price	10	.05	.01
☐ 482 Tony Bernazard	10	.05	.01
☐ 483 Scott McGregor	10	.05	.01
☐ 484 Paul Molitor	75	.35	.09
☐ 485 Mike Ivie	10	.05	.01
☐ 486 Ken Griffey	25	.11	.03
☐ 487 Dennis Eckersley	1.25	.55	.16
☐ 488 Steve Garvey	40	.18	.05
☐ 489 Mike Fischlin	10	.05	.01
☐ 490 U.L. Washington	10	.05	.01
☐ 491 Steve McCatty	10	.05	.01
☐ 492 Roy Johnson	10	.05	.01
☐ 493 Don Baylor	12	.05	.02
☐ 494 Bobby Johnson	10	.05	.01
☐ 495 Mike Squires	10	.05	.01
☐ 496 Bert Roberge	10	.05	.01
☐ 497 Dick Ruthven	10	.05	.01
☐ 498 Tito Landrum	10	.05	.01
☐ 499 Sixto Lezcano	10	.05	.01

☐ 500 Johnny Bench	1.25	.55	.16
☐ 501 Larry Whisenton	10	.05	.01
☐ 502 Manny Sarmiento	10	.05	.01
☐ 503 Fred Breining	10	.05	.01
☐ 504 Bill Campbell	10	.05	.01
☐ 505 Todd Cruz	10	.05	.01
☐ 506 Bob Bailor	10	.05	.01
☐ 507 Dave Stieb	20	.09	.03
☐ 508 Al Williams	10	.05	.01
☐ 509 Dan Ford	10	.05	.01
☐ 510 Gorman Thomas	10	.05	.01
☐ 511 Chet Lemon	10	.05	.01
☐ 512 Mike Torrez	10	.05	.01
☐ 513 Shane Rawley	10	.05	.01
☐ 514 Mark Belanger	10	.05	.01
☐ 515 Rodney Craig	10	.05	.01
☐ 516 Onix Concepcion	10	.05	.01
☐ 517 Mike Heath	10	.05	.01
☐ 518 Andre Dawson UER	1.50	.65	.19
(Middle name Fernando, should be Nolan)			
☐ 519 Luis Sanchez	10	.05	.01
☐ 520 Terry Bogener	10	.05	.01
☐ 521 Rudy Law	10	.05	.01
☐ 522 Ray Knight	12	.05	.02
☐ 523 Joe Lefebvre	10	.05	.01
☐ 524 Jim Wohlford	10	.05	.01
☐ 525 Julio Franco	6.00	2.70	.75
☐ 526 Ron Oester	10	.05	.01
☐ 527 Rick Mahler	10	.05	.01
☐ 528 Steve Nicosia	10	.05	.01
☐ 529 Junior Kennedy	10	.05	.01
☐ 530A Whitey Herzog MG	15	.07	.02
(Bio printed black on white)			
☐ 530B Whitey Herzog MG	15	.07	.02
(Bio printed black on yellow)			
☐ 531A Don Sutton	40	.18	.05
(Blue border on photo)			
☐ 531B Don Sutton	40	.18	.05
(Green border on photo)			
☐ 532 Mark Brouhard	10	.05	.01
☐ 533A Sparky Anderson MG	15	.07	.02
(Bio printed black on white)			
☐ 533B Sparky Anderson MG	15	.07	.02
(Bio printed black on yellow)			
☐ 534 Roger LaFrancois	10	.05	.01
☐ 535 George Frazier	10	.05	.01
☐ 536 Tom Niedenfuer	10	.05	.01
☐ 537 Ed Glynn	10	.05	.01
☐ 538 Lee May	10	.05	.01
☐ 539 Bob Kearney	10	.05	.01

☐ 540	Tim Raines	60	.25	.08	☐ 594	Bill Stein	10	.05	.01
☐ 541	Paul Mirabella	10	.05	.01	☐ 595	Jesse Barfield	20	.09	.03
☐ 542	Luis Tiant	12	.05	.02	☐ 596	Bob Molinaro	10	.05	.01
☐ 543	Ron LeFlore	12	.05	.02	☐ 597	Mike Vail	10	.05	.01
☐ 544	Dave LaPoint	12	.05	.02	☐ 598	Tony Gwynn	25.00	11.50	3.10
☐ 545	Randy Moffitt	10	.05	.01	☐ 599	Gary Rajsich	10	.05	.01
☐ 546	Luis Aguayo	10	.05	.01	☐ 600	Jerry Ujdur	10	.05	.01
☐ 547	Brad Lesley	10	.05	.01	☐ 601	Cliff Johnson	10	.05	.01
☐ 548	Luis Salazar	10	.05	.01	☐ 602	Jerry White	10	.05	.01
☐ 549	John Candelaria	10	.05	.01	☐ 603	Bryan Clark	10	.05	.01
☐ 550	Dave Bergman	10	.05	.01	☐ 604	Joe Ferguson	10	.05	.01
☐ 551	Bob Watson	12	.05	.02	☐ 605	Guy Sularz	10	.05	.01
☐ 552	Pat Tabler	10	.05	.01	☐ 606A	Ozzie Virgil	15	.07	.02
☐ 553	Brent Gaff	10	.05	.01		(Green border			
☐ 554	Al Cowens	10	.05	.01		on photo)			
☐ 555	Tom Brunansky	40	.18	.05	☐ 606B	Ozzie Virgil	15	.07	.02
☐ 556	Lloyd Moseby	10	.05	.01		(Orange border			
☐ 557A	Pascual Perez ERR	2.00	.90	.25		on photo)			
	(Twins in glove)				☐ 607	Terry Harper	10	.05	.01
☐ 557B	Pascual Perez COR	15	.07	.02	☐ 608	Harvey Kuenn MG	12	.05	.02
	(Braves in glove)				☐ 609	Jim Sundberg	10	.05	.01
☐ 558	Willie Upshaw	10	.05	.01	☐ 610	Willie Stargell	60	.25	.08
☐ 559	Richie Zisk	10	.05	.01	☐ 611	Reggie Smith	12	.05	.02
☐ 560	Pat Zachry	10	.05	.01	☐ 612	Rob Wilfong	10	.05	.01
☐ 561	Jay Johnstone	12	.05	.02	☐ 613	The Niekro Brothers	25	.11	.03
☐ 562	Carlos Diaz	10	.05	.01		Joe Niekro			
☐ 563	John Tudor	12	.05	.02		Phil Niekro			
☐ 564	Frank Robinson MG	30	.14	.04	☐ 614	Lee Elia MG	10	.05	.01
☐ 565	Dave Edwards	10	.05	.01	☐ 615	Mickey Hatcher	10	.05	.01
☐ 566	Paul Householder	10	.05	.01	☐ 616	Jerry Hairston	10	.05	.01
☐ 567	Ron Reed	10	.05	.01	☐ 617	John Martin	10	.05	.01
☐ 568	Mike Ramsey	10	.05	.01	☐ 618	Wally Backman	12	.05	.02
☐ 569	Kiko Garcia	10	.05	.01	☐ 619	Storm Davis	20	.09	.03
☐ 570	Tommy John	15	.07	.02	☐ 620	Alan Knicely	10	.05	.01
☐ 571	Tony LaRussa MG	12	.05	.02	☐ 621	John Stuper	10	.05	.01
☐ 572	Joel Youngblood	10	.05	.01	☐ 622	Matt Sinatro	10	.05	.01
☐ 573	Wayne Tolleson	10	.05	.01	☐ 623	Geno Petralli	12	.05	.02
☐ 574	Keith Creel	10	.05	.01	☐ 624	Duane Walker	10	.05	.01
☐ 575	Billy Martin MG	15	.07	.02	☐ 625	Dick Williams MG	10	.05	.01
☐ 576	Jerry Dybzinski	10	.05	.01	☐ 626	Pat Corrales MG	10	.05	.01
☐ 577	Rick Cerone	10	.05	.01	☐ 627	Vern Ruhle	10	.05	.01
☐ 578	Tony Perez	30	.14	.04	☐ 628	Joe Torre MG	12	.05	.02
☐ 579	Greg Brock	12	.05	.02	☐ 629	Anthony Johnson	10	.05	.01
☐ 580	Glenn Wilson	12	.05	.02	☐ 630	Steve Howe	10	.05	.01
☐ 581	Tim Stoddard	10	.05	.01	☐ 631	Gary Woods	10	.05	.01
☐ 582	Bob McClure	10	.05	.01	☐ 632	LaMarr Hoyt	10	.05	.01
☐ 583	Jim Dwyer	10	.05	.01	☐ 633	Steve Swisher	10	.05	.01
☐ 584	Ed Romero	10	.05	.01	☐ 634	Terry Leach	12	.05	.02
☐ 585	Larry Herndon	10	.05	.01	☐ 635	Jeff Newman	10	.05	.01
☐ 586	Wade Boggs	24.00	11.00	3.00	☐ 636	Brett Butler	50	.23	.06
☐ 587	Jay Howell	12	.05	.02	☐ 637	Gary Gray	10	.05	.01
☐ 588	Dave Stewart	75	.35	.09	☐ 638	Lee Mazzilli	10	.05	.01
☐ 589	Bert Blyleven	30	.14	.04	☐ 639A	Ron Jackson ERR	15.00	6.75	1.90
☐ 590	Dick Howser MG	12	.05	.02		(A's in glove)			
☐ 591	Wayne Gross	10	.05	.01	☐ 639B	Ron Jackson COR	12	.05	.02
☐ 592	Terry Francona	10	.05	.01		(Angels in glove,			
☐ 593	Don Werner	10	.05	.01		red border			

	on photo)			
☐	639C Ron Jackson COR........50	.23	.06
	(Angels in glove, green border on photo)			
☐	640 Juan Beniquez................10	.05	!01
☐	641 Dave Rucker 10	.05	.01
☐	642 Luis Pujols.....................10	.05	.01
☐	643 Rick Monday 10	.05	.01
☐	644 Hosken Powell 10	.05	.01
☐	645 The Chicken...................30	.14	.04
☐	646 Dave Engle 10	.05	.01
☐	647 Dick Davis......................10	.05	.01
☐	648 Frank Robinson..............35	.16	.04
	Vida Blue			
	Joe Morgan			
☐	649 Al Chambers..................10	.05	.01
☐	650 Jesus Vega 10	.05	.01
☐	651 Jeff Jones 10	.05	.01
☐	652 Marvis Foley 10	.05	.01
☐	653 Ty Cobb Puzzle Card 15	.07	.02
☐	654A Dick Perez/Diamond 25	.03	.01
	King Checklist (Unnumbered) ERR (Word "checklist" omitted from back)			
☐	654B Dick Perez/Diamond 25	.03	.01
	King Checklist (Unnumbered) COR (Word "checklist" is on back)			
☐	655 Checklist 1 15	.02	.00
	(Unnumbered)			
☐	656 Checklist 2 15	.02	.00
	(Unnumbered)			
☐	657 Checklist 3 15	.02	.00
	(Unnumbered)			
☐	658 Checklist 4 15	.02	.00
	(Unnumbered)			
☐	659 Checklist 5 15	.02	.00
	(Unnumbered)			
☐	660 Checklist 6 15	.02	.00
	(Unnumbered)			

issues. A new feature, Rated Rookies (RR), was introduced with this set with Bill Madden's 20 selections comprising numbers 27 through 46. Two "Living Legend" cards designated A (featuring Gaylord Perry and Rollie Fingers) and B (featuring Johnny Bench and Carl Yastrzemski) were issued as bonus cards in wax packs, but were not issued in the vending sets sold to hobby dealers. The seven unnumbered checklist cards are arbitrarily assigned numbers 652 through 658 and are listed at the end of the list below. The designs on the fronts of the Donruss cards changed considerably from the past two years. The backs contain statistics and are printed in green and black ink. The cards were distributed with a 63-piece puzzle of Duke Snider. There are no extra variation cards included in the complete set price below. The variation cards apparently resulted from a different printing for the factory sets as the Darling and Stenhouse no number variations as well as the Perez-Steel errors were corrected in the factory sets which were released later in the year. The key Rookie Cards in this set are Joe Carter, Ron Darling, Sid Fernandez, Tony Fernandez, Brian Harper, Don Mattingly, Kevin McReynolds, Darryl Strawberry, and Andy Van Slyke.

1984 Donruss

The 1984 Donruss set contains a total of 660 cards, each measuring 2 1/2" by 3 1/2"; however, only 658 are numbered. The first 26 cards in the set are again Diamond Kings (DK), although the drawings this year were styled differently and are easily differentiated from other DK

		NRMT-MT	EXC	G-VG
	COMPLETE SET (658) 325.00	145.00	40.00
	COMPLETE FACT.SET (658) ..400.00	180.00	50.00
	COMMON PLAYER (1-658) 30	.14	.04
☐	1A Robin Yount DK ERR....5.00	2.30	.60
	(Perez Steel)			
☐	1B Robin Yount DK COR....5.00	2.30	.60
☐	2A Dave Concepcion DK 50	.23	.06
	ERR (Perez Steel)			
☐	2B Dave Concepcion DK 50	.23	.06

COR
- ☐ 3A Dwayne Murphy DK..........40 .18 .05
  ERR (Perez Steel)
- ☐ 3B Dwayne Murphy DK..........40 .18 .05
  COR
- ☐ 4A John Castino DK ERR.....40 .18 .05
  (Perez Steel)
- ☐ 4B John Castino DK COR.....40 .18 .05
- ☐ 5A Leon Durham DK ERR.....40 .18 .05
  (Perez Steel)
- ☐ 5B Leon Durham DK COR....:18 .05
- ☐ 6A Rusty Staub DK ERR.....50 .23 .06
  (Perez Steel)
- ☐ 6B Rusty Staub DK COR.....50 .23 .06
- ☐ 7A Jack Clark DK ERR.....50 .23 .06
  (Perez Steel)
- ☐ 7B Jack Clark DK COR.....50 .23 .06
- ☐ 8A Dave Dravecky DK.....50 .23 .06
  ERR (Perez Steel)
- ☐ 8B Dave Dravecky DK.....50 .23 .06
  COR
- ☐ 9A Al Oliver DK ERR.....40 .18 .05
  (Perez Steel)
- ☐ 9B Al Oliver DK COR.....40 .18 .05
- ☐ 10A Dave Righetti DK.....40 .18 .05
  ERR (Perez Steel)
- ☐ 10B Dave Righetti DK.....40 .18 .05
- ☐ 11A Hal McRae DK ERR.....40 .18 .05
  (Perez Steel)
- ☐ 11B Hal McRae DK COR.....40 .18 .05
- ☐ 12A Ray Knight DK ERR.....40 .18 .05
  (Perez Steel)
- ☐ 12B Ray Knight DK COR.....40 .18 .05
- ☐ 13A Bruce Sutter DK ERR.....50 .23 .06
  (Perez Steel)
- ☐ 13B Bruce Sutter DK COR.....50 .23 .06
- ☐ 14A Bob Horner DK ERR.....40 .18 .05
  (Perez Steel)
- ☐ 14B Bob Horner DK COR.....40 .18 .05
- ☐ 15A Lance Parrish DK.....50 .23 .06
  ERR (Perez Steel)
- ☐ 15B Lance Parrish DK.....50 .23 .06
  COR
- ☐ 16A Matt Young DK ERR.....40 .18 .05
  (Perez Steel)
- ☐ 16B Matt Young DK COR.....40 .18 .05
- ☐ 17A Fred Lynn DK ERR.....50 .23 .06
  (Perez Steel)
  (A's logo on back)
- ☐ 17B Fred Lynn DK COR.....50 .23 .06
- ☐ 18A Ron Kittle DK ERR.....40 .18 .05
  (Perez Steel)
- ☐ 18B Ron Kittle DK COR.....40 .18 .05
- ☐ 19A Jim Clancy DK ERR.....40 .18 .05
  (Perez Steel)
- ☐ 19B Jim Clancy DK COR.....40 .18 .05

- ☐ 20A Bill Madlock DK ERR......40 .18 .05
  (Perez Steel)
- ☐ 20B Bill Madlock DK COR.....40 .18 .05
- ☐ 21A Larry Parrish DK.....40 .18 .05
  ERR (Perez Steel)
- ☐ 21B Larry Parrish DK.....40 .18 .05
  COR
- ☐ 22A Eddie Murray DK ERR..2.00 .90 .25
  (Perez Steel)
- ☐ 22B Eddie Murray DK COR .2.00 .90 .25
- ☐ 23A Mike Schmidt DK ERR.4.00 1.80 .50
  (Perez Steel)
- ☐ 23B Mike Schmidt DK COR.4.00 1.80 .50
- ☐ 24A Pedro Guerrero DK.....50 .23 .06
  ERR (Perez Steel)
- ☐ 24B Pedro Guerrero DK.....50 .23 .06
  COR
- ☐ 25A Andre Thornton DK.....40 .18 .05
  ERR (Perez Steel)
- ☐ 25B Andre Thornton DK.....40 .18 .05
  COR
- ☐ 26A Wade Boggs DK ERR...4.50 2.00 .55
  (Perez Steel)
- ☐ 26B Wade Boggs DK COR ..4.50 2.00 .55
- ☐ 27 Joel Skinner RR.....35 .16 .04
- ☐ 28 Tommy Dunbar RR.....35 .16 .04
- ☐ 29A Mike Stenhouse RR.....35 .16 .04
  ERR (No number on back)
- ☐ 29B Mike Stenhouse RR..2.50 1.15 .30
  COR (Numbered on back)
- ☐ 30A Ron Darling RR ERR..3.00 1.35 .40
  (No number on back)
- ☐ 30B Ron Darling RR COR.25.00 11.50 3.10
  (Numbered on back)
- ☐ 31 Dion James RR.....45 .20 .06
- ☐ 32 Tony Fernandez RR.....6.00 2.70 .75
- ☐ 33 Angel Salazar RR.....35 .16 .04
- ☐ 34 Kevin McReynolds RR ...3.50 1.55 .45
- ☐ 35 Dick Schofield RR.....50 .23 .06
- ☐ 36 Brad Komminsk RR.....35 .16 .04
- ☐ 37 Tim Teufel RR.....50 .23 .06
- ☐ 38 Doug Frobel RR.....35 .16 .04
- ☐ 39 Greg Gagne RR.....1.00 .45 .13
- ☐ 40 Mike Fuentes RR.....35 .16 .04
- ☐ 41 Joe Carter RR.....45.00 20.00 5.75
- ☐ 42 Mike Brown RR.....35 .16 .04
  (Angels OF)
- ☐ 43 Mike Jeffcoat RR.....35 .16 .04
- ☐ 44 Sid Fernandez RR.....5.00 2.30 .60
- ☐ 45 Brian Dayett RR.....35 .16 .04
- ☐ 46 Chris Smith RR.....35 .16 .04
- ☐ 47 Eddie Murray.....6.50 2.90 .80
- ☐ 48 Robin Yount.....10.00 4.50 1.25
- ☐ 49 Lance Parrish.....50 .23 .06
- ☐ 50 Jim Rice.....50 .23 .06

☐ 51 Dave Winfield	8.00	3.60	1.00
☐ 52 Fernando Valenzuela	.40	.18	.05
☐ 53 George Brett	10.00	4.50	1.25
☐ 54 Rickey Henderson	14.00	6.25	1.75
☐ 55 Gary Carter	2.00	.90	.25
☐ 56 Buddy Bell	.40	.18	.05
☐ 57 Reggie Jackson	5.00	2.30	.60
☐ 58 Harold Baines	1.00	.45	.13
☐ 59 Ozzie Smith	6.50	2.90	.80
☐ 60 Nolan Ryan	27.00	12.00	3.40
☐ 61 Pete Rose	5.00	2.30	.60
☐ 62 Ron Oester	.30	.14	.04
☐ 63 Steve Garvey	1.50	.65	.19
☐ 64 Jason Thompson	.30	.14	.04
☐ 65 Jack Clark	.40	.18	.05
☐ 66 Dale Murphy	3.00	1.35	.40
☐ 67 Leon Durham	.30	.14	.04
☐ 68 Darryl Strawberry	45.00	20.00	5.75
☐ 69 Richie Zisk	.30	.14	.04
☐ 70 Kent Hrbek	1.00	.45	.13
☐ 71 Dave Stieb	.40	.18	.05
☐ 72 Ken Schrom	.30	.14	.04
☐ 73 George Bell	3.00	1.35	.40
☐ 74 John Moses	.30	.14	.04
☐ 75 Ed Lynch	.30	.14	.04
☐ 76 Chuck Rainey	.30	.14	.04
☐ 77 Biff Pocoroba	.30	.14	.04
☐ 78 Cecilio Guante	.30	.14	.04
☐ 79 Jim Barr	.30	.14	.04
☐ 80 Kurt Bevacqua	.30	.14	.04
☐ 81 Tom Foley	.30	.14	.04
☐ 82 Joe Lefebvre	.30	.14	.04
☐ 83 Andy Van Slyke	12.00	5.50	1.50
☐ 84 Bob Lillis MG	.30	.14	.04
☐ 85 Ricky Adams	.30	.14	.04
☐ 86 Jerry Hairston	.30	.14	.04
☐ 87 Bob James	.30	.14	.04
☐ 88 Joe Aitobelli MG	.30	.14	.04
☐ 89 Ed Romero	.30	.14	.04
☐ 90 John Grubb	.30	.14	.04
☐ 91 John Henry Johnson	.30	.14	.04
☐ 92 Juan Espino	.30	.14	.04
☐ 93 Candy Maldonado	.50	.23	.06
☐ 94 Andre Thornton	.30	.14	.04
☐ 95 Onix Concepcion	.30	.14	.04
☐ 96 Donnie Hill UER (Listed as P, should be 2B)	.40	.18	.05
☐ 97 Andre Dawson UER (Wrong middle name, should be Nolan)	6.50	2.90	.80
☐ 98 Frank Tanana	.40	.18	.05
☐ 99 Curt Wilkerson	.30	.14	.04
☐ 100 Larry Gura	.30	.14	.04
☐ 101 Dwayne Murphy	.30	.14	.04
☐ 102 Tom Brennan	.30	.14	.04
☐ 103 Dave Righetti	.40	.18	.05
☐ 104 Steve Sax	1.25	.55	.16
☐ 105 Dan Petry	.30	.14	.04
☐ 106 Cal Ripken	30.00	13.50	3.80
☐ 107 Paul Molitor UER ('83 stats should say .270 BA, 608 AB, and 164 hits)	3.00	1.35	.40
☐ 108 Fred Lynn	.40	.18	.05
☐ 109 Neil Allen	.30	.14	.04
☐ 110 Joe Niekro	.40	.18	.05
☐ 111 Steve Carlton	5.00	2.30	.60
☐ 112 Terry Kennedy	.30	.14	.04
☐ 113 Bill Madlock	.40	.18	.05
☐ 114 Chili Davis	.60	.25	.08
☐ 115 Jim Gantner	.40	.18	.05
☐ 116 Tom Seaver	7.00	3.10	.85
☐ 117 Bill Buckner	.40	.18	.05
☐ 118 Bill Caudill	.30	.14	.04
☐ 119 Jim Clancy	.30	.14	.04
☐ 120 John Castino	.30	.14	.04
☐ 121 Dave Concepcion	.40	.18	.05
☐ 122 Greg Luzinski	.40	.18	.05
☐ 123 Mike Boddicker	.30	.14	.04
☐ 124 Pete Ladd	.30	.14	.04
☐ 125 Juan Berenguer	.30	.14	.04
☐ 126 John Montefusco	.30	.14	.04
☐ 127 Ed Jurak	.30	.14	.04
☐ 128 Tom Niedenfuer	.30	.14	.04
☐ 129 Bert Blyleven	1.00	.45	.13
☐ 130 Bud Black	.30	.14	.04
☐ 131 Gorman Heimueller	.30	.14	.04
☐ 132 Dan Schatzeder	.30	.14	.04
☐ 133 Ron Jackson	.30	.14	.04
☐ 134 Tom Henke	2.00	.90	.25
☐ 135 Kevin Hickey	.30	.14	.04
☐ 136 Mike Scott	.40	.18	.05
☐ 137 Bo Diaz	.30	.14	.04
☐ 138 Glenn Brummer	.30	.14	.04
☐ 139 Sid Monge	.30	.14	.04
☐ 140 Rich Gale	.30	.14	.04
☐ 141 Brett Butler	1.00	.45	.13
☐ 142 Brian Harper	2.00	.90	.25
☐ 143 John Rabb	.30	.14	.04
☐ 144 Gary Woods	.30	.14	.04
☐ 145 Pat Putnam	.30	.14	.04
☐ 146 Jim Acker	.30	.14	.04
☐ 147 Mickey Hatcher	.30	.14	.04
☐ 148 Todd Cruz	.30	.14	.04
☐ 149 Tom Tellmann	.30	.14	.04
☐ 150 John Wockenfuss	.30	.14	.04
☐ 151 Wade Boggs	15.00	6.75	1.90
☐ 152 Don Baylor	.40	.18	.05
☐ 153 Bob Welch	.50	.23	.06
☐ 154 Alan Bannister	.30	.14	.04
☐ 155 Willie Aikens	.30	.14	.04
☐ 156 Jeff Burroughs	.30	.14	.04
☐ 157 Bryan Little	.30	.14	.04

☐ 158	Bob Boone	.40	.18	.05	☐ 215	Pat Zachry	.30	.14	.04

Card	Player	Col1	Col2	Col3
☐ 158	Bob Boone	.40	.18	.05
☐ 159	Dave Hostetler	.30	.14	.04
☐ 160	Jerry Dybzinski	.30	.14	.04
☐ 161	Mike Madden	.30	.14	.04
☐ 162	Luis DeLeon	.30	.14	.04
☐ 163	Willie Hernandez	.40	.18	.05
☐ 164	Frank Pastore	.30	.14	.04
☐ 165	Rick Camp	.30	.14	.04
☐ 166	Lee Mazzilli	.30	.14	.04
☐ 167	Scot Thompson	.30	.14	.04
☐ 168	Bob Forsch	.30	.14	.04
☐ 169	Mike Flanagan	.30	.14	.04
☐ 170	Rick Manning	.30	.14	.04
☐ 171	Chet Lemon	.30	.14	.04
☐ 172	Jerry Remy	.30	.14	.04
☐ 173	Ron Guidry	.40	.18	.05
☐ 174	Pedro Guerrero	.40	.18	.05
☐ 175	Willie Wilson	.40	.18	.05
☐ 176	Carney Lansford	.40	.18	.05
☐ 177	Al Oliver	.40	.18	.05
☐ 178	Jim Sundberg	.30	.14	.04
☐ 179	Bobby Grich	.40	.18	.05
☐ 180	Rich Dotson	.30	.14	.04
☐ 181	Joaquin Andujar	.30	.14	.04
☐ 182	Jose Cruz	.40	.18	.05
☐ 183	Mike Schmidt	15.00	6.75	1.90
☐ 184	Gary Redus	.50	.23	.06
☐ 185	Garry Templeton	.40	.18	.05
☐ 186	Tony Pena	.40	.18	.05
☐ 187	Greg Minton	.30	.14	.04
☐ 188	Phil Niekro	1.25	.55	.16
☐ 189	Ferguson Jenkins	1.25	.55	.16
☐ 190	Mookie Wilson	.40	.18	.05
☐ 191	Jim Beattie	.30	.14	.04
☐ 192	Gary Ward	.30	.14	.04
☐ 193	Jesse Barfield	.40	.18	.05
☐ 194	Pete Filson	.30	.14	.04
☐ 195	Roy Lee Jackson	.30	.14	.04
☐ 196	Rick Sweet	.30	.14	.04
☐ 197	Jesse Orosco	.30	.14	.04
☐ 198	Steve Lake	.30	.14	.04
☐ 199	Ken Dayley	.30	.14	.04
☐ 200	Manny Sarmiento	.30	.14	.04
☐ 201	Mark Davis	.40	.18	.05
☐ 202	Tim Flannery	.30	.14	.04
☐ 203	Bill Scherrer	.30	.14	.04
☐ 204	Al Holland	.30	.14	.04
☐ 205	Dave Von Ohlen	.30	.14	.04
☐ 206	Mike LaCoss	.30	.14	.04
☐ 207	Juan Beniquez	.30	.14	.04
☐ 208	Juan Agosto	.30	.14	.04
☐ 209	Bobby Ramos	.30	.14	.04
☐ 210	Al Bumbry	.30	.14	.04
☐ 211	Mark Brouhard	.30	.14	.04
☐ 212	Howard Bailey	.30	.14	.04
☐ 213	Bruce Hurst	.40	.18	.05
☐ 214	Bob Shirley	.30	.14	.04
☐ 215	Pat Zachry	.30	.14	.04
☐ 216	Julio Franco	3.00	1.35	.40
☐ 217	Mike Armstrong	.30	.14	.04
☐ 218	Dave Beard	.30	.14	.04
☐ 219	Steve Rogers	.30	.14	.04
☐ 220	John Butcher	.30	.14	.04
☐ 221	Mike Smithson	.30	.14	.04
☐ 222	Frank White	.40	.18	.05
☐ 223	Mike Heath	.30	.14	.04
☐ 224	Chris Bando	.30	.14	.04
☐ 225	Roy Smalley	.30	.14	.04
☐ 226	Dusty Baker	.40	.18	.05
☐ 227	Lou Whitaker	1.75	.80	.22
☐ 228	John Lowenstein	.30	.14	.04
☐ 229	Ben Oglivie	.30	.14	.04
☐ 230	Doug DeCinces	.30	.14	.04
☐ 231	Lonnie Smith	.40	.18	.05
☐ 232	Ray Knight	.40	.18	.05
☐ 233	Gary Matthews	.40	.18	.05
☐ 234	Juan Bonilla	.30	.14	.04
☐ 235	Rod Scurry	.30	.14	.04
☐ 236	Atlee Hammaker	.30	.14	.04
☐ 237	Mike Caldwell	.30	.14	.04
☐ 238	Keith Hernandez	.40	.18	.05
☐ 239	Larry Bowa	.30	.14	.04
☐ 240	Tony Bernazard	.30	.14	.04
☐ 241	Damaso Garcia	.30	.14	.04
☐ 242	Tom Brunansky	.40	.18	.05
☐ 243	Dan Driessen	.30	.14	.04
☐ 244	Ron Kittle	.40	.18	.05
☐ 245	Tim Stoddard	.30	.14	.04
☐ 246	Bob L. Gibson	.30	.14	.04
	(Brewers Pitcher)			
☐ 247	Marty Castillo	.30	.14	.04
☐ 248	Don Mattingly UER	45.00	20.00	5.75
	("Traiing" on back)			
☐ 249	Jeff Newman	.30	.14	.04
☐ 250	Alejandro Pena	.75	.35	.09
☐ 251	Toby Harrah	.30	.14	.04
☐ 252	Cesar Geronimo	.30	.14	.04
☐ 253	Tom Underwood	.30	.14	.04
☐ 254	Doug Flynn	.30	.14	.04
☐ 255	Andy Hassler	.30	.14	.04
☐ 256	Odell Jones	.30	.14	.04
☐ 257	Rudy Law	.30	.14	.04
☐ 258	Harry Spilman	.30	.14	.04
☐ 259	Marty Bystrom	.30	.14	.04
☐ 260	Dave Rucker	.30	.14	.04
☐ 261	Ruppert Jones	.30	.14	.04
☐ 262	Jeff R. Jones	.30	.14	.04
	(Reds OF)			
☐ 263	Gerald Perry	.40	.18	.05
☐ 264	Gene Tenace	.30	.14	.04
☐ 265	Brad Wellman	.30	.14	.04
☐ 266	Dickie Noles	.30	.14	.04
☐ 267	Jamie Allen	.30	.14	.04
☐ 268	Jim Gott	.30	.14	.04

☐ 269	Ron Davis	.30	.14	.04
☐ 270	Benny Ayala	.30	.14	.04
☐ 271	Ned Yost	.30	.14	.04
☐ 272	Dave Rozema	.30	.14	.04
☐ 273	Dave Stapleton	.30	.14	.04
☐ 274	Lou Piniella	.40	.18	.05
☐ 275	Jose Morales	.30	.14	.04
☐ 276	Broderick Perkins	.30	.14	.04
☐ 277	Butch Davis	.30	.14	.04
☐ 278	Tony Phillips	2.50	1.15	.30
☐ 279	Jeff Reardon	2.50	1.15	.30
☐ 280	Ken Forsch	.30	.14	.04
☐ 281	Pete O'Brien	.75	.35	.09
☐ 282	Tom Paciorek	.40	.18	.05
☐ 283	Frank LaCorte	.30	.14	.04
☐ 284	Tim Lollar	.30	.14	.04
☐ 285	Greg Gross	.30	.14	.04
☐ 286	Alex Trevino	.30	.14	.04
☐ 287	Gene Garber	.30	.14	.04
☐ 288	Dave Parker	1.00	.45	.13
☐ 289	Lee Smith	3.00	1.35	.40
☐ 290	Dave LaPoint	.40	.18	.05
☐ 291	John Shelby	.30	.14	.04
☐ 292	Charlie Moore	.30	.14	.04
☐ 293	Alan Trammell	1.75	.80	.22
☐ 294	Tony Armas	.30	.14	.04
☐ 295	Shane Rawley	.30	.14	.04
☐ 296	Greg Brock	.30	.14	.04
☐ 297	Hal McRae	.40	.18	.05
☐ 298	Mike Davis	.30	.14	.04
☐ 299	Tim Raines	1.50	.65	.19
☐ 300	Bucky Dent	.40	.18	.05
☐ 301	Tommy John	.40	.18	.05
☐ 302	Carlton Fisk	5.00	2.30	.60
☐ 303	Darrell Porter	.30	.14	.04
☐ 304	Dickie Thon	.30	.14	.04
☐ 305	Garry Maddox	.30	.14	.04
☐ 306	Cesar Cedeno	.40	.18	.05
☐ 307	Gary Lucas	.30	.14	.04
☐ 308	Johnny Ray	.30	.14	.04
☐ 309	Andy McGaffigan	.30	.14	.04
☐ 310	Claudell Washington	.30	.14	.04
☐ 311	Ryne Sandberg	30.00	13.50	3.80
☐ 312	George Foster	.40	.18	.05
☐ 313	Spike Owen	.50	.23	.06
☐ 314	Gary Gaetti	.40	.18	.05
☐ 315	Willie Upshaw	.30	.14	.04
☐ 316	Al Williams	.30	.14	.04
☐ 317	Jorge Orta	.30	.14	.04
☐ 318	Orlando Mercado	.30	.14	.04
☐ 319	Junior Ortiz	.30	.14	.04
☐ 320	Mike Proly	.30	.14	.04
☐ 321	Randy Johnson UER	.30	.14	.04

('72-'82 stats are
from Twins' Randy John-
son, '83 stats are from
Braves' Randy Johnson)

☐ 322	Jim Morrison	.30	.14	.04
☐ 323	Max Venable	.30	.14	.04
☐ 324	Tony Gwynn	20.00	9.00	2.50
☐ 325	Duane Walker	.30	.14	.04
☐ 326	Ozzie Virgil	.30	.14	.04
☐ 327	Jeff Lahti	.30	.14	.04
☐ 328	Bill Dawley	.30	.14	.04
☐ 329	Rob Wilfong	.30	.14	.04
☐ 330	Marc Hill	.30	.14	.04
☐ 331	Ray Burris	.30	.14	.04
☐ 332	Allan Ramirez	.30	.14	.04
☐ 333	Chuck Porter	.30	.14	.04
☐ 334	Wayne Krenchicki	.30	.14	.04
☐ 335	Gary Allenson	.30	.14	.04
☐ 336	Bobby Meacham	.30	.14	.04
☐ 337	Joe Beckwith	.30	.14	.04
☐ 338	Rick Sutcliffe	.40	.18	.05
☐ 339	Mark Huismann	.30	.14	.04
☐ 340	Tim Conroy	.30	.14	.04
☐ 341	Scott Sanderson	.30	.14	.04
☐ 342	Larry Biittner	.30	.14	.04
☐ 343	Dave Stewart	1.50	.65	.19
☐ 344	Darryl Motley	.30	.14	.04
☐ 345	Chris Codiroli	.30	.14	.04
☐ 346	Rich Behenna	.30	.14	.04
☐ 347	Andre Robertson	.30	.14	.04
☐ 348	Mike Marshall	.40	.18	.05
☐ 349	Larry Herndon	.30	.14	.04
☐ 350	Rich Dauer	.30	.14	.04
☐ 351	Cecil Cooper	.40	.18	.05
☐ 352	Rod Carew	5.00	2.30	.60
☐ 353	Willie McGee	1.25	.55	.16
☐ 354	Phil Garner	.40	.18	.05
☐ 355	Joe Morgan	1.50	.65	.19
☐ 356	Luis Salazar	.30	.14	.04
☐ 357	John Candelaria	.40	.18	.05
☐ 358	Bill Laskey	.30	.14	.04
☐ 359	Bob McClure	.30	.14	.04
☐ 360	Dave Kingman	.40	.18	.05
☐ 361	Ron Cey	.40	.18	.05
☐ 362	Matt Young	.40	.18	.05
☐ 363	Lloyd Moseby	.30	.14	.04
☐ 364	Frank Viola	1.75	.80	.22
☐ 365	Eddie Milner	.30	.14	.04
☐ 366	Floyd Bannister	.30	.14	.04
☐ 367	Dan Ford	.30	.14	.04
☐ 368	Moose Haas	.30	.14	.04
☐ 369	Doug Bair	.30	.14	.04
☐ 370	Ray Fontenot	.30	.14	.04
☐ 371	Luis Aponte	.30	.14	.04
☐ 372	Jack Fimple	.30	.14	.04
☐ 373	Neal Heaton	.40	.18	.05
☐ 374	Greg Pryor	.30	.14	.04
☐ 375	Wayne Gross	.30	.14	.04
☐ 376	Charlie Lea	.30	.14	.04
☐ 377	Steve Lubratich	.30	.14	.04
☐ 378	Jon Matlack	.30	.14	.04

☐	379	Julio Cruz	.30	.14	.04
☐	380	John Mizerock	.30	.14	.04
☐	381	Kevin Gross	.60	.25	.08
☐	382	Mike Ramsey	.30	.14	.04
☐	383	Doug Gwosdz	.30	.14	.04
☐	384	Kelly Paris	.30	.14	.04
☐	385	Pete Falcone	.30	.14	.04
☐	386	Milt May	.30	.14	.04
☐	387	Fred Breining	.30	.14	.04
☐	388	Craig Lefferts	1.00	.45	.13
☐	389	Steve Henderson	.30	.14	.04
☐	390	Randy Moffitt	.30	.14	.04
☐	391	Ron Washington	.30	.14	.04
☐	392	Gary Roenicke	.30	.14	.04
☐	393	Tom Candiotti	1.75	.80	.22
☐	394	Larry Pashnick	.30	.14	.04
☐	395	Dwight Evans	.60	.25	.08
☐	396	Goose Gossage	.40	.18	.05
☐	397	Derrel Thomas	.30	.14	.04
☐	398	Juan Eichelberger	.30	.14	.04
☐	399	Leon Roberts	.30	.14	.04
☐	400	Dave Lopes	.40	.18	.05
☐	401	Bill Gullickson	.40	.18	.05
☐	402	Geoff Zahn	.30	.14	.04
☐	403	Billy Sample	.30	.14	.04
☐	404	Mike Squires	.30	.14	.04
☐	405	Craig Reynolds	.30	.14	.04
☐	406	Eric Show	.30	.14	.04
☐	407	John Denny	.30	.14	.04
☐	408	Dann Bilardello	.30	.14	.04
☐	409	Bruce Benedict	.30	.14	.04
☐	410	Kent Tekulve	.40	.18	.05
☐	411	Mel Hall	.75	.35	.09
☐	412	John Stuper	.30	.14	.04
☐	413	Rick Dempsey	.40	.18	.05
☐	414	Don Sutton	1.25	.55	.16
☐	415	Jack Morris	4.00	1.80	.50
☐	416	John Tudor	.40	.18	.05
☐	417	Willie Randolph	.40	.18	.05
☐	418	Jerry Reuss	.30	.14	.04
☐	419	Don Slaught	.40	.18	.05
☐	420	Steve McCatty	.30	.14	.04
☐	421	Tim Wallach	.40	.18	.05
☐	422	Larry Parrish	.30	.14	.04
☐	423	Brian Downing	.40	.18	.05
☐	424	Britt Burns	.30	.14	.04
☐	425	David Green	.30	.14	.04
☐	426	Jerry Mumphrey	.30	.14	.04
☐	427	Ivan DeJesus	.30	.14	.04
☐	428	Mario Soto	.30	.14	.04
☐	429	Gene Richards	.30	.14	.04
☐	430	Dale Berra	.30	.14	.04
☐	431	Darrell Evans	.40	.18	.05
☐	432	Glenn Hubbard	.30	.14	.04
☐	433	Jody Davis	.30	.14	.04
☐	434	Danny Heep	.30	.14	.04
☐	435	Ed Nunez	.30	.14	.04
☐	436	Bobby Castillo	.30	.14	.04
☐	437	Ernie Whitt	.30	.14	.04
☐	438	Scott Ullger	.30	.14	.04
☐	439	Doyle Alexander	.30	.14	.04
☐	440	Domingo Ramos	.30	.14	.04
☐	441	Craig Swan	.30	.14	.04
☐	442	Warren Brusstar	.30	.14	.04
☐	443	Len Barker	.30	.14	.04
☐	444	Mike Easler	.30	.14	.04
☐	445	Renie Martin	.30	.14	.04
☐	446	Dennis Rasmussen	.40	.18	.05
☐	447	Ted Power	.30	.14	.04
☐	448	Charles Hudson	.30	.14	.04
☐	449	Danny Cox	.40	.18	.05
☐	450	Kevin Bass	.30	.14	.04
☐	451	Daryl Sconiers	.30	.14	.04
☐	452	Scott Fletcher	.30	.14	.04
☐	453	Bryn Smith	.30	.14	.04
☐	454	Jim Dwyer	.30	.14	.04
☐	455	Rob Picciolo	.30	.14	.04
☐	456	Enos Cabell	.30	.14	.04
☐	457	Dennis Boyd	.40	.18	.05
☐	458	Butch Wynegar	.30	.14	.04
☐	459	Burt Hooton	.30	.14	.04
☐	460	Ron Hassey	.30	.14	.04
☐	461	Danny Jackson	.75	.35	.09
☐	462	Bob Kearney	.30	.14	.04
☐	463	Terry Francona	.30	.14	.04
☐	464	Wayne Tolleson	.30	.14	.04
☐	465	Mickey Rivers	.30	.14	.04
☐	466	John Wathan	.30	.14	.04
☐	467	Bill Almon	.30	.14	.04
☐	468	George Vukovich	.30	.14	.04
☐	469	Steve Kemp	.30	.14	.04
☐	470	Ken Landreaux	.30	.14	.04
☐	471	Milt Wilcox	.30	.14	.04
☐	472	Tippy Martinez	.30	.14	.04
☐	473	Ted Simmons	.40	.18	.05
☐	474	Tim Foli	.30	.14	.04
☐	475	George Hendrick	.30	.14	.04
☐	476	Terry Puhl	.30	.14	.04
☐	477	Von Hayes	.40	.18	.05
☐	478	Bobby Brown	.30	.14	.04
☐	479	Lee Lacy	.30	.14	.04
☐	480	Joel Youngblood	.30	.14	.04
☐	481	Jim Slaton	.30	.14	.04
☐	482	Mike Fitzgerald	.30	.14	.04
☐	483	Keith Moreland	.30	.14	.04
☐	484	Ron Roenicke	.30	.14	.04
☐	485	Luis Leal	.30	.14	.04
☐	486	Bryan Oelkers	.30	.14	.04
☐	487	Bruce Berenyi	.30	.14	.04
☐	488	LaMarr Hoyt	.30	.14	.04
☐	489	Joe Nolan	.30	.14	.04
☐	490	Marshall Edwards	.30	.14	.04
☐	491	Mike Laga	.30	.14	.04
☐	492	Rick Cerone	.30	.14	.04

☐ 493	Rick Miller UER (Listed as Mike on card front)	.30	.14	.04		(Listed as P on card front)		
☐ 494	Rick Honeycutt	.30	.14	.04	☐ 547	Tug McGraw	.40	.18	.05
☐ 495	Mike Hargrove	.40	.18	.05	☐ 548	Dave Smith	.30	.14	.04
☐ 496	Joe Simpson	.30	.14	.04	☐ 549	Len Matuszek	.30	.14	.04
☐ 497	Keith Atherton	.30	.14	.04	☐ 550	Tom Hume	.30	.14	.04
☐ 498	Chris Welsh	.30	.14	.04	☐ 551	Dave Dravecky	.50	.23	.06
☐ 499	Bruce Kison	.30	.14	.04	☐ 552	Rick Rhoden	.30	.14	.04
☐ 500	Bobby Johnson	.30	.14	.04	☐ 553	Duane Kuiper	.30	.14	.04
☐ 501	Jerry Koosman	.40	.18	.05	☐ 554	Rusty Staub	.40	.18	.05
☐ 502	Frank DiPino	.30	.14	.04	☐ 555	Bill Campbell	.30	.14	.04
☐ 503	Tony Perez	1.00	.45	.13	☐ 556	Mike Torrez	.30	.14	.04
☐ 504	Ken Oberkfell	.30	.14	.04	☐ 557	Dave Henderson	.60	.25	.08
☐ 505	Mark Thurmond	.30	.14	.04	☐ 558	Len Whitehouse	.30	.14	.04
☐ 506	Joe Price	.30	.14	.04	☐ 559	Barry Bonnell	.30	.14	.04
☐ 507	Pascual Perez	.30	.14	.04	☐ 560	Rick Lysander	.30	.14	.04
☐ 508	Marvell Wynne	.30	.14	.04	☐ 561	Garth Iorg	.30	.14	.04
☐ 509	Mike Krukow	.30	.14	.04	☐ 562	Bryan Clark	.30	.14	.04
☐ 510	Dick Ruthven	.30	.14	.04	☐ 563	Brian Giles	.30	.14	.04
☐ 511	Al Cowens	.30	.14	.04	☐ 564	Vern Ruhle	.30	.14	.04
☐ 512	Cliff Johnson	.30	.14	.04	☐ 565	Steve Bedrosian	.40	.18	.05
☐ 513	Randy Bush	.40	.18	.05	☐ 566	Larry McWilliams	.30	.14	.04
☐ 514	Sammy Stewart	.30	.14	.04	☐ 567	Jeff Leonard UER	.30	.14	.04
☐ 515	Bill Schroeder	.30	.14	.04		(Listed as P on card front)			
☐ 516	Aurelio Lopez	.30	.14	.04					
☐ 517	Mike G. Brown (Red Sox pitcher)	.30	.14	.04	☐ 568	Alan Wiggins	.30	.14	.04
					☐ 569	Jeff Russell	1.00	.45	.13
					☐ 570	Salome Barojas	.30	.14	.04
☐ 518	Graig Nettles	.40	.18	.05	☐ 571	Dane Iorg	.30	.14	.04
☐ 519	Dave Sax	.30	.14	.04	☐ 572	Bob Knepper	.30	.14	.04
☐ 520	Jerry Willard	.30	.14	.04	☐ 573	Gary Lavelle	.30	.14	.04
☐ 521	Paul Splittorff	.30	.14	.04	☐ 574	Gorman Thomas	.30	.14	.04
☐ 522	Tom Burgmeier	.30	.14	.04	☐ 575	Manny Trillo	.30	.14	.04
☐ 523	Chris Speier	.30	.14	.04	☐ 576	Jim Palmer	5.00	2.30	.60
☐ 524	Bobby Clark	.30	.14	.04	☐ 577	Dale Murray	.30	.14	.04
☐ 525	George Wright	.30	.14	.04	☐ 578	Tom Brookens	.30	.14	.04
☐ 526	Dennis Lamp	.30	.14	.04	☐ 579	Rich Gedman	.30	.14	.04
☐ 527	Tony Scott	.30	.14	.04	☐ 580	Bill Doran	.75	.35	.09
☐ 528	Ed Whitson	.30	.14	.04	☐ 581	Steve Yeager	.30	.14	.04
☐ 529	Ron Reed	.30	.14	.04	☐ 582	Dan Spillner	.30	.14	.04
☐ 530	Charlie Puleo	.30	.14	.04	☐ 583	Dan Quisenberry	.40	.18	.05
☐ 531	Jerry Royster	.30	.14	.04	☐ 584	Rance Mulliniks	.30	.14	.04
☐ 532	Don Robinson	.30	.14	.04	☐ 585	Storm Davis	.40	.18	.05
☐ 533	Steve Trout	.30	.14	.04	☐ 586	Dave Schmidt	.30	.14	.04
☐ 534	Bruce Sutter	.40	.18	.05	☐ 587	Bill Russell	.30	.14	.04
☐ 535	Bob Horner	.40	.18	.05	☐ 588	Pat Sheridan	.30	.14	.04
☐ 536	Pat Tabler	.30	.14	.04	☐ 589	Rafael Ramirez UER (A's on front)	.30	.14	.04
☐ 537	Chris Chambliss	.40	.18	.05					
☐ 538	Bob Ojeda	.30	.14	.04	☐ 590	Bud Anderson	.30	.14	.04
☐ 539	Alan Ashby	.30	.14	.04	☐ 591	George Frazier	.30	.14	.04
☐ 540	Jay Johnstone	.40	.18	.05	☐ 592	Lee Tunnell	.30	.14	.04
☐ 541	Bob Dernier	.30	.14	.04	☐ 593	Kirk Gibson	1.00	.45	.13
☐ 542	Brook Jacoby	.50	.23	.06	☐ 594	Scott McGregor	.30	.14	.04
☐ 543	U.L. Washington	.30	.14	.04	☐ 595	Bob Bailor	.30	.14	.04
☐ 544	Danny Darwin	.30	.14	.04	☐ 596	Tommy Herr	.40	.18	.05
☐ 545	Kiko Garcia	.30	.14	.04	☐ 597	Luis Sanchez	.30	.14	.04
☐ 546	Vance Law UER	.30	.14	.04	☐ 598	Dave Engle	.30	.14	.04

☐ 599	Craig McMurtry	.30	.14	.04
☐ 600	Carlos Diaz	.30	.14	.04
☐ 601	Tom O'Malley	.30	.14	.04
☐ 602	Nick Esasky	.40	.18	.05
☐ 603	Ron Hodges	.30	.14	.04
☐ 604	Ed VandeBerg	.30	.14	.04
☐ 605	Alfredo Griffin	.30	.14	.04
☐ 606	Glenn Hoffman	.30	.14	.04
☐ 607	Hubie Brooks	.40	.18	.05
☐ 608	Richard Barnes UER	.30	.14	.04
	(Photo actually			
	Neal Heaton)			
☐ 609	Greg Walker	.40	.18	.05
☐ 610	Ken Singleton	.40	.18	.05
☐ 611	Mark Clear	.30	.14	.04
☐ 612	Buck Martinez	.30	.14	.04
☐ 613	Ken Griffey	.40	.18	.05
☐ 614	Reid Nichols	.30	.14	.04
☐ 615	Doug Sisk	.30	.14	.04
☐ 616	Bob Brenly	.30	.14	.04
☐ 617	Joey McLaughlin	.30	.14	.04
☐ 618	Glenn Wilson	.40	.18	.05
☐ 619	Bob Stoddard	.30	.14	.04
☐ 620	Lenn Sakata UER	.30	.14	.04
	(Listed as Len			
	on card front)			
☐ 621	Mike Young	.30	.14	.04
☐ 622	John Stefero	.30	.14	.04
☐ 623	Carmelo Martinez	.40	.18	.05
☐ 624	Dave Bergman	.30	.14	.04
☐ 625	Runnin' Reds UER	1.25	.55	.16
	(Sic, Redbirds)			
	David Green			
	Willie McGee			
	Lonnie Smith			
	Ozzie Smith			
☐ 626	Rudy May	.30	.14	.04
☐ 627	Matt Keough	.30	.14	.04
☐ 628	Jose DeLeon	.40	.18	.05
☐ 629	Jim Essian	.30	.14	.04
☐ 630	Darnell Coles	.50	.23	.06
☐ 631	Mike Warren	.30	.14	.04
☐ 632	Del Crandall MG	.30	.14	.04
☐ 633	Dennis Martinez	.40	.18	.05
☐ 634	Mike Moore	.50	.23	.06
☐ 635	Lary Sorensen	.30	.14	.04
☐ 636	Ricky Nelson	.30	.14	.04
☐ 637	Omar Moreno	.30	.14	.04
☐ 638	Charlie Hough	.40	.18	.05
☐ 639	Dennis Eckersley	5.00	2.30	.60
☐ 640	Walt Terrell	.50	.23	.06
☐ 641	Denny Walling	.30	.14	.04
☐ 642	Dave Anderson	.40	.18	.05
☐ 643	Jose Oquendo	.40	.18	.05
☐ 644	Bob Stanley	.30	.14	.04
☐ 645	Dave Geisel	.30	.14	.04
☐ 646	Scott Garrelts	.40	.18	.05
☐ 647	Gary Pettis	.40	.18	.05
☐ 648	Duke Snider	.40	.18	.05
	Puzzle Card			
☐ 649	Johnnie LeMaster	.30	.14	.04
☐ 650	Dave Collins	.30	.14	.04
☐ 651	The Chicken	.50	.23	.06
☐ 652	DK Checklist	.35	.04	.01
	(Unnumbered)			
☐ 653	Checklist 1-130	.35	.04	.01
	(Unnumbered)			
☐ 654	Checklist 131-234	.35	.04	.01
	(Unnumbered)			
☐ 655	Checklist 235-338	.35	.04	.01
	(Unnumbered)			
☐ 656	Checklist 339-442	.35	.04	.01
	(Unnumbered)			
☐ 657	Checklist 443-546	.35	.04	.01
	(Unnumbered)			
☐ 658	Checklist 547-651	.35	.04	.01
	(Unnumbered)			
☐ A	Living Legends A	5.00	2.30	.60
	Gaylord Perry			
	Rollie Fingers			
☐ B	Living Legends B	10.00	4.50	1.25
	Carl Yastrzemski			
	Johnny Bench			

1985 Donruss

The cards in this 660-card set measure 2 1/2" by 3 1/2". The 1985 Donruss regular issue cards have fronts that feature jet black borders on which orange lines have been placed. The fronts contain the standard team logo, player's name, position, and Donruss logo. The cards were distributed with puzzle pieces from a Dick Perez rendition of Lou Gehrig. The first 26 cards

of the set feature Diamond Kings (DK), for the fourth year in a row; the artwork on the Diamond Kings was again produced by the Perez-Steele Galleries. Cards 27-46 feature Rated Rookies (RR). The unnumbered checklist cards are arbitrarily numbered below as numbers 654 through 660. This set is noted for containing the Rookie Cards of Roger Clemens, Alvin Davis, Eric Davis, Shawon Dunston, Dwight Gooden, Orel Hershiser, Jimmy Key, Mark Langston, Terry Pendleton, Kirby Puckett, Jose Rijo, Bret Saberhagen, and Danny Tartabull.

	NRMT-MT	EXC	G-VG
COMPLETE SET (660)	200.00	90.00	25.00
COMPLETE FACT.SET (660)	250.00	115.00	31.00
COMMON PLAYER (1-660)	.10	.05	.01

☐ 1	Ryne Sandberg DK	4.00	1.80	.50
☐ 2	Doug DeCinces DK	.15	.07	.02
☐ 3	Richard Dotson DK	.15	.07	.02
☐ 4	Bert Blyleven DK	.15	.07	.02
☐ 5	Lou Whitaker DK	.25	.11	.03
☐ 6	Dan Quisenberry DK	.15	.07	.02
☐ 7	Don Mattingly DK	2.50	1.15	.30
☐ 8	Carney Lansford DK	.15	.07	.02
☐ 9	Frank Tanana DK	.15	.07	.02
☐ 10	Willie Upshaw DK	.15	.07	.02
☐ 11	Claudell Washington DK	.15	.07	.02
☐ 12	Mike Marshall DK	.15	.07	.02
☐ 13	Joaquin Andujar DK	.15	.07	.02
☐ 14	Cal Ripken DK	4.00	1.80	.50
☐ 15	Jim Rice DK	.15	.07	.02
☐ 16	Don Sutton DK	.20	.09	.03
☐ 17	Frank Viola DK	.25	.11	.03
☐ 18	Alvin Davis DK	.15	.07	.02
☐ 19	Mario Soto DK	.15	.07	.02
☐ 20	Jose Cruz DK	.15	.07	.02
☐ 21	Charlie Lea DK	.15	.07	.02
☐ 22	Jesse Orosco DK	.15	.07	.02
☐ 23	Juan Samuel DK	.15	.07	.02
☐ 24	Tony Pena DK	.15	.07	.02
☐ 25	Tony Gwynn DK	2.25	1.00	.30
☐ 26	Bob Brenly DK	.15	.07	.02
☐ 27	Danny Tartabull RR	10.00	4.50	1.25
☐ 28	Mike Bielecki RR	.40	.18	.05
☐ 29	Steve Lyons RR	.15	.07	.02
☐ 30	Jeff Reed RR	.15	.07	.02
☐ 31	Tony Brewer RR	.15	.07	.02
☐ 32	John Morris RR	.15	.07	.02
☐ 33	Daryl Boston RR	.25	.11	.03
☐ 34	Al Pulido RR	.15	.07	.02
☐ 35	Steve Kiefer RR	.15	.07	.02
☐ 36	Larry Sheets RR	.15	.07	.02
☐ 37	Scott Bradley RR	.15	.07	.02
☐ 38	Calvin Schiraldi RR	.15	.07	.02
☐ 39	Shawon Dunston RR	2.00	.90	.25
☐ 40	Charlie Mitchell RR	.15	.07	.02
☐ 41	Billy Hatcher RR	.35	.16	.04
☐ 42	Russ Stephans RR	.15	.07	.02
☐ 43	Alejandro Sanchez RR	.15	.07	.02
☐ 44	Steve Jeltz RR	.15	.07	.02
☐ 45	Jim Traber RR	.15	.07	.02
☐ 46	Doug Loman RR	.15	.07	.02
☐ 47	Eddie Murray	2.00	.90	.25
☐ 48	Robin Yount	4.00	1.80	.50
☐ 49	Lance Parrish	.12	.05	.02
☐ 50	Jim Rice	.20	.09	.03
☐ 51	Dave Winfield	3.50	1.55	.45
☐ 52	Fernando Valenzuela	.12	.05	.02
☐ 53	George Brett	4.00	1.80	.50
☐ 54	Dave Kingman	.12	.05	.02
☐ 55	Gary Carter	.60	.25	.08
☐ 56	Buddy Bell	.12	.05	.02
☐ 57	Reggie Jackson	2.00	.90	.25
☐ 58	Harold Baines	.35	.16	.04
☐ 59	Ozzie Smith	2.00	.90	.25
☐ 60	Nolan Ryan UER	10.00	4.50	*1.25
	(Set strikeout record			
	in 1973, not 1972)			
☐ 61	Mike Schmidt	5.00	2.30	.60
☐ 62	Dave Parker	.40	.18	.05
☐ 63	Tony Gwynn	6.00	2.70	.75
☐ 64	Tony Pena	.12	.05	.02
☐ 65	Jack Clark	.12	.05	.02
☐ 66	Dale Murphy	1.00	.45	.13
☐ 67	Ryne Sandberg	10.00	4.50	1.25
☐ 68	Keith Hernandez	.20	.09	.03
☐ 69	Alvin Davis	.35	.16	.04
☐ 70	Kent Hrbek	.40	.18	.05
☐ 71	Willie Upshaw	.10	.05	.01
☐ 72	Dave Engle	.10	.05	.01
☐ 73	Alfredo Griffin	.10	.05	.01
☐ 74A	Jack Perconte	.10	.05	.01
	(Career Highlights			
	takes four lines)			
☐ 74B	Jack Perconte	.10	.05	.01
	(Career Highlights			
	takes three lines)			
☐ 75	Jesse Orosco	.10	.05	.01
☐ 76	Jody Davis	.10	.05	.01
☐ 77	Bob Horner	.12	.05	.02
☐ 78	Larry McWilliams	.10	.05	.01
☐ 79	Joel Youngblood	.10	.05	.01
☐ 80	Alan Wiggins	.10	.05	.01
☐ 81	Ron Oester	.10	.05	.01
☐ 82	Ozzie Virgil	.10	.05	.01
☐ 83	Ricky Horton	.10	.05	.01
☐ 84	Bill Doran	.12	.05	.02
☐ 85	Rod Carew	1.75	.80	.22
☐ 86	LaMarr Hoyt	.10	.05	.01
☐ 87	Tim Wallach	.12	.05	.02

☐ 88 Mike Flanagan	.10	.05	.01
☐ 89 Jim Sundberg	.12	.05	.02
☐ 90 Chet Lemon	.10	.05	.01
☐ 91 Bob Stanley	.10	.05	.01
☐ 92 Willie Randolph	.12	.05	.02
☐ 93 Bill Russell	.12	.05	.02
☐ 94 Julio Franco	.90	.40	.11
☐ 95 Dan Quisenberry	.12	.05	.02
☐ 96 Bill Caudill	.10	.05	.01
☐ 97 Bill Gullickson	.12	.05	.02
☐ 98 Danny Darwin	.10	.05	.01
☐ 99 Curtis Wilkerson	.10	.05	.01
☐ 100 Bud Black	.10	.05	.01
☐ 101 Tony Phillips	.12	.05	.02
☐ 102 Tony Bernazard	.10	.05	.01
☐ 103 Jay Howell	.12	.05	.02
☐ 104 Burt Hooton	.10	.05	.01
☐ 105 Milt Wilcox	.10	.05	.01
☐ 106 Rich Dauer	.10	.05	.01
☐ 107 Don Sutton	.50	.23	.06
☐ 108 Mike Witt	.10	.05	.01
☐ 109 Bruce Sutter	.12	.05	.02
☐ 110 Enos Cabell	.10	.05	.01
☐ 111 John Denny	.10	.05	.01
☐ 112 Dave Dravecky	.12	.05	.02
☐ 113 Marvell Wynne	.10	.05	.01
☐ 114 Johnnie LeMaster	.10	.05	.01
☐ 115 Chuck Porter	.10	.05	.01
☐ 116 John Gibbons	.10	.05	.01
☐ 117 Keith Moreland	.10	.05	.01
☐ 118 Darnell Coles	.12	.05	.02
☐ 119 Dennis Lamp	.10	.05	.01
☐ 120 Ron Davis	.10	.05	.01
☐ 121 Nick Esasky	.10	.05	.01
☐ 122 Vance Law	.10	.05	.01
☐ 123 Gary Roenicke	.10	.05	.01
☐ 124 Bill Schroeder	.10	.05	.01
☐ 125 Dave Rozema	.10	.05	.01
☐ 126 Bobby Meacham	.10	.05	.01
☐ 127 Marty Barrett	.10	.05	.01
☐ 128 R.J. Reynolds	.10	.05	.01
☐ 129 Ernie Camacho UER	.10	.05	.01
(Photo actually			
Rich Thompson)			
☐ 130 Jorge Orta	.10	.05	.01
☐ 131 Lary Sorensen	.10	.05	.01
☐ 132 Terry Francona	.10	.05	.01
☐ 133 Fred Lynn	.12	.05	.02
☐ 134 Bob Jones	.10	.05	.01
☐ 135 Jerry Hairston	.10	.05	.01
☐ 136 Kevin Bass	.10	.05	.01
☐ 137 Garry Maddox	.10	.05	.01
☐ 138 Dave LaPoint	.10	.05	.01
☐ 139 Kevin McReynolds	.35	.16	.04
☐ 140 Wayne Krenchicki	.10	.05	.01
☐ 141 Rafael Ramirez	.10	.05	.01
☐ 142 Rod Scurry	.10	.05	.01
☐ 143 Greg Minton	.10	.05	.01
☐ 144 Tim Stoddard	.10	.05	.01
☐ 145 Steve Henderson	.10	.05	.01
☐ 146 George Bell	1.00	.45	.13
☐ 147 Dave Meier	.10	.05	.01
☐ 148 Sammy Stewart	.10	.05	.01
☐ 149 Mark Brouhard	.10	.05	.01
☐ 150 Larry Herndon	.10	.05	.01
☐ 151 Oil-Can Boyd	.10	.05	.01
☐ 152 Brian Dayett	.10	.05	.01
☐ 153 Tom Niedenfuer	.10	.05	.01
☐ 154 Brook Jacoby	.12	.05	.02
☐ 155 Onix Concepcion	.10	.05	.01
☐ 156 Tim Conroy	.10	.05	.01
☐ 157 Joe Hesketh	.25	.11	.03
☐ 158 Brian Downing	.12	.05	.02
☐ 159 Tommy Dunbar	.10	.05	.01
☐ 160 Marc Hill	.10	.05	.01
☐ 161 Phil Garner	.12	.05	.02
☐ 162 Jerry Davis	.10	.05	.01
☐ 163 Bill Campbell	.10	.05	.01
☐ 164 John Franco	1.50	.65	.19
☐ 165 Len Barker	.10	.05	.01
☐ 166 Benny Distefano	.10	.05	.01
☐ 167 George Frazier	.10	.05	.01
☐ 168 Tito Landrum	.10	.05	.01
☐ 169 Cal Ripken	10.00	4.50	1.25
☐ 170 Cecil Cooper	.12	.05	.02
☐ 171 Alan Trammell	.50	.23	.06
☐ 172 Wade Boggs	5.00	2.30	.60
☐ 173 Don Baylor	.12	.05	.02
☐ 174 Pedro Guerrero	.15	.07	.02
☐ 175 Frank White	.12	.05	.02
☐ 176 Rickey Henderson	4.00	1.80	.50
☐ 177 Charlie Lea	.10	.05	.01
☐ 178 Pete O'Brien	.12	.05	.01
☐ 179 Doug DeCinces	.10	.05	.01
☐ 180 Ron Kittle	.12	.05	.02
☐ 181 George Hendrick	.10	.05	.01
☐ 182 Joe Niekro	.12	.05	.02
☐ 183 Juan Samuel	.25	.11	.03
☐ 184 Mario Soto	.10	.05	.01
☐ 185 Goose Gossage	.15	.07	.02
☐ 186 Johnny Ray	.10	.05	.01
☐ 187 Bob Brenly	.10	.05	.01
☐ 188 Craig McMurtry	.10	.05	.01
☐ 189 Leon Durham	.10	.05	.01
☐ 190 Dwight Gooden	8.00	3.60	1.00
☐ 191 Barry Bonnell	.10	.05	.01
☐ 192 Tim Teufel	.10	.05	.01
☐ 193 Dave Stieb	.12	.05	.02
☐ 194 Mickey Hatcher	.10	.05	.01
☐ 195 Jesse Barfield	.12	.05	.02
☐ 196 Al Cowens	.10	.05	.01
☐ 197 Hubie Brooks	.12	.05	.02
☐ 198 Steve Trout	.10	.05	.01
☐ 199 Glenn Hubbard	.10	.05	.01

☐ 200 Bill Madlock	12	.05	.02
☐ 201 Jeff D. Robinson	12	.05	.02
(Giants pitcher)			
☐ 202 Eric Show	10	.05	.01
☐ 203 Dave Concepcion	12	.05	.02
☐ 204 Ivan DeJesus	10	.05	.01
☐ 205 Neil Allen	10	.05	.01
☐ 206 Jerry Mumphrey	10	.05	.01
☐ 207 Mike C. Brown	10	.05	.01
(Angels OF)			
☐ 208 Carlton Fisk	1.75	.80	.22
☐ 209 Bryn Smith	10	.05	.01
☐ 210 Tippy Martinez	10	.05	.01
☐ 211 Dion James	10	.05	.01
☐ 212 Willie Hernandez	10	.05	.01
☐ 213 Mike Easler	10	.05	.01
☐ 214 Ron Guidry	12	.05	.02
☐ 215 Rick Honeycutt	10	.05	.01
☐ 216 Brett Butler	40	.18	.05
☐ 217 Larry Gura	10	.05	.01
☐ 218 Ray Burris	10	.05	.01
☐ 219 Steve Rogers	10	.05	.01
☐ 220 Frank Tanana UER	12	.05	.02
(Bats Left listed			
twice on card back)			
☐ 221 Ned Yost	10	.05	.01
☐ 222 Bret Saberhagen UER	5.00	2.30	.60
(18 career IP on back)			
☐ 223 Mike Davis	10	.05	.01
☐ 224 Bert Blyleven	35	.16	.04
☐ 225 Steve Kemp	10	.05	.01
☐ 226 Jerry Reuss	10	.05	.01
☐ 227 Darrell Evans UER	12	.05	.02
(80 homers in 1980)			
☐ 228 Wayne Gross	10	.05	.01
☐ 229 Jim Gantner	10	.05	.01
☐ 230 Bob Boone	12	.05	.02
☐ 231 Lonnie Smith	10	.05	.01
☐ 232 Frank DiPino	10	.05	.01
☐ 233 Jerry Koosman	12	.05	.02
☐ 234 Graig Nettles	12	.05	.02
☐ 235 John Tudor	12	.05	.02
☐ 236 John Rabb	10	.05	.01
☐ 237 Rick Manning	10	.05	.01
☐ 238 Mike Fitzgerald	10	.05	.01
☐ 239 Gary Matthews	10	.05	.01
☐ 240 Jim Presley	10	.05	.01
☐ 241 Dave Collins	10	.05	.01
☐ 242 Gary Gaetti	12	.05	.02
☐ 243 Dann Bilardello	10	.05	.01
☐ 244 Rudy Law	10	.05	.01
☐ 245 John Lowenstein	10	.05	.01
☐ 246 Tom Tellmann	10	.05	.01
☐ 247 Howard Johnson	1.50	.65	.19
☐ 248 Ray Fontenot	10	.05	.01
☐ 249 Tony Armas	10	.05	.01
☐ 250 Candy Maldonado	12	.05	.02
☐ 251 Mike Jeffcoat	10	.05	.01
☐ 252 Dane Iorg	10	.05	.01
☐ 253 Bruce Bochte	10	.05	.01
☐ 254 Pete Rose	1.75	.80	.22
☐ 255 Don Aase	10	.05	.01
☐ 256 George Wright	10	.05	.01
☐ 257 Britt Burns	10	.05	.01
☐ 258 Mike Scott	12	.05	.02
☐ 259 Len Matuszek	10	.05	.01
☐ 260 Dave Rucker	10	.05	.01
☐ 261 Craig Lefferts	12	.05	.02
☐ 262 Jay Tibbs	10	.05	.01
☐ 263 Bruce Benedict	10	.05	.01
☐ 264 Don Robinson	10	.05	.01
☐ 265 Gary Lavelle	10	.05	.01
☐ 266 Scott Sanderson	10	.05	.01
☐ 267 Matt Young	10	.05	.01
☐ 268 Ernie Whitt	10	.05	.01
☐ 269 Houston Jimenez	10	.05	.01
☐ 270 Ken Dixon	10	.05	.01
☐ 271 Pete Ladd	10	.05	.01
☐ 272 Juan Berenguer	10	.05	.01
☐ 273 Roger Clemens	60.00	27.00	7.50
☐ 274 Rick Cerone	10	.05	.01
☐ 275 Dave Anderson	10	.05	.01
☐ 276 George Vukovich	10	.05	.01
☐ 277 Greg Pryor	10	.05	.01
☐ 278 Mike Warren	10	.05	.01
☐ 279 Bob James	10	.05	.01
☐ 280 Bobby Grich	12	.05	.02
☐ 281 Mike Mason	10	.05	.01
☐ 282 Ron Reed	10	.05	.01
☐ 283 Alan Ashby	10	.05	.01
☐ 284 Mark Thurmond	10	.05	.01
☐ 285 Joe Lefebvre	10	.05	.01
☐ 286 Ted Power	10	.05	.01
☐ 287 Chris Chambliss	12	.05	.02
☐ 288 Lee Tunnell	10	.05	.01
☐ 289 Rich Bordi	10	.05	.01
☐ 290 Glenn Brummer	10	.05	.01
☐ 291 Mike Boddicker	10	.05	.01
☐ 292 Rollie Fingers	50	.23	.06
☐ 293 Lou Whitaker	50	.23	.06
☐ 294 Dwight Evans	20	.09	.03
☐ 295 Don Mattingly	7.00	3.10	.85
☐ 296 Mike Marshall	10	.05	.01
☐ 297 Willie Wilson	12	.05	.01
☐ 298 Mike Heath	10	.05	.01
☐ 299 Tim Raines	40	.18	.05
☐ 300 Larry Parrish	10	.05	.01
☐ 301 Geoff Zahn	10	.05	.01
☐ 302 Rich Dotson	10	.05	.01
☐ 303 David Green	10	.05	.01
☐ 304 Jose Cruz	12	.05	.02
☐ 305 Steve Carlton	1.75	.80	.22
☐ 306 Gary Redus	10	.05	.01
☐ 307 Steve Garvey	40	.18	.05

□	#	Player			
□	308	Jose DeLeon	.10	.05	.01
□	309	Randy Lerch	.10	.05	.01
□	310	Claudell Washington	.10	.05	.01
□	311	Lee Smith	1.00	.45	.13
□	312	Darryl Strawberry	7.00	3.10	.85
□	313	Jim Beattie	.10	.05	.01
□	314	John Butcher	.10	.05	.01
□	315	Damaso Garcia	.10	.05	.01
□	316	Mike Smithson	.10	.05	.01
□	317	Luis Leal	.10	.05	.01
□	318	Ken Phelps	.10	.05	.01
□	319	Wally Backman	.10	.05	.01
□	320	Ron Cey	.12	.05	.02
□	321	Brad Komminsk	.10	.05	.01
□	322	Jason Thompson	.10	.05	.01
□	323	Frank Williams	.10	.05	.01
□	324	Tim Lollar	.10	.05	.01
□	325	Eric Davis	8.00	3.60	1.00
□	326	Von Hayes	.10	.05	.01
□	327	Andy Van Slyke	2.00	.90	.25
□	328	Craig Reynolds	.10	.05	.01
□	329	Dick Schofield	.10	.05	.01
□	330	Scott Fletcher	.10	.05	.01
□	331	Jeff Reardon	.90	.40	.11
□	332	Rick Dempsey	.10	.05	.01
□	333	Ben Oglivie	.10	.05	.01
□	334	Dan Petry	.10	.05	.01
□	335	Jackie Gutierrez	.10	.05	.01
□	336	Dave Righetti	.12	.05	.02
□	337	Alejandro Pena	.12	.05	.02
□	338	Mel Hall	.25	.11	.03
□	339	Pat Sheridan	.10	.05	.01
□	340	Keith Atherton	.10	.05	.01
□	341	David Palmer	.10	.05	.01
□	342	Gary Ward	.10	.05	.01
□	343	Dave Stewart	.50	.23	.06
□	344	Mark Gubicza	.75	.35	.09
□	345	Carney Lansford	.12	.05	.02
□	346	Jerry Willard	.10	.05	.01
□	347	Ken Griffey	.15	.07	.02
□	348	Franklin Stubbs	.20	.09	.03
□	349	Aurelio Lopez	.10	.05	.01
□	350	Al Bumbry	.10	.05	.01
□	351	Charlie Moore	.10	.05	.01
□	352	Luis Sanchez	.10	.05	.01
□	353	Darrell Porter	.10	.05	.01
□	354	Bill Dawley	.10	.05	.01
□	355	Charles Hudson	.10	.05	.01
□	356	Garry Templeton	.10	.05	.01
□	357	Cecilio Guante	.10	.05	.01
□	358	Jeff Leonard	.10	.05	.01
□	359	Paul Molitor	1.00	.45	.13
□	360	Ron Gardenhire	.10	.05	.01
□	361	Larry Bowa	.12	.05	.02
□	362	Bob Kearney	.10	.05	.01
□	363	Garth Iorg	.10	.05	.01
□	364	Tom Brunansky	.12	.05	.02
□	365	Brad Gulden	.10	.05	.01
□	366	Greg Walker	.10	.05	.01
□	367	Mike Young	.10	.05	.01
□	368	Rick Waits	.10	.05	.01
□	369	Doug Bair	.10	.05	.01
□	370	Bob Shirley	.10	.05	.01
□	371	Bob Ojeda	.10	.05	.01
□	372	Bob Welch	.20	.09	.03
□	373	Neal Heaton	.10	.05	.01
□	374	Danny Jackson UER (Photo actually Frank Wills)	.12	.05	.02
□	375	Donnie Hill	.10	.05	.01
□	376	Mike Stenhouse	.10	.05	.01
□	377	Bruce Kison	.10	.05	.01
□	378	Wayne Tolleson	.10	.05	.01
□	379	Floyd Bannister	.10	.05	.01
□	380	Vern Ruhle	.10	.05	.01
□	381	Tim Corcoran	.10	.05	.01
□	382	Kurt Kepshire	.10	.05	.01
□	383	Bobby Brown	.10	.05	.01
□	384	Dave Van Gorder	.10	.05	.01
□	385	Rick Mahler	.10	.05	.01
□	386	Lee Mazzilli	.10	.05	.01
□	387	Bill Laskey	.10	.05	.01
□	388	Thad Bosley	.10	.05	.01
□	389	Al Chambers	.10	.05	.01
□	390	Tony Fernandez	.75	.35	.09
□	391	Ron Washington	.10	.05	.01
□	392	Bill Swaggerty	.10	.05	.01
□	393	Bob L. Gibson	.10	.05	.01
□	394	Marty Castillo	.10	.05	.01
□	395	Steve Crawford	.10	.05	.01
□	396	Clay Christiansen	.10	.05	.01
□	397	Bob Bailor	.10	.05	.01
□	398	Mike Hargrove	.12	.05	.02
□	399	Charlie Leibrandt	.12	.05	.02
□	400	Tom Burgmeier	.10	.05	.01
□	401	Razor Shines	.10	.05	.01
□	402	Rob Wilfong	.10	.05	.01
□	403	Tom Henke	.40	.18	.05
□	404	Al Jones	.10	.05	.01
□	405	Mike LaCoss	.10	.05	.01
□	406	Luis DeLeon	.10	.05	.01
□	407	Greg Gross	.10	.05	.01
□	408	Tom Hume	.10	.05	.01
□	409	Rick Camp	.10	.05	.01
□	410	Milt May	.10	.05	.01
□	411	Henry Cotto	.10	.05	.01
□	412	David Von Ohlen	.10	.05	.01
□	413	Scott McGregor	.10	.05	.01
□	414	Ted Simmons	.12	.05	.02
□	415	Jack Morris	1.25	.55	.16
□	416	Bill Buckner	.12	.05	.02
□	417	Butch Wynegar	.10	.05	.01
□	418	Steve Sax	.50	.23	.06
□	419	Steve Balboni	.10	.05	.01

☐ 420	Dwayne Murphy..............10	.05	.01
☐ 421	Andre Dawson 2.00	.90	.25
☐ 422	Charlie Hough..............12	.05	.02
☐ 423	Tommy John..............20	.09	.03
☐ 424A	Tom Seaver ERR 1.75	.80	.22
	(Photo actually		
	Floyd Bannister)		
☐ 424B	Tom Seaver COR 30.00	13.50	3.80
☐ 425	Tommy Herr..............10	.05	.01
☐ 426	Terry Puhl..............10	.05	.01
☐ 427	Al Holland..............10	.05	.01
☐ 428	Eddie Milner..............10	.05	.01
☐ 429	Terry Kennedy..............10	.05	.01
☐ 430	John Candelaria..............10	.05	.01
☐ 431	Manny Trillo..............10	.05	.01
☐ 432	Ken Oberkfell..............10	.05	.01
☐ 433	Rick Sutcliffe..............12	.05	.02
☐ 434	Ron Darling..............50	.23	.06
☐ 435	Spike Owen..............10	.05	.01
☐ 436	Frank Viola..............50	.23	.06
☐ 437	Lloyd Moseby..............10	.05	.01
☐ 438	Kirby Puckett 50.00	23.00	6.25
☐ 439	Jim Clancy..............10	.05	.01
☐ 440	Mike Moore..............25	.11	.03
☐ 441	Doug Sisk..............10	.05	.01
☐ 442	Dennis Eckersley......1.25	.55	.16
☐ 443	Gerald Perry..............10	.05	.01
☐ 444	Dale Berra..............10	.05	.01
☐ 445	Dusty Baker..............12	.05	.02
☐ 446	Ed Whitson..............10	.05	.01
☐ 447	Cesar Cedeno..............12	.05	.02
☐ 448	Rick Schu..............10	.05	.01
☐ 449	Joaquin Andujar..............10	.05	.01
☐ 450	Mark Bailey..............10	.05	.01
☐ 451	Ron Romanick..............10	.05	.01
☐ 452	Julio Cruz..............10	.05	.01
☐ 453	Miguel Dilone..............10	.05	.01
☐ 454	Storm Davis..............10	.05	.01
☐ 455	Jaime Cocanower..............10	.05	.01
☐ 456	Barbaro Garbey..............10	.05	.01
☐ 457	Rich Gedman..............10	.05	.01
☐ 458	Phil Niekro..............50	.23	.06
☐ 459	Mike Scioscia..............12	.05	.02
☐ 460	Pat Tabler..............10	.05	.01
☐ 461	Darryl Motley..............10	.05	.01
☐ 462	Chris Codiroli..............10	.05	.01
☐ 463	Doug Flynn..............10	.05	.01
☐ 464	Billy Sample..............10	.05	.01
☐ 465	Mickey Rivers..............10	.05	.01
☐ 466	John Wathan..............10	.05	.01
☐ 467	Bill Krueger..............15	.07	.02
☐ 468	Andre Thornton..............10	.05	.01
☐ 469	Rex Hudler..............20	.09	.03
☐ 470	Sid Bream..............1.25	.55	.16
☐ 471	Kirk Gibson..............30	.14	.04
☐ 472	John Shelby..............10	.05	.01
☐ 473	Moose Haas..............10	.05	.01
☐ 474	Doug Corbett 10	.05	.01
☐ 475	Willie McGee..............40	.18	.05
☐ 476	Bob Knepper..............10	.05	.01
☐ 477	Kevin Gross..............10	.05	.01
☐ 478	Carmelo Martinez..............10	.05	.01
☐ 479	Kent Tekulve..............10	.05	.01
☐ 480	Chili Davis..............15	.07	.02
☐ 481	Bobby Clark..............10	.05	.01
☐ 482	Mookie Wilson..............12	.05	.02
☐ 483	Dave Owen..............10	.05	.01
☐ 484	Ed Nunez..............10	.05	.01
☐ 485	Rance Mulliniks..............10	.05	.01
☐ 486	Ken Schrom..............10	.05	.01
☐ 487	Jeff Russell..............20	.09	.03
☐ 488	Tom Paciorek..............12	.05	.02
☐ 489	Dan Ford..............10	.05	.01
☐ 490	Mike Caldwell..............10	.05	.01
☐ 491	Scottie Earl..............10	.05	.01
☐ 492	Jose Rijo..............3.50	1.55	.45
☐ 493	Bruce Hurst..............12	.05	.02
☐ 494	Ken Landreaux..............10	.05	.01
☐ 495	Mike Fischlin..............10	.05	.01
☐ 496	Don Slaught..............10	.05	.01
☐ 497	Steve McCatty..............10	.05	.01
☐ 498	Gary Lucas..............10	.05	.01
☐ 499	Gary Pettis..............10	.05	.01
☐ 500	Marvis Foley..............10	.05	.01
☐ 501	Mike Squires..............10	.05	.01
☐ 502	Jim Pankovits..............10	.05	.01
☐ 503	Luis Aguayo..............10	.05	.01
☐ 504	Ralph Citarella..............10	.05	.01
☐ 505	Bruce Bochy..............10	.05	.01
☐ 506	Bob Owchinko..............10	.05	.01
☐ 507	Pascual Perez..............10	.05	.01
☐ 508	Lee Lacy..............10	.05	.01
☐ 509	Atlee Hammaker..............10	.05	.01
☐ 510	Bob Dernier..............10	.05	.01
☐ 511	Ed VandeBerg..............10	.05	.01
☐ 512	Cliff Johnson..............10	.05	.01
☐ 513	Len Whitehouse..............10	.05	.01
☐ 514	Dennis Martinez..............12	.05	.02
☐ 515	Ed Romero..............10	.05	.01
☐ 516	Rusty Kuntz..............10	.05	.01
☐ 517	Rick Miller..............10	.05	.01
☐ 518	Dennis Rasmussen..............10	.05	.01
☐ 519	Steve Yeager..............10	.05	.01
☐ 520	Chris Bando..............10	.05	.01
☐ 521	U.L. Washington..............10	.05	.01
☐ 522	Curt Young..............10	.05	.01
☐ 523	Angel Salazar..............10	.05	.01
☐ 524	Curt Kaufman..............10	.05	.01
☐ 525	Odell Jones..............10	.05	.01
☐ 526	Juan Agosto..............10	.05	.01
☐ 527	Denny Walling..............10	.05	.01
☐ 528	Andy Hawkins..............10	.05	.01
☐ 529	Sixto Lezcano..............10	.05	.01
☐ 530	Skeeter Barnes..............15	.07	.02

☐ 531 Randy Johnson	.10	.05	.01
☐ 532 Jim Morrison	.10	.05	.01
☐ 533 Warren Brusstar	.10	.05	.01
☐ 534A Jeff Pendleton ERR	9.00	4.00	1.15
(Wrong first name)			
☐ 534B Terry Pendleton COR	27.00	12.00	3.40
☐ 535 Vic Rodriguez	.10	.05	.01
☐ 536 Bob McClure	.10	.05	.01
☐ 537 Dave Bergman	.10	.05	.01
☐ 538 Mark Clear	.10	.05	.01
☐ 539 Mike Pagliarulo	.20	.09	.03
☐ 540 Terry Whitfield	.10	.05	.01
☐ 541 Joe Beckwith	.10	.05	.01
☐ 542 Jeff Burroughs	.10	.05	.01
☐ 543 Dan Schatzeder	.10	.05	.01
☐ 544 Donnie Scott	.10	.05	.01
☐ 545 Jim Slaton	.10	.05	.01
☐ 546 Greg Luzinski	.12	.05	.02
☐ 547 Mark Salas	.10	.05	.01
☐ 548 Dave Smith	.10	.05	.01
☐ 549 John Wockenfuss	.10	.05	.01
☐ 550 Frank Pastore	.10	.05	.01
☐ 551 Tim Flannery	.10	.05	.01
☐ 552 Rick Rhoden	.10	.05	.01
☐ 553 Mark Davis	.12	.05	.02
☐ 554 Jeff Dedmon	.10	.05	.01
☐ 555 Gary Woods	.10	.05	.01
☐ 556 Danny Heep	.10	.05	.01
☐ 557 Mark Langston	3.50	1.55	.45
☐ 558 Darrell Brown	.10	.05	.01
☐ 559 Jimmy Key	2.00	.90	.25
☐ 560 Rick Lysander	.10	.05	.01
☐ 561 Doyle Alexander	.10	.05	.01
☐ 562 Mike Stanton	.10	.05	.01
☐ 563 Sid Fernandez	.50	.23	.06
☐ 564 Richie Hebner	.10	.05	.01
☐ 565 Alex Trevino	.10	.05	.01
☐ 566 Brian Harper	.40	.18	.05
☐ 567 Dan Gladden	.40	.18	.05
☐ 568 Luis Salazar	.10	.05	.01
☐ 569 Tom Foley	.10	.05	.01
☐ 570 Larry Andersen	.10	.05	.01
☐ 571 Danny Cox	.10	.05	.01
☐ 572 Joe Sambito	.10	.05	.01
☐ 573 Juan Beniquez	.10	.05	.01
☐ 574 Joel Skinner	.10	.05	.01
☐ 575 Randy St.Claire	.10	.05	.01
☐ 576 Floyd Rayford	.10	.05	.01
☐ 577 Roy Howell	.10	.05	.01
☐ 578 John Grubb	.10	.05	.01
☐ 579 Ed Jurak	.10	.05	.01
☐ 580 John Montefusco	.10	.05	.01
☐ 581 Orel Hershiser	3.50	1.55	.45
☐ 582 Tom Waddell	.10	.05	.01
☐ 583 Mark Huismann	.10	.05	.01
☐ 584 Joe Morgan	.60	.25	.08
☐ 585 Jim Wohlford	.10	.05	.01
☐ 586 Dave Schmidt	.10	.05	.01
☐ 587 Jeff Kunkel	.10	.05	.01
☐ 588 Hal McRae	.12	.05	.02
☐ 589 Bill Almon	.10	.05	.01
☐ 590 Carmen Castillo	.10	.05	.01
☐ 591 Omar Moreno	.10	.05	.01
☐ 592 Ken Howell	.10	.05	.01
☐ 593 Tom Brookens	.10	.05	.01
☐ 594 Joe Nolan	.10	.05	.01
☐ 595 Willie Lozado	.10	.05	.01
☐ 596 Tom Nieto	.10	.05	.01
☐ 597 Walt Terrell	.10	.05	.01
☐ 598 Al Oliver	.12	.05	.02
☐ 599 Shane Rawley	.10	.05	.01
☐ 600 Denny Gonzalez	.10	.05	.01
☐ 601 Mark Grant	.10	.05	.01
☐ 602 Mike Armstrong	.10	.05	.01
☐ 603 George Foster	.12	.05	.02
☐ 604 Dave Lopes	.12	.05	.02
☐ 605 Salome Barojas	.10	.05	.01
☐ 606 Roy Lee Jackson	.10	.05	.01
☐ 607 Pete Filson	.10	.05	.01
☐ 608 Duane Walker	.10	.05	.01
☐ 609 Glenn Wilson	.10	.05	.01
☐ 610 Rafael Santana	.10	.05	.01
☐ 611 Roy Smith	.10	.05	.01
☐ 612 Ruppert Jones	.10	.05	.01
☐ 613 Joe Cowley	.10	.05	.01
☐ 614 Al Nipper UER	.10	.05	.01
(Photo actually			
Mike Brown)			
☐ 615 Gene Nelson	.10	.05	.01
☐ 616 Joe Carter	7.00	3.10	.85
☐ 617 Ray Knight	.12	.05	.02
☐ 618 Chuck Rainey	.10	.05	.01
☐ 619 Dan Driessen	.10	.05	.01
☐ 620 Daryl Sconiers	.10	.05	.01
☐ 621 Bill Stein	.10	.05	.01
☐ 622 Roy Smalley	.10	.05	.01
☐ 623 Ed Lynch	.10	.05	.01
☐ 624 Jeff Stone	.10	.05	.01
☐ 625 Bruce Berenyi	.10	.05	.01
☐ 626 Kelvin Chapman	.10	.05	.01
☐ 627 Joe Price	.10	.05	.01
☐ 628 Steve Bedrosian	.10	.05	.01
☐ 629 Vic Mata	.10	.05	.01
☐ 630 Mike Krukow	.10	.05	.01
☐ 631 Phil Bradley	.12	.05	.02
☐ 632 Jim Gott	.10	.05	.01
☐ 633 Randy Bush	.10	.05	.01
☐ 634 Tom Browning	1.00	.45	.13
☐ 635 Lou Gehrig	.20	.09	.03
Puzzle Card			
☐ 636 Reid Nichols	.10	.05	.01
☐ 637 Dan Pasqua	.40	.18	.05
☐ 638 German Rivera	.10	.05	.01
☐ 639 Don Schulze	.10	.05	.01

☐ 640A	Mike Jones 10	.05	.01
	(Career Highlights,		
	takes five lines)		
☐ 640B	Mike Jones 10	.05	.01
	(Career Highlights,		
	takes four lines)		
☐ 641	Pete Rose 1.75	.80	.22
☐ 642	Wade Rowdon 10	.05	.01
☐ 643	Jerry Narron 10	.05	.01
☐ 644	Darrell Miller 10	.05	.01
☐ 645	Tim Hulett 10	.05	.01
☐ 646	Andy McGaffigan 10	.05	.01
☐ 647	Kurt Bevacqua 10	.05	.01
☐ 648	John Russell 10	.05	.01
☐ 649	Ron Robinson 15	.07	.02
☐ 650	Donnie Moore 10	.05	.01
☐ 651A	Two for the Title 3.00	1.35	.40
	Dave Winfield		
	Don Mattingly		
	(Yellow letters)		
☐ 651B	Two for the Title 10.00	4.50	1.25
	Dave Winfield		
	Don Mattingly		
	(White letters)		
☐ 652	Tim Laudner 10	.05	.01
☐ 653	Steve Farr 75	.35	.09
☐ 654	DK Checklist 1-26 15	.02	.00
	(Unnumbered)		
☐ 655	Checklist 27-130 15	.02	.00
	(Unnumbered)		
☐ 656	Checklist 131-234 15	.02	.00
	(Unnumbered)		
☐ 657	Checklist 235-338 15	.02	.00
	(Unnumbered)		
☐ 658	Checklist 339-442 15	.02	.00
	(Unnumbered)		
☐ 659	Checklist 443-546 15	.02	.00
	(Unnumbered)		
☐ 660	Checklist 547-653 15	.02	.00
	(Unnumbered)		

1986 Donruss

The cards in this 660-card set measure
2 1/2" by 3 1/2". The 1986 Donruss regular
issue cards have fronts that feature blue
borders. The fronts contain the standard
team logo, player's name, position, and
Donruss logo. The cards were distributed
with puzzle pieces from a Dick Perez rendition of Hank Aaron. The first 26 cards of
the set are Diamond Kings (DK), for the
fifth year in a row; the artwork on the

Diamond Kings was again produced by the
Perez-Steele Galleries. Cards 27-46 again
feature Rated Rookies (RR); Danny
Tartabull is included in this subset for the
second year in a row. The unnumbered
checklist cards are arbitrarily numbered
below as numbers 654 through 660. The
key Rookie Cards in this set are Jose
Canseco, Vince Coleman, Kal Daniels,
Cecil Fielder, Fred McGriff, Paul O'Neill,
and Mickey Tettleton.

	MT	EX-MT	VG
COMPLETE SET (660) 140.00		65.00	17.50
COMPLETE FACT.SET (660) ...150.00		70.00	19.00
COMMON PLAYER (1-660) 10		.05	.01

☐ 1	Kirk Gibson DK 20	.09	.03
☐ 2	Gooce Gossage DK 15	.07	.02
☐ 3	Willie McGee DK 15	.07	.02
☐ 4	George Bell DK 20	.09	.03
☐ 5	Tony Armas DK 15	.07	.02
☐ 6	Chili Davis DK 15	.07	.02
☐ 7	Cecil Cooper DK 15	.07	.02
☐ 8	Mike Boddicker DK 15	.07	.02
☐ 9	Dave Lopes DK 15	.07	.02
☐ 10	Bill Doran DK 15	.07	.02
☐ 11	Bret Saberhagen DK 35	.16	.04
☐ 12	Brett Butler DK 15	.07	.02
☐ 13	Harold Baines DK 15	.07	.02
☐ 14	Mike Davis DK 15	.07	.02
☐ 15	Tony Perez DK 15	.07	.02
☐ 16	Willie Randolph DK 15	.07	.02
☐ 17	Bob Boone DK 15	.07	.02
☐ 18	Orel Hershiser DK 25	.11	.03
☐ 19	Johnny Ray DK 15	.07	.02
☐ 20	Gary Ward DK 15	.07	.02
☐ 21	Rick Mahler DK 15	.07	.02
☐ 22	Phil Bradley DK 15	.07	.02
☐ 23	Jerry Koosman DK 15	.07	.02
☐ 24	Tom Brunansky DK 15	.07	.02
☐ 25	Andre Dawson DK 40	.18	.05
☐ 26	Dwight Gooden DK 40	.18	.05

☐ 27	Kal Daniels RR	1.25	.55	.16	☐ 81 Ron Oester	.10	.05	.01

☐	#	Player	Price	Price	Price	☐	#	Player	Price	Price	Price
☐	27	Kal Daniels RR	1.25	.55	.16	☐	81	Ron Oester	.10	.05	.01
☐	28	Fred McGriff RR	28.00	12.50	3.50	☐	82	John Russell	.10	.05	.01
☐	29	Cory Snyder RR	.60	.25	.08	☐	83	Tommy Herr	.10	.05	.01
☐	30	Jose Guzman RR	.75	.35	.09	☐	84	Jerry Mumphrey	.10	.05	.01
☐	31	Ty Gainey RR	.12	.05	.02	☐	85	Ron Romanick	.10	.05	.01
☐	32	Johnny Abrego RR	.12	.05	.02	☐	86	Daryl Boston	.10	.05	.01
☐	33A	Andres Galarraga RR (No accent)	.60	.25	.08	☐	87	Andre Dawson	1.00	.45	.13
						☐	88	Eddie Murray	1.00	.45	.13
☐	33B	Andre's Galarraga RR (Accent over e)	1.25	.55	.16	☐	89	Dion James	.10	.05	.01
						☐	90	Chet Lemon	.10	.05	.01
☐	34	Dave Shipanoff RR	.12	.05	.02	☐	91	Bob Stanley	.10	.05	.01
☐	35	Mark McLemore RR	.20	.09	.03	☐	92	Willie Randolph	.12	.05	.02
☐	36	Marty Clary RR	.12	.05	.02	☐	93	Mike Scioscia	.10	.05	.01
☐	37	Paul O'Neill RR	2.50	1.15	.30	☐	94	Tom Waddell	.10	.05	.01
☐	38	Danny Tartabull RR	2.00	.90	.25	☐	95	Danny Jackson	.10	.05	.01
☐	39	Jose Canseco RR	60.00	27.00	7.50	☐	96	Mike Davis	.10	.05	.01
☐	40	Juan Nieves RR	.12	.05	.02	☐	97	Mike Fitzgerald	.10	.05	.01
☐	41	Lance McCullers RR	.12	.05	.02	☐	98	Gary Ward	.10	.05	.01
☐	42	Rick Surhoff RR	.12	.05	.02	☐	99	Pete O'Brien	.10	.05	.01
☐	43	Todd Worrell RR	.35	.16	.04	☐	100	Bret Saberhagen	.75	.35	.09
☐	44	Bob Kipper RR	.12	.05	.02	☐	101	Alfredo Griffin	.10	.05	.01
☐	45	John Habyan RR	.20	.09	.03	☐	102	Brett Butler	.20	.09	.03
☐	46	Mike Woodard RR	.12	.05	.02	☐	103	Ron Guidry	.12	.05	.02
☐	47	Mike Boddicker	.10	.05	.01	☐	104	Jerry Reuss	.10	.05	.01
☐	48	Robin Yount	2.00	.90	.25	☐	105	Jack Morris	.75	.35	.09
☐	49	Lou Whitaker	.30	.14	.04	☐	106	Rick Dempsey	.10	.05	.01
☐	50	Oil Can Boyd	.10	.05	.01	☐	107	Ray Burris	.10	.05	.01
☐	51	Rickey Henderson	2.00	.90	.25	☐	108	Brian Downing	.12	.05	.02
☐	52	Mike Marshall	.10	.05	.01	☐	109	Willie McGee	.20	.09	.03
☐	53	George Brett	2.00	.90	.25	☐	110	Bill Doran	.10	.05	.01
☐	54	Dave Kingman	.12	.05	.02	☐	111	Kent Tekulve	.10	.05	.01
☐	55	Hubie Brooks	.10	.05	.01	☐	112	Tony Gwynn	3.00	1.35	.40
☐	56	Oddibe McDowell	.10	.05	.01	☐	113	Marvell Wynne	.10	.05	.01
☐	57	Doug DeCinces	.10	.05	.01	☐	114	David Green	.10	.05	.01
☐	58	Britt Burns	.10	.05	.01	☐	115	Jim Gantner	.10	.05	.01
☐	59	Ozzie Smith	1.00	.45	.13	☐	116	George Foster	.12	.05	.02
☐	60	Jose Cruz	.10	.05	.01	☐	117	Steve Trout	.10	.05	.01
☐	61	Mike Schmidt	2.50	1.15	.30	☐	118	Mark Langston	.50	.23	.06
☐	62	Pete Rose	1.00	.45	.13	☐	119	Tony Fernandez	.25	.11	.03
☐	63	Steve Garvey	.35	.16	.04	☐	120	John Butcher	.10	.05	.01
☐	64	Tony Pena	.12	.05	.02	☐	121	Ron Robinson	.10	.05	.01
☐	65	Chili Davis	.12	.05	.02	☐	122	Dan Spillner	.10	.05	.01
☐	66	Dale Murphy	.50	.23	.06	☐	123	Mike Young	.10	.05	.01
☐	67	Ryne Sandberg	4.50	2.00	.55	☐	124	Paul Molitor	.40	.18	.05
☐	68	Gary Carter	.35	.16	.04	☐	125	Kirk Gibson	.15	.07	.02
☐	69	Alvin Davis	.10	.05	.01	☐	126	Ken Griffey	.12	.05	.02
☐	70	Kent Hrbek	.20	.09	.03	☐	127	Tony Armas	.10	.05	.01
☐	71	George Bell	.50	.23	.06	☐	128	Mariano Duncan	.60	.25	.08
☐	72	Kirby Puckett	10.00	4.50	1.25	☐	129	Pat Tabler	.10	.05	.01
☐	73	Lloyd Moseby	.10	.05	.01	☐	130	Frank White	.12	.05	.02
☐	74	Bob Kearney	.10	.05	.01	☐	131	Carney Lansford	.12	.05	.02
☐	75	Dwight Gooden	1.25	.55	.16	☐	132	Vance Law	.10	.05	.01
☐	76	Gary Matthews	.10	.05	.01	☐	133	Dick Schofield	.10	.05	.01
☐	77	Rick Mahler	.10	.05	.01	☐	134	Wayne Tolleson	.10	.05	.01
☐	78	Benny Distefano	.10	.05	.01	☐	135	Greg Walker	.10	.05	.01
☐	79	Jeff Leonard	.10	.05	.01	☐	136	Denny Walling	.10	.05	.01
☐	80	Kevin McReynolds	.12	.05	.02	☐	137	Ozzie Virgil	.10	.05	.01

☐	138 Ricky Horton	.10	.05	.01	☐	194 Frank Viola	.30	.14	.04
☐	139 LaMarr Hoyt	.10	.05	.01	☐	195 Willie Upshaw	.10	.05	.01
☐	140 Wayne Krenchicki	.10	.05	.01	☐	196 Jim Beattie	.10	.05	.01
☐	141 Glenn Hubbard	.10	.05	.01	☐	197 Darryl Strawberry	2.50	1.15	.30
☐	142 Cecilio Guante	.10	.05	.01	☐	198 Ron Cey	.12	.05	.02
☐	143 Mike Krukow	.10	.05	.01	☐	199 Steve Bedrosian	.10	.05	.01
☐	144 Lee Smith	.60	.25	.08	☐	200 Steve Kemp	.10	.05	.01
☐	145 Edwin Nunez	.10	.05	.01	☐	201 Manny Trillo	.10	.05	.01
☐	146 Dave Stieb	.12	.05	.02	☐	202 Garry Templeton	.10	.05	.01
☐	147 Mike Smithson	.10	.05	.01	☐	203 Dave Parker	.20	.09	.03
☐	148 Ken Dixon	.10	.05	.01	☐	204 John Denny	.10	.05	.01
☐	149 Danny Darwin	.10	.05	.01	☐	205 Terry Pendleton	1.50	.65	.19
☐	150 Chris Pittaro	.10	.05	.01	☐	206 Terry Puhl	.10	.05	.01
☐	151 Bill Buckner	.12	.05	.02	☐	207 Bobby Grich	.12	.05	.02
☐	152 Mike Pagliarulo	.10	.05	.01	☐	208 Ozzie Guillen	.60	.25	.08
☐	153 Bill Russell	.12	.05	.02	☐	209 Jeff Reardon	.50	.23	.06
☐	154 Brook Jacoby	.10	.05	.01	☐	210 Cal Ripken	5.00	2.30	.60
☐	155 Pat Sheridan	.10	.05	.01	☐	211 Bill Schroeder	.10	.05	.01
☐	156 Mike Gallego	.20	.09	.03	☐	212 Dan Petry	.10	.05	.01
☐	157 Jim Wohlford	.10	.05	.01	☐	213 Jim Rice	.15	.07	.02
☐	158 Gary Pettis	.10	.05	.01	☐	214 Dave Righetti	.12	.05	.02
☐	159 Toby Harrah	.10	.05	.01	☐	215 Fernando Valenzuela	.12	.05	.02
☐	160 Richard Dotson	.10	.05	.01	☐	216 Julio Franco	.35	.16	.04
☐	161 Bob Knepper	.10	.05	.01	☐	217 Darryl Motley	.10	.05	.01
☐	162 Dave Dravecky	.12	.05	.02	☐	218 Dave Collins	.10	.05	.01
☐	163 Greg Gross	.10	.05	.01	☐	219 Tim Wallach	.12	.05	.02
☐	164 Eric Davis	1.25	.55	.16	☐	220 George Wright	.10	.05	.01
☐	165 Gerald Perry	.10	.05	.01	☐	221 Tommy Dunbar	.10	.05	.01
☐	166 Rick Rhoden	.10	.05	.01	☐	222 Steve Balboni	.10	.05	.01
☐	167 Keith Moreland	.10	.05	.01	☐	223 Jay Howell	.12	.05	.02
☐	168 Jack Clark	.12	.05	.02	☐	224 Joe Carter	2.50	1.15	.30
☐	169 Storm Davis	.10	.05	.01	☐	225 Ed Whitson	.10	.05	.01
☐	170 Cecil Cooper	.12	.05	.02	☐	226 Orel Hershiser	.50	.23	.06
☐	171 Alan Trammell	.30	.14	.04	☐	227 Willie Hernandez	.10	.05	.01
☐	172 Roger Clemens	12.00	5.50	1.50	☐	228 Lee Lacy	.10	.05	.01
☐	173 Don Mattingly	2.50	1.15	.30	☐	229 Rollie Fingers	.40	.18	.05
☐	174 Pedro Guerrero	.12	.05	.02	☐	230 Bob Boone	.12	.05	.02
☐	175 Willie Wilson	.10	.05	.01	☐	231 Joaquin Andujar	.10	.05	.01
☐	176 Dwayne Murphy	.10	.05	.01	☐	232 Craig Reynolds	.10	.05	.01
☐	177 Tim Raines	.30	.14	.04	☐	233 Shane Rawley	.10	.05	.01
☐	178 Larry Parrish	.10	.05	.01	☐	234 Eric Show	.10	.05	.01
☐	179 Mike Witt	.10	.05	.01	☐	235 Jose DeLeon	.10	.05	.01
☐	180 Harold Baines	.25	.11	.03	☐	236 Jose Uribe	.15	.07	.02
☐	181 Vince Coleman UER	1.75	.80	.22	☐	237 Moose Haas	.10	.05	.01
	(BA 2.67 on back)				☐	238 Wally Backman	.10	.05	.01
☐	182 Jeff Heathcock	.10	.05	.01	☐	239 Dennis Eckersley	.75	.35	.09
☐	183 Steve Carlton	.90	.40	.11	☐	240 Mike Moore	.12	.05	.02
☐	184 Mario Soto	.10	.05	.01	☐	241 Damaso Garcia	.10	.05	.01
☐	185 Goose Gossage	.15	.07	.02	☐	242 Tim Teufel	.10	.05	.01
☐	186 Johnny Ray	.10	.05	.01	☐	243 Dave Concepcion	.12	.05	.02
☐	187 Dan Gladden	.10	.05	.01	☐	244 Floyd Bannister	.10	.05	.01
☐	188 Bob Horner	.12	.05	.02	☐	245 Fred Lynn	.12	.05	.02
☐	189 Rick Sutcliffe	.12	.05	.02	☐	246 Charlie Moore	.10	.05	.01
☐	190 Keith Hernandez	.15	.07	.02	☐	247 Walt Terrell	.10	.05	.01
☐	191 Phil Bradley	.10	.05	.01	☐	248 Dave Winfield	1.25	.55	.16
☐	192 Tom Brunansky	.10	.05	.02	☐	249 Dwight Evans	.12	.05	.02
☐	193 Jesse Barfield	.12	.05	.02	☐	250 Dennis Powell	.10	.05	.01

☐	251	Andre Thornton	.10	.05	.01
☐	252	Onix Concepcion	.10	.05	.01
☐	253	Mike Heath	.10	.05	.01
☐	254A	David Palmer ERR	.10	.05	.01
		(Position 2B)			
☐	254B	David Palmer COR	.60	.25	.08
		(Position P)			
☐	255	Donnie Moore	.10	.05	.01
☐	256	Curtis Wilkerson	.10	.05	.01
☐	257	Julio Cruz	.10	.05	.01
☐	258	Nolan Ryan	6.00	2.70	.75
☐	259	Jeff Stone	.10	.05	.01
☐	260	John Tudor	.12	.05	.02
☐	261	Mark Thurmond	.10	.05	.01
☐	262	Jay Tibbs	.10	.05	.01
☐	263	Rafael Ramirez	.10	.05	.01
☐	264	Larry McWilliams	.10	.05	.01
☐	265	Mark Davis	.12	.05	.02
☐	266	Bob Dernier	.10	.05	.01
☐	267	Matt Young	.10	.05	.01
☐	268	Jim Clancy	.10	.05	.01
☐	269	Mickey Hatcher	.10	.05	.01
☐	270	Sammy Stewart	.10	.05	.01
☐	271	Bob L. Gibson	.10	.05	.01
☐	272	Nelson Simmons	.10	.05	.01
☐	273	Rich Gedman	.10	.05	.01
☐	274	Butch Wynegar	.10	.05	.01
☐	275	Ken Howell	.10	.05	.01
☐	276	Mel Hall	.12	.05	.02
☐	277	Jim Sundberg	.12	.05	.02
☐	278	Chris Codiroli	.10	.05	.01
☐	279	Herm Winningham	.20	.09	.03
☐	280	Rod Carew	.90	.40	.11
☐	281	Don Slaught	.10	.05	.01
☐	282	Scott Fletcher	.10	.05	.01
☐	283	Bill Dawley	.10	.05	.01
☐	284	Andy Hawkins	.10	.05	.01
☐	285	Glenn Wilson	.10	.05	.01
☐	286	Nick Esasky	.10	.05	.01
☐	287	Claudell Washington	.10	.05	.01
☐	288	Lee Mazzilli	.10	.05	.01
☐	289	Jody Davis	.10	.05	.01
☐	290	Darrell Porter	.10	.05	.01
☐	291	Scott McGregor	.10	.05	.01
☐	292	Ted Simmons	.12	.05	.02
☐	293	Aurelio Lopez	.10	.05	.01
☐	294	Marty Barrett	.10	.05	.01
☐	295	Dale Berra	.10	.05	.01
☐	296	Greg Brock	.10	.05	.01
☐	297	Charlie Leibrandt	.12	.05	.02
☐	298	Bill Krueger	.10	.05	.01
☐	299	Bryn Smith	.10	.05	.01
☐	300	Burt Hooton	.10	.05	.01
☐	301	Stu Cliburn	.10	.05	.01
☐	302	Luis Salazar	.10	.05	.01
☐	303	Ken Dayley	.10	.05	.01
☐	304	Frank DiPino	.10	.05	.01
☐	305	Von Hayes	.10	.05	.01
☐	306	Gary Redus	.10	.05	.01
☐	307	Craig Lefferts	.12	.05	.02
☐	308	Sammy Khalifa	.10	.05	.01
☐	309	Scott Garrelts	.10	.05	.01
☐	310	Rick Cerone	.10	.05	.01
☐	311	Shawon Dunston	.30	.14	.04
☐	312	Howard Johnson	.60	.25	.08
☐	313	Jim Presley	.10	.05	.01
☐	314	Gary Gaetti	.12	.05	.02
☐	315	Luis Leal	.10	.05	.01
☐	316	Mark Salas	.10	.05	.01
☐	317	Bill Caudill	.10	.05	.01
☐	318	Dave Henderson	.12	.05	.02
☐	319	Rafael Santana	.10	.05	.01
☐	320	Leon Durham	.10	.05	.01
☐	321	Bruce Sutter	.12	.05	.02
☐	322	Jason Thompson	.10	.05	.01
☐	323	Bob Brenly	.10	.05	.01
☐	324	Carmelo Martinez	.10	.05	.01
☐	325	Eddie Milner	.10	.05	.01
☐	326	Juan Samuel	.12	.05	.02
☐	327	Tom Nieto	.10	.05	.01
☐	328	Dave Smith	.10	.05	.01
☐	329	Urbano Lugo	.10	.05	.01
☐	330	Joel Skinner	.10	.05	.01
☐	331	Bill Gullickson	.12	.05	.02
☐	332	Floyd Rayford	.10	.05	.01
☐	333	Ben Oglivie	.10	.05	.01
☐	334	Lance Parrish	.12	.05	.02
☐	335	Jackie Gutierrez	.10	.05	.01
☐	336	Dennis Rasmussen	.10	.05	.01
☐	337	Terry Whitfield	.10	.05	.01
☐	338	Neal Heaton	.10	.05	.01
☐	339	Jorge Orta	.10	.05	.01
☐	340	Donnie Hill	.10	.05	.01
☐	341	Joe Hesketh	.10	.05	.01
☐	342	Charlie Hough	.10	.05	.01
☐	343	Dave Rozema	.10	.05	.01
☐	344	Greg Pryor	.10	.05	.01
☐	345	Mickey Tettleton	2.00	.90	.25
☐	346	George Vukovich	.10	.05	.01
☐	347	Don Baylor	.12	.05	.02
☐	348	Carlos Diaz	.10	.05	.01
☐	349	Barbaro Garbey	.10	.05	.01
☐	350	Larry Sheets	.10	.05	.01
☐	351	Ted Higuera	.20	.09	.03
☐	352	Juan Beniquez	.10	.05	.01
☐	353	Bob Forsch	.10	.05	.01
☐	354	Mark Bailey	.10	.05	.01
☐	355	Larry Andersen	.10	.05	.01
☐	356	Terry Kennedy	.10	.05	.01
☐	357	Don Robinson	.10	.05	.01
☐	358	Jim Gott	.10	.05	.01
☐	359	Earnie Riles	.10	.05	.01
☐	360	John Christensen	.10	.05	.01
☐	361	Ray Fontenot	.10	.05	.01

☐ 362	Spike Owen	10	.05	.01
☐ 363	Jim Acker	10	.05	.01
☐ 364	Ron Davis	10	.05	.01
☐ 365	Tom Hume	10	.05	.01
☐ 366	Carlton Fisk	90	.40	.11
☐ 367	Nate Snell	10	.05	.01
☐ 368	Rick Manning	10	.05	.01
☐ 369	Darrell Evans	12	.05	.02
☐ 370	Ron Hassey	10	.05	.01
☐ 371	Wade Boggs	2.00	.90	.25
☐ 372	Rick Honeycutt	10	.05	.01
☐ 373	Chris Bando	10	.05	.01
☐ 374	Bud Black	10	.05	.01
☐ 375	Steve Henderson	10	.05	.01
☐ 376	Charlie Lea	10	.05	.01
☐ 377	Reggie Jackson	1.00	.45	.13
☐ 378	Dave Schmidt	10	.05	.01
☐ 379	Bob James	10	.05	.01
☐ 380	Glenn Davis	1.00	.45	.13
☐ 381	Tim Corcoran	10	.05	.01
☐ 382	Danny Cox	10	.05	.01
☐ 383	Tim Flannery	10	.05	.01
☐ 384	Tom Browning	25	.11	.03
☐ 385	Rick Camp	10	.05	.01
☐ 386	Jim Morrison	10	.05	.01
☐ 387	Dave LaPoint	10	.05	.01
☐ 388	Dave Lopes	12	.05	.02
☐ 389	Al Cowens	10	.05	.01
☐ 390	Doyle Alexander	10	.05	.01
☐ 391	Tim Laudner	10	.05	.01
☐ 392	Don Aase	10	.05	.01
☐ 393	Jaime Cocanower	10	.05	.01
☐ 394	Randy O'Neal	10	.05	.01
☐ 395	Mike Easler	10	.05	.01
☐ 396	Scott Bradley	10	.05	.01
☐ 397	Tom Niedenfuer	10	.05	.01
☐ 398	Jerry Willard	10	.05	.01
☐ 399	Lonnie Smith	10	.05	.01
☐ 400	Bruce Bochte	10	.05	.01
☐ 401	Terry Francona	10	.05	.01
☐ 402	Jim Slaton	10	.05	.01
☐ 403	Bill Stein	10	.05	.01
☐ 404	Tim Hulett	10	.05	.01
☐ 405	Alan Ashby	10	.05	.01
☐ 406	Tim Stoddard	10	.05	.01
☐ 407	Garry Maddox	10	.05	.01
☐ 408	Ted Power	10	.05	.01
☐ 409	Len Barker	10	.05	.01
☐ 410	Denny Gonzalez	10	.05	.01
☐ 411	George Frazier	10	.05	.01
☐ 412	Andy Van Slyke	75	.35	.09
☐ 413	Jim Dwyer	10	.05	.01
☐ 414	Paul Householder	10	.05	.01
☐ 415	Alejandro Sanchez	10	.05	.01
☐ 416	Steve Crawford	10	.05	.01
☐ 417	Dan Pasqua	12	.05	.02
☐ 418	Enos Cabell	10	.05	.01
☐ 419	Mike Jones	10	.05	.01
☐ 420	Steve Kiefer	10	.05	.01
☐ 421	Tim Burke	20	.09	.03
☐ 422	Mike Mason	10	.05	.01
☐ 423	Ruppert Jones	10	.05	.01
☐ 424	Jerry Hairston	10	.05	.01
☐ 425	Tito Landrum	10	.05	.01
☐ 426	Jeff Calhoun	10	.05	.01
☐ 427	Don Carman	10	.05	.01
☐ 428	Tony Perez	30	.14	.04
☐ 429	Jerry Davis	10	.05	.01
☐ 430	Bob Walk	10	.05	.01
☐ 431	Brad Wellman	10	.05	.01
☐ 432	Terry Forster	10	.05	.01
☐ 433	Billy Hatcher	12	.05	.02
☐ 434	Clint Hurdle	10	.05	.01
☐ 435	Ivan Calderon	1.25	.55	.16
☐ 436	Pete Filson	10	.05	.01
☐ 437	Tom Henke	30	.14	.04
☐ 438	Dave Engle	10	.05	.01
☐ 439	Tom Filer	10	.05	.01
☐ 440	Gorman Thomas	10	.05	.01
☐ 441	Rick Aguilera	1.75	.80	.22
☐ 442	Scott Sanderson	10	.05	.01
☐ 443	Jeff Dedmon	10	.05	.01
☐ 444	Joe Orsulak	35	.16	.04
☐ 445	Atlee Hammaker	10	.05	.01
☐ 446	Jerry Royster	10	.05	.01
☐ 447	Buddy Bell	12	.05	.02
☐ 448	Dave Rucker	10	.05	.01
☐ 449	Ivan DeJesus	10	.05	.01
☐ 450	Jim Pankovits	10	.05	.01
☐ 451	Jerry Narron	10	.05	.01
☐ 452	Bryan Little	10	.05	.01
☐ 453	Gary Lucas	10	.05	.01
☐ 454	Dennis Martinez	12	.05	.02
☐ 455	Ed Romero	10	.05	.01
☐ 456	Bob Melvin	10	.05	.01
☐ 457	Glenn Hoffman	10	.05	.01
☐ 458	Bob Shirley	10	.05	.01
☐ 459	Bob Welch	15	.07	.02
☐ 460	Carmen Castillo	10	.05	.01
☐ 461	Dave Leeper OF	10	.05	.01
☐ 462	Tim Birtsas	10	.05	.01
☐ 463	Randy St.Claire	10	.05	.01
☐ 464	Chris Welsh	10	.05	.01
☐ 465	Greg Harris	10	.05	.01
☐ 466	Lynn Jones	10	.05	.01
☐ 467	Dusty Baker	12	.05	.02
☐ 468	Roy Smith	10	.05	.01
☐ 469	Andre Robertson	10	.05	.01
☐ 470	Ken Landreaux	10	.05	.01
☐ 471	Dave Bergman	10	.05	.01
☐ 472	Gary Roenicke	10	.05	.01
☐ 473	Pete Vuckovich	10	.05	.01
☐ 474	Kirk McCaskill	30	.14	.04
☐ 475	Jeff Lahti	10	.05	.01

☐ 476	Mike Scott	12	.05	.02
☐ 477	Darren Daulton	2.00	.90	.25
☐ 478	Graig Nettles	12	.05	.02
☐ 479	Bill Almon	10	.05	.01
☐ 480	Greg Minton	10	.05	.01
☐ 481	Randy Ready	10	.05	.01
☐ 482	Len Dykstra	1.75	.80	.22
☐ 483	Thad Bosley	10	.05	.01
☐ 484	Harold Reynolds	60	.25	.08
☐ 485	Al Oliver	12	.05	.02
☐ 486	Roy Smalley	10	.05	.01
☐ 487	John Franco	25	.11	.03
☐ 488	Juan Agosto	10	.05	.01
☐ 489	Al Pardo	10	.05	.01
☐ 490	Bill Wegman	50	.23	.06
☐ 491	Frank Tanana	12	.05	.02
☐ 492	Brian Fisher	10	.05	.01
☐ 493	Mark Clear	10	.05	.01
☐ 494	Len Matuszek	10	.05	.01
☐ 495	Ramon Romero	10	.05	.01
☐ 496	John Wathan	10	.05	.01
☐ 497	Rob Picciolo	10	.05	.01
☐ 498	U.L. Washington	10	.05	.01
☐ 499	John Candelaria	10	.05	.01
☐ 500	Duane Walker	10	.05	.01
☐ 501	Gene Nelson	10	.05	.01
☐ 502	John Mizerock	10	.05	.01
☐ 503	Luis Aguayo	10	.05	.01
☐ 504	Kurt Kepshire	10	.05	.01
☐ 505	Ed Wojna	10	.05	.01
☐ 506	Joe Price	10	.05	.01
☐ 507	Milt Thompson	20	.09	.03
☐ 508	Junior Ortiz	10	.05	.01
☐ 509	Vida Blue	12	.05	.02
☐ 510	Steve Engel	10	.05	.01
☐ 511	Karl Best	10	.05	.01
☐ 512	Cecil Fielder	27.00	12.00	3.40
☐ 513	Frank Eufemia	10	.05	.01
☐ 514	Tippy Martinez	10	.05	.01
☐ 515	Billy Joe Robidoux	10	.05	.01
☐ 516	Bill Scherrer	10	.05	.01
☐ 517	Bruce Hurst	12	.05	.02
☐ 518	Rich Bordi	10	.05	.01
☐ 519	Steve Yeager	10	.05	.01
☐ 520	Tony Bernazard	10	.05	.01
☐ 521	Hal McRae	12	.05	.02
☐ 522	Jose Rijo	60	.25	.08
☐ 523	Mitch Webster	10	.05	.01
☐ 524	Jack Howell	10	.05	.01
☐ 525	Alan Bannister	10	.05	.01
☐ 526	Ron Kittle	10	.05	.01
☐ 527	Phil Garner	12	.05	.02
☐ 528	Kurt Bevacqua	10	.05	.01
☐ 529	Kevin Gross	10	.05	.01
☐ 530	Bo Diaz	10	.05	.01
☐ 531	Ken Oberkfell	10	.05	.01
☐ 532	Rick Reuschel	10	.05	.01

☐ 533	Ron Meridith	10	.05	.01
☐ 534	Steve Braun	10	.05	.01
☐ 535	Wayne Gross	10	.05	.01
☐ 536	Ray Searage	10	.05	.01
☐ 537	Tom Brookens	10	.05	.01
☐ 538	Al Nipper	10	.05	.01
☐ 539	Billy Sample	10	.05	.01
☐ 540	Steve Sax	25	.11	.03
☐ 541	Dan Quisenberry	12	.05	.02
☐ 542	Tony Phillips	12	.05	.02
☐ 543	Floyd Youmans	10	.05	.01
☐ 544	Steve Buechele	1.00	.45	.13
☐ 545	Craig Gerber	10	.05	.01
☐ 546	Joe DeSa	10	.05	.01
☐ 547	Brian Harper	25	.11	.03
☐ 548	Kevin Bass	10	.05	.01
☐ 549	Tom Foley	10	.05	.01
☐ 550	Dave Van Gorder	10	.05	.01
☐ 551	Bruce Bochy	10	.05	.01
☐ 552	R.J. Reynolds	10	.05	.01
☐ 553	Chris Brown	10	.05	.01
☐ 554	Bruce Benedict	10	.05	.01
☐ 555	Warren Brusstar	10	.05	.01
☐ 556	Danny Heep	10	.05	.01
☐ 557	Darnell Coles	12	.05	.02
☐ 558	Greg Gagne	12	.05	.02
☐ 559	Ernie Whitt	10	.05	.01
☐ 560	Ron Washington	10	.05	.01
☐ 561	Jimmy Key	25	.11	.03
☐ 562	Billy Swift	40	.18	.05
☐ 563	Ron Darling	20	.09	.03
☐ 564	Dick Ruthven	10	.05	.01
☐ 565	Zane Smith	25	.11	.03
☐ 566	Sid Bream	12	.05	.02
☐ 567A	Joel Youngblood ERR	10	.05	.01
	(Position P)			
☐ 567B	Joel Youngblood COR	60	.25	.08
	(Position IF)			
☐ 568	Mario Ramirez	10	.05	.01
☐ 569	Tom Runnells	12	.05	.02
☐ 570	Rick Schu	10	.05	.01
☐ 571	Bill Campbell	10	.05	.01
☐ 572	Dickie Thon	10	.05	.01
☐ 573	Al Holland	10	.05	.01
☐ 574	Reid Nichols	10	.05	.01
☐ 575	Bert Roberge	10	.05	.01
☐ 576	Mike Flanagan	10	.05	.01
☐ 577	Tim Leary	10	.05	.01
☐ 578	Mike Laga	10	.05	.01
☐ 579	Steve Lyons	10	.05	.01
☐ 580	Phil Niekro	30	.14	.04
☐ 581	Gilberto Reyes	12	.05	.02
☐ 582	Jamie Easterly	10	.05	.01
☐ 583	Mark Gubicza	12	.05	.02
☐ 584	Stan Javier	12	.05	.02
☐ 585	Bill Laskey	10	.05	.01
☐ 586	Jeff Russell	12	.05	.02

☐ 587	Dickie Noles	10	.05	.01
☐ 588	Steve Farr	12	.05	.02
☐ 589	Steve Ontiveros	10	.05	.01
☐ 590	Mike Hargrove	12	.05	.02
☐ 591	Marty Bystrom	10	.05	.01
☐ 592	Franklin Stubbs	10	.05	.01
☐ 593	Larry Herndon	10	.05	.01
☐ 594	Bill Swaggerty	10	.05	.01
☐ 595	Carlos Ponce	10	.05	.01
☐ 596	Pat Perry	10	.05	.01
☐ 597	Ray Knight	12	.05	.02
☐ 598	Steve Lombardozzi	10	.05	.01
☐ 599	Brad Havens	10	.05	.01
☐ 600	Pat Clements	10	.05	.01
☐ 601	Joe Niekro	12	.05	.02
☐ 602	Hank Aaron	15	.07	.02
	Puzzle Card			
☐ 603	Dwayne Henry	10	.05	.01
☐ 604	Mookie Wilson	12	.05	.02
☐ 605	Buddy Biancalana	10	.05	.01
☐ 606	Rance Mulliniks	10	.05	.01
☐ 607	Alan Wiggins	10	.05	.01
☐ 608	Joe Cowley	10	.05	.01
☐ 609A	Tom Seaver	1.00	.45	.13
	(Green borders			
	on name)			
☐ 609B	Tom Seaver	2.50	1.15	.30
	(Yellow borders			
	on name)			
☐ 610	Neil Allen	10	.05	.01
☐ 611	Don Sutton	30	.14	.04
☐ 612	Fred Toliver	10	.05	.01
☐ 613	Jay Baller	10	.05	.01
☐ 614	Marc Sullivan	10	.05	.01
☐ 615	John Grubb	10	.05	.01
☐ 616	Bruce Kison	10	.05	.01
☐ 617	Bill Madlock	12	.05	.02
☐ 618	Chris Chambliss	12	.05	.02
☐ 619	Dave Stewart	20	.09	.03
☐ 620	Tim Lollar	10	.05	.01
☐ 621	Gary Lavelle	10	.05	.01
☐ 622	Charles Hudson	10	.05	.01
☐ 623	Joel Davis	10	.05	.01
☐ 624	Joe Johnson	10	.05	.01
☐ 625	Sid Fernandez	25	.11	.03
☐ 626	Dennis Lamp	10	.05	.01
☐ 627	Terry Harper	10	.05	.01
☐ 628	Jack Lazorko	10	.05	.01
☐ 629	Roger McDowell	25	.11	.03
☐ 630	Mark Funderburk	10	.05	.01
☐ 631	Ed Lynch	10	.05	.01
☐ 632	Rudy Law	10	.05	.01
☐ 633	Roger Mason	20	.09	.03
☐ 634	Mike Felder	25	.11	.03
☐ 635	Ken Schrom	10	.05	.01
☐ 636	Bob Ojeda	10	.05	.01
☐ 637	Ed VandeBerg	10	.05	.01

☐ 638	Bobby Meacham	10	.05	.01
☐ 639	Cliff Johnson	10	.05	.01
☐ 640	Garth Iorg	10	.05	.01
☐ 641	Dan Driessen	10	.05	.01
☐ 642	Mike Brown OF	10	.05	.01
☐ 643	John Shelby	10	.05	.01
☐ 644	Pete Rose	50	.23	.06
	(Ty-Breaking)			
☐ 645	The Knuckle Brothers	10	.05	.01
	Phil Niekro			
	Joe Niekro			
☐ 646	Jesse Orosco	10	.05	.01
☐ 647	Billy Beane	10	.05	.01
☐ 648	Cesar Cedeno	12	.05	.02
☐ 649	Bert Blyleven	20	.09	.03
☐ 650	Max Venable	10	.05	.01
☐ 651	Fleet Feet	30	.14	.04
	Vince Coleman			
	Willie McGee			
☐ 652	Calvin Schiraldi	10	.05	.01
☐ 653	King of Kings	1.00	.45	.13
	(Pete Rose)			
☐ 654	CL: Diamond Kings	15	.02	.00
	(Unnumbered)			
☐ 655A	CL 1: 27-130	15	.02	.00
	(Unnumbered)			
	(45 Beane ERR)			
☐ 655B	CL 1: 27-130	60	.06	.02
	(Unnumbered)			
	(45 Habyan COR)			
☐ 656	CL 2: 131-234	15	.02	.00
	(Unnumbered)			
☐ 657	CL 3: 235-338	15	.02	.00
	(Unnumbered)			
☐ 658	CL 4: 339-442	15	.02	.00
	(Unnumbered)			
☐ 659	CL 5: 443-546	15	.02	.00
	(Unnumbered)			
☐ 660	CL 6: 547-653	15	.02	.00
	(Unnumbered)			

1986 Donruss Rookies

The 1986 Donruss "The Rookies" set features 56 cards plus a 15-piece puzzle of Hank Aaron. Cards are in full color and are standard size, 2 1/2" by 3 1/2". The set was distributed in a small green box with gold lettering. Although the set was wrapped in cellophane, the top card was number 1 Joyner, resulting in a percentage of the Joyner cards arriving in less than perfect condition. Donruss fixed the problem after it was called to their attention and even went so far as to include a customer service phone number in their second printing. Card fronts are similar in design to the 1986 Donruss regular issue except for the presence of "The Rookies" logo in the lower left corner and a bluish green border instead of a blue border. The key (extended) Rookie Cards in this set are Barry Bonds, Bobby Bonilla, Will Clark, Bo Jackson, Wally Joyner, Kevin Mitchell, and Ruben Sierra.

	MT	EX-MT	VG
COMPLETE SET (56)	50.00	23.00	6.25
COMMON PLAYER (1-56)	.10	.05	.01

		MT	EX-MT	VG
☐	1 Wally Joyner	1.75	.80	.22
☐	2 Tracy Jones	.10	.05	.01
☐	3 Allan Anderson	.15	.07	.02
☐	4 Ed Correa	.10	.05	.01
☐	5 Reggie Williams	.10	.05	.01
☐	6 Charlie Kerfeld	.15	.07	.02
☐	7 Andres Galarraga	.30	.14	.04
☐	8 Bob Tewksbury	.90	.40	.11
☐	9 Al Newman	.10	.05	.01
☐	10 Andres Thomas	.10	.05	.01
☐	11 Barry Bonds	13.00	5.75	1.65
☐	12 Juan Nieves	.10	.05	.01
☐	13 Mark Eichhorn	.15	.07	.02
☐	14 Dan Plesac	.20	.09	.03
☐	15 Cory Snyder	.40	.18	.05
☐	16 Kelly Gruber	.90	.40	.11
☐	17 Kevin Mitchell	2.50	1.15	.30
☐	18 Steve Lombardozzi	.10	.05	.01
☐	19 Mitch Williams	.40	.18	.05
☐	20 John Cerutti	.10	.05	.01
☐	21 Todd Worrell	.15	.07	.02
☐	22 Jose Canseco	10.00	4.50	1.25
☐	23 Pete Incaviglia	.40	.18	.05
☐	24 Jose Guzman	.30	.14	.04
☐	25 Scott Bailes	.10	.05	.01
☐	26 Greg Mathews	.10	.05	.01
☐	27 Eric King	.10	.05	.01
☐	28 Paul Assenmacher	.10	.05	.01
☐	29 Jeff Sellers	.10	.05	.01
☐	30 Bobby Bonilla	5.00	2.30	.60
☐	31 Doug Drabek	2.00	.90	.25
☐	32 Will Clark UER	13.00	5.75	1.65
	(Listed as throwing right, should be left)			
☐	33 Bip Roberts	1.25	.55	.16
☐	34 Jim Deshaies	.15	.07	.02
☐	35 Mike LaValliere	.35	.16	.04
☐	36 Scott Bankhead	.15	.07	.02
☐	37 Dale Sveum	.10	.05	.01
☐	38 Bo Jackson	5.00	2.30	.60
☐	39 Robby Thompson	.50	.23	.06
☐	40 Eric Plunk	.10	.05	.01
☐	41 Bill Bathe	.10	.05	.01
☐	42 John Kruk	2.00	.90	.25
☐	43 Andy Allanson	.10	.05	.01
☐	44 Mark Portugal	.20	.09	.03
☐	45 Danny Tartabull	2.00	.90	.25
☐	46 Bob Kipper	.10	.05	.01
☐	47 Gene Walter	.10	.05	.01
☐	48 Rey Quinones UER	.10	.05	.01
	(Misspelled Quinonez)			
☐	49 Bobby Witt	.50	.23	.06
☐	50 Bill Mooneyham	.10	.05	.01
☐	51 John Cangelosi	.10	.05	.01
☐	52 Ruben Sierra	11.00	4.90	1.40
☐	53 Rob Woodward	.10	.05	.01
☐	54 Ed Hearn	.10	.05	.01
☐	55 Joel McKeon	.10	.05	.01
☐	56 Checklist Card	.15	.02	.00

1987 Donruss

This 660-card set was distributed along with a puzzle of Roberto Clemente. The checklist cards are numbered throughout the set as multiples of 100. The wax pack boxes again contain four separate cards printed on the bottom of the box. Cards measure 2 1/2" by 3 1/2" and feature a black and gold border on the front; the backs are also done in black and gold on white card stock. The popular Diamond King subset returns for the sixth consecutive year. Some of the Diamond King (1-26) selections are repeats from prior years; Perez-Steele Galleries has indicated that a five-year rotation will be maintained in order to avoid depleting the pool of available worthy "kings" on some of the teams. Three of the Diamond Kings have a variation (on the reverse) where the yellow strip behind the words "Donruss Diamond Kings" is not printed and, hence, the background is white. The key Rookie Cards in this set are Barry Bonds, Bobby Bonilla, Kevin Brown, Will Clark, David Cone, Chuck Finley, Mike Greenwell, Bo Jackson, Wally Joyner, Barry Larkin, Greg Maddux, Dave Magadan, Kevin Mitchell, Rafael Palmiero, and Ruben Sierra. The backs of the cards in the factory sets are oriented differently than cards taken from wax packs, giving the appearance that one version or the other is upside down when sorting from the card backs.

	MT	EX-MT	VG
COMPLETE SET (660)	60.00	27.00	7.50
COMPLETE FACT.SET (660)	60.00	27.00	7.50
COMMON PLAYER (1-660)	.05	.02	.01

			MT	EX-MT	VG
☐	1	Wally Joyner DK	.30	.14	.04
☐	2	Roger Clemens DK	.90	.40	.11
☐	3	Dale Murphy DK	.15	.07	.02
☐	4	Darryl Strawberry DK	.35	.16	.04
☐	5	Ozzie Smith DK	.20	.09	.03
☐	6	Jose Canseco DK	1.00	.45	.13
☐	7	Charlie Hough DK	.08	.04	.01
☐	8	Brook Jacoby DK	.08	.04	.01
☐	9	Fred Lynn DK	.08	.04	.01
☐	10	Rick Rhoden DK	.08	.04	.01
☐	11	Chris Brown DK	.08	.04	.01
☐	12	Von Hayes DK	.08	.04	.01
☐	13	Jack Morris DK	.15	.07	.02
☐	14A	Kevin McReynolds DK	.50	.23	.06
		ERR (Yellow strip			
		missing on back)			
☐	14B	Kevin McReynolds DK	.08	.04	.01
		COR			
☐	15	George Brett DK	.30	.14	.04
☐	16	Ted Higuera DK	.08	.04	.01
☐	17	Hubie Brooks DK	.08	.04	.01
☐	18	Mike Scott DK	.08	.04	.01
☐	19	Kirby Puckett DK	.75	.35	.09
☐	20	Dave Winfield DK	.30	.14	.04
☐	21	Lloyd Moseby DK	.08	.04	.01
☐	22A	Eric Davis DK ERR	.75	.35	.09
		(Yellow strip			
		missing on back)			
☐	22B	Eric Davis DK COR	.20	.09	.03
☐	23	Jim Presley DK	.08	.04	.01
☐	24	Keith Moreland DK	.08	.04	.01
☐	25A	Greg Walker DK ERR	.50	.23	.06
		(Yellow strip			
		missing on back)			
☐	25B	Greg Walker DK COR	.08	.04	.01
☐	26	Steve Sax DK	.08	.04	.01
☐	27	DK Checklist 1-26	.10	.01	.00
☐	28	B.J. Surhoff RR	.25	.11	.03
☐	29	Randy Myers RR	.35	.16	.04
☐	30	Ken Gerhart RR	.08	.04	.01
☐	31	Benito Santiago RR	.50	.23	.06
☐	32	Greg Swindell RR	1.25	.55	.16
☐	33	Mike Birkbeck RR	.08	.04	.01
☐	34	Terry Steinbach RR	.40	.18	.05
☐	35	Bo Jackson RR	3.00	1.35	.40
☐	36	Greg Maddux RR	6.00	2.70	.75
☐	37	Jim Lindeman RR	.08	.04	.01
☐	38	Devon White RR	1.00	.45	.13
☐	39	Eric Bell RR	.08	.04	.01
☐	40	Willie Fraser RR	.08	.04	.01
☐	41	Jerry Browne RR	.20	.09	.03
☐	42	Chris James RR	.12	.05	.02
☐	43	Rafael Palmeiro RR	4.00	1.80	.50
☐	44	Pat Dodson RR	.08	.04	.01
☐	45	Duane Ward RR	.50	.23	.06
☐	46	Mark McGwire RR	10.00	4.50	1.25
☐	47	Bruce Fields RR UER	.08	.04	.01
		(Photo actually			
		Darnell Coles)			
☐	48	Eddie Murray	.40	.18	.05
☐	49	Ted Higuera	.05	.02	.01
☐	50	Kirk Gibson	.10	.05	.01
☐	51	Oil Can Boyd	.05	.02	.01
☐	52	Don Mattingly	.90	.40	.11
☐	53	Pedro Guerrero	.08	.04	.01
☐	54	George Brett	.75	.35	.09
☐	55	Jose Rijo	.20	.09	.03
☐	56	Tim Raines	.15	.07	.02
☐	57	Ed Correa	.05	.02	.01
☐	58	Mike Witt	.05	.02	.01
☐	59	Greg Walker	.05	.02	.01
☐	60	Ozzie Smith	.40	.18	.05
☐	61	Glenn Davis	.20	.09	.03
☐	62	Glenn Wilson	.05	.02	.01

☐	63	Tom Browning	.08	.04	.01	☐	120	Jim Presley	.05	.02	.01

☐	63	Tom Browning	.08	.04	.01
☐	64	Tony Gwynn	.90	.40	.11
☐	65	R.J. Reynolds	.05	.02	.01
☐	66	Will Clark	8.00	3.60	1.00
☐	67	Ozzie Virgil	.05	.02	.01
☐	68	Rick Sutcliffe	.08	.04	.01
☐	69	Gary Carter	.20	.09	.03
☐	70	Mike Moore	.05	.02	.01
☐	71	Bert Blyleven	.12	.05	.02
☐	72	Tony Fernandez	.12	.05	.02
☐	73	Kent Hrbek	.15	.07	.02
☐	74	Lloyd Moseby	.05	.02	.01
☐	75	Alvin Davis	.05	.02	.01
☐	76	Keith Hernandez	.08	.04	.01
☐	77	Ryne Sandberg	1.25	.55	.16
☐	78	Dale Murphy	.25	.11	.03
☐	79	Sid Bream	.08	.04	.01
☐	80	Chris Brown	.05	.02	.01
☐	81	Steve Garvey	.20	.09	.03
☐	82	Mario Soto	.05	.02	.01
☐	83	Shane Rawley	.05	.02	.01
☐	84	Willie McGee	.08	.04	.01
☐	85	Jose Cruz	.05	.02	.01
☐	86	Brian Downing	.05	.02	.01
☐	87	Ozzie Guillen	.08	.04	.01
☐	88	Hubie Brooks	.05	.02	.01
☐	89	Cal Ripken	1.75	.80	.22
☐	90	Juan Nieves	.05	.02	.01
☐	91	Lance Parrish	.08	.04	.01
☐	92	Jim Rice	.12	.05	.02
☐	93	Ron Guidry	.08	.04	.01
☐	94	Fernando Valenzuela	.08	.04	.01
☐	95	Andy Allanson	.05	.02	.01
☐	96	Willie Wilson	.05	.02	.01
☐	97	Jose Canseco	5.00	2.30	.60
☐	98	Jeff Reardon	.20	.09	.03
☐	99	Bobby Witt	.30	.14	.04
☐	100	Checklist Card	.10	.01	.00
☐	101	Jose Guzman	.08	.04	.01
☐	102	Steve Balboni	.05	.02	.01
☐	103	Tony Phillips	.08	.04	.01
☐	104	Brook Jacoby	.05	.02	.01
☐	105	Dave Winfield	.60	.25	.08
☐	106	Orel Hershiser	.20	.09	.03
☐	107	Lou Whitaker	.15	.07	.02
☐	108	Fred Lynn	.08	.04	.01
☐	109	Bill Wegman	.05	.02	.01
☐	110	Donnie Moore	.05	.02	.01
☐	111	Jack Clark	.08	.04	.01
☐	112	Bob Knepper	.05	.02	.01
☐	113	Von Hayes	.05	.02	.01
☐	114	Bip Roberts	.75	.35	.09
☐	115	Tony Pena	.05	.02	.01
☐	116	Scott Garrelts	.05	.02	.01
☐	117	Paul Molitor	.25	.11	.03
☐	118	Darryl Strawberry	.75	.35	.09
☐	119	Shawon Dunston	.08	.04	.01

☐	120	Jim Presley	.05	.02	.01
☐	121	Jesse Barfield	.08	.04	.01
☐	122	Gary Gaetti	.05	.02	.01
☐	123	Kurt Stillwell	.15	.07	.02
☐	124	Joel Davis	.05	.02	.01
☐	125	Mike Boddicker	.05	.02	.01
☐	126	Robin Yount	.75	.35	.09
☐	127	Alan Trammell	.15	.07	.02
☐	128	Dave Righetti	.08	.04	.01
☐	129	Dwight Evans	.10	.05	.01
☐	130	Mike Scioscia	.05	.02	.01
☐	131	Julio Franco	.25	.11	.03
☐	132	Bret Saberhagen	.25	.11	.03
☐	133	Mike Davis	.05	.02	.01
☐	134	Joe Hesketh	.05	.02	.01
☐	135	Wally Joyner	1.25	.55	.16
☐	136	Don Slaught	.05	.02	.01
☐	137	Daryl Boston	.05	.02	.01
☐	138	Nolan Ryan	2.00	.90	.25
☐	139	Mike Schmidt	1.00	.45	.13
☐	140	Tommy Herr	.05	.02	.01
☐	141	Garry Templeton	.05	.02	.01
☐	142	Kal Daniels	.10	.05	.01
☐	143	Billy Sample	.05	.02	.01
☐	144	Johnny Ray	.05	.02	.01
☐	145	Rob Thompson	.30	.14	.04
☐	146	Bob Dernier	.05	.02	.01
☐	147	Danny Tartabull	.40	.18	.05
☐	148	Ernie Whitt	.05	.02	.01
☐	149	Kirby Puckett	2.00	.90	.25
☐	150	Mike Young	.05	.02	.01
☐	151	Ernest Riles	.05	.02	.01
☐	152	Frank Tanana	.05	.02	.01
☐	153	Rich Gedman	.05	.02	.01
☐	154	Willie Randolph	.08	.04	.01
☐	155	Bill Madlock	.08	.04	.01
☐	156	Joe Carter	.90	.40	.11
☐	157	Danny Jackson	.05	.02	.01
☐	158	Carney Lansford	.08	.04	.01
☐	159	Bryn Smith	.05	.02	.01
☐	160	Gary Pettis	.05	.02	.01
☐	161	Oddibe McDowell	.05	.02	.01
☐	162	John Cangelosi	.05	.02	.01
☐	163	Mike Scott	.08	.04	.01
☐	164	Eric Show	.05	.02	.01
☐	165	Juan Samuel	.05	.02	.01
☐	166	Nick Esasky	.05	.02	.01
☐	167	Zane Smith	.08	.04	.01
☐	168	Mike C. Brown OF	.05	.02	.01
☐	169	Keith Moreland	.05	.02	.01
☐	170	John Tudor	.08	.04	.01
☐	171	Ken Dixon	.05	.02	.01
☐	172	Jim Gantner	.05	.02	.01
☐	173	Jack Morris	.30	.14	.04
☐	174	Bruce Hurst	.08	.04	.01
☐	175	Dennis Rasmussen	.05	.02	.01
☐	176	Mike Marshall	.05	.02	.01

☐	177	Dan Quisenberry	.08	.04	.01			
☐	178	Eric Plunk	.05	.02	.01			
☐	179	Tim Wallach	.08	.04	.01			
☐	180	Steve Buechele	.08	.04	.01			
☐	181	Don Sutton	.15	.07	.02			
☐	182	Dave Schmidt	.05	.02	.01			
☐	183	Terry Pendleton	.40	.18	.05			
☐	184	Jim Deshaies	.12	.05	.02			
☐	185	Steve Bedrosian	.05	.02	.01			
☐	186	Pete Rose	.40	.18	.05			
☐	187	Dave Dravecky	.08	.04	.01			
☐	188	Rick Reuschel	.05	.02	.01			
☐	189	Dan Gladden	.05	.02	.01			
☐	190	Rick Mahler	.05	.02	.01			
☐	191	Thad Bosley	.05	.02	.01			
☐	192	Ron Darling	.08	.04	.01			
☐	193	Matt Young	.05	.02	.01			
☐	194	Tom Brunansky	.08	.04	.01			
☐	195	Dave Stieb	.08	.04	.01			
☐	196	Frank Viola	.15	.07	.02			
☐	197	Tom Henke	.08	.04	.01			
☐	198	Karl Best	.05	.02	.01			
☐	199	Dwight Gooden	.35	.16	.04			
☐	200	Checklist Card	.10	.01	.00			
☐	201	Steve Trout	.05	.02	.01			
☐	202	Rafael Ramirez	.05	.02	.01			
☐	203	Bob Walk	.05	.02	.01			
☐	204	Roger Mason	.08	.04	.01			
☐	205	Terry Kennedy	.05	.02	.01			
☐	206	Ron Oester	.05	.02	.01			
☐	207	John Russell	.05	.02	.01			
☐	208	Charlie Kerfeld	.05	.02	.01			
☐	209	Charlie Kerfeld	.05	.02	.01			
☐	210	Reggie Jackson	.40	.18	.05			
☐	211	Floyd Bannister	.05	.02	.01			
☐	212	Vance Law	.05	.02	.01			
☐	213	Rich Bordi	.05	.02	.01			
☐	214	Dan Plesac	.15	.07	.02			
☐	215	Dave Collins	.05	.02	.01			
☐	216	Bob Stanley	.05	.02	.01			
☐	217	Joe Niekro	.08	.04	.01			
☐	218	Tom Niedenfuer	.05	.02	.01			
☐	219	Brett Butler	.15	.07	.02			
☐	220	Charlie Leibrandt	.08	.04	.01			
☐	221	Steve Ontiveros	.05	.02	.01			
☐	222	Tim Burke	.05	.02	.01			
☐	223	Curtis Wilkerson	.05	.02	.01			
☐	224	Pete Incaviglia	.25	.11	.03			
☐	225	Lonnie Smith	.05	.02	.01			
☐	226	Chris Codiroli	.05	.02	.01			
☐	227	Scott Bailes	.05	.02	.01			
☐	228	Rickey Henderson	.75	.35	.09			
☐	229	Ken Howell	.05	.02	.01			
☐	230	Darnell Coles	.05	.02	.01			
☐	231	Don Aase	.05	.02	.01			
☐	232	Tim Leary	.05	.02	.01			
☐	233	Bob Boone	.08	.04	.01			
☐	234	Ricky Horton	.05	.02	.01			
☐	235	Mark Bailey	.05	.02	.01			
☐	236	Kevin Gross	.05	.02	.01			
☐	237	Lance McCullers	.05	.02	.01			
☐	238	Cecilio Guante	.05	.02	.01			
☐	239	Bob Melvin	.05	.02	.01			
☐	240	Billy Joe Robidoux	.05	.02	.01			
☐	241	Roger McDowell	.05	.02	.01			
☐	242	Leon Durham	.05	.02	.01			
☐	243	Ed Nunez	.05	.02	.01			
☐	244	Jimmy Key	.08	.04	.01			
☐	245	Mike Smithson	.05	.02	.01			
☐	246	Bo Diaz	.05	.02	.01			
☐	247	Carlton Fisk	.40	.18	.05			
☐	248	Larry Sheets	.05	.02	.01			
☐	249	Juan Castillo	.05	.02	.01			
☐	250	Eric King	.05	.02	.01			
☐	251	Doug Drabek	1.25	.55	.16			
☐	252	Wade Boggs	.75	.35	.09			
☐	253	Mariano Duncan	.05	.02	.01			
☐	254	Pat Tabler	.05	.02	.01			
☐	255	Frank White	.05	.02	.01			
☐	256	Alfredo Griffin	.05	.02	.01			
☐	257	Floyd Youmans	.05	.02	.01			
☐	258	Rob Wilfong	.05	.02	.01			
☐	259	Pete O'Brien	.05	.02	.01			
☐	260	Tim Hulett	.05	.02	.01			
☐	261	Dickie Thon	.05	.02	.01			
☐	262	Darren Daulton	.30	.14	.04			
☐	263	Vince Coleman	.20	.09	.03			
☐	264	Andy Hawkins	.05	.02	.01			
☐	265	Eric Davis	.35	.16	.04			
☐	266	Andres Thomas	.05	.02	.01			
☐	267	Mike Diaz	.05	.02	.01			
☐	268	Chili Davis	.08	.04	.01			
☐	269	Jody Davis	.05	.02	.01			
☐	270	Phil Bradley	.05	.02	.01			
☐	271	George Bell	.25	.11	.03			
☐	272	Keith Atherton	.05	.02	.01			
☐	273	Storm Davis	.05	.02	.01			
☐	274	Rob Deer	.25	.11	.03			
☐	275	Walt Terrell	.05	.02	.01			
☐	276	Roger Clemens	2.00	.90	.25			
☐	277	Mike Easler	.05	.02	.01			
☐	278	Steve Sax	.12	.05	.02			
☐	279	Andre Thornton	.05	.02	.01			
☐	280	Jim Sundberg	.05	.02	.01			
☐	281	Bill Bathe	.05	.02	.01			
☐	282	Jay Tibbs	.05	.02	.01			
☐	283	Dick Schofield	.05	.02	.01			
☐	284	Mike Mason	.05	.02	.01			
☐	285	Jerry Hairston	.05	.02	.01			
☐	286	Bill Doran	.05	.02	.01			
☐	287	Tim Flannery	.05	.02	.01			
☐	288	Gary Redus	.05	.02	.01			
☐	289	John Franco	.10	.05	.01			
☐	290	Paul Assenmacher	.05	.02	.01			

☐ 291 Joe Orsulak	.05	.02	.01		
☐ 292 Lee Smith	.25	.11	.03		
☐ 293 Mike Laga	.05	.02	.01		
☐ 294 Rick Dempsey	.05	.02	.01		
☐ 295 Mike Felder	.05	.02	.01		
☐ 296 Tom Brookens	.05	.02	.01		
☐ 297 Al Nipper	.05	.02	.01		
☐ 298 Mike Pagliarulo	.05	.02	.01		
☐ 299 Franklin Stubbs	.05	.02	.01		
☐ 300 Checklist Card	.10	.01	.00		
☐ 301 Steve Farr	.08	.04	.01		
☐ 302 Bill Mooneyham	.05	.02	.01		
☐ 303 Andres Galarraga	.08	.04	.01		
☐ 304 Scott Fletcher	.05	.02	.01		
☐ 305 Jack Howell	.05	.02	.01		
☐ 306 Russ Morman	.05	.02	.01		
☐ 307 Todd Worrell	.08	.04	.01		
☐ 308 Dave Smith	.05	.02	.01		
☐ 309 Jeff Stone	.05	.02	.01		
☐ 310 Ron Robinson	.05	.02	.01*		
☐ 311 Bruce Bochy	.05	.02	.01		
☐ 312 Jim Winn	.05	.02	.01		
☐ 313 Mark Davis	.05	.02	.01		
☐ 314 Jeff Dedmon	.05	.02	.01		
☐ 315 Jamie Moyer	.05	.02	.01		
☐ 316 Wally Backman	.05	.02	.01		
☐ 317 Ken Phelps	.05	.02	.01		
☐ 318 Steve Lombardozzi	.05	.02	.01		
☐ 319 Rance Mulliniks	.05	.02	.01		
☐ 320 Tim Laudner	.05	.02	.01		
☐ 321 Mark Eichhorn	.08	.04	.01		
☐ 322 Lee Guetterman	.05	.02	.01		
☐ 323 Sid Fernandez	.08	.04	.01		
☐ 324 Jerry Mumphrey	.05	.02	.01		
☐ 325 David Palmer	.05	.02	.01		
☐ 326 Bill Almon	.05	.02	.01		
☐ 327 Candy Maldonado	.08	.04	.01		
☐ 328 John Kruk	1.25	.55	.16		
☐ 329 John Denny	.05	.02	.01		
☐ 330 Milt Thompson	.08	.04	.01		
☐ 331 Mike LaValliere	.25	.11	.03		
☐ 332 Alan Ashby	.05	.02	.01		
☐ 333 Doug Corbett	.05	.02	.01		
☐ 334 Ron Karkovice	.08	.04	.01		
☐ 335 Mitch Webster	.05	.02	.01		
☐ 336 Lee Lacy	.05	.02	.01		
☐ 337 Glenn Braggs	.15	.07	.02		
☐ 338 Dwight Lowry	.05	.02	.01		
☐ 339 Don Baylor	.08	.04	.01		
☐ 340 Brian Fisher	.05	.02	.01		
☐ 341 Reggie Williams	.05	.02	.01		
☐ 342 Tom Candiotti	.08	.04	.01		
☐ 343 Rudy Law	.05	.02	.01		
☐ 344 Curt Young	.05	.02	.01		
☐ 345 Mike Fitzgerald	.05	.02	.01		
☐ 346 Ruben Sierra	6.00	2.70	.75		
☐ 347 Mitch Williams	.30	.14	.04		
☐ 348 Jorge Orta	.05	.02	.01		
☐ 349 Mickey Tettleton	.25	.11	.03		
☐ 350 Ernie Camacho	.05	.02	.01		
☐ 351 Ron Kittle	.05	.02	.01		
☐ 352 Ken Landreaux	.05	.02	.01		
☐ 353 Chet Lemon	.05	.02	.01		
☐ 354 John Shelby	.05	.02	.01		
☐ 355 Mark Clear	.05	.02	.01		
☐ 356 Doug DeCinces	.05	.02	.01		
☐ 357 Ken Dayley	.05	.02	.01		
☐ 358 Phil Garner	.08	.04	.01		
☐ 359 Steve Jeltz	.05	.02	.01		
☐ 360 Ed Whitson	.05	.02	.01		
☐ 361 Barry Bonds	8.00	3.60	1.00		
☐ 362 Vida Blue	.08	.04	.01		
☐ 363 Cecil Cooper	.08	.04	.01		
☐ 364 Bob Ojeda	.05	.02	.01		
☐ 365 Dennis Eckersley	.30	.14	.04		
☐ 366 Mike Morgan	.08	.04	.01		
☐ 367 Willie Upshaw	.05	.02	.01		
☐ 368 Allan Anderson	.05	.02	.01		
☐ 369 Bill Gullickson	.08	.04	.01		
☐ 370 Bobby Thigpen	.50	.23	.06		
☐ 371 Juan Beniquez	.05	.02	.01		
☐ 372 Charlie Moore	.05	.02	.01		
☐ 373 Dan Petry	.05	.02	.01		
☐ 374 Rod Scurry	.05	.02	.01		
☐ 375 Tom Seaver	.40	.18	.05		
☐ 376 Ed VandeBerg	.05	.02	.01		
☐ 377 Tony Bernazard	.05	.02	.01		
☐ 378 Greg Pryor	.05	.02	.01		
☐ 379 Dwayne Murphy	.05	.02	.01		
☐ 380 Andy McGaffigan	.05	.02	.01		
☐ 381 Kirk McCaskill	.05	.02	.01		
☐ 382 Greg Harris	.05	.02	.01		
☐ 383 Rich Dotson	.05	.02	.01		
☐ 384 Craig Reynolds	.05	.02	.01		
☐ 385 Greg Gross	.05	.02	.01		
☐ 386 Tito Landrum	.05	.02	.01		
☐ 387 Craig Lefferts	.08	.04	.01		
☐ 388 Dave Parker	.12	.05	.02		
☐ 389 Bob Horner	.08	.04	.01		
☐ 390 Pat Clements	.05	.02	.01		
☐ 391 Jeff Leonard	.05	.02	.01		
☐ 392 Chris Speier	.05	.02	.01		
☐ 393 John Moses	.05	.02	.01		
☐ 394 Garth Iorg	.05	.02	.01		
☐ 395 Greg Gagne	.08	.04	.01		
☐ 396 Nate Snell	.05	.02	.01		
☐ 397 Bryan Clutterbuck	.05	.02	.01		
☐ 398 Darrell Evans	.08	.04	.01		
☐ 399 Steve Crawford	.05	.02	.01		
☐ 400 Checklist Card	.10	.01	.00		
☐ 401 Phil Lombardi	.05	.02	.01		
☐ 402 Rick Honeycutt	.05	.02	.01		
☐ 403 Ken Schrom	.05	.02	.01		
☐ 404 Bud Black	.05	.02	.01		

☐ 405	Donnie Hill	.05	.02	.01
☐ 406	Wayne Krenchicki	.05	.02	.01
☐ 407	Chuck Finley	.50	.23	.06
☐ 408	Toby Harrah	.05	.02	.01
☐ 409	Steve Lyons	.05	.02	.01
☐ 410	Kevin Bass	.05	.02	.01
☐ 411	Marvell Wynne	.05	.02	.01
☐ 412	Ron Roenicke	.05	.02	.01
☐ 413	Tracy Jones	.05	.02	.01
☐ 414	Gene Garber	.05	.02	.01
☐ 415	Mike Bielecki	.05	.02	.01
☐ 416	Frank DiPino	.05	.02	.01
☐ 417	Andy Van Slyke	.30	.14	.04
☐ 418	Jim Dwyer	.05	.02	.01
☐ 419	Ben Oglivie	.05	.02	.01
☐ 420	Dave Bergman	.05	.02	.01
☐ 421	Joe Sambito	.05	.02	.01
☐ 422	Bob Tewksbury	.50	.23	.06
☐ 423	Len Matuszek	.05	.02	.01
☐ 424	Mike Kingery	.05	.02	.01
☐ 425	Dave Kingman	.08	.04	.01
☐ 426	Al Newman	.05	.02	.01
☐ 427	Gary Ward	.05	.02	.01
☐ 428	Ruppert Jones	.05	.02	.01
☐ 429	Harold Baines	.12	.05	.02
☐ 430	Pat Perry	.05	.02	.01
☐ 431	Terry Puhl	.05	.02	.01
☐ 432	Don Carman	.05	.02	.01
☐ 433	Eddie Milner	.05	.02	.01
☐ 434	LaMarr Hoyt	.05	.02	.01
☐ 435	Rick Rhoden	.05	.02	.01
☐ 436	Jose Uribe	.05	.02	.01
☐ 437	Ken Oberkfell	.05	.02	.01
☐ 438	Ron Davis	.05	.02	.01
☐ 439	Jesse Orosco	.05	.02	.01
☐ 440	Scott Bradley	.05	.02	.01
☐ 441	Randy Bush	.05	.02	.01
☐ 442	John Cerutti	.05	.02	.01
☐ 443	Roy Smalley	.05	.02	.01
☐ 444	Kelly Gruber	.60	.25	.08
☐ 445	Bob Kearney	.05	.02	.01
☐ 446	Ed Hearn	.05	.02	.01
☐ 447	Scott Sanderson	.05	.02	.01
☐ 448	Bruce Benedict	.05	.02	.01
☐ 449	Junior Ortiz	.05	.02	.01
☐ 450	Mike Aldrete	.05	.02	.01
☐ 451	Kevin McReynolds	.08	.04	.01
☐ 452	Rob Murphy	.05	.02	.01
☐ 453	Kent Tekulve	.05	.02	.01
☐ 454	Curt Ford	.05	.02	.01
☐ 455	Dave Lopes	.08	.04	.01
☐ 456	Bob Grich	.08	.04	.01
☐ 457	Jose DeLeon	.05	.02	.01
☐ 458	Andre Dawson	.50	.23	.06
☐ 459	Mike Flanagan	.05	.02	.01
☐ 460	Joey Meyer	.05	.02	.01
☐ 461	Chuck Cary	.05	.02	.01
☐ 462	Bill Buckner	.08	.04	.01
☐ 463	Bob Shirley	.05	.02	.01
☐ 464	Jeff Hamilton	.05	.02	.01
☐ 465	Phil Niekro	.15	.07	.02
☐ 466	Mark Gubicza	.05	.02	.01
☐ 467	Jerry Willard	.05	.02	.01
☐ 468	Bob Sebra	.05	.02	.01
☐ 469	Larry Parrish	.05	.02	.01
☐ 470	Charlie Hough	.05	.02	.01
☐ 471	Hal McRae	.08	.04	.01
☐ 472	Dave Leiper	.05	.02	.01
☐ 473	Mel Hall	.08	.04	.01
☐ 474	Dan Pasqua	.08	.04	.01
☐ 475	Bob Welch	.08	.04	.01
☐ 476	Johnny Grubb	.05	.02	.01
☐ 477	Jim Traber	.05	.02	.01
☐ 478	Chris Bosio	.40	.18	.05
☐ 479	Mark McLemore	.05	.02	.01
☐ 480	John Morris	.05	.02	.01
☐ 481	Billy Hatcher	.08	.04	.01
☐ 482	Dan Schatzeder	.05	.02	.01
☐ 483	Rich Gossage	.10	.05	.01
☐ 484	Jim Morrison	.05	.02	.01
☐ 485	Bob Brenly	.05	.02	.01
☐ 486	Bill Schroeder	.05	.02	.01
☐ 487	Mookie Wilson	.08	.04	.01
☐ 488	Dave Martinez	.30	.14	.04
☐ 489	Harold Reynolds	.05	.02	.01
☐ 490	Jeff Hearron	.05	.02	.01
☐ 491	Mickey Hatcher	.05	.02	.01
☐ 492	Barry Larkin	3.50	1.55	.45
☐ 493	Bob James	.05	.02	.01
☐ 494	John Habyan	.05	.02	.01
☐ 495	Jim Adduci	.05	.02	.01
☐ 496	Mike Heath	.05	.02	.01
☐ 497	Tim Stoddard	.05	.02	.01
☐ 498	Tony Armas	.05	.02	.01
☐ 499	Dennis Powell	.05	.02	.01
☐ 500	Checklist Card	.10	.01	.00
☐ 501	Chris Bando	.05	.02	.01
☐ 502	David Cone	3.50	1.55	.45
☐ 503	Jay Howell	.08	.04	.01
☐ 504	Tom Foley	.05	.02	.01
☐ 505	Ray Chadwick	.05	.02	.01
☐ 506	Mike Loynd	.05	.02	.01
☐ 507	Neil Allen	.05	.02	.01
☐ 508	Danny Darwin	.05	.02	.01
☐ 509	Rick Schu	.05	.02	.01
☐ 510	Jose Oquendo	.05	.02	.01
☐ 511	Gene Walter	.05	.02	.01
☐ 512	Terry McGriff	.05	.02	.01
☐ 513	Ken Griffey	.08	.04	.01
☐ 514	Benny Distefano	.05	.02	.01
☐ 515	Terry Mulholland	.50	.23	.06
☐ 516	Ed Lynch	.05	.02	.01
☐ 517	Bill Swift	.12	.05	.02
☐ 518	Manny Lee	.08	.04	.01

☐	519	Andre David	.05	.02	.01			
☐	520	Scott McGregor	.05	.02	.01			
☐	521	Rick Manning	.05	.02	.01			
☐	522	Willie Hernandez	.05	.02	.01			
☐	523	Marty Barrett	.05	.02	.01			
☐	524	Wayne Tolleson	.05	.02	.01			
☐	525	Jose Gonzalez	.05	.02	.01			
☐	526	Cory Snyder	.15	.07	.02			
☐	527	Buddy Biancalana	.05	.02	.01			
☐	528	Moose Haas	.05	.02	.01			
☐	529	Wilfredo Tejada	.05	.02	.01			
☐	530	Stu Cliburn	.05	.02	.01			
☐	531	Dale Mohorcic	.05	.02	.01			
☐	532	Ron Hassey	.05	.02	.01			
☐	533	Ty Gainey	.05	.02	.01			
☐	534	Jerry Royster	.05	.02	.01			
☐	535	Mike Maddux	.05	.02	.01			
☐	536	Ted Power	.05	.02	.01			
☐	537	Ted Simmons	.08	.04	.01			
☐	538	Rafael Belliard	.20	.09	.03			
☐	539	Chico Walker	.08	.04	.01			
☐	540	Bob Forsch	.05	.02	.01			
☐	541	John Stefero	.05	.02	.01			
☐	542	Dale Sveum	.05	.02	.01			
☐	543	Mark Thurmond	.05	.02	.01			
☐	544	Jeff Sellers	.05	.02	.01			
☐	545	Joel Skinner	.05	.02	.01			
☐	546	Alex Trevino	.05	.02	.01			
☐	547	Randy Kutcher	.05	.02	.01			
☐	548	Joaquin Andujar	.05	.02	.01			
☐	549	Casey Candaele	.05	.02	.01			
☐	550	Jeff Russell	.08	.04	.01			
☐	551	John Candelaria	.05	.02	.01			
☐	552	Joe Cowley	.05	.02	.01			
☐	553	Danny Cox	.05	.02	.01			
☐	554	Denny Walling	.05	.02	.01			
☐	555	Bruce Ruffin	.05	.02	.01			
☐	556	Buddy Bell	.08	.04	.01			
☐	557	Jimmy Jones	.20	.09	.03			
☐	558	Bobby Bonilla	3.00	1.35	.40			
☐	559	Jeff D. Robinson	.05	.02	.01			
☐	560	Ed Olwine	.05	.02	.01			
☐	561	Glenallen Hill	.30	.14	.04			
☐	562	Lee Mazzilli	.05	.02	.01			
☐	563	Mike G. Brown P	.05	.02	.01			
☐	564	George Frazier	.05	.02	.01			
☐	565	Mike Sharperson	.15	.07	.02			
☐	566	Mark Portugal	.15	.07	.02			
☐	567	Rick Leach	.05	.02	.01			
☐	568	Mark Langston	.20	.09	.03			
☐	569	Rafael Santana	.05	.02	.01			
☐	570	Manny Trillo	.05	.02	.01			
☐	571	Cliff Speck	.05	.02	.01			
☐	572	Bob Kipper	.05	.02	.01			
☐	573	Kelly Downs	.10	.05	.01			
☐	574	Randy Asadoor	.05	.02	.01			
☐	575	Dave Magadan	.30	.14	.04			
☐	576	Marvin Freeman	.05	.02	.01			
☐	577	Jeff Lahti	.05	.02	.01			
☐	578	Jeff Calhoun	.05	.02	.01			
☐	579	Gus Polidor	.05	.02	.01			
☐	580	Gene Nelson	.05	.02	.01			
☐	581	Tim Teufel	.05	.02	.01			
☐	582	Odell Jones	.05	.02	.01			
☐	583	Mark Ryal	.05	.02	.01			
☐	584	Randy O'Neal	.05	.02	.01			
☐	585	Mike Greenwell	1.00	.45	.13			
☐	586	Ray Knight	.08	.04	.01			
☐	587	Ralph Bryant	.08	.04	.01			
☐	588	Carmen Castillo	.05	.02	.01			
☐	589	Ed Wojna	.05	.02	.01			
☐	590	Stan Javier	.08	.04	.01			
☐	591	Jeff Musselman	.05	.02	.01			
☐	592	Mike Stanley	.05	.02	.01			
☐	593	Darrell Porter	.05	.02	.01			
☐	594	Drew Hall	.05	.02	.01			
☐	595	Rob Nelson	.05	.02	.01			
☐	596	Bryan Oelkers	.05	.02	.01			
☐	597	Scott Nielsen	.05	.02	.01			
☐	598	Brian Holton	.05	.02	.01			
☐	599	Kevin Mitchell	1.50	.65	.19			
☐	600	Checklist Card	.10	.01	.00			
☐	601	Jackie Gutierrez	.05	.02	.01			
☐	602	Barry Jones	.08	.04	.01			
☐	603	Jerry Narron	.05	.02	.01			
☐	604	Steve Lake	.05	.02	.01			
☐	605	Jim Pankovits	.05	.02	.01			
☐	606	Ed Romero	.05	.02	.01			
☐	607	Dave LaPoint	.05	.02	.01			
☐	608	Don Robinson	.05	.02	.01			
☐	609	Mike Krukow	.05	.02	.01			
☐	610	Dave Valle	.05	.02	.01			
☐	611	Len Dykstra	.25	.11	.03			
☐	612	Roberto Clemente PUZ	.15	.07	.02			
☐	613	Mike Trujillo	.05	.02	.01			
☐	614	Damaso Garcia	.05	.02	.01			
☐	615	Neal Heaton	.05	.02	.01			
☐	616	Juan Berenguer	.05	.02	.01			
☐	617	Steve Carlton	.40	.18	.05			
☐	618	Gary Lucas	.05	.02	.01			
☐	619	Geno Petralli	.05	.02	.01			
☐	620	Rick Aguilera	.25	.11	.03			
☐	621	Fred McGriff	3.50	1.55	.45			
☐	622	Dave Henderson	.08	.04	.01			
☐	623	Dave Clark	.05	.02	.01			
☐	624	Angel Salazar	.05	.02	.01			
☐	625	Randy Hunt	.05	.02	.01			
☐	626	John Gibbons	.05	.02	.01			
☐	627	Kevin Brown	2.25	1.00	.30			
☐	628	Bill Dawley	.05	.02	.01			
☐	629	Aurelio Lopez	.05	.02	.01			
☐	630	Charles Hudson	.05	.02	.01			
☐	631	Ray Soff	.05	.02	.01			
☐	632	Ray Hayward	.05	.02	.01			

□	633	Spike Owen	.05	.02	.01
□	634	Glenn Hubbard	.05	.02	.01
□	635	Kevin Elster	.10	.05	.01
□	636	Mike LaCoss	.05	.02	.01
□	637	Dwayne Henry	.05	.02	.01
□	638	Rey Quinones	.05	.02	.01
□	639	Jim Clancy	.05	.02	.01
□	640	Larry Andersen	.05	.02	.01
□	641	Calvin Schiraldi	.05	.02	.01
□	642	Stan Jefferson	.05	.02	.01
□	643	Marc Sullivan	.05	.02	.01
□	644	Mark Grant	.05	.02	.01
□	645	Cliff Johnson	.05	.02	.01
□	646	Howard Johnson	.25	.11	.03
□	647	Dave Sax	.05	.02	.01
□	648	Dave Stewart	.12	.05	.02
□	649	Danny Heep	.05	.02	.01
□	650	Joe Johnson	.05	.02	.01
□	651	Bob Brower	.05	.02	.01
□	652	Rob Woodward	.05	.02	.01
□	653	John Mizerock	.05	.02	.01
□	654	Tim Pyznarski	.05	.02	.01
□	655	Luis Aquino	.05	.02	.01
□	656	Mickey Brantley	.05	.02	.01
□	657	Doyle Alexander	.05	.02	.01
□	658	Sammy Stewart	.05	.02	.01
□	659	Jim Acker	.05	.02	.01
□	660	Pete Ladd	.05	.02	.01

1987 Donruss Rookies

The 1987 Donruss "The Rookies" set features 56 cards plus a 15-piece puzzle of Roberto Clemente. Cards are in full color and are standard size, 2 1/2" by 3 1/2". The set was distributed in a small green

and black box with gold lettering. Card fronts are similar in design to the 1987 Donruss regular issue except for the presence of "The Rookies" logo in the lower left corner and a green border instead of a black border. The key (extended) Rookie Cards in this set are Ellis Burks, Shane Mack, John Smiley, and Matt Williams.

			MT	EX-MT	VG
	COMPLETE SET (56)		20.00	9.00	2.50
	COMMON PLAYER (1-56)		.08	.04	.01

□	1	Mark McGwire	6.00	2.70	.75
□	2	Eric Bell	.08	.04	.01
□	3	Mark Williamson	.08	.04	.01
□	4	Mike Greenwell	.75	.35	.09
□	5	Ellis Burks	.75	.35	.09
□	6	DeWayne Buice	.08	.04	.01
□	7	Mark McLemore	.08	.04	.01
□	8	Devon White	.40	.18	.05
□	9	Willie Fraser	.08	.04	.01
□	10	Les Lancaster	.08	.04	.01
□	11	Ken Williams	.08	.04	.01
□	12	Matt Nokes	.40	.18	.05
□	13	Jeff M. Robinson	.12	.05	.02
□	14	Bo Jackson	2.00	.90	.25
□	15	Kevin Seitzer	.40	.18	.05
□	16	Billy Ripken	.15	.07	.02
□	17	B.J. Surhoff	.12	.05	.02
□	18	Chuck Crim	.08	.04	.01
□	19	Mike Birkbeck	.08	.04	.01
□	20	Chris Bosio	.25	.11	.03
□	21	Les Straker	.08	.04	.01
□	22	Mark Davidson	.08	.04	.01
□	23	Gene Larkin	.20	.09	.03
□	24	Ken Gerhart	.08	.04	.01
□	25	Luis Polonia	.75	.35	.09
□	26	Terry Steinbach	.25	.11	.03
□	27	Mickey Brantley	.08	.04	.01
□	28	Mike Stanley	.08	.04	.01
□	29	Jerry Browne	.12	.05	.02
□	30	Todd Benzinger	.15	.07	.02
□	31	Fred McGriff	3.50	1.55	.45
□	32	Mike Henneman	.30	.14	.04
□	33	Casey Candaele	.08	.04	.01
□	34	Dave Magadan	.15	.07	.02
□	35	David Cone	2.50	1.15	.30
□	36	Mike Jackson	.20	.09	.03
□	37	John Mitchell	.08	.04	.01
□	38	Mike Dunne	.08	.04	.01
□	39	John Smiley	1.00	.45	.13
□	40	Joe Magrane	.15	.07	.02
□	41	Jim Lindeman	.08	.04	.01
□	42	Shane Mack	1.50	.65	.19
□	43	Stan Jefferson	.08	.04	.01
□	44	Benito Santiago	.40	.18	.05

			MT	EX-MT	VG
☐	45	Matt Williams	2.50	1.15	.30
☐	46	Dave Meads	.08	.04	.01
☐	47	Rafael Palmeiro	2.50	1.15	.30
☐	48	Bill Long	.08	.04	.01
☐	49	Bob Brower	.08	.04	.01
☐	50	James Steels	.08	.04	.01
☐	51	Paul Noce	.08	.04	.01
☐	52	Greg Maddux	4.00	1.80	.50
☐	53	Jeff Musselman	.08	.04	.01
☐	54	Brian Holton	.08	.04	.01
☐	55	Chuck Jackson	.08	.04	.01
☐	56	Checklist Card	.08	.01	.00

1988 Donruss

This 660-card set was distributed along with a puzzle of Stan Musial. The six regular checklist cards are numbered throughout the set as multiples of 100. Cards measure 2 1/2" by 3 1/2" and feature a distinctive black and blue border on the front. The popular Diamond King subset returns for the seventh consecutive year. Rated Rookies are featured again as cards 28-47. Cards marked as SP (short printed) from 648-660 are more difficult to find than the other 13 SP's in the lower 600s. These 26 cards listed as SP were apparently pulled from the printing sheet to make room for the 26 Bonus MVP cards. Numbered with the prefix "BC" for bonus card, this 26-card set featuring the most valuable player from each of the 26 teams was randomly inserted in the wax and rack packs. The cards are distinguished by the MVP logo in the upper left corner of the obverse, and cards BC14-BC26 are considered to be more difficult to find than

cards BC1-BC13. Six of the checklist cards were done two different ways to reflect the inclusion or exclusion of the Bonus MVP cards in the wax packs. In the checklist below, the A variations (for the checklist cards) are from the wax packs and the B variations are from the factory-collated sets. The key Rookie Cards in this set are Roberto Alomar, Ellis Burks, Ron Gant, Tom Glavine, Mark Grace, Gregg Jefferies, Roberto Kelly, Jack McDowell, and Matt Williams. There was also a Kirby Puckett card issued as the package back of Donruss blister packs; it uses a different photo from both of Kirby's regular and Bonus MVP cards and is unnumbered on the back. The design pattern of the factory set card fronts is oriented differently from that of the regular wax pack cards.

	MT	EX-MT	VG
COMPLETE SET (660)	20.00	9.00	2.50
COMPLETE FACT.SET (660)	20.00	9.00	2.50
COMMON PLAYER (1-647)	.04	.02	.01
COMMON PLAYER SP (648-660)	.07	.03	.01
COMPLETE MVP SET (26)	3.50	1.55	.45
COMMON MVP (BC1-BC13)	.05	.02	.01
COMMON MVP SP (BC14-BC26)	.08	.04	.01

			MT	EX-MT	VG
☐	1	Mark McGwire DK	.40	.18	.05
☐	2	Tim Raines DK	.08	.04	.01
☐	3	Benito Santiago DK	.08	.04	.01
☐	4	Alan Trammell DK	.08	.04	.01
☐	5	Danny Tartabull DK	.10	.05	.01
☐	6	Ron Darling DK	.05	.02	.01
☐	7	Paul Molitor DK	.08	.04	.01
☐	8	Devon White DK	.08	.04	.01
☐	9	Andre Dawson DK	.10	.05	.01
☐	10	Julio Franco DK	.05	.02	.01
☐	11	Scott Fletcher DK	.05	.02	.01
☐	12	Tony Fernandez DK	.05	.02	.01
☐	13	Shane Rawley DK	.05	.02	.01
☐	14	Kal Daniels DK	.05	.02	.01
☐	15	Jack Clark DK	.05	.02	.01
☐	16	Dwight Evans DK	.05	.02	.01
☐	17	Tommy John DK	.05	.02	.01
☐	18	Andy Van Slyke DK	.08	.04	.01
☐	19	Gary Gaetti DK	.05	.02	.01
☐	20	Mark Langston DK	.05	.02	.01
☐	21	Will Clark DK	.30	.14	.04
☐	22	Glenn Hubbard DK	.05	.02	.01
☐	23	Billy Hatcher DK	.05	.02	.01
☐	24	Bob Welch DK	.05	.02	.01
☐	25	Ivan Calderon DK	.05	.02	.01
☐	26	Cal Ripken DK	.30	.14	.04
☐	27	DK Checklist 1-26	.06	.01	.00
☐	28	Mackey Sasser RR	.10	.05	.01

☐ 29	Jeff Treadway RR	10	.05	.01
☐ 30	Mike Campbell RR	06	.03	.01
☐ 31	Lance Johnson RR	20	.09	.03
☐ 32	Nelson Liriano RR	06	.03	.01
☐ 33	Shawn Abner RR	06	.03	.01
☐ 34	Roberto Alomar RR	5.00	2.30	.60
☐ 35	Shawn Hillegas RR	06	.03	.01
☐ 36	Joey Meyer RR	06	.03	.01
☐ 37	Kevin Elster RR	06	.03	.01
☐ 38	Jose Lind RR	15	.07	.02
☐ 39	Kirt Manwaring RR	10	.05	.01
☐ 40	Mark Grace RR	1.25	.55	.16
☐ 41	Jody Reed RR	25	.11	.03
☐ 42	John Farrell RR	06	.03	.01
☐ 43	Al Leiter RR	06	.03	.01
☐ 44	Gary Thurman RR	06	.03	.01
☐ 45	Vicente Palacios RR	10	.05	.01
☐ 46	Eddie Williams RR	06	.03	.01
☐ 47	Jack McDowell RR	1.25	.55	.16
☐ 48	Ken Dixon	04	.02	.01
☐ 49	Mike Birkbeck	04	.02	.01
☐ 50	Eric King	04	.02	.01
☐ 51	Roger Clemens	50	.23	.06
☐ 52	Pat Clements	04	.02	.01
☐ 53	Fernando Valenzuela	07	.03	.01
☐ 54	Mark Gubicza	04	.02	.01
☐ 55	Jay Howell	04	.02	.01
☐ 56	Floyd Youmans	04	.02	.01
☐ 57	Ed Correa	04	.02	.01
☐ 58	DeWayne Buice	04	.02	.01
☐ 59	Jose DeLeon	04	.02	.01
☐ 60	Danny Cox	04	.02	.01
☐ 61	Nolan Ryan	75	.35	.09
☐ 62	Steve Bedrosian	04	.02	.01
☐ 63	Tom Browning	04	.02	.01
☐ 64	Mark Davis	04	.02	.01
☐ 65	R.J. Reynolds	04	.02	.01
☐ 66	Kevin Mitchell	15	.07	.02
☐ 67	Ken Oberkfell	04	.02	.01
☐ 68	Rick Sutcliffe	07	.03	.01
☐ 69	Dwight Gooden	12	.05	.02
☐ 70	Scott Bankhead	04	.02	.01
☐ 71	Bert Blyleven	07	.03	.01
☐ 72	Jimmy Key	07	.03	.01
☐ 73	Les Straker	04	.02	.01
☐ 74	Jim Clancy	04	.02	.01
☐ 75	Mike Moore	04	.02	.01
☐ 76	Ron Darling	07	.03	.01
☐ 77	Ed Lynch	04	.02	.01
☐ 78	Dale Murphy	10	.05	.01
☐ 79	Doug Drabek	10	.05	.01
☐ 80	Scott Garrelts	04	.02	.01
☐ 81	Ed Whitson	04	.02	.01
☐ 82	Rob Murphy	04	.02	.01
☐ 83	Shane Rawley	04	.02	.01
☐ 84	Greg Mathews	04	.02	.01
☐ 85	Jim Deshaies	04	.02	.01
☐ 86	Mike Witt	04	.02	.01
☐ 87	Donnie Hill	04	.02	.01
☐ 88	Jeff Reed	04	.02	.01
☐ 89	Mike Boddicker	04	.02	.01
☐ 90	Ted Higuera	04	.02	.01
☐ 91	Walt Terrell	04	.02	.01
☐ 92	Bob Stanley	04	.02	.01
☐ 93	Dave Righetti	04	.02	.01
☐ 94	Orel Hershiser	07	.03	.01
☐ 95	Chris Bando	04	.02	.01
☐ 96	Bret Saberhagen	10	.05	.01
☐ 97	Curt Young	04	.02	.01
☐ 98	Tim Burke	04	.02	.01
☐ 99	Charlie Hough	04	.02	.01
☐ 100A	Checklist 28-137	06	.01	.00
☐ 100B	Checklist 28-133	06	.01	.00
☐ 101	Bobby Witt	07	.03	.01
☐ 102	George Brett	25	.11	.03
☐ 103	Mickey Tettleton	12	.05	.02
☐ 104	Scott Bailes	04	.02	.01
☐ 105	Mike Pagliarulo	04	.02	.01
☐ 106	Mike Scioscia	04	.02	.01
☐ 107	Tom Brookens	04	.02	.01
☐ 108	Ray Knight	07	.03	.01
☐ 109	Dan Plesac	04	.02	.01
☐ 110	Wally Joyner	12	.05	.02
☐ 111	Bob Forsch	04	.02	.01
☐ 112	Mike Scott	07	.03	.01
☐ 113	Kevin Gross	04	.02	.01
☐ 114	Benito Santiago	10	.05	.01
☐ 115	Bob Kipper	04	.02	.01
☐ 116	Mike Krukow	04	.02	.01
☐ 117	Chris Bosio	07	.03	.01
☐ 118	Sid Fernandez	07	.03	.01
☐ 119	Jody Davis	04	.02	.01
☐ 120	Mike Morgan	07	.03	.01
☐ 121	Mark Eichhorn	04	.02	.01
☐ 122	Jeff Reardon	12	.05	.02
☐ 123	John Franco	04	.02	.01
☐ 124	Richard Dotson	04	.02	.01
☐ 125	Eric Bell	04	.02	.01
☐ 126	Juan Nieves	04	.02	.01
☐ 127	Jack Morris	12	.05	.02
☐ 128	Rick Rhoden	04	.02	.01
☐ 129	Rich Gedman	04	.02	.01
☐ 130	Ken Howell	04	.02	.01
☐ 131	Brook Jacoby	04	.02	.01
☐ 132	Danny Jackson	04	.02	.01
☐ 133	Gene Nelson	04	.02	.01
☐ 134	Neal Heaton	04	.02	.01
☐ 135	Willie Fraser	04	.02	.01
☐ 136	Jose Guzman	07	.03	.01
☐ 137	Ozzie Guillen	07	.03	.01
☐ 138	Bob Knepper	04	.02	.01
☐ 139	Mike Jackson	10	.05	.01
☐ 140	Joe Magrane	10	.05	.01
☐ 141	Jimmy Jones	04	.02	.01

☐	142	Ted Power	.04	.02	.01	☐	199	Gary Carter	.10	.05	.01
☐	143	Ozzie Virgil	.04	.02	.01	☐	200A	Checklist 138-247	.06	.01	.00
☐	144	Felix Fermin	.04	.02	.01	☐	200B	Checklist 134-239	.06	.01	.00
☐	145	Kelly Downs	.04	.02	.01	☐	201	Keith Moreland	.04	.02	.01
☐	146	Shawon Dunston	.07	.03	.01	☐	202	Ken Griffey	.07	.03	.01
☐	147	Scott Bradley	.04	.02	.01	☐	203	Tommy Gregg	.04	.02	.01
☐	148	Dave Stieb	.07	.03	.01	☐	204	Will Clark	.60	.25	.08
☐	149	Frank Viola	.07	.03	.01	☐	205	John Kruk	.15	.07	.02
☐	150	Terry Kennedy	.04	.02	.01	☐	206	Buddy Bell	.07	.03	.01
☐	151	Bill Wegman	.04	.02	.01	☐	207	Von Hayes	.04	.02	.01
☐	152	Matt Nokes	.20	.09	.03	☐	208	Tommy Herr	.04	.02	.01
☐	153	Wade Boggs	.30	.14	.04	☐	209	Craig Reynolds	.04	.02	.01
☐	154	Wayne Tolleson	.04	.02	.01	☐	210	Gary Pettis	.04	.02	.01
☐	155	Mariano Duncan	.04	.02	.01	☐	211	Harold Baines	.07	.03	.01
☐	156	Julio Franco	.10	.05	.01	☐	212	Vance Law	.04	.02	.01
☐	157	Charlie Leibrandt	.04	.02	.01	☐	213	Ken Gerhart	.04	.02	.01
☐	158	Terry Steinbach	.07	.03	.01	☐	214	Jim Gantner	.04	.02	.01
☐	159	Mike Fitzgerald	.04	.02	.01	☐	215	Chet Lemon	.04	.02	.01
☐	160	Jack Lazorko	.04	.02	.01	☐	216	Dwight Evans	.07	.03	.01
☐	161	Mitch Williams	.07	.03	.01	☐	217	Don Mattingly	.30	.14	.04
☐	162	Greg Walker	.04	.02	.01	☐	218	Franklin Stubbs	.04	.02	.01
☐	163	Alan Ashby	.04	.02	.01	☐	219	Pat Tabler	.04	.02	.01
☐	164	Tony Gwynn	.30	.14	.04	☐	220	Bo Jackson	.30	.14	.04
☐	165	Bruce Ruffin	.04	.02	.01	☐	221	Tony Phillips	.04	.02	.01
☐	166	Ron Robinson	.04	.02	.01	☐	222	Tim Wallach	.07	.03	.01
☐	167	Zane Smith	.04	.02	.01	☐	223	Ruben Sierra	.40	.18	.05
☐	168	Junior Ortiz	.04	.02	.01	☐	224	Steve Buechele	.04	.02	.01
☐	169	Jamie Moyer	.04	.02	.01	☐	225	Frank White	.04	.02	.01
☐	170	Tony Pena	.04	.02	.01	☐	226	Alfredo Griffin	.04	.02	.01
☐	171	Cal Ripken	.60	.25	.08	☐	227	Greg Swindell	.15	.07	.02
☐	172	B.J. Surhoff	.07	.03	.01	☐	228	Willie Randolph	.07	.03	.01
☐	173	Lou Whitaker	.07	.03	.01	☐	229	Mike Marshall	.04	.02	.01
☐	174	Ellis Burks	.25	.11	.03	☐	230	Alan Trammell	.07	.03	.01
☐	175	Ron Guidry	.07	.03	.01	☐	231	Eddie Murray	.20	.09	.03
☐	176	Steve Sax	.07	.03	.01	☐	232	Dale Sveum	.04	.02	.01
☐	177	Danny Tartabull	.15	.07	.02	☐	233	Dick Schofield	.04	.02	.01
☐	178	Carney Lansford	.07	.03	.01	☐	234	Jose Oquendo	.04	.02	.01
☐	179	Casey Candaele	.04	.02	.01	☐	235	Bill Doran	.04	.02	.01
☐	180	Scott Fletcher	.04	.02	.01	☐	236	Milt Thompson	.04	.02	.01
☐	181	Mark McLemore	.04	.02	.01	☐	237	Marvell Wynne	.04	.02	.01
☐	182	Ivan Calderon	.07	.03	.01	☐	238	Bobby Bonilla	.25	.11	.03
☐	183	Jack Clark	.07	.03	.01	☐	239	Chris Speier	.04	.02	.01
☐	184	Glenn Davis	.07	.03	.01	☐	240	Glenn Braggs	.04	.02	.01
☐	185	Luis Aguayo	.04	.02	.01	☐	241	Wally Backman	.04	.02	.01
☐	186	Bo Diaz	.04	.02	.01	☐	242	Ryne Sandberg	.50	.23	.06
☐	187	Stan Jefferson	.04	.02	.01	☐	243	Phil Bradley	.04	.02	.01
☐	188	Sid Bream	.07	.03	.01	☐	244	Kelly Gruber	.07	.03	.01
☐	189	Bob Brenly	.04	.02	.01	☐	245	Tom Brunansky	.07	.03	.01
☐	190	Dion James	.04	.02	.01	☐	246	Ron Oester	.04	.02	.01
☐	191	Leon Durham	.04	.02	.01	☐	247	Bobby Thigpen	.07	.03	.01
☐	192	Jesse Orosco	.04	.02	.01	☐	248	Fred Lynn	.07	.03	.01
☐	193	Alvin Davis	.04	.02	.01	☐	249	Paul Molitor	.12	.05	.02
☐	194	Gary Gaetti	.04	.02	.01	☐	250	Darrell Evans	.07	.03	.01
☐	195	Fred McGriff	.40	.18	.05	☐	251	Gary Ward	.04	.02	.01
☐	196	Steve Lombardozzi	.04	.02	.01	☐	252	Bruce Hurst	.07	.03	.01
☐	197	Rance Mulliniks	.04	.02	.01	☐	253	Bob Welch	.07	.03	.01
☐	198	Rey Quinones	.04	.02	.01	☐	254	Joe Carter	.25	.11	.03

☐	255	Willie Wilson	.04	.02	.01			
☐	256	Mark McGwire	.50	.23	.06			
☐	257	Mitch Webster	.04	.02	.01			
☐	258	Brian Downing	.04	.02	.01			
☐	259	Mike Stanley	.04	.02	.01			
☐	260	Carlton Fisk	.20	.09	.03			
☐	261	Billy Hatcher	.04	.02	.01			
☐	262	Glenn Wilson	.04	.02	.01			
☐	263	Ozzie Smith	.20	.09	.03			
☐	264	Randy Ready	.04	.02	.01			
☐	265	Kurt Stillwell	.04	.02	.01			
☐	266	David Palmer	.04	.02	.01			
☐	267	Mike Diaz	.04	.02	.01			
☐	268	Robby Thompson	.07	.03	.01			
☐	269	Andre Dawson	.20	.09	.03			
☐	270	Lee Guetterman	.04	.02	.01			
☐	271	Willie Upshaw	.04	.02	.01			
☐	272	Randy Bush	.04	.02	.01			
☐	273	Larry Sheets	.04	.02	.01			
☐	274	Rob Deer	.07	.03	.01			
☐	275	Kirk Gibson	.07	.03	.01			
☐	276	Marty Barrett	.04	.02	.01			
☐	277	Rickey Henderson	.30	.14	.04			
☐	278	Pedro Guerrero	.07	.03	.01			
☐	279	Brett Butler	.10	.05	.01			
☐	280	Kevin Seitzer	.07	.03	.01			
☐	281	Mike Davis	.04	.02	.01			
☐	282	Andres Galarraga	.04	.02	.01			
☐	283	Devon White	.10	.05	.01			
☐	284	Pete O'Brien	.04	.02	.01			
☐	285	Jerry Hairston	.04	.02	.01			
☐	286	Kevin Bass	.04	.02	.01			
☐	287	Carmelo Martinez	.04	.02	.01			
☐	288	Juan Samuel	.04	.02	.01			
☐	289	Kal Daniels	.07	.03	.01			
☐	290	Albert Hall	.04	.02	.01			
☐	291	Andy Van Slyke	.10	.05	.01			
☐	292	Lee Smith	.15	.07	.02			
☐	293	Vince Coleman	.07	.03	.01			
☐	294	Tom Niedenfuer	.04	.02	.01			
☐	295	Robin Yount	.25	.11	.03			
☐	296	Jeff M. Robinson	.04	.02	.01			
☐	297	Todd Benzinger	.10	.05	.01			
☐	298	Dave Winfield	.20	.09	.03			
☐	299	Mickey Hatcher	.04	.02	.01			
☐	300A	Checklist 248-357	.06	.01	.00			
☐	300B	Checklist 240-345	.06	.01	.00			
☐	301	Bud Black	.04	.02	.01			
☐	302	Jose Canseco	.60	.25	.08			
☐	303	Tom Foley	.04	.02	.01			
☐	304	Pete Incaviglia	.07	.03	.01			
☐	305	Bob Boone	.07	.03	.01			
☐	306	Bill Long	.04	.02	.01			
☐	307	Willie McGee	.07	.03	.01			
☐	308	Ken Caminiti	.30	.14	.04			
☐	309	Darren Daulton	.07	.03	.01			
☐	310	Tracy Jones	.04	.02	.01			
☐	311	Greg Booker	.04	.02	.01			
☐	312	Mike LaValliere	.04	.02	.01			
☐	313	Chili Davis	.07	.03	.01			
☐	314	Glenn Hubbard	.04	.02	.01			
☐	315	Paul Noce	.04	.02	.01			
☐	316	Keith Hernandez	.07	.03	.01			
☐	317	Mark Langston	.07	.03	.01			
☐	318	Keith Atherton	.04	.02	.01			
☐	319	Tony Fernandez	.07	.03	.01			
☐	320	Kent Hrbek	.07	.03	.01			
☐	321	John Cerutti	.04	.02	.01			
☐	322	Mike Kingery	.04	.02	.01			
☐	323	Dave Magadan	.07	.03	.01			
☐	324	Rafael Palmeiro	.30	.14	.04			
☐	325	Jeff Dedmon	.04	.02	.01			
☐	326	Barry Bonds	.60	.25	.08			
☐	327	Jeffrey Leonard	.04	.02	.01			
☐	328	Tim Flannery	.04	.02	.01			
☐	329	Dave Concepcion	.07	.03	.01			
☐	330	Mike Schmidt	.40	.18	.05			
☐	331	Bill Dawley	.04	.02	.01			
☐	332	Larry Andersen	.04	.02	.01			
☐	333	Jack Howell	.04	.02	.01			
☐	334	Ken Williams	.04	.02	.01			
☐	335	Bryn Smith	.04	.02	.01			
☐	336	Billy Ripken	.10	.05	.01			
☐	337	Greg Brock	.04	.02	.01			
☐	338	Mike Heath	.04	.02	.01			
☐	339	Mike Greenwell	.10	.05	.01			
☐	340	Claudell Washington	.04	.02	.01			
☐	341	Jose Gonzalez	.04	.02	.01			
☐	342	Mel Hall	.04	.02	.01			
☐	343	Jim Eisenreich	.04	.02	.01			
☐	344	Tony Bernazard	.04	.02	.01			
☐	345	Tim Raines	.07	.03	.01			
☐	346	Bob Brower	.04	.02	.01			
☐	347	Larry Parrish	.04	.02	.01			
☐	348	Thad Bosley	.04	.02	.01			
☐	349	Dennis Eckersley	.15	.07	.02			
☐	350	Cory Snyder	.07	.03	.01			
☐	351	Rick Cerone	.04	.02	.01			
☐	352	John Shelby	.04	.02	.01			
☐	353	Larry Herndon	.04	.02	.01			
☐	354	John Habyan	.04	.02	.01			
☐	355	Chuck Crim	.04	.02	.01			
☐	356	Gus Polidor	.04	.02	.01			
☐	357	Ken Dayley	.04	.02	.01			
☐	358	Danny Darwin	.04	.02	.01			
☐	359	Lance Parrish	.07	.03	.01			
☐	360	James Steels	.04	.02	.01			
☐	361	Al Pedrique	.04	.02	.01			
☐	362	Mike Aldrete	.04	.02	.01			
☐	363	Juan Castillo	.04	.02	.01			
☐	364	Len Dykstra	.07	.03	.01			
☐	365	Luis Quinones	.04	.02	.01			
☐	366	Jim Presley	.04	.02	.01			
☐	367	Lloyd Moseby	.04	.02	.01			

☐ 368	Kirby Puckett	.40	.18	.05
☐ 369	Eric Davis	.10	.05	.01
☐ 370	Gary Redus	.04	.02	.01
☐ 371	Dave Schmidt	.04	.02	.01
☐ 372	Mark Clear	.04	.02	.01
☐ 373	Dave Bergman	.04	.02	.01
☐ 374	Charles Hudson	.04	.02	.01
☐ 375	Calvin Schiraldi	.04	.02	.01
☐ 376	Alex Trevino	.04	.02	.01
☐ 377	Tom Candiotti	.04	.02	.01
☐ 378	Steve Farr	.04	.02	.01
☐ 379	Mike Gallego	.04	.02	.01
☐ 380	Andy McGaffigan	.04	.02	.01
☐ 381	Kirk McCaskill	.04	.02	.01
☐ 382	Oddibe McDowell	.04	.02	.01
☐ 383	Floyd Bannister	.04	.02	.01
☐ 384	Denny Walling	.04	.02	.01
☐ 385	Don Carman	.04	.02	.01
☐ 386	Todd Worrell	.07	.03	.01
☐ 387	Eric Show	.04	.02	.01
☐ 388	Dave Parker	.07	.03	.01
☐ 389	Rick Mahler	.04	.02	.01
☐ 390	Mike Dunne	.04	.02	.01
☐ 391	Candy Maldonado	.04	.02	.01
☐ 392	Bob Dernier	.04	.02	.01
☐ 393	Dave Valle	.04	.02	.01
☐ 394	Ernie Whitt	.04	.02	.01
☐ 395	Juan Berenguer	.04	.02	.01
☐ 396	Mike Young	.04	.02	.01
☐ 397	Mike Felder	.04	.02	.01
☐ 398	Willie Hernandez	.04	.02	.01
☐ 399	Jim Rice	.07	.03	.01
☐ 400A	Checklist 358-467	.06	.01	.00
☐ 400B	Checklist 346-451	.06	.01	.00
☐ 401	Tommy John	.07	.03	.01
☐ 402	Brian Holton	.04	.02	.01
☐ 403	Carmen Castillo	.04	.02	.01
☐ 404	Jamie Quirk	.04	.02	.01
☐ 405	Dwayne Murphy	.04	.02	.01
☐ 406	Jeff Parrett	.04	.02	.01
☐ 407	Don Sutton	.10	.05	.01
☐ 408	Jerry Browne	.04	.02	.01
☐ 409	Jim Winn	.04	.02	.01
☐ 410	Dave Smith	.04	.02	.01
☐ 411	Shane Mack	.25	.11	.03
☐ 412	Greg Gross	.04	.02	.01
☐ 413	Nick Esasky	.04	.02	.01
☐ 414	Damaso Garcia	.04	.02	.01
☐ 415	Brian Fisher	.04	.02	.01
☐ 416	Brian Dayett	.04	.02	.01
☐ 417	Curt Ford	.04	.02	.01
☐ 418	Mark Williamson	.04	.02	.01
☐ 419	Bill Schroeder	.04	.02	.01
☐ 420	Mike Henneman	.15	.07	.02
☐ 421	John Marzano	.04	.02	.01
☐ 422	Ron Kittle	.04	.02	.01
☐ 423	Matt Young	.04	.02	.01
☐ 424	Steve Balboni	.04	.02	.01
☐ 425	Luis Polonia	.25	.11	.03
☐ 426	Randy St.Claire	.04	.02	.01
☐ 427	Greg Harris	.04	.02	.01
☐ 428	Johnny Ray	.04	.02	.01
☐ 429	Ray Searage	.04	.02	.01
☐ 430	Ricky Horton	.04	.02	.01
☐ 431	Gerald Young	.04	.02	.01
☐ 432	Rick Schu	.04	.02	.01
☐ 433	Paul O'Neill	.10	.05	.01
☐ 434	Rich Gossage	.07	.03	.01
☐ 435	John Cangelosi	.04	.02	.01
☐ 436	Mike LaCoss	.04	.02	.01
☐ 437	Gerald Perry	.04	.02	.01
☐ 438	Dave Martinez	.07	.03	.01
☐ 439	Darryl Strawberry	.30	.14	.04
☐ 440	John Moses	.04	.02	.01
☐ 441	Greg Gagne	.04	.02	.01
☐ 442	Jesse Barfield	.04	.02	.01
☐ 443	George Frazier	.04	.02	.01
☐ 444	Garth Iorg	.04	.02	.01
☐ 445	Ed Nunez	.04	.02	.01
☐ 446	Rick Aguilera	.07	.03	.01
☐ 447	Jerry Mumphrey	.04	.02	.01
☐ 448	Rafael Ramirez	.04	.02	.01
☐ 449	John Smiley	.40	.18	.05
☐ 450	Atlee Hammaker	.04	.02	.01
☐ 451	Lance McCullers	.04	.02	.01
☐ 452	Guy Hoffman	.04	.02	.01
☐ 453	Chris James	.04	.02	.01
☐ 454	Terry Pendleton	.15	.07	.02
☐ 455	Dave Meads	.04	.02	.01
☐ 456	Bill Buckner	.07	.03	.01
☐ 457	John Pawlowski	.04	.02	.01
☐ 458	Bob Sebra	.04	.02	.01
☐ 459	Jim Dwyer	.04	.02	.01
☐ 460	Jay Aldrich	.04	.02	.01
☐ 461	Frank Tanana	.04	.02	.01
☐ 462	Oil Can Boyd	.04	.02	.01
☐ 463	Dan Pasqua	.04	.02	.01
☐ 464	Tim Crews	.04	.02	.01
☐ 465	Andy Allanson	.04	.02	.01
☐ 466	Bill Pecota	.10	.05	.01
☐ 467	Steve Ontiveros	.04	.02	.01
☐ 468	Hubie Brooks	.04	.02	.01
☐ 469	Paul Kilgus	.04	.02	.01
☐ 470	Dale Mohorcic	.04	.02	.01
☐ 471	Dan Quisenberry	.07	.03	.01
☐ 472	Dave Stewart	.07	.03	.01
☐ 473	Dave Clark	.04	.02	.01
☐ 474	Joel Skinner	.04	.02	.01
☐ 475	Dave Anderson	.04	.02	.01
☐ 476	Dan Petry	.04	.02	.01
☐ 477	Carl Nichols	.04	.02	.01
☐ 478	Ernest Riles	.04	.02	.01
☐ 479	George Hendrick	.04	.02	.01
☐ 480	John Morris	.04	.02	.01

☐ 481	Manny Hernandez	.04	.02	.01
☐ 482	Jeff Stone	.04	.02	.01
☐ 483	Chris Brown	.04	.02	.01
☐ 484	Mike Bielecki	.04	.02	.01
☐ 485	Dave Dravecky	.07	.03	.01
☐ 486	Rick Manning	.04	.02	.01
☐ 487	Bill Almon	.04	.02	.01
☐ 488	Jim Sundberg	.04	.02	.01
☐ 489	Ken Phelps	.04	.02	.01
☐ 490	Tom Henke	.07	.03	.01
☐ 491	Dan Gladden	.04	.02	.01
☐ 492	Barry Larkin	.25	.11	.03
☐ 493	Fred Manrique	.04	.02	.01
☐ 494	Mike Griffin	.04	.02	.01
☐ 495	Mark Knudson	.04	.02	.01
☐ 496	Bill Madlock	.07	.03	.01
☐ 497	Tim Stoddard	.04	.02	.01
☐ 498	Sam Horn	.12	.05	.02
☐ 499	Tracy Woodson	.10	.05	.01
☐ 500A	Checklist 468-577	.06	.01	.00
☐ 500B	Checklist 452-557	.06	.01	.00
☐ 501	Ken Schrom	.04	.02	.01
☐ 502	Angel Salazar	.04	.02	.01
☐ 503	Eric Plunk	.04	.02	.01
☐ 504	Joe Hesketh	.04	.02	.01
☐ 505	Greg Minton	.04	.02	.01
☐ 506	Geno Petralli	.04	.02	.01
☐ 507	Bob James	.04	.02	.01
☐ 508	Robbie Wine	.04	.02	.01
☐ 509	Jeff Calhoun	.04	.02	.01
☐ 510	Steve Lake	.04	.02	.01
☐ 511	Mark Grant	.04	.02	.01
☐ 512	Frank Williams	.04	.02	.01
☐ 513	Jeff Blauser	.25	.11	.03
☐ 514	Bob Walk	.04	.02	.01
☐ 515	Craig Lefferts	.04	.02	.01
☐ 516	Manny Trillo	.04	.02	.01
☐ 517	Jerry Reed	.04	.02	.01
☐ 518	Rick Leach	.04	.02	.01
☐ 519	Mark Davidson	.04	.02	.01
☐ 520	Jeff Ballard	.04	.02	.01
☐ 521	Dave Stapleton	.04	.02	.01
☐ 522	Pat Sheridan	.04	.02	.01
☐ 523	Al Nipper	.04	.02	.01
☐ 524	Steve Trout	.04	.02	.01
☐ 525	Jeff Hamilton	.04	.02	.01
☐ 526	Tommy Hinzo	.04	.02	.01
☐ 527	Lonnie Smith	.04	.02	.01
☐ 528	Greg Cadaret UER	.04	.02	.01
☐ 529	Bob McClure UER	.04	.02	.01
	("Rob" on front)			
☐ 530	Chuck Finley	.07	.03	.01
☐ 531	Jeff Russell	.04	.02	.01
☐ 532	Steve Lyons	.04	.02	.01
☐ 533	Terry Puhl	.04	.02	.01
☐ 534	Eric Nolte	.04	.02	.01
☐ 535	Kent Tekulve	.04	.02	.01
☐ 536	Pat Pacillo	.04	.02	.01
☐ 537	Charlie Puleo	.04	.02	.01
☐ 538	Tom Prince	.04	.02	.01
☐ 539	Greg Maddux	.40	.18	.05
☐ 540	Jim Lindeman	.04	.02	.01
☐ 541	Pete Stanicek	.04	.02	.01
☐ 542	Steve Kiefer	.04	.02	.01
☐ 543A	Jim Morrison ERR	.30	.14	.04
	(No decimal before			
	lifetime average)			
☐ 543B	Jim Morrison COR	.04	.02	.01
☐ 544	Spike Owen	.04	.02	.01
☐ 545	Jay Buhner	.40	.18	.05
☐ 546	Mike Devereaux	.90	.40	.11
☐ 547	Jerry Don Gleaton	.04	.02	.01
☐ 548	Jose Rijo	.10	.05	.01
☐ 549	Dennis Martinez	.07	.03	.01
☐ 550	Mike Loynd	.04	.02	.01
☐ 551	Darrell Miller	.04	.02	.01
☐ 552	Dave LaPoint	.04	.02	.01
☐ 553	John Tudor	.04	.02	.01
☐ 554	Rocky Childress	.04	.02	.01
☐ 555	Wally Ritchie	.04	.02	.01
☐ 556	Terry McGriff	.04	.02	.01
☐ 557	Dave Leiper	.04	.02	.01
☐ 558	Jeff D. Robinson	.04	.02	.01
☐ 559	Jose Uribe	.04	.02	.01
☐ 560	Ted Simmons	.07	.03	.01
☐ 561	Les Lancaster	.04	.02	.01
☐ 562	Keith A. Miller	.20	.09	.03
☐ 563	Harold Reynolds	.04	.02	.01
☐ 564	Gene Larkin	.10	.05	.01
☐ 565	Cecil Fielder	.30	.14	.04
☐ 566	Roy Smalley	.04	.02	.01
☐ 567	Duane Ward	.04	.02	.01
☐ 568	Bill Wilkinson	.04	.02	.01
☐ 569	Howard Johnson	.10	.05	.01
☐ 570	Frank DiPino	.04	.02	.01
☐ 571	Pete Smith	.40	.18	.05
☐ 572	Darnell Coles	.04	.02	.01
☐ 573	Don Robinson	.04	.02	.01
☐ 574	Rob Nelson UER	.04	.02	.01
	(Career 0 RBI,			
	but 1 RBI in '87)			
☐ 575	Dennis Rasmussen	.04	.02	.01
☐ 576	Steve Jeltz UER	.04	.02	.01
	(Photo actually Juan			
	Samuel; Samuel noted			
	for one batting glove			
	and black bat)			
☐ 577	Tom Pagnozzi	.25	.11	.03
☐ 578	Ty Gainey	.04	.02	.01
☐ 579	Gary Lucas	.04	.02	.01
☐ 580	Ron Hassey	.04	.02	.01
☐ 581	Herm Winningham	.04	.02	.01
☐ 582	Rene Gonzales	.12	.05	.02
☐ 583	Brad Komminsk	.04	.02	.01

☐ 584	Doyle Alexander	.04	.02	.01
☐ 585	Jeff Sellers	.04	.02	.01
☐ 586	Bill Gullickson	.04	.02	.01
☐ 587	Tim Belcher	.12	.05	.02
☐ 588	Doug Jones	.25	.11	.03
☐ 589	Melido Perez	.40	.18	.05
☐ 590	Rick Honeycutt	.04	.02	.01
☐ 591	Pascual Perez	.04	.02	.01
☐ 592	Curt Wilkerson	.04	.02	.01
☐ 593	Steve Howe	.04	.02	.01
☐ 594	John Davis	.04	.02	.01
☐ 595	Storm Davis	.04	.02	.01
☐ 596	Sammy Stewart	.04	.02	.01
☐ 597	Neil Allen	.04	.02	.01
☐ 598	Alejandro Pena	.04	.02	.01
☐ 599	Mark Thurmond	.04	.02	.01
☐ 600A	Checklist 578-BC26	.06	.01	.00
☐ 600B	Checklist 558-660	.06	.01	.00
☐ 601	Jose Mesa	.10	.05	.01
☐ 602	Don August	.04	.02	.01
☐ 603	Terry Leach SP	.07	.03	.01
☐ 604	Tom Newell	.04	.02	.01
☐ 605	Randall Byers SP	.07	.03	.01
☐ 606	Jim Gott	.04	.02	.01
☐ 607	Harry Spilman	.04	.02	.01
☐ 608	John Candelaria	.04	.02	.01
☐ 609	Mike Brumley	.04	.02	.01
☐ 610	Mickey Brantley	.04	.02	.01
☐ 611	Jose Nunez SP	.04	.02	.01
☐ 612	Tom Nieto	.04	.02	.01
☐ 613	Rick Reuschel	.04	.02	.01
☐ 614	Lee Mazzilli SP	.07	.03	.01
☐ 615	Scott Lusader	.04	.02	.01
☐ 616	Bobby Meacham	.04	.02	.01
☐ 617	Kevin McReynolds SP	.10	.05	.01
☐ 618	Gene Garber	.04	.02	.01
☐ 619	Barry Lyons SP	.07	.03	.01
☐ 620	Randy Myers	.07	.03	.01
☐ 621	Donnie Moore	.04	.02	.01
☐ 622	Domingo Ramos	.04	.02	.01
☐ 623	Ed Romero	.04	.02	.01
☐ 624	Greg Myers	.10	.05	.01
☐ 625	Ripken Family	.25	.11	.03
	Cal Ripken Sr.			
	Cal Ripken Jr.			
	Billy Ripken			
☐ 626	Pat Perry	.04	.02	.01
☐ 627	Andres Thomas	.07	.03	.01
☐ 628	Matt Williams SP	1.00	.45	.13
☐ 629	Dave Hengel	.04	.02	.01
☐ 630	Jeff Musselman SP	.07	.03	.01
☐ 631	Tim Laudner	.04	.02	.01
☐ 632	Bob Ojeda SP	.04	.02	.01
☐ 633	Rafael Santana	.04	.02	.01
☐ 634	Wes Gardner	.04	.02	.01
☐ 635	Roberto Kelly SP	1.00	.45	.13
☐ 636	Mike Flanagan SP	.07	.03	.01

☐ 637	Jay Bell	.30	.14	.04
☐ 638	Bob Melvin	.04	.02	.01
☐ 639	Damon Berryhill UER	.15	.07	.02
	(Bats: Switch)			
☐ 640	David Wells SP	.15	.07	.02
☐ 641	Stan Musial PUZ	.10	.05	.01
☐ 642	Doug Sisk	.04	.02	.01
☐ 643	Keith Hughes	.04	.02	.01
☐ 644	Tom Glavine	2.25	1.00	.30
☐ 645	Al Newman	.04	.02	.01
☐ 646	Scott Sanderson	.04	.02	.01
☐ 647	Scott Terry	.04	.02	.01
☐ 648	Tim Teufel SP	.07	.03	.01
☐ 649	Garry Templeton SP	.07	.03	.01
☐ 650	Manny Lee SP	.07	.03	.01
☐ 651	Roger McDowell SP	.07	.03	.01
☐ 652	Mookie Wilson SP	.11	.05	.01
☐ 653	David Cone SP	.50	.23	.06
☐ 654	Ron Gant SP	2.25	1.00	.30
☐ 655	Joe Price SP	.07	.03	.01
☐ 656	George Bell SP	.15	.07	.02
☐ 657	Gregg Jefferies SP	1.25	.55	.16
☐ 658	Todd Stottlemyre SP	.35	.16	.04
☐ 659	Geronimo Berroa SP	.12	.05	.02
☐ 660	Jerry Royster SP	.07	.03	.01
☐ BC1	Cal Ripken	.30	.14	.04
☐ BC2	Eric Davis	.10	.05	.01
☐ BC3	Paul Molitor	.08	.04	.01
☐ BC4	Mike Schmidt	.20	.09	.03
☐ BC5	Ivan Calderon	.05	.02	.01
☐ BC6	Tony Gwynn	.15	.07	.02
☐ BC7	Wade Boggs	.15	.07	.02
☐ BC8	Andy Van Slyke	.08	.04	.01
☐ BC9	Joe Carter	.15	.07	.02
☐ BC10	Andre Dawson	.08	.04	.01
☐ BC11	Alan Trammell	.08	.04	.01
☐ BC12	Mike Scott	.05	.02	.01
☐ BC13	Wally Joyner	.10	.05	.01
☐ BC14	Dale Murphy SP	.15	.07	.02
☐ BC15	Kirby Puckett SP	.40	.18	.05
☐ BC16	Pedro Guerrero SP	.08	.04	.01
☐ BC17	Kevin Seitzer SP	.08	.04	.01
☐ BC18	Tim Raines SP	.08	.04	.01
☐ BC19	George Bell SP	.15	.07	.02
☐ BC20	Darryl Strawberry SP	.30	.14	.04
☐ BC21	Don Mattingly SP	.30	.14	.04
☐ BC22	Ozzie Smith SP	.15	.07	.02
☐ BC23	Mark McGwire SP	.50	.23	.06
☐ BC24	Will Clark SP	.60	.25	.08
☐ BC25	Alvin Davis SP	.08	.04	.01
☐ BC26	Ruben Sierra SP	.40	.18	.05

1988 Donruss Rookies

The 1988 Donruss "The Rookies" set features 56 cards plus a 15-piece puzzle of Stan Musial. Cards are in full color and are standard size, 2 1/2" by 3 1/2". The set was distributed in a small green and black box with gold lettering. Card fronts are similar in design to the 1988 Donruss regular issue except for the presence of "The Rookies" logo in the lower right corner and a green and black border instead of a blue and black border on the fronts. The key Rookie Cards in this set are ROY's, Chris Sabo and Walt Weiss. Noteworthy extended Rookie Cards include Roberto Alomar, Brady Anderson, Ron Gant, Edgar Martinez and Jack McDowell.

	MT	EX-MT	VG
COMPLETE SET (56)	20.00	9.00	2.50
COMMON PLAYER (1-56)	.08	.04	.01

		MT	EX-MT	VG
☐	1 Mark Grace	2.00	.90	.25
☐	2 Mike Campbell	.08	.04	.01
☐	3 Todd Frohwirth	.08	.04	.01
☐	4 Dave Stapleton	.08	.04	.01
☐	5 Shawn Abner	.08	.04	.01
☐	6 Jose Cecena	.08	.04	.01
☐	7 Dave Gallagher	.08	.04	.01
☐	8 Mark Parent	.08	.04	.01
☐	9 Cecil Espy	.12	.05	.02
☐	10 Pete Smith	.50	.23	.06
☐	11 Jay Buhner	.60	.25	.08
☐	12 Pat Borders	.60	.25	.08
☐	13 Doug Jennings	.08	.04	.01
☐	14 Brady Anderson	1.50	.65	.19
☐	15 Pete Stanicek	.08	.04	.01
☐	16 Roberto Kelly	1.00	.45	.13
☐	17 Jeff Treadway	.12	.05	.02
☐	18 Walt Weiss	.25	.11	.03
☐	19 Paul Gibson	.08	.04	.01
☐	20 Tim Crews	.08	.04	.01
☐	21 Melido Perez	.50	.23	.06
☐	22 Steve Peters	.08	.04	.01
☐	23 Craig Worthington	.08	.04	.01
☐	24 John Trautwein	.08	.04	.01
☐	25 DeWayne Vaughn	.08	.04	.01
☐	26 David Wells	.08	.04	.01
☐	27 Al Leiter	.08	.04	.01
☐	28 Tim Belcher	.15	.07	.02
☐	29 Johnny Paredes	.08	.04	.01
☐	30 Chris Sabo	.75	.35	.09
☐	31 Damon Berryhill	.12	.05	.02
☐	32 Randy Milligan	.35	.16	.04
☐	33 Gary Thurman	.08	.04	.01
☐	34 Kevin Elster	.08	.04	.01
☐	35 Roberto Alomar	12.00	5.50	1.50
☐	36 Edgar Martinez UER (Photo actually Edwin Nunez)	2.00	.90	.25
☐	37 Todd Stottlemyre	.50	.23	.06
☐	38 Joey Meyer	.08	.04	.01
☐	39 Carl Nichols	.08	.04	.01
☐	40 Jack McDowell	2.00	.90	.25
☐	41 Jose Bautista	.08	.04	.01
☐	42 Sil Campusano	.08	.04	.01
☐	43 John Dopson	.08	.04	.01
☐	44 Jody Reed	.50	.23	.06
☐	45 Darrin Jackson	.50	.23	.06
☐	46 Mike Capel	.08	.04	.01
☐	47 Ron Gant	2.50	1.15	.30
☐	48 John Davis	.08	.04	.01
☐	49 Kevin Coffman	.08	.04	.01
☐	50 Cris Carpenter	.15	.07	.02
☐	51 Mackey Sasser	.12	.05	.02
☐	52 Luis Alicea	.15	.07	.02
☐	53 Bryan Harvey	.60	.25	.08
☐	54 Steve Ellsworth	.08	.04	.01
☐	55 Mike Macfarlane	.40	.18	.05
☐	56 Checklist Card	.08	.01	.00

1989 Donruss

This 660-card set was distributed along with a puzzle of Warren Spahn. The six regular checklist cards are numbered throughout the set as multiples of 100. Cards measure 2 1/2" by 3 1/2" and feature a distinctive black side border with an alternating coating. The popular Diamond King subset returns for the eighth consecutive year. Rated Rookies are featured again as cards 28-47. The Donruss '89 logo appears in the lower left corner of every obverse. There are two variations that occur throughout most of the set. On the card backs "Denotes Led League" can be found with one asterisk to the left or with an asterisk on each side. On the card fronts the horizontal lines on the left and right borders can be glossy or non-glossy. Since both of these variation types are relatively minor and seem equally common, there is no premium value for either type. Rather than short-printing 26 cards in order to make room for printing the Bonus MVP's this year, Donruss apparently chose to double print 106 cards. These double prints are listed below by DP. Numbered with the prefix "BC" for bonus card, the 26-card set featuring the most valuable player from each of the 26 teams was randomly inserted in the wax and rack packs. These cards are distinguished by the bold MVP logo in the upper background of the obverse, and the four doubleprinted cards are denoted by "DP" in the checklist below. The key Rookie Cards in this set are Sandy Alomar Jr., Ken Griffey Jr., Felix Jose, Ramon Martinez, Hal Morris, Gary Sheffield, and John Smoltz.

	MT	EX-MT	VG
COMPLETE SET (660)	20.00	9.00	2.50
COMPLETE FACT.SET (660)	20.00	9.00	2.50
COMMON PLAYER (1-660)	.04	.02	.01
COMMON PLAYER DP	.03	.01	.00
COMPLETE MVP SET (26)	1.25	.55	.16
COMMON MVP (BC1-BC26)	.05	.02	.01

☐ 1 Mike Greenwell DK	.08	.04	.01
☐ 2 Bobby Bonilla DK DP	.08	.04	.01
☐ 3 Pete Incaviglia DK	.05	.02	.01
☐ 4 Chris Sabo DK DP	.08	.04	.01
☐ 5 Robin Yount DK	.10	.05	.01
☐ 6 Tony Gwynn DK DP	.10	.05	.01
☐ 7 Carlton Fisk DK UER (OF on back)	.10	.05	.01
☐ 8 Cory Snyder DK	.05	.02	.01
☐ 9 David Cone DK UER (Sic, "hurdlers")	.08	.04	.01
☐ 10 Kevin Seitzer DK	.05	.02	.01
☐ 11 Rick Reuschel DK	.05	.02	.01
☐ 12 Johnny Ray DK	.05	.02	.01
☐ 13 Dave Schmidt DK	.05	.02	.01
☐ 14 Andres Galarraga DK	.05	.02	.01
☐ 15 Kirk Gibson DK	.05	.02	.01
☐ 16 Fred McGriff DK	.12	.05	.02
☐ 17 Mark Grace DK	.10	.05	.01
☐ 18 Jeff M. Robinson DK	.05	.02	.01
☐ 19 Vince Coleman DK DP	.05	.02	.01
☐ 20 Dave Henderson DK	.05	.02	.01
☐ 21 Harold Reynolds DK	.05	.02	.01
☐ 22 Gerald Perry DK	.05	.02	.01
☐ 23 Frank Viola DK	.05	.02	.01
☐ 24 Steve Bedrosian DK	.05	.02	.01
☐ 25 Glenn Davis DK	.05	.02	.01
☐ 26 Don Mattingly DK UER (Doesn't mention Don's previous DK in 1985)	.12	.05	.02
☐ 27 DK Checklist DP	.05	.01	.00
☐ 28 Sandy Alomar Jr. RR	.25	.11	.03
☐ 29 Steve Searcy RR	.06	.03	.01
☐ 30 Cameron Drew RR	.06	.03	.01
☐ 31 Gary Sheffield RR	2.00	.90	.25
☐ 32 Erik Hanson RR	.20	.09	.03
☐ 33 Ken Griffey Jr. RR	4.50	2.00	.55
☐ 34 Greg W. Harris RR	.10	.05	.01
☐ 35 Gregg Jefferies RR	.20	.09	.03
☐ 36 Luis Medina RR	.06	.03	.01
☐ 37 Carlos Quintana RR	.10	.05	.01
☐ 38 Felix Jose RR	.75	.35	.09
☐ 39 Cris Carpenter RR	.10	.05	.01
☐ 40 Ron Jones RR	.06	.03	.01
☐ 41 Dave West RR	.10	.05	.01
☐ 42 Randy Johnson RR	.35	.16	.04
☐ 43 Mike Harkey RR	.12	.05	.02
☐ 44 Pete Harnisch RR	.15	.07	.02
☐ 45 Tom Gordon RR DP	.10	.05	.01
☐ 46 Gregg Olson RR DP	.35	.16	.04
☐ 47 Alex Sanchez RR DP	.06	.03	.01
☐ 48 Ruben Sierra	.30	.14	.04
☐ 49 Rafael Palmeiro	.20	.09	.03
☐ 50 Ron Gant	.40	.18	.05
☐ 51 Cal Ripken	.50	.23	.06
☐ 52 Wally Joyner	.08	.04	.01
☐ 53 Gary Carter	.06	.03	.01
☐ 54 Andy Van Slyke	.10	.05	.01
☐ 55 Robin Yount	.20	.09	.03

☐ 56 Pete Incaviglia	.03	.01	.00
☐ 57 Greg Brock	.03	.01	.00
☐ 58 Melido Perez	.06	.03	.01
☐ 59 Craig Lefferts	.03	.01	.00
☐ 60 Gary Pettis	.03	.01	.00
☐ 61 Danny Tartabull	.12	.05	.02
☐ 62 Guillermo Hernandez	.03	.01	.00
☐ 63 Ozzie Smith	.15	.07	.02
☐ 64 Gary Gaetti	.03	.01	.00
☐ 65 Mark Davis	.03	.01	.00
☐ 66 Lee Smith	.06	.03	.01
☐ 67 Dennis Eckersley	.12	.05	.02
☐ 68 Wade Boggs	.25	.11	.03
☐ 69 Mike Scott	.03	.01	.00
☐ 70 Fred McGriff	.25	.11	.03
☐ 71 Tom Browning	.06	.03	.01
☐ 72 Claudell Washington	.03	.01	.00
☐ 73 Mel Hall	.03	.01	.00
☐ 74 Don Mattingly	.25	.11	.03
☐ 75 Steve Bedrosian	.03	.01	.00
☐ 76 Juan Samuel	.03	.01	.00
☐ 77 Mike Scioscia	.03	.01	.00
☐ 78 Dave Righetti	.03	.01	.00
☐ 79 Alfredo Griffin	.03	.01	.00
☐ 80 Eric Davis UER	.12	.05	.02
(165 games in 1988,			
should be 135)			
☐ 81 Juan Berenguer	.03	.01	.00
☐ 82 Todd Worrell	.06	.03	.01
☐ 83 Joe Carter	.25	.11	.03
☐ 84 Steve Sax	.06	.03	.01
☐ 85 Frank White	.03	.01	.00
☐ 86 John Kruk	.06	.03	.01
☐ 87 Ranco Mulliniks	.03	.01	.00
☐ 88 Alan Ashby	.03	.01	.00
☐ 89 Charlie Leibrandt	.03	.01	.00
☐ 90 Frank Tanana	.03	.01	.00
☐ 91 Jose Canseco	.40	.18	.05
☐ 92 Barry Bonds	.40	.18	.05
☐ 93 Harold Reynolds	.03	.01	.00
☐ 94 Mark McLemore	.03	.01	.00
☐ 95 Mark McGwire	.35	.16	.04
☐ 96 Eddie Murray	.15	.07	.02
☐ 97 Tim Raines	.06	.03	.01
☐ 98 Robby Thompson	.03	.01	.00
☐ 99 Kevin McReynolds	.06	.03	.01
☐ 100 Checklist Card	.05	.01	.00
☐ 101 Carlton Fisk	.15	.07	.02
☐ 102 Dave Martinez	.06	.03	.01
☐ 103 Glenn Braggs	.03	.01	.00
☐ 104 Dale Murphy	.10	.05	.01
☐ 105 Ryne Sandberg	.40	.18	.05
☐ 106 Dennis Martinez	.06	.03	.01
☐ 107 Pete O'Brien	.03	.01	.00
☐ 108 Dick Schofield	.03	.01	.00
☐ 109 Henry Cotto	.03	.01	.00
☐ 110 Mike Marshall	.03	.01	.00

☐ 111 Keith Moreland	.03	.01	.00
☐ 112 Tom Brunansky	.06	.03	.01
☐ 113 Kelly Gruber UER	.06	.03	.01
(Wrong birthdate)			
☐ 114 Brook Jacoby	.03	.01	.00
☐ 115 Keith Brown	.03	.01	.00
☐ 116 Matt Nokes	.06	.03	.01
☐ 117 Keith Hernandez	.06	.03	.01
☐ 118 Bob Forsch	.03	.01	.00
☐ 119 Bert Blyleven UER	.06	.03	.01
(... 3000 strikeouts in			
1987, should be 1986)			
☐ 120 Willie Wilson	.03	.01	.00
☐ 121 Tommy Gregg	.03	.01	.00
☐ 122 Jim Rice	.06	.03	.01
☐ 123 Bob Knepper	.03	.01	.00
☐ 124 Danny Jackson	.03	.01	.00
☐ 125 Eric Plunk	.03	.01	.00
☐ 126 Brian Fisher	.03	.01	.00
☐ 127 Mike Pagliarulo	.03	.01	.00
☐ 128 Tony Gwynn	.25	.11	.03
☐ 129 Lance McCullers	.03	.01	.00
☐ 130 Andres Galarraga	.03	.01	.00
☐ 131 Jose Uribe	.03	.01	.00
☐ 132 Kirk Gibson UER	.06	.03	.01
(Wrong birthdate)			
☐ 133 David Palmer	.03	.01	.00
☐ 134 R.J. Reynolds	.03	.01	.00
☐ 135 Greg Walker	.03	.01	.00
☐ 136 Kirk McCaskill UER	.03	.01	.00
(Wrong birthdate)			
☐ 137 Shawon Dunston	.06	.03	.01
☐ 138 Andy Allanson	.03	.01	.00
☐ 139 Rob Murphy	.03	.01	.00
☐ 140 Mike Aldrete	.03	.01	.00
☐ 141 Terry Kennedy	.03	.01	.00
☐ 142 Scott Fletcher	.03	.01	.00
☐ 143 Steve Balboni	.03	.01	.00
☐ 144 Bret Saberhagen	.06	.03	.01
☐ 145 Ozzie Virgil	.03	.01	.00
☐ 146 Dale Sveum	.03	.01	.00
☐ 147 Darryl Strawberry	.25	.11	.03
☐ 148 Harold Baines	.06	.03	.01
☐ 149 George Bell	.10	.05	.01
☐ 150 Dave Parker	.06	.03	.01
☐ 151 Bobby Bonilla	.20	.09	.03
☐ 152 Mookie Wilson	.06	.03	.01
☐ 153 Ted Power	.03	.01	.00
☐ 154 Nolan Ryan	.60	.25	.08
☐ 155 Jeff Reardon	.06	.03	.01
☐ 156 Tim Wallach	.06	.03	.01
☐ 157 Jamie Moyer	.03	.01	.00
☐ 158 Rich Gossage	.06	.03	.01
☐ 159 Dave Winfield	.20	.09	.03
☐ 160 Von Hayes	.03	.01	.00
☐ 161 Willie McGee	.06	.03	.01
☐ 162 Rich Gedman	.03	.01	.00

☐ 163	Tony Pena	.03	.01	.00
☐ 164	Mike Morgan	.06	.03	.01
☐ 165	Charlie Hough	.03	.01	.00
☐ 166	Mike Stanley	.03	.01	.00
☐ 167	Andre Dawson	.15	.07	.02
☐ 168	Joe Boever	.03	.01	.00
☐ 169	Pete Stanicek	.03	.01	.00
☐ 170	Bob Boone	.06	.03	.01
☐ 171	Ron Darling	.03	.01	.00
☐ 172	Bob Walk	.03	.01	.00
☐ 173	Rob Deer	.06	.03	.01
☐ 174	Steve Buechele	.03	.01	.00
☐ 175	Ted Higuera	.03	.01	.00
☐ 176	Ozzie Guillen	.03	.01	.00
☐ 177	Candy Maldonado	.03	.01	.00
☐ 178	Doyle Alexander	.03	.01	.00
☐ 179	Mark Gubicza	.03	.01	.00
☐ 180	Alan Trammell	.06	.03	.01
☐ 181	Vince Coleman	.06	.03	.01
☐ 182	Kirby Puckett	.40	.18	.05
☐ 183	Chris Brown	.03	.01	.00
☐ 184	Marty Barrett	.03	.01	.00
☐ 185	Stan Javier	.03	.01	.00
☐ 186	Mike Greenwell	.06	.03	.01
☐ 187	Billy Hatcher	.03	.01	.00
☐ 188	Jimmy Key	.06	.03	.01
☐ 189	Nick Esasky	.03	.01	.00
☐ 190	Don Slaught	.03	.01	.00
☐ 191	Cory Snyder	.03	.01	.00
☐ 192	John Candelaria	.03	.01	.00
☐ 193	Mike Schmidt	.35	.16	.04
☐ 194	Kevin Gross	.03	.01	.00
☐ 195	John Tudor	.03	.01	.00
☐ 196	Neil Allen	.03	.01	.00
☐ 197	Orel Hershiser	.06	.03	.01
☐ 198	Kal Daniels	.06	.03	.01
☐ 199	Kent Hrbek	.06	.03	.01
☐ 200	Checklist Card	.05	.01	.00
☐ 201	Joe Magrane	.03	.01	.00
☐ 202	Scott Bailes	.03	.01	.00
☐ 203	Tim Belcher	.06	.03	.01
☐ 204	George Brett	.20	.09	.03
☐ 205	Benito Santiago	.06	.03	.01
☐ 206	Tony Fernandez	.06	.03	.01
☐ 207	Gerald Young	.03	.01	.00
☐ 208	Bo Jackson	.20	.09	.03
☐ 209	Chet Lemon	.03	.01	.00
☐ 210	Storm Davis	.03	.01	.00
☐ 211	Doug Drabek	.06	.03	.01
☐ 212	Mickey Brantley UER	.03	.01	.00
	(Photo actually			
	Nelson Simmons)			
☐ 213	Devon White	.06	.03	.01
☐ 214	Dave Stewart	.06	.03	.01
☐ 215	Dave Schmidt	.03	.01	.00
☐ 216	Bryn Smith	.03	.01	.00
☐ 217	Brett Butler	.06	.03	.01
☐ 218	Bob Ojeda	.03	.01	.00
☐ 219	Steve Rosenberg	.03	.01	.00
☐ 220	Hubie Brooks	.06	.03	.01
☐ 221	B.J. Surhoff	.03	.01	.00
☐ 222	Rick Mahler	.03	.01	.00
☐ 223	Rick Sutcliffe	.06	.03	.01
☐ 224	Neal Heaton	.03	.01	.00
☐ 225	Mitch Williams	.06	.03	.01
☐ 226	Chuck Finley	.06	.03	.01
☐ 227	Mark Langston	.06	.03	.01
☐ 228	Jesse Orosco	.03	.01	.00
☐ 229	Ed Whitson	.03	.01	.00
☐ 230	Terry Pendleton	.12	.05	.02
☐ 231	Lloyd Moseby	.03	.01	.00
☐ 232	Greg Swindell	.06	.03	.01
☐ 233	John Franco	.06	.03	.01
☐ 234	Jack Morris	.12	.05	.02
☐ 235	Howard Johnson	.06	.03	.01
☐ 236	Glenn Davis	.06	.03	.01
☐ 237	Frank Viola	.06	.03	.01
☐ 238	Kevin Seitzer	.06	.03	.01
☐ 239	Gerald Perry	.03	.01	.00
☐ 240	Dwight Evans	.06	.03	.01
☐ 241	Jim Deshaies	.03	.01	.00
☐ 242	Bo Diaz	.03	.01	.00
☐ 243	Carney Lansford	.06	.03	.01
☐ 244	Mike LaValliere	.03	.01	.00
☐ 245	Rickey Henderson	.25	.11	.03
☐ 246	Roberto Alomar	.75	.35	.09
☐ 247	Jimmy Jones	.03	.01	.00
☐ 248	Pascual Perez	.03	.01	.00
☐ 249	Will Clark	.40	.18	.05
☐ 250	Fernando Valenzuela	.06	.03	.01
☐ 251	Shane Rawley	.03	.01	.00
☐ 252	Sid Bream	.03	.01	.00
☐ 253	Steve Lyons	.03	.01	.00
☐ 254	Brian Downing	.03	.01	.00
☐ 255	Mark Grace	.30	.14	.04
☐ 256	Tom Candiotti	.03	.01	.00
☐ 257	Barry Larkin	.15	.07	.02
☐ 258	Mike Krukow	.03	.01	.00
☐ 259	Billy Ripken	.03	.01	.00
☐ 260	Cecilio Guante	.03	.01	.00
☐ 261	Scott Bradley	.03	.01	.00
☐ 262	Floyd Bannister	.03	.01	.00
☐ 263	Pete Smith	.06	.03	.01
☐ 264	Jim Gantner UER	.03	.01	.00
	(Wrong birthdate)			
☐ 265	Roger McDowell	.03	.01	.00
☐ 266	Bobby Thigpen	.03	.01	.00
☐ 267	Jim Clancy	.03	.01	.00
☐ 268	Terry Steinbach	.06	.03	.01
☐ 269	Mike Dunne	.03	.01	.00
☐ 270	Dwight Gooden	.12	.05	.02
☐ 271	Mike Heath	.03	.01	.00
☐ 272	Dave Smith	.03	.01	.00
☐ 273	Keith Atherton	.03	.01	.00

☐ 274	Tim Burke	.03	.01	.00
☐ 275	Damon Berryhill	.03	.01	.00
☐ 276	Vance Law	.03	.01	.00
☐ 277	Rich Dotson	.03	.01	.00
☐ 278	Lance Parrish	.06	.03	.01
☐ 279	Denny Walling	.03	.01	.00
☐ 280	Roger Clemens	.40	.18	.05
☐ 281	Greg Mathews	.03	.01	.00
☐ 282	Tom Niedenfuer	.03	.01	.00
☐ 283	Paul Kilgus	.03	.01	.00
☐ 284	Jose Guzman	.06	.03	.01
☐ 285	Calvin Schiraldi	.03	.01	.00
☐ 286	Charlie Puleo UER	.03	.01	.00
	(Career ERA 4.24,			
	should be 4.23)			
☐ 287	Joe Orsulak	.03	.01	.00
☐ 288	Jack Howell	.03	.01	.00
☐ 289	Kevin Elster	.03	.01	.00
☐ 290	Jose Lind	.03	.01	.00
☐ 291	Paul Molitor	.10	.05	.01
☐ 292	Cecil Espy	.03	.01	.00
☐ 293	Bill Wegman	.03	.01	.00
☐ 294	Dan Pasqua	.03	.01	.00
☐ 295	Scott Garrelts UER	.03	.01	.00
	(Wrong birthdate)			
☐ 296	Walt Terrell	.03	.01	.00
☐ 297	Ed Hearn	.03	.01	.00
☐ 298	Lou Whitaker	.06	.03	.01
☐ 299	Ken Dayley	.03	.01	.00
☐ 300	Checklist Card	.05	.01	.00
☐ 301	Tommy Herr	.03	.01	.00
☐ 302	Mike Brumley	.03	.01	.00
☐ 303	Ellis Burks	.06	.03	.01
☐ 304	Curt Young UER	.03	.01	.00
	(Wrong birthdate)			
☐ 305	Jody Reed	.03	.01	.00
☐ 306	Bill Doran	.03	.01	.00
☐ 307	David Wells	.03	.01	.00
☐ 308	Ron Robinson	.03	.01	.00
☐ 309	Rafael Santana	.03	.01	.00
☐ 310	Julio Franco	.06	.03	.01
☐ 311	Jack Clark	.06	.03	.01
☐ 312	Chris James	.03	.01	.00
☐ 313	Milt Thompson	.03	.01	.00
☐ 314	John Shelby	.03	.01	.00
☐ 315	Al Leiter	.03	.01	.00
☐ 316	Mike Davis	.03	.01	.00
☐ 317	Chris Sabo	.30	.14	.04
☐ 318	Greg Gagne	.03	.01	.00
☐ 319	Jose Oquendo	.03	.01	.00
☐ 320	John Farrell	.03	.01	.00
☐ 321	Franklin Stubbs	.03	.01	.00
☐ 322	Kurt Stillwell	.03	.01	.00
☐ 323	Shawn Abner	.03	.01	.00
☐ 324	Mike Flanagan	.03	.01	.00
☐ 325	Kevin Bass	.03	.01	.00
☐ 326	Pat Tabler	.03	.01	.00
☐ 327	Mike Henneman	.06	.03	.01
☐ 328	Rick Honeycutt	.03	.01	.00
☐ 329	John Smiley	.06	.03	.01
☐ 330	Rey Quinones	.03	.01	.00
☐ 331	Johnny Ray	.03	.01	.00
☐ 332	Bob Welch	.06	.03	.01
☐ 333	Larry Sheets	.03	.01	.00
☐ 334	Jeff Parrett	.03	.01	.00
☐ 335	Rick Reuschel UER	.03	.01	.00
	(For Don Robinson,			
	should be Jeff)			
☐ 336	Randy Myers	.06	.03	.01
☐ 337	Ken Williams	.03	.01	.00
☐ 338	Andy McGaffigan	.03	.01	.00
☐ 339	Joey Meyer	.03	.01	.00
☐ 340	Dion James	.03	.01	.00
☐ 341	Les Lancaster	.03	.01	.00
☐ 342	Tom Foley	.03	.01	.00
☐ 343	Geno Petralli	.03	.01	.00
☐ 344	Dan Petry	.03	.01	.00
☐ 345	Alvin Davis	.03	.01	.00
☐ 346	Mickey Hatcher	.03	.01	.00
☐ 347	Marvell Wynne	.03	.01	.00
☐ 348	Danny Cox	.03	.01	.00
☐ 349	Dave Stieb	.06	.03	.01
☐ 350	Jay Bell	.06	.03	.01
☐ 351	Jeff Treadway	.03	.01	.00
☐ 352	Luis Salazar	.03	.01	.00
☐ 353	Len Dykstra	.06	.03	.01
☐ 354	Juan Agosto	.03	.01	.00
☐ 355	Gene Larkin	.03	.01	.00
☐ 356	Steve Farr	.03	.01	.00
☐ 357	Paul Assenmacher	.03	.01	.00
☐ 358	Todd Benzinger	.03	.01	.00
☐ 359	Larry Andersen	.03	.01	.00
☐ 360	Paul O'Neill	.06	.03	.01
☐ 361	Ron Hassey	.03	.01	.00
☐ 362	Jim Gott	.03	.01	.00
☐ 363	Ken Phelps	.03	.01	.00
☐ 364	Tim Flannery	.03	.01	.00
☐ 365	Randy Ready	.03	.01	.00
☐ 366	Nelson Santovenia	.03	.01	.00
☐ 367	Kelly Downs	.03	.01	.00
☐ 368	Danny Heep	.03	.01	.00
☐ 369	Phil Bradley	.03	.01	.00
☐ 370	Jeff D. Robinson	.03	.01	.00
☐ 371	Ivan Calderon	.03	.01	.00
☐ 372	Mike Witt	.03	.01	.00
☐ 373	Greg Maddux	.30	.14	.04
☐ 374	Carmen Castillo	.03	.01	.00
☐ 375	Jose Rijo	.06	.03	.01
☐ 376	Joe Price	.03	.01	.00
☐ 377	Rene Gonzales	.03	.01	.00
☐ 378	Oddibe McDowell	.03	.01	.00
☐ 379	Jim Presley	.03	.01	.00
☐ 380	Brad Wellman	.03	.01	.00
☐ 381	Tom Glavine	.50	.23	.06

☐ 382 Dan Plesac	.03	.01	.00
☐ 383 Wally Backman	.03	.01	.00
☐ 384 Dave Gallagher	.03	.01	.00
☐ 385 Tom Henke	.06	.03	.01
☐ 386 Luis Polonia	.06	.03	.01
☐ 387 Junior Ortiz	.03	.01	.00
☐ 388 David Cone	.15	.07	.02
☐ 389 Dave Bergman	.03	.01	.00
☐ 390 Danny Darwin	.03	.01	.00
☐ 391 Dan Gladden	.03	.01	.00
☐ 392 John Dopson	.03	.01	.00
☐ 393 Frank DiPino	.03	.01	.00
☐ 394 Al Nipper	.03	.01	.00
☐ 395 Willie Randolph	.06	.03	.01
☐ 396 Don Carman	.03	.01	.00
☐ 397 Scott Terry	.03	.01	.00
☐ 398 Rick Cerone	.03	.01	.00
☐ 399 Tom Pagnozzi	.03	.01	.00
☐ 400 Checklist Card	.05	.01	.00
☐ 401 Mickey Tettleton	.06	.03	.01
☐ 402 Curtis Wilkerson	.03	.01	.00
☐ 403 Jeff Russell	.03	.01	.00
☐ 404 Pat Perry	.03	.01	.00
☐ 405 Jose Alvarez	.03	.01	.00
☐ 406 Rick Schu	.03	.01	.00
☐ 407 Sherman Corbett	.03	.01	.00
☐ 408 Dave Magadan	.06	.03	.01
☐ 409 Bob Kipper	.03	.01	.00
☐ 410 Don August	.03	.01	.00
☐ 411 Bob Brower	.03	.01	.00
☐ 412 Chris Bosio	.03	.01	.00
☐ 413 Jerry Reuss	.03	.01	.00
☐ 414 Atlee Hammaker	.03	.01	.00
☐ 415 Jim Walewander	.03	.01	.00
☐ 416 Mike Macfarlane	.15	.07	.02
☐ 417 Pat Sheridan	.03	.01	.00
☐ 418 Pedro Guerrero	.06	.03	.01
☐ 419 Allan Anderson	.03	.01	.00
☐ 420 Mark Parent	.03	.01	.00
☐ 421 Bob Stanley	.03	.01	.00
☐ 422 Mike Gallego	.03	.01	.00
☐ 423 Bruce Hurst	.06	.03	.01
☐ 424 Dave Meads	.03	.01	.00
☐ 425 Jesse Barfield	.03	.01	.00
☐ 426 Rob Dibble	.20	.09	.03
☐ 427 Joel Skinner	.03	.01	.00
☐ 428 Ron Kittle	.03	.01	.00
☐ 429 Rick Rhoden	.03	.01	.00
☐ 430 Bob Dernier	.03	.01	.00
☐ 431 Steve Jeltz	.03	.01	.00
☐ 432 Rick Dempsey	.03	.01	.00
☐ 433 Roberto Kelly	.15	.07	.02
☐ 434 Dave Anderson	.03	.01	.00
☐ 435 Herm Winningham	.03	.01	.00
☐ 436 Al Newman	.03	.01	.00
☐ 437 Jose DeLeon	.03	.01	.00
☐ 438 Doug Jones	.06	.03	.01
☐ 439 Brian Holton	.03	.01	.00
☐ 440 Jeff Montgomery	.06	.03	.01
☐ 441 Dickie Thon	.03	.01	.00
☐ 442 Cecil Fielder	.25	.11	.03
☐ 443 John Fishel	.03	.01	.00
☐ 444 Jerry Don Gleaton	.03	.01	.00
☐ 445 Paul Gibson	.03	.01	.00
☐ 446 Walt Weiss	.06	.03	.01
☐ 447 Glenn Wilson	.03	.01	.00
☐ 448 Mike Moore	.03	.01	.00
☐ 449 Chili Davis	.06	.03	.01
☐ 450 Dave Henderson	.06	.03	.01
☐ 451 Jose Bautista	.03	.01	.00
☐ 452 Rex Hudler	.03	.01	.00
☐ 453 Bob Brenly	.03	.01	.00
☐ 454 Mackey Sasser	.03	.01	.00
☐ 455 Daryl Boston	.03	.01	.00
☐ 456 Mike R. Fitzgerald	.03	.01	.00
Montreal Expos			
☐ 457 Jeffrey Leonard	.03	.01	.00
☐ 458 Bruce Sutter	.06	.03	.01
☐ 459 Mitch Webster	.03	.01	.00
☐ 460 Joe Hesketh	.03	.01	.00
☐ 461 Bobby Witt	.06	.03	.01
☐ 462 Stew Cliburn	.03	.01	.00
☐ 463 Scott Bankhead	.03	.01	.00
☐ 464 Ramon Martinez	.50	.23	.06
☐ 465 Dave Leiper	.03	.01	.00
☐ 466 Luis Alicea	.10	.05	.01
☐ 467 John Cerutti	.03	.01	.00
☐ 468 Ron Washington	.03	.01	.00
☐ 469 Jeff Reed	.03	.01	.00
☐ 470 Jeff M. Robinson	.03	.01	.00
☐ 471 Sid Fernandez	.06	.03	.01
☐ 472 Terry Puhl	.03	.01	.00
☐ 473 Charlie Lea	.03	.01	.00
☐ 474 Israel Sanchez	.03	.01	.00
☐ 475 Bruce Benedict	.03	.01	.00
☐ 476 Oil Can Boyd	.03	.01	.00
☐ 477 Craig Reynolds	.03	.01	.00
☐ 478 Frank Williams	.03	.01	.00
☐ 479 Greg Cadaret	.03	.01	.00
☐ 480 Randy Kramer	.03	.01	.00
☐ 481 Dave Eiland	.03	.01	.00
☐ 482 Eric Show	.03	.01	.00
☐ 483 Garry Templeton	.03	.01	.00
☐ 484 Wallace Johnson	.03	.01	.00
☐ 485 Kevin Mitchell	.10	.05	.01
☐ 486 Tim Crews	.03	.01	.00
☐ 487 Mike Maddux	.03	.01	.00
☐ 488 Dave LaPoint	.03	.01	.00
☐ 489 Fred Manrique	.03	.01	.00
☐ 490 Greg Minton	.03	.01	.00
☐ 491 Doug Dascenzo UER	.03	.01	.00
(Photo actually			
Damon Berryhill)			
☐ 492 Willie Upshaw	.03	.01	.00

☐ 493	Jack Armstrong	12	.05	.02
☐ 494	Kirt Manwaring	.03	.01	.00
☐ 495	Jeff Ballard	.03	.01	.00
☐ 496	Jeff Kunkel	.03	.01	.00
☐ 497	Mike Campbell	.03	.01	.00
☐ 498	Gary Thurman	.03	.01	.00
☐ 499	Zane Smith	.03	.01	.00
☐ 500	Checklist Card DP	.05	.02	.01
☐ 501	Mike Birkbeck	.03	.01	.00
☐ 502	Terry Leach	.03	.01	.00
☐ 503	Shawn Hillegas	.03	.01	.00
☐ 504	Manny Lee	.03	.01	.00
☐ 505	Doug Jennings	.03	.01	.00
☐ 506	Ken Oberkfell	.03	.01	.00
☐ 507	Tim Teufel	.03	.01	.00
☐ 508	Tom Brookens	.03	.01	.00
☐ 509	Rafael Ramirez	.03	.01	.00
☐ 510	Fred Toliver	.03	.01	.00
☐ 511	Brian Holman	10	.05	.01
☐ 512	Mike Bielecki	.03	.01	.00
☐ 513	Jeff Pico	.03	.01	.00
☐ 514	Charles Hudson	.03	.01	.00
☐ 515	Bruce Ruffin	.03	.01	.00
☐ 516	Larry McWilliams UER	.03	.01	.00
	(New Richland, should be North Richland)			
☐ 517	Jeff Sellers	.03	.01	.00
☐ 518	John Costello	.03	.01	.00
☐ 519	Brady Anderson	.60	.25	.08
☐ 520	Craig McMurtry	.03	.01	.00
☐ 521	Ray Hayward DP	.03	.01	.00
☐ 522	Drew Hall DP	.03	.01	.00
☐ 523	Mark Lemke DP	12	.05	.02
☐ 524	Oswald Peraza DP	.03	.01	.00
☐ 525	Bryan Harvey DP	.20	.09	.03
☐ 526	Rick Aguilera DP	.03	.01	.00
☐ 527	Tom Prince DP	.03	.01	.00
☐ 528	Mark Clear DP	.03	.01	.00
☐ 529	Jerry Browne DP	.03	.01	.00
☐ 530	Juan Castillo DP	.03	.01	.00
☐ 531	Jack McDowell DP	.25	.11	.03
☐ 532	Chris Speier DP	.03	.01	.00
☐ 533	Darrell Evans DP	.03	.01	.00
☐ 534	Luis Aquino DP	.03	.01	.00
☐ 535	Eric King DP	.03	.01	.00
☐ 536	Ken Hill DP	.35	.16	.04
☐ 537	Randy Bush DP	.03	.01	.00
☐ 538	Shane Mack DP	.06	.03	.01
☐ 539	Tom Bolton DP	.03	.01	.00
☐ 540	Gene Nelson DP	.03	.01	.00
☐ 541	Wes Gardner DP	.03	.01	.00
☐ 542	Ken Caminiti DP	.06	.03	.01
☐ 543	Duane Ward DP	.06	.03	.01
☐ 544	Norm Charlton DP	15	.07	.02
☐ 545	Hal Morris DP	.30	.14	.04
☐ 546	Rich Yett DP	.03	.01	.00
☐ 547	Hensley Meulens DP	12	.05	.02

☐ 548	Greg A. Harris DP	.03	.01	.00
	Philadelphia Phillies			
☐ 549	Darren Daulton DP	.06	.03	.01
	(Posing as right-handed hitter)			
☐ 550	Jeff Hamilton DP	.03	.01	.00
☐ 551	Luis Aguayo DP	.03	.01	.00
☐ 552	Tim Leary DP	.03	.01	.00
	(Resembles M.Marshall)			
☐ 553	Ron Oester DP	.03	.01	.00
☐ 554	Steve Lombardozzi DP	.03	.01	.00
☐ 555	Tim Jones DP	.03	.01	.00
☐ 556	Bud Black DP	.03	.01	.00
☐ 557	Alejandro Pena DP	.03	.01	.00
☐ 558	Jose DeJesus DP	.03	.01	.00
☐ 559	Dennis Rasmussen DP	.03	.01	.00
☐ 560	Pat Borders DP	.25	.11	.03
☐ 561	Craig Biggio DP	30	.14	.04
☐ 562	Luis De Los Santos DP	.03	.01	.00
☐ 563	Fred Lynn DP	.03	.01	.00
☐ 564	Todd Burns DP	.03	.01	.00
☐ 565	Felix Fermin DP	.03	.01	.00
☐ 566	Darnell Coles DP	.03	.01	.00
☐ 567	Willie Fraser DP	.03	.01	.00
☐ 568	Glenn Hubbard DP	.03	.01	.00
☐ 569	Craig Worthington DP	.03	.01	.00
☐ 570	Johnny Paredes DP	.03	.01	.00
☐ 571	Don Robinson DP	.03	.01	.00
☐ 572	Barry Lyons DP	.03	.01	.00
☐ 573	Bill Long DP	.03	.01	.00
☐ 574	Tracy Jones DP	.03	.01	.00
☐ 575	Juan Nieves DP	.03	.01	.00
☐ 576	Andres Thomas DP	.03	.01	.00
☐ 577	Rolando Roomes DP	.03	.01	.00
☐ 578	Luis Rivera UER DP	.03	.01	.00
	(Wrong birthdate)			
☐ 579	Chad Kreuter DP	.03	.01	.00
☐ 580	Tony Armas DP	.03	.01	.00
☐ 581	Jay Buhner	10	.05	.01
☐ 582	Ricky Horton DP	.03	.01	.00
☐ 583	Andy Hawkins DP	.03	.01	.00
☐ 584	Sil Campusano	.03	.01	.00
☐ 585	Dave Clark	.03	.01	.00
☐ 586	Van Snider DP	.03	.01	.00
☐ 587	Todd Frohwirth DP	.03	.01	.00
☐ 588	Warren Spahn DP PUZ	.08	.04	.01
☐ 589	William Brennan	.03	.01	.00
☐ 590	German Gonzalez	.03	.01	.00
☐ 591	Ernie Whitt DP	.03	.01	.00
☐ 592	Jeff Blauser	.06	.03	.01
☐ 593	Spike Owen DP	.03	.01	.00
☐ 594	Matt Williams	15	.07	.02
☐ 595	Lloyd McClendon DP	.03	.01	.00
☐ 596	Steve Ontiveros	.03	.01	.00
☐ 597	Scott Medvin	.03	.01	.00
☐ 598	Hipolito Pena DP	.03	.01	.00
☐ 599	Jerald Clark DP	12	.05	.02

☐ 600A	Checklist Card DP 30	.03	.01
	(635 Kurt Schilling)		
☐ 600B	Checklist Card DP 05	.01	.00
	(635 Curt Schilling; MVP's not listed on checklist card)		
☐ 600C	Checklist Card DP 05	.01	.00
	(635 Curt Schilling; MVP's listed following 660)		
☐ 601	Carmelo Martinez DP 03	.01	.00
☐ 602	Mike LaCoss 03	.01	.00
☐ 603	Mike Devereaux 15	.07	.02
☐ 604	Alex Madrid DP 03	.01	.00
☐ 605	Gary Redus DP 03	.01	.00
☐ 606	Lance Johnson 06	.03	.01
☐ 607	Terry Clark DP 03	.01	.00
☐ 608	Manny Trillo DP 03	.01	.00
☐ 609	Scott Jordan 10	.05	.01
☐ 610	Jay Howell DP 03	.01	.00
☐ 611	Francisco Melendez 03	.01	.00
☐ 612	Mike Boddicker 03	.01	.00
☐ 613	Kevin Brown DP 25	.11	.03
☐ 614	Dave Valle 03	.01	.00
☐ 615	Tim Laudner DP 03	.01	.00
☐ 616	Andy Nezelek UER 03	.01	.00
	(Wrong birthdate)		
☐ 617	Chuck Crim 03	.01	.00
☐ 618	Jack Savage DP 03	.01	.00
☐ 619	Adam Peterson 03	.01	.00
☐ 620	Todd Stottlemyre 10	.05	.01
☐ 621	Lance Blankenship 10	.05	.01
☐ 622	Miguel Garcia DP 03	.01	.00
☐ 623	Keith A. Miller DP 03	.01	.00
☐ 624	Ricky Jordan DP 10	.05	.01
☐ 625	Ernest Riles DP 03	.01	.00
☐ 626	John Moses DP 03	.01	.00
☐ 627	Nelson Liriano DP 03	.01	.00
☐ 628	Mike Smithson DP 03	.01	.00
☐ 629	Scott Sanderson 03	.01	.00
☐ 630	Dale Mohorcic 03	.01	.00
☐ 631	Marvin Freeman DP 03	.01	.00
☐ 632	Mike Young DP 03	.01	.00
☐ 633	Dennis Lamp 03	.01	.00
☐ 634	Dante Bichette DP 25	.11	.03
☐ 635	Curt Schilling DP 30	.14	.04
☐ 636	Scott May DP 03	.01	.00
☐ 637	Mike Schooler 10	.05	.01
☐ 638	Rick Leach 03	.01	.00
☐ 639	Tom Lampkin UER 03	.01	.00
	(Throws Left, should be Throws Right)		
☐ 640	Brian Meyer 03	.01	.00
☐ 641	Brian Harper 06	.03	.01
☐ 642	John Smoltz 60	.25	.08
☐ 643	Jose: 40/40 Club 20	.09	.03
	(Jose Canseco)		

☐ 644	Bill Schroeder 03	.01	.00
☐ 645	Edgar Martinez 40	.18	.05
☐ 646	Dennis Cook 10	.05	.01
☐ 647	Barry Jones 03	.01	.00
☐ 648	Orel: 59 and Counting 06	.03	.01
	(Orel Hershiser)		
☐ 649	Rod Nichols 03	.01	.00
☐ 650	Jody Davis 03	.01	.00
☐ 651	Bob Milacki 10	.05	.01
☐ 652	Mike Jackson 03	.01	.00
☐ 653	Derek Lilliquist 10	.05	.01
☐ 654	Paul Mirabella 03	.01	.00
☐ 655	Mike Diaz 03	.01	.00
☐ 656	Jeff Musselman 03	.01	.00
☐ 657	Jerry Reed 03	.01	.00
☐ 658	Kevin Blankenship 03	.01	.00
☐ 659	Wayne Tolleson 03	.01	.00
☐ 660	Eric Hetzel 03	.01	.00
☐ BC1	Kirby Puckett 20	.09	.03
☐ BC2	Mike Scott 05	.02	.01
☐ BC3	Joe Carter 10	.05	.01
☐ BC4	Orel Hershiser 05	.02	.01
☐ BC5	Jose Canseco 20	.09	.03
☐ BC6	Darryl Strawberry 12	.05	.02
☐ BC7	George Brett 10	.05	.01
☐ BC8	Andre Dawson 10	.05	.01
☐ BC9	Paul Molitor UER 08	.04	.01
	(Brewers logo missing the word Milwaukee)		
☐ BC10	Andy Van Slyke 08	.04	.01
☐ BC11	Dave Winfield 10	.05	.01
☐ BC12	Kevin Gross 05	.02	.01
☐ BC13	Mike Greenwell 08	.04	.01
☐ BC14	Ozzie Smith 10	.05	.01
☐ BC15	Cal Ripken 25	.11	.03
☐ BC16	Andres Galarraga 05	.02	.01
☐ BC17	Alan Trammell 08	.04	.01
☐ BC18	Kal Daniels 05	.02	.01
☐ BC19	Fred McGriff 12	.05	.02
☐ BC20	Tony Gwynn 12	.05	.02
☐ BC21	Wally Joyner DP 08	.04	.01
☐ BC22	Will Clark DP 15	.07	.02
☐ BC23	Ozzie Guillen 05	.02	.01
☐ BC24	Gerald Perry DP 05	.02	.01
☐ BC25	Alvin Davis DP 05	.02	.01
☐ BC26	Ruben Sierra 15	.07	.02

1989 Donruss Rookies

The 1989 Donruss Rookies set contains 56 standard-size (2 1/2" by 3 1/2") cards. The fronts have green and black borders; the backs are green and feature career highlights. The cards were distributed as a boxed set through the Donruss Dealer Network. The key Rookie Cards in this set are Jim Abbott, Junior Felix, Ken Griffey Jr., Steve Finley, Deion Sanders, and Gary Sheffield.

	MT	EX-MT	VG
COMPLETE SET (56)	15.00	6.75	1.90
COMMON PLAYER (1-56)	.05	.02	.01

		MT	EX-MT	VG
☐ 1	Gary Sheffield	3.00	1.35	.40
☐ 2	Gregg Jefferies	.35	.16	.04
☐ 3	Ken Griffey Jr.	8.00	3.60	1.00
☐ 4	Tom Gordon	.10	.05	.01
☐ 5	Billy Spiers	.10	.05	.01
☐ 6	Deion Sanders	2.25	1.00	.30
☐ 7	Donn Pall	.05	.02	.01
☐ 8	Steve Carter	.05	.02	.01
☐ 9	Francisco Oliveras	.05	.02	.01
☐ 10	Steve Wilson	.05	.02	.01
☐ 11	Bob Geren	.05	.02	.01
☐ 12	Tony Castillo	.05	.02	.01
☐ 13	Kenny Rogers	.05	.02	.01
☐ 14	Carlos Martinez	.12	.05	.02
☐ 15	Edgar Martinez	.50	.23	.06
☐ 16	Jim Abbott	1.25	.55	.16
☐ 17	Torey Lovullo	.05	.02	.01
☐ 18	Mark Carreon	.05	.02	.01
☐ 19	Geronimo Berroa	.05	.02	.01
☐ 20	Luis Medina	.05	.02	.01
☐ 21	Sandy Alomar Jr.	.25	.11	.03
☐ 22	Bob Milacki	.10	.05	.01
☐ 23	Joe Girardi	.15	.07	.02
☐ 24	German Gonzalez	.05	.02	.01
☐ 25	Craig Worthington	.05	.02	.01
☐ 26	Jerome Walton	.10	.05	.01
☐ 27	Gary Wayne	.05	.02	.01
☐ 28	Tim Jones	.05	.02	.01
☐ 29	Dante Bichette	.08	.04	.01
☐ 30	Alexis Infante	.05	.02	.01
☐ 31	Ken Hill	.40	.18	.05
☐ 32	Dwight Smith	.10	.05	.01
☐ 33	Luis de los Santos	.05	.02	.01
☐ 34	Eric Yelding	.05	.02	.01
☐ 35	Gregg Olson	.50	.23	.06
☐ 36	Phil Stephenson	.05	.02	.01
☐ 37	Ken Patterson	.05	.02	.01
☐ 38	Rick Wrona	.05	.02	.01
☐ 39	Mike Brumley	.05	.02	.01
☐ 40	Cris Carpenter	.10	.05	.01
☐ 41	Jeff Brantley	.10	.05	.01
☐ 42	Ron Jones	.05	.02	.01
☐ 43	Randy Johnson	.15	.07	.02
☐ 44	Kevin Brown	.30	.14	.04
☐ 45	Ramon Martinez	.50	.23	.06
☐ 46	Greg W.Harris	.08	.04	.01
☐ 47	Steve Finley	.40	.18	.05
☐ 48	Randy Kramer	.05	.02	.01
☐ 49	Erik Hanson	.20	.09	.03
☐ 50	Matt Merullo	.10	.05	.01
☐ 51	Mike Devereaux	.35	.16	.04
☐ 52	Clay Parker	.05	.02	.01
☐ 53	Omar Vizquel	.15	.07	.02
☐ 54	Dorok Lilliquist	.10	.05	.01
☐ 55	Junior Felix	.25	.11	.03
☐ 56	Checklist Card	.08	.01	.00

1990 Donruss

The 1990 Donruss set contains 716 standard-size (2 1/2" by 3 1/2") cards. The front borders are bright red. The horizontally oriented backs are amber. Cards numbered 1-26 are Diamond Kings; cards numbered 28-47 are Rated Rookies (RR). Numbered with the prefix "BC" for bonus card, a 26-card set featuring the most valuable player from each of the 26 teams was randomly inserted in all 1990 Donruss unopened pack formats. Card number 716 was added to the set shortly after the set's initial production, necessitating the checklist variation on card number 700. The set

was the largest ever produced by Donruss, unfortunately it also had a large number of errors which were corrected after the cards were released. Every All-Star selection in the set has two versions, the statistical heading on the back is either "Recent Major League Performance" or "All-Star Game Performance." There are a number of cards that have been discovered to have minor printing flaws, which are insignificant variations, that collectors have found unworthy of price differentials. These very minor variations include numbers 1, 18, 154, 168, 206, 270, 321, 347, 405, 408, 425, 583, 585, 619, 637, 639, 699, 701, and 716. The factory sets were distributed without the Bonus Cards; thus there were again new checklist cards printed to reflect the exclusion of the Bonus Cards. These factory set checklist cards are the B variations below (except for 700C). The key Rookie Cards in this set are Delino DeShields, Juan Gonzalez, Marquis Grissom, Dave Justice, Ben McDonald, John Olerud, and Dean Palmer. The unusual number of cards in the set (716 plus 26 BC's, i.e., not divisible by 132) apparently led to 50 double-printed numbers, which are indicated in the checklists below (1990 Donruss and 1990 Donruss Bonus MVP's) by DP.

	MT	EX-MT	VG
COMPLETE SET (716)	15.00	6.75	1.90
COMPLETE FACT.SET (716)	15.00	6.75	1.90
COMMON PLAYER (1-716)	.04	.02	.01
COMPLETE MVP SET (26)	2.00	.90	.25
COMMON MVP (BC1-BC26)	.05	.02	.01

☐ 1 Bo Jackson DK	.12	.05	.02
☐ 2 Steve Sax DK	.05	.02	.01
☐ 3A Ruben Sierra DK ERR	.50	.23	.06
(No small line on top border on card back)			
☐ 3B Ruben Sierra DK COR	.25	.11	.03
☐ 4 Ken Griffey Jr. DK	.50	.23	.06
☐ 5 Mickey Tettleton DK	.05	.02	.01
☐ 6 Dave Stewart DK	.05	.02	.01
☐ 7 Jim Deshaies DK DP	.05	.02	.01
☐ 8 John Smoltz DK	.12	.05	.02
☐ 9 Mike Bielecki DK	.05	.02	.01
☐ 10A Brian Downing DK	.50	.23	.06
ERR (Reverse negative on card front)			
☐ 10B Brian Downing DK COR	.05	.02	.01
☐ 11 Kevin Mitchell DK	.08	.04	.01
☐ 12 Kelly Gruber DK	.05	.02	.01
☐ 13 Joe Magrane DK	.05	.02	.01
☐ 14 John Franco DK	.05	.02	.01
☐ 15 Ozzie Guillen DK	.05	.02	.01
☐ 16 Lou Whitaker DK	.05	.02	.01
☐ 17 John Smiley DK	.05	.02	.01
☐ 18 Howard Johnson DK	.05	.02	.01
☐ 19 Willie Randolph DK	.05	.02	.01
☐ 20 Chris Bosio DK	.05	.02	.01
☐ 21 Tommy Herr DK DP	.05	.02	.01
☐ 22 Dan Gladden DK	.05	.02	.01
☐ 23 Ellis Burks DK	.05	.02	.01
☐ 24 Pete O'Brien DK	.05	.02	.01
☐ 25 Bryn Smith DK	.05	.02	.01
☐ 26 Ed Whitson DK	.05	.02	.01
☐ 27 DK Checklist DP	.04	.00	.00
(Comments on Perez-Steele on back)			
☐ 28 Robin Ventura RR	.75	.35	.09
☐ 29 Todd Zeile RR	.15	.07	.02
☐ 30 Sandy Alomar Jr. RR	.10	.05	.01
☐ 31 Kent Mercker RR	.12	.05	.02
☐ 32 Ben McDonald RR UER	.50	.23	.06
(Middle name Benard, not Benjamin)			
☐ 33A Juan Gonzalez RR ERR	3.50	1.55	.45
(Reverse negative)			
☐ 33B Juan Gonzalez RR COR	1.75	.80	.22
☐ 34 Eric Anthony RR	.30	.14	.04
☐ 35 Mike Fetters RR	.10	.05	.01
☐ 36 Marquis Grissom RR	.60	.25	.08
☐ 37 Greg Vaughn RR	.15	.07	.02
☐ 38 Brian DuBois RR	.05	.02	.01
☐ 39 Steve Avery RR UER	.75	.35	.09
(Born in MI, not NJ)			
☐ 40 Mark Gardner RR	.12	.05	.02
☐ 41 Andy Benes RR	.20	.09	.03
☐ 42 Delino DeShields RR	.60	.25	.08
☐ 43 Scott Coolbaugh RR	.05	.02	.01
☐ 44 Pat Combs RR DP	.05	.02	.01
☐ 45 Alex Sanchez RR DP	.05	.02	.01
☐ 46 Kelly Mann RR DP	.05	.02	.01
☐ 47 Julio Machado RR DP	.05	.02	.01

☐ 48	Pete Incaviglia	.04	.02	.01			
☐ 49	Shawon Dunston	.07	.03	.01			
☐ 50	Jeff Treadway	.04	.02	.01			
☐ 51	Jeff Ballard	.04	.02	.01			
☐ 52	Claudell Washington	.04	.02	.01			
☐ 53	Juan Samuel	.04	.02	.01			
☐ 54	John Smiley	.07	.03	.01			
☐ 55	Rob Deer	.07	.03	.01			
☐ 56	Geno Petralli	.04	.02	.01			
☐ 57	Chris Bosio	.04	.02	.01			
☐ 58	Carlton Fisk	.10	.05	.01			
☐ 59	Kirt Manwaring	.04	.02	.01			
☐ 60	Chet Lemon	.04	.02	.01			
☐ 61	Bo Jackson	.15	.07	.02			
☐ 62	Doyle Alexander	.04	.02	.01			
☐ 63	Pedro Guerrero	.07	.03	.01			
☐ 64	Allan Anderson	.04	.02	.01			
☐ 65	Greg W. Harris	.04	.02	.01			
☐ 66	Mike Greenwell	.07	.03	.01			
☐ 67	Walt Weiss	.04	.02	.01			
☐ 68	Wade Boggs	.20	.09	.03			
☐ 69	Jim Clancy	.04	.02	.01			
☐ 70	Junior Felix	.07	.03	.01			
☐ 71	Barry Larkin	.12	.05	.02			
☐ 72	Dave LaPoint	.04	.02	.01			
☐ 73	Joel Skinner	.04	.02	.01			
☐ 74	Jesse Barfield	.04	.02	.01			
☐ 75	Tommy Herr	.04	.02	.01			
☐ 76	Ricky Jordan	.04	.02	.01			
☐ 77	Eddie Murray	.10	.05	.01			
☐ 78	Steve Sax	.07	.03	.01			
☐ 79	Tim Belcher	.07	.03	.01			
☐ 80	Danny Jackson	.04	.02	.01			
☐ 81	Kent Hrbek	.07	.03	.01			
☐ 82	Milt Thompson	.04	.02	.01			
☐ 83	Brook Jacoby	.04	.02	.01			
☐ 84	Mike Marshall	.04	.02	.01			
☐ 85	Kevin Seitzer	.07	.03	.01			
☐ 86	Tony Gwynn	.20	.09	.03			
☐ 87	Dave Stieb	.07	.03	.01			
☐ 88	Dave Smith	.04	.02	.01			
☐ 89	Bret Saberhagen	.07	.03	.01			
☐ 90	Alan Trammell	.07	.03	.01			
☐ 91	Tony Phillips	.04	.02	.01			
☐ 92	Doug Drabek	.07	.03	.01			
☐ 93	Jeffrey Leonard	.04	.02	.01			
☐ 94	Wally Joyner	.07	.03	.01			
☐ 95	Carney Lansford	.07	.03	.01			
☐ 96	Cal Ripken	.40	.18	.05			
☐ 97	Andres Galarraga	.04	.02	.01			
☐ 98	Kevin Mitchell	.10	.05	.01			
☐ 99	Howard Johnson	.07	.03	.01			
☐ 100A	Checklist Card (28-129)	.06	.01	.00			
☐ 100B	Checklist Card (28-125)	.06	.01	.00			
☐ 101	Melido Perez	.07	.03	.01			
☐ 102	Spike Owen	.04	.02	.01
☐ 103	Paul Molitor	.10	.05	.01
☐ 104	Geronimo Berroa	.04	.02	.01
☐ 105	Ryne Sandberg	.35	.16	.04
☐ 106	Bryn Smith	.04	.02	.01
☐ 107	Steve Buechele	.04	.02	.01
☐ 108	Jim Abbott	.20	.09	.03
☐ 109	Alvin Davis	.04	.02	.01
☐ 110	Lee Smith	.07	.03	.01
☐ 111	Roberto Alomar	.40	.18	.05
☐ 112	Rick Reuschel	.04	.02	.01
☐ 113A	Kelly Gruber ERR (Born 2/22)	.07	.03	.01
☐ 113B	Kelly Gruber COR (Born 2/26; corrected in factory sets)	.07	.03	.01
☐ 114	Joe Carter	.20	.09	.03
☐ 115	Jose Rijo	.07	.03	.01
☐ 116	Greg Minton	.04	.02	.01
☐ 117	Bob Ojeda	.04	.02	.01
☐ 118	Glenn Davis	.07	.03	.01
☐ 119	Jeff Reardon	.07	.03	.01
☐ 120	Kurt Stillwell	.04	.02	.01
☐ 121	John Smoltz	.25	.11	.03
☐ 122	Dwight Evans	.07	.03	.01
☐ 123	Eric Yelding	.04	.02	.01
☐ 124	John Franco	.07	.03	.01
☐ 125	Jose Canseco	.30	.14	.04
☐ 126	Barry Bonds	.30	.14	.04
☐ 127	Lee Guetterman	.04	.02	.01
☐ 128	Jack Clark	.07	.03	.01
☐ 129	Dave Valle	.04	.02	.01
☐ 130	Hubie Brooks	.04	.02	.01
☐ 131	Ernest Riles	.04	.02	.01
☐ 132	Mike Morgan	.04	.02	.01
☐ 133	Steve Jeltz	.04	.02	.01
☐ 134	Jeff D. Robinson	.04	.02	.01
☐ 135	Ozzie Guillen	.04	.02	.01
☐ 136	Chili Davis	.07	.03	.01
☐ 137	Mitch Webster	.04	.02	.01
☐ 138	Jerry Browne	.04	.02	.01
☐ 139	Bo Diaz	.04	.02	.01
☐ 140	Robby Thompson	.04	.02	.01
☐ 141	Craig Worthington	.04	.02	.01
☐ 142	Julio Franco	.07	.03	.01
☐ 143	Brian Holman	.04	.02	.01
☐ 144	George Brett	.15	.07	.02
☐ 145	Tom Glavine	.25	.11	.03
☐ 146	Robin Yount	.15	.07	.02
☐ 147	Gary Carter	.07	.03	.01
☐ 148	Ron Kittle	.04	.02	.01
☐ 149	Tony Fernandez	.07	.03	.01
☐ 150	Dave Stewart	.07	.03	.01
☐ 151	Gary Gaetti	.04	.02	.01
☐ 152	Kevin Elster	.04	.02	.01
☐ 153	Gerald Perry	.04	.02	.01
☐ 154	Jesse Orosco	.04	.02	.01

☐ 155	Wally Backman	.04	.02	.01
☐ 156	Dennis Martinez	.07	.03	.01
☐ 157	Rick Sutcliffe	.07	.03	.01
☐ 158	Greg Maddux	.20	.09	.03
☐ 159	Andy Hawkins	.04	.02	.01
☐ 160	John Kruk	.07	.03	.01
☐ 161	Jose Oquendo	.04	.02	.01
☐ 162	John Dopson	.04	.02	.01
☐ 163	Joe Magrane	.04	.02	.01
☐ 164	Bill Ripken	.04	.02	.01
☐ 165	Fred Manrique	.04	.02	.01
☐ 166	Nolan Ryan UER	.50	.23	.06
	(Did not lead NL in			
	K's in '89 as he was			
	in AL in '89)			
☐ 167	Damon Berryhill	.04	.02	.01
☐ 168	Dale Murphy	.10	.05	.01
☐ 169	Mickey Tettleton	.07	.03	.01
☐ 170A	Kirk McCaskill ERR	.04	.02	.01
	(Born 4/19)			
☐ 170B	Kirk McCaskill COR	.04	.02	.01
	(Born 4/9; corrected			
	in factory sets)			
☐ 171	Dwight Gooden	.10	.05	.01
☐ 172	Jose Lind	.04	.02	.01
☐ 173	B.J. Surhoff	.04	.02	.01
☐ 174	Ruben Sierra	.20	.09	.03
☐ 175	Dan Plesac	.04	.02	.01
☐ 176	Dan Pasqua	.04	.02	.01
☐ 177	Kelly Downs	.04	.02	.01
☐ 178	Matt Nokes	.04	.02	.01
☐ 179	Luis Aquino	.04	.02	.01
☐ 180	Frank Tanana	.04	.02	.01
☐ 181	Tony Pena	.04	.02	.01
☐ 182	Dan Gladden	.04	.02	.01
☐ 183	Bruce Hurst	.07	.03	.01
☐ 184	Roger Clemens	.35	.16	.04
☐ 185	Mark McGwire	.30	.14	.04
☐ 186	Rob Murphy	.04	.02	.01
☐ 187	Jim Deshaies	.04	.02	.01
☐ 188	Fred McGriff	.20	.09	.03
☐ 189	Rob Dibble	.07	.03	.01
☐ 190	Don Mattingly	.20	.09	.03
☐ 191	Felix Fermin	.04	.02	.01
☐ 192	Roberto Kelly	.10	.05	.01
☐ 193	Dennis Cook	.04	.02	.01
☐ 194	Darren Daulton	.07	.03	.01
☐ 195	Alfredo Griffin	.04	.02	.01
☐ 196	Eric Plunk	.04	.02	.01
☐ 197	Orel Hershiser	.07	.03	.01
☐ 198	Paul O'Neill	.07	.03	.01
☐ 199	Randy Bush	.04	.02	.01
☐ 200A	Checklist Card	.06	.01	.00
	(130-231)			
☐ 200B	Checklist Card	.06	.01	.00
	(126-223)			
☐ 201	Ozzie Smith	.12	.05	.02

☐ 202	Pete O'Brien	.04	.02	.01
☐ 203	Jay Howell	.04	.02	.01
☐ 204	Mark Gubicza	.04	.02	.01
☐ 205	Ed Whitson	.04	.02	.01
☐ 206	George Bell	.07	.03	.01
☐ 207	Mike Scott	.04	.02	.01
☐ 208	Charlie Leibrandt	.04	.02	.01
☐ 209	Mike Heath	.04	.02	.01
☐ 210	Dennis Eckersley	.12	.05	.02
☐ 211	Mike LaValliere	.04	.02	.01
☐ 212	Darnell Coles	.04	.02	.01
☐ 213	Lance Parrish	.07	.03	.01
☐ 214	Mike Moore	.04	.02	.01
☐ 215	Steve Finley	.07	.03	.01
☐ 216	Tim Raines	.07	.03	.01
☐ 217A	Scott Garrelts ERR	.04	.02	.01
	(Born 10/20)			
☐ 217B	Scott Garrelts COR	.04	.02	.01
	(Born 10/30; corrected			
	in factory sets)			
☐ 218	Kevin McReynolds	.07	.03	.01
☐ 219	Dave Gallagher	.04	.02	.01
☐ 220	Tim Wallach	.07	.03	.01
☐ 221	Chuck Crim	.04	.02	.01
☐ 222	Lonnie Smith	.04	.02	.01
☐ 223	Andre Dawson	.12	.05	.02
☐ 224	Nelson Santovenia	.04	.02	.01
☐ 225	Rafael Palmeiro	.10	.05	.01
☐ 226	Devon White	.07	.03	.01
☐ 227	Harold Reynolds	.04	.02	.01
☐ 228	Ellis Burks	.07	.03	.01
☐ 229	Mark Parent	.04	.02	.01
☐ 230	Will Clark	.30	.14	.04
☐ 231	Jimmy Key	.07	.03	.01
☐ 232	John Farrell	.04	.02	.01
☐ 233	Eric Davis	.10	.05	.01
☐ 234	Johnny Ray	.04	.02	.01
☐ 235	Darryl Strawberry	.20	.09	.03
☐ 236	Bill Doran	.04	.02	.01
☐ 237	Greg Gagne	.04	.02	.01
☐ 238	Jim Eisenreich	.04	.02	.01
☐ 239	Tommy Gregg	.04	.02	.01
☐ 240	Marty Barrett	.04	.02	.01
☐ 241	Rafael Ramirez	.04	.02	.01
☐ 242	Chris Sabo	.07	.03	.01
☐ 243	Dave Henderson	.04	.02	.01
☐ 244	Andy Van Slyke	.10	.05	.01
☐ 245	Alvaro Espinoza	.04	.02	.01
☐ 246	Garry Templeton	.04	.02	.01
☐ 247	Gene Harris	.04	.02	.01
☐ 248	Kevin Gross	.04	.02	.01
☐ 249	Brett Butler	.07	.03	.01
☐ 250	Willie Randolph	.07	.03	.01
☐ 251	Roger McDowell	.04	.02	.01
☐ 252	Rafael Belliard	.04	.02	.01
☐ 253	Steve Rosenberg	.04	.02	.01
☐ 254	Jack Howell	.04	.02	.01

☐ 255	Marvell Wynne	.04	.02	.01
☐ 256	Tom Candiotti	.04	.02	.01
☐ 257	Todd Benzinger	.04	.02	.01
☐ 258	Don Robinson	.04	.02	.01
☐ 259	Phil Bradley	.04	.02	.01
☐ 260	Cecil Espy	.04	.02	.01
☐ 261	Scott Bankhead	.04	.02	.01
☐ 262	Frank White	.04	.02	.01
☐ 263	Andres Thomas	.04	.02	.01
☐ 264	Glenn Braggs	.04	.02	.01
☐ 265	David Cone	.12	.05	.02
☐ 266	Bobby Thigpen	.04	.02	.01
☐ 267	Nelson Liriano	.04	.02	.01
☐ 268	Terry Steinbach	.07	.03	.01
☐ 269	Kirby Puckett UER	.30	.14	.04
	(Back doesn't consider			
	Joe Torre's .363 in '71)			
☐ 270	Gregg Jefferies	.12	.05	.02
☐ 271	Jeff Blauser	.07	.03	.01
☐ 272	Cory Snyder	.04	.02	.01
☐ 273	Roy Smith	.04	.02	.01
☐ 274	Tom Foley	.04	.02	.01
☐ 275	Mitch Williams	.07	.03	.01
☐ 276	Paul Kilgus	.04	.02	.01
☐ 277	Don Slaught	.04	.02	.01
☐ 278	Von Hayes	.04	.02	.01
☐ 279	Vince Coleman	.07	.03	.01
☐ 280	Mike Boddicker	.04	.02	.01
☐ 281	Ken Dayley	.04	.02	.01
☐ 282	Mike Devereaux	.07	.03	.01
☐ 283	Kenny Rogers	.04	.02	.01
☐ 284	Jeff Russell	.04	.02	.01
☐ 285	Jerome Walton	.07	.03	.01
☐ 286	Derek Lilliquist	.04	.02	.01
☐ 287	Joe Orsulak	.04	.02	.01
☐ 288	Dick Schofield	.04	.02	.01
☐ 289	Ron Darling	.07	.03	.01
☐ 290	Bobby Bonilla	.12	.05	.02
☐ 291	Jim Gantner	.04	.02	.01
☐ 292	Bobby Witt	.07	.03	.01
☐ 293	Greg Brock	.04	.02	.01
☐ 294	Ivan Calderon	.04	.02	.01
☐ 295	Steve Bedrosian	.04	.02	.01
☐ 296	Mike Henneman	.04	.02	.01
☐ 297	Tom Gordon	.07	.03	.01
☐ 298	Lou Whitaker	.07	.03	.01
☐ 299	Terry Pendleton	.10	.05	.01
☐ 300A	Checklist Card	.06	.01	.00
	(232-333)			
☐ 300B	Checklist Card	.06	.01	.00
	(224-321)			
☐ 301	Juan Berenguer	.04	.02	.01
☐ 302	Mark Davis	.04	.02	.01
☐ 303	Nick Esasky	.04	.02	.01
☐ 304	Rickey Henderson	.20	.09	.03
☐ 305	Rick Cerone	.04	.02	.01
☐ 306	Craig Biggio	.10	.05	.01
☐ 307	Duane Ward	.04	.02	.01
☐ 308	Tom Browning	.04	.02	.01
☐ 309	Walt Terrell	.04	.02	.01
☐ 310	Greg Swindell	.07	.03	.01
☐ 311	Dave Righetti	.04	.02	.01
☐ 312	Mike Maddux	.04	.02	.01
☐ 313	Len Dykstra	.07	.03	.01
☐ 314	Jose Gonzalez	.04	.02	.01
☐ 315	Steve Balboni	.04	.02	.01
☐ 316	Mike Scioscia	.04	.02	.01
☐ 317	Ron Oester	.04	.02	.01
☐ 318	Gary Wayne	.04	.02	.01
☐ 319	Todd Worrell	.04	.02	.01
☐ 320	Doug Jones	.04	.02	.01
☐ 321	Jeff Hamilton	.04	.02	.01
☐ 322	Danny Tartabull	.10	.05	.01
☐ 323	Chris James	.04	.02	.01
☐ 324	Mike Flanagan	.04	.02	.01
☐ 325	Gerald Young	.04	.02	.01
☐ 326	Bob Boone	.07	.03	.01
☐ 327	Frank Williams	.04	.02	.01
☐ 328	Dave Parker	.07	.03	.01
☐ 329	Sid Bream	.04	.02	.01
☐ 330	Mike Schooler	.04	.02	.01
☐ 331	Bert Blyleven	.07	.03	.01
☐ 332	Bob Welch	.07	.03	.01
☐ 333	Bob Milacki	.04	.02	.01
☐ 334	Tim Burke	.04	.02	.01
☐ 335	Jose Uribe	.04	.02	.01
☐ 336	Randy Myers	.04	.02	.01
☐ 337	Eric King	.04	.02	.01
☐ 338	Mark Langston	.07	.03	.01
☐ 339	Teddy Higuera	.04	.02	.01
☐ 340	Oddibe McDowell	.04	.02	.01
☐ 341	Lloyd McClendon	.04	.02	.01
☐ 342	Pascual Perez	.04	.02	.01
☐ 343	Kevin Brown UER	.10	.05	.01
	(Signed is misspelled			
	as signeed on back)			
☐ 344	Chuck Finley	.07	.03	.01
☐ 345	Erik Hanson	.07	.03	.01
☐ 346	Rich Gedman	.04	.02	.01
☐ 347	Bip Roberts	.07	.03	.01
☐ 348	Matt Williams	.10	.05	.01
☐ 349	Tom Henke	.07	.03	.01
☐ 350	Brad Komminsk	.04	.02	.01
☐ 351	Jeff Reed	.04	.02	.01
☐ 352	Brian Downing	.04	.02	.01
☐ 353	Frank Viola	.07	.03	.01
☐ 354	Terry Puhl	.04	.02	.01
☐ 355	Brian Harper	.07	.03	.01
☐ 356	Steve Farr	.04	.02	.01
☐ 357	Joe Boever	.04	.02	.01
☐ 358	Danny Heep	.04	.02	.01
☐ 359	Larry Andersen	.04	.02	.01
☐ 360	Rolando Roomes	.04	.02	.01
☐ 361	Mike Gallego	.04	.02	.01

☐	362	Bob Kipper	.04	.02	.01			
☐	363	Clay Parker	.04	.02	.01			
☐	364	Mike Pagliarulo	.04	.02	.01			
☐	365	Ken Griffey Jr. UER	1.25	.55	.16			
		(Signed through 1990,						
		should be 1991)						
☐	366	Rex Hudler	.04	.02	.01			
☐	367	Pat Sheridan	.04	.02	.01			
☐	368	Kirk Gibson	.07	.03	.01			
☐	369	Jeff Parrett	.04	.02	.01			
☐	370	Bob Walk	.04	.02	.01			
☐	371	Ken Patterson	.04	.02	.01			
☐	372	Bryan Harvey	.07	.03	.01			
☐	373	Mike Bielecki	.04	.02	.01			
☐	374	Tom Magrann	.04	.02	.01			
☐	375	Rick Mahler	.04	.02	.01			
☐	376	Craig Lefferts	.04	.02	.01			
☐	377	Gregg Olson	.10	.05	.01			
☐	378	Jamie Moyer	.04	.02	.01			
☐	379	Randy Johnson	.07	.03	.01			
☐	380	Jeff Montgomery	.07	.03	.01			
☐	381	Marty Clary	.04	.02	.01			
☐	382	Bill Spiers	.04	.02	.01			
☐	383	Dave Magadan	.07	.03	.01			
☐	384	Greg Hibbard	.20	.09	.03			
☐	385	Ernie Whitt	.04	.02	.01			
☐	386	Rick Honeycutt	.04	.02	.01			
☐	387	Dave West	.04	.02	.01			
☐	388	Keith Hernandez	.07	.03	.01			
☐	389	Jose Alvarez	.04	.02	.01			
☐	390	Joey Belle	.50	.23	.06			
☐	391	Rick Aguilera	.07	.03	.01			
☐	392	Mike Fitzgerald	.04	.02	.01			
☐	393	Dwight Smith	.04	.02	.01			
☐	394	Steve Wilson	.04	.02	.01			
☐	395	Bob Geren	.04	.02	.01			
☐	396	Randy Ready	.04	.02	.01			
☐	397	Ken Hill	.12	.05	.02			
☐	398	Jody Reed	.04	.02	.01			
☐	399	Tom Brunansky	.07	.03	.01			
☐	400A	Checklist Card	.06	.01	.00			
		(334-435)						
☐	400B	Checklist Card	.06	.01	.00			
		(322-419)						
☐	401	Rene Gonzales	.04	.02	.01			
☐	402	Harold Baines	.07	.03	.01			
☐	403	Cecilio Guante	.04	.02	.01			
☐	404	Joe Girardi	.04	.02	.01			
☐	405A	Sergio Valdez ERR	.15	.07	.02			
		(Card front shows						
		black line crossing						
		S in Sergio)						
☐	405B	Sergio Valdez COR	.04	.02	.01			
☐	406	Mark Williamson	.04	.02	.01			
☐	407	Glenn Hoffman	.04	.02	.01			
☐	408	Jeff Innis	.04	.02	.01			
☐	409	Randy Kramer	.04	.02	.01			
☐	410	Charlie O'Brien	.04	.02	.01			
☐	411	Charlie Hough	.04	.02	.01			
☐	412	Gus Polidor	.04	.02	.01			
☐	413	Ron Karkovice	.04	.02	.01			
☐	414	Trevor Wilson	.04	.02	.01			
☐	415	Kevin Ritz	.10	.05	.01			
☐	416	Gary Thurman	.04	.02	.01			
☐	417	Jeff M. Robinson	.04	.02	.01			
☐	418	Scott Terry	.04	.02	.01			
☐	419	Tim Laudner	.04	.02	.01			
☐	420	Dennis Rasmussen	.04	.02	.01			
☐	421	Luis Rivera	.04	.02	.01			
☐	422	Jim Corsi	.04	.02	.01			
☐	423	Dennis Lamp	.04	.02	.01			
☐	424	Ken Caminiti	.07	.03	.01			
☐	425	David Wells	.07	.03	.01			
☐	426	Norm Charlton	.07	.03	.01			
☐	427	Deion Sanders	.40	.18	.05			
☐	428	Dion James	.04	.02	.01			
☐	429	Chuck Cary	.04	.02	.01			
☐	430	Ken Howell	.04	.02	.01			
☐	431	Steve Lake	.04	.02	.01			
☐	432	Kal Daniels	.04	.02	.01			
☐	433	Lance McCullers	.04	.02	.01			
☐	434	Lenny Harris	.04	.02	.01			
☐	435	Scott Scudder	.04	.02	.01			
☐	436	Gene Larkin	.04	.02	.01			
☐	437	Dan Quisenberry	.07	.03	.01			
☐	438	Steve Olin	.20	.09	.03			
☐	439	Mickey Hatcher	.04	.02	.01			
☐	440	Willie Wilson	.04	.02	.01			
☐	441	Mark Grant	.04	.02	.01			
☐	442	Mookie Wilson	.04	.02	.01			
☐	443	Alex Trevino	.04	.02	.01			
☐	444	Pat Tabler	.04	.02	.01			
☐	445	Dave Bergman	.04	.02	.01			
☐	446	Todd Burns	.04	.02	.01			
☐	447	R.J. Reynolds	.04	.02	.01			
☐	448	Jay Buhner	.07	.03	.01			
☐	449	Lee Stevens	.10	.05	.01			
☐	450	Ron Hassey	.04	.02	.01			
☐	451	Bob Melvin	.04	.02	.01			
☐	452	Dave Martinez	.07	.03	.01			
☐	453	Greg Litton	.04	.02	.01			
☐	454	Mark Carreon	.04	.02	.01			
☐	455	Scott Fletcher	.04	.02	.01			
☐	456	Otis Nixon	.07	.03	.01			
☐	457	Tony Fossas	.04	.02	.01			
☐	458	John Russell	.04	.02	.01			
☐	459	Paul Assenmacher	.04	.02	.01			
☐	460	Zane Smith	.04	.02	.01			
☐	461	Jack Daugherty	.04	.02	.01			
☐	462	Rich Monteleone	.04	.02	.01			
☐	463	Greg Briley	.04	.02	.01			
☐	464	Mike Smithson	.04	.02	.01			
☐	465	Benito Santiago	.07	.03	.01			
☐	466	Jeff Brantley	.04	.02	.01			

☐ 467 Jose Nunez	.04	.02	.01
☐ 468 Scott Bailes	.04	.02	.01
☐ 469 Ken Griffey Sr.	.07	.03	.01
☐ 470 Bob McClure	.04	.02	.01
☐ 471 Mackey Sasser	.04	.02	.01
☐ 472 Glenn Wilson	.04	.02	.01
☐ 473 Kevin Tapani	.35	.16	.04
☐ 474 Bill Buckner	.07	.03	.01
☐ 475 Ron Gant	.25	.11	.03
☐ 476 Kevin Romine	.04	.02	.01
☐ 477 Juan Agosto	.04	.02	.01
☐ 478 Herm Winningham	.04	.02	.01
☐ 479 Storm Davis	.04	.02	.01
☐ 480 Jeff King	.07	.03	.01
☐ 481 Kevin Mmahat	.07	.03	.01
☐ 482 Carmelo Martinez	.04	.02	.01
☐ 483 Omar Vizquel	.07	.03	.01
☐ 484 Jim Dwyer	.04	.02	.01
☐ 485 Bob Knepper	.04	.02	.01
☐ 486 Dave Anderson	.04	.02	.01
☐ 487 Ron Jones	.04	.02	.01
☐ 488 Jay Bell	.07	.03	.01
☐ 489 Sammy Sosa	.15	.07	.02
☐ 490 Kent Anderson	.04	.02	.01
☐ 491 Domingo Ramos	.04	.02	.01
☐ 492 Dave Clark	.04	.02	.01
☐ 493 Tim Birtsas	.04	.02	.01
☐ 494 Ken Oberkfell	.04	.02	.01
☐ 495 Larry Sheets	.04	.02	.01
☐ 496 Jeff Kunkel	.04	.02	.01
☐ 497 Jim Presley	.04	.02	.01
☐ 498 Mike Macfarlane	.04	.02	.01
☐ 499 Pete Smith	.07	.03	.01
☐ 500A Checklist Card DP	.06	.01	.00
(436-537)			
☐ 500B Checklist Card	.06	.01	.00
(420-517)			
☐ 501 Gary Sheffield	.50	.23	.06
☐ 502 Terry Bross	.04	.02	.01
☐ 503 Jerry Kutzler	.04	.02	.01
☐ 504 Lloyd Moseby	.04	.02	.01
☐ 505 Curt Young	.04	.02	.01
☐ 506 Al Newman	.04	.02	.01
☐ 507 Keith Miller	.04	.02	.01
☐ 508 Mike Stanton	.15	.07	.02
☐ 509 Rich Yett	.04	.02	.01
☐ 510 Tim Drummond	.04	.02	.01
☐ 511 Joe Hesketh	.04	.02	.01
☐ 512 Rick Wrona	.04	.02	.01
☐ 513 Luis Salazar	.04	.02	.01
☐ 514 Hal Morris	.15	.07	.02
☐ 515 Terry Mulholland	.07	.03	.01
☐ 516 John Morris	.04	.02	.01
☐ 517 Carlos Quintana	.07	.03	.01
☐ 518 Frank DiPino	.04	.02	.01
☐ 519 Randy Milligan	.04	.02	.01
☐ 520 Chad Kreuter	.04	.02	.01
☐ 521 Mike Jeffcoat	.04	.02	.01
☐ 522 Mike Harkey	.07	.03	.01
☐ 523A Andy Nezelek ERR	.04	.02	.01
(Wrong birth year)			
☐ 523B Andy Nezelek COR	.15	.07	.02
(Finally corrected			
in factory sets)			
☐ 524 Dave Schmidt	.04	.02	.01
☐ 525 Tony Armas	.04	.02	.01
☐ 526 Barry Lyons	.04	.02	.01
☐ 527 Rick Reed	.04	.02	.01
☐ 528 Jerry Reuss	.04	.02	.01
☐ 529 Dean Palmer	.60	.25	.08
☐ 530 Jeff Peterek	.10	.05	.01
☐ 531 Carlos Martinez	.07	.03	.01
☐ 532 Atlee Hammaker	.04	.02	.01
☐ 533 Mike Brumley	.04	.02	.01
☐ 534 Terry Leach	.04	.02	.01
☐ 535 Doug Strange	.10	.05	.01
☐ 536 Jose DeLeon	.04	.02	.01
☐ 537 Shane Rawley	.04	.02	.01
☐ 538 Joey Cora	.04	.02	.01
☐ 539 Eric Hetzel	.04	.02	.01
☐ 540 Gene Nelson	.04	.02	.01
☐ 541 Wes Gardner	.04	.02	.01
☐ 542 Mark Portugal	.04	.02	.01
☐ 543 Al Leiter	.04	.02	.01
☐ 544 Jack Armstrong	.07	.03	.01
☐ 545 Greg Cadaret	.04	.02	.01
☐ 546 Rod Nichols	.04	.02	.01
☐ 547 Luis Polonia	.07	.03	.01
☐ 548 Charlie Hayes	.12	.05	.02
☐ 549 Dickie Thon	.04	.02	.01
☐ 550 Tim Crews	.04	.02	.01
☐ 551 Dave Winfield	.15	.07	.02
☐ 552 Mike Davis	.04	.02	.01
☐ 553 Ron Robinson	.04	.02	.01
☐ 554 Carmen Castillo	.04	.02	.01
☐ 555 John Costello	.04	.02	.01
☐ 556 Bud Black	.04	.02	.01
☐ 557 Rick Dempsey	.04	.02	.01
☐ 558 Jim Acker	.04	.02	.01
☐ 559 Eric Show	.04	.02	.01
☐ 560 Pat Borders	.07	.03	.01
☐ 561 Danny Darwin	.04	.02	.01
☐ 562 Rick Luecken	.04	.02	.01
☐ 563 Edwin Nunez	.04	.02	.01
☐ 564 Felix Jose	.20	.09	.03
☐ 565 John Cangelosi	.04	.02	.01
☐ 566 Bill Swift	.07	.03	.01
☐ 567 Bill Schroeder	.04	.02	.01
☐ 568 Stan Javier	.04	.02	.01
☐ 569 Jim Traber	.04	.02	.01
☐ 570 Wallace Johnson	.04	.02	.01
☐ 571 Donell Nixon	.04	.02	.01
☐ 572 Sid Fernandez	.07	.03	.01
☐ 573 Lance Johnson	.07	.03	.01

☐ 574 Andy McGaffigan	.04	.02	.01
☐ 575 Mark Knudson	.04	.02	.01
☐ 576 Tommy Greene	.12	.05	.02
☐ 577 Mark Grace	.20	.09	.03
☐ 578 Larry Walker	.90	.40	.11
☐ 579 Mike Stanley	.04	.02	.01
☐ 580 Mike Witt DP	.04	.02	.01
☐ 581 Scott Bradley	.04	.02	.01
☐ 582 Greg A. Harris	.04	.02	.01
☐ 583A Kevin Hickey ERR	.15	.07	.02
☐ 583B Kevin Hickey COR	.04	.02	.01
☐ 584 Lee Mazzilli	.04	.02	.01
☐ 585 Jeff Pico	.04	.02	.01
☐ 586 Joe Oliver	.10	.05	.01
☐ 587 Willie Fraser DP	.04	.02	.01
☐ 588 Carl Yastrzemski	.08	.04	.01
Puzzle Card DP			
☐ 589 Kevin Bass DP	.04	.02	.01
☐ 590 John Moses DP	.04	.02	.01
☐ 591 Tom Pagnozzi DP	.04	.02	.01
☐ 592 Tony Castillo DP	.04	.02	.01
☐ 593 Jerald Clark DP	.04	.02	.01
☐ 594 Dan Schatzeder	.04	.02	.01
☐ 595 Luis Quinones DP	.04	.02	.01
☐ 596 Pete Harnisch DP	.07	.03	.01
☐ 597 Gary Redus	.04	.02	.01
☐ 598 Mel Hall	.04	.02	.01
☐ 599 Rick Schu	.04	.02	.01
☐ 600A Checklist Card	.06	.01	.00
(538-639)			
☐ 600B Checklist Card	.06	.01	.00
(518-617)			
☐ 601 Mike Kingery DP	.04	.02	.01
☐ 602 Terry Kennedy DP	.04	.02	.01
☐ 603 Mike Sharperson DP	.04	.02	.01
☐ 604 Don Carman DP	.04	.02	.01
☐ 605 Jim Gott	.04	.02	.01
☐ 606 Donn Pall DP	.04	.02	.01
☐ 607 Rance Mulliniks	.04	.02	.01
☐ 608 Curt Wilkerson DP	.04	.02	.01
☐ 609 Mike Felder DP	.04	.02	.01
☐ 610 Guillermo Hernandez DP	.04	.02	.01
☐ 611 Candy Maldonado DP	.04	.02	.01
☐ 612 Mark Thurmond DP	.04	.02	.01
☐ 613 Rick Leach DP	.04	.02	.01
☐ 614 Jerry Reed DP	.04	.02	.01
☐ 615 Franklin Stubbs	.04	.02	.01
☐ 616 Billy Hatcher DP	.04	.02	.01
☐ 617 Don August DP	.04	.02	.01
☐ 618 Tim Teufel	.04	.02	.01
☐ 619 Shawn Hillegas DP	.04	.02	.01
☐ 620 Manny Lee	.04	.02	.01
☐ 621 Gary Ward DP	.04	.02	.01
☐ 622 Mark Guthrie DP	.04	.02	.01
☐ 623 Jeff Musselman DP	.04	.02	.01
☐ 624 Mark Lemke DP	.04	.02	.01
☐ 625 Fernando Valenzuela	.07	.03	.01
☐ 626 Paul Sorrento DP	.20	.09	.03
☐ 627 Glenallen Hill DP	.04	.02	.01
☐ 628 Les Lancaster DP	.04	.02	.01
☐ 629 Vance Law DP	.04	.02	.01
☐ 630 Randy Velarde DP	.04	.02	.01
☐ 631 Todd Frohwirth DP	.04	.02	.01
☐ 632 Willie McGee	.07	.03	.01
☐ 633 Dennis Boyd DP	.04	.02	.01
☐ 634 Cris Carpenter DP	.04	.02	.01
☐ 635 Brian Holton	.04	.02	.01
☐ 636 Tracy Jones DP	.04	.02	.01
☐ 637A Terry Steinbach AS	.10	.05	.01
(Recent Major			
League Performance)			
☐ 637B Terry Steinbach AS	.04	.02	.01
(All-Star Game			
Performance)			
☐ 638 Brady Anderson	.12	.05	.02
☐ 639A Jack Morris ERR	.20	.09	.03
(Card front shows			
black line crossing			
J in Jack)			
☐ 639B Jack Morris COR	.10	.05	.01
☐ 640 Jaime Navarro	.20	.09	.03
☐ 641 Darrin Jackson	.07	.03	.01
☐ 642 Mike Dyer	.04	.02	.01
☐ 643 Mike Schmidt	.25	.11	.03
☐ 644 Henry Cotto	.04	.02	.01
☐ 645 John Cerutti	.04	.02	.01
☐ 646 Francisco Cabrera	.19	.05	.01
☐ 647 Scott Sanderson	.04	.02	.01
☐ 648 Brian Meyer	.04	.02	.01
☐ 649 Ray Searage	.04	.02	.01
☐ 650A Bo Jackson AS	.20	.09	.03
(Recent Major			
League Performance)			
☐ 650B Bo Jackson AS	.10	.05	.01
(All-Star Game			
Performance)			
☐ 651 Steve Lyons	.04	.02	.01
☐ 652 Mike LaCoss	.04	.02	.01
☐ 653 Ted Power	.04	.02	.01
☐ 654A Howard Johnson AS	.10	.05	.01
(Recent Major			
League Performance)			
☐ 654B Howard Johnson AS	.04	.02	.01
(All-Star Game			
Performance)			
☐ 655 Mauro Gozzo	.04	.02	.01
☐ 656 Mike Blowers	.04	.02	.01
☐ 657 Paul Gibson	.04	.02	.01
☐ 658 Neal Heaton	.04	.02	.01
☐ 659A Nolan Ryan 5000K	3.00	1.35	.40
(665 King of			
Kings back) ERR			
☐ 659B Nolan Ryan 5000K	.40	.18	.05
COR (Still an error as			

Ryan did not lead AL
in K's in '75
- [ ] 660A Harold Baines AS......2.00 .90 .25
  (Black line through
  star on front;
  Recent Major
  League Performance)
- [ ] 660B Harold Baines AS......4.00 1.80 .50
  (Black line through
  star on front;
  All-Star Game
  Performance)
- [ ] 660C Harold Baines AS......1.00 .45 .13
  (Black line behind
  star on front;
  Recent Major
  League Performance)
- [ ] 660D Harold Baines AS.........04 .02 .01
  (Black line behind
  star on front;
  All-Star Game
  Performance)
- [ ] 661 Gary Pettis ....04 .02 .01
- [ ] 662 Clint Zavaras ....04 .02 .01
- [ ] 663A Rick Reuschel AS ....10 .05 .01
  (Recent Major
  League Performance)
- [ ] 663B Rick Reuschel AS ....04 .02 .01
  (All-Star Game
  Performance)
- [ ] 664 Alejandro Pena............04 .02 .01
- [ ] 665A Nolan Ryan KING....2.50 1.15 .30
  (659 5000 K
  back) ERR
- [ ] 665B Nolan Ryan KING COR..40 .18 .05
- [ ] 665C Nolan Ryan KING ERR..90 .40 .11
  (No number on back;
  in factory sets)
- [ ] 666 Ricky Horton ....04 .02 .01
- [ ] 667 Curt Schilling ....15 .07 .02
- [ ] 668 Bill Landrum ....04 .02 .01
- [ ] 669 Todd Stottlemyre..........07 .03 .01
- [ ] 670 Tim Leary...................04 .02 .01
- [ ] 671 John Wetteland............15 .07 .02
- [ ] 672 Calvin Schiraldi............04 .02 .01
- [ ] 673A Ruben Sierra AS ....25 .11 .03
  (Recent Major
  League Performance)
- [ ] 673B Ruben Sierra AS ....12 .05 .02
  (All-Star Game
  Performance)
- [ ] 674A Pedro Guerrero AS ....10 .05 .01
  (Recent Major
  League Performance)
- [ ] 674B Pedro Guerrero AS ....04 .02 .01
  (All-Star Game
  Performance)

- [ ] 675 Ken Phelps..................04 .02 .01
- [ ] 676A Cal Ripken AS ....40 .18 .05
  (Recent Major
  League Performance)
- [ ] 676B Cal Ripken AS ....20 .09 .03
  (All-Star Game
  Performance)
- [ ] 677 Denny Walling...............04 .02 .01
- [ ] 678 Goose Gossage............07 .03 .01
- [ ] 679 Gary Mielke................04 .02 .01
- [ ] 680 Bill Bathe...................04 .02 .01
- [ ] 681 Tom Lawless...............04 .02 .01
- [ ] 682 Xavier Hernandez.........12 .05 .02
- [ ] 683A Kirby Puckett AS..........25 .11 .03
  (Recent Major
  League Performance)
- [ ] 683B Kirby Puckett AS..........12 .05 .02
  (All-Star Game
  Performance)
- [ ] 684 Mariano Duncan ....04 .02 .01
- [ ] 685 Ramon Martinez ,.........15 .07 .02
- [ ] 686 Tim Jones..................04 .02 .01
- [ ] 687 Tom Filer...................04 .02 .01
- [ ] 688 Steve Lombardozzi ....04 .02 .01
- [ ] 689 Bernie Williams............30 .14 .04
- [ ] 690 Chip Hale...................04 .02 .01
- [ ] 691 Beau Allred ....04 .02 .01
- [ ] 692A Ryne Sandberg AS.......35 .16 .04
  (Recent Major
  League Performance)
- [ ] 692B Ryne Sandberg AS.......20 .09 .03
  (All-Star Game
  Performance)
- [ ] 693 Jeff Huson ....10 .05 .01
- [ ] 694 Curt Ford...................04 .02 .01
- [ ] 695A Eric Davis AS ....20 .09 .03
  (Recent Major
  League Performance)
- [ ] 695B Eric Davis AS ....10 .05 .01
  (All-Star Game
  Performance)
- [ ] 696 Scott Lusader..............04 .02 .01
- [ ] 697A Mark McGwire AS.........30 .14 .04
  (Recent Major
  League Performance)
- [ ] 697B Mark McGwire AS.........15 .07 .02
  (All-Star Game
  Performance)
- [ ] 698 Steve Cummings...........04 .02 .01
- [ ] 699 George Canale.............04 .02 .01
- [ ] 700A Checklist Card.............50 .05 .02
  (640-715/BC1-BC26)
- [ ] 700B Checklist Card.............10 .01 .00
  (640-716/BC1-BC26)
- [ ] 700C Checklist Card.............06 .01 .00
  (618-716)
- [ ] 701A Julio Franco AS ....10 .05 .01

	(Recent Major League Performance)			
☐ 701B	Julio Franco AS	.04	.02	.01
	(All-Star Game Performance)			
☐ 702	Dave Johnson (P)	.04	.02	.01
☐ 703A	Dave Stewart AS	.10	.05	.01
	(Recent Major League Performance)			
☐ 703B	Dave Stewart AS	.04	.02	.01
	(All-Star Game Performance)			
☐ 704	Dave Justice	1.25	.55	.16
☐ 705A	Tony Gwynn AS	.20	.09	.03
	(Recent Major League Performance)			
☐ 705B	Tony Gwynn AS	.10	.05	.01
	(All-Star Game Performance)			
☐ 706	Greg Myers	.04	.02	.01
☐ 707A	Will Clark AS	.30	.14	.04
	(Recent Major League Performance)			
☐ 707B	Will Clark AS	.15	.07	.02
	(All-Star Game Performance)			
☐ 708A	Benito Santiago AS	.10	.05	.01
	(Recent Major League Performance)			
☐ 708B	Benito Santiago AS	.04	.02	.01
	(All-Star Game Performance)			
☐ 709	Larry McWilliams	.04	.02	.01
☐ 710A	Ozzie Smith AS	.10	.05	.01
	(Recent Major League Performance)			
☐ 710B	Ozzie Smith AS	.04	.02	.01
	(All-Star Game Performance)			
☐ 711	John Olerud	.60	.25	.08
☐ 712A	Wade Boggs AS	.15	.07	.02
	(Recent Major League Performance)			
☐ 712B	Wade Boggs AS	.08	.04	.01
	(All-Star Game Performance)			
☐ 713	Gary Eave	.04	.02	.01
☐ 714	Bob Tewksbury	.07	.03	.01
☐ 715A	Kevin Mitchell AS	.10	.05	.01
	(Recent Major League Performance)			
☐ 715B	Kevin Mitchell AS	.04	.02	.01
	(All-Star Game Performance)			
☐ 716	Bart Giamatti COMM	.20	.09	.03
	(In Memoriam)			
☐ BC1	Bo Jackson	.10	.05	.01

☐ BC2	Howard Johnson	.05	.02	.01
☐ BC3	Dave Stewart	.05	.02	.01
☐ BC4	Tony Gwynn	.10	.05	.01
☐ BC5	Orel Hershiser	.05	.02	.01
☐ BC6	Pedro Guerrero	.05	.02	.01
☐ BC7	Tim Raines	.08	.04	.01
☐ BC8	Kirby Puckett	.15	.07	.02
☐ BC9	Alvin Davis	.05	.02	.01
☐ BC10	Ryne Sandberg	.20	.09	.03
☐ BC11	Kevin Mitchell	.08	.04	.01
☐ BC12A	John Smoltz ERR	.40	.18	.05
	(Photo actually Tom Glavine)			
☐ BC12B	John Smoltz COR	1.00	.45	.13
☐ BC13	George Bell	.05	.02	.01
☐ BC14	Julio Franco	.05	.02	.01
☐ BC15	Paul Molitor	.08	.04	.01
☐ BC16	Bobby Bonilla	.08	.04	.01
☐ BC17	Mike Greenwell	.08	.04	.01
☐ BC18	Cal Ripken	.20	.09	.03
☐ BC19	Carlton Fisk	.10	.05	.01
☐ BC20	Chili Davis	.05	.02	.01
☐ BC21	Glenn Davis	.05	.02	.01
☐ BC22	Steve Sax	.05	.02	.01
☐ BC23	Eric Davis DP	.08	.04	.01
☐ BC24	Greg Swindell DP	.05	.02	.01
☐ BC25	Von Hayes DP	.05	.02	.01
☐ BC26	Alan Trammell	.05	.02	.01

1990 Donruss Rookies

The 1990 Donruss Rookies set marked the fifth consecutive year that Donruss issued a boxed set honoring the best rookies of the season. This set, which used the 1990 Donruss design but featured a green bor-

*der, was issued exclusively through the
Donruss dealer network to hobby dealers.
This 56-card, standard size, 2 1/2" by
3 1/2" set came in its own box and the
words "The Rookies" are featured prominently on the front of the cards. The key
Rookie Cards in this set are Carlos Baerga
and Dave Hollins.*

		MT	EX-MT	VG
COMPLETE SET (56)		6.00	2.70	.75
COMMON PLAYER (1-56)		.05	.02	.01

		MT	EX-MT	VG
☐ 1	Sandy Alomar Jr. UER (No stitches on base-ball on Donruss logo on card front)	.10	.05	.01
☐ 2	John Olerud	.60	.25	.08
☐ 3	Pat Combs	.08	.04	.01
☐ 4	Brian DuBois	.05	.02	.01
☐ 5	Felix Jose	.08	.04	.01
☐ 6	Delino DeShields	.60	.25	.08
☐ 7	Mike Stanton	.08	.04	.01
☐ 8	Mike Munoz	.05	.02	.01
☐ 9	Craig Grebeck	.15	.07	.02
☐ 10	Joe Kraemer	.05	.02	.01
☐ 11	Jeff Huson	.05	.02	.01
☐ 12	Bill Sampen	.05	.02	.01
☐ 13	Brian Bohanon	.10	.05	.01
☐ 14	Dave Justice	1.25	.55	.16
☐ 15	Robin Ventura	.60	.25	.08
☐ 16	Greg Vaughn	.20	.09	.03
☐ 17	Wayne Edwards	.05	.02	.01
☐ 18	Shawn Boskie	.10	.05	.01
☐ 19	Carlos Baerga	1.25	.55	.16
☐ 20	Mark Gardner	.12	.05	.02
☐ 21	Kevin Appier	.25	.11	.03
☐ 22	Mike Harkey	.08	.04	.01
☐ 23	Tim Layana	.05	.02	.01
☐ 24	Glenallen Hill	.08	.04	.01
☐ 25	Jerry Kutzler	.05	.02	.01
☐ 26	Mike Blowers	.05	.02	.01
☐ 27	Scott Ruskin	.05	.02	.01
☐ 28	Dana Kiecker	.05	.02	.01
☐ 29	Willie Blair	.10	.05	.01
☐ 30	Ben McDonald	.50	.23	.06
☐ 31	Todd Zeile	.20	.09	.03
☐ 32	Scott Coolbaugh	.05	.02	.01
☐ 33	Xavier Hernandez	.08	.04	.01
☐ 34	Mike Hartley	.05	.02	.01
☐ 35	Kevin Tapani	.35	.16	.04
☐ 36	Kevin Wickander	.05	.02	.01
☐ 37	Carlos Hernandez	.10	.05	.01
☐ 38	Brian Traxler	.10	.05	.01
☐ 39	Marty Brown	.05	.02	.01
☐ 40	Scott Radinsky	.15	.07	.02
☐ 41	Julio Machado	.08	.04	.01
☐ 42	Steve Avery	.60	.25	.08
☐ 43	Mark Lemke	.08	.04	.01
☐ 44	Alan Mills	.12	.05	.02
☐ 45	Marquis Grissom	.60	.25	.08
☐ 46	Greg Olson	.10	.05	.01
☐ 47	Dave Hollins	.60	.25	.08
☐ 48	Jerald Clark	.08	.04	.01
☐ 49	Eric Anthony	.30	.14	.04
☐ 50	Tim Drummond	.05	.02	.01
☐ 51	John Burkett	.10	.05	.01
☐ 52	Brent Knackert	.10	.05	.01
☐ 53	Jeff Shaw	.05	.02	.01
☐ 54	John Orton	.10	.05	.01
☐ 55	Terry Shumpert	.05	.02	.01
☐ 56	Checklist Card	.08	.01	.00

1991 Donruss

*The 1991 Donruss set was issued in two
separate series of 396 cards each. This
set marked the first time Donruss has
issued their cards in series. The cards feature a blue border with some stripes and
the players name in white against a red
background. The cards measure the standard size of 2 1/2" by 3 1/2". Series I contained 386 cards (numbered 1-386) and
another ten cards numbered BC1-BC10.
These bonus cards were randomnly inserted in Donruss packs and highlight outstanding player achievements. The first 26
cards again feature the artwork of Dick
Perez drawing each team's Diamond King.
The first series also contains 20 Rated
Rookie (RR) cards and nine All-Star cards
(the AS cards are all American Leaguers in
this first series). On cards 60, 70, 127, 182,
239, 294, 355, 368, and 377, the border*

stripes are red and yellow. As a separate promotion wax packs were also given away with six and 12-packs of Coke and Diet Coke. The key Rookie Cards in the set are Wes Chamberlain, Brian McRae, Pedro Munoz, and Phil Plantier. The second series was issued approximately three months after the first series was issued. This series features the 26 MVP cards which Donruss had issued for the three previous years as their Bonus Cards, twenty more rated Rookie Cards and nine All-Star Cards (National Leaguers in this series). There were also special cards to honor the award winners and the heroes of the World Series. Bringing the total to 22, 12 additional Bonus Cards were randomly inserted in packs and pick up in time beginning with Valenzuela's no-hitter and continuing until the end of the season.

	MT	EX-MT	VG
COMPLETE SET (792)	15.00	6.75	1.90
COMPLETE W/4 LEAF PRVU	25.00	11.50	3.10
COMPLETE W/4 STUDIO PRVU	20.00	9.00	2.50
COMPLETE BC SET (22)	1.50	.65	.19
COMMON PLAYER (1-386)	.04	.02	.01
COMMON PLAYER (387-770)	.04	.02	.01
COMMON BC (BC1-BC10)	.06	.03	.01
COMMON BC (BC11-BC22)	.06	.03	.01

☐ 1 Dave Stieb DK	.05	.02	.01
☐ 2 Craig Biggio DK	.05	.02	.01
☐ 3 Cecil Fielder DK	.10	.05	.01
☐ 4 Barry Bonds DK	.10	.05	.01
☐ 5 Barry Larkin DK	.08	.04	.01
☐ 6 Dave Parker DK	.05	.02	.01
☐ 7 Len Dykstra DK	.05	.02	.01
☐ 8 Bobby Thigpen DK	.05	.02	.01
☐ 9 Roger Clemens DK	.12	.05	.02
☐ 10 Ron Gant DK UER	.10	.05	.01
(No trademark on team logo on back)			
☐ 11 Delino DeShields DK	.10	.05	.01
☐ 12 Roberto Alomar DK UER	.12	.05	.02
(No trademark on team logo on back)			
☐ 13 Sandy Alomar Jr. DK	.05	.02	.01
☐ 14 Ryne Sandberg DK UER	.12	.05	.02
(Was DK in '85, not '83 as shown)			
☐ 15 Ramon Martinez DK	.05	.02	.01
☐ 16 Edgar Martinez DK	.05	.02	.01
☐ 17 Dave Magadan DK	.05	.02	.01
☐ 18 Matt Williams DK	.05	.02	.01
☐ 19 Rafael Palmeiro DK	.05	.02	.01
UER (No trademark on			

team logo on back)			
☐ 20 Bob Welch DK	.05	.02	.01
☐ 21 Dave Righetti DK	.05	.02	.01
☐ 22 Brian Harper DK	.05	.02	.01
☐ 23 Gregg Olson DK	.05	.02	.01
☐ 24 Kurt Stillwell DK	.05	.02	.01
☐ 25 Pedro Guerrero DK UER	.05	.02	.01
(No trademark on team logo on back)			
☐ 26 Chuck Finley DK UER	.05	.02	.01
(No trademark on team logo on back)			
☐ 27 DK Checklist	.05	.01	.00
☐ 28 Tino Martinez RR	.10	.05	.01
☐ 29 Mark Lewis RR	.12	.05	.02
☐ 30 Bernard Gilkey RR	.15	.07	.02
☐ 31 Hensley Meulens RR	.08	.04	.01
☐ 32 Derek Bell RR	.30	.14	.04
☐ 33 Jose Offerman RR	.10	.05	.01
☐ 34 Terry Bross RR	.05	.02	.01
☐ 35 Leo Gomez RR	.25	.11	.03
☐ 36 Derrick May RR	.10	.05	.01
☐ 37 Kevin Morton RR	.10	.05	.01
☐ 38 Moises Alou RR	.25	.11	.03
☐ 39 Julio Valera RR	.15	.07	.02
☐ 40 Milt Cuyler RR	.10	.05	.01
☐ 41 Phil Plantier RR	.50	.23	.06
☐ 42 Scott Chiamparino RR	.08	.04	.01
☐ 43 Ray Lankford RR	.40	.18	.05
☐ 44 Mickey Morandini RR	.12	.05	.02
☐ 45 Dave Hansen RR	.10	.05	.01
☐ 46 Kevin Belcher RR	.10	.05	.01
☐ 47 Darrin Fletcher RR	.05	.02	.01
☐ 48 Steve Sax AS	.05	.02	.01
☐ 49 Ken Griffey Jr. AS	.25	.11	.03
☐ 50A Jose Canseco AS ERR	.12	.05	.02
(Team in stat box should be AL, not A's)			
☐ 50B Jose Canseco AS COR	1.00	.45	.13
☐ 51 Sandy Alomar Jr. AS	.05	.02	.01
☐ 52 Cal Ripken AS	.15	.07	.02
☐ 53 Rickey Henderson AS	.10	.05	.01
☐ 54 Bob Welch AS	.05	.02	.01
☐ 55 Wade Boggs AS	.10	.05	.01
☐ 56 Mark McGwire AS	.10	.05	.01
☐ 57A Jack McDowell ERR	.10	.05	.01
(Career stats do not include 1990)			
☐ 57B Jack McDowell COR	.50	.23	.06
(Career stats do not include 1990)			
☐ 58 Jose Lind	.04	.02	.01
☐ 59 Alex Fernandez	.15	.07	.02
☐ 60 Pat Combs	.04	.02	.01
☐ 61 Mike Walker	.04	.02	.01
☐ 62 Juan Samuel	.04	.02	.01
☐ 63 Mike Blowers UER	.04	.02	.01

(Last line has
aseball, not baseball)

☐	64	Mark Guthrie	.04	.02	.01
☐	65	Mark Salas	.04	.02	.01
☐	66	Tim Jones	.04	.02	.01
☐	67	Tim Leary	.04	.02	.01
☐	68	Andres Galarraga	.04	.02	.01
☐	69	Bob Milacki	.04	.02	.01
☐	70	Tim Belcher	.07	.03	.01
☐	71	Todd Zeile	.07	.03	.01
☐	72	Jerome Walton	.04	.02	.01
☐	73	Kevin Seitzer	.07	.03	.01
☐	74	Jerald Clark	.04	.02	.01
☐	75	John Smoltz UER	.10	.05	.01

(Born in Detroit,
not Warren)

☐	76	Mike Henneman	.04	.02	.01
☐	77	Ken Griffey Jr.	.50	.23	.06
☐	78	Jim Abbott	.12	.05	.02
☐	79	Gregg Jefferies	.07	.03	.01
☐	80	Kevin Reimer	.10	.05	.01
☐	81	Roger Clemens	.25	.11	.03
☐	82	Mike Fitzgerald	.04	.02	.01
☐	83	Bruce Hurst UER	.07	.03	.01

(Middle name is
Lee, not Vee)

☐	84	Eric Davis	.07	.03	.01
☐	85	Paul Molitor	.10	.05	.01
☐	86	Will Clark	.20	.09	.03
☐	87	Mike Bielecki	.04	.02	.01
☐	88	Bret Saberhagen	.07	.03	.01
☐	89	Nolan Ryan	.40	.18	.05
☐	90	Bobby Thigpen	.04	.02	.01
☐	91	Dickie Thon	.04	.02	.01
☐	92	Duane Ward	.04	.02	.01
☐	93	Luis Polonia	.07	.03	.01
☐	94	Terry Kennedy	.04	.02	.01
☐	95	Kent Hrbek	.07	.03	.01
☐	96	Danny Jackson	.04	.02	.01
☐	97	Sid Fernandez	.07	.03	.01
☐	98	Jimmy Key	.04	.02	.01
☐	99	Franklin Stubbs	.04	.02	.01
☐	100	Checklist Card	.05	.01	.00
☐	101	R.J. Reynolds	.04	.02	.01
☐	102	Dave Stewart	.07	.03	.01
☐	103	Dan Pasqua	.04	.02	.01
☐	104	Dan Plesac	.04	.02	.01
☐	105	Mark McGwire	.20	.09	.03
☐	106	John Farrell	.04	.02	.01
☐	107	Don Mattingly	.15	.07	.02
☐	108	Carlton Fisk	.10	.05	.01
☐	109	Ken Oberkfell	.04	.02	.01
☐	110	Darrel Akerfelds	.04	.02	.01
☐	111	Gregg Olson	.07	.03	.01
☐	112	Mike Scioscia	.04	.02	.01
☐	113	Bryn Smith	.04	.02	.01
☐	114	Bob Geren	.04	.02	.01

☐	115	Tom Candiotti	.04	.02	.01
☐	116	Kevin Tapani	.07	.03	.01
☐	117	Jeff Treadway	.04	.02	.01
☐	118	Alan Trammell	.07	.03	.01
☐	119	Pete O'Brien	.04	.02	.01

(Blue shading goes
through stats)

☐	120	Joel Skinner	.04	.02	.01
☐	121	Mike LaValliere	.04	.02	.01
☐	122	Dwight Evans	.07	.03	.01
☐	123	Jody Reed	.04	.02	.01
☐	124	Lee Guetterman	.04	.02	.01
☐	125	Tim Burke	.04	.02	.01
☐	126	Dave Johnson	.04	.02	.01
☐	127	Fernando Valenzuela	.07	.03	.01

(Lower large stripe
in yellow instead
of blue) UER

☐	128	Jose DeLeon	.04	.02	.01
☐	129	Andre Dawson	.10	.05	.01
☐	130	Gerald Perry	.04	.02	.01
☐	131	Greg W. Harris	.04	.02	.01
☐	132	Tom Glavine	.20	.09	.03
☐	133	Lance McCullers	.04	.02	.01
☐	134	Randy Johnson	.07	.03	.01
☐	135	Lance Parrish UER	.07	.03	.01

(Born in McKeesport,
not Clairton)

☐	136	Mackey Sasser	.04	.02	.01
☐	137	Geno Petralli	.04	.02	.01
☐	138	Dennis Lamp	.04	.02	.01
☐	139	Dennis Martinez	.07	.03	.01
☐	140	Mike Pagliarulo	.04	.02	.01
☐	141	Hal Morris	.07	.03	.01
☐	142	Dave Parker	.07	.03	.01
☐	143	Brett Butler	.07	.03	.01
☐	144	Paul Assenmacher	.04	.02	.01
☐	145	Mark Gubicza	.04	.02	.01
☐	146	Charlie Hough	.04	.02	.01
☐	147	Sammy Sosa	.07	.03	.01
☐	148	Randy Ready	.04	.02	.01
☐	149	Kelly Gruber	.07	.03	.01
☐	150	Devon White	.07	.03	.01
☐	151	Gary Carter	.07	.03	.01
☐	152	Gene Larkin	.04	.02	.01
☐	153	Chris Sabo	.07	.03	.01
☐	154	David Cone	.10	.05	.01
☐	155	Todd Stottlemyre	.07	.03	.01
☐	156	Glenn Wilson	.04	.02	.01
☐	157	Bob Walk	.04	.02	.01
☐	158	Mike Gallego	.04	.02	.01
☐	159	Greg Hibbard	.04	.02	.01
☐	160	Chris Bosio	.04	.02	.01
☐	161	Mike Moore	.04	.02	.01
☐	162	Jerry Browne UER	.04	.02	.01

(Born Christiansted,
should be St. Croix)

☐	163 Steve Sax UER	.07	.03	.01	☐ 214 Walt Weiss	.04	.02	.01

#	Name				#	Name			
163	Steve Sax UER	.07	.03	.01	214	Walt Weiss	.04	.02	.01
	(No asterisk next to				215	Donn Pall	.04	.02	.01
	his 1989 At Bats)				216	Jaime Navarro	.07	.03	.01
164	Melido Perez	.07	.03	.01	217	Willie Randolph	.07	.03	.01
165	Danny Darwin	.04	.02	.01	218	Rudy Seanez	.12	.05	.02
166	Roger McDowell	.04	.02	.01	219	Jim Leyritz	.04	.02	.01
167	Bill Ripken	.04	.02	.01	220	Ron Karkovice	.04	.02	.01
168	Mike Sharperson	.04	.02	.01	221	Ken Caminiti	.07	.03	.01
169	Lee Smith	.07	.03	.01	222	Von Hayes	.04	.02	.01
170	Matt Nokes	.04	.02	.01	223	Cal Ripken	.30	.14	.04
171	Jesse Orosco	.04	.02	.01	224	Lenny Harris	.04	.02	.01
172	Rick Aguilera	.07	.03	.01	225	Milt Thompson	.04	.02	.01
173	Jim Presley	.04	.02	.01	226	Alvaro Espinoza	.04	.02	.01
174	Lou Whitaker	.07	.03	.01	227	Chris James	.04	.02	.01
175	Harold Reynolds	.04	.02	.01	228	Dan Gladden	.04	.02	.01
176	Brook Jacoby	.04	.02	.01	229	Jeff Blauser	.04	.02	.01
177	Wally Backman	.04	.02	.01	230	Mike Heath	.04	.02	.01
178	Wade Boggs	.12	.05	.02	231	Omar Vizquel	.04	.02	.01
179	Chuck Cary	.04	.02	.01	232	Doug Jones	.04	.02	.01
	(Comma after DOB,				233	Jeff King	.04	.02	.01
	not on other cards)				234	Luis Rivera	.04	.02	.01
180	Tom Foley	.04	.02	.01	235	Ellis Burks	.07	.03	.01
181	Pete Harnisch	.07	.03	.01	236	Greg Cadaret	.04	.02	.01
182	Mike Morgan	.04	.02	.01	237	Dave Martinez	.04	.02	.01
183	Bob Tewksbury	.07	.03	.01	238	Mark Williamson	.04	.02	.01
184	Joe Girardi	.04	.02	.01	239	Stan Javier	.04	.02	.01
185	Storm Davis	.04	.02	.01	240	Ozzie Smith	.10	.05	.01
186	Ed Whitson	.04	.02	.01	241	Shawn Boskie	.04	.02	.01
187	Steve Avery UER	.20	.09	.03	242	Tom Gordon	.07	.03	.01
	(Born in New Jersey,				243	Tony Gwynn	.12	.05	.02
	should be Michigan)				244	Tommy Gregg	.04	.02	.01
188	Lloyd Moseby	.04	.02	.01	245	Jeff M. Robinson	.04	.02	.01
189	Scott Bankhead	.04	.02	.01	246	Keith Comstock	.04	.02	.01
190	Mark Langston	.07	.03	.01	247	Jack Howell	.04	.02	.01
191	Kevin McReynolds	.07	.03	.01	248	Keith Miller	.04	.02	.01
192	Julio Franco	.07	.03	.01	249	Bobby Witt	.07	.03	.01
193	John Dopson	.04	.02	.01	250	Rob Murphy UER	.04	.02	.01
194	Dennis Boyd	.04	.02	.01		(Shown as on Reds			
195	Bip Roberts	.07	.03	.01		in '89 stats,			
196	Billy Hatcher	.04	.02	.01		should be Red Sox)			
197	Edgar Diaz	.04	.02	.01	251	Spike Owen	.04	.02	.01
198	Greg Litton	.04	.02	.01	252	Garry Templeton	.04	.02	.01
199	Mark Grace	.10	.05	.01	253	Glenn Braggs	.04	.02	.01
200	Checklist Card	.05	.01	.00	254	Ron Robinson	.04	.02	.01
201	George Brett	.10	.05	.01	255	Kevin Mitchell	.07	.03	.01
202	Jeff Russell	.04	.02	.01	256	Les Lancaster	.04	.02	.01
203	Ivan Calderon	.04	.02	.01	257	Mel Stottlemyre Jr.	.04	.02	.01
204	Ken Howell	.04	.02	.01	258	Kenny Rogers UER	.04	.02	.01
205	Tom Henke	.07	.03	.01		(IP listed as 171,			
206	Bryan Harvey	.04	.02	.01		should be 172)			
207	Steve Bedrosian	.04	.02	.01	259	Lance Johnson	.04	.02	.01
208	Al Newman	.04	.02	.01	260	John Kruk	.07	.03	.01
209	Randy Myers	.07	.03	.01	261	Fred McGriff	.12	.05	.02
210	Daryl Boston	.04	.02	.01	262	Dick Schofield	.04	.02	.01
211	Manny Lee	.04	.02	.01	263	Trevor Wilson	.04	.02	.01
212	Dave Smith	.04	.02	.01	264	David West	.04	.02	.01
213	Don Slaught	.04	.02	.01	265	Scott Scudder	.04	.02	.01

☐	266	Dwight Gooden	.07	.03	.01	☐	310	Bill Spiers	.04	.02	.01

☐	266	Dwight Gooden	.07	.03	.01
☐	267	Willie Blair	.04	.02	.01
☐	268	Mark Portugal	.04	.02	.01
☐	269	Doug Drabek	.07	.03	.01
☐	270	Dennis Eckersley	.12	.05	.02
☐	271	Eric King	.04	.02	.01
☐	272	Robin Yount	.10	.05	.01
☐	273	Carney Lansford	.07	.03	.01
☐	274	Carlos Baerga	.20	.09	.03
☐	275	Dave Righetti	.04	.02	.01
☐	276	Scott Fletcher	.04	.02	.01
☐	277	Eric Yelding	.04	.02	.01
☐	278	Charlie Hayes	.04	.02	.01
☐	279	Jeff Ballard	.04	.02	.01
☐	280	Orel Hershiser	.07	.03	.01
☐	281	Jose Oquendo	.04	.02	.01
☐	282	Mike Witt	.04	.02	.01
☐	283	Mitch Webster	.04	.02	.01
☐	284	Greg Gagne	.04	.02	.01
☐	285	Greg Olson	.04	.02	.01
☐	286	Tony Phillips UER	.04	.02	.01
		(Born 4/15, should be 4/25)			
☐	287	Scott Bradley	.04	.02	.01
☐	288	Cory Snyder UER	.04	.02	.01
		(In text, led is repeated and Inglewood is misspelled as Englewood)			
☐	289	Jay Bell UER	.07	.03	.01
		(Born in Pensacola, not Eglin AFB)			
☐	290	Kevin Romine	.04	.02	.01
☐	291	Jeff D. Robinson	.04	.02	.01
☐	292	Steve Frey UER	.04	.02	.01
		(Bats left, should be right)			
☐	293	Craig Worthington	.04	.02	.01
☐	294	Tim Crews	.04	.02	.01
☐	295	Joe Magrane	.04	.02	.01
☐	296	Hector Villanueva	.04	.02	.01
☐	297	Terry Shumpert	.04	.02	.01
☐	298	Joe Carter	.12	.05	.02
☐	299	Kent Mercker UER	.07	.03	.01
		(IP listed as 53, should be 52)			
☐	300	Checklist Card	.05	.01	.00
☐	301	Chet Lemon	.04	.02	.01
☐	302	Mike Schooler	.04	.02	.01
☐	303	Dante Bichette	.04	.02	.01
☐	304	Kevin Elster	.04	.02	.01
☐	305	Jeff Huson	.04	.02	.01
☐	306	Greg A. Harris	.04	.02	.01
☐	307	Marquis Grissom UER	.15	.07	.02
		(Middle name Deon, should be Dean)			
☐	308	Calvin Schiraldi	.04	.02	.01
☐	309	Mariano Duncan	.04	.02	.01

☐	310	Bill Spiers	.04	.02	.01
☐	311	Scott Garrelts	.04	.02	.01
☐	312	Mitch Williams	.04	.02	.01
☐	313	Mike Macfarlane	.04	.02	.01
☐	314	Kevin Brown	.07	.03	.01
☐	315	Robin Ventura	.20	.09	.03
☐	316	Darren Daulton	.07	.03	.01
☐	317	Pat Borders	.04	.02	.01
☐	318	Mark Eichhorn	.04	.02	.01
☐	319	Jeff Brantley	.04	.02	.01
☐	320	Shane Mack	.07	.03	.01
☐	321	Rob Dibble	.07	.03	.01
☐	322	John Franco	.07	.03	.01
☐	323	Junior Felix	.04	.02	.01
☐	324	Casey Candaele	.04	.02	.01
☐	325	Bobby Bonilla	.10	.05	.01
☐	326	Dave Henderson	.04	.02	.01
☐	327	Wayne Edwards	.04	.02	.01
☐	328	Mark Knudson	.04	.02	.01
☐	329	Terry Steinbach	.07	.03	.01
☐	330	Colby Ward UER	.04	.02	.01
		(No comma between city and state)			
☐	331	Oscar Azocar	.04	.02	.01
☐	332	Scott Radinsky	.04	.02	.01
☐	333	Eric Anthony	.07	.03	.01
☐	334	Steve Lake	.04	.02	.01
☐	335	Bob Melvin	.04	.02	.01
☐	336	Kal Daniels	.04	.02	.01
☐	337	Tom Pagnozzi	.04	.02	.01
☐	338	Alan Mills	.04	.02	.01
☐	339	Steve Olin	.07	.03	.01
☐	340	Juan Berenguer	.04	.02	.01
☐	341	Francisco Cabrera	.04	.02	.01
☐	342	Dave Bergman	.04	.02	.01
☐	343	Henry Cotto	.04	.02	.01
☐	344	Sergio Valdez	.04	.02	.01
☐	345	Bob Patterson	.04	.02	.01
☐	346	John Marzano	.04	.02	.01
☐	347	Dana Kiecker	.04	.02	.01
☐	348	Dion James	.04	.02	.01
☐	349	Hubie Brooks	.04	.02	.01
☐	350	Bill Landrum	.04	.02	.01
☐	351	Bill Sampen	.04	.02	.01
☐	352	Greg Briley	.04	.02	.01
☐	353	Paul Gibson	.04	.02	.01
☐	354	Dave Eiland	.04	.02	.01
☐	355	Steve Finley	.07	.03	.01
☐	356	Bob Boone	.07	.03	.01
☐	357	Steve Buechele	.04	.02	.01
☐	358	Chris Hoiles	.15	.07	.02
☐	359	Larry Walker	.20	.09	.03
☐	360	Frank DiPino	.04	.02	.01
☐	361	Mark Grant	.04	.02	.01
☐	362	Dave Magadan	.07	.03	.01
☐	363	Robby Thompson	.04	.02	.01
☐	364	Lonnie Smith	.04	.02	.01

☐ 365	Steve Farr	.04	.02	.01
☐ 366	Dave Valle	.04	.02	.01
☐ 367	Tim Naehring	.07	.03	.01
☐ 368	Jim Acker	.04	.02	.01
☐ 369	Jeff Reardon UER (Born in Pittsfield, not Dalton)	.07	.03	.01
☐ 370	Tim Teufel	.04	.02	.01
☐ 371	Juan Gonzalez	.35	.16	.04
☐ 372	Luis Salazar	.04	.02	.01
☐ 373	Rick Honeycutt	.04	.02	.01
☐ 374	Greg Maddux	.10	.05	.01
☐ 375	Jose Uribe UER (Middle name Elta, should be Alta)	.04	.02	.01
☐ 376	Donnie Hill	.04	.02	.01
☐ 377	Don Carman	.04	.02	.01
☐ 378	Craig Grebeck	.04	.02	.01
☐ 379	Willie Fraser	.04	.02	.01
☐ 380	Glenallen Hill	.04	.02	.01
☐ 381	Joe Oliver	.04	.02	.01
☐ 382	Randy Bush	.04	.02	.01
☐ 383	Alex Cole	.04	.02	.01
☐ 384	Norm Charlton	.07	.03	.01
☐ 385	Gene Nelson	.04	.02	.01
☐ 386	Checklist Card	.05	.01	.00
☐ 387	Rickey Henderson MVP	.10	.05	.01
☐ 388	Lance Parrish MVP	.05	.02	.01
☐ 389	Fred McGriff MVP	.10	.05	.01
☐ 390	Dave Parker MVP	.05	.02	.01
☐ 391	Candy Maldonado MVP	.05	.02	.01
☐ 392	Ken Griffey Jr. MVP	.25	.11	.03
☐ 393	Gregg Olson MVP	.05	.02	.01
☐ 394	Rafael Palmeiro MVP	.08	.04	.01
☐ 395	Roger Clemens MVP	.12	.05	.02
☐ 396	George Brett MVP	.10	.05	.01
☐ 397	Cecil Fielder MVP	.10	.05	.01
☐ 398	Brian Harper MVP UER (Major League Performance, should be Career)	.05	.02	.01
☐ 399	Bobby Thigpen MVP	.05	.02	.01
☐ 400	Roberto Kelly MVP UER (Second Base on front and OF on back)	.05	.02	.01
☐ 401	Danny Darwin MVP	.05	.02	.01
☐ 402	Dave Justice MVP	.15	.07	.02
☐ 403	Lee Smith MVP	.05	.02	.01
☐ 404	Ryne Sandberg MVP	.12	.05	.02
☐ 405	Eddie Murray MVP	.10	.05	.01
☐ 406	Tim Wallach MVP	.05	.02	.01
☐ 407	Kevin Mitchell MVP	.05	.02	.01
☐ 408	Darryl Strawberry MVP	.10	.05	.01
☐ 409	Joe Carter MVP	.08	.04	.01
☐ 410	Len Dykstra MVP	.05	.02	.01
☐ 411	Doug Drabek MVP	.05	.02	.01
☐ 412	Chris Sabo MVP	.05	.02	.01
☐ 413	Paul Marak RR	.05	.02	.01
☐ 414	Tim McIntosh RR	.05	.02	.01
☐ 415	Brian Barnes RR	.12	.05	.02
☐ 416	Eric Gunderson RR	.05	.02	.01
☐ 417	Mike Gardiner RR	.10	.05	.01
☐ 418	Steve Carter RR	.05	.02	.01
☐ 419	Gerald Alexander RR	.10	.05	.01
☐ 420	Rich Garces RR	.10	.05	.01
☐ 421	Chuck Knoblauch RR	.40	.18	.05
☐ 422	Scott Aldred RR	.10	.05	.01
☐ 423	Wes Chamberlain RR	.20	.09	.03
☐ 424	Lance Dickson RR	.10	.05	.01
☐ 425	Greg Colbrunn RR	.25	.11	.03
☐ 426	Rich DeLucia RR UER (Misspelled Delucia on card)	.05	.02	.01
☐ 427	Jeff Conine RR	.25	.11	.03
☐ 428	Steve Decker RR	.15	.07	.02
☐ 429	Turner Ward RR	.10	.05	.01
☐ 430	Mo Vaughn RR	.20	.09	.03
☐ 431	Steve Chitren RR	.10	.05	.01
☐ 432	Mike Benjamin RR	.05	.02	.01
☐ 433	Ryne Sandberg AS	.12	.05	.02
☐ 434	Len Dykstra AS	.05	.02	.01
☐ 435	Andre Dawson AS	.10	.05	.01
☐ 436A	Mike Scioscia AS (White star by name)	.05	.02	.01
☐ 436B	Mike Scioscia AS (Yellow star by name)	.05	.02	.01
☐ 437	Ozzie Smith AS	.10	.05	.01
☐ 438	Kevin Mitchell AS	.05	.02	.01
☐ 439	Jack Armstrong AS	.05	.02	.01
☐ 440	Chris Sabo AS	.05	.02	.01
☐ 441	Will Clark AS	.10	.05	.01
☐ 442	Mel Hall	.04	.02	.01
☐ 443	Mark Gardner	.04	.02	.01
☐ 444	Mike Devereaux	.07	.03	.01
☐ 445	Kirk Gibson	.07	.03	.01
☐ 446	Terry Pendleton	.10	.05	.01
☐ 447	Mike Harkey	.07	.03	.01
☐ 448	Jim Eisenreich	.04	.02	.01
☐ 449	Benito Santiago	.07	.03	.01
☐ 450	Oddibe McDowell	.04	.02	.01
☐ 451	Cecil Fielder	.12	.05	.02
☐ 452	Ken Griffey Sr.	.07	.03	.01
☐ 453	Bert Blyleven	.07	.03	.01
☐ 454	Howard Johnson	.07	.03	.01
☐ 455	Monty Fariss UER (Misspelled Farris on card)	.15	.07	.02
☐ 456	Tony Pena	.04	.02	.01
☐ 457	Tim Raines	.07	.03	.01
☐ 458	Dennis Rasmussen	.04	.02	.01
☐ 459	Luis Quinones	.04	.02	.01
☐ 460	B.J. Surhoff	.04	.02	.01
☐ 461	Ernest Riles	.04	.02	.01
☐ 462	Rick Sutcliffe	.07	.03	.01

□	#	Player	BA		
□	463	Danny Tartabull	.07	.03	.01
□	464	Pete Incaviglia	.04	.02	.01
□	465	Carlos Martinez	.04	.02	.01
□	466	Ricky Jordan	.04	.02	.01
□	467	John Cerutti	.04	.02	.01
□	468	Dave Winfield	.10	.05	.01
□	469	Francisco Oliveras	.04	.02	.01
□	470	Roy Smith	.04	.02	.01
□	471	Barry Larkin	.10	.05	.01
□	472	Ron Darling	.07	.03	.01
□	473	David Wells	.04	.02	.01
□	474	Glenn Davis	.07	.03	.01
□	475	Neal Heaton	.04	.02	.01
□	476	Ron Hassey	.04	.02	.01
□	477	Frank Thomas	1.25	.55	.16
□	478	Greg Vaughn	.10	.05	.01
□	479	Todd Burns	.04	.02	.01
□	480	Candy Maldonado	.04	.02	.01
□	481	Dave LaPoint	.04	.02	.01
□	482	Alvin Davis	.04	.02	.01
□	483	Mike Scott	.04	.02	.01
□	484	Dale Murphy	.07	.03	.01
□	485	Ben McDonald	.10	.05	.01
□	486	Jay Howell	.04	.02	.01
□	487	Vince Coleman	.07	.03	.01
□	488	Alfredo Griffin	.04	.02	.01
□	489	Sandy Alomar Jr.	.07	.03	.01
□	490	Kirby Puckett	.20	.09	.03
□	491	Andres Thomas	.04	.02	.01
□	492	Jack Morris	.10	.05	.01
□	493	Matt Young	.04	.02	.01
□	494	Greg Myers	.04	.02	.01
□	495	Barry Bonds	.20	.09	.03
□	496	Scott Cooper UER	.25	.11	.03
		(No BA for 1990			
		and career)			
□	497	Dan Schatzeder	.04	.02	.01
□	498	Jesse Barfield	.04	.02	.01
□	499	Jerry Goff	.04	.02	.01
□	500	Checklist Card	.05	.01	.00
□	501	Anthony Telford	.04	.02	.01
□	502	Eddie Murray	.10	.05	.01
□	503	Omar Olivares	.12	.05	.02
□	504	Ryne Sandberg	.25	.11	.03
□	505	Jeff Montgomery	.04	.02	.01
□	506	Mark Parent	.04	.02	.01
□	507	Ron Gant	.12	.05	.02
□	508	Frank Tanana	.04	.02	.01
□	509	Jay Buhner	.07	.03	.01
□	510	Max Venable	.04	.02	.01
□	511	Wally Whitehurst	.04	.02	.01
□	512	Gary Pettis	.04	.02	.01
□	513	Tom Brunansky	.07	.03	.01
□	514	Tim Wallach	.07	.03	.01
□	515	Craig Lefferts	.04	.02	.01
□	516	Tim Layana	.04	.02	.01
□	517	Darryl Hamilton	.07	.03	.01
□	518	Rick Reuschel	.04	.02	.01
□	519	Steve Wilson	.04	.02	.01
□	520	Kurt Stillwell	.04	.02	.01
□	521	Rafael Palmeiro	.10	.05	.01
□	522	Ken Patterson	.04	.02	.01
□	523	Len Dykstra	.07	.03	.01
□	524	Tony Fernandez	.07	.03	.01
□	525	Kent Anderson	.04	.02	.01
□	526	Mark Leonard	.10	.05	.01
□	527	Allan Anderson	.04	.02	.01
□	528	Tom Browning	.04	.02	.01
□	529	Frank Viola	.07	.03	.01
□	530	John Olerud	.15	.07	.02
□	531	Juan Agosto	.04	.02	.01
□	532	Zane Smith	.04	.02	.01
□	533	Scott Sanderson	.04	.02	.01
□	534	Barry Jones	.04	.02	.01
□	535	Mike Felder	.04	.02	.01
□	536	Jose Canseco	.20	.09	.03
□	537	Felix Fermin	.04	.02	.01
□	538	Roberto Kelly	.07	.03	.01
□	539	Brian Holman	.04	.02	.01
□	540	Mark Davidson	.04	.02	.01
□	541	Terry Mulholland	.04	.02	.01
□	542	Randy Milligan	.04	.02	.01
□	543	Jose Gonzalez	.04	.02	.01
□	544	Craig Wilson	.10	.05	.01
□	545	Mike Hartley	.04	.02	.01
□	546	Greg Swindell	.07	.03	.01
□	547	Gary Gaetti	.04	.02	.01
□	548	Dave Justice	.30	.14	.04
□	549	Steve Searcy	.04	.02	.01
□	550	Erik Hanson	.04	.02	.01
□	551	Dave Stieb	.04	.02	.01
□	552	Andy Van Slyke	.10	.05	.01
□	553	Mike Greenwell	.07	.03	.01
□	554	Kevin Maas	.10	.05	.01
□	555	Delino DeShields	.15	.07	.02
□	556	Curt Schilling	.07	.03	.01
□	557	Ramon Martinez	.10	.05	.01
□	558	Pedro Guerrero	.07	.03	.01
□	559	Dwight Smith	.04	.02	.01
□	560	Mark Davis	.04	.02	.01
□	561	Shawn Abner	.04	.02	.01
□	562	Charlie Leibrandt	.04	.02	.01
□	563	John Shelby	.04	.02	.01
□	564	Bill Swift	.04	.02	.01
□	565	Mike Fetters	.04	.02	.01
□	566	Alejandro Pena	.04	.02	.01
□	567	Ruben Sierra	.15	.07	.02
□	568	Carlos Quintana	.04	.02	.01
□	569	Kevin Gross	.04	.02	.01
□	570	Derek Lilliquist	.04	.02	.01
□	571	Jack Armstrong	.04	.02	.01
□	572	Greg Brock	.04	.02	.01
□	573	Mike Kingery	.04	.02	.01
□	574	Greg Smith	.04	.02	.01

☐ 575	Brian McRae 20	.09	.03
☐ 576	Jack Daugherty 04	.02	.01
☐ 577	Ozzie Guillen 04	.02	.01
☐ 578	Joe Boever 04	.02	.01
☐ 579	Luis Sojo 04	.02	.01
☐ 580	Chili Davis 07	.03	.01
☐ 581	Don Robinson 04	.02	.01
☐ 582	Brian Harper 04	.02	.01
☐ 583	Paul O'Neill 07	.03	.01
☐ 584	Bob Ojeda 04	.02	.01
☐ 585	Mookie Wilson 04	.02	.01
☐ 586	Rafael Ramirez 04	.02	.01
☐ 587	Gary Redus 04	.02	.01
☐ 588	Jamie Quirk 04	.02	.01
☐ 589	Shawn Hillegas 04	.02	.01
☐ 590	Tom Edens 10	.05	.01
☐ 591	Joe Klink 04	.02	.01
☐ 592	Charles Nagy 40	.18	.05
☐ 593	Eric Plunk 04	.02	.01
☐ 594	Tracy Jones 04	.02	.01
☐ 595	Craig Biggio 07	.03	.01
☐ 596	Jose DeJesus 04	.02	.01
☐ 597	Mickey Tettleton 07	.03	.01
☐ 598	Chris Gwynn 04	.02	.01
☐ 599	Rex Hudler 04	.02	.01
☐ 600	Checklist Card 05	.01	.00
☐ 601	Jim Gott 04	.02	.01
☐ 602	Jeff Manto 04	.02	.01
☐ 603	Nelson Liriano 04	.02	.01
☐ 604	Mark Lemke 04	.02	.01
☐ 605	Clay Parker 04	.02	.01
☐ 606	Edgar Martinez 07	.03	.01
☐ 607	Mark Whiten 12	.05	.02
☐ 608	Ted Power 04	.02	.01
☐ 609	Tom Bolton 04	.02	.01
☐ 610	Tom Herr 04	.02	.01
☐ 611	Andy Hawkins UER 04	.02	.01
	(Pitched No-Hitter		
	on 7/1, not 7/2)		
☐ 612	Scott Ruskin 04	.02	.01
☐ 613	Ron Kittle 04	.02	.01
☐ 614	John Wetteland 07	.03	.01
☐ 615	Mike Perez 15	.07	.02
☐ 616	Dave Clark 04	.02	.01
☐ 617	Brent Mayne 04	.02	.01
☐ 618	Jack Clark 07	.03	.01
☐ 619	Marvin Freeman 04	.02	.01
☐ 620	Edwin Nunez 04	.02	.01
☐ 621	Russ Swan 04	.02	.01
☐ 622	Johnny Ray 04	.02	.01
☐ 623	Charlie O'Brien 04	.02	.01
☐ 624	Joe Bitker 04	.02	.01
☐ 625	Mike Marshall 04	.02	.01
☐ 626	Otis Nixon 07	.03	.01
☐ 627	Andy Benes 10	.05	.01
☐ 628	Ron Oester 04	.02	.01
☐ 629	Ted Higuera 04	.02	.01

☐ 630	Kevin Bass 04	.02	.01
☐ 631	Damon Berryhill 04	.02	.01
☐ 632	Bo Jackson 12	.05	.02
☐ 633	Brad Arnsberg 04	.02	.01
☐ 634	Jerry Willard 04	.02	.01
☐ 635	Tommy Greene 04	.02	.01
☐ 636	Bob MacDonald 10	.05	.01
☐ 637	Kirk McCaskill 04	.02	.01
☐ 638	John Burkett 04	.02	.01
☐ 639	Paul Abbott 10	.05	.01
☐ 640	Todd Benzinger 04	.02	.01
☐ 641	Todd Hundley 04	.02	.01
☐ 642	George Bell 07	.03	.01
☐ 643	Javier Ortiz 04	.02	.01
☐ 644	Sid Bream 04	.02	.01
☐ 645	Bob Welch 04	.02	.01
☐ 646	Phil Bradley 04	.02	.01
☐ 647	Bill Krueger 04	.02	.01
☐ 648	Rickey Henderson 12	.05	.02
☐ 649	Kevin Wickander 04	.02	.01
☐ 650	Steve Balboni 04	.02	.01
☐ 651	Gene Harris 04	.02	.01
☐ 652	Jim Deshaies 04	.02	.01
☐ 653	Jason Grimsley 10	.05	.01
☐ 654	Joe Orsulak 04	.02	.01
☐ 655	Jim Poole 04	.02	.01
☐ 656	Felix Jose 07	.03	.01
☐ 657	Dennis Cook 04	.02	.01
☐ 658	Tom Brookens 04	.02	.01
☐ 659	Junior Ortiz 04	.02	.01
☐ 660	Jeff Parrett 04	.02	.01
☐ 661	Jerry Don Gleaton 04	.02	.01
☐ 662	Brent Knackert 07	.03	.01
☐ 663	Rance Mulliniks 04	.02	.01
☐ 664	John Smiley 07	.03	.01
☐ 665	Larry Andersen 04	.02	.01
☐ 666	Willie McGee 07	.03	.01
☐ 667	Chris Nabholz 10	.05	.01
☐ 668	Brady Anderson 07	.03	.01
☐ 669	Darren Holmes UER 15	.07	.02
	(19 CG's, should be 0)		
☐ 670	Ken Hill 07	.03	.01
☐ 671	Gary Varsho 04	.02	.01
☐ 672	Bill Pecota 04	.02	.01
☐ 673	Fred Lynn 07	.03	.01
☐ 674	Kevin D. Brown 04	.02	.01
☐ 675	Dan Petry 04	.02	.01
☐ 676	Mike Jackson 04	.02	.01
☐ 677	Wally Joyner 07	.03	.01
☐ 678	Danny Jackson 04	.02	.01
☐ 679	Bill Haselman 10	.05	.01
☐ 680	Mike Boddicker 04	.02	.01
☐ 681	Mel Rojas 10	.05	.01
☐ 682	Roberto Alomar 20	.09	.03
☐ 683	Dave Justice ROY 15	.07	.02
☐ 684	Chuck Crim 04	.02	.01
☐ 685	Matt Williams 07	.03	.01

☐ 686	Shawon Dunston	.07	.03	.01
☐ 687	Jeff Schulz	.04	.02	.01
☐ 688	John Barfield	.04	.02	.01
☐ 689	Gerald Young	.04	.02	.01
☐ 690	Luis Gonzalez	.20	.09	.03
☐ 691	Frank Wills	.04	.02	.01
☐ 692	Chuck Finley	.07	.03	.01
☐ 693	Sandy Alomar Jr. ROY	.07	.03	.01
☐ 694	Tim Drummond	.04	.02	.01
☐ 695	Herm Winningham	.04	.02	.01
☐ 696	Darryl Strawberry	.12	.05	.02
☐ 697	Al Leiter	.04	.02	.01
☐ 698	Karl Rhodes	.04	.02	.01
☐ 699	Stan Belinda	.04	.02	.01
☐ 700	Checklist Card	.05	.01	.00
☐ 701	Lance Blankenship	.04	.02	.01
☐ 702	Willie Stargell PUZ	.04	.02	.01
☐ 703	Jim Gantner	.04	.02	.01
☐ 704	Reggie Harris	.10	.05	.01
☐ 705	Rob Ducey	.04	.02	.01
☐ 706	Tim Hulett	.04	.02	.01
☐ 707	Atlee Hammaker	.04	.02	.01
☐ 708	Xavier Hernandez	.04	.02	.01
☐ 709	Chuck McElroy	.04	.02	.01
☐ 710	John Mitchell	.04	.02	.01
☐ 711	Carlos Hernandez	.04	.02	.01
☐ 712	Geronimo Pena	.10	.05	.01
☐ 713	Jim Neidlinger	.04	.02	.01
☐ 714	John Orton	.04	.02	.01
☐ 715	Terry Leach	.04	.02	.01
☐ 716	Mike Stanton	.04	.02	.01
☐ 717	Walt Terrell	.04	.02	.01
☐ 718	Luis Aquino	.04	.02	.01
☐ 719	Bud Black	.04	.02	.01
	(Blue Jays uniform,			
	but Giants logo)			
☐ 720	Bob Kipper	.04	.02	.01
☐ 721	Jeff Gray	.04	.02	.01
☐ 722	Jose Rijo	.07	.03	.01
☐ 723	Curt Young	.04	.02	.01
☐ 724	Jose Vizcaino	.04	.02	.01
☐ 725	Randy Tomlin	.20	.09	.03
☐ 726	Junior Noboa	.04	.02	.01
☐ 727	Bob Welch CY	.04	.02	.01
☐ 728	Gary Ward	.04	.02	.01
☐ 729	Rob Deer	.07	.03	.01
	(Brewers uniform,			
	but Tigers logo)			
☐ 730	David Segui	.04	.02	.01
☐ 731	Mark Carreon	.04	.02	.01
☐ 732	Vicente Palacios	.04	.02	.01
☐ 733	Sam Horn	.04	.02	.01
☐ 734	Howard Farmer	.04	.02	.01
☐ 735	Ken Dayley	.04	.02	.01
	(Cardinals uniform,			
	but Blue Jays logo)			
☐ 736	Kelly Mann	.04	.02	.01

☐ 737	Joe Grahe	.15	.07	.02
☐ 738	Kelly Downs	.04	.02	.01
☐ 739	Jimmy Kremers	.04	.02	.01
☐ 740	Kevin Appier	.07	.03	.01
☐ 741	Jeff Reed	.04	.02	.01
☐ 742	Jose Rijo WS	.07	.03	.01
☐ 743	Dave Rohde	.04	.02	.01
☐ 744	Dr.Dirt/Mr.Clean	.07	.03	.01
	Len Dykstra			
	Dale Murphy			
	UER (No '91 Donruss			
	logo on card front)			
☐ 745	Paul Sorrento	.07	.03	.01
☐ 746	Thomas Howard	.10	.05	.01
☐ 747	Matt Stark	.10	.05	.01
☐ 748	Harold Baines	.07	.03	.01
☐ 749	Doug Dascenzo	.04	.02	.01
☐ 750	Doug Drabek CY	.07	.03	.01
☐ 751	Gary Sheffield	.25	.11	.03
☐ 752	Terry Lee	.10	.05	.01
☐ 753	Jim Vatcher	.04	.02	.01
☐ 754	Lee Stevens	.04	.02	.01
☐ 755	Randy Veres	.04	.02	.01
☐ 756	Bill Doran	.04	.02	.01
☐ 757	Gary Wayne	.04	.02	.01
☐ 758	Pedro Munoz	.25	.11	.03
☐ 759	Chris Hammond	.10	.05	.01
☐ 760	Checklist Card	.05	.01	.00
☐ 761	Rickey Henderson MVP	.10	.05	.01
☐ 762	Barry Bonds MVP	.10	.05	.01
☐ 763	Billy Hatcher WS	.04	.02	.01
	UER (Line 13, on			
	should be one)			
☐ 764	Julio Machado	.04	.02	.01
☐ 765	Jose Mesa	.04	.02	.01
☐ 766	Willie Randolph WS	.04	.02	.01
☐ 767	Scott Erickson	.20	.09	.03
☐ 768	Travis Fryman	.60	.25	.08
☐ 769	Rich Rodriguez	.10	.05	.01
☐ 770	Checklist Card	.05	.01	.00
☐ BC1	Langston/Witt	.06	.03	.01
	No-Hits Mariners			
☐ BC2	Randy Johnson	.06	.03	.01
	No-Hits Tigers			
☐ BC3	Nolan Ryan	.35	.16	.04
	No-Hits A's			
☐ BC4	Dave Stewart	.06	.03	.01
	No-Hits Blue Jays			
☐ BC5	Cecil Fielder	.10	.05	.01
	50 Homer Club			
☐ BC6	Carlton Fisk	.10	.05	.01
	Record Home Run			
☐ BC7	Ryne Sandberg	.20	.09	.03
	Sets Fielding Records			
☐ BC8	Gary Carter	.06	.03	.01
	Breaks Catching Mark			
☐ BC9	Mark McGwire	.15	.07	.02

Home Run Milestone
(Back says First
Baseman, others say
only base)

☐ BC10 Bo Jackson................12	.05	.02	

Four Consecutive HR's

☐ BC11 Fernando Valenzuela.....06	.03	.01	

No Hits Cardinals

☐ BC12A Andy Hawkins ERR .1.00	.45	.13	

Pitcher

☐ BC12B Andy Hawkins COR....06	.03	.01	

No Hits White Sox

☐ BC13 Melido Perez..............06	.03	.01	

No Hits Yankees

☐ BC14 Terry Mulholland 06	.03	.01	

No Hits Giants
UER (Charlie Hayes is
called Chris Hayes)

☐ BC15 Nolan Ryan................35	.16	.04	

300th Win

☐ BC16 Delino DeShields........15	.07	.02	

4 Hits in Debut

☐ BC17 Cal Ripken 20	.09	.03	

Errorless Games

☐ BC18 Eddie Murray..............10	.05	.01	

Switch Hit Homers

☐ BC19 George Brett...............10	.05	.01	

3 Decade Champ

☐ BC20 Bobby Thigpen 06	.03	.01	

Shatters Save Mark

☐ BC21 Dave Stieb..................06	.03	.01	

No Hits Indians

☐ BC22 Willie McGee 06	.03	.01	

NL Batting Champ

1991 Donruss Rookies

*The 1991 Donruss Rookies set is a boxed
set issued to honor the best rookies of the
season. The cards measure the standard
size (2 1/2" by 3 1/2"), and a mini puzzle
featuring Hall of Famer Willie Stargell was
included with the set. The fronts feature
color action player photos, with white and
red borders. Yellow and green stripes cut
across the bottom of the card face, presenting the player's name and position.
The words "The Rookies" and a baseball
icon appear in the lower left corner of the
picture. The horizontally oriented backs*

*are printed in black on a green and white
background, and present biography, statistics, and career highlights. The cards are
numbered on the back. Outstanding rookies showcased in the set are Jeff Bagwell,
Chito Martinez, Orlando Merced, Dean
Palmer, Ivan Rodriguez, and Todd Van
Poppel.*

	MT	EX-MT	VG
COMPLETE SET (56) 5.00	2.30	.60	
COMMON PLAYER (1-56) 05	.02	.01	

☐ 1 Pat Kelly........................15	.07	.02	
☐ 2 Rich DeLucia..................05	.02	.01	
☐ 3 Wes Chamberlain............20	.09	.03	
☐ 4 Scott Leius.....................10	.05	.01	
☐ 5 Darryl Kile.....................10	.05	.01	
☐ 6 Milt Cuyler.....................08	.04	.01	
☐ 7 Todd Van Poppel 50	.23	.06	
☐ 8 Ray Lankford..................30	.14	.04	
☐ 9 Brian Hunter 25	.11	.03	
☐ 10 Tony Perezchica.............05	.02	.01	
☐ 11 Ced Landrum 10	.05	.01	
☐ 12 Dave Burba 10	.05	.01	
☐ 13 Ramon Garcia................10	.05	.01	
☐ 14 Ed Sprague 20	.09	.03	
☐ 15 Warren Newson 10	.05	.01	
☐ 16 Paul Faries 05	.02	.01	
☐ 17 Luis Gonzalez................20	.09	.03	
☐ 18 Charles Nagy.................25	.11	.03	
☐ 19 Chris Hammond 08	.04	.01	
☐ 20 Frank Castillo 15	.07	.02	
☐ 21 Pedro Munoz..................25	.11	.03	
☐ 22 Orlando Merced..............20	.09	.03	
☐ 23 Jose Melendez 10	.05	.01	
☐ 24 Kirk Dressendorfer..........10	.05	.01	
☐ 25 Heathcliff Slocumb 05	.02	.01	
☐ 26 Doug Simons 05	.02	.01	
☐ 27 Mike Timlin 10	.05	.01	
☐ 28 Jeff Fassero 10	.05	.01	
☐ 29 Mark Leiter 10	.05	.01	
☐ 30 Jeff Bagwell 1.25	.55	.16	

			MT	EX-MT	VG
☐ 31	Brian McRae	.20	.09	.03
☐ 32	Mark Whiten	.10	.05	.01
☐ 33	Ivan Rodriguez	1.25	.55	.16
☐ 34	Wade Taylor	.05	.02	.01
☐ 35	Darren Lewis	.10	.05	.01
☐ 36	Mo Vaughn	.20	.09	.03
☐ 37	Mike Remlinger	.05	.02	.01
☐ 38	Rick Wilkins	.10	.05	.01
☐ 39	Chuck Knoblauch	.30	.14	.04
☐ 40	Kevin Morton	.05	.02	.01
☐ 41	Carlos Rodriguez	.10	.05	.01
☐ 42	Mark Lewis	.10	.05	.01
☐ 43	Brent Mayne	.08	.04	.01
☐ 44	Chris Haney	.10	.05	.01
☐ 45	Denis Boucher	.12	.05	.02
☐ 46	Mike Gardiner	.10	.05	.01
☐ 47	Jeff Johnson	.10	.05	.01
☐ 48	Dean Palmer	.20	.09	.03
☐ 49	Chuck McElroy	.05	.02	.01
☐ 50	Chris Jones	.05	.02	.01
☐ 51	Scott Leius	.10	.05	.01
☐ 52	Al Osuna	.10	.05	.01
☐ 53	Rusty Meacham	.10	.05	.01
☐ 54	Chito Martinez	.10	.05	.01
☐ 55	Reggie Jefferson	.15	.07	.02
☐ 56	Checklist Card	.08	.01	.00

1992 Donruss

The 1992 Donruss set contains two series each featuring 396 cards, measuring the standard size (2 1/2" by 3 1/2"). The front design features glossy color player photos with white borders. Two-toned blue stripes overlay the top and bottom of the picture, with the player's name printed in silver-and-black lettering above the bottom stripe. The horizontally oriented backs

have a color headshot of the player (except on subset cards listed below), biography, career highlights, and recent Major League performance statistics (no earlier than 1987). The set includes Rated Rookies (1-20), AL All-Stars (21-30), Highlights (33, 94, 154, 215, 276), Rated Rookies (397-421), NL All-Stars (422-431), Highlights (434, 449, 555, 616, 677) and a puzzle of Hall of Famer Rod Carew. The cards are numbered on the back and checklisted below accordingly. Thirteen Diamond Kings cards featuring the artwork of Dick Perez were randomly inserted in first series foil packs and 13 more Diamond Kings were randomly inserted in second series foil packs. Inserted in both series foil and rack packs are 5,000 Cal Ripken Signature autographed cards, 7,500 Legend cards of Rickey Henderson, and 10,000 Elite cards each of Wade Boggs, Joe Carter, Will Clark, Dwight Gooden, Ken Griffey Jr., Tony Gwynn, Howard Johnson, Terry Pendleton, Kirby Puckett, and Frank Thomas. Key Rookie Cards in the set are John Jaha, Pat Mahomes, Brian Williams, and Bob Zupcic.

		MT	EX-MT	VG
COMPLETE SET (784)		20.00	9.00	2.50
COMPLETE FACT.SET (788)		30.00	13.50	3.80
COMPLETE SERIES 1 (396)		10.00	4.50	1.25
COMPLETE SERIES 2 (388)		10.00	4.50	1.25
COMPLETE BC SET (8)		1.50	.65	.19
COMMON PLAYER (1-396)		.04	.02	.01
COMMON PLAYER (397-784)		.04	.02	.01
COMMON BC SP (BC1-BC8)		.15	.07	.02

			MT	EX-MT	VG
☐ 1	Mark Wohlers RR	.10	.05	.01
☐ 2	Wilfredo Cordero RR	.15	.07	.02
☐ 3	Kyle Abbott RR	.08	.04	.01
☐ 4	Dave Nilsson RR	.15	.07	.02
☐ 5	Kenny Lofton RR	.40	.18	.05
☐ 6	Luis Mercedes RR	.08	.04	.01
☐ 7	Roger Salkeld RR	.10	.05	.01
☐ 8	Eddie Zosky RR	.08	.04	.01
☐ 9	Todd Van Poppel RR	.20	.09	.03
☐ 10	Frank Seminara RR	.20	.09	.03
☐ 11	Andy Ashby RR	.05	.02	.01
☐ 12	Reggie Jefferson RR	.08	.04	.01
☐ 13	Ryan Klesko RR	.50	.23	.06
☐ 14	Carlos Garcia RR	.08	.04	.01
☐ 15	John Ramos RR	.05	.02	.01
☐ 16	Eric Karros RR	.50	.23	.06
☐ 17	Patrick Lennon RR	.05	.02	.01
☐ 18	Eddie Taubensee RR	.12	.05	.02
☐ 19	Roberto Hernandez RR	.12	.05	.02

☐	20	D.J. Dozier RR	.08	.04	.01		
☐	21	Dave Henderson AS	.05	.02	.01		
☐	22	Cal Ripken AS	.15	.07	.02		
☐	23	Wade Boggs AS	.10	.05	.01		
☐	24	Ken Griffey Jr. AS	.25	.11	.03		
☐	25	Jack Morris AS	.08	.04	.01		
☐	26	Danny Tartabull AS	.08	.04	.01		
☐	27	Cecil Fielder AS	.10	.05	.01		
☐	28	Roberto Alomar AS	.10	.05	.01		
☐	29	Sandy Alomar Jr. AS	.05	.02	.01		
☐	30	Rickey Henderson AS	.10	.05	.01		
☐	31	Ken Hill	.04	.02	.01		
☐	32	John Habyan	.04	.02	.01		
☐	33	Otis Nixon HL	.05	.02	.01		
☐	34	Tim Wallach	.07	.03	.01		
☐	35	Cal Ripken	.25	.11	.03		
☐	36	Gary Carter	.07	.03	.01		
☐	37	Juan Agosto	.04	.02	.01		
☐	38	Doug Dascenzo	.04	.02	.01		
☐	39	Kirk Gibson	.07	.03	.01		
☐	40	Benito Santiago	.07	.03	.01		
☐	41	Otis Nixon	.04	.02	.01		
☐	42	Andy Allanson	.04	.02	.01		
☐	43	Brian Holman	.04	.02	.01		
☐	44	Dick Schofield	.04	.02	.01		
☐	45	Dave Magadan	.07	.03	.01		
☐	46	Rafael Palmeiro	.07	.03	.01		
☐	47	Jody Reed	.04	.02	.01		
☐	48	Ivan Calderon	.04	.02	.01		
☐	49	Greg W. Harris	.04	.02	.01		
☐	50	Chris Sabo	.07	.03	.01		
☐	51	Paul Molitor	.07	.03	.01		
☐	52	Robby Thompson	.04	.02	.01		
☐	53	Dave Smith	.04	.02	.01		
☐	54	Mark Davis	.04	.02	.01		
☐	55	Kevin Brown	.07	.03	.01		
☐	56	Donn Pall	.04	.02	.01		
☐	57	Len Dykstra	.07	.03	.01		
☐	58	Roberto Alomar	.20	.09	.03		
☐	59	Jeff D. Robinson	.04	.02	.01		
☐	60	Willie McGee	.07	.03	.01		
☐	61	Jay Buhner	.07	.03	.01		
☐	62	Mike Pagliarulo	.04	.02	.01		
☐	63	Paul O'Neill	.07	.03	.01		
☐	64	Hubie Brooks	.04	.02	.01		
☐	65	Kelly Gruber	.07	.03	.01		
☐	66	Ken Caminiti	.07	.03	.01		
☐	67	Gary Redus	.04	.02	.01		
☐	68	Harold Baines	.07	.03	.01		
☐	69	Charlie Hough	.04	.02	.01		
☐	70	B.J. Surhoff	.04	.02	.01		
☐	71	Walt Weiss	.04	.02	.01		
☐	72	Shawn Hillegas	.04	.02	.01		
☐	73	Roberto Kelly	.07	.03	.01		
☐	74	Jeff Ballard	.04	.02	.01		
☐	75	Craig Biggio	.07	.03	.01		
☐	76	Pat Combs	.04	.02	.01		
☐	77	Jeff M. Robinson	.04	.02	.01		
☐	78	Tim Belcher	.07	.03	.01		
☐	79	Cris Carpenter	.04	.02	.01		
☐	80	Checklist Card	.05	.01	.00		
☐	81	Steve Avery	.15	.07	.02		
☐	82	Chris James	.04	.02	.01		
☐	83	Brian Harper	.04	.02	.01		
☐	84	Charlie Leibrandt	.04	.02	.01		
☐	85	Mickey Tettleton	.07	.03	.01		
☐	86	Pete O'Brien	.04	.02	.01		
☐	87	Danny Darwin	.04	.02	.01		
☐	88	Bob Walk	.04	.02	.01		
☐	89	Jeff Reardon	.07	.03	.01		
☐	90	Bobby Rose	.04	.02	.01		
☐	91	Danny Jackson	.04	.02	.01		
☐	92	John Morris	.04	.02	.01		
☐	93	Bud Black	.04	.02	.01		
☐	94	Tommy Greene HL	.05	.02	.01		
☐	95	Rick Aguilera	.07	.03	.01		
☐	96	Gary Gaetti	.04	.02	.01		
☐	97	David Cone	.07	.03	.01		
☐	98	John Olerud	.10	.05	.01		
☐	99	Joel Skinner	.04	.02	.01		
☐	100	Jay Bell	.04	.02	.01		
☐	101	Bob Milacki	.04	.02	.01		
☐	102	Norm Charlton	.07	.03	.01		
☐	103	Chuck Crim	.04	.02	.01		
☐	104	Terry Steinbach	.07	.03	.01		
☐	105	Juan Samuel	.04	.02	.01		
☐	106	Steve Howe	.04	.02	.01		
☐	107	Rafael Belliard	.04	.02	.01		
☐	108	Joey Cora	.04	.02	.01		
☐	109	Tommy Greene	.04	.02	.01		
☐	110	Gregg Olson	.07	.03	.01		
☐	111	Frank Tanana	.04	.02	.01		
☐	112	Lee Smith	.07	.03	.01		
☐	113	Greg A. Harris	.04	.02	.01		
☐	114	Dwayne Henry	.04	.02	.01		
☐	115	Chili Davis	.07	.03	.01		
☐	116	Kent Mercker	.04	.02	.01		
☐	117	Brian Barnes	.04	.02	.01		
☐	118	Rich DeLucia	.04	.02	.01		
☐	119	Andre Dawson	.10	.05	.01		
☐	120	Carlos Baerga	.15	.07	.02		
☐	121	Mike LaValliere	.04	.02	.01		
☐	122	Jeff Gray	.04	.02	.01		
☐	123	Bruce Hurst	.07	.03	.01		
☐	124	Alvin Davis	.04	.02	.01		
☐	125	John Candelaria	.04	.02	.01		
☐	126	Matt Nokes	.04	.02	.01		
☐	127	George Bell	.07	.03	.01		
☐	128	Bret Saberhagen	.07	.03	.01		
☐	129	Jeff Russell	.04	.02	.01		
☐	130	Jim Abbott	.12	.05	.02		
☐	131	Bill Gullickson	.04	.02	.01		
☐	132	Todd Zeile	.04	.02	.01		
☐	133	Dave Winfield	.10	.05	.01		

☐ 134	Wally Whitehurst	.04	.02	.01	☐ 191	Alex Fernandez	.07	.03	.01
☐ 135	Matt Williams	.07	.03	.01	☐ 192	Gary Sheffield	.20	.09	.03
☐ 136	Tom Browning	.04	.02	.01	☐ 193	Rickey Henderson	.12	.05	.02
☐ 137	Marquis Grissom	.10	.05	.01	☐ 194	Rod Nichols	.04	.02	.01
☐ 138	Erik Hanson	.04	.02	.01	☐ 195	Scott Kamieniecki	.04	.02	.01
☐ 139	Rob Dibble	.07	.03	.01	☐ 196	Mike Flanagan	.04	.02	.01
☐ 140	Don August	.04	.02	.01	☐ 197	Steve Finley	.07	.03	.01
☐ 141	Tom Henke	.07	.03	.01	☐ 198	Darren Daulton	.07	.03	.01
☐ 142	Dan Pasqua	.04	.02	.01	☐ 199	Leo Gomez	.10	.05	.01
☐ 143	George Brett	.10	.05	.01	☐ 200	Mike Morgan	.04	.02	.01
☐ 144	Jerald Clark	.04	.02	.01	☐ 201	Bob Tewksbury	.07	.03	.01
☐ 145	Robin Ventura	.15	.07	.02	☐ 202	Sid Bream	.04	.02	.01
☐ 146	Dale Murphy	.07	.03	.01	☐ 203	Sandy Alomar Jr.	.07	.03	.01
☐ 147	Dennis Eckersley	.10	.05	.01	☐ 204	Greg Gagne	.04	.02	.01
☐ 148	Eric Yelding	.04	.02	.01	☐ 205	Juan Berenguer	.04	.02	.01
☐ 149	Mario Diaz	.04	.02	.01	☐ 206	Cecil Fielder	.12	.05	.02
☐ 150	Casey Candaele	.04	.02	.01	☐ 207	Randy Johnson	.07	.03	.01
☐ 151	Steve Olin	.04	.02	.01	☐ 208	Tony Pena	.04	.02	.01
☐ 152	Luis Salazar	.04	.02	.01	☐ 209	Doug Drabek	.07	.03	.01
☐ 153	Kevin Maas	.07	.03	.01	☐ 210	Wade Boggs	.12	.05	.02
☐ 154	Nolan Ryan HL	.25	.11	.03	☐ 211	Bryan Harvey	.04	.02	.01
☐ 155	Barry Jones	.04	.02	.01	☐ 212	Jose Vizcaino	.04	.02	.01
☐ 156	Chris Hoiles	.07	.03	.01	☐ 213	Alonzo Powell	.04	.02	.01
☐ 157	Bobby Ojeda	.04	.02	.01	☐ 214	Will Clark	.20	.09	.03
☐ 158	Pedro Guerrero	.07	.03	.01	☐ 215	Rickey Henderson HL	.10	.05	.01
☐ 159	Paul Assenmacher	.04	.02	.01	☐ 216	Jack Morris	.10	.05	.01
☐ 160	Checklist Card	.05	.01	.00	☐ 217	Junior Felix	.04	.02	.01
☐ 161	Mike Macfarlane	.04	.02	.01	☐ 218	Vince Coleman	.07	.03	.01
☐ 162	Craig Lefferts	.04	.02	.01	☐ 219	Jimmy Key	.04	.02	.01
☐ 163	Brian Hunter	.10	.05	.01	☐ 220	Alex Cole	.04	.02	.01
☐ 164	Alan Trammell	.07	.03	.01	☐ 221	Bill Landrum	.04	.02	.01
☐ 165	Ken Griffey Jr.	.50	.23	.06	☐ 222	Randy Milligan	.04	.02	.01
☐ 166	Lance Parrish	.07	.03	.01	☐ 223	Jose Rijo	.07	.03	.01
☐ 167	Brian Downing	.04	.02	.01	☐ 224	Greg Vaughn	.07	.03	.01
☐ 168	John Barfield	.04	.02	.01	☐ 225	Dave Stewart	.07	.03	.01
☐ 169	Jack Clark	.07	.03	.01	☐ 226	Lenny Harris	.04	.02	.01
☐ 170	Chris Nabholz	.07	.03	.01	☐ 227	Scott Sanderson	.04	.02	.01
☐ 171	Tim Teufel	.04	.02	.01	☐ 228	Jeff Blauser	.04	.02	.01
☐ 172	Chris Hammond	.04	.02	.01	☐ 229	Ozzie Guillen	.04	.02	.01
☐ 173	Robin Yount	.10	.05	.01	☐ 230	John Kruk	.07	.03	.01
☐ 174	Dave Righetti	.04	.02	.01	☐ 231	Bob Melvin	.04	.02	.01
☐ 175	Joe Girardi	.04	.02	.01	☐ 232	Milt Cuyler	.07	.03	.01
☐ 176	Mike Boddicker	.04	.02	.01	☐ 233	Felix Jose	.07	.03	.01
☐ 177	Dean Palmer	.12	.05	.02	☐ 234	Ellis Burks	.07	.03	.01
☐ 178	Greg Hibbard	.04	.02	.01	☐ 235	Pete Harnisch	.04	.02	.01
☐ 179	Randy Ready	.04	.02	.01	☐ 236	Kevin Tapani	.04	.02	.01
☐ 180	Devon White	.07	.03	.01	☐ 237	Terry Pendleton	.10	.05	.01
☐ 181	Mark Eichhorn	.04	.02	.01	☐ 238	Mark Gardner	.04	.02	.01
☐ 182	Mike Felder	.04	.02	.01	☐ 239	Harold Reynolds	.04	.02	.01
☐ 183	Joe Klink	.04	.02	.01	☐ 240	Checklist Card	.05	.01	.00
☐ 184	Steve Bedrosian	.04	.02	.01	☐ 241	Mike Harkey	.07	.03	.01
☐ 185	Barry Larkin	.10	.05	.01	☐ 242	Felix Fermin	.04	.02	.01
☐ 186	John Franco	.07	.03	.01	☐ 243	Barry Bonds	.15	.07	.02
☐ 187	Ed Sprague	.07	.03	.01	☐ 244	Roger Clemens	.25	.11	.03
☐ 188	Mark Portugal	.04	.02	.01	☐ 245	Dennis Rasmussen	.04	.02	.01
☐ 189	Jose Lind	.04	.02	.01	☐ 246	Jose DeLeon	.04	.02	.01
☐ 190	Bob Welch	.04	.02	.01	☐ 247	Orel Hershiser	.07	.03	.01

☐ 248 Mel Hall	.04	.02	.01	
☐ 249 Rick Wilkins	.04	.02	.01	
☐ 250 Tom Gordon	.04	.02	.01	
☐ 251 Kevin Reimer	.04	.02	.01	
☐ 252 Luis Polonia	.07	.03	.01	
☐ 253 Mike Henneman	.04	.02	.01	
☐ 254 Tom Pagnozzi	.04	.02	.01	
☐ 255 Chuck Finley	.04	.02	.01	
☐ 256 Mackey Sasser	.04	.02	.01	
☐ 257 John Burkett	.04	.02	.01	
☐ 258 Hal Morris	.07	.03	.01	
☐ 259 Larry Walker	.15	.07	.02	
☐ 260 Billy Swift	.04	.02	.01	
☐ 261 Joe Oliver	.04	.02	.01	
☐ 262 Julio Machado	.04	.02	.01	
☐ 263 Todd Stottlemyre	.07	.03	.01	
☐ 264 Matt Merullo	.04	.02	.01	
☐ 265 Brent Mayne	.04	.02	.01	
☐ 266 Thomas Howard	.04	.02	.01	
☐ 267 Lance Johnson	.04	.02	.01	
☐ 268 Terry Mulholland	.04	.02	.01	
☐ 269 Rick Honeycutt	.04	.02	.01	
☐ 270 Luis Gonzalez	.07	.03	.01	
☐ 271 Jose Guzman	.04	.02	.01	
☐ 272 Jimmy Jones	.04	.02	.01	
☐ 273 Mark Lewis	.07	.03	.01	
☐ 274 Rene Gonzales	.04	.02	.01	
☐ 275 Jeff Johnson	.04	.02	.01	
☐ 276 Dennis Martinez HL	.05	.02	.01	
☐ 277 Delino DeShields	.10	.05	.01	
☐ 278 Sam Horn	.04	.02	.01	
☐ 279 Kevin Gross	.04	.02	.01	
☐ 280 Jose Oquendo	.04	.02	.01	
☐ 281 Mark Grace	.07	.03	.01	
☐ 282 Mark Gubicza	.04	.02	.01	
☐ 283 Fred McGriff	.12	.05	.02	
☐ 284 Ron Gant	.10	.05	.01	
☐ 285 Lou Whitaker	.07	.03	.01	
☐ 286 Edgar Martinez	.07	.03	.01	
☐ 287 Ron Tingley	.04	.02	.01	
☐ 288 Kevin McReynolds	.07	.03	.01	
☐ 289 Ivan Rodriguez	.35	.16	.04	
☐ 290 Mike Gardiner	.04	.02	.01	
☐ 291 Chris Haney	.04	.02	.01	
☐ 292 Darrin Jackson	.07	.03	.01	
☐ 293 Bill Doran	.04	.02	.01	
☐ 294 Ted Higuera	.04	.02	.01	
☐ 295 Jeff Brantley	.04	.02	.01	
☐ 296 Les Lancaster	.04	.02	.01	
☐ 297 Jim Eisenreich	.04	.02	.01	
☐ 298 Ruben Sierra	.15	.07	.02	
☐ 299 Scott Radinsky	.04	.02	.01	
☐ 300 Jose DeJesus	.04	.02	.01	
☐ 301 Mike Timlin	.04	.02	.01	
☐ 302 Luis Sojo	.04	.02	.01	
☐ 303 Kelly Downs	.04	.02	.01	
☐ 304 Scott Bankhead	.04	.02	.01	
☐ 305 Pedro Munoz	.07	.03	.01	
☐ 306 Scott Scudder	.04	.02	.01	
☐ 307 Kevin Elster	.04	.02	.01	
☐ 308 Duane Ward	.04	.02	.01	
☐ 309 Darryl Kile	.07	.03	.01	
☐ 310 Orlando Merced	.07	.03	.01	
☐ 311 Dave Henderson	.04	.02	.01	
☐ 312 Tim Raines	.07	.03	.01	
☐ 313 Mark Lee	.04	.02	.01	
☐ 314 Mike Gallego	.04	.02	.01	
☐ 315 Charles Nagy	.10	.05	.01	
☐ 316 Jesse Barfield	.04	.02	.01	
☐ 317 Todd Frohwirth	.04	.02	.01	
☐ 318 Al Osuna	.04	.02	.01	
☐ 319 Darrin Fletcher	.04	.02	.01	
☐ 320 Checklist Card	.05	.01	.00	
☐ 321 David Segui	.04	.02	.01	
☐ 322 Stan Javier	.04	.02	.01	
☐ 323 Bryn Smith	.04	.02	.01	
☐ 324 Jeff Treadway	.04	.02	.01	
☐ 325 Mark Whiten	.07	.03	.01	
☐ 326 Kent Hrbek	.07	.03	.01	
☐ 327 Dave Justice	.20	.09	.03	
☐ 328 Tony Phillips	.04	.02	.01	
☐ 329 Rob Murphy	.04	.02	.01	
☐ 330 Kevin Morton	.04	.02	.01	
☐ 331 John Smiley	.07	.03	.01	
☐ 332 Luis Rivera	.04	.02	.01	
☐ 333 Wally Joyner	.07	.03	.01	
☐ 334 Heathcliff Slocumb	.04	.02	.01	
☐ 335 Rick Cerone	.04	.02	.01	
☐ 336 Mike Remlinger	.04	.02	.01	
☐ 337 Mike Moore	.04	.02	.01	
☐ 338 Lloyd McClendon	.04	.02	.01	
☐ 339 Al Newman	.04	.02	.01	
☐ 340 Kirk McCaskill	.04	.02	.01	
☐ 341 Howard Johnson	.07	.03	.01	
☐ 342 Greg Myers	.04	.02	.01	
☐ 343 Kal Daniels	.04	.02	.01	
☐ 344 Bernie Williams	.10	.05	.01	
☐ 345 Shane Mack	.07	.03	.01	
☐ 346 Gary Thurman	.04	.02	.01	
☐ 347 Dante Bichette	.04	.02	.01	
☐ 348 Mark McGwire	.20	.09	.03	
☐ 349 Travis Fryman	.30	.14	.04	
☐ 350 Ray Lankford	.15	.07	.02	
☐ 351 Mike Jeffcoat	.04	.02	.01	
☐ 352 Jack McDowell	.07	.03	.01	
☐ 353 Mitch Williams	.04	.02	.01	
☐ 354 Mike Devereaux	.07	.03	.01	
☐ 355 Andres Galarraga	.04	.02	.01	
☐ 356 Henry Cotto	.04	.02	.01	
☐ 357 Scott Bailes	.04	.02	.01	
☐ 358 Jeff Bagwell	.25	.11	.03	
☐ 359 Scott Leius	.04	.02	.01	
☐ 360 Zane Smith	.04	.02	.01	
☐ 361 Bill Pecota	.04	.02	.01	

☐ 362	Tony Fernandez	.07	.03	.01
☐ 363	Glenn Braggs	.04	.02	.01
☐ 364	Bill Spiers	.04	.02	.01
☐ 365	Vicente Palacios	.04	.02	.01
☐ 366	Tim Burke	.04	.02	.01
☐ 367	Randy Tomlin	.04	.02	.01
☐ 368	Kenny Rogers	.04	.02	.01
☐ 369	Brett Butler	.07	.03	.01
☐ 370	Pat Kelly	.07	.03	.01
☐ 371	Bip Roberts	.07	.03	.01
☐ 372	Gregg Jefferies	.07	.03	.01
☐ 373	Kevin Bass	.04	.02	.01
☐ 374	Ron Karkovice	.04	.02	.01
☐ 375	Paul Gibson	.04	.02	.01
☐ 376	Bernard Gilkey	.07	.03	.01
☐ 377	Dave Gallagher	.04	.02	.01
☐ 378	Bill Wegman	.04	.02	.01
☐ 379	Pat Borders	.04	.02	.01
☐ 380	Ed Whitson	.04	.02	.01
☐ 381	Gilberto Reyes	.04	.02	.01
☐ 382	Russ Swan	.04	.02	.01
☐ 383	Andy Van Slyke	.07	.03	.01
☐ 384	Wes Chamberlain	.04	.02	.01
☐ 385	Steve Chitren	.04	.02	.01
☐ 386	Greg Olson	.04	.02	.01
☐ 387	Brian McRae	.07	.03	.01
☐ 388	Rich Rodriguez	.04	.02	.01
☐ 389	Steve Decker	.04	.02	.01
☐ 390	Chuck Knoblauch	.20	.09	.03
☐ 391	Bobby Witt	.04	.02	.01
☐ 392	Eddie Murray	.10	.05	.01
☐ 393	Juan Gonzalez	.35	.16	.04
☐ 394	Scott Ruskin	.04	.02	.01
☐ 395	Jay Howell	.04	.02	.01
☐ 396	Checklist Card	.05	.01	.00
☐ 397	Royce Clayton RR	.15	.07	.02
☐ 398	John Jaha RR	.25	.11	.03
☐ 399	Dan Wilson RR	.05	.02	.01
☐ 400	Archie Corbin RR	.10	.05	.01
☐ 401	Barry Manuel RR	.12	.05	.02
☐ 402	Kim Batiste RR	.05	.02	.01
☐ 403	Pat Mahomes RR	.25	.11	.03
☐ 404	Dave Fleming RR	.50	.23	.06
☐ 405	Jeff Juden RR	.10	.05	.01
☐ 406	Jim Thome RR	.12	.05	.02
☐ 407	Sam Militello RR	.30	.14	.04
☐ 408	Jeff Nelson RR	.12	.05	.02
☐ 409	Anthony Young RR	.08	.04	.01
☐ 410	Tino Martinez RR	.08	.04	.01
☐ 411	Jeff Mutis RR	.10	.05	.01
☐ 412	Rey Sanchez RR	.12	.05	.02
☐ 413	Chris Gardner RR	.10	.05	.01
☐ 414	John VanderWal RR	.15	.07	.02
☐ 415	Reggie Sanders RR	.25	.11	.03
☐ 416	Brian Williams RR	.25	.11	.03
☐ 417	Mo Sanford RR	.05	.02	.01
☐ 418	David Weathers RR	.20	.09	.03
☐ 419	Hector Fajardo RR	.12	.05	.02
☐ 420	Steve Foster RR	.10	.05	.01
☐ 421	Lance Dickson RR	.05	.02	.01
☐ 422	Andre Dawson AS	.10	.05	.01
☐ 423	Ozzie Smith AS	.10	.05	.01
☐ 424	Chris Sabo AS	.05	.02	.01
☐ 425	Tony Gwynn AS	.10	.05	.01
☐ 426	Tom Glavine AS	.10	.05	.01
☐ 427	Bobby Bonilla AS	.08	.04	.01
☐ 428	Will Clark AS	.10	.05	.01
☐ 429	Ryne Sandberg AS	.10	.05	.01
☐ 430	Benito Santiago AS	.05	.02	.01
☐ 431	Ivan Calderon AS	.05	.02	.01
☐ 432	Ozzie Smith	.10	.05	.01
☐ 433	Tim Leary	.04	.02	.01
☐ 434	Bret Saberhagen HL	.07	.03	.01
☐ 435	Mel Rojas	.04	.02	.01
☐ 436	Ben McDonald	.10	.05	.01
☐ 437	Tim Crews	.04	.02	.01
☐ 438	Rex Hudler	.04	.02	.01
☐ 439	Chico Walker	.04	.02	.01
☐ 440	Kurt Stillwell	.04	.02	.01
☐ 441	Tony Gwynn	.12	.05	.02
☐ 442	John Smoltz	.10	.05	.01
☐ 443	Lloyd Moseby	.04	.02	.01
☐ 444	Mike Schooler	.04	.02	.01
☐ 445	Joe Grahe	.04	.02	.01
☐ 446	Dwight Gooden	.07	.03	.01
☐ 447	Oil Can Boyd	.04	.02	.01
☐ 448	John Marzano	.04	.02	.01
☐ 449	Bret Barberie	.07	.03	.01
☐ 450	Mike Maddux	.04	.02	.01
☐ 451	Jeff Reed	.04	.02	.01
☐ 452	Dalo Sveum	.04	.02	.01
☐ 453	Jose Uribe	.04	.02	.01
☐ 454	Bob Scanlan	.04	.02	.01
☐ 455	Kevin Appier	.07	.03	.01
☐ 456	Jeff Huson	.04	.02	.01
☐ 457	Ken Patterson	.04	.02	.01
☐ 458	Ricky Jordan	.04	.02	.01
☐ 459	Tom Candiotti	.04	.02	.01
☐ 460	Lee Stevens	.04	.02	.01
☐ 461	Rod Beck	.12	.05	.02
☐ 462	Dave Valle	.04	.02	.01
☐ 463	Scott Erickson	.10	.05	.01
☐ 464	Chris Jones	.04	.02	.01
☐ 465	Mark Carreon	.04	.02	.01
☐ 466	Rob Ducey	.04	.02	.01
☐ 467	Jim Corsi	.04	.02	.01
☐ 468	Jeff King	.04	.02	.01
☐ 469	Curt Young	.04	.02	.01
☐ 470	Bo Jackson	.12	.05	.02
☐ 471	Chris Bosio	.04	.02	.01
☐ 472	Jamie Quirk	.04	.02	.01
☐ 473	Jesse Orosco	.04	.02	.01
☐ 474	Alvaro Espinoza	.04	.02	.01
☐ 475	Joe Orsulak	.04	.02	.01

☐ 476 Checklist Card	.05	.01	.00
☐ 477 Gerald Young	.04	.02	.01
☐ 478 Wally Backman	.04	.02	.01
☐ 479 Juan Bell	.04	.02	.01
☐ 480 Mike Scioscia	.04	.02	.01
☐ 481 Omar Olivares	.04	.02	.01
☐ 482 Francisco Cabrera	.04	.02	.01
☐ 483 Greg Swindell UER	.07	.03	.01
(Shown on Indians,			
but listed on Reds)			
☐ 484 Terry Leach	.04	.02	.01
☐ 485 Tommy Gregg	.04	.02	.01
☐ 486 Scott Aldred	.04	.02	.01
☐ 487 Greg Briley	.04	.02	.01
☐ 488 Phil Plantier	.15	.07	.02
☐ 489 Curtis Wilkerson	.04	.02	.01
☐ 490 Tom Brunansky	.07	.03	.01
☐ 491 Mike Fetters	.04	.02	.01
☐ 492 Frank Castillo	.10	.05	.01
☐ 493 Joe Boever	.04	.02	.01
☐ 494 Kirt Manwaring	.04	.02	.01
☐ 495 Wilson Alvarez HL	.05	.02	.01
☐ 496 Gene Larkin	.04	.02	.01
☐ 497 Gary DiSarcina	.07	.03	.01
☐ 498 Frank Viola	.07	.03	.01
☐ 499 Manuel Lee	.04	.02	.01
☐ 500 Albert Belle	.12	.05	.02
☐ 501 Stan Belinda	.04	.02	.01
☐ 502 Dwight Evans	.07	.03	.01
☐ 503 Eric Davis	.07	.03	.01
☐ 504 Darren Holmes	.04	.02	.01
☐ 505 Mike Bordick	.10	.05	.01
☐ 506 Dave Hansen	.04	.02	.01
☐ 507 Lee Guetterman	.04	.02	.01
☐ 508 Keith Mitchell	.07	.03	.01
☐ 509 Melido Perez	.07	.03	.01
☐ 510 Dickie Thon	.04	.02	.01
☐ 511 Mark Williamson	.04	.02	.01
☐ 512 Mark Salas	.04	.02	.01
☐ 513 Milt Thompson	.04	.02	.01
☐ 514 Mo Vaughn	.07	.03	.01
☐ 515 Jim Deshaies	.04	.02	.01
☐ 516 Rich Garces	.04	.02	.01
☐ 517 Lonnie Smith	.04	.02	.01
☐ 518 Spike Owen	.04	.02	.01
☐ 519 Tracy Jones	.04	.02	.01
☐ 520 Greg Maddux	.07	.03	.01
☐ 521 Carlos Martinez	.04	.02	.01
☐ 522 Neal Heaton	.04	.02	.01
☐ 523 Mike Greenwell	.07	.03	.01
☐ 524 Andy Benes	.07	.03	.01
☐ 525 Jeff Schaefer UER	.04	.02	.01
(Photo actually			
Tino Martinez)			
☐ 526 Mike Sharperson	.04	.02	.01
☐ 527 Wade Taylor	.04	.02	.01
☐ 528 Jerome Walton	.04	.02	.01

☐ 529 Storm Davis	.04	.02	.01
☐ 530 Jose Hernandez	.10	.05	.01
☐ 531 Mark Langston	.07	.03	.01
☐ 532 Rob Deer	.07	.03	.01
☐ 533 Geronimo Pena	.04	.02	.01
☐ 534 Juan Guzman	.75	.35	.09
☐ 535 Pete Schourek	.07	.03	.01
☐ 536 Todd Benzinger	.04	.02	.01
☐ 537 Billy Hatcher	.04	.02	.01
☐ 538 Tom Foley	.04	.02	.01
☐ 539 Dave Cochrane	.04	.02	.01
☐ 540 Mariano Duncan	.04	.02	.01
☐ 541 Edwin Nunez	.04	.02	.01
☐ 542 Rance Mulliniks	.04	.02	.01
☐ 543 Carlton Fisk	.10	.05	.01
☐ 544 Luis Aquino	.04	.02	.01
☐ 545 Ricky Bones	.10	.05	.01
☐ 546 Craig Grebeck	.04	.02	.01
☐ 547 Charlie Hayes	.04	.02	.01
☐ 548 Jose Canseco	.20	.09	.03
☐ 549 Andujar Cedeno	.07	.03	.01
☐ 550 Geno Petralli	.04	.02	.01
☐ 551 Javier Ortiz	.04	.02	.01
☐ 552 Rudy Seanez	.04	.02	.01
☐ 553 Rich Gedman	.04	.02	.01
☐ 554 Eric Plunk	.04	.02	.01
☐ 555 Nolan Ryan HL	.20	.09	.03
(With Rich Gossage)			
☐ 556 Checklist Card	.05	.01	.00
☐ 557 Greg Colbrunn	.07	.03	.01
☐ 558 Chito Martinez	.04	.02	.01
☐ 559 Darryl Strawberry	.12	.05	.02
☐ 560 Luis Alicea	.04	.02	.01
☐ 561 Dwight Smith	.04	.02	.01
☐ 562 Terry Shumpert	.04	.02	.01
☐ 563 Jim Vatcher	.04	.02	.01
☐ 564 Deion Sanders	.15	.07	.02
☐ 565 Walt Terrell	.04	.02	.01
☐ 566 Dave Burba	.04	.02	.01
☐ 567 Dave Howard	.04	.02	.01
☐ 568 Todd Hundley	.04	.02	.01
☐ 569 Jack Daugherty	.04	.02	.01
☐ 570 Scott Cooper	.07	.03	.01
☐ 571 Bill Sampen	.04	.02	.01
☐ 572 Jose Melendez	.04	.02	.01
☐ 573 Freddie Benavides	.04	.02	.01
☐ 574 Jim Gantner	.04	.02	.01
☐ 575 Trevor Wilson	.04	.02	.01
☐ 576 Ryne Sandberg	.25	.11	.03
☐ 577 Kevin Seitzer	.07	.03	.01
☐ 578 Gerald Alexander	.04	.02	.01
☐ 579 Mike Huff	.04	.02	.01
☐ 580 Von Hayes	.04	.02	.01
☐ 581 Derek Bell	.10	.05	.01
☐ 582 Mike Stanley	.04	.02	.01
☐ 583 Kevin Mitchell	.07	.03	.01
☐ 584 Mike Jackson	.04	.02	.01

☐ 585	Dan Gladden 04	.02	.01
☐ 586	Ted Power UER 04	.02	.01
	(Wrong year given for		
	signing with Reds)		
☐ 587	Jeff Innis.......................04	.02	.01
☐ 588	Bob MacDonald 04	.02	.01
☐ 589	Jose Tolentino 10	.05	.01
☐ 590	Bob Patterson 04	.02	.01
☐ 591	Scott Brosius 10	.05	.01
☐ 592	Frank Thomas 75	.35	.09
☐ 593	Darryl Hamilton..............07	.03	.01
☐ 594	Kirk Dressendorfer..........04	.02	.01
☐ 595	Jeff Shaw 04	.02	.01
☐ 596	Don Mattingly 12	.05	.02
☐ 597	Glenn Davis 07	.03	.01
☐ 598	Andy Mota 04	.02	.01
☐ 599	Jason Grimsley 04	.02	.01
☐ 600	Jimmy Poole...................04	.02	.01
☐ 601	Jim Gott 04	.02	.01
☐ 602	Stan Royer 04	.02	.01
☐ 603	Marvin Freeman 04	.02	.01
☐ 604	Denis Boucher 07	.03	.01
☐ 605	Denny Neagle..................07	.03	.01
☐ 606	Mark Lemke 04	.02	.01
☐ 607	Jerry Don Gleaton 04	.02	.01
☐ 608	Brent Knackert 04	.02	.01
☐ 609	Carlos Quintana 04	.02	.01
☐ 610	Bobby Bonilla.................10	.05	.01
☐ 611	Joe Hesketh 04	.02	.01
☐ 612	Daryl Boston 04	.02	.01
☐ 613	Shawon Dunston 07	.03	.01
☐ 614	Danny Cox 04	.02	.01
☐ 615	Darren Lewis...................07	.03	.01
☐ 616	Braves No-Hitter UER 05	.02	.01
	Kent Mercker		
	(Misspelled Merker		
	on card front)		
	Alejandro Pena		
	Mark Wohlers		
☐ 617	Kirby Puckett.................20	.09	.03
☐ 618	Franklin Stubbs..............04	.02	.01
☐ 619	Chris Donnels 04	.02	.01
☐ 620	David Wells UER 04	.02	.01
	(Career Highlights		
	in black not red)		
☐ 621	Mike Aldrete 04	.02	.01
☐ 622	Bob Kipper 04	.02	.01
☐ 623	Anthony Telford 04	.02	.01
☐ 624	Randy Myers...................07	.03	.01
☐ 625	Willie Randolph...............07	.03	.01
☐ 626	Joe Slusarski..................04	.02	.01
☐ 627	John Wetteland...............04	.02	.01
☐ 628	Greg Cadaret 04	.02	.01
☐ 629	Tom Glavine 12	.05	.02
☐ 630	Wilson Alvarez................04	.02	.01
☐ 631	Wally Ritchie..................04	.02	.01
☐ 632	Mike Mussina.................50	.23	.06

☐ 633	Mark Leiter.....................04	.02	.01
☐ 634	Gerald Perry...................04	.02	.01
☐ 635	Matt Young 04	.02	.01
☐ 636	Checklist Card.................05	.01	.00
☐ 637	Scott Hemond 04	.02	.01
☐ 638	David West 04	.02	.01
☐ 639	Jim Clancy 04	.02	.01
☐ 640	Doug Piatt UER...............04	.02	.01
	(Not born in 1955 as		
	on card; incorrect info		
	on How Acquired)		
☐ 641	Omar Vizquel 04	.02	.01
☐ 642	Rick Sutcliffe.................07	.03	.01
☐ 643	Glenallen Hill.................04	.02	.01
☐ 644	Gary Varsho....................04	.02	.01
☐ 645	Tony Fossas....................04	.02	.01
☐ 646	Jack Howell....................04	.02	.01
☐ 647	Jim Campanis 10	.05	.01
☐ 648	Chris Gwynn 04	.02	.01
☐ 649	Jim Leyritz.....................04	.02	.01
☐ 650	Chuck McElroy................04	.02	.01
☐ 651	Sean Berry 04	.02	.01
☐ 652	Donald Harris..................04	.02	.01
☐ 653	Don Slaught 04	.02	.01
☐ 654	Rusty Meacham 04	.02	.01
☐ 655	Scott Terry 04	.02	.01
☐ 656	Ramon Martinez 07	.03	.01
☐ 657	Keith Miller 04	.02	.01
☐ 658	Ramon Garcia 04	.02	.01
☐ 659	Milt Hill 10	.05	.01
☐ 660	Steve Frey 04	.02	.01
☐ 661	Bob McClure 04	.02	.01
☐ 662	Ced Landrum 04	.02	.01
☐ 663	Doug Henry.....................15	.07	.02
☐ 664	Candy Maldonado 04	.02	.01
☐ 665	Carl Willis 04	.02	.01
☐ 666	Jeff Montgomery 04	.02	.01
☐ 667	Craig Shipley..................10	.05	.01
☐ 668	Warren Newson 04	.02	.01
☐ 669	Mickey Morandini 07	.03	.01
☐ 670	Brook Jacoby 04	.02	.01
☐ 671	Ryan Bowen 07	.03	.01
☐ 672	Bill Krueger 04	.02	.01
☐ 673	Rob Mallicoat..................04	.02	.01
☐ 674	Doug Jones.....................04	.02	.01
☐ 675	Scott Livingstone............05	.01	.01
☐ 676	Danny Tartabull...............07	.03	.01
☐ 677	Joe Carter HL..................10	.05	.01
☐ 678	Cecil Espy 04	.02	.01
☐ 679	Randy Velarde 04	.02	.01
☐ 680	Bruce Ruffin...................04	.02	.01
☐ 681	Ted Wood 10	.05	.01
☐ 682	Dan Plesac.....................04	.02	.01
☐ 683	Eric Bullock 04	.02	.01
☐ 684	Junior Ortiz 04	.02	.01
☐ 685	Dave Hollins 07	.03	.01
☐ 686	Dennis Martinez..............07	.03	.01

☐ 687 Larry Andersen	.04	.02	.01
☐ 688 Doug Simons	.04	.02	.01
☐ 689 Tim Spehr	.04	.02	.01
☐ 690 Calvin Jones	.10	.05	.01
☐ 691 Mark Guthrie	.04	.02	.01
☐ 692 Alfredo Griffin	.04	.02	.01
☐ 693 Joe Carter	.12	.05	.02
☐ 694 Terry Mathews	.10	.05	.01
☐ 695 Pascual Perez	.04	.02	.01
☐ 696 Gene Nelson	.04	.02	.01
☐ 697 Gerald Williams	.10	.05	.01
☐ 698 Chris Cron	.10	.05	.01
☐ 699 Steve Buechele	.04	.02	.01
☐ 700 Paul McClellan	.04	.02	.01
☐ 701 Jim Lindeman	.04	.02	.01
☐ 702 Francisco Oliveras	.04	.02	.01
☐ 703 Rob Maurer	.12	.05	.02
☐ 704 Pat Hentgen	.10	.05	.01
☐ 705 Jaime Navarro	.07	.03	.01
☐ 706 Mike Magnante	.12	.05	.02
☐ 707 Nolan Ryan	.40	.18	.05
☐ 708 Bobby Thigpen	.04	.02	.01
☐ 709 John Cerutti	.04	.02	.01
☐ 710 Steve Wilson	.04	.02	.01
☐ 711 Hensley Meulens	.04	.02	.01
☐ 712 Rheal Cormier	.04	.02	.01
☐ 713 Scott Bradley	.04	.02	.01
☐ 714 Mitch Webster	.04	.02	.01
☐ 715 Roger Mason	.04	.02	.01
☐ 716 Checklist Card	.05	.01	.00
☐ 717 Jeff Fassero	.04	.02	.01
☐ 718 Cal Eldred	.35	.16	.04
☐ 719 Sid Fernandez	.07	.03	.01
☐ 720 Bob Zupcic	.25	.11	.03
☐ 721 Jose Offerman	.07	.03	.01
☐ 722 Cliff Brantley	.10	.05	.01
☐ 723 Ron Darling	.07	.03	.01
☐ 724 Dave Stieb	.04	.02	.01
☐ 725 Hector Villanueva	.04	.02	.01
☐ 726 Mike Hartley	.04	.02	.01
☐ 727 Arthur Rhodes	.15	.07	.02
☐ 728 Randy Bush	.04	.02	.01
☐ 729 Steve Sax	.07	.03	.01
☐ 730 Dave Otto	.04	.02	.01
☐ 731 John Wehner	.07	.03	.01
☐ 732 Dave Martinez	.04	.02	.01
☐ 733 Ruben Amaro	.04	.02	.01
☐ 734 Billy Ripken	.04	.02	.01
☐ 735 Steve Farr	.04	.02	.01
☐ 736 Shawn Abner	.04	.02	.01
☐ 737 Gil Heredia	.10	.05	.01
☐ 738 Ron Jones	.04	.02	.01
☐ 739 Tony Castillo	.04	.02	.01
☐ 740 Sammy Sosa	.04	.02	.01
☐ 741 Julio Franco	.07	.03	.01
☐ 742 Tim Naehring	.07	.03	.01
☐ 743 Steve Wapnick	.04	.02	.01
☐ 744 Craig Wilson	.04	.02	.01
☐ 745 Darrin Chapin	.10	.05	.01
☐ 746 Chris George	.04	.02	.01
☐ 747 Mike Simms	.04	.02	.01
☐ 748 Rosario Rodriguez	.04	.02	.01
☐ 749 Skeeter Barnes	.04	.02	.01
☐ 750 Roger McDowell	.04	.02	.01
☐ 751 Dann Howitt	.04	.02	.01
☐ 752 Paul Sorrento	.07	.03	.01
☐ 753 Braulio Castillo	.15	.07	.02
☐ 754 Yorkis Perez	.15	.07	.02
☐ 755 Willie Fraser	.04	.02	.01
☐ 756 Jeremy Hernandez	.10	.05	.01
☐ 757 Curt Schilling	.07	.03	.01
☐ 758 Steve Lyons	.04	.02	.01
☐ 759 Dave Anderson	.04	.02	.01
☐ 760 Willie Banks	.07	.03	.01
☐ 761 Mark Leonard	.04	.02	.01
☐ 762 Jack Armstrong	.04	.02	.01
(Listed on Indians,			
but shown on Reds)			
☐ 763 Scott Servais	.04	.02	.01
☐ 764 Ray Stephens	.04	.02	.01
☐ 765 Junior Noboa	.04	.02	.01
☐ 766 Jim Olander	.10	.05	.01
☐ 767 Joe Magrane	.04	.02	.01
☐ 768 Lance Blankenship	.04	.02	.01
☐ 769 Mike Humphreys	.07	.03	.01
☐ 770 Jarvis Brown	.10	.05	.01
☐ 771 Damon Berryhill	.04	.02	.01
☐ 772 Alejandro Pena	.04	.02	.01
☐ 773 Jose Mesa	.04	.02	.01
☐ 774 Gary Cooper	.10	.05	.01
☐ 775 Carney Lansford	.07	.03	.01
☐ 776 Mike Bielecki	.04	.02	.01
(Shown on Cubs,			
but listed on Braves)			
☐ 777 Charlie O'Brien	.04	.02	.01
☐ 778 Carlos Hernandez	.04	.02	.01
☐ 779 Howard Farmer	.04	.02	.01
☐ 780 Mike Stanton	.04	.02	.01
☐ 781 Reggie Harris	.04	.02	.01
☐ 782 Xavier Hernandez	.04	.02	.01
☐ 783 Bryan Hickerson	.10	.05	.01
☐ 784 Checklist Card	.05	.01	.00
☐ BC1 Cal Ripken MVP	.40	.18	.05
☐ BC2 Terry Pendleton MVP	.15	.07	.02
☐ BC3 Roger Clemens CY	.30	.14	.04
☐ BC4 Tom Glavine CY	.20	.09	.03
☐ BC5 Chuck Knoblauch ROY	.30	.14	.04
☐ BC6 Jeff Bagwell ROY	.40	.18	.05
☐ BC7 Colorado Rockies	.50	.23	.06
☐ BC8 Florida Marlins	.50	.23	.06

1992 Donruss Diamond Kings

These standard-size (2 1/2" by 3 1/2")
cards were randomly inserted in 1992
Donruss I foil packs (cards 1-13 and the
checklist only) and in 1992 Donruss II foil
packs (cards 14-26). The fronts feature
player portraits by noted sports artist Dick
Perez. The words "Donruss Diamond
Kings" are superimposed at the card top in
a gold-trimmed blue and black banner,
with the player's name in a similarly
designed black stripe at the card bottom.
On a white background with a dark blue
border, the backs present career summary.
The cards are numbered on the back with
a DK prefix.

		MT	EX-MT	VG
COMPLETE SET (27)		40.00	18.00	5.00
COMPLETE SERIES 1 (14)		25.00	11.50	3.10
COMPLETE SERIES 2 (13)		15.00	6.75	1.90
COMMON PLAYER (1-13)		1.00	.45	.13
COMMON PLAYER (14-26)		1.00	.45	.13
☐ 1	Paul Molitor	1.25	.55	.16
☐ 2	Will Clark	4.00	1.80	.50
☐ 3	Joe Carter	2.50	1.15	.30
☐ 4	Julio Franco	1.00	.45	.13
☐ 5	Cal Ripken	6.00	2.70	.75
☐ 6	Dave Justice	3.50	1.55	.45
☐ 7	George Bell	1.00	.45	.13
☐ 8	Frank Thomas	12.00	5.50	1.50
☐ 9	Wade Boggs	2.00	.90	.25
☐ 10	Scott Sanderson	1.00	.45	.13
☐ 11	Jeff Bagwell	4.00	1.80	.50
☐ 12	John Kruk	1.00	.45	.13
☐ 13	Felix Jose	1.00	.45	.13
☐ 14	Harold Baines	1.00	.45	.13
☐ 15	Dwight Gooden	1.25	.55	.16
☐ 16	Brian McRae	1.25	.55	.16
☐ 17	Jay Bell	1.00	.45	.13
☐ 18	Brett Butler	1.00	.45	.13
☐ 19	Hal Morris	1.00	.45	.13
☐ 20	Mark Langston	1.00	.45	.13
☐ 21	Scott Erickson	1.25	.55	.16
☐ 22	Randy Johnson	1.00	.45	.13
☐ 23	Greg Swindell	1.00	.45	.13
☐ 24	Dennis Martinez	1.00	.45	.13
☐ 25	Tony Phillips	1.00	.45	.13
☐ 26	Fred McGriff	2.50	1.15	.30
☐ 27	Checklist Card	.60	.25	.08

1992 Donruss Phenoms

This 20-card set features baseball's most
dynamic young prospects. The first 12
Phenom cards (1-12) were randomly
inserted into 1992 Donruss The Rookies
12-card foil packs. The last eight Phenom
cards (13-20) were randomly inserted in
30-card jumbo packs. The standard-size
(2 1/2" by 3 1/2") cards display non-action
color photos that are accented by gold-foil
border stripes on a predominantly black
card face. The set title "Phenoms" appears
in gold foil lettering above the picture,
while the player's name is given in the bottom border. In a horizontal format, the
backs present biography, career highlights,
and recent career performance statistics in
a white and gray box enclosed by black
and gold borders. The cards are arranged

alphabetically and numbered on the back with a BC prefix.

	MT	EX-MT	VG
COMPLETE SET (20)	50.00	23.00	6.25
COMPLETE FOIL SET (12)	35.00	16.00	4.40
COMPLETE JUMBO SET (8)	20.00	9.00	2.50
COMMON PLAYER (1-12)	1.50	.65	.19
COMMON PLAYER (13-20)	2.00	.90	.25

		MT	EX-MT	VG
☐ 1	Moises Alou	2.00	.90	.25
☐ 2	Bret Boone	5.00	2.30	.60
☐ 3	Jeff Conine	2.00	.90	.25
☐ 4	Dave Fleming	4.00	1.80	.50
☐ 5	Tyler Green	2.50	1.15	.30
☐ 6	Eric Karros	8.00	3.60	1.00
☐ 7	Pat Listach	8.00	3.60	1.00
☐ 8	Kenny Lofton	6.00	2.70	.75
☐ 9	Mike Piazza	4.50	2.00	.55
☐ 10	Tim Salmon	5.00	2.30	.60
☐ 11	Andy Stankiewicz	1.75	.80	.22
☐ 12	Dan Walters	1.50	.65	.19
☐ 13	Ramon Caraballo	2.00	.90	.25
☐ 14	Brian Jordan	3.00	1.35	.40
☐ 15	Ryan Klesko	6.00	2.70	.75
☐ 16	Sam Militello	4.00	1.80	.50
☐ 17	Frank Seminara	3.00	1.35	.40
☐ 18	Salomon Torres	3.00	1.35	.40
☐ 19	John Valentin	2.00	.90	.25
☐ 20	Wilfredo Cordero	3.50	1.55	.45

1992 Donruss Rookies

After six years of issuing "The Rookies" as a 56-card boxed set, Donruss expanded it to a 132-card set available only as a foil

pack product. An additional 20 Phenom cards were randomly inserted in the packs (numbered 1-12 in 12-card foil packs and numbered 13-20 in 30-card jumbo packs). The cards measure the standard size (2 1/2" by 3 1/2"). The card design is the same as the 1992 Donruss regular issue except that the two-tone blue color bars have been replaced by green, as in the previous six Donruss Rookies sets. The cards are arranged in alphabetical order and numbered on the back. The key Rookie Cards in this set are Billy Ashley, Pedro Astacio, Brent Gates, David Nied, Manny Ramirez, and Tim Wakefield.

		MT	EX-MT	VG
COMPLETE SET (132)		12.00	5.50	1.50
COMMON PLAYER (1-132)		.05	.02	.01

		MT	EX-MT	VG
☐ 1	Kyle Abbott	.10	.05	.01
☐ 2	Troy Afenir	.05	.02	.01
☐ 3	Rich Amaral	.10	.05	.01
☐ 4	Ruben Amaro	.05	.02	.01
☐ 5	Billy Ashley	.50	.23	.06
☐ 6	Pedro Astacio	.40	.18	.05
☐ 7	Jim Austin	.10	.05	.01
☐ 8	Robert Ayrault	.10	.05	.01
☐ 9	Kevin Baez	.12	.05	.02
☐ 10	Esteban Beltre	.10	.05	.01
☐ 11	Brian Bohanon	.05	.02	.01
☐ 12	Kent Bottenfield	.15	.07	.02
☐ 13	Jeff Branson	.05	.02	.01
☐ 14	Brad Brink	.10	.05	.01
☐ 15	John Briscoe	.10	.05	.01
☐ 16	Doug Brocail	.10	.05	.01
☐ 17	Rico Brogna	.10	.05	.01
☐ 18	J.T. Bruett	.10	.05	.01
☐ 19	Jacob Brumfield	.10	.05	.01
☐ 20	Jim Bullinger	.10	.05	.01
☐ 21	Kevin Campbell	.10	.05	.01
☐ 22	Pedro Castellano	.15	.07	.02
☐ 23	Mike Christopher	.10	.05	.01
☐ 24	Archi Cianfrocco	.15	.07	.02
☐ 25	Mark Clark	.10	.05	.01
☐ 26	Craig Colbert	.10	.05	.01
☐ 27	Victor Cole	.15	.07	.02
☐ 28	Steve Cooke	.25	.11	.03
☐ 29	Tim Costo	.12	.05	.02
☐ 30	Chad Curtis	.25	.11	.03
☐ 31	Doug Davis	.10	.05	.01
☐ 32	Gary DiSarcina	.08	.04	.01
☐ 33	Mike Doherty	.15	.07	.02
☐ 34	Mike Draper	.10	.05	.01
☐ 35	Monty Fariss	.10	.05	.01
☐ 36	Bien Figueroa	.10	.05	.01
☐ 37	John Flaherty	.10	.05	.01

☐ 38	Tim Fortugno	.10	.05	.01
☐ 39	Eric Fox	.12	.05	.02
☐ 40	Jeff Frye	.10	.05	.01
☐ 41	Ramon Garcia	.05	.02	.01
☐ 42	Brent Gates	.50	.23	.06
☐ 43	Tom Goodwin	.10	.05	.01
☐ 44	Buddy Groom	.10	.05	.01
☐ 45	Jeff Grotewold	.10	.05	.01
☐ 46	Juan Guerrero	.12	.05	.02
☐ 47	Johnny Guzman	.20	.09	.03
☐ 48	Shawn Hare	.10	.05	.01
☐ 49	Ryan Hawblitzel	.20	.09	.03
☐ 50	Bert Heffernan	.10	.05	.01
☐ 51	Butch Henry	.12	.05	.02
☐ 52	Cesar Hernandez	.10	.05	.01
☐ 53	Vince Horsman	.10	.05	.01
☐ 54	Steve Hosey	.30	.14	.04
☐ 55	Pat Howell	.20	.09	.03
☐ 56	Peter Hoy	.10	.05	.01
☐ 57	Jonathan Hurst	.20	.09	.03
☐ 58	Mark Hutton	.25	.11	.03
☐ 59	Shawn Jeter	.12	.05	.02
☐ 60	Joel Johnston	.05	.02	.01
☐ 61	Jeff Kent	.30	.14	.04
☐ 62	Kurt Knudsen	.10	.05	.01
☐ 63	Kevin Koslofski	.10	.05	.01
☐ 64	Danny Leon	.10	.05	.01
☐ 65	Jesse Levis	.15	.07	.02
☐ 66	Tom Marsh	.10	.05	.01
☐ 67	Ed Martel	.15	.07	.02
☐ 68	Al Martin	.35	.16	.04
☐ 69	Podro Martinez	.20	.09	.03
☐ 70	Derrick May	.08	.04	.01
☐ 71	Matt Maysey	.10	.05	.01
☐ 72	Russ McGinnis	.10	.05	.01
☐ 73	Tim McIntosh	.05	.02	.01
☐ 74	Jim McNamara	.10	.05	.01
☐ 75	Jeff McNeely	.10	.05	.01
☐ 76	Rusty Meacham	.05	.02	.01
☐ 77	Tony Menendez	.10	.05	.01
☐ 78	Henry Mercedes	.12	.05	.02
☐ 79	Paul Miller	.10	.05	.01
☐ 80	Joe Millette	.10	.05	.01
☐ 81	Blas Minor	.10	.05	.01
☐ 82	Dennis Moeller	.10	.05	.01
☐ 83	Raul Mondesi	.25	.11	.03
☐ 84	Rob Natal	.10	.05	.01
☐ 85	Troy Neel	.20	.09	.03
☐ 86	David Nied	3.00	1.35	.40
☐ 87	Jerry Nielson	.12	.05	.02
☐ 88	Donovan Osborne	.30	.14	.04
☐ 89	John Patterson	.12	.05	.02
☐ 90	Roger Pavlik	.15	.07	.02
☐ 91	Dan Peltier	.05	.02	.01
☐ 92	Jim Pena	.10	.05	.01
☐ 93	William Pennyfeather	.10	.05	.01
☐ 94	Mike Perez	.05	.02	.01

☐ 95	Hipolito Pichardo	.10	.05	.01
☐ 96	Greg Pirkl	.15	.07	.02
☐ 97	Harvey Pulliam	.10	.05	.01
☐ 98	Manny Ramirez	.60	.25	.08
☐ 99	Pat Rapp	.20	.09	.03
☐ 100	Jeff Reboulet	.10	.05	.01
☐ 101	Darren Reed	.05	.02	.01
☐ 102	Shane Reynolds	.10	.05	.01
☐ 103	Bill Risley	.10	.05	.01
☐ 104	Ben Rivera	.10	.05	.01
☐ 105	Henry Rodriguez	.10	.05	.01
☐ 106	Rico Rossy	.10	.05	.01
☐ 107	Johnny Ruffin	.10	.05	.01
☐ 108	Steve Scarsone	.10	.05	.01
☐ 109	Tim Scott	.12	.05	.02
☐ 110	Steve Shifflett	.10	.05	.01
☐ 111	Dave Silvestri	.15	.07	.02
☐ 112	Matt Stairs	.15	.07	.02
☐ 113	William Suero	.10	.05	.01
☐ 114	Jeff Tackett	.10	.05	.01
☐ 115	Eddie Taubensee	.10	.05	.01
☐ 116	Rick Trlicek	.12	.05	.02
☐ 117	Scooter Tucker	.10	.05	.01
☐ 118	Shane Turner	.08	.04	.01
☐ 119	Julio Valera	.08	.04	.01
☐ 120	Paul Wagner	.10	.05	.01
☐ 121	Tim Wakefield	3.00	1.35	.40
☐ 122	Mike Walker	.10	.05	.01
☐ 123	Bruce Walton	.05	.02	.01
☐ 124	Lenny Webster	.05	.02	.01
☐ 125	Bob Wickman	.30	.14	.04
☐ 126	Mike Williams	.15	.07	.02
☐ 127	Kerry Woodson	.10	.05	.01
☐ 128	Eric Young	.25	.11	.03
☐ 129	Kevin Young	.50	.23	.06
☐ 130	Pete Young	.10	.05	.01
☐ 131	Checklist 1-66	.05	.01	.00
☐ 132	Checklist 67-132	.05	.01	.00

1993 Donruss

The first series of 1993 Donruss consists of 396 standard-size (2 1/2" by 3 1/2") cards. Fifteen Diamond King cards, featuring the artwork of Dick Perez and gold-foil stamped, were randomly inserted into the packs. The ten-card Spirit of the Game random inserts were new in 1993, and they are packed approximately two per box in Series I. Other random inserts featured are the nine-card Elite series, a Will Clark Signature card, and a Legends card honoring Yount. Finally a Rated Rookies subset spotlights 20 top prospects; these Rated Rookies are sprinkled throughout the set and are designated by RR in the checklist below. The fronts feature glossy color action photos bordered in white. At the bottom of the picture, the team logo appears in a team color-coded diamond with the player's name in a color-coded bar extending to the right. The backs have a second color player photo with biography and recent major league statistics filling up the rest of the card. The cards are numbered in a team color-coded home plate icon at the upper right corner.

	MT	EX-MT	VG
COMPLETE SET (396)	15.00	6.75	1.90
COMMON PLAYER (1-396)	.05	.02	.01

		MT	EX-MT	VG
☐ 1	Craig Lefferts	.05	.02	.01
☐ 2	Kent Mercker	.05	.02	.01
☐ 3	Phil Plantier	.07	.03	.01
☐ 4	Alex Arias	.10	.05	.01
☐ 5	Julio Valera	.05	.02	.01
☐ 6	Dan Wilson	.05	.02	.01
☐ 7	Frank Thomas	.75	.35	.09
☐ 8	Eric Anthony	.07	.03	.01
☐ 9	Derek Lilliquist	.05	.02	.01
☐ 10	Rafael Bournigal	.25	.11	.03
☐ 11	Manny Alexander RR	.10	.05	.01
☐ 12	Bret Barberie	.05	.02	.01
☐ 13	Mickey Tettleton	.07	.03	.01
☐ 14	Anthony Young	.07	.03	.01
☐ 15	Tim Spehr	.05	.02	.01
☐ 16	Bob Ayrault	.08	.04	.01
☐ 17	Bill Wegman	.05	.02	.01
☐ 18	Jay Bell	.05	.02	.01
☐ 19	Rick Aguilera	.05	.02	.01
☐ 20	Todd Zeile	.05	.02	.01
☐ 21	Steve Farr	.05	.02	.01
☐ 22	Andy Benes	.07	.03	.01
☐ 23	Lance Blankenship	.05	.02	.01
☐ 24	Ted Wood	.05	.02	.01
☐ 25	Omar Vizquel	.05	.02	.01
☐ 26	Steve Avery	.12	.05	.02
☐ 27	Brian Bohanon	.05	.02	.01
☐ 28	Rick Wilkins	.05	.02	.01
☐ 29	Devon White	.07	.03	.01
☐ 30	Bobby Ayala	.30	.14	.04
☐ 31	Leo Gomez	.07	.03	.01
☐ 32	Mike Simms	.05	.02	.01
☐ 33	Ellis Burks	.07	.03	.01
☐ 34	Steve Wilson	.05	.02	.01
☐ 35	Jim Abbott	.10	.05	.01
☐ 36	Tim Wallach	.07	.03	.01
☐ 37	Wilson Alvarez	.05	.02	.01
☐ 38	Daryl Boston	.05	.02	.01
☐ 39	Sandy Alomar Jr.	.07	.03	.01
☐ 40	Mitch Williams	.05	.02	.01
☐ 41	Rico Brogna	.07	.03	.01
☐ 42	Gary Varsho	.05	.02	.01
☐ 43	Kevin Appier	.07	.03	.01
☐ 44	Eric Wedge RR	.35	.16	.04
☐ 45	Dante Bichette	.05	.02	.01
☐ 46	Jose Oquendo	.05	.02	.01
☐ 47	Mike Trombley	.12	.05	.02
☐ 48	Dan Walters	.08	.04	.01
☐ 49	Gerald Williams	.05	.02	.01
☐ 50	Bud Black	.05	.02	.01
☐ 51	Bobby Witt	.05	.02	.01
☐ 52	Mark Davis	.05	.02	.01
☐ 53	Shawn Barton	.10	.05	.01
☐ 54	Paul Assenmacher	.05	.02	.01
☐ 55	Kevin Reimer	.05	.02	.01
☐ 56	Billy Ashley RR	.20	.09	.03
☐ 57	Eddie Zosky	.05	.02	.01
☐ 58	Chris Sabo	.07	.03	.01
☐ 59	Billy Ripken	.05	.02	.01
☐ 60	Scooter Tucker	.05	.02	.01
☐ 61	Tim Wakefield RR	.60	.25	.08
☐ 62	Mitch Webster	.05	.02	.01
☐ 63	Jack Clark	.07	.03	.01
☐ 64	Mark Gardner	.05	.02	.01
☐ 65	Lee Stevens	.05	.02	.01
☐ 66	Todd Hundley	.05	.02	.01
☐ 67	Bobby Thigpen	.05	.02	.01
☐ 68	Dave Hollins	.07	.03	.01
☐ 69	Jack Armstrong	.05	.02	.01
☐ 70	Alex Cole	.05	.02	.01
☐ 71	Mark Carreon	.05	.02	.01
☐ 72	Todd Worrell	.05	.02	.01
☐ 73	Steve Shifflett	.05	.02	.01
☐ 74	Jerald Clark	.05	.02	.01
☐ 75	Paul Molitor	.07	.03	.01
☐ 76	Larry Carter	.12	.05	.02
☐ 77	Rich Rowland RR	.08	.04	.01
☐ 78	Damon Berryhill	.05	.02	.01
☐ 79	Willie Banks	.07	.03	.01
☐ 80	Hector Villanueva	.05	.02	.01

☐ 81	Mike Gallego	.05	.02	.01
☐ 82	Tim Belcher	.07	.03	.01
☐ 83	Mike Bordick	.05	.02	.01
☐ 84	Craig Biggio	.07	.03	.01
☐ 85	Lance Parrish	.07	.03	.01
☐ 86	Brett Butler	.07	.03	.01
☐ 87	Mike Timlin	.05	.02	.01
☐ 88	Brian Barnes	.05	.02	.01
☐ 89	Brady Anderson	.07	.03	.01
☐ 90	D.J. Dozier	.07	.03	.01
☐ 91	Frank Viola	.07	.03	.01
☐ 92	Darren Daulton	.07	.03	.01
☐ 93	Chad Curtis	.10	.05	.01
☐ 94	Zane Smith	.05	.02	.01
☐ 95	George Bell	.07	.03	.01
☐ 96	Rex Hudler	.05	.02	.01
☐ 97	Mark Whiten	.05	.02	.01
☐ 98	Tim Teufel	.05	.02	.01
☐ 99	Kevin Ritz	.05	.02	.01
☐ 100	Jeff Brantley	.05	.02	.01
☐ 101	Jeff Conine	.05	.02	.01
☐ 102	Vinny Castilla	.05	.02	.01
☐ 103	Greg Vaughn	.07	.03	.01
☐ 104	Steve Buechele	.05	.02	.01
☐ 105	Darren Reed	.05	.02	.01
☐ 106	Bip Roberts	.07	.03	.01
☐ 107	John Habyan	.05	.02	.01
☐ 108	Scott Servais	.05	.02	.01
☐ 109	Walt Weiss	.05	.02	.01
☐ 110	J.T. Snow RR	.50	.23	.06
☐ 111	Jay Buhner	.07	.03	.01
☐ 112	Darryl Strawberry	.12	.05	.02
☐ 113	Roger Pavlik	.05	.02	.01
☐ 114	Chris Nabholz	.07	.03	.01
☐ 115	Pat Borders	.05	.02	.01
☐ 116	Pat Howell	.05	.02	.01
☐ 117	Gregg Olson	.07	.03	.01
☐ 118	Curt Schilling	.05	.02	.01
☐ 119	Roger Clemens	.20	.09	.03
☐ 120	Victor Cole	.05	.02	.01
☐ 121	Gary DiSarcina	.05	.02	.01
☐ 122	Checklist 1-80	.06	.02	.01
	(Gary Carter and			
	Kirt Manwaring)			
☐ 123	Steve Sax	.07	.03	.01
☐ 124	Chuck Carr	.05	.02	.01
☐ 125	Mark Lewis	.05	.02	.01
☐ 126	Tony Gwynn	.12	.05	.02
☐ 127	Travis Fryman	.20	.09	.03
☐ 128	Dave Burba	.05	.02	.01
☐ 129	Wally Joyner	.07	.03	.01
☐ 130	John Smoltz	.10	.05	.01
☐ 131	Cal Eldred	.20	.09	.03
☐ 132	Checklist 81-159	.06	.02	.01
	(Roberto Alomar and			
	Devon White)			
☐ 133	Arthur Rhodes	.07	.03	.01
☐ 134	Jeff Blauser	.05	.02	.01
☐ 135	Scott Cooper	.07	.03	.01
☐ 136	Doug Strange	.05	.02	.01
☐ 137	Luis Sojo	.05	.02	.01
☐ 138	Jeff Branson	.05	.02	.01
☐ 139	Alex Fernandez	.07	.03	.01
☐ 140	Ken Caminiti	.07	.03	.01
☐ 141	Charles Nagy	.07	.03	.01
☐ 142	Tom Candiotti	.05	.02	.01
☐ 143	Willie Greene RR	.15	.07	.02
☐ 144	John Vander Wal	.05	.02	.01
☐ 145	Kurt Knudsen	.05	.02	.01
☐ 146	John Franco	.07	.03	.01
☐ 147	Eddie Pierce	.10	.05	.01
☐ 148	Kim Batiste	.05	.02	.01
☐ 149	Darren Holmes	.05	.02	.01
☐ 150	Steve Cooke	.05	.02	.01
☐ 151	Terry Jorgensen	.05	.02	.01
☐ 152	Mark Clark	.05	.02	.01
☐ 153	Randy Velarde	.05	.02	.01
☐ 154	Greg W. Harris	.05	.02	.01
☐ 155	Kevin Campbell	.05	.02	.01
☐ 156	John Burkett	.05	.02	.01
☐ 157	Kevin Mitchell	.07	.03	.01
☐ 158	Deion Sanders	.12	.05	.02
☐ 159	Jose Canseco	.20	.09	.03
☐ 160	Jeff Hartsock	.10	.05	.01
☐ 161	Tom Quinlan	.12	.05	.02
☐ 162	Tim Pugh	.25	.11	.03
☐ 163	Glenn Davis	.07	.03	.01
☐ 164	Shane Reynolds	.05	.02	.01
☐ 165	Jody Reed	.05	.02	.01
☐ 166	Mike Sharperson	.05	.02	.01
☐ 167	Scott Lewis	.05	.02	.01
☐ 168	Dennis Martinez	.07	.03	.01
☐ 169	Scott Radinsky	.05	.02	.01
☐ 170	Dave Gallagher	.05	.02	.01
☐ 171	Jim Thome	.07	.03	.01
☐ 172	Terry Mulholland	.05	.02	.01
☐ 173	Milt Cuyler	.05	.02	.01
☐ 174	Bob Patterson	.05	.02	.01
☐ 175	Jeff Montgomery	.05	.02	.01
☐ 176	Tim Salmon RR	.25	.11	.03
☐ 177	Franklin Stubbs	.05	.02	.01
☐ 178	Donovan Osborne	.12	.05	.02
☐ 179	Jeff Reboulet	.05	.02	.01
☐ 180	Jeremy Hernandez	.05	.02	.01
☐ 181	Charlie Hayes	.05	.02	.01
☐ 182	Matt Williams	.07	.03	.01
☐ 183	Mike Raczka	.10	.05	.01
☐ 184	Francisco Cabrera	.05	.02	.01
☐ 185	Rich DeLucia	.05	.02	.01
☐ 186	Sammy Sosa	.05	.02	.01
☐ 187	Ivan Rodriguez	.20	.09	.03
☐ 188	Bret Boone RR	.25	.11	.03
☐ 189	Juan Guzman	.30	.14	.04
☐ 190	Tom Browning	.05	.02	.01

☐	191	Randy Milligan	.05	.02	.01			
☐	192	Steve Finley	.05	.02	.01			
☐	193	John Patterson RR	.05	.02	.01			
☐	194	Kip Gross	.05	.02	.01			
☐	195	Tony Fossas	.05	.02	.01			
☐	196	Ivan Calderon	.05	.02	.01			
☐	197	Junior Felix	.05	.02	.01			
☐	198	Pate Schourek	.05	.02	.01			
☐	199	Craig Grebeck	.05	.02	.01			
☐	200	Juan Bell	.05	.02	.01			
☐	201	Glenallen Hill	.05	.02	.01			
☐	202	Danny Jackson	.05	.02	.01			
☐	203	John Kiely	.05	.02	.01			
☐	204	Bob Tewksbury	.05	.02	.01			
☐	205	Kevin Koslofski	.05	.02	.01			
☐	206	Craig Shipley	.05	.02	.01			
☐	207	John Jaha	.10	.05	.01			
☐	208	Royce Clayton	.10	.05	.01			
☐	209	Mike Piazza RR	.35	.16	.04			
☐	210	Ron Gant	.10	.05	.01			
☐	211	Scott Erickson	.07	.03	.01			
☐	212	Doug Dascenzo	.05	.02	.01			
☐	213	Andy Stankiewicz	.05	.02	.01			
☐	214	Geronimo Berroa	.05	.02	.01			
☐	215	Dennis Eckersley	.10	.05	.01			
☐	216	Al Osuna	.05	.02	.01			
☐	217	Tino Martinez	.07	.03	.01			
☐	218	Henry Rodriguez	.05	.02	.01			
☐	219	Ed Sprague	.07	.03	.01			
☐	220	Ken Hill	.05	.02	.01			
☐	221	Chito Martinez	.05	.02	.01			
☐	222	Bret Saberhagen	.07	.03	.01			
☐	223	Mike Greenwell	.07	.03	.01			
☐	224	Mickey Morandini	.05	.02	.01			
☐	225	Chuck Finley	.05	.02	.01			
☐	226	Denny Neagle	.05	.02	.01			
☐	227	Kirk McCaskill	.05	.02	.01			
☐	228	Rheal Cormier	.05	.02	.01			
☐	229	Paul Sorrento	.05	.02	.01			
☐	230	Darrin Jackson	.05	.02	.01			
☐	231	Rob Deer	.07	.03	.01			
☐	232	Bill Swift	.05	.02	.01			
☐	233	Kevin McReynolds	.07	.03	.01			
☐	234	Terry Pendleton	.07	.03	.01			
☐	235	Dave Nilsson	.07	.03	.01			
☐	236	Chuck McElroy	.05	.02	.01			
☐	237	Derek Parks	.05	.02	.01			
☐	238	Norm Charlton	.07	.03	.01			
☐	239	Matt Nokes	.05	.02	.01			
☐	240	Juan Guerrero	.05	.02	.01			
☐	241	Jeff Parrett	.05	.02	.01			
☐	242	Ryan Thompson RR	.25	.11	.03			
☐	243	Dave Fleming	.20	.09	.03			
☐	244	Dave Hansen	.05	.02	.01			
☐	245	Monty Fariss	.05	.02	.01			
☐	246	Archi Cianfrocco	.05	.02	.01			
☐	247	Pat Hentgen	.05	.02	.01			
☐	248	Bill Pecota	.05	.02	.01
☐	249	Ben McDonald	.07	.03	.01
☐	250	Cliff Brantley	.05	.02	.01
☐	251	John Valentin	.12	.05	.02
☐	252	Jeff King	.05	.02	.01
☐	253	Reggie Williams	.05	.02	.01
☐	254	Checklist 160-238	.06	.02	.01
		(Damon Berryhill			
		and Alex Arias)			
☐	255	Ozzie Guillen	.05	.02	.01
☐	256	Mike Perez	.05	.02	.01
☐	257	Thomas Howard	.05	.02	.01
☐	258	Kurt Stillwell	.05	.02	.01
☐	259	Mike Henneman	.05	.02	.01
☐	260	Steve Decker	.05	.02	.01
☐	261	Brent Mayne	.05	.02	.01
☐	262	Otis Nixon	.05	.02	.01
☐	263	Mark Kiefer	.10	.05	.01
☐	264	Checklist 239-317	.06	.02	.01
		(Don Mattingly			
		and Mike Bordick)			
☐	265	Richie Lewis	.15	.07	.02
☐	266	Pat Gomez	.10	.05	.01
☐	267	Scott Taylor	.05	.02	.01
☐	268	Shawon Dunston	.05	.02	.01
☐	269	Greg Myers	.05	.02	.01
☐	270	Tim Costo	.07	.03	.01
☐	271	Greg Hibbard	.05	.02	.01
☐	272	Pete Harnisch	.05	.02	.01
☐	273	Dave Mlicki	.10	.05	.01
☐	274	Orel Hershiser	.07	.03	.01
☐	275	Sean Berry RR	.07	.03	.01
☐	276	Doug Simons	.05	.02	.01
☐	277	John Doherty	.05	.02	.01
☐	278	Eddie Murray	.10	.05	.01
☐	279	Chris Haney	.05	.02	.01
☐	280	Stan Javier	.05	.02	.01
☐	281	Jaime Navarro	.07	.03	.01
☐	282	Orlando Merced	.05	.02	.01
☐	283	Kent Hrbek	.07	.03	.01
☐	284	Bernard Gilkey	.07	.03	.01
☐	285	Russ Springer	.12	.05	.02
☐	286	Mike Maddux	.05	.02	.01
☐	287	Eric Fox	.05	.02	.01
☐	288	Mark Leonard	.05	.02	.01
☐	289	Tim Leary	.05	.02	.01
☐	290	Brian Hunter	.07	.03	.01
☐	291	Donald Harris	.05	.02	.01
☐	292	Bob Scanlan	.05	.02	.01
☐	293	Turner Ward	.05	.02	.01
☐	294	Hal Morris	.07	.03	.01
☐	295	Jimmy Poole	.05	.02	.01
☐	296	Doug Jones	.05	.02	.01
☐	297	Tony Pena	.05	.02	.01
☐	298	Ramon Martinez	.07	.03	.01
☐	299	Tim Fortugno	.05	.02	.01
☐	300	Marquis Grissom	.10	.05	.01

☐ 301	Lance Johnson	.05	.02	.01
☐ 302	Jeff Kent	.07	.03	.01
☐ 303	Reggie Jefferson	.07	.03	.01
☐ 304	Wes Chamberlain	.05	.02	.01
☐ 305	Shawn Hare	.05	.02	.01
☐ 306	Mike LaValliere	.05	.02	.01
☐ 307	Gregg Jefferies	.07	.03	.01
☐ 308	Troy Neel RR	.07	.03	.01
☐ 309	Pat Listach	.50	.23	.06
☐ 310	Geronimo Pena	.05	.02	.01
☐ 311	Pedro Munoz	.07	.03	.01
☐ 312	Guillermo Velasquez	.10	.05	.01
☐ 313	Roberto Kelly	.07	.03	.01
☐ 314	Mike Jackson	.05	.02	.01
☐ 315	Rickey Henderson	.12	.05	.02
☐ 316	Mark Lemke	.05	.02	.01
☐ 317	Erik Hanson	.05	.02	.01
☐ 318	Derrick May	.07	.03	.01
☐ 319	Geno Petralli	.05	.02	.01
☐ 320	Melvin Nieves RR	.40	.18	.05
☐ 321	Doug Linton	.10	.05	.01
☐ 322	Rob Dibble	.07	.03	.01
☐ 323	Chris Hoiles	.07	.03	.01
☐ 324	Jimmy Jones	.05	.02	.01
☐ 325	Dave Staton RR	.10	.05	.01
☐ 326	Pedro Martinez	.12	.05	.02
☐ 327	Paul Quantrill	.10	.05	.01
☐ 328	Greg Colbrunn	.07	.03	.01
☐ 329	Hilly Hathaway	.30	.14	.04
☐ 330	Jeff Innis	.05	.02	.01
☐ 331	Ron Karkovice	.05	.02	.01
☐ 332	Keith Shepherd	.20	.09	.03
☐ 333	Alan Embree	.15	.07	.02
☐ 334	Paul Wagner	.05	.02	.01
☐ 335	Dave Haas	.05	.02	.01
☐ 336	Ozzie Canseco	.05	.02	.01
☐ 337	Bill Sampen	.05	.02	.01
☐ 338	Rich Rodriguez	.05	.02	.01
☐ 339	Dean Palmer	.10	.05	.01
☐ 340	Greg Litton	.05	.02	.01
☐ 341	Jim Tatum RR	.20	.09	.03
☐ 342	Todd Haney	.12	.05	.02
☐ 343	Larry Casian	.05	.02	.01
☐ 344	Ryne Sandberg	.20	.09	.03
☐ 345	Sterling Hitchcock	.35	.16	.04
☐ 346	Chris Hammond	.05	.02	.01
☐ 347	Vince Horsman	.05	.02	.01
☐ 348	Butch Henry	.05	.02	.01
☐ 349	Dann Howitt	.05	.02	.01
☐ 350	Roger McDowell	.05	.02	.01
☐ 351	Jack Morris	.10	.05	.01
☐ 352	Bill Krueger	.05	.02	.01
☐ 353	Cris Colon	.10	.05	.01
☐ 354	Joe Vitko	.15	.07	.02
☐ 355	Willie McGee	.07	.03	.01
☐ 356	Jay Baller	.05	.02	.01
☐ 357	Pat Mahomes	.10	.05	.01

☐ 358	Roger Mason	.05	.02	.01
☐ 359	Jerry Nielsen	.05	.02	.01
☐ 360	Tom Pagnozzi	.05	.02	.01
☐ 361	Kevin Baez	.05	.02	.01
☐ 362	Tim Scott	.07	.03	.01
☐ 363	Domingo Martinez	.25	.11	.03
☐ 364	Kirt Manwaring	.05	.02	.01
☐ 365	Rafael Palmeiro	.07	.03	.01
☐ 366	Ray Lankford	.12	.05	.02
☐ 367	Tim McIntosh	.05	.02	.01
☐ 368	Jessie Hollins	.07	.03	.01
☐ 369	Scott Leius	.05	.02	.01
☐ 370	Bill Doran	.05	.02	.01
☐ 371	Sam Militello	.15	.07	.02
☐ 372	Ryan Bowen	.05	.02	.01
☐ 373	Dave Henderson	.05	.02	.01
☐ 374	Dan Smith RR	.07	.03	.01
☐ 375	Steve Reed RR	.12	.05	.02
☐ 376	Jose Offerman	.07	.03	.01
☐ 377	Kevin Brown	.07	.03	.01
☐ 378	Darrin Fletcher	.05	.02	.01
☐ 379	Duane Ward	.05	.02	.01
☐ 380	Wayne Kirby RR	.05	.02	.01
☐ 381	Steve Scarsone	.05	.02	.01
☐ 382	Mariano Duncan	.05	.02	.01
☐ 383	Ken Ryan	.15	.07	.02
☐ 384	Lloyd McClendon	.05	.02	.01
☐ 385	Brian Holman	.05	.02	.01
☐ 386	Braulio Castillo	.05	.02	.01
☐ 387	Danny Leon	.05	.02	.01
☐ 388	Omar Olivares	.05	.02	.01
☐ 389	Kevin Wickander	.05	.02	.01
☐ 390	Fred McGriff	.12	.05	.02
☐ 391	Phil Clark	.05	.02	.01
☐ 392	Darren Lewis	.05	.02	.01
☐ 393	Phil Hiatt	.20	.09	.03
☐ 394	Mike Morgan	.05	.02	.01
☐ 395	Shane Mack	.07	.03	.01
☐ 396	Checklist 318-396	.06	.02	.01
	(Dennis Eckersley			
	and Art Kusnyer CO)			

1993 Donruss Diamond Kings

These standard-size (2 1/2" by 3 1/2") cards were randomly inserted in 1993 Donruss Series I packs. The cards are gold-foil stamped and feature on the fronts player portraits by noted sports artist Dick Perez. Inside green borders, the backs

present career summary. The first 15 cards (1-15) were available in the first series of the 1993 Donruss. Diamond King numbers 27-28 honor the first draft picks of the new Florida Marlins and Colorado Rockies franchises. The cards are numbered on the back.

early in production, is considered scarce and has even been counterfeited; the fake has a rosy coloration and a cross-hatch pattern visible over the picture area. The card numbering is arranged essentially in chronological order.

	MT	EX-MT	VG
COMPLETE SET (15)	40.00	18.00	5.00
COMMON PLAYER (1-15)	1.50	.65	.19

		MT	EX-MT	VG
☐	1 Ken Griffey Jr.	9.00	4.00	1.15
☐	2 Ryne Sandberg	6.00	2.70	.75
☐	3 Roger Clemens	6.00	2.70	.75
☐	4 Kirby Puckett	5.00	2.30	.60
☐	5 Bill Swift	1.50	.65	.19
☐	6 Larry Walker	3.00	1.35	.40
☐	7 Juan Gonzalez	6.00	2.70	.75
☐	8 Wally Joyner	1.50	.65	.19
☐	9 Andy Van Slyke	2.00	.90	.25
☐	10 Robin Ventura	3.00	1.35	.40
☐	11 Bip Roberts	1.50	.65	.19
☐	12 Roberto Kelly	1.50	.65	.19
☐	13 Carlos Baerga	3.00	1.35	.40
☐	14 Orel Hershiser	1.50	.65	.19
☐	15 Cecil Fielder	3.00	1.35	.40

1959 Fleer

The cards in this 80-card set measure 2 1/2" by 3 1/2". The 1959 Fleer set, with a catalog designation of R418-1, portrays the life of Ted Williams. The wording of the wrapper, "Baseball's Greatest Series," has led to speculation that Fleer contemplated similar sets honoring other baseball immortals, but chose to develop instead the format of the 1960 and 1961 issues. Card number 68, which was withdrawn

	NRMT	VG-E	GOOD
COMPLETE SET (80)	1400.00	650.00	180.00
COMMON CARDS (1-80)	7.50	3.40	.95

		NRMT	VG-E	GOOD
☐	1 The Early Years (Choosing up sides on the sandlots)	50.00	7.50	1.50
☐	2 Ted's Idol Babe Ruth (Meeting boyhood idol, Babe Ruth)	60.00	27.00	7.50
☐	3 Practice Makes Perfect (At place practicing on the sandlots)	7.50	3.40	.95
☐	4 Learns Fine Points (Sliding at Herbert Hoover High)	7.50	3.40	.95
☐	5 Ted's Fame Spreads (At plate at Herbert Hoover High)	7.50	3.40	.95
☐	6 Ted Turns Pro (Portrait, San Diego Padres, PCL League uniform)	15.00	6.75	1.90
☐	7 From Mound to Plate (At plate, San Diego Padres, PCL)	7.50	3.40	.95
☐	8 1937 First Full Season (Making a leaping catch)	9.00	4.00	1.15
☐	9 First Step to Majors (With Eddie Collins)	12.50	5.75	1.55
☐	10 Gunning as Pastime (Wearing hunting gear, taking aim)	7.50	3.40	.95
☐	11 First Spring Training (with Jimmie Foxx)	25.00	11.50	3.10

☐ 12 Burning Up Minors 12.50   5.75   1.55
(Pitching for Minne-
apolis in American
Association)

☐ 13 1939 Shows Will Stay 9.00   4.00   1.15
(Follow-through)

☐ 14 Outstanding Rookie '39 .9.00   4.00   1.15
(Follow-through)

☐ 15 Licks Sophomore Jinx ...9.00   4.00   1.15
(Sliding into third
base for a triple)

☐ 16 1941 Greatest Year 9.00   4.00   1.15
(Follow-through at
plate)

☐ 17 How Ted Hit .400 ....25.00   11.50   3.10
(Youthful Williams,
as he looked in '41)

☐ 18 1941 All Star Hero 9.00   4.00   1.15
(Crossing plate
after home run)

☐ 19 Ted Wins Triple Crown ..9.00   4.00   1.15
(Crossing plate
at Fenway Park)

☐ 20 On to Naval Training ......7.50   3.40   .95
(In training plane
at Amherst College)

☐ 21 Honors for Williams 9.00   4.00   1.15
(Receiving 1942
Sporting News POY)

☐ 22 1944 Ted Solos ....7.50   3.40   .95
(In cockpit at
Pensacola, FL Navy
Air Station)

☐ 23 Williams Wins Wings 9.00   4.00   1.15
(Wearing Naval
Aviation Cadet uniform)

☐ 24 1945 Sharpshooter ....7.50   3.40   .95
(Taking Naval eye test)

☐ 25 1945 Ted Discharged 9.00   4.00   1.15
(In cockpit, giving
the thumbs up)

☐ 26 Off to Flying Start 9.00   4.00   1.15
(In batters box,
spring training 1946)

☐ 27 7/9/46 One Man Show ...9.00   4.00   1.15
(Riding "blooper"
pitch out of park)

☐ 28 The Williams Shift ....7.50   3.40   .95
(Diagram of Cleveland
Indians' position shift
to defense Williams)

☐ 29 Ted Hits for Cycle 12.50   5.75   1.55
(Close-up of follow-
through)

☐ 30 Beating Williams 9.00   4.00   1.15
Shift (Crossing plate
after home run)

☐ 31 Sox Lose Series 9.00   4.00   1.15
(Sliding across plate,
Sept. 14, 1946)

☐ 32 Most Valuable Player 9.00   4.00   1.15
(Receiving MVP Award
from Joseph Cashman)

☐ 33 Another Triple Crown .....7.50   3.40   .95
(Famous "Williams'
Grip")

☐ 34 Runs Scored Record ......7.50   3.40   .95
(Sliding into 2nd
base in 1947 AS Game)

☐ 35 Sox Miss Pennant ....7.50   3.40   .95
(Checking weight on
new 36 oz. hickory bat)

☐ 36 Banner Year for Ted 9.00   4.00   1.15
(Bunting down the
3rd base line)

☐ 37 1949 Sox Miss Again 9.00   4.00   1.15
(Two moods: grim and
determined, smiling
and happy)

☐ 38 1949 Power Rampage ...9.00   4.00   1.15
(Full shot of his
batting follow-
through)

☐ 39 1950 Great Start 12.50   5.75   1.55
(Signing 125,000
contract, shaking
hands with Joe Cronin
and Eddie Collins)

☐ 40 Ted Crashes into Wall 9.00   4.00   1.15
(Making catch in
1950 A-S game and
crashing into wall)

☐ 41 1950 Ted Recovers ....7.50   3.40   .95
(Recuperating from
elbow operation in
hospital)

☐ 42 Slowed by Injury 9.00   4.00   1.15
(With Tom Yawkey)

☐ 43 Double Play Lead 9.00   4.00   1.15
(Leaping high to
make great catch)

☐ 44 Back to Marines 9.00   4.00   1.15
(Hanging up number 9
prior to leaving
for Marines)

☐ 45 Farewell to Baseball 9.00   4.00   1.15
(Honored at Fenway
Park prior to return
to service)

☐ 46 Ready for Combat ....7.50   3.40   .95
(Drawing jet pilot
equipment
in Willow Grove)

☐ 47 Ted Crash Lands Jet ......7.50   3.40   .95

(In flying gear and
jet he crash landed in)

☐ 48 1953 Ted Returns 12.50   5.75   1.55
(Throwing out 1st
ball at AS Game in
Cincinnati; Ford
Frick looks on)

☐ 49 Smash Return ....7.50   3.40   .95
(Giving his arm
whirlpool treatment)

☐ 50 1954 Spring Injury 12.50   5.75   1.55
(Full batting pose
at plate)

☐ 51 Ted is Patched Up ....7.50   3.40   .95
(In first workout
after fractured
collar bone)

☐ 52 1954 Ted's Comeback .12.50   5.75   1.55
(Hitting a home run
against Detroit)

☐ 53 Comeback is Success 9.00   4.00   1.15
(Beating catcher's
tag at home plate)

☐ 54 Ted Hooks Big One 9.00   4.00   1.15
(With prize catch,
1235 lb. black marlin)

☐ 55 Retirement "No Go" 12.50   5.75   1.55
(Returning from
retirement and
signing with
Joe Cronin in '55)

☐ 56 2000th Hit 9.00   4.00   1.15
(2,000th Major
League hit, 8/11/55)

☐ 57 400th Homer 9.00   4.00   1.15
(In locker room after
hitting 400th homerun)

☐ 58 Williams Hits .388 ....9.00   4.00   1.15
(Four-picture
sequence of his
batting swing)

☐ 59 Hot September for Ted ..9.00   4.00   1.15
(Full shot of follow-
through at plate)

☐ 60 More Records for Ted 9.00   4.00   1.15
(Swinging and
missing)

☐ 61 1957 Outfielder Ted 9.00   4.00   1.15
(Warming up prior
to ball game)

☐ 62 1958 Sixth Batting ....7.50   3.40   .95
Title (Slamming pitch
into stands)

☐ 63 Ted's All-Star Record ...45.00   20.00   5.75
(Portrait and
facsimile autograph)

☐ 64 Daughter and Daddy ......7.50   3.40   .95

(In uniform holding
Barbara, his daughter)

☐ 65 1958 August 30 ....9.00   4.00   1.15
(Determination on
face; connecting
with ball)

☐ 66 1958 Powerhouse ....7.50   3.40   .95
(Stance and follow-
through in batters box)

☐ 67 Two Famous Fishermen 20.00   9.00   2.50
(With Sam Snead,
testing fishing
equipment)

☐ 68 Ted Signs for 1959 ....750.00   350.00   95.00
(With Bucky Harris,
signing contract) SP

☐ 69 A Future Ted Williams 9.00   4.00   1.15
(With eager, young
newcomer)

☐ 70 Williams and Thorpe 25.00   11.50   3.10
(With Jim Thorpe,
at Sportsmen's Show)

☐ 71 Hitting Fund. 1 ....7.50   3.40   .95
(Proper gripping of
a baseball bat)

☐ 72 Hitting Fund. 2 ....7.50   3.40   .95
(Checking his swing)

☐ 73 Hitting Fund. 3 ....7.50   3.40   .95
(Stance and follow-
through)

☐ 74 Here's How ....7.50   3.40   .95
(Demonstrating in
locker room an
aspect of hitting)

☐ 75 Williams' Value to 45.00   20.00   5.75
Sox (Ed Collins
and Babe Ruth)

☐ 76 On Base Record ....7.50   3.40   .95
(Awaiting intentional
walk to first base)

☐ 77 Ted Relaxes 9.00   4.00   1.15
(Displaying bone-
fish which he caught)

☐ 78 Honors for Williams 9.00   4.00   1.15
(With Representative
Joe Martin and Chief
Justice Earl Warren;
Clark Griffith Memorial
Award)

☐ 79 Where Ted Stands 12.50   5.75   1.55
(Wielding giant eight-
foot bat when honored
as modern-day Paul
Bunyan)

☐ 80 Ted's Goals for 1959 ...25.00   6.00   1.20
(Admiring his portrait)

1960 Fleer

The cards in this 79-card set measure 2 1/2" by 3 1/2". The cards from the 1960 Fleer series of Baseball Greats are sometimes mistaken for 1930s cards by collectors not familiar with this set. The cards each contain a tinted photo of a baseball immortal, and were issued in one series. There are no known scarcities, although a number 80 card (Pepper Martin reverse with either Eddie Collins or Lefty Grove obverse) exists (this is not considered part of the set). The catalog designation for 1960 Fleer is R418-2. The cards were printed on a 96-card sheet with 17 double prints. These are noted in the checklist below by DP. On the sheet the second Eddie Collins card is typically found in the number 80 position.

	NRMT	VG-E	GOOD
COMPLETE SET (79)	500.00	230.00	65.00
COMMON PLAYER (1-79)	3.50	1.55	.45
COMMON PLAYER DP	3.00	1.35	.40

		NRMT	VG-E	GOOD
☐	1 Napoleon Lajoie DP	20.00	5.00	1.00
☐	2 Christy Mathewson	10.00	4.50	1.25
☐	3 Babe Ruth	90.00	40.00	11.50
☐	4 Carl Hubbell	6.00	2.70	.75
☐	5 Grover Alexander	6.00	2.70	.75
☐	6 Walter Johnson DP	8.00	3.60	1.00
☐	7 Chief Bender	3.50	1.55	.45
☐	8 Roger Bresnahan	3.50	1.55	.45
☐	9 Mordecai Brown	3.50	1.55	.45
☐	10 Tris Speaker	6.00	2.70	.75
☐	11 Arky Vaughan DP	3.00	1.35	.40
☐	12 Zach Wheat	3.50	1.55	.45
☐	13 George Sisler	3.50	1.55	.45
☐	14 Connie Mack	6.00	2.70	.75
☐	15 Clark Griffith	3.50	1.55	.45
☐	16 Lou Boudreau DP	6.00	2.70	.75
☐	17 Ernie Lombardi	3.50	1.55	.45
☐	18 Heinie Manush	3.50	1.55	.45
☐	19 Marty Marion	3.50	1.55	.45
☐	20 Eddie Collins DP	3.00	1.35	.40
☐	21 Rabbit Maranville DP	3.00	1.35	.40
☐	22 Joe Medwick	3.50	1.55	.45
☐	23 Ed Barrow	3.50	1.55	.45
☐	24 Mickey Cochrane	4.50	2.00	.55
☐	25 Jimmy Collins	3.50	1.55	.45
☐	26 Bob Feller DP	12.00	5.50	1.50
☐	27 Luke Appling	6.00	2.70	.75
☐	28 Lou Gehrig	50.00	23.00	6.25
☐	29 Gabby Hartnett	3.50	1.55	.45
☐	30 Chuck Klein	3.50	1.55	.45
☐	31 Tony Lazzeri DP	4.50	2.00	.55
☐	32 Al Simmons	3.50	1.55	.45
☐	33 Wilbert Robinson	3.50	1.55	.45
☐	34 Edgar(Sam) Rice	3.50	1.55	.45
☐	35 Herb Pennock	3.50	1.55	.45
☐	36 Mel Ott DP	6.00	2.70	.75
☐	37 Lefty O'Doul	3.50	1.55	.45
☐	38 Johnny Mize	7.00	3.10	.85
☐	39 Edmund(Bing) Miller	3.50	1.55	.45
☐	40 Joe Tinker	3.50	1.55	.45
☐	41 Frank Baker DP	3.00	1.35	.40
☐	42 Ty Cobb	50.00	23.00	6.25
☐	43 Paul Derringer	3.50	1.55	.45
☐	44 Adrian(Cap) Anson	3.50	1.55	.45
☐	45 Jim Bottomley	3.50	1.55	.45
☐	46 Eddie Plank DP	3.50	1.55	.45
☐	47 Denton(Cy) Young	8.00	3.60	1.00
☐	48 Hack Wilson	6.00	2.70	.75
☐	49 Edward Walsh UER	3.50	1.55	.45
	(Photo actually			
	Ed Walsh Jr.)			
☐	50 Frank Chance	3.50	1.55	.45
☐	51 Dazzy Vance DP	3.00	1.35	.40
☐	52 Bill Terry	6.00	2.70	.75
☐	53 Jimmy Foxx	8.00	3.60	1.00
☐	54 Lefty Gomez	7.00	3.10	.85
☐	55 Branch Rickey	3.50	1.55	.45
☐	56 Ray Schalk DP	3.00	1.35	.40
☐	57 Johnny Evers	3.50	1.55	.45
☐	58 Charles Gehringer	6.00	2.70	.75
☐	59 Burleigh Grimes	3.50	1.55	.45
☐	60 Lefty Grove	7.00	3.10	.85
☐	61 Rube Waddell DP	3.00	1.35	.40
☐	62 John(Honus) Wagner	10.00	4.50	1.25
☐	63 Charles(Red) Ruffing	3.50	1.55	.45
☐	64 Kenesaw M. Landis	3.50	1.55	.45
☐	65 Harry Heilmann	3.50	1.55	.45
☐	66 John McGraw DP	3.00	1.35	.40
☐	67 Hugh Jennings	3.50	1.55	.45
☐	68 Hal Newhouser	4.50	2.00	.55
☐	69 Waite Hoyt	3.50	1.55	.45

		NRMT	VG-E	GOOD
☐ 70	Louis(Bobo) Newsom	3.50	1.55	.45
☐ 71	Earl Averill DP	3.00	1.35	.40
☐ 72	Ted Williams	75.00	34.00	9.50
☐ 73	Warren Giles	3.50	1.55	.45
☐ 74	Ford Frick	3.50	1.55	.45
☐ 75	Hazen(Kiki) Cuyler	3.50	1.55	.45
☐ 76	Paul Waner DP	3.00	1.35	.40
☐ 77	Harold(Pie) Traynor	3.50	1.55	.45
☐ 78	Lloyd Waner	3.50	1.55	.45
☐ 79	Ralph Kiner	9.00	3.00	.75
☐ 80A	Pepper Martin SP	1800.00	750.00	250.00
	(Eddie Collins pictured on obverse)			
☐ 80B	Pepper Martin SP	1200.00	500.00	150.00
	(Lefty Grove pictured on obverse)			

1961 Fleer

The cards in this 154-card set measure 2 1/2" by 3 1/2". In 1961, Fleer continued its Baseball Greats format by issuing this series of cards. The set was released in two distinct series, 1-88 and 89-154 (of which the latter is more difficult to obtain). The players within each series are conveniently numbered in alphabetical order. It appears that this set continued to be issued the following year by Fleer. The catalog number for this set is F418-3. In each first series pack Fleer inserted a Major League team decal and a pennant sticker honoring past World Series winners.

	NRMT	VG-E	GOOD
COMPLETE SET (154)	1000.00	450.00	125.00
COMMON PLAYER (1-88)	3.00	1.35	.40

		NRMT	VG-E	GOOD
COMMON PLAYER (89-154)		6.00	2.70	.75
☐ 1	Baker/Cobb/Wheat	40.00	6.00	1.20
	(Checklist back)			
☐ 2	Grover C. Alexander	6.00	2.70	.75
☐ 3	Nick Altrock	3.00	1.35	.40
☐ 4	Cap Anson	3.00	1.35	.40
☐ 5	Earl Averill	3.00	1.35	.40
☐ 6	Frank Baker	3.00	1.35	.40
☐ 7	Dave Bancroft	3.00	1.35	.40
☐ 8	Chief Bender	3.00	1.35	.40
☐ 9	Jim Bottomley	3.00	1.35	.40
☐ 10	Roger Bresnahan	3.00	1.35	.40
☐ 11	Mordecai Brown	3.00	1.35	.40
☐ 12	Max Carey	3.00	1.35	.40
☐ 13	Jack Chesbro	3.00	1.35	.40
☐ 14	Ty Cobb	40.00	18.00	5.00
☐ 15	Mickey Cochrane	4.00	1.80	.50
☐ 16	Eddie Collins	3.00	1.35	.40
☐ 17	Earle Combs	3.00	1.35	.40
☐ 18	Charles Comiskey	3.00	1.35	.40
☐ 19	Kiki Cuyler	3.00	1.35	.40
☐ 20	Paul Derringer	3.00	1.35	.40
☐ 21	Howard Ehmke	3.00	1.35	.40
☐ 22	Billy Evans	3.00	1.35	.40
☐ 23	Johnny Evers	3.00	1.35	.40
☐ 24	Urban Faber	3.00	1.35	.40
☐ 25	Bob Feller	10.00	4.50	1.25
☐ 26	Wes Ferrell	3.00	1.35	.40
☐ 27	Lew Fonseca	3.00	1.35	.40
☐ 28	Jimmy Foxx	7.00	3.10	.85
☐ 29	Ford Frick	3.00	1.35	.40
☐ 30	Frank Frisch	4.00	1.80	.50
☐ 31	Lou Gehrig	40.00	18.00	5.00
☐ 32	Charlie Gehringer	5.00	2.30	.60
☐ 33	Warren Giles	3.00	1.35	.40
☐ 34	Lefty Gomez	5.00	2.30	.60
☐ 35	Goose Goslin	3.00	1.35	.40
☐ 36	Clark Griffith	3.00	1.35	.40
☐ 37	Burleigh Grimes	3.00	1.35	.40
☐ 38	Lefty Grove	6.00	2.70	.75
☐ 39	Chick Hafey	3.00	1.35	.40
☐ 40	Jesse Haines	3.00	1.35	.40
☐ 41	Gabby Hartnett	3.00	1.35	.40
☐ 42	Harry Heilmann	3.00	1.35	.40
☐ 43	Rogers Hornsby	7.00	3.10	.85
☐ 44	Waite Hoyt	3.00	1.35	.40
☐ 45	Carl Hubbell	5.00	2.30	.60
☐ 46	Miller Huggins	3.00	1.35	.40
☐ 47	Hugh Jennings	3.00	1.35	.40
☐ 48	Ban Johnson	3.00	1.35	.40
☐ 49	Walter Johnson	10.00	4.50	1.25
☐ 50	Ralph Kiner	7.00	3.10	.85
☐ 51	Chuck Klein	3.00	1.35	.40
☐ 52	Johnny Kling	3.00	1.35	.40
☐ 53	Kenesaw M. Landis	3.00	1.35	.40
☐ 54	Tony Lazzeri	4.00	1.80	.50

☐ 55	Ernie Lombardi	3.00	1.35	.40
☐ 56	Dolf Luque	3.00	1.35	.40
☐ 57	Heinie Manush	3.00	1.35	.40
☐ 58	Marty Marion	3.00	1.35	.40
☐ 59	Christy Mathewson	10.00	4.50	1.25
☐ 60	John McGraw	4.00	1.80	.50
☐ 61	Joe Medwick	3.00	1.35	.40
☐ 62	Edmund(Bing) Miller	3.00	1.35	.40
☐ 63	Johnny Mize	6.00	2.70	.75
☐ 64	John Mostil	3.00	1.35	.40
☐ 65	Art Nehf	3.00	1.35	.40
☐ 66	Hal Newhouser	4.00	1.80	.50
☐ 67	Bobo Newsom	3.00	1.35	.40
☐ 68	Mel Ott	5.00	2.30	.60
☐ 69	Allie Reynolds	3.00	1.35	.40
☐ 70	Sam Rice	3.00	1.35	.40
☐ 71	Eppa Rixey	3.00	1.35	.40
☐ 72	Edd Roush	3.00	1.35	.40
☐ 73	Schoolboy Rowe	3.00	1.35	.40
☐ 74	Red Ruffing	3.00	1.35	.40
☐ 75	Babe Ruth	80.00	36.00	10.00
☐ 76	Joe Sewell	3.00	1.35	.40
☐ 77	Al Simmons	3.00	1.35	.40
☐ 78	George Sisler	3.00	1.35	.40
☐ 79	Tris Speaker	6.00	2.70	.75
☐ 80	Fred Toney	3.00	1.35	.40
☐ 81	Dazzy Vance	3.00	1.35	.40
☐ 82	Jim Vaughn	3.00	1.35	.40
☐ 83	Ed Walsh	3.00	1.35	.40
☐ 84	Lloyd Waner	3.00	1.35	.40
☐ 85	Paul Waner	3.00	1.35	.40
☐ 86	Zack Wheat	3.00	1.35	.40
☐ 87	Hack Wilson	4.00	1.80	.50
☐ 88	Jimmy Wilson	3.00	1.35	.40
☐ 89	George Sisler and	30.00	5.00	1.00
	Pie Traynor			
	(Checklist back)			
☐ 90	Babe Adams	6.00	2.70	.75
☐ 91	Dale Alexander	6.00	2.70	.75
☐ 92	Jim Bagby	6.00	2.70	.75
☐ 93	Ossie Bluege	6.00	2.70	.75
☐ 94	Lou Boudreau	10.00	4.50	1.25
☐ 95	Tom Bridges	6.00	2.70	.75
☐ 96	Donie Bush	6.00	2.70	.75
☐ 97	Dolph Camilli	6.00	2.70	.75
☐ 98	Frank Chance	8.00	3.60	1.00
☐ 99	Jimmy Collins	8.00	3.60	1.00
☐ 100	Stan Coveleskie	8.00	3.60	1.00
☐ 101	Hugh Critz	6.00	2.70	.75
☐ 102	Alvin Crowder	6.00	2.70	.75
☐ 103	Joe Dugan	6.00	2.70	.75
☐ 104	Bibb Falk	6.00	2.70	.75
☐ 105	Rick Ferrell	8.00	3.60	1.00
☐ 106	Art Fletcher	6.00	2.70	.75
☐ 107	Dennis Galehouse	6.00	2.70	.75
☐ 108	Chick Galloway	6.00	2.70	.75
☐ 109	Mule Haas	6.00	2.70	.75

☐ 110	Stan Hack	6.00	2.70	.75
☐ 111	Bump Hadley	6.00	2.70	.75
☐ 112	Billy Hamilton	8.00	3.60	1.00
☐ 113	Joe Hauser	6.00	2.70	.75
☐ 114	Babe Herman	6.00	2.70	.75
☐ 115	Travis Jackson	10.00	4.50	1.25
☐ 116	Eddie Joost	6.00	2.70	.75
☐ 117	Addie Joss	10.00	4.50	1.25
☐ 118	Joe Judge	6.00	2.70	.75
☐ 119	Joe Kuhel	6.00	2.70	.75
☐ 120	Napoleon Lajoie	15.00	6.75	1.90
☐ 121	Dutch Leonard	6.00	2.70	.75
☐ 122	Ted Lyons	8.00	3.60	1.00
☐ 123	Connie Mack	15.00	6.75	1.90
☐ 124	Rabbit Maranville	8.00	3.60	1.00
☐ 125	Fred Marberry	6.00	2.70	.75
☐ 126	Joe McGinnity	10.00	4.50	1.25
☐ 127	Oscar Melillo	6.00	2.70	.75
☐ 128	Ray Mueller	6.00	2.70	.75
☐ 129	Kid Nichols	8.00	3.60	1.00
☐ 130	Lefty O'Doul	6.00	2.70	.75
☐ 131	Bob O'Farrell	6.00	2.70	.75
☐ 132	Roger Peckinpaugh	6.00	2.70	.75
☐ 133	Herb Pennock	8.00	3.60	1.00
☐ 134	George Pipgras	6.00	2.70	.75
☐ 135	Eddie Plank	10.00	4.50	1.25
☐ 136	Ray Schalk	8.00	3.60	1.00
☐ 137	Hal Schumacher	6.00	2.70	.75
☐ 138	Luke Sewell	6.00	2.70	.75
☐ 139	Bob Shawkey	6.00	2.70	.75
☐ 140	Riggs Stephenson	6.00	2.70	.75
☐ 141	Billy Sullivan	6.00	2.70	.75
☐ 142	Bill Terry	15.00	6.75	1.90
☐ 143	Joe Tinker	8.00	3.60	1.00
☐ 144	Pie Traynor	10.00	4.50	1.25
☐ 145	Hal Trosky	6.00	2.70	.75
☐ 146	George Uhle	6.00	2.70	.75
☐ 147	Johnny VanderMeer	8.00	3.60	1.00
☐ 148	Arky Vaughan	8.00	3.60	1.00
☐ 149	Rube Waddell	8.00	3.60	1.00
☐ 150	Honus Wagner	40.00	18.00	5.00
☐ 151	Dixie Walker	6.00	2.70	.75
☐ 152	Ted Williams	80.00	36.00	10.00
☐ 153	Cy Young	25.00	11.50	3.10
☐ 154	Ross Youngs	20.00	7.50	1.50

1963 Fleer

The cards in this 66-card set measure 2 1/2" by 3 1/2". The Fleer set of current baseball players was marketed in 1963 in a gum card-style waxed wrapper package which contained a cherry cookie instead of gum. The cards were printed in sheets of 66 with the scarce card of Adcock apparently being replaced by the unnumbered checklist card for the final press run. The complete set price includes the checklist card. The catalog designation for this set is R418-4. The key Rookie Card in this set is Maury Wills. The set is basically arranged numerically in alphabetical order by teams which are also in alphabetical order.

		NRMT	VG-E	GOOD
	COMPLETE SET (67)	1250.00	575.00	160.00
	COMMON PLAYER (1-66)	8.00	3.60	1.00
☐ 1	Steve Barber	16.00	7.25	2.00
☐ 2	Ron Hansen	8.00	3.60	1.00
☐ 3	Milt Pappas	9.00	4.00	1.15
☐ 4	Brooks Robinson	55.00	25.00	7.00
☐ 5	Willie Mays	120.00	55.00	15.00
☐ 6	Lou Clinton	8.00	3.60	1.00
☐ 7	Bill Monbouquette	8.00	3.60	1.00
☐ 8	Carl Yastrzemski	100.00	45.00	12.50
☐ 9	Ray Herbert	8.00	3.60	1.00
☐ 10	Jim Landis	8.00	3.60	1.00
☐ 11	Dick Donovan	8.00	3.60	1.00
☐ 12	Tito Francona	8.00	3.60	1.00
☐ 13	Jerry Kindall	8.00	3.60	1.00
☐ 14	Frank Lary	9.00	4.00	1.15
☐ 15	Dick Howser	9.00	4.00	1.15
☐ 16	Jerry Lumpe	8.00	3.60	1.00
☐ 17	Norm Siebern	8.00	3.60	1.00
☐ 18	Don Lee	8.00	3.60	1.00
☐ 19	Albie Pearson	9.00	4.00	1.15
☐ 20	Bob Rodgers	9.00	4.00	1.15
☐ 21	Leon Wagner	8.00	3.60	1.00
☐ 22	Jim Kaat	15.00	6.75	1.90
☐ 23	Vic Power	9.00	4.00	1.15
☐ 24	Rich Rollins	8.00	3.60	1.00
☐ 25	Bobby Richardson	15.00	6.75	1.90
☐ 26	Ralph Terry	9.00	4.00	1.15
☐ 27	Tom Cheney	8.00	3.60	1.00
☐ 28	Chuck Cottier	8.00	3.60	1.00
☐ 29	Jim Piersall	11.00	4.90	1.40
☐ 30	Dave Stenhouse	8.00	3.60	1.00
☐ 31	Glen Hobbie	8.00	3.60	1.00
☐ 32	Ron Santo	15.00	6.75	1.90
☐ 33	Gene Freese	8.00	3.60	1.00
☐ 34	Vada Pinson	15.00	6.75	1.90
☐ 35	Bob Purkey	8.00	3.60	1.00
☐ 36	Joe Amalfitano	8.00	3.60	1.00
☐ 37	Bob Aspromonte	8.00	3.60	1.00
☐ 38	Dick Farrell	8.00	3.60	1.00
☐ 39	Al Spangler	8.00	3.60	1.00
☐ 40	Tommy Davis	11.00	4.90	1.40
☐ 41	Don Drysdale	40.00	18.00	5.00
☐ 42	Sandy Koufax	135.00	60.00	17.00
☐ 43	Maury Wills	85.00	38.00	10.50
☐ 44	Frank Bolling	8.00	3.60	1.00
☐ 45	Warren Spahn	40.00	18.00	5.00
☐ 46	Joe Adcock SP	165.00	75.00	21.00
☐ 47	Roger Craig	11.00	4.90	1.40
☐ 48	Al Jackson	8.00	3.60	1.00
☐ 49	Rod Kanehl	8.00	3.60	1.00
☐ 50	Ruben Amaro	8.00	3.60	1.00
☐ 51	Johnny Callison	9.00	4.00	1.15
☐ 52	Clay Dalrymple	8.00	3.60	1.00
☐ 53	Don Demeter	8.00	3.60	1.00
☐ 54	Art Mahaffey	8.00	3.60	1.00
☐ 55	Smoky Burgess	9.00	4.00	1.15
☐ 56	Roberto Clemente	130.00	57.50	16.50
☐ 57	Roy Face	11.00	4.90	1.40
☐ 58	Vern Law	9.00	4.00	1.15
☐ 59	Bill Mazeroski	14.00	6.25	1.75
☐ 60	Ken Boyer	15.00	6.75	1.90
☐ 61	Bob Gibson	45.00	20.00	5.75
☐ 62	Gene Oliver	8.00	3.60	1.00
☐ 63	Bill White	15.00	6.75	1.90
☐ 64	Orlando Cepeda	20.00	9.00	2.50
☐ 65	Jim Davenport	8.00	3.60	1.00
☐ 66	Billy O'Dell	16.00	7.25	2.00
☐ NNO	Checklist card	450.00	70.00	23.00

1981 Fleer

The cards in this 660-card set measure 2 1/2" by 3 1/2". This issue of cards marks Fleer's first entry into the current player baseball card market since 1963. Players from the same team are conveniently grouped together by number in the set. The teams are ordered (by 1980 standings) as follows: Philadelphia (1-27), Kansas City (28-50), Houston (51-78),

New York Yankees (79-109), Los Angeles (110-141), Montreal (142-168), Baltimore (169-195), Cincinnati (196-220), Boston (221-241), Atlanta (242-267), California (268-290), Chicago Cubs (291-315), New York Mets (316-338), Chicago White Sox (339-350 and 352-359), Pittsburgh (360-386), Cleveland (387-408), Toronto (409-431), San Francisco (432-458), Detroit (459-483), San Diego (484-506), Milwaukee (507-527), St. Louis (528-550), Minnesota (551-571), Oakland (351 and 572-594), Seattle (595-616), and Texas (617-637). Cards 638-660 feature specials and checklists. The cards of pitchers in this set erroneously show a heading (on the card backs) of "Batting Record" over their career pitching statistics. There were three distinct printings: the two following the primary run were designed to correct numerous errors. The variations caused by these multiple printings are noted in the checklist below (P1, P2, or P3). The C. Nettles variation was corrected before the end of the first printing and thus is not included in the complete set consideration. The key Rookie Cards in this set are Harold Baines, Kirk Gibson, Jeff Reardon, and Fernando Valenzuela, whose first name was erroneously spelled Fernand on the card front.

	NRMT-MT	EXC	G-VG
COMPLETE SET (660)	60.00	27.00	7.50
COMMON PLAYER (1-660)	.10	.05	.01

☐ 1	Pete Rose UER	2.50	1.15	.30
	(270 hits in '63,			
	should be 170)			
☐ 2	Larry Bowa	.12	.05	.02
☐ 3	Manny Trillo	.10	.05	.01
☐ 4	Bob Boone	.12	.05	.02
☐ 5	Mike Schmidt	3.00	1.35	.40
	(See also 640A)			

☐ 6A	Steve Carlton P1	2.00	.90	.25
	Pitcher of Year			
	(See also 660A;			
	Back "1066 Cardinals")			
☐ 6B	Steve Carlton P2	2.00	.90	.25
	Pitcher of Year			
	(Back "1066 Cardinals")			
☐ 6C	Steve Carlton P3	2.00	.90	.25
	("1966 Cardinals")			
☐ 7	Tug McGraw	.12	.05	.02
	(See 657A)			
☐ 8	Larry Christenson	.10	.05	.01
☐ 9	Bake McBride	.10	.05	.01
☐ 10	Greg Luzinski	.12	.05	.02
☐ 11	Ron Reed	.10	.05	.01
☐ 12	Dickie Noles	.10	.05	.01
☐ 13	Keith Moreland	.12	.05	.02
☐ 14	Bob Walk	.35	.16	.04
☐ 15	Lonnie Smith	.15	.07	.02
☐ 16	Dick Ruthven	.10	.05	.01
☐ 17	Sparky Lyle	.12	.05	.02
☐ 18	Greg Gross	.10	.05	.01
☐ 19	Garry Maddox	.10	.05	.01
☐ 20	Nino Espinosa	.10	.05	.01
☐ 21	George Vukovich	.10	.05	.01
☐ 22	John Vukovich	.10	.05	.01
☐ 23	Ramon Aviles	.10	.05	.01
☐ 24A	Ken Saucier P1	.10	.05	.01
	(Name on back "Ken")			
☐ 24B	Ken Saucier P2	.10	.05	.01
	(Name on back "Ken")			
☐ 24C	Kevin Saucier P3	.25	.11	.03
	(Name on back "Kevin")			
☐ 25	Randy Lerch	.10	.05	.01
☐ 26	Del Unser	.10	.05	.01
☐ 27	Tim McCarver	.12	.05	.02
☐ 28	George Brett	4.00	1.80	.50
	(See also 655A)			
☐ 29	Willie Wilson	.20	.09	.03
	(See also 653A)			
☐ 30	Paul Splittorff	.10	.05	.01
☐ 31	Dan Quisenberry	.25	.11	.03
☐ 32A	Amos Otis P1	.15	.07	.02
	(Batting Pose;			
	"Outfield";			
	32 on back)			
☐ 32B	Amos Otis P2	.15	.07	.02
	"Series Starter"			
	(483 on back)			
☐ 33	Steve Busby	.10	.05	.01
☐ 34	U.L. Washington	.10	.05	.01
☐ 35	Dave Chalk	.10	.05	.01
☐ 36	Darrell Porter	.10	.05	.01
☐ 37	Marty Pattin	.10	.05	.01
☐ 38	Larry Gura	.10	.05	.01
☐ 39	Renie Martin	.10	.05	.01
☐ 40	Rich Gale	.10	.05	.01

☐ 41A	Hal McRae P1 ....50 ("Royals" on front in black letters)	.23	.06
☐ 41B	Hal McRae P2 ....15 ("Royals" on front in blue letters)	.07	.02
☐ 42	Dennis Leonard...............10	.05	.01
☐ 43	Willie Aikens 10	.05	.01
☐ 44	Frank White......................12	.05	.02
☐ 45	Clint Hurdle.....................10	.05	.01
☐ 46	John Wathan....................10	.05	.01
☐ 47	Pete LaCock....................10	.05	.01
☐ 48	Rance Mulliniks 10	.05	.01
☐ 49	Jeff Twitty........................10	.05	.01
☐ 50	Jamie Quirk.....................10	.05	.01
☐ 51	Art Howe..........................12	.05	.02
☐ 52	Ken Forsch.......................10	.05	.01
☐ 53	Vern Ruhle.......................10	.05	.01
☐ 54	Joe Niekro.......................12	.05	.02
☐ 55	Frank LaCorte..................10	.05	.01
☐ 56	J.R. Richard.....................12	.05	.02
☐ 57	Nolan Ryan 8.00	3.60	1.00
☐ 58	Enos Cabell......................10	.05	.01
☐ 59	Cesar Cedeno 12	.05	.02
☐ 60	Jose Cruz.........................12	.05	.02
☐ 61	Bill Virdon MG 10	.05	.01
☐ 62	Terry Puhl........................10	.05	.01
☐ 63	Joaquin Andujar...............12	.05	.02
☐ 64	Alan Ashby.......................10	.05	.01
☐ 65	Joe Sambito.....................10	.05	.01
☐ 66	Denny Walling...................10	.05	.01
☐ 67	Jeff Leonard.....................12	.05	.02
☐ 68	Luis Pujols.......................10	.05	.01
☐ 69	Bruce Bochy.....................10	.05	.01
☐ 70	Rafael Landestoy 10	.05	.01
☐ 71	Dave Smith.......................25	.11	.03
☐ 72	Danny Heep......................10	.05	.01
☐ 73	Julio Gonzalez..................10	.05	.01
☐ 74	Craig Reynolds.................10	.05	.01
☐ 75	Gary Woods......................10	.05	.01
☐ 76	Dave Bergman 10	.05	.01
☐ 77	Randy Niemann 10	.05	.01
☐ 78	Joe Morgan....................1.00	.45	.13
☐ 79	Reggie Jackson...........2.50 (See also 650A)	1.15	.30
☐ 80	Bucky Dent.......................12	.05	.02
☐ 81	Tommy John......................20	.09	.03
☐ 82	Luis Tiant.........................12	.05	.02
☐ 83	Rick Cerone 10	.05	.01
☐ 84	Dick Howser MG 12	.05	.02
☐ 85	Lou Piniella......................12	.05	.02
☐ 86	Ron Davis.........................10	.05	.01
☐ 87A	Craig Nettles P1 ....10.00 ERR (Name on back misspelled "Craig")	4.50	1.25
☐ 87B	Graig Nettles P2 COR .....25 ("Graig")	.11	.03
☐ 88	Ron Guidry 25	.11	.03
☐ 89	Rich Gossage...................20	.09	.03
☐ 90	Rudy May 10	.05	.01
☐ 91	Gaylord Perry...................60	.25	.08
☐ 92	Eric Soderholm.................10	.05	.01
☐ 93	Bob Watson 12	.05	.02
☐ 94	Bobby Murcer...................12	.05	.02
☐ 95	Bobby Brown....................10	.05	.01
☐ 96	Jim Spencer 10	.05	.01
☐ 97	Tom Underwood................10	.05	.01
☐ 98	Oscar Gamble 10	.05	.01
☐ 99	Johnny Oates 10	.05	.01
☐ 100	Fred Stanley.....................10	.05	.01
☐ 101	Ruppert Jones 10	.05	.01
☐ 102	Dennis Werth....................10	.05	.01
☐ 103	Joe Lefebvre.....................10	.05	.01
☐ 104	Brian Doyle......................10	.05	.01
☐ 105	Aurelio Rodriguez.............10	.05	.01
☐ 106	Doug Bird.........................10	.05	.01
☐ 107	Mike Griffin......................10	.05	.01
☐ 108	Tim Lollar........................10	.05	.01
☐ 109	Willie Randolph................12	.05	.02
☐ 110	Steve Garvey.....................75	.35	.09
☐ 111	Reggie Smith....................12	.05	.02
☐ 112	Don Sutton.......................60	.25	.08
☐ 113	Burt Hooton.....................10	.05	.01
☐ 114A	Dave Lopes P1.................50 (Small hand on back)	.23	.06
☐ 114B	Dave Lopes P2.................12 (No hand)	.05	.02
☐ 115	Dusty Baker......................12	.05	.02
☐ 116	Tom Lasorda MG 12	.05	.02
☐ 117	Bill Russell.......................12	.05	.02
☐ 118	Jerry Reuss UER.............12 ("Home:" omitted)	.05	.02
☐ 119	Terry Forster....................10	.05	.01
☐ 120A	Bob Welch P1..................40 (Name on back is "Bob")	.18	.05
☐ 120B	Bob Welch P2..................40 (Name on back is "Robert")	.18	.05
☐ 121	Don Stanhouse 10	.05	.01
☐ 122	Rick Monday 12	.05	.02
☐ 123	Derrel Thomas..................10	.05	.01
☐ 124	Joe Ferguson....................10	.05	.01
☐ 125	Rick Sutcliffe...................35	.16	.04
☐ 126A	Ron Cey P1 ....50 (Small hand on back)	.23	.06
☐ 126B	Ron Cey P2 ....12 (No hand)	.05	.02
☐ 127	Dave Goltz.......................10	.05	.01
☐ 128	Jay Johnstone..................12	.05	.02
☐ 129	Steve Yeager....................10	.05	.01
☐ 130	Gary Weiss.......................10	.05	.01
☐ 131	Mike Scioscia...................75	.35	.09
☐ 132	Vic Davalillo 10	.05	.01

☐ 133 Doug Rau	.10	.05	.01	☐ 186 John Lowenstein	.10	.05	.01
☐ 134 Pepe Frias	.10	.05	.01	☐ 187 Gary Roenicke	.10	.05	.01
☐ 135 Mickey Hatcher	.10	.05	.01	☐ 188 Ken Singleton	.12	.05	.02
☐ 136 Steve Howe	.12	.05	.02	☐ 189 Dan Graham	.10	.05	.01
☐ 137 Robert Castillo	.10	.05	.01	☐ 190 Terry Crowley	.10	.05	.01
☐ 138 Gary Thomasson	.10	.05	.01	☐ 191 Kiko Garcia	.10	.05	.01
☐ 139 Rudy Law	.10	.05	.01	☐ 192 Dave Ford	.10	.05	.01
☐ 140 Fernand Valenzuela	2.00	.90	.25	☐ 193 Mark Corey	.10	.05	.01
UER (Sic, Fernando)				☐ 194 Lenn Sakata	.10	.05	.01
☐ 141 Manny Mota	.12	.05	.02	☐ 195 Doug DeCinces	.12	.05	.02
☐ 142 Gary Carter	1.00	.45	.13	☐ 196 Johnny Bench	2.00	.90	.25
☐ 143 Steve Rogers	.10	.05	.01	☐ 197 Dave Concepcion	.15	.07	.02
☐ 144 Warren Cromartie	.10	.05	.01	☐ 198 Ray Knight	.12	.05	.02
☐ 145 Andre Dawson	2.00	.90	.25	☐ 199 Ken Griffey	.35	.16	.04
☐ 146 Larry Parrish	.10	.05	.01	☐ 200 Tom Seaver	2.00	.90	.25
☐ 147 Rowland Office	.10	.05	.01	☐ 201 Dave Collins	.10	.05	.01
☐ 148 Ellis Valentine	.10	.05	.01	☐ 202A George Foster P1	.20	.09	.03
☐ 149 Dick Williams MG	.10	.05	.01	Slugger			
☐ 150 Bill Gullickson	1.00	.45	.13	(Number on back 216)			
☐ 151 Elias Sosa	.10	.05	.01	☐ 202B George Foster P2	.20	.09	.03
☐ 152 John Tamargo	.10	.05	.01	Slugger			
☐ 153 Chris Speier	.10	.05	.01	(Number on back 202)			
☐ 154 Ron LeFlore	.12	.05	.02				
☐ 155 Rodney Scott	.10	.05	.01	☐ 203 Junior Kennedy	.10	.05	.01
☐ 156 Stan Bahnsen	.10	.05	.01	☐ 204 Frank Pastore	.10	.05	.01
☐ 157 Bill Lee	.10	.05	.01	☐ 205 Dan Driessen	.10	.05	.01
☐ 158 Fred Norman	.10	.05	.01	☐ 206 Hector Cruz	.10	.05	.01
☐ 159 Woodie Fryman	.10	.05	.01	☐ 207 Paul Moskau	.10	.05	.01
☐ 160 David Palmer	.10	.05	.01	☐ 208 Charlie Leibrandt	.90	.40	.11
☐ 161 Jerry White	.10	.05	.01	☐ 209 Harry Spilman	.10	.05	.01
☐ 162 Roberto Ramos	.10	.05	.01	☐ 210 Joe Price	.10	.05	.01
☐ 163 John D'Acquisto	.10	.05	.01	☐ 211 Tom Hume	.10	.05	.01
☐ 164 Tommy Hutton	.10	.05	.01	☐ 212 Joe Nolan	.10	.05	.01
☐ 165 Charlie Lea	.10	.05	.01	☐ 213 Doug Bair	.10	.05	.01
☐ 166 Scott Sanderson	.12	.05	.02	☐ 214 Mario Soto	.10	.05	.01
☐ 167 Ken Macha	.10	.05	.01	☐ 215A Bill Bonham P1	.50	.23	.06
☐ 168 Tony Bernazard	.10	.05	.01	(Small hand on back)			
☐ 169 Jim Palmer	1.75	.80	.22	☐ 215B Bill Bonham P2	.10	.05	.01
☐ 170 Steve Stone	.12	.05	.02	(No hand)			
☐ 171 Mike Flanagan	.12	.05	.02	☐ 216 George Foster	.20	.09	.03
☐ 172 Al Bumbry	.10	.05	.01	(See 202)			
☐ 173 Doug DeCinces	.12	.05	.02	☐ 217 Paul Householder	.10	.05	.01
☐ 174 Scott McGregor	.10	.05	.01	☐ 218 Ron Oester	.10	.05	.01
☐ 175 Mark Belanger	.12	.05	.02	☐ 219 Sam Mejias	.10	.05	.01
☐ 176 Tim Stoddard	.10	.05	.01	☐ 220 Sheldon Burnside	.10	.05	.01
☐ 177A Rick Dempsey P1	.50	.23	.06	☐ 221 Carl Yastrzemski	2.00	.90	.25
(Small hand on front)				☐ 222 Jim Rice	.30	.14	.04
☐ 177B Rick Dempsey P2	.12	.05	.02	☐ 223 Fred Lynn	.12	.05	.02
(No hand)				☐ 224 Carlton Fisk	2.00	.90	.25
☐ 178 Earl Weaver MG	.12	.05	.02	☐ 225 Rick Burleson	.10	.05	.01
☐ 179 Tippy Martinez	.12	.05	.02	☐ 226 Dennis Eckersley	1.75	.80	.22
☐ 180 Dennis Martinez	.35	.16	.04	☐ 227 Butch Hobson	.12	.05	.02
☐ 181 Sammy Stewart	.10	.05	.01	☐ 228 Tom Burgmeier	.10	.05	.01
☐ 182 Rich Dauer	.10	.05	.01	☐ 229 Garry Hancock	.10	.05	.01
☐ 183 Lee May	.12	.05	.02	☐ 230 Don Zimmer MG	.10	.05	.01
☐ 184 Eddie Murray	3.00	1.35	.40	☐ 231 Steve Renko	.10	.05	.01
☐ 185 Benny Ayala	.10	.05	.01	☐ 232 Dwight Evans	.35	.16	.04
				☐ 233 Mike Torrez	.10	.05	.01

☐ 234 Bob Stanley	10	.05	.01
☐ 235 Jim Dwyer	10	.05	.01
☐ 236 Dave Stapleton	10	.05	.01
☐ 237 Glenn Hoffman	10	.05	.01
☐ 238 Jerry Remy	10	.05	.01
☐ 239 Dick Drago	10	.05	.01
☐ 240 Bill Campbell	10	.05	.01
☐ 241 Tony Perez	40	.18	.05
☐ 242 Phil Niekro	60	.25	.08
☐ 243 Dale Murphy	1.00	.45	.13
☐ 244 Bob Horner	12	.05	.02
☐ 245 Jeff Burroughs	10	.05	.01
☐ 246 Rick Camp	10	.05	.01
☐ 247 Bobby Cox MG	10	.05	.01
☐ 248 Bruce Benedict	10	.05	.01
☐ 249 Gene Garber	10	.05	.01
☐ 250 Jerry Royster	10	.05	.01
☐ 251A Gary Matthews P1	50	.23	.06
(Small hand on back)			
☐ 251B Gary Matthews P2	12	.05	.02
(No hand)			
☐ 252 Chris Chambliss	12	.05	.02
☐ 253 Luis Gomez	10	.05	.01
☐ 254 Bill Nahorodny	10	.05	.01
☐ 255 Doyle Alexander	10	.05	.01
☐ 256 Brian Asselstine	10	.05	.01
☐ 257 Biff Pocoroba	10	.05	.01
☐ 258 Mike Lum	10	.05	.01
☐ 259 Charlie Spikes	10	.05	.01
☐ 260 Glenn Hubbard	10	.05	.01
☐ 261 Tommy Boggs	10	.05	.01
☐ 262 Al Hrabosky	10	.05	.01
☐ 263 Rick Matula	10	.05	.01
☐ 264 Preston Hanna	10	.05	.01
☐ 265 Larry Bradford	10	.05	.01
☐ 266 Rafael Ramirez	20	.09	.03
☐ 267 Larry McWilliams	10	.05	.01
☐ 268 Rod Carew	2.00	.90	.25
☐ 269 Bobby Grich	12	.05	.02
☐ 270 Carney Lansford	30	.14	.04
☐ 271 Don Baylor	12	.05	.02
☐ 272 Joe Rudi	12	.05	.02
☐ 273 Dan Ford	10	.05	.01
☐ 274 Jim Fregosi MG	10	.05	.01
☐ 275 Dave Frost	10	.05	.01
☐ 276 Frank Tanana	12	.05	.02
☐ 277 Dickie Thon	12	.05	.02
☐ 278 Jason Thompson	10	.05	.01
☐ 279 Rick Miller	10	.05	.01
☐ 280 Bert Campaneris	12	.05	.02
☐ 281 Tom Donohue	10	.05	.01
☐ 282 Brian Downing	12	.05	.02
☐ 283 Fred Patek	10	.05	.01
☐ 284 Bruce Kison	10	.05	.01
☐ 285 Dave LaRoche	10	.05	.01
☐ 286 Don Aase	10	.05	.01
☐ 287 Jim Barr	10	.05	.01
☐ 288 Alfredo Martinez	10	.05	.01
☐ 289 Larry Harlow	10	.05	.01
☐ 290 Andy Hassler	10	.05	.01
☐ 291 Dave Kingman	12	.05	.02
☐ 292 Bill Buckner	12	.05	.02
☐ 293 Rick Reuschel	12	.05	.02
☐ 294 Bruce Sutter	20	.09	.03
☐ 295 Jerry Martin	10	.05	.01
☐ 296 Scot Thompson	10	.05	.01
☐ 297 Ivan DeJesus	10	.05	.01
☐ 298 Steve Dillard	10	.05	.01
☐ 299 Dick Tidrow	10	.05	.01
☐ 300 Randy Martz	10	.05	.01
☐ 301 Lenny Randle	10	.05	.01
☐ 302 Lynn McGlothen	10	.05	.01
☐ 303 Cliff Johnson	10	.05	.01
☐ 304 Tim Blackwell	10	.05	.01
☐ 305 Dennis Lamp	10	.05	.01
☐ 306 Bill Caudill	10	.05	.01
☐ 307 Carlos Lezcano	10	.05	.01
☐ 308 Jim Tracy	10	.05	.01
☐ 309 Doug Capilla UER	10	.05	.01
(Cubs on front but			
Braves on back)			
☐ 310 Willie Hernandez	12	.05	.02
☐ 311 Mike Vail	10	.05	.01
☐ 312 Mike Krukow	10	.05	.01
☐ 313 Barry Foote	10	.05	.01
☐ 314 Larry Biittner	10	.05	.01
☐ 315 Mike Tyson	10	.05	.01
☐ 316 Lee Mazzilli	10	.05	.01
☐ 317 John Stearns	10	.05	.01
☐ 318 Alex Trevino	10	.05	.01
☐ 319 Craig Swan	10	.05	.01
☐ 320 Frank Taveras	10	.05	.01
☐ 321 Steve Henderson	10	.05	.01
☐ 322 Neil Allen	10	.05	.01
☐ 323 Mark Bomback	10	.05	.01
☐ 324 Mike Jorgensen	10	.05	.01
☐ 325 Joe Torre MG	12	.05	.02
☐ 326 Elliott Maddox	10	.05	.01
☐ 327 Pete Falcone	10	.05	.01
☐ 328 Ray Burris	10	.05	.01
☐ 329 Claudell Washington	10	.05	.01
☐ 330 Doug Flynn	10	.05	.01
☐ 331 Joel Youngblood	10	.05	.01
☐ 332 Bill Almon	10	.05	.01
☐ 333 Tom Hausman	10	.05	.01
☐ 334 Pat Zachry	10	.05	.01
☐ 335 Jeff Reardon	6.00	2.70	.75
☐ 336 Wally Backman	15	.07	.02
☐ 337 Dan Norman	10	.05	.01
☐ 338 Jerry Morales	10	.05	.01
☐ 339 Ed Farmer	10	.05	.01
☐ 340 Bob Molinaro	10	.05	.01
☐ 341 Todd Cruz	10	.05	.01
☐ 342A Britt Burns P1	50	.23	.06

(Small hand on front)
☐	342B Britt Burns P2	12	.05	.02

(No hand)
☐	343 Kevin Bell	10	.05	.01
☐	344 Tony LaRussa MG	12	.05	.02
☐	345 Steve Trout	10	.05	.01
☐	346 Harold Baines	2.50	1.15	.30
☐	347 Richard Wortham	10	.05	.01
☐	348 Wayne Nordhagen	10	.05	.01
☐	349 Mike Squires	10	.05	.01
☐	350 Lamar Johnson	10	.05	.01
☐	351 Rickey Henderson	8.00	3.60	1.00

(Most Stolen Bases AL)
☐	352 Francisco Barrios	10	.05	.01
☐	353 Thad Bosley	10	.05	.01
☐	354 Chet Lemon	10	.05	.01
☐	355 Bruce Kimm	10	.05	.01
☐	356 Richard Dotson	12	.05	.02
☐	357 Jim Morrison	10	.05	.01
☐	358 Mike Proly	10	.05	.01
☐	359 Greg Pryor	10	.05	.01
☐	360 Dave Parker	40	.18	.05
☐	361 Omar Moreno	10	.05	.01
☐	362A Kent Tekulve P1	15	.07	.02

(Back "1071 Waterbury"
and "1078 Pirates")
☐	362B Kent Tekulve P2	12	.05	.02

("1971 Waterbury" and
"1978 Pirates")
☐	363 Willie Stargell	1.00	.45	.13
☐	364 Phil Garner	12	.05	.02
☐	365 Ed Ott	10	.05	.01
☐	366 Don Robinson	10	.05	.01
☐	367 Chuck Tanner MG	10	.05	.01
☐	368 Jim Rooker	10	.05	.01
☐	369 Dale Berra	10	.05	.01
☐	370 Jim Bibby	10	.05	.01
☐	371 Steve Nicosia	10	.05	.01
☐	372 Mike Easler	10	.05	.01
☐	373 Bill Robinson	12	.05	.02
☐	374 Lee Lacy	10	.05	.01
☐	375 John Candelaria	12	.05	.02
☐	376 Manny Sanguillen	12	.05	.02
☐	377 Rick Rhoden	10	.05	.01
☐	378 Grant Jackson	10	.05	.01
☐	379 Tim Foli	10	.05	.01
☐	380 Rod Scurry	10	.05	.01
☐	381 Bill Madlock	12	.05	.02
☐	382A Kurt Bevacqua	25	.11	.03

P1 ERR
(P on cap backwards)
☐	382B Kurt Bevacqua P2	10	.05	.01

COR
☐	383 Bert Blyleven	40	.18	.05
☐	384 Eddie Solomon	10	.05	.01
☐	385 Enrique Romo	10	.05	.01
☐	386 John Milner	10	.05	.01

☐	387 Mike Hargrove	12	.05	.02
☐	388 Jorge Orta	10	.05	.01
☐	389 Toby Harrah	12	.05	.02
☐	390 Tom Veryzer	10	.05	.01
☐	391 Miguel Dilone	10	.05	.01
☐	392 Dan Spillner	10	.05	.01
☐	393 Jack Brohamer	10	.05	.01
☐	394 Wayne Garland	10	.05	.01
☐	395 Sid Monge	10	.05	.01
☐	396 Rick Waits	10	.05	.01
☐	397 Joe Charboneau	12	.05	.02
☐	398 Gary Alexander	10	.05	.01
☐	399 Jerry Dybzinski	10	.05	.01
☐	400 Mike Stanton	10	.05	.01
☐	401 Mike Paxton	10	.05	.01
☐	402 Gary Gray	10	.05	.01
☐	403 Rick Manning	10	.05	.01
☐	404 Bo Diaz	10	.05	.01
☐	405 Ron Hassey	10	.05	.01
☐	406 Ross Grimsley	10	.05	.01
☐	407 Victor Cruz	10	.05	.01
☐	408 Len Barker	10	.05	.01
☐	409 Bob Bailor	10	.05	.01
☐	410 Otto Velez	10	.05	.01
☐	411 Ernie Whitt	10	.05	.01
☐	412 Jim Clancy	10	.05	.01
☐	413 Barry Bonnell	10	.05	.01
☐	414 Dave Stieb	35	.16	.04
☐	415 Damaso Garcia	12	.05	.02
☐	416 John Mayberry	10	.05	.01
☐	417 Roy Howell	10	.05	.01
☐	418 Danny Ainge	2.00	.90	.25
☐	419A Jesse Jefferson P1	10	.05	.01

(Back says Pirates)
☐	419B Jesse Jefferson P2	10	.05	.01

(Back says Pirates)
☐	419C Jesse Jefferson P3	25	.11	.03

(Back says Blue Jays)
☐	420 Joey McLaughlin	10	.05	.01
☐	421 Lloyd Moseby	20	.09	.03
☐	422 Alvis Woods	10	.05	.01
☐	423 Garth Iorg	10	.05	.01
☐	424 Doug Ault	10	.05	.01
☐	425 Ken Schrom	10	.05	.01
☐	426 Mike Willis	10	.05	.01
☐	427 Steve Braun	10	.05	.01
☐	428 Bob Davis	10	.05	.01
☐	429 Jerry Garvin	10	.05	.01
☐	430 Alfredo Griffin	10	.05	.01
☐	431 Bob Mattick MG	10	.05	.01
☐	432 Vida Blue	12	.05	.02
☐	433 Jack Clark	25	.11	.03
☐	434 Willie McCovey	1.00	.45	.13
☐	435 Mike Ivie	10	.05	.01
☐	436A Darrel Evans P1 ERR	25	.11	.03

(Name on front
"Darrel")

☐ 436B Darrell Evans P2 COR ...15	.07	.02
(Name on front		
"Darrell")		
☐ 437 Terry Whitfield 10	.05	.01
☐ 438 Rennie Stennett 10	.05	.01
☐ 439 John Montefusco 10	.05	.01
☐ 440 Jim Wohlford 10	.05	.01
☐ 441 Bill North.......................10	.05	.01
☐ 442 Milt May 10	.05	.01
☐ 443 Max Venable 10	.05	.01
☐ 444 Ed Whitson 12	.05	.02
☐ 445 Al Holland 10	.05	.01
☐ 446 Randy Moffitt 10	.05	.01
☐ 447 Bob Knepper 10	.05	.01
☐ 448 Gary Lavelle 10	.05	.01
☐ 449 Greg Minton 10	.05	.01
☐ 450 Johnnie LeMaster 10	.05	.01
☐ 451 Larry Herndon 10	.05	.01
☐ 452 Rich Murray 10	.05	.01
☐ 453 Joe Pettini 10	.05	.01
☐ 454 Allen Ripley 10	.05	.01
☐ 455 Dennis Littlejohn............10	.05	.01
☐ 456 Tom Griffin 10	.05	.01
☐ 457 Alan Hargesheimer 10	.05	.01
☐ 458 Joe Strain 10	.05	.01
☐ 459 Steve Kemp 10	.05	.01
☐ 460 Sparky Anderson MG 12	.05	.02
☐ 461 Alan Trammell.................90	.40	.11
☐ 462 Mark Fidrych 12	.05	.02
☐ 463 Lou Whitaker..................90	.40	.11
☐ 464 Dave Rozema 10	.05	.01
☐ 465 Milt Wilcox....................10	.05	.01
☐ 466 Champ Summers 10	.05	.01
☐ 467 Lance Parrish 25	.11	.03
☐ 468 Dan Petry 12	.05	.02
☐ 469 Pat Underwood 10	.05	.01
☐ 470 Rick Peters 10	.05	.01
☐ 471 Al Cowens 10	.05	.01
☐ 472 John Wockenfuss............10	.05	.01
☐ 473 Tom Brookens 10	.05	.01
☐ 474 Richie Hebner 10	.05	.01
☐ 475 Jack Morris..................2.00	.90	.25
☐ 476 Jim Lentine 10	.05	.01
☐ 477 Bruce Robbins 10	.05	.01
☐ 478 Mark Wagner 10	.05	.01
☐ 479 Tim Corcoran 10	.05	.01
☐ 480A Stan Papi P1................15	.07	.02
(Front as Pitcher)		
☐ 480B Stan Papi P2................10	.05	.01
(Front as Shortstop)		
☐ 481 Kirk Gibson 2.00	.90	.25
☐ 482 Dan Schatzeder 10	.05	.01
☐ 483A Amos Otis P1...............15	.07	.02
(See card 32)		
☐ 483B Amos Otis P2...............15	.07	.02
(See card 32)		
☐ 484 Dave Winfield...............3.00	1.35	.40

☐ 485 Rollie Fingers..............1.00	.45	.13
☐ 486 Gene Richards 10	.05	.01
☐ 487 Randy Jones 10	.05	.01
☐ 488 Ozzie Smith 3.00	1.35	.40
☐ 489 Gene Tenace 10	.05	.01
☐ 490 Bill Fahey 10	.05	.01
☐ 491 John Curtis 10	.05	.01
☐ 492 Dave Cash 10	.05	.01
☐ 493A Tim Flannery P1...........15	.07	.02
(Batting right)		
☐ 493B Tim Flannery P2...........10	.05	.01
(Batting left)		
☐ 494 Jerry Mumphrey 10	.05	.01
☐ 495 Bob Shirley 10	.05	.01
☐ 496 Steve Mura 10	.05	.01
☐ 497 Eric Rasmussen 10	.05	.01
☐ 498 Broderick Perkins 10	.05	.01
☐ 499 Barry Evans 10	.05	.01
☐ 500 Chuck Baker 10	.05	.01
☐ 501 Luis Salazar 20	.09	.03
☐ 502 Gary Lucas 10	.05	.01
☐ 503 Mike Armstrong 10	.05	.01
☐ 504 Jerry Turner 10	.05	.01
☐ 505 Dennis Kinney 10	.05	.01
☐ 506 Willie Montanez UER 10	.05	.01
(Misspelled Willy		
on card front)		
☐ 507 Gorman Thomas 12	.05	.02
☐ 508 Ben Oglivie 12	.05	.02
☐ 509 Larry Hisle 10	.05	.01
☐ 510 Sal Bando 12	.05	.02
☐ 511 Robin Yount 4.00	1.80	.50
☐ 512 Mike Caldwell 10	.05	.01
☐ 513 Sixto Lezcano 10	.05	.01
☐ 514A Bill Travers P1 ERR 15	.07	.02
("Jerry Augustine"		
with Augustine back)		
☐ 514B Bill Travers P2 COR......10	.05	.01
☐ 515 Paul Molitor 1.25	.55	.16
☐ 516 Moose Haas 10	.05	.01
☐ 517 Bill Castro 10	.05	.01
☐ 518 Jim Slaton 10	.05	.01
☐ 519 Lary Sorensen 10	.05	.01
☐ 520 Bob McClure 10	.05	.01
☐ 521 Charlie Moore 10	.05	.01
☐ 522 Jim Gantner 12	.05	.02
☐ 523 Reggie Cleveland 10	.05	.01
☐ 524 Don Money 10	.05	.01
☐ 525 Bill Travers 10	.05	.01
☐ 526 Buck Martinez 10	.05	.01
☐ 527 Dick Davis 10	.05	.01
☐ 528 Ted Simmons 20	.09	.03
☐ 529 Garry Templeton 12	.05	.02
☐ 530 Ken Reitz 10	.05	.01
☐ 531 Tony Scott 10	.05	.01
☐ 532 Ken Oberkfell 10	.05	.01
☐ 533 Bob Sykes 10	.05	.01

☐ 534	Keith Smith	.10	.05	.01
☐ 535	John Littlefield	.10	.05	.01
☐ 536	Jim Kaat	.20	.09	.03
☐ 537	Bob Forsch	.10	.05	.01
☐ 538	Mike Phillips	.10	.05	.01
☐ 539	Terry Landrum	.10	.05	.01
☐ 540	Leon Durham	.12	.05	.02
☐ 541	Terry Kennedy	.12	.05	.02
☐ 542	George Hendrick	.12	.05	.02
☐ 543	Dane Iorg	.10	.05	.01
☐ 544	Mark Littell	.10	.05	.01
☐ 545	Keith Hernandez	.30	.14	.04
☐ 546	Silvio Martinez	.10	.05	.01
☐ 547A	Don Hood P1 ERR	.15	.07	.02

("Pete Vuckovich"
with Vuckovich back)

☐ 547B	Don Hood P2 COR	.10	.05	.01
☐ 548	Bobby Bonds	.12	.05	.02
☐ 549	Mike Ramsey	.10	.05	.01
☐ 550	Tom Herr	.12	.05	.02
☐ 551	Roy Smalley	.10	.05	.01
☐ 552	Jerry Koosman	.12	.05	.02
☐ 553	Ken Landreaux	.10	.05	.01
☐ 554	John Castino	.10	.05	.01
☐ 555	Doug Corbett	.10	.05	.01
☐ 556	Bombo Rivera	.10	.05	.01
☐ 557	Ron Jackson	.10	.05	.01
☐ 558	Butch Wynegar	.10	.05	.01
☐ 559	Hosken Powell	.10	.05	.01
☐ 560	Pete Redfern	.10	.05	.01
☐ 561	Roger Erickson	.10	.05	.01
☐ 562	Glenn Adams	.10	.05	.01
☐ 563	Rick Sofield	.10	.05	.01
☐ 564	Geoff Zahn	.10	.05	.01
☐ 565	Pete Mackanin	.10	.05	.01
☐ 566	Mike Cubbage	.10	.05	.01
☐ 567	Darrell Jackson	.10	.05	.01
☐ 568	Dave Edwards	.10	.05	.01
☐ 569	Rob Wilfong	.10	.05	.01
☐ 570	Sal Butera	.10	.05	.01
☐ 571	Jose Morales	.10	.05	.01
☐ 572	Rick Langford	.10	.05	.01
☐ 573	Mike Norris	.10	.05	.01
☐ 574	Rickey Henderson	13.00	5.75	1.65
☐ 575	Tony Armas	.10	.05	.01
☐ 576	Dave Revering	.10	.05	.01
☐ 577	Jeff Newman	.10	.05	.01
☐ 578	Bob Lacey	.10	.05	.01
☐ 579	Brian Kingman	.10	.05	.01
☐ 580	Mitchell Page	.10	.05	.01
☐ 581	Billy Martin MG	.25	.11	.03
☐ 582	Rob Picciolo	.10	.05	.01
☐ 583	Mike Heath	.10	.05	.01
☐ 584	Mickey Klutts	.10	.05	.01
☐ 585	Orlando Gonzalez	.10	.05	.01
☐ 586	Mike Davis	.12	.05	.02
☐ 587	Wayne Gross	.10	.05	.01

☐ 588	Matt Keough	.10	.05	.01
☐ 589	Steve McCatty	.10	.05	.01
☐ 590	Dwayne Murphy	.10	.05	.01
☐ 591	Mario Guerrero	.10	.05	.01
☐ 592	Dave McKay	.10	.05	.01
☐ 593	Jim Essian	.10	.05	.01
☐ 594	Dave Heaverlo	.10	.05	.01
☐ 595	Maury Wills MG	.12	.05	.02
☐ 596	Juan Beniquez	.10	.05	.01
☐ 597	Rodney Craig	.10	.05	.01
☐ 598	Jim Anderson	.10	.05	.01
☐ 599	Floyd Bannister	.10	.05	.01
☐ 600	Bruce Bochte	.10	.05	.01
☐ 601	Julio Cruz	.10	.05	.01
☐ 602	Ted Cox	.10	.05	.01
☐ 603	Dan Meyer	.10	.05	.01
☐ 604	Larry Cox	.10	.05	.01
☐ 605	Bill Stein	.10	.05	.01
☐ 606	Steve Garvey	.75	.35	.09

(Most Hits NL)

☐ 607	Dave Roberts	.10	.05	.01
☐ 608	Leon Roberts	.10	.05	.01
☐ 609	Reggie Walton	.10	.05	.01
☐ 610	Dave Edler	.10	.05	.01
☐ 611	Larry Milbourne	.10	.05	.01
☐ 612	Kim Allen	.10	.05	.01
☐ 613	Mario Mendoza	.10	.05	.01
☐ 614	Tom Paciorek	.12	.05	.02
☐ 615	Glenn Abbott	.10	.05	.01
☐ 616	Joe Simpson	.10	.05	.01
☐ 617	Mickey Rivers	.12	.05	.02
☐ 618	Jim Kern	.10	.05	.01
☐ 619	Jim Sundberg	.12	.05	.02
☐ 620	Richie Zisk	.10	.05	.01
☐ 621	Jon Matlack	.10	.05	.01
☐ 622	Ferguson Jenkins	.60	.25	.08
☐ 623	Pat Corrales MG	.10	.05	.01
☐ 624	Ed Figueroa	.10	.05	.01
☐ 625	Buddy Bell	.12	.05	.02
☐ 626	Al Oliver	.12	.05	.02
☐ 627	Doc Medich	.10	.05	.01
☐ 628	Bump Wills	.10	.05	.01
☐ 629	Rusty Staub	.12	.05	.02
☐ 630	Pat Putnam	.10	.05	.01
☐ 631	John Grubb	.10	.05	.01
☐ 632	Danny Darwin	.10	.05	.01
☐ 633	Ken Clay	.10	.05	.01
☐ 634	Jim Norris	.10	.05	.01
☐ 635	John Butcher	.10	.05	.01
☐ 636	Dave Roberts	.10	.05	.01
☐ 637	Billy Sample	.10	.05	.01
☐ 638	Carl Yastrzemski	2.00	.90	.25
☐ 639	Cecil Cooper	.12	.05	.02
☐ 640A	Mike Schmidt P1	3.00	1.35	.40

(Portrait;
"Third Base";
number on back 5)

☐ 640B Mike Schmidt P2 ....3.00   1.35   .40
    ("1980 Home Run King";
    640 on back)
☐ 641A CL: Phils/Royals P1 15   .02   .00
    41 is Hal McRae
☐ 641B CL: Phils/Royals P2 15   .02   .00
    (41 is Hal McRae,
    Double Threat)
☐ 642 CL: Astros/Yankees......15   .02   .00
☐ 643 CL: Expos/Dodgers 15   .02   .00
☐ 644A CL: Reds/Orioles P1 15   .02   .00
    (202 is George Foster;
    Joe Nolan pitcher,
    should be catcher)
☐ 644B CL: Reds/Orioles P2 15   .02   .00
    (202 is Foster Slugger;
    Joe Nolan pitcher,
    should be catcher)
☐ 645A Rose/Bowa/Schmidt ..2.50   1.15   .30
    Triple Threat P1
    (No number on back)
☐ 645B Rose/Bowa/Schmidt ..1.75   .80   .22
    Triple Threat P2
    (Back numbered 645)
☐ 646 CL: Braves/Red Sox 15   .02   .00
☐ 647 CL: Cubs/Angels 15   .02   .00
☐ 648 CL: Mets/White Sox 15   .02   .00
☐ 649 CL: Indians/Pirates 15   .02   .00
☐ 650A Reggie Jackson ....2.50   1.15   .30
    Mr. Baseball P1
    (Number on back 79)
☐ 650B Reggie Jackson ....2.50   1.15   .30
    Mr. Baseball P2
    (Number on back 650)
☐ 651 CL: Giants/Blue Jays 15   .02   .00
☐ 652A CL: Tigers/Padres P1 ...15   .02   .00
    (483 is listed)
☐ 652B CL: Tigers/Padres P2 ...15   .02   .00
    (483 is deleted)
☐ 653A Willie Wilson P1 15   .07   .02
    Most Hits Most Runs
    (Number on back 29)
☐ 653B Willie Wilson P2 15   .07   .02
    Most Hits Most Runs
    (Number on back 653)
☐ 654A CL:Brewers/Cards P1....15   .02   .00
    (514 Jerry Augustine;
    547 Pete Vuckovich)
☐ 654B CL:Brewers/Cards P2....15   .02   .00
    (514 Billy Travers;
    547 Don Hood)
☐ 655A George Brett P1 ....3.00   1.35   .40
    .390 Average
    (Number on back 28)
☐ 655B George Brett P2 ....3.00   1.35   .40
    .390 Average
    (Number on back 655)

☐ 656 CL: Twins/Oakland A's 15   .02   .00
☐ 657A Tug McGraw P1 12   .05   .02
    Game Saver
    (Number on back 7)
☐ 657B Tug McGraw P2 12   .05   .02
    Game Saver
    (Number on back 657)
☐ 658 CL: Rangers/Mariners.....15   .02   .00
☐ 659A Checklist P1 15   .02   .00
    of Special Cards
    (Last lines on front,
    Wilson Most Hits)
☐ 659B Checklist P2 15   .02   .00
    of Special Cards
    (Last lines on front,
    Otis Series Starter)
☐ 660A Steve Carlton P1 ....2.00   .90   .25
    Golden Arm
    (Back "1066 Cardinals";
    Number on back 6)
☐ 660B Steve Carlton P2 ....2.00   .90   .25
    Golden Arm
    (Number on back 660;
    Back "1066 Cardinals")
☐ 660C Steve Carlton P3 ....2.00   .90   .25
    Golden Arm
    ("1966 Cardinals")

1982 Fleer

*The cards in this 660-card set measure
2 1/2" by 3 1/2". The 1982 Fleer set is
again ordered by teams; in fact, the players within each team are listed in alphabetical order. The teams are ordered (by 1981
standings) as follows: Los Angeles (1-29),
New York Yankees (30-56), Cincinnati (57-
84), Oakland (85-109), St. Louis (110-132),*

Milwaukee (133-156), Baltimore (157-182), Montreal (183-211), Houston (212-237), Philadelphia (238-262), Detroit (263-286), Boston (287-312), Texas (313-334), Chicago White Sox (335-358), Cleveland (359-382), San Francisco (383-403), Kansas City (404-427), Atlanta (428-449), California (450-474), Pittsburgh (475-501), Seattle (502-519), New York Mets (520-544), Minnesota (545-565), San Diego (566-585), Chicago Cubs (586-607), and Toronto (608-627). Cards numbered 628 through 646 are special cards highlighting some of the stars and leaders of the 1981 season. The last 14 cards in the set (647-660) are checklist cards. The backs feature player statistics and a full-color team logo in the upper right-hand corner of each card. The complete set price below does not include any of the more valuable variation cards listed. The key Rookie Cards in this set are George Bell, Cal Ripken Jr., Steve Sax, Lee Smith, and Dave Stewart.

	NRMT-MT	EXC	G-VG
COMPLETE SET (660)	100.00	45.00	12.50
COMMON PLAYER (1-660)	.10	.05	.01

☐ 1 Dusty Baker	12	.05	.02
☐ 2 Robert Castillo	10	.05	.01
☐ 3 Ron Cey	12	.05	.02
☐ 4 Terry Forster	10	.05	.01
☐ 5 Steve Garvey	60	.25	.08
☐ 6 Dave Goltz	10	.05	.01
☐ 7 Pedro Guerrero	30	.14	.04
☐ 8 Burt Hooton	10	.05	.01
☐ 9 Steve Howe	10	.05	.01
☐ 10 Jay Johnstone	12	.05	.02
☐ 11 Ken Landreaux	10	.05	.01
☐ 12 Dave Lopes	12	.05	.02
☐ 13 Mike A. Marshall OF	20	.09	.03
☐ 14 Bobby Mitchell	10	.05	.01
☐ 15 Rick Monday	10	.05	.01
☐ 16 Tom Niedenfuer	10	.05	.01
☐ 17 Ted Power	15	.07	.02
☐ 18 Jerry Reuss UER	10	.05	.01
("Home:" omitted)			
☐ 19 Ron Roenicke	10	.05	.01
☐ 20 Bill Russell	12	.05	.02
☐ 21 Steve Sax	3.00	1.35	.40
☐ 22 Mike Scioscia	25	.11	.03
☐ 23 Reggie Smith	12	.05	.02
☐ 24 Dave Stewart	3.00	1.35	.40
☐ 25 Rick Sutcliffe	30	.14	.04
☐ 26 Derrel Thomas	10	.05	.01
☐ 27 Fernando Valenzuela	25	.11	.03
☐ 28 Bob Welch	30	.14	.04

☐ 29 Steve Yeager	10	.05	.01
☐ 30 Bobby Brown	10	.05	.01
☐ 31 Rick Cerone	10	.05	.01
☐ 32 Ron Davis	10	.05	.01
☐ 33 Bucky Dent	12	.05	.02
☐ 34 Barry Foote	10	.05	.01
☐ 35 George Frazier	10	.05	.01
☐ 36 Oscar Gamble	10	.05	.01
☐ 37 Rich Gossage	20	.09	.03
☐ 38 Ron Guidry	25	.11	.03
☐ 39 Reggie Jackson	2.00	.90	.25
☐ 40 Tommy John	20	.09	.03
☐ 41 Rudy May	10	.05	.01
☐ 42 Larry Milbourne	10	.05	.01
☐ 43 Jerry Mumphrey	10	.05	.01
☐ 44 Bobby Murcer	12	.05	.02
☐ 45 Gene Nelson	10	.05	.01
☐ 46 Graig Nettles	12	.05	.02
☐ 47 Johnny Oates	10	.05	.01
☐ 48 Lou Piniella	12	.05	.02
☐ 49 Willie Randolph	12	.05	.02
☐ 50 Rick Reuschel	12	.05	.02
☐ 51 Dave Revering	10	.05	.01
☐ 52 Dave Righetti	50	.23	.06
☐ 53 Aurelio Rodriguez	10	.05	.01
☐ 54 Bob Watson	12	.05	.02
☐ 55 Dennis Werth	10	.05	.01
☐ 56 Dave Winfield	2.50	1.15	.30
☐ 57 Johnny Bench	1.50	.65	.19
☐ 58 Bruce Berenyi	10	.05	.01
☐ 59 Larry Biittner	10	.05	.01
☐ 60 Scott Brown	10	.05	.01
☐ 61 Dave Collins	10	.05	.01
☐ 62 Geoff Combe	10	.05	.01
☐ 63 Dave Concepcion	12	.05	.02
☐ 64 Dan Driessen	10	.05	.01
☐ 65 Joe Edelen	10	.05	.01
☐ 66 George Foster	12	.05	.02
☐ 67 Ken Griffey	25	.11	.03
☐ 68 Paul Householder	10	.05	.01
☐ 69 Tom Hume	10	.05	.01
☐ 70 Junior Kennedy	10	.05	.01
☐ 71 Ray Knight	12	.05	.02
☐ 72 Mike LaCoss	10	.05	.01
☐ 73 Rafael Landestoy	10	.05	.01
☐ 74 Charlie Leibrandt	10	.05	.01
☐ 75 Sam Mejias	10	.05	.01
☐ 76 Paul Moskau	10	.05	.01
☐ 77 Joe Nolan	10	.05	.01
☐ 78 Mike O'Berry	10	.05	.01
☐ 79 Ron Oester	10	.05	.01
☐ 80 Frank Pastore	10	.05	.01
☐ 81 Joe Price	10	.05	.01
☐ 82 Tom Seaver	1.50	.65	.19
☐ 83 Mario Soto	10	.05	.01
☐ 84 Mike Vail	10	.05	.01
☐ 85 Tony Armas	10	.05	.01

☐ 86	Shooty Babitt	10	.05	.01
☐ 87	Dave Beard	10	.05	.01
☐ 88	Rick Bosetti	10	.05	.01
☐ 89	Keith Drumwright	10	.05	.01
☐ 90	Wayne Gross	10	.05	.01
☐ 91	Mike Heath	10	.05	.01
☐ 92	Rickey Henderson	4.50	2.00	.55
☐ 93	Cliff Johnson	10	.05	.01
☐ 94	Jeff Jones	10	.05	.01
☐ 95	Matt Keough	10	.05	.01
☐ 96	Brian Kingman	10	.05	.01
☐ 97	Mickey Klutts	10	.05	.01
☐ 98	Rick Langford	10	.05	.01
☐ 99	Steve McCatty	10	.05	.01
☐ 100	Dave McKay	10	.05	.01
☐ 101	Dwayne Murphy	10	.05	.01
☐ 102	Jeff Newman	10	.05	.01
☐ 103	Mike Norris	10	.05	.01
☐ 104	Bob Owchinko	10	.05	.01
☐ 105	Mitchell Page	10	.05	.01
☐ 106	Rob Picciolo	10	.05	.01
☐ 107	Jim Spencer	10	.05	.01
☐ 108	Fred Stanley	10	.05	.01
☐ 109	Tom Underwood	10	.05	.01
☐ 110	Joaquin Andujar	12	.05	.02
☐ 111	Steve Braun	10	.05	.01
☐ 112	Bob Forsch	10	.05	.01
☐ 113	George Hendrick	12	.05	.02
☐ 114	Keith Hernandez	25	.11	.03
☐ 115	Tom Herr	12	.05	.02
☐ 116	Dane Iorg	10	.05	.01
☐ 117	Jim Kaat	15	.07	.02
☐ 118	Tito Landrum	10	.05	.01
☐ 119	Sixto Lezcano	10	.05	.01
☐ 120	Mark Littell	10	.05	.01
☐ 121	John Martin	10	.05	.01
☐ 122	Silvio Martinez	10	.05	.01
☐ 123	Ken Oberkfell	10	.05	.01
☐ 124	Darrell Porter	10	.05	.01
☐ 125	Mike Ramsey	10	.05	.01
☐ 126	Orlando Sanchez	10	.05	.01
☐ 127	Bob Shirley	10	.05	.01
☐ 128	Lary Sorensen	10	.05	.01
☐ 129	Bruce Sutter	20	.09	.03
☐ 130	Bob Sykes	10	.05	.01
☐ 131	Garry Templeton	12	.05	.02
☐ 132	Gene Tenace	10	.05	.01
☐ 133	Jerry Augustine	10	.05	.01
☐ 134	Sal Bando	12	.05	.02
☐ 135	Mark Brouhard	10	.05	.01
☐ 136	Mike Caldwell	10	.05	.01
☐ 137	Reggie Cleveland	10	.05	.01
☐ 138	Cecil Cooper	12	.05	.02
☐ 139	Jamie Easterly	10	.05	.01
☐ 140	Marshall Edwards	10	.05	.01
☐ 141	Rollie Fingers	75	.35	.09
☐ 142	Jim Gantner	12	.05	.02
☐ 143	Moose Haas	10	.05	.01
☐ 144	Larry Hisle	10	.05	.01
☐ 145	Roy Howell	10	.05	.01
☐ 146	Rickey Keeton	10	.05	.01
☐ 147	Randy Lerch	10	.05	.01
☐ 148	Paul Molitor	1.00	.45	.13
☐ 149	Don Money	10	.05	.01
☐ 150	Charlie Moore	10	.05	.01
☐ 151	Ben Oglivie	10	.05	.01
☐ 152	Ted Simmons	12	.05	.02
☐ 153	Jim Slaton	10	.05	.01
☐ 154	Gorman Thomas	10	.05	.01
☐ 155	Robin Yount	3.00	1.35	.40
☐ 156	Pete Vuckovich	12	.05	.02
	(Should precede Yount			
	in the team order)			
☐ 157	Benny Ayala	10	.05	.01
☐ 158	Mark Belanger	12	.05	.02
☐ 159	Al Bumbry	10	.05	.01
☐ 160	Terry Crowley	10	.05	.01
☐ 161	Rich Dauer	10	.05	.01
☐ 162	Doug DeCinces	12	.05	.02
☐ 163	Rick Dempsey	12	.05	.02
☐ 164	Jim Dwyer	10	.05	.01
☐ 165	Mike Flanagan	12	.05	.02
☐ 166	Dave Ford	10	.05	.01
☐ 167	Dan Graham	10	.05	.01
☐ 168	Wayne Krenchicki	10	.05	.01
☐ 169	John Lowenstein	10	.05	.01
☐ 170	Dennis Martinez	25	.11	.03
☐ 171	Tippy Martinez	10	.05	.01
☐ 172	Scott McGregor	10	.05	.01
☐ 173	Jose Morales	10	.05	.01
☐ 174	Eddie Murray	2.00	.90	.25
☐ 175	Jim Palmer	1.25	.55	.16
☐ 176	Cal Ripken	50.00	23.00	6.25
☐ 177	Gary Roenicke	10	.05	.01
☐ 178	Lenn Sakata	10	.05	.01
☐ 179	Ken Singleton	12	.05	.02
☐ 180	Sammy Stewart	10	.05	.01
☐ 181	Tim Stoddard	10	.05	.01
☐ 182	Steve Stone	12	.05	.02
☐ 183	Stan Bahnsen	10	.05	.01
☐ 184	Ray Burris	10	.05	.01
☐ 185	Gary Carter	90	.40	.11
☐ 186	Warren Cromartie	10	.05	.01
☐ 187	Andre Dawson	2.00	.90	.25
☐ 188	Terry Francona	10	.05	.01
☐ 189	Woodie Fryman	10	.05	.01
☐ 190	Bill Gullickson	25	.11	.03
☐ 191	Grant Jackson	10	.05	.01
☐ 192	Wallace Johnson	10	.05	.01
☐ 193	Charlie Lea	10	.05	.01
☐ 194	Bill Lee	10	.05	.01
☐ 195	Jerry Manuel	10	.05	.01
☐ 196	Brad Mills	10	.05	.01
☐ 197	John Milner	10	.05	.01

☐ 198 Rowland Office	10	.05	.01
☐ 199 David Palmer	10	.05	.01
☐ 200 Larry Parrish	10	.05	.01
☐ 201 Mike Phillips	10	.05	.01
☐ 202 Tim Raines	1.75	.80	.22
☐ 203 Bobby Ramos	10	.05	.01
☐ 204 Jeff Reardon	2.00	.90	.25
☐ 205 Steve Rogers	10	.05	.01
☐ 206 Scott Sanderson	12	.05	.02
☐ 207 Rodney Scott UER	20	.09	.03
(Photo actually Tim Raines)			
☐ 208 Elias Sosa	10	.05	.01
☐ 209 Chris Speier	10	.05	.01
☐ 210 Tim Wallach	1.00	.45	.13
☐ 211 Jerry White	10	.05	.01
☐ 212 Alan Ashby	10	.05	.01
☐ 213 Cesar Cedeno	12	.05	.02
☐ 214 Jose Cruz	12	.05	.02
☐ 215 Kiko Garcia	10	.05	.01
☐ 216 Phil Garner	12	.05	.02
☐ 217 Danny Heep	10	.05	.01
☐ 218 Art Howe	10	.05	.01
☐ 219 Bob Knepper	10	.05	.01
☐ 220 Frank LaCorte	10	.05	.01
☐ 221 Joe Niekro	12	.05	.02
☐ 222 Joe Pittman	10	.05	.01
☐ 223 Terry Puhl	10	.05	.01
☐ 224 Luis Pujols	10	.05	.01
☐ 225 Craig Reynolds	10	.05	.01
☐ 226 J.R. Richard	12	.05	.02
☐ 227 Dave Roberts	10	.05	.01
☐ 228 Vern Ruhle	10	.05	.01
☐ 229 Nolan Ryan	8.00	3.60	1.00
☐ 230 Joe Sambito	10	.05	.01
☐ 231 Tony Scott	10	.05	.01
☐ 232 Dave Smith	10	.05	.01
☐ 233 Harry Spilman	10	.05	.01
☐ 234 Don Sutton	40	.18	.05
☐ 235 Dickie Thon	10	.05	.01
☐ 236 Denny Walling	10	.05	.01
☐ 237 Gary Woods	10	.05	.01
☐ 238 Luis Aguayo	10	.05	.01
☐ 239 Ramon Aviles	10	.05	.01
☐ 240 Bob Boone	12	.05	.02
☐ 241 Larry Bowa	12	.05	.02
☐ 242 Warren Brusstar	10	.05	.01
☐ 243 Steve Carlton	1.50	.65	.19
☐ 244 Larry Christenson	10	.05	.01
☐ 245 Dick Davis	10	.05	.01
☐ 246 Greg Gross	10	.05	.01
☐ 247 Sparky Lyle	12	.05	.02
☐ 248 Garry Maddox	10	.05	.01
☐ 249 Gary Matthews	12	.05	.02
☐ 250 Bake McBride	10	.05	.01
☐ 251 Tug McGraw	12	.05	.02
☐ 252 Keith Moreland	10	.05	.01
☐ 253 Dickie Noles	10	.05	.01
☐ 254 Mike Proly	10	.05	.01
☐ 255 Ron Reed	10	.05	.01
☐ 256 Pete Rose	1.50	.65	.19
☐ 257 Dick Ruthven	10	.05	.01
☐ 258 Mike Schmidt	2.50	1.15	.30
☐ 259 Lonnie Smith	12	.05	.02
☐ 260 Manny Trillo	10	.05	.01
☐ 261 Del Unser	10	.05	.01
☐ 262 George Vukovich	10	.05	.01
☐ 263 Tom Brookens	10	.05	.01
☐ 264 George Cappuzzello	10	.05	.01
☐ 265 Marty Castillo	10	.05	.01
☐ 266 Al Cowens	10	.05	.01
☐ 267 Kirk Gibson	50	.23	.06
☐ 268 Richie Hebner	10	.05	.01
☐ 269 Ron Jackson	10	.05	.01
☐ 270 Lynn Jones	10	.05	.01
☐ 271 Steve Kemp	10	.05	.01
☐ 272 Rick Leach	10	.05	.01
☐ 273 Aurelio Lopez	10	.05	.01
☐ 274 Jack Morris	1.50	.65	.19
☐ 275 Kevin Saucier	10	.05	.01
☐ 276 Lance Parrish	25	.11	.03
☐ 277 Rick Peters	10	.05	.01
☐ 278 Dan Petry	10	.05	.01
☐ 279 Dave Rozema	10	.05	.01
☐ 280 Stan Papi	10	.05	.01
☐ 281 Dan Schatzeder	10	.05	.01
☐ 282 Champ Summers	10	.05	.01
☐ 283 Alan Trammell	50	.23	.06
☐ 284 Lou Whitaker	50	.23	.06
☐ 285 Milt Wilcox	10	.05	.01
☐ 286 John Wockenfuss	10	.05	.01
☐ 287 Gary Allenson	10	.05	.01
☐ 288 Tom Burgmeier	10	.05	.01
☐ 289 Bill Campbell	10	.05	.01
☐ 290 Mark Clear	10	.05	.01
☐ 291 Steve Crawford	10	.05	.01
☐ 292 Dennis Eckersley	1.50	.65	.19
☐ 293 Dwight Evans	25	.11	.03
☐ 294 Rich Gedman	15	.07	.02
☐ 295 Garry Hancock	10	.05	.01
☐ 296 Glenn Hoffman	10	.05	.01
☐ 297 Bruce Hurst	75	.35	.09
☐ 298 Carney Lansford	12	.05	.02
☐ 299 Rick Miller	10	.05	.01
☐ 300 Reid Nichols	10	.05	.01
☐ 301 Bob Ojeda	40	.18	.05
☐ 302 Tony Perez	35	.16	.04
☐ 303 Chuck Rainey	10	.05	.01
☐ 304 Jerry Remy	10	.05	.01
☐ 305 Jim Rice	25	.11	.03
☐ 306 Joe Rudi	10	.05	.01
☐ 307 Bob Stanley	10	.05	.01
☐ 308 Dave Stapleton	10	.05	.01
☐ 309 Frank Tanana	12	.05	.02

☐ 310	Mike Torrez	10	.05	.01
☐ 311	John Tudor	12	.05	.02
☐ 312	Carl Yastrzemski	1.50	.65	.19
☐ 313	Buddy Bell	12	.05	.02
☐ 314	Steve Comer	10	.05	.01
☐ 315	Danny Darwin	10	.05	.01
☐ 316	John Ellis	10	.05	.01
☐ 317	John Grubb	10	.05	.01
☐ 318	Rick Honeycutt	10	.05	.01
☐ 319	Charlie Hough	12	.05	.02
☐ 320	Ferguson Jenkins	40	.18	.05
☐ 321	John Henry Johnson	10	.05	.01
☐ 322	Jim Kern	10	.05	.01
☐ 323	Jon Matlack	10	.05	.01
☐ 324	Doc Medich	10	.05	.01
☐ 325	Mario Mendoza	10	.05	.01
☐ 326	Al Oliver	12	.05	.02
☐ 327	Pat Putnam	10	.05	.01
☐ 328	Mickey Rivers	10	.05	.01
☐ 329	Leon Roberts	10	.05	.01
☐ 330	Billy Sample	10	.05	.01
☐ 331	Bill Stein	10	.05	.01
☐ 332	Jim Sundberg	12	.05	.02
☐ 333	Mark Wagner	10	.05	.01
☐ 334	Bump Wills	10	.05	.01
☐ 335	Bill Almon	10	.05	.01
☐ 336	Harold Baines	60	.25	.08
☐ 337	Ross Baumgarten	10	.05	.01
☐ 338	Tony Bernazard	10	.05	.01
☐ 339	Britt Burns	10	.05	.01
☐ 340	Richard Dotson	10	.05	.01
☐ 341	Jim Essian	10	.05	.01
☐ 342	Ed Farmer	10	.05	.01
☐ 343	Carlton Fisk	1.50	.65	.19
☐ 344	Kevin Hickey	10	.05	.01
☐ 345	LaMarr Hoyt	10	.05	.01
☐ 346	Lamar Johnson	10	.05	.01
☐ 347	Jerry Koosman	12	.05	.02
☐ 348	Rusty Kuntz	10	.05	.01
☐ 349	Dennis Lamp	10	.05	.01
☐ 350	Ron LeFlore	12	.05	.02
☐ 351	Chet Lemon	10	.05	.01
☐ 352	Greg Luzinski	12	.05	.02
☐ 353	Bob Molinaro	10	.05	.01
☐ 354	Jim Morrison	10	.05	.01
☐ 355	Wayne Nordhagen	10	.05	.01
☐ 356	Greg Pryor	10	.05	.01
☐ 357	Mike Squires	10	.05	.01
☐ 358	Steve Trout	10	.05	.01
☐ 359	Alan Bannister	10	.05	.01
☐ 360	Len Barker	10	.05	.01
☐ 361	Bert Blyleven	35	.16	.04
☐ 362	Joe Charboneau	10	.05	.01
☐ 363	John Denny	10	.05	.01
☐ 364	Bo Diaz	10	.05	.01
☐ 365	Miguel Dilone	10	.05	.01
☐ 366	Jerry Dybzinski	10	.05	.01
☐ 367	Wayne Garland	10	.05	.01
☐ 368	Mike Hargrove	12	.05	.02
☐ 369	Toby Harrah	12	.05	.02
☐ 370	Ron Hassey	10	.05	.01
☐ 371	Von Hayes	30	.14	.04
☐ 372	Pat Kelly	10	.05	.01
☐ 373	Duane Kuiper	10	.05	.01
☐ 374	Rick Manning	10	.05	.01
☐ 375	Sid Monge	10	.05	.01
☐ 376	Jorge Orta	10	.05	.01
☐ 377	Dave Rosello	10	.05	.01
☐ 378	Dan Spillner	10	.05	.01
☐ 379	Mike Stanton	10	.05	.01
☐ 380	Andre Thornton	12	.05	.02
☐ 381	Tom Veryzer	10	.05	.01
☐ 382	Rick Waits	10	.05	.01
☐ 383	Doyle Alexander	10	.05	.01
☐ 384	Vida Blue	12	.05	.02
☐ 385	Fred Breining	10	.05	.01
☐ 386	Enos Cabell	10	.05	.01
☐ 387	Jack Clark	20	.09	.03
☐ 388	Darrell Evans	12	.05	.02
☐ 389	Tom Griffin	10	.05	.01
☐ 390	Larry Herndon	10	.05	.01
☐ 391	Al Holland	10	.05	.01
☐ 392	Gary Lavelle	10	.05	.01
☐ 393	Johnnie LeMaster	10	.05	.01
☐ 394	Jerry Martin	10	.05	.01
☐ 395	Milt May	10	.05	.01
☐ 396	Greg Minton	10	.05	.01
☐ 397	Joe Morgan	75	.35	.09
☐ 398	Joe Pettini	10	.05	.01
☐ 399	Allen Ripley	10	.05	.01
☐ 400	Billy Smith	10	.05	.01
☐ 401	Rennie Stennett	10	.05	.01
☐ 402	Ed Whitson	10	.05	.01
☐ 403	Jim Wohlford	10	.05	.01
☐ 404	Willie Aikens	10	.05	.01
☐ 405	George Brett	3.00	1.35	.40
☐ 406	Ken Brett	10	.05	.01
☐ 407	Dave Chalk	10	.05	.01
☐ 408	Rich Gale	10	.05	.01
☐ 409	Cesar Geronimo	10	.05	.01
☐ 410	Larry Gura	10	.05	.01
☐ 411	Clint Hurdle	10	.05	.01
☐ 412	Mike Jones	10	.05	.01
☐ 413	Dennis Leonard	10	.05	.01
☐ 414	Renie Martin	10	.05	.01
☐ 415	Lee May	10	.05	.01
☐ 416	Hal McRae	12	.05	.02
☐ 417	Darryl Motley	10	.05	.01
☐ 418	Rance Mulliniks	10	.05	.01
☐ 419	Amos Otis	12	.05	.02
☐ 420	Ken Phelps	10	.05	.01
☐ 421	Jamie Quirk	10	.05	.01
☐ 422	Dan Quisenberry	12	.05	.02
☐ 423	Paul Splittorff	10	.05	.01

☐ 424 U.L. Washington	.10	.05	.01
☐ 425 John Wathan	.10	.05	.01
☐ 426 Frank White	.12	.05	.02
☐ 427 Willie Wilson	.12	.05	.02
☐ 428 Brian Asselstine	.10	.05	.01
☐ 429 Bruce Benedict	.10	.05	.01
☐ 430 Tommy Boggs	.10	.05	.01
☐ 431 Larry Bradford	.10	.05	.01
☐ 432 Rick Camp	.10	.05	.01
☐ 433 Chris Chambliss	.12	.05	.02
☐ 434 Gene Garber	.10	.05	.01
☐ 435 Preston Hanna	.10	.05	.01
☐ 436 Bob Horner	.12	.05	.02
☐ 437 Glenn Hubbard	.10	.05	.01
☐ 438A Al Hrabosky ERR	20.00	9.00	2.50
(Height 5'1",			
All on reverse)			
☐ 438B Al Hrabosky ERR	.75	.35	.09
(Height 5'1")			
☐ 438C Al Hrabosky COR	.12	.05	.02
(Height 5'10")			
☐ 439 Rufino Linares	.10	.05	.01
☐ 440 Rick Mahler	.10	.05	.01
☐ 441 Ed Miller	.10	.05	.01
☐ 442 John Montefusco	.10	.05	.01
☐ 443 Dale Murphy	1.00	.45	.13
☐ 444 Phil Niekro	.40	.18	.05
☐ 445 Gaylord Perry	.40	.18	.05
☐ 446 Biff Pocoroba	.10	.05	.01
☐ 447 Rafael Ramirez	.10	.05	.01
☐ 448 Jerry Royster	.10	.05	.01
☐ 449 Claudell Washington	.10	.05	.01
☐ 450 Don Aase	.10	.05	.01
☐ 451 Don Baylor	.12	.05	.02
☐ 452 Juan Beniquez	.10	.05	.01
☐ 453 Rick Burleson	.10	.05	.01
☐ 454 Bert Campaneris	.12	.05	.02
☐ 455 Rod Carew	1.50	.65	.19
☐ 456 Bob Clark	.10	.05	.01
☐ 457 Brian Downing	.12	.05	.02
☐ 458 Dan Ford	.10	.05	.01
☐ 459 Ken Forsch	.10	.05	.01
☐ 460A Dave Frost (5 mm	.10	.05	.01
space before ERA)			
☐ 460B Dave Frost	.10	.05	.01
(1 mm space)			
☐ 461 Bobby Grich	.12	.05	.02
☐ 462 Larry Harlow	.10	.05	.01
☐ 463 John Harris	.10	.05	.01
☐ 464 Andy Hassler	.10	.05	.01
☐ 465 Butch Hobson	.12	.05	.02
☐ 466 Jesse Jefferson	.10	.05	.01
☐ 467 Bruce Kison	.10	.05	.01
☐ 468 Fred Lynn	.12	.05	.02
☐ 469 Angel Moreno	.10	.05	.01
☐ 470 Ed Ott	.10	.05	.01
☐ 471 Fred Patek	.10	.05	.01
☐ 472 Steve Renko	.10	.05	.01
☐ 473 Mike Witt	.15	.07	.02
☐ 474 Geoff Zahn	.10	.05	.01
☐ 475 Gary Alexander	.10	.05	.01
☐ 476 Dale Berra	.10	.05	.01
☐ 477 Kurt Bevacqua	.10	.05	.01
☐ 478 Jim Bibby	.10	.05	.01
☐ 479 John Candelaria	.10	.05	.01
☐ 480 Victor Cruz	.10	.05	.01
☐ 481 Mike Easler	.10	.05	.01
☐ 482 Tim Foli	.10	.05	.01
☐ 483 Lee Lacy	.10	.05	.01
☐ 484 Vance Law	.10	.05	.01
☐ 485 Bill Madlock	.12	.05	.02
☐ 486 Willie Montanez	.10	.05	.01
☐ 487 Omar Moreno	.10	.05	.01
☐ 488 Steve Nicosia	.10	.05	.01
☐ 489 Dave Parker	.35	.16	.04
☐ 490 Tony Pena	.20	.09	.03
☐ 491 Pascual Perez	.10	.05	.01
☐ 492 Johnny Ray	.15	.07	.02
☐ 493 Rick Rhoden	.10	.05	.01
☐ 494 Bill Robinson	.12	.05	.02
☐ 495 Don Robinson	.10	.05	.01
☐ 496 Enrique Romo	.10	.05	.01
☐ 497 Rod Scurry	.10	.05	.01
☐ 498 Eddie Solomon	.10	.05	.01
☐ 499 Willie Stargell	.75	.35	.09
☐ 500 Kent Tekulve	.12	.05	.02
☐ 501 Jason Thompson	.10	.05	.01
☐ 502 Glenn Abbott	.10	.05	.01
☐ 503 Jim Anderson	.10	.05	.01
☐ 504 Floyd Bannister	.10	.05	.01
☐ 505 Bruce Bochte	.10	.05	.01
☐ 506 Jeff Burroughs	.10	.05	.01
☐ 507 Bryan Clark	.10	.05	.01
☐ 508 Ken Clay	.10	.05	.01
☐ 509 Julio Cruz	.10	.05	.01
☐ 510 Dick Drago	.10	.05	.01
☐ 511 Gary Gray	.10	.05	.01
☐ 512 Dan Meyer	.10	.05	.01
☐ 513 Jerry Narron	.10	.05	.01
☐ 514 Tom Paciorek	.12	.05	.02
☐ 515 Casey Parsons	.10	.05	.01
☐ 516 Lenny Randle	.10	.05	.01
☐ 517 Shane Rawley	.10	.05	.01
☐ 518 Joe Simpson	.10	.05	.01
☐ 519 Richie Zisk	.10	.05	.01
☐ 520 Neil Allen	.10	.05	.01
☐ 521 Bob Bailor	.10	.05	.01
☐ 522 Hubie Brooks	.35	.16	.04
☐ 523 Mike Cubbage	.10	.05	.01
☐ 524 Pete Falcone	.10	.05	.01
☐ 525 Doug Flynn	.10	.05	.01
☐ 526 Tom Hausman	.10	.05	.01
☐ 527 Ron Hodges	.10	.05	.01
☐ 528 Randy Jones	.10	.05	.01

□	529	Mike Jorgensen	.10	.05	.01
□	530	Dave Kingman	.12	.05	.02
□	531	Ed Lynch	.10	.05	.01
□	532	Mike G. Marshall P.	.12	.05	.02
□	533	Lee Mazzilli	.10	.05	.01
□	534	Dyar Miller	.10	.05	.01
□	535	Mike Scott	.12	.05	.02
□	536	Rusty Staub	.12	.05	.02
□	537	John Stearns	.10	.05	.01
□	538	Craig Swan	.10	.05	.01
□	539	Frank Taveras	.10	.05	.01
□	540	Alex Trevino	.10	.05	.01
□	541	Ellis Valentine	.10	.05	.01
□	542	Mookie Wilson	.12	.05	.02
□	543	Joel Youngblood	.10	.05	.01
□	544	Pat Zachry	.10	.05	.01
□	545	Glenn Adams	.10	.05	.01
□	546	Fernando Arroyo	.10	.05	.01
□	547	John Verhoeven	.10	.05	.01
□	548	Sal Butera	.10	.05	.01
□	549	John Castino	.10	.05	.01
□	550	Don Cooper	.10	.05	.01
□	551	Doug Corbett	.10	.05	.01
□	552	Dave Engle	.10	.05	.01
□	553	Roger Erickson	.10	.05	.01
□	554	Danny Goodwin	.10	.05	.01
□	555A	Darrell Jackson	.75	.35	.09
		(Black cap)			
□	555B	Darrell Jackson	.12	.05	.02
		(Red cap with T)			
□	555C	Darrell Jackson	4.00	1.80	.50
		(Red cap, no emblem)			
□	556	Pete Mackanin	.10	.05	.01
□	557	Jack O'Connor	.10	.05	.01
□	558	Hosken Powell	.10	.05	.01
□	559	Pete Redfern	.10	.05	.01
□	560	Roy Smalley	.12	.05	.02
□	561	Chuck Baker UER	.10	.05	.01
		(Shortshop on front)			
□	562	Gary Ward	.10	.05	.01
□	563	Rob Wilfong	.10	.05	.01
□	564	Al Williams	.10	.05	.01
□	565	Butch Wynegar	.10	.05	.01
□	566	Randy Bass	.10	.05	.01
□	567	Juan Bonilla	.10	.05	.01
□	568	Danny Boone	.10	.05	.01
□	569	John Curtis	.10	.05	.01
□	570	Juan Eichelberger	.10	.05	.01
□	571	Barry Evans	.10	.05	.01
□	572	Tim Flannery	.10	.05	.01
□	573	Ruppert Jones	.10	.05	.01
□	574	Terry Kennedy	.10	.05	.01
□	575	Joe Lefebvre	.10	.05	.01
□	576A	John Littlefield	300.00	135.00	38.00
		ERR (Left handed; reverse negative)			
□	576B	John Littlefield COR	.12	.05	.02

		(Right handed)			
□	577	Gary Lucas	.10	.05	.01
□	578	Steve Mura	.10	.05	.01
□	579	Broderick Perkins	.10	.05	.01
□	580	Gene Richards	.10	.05	.01
□	581	Luis Salazar	.10	.05	.01
□	582	Ozzie Smith	2.00	.90	.25
□	583	John Urrea	.10	.05	.01
□	584	Chris Welsh	.10	.05	.01
□	585	Rick Wise	.10	.05	.01
□	586	Doug Bird	.10	.05	.01
□	587	Tim Blackwell	.10	.05	.01
□	588	Bobby Bonds	.12	.05	.02
□	589	Bill Buckner	.12	.05	.02
□	590	Bill Caudill	.10	.05	.01
□	591	Hector Cruz	.10	.05	.01
□	592	Jody Davis	.12	.05	.02
□	593	Ivan DeJesus	.10	.05	.01
□	594	Steve Dillard	.10	.05	.01
□	595	Leon Durham	.10	.05	.01
□	596	Rawly Eastwick	.10	.05	.01
□	597	Steve Henderson	.10	.05	.01
□	598	Mike Krukow	.10	.05	.01
□	599	Mike Lum	.10	.05	.01
□	600	Randy Martz	.10	.05	.01
□	601	Jerry Morales	.10	.05	.01
□	602	Ken Reitz	.10	.05	.01
□	603A	Lee Smith ERR	7.00	3.10	.85
		(Cubs logo reversed)			
□	603B	Lee Smith COR	7.00	3.10	.85
□	604	Dick Tidrow	.10	.05	.01
□	605	Jim Tracy	.10	.05	.01
□	606	Mike Tyson	.10	.05	.01
□	607	Ty Waller	.10	.05	.01
□	608	Danny Ainge	.75	.35	.09
□	609	Jorge Bell	6.00	2.70	.75
□	610	Mark Bomback	.10	.05	.01
□	611	Barry Bonnell	.10	.05	.01
□	612	Jim Clancy	.10	.05	.01
□	613	Damaso Garcia	.10	.05	.01
□	614	Jerry Garvin	.10	.05	.01
□	615	Alfredo Griffin	.10	.05	.01
□	616	Garth Iorg	.10	.05	.01
□	617	Luis Leal	.10	.05	.01
□	618	Ken Macha	.10	.05	.01
□	619	John Mayberry	.10	.05	.01
□	620	Joey McLaughlin	.10	.05	.01
□	621	Lloyd Moseby	.10	.05	.01
□	622	Dave Stieb	.20	.09	.03
□	623	Jackson Todd	.10	.05	.01
□	624	Willie Upshaw	.10	.05	.01
□	625	Otto Velez	.10	.05	.01
□	626	Ernie Whitt	.10	.05	.01
□	627	Alvis Woods	.10	.05	.01
□	628	All Star Game	.15	.07	.02
		Cleveland, Ohio			
□	629	All Star Infielders	.15	.07	.02

Frank White and
Bucky Dent
- ☐ 630 Big Red Machine............15 .07 .02
Dan Driessen
Dave Concepcion
George Foster
- ☐ 631 Bruce Sutter...................15 .07 .02
Top NL Relief Pitcher
- ☐ 632 "Steve and Carlton".......75 .35 .09
Steve Carlton and
Carlton Fisk
- ☐ 633 Carl Yastrzemski...........75 .35 .09
3000th Game
- ☐ 634 Dynamic Duo...............1.50 .65 .19
Johnny Bench and
Tom Seaver
- ☐ 635 West Meets East............15 .07 .02
Fernando Valenzuela
and Gary Carter
- ☐ 636A Fernando Valenzuela:....30 .14 .04
NL SO King ("he" NL)
- ☐ 636B Fernando Valenzuela:....15 .07 .02
NL SO King ("the" NL)
- ☐ 637 Mike Schmidt...............1.25 .55 .16
Home Run King
- ☐ 638 NL All Stars...................30 .14 .04
Gary Carter and
Dave Parker
- ☐ 639 Perfect Game UER ....15 .07 .02
Len Barker and
Bo Diaz
(Catcher actually
Ron Hassey)
- ☐ 640 Pete and Re-Pete ....1.50 .65 .19
Pete Rose and Son
- ☐ 641 Phillies Finest...............75 .35 .09
Lonnie Smith
Mike Schmidt
Steve Carlton
- ☐ 642 Red Sox Reunion ....15 .07 .02
Fred Lynn and
Dwight Evans
- ☐ 643 Rickey Henderson.......2.50 1.15 .30
Most Hits and Runs
- ☐ 644 Rollie Fingers.................40 .18 .05
Most Saves AL
- ☐ 645 Tom Seaver...................75 .35 .09
Most 1981 Wins
- ☐ 646A Yankee Powerhouse ..1.75 .80 .22
Reggie Jackson and
Dave Winfield
(Comma on back
after outfielder)
- ☐ 646B Yankee Powerhouse ..1.75 .80 .22
Reggie Jackson and
Dave Winfield
(No comma)

- ☐ 647 CL: Yankees/Dodgers......15 .02 .00
- ☐ 648 CL: A's/Reds.................15 .02 .00
- ☐ 649 CL: Cards/Brewers.........15 .02 .00
- ☐ 650 CL: Expos/Orioles ....15 .02 .00
- ☐ 651 CL: Astros/Phillies..........15 .02 .00
- ☐ 652 CL: Tigers/Red Sox.........15 .02 .00
- ☐ 653 CL: Rangers/White Sox...15 .02 .00
- ☐ 654 CL: Giants/Indians..........15 .02 .00
- ☐ 655 CL: Royals/Braves..........15 .02 .00
- ☐ 656 CL: Angels/Pirates..........15 .02 .00
- ☐ 657 CL: Mariners/Mets..........15 .02 .00
- ☐ 658 CL: Padres/Twins............15 .02 .00
- ☐ 659 CL: Blue Jays/Cubs.........15 .02 .00
- ☐ 660 Specials Checklist............15 .02 .00

1983 Fleer

The cards in this 660-card set measure 2 1/2" by 3 1/2". In 1983, for the third straight year, Fleer has produced a base-ball series numbering 660 cards. Of these, 1-628 are player cards, 629-646 are spe-cial cards, and 647-660 are checklist cards. The player cards are again ordered alphabetically within team. The team order relates back to each team's on-field perfor-mance during the previous year, i.e., World Champion Cardinals (1-25), AL Champion Brewers (26-51), Baltimore (52-75), California (76-103), Kansas City (104-128), Atlanta (129-152), Philadelphia (153-176), Boston (177-200), Los Angeles (201-227), Chicago White Sox (228-251), San Francisco (252-276), Montreal (277-301), Pittsburgh (302-326), Detroit (327-351), San Diego (352-375), New York Yankees (376-399), Cleveland (400-423), Toronto (424-444), Houston (445-469), Seattle

(470-489), Chicago Cubs (490-512), Oakland (513-535), New York Mets (536-561), Texas (562-583), Cincinnati (584-606), and Minnesota (607-628). The front of each card has a colorful team logo at bottom left and the player's name and position at lower right. The reverses are done in shades of brown on white. The cards are numbered on the back next to a small black and white photo of the player. The key Rookie Cards in this set are Wade Boggs, Tony Gwynn, Howard Johnson, Willie McGee, Ryne Sandberg, and Frank Viola.

	NRMT-MT	EXC	G-VG
COMPLETE SET (660)	130.00	57.50	16.50
COMMON PLAYER (1-660)	.10	.05	.01
☐ 1 Joaquin Andujar	.12	.05	.02
☐ 2 Doug Bair	.10	.05	.01
☐ 3 Steve Braun	.10	.05	.01
☐ 4 Glenn Brummer	.10	.05	.01
☐ 5 Bob Forsch	.10	.05	.01
☐ 6 David Green	.10	.05	.01
☐ 7 George Hendrick	.12	.05	.02
☐ 8 Keith Hernandez	.20	.09	.03
☐ 9 Tom Herr	.12	.05	.02
☐ 10 Dane Iorg	.10	.05	.01
☐ 11 Jim Kaat	.15	.07	.02
☐ 12 Jeff Lahti	.10	.05	.01
☐ 13 Tito Landrum	.10	.05	.01
☐ 14 Dave LaPoint	.12	.05	.02
☐ 15 Willie McGee	2.50	1.15	.30
☐ 16 Steve Mura	.10	.05	.01
☐ 17 Ken Oberkfell	.10	.05	.01
☐ 18 Darrell Porter	.10	.05	.01
☐ 19 Mike Ramsey	.10	.05	.01
☐ 20 Gene Roof	.10	.05	.01
☐ 21 Lonnie Smith	.12	.05	.02
☐ 22 Ozzie Smith	1.50	.65	.19
☐ 23 John Stuper	.10	.05	.01
☐ 24 Bruce Sutter	.20	.09	.03
☐ 25 Gene Tenace	.10	.05	.01
☐ 26 Jerry Augustine	.10	.05	.01
☐ 27 Dwight Bernard	.10	.05	.01
☐ 28 Mark Brouhard	.10	.05	.01
☐ 29 Mike Caldwell	.10	.05	.01
☐ 30 Cecil Cooper	.12	.05	.02
☐ 31 Jamie Easterly	.10	.05	.01
☐ 32 Marshall Edwards	.10	.05	.01
☐ 33 Rollie Fingers	.60	.25	.08
☐ 34 Jim Gantner	.10	.05	.02
☐ 35 Moose Haas	.10	.05	.01
☐ 36 Roy Howell	.10	.05	.01
☐ 37 Pete Ladd	.10	.05	.01
☐ 38 Bob McClure	.10	.05	.01
☐ 39 Doc Medich	.10	.05	.01
☐ 40 Paul Molitor	.90	.40	.11
☐ 41 Don Money	.10	.05	.01
☐ 42 Charlie Moore	.10	.05	.01
☐ 43 Ben Oglivie	.10	.05	.01
☐ 44 Ed Romero	.10	.05	.01
☐ 45 Ted Simmons	.12	.05	.02
☐ 46 Jim Slaton	.10	.05	.01
☐ 47 Don Sutton	.40	.18	.05
☐ 48 Gorman Thomas	.10	.05	.01
☐ 49 Pete Vuckovich	.10	.05	.01
☐ 50 Ned Yost	.10	.05	.01
☐ 51 Robin Yount	2.50	1.15	.30
☐ 52 Benny Ayala	.10	.05	.01
☐ 53 Bob Bonner	.10	.05	.01
☐ 54 Al Bumbry	.10	.05	.01
☐ 55 Terry Crowley	.10	.05	.01
☐ 56 Storm Davis	.20	.09	.03
☐ 57 Rich Dauer	.10	.05	.01
☐ 58 Rick Dempsey UER	.12	.05	.02
(Posing batting lefty)			
☐ 59 Jim Dwyer	.10	.05	.01
☐ 60 Mike Flanagan	.12	.05	.02
☐ 61 Dan Ford	.10	.05	.01
☐ 62 Glenn Gulliver	.10	.05	.01
☐ 63 John Lowenstein	.10	.05	.01
☐ 64 Dennis Martinez	.12	.05	.02
☐ 65 Tippy Martinez	.10	.05	.01
☐ 66 Scott McGregor	.10	.05	.01
☐ 67 Eddie Murray	1.75	.80	.22
☐ 68 Joe Nolan	.10	.05	.01
☐ 69 Jim Palmer	1.00	.45	.13
☐ 70 Cal Ripken Jr.	18.00	8.00	2.30
☐ 71 Gary Roenicke	.10	.05	.01
☐ 72 Lenn Sakata	.10	.05	.01
☐ 73 Ken Singleton	.12	.05	.02
☐ 74 Sammy Stewart	.10	.05	.01
☐ 75 Tim Stoddard	.10	.05	.01
☐ 76 Don Aase	.10	.05	.01
☐ 77 Don Baylor	.12	.05	.02
☐ 78 Juan Beniquez	.10	.05	.01
☐ 79 Bob Boone	.12	.05	.02
☐ 80 Rick Burleson	.10	.05	.01
☐ 81 Rod Carew	1.25	.55	.16
☐ 82 Bobby Clark	.10	.05	.01
☐ 83 Doug Corbett	.10	.05	.01
☐ 84 John Curtis	.10	.05	.01
☐ 85 Doug DeCinces	.12	.05	.02
☐ 86 Brian Downing	.12	.05	.02
☐ 87 Joe Ferguson	.10	.05	.01
☐ 88 Tim Foli	.10	.05	.01
☐ 89 Ken Forsch	.10	.05	.01
☐ 90 Dave Goltz	.10	.05	.01
☐ 91 Bobby Grich	.12	.05	.02
☐ 92 Andy Hassler	.10	.05	.01
☐ 93 Reggie Jackson	1.50	.65	.19
☐ 94 Ron Jackson	.10	.05	.01

☐	95	Tommy John	15	.07	.02
☐	96	Bruce Kison	10	.05	.01
☐	97	Fred Lynn	12	.05	.02
☐	98	Ed Ott	10	.05	.01
☐	99	Steve Renko	10	.05	.01
☐	100	Luis Sanchez	10	.05	.01
☐	101	Rob Wilfong	10	.05	.01
☐	102	Mike Witt	10	.05	.01
☐	103	Geoff Zahn	10	.05	.01
☐	104	Willie Aikens	10	.05	.01
☐	105	Mike Armstrong	10	.05	.01
☐	106	Vida Blue	12	.05	.02
☐	107	Bud Black	40	.18	.05
☐	108	George Brett	2.50	1.15	.30
☐	109	Bill Castro	10	.05	.01
☐	110	Onix Concepcion	10	.05	.01
☐	111	Dave Frost	10	.05	.01
☐	112	Cesar Geronimo	10	.05	.01
☐	113	Larry Gura	10	.05	.01
☐	114	Steve Hammond	10	.05	.01
☐	115	Don Hood	10	.05	.01
☐	116	Dennis Leonard	10	.05	.01
☐	117	Jerry Martin	10	.05	.01
☐	118	Lee May	10	.05	.01
☐	119	Hal McRae	12	.05	.02
☐	120	Amos Otis	12	.05	.02
☐	121	Greg Pryor	10	.05	.01
☐	122	Dan Quisenberry	12	.05	.02
☐	123	Don Slaught	50	.23	.06
☐	124	Paul Splittorff	10	.05	.01
☐	125	U.L. Washington	10	.05	.01
☐	126	John Wathan	10	.05	.01
☐	127	Frank White	12	.05	.02
☐	128	Willie Wilson	12	.05	.02
☐	129	Steve Bedrosian UER (Height 6'33")	12	.05	.02
☐	130	Bruce Benedict	10	.05	.01
☐	131	Tommy Boggs	10	.05	.01
☐	132	Brett Butler	75	.35	.09
☐	133	Rick Camp	10	.05	.01
☐	134	Chris Chambliss	12	.05	.02
☐	135	Ken Dayley	10	.05	.01
☐	136	Gene Garber	10	.05	.01
☐	137	Terry Harper	10	.05	.01
☐	138	Bob Horner	12	.05	.02
☐	139	Glenn Hubbard	10	.05	.01
☐	140	Rufino Linares	10	.05	.01
☐	141	Rick Mahler	10	.05	.01
☐	142	Dale Murphy	75	.35	.09
☐	143	Phil Niekro	40	.18	.05
☐	144	Pascual Perez	10	.05	.01
☐	145	Biff Pocoroba	10	.05	.01
☐	146	Rafael Ramirez	10	.05	.01
☐	147	Jerry Royster	10	.05	.01
☐	148	Ken Smith	10	.05	.01
☐	149	Bob Walk	10	.05	.01
☐	150	Claudell Washington	10	.05	.01
☐	151	Bob Watson	12	.05	.02
☐	152	Larry Whisenton	10	.05	.01
☐	153	Porfirio Altamirano	10	.05	.01
☐	154	Marty Bystrom	10	.05	.01
☐	155	Steve Carlton	1.25	.55	.16
☐	156	Larry Christenson	10	.05	.01
☐	157	Ivan DeJesus	10	.05	.01
☐	158	John Denny	10	.05	.01
☐	159	Bob Dernier	10	.05	.01
☐	160	Bo Diaz	10	.05	.01
☐	161	Ed Farmer	10	.05	.01
☐	162	Greg Gross	10	.05	.01
☐	163	Mike Krukow	10	.05	.01
☐	164	Garry Maddox	10	.05	.01
☐	165	Gary Matthews	12	.05	.02
☐	166	Tug McGraw	12	.05	.02
☐	167	Bob Molinaro	10	.05	.01
☐	168	Sid Monge	10	.05	.01
☐	169	Ron Reed	10	.05	.01
☐	170	Bill Robinson	12	.05	.02
☐	171	Pete Rose	1.25	.55	.16
☐	172	Dick Ruthven	10	.05	.01
☐	173	Mike Schmidt	2.00	.90	.25
☐	174	Manny Trillo	10	.05	.01
☐	175	Ozzie Virgil	10	.05	.01
☐	176	George Vukovich	10	.05	.01
☐	177	Gary Allenson	10	.05	.01
☐	178	Luis Aponte	10	.05	.01
☐	179	Wade Boggs	24.00	11.00	3.00
☐	180	Tom Burgmeier	10	.05	.01
☐	181	Mark Clear	10	.05	.01
☐	182	Dennis Eckersley	1.25	.55	.16
☐	183	Dwight Evans	25	.11	.03
☐	184	Rich Gedman	10	.05	.01
☐	185	Glenn Hoffman	10	.05	.01
☐	186	Bruce Hurst	12	.05	.02
☐	187	Carney Lansford	12	.05	.02
☐	188	Rick Miller	10	.05	.01
☐	189	Reid Nichols	10	.05	.01
☐	190	Bob Ojeda	12	.05	.02
☐	191	Tony Perez	30	.14	.04
☐	192	Chuck Rainey	10	.05	.01
☐	193	Jerry Remy	10	.05	.01
☐	194	Jim Rice	20	.09	.03
☐	195	Bob Stanley	10	.05	.01
☐	196	Dave Stapleton	10	.05	.01
☐	197	Mike Torrez	10	.05	.01
☐	198	John Tudor	12	.05	.02
☐	199	Julio Valdez	10	.05	.01
☐	200	Carl Yastrzemski	1.25	.55	.16
☐	201	Dusty Baker	12	.05	.02
☐	202	Joe Beckwith	10	.05	.01
☐	203	Greg Brock	12	.05	.02
☐	204	Ron Cey	12	.05	.02
☐	205	Terry Forster	10	.05	.01
☐	206	Steve Garvey	40	.18	.05
☐	207	Pedro Guerrero	25	.11	.03

☐ 208	Burt Hooton	.10	.05	.01
☐ 209	Steve Howe	.10	.05	.01
☐ 210	Ken Landreaux	.10	.05	.01
☐ 211	Mike Marshall	.12	.05	.02
☐ 212	Candy Maldonado	1.00	.45	.13
☐ 213	Rick Monday	.10	.05	.01
☐ 214	Tom Niedenfuer	.10	.05	.01
☐ 215	Jorge Orta	.10	.05	.01
☐ 216	Jerry Reuss UER	.10	.05	.01
	("Home:" omitted)			
☐ 217	Ron Roenicke	.10	.05	.01
☐ 218	Vicente Romo	.10	.05	.01
☐ 219	Bill Russell	.12	.05	.02
☐ 220	Steve Sax	.75	.35	.09
☐ 221	Mike Scioscia	.12	.05	.02
☐ 222	Dave Stewart	.75	.35	.09
☐ 223	Derrel Thomas	.10	.05	.01
☐ 224	Fernando Valenzuela	.15	.07	.02
☐ 225	Bob Welch	.25	.11	.03
☐ 226	Ricky Wright	.10	.05	.01
☐ 227	Steve Yeager	.10	.05	.01
☐ 228	Bill Almon	.10	.05	.01
☐ 229	Harold Baines	.50	.23	.06
☐ 230	Salome Barojas	.10	.05	.01
☐ 231	Tony Bernazard	.10	.05	.01
☐ 232	Britt Burns	.10	.05	.01
☐ 233	Richard Dotson	.10	.05	.01
☐ 234	Ernesto Escarrega	.10	.05	.01
☐ 235	Carlton Fisk	1.25	.55	.16
☐ 236	Jerry Hairston	.10	.05	.01
☐ 237	Kevin Hickey	.10	.05	.01
☐ 238	LaMarr Hoyt	.10	.05	.01
☐ 239	Steve Kemp	.10	.05	.01
☐ 240	Jim Kern	.10	.05	.01
☐ 241	Ron Kittle	.25	.11	.03
☐ 242	Jerry Koosman	.12	.05	.02
☐ 243	Dennis Lamp	.10	.05	.01
☐ 244	Rudy Law	.10	.05	.01
☐ 245	Vance Law	.10	.05	.01
☐ 246	Ron LeFlore	.12	.05	.02
☐ 247	Greg Luzinski	.12	.05	.02
☐ 248	Tom Paciorek	.12	.05	.02
☐ 249	Aurelio Rodriguez	.10	.05	.01
☐ 250	Mike Squires	.10	.05	.01
☐ 251	Steve Trout	.10	.05	.01
☐ 252	Jim Barr	.10	.05	.01
☐ 253	Dave Bergman	.10	.05	.01
☐ 254	Fred Breining	.10	.05	.01
☐ 255	Bob Brenly	.10	.05	.01
☐ 256	Jack Clark	.15	.07	.02
☐ 257	Chili Davis	.50	.23	.06
☐ 258	Darrell Evans	.12	.05	.02
☐ 259	Alan Fowlkes	.10	.05	.01
☐ 260	Rich Gale	.10	.05	.01
☐ 261	Atlee Hammaker	.10	.05	.01
☐ 262	Al Holland	.10	.05	.01
☐ 263	Duane Kuiper	.10	.05	.01
☐ 264	Bill Laskey	.10	.05	.01
☐ 265	Gary Lavelle	.10	.05	.01
☐ 266	Johnnie LeMaster	.10	.05	.01
☐ 267	Renie Martin	.10	.05	.01
☐ 268	Milt May	.10	.05	.01
☐ 269	Greg Minton	.10	.05	.01
☐ 270	Joe Morgan	.60	.25	.08
☐ 271	Tom O'Malley	.10	.05	.01
☐ 272	Reggie Smith	.12	.05	.02
☐ 273	Guy Sularz	.10	.05	.01
☐ 274	Champ Summers	.10	.05	.01
☐ 275	Max Venable	.10	.05	.01
☐ 276	Jim Wohlford	.10	.05	.01
☐ 277	Ray Burris	.10	.05	.01
☐ 278	Gary Carter	.75	.35	.09
☐ 279	Warren Cromartie	.10	.05	.01
☐ 280	Andre Dawson	1.50	.65	.19
☐ 281	Terry Francona	.10	.05	.01
☐ 282	Doug Flynn	.10	.05	.01
☐ 283	Woodie Fryman	.10	.05	.01
☐ 284	Bill Gullickson	.20	.09	.03
☐ 285	Wallace Johnson	.10	.05	.01
☐ 286	Charlie Lea	.10	.05	.01
☐ 287	Randy Lerch	.10	.05	.01
☐ 288	Brad Mills	.10	.05	.01
☐ 289	Dan Norman	.10	.05	.01
☐ 290	Al Oliver	.12	.05	.02
☐ 291	David Palmer	.10	.05	.01
☐ 292	Tim Raines	.60	.25	.08
☐ 293	Jeff Reardon	1.25	.55	.16
☐ 294	Steve Rogers	.10	.05	.01
☐ 295	Scott Sanderson	.10	.05	.01
☐ 296	Dan Schatzeder	.10	.05	.01
☐ 297	Bryn Smith	.12	.05	.02
☐ 298	Chris Speier	.10	.05	.01
☐ 299	Tim Wallach	.20	.09	.03
☐ 300	Jerry White	.10	.05	.01
☐ 301	Joel Youngblood	.10	.05	.01
☐ 302	Ross Baumgarten	.10	.05	.01
☐ 303	Dale Berra	.10	.05	.01
☐ 304	John Candelaria	.10	.05	.01
☐ 305	Dick Davis	.10	.05	.01
☐ 306	Mike Easler	.10	.05	.01
☐ 307	Richie Hebner	.10	.05	.01
☐ 308	Lee Lacy	.10	.05	.01
☐ 309	Bill Madlock	.12	.05	.02
☐ 310	Larry McWilliams	.10	.05	.01
☐ 311	John Milner	.10	.05	.01
☐ 312	Omar Moreno	.10	.05	.01
☐ 313	Jim Morrison	.10	.05	.01
☐ 314	Steve Nicosia	.10	.05	.01
☐ 315	Dave Parker	.35	.16	.04
☐ 316	Tony Pena	.12	.05	.02
☐ 317	Johnny Ray	.10	.05	.01
☐ 318	Rick Rhoden	.10	.05	.01
☐ 319	Don Robinson	.10	.05	.01
☐ 320	Enrique Romo	.10	.05	.01

☐ 321	Manny Sarmiento	.10	.05	.01
☐ 322	Rod Scurry	.10	.05	.01
☐ 323	Jimmy Smith	.10	.05	.01
☐ 324	Willie Stargell	.60	.25	.08
☐ 325	Jason Thompson	.10	.05	.01
☐ 326	Kent Tekulve	.12	.05	.02
☐ 327A	Tom Brookens	.10	.05	.01
	(Short .375" brown box			
	shaded in on card back)			
☐ 327B	Tom Brookens	.10	.05	.01
	(Longer 1.25" brown box			
	shaded in on card back)			
☐ 328	Enos Cabell	.10	.05	.01
☐ 329	Kirk Gibson	.35	.16	.04
☐ 330	Larry Herndon	.10	.05	.01
☐ 331	Mike Ivie	.10	.05	.01
☐ 332	Howard Johnson	6.00	2.70	.75
☐ 333	Lynn Jones	.10	.05	.01
☐ 334	Rick Leach	.10	.05	.01
☐ 335	Chet Lemon	.10	.05	.01
☐ 336	Jack Morris	1.25	.55	.16
☐ 337	Lance Parrish	.15	.07	.02
☐ 338	Larry Pashnick	.10	.05	.01
☐ 339	Dan Petry	.10	.05	.01
☐ 340	Dave Rozema	.10	.05	.01
☐ 341	Dave Rucker	.10	.05	.01
☐ 342	Elias Sosa	.10	.05	.01
☐ 343	Dave Tobik	.10	.05	.01
☐ 344	Alan Trammell	.50	.23	.06
☐ 345	Jerry Turner	.10	.05	.01
☐ 346	Jerry Ujdur	.10	.05	.01
☐ 347	Pat Underwood	.10	.05	.01
☐ 348	Lou Whitaker	.50	.23	.06
☐ 349	Milt Wilcox	.10	.05	.01
☐ 350	Glenn Wilson	.12	.05	.02
☐ 351	John Wockenfuss	.10	.05	.01
☐ 352	Kurt Bevacqua	.10	.05	.01
☐ 353	Juan Bonilla	.10	.05	.01
☐ 354	Floyd Chiffer	.10	.05	.01
☐ 355	Luis DeLeon	.10	.05	.01
☐ 356	Dave Dravecky	.60	.25	.08
☐ 357	Dave Edwards	.10	.05	.01
☐ 358	Juan Eichelberger	.10	.05	.01
☐ 359	Tim Flannery	.10	.05	.01
☐ 360	Tony Gwynn	25.00	11.50	3.10
☐ 361	Ruppert Jones	.10	.05	.01
☐ 362	Terry Kennedy	.10	.05	.01
☐ 363	Joe Lefebvre	.10	.05	.01
☐ 364	Sixto Lezcano	.10	.05	.01
☐ 365	Tim Lollar	.10	.05	.01
☐ 366	Gary Lucas	.10	.05	.01
☐ 367	John Montefusco	.10	.05	.01
☐ 368	Broderick Perkins	.10	.05	.01
☐ 369	Joe Pittman	.10	.05	.01
☐ 370	Gene Richards	.10	.05	.01
☐ 371	Luis Salazar	.10	.05	.01
☐ 372	Eric Show	.10	.05	.01
☐ 373	Garry Templeton	.12	.05	.02
☐ 374	Chris Welsh	.10	.05	.01
☐ 375	Alan Wiggins	.10	.05	.01
☐ 376	Rick Cerone	.10	.05	.01
☐ 377	Dave Collins	.10	.05	.01
☐ 378	Roger Erickson	.10	.05	.01
☐ 379	George Frazier	.10	.05	.01
☐ 380	Oscar Gamble	.10	.05	.01
☐ 381	Rich Gossage	.20	.09	.03
☐ 382	Ken Griffey	.25	.11	.03
☐ 383	Ron Guidry	.20	.09	.03
☐ 384	Dave LaRoche	.10	.05	.01
☐ 385	Rudy May	.10	.05	.01
☐ 386	John Mayberry	.10	.05	.01
☐ 387	Lee Mazzilli	.10	.05	.01
☐ 388	Mike Morgan	.35	.16	.04
☐ 389	Jerry Mumphrey	.10	.05	.01
☐ 390	Bobby Murcer	.12	.05	.02
☐ 391	Graig Nettles	.12	.05	.02
☐ 392	Lou Piniella	.12	.05	.02
☐ 393	Willie Randolph	.12	.05	.02
☐ 394	Shane Rawley	.10	.05	.01
☐ 395	Dave Righetti	.15	.07	.02
☐ 396	Andre Robertson	.10	.05	.01
☐ 397	Roy Smalley	.10	.05	.01
☐ 398	Dave Winfield	2.00	.90	.25
☐ 399	Butch Wynegar	.10	.05	.01
☐ 400	Chris Bando	.10	.05	.01
☐ 401	Alan Bannister	.10	.05	.01
☐ 402	Len Barker	.10	.05	.01
☐ 403	Tom Brennan	.10	.05	.01
☐ 404	Carmelo Castillo	.10	.05	.01
☐ 405	Miguel Dilone	.10	.05	.01
☐ 406	Jerry Dybzinski	.10	.05	.01
☐ 407	Mike Fischlin	.10	.05	.01
☐ 408	Ed Glynn UER	.10	.05	.01
	(Photo actually			
	Bud Anderson)			
☐ 409	Mike Hargrove	.12	.05	.02
☐ 410	Toby Harrah	.10	.05	.01
☐ 411	Ron Hassey	.10	.05	.01
☐ 412	Von Hayes	.12	.05	.02
☐ 413	Rick Manning	.10	.05	.01
☐ 414	Bake McBride	.10	.05	.01
☐ 415	Larry Milbourne	.10	.05	.01
☐ 416	Bill Nahorodny	.10	.05	.01
☐ 417	Jack Perconte	.10	.05	.01
☐ 418	Lary Sorensen	.10	.05	.01
☐ 419	Dan Spillner	.10	.05	.01
☐ 420	Rick Sutcliffe	.25	.11	.03
☐ 421	Andre Thornton	.10	.05	.01
☐ 422	Rick Waits	.10	.05	.01
☐ 423	Eddie Whitson	.10	.05	.01
☐ 424	Jesse Barfield	.20	.09	.03
☐ 425	Barry Bonnell	.10	.05	.01
☐ 426	Jim Clancy	.10	.05	.01
☐ 427	Damaso Garcia	.10	.05	.01

☐	428	Jerry Garvin	10	.05	.01
☐	429	Alfredo Griffin	10	.05	.01
☐	430	Garth Iorg	10	.05	.01
☐	431	Roy Lee Jackson	10	.05	.01
☐	432	Luis Leal	10	.05	.01
☐	433	Buck Martinez	10	.05	.01
☐	434	Joey McLaughlin	10	.05	.01
☐	435	Lloyd Moseby	10	.05	.01
☐	436	Rance Mulliniks	10	.05	.01
☐	437	Dale Murray	10	.05	.01
☐	438	Wayne Nordhagen	10	.05	.01
☐	439	Geno Petralli	12	.05	.02
☐	440	Hosken Powell	10	.05	.01
☐	441	Dave Stieb	20	.09	.03
☐	442	Willie Upshaw	10	.05	.01
☐	443	Ernie Whitt	10	.05	.01
☐	444	Alvis Woods	10	.05	.01
☐	445	Alan Ashby	10	.05	.01
☐	446	Jose Cruz	12	.05	.02
☐	447	Kiko Garcia	10	.05	.01
☐	448	Phil Garner	12	.05	.02
☐	449	Danny Heep	10	.05	.01
☐	450	Art Howe	10	.05	.01
☐	451	Bob Knepper	10	.05	.01
☐	452	Alan Knicely	10	.05	.01
☐	453	Ray Knight	12	.05	.02
☐	454	Frank LaCorte	10	.05	.01
☐	455	Mike LaCoss	10	.05	.01
☐	456	Randy Moffitt	10	.05	.01
☐	457	Joe Niekro	12	.05	.02
☐	458	Terry Puhl	10	.05	.01
☐	459	Luis Pujols	10	.05	.01
☐	460	Craig Reynolds	10	.05	.01
☐	461	Bert Roberge	10	.05	.01
☐	462	Vern Ruhle	10	.05	.01
☐	463	Nolan Ryan	7.00	3.10	.85
☐	464	Joe Sambito	10	.05	.01
☐	465	Tony Scott	10	.05	.01
☐	466	Dave Smith	10	.05	.01
☐	467	Harry Spilman	10	.05	.01
☐	468	Dickie Thon	10	.05	.01
☐	469	Denny Walling	10	.05	.01
☐	470	Larry Andersen	10	.05	.01
☐	471	Floyd Bannister	10	.05	.01
☐	472	Jim Beattie	10	.05	.01
☐	473	Bruce Bochte	10	.05	.01
☐	474	Manny Castillo	10	.05	.01
☐	475	Bill Caudill	10	.05	.01
☐	476	Bryan Clark	10	.05	.01
☐	477	Al Cowens	10	.05	.01
☐	478	Julio Cruz	10	.05	.01
☐	479	Todd Cruz	10	.05	.01
☐	480	Gary Gray	10	.05	.01
☐	481	Dave Henderson	50	.23	.06
☐	482	Mike Moore	1.00	.45	.13
☐	483	Gaylord Perry	40	.18	.05
☐	484	Dave Revering	10	.05	.01
☐	485	Joe Simpson	10	.05	.01
☐	486	Mike Stanton	10	.05	.01
☐	487	Rick Sweet	10	.05	.01
☐	488	Ed VandeBerg	10	.05	.01
☐	489	Richie Zisk	10	.05	.01
☐	490	Doug Bird	10	.05	.01
☐	491	Larry Bowa	12	.05	.02
☐	492	Bill Buckner	12	.05	.02
☐	493	Bill Campbell	10	.05	.01
☐	494	Jody Davis	10	.05	.01
☐	495	Leon Durham	10	.05	.01
☐	496	Steve Henderson	10	.05	.01
☐	497	Willie Hernandez	12	.05	.02
☐	498	Ferguson Jenkins	40	.18	.05
☐	499	Jay Johnstone	12	.05	.02
☐	500	Junior Kennedy	10	.05	.01
☐	501	Randy Martz	10	.05	.01
☐	502	Jerry Morales	10	.05	.01
☐	503	Keith Moreland	10	.05	.01
☐	504	Dickie Noles	10	.05	.01
☐	505	Mike Proly	10	.05	.01
☐	506	Allen Ripley	10	.05	.01
☐	507	Ryne Sandberg UER	40.00	18.00	5.00
		(Should say High School			
		in Spokane, Washington)			
☐	508	Lee Smith	2.25	1.00	.30
☐	509	Pat Tabler	10	.05	.01
☐	510	Dick Tidrow	10	.05	.01
☐	511	Bump Wills	10	.05	.01
☐	512	Gary Woods	10	.05	.01
☐	513	Tony Armas	10	.05	.01
☐	514	Dave Beard	10	.05	.01
☐	515	Jeff Burroughs	10	.05	.01
☐	516	John D'Acquisto	10	.05	.01
☐	517	Wayne Gross	10	.05	.01
☐	518	Mike Heath	10	.05	.01
☐	519	Rickey Henderson	3.50	1.55	.45
		UER (Brock record			
		listed as 120 steals)			
☐	520	Cliff Johnson	10	.05	.01
☐	521	Matt Keough	10	.05	.01
☐	522	Brian Kingman	10	.05	.01
☐	523	Rick Langford	10	.05	.01
☐	524	Dave Lopes	12	.05	.02
☐	525	Steve McCatty	10	.05	.01
☐	526	Dave McKay	10	.05	.01
☐	527	Dan Meyer	10	.05	.01
☐	528	Dwayne Murphy	10	.05	.01
☐	529	Jeff Newman	10	.05	.01
☐	530	Mike Norris	10	.05	.01
☐	531	Bob Owchinko	10	.05	.01
☐	532	Joe Rudi	10	.05	.01
☐	533	Jimmy Sexton	10	.05	.01
☐	534	Fred Stanley	10	.05	.01
☐	535	Tom Underwood	10	.05	.01
☐	536	Neil Allen	10	.05	.01
☐	537	Wally Backman	12	.05	.02

☐ 538 Bob Bailor	10	.05	.01
☐ 539 Hubie Brooks	15	.07	.02
☐ 540 Carlos Diaz	10	.05	.01
☐ 541 Pete Falcone	10	.05	.01
☐ 542 George Foster	12	.05	.02
☐ 543 Ron Gardenhire	10	.05	.01
☐ 544 Brian Giles	10	.05	.01
☐ 545 Ron Hodges	10	.05	.01
☐ 546 Randy Jones	10	.05	.01
☐ 547 Mike Jorgensen	10	.05	.01
☐ 548 Dave Kingman	12	.05	.02
☐ 549 Ed Lynch	10	.05	.01
☐ 550 Jesse Orosco	10	.05	.01
☐ 551 Rick Ownbey	10	.05	.01
☐ 552 Charlie Puleo	10	.05	.01
☐ 553 Gary Rajsich	10	.05	.01
☐ 554 Mike Scott	12	.05	.02
☐ 555 Rusty Staub	12	.05	.02
☐ 556 John Stearns	10	.05	.01
☐ 557 Craig Swan	10	.05	.01
☐ 558 Ellis Valentine	10	.05	.01
☐ 559 Tom Veryzer	10	.05	.01
☐ 560 Mookie Wilson	12	.05	.02
☐ 561 Pat Zachry	10	.05	.01
☐ 562 Buddy Bell	12	.05	.02
☐ 563 John Butcher	10	.05	.01
☐ 564 Steve Comer	10	.05	.01
☐ 565 Danny Darwin	10	.05	.01
☐ 566 Bucky Dent	12	.05	.02
☐ 567 John Grubb	10	.05	.01
☐ 568 Rick Honeycutt	10	.05	.01
☐ 569 Dave Hostetler	10	.05	.01
☐ 570 Charlie Hough	12	.05	.02
☐ 571 Lamar Johnson	10	.05	.01
☐ 572 Jon Matlack	10	.05	.01
☐ 573 Paul Mirabella	10	.05	.01
☐ 574 Larry Parrish	10	.05	.01
☐ 575 Mike Richardt	10	.05	.01
☐ 576 Mickey Rivers	10	.05	.01
☐ 577 Billy Sample	10	.05	.01
☐ 578 Dave Schmidt	10	.05	.01
☐ 579 Bill Stein	10	.05	.01
☐ 580 Jim Sundberg	12	.05	.02
☐ 581 Frank Tanana	12	.05	.02
☐ 582 Mark Wagner	10	.05	.01
☐ 583 George Wright	10	.05	.01
☐ 584 Johnny Bench	1.25	.55	.16
☐ 585 Bruce Berenyi	10	.05	.01
☐ 586 Larry Biittner	10	.05	.01
☐ 587 Cesar Cedeno	12	.05	.02
☐ 588 Dave Concepcion	12	.05	.02
☐ 589 Dan Driessen	10	.05	.01
☐ 590 Greg Harris	10	.05	.01
☐ 591 Ben Hayes	10	.05	.01
☐ 592 Paul Householder	10	.05	.01
☐ 593 Tom Hume	10	.05	.01
☐ 594 Wayne Krenchicki	10	.05	.01
☐ 595 Rafael Landestoy	10	.05	.01
☐ 596 Charlie Leibrandt	12	.05	.02
☐ 597 Eddie Milner	10	.05	.01
☐ 598 Ron Oester	10	.05	.01
☐ 599 Frank Pastore	10	.05	.01
☐ 600 Joe Price	10	.05	.01
☐ 601 Tom Seaver	1.25	.55	.16
☐ 602 Bob Shirley	10	.05	.01
☐ 603 Mario Soto	10	.05	.01
☐ 604 Alex Trevino	10	.05	.01
☐ 605 Mike Vail	10	.05	.01
☐ 606 Duane Walker	10	.05	.01
☐ 607 Tom Brunansky	40	.18	.05
☐ 608 Bobby Castillo	10	.05	.01
☐ 609 John Castino	10	.05	.01
☐ 610 Ron Davis	10	.05	.01
☐ 611 Lenny Faedo	10	.05	.01
☐ 612 Terry Felton	10	.05	.01
☐ 613 Gary Gaetti	40	.18	.05
☐ 614 Mickey Hatcher	10	.05	.01
☐ 615 Brad Havens	10	.05	.01
☐ 616 Kent Hrbek	75	.35	.09
☐ 617 Randy Johnson	10	.05	.01
☐ 618 Tim Laudner	10	.05	.01
☐ 619 Jeff Little	10	.05	.01
☐ 620 Bobby Mitchell	10	.05	.01
☐ 621 Jack O'Connor	10	.05	.01
☐ 622 John Pacella	10	.05	.01
☐ 623 Pete Redfern	10	.05	.01
☐ 624 Jesus Vega	10	.05	.01
☐ 625 Frank Viola	3.00	1.35	.40
☐ 626 Ron Washington	10	.05	.01
☐ 627 Gary Ward	10	.05	.01
☐ 628 Al Williams	10	.05	.01
☐ 629 Red Sox All-Stars	75	.35	.09
Carl Yastrzemski			
Dennis Eckersley			
Mark Clear			
☐ 630 "300 Career Wins"	15	.07	.02
Gaylord Perry and			
Terry Bulling 5/6/82			
☐ 631 Pride of Venezuela	15	.07	.02
Dave Concepcion and			
Manny Trillo			
☐ 632 All-Star Infielders	60	.25	.08
Robin Yount and			
Buddy Bell			
☐ 633 Mr.Vet and Mr.Rookie	60	.25	.08
Dave Winfield and			
Kent Hrbek			
☐ 634 Fountain of Youth	60	.25	.08
Willie Stargell and			
Pete Rose			
☐ 635 Big Chiefs	15	.07	.02
Toby Harrah and			
Andre Thornton			
☐ 636 Smith Brothers	50	.23	.06

☐ 637	Ozzie and Lonnie Base Stealers' Threat ......15 Bo Diaz and Gary Carter	.07	.02
☐ 638	All-Star Catchers ....25 Carlton Fisk and Gary Carter	.11	.03
☐ 639	The Silver Shoe ....2.00 Rickey Henderson	.90	.25
☐ 640	Home Run Threats ....40 Ben Oglivie and Reggie Jackson	.18	.05
☐ 641	Two Teams Same Day ....15 Joel Youngblood August 4, 1982	.07	.02
☐ 642	Last Perfect Game ....15 Ron Hassey and Len Barker	.07	.02
☐ 643	Black and Blue ....15 Vida Blue	.07	.02
☐ 644	Black and Blue ....15 Bud Black	.07	.02
☐ 645	Speed and Power ....75 Reggie Jackson	.35	.09
☐ 646	Speed and Power ....1.50 Rickey Henderson	.65	.19
☐ 647	CL: Cards/Brewers 15	.02	.00
☐ 648	CL: Orioles/Angels 15	.02	.00
☐ 649	CL: Royals/Braves 15	.02	.00
☐ 650	CL: Phillies/Red Sox 15	.02	.00
☐ 651	CL: Dodgers/White Sox ...15	.02	.00
☐ 652	CL: Giants/Expos 15	.02	.00
☐ 653	CL: Pirates/Tigers 15	.02	.00
☐ 654	CL: Padres/Yankees 15	.02	.00
☐ 655	CL: Indians/Blue Jays 15	.02	.00
☐ 656	CL: Astros/Mariners 15	.02	.00
☐ 657	CL: Cubs/A's 15	.02	.00
☐ 658	CL: Mets/Rangers 15	.02	.00
☐ 659	CL: Reds/Twins 15	.02	.00
☐ 660	CL: Specials/Teams 15	.02	.00

1984 Fleer

The cards in this 660-card set measure 2 1/2" by 3 1/2". The 1984 Fleer card set featured fronts with full-color team logos along with the player's name and position and the Fleer identification. The set features many imaginative photos, several multi-player cards, and many more action shots than the 1983 card set. The backs are quite similar to the 1983 backs except that blue rather than brown ink is used.

The player cards are alphabetized within team and the teams are ordered by their 1983 season finish and won-lost record, e.g., Baltimore (1-23), Philadelphia (24-49), Chicago White Sox (50-73), Detroit (74-95), Los Angeles (96-118), New York Yankees (119-144), Toronto (145-169), Atlanta (170-193), Milwaukee (194-219), Houston (220-244), Pittsburgh (245-269), Montreal (270-293), San Diego (294-317), St. Louis (318-340), Kansas City (341-364), San Francisco (365-387), Boston (388-412), Texas (413-435), Oakland (436-461), Cincinnati (462-485), Chicago (486-507), California (508-532), Cleveland (533-555), Minnesota (556-579), New York Mets (580-603), and Seattle (604-625). Specials (626-646) and checklist cards (647-660) make up the end of the set. The key Rookie Cards in this set are Tony Fernandez, Don Mattingly, Kevin McReynolds, Juan Samuel, Darryl Strawberry, and Andy Van Slyke.

		NRMT-MT	EXC	G-VG
	COMPLETE SET (660) 200.00		90.00	25.00
	COMMON PLAYER (1-660) 15		.07	.02
☐ 1	Mike Boddicker 20		.09	.03
☐ 2	Al Bumbry 15		.07	.02
☐ 3	Todd Cruz 15		.07	.02
☐ 4	Rich Dauer 15		.07	.02
☐ 5	Storm Davis 15		.07	.02
☐ 6	Rick Dempsey 15		.07	.02
☐ 7	Jim Dwyer 15		.07	.02
☐ 8	Mike Flanagan 15		.07	.02
☐ 9	Dan Ford 15		.07	.02
☐ 10	John Lowenstein 15		.09	.03
☐ 11	Dennis Martinez 20		.09	.03
☐ 12	Tippy Martinez 15		.07	.02
☐ 13	Scott McGregor 15		.07	.02
☐ 14	Eddie Murray 4.00		1.80	.50

☐ 15	Joe Nolan	15	.07	.02
☐ 16	Jim Palmer	3.00	1.35	.40
☐ 17	Cal Ripken	20.00	9.00	2.50
☐ 18	Gary Roenicke	15	.07	.02
☐ 19	Lenn Sakata	15	.07	.02
☐ 20	John Shelby	15	.07	.02
☐ 21	Ken Singleton	20	.09	.03
☐ 22	Sammy Stewart	15	.07	.02
☐ 23	Tim Stoddard	15	.07	.02
☐ 24	Marty Bystrom	15	.07	.02
☐ 25	Steve Carlton	3.00	1.35	.40
☐ 26	Ivan DeJesus	15	.07	.02
☐ 27	John Denny	15	.07	.02
☐ 28	Bob Dernier	15	.07	.02
☐ 29	Bo Diaz	15	.07	.02
☐ 30	Kiko Garcia	15	.07	.02
☐ 31	Greg Gross	15	.07	.02
☐ 32	Kevin Gross	40	.18	.05
☐ 33	Von Hayes	20	.09	.03
☐ 34	Willie Hernandez	20	.09	.03
☐ 35	Al Holland	15	.07	.02
☐ 36	Charles Hudson	15	.07	.02
☐ 37	Joe Lefebvre	15	.07	.02
☐ 38	Sixto Lezcano	15	.07	.02
☐ 39	Garry Maddox	15	.07	.02
☐ 40	Gary Matthews	20	.09	.03
☐ 41	Len Matuszek	15	.07	.02
☐ 42	Tug McGraw	20	.09	.03
☐ 43	Joe Morgan	1.00	.45	.13
☐ 44	Tony Perez	75	.35	.09
☐ 45	Ron Reed	15	.07	.02
☐ 46	Pete Rose	3.00	1.35	.40
☐ 47	Juan Samuel	1.00	.45	.13
☐ 48	Mike Schmidt	9.00	4.00	1.15
☐ 49	Ozzie Virgil	15	.07	.02
☐ 50	Juan Agosto	15	.07	.02
☐ 51	Harold Baines	60	.25	.08
☐ 52	Floyd Bannister	15	.07	.02
☐ 53	Salome Barojas	15	.07	.02
☐ 54	Britt Burns	15	.07	.02
☐ 55	Julio Cruz	15	.07	.02
☐ 56	Richard Dotson	15	.07	.02
☐ 57	Jerry Dybzinski	15	.07	.02
☐ 58	Carlton Fisk	3.00	1.35	.40
☐ 59	Scott Fletcher	15	.07	.02
☐ 60	Jerry Hairston	15	.07	.02
☐ 61	Kevin Hickey	15	.07	.02
☐ 62	Marc Hill	15	.07	.02
☐ 63	LaMarr Hoyt	15	.07	.02
☐ 64	Ron Kittle	20	.09	.03
☐ 65	Jerry Koosman	20	.09	.03
☐ 66	Dennis Lamp	15	.07	.02
☐ 67	Rudy Law	15	.07	.02
☐ 68	Vance Law	15	.07	.02
☐ 69	Greg Luzinski	20	.09	.03
☐ 70	Tom Paciorek	20	.09	.03
☐ 71	Mike Squires	15	.07	.02
☐ 72	Dick Tidrow	15	.07	.02
☐ 73	Greg Walker	20	.09	.03
☐ 74	Glenn Abbott	15	.07	.02
☐ 75	Howard Bailey	15	.07	.02
☐ 76	Doug Bair	15	.07	.02
☐ 77	Juan Berenguer	15	.07	.02
☐ 78	Tom Brookens	15	.07	.02
☐ 79	Enos Cabell	15	.07	.02
☐ 80	Kirk Gibson	60	.25	.08
☐ 81	John Grubb	15	.07	.02
☐ 82	Larry Herndon	15	.07	.02
☐ 83	Wayne Krenchicki	15	.07	.02
☐ 84	Rick Leach	15	.07	.02
☐ 85	Chet Lemon	15	.07	.02
☐ 86	Aurelio Lopez	15	.07	.02
☐ 87	Jack Morris	2.50	1.15	.30
☐ 88	Lance Parrish	25	.11	.03
☐ 89	Dan Petry	15	.07	.02
☐ 90	Dave Rozema	15	.07	.02
☐ 91	Alan Trammell	1.00	.45	.13
☐ 92	Lou Whitaker	1.00	.45	.13
☐ 93	Milt Wilcox	15	.07	.02
☐ 94	Glenn Wilson	15	.07	.02
☐ 95	John Wockenfuss	15	.07	.02
☐ 96	Dusty Baker	20	.09	.03
☐ 97	Joe Beckwith	15	.07	.02
☐ 98	Greg Brock	15	.07	.02
☐ 99	Jack Fimple	15	.07	.02
☐ 100	Pedro Guerrero	25	.11	.03
☐ 101	Rick Honeycutt	15	.07	.02
☐ 102	Burt Hooton	15	.07	.02
☐ 103	Steve Howe	15	.07	.02
☐ 104	Ken Landreaux	15	.07	.02
☐ 105	Mike Marshall	20	.09	.03
☐ 106	Rick Monday	15	.07	.02
☐ 107	Jose Morales	15	.07	.02
☐ 108	Tom Niedenfuer	15	.07	.02
☐ 109	Alejandro Pena	50	.23	.06
☐ 110	Jerry Reuss UER	15	.07	.02
	("Home:" omitted)			
☐ 111	Bill Russell	20	.09	.03
☐ 112	Steve Sax	75	.35	.09
☐ 113	Mike Scioscia	20	.09	.03
☐ 114	Derrel Thomas	15	.07	.02
☐ 115	Fernando Valenzuela	20	.09	.03
☐ 116	Bob Welch	30	.14	.04
☐ 117	Steve Yeager	15	.07	.02
☐ 118	Pat Zachry	15	.07	.02
☐ 119	Don Baylor	20	.09	.03
☐ 120	Bert Campaneris	20	.09	.03
☐ 121	Rick Cerone	15	.07	.02
☐ 122	Ray Fontenot	15	.07	.02
☐ 123	George Frazier	15	.07	.02
☐ 124	Oscar Gamble	15	.07	.02
☐ 125	Rich Gossage	25	.11	.03
☐ 126	Ken Griffey	25	.11	.03
☐ 127	Ron Guidry	20	.09	.03

☐	128	Jay Howell	.20	.09	.03			
☐	129	Steve Kemp	.15	.07	.02			
☐	130	Matt Keough	.15	.07	.02			
☐	131	Don Mattingly	25.00	11.50	3.10			
☐	132	John Montefusco	.15	.07	.02			
☐	133	Omar Moreno	.15	.07	.02			
☐	134	Dale Murray	.15	.07	.02			
☐	135	Graig Nettles	.20	.09	.03			
☐	136	Lou Piniella	.20	.09	.03			
☐	137	Willie Randolph	.20	.09	.03			
☐	138	Shane Rawley	.15	.07	.02			
☐	139	Dave Righetti	.20	.09	.03			
☐	140	Andre Robertson	.15	.07	.02			
☐	141	Bob Shirley	.15	.07	.02			
☐	142	Roy Smalley	.15	.07	.02			
☐	143	Dave Winfield	5.00	2.30	.60			
☐	144	Butch Wynegar	.15	.07	.02			
☐	145	Jim Acker	.15	.07	.02			
☐	146	Doyle Alexander	.15	.07	.02			
☐	147	Jesse Barfield	.20	.09	.03			
☐	148	Jorge Bell	1.75	.80	.22			
☐	149	Barry Bonnell	.15	.07	.02			
☐	150	Jim Clancy	.15	.07	.02			
☐	151	Dave Collins	.15	.07	.02			
☐	152	Tony Fernandez	4.00	1.80	.50			
☐	153	Damaso Garcia	.15	.07	.02			
☐	154	Dave Geisel	.15	.07	.02			
☐	155	Jim Gott	.15	.07	.02			
☐	156	Alfredo Griffin	.15	.07	.02			
☐	157	Garth Iorg	.15	.07	.02			
☐	158	Roy Lee Jackson	.15	.07	.02			
☐	159	Cliff Johnson	.15	.07	.02			
☐	160	Luis Leal	.15	.07	.02			
☐	161	Buck Martinez	.15	.07	.02			
☐	162	Joey McLaughlin	.15	.07	.02			
☐	163	Randy Moffitt	.15	.07	.02			
☐	164	Lloyd Moseby	.15	.07	.02			
☐	165	Rance Mulliniks	.15	.07	.02			
☐	166	Jorge Orta	.15	.07	.02			
☐	167	Dave Stieb	.20	.09	.03			
☐	168	Willie Upshaw	.15	.07	.02			
☐	169	Ernie Whitt	.15	.07	.02			
☐	170	Len Barker	.15	.07	.02			
☐	171	Steve Bedrosian	.20	.09	.03			
☐	172	Bruce Benedict	.15	.07	.02			
☐	173	Brett Butler	.60	.25	.08			
☐	174	Rick Camp	.15	.07	.02			
☐	175	Chris Chambliss	.20	.09	.03			
☐	176	Ken Dayley	.15	.07	.02			
☐	177	Pete Falcone	.15	.07	.02			
☐	178	Terry Forster	.15	.07	.02			
☐	179	Gene Garber	.15	.07	.02			
☐	180	Terry Harper	.15	.07	.02			
☐	181	Bob Horner	.20	.09	.03			
☐	182	Glenn Hubbard	.15	.07	.02			
☐	183	Randy Johnson	.15	.07	.02			
☐	184	Craig McMurtry	.15	.07	.02			
☐	185	Donnie Moore	.15	.07	.02			
☐	186	Dale Murphy	1.75	.80	.22			
☐	187	Phil Niekro	.75	.35	.09			
☐	188	Pascual Perez	.15	.07	.02			
☐	189	Biff Pocoroba	.15	.07	.02			
☐	190	Rafael Ramirez	.15	.07	.02			
☐	191	Jerry Royster	.15	.07	.02			
☐	192	Claudell Washington	.15	.07	.02			
☐	193	Bob Watson	.20	.09	.03			
☐	194	Jerry Augustine	.15	.07	.02			
☐	195	Mark Brouhard	.15	.07	.02			
☐	196	Mike Caldwell	.15	.07	.02			
☐	197	Tom Candiotti	1.00	.45	.13			
☐	198	Cecil Cooper	.20	.09	.03			
☐	199	Rollie Fingers	1.00	.45	.13			
☐	200	Jim Gantner	.20	.09	.03			
☐	201	Bob L. Gibson	.15	.07	.02			
☐	202	Moose Haas	.15	.07	.02			
☐	203	Roy Howell	.15	.07	.02			
☐	204	Pete Ladd	.15	.07	.02			
☐	205	Rick Manning	.15	.07	.02			
☐	206	Bob McClure	.15	.07	.02			
☐	207	Paul Molitor UER	1.25	.55	.16			
		('83 stats should say						
		.270 BA and 608 AB)						
☐	208	Don Money	.15	.07	.02			
☐	209	Charlie Moore	.15	.07	.02			
☐	210	Ben Oglivie	.15	.07	.02			
☐	211	Chuck Porter	.15	.07	.02			
☐	212	Ed Romero	.15	.07	.02			
☐	213	Ted Simmons	.20	.09	.03			
☐	214	Jim Slaton	.15	.07	.02			
☐	215	Don Sutton	.75	.35	.09			
☐	216	Tom Tellmann	.15	.07	.02			
☐	217	Pete Vuckovich	.15	.07	.02			
☐	218	Ned Yost	.15	.07	.02			
☐	219	Robin Yount	6.00	2.70	.75			
☐	220	Alan Ashby	.15	.07	.02			
☐	221	Kevin Bass	.15	.07	.02			
☐	222	Jose Cruz	.20	.09	.03			
☐	223	Bill Dawley	.15	.07	.02			
☐	224	Frank DiPino	.15	.07	.02			
☐	225	Bill Doran	.50	.23	.06			
☐	226	Phil Garner	.20	.09	.03			
☐	227	Art Howe	.15	.07	.02			
☐	228	Bob Knepper	.15	.07	.02			
☐	229	Ray Knight	.20	.09	.03			
☐	230	Frank LaCorte	.15	.07	.02			
☐	231	Mike LaCoss	.15	.07	.02			
☐	232	Mike Madden	.15	.07	.02			
☐	233	Jerry Mumphrey	.15	.07	.02			
☐	234	Joe Niekro	.20	.09	.03			
☐	235	Terry Puhl	.15	.07	.02			
☐	236	Luis Pujols	.15	.07	.02			
☐	237	Craig Reynolds	.15	.07	.02			
☐	238	Vern Ruhle	.15	.07	.02			
☐	239	Nolan Ryan	18.00	8.00	2.30			

☐	240	Mike Scott	.20	.09	.03			
☐	241	Tony Scott	.15	.07	.02			
☐	242	Dave Smith	.15	.07	.02			
☐	243	Dickie Thon	.15	.07	.02			
☐	244	Denny Walling	.15	.07	.02			
☐	245	Dale Berra	.15	.07	.02			
☐	246	Jim Bibby	.15	.07	.02			
☐	247	John Candelaria	.15	.07	.02			
☐	248	Jose DeLeon	.20	.09	.03			
☐	249	Mike Easler	.15	.07	.02			
☐	250	Cecilio Guante	.15	.07	.02			
☐	251	Richie Hebner	.15	.07	.02			
☐	252	Lee Lacy	.15	.07	.02			
☐	253	Bill Madlock	.20	.09	.03			
☐	254	Milt May	.15	.07	.02			
☐	255	Lee Mazzilli	.15	.07	.02			
☐	256	Larry McWilliams	.15	.07	.02			
☐	257	Jim Morrison	.15	.07	.02			
☐	258	Dave Parker	.60	.25	.08			
☐	259	Tony Pena	.20	.09	.03			
☐	260	Johnny Ray	.15	.07	.02			
☐	261	Rick Rhoden	.15	.07	.02			
☐	262	Don Robinson	.15	.07	.02			
☐	263	Manny Sarmiento	.15	.07	.02			
☐	264	Rod Scurry	.15	.07	.02			
☐	265	Kent Tekulve	.20	.09	.03			
☐	266	Gene Tenace	.15	.07	.02			
☐	267	Jason Thompson	.15	.07	.02			
☐	268	Lee Tunnell	.15	.07	.02			
☐	269	Marvell Wynne	.15	.07	.02			
☐	270	Ray Burris	.15	.07	.02			
☐	271	Gary Carter	1.00	.45	.13			
☐	272	Warren Cromartie	.15	.07	.02			
☐	273	Andre Dawson	4.00	1.80	.50			
☐	274	Doug Flynn	.15	.07	.02			
☐	275	Terry Francona	.15	.07	.02			
☐	276	Bill Gullickson	.20	.09	.03			
☐	277	Bob James	.15	.07	.02			
☐	278	Charlie Lea	.15	.07	.02			
☐	279	Bryan Little	.15	.07	.02			
☐	280	Al Oliver	.20	.09	.03			
☐	281	Tim Raines	1.00	.45	.13			
☐	282	Bobby Ramos	.15	.07	.02			
☐	283	Jeff Reardon	1.75	.80	.22			
☐	284	Steve Rogers	.15	.07	.02			
☐	285	Scott Sanderson	.15	.07	.02			
☐	286	Dan Schatzeder	.15	.07	.02			
☐	287	Bryn Smith	.15	.07	.02			
☐	288	Chris Speier	.15	.07	.02			
☐	289	Manny Trillo	.15	.07	.02			
☐	290	Mike Vail	.15	.07	.02			
☐	291	Tim Wallach	.20	.09	.03			
☐	292	Chris Welsh	.15	.07	.02			
☐	293	Jim Wohlford	.15	.07	.02			
☐	294	Kurt Bevacqua	.15	.07	.02			
☐	295	Juan Bonilla	.15	.07	.02			
☐	296	Bobby Brown	.15	.07	.02			
☐	297	Luis DeLeon	.15	.07	.02			
☐	298	Dave Dravecky	.20	.09	.03			
☐	299	Tim Flannery	.15	.07	.02			
☐	300	Steve Garvey	.90	.40	.11			
☐	301	Tony Gwynn	13.00	5.75	1.65			
☐	302	Andy Hawkins	.20	.09	.03			
☐	303	Ruppert Jones	.15	.07	.02			
☐	304	Terry Kennedy	.15	.07	.02			
☐	305	Tim Lollar	.15	.07	.02			
☐	306	Gary Lucas	.15	.07	.02			
☐	307	Kevin McReynolds	2.00	.90	.25			
☐	308	Sid Monge	.15	.07	.02			
☐	309	Mario Ramirez	.15	.07	.02			
☐	310	Gene Richards	.15	.07	.02			
☐	311	Luis Salazar	.15	.07	.02			
☐	312	Eric Show	.15	.07	.02			
☐	313	Elias Sosa	.15	.07	.02			
☐	314	Garry Templeton	.20	.09	.03			
☐	315	Mark Thurmond	.15	.07	.02			
☐	316	Ed Whitson	.15	.07	.02			
☐	317	Alan Wiggins	.15	.07	.02			
☐	318	Neil Allen	.15	.07	.02			
☐	319	Joaquin Andujar	.15	.07	.02			
☐	320	Steve Braun	.15	.07	.02			
☐	321	Glenn Brummer	.15	.07	.02			
☐	322	Bob Forsch	.15	.07	.02			
☐	323	David Green	.15	.07	.02			
☐	324	George Hendrick	.15	.07	.02			
☐	325	Tom Herr	.20	.09	.03			
☐	326	Dane Iorg	.15	.07	.02			
☐	327	Jeff Lahti	.15	.07	.02			
☐	328	Dave LaPoint	.20	.09	.03			
☐	329	Willie McGee	.75	.35	.09			
☐	330	Ken Oberkfell	.15	.07	.02			
☐	331	Darrell Porter	.15	.07	.02			
☐	332	Jamie Quirk	.15	.07	.02			
☐	333	Mike Ramsey	.15	.07	.02			
☐	334	Floyd Rayford	.15	.07	.02			
☐	335	Lonnie Smith	.20	.09	.03			
☐	336	Ozzie Smith	4.00	1.80	.50			
☐	337	John Stuper	.15	.07	.02			
☐	338	Bruce Sutter	.25	.11	.03			
☐	339	Andy Van Slyke UER	8.00	3.60	1.00			
		(Batting and throwing both wrong on card back)						
☐	340	Dave Von Ohlen	.15	.07	.02			
☐	341	Willie Aikens	.15	.07	.02			
☐	342	Mike Armstrong	.15	.07	.02			
☐	343	Bud Black	.15	.07	.02			
☐	344	George Brett	6.00	2.70	.75			
☐	345	Onix Concepcion	.15	.07	.02			
☐	346	Keith Creel	.15	.07	.02			
☐	347	Larry Gura	.15	.07	.02			
☐	348	Don Hood	.15	.07	.02			
☐	349	Dennis Leonard	.15	.07	.02			
☐	350	Hal McRae	.20	.09	.03			
☐	351	Amos Otis	.20	.09	.03			

☐ 352	Gaylord Perry	75	.35	.09
☐ 353	Greg Pryor	.15	.07	.02
☐ 354	Dan Quisenberry	.20	.09	.03
☐ 355	Steve Renko	.15	.07	.02
☐ 356	Leon Roberts	.15	.07	.02
☐ 357	Pat Sheridan	.15	.07	.02
☐ 358	Joe Simpson	.15	.07	.02
☐ 359	Don Slaught	.20	.09	.03
☐ 360	Paul Splittorff	.15	.07	.02
☐ 361	U.L. Washington	.15	.07	.02
☐ 362	John Wathan	.15	.07	.02
☐ 363	Frank White	.20	.09	.03
☐ 364	Willie Wilson	.20	.09	.03
☐ 365	Jim Barr	.15	.07	.02
☐ 366	Dave Bergman	.15	.07	.02
☐ 367	Fred Breining	.15	.07	.02
☐ 368	Bob Brenly	.15	.07	.02
☐ 369	Jack Clark	.20	.09	.03
☐ 370	Chili Davis	.30	.14	.04
☐ 371	Mark Davis	.20	.09	.03
☐ 372	Darrell Evans	.20	.09	.03
☐ 373	Atlee Hammaker	.15	.07	.02
☐ 374	Mike Krukow	.15	.07	.02
☐ 375	Duane Kuiper	.15	.07	.02
☐ 376	Bill Laskey	.15	.07	.02
☐ 377	Gary Lavelle	.15	.07	.02
☐ 378	Johnnie LeMaster	.15	.07	.02
☐ 379	Jeff Leonard	.15	.07	.02
☐ 380	Randy Lerch	.15	.07	.02
☐ 381	Renie Martin	.15	.07	.02
☐ 382	Andy McGaffigan	.15	.07	.02
☐ 383	Greg Minton	.15	.07	.02
☐ 384	Tom O'Malley	.15	.07	.02
☐ 385	Max Venable	.15	.07	.02
☐ 386	Brad Wellman	.15	.07	.02
☐ 387	Joel Youngblood	.15	.07	.02
☐ 388	Gary Allenson	.15	.07	.02
☐ 389	Luis Aponte	.15	.07	.02
☐ 390	Tony Armas	.15	.07	.02
☐ 391	Doug Bird	.15	.07	.02
☐ 392	Wade Boggs	10.00	4.50	1.25
☐ 393	Dennis Boyd	.20	.09	.03
☐ 394	Mike Brown UER P	.15	.07	.02
	(shown with record			
	of 31-104)			
☐ 395	Mark Clear	.15	.07	.02
☐ 396	Dennis Eckersley	3.50	1.55	.45
☐ 397	Dwight Evans	.35	.16	.04
☐ 398	Rich Gedman	.15	.07	.02
☐ 399	Glenn Hoffman	.15	.07	.02
☐ 400	Bruce Hurst	.20	.09	.03
☐ 401	John Henry Johnson	.15	.07	.02
☐ 402	Ed Jurak	.15	.07	.02
☐ 403	Rick Miller	.15	.07	.02
☐ 404	Jeff Newman	.15	.07	.02
☐ 405	Reid Nichols	.15	.07	.02
☐ 406	Bob Ojeda	.15	.07	.02
☐ 407	Jerry Remy	.15	.07	.02
☐ 408	Jim Rice	.30	.14	.04
☐ 409	Bob Stanley	.15	.07	.02
☐ 410	Dave Stapleton	.15	.07	.02
☐ 411	John Tudor	.20	.09	.03
☐ 412	Carl Yastrzemski	3.00	1.35	.40
☐ 413	Buddy Bell	.20	.09	.03
☐ 414	Larry Biittner	.15	.07	.02
☐ 415	John Butcher	.15	.07	.02
☐ 416	Danny Darwin	.15	.07	.02
☐ 417	Bucky Dent	.20	.09	.03
☐ 418	Dave Hostetler	.15	.07	.02
☐ 419	Charlie Hough	.20	.09	.03
☐ 420	Bobby Johnson	.15	.07	.02
☐ 421	Odell Jones	.15	.07	.02
☐ 422	Jon Matlack	.15	.07	.02
☐ 423	Pete O'Brien	.40	.18	.05
☐ 424	Larry Parrish	.15	.07	.02
☐ 425	Mickey Rivers	.15	.07	.02
☐ 426	Billy Sample	.15	.07	.02
☐ 427	Dave Schmidt	.15	.07	.02
☐ 428	Mike Smithson	.15	.07	.02
☐ 429	Bill Stein	.15	.07	.02
☐ 430	Dave Stewart	.90	.40	.11
☐ 431	Jim Sundberg	.20	.09	.03
☐ 432	Frank Tanana	.20	.09	.03
☐ 433	Dave Tobik	.15	.07	.02
☐ 434	Wayne Tolleson	.15	.07	.02
☐ 435	George Wright	.15	.07	.02
☐ 436	Bill Almon	.15	.07	.02
☐ 437	Keith Atherton	.15	.07	.02
☐ 438	Dave Beard	.15	.07	.02
☐ 439	Tom Burgmeier	.15	.07	.02
☐ 440	Jeff Burroughs	.15	.07	.02
☐ 441	Chris Codiroli	.15	.07	.02
☐ 442	Tim Conroy	.15	.07	.02
☐ 443	Mike Davis	.15	.07	.02
☐ 444	Wayne Gross	.15	.07	.02
☐ 445	Garry Hancock	.15	.07	.02
☐ 446	Mike Heath	.15	.07	.02
☐ 447	Rickey Henderson	9.00	4.00	1.15
☐ 448	Donnie Hill	.15	.07	.02
☐ 449	Bob Kearney	.15	.07	.02
☐ 450	Bill Krueger	.40	.18	.05
☐ 451	Rick Langford	.15	.07	.02
☐ 452	Carney Lansford	.20	.09	.03
☐ 453	Dave Lopes	.20	.09	.03
☐ 454	Steve McCatty	.15	.07	.02
☐ 455	Dan Meyer	.15	.07	.02
☐ 456	Dwayne Murphy	.15	.07	.02
☐ 457	Mike Norris	.15	.07	.02
☐ 458	Ricky Peters	.15	.07	.02
☐ 459	Tony Phillips	1.50	.65	.19
☐ 460	Tom Underwood	.15	.07	.02
☐ 461	Mike Warren	.15	.07	.02
☐ 462	Johnny Bench	3.00	1.35	.40
☐ 463	Bruce Berenyi	.15	.07	.02

☐	464	Dann Bilardello	.15	.07	.02		
☐	465	Cesar Cedeno	.20	.09	.03		
☐	466	Dave Concepcion	.20	.09	.03		
☐	467	Dan Driessen	.15	.07	.02		
☐	468	Nick Esasky	.20	.09	.03		
☐	469	Rich Gale	.15	.07	.02		
☐	470	Ben Hayes	.15	.07	.02		
☐	471	Paul Householder	.15	.07	.02		
☐	472	Tom Hume	.15	.07	.02		
☐	473	Alan Knicely	.15	.07	.02		
☐	474	Eddie Milner	.15	.07	.02		
☐	475	Ron Oester	.15	.07	.02		
☐	476	Kelly Paris	.15	.07	.02		
☐	477	Frank Pastore	.15	.07	.02		
☐	478	Ted Power	.15	.07	.02		
☐	479	Joe Price	.15	.07	.02		
☐	480	Charlie Puleo	.15	.07	.02		
☐	481	Gary Redus	.30	.14	.04		
☐	482	Bill Scherrer	.15	.07	.02		
☐	483	Mario Soto	.15	.07	.02		
☐	484	Alex Trevino	.15	.07	.02		
☐	485	Duane Walker	.15	.07	.02		
☐	486	Larry Bowa	.20	.09	.03		
☐	487	Warren Brusstar	.15	.07	.02		
☐	488	Bill Buckner	.20	.09	.03		
☐	489	Bill Campbell	.15	.07	.02		
☐	490	Ron Cey	.20	.09	.03		
☐	491	Jody Davis	.15	.07	.02		
☐	492	Leon Durham	.15	.07	.02		
☐	493	Mel Hall	.75	.35	.09		
☐	494	Ferguson Jenkins	.75	.35	.09		
☐	495	Jay Johnstone	.20	.09	.03		
☐	496	Craig Lefferts	.75	.35	.09		
☐	497	Carmelo Martinez	.20	.09	.03		
☐	498	Jerry Morales	.15	.07	.02		
☐	499	Keith Moreland	.15	.07	.02		
☐	500	Dickie Noles	.15	.07	.02		
☐	501	Mike Proly	.15	.07	.02		
☐	502	Chuck Rainey	.15	.07	.02		
☐	503	Dick Ruthven	.15	.07	.02		
☐	504	Ryne Sandberg	20.00	9.00	2.50		
☐	505	Lee Smith	1.75	.80	.22		
☐	506	Steve Trout	.15	.07	.02		
☐	507	Gary Woods	.15	.07	.02		
☐	508	Juan Beniquez	.15	.07	.02		
☐	509	Bob Boone	.20	.09	.03		
☐	510	Rick Burleson	.15	.07	.02		
☐	511	Rod Carew	3.00	1.35	.40		
☐	512	Bobby Clark	.15	.07	.02		
☐	513	John Curtis	.15	.07	.02		
☐	514	Doug DeCinces	.15	.07	.02		
☐	515	Brian Downing	.20	.09	.03		
☐	516	Tim Foli	.15	.07	.02		
☐	517	Ken Forsch	.15	.07	.02		
☐	518	Bobby Grich	.20	.09	.03		
☐	519	Andy Hassler	.15	.07	.02		
☐	520	Reggie Jackson	3.50	1.55	.45		
☐	521	Ron Jackson	.15	.07	.02		
☐	522	Tommy John	.25	.11	.03		
☐	523	Bruce Kison	.15	.07	.02		
☐	524	Steve Lubratich	.15	.07	.02		
☐	525	Fred Lynn	.20	.09	.03		
☐	526	Gary Pettis	.20	.09	.03		
☐	527	Luis Sanchez	.15	.07	.02		
☐	528	Daryl Sconiers	.15	.07	.02		
☐	529	Ellis Valentine	.15	.07	.02		
☐	530	Rob Wilfong	.15	.07	.02		
☐	531	Mike Witt	.15	.07	.02		
☐	532	Geoff Zahn	.15	.07	.02		
☐	533	Bud Anderson	.15	.07	.02		
☐	534	Chris Bando	.15	.07	.02		
☐	535	Alan Bannister	.15	.07	.02		
☐	536	Bert Blyleven	.50	.23	.06		
☐	537	Tom Brennan	.15	.07	.02		
☐	538	Jamie Easterly	.15	.07	.02		
☐	539	Juan Eichelberger	.15	.07	.02		
☐	540	Jim Essian	.15	.07	.02		
☐	541	Mike Fischlin	.15	.07	.02		
☐	542	Julio Franco	2.25	1.00	.30		
☐	543	Mike Hargrove	.20	.09	.03		
☐	544	Toby Harrah	.15	.07	.02		
☐	545	Ron Hassey	.15	.07	.02		
☐	546	Neal Heaton	.20	.09	.03		
☐	547	Bake McBride	.15	.07	.02		
☐	548	Broderick Perkins	.15	.07	.02		
☐	549	Lary Sorensen	.15	.07	.02		
☐	550	Dan Spillner	.15	.07	.02		
☐	551	Rick Sutcliffe	.25	.11	.03		
☐	552	Pat Tabler	.15	.07	.02		
☐	553	Gorman Thomas	.15	.07	.02		
☐	554	Andre Thornton	.15	.07	.02		
☐	555	George Vukovich	.15	.07	.02		
☐	556	Darrell Brown	.15	.07	.02		
☐	557	Tom Brunansky	.25	.11	.03		
☐	558	Randy Bush	.15	.07	.02		
☐	559	Bobby Castillo	.15	.07	.02		
☐	560	John Castino	.15	.07	.02		
☐	561	Ron Davis	.15	.07	.02		
☐	562	Dave Engle	.15	.07	.02		
☐	563	Lenny Faedo	.15	.07	.02		
☐	564	Pete Filson	.15	.07	.02		
☐	565	Gary Gaetti	.20	.09	.03		
☐	566	Mickey Hatcher	.15	.07	.02		
☐	567	Kent Hrbek	.60	.25	.08		
☐	568	Rusty Kuntz	.15	.07	.02		
☐	569	Tim Laudner	.15	.07	.02		
☐	570	Rick Lysander	.15	.07	.02		
☐	571	Bobby Mitchell	.15	.07	.02		
☐	572	Ken Schrom	.15	.07	.02		
☐	573	Ray Smith	.15	.07	.02		
☐	574	Tim Teufel	.30	.14	.04		
☐	575	Frank Viola	1.00	.45	.13		
☐	576	Gary Ward	.15	.07	.02		
☐	577	Ron Washington	.15	.07	.02		

☐ 578	Len Whitehouse	.15	.07	.02
☐ 579	Al Williams	.15	.07	.02
☐ 580	Bob Bailor	.15	.07	.02
☐ 581	Mark Bradley	.15	.07	.02
☐ 582	Hubie Brooks	.20	.09	.03
☐ 583	Carlos Diaz	.15	.07	.02
☐ 584	George Foster	.20	.09	.03
☐ 585	Brian Giles	.15	.07	.02
☐ 586	Danny Heep	.15	.07	.02
☐ 587	Keith Hernandez	.25	.11	.03
☐ 588	Ron Hodges	.15	.07	.02
☐ 589	Scott Holman	.15	.07	.02
☐ 590	Dave Kingman	.20	.09	.03
☐ 591	Ed Lynch	.15	.07	.02
☐ 592	Jose Oquendo	.25	.11	.03
☐ 593	Jesse Orosco	.15	.07	.02
☐ 594	Junior Ortiz	.15	.07	.02
☐ 595	Tom Seaver	4.00	1.80	.50
☐ 596	Doug Sisk	.15	.07	.02
☐ 597	Rusty Staub	.20	.09	.03
☐ 598	John Stearns	.15	.07	.02
☐ 599	Darryl Strawberry	25.00	11.50	3.10
☐ 600	Craig Swan	.15	.07	.02
☐ 601	Walt Terrell	.25	.11	.03
☐ 602	Mike Torrez	.15	.07	.02
☐ 603	Mookie Wilson	.20	.09	.03
☐ 604	Jamie Allen	.15	.07	.02
☐ 605	Jim Beattie	.15	.07	.02
☐ 606	Tony Bernazard	.15	.07	.02
☐ 607	Manny Castillo	.15	.07	.02
☐ 608	Bill Caudill	.15	.07	.02
☐ 609	Bryan Clark	.15	.07	.02
☐ 610	Al Cowens	.15	.07	.02
☐ 611	Dave Henderson	.25	.11	.03
☐ 612	Steve Henderson	.15	.07	.02
☐ 613	Orlando Mercado	.15	.07	.02
☐ 614	Mike Moore	.35	.16	.04
☐ 615	Ricky Nelson UER	.15	.07	.02
	(Jamie Nelson's			
	stats on back)			
☐ 616	Spike Owen	.30	.14	.04
☐ 617	Pat Putnam	.15	.07	.02
☐ 618	Ron Roenicke	.15	.07	.02
☐ 619	Mike Stanton	.15	.07	.02
☐ 620	Bob Stoddard	.15	.07	.02
☐ 621	Rick Sweet	.15	.07	.02
☐ 622	Roy Thomas	.15	.07	.02
☐ 623	Ed VandeBerg	.15	.07	.02
☐ 624	Matt Young	.20	.09	.03
☐ 625	Richie Zisk	.15	.07	.02
☐ 626	Fred Lynn	.20	.09	.03
	1982 AS Game RB			
☐ 627	Manny Trillo	.20	.09	.03
	1983 AS Game RB			
☐ 628	Steve Garvey	.40	.18	.05
	NL Iron Man			
☐ 629	Rod Carew	.60	.25	.08

	AL Batting Runner-Up			
☐ 630	Wade Boggs	2.00	.90	.25
	AL Batting Champion			
☐ 631	Tim Raines: Letting	.40	.18	.05
	Go of the Raines			
☐ 632	Al Oliver	.20	.09	.03
	Double Trouble			
☐ 633	Steve Sax	.20	.09	.03
	AS Second Base			
☐ 634	Dickie Thon	.20	.09	.03
	AS Shortstop			
☐ 635	Ace Firemen	.20	.09	.03
	Dan Quisenberry			
	and Tippy Martinez			
☐ 636	Reds Reunited	.75	.35	.09
	Joe Morgan			
	Pete Rose			
	Tony Perez			
☐ 637	Backstop Stars	.20	.09	.03
	Lance Parrish			
	Bob Boone			
☐ 638	George Brett and	1.25	.55	.16
	Gaylord Perry			
	Pine Tar 7/24/83			
☐ 639	1983 No Hitters	.20	.09	.03
	Dave Righetti			
	Mike Warren			
	Bob Forsch			
☐ 640	Johnny Bench and	3.00	1.35	.40
	Carl Yastrzemski			
	Retiring Superstars			
☐ 641	Gaylord Perry	.35	.16	.04
	Going Out In Style			
☐ 642	Steve Carlton	.75	.35	.09
	300 Club and			
	Strikeout Record			
☐ 643	Joe Altobelli and	.20	.09	.03
	Paul Owens			
	World Series Managers			
☐ 644	Rick Dempsey	.20	.09	.03
	World Series MVP			
☐ 645	Mike Boddicker	.20	.09	.03
	WS Rookie Winner			
☐ 646	Scott McGregor	.20	.09	.03
	WS Clincher			
☐ 647	CL: Orioles/Royals	.20	.02	.01
☐ 648	CL: Phillies/Giants	.20	.02	.01
☐ 649	CL: White Sox/Red Sox	.20	.02	.01
☐ 650	CL: Tigers/Rangers	.20	.02	.01
☐ 651	CL: Dodgers/A's	.20	.02	.01
☐ 652	CL: Yankees/Reds	.20	.02	.01
☐ 653	CL: Blue Jays/Cubs	.20	.02	.01
☐ 654	CL: Braves/Angels	.20	.02	.01
☐ 655	CL: Brewers/Indians	.20	.02	.01
☐ 656	CL: Astros/Twins	.20	.02	.01
☐ 657	CL: Pirates/Mets	.20	.02	.01
☐ 658	CL: Expos/Mariners	.20	.02	.01

			NRMT-MT	EXC	G-VG
☐ 659	CL: Padres/Specials	.20	.02		.01
☐ 660	CL: Cardinals/Teams	.20	.02		.01

1984 Fleer Update

The cards in this 132-card set measure 2 1/2" by 3 1/2". For the first time, the Fleer Gum Company issued a traded, extended, or update set. The purpose of the set was the same as the traded sets issued by Topps over the past four years, i.e., to portray players with their proper team for the current year and to portray rookies who were not in their regular issue. Like the Topps Traded sets of the past four years, the Fleer Update sets were distributed through hobby dealers only. The set was quite popular with collectors, and, apparently, the print run was relatively short, as the set was quickly in short supply and exhibited a rapid and dramatic price increase. The cards are numbered on the back with a U prefix; the order corresponds to the alphabetical order of the subjects' names. The key (extended) Rookie Cards in this set are Roger Clemens, Ron Darling, Alvin Davis, John Franco, Dwight Gooden, Jimmy Key, Mark Langston, Kirby Puckett, Jose Rijo, and Bret Saberhagen. Collectors are urged to be careful if purchasing single cards of Clemens, Darling, Gooden, Puckett, Rose, or Saberhagen as these specific cards have been illegally reprinted. These fakes are blurry when compared to the real thing.

		NRMT-MT	EXC	G-VG
COMPLETE SET (132)		950.00	425.00	120.00
COMMON PLAYER (1-132)		1.00	.45	.13
☐ 1	Willie Aikens	1.00	.45	.13
☐ 2	Luis Aponte	1.00	.45	.13
☐ 3	Mark Bailey	1.00	.45	.13
☐ 4	Bob Bailor	1.00	.45	.13
☐ 5	Dusty Baker	1.25	.55	.16
☐ 6	Steve Balboni	1.00	.45	.13
☐ 7	Alan Bannister	1.00	.45	.13
☐ 8	Marty Barrett	1.25	.55	.16
☐ 9	Dave Beard	1.00	.45	.13
☐ 10	Joe Beckwith	1.00	.45	.13
☐ 11	Dave Bergman	1.00	.45	.13
☐ 12	Tony Bernazard	1.00	.45	.13
☐ 13	Bruce Bochte	1.00	.45	.13
☐ 14	Barry Bonnell	1.00	.45	.13
☐ 15	Phil Bradley	1.25	.55	.16
☐ 16	Fred Breining	1.00	.45	.13
☐ 17	Mike C. Brown OF	1.00	.45	.13
☐ 18	Bill Buckner	1.25	.55	.16
☐ 19	Ray Burris	1.00	.45	.13
☐ 20	John Butcher	1.00	.45	.13
☐ 21	Brett Butler	3.00	1.35	.40
☐ 22	Enos Cabell	1.00	.45	.13
☐ 23	Bill Campbell	1.00	.45	.13
☐ 24	Bill Caudill	1.00	.45	.13
☐ 25	Bobby Clark	1.00	.45	.13
☐ 26	Bryan Clark	1.00	.45	.13
☐ 27	Roger Clemens	450.00	200.00	57.50
☐ 28	Jaime Cocanower	1.00	.45	.13
☐ 29	Ron Darling	10.00	4.50	1.25
☐ 30	Alvin Davis	2.00	.90	.25
☐ 31	Bob Dernier	1.00	.45	.13
☐ 32	Carlos Diaz	1.00	.45	.13
☐ 33	Mike Easler	1.00	.45	.13
☐ 34	Dennis Eckersley	20.00	9.00	2.50
☐ 35	Jim Essian	1.00	.45	.13
☐ 36	Darrell Evans	1.25	.55	.16
☐ 37	Mike Fitzgerald	1.00	.45	.13
☐ 38	Tim Foli	1.00	.45	.13
☐ 39	John Franco	10.00	4.50	1.25
☐ 40	George Frazier	1.00	.45	.13
☐ 41	Rich Gale	1.00	.45	.13
☐ 42	Barbaro Garbey	1.00	.45	.13
☐ 43	Dwight Gooden	90.00	40.00	11.50
☐ 44	Rich Gossage	1.50	.65	.19
☐ 45	Wayne Gross	1.00	.45	.13
☐ 46	Mark Gubicza	4.00	1.80	.50
☐ 47	Jackie Gutierrez	1.00	.45	.13
☐ 48	Toby Harrah	1.00	.45	.13
☐ 49	Ron Hassey	1.00	.45	.13
☐ 50	Richie Hebner	1.00	.45	.13
☐ 51	Willie Hernandez	1.25	.55	.16
☐ 52	Ed Hodge	1.00	.45	.13
☐ 53	Ricky Horton	1.00	.45	.13

☐	54 Art Howe	1.00	.45	.13
☐	55 Dane Iorg	1.00	.45	.13
☐	56 Brook Jacoby	1.50	.65	.19
☐	57 Dion James	1.25	.55	.16
☐	58 Mike Jeffcoat	1.00	.45	.13
☐	59 Ruppert Jones	1.00	.45	.13
☐	60 Bob Kearney	1.00	.45	.13
☐	61 Jimmy Key	12.00	5.50	1.50
☐	62 Dave Kingman	1.25	.55	.16
☐	63 Brad Kominsk	1.00	.45	.13
☐	64 Jerry Koosman	1.25	.55	.16
☐	65 Wayne Krenchicki	1.00	.45	.13
☐	66 Rusty Kuntz	1.00	.45	.13
☐	67 Frank LaCorte	1.00	.45	.13
☐	68 Dennis Lamp	1.00	.45	.13
☐	69 Tito Landrum	1.00	.45	.13
☐	70 Mark Langston	25.00	11.50	3.10
☐	71 Rick Leach	1.00	.45	.13
☐	72 Craig Lefferts	1.50	.65	.19
☐	73 Gary Lucas	1.00	.45	.13
☐	74 Jerry Martin	1.00	.45	.13
☐	75 Carmelo Martinez	1.25	.55	.16
☐	76 Mike Mason	1.00	.45	.13
☐	77 Gary Matthews	1.25	.55	.16
☐	78 Andy McGaffigan	1.00	.45	.13
☐	79 Joey McLaughlin	1.00	.45	.13
☐	80 Joe Morgan	10.00	4.50	1.25
☐	81 Darryl Motley	1.00	.45	.13
☐	82 Graig Nettles	1.25	.55	.16
☐	83 Phil Niekro	8.00	3.60	1.00
☐	84 Ken Oberkfell	1.00	.45	.13
☐	85 Al Oliver	1.25	.55	.16
☐	86 Jorge Orta	1.00	.45	.13
☐	87 Amos Otis	1.25	.55	.16
☐	88 Bob Owchinko	1.00	.45	.13
☐	89 Dave Parker	5.00	2.30	.60
☐	90 Jack Perconte	1.00	.45	.13
☐	91 Tony Perez	8.00	3.60	1.00
☐	92 Gerald Perry	1.25	.55	.16
☐	93 Kirby Puckett	375.00	170.00	47.50
☐	94 Shane Rawley	1.00	.45	.13
☐	95 Floyd Rayford	1.00	.45	.13
☐	96 Ron Reed	1.00	.45	.13
☐	97 R.J. Reynolds	1.00	.45	.13
☐	98 Gene Richards	1.00	.45	.13
☐	99 Jose Rijo	27.00	12.00	3.40
☐	100 Jeff D. Robinson	1.25	.55	.16
☐	101 Ron Romanick	1.00	.45	.13
☐	102 Pete Rose	25.00	11.50	3.10
☐	103 Bret Saberhagen	35.00	16.00	4.40
☐	104 Scott Sanderson	1.00	.45	.13
☐	105 Dick Schofield	1.50	.65	.19
☐	106 Tom Seaver	25.00	11.50	3.10
☐	107 Jim Slaton	1.00	.45	.13
☐	108 Mike Smithson	1.00	.45	.13
☐	109 Lary Sorensen	1.00	.45	.13
☐	110 Tim Stoddard	1.00	.45	.13

☐	111 Jeff Stone	1.00	.45	.13
☐	112 Champ Summers	1.00	.45	.13
☐	113 Jim Sundberg	1.25	.55	.16
☐	114 Rick Sutcliffe	1.50	.65	.19
☐	115 Craig Swan	1.00	.45	.13
☐	116 Derrel Thomas	1.00	.45	.13
☐	117 Gorman Thomas	1.00	.45	.13
☐	118 Alex Trevino	1.00	.45	.13
☐	119 Manny Trillo	1.00	.45	.13
☐	120 John Tudor	1.25	.55	.16
☐	121 Tom Underwood	1.00	.45	.13
☐	122 Mike Vail	1.00	.45	.13
☐	123 Tom Waddell	1.00	.45	.13
☐	124 Gary Ward	1.00	.45	.13
☐	125 Terry Whitfield	1.00	.45	.13
☐	126 Curtis Wilkerson	1.00	.45	.13
☐	127 Frank Williams	1.00	.45	.13
☐	128 Glenn Wilson	1.00	.45	.13
☐	129 John Wockenfuss	1.00	.45	.13
☐	130 Ned Yost	1.00	.45	.13
☐	131 Mike Young	1.00	.45	.13
☐	132 Checklist: 1-132	1.25	.13	.04

1985 Fleer

The cards in this 660-card set measure 2 1/2" by 3 1/2". The 1985 Fleer set features fronts that contain the team logo along with the player's name and position. The borders enclosing the photo are color-coded to correspond to the player's team. In each case, the color is one of the standard colors of that team, e.g., orange for Baltimore, red for St. Louis, etc. The backs feature the same name, number, and statistics format that Fleer has been using over the past few years. The cards are ordered alphabetically within team. The

teams are ordered based on their respective performance during the prior year, e.g., World Champion Detroit Tigers (1-25), NL Champion San Diego (26-48), Chicago Cubs (49-71), New York Mets (72-95), Toronto (96-119), New York Yankees (120-147), Boston (148-169), Baltimore (170-195), Kansas City (196-218), St. Louis (219-243), Philadelphia (244-269), Minnesota (270-292), California (293-317), Atlanta (318-342), Houston (343-365), Los Angeles (366-391), Montreal (392-413), Oakland (414-436), Cleveland (437-460), Pittsburgh (461-481), Seattle (482-505), Chicago White Sox (506-530), Cincinnati (531-554), Texas (555-575), Milwaukee (576-601), and San Francisco (602-625). Specials (626-643), Major League Prospects (644-653), and checklist cards (654-660) complete the set. The black and white photo on the reverse is included for the third straight year. This set is noted for containing the Rookie Cards of Roger Clemens, Alvin Davis, Eric Davis, Glenn Davis, Rob Deer, Shawon Dunston, Dwight Gooden, Kelly Gruber, Orel Hershiser, Jimmy Key, Mark Langston, Terry Pendleton, Kirby Puckett, Jose Rijo, Bret Saberhagen, and Danny Tartabull.

	NRMT-MT	EXC	G-VG
COMPLETE SET (660)	200.00	90.00	25.00
COMMON PLAYER (1-660)	.10	.05	.01

☐ 1 Doug Bair	.10	.05	.01
☐ 2 Juan Berenguer	.10	.05	.01
☐ 3 Dave Bergman	.10	.05	.01
☐ 4 Tom Brookens	.10	.05	.01
☐ 5 Marty Castillo	.10	.05	.01
☐ 6 Darrell Evans	.12	.05	.02
☐ 7 Barbaro Garbey	.10	.05	.01
☐ 8 Kirk Gibson	.30	.14	.04
☐ 9 John Grubb	.10	.05	.01
☐ 10 Willie Hernandez	.10	.05	.01
☐ 11 Larry Herndon	.10	.05	.01
☐ 12 Howard Johnson	1.50	.65	.19
☐ 13 Ruppert Jones	.10	.05	.01
☐ 14 Rusty Kuntz	.10	.05	.01
☐ 15 Chet Lemon	.10	.05	.01
☐ 16 Aurelio Lopez	.10	.05	.01
☐ 17 Sid Monge	.10	.05	.01
☐ 18 Jack Morris	1.25	.55	.16
☐ 19 Lance Parrish	.12	.05	.02
☐ 20 Dan Petry	.10	.05	.01
☐ 21 Dave Rozema	.10	.05	.01
☐ 22 Bill Scherrer	.10	.05	.01
☐ 23 Alan Trammell	.50	.23	.06
☐ 24 Lou Whitaker	.50	.23	.06
☐ 25 Milt Wilcox	.10	.05	.01
☐ 26 Kurt Bevacqua	.10	.05	.01
☐ 27 Greg Booker	.10	.05	.01
☐ 28 Bobby Brown	.10	.05	.01
☐ 29 Luis DeLeon	.10	.05	.01
☐ 30 Dave Dravecky	.12	.05	.02
☐ 31 Tim Flannery	.10	.05	.01
☐ 32 Steve Garvey	.40	.18	.05
☐ 33 Rich Gossage	.15	.07	.02
☐ 34 Tony Gwynn	6.00	2.70	.75
☐ 35 Greg Harris	.10	.05	.01
☐ 36 Andy Hawkins	.10	.05	.01
☐ 37 Terry Kennedy	.10	.05	.01
☐ 38 Craig Lefferts	.12	.05	.02
☐ 39 Tim Lollar	.10	.05	.01
☐ 40 Carmelo Martinez	.10	.05	.01
☐ 41 Kevin McReynolds	.35	.16	.04
☐ 42 Graig Nettles	.12	.05	.02
☐ 43 Luis Salazar	.10	.05	.01
☐ 44 Eric Show	.10	.05	.01
☐ 45 Garry Templeton	.10	.05	.01
☐ 46 Mark Thurmond	.10	.05	.01
☐ 47 Ed Whitson	.10	.05	.01
☐ 48 Alan Wiggins	.10	.05	.01
☐ 49 Rich Bordi	.10	.05	.01
☐ 50 Larry Bowa	.12	.05	.02
☐ 51 Warren Brusstar	.10	.05	.01
☐ 52 Ron Cey	.12	.05	.02
☐ 53 Henry Cotto	.10	.05	.01
☐ 54 Jody Davis	.10	.05	.01
☐ 55 Bob Dernier	.10	.05	.01
☐ 56 Leon Durham	.10	.05	.01
☐ 57 Dennis Eckersley	1.25	.55	.16
☐ 58 George Frazier	.10	.05	.01
☐ 59 Richie Hebner	.10	.05	.01
☐ 60 Dave Lopes	.12	.05	.02
☐ 61 Gary Matthews	.10	.05	.01
☐ 62 Keith Moreland	.10	.05	.01
☐ 63 Rick Reuschel	.12	.05	.02
☐ 64 Dick Ruthven	.10	.05	.01
☐ 65 Ryne Sandberg	10.00	4.50	1.25
☐ 66 Scott Sanderson	.10	.05	.01
☐ 67 Lee Smith	1.00	.45	.13
☐ 68 Tim Stoddard	.10	.05	.01
☐ 69 Rick Sutcliffe	.12	.05	.02
☐ 70 Steve Trout	.10	.05	.01
☐ 71 Gary Woods	.10	.05	.01
☐ 72 Wally Backman	.10	.05	.01
☐ 73 Bruce Berenyi	.10	.05	.01
☐ 74 Hubie Brooks UER	.12	.05	.02
(Kelvin Chapman's stats on card back)			
☐ 75 Kelvin Chapman	.10	.05	.01
☐ 76 Ron Darling	.60	.25	.08
☐ 77 Sid Fernandez	.60	.25	.08

☐ 78	Mike Fitzgerald	.10	.05	.01	☐ 135	John Montefusco	.10	.05	.01
☐ 79	George Foster	.12	.05	.02	☐ 136	Omar Moreno	.10	.05	.01
☐ 80	Brent Gaff	.10	.05	.01	☐ 137	Dale Murray	.10	.05	.01
☐ 81	Ron Gardenhire	.10	.05	.01	☐ 138	Phil Niekro	.50	.23	.06
☐ 82	Dwight Gooden	8.00	3.60	1.00	☐ 139	Mike Pagliarulo	.20	.09	.03
☐ 83	Tom Gorman	.10	.05	.01	☐ 140	Willie Randolph	.12	.05	.02
☐ 84	Danny Heep	.10	.05	.01	☐ 141	Dennis Rasmussen	.10	.05	.01
☐ 85	Keith Hernandez	.20	.09	.03	☐ 142	Dave Righetti	.12	.05	.02
☐ 86	Ray Knight	.12	.05	.02	☐ 143	Jose Rijo	3.50	1.55	.45
☐ 87	Ed Lynch	.10	.05	.01	☐ 144	Andre Robertson	.10	.05	.01
☐ 88	Jose Oquendo	.12	.05	.02	☐ 145	Bob Shirley	.10	.05	.01
☐ 89	Jesse Orosco	.10	.05	.01	☐ 146	Dave Winfield	3.50	1.55	.45
☐ 90	Rafael Santana	.10	.05	.01	☐ 147	Butch Wynegar	.10	.05	.01
☐ 91	Doug Sisk	.10	.05	.01	☐ 148	Gary Allenson	.10	.05	.01
☐ 92	Rusty Staub	.12	.05	.02	☐ 149	Tony Armas	.10	.05	.01
☐ 93	Darryl Strawberry	7.00	3.10	.85	☐ 150	Marty Barrett	.10	.05	.01
☐ 94	Walt Terrell	.10	.05	.01	☐ 151	Wade Boggs	5.00	2.30	.60
☐ 95	Mookie Wilson	.12	.05	.02	☐ 152	Dennis Boyd	.10	.05	.01
☐ 96	Jim Acker	.10	.05	.01	☐ 153	Bill Buckner	.12	.05	.02
☐ 97	Willie Aikens	.10	.05	.01	☐ 154	Mark Clear	.10	.05	.01
☐ 98	Doyle Alexander	.10	.05	.01	☐ 155	Roger Clemens	60.00	27.00	7.50
☐ 99	Jesse Barfield	.12	.05	.02	☐ 156	Steve Crawford	.10	.05	.01
☐ 100	George Bell	1.00	.45	.13	☐ 157	Mike Easler	.10	.05	.01
☐ 101	Jim Clancy	.10	.05	.01	☐ 158	Dwight Evans	.20	.09	.03
☐ 102	Dave Collins	.10	.05	.01	☐ 159	Rich Gedman	.10	.05	.01
☐ 103	Tony Fernandez	.75	.35	.09	☐ 160	Jackie Gutierrez	.12	.05	.02
☐ 104	Damaso Garcia	.10	.05	.01		(Wade Boggs			
☐ 105	Jim Gott	.10	.05	.01		shown on deck)			
☐ 106	Alfredo Griffin	.10	.05	.01	☐ 161	Bruce Hurst	.12	.05	.02
☐ 107	Garth Iorg	.10	.05	.01	☐ 162	John Henry Johnson	.10	.05	.01
☐ 108	Roy Lee Jackson	.10	.05	.01	☐ 163	Rick Miller	.10	.05	.01
☐ 109	Cliff Johnson	.10	.05	.01	☐ 164	Reid Nichols	.10	.05	.01
☐ 110	Jimmy Key	2.00	.90	.25	☐ 165	Al Nipper	.10	.05	.01
☐ 111	Dennis Lamp	.10	.05	.01	☐ 166	Bob Ojeda	.10	.05	.01
☐ 112	Rick Leach	.10	.05	.01	☐ 167	Jerry Remy	.10	.05	.01
☐ 113	Luis Leal	.10	.05	.01	☐ 168	Jim Rice	.20	.09	.03
☐ 114	Buck Martinez	.10	.05	.01	☐ 169	Bob Stanley	.10	.05	.01
☐ 115	Lloyd Moseby	.10	.05	.01	☐ 170	Mike Boddicker	.10	.05	.01
☐ 116	Rance Mulliniks	.10	.05	.01	☐ 171	Al Bumbry	.10	.05	.01
☐ 117	Dave Stieb	.12	.05	.02	☐ 172	Todd Cruz	.10	.05	.01
☐ 118	Willie Upshaw	.10	.05	.01	☐ 173	Rich Dauer	.10	.05	.01
☐ 119	Ernie Whitt	.10	.05	.01	☐ 174	Storm Davis	.10	.05	.01
☐ 120	Mike Armstrong	.10	.05	.01	☐ 175	Rick Dempsey	.10	.05	.01
☐ 121	Don Baylor	.12	.05	.02	☐ 176	Jim Dwyer	.10	.05	.01
☐ 122	Marty Bystrom	.10	.05	.01	☐ 177	Mike Flanagan	.10	.05	.01
☐ 123	Rick Cerone	.10	.05	.01	☐ 178	Dan Ford	.10	.05	.01
☐ 124	Joe Cowley	.10	.05	.01	☐ 179	Wayne Gross	.10	.05	.01
☐ 125	Brian Dayett	.10	.05	.01	☐ 180	John Lowenstein	.10	.05	.01
☐ 126	Tim Foli	.10	.05	.01	☐ 181	Dennis Martinez	.12	.05	.02
☐ 127	Ray Fontenot	.10	.05	.01	☐ 182	Tippy Martinez	.10	.05	.01
☐ 128	Ken Griffey	.15	.07	.02	☐ 183	Scott McGregor	.10	.05	.01
☐ 129	Ron Guidry	.12	.05	.02	☐ 184	Eddie Murray	2.00	.90	.25
☐ 130	Toby Harrah	.10	.05	.01	☐ 185	Joe Nolan	.10	.05	.01
☐ 131	Jay Howell	.12	.05	.02	☐ 186	Floyd Rayford	.10	.05	.01
☐ 132	Steve Kemp	.10	.05	.01	☐ 187	Cal Ripken	10.00	4.50	1.25
☐ 133	Don Mattingly	7.00	3.10	.85	☐ 188	Gary Roenicke	.10	.05	.01
☐ 134	Bobby Meacham	.10	.05	.01	☐ 189	Lenn Sakata	.10	.05	.01

☐	190	John Shelby	.10	.05	.01			
☐	191	Ken Singleton	.12	.05	.02			
☐	192	Sammy Stewart	.10	.05	.01			
☐	193	Bill Swaggerty	.10	.05	.01			
☐	194	Tom Underwood	.10	.05	.01			
☐	195	Mike Young	.10	.05	.01			
☐	196	Steve Balboni	.10	.05	.01			
☐	197	Joe Beckwith	.10	.05	.01			
☐	198	Bud Black	.10	.05	.01			
☐	199	George Brett	4.00	1.80	.50			
☐	200	Onix Concepcion	.10	.05	.01			
☐	201	Mark Gubicza	.75	.35	.09			
☐	202	Larry Gura	.10	.05	.01			
☐	203	Mark Huismann	.10	.05	.01			
☐	204	Dane Iorg	.10	.05	.01			
☐	205	Danny Jackson	.10	.05	.01			
☐	206	Charlie Leibrandt	.12	.05	.02			
☐	207	Hal McRae	.12	.05	.02			
☐	208	Darryl Motley	.10	.05	.01			
☐	209	Jorge Orta	.10	.05	.01			
☐	210	Greg Pryor	.10	.05	.01			
☐	211	Dan Quisenberry	.12	.05	.02			
☐	212	Bret Saberhagen	5.00	2.30	.60			
☐	213	Pat Sheridan	.10	.05	.01			
☐	214	Don Slaught	.12	.05	.02			
☐	215	U.L. Washington	.10	.05	.01			
☐	216	John Wathan	.10	.05	.01			
☐	217	Frank White	.12	.05	.02			
☐	218	Willie Wilson	.12	.05	.02			
☐	219	Neil Allen	.10	.05	.01			
☐	220	Joaquin Andujar	.10	.05	.01			
☐	221	Steve Braun	.10	.05	.01			
☐	222	Danny Cox	.10	.05	.01			
☐	223	Bob Forsch	.10	.05	.01			
☐	224	David Green	.10	.05	.01			
☐	225	George Hendrick	.10	.05	.01			
☐	226	Tom Herr	.10	.05	.01			
☐	227	Ricky Horton	.10	.05	.01			
☐	228	Art Howe	.10	.05	.01			
☐	229	Mike Jorgensen	.10	.05	.01			
☐	230	Kurt Kepshire	.10	.05	.01			
☐	231	Jeff Lahti	.10	.05	.01			
☐	232	Tito Landrum	.10	.05	.01			
☐	233	Dave LaPoint	.10	.05	.01			
☐	234	Willie McGee	.40	.18	.05			
☐	235	Tom Nieto	.10	.05	.01			
☐	236	Terry Pendleton	9.00	4.00	1.15			
☐	237	Darrell Porter	.10	.05	.01			
☐	238	Dave Rucker	.10	.05	.01			
☐	239	Lonnie Smith	.10	.05	.01			
☐	240	Ozzie Smith	2.00	.90	.25			
☐	241	Bruce Sutter	.12	.05	.02			
☐	242	Andy Van Slyke UER	2.00	.90	.25			
		(Bats Right,						
		Throws Left)						
☐	243	Dave Von Ohlen	.10	.05	.01			
☐	244	Larry Andersen	.10	.05	.01			
☐	245	Bill Campbell	.10	.05	.01			
☐	246	Steve Carlton	1.75	.80	.22			
☐	247	Tim Corcoran	.10	.05	.01			
☐	248	Ivan DeJesus	.10	.05	.01			
☐	249	John Denny	.10	.05	.01			
☐	250	Bo Diaz	.10	.05	.01			
☐	251	Greg Gross	.10	.05	.01			
☐	252	Kevin Gross	.10	.05	.01			
☐	253	Von Hayes	.10	.05	.01			
☐	254	Al Holland	.10	.05	.01			
☐	255	Charles Hudson	.10	.05	.01			
☐	256	Jerry Koosman	.12	.05	.02			
☐	257	Joe Lefebvre	.10	.05	.01			
☐	258	Sixto Lezcano	.10	.05	.01			
☐	259	Garry Maddox	.10	.05	.01			
☐	260	Len Matuszek	.10	.05	.01			
☐	261	Tug McGraw	.12	.05	.02			
☐	262	Al Oliver	.12	.05	.02			
☐	263	Shane Rawley	.10	.05	.01			
☐	264	Juan Samuel	.20	.09	.03			
☐	265	Mike Schmidt	5.00	2.30	.60			
☐	266	Jeff Stone	.10	.05	.01			
☐	267	Ozzie Virgil	.10	.05	.01			
☐	268	Glenn Wilson	.10	.05	.01			
☐	269	John Wockenfuss	.10	.05	.01			
☐	270	Darrell Brown	.10	.05	.01			
☐	271	Tom Brunansky	.12	.05	.02			
☐	272	Randy Bush	.10	.05	.01			
☐	273	John Butcher	.10	.05	.01			
☐	274	Bobby Castillo	.10	.05	.01			
☐	275	Ron Davis	.10	.05	.01			
☐	276	Dave Engle	.10	.05	.01			
☐	277	Pete Filson	.10	.05	.01			
☐	278	Gary Gaetti	.12	.05	.02			
☐	279	Mickey Hatcher	.10	.05	.01			
☐	280	Ed Hodge	.10	.05	.01			
☐	281	Kent Hrbek	.40	.18	.05			
☐	282	Houston Jimenez	.10	.05	.01			
☐	283	Tim Laudner	.10	.05	.01			
☐	284	Rick Lysander	.10	.05	.01			
☐	285	Dave Meier	.10	.05	.01			
☐	286	Kirby Puckett	50.00	23.00	6.25			
☐	287	Pat Putnam	.10	.05	.01			
☐	288	Ken Schrom	.10	.05	.01			
☐	289	Mike Smithson	.10	.05	.01			
☐	290	Tim Teufel	.10	.05	.01			
☐	291	Frank Viola	.50	.23	.06			
☐	292	Ron Washington	.10	.05	.01			
☐	293	Don Aase	.10	.05	.01			
☐	294	Juan Beniquez	.10	.05	.01			
☐	295	Bob Boone	.12	.05	.02			
☐	296	Mike C. Brown OF	.10	.05	.01			
☐	297	Rod Carew	1.75	.80	.22			
☐	298	Doug Corbett	.10	.05	.01			
☐	299	Doug DeCinces	.10	.05	.01			
☐	300	Brian Downing	.12	.05	.02			
☐	301	Ken Forsch	.10	.05	.01			

☐ 302 Bobby Grich	.12	.05	.02
☐ 303 Reggie Jackson	2.00	.90	.25
☐ 304 Tommy John	.20	.09	.03
☐ 305 Curt Kaufman	.10	.05	.01
☐ 306 Bruce Kison	.10	.05	.01
☐ 307 Fred Lynn	.12	.05	.02
☐ 308 Gary Pettis	.10	.05	.01
☐ 309 Ron Romanick	.10	.05	.01
☐ 310 Luis Sanchez	.10	.05	.01
☐ 311 Dick Schofield	.10	.05	.01
☐ 312 Daryl Sconiers	.10	.05	.01
☐ 313 Jim Slaton	.10	.05	.01
☐ 314 Derrel Thomas	.10	.05	.01
☐ 315 Rob Wilfong	.10	.05	.01
☐ 316 Mike Witt	.10	.05	.01
☐ 317 Geoff Zahn	.10	.05	.01
☐ 318 Len Barker	.10	.05	.01
☐ 319 Steve Bedrosian	.10	.05	.01
☐ 320 Bruce Benedict	.10	.05	.01
☐ 321 Rick Camp	.10	.05	.01
☐ 322 Chris Chambliss	.12	.05	.02
☐ 323 Jeff Dedmon	.10	.05	.01
☐ 324 Terry Forster	.10	.05	.01
☐ 325 Gene Garber	.10	.05	.01
☐ 326 Albert Hall	.10	.05	.01
☐ 327 Terry Harper	.10	.05	.01
☐ 328 Bob Horner	.12	.05	.02
☐ 329 Glenn Hubbard	.10	.05	.01
☐ 330 Randy Johnson	.10	.05	.01
☐ 331 Brad Komminsk	.10	.05	.01
☐ 332 Rick Mahler	.10	.05	.01
☐ 333 Craig McMurtry	.10	.05	.01
☐ 334 Donnie Moore	.10	.05	.01
☐ 335 Dale Murphy	1.00	.45	.13
☐ 336 Ken Oberkfell	.10	.05	.01
☐ 337 Pascual Perez	.10	.05	.01
☐ 338 Gerald Perry	.10	.05	.01
☐ 339 Rafael Ramirez	.10	.05	.01
☐ 340 Jerry Royster	.10	.05	.01
☐ 341 Alex Trevino	.10	.05	.01
☐ 342 Claudell Washington	.10	.05	.01
☐ 343 Alan Ashby	.10	.05	.01
☐ 344 Mark Bailey	.10	.05	.01
☐ 345 Kevin Bass	.10	.05	.01
☐ 346 Enos Cabell	.10	.05	.01
☐ 347 Jose Cruz	.12	.05	.02
☐ 348 Bill Dawley	.10	.05	.01
☐ 349 Frank DiPino	.10	.05	.01
☐ 350 Bill Doran	.12	.05	.02
☐ 351 Phil Garner	.12	.05	.02
☐ 352 Bob Knepper	.10	.05	.01
☐ 353 Mike LaCoss	.10	.05	.01
☐ 354 Jerry Mumphrey	.10	.05	.01
☐ 355 Joe Niekro	.12	.05	.02
☐ 356 Terry Puhl	.10	.05	.01
☐ 357 Craig Reynolds	.10	.05	.01
☐ 358 Vern Ruhle	.10	.05	.01
☐ 359 Nolan Ryan	10.00	4.50	1.25
☐ 360 Joe Sambito	.10	.05	.01
☐ 361 Mike Scott	.12	.05	.02
☐ 362 Dave Smith	.10	.05	.01
☐ 363 Julio Solano	.10	.05	.01
☐ 364 Dickie Thon	.10	.05	.01
☐ 365 Denny Walling	.10	.05	.01
☐ 366 Dave Anderson	.10	.05	.01
☐ 367 Bob Bailor	.10	.05	.01
☐ 368 Greg Brock	.10	.05	.01
☐ 369 Carlos Diaz	.10	.05	.01
☐ 370 Pedro Guerrero	.15	.07	.02
☐ 371 Orel Hershiser	3.50	1.55	.45
☐ 372 Rick Honeycutt	.10	.05	.01
☐ 373 Burt Hooton	.10	.05	.01
☐ 374 Ken Howell	.10	.05	.01
☐ 375 Ken Landreaux	.10	.05	.01
☐ 376 Candy Maldonado	.12	.05	.02
☐ 377 Mike Marshall	.10	.05	.01
☐ 378 Tom Niedenfuer	.10	.05	.01
☐ 379 Alejandro Pena	.10	.05	.01
☐ 380 Jerry Reuss UER	.10	.05	.01
("Home:" omitted)			
☐ 381 R.J. Reynolds	.10	.05	.01
☐ 382 German Rivera	.10	.05	.01
☐ 383 Bill Russell	.12	.05	.02
☐ 384 Steve Sax	.50	.23	.06
☐ 385 Mike Scioscia	.12	.05	.02
☐ 386 Franklin Stubbs	.20	.09	.03
☐ 387 Fernando Valenzuela	.12	.05	.02
☐ 388 Bob Welch	.20	.09	.03
☐ 389 Terry Whitfield	.10	.05	.01
☐ 390 Steve Yeager	.10	.05	.01
☐ 391 Pat Zachry	.10	.05	.01
☐ 392 Fred Breining	.10	.05	.01
☐ 393 Gary Carter	.60	.25	.08
☐ 394 Andre Dawson	2.00	.90	.25
☐ 395 Miguel Dilone	.10	.05	.01
☐ 396 Dan Driessen	.10	.05	.01
☐ 397 Doug Flynn	.10	.05	.01
☐ 398 Terry Francona	.10	.05	.01
☐ 399 Bill Gullickson	.12	.05	.02
☐ 400 Bob James	.10	.05	.01
☐ 401 Charlie Lea	.10	.05	.01
☐ 402 Bryan Little	.10	.05	.01
☐ 403 Gary Lucas	.10	.05	.01
☐ 404 David Palmer	.10	.05	.01
☐ 405 Tim Raines	.40	.18	.05
☐ 406 Mike Ramsey	.10	.05	.01
☐ 407 Jeff Reardon	.90	.40	.11
☐ 408 Steve Rogers	.10	.05	.01
☐ 409 Dan Schatzeder	.10	.05	.01
☐ 410 Bryn Smith	.10	.05	.01
☐ 411 Mike Stenhouse	.10	.05	.01
☐ 412 Tim Wallach	.12	.05	.02
☐ 413 Jim Wohlford	.10	.05	.01
☐ 414 Bill Almon	.10	.05	.01

☐ 415 Keith Atherton	10	.05	.01
☐ 416 Bruce Bochte	10	.05	.01
☐ 417 Tom Burgmeier	10	.05	.01
☐ 418 Ray Burris	10	.05	.01
☐ 419 Bill Caudill	10	.05	.01
☐ 420 Chris Codiroli	10	.05	.01
☐ 421 Tim Conroy	10	.05	.01
☐ 422 Mike Davis	10	.05	.01
☐ 423 Jim Essian	10	.05	.01
☐ 424 Mike Heath	10	.05	.01
☐ 425 Rickey Henderson	4.00	1.80	.50
☐ 426 Donnie Hill	10	.05	.01
☐ 427 Dave Kingman	12	.05	.02
☐ 428 Bill Krueger	12	.05	.02
☐ 429 Carney Lansford	12	.05	.02
☐ 430 Steve McCatty	10	.05	.01
☐ 431 Joe Morgan	60	.25	.08
☐ 432 Dwayne Murphy	10	.05	.01
☐ 433 Tony Phillips	12	.05	.02
☐ 434 Lary Sorensen	10	.05	.01
☐ 435 Mike Warren	10	.05	.01
☐ 436 Curt Young	10	.05	.01
☐ 437 Luis Aponte	10	.05	.01
☐ 438 Chris Bando	10	.05	.01
☐ 439 Tony Bernazard	10	.05	.01
☐ 440 Bert Blyleven	35	.16	.04
☐ 441 Brett Butler	40	.18	.05
☐ 442 Ernie Camacho	10	.05	.01
☐ 443 Joe Carter	9.00	4.00	1.15
☐ 444 Carmelo Castillo	10	.05	.01
☐ 445 Jamie Easterly	10	.05	.01
☐ 446 Steve Farr	75	.35	.09
☐ 447 Mike Fischlin	10	.05	.01
☐ 448 Julio Franco	75	.35	.09
☐ 449 Mel Hall	25	.11	.03
☐ 450 Mike Hargrove	12	.05	.02
☐ 451 Neal Heaton	10	.05	.01
☐ 452 Brook Jacoby	10	.05	.01
☐ 453 Mike Jeffcoat	10	.05	.01
☐ 454 Don Schulze	10	.05	.01
☐ 455 Roy Smith	10	.05	.01
☐ 456 Pat Tabler	10	.05	.01
☐ 457 Andre Thornton	10	.05	.01
☐ 458 George Vukovich	10	.05	.01
☐ 459 Tom Waddell	10	.05	.01
☐ 460 Jerry Willard	10	.05	.01
☐ 461 Dale Berra	10	.05	.01
☐ 462 John Candelaria	10	.05	.01
☐ 463 Jose DeLeon	10	.05	.01
☐ 464 Doug Frobel	10	.05	.01
☐ 465 Cecilio Guante	10	.05	.01
☐ 466 Brian Harper	50	.23	.06
☐ 467 Lee Lacy	10	.05	.01
☐ 468 Bill Madlock	12	.05	.02
☐ 469 Lee Mazzilli	10	.05	.01
☐ 470 Larry McWilliams	10	.05	.01
☐ 471 Jim Morrison	10	.05	.01
☐ 472 Tony Pena	12	.05	.02
☐ 473 Johnny Ray	10	.05	.01
☐ 474 Rick Rhoden	10	.05	.01
☐ 475 Don Robinson	10	.05	.01
☐ 476 Rod Scurry	10	.05	.01
☐ 477 Kent Tekulve	10	.05	.01
☐ 478 Jason Thompson	10	.05	.01
☐ 479 John Tudor	12	.05	.02
☐ 480 Lee Tunnell	10	.05	.01
☐ 481 Marvell Wynne	10	.05	.01
☐ 482 Salome Barojas	10	.05	.01
☐ 483 Dave Beard	10	.05	.01
☐ 484 Jim Beattie	10	.05	.01
☐ 485 Barry Bonnell	10	.05	.01
☐ 486 Phil Bradley	12	.05	.02
☐ 487 Al Cowens	10	.05	.01
☐ 488 Alvin Davis	30	.14	.04
☐ 489 Dave Henderson	15	.07	.02
☐ 490 Steve Henderson	10	.05	.01
☐ 491 Bob Kearney	10	.05	.01
☐ 492 Mark Langston	3.50	1.55	.45
☐ 493 Larry Milbourne	10	.05	.01
☐ 494 Paul Mirabella	10	.05	.01
☐ 495 Mike Moore	25	.11	.03
☐ 496 Edwin Nunez	10	.05	.01
☐ 497 Spike Owen	10	.05	.01
☐ 498 Jack Perconte	10	.05	.01
☐ 499 Ken Phelps	10	.05	.01
☐ 500 Jim Presley	10	.05	.01
☐ 501 Mike Stanton	10	.05	.01
☐ 502 Bob Stoddard	10	.05	.01
☐ 503 Gorman Thomas	10	.05	.01
☐ 504 Ed VandeBerg	10	.05	.01
☐ 505 Matt Young	10	.05	.01
☐ 506 Juan Agosto	10	.05	.01
☐ 507 Harold Baines	35	.16	.04
☐ 508 Floyd Bannister	10	.05	.01
☐ 509 Britt Burns	10	.05	.01
☐ 510 Julio Cruz	10	.05	.01
☐ 511 Richard Dotson	10	.05	.01
☐ 512 Jerry Dybzinski	10	.05	.01
☐ 513 Carlton Fisk	1.75	.80	.22
☐ 514 Scott Fletcher	10	.05	.01
☐ 515 Jerry Hairston	10	.05	.01
☐ 516 Marc Hill	10	.05	.01
☐ 517 LaMarr Hoyt	10	.05	.01
☐ 518 Ron Kittle	12	.05	.02
☐ 519 Rudy Law	10	.05	.01
☐ 520 Vance Law	10	.05	.01
☐ 521 Greg Luzinski	12	.05	.02
☐ 522 Gene Nelson	10	.05	.01
☐ 523 Tom Paciorek	12	.05	.02
☐ 524 Ron Reed	10	.05	.01
☐ 525 Bert Roberge	10	.05	.01
☐ 526 Tom Seaver	1.75	.80	.22
☐ 527 Roy Smalley	10	.05	.01
☐ 528 Dan Spillner	10	.05	.01

☐	529	Mike Squires	.10	.05	.01	☐	584	Dion James	.10	.05	.01

□	#	Name				□	#	Name			
□	529	Mike Squires	.10	.05	.01	□	584	Dion James	.10	.05	.01
□	530	Greg Walker	.10	.05	.01	□	585	Pete Ladd	.10	.05	.01
□	531	Cesar Cedeno	.12	.05	.02	□	586	Rick Manning	.10	.05	.01
□	532	Dave Concepcion	.12	.05	.02	□	587	Bob McClure	.10	.05	.01
□	533	Eric Davis	8.00	3.60	1.00	□	588	Paul Molitor	1.00	.45	.13
□	534	Nick Esasky	.10	.05	.01	□	589	Charlie Moore	.10	.05	.01
□	535	Tom Foley	.10	.05	.01	□	590	Ben Oglivie	.10	.05	.01
□	536	John Franco UER	1.50	.65	.19	□	591	Chuck Porter	.10	.05	.01
		(Koufax misspelled				□	592	Randy Ready	.15	.07	.02
		as Kofax on back)				□	593	Ed Romero	.10	.05	.01
□	537	Brad Gulden	.10	.05	.01	□	594	Bill Schroeder	.10	.05	.01
□	538	Tom Hume	.10	.05	.01	□	595	Ray Searage	.10	.05	.01
□	539	Wayne Krenchicki	.10	.05	.01	□	596	Ted Simmons	.12	.05	.02
□	540	Andy McGaffigan	.10	.05	.01	□	597	Jim Sundberg	.12	.05	.02
□	541	Eddie Milner	.10	.05	.01	□	598	Don Sutton	.50	.23	.06
□	542	Ron Oester	.10	.05	.01	□	599	Tom Tellmann	.10	.05	.01
□	543	Bob Owchinko	.10	.05	.01	□	600	Rick Waits	.10	.05	.01
□	544	Dave Parker	.40	.18	.05	□	601	Robin Yount	4.00	1.80	.50
□	545	Frank Pastore	.10	.05	.01	□	602	Dusty Baker	.12	.05	.02
□	546	Tony Perez	.40	.18	.05	□	603	Bob Brenly	.10	.05	.01
□	547	Ted Power	.10	.05	.01	□	604	Jack Clark	.12	.05	.02
□	548	Joe Price	.10	.05	.01	□	605	Chili Davis	.15	.07	.02
□	549	Gary Redus	.10	.05	.01	□	606	Mark Davis	.12	.05	.02
□	550	Pete Rose	1.75	.80	.22	□	607	Dan Gladden	.40	.18	.05
□	551	Jeff Russell	.20	.09	.03	□	608	Atlee Hammaker	.10	.05	.01
□	552	Mario Soto	.10	.05	.01	□	609	Mike Krukow	.10	.05	.01
□	553	Jay Tibbs	.10	.05	.01	□	610	Duane Kuiper	.10	.05	.01
□	554	Duane Walker	.10	.05	.01	□	611	Bob Lacey	.10	.05	.01
□	555	Alan Bannister	.10	.05	.01	□	612	Bill Laskey	.10	.05	.01
□	556	Buddy Bell	.12	.05	.02	□	613	Gary Lavelle	.10	.05	.01
□	557	Danny Darwin	.10	.05	.01	□	614	Johnnie LeMaster	.10	.05	.01
□	558	Charlie Hough	.12	.05	.02	□	615	Jeff Leonard	.10	.05	.01
□	559	Bobby Jones	.10	.05	.01	□	616	Randy Lerch	.10	.05	.01
□	560	Odell Jones	.10	.05	.01	□	617	Greg Minton	.10	.05	.01
□	561	Jeff Kunkel	.10	.05	.01	□	618	Steve Nicosia	.10	.05	.01
□	562	Mike Mason	.10	.05	.01	□	619	Gene Richards	.10	.05	.01
□	563	Pete O'Brien	.12	.05	.02	□	620	Jeff D. Robinson	.12	.05	.02
□	564	Larry Parrish	.10	.05	.01	□	621	Scot Thompson	.10	.05	.01
□	565	Mickey Rivers	.10	.05	.01	□	622	Manny Trillo	.10	.05	.01
□	566	Billy Sample	.10	.05	.01	□	623	Brad Wellman	.10	.05	.01
□	567	Dave Schmidt	.10	.05	.01	□	624	Frank Williams	.10	.05	.01
□	568	Donnie Scott	.10	.05	.01	□	625	Joel Youngblood	.10	.05	.01
□	569	Dave Stewart	.50	.23	.06	□	626	Cal Ripken IA	4.00	1.80	.50
□	570	Frank Tanana	.12	.05	.02	□	627	Mike Schmidt IA	2.00	.90	.25
□	571	Wayne Tolleson	.10	.05	.01	□	628	Giving The Signs	.15	.07	.02
□	572	Gary Ward	.10	.05	.01			Sparky Anderson			
□	573	Curtis Wilkerson	.10	.05	.01	□	629	AL Pitcher's Nightmare	1.75	.80	.22
□	574	George Wright	.10	.05	.01			Dave Winfield			
□	575	Ned Yost	.10	.05	.01			Rickey Henderson			
□	576	Mark Brouhard	.10	.05	.01	□	630	NL Pitcher's Nightmare	2.00	.90	.25
□	577	Mike Caldwell	.10	.05	.01			Mike Schmidt			
□	578	Bobby Clark	.10	.05	.01			Ryne Sandberg			
□	579	Jaime Cocanower	.10	.05	.01	□	631	NL All-Stars	1.00	.45	.13
□	580	Cecil Cooper	.12	.05	.02			Darryl Strawberry			
□	581	Rollie Fingers	.50	.23	.06			Gary Carter			
□	582	Jim Gantner	.10	.05	.01			Steve Garvey			
□	583	Moose Haas	.10	.05	.01			Ozzie Smith			

☐ 632	A-S Winning Battery ....15 Gary Carter Charlie Lea	.07	.02
☐ 633	NL Pennant Clinchers .....15 Steve Garvey Rich Gossage	.07	.02
☐ 634	NL Rookie Phenoms ....50 Dwight Gooden Juan Samuel	.23	.06
☐ 635	Toronto's Big Guns.........15 Willie Upshaw	.07	.02
☐ 636	Toronto's Big Guns.........15 Lloyd Moseby	.07	.02
☐ 637	HOLLAND: Al Holland 15	.07	.02
☐ 638	TUNNELL: Lee Tunnell....15	.07	.02
☐ 639	500th Homer.....................90 Reggie Jackson	.40	.11
☐ 640	4000th Hit......................75 Pete Rose	.35	.09
☐ 641	Father and Son.........3.50 Cal Ripken Jr. and Sr.	1.55	.45
☐ 642	Cubs: Division Champs...15	.07	.02
☐ 643	Two Perfect Games........15 and One No-Hitter: Mike Witt David Palmer Jack Morris	.07	.02
☐ 644	Willie Lozado and............15 Vic Mata	.07	.02
☐ 645	Kelly Gruber and ....4.00 Randy O'Neal	1.80	.50
☐ 646	Jose Roman and............15 Joel Skinner	.07	.02
☐ 647	Steve Kiefer and ....9.00 Danny Tartabull	4.00	1.15
☐ 648	Rob Deer and.............2.00 Alejandro Sanchez	.90	.25
☐ 649	Billy Hatcher and.........2.00 Shawon Dunston	.90	.25
☐ 650	Ron Robinson and.........40 Mike Bielecki	.18	.05
☐ 651	Zane Smith and.............90 Paul Zuvella	.40	.11
☐ 652	Joe Hesketh and ....4.00 Glenn Davis	1.80	.50
☐ 653	John Russell and ....15 Steve Jeltz	.07	.02
☐ 654	CL: Tigers/Padres ....15 and Cubs/Mets	.02	.00
☐ 655	CL: Blue Jays/Yankees....15 and Red Sox/Orioles	.02	.00
☐ 656	CL: Royals/Cardinals.....15 and Phillies/Twins	.02	.00
☐ 657	CL: Angels/Braves........15 and Astros/Dodgers	.02	.00
☐ 658	CL: Expos/A's ....15 and Indians/Pirates	.02	.00
☐ 659	CL: Mariners/White Sox..15 and Reds/Rangers	.02	.00
☐ 660	CL: Brewers/Giants.........15 and Special Cards	.02	.00

1985 Fleer Update

This 132-card set was issued late in the collecting year and features new players and players on new teams compared to the 1985 Fleer regular issue cards. Cards measure 2 1/2" by 3 1/2" and were distributed together as a complete set in a special box. The cards are numbered with a U prefix and are ordered alphabetically by the player's name. This set features the Extended Rookie Cards of Ivan Calderon, Vince Coleman, Darren Daulton, Ozzie Guillen, Teddy Higuera, and Mickey Tettleton.

	NRMT-MT	EXC	G-VG
COMPLETE SET (132) 33.00	15.00	4.10
COMMON PLAYER (1-132) 15	.07	.02

☐ 1	Don Aase 15	.07	.02
☐ 2	Bill Almon 15	.07	.02
☐ 3	Dusty Baker 25	.11	.03
☐ 4	Dale Berra 15	.07	.02
☐ 5	Karl Best 15	.07	.02
☐ 6	Tim Birtsas 15	.07	.02
☐ 7	Vida Blue 25	.11	.03
☐ 8	Rich Bordi 15	.07	.02
☐ 9	Daryl Boston 25	.11	.03
☐ 10	Hubie Brooks 25	.11	.03
☐ 11	Chris Brown 15	.07	.02
☐ 12	Tom Browning 1.00	.45	.13
☐ 13	Al Bumbry 15	.07	.02

☐	14	Tim Burke	.25	.11	.03
☐	15	Ray Burris	.15	.07	.02
☐	16	Jeff Burroughs	.15	.07	.02
☐	17	Ivan Calderon	1.75	.80	.22
☐	18	Jeff Calhoun	.15	.07	.02
☐	19	Bill Campbell	.15	.07	.02
☐	20	Don Carman	.15	.07	.02
☐	21	Gary Carter	1.00	.45	.13
☐	22	Bobby Castillo	.15	.07	.02
☐	23	Bill Caudill	.15	.07	.02
☐	24	Rick Cerone	.15	.07	.02
☐	25	Jack Clark	.25	.11	.03
☐	26	Pat Clements	.15	.07	.02
☐	27	Stewart Cliburn	.15	.07	.02
☐	28	Vince Coleman	4.00	1.80	.50
☐	29	Dave Collins	.15	.07	.02
☐	30	Fritz Connally	.15	.07	.02
☐	31	Henry Cotto	.15	.07	.02
☐	32	Danny Darwin	.15	.07	.02
☐	33	Darren Daulton	5.00	2.30	.60
☐	34	Jerry Davis	.15	.07	.02
☐	35	Brian Dayett	.15	.07	.02
☐	36	Ken Dixon	.15	.07	.02
☐	37	Tommy Dunbar	.15	.07	.02
☐	38	Mariano Duncan	1.25	.55	.16
☐	39	Bob Fallon	.15	.07	.02
☐	40	Brian Fisher	.15	.07	.02
☐	41	Mike Fitzgerald	.15	.07	.02
☐	42	Ray Fontenot	.15	.07	.02
☐	43	Greg Gagne	.40	.18	.05
☐	44	Oscar Gamble	.15	.07	.02
☐	45	Jim Gott	.15	.07	.02
☐	46	David Green	.15	.07	.02
☐	47	Alfredo Griffin	.15	.07	.02
☐	48	Ozzie Guillen	1.25	.55	.16
☐	49	Toby Harrah	.15	.07	.02
☐	50	Ron Hassey	.15	.07	.02
☐	51	Rickey Henderson	5.00	2.30	.60
☐	52	Steve Henderson	.15	.07	.02
☐	53	George Hendrick	.15	.07	.02
☐	54	Teddy Higuera	.25	.11	.03
☐	55	Al Holland	.15	.07	.02
☐	56	Burt Hooton	.15	.07	.02
☐	57	Jay Howell	.25	.11	.03
☐	58	LaMarr Hoyt	.15	.07	.02
☐	59	Tim Hulett	.15	.07	.02
☐	60	Bob James	.15	.07	.02
☐	61	Cliff Johnson	.15	.07	.02
☐	62	Howard Johnson	2.00	.90	.25
☐	63	Ruppert Jones	.15	.07	.02
☐	64	Steve Kemp	.15	.07	.02
☐	65	Bruce Kison	.15	.07	.02
☐	66	Mike LaCoss	.15	.07	.02
☐	67	Lee Lacy	.15	.07	.02
☐	68	Dave LaPoint	.15	.07	.02
☐	69	Gary Lavelle	.15	.07	.02
☐	70	Vance Law	.15	.07	.02
☐	71	Manny Lee	.75	.35	.09
☐	72	Sixto Lezcano	.15	.07	.02
☐	73	Tim Lollar	.15	.07	.02
☐	74	Urbano Lugo	.15	.07	.02
☐	75	Fred Lynn	.25	.11	.03
☐	76	Steve Lyons	.25	.11	.03
☐	77	Mickey Mahler	.15	.07	.02
☐	78	Ron Mathis	.15	.07	.02
☐	79	Len Matuszek	.15	.07	.02
☐	80	Oddibe McDowell UER	.25	.11	.03
		(Part of bio			
		actually Roger's)			
☐	81	Roger McDowell UER	.40	.18	.05
		(Part of bio			
		actually Oddibe's)			
☐	82	Donnie Moore	.15	.07	.02
☐	83	Ron Musselman	.15	.07	.02
☐	84	Al Oliver	.25	.11	.03
☐	85	Joe Orsulak	.60	.25	.08
☐	86	Dan Pasqua	.40	.18	.05
☐	87	Chris Pittaro	.15	.07	.02
☐	88	Rick Reuschel	.25	.11	.03
☐	89	Earnie Riles	.15	.07	.02
☐	90	Jerry Royster	.15	.07	.02
☐	91	Dave Rozema	.15	.07	.02
☐	92	Dave Rucker	.15	.07	.02
☐	93	Vern Ruhle	.15	.07	.02
☐	94	Mark Salas	.15	.07	.02
☐	95	Luis Salazar	.15	.07	.02
☐	96	Joe Sambito	.15	.07	.02
☐	97	Billy Sample	.15	.07	.02
☐	98	Alejandro Sanchez	.15	.07	.02
☐	99	Calvin Schiraldi	.15	.07	.02
☐	100	Rick Schu	.15	.07	.02
☐	101	Larry Sheets	.15	.07	.02
☐	102	Ron Shephard	.15	.07	.02
☐	103	Nelson Simmons	.15	.07	.02
☐	104	Don Slaught	.15	.07	.02
☐	105	Roy Smalley	.15	.07	.02
☐	106	Lonnie Smith	.25	.11	.03
☐	107	Nate Snell	.15	.07	.02
☐	108	Lary Sorensen	.15	.07	.02
☐	109	Chris Speier	.15	.07	.02
☐	110	Mike Stenhouse	.15	.07	.02
☐	111	Tim Stoddard	.15	.07	.02
☐	112	John Stuper	.15	.07	.02
☐	113	Jim Sundberg	.25	.11	.03
☐	114	Bruce Sutter	.25	.11	.03
☐	115	Don Sutton	.75	.35	.09
☐	116	Bruce Tanner	.15	.07	.02
☐	117	Kent Tekulve	.15	.07	.02
☐	118	Walt Terrell	.15	.07	.02
☐	119	Mickey Tettleton	5.00	2.30	.60
☐	120	Rich Thompson	.15	.07	.02
☐	121	Louis Thornton	.15	.07	.02
☐	122	Alex Trevino	.15	.07	.02
☐	123	John Tudor	.25	.11	.03

☐	124	Jose Uribe	.25	.11	.03
☐	125	Dave Valle	.15	.07	.02
☐	126	Dave Von Ohlen	.15	.07	.02
☐	127	Curt Wardle	.15	.07	.02
☐	128	U.L. Washington	.15	.07	.02
☐	129	Ed Whitson	.15	.07	.02
☐	130	Herm Winningham	.30	.14	.04
☐	131	Rich Yett	.15	.07	.02
☐	132	Checklist U1-U132	.25	.03	.01

and statistics format that Fleer has been using over the past few years. The Dennis and Tippy Martinez cards were apparently switched in the set numbering, as their adjacent numbers (279 and 280) were reversed on the Orioles checklist card. The set includes the Rookie Cards of Jose Canseco, Vince Coleman, Kal Daniels, Len Dykstra, Cecil Fielder, Benito Santiago, and Mickey Tettleton.

1986 Fleer

The cards in this 660-card set measure 2 1/2" by 3 1/2". The 1986 Fleer set features fronts that contain the team logo along with the player's name and position. The player cards are alphabetized within team and the teams are ordered by their 1985 season finish and won-lost record, e.g., Kansas City (1-25), St. Louis (26-49), Toronto (50-73), New York Mets (74-97), New York Yankees (98-122), Los Angeles (123-147), California (148-171), Cincinnati (172-196), Chicago White Sox (197-220), Detroit (221-243), Montreal (244-267), Baltimore (268-291), Houston (292-314), San Diego (315-338), Boston (339-360), Chicago Cubs (361-385), Minnesota (386-409), Oakland (410-432), Philadelphia (433-457), Seattle (458-481), Milwaukee (482-506), Atlanta (507-532), San Francisco (533-555), Texas (556-578), Cleveland (579-601), and Pittsburgh (602-625). Specials (626-643), Major League Prospects (644-653), and checklist cards (654-660) complete the set. The border enclosing the photo is dark blue. The backs feature the same name, number,

			MT	EX-MT	VG
	COMPLETE SET (660)		125.00	57.50	15.50
	COMPLETE FACT.SET (660)		130.00	57.50	16.50
	COMMON PLAYER (1-660)		.10	.05	.01
☐	1	Steve Balboni	.15	.05	.02
☐	2	Joe Beckwith	.10	.05	.01
☐	3	Buddy Biancalana	.10	.05	.01
☐	4	Bud Black	.10	.05	.01
☐	5	George Brett	2.00	.90	.25
☐	6	Onix Concepcion	.10	.05	.01
☐	7	Steve Farr	.15	.07	.02
☐	8	Mark Gubicza	.15	.07	.02
☐	9	Dane Iorg	.10	.05	.01
☐	10	Danny Jackson	.15	.05	.01
☐	11	Lynn Jones	.10	.05	.01
☐	12	Mike Jones	.10	.05	.01
☐	13	Charlie Leibrandt	.15	.07	.02
☐	14	Hal McRae	.15	.07	.02
☐	15	Omar Moreno	.10	.05	.01
☐	16	Darryl Motley	.10	.05	.01
☐	17	Jorge Orta	.10	.05	.01
☐	18	Dan Quisenberry	.15	.07	.02
☐	19	Bret Saberhagen	.75	.35	.09
☐	20	Pat Sheridan	.10	.05	.01
☐	21	Lonnie Smith	.10	.05	.01
☐	22	Jim Sundberg	.15	.07	.02
☐	23	John Wathan	.10	.05	.01
☐	24	Frank White	.15	.07	.02
☐	25	Willie Wilson	.10	.05	.01
☐	26	Joaquin Andujar	.10	.05	.01
☐	27	Steve Braun	.10	.05	.01
☐	28	Bill Campbell	.10	.05	.01
☐	29	Cesar Cedeno	.15	.07	.02
☐	30	Jack Clark	.15	.07	.02
☐	31	Vince Coleman	1.75	.80	.22
☐	32	Danny Cox	.10	.05	.01
☐	33	Ken Dayley	.10	.05	.01
☐	34	Ivan DeJesus	.10	.05	.01
☐	35	Bob Forsch	.10	.05	.01
☐	36	Brian Harper	.25	.11	.03
☐	37	Tom Herr	.10	.05	.01
☐	38	Ricky Horton	.10	.05	.01
☐	39	Kurt Kepshire	.10	.05	.01
☐	40	Jeff Lahti	.10	.05	.01
☐	41	Tito Landrum	.10	.05	.01

☐ 42	Willie McGee	.20	.09	.03
☐ 43	Tom Nieto	.10	.05	.01
☐ 44	Terry Pendleton	1.50	.65	.19
☐ 45	Darrell Porter	.10	.05	.01
☐ 46	Ozzie Smith	1.00	.45	.13
☐ 47	John Tudor	.15	.07	.02
☐ 48	Andy Van Slyke	.75	.35	.09
☐ 49	Todd Worrell	.35	.16	.04
☐ 50	Jim Acker	.10	.05	.01
☐ 51	Doyle Alexander	.10	.05	.01
☐ 52	Jesse Barfield	.15	.07	.02
☐ 53	George Bell	.50	.23	.06
☐ 54	Jeff Burroughs	.10	.05	.01
☐ 55	Bill Caudill	.10	.05	.01
☐ 56	Jim Clancy	.10	.05	.01
☐ 57	Tony Fernandez	.25	.11	.03
☐ 58	Tom Filer	.10	.05	.01
☐ 59	Damaso Garcia	.10	.05	.01
☐ 60	Tom Henke	.50	.23	.06
☐ 61	Garth Iorg	.10	.05	.01
☐ 62	Cliff Johnson	.10	.05	.01
☐ 63	Jimmy Key	.25	.11	.03
☐ 64	Dennis Lamp	.10	.05	.01
☐ 65	Gary Lavelle	.10	.05	.01
☐ 66	Buck Martinez	.10	.05	.01
☐ 67	Lloyd Moseby	.10	.05	.01
☐ 68	Rance Mulliniks	.10	.05	.01
☐ 69	Al Oliver	.15	.07	.02
☐ 70	Dave Stieb	.15	.07	.02
☐ 71	Louis Thornton	.10	.05	.01
☐ 72	Willie Upshaw	.10	.05	.01
☐ 73	Ernie Whitt	.10	.05	.01
☐ 74	Rick Aguilera	1.75	.80	.22
☐ 75	Wally Backman	.10	.05	.01
☐ 76	Gary Carter	.35	.16	.04
☐ 77	Ron Darling	.20	.09	.03
☐ 78	Len Dykstra	1.75	.80	.22
☐ 79	Sid Fernandez	.25	.11	.03
☐ 80	George Foster	.15	.07	.02
☐ 81	Dwight Gooden	1.25	.55	.16
☐ 82	Tom Gorman	.10	.05	.01
☐ 83	Danny Heep	.10	.05	.01
☐ 84	Keith Hernandez	.15	.07	.02
☐ 85	Howard Johnson	.60	.25	.08
☐ 86	Ray Knight	.15	.07	.02
☐ 87	Terry Leach	.10	.05	.01
☐ 88	Ed Lynch	.10	.05	.01
☐ 89	Roger McDowell	.25	.11	.03
☐ 90	Jesse Orosco	.10	.05	.01
☐ 91	Tom Paciorek	.15	.07	.02
☐ 92	Ronn Reynolds	.10	.05	.01
☐ 93	Rafael Santana	.10	.05	.01
☐ 94	Doug Sisk	.10	.05	.01
☐ 95	Rusty Staub	.15	.07	.02
☐ 96	Darryl Strawberry	2.50	1.15	.30
☐ 97	Mookie Wilson	.15	.07	.02
☐ 98	Neil Allen	.10	.05	.01
☐ 99	Don Baylor	.15	.07	.02
☐ 100	Dale Berra	.10	.05	.01
☐ 101	Rich Bordi	.10	.05	.01
☐ 102	Marty Bystrom	.10	.05	.01
☐ 103	Joe Cowley	.10	.05	.01
☐ 104	Brian Fisher	.10	.05	.01
☐ 105	Ken Griffey	.15	.07	.02
☐ 106	Ron Guidry	.15	.07	.02
☐ 107	Ron Hassey	.10	.05	.01
☐ 108	Rickey Henderson UER (SB Record of 120, sic)	2.00	.90	.25
☐ 109	Don Mattingly	2.50	1.15	.30
☐ 110	Bobby Meacham	.10	.05	.01
☐ 111	John Montefusco	.10	.05	.01
☐ 112	Phil Niekro	.30	.14	.04
☐ 113	Mike Pagliarulo	.10	.05	.01
☐ 114	Dan Pasqua	.15	.07	.02
☐ 115	Willie Randolph	.15	.07	.02
☐ 116	Dave Righetti	.15	.07	.02
☐ 117	Andre Robertson	.10	.05	.01
☐ 118	Billy Sample	.10	.05	.01
☐ 119	Bob Shirley	.10	.05	.01
☐ 120	Ed Whitson	.10	.05	.01
☐ 121	Dave Winfield	1.25	.55	.16
☐ 122	Butch Wynegar	.10	.05	.01
☐ 123	Dave Anderson	.10	.05	.01
☐ 124	Bob Bailor	.10	.05	.01
☐ 125	Greg Brock	.10	.05	.01
☐ 126	Enos Cabell	.10	.05	.01
☐ 127	Bobby Castillo	.10	.05	.01
☐ 128	Carlos Diaz	.10	.05	.01
☐ 129	Mariano Duncan	.60	.25	.08
☐ 130	Pedro Guerrero	.12	.05	.02
☐ 131	Orel Hershiser	.50	.23	.06
☐ 132	Rick Honeycutt	.10	.05	.01
☐ 133	Ken Howell	.10	.05	.01
☐ 134	Ken Landreaux	.10	.05	.01
☐ 135	Bill Madlock	.15	.07	.02
☐ 136	Candy Maldonado	.15	.07	.02
☐ 137	Mike Marshall	.15	.07	.02
☐ 138	Len Matuszek	.10	.05	.01
☐ 139	Tom Niedenfuer	.10	.05	.01
☐ 140	Alejandro Pena	.10	.05	.01
☐ 141	Jerry Reuss	.10	.05	.01
☐ 142	Bill Russell	.15	.07	.02
☐ 143	Steve Sax	.25	.11	.03
☐ 144	Mike Scioscia	.10	.05	.01
☐ 145	Fernando Valenzuela	.15	.07	.02
☐ 146	Bob Welch	.15	.07	.02
☐ 147	Terry Whitfield	.10	.05	.01
☐ 148	Juan Beniquez	.10	.05	.01
☐ 149	Bob Boone	.15	.07	.02
☐ 150	John Candelaria	.10	.05	.01
☐ 151	Rod Carew	.90	.40	.11
☐ 152	Stewart Cliburn	.10	.05	.01
☐ 153	Doug DeCinces	.10	.05	.01

☐ 154 Brian Downing	15	.07	.02
☐ 155 Ken Forsch	10	.05	.01
☐ 156 Craig Gerber	10	.05	.01
☐ 157 Bobby Grich	15	.07	.02
☐ 158 George Hendrick	10	.05	.01
☐ 159 Al Holland	10	.05	.01
☐ 160 Reggie Jackson	1.00	.45	.13
☐ 161 Ruppert Jones	10	.05	.01
☐ 162 Urbano Lugo	10	.05	.01
☐ 163 Kirk McCaskill	30	.14	.04
☐ 164 Donnie Moore	10	.05	.01
☐ 165 Gary Pettis	10	.05	.01
☐ 166 Ron Romanick	10	.05	.01
☐ 167 Dick Schofield	10	.05	.01
☐ 168 Daryl Sconiers	10	.05	.01
☐ 169 Jim Slaton	10	.05	.01
☐ 170 Don Sutton	30	.14	.04
☐ 171 Mike Witt	10	.05	.01
☐ 172 Buddy Bell	15	.07	.02
☐ 173 Tom Browning	25	.11	.03
☐ 174 Dave Concepcion	15	.07	.02
☐ 175 Eric Davis	1.00	.45	.13
☐ 176 Bo Diaz	10	.05	.01
☐ 177 Nick Esasky	10	.05	.01
☐ 178 John Franco	25	.11	.03
☐ 179 Tom Hume	10	.05	.01
☐ 180 Wayne Krenchicki	10	.05	.01
☐ 181 Andy McGaffigan	10	.05	.01
☐ 182 Eddie Milner	10	.05	.01
☐ 183 Ron Oester	10	.05	.01
☐ 184 Dave Parker	20	.09	.03
☐ 185 Frank Pastore	10	.05	.01
☐ 186 Tony Perez	30	.14	.04
☐ 187 Ted Power	10	.05	.01
☐ 188 Joe Price	10	.05	.01
☐ 189 Gary Redus	10	.05	.01
☐ 190 Ron Robinson	10	.05	.01
☐ 191 Pete Rose	1.00	.45	.13
☐ 192 Mario Soto	10	.05	.01
☐ 193 John Stuper	10	.05	.01
☐ 194 Jay Tibbs	10	.05	.01
☐ 195 Dave Van Gorder	10	.05	.01
☐ 196 Max Venable	10	.05	.01
☐ 197 Juan Agosto	10	.05	.01
☐ 198 Harold Baines	25	.11	.03
☐ 199 Floyd Bannister	10	.05	.01
☐ 200 Britt Burns	10	.05	.01
☐ 201 Julio Cruz	10	.05	.01
☐ 202 Joel Davis	10	.05	.01
☐ 203 Richard Dotson	10	.05	.01
☐ 204 Carlton Fisk	90	.40	.11
☐ 205 Scott Fletcher	10	.05	.01
☐ 206 Ozzie Guillen	60	.25	.08
☐ 207 Jerry Hairston	10	.05	.01
☐ 208 Tim Hulett	10	.05	.01
☐ 209 Bob James	10	.05	.01
☐ 210 Ron Kittle	10	.05	.01
☐ 211 Rudy Law	10	.05	.01
☐ 212 Bryan Little	10	.05	.01
☐ 213 Gene Nelson	10	.05	.01
☐ 214 Reid Nichols	10	.05	.01
☐ 215 Luis Salazar	10	.05	.01
☐ 216 Tom Seaver	90	.40	.11
☐ 217 Dan Spillner	10	.05	.01
☐ 218 Bruce Tanner	10	.05	.01
☐ 219 Greg Walker	10	.05	.01
☐ 220 Dave Wehrmeister	10	.05	.01
☐ 221 Juan Berenguer	10	.05	.01
☐ 222 Dave Bergman	10	.05	.01
☐ 223 Tom Brookens	10	.05	.01
☐ 224 Darrell Evans	15	.07	.02
☐ 225 Barbaro Garbey	10	.05	.01
☐ 226 Kirk Gibson	15	.07	.02
☐ 227 John Grubb	10	.05	.01
☐ 228 Willie Hernandez	10	.05	.01
☐ 229 Larry Herndon	10	.05	.01
☐ 230 Chet Lemon	10	.05	.01
☐ 231 Aurelio Lopez	10	.05	.01
☐ 232 Jack Morris	60	.25	.08
☐ 233 Randy O'Neal	10	.05	.01
☐ 234 Lance Parrish	15	.07	.02
☐ 235 Dan Petry	10	.05	.01
☐ 236 Alejandro Sanchez	10	.05	.01
☐ 237 Bill Scherrer	10	.05	.01
☐ 238 Nelson Simmons	10	.05	.01
☐ 239 Frank Tanana	15	.07	.02
☐ 240 Walt Terrell	10	.05	.01
☐ 241 Alan Trammell	30	.14	.04
☐ 242 Lou Whitaker	30	.14	.04
☐ 243 Milt Wilcox	10	.05	.01
☐ 244 Hubie Brooks	10	.05	.01
☐ 245 Tim Burke	20	.09	.03
☐ 246 Andre Dawson	1.00	.45	.13
☐ 247 Mike Fitzgerald	10	.05	.01
☐ 248 Terry Francona	10	.05	.01
☐ 249 Bill Gullickson	15	.07	.02
☐ 250 Joe Hesketh	10	.05	.01
☐ 251 Bill Laskey	10	.05	.01
☐ 252 Vance Law	10	.05	.01
☐ 253 Charlie Lea	10	.05	.01
☐ 254 Gary Lucas	10	.05	.01
☐ 255 David Palmer	10	.05	.01
☐ 256 Tim Raines	30	.14	.04
☐ 257 Jeff Reardon	50	.23	.06
☐ 258 Bert Roberge	10	.05	.01
☐ 259 Dan Schatzeder	10	.05	.01
☐ 260 Bryn Smith	10	.05	.01
☐ 261 Randy St.Claire	10	.05	.01
☐ 262 Scot Thompson	10	.05	.01
☐ 263 Tim Wallach	15	.07	.02
☐ 264 U.L. Washington	10	.05	.01
☐ 265 Mitch Webster	10	.05	.01
☐ 266 Herm Winningham	20	.09	.03
☐ 267 Floyd Youmans	10	.05	.01

☐ 382	Chris Speier	.10	.05	.01
☐ 383	Rick Sutcliffe	.15	.07	.02
☐ 384	Steve Trout	.10	.05	.01
☐ 385	Gary Woods	.10	.05	.01
☐ 386	Bert Blyleven	.20	.09	.03
☐ 387	Tom Brunansky	.15	.07	.02
☐ 388	Randy Bush	.10	.05	.01
☐ 389	John Butcher	.10	.05	.01
☐ 390	Ron Davis	.10	.05	.01
☐ 391	Dave Engle	.10	.05	.01
☐ 392	Frank Eufemia	.10	.05	.01
☐ 393	Pete Filson	.10	.05	.01
☐ 394	Gary Gaetti	.15	.07	.02
☐ 395	Greg Gagne	.15	.07	.02
☐ 396	Mickey Hatcher	.10	.05	.01
☐ 397	Kent Hrbek	.20	.09	.03
☐ 398	Tim Laudner	.10	.05	.01
☐ 399	Rick Lysander	.10	.05	.01
☐ 400	Dave Meier	.10	.05	.01
☐ 401	Kirby Puckett UER (Card has him in NL, should be AL)	10.00	4.50	1.25
☐ 402	Mark Salas	.10	.05	.01
☐ 403	Ken Schrom	.10	.05	.01
☐ 404	Roy Smalley	.10	.05	.01
☐ 405	Mike Smithson	.10	.05	.01
☐ 406	Mike Stenhouse	.10	.05	.01
☐ 407	Tim Teufel	.10	.05	.01
☐ 408	Frank Viola	.30	.14	.04
☐ 409	Ron Washington	.10	.05	.01
☐ 410	Keith Atherton	.10	.05	.01
☐ 411	Dusty Baker	.15	.07	.02
☐ 412	Tim Birtsas	.10	.05	.01
☐ 413	Bruce Bochte	.10	.05	.01
☐ 414	Chris Codiroli	.10	.05	.01
☐ 415	Dave Collins	.10	.05	.01
☐ 416	Mike Davis	.10	.05	.01
☐ 417	Alfredo Griffin	.10	.05	.01
☐ 418	Mike Heath	.10	.05	.01
☐ 419	Steve Henderson	.10	.05	.01
☐ 420	Donnie Hill	.10	.05	.01
☐ 421	Jay Howell	.15	.07	.02
☐ 422	Tommy John	.15	.07	.02
☐ 423	Dave Kingman	.15	.07	.02
☐ 424	Bill Krueger	.10	.05	.01
☐ 425	Rick Langford	.10	.05	.01
☐ 426	Carney Lansford	.15	.07	.02
☐ 427	Steve McCatty	.10	.05	.01
☐ 428	Dwayne Murphy	.10	.05	.01
☐ 429	Steve Ontiveros	.10	.05	.01
☐ 430	Tony Phillips	.15	.07	.02
☐ 431	Jose Rijo	.60	.25	.08
☐ 432	Mickey Tettleton	2.00	.90	.25
☐ 433	Luis Aguayo	.10	.05	.01
☐ 434	Larry Andersen	.10	.05	.01
☐ 435	Steve Carlton	.90	.40	.11
☐ 436	Don Carman	.10	.05	.01
☐ 437	Tim Corcoran	.10	.05	.01
☐ 438	Darren Daulton	2.00	.90	.25
☐ 439	John Denny	.10	.05	.01
☐ 440	Tom Foley	.10	.05	.01
☐ 441	Greg Gross	.10	.05	.01
☐ 442	Kevin Gross	.10	.05	.01
☐ 443	Von Hayes	.10	.05	.01
☐ 444	Charles Hudson	.10	.05	.01
☐ 445	Garry Maddox	.10	.05	.01
☐ 446	Shane Rawley	.10	.05	.01
☐ 447	Dave Rucker	.10	.05	.01
☐ 448	John Russell	.10	.05	.01
☐ 449	Juan Samuel	.15	.07	.02
☐ 450	Mike Schmidt	2.50	1.15	.30
☐ 451	Rick Schu	.10	.05	.01
☐ 452	Dave Shipanoff	.10	.05	.01
☐ 453	Dave Stewart	.20	.09	.03
☐ 454	Jeff Stone	.10	.05	.01
☐ 455	Kent Tekulve	.10	.05	.01
☐ 456	Ozzie Virgil	.10	.05	.01
☐ 457	Glenn Wilson	.10	.05	.01
☐ 458	Jim Beattie	.10	.05	.01
☐ 459	Karl Best	.10	.05	.01
☐ 460	Barry Bonnell	.10	.05	.01
☐ 461	Phil Bradley	.10	.05	.01
☐ 462	Ivan Calderon	1.25	.55	.16
☐ 463	Al Cowens	.10	.05	.01
☐ 464	Alvin Davis	.10	.05	.01
☐ 465	Dave Henderson	.12	.05	.02
☐ 466	Bob Kearney	.10	.05	.01
☐ 467	Mark Langston	.50	.23	.06
☐ 468	Bob Long	.10	.05	.01
☐ 469	Mike Moore	.15	.07	.02
☐ 470	Edwin Nunez	.10	.05	.01
☐ 471	Spike Owen	.10	.05	.01
☐ 472	Jack Perconte	.10	.05	.01
☐ 473	Jim Presley	.10	.05	.01
☐ 474	Donnie Scott	.10	.05	.01
☐ 475	Bill Swift	.40	.18	.05
☐ 476	Danny Tartabull	2.00	.90	.25
☐ 477	Gorman Thomas	.10	.05	.01
☐ 478	Roy Thomas	.10	.05	.01
☐ 479	Ed VandeBerg	.10	.05	.01
☐ 480	Frank Wills	.10	.05	.01
☐ 481	Matt Young	.10	.05	.01
☐ 482	Ray Burris	.10	.05	.01
☐ 483	Jaime Cocanower	.10	.05	.01
☐ 484	Cecil Cooper	.15	.07	.02
☐ 485	Danny Darwin	.10	.05	.01
☐ 486	Rollie Fingers	.40	.18	.05
☐ 487	Jim Gantner	.10	.05	.01
☐ 488	Bob L. Gibson	.10	.05	.01
☐ 489	Moose Haas	.10	.05	.01
☐ 490	Teddy Higuera	.20	.09	.03
☐ 491	Paul Householder	.10	.05	.01
☐ 492	Pete Ladd	.10	.05	.01
☐ 493	Rick Manning	.10	.05	.01

☐	494	Bob McClure	10	.05	.01			
☐	495	Paul Molitor	40	.18	.05			
☐	496	Charlie Moore	12	.05	.02			
☐	497	Ben Oglivie	10	.05	.01			
☐	498	Randy Ready	10	.05	.01			
☐	499	Earnie Riles	10	.05	.01			
☐	500	Ed Romero	10	.05	.01			
☐	501	Bill Schroeder	10	.05	.01			
☐	502	Ray Searage	10	.05	.01			
☐	503	Ted Simmons	15	.07	.02			
☐	504	Pete Vuckovich	10	.05	.01			
☐	505	Rick Waits	10	.05	.01			
☐	506	Robin Yount	2.00	.90	.25			
☐	507	Len Barker	10	.05	.01			
☐	508	Steve Bedrosian	10	.05	.01			
☐	509	Bruce Benedict	10	.05	.01			
☐	510	Rick Camp	10	.05	.01			
☐	511	Rick Cerone	10	.05	.01			
☐	512	Chris Chambliss	15	.07	.02			
☐	513	Jeff Dedmon	10	.05	.01			
☐	514	Terry Forster	10	.05	.01			
☐	515	Gene Garber	10	.05	.01			
☐	516	Terry Harper	10	.05	.01			
☐	517	Bob Horner	15	.07	.02			
☐	518	Glenn Hubbard	10	.05	.01			
☐	519	Joe Johnson	10	.05	.01			
☐	520	Brad Komminsk	10	.05	.01			
☐	521	Rick Mahler	10	.05	.01			
☐	522	Dale Murphy	50	.23	.06			
☐	523	Ken Oberkfell	10	.05	.01			
☐	524	Pascual Perez	10	.05	.01			
☐	525	Gerald Perry	10	.05	.01			
☐	526	Rafael Ramirez	10	.05	.01			
☐	527	Steve Shields	10	.05	.01			
☐	528	Zane Smith	25	.11	.03			
☐	529	Bruce Sutter	15	.07	.02			
☐	530	Milt Thompson	20	.09	.03			
☐	531	Claudell Washington	10	.05	.01			
☐	532	Paul Zuvella	10	.05	.01			
☐	533	Vida Blue	15	.07	.02			
☐	534	Bob Brenly	10	.05	.01			
☐	535	Chris Brown	10	.05	.01			
☐	536	Chili Davis	15	.07	.02			
☐	537	Mark Davis	15	.07	.02			
☐	538	Rob Deer	30	.14	.04			
☐	539	Dan Driessen	10	.05	.01			
☐	540	Scott Garrelts	10	.05	.01			
☐	541	Dan Gladden	10	.05	.01			
☐	542	Jim Gott	10	.05	.01			
☐	543	David Green	10	.05	.01			
☐	544	Atlee Hammaker	10	.05	.01			
☐	545	Mike Jeffcoat	10	.05	.01			
☐	546	Mike Krukow	10	.05	.01			
☐	547	Dave LaPoint	10	.05	.01			
☐	548	Jeff Leonard	10	.05	.01			
☐	549	Greg Minton	10	.05	.01			
☐	550	Alex Trevino	10	.05	.01			
☐	551	Manny Trillo	10	.05	.01			
☐	552	Jose Uribe	15	.07	.02			
☐	553	Brad Wellman	10	.05	.01			
☐	554	Frank Williams	10	.05	.01			
☐	555	Joel Youngblood	10	.05	.01			
☐	556	Alan Bannister	10	.05	.01			
☐	557	Glenn Brummer	10	.05	.01			
☐	558	Steve Buechele	1.00	.45	.13			
☐	559	Jose Guzman	75	.35	.09			
☐	560	Toby Harrah	10	.05	.01			
☐	561	Greg Harris	10	.05	.01			
☐	562	Dwayne Henry	10	.05	.01			
☐	563	Burt Hooton	10	.05	.01			
☐	564	Charlie Hough	10	.05	.01			
☐	565	Mike Mason	10	.05	.01			
☐	566	Oddibe McDowell	10	.05	.01			
☐	567	Dickie Noles	10	.05	.01			
☐	568	Pete O'Brien	10	.05	.01			
☐	569	Larry Parrish	10	.05	.01			
☐	570	Dave Rozema	10	.05	.01			
☐	571	Dave Schmidt	10	.05	.01			
☐	572	Don Slaught	10	.05	.01			
☐	573	Wayne Tolleson	10	.05	.01			
☐	574	Duane Walker	10	.05	.01			
☐	575	Gary Ward	10	.05	.01			
☐	576	Chris Welsh	10	.05	.01			
☐	577	Curtis Wilkerson	10	.05	.01			
☐	578	George Wright	10	.05	.01			
☐	579	Chris Bando	10	.05	.01			
☐	580	Tony Bernazard	10	.05	.01			
☐	581	Brett Butler	20	.09	.03			
☐	582	Ernie Camacho	10	.05	.01			
☐	583	Joe Carter	2.50	1.15	.30			
☐	584	Carmen Castillo	10	.05	.01			
☐	585	Jamie Easterly	10	.05	.01			
☐	586	Julio Franco	35	.16	.04			
☐	587	Mel Hall	12	.05	.02			
☐	588	Mike Hargrove	15	.07	.02			
☐	589	Neal Heaton	10	.05	.01			
☐	590	Brook Jacoby	10	.05	.01			
☐	591	Otis Nixon	1.25	.55	.16			
☐	592	Jerry Reed	10	.05	.01			
☐	593	Vern Ruhle	10	.05	.01			
☐	594	Pat Tabler	10	.05	.01			
☐	595	Rich Thompson	10	.05	.01			
☐	596	Andre Thornton	10	.05	.01			
☐	597	Dave Von Ohlen	10	.05	.01			
☐	598	George Vukovich	10	.05	.01			
☐	599	Tom Waddell	10	.05	.01			
☐	600	Curt Wardle	10	.05	.01			
☐	601	Jerry Willard	10	.05	.01			
☐	602	Bill Almon	10	.05	.01			
☐	603	Mike Bielecki	15	.07	.02			
☐	604	Sid Bream	15	.07	.02			
☐	605	Mike C. Brown OF	10	.05	.01			
☐	606	Pat Clements	10	.05	.01			
☐	607	Jose DeLeon	10	.05	.01			

☐	608	Denny Gonzalez 10	.05	.01
☐	609	Cecilio Guante 10	.05	.01
☐	610	Steve Kemp....................10	.05	.01
☐	611	Sammy Khalifa................10	.05	.01
☐	612	Lee Mazzilli...................10	.05	.01
☐	613	Larry McWilliams.............10	.05	.01
☐	614	Jim Morrison..................10	.05	.01
☐	615	Joe Orsulak....................35	.16	.04
☐	616	Tony Pena......................15	.07	.02
☐	617	Johnny Ray.....................10	.05	.01
☐	618	Rick Reuschel.................10	.05	.01
☐	619	R.J. Reynolds.................10	.05	.01
☐	620	Rick Rhoden...................10	.05	.01
☐	621	Don Robinson.................10	.05	.01
☐	622	Jason Thompson 10	.05	.01
☐	623	Lee Tunnell....................10	.05	.01
☐	624	Jim Winn.......................10	.05	.01
☐	625	Marvell Wynne 10	.05	.01
☐	626	Dwight Gooden IA...........40	.18	.05
☐	627	Don Mattingly IA........1.25	.55	.16
☐	628	4192 (Pete Rose)............60	.25	.08
☐	629	3000 Career Hits.............45	.20	.06
		Rod Carew		
☐	630	300 Career Wins.............40	.18	.05
		Tom Seaver		
		Phil Niekro		
☐	631	Ouch (Don Baylor)..........15	.07	.02
☐	632	Instant Offense 50	.23	.06
		Darryl Strawberry		
		Tim Raines		
☐	633	Shortstops Supreme...1.25	.55	.16
		Cal Ripken		
		Alan Trammell		
☐	634	Boggs and "Hero"......1.00	.45	.13
		Wade Boggs		
		George Brett		
☐	635	Braves Dynamic Duo 15	.07	.02
		Bob Horner		
		Dale Murphy		
☐	636	Cardinal Ignitors 30	.14	.04
		Willie McGee		
		Vince Coleman		
☐	637	Terror on Basepaths 30	.14	.04
		Vince Coleman		
☐	638	Charlie Hustle / Dr.K......60	.25	.08
		Pete Rose		
		Dwight Gooden		
☐	639	1984 and 1985 AL 1.25	.55	.16
		Batting Champs		
		Wade Boggs		
		Don Mattingly		
☐	640	NL West Sluggers............30	.14	.04
		Dale Murphy		
		Steve Garvey		
		Dave Parker		
☐	641	Staff Aces 20	.09	.03
		Fernando Valenzuela		

		Dwight Gooden		
☐	642	Blue Jay Stoppers...........15	.07	.02
		Jimmy Key		
		Dave Stieb		
☐	643	AL All-Star Backstops 15	.07	.02
		Carlton Fisk		
		Rich Gedman		
☐	644	Gene Walter and 3.50	1.55	.45
		Benito Santiago		
☐	645	Mike Woodard and..........12	.05	.02
		Colin Ward		
☐	646	Kal Daniels and 3.50	1.55	.45
		Paul O'Neill		
☐	647	Andres Galarraga and 60	.25	.08
		Fred Toliver		
☐	648	Bob Kipper and 12	.05	.02
		Curt Ford		
☐	649	Jose Canseco and 40.00	18.00	5.00
		Eric Plunk		
☐	650	Mark McLemore and........20	.09	.03
		Gus Polidor		
☐	651	Rob Woodward and..........12	.05	.02
		Mickey Brantley		
☐	652	Billy Joe Robidoux and ...12	.05	.02
		Mark Funderburk		
☐	653	Cecil Fielder and........20.00	9.00	2.50
		Cory Snyder		
☐	654	CL: Royals/Cardinals......12	.01	.00
		Blue Jays/Mets		
☐	655	CL: Yankees/Dodgers......12	.01	.00
		Angels/Reds UER		
		(168 Darly Sconiers)		
☐	656	CL: White Sox/Tigers 12	.01	.00
		Expos/Orioles		
		(279 Dennis,		
		280 Tippy)		
☐	657	CL: Astros/Padres..........12	.01	.00
		Red Sox/Cubs		
☐	658	CL: Twins/A's................12	.01	.00
		Phillies/Mariners		
☐	659	CL: Brewers/Braves 12	.01	.00
		Giants/Rangers		
☐	660	CL: Indians/Pirates.........12	.01	.00
		Special Cards		

1986 Fleer Update

This 132-card set was distributed by Fleer to dealers as a complete set in a custom box. In addition to the complete set of 132 cards, the box also contains 25 Team Logo Stickers. The card fronts look very similar to the 1986 Fleer regular issue. The

*cards are numbered (with a U prefix)
alphabetically according to player's last
name. Cards measure the standard size,
2 1/2" by 3 1/2". The key (extended)
Rookie Cards in this set are Barry Bonds,
Bobby Bonilla, Will Clark, Doug Drabek,
Wally Joyner, John Kruk, Kevin Mitchell,
and Ruben Sierra.*

	MT	EX-MT	VG
COMPLETE SET (132)	30.00	13.50	3.80
COMMON PLAYER (1-132)	.07	.03	.01
☐ 1 Mike Aldrete	.10	.05	.01
☐ 2 Andy Allanson	.07	.03	.01
☐ 3 Neil Allen	.07	.03	.01
☐ 4 Joaquin Andujar	.07	.03	.01
☐ 5 Paul Assenmacher	.07	.03	.01
☐ 6 Scott Bailes	.07	.03	.01
☐ 7 Jay Baller	.07	.03	.01
☐ 8 Scott Bankhead	.10	.05	.01
☐ 9 Bill Bathe	.07	.03	.01
☐ 10 Don Baylor	.10	.05	.01
☐ 11 Billy Beane	.07	.03	.01
☐ 12 Steve Bedrosian	.07	.03	.01
☐ 13 Juan Beniquez	.07	.03	.01
☐ 14 Barry Bonds	9.00	4.00	1.15
☐ 15 Bobby Bonilla UER	4.00	1.80	.50
(Wrong birthday)			
☐ 16 Rich Bordi	.07	.03	.01
☐ 17 Bill Campbell	.07	.03	.01
☐ 18 Tom Candiotti	.15	.07	.02
☐ 19 John Cangelosi	.07	.03	.01
☐ 20 Jose Canseco UER	7.00	3.10	.85
(Headings on back			
for a pitcher)			
☐ 21 Chuck Cary	.07	.03	.01
☐ 22 Juan Castillo	.07	.03	.01
☐ 23 Rick Cerone	.07	.03	.01
☐ 24 John Cerutti	.07	.03	.01
☐ 25 Will Clark	9.00	4.00	1.15
☐ 26 Mark Clear	.07	.03	.01
☐ 27 Darnell Coles	.10	.05	.01
☐ 28 Dave Collins	.07	.03	.01
☐ 29 Tim Conroy	.07	.03	.01
☐ 30 Ed Correa	.07	.03	.01
☐ 31 Joe Cowley	.07	.03	.01
☐ 32 Bill Dawley	.07	.03	.01
☐ 33 Rob Deer	.30	.14	.04
☐ 34 John Denny	.07	.03	.01
☐ 35 Jim Deshaies	.12	.05	.02
☐ 36 Doug Drabek	1.75	.80	.22
☐ 37 Mike Easler	.07	.03	.01
☐ 38 Mark Eichhorn	.10	.05	.01
☐ 39 Dave Engle	.07	.03	.01
☐ 40 Mike Fischlin	.07	.03	.01
☐ 41 Scott Fletcher	.07	.03	.01
☐ 42 Terry Forster	.07	.03	.01
☐ 43 Terry Francona	.07	.03	.01
☐ 44 Andres Galarraga	.20	.09	.03
☐ 45 Lee Guetterman	.07	.03	.01
☐ 46 Bill Gullickson	.10	.05	.01
☐ 47 Jackie Gutierrez	.07	.03	.01
☐ 48 Moose Haas	.07	.03	.01
☐ 49 Billy Hatcher	.10	.05	.01
☐ 50 Mike Heath	.07	.03	.01
☐ 51 Guy Hoffman	.07	.03	.01
☐ 52 Tom Hume	.07	.03	.01
☐ 53 Pete Incaviglia	.30	.14	.04
☐ 54 Dane Iorg	.07	.03	.01
☐ 55 Chris James	.15	.07	.02
☐ 56 Stan Javier	.12	.05	.02
☐ 57 Tommy John	.15	.07	.02
☐ 58 Tracy Jones	.07	.03	.01
☐ 59 Wally Joyner	1.50	.65	.19
☐ 60 Wayne Krenchicki	.07	.03	.01
☐ 61 John Kruk	1.25	.55	.16
☐ 62 Mike LaCoss	.07	.03	.01
☐ 63 Pete Ladd	.07	.03	.01
☐ 64 Dave LaPoint	.07	.03	.01
☐ 65 Mike LaValliere	.30	.14	.04
☐ 66 Rudy Law	.07	.03	.01
☐ 67 Dennis Leonard	.07	.03	.01
☐ 68 Steve Lombardozzi	.07	.03	.01
☐ 69 Aurelio Lopez	.07	.03	.01
☐ 70 Mickey Mahler	.07	.03	.01
☐ 71 Candy Maldonado	.10	.05	.01
☐ 72 Roger Mason	.15	.07	.02
☐ 73 Greg Mathews	.10	.05	.01
☐ 74 Andy McGaffigan	.07	.03	.01
☐ 75 Joel McKeon	.07	.03	.01
☐ 76 Kevin Mitchell	2.00	.90	.25
☐ 77 Bill Mooneyham	.07	.03	.01
☐ 78 Omar Moreno	.07	.03	.01
☐ 79 Jerry Mumphrey	.07	.03	.01
☐ 80 Al Newman	.07	.03	.01
☐ 81 Phil Niekro	.30	.14	.04
☐ 82 Randy Niemann	.07	.03	.01
☐ 83 Juan Nieves	.07	.03	.01
☐ 84 Bob Ojeda	.07	.03	.01

☐	85 Rick Ownbey	.07	.03	.01
☐	86 Tom Paciorek	.10	.05	.01
☐	87 David Palmer	.07	.03	.01
☐	88 Jeff Parrett	.30	.14	.04
☐	89 Pat Perry	.07	.03	.01
☐	90 Dan Plesac	.15	.07	.02
☐	91 Darrell Porter	.07	.03	.01
☐	92 Luis Quinones	.07	.03	.01
☐	93 Rey Quinones UER	.07	.03	.01
	(Misspelled Quinonez)			
☐	94 Gary Redus	.07	.03	.01
☐	95 Jeff Reed	.07	.03	.01
☐	96 Bip Roberts	1.00	.45	.13
☐	97 Billy Joe Robidoux	.07	.03	.01
☐	98 Gary Roenicke	.07	.03	.01
☐	99 Ron Roenicke	.07	.03	.01
☐	100 Angel Salazar	.07	.03	.01
☐	101 Joe Sambito	.07	.03	.01
☐	102 Billy Sample	.07	.03	.01
☐	103 Dave Schmidt	.07	.03	.01
☐	104 Ken Schrom	.07	.03	.01
☐	105 Ruben Sierra	7.00	3.10	.85
☐	106 Ted Simmons	.10	.05	.01
☐	107 Sammy Stewart	.07	.03	.01
☐	108 Kurt Stillwell	.20	.09	.03
☐	109 Dale Sveum	.07	.03	.01
☐	110 Tim Teufel	.07	.03	.01
☐	111 Bob Tewksbury	.60	.25	.08
☐	112 Andres Thomas	.07	.03	.01
☐	113 Jason Thompson	.07	.03	.01
☐	114 Milt Thompson	.10	.05	.01
☐	115 Robby Thompson	.40	.18	.05
☐	116 Jay Tibbs	.07	.03	.01
☐	117 Fred Toliver	.07	.03	.01
☐	118 Wayne Tolleson	.07	.03	.01
☐	119 Alex Trevino	.07	.03	.01
☐	120 Manny Trillo	.07	.03	.01
☐	121 Ed VandeBerg	.07	.03	.01
☐	122 Ozzie Virgil	.07	.03	.01
☐	123 Tony Walker	.07	.03	.01
☐	124 Gene Walter	.07	.03	.01
☐	125 Duane Ward	.75	.35	.09
☐	126 Jerry Willard	.07	.03	.01
☐	127 Mitch Williams	.35	.16	.04
☐	128 Reggie Williams	.07	.03	.01
☐	129 Bobby Witt	.40	.18	.05
☐	130 Marvell Wynne	.07	.03	.01
☐	131 Steve Yeager	.07	.03	.01
☐	132 Checklist 1-132	.10	.01	.00

1987 Fleer

This 660-card set features a distinctive blue border, which fades to white on the card fronts. The backs are printed in blue, red, and pink on white card stock. The bottom of the card back shows an innovative graph of the player's ability, e.g., "He's got the stuff" for pitchers and "How he's hitting 'em," for hitters. Cards are numbered on the back and are again the standard 2 1/2" by 3 1/2". Cards are again organized numerically by teams, i.e., World Champion Mets (1-25), Boston Red Sox (26-48), Houston Astros (49-72), California Angels (73-95), New York Yankees (96-120), Texas Rangers (121-143), Detroit Tigers (144-168), Philadelphia Phillies (169-192), Cincinnati Reds (193-218), Toronto Blue Jays (219-240), Cleveland Indians (241-263), San Francisco Giants (264-288), St. Louis Cardinals (289-312), Montreal Expos (313-337), Milwaukee Brewers (338-361), Kansas City Royals (362-384), Oakland A's (385-410), San Diego Padres (411-435), Los Angeles Dodgers (436-460), Baltimore Orioles (461-483), Chicago White Sox (484-508), Atlanta Braves (509-532), Minnesota Twins (533-554), Chicago Cubs (555-578), Seattle Mariners (579-600), and Pittsburgh Pirates (601-624). The last 36 cards in the set consist of Specials (625-643), Rookie Pairs (644-653), and checklists (654-660). The key Rookie Cards in this set are Barry Bonds, Bobby Bonilla, Will Clark, Doug Drabek, Chuck Finley, Bo Jackson, John Kruk, Barry Larkin, Dave Magadan, Kevin Mitchell, Kevin Seitzer, Ruben Sierra, and Greg Swindell. Fleer also produced a "lim-

ited" edition version of this set with glossy coating and packaged in a "tin." However, this glossy tin set was apparently not limited enough (estimated between 75,000 and 100,000 1987 tin sets produced by Fleer), since the values of the "tin" glossy cards are now the same as the values of the regular set cards.

	MT	EX-MT	VG
COMPLETE SET (660)	90.00	40.00	11.50
COMPLETE FACT.SET (672)	90.00	40.00	11.50
COMMON PLAYER (1-660)	.07	.03	.01
COMPLETE WS SET (12)	4.00	1.80	.50

☐	1 Rick Aguilera	.40	.18	.05
☐	2 Richard Anderson	.07	.03	.01
☐	3 Wally Backman	.07	.03	.01
☐	4 Gary Carter	.30	.14	.04
☐	5 Ron Darling	.10	.05	.01
☐	6 Len Dykstra	.35	.16	.04
☐	7 Kevin Elster	.12	.05	.02
☐	8 Sid Fernandez	.10	.05	.01
☐	9 Dwight Gooden	.60	.25	.08
☐	10 Ed Hearn	.07	.03	.01
☐	11 Danny Heep	.07	.03	.01
☐	12 Keith Hernandez	.07	.03	.01
☐	13 Howard Johnson	.45	.20	.06
☐	14 Ray Knight	.10	.05	.01
☐	15 Lee Mazzilli	.07	.03	.01
☐	16 Roger McDowell	.07	.03	.01
☐	17 Kevin Mitchell	3.00	1.35	.40
☐	18 Randy Niemann	.07	.03	.01
☐	19 Bob Ojeda	.07	.03	.01
☐	20 Jesse Orosco	.07	.03	.01
☐	21 Rafael Santana	.07	.03	.01
☐	22 Doug Sisk	.07	.03	.01
☐	23 Darryl Strawberry	1.25	.55	.16
☐	24 Tim Teufel	.07	.03	.01
☐	25 Mookie Wilson	.10	.05	.01
☐	26 Tony Armas	.07	.03	.01
☐	27 Marty Barrett	.07	.03	.01
☐	28 Don Baylor	.10	.05	.01
☐	29 Wade Boggs	1.50	.65	.19
☐	30 Oil Can Boyd	.07	.03	.01
☐	31 Bill Buckner	.10	.05	.01
☐	32 Roger Clemens	4.50	2.00	.55
☐	33 Steve Crawford	.07	.03	.01
☐	34 Dwight Evans	.12	.05	.02
☐	35 Rich Gedman	.07	.03	.01
☐	36 Dave Henderson	.10	.05	.01
☐	37 Bruce Hurst	.10	.05	.01
☐	38 Tim Lollar	.07	.03	.01
☐	39 Al Nipper	.07	.03	.01
☐	40 Spike Owen	.07	.03	.01
☐	41 Jim Rice	.15	.07	.02
☐	42 Ed Romero	.07	.03	.01
☐	43 Joe Sambito	.07	.03	.01
☐	44 Calvin Schiraldi	.07	.03	.01
☐	45 Tom Seaver	.75	.35	.09
☐	46 Jeff Sellers	.07	.03	.01
☐	47 Bob Stanley	.07	.03	.01
☐	48 Sammy Stewart	.07	.03	.01
☐	49 Larry Andersen	.07	.03	.01
☐	50 Alan Ashby	.07	.03	.01
☐	51 Kevin Bass	.07	.03	.01
☐	52 Jeff Calhoun	.07	.03	.01
☐	53 Jose Cruz	.07	.03	.01
☐	54 Danny Darwin	.07	.03	.01
☐	55 Glenn Davis	.35	.16	.04
☐	56 Jim Deshaies	.20	.09	.03
☐	57 Bill Doran	.07	.03	.01
☐	58 Phil Garner	.10	.05	.01
☐	59 Billy Hatcher	.10	.05	.01
☐	60 Charlie Kerfeld	.07	.03	.01
☐	61 Bob Knepper	.07	.03	.01
☐	62 Dave Lopes	.10	.05	.01
☐	63 Aurelio Lopez	.07	.03	.01
☐	64 Jim Pankovits	.07	.03	.01
☐	65 Terry Puhl	.07	.03	.01
☐	66 Craig Reynolds	.07	.03	.01
☐	67 Nolan Ryan	4.00	1.80	.50
☐	68 Mike Scott	.10	.05	.01
☐	69 Dave Smith	.07	.03	.01
☐	70 Dickie Thon	.07	.03	.01
☐	71 Tony Walker	.07	.03	.01
☐	72 Denny Walling	.07	.03	.01
☐	73 Bob Boone	.10	.05	.01
☐	74 Rick Burleson	.07	.03	.01
☐	75 John Candelaria	.07	.03	.01
☐	76 Doug Corbett	.07	.03	.01
☐	77 Doug DeCinces	.07	.03	.01
☐	78 Brian Downing	.07	.03	.01
☐	79 Chuck Finley	1.00	.45	.13
☐	80 Terry Forster	.07	.03	.01
☐	81 Bob Grich	.10	.05	.01
☐	82 George Hendrick	.07	.03	.01
☐	83 Jack Howell	.07	.03	.01
☐	84 Reggie Jackson	.90	.40	.11
☐	85 Ruppert Jones	.07	.03	.01
☐	86 Wally Joyner	2.00	.90	.25
☐	87 Gary Lucas	.07	.03	.01
☐	88 Kirk McCaskill	.07	.03	.01
☐	89 Donnie Moore	.07	.03	.01
☐	90 Gary Pettis	.07	.03	.01
☐	91 Vern Ruhle	.07	.03	.01
☐	92 Dick Schofield	.07	.03	.01
☐	93 Don Sutton	.25	.11	.03
☐	94 Rob Wilfong	.07	.03	.01
☐	95 Mike Witt	.07	.03	.01
☐	96 Doug Drabek	2.50	1.15	.30
☐	97 Mike Easler	.07	.03	.01
☐	98 Mike Fischlin	.07	.03	.01
☐	99 Brian Fisher	.07	.03	.01

☐ 100	Ron Guidry	.10	.05	.01
☐ 101	Rickey Henderson	1.50	.65	.19
☐ 102	Tommy John	.10	.05	.01
☐ 103	Ron Kittle	.07	.03	.01
☐ 104	Don Mattingly	1.25	.55	.16
☐ 105	Bobby Meacham	.07	.03	.01
☐ 106	Joe Niekro	.10	.05	.01
☐ 107	Mike Pagliarulo	.07	.03	.01
☐ 108	Dan Pasqua	.10	.05	.01
☐ 109	Willie Randolph	.10	.05	.01
☐ 110	Dennis Rasmussen	.07	.03	.01
☐ 111	Dave Righetti	.10	.05	.01
☐ 112	Gary Roenicke	.07	.03	.01
☐ 113	Rod Scurry	.07	.03	.01
☐ 114	Bob Shirley	.07	.03	.01
☐ 115	Joel Skinner	.07	.03	.01
☐ 116	Tim Stoddard	.07	.03	.01
☐ 117	Bob Tewksbury	1.00	.45	.13
☐ 118	Wayne Tolleson	.07	.03	.01
☐ 119	Claudell Washington	.07	.03	.01
☐ 120	Dave Winfield	1.00	.45	.13
☐ 121	Steve Buechele	.10	.05	.01
☐ 122	Ed Correa	.07	.03	.01
☐ 123	Scott Fletcher	.07	.03	.01
☐ 124	Jose Guzman	.10	.05	.01
☐ 125	Toby Harrah	.07	.03	.01
☐ 126	Greg Harris	.07	.03	.01
☐ 127	Charlie Hough	.07	.03	.01
☐ 128	Pete Incaviglia	.50	.23	.06
☐ 129	Mike Mason	.07	.03	.01
☐ 130	Oddibe McDowell	.07	.03	.01
☐ 131	Dale Mohorcic	.07	.03	.01
☐ 132	Pete O'Brien	.07	.03	.01
☐ 133	Tom Paciorek	.10	.05	.01
☐ 134	Larry Parrish	.07	.03	.01
☐ 135	Geno Petralli	.07	.03	.01
☐ 136	Darrell Porter	.07	.03	.01
☐ 137	Jeff Russell	.10	.05	.01
☐ 138	Ruben Sierra	13.00	5.75	1.65
☐ 139	Don Slaught	.07	.03	.01
☐ 140	Gary Ward	.07	.03	.01
☐ 141	Curtis Wilkerson	.07	.03	.01
☐ 142	Mitch Williams	.50	.23	.06
☐ 143	Bobby Witt UER	.60	.25	.08
	(Tulsa misspelled as Tusla; ERA should be 6.43, not .643)			
☐ 144	Dave Bergman	.07	.03	.01
☐ 145	Tom Brookens	.07	.03	.01
☐ 146	Bill Campbell	.07	.03	.01
☐ 147	Chuck Cary	.07	.03	.01
☐ 148	Darnell Coles	.07	.03	.01
☐ 149	Dave Collins	.07	.03	.01
☐ 150	Darrell Evans	.10	.05	.01
☐ 151	Kirk Gibson	.10	.05	.01
☐ 152	John Grubb	.07	.03	.01
☐ 153	Willie Hernandez	.07	.03	.01
☐ 154	Larry Herndon	.07	.03	.01
☐ 155	Eric King	.07	.03	.01
☐ 156	Chet Lemon	.07	.03	.01
☐ 157	Dwight Lowry	.07	.03	.01
☐ 158	Jack Morris	.60	.25	.08
☐ 159	Randy O'Neal	.07	.03	.01
☐ 160	Lance Parrish	.10	.05	.01
☐ 161	Dan Petry	.07	.03	.01
☐ 162	Pat Sheridan	.07	.03	.01
☐ 163	Jim Slaton	.07	.03	.01
☐ 164	Frank Tanana	.07	.03	.01
☐ 165	Walt Terrell	.07	.03	.01
☐ 166	Mark Thurmond	.07	.03	.01
☐ 167	Alan Trammell	.25	.11	.03
☐ 168	Lou Whitaker	.25	.11	.03
☐ 169	Luis Aguayo	.07	.03	.01
☐ 170	Steve Bedrosian	.07	.03	.01
☐ 171	Don Carman	.07	.03	.01
☐ 172	Darren Daulton	.50	.23	.06
☐ 173	Greg Gross	.07	.03	.01
☐ 174	Kevin Gross	.07	.03	.01
☐ 175	Von Hayes	.07	.03	.01
☐ 176	Charles Hudson	.07	.03	.01
☐ 177	Tom Hume	.07	.03	.01
☐ 178	Steve Jeltz	.07	.03	.01
☐ 179	Mike Maddux	.07	.03	.01
☐ 180	Shane Rawley	.07	.03	.01
☐ 181	Gary Redus	.07	.03	.01
☐ 182	Ron Roenicke	.07	.03	.01
☐ 183	Bruce Ruffin	.07	.03	.01
☐ 184	John Russell	.07	.03	.01
☐ 185	Juan Samuel	.07	.03	.01
☐ 186	Dan Schatzeder	.07	.03	.01
☐ 187	Mike Schmidt	1.75	.80	.22
☐ 188	Rick Schu	.07	.03	.01
☐ 189	Jeff Stone	.07	.03	.01
☐ 190	Kent Tekulve	.07	.03	.01
☐ 191	Milt Thompson	.10	.05	.01
☐ 192	Glenn Wilson	.07	.03	.01
☐ 193	Buddy Bell	.10	.05	.01
☐ 194	Tom Browning	.10	.05	.01
☐ 195	Sal Butera	.07	.03	.01
☐ 196	Dave Concepcion	.10	.05	.01
☐ 197	Kal Daniels	.12	.05	.02
☐ 198	Eric Davis	.60	.25	.08
☐ 199	John Denny	.07	.03	.01
☐ 200	Bo Diaz	.07	.03	.01
☐ 201	Nick Esasky	.07	.03	.01
☐ 202	John Franco	.15	.07	.02
☐ 203	Bill Gullickson	.10	.05	.01
☐ 204	Barry Larkin	7.00	3.10	.85
☐ 205	Eddie Milner	.07	.03	.01
☐ 206	Rob Murphy	.07	.03	.01
☐ 207	Ron Oester	.07	.03	.01
☐ 208	Dave Parker	.20	.09	.03
☐ 209	Tony Perez	.20	.09	.03
☐ 210	Ted Power	.07	.03	.01

☐	211	Joe Price	.07	.03	.01
☐	212	Ron Robinson	.07	.03	.01
☐	213	Pete Rose	.75	.35	.09
☐	214	Mario Soto	.07	.03	.01
☐	215	Kurt Stillwell	.30	.14	.04
☐	216	Max Venable	.07	.03	.01
☐	217	Chris Welsh	.07	.03	.01
☐	218	Carl Willis	.15	.07	.02
☐	219	Jesse Barfield	.10	.05	.01
☐	220	George Bell	.50	.23	.06
☐	221	Bill Caudill	.07	.03	.01
☐	222	John Cerutti	.07	.03	.01
☐	223	Jim Clancy	.07	.03	.01
☐	224	Mark Eichhorn	.10	.05	.01
☐	225	Tony Fernandez	.20	.09	.03
☐	226	Damaso Garcia	.07	.03	.01
☐	227	Kelly Gruber ERR	.35	.16	.04
		(Wrong birth year)			
☐	228	Tom Henke	.10	.05	.01
☐	229	Garth Iorg	.07	.03	.01
☐	230	Joe Johnson	.07	.03	.01
☐	231	Cliff Johnson	.07	.03	.01
☐	232	Jimmy Key	.10	.05	.01
☐	233	Dennis Lamp	.07	.03	.01
☐	234	Rick Leach	.07	.03	.01
☐	235	Buck Martinez	.07	.03	.01
☐	236	Lloyd Moseby	.07	.03	.01
☐	237	Rance Mulliniks	.07	.03	.01
☐	238	Dave Stieb	.10	.05	.01
☐	239	Willie Upshaw	.07	.03	.01
☐	240	Ernie Whitt	.07	.03	.01
☐	241	Andy Allanson	.07	.03	.01
☐	242	Scott Bailes	.07	.03	.01
☐	243	Chris Bando	.07	.03	.01
☐	244	Tony Bernazard	.07	.03	.01
☐	245	John Butcher	.07	.03	.01
☐	246	Brett Butler	.20	.09	.03
☐	247	Ernie Camacho	.07	.03	.01
☐	248	Tom Candiotti	.10	.05	.01
☐	249	Joe Carter	1.50	.65	.19
☐	250	Carmen Castillo	.07	.03	.01
☐	251	Julio Franco	.35	.16	.04
☐	252	Mel Hall	.10	.05	.01
☐	253	Brook Jacoby	.07	.03	.01
☐	254	Phil Niekro	.25	.11	.03
☐	255	Otis Nixon	.35	.16	.04
☐	256	Dickie Noles	.07	.03	.01
☐	257	Bryan Oelkers	.07	.03	.01
☐	258	Ken Schrom	.07	.03	.01
☐	259	Don Schulze	.07	.03	.01
☐	260	Cory Snyder	.20	.09	.03
☐	261	Pat Tabler	.07	.03	.01
☐	262	Andre Thornton	.07	.03	.01
☐	263	Rich Yett	.07	.03	.01
☐	264	Mike Aldrete	.07	.03	.01
☐	265	Juan Berenguer	.07	.03	.01
☐	266	Vida Blue	.10	.05	.01

☐	267	Bob Brenly	.07	.03	.01
☐	268	Chris Brown	.07	.03	.01
☐	269	Will Clark	20.00	9.00	2.50
☐	270	Chili Davis	.10	.05	.01
☐	271	Mark Davis	.07	.03	.01
☐	272	Kelly Downs	.12	.05	.02
☐	273	Scott Garrelts	.07	.03	.01
☐	274	Dan Gladden	.07	.03	.01
☐	275	Mike Krukow	.07	.03	.01
☐	276	Randy Kutcher	.07	.03	.01
☐	277	Mike LaCoss	.07	.03	.01
☐	278	Jeff Leonard	.07	.03	.01
☐	279	Candy Maldonado	.10	.05	.01
☐	280	Roger Mason	.10	.05	.01
☐	281	Bob Melvin	.07	.03	.01
☐	282	Greg Minton	.07	.03	.01
☐	283	Jeff D. Robinson	.07	.03	.01
☐	284	Harry Spilman	.07	.03	.01
☐	285	Robby Thompson	.60	.25	.08
☐	286	Jose Uribe	.07	.03	.01
☐	287	Frank Williams	.07	.03	.01
☐	288	Joel Youngblood	.07	.03	.01
☐	289	Jack Clark	.10	.05	.01
☐	290	Vince Coleman	.35	.16	.04
☐	291	Tim Conroy	.07	.03	.01
☐	292	Danny Cox	.07	.03	.01
☐	293	Ken Dayley	.07	.03	.01
☐	294	Curt Ford	.07	.03	.01
☐	295	Bob Forsch	.07	.03	.01
☐	296	Tom Herr	.07	.03	.01
☐	297	Ricky Horton	.07	.03	.01
☐	298	Clint Hurdle	.07	.03	.01
☐	299	Jeff Lahti	.07	.03	.01
☐	300	Steve Lake	.07	.03	.01
☐	301	Tito Landrum	.07	.03	.01
☐	302	Mike LaValliere	.35	.16	.04
☐	303	Greg Mathews	.07	.03	.01
☐	304	Willie McGee	.10	.05	.01
☐	305	Jose Oquendo	.07	.03	.01
☐	306	Terry Pendleton	.75	.35	.09
☐	307	Pat Perry	.07	.03	.01
☐	308	Ozzie Smith	.75	.35	.09
☐	309	Ray Soff	.07	.03	.01
☐	310	John Tudor	.10	.05	.01
☐	311	Andy Van Slyke UER	.50	.23	.06
		(Bats R, Throws L)			
☐	312	Todd Worrell	.10	.05	.01
☐	313	Dann Bilardello	.07	.03	.01
☐	314	Hubie Brooks	.07	.03	.01
☐	315	Tim Burke	.07	.03	.01
☐	316	Andre Dawson	.90	.40	.11
☐	317	Mike Fitzgerald	.07	.03	.01
☐	318	Tom Foley	.07	.03	.01
☐	319	Andres Galarraga	.10	.05	.01
☐	320	Joe Hesketh	.07	.03	.01
☐	321	Wallace Johnson	.07	.03	.01
☐	322	Wayne Krenchicki	.07	.03	.01

☐ 323 Vance Law	.07	.03	.01
☐ 324 Dennis Martinez	.10	.05	.01
☐ 325 Bob McClure	.07	.03	.01
☐ 326 Andy McGaffigan	.07	.03	.01
☐ 327 Al Newman	.07	.03	.01
☐ 328 Tim Raines	.25	.11	.03
☐ 329 Jeff Reardon	.40	.18	.05
☐ 330 Luis Rivera	.07	.03	.01
☐ 331 Bob Sebra	.07	.03	.01
☐ 332 Bryn Smith	.07	.03	.01
☐ 333 Jay Tibbs	.07	.03	.01
☐ 334 Tim Wallach	.10	.05	.01
☐ 335 Mitch Webster	.07	.03	.01
☐ 336 Jim Wohlford	.07	.03	.01
☐ 337 Floyd Youmans	.07	.03	.01
☐ 338 Chris Bosio	.75	.35	.09
☐ 339 Glenn Braggs	.25	.11	.03
☐ 340 Rick Cerone	.07	.03	.01
☐ 341 Mark Clear	.07	.03	.01
☐ 342 Bryan Clutterbuck	.07	.03	.01
☐ 343 Cecil Cooper	.10	.05	.01
☐ 344 Rob Deer	.20	.09	.03
☐ 345 Jim Gantner	.07	.03	.01
☐ 346 Ted Higuera	.07	.03	.01
☐ 347 John Henry Johnson	.07	.03	.01
☐ 348 Tim Leary	.07	.03	.01
☐ 349 Rick Manning	.07	.03	.01
☐ 350 Paul Molitor	.40	.18	.05
☐ 351 Charlie Moore	.07	.03	.01
☐ 352 Juan Nieves	.07	.03	.01
☐ 353 Ben Oglivie	.07	.03	.01
☐ 354 Dan Plesac	.20	.09	.03
☐ 355 Ernest Riles	.07	.03	.01
☐ 356 Billy Joe Robidoux	.07	.03	.01
☐ 357 Bill Schroeder	.07	.03	.01
☐ 358 Dale Sveum	.07	.03	.01
☐ 359 Gorman Thomas	.07	.03	.01
☐ 360 Bill Wegman	.20	.09	.03
☐ 361 Robin Yount	1.25	.55	.16
☐ 362 Steve Balboni	.07	.03	.01
☐ 363 Scott Bankhead	.07	.03	.01
☐ 364 Buddy Biancalana	.07	.03	.01
☐ 365 Bud Black	.07	.03	.01
☐ 366 George Brett	1.25	.55	.16
☐ 367 Steve Farr	.10	.05	.01
☐ 368 Mark Gubicza	.07	.03	.01
☐ 369 Bo Jackson	5.00	2.30	.60
☐ 370 Danny Jackson	.07	.03	.01
☐ 371 Mike Kingery	.07	.03	.01
☐ 372 Rudy Law	.07	.03	.01
☐ 373 Charlie Leibrandt	.10	.05	.01
☐ 374 Dennis Leonard	.07	.03	.01
☐ 375 Hal McRae	.10	.05	.01
☐ 376 Jorge Orta	.07	.03	.01
☐ 377 Jamie Quirk	.07	.03	.01
☐ 378 Dan Quisenberry	.10	.05	.01
☐ 379 Bret Saberhagen	.40	.18	.05
☐ 380 Angel Salazar	.07	.03	.01
☐ 381 Lonnie Smith	.07	.03	.01
☐ 382 Jim Sundberg	.07	.03	.01
☐ 383 Frank White	.07	.03	.01
☐ 384 Willie Wilson	.07	.03	.01
☐ 385 Joaquin Andujar	.07	.03	.01
☐ 386 Doug Bair	.07	.03	.01
☐ 387 Dusty Baker	.10	.05	.01
☐ 388 Bruce Bochte	.07	.03	.01
☐ 389 Jose Canseco	10.00	4.50	1.25
☐ 390 Chris Codiroli	.07	.03	.01
☐ 391 Mike Davis	.07	.03	.01
☐ 392 Alfredo Griffin	.07	.03	.01
☐ 393 Moose Haas	.07	.03	.01
☐ 394 Donnie Hill	.07	.03	.01
☐ 395 Jay Howell	.10	.05	.01
☐ 396 Dave Kingman	.10	.05	.01
☐ 397 Carney Lansford	.10	.05	.01
☐ 398 Dave Leiper	.07	.03	.01
☐ 399 Bill Mooneyham	.07	.03	.01
☐ 400 Dwayne Murphy	.07	.03	.01
☐ 401 Steve Ontiveros	.07	.03	.01
☐ 402 Tony Phillips	.10	.05	.01
☐ 403 Eric Plunk	.07	.03	.01
☐ 404 Jose Rijo	.35	.16	.04
☐ 405 Terry Steinbach	.75	.35	.09
☐ 406 Dave Stewart	.25	.11	.03
☐ 407 Mickey Tettleton	.40	.18	.05
☐ 408 Dave Von Ohlen	.07	.03	.01
☐ 409 Jerry Willard	.07	.03	.01
☐ 410 Curt Young	.07	.03	.01
☐ 411 Bruce Bochy	.07	.03	.01
☐ 412 Dave Dravecky	.10	.05	.01
☐ 413 Tim Flannery	.07	.03	.01
☐ 414 Steve Garvey	.35	.16	.04
☐ 415 Rich Gossage	.12	.05	.02
☐ 416 Tony Gwynn	1.75	.80	.22
☐ 417 Andy Hawkins	.07	.03	.01
☐ 418 LaMarr Hoyt	.07	.03	.01
☐ 419 Terry Kennedy	.07	.03	.01
☐ 420 John Kruk	2.50	1.15	.30
☐ 421 Dave LaPoint	.07	.03	.01
☐ 422 Craig Lefferts	.10	.05	.01
☐ 423 Carmelo Martinez	.07	.03	.01
☐ 424 Lance McCullers	.07	.03	.01
☐ 425 Kevin McReynolds	.10	.05	.01
☐ 426 Graig Nettles	.10	.05	.01
☐ 427 Bip Roberts	1.50	.65	.19
☐ 428 Jerry Royster	.07	.03	.01
☐ 429 Benito Santiago	.50	.23	.06
☐ 430 Eric Show	.07	.03	.01
☐ 431 Bob Stoddard	.07	.03	.01
☐ 432 Garry Templeton	.07	.03	.01
☐ 433 Gene Walter	.07	.03	.01
☐ 434 Ed Whitson	.07	.03	.01
☐ 435 Marvell Wynne	.07	.03	.01
☐ 436 Dave Anderson	.07	.03	.01

☐ 437	Greg Brock	.07	.03	.01
☐ 438	Enos Cabell	.07	.03	.01
☐ 439	Mariano Duncan	.07	.03	.01
☐ 440	Pedro Guerrero	.10	.05	.01
☐ 441	Orel Hershiser	.30	.14	.04
☐ 442	Rick Honeycutt	.07	.03	.01
☐ 443	Ken Howell	.07	.03	.01
☐ 444	Ken Landreaux	.07	.03	.01
☐ 445	Bill Madlock	.10	.05	.01
☐ 446	Mike Marshall	.07	.03	.01
☐ 447	Len Matuszek	.07	.03	.01
☐ 448	Tom Niedenfuer	.07	.03	.01
☐ 449	Alejandro Pena	.07	.03	.01
☐ 450	Dennis Powell	.07	.03	.01
☐ 451	Jerry Reuss	.07	.03	.01
☐ 452	Bill Russell	.10	.05	.01
☐ 453	Steve Sax	.20	.09	.03
☐ 454	Mike Scioscia	.07	.03	.01
☐ 455	Franklin Stubbs	.07	.03	.01
☐ 456	Alex Trevino	.07	.03	.01
☐ 457	Fernando Valenzuela	.10	.05	.01
☐ 458	Ed VandeBerg	.07	.03	.01
☐ 459	Bob Welch	.10	.05	.01
☐ 460	Reggie Williams	.07	.03	.01
☐ 461	Don Aase	.07	.03	.01
☐ 462	Juan Beniquez	.07	.03	.01
☐ 463	Mike Boddicker	.07	.03	.01
☐ 464	Juan Bonilla	.07	.03	.01
☐ 465	Rich Bordi	.07	.03	.01
☐ 466	Storm Davis	.07	.03	.01
☐ 467	Rick Dempsey	.07	.03	.01
☐ 468	Ken Dixon	.07	.03	.01
☐ 469	Jim Dwyer	.07	.03	.01
☐ 470	Mike Flanagan	.07	.03	.01
☐ 471	Jackie Gutierrez	.07	.03	.01
☐ 472	Brad Havens	.07	.03	.01
☐ 473	Lee Lacy	.07	.03	.01
☐ 474	Fred Lynn	.10	.05	.01
☐ 475	Scott McGregor	.07	.03	.01
☐ 476	Eddie Murray	.75	.35	.09
☐ 477	Tom O'Malley	.07	.03	.01
☐ 478	Cal Ripken Jr.	3.50	1.55	.45
☐ 479	Larry Sheets	.07	.03	.01
☐ 480	John Shelby	.07	.03	.01
☐ 481	Nate Snell	.07	.03	.01
☐ 482	Jim Traber	.07	.03	.01
☐ 483	Mike Young	.07	.03	.01
☐ 484	Neil Allen	.07	.03	.01
☐ 485	Harold Baines	.15	.07	.02
☐ 486	Floyd Bannister	.07	.03	.01
☐ 487	Daryl Boston	.07	.03	.01
☐ 488	Ivan Calderon	.15	.07	.02
☐ 489	John Cangelosi	.07	.03	.01
☐ 490	Steve Carlton	.75	.35	.09
☐ 491	Joe Cowley	.07	.03	.01
☐ 492	Julio Cruz	.07	.03	.01
☐ 493	Bill Dawley	.07	.03	.01
☐ 494	Jose DeLeon	.07	.03	.01
☐ 495	Richard Dotson	.07	.03	.01
☐ 496	Carlton Fisk	.75	.35	.09
☐ 497	Ozzie Guillen	.10	.05	.01
☐ 498	Jerry Hairston	.07	.03	.01
☐ 499	Ron Hassey	.07	.03	.01
☐ 500	Tim Hulett	.07	.03	.01
☐ 501	Bob James	.07	.03	.01
☐ 502	Steve Lyons	.07	.03	.01
☐ 503	Joel McKeon	.07	.03	.01
☐ 504	Gene Nelson	.07	.03	.01
☐ 505	Dave Schmidt	.07	.03	.01
☐ 506	Ray Searage	.07	.03	.01
☐ 507	Bobby Thigpen	1.00	.45	.13
☐ 508	Greg Walker	.07	.03	.01
☐ 509	Jim Acker	.07	.03	.01
☐ 510	Doyle Alexander	.07	.03	.01
☐ 511	Paul Assenmacher	.07	.03	.01
☐ 512	Bruce Benedict	.07	.03	.01
☐ 513	Chris Chambliss	.10	.05	.01
☐ 514	Jeff Dedmon	.07	.03	.01
☐ 515	Gene Garber	.07	.03	.01
☐ 516	Ken Griffey	.10	.05	.01
☐ 517	Terry Harper	.07	.03	.01
☐ 518	Bob Horner	.10	.05	.01
☐ 519	Glenn Hubbard	.07	.03	.01
☐ 520	Rick Mahler	.07	.03	.01
☐ 521	Omar Moreno	.07	.03	.01
☐ 522	Dale Murphy	.40	.18	.05
☐ 523	Ken Oberkfell	.07	.03	.01
☐ 524	Ed Olwine	.07	.03	.01
☐ 525	David Palmer	.07	.03	.01
☐ 526	Rafael Ramirez	.07	.03	.01
☐ 527	Billy Sample	.07	.03	.01
☐ 528	Ted Simmons	.10	.05	.01
☐ 529	Zane Smith	.10	.05	.01
☐ 530	Bruce Sutter	.10	.05	.01
☐ 531	Andres Thomas	.07	.03	.01
☐ 532	Ozzie Virgil	.07	.03	.01
☐ 533	Allan Anderson	.07	.03	.01
☐ 534	Keith Atherton	.07	.03	.01
☐ 535	Billy Beane	.07	.03	.01
☐ 536	Bert Blyleven	.15	.07	.02
☐ 537	Tom Brunansky	.10	.05	.01
☐ 538	Randy Bush	.07	.03	.01
☐ 539	George Frazier	.07	.03	.01
☐ 540	Gary Gaetti	.07	.03	.01
☐ 541	Greg Gagne	.10	.05	.01
☐ 542	Mickey Hatcher	.07	.03	.01
☐ 543	Neal Heaton	.07	.03	.01
☐ 544	Kent Hrbek	.20	.09	.03
☐ 545	Roy Lee Jackson	.07	.03	.01
☐ 546	Tim Laudner	.07	.03	.01
☐ 547	Steve Lombardozzi	.07	.03	.01
☐ 548	Mark Portugal	.30	.14	.04
☐ 549	Kirby Puckett	4.00	1.80	.50
☐ 550	Jeff Reed	.07	.03	.01

☐ 551	Mark Salas....................07	.03	.01
☐ 552	Roy Smalley....................07	.03	.01
☐ 553	Mike Smithson....................07	.03	.01
☐ 554	Frank Viola....................30	.14	.04
☐ 555	Thad Bosley....................07	.03	.01
☐ 556	Ron Cey........................10	.05	.01
☐ 557	Jody Davis....................07	.03	.01
☐ 558	Ron Davis....................07	.03	.01
☐ 559	Bob Dernier....................07	.03	.01
☐ 560	Frank DiPino 07	.03	.01
☐ 561	Shawon Dunston UER 10	.05	.01
	(Wrong birth year		
	listed on card back)		
☐ 562	Leon Durham....................07	.03	.01
☐ 563	Dennis Eckersley..............60	.25	.08
☐ 564	Terry Francona....................07	.03	.01
☐ 565	Dave Gumpert....................07	.03	.01
☐ 566	Guy Hoffman....................07	.03	.01
☐ 567	Ed Lynch....................07	.03	.01
☐ 568	Gary Matthews....................07	.03	.01
☐ 569	Keith Moreland....................07	.03	.01
☐ 570	Jamie Moyer....................07	.03	.01
☐ 571	Jerry Mumphrey....................07	.03	.01
☐ 572	Ryne Sandberg...........2.50	1.15	.30
☐ 573	Scott Sanderson....................07	.03	.01
☐ 574	Lee Smith 40	.18	.05
☐ 575	Chris Speier....................07	.03	.01
☐ 576	Rick Sutcliffe....................10	.05	.01
☐ 577	Manny Trillo....................07	.03	.01
☐ 578	Steve Trout....................07	.03	.01
☐ 579	Karl Best....................07	.03	.01
☐ 580	Scott Bradley....................07	.03	.01
☐ 581	Phil Bradley....................07	.03	.01
☐ 582	Mickey Brantley....................07	.03	.01
☐ 583	Mike G. Brown P....................07	.03	.01
☐ 584	Alvin Davis....................07	.03	.01
☐ 585	Lee Guetterman....................07	.03	.01
☐ 586	Mark Huismann....................07	.03	.01
☐ 587	Bob Kearney....................07	.03	.01
☐ 588	Pete Ladd....................07	.03	.01
☐ 589	Mark Langston....................35	.16	.04
☐ 590	Mike Moore....................07	.03	.01
☐ 591	Mike Morgan....................10	.05	.01
☐ 592	John Moses....................07	.03	.01
☐ 593	Ken Phelps....................07	.03	.01
☐ 594	Jim Presley....................07	.03	.01
☐ 595	Rey Quinones UER....................07	.03	.01
	(Quinonez on front)		
☐ 596	Harold Reynolds....................10	.05	.01
☐ 597	Billy Swift....................12	.05	.02
☐ 598	Danny Tartabull....................75	.35	.09
☐ 599	Steve Yeager....................07	.03	.01
☐ 600	Matt Young....................07	.03	.01
☐ 601	Bill Almon....................07	.03	.01
☐ 602	Rafael Belliard....................35	.16	.04
☐ 603	Mike Bielecki....................07	.03	.01

☐ 604	Barry Bonds..............20.00	9.00	2.50
☐ 605	Bobby Bonilla..............5.00	2.30	.60
☐ 606	Sid Bream....................10	.05	.01
☐ 607	Mike C. Brown OF....................07	.03	.01
☐ 608	Pat Clements....................07	.03	.01
☐ 609	Mike Diaz....................07	.03	.01
☐ 610	Cecilio Guante....................07	.03	.01
☐ 611	Barry Jones....................10	.05	.01
☐ 612	Bob Kipper....................07	.03	.01
☐ 613	Larry McWilliams....................07	.03	.01
☐ 614	Jim Morrison....................07	.03	.01
☐ 615	Joe Orsulak....................07	.03	.01
☐ 616	Junior Ortiz....................07	.03	.01
☐ 617	Tony Pena....................07	.03	.01
☐ 618	Johnny Ray....................07	.03	.01
☐ 619	Rick Reuschel....................07	.03	.01
☐ 620	R.J. Reynolds....................07	.03	.01
☐ 621	Rick Rhoden....................07	.03	.01
☐ 622	Don Robinson....................07	.03	.01
☐ 623	Bob Walk....................07	.03	.01
☐ 624	Jim Winn....................07	.03	.01
☐ 625	Youthful Power....................75	.35	.09
	Pete Incaviglia		
	Jose Canseco		
☐ 626	300 Game Winners.........10	.05	.01
	Don Sutton		
	Phil Niekro		
☐ 627	AL Firemen....................10	.05	.01
	Dave Righetti		
	Don Aase		
☐ 628	Rookie All-Stars.........1.00	.45	.13
	Wally Joyner		
	Jose Canseco		
☐ 629	Magic Mets....................30	.14	.04
	Gary Carter		
	Sid Fernandez		
	Dwight Gooden		
	Keith Hernandez		
	Darryl Strawberry		
☐ 630	NL Best Righties.............10	.05	.01
	Mike Scott		
	Mike Krukow		
☐ 631	Sensational Southpaws...10	.05	.01
	Fernando Valenzuela		
	John Franco		
☐ 632	Count'Em....................10	.05	.01
	Bob Horner		
☐ 633	AL Pitcher's Nightmare 1.25	.55	.16
	Jose Canseco		
	Jim Rice		
	Kirby Puckett		
☐ 634	All-Star Battery.............60	.25	.08
	Gary Carter		
	Roger Clemens		
☐ 635	4000 Strikeouts.............15	.07	.02
	Steve Carlton		

☐ 636	Big Bats at First................10	.05	.01	
	Glenn Davis			
	Eddie Murray			
☐ 637	On Base 20	.09	.03	
	Wade Boggs			
	Keith Hernandez			
☐ 638	Sluggers Left Side 75	.35	.09	
	Don Mattingly			
	Darryl Strawberry			
☐ 639	Former MVP's.................20	.09	.03	
	Dave Parker			
	Ryne Sandberg			
☐ 640	Dr. K and Super K.......1.25	.55	.16	
	Dwight Gooden			
	Roger Clemens			
☐ 641	AL West Stoppers...........10	.05	.01	
	Mike Witt			
	Charlie Hough			
☐ 642	Doubles and Triples........10	.05	.01	
	Juan Samuel			
	Tim Raines			
☐ 643	Outfielders with Punch....10	.05	.01	
	Harold Baines			
	Jesse Barfield			
☐ 644	Dave Clark and.............3.00	1.35	.40	
	Greg Swindell			
☐ 645	Ron Karkovice and..........10	.05	.01	
	Russ Morman			
☐ 646	Devon White and 1.75	.80	.22	
	Willie Fraser			
☐ 647	Mike Stanley and 20	.09	.03	
	Jerry Browne			
☐ 648	Dave Magadan and 60	.25	.08	
	Phil Lombardi			
☐ 649	Jose Gonzalez and 10	.05	.01	
	Ralph Bryant			
☐ 650	Jimmy Jones and............30	.14	.04	
	Randy Asadoor			
☐ 651	Tracy Jones and.............10	.05	.01	
	Marvin Freeman			
☐ 652	John Stefero and 1.00	.45	.13	
	Kevin Seitzer			
☐ 653	Rob Nelson and 10	.05	.01	
	Steve Fireovid			
☐ 654	CL: Mets/Red Sox...........10	.01	.00	
	Astros/Angels			
☐ 655	CL: Yankees/Rangers......10	.01	.00	
	Tigers/Phillies			
☐ 656	CL: Reds/Blue Jays.........10	.01	.00	
	Indians/Giants			
	UER (230/231 wrong)			
☐ 657	CL: Cardinals/Expos........10	.01	.00	
	Brewers/Royals			
☐ 658	CL: A's/Padres 10	.01	.00	
	Dodgers/Orioles			
☐ 659	CL: White Sox/Braves 10	.01	.00	

	Twins/Cubs			
☐ 660	CL: Mariners/Pirates 10	.01	.00	
	Special Cards			
	UER (580/581 wrong)			

1987 Fleer Update

This 132-card set was distributed by Fleer to dealers as a complete set in a custom box. In addition to the complete set of 132 cards, the box also contains 25 Team Logo stickers. The card fronts look very similar to the 1987 Fleer regular issue. The cards are numbered (with a U prefix) alphabetically according to player's last name. Cards measure the standard size, 2 1/2" by 3 1/2". Fleer misalphabetized Jim Winn in their set numbering by putting him ahead of the next four players listed. The key (extended) Rookie Cards in this set are Ellis Burks, Mike Greenwell, Fred McGriff, Mark McGwire and Matt Williams. Fleer also produced a "limited" edition version of this set with glossy coating and packaged in a "tin." However, this glossy tin set was apparently not limited enough (estimated between 75,000 and 100,000 1987 Update tin sets produced by Fleer), since the values of the "tin" glossy cards are now the same as the values of the cards in the regular set.

	MT	EX-MT	VG
COMPLETE SET (132) 14.00		6.25	1.75
COMMON PLAYER (1-132) 05		.02	.01
☐ 1 Scott Bankhead..................05		.02	.01

☐ 2 Eric Bell	.05	.02	.01
☐ 3 Juan Beniquez	.05	.02	.01
☐ 4 Juan Berenguer	.05	.02	.01
☐ 5 Mike Birkbeck	.05	.02	.01
☐ 6 Randy Bockus	.05	.02	.01
☐ 7 Rod Booker	.05	.02	.01
☐ 8 Thad Bosley	.05	.02	.01
☐ 9 Greg Brock	.05	.02	.01
☐ 10 Bob Brower	.05	.02	.01
☐ 11 Chris Brown	.05	.02	.01
☐ 12 Jerry Browne	.08	.04	.01
☐ 13 Ralph Bryant	.08	.04	.01
☐ 14 DeWayne Buice	.05	.02	.01
☐ 15 Ellis Burks	.75	.35	.09
☐ 16 Casey Candaele	.05	.02	.01
☐ 17 Steve Carlton	.40	.18	.05
☐ 18 Juan Castillo	.05	.02	.01
☐ 19 Chuck Crim	.05	.02	.01
☐ 20 Mark Davidson	.05	.02	.01
☐ 21 Mark Davis	.05	.02	.01
☐ 22 Storm Davis	.05	.02	.01
☐ 23 Bill Dawley	.05	.02	.01
☐ 24 Andre Dawson	.40	.18	.05
☐ 25 Brian Dayett	.05	.02	.01
☐ 26 Rick Dempsey	.05	.02	.01
☐ 27 Ken Dowell	.05	.02	.01
☐ 28 Dave Dravecky	.08	.04	.01
☐ 29 Mike Dunne	.05	.02	.01
☐ 30 Dennis Eckersley	.35	.16	.04
☐ 31 Cecil Fielder	1.50	.65	.19
☐ 32 Brian Fisher	.05	.02	.01
☐ 33 Willie Fraser	.05	.02	.01
☐ 34 Ken Gerhart	.05	.02	.01
☐ 35 Jim Gott	.05	.02	.01
☐ 36 Dan Gladden	.05	.02	.01
☐ 37 Mike Greenwell	.75	.35	.09
☐ 38 Cecilio Guante	.05	.02	.01
☐ 39 Albert Hall	.05	.02	.01
☐ 40 Atlee Hammaker	.05	.02	.01
☐ 41 Mickey Hatcher	.05	.02	.01
☐ 42 Mike Heath	.05	.02	.01
☐ 43 Neal Heaton	.05	.02	.01
☐ 44 Mike Henneman	.30	.14	.04
☐ 45 Guy Hoffman	.05	.02	.01
☐ 46 Charles Hudson	.05	.02	.01
☐ 47 Chuck Jackson	.05	.02	.01
☐ 48 Mike Jackson	.20	.09	.03
☐ 49 Reggie Jackson	.50	.23	.06
☐ 50 Chris James	.05	.02	.01
☐ 51 Dion James	.05	.02	.01
☐ 52 Stan Javier	.05	.02	.01
☐ 53 Stan Jefferson	.05	.02	.01
☐ 54 Jimmy Jones	.05	.02	.01
☐ 55 Tracy Jones	.05	.02	.01
☐ 56 Terry Kennedy	.05	.02	.01
☐ 57 Mike Kingery	.05	.02	.01
☐ 58 Ray Knight	.08	.04	.01
☐ 59 Gene Larkin	.20	.09	.03
☐ 60 Mike LaValliere	.08	.04	.01
☐ 61 Jack Lazorko	.05	.02	.01
☐ 62 Terry Leach	.05	.02	.01
☐ 63 Rick Leach	.05	.02	.01
☐ 64 Craig Lefferts	.05	.02	.01
☐ 65 Jim Lindeman	.05	.02	.01
☐ 66 Bill Long	.05	.02	.01
☐ 67 Mike Loynd	.05	.02	.01
☐ 68 Greg Maddux	4.00	1.80	.50
☐ 69 Bill Madlock	.08	.04	.01
☐ 70 Dave Magadan	.15	.07	.02
☐ 71 Joe Magrane	.15	.07	.02
☐ 72 Fred Manrique	.05	.02	.01
☐ 73 Mike Mason	.05	.02	.01
☐ 74 Lloyd McClendon	.05	.02	.01
☐ 75 Fred McGriff	3.50	1.55	.45
☐ 76 Mark McGwire	6.00	2.70	.75
☐ 77 Mark McLemore	.05	.02	.01
☐ 78 Kevin McReynolds	.08	.04	.01
☐ 79 Dave Meads	.05	.02	.01
☐ 80 Greg Minton	.05	.02	.01
☐ 81 John Mitchell	.05	.02	.01
☐ 82 Kevin Mitchell	.75	.35	.09
☐ 83 John Morris	.05	.02	.01
☐ 84 Jeff Musselman	.05	.02	.01
☐ 85 Randy Myers	.30	.14	.04
☐ 86 Gene Nelson	.05	.02	.01
☐ 87 Joe Niekro	.08	.04	.01
☐ 88 Tom Nieto	.05	.02	.01
☐ 89 Reid Nichols	.05	.02	.01
☐ 90 Matt Nokes	.35	.16	.04
☐ 91 Dickie Noles	.05	.02	.01
☐ 92 Edwin Nunez	.05	.02	.01
☐ 93 Jose Nunez	.05	.02	.01
☐ 94 Paul O'Neill	.30	.14	.04
☐ 95 Jim Paciorek	.05	.02	.01
☐ 96 Lance Parrish	.08	.04	.01
☐ 97 Bill Pecota	.12	.05	.02
☐ 98 Tony Pena	.05	.02	.01
☐ 99 Luis Polonia	.50	.23	.06
☐ 100 Randy Ready	.05	.02	.01
☐ 101 Jeff Reardon	.20	.09	.03
☐ 102 Gary Redus	.05	.02	.01
☐ 103 Rick Rhoden	.05	.02	.01
☐ 104 Wally Ritchie	.05	.02	.01
☐ 105 Jeff Robinson UER	.08	.04	.01
(Wrong Jeff's			
stats on back)			
☐ 106 Mark Salas	.05	.02	.01
☐ 107 Dave Schmidt	.05	.02	.01
☐ 108 Kevin Seitzer UER	.25	.11	.03
(Wrong birth year)			
☐ 109 John Shelby	.05	.02	.01
☐ 110 John Smiley	1.00	.45	.13
☐ 111 Lary Sorensen	.05	.02	.01
☐ 112 Chris Speier	.05	.02	.01

☐ 113 Randy St.Claire	.05	.02	.01
☐ 114 Jim Sundberg	.05	.02	.01
☐ 115 B.J. Surhoff	.20	.09	.03
☐ 116 Greg Swindell	.75	.35	.09
☐ 117 Danny Tartabull	.40	.18	.05
☐ 118 Dorn Taylor	.05	.02	.01
☐ 119 Lee Tunnell	.05	.02	.01
☐ 120 Ed VandeBerg	.05	.02	.01
☐ 121 Andy Van Slyke	.30	.14	.04
☐ 122 Gary Ward	.05	.02	.01
☐ 123 Devon White	.35	.16	.04
☐ 124 Alan Wiggins	.05	.02	.01
☐ 125 Bill Wilkinson	.05	.02	.01
☐ 126 Jim Winn	.05	.02	.01
☐ 127 Frank Williams	.05	.02	.01
☐ 128 Ken Williams	.05	.02	.01
☐ 129 Matt Williams	2.25	1.00	.30
☐ 130 Herm Willingham	.05	.02	.01
☐ 131 Matt Young	.05	.02	.01
☐ 132 Checklist Card	.08	.01	.00

1988 Fleer

This 660-card set features a distinctive white background with red and blue diagonal stripes across the card. The backs are printed in gray and red on white card stock. The bottom of the card back shows an innovative breakdown of the player's demonstrated ability with respect to day, night, home, and road games. Cards are numbered on the back and are again the standard 2 1/2" by 3 1/2". Cards are again organized numerically by teams, i.e., World Champion Twins (1-25), St. Louis Cardinals (26-50), Detroit Tigers (51-75), San Francisco Giants (76-101), Toronto Blue Jays (102-126), New York Mets (127-

154), Milwaukee Brewers (155-178), Montreal Expos (179-201), New York Yankees (202-226), Cincinnati Reds (227-250), Kansas City Royals (251-274), Oakland A's (275-296), Philadelphia Phillies (297-320), Pittsburgh Pirates (321-342), Boston Red Sox (343-367), Seattle Mariners (368-390), Chicago White Sox (391-413), Chicago Cubs (414-436), Houston Astros (437-460), Texas Rangers (461-483), California Angels (484-507), Los Angeles Dodgers (508-530), Atlanta Braves (531-552), Baltimore Orioles (553-575), San Diego Padres (576-599), and Cleveland Indians (600-621). The last 39 cards in the set consist of Specials (622-640), Rookie Pairs (641-653), and checklists (654-660). Cards 90 and 91 are incorrectly numbered on the checklist card number 654. The key Rookie Cards in this set are Ellis Burks, Ron Gant, Tom Glavine, Mark Grace, Gregg Jefferies, Roberto Kelly, Edgar Martinez, Jack McDowell, and Matt Williams. A subset of "Stadium Cards" was randomly inserted throughout the packs. These cards pictured all 26 stadiums used by Major League Baseball and presented facts about these ballparks. Fleer also produced a "limited" edition version of this set with glossy coating and packaged in a "tin." However, this tin set was apparently not limited enough (estimated between 40,000 and 60,000 1988 tin sets produced by Fleer), since the values of the "tin" glossy cards are now only double the values of the respective cards in the regular set.

	MT	EX-MT	VG
COMPLETE SET (660)	33.00	15.00	4.10
COMPLETE FACT.SET (672)	35.00	16.00	4.40
COMMON PLAYER (1-660)	.05	.02	.01
COMPLETE WS SET (12)	2.50	1.15	.30

☐ 1 Keith Atherton	.05	.02	.01
☐ 2 Don Baylor	.08	.04	.01
☐ 3 Juan Berenguer	.05	.02	.01
☐ 4 Bert Blyleven	.08	.04	.01
☐ 5 Tom Brunansky	.08	.04	.01
☐ 6 Randy Bush	.05	.02	.01
☐ 7 Steve Carlton	.30	.14	.04
☐ 8 Mark Davidson	.05	.02	.01
☐ 9 George Frazier	.05	.02	.01
☐ 10 Gary Gaetti	.05	.02	.01
☐ 11 Greg Gagne	.05	.02	.01
☐ 12 Dan Gladden	.05	.02	.01
☐ 13 Kent Hrbek	.08	.04	.01

☐	268	Don Aase	.10	.05	.01	☐	325	LaMarr Hoyt
☐	269	Mike Boddicker	.10	.05	.01	☐	326	Roy Lee Jackson
☐	270	Rich Dauer	.10	.05	.01	☐	327	Terry Kennedy
☐	271	Storm Davis	.10	.05	.01	☐	328	Craig Lefferts
☐	272	Rick Dempsey	.10	.05	.01	☐	329	Carmelo Martinez
☐	273	Ken Dixon	.10	.05	.01	☐	330	Lance McCullers
☐	274	Jim Dwyer	.10	.05	.01	☐	331	Kevin McReynolds
☐	275	Mike Flanagan	.10	.05	.01	☐	332	Graig Nettles
☐	276	Wayne Gross	.10	.05	.01	☐	333	Jerry Royster
☐	277	Lee Lacy	.10	.05	.01	☐	334	Eric Show
☐	278	Fred Lynn	.15	.07	.02	☐	335	Tim Stoddard
☐	279	Tippy Martinez	.10	.05	.01	☐	336	Garry Templeton
☐	280	Dennis Martinez	.15	.07	.02	☐	337	Mark Thurmond
☐	281	Scott McGregor	.10	.05	.01	☐	338	Ed Wojna
☐	282	Eddie Murray	1.00	.45	.13	☐	339	Tony Armas
☐	283	Floyd Rayford	.10	.05	.01	☐	340	Marty Barrett
☐	284	Cal Ripken	5.00	2.30	.60	☐	341	Wade Boggs
☐	285	Gary Roenicke	.10	.05	.01	☐	342	Dennis Boyd
☐	286	Larry Sheets	.10	.05	.01	☐	343	Bill Buckner
☐	287	John Shelby	.10	.05	.01	☐	344	Mark Clear
☐	288	Nate Snell	.10	.05	.01	☐	345	Roger Clemens
☐	289	Sammy Stewart	.10	.05	.01	☐	346	Steve Crawford
☐	290	Alan Wiggins	.10	.05	.01	☐	347	Mike Easler
☐	291	Mike Young	.10	.05	.01	☐	348	Dwight Evans
☐	292	Alan Ashby	.10	.05	.01	☐	349	Rich Gedman
☐	293	Mark Bailey	.10	.05	.01	☐	350	Jackie Gutierrez
☐	294	Kevin Bass	.10	.05	.01	☐	351	Glenn Hoffman
☐	295	Jeff Calhoun	.10	.05	.01	☐	352	Bruce Hurst
☐	296	Jose Cruz	.10	.05	.01	☐	353	Bruce Kison
☐	297	Glenn Davis	.75	.35	.09	☐	354	Tim Lollar
☐	298	Bill Dawley	.10	.05	.01	☐	355	Steve Lyons
☐	299	Frank DiPino	.10	.05	.01	☐	356	Al Nipper
☐	300	Bill Doran	.10	.05	.01	☐	357	Bob Ojeda
☐	301	Phil Garner	.15	.07	.02	☐	358	Jim Rice
☐	302	Jeff Heathcock	.10	.05	.01	☐	359	Bob Stanley
☐	303	Charlie Kerfeld	.10	.05	.01	☐	360	Mike Trujillo
☐	304	Bob Knepper	.10	.05	.01	☐	361	Thad Bosley
☐	305	Ron Mathis	.10	.05	.01	☐	362	Warren Brusstar
☐	306	Jerry Mumphrey	.10	.05	.01	☐	363	Ron Cey
☐	307	Jim Pankovits	.10	.05	.01	☐	364	Jody Davis
☐	308	Terry Puhl	.10	.05	.01	☐	365	Bob Dernier
☐	309	Craig Reynolds	.10	.05	.01	☐	366	Shawon Dunston
☐	310	Nolan Ryan	6.00	2.70	.75	☐	367	Leon Durham
☐	311	Mike Scott	.15	.07	.02	☐	368	Dennis Eckersley
☐	312	Dave Smith	.10	.05	.01	☐	369	Ray Fontenot
☐	313	Dickie Thon	.10	.05	.01	☐	370	George Frazier
☐	314	Denny Walling	.10	.05	.01	☐	371	Billy Hatcher
☐	315	Kurt Bevacqua	.10	.05	.01	☐	372	Dave Lopes
☐	316	Al Bumbry	.10	.05	.01	☐	373	Gary Matthews
☐	317	Jerry Davis	.10	.05	.01	☐	374	Ron Meridith
☐	318	Luis DeLeon	.10	.05	.01	☐	375	Keith Moreland
☐	319	Dave Dravecky	.15	.07	.02	☐	376	Reggie Patterson
☐	320	Tim Flannery	.10	.05	.01	☐	377	Dick Ruthven
☐	321	Steve Garvey	.35	.16	.04	☐	378	Ryne Sandberg
☐	322	Rich Gossage	.15	.07	.02	☐	379	Scott Sanderson
☐	323	Tony Gwynn	3.00	1.35	.40	☐	380	Lee Smith
☐	324	Andy Hawkins	.10	.05	.01	☐	381	Lary Sorensen

Right column values:

☐	325	LaMarr Hoyt	.10	.05	.01
☐	326	Roy Lee Jackson	.10	.05	.01
☐	327	Terry Kennedy	.10	.05	.01
☐	328	Craig Lefferts	.15	.07	.02
☐	329	Carmelo Martinez	.10	.05	.01
☐	330	Lance McCullers	.10	.05	.01
☐	331	Kevin McReynolds	.12	.05	.02
☐	332	Graig Nettles	.15	.07	.02
☐	333	Jerry Royster	.10	.05	.01
☐	334	Eric Show	.10	.05	.01
☐	335	Tim Stoddard	.10	.05	.01
☐	336	Garry Templeton	.10	.05	.01
☐	337	Mark Thurmond	.10	.05	.01
☐	338	Ed Wojna	.10	.05	.01
☐	339	Tony Armas	.10	.05	.01
☐	340	Marty Barrett	.10	.05	.01
☐	341	Wade Boggs	2.00	.90	.25
☐	342	Dennis Boyd	.10	.05	.01
☐	343	Bill Buckner	.15	.07	.02
☐	344	Mark Clear	.10	.05	.01
☐	345	Roger Clemens	12.00	5.50	1.50
☐	346	Steve Crawford	.10	.05	.01
☐	347	Mike Easler	.10	.05	.01
☐	348	Dwight Evans	.12	.05	.02
☐	349	Rich Gedman	.10	.05	.01
☐	350	Jackie Gutierrez	.10	.05	.01
☐	351	Glenn Hoffman	.10	.05	.01
☐	352	Bruce Hurst	.15	.07	.02
☐	353	Bruce Kison	.10	.05	.01
☐	354	Tim Lollar	.10	.05	.01
☐	355	Steve Lyons	.10	.05	.01
☐	356	Al Nipper	.10	.05	.01
☐	357	Bob Ojeda	.10	.05	.01
☐	358	Jim Rice	.15	.07	.02
☐	359	Bob Stanley	.10	.05	.01
☐	360	Mike Trujillo	.10	.05	.01
☐	361	Thad Bosley	.10	.05	.01
☐	362	Warren Brusstar	.10	.05	.01
☐	363	Ron Cey	.15	.07	.02
☐	364	Jody Davis	.10	.05	.01
☐	365	Bob Dernier	.10	.05	.01
☐	366	Shawon Dunston	.30	.14	.04
☐	367	Leon Durham	.10	.05	.01
☐	368	Dennis Eckersley	.75	.35	.09
☐	369	Ray Fontenot	.10	.05	.01
☐	370	George Frazier	.10	.05	.01
☐	371	Billy Hatcher	.15	.07	.02
☐	372	Dave Lopes	.15	.07	.02
☐	373	Gary Matthews	.10	.05	.01
☐	374	Ron Meridith	.10	.05	.01
☐	375	Keith Moreland	.10	.05	.01
☐	376	Reggie Patterson	.10	.05	.01
☐	377	Dick Ruthven	.10	.05	.01
☐	378	Ryne Sandberg	4.50	2.00	.55
☐	379	Scott Sanderson	.10	.05	.01
☐	380	Lee Smith	.60	.25	.08
☐	381	Lary Sorensen	.10	.05	.01

☐ 14 Gene Larkin	12	.05	.02
☐ 15 Tim Laudner	.05	.02	.01
☐ 16 Steve Lombardozzi	.05	.02	.01
☐ 17 Al Newman	.05	.02	.01
☐ 18 Joe Niekro	.08	.04	.01
☐ 19 Kirby Puckett	1.00	.45	.13
☐ 20 Jeff Reardon	.20	.09	.03
☐ 21A Dan Schatzeder ERR	.10	.05	.01
(Misspelled Schatzader			
on card front)			
☐ 21B Dan Schatzeder COR	.05	.02	.01
☐ 22 Roy Smalley	.05	.02	.01
☐ 23 Mike Smithson	.05	.02	.01
☐ 24 Les Straker	.05	.02	.01
☐ 25 Frank Viola	.08	.04	.01
☐ 26 Jack Clark	.08	.04	.01
☐ 27 Vince Coleman	.08	.04	.01
☐ 28 Danny Cox	.05	.02	.01
☐ 29 Bill Dawley	.05	.02	.01
☐ 30 Ken Dayley	.05	.02	.01
☐ 31 Doug DeCinces	.05	.02	.01
☐ 32 Curt Ford	.05	.02	.01
☐ 33 Bob Forsch	.05	.02	.01
☐ 34 David Green	.05	.02	.01
☐ 35 Tom Herr	.05	.02	.01
☐ 36 Ricky Horton	.05	.02	.01
☐ 37 Lance Johnson	.40	.18	.05
☐ 38 Steve Lake	.05	.02	.01
☐ 39 Jim Lindeman	.05	.02	.01
☐ 40 Joe Magrane	.15	.07	.02
☐ 41 Greg Mathews	.05	.02	.01
☐ 42 Willie McGee	.08	.04	.01
☐ 43 John Morris	.05	.02	.01
☐ 44 Jose Oquendo	.05	.02	.01
☐ 45 Tony Pena	.05	.02	.01
☐ 46 Terry Pendleton	.25	.11	.03
☐ 47 Ozzie Smith	.40	.18	.05
☐ 48 John Tudor	.05	.02	.01
☐ 49 Lee Tunnell	.05	.02	.01
☐ 50 Todd Worrell	.08	.04	.01
☐ 51 Doyle Alexander	.05	.02	.01
☐ 52 Dave Bergman	.05	.02	.01
☐ 53 Tom Brookens	.05	.02	.01
☐ 54 Darrell Evans	.08	.04	.01
☐ 55 Kirk Gibson	.08	.04	.01
☐ 56 Mike Heath	.05	.02	.01
☐ 57 Mike Henneman	.30	.14	.04
☐ 58 Willie Hernandez	.05	.02	.01
☐ 59 Larry Herndon	.05	.02	.01
☐ 60 Eric King	.05	.02	.01
☐ 61 Chet Lemon	.05	.02	.01
☐ 62 Scott Lusader	.05	.02	.01
☐ 63 Bill Madlock	.05	.02	.01
☐ 64 Jack Morris	.15	.07	.02
☐ 65 Jim Morrison	.05	.02	.01
☐ 66 Matt Nokes	.40	.18	.05
☐ 67 Dan Petry	.05	.02	.01

☐ 68A Jeff M. Robinson ERR	.25	.11	.03
(Stats for Jeff D.			
Robinson on card back,			
Born 12-13-60)			
☐ 68B Jeff M. Robinson COR	.08	.04	.01
(Born 12-14-61)			
☐ 69 Pat Sheridan	.05	.02	.01
☐ 70 Nate Snell	.05	.02	.01
☐ 71 Frank Tanana	.05	.02	.01
☐ 72 Walt Terrell	.05	.02	.01
☐ 73 Mark Thurmond	.05	.02	.01
☐ 74 Alan Trammell	.08	.04	.01
☐ 75 Lou Whitaker	.08	.04	.01
☐ 76 Mike Aldrete	.05	.02	.01
☐ 77 Bob Brenly	.05	.02	.01
☐ 78 Will Clark	1.50	.65	.19
☐ 79 Chili Davis	.08	.04	.01
☐ 80 Kelly Downs	.05	.02	.01
☐ 81 Dave Dravecky	.08	.04	.01
☐ 82 Scott Garrelts	.05	.02	.01
☐ 83 Atlee Hammaker	.05	.02	.01
☐ 84 Dave Henderson	.05	.02	.01
☐ 85 Mike Krukow	.05	.02	.01
☐ 86 Mike LaCoss	.05	.02	.01
☐ 87 Craig Lefferts	.05	.02	.01
☐ 88 Jeff Leonard	.05	.02	.01
☐ 89 Candy Maldonado	.05	.02	.01
☐ 90 Eddie Milner	.05	.02	.01
☐ 91 Bob Melvin	.05	.02	.01
☐ 92 Kevin Mitchell	.25	.11	.03
☐ 93 Jon Perlman	.05	.02	.01
☐ 94 Rick Reuschel	.05	.02	.01
☐ 95 Don Robinson	.05	.02	.01
☐ 96 Chris Speier	.05	.02	.01
☐ 97 Harry Spilman	.05	.02	.01
☐ 98 Robby Thompson	.08	.04	.01
☐ 99 Jose Uribe	.05	.02	.01
☐ 100 Mark Wasinger	.05	.02	.01
☐ 101 Matt Williams	2.00	.90	.25
☐ 102 Jesse Barfield	.05	.02	.01
☐ 103 George Bell	.15	.07	.02
☐ 104 Juan Beniquez	.05	.02	.01
☐ 105 John Cerutti	.05	.02	.01
☐ 106 Jim Clancy	.05	.02	.01
☐ 107 Rob Ducey	.05	.02	.01
☐ 108 Mark Eichhorn	.05	.02	.01
☐ 109 Tony Fernandez	.08	.04	.01
☐ 110 Cecil Fielder	.60	.25	.08
☐ 111 Kelly Gruber	.08	.04	.01
☐ 112 Tom Henke	.08	.04	.01
☐ 113A Garth Iorg ERR	.25	.11	.03
(Misspelled Iorq			
on card front)			
☐ 113B Garth Iorg COR	.05	.02	.01
☐ 114 Jimmy Key	.08	.04	.01
☐ 115 Rick Leach	.05	.02	.01
☐ 116 Manny Lee	.05	.02	.01

□	117	Nelson Liriano	.05	.02	.01
□	118	Fred McGriff	1.50	.65	.19
□	119	Lloyd Moseby	.05	.02	.01
□	120	Rance Mulliniks	.05	.02	.01
□	121	Jeff Musselman	.05	.02	.01
□	122	Jose Nunez	.05	.02	.01
□	123	Dave Stieb	.08	.04	.01
□	124	Willie Upshaw	.05	.02	.01
□	125	Duane Ward	.25	.11	.03
□	126	Ernie Whitt	.05	.02	.01
□	127	Rick Aguilera	.08	.04	.01
□	128	Wally Backman	.05	.02	.01
□	129	Mark Carreon	.15	.07	.02
□	130	Gary Carter	.10	.05	.01
□	131	David Cone	1.25	.55	.16
□	132	Ron Darling	.08	.04	.01
□	133	Len Dykstra	.08	.04	.01
□	134	Sid Fernandez	.08	.04	.01
□	135	Dwight Gooden	.15	.07	.02
□	136	Keith Hernandez	.08	.04	.01
□	137	Gregg Jefferies	2.00	.90	.25
□	138	Howard Johnson	.15	.07	.02
□	139	Terry Leach	.05	.02	.01
□	140	Barry Lyons	.05	.02	.01
□	141	Dave Magadan	.08	.04	.01
□	142	Roger McDowell	.05	.02	.01
□	143	Kevin McReynolds	.08	.04	.01
□	144	Keith A. Miller	.35	.16	.04
□	145	John Mitchell	.05	.02	.01
□	146	Randy Myers	.12	.05	.02
□	147	Bob Ojeda	.05	.02	.01
□	148	Jesse Orosco	.05	.02	.01
□	149	Rafael Santana	.05	.02	.01
□	150	Doug Sisk	.05	.02	.01
□	151	Darryl Strawberry	.60	.25	.08
□	152	Tim Teufel	.05	.02	.01
□	153	Gene Walter	.05	.02	.01
□	154	Mookie Wilson	.08	.04	.01
□	155	Jay Aldrich	.05	.02	.01
□	156	Chris Bosio	.08	.04	.01
□	157	Glenn Braggs	.05	.02	.01
□	158	Greg Brock	.05	.02	.01
□	159	Juan Castillo	.05	.02	.01
□	160	Mark Clear	.05	.02	.01
□	161	Cecil Cooper	.08	.04	.01
□	162	Chuck Crim	.05	.02	.01
□	163	Rob Deer	.08	.04	.01
□	164	Mike Felder	.05	.02	.01
□	165	Jim Gantner	.05	.02	.01
□	166	Ted Higuera	.05	.02	.01
□	167	Steve Kiefer	.05	.02	.01
□	168	Rick Manning	.05	.02	.01
□	169	Paul Molitor	.25	.11	.03
□	170	Juan Nieves	.05	.02	.01
□	171	Dan Plesac	.05	.02	.01
□	172	Earnest Riles	.05	.02	.01
□	173	Bill Schroeder	.05	.02	.01
□	174	Steve Stanicek	.05	.02	.01
□	175	B.J. Surhoff	.05	.02	.01
□	176	Dale Sveum	.05	.02	.01
□	177	Bill Wegman	.05	.02	.01
□	178	Robin Yount	.50	.23	.06
□	179	Hubie Brooks	.05	.02	.01
□	180	Tim Burke	.05	.02	.01
□	181	Casey Candaele	.05	.02	.01
□	182	Mike Fitzgerald	.05	.02	.01
□	183	Tom Foley	.05	.02	.01
□	184	Andres Galarraga	.05	.02	.01
□	185	Neal Heaton	.05	.02	.01
□	186	Wallace Johnson	.05	.02	.01
□	187	Vance Law	.05	.02	.01
□	188	Dennis Martinez	.08	.04	.01
□	189	Bob McClure	.05	.02	.01
□	190	Andy McGaffigan	.05	.02	.01
□	191	Reid Nichols	.05	.02	.01
□	192	Pascual Perez	.05	.02	.01
□	193	Tim Raines	.08	.04	.01
□	194	Jeff Reed	.05	.02	.01
□	195	Bob Sebra	.05	.02	.01
□	196	Bryn Smith	.05	.02	.01
□	197	Randy St.Claire	.05	.02	.01
□	198	Tim Wallach	.08	.04	.01
□	199	Mitch Webster	.05	.02	.01
□	200	Herm Winningham	.05	.02	.01
□	201	Floyd Youmans	.05	.02	.01
□	202	Brad Arnsberg	.05	.02	.01
□	203	Rick Cerone	.05	.02	.01
□	204	Pat Clements	.05	.02	.01
□	205	Henry Cotto	.05	.02	.01
□	206	Mike Easler	.05	.02	.01
□	207	Ron Guidry	.08	.04	.01
□	208	Bill Gullickson	.05	.02	.01
□	209	Rickey Henderson	.60	.25	.08
□	210	Charles Hudson	.05	.02	.01
□	211	Tommy John	.08	.04	.01
□	212	Roberto Kelly	2.00	.90	.25
□	213	Ron Kittle	.05	.02	.01
□	214	Don Mattingly	.60	.25	.08
□	215	Bobby Meacham	.05	.02	.01
□	216	Mike Pagliarulo	.05	.02	.01
□	217	Dan Pasqua	.05	.02	.01
□	218	Willie Randolph	.08	.04	.01
□	219	Rick Rhoden	.05	.02	.01
□	220	Dave Righetti	.05	.02	.01
□	221	Jerry Royster	.05	.02	.01
□	222	Tim Stoddard	.05	.02	.01
□	223	Wayne Tolleson	.05	.02	.01
□	224	Gary Ward	.05	.02	.01
□	225	Claudell Washington	.05	.02	.01
□	226	Dave Winfield	.40	.18	.05
□	227	Buddy Bell	.08	.04	.01
□	228	Tom Browning	.05	.02	.01
□	229	Dave Concepcion	.08	.04	.01
□	230	Kal Daniels	.08	.04	.01

☐	231 Eric Davis	15	.07	.02
☐	232 Bo Diaz	05	.02	.01
☐	233 Nick Esasky UER	05	.02	.01
	(Has a dollar sign before '87 SB totals)			
☐	234 John Franco	08	.04	.01
☐	235 Guy Hoffman	05	.02	.01
☐	236 Tom Hume	05	.02	.01
☐	237 Tracy Jones	05	.02	.01
☐	238 Bill Landrum	08	.04	.01
☐	239 Barry Larkin	35	.16	.04
☐	240 Terry McGriff	05	.02	.01
☐	241 Rob Murphy	05	.02	.01
☐	242 Ron Oester	05	.02	.01
☐	243 Dave Parker	08	.04	.01
☐	244 Pat Perry	05	.02	.01
☐	245 Ted Power	05	.02	.01
☐	246 Dennis Rasmussen	05	.02	.01
☐	247 Ron Robinson	05	.02	.01
☐	248 Kurt Stillwell	05	.02	.01
☐	249 Jeff Treadway	12	.05	.02
☐	250 Frank Williams	05	.02	.01
☐	251 Steve Balboni	05	.02	.01
☐	252 Bud Black	05	.02	.01
☐	253 Thad Bosley	05	.02	.01
☐	254 George Brett	50	.23	.06
☐	255 John Davis	05	.02	.01
☐	256 Steve Farr	05	.02	.01
☐	257 Gene Garber	05	.02	.01
☐	258 Jerry Don Gleaton	05	.02	.01
☐	259 Mark Gubicza	05	.02	.01
☐	260 Bo Jackson	75	.35	.09
☐	261 Danny Jackson	05	.02	.01
☐	262 Ross Jones	05	.02	.01
☐	263 Charlie Leibrandt	05	.02	.01
☐	264 Bill Pecota	15	.07	.02
☐	265 Melido Perez	75	.35	.09
☐	266 Jamie Quirk	05	.02	.01
☐	267 Dan Quisenberry	08	.04	.01
☐	268 Bret Saberhagen	12	.05	.02
☐	269 Angel Salazar	05	.02	.01
☐	270 Kevin Seitzer UER	08	.04	.01
	(Wrong birth year)			
☐	271 Danny Tartabull	25	.11	.03
☐	272 Gary Thurman	05	.02	.01
☐	273 Frank White	05	.02	.01
☐	274 Willie Wilson	05	.02	.01
☐	275 Tony Bernazard	05	.02	.01
☐	276 Jose Canseco	1.50	.65	.19
☐	277 Mike Davis	05	.02	.01
☐	278 Storm Davis	05	.02	.01
☐	279 Dennis Eckersley	30	.14	.04
☐	280 Alfredo Griffin	05	.02	.01
☐	281 Rick Honeycutt	05	.02	.01
☐	282 Jay Howell	05	.02	.01
☐	283 Reggie Jackson	50	.23	.06
☐	284 Dennis Lamp	05	.02	.01

☐	285 Carney Lansford	08	.04	.01
☐	286 Mark McGwire	2.00	.90	.25
☐	287 Dwayne Murphy	05	.02	.01
☐	288 Gene Nelson	05	.02	.01
☐	289 Steve Ontiveros	05	.02	.01
☐	290 Tony Phillips	05	.02	.01
☐	291 Eric Plunk	05	.02	.01
☐	292 Luis Polonia	60	.25	.08
☐	293 Rick Rodriguez	05	.02	.01
☐	294 Terry Steinbach	08	.04	.01
☐	295 Dave Stewart	08	.04	.01
☐	296 Curt Young	05	.02	.01
☐	297 Luis Aguayo	05	.02	.01
☐	298 Steve Bedrosian	05	.02	.01
☐	299 Jeff Calhoun	05	.02	.01
☐	300 Don Carman	05	.02	.01
☐	301 Todd Frohwirth	05	.02	.01
☐	302 Greg Gross	05	.02	.01
☐	303 Kevin Gross	05	.02	.01
☐	304 Von Hayes	05	.02	.01
☐	305 Keith Hughes	05	.02	.01
☐	306 Mike Jackson	15	.07	.02
☐	307 Chris James	05	.02	.01
☐	308 Steve Jeltz	05	.02	.01
☐	309 Mike Maddux	05	.02	.01
☐	310 Lance Parrish	08	.04	.01
☐	311 Shane Rawley	05	.02	.01
☐	312 Wally Ritchie	05	.02	.01
☐	313 Bruce Ruffin	05	.02	.01
☐	314 Juan Samuel	05	.02	.01
☐	315 Mike Schmidt	90	.40	.11
☐	316 Rick Schu	05	.02	.01
☐	317 Jeff Stone	05	.02	.01
☐	318 Kent Tekulve	05	.02	.01
☐	319 Milt Thompson	05	.02	.01
☐	320 Glenn Wilson	05	.02	.01
☐	321 Rafael Belliard	05	.02	.01
☐	322 Barry Bonds	1.50	.65	.19
☐	323 Bobby Bonilla UER	50	.23	.06
	(Wrong birth year)			
☐	324 Sid Bream	08	.04	.01
☐	325 John Cangelosi	05	.02	.01
☐	326 Mike Diaz	05	.02	.01
☐	327 Doug Drabek	20	.09	.03
☐	328 Mike Dunne	05	.02	.01
☐	329 Brian Fisher	05	.02	.01
☐	330 Brett Gideon	05	.02	.01
☐	331 Terry Harper	05	.02	.01
☐	332 Bob Kipper	05	.02	.01
☐	333 Mike LaValliere	05	.02	.01
☐	334 Jose Lind	30	.14	.04
☐	335 Junior Ortiz	05	.02	.01
☐	336 Vicente Palacios	12	.05	.02
☐	337 Bob Patterson	05	.02	.01
☐	338 Al Pedrique	05	.02	.01
☐	339 R.J. Reynolds	05	.02	.01
☐	340 John Smiley	1.00	.45	.13

☐ 341	Andy Van Slyke UER 20	.09	.03
	(Wrong batting and		
	throwing listed)		
☐ 342	Bob Walk 05	.02	.01
☐ 343	Marty Barrett 05	.02	.01
☐ 344	Todd Benzinger 15	.07	.02
☐ 345	Wade Boggs 50	.23	.06
☐ 346	Tom Bolton 05	.02	.01
☐ 347	Oil Can Boyd 05	.02	.01
☐ 348	Ellis Burks 75	.35	.09
☐ 349	Roger Clemens 1.00	.45	.13
☐ 350	Steve Crawford 05	.02	.01
☐ 351	Dwight Evans 08	.04	.01
☐ 352	Wes Gardner 05	.02	.01
☐ 353	Rich Gedman 05	.02	.01
☐ 354	Mike Greenwell 30	.14	.04
☐ 355	Sam Horn 09	.09	.03
☐ 356	Bruce Hurst 08	.04	.01
☐ 357	John Marzano 05	.02	.01
☐ 358	Al Nipper 05	.02	.01
☐ 359	Spike Owen 05	.02	.01
☐ 360	Jody Reed 60	.25	.08
☐ 361	Jim Rice 05	.02	.01
☐ 362	Ed Romero 05	.02	.01
☐ 363	Kevin Romine 05	.02	.01
☐ 364	Joe Sambito 05	.02	.01
☐ 365	Calvin Schiraldi 05	.02	.01
☐ 366	Jeff Sellers 05	.02	.01
☐ 367	Bob Stanley 05	.02	.01
☐ 368	Scott Bankhead 05	.02	.01
☐ 369	Phil Bradley 05	.02	.01
☐ 370	Scott Bradley 05	.02	.01
☐ 371	Mickey Brantley 05	.02	.01
☐ 372	Mike Campbell 05	.02	.01
☐ 373	Alvin Davis 05	.02	.01
☐ 374	Lee Guetterman 05	.02	.01
☐ 375	Dave Hengel 05	.02	.01
☐ 376	Mike Kingery 05	.02	.01
☐ 377	Mark Langston 08	.04	.01
☐ 378	Edgar Martinez 3.50	1.55	.45
☐ 379	Mike Moore 05	.02	.01
☐ 380	Mike Morgan 08	.04	.01
☐ 381	John Moses 05	.02	.01
☐ 382	Donell Nixon 05	.02	.01
☐ 383	Edwin Nunez 05	.02	.01
☐ 384	Ken Phelps 05	.02	.01
☐ 385	Jim Presley 05	.02	.01
☐ 386	Rey Quinones 05	.02	.01
☐ 387	Jerry Reed 05	.02	.01
☐ 388	Harold Reynolds 05	.02	.01
☐ 389	Dave Valle 05	.02	.01
☐ 390	Bill Wilkinson 05	.02	.01
☐ 391	Harold Baines 08	.04	.01
☐ 392	Floyd Bannister 05	.02	.01
☐ 393	Daryl Boston 05	.02	.01
☐ 394	Ivan Calderon 08	.04	.01
☐ 395	Jose DeLeon 05	.02	.01

☐ 396	Richard Dotson 05	.02	.01
☐ 397	Carlton Fisk 35	.16	.04
☐ 398	Ozzie Guillen 08	.04	.01
☐ 399	Ron Hassey 05	.02	.01
☐ 400	Donnie Hill 05	.02	.01
☐ 401	Bob James 05	.02	.01
☐ 402	Dave LaPoint 05	.02	.01
☐ 403	Bill Lindsey 05	.02	.01
☐ 404	Bill Long 05	.02	.01
☐ 405	Steve Lyons 05	.02	.01
☐ 406	Fred Manrique 05	.02	.01
☐ 407	Jack McDowell 3.50	1.55	.45
☐ 408	Gary Redus 05	.02	.01
☐ 409	Ray Searage 05	.02	.01
☐ 410	Bobby Thigpen 08	.04	.01
☐ 411	Greg Walker 05	.02	.01
☐ 412	Ken Williams 05	.02	.01
☐ 413	Jim Winn 05	.02	.01
☐ 414	Jody Davis 05	.02	.01
☐ 415	Andre Dawson 40	.18	.05
☐ 416	Brian Dayett 05	.02	.01
☐ 417	Bob Dernier 05	.02	.01
☐ 418	Frank DiPino 05	.02	.01
☐ 419	Shawon Dunston 08	.04	.01
☐ 420	Leon Durham 05	.02	.01
☐ 421	Les Lancaster 05	.02	.01
☐ 422	Ed Lynch 05	.02	.01
☐ 423	Greg Maddux 1.50	.65	.19
☐ 424	Dave Martinez 12	.05	.02
☐ 425A	Keith Moreland ERR ..1.50	.65	.19
	(Photo actually		
	Jody Davis)		
☐ 425B	Keith Moreland COR 12	.05	.02
	(Bat on shoulder)		
☐ 426	Jamie Moyer 05	.02	.01
☐ 427	Jerry Mumphrey 05	.02	.01
☐ 428	Paul Noce 05	.02	.01
☐ 429	Rafael Palmeiro 1.00	.45	.13
☐ 430	Wade Rowdon 05	.02	.01
☐ 431	Ryne Sandberg 1.00	.45	.13
☐ 432	Scott Sanderson 05	.02	.01
☐ 433	Lee Smith 25	.11	.03
☐ 434	Jim Sundberg 05	.02	.01
☐ 435	Rick Sutcliffe 08	.04	.01
☐ 436	Manny Trillo 05	.02	.01
☐ 437	Juan Agosto 05	.02	.01
☐ 438	Larry Andersen 05	.02	.01
☐ 439	Alan Ashby 05	.02	.01
☐ 440	Kevin Bass 05	.02	.01
☐ 441	Ken Caminiti 60	.25	.08
☐ 442	Rocky Childress 05	.02	.01
☐ 443	Jose Cruz 05	.02	.01
☐ 444	Danny Darwin 05	.02	.01
☐ 445	Glenn Davis 08	.04	.01
☐ 446	Jim Deshaies 05	.02	.01
☐ 447	Bill Doran 05	.02	.01
☐ 448	Ty Gainey 05	.02	.01

☐ 449	Billy Hatcher	.05	.02	.01
☐ 450	Jeff Heathcock	.05	.02	.01
☐ 451	Bob Knepper	.05	.02	.01
☐ 452	Rob Mallicoat	.05	.02	.01
☐ 453	Dave Meads	.05	.02	.01
☐ 454	Craig Reynolds	.05	.02	.01
☐ 455	Nolan Ryan	1.50	.65	.19
☐ 456	Mike Scott	.08	.04	.01
☐ 457	Dave Smith	.05	.02	.01
☐ 458	Denny Walling	.05	.02	.01
☐ 459	Robbie Wine	.05	.02	.01
☐ 460	Gerald Young	.05	.02	.01
☐ 461	Bob Brower	.05	.02	.01
☐ 462A	Jerry Browne ERR	1.50	.65	.19
	(Photo actually			
	Bob Brower,			
	white player)			
☐ 462B	Jerry Browne COR	.12	.05	.02
	(Black player)			
☐ 463	Steve Buechele	.05	.02	.01
☐ 464	Edwin Correa	.05	.02	.01
☐ 465	Cecil Espy	.10	.05	.01
☐ 466	Scott Fletcher	.05	.02	.01
☐ 467	Jose Guzman	.08	.04	.01
☐ 468	Greg Harris	.05	.02	.01
☐ 469	Charlie Hough	.05	.02	.01
☐ 470	Pete Incaviglia	.08	.04	.01
☐ 471	Paul Kilgus	.05	.02	.01
☐ 472	Mike Loynd	.05	.02	.01
☐ 473	Oddibe McDowell	.05	.02	.01
☐ 474	Dale Mohorcic	.05	.02	.01
☐ 475	Pete O'Brien	.05	.02	.01
☐ 476	Larry Parrish	.05	.02	.01
☐ 477	Geno Petralli	.05	.02	.01
☐ 478	Jeff Russell	.05	.02	.01
☐ 479	Ruben Sierra	1.00	.45	.13
☐ 480	Mike Stanley	.05	.02	.01
☐ 481	Curtis Wilkerson	.05	.02	.01
☐ 482	Mitch Williams	.08	.04	.01
☐ 483	Bobby Witt	.08	.04	.01
☐ 484	Tony Armas	.05	.02	.01
☐ 485	Bob Boone	.08	.04	.01
☐ 486	Bill Buckner	.08	.04	.01
☐ 487	DeWayne Buice	.05	.02	.01
☐ 488	Brian Downing	.05	.02	.01
☐ 489	Chuck Finley	.08	.04	.01
☐ 490	Willie Fraser UER	.05	.02	.01
	(Wrong bio stats,			
	for George Hendrick)			
☐ 491	Jack Howell	.05	.02	.01
☐ 492	Ruppert Jones	.05	.02	.01
☐ 493	Wally Joyner	.20	.09	.03
☐ 494	Jack Lazorko	.05	.02	.01
☐ 495	Gary Lucas	.05	.02	.01
☐ 496	Kirk McCaskill	.05	.02	.01
☐ 497	Mark McLemore	.05	.02	.01
☐ 498	Darrell Miller	.05	.02	.01
☐ 499	Greg Minton	.05	.02	.01
☐ 500	Donnie Moore	.05	.02	.01
☐ 501	Gus Polidor	.05	.02	.01
☐ 502	Johnny Ray	.05	.02	.01
☐ 503	Mark Ryal	.05	.02	.01
☐ 504	Dick Schofield	.05	.02	.01
☐ 505	Don Sutton	.15	.07	.02
☐ 506	Devon White	.12	.05	.02
☐ 507	Mike Witt	.05	.02	.01
☐ 508	Dave Anderson	.05	.02	.01
☐ 509	Tim Belcher	.25	.11	.03
☐ 510	Ralph Bryant	.05	.02	.01
☐ 511	Tim Crews	.05	.02	.01
☐ 512	Mike Devereaux	2.00	.90	.25
☐ 513	Mariano Duncan	.05	.02	.01
☐ 514	Pedro Guerrero	.08	.04	.01
☐ 515	Jeff Hamilton	.05	.02	.01
☐ 516	Mickey Hatcher	.05	.02	.01
☐ 517	Brad Havens	.05	.02	.01
☐ 518	Orel Hershiser	.08	.04	.01
☐ 519	Shawn Hillegas	.05	.02	.01
☐ 520	Ken Howell	.05	.02	.01
☐ 521	Tim Leary	.05	.02	.01
☐ 522	Mike Marshall	.05	.02	.01
☐ 523	Steve Sax	.08	.04	.01
☐ 524	Mike Scioscia	.05	.02	.01
☐ 525	Mike Sharperson	.05	.02	.01
☐ 526	John Shelby	.05	.02	.01
☐ 527	Franklin Stubbs	.05	.02	.01
☐ 528	Fernando Valenzuela	.08	.04	.01
☐ 529	Bob Welch	.08	.04	.01
☐ 530	Matt Young	.05	.02	.01
☐ 531	Jim Acker	.05	.02	.01
☐ 532	Paul Assenmacher	.05	.02	.01
☐ 533	Jeff Blauser	.60	.25	.08
☐ 534	Joe Boever	.05	.02	.01
☐ 535	Martin Clary	.05	.02	.01
☐ 536	Kevin Coffman	.05	.02	.01
☐ 537	Jeff Dedmon	.05	.02	.01
☐ 538	Ron Gant	5.00	2.30	.60
☐ 539	Tom Glavine	9.00	4.00	1.15
☐ 540	Ken Griffey	.08	.04	.01
☐ 541	Albert Hall	.05	.02	.01
☐ 542	Glenn Hubbard	.05	.02	.01
☐ 543	Dion James	.05	.02	.01
☐ 544	Dale Murphy	.15	.07	.02
☐ 545	Ken Oberkfell	.05	.02	.01
☐ 546	David Palmer	.05	.02	.01
☐ 547	Gerald Perry	.05	.02	.01
☐ 548	Charlie Puleo	.05	.02	.01
☐ 549	Ted Simmons	.08	.04	.01
☐ 550	Zane Smith	.05	.02	.01
☐ 551	Andres Thomas	.05	.02	.01
☐ 552	Ozzie Virgil	.05	.02	.01
☐ 553	Don Aase	.05	.02	.01
☐ 554	Jeff Ballard	.05	.02	.01
☐ 555	Eric Bell	.05	.02	.01

☐ 556	Mike Boddicker 05	.02	.01
☐ 557	Ken Dixon 05	.02	.01
☐ 558	Jim Dwyer.....................05	.02	.01
☐ 559	Ken Gerhart...................05	.02	.01
☐ 560	Rene Gonzales 20	.09	.03
☐ 561	Mike Griffin 05	.02	.01
☐ 562	John Habyan UER 05	.02	.01
	(Misspelled Hayban on		
	both sides of card)		
☐ 563	Terry Kennedy 05	.02	.01
☐ 564	Ray Knight 08	.04	.01
☐ 565	Lee Lacy 05	.02	.01
☐ 566	Fred Lynn.....................08	.04	.01
☐ 567	Eddie Murray 35	.16	.04
☐ 568	Tom Niedenfuer 05	.02	.01
☐ 569	Bill Ripken...................15	.07	.02
☐ 570	Cal Ripken..................1.25	.55	.16
☐ 571	Dave Schmidt 05	.02	.01
☐ 572	Larry Sheets 05	.02	.01
☐ 573	Pete Stanicek 05	.02	.01
☐ 574	Mark Williamson 05	.02	.01
☐ 575	Mike Young...................05	.02	.01
☐ 576	Shawn Abner 05	.02	.01
☐ 577	Greg Booker..................05	.02	.01
☐ 578	Chris Brown 05	.02	.01
☐ 579	Keith Comstock 05	.02	.01
☐ 580	Joey Cora.....................08	.04	.01
☐ 581	Mark Davis....................05	.02	.01
☐ 582	Tim Flannery.................08	.04	.01
	(With surfboard)		
☐ 583	Goose Gossage.............08	.04	.01
☐ 584	Mark Grant...................05	.02	.01
☐ 585	Tony Gwynn...................60	.25	.08
☐ 586	Andy Hawkins................05	.02	.01
☐ 587	Stan Jefferson 05	.02	.01
☐ 588	Jimmy Jones 05	.02	.01
☐ 589	John Kruk.....................25	.11	.03
☐ 590	Shane Mack................1.00	.45	.13
☐ 591	Carmelo Martinez...........05	.02	.01
☐ 592	Lance McCullers UER 05	.02	.01
	(6'11" tall)		
☐ 593	Eric Nolte....................05	.02	.01
☐ 594	Randy Ready.................05	.02	.01
☐ 595	Luis Salazar 05	.02	.01
☐ 596	Benito Santiago.............15	.07	.02
☐ 597	Eric Show 05	.02	.01
☐ 598	Garry Templeton 05	.02	.01
☐ 599	Ed Whitson 05	.02	.01
☐ 600	Scott Bailes..................05	.02	.01
☐ 601	Chris Bando 05	.02	.01
☐ 602	Jay Bell 75	.35	.09
☐ 603	Brett Butler 12	.05	.02
☐ 604	Tom Candiotti................05	.02	.01
☐ 605	Joe Carter 60	.25	.08
☐ 606	Carmen Castillo.............05	.02	.01
☐ 607	Brian Dorsett................05	.02	.01
☐ 608	John Farrell..................05	.02	.01
☐ 609	Julio Franco 12	.05	.02
☐ 610	Mel Hall 05	.02	.01
☐ 611	Tommy Hinzo 05	.02	.01
☐ 612	Brook Jacoby.................05	.02	.01
☐ 613	Doug Jones 50	.23	.06
☐ 614	Ken Schrom 05	.02	.01
☐ 615	Cory Snyder..................08	.04	.01
☐ 616	Sammy Stewart 05	.02	.01
☐ 617	Greg Swindell 25	.11	.03
☐ 618	Pat Tabler 05	.02	.01
☐ 619	Ed VandeBerg 05	.02	.01
☐ 620	Eddie Williams...............05	.02	.01
☐ 621	Rich Yett 05	.02	.01
☐ 622	Slugging Sophomores 05	.02	.01
	Wally Joyner		
	Cory Snyder		
☐ 623	Dominican Dynamite.......05	.02	.01
	George Bell		
	Pedro Guerrero		
☐ 624	Oakland's Power Team 1.00	.45	.13
	Mark McGwire		
	Jose Canseco		
☐ 625	Classic Relief 05	.02	.01
	Dave Righetti		
	Dan Plesac		
☐ 626	All Star Righties 05	.02	.01
	Bret Saberhagen		
	Mike Witt		
	Jack Morris		
☐ 627	Game Closers 05	.02	.01
	John Franco		
	Steve Bedrosian		
☐ 628	Masters/Double Play.......40	.18	.05
	Ozzie Smith		
	Ryne Sandberg		
☐ 629	Rookie Record Setter......60	.25	.08
	Mark McGwire		
☐ 630	Changing the Guard........15	.07	.02
	Mike Greenwell		
	Ellis Burks		
	Todd Benzinger		
☐ 631	NL Batting Champs.........20	.09	.03
	Tony Gwynn		
	Tim Raines		
☐ 632	Pitching Magic...............05	.02	.01
	Mike Scott		
	Orel Hershiser		
☐ 633	Big Bats at First.............30	.14	.04
	Pat Tabler		
	Mark McGwire		
☐ 634	Hitting King/Thief...........20	.09	.03
	Tony Gwynn		
	Vince Coleman		
☐ 635	Slugging Shortstops 35	.16	.04
	Tony Fernandez		
	Cal Ripken		
	Alan Trammell		

☐ 636	Tried/True Sluggers ....30 Mike Schmidt Gary Carter	.14	.04
☐ 637	Crunch Time ....25 Darryl Strawberry Eric Davis	.11	.03
☐ 638	AL All-Stars ....25 Matt Nokes Kirby Puckett	.11	.03
☐ 639	NL All-Stars ....05 Keith Hernandez Dale Murphy	.02	.01
☐ 640	The O's Brothers ....50 Billy Ripken Cal Ripken	.23	.06
☐ 641	Mark Grace and ....4.00 Darrin Jackson	1.80	.50
☐ 642	Damon Berryhill and .....75 Jeff Montgomery	.35	.09
☐ 643	Felix Fermin and ....08 Jesse Reid	.04	.01
☐ 644	Greg Myers and ....15 Greg Tabor	.07	.02
☐ 645	Joey Meyer and ....08 Jim Eppard	.04	.01
☐ 646	Adam Peterson and ....08 Randy Velarde	.04	.01
☐ 647	Peter Smith and ....75 Chris Gwynn	.35	.09
☐ 648	Tom Newell and ....08 Greg Jelks	.04	.01
☐ 649	Mario Diaz and ....08 Clay Parker	.04	.01
☐ 650	Jack Savage and ....08 Todd Simmons	.04	.01
☐ 651	John Burkett and ....35 Kirt Manwaring	.16	.04
☐ 652	Dave Otto and ....35 Walt Weiss	.16	.04
☐ 653	Jeff King and ....40 Randell Byers	.18	.05
☐ 654	CL: Twins/Cards ....06 Tigers/Giants UER (90 Bob Melvin, 91 Eddie Milner)	.01	.00
☐ 655	CL: Blue Jays/Mets ....06 Brewers/Expos UER (Mets listed before Blue Jays on card)	.01	.00
☐ 656	CL: Yankees/Reds ....06 Royals/A's	.01	.00
☐ 657	CL: Phillies/Pirates ....06 Red Sox/Mariners	.01	.00
☐ 658	CL: White Sox/Cubs ....06 Astros/Rangers	.01	.00
☐ 659	CL: Angels/Dodgers ....06 Braves/Orioles	.01	.00

☐ 660	CL: Padres/Indians ....06 — .01 Rookies/Specials		.00

1988 Fleer Update

This 132-card set was distributed by Fleer to dealers as a complete set in a custom box. In addition to the complete set of 132 cards, the box also contains 25 Team Logo stickers. The card fronts look very similar to the 1988 Fleer regular issue. The cards are numbered (with a U prefix) alphabetically according to player's last name. Cards measure the standard size, 2 1/2" by 3 1/2". This was the first Fleer Update set to adopt the Fleer "alphabetical within team" numbering system. Tho key (extended) Rookie Cards in this set are Roberto Alomar, Craig Biggio, Chris Sabo, and John Smoltz. Fleer also produced a "limited" edition version of this set with glossy coating and packaged in a "tin." However, this tin set was apparently not limited enough (estimated between 40,000 and 60,000 1988 Update tin sets produced by Fleer), since the values of the "tin" glossy cards are now only double the values of the respective cards in the regular set.

	MT	EX-MT	VG
COMPLETE SET (132) 18.00		8.00	2.30
COMMON PLAYER (1-132) 06		.03	.01
☐ 1 Jose Bautista 06		.03	.01
☐ 2 Joe Orsulak 06		.03	.01
☐ 3 Doug Sisk 06		.03	.01
☐ 4 Craig Worthington 06		.03	.01

☐ 5	Mike Boddicker	.06	.03	.01
☐ 6	Rick Cerone	.06	.03	.01
☐ 7	Larry Parrish	.06	.03	.01
☐ 8	Lee Smith	.20	.09	.03
☐ 9	Mike Smithson	.06	.03	.01
☐ 10	John Trautwein	.06	.03	.01
☐ 11	Sherman Corbett	.06	.03	.01
☐ 12	Chili Davis	.10	.04	.01
☐ 13	Jim Eppard	.06	.03	.01
☐ 14	Bryan Harvey	.60	.25	.08
☐ 15	John Davis	.06	.03	.01
☐ 16	Dave Gallagher	.06	.03	.01
☐ 17	Ricky Horton	.06	.03	.01
☐ 18	Dan Pasqua	.06	.03	.01
☐ 19	Melido Perez	.40	.18	.05
☐ 20	Jose Segura	.06	.03	.01
☐ 21	Andy Allanson	.06	.03	.01
☐ 22	Jon Perlman	.06	.03	.01
☐ 23	Domingo Ramos	.06	.03	.01
☐ 24	Rick Rodriguez	.06	.03	.01
☐ 25	Willie Upshaw	.06	.03	.01
☐ 26	Paul Gibson	.06	.03	.01
☐ 27	Don Heinkel	.06	.03	.01
☐ 28	Ray Knight	.10	.04	.01
☐ 29	Gary Pettis	.06	.03	.01
☐ 30	Luis Salazar	.06	.03	.01
☐ 31	Mike Macfarlane	.40	.18	.05
☐ 32	Jeff Montgomery	.25	.11	.03
☐ 33	Ted Power	.06	.03	.01
☐ 34	Israel Sanchez	.06	.03	.01
☐ 35	Kurt Stillwell	.06	.03	.01
☐ 36	Pat Tabler	.06	.03	.01
☐ 37	Don August	.06	.03	.01
☐ 38	Darryl Hamilton	.40	.18	.05
☐ 39	Jeff Leonard	.06	.03	.01
☐ 40	Joey Meyer	.06	.03	.01
☐ 41	Allan Anderson	.06	.03	.01
☐ 42	Brian Harper	.10	.04	.01
☐ 43	Tom Herr	.06	.03	.01
☐ 44	Charlie Lea	.06	.03	.01
☐ 45	John Moses	.06	.03	.01
	(Listed as Hohn on			
	checklist card)			
☐ 46	John Candelaria	.06	.03	.01
☐ 47	Jack Clark	.10	.04	.01
☐ 48	Richard Dotson	.06	.03	.01
☐ 49	Al Leiter	.06	.03	.01
☐ 50	Rafael Santana	.06	.03	.01
☐ 51	Don Slaught	.06	.03	.01
☐ 52	Todd Burns	.06	.03	.01
☐ 53	Dave Henderson	.10	.04	.01
☐ 54	Doug Jennings	.06	.03	.01
☐ 55	Dave Parker	.10	.04	.01
☐ 56	Walt Weiss	.25	.11	.03
☐ 57	Bob Welch	.10	.04	.01
☐ 58	Henry Cotto	.06	.03	.01
☐ 59	Mario Diaz UER	.06	.03	.01

	(Listed as Marion			
	on card front)			
☐ 60	Mike Jackson	.06	.03	.01
☐ 61	Bill Swift	.10	.05	.01
☐ 62	Jose Cecena	.06	.03	.01
☐ 63	Ray Hayward	.06	.03	.01
☐ 64	Jim Steels UER	.06	.03	.01
	(Listed as Jim Steele			
	on card back)			
☐ 65	Pat Borders	.60	.25	.08
☐ 66	Sil Campusano	.06	.03	.01
☐ 67	Mike Flanagan	.06	.03	.01
☐ 68	Todd Stottlemyre	.50	.23	.06
☐ 69	David Wells	.20	.09	.03
☐ 70	Jose Alvarez	.06	.03	.01
☐ 71	Paul Runge	.06	.03	.01
☐ 72	Cesar Jimenez UER	.06	.03	.01
	(Card was intended			
	for German Jiminez,			
	it's his photo)			
☐ 73	Pete Smith	.50	.23	.06
☐ 74	John Smoltz	5.00	2.30	.60
☐ 75	Damon Berryhill	.15	.07	.02
☐ 76	Goose Gossage	.10	.04	.01
☐ 77	Mark Grace	2.00	.90	.25
☐ 78	Darrin Jackson	.10	.04	.01
☐ 79	Vance Law	.06	.03	.01
☐ 80	Jeff Pico	.06	.03	.01
☐ 81	Gary Varsho	.06	.03	.01
☐ 82	Tim Birtsas	.06	.03	.01
☐ 83	Rob Dibble	.60	.25	.08
☐ 84	Danny Jackson	.06	.03	.01
☐ 85	Paul O'Neill	.15	.07	.02
☐ 86	Jose Rijo	.15	.07	.02
☐ 87	Chris Sabo	.75	.35	.09
☐ 88	John Fishel	.06	.03	.01
☐ 89	Craig Biggio	1.25	.55	.16
☐ 90	Terry Puhl	.06	.03	.01
☐ 91	Rafael Ramirez	.06	.03	.01
☐ 92	Louie Meadows	.06	.03	.01
☐ 93	Kirk Gibson	.10	.04	.01
☐ 94	Alfredo Griffin	.06	.03	.01
☐ 95	Jay Howell	.06	.03	.01
☐ 96	Jesse Orosco	.06	.03	.01
☐ 97	Alejandro Pena	.06	.03	.01
☐ 98	Tracy Woodson	.12	.05	.02
☐ 99	John Dopson	.06	.03	.01
☐ 100	Brian Holman	.15	.07	.02
☐ 101	Rex Hudler	.06	.03	.01
☐ 102	Jeff Parrett	.06	.03	.01
☐ 103	Nelson Santovenia	.06	.03	.01
☐ 104	Kevin Elster	.06	.03	.01
☐ 105	Jeff Innis	.06	.03	.01
☐ 106	Mackey Sasser	.10	.05	.01
☐ 107	Phil Bradley	.06	.03	.01
☐ 108	Danny Clay	.06	.03	.01
☐ 109	Greg Harris	.06	.03	.01

☐	110	Ricky Jordan	.20	.09	.03
☐	111	David Palmer	.06	.03	.01
☐	112	Jim Gott	.06	.03	.01
☐	113	Tommy Gregg UER	.10	.04	.01
		(Photo actually			
		Randy Milligan)			
☐	114	Barry Jones	.06	.03	.01
☐	115	Randy Milligan	.30	.14	.04
☐	116	Luis Alicea	.15	.07	.02
☐	117	Tom Brunansky	.10	.04	.01
☐	118	John Costello	.06	.03	.01
☐	119	Jose DeLeon	.06	.03	.01
☐	120	Bob Horner	.10	.04	.01
☐	121	Scott Terry	.06	.03	.01
☐	122	Roberto Alomar	11.00	4.90	1.40
☐	123	Dave Leiper	.06	.03	.01
☐	124	Keith Moreland	.06	.03	.01
☐	125	Mark Parent	.06	.03	.01
☐	126	Dennis Rasmussen	.06	.03	.01
☐	127	Randy Bockus	.06	.03	.01
☐	128	Brett Butler	.10	.05	.01
☐	129	Donell Nixon	.06	.03	.01
☐	130	Earnest Riles	.06	.03	.01
☐	131	Roger Samuels	.06	.03	.01
☐	132	Checklist U1-U132	.10	.01	.00

1989 Fleer

This 660-card set features a distinctive gray border background with white and yellow trim. The backs are printed in gray, black, and yellow on white card stock. The bottom of the card back shows an innovative breakdown of the player's demonstrated ability with respect to his performance before and after the All-Star break. Cards are numbered on the back and are again

the standard 2 1/2" by 3 1/2". Cards are again organized numerically by teams and alphabetically within teams: Oakland A's (1-26), New York Mets (27-52), Los Angeles Dodgers (53-77), Boston Red Sox (78-101), Minnesota Twins (102-127), Detroit Tigers (128-151), Cincinnati Reds (152-175), Milwaukee Brewers (176-200), Pittsburgh Pirates (201-224), Toronto Blue Jays (225-248), New York Yankees (249-274), Kansas City Royals (275-298), San Diego Padres (299-322), San Francisco Giants (323-347), Houston Astros (348-370), Montreal Expos (371-395), Cleveland Indians (396-417), Chicago Cubs (418-442), St. Louis Cardinals (443-466), California Angels (467-490), Chicago White Sox (491-513), Texas Rangers (514-537), Seattle Mariners (538-561), Philadelphia Phillies (562-584), Atlanta Braves (585-605), and Baltimore Orioles (606-627). However, pairs 148/149, 153/154, 272/273, 283/284, and 367/368 were apparently mis-alphabetized by Fleer. The last 33 cards in the set consist of Specials (628-639), Rookie Pairs (640-653), and checklists (654-660). Due to the early beginning of production of this set, it seemed Fleer "presumed" that the A's would win the World Series, since they are listed as the first team in the numerical order; in fact, Fleer had the Mets over the underdog (but eventual World Champion) Dodgers as well. Fleer later reported that they merely arranged the teams according to team record due to the early printing date. Approximately half of the California Angels players have white rather than yellow halos. Certain Oakland A's player cards have red instead of green lines for front photo borders. Checklist cards are available either with or without positions listed for each player. The key rookies in this set are Sandy Alomar Jr., Ken Griffey Jr., Felix Jose, Ramon Martinez, Hal Morris, and Gary Sheffield. Fleer also produced the last of their three-year run of "limited" edition glossy, tin sets. This tin set was limited, but only compared to the previous year, as collector and dealer interest in the tin sets was apparently waning. It has been estimated that approximately 30,000 1989 Fleer tin sets were produced by Fleer; as a result, the price of the "tin" glossy cards now ranges from double to triple the price of the regular set cards.

		MT	EX-MT	VG
	COMPLETE SET (660)	20.00	9.00	2.50
	COMPLETE FACT.SET (660)	20.00	9.00	2.50
	COMPLETE FACT.SET (672)	22.00	10.00	2.80
	COMMON PLAYER (1-660)	.04	.02	.01
	COMPLETE WS SET (12)	2.00	.90	.25
☐ 1	Don Baylor	.07	.03	.01
☐ 2	Lance Blankenship	.10	.05	.01
☐ 3	Todd Burns UER	.04	.02	.01
	(Wrong birthdate; before/after All-Star stats missing)			
☐ 4	Greg Cadaret UER	.04	.02	.01
	(All-Star Break stats show 3 losses, should be 2)			
☐ 5	Jose Canseco	.40	.18	.05
☐ 6	Storm Davis	.04	.02	.01
☐ 7	Dennis Eckersley	.12	.05	.02
☐ 8	Mike Gallego	.04	.02	.01
☐ 9	Ron Hassey	.04	.02	.01
☐ 10	Dave Henderson	.07	.03	.01
☐ 11	Rick Honeycutt	.04	.02	.01
☐ 12	Glenn Hubbard	.04	.02	.01
☐ 13	Stan Javier	.04	.02	.01
☐ 14	Doug Jennings	.04	.02	.01
☐ 15	Felix Jose	.75	.35	.09
☐ 16	Carney Lansford	.07	.03	.01
☐ 17	Mark McGwire	.40	.18	.05
☐ 18	Gene Nelson	.04	.02	.01
☐ 19	Dave Parker	.07	.03	.01
☐ 20	Eric Plunk	.04	.02	.01
☐ 21	Luis Polonia	.07	.03	.01
☐ 22	Terry Steinbach	.07	.03	.01
☐ 23	Dave Stewart	.07	.03	.01
☐ 24	Walt Weiss	.07	.03	.01
☐ 25	Bob Welch	.07	.03	.01
☐ 26	Curt Young	.04	.02	.01
☐ 27	Rick Aguilera	.07	.03	.01
☐ 28	Wally Backman	.04	.02	.01
☐ 29	Mark Carreon UER	.04	.02	.01
	(After All-Star Break batting 7.14)			
☐ 30	Gary Carter	.07	.03	.01
☐ 31	David Cone	.15	.07	.02
☐ 32	Ron Darling	.07	.03	.01
☐ 33	Len Dykstra	.07	.03	.01
☐ 34	Kevin Elster	.04	.02	.01
☐ 35	Sid Fernandez	.07	.03	.01
☐ 36	Dwight Gooden	.12	.05	.02
☐ 37	Keith Hernandez	.07	.03	.01
☐ 38	Gregg Jefferies	.20	.09	.03
☐ 39	Howard Johnson	.07	.03	.01
☐ 40	Terry Leach	.04	.02	.01
☐ 41	Dave Magadan UER	.07	.03	.01
	(Bio says 15 doubles, should be 13)			
☐ 42	Bob McClure	.04	.02	.01
☐ 43	Roger McDowell UER	.04	.02	.01
	(Led Mets with 58, should be 62)			
☐ 44	Kevin McReynolds	.07	.03	.01
☐ 45	Keith A. Miller	.04	.02	.01
☐ 46	Randy Myers	.07	.03	.01
☐ 47	Bob Ojeda	.04	.02	.01
☐ 48	Mackey Sasser	.04	.02	.01
☐ 49	Darryl Strawberry	.25	.11	.03
☐ 50	Tim Teufel	.04	.02	.01
☐ 51	Dave West	.10	.05	.01
☐ 52	Mookie Wilson	.07	.03	.01
☐ 53	Dave Anderson	.04	.02	.01
☐ 54	Tim Belcher	.07	.03	.01
☐ 55	Mike Davis	.04	.02	.01
☐ 56	Mike Devereaux	.15	.07	.02
☐ 57	Kirk Gibson	.07	.03	.01
☐ 58	Alfredo Griffin	.04	.02	.01
☐ 59	Chris Gwynn	.04	.02	.01
☐ 60	Jeff Hamilton	.04	.02	.01
☐ 61A	Danny Heep	.40	.18	.05
	(Home: Lake Hills)			
☐ 61B	Danny Heep	.10	.05	.01
	(Home: San Antonio)			
☐ 62	Orel Hershiser	.07	.03	.01
☐ 63	Brian Holton	.04	.02	.01
☐ 64	Jay Howell	.04	.02	.01
☐ 65	Tim Leary	.04	.02	.01
☐ 66	Mike Marshall	.04	.02	.01
☐ 67	Ramon Martinez	.50	.23	.06
☐ 68	Jesse Orosco	.04	.02	.01
☐ 69	Alejandro Pena	.04	.02	.01
☐ 70	Steve Sax	.07	.03	.01
☐ 71	Mike Scioscia	.04	.02	.01
☐ 72	Mike Sharperson	.04	.02	.01
☐ 73	John Shelby	.04	.02	.01
☐ 74	Franklin Stubbs	.04	.02	.01
☐ 75	John Tudor	.04	.02	.01
☐ 76	Fernando Valenzuela	.07	.03	.01
☐ 77	Tracy Woodson	.04	.02	.01
☐ 78	Marty Barrett	.04	.02	.01
☐ 79	Todd Benzinger	.04	.02	.01
☐ 80	Mike Boddicker UER	.04	.02	.01
	(Rochester in '76, should be '78)			
☐ 81	Wade Boggs	.25	.11	.03
☐ 82	Oil Can Boyd	.04	.02	.01
☐ 83	Ellis Burks	.07	.03	.01
☐ 84	Rick Cerone	.04	.02	.01
☐ 85	Roger Clemens	.40	.18	.05
☐ 86	Steve Curry	.04	.02	.01
☐ 87	Dwight Evans	.07	.03	.01
☐ 88	Wes Gardner	.04	.02	.01
☐ 89	Rich Gedman	.04	.02	.01
☐ 90	Mike Greenwell	.07	.03	.01

☐ 91 Bruce Hurst	.07	.03	.01
☐ 92 Dennis Lamp	.04	.02	.01
☐ 93 Spike Owen	.04	.02	.01
☐ 94 Larry Parrish UER	.04	.02	.01
(Before All-Star Break			
batting 1.90)			
☐ 95 Carlos Quintana	.10	.05	.01
☐ 96 Jody Reed	.04	.02	.01
☐ 97 Jim Rice	.07	.03	.01
☐ 98A Kevin Romine ERR	.40	.18	.05
(Photo actually			
Randy Kutcher batting)			
☐ 98B Kevin Romine COR	.10	.05	.01
(Arms folded)			
☐ 99 Lee Smith	.07	.03	.01
☐ 100 Mike Smithson	.04	.02	.01
☐ 101 Bob Stanley	.04	.02	.01
☐ 102 Allan Anderson	.04	.02	.01
☐ 103 Keith Atherton	.04	.02	.01
☐ 104 Juan Berenguer	.04	.02	.01
☐ 105 Bert Blyleven	.07	.03	.01
☐ 106 Eric Bullock UER	.04	.02	.01
(Bats/Throws Right,			
should be Left)			
☐ 107 Randy Bush	.04	.02	.01
☐ 108 John Christensen	.04	.02	.01
☐ 109 Mark Davidson	.04	.02	.01
☐ 110 Gary Gaetti	.04	.02	.01
☐ 111 Greg Gagne	.04	.02	.01
☐ 112 Dan Gladden	.04	.02	.01
☐ 113 German Gonzalez	.04	.02	.01
☐ 114 Brian Harper	.07	.03	.01
☐ 115 Tom Herr	.04	.02	.01
☐ 116 Kent Hrbek	.07	.03	.01
☐ 117 Gene Larkin	.04	.02	.01
☐ 118 Tim Laudner	.04	.02	.01
☐ 119 Charlie Lea	.04	.02	.01
☐ 120 Steve Lombardozzi	.04	.02	.01
☐ 121A John Moses	.40	.18	.05
(Home: Tempe)			
☐ 121B John Moses	.10	.05	.01
(Home: Phoenix)			
☐ 122 Al Newman	.04	.02	.01
☐ 123 Mark Portugal	.04	.02	.01
☐ 124 Kirby Puckett	.40	.18	.05
☐ 125 Jeff Reardon	.07	.03	.01
☐ 126 Fred Toliver	.04	.02	.01
☐ 127 Frank Viola	.07	.03	.01
☐ 128 Doyle Alexander	.04	.02	.01
☐ 129 Dave Bergman	.04	.02	.01
☐ 130A Tom Brookens ERR	.75	.35	.09
(Mike Heath back)			
☐ 130B Tom Brookens COR	.10	.05	.01
☐ 131 Paul Gibson	.04	.02	.01
☐ 132A Mike Heath ERR	.75	.35	.09
(Tom Brookens back)			
☐ 132B Mike Heath COR	.10	.05	.01

☐ 133 Don Heinkel	.04	.02	.01
☐ 134 Mike Henneman	.07	.03	.01
☐ 135 Guillermo Hernandez	.04	.02	.01
☐ 136 Eric King	.04	.02	.01
☐ 137 Chet Lemon	.04	.02	.01
☐ 138 Fred Lynn UER	.07	.03	.01
('74, '75 stats			
missing)			
☐ 139 Jack Morris	.12	.05	.02
☐ 140 Matt Nokes	.07	.03	.01
☐ 141 Gary Pettis	.04	.02	.01
☐ 142 Ted Power	.04	.02	.01
☐ 143 Jeff M. Robinson	.04	.02	.01
☐ 144 Luis Salazar	.04	.02	.01
☐ 145 Steve Searcy	.04	.02	.01
☐ 146 Pat Sheridan	.04	.02	.01
☐ 147 Frank Tanana	.04	.02	.01
☐ 148 Alan Trammell	.07	.03	.01
☐ 149 Walt Terrell	.04	.02	.01
☐ 150 Jim Walewander	.04	.02	.01
☐ 151 Lou Whitaker	.07	.03	.01
☐ 152 Tim Birtsas	.04	.02	.01
☐ 153 Tom Browning	.04	.02	.01
☐ 154 Keith Brown	.04	.02	.01
☐ 155 Norm Charlton	.20	.09	.03
☐ 156 Dave Concepcion	.07	.03	.01
☐ 157 Kal Daniels	.07	.03	.01
☐ 158 Eric Davis	.12	.05	.02
☐ 159 Bo Diaz	.04	.02	.01
☐ 160 Rob Dibble	.20	.09	.03
☐ 161 Nick Esasky	.04	.02	.01
☐ 162 John Franco	.07	.03	.01
☐ 163 Danny Jackson	.04	.02	.01
☐ 164 Barry Larkin	.15	.07	.02
☐ 165 Rob Murphy	.04	.02	.01
☐ 166 Paul O'Neill	.07	.03	.01
☐ 167 Jeff Reed	.04	.02	.01
☐ 168 Jose Rijo	.07	.03	.01
☐ 169 Ron Robinson	.04	.02	.01
☐ 170 Chris Sabo	.30	.14	.04
☐ 171 Candy Sierra	.04	.02	.01
☐ 172 Van Snider	.04	.02	.01
☐ 173A Jeff Treadway	9.00	4.00	1.15
(Target registration			
mark above head			
on front in			
light blue)			
☐ 173B Jeff Treadway	.04	.02	.01
(No target on front)			
☐ 174 Frank Williams	.04	.02	.01
(After All-Star Break			
stats are jumbled)			
☐ 175 Herm Winningham	.04	.02	.01
☐ 176 Jim Adduci	.04	.02	.01
☐ 177 Don August	.04	.02	.01
☐ 178 Mike Birkbeck	.04	.02	.01
☐ 179 Chris Bosio	.04	.02	.01

☐	180	Glenn Braggs	.04	.02	.01	☐	237	Rick Leach	.04	.02	.01

☐	180	Glenn Braggs	.04	.02	.01
☐	181	Greg Brock	.04	.02	.01
☐	182	Mark Clear	.04	.02	.01
☐	183	Chuck Crim	.04	.02	.01
☐	184	Rob Deer	.07	.03	.01
☐	185	Tom Filer	.04	.02	.01
☐	186	Jim Gantner	.04	.02	.01
☐	187	Darryl Hamilton	.20	.09	.03
☐	188	Ted Higuera	.04	.02	.01
☐	189	Odell Jones	.04	.02	.01
☐	190	Jeffrey Leonard	.04	.02	.01
☐	191	Joey Meyer	.04	.02	.01
☐	192	Paul Mirabella	.04	.02	.01
☐	193	Paul Molitor	.10	.05	.01
☐	194	Charlie O'Brien	.04	.02	.01
☐	195	Dan Plesac	.04	.02	.01
☐	196	Gary Sheffield	2.50	1.15	.30
☐	197	B.J. Surhoff	.04	.02	.01
☐	198	Dale Sveum	.04	.02	.01
☐	199	Bill Wegman	.04	.02	.01
☐	200	Robin Yount	.20	.09	.03
☐	201	Rafael Belliard	.04	.02	.01
☐	202	Barry Bonds	.40	.18	.05
☐	203	Bobby Bonilla	.20	.09	.03
☐	204	Sid Bream	.04	.02	.01
☐	205	Benny Distefano	.04	.02	.01
☐	206	Doug Drabek	.07	.03	.01
☐	207	Mike Dunne	.04	.02	.01
☐	208	Felix Fermin	.04	.02	.01
☐	209	Brian Fisher	.04	.02	.01
☐	210	Jim Gott	.04	.02	.01
☐	211	Bob Kipper	.04	.02	.01
☐	212	Dave LaPoint	.04	.02	.01
☐	213	Mike LaValliere	.04	.02	.01
☐	214	Jose Lind	.04	.02	.01
☐	215	Junior Ortiz	.04	.02	.01
☐	216	Vicente Palacios	.04	.02	.01
☐	217	Tom Prince	.04	.02	.01
☐	218	Gary Redus	.04	.02	.01
☐	219	R.J. Reynolds	.04	.02	.01
☐	220	Jeff D. Robinson	.04	.02	.01
☐	221	John Smiley	.07	.03	.01
☐	222	Andy Van Slyke	.10	.05	.01
☐	223	Bob Walk	.04	.02	.01
☐	224	Glenn Wilson	.04	.02	.01
☐	225	Jesse Barfield	.04	.02	.01
☐	226	George Bell	.10	.05	.01
☐	227	Pat Borders	.30	.14	.04
☐	228	John Cerutti	.04	.02	.01
☐	229	Jim Clancy	.04	.02	.01
☐	230	Mark Eichhorn	.04	.02	.01
☐	231	Tony Fernandez	.07	.03	.01
☐	232	Cecil Fielder	.25	.11	.03
☐	233	Mike Flanagan	.04	.02	.01
☐	234	Kelly Gruber	.07	.03	.01
☐	235	Tom Henke	.07	.03	.01
☐	236	Jimmy Key	.07	.03	.01

☐	237	Rick Leach	.04	.02	.01
☐	238	Manny Lee UER	.04	.02	.01
		(Bio says regular			
		shortstop, sic,			
		Tony Fernandez)			
☐	239	Nelson Liriano	.04	.02	.01
☐	240	Fred McGriff	.25	.11	.03
☐	241	Lloyd Moseby	.04	.02	.01
☐	242	Rance Mulliniks	.04	.02	.01
☐	243	Jeff Musselman	.04	.02	.01
☐	244	Dave Stieb	.07	.03	.01
☐	245	Todd Stottlemyre	.10	.05	.01
☐	246	Duane Ward	.07	.03	.01
☐	247	David Wells	.10	.05	.01
☐	248	Ernie Whitt UER	.04	.02	.01
		(HR total 21,			
		should be 121)			
☐	249	Luis Aguayo	.04	.02	.01
☐	250A	Neil Allen	.75	.35	.09
		(Home: Sarasota, FL)			
☐	250B	Neil Allen	.10	.05	.01
		(Home: Syosset, NY)			
☐	251	John Candelaria	.04	.02	.01
☐	252	Jack Clark	.07	.03	.01
☐	253	Richard Dotson	.04	.02	.01
☐	254	Rickey Henderson	.25	.11	.03
☐	255	Tommy John	.07	.03	.01
☐	256	Roberto Kelly	.15	.07	.02
☐	257	Al Leiter	.04	.02	.01
☐	258	Don Mattingly	.25	.11	.03
☐	259	Dale Mohorcic	.04	.02	.01
☐	260	Hal Morris	.60	.25	.08
☐	261	Scott Nielsen	.04	.02	.01
☐	262	Mike Pagliarulo UER	.04	.02	.01
		(Wrong birthdate)			
☐	263	Hipolito Pena	.04	.02	.01
☐	264	Ken Phelps	.04	.02	.01
☐	265	Willie Randolph	.07	.03	.01
☐	266	Rick Rhoden	.04	.02	.01
☐	267	Dave Righetti	.04	.02	.01
☐	268	Rafael Santana	.04	.02	.01
☐	269	Steve Shields	.04	.02	.01
☐	270	Joel Skinner	.04	.02	.01
☐	271	Don Slaught	.04	.02	.01
☐	272	Claudell Washington	.04	.02	.01
☐	273	Gary Ward	.04	.02	.01
☐	274	Dave Winfield	.20	.09	.03
☐	275	Luis Aquino	.04	.02	.01
☐	276	Floyd Bannister	.04	.02	.01
☐	277	George Brett	.20	.09	.03
☐	278	Bill Buckner	.07	.03	.01
☐	279	Nick Capra	.04	.02	.01
☐	280	Jose DeJesus	.04	.02	.01
☐	281	Steve Farr	.04	.02	.01
☐	282	Jerry Don Gleaton	.04	.02	.01
☐	283	Mark Gubicza	.04	.02	.01
☐	284	Tom Gordon UER	.10	.05	.01

(16.2 innings in '88,
should be 15.2)

☐ 285 Bo Jackson	.20	.09	.03
☐ 286 Charlie Leibrandt	.04	.02	.01
☐ 287 Mike Macfarlane	.15	.07	.02
☐ 288 Jeff Montgomery	.07	.03	.01
☐ 289 Bill Pecota UER	.04	.02	.01

(Photo actually
Brad Wellman)

☐ 290 Jamie Quirk	.04	.02	.01
☐ 291 Bret Saberhagen	.07	.03	.01
☐ 292 Kevin Seitzer	.07	.03	.01
☐ 293 Kurt Stillwell	.04	.02	.01
☐ 294 Pat Tabler	.04	.02	.01
☐ 295 Danny Tartabull	.12	.05	.02
☐ 296 Gary Thurman	.04	.02	.01
☐ 297 Frank White	.04	.02	.01
☐ 298 Willie Wilson	.04	.02	.01
☐ 299 Roberto Alomar	.75	.35	.09
☐ 300 Sandy Alomar Jr. UER	.25	.11	.03

(Wrong birthdate, says
6/16/66, should say
6/18/66)

☐ 301 Chris Brown	.04	.02	.01
☐ 302 Mike Brumley UER	.04	.02	.01

(133 hits in '88,
should be 134)

☐ 303 Mark Davis	.04	.02	.01
☐ 304 Mark Grant	.04	.02	.01
☐ 305 Tony Gwynn	.25	.11	.03
☐ 306 Greg W. Harris	.10	.05	.01
☐ 307 Andy Hawkins	.04	.02	.01
☐ 308 Jimmy Jones	.04	.02	.01
☐ 309 John Kruk	.07	.03	.01
☐ 310 Dave Leiper	.04	.02	.01
☐ 311 Carmelo Martinez	.04	.02	.01
☐ 312 Lance McCullers	.04	.02	.01
☐ 313 Keith Moreland	.04	.02	.01
☐ 314 Dennis Rasmussen	.04	.02	.01
☐ 315 Randy Ready UER	.04	.02	.01

(1214 games in '88,
should be 114)

☐ 316 Benito Santiago	.07	.03	.01
☐ 317 Eric Show	.04	.02	.01
☐ 318 Todd Simmons	.04	.02	.01
☐ 319 Garry Templeton	.04	.02	.01
☐ 320 Dickie Thon	.04	.02	.01
☐ 321 Ed Whitson	.04	.02	.01
☐ 322 Marvell Wynne	.04	.02	.01
☐ 323 Mike Aldrete	.04	.02	.01
☐ 324 Brett Butler	.07	.03	.01
☐ 325 Will Clark UER	.40	.18	.05

(Three consecutive
100 RBI seasons)

☐ 326 Kelly Downs UER	.04	.02	.01

('88 stats missing)

☐ 327 Dave Dravecky	.07	.03	.01
☐ 328 Scott Garrelts	.04	.02	.01
☐ 329 Atlee Hammaker	.04	.02	.01
☐ 330 Charlie Hayes	.25	.11	.03
☐ 331 Mike Krukow	.04	.02	.01
☐ 332 Craig Lefferts	.04	.02	.01
☐ 333 Candy Maldonado	.04	.02	.01
☐ 334 Kirt Manwaring UER	.04	.02	.01

(Bats Rights)

☐ 335 Bob Melvin	.04	.02	.01
☐ 336 Kevin Mitchell	.10	.05	.01
☐ 337 Donell Nixon	.04	.02	.01
☐ 338 Tony Perezchica	.04	.02	.01
☐ 339 Joe Price	.04	.02	.01
☐ 340 Rick Reuschel	.04	.02	.01
☐ 341 Earnest Riles	.04	.02	.01
☐ 342 Don Robinson	.04	.02	.01
☐ 343 Chris Speier	.04	.02	.01
☐ 344 Robby Thompson UER	.04	.02	.01

(West Plam Beach)

☐ 345 Jose Uribe	.04	.02	.01
☐ 346 Matt Williams	.15	.07	.02
☐ 347 Trevor Wilson	.12	.05	.02
☐ 348 Juan Agosto	.04	.02	.01
☐ 349 Larry Andersen	.04	.02	.01
☐ 350A Alan Ashby ERR	3.00	1.35	.40

(Throws Rig)

☐ 350B Alan Ashby COR	.04	.02	.01
☐ 351 Kevin Bass	.04	.02	.01
☐ 352 Buddy Bell	.07	.03	.01
☐ 353 Craig Biggio	.40	.18	.05
☐ 354 Danny Darwin	.04	.02	.01
☐ 355 Glenn Davis	.07	.03	.01
☐ 356 Jim Deshaies	.04	.02	.01
☐ 357 Bill Duran	.04	.02	.01
☐ 358 John Fishel	.04	.02	.01
☐ 359 Billy Hatcher	.04	.02	.01
☐ 360 Bob Knepper	.04	.02	.01
☐ 361 Louie Meadows UER	.04	.02	.01

(Bio says 10 EBH's
and 6 SB's in '88,
should be 3 and 4)

☐ 362 Dave Meads	.04	.02	.01
☐ 363 Jim Pankovits	.04	.02	.01
☐ 364 Terry Puhl	.04	.02	.01
☐ 365 Rafael Ramirez	.04	.02	.01
☐ 366 Craig Reynolds	.04	.02	.01
☐ 367 Mike Scott	.04	.02	.01

(Card number listed
as 368 on Astros CL)

☐ 368 Nolan Ryan	.60	.25	.08

(Card number listed
as 367 on Astros CL)

☐ 369 Dave Smith	.04	.02	.01
☐ 370 Gerald Young	.04	.02	.01
☐ 371 Hubie Brooks	.04	.02	.01
☐ 372 Tim Burke	.04	.02	.01
☐ 373 John Dopson	.04	.02	.01

□	374	Mike R. Fitzgerald 04	.02	.01
		Montreal Expos		
□	375	Tom Foley 04	.02	.01
□	376	Andres Galarraga UER 04	.02	.01
		(Home: Caracus)		
□	377	Neal Heaton 04	.02	.01
□	378	Joe Hesketh 04	.02	.01
□	379	Brian Holman 10	.05	.01
□	380	Rex Hudler 04	.02	.01
□	381	Randy Johnson UER 35	.16	.04
		(Innings for '85 and		
		'86 shown as 27 and		
		120, should be 27.1		
		and 119.2)		
□	382	Wallace Johnson 04	.02	.01
□	383	Tracy Jones 04	.02	.01
□	384	Dave Martinez 07	.03	.01
□	385	Dennis Martinez 07	.03	.01
□	386	Andy McGaffigan 04	.02	.01
□	387	Otis Nixon 07	.03	.01
□	388	Johnny Paredes 04	.02	.01
□	389	Jeff Parrett 04	.02	.01
□	390	Pascual Perez 04	.02	.01
□	391	Tim Raines 07	.03	.01
□	392	Luis Rivera 04	.02	.01
□	393	Nelson Santovenia 04	.02	.01
□	394	Bryn Smith 04	.02	.01
□	395	Tim Wallach 07	.03	.01
□	396	Andy Allanson UER 04	.02	.01
		(1214 hits in '88,		
		should be 114)		
□	397	Rod Allen 04	.02	.01
□	398	Scott Bailes 04	.02	.01
□	399	Tom Candiotti 04	.02	.01
□	400	Joe Carter 25	.11	.03
□	401	Carmen Castillo UER 04	.02	.01
		(After All-Star Break		
		batting 2.50)		
□	402	Dave Clark UER 04	.02	.01
		(Card front shows		
		position as Rookie;		
		after All-Star Break		
		batting 3.14)		
□	403	John Farrell UER 04	.02	.01
		(Typo in runs		
		allowed in '88)		
□	404	Julio Franco 07	.03	.01
□	405	Don Gordon 04	.02	.01
□	406	Mel Hall 04	.02	.01
□	407	Brad Havens 04	.02	.01
□	408	Brook Jacoby 04	.02	.01
□	409	Doug Jones 07	.03	.01
□	410	Jeff Kaiser 04	.02	.01
□	411	Luis Medina 04	.02	.01
□	412	Cory Snyder 04	.02	.01
□	413	Greg Swindell 07	.03	.01
□	414	Ron Tingley UER 04	.02	.01

		(Hit HR in first ML		
		at-bat, should be		
		first AL at-bat)		
□	415	Willie Upshaw 04	.02	.01
□	416	Ron Washington 04	.02	.01
□	417	Rich Yett 04	.02	.01
□	418	Damon Berryhill 04	.02	.01
□	419	Mike Bielecki 04	.02	.01
□	420	Doug Dascenzo 04	.02	.01
□	421	Jody Davis UER 04	.02	.01
		(Braves stats for		
		'88 missing)		
□	422	Andre Dawson 15	.07	.02
□	423	Frank DiPino 04	.02	.01
□	424	Shawon Dunston 07	.03	.01
□	425	Rich Gossage 07	.03	.01
□	426	Mark Grace UER 30	.14	.04
		(Minor League stats		
		for '88 missing)		
□	427	Mike Harkey 12	.05	.02
□	428	Darrin Jackson 15	.07	.02
□	429	Les Lancaster 04	.02	.01
□	430	Vance Law 04	.02	.01
□	431	Greg Maddux 30	.14	.04
□	432	Jamie Moyer 04	.02	.01
□	433	Al Nipper 04	.02	.01
□	434	Rafael Palmeiro UER 20	.09	.03
		(170 hits in '88,		
		should be 178)		
□	435	Pat Perry 04	.02	.01
□	436	Jeff Pico 04	.02	.01
□	437	Ryne Sandberg 40	.18	.05
□	438	Calvin Schiraldi 04	.02	.01
□	439	Rick Sutcliffe 07	.03	.01
□	440A	Manny Trillo ERR 3.00	1.35	.40
		(Throws Rig)		
□	440B	Manny Trillo COR 04	.02	.01
□	441	Gary Varsho UER 04	.02	.01
		(Wrong birthdate;		
		.303 should be .302;		
		11/28 should be 9/19)		
□	442	Mitch Webster 04	.02	.01
□	443	Luis Alicea 10	.05	.01
□	444	Tom Brunansky 07	.03	.01
□	445	Vince Coleman 07	.03	.01
		(Third straight with		
		83, should be fourth		
		straight with 81)		
□	446	John Costello UER 04	.02	.01
		(Home California,		
		should be New York)		
□	447	Danny Cox 04	.02	.01
□	448	Ken Dayley 04	.02	.01
□	449	Jose DeLeon 04	.02	.01
□	450	Curt Ford 04	.02	.01
□	451	Pedro Guerrero 07	.03	.01
□	452	Bob Horner 04	.02	.01

☐ 453	Tim Jones	.04	.02	.01
☐ 454	Steve Lake	.04	.02	.01
☐ 455	Joe Magrane UER	.04	.02	.01
	(Des Moines, IO)			
☐ 456	Greg Mathews	.04	.02	.01
☐ 457	Willie McGee	.07	.03	.01
☐ 458	Larry McWilliams	.04	.02	.01
☐ 459	Jose Oquendo	.04	.02	.01
☐ 460	Tony Pena	.04	.02	.01
☐ 461	Terry Pendleton	.12	.05	.02
☐ 462	Steve Peters UER	.04	.02	.01
	(Lives in Harrah,			
	not Harah)			
☐ 463	Ozzie Smith	.15	.07	.02
☐ 464	Scott Terry	.04	.02	.01
☐ 465	Denny Walling	.04	.02	.01
☐ 466	Todd Worrell	.07	.03	.01
☐ 467	Tony Armas UER	.04	.02	.01
	(Before All-Star Break			
	batting 2.39)			
☐ 468	Dante Bichette	.25	.11	.03
☐ 469	Bob Boone	.07	.03	.01
☐ 470	Terry Clark	.04	.02	.01
☐ 471	Stew Cliburn	.04	.02	.01
☐ 472	Mike Cook UER	.04	.02	.01
	(TM near Angels logo			
	missing from front)			
☐ 473	Sherman Corbett	.04	.02	.01
☐ 474	Chili Davis	.07	.03	.01
☐ 475	Brian Downing	.04	.02	.01
☐ 476	Jim Eppard	.04	.02	.01
☐ 477	Chuck Finley	.07	.03	.01
☐ 478	Willie Fraser	.04	.02	.01
☐ 479	Bryan Harvey UER	.25	.11	.03
	(ML record shows 0-0,			
	should be 7-5)			
☐ 480	Jack Howell	.04	.02	.01
☐ 481	Wally Joyner UER	.10	.05	.01
	(Yorba Linda, GA)			
☐ 482	Jack Lazorko	.04	.02	.01
☐ 483	Kirk McCaskill	.04	.02	.01
☐ 484	Mark McLemore	.04	.02	.01
☐ 485	Greg Minton	.04	.02	.01
☐ 486	Dan Petry	.04	.02	.01
☐ 487	Johnny Ray	.04	.02	.01
☐ 488	Dick Schofield	.04	.02	.01
☐ 489	Devon White	.07	.03	.01
☐ 490	Mike Witt	.04	.02	.01
☐ 491	Harold Baines	.07	.03	.01
☐ 492	Daryl Boston	.04	.02	.01
☐ 493	Ivan Calderon UER	.04	.02	.01
	('80 stats shifted)			
☐ 494	Mike Diaz	.04	.02	.01
☐ 495	Carlton Fisk	.15	.07	.02
☐ 496	Dave Gallagher	.04	.02	.01
☐ 497	Ozzie Guillen	.04	.02	.01
☐ 498	Shawn Hillegas	.04	.02	.01
☐ 499	Lance Johnson	.07	.03	.01
☐ 500	Barry Jones	.04	.02	.01
☐ 501	Bill Long	.04	.02	.01
☐ 502	Steve Lyons	.04	.02	.01
☐ 503	Fred Manrique	.04	.02	.01
☐ 504	Jack McDowell	.30	.14	.04
☐ 505	Donn Pall	.04	.02	.01
☐ 506	Kelly Paris	.04	.02	.01
☐ 507	Dan Pasqua	.04	.02	.01
☐ 508	Ken Patterson	.04	.02	.01
☐ 509	Melido Perez	.07	.03	.01
☐ 510	Jerry Reuss	.04	.02	.01
☐ 511	Mark Salas	.04	.02	.01
☐ 512	Bobby Thigpen UER	.04	.02	.01
	('86 ERA 4.69,			
	should be 4.68)			
☐ 513	Mike Woodard	.04	.02	.01
☐ 514	Bob Brower	.04	.02	.01
☐ 515	Steve Buechele	.04	.02	.01
☐ 516	Jose Cecena	.04	.02	.01
☐ 517	Cecil Espy	.04	.02	.01
☐ 518	Scott Fletcher	.04	.02	.01
☐ 519	Cecilio Guante	.04	.02	.01
	('87 Yankee stats			
	are off-centered)			
☐ 520	Jose Guzman	.07	.03	.01
☐ 521	Ray Hayward	.04	.02	.01
☐ 522	Charlie Hough	.04	.02	.01
☐ 523	Pete Incaviglia	.04	.02	.01
☐ 524	Mike Jeffcoat	.04	.02	.01
☐ 525	Paul Kilgus	.04	.02	.01
☐ 526	Chad Kreuter	.04	.02	.01
☐ 527	Jeff Kunkel	.04	.02	.01
☐ 528	Oddibe McDowell	.04	.02	.01
☐ 529	Pete O'Brien	.04	.02	.01
☐ 530	Geno Petralli	.04	.02	.01
☐ 531	Jeff Russell	.04	.02	.01
☐ 532	Ruben Sierra	.30	.14	.04
☐ 533	Mike Stanley	.04	.02	.01
☐ 534A	Ed VandeBerg ERR	3.00	1.35	.40
	(Throws Lef)			
☐ 534B	Ed VandeBerg COR	.04	.02	.01
☐ 535	Curtis Wilkerson ERR	.04	.02	.01
	(Pitcfter headings			
	at bottom)			
☐ 536	Mitch Williams	.07	.03	.01
☐ 537	Bobby Witt UER	.07	.03	.01
	('85 ERA .643,			
	should be 6.43)			
☐ 538	Steve Balboni	.04	.02	.01
☐ 539	Scott Bankhead	.04	.02	.01
☐ 540	Scott Bradley	.04	.02	.01
☐ 541	Mickey Brantley	.04	.02	.01
☐ 542	Jay Buhner	.10	.05	.01
☐ 543	Mike Campbell	.04	.02	.01
☐ 544	Darnell Coles	.04	.02	.01
☐ 545	Henry Cotto	.04	.02	.01

☐ 546	Alvin Davis	.04	.02	.01
☐ 547	Mario Diaz	.04	.02	.01
☐ 548	Ken Griffey Jr.	6.00	2.70	.75
☐ 549	Erik Hanson	.20	.09	.03
☐ 550	Mike Jackson UER	.04	.02	.01
	(Lifetime ERA 3.345, should be 3.45)			
☐ 551	Mark Langston	.07	.03	.01
☐ 552	Edgar Martinez	.35	.16	.04
☐ 553	Bill McGuire	.04	.02	.01
☐ 554	Mike Moore	.04	.02	.01
☐ 555	Jim Presley	.04	.02	.01
☐ 556	Rey Quinones	.04	.02	.01
☐ 557	Jerry Reed	.04	.02	.01
☐ 558	Harold Reynolds	.04	.02	.01
☐ 559	Mike Schooler	.10	.05	.01
☐ 560	Bill Swift	.07	.03	.01
☐ 561	Dave Valle	.04	.02	.01
☐ 562	Steve Bedrosian	.04	.02	.01
☐ 563	Phil Bradley	.04	.02	.01
☐ 564	Don Carman	.04	.02	.01
☐ 565	Bob Dernier	.04	.02	.01
☐ 566	Marvin Freeman	.04	.02	.01
☐ 567	Todd Frohwirth	.04	.02	.01
☐ 568	Greg Gross	.04	.02	.01
☐ 569	Kevin Gross	.04	.02	.01
☐ 570	Greg A. Harris	.04	.02	.01
☐ 571	Von Hayes	.04	.02	.01
☐ 572	Chris James	.04	.02	.01
☐ 573	Steve Jeltz	.04	.02	.01
☐ 574	Ron Jones UER	.04	.02	.01
	(Led IL in '88 with 85, should be 75)			
☐ 575	Ricky Jordan	.10	.05	.01
☐ 576	Mike Maddux	.04	.02	.01
☐ 577	David Palmer	.04	.02	.01
☐ 578	Lance Parrish	.07	.03	.01
☐ 579	Shane Rawley	.04	.02	.01
☐ 580	Bruce Ruffin	.04	.02	.01
☐ 581	Juan Samuel	.04	.02	.01
☐ 582	Mike Schmidt	.40	.18	.05
☐ 583	Kent Tekulve	.04	.02	.01
☐ 584	Milt Thompson UER	.04	.02	.01
	(19 hits in '88, should be 109)			
☐ 585	Jose Alvarez	.04	.02	.01
☐ 586	Paul Assenmacher	.04	.02	.01
☐ 587	Bruce Benedict	.04	.02	.01
☐ 588	Jeff Blauser	.07	.03	.01
☐ 589	Terry Blocker	.04	.02	.01
☐ 590	Ron Gant	.40	.18	.05
☐ 591	Tom Glavine	.50	.23	.06
☐ 592	Tommy Gregg	.04	.02	.01
☐ 593	Albert Hall	.04	.02	.01
☐ 594	Dion James	.04	.02	.01
☐ 595	Rick Mahler	.04	.02	.01
☐ 596	Dale Murphy	.10	.05	.01
☐ 597	Gerald Perry	.04	.02	.01
☐ 598	Charlie Puleo	.04	.02	.01
☐ 599	Ted Simmons	.07	.03	.01
☐ 600	Pete Smith	.07	.03	.01
☐ 601	Zane Smith	.04	.02	.01
☐ 602	John Smoltz	.75	.35	.09
☐ 603	Bruce Sutter	.07	.03	.01
☐ 604	Andres Thomas	.04	.02	.01
☐ 605	Ozzie Virgil	.04	.02	.01
☐ 606	Brady Anderson	.60	.25	.08
☐ 607	Jeff Ballard	.04	.02	.01
☐ 608	Jose Bautista	.04	.02	.01
☐ 609	Ken Gerhart	.04	.02	.01
☐ 610	Terry Kennedy	.04	.02	.01
☐ 611	Eddie Murray	.15	.07	.02
☐ 612	Carl Nichols UER	.04	.02	.01
	(Before All-Star Break batting 1.88)			
☐ 613	Tom Niedenfuer	.04	.02	.01
☐ 614	Joe Orsulak	.04	.02	.01
☐ 615	Oswald Peraza UER	.04	.02	.01
	(Shown as Oswaldo)			
☐ 616A	Bill Ripken ERR	10.00	4.50	1.25
	(Rick Face written on knob of bat)			
☐ 616B	Bill Ripken	40.00	18.00	5.00
	(Bat knob whited out)			
☐ 616C	Bill Ripken	10.00	4.50	1.25
	(Words on bat knob scribbled out)			
☐ 616D	Bill Ripken DP	.10	.05	.01
	(Black box covering bat knob)			
☐ 617	Cal Ripken	.50	.23	.06
☐ 618	Dave Schmidt	.04	.02	.01
☐ 619	Rick Schu	.04	.02	.01
☐ 620	Larry Sheets	.04	.02	.01
☐ 621	Doug Sisk	.04	.02	.01
☐ 622	Pete Stanicek	.04	.02	.01
☐ 623	Mickey Tettleton	.07	.03	.01
☐ 624	Jay Tibbs	.04	.02	.01
☐ 625	Jim Traber	.04	.02	.01
☐ 626	Mark Williamson	.04	.02	.01
☐ 627	Craig Worthington	.04	.02	.01
☐ 628	Speed/Power	.20	.09	.03
	Jose Canseco			
☐ 629	Pitcher Perfect	.06	.03	.01
	Tom Browning			
☐ 630	Like Father/Like Sons	.40	.18	.05
	Roberto Alomar Jr. Sandy Alomar Jr. (Names on card listed in wrong order) UER			
☐ 631	NL All Stars UER	.20	.09	.03
	Will Clark Rafael Palmeiro			

(Gallaraga, sic;
Clark 3 consecutive
100 RBI seasons;
third with 102 RBI's)

☐ 632 Homeruns - Coast...........20 .09 .03
to Coast UER
Darryl Strawberry
Will Clark (Homeruns
should be two words)

☐ 633 Hot Corners - Hot ....10 .05 .01
Hitters UER
Wade Boggs
Carney Lansford
(Boggs hit .366 in
'86, should be '88)

☐ 634 Triple A's ....30 .14 .04
Jose Canseco
Terry Steinbach
Mark McGwire

☐ 635 Dual Heat ....06 .03 .01
Mark Davis
Dwight Gooden

☐ 636 NL Pitching Power UER ..06 .03 .01
Danny Jackson
David Cone
(Hersheiser, sic)

☐ 637 Cannon Arms UER ....10 .05 .01
Chris Sabo
Bobby Bonilla
(Bobby Bonds, sic)

☐ 638 Double Trouble UER ....06 .03 .01
Andres Galarraga
(Misspellod Gallaraga
on card back)
Gerald Perry

☐ 639 Power Center ....15 .07 .02
Kirby Puckett
Eric Davis

☐ 640 Steve Wilson and ....06 .03 .01
Cameron Drew

☐ 641 Kevin Brown and............90 .40 .11
Kevin Reimer

☐ 642 Brad Pounders and ....12 .05 .02
Jerald Clark

☐ 643 Mike Capel and ....06 .03 .01
Drew Hall

☐ 644 Joe Girardi and ....12 .05 .02
Rolando Roomes

☐ 645 Lenny Harris and ....12 .05 .02
Marty Brown

☐ 646 Luis De Los Santos........06 .03 .01
and Jim Campbell

☐ 647 Randy Kramer and..........06 .03 .01
Miguel Garcia

☐ 648 Torey Lovullo and ....06 .03 .01
Robert Palacios

☐ 649 Jim Corsi and.................12 .05 .02

Bob Milacki

☐ 650 Grady Hall and ....06 .03 .01
Mike Rochford

☐ 651 Terry Taylor and.............06 .03 .01
Vance Lovelace

☐ 652 Ken Hill and ....:....50 .23 .06
Dennis Cook

☐ 653 Scott Service and ....06 .03 .01
Shane Turner

☐ 654 CL: Oakland/Mets............05 .01 .00
Dodgers/Red Sox
(10 Henderson;
68 Jess Orosco)

☐ 655A CL: Twins/Tigers ERR....10 .01 .00
Reds/Brewers
(179 Boslo and
Twins/Tigers positions
listed)

☐ 655B CL: Twins/Tigers COR....10 .01 .00
Reds/Brewers
(179 Boslo but
Twins/Tigers positions
not listed)

☐ 656 CL: Pirates/Blue Jays ......05 .01 .00
Yankees/Royals
(225 Jess Barfield)

☐ 657 CL: Padres/Giants ....05 .01 .00
Astros/Expos
(367/368 wrong)

☐ 658 CL: Indians/Cubs ....05 .01 .00
Cardinals/Angels
(449 Deleon)

☐ 659 CL: White Sox/Rangers ...05 .01 .00
Mariners/Phillies

☐ 660 CL: Braves/Orloles ....05 .01 .00
Specials/Checklists
(632 hyphenated diff-
erently and 650 Hall;
595 Rich Mahler;
619 Rich Schu)

1989 Fleer Update

The 1989 Fleer Update set contains 132
standard-size (2 1/2" by 3 1/2") cards. The
fronts are gray with white pinstripes. The
vertically oriented backs show lifetime stats
and performance "Before and After the All-
Star Break". The set numbering is in team
order with players within teams ordered
alphabetically. The set does not include a
card of 1989 AL Rookie of the Year Gregg
Olson, but contains the first major card of

Greg Vaughn and special cards for Nolan Ryan's 5,000th strikeout and Mike Schmidt's retirement. Other key rookies in this set are Kevin Appier, Joey (Albert) Belle, Junior Felix, Jaime Navarro, Deion Sanders, Robin Ventura, Jerome Walton and Todd Zeile. Fleer did NOT produce a limited (tin) edition version of this set with glossy coating. The card numbering is in alphabetical order within teams with the teams themselves alphabetized within league. Cards are numbered with a U prefix.

	MT	EX-MT	VG
COMPLETE SET (132)	10.00	4.50	1.25
COMMON PLAYER (1-132)	.05	.02	.01

		MT	EX-MT	VG
☐ 1	Phil Bradley	.05	.02	.01
☐ 2	Mike Devereaux	.20	.09	.03
☐ 3	Steve Finley	.40	.18	.05
☐ 4	Kevin Hickey	.05	.02	.01
☐ 5	Brian Holton	.05	.02	.01
☐ 6	Bob Milacki	.10	.05	.01
☐ 7	Randy Milligan	.05	.02	.01
☐ 8	John Dopson	.05	.02	.01
☐ 9	Nick Esasky	.05	.02	.01
☐ 10	Rob Murphy	.05	.02	.01
☐ 11	Jim Abbott	1.25	.55	.16
☐ 12	Bert Blyleven	.08	.04	.01
☐ 13	Jeff Manto	.10	.05	.01
☐ 14	Bob McClure	.05	.02	.01
☐ 15	Lance Parrish	.08	.04	.01
☐ 16	Lee Stevens	.20	.09	.03
☐ 17	Claudell Washington	.05	.02	.01
☐ 18	Mark Davis	.05	.02	.01
☐ 19	Eric King	.05	.02	.01
☐ 20	Ron Kittle	.05	.02	.01
☐ 21	Matt Merullo	.05	.02	.01
☐ 22	Steve Rosenberg	.05	.02	.01
☐ 23	Robin Ventura	2.50	1.15	.30
☐ 24	Keith Atherton	.05	.02	.01
☐ 25	Joey Belle	2.00	.90	.25
☐ 26	Jerry Browne	.05	.02	.01
☐ 27	Felix Fermin	.05	.02	.01
☐ 28	Brad Komminsk	.05	.02	.01
☐ 29	Pete O'Brien	.05	.02	.01
☐ 30	Mike Brumley	.05	.02	.01
☐ 31	Tracy Jones	.05	.02	.01
☐ 32	Mike Schwabe	.05	.02	.01
☐ 33	Gary Ward	.05	.02	.01
☐ 34	Frank Williams	.05	.02	.01
☐ 35	Kevin Appier	1.00	.45	.13
☐ 36	Bob Boone	.08	.04	.01
☐ 37	Luis de los Santos	.05	.02	.01
☐ 38	Jim Eisenreich	.05	.02	.01
☐ 39	Jaime Navarro	.75	.35	.09
☐ 40	Bill Spiers	.10	.05	.01
☐ 41	Greg Vaughn	.75	.35	.09
☐ 42	Randy Veres	.05	.02	.01
☐ 43	Wally Backman	.05	.02	.01
☐ 44	Shane Rawley	.05	.02	.01
☐ 45	Steve Balboni	.05	.02	.01
☐ 46	Jesse Barfield	.05	.02	.01
☐ 47	Alvaro Espinoza	.05	.02	.01
☐ 48	Bob Geren	.05	.02	.01
☐ 49	Mel Hall	.05	.02	.01
☐ 50	Andy Hawkins	.05	.02	.01
☐ 51	Hensley Meulens	.12	.05	.02
☐ 52	Steve Sax	.08	.04	.01
☐ 53	Deion Sanders	2.25	1.00	.30
☐ 54	Rickey Henderson	.25	.11	.03
☐ 55	Mike Moore	.05	.02	.01
☐ 56	Tony Phillips	.05	.02	.01
☐ 57	Greg Briley	.10	.05	.01
☐ 58	Gene Harris	.10	.05	.01
☐ 59	Randy Johnson	.15	.07	.02
☐ 60	Jeffrey Leonard	.05	.02	.01
☐ 61	Dennis Powell	.05	.02	.01
☐ 62	Omar Vizquel	.15	.07	.02
☐ 63	Kevin Brown	.25	.11	.03
☐ 64	Julio Franco	.08	.04	.01
☐ 65	Jamie Moyer	.05	.02	.01
☐ 66	Rafael Palmeiro	.20	.09	.03
☐ 67	Nolan Ryan	1.50	.65	.19
☐ 68	Francisco Cabrera	.30	.14	.04
☐ 69	Junior Felix	.25	.11	.03
☐ 70	Al Leiter	.05	.02	.01
☐ 71	Alex Sanchez	.05	.02	.01
☐ 72	Geronimo Berroa	.05	.02	.01
☐ 73	Derek Lilliquist	.10	.05	.01
☐ 74	Lonnie Smith	.05	.02	.01
☐ 75	Jeff Treadway	.08	.04	.01
☐ 76	Paul Kilgus	.05	.02	.01
☐ 77	Lloyd McClendon	.05	.02	.01
☐ 78	Scott Sanderson	.05	.02	.01
☐ 79	Dwight Smith	.10	.05	.01
☐ 80	Jerome Walton	.10	.05	.01
☐ 81	Mitch Williams	.08	.04	.01
☐ 82	Steve Wilson	.05	.02	.01

☐ 83	Todd Benzinger	.05	.02	.01
☐ 84	Ken Griffey Sr.	.08	.04	.01
☐ 85	Rick Mahler	.05	.02	.01
☐ 86	Rolando Roomes	.05	.02	.01
☐ 87	Scott Scudder	.12	.05	.02
☐ 88	Jim Clancy	.05	.02	.01
☐ 89	Rick Rhoden	.05	.02	.01
☐ 90	Dan Schatzeder	.05	.02	.01
☐ 91	Mike Morgan	.08	.04	.01
☐ 92	Eddie Murray	.15	.07	.02
☐ 93	Willie Randolph	.08	.04	.01
☐ 94	Ray Searage	.05	.02	.01
☐ 95	Mike Aldrete	.05	.02	.01
☐ 96	Kevin Gross	.05	.02	.01
☐ 97	Mark Langston	.08	.04	.01
☐ 98	Spike Owen	.05	.02	.01
☐ 99	Zane Smith	.05	.02	.01
☐ 100	Don Aase	.05	.02	.01
☐ 101	Barry Lyons	.05	.02	.01
☐ 102	Juan Samuel	.05	.02	.01
☐ 103	Wally Whitehurst	.10	.05	.01
☐ 104	Dennis Cook	.08	.04	.01
☐ 105	Len Dykstra	.08	.04	.01
☐ 106	Charlie Hayes	.20	.09	.03
☐ 107	Tommy Herr	.05	.02	.01
☐ 108	Ken Howell	.05	.02	.01
☐ 109	John Kruk	.08	.04	.01
☐ 110	Roger McDowell	.05	.02	.01
☐ 111	Terry Mulholland	.10	.05	.01
☐ 112	Jeff Parrett	.05	.02	.01
☐ 113	Neal Heaton	.05	.02	.01
☐ 114	Jeff King	.08	.04	.01
☐ 115	Randy Kramer	.05	.02	.01
☐ 116	Bill Landrum	.05	.02	.01
☐ 117	Cris Carpenter	.10	.05	.01
☐ 118	Frank DiPino	.05	.02	.01
☐ 119	Ken Hill	.25	.11	.03
☐ 120	Dan Quisenberry	.08	.04	.01
☐ 121	Milt Thompson	.05	.02	.01
☐ 122	Todd Zeile	.60	.25	.08
☐ 123	Jack Clark	.08	.04	.01
☐ 124	Bruce Hurst	.08	.04	.01
☐ 125	Mark Parent	.05	.02	.01
☐ 126	Bip Roberts	.08	.04	.01
☐ 127	Jeff Brantley UER	.10	.05	.01
	(Photo actually			
	Joe Kmak)			
☐ 128	Terry Kennedy	.05	.02	.01
☐ 129	Mike LaCoss	.05	.02	.01
☐ 130	Greg Litton	.05	.02	.01
☐ 131	Mike Schmidt	.50	.23	.06
☐ 132	Checklist 1-132	.08	.01	.00

1990 Fleer

The 1990 Fleer set contains 660 standard-size (2 1/2" by 3 1/2") cards. The outer front borders are white; the inner, ribbon-like borders are different depending on the team. The vertically oriented backs are white, red, pink, and navy. The set is again ordered numerically by teams, followed by combination cards, rookie prospect pairs, and checklists. Just as with the 1989 set, Fleer incorrectly anticipated the outcome of the 1989 Playoffs according to the team ordering. The A's, listed first, did win the World Series, but their opponents were the Giants, not the Cubs. Fleer later reported that they merely arranged the teams according to regular season team record due to the early printing date. The complete team ordering is as follows: Oakland A's (1-24), Chicago Cubs (25-49), San Francisco Giants (50-75), Toronto Blue Jays (76-99), Kansas City Royals (100-124), California Angels (125-148), San Diego Padres (149-171), Baltimore Orioles (172-195), New York Mets (196-219), Houston Astros (220-241), St. Louis Cardinals (242-265), Boston Red Sox (266-289), Texas Rangers (290-315), Milwaukee Brewers (316-340), Montreal Expos (341-364), Minnesota Twins (365-388), Los Angeles Dodgers (389-411), Cincinnati Reds (412-435), New York Yankees (436-458), Pittsburgh Pirates (459-482), Cleveland Indians (483-504), Seattle Mariners (505-528), Chicago White Sox (529-551), Philadelphia Phillies (552-573), Atlanta Braves (574-598), and Detroit Tigers (599-620). The key Rookie Cards in this set are Alex Cole, Delino

DeShields, Juan Gonzalez, Marquis Grissom, Dave Justice, Kevin Maas, Ben McDonald, and Larry Walker. The following five cards have minor printing differences, 6, 162, 260, 469, and 550; these differences are so minor that collectors have deemed them not significant enough to effect a price differential. Fleer also produced a separate set for Canada. The Canadian set only differs from the regular set in that it shows copyright "FLEER LTD./LTEE PTD. IN CANADA" on the card backs. Although these Canadian cards were undoubtedly produced in much lesser quantities compared to the U.S. issue, the fact that the versions are so similar has kept the demand (and the price differential) for the Canadian cards down.

	MT	EX-MT	VG
COMPLETE SET (660)	15.00	6.75	1.90
COMPLETE FACT.SET (672)	15.00	6.75	1.90
COMMON PLAYER (1-660)	.04	.02	.01

		MT	EX-MT	VG
☐ 1	Lance Blankenship	.04	.02	.01
☐ 2	Todd Burns	.04	.02	.01
☐ 3	Jose Canseco	.30	.14	.04
☐ 4	Jim Corsi	.04	.02	.01
☐ 5	Storm Davis	.04	.02	.01
☐ 6	Dennis Eckersley	.12	.05	.02
☐ 7	Mike Gallego	.04	.02	.01
☐ 8	Ron Hassey	.04	.02	.01
☐ 9	Dave Henderson	.04	.02	.01
☐ 10	Rickey Henderson	.20	.09	.03
☐ 11	Rick Honeycutt	.04	.02	.01
☐ 12	Stan Javier	.04	.02	.01
☐ 13	Felix Jose	.20	.09	.03
☐ 14	Carney Lansford	.07	.03	.01
☐ 15	Mark McGwire UER	.30	.14	.04
	(1989 runs listed as 4, should be 74)			
☐ 16	Mike Moore	.04	.02	.01
☐ 17	Gene Nelson	.04	.02	.01
☐ 18	Dave Parker	.07	.03	.01
☐ 19	Tony Phillips	.04	.02	.01
☐ 20	Terry Steinbach	.07	.03	.01
☐ 21	Dave Stewart	.07	.03	.01
☐ 22	Walt Weiss	.04	.02	.01
☐ 23	Bob Welch	.07	.03	.01
☐ 24	Curt Young	.04	.02	.01
☐ 25	Paul Assenmacher	.04	.02	.01
☐ 26	Damon Berryhill	.04	.02	.01
☐ 27	Mike Bielecki	.04	.02	.01
☐ 28	Kevin Blankenship	.04	.02	.01
☐ 29	Andre Dawson	.12	.05	.02
☐ 30	Shawon Dunston	.07	.03	.01
☐ 31	Joe Girardi	.04	.02	.01

		MT	EX-MT	VG
☐ 32	Mark Grace	.20	.09	.03
☐ 33	Mike Harkey	.07	.03	.01
☐ 34	Paul Kilgus	.04	.02	.01
☐ 35	Les Lancaster	.04	.02	.01
☐ 36	Vance Law	.04	.02	.01
☐ 37	Greg Maddux	.20	.09	.03
☐ 38	Lloyd McClendon	.04	.02	.01
☐ 39	Jeff Pico	.04	.02	.01
☐ 40	Ryne Sandberg	.35	.16	.04
☐ 41	Scott Sanderson	.04	.02	.01
☐ 42	Dwight Smith	.04	.02	.01
☐ 43	Rick Sutcliffe	.07	.03	.01
☐ 44	Jerome Walton	.07	.03	.01
☐ 45	Mitch Webster	.04	.02	.01
☐ 46	Curt Wilkerson	.04	.02	.01
☐ 47	Dean Wilkins	.04	.02	.01
☐ 48	Mitch Williams	.07	.03	.01
☐ 49	Steve Wilson	.04	.02	.01
☐ 50	Steve Bedrosian	.04	.02	.01
☐ 51	Mike Benjamin	.10	.05	.01
☐ 52	Jeff Brantley	.04	.02	.01
☐ 53	Brett Butler	.07	.03	.01
☐ 54	Will Clark UER	.30	.14	.04
	("Did You Know" says first in runs, should say tied for first)			
☐ 55	Kelly Downs	.04	.02	.01
☐ 56	Scott Garrelts	.04	.02	.01
☐ 57	Atlee Hammaker	.04	.02	.01
☐ 58	Terry Kennedy	.04	.02	.01
☐ 59	Mike LaCoss	.04	.02	.01
☐ 60	Craig Lefferts	.04	.02	.01
☐ 61	Greg Litton	.04	.02	.01
☐ 62	Candy Maldonado	.04	.02	.01
☐ 63	Kirt Manwaring UER	.04	.02	.01
	(No '88 Phoenix stats as noted in box)			
☐ 64	Randy McCament	.04	.02	.01
☐ 65	Kevin Mitchell	.10	.05	.01
☐ 66	Donell Nixon	.04	.02	.01
☐ 67	Ken Oberkfell	.04	.02	.01
☐ 68	Rick Reuschel	.04	.02	.01
☐ 69	Ernest Riles	.04	.02	.01
☐ 70	Don Robinson	.04	.02	.01
☐ 71	Pat Sheridan	.04	.02	.01
☐ 72	Chris Speier	.04	.02	.01
☐ 73	Robby Thompson	.04	.02	.01
☐ 74	Jose Uribe	.04	.02	.01
☐ 75	Matt Williams	.10	.05	.01
☐ 76	George Bell	.07	.03	.01
☐ 77	Pat Borders	.07	.03	.01
☐ 78	John Cerutti	.04	.02	.01
☐ 79	Junior Felix	.07	.03	.01
☐ 80	Tony Fernandez	.07	.03	.01
☐ 81	Mike Flanagan	.04	.02	.01
☐ 82	Mauro Gozzo	.04	.02	.01
☐ 83	Kelly Gruber	.07	.03	.01

☐ 84	Tom Henke	.07	.03	.01
☐ 85	Jimmy Key	.07	.03	.01
☐ 86	Manny Lee	.04	.02	.01
☐ 87	Nelson Liriano UER	.04	.02	.01
	(Should say "led the IL" instead of "led the TL")			
☐ 88	Lee Mazzilli	.04	.02	.01
☐ 89	Fred McGriff	.20	.09	.03
☐ 90	Lloyd Moseby	.04	.02	.01
☐ 91	Rance Mulliniks	.04	.02	.01
☐ 92	Alex Sanchez	.04	.02	.01
☐ 93	Dave Stieb	.07	.03	.01
☐ 94	Todd Stottlemyre	.07	.03	.01
☐ 95	Duane Ward UER	.04	.02	.01
	(Double line of '87 Syracuse stats)			
☐ 96	David Wells	.07	.03	.01
☐ 97	Ernie Whitt	.04	.02	.01
☐ 98	Frank Wills	.04	.02	.01
☐ 99	Mookie Wilson	.04	.02	.01
☐ 100	Kevin Appier	.25	.11	.03
☐ 101	Luis Aquino	.04	.02	.01
☐ 102	Bob Boone	.07	.03	.01
☐ 103	George Brett	.15	.07	.02
☐ 104	Jose DeJesus	.04	.02	.01
☐ 105	Luis De Los Santos	.04	.02	.01
☐ 106	Jim Eisenreich	.04	.02	.01
☐ 107	Steve Farr	.04	.02	.01
☐ 108	Tom Gordon	.07	.03	.01
☐ 109	Mark Gubicza	.04	.02	.01
☐ 110	Bo Jackson	.15	.07	.02
☐ 111	Terry Leach	.04	.02	.01
☐ 112	Charlie Leibrandt	.04	.02	.01
☐ 113	Rick Luecken	.04	.02	.01
☐ 114	Mike Macfarlane	.04	.02	.01
☐ 115	Jeff Montgomery	.07	.03	.01
☐ 116	Bret Saberhagen	.07	.03	.01
☐ 117	Kevin Seitzer	.07	.03	.01
☐ 118	Kurt Stillwell	.04	.02	.01
☐ 119	Pat Tabler	.04	.02	.01
☐ 120	Danny Tartabull	.10	.05	.01
☐ 121	Gary Thurman	.04	.02	.01
☐ 122	Frank White	.04	.02	.01
☐ 123	Willie Wilson	.04	.02	.01
☐ 124	Matt Winters	.04	.02	.01
☐ 125	Jim Abbott	.20	.09	.03
☐ 126	Tony Armas	.04	.02	.01
☐ 127	Dante Bichette	.07	.03	.01
☐ 128	Bert Blyleven	.07	.03	.01
☐ 129	Chili Davis	.07	.03	.01
☐ 130	Brian Downing	.04	.02	.01
☐ 131	Mike Fetters	.10	.05	.01
☐ 132	Chuck Finley	.07	.03	.01
☐ 133	Willie Fraser	.04	.02	.01
☐ 134	Bryan Harvey	.07	.03	.01
☐ 135	Jack Howell	.04	.02	.01
☐ 136	Wally Joyner	.07	.03	.01
☐ 137	Jeff Manto	.04	.02	.01
☐ 138	Kirk McCaskill	.04	.02	.01
☐ 139	Bob McClure	.04	.02	.01
☐ 140	Greg Minton	.04	.02	.01
☐ 141	Lance Parrish	.07	.03	.01
☐ 142	Dan Petry	.04	.02	.01
☐ 143	Johnny Ray	.04	.02	.01
☐ 144	Dick Schofield	.04	.02	.01
☐ 145	Lee Stevens	.08	.04	.01
☐ 146	Claudell Washington	.04	.02	.01
☐ 147	Devon White	.07	.03	.01
☐ 148	Mike Witt	.04	.02	.01
☐ 149	Roberto Alomar	.40	.18	.05
☐ 150	Sandy Alomar Jr.	.10	.05	.01
☐ 151	Andy Benes	.20	.09	.03
☐ 152	Jack Clark	.07	.03	.01
☐ 153	Pat Clements	.04	.02	.01
☐ 154	Joey Cora	.04	.02	.01
☐ 155	Mark Davis	.04	.02	.01
☐ 156	Mark Grant	.04	.02	.01
☐ 157	Tony Gwynn	.20	.09	.03
☐ 158	Greg W. Harris	.04	.02	.01
☐ 159	Bruce Hurst	.07	.03	.01
☐ 160	Darrin Jackson	.07	.03	.01
☐ 161	Chris James	.04	.02	.01
☐ 162	Carmelo Martinez	.04	.02	.01
☐ 163	Mike Pagliarulo	.04	.02	.01
☐ 164	Mark Parent	.04	.02	.01
☐ 165	Dennis Rasmussen	.04	.02	.01
☐ 166	Bip Roberts	.07	.03	.01
☐ 167	Benito Santiago	.07	.03	.01
☐ 168	Calvin Schiraldi	.04	.02	.01
☐ 169	Eric Show	.04	.02	.01
☐ 170	Garry Templeton	.04	.02	.01
☐ 171	Ed Whitson	.04	.02	.01
☐ 172	Brady Anderson	.12	.05	.02
☐ 173	Jeff Ballard	.04	.02	.01
☐ 174	Phil Bradley	.04	.02	.01
☐ 175	Mike Devereaux	.07	.03	.01
☐ 176	Steve Finley	.07	.03	.01
☐ 177	Pete Harnisch	.10	.05	.01
☐ 178	Kevin Hickey	.04	.02	.01
☐ 179	Brian Holton	.04	.02	.01
☐ 180	Ben McDonald	.50	.23	.06
☐ 181	Bob Melvin	.04	.02	.01
☐ 182	Bob Milacki	.04	.02	.01
☐ 183	Randy Milligan UER	.04	.02	.01
	(Double line of '87 stats)			
☐ 184	Gregg Olson	.10	.05	.01
☐ 185	Joe Orsulak	.04	.02	.01
☐ 186	Bill Ripken	.04	.02	.01
☐ 187	Cal Ripken	.40	.18	.05
☐ 188	Dave Schmidt	.04	.02	.01
☐ 189	Larry Sheets	.04	.02	.01
☐ 190	Mickey Tettleton	.07	.03	.01

☐ 191	Mark Thurmond	04	.02	.01
☐ 192	Jay Tibbs	04	.02	.01
☐ 193	Jim Traber	04	.02	.01
☐ 194	Mark Williamson	04	.02	.01
☐ 195	Craig Worthington	04	.02	.01
☐ 196	Don Aase	04	.02	.01
☐ 197	Blaine Beatty	04	.02	.01
☐ 198	Mark Carreon	04	.02	.01
☐ 199	Gary Carter	07	.03	.01
☐ 200	David Cone	12	.05	.02
☐ 201	Ron Darling	07	.03	.01
☐ 202	Kevin Elster	04	.02	.01
☐ 203	Sid Fernandez	07	.03	.01
☐ 204	Dwight Gooden	10	.05	.01
☐ 205	Keith Hernandez	07	.03	.01
☐ 206	Jeff Innis	04	.02	.01
☐ 207	Gregg Jefferies	12	.05	.02
☐ 208	Howard Johnson	07	.03	.01
☐ 209	Barry Lyons UER	04	.02	.01
	(Double line of			
	'87 stats)			
☐ 210	Dave Magadan	07	.03	.01
☐ 211	Kevin McReynolds	07	.03	.01
☐ 212	Jeff Musselman	04	.02	.01
☐ 213	Randy Myers	07	.03	.01
☐ 214	Bob Ojeda	04	.02	.01
☐ 215	Juan Samuel	04	.02	.01
☐ 216	Mackey Sasser	04	.02	.01
☐ 217	Darryl Strawberry	20	.09	.03
☐ 218	Tim Teufel	04	.02	.01
☐ 219	Frank Viola	07	.03	.01
☐ 220	Juan Agosto	04	.02	.01
☐ 221	Larry Andersen	04	.02	.01
☐ 222	Eric Anthony	30	.14	.04
☐ 223	Kevin Bass	04	.02	.01
☐ 224	Craig Biggio	10	.05	.01
☐ 225	Ken Caminiti	07	.03	.01
☐ 226	Jim Clancy	04	.02	.01
☐ 227	Danny Darwin	04	.02	.01
☐ 228	Glenn Davis	07	.03	.01
☐ 229	Jim Deshaies	04	.02	.01
☐ 230	Bill Doran	04	.02	.01
☐ 231	Bob Forsch	04	.02	.01
☐ 232	Brian Meyer	04	.02	.01
☐ 233	Terry Puhl	04	.02	.01
☐ 234	Rafael Ramirez	04	.02	.01
☐ 235	Rick Rhoden	04	.02	.01
☐ 236	Dan Schatzeder	04	.02	.01
☐ 237	Mike Scott	04	.02	.01
☐ 238	Dave Smith	04	.02	.01
☐ 239	Alex Trevino	04	.02	.01
☐ 240	Glenn Wilson	04	.02	.01
☐ 241	Gerald Young	04	.02	.01
☐ 242	Tom Brunansky	07	.03	.01
☐ 243	Cris Carpenter	04	.02	.01
☐ 244	Alex Cole	15	.07	.02
☐ 245	Vince Coleman	07	.03	.01
☐ 246	John Costello	04	.02	.01
☐ 247	Ken Dayley	04	.02	.01
☐ 248	Jose DeLeon	04	.02	.01
☐ 249	Frank DiPino	04	.02	.01
☐ 250	Pedro Guerrero	07	.03	.01
☐ 251	Ken Hill	12	.05	.02
☐ 252	Joe Magrane	04	.02	.01
☐ 253	Willie McGee UER	07	.03	.01
	(No decimal point			
	before 353)			
☐ 254	John Morris	04	.02	.01
☐ 255	Jose Oquendo	04	.02	.01
☐ 256	Tony Pena	04	.02	.01
☐ 257	Terry Pendleton	10	.05	.01
☐ 258	Ted Power	04	.02	.01
☐ 259	Dan Quisenberry	07	.03	.01
☐ 260	Ozzie Smith	12	.05	.02
☐ 261	Scott Terry	04	.02	.01
☐ 262	Milt Thompson	04	.02	.01
☐ 263	Denny Walling	04	.02	.01
☐ 264	Todd Worrell	04	.02	.01
☐ 265	Todd Zeile	15	.07	.02
☐ 266	Marty Barrett	04	.02	.01
☐ 267	Mike Boddicker	04	.02	.01
☐ 268	Wade Boggs	20	.09	.03
☐ 269	Ellis Burks	07	.03	.01
☐ 270	Rick Cerone	04	.02	.01
☐ 271	Roger Clemens	35	.16	.04
☐ 272	John Dopson	04	.02	.01
☐ 273	Nick Esasky	04	.02	.01
☐ 274	Dwight Evans	07	.03	.01
☐ 275	Wes Gardner	04	.02	.01
☐ 276	Rich Gedman	04	.02	.01
☐ 277	Mike Greenwell	07	.03	.01
☐ 278	Danny Heep	04	.02	.01
☐ 279	Eric Hetzel	04	.02	.01
☐ 280	Dennis Lamp	04	.02	.01
☐ 281	Rob Murphy UER	04	.02	.01
	('89 stats say Reds,			
	should say Red Sox)			
☐ 282	Joe Price	04	.02	.01
☐ 283	Carlos Quintana	07	.03	.01
☐ 284	Jody Reed	04	.02	.01
☐ 285	Luis Rivera	04	.02	.01
☐ 286	Kevin Romine	04	.02	.01
☐ 287	Lee Smith	07	.03	.01
☐ 288	Mike Smithson	04	.02	.01
☐ 289	Bob Stanley	04	.02	.01
☐ 290	Harold Baines	07	.03	.01
☐ 291	Kevin Brown	10	.05	.01
☐ 292	Steve Buechele	04	.02	.01
☐ 293	Scott Coolbaugh	04	.02	.01
☐ 294	Jack Daugherty	04	.02	.01
☐ 295	Cecil Espy	04	.02	.01
☐ 296	Julio Franco	07	.03	.01
☐ 297	Juan Gonzalez	2.00	.90	.25
☐ 298	Cecilio Guante	04	.02	.01

☐ 299 Drew Hall	.04	.02	.01
☐ 300 Charlie Hough	.04	.02	.01
☐ 301 Pete Incaviglia	.04	.02	.01
☐ 302 Mike Jeffcoat	.04	.02	.01
☐ 303 Chad Kreuter	.04	.02	.01
☐ 304 Jeff Kunkel	.04	.02	.01
☐ 305 Rick Leach	.04	.02	.01
☐ 306 Fred Manrique	.04	.02	.01
☐ 307 Jamie Moyer	.04	.02	.01
☐ 308 Rafael Palmeiro	.10	.05	.01
☐ 309 Geno Petralli	.04	.02	.01
☐ 310 Kevin Reimer	.04	.02	.01
☐ 311 Kenny Rogers	.04	.02	.01
☐ 312 Jeff Russell	.04	.02	.01
☐ 313 Nolan Ryan	.50	.23	.06
☐ 314 Ruben Sierra	.20	.09	.03
☐ 315 Bobby Witt	.07	.03	.01
☐ 316 Chris Bosio	.04	.02	.01
☐ 317 Glenn Braggs UER	.04	.02	.01
(Stats say 111 K's,			
but bio says 117 K's)			
☐ 318 Greg Brock	.04	.02	.01
☐ 319 Chuck Crim	.04	.02	.01
☐ 320 Rob Deer	.07	.03	.01
☐ 321 Mike Felder	.04	.02	.01
☐ 322 Tom Filer	.04	.02	.01
☐ 323 Tony Fossas	.04	.02	.01
☐ 324 Jim Gantner	.04	.02	.01
☐ 325 Darryl Hamilton	.07	.03	.01
☐ 326 Teddy Higuera	.04	.02	.01
☐ 327 Mark Knudson	.04	.02	.01
☐ 328 Bill Krueger UER	.04	.02	.01
('86 stats missing)			
☐ 329 Tim McIntosh	.10	.05	.01
☐ 330 Paul Molitor	.10	.05	.01
☐ 331 Jaime Navarro	.07	.03	.01
☐ 332 Charlie O'Brien	.04	.02	.01
☐ 333 Jeff Peterek	.10	.05	.01
☐ 334 Dan Plesac	.04	.02	.01
☐ 335 Jerry Reuss	.04	.02	.01
☐ 336 Gary Sheffield UER	.50	.23	.06
(Bio says played for			
3 teams in '87, but			
stats say in '88)			
☐ 337 Bill Spiers	.04	.02	.01
☐ 338 B.J. Surhoff	.04	.02	.01
☐ 339 Greg Vaughn	.20	.09	.03
☐ 340 Robin Yount	.15	.07	.02
☐ 341 Hubie Brooks	.04	.02	.01
☐ 342 Tim Burke	.04	.02	.01
☐ 343 Mike Fitzgerald	.04	.02	.01
☐ 344 Tom Foley	.04	.02	.01
☐ 345 Andres Galarraga	.04	.02	.01
☐ 346 Damaso Garcia	.04	.02	.01
☐ 347 Marquis Grissom	.60	.25	.08
☐ 348 Kevin Gross	.04	.02	.01
☐ 349 Joe Hesketh	.04	.02	.01

☐ 350 Jeff Huson	.10	.05	.01
☐ 351 Wallace Johnson	.04	.02	.01
☐ 352 Mark Langston	.07	.03	.01
☐ 353A Dave Martinez	3.00	1.35	.40
(Yellow on front)			
☐ 353B Dave Martinez	.07	.03	.01
(Red on front)			
☐ 354 Dennis Martinez UER	.07	.03	.01
('87 ERA is 616,			
should be 6.16)			
☐ 355 Andy McGaffigan	.04	.02	.01
☐ 356 Otis Nixon	.07	.03	.01
☐ 357 Spike Owen	.04	.02	.01
☐ 358 Pascual Perez	.04	.02	.01
☐ 359 Tim Raines	.07	.03	.01
☐ 360 Nelson Santovenia	.04	.02	.01
☐ 361 Bryn Smith	.04	.02	.01
☐ 362 Zane Smith	.04	.02	.01
☐ 363 Larry Walker	.90	.40	.11
☐ 364 Tim Wallach	.07	.03	.01
☐ 365 Rick Aguilera	.07	.03	.01
☐ 366 Allan Anderson	.04	.02	.01
☐ 367 Wally Backman	.04	.02	.01
☐ 368 Doug Baker	.04	.02	.01
☐ 369 Juan Berenguer	.04	.02	.01
☐ 370 Randy Bush	.04	.02	.01
☐ 371 Carmen Castillo	.04	.02	.01
☐ 372 Mike Dyer	.04	.02	.01
☐ 373 Gary Gaetti	.04	.02	.01
☐ 374 Greg Gagne	.04	.02	.01
☐ 375 Dan Gladden	.04	.02	.01
☐ 376 German Gonzalez UER	.04	.02	.01
(Bio says 31 saves in			
'88, but stats say 30)			
☐ 377 Brian Harper	.07	.03	.01
☐ 378 Kent Hrbek	.07	.03	.01
☐ 379 Gene Larkin	.04	.02	.01
☐ 380 Tim Laudner UER	.04	.02	.01
(No decimal point			
before '85 BA of 238)			
☐ 381 John Moses	.04	.02	.01
☐ 382 Al Newman	.04	.02	.01
☐ 383 Kirby Puckett	.30	.14	.04
☐ 384 Shane Rawley	.04	.02	.01
☐ 385 Jeff Reardon	.07	.03	.01
☐ 386 Roy Smith	.04	.02	.01
☐ 387 Gary Wayne	.04	.02	.01
☐ 388 Dave West	.04	.02	.01
☐ 389 Tim Belcher	.07	.03	.01
☐ 390 Tim Crews UER	.04	.02	.01
(Stats say 163 IP for			
'83, but bio says 136)			
☐ 391 Mike Davis	.04	.02	.01
☐ 392 Rick Dempsey	.04	.02	.01
☐ 393 Kirk Gibson	.07	.03	.01
☐ 394 Jose Gonzalez	.04	.02	.01
☐ 395 Alfredo Griffin	.04	.02	.01

☐ 396	Jeff Hamilton 04	.02	.01
☐ 397	Lenny Harris 04	.02	.01
☐ 398	Mickey Hatcher 04	.02	.01
☐ 399	Orel Hershiser 07	.03	.01
☐ 400	Jay Howell 04	.02	.01
☐ 401	Mike Marshall 04	.02	.01
☐ 402	Ramon Martinez 15	.07	.02
☐ 403	Mike Morgan 04	.02	.01
☐ 404	Eddie Murray 10	.05	.01
☐ 405	Alejandro Pena 04	.02	.01
☐ 406	Willie Randolph 07	.03	.01
☐ 407	Mike Scioscia 04	.02	.01
☐ 408	Ray Searage..................04	.02	.01
☐ 409	Fernando Valenzuela 07	.03	.01
☐ 410	Jose Vizcaino 10	.05	.01
☐ 411	John Wetteland 07	.03	.01
☐ 412	Jack Armstrong 07	.03	.01
☐ 413	Todd Benzinger UER 04	.02	.01
	(Bio says .323 at		
	Pawtucket, but		
	stats say .321)		
☐ 414	Tim Birtsas..................04	.02	.01
☐ 415	Tom Browning 04	.02	.01
☐ 416	Norm Charlton 07	.03	.01
☐ 417	Eric Davis....................10	.05	.01
☐ 418	Rob Dibble....................07	.03	.01
☐ 419	John Franco..................07	.03	.01
☐ 420	Ken Griffey Sr................07	.03	.01
☐ 421	Chris Hammond.............20	.09	.03
	(No 1989 used for		
	"Did Not Play" stat,		
	actually did play for		
	Nashville in 1989)		
☐ 422	Danny Jackson 04	.02	.01
☐ 423	Barry Larkin 12	.05	.02
☐ 424	Tim Leary 04	.02	.01
☐ 425	Rick Mahler..................04	.02	.01
☐ 426	Joe Oliver 10	.05	.01
☐ 427	Paul O'Neill 07	.03	.01
☐ 428	Luis Quinones UER 04	.02	.01
	('86-'88 stats are		
	omitted from card but		
	included in totals)		
☐ 429	Jeff Reed.....................04	.02	.01
☐ 430	Jose Rijo.....................07	.03	.01
☐ 431	Ron Robinson 04	.02	.01
☐ 432	Rolando Roomes 04	.02	.01
☐ 433	Chris Sabo 07	.03	.01
☐ 434	Scott Scudder...............04	.02	.01
☐ 435	Herm Winningham 04	.02	.01
☐ 436	Steve Balboni................04	.02	.01
☐ 437	Jesse Barfield 04	.02	.01
☐ 438	Mike Blowers 04	.02	.01
☐ 439	Tom Brookens 04	.02	.01
☐ 440	Greg Cadaret................04	.02	.01
☐ 441	Alvaro Espinoza UER 04	.02	.01
	(Career games say		

	218, should be 219)		
☐ 442	Bob Geren....................04	.02	.01
☐ 443	Lee Guetterman 04	.02	.01
☐ 444	Mel Hall.......................04	.02	.01
☐ 445	Andy Hawkins 04	.02	.01
☐ 446	Roberto Kelly 10	.05	.01
☐ 447	Don Mattingly................20	.09	.03
☐ 448	Lance McCullers............04	.02	.01
☐ 449	Hensley Meulens...........07	.03	.01
☐ 450	Dale Mohorcic................04	.02	.01
☐ 451	Clay Parker 04	.02	.01
☐ 452	Eric Plunk....................04	.02	.01
☐ 453	Dave Righetti 04	.02	.01
☐ 454	Deion Sanders 40	.18	.05
☐ 455	Steve Sax 07	.03	.01
☐ 456	Don Slaught..................04	.02	.01
☐ 457	Walt Terrell 04	.02	.01
☐ 458	Dave Winfield................15	.07	.02
☐ 459	Jay Bell 07	.03	.01
☐ 460	Rafael Belliard...............04	.02	.01
☐ 461	Barry Bonds..................30	.14	.04
☐ 462	Bobby Bonilla................12	.05	.02
☐ 463	Sid Bream 04	.02	.01
☐ 464	Benny Distefano 04	.02	.01
☐ 465	Doug Drabek.................07	.03	.01
☐ 466	Jim Gott 04	.02	.01
☐ 467	Billy Hatcher UER 04	.02	.01
	(.1 hits for Cubs		
	in 1984)		
☐ 468	Neal Heaton 04	.02	.01
☐ 469	Jeff King 07	.03	.01
☐ 470	Bob Kipper 04	.02	.01
☐ 471	Randy Kramer 04	.02	.01
☐ 472	Bill Landrum 04	.02	.01
☐ 473	Mike LaValliere 04	.02	.01
☐ 474	Jose Lind 04	.02	.01
☐ 475	Junior Ortiz 04	.02	.01
☐ 476	Gary Redus 04	.02	.01
☐ 477	Rick Reed 04	.02	.01
☐ 478	R.J. Reynolds................04	.02	.01
☐ 479	Jeff D. Robinson............04	.02	.01
☐ 480	John Smiley 07	.03	.01
☐ 481	Andy Van Slyke 10	.05	.01
☐ 482	Bob Walk 04	.02	.01
☐ 483	Andy Allanson...............04	.02	.01
☐ 484	Scott Bailes..................04	.02	.01
☐ 485	Joey Belle UER 50	.23	.06
	(Has Jay Bell		
	"Did You Know")		
☐ 486	Bud Black.....................04	.02	.01
☐ 487	Jerry Browne 04	.02	.01
☐ 488	Tom Candiotti 04	.02	.01
☐ 489	Joe Carter 20	.09	.03
☐ 490	Dave Clark....................04	.02	.01
	(No '84 stats)		
☐ 491	John Farrell 04	.02	.01
☐ 492	Felix Fermin..................04	.02	.01

☐ 493	Brook Jacoby	.04	.02	.01
☐ 494	Dion James	.04	.02	.01
☐ 495	Doug Jones	.07	.03	.01
☐ 496	Brad Komminsk	.04	.02	.01
☐ 497	Rod Nichols	.04	.02	.01
☐ 498	Pete O'Brien	.04	.02	.01
☐ 499	Steve Olin	.20	.09	.03
☐ 500	Jesse Orosco	.04	.02	.01
☐ 501	Joel Skinner	.04	.02	.01
☐ 502	Cory Snyder	.04	.02	.01
☐ 503	Greg Swindell	.07	.03	.01
☐ 504	Rich Yett	.04	.02	.01
☐ 505	Scott Bankhead	.04	.02	.01
☐ 506	Scott Bradley	.04	.02	.01
☐ 507	Greg Briley UER	.04	.02	.01
	(28 SB's in bio, but 27 in stats)			
☐ 508	Jay Buhner	.07	.03	.01
☐ 509	Darnell Coles	.04	.02	.01
☐ 510	Keith Comstock	.04	.02	.01
☐ 511	Henry Cotto	.04	.02	.01
☐ 512	Alvin Davis	.04	.02	.01
☐ 513	Ken Griffey Jr.	1.25	.55	.16
☐ 514	Erik Hanson	.07	.03	.01
☐ 515	Gene Harris	.04	.02	.01
☐ 516	Brian Holman	.04	.02	.01
☐ 517	Mike Jackson	.04	.02	.01
☐ 518	Randy Johnson	.07	.03	.01
☐ 519	Jeffrey Leonard	.04	.02	.01
☐ 520	Edgar Martinez	.20	.09	.03
☐ 521	Dennis Powell	.04	.02	.01
☐ 522	Jim Presley	.04	.02	.01
☐ 523	Jerry Reed	.04	.02	.01
☐ 524	Harold Reynolds	.04	.02	.01
☐ 525	Mike Schooler	.04	.02	.01
☐ 526	Bill Swift	.07	.03	.01
☐ 527	Dave Valle	.04	.02	.01
☐ 528	Omar Vizquel	.07	.03	.01
☐ 529	Ivan Calderon	.04	.02	.01
☐ 530	Carlton Fisk UER	.10	.05	.01
	(Bellow Falls, should be Bellows Falls)			
☐ 531	Scott Fletcher	.04	.02	.01
☐ 532	Dave Gallagher	.04	.02	.01
☐ 533	Ozzie Guillen	.04	.02	.01
☐ 534	Greg Hibbard	.20	.09	.03
☐ 535	Shawn Hillegas	.04	.02	.01
☐ 536	Lance Johnson	.07	.03	.01
☐ 537	Eric King	.04	.02	.01
☐ 538	Ron Kittle	.04	.02	.01
☐ 539	Steve Lyons	.04	.02	.01
☐ 540	Carlos Martinez	.04	.02	.01
☐ 541	Tom McCarthy	.04	.02	.01
☐ 542	Matt Merullo	.04	.02	.01
	(Had 5 ML runs scored entering '90, not 6)			
☐ 543	Donn Pall UER	.04	.02	.01

	(Stats say pro career began in '85, bio says '88)			
☐ 544	Dan Pasqua	.04	.02	.01
☐ 545	Ken Patterson	.04	.02	.01
☐ 546	Melido Perez	.07	.03	.01
☐ 547	Steve Rosenberg	.04	.02	.01
☐ 548	Sammy Sosa	.15	.07	.02
☐ 549	Bobby Thigpen	.04	.02	.01
☐ 550	Robin Ventura	.60	.25	.08
☐ 551	Greg Walker	.04	.02	.01
☐ 552	Don Carman	.04	.02	.01
☐ 553	Pat Combs	.07	.03	.01
	(6 walks for Phillies in '89 in stats, brief bio says 4)			
☐ 554	Dennis Cook	.04	.02	.01
☐ 555	Darren Daulton	.07	.03	.01
☐ 556	Len Dykstra	.07	.03	.01
☐ 557	Curt Ford	.04	.02	.01
☐ 558	Charlie Hayes	.07	.03	.01
☐ 559	Von Hayes	.04	.02	.01
☐ 560	Tommy Herr	.04	.02	.01
☐ 561	Ken Howell	.04	.02	.01
☐ 562	Steve Jeltz	.04	.02	.01
☐ 563	Ron Jones	.04	.02	.01
☐ 564	Ricky Jordan UER	.04	.02	.01
	(Duplicate line of statistics on back)			
☐ 565	John Kruk	.07	.03	.01
☐ 566	Steve Lake	.04	.02	.01
☐ 567	Roger McDowell	.04	.02	.01
☐ 568	Terry Mulholland UER	.07	.03	.01
	("Did You Know" refers to Dave Magadan)			
☐ 569	Dwayne Murphy	.04	.02	.01
☐ 570	Jeff Parrett	.04	.02	.01
☐ 571	Randy Ready	.04	.02	.01
☐ 572	Bruce Ruffin	.04	.02	.01
☐ 573	Dickie Thon	.04	.02	.01
☐ 574	Jose Alvarez UER	.04	.02	.01
	('78 and '79 stats are reversed)			
☐ 575	Geronimo Berroa	.04	.02	.01
☐ 576	Jeff Blauser	.07	.03	.01
☐ 577	Joe Boever	.04	.02	.01
☐ 578	Marty Clary UER	.04	.02	.01
	(No comma between city and state)			
☐ 579	Jody Davis	.04	.02	.01
☐ 580	Mark Eichhorn	.04	.02	.01
☐ 581	Darrell Evans	.07	.03	.01
☐ 582	Ron Gant	.25	.11	.03
☐ 583	Tom Glavine	.25	.11	.03
☐ 584	Tommy Greene	.12	.05	.02
☐ 585	Tommy Gregg	.04	.02	.01
☐ 586	Dave Justice UER	1.25	.55	.16

(Actually had 16 doubles
in Sumter in '86)

☐	587	Mark Lemke....................07	.03	.01
☐	588	Derek Lilliquist...............04	.02	.01
☐	589	Oddibe McDowell............04	.02	.01
☐	590	Kent Mercker ERA..........12	.05	.02

(Bio says 2.75 ERA,
stats say 2.68 ERA)

☐	591	Dale Murphy 10	.05	.01
☐	592	Gerald Perry 04	.02	.01
☐	593	Lonnie Smith 04	.02	.01
☐	594	Pete Smith 07	.03	.01
☐	595	John Smoltz....................25	.11	.03
☐	596	Mike Stanton UER...........15	.07	.02

(No comma between
city and state)

☐	597	Andres Thomas...............04	.02	.01
☐	598	Jeff Treadway 04	.02	.01
☐	599	Doyle Alexander.............04	.02	.01
☐	600	Dave Bergman 04	.02	.01
☐	601	Brian DuBois..................04	.02	.01
☐	602	Paul Gibson 04	.02	.01
☐	603	Mike Heath.....................04	.02	.01
☐	604	Mike Henneman...............04	.02	.01
☐	605	Guillermo Hernandez 04	.02	.01
☐	606	Shawn Holman 04	.02	.01
☐	607	Tracy Jones 04	.02	.01
☐	608	Chet Lemon 04	.02	.01
☐	609	Fred Lynn......................07	.03	.01
☐	610	Jack Morris....................10	.05	.01
☐	611	Matt Nokes 04	.02	.01
☐	612	Gary Pettis 04	.02	.01
☐	613	Kevin Ritz......................10	.05	.01
☐	614	Jeff M. Robinson............04	.02	.01

('88 stats are
not in line)

☐	615	Steve Searcy 04	.02	.01
☐	616	Frank Tanana 04	.02	.01
☐	617	Alan Trammell.................07	.03	.01
☐	618	Gary Ward......................04	.02	.01
☐	619	Lou Whitaker..................07	.03	.01
☐	620	Frank Williams................04	.02	.01
☐	621A	George Brett '80 ....1.25	.55	.16

ERR (Had 10 .390
hitting seasons)

☐	621B	George Brett '80 10	.05	.01

COR

☐	622	Fern.Valenzuela '81 05	.02	.01
☐	623	Dale Murphy '82 10	.05	.01
☐	624A	Cal Ripken '83 ERR ...3.50	1.55	.45

(Misspelled Ripkin
on card back)

☐	624B	Cal Ripken '83 COR 20	.09	.03
☐	625	Ryne Sandberg '84 20	.09	.03
☐	626	Don Mattingly '85 10	.05	.01
☐	627	Roger Clemens '86 20	.09	.03
☐	628	George Bell '87 05	.02	.01

☐	629	Jose Canseco '88 UER....15	.07	.02

(Reggie won MVP in
'83, should say '73)

☐	630A	Will Clark '89 ERR 1.25	.55	.16

(32 total bases
on card back)

☐	630B	Will Clark '89 COR 15	.07	.02

(321 total bases;
technically still
an error, listing
only 24 runs)

☐	631	Game Savers....................05	.02	.01

Mark Davis
Mitch Williams

☐	632	Boston Igniters 10	.05	.01

Wade Boggs
Mike Greenwell

☐	633	Starter and Stopper 05	.02	.01

Mark Gubicza
Jeff Russell

☐	634	League's Best 15	.07	.02

Shortstops
Tony Fernandez
Cal Ripken

☐	635	Human Dynamos 15	.07	.02

Kirby Puckett
Bo Jackson

☐	636	300 Strikeout Club 20	.09	.03

Nolan Ryan
Mike Scott

☐	637	The Dynamic Duo 10	.05	.01

Will Clark
Kevin Mitchell

☐	638	AL All-Stars...................15	.07	.02

Don Mattingly
Mark McGwire

☐	639	NL East Rivals...............10	.05	.01

Howard Johnson
Ryne Sandberg

☐	640	Rudy Seanez 15	.07	.02

Colin Charland

☐	641	George Canale.................30	.14	.04

Kevin Maas UER
(Canale listed as INF
on front, 1B on back)

☐	642	Kelly Mann.....................15	.07	.02

and Dave Hansen

☐	643	Greg Smith 05	.02	.01

and Stu Tate

☐	644	Tom Drees......................05	.02	.01

and Dann Howitt

☐	645	Mike Roesler...................30	.14	.04

and Derrick May

☐	646	Scott Hemond.................15	.07	.02

and Mark Gardner

☐	647	John Orton.....................25	.11	.03

and Scott Leius

☐ 648	Rich Monteleone............05 and Dana Williams	.02	.01
☐ 649	Mike Huff......................05 and Steve Frey	.02	.01
☐ 650	Chuck McElroy.............50 and Moises Alou	.23	.06
☐ 651	Bobby Rose ....05 and Mike Hartley	.02	.01
☐ 652	Matt Kinzer ....05 and Wayne Edwards	.02	.01
☐ 653	Delino DeShields.........60 and Jason Grimsley	.25	.08
☐ 654	CL: A's/Cubs................05 Giants/Blue Jays	.01	.00
☐ 655	CL: Royals/Angels........05 Padres/Orioles	.01	.00
☐ 656	CL: Mets/Astros............05 Cards/Red Sox	.01	.00
☐ 657	CL: Rangers/Brewers....05 Expos/Twins	.01	.00
☐ 658	CL: Dodgers/Reds.........05 Yankees/Pirates	.01	.00
☐ 659	CL: Indians/Mariners ....05 White Sox/Phillies	.01	.00
☐ 660A	CL: Braves/Tigers ....10 Specials/Checklists (Checklist-660 in small-er print on card front)	.01	.00
☐ 660B	CL: Braves/Tigers ....10 Specials/Checklists (Checklist-660 in nor-mal print on card front)	.01	.00

1990 Fleer Update

The 1990 Fleer Update set contains 132 standard-size (2 1/2" by 3 1/2") cards. This set marked the seventh consecutive year

Fleer issued an end of season Update set. The set was issued exclusively as a boxed set through hobby dealers. The set is checklisted alphabetically by team for each league and then alphabetically within each team. The fronts are styled the same as the 1990 Fleer regular issue set. The backs are numbered with the prefix U for Update. The key rookies in this set are Carlos Baerga, Alex Fernandez, Travis Fryman, Dave Hollins, Jose Offerman, John Olerud, Frank Thomas, and Mark Whiten.

	MT	EX-MT	VG
COMPLETE SET (132) 7.00		3.10	.85
COMMON PLAYER (1-132) 05		.02	.01
☐ 1 Steve Avery.........................75		.35	.09
☐ 2 Francisco Cabrera 10		.05	.01
☐ 3 Nick Esasky.......................05		.02	.01
☐ 4 Jim Kremers 05		.02	.01
☐ 5 Greg Olson........................10		.05	.01
☐ 6 Jim Presley........................05		.02	.01
☐ 7 Shawn Boskie....................10		.05	.01
☐ 8 Joe Kraemer 05		.02	.01
☐ 9 Luis Salazar.......................05		.02	.01
☐ 10 Hector Villanueva..............10		.05	.01
☐ 11 Glenn Braggs 05		.02	.01
☐ 12 Mariano Duncan 05		.02	.01
☐ 13 Billy Hatcher 05		.02	.01
☐ 14 Tim Layana 05		.02	.01
☐ 15 Hal Morris.........................15		.07	.02
☐ 16 Javier Ortiz........................10		.05	.01
☐ 17 Dave Rohde.......................05		.02	.01
☐ 18 Eric Yelding 05		.02	.01
☐ 19 Hubie Brooks.....................05		.02	.01
☐ 20 Kal Daniels 05		.02	.01
☐ 21 Dave Hansen.....................15		.07	.02
☐ 22 Mike Hartley......................05		.02	.01
☐ 23 Stan Javier........................05		.02	.01
☐ 24 Jose Offerman 20		.09	.03
☐ 25 Juan Samuel......................05		.02	.01
☐ 26 Dennis Boyd 05		.02	.01
☐ 27 Delino DeShields...............60		.25	.08
☐ 28 Steve Frey.........................05		.02	.01
☐ 29 Mark Gardner.....................08		.04	.01
☐ 30 Chris Nabholz.....................20		.09	.03
☐ 31 Bill Sampen.......................05		.02	.01
☐ 32 Dave Schmidt 05		.02	.01
☐ 33 Daryl Boston......................05		.02	.01
☐ 34 Chuck Carr 12		.05	.02
☐ 35 John Franco.......................08		.04	.01
☐ 36 Todd Hundley 15		.07	.02
☐ 37 Julio Machado 08		.04	.01
☐ 38 Alejandro Pena..................05		.02	.01
☐ 39 Darren Reed.......................10		.05	.01

☐ 40 Kelvin Torve	.05	.02	.01
☐ 41 Darrel Akerfelds	.05	.02	.01
☐ 42 Jose DeJesus	.05	.02	.01
☐ 43 Dave Hollins	.60	.25	.08
(Misspelled Dane on card back)			
☐ 44 Carmelo Martinez	.05	.02	.01
☐ 45 Brad Moore	.05	.02	.01
☐ 46 Dale Murphy	.10	.05	.01
☐ 47 Wally Backman	.05	.02	.01
☐ 48 Stan Belinda	.15	.07	.02
☐ 49 Bob Patterson	.05	.02	.01
☐ 50 Ted Power	.05	.02	.01
☐ 51 Don Slaught	.05	.02	.01
☐ 52 Geronimo Pena	.15	.07	.02
☐ 53 Lee Smith	.08	.04	.01
☐ 54 John Tudor	.05	.02	.01
☐ 55 Joe Carter	.20	.09	.03
☐ 56 Thomas Howard	.12	.05	.02
☐ 57 Craig Lefferts	.05	.02	.01
☐ 58 Rafael Valdez	.10	.05	.01
☐ 59 Dave Anderson	.05	.02	.01
☐ 60 Kevin Bass	.05	.02	.01
☐ 61 John Burkett	.10	.05	.01
☐ 62 Gary Carter	.08	.04	.01
☐ 63 Rick Parker	.05	.02	.01
☐ 64 Trevor Wilson	.05	.02	.01
☐ 65 Chris Hoiles	.40	.18	.05
☐ 66 Tim Hulett	.05	.02	.01
☐ 67 Dave Johnson	.05	.02	.01
☐ 68 Curt Schilling	.15	.07	.02
☐ 69 David Segui	.10	.05	.01
☐ 70 Tom Brunansky	.08	.04	.01
☐ 71 Greg A. Harris	.05	.02	.01
☐ 72 Dana Kiecker	.05	.02	.01
☐ 73 Tim Naehring	.15	.07	.02
☐ 74 Tony Pena	.05	.02	.01
☐ 75 Jeff Reardon	.08	.04	.01
☐ 76 Jerry Reed	.05	.02	.01
☐ 77 Mark Eichhorn	.05	.02	.01
☐ 78 Mark Langston	.08	.04	.01
☐ 79 John Orton	.05	.02	.01
☐ 80 Luis Polonia	.08	.04	.01
☐ 81 Dave Winfield	.15	.07	.02
☐ 82 Cliff Young	.10	.05	.01
☐ 83 Wayne Edwards	.05	.02	.01
☐ 84 Alex Fernandez	.40	.18	.05
☐ 85 Craig Grebeck	.15	.07	.02
☐ 86 Scott Radinsky	.15	.07	.02
☐ 87 Frank Thomas	4.00	1.80	.50
☐ 88 Beau Allred	.05	.02	.01
☐ 89 Sandy Alomar Jr.	.10	.05	.01
☐ 90 Carlos Baerga	1.25	.55	.16
☐ 91 Kevin Bearse	.05	.02	.01
☐ 92 Chris James	.05	.02	.01
☐ 93 Candy Maldonado	.05	.02	.01
☐ 94 Jeff Manto	.05	.02	.01

☐ 95 Cecil Fielder	.20	.09	.03
☐ 96 Travis Fryman	1.50	.65	.19
☐ 97 Lloyd Moseby	.05	.02	.01
☐ 98 Edwin Nunez	.05	.02	.01
☐ 99 Tony Phillips	.05	.02	.01
☐ 100 Larry Sheets	.05	.02	.01
☐ 101 Mark Davis	.05	.02	.01
☐ 102 Storm Davis	.05	.02	.01
☐ 103 Gerald Perry	.05	.02	.01
☐ 104 Terry Shumpert	.05	.02	.01
☐ 105 Edgar Diaz	.05	.02	.01
☐ 106 Dave Parker	.08	.04	.01
☐ 107 Tim Drummond	.05	.02	.01
☐ 108 Junior Ortiz	.05	.02	.01
☐ 109 Park Pittman	.05	.02	.01
☐ 110 Kevin Tapani	.35	.16	.04
☐ 111 Oscar Azocar	.10	.05	.01
☐ 112 Jim Leyritz	.10	.05	.01
☐ 113 Kevin Maas	.25	.11	.03
☐ 114 Alan Mills	.12	.05	.02
☐ 115 Matt Nokes	.05	.02	.01
☐ 116 Pascual Perez	.05	.02	.01
☐ 117 Ozzie Canseco	.10	.05	.01
☐ 118 Scott Sanderson	.05	.02	.01
☐ 119 Tino Martinez	.15	.07	.02
☐ 120 Jeff Schaefer	.05	.02	.01
☐ 121 Matt Young	.05	.02	.01
☐ 122 Brian Bohanon	.10	.05	.01
☐ 123 Jeff Huson	.05	.02	.01
☐ 124 Ramon Manon	.05	.02	.01
☐ 125 Gary Mielke UER	.05	.02	.01
(Shown as Blue Jay on front)			
☐ 126 Willie Blair	.10	.05	.01
☐ 127 Glenallen Hill	.08	.04	.01
☐ 128 John Olerud	.60	.25	.08
☐ 129 Luis Sojo	.15	.07	.02
☐ 130 Mark Whiten	.35	.16	.04
☐ 131 Nolan Ryan	.60	.25	.08
☐ 132 Checklist 1-132	.08	.01	.00

1991 Fleer

The 1991 Fleer set consists of 720 cards which measure the now standard size of 2 1/2" by 3 1/2". This set marks Fleer's eleventh consecutive year of issuing sets of current players. This set does not have what has been a Fleer tradition in recent years, the two-player Rookie Cards and there are less two-player special cards than in prior years. Apparently this was an

attempt by Fleer to increase the number of single player cards in the set. The design features solid yellow borders with the information in black indicating name, position, and team. The backs feature beautiful full-color photos along with the career statistics and a biography for those players where there is room. The set is again ordered numerically by teams, followed by combination cards, rookie prospect pairs, and checklists. Again Fleer incorrectly anticipated the outcome of the 1990 Playoffs according to the team ordering. The A's, listed first, did not win the World Series and their opponents (and Series winners) were the Reds, not the Pirates. Fleer later reported that they merely arranged the teams according to regular season team record due to the early printing date. The complete team ordering is as follows: Oakland A's (1-28), Pittsburgh Pirates (29-54), Cincinnati Reds (55-82), Boston Red Sox (83-113), Chicago White Sox (114-139), New York Mets (140-166), Toronto Blue Jays (167-192), Los Angeles Dodgers (193-223), Montreal Expos (224-251), San Francisco Giants (252-277), Texas Rangers (278-304), California Angels (305-330), Detroit Tigers (331-357), Cleveland Indians (358-385), Philadelphia Phillies (386-412), Chicago Cubs (413-441), Seattle Mariners (442-465), Baltimore Orioles (466-496), Houston Astros (497-522) San Diego Padres (523-548), Kansas City Royals (549-575), Milwaukee Brewers (576-601), Minnesota Twins (602-627), St. Louis Cardinals (628-654), New York Yankees (655-680), and Atlanta Braves (681-708). A number of the cards in the set can be found with photos cropped (very slightly) differently as Fleer used two separate printers in their attempt to maximize production. The key Rookie

Cards in this set are Wes Chamberlain, Luis Gonzalez, Brian McRae, Pedro Munoz, Phil Plantier, and Randy Tomlin. The 724-card factory set includes four Pro-Vision cards.

	MT	EX-MT	VG
COMPLETE SET (720)	15.00	6.75	1.90
COMPLETE FACT.SET (724)	18.00	8.00	2.30
COMMON PLAYER (1-720)	.04	.02	.01

		MT	EX-MT	VG
☐ 1	Troy Afenir	.10	.05	.01
☐ 2	Harold Baines	.07	.03	.01
☐ 3	Lance Blankenship	.04	.02	.01
☐ 4	Todd Burns	.04	.02	.01
☐ 5	Jose Canseco	.20	.09	.03
☐ 6	Dennis Eckersley	.12	.05	.02
☐ 7	Mike Gallego	.04	.02	.01
☐ 8	Ron Hassey	.04	.02	.01
☐ 9	Dave Henderson	.04	.02	.01
☐ 10	Rickey Henderson	.12	.05	.02
☐ 11	Rick Honeycutt	.04	.02	.01
☐ 12	Doug Jennings	.04	.02	.01
☐ 13	Joe Klink	.04	.02	.01
☐ 14	Carney Lansford	.07	.03	.01
☐ 15	Darren Lewis	.10	.05	.01
☐ 16	Willie McGee UER	.07	.03	.01
	(Height 6'11")			
☐ 17	Mark McGwire UER	.20	.09	.03
	(183 extra base hits in 1987)			
☐ 18	Mike Moore	.04	.02	.01
☐ 19	Gene Nelson	.04	.02	.01
☐ 20	Dave Otto	.04	.02	.01
☐ 21	Jamie Quirk	.04	.02	.01
☐ 22	Willie Randolph	.07	.03	.01
☐ 23	Scott Sanderson	.04	.02	.01
☐ 24	Terry Steinbach	.07	.03	.01
☐ 25	Dave Stewart	.07	.03	.01
☐ 26	Walt Weiss	.04	.02	.01
☐ 27	Bob Welch	.07	.03	.01
☐ 28	Curt Young	.04	.02	.01
☐ 29	Wally Backman	.04	.02	.01
☐ 30	Stan Belinda UER	.04	.02	.01
	(Born in Huntington, should be State College)			
☐ 31	Jay Bell	.07	.03	.01
☐ 32	Rafael Belliard	.04	.02	.01
☐ 33	Barry Bonds	.20	.09	.03
☐ 34	Bobby Bonilla	.10	.05	.01
☐ 35	Sid Bream	.04	.02	.01
☐ 36	Doug Drabek	.07	.03	.01
☐ 37	Carlos Garcia	.20	.09	.03
☐ 38	Neal Heaton	.04	.02	.01
☐ 39	Jeff King	.04	.02	.01
☐ 40	Bob Kipper	.04	.02	.01
☐ 41	Bill Landrum	.04	.02	.01

☐ 42 Mike LaValliere	.04	.02	.01
☐ 43 Jose Lind	.04	.02	.01
☐ 44 Carmelo Martinez	.04	.02	.01
☐ 45 Bob Patterson	.04	.02	.01
☐ 46 Ted Power	.04	.02	.01
☐ 47 Gary Redus	.04	.02	.01
☐ 48 R.J. Reynolds	.04	.02	.01
☐ 49 Don Slaught	.04	.02	.01
☐ 50 John Smiley	.07	.03	.01
☐ 51 Zane Smith	.04	.02	.01
☐ 52 Randy Tomlin	.20	.09	.03
☐ 53 Andy Van Slyke	.10	.05	.01
☐ 54 Bob Walk	.04	.02	.01
☐ 55 Jack Armstrong	.04	.02	.01
☐ 56 Todd Benzinger	.04	.02	.01
☐ 57 Glenn Braggs	.04	.02	.01
☐ 58 Keith Brown	.04	.02	.01
☐ 59 Tom Browning	.04	.02	.01
☐ 60 Norm Charlton	.07	.03	.01
☐ 61 Eric Davis	.07	.03	.01
☐ 62 Rob Dibble	.07	.03	.01
☐ 63 Bill Doran	.04	.02	.01
☐ 64 Mariano Duncan	.04	.02	.01
☐ 65 Chris Hammond	.10	.05	.01
☐ 66 Billy Hatcher	.04	.02	.01
☐ 67 Danny Jackson	.04	.02	.01
☐ 68 Barry Larkin	.10	.05	.01
☐ 69 Tim Layana	.04	.02	.01
(Black line over made			
in first text line)			
☐ 70 Terry Lee	.10	.05	.01
☐ 71 Rick Mahler	.04	.02	.01
☐ 72 Hal Morris	.07	.03	.01
☐ 73 Randy Myers	.07	.03	.01
☐ 74 Ron Oester	.04	.02	.01
☐ 75 Joe Oliver	.04	.02	.01
☐ 76 Paul O'Neill	.07	.03	.01
☐ 77 Luis Quinones	.04	.02	.01
☐ 78 Jeff Reed	.04	.02	.01
☐ 79 Jose Rijo	.07	.03	.01
☐ 80 Chris Sabo	.07	.03	.01
☐ 81 Scott Scudder	.04	.02	.01
☐ 82 Herm Winningham	.04	.02	.01
☐ 83 Larry Andersen	.04	.02	.01
☐ 84 Marty Barrett	.04	.02	.01
☐ 85 Mike Boddicker	.04	.02	.01
☐ 86 Wade Boggs	.12	.05	.02
☐ 87 Tom Bolton	.04	.02	.01
☐ 88 Tom Brunansky	.07	.03	.01
☐ 89 Ellis Burks	.07	.03	.01
☐ 90 Roger Clemens	.25	.11	.03
☐ 91 Scott Cooper	.25	.11	.03
☐ 92 John Dopson	.04	.02	.01
☐ 93 Dwight Evans	.07	.03	.01
☐ 94 Wes Gardner	.04	.02	.01
☐ 95 Jeff Gray	.04	.02	.01
☐ 96 Mike Greenwell	.07	.03	.01
☐ 97 Greg A. Harris	.04	.02	.01
☐ 98 Daryl Irvine	.04	.02	.01
☐ 99 Dana Kiecker	.04	.02	.01
☐ 100 Randy Kutcher	.04	.02	.01
☐ 101 Dennis Lamp	.04	.02	.01
☐ 102 Mike Marshall	.04	.02	.01
☐ 103 John Marzano	.04	.02	.01
☐ 104 Rob Murphy	.04	.02	.01
☐ 105 Tim Naehring	.07	.03	.01
☐ 106 Tony Pena	.04	.02	.01
☐ 107 Phil Plantier	.50	.23	.06
☐ 108 Carlos Quintana	.04	.02	.01
☐ 109 Jeff Reardon	.07	.03	.01
☐ 110 Jerry Reed	.04	.02	.01
☐ 111 Jody Reed	.04	.02	.01
☐ 112 Luis Rivera UER	.04	.02	.01
(Born 1/3/84)			
☐ 113 Kevin Romine	.04	.02	.01
☐ 114 Phil Bradley	.04	.02	.01
☐ 115 Ivan Calderon	.04	.02	.01
☐ 116 Wayne Edwards	.04	.02	.01
☐ 117 Alex Fernandez	.12	.05	.02
☐ 118 Carlton Fisk	.10	.05	.01
☐ 119 Scott Fletcher	.04	.02	.01
☐ 120 Craig Grebeck	.04	.02	.01
☐ 121 Ozzie Guillen	.04	.02	.01
☐ 122 Greg Hibbard	.04	.02	.01
☐ 123 Lance Johnson UER	.04	.02	.01
(Born Cincinnati, should			
be Lincoln Heights)			
☐ 124 Barry Jones	.04	.02	.01
☐ 125 Ron Karkovice	.04	.02	.01
☐ 126 Eric King	.04	.02	.01
☐ 127 Steve Lyons	.04	.02	.01
☐ 128 Carlos Martinez	.04	.02	.01
☐ 129 Jack McDowell UER	.10	.05	.01
(Stanford misspelled			
as Standford on back)			
☐ 130 Donn Pall	.04	.02	.01
(No dots over any			
i's in text)			
☐ 131 Dan Pasqua	.04	.02	.01
☐ 132 Ken Patterson	.04	.02	.01
☐ 133 Melido Perez	.07	.03	.01
☐ 134 Adam Peterson	.04	.02	.01
☐ 135 Scott Radinsky	.04	.02	.01
☐ 136 Sammy Sosa	.07	.03	.01
☐ 137 Bobby Thigpen	.04	.02	.01
☐ 138 Frank Thomas	1.25	.55	.16
☐ 139 Robin Ventura	.20	.09	.03
☐ 140 Daryl Boston	.04	.02	.01
☐ 141 Chuck Carr	.04	.02	.01
☐ 142 Mark Carreon	.04	.02	.01
☐ 143 David Cone	.10	.05	.01
☐ 144 Ron Darling	.04	.02	.01
☐ 145 Kevin Elster	.04	.02	.01
☐ 146 Sid Fernandez	.07	.03	.01

☐ 147	John Franco	.07	.03	.01
☐ 148	Dwight Gooden	.07	.03	.01
☐ 149	Tom Herr	.04	.02	.01
☐ 150	Todd Hundley	.04	.02	.01
☐ 151	Gregg Jefferies	.07	.03	.01
☐ 152	Howard Johnson	.07	.03	.01
☐ 153	Dave Magadan	.07	.03	.01
☐ 154	Kevin McReynolds	.07	.03	.01
☐ 155	Keith Miller UER	.04	.02	.01

(Text says Rochester in
'87, stats say Tide-
water, mixed up with
other Keith Miller)

☐ 156	Bob Ojeda	.04	.02	.01
☐ 157	Tom O'Malley	.04	.02	.01
☐ 158	Alejandro Pena	.04	.02	.01
☐ 159	Darren Reed	.04	.02	.01
☐ 160	Mackey Sasser	.04	.02	.01
☐ 161	Darryl Strawberry	.12	.05	.02
☐ 162	Tim Teufel	.04	.02	.01
☐ 163	Kelvin Torve	.04	.02	.01
☐ 164	Julio Valera	.15	.07	.02
☐ 165	Frank Viola	.07	.03	.01
☐ 166	Wally Whitehurst	.04	.02	.01
☐ 167	Jim Acker	.04	.02	.01
☐ 168	Derek Bell	.30	.14	.04
☐ 169	George Bell	.07	.03	.01
☐ 170	Willie Blair	.04	.02	.01
☐ 171	Pat Borders	.04	.02	.01
☐ 172	John Cerutti	.04	.02	.01
☐ 173	Junior Felix	.04	.02	.01
☐ 174	Tony Fernandez	.07	.03	.01
☐ 175	Kelly Gruber UER	.07	.03	.01

(Born in Houston,
should be Bellaire)

☐ 176	Tom Henke	.07	.03	.01
☐ 177	Glenallen Hill	.04	.02	.01
☐ 178	Jimmy Key	.04	.02	.01
☐ 179	Manny Lee	.04	.02	.01
☐ 180	Fred McGriff	.12	.05	.02
☐ 181	Rance Mulliniks	.04	.02	.01
☐ 182	Greg Myers	.04	.02	.01
☐ 183	John Olerud	.15	.07	.02
☐ 184	Luis Sojo	.04	.02	.01
☐ 185	Dave Stieb	.04	.02	.01
☐ 186	Todd Stottlemyre	.07	.03	.01
☐ 187	Duane Ward	.04	.02	.01
☐ 188	David Wells	.04	.02	.01
☐ 189	Mark Whiten	.10	.05	.01
☐ 190	Ken Williams	.04	.02	.01
☐ 191	Frank Wills	.04	.02	.01
☐ 192	Mookie Wilson	.04	.02	.01
☐ 193	Don Aase	.04	.02	.01
☐ 194	Tim Belcher UER	.07	.03	.01

(Born Sparta, Ohio,
should say Mt. Gilead)

☐ 195	Hubie Brooks	.04	.02	.01

☐ 196	Dennis Cook	.04	.02	.01
☐ 197	Tim Crews	.04	.02	.01
☐ 198	Kal Daniels	.04	.02	.01
☐ 199	Kirk Gibson	.07	.03	.01
☐ 200	Jim Gott	.04	.02	.01
☐ 201	Alfredo Griffin	.04	.02	.01
☐ 202	Chris Gwynn	.04	.02	.01
☐ 203	Dave Hansen	.04	.02	.01
☐ 204	Lenny Harris	.04	.02	.01
☐ 205	Mike Hartley	.04	.02	.01
☐ 206	Mickey Hatcher	.04	.02	.01
☐ 207	Carlos Hernandez	.10	.05	.01
☐ 208	Orel Hershiser	.07	.03	.01
☐ 209	Jay Howell UER	.04	.02	.01

(No 1982 Yankee stats)

☐ 210	Mike Huff	.04	.02	.01
☐ 211	Stan Javier	.04	.02	.01
☐ 212	Ramon Martinez	.10	.05	.01
☐ 213	Mike Morgan	.04	.02	.01
☐ 214	Eddie Murray	.10	.05	.01
☐ 215	Jim Neidlinger	.04	.02	.01
☐ 216	Jose Offerman	.10	.05	.01
☐ 217	Jim Poole	.04	.02	.01
☐ 218	Juan Samuel	.04	.02	.01
☐ 219	Mike Scioscia	.04	.02	.01
☐ 220	Ray Searage	.04	.02	.01
☐ 221	Mike Sharperson	.04	.02	.01
☐ 222	Fernando Valenzuela	.07	.03	.01
☐ 223	Jose Vizcaino	.04	.02	.01
☐ 224	Mike Aldrete	.04	.02	.01
☐ 225	Scott Anderson	.10	.05	.01
☐ 226	Dennis Boyd	.04	.02	.01
☐ 227	Tim Burke	.04	.02	.01
☐ 228	Delino DeShields	.15	.07	.02
☐ 229	Mike Fitzgerald	.04	.02	.01
☐ 230	Tom Foley	.04	.02	.01
☐ 231	Steve Frey	.04	.02	.01
☐ 232	Andres Galarraga	.04	.02	.01
☐ 233	Mark Gardner	.04	.02	.01
☐ 234	Marquis Grissom	.15	.07	.02
☐ 235	Kevin Gross UER	.04	.02	.01

(No date given for
first Expos win)

☐ 236	Drew Hall	.04	.02	.01
☐ 237	Dave Martinez	.04	.02	.01
☐ 238	Dennis Martinez	.07	.03	.01
☐ 239	Dale Mohorcic	.04	.02	.01
☐ 240	Chris Nabholz	.07	.03	.01
☐ 241	Otis Nixon	.04	.02	.01
☐ 242	Junior Noboa	.04	.02	.01
☐ 243	Spike Owen	.04	.02	.01
☐ 244	Tim Raines	.07	.03	.01
☐ 245	Mel Rojas UER	.10	.05	.01

(Stats show 3.60 ERA,
bio says 3.19 ERA)

☐ 246	Scott Ruskin	.04	.02	.01
☐ 247	Bill Sampen	.04	.02	.01

☐ 248	Nelson Santovenia	.04	.02	.01
☐ 249	Dave Schmidt	.04	.02	.01
☐ 250	Larry Walker	.20	.09	.03
☐ 251	Tim Wallach	.07	.03	.01
☐ 252	Dave Anderson	.04	.02	.01
☐ 253	Kevin Bass	.04	.02	.01
☐ 254	Steve Bedrosian	.04	.02	.01
☐ 255	Jeff Brantley	.04	.02	.01
☐ 256	John Burkett	.04	.02	.01
☐ 257	Brett Butler	.07	.03	.01
☐ 258	Gary Carter	.07	.03	.01
☐ 259	Will Clark	.20	.09	.03
☐ 260	Steve Decker	.15	.07	.02
☐ 261	Kelly Downs	.04	.02	.01
☐ 262	Scott Garrelts	.04	.02	.01
☐ 263	Terry Kennedy	.04	.02	.01
☐ 264	Mike LaCoss	.04	.02	.01
☐ 265	Mark Leonard	.10	.05	.01
☐ 266	Greg Litton	.04	.02	.01
☐ 267	Kevin Mitchell	.07	.03	.01
☐ 268	Randy O'Neal	.04	.02	.01
☐ 269	Rick Parker	.04	.02	.01
☐ 270	Rick Reuschel	.04	.02	.01
☐ 271	Ernest Riles	.04	.02	.01
☐ 272	Don Robinson	.04	.02	.01
☐ 273	Robby Thompson	.04	.02	.01
☐ 274	Mark Thurmond	.04	.02	.01
☐ 275	Jose Uribe	.04	.02	.01
☐ 276	Matt Williams	.07	.03	.01
☐ 277	Trevor Wilson	.04	.02	.01
☐ 278	Gerald Alexander	.10	.05	.01
☐ 279	Brad Arnsberg	.04	.02	.01
☐ 280	Kevin Belcher	.10	.05	.01
☐ 281	Joe Bitker	.04	.02	.01
☐ 282	Kevin Brown	.07	.03	.01
☐ 283	Steve Buechele	.04	.02	.01
☐ 284	Jack Daugherty	.04	.02	.01
☐ 285	Julio Franco	.07	.03	.01
☐ 286	Juan Gonzalez	.35	.16	.04
☐ 287	Bill Haselman	.10	.05	.01
☐ 288	Charlie Hough	.04	.02	.01
☐ 289	Jeff Huson	.04	.02	.01
☐ 290	Pete Incaviglia	.04	.02	.01
☐ 291	Mike Jeffcoat	.04	.02	.01
☐ 292	Jeff Kunkel	.04	.02	.01
☐ 293	Gary Mielke	.04	.02	.01
☐ 294	Jamie Moyer	.04	.02	.01
☐ 295	Rafael Palmeiro	.10	.05	.01
☐ 296	Geno Petralli	.04	.02	.01
☐ 297	Gary Pettis	.04	.02	.01
☐ 298	Kevin Reimer	.10	.05	.01
☐ 299	Kenny Rogers	.04	.02	.01
☐ 300	Jeff Russell	.04	.02	.01
☐ 301	John Russell	.04	.02	.01
☐ 302	Nolan Ryan	.40	.18	.05
☐ 303	Ruben Sierra	.15	.07	.02
☐ 304	Bobby Witt	.04	.02	.01
☐ 305	Jim Abbott	.12	.05	.02
☐ 306	Kent Anderson	.04	.02	.01
☐ 307	Dante Bichette	.04	.02	.01
☐ 308	Bert Blyleven	.07	.03	.01
☐ 309	Chili Davis	.07	.03	.01
☐ 310	Brian Downing	.04	.02	.01
☐ 311	Mark Eichhorn	.04	.02	.01
☐ 312	Mike Fetters	.04	.02	.01
☐ 313	Chuck Finley	.07	.03	.01
☐ 314	Willie Fraser	.04	.02	.01
☐ 315	Bryan Harvey	.04	.02	.01
☐ 316	Donnie Hill	.04	.02	.01
☐ 317	Wally Joyner	.07	.03	.01
☐ 318	Mark Langston	.07	.03	.01
☐ 319	Kirk McCaskill	.04	.02	.01
☐ 320	John Orton	.04	.02	.01
☐ 321	Lance Parrish	.07	.03	.01
☐ 322	Luis Polonia UER	.07	.03	.01
	(1984 Madison,			
	should be Madison)			
☐ 323	Johnny Ray	.04	.02	.01
☐ 324	Bobby Rose	.04	.02	.01
☐ 325	Dick Schofield	.04	.02	.01
☐ 326	Rick Schu	.04	.02	.01
☐ 327	Lee Stevens	.04	.02	.01
☐ 328	Devon White	.07	.03	.01
☐ 329	Dave Winfield	.10	.05	.01
☐ 330	Cliff Young	.04	.02	.01
☐ 331	Dave Bergman	.04	.02	.01
☐ 332	Phil Clark	.15	.07	.02
☐ 333	Darnell Coles	.04	.02	.01
☐ 334	Milt Cuyler	.10	.05	.01
☐ 335	Cecil Fielder	.12	.05	.02
☐ 336	Travis Fryman	.50	.23	.06
☐ 337	Paul Gibson	.04	.02	.01
☐ 338	Jerry Don Gleaton	.04	.02	.01
☐ 339	Mike Heath	.04	.02	.01
☐ 340	Mike Henneman	.04	.02	.01
☐ 341	Chet Lemon	.04	.02	.01
☐ 342	Lance McCullers	.04	.02	.01
☐ 343	Jack Morris	.10	.05	.01
☐ 344	Lloyd Moseby	.04	.02	.01
☐ 345	Edwin Nunez	.04	.02	.01
☐ 346	Clay Parker	.04	.02	.01
☐ 347	Dan Petry	.04	.02	.01
☐ 348	Tony Phillips	.04	.02	.01
☐ 349	Jeff M. Robinson	.04	.02	.01
☐ 350	Mark Salas	.04	.02	.01
☐ 351	Mike Schwabe	.04	.02	.01
☐ 352	Larry Sheets	.04	.02	.01
☐ 353	John Shelby	.04	.02	.01
☐ 354	Frank Tanana	.04	.02	.01
☐ 355	Alan Trammell	.07	.03	.01
☐ 356	Gary Ward	.04	.02	.01
☐ 357	Lou Whitaker	.07	.03	.01
☐ 358	Beau Allred	.04	.02	.01
☐ 359	Sandy Alomar Jr.	.07	.03	.01

☐ 360 Carlos Baerga	.20	.09	.03
☐ 361 Kevin Bearse	.04	.02	.01
☐ 362 Tom Brookens	.04	.02	.01
☐ 363 Jerry Browne UER	.04	.02	.01
(No dot over i in			
first text line)			
☐ 364 Tom Candiotti	.04	.02	.01
☐ 365 Alex Cole	.04	.02	.01
☐ 366 John Farrell UER	.04	.02	.01
(Born in Neptune,			
should be Monmouth)			
☐ 367 Felix Fermin	.04	.02	.01
☐ 368 Keith Hernandez	.07	.03	.01
☐ 369 Brook Jacoby	.04	.02	.01
☐ 370 Chris James	.04	.02	.01
☐ 371 Dion James	.04	.02	.01
☐ 372 Doug Jones	.04	.02	.01
☐ 373 Candy Maldonado	.04	.02	.01
☐ 374 Steve Olin	.07	.03	.01
☐ 375 Jesse Orosco	.04	.02	.01
☐ 376 Rudy Seanez	.07	.03	.01
☐ 377 Joel Skinner	.04	.02	.01
☐ 378 Cory Snyder	.04	.02	.01
☐ 379 Greg Swindell	.07	.03	.01
☐ 380 Sergio Valdez	.04	.02	.01
☐ 381 Mike Walker	.04	.02	.01
☐ 382 Colby Ward	.04	.02	.01
☐ 383 Turner Ward	.10	.05	.01
☐ 384 Mitch Webster	.04	.02	.01
☐ 385 Kevin Wickander	.04	.02	.01
☐ 386 Darrel Akerfelds	.04	.02	.01
☐ 387 Joe Boever	.04	.02	.01
☐ 388 Rod Booker	.04	.02	.01
☐ 389 Sil Campusano	.04	.02	.01
☐ 390 Don Carman	.04	.02	.01
☐ 391 Wes Chamberlain	.20	.09	.03
☐ 392 Pat Combs	.04	.02	.01
☐ 393 Darren Daulton	.07	.03	.01
☐ 394 Jose DeJesus	.04	.02	.01
☐ 395 Len Dykstra	.07	.03	.01
☐ 396 Jason Grimsley	.04	.02	.01
☐ 397 Charlie Hayes	.04	.02	.01
☐ 398 Von Hayes	.04	.02	.01
☐ 399 David Hollins UER	.12	.05	.02
(Atl-bats, should			
say at-bats)			
☐ 400 Ken Howell	.04	.02	.01
☐ 401 Ricky Jordan	.04	.02	.01
☐ 402 John Kruk	.07	.03	.01
☐ 403 Steve Lake	.04	.02	.01
☐ 404 Chuck Malone	.04	.02	.01
☐ 405 Roger McDowell UER	.04	.02	.01
(Says Phillies is			
saves, should say in)			
☐ 406 Chuck McElroy	.04	.02	.01
☐ 407 Mickey Morandini	.12	.05	.02
☐ 408 Terry Mulholland	.04	.02	.01

☐ 409 Dale Murphy	.07	.03	.01
☐ 410A Randy Ready ERR	.04	.02	.01
(No Brewers stats			
listed for 1983)			
☐ 410B Randy Ready COR	.04	.02	.01
☐ 411 Bruce Ruffin	.04	.02	.01
☐ 412 Dickie Thon	.04	.02	.01
☐ 413 Paul Assenmacher	.04	.02	.01
☐ 414 Damon Berryhill	.04	.02	.01
☐ 415 Mike Bielecki	.04	.02	.01
☐ 416 Shawn Boskie	.04	.02	.01
☐ 417 Dave Clark	.04	.02	.01
☐ 418 Doug Dascenzo	.04	.02	.01
☐ 419A Andre Dawson ERR	.10	.05	.01
(No stats for 1976)			
☐ 419B Andre Dawson COR	.10	.05	.01
☐ 420 Shawon Dunston	.07	.03	.01
☐ 421 Joe Girardi	.04	.02	.01
☐ 422 Mark Grace	.10	.05	.01
☐ 423 Mike Harkey	.07	.03	.01
☐ 424 Les Lancaster	.04	.02	.01
☐ 425 Bill Long	.04	.02	.01
☐ 426 Greg Maddux	.10	.05	.01
☐ 427 Derrick May	.07	.03	.01
☐ 428 Jeff Pico	.04	.02	.01
☐ 429 Domingo Ramos	.04	.02	.01
☐ 430 Luis Salazar	.04	.02	.01
☐ 431 Ryne Sandberg	.25	.11	.03
☐ 432 Dwight Smith	.04	.02	.01
☐ 433 Greg Smith	.04	.02	.01
☐ 434 Rick Sutcliffe	.07	.03	.01
☐ 435 Gary Varsho	.04	.02	.01
☐ 436 Hector Villanueva	.04	.02	.01
☐ 437 Jerome Walton	.04	.02	.01
☐ 438 Curtis Wilkerson	.04	.02	.01
☐ 439 Mitch Williams	.04	.02	.01
☐ 440 Steve Wilson	.04	.02	.01
☐ 441 Marvell Wynne	.04	.02	.01
☐ 442 Scott Bankhead	.04	.02	.01
☐ 443 Scott Bradley	.04	.02	.01
☐ 444 Greg Briley	.04	.02	.01
☐ 445 Mike Brumley UER	.04	.02	.01
(Text 40 SB's in 1988,			
stats say 41)			
☐ 446 Jay Buhner	.07	.03	.01
☐ 447 Dave Burba	.10	.05	.01
☐ 448 Henry Cotto	.04	.02	.01
☐ 449 Alvin Davis	.04	.02	.01
☐ 450A Ken Griffey Jr. ERR	.50	.23	.06
(Bat .300)			
☐ 450B Ken Griffey Jr. COR	.50	.23	.06
(Bat around .300)			
☐ 451 Erik Hanson	.04	.02	.01
☐ 452 Gene Harris UER	.04	.02	.01
(63 career runs,			
should be 73)			
☐ 453 Brian Holman	.04	.02	.01

☐ 454	Mike Jackson................04	.02	.01
☐ 455	Randy Johnson...............07	.03	.01
☐ 456	Jeffrey Leonard............04	.02	.01
☐ 457	Edgar Martinez............07	.03	.01
☐ 458	Tino Martinez................10	.05	.01
☐ 459	Pete O'Brien UER........04	.02	.01
	(1987 BA .266,		
	should be .286)		
☐ 460	Harold Reynolds.........04	.02	.01
☐ 461	Mike Schooler..............04	.02	.01
☐ 462	Bill Swift.....................04	.02	.01
☐ 463	David Valle...................04	.02	.01
☐ 464	Omar Vizquel...............04	.02	.01
☐ 465	Matt Young...................04	.02	.01
☐ 466	Brady Anderson...........07	.03	.01
☐ 467	Jeff Ballard UER...........04	.02	.01
	(Missing top of right		
	parenthesis after		
	Saberhagen in last		
	text line)		
☐ 468	Juan Bell....................04	.02	.01
☐ 469A	Mike Devereaux ERR 07	.03	.01
	(First line of text		
	ends with six)		
☐ 469B	Mike Devereaux COR 07	.03	.01
	(First line of text		
	ends with runs)		
☐ 470	Steve Finley................07	.03	.01
☐ 471	Dave Gallagher............04	.02	.01
☐ 472	Leo Gomez...................25	.11	.03
☐ 473	Rene Gonzales.............04	.02	.01
☐ 474	Pete Harnisch..............07	.03	.01
☐ 475	Kevin Hickey................04	.02	.01
☐ 476	Chris Hoiles.................10	.05	.01
☐ 477	Sam Horn....................04	.02	.01
☐ 478	Tim Hulett....................04	.02	.01
	(Photo shows National		
	Leaguer sliding into		
	second base)		
☐ 479	Dave Johnson...............04	.02	.01
☐ 480	Ron Kittle UER............04	.02	.01
	(Edmonton misspelled		
	as Edmundton)		
☐ 481	Ben McDonald..............10	.05	.01
☐ 482	Bob Melvin...................04	.02	.01
☐ 483	Bob Milacki..................04	.02	.01
☐ 484	Randy Milligan.............04	.02	.01
☐ 485	John Mitchell................04	.02	.01
☐ 486	Gregg Olson.................07	.03	.01
☐ 487	Joe Orsulak.................04	.02	.01
☐ 488	Joe Price.....................04	.02	.01
☐ 489	Bill Ripken...................04	.02	.01
☐ 490	Cal Ripken...................30	.14	.04
☐ 491	Curt Schilling...............07	.03	.01
☐ 492	David Segui..................04	.02	.01
☐ 493	Anthony Telford............04	.02	.01
☐ 494	Mickey Tettleton...........07	.03	.01
☐ 495	Mark Williamson..........04	.02	.01
☐ 496	Craig Worthington 04	.02	.01
☐ 497	Juan Agosto.................04	.02	.01
☐ 498	Eric Anthony................07	.03	.01
☐ 499	Craig Biggio.................07	.03	.01
☐ 500	Ken Caminiti UER.........07	.03	.01
	(Born 4/4, should		
	be 4/21)		
☐ 501	Casey Candaele...........04	.02	.01
☐ 502	Andujar Cedeno 12	.05	.02
☐ 503	Danny Darwin...............04	.02	.01
☐ 504	Mark Davidson.............04	.02	.01
☐ 505	Glenn Davis..................07	.03	.01
☐ 506	Jim Deshaies...............04	.02	.01
☐ 507	Luis Gonzalez...............20	.09	.03
☐ 508	Bill Gullickson.............04	.02	.01
☐ 509	Xavier Hernandez.........04	.02	.01
☐ 510	Brian Meyer.................04	.02	.01
☐ 511	Ken Oberkfell................04	.02	.01
☐ 512	Mark Portugal...............04	.02	.01
☐ 513	Rafael Ramirez.............04	.02	.01
☐ 514	Karl Rhodes.................04	.02	.01
☐ 515	Mike Scott...................04	.02	.01
☐ 516	Mike Simms..................10	.05	.01
☐ 517	Dave Smith...................04	.02	.01
☐ 518	Franklin Stubbs............04	.02	.01
☐ 519	Glenn Wilson................04	.02	.01
☐ 520	Eric Yelding UER...........04	.02	.01
	(Text has 63 steals,		
	stats have 64,		
	which is correct)		
☐ 521	Gerald Young................04	.02	.01
☐ 522	Shawn Abner................04	.02	.01
☐ 523	Roberto Alomar 20	.09	.03
☐ 524	Andy Benes..................10	.05	.01
☐ 525	Joe Carter....................12	.05	.02
☐ 526	Jack Clark...................07	.03	.01
☐ 527	Joey Cora....................04	.02	.01
☐ 528	Paul Faries...................04	.02	.01
☐ 529	Tony Gwynn..................12	.05	.02
☐ 530	Atlee Hammaker............04	.02	.01
☐ 531	Greg W. Harris..............04	.02	.01
☐ 532	Thomas Howard............04	.02	.01
☐ 533	Bruce Hurst.................07	.03	.01
☐ 534	Craig Lefferts..............04	.02	.01
☐ 535	Derek Lilliquist............04	.02	.01
☐ 536	Fred Lynn....................07	.03	.01
☐ 537	Mike Pagliarulo............04	.02	.01
☐ 538	Mark Parent.................04	.02	.01
☐ 539	Dennis Rasmussen 04	.02	.01
☐ 540	Bip Roberts..................07	.03	.01
☐ 541	Richard Rodriguez.........04	.02	.01
☐ 542	Benito Santiago...........07	.03	.01
☐ 543	Calvin Schiraldi............04	.02	.01
☐ 544	Eric Show.....................04	.02	.01
☐ 545	Phil Stephenson...........04	.02	.01
☐ 546	Garry Templeton UER....04	.02	.01

(Born 3/24/57,
should be 3/24/56)

☐ 547	Ed Whitson	.04	.02	.01
☐ 548	Eddie Williams	.04	.02	.01
☐ 549	Kevin Appier	.07	.03	.01
☐ 550	Luis Aquino	.04	.02	.01
☐ 551	Bob Boone	.07	.03	.01
☐ 552	George Brett	.10	.05	.01
☐ 553	Jeff Conine	.25	.11	.03
☐ 554	Steve Crawford	.04	.02	.01
☐ 555	Mark Davis	.04	.02	.01
☐ 556	Storm Davis	.04	.02	.01
☐ 557	Jim Eisenreich	.04	.02	.01
☐ 558	Steve Farr	.04	.02	.01
☐ 559	Tom Gordon	.07	.03	.01
☐ 560	Mark Gubicza	.04	.02	.01
☐ 561	Bo Jackson	.12	.05	.02
☐ 562	Mike Macfarlane	.04	.02	.01
☐ 563	Brian McRae	.20	.09	.03
☐ 564	Jeff Montgomery	.04	.02	.01
☐ 565	Bill Pecota	.04	.02	.01
☐ 566	Gerald Perry	.04	.02	.01
☐ 567	Bret Saberhagen	.07	.03	.01
☐ 568	Jeff Schulz	.04	.02	.01
☐ 569	Kevin Seitzer	.07	.03	.01
☐ 570	Terry Shumpert	.04	.02	.01
☐ 571	Kurt Stillwell	.04	.02	.01
☐ 572	Danny Tartabull	.07	.03	.01
☐ 573	Gary Thurman	.04	.02	.01
☐ 574	Frank White	.04	.02	.01
☐ 575	Willie Wilson	.04	.02	.01
☐ 576	Chris Bosio	.04	.02	.01
☐ 577	Greg Brock	.04	.02	.01
☐ 578	George Canale	.04	.02	.01
☐ 579	Chuck Crim	.04	.02	.01
☐ 580	Rob Deer	.07	.03	.01
☐ 581	Edgar Diaz	.04	.02	.01
☐ 582	Tom Edens	.10	.05	.01
☐ 583	Mike Felder	.04	.02	.01
☐ 584	Jim Gantner	.04	.02	.01
☐ 585	Darryl Hamilton	.07	.03	.01
☐ 586	Ted Higuera	.04	.02	.01
☐ 587	Mark Knudson	.04	.02	.01
☐ 588	Bill Krueger	.04	.02	.01
☐ 589	Tim McIntosh	.04	.02	.01
☐ 590	Paul Mirabella	.04	.02	.01
☐ 591	Paul Molitor	.10	.05	.01
☐ 592	Jaime Navarro	.07	.03	.01
☐ 593	Dave Parker	.07	.03	.01
☐ 594	Dan Plesac	.04	.02	.01
☐ 595	Ron Robinson	.04	.02	.01
☐ 596	Gary Sheffield	.25	.11	.03
☐ 597	Bill Spiers	.04	.02	.01
☐ 598	B.J. Surhoff	.04	.02	.01
☐ 599	Greg Vaughn	.10	.05	.01
☐ 600	Randy Veres	.04	.02	.01
☐ 601	Robin Yount	.10	.05	.01

☐ 602	Rick Aguilera	.07	.03	.01
☐ 603	Allan Anderson	.04	.02	.01
☐ 604	Juan Berenguer	.04	.02	.01
☐ 605	Randy Bush	.04	.02	.01
☐ 606	Carmen Castillo	.04	.02	.01
☐ 607	Tim Drummond	.04	.02	.01
☐ 608	Scott Erickson	.20	.09	.03
☐ 609	Gary Gaetti	.04	.02	.01
☐ 610	Greg Gagne	.04	.02	.01
☐ 611	Dan Gladden	.04	.02	.01
☐ 612	Mark Guthrie	.04	.02	.01
☐ 613	Brian Harper	.04	.02	.01
☐ 614	Kent Hrbek	.07	.03	.01
☐ 615	Gene Larkin	.04	.02	.01
☐ 616	Terry Leach	.04	.02	.01
☐ 617	Nelson Liriano	.04	.02	.01
☐ 618	Shane Mack	.07	.03	.01
☐ 619	John Moses	.04	.02	.01
☐ 620	Pedro Munoz	.25	.11	.03
☐ 621	Al Newman	.04	.02	.01
☐ 622	Junior Ortiz	.04	.02	.01
☐ 623	Kirby Puckett	.20	.09	.03
☐ 624	Roy Smith	.04	.02	.01
☐ 625	Kevin Tapani	.07	.03	.01
☐ 626	Gary Wayne	.04	.02	.01
☐ 627	David West	.04	.02	.01
☐ 628	Cris Carpenter	.04	.02	.01
☐ 629	Vince Coleman	.07	.03	.01
☐ 630	Ken Dayley	.04	.02	.01
☐ 631	Jose DeLeon	.04	.02	.01
☐ 632	Frank DiPino	.04	.02	.01
☐ 633	Bernard Gilkey	.15	.07	.02
☐ 634	Pedro Guerrero	.07	.03	.01
☐ 635	Ken Hill	.07	.03	.01
☐ 636	Felix Jose	.07	.03	.01
☐ 637	Ray Lankford	.40	.18	.05
☐ 638	Joe Magrane	.04	.02	.01
☐ 639	Tom Niedenfuer	.04	.02	.01
☐ 640	Jose Oquendo	.04	.02	.01
☐ 641	Tom Pagnozzi	.04	.02	.01
☐ 642	Terry Pendleton	.10	.05	.01
☐ 643	Mike Perez	.15	.07	.02
☐ 644	Bryn Smith	.04	.02	.01
☐ 645	Lee Smith	.07	.03	.01
☐ 646	Ozzie Smith	.10	.05	.01
☐ 647	Scott Terry	.04	.02	.01
☐ 648	Bob Tewksbury	.07	.03	.01
☐ 649	Milt Thompson	.04	.02	.01
☐ 650	John Tudor	.04	.02	.01
☐ 651	Denny Walling	.04	.02	.01
☐ 652	Craig Wilson	.10	.05	.01
☐ 653	Todd Worrell	.04	.02	.01
☐ 654	Todd Zeile	.07	.03	.01
☐ 655	Oscar Azocar	.04	.02	.01
☐ 656	Steve Balboni UER	.04	.02	.01

(Born 1/5/57,
should be 1/16)

☐	657 Jesse Barfield 04	.02	.01
☐	658 Greg Cadaret 04	.02	.01
☐	659 Chuck Cary 04	.02	.01
☐	660 Rick Cerone 04	.02	.01
☐	661 Dave Eiland 04	.02	.01
☐	662 Alvaro Espinoza 04	.02	.01
☐	663 Bob Geren 04	.02	.01
☐	664 Lee Guetterman 04	.02	.01
☐	665 Mel Hall 04	.02	.01
☐	666 Andy Hawkins 04	.02	.01
☐	667 Jimmy Jones 04	.02	.01
☐	668 Roberto Kelly 07	.03	.01
☐	669 Dave LaPoint UER 04	.02	.01
	(No '81 Brewers stats, totals also are wrong)		
☐	670 Tim Leary 04	.02	.01
☐	671 Jim Leyritz 04	.02	.01
☐	672 Kevin Maas 10	.05	.01
☐	673 Don Mattingly 15	.07	.02
☐	674 Matt Nokes 04	.02	.01
☐	675 Pascual Perez 04	.02	.01
☐	676 Eric Plunk 04	.02	.01
☐	677 Dave Righetti 04	.02	.01
☐	678 Jeff D. Robinson 04	.02	.01
☐	679 Steve Sax 07	.03	.01
☐	680 Mike Witt 04	.02	.01
☐	681 Steve Avery UER 20	.09	.03
	(Born in New Jersey, should say Michigan)		
☐	682 Mike Bell 10	.05	.01
☐	683 Jeff Blauser 04	.02	.01
☐	684 Francisco Cabrera UER ...04	.02	.01
	(Born 10/16, should say 10/10)		
☐	685 Tony Castillo 04	.02	.01
☐	686 Marty Clary UER 04	.02	.01
	(Shown pitching righty, but bio has left)		
☐	687 Nick Esasky 04	.02	.01
☐	688 Ron Gant 12	.05	.02
☐	689 Tom Glavine 20	.09	.03
☐	690 Mark Grant 04	.02	.01
☐	691 Tommy Gregg 04	.02	.01
☐	692 Dwayne Henry 04	.02	.01
☐	693 Dave Justice 30	.14	.04
☐	694 Jimmy Kremers 04	.02	.01
☐	695 Charlie Leibrandt 04	.02	.01
☐	696 Mark Lemke 04	.02	.01
☐	697 Oddibe McDowell 04	.02	.01
☐	698 Greg Olson 04	.02	.01
☐	699 Jeff Parrett 04	.02	.01
☐	700 Jim Presley 04	.02	.01
☐	701 Victor Rosario 10	.05	.01
☐	702 Lonnie Smith 04	.02	.01
☐	703 Pete Smith 07	.03	.01
☐	704 John Smoltz 10	.05	.01
☐	705 Mike Stanton 04	.02	.01

☐	706 Andres Thomas............04	.02	.01
☐	707 Jeff Treadway 04	.02	.01
☐	708 Jim Vatcher 04	.02	.01
☐	709 Home Run Kings...........12	.05	.02
	Ryne Sandberg		
	Cecil Fielder		
☐	710 2nd Generation Stars......25	.11	.03
	Barry Bonds		
	Ken Griffey Jr.		
☐	711 NLCS Team Leaders 08	.04	.01
	Bobby Bonilla		
	Barry Larkin		
☐	712 Top Game Savers...........05	.02	.01
	Bobby Thigpen		
	John Franco		
☐	713 Chicago's 100 Club........10	.05	.01
	Andre Dawson		
	Ryne Sandberg UER		
	(Ryno misspelled Rhino)		
☐	714 CL:A's/Pirates.............05	.01	.00
	Reds/Red Sox		
☐	715 CL:White Sox/Mets.......05	.01	.00
	Blue Jays/Dodgers		
☐	716 CL:Expos/Giants...........05	.01	.00
	Rangers/Angels		
☐	717 CL:Tigers/Indians.........05	.01	.00
	Phillies/Cubs		
☐	718 CL:Mariners/Orioles.......05	.01	.00
	Astros/Padres		
☐	719 CL:Royals/Brewers........05	.01	.00
	Twins/Canada		
☐	720 CL:Yankees/Braves........05	.01	.00
	Superstars/Specials		

1991 Fleer All-Star Inserts

For the sixth consecutive year Fleer issued an All-Star insert set. This year the cards were only available in Fleer cello packs. This ten-card set measures the standard size of 2 1/2" by 3 1/2" and is reminiscent of the 1971 Topps Greatest Moments set with two pictures on the (black-bordered) front as well as a photo on the back.

	MT	EX-MT	VG
COMPLETE SET (10) 16.00	7.25	2.00
COMMON PLAYER (1-10) 40	.18	.05

☐ 1 Ryne Sandberg 2.50	1.15	.30

Chicago White Sox (11-15), Cleveland Indians (16-21), Detroit Tigers (22-24), Kansas City Royals (25-28), Milwaukee Brewers (29-35), Minnesota Twins (36-41), New York Yankees (42-49), Oakland Athletics (50-51), Seattle Mariners (52-57), Texas Rangers (58-62), Toronto Blue Jays (63-69), Atlanta Braves (70-76), Chicago Cubs (77-83), Cincinnati Reds (84-86), Houston Astros (87-90), Los Angeles Dodgers (91-96), Montreal Expos (97-99), New York Mets (100-104), Philadelphia Phillies (105-110), Pittsburgh Pirates (111-115), St. Louis Cardinals (116-119), San Diego Padres (120-127), and San Francisco Giants (128-131). The key Rookie Cards in this set are Jeff Bagwell and Ivan Rodriguez. Cards are numbered with a U prefix.

		MT	EX-MT	VG
□ 2	Barry Larkin	.75	.35	.09
□ 3	Matt Williams	.50	.23	.06
□ 4	Cecil Fielder	1.25	.55	.16
□ 5	Barry Bonds	2.00	.90	.25
□ 6	Rickey Henderson	1.50	.65	.19
□ 7	Ken Griffey Jr.	6.00	2.70	.75
□ 8	Jose Canseco	2.00	.90	.25
□ 9	Benito Santiago	.40	.18	.05
□ 10	Roger Clemens	2.50	1.15	.30

1991 Fleer Update

The 1991 Fleer Update set contains 132 cards measuring the standard size (2 1/2" by 3 1/2"). The glossy color action photos on the fronts are placed on a yellow card face and accentuated by black lines above and below. The backs have a head shot (circular format), biography, and complete Major League statistics. The cards are checklisted below alphabetically within and according to teams for each league as follows: Baltimore Orioles (1-3), Boston Red Sox (4-7), California Angels (8-10),

		MT	EX-MT	VG
	COMPLETE SET (132)	6.00	2.70	.75
	COMMON PLAYER (1-132)	.05	.02	.01
□ 1	Glenn Davis	.08	.04	.01
□ 2	Dwight Evans	.08	.04	.01
□ 3	Jose Mesa	.05	.02	.01
□ 4	Jack Clark	.08	.04	.01
□ 5	Danny Darwin	.05	.02	.01
□ 6	Steve Lyons	.05	.02	.01
□ 7	Mo Vaughn	.20	.09	.03
□ 8	Floyd Bannister	.05	.02	.01
□ 9	Gary Gaetti	.05	.02	.01
□ 10	Dave Parker	.08	.04	.01
□ 11	Joey Cora	.05	.02	.01
□ 12	Charlie Hough	.05	.02	.01
□ 13	Matt Merullo	.05	.02	.01
□ 14	Warren Newson	.10	.05	.01
□ 15	Tim Raines	.08	.04	.01
□ 16	Albert Belle	.15	.07	.02
□ 17	Glenallen Hill	.05	.02	.01
□ 18	Shawn Hillegas	.05	.02	.01
□ 19	Mark Lewis	.12	.05	.02
□ 20	Charles Nagy	.40	.18	.05
□ 21	Mark Whiten	.10	.05	.01
□ 22	John Cerutti	.05	.02	.01
□ 23	Rob Deer	.08	.04	.01
□ 24	Mickey Tettleton	.08	.04	.01
□ 25	Warren Cromartie	.05	.02	.01
□ 26	Kirk Gibson	.08	.04	.01
□ 27	David Howard	.10	.05	.01
□ 28	Brent Mayne	.05	.02	.01
□ 29	Dante Bichette	.05	.02	.01
□ 30	Mark Lee	.10	.05	.01
□ 31	Julio Machado	.05	.02	.01
□ 32	Edwin Nunez	.05	.02	.01
□ 33	Willie Randolph	.08	.04	.01

☐ 34 Franklin Stubbs	.05	.02	.01
☐ 35 Bill Wegman	.05	.02	.01
☐ 36 Chili Davis	.08	.04	.01
☐ 37 Chuck Knoblauch	.40	.18	.05
☐ 38 Scott Leius	.10	.05	.01
☐ 39 Jack Morris	.10	.05	.01
☐ 40 Mike Pagliarulo	.05	.02	.01
☐ 41 Lenny Webster	.05	.02	.01
☐ 42 John Habyan	.05	.02	.01
☐ 43 Steve Howe	.05	.02	.01
☐ 44 Jeff Johnson	.10	.05	.01
☐ 45 Scott Kamieniecki	.10	.05	.01
☐ 46 Pat Kelly	.15	.07	.02
☐ 47 Hensley Meulens	.08	.04	.01
☐ 48 Wade Taylor	.05	.02	.01
☐ 49 Bernie Williams	.20	.09	.03
☐ 50 Kirk Dressendorfer	.10	.05	.01
☐ 51 Ernest Riles	.05	.02	.01
☐ 52 Rich DeLucia	.05	.02	.01
☐ 53 Tracy Jones	.05	.02	.01
☐ 54 Bill Krueger	.05	.02	.01
☐ 55 Alonzo Powell	.10	.05	.01
☐ 56 Jeff Schaefer	.05	.02	.01
☐ 57 Russ Swan	.05	.02	.01
☐ 58 John Barfield	.05	.02	.01
☐ 59 Rich Gossage	.08	.04	.01
☐ 60 Jose Guzman	.05	.02	.01
☐ 61 Dean Palmer	.20	.09	.03
☐ 62 Ivan Rodriguez	1.25	.55	.16
☐ 63 Roberto Alomar	.20	.09	.03
☐ 64 Tom Candiotti	.05	.02	.01
☐ 65 Joe Carter	.12	.05	.02
☐ 66 Ed Sprague	.20	.09	.03
☐ 67 Pat Tabler	.05	.02	.01
☐ 68 Mike Timlin	.10	.05	.01
☐ 69 Devon White	.08	.04	.01
☐ 70 Rafael Belliard	.05	.02	.01
☐ 71 Juan Berenguer	.05	.02	.01
☐ 72 Sid Bream	.05	.02	.01
☐ 73 Marvin Freeman	.05	.02	.01
☐ 74 Kent Mercker	.08	.04	.01
☐ 75 Otis Nixon	.08	.04	.01
☐ 76 Terry Pendleton	.10	.05	.01
☐ 77 George Bell	.08	.04	.01
☐ 78 Danny Jackson	.05	.02	.01
☐ 79 Chuck McElroy	.05	.02	.01
☐ 80 Gary Scott	.15	.07	.02
☐ 81 Heathcliff Slocumb	.05	.02	.01
☐ 82 Dave Smith	.05	.02	.01
☐ 83 Rick Wilkins	.10	.05	.01
☐ 84 Freddie Benavides	.05	.02	.01
☐ 85 Ted Power	.05	.02	.01
☐ 86 Mo Sanford	.15	.07	.02
☐ 87 Jeff Bagwell	1.25	.55	.16
☐ 88 Steve Finley	.08	.04	.01
☐ 89 Pete Harnisch	.08	.04	.01
☐ 90 Darryl Kile	.10	.05	.01

☐ 91 Brett Butler	.08	.04	.01
☐ 92 John Candelaria	.05	.02	.01
☐ 93 Gary Carter	.08	.04	.01
☐ 94 Kevin Gross	.05	.02	.01
☐ 95 Bob Ojeda	.05	.02	.01
☐ 96 Darryl Strawberry	.12	.05	.02
☐ 97 Ivan Calderon	.05	.02	.01
☐ 98 Ron Hassey	.05	.02	.01
☐ 99 Gilberto Reyes	.05	.02	.01
☐ 100 Hubie Brooks	.05	.02	.01
☐ 101 Rick Cerone	.05	.02	.01
☐ 102 Vince Coleman	.08	.04	.01
☐ 103 Jeff Innis	.05	.02	.01
☐ 104 Pete Schourek	.12	.05	.02
☐ 105 Andy Ashby	.12	.05	.02
☐ 106 Wally Backman	.05	.02	.01
☐ 107 Darrin Fletcher	.05	.02	.01
☐ 108 Tommy Greene	.05	.02	.01
☐ 109 John Morris	.05	.02	.01
☐ 110 Mitch Williams	.05	.02	.01
☐ 111 Lloyd McClendon	.05	.02	.01
☐ 112 Orlando Merced	.20	.09	.03
☐ 113 Vicente Palacios	.05	.02	.01
☐ 114 Gary Varsho	.05	.02	.01
☐ 115 John Wehner	.10	.05	.01
☐ 116 Rex Hudler	.05	.02	.01
☐ 117 Tim Jones	.05	.02	.01
☐ 118 Geronimo Pena	.05	.02	.01
☐ 119 Gerald Perry	.05	.02	.01
☐ 120 Larry Andersen	.05	.02	.01
☐ 121 Jerald Clark	.05	.02	.01
☐ 122 Scott Coolbaugh	.05	.02	.01
☐ 123 Tony Fernandez	.08	.04	.01
☐ 124 Darrin Jackson	.08	.04	.01
☐ 125 Fred McGriff	.12	.05	.02
☐ 126 Jose Mota	.10	.05	.01
☐ 127 Tim Teufel	.05	.02	.01
☐ 128 Bud Black	.05	.02	.01
☐ 129 Mike Felder	.05	.02	.01
☐ 130 Willie McGee	.08	.04	.01
☐ 131 Dave Righetti	.05	.02	.01
☐ 132 Checklist Card	.08	.01	.00

1992 Fleer

The 1992 Fleer set contains 720 cards measuring the standard size (2 1/2" by 3 1/2"). The card fronts shade from metallic pale green to white as one moves down the face. The team logo and player's name appear to the right of the picture, running the length of the card. The top portion of

the back has a different color player photo and biography, while the bottom portion includes statistics and player profile. The cards are checklisted below alphabetically within and according to teams for each league as follows: Baltimore Orioles (1-31), Boston Red Sox (32-49), California Angels (50-73), Chicago White Sox (74-101), Cleveland Indians (102-126), Detroit Tigers (127-149), Kansas City Royals (150-172), Milwaukee Brewers (173-194), Minnesota Twins (195-220), New York Yankees (221-247), Oakland Athletics (248-272), Seattle Mariners (273-296), Texas Rangers (297-321), Toronto Blue Jays (322-348), Atlanta Braves (349-374), Chicago Cubs (375-397), Cincinnati Reds (398-423), Houston Astros (424-446), Los Angeles Dodgers (447-471), Montreal Expos (472-494), New York Mets (495-520), Philadelphia Phillies (521-547), Pittsburgh Pirates (548-573), St. Louis Cardinals (574-596), San Diego Padres (597-624), and San Francisco Giants (625-651). Topical subsets feature Major League Prospects (652-680), Record Setters (681-687), League Leaders (688-697), Super Star Specials (698-707), Pro Visions (708-713), and Checklists (714-720). The only noteworthy Rookie Card in the set is Rob Maurer. Hobby factory sets included a 9-card Lumber Company subset and three Roger Clemens cards; retail factory sets included a 12-card "Smoke 'n Heat" subset.

	MT	EX-MT	VG
COMPLETE SET (720)	20.00	9.00	2.50
COMPLETE HOBBY SET (732)	40.00	18.00	5.00
COMPLETE RETAIL SET (732)	30.00	13.50	3.80
COMMON PLAYER (1-720)	.04	.02	.01
☐ 1 Brady Anderson	.07	.03	.01
☐ 2 Jose Bautista	.04	.02	.01

☐ 3 Juan Bell	.04	.02	.01
☐ 4 Glenn Davis	.07	.03	.01
☐ 5 Mike Devereaux	.07	.03	.01
☐ 6 Dwight Evans	.07	.03	.01
☐ 7 Mike Flanagan	.04	.02	.01
☐ 8 Leo Gomez	.10	.05	.01
☐ 9 Chris Hoiles	.07	.03	.01
☐ 10 Sam Horn	.04	.02	.01
☐ 11 Tim Hulett	.04	.02	.01
☐ 12 Dave Johnson	.04	.02	.01
☐ 13 Chito Martinez	.04	.02	.01
☐ 14 Ben McDonald	.10	.05	.01
☐ 15 Bob Melvin	.04	.02	.01
☐ 16 Luis Mercedes	.04	.02	.01
☐ 17 Jose Mesa	.04	.02	.01
☐ 18 Bob Milacki	.04	.02	.01
☐ 19 Randy Milligan	.04	.02	.01
☐ 20 Mike Mussina UER	.50	.23	.06
(Card back refers			
to him as Jeff)			
☐ 21 Gregg Olson	.07	.03	.01
☐ 22 Joe Orsulak	.04	.02	.01
☐ 23 Jim Poole	.04	.02	.01
☐ 24 Arthur Rhodes	.15	.07	.02
☐ 25 Billy Ripken	.04	.02	.01
☐ 26 Cal Ripken	.25	.11	.03
☐ 27 David Segui	.04	.02	.01
☐ 28 Roy Smith	.04	.02	.01
☐ 29 Anthony Telford	.04	.02	.01
☐ 30 Mark Williamson	.04	.02	.01
☐ 31 Craig Worthington	.04	.02	.01
☐ 32 Wade Boggs	.12	.05	.02
☐ 33 Tom Bolton	.04	.02	.01
☐ 34 Tom Brunansky	.07	.03	.01
☐ 35 Ellis Burks	.07	.03	.01
☐ 36 Jack Clark	.07	.03	.01
☐ 37 Roger Clemens	.25	.11	.03
☐ 38 Danny Darwin	.04	.02	.01
☐ 39 Mike Greenwell	.07	.03	.01
☐ 40 Joe Hesketh	.04	.02	.01
☐ 41 Daryl Irvine	.04	.02	.01
☐ 42 Dennis Lamp	.04	.02	.01
☐ 43 Tony Pena	.04	.02	.01
☐ 44 Phil Plantier	.15	.07	.02
☐ 45 Carlos Quintana	.04	.02	.01
☐ 46 Jeff Reardon	.07	.03	.01
☐ 47 Jody Reed	.04	.02	.01
☐ 48 Luis Rivera	.04	.02	.01
☐ 49 Mo Vaughn	.07	.03	.01
☐ 50 Jim Abbott	.12	.05	.02
☐ 51 Kyle Abbott	.07	.03	.01
☐ 52 Ruben Amaro Jr.	.04	.02	.01
☐ 53 Scott Bailes	.04	.02	.01
☐ 54 Chris Beasley	.10	.05	.01
☐ 55 Mark Eichhorn	.04	.02	.01
☐ 56 Mike Fetters	.04	.02	.01
☐ 57 Chuck Finley	.04	.02	.01

☐ 58	Gary Gaetti	.04	.02	.01		
☐ 59	Dave Gallagher	.04	.02	.01		
☐ 60	Donnie Hill	.04	.02	.01		
☐ 61	Bryan Harvey UER	.04	.02	.01		
	(Lee Smith led the					
	Majors with 47 saves)					
☐ 62	Wally Joyner	.07	.03	.01		
☐ 63	Mark Langston	.07	.03	.01		
☐ 64	Kirk McCaskill	.04	.02	.01		
☐ 65	John Orton	.04	.02	.01		
☐ 66	Lance Parrish	.07	.03	.01		
☐ 67	Luis Polonia	.07	.03	.01		
☐ 68	Bobby Rose	.04	.02	.01		
☐ 69	Dick Schofield	.04	.02	.01		
☐ 70	Luis Sojo	.04	.02	.01		
☐ 71	Lee Stevens	.04	.02	.01		
☐ 72	Dave Winfield	.10	.05	.01		
☐ 73	Cliff Young	.04	.02	.01		
☐ 74	Wilson Alvarez	.04	.02	.01		
☐ 75	Esteban Beltre	.10	.05	.01		
☐ 76	Joey Cora	.04	.02	.01		
☐ 77	Brian Drahman	.04	.02	.01		
☐ 78	Alex Fernandez	.07	.03	.01		
☐ 79	Carlton Fisk	.10	.05	.01		
☐ 80	Scott Fletcher	.04	.02	.01		
☐ 81	Craig Grebeck	.04	.02	.01		
☐ 82	Ozzie Guillen	.04	.02	.01		
☐ 83	Greg Hibbard	.04	.02	.01		
☐ 84	Charlie Hough	.04	.02	.01		
☐ 85	Mike Huff	.04	.02	.01		
☐ 86	Bo Jackson	.12	.05	.02		
☐ 87	Lance Johnson	.04	.02	.01		
☐ 88	Ron Karkovice	.04	.02	.01		
☐ 89	Jack McDowell	.07	.03	.01		
☐ 90	Matt Merullo	.04	.02	.01		
☐ 91	Warren Newson	.04	.02	.01		
☐ 92	Donn Pall UER	.04	.02	.01		
	(Called Dunn on					
	card back)					
☐ 93	Dan Pasqua	.04	.02	.01		
☐ 94	Ken Patterson	.04	.02	.01		
☐ 95	Melido Perez	.07	.03	.01		
☐ 96	Scott Radinsky	.04	.02	.01		
☐ 97	Tim Raines	.07	.03	.01		
☐ 98	Sammy Sosa	.04	.02	.01		
☐ 99	Bobby Thigpen	.04	.02	.01		
☐ 100	Frank Thomas	.75	.35	.09		
☐ 101	Robin Ventura	.15	.07	.02		
☐ 102	Mike Aldrete	.04	.02	.01		
☐ 103	Sandy Alomar Jr.	.07	.03	.01		
☐ 104	Carlos Baerga	.15	.07	.02		
☐ 105	Albert Belle	.12	.05	.02		
☐ 106	Willie Blair	.04	.02	.01		
☐ 107	Jerry Browne	.04	.02	.01		
☐ 108	Alex Cole	.04	.02	.01		
☐ 109	Felix Fermin	.04	.02	.01		
☐ 110	Glenallen Hill	.04	.02	.01		
☐ 111	Shawn Hillegas	.04	.02	.01		
☐ 112	Chris James	.04	.02	.01		
☐ 113	Reggie Jefferson	.07	.03	.01		
☐ 114	Doug Jones	.04	.02	.01		
☐ 115	Eric King	.04	.02	.01		
☐ 116	Mark Lewis	.07	.03	.01		
☐ 117	Carlos Martinez	.04	.02	.01		
☐ 118	Charles Nagy UER	.10	.05	.01		
	(Throws right, but					
	card says left)					
☐ 119	Rod Nichols	.04	.02	.01		
☐ 120	Steve Olin	.04	.02	.01		
☐ 121	Jesse Orosco	.04	.02	.01		
☐ 122	Rudy Seanez	.04	.02	.01		
☐ 123	Joel Skinner	.04	.02	.01		
☐ 124	Greg Swindell	.07	.03	.01		
☐ 125	Jim Thome	.12	.05	.02		
☐ 126	Mark Whiten	.07	.03	.01		
☐ 127	Scott Aldred	.04	.02	.01		
☐ 128	Andy Allanson	.04	.02	.01		
☐ 129	John Cerutti	.04	.02	.01		
☐ 130	Milt Cuyler	.04	.02	.01		
☐ 131	Mike Dalton	.10	.05	.01		
☐ 132	Rob Deer	.07	.03	.01		
☐ 133	Cecil Fielder	.12	.05	.02		
☐ 134	Travis Fryman	.30	.14	.04		
☐ 135	Dan Gakeler	.04	.02	.01		
☐ 136	Paul Gibson	.04	.02	.01		
☐ 137	Bill Gullickson	.04	.02	.01		
☐ 138	Mike Henneman	.04	.02	.01		
☐ 139	Pete Incaviglia	.04	.02	.01		
☐ 140	Mark Leiter	.04	.02	.01		
☐ 141	Scott Livingstone	.10	.05	.01		
☐ 142	Lloyd Moseby	.04	.02	.01		
☐ 143	Tony Phillips	.04	.02	.01		
☐ 144	Mark Salas	.04	.02	.01		
☐ 145	Frank Tanana	.04	.02	.01		
☐ 146	Walt Terrell	.04	.02	.01		
☐ 147	Mickey Tettleton	.07	.03	.01		
☐ 148	Alan Trammell	.07	.03	.01		
☐ 149	Lou Whitaker	.07	.03	.01		
☐ 150	Kevin Appier	.07	.03	.01		
☐ 151	Luis Aquino	.04	.02	.01		
☐ 152	Todd Benzinger	.04	.02	.01		
☐ 153	Mike Boddicker	.04	.02	.01		
☐ 154	George Brett	.10	.05	.01		
☐ 155	Storm Davis	.04	.02	.01		
☐ 156	Jim Eisenreich	.04	.02	.01		
☐ 157	Kirk Gibson	.07	.03	.01		
☐ 158	Tom Gordon	.04	.02	.01		
☐ 159	Mark Gubicza	.04	.02	.01		
☐ 160	David Howard	.04	.02	.01		
☐ 161	Mike Macfarlane	.04	.02	.01		
☐ 162	Brent Mayne	.04	.02	.01		
☐ 163	Brian McRae	.07	.03	.01		
☐ 164	Jeff Montgomery	.04	.02	.01		
☐ 165	Bill Pecota	.04	.02	.01		

☐ 166 Harvey Pulliam .10	.05	.01
☐ 167 Bret Saberhagen .07	.03	.01
☐ 168 Kevin Seitzer .07	.03	.01
☐ 169 Terry Shumpert .04	.02	.01
☐ 170 Kurt Stillwell .04	.02	.01
☐ 171 Danny Tartabull .07	.03	.01
☐ 172 Gary Thurman .04	.02	.01
☐ 173 Dante Bichette .04	.02	.01
☐ 174 Kevin D. Brown .04	.02	.01
☐ 175 Chuck Crim .04	.02	.01
☐ 176 Jim Gantner .04	.02	.01
☐ 177 Darryl Hamilton .07	.03	.01
☐ 178 Ted Higuera .04	.02	.01
☐ 179 Darren Holmes .04	.02	.01
☐ 180 Mark Lee .04	.02	.01
☐ 181 Julio Machado .04	.02	.01
☐ 182 Paul Molitor .07	.03	.01
☐ 183 Jaime Navarro .07	.03	.01
☐ 184 Edwin Nunez .04	.02	.01
☐ 185 Dan Plesac .04	.02	.01
☐ 186 Willie Randolph .07	.03	.01
☐ 187 Ron Robinson .04	.02	.01
☐ 188 Gary Sheffield .20	.09	.03
☐ 189 Bill Spiers .04	.02	.01
☐ 190 B.J. Surhoff .04	.02	.01
☐ 191 Dale Sveum .04	.02	.01
☐ 192 Greg Vaughn .07	.03	.01
☐ 193 Bill Wegman .04	.02	.01
☐ 194 Robin Yount .10	.05	.01
☐ 195 Rick Aguilera .07	.03	.01
☐ 196 Allan Anderson .04	.02	.01
☐ 197 Steve Bedrosian .04	.02	.01
☐ 198 Randy Bush .04	.02	.01
☐ 199 Larry Casian .04	.02	.01
☐ 200 Chili Davis .07	.03	.01
☐ 201 Scott Erickson .10	.05	.01
☐ 202 Greg Gagne .04	.02	.01
☐ 203 Dan Gladden .04	.02	.01
☐ 204 Brian Harper .04	.02	.01
☐ 205 Kent Hrbek .07	.03	.01
☐ 206 Chuck Knoblauch UER .20	.09	.03
(Career hit total of 59 is wrong)		
☐ 207 Gene Larkin .04	.02	.01
☐ 208 Terry Leach .04	.02	.01
☐ 209 Scott Leius .04	.02	.01
☐ 210 Shane Mack .07	.03	.01
☐ 211 Jack Morris .10	.05	.01
☐ 212 Pedro Munoz .07	.03	.01
☐ 213 Denny Neagle .07	.03	.01
☐ 214 Al Newman .04	.02	.01
☐ 215 Junior Ortiz .04	.02	.01
☐ 216 Mike Pagliarulo .04	.02	.01
☐ 217 Kirby Puckett .20	.09	.03
☐ 218 Paul Sorrento .07	.03	.01
☐ 219 Kevin Tapani .07	.03	.01
☐ 220 Lenny Webster .04	.02	.01

☐ 221 Jesse Barfield .04	.02	.01
☐ 222 Greg Cadaret .04	.02	.01
☐ 223 Dave Eiland .04	.02	.01
☐ 224 Alvaro Espinoza .04	.02	.01
☐ 225 Steve Farr .04	.02	.01
☐ 226 Bob Geren .04	.02	.01
☐ 227 Lee Guetterman .04	.02	.01
☐ 228 John Habyan .04	.02	.01
☐ 229 Mel Hall .04	.02	.01
☐ 230 Steve Howe .04	.02	.01
☐ 231 Mike Humphreys .07	.03	.01
☐ 232 Scott Kamieniecki .04	.02	.01
☐ 233 Pat Kelly .07	.03	.01
☐ 234 Roberto Kelly .07	.03	.01
☐ 235 Tim Leary .04	.02	.01
☐ 236 Kevin Maas .07	.03	.01
☐ 237 Don Mattingly .12	.05	.02
☐ 238 Hensley Meulens .04	.02	.01
☐ 239 Matt Nokes .04	.02	.01
☐ 240 Pascual Perez .04	.02	.01
☐ 241 Eric Plunk .04	.02	.01
☐ 242 John Ramos .04	.02	.01
☐ 243 Scott Sanderson .04	.02	.01
☐ 244 Steve Sax .07	.03	.01
☐ 245 Wade Taylor .04	.02	.01
☐ 246 Randy Velarde .04	.02	.01
☐ 247 Bernie Williams .10	.05	.01
☐ 248 Troy Afenir .04	.02	.01
☐ 249 Harold Baines .07	.03	.01
☐ 250 Lance Blankenship .04	.02	.01
☐ 251 Mike Bordick .10	.05	.01
☐ 252 Jose Canseco .20	.09	.03
☐ 253 Steve Chitren .04	.02	.01
☐ 254 Ron Darling .07	.03	.01
☐ 255 Dennis Eckersley .10	.05	.01
☐ 256 Mike Gallego .04	.02	.01
☐ 257 Dave Henderson .04	.02	.01
☐ 258 Rickey Henderson UFR .12	.05	.02
(Wearing 24 on front and 22 on back)		
☐ 259 Rick Honeycutt .04	.02	.01
☐ 260 Brook Jacoby .04	.02	.01
☐ 261 Carney Lansford .07	.03	.01
☐ 262 Mark McGwire .20	.09	.03
☐ 263 Mike Moore .04	.02	.01
☐ 264 Gene Nelson .04	.02	.01
☐ 265 Jamie Quirk .04	.02	.01
☐ 266 Joe Slusarski .04	.02	.01
☐ 267 Terry Steinbach .07	.03	.01
☐ 268 Dave Stewart .07	.03	.01
☐ 269 Todd Van Poppel .20	.09	.03
☐ 270 Walt Weiss .04	.02	.01
☐ 271 Bob Welch .04	.02	.01
☐ 272 Curt Young .04	.02	.01
☐ 273 Scott Bradley .04	.02	.01
☐ 274 Greg Briley .04	.02	.01
☐ 275 Jay Buhner .07	.03	.01

☐ 276	Henry Cotto	.04	.02	.01
☐ 277	Alvin Davis	.04	.02	.01
☐ 278	Rich DeLucia	.04	.02	.01
☐ 279	Ken Griffey Jr.	.50	.23	.06
☐ 280	Erik Hanson	.04	.02	.01
☐ 281	Brian Holman	.04	.02	.01
☐ 282	Mike Jackson	.04	.02	.01
☐ 283	Randy Johnson	.07	.03	.01
☐ 284	Tracy Jones	.04	.02	.01
☐ 285	Bill Krueger	.04	.02	.01
☐ 286	Edgar Martinez	.07	.03	.01
☐ 287	Tino Martinez	.07	.03	.01
☐ 288	Rob Murphy	.04	.02	.01
☐ 289	Pete O'Brien	.04	.02	.01
☐ 290	Alonzo Powell	.04	.02	.01
☐ 291	Harold Reynolds	.04	.02	.01
☐ 292	Mike Schooler	.04	.02	.01
☐ 293	Russ Swan	.04	.02	.01
☐ 294	Bill Swift	.04	.02	.01
☐ 295	Dave Valle	.04	.02	.01
☐ 296	Omar Vizquel	.04	.02	.01
☐ 297	Gerald Alexander	.04	.02	.01
☐ 298	Brad Arnsberg	.04	.02	.01
☐ 299	Kevin Brown	.07	.03	.01
☐ 300	Jack Daugherty	.04	.02	.01
☐ 301	Mario Diaz	.04	.02	.01
☐ 302	Brian Downing	.04	.02	.01
☐ 303	Julio Franco	.07	.03	.01
☐ 304	Juan Gonzalez	.35	.16	.04
☐ 305	Rich Gossage	.07	.03	.01
☐ 306	Jose Guzman	.04	.02	.01
☐ 307	Jose Hernandez	.10	.05	.01
☐ 308	Jeff Huson	.04	.02	.01
☐ 309	Mike Jeffcoat	.04	.02	.01
☐ 310	Terry Mathews	.10	.05	.01
☐ 311	Rafael Palmeiro	.07	.03	.01
☐ 312	Dean Palmer	.12	.05	.02
☐ 313	Geno Petralli	.04	.02	.01
☐ 314	Gary Pettis	.04	.02	.01
☐ 315	Kevin Reimer	.07	.03	.01
☐ 316	Ivan Rodriguez	.30	.14	.04
☐ 317	Kenny Rogers	.04	.02	.01
☐ 318	Wayne Rosenthal	.10	.05	.01
☐ 319	Jeff Russell	.04	.02	.01
☐ 320	Nolan Ryan	.40	.18	.05
☐ 321	Ruben Sierra	.15	.07	.02
☐ 322	Jim Acker	.04	.02	.01
☐ 323	Roberto Alomar	.20	.09	.03
☐ 324	Derek Bell	.10	.05	.01
☐ 325	Pat Borders	.04	.02	.01
☐ 326	Tom Candiotti	.04	.02	.01
☐ 327	Joe Carter	.12	.05	.02
☐ 328	Rob Ducey	.04	.02	.01
☐ 329	Kelly Gruber	.07	.03	.01
☐ 330	Juan Guzman	.75	.35	.09
☐ 331	Tom Henke	.07	.03	.01
☐ 332	Jimmy Key	.04	.02	.01
☐ 333	Manny Lee	.04	.02	.01
☐ 334	Al Leiter	.04	.02	.01
☐ 335	Bob MacDonald	.04	.02	.01
☐ 336	Candy Maldonado	.04	.02	.01
☐ 337	Rance Mulliniks	.04	.02	.01
☐ 338	Greg Myers	.04	.02	.01
☐ 339	John Olerud UER	.10	.05	.01
	(1991 BA has .256,			
	but text says .258)			
☐ 340	Ed Sprague	.07	.03	.01
☐ 341	Dave Stieb	.04	.02	.01
☐ 342	Todd Stottlemyre	.07	.03	.01
☐ 343	Mike Timlin	.04	.02	.01
☐ 344	Duane Ward	.04	.02	.01
☐ 345	David Wells	.04	.02	.01
☐ 346	Devon White	.07	.03	.01
☐ 347	Mookie Wilson	.04	.02	.01
☐ 348	Eddie Zosky	.07	.03	.01
☐ 349	Steve Avery	.15	.07	.02
☐ 350	Mike Bell	.04	.02	.01
☐ 351	Rafael Belliard	.04	.02	.01
☐ 352	Juan Berenguer	.04	.02	.01
☐ 353	Jeff Blauser	.04	.02	.01
☐ 354	Sid Bream	.04	.02	.01
☐ 355	Francisco Cabrera	.04	.02	.01
☐ 356	Marvin Freeman	.04	.02	.01
☐ 357	Ron Gant	.10	.05	.01
☐ 358	Tom Glavine	.12	.05	.02
☐ 359	Brian Hunter	.10	.05	.01
☐ 360	Dave Justice	.20	.09	.03
☐ 361	Charlie Leibrandt	.04	.02	.01
☐ 362	Mark Lemke	.04	.02	.01
☐ 363	Kent Mercker	.04	.02	.01
☐ 364	Keith Mitchell	.07	.03	.01
☐ 365	Greg Olson	.04	.02	.01
☐ 366	Terry Pendleton	.10	.05	.01
☐ 367	Armando Reynoso	.10	.05	.01
☐ 368	Deion Sanders	.15	.07	.02
☐ 369	Lonnie Smith	.07	.03	.01
☐ 370	Pete Smith	.07	.03	.01
☐ 371	John Smoltz	.10	.05	.01
☐ 372	Mike Stanton	.04	.02	.01
☐ 373	Jeff Treadway	.04	.02	.01
☐ 374	Mark Wohlers	.10	.05	.01
☐ 375	Paul Assenmacher	.04	.02	.01
☐ 376	George Bell	.07	.03	.01
☐ 377	Shawn Boskie	.04	.02	.01
☐ 378	Frank Castillo	.04	.02	.01
☐ 379	Andre Dawson	.10	.05	.01
☐ 380	Shawon Dunston	.07	.03	.01
☐ 381	Mark Grace	.07	.03	.01
☐ 382	Mike Harkey	.07	.03	.01
☐ 383	Danny Jackson	.04	.02	.01
☐ 384	Les Lancaster	.04	.02	.01
☐ 385	Ced Landrum	.07	.03	.01
☐ 386	Greg Maddux	.07	.03	.01
☐ 387	Derrick May	.07	.03	.01

☐ 388	Chuck McElroy	.04	.02	.01
☐ 389	Ryne Sandberg	.20	.09	.03
☐ 390	Heathcliff Slocumb	.04	.02	.01
☐ 391	Dave Smith	.04	.02	.01
☐ 392	Dwight Smith	.04	.02	.01
☐ 393	Rick Sutcliffe	.07	.03	.01
☐ 394	Hector Villanueva	.04	.02	.01
☐ 395	Chico Walker	.04	.02	.01
☐ 396	Jerome Walton	.04	.02	.01
☐ 397	Rick Wilkins	.04	.02	.01
☐ 398	Jack Armstrong	.04	.02	.01
☐ 399	Freddie Benavides	.04	.02	.01
☐ 400	Glenn Braggs	.04	.02	.01
☐ 401	Tom Browning	.04	.02	.01
☐ 402	Norm Charlton	.07	.03	.01
☐ 403	Eric Davis	.07	.03	.01
☐ 404	Rob Dibble	.07	.03	.01
☐ 405	Bill Doran	.04	.02	.01
☐ 406	Mariano Duncan	.04	.02	.01
☐ 407	Kip Gross	.10	.05	.01
☐ 408	Chris Hammond	.04	.02	.01
☐ 409	Billy Hatcher	.04	.02	.01
☐ 410	Chris Jones	.04	.02	.01
☐ 411	Barry Larkin	.10	.05	.01
☐ 412	Hal Morris	.07	.03	.01
☐ 413	Randy Myers	.07	.03	.01
☐ 414	Joe Oliver	.04	.02	.01
☐ 415	Paul O'Neill	.07	.03	.01
☐ 416	Ted Power	.04	.02	.01
☐ 417	Luis Quinones	.04	.02	.01
☐ 418	Jeff Reed	.04	.02	.01
☐ 419	Jose Rijo	.07	.03	.01
☐ 420	Chris Sabo	.07	.03	.01
☐ 421	Reggie Sanders	.25	.11	.03
☐ 422	Scott Scudder	.04	.02	.01
☐ 423	Glenn Sutko	.04	.02	.01
☐ 424	Eric Anthony	.07	.03	.01
☐ 425	Jeff Bagwell	.25	.11	.03
☐ 426	Craig Biggio	.07	.03	.01
☐ 427	Ken Caminiti	.07	.03	.01
☐ 428	Casey Candaele	.04	.02	.01
☐ 429	Mike Capel	.04	.02	.01
☐ 430	Andujar Cedeno	.07	.03	.01
☐ 431	Jim Corsi	.04	.02	.01
☐ 432	Mark Davidson	.04	.02	.01
☐ 433	Steve Finley	.07	.03	.01
☐ 434	Luis Gonzalez	.07	.03	.01
☐ 435	Pete Harnisch	.04	.02	.01
☐ 436	Dwayne Henry	.04	.02	.01
☐ 437	Xavier Hernandez	.04	.02	.01
☐ 438	Jimmy Jones	.04	.02	.01
☐ 439	Darryl Kile	.07	.03	.01
☐ 440	Rob Mallicoat	.04	.02	.01
☐ 441	Andy Mota	.04	.02	.01
☐ 442	Al Osuna	.04	.02	.01
☐ 443	Mark Portugal	.04	.02	.01
☐ 444	Scott Servais	.04	.02	.01
☐ 445	Mike Simms	.04	.02	.01
☐ 446	Gerald Young	.04	.02	.01
☐ 447	Tim Belcher	.07	.03	.01
☐ 448	Brett Butler	.07	.03	.01
☐ 449	John Candelaria	.04	.02	.01
☐ 450	Gary Carter	.07	.03	.01
☐ 451	Dennis Cook	.04	.02	.01
☐ 452	Tim Crews	.04	.02	.01
☐ 453	Kal Daniels	.04	.02	.01
☐ 454	Jim Gott	.04	.02	.01
☐ 455	Alfredo Griffin	.04	.02	.01
☐ 456	Kevin Gross	.04	.02	.01
☐ 457	Chris Gwynn	.04	.02	.01
☐ 458	Lenny Harris	.04	.02	.01
☐ 459	Orel Hershiser	.07	.03	.01
☐ 460	Jay Howell	.04	.02	.01
☐ 461	Stan Javier	.04	.02	.01
☐ 462	Eric Karros	.50	.23	.06
☐ 463	Ramon Martinez UER	.07	.03	.01
	(Card says bats right,			
	should be left)			
☐ 464	Roger McDowell UER	.04	.02	.01
	(Wins add up to 54,			
	totals have 51)			
☐ 465	Mike Morgan	.04	.02	.01
☐ 466	Eddie Murray	.10	.05	.01
☐ 467	Jose Offerman	.07	.03	.01
☐ 468	Bob Ojeda	.04	.02	.01
☐ 469	Juan Samuel	.04	.02	.01
☐ 470	Mike Scioscia	.04	.02	.01
☐ 471	Darryl Strawberry	.12	.05	.02
☐ 472	Bret Barberie	.04	.02	.01
☐ 473	Brian Barnes	.04	.02	.01
☐ 474	Eric Bullock	.04	.02	.01
☐ 475	Ivan Calderon	.04	.02	.01
☐ 476	Delino DeShields	.10	.05	.01
☐ 477	Jeff Fassero	.04	.02	.01
☐ 478	Mike Fitzgerald	.04	.02	.01
☐ 479	Steve Frey	.04	.02	.01
☐ 480	Andres Galarraga	.04	.02	.01
☐ 481	Mark Gardner	.04	.02	.01
☐ 482	Marquis Grissom	.10	.05	.01
☐ 483	Chris Haney	.04	.02	.01
☐ 484	Barry Jones	.04	.02	.01
☐ 485	Dave Martinez	.04	.02	.01
☐ 486	Dennis Martinez	.07	.03	.01
☐ 487	Chris Nabholz	.07	.03	.01
☐ 488	Spike Owen	.04	.02	.01
☐ 489	Gilberto Reyes	.04	.02	.01
☐ 490	Mel Rojas	.04	.02	.01
☐ 491	Scott Ruskin	.04	.02	.01
☐ 492	Bill Sampen	.04	.02	.01
☐ 493	Larry Walker	.15	.07	.02
☐ 494	Tim Wallach	.07	.03	.01
☐ 495	Daryl Boston	.04	.02	.01
☐ 496	Hubie Brooks	.04	.02	.01
☐ 497	Tim Burke	.04	.02	.01

☐ 498	Mark Carreon	.04	.02	.01
☐ 499	Tony Castillo	.04	.02	.01
☐ 500	Vince Coleman	.07	.03	.01
☐ 501	David Cone	.07	.03	.01
☐ 502	Kevin Elster	.04	.02	.01
☐ 503	Sid Fernandez	.07	.03	.01
☐ 504	John Franco	.07	.03	.01
☐ 505	Dwight Gooden	.07	.03	.01
☐ 506	Todd Hundley	.04	.02	.01
☐ 507	Jeff Innis	.04	.02	.01
☐ 508	Gregg Jefferies	.07	.03	.01
☐ 509	Howard Johnson	.07	.03	.01
☐ 510	Dave Magadan	.07	.03	.01
☐ 511	Terry McDaniel	.10	.05	.01
☐ 512	Kevin McReynolds	.07	.03	.01
☐ 513	Keith Miller	.04	.02	.01
☐ 514	Charlie O'Brien	.04	.02	.01
☐ 515	Mackey Sasser	.04	.02	.01
☐ 516	Pete Schourek	.07	.03	.01
☐ 517	Julio Valera	.04	.02	.01
☐ 518	Frank Viola	.07	.03	.01
☐ 519	Wally Whitehurst	.04	.02	.01
☐ 520	Anthony Young	.07	.03	.01
☐ 521	Andy Ashby	.04	.02	.01
☐ 522	Kim Batiste	.04	.02	.01
☐ 523	Joe Boever	.04	.02	.01
☐ 524	Wes Chamberlain	.04	.02	.01
☐ 525	Pat Combs	.04	.02	.01
☐ 526	Danny Cox	.04	.02	.01
☐ 527	Darren Daulton	.07	.03	.01
☐ 528	Jose DeJesus	.04	.02	.01
☐ 529	Len Dykstra	.07	.03	.01
☐ 530	Darrin Fletcher	.04	.02	.01
☐ 531	Tommy Greene	.04	.02	.01
☐ 532	Jason Grimsley	.04	.02	.01
☐ 533	Charlie Hayes	.04	.02	.01
☐ 534	Von Hayes	.04	.02	.01
☐ 535	Dave Hollins	.07	.03	.01
☐ 536	Ricky Jordan	.04	.02	.01
☐ 537	John Kruk	.07	.03	.01
☐ 538	Jim Lindeman	.04	.02	.01
☐ 539	Mickey Morandini	.07	.03	.01
☐ 540	Terry Mulholland	.04	.02	.01
☐ 541	Dale Murphy	.07	.03	.01
☐ 542	Randy Ready	.04	.02	.01
☐ 543	Wally Ritchie UER	.04	.02	.01
	(Letters in data are			
	cut off on card)			
☐ 544	Bruce Ruffin	.04	.02	.01
☐ 545	Steve Searcy	.04	.02	.01
☐ 546	Dickie Thon	.04	.02	.01
☐ 547	Mitch Williams	.04	.02	.01
☐ 548	Stan Belinda	.04	.02	.01
☐ 549	Jay Bell	.04	.02	.01
☐ 550	Barry Bonds	.15	.07	.02
☐ 551	Bobby Bonilla	.10	.05	.01
☐ 552	Steve Buechele	.04	.02	.01

☐ 553	Doug Drabek	.07	.03	.01
☐ 554	Neal Heaton	.04	.02	.01
☐ 555	Jeff King	.04	.02	.01
☐ 556	Bob Kipper	.04	.02	.01
☐ 557	Bill Landrum	.04	.02	.01
☐ 558	Mike LaValliere	.04	.02	.01
☐ 559	Jose Lind	.04	.02	.01
☐ 560	Lloyd McClendon	.04	.02	.01
☐ 561	Orlando Merced	.07	.03	.01
☐ 562	Bob Patterson	.04	.02	.01
☐ 563	Joe Redfield	.10	.05	.01
☐ 564	Gary Redus	.04	.02	.01
☐ 565	Rosario Rodriguez	.04	.02	.01
☐ 566	Don Slaught	.04	.02	.01
☐ 567	John Smiley	.07	.03	.01
☐ 568	Zane Smith	.04	.02	.01
☐ 569	Randy Tomlin	.04	.02	.01
☐ 570	Andy Van Slyke	.07	.03	.01
☐ 571	Gary Varsho	.04	.02	.01
☐ 572	Bob Walk	.04	.02	.01
☐ 573	John Wehner UER	.07	.03	.01
	(Actually played for			
	Carolina in 1991,			
	not Cards)			
☐ 574	Juan Agosto	.04	.02	.01
☐ 575	Cris Carpenter	.04	.02	.01
☐ 576	Jose DeLeon	.04	.02	.01
☐ 577	Rich Gedman	.04	.02	.01
☐ 578	Bernard Gilkey	.07	.03	.01
☐ 579	Pedro Guerrero	.07	.03	.01
☐ 580	Ken Hill	.07	.03	.01
☐ 581	Rex Hudler	.04	.02	.01
☐ 582	Felix Jose	.07	.03	.01
☐ 583	Ray Lankford	.15	.07	.02
☐ 584	Omar Olivares	.04	.02	.01
☐ 585	Jose Oquendo	.04	.02	.01
☐ 586	Tom Pagnozzi	.04	.02	.01
☐ 587	Geronimo Pena	.04	.02	.01
☐ 588	Mike Perez	.04	.02	.01
☐ 589	Gerald Perry	.04	.02	.01
☐ 590	Bryn Smith	.04	.02	.01
☐ 591	Lee Smith	.07	.03	.01
☐ 592	Ozzie Smith	.10	.05	.01
☐ 593	Scott Terry	.04	.02	.01
☐ 594	Bob Tewksbury	.07	.03	.01
☐ 595	Milt Thompson	.04	.02	.01
☐ 596	Todd Zeile	.04	.02	.01
☐ 597	Larry Andersen	.04	.02	.01
☐ 598	Oscar Azocar	.04	.02	.01
☐ 599	Andy Benes	.07	.03	.01
☐ 600	Ricky Bones	.10	.05	.01
☐ 601	Jerald Clark	.04	.02	.01
☐ 602	Pat Clements	.04	.02	.01
☐ 603	Paul Faries	.04	.02	.01
☐ 604	Tony Fernandez	.07	.03	.01
☐ 605	Tony Gwynn	.12	.05	.02
☐ 606	Greg W. Harris	.04	.02	.01

☐ 607 Thomas Howard	.04	.02	.01
☐ 608 Bruce Hurst	.07	.03	.01
☐ 609 Darrin Jackson	.07	.03	.01
☐ 610 Tom Lampkin	.04	.02	.01
☐ 611 Craig Lefferts	.04	.02	.01
☐ 612 Jim Lewis	.10	.05	.01
☐ 613 Mike Maddux	.04	.02	.01
☐ 614 Fred McGriff	.12	.05	.02
☐ 615 Jose Melendez	.04	.02	.01
☐ 616 Jose Mota	.04	.02	.01
☐ 617 Dennis Rasmussen	.04	.02	.01
☐ 618 Bip Roberts	.07	.03	.01
☐ 619 Rich Rodriguez	.04	.02	.01
☐ 620 Benito Santiago	.07	.03	.01
☐ 621 Craig Shipley	.10	.05	.01
☐ 622 Tim Teufel	.04	.02	.01
☐ 623 Kevin Ward	.10	.05	.01
☐ 624 Ed Whitson	.04	.02	.01
☐ 625 Dave Anderson	.04	.02	.01
☐ 626 Kevin Bass	.04	.02	.01
☐ 627 Rod Beck	.12	.05	.02
☐ 628 Bud Black	.04	.02	.01
☐ 629 Jeff Brantley	.04	.02	.01
☐ 630 John Burkett	.04	.02	.01
☐ 631 Will Clark	.20	.09	.03
☐ 632 Royce Clayton	.15	.07	.02
☐ 633 Steve Decker	.04	.02	.01
☐ 634 Kelly Downs	.04	.02	.01
☐ 635 Mike Felder	.04	.02	.01
☐ 636 Scott Garrelts	.04	.02	.01
☐ 637 Eric Gunderson	.04	.02	.01
☐ 638 Bryan Hickerson	.10	.05	.01
☐ 639 Darren Lewis	.07	.03	.01
☐ 640 Greg Litton	.04	.02	.01
☐ 641 Kirt Manwaring	.04	.02	.01
☐ 642 Paul McClellan	.04	.02	.01
☐ 643 Willie McGee	.07	.03	.01
☐ 644 Kevin Mitchell	.07	.03	.01
☐ 645 Francisco Oliveras	.04	.02	.01
☐ 646 Mike Remlinger	.04	.02	.01
☐ 647 Dave Righetti	.04	.02	.01
☐ 648 Robby Thompson	.04	.02	.01
☐ 649 Jose Uribe	.04	.02	.01
☐ 650 Matt Williams	.07	.03	.01
☐ 651 Trevor Wilson	.04	.02	.01
☐ 652 Tom Goodwin MLP UER	.05	.02	.01
(Timed in 3.5, should be be timed)			
☐ 653 Terry Bross MLP	.05	.02	.01
☐ 654 Mike Christopher MLP	.10	.05	.01
☐ 655 Kenny Lofton MLP	.40	.18	.05
☐ 656 Chris Cron MLP	.10	.05	.01
☐ 657 Willie Banks MLP	.08	.04	.01
☐ 658 Pat Rice MLP	.10	.05	.01
☐ 659A Rob Maurer MLP ERR	.75	.35	.09
(Name misspelled as Mauer on card front)			

☐ 659B Rob Maurer MLP COR	.15	.07	.02
☐ 660 Don Harris MLP	.05	.02	.01
☐ 661 Henry Rodriguez MLP	.10	.05	.01
☐ 662 Cliff Brantley MLP	.10	.05	.01
☐ 663 Mike Linskey MLP UER	.05	.02	.01
(220 pounds in data, 200 in text)			
☐ 664 Gary DiSarcina MLP	.08	.04	.01
☐ 665 Gil Heredia MLP	.10	.05	.01
☐ 666 Vinny Castilla MLP	.10	.05	.01
☐ 667 Paul Abbott MLP	.05	.02	.01
☐ 668 Monty Fariss MLP UER	.10	.05	.01
(Called Paul on back)			
☐ 669 Jarvis Brown MLP	.10	.05	.01
☐ 670 Wayne Kirby MLP	.10	.05	.01
☐ 671 Scott Brosius MLP	.10	.05	.01
☐ 672 Bob Hamelin MLP	.08	.04	.01
☐ 673 Joel Johnston MLP	.05	.02	.01
☐ 674 Tim Spehr MLP	.05	.02	.01
☐ 675A Jeff Gardner MLP ERR	.10	.05	.01
(Shortstop on back, should say Pitcher)			
☐ 675B Jeff Gardner MLP COR	.10	.05	.01
☐ 676 Rico Rossy MLP	.10	.05	.01
☐ 677 Roberto Hernandez MLP	.12	.05	.02
☐ 678 Ted Wood MLP	.10	.05	.01
☐ 679 Cal Eldred MLP	.35	.16	.04
☐ 680 Sean Berry MLP	.08	.04	.01
☐ 681 Rickey Henderson RS	.10	.05	.01
☐ 682 Nolan Ryan RS	.25	.11	.03
☐ 683 Dennis Martinez RS	.05	.02	.01
☐ 684 Wilson Alvarez RS	.05	.02	.01
☐ 685 Joe Carter RS	.10	.05	.01
☐ 686 Dave Winfield RS	.10	.05	.01
☐ 687 David Cone RS	.08	.04	.01
☐ 688 Jose Canseco LL	.12	.05	.02
☐ 689 Howard Johnson LL	.05	.02	.01
☐ 690 Julio Franco LL	.05	.02	.01
☐ 691 Terry Pendleton LL	.10	.05	.01
☐ 692 Cecil Fielder LL	.10	.05	.01
☐ 693 Scott Erickson LL	.10	.05	.01
☐ 694 Tom Glavine LL	.10	.05	.01
☐ 695 Dennis Martinez LL	.05	.02	.01
☐ 696 Bryan Harvey LL	.05	.02	.01
☐ 697 Lee Smith LL	.05	.02	.01
☐ 698 Super Siblings	.15	.07	.02
Roberto Alomar Sandy Alomar Jr.			
☐ 699 The Indispensables	.12	.05	.02
Bobby Bonilla Will Clark			
☐ 700 Teamwork	.05	.02	.01
Mark Wohlers Kent Mercker Alejandro Pena			
☐ 701 Tiger Tandems	.20	.09	.03
Stacy Jones			

Bo Jackson
Gregg Olson
Frank Thomas

☐ 702	The Ignitors	.05	.02	.01
	Paul Molitor			
	Brett Butler			
☐ 703	Indispensables II	.15	.07	.02
	Cal Ripken			
	Joe Carter			
☐ 704	Power Packs	.10	.05	.01
	Barry Larkin			
	Kirby Puckett			
☐ 705	Today and Tomorrow	.10	.05	.01
	Mo Vaughn			
	Cecil Fielder			
☐ 706	Teenage Sensations	.05	.02	.01
	Ramon Martinez			
	Ozzie Guillen			
☐ 707	Designated Hitters	.05	.02	.01
	Harold Baines			
	Wade Boggs			
☐ 708	Robin Yount PV	.15	.07	.02
☐ 709	Ken Griffey Jr. PV UER	.75	.35	.09
	(Missing quotations on			
	back; BA has .322, but			
	was actually .327)			
☐ 710	Nolan Ryan PV	.60	.25	.08
☐ 711	Cal Ripken PV	.50	.23	.06
☐ 712	Frank Thomas PV	.75	.35	.09
☐ 713	Dave Justice PV	.35	.16	.04
☐ 714	Checklist Card	.05	.01	.00
☐ 715	Checklist Card	.05	.01	.00
☐ 716	Checklist Card	.05	.01	.00
☐ 717	Checklist Card	.05	.01	.00
☐ 718	Checklist Card	.05	.01	.00
☐ 719	Checklist Card	.05	.01	.00
☐ 720A	Checklist Card ERR	.05	.01	.00
	(659 Rob Mauer)			
☐ 720B	Checklist Card COR	.05	.01	.00
	(659 Rob Maurer)			

1992 Fleer All-Stars

The 24-card All-Stars series was randomly inserted in 1992 Fleer wax packs (fin-sealed single packs). The cards measure the standard size (2 1/2" by 3 1/2"). The glossy color photos on the fronts are bor-dered in black and accented above and below with gold stripes and lettering. A dia-mond with a color head shot of the player is superimposed at the lower right corner of the picture. The player's name and the

words "Fleer '92 All-Stars" appear above and below the picture respectively in gold foil lettering. On a white background with black borders, the back has career high-lights with the words "Fleer '92 All-Stars" appearing at the top in yellow lettering. The cards are numbered on the back.

	MT	EX-MT	VG
COMPLETE SET (24)	40.00	18.00	5.00
COMMON PLAYER (1-24)	1.00	.45	.13

☐ 1	Felix Jose	1.25	.55	.16
☐ 2	Tony Gwynn	2.00	.90	.25
☐ 3	Barry Bonds	3.00	1.35	.40
☐ 4	Bobby Bonilla	1.25	.55	.16
☐ 5	Mike LaValliere	1.00	.45	.13
☐ 6	Tom Glavine	2.00	.90	.25
☐ 7	Ramon Martinez	1.25	.55	.16
☐ 8	Lee Smith	1.00	.45	.13
☐ 9	Mickey Tettleton	1.00	.45	.13
☐ 10	Scott Erickson	1.25	.55	.16
☐ 11	Frank Thomas	10.00	4.50	1.25
☐ 12	Danny Tartabull	1.25	.55	.16
☐ 13	Will Clark	3.00	1.35	.40
☐ 14	Ryne Sandberg	3.50	1.55	.45
☐ 15	Terry Pendleton	1.00	.45	.13
☐ 16	Barry Larkin	1.50	.65	.19
☐ 17	Rafael Palmeiro	1.25	.55	.16
☐ 18	Julio Franco	1.00	.45	.13
☐ 19	Robin Ventura	3.00	1.35	.40
☐ 20	Cal Ripken UER	5.00	2.30	.60
	(Candidte; total bases			
	misspelled as based)			
☐ 21	Joe Carter	2.00	.90	.25
☐ 22	Kirby Puckett	3.00	1.35	.40
☐ 23	Ken Griffey Jr.	7.00	3.10	.85
☐ 24	Jose Canseco	3.00	1.35	.40

1992 Fleer Lumber Company

1992 Fleer Rookie Sensations

The 1992 Fleer Lumber Company set features nine outstanding hitters in Major League Baseball. The cards measure the standard size (2 1/2" by 3 1/2"). Inside a black glossy frame, the fronts display color action player photos, with the player's name printed in black in a gold foil bar beneath the picture. The wider right border contains the catch phrase "The Lumber Co." in the shape of a baseball bat, complete with woodgrain streaks. The backs carry a color head shot and, on a tan panel, a summary of the player's hitting performance and records. The cards are numbered on the back with an L prefix.

	MT	EX-MT	VG
COMPLETE SET (9)	20.00	9.00	2.50
COMMON PLAYER (L1-L9)	1.50	.65	.19
☐ L1 Cecil Fielder	2.50	1.15	.30
☐ L2 Mickey Tettleton	1.50	.65	.19
☐ L3 Darryl Strawberry	2.50	1.15	.30
☐ L4 Ryne Sandberg	4.50	2.00	.55
☐ L5 Jose Canseco	4.00	1.80	.50
☐ L6 Matt Williams	1.50	.65	.19
☐ L7 Cal Ripken	7.00	3.10	.85
☐ L8 Barry Bonds	4.00	1.80	.50
☐ L9 Ron Gant	2.00	.90	.25

The 20-card Fleer Rookie Sensations series was randomly inserted in 1992 Fleer 35-card cello packs. The cards measure the standard size (2 1/2" by 3 1/2"). The glossy color photos on the fronts have a white border on a royal blue card face. The words "Rookie Sensations" appear above the picture in gold foil lettering, while the player's name appears on a gold foil plaque beneath the picture. On a light blue background with royal blue borders, the backs have career summary. The cards are numbered on the back. Through a mail-in offer for ten Fleer baseball card wrappers and 1.00 for postage and handling, Fleer offered an uncut 8 1/2" by 11" numbered promo sheet picturing ten of the 20-card set on each side in a reduced-size front-only format. The offer indicated an expiration date of July 31, 1992, or whenever the production quantity of 250,000 sheets was exhausted.

	MT	EX-MT	VG
COMPLETE SET (20)	100.00	45.00	12.50
COMMON PLAYER (1-20)	2.00	.90	.25
☐ 1 Frank Thomas	50.00	23.00	6.25
☐ 2 Todd Van Poppel	7.00	3.10	.85
☐ 3 Orlando Merced	3.00	1.35	.40
☐ 4 Jeff Bagwell	16.00	7.25	2.00
☐ 5 Jeff Fassero	2.00	.90	.25
☐ 6 Darren Lewis	2.50	1.15	.30
☐ 7 Milt Cuyler	2.00	.90	.25
☐ 8 Mike Timlin	2.00	.90	.25
☐ 9 Brian McRae	3.00	1.35	.40

		MT	EX-MT	VG
☐	10 Chuck Knoblauch	12.00	5.50	1.50
☐	11 Rich DeLucia	2.00	.90	.25
☐	12 Ivan Rodriguez	16.00	7.25	2.00
☐	13 Juan Guzman	20.00	9.00	2.50
☐	14 Steve Chitren	2.00	.90	.25
☐	15 Mark Wohlers	3.00	1.35	.40
☐	16 Wes Chamberlain	3.00	1.35	.40
☐	17 Ray Lankford	11.00	4.90	1.40
☐	18 Chito Martinez	2.00	.90	.25
☐	19 Phil Plantier	10.00	4.50	1.25
☐	20 Scott Leius UER	2.00	.90	.25
	(Misspelled Lieus			
	on card front)			

		MT	EX-MT	VG
COMPLETE SET (12)		10.00	4.50	1.25
COMMON PLAYER (S1-S12)		.75	.35	.09
☐	S1 Lee Smith	.75	.35	.09
☐	S2 Jack McDowell	1.00	.45	.13
☐	S3 David Cone	1.00	.45	.13
☐	S4 Roger Clemens	3.00	1.35	.40
☐	S5 Nolan Ryan	5.00	2.30	.60
☐	S6 Scott Erickson	1.00	.45	.13
☐	S7 Tom Glavine	1.25	.55	.16
☐	S8 Dwight Gooden	1.00	.45	.13
☐	S9 Andy Benes	1.00	.45	.13
☐	S10 Steve Avery	1.50	.65	.19
☐	S11 Randy Johnson	.75	.35	.09
☐	S12 Jim Abbott	1.00	.45	.13

1992 Fleer Smoke 'n Heat

This 12-card set features outstanding major league pitchers, especially the premier fastball pitchers in both leagues. The cards were randomly inserted in Fleer's 1992 Christmas baseball set. The cards measure the standard size (2 1/2" by 3 1/2"). The front design features color action player photos bordered in black. The player's name appears in a gold foil bar beneath the picture, and the words "Smoke 'n Heat" are printed vertically in the wider right border. Within black borders and on a background of yellow shading to orange, the backs carry a color head shot and player profile. The cards are numbered on the back.

1992 Fleer Update

The 1992 Fleer Update set contains 132 cards measuring the standard size (2 1/2" by 3 1/2"). This year's set, which was available only through hobby dealers, included a four-card, black-bordered "92 Headliners" insert subset. For the Headliners the lettering above the photos and stripe carrying the player's name at the card bottom are both in gold foil. The front design of the regular cards in the update set has color action player photos, with a metallic blue-green border that fades to white as one moves down the card face. The team logo, player's name, and his position appear in the wider right border. The top half of the backs has a close-up photo, while the bottom half carry biography and complete career statistics.

The cards are checklisted below alphabetically within and according to teams for each league as follows: Baltimore Orioles (1-3), Boston Red Sox (4-6), California Angels (7-11), Chicago White Sox (12-14), Cleveland Indians (15-18), Detroit Tigers (19-25), Kansas City Royals (26-32), Milwaukee Brewers (33-38), Minnesota Twins (39-41), New York Yankees (42-46), Oakland Athletics (47-53), Seattle Mariners (54-58), Texas Rangers (59-62), Toronto Blue Jays (63-67), Atlanta Braves (68-71), Chicago Cubs (72-77), Cincinnati Reds (78-84), Houston Astros (85-88), Los Angeles Dodgers (89-94), Montreal Expos (95-100), New York Mets (101-107), Philadelphia Phillies (108-112), Pittsburgh Pirates (113-117), St. Louis Cardinals (118-121), San Diego Padres (122-126), and San Francisco Giants (127-132). The cards are numbered on the back with a U prefix. The key Rookie Cards in this set are Pat Listach, David Nied, Mike Piazza, and Tim Wakefield.

	MT	EX-MT	VG
COMPLETE FACT.SET (136)	27.00	12.00	3.40
COMPLETE SET (132)	17.00	7.75	2.10
COMMON PLAYER (1-132)	.05	.02	.01
COMPLETE HEADLINERS SET (4)	10.00	4.50	1.25
COMMON HEADLINERS (H1-H4)	.50	.23	.06

☐	1 Todd Frohwirth	.05	.02	.01
☐	2 Alan Mills	.05	.02	.01
☐	3 Rick Sutcliffe	.08	.04	.01
☐	4 John Valentin	.25	.11	.03
☐	5 Frank Viola	.08	.04	.01
☐	6 Bob Zupcic	.25	.11	.03
☐	7 Mike Butcher	.10	.05	.01
☐	8 Chad Curtis	.30	.14	.04
☐	9 Damion Easley	.40	.18	.05
☐	10 Tim Salmon	.60	.25	.08
☐	11 Julio Valera	.08	.04	.01
☐	12 George Bell	.08	.04	.01
☐	13 Roberto Hernandez	.12	.05	.02
☐	14 Shawn Jeter	.15	.07	.02
☐	15 Thomas Howard	.05	.02	.01
☐	16 Jesse Levis	.15	.07	.02
☐	17 Kenny Lofton	.40	.18	.05
☐	18 Paul Sorrento	.08	.04	.01
☐	19 Rico Brogna	.10	.05	.01
☐	20 John Doherty	.15	.07	.02
☐	21 Dan Gladden	.05	.02	.01
☐	22 Buddy Groom	.10	.05	.01
☐	23 Shawn Hare	.10	.05	.01
☐	24 John Kiely	.10	.05	.01
☐	25 Kurt Knudsen	.10	.05	.01
☐	26 Gregg Jefferies	.08	.04	.01
☐	27 Wally Joyner	.08	.04	.01
☐	28 Kevin Koslofski	.10	.05	.01
☐	29 Kevin McReynolds	.08	.04	.01
☐	30 Rusty Meacham	.05	.02	.01
☐	31 Keith Miller	.05	.02	.01
☐	32 Hipolito Pichardo	.10	.05	.01
☐	33 James Austin	.10	.05	.01
☐	34 Scott Fletcher	.05	.02	.01
☐	35 John Jaha	.30	.14	.04
☐	36 Pat Listach	1.50	.65	.19
☐	37 Dave Nilsson	.15	.07	.02
☐	38 Kevin Seitzer	.08	.04	.01
☐	39 Tom Edens	.05	.02	.01
☐	40 Pat Mahomes	.25	.11	.03
☐	41 John Smiley	.08	.04	.01
☐	42 Charlie Hayes	.08	.04	.01
☐	43 Sam Militello	.30	.14	.04
☐	44 Andy Stankiewicz	.15	.07	.02
☐	45 Danny Tartabull	.08	.04	.01
☐	46 Bob Wickman	.30	.14	.04
☐	47 Jerry Browne	.05	.02	.01
☐	48 Kevin Campbell	.10	.05	.01
☐	49 Vince Horsman	.10	.05	.01
☐	50 Troy Neel	.25	.11	.03
☐	51 Ruben Sierra	.15	.07	.02
☐	52 Bruce Walton	.05	.02	.01
☐	53 Willie Wilson	.05	.02	.01
☐	54 Bret Boone	.50	.23	.06
☐	55 Dave Fleming	.50	.23	.06
☐	56 Kevin Mitchell	.08	.04	.01
☐	57 Jeff Nelson	.12	.05	.02
☐	58 Shane Turner	.05	.02	.01
☐	59 Jose Canseco	.25	.11	.03
☐	60 Jeff Frye	.10	.05	.01
☐	61 Danny Leon	.10	.05	.01
☐	62 Roger Pavlik	.15	.07	.02
☐	63 David Cone	.10	.05	.01
☐	64 Pat Hentgen	.10	.05	.01
☐	65 Randy Knorr	.10	.05	.01
☐	66 Jack Morris	.10	.05	.01
☐	67 Dave Winfield	.10	.05	.01
☐	68 David Nied	3.00	1.35	.40
☐	69 Otis Nixon	.08	.04	.01
☐	70 Alejandro Pena	.05	.02	.01
☐	71 Jeff Reardon	.10	.05	.01
☐	72 Alex Arias	.20	.09	.03
☐	73 Jim Bullinger	.10	.05	.01
☐	74 Mike Morgan	.05	.02	.01
☐	75 Rey Sanchez	.12	.05	.02
☐	76 Bob Scanlan	.05	.02	.01
☐	77 Sammy Sosa	.05	.02	.01
☐	78 Scott Bankhead	.05	.02	.01
☐	79 Tim Belcher	.08	.04	.01
☐	80 Steve Foster	.10	.05	.01
☐	81 Willie Greene	.40	.18	.05
☐	82 Bip Roberts	.08	.04	.01

☐ 83 Scott Ruskin	.05	.02	.01
☐ 84 Greg Swindell	.08	.04	.01
☐ 85 Juan Guerrero	.12	.05	.02
☐ 86 Butch Henry	.12	.05	.02
☐ 87 Doug Jones	.05	.02	.01
☐ 88 Brian Williams	.25	.11	.03
☐ 89 Tom Candiotti	.05	.02	.01
☐ 90 Eric Davis	.08	.04	.01
☐ 91 Carlos Hernandez	.05	.02	.01
☐ 92 Mike Piazza	.60	.25	.08
☐ 93 Mike Sharperson	.05	.02	.01
☐ 94 Eric Young	.25	.11	.03
☐ 95 Moises Alou	.10	.05	.01
☐ 96 Greg Colbrunn	.10	.05	.01
☐ 97 Wilfredo Cordero	.15	.07	.02
☐ 98 Ken Hill	.08	.04	.01
☐ 99 John Vander Wal	.15	.07	.02
☐ 100 John Wetteland	.05	.02	.01
☐ 101 Bobby Bonilla	.10	.05	.01
☐ 102 Eric Hillman	.20	.09	.03
☐ 103 Pat Howell	.20	.09	.03
☐ 104 Jeff Kent	.30	.14	.04
☐ 105 Dick Schofield	.05	.02	.01
☐ 106 Ryan Thompson	.60	.25	.08
☐ 107 Chico Walker	.05	.02	.01
☐ 108 Juan Bell	.05	.02	.01
☐ 109 Mariano Duncan	.05	.02	.01
☐ 110 Jeff Grotewold	.10	.05	.01
☐ 111 Ben Rivera	.10	.05	.01
☐ 112 Curt Schilling	.08	.04	.01
☐ 113 Victor Cole	.15	.07	.02
☐ 114 Albert Martin	.35	.16	.04
☐ 115 Roger Mason	.05	.02	.01
☐ 116 Blas Minor	.10	.05	.01
☐ 117 Tim Wakefield	3.00	1.35	.40
☐ 118 Mark Clark	.10	.05	.01
☐ 119 Rheal Cormier	.10	.05	.01
☐ 120 Donovan Osborne	.30	.14	.04
☐ 121 Todd Worrell	.05	.02	.01
☐ 122 Jeremy Hernandez	.10	.05	.01
☐ 123 Randy Myers	.08	.04	.01
☐ 124 Frank Seminara	.20	.09	.03
☐ 125 Gary Sheffield	.25	.11	.03
☐ 126 Dan Walters	.15	.07	.02
☐ 127 Steve Hosey	.30	.14	.04
☐ 128 Mike Jackson	.05	.02	.01
☐ 129 Jim Pena	.10	.05	.01
☐ 130 Cory Snyder	.05	.02	.01
☐ 131 Bill Swift	.05	.02	.01
☐ 132 Checklist 1-132	.08	.01	.00
☐ H1 Ken Griffey Jr.	7.00	3.10	.85
1992 All-Star Game MVP			
☐ H2 Robin Yount	2.00	.90	.25
3000 Career Hits			
☐ H3 Jeff Reardon	.50	.23	.06
ML Career Saves Record			

☐ H4 Cecil Fielder	2.00	.90	.25
Record RBI Performance			

1993 Fleer

The first series of the 1993 Fleer baseball set comprises 360 cards measuring the standard size (2 1/2" by 3 1/2"). Randomly inserted in the wax packs were a three-card Golden Moments subset, a 12-card NL All-Stars subset, an 18-card Major League Prospects subset, and three Pro-Visions cards. The fronts show glossy color action player photos bordered in silver. A team color-coded stripe edges the left side of the picture and carries the player's name and team name. On a background that shades from white to silver, the horizontally oriented backs have the player's last name in team-color coded block lettering, a cut out color player photo, and a box displaying biographical and statistical information. The cards are check-listed below alphabetically within and according to teams for each league as follows: Atlanta Braves (1-16), Chicago Cubs (17-28), Cincinnati Reds (29-44), Houston Astros (45-56), Los Angeles Dodgers (57-69), Montreal Expos (70-83), New York Mets (84-96), Philadelphia Phillies (97-109), Pittsburgh Pirates (110-123), St. Louis Cardinals (124-136), San Diego Padres (137-149), San Francisco Giants (150-162), Baltimore Orioles (163-175), Boston Red Sox (176-186), California Angels (187-198), Chicago White Sox (199-211), Cleveland Indians (212-223), Detroit Tigers (224-234), Kansas City

Royals (235-246), Milwaukee Brewers (247-260), Minnesota Twins (261-275), New York Yankees (276-289), Oakland Athletics (290-303), Seattle Mariners (304-316), Texas Rangers (317-329), and Toronto Blue Jays (330-343). Topical subsets featured include League Leaders (344-348), NL Round Trippers (349-353), and Super Star Specials (354-357). The set concludes with checklists (358-360).

		MT	EX-MT	VG
COMPLETE SET (360)		15.00	6.75	1.90
COMMON PLAYER (1-360)		.04	.02	.01
☐ 1	Steve Avery	.15	.07	.02
☐ 2	Sid Bream	.04	.02	.01
☐ 3	Ron Gant	.06	.03	.01
☐ 4	Tom Glavine	.12	.05	.02
☐ 5	Brian Hunter	.06	.03	.01
☐ 6	Ryan Klesko	.30	.14	.04
☐ 7	Charlie Leibrandt	.04	.02	.01
☐ 8	Kent Mercker	.04	.02	.01
☐ 9	David Nied	1.00	.45	.13
☐ 10	Otis Nixon	.04	.02	.01
☐ 11	Greg Olson	.04	.02	.01
☐ 12	Terry Pendleton	.06	.03	.01
☐ 13	Deion Sanders	.12	.05	.02
☐ 14	John Smoltz	.10	.05	.01
☐ 15	Mike Stanton	.04	.02	.01
☐ 16	Mark Wohlers	.06	.03	.01
☐ 17	Paul Assenmacher	.04	.02	.01
☐ 18	Steve Buechele	.04	.02	.01
☐ 19	Shawon Dunston	.06	.03	.01
☐ 20	Mark Grace	.06	.03	.01
☐ 21	Derrick May	.06	.03	.01
☐ 22	Chuck McElroy	.04	.02	.01
☐ 23	Mike Morgan	.04	.02	.01
☐ 24	Rey Sanchez	.04	.02	.01
☐ 25	Ryne Sandberg	.20	.09	.03
☐ 26	Bob Scanlan	.04	.02	.01
☐ 27	Sammy Sosa	.04	.02	.01
☐ 28	Rick Wilkins	.04	.02	.01
☐ 29	Bobby Ayala	.20	.09	.03
☐ 30	Tim Belcher	.06	.03	.01
☐ 31	Jeff Branson	.04	.02	.01
☐ 32	Norm Charlton	.04	.02	.01
☐ 33	Steve Foster	.04	.02	.01
☐ 34	Willie Greene	.08	.04	.01
☐ 35	Chris Hammond	.04	.02	.01
☐ 36	Milt Hill	.04	.02	.01
☐ 37	Hal Morris	.06	.03	.01
☐ 38	Joe Oliver	.04	.02	.01
☐ 39	Paul O'Neill	.06	.03	.01
☐ 40	Tim Pugh	.25	.11	.03
☐ 41	Jose Rijo	.06	.03	.01
☐ 42	Bip Roberts	.06	.03	.01
☐ 43	Chris Sabo	.06	.03	.01
☐ 44	Reggie Sanders	.12	.05	.02
☐ 45	Eric Anthony	.06	.03	.01
☐ 46	Jeff Bagwell	.20	.09	.03
☐ 47	Craig Biggio	.06	.03	.01
☐ 48	Joe Boever	.04	.02	.01
☐ 49	Casey Candaele	.04	.02	.01
☐ 50	Steve Finley	.04	.02	.01
☐ 51	Luis Gonzalez	.06	.03	.01
☐ 52	Pete Harnisch	.04	.02	.01
☐ 53	Xavier Hernandez	.04	.02	.01
☐ 54	Doug Jones	.04	.02	.01
☐ 55	Eddie Taubensee	.06	.03	.01
☐ 56	Brian Williams	.06	.03	.01
☐ 57	Pedro Astacio	.20	.09	.03
☐ 58	Todd Benzinger	.04	.02	.01
☐ 59	Brett Butler	.06	.03	.01
☐ 60	Tom Candiotti	.04	.02	.01
☐ 61	Lenny Harris	.04	.02	.01
☐ 62	Carlos Hernandez	.06	.03	.01
☐ 63	Orel Hershiser	.06	.03	.01
☐ 64	Eric Karros	.35	.16	.04
☐ 65	Ramon Martinez	.06	.03	.01
☐ 66	Jose Offerman	.06	.03	.01
☐ 67	Mike Scioscia	.04	.02	.01
☐ 68	Mike Sharperson	.04	.02	.01
☐ 69	Eric Young	.12	.05	.02
☐ 70	Moises Alou	.06	.03	.01
☐ 71	Ivan Calderon	.04	.02	.01
☐ 72	Archi Cianfrocco	.06	.03	.01
☐ 73	Wilfredo Cordero	.06	.03	.01
☐ 74	Delino DeShields	.10	.05	.01
☐ 75	Mark Gardner	.04	.02	.01
☐ 76	Ken Hill	.06	.03	.01
☐ 77	Tim Laker	.12	.05	.02
☐ 78	Chris Nabholz	.06	.03	.01
☐ 79	Mel Rojas	.04	.02	.01
☐ 80	John Vander Wal	.04	.02	.01
☐ 81	Larry Walker	.12	.05	.02
☐ 82	Tim Wallach	.06	.03	.01
☐ 83	John Wetteland	.04	.02	.01
☐ 84	Bobby Bonilla	.10	.05	.01
☐ 85	Daryl Boston	.04	.02	.01
☐ 86	Sid Fernandez	.06	.03	.01
☐ 87	Eric Hillman	.15	.07	.02
☐ 88	Todd Hundley	.04	.02	.01
☐ 89	Howard Johnson	.06	.03	.01
☐ 90	Jeff Kent	.12	.05	.02
☐ 91	Eddie Murray	.10	.05	.01
☐ 92	Bill Pecota	.04	.02	.01
☐ 93	Bret Saberhagen	.06	.03	.01
☐ 94	Dick Schofield	.04	.02	.01
☐ 95	Pete Schourek	.06	.03	.01
☐ 96	Anthony Young	.06	.03	.01
☐ 97	Ruben Amaro Jr.	.04	.02	.01
☐ 98	Juan Bell	.04	.02	.01
☐ 99	Wes Chamberlain	.04	.02	.01

☐ 100 Darren Daulton	.06	.03	.01
☐ 101 Mariano Duncan	.04	.02	.01
☐ 102 Mike Hartley	.04	.02	.01
☐ 103 Ricky Jordan	.04	.02	.01
☐ 104 John Kruk	.06	.03	.01
☐ 105 Mickey Morandini	.06	.03	.01
☐ 106 Terry Mulholland	.04	.02	.01
☐ 107 Ben Rivera	.06	.03	.01
☐ 108 Curt Schilling	.04	.02	.01
☐ 109 Keith Shepherd	.20	.09	.03
☐ 110 Stan Belinda	.04	.02	.01
☐ 111 Jay Bell	.04	.02	.01
☐ 112 Barry Bonds	.20	.09	.03
☐ 113 Jeff King	.04	.02	.01
☐ 114 Mike LaValliere	.04	.02	.01
☐ 115 Jose Lind	.04	.02	.01
☐ 116 Roger Mason	.04	.02	.01
☐ 117 Orlando Merced	.06	.03	.01
☐ 118 Bob Patterson	.04	.02	.01
☐ 119 Don Slaught	.04	.02	.01
☐ 120 Zane Smith	.04	.02	.01
☐ 121 Randy Tomlin	.04	.02	.01
☐ 122 Andy Van Slyke	.06	.03	.01
☐ 123 Tim Wakefield	.60	.25	.08
☐ 124 Rheal Cormier	.04	.02	.01
☐ 125 Bernard Gilkey	.06	.03	.01
☐ 126 Felix Jose	.06	.03	.01
☐ 127 Ray Lankford	.10	.05	.01
☐ 128 Bob McClure	.04	.02	.01
☐ 129 Donovan Osborne	.12	.05	.02
☐ 130 Tom Pagnozzi	.04	.02	.01
☐ 131 Geronimo Pena	.04	.02	.01
☐ 132 Mike Perez	.06	.03	.01
☐ 133 Lee Smith	.06	.03	.01
☐ 134 Bob Tewksbury	.06	.03	.01
☐ 135 Todd Worrell	.04	.02	.01
☐ 136 Todd Zeile	.06	.03	.01
☐ 137 Jerald Clark	.04	.02	.01
☐ 138 Tony Gwynn	.12	.05	.02
☐ 139 Greg W. Harris	.04	.02	.01
☐ 140 Jeremy Hernandez	.04	.02	.01
☐ 141 Darrin Jackson	.04	.02	.01
☐ 142 Mike Maddux	.04	.02	.01
☐ 143 Fred McGriff	.12	.05	.02
☐ 144 Jose Melendez	.04	.02	.01
☐ 145 Rich Rodriguez	.04	.02	.01
☐ 146 Frank Seminara	.04	.02	.01
☐ 147 Gary Sheffield	.20	.09	.03
☐ 148 Kurt Stillwell	.04	.02	.01
☐ 149 Dan Walters	.04	.02	.01
☐ 150 Rod Beck	.06	.03	.01
☐ 151 Bud Black	.04	.02	.01
☐ 152 Jeff Brantley	.04	.02	.01
☐ 153 John Burkett	.04	.02	.01
☐ 154 Will Clark	.20	.09	.03
☐ 155 Royce Clayton	.06	.03	.01
☐ 156 Mike Jackson	.04	.02	.01
☐ 157 Darren Lewis	.04	.02	.01
☐ 158 Kirt Manwaring	.04	.02	.01
☐ 159 Willie McGee	.06	.03	.01
☐ 160 Cory Snyder	.04	.02	.01
☐ 161 Bill Swift	.04	.02	.01
☐ 162 Trevor Wilson	.04	.02	.01
☐ 163 Brady Anderson	.06	.03	.01
☐ 164 Glenn Davis	.06	.03	.01
☐ 165 Mike Devereaux	.06	.03	.01
☐ 166 Todd Frohwirth	.04	.02	.01
☐ 167 Leo Gomez	.06	.03	.01
☐ 168 Chris Hoiles	.06	.03	.01
☐ 169 Ben McDonald	.06	.03	.01
☐ 170 Randy Milligan	.04	.02	.01
☐ 171 Alan Mills	.04	.02	.01
☐ 172 Mike Mussina	.30	.14	.04
☐ 173 Gregg Olson	.06	.03	.01
☐ 174 Arthur Rhodes	.10	.05	.01
☐ 175 David Segui	.04	.02	.01
☐ 176 Ellis Burks	.04	.02	.01
☐ 177 Roger Clemens	.20	.09	.03
☐ 178 Scott Cooper	.06	.03	.01
☐ 179 Danny Darwin	.04	.02	.01
☐ 180 Tony Fossas	.04	.02	.01
☐ 181 Paul Quantrill	.10	.05	.01
☐ 182 Jody Reed	.04	.02	.01
☐ 183 John Valentin	.12	.05	.02
☐ 184 Mo Vaughn	.06	.03	.01
☐ 185 Frank Viola	.06	.03	.01
☐ 186 Bob Zupcic	.06	.03	.01
☐ 187 Jim Abbott	.10	.05	.01
☐ 188 Gary DiSarcina	.06	.03	.01
☐ 189 Damion Easley	.15	.07	.02
☐ 190 Junior Felix	.04	.02	.01
☐ 191 Chuck Finley	.04	.02	.01
☐ 192 Joe Grahe	.04	.02	.01
☐ 193 Bryan Harvey	.04	.02	.01
☐ 194 Mark Langston	.06	.03	.01
☐ 195 John Orton	.04	.02	.01
☐ 196 Luis Polonia	.04	.02	.01
☐ 197 Tim Salmon	.30	.14	.04
☐ 198 Luis Sojo	.04	.02	.01
☐ 199 Wilson Alvarez	.04	.02	.01
☐ 200 George Bell	.06	.03	.01
☐ 201 Alex Fernandez	.06	.03	.01
☐ 202 Craig Grebeck	.04	.02	.01
☐ 203 Ozzie Guillen	.04	.02	.01
☐ 204 Lance Johnson	.04	.02	.01
☐ 205 Ron Karkovice	.04	.02	.01
☐ 206 Kirk McCaskill	.04	.02	.01
☐ 207 Jack McDowell	.06	.03	.01
☐ 208 Scott Radinsky	.04	.02	.01
☐ 209 Tim Raines	.06	.03	.01
☐ 210 Frank Thomas	.75	.35	.09
☐ 211 Robin Ventura	.15	.07	.02
☐ 212 Sandy Alomar Jr.	.06	.03	.01
☐ 213 Carlos Baerga	.15	.07	.02

☐ 214 Dennis Cook	.04	.02	.01
☐ 215 Thomas Howard	.04	.02	.01
☐ 216 Mark Lewis	.06	.03	.01
☐ 217 Derek Lilliquist	.04	.02	.01
☐ 218 Kenny Lofton	.20	.09	.03
☐ 219 Charles Nagy	.06	.03	.01
☐ 220 Steve Olin	.04	.02	.01
☐ 221 Paul Sorrento	.04	.02	.01
☐ 222 Jim Thome	.06	.03	.01
☐ 223 Mark Whiten	.06	.03	.01
☐ 224 Milt Cuyler	.04	.02	.01
☐ 225 Rob Deer	.06	.03	.01
☐ 226 John Doherty	.04	.02	.01
☐ 227 Cecil Fielder	.12	.05	.02
☐ 228 Travis Fryman	.20	.09	.03
☐ 229 Mike Henneman	.04	.02	.01
☐ 230 John Kiely	.04	.02	.01
☐ 231 Kurt Knudsen	.04	.02	.01
☐ 232 Scott Livingstone	.06	.03	.01
☐ 233 Tony Phillips	.04	.02	.01
☐ 234 Mickey Tettleton	.06	.03	.01
☐ 235 Kevin Appier	.06	.03	.01
☐ 236 George Brett	.10	.05	.01
☐ 237 Tom Gordon	.04	.02	.01
☐ 238 Gregg Jefferies	.06	.03	.01
☐ 239 Wally Joyner	.06	.03	.01
☐ 240 Kevin Koslofski	.04	.02	.01
☐ 241 Mike Macfarlane	.04	.02	.01
☐ 242 Brian McRae	.04	.02	.01
☐ 243 Rusty Meacham	.04	.02	.01
☐ 244 Keith Miller	.04	.02	.01
☐ 245 Jeff Montgomery	.04	.02	.01
☐ 246 Hipolito Pichardo	.04	.02	.01
☐ 247 Ricky Bones	.04	.02	.01
☐ 248 Cal Eldred	.20	.09	.03
☐ 249 Mike Fetters	.04	.02	.01
☐ 250 Darryl Hamilton	.06	.03	.01
☐ 251 Doug Henry	.04	.02	.01
☐ 252 John Jaha	.15	.07	.02
☐ 253 Pat Listach	.50	.23	.06
☐ 254 Paul Molitor	.06	.03	.01
☐ 255 Jaime Navarro	.06	.03	.01
☐ 256 Kevin Seitzer	.06	.03	.01
☐ 257 B.J. Surhoff	.04	.02	.01
☐ 258 Greg Vaughn	.06	.03	.01
☐ 259 Bill Wegman	.04	.02	.01
☐ 260 Robin Yount	.10	.05	.01
☐ 261 Rick Aguilera	.06	.03	.01
☐ 262 Chili Davis	.06	.03	.01
☐ 263 Scott Erickson	.04	.02	.01
☐ 264 Greg Gagne	.04	.02	.01
☐ 265 Mark Guthrie	.04	.02	.01
☐ 266 Brian Harper	.04	.02	.01
☐ 267 Kent Hrbek	.06	.03	.01
☐ 268 Terry Jorgensen	.04	.02	.01
☐ 269 Gene Larkin	.04	.02	.01
☐ 270 Scott Leius	.04	.02	.01
☐ 271 Pat Mahomes	.06	.03	.01
☐ 272 Pedro Munoz	.06	.03	.01
☐ 273 Kirby Puckett	.20	.09	.03
☐ 274 Kevin Tapani	.06	.03	.01
☐ 275 Carl Willis	.04	.02	.01
☐ 276 Steve Farr	.04	.02	.01
☐ 277 John Habyan	.04	.02	.01
☐ 278 Mel Hall	.04	.02	.01
☐ 279 Charlie Hayes	.04	.02	.01
☐ 280 Pat Kelly	.06	.03	.01
☐ 281 Don Mattingly	.12	.05	.02
☐ 282 Sam Militello	.15	.07	.02
☐ 283 Matt Nokes	.04	.02	.01
☐ 284 Melido Perez	.04	.02	.01
☐ 285 Andy Stankiewicz	.06	.03	.01
☐ 286 Danny Tartabull	.06	.03	.01
☐ 287 Randy Velarde	.04	.02	.01
☐ 288 Bob Wickman	.20	.09	.03
☐ 289 Bernie Williams	.06	.03	.01
☐ 290 Lance Blankenship	.04	.02	.01
☐ 291 Mike Bordick	.06	.03	.01
☐ 292 Jerry Browne	.04	.02	.01
☐ 293 Dennis Eckersley	.10	.05	.01
☐ 294 Rickey Henderson	.12	.05	.02
☐ 295 Vince Horsman	.04	.02	.01
☐ 296 Mark McGwire	.20	.09	.03
☐ 297 Jeff Parrett	.04	.02	.01
☐ 298 Ruben Sierra	.15	.07	.02
☐ 299 Terry Steinbach	.06	.03	.01
☐ 300 Walt Weiss	.06	.03	.01
☐ 301 Bob Welch	.04	.02	.01
☐ 302 Willie Wilson	.04	.02	.01
☐ 303 Bobby Witt	.04	.02	.01
☐ 304 Bret Boone	.25	.11	.03
☐ 305 Jay Buhner	.06	.03	.01
☐ 306 Dave Fleming	.20	.09	.03
☐ 307 Ken Griffey Jr.	.50	.23	.06
☐ 308 Erik Hanson	.04	.02	.01
☐ 309 Edgar Martinez	.06	.03	.01
☐ 310 Tino Martinez	.06	.03	.01
☐ 311 Jeff Nelson	.04	.02	.01
☐ 312 Dennis Powell	.04	.02	.01
☐ 313 Mike Schooler	.04	.02	.01
☐ 314 Russ Swan	.04	.02	.01
☐ 315 Dave Valle	.04	.02	.01
☐ 316 Omar Vizquel	.04	.02	.01
☐ 317 Kevin Brown	.06	.03	.01
☐ 318 Todd Burns	.04	.02	.01
☐ 319 Jose Canseco	.20	.09	.03
☐ 320 Julio Franco	.06	.03	.01
☐ 321 Jeff Frye	.04	.02	.01
☐ 322 Juan Gonzalez	.30	.14	.04
☐ 323 Jose Guzman	.06	.03	.01
☐ 324 Jeff Huson	.04	.02	.01
☐ 325 Dean Palmer	.06	.03	.01
☐ 326 Kevin Reimer	.06	.03	.01
☐ 327 Ivan Rodriguez	.20	.09	.03

☐ 328	Kenny Rogers 04	.02	.01
☐ 329	Dan Smith...................12	.05	.02
☐ 330	Roberto Alomar 20	.09	.03
☐ 331	Derek Bell 06	.03	.01
☐ 332	Pat Borders.................04	.02	.01
☐ 333	Joe Carter 12	.05	.02
☐ 334	Kelly Gruber 06	.03	.01
☐ 335	Tom Henke 06	.03	.01
☐ 336	Jimmy Key 04	.02	.01
☐ 337	Manuel Lee 04	.02	.01
☐ 338	Candy Maldonado 04	.02	.01
☐ 339	John Olerud 10	.05	.01
☐ 340	Todd Stottlemyre 06	.03	.01
☐ 341	Duane Ward 04	.02	.01
☐ 342	Devon White 06	.03	.01
☐ 343	Dave Winfield 10	.05	.01
☐ 344	Edgar Martinez LL...........05	.02	.01
☐ 345	Cecil Fielder LL 10	.05	.01
☐ 346	Kenny Lofton LL 10	.05	.01
☐ 347	Jack Morris LL 10	.05	.01
☐ 348	Roger Clemens LL 12	.05	.02
☐ 349	Fred McGriff RT 10	.05	.01
☐ 350	Barry Bonds RT 10	.05	.01
☐ 351	Gary Sheffield RT...........10	.05	.01
☐ 352	Darren Daulton RT 05	.02	.01
☐ 353	Dave Hollins RT 05	.02	.01
☐ 354	Brothers in Blue 10	.05	.01
	Pedro Martinez		
	Ramon Martinez		
☐ 355	Power Packs 15	.07	.02
	Ivan Rodriguez		
	Kirby Puckett		
☐ 356	Triple Threats................15	.07	.02
	Ryne Sandberg		
	Gary Sheffield		
☐ 357	Infield Trifecta..............15	.07	.02
	Roberto Alomar		
	Chuck Knoblauch		
	Carlos Baerga		
☐ 358	Checklist 1-120 05	.01	.00
☐ 359	Checklist 121-240 05	.01	.00
☐ 360	Checklist 241-360 05	.01	.00

1993 Fleer All-Stars

This 12-card standard-size (2 1/2" by 3 1/2") set was randomly inserted in 1993 Fleer series I wax packs. Cards 1-12 feature National League All-Stars. The horizontal fronts feature a color close-up photo cut out and superimposed on a black-and-white action scene framed by white

borders. The player's name and the word "All-Stars" are printed in gold foil lettering across the bottom of the picture. On a pastel yellow panel, the horizontal backs carry career summary. The cards are numbered on the back "No. X of 12."

	MT	EX-MT	VG
COMPLETE SET (12) 20.00		9.00	2.50
COMMON PLAYER (1-12) ..1.00		.45	.13
☐ 1 Fred McGriff 2.50		1.15	.30
☐ 2 Delino DeShields.........2.00		.90	.25
☐ 3 Gary Sheffield 3.50		1.55	.45
☐ 4 Barry Larkin 2.00		.90	.25
☐ 5 Felix Jose 1.00		.45	.13
☐ 6 Larry Walker 2.00		.90	.25
☐ 7 Barry Bonds 4.00		1.80	.50
☐ 8 Andy Van Slyke 1.50		.65	.19
☐ 9 Darren Daulton 1.00		.45	.13
☐ 10 Greg Maddux 2.50		1.15	.30
☐ 11 Tom Glavine 2.50		1.15	.30
☐ 12 Lee Smith 1.00		.45	.13

1993 Fleer Golden Moments

This three-card standard-size (2 1/2" by 3 1/2") set was randomly inserted in 1993 Fleer series I wax packs. The fronts feature glossy color action photos framed by thin aqua and white lines and a black outer border. A gold foil baseball icon appears at each corner of the picture, and the player's name and the set title "Golden Moments" appears in a gold foil bar toward the bottom of the picture. The backs have a simi-

lar design to that on the fronts, only with a small color head shot and a summary of the player's outstanding achievement on a white panel. The cards are unnumbered and checklisted below in alphabetical order.

	MT	EX-MT	VG
COMPLETE SET (3)	6.00	2.70	.75
COMMON PLAYER (1-3)	1.00	.45	.13
☐ 1 George Brett	3.50	1.55	.45
3,000 Hits			
☐ 2 Mickey Morandini	1.00	.45	.13
Unassisted Triple Play			
☐ 3 Dave Winfield	3.00	1.35	.40
Oldest Player with			
100 RBI Season			

1993 Fleer Major League Prospects

This 18-card standard-size (2 1/2" by 3 1/2") set was randomly inserted in 1993 Fleer series I wax packs. The fronts display glossy color action photos bordered in black. The player's name is printed in gold foil lettering across the top of the picture. At the bottom center, a black and gold foil triangle carries a baseball icon and the words "Major League Prospects." Inside black borders on a white panel, the backs show a color close-up photo, biography, and player profile. The cards are numbered on the back "X of 18."

	MT	EX-MT	VG
COMPLETE SET (18)	25.00	11.50	3.10
COMMON PLAYER (1-18)	1.00	.45	.13
☐ 1 Melvin Nieves	4.00	1.80	.50
☐ 2 Sterling Hitchcock	3.00	1.35	.40
☐ 3 Tim Costo	1.25	.55	.16
☐ 4 Manny Alexander	1.25	.55	.16
☐ 5 Alan Embree	3.00	1.35	.40
☐ 6 Kevin Young	3.00	1.35	.40
☐ 7 J.T. Snow	4.00	1.80	.50
☐ 8 Russ Springer	1.50	.65	.19
☐ 9 Billy Ashley	3.00	1.35	.40
☐ 10 Kevin Rogers	1.00	.45	.13
☐ 11 Steve Hosey	2.00	.90	.25
☐ 12 Eric Wedge	3.00	1.35	.40
☐ 13 Mike Piazza	3.50	1.55	.45
☐ 14 Jesse Levis	1.00	.45	.13
☐ 15 Rico Brogna	1.00	.45	.13
☐ 16 Alex Arias	1.00	.45	.13
☐ 17 Rod Brewer	1.25	.55	.16
☐ 18 Troy Neel	1.25	.55	.16

1993 Fleer Pro-Visions

This three-card standard-size (2 1/2" by 3 1/2") set was randomly inserted in 1993 Fleer series I wax packs. Inside a black border, the fronts display surrealistic artistic drawings of the featured player. His name is printed in gold foil block lettering in the wider bottom black border. Inside black borders on a white panel, the backs give the player a nickname illustrated by the front drawing and describes the

player's career. The cards are numbered on the back "X of 3."

	MT	EX-MT	VG
COMPLETE SET (3)	7.00	3.10	.85
COMMON PLAYER (1-3)	1.25	.55	.16
☐ 1 Roberto Alomar	4.00	1.80	.50
☐ 2 Dennis Eckersley	1.25	.55	.16
☐ 3 Gary Sheffield	3.00	1.35	.40

1948-49 Leaf

The cards in this 98-card set measure 2 3/8" by 2 7/8". The 1948-49 Leaf set was the first post-war baseball series issued in color. This effort was not entirely successful due to a lack of refinement which resulted in many color variations and cards out of register. In addition, the set was skip numbered from 1-168, with 49 of the 98 cards printed in limited quantities (marked with SP in the checklist). Cards 102 and 136 have variations, and cards are sometimes found with overprinted or incorrect backs. The notable Rookie Cards in this

set include Stan Musial, Satchel Paige, and Jackie Robinson.

	NRMT	VG-E	GOOD
COMPLETE SET (98)	28000.	12600.	3500.
COMMON PLAYER (1-168)	25.00	11.50	3.10
☐ 1 Joe DiMaggio	2150.00	950.00	275.00
☐ 3 Babe Ruth	2400.00	1100.00	300.00
☐ 4 Stan Musial	800.00	350.00	100.00
☐ 5 Virgil Trucks SP	425.00	190.00	52.50
☐ 8 Satchel Paige SP	2250.00	1000.00	275.00
☐ 10 Dizzy Trout	28.00	12.50	3.50
☐ 11 Phil Rizzuto	210.00	95.00	26.00
☐ 13 Cass Michaels SP	350.00	160.00	45.00
☐ 14 Billy Johnson	28.00	12.50	3.50
☐ 17 Frank Overmire	25.00	11.50	3.10
☐ 19 Johnny Wyrostek SP	350.00	160.00	45.00
☐ 20 Hank Sauer SP	450.00	200.00	57.50
☐ 22 Al Evans	25.00	11.50	3.10
☐ 26 Sam Chapman	25.00	11.50	3.10
☐ 27 Mickey Harris	25.00	11.50	3.10
☐ 28 Jim Hegan	30.00	13.50	3.80
☐ 29 Elmer Valo	30.00	13.50	3.80
☐ 30 Billy Goodman SP	400.00	180.00	50.00
☐ 31 Lou Brissie	25.00	11.50	3.10
☐ 32 Warren Spahn	275.00	125.00	34.00
☐ 33 Peanuts Lowrey SP	350.00	160.00	45.00
☐ 36 Al Zarilla SP	350.00	160.00	45.00
☐ 38 Ted Kluszewski	95.00	42.50	12.00
☐ 39 Ewell Blackwell	55.00	25.00	7.00
☐ 42 Kent Peterson	25.00	11.50	3.10
☐ 43 Ed Stevens SP	350.00	160.00	45.00
☐ 45 Ken Keltner SP	350.00	160.00	45.00
☐ 46 Johnny Mize	110.00	50.00	14.00
☐ 47 George Vico	25.00	11.50	3.10
☐ 48 Johnny Schmitz SP	350.00	160.00	45.00
☐ 49 Del Ennis	40.00	18.00	5.00
☐ 50 Dick Wakefield	25.00	11.50	3.10
☐ 51 Al Dark SP	450.00	200.00	57.50
☐ 53 Johnny VanderMeer	45.00	20.00	5.75
☐ 54 Bobby Adams SP	350.00	160.00	45.00
☐ 55 Tommy Henrich SP	450.00	200.00	57.50
☐ 56 Larry Jansen	30.00	13.50	3.80
☐ 57 Bob McCall	25.00	11.50	3.10
☐ 59 Luke Appling	90.00	40.00	11.50
☐ 61 Jake Early	25.00	11.50	3.10
☐ 62 Eddie Joost SP	350.00	160.00	45.00
☐ 63 Barney McCosky SP	350.00	160.00	45.00
☐ 65 Robert Elliott UER	40.00	18.00	5.00
(Misspelled Elliot			
on card front)			
☐ 66 Orval Grove SP	350.00	160.00	45.00
☐ 68 Eddie Miller SP	350.00	160.00	45.00
☐ 70 Honus Wagner	300.00	135.00	38.00
☐ 72 Hank Edwards	25.00	11.50	3.10
☐ 73 Pat Seerey	25.00	11.50	3.10

☐	75	Dom DiMaggio SP	575.00	250.00	70.00
☐	76	Ted Williams	750.00	350.00	95.00
☐	77	Roy Smalley	30.00	13.50	3.80
☐	78	Hoot Evers SP	350.00	160.00	45.00
☐	79	Jackie Robinson	825.00	375.00	105.00
☐	81	Whitey Kurowski SP	350.00	160.00	45.00
☐	82	Johnny Lindell	28.00	12.50	3.50
☐	83	Bobby Doerr	125.00	57.50	15.50
☐	84	Sid Hudson	25.00	11.50	3.10
☐	85	Dave Philley SP	400.00	180.00	50.00
☐	86	Ralph Weigel	25.00	11.50	3.10
☐	88	Frank Gustine SP	350.00	160.00	45.00
☐	91	Ralph Kiner	200.00	90.00	25.00
☐	93	Bob Feller SP	1500.00	700.00	190.00
☐	95	George Stirnweiss	30.00	13.50	3.80
☐	97	Marty Marion	55.00	25.00	7.00
☐	98	Hal Newhouser SP	675.00	300.00	85.00
☐	102A	Gene Hermanski ERR	300.00	135.00	38.00
☐	102B	Gene Hermanski COR	28.00	12.50	3.50
☐	104	Eddie Stewart SP	350.00	160.00	45.00
☐	106	Lou Boudreau	110.00	50.00	14.00
☐	108	Matt Batts SP	350.00	160.00	45.00
☐	111	Jerry Priddy	25.00	11.50	3.10
☐	113	Dutch Leonard SP	350.00	160.00	45.00
☐	117	Joe Gordon	40.00	18.00	5.00
☐	120	George Kell SP	650.00	300.00	80.00
☐	121	Johnny Pesky SP	425.00	190.00	52.50
☐	123	Cliff Fannin SP	350.00	160.00	45.00
☐	125	Andy Pafko	30.00	13.50	3.80
☐	127	Enos Slaughter SP	775.00	350.00	95.00
☐	128	Buddy Rosar	25.00	11.50	3.10
☐	129	Kirby Higbe SP	350.00	160.00	45.00
☐	131	Sid Gordon SP	350.00	160.00	45.00
☐	133	Tommy Holmes SP	425.00	190.00	52.50
☐	136A	Cliff Aberson	25.00	11.50	3.10
		(Full sleeve)			
☐	136B	Cliff Aberson	300.00	135.00	38.00
		(Short sleeve)			
☐	137	Harry Walker SP	350.00	160.00	45.00
☐	138	Larry Doby SP	550.00	250.00	70.00
☐	139	Johnny Hopp	30.00	13.50	3.80
☐	142	Danny Murtaugh SP	425.00	190.00	52.50
☐	143	Dick Sisler SP	350.00	160.00	45.00
☐	144	Bob Dillinger SP	350.00	160.00	45.00
☐	146	Pete Reiser SP	450.00	200.00	57.50
☐	149	Hank Majeski SP	350.00	160.00	45.00
☐	153	Floyd Baker SP	350.00	160.00	45.00
☐	158	Harry Brecheen SP	425.00	190.00	52.50
☐	159	Mizell Platt	25.00	11.50	3.10
☐	160	Bob Scheffing SP	350.00	160.00	45.00
☐	161	Vern Stephens SP	425.00	190.00	52.50
☐	163	Fred Hutchinson SP	450.00	200.00	57.50
☐	165	Dale Mitchell SP	425.00	190.00	52.50
☐	168	Phil Cavarretta SP	450.00	200.00	57.50

1960 Leaf

The cards in this 144-card set measure
2 1/2" by 3 1/2". The 1960 Leaf set was
issued in a regular gum package style but
with a marble instead of gum. The series
was a joint production by Sports Novelties,
Inc., and Leaf, two Chicago-based companies. Cards 73-144 are more difficult to
find than the lower numbers. Photo variations exist (probably proof cards) for the
seven cards listed with an asterisk and
there is a well-known error card, number
25 showing Brooks Lawrence (in a Reds
uniform) with Jim Grant's name on front,
and Grant's biography and record on back.
The corrected version with Grant's photo is
the more difficult variety. The only notable
Rookie Card in this set is Dallas Green.
The complete set price below includes
both versions of Jim Grant.

		NRMT	VG-E	GOOD
COMPLETE SET (145)		1200.00	550.00	150.00
COMMON PLAYER (1-72)		2.50	1.15	.30
COMMON PLAYER (73-144)		14.00	6.25	1.75

			NRMT	VG-E	GOOD
☐	1	Luis Aparicio *	20.00	5.00	1.60
☐	2	Woody Held	2.50	1.15	.30
☐	3	Frank Lary	3.00	1.35	.40
☐	4	Camilo Pascual	3.00	1.35	.40
☐	5	Pancho Herrera	2.50	1.15	.30
☐	6	Felipe Alou	6.50	2.90	.80
☐	7	Benjamin Daniels	2.50	1.15	.30
☐	8	Roger Craig	5.50	2.50	.70
☐	9	Eddie Kasko	2.50	1.15	.30
☐	10	Bob Grim	2.50	1.35	.40
☐	11	Jim Busby	2.50	1.15	.30
☐	12	Ken Boyer	8.00	3.60	1.00
☐	13	Bob Boyd	2.50	1.15	.30

☐	14 Sam Jones	3.00	1.35	.40
☐	15 Larry Jackson	3.00	1.35	.40
☐	16 Elroy Face	4.50	2.00	.55
☐	17 Walt Moryn *	2.50	1.15	.30
☐	18 Jim Gilliam	4.50	2.00	.55
☐	19 Don Newcombe	4.50	2.00	.55
☐	20 Glen Hobbie	2.50	1.15	.30
☐	21 Pedro Ramos	2.50	1.15	.30
☐	22 Ryne Duren	4.50	2.00	.55
☐	23 Joey Jay *	3.00	1.35	.40
☐	24 Lou Berberet	2.50	1.15	.30
☐	25A Jim Grant ERR	13.50	6.00	1.70
	(Photo actually			
	Brooks Lawrence)			
☐	25B Jim Grant COR	20.00	9.00	2.50
☐	26 Tom Borland	2.50	1.15	.30
☐	27 Brooks Robinson	35.00	16.00	4.40
☐	28 Jerry Adair	2.50	1.15	.30
☐	29 Ron Jackson	2.50	1.15	.30
☐	30 George Strickland	2.50	1.15	.30
☐	31 Rocky Bridges	2.50	1.15	.30
☐	32 Bill Tuttle	2.50	1.15	.30
☐	33 Ken Hunt	2.50	1.15	.30
☐	34 Hal Griggs	2.50	1.15	.30
☐	35 Jim Coates *	2.50	1.15	.30
☐	36 Brooks Lawrence	2.50	1.15	.30
☐	37 Duke Snider	48.00	22.00	6.00
☐	38 Al Spangler	2.50	1.15	.30
☐	39 Jim Owens	2.50	1.15	.30
☐	40 Bill Virdon	4.50	2.00	.55
☐	41 Ernie Broglio	3.00	1.35	.40
☐	42 Andre Rodgers	2.50	1.15	.30
☐	43 Julio Becquer	2.50	1.15	.30
☐	44 Tony Taylor	3.00	1.35	.40
☐	45 Jerry Lynch	3.00	1.35	.40
☐	46 Cletis Boyer	4.50	2.00	.55
☐	47 Jerry Lumpe	2.50	1.15	.30
☐	48 Charlie Maxwell	3.00	1.35	.40
☐	49 Jim Perry	4.50	2.00	.55
☐	50 Danny McDevitt	2.50	1.15	.30
☐	51 Juan Pizarro	2.50	1.15	.30
☐	52 Dallas Green	6.50	2.90	.80
☐	53 Bob Friend	3.00	1.35	.40
☐	54 Jack Sanford	3.00	1.35	.40
☐	55 Jim Rivera	2.50	1.15	.30
☐	56 Ted Wills	2.50	1.15	.30
☐	57 Milt Pappas	3.00	1.35	.40
☐	58 Hal Smith *	2.50	1.15	.30
☐	59 Bobby Avila	2.50	1.15	.30
☐	60 Clem Labine	3.00	1.35	.40
☐	61 Norman Rehm *	2.50	1.15	.30
☐	62 John Gabler	2.50	1.15	.30
☐	63 John Tsitouris	2.50	1.15	.30
☐	64 Dave Sisler	2.50	1.15	.30
☐	65 Vic Power	3.00	1.35	.40
☐	66 Earl Battey	2.50	1.15	.30
☐	67 Bob Purkey	2.50	1.15	.30
☐	68 Moe Drabowsky	3.00	1.35	.40
☐	69 Hoyt Wilhelm	15.00	6.75	1.90
☐	70 Humberto Robinson	2.50	1.15	.30
☐	71 Whitey Herzog	6.00	2.70	.75
☐	72 Dick Donovan *	2.50	1.15	.30
☐	73 Gordon Jones	16.00	7.25	2.00
☐	74 Joe Hicks	14.00	6.25	1.75
☐	75 Ray Culp	18.00	8.00	2.30
☐	76 Dick Drott	14.00	6.25	1.75
☐	77 Bob Duliba	14.00	6.25	1.75
☐	78 Art Ditmar	14.00	6.25	1.75
☐	79 Steve Korcheck	14.00	6.25	1.75
☐	80 Henry Mason	14.00	6.25	1.75
☐	81 Harry Simpson	14.00	6.25	1.75
☐	82 Gene Green	14.00	6.25	1.75
☐	83 Bob Shaw	14.00	6.25	1.75
☐	84 Howard Reed	14.00	6.25	1.75
☐	85 Dick Stigman	14.00	6.25	1.75
☐	86 Rip Repulski	14.00	6.25	1.75
☐	87 Seth Morehead	14.00	6.25	1.75
☐	88 Camilo Carreon	14.00	6.25	1.75
☐	89 John Blanchard	18.00	8.00	2.30
☐	90 Billy Hoeft	14.00	6.25	1.75
☐	91 Fred Hopke	14.00	6.25	1.75
☐	92 Joe Martin	14.00	6.25	1.75
☐	93 Wally Shannon	14.00	6.25	1.75
☐	94 Two Hal Smith's	20.00	9.00	2.50
	Hal R. Smith			
	Hal W. Smith			
☐	95 Al Schroll	14.00	6.25	1.75
☐	96 John Kucks	14.00	6.25	1.75
☐	97 Tom Morgan	14.00	6.25	1.75
☐	98 Willie Jones	14.00	6.25	1.75
☐	99 Marshall Renfroe	14.00	6.25	1.75
☐	100 Willie Tasby	14.00	6.25	1.75
☐	101 Irv Noren	14.00	6.25	1.75
☐	102 Russ Snyder	14.00	6.25	1.75
☐	103 Bob Turley	16.50	7.50	2.10
☐	104 Jim Woods	14.00	6.25	1.75
☐	105 Ronnie Kline	14.00	6.25	1.75
☐	106 Steve Bilko	14.00	6.25	1.75
☐	107 Elmer Valo	14.00	6.25	1.75
☐	108 Tom McAvoy	14.00	6.25	1.75
☐	109 Stan Williams	16.00	7.25	2.00
☐	110 Earl Averill Jr.	14.00	6.25	1.75
☐	111 Lee Walls	14.00	6.25	1.75
☐	112 Paul Richards MG	16.00	7.25	2.00
☐	113 Ed Sadowski	14.00	6.25	1.75
☐	114 Stover McIlwain	14.00	6.25	1.75
☐	115 Chuck Tanner UER	16.50	7.50	2.10
	(Photo actually			
	Ken Kuhn)			
☐	116 Lou Klimchock	14.00	6.25	1.75
☐	117 Neil Chrisley	14.00	6.25	1.75
☐	118 John Callison	16.50	7.50	2.10
☐	119 Hal Smith	14.00	6.25	1.75
☐	120 Carl Sawatski	14.00	6.25	1.75

☐	121	Frank Leja	14.00	6.25	1.75
☐	122	Earl Torgeson	14.00	6.25	1.75
☐	123	Art Schult	14.00	6.25	1.75
☐	124	Jim Brosnan	16.00	7.25	2.00
☐	125	Sparky Anderson	40.00	18.00	5.00
☐	126	Joe Pignatano	14.00	6.25	1.75
☐	127	Rocky Nelson	14.00	6.25	1.75
☐	128	Orlando Cepeda	50.00	23.00	6.25
☐	129	Daryl Spencer	14.00	6.25	1.75
☐	130	Ralph Lumenti	14.00	6.25	1.75
☐	131	Sam Taylor	14.00	6.25	1.75
☐	132	Harry Brecheen CO	16.00	7.25	2.00
☐	133	Johnny Groth	14.00	6.25	1.75
☐	134	Wayne Terwilliger	14.00	6.25	1.75
☐	135	Kent Hadley	14.00	6.25	1.75
☐	136	Faye Throneberry	14.00	6.25	1.75
☐	137	Jack Meyer	14.00	6.25	1.75
☐	138	Chuck Cottier	16.50	7.50	2.10
☐	139	Joe DeMaestri	14.00	6.25	1.75
☐	140	Gene Freese	14.00	6.25	1.75
☐	141	Curt Flood	25.00	11.50	3.10
☐	142	Gino Cimoli	14.00	6.25	1.75
☐	143	Clay Dalrymple	14.00	6.25	1.75
☐	144	Jim Bunning	50.00	23.00	6.25

1990 Leaf

The 1990 Leaf set was another major, premium set introduced by Donruss in 1990. This set, which was produced on high quality paper stock, was issued in two separate series of 264 cards each. The second series was issued approximately six weeks after the release of the first series. The cards are in the standard size of 2 1/2" by 3 1/2" and have full-color photos on both the front and the back of the cards. The first card of the set includes a brief his-

tory of the Leaf company and the checklists feature player photos in a style very reminiscent to the Topps checklists of the late 1960s. The card style is very similar to Upper Deck, but the Leaf sets were only distributed through hobby channels and were not available in factory sets. The key Rookie Cards in the first series are Eric Anthony, Delino DeShields, Marquis Grissom, Ben McDonald, John Olerud, and Sammy Sosa. The key Rookie Cards in the second series are Carlos Baerga, Chris Hoiles, Dave Justice, Kevin Maas, Jose Offerman, Kevin Tapani, Frank Thomas, Larry Walker, and Mark Whiten. Each pack contained 15 cards and one three-piece puzzle card of a 63-piece Yogi Berra "Donruss Hall of Fame Diamond King" puzzle.

	MT	EX-MT	VG
COMPLETE SET (528)	250.00	115.00	31.00
COMPLETE SERIES 1 (264)	120.00	55.00	15.00
COMPLETE SERIES 2 (264)	130.00	57.50	16.50
COMMON PLAYER (1-264)	.25	.11	.03
COMMON PLAYER (265-528)	.25	.11	.03

☐	1	Introductory Card	.25	.11	.03
☐	2	Mike Henneman	.25	.11	.03
☐	3	Steve Bedrosian	.25	.11	.03
☐	4	Mike Scott	.25	.11	.03
☐	5	Allan Anderson	.25	.11	.03
☐	6	Rick Sutcliffe	.30	.14	.04
☐	7	Gregg Olson	1.50	.65	.19
☐	8	Kevin Elster	.25	.11	.03
☐	9	Pete O'Brien	.25	.11	.03
☐	10	Carlton Fisk	1.00	.45	.13
☐	11	Joe Magrane	.25	.11	.03
☐	12	Roger Clemens	4.00	1.80	.50
☐	13	Tom Glavine	9.00	4.00	1.15
☐	14	Tom Gordon	.30	.14	.04
☐	15	Todd Benzinger	.25	.11	.03
☐	16	Hubie Brooks	.25	.11	.03
☐	17	Roberto Kelly	1.00	.45	.13
☐	18	Barry Larkin	1.50	.65	.19
☐	19	Mike Boddicker	.25	.11	.03
☐	20	Roger McDowell	.25	.11	.03
☐	21	Nolan Ryan	7.00	3.10	.85
☐	22	John Farrell	.25	.11	.03
☐	23	Bruce Hurst	.30	.14	.04
☐	24	Wally Joyner	.35	.16	.04
☐	25	Greg Maddux	4.00	1.80	.50
☐	26	Chris Bosio	.25	.11	.03
☐	27	John Cerutti	.25	.11	.03
☐	28	Tim Burke	.25	.11	.03
☐	29	Dennis Eckersley	.90	.40	.11
☐	30	Glenn Davis	.30	.14	.04

☐ 31	Jim Abbott	4.00	1.80	.50
☐ 32	Mike LaValliere	.25	.11	.03
☐ 33	Andres Thomas	.25	.11	.03
☐ 34	Lou Whitaker	.30	.14	.04
☐ 35	Alvin Davis	.25	.11	.03
☐ 36	Melido Perez	.30	.14	.04
☐ 37	Craig Biggio	.75	.35	.09
☐ 38	Rick Aguilera	.30	.14	.04
☐ 39	Pete Harnisch	.40	.18	.05
☐ 40	David Cone	1.75	.80	.22
☐ 41	Scott Garrelts	.25	.11	.03
☐ 42	Jay Howell	.25	.11	.03
☐ 43	Eric King	.25	.11	.03
☐ 44	Pedro Guerrero	.30	.14	.04
☐ 45	Mike Bielecki	.25	.11	.03
☐ 46	Bob Boone	.30	.14	.04
☐ 47	Kevin Brown	1.25	.55	.16
☐ 48	Jerry Browne	.25	.11	.03
☐ 49	Mike Scioscia	.25	.11	.03
☐ 50	Chuck Cary	.25	.11	.03
☐ 51	Wade Boggs	1.75	.80	.22
☐ 52	Von Hayes	.25	.11	.03
☐ 53	Tony Fernandez	.30	.14	.04
☐ 54	Dennis Martinez	.30	.14	.04
☐ 55	Tom Candiotti	.25	.11	.03
☐ 56	Andy Benes	3.00	1.35	.40
☐ 57	Rob Dibble	.50	.23	.06
☐ 58	Chuck Crim	.25	.11	.03
☐ 59	John Smoltz	5.00	2.30	.60
☐ 60	Mike Heath	.25	.11	.03
☐ 61	Kevin Gross	.25	.11	.03
☐ 62	Mark McGwire	3.50	1.55	.45
☐ 63	Bert Blyleven	.30	.14	.04
☐ 64	Bob Walk	.25	.11	.03
☐ 65	Mickey Tettleton	.40	.18	.05
☐ 66	Sid Fernandez	.30	.14	.04
☐ 67	Terry Kennedy	.25	.11	.03
☐ 68	Fernando Valenzuela	.30	.14	.04
☐ 69	Don Mattingly	2.00	.90	.25
☐ 70	Paul O'Neill	.30	.14	.04
☐ 71	Robin Yount	1.75	.80	.22
☐ 72	Bret Saberhagen	.30	.14	.04
☐ 73	Geno Petralli	.25	.11	.03
☐ 74	Brook Jacoby	.25	.11	.03
☐ 75	Roberto Alomar	7.00	3.10	.85
☐ 76	Devon White	.30	.14	.04
☐ 77	Jose Lind	.25	.11	.03
☐ 78	Pat Combs	.30	.14	.04
☐ 79	Dave Stieb	.30	.14	.04
☐ 80	Tim Wallach	.30	.14	.04
☐ 81	Dave Stewart	.30	.14	.04
☐ 82	Eric Anthony	2.00	.90	.25
☐ 83	Randy Bush	.25	.11	.03
☐ 84	Checklist Card	.35	.16	.04
	(Rickey Henderson)			
☐ 85	Jaime Navarro	2.00	.90	.25
☐ 86	Tommy Gregg	.25	.11	.03
☐ 87	Frank Tanana	.25	.11	.03
☐ 88	Omar Vizquel	.40	.18	.05
☐ 89	Ivan Calderon	.25	.11	.03
☐ 90	Vince Coleman	.30	.14	.04
☐ 91	Barry Bonds	3.50	1.55	.45
☐ 92	Randy Milligan	.25	.11	.03
☐ 93	Frank Viola	.30	.14	.04
☐ 94	Matt Williams	1.00	.45	.13
☐ 95	Alfredo Griffin	.25	.11	.03
☐ 96	Steve Sax	.30	.14	.04
☐ 97	Gary Gaetti	.25	.11	.03
☐ 98	Ryne Sandberg	4.00	1.80	.50
☐ 99	Danny Tartabull	.75	.35	.09
☐ 100	Rafael Palmeiro	1.25	.55	.16
☐ 101	Jesse Orosco	.25	.11	.03
☐ 102	Garry Templeton	.25	.11	.03
☐ 103	Frank DiPino	.25	.11	.03
☐ 104	Tony Pena	.25	.11	.03
☐ 105	Dickie Thon	.25	.11	.03
☐ 106	Kelly Gruber	.30	.14	.04
☐ 107	Marquis Grissom	6.00	2.70	.75
☐ 108	Jose Canseco	3.50	1.55	.45
☐ 109	Mike Blowers	.25	.11	.03
☐ 110	Tom Browning	.25	.11	.03
☐ 111	Greg Vaughn	1.50	.65	.19
☐ 112	Oddibe McDowell	.25	.11	.03
☐ 113	Gary Ward	.25	.11	.03
☐ 114	Jay Buhner	.35	.16	.04
☐ 115	Eric Show	.25	.11	.03
☐ 116	Bryan Harvey	.35	.16	.04
☐ 117	Andy Van Slyke	.50	.23	.06
☐ 118	Jeff Ballard	.25	.11	.03
☐ 119	Barry Lyons	.25	.11	.03
☐ 120	Kevin Mitchell	.50	.23	.06
☐ 121	Mike Gallego	.25	.11	.03
☐ 122	Dave Smith	.25	.11	.03
☐ 123	Kirby Puckett	3.50	1.55	.45
☐ 124	Jerome Walton	.30	.14	.04
☐ 125	Bo Jackson	1.25	.55	.16
☐ 126	Harold Baines	.30	.14	.04
☐ 127	Scott Bankhead	.25	.11	.03
☐ 128	Ozzie Guillen	.25	.11	.03
☐ 129	Jose Oquendo UER	.25	.11	.03
	(League misspelled			
	as Legue)			
☐ 130	John Dopson	.25	.11	.03
☐ 131	Charlie Hayes	.50	.23	.06
☐ 132	Fred McGriff	2.00	.90	.25
☐ 133	Chet Lemon	.25	.11	.03
☐ 134	Gary Carter	.35	.16	.04
☐ 135	Rafael Ramirez	.25	.11	.03
☐ 136	Shane Mack	1.00	.45	.13
☐ 137	Mark Grace UER	2.00	.90	.25
	(Card back has OB:L,			
	should be B:L)			
☐ 138	Phil Bradley	.25	.11	.03
☐ 139	Dwight Gooden	.50	.23	.06

□	140	Harold Reynolds	.25	.11	.03
□	141	Scott Fletcher	.25	.11	.03
□	142	Ozzie Smith	1.00	.45	.13
□	143	Mike Greenwell	.30	.14	.04
□	144	Pete Smith	.75	.35	.09
□	145	Mark Gubicza	.25	.11	.03
□	146	Chris Sabo	.40	.18	.05
□	147	Ramon Martinez	1.75	.80	.22
□	148	Tim Leary	.25	.11	.03
□	149	Randy Myers	.30	.14	.04
□	150	Jody Reed	.25	.11	.03
□	151	Bruce Ruffin	.25	.11	.03
□	152	Jeff Russell	.25	.11	.03
□	153	Doug Jones	.30	.14	.04
□	154	Tony Gwynn	2.00	.90	.25
□	155	Mark Langston	.30	.14	.04
□	156	Mitch Williams	.30	.14	.04
□	157	Gary Sheffield	15.00	6.75	1.90
□	158	Tom Henke	.30	.14	.04
□	159	Oil Can Boyd	.25	.11	.03
□	160	Rickey Henderson	2.00	.90	.25
□	161	Bill Doran	.25	.11	.03
□	162	Chuck Finley	.30	.14	.04
□	163	Jeff King	.30	.14	.04
□	164	Nick Esasky	.25	.11	.03
□	165	Cecil Fielder	2.00	.90	.25
□	166	Dave Valle	.25	.11	.03
□	167	Robin Ventura	11.00	4.90	1.40
□	168	Jim Deshaies	.25	.11	.03
□	169	Juan Berenguer	.25	.11	.03
□	170	Craig Worthington	.25	.11	.03
□	171	Gregg Jefferies	1.25	.55	.16
□	172	Will Clark	3.50	1.55	.45
□	173	Kirk Gibson	.30	.14	.04
□	174	Checklist Card (Carlton Fisk)	.30	.14	.04
□	175	Bobby Thigpen	.25	.11	.03
□	176	John Tudor	.25	.11	.03
□	177	Andre Dawson	1.00	.45	.13
□	178	George Brett	1.75	.80	.22
□	179	Steve Buechele	.25	.11	.03
□	180	Joey Belle	8.00	3.60	1.00
□	181	Eddie Murray	1.00	.45	.13
□	182	Bob Geren	.25	.11	.03
□	183	Rob Murphy	.25	.11	.03
□	184	Tom Herr	.25	.11	.03
□	185	George Bell	.30	.14	.04
□	186	Spike Owen	.25	.11	.03
□	187	Cory Snyder	.25	.11	.03
□	188	Fred Lynn	.30	.14	.04
□	189	Eric Davis	.50	.23	.06
□	190	Dave Parker	.30	.14	.04
□	191	Jeff Blauser	.30	.14	.04
□	192	Matt Nokes	.25	.11	.03
□	193	Delino DeShields	6.00	2.70	.75
□	194	Scott Sanderson	.25	.11	.03
□	195	Lance Parrish	.30	.14	.04
□	196	Bobby Bonilla	1.25	.55	.16
□	197	Cal Ripken UER (Reistertown, should be Reisterstown)	5.00	2.30	.60
□	198	Kevin McReynolds	.30	.14	.04
□	199	Robby Thompson	.25	.11	.03
□	200	Tim Belcher	.30	.14	.04
□	201	Jesse Barfield	.25	.11	.03
□	202	Mariano Duncan	.25	.11	.03
□	203	Bill Spiers	.25	.11	.03
□	204	Frank White	.25	.11	.03
□	205	Julio Franco	.30	.14	.04
□	206	Greg Swindell	.50	.23	.06
□	207	Benito Santiago	.30	.14	.04
□	208	Johnny Ray	.25	.11	.03
□	209	Gary Redus	.25	.11	.03
□	210	Jeff Parrett	.25	.11	.03
□	211	Jimmy Key	.30	.14	.04
□	212	Tim Raines	.30	.14	.04
□	213	Carney Lansford	.30	.14	.04
□	214	Gerald Young	.25	.11	.03
□	215	Gene Larkin	.25	.11	.03
□	216	Dan Plesac	.25	.11	.03
□	217	Lonnie Smith	.30	.14	.04
□	218	Alan Trammell	.30	.14	.04
□	219	Jeffrey Leonard	.25	.11	.03
□	220	Sammy Sosa	.75	.35	.09
□	221	Todd Zeile	1.00	.45	.13
□	222	Bill Landrum	.25	.11	.03
□	223	Mike Devereaux	1.00	.45	.13
□	224	Mike Marshall	.25	.11	.03
□	225	Jose Uribe	.25	.11	.03
□	226	Juan Samuel	.25	.11	.03
□	227	Mel Hall	.25	.11	.03
□	228	Kent Hrbek	.30	.14	.04
□	229	Shawon Dunston	.30	.14	.04
□	230	Kevin Seitzer	.30	.14	.04
□	231	Pete Incaviglia	.25	.11	.03
□	232	Sandy Alomar Jr.	.50	.23	.06
□	233	Bip Roberts	.30	.14	.04
□	234	Scott Terry	.25	.11	.03
□	235	Dwight Evans	.30	.14	.04
□	236	Ricky Jordan	.30	.14	.04
□	237	John Olerud	6.00	2.70	.75
□	238	Zane Smith	.25	.11	.03
□	239	Walt Weiss	.25	.11	.03
□	240	Alvaro Espinoza	.25	.11	.03
□	241	Billy Hatcher	.25	.11	.03
□	242	Paul Molitor	.50	.23	.06
□	243	Dale Murphy	.50	.23	.06
□	244	Dave Bergman	.25	.11	.03
□	245	Ken Griffey Jr.	24.00	11.00	3.00
□	246	Ed Whitson	.25	.11	.03
□	247	Kirk McCaskill	.25	.11	.03
□	248	Jay Bell	.30	.14	.04
□	249	Ben McDonald	4.00	1.80	.50
□	250	Darryl Strawberry	2.00	.90	.25

□	251	Brett Butler	.30	.14	.04
□	252	Terry Steinbach	.30	.14	.04
□	253	Ken Caminiti	.30	.14	.04
□	254	Dan Gladden	.25	.11	.03
□	255	Dwight Smith	.25	.11	.03
□	256	Kurt Stillwell	.25	.11	.03
□	257	Ruben Sierra	2.00	.90	.25
□	258	Mike Schooler	.25	.11	.03
□	259	Lance Johnson	.30	.14	.04
□	260	Terry Pendleton	.60	.25	.08
□	261	Ellis Burks	.30	.14	.04
□	262	Len Dykstra	.30	.14	.04
□	263	Mookie Wilson	.25	.11	.03
□	264	Checklist Card (Nolan Ryan) UER (No TM after Ranger logo)	.50	.23	.06
□	265	No Hit King (Nolan Ryan)	5.00	2.30	.60
□	266	Brian DuBois	.25	.11	.03
□	267	Don Robinson	.25	.11	.03
□	268	Glenn Wilson	.25	.11	.03
□	269	Kevin Tapani	2.50	1.15	.30
□	270	Marvell Wynne	.25	.11	.03
□	271	Billy Ripken	.25	.11	.03
□	272	Howard Johnson	.30	.14	.04
□	273	Brian Holman	.25	.11	.03
□	274	Dan Pasqua	.25	.11	.03
□	275	Ken Dayley	.25	.11	.03
□	276	Jeff Reardon	.40	.18	.05
□	277	Jim Presley	.25	.11	.03
□	278	Jim Eisenreich	.25	.11	.03
□	279	Danny Jackson	.25	.11	.03
□	280	Orel Hershiser	.30	.14	.04
□	281	Andy Hawkins	.25	.11	.03
□	282	Jose Rijo	.35	.16	.04
□	283	Luis Rivera	.25	.11	.03
□	284	John Kruk	.40	.18	.05
□	285	Jeff Huson	.35	.16	.04
□	286	Joel Skinner	.25	.11	.03
□	287	Jack Clark	.30	.14	.04
□	288	Chili Davis	.30	.14	.04
□	289	Joe Girardi	.25	.11	.03
□	290	B.J. Surhoff	.25	.11	.03
□	291	Luis Sojo	.25	.23	.06
□	292	Tom Foley	.25	.11	.03
□	293	Mike Moore	.25	.11	.03
□	294	Ken Oberkfell	.25	.11	.03
□	295	Luis Polonia	.30	.14	.04
□	296	Doug Drabek	.35	.16	.04
□	297	Dave Justice	20.00	9.00	2.50
□	298	Paul Gibson	.25	.11	.03
□	299	Edgar Martinez	2.50	1.15	.30
□	300	Frank Thomas UER (No B in front of birthdate)	60.00	27.00	7.50
□	301	Eric Yelding	.25	.11	.03
□	302	Greg Gagne	.25	.11	.03
□	303	Brad Komminsk	.25	.11	.03
□	304	Ron Darling	.30	.14	.04
□	305	Kevin Bass	.25	.11	.03
□	306	Jeff Hamilton	.25	.11	.03
□	307	Ron Karkovice	.25	.11	.03
□	308	Milt Thompson UER (Ray Lankford pictured on card back)	.40	.18	.05
□	309	Mike Harkey	.30	.14	.04
□	310	Mel Stottlemyre Jr.	.25	.11	.03
□	311	Kenny Rogers	.25	.11	.03
□	312	Mitch Webster	.25	.11	.03
□	313	Kal Daniels	.25	.11	.03
□	314	Matt Nokes	.30	.14	.04
□	315	Dennis Lamp	.25	.11	.03
□	316	Ken Howell	.25	.11	.03
□	317	Glenallen Hill	.30	.14	.04
□	318	Dave Martinez	.30	.14	.04
□	319	Chris James	.25	.11	.03
□	320	Mike Pagliarulo	.25	.11	.03
□	321	Hal Morris	1.50	.65	.19
□	322	Rob Deer	.30	.14	.04
□	323	Greg Olson	.35	.16	.04
□	324	Tony Phillips	.25	.11	.03
□	325	Larry Walker	10.00	4.50	1.25
□	326	Ron Hassey	.25	.11	.03
□	327	Jack Howell	.25	.11	.03
□	328	John Smiley	.30	.14	.04
□	329	Steve Finley	.60	.25	.08
□	330	Dave Magadan	.30	.14	.04
□	331	Greg Litton	.25	.11	.03
□	332	Mickey Hatcher	.25	.11	.03
□	333	Lee Guetterman	.25	.11	.03
□	334	Norm Charlton	.40	.18	.05
□	335	Edgar Diaz	.25	.11	.03
□	336	Willie Wilson	.25	.11	.03
□	337	Bobby Witt	.30	.14	.04
□	338	Candy Maldonado	.25	.11	.03
□	339	Craig Lefferts	.25	.11	.03
□	340	Dante Bichette	.50	.23	.06
□	341	Wally Backman	.25	.11	.03
□	342	Dennis Cook	.25	.11	.03
□	343	Pat Borders	.60	.25	.08
□	344	Wallace Johnson	.25	.11	.03
□	345	Willie Randolph	.30	.14	.04
□	346	Danny Darwin	.25	.11	.03
□	347	Al Newman	.25	.11	.03
□	348	Mark Knudson	.25	.11	.03
□	349	Joe Boever	.25	.11	.03
□	350	Larry Sheets	.25	.11	.03
□	351	Mike Jackson	.25	.11	.03
□	352	Wayne Edwards	.25	.11	.03
□	353	Bernard Gilkey	1.50	.65	.19
□	354	Don Slaught	.25	.11	.03
□	355	Joe Orsulak	.25	.11	.03
□	356	John Franco	.30	.14	.04

☐ 357	Jeff Brantley	.25	.11	.03
☐ 358	Mike Morgan	.30	.14	.04
☐ 359	Deion Sanders	8.00	3.60	1.00
☐ 360	Terry Leach	.25	.11	.03
☐ 361	Les Lancaster	.25	.11	.03
☐ 362	Storm Davis	.25	.11	.03
☐ 363	Scott Coolbaugh	.25	.11	.03
☐ 364	Checklist Card	.30	.14	.04
	(Ozzie Smith)			
☐ 365	Cecilio Guante	.25	.11	.03
☐ 366	Joey Cora	.25	.11	.03
☐ 367	Willie McGee	.30	.14	.04
☐ 368	Jerry Reed	.25	.11	.03
☐ 369	Darren Daulton	.50	.23	.06
☐ 370	Manny Lee	.25	.11	.03
☐ 371	Mark Gardner	.60	.25	.08
☐ 372	Rick Honeycutt	.25	.11	.03
☐ 373	Steve Balboni	.25	.11	.03
☐ 374	Jack Armstrong	.30	.14	.04
☐ 375	Charlie O'Brien	.25	.11	.03
☐ 376	Ron Gant	3.00	1.35	.40
☐ 377	Lloyd Moseby	.25	.11	.03
☐ 378	Gene Harris	.25	.11	.03
☐ 379	Joe Carter	2.00	.90	.25
☐ 380	Scott Bailes	.25	.11	.03
☐ 381	R.J. Reynolds	.25	.11	.03
☐ 382	Bob Melvin	.25	.11	.03
☐ 383	Tim Teufel	.25	.11	.03
☐ 384	John Burkett	.35	.16	.04
☐ 385	Felix Jose	1.75	.80	.22
☐ 386	Larry Andersen	.25	.11	.03
☐ 387	David West	.25	.11	.03
☐ 388	Luis Salazar	.25	.11	.03
☐ 389	Mike Macfarlane	.35	.16	.04
☐ 390	Charlie Hough	.25	.11	.03
☐ 391	Greg Briley	.30	.14	.04
☐ 392	Donn Pall	.25	.11	.03
☐ 393	Bryn Smith	.25	.11	.03
☐ 394	Carlos Quintana	.30	.14	.04
☐ 395	Steve Lake	.25	.11	.03
☐ 396	Mark Whiten	1.50	.65	.19
☐ 397	Edwin Nunez	.25	.11	.03
☐ 398	Rick Parker	.25	.11	.03
☐ 399	Mark Portugal	.25	.11	.03
☐ 400	Roy Smith	.25	.11	.03
☐ 401	Hector Villanueva	.35	.16	.04
☐ 402	Bob Milacki	.25	.11	.03
☐ 403	Alejandro Pena	.25	.11	.03
☐ 404	Scott Bradley	.25	.11	.03
☐ 405	Ron Kittle	.25	.11	.03
☐ 406	Bob Tewksbury	.30	.14	.04
☐ 407	Wes Gardner	.25	.11	.03
☐ 408	Ernie White	.25	.11	.03
☐ 409	Terry Shumpert	.25	.11	.03
☐ 410	Tim Layana	.25	.11	.03
☐ 411	Chris Gwynn	.30	.14	.04
☐ 412	Jeff Robinson	.25	.11	.03
☐ 413	Scott Scudder	.35	.16	.04
☐ 414	Kevin Romine	.25	.11	.03
☐ 415	Jose DeJesus	.25	.11	.03
☐ 416	Mike Jeffcoat	.25	.11	.03
☐ 417	Rudy Seanez	.40	.18	.05
☐ 418	Mike Dunne	.25	.11	.03
☐ 419	Dick Schofield	.25	.11	.03
☐ 420	Steve Wilson	.25	.11	.03
☐ 421	Bill Krueger	.25	.11	.03
☐ 422	Junior Felix	.50	.23	.06
☐ 423	Drew Hall	.25	.11	.03
☐ 424	Curt Young	.25	.11	.03
☐ 425	Franklin Stubbs	.25	.11	.03
☐ 426	Dave Winfield	1.50	.65	.19
☐ 427	Rick Reed	.25	.11	.03
☐ 428	Charlie Leibrandt	.25	.11	.03
☐ 429	Jeff Robinson	.25	.11	.03
☐ 430	Erik Hanson	.30	.14	.04
☐ 431	Barry Jones	.25	.11	.03
☐ 432	Alex Trevino	.25	.11	.03
☐ 433	John Moses	.25	.11	.03
☐ 434	Dave Johnson	.25	.11	.03
☐ 435	Mackey Sasser	.25	.11	.03
☐ 436	Rick Leach	.25	.11	.03
☐ 437	Lenny Harris	.30	.14	.04
☐ 438	Carlos Martinez	.30	.14	.04
☐ 439	Rex Hudler	.25	.11	.03
☐ 440	Domingo Ramos	.25	.11	.03
☐ 441	Gerald Perry	.25	.11	.03
☐ 442	Jeff Russell	.25	.11	.03
☐ 443	Carlos Baerga	11.00	4.90	1.40
☐ 444	Checklist Card	.35	.16	.04
	(Will Clark)			
☐ 445	Stan Javier	.25	.11	.03
☐ 446	Kevin Maas	1.50	.65	.19
☐ 447	Tom Brunansky	.30	.14	.04
☐ 448	Carmelo Martinez	.25	.11	.03
☐ 449	Willie Blair	.35	.16	.04
☐ 450	Andres Galarraga	.30	.14	.04
☐ 451	Bud Black	.25	.11	.03
☐ 452	Greg W. Harris	.30	.14	.04
☐ 453	Joe Oliver	.35	.16	.04
☐ 454	Greg Brock	.25	.11	.03
☐ 455	Jeff Treadway	.25	.11	.03
☐ 456	Lance McCullers	.25	.11	.03
☐ 457	Dave Schmidt	.25	.11	.03
☐ 458	Todd Burns	.25	.11	.03
☐ 459	Max Venable	.25	.11	.03
☐ 460	Neal Heaton	.25	.11	.03
☐ 461	Mark Williamson	.25	.11	.03
☐ 462	Keith Miller	.25	.11	.03
☐ 463	Mike LaCoss	.25	.11	.03
☐ 464	Jose Offerman	.90	.40	.11
☐ 465	Jim Leyritz	.35	.16	.04
☐ 466	Glenn Braggs	.25	.11	.03
☐ 467	Ron Robinson	.25	.11	.03
☐ 468	Mark Davis	.25	.11	.03

☐ 469	Gary Pettis	.25	.11	.03
☐ 470	Keith Hernandez	.30	.14	.04
☐ 471	Dennis Rasmussen	.25	.11	.03
☐ 472	Mark Eichhorn	.25	.11	.03
☐ 473	Ted Power	.25	.11	.03
☐ 474	Terry Mulholland	.30	.14	.04
☐ 475	Todd Stottlemyre	.40	.18	.05
☐ 476	Jerry Goff	.25	.11	.03
☐ 477	Gene Nelson	.25	.11	.03
☐ 478	Rich Gedman	.25	.11	.03
☐ 479	Brian Harper	.30	.14	.04
☐ 480	Mike Felder	.25	.11	.03
☐ 481	Steve Avery	11.00	4.90	1.40
☐ 482	Jack Morris	.75	.35	.09
☐ 483	Randy Johnson	1.00	.45	.13
☐ 484	Scott Radinsky	.75	.35	.09
☐ 485	Jose DeLeon	.25	.11	.03
☐ 486	Stan Belinda	.60	.25	.08
☐ 487	Brian Holton	.25	.11	.03
☐ 488	Mark Carreon	.25	.11	.03
☐ 489	Trevor Wilson	.25	.11	.03
☐ 490	Mike Sharperson	.25	.11	.03
☐ 491	Alan Mills	.50	.23	.06
☐ 492	John Candelaria	.25	.11	.03
☐ 493	Paul Assenmacher	.25	.11	.03
☐ 494	Steve Crawford	.25	.11	.03
☐ 495	Brad Arnsberg	.25	.11	.03
☐ 496	Sergio Valdez	.25	.11	.03
☐ 497	Mark Parent	.25	.11	.03
☐ 498	Tom Pagnozzi	.30	.14	.04
☐ 499	Greg A. Harris	.25	.11	.03
☐ 500	Randy Ready	.25	.11	.03
☐ 501	Duane Ward	.25	.11	.03
☐ 502	Nelson Santovenia	.25	.11	.03
☐ 503	Joe Klink	.25	.11	.03
☐ 504	Eric Plunk	.25	.11	.03
☐ 505	Jeff Reed	.25	.11	.03
☐ 506	Ted Higuera	.25	.11	.03
☐ 507	Joe Hesketh	.25	.11	.03
☐ 508	Dan Petry	.25	.11	.03
☐ 509	Matt Young	.25	.11	.03
☐ 510	Jerald Clark	.35	.16	.04
☐ 511	John Orton	.35	.16	.04
☐ 512	Scott Ruskin	.25	.11	.03
☐ 513	Chris Hoiles	3.00	1.35	.40
☐ 514	Daryl Boston	.25	.11	.03
☐ 515	Francisco Oliveras	.25	.11	.03
☐ 516	Ozzie Canseco	.40	.18	.05
☐ 517	Xavier Hernandez	.35	.16	.04
☐ 518	Fred Manrique	.25	.11	.03
☐ 519	Shawn Boskie	.40	.18	.05
☐ 520	Jeff Montgomery	.30	.14	.04
☐ 521	Jack Daugherty	.25	.11	.03
☐ 522	Keith Comstock	.25	.11	.03
☐ 523	Greg Hibbard	.75	.35	.09
☐ 524	Lee Smith	.50	.23	.06
☐ 525	Dana Kiecker	.25	.11	.03

☐ 526	Darrel Akerfelds	.25	.11	.03
☐ 527	Greg Myers	.25	.11	.03
☐ 528	Checklist Card	.35	.16	.04
	(Ryne Sandberg)			

1991 Leaf

*This 528-card standard size 2 1/2" by
3 1/2" set marks the second year Donruss
has produced a two-series premium set
using the Leaf name. This set features a
photo of the player which is surrounded by
black and white borders. The whole card is
framed in gray borders. The Leaf logo is in
the upper right corner of the card. The
back of the card features a gray, red and
black back with white lettering on the black
background and black lettering on the gray
and red backgrounds. The backs of the
cards also features biographical and statistical information along with a write-up
when room is provided. The set was
issued using the Donruss dealer distribution network with very little Leaf product
being released in other fashions. The
cards are numbered on the back. The key
Rookie Cards in the first series are Wes
Chamberlain, Brian McRae, and Randy
Tomlin. The key Rookie Cards in the second series are Orlando Merced and Denny
Neagle.*

	MT	EX-MT	VG
COMPLETE SET (528)	45.00	20.00	5.75
COMPLETE SERIES 1 (264)	22.50	10.00	2.80
COMPLETE SERIES 2 (264)	22.50	10.00	2.80
COMMON PLAYER (1-264)	.08	.04	.01
COMMON PLAYER (265-528)	.08	.04	.01

☐	1 The Leaf Card	.10	.04	.01	☐	58 Jose Oquendo	.08	.04	.01
☐	2 Kurt Stillwell	.08	.04	.01	☐	59 Dick Schofield	.08	.04	.01
☐	3 Bobby Witt	.08	.04	.01	☐	60 Dickie Thon	.08	.04	.01
☐	4 Tony Phillips	.08	.04	.01	☐	61 Ramon Martinez	.15	.07	.02
☐	5 Scott Garrelts	.08	.04	.01	☐	62 Jay Buhner	.10	.04	.01
☐	6 Greg Swindell	.10	.04	.01	☐	63 Mark Portugal	.08	.04	.01
☐	7 Billy Ripken	.08	.04	.01	☐	64 Bob Welch	.08	.04	.01
☐	8 Dave Martinez	.08	.04	.01	☐	65 Chris Sabo	.10	.04	.01
☐	9 Kelly Gruber	.10	.04	.01	☐	66 Chuck Cary	.08	.04	.01
☐	10 Juan Samuel	.08	.04	.01	☐	67 Mark Langston	.10	.04	.01
☐	11 Brian Holman	.08	.04	.01	☐	68 Joe Boever	.08	.04	.01
☐	12 Craig Biggio	.15	.07	.02	☐	69 Jody Reed	.08	.04	.01
☐	13 Lonnie Smith	.08	.04	.01	☐	70 Alejandro Pena	.08	.04	.01
☐	14 Ron Robinson	.08	.04	.01	☐	71 Jeff King	.08	.04	.01
☐	15 Mike LaValliere	.08	.04	.01	☐	72 Tom Pagnozzi	.08	.04	.01
☐	16 Mark Davis	.08	.04	.01	☐	73 Joe Oliver	.08	.04	.01
☐	17 Jack Daugherty	.08	.04	.01	☐	74 Mike Witt	.08	.04	.01
☐	18 Mike Henneman	.08	.04	.01	☐	75 Hector Villanueva	.08	.04	.01
☐	19 Mike Greenwell	.12	.05	.02	☐	76 Dan Gladden	.08	.04	.01
☐	20 Dave Magadan	.10	.04	.01	☐	77 Dave Justice	2.00	.90	.25
☐	21 Mark Williamson	.08	.04	.01	☐	78 Mike Gallego	.08	.04	.01
☐	22 Marquis Grissom	.50	.23	.06	☐	79 Tom Candiotti	.08	.04	.01
☐	23 Pat Borders	.08	.04	.01	☐	80 Ozzie Smith	.25	.11	.03
☐	24 Mike Scioscia	.08	.04	.01	☐	81 Luis Polonia	.10	.04	.01
☐	25 Shawon Dunston	.10	.04	.01	☐	82 Randy Ready	.08	.04	.01
☐	26 Randy Bush	.08	.04	.01	☐	83 Greg A. Harris	.08	.04	.01
☐	27 John Smoltz	.40	.18	.05	☐	84 Checklist Card	.15	.07	.02
☐	28 Chuck Crim	.08	.04	.01		Dave Justice			
☐	29 Don Slaught	.08	.04	.01	☐	85 Kevin Mitchell	.12	.05	.02
☐	30 Mike Macfarlane	.08	.04	.01	☐	86 Mark McLemore	.08	.04	.01
☐	31 Wally Joyner	.10	.04	.01	☐	87 Terry Steinbach	.10	.04	.01
☐	32 Pat Combs	.08	.04	.01	☐	88 Tom Browning	.08	.04	.01
☐	33 Tony Pena	.08	.04	.01	☐	89 Matt Nokes	.08	.04	.01
☐	34 Howard Johnson	.10	.04	.01	☐	90 Mike Harkey	.10	.04	.01
☐	35 Leo Gomez	.75	.35	.09	☐	91 Omar Vizquel	.08	.04	.01
☐	36 Spike Owen	.08	.04	.01	☐	92 Dave Bergman	.08	.04	.01
☐	37 Eric Davis	.15	.07	.02	☐	93 Matt Williams	.12	.05	.02
☐	38 Roberto Kelly	.12	.05	.02	☐	94 Steve Olin	.10	.04	.01
☐	39 Jerome Walton	.08	.04	.01	☐	95 Craig Wilson	.10	.07	.02
☐	40 Shane Mack	.10	.04	.01	☐	96 Dave Stieb	.08	.04	.01
☐	41 Kent Mercker	.08	.04	.01	☐	97 Ruben Sierra	.50	.23	.06
☐	42 B.J. Surhoff	.08	.04	.01	☐	98 Jay Howell	.08	.04	.01
☐	43 Jerry Browne	.08	.04	.01	☐	99 Scott Bradley	.08	.04	.01
☐	44 Lee Smith	.10	.04	.01	☐	100 Eric Yelding	.08	.04	.01
☐	45 Chuck Finley	.10	.04	.01	☐	101 Rickey Henderson	.40	.18	.05
☐	46 Terry Mulholland	.08	.04	.01	☐	102 Jeff Reed	.08	.04	.01
☐	47 Tom Bolton	.08	.04	.01	☐	103 Jimmy Key	.08	.04	.01
☐	48 Tom Herr	.08	.04	.01	☐	104 Terry Shumpert	.08	.04	.01
☐	49 Jim Deshaies	.08	.04	.01	☐	105 Kenny Rogers	.08	.04	.01
☐	50 Walt Weiss	.08	.04	.01	☐	106 Cecil Fielder	.40	.18	.05
☐	51 Hal Morris	.10	.04	.01	☐	107 Robby Thompson	.08	.04	.01
☐	52 Lee Guetterman	.08	.04	.01	☐	108 Alex Cole	.08	.04	.01
☐	53 Paul Assenmacher	.08	.04	.01	☐	109 Randy Milligan	.08	.04	.01
☐	54 Brian Harper	.08	.04	.01	☐	110 Andres Galarraga	.08	.04	.01
☐	55 Paul Gibson	.08	.04	.01	☐	111 Bill Spiers	.08	.04	.01
☐	56 John Burkett	.08	.04	.01	☐	112 Kal Daniels	.08	.04	.01
☐	57 Doug Jones	.08	.04	.01	☐	113 Henry Cotto	.08	.04	.01

☐ 114	Casey Candaele	.08	.04	.01
☐ 115	Jeff Blauser	.08	.04	.01
☐ 116	Robin Yount	.35	.16	.04
☐ 117	Ben McDonald	.25	.11	.03
☐ 118	Bret Saberhagen	.10	.04	.01
☐ 119	Juan Gonzalez	4.00	1.80	.50
☐ 120	Lou Whitaker	.10	.04	.01
☐ 121	Ellis Burks	.10	.04	.01
☐ 122	Charlie O'Brien	.08	.04	.01
☐ 123	John Smiley	.10	.04	.01
☐ 124	Tim Burke	.08	.04	.01
☐ 125	John Olerud	.50	.23	.06
☐ 126	Eddie Murray	.25	.11	.03
☐ 127	Greg Maddux	.30	.14	.04
☐ 128	Kevin Tapani	.25	.11	.03
☐ 129	Ron Gant	.40	.18	.05
☐ 130	Jay Bell	.10	.04	.01
☐ 131	Chris Hoiles	.30	.14	.04
☐ 132	Tom Gordon	.10	.04	.01
☐ 133	Kevin Seitzer	.10	.04	.01
☐ 134	Jeff Huson	.08	.04	.01
☐ 135	Jerry Don Gleaton	.08	.04	.01
☐ 136	Jeff Brantley UER	.08	.04	.01
	(Photo actually Rick Leach on back)			
☐ 137	Felix Fermin	.08	.04	.01
☐ 138	Mike Devereaux	.10	.04	.01
☐ 139	Delino DeShields	.50	.23	.06
☐ 140	David Wells	.08	.04	.01
☐ 141	Tim Crews	.08	.04	.01
☐ 142	Erik Hanson	.08	.04	.01
☐ 143	Mark Davidson	.08	.04	.01
☐ 144	Tommy Gregg	.08	.04	.01
☐ 145	Jim Gantner	.08	.04	.01
☐ 146	Jose Lind	.08	.04	.01
☐ 147	Danny Tartabull	.15	.07	.02
☐ 148	Geno Petralli	.08	.04	.01
☐ 149	Travis Fryman	3.50	1.55	.45
☐ 150	Tim Naehring	.15	.07	.02
☐ 151	Kevin McReynolds	.10	.04	.01
☐ 152	Joe Orsulak	.08	.04	.01
☐ 153	Steve Frey	.08	.04	.01
☐ 154	Duane Ward	.08	.04	.01
☐ 155	Stan Javier	.08	.04	.01
☐ 156	Damon Berryhill	.08	.04	.01
☐ 157	Gene Larkin	.08	.04	.01
☐ 158	Greg Olson	.08	.04	.01
☐ 159	Mark Knudson	.08	.04	.01
☐ 160	Carmelo Martinez	.08	.04	.01
☐ 161	Storm Davis	.08	.04	.01
☐ 162	Jim Abbott	.35	.16	.04
☐ 163	Len Dykstra	.10	.04	.01
☐ 164	Tom Brunansky	.10	.04	.01
☐ 165	Dwight Gooden	.15	.07	.02
☐ 166	Jose Mesa	.08	.04	.01
☐ 167	Oil Can Boyd	.08	.04	.01
☐ 168	Barry Larkin	.25	.11	.03
☐ 169	Scott Sanderson	.08	.04	.01
☐ 170	Mark Grace	.30	.14	.04
☐ 171	Mark Guthrie	.08	.04	.01
☐ 172	Tom Glavine	.75	.35	.09
☐ 173	Gary Sheffield	1.25	.55	.16
☐ 174	Checklist Card	.15	.07	.02
	Roger Clemens			
☐ 175	Chris James	.08	.04	.01
☐ 176	Milt Thompson	.08	.04	.01
☐ 177	Donnie Hill	.08	.04	.01
☐ 178	Wes Chamberlain	.60	.25	.08
☐ 179	John Marzano	.08	.04	.01
☐ 180	Frank Viola	.10	.04	.01
☐ 181	Eric Anthony	.12	.05	.02
☐ 182	Jose Canseco	.75	.35	.09
☐ 183	Scott Scudder	.08	.04	.01
☐ 184	Dave Eiland	.08	.04	.01
☐ 185	Luis Salazar	.08	.04	.01
☐ 186	Pedro Munoz	.75	.35	.09
☐ 187	Steve Searcy	.08	.04	.01
☐ 188	Don Robinson	.08	.04	.01
☐ 189	Sandy Alomar Jr.	.10	.04	.01
☐ 190	Jose DeLeon	.08	.04	.01
☐ 191	John Orton	.08	.04	.01
☐ 192	Darren Daulton	.10	.04	.01
☐ 193	Mike Morgan	.08	.04	.01
☐ 194	Greg Briley	.08	.04	.01
☐ 195	Karl Rhodes	.08	.04	.01
☐ 196	Harold Baines	.10	.04	.01
☐ 197	Bill Doran	.08	.04	.01
☐ 198	Alvaro Espinoza	.08	.04	.01
☐ 199	Kirk McCaskill	.08	.04	.01
☐ 200	Jose DeJesus	.08	.04	.01
☐ 201	Jack Clark	.10	.04	.01
☐ 202	Daryl Boston	.08	.04	.01
☐ 203	Randy Tomlin	.50	.23	.06
☐ 204	Pedro Guerrero	.08	.04	.01
☐ 205	Billy Hatcher	.08	.04	.01
☐ 206	Tim Leary	.08	.04	.01
☐ 207	Ryne Sandberg	.90	.40	.11
☐ 208	Kirby Puckett	.75	.35	.09
☐ 209	Charlie Leibrandt	.08	.04	.01
☐ 210	Rick Honeycutt	.08	.04	.01
☐ 211	Joel Skinner	.08	.04	.01
☐ 212	Rex Hudler	.08	.04	.01
☐ 213	Bryan Harvey	.08	.04	.01
☐ 214	Charlie Hayes	.08	.04	.01
☐ 215	Matt Young	.08	.04	.01
☐ 216	Terry Kennedy	.08	.04	.01
☐ 217	Carl Nichols	.08	.04	.01
☐ 218	Mike Moore	.08	.04	.01
☐ 219	Paul O'Neill	.10	.04	.01
☐ 220	Steve Sax	.10	.04	.01
☐ 221	Shawn Boskie	.08	.04	.01
☐ 222	Rich DeLucia	.08	.04	.01
☐ 223	Lloyd Moseby	.08	.04	.01
☐ 224	Mike Kingery	.08	.04	.01

☐	225 Carlos Baerga	.90	.40	.11
☐	226 Bryn Smith	.08	.04	.01
☐	227 Todd Stottlemyre	.10	.04	.01
☐	228 Julio Franco	.10	.04	.01
☐	229 Jim Gott	.08	.04	.01
☐	230 Mike Schooler	.08	.04	.01
☐	231 Steve Finley	.10	.04	.01
☐	232 Dave Henderson	.08	.04	.01
☐	233 Luis Quinones	.08	.04	.01
☐	234 Mark Whiten	.20	.09	.03
☐	235 Brian McRae	.60	.25	.08
☐	236 Rich Gossage	.10	.04	.01
☐	237 Rob Deer	.10	.04	.01
☐	238 Will Clark	.75	.35	.09
☐	239 Albert Belle	.75	.35	.09
☐	240 Bob Melvin	.08	.04	.01
☐	241 Larry Walker	.75	.35	.09
☐	242 Dante Bichette	.08	.04	.01
☐	243 Orel Hershiser	.12	.05	.02
☐	244 Pete O'Brien	.08	.04	.01
☐	245 Pete Harnisch	.10	.04	.01
☐	246 Jeff Treadway	.08	.04	.01
☐	247 Julio Machado	.08	.04	.01
☐	248 Dave Johnson	.08	.04	.01
☐	249 Kirk Gibson	.10	.04	.01
☐	250 Kevin Brown	.10	.04	.01
☐	251 Milt Cuyler	.15	.07	.02
☐	252 Jeff Reardon	.12	.05	.02
☐	253 David Cone	.20	.09	.03
☐	254 Gary Redus	.08	.04	.01
☐	255 Junior Noboa	.08	.04	.01
☐	256 Greg Myers	.08	.04	.01
☐	257 Dennis Cook	.08	.04	.01
☐	258 Joe Girardi	.08	.04	.01
☐	259 Allan Anderson	.08	.04	.01
☐	260 Paul Marak	.08	.04	.01
☐	261 Barry Bonds	.60	.25	.08
☐	262 Juan Bell	.08	.04	.01
☐	263 Russ Morman	.08	.04	.01
☐	264 Checklist Card	.15	.07	.02
	George Brett			
☐	265 Jerald Clark	.08	.04	.01
☐	266 Dwight Evans	.10	.04	.01
☐	267 Roberto Alomar	1.00	.45	.13
☐	268 Danny Jackson	.08	.04	.01
☐	269 Brian Downing	.08	.04	.01
☐	270 John Cerutti	.08	.04	.01
☐	271 Robin Ventura	.90	.40	.11
☐	272 Gerald Perry	.08	.04	.01
☐	273 Wade Boggs	.40	.18	.05
☐	274 Dennis Martinez	.10	.04	.01
☐	275 Andy Benes	.30	.14	.04
☐	276 Tony Fossas	.08	.04	.01
☐	277 Franklin Stubbs	.08	.04	.01
☐	278 John Kruk	.10	.04	.01
☐	279 Kevin Gross	.08	.04	.01
☐	280 Von Hayes	.08	.04	.01
☐	281 Frank Thomas	6.00	2.70	.75
☐	282 Rob Dibble	.10	.04	.01
☐	283 Mel Hall	.08	.04	.01
☐	284 Rick Mahler	.08	.04	.01
☐	285 Dennis Eckersley	.15	.07	.02
☐	286 Bernard Gilkey	.30	.14	.04
☐	287 Dan Plesac	.08	.04	.01
☐	288 Jason Grimsley	.15	.07	.02
☐	289 Mark Lewis	.30	.14	.04
☐	290 Tony Gwynn	.40	.18	.05
☐	291 Jeff Russell	.08	.04	.01
☐	292 Curt Schilling	.10	.04	.01
☐	293 Pascual Perez	.08	.04	.01
☐	294 Jack Morris	.20	.09	.03
☐	295 Hubie Brooks	.08	.04	.01
☐	296 Alex Fernandez	.30	.14	.04
☐	297 Harold Reynolds	.08	.04	.01
☐	298 Craig Worthington	.08	.04	.01
☐	299 Willie Wilson	.08	.04	.01
☐	300 Mike Maddux	.08	.04	.01
☐	301 Dave Righetti	.08	.04	.01
☐	302 Paul Molitor	.15	.07	.02
☐	303 Gary Gaetti	.08	.04	.01
☐	304 Terry Pendleton	.15	.07	.02
☐	305 Kevin Elster	.08	.04	.01
☐	306 Scott Fletcher	.08	.04	.01
☐	307 Jeff Robinson	.08	.04	.01
☐	308 Jesse Barfield	.08	.04	.01
☐	309 Mike LaCoss	.08	.04	.01
☐	310 Andy Van Slyke	.20	.09	.03
☐	311 Glenallen Hill	.08	.04	.01
☐	312 Bud Black	.08	.04	.01
☐	313 Kent Hrbek	.10	.04	.01
☐	314 Tim Teufel	.08	.04	.01
☐	315 Tony Fernandez	.10	.04	.01
☐	316 Beau Allred	.08	.04	.01
☐	317 Curtis Wilkerson	.08	.04	.01
☐	318 Bill Sampen	.08	.04	.01
☐	319 Randy Johnson	.10	.04	.01
☐	320 Mike Heath	.08	.04	.01
☐	321 Sammy Sosa	.10	.04	.01
☐	322 Mickey Tettleton	.10	.04	.01
☐	323 Jose Vizcaino	.08	.04	.01
☐	324 John Candelaria	.08	.04	.01
☐	325 Dave Howard	.15	.07	.02
☐	326 Jose Rijo	.10	.04	.01
☐	327 Todd Zeile	.15	.07	.02
☐	328 Gene Nelson	.08	.04	.01
☐	329 Dwayne Henry	.08	.04	.01
☐	330 Mike Boddicker	.08	.04	.01
☐	331 Ozzie Guillen	.08	.04	.01
☐	332 Sam Horn	.08	.04	.01
☐	333 Wally Whitehurst	.08	.04	.01
☐	334 Dave Parker	.10	.04	.01
☐	335 George Brett	.35	.16	.04
☐	336 Bobby Thigpen	.08	.04	.01
☐	337 Ed Whitson	.08	.04	.01

□	338 Ivan Calderon	.08	.04	.01
□	339 Mike Pagliarulo	.08	.04	.01
□	340 Jack McDowell	.30	.14	.04
□	341 Dana Kiecker	.08	.04	.01
□	342 Fred McGriff	.40	.18	.05
□	343 Mark Lee	.15	.07	.02
□	344 Alfredo Griffin	.08	.04	.01
□	345 Scott Bankhead	.08	.04	.01
□	346 Darrin Jackson	.10	.04	.01
□	347 Rafael Palmeiro	.20	.09	.03
□	348 Steve Farr	.08	.04	.01
□	349 Hensley Meulens	.10	.04	.01
□	350 Danny Cox	.08	.04	.01
□	351 Alan Trammell	.10	.04	.01
□	352 Edwin Nunez	.08	.04	.01
□	353 Joe Carter	.40	.18	.05
□	354 Eric Show	.08	.04	.01
□	355 Vance Law	.08	.04	.01
□	356 Jeff Gray	.08	.04	.01
□	357 Bobby Bonilla	.25	.11	.03
□	358 Ernest Riles	.08	.04	.01
□	359 Ron Hassey	.08	.04	.01
□	360 Willie McGee	.10	.04	.01
□	361 Mackey Sasser	.08	.04	.01
□	362 Glenn Braggs	.08	.04	.01
□	363 Mario Diaz	.08	.04	.01
□	364 Checklist Card	.12	.05	.02
	Barry Bonds			
□	365 Kevin Bass	.08	.04	.01
□	366 Pete Incaviglia	.08	.04	.01
□	367 Luis Sojo UER	.08	.04	.01
	(1989 stats inter-			
	spersed with 1990's)			
□	368 Lance Parrish	.10	.04	.01
□	369 Mark Leonard	.20	.09	.03
□	370 Heathcliff Slocumb	.08	.04	.01
□	371 Jimmy Jones	.08	.04	.01
□	372 Ken Griffey Jr.	2.00	.90	.25
□	373 Chris Hammond	.20	.09	.03
□	374 Chili Davis	.10	.04	.01
□	375 Joey Cora	.08	.04	.01
□	376 Ken Hill	.10	.04	.01
□	377 Darryl Strawberry	.40	.18	.05
□	378 Ron Darling	.10	.04	.01
□	379 Sid Bream	.08	.04	.01
□	380 Bill Swift	.08	.04	.01
□	381 Shawn Abner	.08	.04	.01
□	382 Eric King	.08	.04	.01
□	383 Mickey Morandini	.25	.11	.03
□	384 Carlton Fisk	.30	.14	.04
□	385 Steve Lake	.08	.04	.01
□	386 Mike Jeffcoat	.08	.04	.01
□	387 Darren Holmes	.30	.14	.04
□	388 Tim Wallach	.10	.04	.01
□	389 George Bell	.10	.04	.01
□	390 Craig Lefferts	.08	.04	.01
□	391 Ernie Whitt	.08	.04	.01

□	392 Felix Jose	.15	.07	.02
□	393 Kevin Maas	.15	.07	.02
□	394 Devon White	.10	.04	.01
□	395 Otis Nixon	.10	.04	.01
□	396 Chuck Knoblauch	1.75	.80	.22
□	397 Scott Coolbaugh	.08	.04	.01
□	398 Glenn Davis	.10	.04	.01
□	399 Manny Lee	.08	.04	.01
□	400 Andre Dawson	.25	.11	.03
□	401 Scott Chiamparino	.10	.04	.01
□	402 Bill Gullickson	.08	.04	.01
□	403 Lance Johnson	.08	.04	.01
□	404 Juan Agosto	.08	.04	.01
□	405 Danny Darwin	.08	.04	.01
□	406 Barry Jones	.08	.04	.01
□	407 Larry Andersen	.08	.04	.01
□	408 Luis Rivera	.08	.04	.01
□	409 Jaime Navarro	.10	.04	.01
□	410 Roger McDowell	.08	.04	.01
□	411 Brett Butler	.08	.04	.01
□	412 Dale Murphy	.12	.05	.02
□	413 Tim Raines UER	.12	.05	.02
	(Listed as hitting .500			
	in 1980, should be .050)			
□	414 Norm Charlton	.10	.04	.01
□	415 Greg Cadaret	.08	.04	.01
□	416 Chris Nabholz	.20	.09	.03
□	417 Dave Stewart	.10	.04	.01
□	418 Rich Gedman	.08	.04	.01
□	419 Willie Randolph	.08	.04	.01
□	420 Mitch Williams	.08	.04	.01
□	421 Brook Jacoby	.08	.04	.01
□	422 Greg W. Harris	.08	.04	.01
□	423 Nolan Ryan	2.00	.90	.25
□	424 Dave Rohde	.08	.04	.01
□	425 Don Mattingly	.40	.18	.05
□	426 Greg Gagne	.08	.04	.01
□	427 Vince Coleman	.10	.04	.01
□	428 Dan Pasqua	.08	.04	.01
□	429 Alvin Davis	.08	.04	.01
□	430 Cal Ripken	1.25	.55	.16
□	431 Jamie Quirk	.08	.04	.01
□	432 Benito Santiago	.10	.04	.01
□	433 Jose Uribe	.08	.04	.01
□	434 Candy Maldonado	.08	.04	.01
□	435 Junior Felix	.08	.04	.01
□	436 Deion Sanders	.75	.35	.09
□	437 John Franco	.10	.04	.01
□	438 Greg Hibbard	.08	.04	.01
□	439 Floyd Bannister	.08	.04	.01
□	440 Steve Howe	.08	.04	.01
□	441 Steve Decker	.35	.16	.04
□	442 Vicente Palacios	.08	.04	.01
□	443 Pat Tabler	.08	.04	.01
□	444 Checklist Card	.12	.05	.02
	Darryl Strawberry			
□	445 Mike Felder	.08	.04	.01

☐ 446	Al Newman	.08	.04	.01
☐ 447	Chris Donnels	.20	.09	.03
☐ 448	Rich Rodriguez	.12	.05	.02
☐ 449	Turner Ward	.15	.07	.02
☐ 450	Bob Walk	.08	.04	.01
☐ 451	Gilberto Reyes	.08	.04	.01
☐ 452	Mike Jackson	.08	.04	.01
☐ 453	Rafael Belliard	.08	.04	.01
☐ 454	Wayne Edwards	.08	.04	.01
☐ 455	Andy Allanson	.08	.04	.01
☐ 456	Dave Smith	.08	.04	.01
☐ 457	Gary Carter	.10	.04	.01
☐ 458	Warren Cromartie	.08	.04	.01
☐ 459	Jack Armstrong	.08	.04	.01
☐ 460	Bob Tewksbury	.10	.04	.01
☐ 461	Joe Klink	.08	.04	.01
☐ 462	Xavier Hernandez	.08	.04	.01
☐ 463	Scott Radinsky	.08	.04	.01
☐ 464	Jeff Robinson	.08	.04	.01
☐ 465	Gregg Jefferies	.20	.09	.03
☐ 466	Denny Neagle	.40	.18	.05
☐ 467	Carmelo Martinez	.08	.04	.01
☐ 468	Donn Pall	.08	.04	.01
☐ 469	Bruce Hurst	.10	.04	.01
☐ 470	Eric Bullock	.08	.04	.01
☐ 471	Rick Aguilera	.10	.04	.01
☐ 472	Charlie Hough	.08	.04	.01
☐ 473	Carlos Quintana	.08	.04	.01
☐ 474	Marty Barrett	.08	.04	.01
☐ 475	Kevin D. Brown	.08	.04	.01
☐ 476	Bobby Ojeda	.08	.04	.01
☐ 477	Edgar Martinez	.25	.11	.03
☐ 478	Bip Roberts	.10	.04	.01
☐ 479	Mike Flanagan	.08	.04	.01
☐ 480	John Habyan	.08	.04	.01
☐ 481	Larry Casian	.08	.04	.01
☐ 482	Wally Backman	.08	.04	.01
☐ 483	Doug Dascenzo	.08	.04	.01
☐ 484	Rick Dempsey	.08	.04	.01
☐ 485	Ed Sprague	.35	.16	.04
☐ 486	Steve Chitren	.12	.05	.02
☐ 487	Mark McGwire	.75	.35	.09
☐ 488	Roger Clemens	1.00	.45	.13
☐ 489	Orlando Merced	.50	.23	.06
☐ 490	Rene Gonzales	.08	.04	.01
☐ 491	Mike Stanton	.08	.04	.01
☐ 492	Al Osuna	.15	.07	.02
☐ 493	Rick Cerone	.08	.04	.01
☐ 494	Mariano Duncan	.08	.04	.01
☐ 495	Zane Smith	.08	.04	.01
☐ 496	John Morris	.08	.04	.01
☐ 497	Frank Tanana	.08	.04	.01
☐ 498	Junior Ortiz	.08	.04	.01
☐ 499	Dave Winfield	.25	.11	.03
☐ 500	Gary Varsho	.08	.04	.01
☐ 501	Chico Walker	.08	.04	.01
☐ 502	Ken Caminiti	.10	.04	.01

☐ 503	Ken Griffey Sr.	.10	.04	.01
☐ 504	Randy Myers	.10	.04	.01
☐ 505	Steve Bedrosian	.08	.04	.01
☐ 506	Cory Snyder	.08	.04	.01
☐ 507	Cris Carpenter	.08	.04	.01
☐ 508	Tim Belcher	.10	.04	.01
☐ 509	Jeff Hamilton	.08	.04	.01
☐ 510	Steve Avery	.90	.40	.11
☐ 511	Dave Valle	.08	.04	.01
☐ 512	Tom Lampkin	.08	.04	.01
☐ 513	Shawn Hillegas	.08	.04	.01
☐ 514	Reggie Jefferson	.50	.23	.06
☐ 515	Ron Karkovice	.08	.04	.01
☐ 516	Doug Drabek	.10	.04	.01
☐ 517	Tom Henke	.10	.04	.01
☐ 518	Chris Bosio	.08	.04	.01
☐ 519	Gregg Olson	.10	.04	.01
☐ 520	Bob Scanlan	.20	.09	.03
☐ 521	Alonzo Powell	.12	.05	.02
☐ 522	Jeff Ballard	.08	.04	.01
☐ 523	Ray Lankford	1.50	.65	.19
☐ 524	Tommy Greene	.08	.04	.01
☐ 525	Mike Timlin	.25	.11	.03
☐ 526	Juan Berenguer	.08	.04	.01
☐ 527	Scott Erickson	.60	.25	.08
☐ 528	Checklist Card	.12	.05	.02
	Sandy Alomar Jr.			

1991 Leaf
Gold Rookies

This 26-card standard size (2 1/2" by 3 1/2") set was issued by Leaf as an adjunct (inserted in packs) to its 1991 Leaf regular issue. The set features some of the most popular prospects active in baseball. This set marks the first time Leaf Inc.

and/or Donruss had produced a card utilizing any of the first 24 young players. The first twelve cards were issued as random inserts in with the first series of 1991 Leaf foil packs. The rest were issued as random inserts in with the second series. The card numbers have a BC prefix. The earliest Leaf Gold Rookie cards issued with the first series can sometimes be found with erroneous regular numbered backs 265 through 276 instead of the correct BC1 through BC12. These numbered variations are very tough to find and are valued at ten times the values listed below.

1992 Leaf

	MT	EX-MT	VG
COMPLETE SET (26)	50.00	23.00	6.25
COMMON PLAYER (1-12)	1.00	.45	.13
COMMON PLAYER (13-26)	1.00	.45	.13

		MT	EX-MT	VG
☐ 1	Scott Leius	1.00	.45	.13
☐ 2	Luis Gonzalez	2.00	.90	.25
☐ 3	Wilfredo Cordero	5.00	2.30	.60
☐ 4	Gary Scott	2.00	.90	.25
☐ 5	Willie Banks	2.50	1.15	.30
☐ 6	Arthur Rhodes	4.50	2.00	.55
☐ 7	Mo Vaughn	2.50	1.15	.30
☐ 8	Henry Rodriguez	2.00	.90	.25
☐ 9	Todd Van Poppel	5.00	2.30	.60
☐ 10	Reggie Sanders	7.00	3.10	.85
☐ 11	Rico Brogna	2.00	.90	.25
☐ 12	Mike Mussina	13.00	5.75	1.65
☐ 13	Kirk Dressendorfer	1.00	.45	.13
☐ 14	Jeff Bagwell	10.00	4.50	1.25
☐ 15	Pete Schourek	1.50	.65	.19
☐ 16	Wade Taylor	1.00	.45	.13
☐ 17	Pat Kelly	1.50	.65	.19
☐ 18	Tim Costo	2.50	1.15	.30
☐ 19	Roger Salkeld	2.50	1.15	.30
☐ 20	Andujar Cedeno	2.00	.90	.25
☐ 21	Ryan Klesko UER (1990 Sumter BA .289; should be .368)	10.00	4.50	1.25
☐ 22	Mike Huff	1.00	.45	.13
☐ 23	Anthony Young	2.00	.90	.25
☐ 24	Eddie Zosky	1.50	.65	.19
☐ 25	Nolan Ryan UER No Hitter 7 (Word other repeated in 7th line)	5.00	2.30	.60
☐ 26	Rickey Henderson Record Steal	1.75	.80	.22

The 1992 Leaf set consists of 528 cards, issued in two series each with 264 cards measuring the standard size (2 1/2" by 3 1/2"). The fronts feature color action player photos on a silver card face. The player's name appears in a black bar edged at the bottom by a thin red stripe. The team logo overlaps the bar at the right corner. The horizontally oriented backs have color action player photos on left portion of the card. The right portion carries the player's name and team logo in a black bar as well as career statistics and career highlights in a white box. The card backs have a silver background. The cards are numbered on the back. Leaf also produced a Gold Foil Version of the complete set (series I and II), featuring gold metallic ink and gold foil highlights instead of the traditional silver. One of these "black gold inserts" was included in each 15-card foil pack. Twelve "Gold Leaf Rookie" bonus cards, numbered BC1-BC12, were randomly inserted in first series foil packs and twelve, numbered BC13-24, were randomly inserted in second series foil packs. The most noteworthy Rookie Card in the first series is Chris Gardner. The most noteworthy Rookie Cards in the second series are Archi Cianfrocco and Pat Listach.

	MT	EX-MT	VG
COMPLETE SET (528)	40.00	18.00	5.00
COMPLETE SERIES 1 (264)	20.00	9.00	2.50
COMPLETE SERIES 2 (264)	20.00	9.00	2.50
COMMON PLAYER (1-264)	.07	.03	.01
COMMON PLAYER (265-528)	.07	.03	.01

☐	1	Jim Abbott	.20	.09	.03	☐	58	Roger McDowell	.07	.03	.01
☐	2	Cal Eldred	1.00	.45	.13	☐	59	Steve Avery	.50	.23	.06
☐	3	Bud Black	.07	.03	.01	☐	60	John Olerud	.25	.11	.03
☐	4	Dave Howard	.07	.03	.01	☐	61	Bill Gullickson	.07	.03	.01
☐	5	Luis Sojo	.07	.03	.01	☐	62	Juan Gonzalez	1.25	.55	.16
☐	6	Gary Scott	.10	.05	.01	☐	63	Felix Jose	.10	.05	.01
☐	7	Joe Oliver	.07	.03	.01	☐	64	Robin Yount	.25	.11	.03
☐	8	Chris Gardner	.15	.07	.02	☐	65	Greg Briley	.07	.03	.01
☐	9	Sandy Alomar Jr.	.10	.05	.01	☐	66	Steve Finley	.10	.05	.01
☐	10	Greg W. Harris	.07	.03	.01	☐	67	Checklist	.10	.01	.00
☐	11	Doug Drabek	.10	.05	.01	☐	68	Tom Gordon	.07	.03	.01
☐	12	Darryl Hamilton	.10	.05	.01	☐	69	Rob Dibble	.10	.05	.01
☐	13	Mike Mussina	1.75	.80	.22	☐	70	Glenallen Hill	.07	.03	.01
☐	14	Kevin Tapani	.10	.05	.01	☐	71	Calvin Jones	.12	.05	.02
☐	15	Ron Gant	.20	.09	.03	☐	72	Joe Girardi	.07	.03	.01
☐	16	Mark McGwire	.50	.23	.06	☐	73	Barry Larkin	.20	.09	.03
☐	17	Robin Ventura	.50	.23	.06	☐	74	Andy Benes	.12	.05	.02
☐	18	Pedro Guerrero	.10	.05	.01	☐	75	Milt Cuyler	.07	.03	.01
☐	19	Roger Clemens	.60	.25	.08	☐	76	Kevin Bass	.07	.03	.01
☐	20	Steve Farr	.07	.03	.01	☐	77	Pete Harnisch	.07	.03	.01
☐	21	Frank Tanana	.07	.03	.01	☐	78	Wilson Alvarez	.07	.03	.01
☐	22	Joe Hesketh	.07	.03	.01	☐	79	Mike Devereaux	.10	.05	.01
☐	23	Erik Hanson	.07	.03	.01	☐	80	Doug Henry	.30	.14	.04
☐	24	Greg Cadaret	.07	.03	.01	☐	81	Orel Hershiser	.12	.05	.02
☐	25	Rex Hudler	.07	.03	.01	☐	82	Shane Mack	.10	.05	.01
☐	26	Mark Grace	.12	.05	.02	☐	83	Mike Macfarlane	.07	.03	.01
☐	27	Kelly Gruber	.10	.05	.01	☐	84	Thomas Howard	.07	.03	.01
☐	28	Jeff Bagwell	.75	.35	.09	☐	85	Alex Fernandez	.10	.05	.01
☐	29	Darryl Strawberry	.30	.14	.04	☐	86	Reggie Jefferson	.15	.07	.02
☐	30	Dave Smith	.07	.03	.01	☐	87	Leo Gomez	.20	.09	.03
☐	31	Kevin Appier	.10	.05	.01	☐	88	Mel Hall	.07	.03	.01
☐	32	Steve Chitren	.07	.03	.01	☐	89	Mike Greenwell	.12	.05	.02
☐	33	Kevin Gross	.07	.03	.01	☐	90	Jeff Russell	.07	.03	.01
☐	34	Rick Aguilera	.10	.05	.01	☐	91	Steve Buechele	.07	.03	.01
☐	35	Juan Guzman	1.75	.80	.22	☐	92	David Cone	.12	.05	.02
☐	36	Joe Orsulak	.07	.03	.01	☐	93	Kevin Reimer	.10	.05	.01
☐	37	Tim Raines	.12	.05	.02	☐	94	Mark Lemke	.07	.03	.01
☐	38	Harold Reynolds	.07	.03	.01	☐	95	Bob Tewksbury	.10	.05	.01
☐	39	Charlie Hough	.07	.03	.01	☐	96	Zane Smith	.07	.03	.01
☐	40	Tony Phillips	.07	.03	.01	☐	97	Mark Eichhorn	.07	.03	.01
☐	41	Nolan Ryan	1.50	.65	.19	☐	98	Kirby Puckett	.50	.23	.06
☐	42	Vince Coleman	.10	.05	.01	☐	99	Paul O'Neill	.10	.05	.01
☐	43	Andy Van Slyke	.12	.05	.02	☐	100	Dennis Eckersley	.15	.07	.02
☐	44	Tim Burke	.07	.03	.01	☐	101	Duane Ward	.07	.03	.01
☐	45	Luis Polonia	.10	.05	.01	☐	102	Matt Nokes	.07	.03	.01
☐	46	Tom Browning	.07	.03	.01	☐	103	Mo Vaughn	.12	.05	.02
☐	47	Willie McGee	.10	.05	.01	☐	104	Pat Kelly	.12	.05	.02
☐	48	Gary DiSarcina	.10	.05	.01	☐	105	Ron Karkovice	.07	.03	.01
☐	49	Mark Lewis	.10	.05	.01	☐	106	Bill Spiers	.07	.03	.01
☐	50	Phil Plantier	.30	.14	.04	☐	107	Gary Gaetti	.07	.03	.01
☐	51	Doug Dascenzo	.07	.03	.01	☐	108	Mackey Sasser	.07	.03	.01
☐	52	Cal Ripken	.75	.35	.09	☐	109	Robby Thompson	.07	.03	.01
☐	53	Pedro Munoz	.12	.05	.02	☐	110	Marvin Freeman	.07	.03	.01
☐	54	Carlos Hernandez	.07	.03	.01	☐	111	Jimmy Key	.07	.03	.01
☐	55	Jerald Clark	.07	.03	.01	☐	112	Dwight Gooden	.12	.05	.02
☐	56	Jeff Brantley	.07	.03	.01	☐	113	Charlie Leibrandt	.07	.03	.01
☐	57	Don Mattingly	.30	.14	.04	☐	114	Devon White	.10	.05	.01

☐	115 Charles Nagy	25	.11	.03		
☐	116 Rickey Henderson	25	.11	.03		
☐	117 Paul Assenmacher	07	.03	.01		
☐	118 Junior Felix	07	.03	.01		
☐	119 Julio Franco	10	.05	.01		
☐	120 Norm Charlton	10	.05	.01		
☐	121 Scott Servais	07	.03	.01		
☐	122 Gerald Perry	07	.03	.01		
☐	123 Brian McRae	12	.05	.02		
☐	124 Don Slaught	07	.03	.01		
☐	125 Juan Samuel	07	.03	.01		
☐	126 Harold Baines	10	.05	.01		
☐	127 Scott Livingstone	20	.09	.03		
☐	128 Jay Buhner	10	.05	.01		
☐	129 Darrin Jackson	10	.05	.01		
☐	130 Luis Mercedes	25	.11	.03		
☐	131 Brian Harper	07	.03	.01		
☐	132 Howard Johnson	10	.05	.01		
☐	133 Checklist	10	.01	.00		
☐	134 Dante Bichette	07	.03	.01		
☐	135 Dave Righetti	07	.03	.01		
☐	136 Jeff Montgomery	07	.03	.01		
☐	137 Joe Grahe	07	.03	.01		
☐	138 Delino DeShields	25	.11	.03		
☐	139 Jose Rijo	10	.05	.01		
☐	140 Ken Caminiti	10	.05	.01		
☐	141 Steve Olin	07	.03	.01		
☐	142 Kurt Stillwell	07	.03	.01		
☐	143 Jay Bell	07	.03	.01		
☐	144 Jaime Navarro	10	.05	.01		
☐	145 Ben McDonald	15	.07	.02		
☐	146 Greg Gagne	07	.03	.01		
☐	147 Jeff Blauser	07	.03	.01		
☐	148 Carney Lansford	10	.05	.01		
☐	149 Ozzie Guillen	07	.03	.01		
☐	150 Milt Thompson	07	.03	.01		
☐	151 Jeff Reardon	12	.05	.02		
☐	152 Scott Sanderson	07	.03	.01		
☐	153 Cecil Fielder	30	.14	.04		
☐	154 Greg A. Harris	07	.03	.01		
☐	155 Rich DeLucia	07	.03	.01		
☐	156 Roberto Kelly	12	.05	.02		
☐	157 Bryn Smith	07	.03	.01		
☐	158 Chuck McElroy	07	.03	.01		
☐	159 Tom Henke	10	.05	.01		
☐	160 Luis Gonzalez	12	.05	.02		
☐	161 Steve Wilson	07	.03	.01		
☐	162 Shawn Boskie	07	.03	.01		
☐	163 Mark Davis	07	.03	.01		
☐	164 Mike Moore	07	.03	.01		
☐	165 Mike Scioscia	07	.03	.01		
☐	166 Scott Erickson	15	.07	.02		
☐	167 Todd Stottlemyre	10	.05	.01		
☐	168 Alvin Davis	07	.03	.01		
☐	169 Greg Hibbard	07	.03	.01		
☐	170 David Valle	07	.03	.01		
☐	171 Dave Winfield	20	.09	.03		
☐	172 Alan Trammell	12	.05	.02		
☐	173 Kenny Rogers	07	.03	.01		
☐	174 John Franco	10	.05	.01		
☐	175 Jose Lind	07	.03	.01		
☐	176 Pete Schourek	10	.05	.01		
☐	177 Von Hayes	07	.03	.01		
☐	178 Chris Hammond	07	.03	.01		
☐	179 John Burkett	07	.03	.01		
☐	180 Dickie Thon	07	.03	.01		
☐	181 Joel Skinner	07	.03	.01		
☐	182 Scott Cooper	25	.11	.03		
☐	183 Andre Dawson	15	.07	.02		
☐	184 Billy Ripken	07	.03	.01		
☐	185 Kevin Mitchell	12	.05	.02		
☐	186 Brett Butler	10	.05	.01		
☐	187 Tony Fernandez	10	.05	.01		
☐	188 Cory Snyder	07	.03	.01		
☐	189 John Habyan	07	.03	.01		
☐	190 Dennis Martinez	10	.05	.01		
☐	191 John Smoltz	20	.09	.03		
☐	192 Greg Myers	07	.03	.01		
☐	193 Rob Deer	10	.05	.01		
☐	194 Ivan Rodriguez	1.00	.45	.13		
☐	195 Ray Lankford	40	.18	.05		
☐	196 Bill Wegman	07	.03	.01		
☐	197 Edgar Martinez	10	.05	.01		
☐	198 Darryl Kile	10	.05	.01		
☐	199 Checklist	10	.01	.00		
☐	200 Brent Mayne	07	.03	.01		
☐	201 Larry Walker	35	.16	.04		
☐	202 Carlos Baerga	40	.18	.05		
☐	203 Russ Swan	07	.03	.01		
☐	204 Mike Morgan	07	.03	.01		
☐	205 Hal Morris	10	.05	.01		
☐	206 Tony Gwynn	30	.14	.04		
☐	207 Mark Leiter	07	.03	.01		
☐	208 Kirt Manwaring	07	.03	.01		
☐	209 Al Osuna	07	.03	.01		
☐	210 Bobby Thigpen	07	.03	.01		
☐	211 Chris Hoiles	12	.05	.02		
☐	212 B.J. Surhoff	07	.03	.01		
☐	213 Lenny Harris	07	.03	.01		
☐	214 Scott Leius	07	.03	.01		
☐	215 Gregg Jefferies	10	.05	.01		
☐	216 Bruce Hurst	10	.05	.01		
☐	217 Steve Sax	10	.05	.01		
☐	218 Dave Otto	07	.03	.01		
☐	219 Sam Horn	07	.03	.01		
☐	220 Charlie Hayes	07	.03	.01		
☐	221 Frank Viola	10	.05	.01		
☐	222 Jose Guzman	07	.03	.01		
☐	223 Gary Redus	07	.03	.01		
☐	224 Dave Gallagher	07	.03	.01		
☐	225 Dean Palmer	40	.18	.05		
☐	226 Greg Olson	07	.03	.01		
☐	227 Jose DeLeon	07	.03	.01		
☐	228 Mike LaValliere	07	.03	.01		

☐	229	Mark Langston	.10	.05	.01	☐ 286	Wade Boggs	.30	.14	.04

☐	229	Mark Langston	.10	.05	.01
☐	230	Chuck Knoblauch	.40	.18	.05
☐	231	Bill Doran	.07	.03	.01
☐	232	Dave Henderson	.07	.03	.01
☐	233	Roberto Alomar	.50	.23	.06
☐	234	Scott Fletcher	.07	.03	.01
☐	235	Tim Naehring	.07	.03	.01
☐	236	Mike Gallego	.07	.03	.01
☐	237	Lance Johnson	.07	.03	.01
☐	238	Paul Molitor	.12	.05	.02
☐	239	Dan Gladden	.07	.03	.01
☐	240	Willie Randolph	.10	.05	.01
☐	241	Will Clark	.50	.23	.06
☐	242	Sid Bream	.07	.03	.01
☐	243	Derek Bell	.30	.14	.04
☐	244	Bill Pecota	.07	.03	.01
☐	245	Terry Pendleton	.12	.05	.02
☐	246	Randy Ready	.07	.03	.01
☐	247	Jack Armstrong	.07	.03	.01
☐	248	Todd Van Poppel	.40	.18	.05
☐	249	Shawon Dunston	.10	.05	.01
☐	250	Bobby Rose	.07	.03	.01
☐	251	Jeff Huson	.07	.03	.01
☐	252	Bip Roberts	.10	.05	.01
☐	253	Doug Jones	.07	.03	.01
☐	254	Lee Smith	.10	.05	.01
☐	255	George Brett	.25	.11	.03
☐	256	Randy Tomlin	.12	.05	.02
☐	257	Todd Benzinger	.07	.03	.01
☐	258	Dave Stewart	.10	.05	.01
☐	259	Mark Carreon	.07	.03	.01
☐	260	Pete O'Brien	.07	.03	.01
☐	261	Tim Teufel	.07	.03	.01
☐	262	Bob Milacki	.07	.03	.01
☐	263	Mark Guthrie	.07	.03	.01
☐	264	Darrin Fletcher	.07	.03	.01
☐	265	Omar Vizquel	.07	.03	.01
☐	266	Chris Bosio	.07	.03	.01
☐	267	Jose Canseco	.50	.23	.06
☐	268	Mike Boddicker	.07	.03	.01
☐	269	Lance Parrish	.10	.05	.01
☐	270	Jose Vizcaino	.07	.03	.01
☐	271	Chris Sabo	.10	.05	.01
☐	272	Royce Clayton	.40	.18	.05
☐	273	Marquis Grissom	.25	.11	.03
☐	274	Fred McGriff	.30	.14	.04
☐	275	Barry Bonds	.50	.23	.06
☐	276	Greg Vaughn	.10	.05	.01
☐	277	Gregg Olson	.10	.05	.01
☐	278	Dave Hollins	.25	.11	.03
☐	279	Tom Glavine	.30	.14	.04
☐	280	Bryan Hickerson	.07	.03	.01
☐	281	Scott Radinsky	.07	.03	.01
☐	282	Omar Olivares	.07	.03	.01
☐	283	Ivan Calderon	.07	.03	.01
☐	284	Kevin Maas	.10	.05	.01
☐	285	Mickey Tettleton	.10	.05	.01
☐	286	Wade Boggs	.30	.14	.04
☐	287	Stan Belinda	.07	.03	.01
☐	288	Bret Barberie	.12	.05	.02
☐	289	Jose Oquendo	.07	.03	.01
☐	290	Frank Castillo	.15	.07	.02
☐	291	Dave Stieb	.07	.03	.01
☐	292	Tommy Greene	.07	.03	.01
☐	293	Eric Karros	1.75	.80	.22
☐	294	Greg Maddux	.15	.07	.02
☐	295	Jim Eisenreich	.07	.03	.01
☐	296	Rafael Palmeiro	.12	.05	.02
☐	297	Ramon Martinez	.12	.05	.02
☐	298	Tim Wallach	.10	.05	.01
☐	299	Jim Thome	.25	.11	.03
☐	300	Chito Martinez	.07	.03	.01
☐	301	Mitch Williams	.07	.03	.01
☐	302	Randy Johnson	.10	.05	.01
☐	303	Carlton Fisk	.20	.09	.03
☐	304	Travis Fryman	1.00	.45	.13
☐	305	Bobby Witt	.07	.03	.01
☐	306	Dave Magadan	.10	.05	.01
☐	307	Alex Cole	.07	.03	.01
☐	308	Bobby Bonilla	.15	.07	.02
☐	309	Bryan Harvey	.07	.03	.01
☐	310	Rafael Belliard	.07	.03	.01
☐	311	Mariano Duncan	.07	.03	.01
☐	312	Chuck Crim	.07	.03	.01
☐	313	John Kruk	.10	.05	.01
☐	314	Ellis Burks	.10	.05	.01
☐	315	Craig Biggio	.10	.05	.01
☐	316	Glenn Davis	.10	.05	.01
☐	317	Ryne Sandberg	.60	.25	.08
☐	318	Mike Sharperson	.07	.03	.01
☐	319	Rich Rodriguez	.07	.03	.01
☐	320	Lee Guetterman	.07	.03	.01
☐	321	Benito Santiago	.12	.05	.02
☐	322	Jose Offerman	.10	.05	.01
☐	323	Tony Pena	.07	.03	.01
☐	324	Pat Borders	.07	.03	.01
☐	325	Mike Henneman	.07	.03	.01
☐	326	Kevin Brown	.10	.05	.01
☐	327	Chris Nabholz	.07	.03	.01
☐	328	Franklin Stubbs	.07	.03	.01
☐	329	Tino Martinez	.12	.05	.02
☐	330	Mickey Morandini	.07	.03	.01
☐	331	Checklist	.10	.01	.00
☐	332	Mark Gubicza	.07	.03	.01
☐	333	Bill Landrum	.07	.03	.01
☐	334	Mark Whiten	.07	.03	.01
☐	335	Darren Daulton	.10	.05	.01
☐	336	Rick Wilkins	.07	.03	.01
☐	337	Brian Jordan	.40	.18	.05
☐	338	Kevin Ward	.12	.05	.02
☐	339	Ruben Amaro	.12	.05	.02
☐	340	Trevor Wilson	.07	.03	.01
☐	341	Andujar Cedeno	.12	.05	.02
☐	342	Michael Huff	.07	.03	.01

☐ 343	Brady Anderson	10	.05	.01	☐ 398	Dave Cochrane	07	.03	.01
☐ 344	Craig Grebeck	07	.03	.01	☐ 399	Kevin Seitzer	10	.05	.01
☐ 345	Bobby Ojeda	07	.03	.01	☐ 400	Ozzie Smith	20	.09	.03
☐ 346	Mike Pagliarulo	07	.03	.01	☐ 401	Paul Sorrento	10	.05	.01
☐ 347	Terry Shumpert	07	.03	.01	☐ 402	Les Lancaster	07	.03	.01
☐ 348	Dann Bilardello	07	.03	.01	☐ 403	Junior Noboa	07	.03	.01
☐ 349	Frank Thomas	3.00	1.35	.40	☐ 404	David Justice	75	.35	.09
☐ 350	Albert Belle	30	.14	.04	☐ 405	Andy Ashby	15	.07	.02
☐ 351	Jose Mesa	07	.03	.01	☐ 406	Danny Tartabull	12	.05	.02
☐ 352	Rich Monteleone	07	.03	.01	☐ 407	Bill Swift	07	.03	.01
☐ 353	Bob Walk	07	.03	.01	☐ 408	Craig Lefferts	07	.03	.01
☐ 354	Monty Fariss	15	.07	.02	☐ 409	Tom Candiotti	07	.03	.01
☐ 355	Luis Rivera	07	.03	.01	☐ 410	Lance Blankenship	07	.03	.01
☐ 356	Anthony Young	12	.05	.02	☐ 411	Jeff Tackett	12	.05	.02
☐ 357	Geno Petralli	07	.03	.01	☐ 412	Sammy Sosa	07	.03	.01
☐ 358	Otis Nixon	10	.05	.01	☐ 413	Jody Reed	07	.03	.01
☐ 359	Tom Pagnozzi	07	.03	.01	☐ 414	Bruce Ruffin	07	.03	.01
☐ 360	Reggie Sanders	75	.35	.09	☐ 415	Gene Larkin	07	.03	.01
☐ 361	Lee Stevens	07	.03	.01	☐ 416	John Vander Wal	25	.11	.03
☐ 362	Kent Hrbek	10	.05	.01	☐ 417	Tim Belcher	10	.05	.01
☐ 363	Orlando Merced	12	.05	.02	☐ 418	Steve Frey	07	.03	.01
☐ 364	Mike Bordick	15	.07	.02	☐ 419	Dick Schofield	07	.03	.01
☐ 365	Dion James UER	07	.03	.01	☐ 420	Jeff King	07	.03	.01
	(Blue Jays logo				☐ 421	Kim Batiste	15	.07	.02
	on card back)				☐ 422	Jack McDowell	12	.05	.02
☐ 366	Jack Clark	10	.05	.01	☐ 423	Damon Berryhill	07	.03	.01
☐ 367	Mike Stanley	07	.03	.01	☐ 424	Gary Wayne	07	.03	.01
☐ 368	Randy Velarde	07	.03	.01	☐ 425	Jack Morris	15	.07	.02
☐ 369	Dan Pasqua	07	.03	.01	☐ 426	Moises Alou	20	.09	.03
☐ 370	Pat Listach	2.50	1.15	.30	☐ 427	Mark McLemore	07	.03	.01
☐ 371	Mike Fitzgerald	07	.03	.01	☐ 428	Juan Guerrero	20	.09	.03
☐ 372	Tom Foley	07	.03	.01	☐ 429	Scott Scudder	07	.03	.01
☐ 373	Matt Williams	12	.05	.02	☐ 430	Eric Davis	12	.05	.02
☐ 374	Brian Hunter	20	.09	.03	☐ 431	Joe Slusarski	07	.03	.01
☐ 375	Joe Carter	30	.14	.04	☐ 432	Todd Zeile	07	.03	.01
☐ 376	Bret Saberhagen	12	.05	.02	☐ 433	Dwayne Henry	07	.03	.01
☐ 377	Mike Stanton	07	.03	.01	☐ 434	Cliff Brantley	12	.05	.02
☐ 378	Hubie Brooks	07	.03	.01	☐ 435	Butch Henry	20	.09	.03
☐ 379	Eric Bell	07	.03	.01	☐ 436	Todd Worrell	07	.03	.01
☐ 380	Walt Weiss	07	.03	.01	☐ 437	Bob Scanlan	07	.03	.01
☐ 381	Danny Jackson	07	.03	.01	☐ 438	Wally Joyner	10	.05	.01
☐ 382	Manuel Lee	07	.03	.01	☐ 439	John Flaherty	12	.05	.02
☐ 383	Ruben Sierra	40	.18	.05	☐ 440	Brian Downing	07	.03	.01
☐ 384	Greg Swindell	10	.05	.01	☐ 441	Darren Lewis	10	.05	.01
☐ 385	Ryan Bowen	15	.07	.02	☐ 442	Gary Carter	10	.05	.01
☐ 386	Kevin Ritz	07	.03	.01	☐ 443	Wally Ritchie	07	.03	.01
☐ 387	Curtis Wilkerson	07	.03	.01	☐ 444	Chris Jones	07	.03	.01
☐ 388	Gary Varsho	07	.03	.01	☐ 445	Jeff Kent	50	.23	.06
☐ 389	Dave Hansen	12	.05	.02	☐ 446	Gary Sheffield	75	.35	.09
☐ 390	Bob Welch	07	.03	.01	☐ 447	Ron Darling	10	.05	.01
☐ 391	Lou Whitaker	12	.05	.02	☐ 448	Deion Sanders	40	.18	.05
☐ 392	Ken Griffey Jr.	2.00	.90	.25	☐ 449	Andres Galarraga	07	.03	.01
☐ 393	Mike Maddux	07	.03	.01	☐ 450	Chuck Finley	07	.03	.01
☐ 394	Arthur Rhodes	40	.18	.05	☐ 451	Derek Lilliquist	07	.03	.01
☐ 395	Chili Davis	10	.05	.01	☐ 452	Carl Willis	07	.03	.01
☐ 396	Eddie Murray	20	.09	.03	☐ 453	Wes Chamberlain	12	.05	.02
☐ 397	Checklist	10	.01	.00	☐ 454	Roger Mason	07	.03	.01

☐ 455	Spike Owen	.07	.03	.01
☐ 456	Thomas Howard	.07	.03	.01
☐ 457	Dave Martinez	.07	.03	.01
☐ 458	Pete Incaviglia	.07	.03	.01
☐ 459	Keith A. Miller	.07	.03	.01
☐ 460	Mike Fetters	.07	.03	.01
☐ 461	Paul Gibson	.07	.03	.01
☐ 462	George Bell	.10	.05	.01
☐ 463	Checklist	.10	.01	.00
☐ 464	Terry Mulholland	.07	.03	.01
☐ 465	Storm Davis	.07	.03	.01
☐ 466	Gary Pettis	.07	.03	.01
☐ 467	Randy Bush	.07	.03	.01
☐ 468	Ken Hill	.07	.03	.01
☐ 469	Rheal Cormier	.15	.07	.02
☐ 470	Andy Stankiewicz	.25	.11	.03
☐ 471	Dave Burba	.07	.03	.01
☐ 472	Henry Cotto	.07	.03	.01
☐ 473	Dale Sveum	.07	.03	.01
☐ 474	Rich Gossage	.10	.05	.01
☐ 475	William Suero	.12	.05	.02
☐ 476	Doug Strange	.07	.03	.01
☐ 477	Bill Krueger	.07	.03	.01
☐ 478	John Wetteland	.07	.03	.01
☐ 479	Melido Perez	.10	.05	.01
☐ 480	Lonnie Smith	.07	.03	.01
☐ 481	Mike Jackson	.07	.03	.01
☐ 482	Mike Gardiner	.07	.03	.01
☐ 483	David Wells	.07	.03	.01
☐ 484	Barry Jones	.07	.03	.01
☐ 485	Scott Bankhead	.07	.03	.01
☐ 486	Torry Leach	.07	.03	.01
☐ 487	Vince Horsman	.12	.05	.02
☐ 488	Dave Eiland	.07	.03	.01
☐ 489	Alejandro Pena	.07	.03	.01
☐ 490	Julio Valera	.15	.07	.02
☐ 491	Joe Boever	.07	.03	.01
☐ 492	Paul Miller	.15	.07	.02
☐ 493	Archi Cianfrocco	.25	.11	.03
☐ 494	Dave Fleming	1.00	.45	.13
☐ 495	Kyle Abbott	.15	.07	.02
☐ 496	Chad Kreuter	.07	.03	.01
☐ 497	Chris James	.07	.03	.01
☐ 498	Donnie Hill	.07	.03	.01
☐ 499	Jacob Brumfield	.12	.05	.02
☐ 500	Ricky Bones	.15	.07	.02
☐ 501	Terry Steinbach	.10	.05	.01
☐ 502	Bernard Gilkey	.12	.05	.02
☐ 503	Dennis Cook	.07	.03	.01
☐ 504	Len Dykstra	.10	.05	.01
☐ 505	Mike Bielecki	.07	.03	.01
☐ 506	Bob Kipper	.07	.03	.01
☐ 507	Jose Melendez	.12	.05	.02
☐ 508	Rick Sutcliffe	.10	.05	.01
☐ 509	Ken Patterson	.07	.03	.01
☐ 510	Andy Allanson	.07	.03	.01
☐ 511	Al Newman	.07	.03	.01
☐ 512	Mark Gardner	.07	.03	.01
☐ 513	Jeff Schaefer	.07	.03	.01
☐ 514	Jim McNamara	.12	.05	.02
☐ 515	Peter Hoy	.12	.05	.02
☐ 516	Curt Schilling	.10	.05	.01
☐ 517	Kirk McCaskill	.07	.03	.01
☐ 518	Chris Gwynn	.07	.03	.01
☐ 519	Sid Fernandez	.10	.05	.01
☐ 520	Jeff Parrett	.07	.03	.01
☐ 521	Scott Ruskin	.07	.03	.01
☐ 522	Kevin McReynolds	.10	.05	.01
☐ 523	Rick Cerone	.07	.03	.01
☐ 524	Jesse Orosco	.07	.03	.01
☐ 525	Troy Afenir	.07	.03	.01
☐ 526	John Smiley	.10	.05	.01
☐ 527	Dale Murphy	.12	.05	.02
☐ 528	Leaf Set Card	.15	.07	.02

1992 Leaf Gold Rookies

This 24-card standard-size (2 1/2" by 3 1/2") set honors 1992's most promising newcomers. The first 12 cards were randomly inserted in Leaf series I foil packs, while the second 12 cards were featured only in series II packs. The card numbers show a BC prefix. The fronts display full-bleed color action photos highlighted by gold foil border stripes. A gold foil diamond appears at the corners of the picture frame, and the player's name appears in a black bar that extends between the bottom two diamonds. On a gold background, the horizontally oriented backs feature a second color player photo, biography, and, on a white panel, career statistics and career

summary. The cards are numbered on the back.

	MT	EX-MT	VG
COMPLETE SET (24)	60.00	27.00	7.50
COMPLETE SERIES 1 (12)	30.00	13.50	3.80
COMPLETE SERIES 2 (12)	30.00	13.50	3.80
COMMON PLAYER (1-12)	1.50	.65	.19
COMMON PLAYER (13-24)	1.50	.65	.19

		MT	EX-MT	VG
☐	1 Chad Curtis	4.00	1.80	.50
☐	2 Brent Gates	4.50	2.00	.55
☐	3 Pedro Martinez	4.00	1.80	.50
☐	4 Kenny Lofton	6.00	2.70	.75
☐	5 Turk Wendell	1.75	.80	.22
☐	6 Mark Hutton	2.50	1.15	.30
☐	7 Todd Hundley	1.50	.65	.19
☐	8 Matt Stairs	2.00	.90	.25
☐	9 Eddie Taubensee	2.00	.90	.25
☐	10 David Nied	10.00	4.50	1.25
☐	11 Salomon Torres	3.00	1.35	.40
☐	12 Bret Boone	5.00	2.30	.60
☐	13 Johnny Ruffin	2.00	.90	.25
☐	14 Ed Martel	1.75	.80	.22
☐	15 Rick Trlicek	2.00	.90	.25
☐	16 Raul Mondesi	4.00	1.80	.50
☐	17 Pat Mahomes	3.00	1.35	.40
☐	18 Dan Wilson	2.00	.90	.25
☐	19 Donovan Osborne	4.00	1.80	.50
☐	20 Dave Silvestri	2.50	1.15	.30
☐	21 Gary DiSarcina	1.50	.65	.19
☐	22 Denny Neagle	1.50	.65	.19
☐	23 Steve Hosey	4.00	1.80	.50
☐	24 John Doherty	2.00	.90	.25

1992 Pinnacle

The 1992 Score Pinnacle baseball set consists of two series each with 310 cards measuring the standard size (2 1/2" by 3 1/2"). Series I count goods pack had 16 cards per pack, while the cello pack featured 27 cards. Two 12-card bonus subsets, displaying the artwork of Chris Greco, were randomly inserted in series I and II count goods packs. The fronts feature glossy color player photos, on a black background accented by thin white borders. On a black background, the horizontally oriented backs carry a close-up portrait, statistics (1991 and career), and an in-depth player profile. An anti-counterfeit

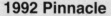

device appears in the bottom border of each card back. Special subsets featured include '92 Rookie Prospects (52, 55, 168, 247-261, 263-280), Idols (281-286), Sidelines (287-294), Draft Picks (295-304), Shades (305-310), Idols (584-591), Sidelines (592-596), Shades (601-605), Grips (606-612), and Technicians (614-620). The cards are numbered on the back. Key Rookie Cards in the set include Cliff Floyd, Tyler Green, Pat Listach, Manny Ramirez, Al Shirley, and Bob Zupcic.

	MT	EX-MT	VG
COMPLETE SET (620)	60.00	27.00	7.50
COMPLETE SERIES 1 (310)	35.00	16.00	4.40
COMPLETE SERIES 2 (310)	25.00	11.50	3.10
COMMON PLAYER (1-310)	.08	.04	.01
COMMON PLAYER (311-620)	.08	.04	.01

		MT	EX-MT	VG
☐	1 Frank Thomas	3.00	1.35	.40
☐	2 Benito Santiago	.12	.05	.02
☐	3 Carlos Baerga	.50	.23	.06
☐	4 Cecil Fielder	.30	.14	.04
☐	5 Barry Larkin	.20	.09	.03
☐	6 Ozzie Smith	.20	.09	.03
☐	7 Willie McGee	.10	.04	.01
☐	8 Paul Molitor	.12	.05	.02
☐	9 Andy Van Slyke	.12	.05	.02
☐	10 Ryne Sandberg	.60	.25	.08
☐	11 Kevin Seitzer	.10	.04	.01
☐	12 Len Dykstra	.10	.04	.01
☐	13 Edgar Martinez	.10	.04	.01
☐	14 Ruben Sierra	.40	.18	.05
☐	15 Howard Johnson	.10	.04	.01
☐	16 Dave Henderson	.08	.04	.01
☐	17 Devon White	.10	.04	.01
☐	18 Terry Pendleton	.12	.05	.02
☐	19 Steve Finley	.10	.04	.01
☐	20 Kirby Puckett	.60	.25	.08
☐	21 Orel Hershiser	.12	.05	.02
☐	22 Hal Morris	.10	.04	.01

☐ 23 Don Mattingly	.30	.14	.04
☐ 24 Delino DeShields	.25	.11	.03
☐ 25 Dennis Eckersley	.15	.07	.02
☐ 26 Ellis Burks	.10	.04	.01
☐ 27 Jay Buhner	.10	.04	.01
☐ 28 Matt Williams	.12	.05	.02
☐ 29 Lou Whitaker	.12	.05	.02
☐ 30 Alex Fernandez	.10	.04	.01
☐ 31 Albert Belle	.30	.14	.04
☐ 32 Todd Zeile	.08	.04	.01
☐ 33 Tony Pena	.08	.04	.01
☐ 34 Jay Bell	.08	.04	.01
☐ 35 Rafael Palmeiro	.12	.05	.02
☐ 36 Wes Chamberlain	.12	.05	.02
☐ 37 George Bell	.10	.04	.01
☐ 38 Robin Yount	.25	.11	.03
☐ 39 Vince Coleman	.10	.04	.01
☐ 40 Bruce Hurst	.10	.04	.01
☐ 41 Harold Baines	.10	.04	.01
☐ 42 Chuck Finley	.08	.04	.01
☐ 43 Ken Caminiti	.10	.04	.01
☐ 44 Ben McDonald	.15	.07	.02
☐ 45 Roberto Alomar	.50	.23	.06
☐ 46 Chili Davis	.10	.04	.01
☐ 47 Bill Doran	.08	.04	.01
☐ 48 Jerald Clark	.08	.04	.01
☐ 49 Jose Lind	.08	.04	.01
☐ 50 Nolan Ryan	1.50	.65	.19
☐ 51 Phil Plantier	.30	.14	.04
☐ 52 Gary DiSarcina	.10	.04	.01
☐ 53 Kevin Bass	.08	.04	.01
☐ 54 Pat Kelly	.12	.05	.02
☐ 55 Mark Wohlers	.20	.09	.03
☐ 56 Walt Weiss	.08	.04	.01
☐ 57 Lenny Harris	.08	.04	.01
☐ 58 Ivan Calderon	.08	.04	.01
☐ 59 Harold Reynolds	.08	.04	.01
☐ 60 George Brett	.25	.11	.03
☐ 61 Gregg Olson	.10	.04	.01
☐ 62 Orlando Merced	.12	.05	.02
☐ 63 Steve Decker	.08	.04	.01
☐ 64 John Franco	.10	.04	.01
☐ 65 Greg Maddux	.15	.07	.02
☐ 66 Alex Cole	.08	.04	.01
☐ 67 Dave Hollins	.25	.11	.03
☐ 68 Kent Hrbek	.10	.04	.01
☐ 69 Tom Pagnozzi	.08	.04	.01
☐ 70 Jeff Bagwell	.75	.35	.09
☐ 71 Jim Gantner	.08	.04	.01
☐ 72 Matt Nokes	.08	.04	.01
☐ 73 Brian Harper	.08	.04	.01
☐ 74 Andy Benes	.12	.05	.02
☐ 75 Tom Glavine	.30	.14	.04
☐ 76 Terry Steinbach	.10	.04	.01
☐ 77 Dennis Martinez	.10	.04	.01
☐ 78 John Olerud	.25	.11	.03
☐ 79 Ozzie Guillen	.08	.04	.01
☐ 80 Darryl Strawberry	.30	.14	.04
☐ 81 Gary Gaetti	.08	.04	.01
☐ 82 Dave Righetti	.08	.04	.01
☐ 83 Chris Hoiles	.12	.05	.02
☐ 84 Andujar Cedeno	.12	.05	.02
☐ 85 Jack Clark	.10	.04	.01
☐ 86 David Howard	.08	.04	.01
☐ 87 Bill Gullickson	.08	.04	.01
☐ 88 Bernard Gilkey	.12	.05	.02
☐ 89 Kevin Elster	.08	.04	.01
☐ 90 Kevin Maas	.10	.04	.01
☐ 91 Mark Lewis	.08	.04	.01
☐ 92 Greg Vaughn	.10	.04	.01
☐ 93 Bret Barberie	.12	.05	.02
☐ 94 Dave Smith	.08	.04	.01
☐ 95 Roger Clemens	.60	.25	.08
☐ 96 Doug Drabek	.10	.04	.01
☐ 97 Omar Vizquel	.08	.04	.01
☐ 98 Jose Guzman	.08	.04	.01
☐ 99 Juan Samuel	.08	.04	.01
☐ 100 Dave Justice	.75	.35	.09
☐ 101 Tom Browning	.08	.04	.01
☐ 102 Mark Gubicza	.08	.04	.01
☐ 103 Mickey Morandini	.10	.04	.01
☐ 104 Ed Whitson	.08	.04	.01
☐ 105 Lance Parrish	.10	.04	.01
☐ 106 Scott Erickson	.15	.07	.02
☐ 107 Jack McDowell	.12	.05	.02
☐ 108 Dave Stieb	.08	.04	.01
☐ 109 Mike Moore	.08	.04	.01
☐ 110 Travis Fryman	1.00	.45	.13
☐ 111 Dwight Gooden	.12	.05	.02
☐ 112 Fred McGriff	.30	.14	.04
☐ 113 Alan Trammell	.12	.05	.02
☐ 114 Roberto Kelly	.12	.05	.02
☐ 115 Andre Dawson	.20	.09	.03
☐ 116 Bill Landrum	.08	.04	.01
☐ 117 Brian McRae	.12	.05	.02
☐ 118 B.J. Surhoff	.08	.04	.01
☐ 119 Chuck Knoblauch	.50	.23	.06
☐ 120 Steve Olin	.08	.04	.01
☐ 121 Robin Ventura	.50	.23	.06
☐ 122 Will Clark	.50	.23	.06
☐ 123 Tino Martinez	.12	.05	.02
☐ 124 Dale Murphy	.12	.05	.02
☐ 125 Pete O'Brien	.08	.04	.01
☐ 126 Ray Lankford	.40	.18	.05
☐ 127 Juan Gonzalez	1.25	.55	.16
☐ 128 Ron Gant	.20	.09	.03
☐ 129 Marquis Grissom	.25	.11	.03
☐ 130 Jose Canseco	.50	.23	.06
☐ 131 Mike Greenwell	.12	.05	.02
☐ 132 Mark Langston	.10	.04	.01
☐ 133 Brett Butler	.10	.04	.01
☐ 134 Kelly Gruber	.10	.04	.01
☐ 135 Chris Sabo	.10	.04	.01
☐ 136 Mark Grace	.12	.05	.02

☐	137	Tony Fernandez	.10	.04	.01
☐	138	Glenn Davis	.10	.04	.01
☐	139	Pedro Munoz	.12	.05	.02
☐	140	Craig Biggio	.10	.04	.01
☐	141	Pete Schourek	.10	.04	.01
☐	142	Mike Boddicker	.08	.04	.01
☐	143	Robby Thompson	.08	.04	.01
☐	144	Mel Hall	.08	.04	.01
☐	145	Bryan Harvey	.08	.04	.01
☐	146	Mike LaValliere	.08	.04	.01
☐	147	John Kruk	.10	.04	.01
☐	148	Joe Carter	.30	.14	.04
☐	149	Greg Olson	.08	.04	.01
☐	150	Julio Franco	.10	.04	.01
☐	151	Darryl Hamilton	.10	.04	.01
☐	152	Felix Fermin	.08	.04	.01
☐	153	Jose Offerman	.10	.04	.01
☐	154	Paul O'Neill	.10	.04	.01
☐	155	Tommy Greene	.08	.04	.01
☐	156	Ivan Rodriguez	1.00	.45	.13
☐	157	Dave Stewart	.10	.04	.01
☐	158	Jeff Reardon	.12	.05	.02
☐	159	Felix Jose	.10	.04	.01
☐	160	Doug Dascenzo	.08	.04	.01
☐	161	Tim Wallach	.10	.04	.01
☐	162	Dan Plesac	.08	.04	.01
☐	163	Luis Gonzalez	.12	.05	.02
☐	164	Mike Henneman	.08	.04	.01
☐	165	Mike Devereaux	.10	.04	.01
☐	166	Luis Polonia	.10	.04	.01
☐	167	Mike Sharperson	.08	.04	.01
☐	168	Chris Donnels	.08	.04	.01
☐	169	Greg W. Harris	.08	.04	.01
☐	170	Deion Sanders	.40	.18	.05
☐	171	Mike Schooler	.08	.04	.01
☐	172	Jose DeJesus	.08	.04	.01
☐	173	Jeff Montgomery	.08	.04	.01
☐	174	Milt Cuyler	.08	.04	.01
☐	175	Wade Boggs	.30	.14	.04
☐	176	Kevin Tapani	.10	.04	.01
☐	177	Bill Spiers	.08	.04	.01
☐	178	Tim Raines	.12	.05	.02
☐	179	Randy Milligan	.08	.04	.01
☐	180	Rob Dibble	.10	.04	.01
☐	181	Kirt Manwaring	.08	.04	.01
☐	182	Pascual Perez	.08	.04	.01
☐	183	Juan Guzman	1.75	.80	.22
☐	184	John Smiley	.10	.04	.01
☐	185	David Segui	.08	.04	.01
☐	186	Omar Olivares	.08	.04	.01
☐	187	Joe Slusarski	.08	.04	.01
☐	188	Erik Hanson	.08	.04	.01
☐	189	Mark Portugal	.08	.04	.01
☐	190	Walt Terrell	.08	.04	.01
☐	191	John Smoltz	.20	.09	.03
☐	192	Wilson Alvarez	.08	.04	.01
☐	193	Jimmy Key	.08	.04	.01
☐	194	Larry Walker	.35	.16	.04
☐	195	Lee Smith	.10	.04	.01
☐	196	Pete Harnisch	.10	.04	.01
☐	197	Mike Harkey	.10	.04	.01
☐	198	Frank Tanana	.08	.04	.01
☐	199	Terry Mulholland	.08	.04	.01
☐	200	Cal Ripken	.75	.35	.09
☐	201	Dave Magadan	.10	.04	.01
☐	202	Bud Black	.08	.04	.01
☐	203	Terry Shumpert	.08	.04	.01
☐	204	Mike Mussina	1.75	.80	.22
☐	205	Mo Vaughn	.12	.05	.02
☐	206	Steve Farr	.08	.04	.01
☐	207	Darrin Jackson	.10	.04	.01
☐	208	Jerry Browne	.08	.04	.01
☐	209	Jeff Russell	.08	.04	.01
☐	210	Mike Scioscia	.08	.04	.01
☐	211	Rick Aguilera	.10	.04	.01
☐	212	Jaime Navarro	.10	.04	.01
☐	213	Randy Tomlin	.12	.05	.02
☐	214	Bobby Thigpen	.08	.04	.01
☐	215	Mark Gardner	.08	.04	.01
☐	216	Norm Charlton	.10	.04	.01
☐	217	Mark McGwire	.50	.23	.06
☐	218	Skeeter Barnes	.08	.04	.01
☐	219	Bob Tewksbury	.10	.04	.01
☐	220	Junior Felix	.08	.04	.01
☐	221	Sam Horn	.08	.04	.01
☐	222	Jody Reed	.08	.04	.01
☐	223	Luis Sojo	.08	.04	.01
☐	224	Jerome Walton	.08	.04	.01
☐	225	Darryl Kile	.10	.04	.01
☐	226	Mickey Tettleton	.10	.04	.01
☐	227	Dan Pasqua	.08	.04	.01
☐	228	Jim Gott	.08	.04	.01
☐	229	Bernie Williams	.25	.11	.03
☐	230	Shane Mack	.10	.04	.01
☐	231	Steve Avery	.50	.23	.06
☐	232	Dave Valle	.08	.04	.01
☐	233	Mark Leonard	.08	.04	.01
☐	234	Spike Owen	.08	.04	.01
☐	235	Gary Sheffield	.75	.35	.09
☐	236	Steve Chitren	.08	.04	.01
☐	237	Zane Smith	.08	.04	.01
☐	238	Tom Gordon	.08	.04	.01
☐	239	Jose Oquendo	.08	.04	.01
☐	240	Todd Stottlemyre	.10	.04	.01
☐	241	Darren Daulton	.10	.04	.01
☐	242	Tim Naehring	.10	.04	.01
☐	243	Tony Phillips	.08	.04	.01
☐	244	Shawon Dunston	.10	.04	.01
☐	245	Manuel Lee	.08	.04	.01
☐	246	Mike Pagliarulo	.08	.04	.01
☐	247	Jim Thome	.25	.11	.03
☐	248	Luis Mercedes	.25	.11	.03
☐	249	Cal Eldred	1.00	.45	.13
☐	250	Derek Bell	.30	.14	.04

☐ 251	Arthur Rhodes	.40	.18	.05
☐ 252	Scott Cooper	.25	.11	.03
☐ 253	Roberto Hernandez	.20	.09	.03
☐ 254	Mo Sanford	.15	.07	.02
☐ 255	Scott Servais	.08	.04	.01
☐ 256	Eric Karros	1.75	.80	.22
☐ 257	Andy Mota	.08	.04	.01
☐ 258	Keith Mitchell	.15	.07	.02
☐ 259	Joel Johnston	.08	.04	.01
☐ 260	John Wehner	.12	.05	.02
☐ 261	Gino Minutelli	.08	.04	.01
☐ 262	Greg Gagne	.08	.04	.01
☐ 263	Stan Royer	.15	.07	.02
☐ 264	Carlos Garcia	.20	.09	.03
☐ 265	Andy Ashby	.08	.04	.01
☐ 266	Kim Batiste	.15	.07	.02
☐ 267	Julio Valera	.15	.07	.02
☐ 268	Royce Clayton	.40	.18	.05
☐ 269	Gary Scott	.10	.04	.01
☐ 270	Kirk Dressendorfer	.08	.04	.01
☐ 271	Sean Berry	.12	.05	.02
☐ 272	Lance Dickson	.12	.05	.02
☐ 273	Rob Maurer	.20	.09	.03
☐ 274	Scott Brosius	.12	.05	.02
☐ 275	Dave Fleming	1.00	.45	.13
☐ 276	Lenny Webster	.08	.04	.01
☐ 277	Mike Humphreys	.10	.04	.01
☐ 278	Freddie Benavides	.08	.04	.01
☐ 279	Harvey Pulliam	.12	.05	.02
☐ 280	Jeff Carter	.08	.04	.01
☐ 281	Jim Abbott I	.40	.18	.05
☐ 282	Wade Boggs I	.20	.09	.03
☐ 283	Ken Griffey Jr. I	.75	.35	.09
☐ 284	Wally Joyner I	.08	.04	.01
☐ 285	Chuck Knoblauch I	.25	.11	.03
☐ 286	Robin Ventura I	.30	.14	.04
☐ 287	Robin Yount SI	.20	.09	.03
☐ 288	Bob Tewksbury SI	.08	.04	.01
☐ 289	Kirby Puckett SI	.25	.11	.03
☐ 290	Kenny Lofton SI	.40	.18	.05
☐ 291	Jack McDowell SI	.12	.05	.02
☐ 292	John Burkett SI	.08	.04	.01
☐ 293	Dwight Smith SI	.08	.04	.01
☐ 294	Nolan Ryan SI	.75	.35	.09
☐ 295	Manny Ramirez DP	1.25	.55	.16
☐ 296	Cliff Floyd DP	1.50	.65	.19
☐ 297	Al Shirley DP	.40	.18	.05
☐ 298	Brian Barber DP	.40	.18	.05
☐ 299	Jon Farrell DP	.20	.09	.03
☐ 300	Scott Ruffcorn DP	.50	.23	.06
☐ 301	Tyrone Hill DP	.75	.35	.09
☐ 302	Benji Gil DP	.40	.18	.05
☐ 303	Tyler Green DP	.60	.25	.08
☐ 304	Allen Watson DP	.50	.23	.06
☐ 305	Jay Buhner SH	.08	.04	.01
☐ 306	Roberto Alomar SH	.30	.14	.04
☐ 307	Chuck Knoblauch SH	.25	.11	.03
☐ 308	Darryl Strawberry SH	.20	.09	.03
☐ 309	Danny Tartabull SH	.08	.04	.01
☐ 310	Bobby Bonilla SH	.10	.04	.01
☐ 311	Mike Felder	.08	.04	.01
☐ 312	Storm Davis	.08	.04	.01
☐ 313	Tim Teufel	.08	.04	.01
☐ 314	Tom Brunansky	.10	.04	.01
☐ 315	Rex Hudler	.08	.04	.01
☐ 316	Dave Otto	.08	.04	.01
☐ 317	Jeff King	.08	.04	.01
☐ 318	Dan Gladden	.08	.04	.01
☐ 319	Bill Pecota	.08	.04	.01
☐ 320	Franklin Stubbs	.08	.04	.01
☐ 321	Gary Carter	.10	.04	.01
☐ 322	Melido Perez	.10	.04	.01
☐ 323	Eric Davis	.12	.05	.02
☐ 324	Greg Myers	.08	.04	.01
☐ 325	Pete Incaviglia	.08	.04	.01
☐ 326	Von Hayes	.08	.04	.01
☐ 327	Greg Swindell	.10	.04	.01
☐ 328	Steve Sax	.10	.04	.01
☐ 329	Chuck McElroy	.08	.04	.01
☐ 330	Gregg Jefferies	.10	.04	.01
☐ 331	Joe Oliver	.08	.04	.01
☐ 332	Paul Faries	.08	.04	.01
☐ 333	David West	.08	.04	.01
☐ 334	Craig Grebeck	.08	.04	.01
☐ 335	Chris Hammond	.08	.04	.01
☐ 336	Billy Ripken	.08	.04	.01
☐ 337	Scott Sanderson	.08	.04	.01
☐ 338	Dick Schofield	.08	.04	.01
☐ 339	Bob Milacki	.08	.04	.01
☐ 340	Kevin Reimer	.08	.04	.01
☐ 341	Jose DeLeon	.08	.04	.01
☐ 342	Henry Cotto	.08	.04	.01
☐ 343	Daryl Boston	.08	.04	.01
☐ 344	Kevin Gross	.08	.04	.01
☐ 345	Milt Thompson	.08	.04	.01
☐ 346	Luis Rivera	.08	.04	.01
☐ 347	Al Osuna	.08	.04	.01
☐ 348	Rob Deer	.10	.04	.01
☐ 349	Tim Leary	.08	.04	.01
☐ 350	Mike Stanton	.08	.04	.01
☐ 351	Dean Palmer	.12	.05	.02
☐ 352	Trevor Wilson	.08	.04	.01
☐ 353	Mark Eichhorn	.08	.04	.01
☐ 354	Scott Aldred	.08	.04	.01
☐ 355	Mark Whiten	.08	.04	.01
☐ 356	Leo Gomez	.20	.09	.03
☐ 357	Rafael Belliard	.08	.04	.01
☐ 358	Carlos Quintana	.08	.04	.01
☐ 359	Mark Davis	.08	.04	.01
☐ 360	Chris Nabholz	.10	.04	.01
☐ 361	Carlton Fisk	.20	.09	.03
☐ 362	Joe Orsulak	.08	.04	.01
☐ 363	Eric Anthony	.12	.05	.02
☐ 364	Greg Hibbard	.08	.04	.01

☐ 365	Scott Leius	.08	.04	.01	☐ 422	Charlie Hough	.08	.04	.01
☐ 366	Hensley Meulens	.08	.04	.01	☐ 423	Charlie Leibrandt	.08	.04	.01
☐ 367	Chris Bosio	.08	.04	.01	☐ 424	Eddie Murray	.20	.09	.03
☐ 368	Brian Downing	.08	.04	.01	☐ 425	Jesse Barfield	.08	.04	.01
☐ 369	Sammy Sosa	.08	.04	.01	☐ 426	Mark Lemke	.08	.04	.01
☐ 370	Stan Belinda	.08	.04	.01	☐ 427	Kevin McReynolds	.10	.04	.01
☐ 371	Joe Grahe	.08	.04	.01	☐ 428	Gilberto Reyes	.08	.04	.01
☐ 372	Luis Salazar	.08	.04	.01	☐ 429	Ramon Martinez	.12	.05	.02
☐ 373	Lance Johnson	.08	.04	.01	☐ 430	Steve Buechele	.08	.04	.01
☐ 374	Kal Daniels	.08	.04	.01	☐ 431	David Wells	.08	.04	.01
☐ 375	Dave Winfield	.20	.09	.03	☐ 432	Kyle Abbott	.15	.07	.02
☐ 376	Brook Jacoby	.08	.04	.01	☐ 433	John Habyan	.08	.04	.01
☐ 377	Mariano Duncan	.08	.04	.01	☐ 434	Kevin Appier	.10	.04	.01
☐ 378	Ron Darling	.10	.04	.01	☐ 435	Gene Larkin	.08	.04	.01
☐ 379	Randy Johnson	.10	.04	.01	☐ 436	Sandy Alomar Jr.	.10	.04	.01
☐ 380	Chito Martinez	.08	.04	.01	☐ 437	Mike Jackson	.08	.04	.01
☐ 381	Andres Galarraga	.08	.04	.01	☐ 438	Todd Benzinger	.08	.04	.01
☐ 382	Willie Randolph	.10	.04	.01	☐ 439	Teddy Higuera	.08	.04	.01
☐ 383	Charles Nagy	.25	.11	.03	☐ 440	Reggie Sanders	.75	.35	.09
☐ 384	Tim Belcher	.10	.04	.01	☐ 441	Mark Carreon	.08	.04	.01
☐ 385	Duane Ward	.08	.04	.01	☐ 442	Bret Saberhagen	.10	.04	.01
☐ 386	Vicente Palacios	.08	.04	.01	☐ 443	Gene Nelson	.08	.04	.01
☐ 387	Mike Gallego	.08	.04	.01	☐ 444	Jay Howell	.08	.04	.01
☐ 388	Rich DeLucia	.08	.04	.01	☐ 445	Roger McDowell	.08	.04	.01
☐ 389	Scott Radinsky	.08	.04	.01	☐ 446	Sid Bream	.08	.04	.01
☐ 390	Damon Berryhill	.08	.04	.01	☐ 447	Mackey Sasser	.08	.04	.01
☐ 391	Kirk McCaskill	.08	.04	.01	☐ 448	Bill Swift	.08	.04	.01
☐ 392	Pedro Guerrero	.10	.04	.01	☐ 449	Hubie Brooks	.08	.04	.01
☐ 393	Kevin Mitchell	.12	.05	.02	☐ 450	David Cone	.12	.05	.02
☐ 394	Dickie Thon	.08	.04	.01	☐ 451	Bobby Witt	.08	.04	.01
☐ 395	Bobby Bonilla	.15	.07	.02	☐ 452	Brady Anderson	.10	.04	.01
☐ 396	Bill Wegman	.08	.04	.01	☐ 453	Lee Stevens	.08	.04	.01
☐ 397	Dave Martinez	.08	.04	.01	☐ 454	Luis Aquino	.08	.04	.01
☐ 398	Rick Sutcliffe	.10	.04	.01	☐ 455	Carney Lansford	.10	.04	.01
☐ 399	Larry Andersen	.08	.04	.01	☐ 456	Carlos Hernandez	.08	.04	.01
☐ 400	Tony Gwynn	.35	.16	.04	☐ 457	Danny Jackson	.08	.04	.01
☐ 401	Rickey Henderson	.25	.11	.03	☐ 458	Gerald Young	.08	.04	.01
☐ 402	Greg Cadaret	.08	.04	.01	☐ 459	Tom Candiotti	.08	.04	.01
☐ 403	Keith Miller	.08	.04	.01	☐ 460	Billy Hatcher	.08	.04	.01
☐ 404	Bip Roberts	.10	.04	.01	☐ 461	John Wetteland	.08	.04	.01
☐ 405	Kevin Brown	.10	.04	.01	☐ 462	Mike Bordick	.15	.07	.02
☐ 406	Mitch Williams	.08	.04	.01	☐ 463	Don Robinson	.08	.04	.01
☐ 407	Frank Viola	.10	.04	.01	☐ 464	Jeff Johnson	.08	.04	.01
☐ 408	Darren Lewis	.10	.04	.01	☐ 465	Lonnie Smith	.08	.04	.01
☐ 409	Bob Welch	.08	.04	.01	☐ 466	Paul Assenmacher	.08	.04	.01
☐ 410	Bob Walk	.08	.04	.01	☐ 467	Alvin Davis	.08	.04	.01
☐ 411	Todd Frohwirth	.08	.04	.01	☐ 468	Jim Eisenreich	.08	.04	.01
☐ 412	Brian Hunter	.20	.09	.03	☐ 469	Brent Mayne	.08	.04	.01
☐ 413	Ron Karkovice	.08	.04	.01	☐ 470	Jeff Brantley	.08	.04	.01
☐ 414	Mike Morgan	.08	.04	.01	☐ 471	Tim Burke	.08	.04	.01
☐ 415	Joe Hesketh	.08	.04	.01	☐ 472	Pat Mahomes	.40	.18	.05
☐ 416	Don Slaught	.08	.04	.01	☐ 473	Ryan Bowen	.15	.07	.02
☐ 417	Tom Henke	.10	.04	.01	☐ 474	Bryn Smith	.08	.04	.01
☐ 418	Kurt Stillwell	.08	.04	.01	☐ 475	Mike Flanagan	.08	.04	.01
☐ 419	Hector Villanueva	.08	.04	.01	☐ 476	Reggie Jefferson	.12	.05	.02
☐ 420	Glenallen Hill	.08	.04	.01	☐ 477	Jeff Blauser	.08	.04	.01
☐ 421	Pat Borders	.08	.04	.01	☐ 478	Craig Lefferts	.08	.04	.01

479 Todd Worrell	.08	.04	.01
480 Scott Scudder	.08	.04	.01
481 Kirk Gibson	.10	.04	.01
482 Kenny Rogers	.08	.04	.01
483 Jack Morris	.15	.07	.02
484 Russ Swan	.08	.04	.01
485 Mike Huff	.08	.04	.01
486 Ken Hill	.08	.04	.01
487 Geronimo Pena	.12	.05	.02
488 Charlie O'Brien	.08	.04	.01
489 Mike Maddux	.08	.04	.01
490 Scott Livingstone	.20	.09	.03
491 Carl Willis	.08	.04	.01
492 Kelly Downs	.08	.04	.01
493 Dennis Cook	.08	.04	.01
494 Joe Magrane	.08	.04	.01
495 Bob Kipper	.08	.04	.01
496 Jose Mesa	.08	.04	.01
497 Charlie Hayes	.08	.04	.01
498 Joe Girardi	.08	.04	.01
499 Doug Jones	.08	.04	.01
500 Barry Bonds	.50	.23	.06
501 Bill Krueger	.08	.04	.01
502 Glenn Braggs	.08	.04	.01
503 Eric King	.08	.04	.01
504 Frank Castillo	.15	.07	.02
505 Mike Gardiner	.08	.04	.01
506 Cory Snyder	.08	.04	.01
507 Steve Howe	.08	.04	.01
508 Jose Rijo	.10	.04	.01
509 Sid Fernandez	.10	.04	.01
510 Archi Cianfrocco	.25	.11	.03
511 Mark Guthrie	.08	.04	.01
512 Bob Ojeda	.08	.04	.01
513 John Doherty	.08	.04	.01
514 Dante Bichette	.08	.04	.01
515 Juan Berenguer	.08	.04	.01
516 Jeff M. Robinson	.08	.04	.01
517 Mike Macfarlane	.08	.04	.01
518 Matt Young	.08	.04	.01
519 Otis Nixon	.08	.04	.01
520 Brian Holman	.08	.04	.01
521 Chris Haney	.12	.05	.02
522 Jeff Kent	.50	.23	.06
523 Chad Curtis	.50	.23	.06
524 Vince Horsman	.12	.05	.02
525 Rod Nichols	.08	.04	.01
526 Peter Hoy	.12	.05	.02
527 Shawn Boskie	.08	.04	.01
528 Alejandro Pena	.08	.04	.01
529 Dave Burba	.08	.04	.01
530 Ricky Jordan	.08	.04	.01
531 Dave Silvestri	.30	.14	.04
532 John Patterson	.20	.09	.03
533 Jeff Branson	.08	.04	.01
534 Derrick May	.10	.04	.01
535 Esteban Beltre	.15	.07	.02
536 Jose Melendez	.12	.05	.02
537 Wally Joyner	.10	.04	.01
538 Eddie Taubensee	.20	.09	.03
539 Jim Abbott	.20	.09	.03
540 Brian Williams	.50	.23	.06
541 Donovan Osborne	.60	.25	.08
542 Patrick Lennon	.12	.05	.02
543 Mike Groppuso	.15	.07	.02
544 Jarvis Brown	.12	.05	.02
545 Shawn Livsey	.20	.09	.03
546 Jeff Ware	.25	.11	.03
547 Danny Tartabull	.12	.05	.02
548 Bobby Jones	.75	.35	.09
549 Ken Griffey Jr.	2.00	.90	.25
550 Rey Sanchez	.20	.09	.03
551 Pedro Astacio	.75	.35	.09
552 Juan Guerrero	.20	.09	.03
553 Jacob Brumfield	.12	.05	.02
554 Ben Rivera	.15	.07	.02
555 Brian Jordan	.40	.18	.05
556 Denny Neagle	.12	.05	.02
557 Cliff Brantley	.08	.04	.01
558 Anthony Young	.12	.05	.02
559 John Vander Wal	.25	.11	.03
560 Monty Fariss	.15	.07	.02
561 Russ Springer	.30	.14	.04
562 Pat Listach	2.50	1.15	.30
563 Pat Hentgen	.15	.07	.02
564 Andy Stankiewicz	.25	.11	.03
565 Mike Perez	.15	.07	.02
566 Mike Bielecki	.08	.04	.01
567 Butch Henry	.20	.09	.03
568 Dave Nilsson	.40	.18	.05
569 Scott Hatteberg	.20	.09	.03
570 Ruben Amaro Jr.	.12	.05	.02
571 Todd Hundley	.08	.04	.01
572 Moises Alou	.10	.04	.01
573 Hector Fajardo	.25	.11	.03
574 Todd Van Poppel	.40	.18	.05
575 Willie Banks	.20	.09	.03
576 Bob Zupcic	.50	.23	.06
577 J.J. Johnson	.30	.14	.04
578 John Burkett	.08	.04	.01
579 Trever Miller	.15	.07	.02
580 Scott Bankhead	.08	.04	.01
581 Rich Amaral	.08	.04	.01
582 Kenny Lofton	1.25	.55	.16
583 Matt Stairs	.30	.14	.04
584 Rod Carew	.20	.09	.03
Don Mattingly
585 Jack Morris	.25	.11	.03
Steve Avery
586 Sandy Alomar	.25	.11	.03
Roberto Alomar
587 Catfish Hunter	.08	.04	.01
Scott Sanderson
588 Dave Justice	.40	.18	.05

Willie Stargell
☐ 589	Roger Staubach	.20	.09	.03
	Rex Hudler			
☐ 590	Jackie Gleason	.12	.05	.02
	David Cone			
☐ 591	Tony Gwynn	.20	.09	.03
	Willie Davis			
☐ 592	Orel Hershiser	.12	.05	.02
☐ 593	John Wetteland	.08	.04	.01
☐ 594	Tom Glavine	.20	.09	.03
☐ 595	Randy Johnson	.10	.04	.01
☐ 596	Jim Gott	.08	.04	.01
☐ 597	Donald Harris	.08	.04	.01
☐ 598	Shawn Hare	.12	.05	.02
☐ 599	Chris Gardner	.15	.07	.02
☐ 600	Rusty Meacham	.08	.04	.01
☐ 601	Benito Santiago	.12	.05	.02
☐ 602	Eric Davis	.12	.05	.02
☐ 603	Jose Lind	.08	.04	.01
☐ 604	Dave Justice	.40	.18	.05
☐ 605	Tim Raines	.12	.05	.02
☐ 606	Randy Tomlin	.08	.04	.01
☐ 607	Jack McDowell	.12	.05	.02
☐ 608	Greg Maddux	.12	.05	.02
☐ 609	Charles Nagy	.12	.05	.02
☐ 610	Tom Candiotti	.08	.04	.01
☐ 611	David Cone	.12	.05	.02
☐ 612	Steve Avery	.20	.09	.03
☐ 613	Rod Beck	.20	.09	.03
☐ 614	Rickey Henderson	.25	.11	.03
☐ 615	Benito Santiago	.12	.05	.02
☐ 616	Ruben Sierra	.25	.11	.03
☐ 617	Ryne Sandberg	.35	.16	.04
☐ 618	Nolan Ryan	.60	.25	.08
☐ 619	Brett Butler	.10	.04	.01
☐ 620	Dave Justice	.40	.18	.05

1992 Pinnacle Rookie Idols

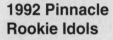

This 18-card insert set is a spin-off on the Idols subset featured in the regular series. The set features full-bleed color photos of 18 rookies along with their pick of sports figures or other individuals who had the greatest impact on their careers. The standard-size (2 1/2" by 3 1/2") cards were randomly inserted in Series II wax packs. Both sides of the cards are horizontally oriented. The fronts carry a close-up photo of the rookie superimposed on an action game

shot of his idol. On a background that shades from white to light blue, the backs feature text comparing the two players flanked by a color photo of each player. The cards are numbered on the back.

	MT	EX-MT	VG
COMPLETE SET (18)	250.00	115.00	31.00
COMMON PAIR (1-18)	12.00	5.50	1.50

		MT	EX-MT	VG
☐ 1	Reggie Sanders and Eric Davis	20.00	9.00	2.50
☐ 2	Hector Fajardo and Jim Abbott	15.00	6.75	1.90
☐ 3	Gary Cooper and George Brett	20.00	9.00	2.50
☐ 4	Mark Wohlers and Roger Clemens	30.00	13.50	3.80
☐ 5	Luis Mercedes and Julio Franco	15.00	6.75	1.90
☐ 6	Willie Banks and Doc Gooden	15.00	6.75	1.90
☐ 7	Kenny Lofton and Rickey Henderson	30.00	13.50	3.80
☐ 8	Keith Mitchell and Dave Henderson	12.00	5.50	1.50
☐ 9	Kim Batiste and Barry Larkin	15.00	6.75	1.90
☐ 10	Todd Hundley and Thurman Munson	15.00	6.75	1.90
☐ 11	Eddie Zosky and Cal Ripken	30.00	13.50	3.80
☐ 12	Todd Van Poppel and Nolan Ryan	50.00	23.00	6.25
☐ 13	Jim Thome and Ryne Sandberg	30.00	13.50	3.80
☐ 14	Dave Fleming and Bobby Murcer	20.00	9.00	2.50
☐ 15	Royce Clayton and Ozzie Smith	20.00	9.00	2.50
☐ 16	Donald Harris and Darryl Strawberry	15.00	6.75	1.90
☐ 17	Chad Curtis	15.00	6.75	1.90

and Alan Trammell
☐ 18 Derek Bell 20.00   9.00   2.50
and Dave Winfield

1992 Pinnacle Rookies

This 30-card boxed set features top rookies of the 1992 season, with at least one
player from each team. Each of the 3,000
sequentially numbered cases contained 60
sets. The fronts feature full-bleed color
action player photos except at the bottom
where a team-color coded bar carries the
player's name (in gold foil lettering) and a
black bar has the words "1992 Rookie."
The team logo appears in a gold foil circle
at the lower right corner. The horizontally
oriented backs carry a second large color
player photo, again edged at the bottom by
a team-color coded bar with the player's
name and a black bar carrying a player
profile. The cards are numbered on the
back. The key Rookie Cards in this set are
Chad Curtis, Pat Mahomes, and Brian
Williams.

	MT	EX-MT	VG
COMPLETE SET (30) 12.00		5.50	1.50
COMMON PLAYER (1-30) 10		.05	.01
☐ 1 Luis Mercedes 30		.14	.04
☐ 2 Scott Cooper 30		.14	.04
☐ 3. Kenny Lofton 1.75		.80	.22
☐ 4 John Doherty 25		.11	.03
☐ 5 Pat Listach 3.50		1.55	.45
☐ 6 Andy Stankiewicz 30		.14	.04

☐ 7 Derek Bell 40	.18	.05
☐ 8 Gary DiSarcina 10	.05	.01
☐ 9 Roberto Hernandez 25	.11	.03
☐ 10 Joel Johnston 10	.05	.01
☐ 11 Pat Mahomes 60	.25	.08
☐ 12 Todd Van Poppel 75	.35	.09
☐ 13 Dave Fleming 1.50	.65	.19
☐ 14 Monty Fariss 20	.09	.03
☐ 15 Gary Scott 15	.07	.02
☐ 16 Moises Alou 25	.11	.03
☐ 17 Todd Hundley 10	.05	.01
☐ 18 Kim Batiste 20	.09	.03
☐ 19 Denny Neagle 15	.07	.02
☐ 20 Donovan Osborne 75	.35	.09
☐ 21 Mark Wohlers 25	.11	.03
☐ 22 Reggie Sanders 1.00	.45	.13
☐ 23 Brian Williams 60	.25	.08
☐ 24 Eric Karros 3.00	1.35	.40
☐ 25 Frank Seminara 50	.23	.06
☐ 26 Royce Clayton 50	.23	.06
☐ 27 Dave Nilsson 50	.23	.06
☐ 28 Matt Stairs 35	.16	.04
☐ 29 Chad Curtis 60	.25	.08
☐ 30 Carlos Hernandez 10	.05	.01

1992 Pinnacle Slugfest

This 15-card set measures the standard
size (2 1/2" by 3 1/2"). The horizontally oriented fronts feature glossy photos of players at bat. The player's name is printed in
gold and the word "Slugfest" is printed in
red in a black border across the bottom of
the picture. The back design includes a
color action player photo on the right half
of the card, and statistics and a career

summary on the left. The cards are numbered on the back. The cards were issued as an insert with specially marked cello packs.

		MT	EX-MT	VG
COMPLETE SET (15)		40.00	18.00	5.00
COMMON PLAYER (1-15)		1.50	.65	.19
☐ 1	Cecil Fielder	2.00	.90	.25
☐ 2	Mark McGwire	3.50	1.55	.45
☐ 3	Jose Canseco	3.50	1.55	.45
☐ 4	Barry Bonds	3.50	1.55	.45
☐ 5	Dave Justice	3.00	1.35	.40
☐ 6	Bobby Bonilla	1.50	.65	.19
☐ 7	Ken Griffey Jr.	7.00	3.10	.85
☐ 8	Ron Gant	1.50	.65	.19
☐ 9	Ryne Sandberg	3.50	1.55	.45
☐ 10	Ruben Sierra	2.50	1.15	.30
☐ 11	Frank Thomas	10.00	4.50	1.25
☐ 12	Will Clark	3.50	1.55	.45
☐ 13	Kirby Puckett	3.50	1.55	.45
☐ 14	Cal Ripken	5.00	2.30	.60
☐ 15	Jeff Bagwell	3.00	1.35	.40

1992 Pinnacle Team Pinnacle

This 12-card, double-sided subset features the National League and American League All-Star team as selected by Pinnacle. The standard-size (2 1/2" by 3 1/2") were randomly inserted in Series I wax packs. There is one card per position, including two cards for pitchers and two cards for relief pitchers for a total set of twelve. The cards feature illustrations by sports artist

Chris Greco of the National League All-Star on one side and the American League All-Star on the other. The words "Team Pinnacle" are printed vertically down the left side of the card in red for American League and blue for National League on the other. The player's name appears in a gold stripe at the bottom. There is no text. The cards are numbered in the black bottom stripe on the side featuring the National League All-Star.

		MT	EX-MT	VG
COMPLETE SET (12)		450.00	200.00	57.50
COMMON PAIR (1-12)		20.00	9.00	2.50
☐ 1	Roger Clemens and Ramon Martinez	50.00	23.00	6.25
☐ 2	Jim Abbott and Steve Avery	40.00	18.00	5.00
☐ 3	Ivan Rodriguez and Benito Santiago	40.00	18.00	5.00
☐ 4	Frank Thomas and Will Clark	100.00	45.00	12.50
☐ 5	Roberto Alomar and Ryne Sandberg	75.00	34.00	9.50
☐ 6	Robin Ventura and Matt Williams	35.00	16.00	4.40
☐ 7	Cal Ripken and Barry Larkin	75.00	34.00	9.50
☐ 8	Danny Tartabull and Barry Bonds	45.00	20.00	5.75
☐ 9	Ken Griffey Jr. and Brett Butler	75.00	34.00	9.50
☐ 10	Ruben Sierra and Dave Justice	45.00	20.00	5.75
☐ 11	Dennis Eckersley and Rob Dibble	30.00	13.50	3.80
☐ 12	Scott Radinsky and John Franco	20.00	9.00	2.50

1992 Pinnacle Team 2000

This 80-card standard-size (2 1/2" by 3 1/2") set focuses on young players who will be still be stars in the year 2000. Cards 1-40 were inserted in Series 1 jumbo packs while cards 41-80 were featured in Series 2 jumbo packs. The fronts features action color player photos. The cards are

bordered by a 1/2" black stripe that runs along the left edge and bottom forming a right angle. The two ends of the black stripe are sloped. The words "Team 2000" and the player's name appear in gold foil in the stripe. The team logo is displayed in the lower left corner. The horizontally oriented backs show a close-up color player photo and a career summary on a black background. The cards are numbered on the back.

	MT	EX-MT	VG
COMPLETE SET (80)	50.00	23.00	6.25
COMPLETE SERIES 1 (40)	30.00	13.50	3.80
COMPLETE SERIES 2 (40)	20.00	9.00	2.50
COMMON PLAYER (1-40)	.15	.07	.02
COMMON PLAYER (41-80)	.15	.07	.02

		MT	EX-MT	VG
☐ 1	Mike Mussina	3.50	1.55	.45
☐ 2	Phil Plantier	.60	.25	.08
☐ 3	Frank Thomas	6.00	2.70	.75
☐ 4	Travis Fryman	2.00	.90	.25
☐ 5	Kevin Appier	.15	.07	.02
☐ 6	Chuck Knoblauch	1.00	.45	.13
☐ 7	Pat Kelly	.15	.07	.02
☐ 8	Ivan Rodriguez	2.00	.90	.25
☐ 9	Dave Justice	1.50	.65	.19
☐ 10	Jeff Bagwell	1.50	.65	.19
☐ 11	Marquis Grissom	.50	.23	.06
☐ 12	Andy Benes	.15	.07	.02
☐ 13	Gregg Olson	.15	.07	.02
☐ 14	Kevin Morton	.15	.07	.02
☐ 15	Tim Naehring	.15	.07	.02
☐ 16	Dave Hollins	.50	.23	.06
☐ 17	Sandy Alomar Jr.	.15	.07	.02
☐ 18	Albert Belle	.60	.25	.08
☐ 19	Charles Nagy	.50	.23	.06
☐ 20	Brian McRae	.20	.09	.03
☐ 21	Larry Walker	.75	.35	.09
☐ 22	Delino DeShields	.50	.23	.06
☐ 23	Jeff Johnson	.15	.07	.02
☐ 24	Bernie Williams	.50	.23	.06
☐ 25	Jose Offerman	.15	.07	.02
☐ 26	Juan Gonzalez	2.50	1.15	.30
☐ 27A	Juan Guzman	3.50	1.55	.45
	(Pinnacle logo at top)			
☐ 27B	Juan Guzman	3.50	1.55	.45
	(Pinnacle logo at bottom)			
☐ 28	Eric Anthony	.15	.07	.02
☐ 29	Brian Hunter	.40	.18	.05
☐ 30	John Smoltz	.35	.16	.04
☐ 31	Deion Sanders	.75	.35	.09
☐ 32	Greg Maddux	.30	.14	.04
☐ 33	Andujar Cedeno	.20	.09	.03
☐ 34	Royce Clayton	.75	.35	.09
☐ 35	Kenny Lofton	2.50	1.15	.30
☐ 36	Cal Eldred	2.00	.90	.25
☐ 37	Jim Thome	.40	.18	.05
☐ 38	Gary DiSarcina	.15	.07	.02
☐ 39	Brian Jordan	.75	.35	.09
☐ 40	Chad Curtis	1.00	.45	.13
☐ 41	Ben McDonald	.30	.14	.04
☐ 42	Jim Abbott	.40	.18	.05
☐ 43	Robin Ventura	1.00	.45	.13
☐ 44	Milt Cuyler	.15	.07	.02
☐ 45	Gregg Jefferies	.15	.07	.02
☐ 46	Scott Radinsky	.15	.07	.02
☐ 47	Ken Griffey Jr.	4.00	1.80	.50
☐ 48	Roberto Alomar	1.00	.45	.13
☐ 49	Ramon Martinez	.15	.07	.02
☐ 50	Bret Barberie	.20	.09	.03
☐ 51	Ray Lankford	.75	.35	.09
☐ 52	Leo Gomez	.40	.18	.05
☐ 53	Tommy Greene	.15	.07	.02
☐ 54	Mo Vaughn	.25	.11	.03
☐ 55	Sammy Sosa	.15	.07	.02
☐ 56	Carlos Baerga	.75	.35	.09
☐ 57	Mark Lewis	.15	.07	.02
☐ 58	Tom Gordon	.15	.07	.02
☐ 59	Gary Sheffield	1.50	.65	.19
☐ 60	Scott Erickson	.30	.14	.04
☐ 61	Pedro Munoz	.25	.11	.03
☐ 62	Tino Martinez	.20	.09	.03
☐ 63	Darren Lewis	.15	.07	.02
☐ 64	Dean Palmer	.50	.23	.06
☐ 65	John Olerud	.50	.23	.06
☐ 66	Steve Avery	.90	.40	.11
☐ 67	Pete Harnisch	.15	.07	.02
☐ 68	Luis Gonzalez	.25	.11	.03
☐ 69	Kim Batiste	.30	.14	.04
☐ 70	Reggie Sanders	1.50	.65	.19
☐ 71	Luis Mercedes	.50	.23	.06
☐ 72	Todd Van Poppel	1.00	.45	.13
☐ 73	Gary Scott	.15	.07	.02
☐ 74	Monty Fariss	.30	.14	.04
☐ 75	Kyle Abbott	.15	.07	.02
☐ 76	Eric Karros	3.50	1.55	.45
☐ 77	Mo Sanford	.15	.07	.02
☐ 78	Todd Hundley	.15	.07	.02

	79 Reggie Jefferson	.35	.16	.04
	80 Pat Mahomes	.75	.35	.09

1988 Score

This 660-card set was distributed by Major League Marketing. Cards measure 2 1/2" by 3 1/2" and feature six distinctive border colors on the front. Highlights (652-660) and Rookie Prospects (623-647) are included in the set. Reggie Jackson's career is honored with a five-card subset on cards 500-504. Card number 501, showing Reggie as a member of the Baltimore Orioles, is one of the few opportunities collectors have to visually remember (on a regular card) Reggie's one-year stay with the Orioles. The set is distinguished by the fact that each card back shows a full-color picture of the player. The key Rookie Cards in this set are Ellis Burks, Ron Gant, Tom Glavine, Gregg Jefferies, Roberto Kelly and Matt Williams. The company also produced a very limited "glossy" set, that is valued at eight times the value of the regular (non-glossy) set. Although exact production quantities of this glossy set are not known, it has been speculated, but not confirmed, that 5,000 glossy sets were produced. It is generally accepted that the number of Score glossy sets produced in 1988 was much smaller (estimated only 10 percent to 15 percent as many) than the number of Topps Tiffany or Fleer Tin sets. These Score glossy cards, when bought or sold individually, are valued approximately five to ten times the values listed below.

		MT	EX-MT	VG
	COMPLETE SET (660)	20.00	9.00	2.50
	COMPLETE FACT.SET (660)	20.00	9.00	2.50
	COMMON PLAYER (1-660)	.04	.02	.01

☐	1 Don Mattingly	.30	.14	.04
☐	2 Wade Boggs	.30	.14	.04
☐	3 Tim Raines	.07	.03	.01
☐	4 Andre Dawson	.20	.09	.03
☐	5 Mark McGwire	.50	.23	.06
☐	6 Kevin Seitzer	.07	.03	.01
☐	7 Wally Joyner	.12	.05	.02
☐	8 Jesse Barfield	.04	.02	.01
☐	9 Pedro Guerrero	.07	.03	.01
☐	10 Eric Davis	.10	.05	.01
☐	11 George Brett	.25	.11	.03
☐	12 Ozzie Smith	.20	.09	.03
☐	13 Rickey Henderson	.30	.14	.04
☐	14 Jim Rice	.07	.03	.01
☐	15 Matt Nokes	.20	.09	.03
☐	16 Mike Schmidt	.40	.18	.05
☐	17 Dave Parker	.07	.03	.01
☐	18 Eddie Murray	.20	.09	.03
☐	19 Andres Galarraga	.04	.02	.01
☐	20 Tony Fernandez	.07	.03	.01
☐	21 Kevin McReynolds	.07	.03	.01
☐	22 B.J. Surhoff	.07	.03	.01
☐	23 Pat Tabler	.04	.02	.01
☐	24 Kirby Puckett	.40	.18	.05
☐	25 Benny Santiago	.10	.05	.01
☐	26 Ryne Sandberg	.50	.23	.06
☐	27 Kelly Downs	.07	.03	.01
	(Will Clark in background, out of focus)			
☐	28 Jose Cruz	.04	.02	.01
☐	29 Pete O'Brien	.04	.02	.01
☐	30 Mark Langston	.07	.03	.01
☐	31 Lee Smith	.15	.07	.02
☐	32 Juan Samuel	.04	.02	.01
☐	33 Kevin Bass	.04	.02	.01
☐	34 R.J. Reynolds	.04	.02	.01
☐	35 Steve Sax	.07	.03	.01
☐	36 John Kruk	.15	.07	.02
☐	37 Alan Trammell	.07	.03	.01
☐	38 Chris Bosio	.07	.03	.01
☐	39 Brook Jacoby	.04	.02	.01
☐	40 Willie McGee UER	.07	.03	.01
	(Excited misspelled as excitd)			
☐	41 Dave Magadan	.07	.03	.01
☐	42 Fred Lynn	.07	.03	.01
☐	43 Kent Hrbek	.07	.03	.01
☐	44 Brian Downing	.04	.02	.01
☐	45 Jose Canseco	.60	.25	.08
☐	46 Jim Presley	.04	.02	.01
☐	47 Mike Stanley	.04	.02	.01
☐	48 Tony Pena	.04	.02	.01

☐ 49	David Cone	50	.23	.06
☐ 50	Rick Sutcliffe	07	.03	.01
☐ 51	Doug Drabek	10	.05	.01
☐ 52	Bill Doran	04	.02	.01
☐ 53	Mike Scioscia	04	.02	.01
☐ 54	Candy Maldonado	04	.02	.01
☐ 55	Dave Winfield	25	.11	.03
☐ 56	Lou Whitaker	04	.02	.01
☐ 57	Tom Henke	07	.03	.01
☐ 58	Ken Gerhart	04	.02	.01
☐ 59	Glenn Braggs	04	.02	.01
☐ 60	Julio Franco	10	.05	.01
☐ 61	Charlie Leibrandt	04	.02	.01
☐ 62	Gary Gaetti	04	.02	.01
☐ 63	Bob Boone	07	.03	.01
☐ 64	Luis Polonia	25	.11	.03
☐ 65	Dwight Evans	07	.03	.01
☐ 66	Phil Bradley	04	.02	.01
☐ 67	Mike Boddicker	04	.02	.01
☐ 68	Vince Coleman	07	.03	.01
☐ 69	Howard Johnson	10	.05	.01
☐ 70	Tim Wallach	07	.03	.01
☐ 71	Keith Moreland	04	.02	.01
☐ 72	Barry Larkin	25	.11	.03
☐ 73	Alan Ashby	04	.02	.01
☐ 74	Rick Rhoden	04	.02	.01
☐ 75	Darrell Evans	07	.03	.01
☐ 76	Dave Stieb	07	.03	.01
☐ 77	Dan Plesac	04	.02	.01
☐ 78	Will Clark UER	60	.25	.08
	(Born 3/17/64,			
	should be 3/13/64)			
☐ 79	Frank White	04	.02	.01
☐ 80	Joe Carter	25	.11	.03
☐ 81	Mike Witt	04	.02	.01
☐ 82	Terry Steinbach	07	.03	.01
☐ 83	Alvin Davis	04	.02	.01
☐ 84	Tommy Herr	07	.03	.01
	(Will Clark shown			
	sliding into second)			
☐ 85	Vance Law	04	.02	.01
☐ 86	Kal Daniels	07	.03	.01
☐ 87	Rick Honeycutt UER	04	.02	.01
	(Wrong years for			
	stats on back)			
☐ 88	Alfredo Griffin	04	.02	.01
☐ 89	Bret Saberhagen	10	.05	.01
☐ 90	Bert Blyleven	07	.03	.01
☐ 91	Jeff Reardon	12	.05	.02
☐ 92	Cory Snyder	07	.03	.01
☐ 93A	Greg Walker ERR	3.00	1.35	.40
	(93 of 66)			
☐ 93B	Greg Walker COR	04	.02	.01
	(93 of 660)			
☐ 94	Joe Magrane	10	.05	.01
☐ 95	Rob Deer	07	.03	.01
☐ 96	Ray Knight	07	.03	.01

☐ 97	Casey Candaele	04	.02	.01
☐ 98	John Cerutti	04	.02	.01
☐ 99	Buddy Bell	07	.03	.01
☐ 100	Jack Clark	07	.03	.01
☐ 101	Eric Bell	04	.02	.01
☐ 102	Willie Wilson	04	.02	.01
☐ 103	Dave Schmidt	04	.02	.01
☐ 104	Dennis Eckersley UER	15	.07	.02
	(Complete games stats			
	are wrong)			
☐ 105	Don Sutton	10	.05	.01
☐ 106	Danny Tartabull	15	.07	.02
☐ 107	Fred McGriff	40	.18	.05
☐ 108	Les Straker	04	.02	.01
☐ 109	Lloyd Moseby	04	.02	.01
☐ 110	Roger Clemens	50	.23	.06
☐ 111	Glenn Hubbard	04	.02	.01
☐ 112	Ken Williams	04	.02	.01
☐ 113	Ruben Sierra	40	.18	.05
☐ 114	Stan Jefferson	04	.02	.01
☐ 115	Milt Thompson	04	.02	.01
☐ 116	Bobby Bonilla	25	.11	.03
☐ 117	Wayne Tolleson	04	.02	.01
☐ 118	Matt Williams	90	.40	.11
☐ 119	Chet Lemon	04	.02	.01
☐ 120	Dale Sveum	04	.02	.01
☐ 121	Dennis Boyd	04	.02	.01
☐ 122	Brett Butler	10	.05	.01
☐ 123	Terry Kennedy	04	.02	.01
☐ 124	Jack Howell	04	.02	.01
☐ 125	Curt Young	04	.02	.01
☐ 126A	Dave Valle ERR	12	.05	.02
	(Misspelled Dale			
	on card front)			
☐ 126B	Dave Valle COR	04	.02	.01
☐ 127	Curt Wilkerson	04	.02	.01
☐ 128	Tim Teufel	04	.02	.01
☐ 129	Ozzie Virgil	04	.02	.01
☐ 130	Brian Fisher	04	.02	.01
☐ 131	Lance Parrish	07	.03	.01
☐ 132	Tom Browning	04	.02	.01
☐ 133A	Larry Andersen ERR	12	.05	.02
	(Misspelled Anderson			
	on card front)			
☐ 133B	Larry Andersen COR	04	.02	.01
☐ 134A	Bob Brenly ERR	12	.05	.02
	(Misspelled Brenley			
	on card front)			
☐ 134B	Bob Brenly COR	04	.02	.01
☐ 135	Mike Marshall	04	.02	.01
☐ 136	Gerald Perry	04	.02	.01
☐ 137	Bobby Meacham	04	.02	.01
☐ 138	Larry Herndon	04	.02	.01
☐ 139	Fred Manrique	04	.02	.01
☐ 140	Charlie Hough	04	.02	.01
☐ 141	Ron Darling	07	.03	.01
☐ 142	Herm Winningham	04	.02	.01

☐ 143	Mike Diaz	.04	.02	.01
☐ 144	Mike Jackson	.10	.05	.01
☐ 145	Denny Walling	.04	.02	.01
☐ 146	Robby Thompson	.07	.03	.01
☐ 147	Franklin Stubbs	.04	.02	.01
☐ 148	Albert Hall	.04	.02	.01
☐ 149	Bobby Witt	.07	.03	.01
☐ 150	Lance McCullers	.04	.02	.01
☐ 151	Scott Bradley	.04	.02	.01
☐ 152	Mark McLemore	.04	.02	.01
☐ 153	Tim Laudner	.04	.02	.01
☐ 154	Greg Swindell	.15	.07	.02
☐ 155	Marty Barrett	.04	.02	.01
☐ 156	Mike Heath	.04	.02	.01
☐ 157	Gary Ward	.04	.02	.01
☐ 158A	Lee Mazzilli ERR	.12	.05	.02
	(Misspelled Mazilli			
	on card front)			
☐ 158B	Lee Mazzilli COR	.04	.02	.01
☐ 159	Tom Foley	.04	.02	.01
☐ 160	Robin Yount	.25	.11	.03
☐ 161	Steve Bedrosian	.04	.02	.01
☐ 162	Bob Walk	.04	.02	.01
☐ 163	Nick Esasky	.04	.02	.01
☐ 164	Ken Caminiti	.30	.14	.04
☐ 165	Jose Uribe	.04	.02	.01
☐ 166	Dave Anderson	.04	.02	.01
☐ 167	Ed Whitson	.04	.02	.01
☐ 168	Ernie Whitt	.04	.02	.01
☐ 169	Cecil Cooper	.07	.03	.01
☐ 170	Mike Pagliarulo	.04	.02	.01
☐ 171	Pat Sheridan	.04	.02	.01
☐ 172	Chris Bando	.04	.02	.01
☐ 173	Lee Lacy	.04	.02	.01
☐ 174	Steve Lombardozzi	.04	.02	.01
☐ 175	Mike Greenwell	.10	.05	.01
☐ 176	Greg Minton	.04	.02	.01
☐ 177	Moose Haas	.04	.02	.01
☐ 178	Mike Kingery	.04	.02	.01
☐ 179	Greg A. Harris	.04	.02	.01
☐ 180	Bo Jackson	.30	.14	.04
☐ 181	Carmelo Martinez	.04	.02	.01
☐ 182	Alex Trevino	.04	.02	.01
☐ 183	Ron Oester	.04	.02	.01
☐ 184	Danny Darwin	.04	.02	.01
☐ 185	Mike Krukow	.04	.02	.01
☐ 186	Rafael Palmeiro	.30	.14	.04
☐ 187	Tim Burke	.04	.02	.01
☐ 188	Roger McDowell	.04	.02	.01
☐ 189	Garry Templeton	.04	.02	.01
☐ 190	Terry Pendleton	.15	.07	.02
☐ 191	Larry Parrish	.04	.02	.01
☐ 192	Rey Quinones	.04	.02	.01
☐ 193	Joaquin Andujar	.04	.02	.01
☐ 194	Tom Brunansky	.07	.03	.01
☐ 195	Donnie Moore	.04	.02	.01
☐ 196	Dan Pasqua	.04	.02	.01
☐ 197	Jim Gantner	.04	.02	.01
☐ 198	Mark Eichhorn	.04	.02	.01
☐ 199	John Grubb	.04	.02	.01
☐ 200	Bill Ripken	.10	.05	.01
☐ 201	Sam Horn	.12	.05	.02
☐ 202	Todd Worrell	.07	.03	.01
☐ 203	Terry Leach	.04	.02	.01
☐ 204	Garth Iorg	.04	.02	.01
☐ 205	Brian Dayett	.04	.02	.01
☐ 206	Bo Diaz	.04	.02	.01
☐ 207	Craig Reynolds	.04	.02	.01
☐ 208	Brian Holton	.04	.02	.01
☐ 209	Marvell Wynne UER	.04	.02	.01
	(Misspelled Marvelle			
	on card front)			
☐ 210	Dave Concepcion	.07	.03	.01
☐ 211	Mike Davis	.04	.02	.01
☐ 212	Devon White	.10	.05	.01
☐ 213	Mickey Brantley	.04	.02	.01
☐ 214	Greg Gagne	.07	.03	.01
☐ 215	Oddibe McDowell	.04	.02	.01
☐ 216	Jimmy Key	.07	.03	.01
☐ 217	Dave Bergman	.04	.02	.01
☐ 218	Calvin Schiraldi	.04	.02	.01
☐ 219	Larry Sheets	.04	.02	.01
☐ 220	Mike Easler	.04	.02	.01
☐ 221	Kurt Stillwell	.04	.02	.01
☐ 222	Chuck Jackson	.04	.02	.01
☐ 223	Dave Martinez	.07	.03	.01
☐ 224	Tim Leary	.04	.02	.01
☐ 225	Steve Garvey	.12	.05	.02
☐ 226	Greg Mathews	.04	.02	.01
☐ 227	Doug Sisk	.04	.02	.01
☐ 228	Dave Henderson	.07	.03	.01
☐ 229	Jimmy Dwyer	.04	.02	.01
☐ 230	Larry Owen	.04	.02	.01
☐ 231	Andre Thornton	.04	.02	.01
☐ 232	Mark Salas	.04	.02	.01
☐ 233	Tom Brookens	.04	.02	.01
☐ 234	Greg Brock	.04	.02	.01
☐ 235	Rance Mulliniks	.04	.02	.01
☐ 236	Bob Brower	.04	.02	.01
☐ 237	Joe Niekro	.07	.03	.01
☐ 238	Scott Bankhead	.04	.02	.01
☐ 239	Doug DeCinces	.04	.02	.01
☐ 240	Tommy John	.07	.03	.01
☐ 241	Rich Gedman	.04	.02	.01
☐ 242	Ted Power	.04	.02	.01
☐ 243	Dave Meads	.04	.02	.01
☐ 244	Jim Sundberg	.04	.02	.01
☐ 245	Ken Oberkfell	.04	.02	.01
☐ 246	Jimmy Jones	.04	.02	.01
☐ 247	Ken Landreaux	.04	.02	.01
☐ 248	Jose Oquendo	.04	.02	.01
☐ 249	John Mitchell	.04	.02	.01
☐ 250	Don Baylor	.07	.03	.01
☐ 251	Scott Fletcher	.04	.02	.01

☐ 252 Al Newman	.04	.02	.01
☐ 253 Carney Lansford	.07	.03	.01
☐ 254 Johnny Ray	.04	.02	.01
☐ 255 Gary Pettis	.04	.02	.01
☐ 256 Ken Phelps	.04	.02	.01
☐ 257 Rick Leach	.04	.02	.01
☐ 258 Tim Stoddard	.04	.02	.01
☐ 259 Ed Romero	.04	.02	.01
☐ 260 Sid Bream	.07	.03	.01
☐ 261A Tom Niedenfuer ERR	.12	.05	.02
(Misspelled Neidenfuer			
on card front)			
☐ 261B Tom Niedenfuer COR	.04	.02	.01
☐ 262 Rick Dempsey	.04	.02	.01
☐ 263 Lonnie Smith	.04	.02	.01
☐ 264 Bob Forsch	.04	.02	.01
☐ 265 Barry Bonds	.60	.25	.08
☐ 266 Willie Randolph	.07	.03	.01
☐ 267 Mike Ramsey	.04	.02	.01
☐ 268 Don Slaught	.04	.02	.01
☐ 269 Mickey Tettleton	.12	.05	.02
☐ 270 Jerry Reuss	.04	.02	.01
☐ 271 Marc Sullivan	.04	.02	.01
☐ 272 Jim Morrison	.04	.02	.01
☐ 273 Steve Balboni	.04	.02	.01
☐ 274 Dick Schofield	.04	.02	.01
☐ 275 John Tudor	.04	.02	.01
☐ 276 Gene Larkin	.10	.05	.01
☐ 277 Harold Reynolds	.04	.02	.01
☐ 278 Jerry Browne	.04	.02	.01
☐ 279 Willie Upshaw	.04	.02	.01
☐ 280 Ted Higuera	.04	.02	.01
☐ 281 Terry McGriff	.04	.02	.01
☐ 282 Terry Puhl	.04	.02	.01
☐ 283 Mark Wasinger	.04	.02	.01
☐ 284 Luis Salazar	.04	.02	.01
☐ 285 Ted Simmons	.07	.03	.01
☐ 286 John Shelby	.04	.02	.01
☐ 287 John Smiley	.40	.18	.05
☐ 288 Curt Ford	.04	.02	.01
☐ 289 Steve Crawford	.04	.02	.01
☐ 290 Dan Quisenberry	.07	.03	.01
☐ 291 Alan Wiggins	.04	.02	.01
☐ 292 Randy Bush	.04	.02	.01
☐ 293 John Candelaria	.04	.02	.01
☐ 294 Tony Phillips	.04	.02	.01
☐ 295 Mike Morgan	.07	.03	.01
☐ 296 Bill Wegman	.04	.02	.01
☐ 297A Terry Francona ERR	.12	.05	.02
(Misspelled Franconia			
on card front)			
☐ 297B Terry Francona COR	.04	.02	.01
☐ 298 Mickey Hatcher	.04	.02	.01
☐ 299 Andres Thomas	.04	.02	.01
☐ 300 Bob Stanley	.04	.02	.01
☐ 301 Al Pedrique	.04	.02	.01
☐ 302 Jim Lindeman	.04	.02	.01

☐ 303 Wally Backman	.04	.02	.01
☐ 304 Paul O'Neill	.10	.05	.01
☐ 305 Hubie Brooks	.04	.02	.01
☐ 306 Steve Buechele	.04	.02	.01
☐ 307 Bobby Thigpen	.07	.03	.01
☐ 308 George Hendrick	.04	.02	.01
☐ 309 John Moses	.04	.02	.01
☐ 310 Ron Guidry	.07	.03	.01
☐ 311 Bill Schroeder	.04	.02	.01
☐ 312 Jose Nunez	.04	.02	.01
☐ 313 Bud Black	.04	.02	.01
☐ 314 Joe Sambito	.04	.02	.01
☐ 315 Scott McGregor	.04	.02	.01
☐ 316 Rafael Santana	.04	.02	.01
☐ 317 Frank Williams	.04	.02	.01
☐ 318 Mike Fitzgerald	.04	.02	.01
☐ 319 Rick Mahler	.04	.02	.01
☐ 320 Jim Gott	.04	.02	.01
☐ 321 Mariano Duncan	.04	.02	.01
☐ 322 Jose Guzman	.07	.03	.01
☐ 323 Lee Guetterman	.04	.02	.01
☐ 324 Dan Gladden	.04	.02	.01
☐ 325 Gary Carter	.10	.05	.01
☐ 326 Tracy Jones	.04	.02	.01
☐ 327 Floyd Youmans	.04	.02	.01
☐ 328 Bill Dawley	.04	.02	.01
☐ 329 Paul Noce	.04	.02	.01
☐ 330 Angel Salazar	.04	.02	.01
☐ 331 Goose Gossage	.07	.03	.01
☐ 332 George Frazier	.04	.02	.01
☐ 333 Ruppert Jones	.04	.02	.01
☐ 334 Billy Joe Robidoux	.04	.02	.01
☐ 335 Mike Scott	.07	.03	.01
☐ 336 Randy Myers	.07	.03	.01
☐ 337 Rob Sebra	.04	.02	.01
☐ 338 Eric Show	.04	.02	.01
☐ 339 Mitch Williams	.07	.03	.01
☐ 340 Paul Molitor	.12	.05	.02
☐ 341 Gus Polidor	.04	.02	.01
☐ 342 Steve Trout	.04	.02	.01
☐ 343 Jerry Don Gleaton	.04	.02	.01
☐ 344 Bob Knepper	.04	.02	.01
☐ 345 Mitch Webster	.04	.02	.01
☐ 346 John Morris	.04	.02	.01
☐ 347 Andy Hawkins	.04	.02	.01
☐ 348 Dave Leiper	.04	.02	.01
☐ 349 Ernest Riles	.04	.02	.01
☐ 350 Dwight Gooden	.12	.05	.02
☐ 351 Dave Righetti	.04	.02	.01
☐ 352 Pat Dodson	.04	.02	.01
☐ 353 John Habyan	.04	.02	.01
☐ 354 Jim Deshaies	.04	.02	.01
☐ 355 Butch Wynegar	.04	.02	.01
☐ 356 Bryn Smith	.04	.02	.01
☐ 357 Matt Young	.04	.02	.01
☐ 358 Tom Pagnozzi	.25	.11	.03
☐ 359 Floyd Rayford	.04	.02	.01

☐	360	Darryl Strawberry	.30	.14	.04	☐	417	Danny Heep	.04	.02	.01
☐	361	Sal Butera	.04	.02	.01	☐	418	John Cangelosi	.04	.02	.01
☐	362	Domingo Ramos	.04	.02	.01	☐	419A	John Christensen ERR	.12	.05	.02
☐	363	Chris Brown	.04	.02	.01			(Christiansen			
☐	364	Jose Gonzalez	.04	.02	.01			on card front)			
☐	365	Dave Smith	.04	.02	.01	☐	419B	John Christensen COR	.04	.02	.01
☐	366	Andy McGaffigan	.04	.02	.01	☐	420	Joey Cora	.07	.03	.01
☐	367	Stan Javier	.04	.02	.01	☐	421	Mike LaValliere	.04	.02	.01
☐	368	Henry Cotto	.04	.02	.01	☐	422	Kelly Gruber	.07	.03	.01
☐	369	Mike Birkbeck	.04	.02	.01	☐	423	Bruce Benedict	.04	.02	.01
☐	370	Len Dykstra	.07	.03	.01	☐	424	Len Matuszek	.04	.02	.01
☐	371	Dave Collins	.04	.02	.01	☐	425	Kent Tekulve	.04	.02	.01
☐	372	Spike Owen	.04	.02	.01	☐	426	Rafael Ramirez	.04	.02	.01
☐	373	Geno Petralli	.04	.02	.01	☐	427	Mike Flanagan	.04	.02	.01
☐	374	Ron Karkovice	.04	.02	.01	☐	428	Mike Gallego	.04	.02	.01
☐	375	Shane Rawley	.04	.02	.01	☐	429	Juan Castillo	.04	.02	.01
☐	376	DeWayne Buice	.04	.02	.01	☐	430	Neal Heaton	.04	.02	.01
☐	377	Bill Pecota	.10	.05	.01	☐	431	Phil Garner	.07	.03	.01
☐	378	Leon Durham	.04	.02	.01	☐	432	Mike Dunne	.04	.02	.01
☐	379	Ed Olwine	.04	.02	.01	☐	433	Wallace Johnson	.04	.02	.01
☐	380	Bruce Hurst	.07	.03	.01	☐	434	Jack O'Connor	.04	.02	.01
☐	381	Bob McClure	.04	.02	.01	☐	435	Steve Jeltz	.04	.02	.01
☐	382	Mark Thurmond	.04	.02	.01	☐	436	Donell Nixon	.04	.02	.01
☐	383	Buddy Biancalana	.04	.02	.01	☐	437	Jack Lazorko	.04	.02	.01
☐	384	Tim Conroy	.04	.02	.01	☐	438	Keith Comstock	.04	.02	.01
☐	385	Tony Gwynn	.30	.14	.04	☐	439	Jeff D. Robinson	.04	.02	.01
☐	386	Greg Gross	.04	.02	.01			(Pirates pitcher)			
☐	387	Barry Lyons	.04	.02	.01	☐	440	Graig Nettles	.07	.03	.01
☐	388	Mike Felder	.04	.02	.01	☐	441	Mel Hall	.04	.02	.01
☐	389	Pat Clements	.04	.02	.01	☐	442	Gerald Young	.04	.02	.01
☐	390	Ken Griffey	.07	.03	.01	☐	443	Gary Redus	.04	.02	.01
☐	391	Mark Davis	.04	.02	.01	☐	444	Charlie Moore	.04	.02	.01
☐	392	Jose Rijo	.10	.05	.01	☐	445	Bill Madlock	.07	.03	.01
☐	393	Mike Young	.04	.02	.01	☐	446	Mark Clear	.04	.02	.01
☐	394	Willie Fraser	.04	.02	.01	☐	447	Greg Booker	.04	.02	.01
☐	395	Dion James	.04	.02	.01	☐	448	Rick Schu	.04	.02	.01
☐	396	Steve Shields	.04	.02	.01	☐	449	Ron Kittle	.04	.02	.01
☐	397	Randy St.Claire	.04	.02	.01	☐	450	Dale Murphy	.10	.05	.01
☐	398	Danny Jackson	.04	.02	.01	☐	451	Bob Dernier	.04	.02	.01
☐	399	Cecil Fielder	.30	.14	.04	☐	452	Dale Mohorcic	.04	.02	.01
☐	400	Keith Hernandez	.07	.03	.01	☐	453	Rafael Belliard	.04	.02	.01
☐	401	Don Carman	.04	.02	.01	☐	454	Charlie Puleo	.04	.02	.01
☐	402	Chuck Crim	.04	.02	.01	☐	455	Dwayne Murphy	.04	.02	.01
☐	403	Rob Woodward	.04	.02	.01	☐	456	Jim Eisenreich	.04	.02	.01
☐	404	Junior Ortiz	.04	.02	.01	☐	457	David Palmer	.04	.02	.01
☐	405	Glenn Wilson	.04	.02	.01	☐	458	Dave Stewart	.07	.03	.01
☐	406	Ken Howell	.04	.02	.01	☐	459	Pascual Perez	.04	.02	.01
☐	407	Jeff Kunkel	.04	.02	.01	☐	460	Glenn Davis	.07	.03	.01
☐	408	Jeff Reed	.04	.02	.01	☐	461	Dan Petry	.04	.02	.01
☐	409	Chris James	.04	.02	.01	☐	462	Jim Winn	.04	.02	.01
☐	410	Zane Smith	.04	.02	.01	☐	463	Darrell Miller	.04	.02	.01
☐	411	Ken Dixon	.04	.02	.01	☐	464	Mike Moore	.04	.02	.01
☐	412	Ricky Horton	.04	.02	.01	☐	465	Mike LaCoss	.04	.02	.01
☐	413	Frank DiPino	.04	.02	.01	☐	466	Steve Farr	.04	.02	.01
☐	414	Shane Mack	.30	.14	.04	☐	467	Jerry Mumphrey	.04	.02	.01
☐	415	Danny Cox	.04	.02	.01	☐	468	Kevin Gross	.04	.02	.01
☐	416	Andy Van Slyke	.10	.05	.01	☐	469	Bruce Bochy	.04	.02	.01

☐ 470 Orel Hershiser	.07	.03	.01
☐ 471 Eric King	.04	.02	.01
☐ 472 Ellis Burks	.25	.11	.03
☐ 473 Darren Daulton	.07	.03	.01
☐ 474 Mookie Wilson	.07	.03	.01
☐ 475 Frank Viola	.07	.03	.01
☐ 476 Ron Robinson	.04	.02	.01
☐ 477 Bob Melvin	.04	.02	.01
☐ 478 Jeff Musselman	.04	.02	.01
☐ 479 Charlie Kerfeld	.04	.02	.01
☐ 480 Richard Dotson	.04	.02	.01
☐ 481 Kevin Mitchell	.15	.07	.02
☐ 482 Gary Roenicke	.04	.02	.01
☐ 483 Tim Flannery	.04	.02	.01
☐ 484 Rich Yett	.04	.02	.01
☐ 485 Pete Incaviglia	.07	.03	.01
☐ 486 Rick Cerone	.04	.02	.01
☐ 487 Tony Armas	.04	.02	.01
☐ 488 Jerry Reed	.04	.02	.01
☐ 489 Dave Lopes	.07	.03	.01
☐ 490 Frank Tanana	.04	.02	.01
☐ 491 Mike Loynd	.04	.02	.01
☐ 492 Bruce Ruffin	.04	.02	.01
☐ 493 Chris Speier	.04	.02	.01
☐ 494 Tom Hume	.04	.02	.01
☐ 495 Jesse Orosco	.04	.02	.01
☐ 496 Robbie Wine UER	.04	.02	.01
(Misspelled Robby on card front)			
☐ 497 Jeff Montgomery	.35	.16	.04
☐ 498 Jeff Dedmon	.04	.02	.01
☐ 499 Luis Aguayo	.04	.02	.01
☐ 500 Reggie Jackson	.30	.14	.04
(Oakland A's)			
☐ 501 Reggie Jackson	.30	.14	.04
(Baltimore Orioles)			
☐ 502 Reggie Jackson	.30	.14	.04
(New York Yankees)			
☐ 503 Reggie Jackson	.30	.14	.04
(California Angels)			
☐ 504 Reggie Jackson	.30	.14	.04
(Oakland A's)			
☐ 505 Billy Hatcher	.04	.02	.01
☐ 506 Ed Lynch	.04	.02	.01
☐ 507 Willie Hernandez	.04	.02	.01
☐ 508 Jose DeLeon	.04	.02	.01
☐ 509 Joel Youngblood	.04	.02	.01
☐ 510 Bob Welch	.07	.03	.01
☐ 511 Steve Ontiveros	.04	.02	.01
☐ 512 Randy Ready	.04	.02	.01
☐ 513 Juan Nieves	.04	.02	.01
☐ 514 Jeff Russell	.04	.02	.01
☐ 515 Von Hayes	.04	.02	.01
☐ 516 Mark Gubicza	.04	.02	.01
☐ 517 Ken Dayley	.04	.02	.01
☐ 518 Don Aase	.04	.02	.01
☐ 519 Rick Reuschel	.04	.02	.01

☐ 520 Mike Henneman	.15	.07	.02
☐ 521 Rick Aguilera	.07	.03	.01
☐ 522 Jay Howell	.04	.02	.01
☐ 523 Ed Correa	.04	.02	.01
☐ 524 Manny Trillo	.04	.02	.01
☐ 525 Kirk Gibson	.07	.03	.01
☐ 526 Wally Ritchie	.04	.02	.01
☐ 527 Al Nipper	.04	.02	.01
☐ 528 Atlee Hammaker	.04	.02	.01
☐ 529 Shawon Dunston	.07	.03	.01
☐ 530 Jim Clancy	.07	.03	.01
☐ 531 Tom Paciorek	.07	.03	.01
☐ 532 Joel Skinner	.04	.02	.01
☐ 533 Scott Garrelts	.04	.02	.01
☐ 534 Tom O'Malley	.04	.02	.01
☐ 535 John Franco	.07	.03	.01
☐ 536 Paul Kilgus	.04	.02	.01
☐ 537 Darrell Porter	.04	.02	.01
☐ 538 Walt Terrell	.04	.02	.01
☐ 539 Bill Long	.04	.02	.01
☐ 540 George Bell	.10	.05	.01
☐ 541 Jeff Sellers	.04	.02	.01
☐ 542 Joe Boever	.04	.02	.01
☐ 543 Steve Howe	.04	.02	.01
☐ 544 Scott Sanderson	.04	.02	.01
☐ 545 Jack Morris	.12	.05	.02
☐ 546 Todd Benzinger	.10	.05	.01
☐ 547 Steve Henderson	.04	.02	.01
☐ 548 Eddie Milner	.04	.02	.01
☐ 549 Jeff M. Robinson	.04	.02	.01
☐ 550 Cal Ripken	.60	.25	.08
☐ 551 Jody Davis	.04	.02	.01
☐ 552 Kirk McCaskill	.04	.02	.01
☐ 553 Craig Lefferts	.04	.02	.01
☐ 554 Darnell Coles	.04	.02	.01
☐ 555 Phil Niekro	.15	.07	.02
☐ 556 Mike Aldrete	.04	.02	.01
☐ 557 Pat Perry	.04	.02	.01
☐ 558 Juan Agosto	.04	.02	.01
☐ 559 Rob Murphy	.04	.02	.01
☐ 560 Dennis Rasmussen	.04	.02	.01
☐ 561 Manny Lee	.04	.02	.01
☐ 562 Jeff Blauser	.25	.11	.03
☐ 563 Bob Ojeda	.04	.02	.01
☐ 564 Dave Dravecky	.07	.03	.01
☐ 565 Gene Garber	.04	.02	.01
☐ 566 Ron Roenicke	.04	.02	.01
☐ 567 Tommy Hinzo	.04	.02	.01
☐ 568 Eric Nolte	.04	.02	.01
☐ 569 Ed Hearn	.04	.02	.01
☐ 570 Mark Davidson	.04	.02	.01
☐ 571 Jim Walewander	.04	.02	.01
☐ 572 Donnie Hill	.04	.02	.01
☐ 573 Jamie Moyer	.04	.02	.01
☐ 574 Ken Schrom	.04	.02	.01
☐ 575 Nolan Ryan	.75	.35	.09
☐ 576 Jim Acker	.04	.02	.01

☐ 577	Jamie Quirk	.04	.02	.01
☐ 578	Jay Aldrich	.04	.02	.01
☐ 579	Claudell Washington	.04	.02	.01
☐ 580	Jeff Leonard	.04	.02	.01
☐ 581	Carmen Castillo	.04	.02	.01
☐ 582	Daryl Boston	.04	.02	.01
☐ 583	Jeff DeWillis	.04	.02	.01
☐ 584	John Marzano	.04	.02	.01
☐ 585	Bill Gullickson	.04	.02	.01
☐ 586	Andy Allanson	.04	.02	.01
☐ 587	Lee Tunnell UER	.04	.02	.01
	(1987 stat line reads .4.84 ERA)			
☐ 588	Gene Nelson	.04	.02	.01
☐ 589	Dave LaPoint	.04	.02	.01
☐ 590	Harold Baines	.07	.03	.01
☐ 591	Bill Buckner	.07	.03	.01
☐ 592	Carlton Fisk	.20	.09	.03
☐ 593	Rick Manning	.04	.02	.01
☐ 594	Doug Jones	.25	.11	.03
☐ 595	Tom Candiotti	.04	.02	.01
☐ 596	Steve Lake	.04	.02	.01
☐ 597	Jose Lind	.15	.07	.02
☐ 598	Ross Jones	.04	.02	.01
☐ 599	Gary Matthews	.04	.02	.01
☐ 600	Fernando Valenzuela	.07	.03	.01
☐ 601	Dennis Martinez	.07	.03	.01
☐ 602	Les Lancaster	.04	.02	.01
☐ 603	Ozzie Guillen	.07	.03	.01
☐ 604	Tony Bernazard	.04	.02	.01
☐ 605	Chili Davis	.07	.03	.01
☐ 606	Roy Smalley	.04	.02	.01
☐ 607	Ivan Calderon	.07	.03	.01
☐ 608	Jay Tibbs	.04	.02	.01
☐ 609	Guy Hoffman	.04	.02	.01
☐ 610	Doyle Alexander	.04	.02	.01
☐ 611	Mike Bielecki	.04	.02	.01
☐ 612	Shawn Hillegas	.04	.02	.01
☐ 613	Keith Atherton	.04	.02	.01
☐ 614	Eric Plunk	.04	.02	.01
☐ 615	Sid Fernandez	.07	.03	.01
☐ 616	Dennis Lamp	.04	.02	.01
☐ 617	Dave Engle	.04	.02	.01
☐ 618	Harry Spilman	.04	.02	.01
☐ 619	Don Robinson	.04	.02	.01
☐ 620	John Farrell	.04	.02	.01
☐ 621	Nelson Liriano	.04	.02	.01
☐ 622	Floyd Bannister	.04	.02	.01
☐ 623	Randy Milligan	.25	.11	.03
☐ 624	Kevin Elster	.05	.02	.01
☐ 625	Jody Reed	.25	.11	.03
☐ 626	Shawn Abner	.05	.02	.01
☐ 627	Kirt Manwaring	.10	.05	.01
☐ 628	Pete Stanicek	.05	.02	.01
☐ 629	Rob Ducey	.05	.02	.01
☐ 630	Steve Kiefer	.05	.02	.01
☐ 631	Gary Thurman	.05	.02	.01

☐ 632	Darrel Akerfelds	.05	.02	.01
☐ 633	Dave Clark	.05	.02	.01
☐ 634	Roberto Kelly	.90	.40	.11
☐ 635	Keith Hughes	.05	.02	.01
☐ 636	John Davis	.05	.02	.01
☐ 637	Mike Devereaux	.90	.40	.11
☐ 638	Tom Glavine	2.25	1.00	.30
☐ 639	Keith A. Miller	.20	.09	.03
☐ 640	Chris Gwynn UER	.12	.05	.02
	(Wrong batting and throwing on back)			
☐ 641	Tim Crews	.05	.02	.01
☐ 642	Mackey Sasser	.10	.05	.01
☐ 643	Vicente Palacios	.10	.05	.01
☐ 644	Kevin Romine	.05	.02	.01
☐ 645	Gregg Jefferies	1.00	.45	.13
☐ 646	Jeff Treadway	.10	.05	.01
☐ 647	Ron Gant	1.50	.65	.19
☐ 648	Mark McGwire and Matt Nokes (Rookie Sluggers)	.20	.09	.03
☐ 649	Eric Davis and Tim Raines (Speed and Power)	.08	.04	.01
☐ 650	Don Mattingly and Jack Clark	.10	.05	.01
☐ 651	Tony Fernandez, Alan Trammell, and Cal Ripken	.20	.09	.03
☐ 652	Vince Coleman HL 100 Stolen Bases	.05	.02	.01
☐ 653	Kirby Puckett HL 10 Hits in a Row	.20	.09	.03
☐ 654	Benito Santiago HL Hitting Streak	.05	.02	.01
☐ 655	Juan Nieves HL No Hitter	.05	.02	.01
☐ 656	Steve Bedrosian HL Saves Record	.05	.02	.01
☐ 657	Mike Schmidt HL 500 Homers	.20	.09	.03
☐ 658	Don Mattingly HL Home Run Streak	.15	.07	.02
☐ 659	Mark McGwire HL Rookie HR Record	.25	.11	.03
☐ 660	Paul Molitor HL Hitting Streak	.08	.04	.01

1988 Score Rookie/Traded

This 110-card set featured traded players (1-65) and rookies (66-110) for the 1988 season. The cards are distinguishable from the regular Score set by the orange borders and by the fact that the numbering on the back has a T suffix. The cards are standard size, 2 1/2" by 3 1/2", and were distributed by Score as a collated set in a special collector box along with some trivia cards. Score also produced a limited "glossy" Rookie and Traded set, that is valued at two to three times the value of the regular (non-glossy) set. It should be noted that the set itself (non-glossy) is now considered somewhat scarce. Apparently Score's first attempt at a Rookie/Traded set was produced very conservatively, resulting in a set which is now recognized as being much tougher to find than the other Rookie/Traded sets from the other major companies of that year. The key (extended) Rookie Cards in this set are Roberto Alomar, Brady Anderson, Craig Biggio, Jay Buhner, Rob Dibble, Mark Grace, Bryan Harvey, Jack McDowell, Melido Perez, Chris Sabo, Todd Stottlemyre, Pat Borders, and Walt Weiss.

	MT	EX-MT	VG
COMPLETE SET (110)	90.00	40.00	11.50
COMMON PLAYER (1T-65T)	.15	.07	.02
COMMON PLAYER (66T-110T)	.15	.07	.02

		MT	EX-MT	VG
☐ 1T	Jack Clark	.25	.11	.03
☐ 2T	Danny Jackson	.15	.07	.02
☐ 3T	Brett Butler	.40	.18	.05
☐ 4T	Kurt Stillwell	.15	.07	.02
☐ 5T	Tom Brunansky	.25	.11	.03
☐ 6T	Dennis Lamp	.15	.07	.02
☐ 7T	Jose DeLeon	.15	.07	.02
☐ 8T	Tom Herr	.15	.07	.02
☐ 9T	Keith Moreland	.15	.07	.02
☐ 10T	Kirk Gibson	.25	.11	.03
☐ 11T	Bud Black	.15	.07	.02
☐ 12T	Rafael Ramirez	.15	.07	.02
☐ 13T	Luis Salazar	.15	.07	.02
☐ 14T	Goose Gossage	.25	.11	.03
☐ 15T	Bob Welch	.25	.11	.03
☐ 16T	Vance Law	.15	.07	.02
☐ 17T	Ray Knight	.25	.11	.03
☐ 18T	Dan Quisenberry	.25	.11	.03
☐ 19T	Don Slaught	.15	.07	.02
☐ 20T	Lee Smith	1.00	.45	.13
☐ 21T	Rick Cerone	.15	.07	.02
☐ 22T	Pat Tabler	.15	.07	.02
☐ 23T	Larry McWilliams	.15	.07	.02
☐ 24T	Ricky Horton	.15	.07	.02
☐ 25T	Graig Nettles	.25	.11	.03
☐ 26T	Dan Petry	.15	.07	.02
☐ 27T	Jose Rijo	.40	.18	.05
☐ 28T	Chili Davis	.25	.11	.03
☐ 29T	Dickie Thon	.15	.07	.02
☐ 30T	Mackey Sasser	.25	.11	.03
☐ 31T	Mickey Tettleton	.40	.18	.05
☐ 32T	Rick Dempsey	.15	.07	.02
☐ 33T	Ron Hassey	.15	.07	.02
☐ 34T	Phil Bradley	.15	.07	.02
☐ 35T	Jay Howell	.15	.07	.02
☐ 36T	Bill Buckner	.25	.11	.03
☐ 37T	Alfredo Griffin	.15	.07	.02
☐ 38T	Gary Pettis	.15	.07	.02
☐ 39T	Calvin Schiraldi	.15	.07	.02
☐ 40T	John Candelaria	.15	.07	.02
☐ 41T	Joe Orsulak	.15	.07	.02
☐ 42T	Willie Upshaw	.15	.07	.02
☐ 43T	Herm Winningham	.15	.07	.02
☐ 44T	Ron Kittle	.15	.07	.02
☐ 45T	Bob Dernier	.15	.07	.02
☐ 46T	Steve Balboni	.15	.07	.02
☐ 47T	Steve Shields	.15	.07	.02
☐ 48T	Henry Cotto	.15	.07	.02
☐ 49T	Dave Henderson	.25	.11	.03
☐ 50T	Dave Parker	.25	.11	.03
☐ 51T	Mike Young	.15	.07	.02
☐ 52T	Mark Salas	.15	.07	.02
☐ 53T	Mike Davis	.15	.07	.02
☐ 54T	Rafael Santana	.15	.07	.02
☐ 55T	Don Baylor	.25	.11	.03
☐ 56T	Dan Pasqua	.15	.07	.02
☐ 57T	Ernest Riles	.15	.07	.02
☐ 58T	Glenn Hubbard	.15	.07	.02
☐ 59T	Mike Smithson	.15	.07	.02
☐ 60T	Richard Dotson	.15	.07	.02

1989 Score

☐ 61T Jerry Reuss	.15	.07	.02
☐ 62T Mike Jackson	.15	.07	.02
☐ 63T Floyd Bannister	.15	.07	.02
☐ 64T Jesse Orosco	.15	.07	.02
☐ 65T Larry Parrish	.15	.07	.02
☐ 66T Jeff Bittiger	.15	.07	.02
☐ 67T Ray Hayward	.15	.07	.02
☐ 68T Ricky Jordan	.50	.23	.06
☐ 69T Tommy Gregg	.15	.07	.02
☐ 70T Brady Anderson	8.00	3.60	1.00
☐ 71T Jeff Montgomery	.50	.23	.06
☐ 72T Darryl Hamilton	1.50	.65	.19
☐ 73T Cecil Espy	.30	.14	.04
☐ 74T Greg Briley	.30	.14	.04
☐ 75T Joey Meyer	.15	.07	.02
☐ 76T Mike Macfarlane	1.50	.65	.19
☐ 77T Oswald Peraza	.15	.07	.02
☐ 78T Jack Armstrong	.60	.25	.08
☐ 79T Don Heinkel	.15	.07	.02
☐ 80T Mark Grace	15.00	6.75	1.90
☐ 81T Steve Curry	.15	.07	.02
☐ 82T Damon Berryhill	.60	.25	.08
☐ 83T Steve Ellsworth	.15	.07	.02
☐ 84T Pete Smith	2.50	1.15	.30
☐ 85T Jack McDowell	15.00	6.75	1.90
☐ 86T Rob Dibble	2.50	1.15	.30
☐ 87T Bryan Harvey	2.00	.90	.25
☐ 88T John Dopson	.15	.07	.02
☐ 89T Dave Gallagher	.15	.07	.02
☐ 90T Todd Stottlemyre	2.00	.90	.25
☐ 91T Mike Schooler	.50	.23	.06
☐ 92T Don Gordon	.15	.07	.02
☐ 93T Sil Campusano	.15	.07	.02
☐ 94T Jeff Pico	.15	.07	.02
☐ 95T Jay Buhner	3.00	1.35	.40
☐ 96T Nelson Santovenia	.15	.07	.02
☐ 97T Al Leiter	.15	.07	.02
☐ 98T Luis Alicea	.35	.16	.04
☐ 99T Pat Borders	3.00	1.35	.40
☐ 100T Chris Sabo	3.50	1.55	.45
☐ 101T Tim Belcher	.60	.25	.08
☐ 102T Walt Weiss	.60	.25	.08
☐ 103T Craig Biggio	5.50	2.50	.70
☐ 104T Don August	.15	.07	.02
☐ 105T Roberto Alomar	60.00	27.00	7.50
☐ 106T Todd Burns	.15	.07	.02
☐ 107T John Costello	.15	.07	.02
☐ 108T Melido Perez	2.00	.90	.25
☐ 109T Darrin Jackson	2.00	.90	.25
☐ 110T Orestes Destrade	.90	.40	.11

This 660-card set was distributed by Major League Marketing. Cards measure 2 1/2" by 3 1/2" and feature six distinctive inner border (inside a white outer border) colors on the front. Highlights (652-660) and Rookie Prospects (621-651) are included in the set. The set is distinguished by the fact that each card back shows a full-color picture (portrait) of the player. Score "missed" many of the mid-season and later trades; there are numerous examples of inconsistency with regard to the treatment of these players. Study as examples of this inconsistency of handling of late trades, cards numbered 49, 71, 77, 83, 106, 126, 139, 145, 173, 177, 242, 348, 384, 420, 439, 488, 494, and 525. The key Rookie Cards in this set are Sandy Alomar Jr., Felix Jose, Ramon Martinez, Gary Sheffield, and John Smoltz.

	MT	EX-MT	VG
COMPLETE SET (660)	20.00	9.00	2.50
COMPLETE FACT.SET (660)	20.00	9.00	2.50
COMMON PLAYER (1-660)	.04	.02	.01
☐ 1 Jose Canseco	.40	.18	.05
☐ 2 Andre Dawson	.15	.07	.02
☐ 3 Mark McGwire UER	.40	.18	.05
(Bio says 116 RBI's, should be 118)			
☐ 4 Benito Santiago	.07	.03	.01
☐ 5 Rick Reuschel	.04	.02	.01
☐ 6 Fred McGriff	.25	.11	.03
☐ 7 Kal Daniels	.07	.03	.01
☐ 8 Gary Gaetti	.04	.02	.01
☐ 9 Ellis Burks	.07	.03	.01
☐ 10 Darryl Strawberry	.25	.11	.03

☐ 11	Julio Franco	.07	.03	.01
☐ 12	Lloyd Moseby	.04	.02	.01
☐ 13	Jeff Pico	.04	.02	.01
☐ 14	Johnny Ray	.04	.02	.01
☐ 15	Cal Ripken	.50	.23	.06
☐ 16	Dick Schofield	.04	.02	.01
☐ 17	Mel Hall	.04	.02	.01
☐ 18	Bill Ripken	.04	.02	.01
☐ 19	Brook Jacoby	.04	.02	.01
☐ 20	Kirby Puckett	.40	.18	.05
☐ 21	Bill Doran	.04	.02	.01
☐ 22	Pete O'Brien	.04	.02	.01
☐ 23	Matt Nokes	.07	.03	.01
☐ 24	Brian Fisher	.04	.02	.01
☐ 25	Jack Clark	.07	.03	.01
☐ 26	Gary Pettis	.04	.02	.01
☐ 27	Dave Valle	.04	.02	.01
☐ 28	Willie Wilson	.04	.02	.01
☐ 29	Curt Young	.04	.02	.01
☐ 30	Dale Murphy	.10	.05	.01
☐ 31	Barry Larkin	.15	.07	.02
☐ 32	Dave Stewart	.07	.03	.01
☐ 33	Mike LaValliere	.04	.02	.01
☐ 34	Glenn Hubbard	.04	.02	.01
☐ 35	Ryne Sandberg	.40	.18	.05
☐ 36	Tony Pena	.04	.02	.01
☐ 37	Greg Walker	.04	.02	.01
☐ 38	Von Hayes	.04	.02	.01
☐ 39	Kevin Mitchell	.10	.05	.01
☐ 40	Tim Raines	.07	.03	.01
☐ 41	Keith Hernandez	.07	.03	.01
☐ 42	Keith Moreland	.04	.02	.01
☐ 43	Ruben Sierra	.30	.14	.04
☐ 44	Chet Lemon	.04	.02	.01
☐ 45	Willie Randolph	.07	.03	.01
☐ 46	Andy Allanson	.04	.02	.01
☐ 47	Candy Maldonado	.04	.02	.01
☐ 48	Sid Bream	.04	.02	.01
☐ 49	Denny Walling	.04	.02	.01
☐ 50	Dave Winfield	.20	.09	.03
☐ 51	Alvin Davis	.04	.02	.01
☐ 52	Cory Snyder	.04	.02	.01
☐ 53	Hubie Brooks	.04	.02	.01
☐ 54	Chili Davis	.07	.03	.01
☐ 55	Kevin Seitzer	.07	.03	.01
☐ 56	Jose Uribe	.04	.02	.01
☐ 57	Tony Fernandez	.07	.03	.01
☐ 58	Tim Teufel	.04	.02	.01
☐ 59	Oddibe McDowell	.04	.02	.01
☐ 60	Les Lancaster	.04	.02	.01
☐ 61	Billy Hatcher	.04	.02	.01
☐ 62	Dan Gladden	.04	.02	.01
☐ 63	Marty Barrett	.04	.02	.01
☐ 64	Nick Esasky	.04	.02	.01
☐ 65	Wally Joyner	.08	.04	.01
☐ 66	Mike Greenwell	.07	.03	.01
☐ 67	Ken Williams	.04	.02	.01

☐ 68	Bob Horner	.04	.02	.01
☐ 69	Steve Sax	.07	.03	.01
☐ 70	Rickey Henderson	.25	.11	.03
☐ 71	Mitch Webster	.04	.02	.01
☐ 72	Rob Deer	.07	.03	.01
☐ 73	Jim Presley	.04	.02	.01
☐ 74	Albert Hall	.04	.02	.01
☐ 75A	George Brett ERR (At age 33)	.75	.35	.09
☐ 75B	George Brett COR (At age 35)	.20	.09	.03
☐ 76	Brian Downing	.04	.02	.01
☐ 77	Dave Martinez	.07	.03	.01
☐ 78	Scott Fletcher	.04	.02	.01
☐ 79	Phil Bradley	.04	.02	.01
☐ 80	Ozzie Smith	.15	.07	.02
☐ 81	Larry Sheets	.04	.02	.01
☐ 82	Mike Aldrete	.04	.02	.01
☐ 83	Darnell Coles	.04	.02	.01
☐ 84	Len Dykstra	.07	.03	.01
☐ 85	Jim Rice	.07	.03	.01
☐ 86	Jeff Treadway	.04	.02	.01
☐ 87	Jose Lind	.04	.02	.01
☐ 88	Willie McGee	.07	.03	.01
☐ 89	Mickey Brantley	.04	.02	.01
☐ 90	Tony Gwynn	.25	.11	.03
☐ 91	R.J. Reynolds	.04	.02	.01
☐ 92	Milt Thompson	.04	.02	.01
☐ 93	Kevin McReynolds	.07	.03	.01
☐ 94	Eddie Murray UER ('86 batting .205, should be .305)	.15	.07	.02
☐ 95	Lance Parrish	.07	.03	.01
☐ 96	Ron Kittle	.04	.02	.01
☐ 97	Gerald Young	.04	.02	.01
☐ 98	Ernie Whitt	.04	.02	.01
☐ 99	Jeff Reed	.04	.02	.01
☐ 100	Don Mattingly	.25	.11	.03
☐ 101	Gerald Perry	.04	.02	.01
☐ 102	Vance Law	.04	.02	.01
☐ 103	John Shelby	.04	.02	.01
☐ 104	Chris Sabo	.30	.14	.04
☐ 105	Danny Tartabull	.12	.05	.02
☐ 106	Glenn Wilson	.04	.02	.01
☐ 107	Mark Davidson	.04	.02	.01
☐ 108	Dave Parker	.07	.03	.01
☐ 109	Eric Davis	.12	.05	.02
☐ 110	Alan Trammell	.07	.03	.01
☐ 111	Ozzie Virgil	.04	.02	.01
☐ 112	Frank Tanana	.04	.02	.01
☐ 113	Rafael Ramirez	.04	.02	.01
☐ 114	Dennis Martinez	.07	.03	.01
☐ 115	Jose DeLeon	.04	.02	.01
☐ 116	Bob Ojeda	.04	.02	.01
☐ 117	Doug Drabek	.07	.03	.01
☐ 118	Andy Hawkins	.04	.02	.01
☐ 119	Greg Maddux	.30	.14	.04

☐ 120	Cecil Fielder UER 25	.11	.03
	(Photo on back reversed)		
☐ 121	Mike Scioscia 04	.02	.01
☐ 122	Dan Petry......................04	.02	.01
☐ 123	Terry Kennedy................04	.02	.01
☐ 124	Kelly Downs...................04	.02	.01
☐ 125	Greg Gross UER 04	.02	.01
	(Gregg on back)		
☐ 126	Fred Lynn......................07	.03	.01
☐ 127	Barry Bonds...................40	.18	.05
☐ 128	Harold Baines 07	.03	.01
☐ 129	Doyle Alexander 04	.02	.01
☐ 130	Kevin Elster 04	.02	.01
☐ 131	Mike Heath.....................04	.02	.01
☐ 132	Teddy Higuera................04	.02	.01
☐ 133	Charlie Leibrandt............04	.02	.01
☐ 134	Tim Laudner...................04	.02	.01
☐ 135A	Ray Knight ERR 60	.25	.08
	(Reverse negative)		
☐ 135B	Ray Knight COR 15	.07	.02
☐ 136	Howard Johnson.............07	.03	.01
☐ 137	Terry Pendleton 12	.05	.02
☐ 138	Andy McGaffigan 04	.02	.01
☐ 139	Ken Oberkfell.................04	.02	.01
☐ 140	Butch Wynegar...............04	.02	.01
☐ 141	Rob Murphy....................04	.02	.01
☐ 142	Rich Renteria.................04	.02	.01
☐ 143	Jose Guzman 07	.03	.01
☐ 144	Andres Galarraga............04	.02	.01
☐ 145	Ricky Horton..................04	.02	.01
☐ 146	Frank DiPino..................04	.02	.01
☐ 147	Glenn Braggs.................04	.02	.01
☐ 148	John Kruk......................07	.03	.01
☐ 149	Mike Schmidt.................40	.18	.05
☐ 150	Lee Smith......................07	.03	.01
☐ 151	Robin Yount...................20	.09	.03
☐ 152	Mark Eichhorn................04	.02	.01
☐ 153	DeWayne Buice...............04	.02	.01
☐ 154	B.J. Surhoff...................04	.02	.01
☐ 155	Vince Coleman................07	.03	.01
☐ 156	Tony Phillips..................04	.02	.01
☐ 157	Willie Fraser..................04	.02	.01
☐ 158	Lance McCullers............04	.02	.01
☐ 159	Greg Gagne...................04	.02	.01
☐ 160	Jesse Barfield................04	.02	.01
☐ 161	Mark Langston................07	.03	.01
☐ 162	Kurt Stillwell.................04	.02	.01
☐ 163	Dion James....................04	.02	.01
☐ 164	Glenn Davis...................07	.03	.01
☐ 165	Walt Weiss.....................07	.03	.01
☐ 166	Dave Concepcion............07	.03	.01
☐ 167	Alfredo Griffin 04	.02	.01
☐ 168	Don Heinkel...................04	.02	.01
☐ 169	Luis Rivera....................04	.02	.01
☐ 170	Shane Rawley.................04	.02	.01
☐ 171	Darrell Evans.................07	.03	.01

☐ 172	Robby Thompson 04	.02	.01
☐ 173	Jody Davis 04	.02	.01
☐ 174	Andy Van Slyke 10	.05	.01
☐ 175	Wade Boggs UER 25	.11	.03
	(Bio says .364, should be .356)		
☐ 176	Garry Templeton 04	.02	.01
	('85 stats off-centered)		
☐ 177	Gary Redus 04	.02	.01
☐ 178	Craig Lefferts 04	.02	.01
☐ 179	Carney Lansford 07	.03	.01
☐ 180	Ron Darling....................07	.03	.01
☐ 181	Kirk McCaskill 04	.02	.01
☐ 182	Tony Armas....................04	.02	.01
☐ 183	Steve Farr 04	.02	.01
☐ 184	Tom Brunansky 07	.03	.01
☐ 185	Bryan Harvey UER 25	.11	.03
	('87 games 47, should be 3)		
☐ 186	Mike Marshall 04	.02	.01
☐ 187	Bo Diaz.........................04	.02	.01
☐ 188	Willie Upshaw.................04	.02	.01
☐ 189	Mike Pagliarulo..............04	.02	.01
☐ 190	Mike Krukow...................04	.02	.01
☐ 191	Tommy Herr 04	.02	.01
☐ 192	Jim Pankovits.................04	.02	.01
☐ 193	Dwight Evans 07	.03	.01
☐ 194	Kelly Gruber 07	.03	.01
☐ 195	Bobby Bonilla.................20	.09	.03
☐ 196	Wallace Johnson.............04	.02	.01
☐ 197	Dave Stieb.....................07	.03	.01
☐ 198	Pat Borders...................30	.14	.04
☐ 199	Rafael Palmeiro..............20	.09	.03
☐ 200	Dwight Gooden................12	.05	.02
☐ 201	Pete Incaviglia...............04	.02	.01
☐ 202	Chris James...................04	.02	.01
☐ 203	Marvell Wynne 04	.02	.01
☐ 204	Pat Sheridan..................04	.02	.01
☐ 205	Don Baylor.....................07	.03	.01
☐ 206	Paul O'Neill...................07	.03	.01
☐ 207	Pete Smith.....................07	.03	.01
☐ 208	Mark McLemore 04	.02	.01
☐ 209	Henry Cotto 04	.02	.01
☐ 210	Kirk Gibson....................07	.03	.01
☐ 211	Claudell Washington........04	.02	.01
☐ 212	Randy Bush....................04	.02	.01
☐ 213	Joe Carter 25	.11	.03
☐ 214	Bill Buckner...................07	.03	.01
☐ 215	Bert Blyleven UER 07	.03	.01
	(Wrong birth year)		
☐ 216	Brett Butler 07	.03	.01
☐ 217	Lee Mazzilli...................04	.02	.01
☐ 218	Spike Owen 04	.02	.01
☐ 219	Bill Swift.......................07	.03	.01
☐ 220	Tim Wallach 07	.03	.01
☐ 221	David Cone 15	.07	.02

332 / 1989 Score

☐	222	Don Carman	04	.02	.01	☐ 274 Mike Moore	04	.02	.01

☐	222	Don Carman	.04	.02	.01
☐	223	Rich Gossage	.07	.03	.01
☐	224	Bob Walk	.04	.02	.01
☐	225	Dave Righetti	.04	.02	.01
☐	226	Kevin Bass	.04	.02	.01
☐	227	Kevin Gross	.04	.02	.01
☐	228	Tim Burke	.04	.02	.01
☐	229	Rick Mahler	.04	.02	.01
☐	230	Lou Whitaker UER	.07	.03	.01
		(252 games in '85, should be 152)			
☐	231	Luis Alicea	.10	.05	.01
☐	232	Roberto Alomar	.75	.35	.09
☐	233	Bob Boone	.07	.03	.01
☐	234	Dickie Thon	.04	.02	.01
☐	235	Shawon Dunston	.07	.03	.01
☐	236	Pete Stanicek	.04	.02	.01
☐	237	Craig Biggio	.40	.18	.05
		(Inconsistent design, portrait on front)			
☐	238	Dennis Boyd	.04	.02	.01
☐	239	Tom Candiotti	.04	.02	.01
☐	240	Gary Carter	.07	.03	.01
☐	241	Mike Stanley	.04	.02	.01
☐	242	Ken Phelps	.04	.02	.01
☐	243	Chris Bosio	.04	.02	.01
☐	244	Les Straker	.04	.02	.01
☐	245	Dave Smith	.04	.02	.01
☐	246	John Candelaria	.04	.02	.01
☐	247	Joe Orsulak	.04	.02	.01
☐	248	Storm Davis	.04	.02	.01
☐	249	Floyd Bannister UER	.04	.02	.01
		(ML Batting Record)			
☐	250	Jack Morris	.12	.05	.02
☐	251	Bret Saberhagen	.07	.03	.01
☐	252	Tom Niedenfuer	.04	.02	.01
☐	253	Neal Heaton	.04	.02	.01
☐	254	Eric Show	.04	.02	.01
☐	255	Juan Samuel	.04	.02	.01
☐	256	Dale Sveum	.04	.02	.01
☐	257	Jim Gott	.04	.02	.01
☐	258	Scott Garrelts	.04	.02	.01
☐	259	Larry McWilliams	.04	.02	.01
☐	260	Steve Bedrosian	.04	.02	.01
☐	261	Jack Howell	.04	.02	.01
☐	262	Jay Tibbs	.04	.02	.01
☐	263	Jamie Moyer	.04	.02	.01
☐	264	Doug Sisk	.04	.02	.01
☐	265	Todd Worrell	.07	.03	.01
☐	266	John Farrell	.04	.02	.01
☐	267	Dave Collins	.04	.02	.01
☐	268	Sid Fernandez	.07	.03	.01
☐	269	Tom Brookens	.04	.02	.01
☐	270	Shane Mack	.07	.03	.01
☐	271	Paul Kilgus	.04	.02	.01
☐	272	Chuck Crim	.04	.02	.01
☐	273	Bob Knepper	.04	.02	.01
☐	274	Mike Moore	.04	.02	.01
☐	275	Guillermo Hernandez	.04	.02	.01
☐	276	Dennis Eckersley	.12	.05	.02
☐	277	Graig Nettles	.07	.03	.01
☐	278	Rich Dotson	.04	.02	.01
☐	279	Larry Herndon	.04	.02	.01
☐	280	Gene Larkin	.04	.02	.01
☐	281	Roger McDowell	.04	.02	.01
☐	282	Greg Swindell	.07	.03	.01
☐	283	Juan Agosto	.04	.02	.01
☐	284	Jeff M. Robinson	.04	.02	.01
☐	285	Mike Dunne	.04	.02	.01
☐	286	Greg Mathews	.04	.02	.01
☐	287	Kent Tekulve	.04	.02	.01
☐	288	Jerry Mumphrey	.04	.02	.01
☐	289	Jack McDowell	.40	.18	.05
☐	290	Frank Viola	.07	.03	.01
☐	291	Mark Gubicza	.04	.02	.01
☐	292	Dave Schmidt	.04	.02	.01
☐	293	Mike Henneman	.07	.03	.01
☐	294	Jimmy Jones	.04	.02	.01
☐	295	Charlie Hough	.04	.02	.01
☐	296	Rafael Santana	.04	.02	.01
☐	297	Chris Speier	.04	.02	.01
☐	298	Mike Witt	.04	.02	.01
☐	299	Pascual Perez	.04	.02	.01
☐	300	Nolan Ryan	.60	.25	.08
☐	301	Mitch Williams	.07	.03	.01
☐	302	Mookie Wilson	.07	.03	.01
☐	303	Mackey Sasser	.04	.02	.01
☐	304	John Cerutti	.04	.02	.01
☐	305	Jeff Reardon	.07	.03	.01
☐	306	Randy Myers UER	.07	.03	.01
		(6 hits in '87, should be 61)			
☐	307	Greg Brock	.04	.02	.01
☐	308	Bob Welch	.07	.03	.01
☐	309	Jeff D. Robinson	.04	.02	.01
☐	310	Harold Reynolds	.04	.02	.01
☐	311	Jim Walewander	.04	.02	.01
☐	312	Dave Magadan	.07	.03	.01
☐	313	Jim Gantner	.04	.02	.01
☐	314	Walt Terrell	.04	.02	.01
☐	315	Wally Backman	.04	.02	.01
☐	316	Luis Salazar	.04	.02	.01
☐	317	Rick Rhoden	.04	.02	.01
☐	318	Tom Henke	.07	.03	.01
☐	319	Mike Macfarlane	.15	.07	.02
☐	320	Dan Plesac	.04	.02	.01
☐	321	Calvin Schiraldi	.04	.02	.01
☐	322	Stan Javier	.04	.02	.01
☐	323	Devon White	.07	.03	.01
☐	324	Scott Bradley	.04	.02	.01
☐	325	Bruce Hurst	.07	.03	.01
☐	326	Manny Lee	.04	.02	.01
☐	327	Rick Aguilera	.07	.03	.01
☐	328	Bruce Ruffin	.04	.02	.01

☐					☐				
329	Ed Whitson	.04	.02	.01	381	Keith Atherton	.04	.02	.01
330	Bo Jackson	.20	.09	.03	382	Kent Hrbek	.07	.03	.01
331	Ivan Calderon	.04	.02	.01	383	Bob Stanley	.04	.02	.01
332	Mickey Hatcher	.04	.02	.01	384	Dave LaPoint	.04	.02	.01
333	Barry Jones	.04	.02	.01	385	Rance Mulliniks	.04	.02	.01
334	Ron Hassey	.04	.02	.01	386	Melido Perez	.15	.07	.02
335	Bill Wegman	.04	.02	.01	387	Doug Jones	.07	.03	.01
336	Damon Berryhill	.04	.02	.01	388	Steve Lyons	.04	.02	.01
337	Steve Ontiveros	.04	.02	.01	389	Alejandro Pena	.04	.02	.01
338	Dan Pasqua	.04	.02	.01	390	Frank White	.04	.02	.01
339	Bill Pecota	.04	.02	.01	391	Pat Tabler	.04	.02	.01
340	Greg Cadaret	.04	.02	.01	392	Eric Plunk	.04	.02	.01
341	Scott Bankhead	.04	.02	.01	393	Mike Maddux	.04	.02	.01
342	Ron Guidry	.07	.03	.01	394	Allan Anderson	.04	.02	.01
343	Danny Heep	.04	.02	.01	395	Bob Brenly	.04	.02	.01
344	Bob Brower	.04	.02	.01	396	Rick Cerone	.04	.02	.01
345	Rich Gedman	.04	.02	.01	397	Scott Terry	.04	.02	.01
346	Nelson Santovenia	.04	.02	.01	398	Mike Jackson	.04	.02	.01
347	George Bell	.10	.05	.01	399	Bobby Thigpen UER	.04	.02	.01
348	Ted Power	.04	.02	.01		(Bio says 37 saves in			
349	Mark Grant	.04	.02	.01		'88, should be 34)			
350A	Roger Clemens ERR	3.50	1.55	.45	400	Don Sutton	.10	.05	.01
	(778 career wins)				401	Cecil Espy	.04	.02	.01
350B	Roger Clemens COR	.40	.18	.05	402	Junior Ortiz	.04	.02	.01
	(78 career wins)				403	Mike Smithson	.04	.02	.01
351	Bill Long	.04	.02	.01	404	Bud Black	.04	.02	.01
352	Jay Bell	.07	.03	.01	405	Tom Foley	.04	.02	.01
353	Steve Balboni	.04	.02	.01	406	Andres Thomas	.04	.02	.01
354	Bob Kipper	.04	.02	.01	407	Rick Sutcliffe	.07	.03	.01
355	Steve Jeltz	.04	.02	.01	408	Brian Harper	.07	.03	.01
356	Jesse Orosco	.04	.02	.01	409	John Smiley	.07	.03	.01
357	Bob Dernier	.04	.02	.01	410	Juan Nieves	.04	.02	.01
358	Mickey Tettleton	.07	.03	.01	411	Shawn Abner	.04	.02	.01
359	Duane Ward	.07	.03	.01	412	Wes Gardner	.04	.02	.01
360	Darrin Jackson	.15	.07	.02	413	Darren Daulton	.07	.03	.01
361	Rey Quinones	.04	.02	.01	414	Juan Berenguer	.04	.02	.01
362	Mark Grace	.40	.18	.05	415	Charles Hudson	.04	.02	.01
363	Steve Lake	.04	.02	.01	416	Rick Honeycutt	.04	.02	.01
364	Pat Perry	.04	.02	.01	417	Greg Booker	.04	.02	.01
365	Terry Steinbach	.07	.03	.01	418	Tim Belcher	.07	.03	.01
366	Alan Ashby	.04	.02	.01	419	Don August	.04	.02	.01
367	Jeff Montgomery	.07	.03	.01	420	Dale Mohorcic	.04	.02	.01
368	Steve Buechele	.04	.02	.01	421	Steve Lombardozzi	.04	.02	.01
369	Chris Brown	.04	.02	.01	422	Atlee Hammaker	.04	.02	.01
370	Orel Hershiser	.07	.03	.01	423	Jerry Don Gleaton	.04	.02	.01
371	Todd Benzinger	.04	.02	.01	424	Scott Bailes	.04	.02	.01
372	Ron Gant	.40	.18	.05	425	Bruce Sutter	.07	.03	.01
373	Paul Assenmacher	.04	.02	.01	426	Randy Ready	.04	.02	.01
374	Joey Meyer	.04	.02	.01	427	Jerry Reed	.04	.02	.01
375	Neil Allen	.04	.02	.01	428	Bryn Smith	.04	.02	.01
376	Mike Davis	.04	.02	.01	429	Tim Leary	.04	.02	.01
377	Jeff Parrett	.04	.02	.01	430	Mark Clear	.04	.02	.01
378	Jay Howell	.04	.02	.01	431	Terry Leach	.04	.02	.01
379	Rafael Belliard	.04	.02	.01	432	John Moses	.04	.02	.01
380	Luis Polonia UER	.07	.03	.01	433	Ozzie Guillen	.04	.02	.01
	(2 triples in '87,				434	Gene Nelson	.04	.02	.01
	should be 10)				435	Gary Ward	.04	.02	.01

☐ 436	Luis Aguayo	.04	.02	.01
☐ 437	Fernando Valenzuela	.07	.03	.01
☐ 438	Jeff Russell UER	.04	.02	.01
	(Saves total does			
	not add up correctly)			
☐ 439	Cecilio Guante	.04	.02	.01
☐ 440	Don Robinson	.04	.02	.01
☐ 441	Rick Anderson	.04	.02	.01
☐ 442	Tom Glavine	.50	.23	.06
☐ 443	Daryl Boston	.04	.02	.01
☐ 444	Joe Price	.04	.02	.01
☐ 445	Stewart Cliburn	.04	.02	.01
☐ 446	Manny Trillo	.04	.02	.01
☐ 447	Joel Skinner	.04	.02	.01
☐ 448	Charlie Puleo	.04	.02	.01
☐ 449	Carlton Fisk	.15	.07	.02
☐ 450	Will Clark	.40	.18	.05
☐ 451	Otis Nixon	.07	.03	.01
☐ 452	Rick Schu	.04	.02	.01
☐ 453	Todd Stottlemyre UER	.10	.05	.01
	(ML Batting Record)			
☐ 454	Tim Birtsas	.04	.02	.01
☐ 455	Dave Gallagher	.04	.02	.01
☐ 456	Barry Lyons	.04	.02	.01
☐ 457	Fred Manrique	.04	.02	.01
☐ 458	Ernest Riles	.04	.02	.01
☐ 459	Doug Jennings	.04	.02	.01
☐ 460	Joe Magrane	.04	.02	.01
☐ 461	Jamie Quirk	.04	.02	.01
☐ 462	Jack Armstrong	.12	.05	.02
☐ 463	Bobby Witt	.07	.03	.01
☐ 464	Keith A. Miller	.04	.02	.01
☐ 465	Todd Burns	.04	.02	.01
☐ 466	John Dopson	.04	.02	.01
☐ 467	Rich Yett	.04	.02	.01
☐ 468	Craig Reynolds	.04	.02	.01
☐ 469	Dave Bergman	.04	.02	.01
☐ 470	Rex Hudler	.04	.02	.01
☐ 471	Eric King	.04	.02	.01
☐ 472	Joaquin Andujar	.04	.02	.01
☐ 473	Sil Campusano	.04	.02	.01
☐ 474	Terry Mulholland	.10	.05	.01
☐ 475	Mike Flanagan	.04	.02	.01
☐ 476	Greg A. Harris	.04	.02	.01
☐ 477	Tommy John	.07	.03	.01
☐ 478	Dave Anderson	.04	.02	.01
☐ 479	Fred Toliver	.04	.02	.01
☐ 480	Jimmy Key	.07	.03	.01
☐ 481	Donell Nixon	.04	.02	.01
☐ 482	Mark Portugal	.04	.02	.01
☐ 483	Tom Pagnozzi	.04	.02	.01
☐ 484	Jeff Kunkel	.04	.02	.01
☐ 485	Frank Williams	.04	.02	.01
☐ 486	Jody Reed	.04	.02	.01
☐ 487	Roberto Kelly	.15	.07	.02
☐ 488	Shawn Hillegas UER	.04	.02	.01
	(165 innings in '87,			
	should be 165.2)			
☐ 489	Jerry Reuss	.04	.02	.01
☐ 490	Mark Davis	.04	.02	.01
☐ 491	Jeff Sellers	.04	.02	.01
☐ 492	Zane Smith	.04	.02	.01
☐ 493	Al Newman	.04	.02	.01
☐ 494	Mike Young	.04	.02	.01
☐ 495	Larry Parrish	.04	.02	.01
☐ 496	Herm Winningham	.04	.02	.01
☐ 497	Carmen Castillo	.04	.02	.01
☐ 498	Joe Hesketh	.04	.02	.01
☐ 499	Darrell Miller	.04	.02	.01
☐ 500	Mike LaCoss	.04	.02	.01
☐ 501	Charlie Lea	.04	.02	.01
☐ 502	Bruce Benedict	.04	.02	.01
☐ 503	Chuck Finley	.07	.03	.01
☐ 504	Brad Wellman	.04	.02	.01
☐ 505	Tim Crews	.04	.02	.01
☐ 506	Ken Gerhart	.04	.02	.01
☐ 507A	Brian Holton ERR	.04	.02	.01
	(Born 1/25/65 Denver,			
	should be 11/29/59			
	in McKeesport)			
☐ 507B	Brian Holton COR	3.00	1.35	.40
☐ 508	Dennis Lamp	.04	.02	.01
☐ 509	Bobby Meacham UER	.04	.02	.01
	('84 games 099)			
☐ 510	Tracy Jones	.04	.02	.01
☐ 511	Mike R. Fitzgerald	.04	.02	.01
	Montreal Expos			
☐ 512	Jeff Bittiger	.04	.02	.01
☐ 513	Tim Flannery	.04	.02	.01
☐ 514	Ray Hayward	.04	.02	.01
☐ 515	Dave Leiper	.04	.02	.01
☐ 516	Rod Scurry	.04	.02	.01
☐ 517	Carmelo Martinez	.04	.02	.01
☐ 518	Curtis Wilkerson	.04	.02	.01
☐ 519	Stan Jefferson	.04	.02	.01
☐ 520	Dan Quisenberry	.07	.03	.01
☐ 521	Lloyd McClendon	.04	.02	.01
☐ 522	Steve Trout	.04	.02	.01
☐ 523	Larry Andersen	.04	.02	.01
☐ 524	Don Aase	.04	.02	.01
☐ 525	Bob Forsch	.04	.02	.01
☐ 526	Geno Petralli	.04	.02	.01
☐ 527	Angel Salazar	.04	.02	.01
☐ 528	Mike Schooler	.10	.05	.01
☐ 529	Jose Oquendo	.04	.02	.01
☐ 530	Jay Buhner	.12	.05	.02
☐ 531	Tom Bolton	.04	.02	.01
☐ 532	Al Nipper	.04	.02	.01
☐ 533	Dave Henderson	.07	.03	.01
☐ 534	John Costello	.04	.02	.01
☐ 535	Donnie Moore	.04	.02	.01
☐ 536	Mike Laga	.04	.02	.01
☐ 537	Mike Gallego	.04	.02	.01
☐ 538	Jim Clancy	.04	.02	.01

☐ 539	Joel Youngblood	.04	.02	.01
☐ 540	Rick Leach	.04	.02	.01
☐ 541	Kevin Romine	.04	.02	.01
☐ 542	Mark Salas	.04	.02	.01
☐ 543	Greg Minton	.04	.02	.01
☐ 544	Dave Palmer	.04	.02	.01
☐ 545	Dwayne Murphy UER	.04	.02	.01
	(Game-sinning)			
☐ 546	Jim Deshaies	.04	.02	.01
☐ 547	Don Gordon	.04	.02	.01
☐ 548	Ricky Jordan	.10	.05	.01
☐ 549	Mike Boddicker	.04	.02	.01
☐ 550	Mike Scott	.04	.02	.01
☐ 551	Jeff Ballard	.04	.02	.01
☐ 552A	Jose Rijo ERR	.60	.25	.08
	(Uniform listed as 27 on back)			
☐ 552B	Jose Rijo COR	.15	.07	.02
	(Uniform listed as 24 on back)			
☐ 553	Danny Darwin	.04	.02	.01
☐ 554	Tom Browning	.07	.03	.01
☐ 555	Danny Jackson	.04	.02	.01
☐ 556	Rick Dempsey	.04	.02	.01
☐ 557	Jeffrey Leonard	.04	.02	.01
☐ 558	Jeff Musselman	.04	.02	.01
☐ 559	Ron Robinson	.04	.02	.01
☐ 560	John Tudor	.04	.02	.01
☐ 561	Don Slaught UER	.04	.02	.01
	(237 games in 1987)			
☐ 562	Dennis Rasmussen	.04	.02	.01
☐ 563	Brady Anderson	.60	.25	.08
☐ 564	Pedro Guerrero	.07	.03	.01
☐ 565	Paul Molitor	.10	.05	.01
☐ 566	Terry Clark	.04	.02	.01
☐ 567	Terry Puhl	.04	.02	.01
☐ 568	Mike Campbell	.04	.02	.01
☐ 569	Paul Mirabella	.04	.02	.01
☐ 570	Jeff Hamilton	.04	.02	.01
☐ 571	Oswald Peraza	.04	.02	.01
☐ 572	Bob McClure	.04	.02	.01
☐ 573	Jose Bautista	.04	.02	.01
☐ 574	Alex Trevino	.04	.02	.01
☐ 575	John Franco	.07	.03	.01
☐ 576	Mark Parent	.04	.02	.01
☐ 577	Nelson Liriano	.04	.02	.01
☐ 578	Steve Shields	.04	.02	.01
☐ 579	Odell Jones	.04	.02	.01
☐ 580	Al Leiter	.04	.02	.01
☐ 581	Dave Stapleton	.04	.02	.01
☐ 582	World Series '88	.07	.03	.01
	Orel Hershiser Jose Canseco Kirk Gibson Dave Stewart			
☐ 583	Donnie Hill	.04	.02	.01
☐ 584	Chuck Jackson	.04	.02	.01
☐ 585	Rene Gonzales	.04	.02	.01
☐ 586	Tracy Woodson	.04	.02	.01
☐ 587	Jim Adduci	.04	.02	.01
☐ 588	Mario Soto	.04	.02	.01
☐ 589	Jeff Blauser	.07	.03	.01
☐ 590	Jim Traber	.04	.02	.01
☐ 591	Jon Perlman	.04	.02	.01
☐ 592	Mark Williamson	.04	.02	.01
☐ 593	Dave Meads	.04	.02	.01
☐ 594	Jim Eisenreich	.04	.02	.01
☐ 595A	Paul Gibson P1	1.00	.45	.13
☐ 595B	Paul Gibson P2	.04	.02	.01
	(Airbrushed leg on player in background)			
☐ 596	Mike Birkbeck	.04	.02	.01
☐ 597	Terry Francona	.04	.02	.01
☐ 598	Paul Zuvella	.04	.02	.01
☐ 599	Franklin Stubbs	.04	.02	.01
☐ 600	Gregg Jefferies	.20	.09	.03
☐ 601	John Cangelosi	.04	.02	.01
☐ 602	Mike Sharperson	.04	.02	.01
☐ 603	Mike Diaz	.04	.02	.01
☐ 604	Gary Varsho	.04	.02	.01
☐ 605	Terry Blocker	.04	.02	.01
☐ 606	Charlie O'Brien	.04	.02	.01
☐ 607	Jim Eppard	.04	.02	.01
☐ 608	John Davis	.04	.02	.01
☐ 609	Ken Griffey Sr.	.07	.03	.01
☐ 610	Buddy Bell	.07	.03	.01
☐ 611	Ted Simmons UER	.07	.03	.01
	('78 stats Cardinal)			
☐ 612	Matt Williams	.15	.07	.02
☐ 613	Danny Cox	.04	.02	.01
☐ 614	Al Pedrique	.04	.02	.01
☐ 615	Ron Oester	.04	.02	.01
☐ 616	John Smoltz	.60	.25	.08
☐ 617	Bob Melvin	.04	.02	.01
☐ 618	Rob Dibble	.20	.09	.03
☐ 619	Kirt Manwaring	.04	.02	.01
☐ 620	Felix Fermin	.04	.02	.01
☐ 621	Doug Dascenzo	.05	.02	.01
☐ 622	Bill Brennan	.05	.02	.01
☐ 623	Carlos Quintana	.10	.05	.01
☐ 624	Mike Harkey UER	.12	.05	.02
	(13 and 31 walks in '88, should be 35 and 33)			
☐ 625	Gary Sheffield	2.00	.90	.25
☐ 626	Tom Prince	.05	.02	.01
☐ 627	Steve Searcy	.05	.02	.01
☐ 628	Charlie Hayes	.25	.11	.03
	(Listed as outfielder)			
☐ 629	Felix Jose UER	.75	.35	.09
	(Modesto misspelled as Modesta)			
☐ 630	Sandy Alomar Jr.	.25	.11	.03
	(Inconsistent design,			

portrait on front)

			MT	EX-MT	VG
☐	631	Derek Lilliquist................10	.05	.01
☐	632	Geronimo Berroa 05	.02	.01
☐	633	Luis Medina 05	.02	.01
☐	634	Tom Gordon UER............10	.05	.01
		(Height 6'0")		
☐	635	Ramon Martinez 50	.23	.06
☐	636	Craig Worthington..........05	.02	.01
☐	637	Edgar Martinez 40	.18	.05
☐	638	Chad Kreuter..................05	.02	.01
☐	639	Ron Jones......................05	.02	.01
☐	640	Van Snider......................05	.02	.01
☐	641	Lance Blankenship.........10	.05	.01
☐	642	Dwight Smith UER 10	.05	.01
		(10 HR's in '87, should be 18)		
☐	643	Cameron Drew 05	.02	.01
☐	644	Jerald Clark...................15	.07	.02
☐	645	Randy Johnson...............35	.16	.04
☐	646	Norm Charlton 20	.09	.03
☐	647	Todd Frohwirth UER 05	.02	.01
		(Southpaw on back)		
☐	648	Luis De Los Santos.........05	.02	.01
☐	649	Tim Jones.......................05	.02	.01
☐	650	Dave West UER 10	.05	.01
		(ML hits 3, should be 6)		
☐	651	Bob Milacki 10	.05	.01
☐	652	Wrigley Field HL.............05	.02	.01
		(Let There Be Lights)		
☐	653	Orel Hershiser HL 08	.04	.01
		(The Streak)		
☐	654A	Wade Boggs HL ERR.3.00	1.35	.40
		(Wade Whacks 'Em) ("seaason" on back)		
☐	654B	Wade Boggs HL COR.......12	.05	.02
		(Wade Whacks 'Em)		
☐	655	Jose Canseco HL 20	.09	.03
		(One of a Kind)		
☐	656	Doug Jones HL 05	.02	.01
		(Doug Sets Saves)		
☐	657	Rickey Henderson HL 12	.05	.02
		(Rickey Rocks 'Em)		
☐	658	Tom Browning HL............05	.02	.01
		(Tom Perfect Pitches)		
☐	659	Mike Greenwell HL..........08	.04	.01
		(Greenwell Gamers)		
☐	660	Boston Red Sox HL..........05	.02	.01
		(Joe Morgan MG, Sox Sock 'Em)		

1989 Score Rookie/Traded

The 1989 Score Rookie and Traded set contains 110 standard-size (2 1/2" by 3 1/2") cards. The fronts have coral green borders with pink diamonds at the bottom. The vertically oriented backs have color facial shots, career stats, and biographical information. Cards 1-80 feature traded players; cards 81-110 feature 1989 rookies. The set was distributed in a blue box with 10 Magic Motion trivia cards. The key Rookie Cards in this set are Jim Abbott, Joey (Albert) Belle, Junior Felix, Ken Griffey Jr., and Jerome Walton.

		MT	EX-MT	VG
COMPLETE SET (110) 10.00			4.50	1.25
COMMON PLAYER (1T-80T)....05			.02	.01
COMMON PLAYER (81T-110T)....05			.02	.01

			MT	EX-MT	VG
☐	1T	Rafael Palmeiro...............20	.09	.03
☐	2T	Nolan Ryan 1.50	.65	.19
☐	3T	Jack Clark.......................08	.04	.01
☐	4T	Dave LaPoint...................05	.02	.01
☐	5T	Mike Moore.....................05	.02	.01
☐	6T	Pete O'Brien....................05	.02	.01
☐	7T	Jeffrey Leonard 05	.02	.01
☐	8T	Rob Murphy.....................05	.02	.01
☐	9T	Tom Herr........................05	.02	.01
☐	10T	Claudell Washington.......05	.02	.01
☐	11T	Mike Pagliarulo...............05	.02	.01
☐	12T	Steve Lake......................05	.02	.01
☐	13T	Spike Owen.....................05	.02	.01
☐	14T	Andy Hawkins..................05	.02	.01
☐	15T	Todd Benzinger...............05	.02	.01
☐	16T	Mookie Wilson.................08	.04	.01
☐	17T	Bert Blyleven...................08	.04	.01

☐ 18T	Jeff Treadway	.08	.04	.01
☐ 19T	Bruce Hurst	.08	.04	.01
☐ 20T	Steve Sax	.08	.04	.01
☐ 21T	Juan Samuel	.05	.02	.01
☐ 22T	Jesse Barfield	.05	.02	.01
☐ 23T	Carmen Castillo	.05	.02	.01
☐ 24T	Terry Leach	.05	.02	.01
☐ 25T	Mark Langston	.08	.04	.01
☐ 26T	Eric King	.05	.02	.01
☐ 27T	Steve Balboni	.05	.02	.01
☐ 28T	Len Dykstra	.08	.04	.01
☐ 29T	Keith Moreland	.05	.02	.01
☐ 30T	Terry Kennedy	.05	.02	.01
☐ 31T	Eddie Murray	.15	.07	.02
☐ 32T	Mitch Williams	.08	.04	.01
☐ 33T	Jeff Parrett	.05	.02	.01
☐ 34T	Wally Backman	.05	.02	.01
☐ 35T	Julio Franco	.08	.04	.01
☐ 36T	Lance Parrish	.08	.04	.01
☐ 37T	Nick Esasky	.05	.02	.01
☐ 38T	Luis Polonia	.08	.04	.01
☐ 39T	Kevin Gross	.05	.02	.01
☐ 40T	John Dopson	.05	.02	.01
☐ 41T	Willie Randolph	.08	.04	.01
☐ 42T	Jim Clancy	.05	.02	.01
☐ 43T	Tracy Jones	.05	.02	.01
☐ 44T	Phil Bradley	.05	.02	.01
☐ 45T	Milt Thompson	.05	.02	.01
☐ 46T	Chris James	.05	.02	.01
☐ 47T	Scott Fletcher	.05	.02	.01
☐ 48T	Kal Daniels	.05	.02	.01
☐ 49T	Steve Bedrosian	.05	.02	.01
☐ 50T	Rickey Henderson	.25	.11	.03
☐ 51T	Dion James	.05	.02	.01
☐ 52T	Tim Leary	.05	.02	.01
☐ 53T	Roger McDowell	.05	.02	.01
☐ 54T	Mel Hall	.05	.02	.01
☐ 55T	Dickie Thon	.05	.02	.01
☐ 56T	Zane Smith	.05	.02	.01
☐ 57T	Danny Heep	.05	.02	.01
☐ 58T	Bob McClure	.05	.02	.01
☐ 59T	Brian Holton	.05	.02	.01
☐ 60T	Randy Ready	.05	.02	.01
☐ 61T	Bob Melvin	.05	.02	.01
☐ 62T	Harold Baines	.08	.04	.01
☐ 63T	Lance McCullers	.05	.02	.01
☐ 64T	Jody Davis	.05	.02	.01
☐ 65T	Darrell Evans	.08	.04	.01
☐ 66T	Joel Youngblood	.05	.02	.01
☐ 67T	Frank Viola	.08	.04	.01
☐ 68T	Mike Aldrete	.05	.02	.01
☐ 69T	Greg Cadaret	.05	.02	.01
☐ 70T	John Kruk	.08	.04	.01
☐ 71T	Pat Sheridan	.05	.02	.01
☐ 72T	Oddibe McDowell	.05	.02	.01
☐ 73T	Tom Brookens	.05	.02	.01
☐ 74T	Bob Boone	.08	.04	.01

☐ 75T	Walt Terrell	.05	.02	.01
☐ 76T	Joel Skinner	.05	.02	.01
☐ 77T	Randy Johnson	.15	.07	.02
☐ 78T	Felix Fermin	.05	.02	.01
☐ 79T	Rick Mahler	.05	.02	.01
☐ 80T	Richard Dotson	.05	.02	.01
☐ 81T	Cris Carpenter	.10	.05	.01
☐ 82T	Bill Spiers	.10	.05	.01
☐ 83T	Junior Felix	.25	.11	.03
☐ 84T	Joe Girardi	.15	.07	.02
☐ 85T	Jerome Walton	.10	.05	.01
☐ 86T	Greg Litton	.05	.02	.01
☐ 87T	Greg W.Harris	.10	.05	.01
☐ 88T	Jim Abbott	1.25	.55	.16
☐ 89T	Kevin Brown	.30	.14	.04
☐ 90T	John Wetteland	.40	.18	.05
☐ 91T	Gary Wayne	.05	.02	.01
☐ 92T	Rich Monteleone	.05	.02	.01
☐ 93T	Bob Geren	.05	.02	.01
☐ 94T	Clay Parker	.05	.02	.01
☐ 95T	Steve Finley	.40	.18	.05
☐ 96T	Gregg Olson	.50	.23	.06
☐ 97T	Ken Patterson	.05	.02	.01
☐ 98T	Ken Hill	.40	.18	.05
☐ 99T	Scott Scudder	.12	.05	.02
☐ 100T	Ken Griffey Jr.	5.00	2.30	.60
☐ 101T	Jeff Brantley	.10	.05	.01
☐ 102T	Donn Pall	.05	.02	.01
☐ 103T	Carlos Martinez	.10	.05	.01
☐ 104T	Joe Oliver	.20	.09	.03
☐ 105T	Omar Vizquel	.15	.07	.02
☐ 106T	Joey Belle	2.00	.90	.25
☐ 107T	Kenny Rogers	.08	.04	.01
☐ 108T	Mark Carreon	.05	.02	.01
☐ 109T	Rolando Roomes	.05	.02	.01
☐ 110T	Pete Harnisch	.25	.11	.03

1990 Score

The 1990 Score set contains 704 standard-size (2 1/2" by 3 1/2") cards. The front borders are red, blue, green or white. The vertically oriented backs are white with borders that match the fronts, and feature color mugshots. Cards numbered 661-682 contain the first round draft picks subset noted as DC for "draft choice" in the checklist below. Cards numbered 683-695 contain the "Dream Team" subset noted by DT in the checklist below. The key Rookie Cards in this set are Delino DeShields, Cal Eldred, Juan Gonzalez, Dave Justice,

Chuck Knoblauch, Kevin Maas, Ben McDonald, John Olerud, Dean Palmer, Frank Thomas, Mo Vaughn, and Larry Walker. A ten-card set of Dream Team Rookies was inserted into each hobby factory set, but was not included in retail factory sets. These cards carry a B prefix on the card number and include a player at each position plus a commemorative card honoring the late Baseball Commissioner A. Bartlett Giamatti.

	MT	EX-MT	VG
COMPLETE SET (704)	20.00	9.00	2.50
COMPLETE FACT.SET (704)	20.00	9.00	2.50
COMPLETE FACT.SET (714)	30.00	13.50	3.80
COMMON PLAYER (1-704)	.04	.02	.01
COMMON PLAYER (B1-B10)	.25	.11	.03

		MT	EX-MT	VG
☐	1 Don Mattingly	.20	.09	.03
☐	2 Cal Ripken	.40	.18	.05
☐	3 Dwight Evans	.07	.03	.01
☐	4 Barry Bonds	.30	.14	.04
☐	5 Kevin McReynolds	.07	.03	.01
☐	6 Ozzie Guillen	.04	.02	.01
☐	7 Terry Kennedy	.04	.02	.01
☐	8 Bryan Harvey	.07	.03	.01
☐	9 Alan Trammell	.07	.03	.01
☐	10 Cory Snyder	.04	.02	.01
☐	11 Jody Reed	.04	.02	.01
☐	12 Roberto Alomar	.40	.18	.05
☐	13 Pedro Guerrero	.07	.03	.01
☐	14 Gary Redus	.04	.02	.01
☐	15 Marty Barrett	.04	.02	.01
☐	16 Ricky Jordan	.04	.02	.01
☐	17 Joe Magrane	.04	.02	.01
☐	18 Sid Fernandez	.07	.03	.01
☐	19 Richard Dotson	.04	.02	.01
☐	20 Jack Clark	.07	.03	.01
☐	21 Bob Walk	.04	.02	.01
☐	22 Ron Karkovice	.04	.02	.01
☐	23 Lenny Harris	.04	.02	.01
☐	24 Phil Bradley	.04	.02	.01
☐	25 Andres Galarraga	.04	.02	.01
☐	26 Brian Downing	.04	.02	.01
☐	27 Dave Martinez	.07	.03	.01
☐	28 Eric King	.04	.02	.01
☐	29 Barry Lyons	.04	.02	.01
☐	30 Dave Schmidt	.04	.02	.01
☐	31 Mike Boddicker	.04	.02	.01
☐	32 Tom Foley	.04	.02	.01
☐	33 Brady Anderson	.12	.05	.02
☐	34 Jim Presley	.04	.02	.01
☐	35 Lance Parrish	.07	.03	.01
☐	36 Von Hayes	.04	.02	.01
☐	37 Lee Smith	.07	.03	.01
☐	38 Herm Winningham	.04	.02	.01
☐	39 Alejandro Pena	.04	.02	.01
☐	40 Mike Scott	.04	.02	.01
☐	41 Joe Orsulak	.04	.02	.01
☐	42 Rafael Ramirez	.04	.02	.01
☐	43 Gerald Young	.04	.02	.01
☐	44 Dick Schofield	.04	.02	.01
☐	45 Dave Smith	.04	.02	.01
☐	46 Dave Magadan	.07	.03	.01
☐	47 Dennis Martinez	.07	.03	.01
☐	48 Greg Minton	.04	.02	.01
☐	49 Milt Thompson	.04	.02	.01
☐	50 Orel Hershiser	.07	.03	.01
☐	51 Bip Roberts	.07	.03	.01
☐	52 Jerry Browne	.04	.02	.01
☐	53 Bob Ojeda	.04	.02	.01
☐	54 Fernando Valenzuela	.07	.03	.01
☐	55 Matt Nokes	.04	.02	.01
☐	56 Brook Jacoby	.04	.02	.01
☐	57 Frank Tanana	.04	.02	.01
☐	58 Scott Fletcher	.04	.02	.01
☐	59 Ron Oester	.04	.02	.01
☐	60 Bob Boone	.07	.03	.01
☐	61 Dan Gladden	.04	.02	.01
☐	62 Darnell Coles	.04	.02	.01
☐	63 Gregg Olson	.10	.05	.01
☐	64 Todd Burns	.04	.02	.01
☐	65 Todd Benzinger	.04	.02	.01
☐	66 Dale Murphy	.10	.05	.01
☐	67 Mike Flanagan	.04	.02	.01
☐	68 Jose Oquendo	.04	.02	.01
☐	69 Cecil Espy	.04	.02	.01
☐	70 Chris Sabo	.07	.03	.01
☐	71 Shane Rawley	.04	.02	.01
☐	72 Tom Brunansky	.07	.03	.01
☐	73 Vance Law	.04	.02	.01
☐	74 B.J. Surhoff	.04	.02	.01
☐	75 Lou Whitaker	.07	.03	.01
☐	76 Ken Caminiti UER	.07	.03	.01
	(Euclid, Ohio should			
	be Hanford, California)			
☐	77 Nelson Liriano	.04	.02	.01
☐	78 Tommy Gregg	.04	.02	.01
☐	79 Don Slaught	.04	.02	.01

☐	80	Eddie Murray	.10	.05	.01	☐	134	John Morris	.04	.02	.01

☐ 80	Eddie Murray	.10	.05	.01
☐ 81	Joe Boever	.04	.02	.01
☐ 82	Charlie Leibrandt	.04	.02	.01
☐ 83	Jose Lind	.04	.02	.01
☐ 84	Tony Phillips	.04	.02	.01
☐ 85	Mitch Webster	.04	.02	.01
☐ 86	Dan Plesac	.04	.02	.01
☐ 87	Rick Mahler	.04	.02	.01
☐ 88	Steve Lyons	.04	.02	.01
☐ 89	Tony Fernandez	.07	.03	.01
☐ 90	Ryne Sandberg	.35	.16	.04
☐ 91	Nick Esasky	.04	.02	.01
☐ 92	Luis Salazar	.04	.02	.01
☐ 93	Pete Incaviglia	.04	.02	.01
☐ 94	Ivan Calderon	.04	.02	.01
☐ 95	Jeff Treadway	.04	.02	.01
☐ 96	Kurt Stillwell	.04	.02	.01
☐ 97	Gary Sheffield	.50	.23	.06
☐ 98	Jeffrey Leonard	.04	.02	.01
☐ 99	Andres Thomas	.04	.02	.01
☐ 100	Roberto Kelly	.10	.05	.01
☐ 101	Alvaro Espinoza	.04	.02	.01
☐ 102	Greg Gagne	.04	.02	.01
☐ 103	John Farrell	.04	.02	.01
☐ 104	Willie Wilson	.04	.02	.01
☐ 105	Glenn Braggs	.04	.02	.01
☐ 106	Chet Lemon	.04	.02	.01
☐ 107A	Jamie Moyer ERR	.04	.02	.01
	(Scintilating)			
☐ 107B	Jamie Moyer COR	.25	.11	.03
	(Scintillating)			
☐ 108	Chuck Crim	.04	.02	.01
☐ 109	Dave Valle	.04	.02	.01
☐ 110	Walt Weiss	.04	.02	.01
☐ 111	Larry Sheets	.04	.02	.01
☐ 112	Don Robinson	.04	.02	.01
☐ 113	Danny Heep	.04	.02	.01
☐ 114	Carmelo Martinez	.04	.02	.01
☐ 115	Dave Gallagher	.04	.02	.01
☐ 116	Mike LaValliere	.04	.02	.01
☐ 117	Bob McClure	.04	.02	.01
☐ 118	Rene Gonzales	.04	.02	.01
☐ 119	Mark Parent	.04	.02	.01
☐ 120	Wally Joyner	.07	.03	.01
☐ 121	Mark Gubicza	.04	.02	.01
☐ 122	Tony Pena	.04	.02	.01
☐ 123	Carmen Castillo	.04	.02	.01
☐ 124	Howard Johnson	.07	.03	.01
☐ 125	Steve Sax	.07	.03	.01
☐ 126	Tim Belcher	.07	.03	.01
☐ 127	Tim Burke	.04	.02	.01
☐ 128	Al Newman	.04	.02	.01
☐ 129	Dennis Rasmussen	.04	.02	.01
☐ 130	Doug Jones	.07	.03	.01
☐ 131	Fred Lynn	.07	.03	.01
☐ 132	Jeff Hamilton	.04	.02	.01
☐ 133	German Gonzalez	.04	.02	.01
☐ 134	John Morris	.04	.02	.01
☐ 135	Dave Parker	.07	.03	.01
☐ 136	Gary Pettis	.04	.02	.01
☐ 137	Dennis Boyd	.04	.02	.01
☐ 138	Candy Maldonado	.04	.02	.01
☐ 139	Rick Cerone	.04	.02	.01
☐ 140	George Brett	.15	.07	.02
☐ 141	Dave Clark	.04	.02	.01
☐ 142	Dickie Thon	.04	.02	.01
☐ 143	Junior Ortiz	.04	.02	.01
☐ 144	Don August	.04	.02	.01
☐ 145	Gary Gaetti	.04	.02	.01
☐ 146	Kirt Manwaring	.04	.02	.01
☐ 147	Jeff Reed	.04	.02	.01
☐ 148	Jose Alvarez	.04	.02	.01
☐ 149	Mike Schooler	.04	.02	.01
☐ 150	Mark Grace	.20	.09	.03
☐ 151	Geronimo Berroa	.04	.02	.01
☐ 152	Barry Jones	.04	.02	.01
☐ 153	Geno Petralli	.04	.02	.01
☐ 154	Jim Deshaies	.04	.02	.01
☐ 155	Barry Larkin	.12	.05	.02
☐ 156	Alfredo Griffin	.04	.02	.01
☐ 157	Tom Henke	.07	.03	.01
☐ 158	Mike Jeffcoat	.04	.02	.01
☐ 159	Bob Welch	.07	.03	.01
☐ 160	Julio Franco	.07	.03	.01
☐ 161	Henry Cotto	.04	.02	.01
☐ 162	Terry Steinbach	.07	.03	.01
☐ 163	Damon Berryhill	.04	.02	.01
☐ 164	Tim Crews	.04	.02	.01
☐ 165	Tom Browning	.04	.02	.01
☐ 166	Fred Manrique	.04	.02	.01
☐ 167	Harold Reynolds	.04	.02	.01
☐ 168A	Ron Hassey ERR	.04	.02	.01
	(27 on back)			
☐ 168B	Ron Hassey COR	1.00	.45	.13
	(24 on back)			
☐ 169	Shawon Dunston	.07	.03	.01
☐ 170	Bobby Bonilla	.12	.05	.02
☐ 171	Tommy Herr	.04	.02	.01
☐ 172	Mike Heath	.04	.02	.01
☐ 173	Rich Gedman	.04	.02	.01
☐ 174	Bill Ripken	.04	.02	.01
☐ 175	Pete O'Brien	.04	.02	.01
☐ 176A	Lloyd McClendon ERR	.75	.35	.09
	(Uniform number on back listed as 1)			
☐ 176B	Lloyd McClendon COR	.04	.02	.01
	(Uniform number on back listed as 10)			
☐ 177	Brian Holton	.04	.02	.01
☐ 178	Jeff Blauser	.07	.03	.01
☐ 179	Jim Eisenreich	.04	.02	.01
☐ 180	Bert Blyleven	.07	.03	.01
☐ 181	Rob Murphy	.04	.02	.01
☐ 182	Bill Doran	.04	.02	.01

☐ 183 Curt Ford.....................04	.02	.01
☐ 184 Mike Henneman............04	.02	.01
☐ 185 Eric Davis....................10	.05	.01
☐ 186 Lance McCullers...........04	.02	.01
☐ 187 Steve Davis.................04	.02	.01
☐ 188 Bill Wegman................04	.02	.01
☐ 189 Brian Harper...............07	.03	.01
☐ 190 Mike Moore.................04	.02	.01
☐ 191 Dale Mohorcic.............04	.02	.01
☐ 192 Tim Wallach.................07	.03	.01
☐ 193 Keith Hernandez..........07	.03	.01
☐ 194 Dave Righetti...............04	.02	.01
☐ 195A Bret Saberhagen ERR..08	.04	.01
(Joke)		
☐ 195B Bret Saberhagen COR..25	.11	.03
(Joker)		
☐ 196 Paul Kilgus..................04	.02	.01
☐ 197 Bud Black....................04	.02	.01
☐ 198 Juan Samuel................04	.02	.01
☐ 199 Kevin Seitzer...............07	.03	.01
☐ 200 Darryl Strawberry 20	.09	.03
☐ 201 Dave Stieb..................07	.03	.01
☐ 202 Charlie Hough..............04	.02	.01
☐ 203 Jack Morris.................10	.05	.01
☐ 204 Rance Mulliniks 04	.02	.01
☐ 205 Alvin Davis..................04	.02	.01
☐ 206 Jack Howell.................04	.02	.01
☐ 207 Ken Patterson..............04	.02	.01
☐ 208 Terry Pendleton 10	.05	.01
☐ 209 Craig Lefferts..............04	.02	.01
☐ 210 Kevin Brown UER..........10	.05	.01
(First mention of '89		
Rangers should be '88)		
☐ 211 Dan Petry...................04	.02	.01
☐ 212 Dave Leiper.................04	.02	.01
☐ 213 Daryl Boston...............04	.02	.01
☐ 214 Kevin Hickey...............04	.02	.01
☐ 215 Mike Krukow................04	.02	.01
☐ 216 Terry Francona.............04	.02	.01
☐ 217 Kirk McCaskill..............04	.02	.01
☐ 218 Scott Bailes.................04	.02	.01
☐ 219 Bob Forsch..................04	.02	.01
☐ 220A Mike Aldrete ERR..........04	.02	.01
(25 on back)		
☐ 220B Mike Aldrete COR 25	.11	.03
(24 on back)		
☐ 221 Steve Buechele............04	.02	.01
☐ 222 Jesse Barfield..............04	.02	.01
☐ 223 Juan Berenguer...........04	.02	.01
☐ 224 Andy McGaffigan..........04	.02	.01
☐ 225 Pete Smith..................07	.03	.01
☐ 226 Mike Witt....................04	.02	.01
☐ 227 Jay Howell..................04	.02	.01
☐ 228 Scott Bradley...............04	.02	.01
☐ 229 Jerome Walton.............07	.03	.01
☐ 230 Greg Swindell...............07	.03	.01
☐ 231 Atlee Hammaker...........04	.02	.01

☐ 232A Mike Devereaux ERR 08	.04	.01
(RF on front)		
☐ 232B Mike Devereaux COR.1.00	.45	.13
(CF on front)		
☐ 233 Ken Hill......................15	.07	.02
☐ 234 Craig Worthington.........04	.02	.01
☐ 235 Scott Terry.................04	.02	.01
☐ 236 Brett Butler.................07	.03	.01
☐ 237 Doyle Alexander...........04	.02	.01
☐ 238 Dave Anderson............04	.02	.01
☐ 239 Bob Milacki.................04	.02	.01
☐ 240 Dwight Smith...............04	.02	.01
☐ 241 Otis Nixon...................07	.03	.01
☐ 242 Pat Tabler...................04	.02	.01
☐ 243 Derek Lilliquist.............04	.02	.01
☐ 244 Danny Tartabull............10	.05	.01
☐ 245 Wade Boggs................20	.09	.03
☐ 246 Scott Garrelts..............04	.02	.01
(Should say Relief		
Pitcher on front)		
☐ 247 Spike Owen.................04	.02	.01
☐ 248 Norm Charlton.............07	.03	.01
☐ 249 Gerald Perry................04	.02	.01
☐ 250 Nolan Ryan.................50	.23	.06
☐ 251 Kevin Gross.................04	.02	.01
☐ 252 Randy Milligan.............04	.02	.01
☐ 253 Mike LaCoss................04	.02	.01
☐ 254 Dave Bergman.............04	.02	.01
☐ 255 Tony Gwynn.................20	.09	.03
☐ 256 Felix Fermin................04	.02	.01
☐ 257 Greg W. Harris............04	.02	.01
☐ 258 Junior Felix.................07	.03	.01
☐ 259 Mark Davis..................04	.02	.01
☐ 260 Vince Coleman.............07	.03	.01
☐ 261 Paul Gibson................04	.02	.01
☐ 262 Mitch Williams 07	.03	.01
☐ 263 Jeff Russell.................04	.02	.01
☐ 264 Omar Vizquel..............07	.03	.01
☐ 265 Andre Dawson 12	.05	.02
☐ 266 Storm Davis................04	.02	.01
☐ 267 Guillermo Hernandez....04	.02	.01
☐ 268 Mike Felder.................04	.02	.01
☐ 269 Tom Candiotti..............04	.02	.01
☐ 270 Bruce Hurst.................07	.03	.01
☐ 271 Fred McGriff................20	.09	.03
☐ 272 Glenn Davis.................07	.03	.01
☐ 273 John Franco.................07	.03	.01
☐ 274 Rich Yett....................04	.02	.01
☐ 275 Craig Biggio.................10	.05	.01
☐ 276 Gene Larkin................04	.02	.01
☐ 277 Rob Dibble..................07	.03	.01
☐ 278 Randy Bush.................04	.02	.01
☐ 279 Kevin Bass..................04	.02	.01
☐ 280A Bo Jackson ERR...........12	.05	.02
(Watham)		
☐ 280B Bo Jackson COR...........50	.23	.06
(Wathan)		

☐ 281	Wally Backman	.04	.02	.01
☐ 282	Larry Andersen	.04	.02	.01
☐ 283	Chris Bosio	.04	.02	.01
☐ 284	Juan Agosto	.04	.02	.01
☐ 285	Ozzie Smith	.12	.05	.02
☐ 286	George Bell	.07	.03	.01
☐ 287	Rex Hudler	.04	.02	.01
☐ 288	Pat Borders	.07	.03	.01
☐ 289	Danny Jackson	.04	.02	.01
☐ 290	Carlton Fisk	.10	.05	.01
☐ 291	Tracy Jones	.04	.02	.01
☐ 292	Allan Anderson	.04	.02	.01
☐ 293	Johnny Ray	.04	.02	.01
☐ 294	Lee Guetterman	.04	.02	.01
☐ 295	Paul O'Neill	.07	.03	.01
☐ 296	Carney Lansford	.07	.03	.01
☐ 297	Tom Brookens	.04	.02	.01
☐ 298	Claudell Washington	.04	.02	.01
☐ 299	Hubie Brooks	.04	.02	.01
☐ 300	Will Clark	.30	.14	.04
☐ 301	Kenny Rogers	.04	.02	.01
☐ 302	Darrell Evans	.07	.03	.01
☐ 303	Greg Briley	.04	.02	.01
☐ 304	Donn Pall	.04	.02	.01
☐ 305	Teddy Higuera	.04	.02	.01
☐ 306	Dan Pasqua	.04	.02	.01
☐ 307	Dave Winfield	.15	.07	.02
☐ 308	Dennis Powell	.04	.02	.01
☐ 309	Jose DeLeon	.04	.02	.01
☐ 310	Roger Clemens UER	.35	.16	.04
	(Dominate, should			
	say dominant)			
☐ 311	Melido Perez	.07	.03	.01
☐ 312	Devon White	.07	.03	.01
☐ 313	Dwight Gooden	.10	.05	.01
☐ 314	Carlos Martinez	.04	.02	.01
☐ 315	Dennis Eckersley	.12	.05	.02
☐ 316	Clay Parker UER	.04	.02	.01
	(Height 6'11")			
☐ 317	Rick Honeycutt	.04	.02	.01
☐ 318	Tim Laudner	.04	.02	.01
☐ 319	Joe Carter	.20	.09	.03
☐ 320	Robin Yount	.15	.07	.02
☐ 321	Felix Jose	.20	.09	.03
☐ 322	Mickey Tettleton	.07	.03	.01
☐ 323	Mike Gallego	.04	.02	.01
☐ 324	Edgar Martinez	.20	.09	.03
☐ 325	Dave Henderson	.04	.02	.01
☐ 326	Chili Davis	.07	.03	.01
☐ 327	Steve Balboni	.04	.02	.01
☐ 328	Jody Davis	.04	.02	.01
☐ 329	Shawn Hillegas	.04	.02	.01
☐ 330	Jim Abbott	.20	.09	.03
☐ 331	John Dopson	.04	.02	.01
☐ 332	Mark Williamson	.04	.02	.01
☐ 333	Jeff D. Robinson	.04	.02	.01
☐ 334	John Smiley	.07	.03	.01
☐ 335	Bobby Thigpen	.04	.02	.01
☐ 336	Garry Templeton	.04	.02	.01
☐ 337	Marvell Wynne	.04	.02	.01
☐ 338A	Ken Griffey Sr. ERR	.08	.04	.01
	(Uniform number on			
	back listed as 25)			
☐ 338B	Ken Griffey Sr. COR	1.50	.65	.19
	(Uniform number on			
	back listed as 30)			
☐ 339	Steve Finley	.07	.03	.01
☐ 340	Ellis Burks	.07	.03	.01
☐ 341	Frank Williams	.04	.02	.01
☐ 342	Mike Morgan	.04	.02	.01
☐ 343	Kevin Mitchell	.10	.05	.01
☐ 344	Joel Youngblood	.04	.02	.01
☐ 345	Mike Greenwell	.07	.03	.01
☐ 346	Glenn Wilson	.04	.02	.01
☐ 347	John Costello	.04	.02	.01
☐ 348	Wes Gardner	.04	.02	.01
☐ 349	Jeff Ballard	.04	.02	.01
☐ 350	Mark Thurmond UER	.04	.02	.01
	(ERA is 192,			
	should be 1.92)			
☐ 351	Randy Myers	.07	.03	.01
☐ 352	Shawn Abner	.04	.02	.01
☐ 353	Jesse Orosco	.04	.02	.01
☐ 354	Greg Walker	.04	.02	.01
☐ 355	Pete Harnisch	.07	.03	.01
☐ 356	Steve Farr	.04	.02	.01
☐ 357	Dave LaPoint	.04	.02	.01
☐ 358	Willie Fraser	.04	.02	.01
☐ 359	Mickey Hatcher	.04	.02	.01
☐ 360	Rickey Henderson	.20	.09	.03
☐ 361	Mike Fitzgerald	.04	.02	.01
☐ 362	Bill Schroeder	.04	.02	.01
☐ 363	Mark Carreon	.04	.02	.01
☐ 364	Ron Jones	.04	.02	.01
☐ 365	Jeff Montgomery	.07	.03	.01
☐ 366	Bill Krueger	.04	.02	.01
☐ 367	John Cangelosi	.04	.02	.01
☐ 368	Jose Gonzalez	.04	.02	.01
☐ 369	Greg Hibbard	.20	.09	.03
☐ 370	John Smoltz	.25	.11	.03
☐ 371	Jeff Brantley	.04	.02	.01
☐ 372	Frank White	.04	.02	.01
☐ 373	Ed Whitson	.04	.02	.01
☐ 374	Willie McGee	.07	.03	.01
☐ 375	Jose Canseco	.30	.14	.04
☐ 376	Randy Ready	.04	.02	.01
☐ 377	Don Aase	.04	.02	.01
☐ 378	Tony Armas	.04	.02	.01
☐ 379	Steve Bedrosian	.04	.02	.01
☐ 380	Chuck Finley	.07	.03	.01
☐ 381	Kent Hrbek	.07	.03	.01
☐ 382	Jim Gantner	.04	.02	.01
☐ 383	Mel Hall	.04	.02	.01
☐ 384	Mike Marshall	.04	.02	.01

☐ 385 Mark McGwire	.30	.14	.04
☐ 386 Wayne Tolleson	.04	.02	.01
☐ 387 Brian Holman	.04	.02	.01
☐ 388 John Wetteland	.07	.03	.01
☐ 389 Darren Daulton	.07	.03	.01
☐ 390 Rob Deer	.07	.03	.01
☐ 391 John Moses	.04	.02	.01
☐ 392 Todd Worrell	.04	.02	.01
☐ 393 Chuck Cary	.04	.02	.01
☐ 394 Stan Javier	.04	.02	.01
☐ 395 Willie Randolph	.07	.03	.01
☐ 396 Bill Buckner	.07	.03	.01
☐ 397 Robby Thompson	.04	.02	.01
☐ 398 Mike Scioscia	.04	.02	.01
☐ 399 Lonnie Smith	.04	.02	.01
☐ 400 Kirby Puckett	.30	.14	.04
☐ 401 Mark Langston	.07	.03	.01
☐ 402 Danny Darwin	.04	.02	.01
☐ 403 Greg Maddux	.20	.09	.03
☐ 404 Lloyd Moseby	.04	.02	.01
☐ 405 Rafael Palmeiro	.10	.05	.01
☐ 406 Chad Kreuter	.04	.02	.01
☐ 407 Jimmy Key	.07	.03	.01
☐ 408 Tim Birtsas	.04	.02	.01
☐ 409 Tim Raines	.07	.03	.01
☐ 410 Dave Stewart	.07	.03	.01
☐ 411 Eric Yelding	.04	.02	.01
☐ 412 Kent Anderson	.04	.02	.01
☐ 413 Les Lancaster	.04	.02	.01
☐ 414 Rick Dempsey	.04	.02	.01
☐ 415 Randy Johnson	.07	.03	.01
☐ 416 Gary Carter	.07	.03	.01
☐ 417 Rolando Roomes	.04	.02	.01
☐ 418 Dan Schatzeder	.04	.02	.01
☐ 419 Bryn Smith	.04	.02	.01
☐ 420 Ruben Sierra	.20	.09	.03
☐ 421 Steve Jeltz	.04	.02	.01
☐ 422 Ken Oberkfell	.04	.02	.01
☐ 423 Sid Bream	.04	.02	.01
☐ 424 Jim Clancy	.04	.02	.01
☐ 425 Kelly Gruber	.07	.03	.01
☐ 426 Rick Leach	.04	.02	.01
☐ 427 Len Dykstra	.07	.03	.01
☐ 428 Jeff Pico	.04	.02	.01
☐ 429 John Cerutti	.04	.02	.01
☐ 430 David Cone	.12	.05	.02
☐ 431 Jeff Kunkel	.04	.02	.01
☐ 432 Luis Aquino	.04	.02	.01
☐ 433 Ernie Whitt	.04	.02	.01
☐ 434 Bo Diaz	.04	.02	.01
☐ 435 Steve Lake	.04	.02	.01
☐ 436 Pat Perry	.04	.02	.01
☐ 437 Mike Davis	.04	.02	.01
☐ 438 Cecilio Guante	.04	.02	.01
☐ 439 Duane Ward	.04	.02	.01
☐ 440 Andy Van Slyke	.10	.05	.01
☐ 441 Gene Nelson	.04	.02	.01
☐ 442 Luis Polonia	.07	.03	.01
☐ 443 Kevin Elster	.04	.02	.01
☐ 444 Keith Moreland	.04	.02	.01
☐ 445 Roger McDowell	.04	.02	.01
☐ 446 Ron Darling	.07	.03	.01
☐ 447 Ernest Riles	.04	.02	.01
☐ 448 Mookie Wilson	.04	.02	.01
☐ 449A Billy Spiers ERR	.75	.35	.09
(No birth year)			
☐ 449B Billy Spiers COR	.04	.02	.01
(Born in 1966)			
☐ 450 Rick Sutcliffe	.07	.03	.01
☐ 451 Nelson Santovenia	.04	.02	.01
☐ 452 Andy Allanson	.04	.02	.01
☐ 453 Bob Melvin	.04	.02	.01
☐ 454 Benito Santiago	.07	.03	.01
☐ 455 Jose Uribe	.04	.02	.01
☐ 456 Bill Landrum	.04	.02	.01
☐ 457 Bobby Witt	.07	.03	.01
☐ 458 Kevin Romine	.04	.02	.01
☐ 459 Lee Mazzilli	.04	.02	.01
☐ 460 Paul Molitor	.10	.05	.01
☐ 461 Ramon Martinez	.15	.07	.02
☐ 462 Frank DiPino	.04	.02	.01
☐ 463 Walt Terrell	.04	.02	.01
☐ 464 Bob Geren	.04	.02	.01
☐ 465 Rick Reuschel	.04	.02	.01
☐ 466 Mark Grant	.04	.02	.01
☐ 467 John Kruk	.07	.03	.01
☐ 468 Gregg Jefferies	.12	.05	.02
☐ 469 R.J. Reynolds	.04	.02	.01
☐ 470 Harold Baines	.07	.03	.01
☐ 471 Dennis Lamp	.04	.02	.01
☐ 472 Tom Gordon	.07	.03	.01
☐ 473 Terry Puhl	.04	.02	.01
☐ 474 Curt Wilkerson	.04	.02	.01
☐ 475 Dan Quisenberry	.07	.03	.01
☐ 476 Oddibe McDowell	.04	.02	.01
☐ 477 Zane Smith UER	.04	.02	.01
(Career ERA .393)			
☐ 478 Franklin Stubbs	.04	.02	.01
☐ 479 Wallace Johnson	.04	.02	.01
☐ 480 Jay Tibbs	.04	.02	.01
☐ 481 Tom Glavine	.25	.11	.03
☐ 482 Manny Lee	.04	.02	.01
☐ 483 Joe Hesketh UER	.04	.02	.01
(Says Rookiess on back,			
should say Rookies)			
☐ 484 Mike Bielecki	.04	.02	.01
☐ 485 Greg Brock	.04	.02	.01
☐ 486 Pascual Perez	.04	.02	.01
☐ 487 Kirk Gibson	.07	.03	.01
☐ 488 Scott Sanderson	.04	.02	.01
☐ 489 Domingo Ramos	.04	.02	.01
☐ 490 Kal Daniels	.04	.02	.01
☐ 491A David Wells ERR	1.50	.65	.19
(Reverse negative			

photo on card back)

☐ 491B	David Wells COR	.07	.03	.01
☐ 492	Jerry Reed	.04	.02	.01
☐ 493	Eric Show	.04	.02	.01
☐ 494	Mike Pagliarulo	.04	.02	.01
☐ 495	Ron Robinson	.04	.02	.01
☐ 496	Brad Komminsk	.04	.02	.01
☐ 497	Greg Litton	.04	.02	.01
☐ 498	Chris James	.04	.02	.01
☐ 499	Luis Quinones	.04	.02	.01
☐ 500	Frank Viola	.04	.02	.01
☐ 501	Tim Teufel UER	.04	.02	.01

(Twins '85, the s is
lower case, should
be upper case)

☐ 502	Terry Leach	.04	.02	.01
☐ 503	Matt Williams	.10	.05	.01
☐ 504	Tim Leary	.04	.02	.01
☐ 505	Doug Drabek	.07	.03	.01
☐ 506	Mariano Duncan	.04	.02	.01
☐ 507	Charlie Hayes	.07	.03	.01
☐ 508	Joey Belle	.50	.23	.06
☐ 509	Pat Sheridan	.04	.02	.01
☐ 510	Mackey Sasser	.04	.02	.01
☐ 511	Jose Rijo	.07	.03	.01
☐ 512	Mike Smithson	.04	.02	.01
☐ 513	Gary Ward	.04	.02	.01
☐ 514	Dion James	.04	.02	.01
☐ 515	Jim Gott	.04	.02	.01
☐ 516	Drew Hall	.04	.02	.01
☐ 517	Doug Bair	.04	.02	.01
☐ 518	Scott Scudder	.04	.02	.01
☐ 519	Rick Aguilera	.07	.03	.01
☐ 520	Rafael Belliard	.04	.02	.01
☐ 521	Jay Buhner	.07	.03	.01
☐ 522	Jeff Reardon	.07	.03	.01
☐ 523	Steve Rosenberg	.04	.02	.01
☐ 524	Randy Velarde	.04	.02	.01
☐ 525	Jeff Musselman	.04	.02	.01
☐ 526	Bill Long	.04	.02	.01
☐ 527	Gary Wayne	.04	.02	.01
☐ 528	Dave Johnson (P)	.04	.02	.01
☐ 529	Ron Kittle	.04	.02	.01
☐ 530	Erik Hanson UER	.07	.03	.01

(5th line on back
says seson, should
say season)

☐ 531	Steve Wilson	.04	.02	.01
☐ 532	Joey Meyer	.04	.02	.01
☐ 533	Curt Young	.04	.02	.01
☐ 534	Kelly Downs	.04	.02	.01
☐ 535	Joe Girardi	.04	.02	.01
☐ 536	Lance Blankenship	.04	.02	.01
☐ 537	Greg Mathews	.04	.02	.01
☐ 538	Donell Nixon	.04	.02	.01
☐ 539	Mark Knudson	.04	.02	.01
☐ 540	Jeff Wetherby	.04	.02	.01
☐ 541	Darrin Jackson	.07	.03	.01
☐ 542	Terry Mulholland	.07	.03	.01
☐ 543	Eric Hetzel	.04	.02	.01
☐ 544	Rick Reed	.04	.02	.01
☐ 545	Dennis Cook	.04	.02	.01
☐ 546	Mike Jackson	.04	.02	.01
☐ 547	Brian Fisher	.04	.02	.01
☐ 548	Gene Harris	.07	.03	.01
☐ 549	Jeff King	.07	.03	.01
☐ 550	Dave Dravecky	.07	.03	.01
☐ 551	Randy Kutcher	.04	.02	.01
☐ 552	Mark Portugal	.04	.02	.01
☐ 553	Jim Corsi	.04	.02	.01
☐ 554	Todd Stottlemyre	.07	.03	.01
☐ 555	Scott Bankhead	.04	.02	.01
☐ 556	Ken Dayley	.04	.02	.01
☐ 557	Rick Wrona	.04	.02	.01
☐ 558	Sammy Sosa	.15	.07	.02
☐ 559	Keith Miller	.04	.02	.01
☐ 560	Ken Griffey Jr.	1.25	.55	.16
☐ 561A	Ryne Sandberg HL	10.00	4.50	1.25

(Position on front
listed as 3B) ERR

☐ 561B	Ryne Sandberg HL COR	.20	.09	.03
☐ 562	Billy Hatcher	.04	.02	.01
☐ 563	Jay Bell	.07	.03	.01
☐ 564	Jack Daugherty	.04	.02	.01
☐ 565	Rich Monteleone	.04	.02	.01
☐ 566	Bo Jackson AS-MVP	.12	.05	.02
☐ 567	Tony Fossas	.04	.02	.01
☐ 568	Roy Smith	.04	.02	.01
☐ 569	Jaime Navarro	.20	.09	.03
☐ 570	Lance Johnson	.07	.03	.01
☐ 571	Mike Dyer	.04	.02	.01
☐ 572	Kevin Ritz	.10	.05	.01
☐ 573	Dave West	.04	.02	.01
☐ 574	Gary Mielke	.04	.02	.01
☐ 575	Scott Lusader	.04	.02	.01
☐ 576	Joe Oliver	.04	.02	.01
☐ 577	Sandy Alomar Jr.	.10	.05	.01
☐ 578	Andy Benes UER	.20	.09	.03

(Extra comma between
day and year)

☐ 579	Tim Jones	.04	.02	.01
☐ 580	Randy McCament	.04	.02	.01
☐ 581	Curt Schilling	.15	.07	.02
☐ 582	John Orton	.10	.05	.01
☐ 583A	Milt Cuyler ERR	1.00	.45	.13

(998 games)

☐ 583B	Milt Cuyler COR	.20	.09	.03

(98 games)

☐ 584	Eric Anthony	.30	.14	.04
☐ 585	Greg Vaughn	.15	.07	.02
☐ 586	Deion Sanders	.50	.23	.06
☐ 587	Jose DeJesus	.04	.02	.01
☐ 588	Chip Hale	.04	.02	.01
☐ 589	John Olerud	.60	.25	.08

☐ 590	Steve Olin	20	.09	.03
☐ 591	Marquis Grissom	60	.25	.08
☐ 592	Moises Alou	50	.23	.06
☐ 593	Mark Lemke	07	.03	.01
☐ 594	Dean Palmer	60	.25	.08
☐ 595	Robin Ventura	75	.35	.09
☐ 596	Tino Martinez	12	.05	.02
☐ 597	Mike Huff	10	.05	.01
☐ 598	Scott Hemond	10	.05	.01
☐ 599	Wally Whitehurst	04	.02	.01
☐ 600	Todd Zeile	15	.07	.02
☐ 601	Glenallen Hill	07	.03	.01
☐ 602	Hal Morris	15	.07	.02
☐ 603	Juan Bell	04	.02	.01
☐ 604	Bobby Rose	07	.03	.01
☐ 605	Matt Merullo	04	.02	.01
☐ 606	Kevin Maas	25	.11	.03
☐ 607	Randy Nosek	04	.02	.01
☐ 608A	Billy Bates	10	.05	.01
	(Text mentions 12 triples in tenth line)			
☐ 608B	Billy Bates	10	.05	.01
	(Text has no mention of triples)			
☐ 609	Mike Stanton	15	.07	.02
☐ 610	Mauro Gozzo	04	.02	.01
☐ 611	Charles Nagy	50	.23	.06
☐ 612	Scott Coolbaugh	04	.02	.01
☐ 613	Jose Vizcaino	10	.05	.01
☐ 614	Greg Smith	10	.05	.01
☐ 615	Jeff Huson	10	.05	.01
☐ 616	Mickey Weston	04	.02	.01
☐ 617	John Pawlowski	04	.02	.01
☐ 618A	Joe Skalski ERR	04	.02	.01
	(27 on back)			
☐ 618B	Joe Skalski COR	1.00	.45	.13
	(67 on back)			
☐ 619	Bernie Williams	30	.14	.04
☐ 620	Shawn Holman	04	.02	.01
☐ 621	Gary Eave	04	.02	.01
☐ 622	Darrin Fletcher UER	10	.05	.01
	(Elmherst, should be Elmhurst)			
☐ 623	Pat Combs	07	.03	.01
☐ 624	Mike Blowers	04	.02	.01
☐ 625	Kevin Appier	25	.11	.03
☐ 626	Pat Austin	04	.02	.01
☐ 627	Kelly Mann	04	.02	.01
☐ 628	Matt Kinzer	07	.03	.01
☐ 629	Chris Hammond	20	.09	.03
☐ 630	Dean Wilkins	04	.02	.01
☐ 631	Larry Walker UER	90	.40	.11
	(Uniform number 55 on front and 33 on back)			
☐ 632	Blaine Beatty	04	.02	.01
☐ 633A	Tommy Barrett ERR	04	.02	.01
	(29 on back)			
☐ 633B	Tommy Barrett COR	2.00	.90	.25
	(14 on back)			
☐ 634	Stan Belinda	15	.07	.02
☐ 635	Mike (Tex) Smith	04	.02	.01
☐ 636	Hensley Meulens	07	.03	.01
☐ 637	Juan Gonzalez	2.00	.90	.25
☐ 638	Lenny Webster	10	.05	.01
☐ 639	Mark Gardner	12	.05	.02
☐ 640	Tommy Greene	12	.05	.02
☐ 641	Mike Hartley	04	.02	.01
☐ 642	Phil Stephenson	04	.02	.01
☐ 643	Kevin Mmahat	04	.02	.01
☐ 644	Ed Whited	04	.02	.01
☐ 645	Delino DeShields	60	.25	.08
☐ 646	Kevin Blankenship	04	.02	.01
☐ 647	Paul Sorrento	25	.11	.03
☐ 648	Mike Roesler	04	.02	.01
☐ 649	Jason Grimsley	10	.05	.01
☐ 650	Dave Justice	1.25	.55	.16
☐ 651	Scott Cooper	40	.18	.05
☐ 652	Dave Eiland	04	.02	.01
☐ 653	Mike Munoz	04	.02	.01
☐ 654	Jeff Fischer	04	.02	.01
☐ 655	Terry Jorgensen	04	.02	.01
☐ 656	George Canale	04	.02	.01
☐ 657	Brian DuBois UER	10	.05	.01
	(Misspelled Dubois on card)			
☐ 658	Carlos Quintana	07	.03	.01
☐ 659	Luis de los Santos	04	.02	.01
☐ 660	Jerald Clark	07	.03	.01
☐ 661	Donald Harris DC	10	.05	.01
☐ 662	Paul Coleman DC	12	.05	.02
☐ 663	Frank Thomas DC	6.00	2.70	.75
☐ 664	Brent Mayne DC	15	.07	.02
☐ 665	Eddie Zosky DC	15	.07	.02
☐ 666	Steve Hosey DC	60	.25	.08
☐ 667	Scott Bryant DC	12	.05	.02
☐ 668	Tom Goodwin DC	15	.07	.02
☐ 669	Cal Eldred DC	1.25	.55	.16
☐ 670	Earl Cunningham DC	12	.05	.02
☐ 671	Alan Zinter DC	10	.05	.01
☐ 672	Chuck Knoblauch DC	1.25	.55	.16
☐ 673	Kyle Abbott DC	20	.09	.03
☐ 674	Roger Salkeld DC	20	.09	.03
☐ 675	Maurice Vaughn DC	40	.18	.05
☐ 676	Keith(Kiki) Jones DC	10	.05	.01
☐ 677	Tyler Houston DC	10	.05	.01
☐ 678	Jeff Jackson DC	10	.05	.01
☐ 679	Greg Gohr DC	15	.07	.02
☐ 680	Ben McDonald DC	50	.23	.06
☐ 681	Greg Blosser DC	25	.11	.03
☐ 682	Willie Green DC UER	50	.23	.06
	(Name misspelled on card, should be Greene)			
☐ 683	Wade Boggs DT UER	10	.05	.01
	(Text says 215 hits in			

☐ 684	Will Clark DT..................15	.07	.02
	'89, should be 205)		
☐ 685	Tony Gwynn DT UER 12	.05	.02
	(Text reads battling		
	instead of batting)		
☐ 686	Rickey Henderson DT 10	.05	.01
☐ 687	Bo Jackson DT...............15	.07	.02
☐ 688	Mark Langston DT 05	.02	.01
☐ 689	Barry Larkin DT...............10	.05	.01
☐ 690	Kirby Puckett DT 12	.05	.02
☐ 691	Ryne Sandberg DT..........20	.09	.03
☐ 692	Mike Scott DT 05	.02	.01
☐ 693A	Terry Steinbach DT........05	.02	.01
	ERR (cathers)		
☐ 693B	Terry Steinbach DT........25	.11	.03
	COR (catchers)		
☐ 694	Bobby Thigpen DT 05	.02	.01
☐ 695	Mitch Williams DT 05	.02	.01
☐ 696	Nolan Ryan HL.................30	.14	.04
☐ 697	Bo Jackson FB/BB...1.50	.65	.19
☐ 698	Rickey Henderson..........10	.05	.01
	ALCS-MVP		
☐ 699	Will Clark 12	.05	.02
	NLCS-MVP		
☐ 700	WS Games 1/2................05	.02	.01
	(Dave Stewart and		
	Mike Moore)		
☐ 701	Lights Out:......................08	.04	.01
	Candlestick		
	5:04pm (10/17/89)		
☐ 702	WS Game 3.....................05	.02	.01
	Bashers Blast Giants		
	(Carney Lansford,		
	Ricky Henderson,		
	Jose Canseco,		
	Dave Henderson)		
☐ 703	WS Game 4/Wrap-up.....05	.02	.01
	A's Sweep Battle of		
	of the Bay		
	(A's Celebrate)		
☐ 704	Wade Boggs HL...............10	.05	.01
	Wade Raps 200		
☐ B1	A.Bartlett Giamatti 1.00	.45	.13
	COMM MEM		
☐ B2	Pat Combs......................25	.11	.03
☐ B3	Todd Zeile.......................90	.40	.11
☐ B4	Luis de los Santos 25	.11	.03
☐ B5	Mark Lemke.....................40	.18	.05
☐ B6	Robin Ventura.............8.00	3.60	1.00
☐ B7	Jeff Huson......................25	.11	.03
☐ B8	Greg Vaughn................1.00	.45	.13
☐ B9	Marquis Grissom........4.00	1.80	.50
☐ B10	Eric Anthony................1.50	.65	.19

1990 Score Rookie/Traded

*The 1990 Score Rookie and Traded set
marks the third consecutive year Score
has issued an end of the year set to mark
trades and give rookies early cards. The
set consists of 110 cards each measuring
the standard size of 2 1/2" by 3 1/2". The
first 66 cards are traded players while the
last 44 cards are Rookie Cards. Included
in the rookie part of the set are cross-ath-
letes Eric Lindros (hockey) and D.J. Dozier
(football). The key baseball player Rookie
Cards in the set are Carlos Baerga, Derek
Bell, and Ray Lankford.*

	MT	EX-MT	VG
COMPLETE SET (110) 16.00		7.25	2.00
COMMON PLAYER (1T-66T) 05		.02	.01
COMMON PLAYER (67T-110T)....05		.02	.01
☐ 1T Dave Winfield..................15		.07	.02
☐ 2T Kevin Bass.....................05		.02	.01
☐ 3T Nick Esasky....................05		.02	.01
☐ 4T Mitch Webster................05		.02	.01
☐ 5T Pascual Perez 05		.02	.01
☐ 6T Gary Pettis.....................05		.02	.01
☐ 7T Tony Pena......................05		.02	.01
☐ 8T Candy Maldonado..........05		.02	.01
☐ 9T Cecil Fielder...................20		.09	.03
☐ 10T Carmelo Martinez..........05		.02	.01
☐ 11T Mark Langston................08		.04	.01
☐ 12T Dave Parker....................08		.04	.01
☐ 13T Don Slaught....................05		.02	.01
☐ 14T Tony Phillips...................05		.02	.01
☐ 15T John Franco....................08		.04	.01
☐ 16T Randy Myers...................08		.04	.01
☐ 17T Jeff Reardon...................08		.04	.01

☐ 18T	Sandy Alomar Jr.	.10	.05	.01
☐ 19T	Joe Carter	.20	.09	.03
☐ 20T	Fred Lynn	.08	.04	.01
☐ 21T	Storm Davis	.05	.02	.01
☐ 22T	Craig Lefferts	.05	.02	.01
☐ 23T	Pete O'Brien	.05	.02	.01
☐ 24T	Dennis Boyd	.05	.02	.01
☐ 25T	Lloyd Moseby	.05	.02	.01
☐ 26T	Mark Davis	.05	.02	.01
☐ 27T	Tim Leary	.05	.02	.01
☐ 28T	Gerald Perry	.05	.02	.01
☐ 29T	Don Aase	.05	.02	.01
☐ 30T	Ernie Whitt	.05	.02	.01
☐ 31T	Dale Murphy	.08	.04	.01
☐ 32T	Alejandro Pena	.05	.02	.01
☐ 33T	Juan Samuel	.05	.02	.01
☐ 34T	Hubie Brooks	.05	.02	.01
☐ 35T	Gary Carter	.08	.04	.01
☐ 36T	Jim Presley	.05	.02	.01
☐ 37T	Wally Backman	.05	.02	.01
☐ 38T	Matt Nokes	.05	.02	.01
☐ 39T	Dan Petry	.05	.02	.01
☐ 40T	Franklin Stubbs	.05	.02	.01
☐ 41T	Jeff Huson	.05	.02	.01
☐ 42T	Billy Hatcher	.05	.02	.01
☐ 43T	Terry Leach	.05	.02	.01
☐ 44T	Phil Bradley	.05	.02	.01
☐ 45T	Claudell Washington	.05	.02	.01
☐ 46T	Luis Polonia	.08	.04	.01
☐ 47T	Daryl Boston	.05	.02	.01
☐ 48T	Lee Smith	.08	.04	.01
☐ 49T	Tom Brunansky	.08	.04	.01
☐ 50T	Mike Witt	.06	.02	.01
☐ 51T	Willie Randolph	.08	.04	.01
☐ 52T	Stan Javier	.05	.02	.01
☐ 53T	Brad Komminsk	.05	.02	.01
☐ 54T	John Candelaria	.05	.02	.01
☐ 55T	Bryn Smith	.05	.02	.01
☐ 56T	Glenn Braggs	.05	.02	.01
☐ 57T	Keith Hernandez	.08	.04	.01
☐ 58T	Ken Oberkfell	.05	.02	.01
☐ 59T	Steve Jeltz	.05	.02	.01
☐ 60T	Chris James	.05	.02	.01
☐ 61T	Scott Sanderson	.05	.02	.01
☐ 62T	Bill Long	.05	.02	.01
☐ 63T	Rick Cerone	.05	.02	.01
☐ 64T	Scott Bailes	.05	.02	.01
☐ 65T	Larry Sheets	.05	.02	.01
☐ 66T	Junior Ortiz	.05	.02	.01
☐ 67T	Francisco Cabrera	.10	.05	.01
☐ 68T	Gary DiSarcina	.20	.09	.03
☐ 69T	Greg Olson	.10	.05	.01
☐ 70T	Beau Allred	.05	.02	.01
☐ 71T	Oscar Azocar	.05	.02	.01
☐ 72T	Kent Mercker	.12	.05	.02
☐ 73T	John Burkett	.10	.05	.01
☐ 74T	Carlos Baerga	1.25	.55	.16

☐ 75T	Dave Hollins	.60	.25	.08
☐ 76T	Todd Hundley	.15	.07	.02
☐ 77T	Rick Parker	.05	.02	.01
☐ 78T	Steve Cummings	.05	.02	.01
☐ 79T	Bill Sampen	.05	.02	.01
☐ 80T	Jerry Kutzler	.05	.02	.01
☐ 81T	Derek Bell	1.00	.45	.13
☐ 82T	Kevin Tapani	.35	.16	.04
☐ 83T	Jim Leyritz	.10	.05	.01
☐ 84T	Ray Lankford	1.00	.45	.13
☐ 85T	Wayne Edwards	.05	.02	.01
☐ 86T	Frank Thomas	6.50	2.90	.80
☐ 87T	Tim Naehring	.15	.07	.02
☐ 88T	Willie Blair	.05	.02	.01
☐ 89T	Alan Mills	.12	.05	.02
☐ 90T	Scott Radinsky	.15	.07	.02
☐ 91T	Howard Farmer	.05	.02	.01
☐ 92T	Julio Machado	.08	.04	.01
☐ 93T	Rafael Valdez	.10	.05	.01
☐ 94T	Shawn Boskie	.10	.05	.01
☐ 95T	David Segui	.10	.05	.01
☐ 96T	Chris Hoiles	.40	.18	.05
☐ 97T	D.J. Dozier	.20	.09	.03
☐ 98T	Hector Villanueva	.10	.05	.01
☐ 99T	Eric Gunderson	.10	.05	.01
☐ 100T	Eric Lindros	7.00	3.10	.85
☐ 101T	Dave Otto	.05	.02	.01
☐ 102T	Dana Kiecker	.05	.02	.01
☐ 103T	Tim Drummond	.05	.02	.01
☐ 104T	Mickey Pina	.05	.02	.01
☐ 105T	Craig Grebeck	.15	.07	.02
☐ 106T	Bernard Gilkey	.40	.18	.05
☐ 107T	Tim Layana	.05	.02	.01
☐ 108T	Scott Chiamparino	.10	.05	.01
☐ 109T	Steve Avery	1.00	.45	.13
☐ 110T	Terry Shumpert	.08	.04	.01

1991 Score

The 1991 Score set contains 893 cards. The cards feature a solid color border framing the full-color photo of the cards. The cards measure the standard card size of 2 1/2" by 3 1/2" and also feature Score trademark full-color photos on the back. The backs also include a brief biography on each player. This set marks the fourth consecutive year that Score has issued a major set but the first time Score issued the set in two series. Score also reused their successful Dream Team concept by using non-baseball photos of Today's stars. Series one contains 441 cards and ends with the Annie Leibowitz photo of Jose Canseco used in American Express ads. This first series also includes 49 Rookie prospects, 12 First Round Draft Picks and five each of the Master Blaster, K-Man, and Rifleman subsets. The All-Star sets in the first series are all American Leaguers (which are all caricatures). The key Rookie Cards in the set are Jeromy Burnitz, Wes Chamberlain, Brian McRae, Mike Mussina, Marc Newfield, Phil Plantier, and Todd Van Poppel. There are a number of pitchers whose card backs show Innings Pitched totals which do not equal the added year-by-year total; the following card numbers were affected; 4, 24, 29, 30, 51, 81, 109, 111, 118, 141, 150, 156, 177, 204, 218, 232, 235, 255, 287, 289, 311, and 328. The second series was issued approximately three months after the release of series one and included many of the special cards Score is noted for, e.g., the continuation of the Dream Team set begun in Series One, All-Star Cartoons featuring National Leaguers, a continuation of the 1990 first round draft picks, and 61 rookie prospects.

	MT	EX-MT	VG
COMPLETE SET (893)	20.00	9.00	2.50
COMPLETE FACT.SET (900)	25.00	11.50	3.10
COMMON PLAYER (1-441)	.04	.02	.01
COMMON PLAYER (442-893)	.04	.02	.01

☐	1 Jose Canseco	20	.09	.03
☐	2 Ken Griffey Jr.	50	.23	.06
☐	3 Ryne Sandberg	25	.11	.03
☐	4 Nolan Ryan	40	.18	.05
☐	5 Bo Jackson	12	.05	.02
☐	6 Bret Saberhagen UER	07	.03	.01
	(In bio, missed			
	misspelled as mised)			
☐	7 Will Clark	20	.09	.03
☐	8 Ellis Burks	07	.03	.01
☐	9 Joe Carter	12	.05	.02
☐	10 Rickey Henderson	12	.05	.02
☐	11 Ozzie Guillen	04	.02	.01
☐	12 Wade Boggs	12	.05	.02
☐	13 Jerome Walton	04	.02	.01
☐	14 John Franco	07	.03	.01
☐	15 Ricky Jordan UER	04	.02	.01
	(League misspelled			
	as legue)			
☐	16 Wally Backman	04	.02	.01
☐	17 Rob Dibble	07	.03	.01
☐	18 Glenn Braggs	04	.02	.01
☐	19 Cory Snyder	04	.02	.01
☐	20 Kal Daniels	04	.02	.01
☐	21 Mark Langston	07	.03	.01
☐	22 Kevin Gross	04	.02	.01
☐	23 Don Mattingly UER	15	.07	.02
	(First line, is			
	missing from Yankee)			
☐	24 Dave Righetti	04	.02	.01
☐	25 Roberto Alomar	20	.09	.03
☐	26 Robby Thompson	04	.02	.01
☐	27 Jack McDowell	10	.05	.01
☐	28 Bip Roberts UER	07	.03	.01
	(Bio reads playd)			
☐	29 Jay Howell	04	.02	.01
☐	30 Dave Stieb UER	04	.02	.01
	(17 wins in bio,			
	18 in stats)			
☐	31 Johnny Ray	04	.02	.01
☐	32 Steve Sax	07	.03	.01
☐	33 Terry Mulholland	04	.02	.01
☐	34 Lee Guetterman	04	.02	.01
☐	35 Tim Raines	07	.03	.01
☐	36 Scott Fletcher	04	.02	.01
☐	37 Lance Parrish	07	.03	.01
☐	38 Tony Phillips UER	04	.02	.01
	(Born 4/15,			
	should be 4/25)			
☐	39 Todd Stottlemyre	07	.03	.01
☐	40 Alan Trammell	07	.03	.01
☐	41 Todd Burns	04	.02	.01
☐	42 Mookie Wilson	04	.02	.01
☐	43 Chris Bosio	04	.02	.01
☐	44 Jeffrey Leonard	04	.02	.01
☐	45 Doug Jones	04	.02	.01
☐	46 Mike Scott UER	04	.02	.01
	(In first line,			
	dominate should			
	read dominating)			
☐	47 Andy Hawkins	04	.02	.01
☐	48 Harold Reynolds	04	.02	.01
☐	49 Paul Molitor	10	.05	.01
☐	50 John Farrell	04	.02	.01
☐	51 Danny Darwin	04	.02	.01

☐ 52 Jeff Blauser	.04	.02	.01
☐ 53 John Tudor UER	.04	.02	.01
(41 wins in '81)			
☐ 54 Milt Thompson	.04	.02	.01
☐ 55 Dave Justice	.30	.14	.04
☐ 56 Greg Olson	.04	.02	.01
☐ 57 Willie Blair	.04	.02	.01
☐ 58 Rick Parker	.04	.02	.01
☐ 59 Shawn Boskie	.04	.02	.01
☐ 60 Kevin Tapani	.07	.03	.01
☐ 61 Dave Hollins	.12	.05	.02
☐ 62 Scott Radinsky	.04	.02	.01
☐ 63 Francisco Cabrera	.04	.02	.01
☐ 64 Tim Layana	.04	.02	.01
☐ 65 Jim Leyritz	.04	.02	.01
☐ 66 Wayne Edwards	.04	.02	.01
☐ 67 Lee Stevens	.04	.02	.01
☐ 68 Bill Sampen UER	.04	.02	.01
(Fourth line, long			
is spelled along)			
☐ 69 Craig Grebeck UER	.04	.02	.01
(Born in Cerritos,			
not Johnstown)			
☐ 70 John Burkett	.04	.02	.01
☐ 71 Hector Villanueva	.04	.02	.01
☐ 72 Oscar Azocar	.04	.02	.01
☐ 73 Alan Mills	.04	.02	.01
☐ 74 Carlos Baerga	.20	.09	.03
☐ 75 Charles Nagy	.25	.11	.03
☐ 76 Tim Drummond	.04	.02	.01
☐ 77 Dana Kiecker	.04	.02	.01
☐ 78 Tom Edens	.10	.05	.01
☐ 79 Kent Mercker	.07	.03	.01
☐ 80 Steve Avery	.20	.09	.03
☐ 81 Lee Smith	.07	.03	.01
☐ 82 Dave Martinez	.04	.02	.01
☐ 83 Dave Winfield	.10	.05	.01
☐ 84 Bill Spiers	.04	.02	.01
☐ 85 Dan Pasqua	.04	.02	.01
☐ 86 Randy Milligan	.04	.02	.01
☐ 87 Tracy Jones	.04	.02	.01
☐ 88 Greg Myers	.04	.02	.01
☐ 89 Keith Hernandez	.07	.03	.01
☐ 90 Todd Benzinger	.04	.02	.01
☐ 91 Mike Jackson	.04	.02	.01
☐ 92 Mike Stanley	.04	.02	.01
☐ 93 Candy Maldonado	.04	.02	.01
☐ 94 John Kruk UER	.07	.03	.01
(No decimal point			
before 1990 BA)			
☐ 95 Cal Ripken UER	.30	.14	.04
(Genius spelled genuis)			
☐ 96 Willie Fraser	.04	.02	.01
☐ 97 Mike Felder	.04	.02	.01
☐ 98 Bill Landrum	.04	.02	.01
☐ 99 Chuck Crim	.04	.02	.01
☐ 100 Chuck Finley	.07	.03	.01
☐ 101 Kirt Manwaring	.04	.02	.01
☐ 102 Jaime Navarro	.07	.03	.01
☐ 103 Dickie Thon	.04	.02	.01
☐ 104 Brian Downing	.04	.02	.01
☐ 105 Jim Abbott	.12	.05	.02
☐ 106 Tom Brookens	.04	.02	.01
☐ 107 Darryl Hamilton UER	.07	.03	.01
(Bio info is for			
Jeff Hamilton)			
☐ 108 Bryan Harvey	.04	.02	.01
☐ 109 Greg A. Harris UER	.04	.02	.01
(Shown pitching lefty,			
bio says righty)			
☐ 110 Greg Swindell	.07	.03	.01
☐ 111 Juan Berenguer	.04	.02	.01
☐ 112 Mike Heath	.04	.02	.01
☐ 113 Scott Bradley	.04	.02	.01
☐ 114 Jack Morris	.10	.05	.01
☐ 115 Barry Jones	.04	.02	.01
☐ 116 Kevin Romine	.04	.02	.01
☐ 117 Garry Templeton	.04	.02	.01
☐ 118 Scott Sanderson	.04	.02	.01
☐ 119 Roberto Kelly	.07	.03	.01
☐ 120 George Brett	.10	.05	.01
☐ 121 Oddibe McDowell	.04	.02	.01
☐ 122 Jim Acker	.04	.02	.01
☐ 123 Bill Swift UER	.04	.02	.01
(Born 12/27/61,			
should be 10/27)			
☐ 124 Eric King	.04	.02	.01
☐ 125 Jay Buhner	.07	.03	.01
☐ 126 Matt Young	.04	.02	.01
☐ 127 Alvaro Espinoza	.04	.02	.01
☐ 128 Greg Hibbard	.04	.02	.01
☐ 129 Jeff M. Robinson	.04	.02	.01
☐ 130 Mike Greenwell	.07	.03	.01
☐ 131 Dion James	.04	.02	.01
☐ 132 Donn Pall UER	.04	.02	.01
(1988 ERA in stats 0.00)			
☐ 133 Lloyd Moseby	.04	.02	.01
☐ 134 Randy Velarde	.04	.02	.01
☐ 135 Allan Anderson	.04	.02	.01
☐ 136 Mark Davis	.04	.02	.01
☐ 137 Eric Davis	.07	.03	.01
☐ 138 Phil Stephenson	.04	.02	.01
☐ 139 Felix Fermin	.04	.02	.01
☐ 140 Pedro Guerrero	.07	.03	.01
☐ 141 Charlie Hough	.04	.02	.01
☐ 142 Mike Henneman	.04	.02	.01
☐ 143 Jeff Montgomery	.04	.02	.01
☐ 144 Lenny Harris	.04	.02	.01
☐ 145 Bruce Hurst	.07	.03	.01
☐ 146 Eric Anthony	.07	.03	.01
☐ 147 Paul Assenmacher	.04	.02	.01
☐ 148 Jesse Barfield	.04	.02	.01
☐ 149 Carlos Quintana	.04	.02	.01
☐ 150 Dave Stewart	.07	.03	.01

☐ 151 Roy Smith	.04	.02	.01
☐ 152 Paul Gibson	.04	.02	.01
☐ 153 Mickey Hatcher	.04	.02	.01
☐ 154 Jim Eisenreich	.04	.02	.01
☐ 155 Kenny Rogers	.04	.02	.01
☐ 156 Dave Schmidt	.04	.02	.01
☐ 157 Lance Johnson	.04	.02	.01
☐ 158 Dave West	.04	.02	.01
☐ 159 Steve Balboni	.04	.02	.01
☐ 160 Jeff Brantley	.04	.02	.01
☐ 161 Craig Biggio	.07	.03	.01
☐ 162 Brook Jacoby	.04	.02	.01
☐ 163 Dan Gladden	.04	.02	.01
☐ 164 Jeff Reardon UER	.07	.03	.01
(Total IP shown as			
943.2, should be 943.1)			
☐ 165 Mark Carreon	.04	.02	.01
☐ 166 Mel Hall	.04	.02	.01
☐ 167 Gary Mielke	.04	.02	.01
☐ 168 Cecil Fielder	.12	.05	.02
☐ 169 Darrin Jackson	.07	.03	.01
☐ 170 Rick Aguilera	.07	.03	.01
☐ 171 Walt Weiss	.04	.02	.01
☐ 172 Steve Farr	.04	.02	.01
☐ 173 Jody Reed	.04	.02	.01
☐ 174 Mike Jeffcoat	.04	.02	.01
☐ 175 Mark Grace	.10	.05	.01
☐ 176 Larry Sheets	.04	.02	.01
☐ 177 Bill Gullickson	.04	.02	.01
☐ 178 Chris Gwynn	.04	.02	.01
☐ 179 Melido Perez	.07	.03	.01
☐ 180 Sid Fernandez UER	.07	.03	.01
(779 runs in 1990)			
☐ 181 Tim Burke	.04	.02	.01
☐ 182 Gary Pettis	.04	.02	.01
☐ 183 Rob Murphy	.04	.02	.01
☐ 184 Craig Lefferts	.04	.02	.01
☐ 185 Howard Johnson	.07	.03	.01
☐ 186 Ken Caminiti	.07	.03	.01
☐ 187 Tim Belcher	.07	.03	.01
☐ 188 Greg Cadaret	.04	.02	.01
☐ 189 Matt Williams	.07	.03	.01
☐ 190 Dave Magadan	.07	.03	.01
☐ 191 Geno Petralli	.04	.02	.01
☐ 192 Jeff D. Robinson	.04	.02	.01
☐ 193 Jim Deshaies	.04	.02	.01
☐ 194 Willie Randolph	.07	.03	.01
☐ 195 George Bell	.07	.03	.01
☐ 196 Hubie Brooks	.04	.02	.01
☐ 197 Tom Gordon	.07	.03	.01
☐ 198 Mike Fitzgerald	.04	.02	.01
☐ 199 Mike Pagliarulo	.04	.02	.01
☐ 200 Kirby Puckett	.20	.09	.03
☐ 201 Shawon Dunston	.07	.03	.01
☐ 202 Dennis Boyd	.04	.02	.01
☐ 203 Junior Felix UER	.04	.02	.01
(Text has him in NL)			

☐ 204 Alejandro Pena	.04	.02	.01
☐ 205 Pete Smith	.07	.03	.01
☐ 206 Tom Glavine UER	.20	.09	.03
(Lefty spelled leftie)			
☐ 207 Luis Salazar	.04	.02	.01
☐ 208 John Smoltz	.10	.05	.01
☐ 209 Doug Dascenzo	.04	.02	.01
☐ 210 Tim Wallach	.07	.03	.01
☐ 211 Greg Gagne	.04	.02	.01
☐ 212 Mark Gubicza	.04	.02	.01
☐ 213 Mark Parent	.04	.02	.01
☐ 214 Ken Oberkfell	.04	.02	.01
☐ 215 Gary Carter	.07	.03	.01
☐ 216 Rafael Palmeiro	.10	.05	.01
☐ 217 Tom Niedenfuer	.04	.02	.01
☐ 218 Dave LaPoint	.04	.02	.01
☐ 219 Jeff Treadway	.04	.02	.01
☐ 220 Mitch Williams UER	.04	.02	.01
('89 ERA shown as 2.76,			
should be 2.64)			
☐ 221 Jose DeLeon	.04	.02	.01
☐ 222 Mike LaValliere	.04	.02	.01
☐ 223 Darrel Akerfelds	.04	.02	.01
☐ 224A Kent Anderson ERR	.08	.04	.01
(First line, flachy			
should read flashy)			
☐ 224B Kent Anderson COR	.08	.04	.01
(Corrected in			
factory sets)			
☐ 225 Dwight Evans	.07	.03	.01
☐ 226 Gary Redus	.04	.02	.01
☐ 227 Paul O'Neill	.07	.03	.01
☐ 228 Marty Barrett	.04	.02	.01
☐ 229 Tom Browning	.04	.02	.01
☐ 230 Terry Pendleton	.10	.05	.01
☐ 231 Jack Armstrong	.04	.02	.01
☐ 232 Mike Boddicker	.04	.02	.01
☐ 233 Neal Heaton	.04	.02	.01
☐ 234 Marquis Grissom	.15	.07	.02
☐ 235 Bert Blyleven	.07	.03	.01
☐ 236 Curt Young	.04	.02	.01
☐ 237 Don Carman	.04	.02	.01
☐ 238 Charlie Hayes	.04	.02	.01
☐ 239 Mark Knudson	.04	.02	.01
☐ 240 Todd Zeile	.07	.03	.01
☐ 241 Larry Walker UER	.20	.09	.03
(Maple River, should			
be Maple Ridge)			
☐ 242 Jerald Clark	.04	.02	.01
☐ 243 Jeff Ballard	.04	.02	.01
☐ 244 Jeff King	.04	.02	.01
☐ 245 Tom Brunansky	.04	.02	.01
☐ 246 Darren Daulton	.07	.03	.01
☐ 247 Scott Terry	.04	.02	.01
☐ 248 Rob Deer	.07	.03	.01
☐ 249 Brady Anderson UER	.07	.03	.01
(1990 Hagerstown 1 hit,			

should say 13 hits)			
☐ 250 Len Dykstra	07	.03	.01
☐ 251 Greg W. Harris	04	.02	.01
☐ 252 Mike Hartley	04	.02	.01
☐ 253 Joey Cora	04	.02	.01
☐ 254 Ivan Calderon	04	.02	.01
☐ 255 Ted Power	04	.02	.01
☐ 256 Sammy Sosa	07	.03	.01
☐ 257 Steve Buechele	04	.02	.01
☐ 258 Mike Devereaux UER	07	.03	.01
(No comma between			
city and state)			
☐ 259 Brad Komminsk UER	04	.02	.01
(Last text line,			
Ba should be BA)			
☐ 260 Teddy Higuera	04	.02	.01
☐ 261 Shawn Abner	04	.02	.01
☐ 262 Dave Valle	04	.02	.01
☐ 263 Jeff Huson	04	.02	.01
☐ 264 Edgar Martinez	07	.03	.01
☐ 265 Carlton Fisk	10	.05	.01
☐ 266 Steve Finley	07	.03	.01
☐ 267 John Wetteland	07	.03	.01
☐ 268 Kevin Appier	07	.03	.01
☐ 269 Steve Lyons	04	.02	.01
☐ 270 Mickey Tettleton	07	.03	.01
☐ 271 Luis Rivera	04	.02	.01
☐ 272 Steve Jeltz	04	.02	.01
☐ 273 R.J. Reynolds	04	.02	.01
☐ 274 Carlos Martinez	04	.02	.01
☐ 275 Dan Plesac	04	.02	.01
☐ 276 Mike Morgan UER	04	.02	.01
(Total IP shown as			
1149.1, should be 1149)			
☐ 277 Jeff Russell	04	.02	.01
☐ 278 Pete Incaviglia	04	.02	.01
☐ 279 Kevin Seitzer UER	07	.03	.01
(Bio has 200 hits twice			
and .300 four times,			
should be once and			
three times)			
☐ 280 Bobby Thigpen	04	.02	.01
☐ 281 Stan Javier UER	04	.02	.01
(Born 1/9,			
should say 9/1)			
☐ 282 Henry Cotto	04	.02	.01
☐ 283 Gary Wayne	04	.02	.01
☐ 284 Shane Mack	07	.03	.01
☐ 285 Brian Holman	04	.02	.01
☐ 286 Gerald Perry	04	.02	.01
☐ 287 Steve Crawford	04	.02	.01
☐ 288 Nelson Liriano	04	.02	.01
☐ 289 Don Aase	04	.02	.01
☐ 290 Randy Johnson	07	.03	.01
☐ 291 Harold Baines	07	.03	.01
☐ 292 Kent Hrbek	07	.03	.01
☐ 293A Les Lancaster ERR	04	.02	.01

(No comma between			
Dallas and Texas)			
☐ 293B Les Lancaster COR	04	.02	.01
(Corrected in			
factory sets)			
☐ 294 Jeff Musselman	04	.02	.01
☐ 295 Kurt Stillwell	04	.02	.01
☐ 296 Stan Belinda	04	.02	.01
☐ 297 Lou Whitaker	07	.03	.01
☐ 298 Glenn Wilson	04	.02	.01
☐ 299 Omar Vizquel UER	04	.02	.01
(Born 5/15, should be			
4/24, there is a decimal			
before GP total for '90)			
☐ 300 Ramon Martinez	10	.05	.01
☐ 301 Dwight Smith	04	.02	.01
☐ 302 Tim Crews	04	.02	.01
☐ 303 Lance Blankenship	04	.02	.01
☐ 304 Sid Bream	04	.02	.01
☐ 305 Rafael Ramirez	04	.02	.01
☐ 306 Steve Wilson	04	.02	.01
☐ 307 Mackey Sasser	04	.02	.01
☐ 308 Franklin Stubbs	04	.02	.01
☐ 309 Jack Daugherty UER	04	.02	.01
(Born 6/3/60,			
should say July)			
☐ 310 Eddie Murray	10	.05	.01
☐ 311 Bob Welch	04	.02	.01
☐ 312 Brian Harper	04	.02	.01
☐ 313 Lance McCullers	04	.02	.01
☐ 314 Dave Smith	04	.02	.01
☐ 315 Bobby Bonilla	10	.05	.01
☐ 316 Jerry Don Gleaton	04	.02	.01
☐ 317 Greg Maddux	10	.05	.01
☐ 318 Keith Miller	04	.02	.01
☐ 319 Mark Portugal	04	.02	.01
☐ 320 Robin Ventura	20	.09	.03
☐ 321 Bob Ojeda	04	.02	.01
☐ 322 Mike Harkey	07	.03	.01
☐ 323 Jay Bell	07	.03	.01
☐ 324 Mark McGwire	20	.09	.03
☐ 325 Gary Gaetti	04	.02	.01
☐ 326 Jeff Pico	04	.02	.01
☐ 327 Kevin McReynolds	07	.03	.01
☐ 328 Frank Tanana	04	.02	.01
☐ 329 Eric Yelding UER	04	.02	.01
(Listed as 6'3",			
should be 5'11")			
☐ 330 Barry Bonds	20	.09	.03
☐ 331 Brian McRae RP UER	20	.09	.03
(No comma between			
city and state)			
☐ 332 Pedro Munoz RP	25	.11	.03
☐ 333 Daryl Irvine RP	05	.02	.01
☐ 334 Chris Hoiles RP	10	.05	.01
☐ 335 Thomas Howard RP	10	.05	.01
☐ 336 Jeff Schulz RP	05	.02	.01

☐ 337	Jeff Manto RP 05	.02	.01
☐ 338	Beau Allred RP 05	.02	.01
☐ 339	Mike Bordick RP 35	.16	.04
☐ 340	Todd Hundley RP 08	.04	.01
☐ 341	Jim Vatcher RP UER ..05	.02	.01
	(Height 6'9",		
	should be 5'9")		
☐ 342	Luis Sojo RP 08	.04	.01
☐ 343	Jose Offerman RP UER ..10	.05	.01
	(Born 1969, should		
	say 1968)		
☐ 344	Pete Coachman RP 05	.02	.01
☐ 345	Mike Benjamin RP 05	.02	.01
☐ 346	Ozzie Canseco RP 10	.05	.01
☐ 347	Tim McIntosh RP 05	.02	.01
☐ 348	Phil Plantier RP 50	.23	.06
☐ 349	Terry Shumpert RP 05	.02	.01
☐ 350	Darren Lewis RP 10	.05	.01
☐ 351	David Walsh RP 10	.05	.01
☐ 352A	Scott Chiamparino RP ..05	.02	.01
	ERR (Bats left,		
	should be right)		
☐ 352B	Scott Chiamparino RP ..05	.02	.01
	COR (corrected in		
	factory sets)		
☐ 353	Julio Valera RP 15	.07	.02
	UER (Progressed mis-		
	spelled as progessed)		
☐ 354	Anthony Telford RP 05	.02	.01
☐ 355	Kevin Wickander RP 05	.02	.01
☐ 356	Tim Naehring RP 08	.04	.01
☐ 357	Jim Poole RP 05	.02	.01
☐ 358	Mark Whiten RP UER 12	.05	.02
	(Shown hitting lefty,		
	bio says righty)		
☐ 359	Terry Wells RP 10	.05	.01
☐ 360	Rafael Valdez RP........05	.02	.01
☐ 361	Mel Stottlemyre Jr. RP 05	.02	.01
☐ 362	David Segui RP 05	.02	.01
☐ 363	Paul Abbott RP 10	.05	.01
☐ 364	Steve Howard RP 08	.04	.01
☐ 365	Karl Rhodes RP 05	.02	.01
☐ 366	Rafael Novoa RP 10	.05	.01
☐ 367	Joe Grahe RP 15	.07	.02
☐ 368	Darren Reed RP 05	.02	.01
☐ 369	Jeff McKnight RP 05	.02	.01
☐ 370	Scott Leius RP 10	.05	.01
☐ 371	Mark Dewey RP 10	.05	.01
☐ 372	Mark Lee RP UER 10	.05	.01
	(Shown hitting lefty,		
	bio says righty, born		
	in Dakota, should		
	say North Dakota)		
☐ 373	Rosario Rodriguez RP 10	.05	.01
	(Shown hitting lefty,		
	bio says righty) UER		
☐ 374	Chuck McElroy RP 05	.02	.01

☐ 375	Mike Bell RP 10	.05	.01
☐ 376	Mickey Morandini RP....12	.05	.02
☐ 377	Bill Haselman RP 10	.05	.01
☐ 378	Dave Pavlas RP 10	.05	.01
☐ 379	Derrick May RP 10	.05	.01
☐ 380	Jeromy Burnitz FDP 30	.14	.04
☐ 381	Donald Peters FDP 10	.05	.01
☐ 382	Alex Fernandez FDP 15	.07	.02
☐ 383	Mike Mussina FDP 1.50	.65	.19
☐ 384	Dan Smith FDP 20	.09	.03
☐ 385	Lance Dickson FDP 10	.05	.01
☐ 386	Carl Everett FDP 25	.11	.03
☐ 387	Thomas Nevers FDP 12	.05	.02
☐ 388	Adam Hyzdu FDP 15	.07	.02
☐ 389	Todd Van Poppel FDP 50	.23	.06
☐ 390	Rondell White FDP 50	.23	.06
☐ 391	Marc Newfield FDP 40	.18	.05
☐ 392	Julio Franco AS 05	.02	.01
☐ 393	Wade Boggs AS 10	.05	.01
☐ 394	Ozzie Guillen AS 05	.02	.01
☐ 395	Cecil Fielder AS 10	.05	.01
☐ 396	Ken Griffey Jr. AS 25	.11	.03
☐ 397	Rickey Henderson AS 10	.05	.01
☐ 398	Jose Canseco AS 12	.05	.02
☐ 399	Roger Clemens AS 12	.05	.02
☐ 400	Sandy Alomar Jr. AS 05	.02	.01
☐ 401	Bobby Thigpen AS 05	.02	.01
☐ 402	Bobby Bonilla MB 08	.04	.01
☐ 403	Eric Davis MB 08	.04	.01
☐ 404	Fred McGriff MB 10	.05	.01
☐ 405	Glenn Davis MB 05	.02	.01
☐ 406	Kevin Mitchell MB 08	.04	.01
☐ 407	Rob Dibble MB 05	.02	.01
☐ 408	Ramon Martinez KM 05	.02	.01
☐ 409	David Cone KM 08	.04	.01
☐ 410	Bobby Witt KM 05	.02	.01
☐ 411	Mark Langston KM 05	.02	.01
☐ 412	Bo Jackson RIF 10	.05	.01
☐ 413	Shawon Dunston RIF 05	.02	.01
	UER (In the baseball,		
	should say in baseball)		
☐ 414	Jesse Barfield RIF 05	.02	.01
☐ 415	Ken Caminiti RIF 05	.02	.01
☐ 416	Benito Santiago RIF 05	.02	.01
☐ 417	Nolan Ryan HL 25	.11	.03
☐ 418	Bobby Thigpen HL UER ..05	.02	.01
	(Back refers to Hal		
	McRae Jr., should		
	say Brian McRae)		
☐ 419	Ramon Martinez HL......05	.02	.01
☐ 420	Bo Jackson HL 10	.05	.01
☐ 421	Carlton Fisk HL 10	.05	.01
☐ 422	Jimmy Key 04	.02	.01
☐ 423	Junior Noboa 04	.02	.01
☐ 424	Al Newman 04	.02	.01
☐ 425	Pat Borders 04	.02	.01
☐ 426	Von Hayes 04	.02	.01

☐	427 Tim Teufel	.04	.02	.01
☐	428 Eric Plunk UER	.04	.02	.01
	(Text says Eric's had,			
	no apostrophe needed)			
☐	429 John Moses	.04	.02	.01
☐	430 Mike Witt	.04	.02	.01
☐	431 Otis Nixon	.03	.01	
☐	432 Tony Fernandez	.07	.03	.01
☐	433 Rance Mulliniks	.04	.02	.01
☐	434 Dan Petry	.04	.02	.01
☐	435 Bob Geren	.04	.02	.01
☐	436 Steve Frey	.04	.02	.01
☐	437 Jamie Moyer	.04	.02	.01
☐	438 Junior Ortiz	.04	.02	.01
☐	439 Tom O'Malley	.04	.02	.01
☐	440 Pat Combs	.04	.02	.01
☐	441 Jose Canseco DT	1.25	.55	.16
☐	442 Alfredo Griffin	.04	.02	.01
☐	443 Andres Galarraga	.04	.02	.01
☐	444 Bryn Smith	.04	.02	.01
☐	445 Andre Dawson	.10	.05	.01
☐	446 Juan Samuel	.04	.02	.01
☐	447 Mike Aldrete	.04	.02	.01
☐	448 Ron Gant	.12	.05	.02
☐	449 Fernando Valenzuela	.07	.03	.01
☐	450 Vince Coleman UER	.07	.03	.01
	(Should say topped			
	majors in steals four			
	times, not three times)			
☐	451 Kevin Mitchell	.07	.03	.01
☐	452 Spike Owen	.04	.02	.01
☐	453 Mike Bielecki	.04	.02	.01
☐	454 Dennis Martinez	.07	.03	.01
☐	455 Brett Butler	.07	.03	.01
☐	456 Ron Darling	.07	.03	.01
☐	457 Dennis Rasmussen	.04	.02	.01
☐	458 Ken Howell	.04	.02	.01
☐	459 Steve Bedrosian	.04	.02	.01
☐	460 Frank Viola	.07	.03	.01
☐	461 Jose Lind	.04	.02	.01
☐	462 Chris Sabo	.07	.03	.01
☐	463 Dante Bichette	.04	.02	.01
☐	464 Rick Mahler	.04	.02	.01
☐	465 John Smiley	.07	.03	.01
☐	466 Devon White	.07	.03	.01
☐	467 John Orton	.04	.02	.01
☐	468 Mike Stanton	.04	.02	.01
☐	469 Billy Hatcher	.04	.02	.01
☐	470 Wally Joyner	.07	.03	.01
☐	471 Gene Larkin	.04	.02	.01
☐	472 Doug Drabek	.07	.03	.01
☐	473 Gary Sheffield	.25	.11	.03
☐	474 David Wells	.04	.02	.01
☐	475 Andy Van Slyke	.10	.05	.01
☐	476 Mike Gallego	.04	.02	.01
☐	477 B.J. Surhoff	.04	.02	.01
☐	478 Gene Nelson	.04	.02	.01
☐	479 Mariano Duncan	.04	.02	.01
☐	480 Fred McGriff	.12	.05	.02
☐	481 Jerry Browne	.04	.02	.01
☐	482 Alvin Davis	.04	.02	.01
☐	483 Bill Wegman	.04	.02	.01
☐	484 Dave Parker	.07	.03	.01
☐	485 Dennis Eckersley	.10	.05	.01
☐	486 Erik Hanson UER	.04	.02	.01
	(Basketball misspelled			
	as basketball)			
☐	487 Bill Ripken	.04	.02	.01
☐	488 Tom Candiotti	.04	.02	.01
☐	489 Mike Schooler	.04	.02	.01
☐	490 Gregg Olson	.07	.03	.01
☐	491 Chris James	.04	.02	.01
☐	492 Pete Harnisch	.07	.03	.01
☐	493 Julio Franco	.07	.03	.01
☐	494 Greg Briley	.04	.02	.01
☐	495 Ruben Sierra	.15	.07	.02
☐	496 Steve Olin	.07	.03	.01
☐	497 Mike Fetters	.04	.02	.01
☐	498 Mark Williamson	.04	.02	.01
☐	499 Bob Tewksbury	.07	.03	.01
☐	500 Tony Gwynn	.12	.05	.02
☐	501 Randy Myers	.07	.03	.01
☐	502 Keith Comstock	.04	.02	.01
☐	503 Craig Worthington UER	.04	.02	.01
	(DeCinces misspelled			
	DiCinces on back)			
☐	504 Mark Eichhorn UER	.04	.02	.01
	(Stats incomplete,			
	doesn't have '89			
	Braves stint)			
☐	505 Barry Larkin	.10	.05	.01
☐	506 Dave Johnson	.04	.02	.01
☐	507 Bobby Witt	.04	.02	.01
☐	508 Joe Orsulak	.04	.02	.01
☐	509 Pete O'Brien	.04	.02	.01
☐	510 Brad Arnsberg	.04	.02	.01
☐	511 Storm Davis	.04	.02	.01
☐	512 Bob Milacki	.04	.02	.01
☐	513 Bill Pecota	.04	.02	.01
☐	514 Glenallen Hill	.07	.03	.01
☐	515 Danny Tartabull	.07	.03	.01
☐	516 Mike Moore	.04	.02	.01
☐	517 Ron Robinson UER	.04	.02	.01
	(577 K's in 1990)			
☐	518 Mark Gardner	.04	.02	.01
☐	519 Rick Wrona	.04	.02	.01
☐	520 Mike Scioscia	.04	.02	.01
☐	521 Frank Wills	.04	.02	.01
☐	522 Greg Brock	.04	.02	.01
☐	523 Jack Clark	.07	.03	.01
☐	524 Bruce Ruffin	.04	.02	.01
☐	525 Robin Yount	.10	.05	.01
☐	526 Tom Foley	.04	.02	.01
☐	527 Pat Perry	.04	.02	.01

☐ 528	Greg Vaughn	.08	.04	.01
☐ 529	Wally Whitehurst	.04	.02	.01
☐ 530	Norm Charlton	.07	.03	.01
☐ 531	Marvell Wynne	.04	.02	.01
☐ 532	Jim Gantner	.04	.02	.01
☐ 533	Greg Litton	.04	.02	.01
☐ 534	Manny Lee	.04	.02	.01
☐ 535	Scott Bailes	.04	.02	.01
☐ 536	Charlie Leibrandt	.04	.02	.01
☐ 537	Roger McDowell	.04	.02	.01
☐ 538	Andy Benes	.10	.05	.01
☐ 539	Rick Honeycutt	.04	.02	.01
☐ 540	Dwight Gooden	.07	.03	.01
☐ 541	Scott Garrelts	.04	.02	.01
☐ 542	Dave Clark	.04	.02	.01
☐ 543	Lonnie Smith	.04	.02	.01
☐ 544	Rick Reuschel	.04	.02	.01
☐ 545	Delino DeShields UER	.15	.07	.02
	(Rockford misspelled			
	as Rock Ford in '88)			
☐ 546	Mike Sharperson	.04	.02	.01
☐ 547	Mike Kingery	.04	.02	.01
☐ 548	Terry Kennedy	.04	.02	.01
☐ 549	David Cone	.10	.05	.01
☐ 550	Orel Hershiser	.07	.03	.01
☐ 551	Matt Nokes	.04	.02	.01
☐ 552	Eddie Williams	.04	.02	.01
☐ 553	Frank DiPino	.04	.02	.01
☐ 554	Fred Lynn	.07	.03	.01
☐ 555	Alex Cole	.04	.02	.01
☐ 556	Terry Leach	.04	.02	.01
☐ 557	Chet Lemon	.04	.02	.01
☐ 558	Paul Mirabella	.04	.02	.01
☐ 559	Bill Long	.04	.02	.01
☐ 560	Phil Bradley	.04	.02	.01
☐ 561	Duane Ward	.04	.02	.01
☐ 562	Dave Bergman	.04	.02	.01
☐ 563	Eric Show	.04	.02	.01
☐ 564	Xavier Hernandez	.04	.02	.01
☐ 565	Jeff Parrett	.04	.02	.01
☐ 566	Chuck Cary	.04	.02	.01
☐ 567	Ken Hill	.07	.03	.01
☐ 568	Bob Welch Hand	.04	.02	.01
	(Complement should be			
	compliment) UER			
☐ 569	John Mitchell	.04	.02	.01
☐ 570	Travis Fryman	.60	.25	.08
☐ 571	Derek Lilliquist	.04	.02	.01
☐ 572	Steve Lake	.04	.02	.01
☐ 573	John Barfield	.04	.02	.01
☐ 574	Randy Bush	.04	.02	.01
☐ 575	Joe Magrane	.04	.02	.01
☐ 576	Eddie Diaz	.04	.02	.01
☐ 577	Casey Candaele	.04	.02	.01
☐ 578	Jesse Orosco	.04	.02	.01
☐ 579	Tom Henke	.07	.03	.01
☐ 580	Rick Cerone UER	.04	.02	.01

	(Actually his third			
	go-round with Yankees)			
☐ 581	Drew Hall	.04	.02	.01
☐ 582	Tony Castillo	.04	.02	.01
☐ 583	Jimmy Jones	.04	.02	.01
☐ 584	Rick Reed	.04	.02	.01
☐ 585	Joe Girardi	.04	.02	.01
☐ 586	Jeff Gray	.04	.02	.01
☐ 587	Luis Polonia	.07	.03	.01
☐ 588	Joe Klink	.04	.02	.01
☐ 589	Rex Hudler	.04	.02	.01
☐ 590	Kirk McCaskill	.04	.02	.01
☐ 591	Juan Agosto	.04	.02	.01
☐ 592	Wes Gardner	.04	.02	.01
☐ 593	Rich Rodriguez	.10	.05	.01
☐ 594	Mitch Webster	.04	.02	.01
☐ 595	Kelly Gruber	.07	.03	.01
☐ 596	Dale Mohorcic	.04	.02	.01
☐ 597	Willie McGee	.07	.03	.01
☐ 598	Bill Krueger	.04	.02	.01
☐ 599	Bob Walk UER	.04	.02	.01
	(Cards says he's 33,			
	but actually he's 34)			
☐ 600	Kevin Maas	.08	.04	.01
☐ 601	Danny Jackson	.04	.02	.01
☐ 602	Craig McMurtry UER	.04	.02	.01
	(Anonymously misspelled			
	anonimously)			
☐ 603	Curtis Wilkerson	.04	.02	.01
☐ 604	Adam Peterson	.04	.02	.01
☐ 605	Sam Horn	.04	.02	.01
☐ 606	Tommy Gregg	.04	.02	.01
☐ 607	Ken Dayley	.04	.02	.01
☐ 608	Carmelo Castillo	.04	.02	.01
☐ 609	John Shelby	.04	.02	.01
☐ 610	Don Slaught	.04	.02	.01
☐ 611	Calvin Schiraldi	.04	.02	.01
☐ 612	Dennis Lamp	.04	.02	.01
☐ 613	Andres Thomas	.04	.02	.01
☐ 614	Jose Gonzalez	.04	.02	.01
☐ 615	Randy Ready	.04	.02	.01
☐ 616	Kevin Bass	.04	.02	.01
☐ 617	Mike Marshall	.04	.02	.01
☐ 618	Daryl Boston	.04	.02	.01
☐ 619	Andy McGaffigan	.04	.02	.01
☐ 620	Joe Oliver	.04	.02	.01
☐ 621	Jim Gott	.04	.02	.01
☐ 622	Jose Oquendo	.04	.02	.01
☐ 623	Jose DeJesus	.04	.02	.01
☐ 624	Mike Brumley	.04	.02	.01
☐ 625	John Olerud	.15	.07	.02
☐ 626	Ernest Riles	.04	.02	.01
☐ 627	Gene Harris	.04	.02	.01
☐ 628	Jose Uribe	.04	.02	.01
☐ 629	Darnell Coles	.04	.02	.01
☐ 630	Carney Lansford	.07	.03	.01
☐ 631	Tim Leary	.04	.02	.01

☐ 632	Tim Hulett	.04	.02	.01
☐ 633	Kevin Elster	.04	.02	.01
☐ 634	Tony Fossas	.04	.02	.01
☐ 635	Francisco Oliveras	.04	.02	.01
☐ 636	Bob Patterson	.04	.02	.01
☐ 637	Gary Ward	.04	.02	.01
☐ 638	Rene Gonzales	.04	.02	.01
☐ 639	Don Robinson	.04	.02	.01
☐ 640	Darryl Strawberry	.12	.05	.02
☐ 641	Dave Anderson	.04	.02	.01
☐ 642	Scott Scudder	.04	.02	.01
☐ 643	Reggie Harris UER	.10	.05	.01
	(Hepatitis misspelled as hepititis)			
☐ 644	Dave Henderson	.04	.02	.01
☐ 645	Ben McDonald	.10	.05	.01
☐ 646	Bob Kipper	.04	.02	.01
☐ 647	Hal Morris UER	.07	.03	.01
	(It's should be its)			
☐ 648	Tim Birtsas	.04	.02	.01
☐ 649	Steve Searcy	.04	.02	.01
☐ 650	Dale Murphy	.07	.03	.01
☐ 651	Ron Oester	.04	.02	.01
☐ 652	Mike LaCoss	.04	.02	.01
☐ 653	Ron Jones	.04	.02	.01
☐ 654	Kelly Downs	.04	.02	.01
☐ 655	Roger Clemens	.25	.11	.03
☐ 656	Herm Winningham	.04	.02	.01
☐ 657	Trevor Wilson	.04	.02	.01
☐ 658	Jose Rijo	.07	.03	.01
☐ 659	Dann Bilardello UER	.04	.02	.01
	(Bio has 13 games, 1 hit, and 32 AB, stats show 19, 2, and 37)			
☐ 660	Gregg Jefferies	.07	.03	.01
☐ 661	Doug Drabek AS UER	.05	.02	.01
	(Through is misspelled though)			
☐ 662	Randy Myers AS	.05	.02	.01
☐ 663	Benny Santiago AS	.05	.02	.01
☐ 664	Will Clark AS	.10	.05	.01
☐ 665	Ryne Sandberg AS	.12	.05	.02
☐ 666	Barry Larkin AS UER	.08	.04	.01
	(Line 13, coolly misspelled cooly)			
☐ 667	Matt Williams AS	.05	.02	.01
☐ 668	Barry Bonds AS	.10	.05	.01
☐ 669	Eric Davis AS	.05	.02	.01
☐ 670	Bobby Bonilla AS	.08	.04	.01
☐ 671	Chipper Jones FDP	.75	.35	.09
☐ 672	Eric Christopherson FDP	.15	.07	.02
☐ 673	Robbie Beckett FDP	.12	.05	.02
☐ 674	Shane Andrews FDP	.20	.09	.03
☐ 675	Steve Karsay FDP	.25	.11	.03
☐ 676	Aaron Holbert FDP	.12	.05	.02
☐ 677	Donovan Osborne FDP	.50	.23	.06

☐ 678	Todd Ritchie FDP	.10	.05	.01
☐ 679	Ron Walden FDP	.10	.05	.01
☐ 680	Tim Costo FDP	.20	.09	.03
☐ 681	Dan Wilson FDP	.15	.07	.02
☐ 682	Kurt Miller FDP	.25	.11	.03
☐ 683	Mike Lieberthal FDP	.20	.09	.03
☐ 684	Roger Clemens KM	.12	.05	.02
☐ 685	Doc Gooden KM	.08	.04	.01
☐ 686	Nolan Ryan KM	.25	.11	.03
☐ 687	Frank Viola KM	.05	.02	.01
☐ 688	Erik Hanson KM	.05	.02	.01
☐ 689	Matt Williams MB	.05	.02	.01
☐ 690	Jose Canseco MB UER	.12	.05	.02
	(Mammoth misspelled as monmouth)			
☐ 691	Darryl Strawberry MB	.10	.05	.01
☐ 692	Bo Jackson MB	.10	.05	.01
☐ 693	Cecil Fielder MB	.10	.05	.01
☐ 694	Sandy Alomar Jr. RF	.05	.02	.01
☐ 695	Cory Snyder RF	.05	.02	.01
☐ 696	Eric Davis RF	.08	.04	.01
☐ 697	Ken Griffey Jr. RF	.25	.11	.03
☐ 698	Andy Van Slyke RF UER	.05	.02	.01
	(Line 2, outfielders does not need)			
☐ 699	Langston/Witt NH	.05	.02	.01
	Mark Langston Mike Witt			
☐ 700	Randy Johnson NH	.05	.02	.01
☐ 701	Nolan Ryan NH	.25	.11	.03
☐ 702	Dave Stewart NH	.05	.02	.01
☐ 703	Fernando Valenzuela NH	.05	.02	.01
☐ 704	Andy Hawkins NH	.05	.02	.01
☐ 705	Melido Perez NH	.05	.02	.01
☐ 706	Terry Mulholland NH	.05	.02	.01
☐ 707	Dave Stieb NH	.05	.02	.01
☐ 708	Brian Barnes RP	.12	.05	.02
☐ 709	Bernard Gilkey RP	.12	.05	.02
☐ 710	Steve Decker RP	.15	.07	.02
☐ 711	Paul Faries RP	.04	.02	.01
☐ 712	Paul Marak RP	.04	.02	.01
☐ 713	Wes Chamberlain RP	.20	.09	.03
☐ 714	Kevin Belcher RP	.10	.05	.01
☐ 715	Dan Boone RP UER	.04	.02	.01
	(IP adds up to 101, but card has 101.2)			
☐ 716	Steve Adkins RP	.10	.05	.01
☐ 717	Geronimo Pena RP	.10	.05	.01
☐ 718	Howard Farmer RP	.04	.02	.01
☐ 719	Mark Leonard RP	.10	.05	.01
☐ 720	Tom Lampkin RP	.04	.02	.01
☐ 721	Mike Gardiner RP	.10	.05	.01
☐ 722	Jeff Conine RP	.25	.11	.03
☐ 723	Efrain Valdez RP	.04	.02	.01
☐ 724	Chuck Malone RP	.04	.02	.01
☐ 725	Leo Gomez RP	.25	.11	.03
☐ 726	Paul McClellan RP	.04	.02	.01

☐ 727	Mark Leiter RP	.10	.05	.01
☐ 728	Rich DeLucia RP UER	.04	.02	.01
	(Line 2, all told is written alltold)			
☐ 729	Mel Rojas RP	.10	.05	.01
☐ 730	Hector Wagner RP	.04	.02	.01
☐ 731	Ray Lankford RP	.30	.14	.04
☐ 732	Turner Ward RP	.10	.05	.01
☐ 733	Gerald Alexander RP	.10	.05	.01
☐ 734	Scott Anderson RP	.10	.05	.01
☐ 735	Tony Perezchica RP	.04	.02	.01
☐ 736	Jimmy Kremers RP	.04	.02	.01
☐ 737	American Flag	.30	.14	.04
	(Pray for Peace)			
☐ 738	Mike York RP	.04	.02	.01
☐ 739	Mike Rochford RP	.04	.02	.01
☐ 740	Scott Aldred RP	.10	.05	.01
☐ 741	Rico Brogna RP	.12	.05	.02
☐ 742	Dave Burba RP	.10	.05	.01
☐ 743	Ray Stephens RP	.10	.05	.01
☐ 744	Eric Gunderson RP	.04	.02	.01
☐ 745	Troy Afenir RP	.10	.05	.01
☐ 746	Jeff Shaw RP	.04	.02	.01
☐ 747	Orlando Merced RP	.20	.09	.03
☐ 748	Omar Olivares RP UER	.12	.05	.02
	(Line 9, league is misspelled leagueu)			
☐ 749	Jerry Kutzler RP	.04	.02	.01
☐ 750	Mo Vaughn RP UER	.20	.09	.03
	(44 SB's in 1990)			
☐ 751	Matt Stark RP	.10	.05	.01
☐ 752	Randy Hennis RP	.10	.05	.01
☐ 753	Andujar Cedeno RP	.12	.05	.02
☐ 754	Kelvin Torve RP	.04	.02	.01
☐ 755	Joe Kraemer RP	.04	.02	.01
☐ 756	Phil Clark RP	.15	.07	.02
☐ 757	Ed Vosberg RP	.10	.05	.01
☐ 758	Mike Perez RP	.15	.07	.02
☐ 759	Scott Lewis RP	.10	.05	.01
☐ 760	Steve Chitren RP	.10	.05	.01
☐ 761	Ray Young RP	.10	.05	.01
☐ 762	Andres Santana RP	.10	.05	.01
☐ 763	Rodney McCray RP	.04	.02	.01
☐ 764	Sean Berry RP UER	.12	.05	.02
	(Name misspelled Barry on card front)			
☐ 765	Brent Mayne RP	.07	.03	.01
☐ 766	Mike Simms RP	.10	.05	.01
☐ 767	Glenn Sutko RP	.04	.02	.01
☐ 768	Gary DiSarcina RP	.07	.03	.01
☐ 769	George Brett HL	.10	.05	.01
☐ 770	Cecil Fielder HL	.10	.05	.01
☐ 771	Jim Presley	.04	.02	.01
☐ 772	John Dopson	.04	.02	.01
☐ 773	Bo Jackson Breaker	.15	.07	.02
☐ 774	Brent Knackert UER	.07	.03	.01
	(Born in 1954, shown throwing righty, but bio says lefty)			
☐ 775	Bill Doran UER	.04	.02	.01
	(Reds in NL East)			
☐ 776	Dick Schofield	.04	.02	.01
☐ 777	Nelson Santovenia	.04	.02	.01
☐ 778	Mark Guthrie	.04	.02	.01
☐ 779	Mark Lemke	.04	.02	.01
☐ 780	Terry Steinbach	.07	.03	.01
☐ 781	Tom Bolton	.04	.02	.01
☐ 782	Randy Tomlin	.20	.09	.03
☐ 783	Jeff Kunkel	.04	.02	.01
☐ 784	Felix Jose	.07	.03	.01
☐ 785	Rick Sutcliffe	.07	.03	.01
☐ 786	John Cerutti	.04	.02	.01
☐ 787	Jose Vizcaino UER	.04	.02	.01
	(Offerman not Opperman)			
☐ 788	Curt Schilling	.07	.03	.01
☐ 789	Ed Whitson	.04	.02	.01
☐ 790	Tony Pena	.04	.02	.01
☐ 791	John Candelaria	.04	.02	.01
☐ 792	Carmelo Martinez	.04	.02	.01
☐ 793	Sandy Alomar Jr. UER	.07	.03	.01
	(Indian's should say Indians')			
☐ 794	Jim Neidlinger	.04	.02	.01
☐ 795	Barry Larkin WS	.07	.03	.01
	and Chris Sabo			
☐ 796	Paul Sorrento	.07	.03	.01
☐ 797	Tom Pagnozzi	.04	.02	.01
☐ 798	Tino Martinez	.08	.04	.01
☐ 799	Scott Ruskin UER	.04	.02	.01
	(Text says first three seasons but lists averages for four)			
☐ 800	Kirk Gibson	.07	.03	.01
☐ 801	Walt Terrell	.04	.02	.01
☐ 802	John Russell	.04	.02	.01
☐ 803	Chili Davis	.07	.03	.01
☐ 804	Chris Nabholz	.10	.05	.01
☐ 805	Juan Gonzalez	.35	.16	.04
☐ 806	Ron Hassey	.04	.02	.01
☐ 807	Todd Worrell	.04	.02	.01
☐ 808	Tommy Greene	.04	.02	.01
☐ 809	Joel Skinner UER	.04	.02	.01
	(Joel, not Bob, was drafted in 1979)			
☐ 810	Benito Santiago	.07	.03	.01
☐ 811	Pat Tabler UER	.04	.02	.01
	(Line 3, always misspelled alway)			
☐ 812	Scott Erickson UER	.20	.09	.03
	(Record spelled rcord)			
☐ 813	Moises Alou	.15	.07	.02
☐ 814	Dale Sveum	.04	.02	.01
☐ 815	Ryne Sandberg MANYR	.20	.09	.03
☐ 816	Rick Dempsey	.04	.02	.01

		MT	EX-MT	VG
☐ 817	Scott Bankhead....04	.02	.01
☐ 818	Jason Grimsley....04	.02	.01
☐ 819	Doug Jennings....04	.02	.01
☐ 820	Tom Herr....04	.02	.01
☐ 821	Rob Ducey....04	.02	.01
☐ 822	Luis Quinones....04	.02	.01
☐ 823	Greg Minton....04	.02	.01
☐ 824	Mark Grant....04	.02	.01
☐ 825	Ozzie Smith UER....10	.05	.01
	(Shortstop misspelled shortsop)		
☐ 826	Dave Eiland....04	.02	.01
☐ 827	Danny Heep....04	.02	.01
☐ 828	Hensley Meulens....07	.03	.01
☐ 829	Charlie O'Brien....04	.02	.01
☐ 830	Glenn Davis....07	.03	.01
☐ 831	John Marzano UER....04	.02	.01
	(International misspelled Internaional)		
☐ 832	Steve Ontiveros....04	.02	.01
☐ 833	Ron Karkovice....04	.02	.01
☐ 834	Jerry Goff....04	.02	.01
☐ 835	Ken Griffey Sr.....07	.03	.01
☐ 836	Kevin Reimer....10	.05	.01
☐ 837	Randy Kutcher UER....04	.02	.01
	(Infectious misspelled infectous)		
☐ 838	Mike Blowers....04	.02	.01
☐ 839	Mike Macfarlane....04	.02	.01
☐ 840	Frank Thomas UER....1.25	.55	.16
	(1989 Sarasota stats, 15 games but 188 AB)		
☐ 841	The Griffeys....50	.23	.06
	Ken Griffey Jr. Ken Griffey Sr.		
☐ 842	Jack Howell....04	.02	.01
☐ 843	Goose Gozzo....04	.02	.01
☐ 844	Gerald Young....04	.02	.01
☐ 845	Zane Smith....04	.02	.01
☐ 846	Kevin Brown....07	.03	.01
☐ 847	Sil Campusano....04	.02	.01
☐ 848	Larry Andersen....04	.02	.01
☐ 849	Cal Ripken FRAN....15	.07	.02
☐ 850	Roger Clemens FRAN....12	.05	.02
☐ 851	Sandy Alomar Jr. FRAN....05	.02	.01
☐ 852	Alan Trammell FRAN....08	.04	.01
☐ 853	George Brett FRAN....10	.05	.01
☐ 854	Robin Yount FRAN....10	.05	.01
☐ 855	Kirby Puckett FRAN....12	.05	.02
☐ 856	Don Mattingly FRAN....10	.05	.01
☐ 857	Rickey Henderson FRAN....10	.05	.01
☐ 858	Ken Griffey Jr. FRAN....25	.11	.03
☐ 859	Ruben Sierra FRAN....10	.05	.01
☐ 860	John Olerud FRAN....10	.05	.01
☐ 861	Dave Justice FRAN....15	.07	.02
☐ 862	Ryne Sandberg FRAN....12	.05	.02
☐ 863	Eric Davis FRAN....08	.04	.01
☐ 864	Darryl Strawberry FRAN....10	.05	.01
☐ 865	Tim Wallach FRAN....05	.02	.01
☐ 866	Doc Gooden FRAN....08	.04	.01
☐ 867	Len Dykstra FRAN....05	.02	.01
☐ 868	Barry Bonds FRAN....10	.05	.01
☐ 869	Todd Zeile FRAN UER....05	.02	.01
	(Powerful misspelled as poweful)		
☐ 870	Benito Santiago FRAN....05	.02	.01
☐ 871	Will Clark FRAN....10	.05	.01
☐ 872	Craig Biggio FRAN....05	.02	.01
☐ 873	Wally Joyner FRAN....05	.02	.01
☐ 874	Frank Thomas FRAN....75	.35	.09
☐ 875	Rickey Henderson MVP....10	.05	.01
☐ 876	Barry Bonds MVP....10	.05	.01
☐ 877	Bob Welch CY....05	.02	.01
☐ 878	Doug Drabek CY....05	.02	.01
☐ 879	Sandy Alomar Jr ROY....05	.02	.01
☐ 880	Dave Justice ROY....15	.07	.02
☐ 881	Damon Berryhill....04	.02	.01
☐ 882	Frank Viola DT....10	.05	.01
☐ 883	Dave Stewart DT....10	.05	.01
☐ 884	Doug Jones DT....10	.05	.01
☐ 885	Randy Myers DT....10	.05	.01
☐ 886	Will Clark DT....40	.18	.05
☐ 887	Roberto Alomar DT....40	.18	.05
☐ 888	Barry Larkin DT....10	.05	.01
☐ 889	Wade Boggs DT....20	.09	.03
☐ 890	Rickey Henderson DT....30	.14	.04
☐ 891	Kirby Puckett DT....40	.18	.05
☐ 892	Ken Griffey Jr DT....1.25	.55	.16
☐ 893	Benny Santiago DT....10	.05	.01

1991 Score Cooperstown

This seven-card set measures the standard 2 1/2" by 3 1/2" and was available only as an insert with 1991 Score factory sets. The card design is not like the regular 1991 Score cards. The card front features a portrait of the player in an oval on a white background. The words "Cooperstown Card" are prominently displayed on the card front. The cards are numbered on the back with a B prefix.

	MT	EX-MT	VG
COMPLETE SET (7)....8.00	3.60	1.00
COMMON PLAYER (B1-B7)....75	.35	.09

player profile on a pale yellow background. The cards are numbered on the back. Cards 1-80 feature traded players, while cards 81-110 focus on rookies. The only noteworthy Rookie Cards in the set are Jeff Bagwell and Ivan Rodriguez.

	MT	EX-MT	VG
COMPLETE SET (110) 6.00		2.70	.75
COMMON PLAYER (1T-80T) 05		.02	.01
COMMON PLAYER (81T-110T) ...05		.02	.01

	B1 Wade Boggs 1.00	.45	.13
☐	B1 Wade Boggs 1.00	.45	.13
☐	B2 Barry Larkin 75	.35	.09
☐	B3 Ken Griffey Jr. 3.00	1.35	.40
☐	B4 Rickey Henderson 1.00	.45	.13
☐	B5 George Brett 1.00	.45	.13
☐	B6 Will Clark 1.50	.65	.19
☐	B7 Nolan Ryan 3.00	1.35	.40

1991 Score Rookie/Traded

The 1991 Score Rookie and Traded set contains 110 standard-size (2 1/2" by 3 1/2") player cards and 10 "World Series II" magic motion trivia cards. The front design features glossy color action photos, with white and purple borders on a mauve card face. The player's name, team, and position are given above the pictures. In a horizontal format, the left portion of the back has a color head shot and biography, while the right portion has statistics and

☐	1T Bo Jackson 15	.07	.02
☐	2T Mike Flanagan 05	.02	.01
☐	3T Pete Incaviglia 05	.02	.01
☐	4T Jack Clark 08	.04	.01
☐	5T Hubie Brooks 05	.02	.01
☐	6T Ivan Calderon 05	.02	.01
☐	7T Glenn Davis 08	.04	.01
☐	8T Wally Backman 05	.02	.01
☐	9T Dave Smith 05	.02	.01
☐	10T Tim Raines 08	.04	.01
☐	11T Joe Carter 12	.05	.02
☐	12T Sid Bream 05	.02	.01
☐	13T George Bell 08	.04	.01
☐	14T Steve Bedrosian 05	.02	.01
☐	15T Willie Wilson 05	.02	.01
☐	16T Darryl Strawberry 12	.05	.02
☐	17T Danny Jackson 05	.02	.01
☐	18T Kirk Gibson 08	.04	.01
☐	19T Willie McGee 08	.04	.01
☐	20T Junior Felix 05	.02	.01
☐	21T Steve Farr 05	.02	.01
☐	22T Pat Tabler 05	.02	.01
☐	23T Brett Butler 08	.04	.01
☐	24T Danny Darwin 05	.02	.01
☐	25T Mickey Tettleton 08	.04	.01
☐	26T Gary Carter 08	.04	.01
☐	27T Mitch Williams 05	.02	.01
☐	28T Candy Maldonado 05	.02	.01
☐	29T Otis Nixon 08	.04	.01
☐	30T Brian Downing 05	.02	.01
☐	31T Tom Candiotti 05	.02	.01
☐	32T John Candelaria 05	.02	.01
☐	33T Rob Murphy 05	.02	.01
☐	34T Deion Sanders 20	.09	.03
☐	35T Willie Randolph 08	.04	.01
☐	36T Pete Harnisch 08	.04	.01
☐	37T Dante Bichette 05	.02	.01
☐	38T Garry Templeton 05	.02	.01
☐	39T Gary Gaetti 05	.02	.01
☐	40T John Cerutti 05	.02	.01
☐	41T Rick Cerone 05	.02	.01
☐	42T Mike Pagliarulo 05	.02	.01
☐	43T Ron Hassey 05	.02	.01
☐	44T Roberto Alomar 20	.09	.02
☐	45T Mike Boddicker 05	.02	.01

☐ 46T	Bud Black	.05	.02	.01
☐ 47T	Rob Deer	.08	.04	.01
☐ 48T	Devon White	.08	.04	.01
☐ 49T	Luis Sojo	.05	.02	.01
☐ 50T	Terry Pendleton	.10	.05	.01
☐ 51T	Kevin Gross	.05	.02	.01
☐ 52T	Mike Huff	.05	.02	.01
☐ 53T	Dave Righetti	.05	.02	.01
☐ 54T	Matt Young	.05	.02	.01
☐ 55T	Earnest Riles	.05	.02	.01
☐ 56T	Bill Gullickson	.05	.02	.01
☐ 57T	Vince Coleman	.08	.04	.01
☐ 58T	Fred McGriff	.15	.07	.02
☐ 59T	Franklin Stubbs	.05	.02	.01
☐ 60T	Eric King	.05	.02	.01
☐ 61T	Cory Snyder	.05	.02	.01
☐ 62T	Dwight Evans	.08	.04	.01
☐ 63T	Gerald Perry	.05	.02	.01
☐ 64T	Eric Show	.05	.02	.01
☐ 65T	Shawn Hillegas	.05	.02	.01
☐ 66T	Tony Fernandez	.08	.04	.01
☐ 67T	Tim Teufel	.05	.02	.01
☐ 68T	Mitch Webster	.05	.02	.01
☐ 69T	Mike Heath	.05	.02	.01
☐ 70T	Chili Davis	.08	.04	.01
☐ 71T	Larry Andersen	.05	.02	.01
☐ 72T	Gary Varsho	.05	.02	.01
☐ 73T	Juan Berenguer	.05	.02	.01
☐ 74T	Jack Morris	.10	.05	.01
☐ 75T	Barry Jones	.05	.02	.01
☐ 76T	Rafael Belliard	.05	.02	.01
☐ 77T	Steve Buechele	.05	.02	.01
☐ 78T	Scott Sanderson	.05	.02	.01
☐ 79T	Bob Ojeda	.05	.02	.01
☐ 80T	Curt Schilling	.08	.04	.01
☐ 81T	Brian Drahman	.10	.05	.01
☐ 82T	Ivan Rodriguez	1.25	.55	.16
☐ 83T	David Howard	.10	.05	.01
☐ 84T	Heathcliff Slocumb	.05	.02	.01
☐ 85T	Mike Timlin	.10	.05	.01
☐ 86T	Darryl Kile	.10	.05	.01
☐ 87T	Pete Schourek	.12	.05	.02
☐ 88T	Bruce Walton	.05	.02	.01
☐ 89T	Al Osuna	.10	.05	.01
☐ 90T	Gary Scott	.15	.07	.02
☐ 91T	Doug Simons	.05	.02	.01
☐ 92T	Chris Jones	.05	.02	.01
☐ 93T	Chuck Knoblauch	.30	.14	.04
☐ 94T	Dana Allison	.10	.05	.01
☐ 95T	Erik Pappas	.05	.02	.01
☐ 96T	Jeff Bagwell	1.25	.55	.16
☐ 97T	Kirk Dressendorfer	.10	.05	.01
☐ 98T	Freddie Benavides	.05	.02	.01
☐ 99T	Luis Gonzalez	.20	.09	.03
☐ 100T	Wade Taylor	.05	.02	.01
☐ 101T	Ed Sprague	.20	.09	.03
☐ 102T	Bob Scanlan	.10	.05	.01
☐ 103T	Rick Wilkins	.10	.05	.01
☐ 104T	Chris Donnels	.12	.05	.02
☐ 105T	Joe Slusarski	.10	.05	.01
☐ 106T	Mark Lewis	.12	.05	.02
☐ 107T	Pat Kelly	.15	.07	.02
☐ 108T	John Briscoe	.10	.05	.01
☐ 109T	Luis Lopez	.10	.05	.01
☐ 110T	Jeff Johnson	.10	.05	.01

1992 Score

The 1992 Score set marked the second year that Score released their set in two different series. The first series contains 442 cards measuring the standard size (2 1/2" by 3 1/2"). The second series contains 451 more cards sequentially numbered. The glossy color action photos on the fronts are bordered above and below by stripes of the same color, and a thicker, different color stripe runs the length of the card to one side of the picture. The backs have a color close-up shot in the upper right corner, with biography, complete career statistics, and player profile printed on a yellow background. Hall of Famer Joe DiMaggio is remembered in a five-card subset. He autographed 2,500 cards; 2,495 of these were randomly inserted in Series I packs, while the other five were given away through a mail-in sweepstakes. Another 150,000 unsigned DiMaggio cards were inserted in Series I Count Goods packs only. Score later extended its DiMaggio promotion to Series I blister packs; one hundred signed and twelve thousand unsigned cards were randomly inserted in these packs. Also a special

"World Series II" trivia card was inserted into each pack. These cards highlight crucial games and heroes from past Octobers. Topical subsets included in the set focus on Rookie Prospects (395-424), No-Hit Club (425-428), Highlights (429-430), AL All-Stars (431-440; with color montages displaying Chris Greco's player caricatures), Dream Team (441-442), Rookie Prospects (736-772, 814-877), NL All-Stars (773-782), Highlights (783, 795-797), No-Hit Club (784-787), Draft Picks (799-810), Memorabilia (878-882), and Dream Team (883-893). All of the Rookie Prospects (736-772) can be found with or without the Rookie Prospect stripe. The cards are numbered on the back. Key Rookie Cards in the set include Cliff Floyd, Brent Gates, Tyler Green, Manny Ramirez, Aaron Sele, and Bob Zupcic. Chuck Knoblauch, 1991 American League Rookie of the Year, autographed 3,000 of his own 1990 Score Draft Pick cards (card number 672) in gold ink, 2,989 were randomly inserted in Series 2 poly packs, while the other 11 were given away in a sweepstakes. The backs of these Knoblauch autograph cards have special holograms to differentiate them. Factory sets included a 17-card insert set, consisting of 7 World Series cards, 4 Cooperstown cards, and two 3-card subsets honoring DiMaggio and Carl Yastrzemski respectively.

	MT	EX-MT	VG
COMPLETE SET (893)	20.00	9.00	2.50
COMPLETE FACT.SET (910)	30.00	13.50	3.80
COMPLETE SERIES 1 (442)	10.00	4.50	1.25
COMPLETE SERIES 2 (451)	10.00	4.50	1.25
COMMON PLAYER (1-442)	.04	.02	.01
COMMON PLAYER (443-893)	.04	.02	.01

		MT	EX-MT	VG
☐ 1	Ken Griffey Jr.	.50	.23	.06
☐ 2	Nolan Ryan	.40	.18	.05
☐ 3	Will Clark	.20	.09	.03
☐ 4	Dave Justice	.20	.09	.03
☐ 5	Dave Henderson	.04	.02	.01
☐ 6	Bret Saberhagen	.07	.03	.01
☐ 7	Fred McGriff	.12	.05	.02
☐ 8	Erik Hanson	.04	.02	.01
☐ 9	Darryl Strawberry	.12	.05	.02
☐ 10	Dwight Gooden	.07	.03	.01
☐ 11	Juan Gonzalez	.35	.16	.04
☐ 12	Mark Langston	.07	.03	.01
☐ 13	Lonnie Smith	.04	.02	.01
☐ 14	Jeff Montgomery	.04	.02	.01
☐ 15	Roberto Alomar	.20	.09	.03
☐ 16	Delino DeShields	.10	.05	.01
☐ 17	Steve Bedrosian	.04	.02	.01
☐ 18	Terry Pendleton	.10	.05	.01
☐ 19	Mark Carreon	.04	.02	.01
☐ 20	Mark McGwire	.20	.09	.03
☐ 21	Roger Clemens	.25	.11	.03
☐ 22	Chuck Crim	.04	.02	.01
☐ 23	Don Mattingly	.12	.05	.02
☐ 24	Dickie Thon	.04	.02	.01
☐ 25	Ron Gant	.10	.05	.01
☐ 26	Milt Cuyler	.04	.02	.01
☐ 27	Mike Macfarlane	.04	.02	.01
☐ 28	Dan Gladden	.04	.02	.01
☐ 29	Melido Perez	.07	.03	.01
☐ 30	Willie Randolph	.07	.03	.01
☐ 31	Albert Belle	.12	.05	.02
☐ 32	Dave Winfield	.10	.05	.01
☐ 33	Jimmy Jones	.04	.02	.01
☐ 34	Kevin Gross	.04	.02	.01
☐ 35	Andres Galarraga	.04	.02	.01
☐ 36	Mike Devereaux	.07	.03	.01
☐ 37	Chris Bosio	.04	.02	.01
☐ 38	Mike LaValliere	.04	.02	.01
☐ 39	Gary Gaetti	.04	.02	.01
☐ 40	Felix Jose	.07	.03	.01
☐ 41	Alvaro Espinoza	.04	.02	.01
☐ 42	Rick Aguilera	.07	.03	.01
☐ 43	Mike Gallego	.04	.02	.01
☐ 44	Eric Davis	.07	.03	.01
☐ 45	George Bell	.07	.03	.01
☐ 46	Tom Brunansky	.07	.03	.01
☐ 47	Steve Farr	.04	.02	.01
☐ 48	Duane Ward	.04	.02	.01
☐ 49	David Wells	.04	.02	.01
☐ 50	Cecil Fielder	.12	.05	.02
☐ 51	Walt Weiss	.04	.02	.01
☐ 52	Todd Zeile	.04	.02	.01
☐ 53	Doug Jones	.04	.02	.01
☐ 54	Bob Walk	.04	.02	.01
☐ 55	Rafael Palmeiro	.07	.03	.01
☐ 56	Rob Deer	.07	.03	.01
☐ 57	Paul O'Neill	.07	.03	.01
☐ 58	Jeff Reardon	.07	.03	.01
☐ 59	Randy Ready	.04	.02	.01
☐ 60	Scott Erickson	.10	.05	.01
☐ 61	Paul Molitor	.07	.03	.01
☐ 62	Jack McDowell	.07	.03	.01
☐ 63	Jim Acker	.04	.02	.01
☐ 64	Jay Buhner	.07	.03	.01
☐ 65	Travis Fryman	.30	.14	.04
☐ 66	Marquis Grissom	.10	.05	.01
☐ 67	Mike Harkey	.07	.03	.01
☐ 68	Luis Polonia	.07	.03	.01
☐ 69	Ken Caminiti	.07	.03	.01
☐ 70	Chris Sabo	.07	.03	.01
☐ 71	Gregg Olson	.07	.03	.01
☐ 72	Carlton Fisk	.10	.05	.01

☐ 73	Juan Samuel	.04	.02	.01
☐ 74	Todd Stottlemyre	.07	.03	.01
☐ 75	Andre Dawson	.10	.05	.01
☐ 76	Alvin Davis	.04	.02	.01
☐ 77	Bill Doran	.04	.02	.01
☐ 78	B.J. Surhoff	.04	.02	.01
☐ 79	Kirk McCaskill	.04	.02	.01
☐ 80	Dale Murphy	.07	.03	.01
☐ 81	Jose DeLeon	.04	.02	.01
☐ 82	Alex Fernandez	.07	.03	.01
☐ 83	Ivan Calderon	.04	.02	.01
☐ 84	Brent Mayne	.04	.02	.01
☐ 85	Jody Reed	.04	.02	.01
☐ 86	Randy Tomlin	.04	.02	.01
☐ 87	Randy Milligan	.04	.02	.01
☐ 88	Pascual Perez	.04	.02	.01
☐ 89	Hensley Meulens	.04	.02	.01
☐ 90	Joe Carter	.12	.05	.02
☐ 91	Mike Moore	.04	.02	.01
☐ 92	Ozzie Guillen	.04	.02	.01
☐ 93	Shawn Hillegas	.04	.02	.01
☐ 94	Chili Davis	.07	.03	.01
☐ 95	Vince Coleman	.07	.03	.01
☐ 96	Jimmy Key	.04	.02	.01
☐ 97	Billy Ripken	.04	.02	.01
☐ 98	Dave Smith	.04	.02	.01
☐ 99	Tom Bolton	.04	.02	.01
☐ 100	Barry Larkin	.10	.05	.01
☐ 101	Kenny Rogers	.04	.02	.01
☐ 102	Mike Boddicker	.04	.02	.01
☐ 103	Kevin Elster	.04	.02	.01
☐ 104	Ken Hill	.04	.02	.01
☐ 105	Charlie Leibrandt	.04	.02	.01
☐ 106	Pat Combs	.04	.02	.01
☐ 107	Hubie Brooks	.04	.02	.01
☐ 108	Julio Franco	.07	.03	.01
☐ 109	Vicente Palacios	.04	.02	.01
☐ 110	Kal Daniels	.04	.02	.01
☐ 111	Bruce Hurst	.07	.03	.01
☐ 112	Willie McGee	.07	.03	.01
☐ 113	Ted Power	.04	.02	.01
☐ 114	Milt Thompson	.04	.02	.01
☐ 115	Doug Drabek	.07	.03	.01
☐ 116	Rafael Belliard	.04	.02	.01
☐ 117	Scott Garrelts	.04	.02	.01
☐ 118	Terry Mulholland	.04	.02	.01
☐ 119	Jay Howell	.04	.02	.01
☐ 120	Danny Jackson	.04	.02	.01
☐ 121	Scott Ruskin	.04	.02	.01
☐ 122	Robin Ventura	.15	.07	.02
☐ 123	Bip Roberts	.07	.03	.01
☐ 124	Jeff Russell	.04	.02	.01
☐ 125	Hal Morris	.07	.03	.01
☐ 126	Teddy Higuera	.04	.02	.01
☐ 127	Luis Sojo	.04	.02	.01
☐ 128	Carlos Baerga	.15	.07	.02
☐ 129	Jeff Ballard	.04	.02	.01
☐ 130	Tom Gordon	.04	.02	.01
☐ 131	Sid Bream	.04	.02	.01
☐ 132	Rance Mulliniks	.04	.02	.01
☐ 133	Andy Benes	.07	.03	.01
☐ 134	Mickey Tettleton	.07	.03	.01
☐ 135	Rich DeLucia	.04	.02	.01
☐ 136	Tom Pagnozzi	.04	.02	.01
☐ 137	Harold Baines	.07	.03	.01
☐ 138	Danny Darwin	.04	.02	.01
☐ 139	Kevin Bass	.04	.02	.01
☐ 140	Chris Nabholz	.07	.03	.01
☐ 141	Pete O'Brien	.04	.02	.01
☐ 142	Jeff Treadway	.04	.02	.01
☐ 143	Mickey Morandini	.07	.03	.01
☐ 144	Eric King	.04	.02	.01
☐ 145	Danny Tartabull	.07	.03	.01
☐ 146	Lance Johnson	.04	.02	.01
☐ 147	Casey Candaele	.04	.02	.01
☐ 148	Felix Fermin	.04	.02	.01
☐ 149	Rich Rodriguez	.04	.02	.01
☐ 150	Dwight Evans	.07	.03	.01
☐ 151	Joe Klink	.04	.02	.01
☐ 152	Kevin Reimer	.07	.03	.01
☐ 153	Orlando Merced	.07	.03	.01
☐ 154	Mel Hall	.04	.02	.01
☐ 155	Randy Myers	.07	.03	.01
☐ 156	Greg A. Harris	.04	.02	.01
☐ 157	Jeff Brantley	.04	.02	.01
☐ 158	Jim Eisenreich	.04	.02	.01
☐ 159	Luis Rivera	.04	.02	.01
☐ 160	Cris Carpenter	.04	.02	.01
☐ 161	Bruce Ruffin	.04	.02	.01
☐ 162	Omar Vizquel	.04	.02	.01
☐ 163	Gerald Alexander	.04	.02	.01
☐ 164	Mark Guthrie	.04	.02	.01
☐ 165	Scott Lewis	.04	.02	.01
☐ 166	Bill Sampen	.04	.02	.01
☐ 167	Dave Anderson	.04	.02	.01
☐ 168	Kevin McReynolds	.07	.03	.01
☐ 169	Jose Vizcaino	.04	.02	.01
☐ 170	Bob Geren	.04	.02	.01
☐ 171	Mike Morgan	.04	.02	.01
☐ 172	Jim Gott	.04	.02	.01
☐ 173	Mike Pagliarulo	.04	.02	.01
☐ 174	Mike Jeffcoat	.04	.02	.01
☐ 175	Craig Lefferts	.04	.02	.01
☐ 176	Steve Finley	.07	.03	.01
☐ 177	Wally Backman	.04	.02	.01
☐ 178	Kent Mercker	.04	.02	.01
☐ 179	John Cerutti	.04	.02	.01
☐ 180	Jay Bell	.04	.02	.01
☐ 181	Dale Sveum	.04	.02	.01
☐ 182	Greg Gagne	.04	.02	.01
☐ 183	Donnie Hill	.04	.02	.01
☐ 184	Rex Hudler	.04	.02	.01
☐ 185	Pat Kelly	.07	.03	.01
☐ 186	Jeff D. Robinson	.04	.02	.01

□ 187	Jeff Gray	.04	.02	.01
□ 188	Jerry Willard	.04	.02	.01
□ 189	Carlos Quintana	.04	.02	.01
□ 190	Dennis Eckersley	.10	.05	.01
□ 191	Kelly Downs	.04	.02	.01
□ 192	Gregg Jefferies	.07	.03	.01
□ 193	Darrin Fletcher	.04	.02	.01
□ 194	Mike Jackson	.04	.02	.01
□ 195	Eddie Murray	.10	.05	.01
□ 196	Bill Landrum	.04	.02	.01
□ 197	Eric Yelding	.04	.02	.01
□ 198	Devon White	.07	.03	.01
□ 199	Larry Walker	.15	.07	.02
□ 200	Ryne Sandberg	.25	.11	.03
□ 201	Dave Magadan	.07	.03	.01
□ 202	Steve Chitren	.04	.02	.01
□ 203	Scott Fletcher	.04	.02	.01
□ 204	Dwayne Henry	.04	.02	.01
□ 205	Scott Coolbaugh	.04	.02	.01
□ 206	Tracy Jones	.04	.02	.01
□ 207	Von Hayes	.04	.02	.01
□ 208	Bob Melvin	.04	.02	.01
□ 209	Scott Scudder	.04	.02	.01
□ 210	Luis Gonzalez	.07	.03	.01
□ 211	Scott Sanderson	.04	.02	.01
□ 212	Chris Donnels	.04	.02	.01
□ 213	Heathcliff Slocumb	.04	.02	.01
□ 214	Mike Timlin	.04	.02	.01
□ 215	Brian Harper	.04	.02	.01
□ 216	Juan Berenguer UER	.04	.02	.01
	(Decimal point missing			
	in IP total)			
□ 217	Mike Henneman	.04	.02	.01
□ 218	Bill Spiers	.04	.02	.01
□ 219	Scott Terry	.04	.02	.01
□ 220	Frank Viola	.07	.03	.01
□ 221	Mark Eichhorn	.04	.02	.01
□ 222	Ernest Riles	.04	.02	.01
□ 223	Ray Lankford	.15	.07	.02
□ 224	Pete Harnisch	.04	.02	.01
□ 225	Bobby Bonilla	.10	.05	.01
□ 226	Mike Scioscia	.04	.02	.01
□ 227	Joel Skinner	.04	.02	.01
□ 228	Brian Holman	.04	.02	.01
□ 229	Gilberto Reyes	.04	.02	.01
□ 230	Matt Williams	.07	.03	.01
□ 231	Jaime Navarro	.07	.03	.01
□ 232	Jose Rijo	.07	.03	.01
□ 233	Atlee Hammaker	.04	.02	.01
□ 234	Tim Teufel	.04	.02	.01
□ 235	John Kruk	.07	.03	.01
□ 236	Kurt Stillwell	.04	.02	.01
□ 237	Dan Pasqua	.04	.02	.01
□ 238	Tim Crews	.04	.02	.01
□ 239	Dave Gallagher	.04	.02	.01
□ 240	Leo Gomez	.10	.05	.01
□ 241	Steve Avery	.15	.07	.02
□ 242	Bill Gullickson	.04	.02	.01
□ 243	Mark Portugal	.04	.02	.01
□ 244	Lee Guetterman	.04	.02	.01
□ 245	Benito Santiago	.07	.03	.01
□ 246	Jim Gantner	.04	.02	.01
□ 247	Robby Thompson	.04	.02	.01
□ 248	Terry Shumpert	.04	.02	.01
□ 249	Mike Bell	.04	.02	.01
□ 250	Harold Reynolds	.04	.02	.01
□ 251	Mike Felder	.04	.02	.01
□ 252	Bill Pecota	.04	.02	.01
□ 253	Bill Krueger	.04	.02	.01
□ 254	Alfredo Griffin	.04	.02	.01
□ 255	Lou Whitaker	.07	.03	.01
□ 256	Roy Smith	.04	.02	.01
□ 257	Jerald Clark	.04	.02	.01
□ 258	Sammy Sosa	.04	.02	.01
□ 259	Tim Naehring	.07	.03	.01
□ 260	Dave Righetti	.04	.02	.01
□ 261	Paul Gibson	.04	.02	.01
□ 262	Chris James	.04	.02	.01
□ 263	Larry Andersen	.04	.02	.01
□ 264	Storm Davis	.04	.02	.01
□ 265	Jose Lind	.04	.02	.01
□ 266	Greg Hibbard	.04	.02	.01
□ 267	Norm Charlton	.07	.03	.01
□ 268	Paul Kilgus	.04	.02	.01
□ 269	Greg Maddux	.07	.03	.01
□ 270	Ellis Burks	.07	.03	.01
□ 271	Frank Tanana	.04	.02	.01
□ 272	Gene Larkin	.04	.02	.01
□ 273	Ron Hassey	.04	.02	.01
□ 274	Jeff M. Robinson	.04	.02	.01
□ 275	Steve Howe	.04	.02	.01
□ 276	Daryl Boston	.04	.02	.01
□ 277	Mark Lee	.04	.02	.01
□ 278	Jose Segura	.10	.05	.01
□ 279	Lance Blankenship	.04	.02	.01
□ 280	Don Slaught	.04	.02	.01
□ 281	Russ Swan	.04	.02	.01
□ 282	Bob Tewksbury	.07	.03	.01
□ 283	Geno Petralli	.04	.02	.01
□ 284	Shane Mack	.07	.03	.01
□ 285	Bob Scanlan	.04	.02	.01
□ 286	Tim Leary	.04	.02	.01
□ 287	John Smoltz	.10	.05	.01
□ 288	Pat Borders	.04	.02	.01
□ 289	Mark Davidson	.04	.02	.01
□ 290	Sam Horn	.04	.02	.01
□ 291	Lenny Harris	.04	.02	.01
□ 292	Franklin Stubbs	.04	.02	.01
□ 293	Thomas Howard	.04	.02	.01
□ 294	Steve Lyons	.04	.02	.01
□ 295	Francisco Oliveras	.04	.02	.01
□ 296	Terry Leach	.04	.02	.01
□ 297	Barry Jones	.04	.02	.01
□ 298	Lance Parrish	.07	.03	.01

☐ 299 Wally Whitehurst	.04	.02	.01		
☐ 300 Bob Welch	.04	.02	.01		
☐ 301 Charlie Hayes	.04	.02	.01		
☐ 302 Charlie Hough	.04	.02	.01		
☐ 303 Gary Redus	.04	.02	.01		
☐ 304 Scott Bradley	.04	.02	.01		
☐ 305 Jose Oquendo	.04	.02	.01		
☐ 306 Pete Incaviglia	.04	.02	.01		
☐ 307 Marvin Freeman	.04	.02	.01		
☐ 308 Gary Pettis	.04	.02	.01		
☐ 309 Joe Slusarski	.04	.02	.01		
☐ 310 Kevin Seitzer	.07	.03	.01		
☐ 311 Jeff Reed	.04	.02	.01		
☐ 312 Pat Tabler	.04	.02	.01		
☐ 313 Mike Maddux	.04	.02	.01		
☐ 314 Bob Milacki	.04	.02	.01		
☐ 315 Eric Anthony	.07	.03	.01		
☐ 316 Dante Bichette	.04	.02	.01		
☐ 317 Steve Decker	.07	.03	.01		
☐ 318 Jack Clark	.07	.03	.01		
☐ 319 Doug Dascenzo	.04	.02	.01		
☐ 320 Scott Leius	.04	.02	.01		
☐ 321 Jim Lindeman	.04	.02	.01		
☐ 322 Bryan Harvey	.04	.02	.01		
☐ 323 Spike Owen	.04	.02	.01		
☐ 324 Roberto Kelly	.07	.03	.01		
☐ 325 Stan Belinda	.04	.02	.01		
☐ 326 Joey Cora	.04	.02	.01		
☐ 327 Jeff Innis	.04	.02	.01		
☐ 328 Willie Wilson	.04	.02	.01		
☐ 329 Juan Agosto	.04	.02	.01		
☐ 330 Charles Nagy	.10	.05	.01		
☐ 331 Scott Bailes	.04	.02	.01		
☐ 332 Pete Schourek	.07	.03	.01		
☐ 333 Mike Flanagan	.04	.02	.01		
☐ 334 Omar Olivares	.04	.02	.01		
☐ 335 Dennis Lamp	.04	.02	.01		
☐ 336 Tommy Greene	.04	.02	.01		
☐ 337 Randy Velarde	.04	.02	.01		
☐ 338 Tom Lampkin	.04	.02	.01		
☐ 339 John Russell	.04	.02	.01		
☐ 340 Bob Kipper	.04	.02	.01		
☐ 341 Todd Burns	.04	.02	.01		
☐ 342 Ron Jones	.04	.02	.01		
☐ 343 Dave Valle	.04	.02	.01		
☐ 344 Mike Heath	.04	.02	.01		
☐ 345 John Olerud	.10	.05	.01		
☐ 346 Gerald Young	.04	.02	.01		
☐ 347 Ken Patterson	.04	.02	.01		
☐ 348 Les Lancaster	.04	.02	.01		
☐ 349 Steve Crawford	.04	.02	.01		
☐ 350 John Candelaria	.04	.02	.01		
☐ 351 Mike Aldrete	.04	.02	.01		
☐ 352 Mariano Duncan	.04	.02	.01		
☐ 353 Julio Machado	.04	.02	.01		
☐ 354 Ken Williams	.04	.02	.01		
☐ 355 Walt Terrell	.04	.02	.01		
☐ 356 Mitch Williams	.04	.02	.01		
☐ 357 Al Newman	.04	.02	.01		
☐ 358 Bud Black	.04	.02	.01		
☐ 359 Joe Hesketh	.04	.02	.01		
☐ 360 Paul Assenmacher	.04	.02	.01		
☐ 361 Bo Jackson	.12	.05	.02		
☐ 362 Jeff Blauser	.04	.02	.01		
☐ 363 Mike Brumley	.04	.02	.01		
☐ 364 Jim Deshaies	.04	.02	.01		
☐ 365 Brady Anderson	.07	.03	.01		
☐ 366 Chuck McElroy	.04	.02	.01		
☐ 367 Matt Merullo	.04	.02	.01		
☐ 368 Tim Belcher	.07	.03	.01		
☐ 369 Luis Aquino	.04	.02	.01		
☐ 370 Joe Oliver	.04	.02	.01		
☐ 371 Greg Swindell	.07	.03	.01		
☐ 372 Lee Stevens	.04	.02	.01		
☐ 373 Mark Knudson	.04	.02	.01		
☐ 374 Bill Wegman	.04	.02	.01		
☐ 375 Jerry Don Gleaton	.04	.02	.01		
☐ 376 Pedro Guerrero	.07	.03	.01		
☐ 377 Randy Bush	.04	.02	.01		
☐ 378 Greg W. Harris	.04	.02	.01		
☐ 379 Eric Plunk	.04	.02	.01		
☐ 380 Jose DeJesus	.04	.02	.01		
☐ 381 Bobby Witt	.04	.02	.01		
☐ 382 Curtis Wilkerson	.04	.02	.01		
☐ 383 Gene Nelson	.04	.02	.01		
☐ 384 Wes Chamberlain	.07	.03	.01		
☐ 385 Tom Henke	.07	.03	.01		
☐ 386 Mark Lemke	.04	.02	.01		
☐ 387 Greg Briley	.04	.02	.01		
☐ 388 Rafael Ramirez	.04	.02	.01		
☐ 389 Tony Fossas	.04	.02	.01		
☐ 390 Henry Cotto	.04	.02	.01		
☐ 391 Tim Hulett	.04	.02	.01		
☐ 392 Dean Palmer	.10	.05	.01		
☐ 393 Glenn Braggs	.04	.02	.01		
☐ 394 Mark Salas	.04	.02	.01		
☐ 395 Rusty Meacham	.05	.02	.01		
☐ 396 Andy Ashby	.05	.02	.01		
☐ 397 Jose Melendez	.05	.02	.01		
☐ 398 Warren Newson	.05	.02	.01		
☐ 399 Frank Castillo	.08	.04	.01		
☐ 400 Chito Martinez	.05	.02	.01		
☐ 401 Bernie Williams	.10	.05	.01		
☐ 402 Derek Bell	.10	.05	.01		
☐ 403 Javier Ortiz	.05	.02	.01		
☐ 404 Tim Sherrill	.05	.02	.01		
☐ 405 Rob MacDonald	.05	.02	.01		
☐ 406 Phil Plantier	.15	.07	.02		
☐ 407 Troy Afenir	.05	.02	.01		
☐ 408 Gino Minutelli	.05	.02	.01		
☐ 409 Reggie Jefferson	.10	.05	.01		
☐ 410 Mike Remlinger	.05	.02	.01		
☐ 411 Carlos Rodriguez	.05	.02	.01		
☐ 412 Joe Redfield	.10	.05	.01		

☐ 413	Alonzo Powell 05	.02	.01
☐ 414	Scott Livingstone UER 10	.05	.01
	(Travis Fryman,		
	not Woody, should be		
	referenced on back)		
☐ 415	Scott Kamieniecki 05	.02	.01
☐ 416	Tim Spehr 05	.02	.01
☐ 417	Brian Hunter 10	.05	.01
☐ 418	Ced Landrum 05	.02	.01
☐ 419	Bret Barberie 05	.02	.01
☐ 420	Kevin Morton 05	.02	.01
☐ 421	Doug Henry 15	.07	.02
☐ 422	Doug Piatt 05	.02	.01
☐ 423	Pat Rice 10	.05	.01
☐ 424	Juan Guzman 75	.35	.09
☐ 425	Nolan Ryan NH 25	.11	.03
☐ 426	Tommy Greene NH 05	.02	.01
☐ 427	Bob Milacki and 05	.02	.01
	Mike Flanagan NH		
	(Mark Williamson		
	and Gregg Olson)		
☐ 428	Wilson Alvarez NH 05	.02	.01
☐ 429	Otis Nixon HL 05	.02	.01
☐ 430	Rickey Henderson HL 10	.05	.01
☐ 431	Cecil Fielder AS 10	.05	.01
☐ 432	Julio Franco AS 05	.02	.01
☐ 433	Cal Ripken AS 15	.07	.02
☐ 434	Wade Boggs AS 10	.05	.01
☐ 435	Joe Carter AS 10	.05	.01
☐ 436	Ken Griffey Jr. AS 25	.11	.03
☐ 437	Ruben Sierra AS 10	.05	.01
☐ 438	Scott Erickson AS 08	.04	.01
☐ 439	Tom Henke AS 05	.02	.01
☐ 440	Terry Steinbach AS 05	.02	.01
☐ 441	Rickey Henderson DT 20	.09	.03
☐ 442	Ryne Sandberg DT 40	.18	.05
☐ 443	Otis Nixon ....04.	.02	.01
☐ 444	Scott Radinsky 04	.02	.01
☐ 445	Mark Grace 07	.03	.01
☐ 446	Tony Pena 04	.02	.01
☐ 447	Billy Hatcher 04	.02	.01
☐ 448	Glenallen Hill 04	.02	.01
☐ 449	Chris Gwynn 04	.02	.01
☐ 450	Tom Glavine 12	.05	.02
☐ 451	John Habyan 04	.02	.01
☐ 452	Al Osuna 04	.02	.01
☐ 453	Tony Phillips 04	.02	.01
☐ 454	Greg Cadaret 04	.02	.01
☐ 455	Rob Dibble 04	.02	.01
☐ 456	Rick Honeycutt 04	.02	.01
☐ 457	Jerome Walton 04	.02	.01
☐ 458	Mookie Wilson 04	.02	.01
☐ 459	Mark Gubicza 04	.02	.01
☐ 460	Craig Biggio 07	.03	.01
☐ 461	Dave Cochrane 04	.02	.01
☐ 462	Keith Miller 04	.02	.01
☐ 463	Alex Cole 04	.02	.01

☐ 464	Pete Smith 07	.03	.01
☐ 465	Brett Butler 07	.03	.01
☐ 466	Jeff Huson 04	.02	.01
☐ 467	Steve Lake 04	.02	.01
☐ 468	Lloyd Moseby 04	.02	.01
☐ 469	Tim McIntosh 04	.02	.01
☐ 470	Dennis Martinez 07	.03	.01
☐ 471	Greg Myers 04	.02	.01
☐ 472	Mackey Sasser 04	.02	.01
☐ 473	Junior Ortiz 04	.02	.01
☐ 474	Greg Olson 04	.02	.01
☐ 475	Steve Sax 07	.03	.01
☐ 476	Ricky Jordan 04	.02	.01
☐ 477	Max Venable 04	.02	.01
☐ 478	Brian McRae 07	.03	.01
☐ 479	Doug Simons 04	.02	.01
☐ 480	Rickey Henderson 12	.05	.02
☐ 481	Gary Varsho 04	.02	.01
☐ 482	Carl Willis 04	.02	.01
☐ 483	Rick Wilkins 04	.02	.01
☐ 484	Donn Pall 04	.02	.01
☐ 485	Edgar Martinez 07	.03	.01
☐ 486	Tom Foley 04	.02	.01
☐ 487	Mark Williamson 04	.02	.01
☐ 488	Jack Armstrong 04	.02	.01
☐ 489	Gary Carter 07	.03	.01
☐ 490	Ruben Sierra 15	.07	.02
☐ 491	Gerald Perry 04	.02	.01
☐ 492	Rob Murphy 04	.02	.01
☐ 493	Zane Smith 04	.02	.01
☐ 494	Darryl Kile 04	.02	.01
☐ 495	Kelly Gruber 07	.03	.01
☐ 496	Jerry Browne 04	.02	.01
☐ 497	Darryl Hamilton 07	.03	.01
☐ 498	Mike Stanton 04	.02	.01
☐ 499	Mark Leonard 04	.02	.01
☐ 500	Jose Canseco 20	.09	.03
☐ 501	Dave Martinez 04	.02	.01
☐ 502	Jose Guzman 04	.02	.01
☐ 503	Terry Kennedy 04	.02	.01
☐ 504	Ed Sprague 07	.03	.01
☐ 505	Frank Thomas UER 75	.35	.09
	(His Gulf Coast League		
	stats are wrong)		
☐ 506	Darren Daulton 07	.03	.01
☐ 507	Kevin Tapani 07	.03	.01
☐ 508	Luis Salazar 04	.02	.01
☐ 509	Paul Faries 04	.02	.01
☐ 510	Sandy Alomar Jr. 07	.03	.01
☐ 511	Jeff King 04	.02	.01
☐ 512	Gary Thurman 04	.02	.01
☐ 513	Chris Hammond................04	.02	.01
☐ 514	Pedro Munoz 07	.03	.01
☐ 515	Alan Trammell 07	.03	.01
☐ 516	Geronimo Pena 04	.02	.01
☐ 517	Rodney McCray UER 04	.02	.01
	(Stole 6 bases in		

1990, not 5; career
totals are correct at 7)

☐ 518	Manny Lee	.04	.02	.01
☐ 519	Junior Felix	.04	.02	.01
☐ 520	Kirk Gibson	.07	.03	.01
☐ 521	Darrin Jackson	.07	.03	.01
☐ 522	John Burkett	.04	.02	.01
☐ 523	Jeff Johnson	.04	.02	.01
☐ 524	Jim Corsi	.04	.02	.01
☐ 525	Robin Yount	.10	.05	.01
☐ 526	Jamie Quirk	.04	.02	.01
☐ 527	Bob Ojeda	.04	.02	.01
☐ 528	Mark Lewis	.04	.02	.01
☐ 529	Bryn Smith	.04	.02	.01
☐ 530	Kent Hrbek	.07	.03	.01
☐ 531	Dennis Boyd	.04	.02	.01
☐ 532	Ron Karkovice	.04	.02	.01
☐ 533	Don August	.04	.02	.01
☐ 534	Todd Frohwirth	.04	.02	.01
☐ 535	Wally Joyner	.07	.03	.01
☐ 536	Dennis Rasmussen	.04	.02	.01
☐ 537	Andy Allanson	.04	.02	.01
☐ 538	Goose Gossage	.07	.03	.01
☐ 539	John Marzano	.04	.02	.01
☐ 540	Cal Ripken	.25	.11	.03
☐ 541	Bill Swift UER	.04	.02	.01
	(Brewers logo on front)			
☐ 542	Kevin Appier	.07	.03	.01
☐ 543	Dave Bergman	.04	.02	.01
☐ 544	Bernard Gilkey	.07	.03	.01
☐ 545	Mike Greenwell	.07	.03	.01
☐ 546	Jose Uribe	.04	.02	.01
☐ 547	Jesse Orosco	.04	.02	.01
☐ 548	Bob Patterson	.04	.02	.01
☐ 549	Mike Stanley	.04	.02	.01
☐ 550	Howard Johnson	.07	.03	.01
☐ 551	Joe Orsulak	.04	.02	.01
☐ 552	Dick Schofield	.04	.02	.01
☐ 553	Dave Hollins	.07	.03	.01
☐ 554	David Segui	.04	.02	.01
☐ 555	Barry Bonds	.15	.07	.02
☐ 556	Mo Vaughn	.07	.03	.01
☐ 557	Craig Wilson	.04	.02	.01
☐ 558	Bobby Rose	.04	.02	.01
☐ 559	Rod Nichols	.04	.02	.01
☐ 560	Len Dykstra	.07	.03	.01
☐ 561	Craig Grebeck	.04	.02	.01
☐ 562	Darren Lewis	.07	.03	.01
☐ 563	Todd Benzinger	.04	.02	.01
☐ 564	Ed Whitson	.04	.02	.01
☐ 565	Jesse Barfield	.04	.02	.01
☐ 566	Lloyd McClendon	.04	.02	.01
☐ 567	Dan Plesac	.04	.02	.01
☐ 568	Danny Cox	.04	.02	.01
☐ 569	Skeeter Barnes	.04	.02	.01
☐ 570	Bobby Thigpen	.04	.02	.01
☐ 571	Deion Sanders	.15	.07	.02
☐ 572	Chuck Knoblauch	.20	.09	.03
☐ 573	Matt Nokes	.04	.02	.01
☐ 574	Herm Winningham	.04	.02	.01
☐ 575	Tom Candiotti	.04	.02	.01
☐ 576	Jeff Bagwell	.25	.11	.03
☐ 577	Brook Jacoby	.04	.02	.01
☐ 578	Chico Walker	.04	.02	.01
☐ 579	Brian Downing	.04	.02	.01
☐ 580	Dave Stewart	.07	.03	.01
☐ 581	Francisco Cabrera	.04	.02	.01
☐ 582	Rene Gonzales	.04	.02	.01
☐ 583	Stan Javier	.04	.02	.01
☐ 584	Randy Johnson	.07	.03	.01
☐ 585	Chuck Finley	.04	.02	.01
☐ 586	Mark Gardner	.04	.02	.01
☐ 587	Mark Whiten	.04	.02	.01
☐ 588	Garry Templeton	.04	.02	.01
☐ 589	Gary Sheffield	.20	.09	.03
☐ 590	Ozzie Smith	.10	.05	.01
☐ 591	Candy Maldonado	.04	.02	.01
☐ 592	Mike Sharperson	.04	.02	.01
☐ 593	Carlos Martinez	.04	.02	.01
☐ 594	Scott Bankhead	.04	.02	.01
☐ 595	Tim Wallach	.07	.03	.01
☐ 596	Tino Martinez	.07	.03	.01
☐ 597	Roger McDowell	.04	.02	.01
☐ 598	Cory Snyder	.04	.02	.01
☐ 599	Andujar Cedeno	.07	.03	.01
☐ 600	Kirby Puckett	.20	.09	.03
☐ 601	Rick Parker	.04	.02	.01
☐ 602	Todd Hundley	.04	.02	.01
☐ 603	Greg Litton	.04	.02	.01
☐ 604	Dave Johnson	.04	.02	.01
☐ 605	John Franco	.07	.03	.01
☐ 606	Mike Fetters	.04	.02	.01
☐ 607	Luis Alicea	.04	.02	.01
☐ 608	Trevor Wilson	.04	.02	.01
☐ 609	Rob Ducey	.04	.02	.01
☐ 610	Ramon Martinez	.07	.03	.01
☐ 611	Dave Burba	.04	.02	.01
☐ 612	Dwight Smith	.04	.02	.01
☐ 613	Kevin Maas	.07	.03	.01
☐ 614	John Costello	.04	.02	.01
☐ 615	Glenn Davis	.07	.03	.01
☐ 616	Shawn Abner	.04	.02	.01
☐ 617	Scott Hemond	.04	.02	.01
☐ 618	Tom Prince	.04	.02	.01
☐ 619	Wally Ritchie	.04	.02	.01
☐ 620	Jim Abbott	.12	.05	.02
☐ 621	Charlie O'Brien	.04	.02	.01
☐ 622	Jack Daugherty	.04	.02	.01
☐ 623	Tommy Gregg	.04	.02	.01
☐ 624	Jeff Shaw	.04	.02	.01
☐ 625	Tony Gwynn	.12	.05	.02
☐ 626	Mark Leiter	.04	.02	.01
☐ 627	Jim Clancy	.04	.02	.01
☐ 628	Tim Layana	.04	.02	.01

☐ 629	Jeff Schaefer	.04	.02	.01
☐ 630	Lee Smith	.07	.03	.01
☐ 631	Wade Taylor	.04	.02	.01
☐ 632	Mike Simms	.04	.02	.01
☐ 633	Terry Steinbach	.07	.03	.01
☐ 634	Shawon Dunston	.07	.03	.01
☐ 635	Tim Raines	.07	.03	.01
☐ 636	Kirt Manwaring	.04	.02	.01
☐ 637	Warren Cromartie	.04	.02	.01
☐ 638	Luis Quinones	.04	.02	.01
☐ 639	Greg Vaughn	.07	.03	.01
☐ 640	Kevin Mitchell	.07	.03	.01
☐ 641	Chris Hoiles	.07	.03	.01
☐ 642	Tom Browning	.04	.02	.01
☐ 643	Mitch Webster	.04	.02	.01
☐ 644	Steve Olin	.04	.02	.01
☐ 645	Tony Fernandez	.07	.03	.01
☐ 646	Juan Bell	.04	.02	.01
☐ 647	Joe Boever	.04	.02	.01
☐ 648	Carney Lansford	.07	.03	.01
☐ 649	Mike Benjamin	.04	.02	.01
☐ 650	George Brett	.10	.05	.01
☐ 651	Tim Burke	.04	.02	.01
☐ 652	Jack Morris	.10	.05	.01
☐ 653	Orel Hershiser	.07	.03	.01
☐ 654	Mike Schooler	.04	.02	.01
☐ 655	Andy Van Slyke	.07	.03	.01
☐ 656	Dave Stieb	.04	.02	.01
☐ 657	Dave Clark	.04	.02	.01
☐ 658	Ben McDonald	.10	.05	.01
☐ 659	John Smiley	.07	.03	.01
☐ 660	Wade Boggs	.12	.05	.02
☐ 661	Eric Bullock	.04	.02	.01
☐ 662	Eric Show	.04	.02	.01
☐ 663	Lenny Webster	.04	.02	.01
☐ 664	Mike Huff	.04	.02	.01
☐ 665	Rick Sutcliffe	.07	.03	.01
☐ 666	Jeff Manto	.04	.02	.01
☐ 667	Mike Fitzgerald	.04	.02	.01
☐ 668	Matt Young	.04	.02	.01
☐ 669	Dave West	.04	.02	.01
☐ 670	Mike Hartley	.04	.02	.01
☐ 671	Curt Schilling	.07	.03	.01
☐ 672	Brian Bohanon	.04	.02	.01
☐ 673	Cecil Espy	.04	.02	.01
☐ 674	Joe Grahe	.04	.02	.01
☐ 675	Sid Fernandez	.07	.03	.01
☐ 676	Edwin Nunez	.04	.02	.01
☐ 677	Hector Villanueva	.04	.02	.01
☐ 678	Sean Berry	.04	.02	.01
☐ 679	Dave Eiland	.04	.02	.01
☐ 680	Dave Cone	.07	.03	.01
☐ 681	Mike Bordick	.08	.04	.01
☐ 682	Tony Castillo	.04	.02	.01
☐ 683	John Barfield	.04	.02	.01
☐ 684	Jeff Hamilton	.04	.02	.01
☐ 685	Ken Dayley	.04	.02	.01
☐ 686	Carmelo Martinez	.04	.02	.01
☐ 687	Mike Capel	.04	.02	.01
☐ 688	Scott Chiamparino	.04	.02	.01
☐ 689	Rich Gedman	.04	.02	.01
☐ 690	Rich Monteleone	.04	.02	.01
☐ 691	Alejandro Pena	.04	.02	.01
☐ 692	Oscar Azocar	.04	.02	.01
☐ 693	Jim Poole	.04	.02	.01
☐ 694	Mike Gardiner	.04	.02	.01
☐ 695	Steve Buechele	.04	.02	.01
☐ 696	Rudy Seanez	.04	.02	.01
☐ 697	Paul Abbott	.04	.02	.01
☐ 698	Steve Searcy	.04	.02	.01
☐ 699	Jose Offerman	.07	.03	.01
☐ 700	Ivan Rodriguez	.30	.14	.04
☐ 701	Joe Girardi	.04	.02	.01
☐ 702	Tony Perezchica	.04	.02	.01
☐ 703	Paul McClellan	.04	.02	.01
☐ 704	David Howard	.04	.02	.01
☐ 705	Dan Petry	.04	.02	.01
☐ 706	Jack Howell	.04	.02	.01
☐ 707	Jose Mesa	.04	.02	.01
☐ 708	Randy St. Claire	.04	.02	.01
☐ 709	Kevin Brown	.07	.03	.01
☐ 710	Ron Darling	.07	.03	.01
☐ 711	Jason Grimsley	.04	.02	.01
☐ 712	John Orton	.04	.02	.01
☐ 713	Shawn Boskie	.04	.02	.01
☐ 714	Pat Clements	.04	.02	.01
☐ 715	Brian Barnes	.04	.02	.01
☐ 716	Luis Lopez	.04	.02	.01
☐ 717	Bob McClure	.04	.02	.01
☐ 718	Mark Davis	.04	.02	.01
☐ 719	Dann Bilardello	.04	.02	.01
☐ 720	Tom Edens	.04	.02	.01
☐ 721	Willie Fraser	.04	.02	.01
☐ 722	Curt Young	.04	.02	.01
☐ 723	Neal Heaton	.04	.02	.01
☐ 724	Craig Worthington	.04	.02	.01
☐ 725	Mel Rojas	.04	.02	.01
☐ 726	Daryl Irvine	.04	.02	.01
☐ 727	Roger Mason	.04	.02	.01
☐ 728	Kirk Dressendorfer	.04	.02	.01
☐ 729	Scott Aldred	.04	.02	.01
☐ 730	Willie Blair	.04	.02	.01
☐ 731	Allan Anderson	.04	.02	.01
☐ 732	Dana Kiecker	.04	.02	.01
☐ 733	Jose Gonzalez	.04	.02	.01
☐ 734	Brian Drahman	.04	.02	.01
☐ 735	Brad Komminsk	.04	.02	.01
☐ 736	Arthur Rhodes	.15	.07	.02
☐ 737	Terry Mathews	.10	.05	.01
☐ 738	Jeff Fassero	.05	.02	.01
☐ 739	Mike Magnante	.12	.05	.02
☐ 740	Kip Gross	.10	.05	.01
☐ 741	Jim Hunter	.10	.05	.01
☐ 742	Jose Mota	.05	.02	.01/

☐ 743 Joe Bitker	.05	.02	.01
☐ 744 Tim Mauser	.10	.05	.01
☐ 745 Ramon Garcia	.05	.02	.01
☐ 746 Rod Beck	.12	.05	.02
☐ 747 Jim Austin	.10	.05	.01
☐ 748 Keith Mitchell	.08	.04	.01
☐ 749 Wayne Rosenthal	.10	.05	.01
☐ 750 Bryan Hickerson	.10	.05	.01
☐ 751 Bruce Egloff	.05	.02	.01
☐ 752 John Wehner	.05	.02	.01
☐ 753 Darren Holmes	.05	.02	.01
☐ 754 Dave Hansen	.05	.02	.01
☐ 755 Mike Mussina	.50	.23	.06
☐ 756 Anthony Young	.08	.04	.01
☐ 757 Ron Tingley	.05	.02	.01
☐ 758 Ricky Bones	.08	.04	.01
☐ 759 Mark Wohlers	.10	.05	.01
☐ 760 Wilson Alvarez	.05	.02	.01
☐ 761 Harvey Pulliam	.08	.04	.01
☐ 762 Ryan Bowen	.08	.04	.01
☐ 763 Terry Bross	.05	.02	.01
☐ 764 Joel Johnston	.05	.02	.01
☐ 765 Terry McDaniel	.10	.05	.01
☐ 766 Esteban Beltre	.10	.05	.01
☐ 767 Rob Maurer	.12	.05	.02
☐ 768 Ted Wood	.10	.05	.01
☐ 769 Mo Sanford	.05	.02	.01
☐ 770 Jeff Carter	.05	.02	.01
☐ 771 Gil Heredia	.10	.05	.01
☐ 772 Monty Fariss	.08	.04	.01
☐ 773 Will Clark AS	.10	.05	.01
☐ 774 Ryne Sandberg AS	.12	.05	.02
☐ 775 Barry Larkin AS	.08	.04	.01
☐ 776 Howard Johnson AS	.05	.02	.01
☐ 777 Barry Bonds AS	.10	.05	.01
☐ 778 Brett Butler AS	.05	.02	.01
☐ 779 Tony Gwynn AS	.10	.05	.01
☐ 780 Ramon Martinez AS	.05	.02	.01
☐ 781 Lee Smith AS	.05	.02	.01
☐ 782 Mike Scioscia AS	.05	.02	.01
☐ 783 Dennis Martinez HL UER	.05	.02	.01
(Card has both 13th			
and 15th perfect game			
in Major League history)			
☐ 784 Dennis Martinez	.05	.02	.01
No-Hit Club			
☐ 785 Mark Gardner	.05	.02	.01
No-Hit Club			
☐ 786 Bret Saberhagen	.05	.02	.01
No-Hit Club			
☐ 787 Kent Mercker	.05	.02	.01
Mark Wohlers			
Alejandro Pena			
No-Hit Club			
☐ 788 Cal Ripken MVP	.15	.07	.02
☐ 789 Terry Pendleton MVP	.08	.04	.01
☐ 790 Roger Clemens CY	.12	.05	.02
☐ 791 Tom Glavine CY	.10	.05	.01
☐ 792 Chuck Knoblauch ROY	.15	.07	.02
☐ 793 Jeff Bagwell ROY	.15	.07	.02
☐ 794 Cal Ripken	.15	.07	.02
Man of the Year			
☐ 795 David Cone HL	.08	.04	.01
☐ 796 Kirby Puckett HL	.12	.05	.02
☐ 797 Steve Avery HL	.10	.05	.01
☐ 798 Jack Morris HL	.08	.04	.01
☐ 799 Allen Watson Draft	.25	.11	.03
☐ 800 Manny Ramirez Draft	.60	.25	.08
☐ 801 Cliff Floyd Draft	.75	.35	.09
☐ 802 Al Shirley Draft	.25	.11	.03
☐ 803 Brian Barber Draft	.20	.09	.03
☐ 804 Jon Farrell Draft	.10	.05	.01
☐ 805 Brent Gates Draft	.50	.23	.06
☐ 806 Scott Ruffcorn Draft	.25	.11	.03
☐ 807 Tyrone Hill Draft	.35	.16	.04
☐ 808 Benji Gil Draft	.20	.09	.03
☐ 809 Aaron Sele Draft	.40	.18	.05
☐ 810 Tyler Green Draft	.25	.11	.03
☐ 811 Chris Jones	.04	.02	.01
☐ 812 Steve Wilson	.04	.02	.01
☐ 813 Freddie Benavides	.04	.02	.01
☐ 814 Don Wakamatsu	.10	.05	.01
☐ 815 Mike Humphreys	.08	.04	.01
☐ 816 Scott Servais	.05	.02	.01
☐ 817 Rico Rossy	.10	.05	.01
☐ 818 John Ramos	.05	.02	.01
☐ 819 Rob Mallicoat	.05	.02	.01
☐ 820 Milt Hill	.10	.05	.01
☐ 821 Carlos Garcia	.10	.05	.01
☐ 822 Stan Royer	.05	.02	.01
☐ 823 Jeff Plympton	.10	.05	.01
☐ 824 Braulio Castillo	.15	.07	.02
☐ 825 David Haas	.05	.02	.01
☐ 826 Luis Mercedes	.08	.04	.01
☐ 827 Eric Karros	.50	.23	.06
☐ 828 Shawn Hare	.10	.05	.01
☐ 829 Reggie Sanders	.25	.11	.03
☐ 830 Tom Goodwin	.05	.02	.01
☐ 831 Dan Gakeler	.05	.02	.01
☐ 832 Stacy Jones	.10	.05	.01
☐ 833 Kim Batiste	.05	.02	.01
☐ 834 Cal Eldred	.35	.16	.04
☐ 835 Chris George	.05	.02	.01
☐ 836 Wayne Housie	.10	.05	.01
☐ 837 Mike Ignasiak	.12	.05	.02
☐ 838 Josias Manzanillo	.10	.05	.01
☐ 839 Jim Olander	.10	.05	.01
☐ 840 Gary Cooper	.10	.05	.01
☐ 841 Royce Clayton	.15	.07	.02
☐ 842 Hector Fajardo	.12	.05	.02
☐ 843 Blaine Beatty	.05	.02	.01
☐ 844 Jorge Pedre	.10	.05	.01
☐ 845 Kenny Lofton	.40	.18	.05
☐ 846 Scott Brosius	.10	.05	.01

			MT	EX-MT
☐ 847	Chris Cron	.10	.05	.01
☐ 848	Denis Boucher	.05	.02	.01
☐ 849	Kyle Abbott	.08	.04	.01
☐ 850	Robert Zupcic	.25	.11	.03
☐ 851	Rheal Cormier	.05	.02	.01
☐ 852	Jim Lewis	.10	.05	.01
☐ 853	Anthony Telford	.05	.02	.01
☐ 854	Cliff Brantley	.10	.05	.01
☐ 855	Kevin Campbell	.10	.05	.01
☐ 856	Craig Shipley	.10	.05	.01
☐ 857	Chuck Carr	.08	.04	.01
☐ 858	Tony Eusebio	.10	.05	.01
☐ 859	Jim Thome	.12	.05	.02
☐ 860	Vinny Castilla	.10	.05	.01
☐ 861	Dann Howitt	.05	.02	.01
☐ 862	Kevin Ward	.10	.05	.01
☐ 863	Steve Wapnick	.05	.02	.01
☐ 864	Rod Brewer	.15	.07	.02
☐ 865	Todd Van Poppel	.20	.09	.03
☐ 866	Jose Hernandez	.10	.05	.01
☐ 867	Amalio Carreno	.10	.05	.01
☐ 868	Calvin Jones	.10	.05	.01
☐ 869	Jeff Gardner	.10	.05	.01
☐ 870	Jarvis Brown	.10	.05	.01
☐ 871	Eddie Taubensee	.12	.05	.02
☐ 872	Andy Mota	.05	.02	.01
☐ 873	Chris Haney	.05	.02	.01
☐ 874	Roberto Hernandez	.12	.05	.02
☐ 875	Laddie Renfroe	.10	.05	.01
☐ 876	Scott Cooper	.08	.04	.01
☐ 877	Armando Reynoso	.10	.05	.01
☐ 878	Ty Cobb (Memorabilia)	.30	.14	.04
☐ 879	Babe Ruth (Memorabilia)	.40	.18	.05
☐ 880	Honus Wagner (Memorabilia)	.20	.09	.03
☐ 881	Lou Gehrig (Memorabilia)	.35	.16	.04
☐ 882	Satchel Paige (Memorabilia)	.20	.09	.03
☐ 883	Will Clark DT	.30	.14	.04
☐ 884	Cal Ripken DT	.50	.23	.06
☐ 885	Wade Boggs DT	.20	.09	.03
☐ 886	Kirby Puckett DT	.30	.14	.04
☐ 887	Tony Gwynn DT	.20	.09	.03
☐ 888	Craig Biggio DT	.10	.05	.01
☐ 889	Scott Erickson DT	.12	.05	.02
☐ 890	Tom Glavine DT	.20	.09	.03
☐ 891	Rob Dibble DT	.10	.05	.01
☐ 892	Mitch Williams DT	.10	.05	.01
☐ 893	Frank Thomas DT	1.00	.45	.13
☐ X672	Chuck Knoblauch	125.00	57.50	15.50
	(1990 Score card, autographed with special hologram on back)			

1992 Score Factory Inserts

This 17-card insert set was included in 1992 Score factory sets and consists of four topical subsets. Cards B1-B7 capture a moment from each game of the 1991 World Series. Cards B8-B11 are Cooperstown cards, honoring future Hall of Famers. Cards B12-B14 form a "Joe D" subset paying tribute to Joe DiMaggio. Cards B15-B17, subtitled "Yaz," conclude the set by commemorating Carl Yastrzemski's heroic feats twenty-five years ago in winning the Triple Crown and lifting the Red Sox to their first American League pennant in 21 years. The cards measure the standard size (2 1/2" by 3 1/2"), and each subset displays a different front design. The World Series cards carry full-bleed color action photos except for a blue stripe at the bottom, while the Cooperstown cards have a color portrait on a white card face. Both the DiMaggio and Yastrzemski subsets have action photos with silver borders; they differ in that the DiMaggio photos are black and white, the Yastrzemski photos are color. The DiMaggio and Yastrzemski subsets are numbered on the back within each subset (e.g., "1 of 3") and as a part of the 17-card insert set (e.g., "B1").

	MT	EX-MT	VG
COMPLETE SET (17)	10.00	4.50	1.25
COMMON WS (B1-B7)	.25	.11	.03
COM COOPERSTOWN (B8-B11)	1.25	.55	.16
COMMON DIMAGGIO (B12-B14)	1.50	.65	.19
COMMON YAZ (B15-B17)	.75	.35	.09

☐	B1	1991 WS Game 1 25	.11	.03
		(Greg) Gagne powers		
		Twins to win		
☐	B2	1991 WS Game 2 25	.11	.03
		(Scott) Leius lifts		
		Twins to 2-0 lead		
☐	B3	1991 WS Game 3 25	.11	.03
		(Mark) Lemke leaves		
		Twins limp		
		(David Justice)		
☐	B4	1991 WS Game 4 25	.11	.03
		Braves gain series tie		
		(Lonnie Smith and		
		Brian Harper)		
☐	B5	1991 WS Game 5 60	.25	.08
		Braves bomb Twins		
		(David Justice)		
☐	B6	1991 WS Game 6 ....1.50	.65	.19
		Kirby (Puckett) keeps		
		the Twins alive		
☐	B7	1991 WS Game 7 25	.11	.03
		A Classic win for the		
		Twins (Gene Larkin)		
☐	B8	Carlton Fisk..................1.25	.55	.16
		Cooperstown Card		
☐	B9	Ozzie Smith....................1.25	.55	.16
		Cooperstown Card		
☐	B10	Dave Winfield..............1.25	.55	.16
		Cooperstown Card		
☐	B11	Robin Yount................1.50	.65	.19
		Cooperstown Card		
☐	D12	Joe DiMaggio 1.50	.65	.19
		The Hard Hitter		
☐	B13	Joe DiMaggio 1.50	.65	.19
		The Stylish Fielder		
☐	B14	Joe DiMaggio 1.50	.65	.19
		The Championship Player		
☐	B15	Carl Yastrzemski..........75	.35	.09
		The Impossible Dream		
☐	B16	Carl Yastrzemski..........75	.35	.09
		The Triple Crown		
☐	B17	Carl Yastrzemski..........75	.35	.09
		The World Series		

1992 Score Impact Players

The 1992 Score Impact Players insert set was issued in two series each with 45 cards with the respective series of the

1992 regular issue Score cards. Five cards from the 45-card first (second) series were randomly inserted in each 1992 Score I (II) jumbo pack. The cards measure the standard size (2 1/2" by 3 1/2") and the fronts feature full-bleed color action player photos. The pictures are enhanced by a wide vertical stripe running near the left edge containing the words "90's Impact Player" and a narrower stripe at the bottom printed with the player's name. The stripes are team color-coded and intersect at the team logo in the lower left corner. The backs display close-up color player photos. The picture borders and background colors reflect the team's colors. A white box below the photo contains biographical and statistical information as well as a career summary. The cards are numbered on the back.

	MT	EX-MT	VG
COMPLETE SET (90) 20.00	9.00	2.50
COMPLETE SERIES 1 (45)..13.00	5.75	1.65
COMPLETE SERIES 2 (45)....7.00	3.10	.85
COMMON PLAYER (1-45)..........10	.05	.01
COMMON PLAYER (46-90)........10	.05	.01

☐	1	Chuck Knoblauch..............50	.23	.06
☐	2	Jeff Bagwell......................75	.35	.09
☐	3	Juan Guzman................1.75	.80	.22
☐	4	Milt Cuyler........................10	.05	.01
☐	5	Ivan Rodriguez..............1.00	.45	.13
☐	6	Rich DeLucia....................10	.05	.01
☐	7	Orlando Merced................12	.05	.02
☐	8	Ray Lankford....................40	.18	.05
☐	9	Brian Hunter....................20	.09	.03
☐	10	Roberto Alomar................50	.23	.06
☐	11	Wes Chamberlain............12	.05	.02
☐	12	Steve Avery......................50	.23	.06
☐	13	Scott Erickson..................15	.07	.02
☐	14	Jim Abbott........................20	.09	.03
☐	15	Mark Whiten......................10	.05	.01
☐	16	Leo Gomez........................20	.09	.03

☐ 17	Doug Henry	.30	.14	.04
☐ 18	Brent Mayne	.10	.05	.01
☐ 19	Charles Nagy	.12	.05	.02
☐ 20	Phil Plantier	.30	.14	.04
☐ 21	Mo Vaughn	.12	.05	.02
☐ 22	Craig Biggio	.12	.05	.02
☐ 23	Derek Bell	.30	.14	.04
☐ 24	Royce Clayton	.40	.18	.05
☐ 25	Gary Cooper	.15	.07	.02
☐ 26	Scott Cooper	.25	.11	.03
☐ 27	Juan Gonzalez	1.25	.55	.16
☐ 28	Ken Griffey Jr.	2.00	.90	.25
☐ 29	Larry Walker	.40	.18	.05
☐ 30	John Smoltz	.20	.09	.03
☐ 31	Todd Hundley	.10	.05	.01
☐ 32	Kenny Lofton	1.25	.55	.16
☐ 33	Andy Mota	.10	.05	.01
☐ 34	Todd Zeile	.10	.05	.01
☐ 35	Arthur Rhodes	.40	.18	.05
☐ 36	Jim Thome	.25	.11	.03
☐ 37	Todd Van Poppel	.40	.18	.05
☐ 38	Mark Wohlers	.20	.09	.03
☐ 39	Anthony Young	.12	.05	.02
☐ 40	Sandy Alomar Jr.	.12	.05	.02
☐ 41	John Olerud	.25	.11	.03
☐ 42	Robin Ventura	.50	.23	.06
☐ 43	Frank Thomas	3.00	1.35	.40
☐ 44	Dave Justice	.75	.35	.09
☐ 45	Hal Morris	.12	.05	.02
☐ 46	Ruben Sierra	.40	.18	.05
☐ 47	Travis Fryman	1.00	.45	.13
☐ 48	Mike Mussina	1.75	.80	.22
☐ 49	Tom Glavine	.30	.14	.04
☐ 50	Barry Larkin	.20	.09	.03
☐ 51	Will Clark	.50	.23	.06
☐ 52	Jose Canseco	.50	.23	.06
☐ 53	Bo Jackson	.25	.11	.03
☐ 54	Dwight Gooden	.12	.05	.02
☐ 55	Barry Bonds	.50	.23	.06
☐ 56	Fred McGriff	.30	.14	.04
☐ 57	Roger Clemens	.60	.25	.08
☐ 58	Benito Santiago	.12	.05	.02
☐ 59	Darryl Strawberry	.30	.14	.04
☐ 60	Cecil Fielder	.30	.14	.04
☐ 61	John Franco	.10	.05	.01
☐ 62	Matt Williams	.12	.05	.02
☐ 63	Marquis Grissom	.25	.11	.03
☐ 64	Danny Tartabull	.12	.05	.02
☐ 65	Ron Gant	.20	.09	.03
☐ 66	Paul O'Neill	.10	.05	.01
☐ 67	Devon White	.10	.05	.01
☐ 68	Rafael Palmeiro	.12	.05	.02
☐ 69	Tom Gordon	.10	.05	.01
☐ 70	Shawon Dunston	.10	.05	.01
☐ 71	Rob Dibble	.10	.05	.01
☐ 72	Eddie Zosky	.10	.05	.01
☐ 73	Jack McDowell	.12	.05	.02

☐ 74	Len Dykstra	.10	.05	.01
☐ 75	Ramon Martinez	.12	.05	.02
☐ 76	Reggie Sanders	.75	.35	.09
☐ 77	Greg Maddux	.12	.05	.02
☐ 78	Ellis Burks	.10	.05	.01
☐ 79	John Smiley	.10	.05	.01
☐ 80	Roberto Kelly	.10	.05	.01
☐ 81	Ben McDonald	.15	.07	.02
☐ 82	Mark Lewis	.10	.05	.01
☐ 83	Jose Rijo	.10	.05	.01
☐ 84	Ozzie Guillen	.10	.05	.01
☐ 85	Lance Dickson	.10	.05	.01
☐ 86	Kim Batiste	.15	.07	.02
☐ 87	Gregg Olson	.10	.05	.01
☐ 88	Andy Benes	.12	.05	.02
☐ 89	Cal Eldred	1.00	.45	.13
☐ 90	David Cone	.12	.05	.02

1992 Score
Rookie/Traded

The 1992 Score Rookie and Traded set contains 110 standard-size (2 1/2" by 3 1/2") cards featuring traded veterans and rookies. The fronts display color action player photos edged on one side by an orange stripe that fades to white as one moves down the card face. The player's name appears in a purple bar above the picture, while his position is printed in a purple bar below the picture. The backs carry a color close-up photo, biography, and on a yellow panel, batting or pitching statistics and career summary. The cards are numbered on the back with the "T" suffix. The set is arranged numerically such

that cards 1-79 are traded players and cards 80-110 feature rookies.

	MT	EX-MT	VG
COMPLETE SET (110)	14.00	6.25	1.75
COMMON PLAYER (1T-79T)	.05	.02	.01
COMMON PLAYER (80T-110T)	.05	.02	.01

☐ 1T Gary Sheffield	.25	.11	.03
☐ 2T Kevin Seitzer	.08	.04	.01
☐ 3T Danny Tartabull	.08	.04	.01
☐ 4T Steve Sax	.08	.04	.01
☐ 5T Bobby Bonilla	.10	.05	.01
☐ 6T Frank Viola	.08	.04	.01
☐ 7T Dave Winfield	.10	.05	.01
☐ 8T Rick Sutcliffe	.08	.04	.01
☐ 9T Jose Canseco	.25	.11	.03
☐ 10T Greg Swindell	.08	.04	.01
☐ 11T Eddie Murray	.10	.05	.01
☐ 12T Randy Myers	.08	.04	.01
☐ 13T Wally Joyner	.08	.04	.01
☐ 14T Kenny Lofton	.35	.16	.04
☐ 15T Jack Morris	.10	.05	.01
☐ 16T Charlie Hayes	.05	.02	.01
☐ 17T Pete Incaviglia	.05	.02	.01
☐ 18T Kevin Mitchell	.08	.04	.01
☐ 19T Kurt Stillwell	.05	.02	.01
☐ 20T Bret Saberhagen	.08	.04	.01
☐ 21T Steve Buechele	.05	.02	.01
☐ 22T John Smiley	.08	.04	.01
☐ 23T Sammy Sosa	.05	.02	.01
☐ 24T George Bell	.08	.04	.01
☐ 25T Curt Schilling	.08	.04	.01
☐ 26T Dick Schofield	.05	.02	.01
☐ 27T David Cone	.08	.04	.01
☐ 28T Dan Gladden	.05	.02	.01
☐ 29T Kirk McCaskill	.05	.02	.01
☐ 30T Mike Gallego	.05	.02	.01
☐ 31T Kevin McReynolds	.08	.04	.01
☐ 32T Bill Swift	.05	.02	.01
☐ 33T Dave Martinez	.05	.02	.01
☐ 34T Storm Davis	.05	.02	.01
☐ 35T Willie Randolph	.08	.04	.01
☐ 36T Melido Perez	.08	.04	.01
☐ 37T Mark Carreon	.05	.02	.01
☐ 38T Doug Jones	.05	.02	.01
☐ 39T Gregg Jefferies	.08	.04	.01
☐ 40T Mike Jackson	.05	.02	.01
☐ 41T Dickie Thon	.05	.02	.01
☐ 42T Eric King	.05	.02	.01
☐ 43T Herm Winningham	.05	.02	.01
☐ 44T Derek Lilliquist	.05	.02	.01
☐ 45T Dave Anderson	.05	.02	.01
☐ 46T Jeff Reardon	.08	.04	.01
☐ 47T Scott Bankhead	.05	.02	.01
☐ 48T Cory Snyder	.05	.02	.01
☐ 49T Al Newman	.05	.02	−.01
☐ 50T Keith Miller	.05	.02	.01
☐ 51T Dave Burba	.05	.02	.01
☐ 52T Bill Pecota	.05	.02	.01
☐ 53T Chuck Crim	.05	.02	.01
☐ 54T Mariano Duncan	.05	.02	.01
☐ 55T Dave Gallagher	.05	.02	.01
☐ 56T Chris Gwynn	.05	.02	.01
☐ 57T Scott Ruskin	.05	.02	.01
☐ 58T Jack Armstrong	.05	.02	.01
☐ 59T Gary Carter	.08	.04	.01
☐ 60T Andres Galarraga	.05	.02	.01
☐ 61T Ken Hill	.08	.04	.01
☐ 62T Eric Davis	.08	.04	.01
☐ 63T Ruben Sierra	.20	.09	.03
☐ 64T Darrin Fletcher	.05	.02	.01
☐ 65T Tim Belcher	.08	.04	.01
☐ 66T Mike Morgan	.05	.02	.01
☐ 67T Scott Scudder	.05	.02	.01
☐ 68T Tom Candiotti	.05	.02	.01
☐ 69T Hubie Brooks	.05	.02	.01
☐ 70T Kal Daniels	.05	.02	.01
☐ 71T Bruce Ruffin	.05	.02	.01
☐ 72T Billy Hatcher	.05	.02	.01
☐ 73T Bob Melvin	.05	.02	.01
☐ 74T Lee Guetterman	.05	.02	.01
☐ 75T Rene Gonzales	.05	.02	.01
☐ 76T Kevin Bass	.05	.02	.01
☐ 77T Tom Bolton	.05	.02	.01
☐ 78T John Wetteland	.05	.02	.01
☐ 79T Bip Roberts	.08	.04	.01
☐ 80T Pat Listach	1.50	.65	.19
☐ 81T John Doherty	.15	.07	.02
☐ 82T Sam Militello	.30	.14	.04
☐ 83T Brian Jordan	.25	.11	.03
☐ 84T Jeff Kent	.25	.11	.03
☐ 85T Dave Fleming	.50	.23	.06
☐ 86T Jeff Tackett	.10	.05	.01
☐ 87T Chad Curtis	.30	.14	.04
☐ 88T Eric Fox	.12	.05	.02
☐ 89T Denny Neagle	.05	.02	.01
☐ 90T Donovan Osborne	.30	.14	.04
☐ 91T Carlos Hernandez	.05	.02	.01
☐ 92T Tim Wakefield	3.00	1.35	.40
☐ 93T Tim Salmon	.50	.23	.06
☐ 94T Dave Nilsson	.15	.07	.02
☐ 95T Mike Perez	.08	.04	.01
☐ 96T Pat Hentgen	.10	.05	.01
☐ 97T Frank Seminara	.20	.09	.03
☐ 98T Ruben Amaro Jr	.05	.02	.01
☐ 99T Archi Cianfrocco	.15	.07	.02
☐ 100T Andy Stankiewicz	.15	.07	.02
☐ 101T Jim Bullinger	.10	.05	.01
☐ 102T Pat Mahomes	.25	.11	.03
☐ 103T Hipolito Pichardo	.10	.05	.01
☐ 104T Bret Boone	.50	.23	.06
☐ 105T John Vander Wal	.15	.07	.02
☐ 106T Vince Horsman	.10	.05	.01

☐ 107T	James Austin	10	.05	.01
☐ 108T	Brian Williams	25	.11	.03
☐ 109T	Dan Walters	15	.07	.02
☐ 110T	Wilfredo Cordero	15	.07	.02

1993 Score Select

Seeking a niche in the premium, mid-price market, Score has produced a new 405-card baseball set. The set includes regular players, rookies, and draft picks, and was sold in 15-card packs and 28-card super packs. Themed Chase Cards (24 in all) were randomly inserted into the 15-card packs. The cards measure the standard size (2 1/2" by 3 1/2"). The front photos, composed either horizontally or vertically, are ultra-violet coated while the two-toned green borders received a matte finish. The player's name appears in mustard-colored lettering in the bottom border. The backs carry a second color photo as well as 1992 statistics, career totals, and an in-depth player profile, all on a two-toned green background. The cards are numbered on the back. The set includes Draft Pick (291, 297, 303, 310, 352-360) and Rookie (271-290, 292-296, 298-302, 304-309, 311-351, 383, 385, 391, 394, 400-405) subsets.

	MT	EX-MT	VG
COMPLETE SET (405)	30.00	13.50	3.80
COMMON PLAYER (1-405)	.07	.03	.01

☐ 1	Barry Bonds	30	.14	.04
☐ 2	Ken Griffey Jr.	75	.35	.09
☐ 3	Will Clark	30	.14	.04
☐ 4	Kirby Puckett	30	.14	.04

☐ 5	Tony Gwynn	20	.09	.03
☐ 6	Frank Thomas	1.00	.45	.13
☐ 7	Tom Glavine	20	.09	.03
☐ 8	Roberto Alomar	35	.16	.04
☐ 9	Andre Dawson	15	.07	.02
☐ 10	Ron Darling	10	.05	.01
☐ 11	Bobby Bonilla	15	.07	.02
☐ 12	Danny Tartabull	10	.05	.01
☐ 13	Darren Daulton	10	.05	.01
☐ 14	Roger Clemens	35	.16	.04
☐ 15	Ozzie Smith	15	.07	.02
☐ 16	Mark McGwire	30	.14	.04
☐ 17	Terry Pendleton	10	.05	.01
☐ 18	Cal Ripken	40	.18	.05
☐ 19	Fred McGriff	15	.07	.02
☐ 20	Cecil Fielder	20	.09	.03
☐ 21	Darryl Strawberry	20	.09	.03
☐ 22	Robin Yount	15	.07	.02
☐ 23	Barry Larkin	15	.07	.02
☐ 24	Don Mattingly	20	.09	.03
☐ 25	Craig Biggio	10	.05	.01
☐ 26	Sandy Alomar Jr.	10	.05	.01
☐ 27	Larry Walker	20	.09	.03
☐ 28	Junior Felix	07	.03	.01
☐ 29	Eddie Murray	15	.07	.02
☐ 30	Robin Ventura	25	.11	.03
☐ 31	Greg Maddux	15	.07	.02
☐ 32	Dave Winfield	15	.07	.02
☐ 33	John Kruk	10	.05	.01
☐ 34	Wally Joyner	10	.05	.01
☐ 35	Andy Van Slyke	10	.05	.01
☐ 36	Chuck Knoblauch	25	.11	.03
☐ 37	Tom Pagnozzi	07	.03	.01
☐ 38	Dennis Eckersley	12	.05	.02
☐ 39	Dave Justice	30	.14	.04
☐ 40	Juan Gonzalez	40	.18	.05
☐ 41	Gary Sheffield	25	.11	.03
☐ 42	Paul Molitor	10	.05	.01
☐ 43	Delino DeShields	15	.07	.02
☐ 44	Travis Fryman	30	.14	.04
☐ 45	Hal Morris	10	.05	.01
☐ 46	Greg Olson	10	.05	.01
☐ 47	Ken Caminiti	07	.03	.01
☐ 48	Wade Boggs	20	.09	.03
☐ 49	Orel Hershiser	07	.03	.01
☐ 50	Albert Belle	20	.09	.03
☐ 51	Bill Swift	07	.03	.01
☐ 52	Mark Langston	10	.05	.01
☐ 53	Joe Girardi	07	.03	.01
☐ 54	Keith Miller	07	.03	.01
☐ 55	Gary Carter	10	.05	.01
☐ 56	Brady Anderson	10	.05	.01
☐ 57	Dwight Gooden	10	.05	.01
☐ 58	Julio Franco	10	.05	.01
☐ 59	Lenny Dykstra	10	.05	.01
☐ 60	Mickey Tettleton	10	.05	.01
☐ 61	Randy Tomlin	07	.03	.01

☐	62	B.J. Surhoff	.07	.03	.01			
☐	63	Todd Zeile	.07	.03	.01			
☐	64	Roberto Kelly	.10	.05	.01			
☐	65	Rob Dibble	.10	.05	.01			
☐	66	Leo Gomez	.10	.05	.01			
☐	67	Doug Jones	.07	.03	.01			
☐	68	Ellis Burks	.10	.05	.01			
☐	69	Mike Scioscia	.07	.03	.01			
☐	70	Charles Nagy	.10	.05	.01			
☐	71	Cory Snyder	.07	.03	.01			
☐	72	Devon White	.10	.05	.01			
☐	73	Mark Grace	.10	.05	.01			
☐	74	Luis Polonia	.07	.03	.01			
☐	75	John Smiley	.10	.05	.01			
☐	76	Carlton Fisk	.15	.07	.02			
☐	77	Luis Sojo	.07	.03	.01			
☐	78	George Brett	.15	.07	.02			
☐	79	Mitch Williams	.07	.03	.01			
☐	80	Kent Hrbek	.10	.05	.01			
☐	81	Jay Bell	.07	.03	.01			
☐	82	Edgar Martinez	.10	.05	.01			
☐	83	Lee Smith	.10	.05	.01			
☐	84	Deion Sanders	.20	.09	.03			
☐	85	Bill Gullickson	.07	.03	.01			
☐	86	Paul O'Neill	.10	.05	.01			
☐	87	Kevin Seitzer	.10	.05	.01			
☐	88	Steve Finley	.07	.03	.01			
☐	89	Mel Hall	.07	.03	.01			
☐	90	Nolan Ryan	.60	.25	.08			
☐	91	Eric Davis	.10	.05	.01			
☐	92	Mike Mussina	.40	.18	.05			
☐	93	Tony Fernandez	.10	.05	.01			
☐	94	Frank Viola	.10	.05	.01			
☐	95	Matt Williams	.10	.05	.01			
☐	96	Joe Carter	.20	.09	.03			
☐	97	Ryne Sandberg	.35	.16	.04			
☐	98	Jim Abbott	.15	.07	.02			
☐	99	Marquis Grissom	.15	.07	.02			
☐	100	George Bell	.10	.05	.01			
☐	101	Howard Johnson	.10	.05	.01			
☐	102	Kevin Appier	.10	.05	.01			
☐	103	Dale Murphy	.10	.05	.01			
☐	104	Shane Mack	.10	.05	.01			
☐	105	Jose Lind	.07	.03	.01			
☐	106	Rickey Henderson	.20	.09	.03			
☐	107	Bob Tewksbury	.07	.03	.01			
☐	108	Kevin Mitchell	.10	.05	.01			
☐	109	Steve Avery	.20	.09	.03			
☐	110	Candy Maldonado	.07	.03	.01			
☐	111	Bip Roberts	.10	.05	.01			
☐	112	Lou Whitaker	.10	.05	.01			
☐	113	Jeff Bagwell	.30	.14	.04			
☐	114	Dante Bichette	.07	.03	.01			
☐	115	Brett Butler	.10	.05	.01			
☐	116	Melido Perez	.07	.03	.01			
☐	117	Andy Benes	.10	.05	.01			
☐	118	Randy Johnson	.10	.05	.01			
☐	119	Willie McGee	.10	.05	.01			
☐	120	Jody Reed	.07	.03	.01			
☐	121	Shawon Dunston	.10	.05	.01			
☐	122	Carlos Baerga	.25	.11	.03			
☐	123	Bret Saberhagen	.07	.03	.01			
☐	124	John Olerud	.15	.07	.02			
☐	125	Ivan Calderon	.07	.03	.01			
☐	126	Bryan Harvey	.07	.03	.01			
☐	127	Terry Mulholland	.07	.03	.01			
☐	128	Ozzie Guillen	.07	.03	.01			
☐	129	Steve Buechele	.07	.03	.01			
☐	130	Kevin Tapani	.10	.05	.01			
☐	131	Felix Jose	.10	.05	.01			
☐	132	Terry Steinbach	.10	.05	.01			
☐	133	Ron Gant	.12	.05	.02			
☐	134	Harold Reynolds	.07	.03	.01			
☐	135	Chris Sabo	.10	.05	.01			
☐	136	Ivan Rodriguez	.30	.14	.04			
☐	137	Eric Anthony	.10	.05	.01			
☐	138	Mike Henneman	.07	.03	.01			
☐	139	Robby Thompson	.07	.03	.01			
☐	140	Scott Fletcher	.07	.03	.01			
☐	141	Bruce Hurst	.10	.05	.01			
☐	142	Kevin Maas	.10	.05	.01			
☐	143	Tom Candiotti	.07	.03	.01			
☐	144	Chris Hoiles	.10	.05	.01			
☐	145	Mike Morgan	.07	.03	.01			
☐	146	Mark Whiten	.07	.03	.01			
☐	147	Dennis Martinez	.10	.05	.01			
☐	148	Tony Pena	.07	.03	.01			
☐	149	Dave Magadan	.07	.03	.01			
☐	150	Mark Lewis	.07	.03	.01			
☐	151	Mariano Duncan	.07	.03	.01			
☐	152	Gregg Jefferies	.10	.05	.01			
☐	153	Doug Drabek	.10	.05	.01			
☐	154	Brian Harper	.07	.03	.01			
☐	155	Ray Lankford	.15	.07	.02			
☐	156	Carney Lansford	.10	.05	.01			
☐	157	Mike Sharperson	.07	.03	.01			
☐	158	Jack Morris	.12	.05	.02			
☐	159	Otis Nixon	.07	.03	.01			
☐	160	Steve Sax	.10	.05	.01			
☐	161	Mark Lemke	.07	.03	.01			
☐	162	Rafael Palmeiro	.10	.05	.01			
☐	163	Jose Rijo	.10	.05	.01			
☐	164	Omar Vizquel	.07	.03	.01			
☐	165	Sammy Sosa	.07	.03	.01			
☐	166	Milt Cuyler	.07	.03	.01			
☐	167	John Franco	.07	.03	.01			
☐	168	Darryl Hamilton	.07	.03	.01			
☐	169	Ken Hill	.07	.03	.01			
☐	170	Mike Devereaux	.10	.05	.01			
☐	171	Don Slaught	.07	.03	.01			
☐	172	Steve Farr	.07	.03	.01			
☐	173	Bernard Gilkey	.10	.05	.01			
☐	174	Mike Fetters	.07	.03	.01			
☐	175	Vince Coleman	.10	.05	.01			

□	176	Kevin McReynolds	.10	.05	.01
□	177	John Smoltz	.12	.05	.02
□	178	Greg Gagne	.07	.03	.01
□	179	Greg Swindell	.10	.05	.01
□	180	Juan Guzman	.40	.18	.05
□	181	Kal Daniels	.07	.03	.01
□	182	Rick Sutcliffe	.10	.05	.01
□	183	Orlando Merced	.07	.03	.01
□	184	Bill Wegman	.07	.03	.01
□	185	Mark Gardner	.07	.03	.01
□	186	Rob Deer	.10	.05	.01
□	187	Dave Hollins	.10	.05	.01
□	188	Jack Clark	.10	.05	.01
□	189	Brian Hunter	.10	.05	.01
□	190	Tim Wallach	.07	.03	.01
□	191	Tim Belcher	.10	.05	.01
□	192	Walt Weiss	.07	.03	.01
□	193	Kurt Stillwell	.07	.03	.01
□	194	Charlie Hayes	.07	.03	.01
□	195	Willie Randolph	.10	.05	.01
□	196	Jack McDowell	.10	.05	.01
□	197	Jose Offerman	.10	.05	.01
□	198	Chuck Finley	.07	.03	.01
□	199	Darrin Jackson	.07	.03	.01
□	200	Kelly Gruber	.10	.05	.01
□	201	John Wetteland	.07	.03	.01
□	202	Jay Buhner	.10	.05	.01
□	203	Mike LaValliere	.07	.03	.01
□	204	Kevin Brown	.10	.05	.01
□	205	Luis Gonzalez	.10	.05	.01
□	206	Rick Aguilera	.07	.03	.01
□	207	Norm Charlton	.10	.05	.01
□	208	Mike Bordick	.10	.05	.01
□	209	Charlie Leibrandt	.07	.03	.01
□	210	Tom Brunansky	.10	.05	.01
□	211	Tom Henke	.10	.05	.01
□	212	Randy Milligan	.07	.03	.01
□	213	Ramon Martinez	.10	.05	.01
□	214	Mo Vaughn	.10	.05	.01
□	215	Randy Myers	.10	.05	.01
□	216	Greg Hibbard	.07	.03	.01
□	217	Wes Chamberlain	.07	.03	.01
□	218	Tony Phillips	.07	.03	.01
□	219	Pete Harnisch	.07	.03	.01
□	220	Mike Gallego	.07	.03	.01
□	221	Bud Black	.07	.03	.01
□	222	Greg Vaughn	.10	.05	.01
□	223	Milt Thompson	.07	.03	.01
□	224	Ben McDonald	.10	.05	.01
□	225	Billy Hatcher	.07	.03	.01
□	226	Paul Sorrento	.07	.03	.01
□	227	Mark Gubicza	.07	.03	.01
□	228	Mike Greenwell	.10	.05	.01
□	229	Curt Schilling	.07	.03	.01
□	230	Alan Trammell	.10	.05	.01
□	231	Zane Smith	.07	.03	.01
□	232	Bobby Thigpen	.07	.03	.01
□	233	Greg Olson	.07	.03	.01
□	234	Joe Orsulak	.07	.03	.01
□	235	Joe Oliver	.07	.03	.01
□	236	Tim Raines	.10	.05	.01
□	237	Juan Samuel	.07	.03	.01
□	238	Chili Davis	.10	.05	.01
□	239	Spike Owen	.07	.03	.01
□	240	Dave Stewart	.10	.05	.01
□	241	Jim Eisenreich	.07	.03	.01
□	242	Phil Plantier	.10	.05	.01
□	243	Sid Fernandez	.10	.05	.01
□	244	Dan Gladden	.07	.03	.01
□	245	Mickey Morandini	.07	.03	.01
□	246	Tino Martinez	.10	.05	.01
□	247	Kirt Manwaring	.07	.03	.01
□	248	Dean Palmer	.12	.05	.02
□	249	Tom Browning	.07	.03	.01
□	250	Brian McRae	.07	.03	.01
□	251	Scott Leius	.07	.03	.01
□	252	Bert Blyleven	.10	.05	.01
□	253	Scott Erickson	.10	.05	.01
□	254	Bob Welch	.07	.03	.01
□	255	Pat Kelly	.10	.05	.01
□	256	Felix Fermin	.07	.03	.01
□	257	Harold Baines	.10	.05	.01
□	258	Duane Ward	.07	.03	.01
□	259	Bill Spiers	.07	.03	.01
□	260	Jaime Navarro	.10	.05	.01
□	261	Scott Sanderson	.07	.03	.01
□	262	Gary Gaetti	.07	.03	.01
□	263	Bob Ojeda	.07	.03	.01
□	264	Jeff Montgomery	.07	.03	.01
□	265	Scott Bankhead	.07	.03	.01
□	266	Lance Johnson	.07	.03	.01
□	267	Rafael Belliard	.07	.03	.01
□	268	Kevin Reimer	.07	.03	.01
□	269	Benito Santiago	.10	.05	.01
□	270	Mike Moore	.07	.03	.01
□	271	Dave Fleming	.30	.14	.04
□	272	Moises Alou	.10	.05	.01
□	273	Pat Listach	.60	.25	.08
□	274	Reggie Sanders	.20	.09	.03
□	275	Kenny Lofton	.30	.14	.04
□	276	Donovan Osborne	.20	.09	.03
□	277	Rusty Meacham	.07	.03	.01
□	278	Eric Karros	.50	.23	.06
□	279	Andy Stankiewicz	.07	.03	.01
□	280	Brian Jordan	.15	.07	.02
□	281	Gary DiSarcina	.07	.03	.01
□	282	Mark Wohlers	.10	.05	.01
□	283	Dave Nilsson	.10	.05	.01
□	284	Anthony Young	.10	.05	.01
□	285	Jim Bullinger	.07	.03	.01
□	286	Derek Bell	.10	.05	.01
□	287	Brian Williams	.12	.05	.02
□	288	Julio Valera	.07	.03	.01
□	289	Dan Walters	.10	.05	.01

☐	290	Chad Curtis	.15	.07	.02	☐ 347 Mike Piazza	.40	.18	.05

☐	No.	Name				☐	No.	Name			
☐	290	Chad Curtis	.15	.07	.02	☐	347	Mike Piazza	.40	.18	.05
☐	291	Michael Tucker DP	1.00	.45	.13	☐	348	Willie Greene	.25	.11	.03
☐	292	Bob Zupcic	.05	.01		☐	349	Tom Goodwin	.07	.03	.01
☐	293	Todd Hundley	.07	.03	.01	☐	350	Eric Hillman	.15	.07	.02
☐	294	Jeff Tackett	.07	.03	.01	☐	351	Steve Reed	.15	.07	.02
☐	295	Greg Colbrunn	.10	.05	.01	☐	352	Dan Serafini DP	.40	.18	.05
☐	296	Cal Eldred	.30	.14	.04	☐	353	Todd Steverson DP	.30	.14	.04
☐	297	Chris Roberts DP	.40	.18	.05	☐	354	Benji Grigsby DP	.30	.14	.04
☐	298	John Doherty	.07	.03	.01	☐	355	Shannon Stewart DP	.40	.18	.05
☐	299	Denny Neagle	.07	.03	.01	☐	356	Sean Lowe DP	.35	.16	.04
☐	300	Arthur Rhodes	.10	.05	.01	☐	357	Derek Wallace DP	.35	.16	.04
☐	301	Mark Clark	.07	.03	.01	☐	358	Rick Helling DP	.15	.07	.02
☐	302	Scott Cooper	.10	.05	.01	☐	359	Jason Kendall DP	.35	.16	.04
☐	303	Jamie Arnold DP	.30	.14	.04	☐	360	Derek Jeter DP	.50	.23	.06
☐	304	Jim Thome	.10	.05	.01	☐	361	David Cone	.10	.05	.01
☐	305	Frank Seminara	.07	.03	.01	☐	362	Jeff Reardon	.10	.05	.01
☐	306	Kurt Knudsen	.07	.03	.01	☐	363	Bobby Witt	.07	.03	.01
☐	307	Tim Wakefield	.90	.40	.11	☐	364	Jose Canseco	.35	.16	.04
☐	308	John Jaha	.15	.07	.02	☐	365	Jeff Russell	.07	.03	.01
☐	309	Pat Hentgen	.07	.03	.01	☐	366	Ruben Sierra	.20	.09	.03
☐	310	B.J. Wallace DP	.60	.25	.08	☐	367	Alan Mills	.07	.03	.01
☐	311	Roberto Hernandez	.10	.05	.01	☐	368	Matt Nokes	.07	.03	.01
☐	312	Hipolito Pichardo	.07	.03	.01	☐	369	Pat Borders	.07	.03	.01
☐	313	Eric Fox	.07	.03	.01	☐	370	Pedro Munoz	.10	.05	.01
☐	314	Willie Banks	.10	.05	.01	☐	371	Danny Jackson	.07	.03	.01
☐	315	Sam Militello	.25	.11	.03	☐	372	Geronimo Pena	.07	.03	.01
☐	316	Vince Horsman	.07	.03	.01	☐	373	Craig Lefferts	.07	.03	.01
☐	317	Carlos Hernandez	.07	.03	.01	☐	374	Joe Grahe	.07	.03	.01
☐	318	Jeff Kent	.10	.05	.01	☐	375	Roger McDowell	.07	.03	.01
☐	319	Mike Perez	.07	.03	.01	☐	376	Jimmy Key	.07	.03	.01
☐	320	Scott Livingstone	.07	.03	.01	☐	377	Steve Olin	.07	.03	.01
☐	321	Jeff Conine	.10	.05	.01	☐	378	Glenn Davis	.10	.05	.01
☐	322	James Austin	.07	.03	.01	☐	379	Rene Gonzales	.07	.03	.01
☐	323	John Vander Wal	.07	.03	.01	☐	380	Manuel Lee	.07	.03	.01
☐	324	Pat Mahomes	.12	.05	.02	☐	381	Ron Karkovice	.07	.03	.01
☐	325	Pedro Astacio	.25	.11	.03	☐	382	Sid Bream	.07	.03	.01
☐	326	Bret Boone	.40	.18	.05	☐	383	Gerald Williams	.12	.05	.02
☐	327	Matt Stairs	.07	.03	.01	☐	384	Lenny Harris	.07	.03	.01
☐	328	Damion Easley	.20	.09	.03	☐	385	J.T. Snow	.75	.35	.09
☐	329	Ben Rivera	.10	.05	.01	☐	386	Dave Stieb	.07	.03	.01
☐	330	Reggie Jefferson	.10	.05	.01	☐	387	Kirk McCaskill	.07	.03	.01
☐	331	Luis Mercedes	.10	.05	.01	☐	388	Lance Parrish	.10	.05	.01
☐	332	Kyle Abbott	.07	.03	.01	☐	389	Craig Grebeck	.07	.03	.01
☐	333	Eddie Taubensee	.07	.03	.01	☐	390	Rick Wilkins	.07	.03	.01
☐	334	Tim McIntosh	.07	.03	.01	☐	391	Manny Alexander	.15	.07	.02
☐	335	Phil Clark	.07	.03	.01	☐	392	Mike Schooler	.07	.03	.01
☐	336	Wilfredo Cordero	.15	.07	.02	☐	393	Bernie Williams	.10	.05	.01
☐	337	Russ Springer	.15	.07	.02	☐	394	Kevin Koslofski	.07	.03	.01
☐	338	Craig Colbert	.07	.03	.01	☐	395	Willie Wilson	.07	.03	.01
☐	339	Tim Salmon	.40	.18	.05	☐	396	Jeff Parrett	.07	.03	.01
☐	340	Braulio Castillo	.10	.05	.01	☐	397	Mike Harkey	.07	.03	.01
☐	341	Donald Harris	.07	.03	.01	☐	398	Frank Tanana	.07	.03	.01
☐	342	Eric Young	.20	.09	.03	☐	399	Doug Henry	.07	.03	.01
☐	343	Bob Wickman	.25	.11	.03	☐	400	Royce Clayton	.15	.07	.02
☐	344	John Valentin	.15	.07	.02	☐	401	Eric Wedge	.50	.23	.06
☐	345	Dan Wilson	.07	.03	.01	☐	402	Derrick May	.10	.05	.01
☐	346	Steve Hosey	.20	.09	.03	☐	403	Carlos Garcia	.10	.05	.01

		MT	EX-MT	VG
☐ 404	Henry Rodriguez	.10	.05	.01
☐ 405	Ryan Klesko	.40	.18	.05

1993 Score Select Aces

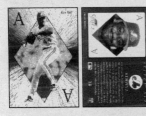

This standard size (2 1/2" by 3 1/2") 24-card set of the top starting pitchers in both leagues was randomly inserted in 1993 Score Select 28-card super packs. According to Score, the chances of finding an Ace card are not less than one in eight packs. The fronts display an action player pose cut out and superimposed on a metallic variegated red and silver diamond design. The diamond itself rests on a background consisting of silver metallic streaks that emanate from the center of the card. In imitation of playing card design, the fronts have a large "A" for Ace in upper left and lower right corners. The player's name in the upper right corner rounds out the card face. On a red background, the horizontal backs have a white "Ace" playing card with a color head shot emanating from a diamond, team logo, and player profile. The cards are numbered on the back.

		MT	EX-MT	VG
COMPLETE SET (24)		80.00	36.00	10.00
COMMON PLAYER (1-24)		3.00	1.35	.40
☐ 1	Roger Clemens	9.00	4.00	1.15
☐ 2	Tom Glavine	5.00	2.30	.60
☐ 3	Jack McDowell	4.00	1.80	.50
☐ 4	Greg Maddux	5.00	2.30	.60
☐ 5	Jack Morris	4.00	1.80	.50
☐ 6	Dennis Martinez	3.00	1.35	.40
☐ 7	Kevin Brown	3.50	1.55	.45
☐ 8	Dwight Gooden	3.50	1.55	.45
☐ 9	Kevin Appier	3.50	1.55	.45
☐ 10	Mike Morgan	3.00	1.35	.40
☐ 11	Juan Guzman	10.00	4.50	1.25
☐ 12	Charles Nagy	4.00	1.80	.50
☐ 13	John Smiley	3.00	1.35	.40
☐ 14	Ken Hill	3.00	1.35	.40
☐ 15	Bob Tewksbury	3.00	1.35	.40
☐ 16	Doug Drabek	3.50	1.55	.45
☐ 17	John Smoltz	4.00	1.80	.50
☐ 18	Greg Swindell	3.50	1.55	.45
☐ 19	Bruce Hurst	3.00	1.35	.40
☐ 20	Mike Mussina	10.00	4.50	1.25
☐ 21	Cal Eldred	7.00	3.10	.85
☐ 22	Melido Perez	3.00	1.35	.40
☐ 23	Dave Fleming	7.00	3.10	.85
☐ 24	Kevin Tapani	3.00	1.35	.40

1993 Score Select Chase Rookies

This 21-card set showcases rookies. The cards were randomly inserted in hobby packs only with at least two cards per box of 36 15-card packs. The fronts exhibit Score's "dufex" printing process, in which a color photo is printed on a metallic base creating an unusual, three-dimensional look. The pictures are tilted slightly to the left and edged on the left and bottom by red metallic borders. On a two-toned red background, the backs present a color headshot in a triangular design and player profile. The cards measure the standard size (2 1/2" by 3 1/2") and are numbered on the back at the bottom center.

	MT	EX-MT	VG
COMPLETE SET (21)	90.00	40.00	11.50
COMMON PLAYER (1-21)	3.00	1.35	.40
☐ 1 Pat Listach	10.00	4.50	1.25
☐ 2 Moises Alou	3.50	1.55	.45
☐ 3 Reggie Sanders	7.00	3.10	.85
☐ 4 Kenny Lofton	8.00	3.60	1.00
☐ 5 Eric Karros	10.00	4.50	1.25
☐ 6 Brian Williams	5.00	2.30	.60
☐ 7 Donovan Osborne	6.00	2.70	.75
☐ 8 Sam Militello	6.00	2.70	.75
☐ 9 Chad Curtis	4.00	1.80	.50
☐ 10 Bob Zupcic	4.00	1.80	.50
☐ 11 Tim Salmon	7.00	3.10	.85
☐ 12 Jeff Conine	3.50	1.55	.45
☐ 13 Pedro Astacio	5.00	2.30	.60
☐ 14 Arthur Rhodes	4.00	1.80	.50
☐ 15 Cal Eldred	7.00	3.10	.85
☐ 16 Tim Wakefield	10.00	4.50	1.25
☐ 17 Andy Stankiewicz	3.00	1.35	.40
☐ 18 Wilfredo Cordero	4.00	1.80	.50
☐ 19 Todd Hundley	3.00	1.35	.40
☐ 20 Dave Fleming	7.00	3.10	.85
☐ 21 Bret Boone	7.00	3.10	.85

1993 Score Select Chase Stars

This 24-card set showcases the top players in Major League Baseball. The cards were randomly inserted in retail packs only with at least two cards per box of 36 15-card packs. The fronts exhibit Score's "dufex" printing process, in which a color photo is printed on a metallic base creating an unusual, three-dimensional look. The pictures are tilted slightly to the left and edged on the left and bottom by green metallic borders. On a two-toned green background, the backs present a color headshot in a triangular design and player profile. The cards measure the standard size (2 1/2" by 3 1/2") and are numbered on the back at the bottom center.

	MT	EX-MT	VG
COMPLETE SET (24)	100.00	45.00	12.50
COMMON PLAYER (1-24)	3.00	1.35	.40
☐ 1 Fred McGriff	6.00	2.70	.75
☐ 2 Ryne Sandberg	8.00	3.60	1.00
☐ 3 Ozzie Smith	4.50	2.00	.55
☐ 4 Gary Sheffield	6.00	2.70	.75
☐ 5 Darren Daulton	3.00	1.35	.40
☐ 6 Andy Van Slyke	3.50	1.55	.45
☐ 7 Barry Bonds	7.00	3.10	.85
☐ 8 Tony Gwynn	6.00	2.70	.75
☐ 9 Greg Maddux	5.00	2.30	.60
☐ 10 Tom Glavine	5.00	2.30	.60
☐ 11 John Franco	3.00	1.35	.40
☐ 12 Lee Smith	3.50	1.55	.45
☐ 13 Cecil Fielder	6.00	2.70	.75
☐ 14 Roberto Alomar	8.00	3.60	1.00
☐ 15 Cal Ripken	9.00	4.00	1.15
☐ 16 Edgar Martinez	3.50	1.55	.45
☐ 17 Ivan Rodriguez	8.00	3.60	1.00
☐ 18 Kirby Puckett	7.00	3.10	.85
☐ 19 Ken Griffey Jr.	10.00	4.50	1.25
☐ 20 Joe Carter	6.00	2.70	.75
☐ 21 Roger Clemens	8.00	3.60	1.00
☐ 22 Dave Fleming	7.00	3.10	.85
☐ 23 Paul Molitor	3.50	1.55	.45
☐ 24 Dennis Eckersley	3.50	1.55	.45

1993 Score Select Triple Crown

Honoring Triple Crown winners, this 3-card set was randomly inserted in hobby packs only with at least two cards per box of 36 15-card packs. The fronts exhibit Score's "dufex" printing process, in which a color photo is printed on a metallic base creating

an unusual, three-dimensional look. The color player photos on the fronts have a forest green metallic border. The player's name and the year he won the Triple Crown appear above the picture, while the words "Triple Crown" are written in script beneath it. On a forest green background, the backs carry a black and white close-up photo of the player wearing a crown and a summary of the player's award winning performance. The cards, which measure the standard 2 1/2" by 3 1/2", are numbered on the back "X of 3" at the lower right corner.

	MT	EX-MT	VG
COMPLETE SET (3)	25.00	11.50	3.10
COMMON PLAYER (1-3)	6.50	2.90	.80
☐ 1 Mickey Mantle	15.00	6.75	1.90
☐ 2 Carl Yastrzemski	6.50	2.90	.80
☐ 3 Frank Robinson	6.50	2.90	.80

1991 Stadium Club

This 600-card standard size (2 1/2" by 3 1/2") set marked Topps first entry into the mass market with a premium quality set. The set features borderless full-color action photos on the front with the name of the player and the Topps Stadium club logo on the bottom of the card, while the back of the card has the basic biographical information as well as making use of the Fastball BARS system and an inset photo of the player's Topps Rookie Card. The set was issued in two series of 300 cards each. The cards are numbered on the back. The key Rookie Cards in the first

series are Greg Colbrunn, Lance Dickson, and Randy Tomlin; however the key cards in the first series are those of Steve Avery, Juan Gonzalez, Ken Griffey Jr., Dave Justice, Nolan Ryan, and Frank Thomas. Series II cards were also available at McDonald's restaurants in the Northeast at three cards per pack. The key Rookie Cards in the second series are Jeff Bagwell, Wes Chamberlain, Pedro Munoz, and Phil Plantier.

	MT	EX-MT	VG
COMPLETE SET (600)	225.00	100.00	28.00
COMPLETE SERIES 1 (300)	135.00	60.00	17.00
COMPLETE SERIES 2 (300)	90.00	40.00	11.50
COMMON PLAYER (1-300)	.25	.11	.03
COMMON PLAYER (301-600)	.25	.11	.03
☐ 1 Dave Stewart (Wearing Tuxedo)	.60	.25	.08
☐ 2 Wally Joyner	.30	.14	.04
☐ 3 Shawon Dunston	.30	.14	.04
☐ 4 Darren Daulton	.35	.16	.04
☐ 5 Will Clark	3.00	1.35	.40
☐ 6 Sammy Sosa	.30	.14	.04
☐ 7 Dan Plesac	.25	.11	.03
☐ 8 Marquis Grissom	2.00	.90	.25
☐ 9 Erik Hanson	.25	.11	.03
☐ 10 Geno Petralli	.25	.11	.03
☐ 11 Jose Rijo	.30	.14	.04
☐ 12 Carlos Quintana	.25	.11	.03
☐ 13 Junior Ortiz	.25	.11	.03
☐ 14 Bob Walk	.25	.11	.03
☐ 15 Mike Macfarlane	.25	.11	.03
☐ 16 Eric Yelding	.25	.11	.03
☐ 17 Bryn Smith	.25	.11	.03
☐ 18 Bip Roberts	.30	.14	.04
☐ 19 Mike Scioscia	.25	.11	.03
☐ 20 Mark Williamson	.25	.11	.03
☐ 21 Don Mattingly	1.50	.65	.19
☐ 22 John Franco	.30	.14	.04
☐ 23 Chet Lemon	.25	.11	.03

☐ 24 Tom Henke	.30	.14	.04
☐ 25 Jerry Browne	.25	.11	.03
☐ 26 Dave Justice	9.00	4.00	1.15
☐ 27 Mark Langston	.30	.14	.04
☐ 28 Damon Berryhill	.25	.11	.03
☐ 29 Kevin Bass	.25	.11	.03
☐ 30 Scott Fletcher	.25	.11	.03
☐ 31 Moises Alou	1.50	.65	.19
☐ 32 Dave Valle	.25	.11	.03
☐ 33 Jody Reed	.25	.11	.03
☐ 34 Dave West	.25	.11	.03
☐ 35 Kevin McReynolds	.30	.14	.04
☐ 36 Pat Combs	.25	.11	.03
☐ 37 Eric Davis	.40	.18	.05
☐ 38 Bret Saberhagen	.30	.14	.04
☐ 39 Stan Javier	.25	.11	.03
☐ 40 Chuck Cary	.25	.11	.03
☐ 41 Tony Phillips	.25	.11	.03
☐ 42 Lee Smith	.40	.18	.05
☐ 43 Tim Teufel	.25	.11	.03
☐ 44 Lance Dickson	.40	.18	.05
☐ 45 Greg Litton	.25	.11	.03
☐ 46 Teddy Higuera	.25	.11	.03
☐ 47 Edgar Martinez	.90	.40	.11
☐ 48 Steve Avery	4.00	1.80	.50
☐ 49 Walt Weiss	.25	.11	.03
☐ 50 David Segui	.25	.11	.03
☐ 51 Andy Benes	1.00	.45	.13
☐ 52 Karl Rhodes	.25	.11	.03
☐ 53 Neal Heaton	.25	.11	.03
☐ 54 Danny Gladden	.25	.11	.03
☐ 55 Luis Rivera	.25	.11	.03
☐ 56 Kevin Brown	.50	.23	.06
☐ 57 Frank Thomas	30.00	13.50	3.80
☐ 58 Terry Mulholland	.25	.11	.03
☐ 59 Dick Schofield	.25	.11	.03
☐ 60 Ron Darling	.30	.14	.04
☐ 61 Sandy Alomar Jr.	.30	.14	.04
☐ 62 Dave Stieb	.25	.11	.03
☐ 63 Alan Trammell	.30	.14	.04
☐ 64 Matt Nokes	.25	.11	.03
☐ 65 Lenny Harris	.25	.11	.03
☐ 66 Milt Thompson	.25	.11	.03
☐ 67 Storm Davis	.25	.11	.03
☐ 68 Joe Oliver	.25	.11	.03
☐ 69 Andres Galarraga	.25	.11	.03
☐ 70 Ozzie Guillen	.25	.11	.03
☐ 71 Ken Howell	.25	.11	.03
☐ 72 Garry Templeton	.25	.11	.03
☐ 73 Derrick May	.30	.14	.04
☐ 74 Xavier Hernandez	.25	.11	.03
☐ 75 Dave Parker	.30	.14	.04
☐ 76 Rick Aguilera	.30	.14	.04
☐ 77 Robby Thompson	.25	.11	.03
☐ 78 Pete Incaviglia	.25	.11	.03
☐ 79 Bob Welch	.25	.11	.03
☐ 80 Randy Milligan	.25	.11	.03

☐ 81 Chuck Finley	.30	.14	.04
☐ 82 Alvin Davis	.25	.11	.03
☐ 83 Tim Naehring	.35	.16	.04
☐ 84 Jay Bell	.30	.14	.04
☐ 85 Joe Magrane	.25	.11	.03
☐ 86 Howard Johnson	.30	.14	.04
☐ 87 Jack McDowell	1.25	.55	.16
☐ 88 Kevin Seitzer	.30	.14	.04
☐ 89 Bruce Ruffin	.25	.11	.03
☐ 90 Fernando Valenzuela	.30	.14	.04
☐ 91 Terry Kennedy	.25	.11	.03
☐ 92 Barry Larkin	1.25	.55	.16
☐ 93 Larry Walker	3.00	1.35	.40
☐ 94 Luis Salazar	.25	.11	.03
☐ 95 Gary Sheffield	5.00	2.30	.60
☐ 96 Bobby Witt	.25	.11	.03
☐ 97 Lonnie Smith	.25	.11	.03
☐ 98 Bryan Harvey	.25	.11	.03
☐ 99 Mookie Wilson	.25	.11	.03
☐ 100 Dwight Gooden	.40	.18	.05
☐ 101 Lou Whitaker	.30	.14	.04
☐ 102 Ron Karkovice	.25	.11	.03
☐ 103 Jesse Barfield	.25	.11	.03
☐ 104 Jose DeJesus	.25	.11	.03
☐ 105 Benito Santiago	.30	.14	.04
☐ 106 Brian Holman	.25	.11	.03
☐ 107 Rafael Ramirez	.25	.11	.03
☐ 108 Ellis Burks	.30	.14	.04
☐ 109 Mike Bielecki	.25	.11	.03
☐ 110 Kirby Puckett	3.00	1.35	.40
☐ 111 Terry Shumpert	.25	.11	.03
☐ 112 Chuck Crim	.25	.11	.03
☐ 113 Todd Benzinger	.25	.11	.03
☐ 114 Brian Barnes	.50	.23	.06
☐ 115 Carlos Baerga	4.00	1.80	.50
☐ 116 Kal Daniels	.25	.11	.03
☐ 117 Dave Johnson	.25	.11	.03
☐ 118 Andy Van Slyke	.40	.18	.05
☐ 119 John Burkett	.25	.11	.03
☐ 120 Rickey Henderson	1.50	.65	.19
☐ 121 Tim Jones	.25	.11	.03
☐ 122 Daryl Irvine	.25	.11	.03
☐ 123 Ruben Sierra	2.00	.90	.25
☐ 124 Jim Abbott	1.50	.65	.19
☐ 125 Daryl Boston	.25	.11	.03
☐ 126 Greg Maddux	1.50	.65	.19
☐ 127 Von Hayes	.25	.11	.03
☐ 128 Mike Fitzgerald	.25	.11	.03
☐ 129 Wayne Edwards	.25	.11	.03
☐ 130 Greg Briley	.25	.11	.03
☐ 131 Rob Dibble	.30	.14	.04
☐ 132 Gene Larkin	.25	.11	.03
☐ 133 David Wells	.25	.11	.03
☐ 134 Steve Balboni	.25	.11	.03
☐ 135 Greg Vaughn	.50	.23	.06
☐ 136 Mark Davis	.25	.11	.03
☐ 137 Dave Rhode	.25	.11	.03

☐ 138 Eric Show	.25	.11	.03
☐ 139 Bobby Bonilla	1.00	.45	.13
☐ 140 Dana Kiecker	.25	.11	.03
☐ 141 Gary Pettis	.25	.11	.03
☐ 142 Dennis Boyd	.25	.11	.03
☐ 143 Mike Benjamin	.25	.11	.03
☐ 144 Luis Polonia	.30	.14	.04
☐ 145 Doug Jones	.25	.11	.03
☐ 146 Al Newman	.25	.11	.03
☐ 147 Alex Fernandez	.75	.35	.09
☐ 148 Bill Doran	.25	.11	.03
☐ 149 Kevin Elster	.25	.11	.03
☐ 150 Len Dykstra	.30	.14	.04
☐ 151 Mike Gallego	.25	.11	.03
☐ 152 Tim Belcher	.30	.14	.04
☐ 153 Jay Buhner	.30	.14	.04
☐ 154 Ozzie Smith UER	.90	.40	.11
(Rookie card is 1979,			
but card back says '78)			
☐ 155 Jose Canseco	3.00	1.35	.40
☐ 156 Gregg Olson	.30	.14	.04
☐ 157 Charlie O'Brien	.25	.11	.03
☐ 158 Frank Tanana	.25	.11	.03
☐ 159 George Brett	1.25	.55	.16
☐ 160 Jeff Huson	.25	.11	.03
☐ 161 Kevin Tapani	.75	.35	.09
☐ 162 Jerome Walton	.25	.11	.03
☐ 163 Charlie Hayes	.25	.11	.03
☐ 164 Chris Bosio	.25	.11	.03
☐ 165 Chris Sabo	.30	.14	.04
☐ 166 Lance Parrish	.30	.14	.04
☐ 167 Don Robinson	.25	.11	.03
☐ 168 Manny Lee	.25	.11	.03
☐ 169 Dennis Rasmussen	.25	.11	.03
☐ 170 Wade Boggs	1.50	.65	.19
☐ 171 Bob Geren	.25	.11	.03
☐ 172 Mackey Sasser	.25	.11	.03
☐ 173 Julio Franco	.30	.14	.04
☐ 174 Otis Nixon	.30	.14	.04
☐ 175 Bert Blyleven	.30	.14	.04
☐ 176 Craig Biggio	.50	.23	.06
☐ 177 Eddie Murray	.90	.40	.11
☐ 178 Randy Tomlin	1.25	.55	.16
☐ 179 Tino Martinez	.75	.35	.09
☐ 180 Carlton Fisk	.90	.40	.11
☐ 181 Dwight Smith	.25	.11	.03
☐ 182 Scott Garrelts	.25	.11	.03
☐ 183 Jim Gantner	.25	.11	.03
☐ 184 Dickie Thon	.25	.11	.03
☐ 185 John Farrell	.25	.11	.03
☐ 186 Cecil Fielder	1.50	.65	.19
☐ 187 Glenn Braggs	.25	.11	.03
☐ 188 Allan Anderson	.25	.11	.03
☐ 189 Kurt Stillwell	.25	.11	.03
☐ 190 Jose Oquendo	.25	.11	.03
☐ 191 Joe Orsulak	.25	.11	.03
☐ 192 Ricky Jordan	.25	.11	.03

☐ 193 Kelly Downs	.25	.11	.03
☐ 194 Delino DeShields	2.00	.90	.25
☐ 195 Omar Vizquel	.25	.11	.03
☐ 196 Mark Carreon	.25	.11	.03
☐ 197 Mike Harkey	.30	.14	.04
☐ 198 Jack Howell	.25	.11	.03
☐ 199 Lance Johnson	.25	.11	.03
☐ 200 Nolan Ryan	12.00	5.50	1.50
(Wearing Tuxedo)			
☐ 201 John Marzano	.25	.11	.03
☐ 202 Doug Drabek	.30	.14	.04
☐ 203 Mark Lemke	.25	.11	.03
☐ 204 Steve Sax	.30	.14	.04
☐ 205 Greg Harris	.25	.11	.03
☐ 206 B.J. Surhoff	.25	.11	.03
☐ 207 Todd Burns	.25	.11	.03
☐ 208 Jose Gonzalez	.25	.11	.03
☐ 209 Mike Scott	.25	.11	.03
☐ 210 Dave Magadan	.30	.14	.04
☐ 211 Dante Bichette	.35	.16	.04
☐ 212 Trevor Wilson	.25	.11	.03
☐ 213 Hector Villanueva	.25	.11	.03
☐ 214 Dan Pasqua	.25	.11	.03
☐ 215 Greg Colbrunn	1.25	.55	.16
☐ 216 Mike Jeffcoat	.25	.11	.03
☐ 217 Harold Reynolds	.25	.11	.03
☐ 218 Paul O'Neill	.30	.14	.04
☐ 219 Mark Guthrie	.25	.11	.03
☐ 220 Barry Bonds	3.00	1.35	.40
☐ 221 Jimmy Key	.25	.11	.03
☐ 222 Billy Ripken	.25	.11	.03
☐ 223 Tom Pagnozzi	.25	.11	.03
☐ 224 Bo Jackson	1.00	.45	.13
☐ 225 Sid Fernandez	.30	.14	.04
☐ 226 Mike Marshall	.25	.11	.03
☐ 227 John Kruk	.35	.16	.04
☐ 228 Mike Fetters	.25	.11	.03
☐ 229 Eric Anthony	.30	.14	.04
☐ 230 Ryne Sandberg	3.50	1.55	.45
☐ 231 Carney Lansford	.30	.14	.04
☐ 232 Melido Perez	.30	.14	.04
☐ 233 Jose Lind	.25	.11	.03
☐ 234 Darryl Hamilton	.30	.14	.04
☐ 235 Tom Browning	.25	.11	.03
☐ 236 Spike Owen	.25	.11	.03
☐ 237 Juan Gonzalez	18.00	8.00	2.30
☐ 238 Felix Fermin	.25	.11	.03
☐ 239 Keith Miller	.25	.11	.03
☐ 240 Mark Gubicza	.25	.11	.03
☐ 241 Kent Anderson	.25	.11	.03
☐ 242 Alvaro Espinoza	.25	.11	.03
☐ 243 Dale Murphy	.40	.18	.05
☐ 244 Orel Hershiser	.30	.14	.04
☐ 245 Paul Molitor	.50	.23	.06
☐ 246 Eddie Whitson	.25	.11	.03
☐ 247 Joe Girardi	.25	.11	.03
☐ 248 Kent Hrbek	.30	.14	.04

☐	249	Bill Sampen	.25	.11	.03			
☐	250	Kevin Mitchell	.35	.16	.04			
☐	251	Mariano Duncan	.25	.11	.03			
☐	252	Scott Bradley	.25	.11	.03			
☐	253	Mike Greenwell	.30	.14	.04			
☐	254	Tom Gordon	.30	.14	.04			
☐	255	Todd Zeile	.40	.18	.05			
☐	256	Bobby Thigpen	.25	.11	.03			
☐	257	Gregg Jefferies	.60	.25	.08			
☐	258	Kenny Rogers	.25	.11	.03			
☐	259	Shane Mack	.50	.23	.06			
☐	260	Zane Smith	.25	.11	.03			
☐	261	Mitch Williams	.25	.11	.03			
☐	262	Jim Deshaies	.25	.11	.03			
☐	263	Dave Winfield	1.00	.45	.13			
☐	264	Ben McDonald	1.25	.55	.16			
☐	265	Randy Ready	.25	.11	.03			
☐	266	Pat Borders	.25	.11	.03			
☐	267	Jose Uribe	.25	.11	.03			
☐	268	Derek Lilliquist	.25	.11	.03			
☐	269	Greg Brock	.25	.11	.03			
☐	270	Ken Griffey Jr.	12.00	5.50	1.50			
☐	271	Jeff Gray	.25	.11	.03			
☐	272	Danny Tartabull	.50	.23	.06			
☐	273	Denny Martinez	.30	.14	.04			
☐	274	Robin Ventura	4.00	1.80	.50			
☐	275	Randy Myers	.30	.14	.04			
☐	276	Jack Daugherty	.25	.11	.03			
☐	277	Greg Gagne	.25	.11	.03			
☐	278	Jay Howell	.25	.11	.03			
☐	279	Mike LaValliere	.25	.11	.03			
☐	280	Rex Hudler	.25	.11	.03			
☐	281	Mike Simms	.35	.16	.04			
☐	282	Kevin Maas	.50	.23	.06			
☐	283	Jeff Ballard	.25	.11	.03			
☐	284	Dave Henderson	.25	.11	.03			
☐	285	Pete O'Brien	.25	.11	.03			
☐	286	Brook Jacoby	.25	.11	.03			
☐	287	Mike Henneman	.25	.11	.03			
☐	288	Greg Olson	.25	.11	.03			
☐	289	Greg Myers	.25	.11	.03			
☐	290	Mark Grace	1.25	.55	.16			
☐	291	Shawn Abner	.25	.11	.03			
☐	292	Frank Viola	.30	.14	.04			
☐	293	Lee Stevens	.35	.16	.04			
☐	294	Jason Grimsley	.25	.11	.03			
☐	295	Matt Williams	.50	.23	.06			
☐	296	Ron Robinson	.25	.11	.03			
☐	297	Tom Brunansky	.30	.14	.04			
☐	298	Checklist 1-100	.25	.03	.01			
☐	299	Checklist 101-200	.25	.03	.01			
☐	300	Checklist 201-300	.25	.03	.01			
☐	301	Darryl Strawberry	1.50	.65	.19			
☐	302	Bud Black	.25	.11	.03			
☐	303	Harold Baines	.30	.14	.04			
☐	304	Roberto Alomar	5.00	2.30	.60			
☐	305	Norm Charlton	.30	.14	.04			
☐	306	Gary Thurman	.25	.11	.03
☐	307	Mike Felder	.25	.11	.03
☐	308	Tony Gwynn	1.50	.65	.19
☐	309	Roger Clemens	3.50	1.55	.45
☐	310	Andre Dawson	.90	.40	.11
☐	311	Scott Radinsky	.25	.11	.03
☐	312	Bob Melvin	.25	.11	.03
☐	313	Kirk McCaskill	.25	.11	.03
☐	314	Pedro Guerrero	.30	.14	.04
☐	315	Walt Terrell	.25	.11	.03
☐	316	Sam Horn	.25	.11	.03
☐	317	Wes Chamberlain	1.25	.55	.16
☐	318	Pedro Munoz	1.50	.65	.19
☐	319	Roberto Kelly	.40	.18	.05
☐	320	Mark Portugal	.25	.11	.03
☐	321	Tim McIntosh	.25	.11	.03
☐	322	Jesse Orosco	.25	.11	.03
☐	323	Gary Green	.25	.11	.03
☐	324	Greg Harris	.25	.11	.03
☐	325	Hubie Brooks	.25	.11	.03
☐	326	Chris Nabholz	.40	.18	.05
☐	327	Terry Pendleton	.60	.25	.08
☐	328	Eric King	.25	.11	.03
☐	329	Chili Davis	.30	.14	.04
☐	330	Anthony Telford	.25	.11	.03
☐	331	Kelly Gruber	.30	.14	.04
☐	332	Dennis Eckersley	.50	.23	.06
☐	333	Mel Hall	.25	.11	.03
☐	334	Bob Kipper	.25	.11	.03
☐	335	Willie McGee	.30	.14	.04
☐	336	Steve Olin	.25	.11	.03
☐	337	Steve Buechele	.25	.11	.03
☐	338	Scott Leius	.40	.18	.05
☐	339	Hal Morris	.40	.18	.05
☐	340	Jose Offerman	.40	.18	.05
☐	341	Kent Mercker	.30	.14	.04
☐	342	Ken Griffey Sr.	.30	.14	.04
☐	343	Pete Harnisch	.25	.11	.03
☐	344	Kirk Gibson	.30	.14	.04
☐	345	Dave Smith	.25	.11	.03
☐	346	Dave Martinez	.25	.11	.03
☐	347	Atlee Hammaker	.25	.11	.03
☐	348	Brian Downing	.25	.11	.03
☐	349	Todd Hundley	.35	.16	.04
☐	350	Candy Maldonado	.25	.11	.03
☐	351	Dwight Evans	.30	.14	.04
☐	352	Steve Searcy	.25	.11	.03
☐	353	Gary Gaetti	.25	.11	.03
☐	354	Jeff Reardon	.35	.16	.04
☐	355	Travis Fryman	12.00	5.50	1.50
☐	356	Dave Righetti	.25	.11	.03
☐	357	Fred McGriff	1.50	.65	.19
☐	358	Don Slaught	.25	.11	.03
☐	359	Gene Nelson	.25	.11	.03
☐	360	Billy Spiers	.25	.11	.03
☐	361	Lee Guetterman	.25	.11	.03
☐	362	Darren Lewis	.40	.18	.05

□	#	Player			
□	363	Duane Ward	.25	.11	.03
□	364	Lloyd Moseby	.25	.11	.03
□	365	John Smoltz	1.50	.65	.19
□	366	Felix Jose	.60	.25	.08
□	367	David Cone	.75	.35	.09
□	368	Wally Backman	.25	.11	.03
□	369	Jeff Montgomery	.25	.11	.03
□	370	Rich Garces	.35	.16	.04
□	371	Billy Hatcher	.25	.11	.03
□	372	Bill Swift	.25	.11	.03
□	373	Jim Eisenreich	.25	.11	.03
□	374	Rob Ducey	.25	.11	.03
□	375	Tim Crews	.25	.11	.03
□	376	Steve Finley	.30	.14	.04
□	377	Jeff Blauser	.25	.11	.03
□	378	Willie Wilson	.25	.11	.03
□	379	Gerald Perry	.25	.11	.03
□	380	Jose Mesa	.25	.11	.03
□	381	Pat Kelly	.60	.25	.08
□	382	Matt Merullo	.25	.11	.03
□	383	Ivan Calderon	.25	.11	.03
□	384	Scott Chiamparino	.30	.14	.04
□	385	Lloyd McClendon	.25	.11	.03
□	386	Dave Bergman	.25	.11	.03
□	387	Ed Sprague	.75	.35	.09
□	388	Jeff Bagwell	9.00	4.00	1.15
□	389	Brett Butler	.30	.14	.04
□	390	Larry Andersen	.25	.11	.03
□	391	Glenn Davis	.30	.14	.04
□	392	Alex Cole UER	.25	.11	.03
		(Front photo actually			
		Otis Nixon)			
□	393	Mike Heath	.25	.11	.03
□	394	Danny Darwin	.25	.11	.03
□	395	Steve Lake	.25	.11	.03
□	396	Tim Layana	.25	.11	.03
□	397	Terry Leach	.25	.11	.03
□	398	Bill Wegman	.25	.11	.03
□	399	Mark McGwire	3.00	1.35	.40
□	400	Mike Boddicker	.25	.11	.03
□	401	Steve Howe	.25	.11	.03
□	402	Bernard Gilkey	.60	.25	.08
□	403	Thomas Howard	.35	.16	.04
□	404	Rafael Belliard	.25	.11	.03
□	405	Tom Candiotti	.25	.11	.03
□	406	Rene Gonzales	.25	.11	.03
□	407	Chuck McElroy	.25	.11	.03
□	408	Paul Sorrento	.50	.23	.06
□	409	Randy Johnson	.30	.14	.04
□	410	Brady Anderson	.60	.25	.08
□	411	Dennis Cook	.25	.11	.03
□	412	Mickey Tettleton	.35	.16	.04
□	413	Mike Stanton	.25	.11	.03
□	414	Ken Oberkfell	.25	.11	.03
□	415	Rick Honeycutt	.25	.11	.03
□	416	Nelson Santovenia	.25	.11	.03
□	417	Bob Tewksbury	.30	.14	.04
□	418	Brent Mayne	.35	.16	.04
□	419	Steve Farr	.25	.11	.03
□	420	Phil Stephenson	.25	.11	.03
□	421	Jeff Russell	.25	.11	.03
□	422	Chris James	.25	.11	.03
□	423	Tim Leary	.25	.11	.03
□	424	Gary Carter	.30	.14	.04
□	425	Glenallen Hill	.25	.11	.03
□	426	Matt Young UER	.25	.11	.03
		(Card mentions 83T/Tr			
		as RC, but 84T shown)			
□	427	Sid Bream	.25	.11	.03
□	428	Greg Swindell	.35	.16	.04
□	429	Scott Aldred	.40	.18	.05
□	430	Cal Ripken	4.00	1.80	.50
□	431	Bill Landrum	.25	.11	.03
□	432	Earnest Riles	.25	.11	.03
□	433	Danny Jackson	.25	.11	.03
□	434	Casey Candaele	.25	.11	.03
□	435	Ken Hill	.30	.14	.04
□	436	Jaime Navarro	.75	.35	.09
□	437	Lance Blankenship	.25	.11	.03
□	438	Randy Velarde	.25	.11	.03
□	439	Frank DiPino	.25	.11	.03
□	440	Carl Nichols	.25	.11	.03
□	441	Jeff M. Robinson	.25	.11	.03
□	442	Deion Sanders	2.50	1.15	.30
□	443	Vicente Palacios	.25	.11	.03
□	444	Devon White	.30	.14	.04
□	445	John Cerutti	.25	.11	.03
□	446	Tracy Jones	.25	.11	.03
□	447	Jack Morris	.60	.25	.08
□	448	Mitch Webster	.25	.11	.03
□	449	Bob Ojeda	.25	.11	.03
□	450	Oscar Azocar	.25	.11	.03
□	451	Luis Aquino	.25	.11	.03
□	452	Mark Whiten	.50	.23	.06
□	453	Stan Belinda	.25	.11	.03
□	454	Ron Gant	1.50	.65	.19
□	455	Jose DeLeon	.25	.11	.03
□	456	Mark Salas UER	.25	.11	.03
		(Back has 85T photo,			
		but calls it 86T)			
□	457	Junior Felix	.25	.11	.03
□	458	Wally Whitehurst	.25	.11	.03
□	459	Phil Plantier	5.00	2.30	.60
□	460	Juan Berenguer	.25	.11	.03
□	461	Franklin Stubbs	.25	.11	.03
□	462	Joe Boever	.25	.11	.03
□	463	Tim Wallach	.30	.14	.04
□	464	Mike Moore	.25	.11	.03
□	465	Albert Belle	2.50	1.15	.30
□	466	Mike Witt	.25	.11	.03
□	467	Craig Worthington	.25	.11	.03
□	468	Jerald Clark	.25	.11	.03
□	469	Scott Terry	.25	.11	.03
□	470	Milt Cuyler	.35	.16	.04

☐ 471 John Smiley	.30	.14	.04
☐ 472 Charles Nagy	2.50	1.15	.30
☐ 473 Alan Mills	.35	.16	.04
☐ 474 John Russell	.25	.11	.03
☐ 475 Bruce Hurst	.30	.14	.04
☐ 476 Andujar Cedeno	.75	.35	.09
☐ 477 Dave Eiland	.25	.11	.03
☐ 478 Brian McRae	1.25	.55	.16
☐ 479 Mike LaCoss	.25	.11	.03
☐ 480 Chris Gwynn	.25	.11	.03
☐ 481 Jamie Moyer	.25	.11	.03
☐ 482 John Olerud	2.00	.90	.25
☐ 483 Efrain Valdez	.25	.11	.03
☐ 484 Sil Campusano	.25	.11	.03
☐ 485 Pascual Perez	.25	.11	.03
☐ 486 Gary Redus	.25	.11	.03
☐ 487 Andy Hawkins	.25	.11	.03
☐ 488 Cory Snyder	.25	.11	.03
☐ 489 Chris Hoiles	1.00	.45	.13
☐ 490 Ron Hassey	.25	.11	.03
☐ 491 Gary Wayne	.25	.11	.03
☐ 492 Mark Lewis	.75	.35	.09
☐ 493 Scott Coolbaugh	.25	.11	.03
☐ 494 Gerald Young	.25	.11	.03
☐ 495 Juan Samuel	.25	.11	.03
☐ 496 Willie Fraser	.25	.11	.03
☐ 497 Jeff Treadway	.25	.11	.03
☐ 498 Vince Coleman	.30	.14	.04
☐ 499 Cris Carpenter	.25	.11	.03
☐ 500 Jack Clark	.30	.14	.04
☐ 501 Kevin Appier	1.25	.55	.16
☐ 502 Rafael Palmeiro	.75	.35	.09
☐ 503 Hensley Meulens	.30	.14	.04
☐ 504 George Bell	.35	.16	.04
☐ 505 Tony Pena	.25	.11	.03
☐ 506 Roger McDowell	.25	.11	.03
☐ 507 Luis Sojo	.25	.11	.03
☐ 508 Mike Schooler	.25	.11	.03
☐ 509 Robin Yount	1.25	.55	.16
☐ 510 Jack Armstrong	.25	.11	.03
☐ 511 Rick Cerone	.25	.11	.03
☐ 512 Curt Wilkerson	.25	.11	.03
☐ 513 Joe Carter	1.50	.65	.19
☐ 514 Tim Burke	.25	.11	.03
☐ 515 Tony Fernandez	.30	.14	.04
☐ 516 Ramon Martinez	.60	.25	.08
☐ 517 Tim Hulett	.25	.11	.03
☐ 518 Terry Steinbach	.30	.14	.04
☐ 519 Pete Smith	.40	.18	.05
☐ 520 Ken Caminiti	.30	.14	.04
☐ 521 Shawn Boskie	.25	.11	.03
☐ 522 Mike Pagliarulo	.25	.11	.03
☐ 523 Tim Raines	.30	.14	.04
☐ 524 Alfredo Griffin	.25	.11	.03
☐ 525 Henry Cotto	.25	.11	.03
☐ 526 Mike Stanley	.25	.11	.03
☐ 527 Charlie Leibrandt	.25	.11	.03
☐ 528 Jeff King	.25	.11	.03
☐ 529 Eric Plunk	.25	.11	.03
☐ 530 Tom Lampkin	.25	.11	.03
☐ 531 Steve Bedrosian	.25	.11	.03
☐ 532 Tom Herr	.25	.11	.03
☐ 533 Craig Lefferts	.25	.11	.03
☐ 534 Jeff Reed	.25	.11	.03
☐ 535 Mickey Morandini	.50	.23	.06
☐ 536 Greg Cadaret	.25	.11	.03
☐ 537 Ray Lankford	5.00	2.30	.60
☐ 538 John Candelaria	.25	.11	.03
☐ 539 Rob Deer	.30	.14	.04
☐ 540 Brad Arnsberg	.25	.11	.03
☐ 541 Mike Sharperson	.25	.11	.03
☐ 542 Jeff D. Robinson	.25	.11	.03
☐ 543 Mo Vaughn	1.25	.55	.16
☐ 544 Jeff Parrett	.25	.11	.03
☐ 545 Willie Randolph	.30	.14	.04
☐ 546 Herm Winningham	.25	.11	.03
☐ 547 Jeff Innis	.25	.11	.03
☐ 548 Chuck Knoblauch	6.00	2.70	.75
☐ 549 Tommy Greene UER	.25	.11	.03
(Born in North Carolina,			
not South Carolina)			
☐ 550 Jeff Hamilton	.25	.11	.03
☐ 551 Barry Jones	.25	.11	.03
☐ 552 Ken Dayley	.25	.11	.03
☐ 553 Rick Dempsey	.25	.11	.03
☐ 554 Greg Smith	.25	.11	.03
☐ 555 Mike Devereaux	.50	.23	.06
☐ 556 Keith Comstock	.25	.11	.03
☐ 557 Paul Faries	.25	.11	.03
☐ 558 Tom Glavine	2.50	1.15	.30
☐ 559 Craig Grebeck	.25	.11	.03
☐ 560 Scott Erickson	1.50	.65	.19
☐ 561 Joel Skinner	.25	.11	.03
☐ 562 Mike Morgan	.25	.11	.03
☐ 563 Dave Gallagher	.25	.11	.03
☐ 564 Todd Stottlemyre	.30	.14	.04
☐ 565 Rich Rodriguez	.35	.16	.04
☐ 566 Craig Wilson	.35	.16	.04
☐ 567 Jeff Brantley	.25	.11	.03
☐ 568 Scott Kamieniecki	.35	.16	.04
☐ 569 Steve Decker	.60	.25	.08
☐ 570 Juan Agosto	.25	.11	.03
☐ 571 Tommy Gregg	.25	.11	.03
☐ 572 Kevin Wickander	.25	.11	.03
☐ 573 Jamie Quirk UER	.25	.11	.03
(Rookie card is 1976,			
but card back is 1990)			
☐ 574 Jerry Don Gleaton	.25	.11	.03
☐ 575 Chris Hammond	.50	.23	.06
☐ 576 Luis Gonzalez	1.25	.55	.16
☐ 577 Russ Swan	.25	.11	.03
☐ 578 Jeff Conine	1.25	.55	.16
☐ 579 Charlie Hough	.25	.11	.03
☐ 580 Jeff Kunkel	.25	.11	.03

□ 581	Darrel Akerfelds	.25	.11	.03
□ 582	Jeff Manto	.25	.11	.03
□ 583	Alejandro Pena	.25	.11	.03
□ 584	Mark Davidson	.25	.11	.03
□ 585	Bob MacDonald	.35	.16	.04
□ 586	Paul Assenmacher	.25	.11	.03
□ 587	Dan Wilson	.60	.25	.08
□ 588	Tom Bolton	.25	.11	.03
□ 589	Brian Harper	.25	.11	.03
□ 590	John Habyan	.25	.11	.03
□ 591	John Orton	.25	.11	.03
□ 592	Mark Gardner	.25	.11	.03
□ 593	Turner Ward	.35	.16	.04
□ 594	Bob Patterson	.25	.11	.03
□ 595	Ed Nunez	.25	.11	.03
□ 596	Gary Scott UER	.75	.35	.09
	(Major League Batting			
	Record should be			
	Minor League)			
□ 597	Scott Bankhead	.25	.11	.03
□ 598	Checklist 301-400	.25	.03	.01
□ 599	Checklist 401-500	.25	.03	.01
□ 600	Checklist 501-600	.25	.03	.01

1992 Stadium Club Dome

The 1992 Topps Stadium Club Special Stadium set features 100 top draft picks, 56 1991 All-Star Game cards, 25 1991 Team U.S.A. cards, and 19 1991 Championship and World Series cards, all packaged in a set box inside a molded-plastic SkyDome display. Topps actually references this set as a 1991 set and the copyright lines on the card backs say

1991, but the set was released well into 1992. The standard-size (2 1/2" by 3 1/2") cards display full-bleed glossy player photos on the fronts. The player's name appears in a sky-blue stripe that is accented by parallel gold stripes. These stripes intersect the Topps Stadium Club logo. The horizontally oriented backs present biography, statistics, or highlights on a colorful artwork background depicting a scene from baseball. The cards are numbered on the back. The key Rookie Cards in this set are Cliff Floyd, Tyler Green, Tyrone Hill, Manny Ramirez, Aaron Sele, and Brien Taylor.

		MT	EX-MT	VG
COMPLETE SET (200)		40.00	18.00	5.00
COMMON PLAYER (1-200)		.15	.07	.02

□ 1	Terry Adams	.20	.09	.03
□ 2	Tommy Adams	.60	.25	.08
□ 3	Rick Aguilera	.15	.07	.02
□ 4	Ron Allen	.25	.11	.03
□ 5	Roberto Alomar	.50	.23	.06
□ 6	Sandy Alomar	.15	.07	.02
□ 7	Greg Anthony	.40	.18	.05
□ 8	James Austin	.20	.09	.03
□ 9	Steve Avery	.60	.25	.08
□ 10	Harold Baines	.15	.07	.02
□ 11	Brian Barber	.90	.40	.11
□ 12	Jon Barnes	.20	.09	.03
□ 13	George Bell	.15	.07	.02
□ 14	Doug Bennett	.25	.11	.03
□ 15	Sean Bergman	.25	.11	.03
□ 16	Craig Biggio	.15	.07	.02
□ 17	Bill Bliss	.20	.09	.03
□ 18	Wade Boggs	.35	.16	.04
□ 19	Bobby Bonilla	.15	.07	.02
□ 20	Russell Brock	.20	.09	.03
□ 21	Tarrik Brock	.20	.09	.03
□ 22	Tom Browning	.15	.07	.02
□ 23	Brett Butler	.15	.07	.02
□ 24	Ivan Calderon	.15	.07	.02
□ 25	Joe Carter	.30	.14	.04
□ 26	Joe Caruso	.40	.18	.05
□ 27	Dan Cholowsky	.60	.25	.08
□ 28	Will Clark	.60	.25	.08
□ 29	Roger Clemens	.75	.35	.09
□ 30	Shawn Curran	.20	.09	.03
□ 31	Chris Curtis	.20	.09	.03
□ 32	Chili Davis	.15	.07	.02
□ 33	Andre Dawson	.20	.09	.03
□ 34	Joe DeBerry	.30	.14	.04
□ 35	John Dettmer	.40	.18	.05
□ 36	Rob Dibble	.15	.07	.02
□ 37	John Donati	.20	.09	.03

☐ 38	Dave Doorneweerd	.40	.18	.05
☐ 39	Darren Dreifort	.75	.35	.09
☐ 40	Mike Durant	.35	.16	.04
☐ 41	Chris Durkin	.30	.14	.04
☐ 42	Dennis Eckersley	.25	.11	.03
☐ 43	Brian Edmondson	.30	.14	.04
☐ 44	Vaughn Eshelman	.20	.09	.03
☐ 45	Shawn Estes	.60	.25	.08
☐ 46	Jorge Fabregas	.35	.16	.04
☐ 47	Jon Farrell	.40	.18	.05
☐ 48	Cecil Fielder	.35	.16	.04
☐ 49	Carlton Fisk	.20	.09	.03
☐ 50	Tim Flannelly	.25	.11	.03
☐ 51	Cliff Floyd	3.00	1.35	.40
☐ 52	Julio Franco	.15	.07	.02
☐ 53	Greg Gagne	.15	.07	.02
☐ 54	Chris Gambs	.20	.09	.03
☐ 55	Ron Gant	.25	.11	.03
☐ 56	Brent Gates	1.50	.65	.19
☐ 57	Dwayne Gerald	.20	.09	.03
☐ 58	Jason Giambi	.90	.40	.11
☐ 59	Benji Gil	.75	.35	.09
☐ 60	Mark Gipner	.20	.09	.03
☐ 61	Danny Gladden	.15	.07	.02
☐ 62	Tom Glavine	.35	.16	.04
☐ 63	Jimmy Gonzalez	.20	.09	.03
☐ 64	Jeff Granger	.60	.25	.08
☐ 65	Dan Grapenthien	.20	.09	.03
☐ 66	Dennis Gray	.25	.11	.03
☐ 67	Shawn Green	1.00	.45	.13
☐ 68	Tyler Green	1.25	.55	.16
☐ 69	Todd Greene	.60	.25	.08
☐ 70	Ken Griffey Jr.	2.00	.90	.25
☐ 71	Kelly Gruber	.15	.07	.02
☐ 72	Ozzie Guillen	.15	.07	.02
☐ 73	Tony Gwynn	.40	.18	.05
☐ 74	Shane Halter	.20	.09	.03
☐ 75	Jeffrey Hammonds	5.00	2.30	.60
☐ 76	Larry Hanlon	.20	.09	.03
☐ 77	Pete Harnisch	.15	.07	.02
☐ 78	Mike Harrison	.25	.11	.03
☐ 79	Bryan Harvey	.15	.07	.02
☐ 80	Scott Hatteberg	.30	.14	.04
☐ 81	Rick Helling	.75	.35	.09
☐ 82	Dave Henderson	.15	.07	.02
☐ 83	Rickey Henderson	.30	.14	.04
☐ 84	Tyrone Hill	1.50	.65	.19
☐ 85	Todd Hollandsworth	.50	.23	.06
☐ 86	Brian Holliday	.20	.09	.03
☐ 87	Terry Horn	.20	.09	.03
☐ 88	Jeff Hostetler	.40	.18	.05
☐ 89	Kent Hrbek	.15	.07	.02
☐ 90	Mark Hubbard	.20	.09	.03
☐ 91	Charles Johnson	4.00	1.80	.50
☐ 92	Howard Johnson	.15	.07	.02
☐ 93	Todd Johnson	.50	.23	.06
☐ 94	Bobby Jones	1.50	.65	.19
☐ 95	Dan Jones	.25	.11	.03
☐ 96	Felix Jose	.15	.07	.02
☐ 97	David Justice	1.00	.45	.13
☐ 98	Jimmy Key	.15	.07	.02
☐ 99	Marc Kroon	.20	.09	.03
☐ 100	John Kruk	.15	.07	.02
☐ 101	Mark Langston	.15	.07	.02
☐ 102	Barry Larkin	.20	.09	.03
☐ 103	Mike LaValliere	.15	.07	.02
☐ 104	Scott Leius	.15	.07	.02
☐ 105	Mark Lemke	.15	.07	.02
☐ 106	Donnie Leshnock	.50	.23	.06
☐ 107	Jimmy Lewis	.40	.18	.05
☐ 108	Shane Livesy	.35	.16	.04
☐ 109	Ryan Long	.35	.16	.04
☐ 110	Trevor Mallory	.20	.09	.03
☐ 111	Denny Martinez	.15	.07	.02
☐ 112	Justin Mashore	.20	.09	.03
☐ 113	Jason McDonald	.40	.18	.05
☐ 114	Jack McDowell	.20	.09	.03
☐ 115	Tom McKinnon	.30	.14	.04
☐ 116	Billy McMillon	.35	.16	.04
☐ 117	Buck McNabb	.30	.14	.04
☐ 118	Jim Mecir	.20	.09	.03
☐ 119	Dan Melendez	.60	.25	.08
☐ 120	Shawn Miller	.20	.09	.03
☐ 121	Trever Miller	.30	.14	.04
☐ 122	Paul Molitor	.20	.09	.03
☐ 123	Vincent Moore	.25	.11	.03
☐ 124	Mike Morgan	.15	.07	.02
☐ 125	Jack Morris WS	.15	.07	.02
☐ 126	Jack Morris AS	.15	.07	.02
☐ 127	Sean Mulligan	.30	.14	.04
☐ 128	Eddie Murray	.25	.11	.03
☐ 129	Mike Neill	1.50	.65	.19
☐ 130	Phil Nevin	6.00	2.70	.75
☐ 131	Mark O'Brien	.25	.11	.03
☐ 132	Alex Ochoa	.35	.16	.04
☐ 133	Chad Ogea	1.25	.55	.16
☐ 134	Greg Olson	.15	.07	.02
☐ 135	Paul O'Neill	.15	.07	.02
☐ 136	Jared Osentowski	.20	.09	.03
☐ 137	Mike Pagliarulo	.15	.07	.02
☐ 138	Rafael Palmeiro	.20	.09	.03
☐ 139	Rodney Pedraza	.30	.14	.04
☐ 140	Tony Phillips (P)	.30	.14	.04
☐ 141	Scott Pisciotta	.50	.23	.06
☐ 142	Christopher Pritchett	.40	.18	.05
☐ 143	Jason Pruitt	.20	.09	.03
☐ 144	Kirby Puckett WS UER	.75	.35	.09
	(Championship series			
	AB and BA is wrong)			
☐ 145	Kirby Puckett AS	.75	.35	.09
☐ 146	Manny Ramirez	2.50	1.15	.30
☐ 147	Eddie Ramos	.30	.14	.04
☐ 148	Mark Ratekin	.20	.09	.03
☐ 149	Jeff Reardon	.20	.09	.03

☐	150	Sean Rees	.20	.09	.03
☐	151	Calvin Reese	.60	.25	.08
☐	152	Desmond Relaford	.20	.09	.03
☐	153	Eric Richardson	.25	.11	.03
☐	154	Cal Ripken	1.00	.45	.13
☐	155	Chris Roberts	1.50	.65	.19
☐	156	Mike Robertson	.40	.18	.05
☐	157	Steve Rodriguez	.40	.18	.05
☐	158	Mike Rossiter	.25	.11	.03
☐	159	Scott Ruffcorn	1.25	.55	.16
☐	160	Chris Sabo	.20	.09	.03
☐	161	Juan Samuel	.15	.07	.02
☐	162	Ryne Sandberg UER	.75	.35	.09
		(On 5th line, prior misspelled as prilor)			
☐	163	Scott Sanderson	.15	.07	.02
☐	164	Benny Santiago	.20	.09	.03
☐	165	Gene Schall	.25	.11	.03
☐	166	Chad Schoenvogel	.20	.09	.03
☐	167	Chris Seelbach	.30	.14	.04
☐	168	Aaron Sele	1.50	.65	.19
☐	169	Basil Shabazz	.50	.23	.06
☐	170	Al Shirley	.75	.35	.09
☐	171	Paul Shuey	1.00	.45	.13
☐	172	Ruben Sierra	.35	.16	.04
☐	173	John Smiley	.15	.07	.02
☐	174	Lee Smith	.15	.07	.02
☐	175	Ozzie Smith	.20	.09	.03
☐	176	Tim Smith	.20	.09	.03
☐	177	Zane Smith	.15	.07	.02
☐	178	John Smoltz	.20	.09	.03
☐	179	Scott Stahoviak	.75	.35	.09
☐	180	Kennie Steenstra	.40	.18	.05
☐	181	Kevin Stocker	.25	.11	.03
☐	182	Chris Stynes	.35	.16	.04
☐	183	Danny Tartabull	.20	.09	.03
☐	184	Brien Taylor	10.00	4.50	1.25
☐	185	Todd Taylor	.40	.18	.05
☐	186	Larry Thomas	.90	.40	.11
☐	187	Ozzie Timmons	.60	.25	.08
		(See also 188)			
☐	188	David Tuttle UER	.40	.18	.05
		(Mistakenly numbered as 187 on card)			
☐	189	Andy Van Slyke	.20	.09	.03
☐	190	Frank Viola	.15	.07	.02
☐	191	Michael Walkden	.30	.14	.04
☐	192	Jeff Ware	.50	.23	.06
☐	193	Allen Watson	1.25	.55	.16
☐	194	Steve Whitaker	.20	.09	.03
☐	195	Jerry Willard	.15	.07	.02
☐	196	Craig Wilson	.50	.23	.06
☐	197	Chris Wimmer	.75	.35	.09
☐	198	Steve Wojciechowski	.25	.11	.03
☐	199	Joel Wolfe	.30	.14	.04
☐	200	Ivan Zweig	.40	.18	.05

1992 Stadium Club

The 1992 Topps Stadium Club baseball card set consists of 900 standard-size (2 1/2" by 3 1/2") cards issued in three series of 300 cards each. The glossy color player photos on the fronts are full-bleed. The "Topps Stadium Club" logo is superimposed at the bottom of the card face, with the player's name appearing immediately below the logo. Some cards in the set have the Stadium Club logo printed upside down. The backs display a mini reprint of the player's Rookie Card and "BARS" (Baseball Analysis and Reporting System) statistics. A card-like application form for membership in Topps Stadium Club was inserted in each wax pack. The cards are numbered on the back. The only noteworthy Rookie Card in the first series is Braulio Castillo. Card numbers 591-600 in the second series form a "Members Choice" subset. The only noteworthy Rookie Card in the second series is Rob Maurer. Card numbers 601-610 in the third series form a "Members Choice" subset. The only noteworthy Rookie Cards in the third series are Pat Listach and Bob Zupcic.

	MT	EX-MT	VG
COMPLETE SET (900)	90.00	40.00	11.50
COMPLETE SERIES 1 (300)	32.00	14.50	4.00
COMPLETE SERIES 2 (300)	32.00	14.50	4.00
COMPLETE SERIES 3 (300)	32.00	14.50	4.00
COMMON PLAYER (1-300)	.15	.07	.02
COMMON PLAYER (301-600)	.15	.07	.02
COMMON PLAYER (601-900)	.15	.07	.02

☐ 1 Cal Ripken UER	2.50	1.15	.30
(Misspelled Ripkin on card back)			
☐ 2 Eric Yelding	.15	.07	.02
☐ 3 Geno Petralli	.15	.07	.02
☐ 4 Wally Backman	.15	.07	.02
☐ 5 Milt Cuyler	.15	.07	.02
☐ 6 Kevin Bass	.15	.07	.02
☐ 7 Dante Bichette	.15	.07	.02
☐ 8 Ray Lankford	.75	.35	.09
☐ 9 Mel Hall	.15	.07	.02
☐ 10 Joe Carter	.60	.25	.08
☐ 11 Juan Samuel	.15	.07	.02
☐ 12 Jeff Montgomery	.15	.07	.02
☐ 13 Glenn Braggs	.15	.07	.02
☐ 14 Henry Cotto	.15	.07	.02
☐ 15 Deion Sanders	.75	.35	.09
☐ 16 Dick Schofield	.15	.07	.02
☐ 17 David Cone	.25	.11	.03
☐ 18 Chili Davis	.20	.09	.03
☐ 19 Tom Foley	.15	.07	.02
☐ 20 Ozzie Guillen	.15	.07	.02
☐ 21 Luis Salazar	.15	.07	.02
☐ 22 Terry Steinbach	.20	.09	.03
☐ 23 Chris James	.15	.07	.02
☐ 24 Jeff King	.15	.07	.02
☐ 25 Carlos Quintana	.15	.07	.02
☐ 26 Mike Maddux	.15	.07	.02
☐ 27 Tommy Greene	.15	.07	.02
☐ 28 Jeff Russell	.15	.07	.02
☐ 29 Steve Finley	.20	.09	.03
☐ 30 Mike Flanagan	.15	.07	.02
☐ 31 Darren Lewis	.20	.09	.03
☐ 32 Mark Lee	.15	.07	.02
☐ 33 Willie Fraser	.15	.07	.02
☐ 34 Mike Henneman	.15	.07	.02
☐ 35 Kevin Maas	.20	.09	.03
☐ 36 Dave Hansen	.20	.09	.03
☐ 37 Erik Hanson	.15	.07	.02
☐ 38 Bill Doran	.15	.07	.02
☐ 39 Mike Boddicker	.15	.07	.02
☐ 40 Vince Coleman	.20	.09	.03
☐ 41 Devon White	.20	.09	.03
☐ 42 Mark Gardner	.15	.07	.02
☐ 43 Scott Lewis	.15	.07	.02
☐ 44 Juan Berenguer	.15	.07	.02
☐ 45 Carney Lansford	.20	.09	.03
☐ 46 Curt Wilkerson	.15	.07	.02
☐ 47 Shane Mack	.20	.09	.03
☐ 48 Bip Roberts	.20	.09	.03
☐ 49 Greg A. Harris	.15	.07	.02
☐ 50 Ryne Sandberg	1.25	.55	.16
☐ 51 Mark Whiten	.20	.09	.03
☐ 52 Jack McDowell	.25	.11	.03
☐ 53 Jimmy Jones	.15	.07	.02
☐ 54 Steve Lake	.15	.07	.02
☐ 55 Bud Black	.15	.07	.02
☐ 56 Dave Valle	.15	.07	.02
☐ 57 Kevin Reimer	.20	.09	.03
☐ 58 Rich Gedman UER	.15	.07	.02
(Wrong BARS chart used)			
☐ 59 Travis Fryman	2.00	.90	.25
☐ 60 Steve Avery	.90	.40	.11
☐ 61 Francisco de la Rosa	.20	.09	.03
☐ 62 Scott Hemond	.15	.07	.02
☐ 63 Hal Morris	.20	.09	.03
☐ 64 Hensley Meulens	.15	.07	.02
☐ 65 Frank Castillo	.30	.14	.04
☐ 66 Gene Larkin	.15	.07	.02
☐ 67 Jose DeLeon	.15	.07	.02
☐ 68 Al Osuna	.15	.07	.02
☐ 69 Dave Cochrane	.15	.07	.02
☐ 70 Robin Ventura	1.00	.45	.13
☐ 71 John Cerutti	.15	.07	.02
☐ 72 Kevin Gross	.15	.07	.02
☐ 73 Ivan Calderon	.15	.07	.02
☐ 74 Mike Macfarlane	.15	.07	.02
☐ 75 Stan Belinda	.15	.07	.02
☐ 76 Shawn Hillegas	.15	.07	.02
☐ 77 Pat Borders	.15	.07	.02
☐ 78 Jim Vatcher	.15	.07	.02
☐ 79 Bobby Rose	.15	.07	.02
☐ 80 Roger Clemens	1.25	.55	.16
☐ 81 Craig Worthington	.15	.07	.02
☐ 82 Jeff Treadway	.15	.07	.02
☐ 83 Jamie Quirk	.15	.07	.02
☐ 84 Randy Bush	.15	.07	.02
☐ 85 Anthony Young	.30	.14	.04
☐ 86 Trevor Wilson	.15	.07	.02
☐ 87 Jaime Navarro	.20	.09	.03
☐ 88 Les Lancaster	.15	.07	.02
☐ 89 Pat Kelly	.20	.09	.03
☐ 90 Alvin Davis	.15	.07	.02
☐ 91 Larry Andersen	.15	.07	.02
☐ 92 Rob Deer	.20	.09	.03
☐ 93 Mike Sharperson	.15	.07	.02
☐ 94 Lance Parrish	.20	.09	.03
☐ 95 Cecil Espy	.15	.07	.02
☐ 96 Tim Spehr	.15	.07	.02
☐ 97 Dave Stieb	.15	.07	.02
☐ 98 Terry Mulholland	.15	.07	.02
☐ 99 Dennis Boyd	.15	.07	.02
☐ 100 Barry Larkin	.35	.16	.04
☐ 101 Ryan Bowen	.30	.14	.04
☐ 102 Felix Fermin	.15	.07	.02
☐ 103 Luis Alicea	.15	.07	.02
☐ 104 Tim Hulett	.15	.07	.02
☐ 105 Rafael Belliard	.15	.07	.02
☐ 106 Mike Gallego	.15	.07	.02
☐ 107 Dave Righetti	.15	.07	.02
☐ 108 Jeff Schaefer	.15	.07	.02
☐ 109 Ricky Bones	.35	.16	.04
☐ 110 Scott Erickson	.25	.11	.03
☐ 111 Matt Nokes	.15	.07	.02

☐ 112	Bob Scanlan	.15	.07	.02
☐ 113	Tom Candiotti	.15	.07	.02
☐ 114	Sean Berry	.30	.14	.04
☐ 115	Kevin Morton	.15	.07	.02
☐ 116	Scott Fletcher	.15	.07	.02
☐ 117	B.J. Surhoff	.15	.07	.02
☐ 118	Dave Magadan UER	.20	.09	.03
	(Born Tampa, not Tamps)			
☐ 119	Bill Gullickson	.15	.07	.02
☐ 120	Marquis Grissom	.50	.23	.06
☐ 121	Lenny Harris	.15	.07	.02
☐ 122	Wally Joyner	.20	.09	.03
☐ 123	Kevin Brown	.20	.09	.03
☐ 124	Braulio Castillo	.40	.18	.05
☐ 125	Eric King	.15	.07	.02
☐ 126	Mark Portugal	.15	.07	.02
☐ 127	Calvin Jones	.30	.14	.04
☐ 128	Mike Heath	.15	.07	.02
☐ 129	Todd Van Poppel	.90	.40	.11
☐ 130	Benny Santiago	.25	.11	.03
☐ 131	Gary Thurman	.15	.07	.02
☐ 132	Joe Girardi	.15	.07	.02
☐ 133	Dave Eiland	.15	.07	.02
☐ 134	Orlando Merced	.30	.14	.04
☐ 135	Joe Orsulak	.15	.07	.02
☐ 136	John Burkett	.15	.07	.02
☐ 137	Ken Dayley	.15	.07	.02
☐ 138	Ken Hill	.20	.09	.03
☐ 139	Walt Terrell	.15	.07	.02
☐ 140	Mike Scioscia	.15	.07	.02
☐ 141	Junior Felix	.15	.07	.02
☐ 142	Ken Caminiti	.20	.09	.03
☐ 143	Carlos Baerga	1.00	.45	.13
☐ 144	Tony Fossas	.15	.07	.02
☐ 145	Craig Grebeck	.15	.07	.02
☐ 146	Scott Bradley	.15	.07	.02
☐ 147	Kent Mercker	.15	.07	.02
☐ 148	Derrick May	.20	.09	.03
☐ 149	Jerald Clark	.15	.07	.02
☐ 150	George Brett	.50	.23	.06
☐ 151	Luis Quinones	.15	.07	.02
☐ 152	Mike Pagliarulo	.15	.07	.02
☐ 153	Jose Guzman	.15	.07	.02
☐ 154	Charlie O'Brien	.15	.07	.02
☐ 155	Darren Holmes	.15	.07	.02
☐ 156	Joe Boever	.15	.07	.02
☐ 157	Rich Monteleone	.15	.07	.02
☐ 158	Reggie Harris	.15	.07	.02
☐ 159	Roberto Alomar	1.00	.45	.13
☐ 160	Robby Thompson	.15	.07	.02
☐ 161	Chris Hoiles	.20	.09	.03
☐ 162	Tom Pagnozzi	.15	.07	.02
☐ 163	Omar Vizquel	.15	.07	.02
☐ 164	John Candelaria	.15	.07	.02
☐ 165	Terry Shumpert	.15	.07	.02
☐ 166	Andy Mota	.20	.09	.03
☐ 167	Scott Bailes	.15	.07	.02
☐ 168	Jeff Blauser	.15	.07	.02
☐ 169	Steve Olin	.15	.07	.02
☐ 170	Doug Drabek	.20	.09	.03
☐ 171	Dave Bergman	.15	.07	.02
☐ 172	Eddie Whitson	.15	.07	.02
☐ 173	Gilberto Reyes	.15	.07	.02
☐ 174	Mark Grace	.25	.11	.03
☐ 175	Paul O'Neill	.20	.09	.03
☐ 176	Greg Cadaret	.15	.07	.02
☐ 177	Mark Williamson	.15	.07	.02
☐ 178	Casey Candaele	.15	.07	.02
☐ 179	Candy Maldonado	.15	.07	.02
☐ 180	Lee Smith	.20	.09	.03
☐ 181	Harold Reynolds	.15	.07	.02
☐ 182	David Justice	1.50	.65	.19
☐ 183	Lenny Webster	.15	.07	.02
☐ 184	Donn Pall	.15	.07	.02
☐ 185	Gerald Alexander	.15	.07	.02
☐ 186	Jack Clark	.20	.09	.03
☐ 187	Stan Javier	.15	.07	.02
☐ 188	Ricky Jordan	.15	.07	.02
☐ 189	Franklin Stubbs	.15	.07	.02
☐ 190	Dennis Eckersley	.25	.11	.03
☐ 191	Danny Tartabull	.20	.09	.03
☐ 192	Pete O'Brien	.15	.07	.02
☐ 193	Mark Lewis	.20	.09	.03
☐ 194	Mike Felder	.15	.07	.02
☐ 195	Mickey Tettleton	.20	.09	.03
☐ 196	Dwight Smith	.15	.07	.02
☐ 197	Shawn Abner	.15	.07	.02
☐ 198	Jim Leyritz UER	.15	.07	.02
	(Career totals less			
	than 1991 totals)			
☐ 199	Mike Devereaux	.20	.09	.03
☐ 200	Craig Biggio	.20	.09	.03
☐ 201	Kevin Elster	.15	.07	.02
☐ 202	Rance Mulliniks	.15	.07	.02
☐ 203	Tony Fernandez	.20	.09	.03
☐ 204	Allan Anderson	.15	.07	.02
☐ 205	Herm Winningham	.15	.07	.02
☐ 206	Tim Jones	.15	.07	.02
☐ 207	Ramon Martinez	.25	.11	.03
☐ 208	Teddy Higuera	.15	.07	.02
☐ 209	John Kruk	.20	.09	.03
☐ 210	Jim Abbott	.35	.16	.04
☐ 211	Dean Palmer	1.00	.45	.13
☐ 212	Mark Davis	.15	.07	.02
☐ 213	Jay Buhner	.20	.09	.03
☐ 214	Jesse Barfield	.15	.07	.02
☐ 215	Kevin Mitchell	.25	.11	.03
☐ 216	Mike LaValliere	.15	.07	.02
☐ 217	Mark Wohlers	.40	.18	.05
☐ 218	Dave Henderson	.15	.07	.02
☐ 219	Dave Smith	.15	.07	.02
☐ 220	Albert Belle	.60	.25	.08
☐ 221	Spike Owen	.15	.07	.02
☐ 222	Jeff Gray	.15	.07	.02

☐ 223 Paul Gibson	.15	.07	.02
☐ 224 Bobby Thigpen	.15	.07	.02
☐ 225 Mike Mussina	3.50	1.55	.45
☐ 226 Darrin Jackson	.20	.09	.03
☐ 227 Luis Gonzalez	.25	.11	.03
☐ 228 Greg Briley	.15	.07	.02
☐ 229 Brent Mayne	.15	.07	.02
☐ 230 Paul Molitor	.25	.11	.03
☐ 231 Al Leiter	.15	.07	.02
☐ 232 Andy Van Slyke	.25	.11	.03
☐ 233 Ron Tingley	.15	.07	.02
☐ 234 Bernard Gilkey	.20	.09	.03
☐ 235 Kent Hrbek	.20	.09	.03
☐ 236 Eric Karros	3.50	1.55	.45
☐ 237 Randy Velarde	.15	.07	.02
☐ 238 Andy Allanson	.15	.07	.02
☐ 239 Willie McGee	.20	.09	.03
☐ 240 Juan Gonzalez	2.50	1.15	.30
☐ 241 Karl Rhodes	.15	.07	.02
☐ 242 Luis Mercedes	.50	.23	.06
☐ 243 Billy Swift	.15	.07	.02
☐ 244 Tommy Gregg	.15	.07	.02
☐ 245 David Howard	.15	.07	.02
☐ 246 Dave Hollins	.50	.23	.06
☐ 247 Kip Gross	.20	.09	.03
☐ 248 Walt Weiss	.15	.07	.02
☐ 249 Mackey Sasser	.15	.07	.02
☐ 250 Cecil Fielder	.60	.25	.08
☐ 251 Jerry Browne	.15	.07	.02
☐ 252 Doug Dascenzo	.15	.07	.02
☐ 253 Darryl Hamilton	.20	.09	.03
☐ 254 Dann Bilardello	.15	.07	.02
☐ 255 Luis Rivera	.15	.07	.02
☐ 256 Larry Walker	.75	.35	.09
☐ 257 Ron Karkovice	.15	.07	.02
☐ 258 Bob Tewksbury	.20	.09	.03
☐ 259 Jimmy Key	.15	.07	.02
☐ 260 Bernie Williams	.50	.23	.06
☐ 261 Gary Wayne	.15	.07	.02
☐ 262 Mike Simms UER	.15	.07	.02
(Reversed negative)			
☐ 263 John Orton	.15	.07	.02
☐ 264 Marvin Freeman	.15	.07	.02
☐ 265 Mike Jeffcoat	.15	.07	.02
☐ 266 Roger Mason	.15	.07	.02
☐ 267 Edgar Martinez	.20	.09	.03
☐ 268 Henry Rodriguez	.40	.18	.05
☐ 269 Sam Horn	.15	.07	.02
☐ 270 Brian McRae	.20	.09	.03
☐ 271 Kirt Manwaring	.15	.07	.02
☐ 272 Mike Bordick	.30	.14	.04
☐ 273 Chris Sabo	.20	.09	.03
☐ 274 Jim Olander	.20	.09	.03
☐ 275 Greg W. Harris	.15	.07	.02
☐ 276 Dan Gakeler	.15	.07	.02
☐ 277 Bill Sampen	.15	.07	.02
☐ 278 Joel Skinner	.15	.07	.02
☐ 279 Curt Schilling	.20	.09	.03
☐ 280 Dale Murphy	.25	.11	.03
☐ 281 Lee Stevens	.15	.07	.02
☐ 282 Lonnie Smith	.15	.07	.02
☐ 283 Manuel Lee	.15	.07	.02
☐ 284 Shawn Boskie	.15	.07	.02
☐ 285 Kevin Seitzer	.20	.09	.03
☐ 286 Stan Royer	.25	.11	.03
☐ 287 John Dopson	.15	.07	.02
☐ 288 Scott Bullett	.30	.14	.04
☐ 289 Ken Patterson	.15	.07	.02
☐ 290 Todd Hundley	.15	.07	.02
☐ 291 Tim Leary	.15	.07	.02
☐ 292 Brett Butler	.20	.09	.03
☐ 293 Gregg Olson	.20	.09	.03
☐ 294 Jeff Brantley	.15	.07	.02
☐ 295 Brian Holman	.15	.07	.02
☐ 296 Brian Harper	.15	.07	.02
☐ 297 Brian Bohanon	.15	.07	.02
☐ 298 Checklist 1-100	.15	.02	.00
☐ 299 Checklist 101-200	.15	.02	.00
☐ 300 Checklist 201-300	.15	.02	.00
☐ 301 Frank Thomas	6.00	2.70	.75
☐ 302 Lloyd McClendon	.15	.07	.02
☐ 303 Brady Anderson	.20	.09	.03
☐ 304 Julio Valera	.30	.14	.04
☐ 305 Mike Aldrete	.15	.07	.02
☐ 306 Joe Oliver	.15	.07	.02
☐ 307 Todd Stottlemyre	.20	.09	.03
☐ 308 Rey Sanchez	.35	.16	.04
☐ 309 Gary Sheffield UER	1.50	.65	.19
(Listed as 5'1",			
should be 5'11")			
☐ 310 Andujar Cedeno	.20	.09	.03
☐ 311 Kenny Rogers	.15	.07	.02
☐ 312 Bruce Hurst	.20	.09	.03
☐ 313 Mike Schooler	.15	.07	.02
☐ 314 Mike Benjamin	.15	.07	.02
☐ 315 Chuck Finley	.15	.07	.02
☐ 316 Mark Lemke	.15	.07	.02
☐ 317 Scott Livingstone	.40	.18	.05
☐ 318 Chris Nabholz	.20	.09	.03
☐ 319 Mike Humphreys	.20	.09	.03
☐ 320 Pedro Guerrero	.20	.09	.03
☐ 321 Willie Banks	.50	.23	.06
☐ 322 Tom Goodwin	.30	.14	.04
☐ 323 Hector Wagner	.15	.07	.02
☐ 324 Wally Ritchie	.15	.07	.02
☐ 325 Mo Vaughn	.25	.11	.03
☐ 326 Joe Klink	.15	.07	.02
☐ 327 Cal Eldred	2.00	.90	.25
☐ 328 Daryl Boston	.15	.07	.02
☐ 329 Mike Huff	.15	.07	.02
☐ 330 Jeff Bagwell	1.50	.65	.19
☐ 331 Bob Milacki	.15	.07	.02
☐ 332 Tom Prince	.15	.07	.02
☐ 333 Pat Tabler	.15	.07	.02

☐ 334 Ced Landrum	.15	.07	.02
☐ 335 Reggie Jefferson	.40	.18	.05
☐ 336 Mo Sanford	.30	.14	.04
☐ 337 Kevin Ritz	.15	.07	.02
☐ 338 Gerald Perry	.15	.07	.02
☐ 339 Jeff Hamilton	.15	.07	.02
☐ 340 Tim Wallach	.20	.09	.03
☐ 341 Jeff Huson	.15	.07	.02
☐ 342 Jose Melendez	.15	.07	.02
☐ 343 Willie Wilson	.15	.07	.02
☐ 344 Mike Stanton	.15	.07	.02
☐ 345 Joel Johnston	.15	.07	.02
☐ 346 Lee Guetterman	.15	.07	.02
☐ 347 Francisco Oliveras	.15	.07	.02
☐ 348 Dave Burba	.15	.07	.02
☐ 349 Tim Crews	.15	.07	.02
☐ 350 Scott Leius	.15	.07	.02
☐ 351 Danny Cox	.15	.07	.02
☐ 352 Wayne Housie	.25	.11	.03
☐ 353 Chris Donnels	.15	.07	.02
☐ 354 Chris George	.15	.07	.02
☐ 355 Gerald Young	.15	.07	.02
☐ 356 Roberto Hernandez	.40	.18	.05
☐ 357 Neal Heaton	.15	.07	.02
☐ 358 Todd Frohwirth	.15	.07	.02
☐ 359 Jose Vizcaino	.15	.07	.02
☐ 360 Jim Thome	.50	.23	.06
☐ 361 Craig Wilson	.15	.07	.02
☐ 362 Dave Haas	.15	.07	.02
☐ 363 Billy Hatcher	.15	.07	.02
☐ 364 John Barfield	.15	.07	.02
☐ 365 Luis Aquino	.15	.07	.02
☐ 366 Charlie Leibrandt	.15	.07	.02
☐ 367 Howard Farmer	.15	.07	.02
☐ 368 Bryn Smith	.15	.07	.02
☐ 369 Mickey Morandini	.20	.09	.03
☐ 370 Jose Canseco	1.00	.45	.13
(See also 597)			
☐ 371 Jose Uribe	.15	.07	.02
☐ 372 Bob MacDonald	.15	.07	.02
☐ 373 Luis Sojo	.15	.07	.02
☐ 374 Craig Shipley	.20	.09	.03
☐ 375 Scott Bankhead	.15	.07	.02
☐ 376 Greg Gagne	.15	.07	.02
☐ 377 Scott Cooper	.50	.23	.06
☐ 378 Jose Offerman	.20	.09	.03
☐ 379 Billy Spiers	.15	.07	.02
☐ 380 John Smiley	.20	.09	.03
☐ 381 Jeff Carter	.15	.07	.02
☐ 382 Heathcliff Slocumb	.15	.07	.02
☐ 383 Jeff Tackett	.25	.11	.03
☐ 384 John Kiely	.20	.09	.03
☐ 385 John Vander Wal	.40	.18	.05
☐ 386 Omar Olivares	.15	.07	.02
☐ 387 Ruben Sierra	.75	.35	.09
☐ 388 Tom Gordon	.15	.07	.02
☐ 389 Charles Nagy	.50	.23	.06

☐ 390 Dave Stewart	.20	.09	.03
☐ 391 Pete Harnisch	.20	.09	.03
☐ 392 Tim Burke	.15	.07	.02
☐ 393 Roberto Kelly	.20	.09	.03
☐ 394 Freddie Benavides	.15	.07	.02
☐ 395 Tom Glavine	.60	.25	.08
☐ 396 Wes Chamberlain	.20	.09	.03
☐ 397 Eric Gunderson	.15	.07	.02
☐ 398 Dave West	.15	.07	.02
☐ 399 Ellis Burks	.20	.09	.03
☐ 400 Ken Griffey Jr.	4.00	1.80	.50
☐ 401 Thomas Howard	.15	.07	.02
☐ 402 Juan Guzman	3.50	1.55	.45
☐ 403 Mitch Webster	.15	.07	.02
☐ 404 Matt Merullo	.15	.07	.02
☐ 405 Steve Buechele	.15	.07	.02
☐ 406 Danny Jackson	.15	.07	.02
☐ 407 Felix Jose	.20	.09	.03
☐ 408 Doug Piatt	.15	.07	.02
☐ 409 Jim Eisenreich	.15	.07	.02
☐ 410 Bryan Harvey	.15	.07	.02
☐ 411 Jim Austin	.20	.09	.03
☐ 412 Jim Poole	.15	.07	.02
☐ 413 Glenallen Hill	.15	.07	.02
☐ 414 Gene Nelson	.15	.07	.02
☐ 415 Ivan Rodriguez	2.00	.90	.25
☐ 416 Frank Tanana	.15	.07	.02
☐ 417 Steve Decker	.15	.07	.02
☐ 418 Jason Grimsley	.15	.07	.02
☐ 419 Tim Layana	.15	.07	.02
☐ 420 Don Mattingly	.60	.25	.08
☐ 421 Jerome Walton	.15	.07	.02
☐ 422 Rob Ducey	.15	.07	.02
☐ 423 Andy Benes	.25	.11	.03
☐ 424 John Marzano	.15	.07	.02
☐ 425 Gene Harris	.15	.07	.02
☐ 426 Tim Raines	.25	.11	.03
☐ 427 Bret Barberie	.20	.09	.03
☐ 428 Harvey Pulliam	.25	.11	.03
☐ 429 Cris Carpenter	.15	.07	.02
☐ 430 Howard Johnson	.20	.09	.03
☐ 431 Orel Hershiser	.25	.11	.03
☐ 432 Brian Hunter	.40	.18	.05
☐ 433 Kevin Tapani	.20	.09	.03
☐ 434 Rick Reed	.15	.07	.02
☐ 435 Ron Witmeyer	.20	.09	.03
☐ 436 Gary Gaetti	.15	.07	.02
☐ 437 Alex Cole	.15	.07	.02
☐ 438 Chito Martinez	.15	.07	.02
☐ 439 Greg Litton	.15	.07	.02
☐ 440 Julio Franco	.20	.09	.03
☐ 441 Mike Munoz	.15	.07	.02
☐ 442 Erik Pappas	.15	.07	.02
☐ 443 Pat Combs	.15	.07	.02
☐ 444 Lance Johnson	.15	.07	.02
☐ 445 Ed Sprague	.20	.09	.03
☐ 446 Mike Greenwell	.25	.11	.03

☐ 447	Milt Thompson	.15	.07	.02
☐ 448	Mike Magnante	.30	.14	.04
☐ 449	Chris Haney	.20	.09	.03
☐ 450	Robin Yount	.50	.23	.06
☐ 451	Rafael Ramirez	.15	.07	.02
☐ 452	Gino Minutelli	.15	.07	.02
☐ 453	Tom Lampkin	.15	.07	.02
☐ 454	Tony Perezchica	.15	.07	.02
☐ 455	Dwight Gooden	.25	.11	.03
☐ 456	Mark Guthrie	.15	.07	.02
☐ 457	Jay Howell	.15	.07	.02
☐ 458	Gary DiSarcina	.15	.07	.02
☐ 459	John Smoltz	.35	.16	.04
☐ 460	Will Clark	1.00	.45	.13
☐ 461	Dave Otto	.15	.07	.02
☐ 462	Rob Maurer	.40	.18	.05
☐ 463	Dwight Evans	.20	.09	.03
☐ 464	Tom Brunansky	.20	.09	.03
☐ 465	Shawn Hare	.15	.11	.03
☐ 466	Geronimo Pena	.25	.11	.03
☐ 467	Alex Fernandez	.20	.09	.03
☐ 468	Greg Myers	.15	.07	.02
☐ 469	Jeff Fassero	.15	.07	.02
☐ 470	Len Dykstra	.20	.09	.03
☐ 471	Jeff Johnson	.15	.07	.02
☐ 472	Russ Swan	.15	.07	.02
☐ 473	Archie Corbin	.30	.14	.04
☐ 474	Chuck McElroy	.15	.07	.02
☐ 475	Mark McGwire	1.00	.45	.13
☐ 476	Wally Whitehurst	.15	.07	.02
☐ 477	Tim McIntosh	.15	.07	.02
☐ 478	Sid Bream	.15	.07	.02
☐ 479	Jeff Juden	.30	.14	.04
☐ 480	Carlton Fisk	.40	.18	.05
☐ 481	Jeff Plympton	.20	.09	.03
☐ 482	Carlos Martinez	.15	.07	.02
☐ 483	Jim Gott	.15	.07	.02
☐ 484	Bob McClure	.15	.07	.02
☐ 485	Tim Teufel	.15	.07	.02
☐ 486	Vicente Palacios	.15	.07	.02
☐ 487	Jeff Reed	.15	.07	.02
☐ 488	Tony Phillips	.15	.07	.02
☐ 489	Mel Rojas	.15	.07	.02
☐ 490	Ben McDonald	.30	.14	.04
☐ 491	Andres Santana	.20	.09	.03
☐ 492	Chris Beasley	.20	.09	.03
☐ 493	Mike Timlin	.15	.07	.02
☐ 494	Brian Downing	.15	.07	.02
☐ 495	Kirk Gibson	.20	.09	.03
☐ 496	Scott Sanderson	.15	.07	.02
☐ 497	Nick Esasky	.15	.07	.02
☐ 498	Johnny Guzman	.50	.23	.06
☐ 499	Mitch Williams	.15	.07	.02
☐ 500	Kirby Puckett	1.00	.45	.13
☐ 501	Mike Harkey	.20	.09	.03
☐ 502	Jim Gantner	.15	.07	.02
☐ 503	Bruce Egloff	.15	.07	.02
☐ 504	Josias Manzanillo	.25	.11	.03
☐ 505	Delino DeShields	.50	.23	.06
☐ 506	Rheal Cormier	.30	.14	.04
☐ 507	Jay Bell	.15	.07	.02
☐ 508	Rich Rowland	.25	.11	.03
☐ 509	Scott Servais	.15	.07	.02
☐ 510	Terry Pendleton	.20	.09	.03
☐ 511	Rich DeLucia	.15	.07	.02
☐ 512	Warren Newson	.15	.07	.02
☐ 513	Paul Faries	.15	.07	.02
☐ 514	Kal Daniels	.15	.07	.02
☐ 515	Jarvis Brown	.20	.09	.03
☐ 516	Rafael Palmeiro	.25	.11	.03
☐ 517	Kelly Downs	.15	.07	.02
☐ 518	Steve Chitren	.15	.07	.02
☐ 519	Moises Alou	.25	.11	.03
☐ 520	Wade Boggs	.60	.25	.08
☐ 521	Pete Schourek	.20	.09	.03
☐ 522	Scott Terry	.15	.07	.02
☐ 523	Kevin Appier	.20	.09	.03
☐ 524	Gary Redus	.15	.07	.02
☐ 525	George Bell	.20	.09	.03
☐ 526	Jeff Kaiser	.15	.07	.02
☐ 527	Alvaro Espinoza	.15	.07	.02
☐ 528	Luis Polonia	.20	.09	.03
☐ 529	Darren Daulton	.20	.09	.03
☐ 530	Norm Charlton	.20	.09	.03
☐ 531	John Olerud	.50	.23	.06
☐ 532	Dan Plesac	.15	.07	.02
☐ 533	Billy Ripken	.15	.07	.02
☐ 534	Rod Nichols	.15	.07	.02
☐ 535	Joey Cora	.15	.07	.02
☐ 536	Harold Baines	.20	.09	.03
☐ 537	Bob Ojeda	.15	.07	.02
☐ 538	Mark Leonard	.15	.07	.02
☐ 539	Danny Darwin	.15	.07	.02
☐ 540	Shawon Dunston	.20	.09	.03
☐ 541	Pedro Munoz	.25	.11	.03
☐ 542	Mark Gubicza	.15	.07	.02
☐ 543	Kevin Baez	.20	.09	.03
☐ 544	Todd Zeile	.15	.07	.02
☐ 545	Don Slaught	.15	.07	.02
☐ 546	Tony Eusebio	.20	.09	.03
☐ 547	Alonzo Powell	.15	.07	.02
☐ 548	Gary Pettis	.15	.07	.02
☐ 549	Brian Barnes	.15	.07	.02
☐ 550	Lou Whitaker	.25	.11	.03
☐ 551	Keith Mitchell	.30	.14	.04
☐ 552	Oscar Azocar	.15	.07	.02
☐ 553	Stu Cole	.25	.11	.03
☐ 554	Steve Wapnick	.15	.07	.02
☐ 555	Derek Bell	.60	.25	.08
☐ 556	Luis Lopez	.20	.09	.03
☐ 557	Anthony Telford	.15	.07	.02
☐ 558	Tim Mauser	.20	.09	.03
☐ 559	Glen Sutko	.15	.07	.02
☐ 560	Darryl Strawberry	.60	.25	.08

□	561	Tom Bolton	.15	.07	.02
□	562	Cliff Young	.15	.07	.02
□	563	Bruce Walton	.15	.07	.02
□	564	Chico Walker	.15	.07	.02
□	565	John Franco	.20	.09	.03
□	566	Paul McClellan	.15	.07	.02
□	567	Paul Abbott	.15	.07	.02
□	568	Gary Varsho	.15	.07	.02
□	569	Carlos Maldonado	.20	.09	.03
□	570	Kelly Gruber	.20	.09	.03
□	571	Jose Oquendo	.15	.07	.02
□	572	Steve Frey	.15	.07	.02
□	573	Tino Martinez	.20	.09	.03
□	574	Bill Haselman	.15	.07	.02
□	575	Eric Anthony	.25	.11	.03
□	576	John Habyan	.15	.07	.02
□	577	Jeff McNeeley	.40	.18	.05
□	578	Chris Bosio	.15	.07	.02
□	579	Joe Grahe	.15	.07	.02
□	580	Fred McGriff	.60	.25	.08
□	581	Rick Honeycutt	.15	.07	.02
□	582	Matt Williams	.20	.09	.03
□	583	Cliff Brantley	.20	.09	.03
□	584	Rob Dibble	.20	.09	.03
□	585	Skeeter Barnes	.15	.07	.02
□	586	Greg Hibbard	.15	.07	.02
□	587	Randy Milligan	.15	.07	.02
□	588	Checklist 301-400	.15	.02	.00
□	589	Checklist 401-500	.15	.02	.00
□	590	Checklist 501-600	.15	.02	.00
□	591	Frank Thomas MC	4.00	1.80	.50
□	592	David Justice MC	1.00	.45	.13
□	593	Roger Clemens MC	1.00	.45	.13
□	594	Steve Avery MC	.75	.35	.09
□	595	Cal Ripken MC	1.50	.65	.19
□	596	Barry Larkin MC UER	.20	.09	.03
		(Ranked in AL,			
		should be NL)			
□	597	Jose Canseco MC UER	.90	.40	.11
		(Mistakenly numbered			
		370 on card back)			
□	598	Will Clark MC	.75	.35	.09
□	599	Cecil Fielder MC	.50	.23	.06
□	600	Ryne Sandberg MC	1.00	.45	.13
□	601	Chuck Knoblauch MC	.75	.35	.09
□	602	Doc Gooden MC	.20	.09	.03
□	603	Ken Griffey Jr. MC	3.00	1.35	.40
□	604	Barry Bonds MC	.75	.35	.09
□	605	Nolan Ryan MC	2.50	1.15	.30
□	606	Jeff Bagwell MC	1.00	.45	.13
□	607	Robin Yount MC	.40	.18	.05
□	608	Bobby Bonilla MC	.20	.09	.03
□	609	George Brett MC	.40	.18	.05
□	610	Howard Johnson MC	.20	.09	.03
□	611	Esteban Beltre	.30	.14	.04
□	612	Mike Christopher	.20	.09	.03
□	613	Troy Afenir	.15	.07	.02
□	614	Mariano Duncan	.15	.07	.02
□	615	Doug Henry	.60	.25	.08
□	616	Doug Jones	.15	.07	.02
□	617	Alvin Davis	.15	.07	.02
□	618	Craig Lefferts	.15	.07	.02
□	619	Kevin McReynolds	.20	.09	.03
□	620	Barry Bonds	1.00	.45	.13
□	621	Turne; Ward	.15	.07	.02
□	622	Joe Magrane	.15	.07	.02
□	623	Mark Parent	.15	.07	.02
□	624	Tom Browning	.15	.07	.02
□	625	John Smiley	.20	.09	.03
□	626	Steve Wilson	.15	.07	.02
□	627	Mike Gallego	.15	.07	.02
□	628	Sammy Sosa	.15	.07	.02
□	629	Rico Rossy	.20	.09	.03
□	630	Royce Clayton	.75	.35	.09
□	631	Clay Parker	.15	.07	.02
□	632	Pete Smith	.20	.09	.03
□	633	Jeff McKnight	.15	.07	.02
□	634	Jack Daugherty	.15	.07	.02
□	635	Steve Sax	.20	.09	.03
□	636	Joe Hesketh	.15	.07	.02
□	637	Vince Horsman	.20	.09	.03
□	638	Eric King	.15	.07	.02
□	639	Joe Boever	.15	.07	.02
□	640	Jack Morris	.30	.14	.04
□	641	Arthur Rhodes	.75	.35	.09
□	642	Bob Melvin	.15	.07	.02
□	643	Rick Wilkins	.15	.07	.02
□	644	Scott Scudder	.15	.07	.02
□	645	Bip Roberts	.20	.09	.03
□	646	Julio Valera	.30	.14	.04
□	647	Kevin Campbell	.20	.09	.03
□	648	Steve Searcy	.15	.07	.02
□	649	Scott Kamieniecki	.15	.07	.02
□	650	Kurt Stillwell	.15	.07	.02
□	651	Bob Welch	.15	.07	.02
□	652	Andres Galarraga	.15	.07	.02
□	653	Mike Jackson	.15	.07	.02
□	654	Bo Jackson	.50	.23	.06
□	655	Sid Fernandez	.20	.09	.03
□	656	Mike Bielecki	.15	.07	.02
□	657	Jeff Reardon	.20	.09	.03
□	658	Wayne Rosenthal	.20	.09	.03
□	659	Eric Bullock	.15	.07	.02
□	660	Eric Davis	.25	.11	.03
□	661	Randy Tomlin	.20	.09	.03
□	662	Tom Edens	.15	.07	.02
□	663	Rob Murphy	.15	.07	.02
□	664	Leo Gomez	.40	.18	.05
□	665	Greg Maddux	.30	.14	.04
□	666	Greg Vaughn	.20	.09	.03
□	667	Wade Taylor	.15	.07	.02
□	668	Brad Arnsberg	.15	.07	.02
□	669	Mike Moore	.15	.07	.02
□	670	Mark Langston	.20	.09	.03

☐ 671 Barry Jones	15	.07	.02
☐ 672 Bill Landrum	15	.07	.02
☐ 673 Greg Swindell	20	.09	.03
☐ 674 Wayne Edwards	15	.07	.02
☐ 675 Greg Olson	15	.07	.02
☐ 676 Bill Pulsipher	25	.11	.03
☐ 677 Bobby Witt	15	.07	.02
☐ 678 Mark Carreon	15	.07	.02
☐ 679 Patrick Lennon	25	.11	.03
☐ 680 Ozzie Smith	40	.18	.05
☐ 681 John Briscoe	20	.09	.03
☐ 682 Matt Young	15	.07	.02
☐ 683 Jeff Conine	15	.07	.02
☐ 684 Phil Stephenson	15	.07	.02
☐ 685 Ron Darling	20	.09	.03
☐ 686 Bryan Hickerson	20	.09	.03
☐ 687 Dale Sveum	15	.07	.02
☐ 688 Kirk McCaskill	15	.07	.02
☐ 689 Rich Amaral	20	.09	.03
☐ 690 Danny Tartabull	25	.11	.03
☐ 691 Donald Harris	15	.07	.02
☐ 692 Doug Davis	20	.09	.03
☐ 693 John Farrell	15	.07	.02
☐ 694 Paul Gibson	15	.07	.02
☐ 695 Kenny Lofton	2.50	1.15	.30
☐ 696 Mike Fetters	15	.07	.02
☐ 697 Rosario Rodriguez	20	.09	.03
☐ 698 Chris Jones	15	.07	.02
☐ 699 Jeff Manto	15	.07	.02
☐ 700 Rick Sutcliffe	20	.09	.03
☐ 701 Scott Bankhead	15	.07	.02
☐ 702 Donnie Hill	15	.07	.02
☐ 703 Todd Worrell	15	.07	.02
☐ 704 Rene Gonzales	15	.07	.02
☐ 705 Rick Cerone	15	.07	.02
☐ 706 Tony Pena	15	.07	.02
☐ 707 Paul Sorrento	20	.09	.03
☐ 708 Gary Scott	20	.09	.03
☐ 709 Junior Noboa	15	.07	.02
☐ 710 Wally Joyner	20	.09	.03
☐ 711 Charlie Hayes	15	.07	.02
☐ 712 Rich Rodriguez	20	.09	.03
☐ 713 Rudy Seanez	20	.09	.03
☐ 714 Jim Bullinger	30	.14	.04
☐ 715 Jeff M. Robinson	15	.07	.02
☐ 716 Jeff Branson	15	.07	.02
☐ 717 Andy Ashby	25	.11	.03
☐ 718 Dave Burba	15	.07	.02
☐ 719 Rich Gossage	20	.09	.03
☐ 720 Randy Johnson	20	.09	.03
☐ 721 David Wells	15	.07	.02
☐ 722 Paul Kilgus	15	.07	.02
☐ 723 Dave Martinez	15	.07	.02
☐ 724 Denny Neagle	25	.11	.03
☐ 725 Andy Stankiewicz	40	.18	.05
☐ 726 Rick Aguilera	20	.09	.03
☐ 727 Junior Ortiz	15	.07	.02
☐ 728 Storm Davis	15	.07	.02
☐ 729 Don Robinson	15	.07	.02
☐ 730 Ron Gant	35	.16	.04
☐ 731 Paul Assenmacher	15	.07	.02
☐ 732 Mike Gardiner	15	.07	.02
☐ 733 Milt Hill	20	.09	.03
☐ 734 Jeremy Hernandez	25	.11	.03
☐ 735 Ken Hill	20	.09	.03
☐ 736 Xavier Hernandez	15	.07	.02
☐ 737 Gregg Jefferies	20	.09	.03
☐ 738 Dick Schofield	15	.07	.02
☐ 739 Ron Robinson	15	.07	.02
☐ 740 Sandy Alomar	20	.09	.03
☐ 741 Mike Stanley	15	.07	.02
☐ 742 Butch Henry	40	.18	.05
☐ 743 Floyd Bannister	15	.07	.02
☐ 744 Brian Drahman	15	.07	.02
☐ 745 Dave Winfield	40	.18	.05
☐ 746 Bob Walk	15	.07	.02
☐ 747 Chris James	15	.07	.02
☐ 748 Don Prybylinski	20	.09	.03
☐ 749 Dennis Rasmussen	15	.07	.02
☐ 750 Rickey Henderson	50	.23	.06
☐ 751 Chris Hammond	15	.07	.02
☐ 752 Bob Kipper	15	.07	.02
☐ 753 Dave Rohde	15	.07	.02
☐ 754 Hubie Brooks	15	.07	.02
☐ 755 Bret Saberhagen	25	.11	.03
☐ 756 Jeff D. Robinson	15	.07	.02
☐ 757 Pat Listach	4.00	1.80	.50
☐ 758 Bill Wegman	15	.07	.02
☐ 759 John Wetteland	15	.07	.02
☐ 760 Phil Plantier	60	.25	.08
☐ 761 Wilson Alvarez	15	.07	.02
☐ 762 Scott Aldred	15	.07	.02
☐ 763 Armando Reynoso	25	.11	.03
☐ 764 Todd Benzinger	15	.07	.02
☐ 765 Kevin Mitchell	25	.11	.03
☐ 766 Gary Sheffield	1.50	.65	.19
☐ 767 Allan Anderson	15	.07	.02
☐ 768 Rusty Meacham	15	.07	.02
☐ 769 Rick Parker	15	.07	.02
☐ 770 Nolan Ryan	3.00	1.35	.40
☐ 771 Jeff Ballard	15	.07	.02
☐ 772 Cory Snyder	15	.07	.02
☐ 773 Denis Boucher	20	.09	.03
☐ 774 Jose Gonzalez	15	.07	.02
☐ 775 Juan Guerrero	40	.18	.05
☐ 776 Ed Nunez	15	.07	.02
☐ 777 Scott Ruskin	15	.07	.02
☐ 778 Terry Leach	15	.07	.02
☐ 779 Carl Willis	15	.07	.02
☐ 780 Bobby Bonilla	35	.16	.04
☐ 781 Duane Ward	15	.07	.02
☐ 782 Joe Slusarski	15	.07	.02
☐ 783 David Segui	15	.07	.02
☐ 784 Kirk Gibson	20	.09	.03

☐	785	Frank Viola	.20	.09	.03	☐	842	Tim Belcher	.20	.09	.03
☐	786	Keith Miller	.15	.07	.02	☐	843	Jeff Shaw	.15	.07	.02
☐	787	Mike Morgan	.15	.07	.02	☐	844	Mike Fitzgerald	.15	.07	.02
☐	788	Kim Batiste	.30	.14	.04	☐	845	Gary Carter	.20	.09	.03
☐	789	Sergio Valdez	.15	.07	.02	☐	846	John Russell	.15	.07	.02
☐	790	Eddie Taubensee	.40	.18	.05	☐	847	Eric Hillman	.60	.25	.08
☐	791	Jack Armstrong	.15	.07	.02	☐	848	Mike Witt	.15	.07	.02
☐	792	Scott Fletcher	.15	.07	.02	☐	849	Curt Wilkerson	.15	.07	.02
☐	793	Steve Farr	.15	.07	.02	☐	850	Alan Trammell	.25	.11	.03
☐	794	Dan Pasqua	.15	.07	.02	☐	851	Rex Hudler	.15	.07	.02
☐	795	Eddie Murray	.40	.18	.05	☐	852	Mike Walkden	.30	.14	.04
☐	796	John Morris	.15	.07	.02	☐	853	Kevin Ward	.20	.09	.03
☐	797	Francisco Cabrera	.15	.07	.02	☐	854	Tim Naehring	.15	.07	.02
☐	798	Mike Perez	.30	.14	.04	☐	855	Bill Swift	.15	.07	.02
☐	799	Ted Wood	.30	.14	.04	☐	856	Damon Berryhill	.15	.07	.02
☐	800	Jose Rijo	.20	.09	.03	☐	857	Mark Eichhorn	.15	.07	.02
☐	801	Danny Gladden	.15	.07	.02	☐	858	Hector Villanueva	.15	.07	.02
☐	802	Archi Cianfrocco	.50	.23	.06	☐	859	Jose Lind	.15	.07	.02
☐	803	Monty Fariss	.30	.14	.04	☐	860	Denny Martinez	.20	.09	.03
☐	804	Roger McDowell	.15	.07	.02	☐	861	Bill Krueger	.15	.07	.02
☐	805	Randy Myers	.20	.09	.03	☐	862	Mike Kingery	.15	.07	.02
☐	806	Kirk Dressendorfer	.15	.07	.02	☐	863	Jeff Innis	.15	.07	.02
☐	807	Zane Smith	.15	.07	.02	☐	864	Derek Lilliquist	.15	.07	.02
☐	808	Glenn Davis	.20	.09	.03	☐	865	Reggie Sanders	1.50	.65	.19
☐	809	Torey Lovullo	.15	.07	.02	☐	866	Ramon Garcia	.15	.07	.02
☐	810	Andre Dawson	.40	.18	.05	☐	867	Bruce Ruffin	.15	.07	.02
☐	811	Bill Pecota	.15	.07	.02	☐	868	Dickie Thon	.15	.07	.02
☐	812	Ted Power	.15	.07	.02	☐	869	Melido Perez	.20	.09	.03
☐	813	Willie Blair	.15	.07	.02	☐	870	Ruben Amaro	.20	.09	.03
☐	814	Dave Fleming	2.00	.90	.25	☐	871	Alan Mills	.15	.07	.02
☐	815	Chris Gwynn	.15	.07	.02	☐	872	Matt Sinatro	.15	.07	.02
☐	816	Jody Reed	.15	.07	.02	☐	873	Eddie Zosky	.30	.14	.04
☐	817	Mark Dewey	.20	.09	.03	☐	874	Pete Incaviglia	.15	.07	.02
☐	818	Kyle Abbott	.30	.14	.04	☐	875	Tom Candiotti	.15	.07	.02
☐	819	Tom Henke	.20	.09	.03	☐	876	Bob Patterson	.15	.07	.02
☐	820	Kevin Seitzer	.20	.09	.03	☐	877	Neal Heaton	.15	.07	.02
☐	821	Al Newman	.15	.07	.02	☐	878	Terrel Hansen	.40	.18	.05
☐	822	Tim Sherrill	.20	.09	.03	☐	879	Dave Eiland	.15	.07	.02
☐	823	Chuck Crim	.15	.07	.02	☐	880	Von Hayes	.15	.07	.02
☐	824	Darren Reed	.15	.07	.02	☐	881	Tim Scott	.25	.11	.03
☐	825	Tony Gwynn	.60	.25	.08	☐	882	Otis Nixon	.20	.09	.03
☐	826	Steve Foster	.25	.11	.03	☐	883	Herm Winningham	.15	.07	.02
☐	827	Steve Howe	.15	.07	.02	☐	884	Dion James	.15	.07	.02
☐	828	Brook Jacoby	.15	.07	.02	☐	885	Dave Wainhouse	.20	.09	.03
☐	829	Rodney McCray	.15	.07	.02	☐	886	Frank DiPino	.15	.07	.02
☐	830	Chuck Knoblauch	1.00	.45	.13	☐	887	Dennis Cook	.15	.07	.02
☐	831	John Wehner	.20	.09	.03	☐	888	Jose Mesa	.15	.07	.02
☐	832	Scott Garrelts	.15	.07	.02	☐	889	Mark Leiter	.15	.07	.02
☐	833	Alejandro Pena	.15	.07	.02	☐	890	Willie Randolph	.20	.09	.03
☐	834	Jeff Parrett	.15	.07	.02	☐	891	Craig Colbert	.20	.09	.03
☐	835	Juan Bell	.15	.07	.02	☐	892	Dwayne Henry	.15	.07	.02
☐	836	Lance Dickson	.20	.09	.03	☐	893	Jim Lindeman	.15	.07	.02
☐	837	Darryl Kile	.30	.14	.04	☐	894	Charlie Hough	.15	.07	.02
☐	838	Efrain Valdez	.15	.07	.02	☐	895	Gil Heredia	.20	.09	.03
☐	839	Bob Zupcic	.75	.35	.09	☐	896	Scott Chiamparino	.15	.07	.02
☐	840	George Bell	.20	.09	.03	☐	897	Lance Blankenship	.15	.07	.02
☐	841	Dave Gallagher	.15	.07	.02	☐	898	Checklist 601-700	.15	.02	.00

			MT	EX-MT	VG
☐ 899	Checklist 701-800	.15	.02		.00
☐ 900	Checklist 801-900	.15	.02		.00

	MT	EX-MT	VG
COMPLETE SET (3)	24.00	11.00	3.00
COMMON PLAYER (1-3)	8.00	3.60	1.00
☐ 1 Chipper Jones	8.00	3.60	1.00
☐ 2 Brien Taylor	10.00	4.50	1.25
☐ 3 Phil Nevin	8.00	3.60	1.00

1992 Stadium Club First Draft Picks

1991 Studio

This three-card subset, featuring Major League Baseball's Number 1 draft pick for 1990, 1991, and 1992, was randomly inserted into 1992 Topps Stadium Club Series III packs. Topps estimated that one of these cards can be found in every 72 packs. One card also was mailed to each member of Topps Stadium Club. The cards measure the standard size (2 1/2" by 3 1/2") and feature on the fronts full-bleed posed color player photos. The player's draft year is printed on an orange circle in the upper right corner and is accented by gold foil stripes of varying lengths that run vertically down the right edge of the card. The player's name appears on the Stadium Club logo at the bottom. The number "1" is gold-foil stamped in a black diamond at the lower left and is followed by a red stripe gold-foil stamped with the words "Draft Pick of the '90s". The back design features color photos on a black and red background with the player's signature gold-foil stamped across the bottom of the photo and gold foil bars running down the right edge of the picture. The team name and biographical information is included in a yellow and white box. The cards are numbered on the back.

The 1991 Leaf Studio set contains 264 cards and a puzzle of recently inducted Hall of Famer Rod Carew. The Carew puzzle was issued on twenty-one 2 1/2" by 3 1/2" cards, with 3 puzzle pieces per card, for a total of 63 pieces. The player cards measure the standard-size (2 1/2" by 3 1/2"), and the fronts feature posed black and white head-and-shoulders player photos with mauve borders. The team logo, player's name, and position appear along the bottom of the card face. The backs are printed in black and white and have four categories of information: personal, career, hobbies and interests, and heroes. The cards are numbered on the back. The cards are checklisted below alphabetically within and according to teams for each league as follows: Baltimore Orioles (1-10), Boston Red Sox (11-20), California Angels (21-30), Chicago White Sox (31-40), Cleveland Indians (41-50), Detroit Tigers (51-60), Kansas City Royals (61-70), Milwaukee Brewers (71-80), Minnesota Twins (81-90), New York Yankees (91-100), Oakland Athletics (101-110), Seattle Mariners (111-120), Texas Rangers (121-130), Toronto Blue Jays (131-140), Atlanta

Braves (141-150), Chicago Cubs (151-160), Cincinnati Reds (161-170), Houston Astros (171-180), Los Angeles Dodgers (181-190), Montreal Expos (191-200), New York Mets (201-210), Philadelphia Phillies (211-220), Pittsburgh Pirates (221-230), St. Louis Cardinals (231-240), San Diego Padres (241-250), and San Francisco Giants (251-260). The key Rookie Cards in the set are Jeff Bagwell, Wes Chamberlain, Phil Plantier, and Todd Van Poppel. Among the other notable cards are Frank Thomas, Juan Gonzalez, and Dave Justice.

	MT	EX-MT	VG
COMPLETE SET (264)	32.00	14.50	4.00
COMMON PLAYER (1-263)	.08	.04	.01

		MT	EX-MT	VG
☐ 1	Glenn Davis	.10	.04	.01
☐ 2	Dwight Evans	.10	.04	.01
☐ 3	Leo Gomez	.75	.35	.09
☐ 4	Chris Hoiles	.30	.14	.04
☐ 5	Sam Horn	.08	.04	.01
☐ 6	Ben McDonald	.25	.11	.03
☐ 7	Randy Milligan	.08	.04	.01
☐ 8	Gregg Olson	.10	.04	.01
☐ 9	Cal Ripken	1.00	.45	.13
☐ 10	David Segui	.08	.04	.01
☐ 11	Wade Boggs	.40	.18	.05
☐ 12	Ellis Burks	.10	.04	.01
☐ 13	Jack Clark	.10	.04	.01
☐ 14	Roger Clemens	.90	.40	.11
☐ 15	Mike Greenwell	.12	.05	.02
☐ 16	Tim Naehring	.15	.07	.02
☐ 17	Tony Pena	.08	.04	.01
☐ 18	Phil Plantier	1.50	.65	.19
☐ 19	Jeff Reardon	.12	.05	.02
☐ 20	Mo Vaughn	.60	.25	.08
☐ 21	Jimmy Reese CO	.10	.04	.01
☐ 22	Jim Abbott UER	.40	.18	.05
	(Born in 1967, not 1969)			
☐ 23	Bert Blyleven	.10	.04	.01
☐ 24	Chuck Finley	.10	.04	.01
☐ 25	Gary Gaetti	.08	.04	.01
☐ 26	Wally Joyner	.10	.04	.01
☐ 27	Mark Langston	.10	.04	.01
☐ 28	Kirk McCaskill	.08	.04	.01
☐ 29	Lance Parrish	.10	.04	.01
☐ 30	Dave Winfield	.25	.11	.03
☐ 31	Alex Fernandez	.30	.14	.04
☐ 32	Carlton Fisk	.30	.14	.04
☐ 33	Scott Fletcher	.08	.04	.01
☐ 34	Greg Hibbard	.08	.04	.01
☐ 35	Charlie Hough	.08	.04	.01
☐ 36	Jack McDowell	.30	.14	.04
☐ 37	Tim Raines	.12	.05	.02
☐ 38	Sammy Sosa	.10	.04	.01
☐ 39	Bobby Thigpen	.08	.04	.01
☐ 40	Frank Thomas	6.00	2.70	.75
☐ 41	Sandy Alomar Jr.	.10	.04	.01
☐ 42	John Farrell	.08	.04	.01
☐ 43	Glenallen Hill	.08	.04	.01
☐ 44	Brook Jacoby	.08	.04	.01
☐ 45	Chris James	.08	.04	.01
☐ 46	Doug Jones	.08	.04	.01
☐ 47	Eric King	.08	.04	.01
☐ 48	Mark Lewis	.25	.11	.03
☐ 49	Greg Swindell UER	.10	.04	.01
	(Photo actually Turner Ward)			
☐ 50	Mark Whiten	.20	.09	.03
☐ 51	Milt Cuyler	.15	.07	.02
☐ 52	Rob Deer	.10	.04	.01
☐ 53	Cecil Fielder	.40	.18	.05
☐ 54	Travis Fryman	3.50	1.55	.45
☐ 55	Bill Gullickson	.08	.04	.01
☐ 56	Lloyd Moseby	.08	.04	.01
☐ 57	Frank Tanana	.08	.04	.01
☐ 58	Mickey Tettleton	.10	.04	.01
☐ 59	Alan Trammell	.12	.05	.02
☐ 60	Lou Whitaker	.12	.05	.02
☐ 61	Mike Boddicker	.08	.04	.01
☐ 62	George Brett	.35	.16	.04
☐ 63	Jeff Conine	.60	.25	.08
☐ 64	Warren Cromartie	.08	.04	.01
☐ 65	Storm Davis	.08	.04	.01
☐ 66	Kirk Gibson	.10	.04	.01
☐ 67	Mark Gubicza	.08	.04	.01
☐ 68	Brian McRae	.60	.25	.08
☐ 69	Bret Saberhagen	.10	.04	.01
☐ 70	Kurt Stillwell	.08	.04	.01
☐ 71	Tim McIntosh	.08	.04	.01
☐ 72	Candy Maldonado	.08	.04	.01
☐ 73	Paul Molitor	.15	.07	.02
☐ 74	Willie Randolph	.10	.04	.01
☐ 75	Ron Robinson	.08	.04	.01
☐ 76	Gary Sheffield	1.25	.55	.16
☐ 77	Franklin Stubbs	.08	.04	.01
☐ 78	B.J. Surhoff	.08	.04	.01
☐ 79	Greg Vaughn	.15	.07	.02
☐ 80	Robin Yount	.35	.16	.04
☐ 81	Rick Aguilera	.10	.04	.01
☐ 82	Steve Bedrosian	.08	.04	.01
☐ 83	Scott Erickson	.60	.25	.08
☐ 84	Greg Gagne	.08	.04	.01
☐ 85	Dan Gladden	.08	.04	.01
☐ 86	Brian Harper	.08	.04	.01
☐ 87	Kent Hrbek	.10	.04	.01
☐ 88	Shane Mack	.10	.04	.01
☐ 89	Jack Morris	.12	.05	.02
☐ 90	Kirby Puckett	.75	.35	.09
☐ 91	Jesse Barfield	.08	.04	.01
☐ 92	Steve Farr	.08	.04	.01

☐ 93 Steve Howe	.08	.04	.01
☐ 94 Roberto Kelly	.12	.05	.02
☐ 95 Tim Leary	.08	.04	.01
☐ 96 Kevin Maas	.15	.07	.02
☐ 97 Don Mattingly	.40	.18	.05
☐ 98 Hensley Meulens	.10	.04	.01
☐ 99 Scott Sanderson	.08	.04	.01
☐ 100 Steve Sax	.10	.04	.01
☐ 101 Jose Canseco	.75	.35	.09
☐ 102 Dennis Eckersley	.15	.07	.02
☐ 103 Dave Henderson	.08	.04	.01
☐ 104 Rickey Henderson	.40	.18	.05
☐ 105 Rick Honeycutt	.08	.04	.01
☐ 106 Mark McGwire	.75	.35	.09
☐ 107 Dave Stewart UER	.10	.04	.01
(No-hitter against			
Toronto, not Texas)			
☐ 108 Eric Show	.08	.04	.01
☐ 109 Todd Van Poppel	2.00	.90	.25
☐ 110 Bob Welch	.08	.04	.01
☐ 111 Alvin Davis	.08	.04	.01
☐ 112 Ken Griffey Jr.	2.00	.90	.25
☐ 113 Ken Griffey Sr.	.10	.04	.01
☐ 114 Erik Hanson UER	.08	.04	.01
(Misspelled Eric)			
☐ 115 Brian Holman	.08	.04	.01
☐ 116 Randy Johnson	.10	.04	.01
☐ 117 Edgar Martinez	.25	.11	.03
☐ 118 Tino Martinez	.25	.11	.03
☐ 119 Harold Reynolds	.08	.04	.01
☐ 120 David Valle	.08	.04	.01
☐ 121 Kevin Belcher	.15	.07	.02
☐ 122 Scott Chiamparino	.10	.04	.01
☐ 123 Julio Franco	.10	.04	.01
☐ 124 Juan Gonzalez	4.00	1.80	.50
☐ 125 Rich Gossage	.10	.04	.01
☐ 126 Jeff Kunkel	.08	.04	.01
☐ 127 Rafael Palmeiro	.20	.09	.03
☐ 128 Nolan Ryan	2.00	.90	.25
☐ 129 Ruben Sierra	.50	.23	.06
☐ 130 Bobby Witt	.08	.04	.01
☐ 131 Roberto Alomar	1.00	.45	.13
☐ 132 Tom Candiotti	.08	.04	.01
☐ 133 Joe Carter	.40	.18	.05
☐ 134 Ken Dayley	.08	.04	.01
☐ 135 Kelly Gruber	.10	.04	.01
☐ 136 John Olerud	.50	.23	.06
☐ 137 Dave Stieb	.08	.04	.01
☐ 138 Turner Ward	.15	.07	.02
☐ 139 Devon White	.10	.04	.01
☐ 140 Mookie Wilson	.08	.04	.01
☐ 141 Steve Avery	.90	.40	.11
☐ 142 Sid Bream	.08	.04	.01
☐ 143 Nick Esasky UER	.08	.04	.01
(Homers abbreviated RH)			
☐ 144 Ron Gant	.40	.18	.05
☐ 145 Tom Glavine	.75	.35	.09
☐ 146 David Justice	2.00	.90	.25
☐ 147 Kelly Mann	.08	.04	.01
☐ 148 Terry Pendleton	.15	.07	.02
☐ 149 John Smoltz	.40	.18	.05
☐ 150 Jeff Treadway	.08	.04	.01
☐ 151 George Bell	.10	.04	.01
☐ 152 Shawn Boskie	.08	.04	.01
☐ 153 Andre Dawson	.25	.11	.03
☐ 154 Lance Dickson	.20	.09	.03
☐ 155 Shawon Dunston	.10	.04	.01
☐ 156 Joe Girardi	.08	.04	.01
☐ 157 Mark Grace	.30	.14	.04
☐ 158 Ryne Sandberg	.90	.40	.11
☐ 159 Gary Scott	.35	.16	.04
☐ 160 Dave Smith	.08	.04	.01
☐ 161 Tom Browning	.08	.04	.01
☐ 162 Eric Davis	.15	.07	.02
☐ 163 Rob Dibble	.10	.04	.01
☐ 164 Mariano Duncan	.08	.04	.01
☐ 165 Chris Hammond	.15	.07	.02
☐ 166 Billy Hatcher	.08	.04	.01
☐ 167 Barry Larkin	.25	.11	.03
☐ 168 Hal Morris	.10	.04	.01
☐ 169 Paul O'Neill	.10	.04	.01
☐ 170 Chris Sabo	.10	.04	.01
☐ 171 Eric Anthony	.12	.05	.02
☐ 172 Jeff Bagwell	3.00	1.35	.40
☐ 173 Craig Biggio	.15	.07	.02
☐ 174 Ken Caminiti	.12	.05	.02
☐ 175 Jim Deshaies	.08	.04	.01
☐ 176 Steve Finley	.10	.04	.01
☐ 177 Pete Harnisch	.10	.04	.01
☐ 178 Darryl Kile	.30	.14	.04
☐ 179 Curt Schilling	.10	.04	.01
☐ 180 Mike Scott	.08	.04	.01
☐ 181 Brett Butler	.10	.04	.01
☐ 182 Gary Carter	.10	.04	.01
☐ 183 Orel Hershiser	.12	.05	.02
☐ 184 Ramon Martinez	.15	.07	.02
☐ 185 Eddie Murray	.25	.11	.03
☐ 186 Jose Offerman	.15	.07	.02
☐ 187 Bob Ojeda	.08	.04	.01
☐ 188 Juan Samuel	.08	.04	.01
☐ 189 Mike Scioscia	.08	.04	.01
☐ 190 Darryl Strawberry	.40	.18	.05
☐ 191 Moises Alou	.50	.23	.06
☐ 192 Brian Barnes	.25	.11	.03
☐ 193 Oil Can Boyd	.08	.04	.01
☐ 194 Ivan Calderon	.08	.04	.01
☐ 195 Delino DeShields	.50	.23	.06
☐ 196 Mike Fitzgerald	.08	.04	.01
☐ 197 Andres Galarraga	.08	.04	.01
☐ 198 Marquis Grissom	.50	.23	.06
☐ 199 Bill Sampen	.08	.04	.01
☐ 200 Tim Wallach	.10	.04	.01
☐ 201 Daryl Boston	.08	.04	.01
☐ 202 Vince Coleman	.10	.04	.01

☐	203 John Franco	10	.04	.01
☐	204 Dwight Gooden	15	.07	.02
☐	205 Tom Herr	08	.04	.01
☐	206 Gregg Jefferies	20	.09	.03
☐	207 Howard Johnson	10	.04	.01
☐	208 Dave Magadan UER	10	.04	.01
	(Born 1862, should be 1962)			
☐	209 Kevin McReynolds	10	.04	.01
☐	210 Frank Viola	10	.04	.01
☐	211 Wes Chamberlain	60	.25	.08
☐	212 Darren Daulton	10	.04	.01
☐	213 Len Dykstra	10	.04	.01
☐	214 Charlie Hayes	08	.04	.01
☐	215 Ricky Jordan	08	.04	.01
☐	216 Steve Lake	08	.04	.01
	(Pictured with parrot on his shoulder)			
☐	217 Roger McDowell	08	.04	.01
☐	218 Mickey Morandini	25	.11	.03
☐	219 Terry Mulholland	08	.04	.01
☐	220 Dale Murphy	12	.05	.02
☐	221 Jay Bell	10	.04	.01
☐	222 Barry Bonds	60	.25	.08
☐	223 Bobby Bonilla	25	.11	.03
☐	224 Doug Drabek	10	.04	.01
☐	225 Bill Landrum	08	.04	.01
☐	226 Mike LaValliere	08	.04	.01
☐	227 Jose Lind	08	.04	.01
☐	228 Don Slaught	08	.04	.01
☐	229 John Smiley	10	.04	.01
☐	230 Andy Van Slyke	20	.09	.03
☐	231 Bernard Gilkey	30	.14	.04
☐	232 Pedro Guerrero	10	.04	.01
☐	233 Rex Hudler	08	.04	.01
☐	234 Ray Lankford	1.50	.65	.19
☐	235 Joe Magrane	08	.04	.01
☐	236 Jose Oquendo	08	.04	.01
☐	237 Lee Smith	10	.04	.01
☐	238 Ozzie Smith	25	.11	.03
☐	239 Milt Thompson	08	.04	.01
☐	240 Todd Zeile	15	.07	.02
☐	241 Larry Andersen	08	.04	.01
☐	242 Andy Benes	30	.14	.04
☐	243 Paul Faries	08	.04	.01
☐	244 Tony Fernandez	10	.04	.01
☐	245 Tony Gwynn	40	.18	.05
☐	246 Atlee Hammaker	08	.04	.01
☐	247 Fred McGriff	40	.18	.05
☐	248 Bip Roberts	10	.04	.01
☐	249 Benito Santiago	12	.05	.02
☐	250 Ed Whitson	08	.04	.01
☐	251 Dave Anderson	08	.04	.01
☐	252 Mike Benjamin	08	.04	.01
☐	253 John Burkett UER	08	.04	.01
	(Front photo actually Trevor Wilson)			

☐	254 Will Clark	75	.35	.09
☐	255 Scott Garrelts	08	.04	.01
☐	256 Willie McGee	10	.04	.01
☐	257 Kevin Mitchell	12	.05	.02
☐	258 Dave Righetti	08	.04	.01
☐	259 Matt Williams	12	.05	.02
☐	260 Black and Decker	08	.04	.01
	Bud Black Steve Decker			
☐	261 Checklist Card 1-88	10	.01	.00
	Sparky Anderson MG			
☐	262 Checklist Card 89-176	10	.01	.00
	Tom Lasorda MG			
☐	263 Checklist Card 177-263	10	.01	.00
	Tony LaRussa MG			
☐	NNO Title Card	10	.05	.01

1992 Studio

The 1992 Leaf Studio set consists of ten players from each of the 26 major league teams, three checklists, and an introduction card for a total of 264 cards. A Heritage series eight-card subset, featuring today's star players dressed in vintage uniforms, was randomly inserted in 12-card foil packs. The cards measure the standard size (2 1/2" by 3 1/2"). Inside champagne color metallic borders, the fronts carry a color close-up shot superimposed on a black and white action player photo. The backs focus on the personal side of each player by providing an up-close look, and unusual statistics show the batter or pitcher each player "Loves to Face" or "Hates to Face". The cards are numbered on the back. The key Rookie

Cards in this set are Chad Curtis and Pat Mahomes.

	MT	EX-MT	VG
COMPLETE SET (264)	25.00	11.50	3.10
COMMON PLAYER (1-264)	.08	.04	.01

		MT	EX-MT	VG
☐ 1	Steve Avery	.50	.23	.06
☐ 2	Sid Bream	.08	.04	.01
☐ 3	Ron Gant	.20	.09	.03
☐ 4	Tom Glavine	.30	.14	.04
☐ 5	David Justice	.75	.35	.09
☐ 6	Mark Lemke	.08	.04	.01
☐ 7	Greg Olson	.08	.04	.01
☐ 8	Terry Pendleton	.12	.05	.02
☐ 9	Deion Sanders	.40	.18	.05
☐ 10	John Smoltz	.20	.09	.03
☐ 11	Doug Dascenzo	.08	.04	.01
☐ 12	Andre Dawson	.20	.09	.03
☐ 13	Joe Girardi	.08	.04	.01
☐ 14	Mark Grace	.15	.07	.02
☐ 15	Greg Maddux	.15	.07	.02
☐ 16	Chuck McElroy	.08	.04	.01
☐ 17	Mike Morgan	.08	.04	.01
☐ 18	Ryne Sandberg	.60	.25	.08
☐ 19	Gary Scott	.10	.04	.01
☐ 20	Sammy Sosa	.08	.04	.01
☐ 21	Norm Charlton	.10	.04	.01
☐ 22	Rob Dibble	.10	.04	.01
☐ 23	Barry Larkin	.20	.09	.03
☐ 24	Hal Morris	.10	.04	.01
☐ 25	Paul O'Neill	.10	.04	.01
☐ 26	Jose Rijo	.10	.04	.01
☐ 27	Bip Roberts	.10	.04	.01
☐ 28	Chris Sabo	.10	.04	.01
☐ 29	Reggie Sanders	.75	.35	.09
☐ 30	Greg Swindell	.10	.04	.01
☐ 31	Jeff Bagwell	.75	.35	.09
☐ 32	Craig Biggio	.10	.04	.01
☐ 33	Ken Caminiti	.10	.04	.01
☐ 34	Andujar Cedeno	.10	.05	.01
☐ 35	Steve Finley	.10	.04	.01
☐ 36	Pete Harnisch	.08	.04	.01
☐ 37	Butch Henry	.20	.09	.03
☐ 38	Doug Jones	.10	.04	.01
☐ 39	Darryl Kile	.15	.07	.02
☐ 40	Eddie Taubensee	.20	.09	.03
☐ 41	Brett Butler	.10	.04	.01
☐ 42	Tom Candiotti	.08	.04	.01
☐ 43	Eric Davis	.12	.05	.02
☐ 44	Orel Hershiser	.12	.05	.02
☐ 45	Eric Karros	1.75	.80	.22
☐ 46	Ramon Martinez	.12	.05	.02
☐ 47	Jose Offerman	.10	.04	.01
☐ 48	Mike Scioscia	.08	.04	.01
☐ 49	Mike Sharperson	.08	.04	.01
☐ 50	Darryl Strawberry	.30	.14	.04
☐ 51	Bret Barberie	.12	.05	.02
☐ 52	Ivan Calderon	.08	.04	.01
☐ 53	Gary Carter	.10	.04	.01
☐ 54	Delino DeShields	.25	.11	.03
☐ 55	Marquis Grissom	.25	.11	.03
☐ 56	Ken Hill	.08	.04	.01
☐ 57	Dennis Martinez	.10	.04	.01
☐ 58	Spike Owen	.08	.04	.01
☐ 59	Larry Walker	.35	.16	.04
☐ 60	Tim Wallach	.10	.04	.01
☐ 61	Bobby Bonilla	.15	.07	.02
☐ 62	Tim Burke	.08	.04	.01
☐ 63	Vince Coleman	.10	.04	.01
☐ 64	John Franco	.10	.04	.01
☐ 65	Dwight Gooden	.12	.05	.02
☐ 66	Todd Hundley	.08	.04	.01
☐ 67	Howard Johnson	.10	.04	.01
☐ 68	Eddie Murray	.20	.09	.03
☐ 69	Bret Saberhagen	.12	.05	.02
☐ 70	Anthony Young	.12	.05	.02
☐ 71	Kim Batiste	.15	.07	.02
☐ 72	Wes Chamberlain	.12	.05	.02
☐ 73	Darren Daulton	.10	.04	.01
☐ 74	Mariano Duncan	.08	.04	.01
☐ 75	Len Dykstra	.10	.04	.01
☐ 76	John Kruk	.10	.04	.01
☐ 77	Mickey Morandini	.10	.04	.01
☐ 78	Terry Mulholland	.08	.04	.01
☐ 79	Dale Murphy	.12	.05	.02
☐ 80	Mitch Williams	.08	.04	.01
☐ 81	Jay Bell	.08	.04	.01
☐ 82	Barry Bonds	.50	.23	.06
☐ 83	Steve Buechele	.08	.04	.01
☐ 84	Doug Drabek	.10	.04	.01
☐ 85	Mike LaValliere	.08	.04	.01
☐ 86	Jose Lind	.08	.04	.01
☐ 87	Denny Neagle	.12	.05	.02
☐ 88	Randy Tomlin	.12	.05	.02
☐ 89	Andy Van Slyke	.12	.05	.02
☐ 90	Gary Varsho	.08	.04	.01
☐ 91	Pedro Guerrero	.10	.04	.01
☐ 92	Rex Hudler	.08	.04	.01
☐ 93	Brian Jordan	.40	.18	.05
☐ 94	Felix Jose	.10	.04	.01
☐ 95	Donovan Osborne	.60	.25	.08
☐ 96	Tom Pagnozzi	.08	.04	.01
☐ 97	Lee Smith	.10	.04	.01
☐ 98	Ozzie Smith	.20	.09	.03
☐ 99	Todd Worrell	.08	.04	.01
☐ 100	Todd Zeile	.08	.04	.01
☐ 101	Andy Benes	.12	.05	.02
☐ 102	Jerald Clark	.08	.04	.01
☐ 103	Tony Fernandez	.10	.04	.01
☐ 104	Tony Gwynn	.30	.14	.04
☐ 105	Greg W. Harris	.08	.04	.01
☐ 106	Fred McGriff	.30	.14	.04
☐ 107	Benito Santiago	.12	.05	.02

☐	108	Gary Sheffield	.75	.35	.09
☐	109	Kurt Stillwell	.08	.04	.01
☐	110	Tim Teufel	.08	.04	.01
☐	111	Kevin Bass	.08	.04	.01
☐	112	Jeff Brantley	.08	.04	.01
☐	113	John Burkett	.08	.04	.01
☐	114	Will Clark	.50	.23	.06
☐	115	Royce Clayton	.40	.18	.05
☐	116	Mike Jackson	.08	.04	.01
☐	117	Darren Lewis	.10	.04	.01
☐	118	Bill Swift	.08	.04	.01
☐	119	Robby Thompson	.08	.04	.01
☐	120	Matt Williams	.10	.05	.01
☐	121	Brady Anderson	.10	.04	.01
☐	122	Glenn Davis	.10	.04	.01
☐	123	Mike Devereaux	.10	.04	.01
☐	124	Chris Hoiles	.12	.05	.02
☐	125	Sam Horn	.08	.04	.01
☐	126	Ben McDonald	.15	.07	.02
☐	127	Mike Mussina	1.75	.80	.22
☐	128	Gregg Olson	.10	.04	.01
☐	129	Cal Ripken Jr.	.75	.35	.09
☐	130	Rick Sutcliffe	.10	.04	.01
☐	131	Wade Boggs	.30	.14	.04
☐	132	Roger Clemens	.60	.25	.08
☐	133	Greg A. Harris	.08	.04	.01
☐	134	Tim Naehring	.10	.04	.01
☐	135	Tony Pena	.08	.04	.01
☐	136	Phil Plantier	.30	.14	.04
☐	137	Jeff Reardon	.12	.05	.02
☐	138	Jody Reed	.08	.04	.01
☐	139	Mo Vaughn	.12	.05	.02
☐	140	Frank Viola	.10	.04	.01
☐	141	Jim Abbott	.20	.09	.03
☐	142	Hubie Brooks	.08	.04	.01
☐	143	Chad Curtis	.50	.23	.06
☐	144	Gary DiSarcina	.08	.04	.01
☐	145	Chuck Finley	.08	.04	.01
☐	146	Bryan Harvey	.08	.04	.01
☐	147	Von Hayes	.08	.04	.01
☐	148	Mark Langston	.10	.04	.01
☐	149	Lance Parrish	.10	.04	.01
☐	150	Lee Stevens	.08	.04	.01
☐	151	George Bell	.10	.04	.01
☐	152	Alex Fernandez	.10	.04	.01
☐	153	Greg Hibbard	.08	.04	.01
☐	154	Lance Johnson	.08	.04	.01
☐	155	Kirk McCaskill	.08	.04	.01
☐	156	Tim Raines	.12	.05	.02
☐	157	Steve Sax	.10	.04	.01
☐	158	Bobby Thigpen	.08	.04	.01
☐	159	Frank Thomas	3.00	1.35	.40
☐	160	Robin Ventura	.50	.23	.06
☐	161	Sandy Alomar Jr.	.10	.04	.01
☐	162	Jack Armstrong	.08	.04	.01
☐	163	Carlos Baerga	.40	.18	.05
☐	164	Albert Belle	.30	.14	.04
☐	165	Alex Cole	.08	.04	.01
☐	166	Glenallen Hill	.08	.04	.01
☐	167	Mark Lewis	.10	.04	.01
☐	168	Kenny Lofton	1.25	.55	.16
☐	169	Paul Sorrento	.10	.04	.01
☐	170	Mark Whiten	.08	.04	.01
☐	171	Milt Cuyler	.08	.04	.01
☐	172	Rob Deer	.10	.04	.01
☐	173	Cecil Fielder	.30	.14	.04
☐	174	Travis Fryman	1.00	.45	.13
☐	175	Mike Henneman	.08	.04	.01
☐	176	Tony Phillips	.08	.04	.01
☐	177	Frank Tanana	.08	.04	.01
☐	178	Mickey Tettleton	.10	.04	.01
☐	179	Alan Trammell	.12	.05	.02
☐	180	Lou Whitaker	.12	.05	.02
☐	181	George Brett	.25	.11	.03
☐	182	Tom Gordon	.08	.04	.01
☐	183	Mark Gubicza	.08	.04	.01
☐	184	Gregg Jefferies	.10	.04	.01
☐	185	Wally Joyner	.10	.04	.01
☐	186	Brent Mayne	.08	.04	.01
☐	187	Brian McRae	.12	.05	.02
☐	188	Kevin McReynolds	.10	.04	.01
☐	189	Keith Miller	.08	.04	.01
☐	190	Jeff Montgomery	.08	.04	.01
☐	191	Dante Bichette	.08	.04	.01
☐	192	Ricky Bones	.15	.07	.02
☐	193	Scott Fletcher	.08	.04	.01
☐	194	Paul Molitor	.12	.05	.02
☐	195	Jaime Navarro	.10	.04	.01
☐	196	Franklin Stubbs	.08	.04	.01
☐	197	B.J. Surhoff	.08	.04	.01
☐	198	Greg Vaughn	.10	.04	.01
☐	199	Bill Wegman	.08	.04	.01
☐	200	Robin Yount	.25	.11	.03
☐	201	Rick Aguilera	.10	.04	.01
☐	202	Scott Erickson	.15	.07	.02
☐	203	Greg Gagne	.08	.04	.01
☐	204	Brian Harper	.08	.04	.01
☐	205	Kent Hrbek	.10	.04	.01
☐	206	Scott Leius	.08	.04	.01
☐	207	Shane Mack	.10	.04	.01
☐	208	Pat Mahomes	.40	.18	.05
☐	209	Kirby Puckett	.50	.23	.06
☐	210	John Smiley	.10	.04	.01
☐	211	Mike Gallego	.08	.04	.01
☐	212	Charlie Hayes	.08	.04	.01
☐	213	Pat Kelly	.10	.05	.01
☐	214	Roberto Kelly	.10	.05	.01
☐	215	Kevin Maas	.10	.04	.01
☐	216	Don Mattingly	.30	.14	.04
☐	217	Matt Nokes	.08	.04	.01
☐	218	Melido Perez	.10	.04	.01
☐	219	Scott Sanderson	.08	.04	.01
☐	220	Danny Tartabull	.12	.05	.02
☐	221	Harold Baines	.10	.04	.01

☐ 222	Jose Canseco	.50	.23	.06
☐ 223	Dennis Eckersley	.15	.07	.02
☐ 224	Dave Henderson	.08	.04	.01
☐ 225	Carney Lansford	.10	.04	.01
☐ 226	Mark McGwire	.50	.23	.06
☐ 227	Mike Moore	.08	.04	.01
☐ 228	Randy Ready	.08	.04	.01
☐ 229	Terry Steinbach	.10	.04	.01
☐ 230	Dave Stewart	.10	.04	.01
☐ 231	Jay Buhner	.10	.04	.01
☐ 232	Ken Griffey Jr.	2.00	.90	.25
☐ 233	Erik Hanson	.08	.04	.01
☐ 234	Randy Johnson	.10	.04	.01
☐ 235	Edgar Martinez	.10	.04	.01
☐ 236	Tino Martinez	.10	.05	.01
☐ 237	Kevin Mitchell	.12	.05	.02
☐ 238	Pete O'Brien	.08	.04	.01
☐ 239	Harold Reynolds	.08	.04	.01
☐ 240	David Valle	.08	.04	.01
☐ 241	Julio Franco	.10	.04	.01
☐ 242	Juan Gonzalez	1.25	.55	.16
☐ 243	Jose Guzman	.08	.04	.01
☐ 244	Rafael Palmeiro	.12	.05	.02
☐ 245	Dean Palmer	.50	.23	.06
☐ 246	Ivan Rodriguez	1.00	.45	.13
☐ 247	Jeff Russell	.08	.04	.01
☐ 248	Nolan Ryan	1.50	.65	.19
☐ 249	Ruben Sierra	.40	.18	.05
☐ 250	Dickie Thon	.08	.04	.01
☐ 251	Roberto Alomar	.50	.23	.06
☐ 252	Derek Bell	.30	.14	.04
☐ 253	Pat Borders	.08	.04	.01
☐ 254	Joe Carter	.30	.14	.04
☐ 255	Kelly Gruber	.10	.04	.01
☐ 256	Juan Guzman	1.75	.80	.22
☐ 257	Jack Morris	.15	.07	.02
☐ 258	John Olerud	.25	.11	.03
☐ 259	Devon White	.10	.04	.01
☐ 260	Dave Winfield	.20	.09	.03
☐ 261	Checklist	.10	.01	.00
☐ 262	Checklist	.10	.01	.00
☐ 263	Checklist	.10	.01	.00
☐ 264	History Card	.15	.07	.02

1992 Studio Heritage

The 1992 Leaf Studio Heritage series sub-set presents today's star players dressed in vintage uniforms. Cards numbered 1-8 were randomly inserted in 12-card Leaf

Studio foil packs while cards numbered 9-14 were featured only in 28-card Leaf Studio jumbo packs and issued one per pack. The cards measure the standard size (2 1/2" by 3 1/2"). The fronts display sepia-toned portraits of the players dressed in vintage uniforms of their current teams. The pictures are bordered by dark turquoise and have bronze foil picture holders at each corner. The set title "Heritage Series" also appears in bronze foil lettering above the pictures. Within a bronze picture frame design on dark turquoise, the backs give a brief history of the team with special reference to the year of the vintage uniform. The cards are numbered on the back with a BC prefix.

	MT	EX-MT	VG
COMPLETE SET (14)	35.00	16.00	4.40
COMPLETE FOIL SET (8)	25.00	11.50	3.10
COMPLETE JUMBO SET (6)	10.00	4.50	1.25
COMMON PLAYER (1-8)	2.00	.90	.25
COMMON PLAYER (9-14)	.75	.35	.09

☐ 1	Ryne Sandberg 1908 Cubs	5.00	2.30	.60
☐ 2	Carlton Fisk 1917 White Sox	2.00	.90	.25
☐ 3	Wade Boggs 1918 Red Sox	2.50	1.15	.30
☐ 4	Jose Canseco 1929 Athletics	4.00	1.80	.50
☐ 5	Don Mattingly 1939 Yankees	2.50	1.15	.30
☐ 6	Darryl Strawberry 1944 Dodgers	2.50	1.15	.30
☐ 7	Cal Ripken 1951 Browns	6.00	2.70	.75
☐ 8	Will Clark 1951 Giants	4.00	1.80	.50
☐ 9	Andre Dawson 1944 Cubs	1.75	.80	.22

		NRMT	VG-E	GOOD
☐	10 Andy Van Slyke	1.00	.45	.13
	1960 Pirates			
☐	11 Paul Molitor	1.00	.45	.13
	1969 Pilots			
☐	12 Jeff Bagwell	3.00	1.35	.40
	1962 Colt 45s			
☐	13 Darren Daulton	.75	.35	.09
	1945 Phillies			
☐	14 Kirby Puckett	4.00	1.80	.50
	1960 Senators			

1951 Topps Blue Backs

The cards in this 52-card set measure 2" by 2 5/8". The 1951 Topps series of blue-backed baseball cards could be used to play a baseball game by shuffling the cards and drawing them from a pile. These cards were marketed with a piece of caramel candy, which often melted or was squashed in such a way as to damage the card and wrapper (despite the fact that a paper shield was inserted between candy and card). Blue Backs are more difficult to obtain than the similarly styled Red Backs. The set is denoted on the cards as "Set B" and the Red Back set is correspondingly Set A. Appropriately leading off the set is Eddie Yost. The only notable Rookie Cardin the set is Billy Pierce.

	NRMT	VG-E	GOOD
COMPLETE SET (52)	2100.00	950.00	275.00
COMMON PLAYER (1-52)	35.00	16.00	4.40
☐ 1 Eddie Yost	55.00	25.00	7.00

☐ 2 Hank Majeski	35.00	16.00	4.40
☐ 3 Richie Ashburn	170.00	75.00	21.00
☐ 4 Del Ennis	40.00	18.00	5.00
☐ 5 Johnny Pesky	40.00	18.00	5.00
☐ 6 Red Schoendienst	125.00	57.50	15.50
☐ 7 Gerry Staley	35.00	16.00	4.40
☐ 8 Dick Sisler	35.00	16.00	4.40
☐ 9 Johnny Sain	45.00	20.00	5.75
☐ 10 Joe Page	40.00	18.00	5.00
☐ 11 Johnny Groth	35.00	16.00	4.40
☐ 12 Sam Jethroe	37.50	17.00	4.70
☐ 13 Mickey Vernon	40.00	18.00	5.00
☐ 14 Red Munger	35.00	16.00	4.40
☐ 15 Eddie Joost	35.00	16.00	4.40
☐ 16 Murry Dickson	35.00	16.00	4.40
☐ 17 Roy Smalley	35.00	16.00	4.40
☐ 18 Ned Garver	35.00	16.00	4.40
☐ 19 Phil Masi	35.00	16.00	4.40
☐ 20 Ralph Branca	45.00	20.00	5.75
☐ 21 Billy Johnson	35.00	16.00	4.40
☐ 22 Bob Kuzava	35.00	16.00	4.40
☐ 23 Dizzy Trout	37.50	17.00	4.70
☐ 24 Sherman Lollar	37.50	17.00	4.70
☐ 25 Sam Mele	35.00	16.00	4.40
☐ 26 Chico Carrasquel	40.00	18.00	5.00
☐ 27 Andy Pafko	37.50	17.00	4.70
☐ 28 Harry Brecheen	37.50	17.00	4.70
☐ 29 Granville Hamner	35.00	16.00	4.40
☐ 30 Enos Slaughter	130.00	57.50	16.50
☐ 31 Lou Brissie	35.00	16.00	4.40
☐ 32 Bob Elliott	37.50	17.00	4.70
☐ 33 Don Lenhardt	35.00	16.00	4.40
☐ 34 Earl Torgeson	35.00	16.00	4.40
☐ 35 Tommy Byrne	35.00	16.00	4.40
☐ 36 Cliff Fannin	35.00	16.00	4.40
☐ 37 Bobby Doerr	110.00	50.00	14.00
☐ 38 Irv Noren	37.50	17.00	4.70
☐ 39 Ed Lopat	45.00	20.00	5.75
☐ 40 Vic Wertz	37.50	17.00	4.70
☐ 41 Johnny Schmitz	35.00	16.00	4.40
☐ 42 Bruce Edwards	35.00	16.00	4.40
☐ 43 Willie Jones	35.00	16.00	4.40
☐ 44 Johnny Wyrostek	35.00	16.00	4.40
☐ 45 Billy Pierce	50.00	23.00	6.25
☐ 46 Gerry Priddy	35.00	16.00	4.40
☐ 47 Herman Wehmeier	35.00	16.00	4.40
☐ 48 Billy Cox	40.00	18.00	5.00
☐ 49 Hank Sauer	40.00	18.00	5.00
☐ 50 Johnny Mize	150.00	70.00	19.00
☐ 51 Eddie Waitkus	35.00	16.00	4.40
☐ 52 Sam Chapman	50.00	23.00	6.25

1951 Topps
Red Backs

The cards in this 52-card set measure 2" by 2 5/8". The 1951 Topps Red Back set is identical in style to the Blue Back set of the same year. The cards have rounded corners and were designed to be used as a baseball game. Zernial, number 36, is listed with either the White Sox or Athletics, and Holmes, number 52, with either the Braves or Hartford. The set is denoted on the cards as "Set A" and the Blue Back set is correspondingly Set B. The only notable Rookie Cardin the set is Monte Irvin.

	NRMT	VG-E	GOOD
COMPLETE SET (54)	750.00	350.00	95.00
COMMON PLAYER (1-52)	7.00	3.10	.85

		NRMT	VG-E	GOOD
☐ 1	Yogi Berra	140.00	65.00	17.50
☐ 2	Sid Gordon	7.00	3.10	.85
☐ 3	Ferris Fain	8.00	3.60	1.00
☐ 4	Vern Stephens	8.00	3.60	1.00
☐ 5	Phil Rizzuto	36.00	16.00	4.50
☐ 6	Allie Reynolds	12.00	5.50	1.50
☐ 7	Howie Pollet	7.00	3.10	.85
☐ 8	Early Wynn	21.00	9.50	2.60
☐ 9	Roy Sievers	8.00	3.60	1.00
☐ 10	Mel Parnell	8.00	3.60	1.00
☐ 11	Gene Hermanski	7.00	3.10	.85
☐ 12	Jim Hegan	8.00	3.60	1.00
☐ 13	Dale Mitchell	8.00	3.60	1.00
☐ 14	Wayne Terwilliger	7.00	3.10	.85
☐ 15	Ralph Kiner	30.00	13.50	3.80
☐ 16	Preacher Roe	10.00	4.50	1.25
☐ 17	Gus Bell	10.00	4.50	1.25
☐ 18	Jerry Coleman	10.00	4.50	1.25
☐ 19	Dick Kokos	7.00	3.10	.85
☐ 20	Dom DiMaggio	14.00	6.25	1.75
☐ 21	Larry Jansen	8.00	3.60	1.00
☐ 22	Bob Feller	50.00	23.00	6.25
☐ 23	Ray Boone	12.00	5.50	1.50
☐ 24	Hank Bauer	14.00	6.25	1.75
☐ 25	Cliff Chambers	7.00	3.10	.85
☐ 26	Luke Easter	10.00	4.50	1.25
☐ 27	Wally Westlake	7.00	3.10	.85
☐ 28	Elmer Valo	7.00	3.10	.85
☐ 29	Bob Kennedy	8.00	3.60	1.00
☐ 30	Warren Spahn	50.00	23.00	6.25
☐ 31	Gil Hodges	36.00	16.00	4.50
☐ 32	Henry Thompson	8.00	3.60	1.00
☐ 33	William Werle	7.00	3.10	.85
☐ 34	Grady Hatton	7.00	3.10	.85
☐ 35	Al Rosen	14.00	6.25	1.75
☐ 36A	Gus Zernial (Chicago)	36.00	16.00	4.50
☐ 36B	Gus Zernial (Philadelphia)	20.00	9.00	2.50
☐ 37	Wes Westrum	8.00	3.60	1.00
☐ 38	Duke Snider	80.00	36.00	10.00
☐ 39	Ted Kluszewski	18.00	8.00	2.30
☐ 40	Mike Garcia	8.00	3.60	1.00
☐ 41	Whitey Lockman	8.00	3.60	1.00
☐ 42	Ray Scarborough	7.00	3.10	.85
☐ 43	Maurice McDermott	7.00	3.10	.85
☐ 44	Sid Hudson	7.00	3.10	.85
☐ 45	Andy Seminick	7.00	3.10	.85
☐ 46	Billy Goodman	8.00	3.60	1.00
☐ 47	Tommy Glaviano	7.00	3.10	.85
☐ 48	Eddie Stanky	8.00	3.60	1.00
☐ 49	Al Zarilla	7.00	3.10	.85
☐ 50	Monte Irvin	45.00	20.00	5.75
☐ 51	Eddie Robinson	7.00	3.10	.85
☐ 52A	Tommy Holmes (Boston)	36.00	16.00	4.50
☐ 52B	Tommy Holmes (Hartford)	22.00	10.00	2.80

1952 Topps

The cards in this 407-card set measure approximately 2 5/8" by 3 3/4". The 1952 Topps set is Topps' first truly major set. Card numbers 1 to 80 were issued with red or black backs, both of which are less plentiful than card numbers 81 to 250. In fact, the first series is considered the most difficult with respect to finding perfect condition cards. Card number 48 (Joe Page) and number 49 (Johnny Sain) can be found with each other's write-up on their

back. Card numbers 251 to 310 are somewhat scarce and numbers 311 to 407 are quite scarce. Cards 281-300 were single printed compared to the other cards in the next to last series. Cards 311-313 were double printed on the last high number printing sheet. The key card in the set is obviously Mickey Mantle, number 311, Mickey's first of many Topps cards. Although rarely seen, there exist salesman sample panels of three cards containing the fronts of regular cards with ad information on the back. Two such panels seen are Bob Mahoney/Robin Roberts/Sid Hudson and Wally Westlake/Dizzy Trout/Irv Noren. The key rookies in this set are Billy Martin, Eddie Mathews, and Hoyt Wilhelm.

	NRMT	VG-E	GOOD
COMPLETE SET (407)	66000.	29700.	8300.
COMMON PLAYER (1-80)	60.00	27.00	7.50
COMMON PLAYER (81-250)	30.00	13.50	3.80
COMMON PLAYER (251-280)	50.00	23.00	6.25
COMMON PLAYER (281-300)	60.00	27.00	7.50
COMMON PLAYER (301-310)	50.00	23.00	6.25
COMMON PLAYER (311-407)	190.00	85.00	24.00

		NRMT	VG-E	GOOD
☐ 1	Andy Pafko	1300.00	130.00	39.00
☐ 2	Pete Runnels	70.00	32.00	8.75
☐ 3	Hank Thompson	65.00	29.00	8.25
☐ 4	Don Lenhardt	60.00	27.00	7.50
☐ 5	Larry Jansen	65.00	29.00	8.25
☐ 6	Grady Hatton	60.00	27.00	7.50
☐ 7	Wayne Terwilliger	60.00	27.00	7.50
☐ 8	Fred Marsh	60.00	27.00	7.50
☐ 9	Robert Hogue	60.00	27.00	7.50
☐ 10	Al Rosen	90.00	40.00	11.50
☐ 11	Phil Rizzuto	190.00	85.00	24.00
☐ 12	Monty Basgall	60.00	27.00	7.50
☐ 13	Johnny Wyrostek	60.00	27.00	7.50
☐ 14	Bob Elliott	65.00	29.00	8.25
☐ 15	Johnny Pesky	65.00	29.00	8.25
☐ 16	Gene Hermanski	60.00	27.00	7.50
☐ 17	Jim Hegan	65.00	29.00	8.25
☐ 18	Merrill Combs	60.00	27.00	7.50
☐ 19	Johnny Bucha	60.00	27.00	7.50
☐ 20	Billy Loes	115.00	52.50	14.50
☐ 21	Ferris Fain	65.00	29.00	8.25
☐ 22	Dom DiMaggio	100.00	45.00	12.50
☐ 23	Billy Goodman	65.00	29.00	8.25
☐ 24	Luke Easter	65.00	29.00	8.25
☐ 25	Johnny Groth	60.00	27.00	7.50
☐ 26	Monte Irvin	110.00	50.00	14.00
☐ 27	Sam Jethroe	65.00	29.00	8.25
☐ 28	Jerry Priddy	60.00	27.00	7.50
☐ 29	Ted Kluszewski	100.00	45.00	12.50
☐ 30	Mel Parnell	65.00	29.00	8.25
☐ 31	Gus Zernial	70.00	32.00	8.75
☐ 32	Eddie Robinson	60.00	27.00	7.50
☐ 33	Warren Spahn	250.00	115.00	31.00
☐ 34	Elmer Valo	60.00	27.00	7.50
☐ 35	Hank Sauer	70.00	32.00	8.75
☐ 36	Gil Hodges	175.00	80.00	22.00
☐ 37	Duke Snider	300.00	135.00	38.00
☐ 38	Wally Westlake	60.00	27.00	7.50
☐ 39	Dizzy Trout	65.00	29.00	8.25
☐ 40	Irv Noren	65.00	29.00	8.25
☐ 41	Bob Wellman	60.00	27.00	7.50
☐ 42	Lou Kretlow	60.00	27.00	7.50
☐ 43	Ray Scarborough	60.00	27.00	7.50
☐ 44	Con Dempsey	60.00	27.00	7.50
☐ 45	Eddie Joost	60.00	27.00	7.50
☐ 46	Gordon Goldsberry	60.00	27.00	7.50
☐ 47	Willie Jones	60.00	27.00	7.50
☐ 48A	Joe Page COR	80.00	36.00	10.00
☐ 48B	Joe Page ERR (Bio for Sain)	300.00	135.00	38.00
☐ 49A	Johnny Sain COR	110.00	50.00	14.00
☐ 49B	Johnny Sain ERR (Bio for Page)	325.00	145.00	40.00
☐ 50	Marv Rickert	60.00	27.00	7.50
☐ 51	Jim Russell	60.00	27.00	7.50
☐ 52	Don Mueller	65.00	29.00	8.25
☐ 53	Chris Van Cuyk	60.00	27.00	7.50
☐ 54	Leo Kiely	60.00	27.00	7.50
☐ 55	Ray Boone	65.00	29.00	8.25
☐ 56	Tommy Glaviano	60.00	27.00	7.50
☐ 57	Ed Lopat	110.00	50.00	14.00
☐ 58	Bob Mahoney	60.00	27.00	7.50
☐ 59	Robin Roberts	175.00	80.00	22.00
☐ 60	Sid Hudson	60.00	27.00	7.50
☐ 61	Tookie Gilbert	60.00	27.00	7.50
☐ 62	Chuck Stobbs	60.00	27.00	7.50
☐ 63	Howie Pollet	60.00	27.00	7.50
☐ 64	Roy Sievers	65.00	29.00	8.25
☐ 65	Enos Slaughter	150.00	70.00	19.00
☐ 66	Preacher Roe	110.00	50.00	14.00
☐ 67	Allie Reynolds	115.00	52.50	14.50

☐	68	Cliff Chambers	60.00	27.00	7.50
☐	69	Virgil Stallcup	60.00	27.00	7.50
☐	70	Al Zarilla	60.00	27.00	7.50
☐	71	Tom Upton	60.00	27.00	7.50
☐	72	Karl Olson	60.00	27.00	7.50
☐	73	Bill Werle	60.00	27.00	7.50
☐	74	Andy Hansen	60.00	27.00	7.50
☐	75	Wes Westrum	65.00	29.00	8.25
☐	76	Eddie Stanky	70.00	32.00	8.75
☐	77	Bob Kennedy	65.00	29.00	8.25
☐	78	Ellis Kinder	60.00	27.00	7.50
☐	79	Gerry Staley	60.00	27.00	7.50
☐	80	Herman Wehmeier	60.00	27.00	7.50
☐	81	Vernon Law	35.00	16.00	4.40
☐	82	Duane Pillette	30.00	13.50	3.80
☐	83	Billy Johnson	30.00	13.50	3.80
☐	84	Vern Stephens	33.00	15.00	4.10
☐	85	Bob Kuzava	33.00	15.00	4.10
☐	86	Ted Gray	30.00	13.50	3.80
☐	87	Dale Coogan	30.00	13.50	3.80
☐	88	Bob Feller	175.00	80.00	22.00
☐	89	Johnny Lipon	30.00	13.50	3.80
☐	90	Mickey Grasso	30.00	13.50	3.80
☐	91	Red Schoendienst	90.00	40.00	11.50
☐	92	Dale Mitchell	33.00	15.00	4.10
☐	93	Al Sima	30.00	13.50	3.80
☐	94	Sam Mele	30.00	13.50	3.80
☐	95	Ken Holcombe	30.00	13.50	3.80
☐	96	Willard Marshall	30.00	13.50	3.80
☐	97	Earl Torgeson	30.00	13.50	3.80
☐	98	Billy Pierce	35.00	16.00	4.40
☐	99	Gene Woodling	60.00	27.00	7.50
☐	100	Del Rice	30.00	13.50	3.80
☐	101	Max Lanier	30.00	13.50	3.80
☐	102	Bill Kennedy	30.00	13.50	3.80
☐	103	Cliff Mapes	30.00	13.50	3.80
☐	104	Don Kolloway	30.00	13.50	3.80
☐	105	Johnny Pramesa	30.00	13.50	3.80
☐	106	Mickey Vernon	35.00	16.00	4.40
☐	107	Connie Ryan	30.00	13.50	3.80
☐	108	Jim Konstanty	35.00	16.00	4.40
☐	109	Ted Wilks	30.00	13.50	3.80
☐	110	Dutch Leonard	30.00	13.50	3.80
☐	111	Peanuts Lowrey	30.00	13.50	3.80
☐	112	Hank Majeski	30.00	13.50	3.80
☐	113	Dick Sisler	33.00	15.00	4.10
☐	114	Willard Ramsdell	30.00	13.50	3.80
☐	115	Red Munger	30.00	13.50	3.80
☐	116	Carl Scheib	30.00	13.50	3.80
☐	117	Sherm Lollar	33.00	15.00	4.10
☐	118	Ken Raffensberger	30.00	13.50	3.80
☐	119	Mickey McDermott	30.00	13.50	3.80
☐	120	Bob Chakales	30.00	13.50	3.80
☐	121	Gus Niarhos	30.00	13.50	3.80
☐	122	Jackie Jensen	75.00	34.00	9.50
☐	123	Eddie Yost	33.00	15.00	4.10
☐	124	Monte Kennedy	30.00	13.50	3.80
☐	125	Bill Rigney	30.00	13.50	3.80
☐	126	Fred Hutchinson	33.00	15.00	4.10
☐	127	Paul Minner	30.00	13.50	3.80
☐	128	Don Bollweg	30.00	13.50	3.80
☐	129	Johnny Mize	90.00	40.00	11.50
☐	130	Sheldon Jones	30.00	13.50	3.80
☐	131	Morrie Martin	30.00	13.50	3.80
☐	132	Clyde Kluttz	30.00	13.50	3.80
☐	133	Al Widmar	30.00	13.50	3.80
☐	134	Joe Tipton	30.00	13.50	3.80
☐	135	Dixie Howell	30.00	13.50	3.80
☐	136	Johnny Schmitz	30.00	13.50	3.80
☐	137	Roy McMillan	35.00	16.00	4.40
☐	138	Bill MacDonald	30.00	13.50	3.80
☐	139	Ken Wood	30.00	13.50	3.80
☐	140	Johnny Antonelli	33.00	15.00	4.10
☐	141	Clint Hartung	30.00	13.50	3.80
☐	142	Harry Perkowski	30.00	13.50	3.80
☐	143	Les Moss	30.00	13.50	3.80
☐	144	Ed Blake	30.00	13.50	3.80
☐	145	Joe Haynes	30.00	13.50	3.80
☐	146	Frank House	30.00	13.50	3.80
☐	147	Bob Young	30.00	13.50	3.80
☐	148	Johnny Klippstein	30.00	13.50	3.80
☐	149	Dick Kryhoski	30.00	13.50	3.80
☐	150	Ted Beard	30.00	13.50	3.80
☐	151	Wally Post	35.00	16.00	4.40
☐	152	Al Evans	30.00	13.50	3.80
☐	153	Bob Rush	30.00	13.50	3.80
☐	154	Joe Muir	30.00	13.50	3.80
☐	155	Frank Overmire	30.00	13.50	3.80
☐	156	Frank Hiller	30.00	13.50	3.80
☐	157	Bob Usher	30.00	13.50	3.80
☐	158	Eddie Waitkus	30.00	13.50	3.80
☐	159	Saul Rogovin	30.00	13.50	3.80
☐	160	Owen Friend	30.00	13.50	3.80
☐	161	Bud Byerly	30.00	13.50	3.80
☐	162	Del Crandall	33.00	15.00	4.10
☐	163	Stan Rojek	30.00	13.50	3.80
☐	164	Walt Dubiel	30.00	13.50	3.80
☐	165	Eddie Kazak	30.00	13.50	3.80
☐	166	Paul LaPalme	30.00	13.50	3.80
☐	167	Bill Howerton	30.00	13.50	3.80
☐	168	Charlie Silvera	35.00	16.00	4.40
☐	169	Howie Judson	30.00	13.50	3.80
☐	170	Gus Bell	33.00	15.00	4.10
☐	171	Ed Erautt	30.00	13.50	3.80
☐	172	Eddie Miksis	30.00	13.50	3.80
☐	173	Roy Smalley	30.00	13.50	3.80
☐	174	Clarence Marshall	30.00	13.50	3.80
☐	175	Billy Martin	380.00	170.00	47.50
☐	176	Hank Edwards	30.00	13.50	3.80
☐	177	Bill Wight	30.00	13.50	3.80
☐	178	Cass Michaels	30.00	13.50	3.80
☐	179	Frank Smith	30.00	13.50	3.80
☐	180	Charlie Maxwell	35.00	16.00	4.40
☐	181	Bob Swift	30.00	13.50	3.80

☐ 182 Billy Hitchcock	30.00	13.50	3.80
☐ 183 Erv Dusak	30.00	13.50	3.80
☐ 184 Bob Ramazzotti	30.00	13.50	3.80
☐ 185 Bill Nicholson	33.00	15.00	4.10
☐ 186 Walt Masterson	30.00	13.50	3.80
☐ 187 Bob Miller	30.00	13.50	3.80
☐ 188 Clarence Podbielan	30.00	13.50	3.80
☐ 189 Pete Reiser	35.00	16.00	4.40
☐ 190 Don Johnson	30.00	13.50	3.80
☐ 191 Yogi Berra	425.00	190.00	52.50
☐ 192 Myron Ginsberg	30.00	13.50	3.80
☐ 193 Harry Simpson	33.00	15.00	4.10
☐ 194 Joe Hatton	30.00	13.50	3.80
☐ 195 Minnie Minoso	125.00	57.50	15.50
☐ 196 Solly Hemus	35.00	16.00	4.40
☐ 197 George Strickland	30.00	13.50	3.80
☐ 198 Phil Haugstad	30.00	13.50	3.80
☐ 199 George Zuverink	30.00	13.50	3.80
☐ 200 Ralph Houk	65.00	29.00	8.25
☐ 201 Alex Kellner	30.00	13.50	3.80
☐ 202 Joe Collins	40.00	18.00	5.00
☐ 203 Curt Simmons	35.00	16.00	4.40
☐ 204 Ron Northey	30.00	13.50	3.80
☐ 205 Clyde King	30.00	13.50	3.80
☐ 206 Joe Ostrowski	30.00	13.50	3.80
☐ 207 Mickey Harris	30.00	13.50	3.80
☐ 208 Marlin Stuart	30.00	13.50	3.80
☐ 209 Howie Fox	30.00	13.50	3.80
☐ 210 Dick Fowler	30.00	13.50	3.80
☐ 211 Ray Coleman	30.00	13.50	3.80
☐ 212 Ned Garver	30.00	13.50	3.80
☐ 213 Nippy Jones	30.00	13.50	3.80
☐ 214 Johnny Hopp	33.00	15.00	4.10
☐ 215 Hank Bauer	55.00	25.00	7.00
☐ 216 Richie Ashburn	110.00	50.00	14.00
☐ 217 Snuffy Stirnweiss	33.00	15.00	4.10
☐ 218 Clyde McCullough	30.00	13.50	3.80
☐ 219 Bobby Shantz	40.00	18.00	5.00
☐ 220 Joe Presko	30.00	13.50	3.80
☐ 221 Granny Hamner	30.00	13.50	3.80
☐ 222 Hoot Evers	30.00	13.50	3.80
☐ 223 Del Ennis	33.00	15.00	4.10
☐ 224 Bruce Edwards	30.00	13.50	3.80
☐ 225 Frank Baumholtz	30.00	13.50	3.80
☐ 226 Dave Philley	30.00	13.50	3.80
☐ 227 Joe Garagiola	125.00	57.50	15.50
☐ 228 Al Brazle	30.00	13.50	3.80
☐ 229 Gene Bearden UER	30.00	13.50	3.80
(Misspelled Beardon)			
☐ 230 Matt Batts	30.00	13.50	3.80
☐ 231 Sam Zoldak	30.00	13.50	3.80
☐ 232 Billy Cox	33.00	15.00	4.10
☐ 233 Bob Friend	40.00	18.00	5.00
☐ 234 Steve Souchock	30.00	13.50	3.80
☐ 235 Walt Dropo	33.00	15.00	4.10
☐ 236 Ed Fitzgerald	30.00	13.50	3.80
☐ 237 Jerry Coleman	33.00	15.00	4.10
☐ 238 Art Houtteman	30.00	13.50	3.80
☐ 239 Rocky Bridges	30.00	13.50	3.80
☐ 240 Jack Phillips	30.00	13.50	3.80
☐ 241 Tommy Byrne	30.00	13.50	3.80
☐ 242 Tom Poholsky	30.00	13.50	3.80
☐ 243 Larry Doby	40.00	18.00	5.00
☐ 244 Vic Wertz	33.00	15.00	4.10
☐ 245 Sherry Robertson	30.00	13.50	3.80
☐ 246 George Kell	85.00	38.00	10.50
☐ 247 Randy Gumpert	30.00	13.50	3.80
☐ 248 Frank Shea	30.00	13.50	3.80
☐ 249 Bobby Adams	30.00	13.50	3.80
☐ 250 Carl Erskine	70.00	32.00	8.75
☐ 251 Chico Carrasquel	50.00	23.00	6.25
☐ 252 Vern Bickford	50.00	23.00	6.25
☐ 253 Johnny Berardino	55.00	25.00	7.00
☐ 254 Joe Dobson	50.00	23.00	6.25
☐ 255 Clyde Vollmer	50.00	23.00	6.25
☐ 256 Pete Suder	50.00	23.00	6.25
☐ 257 Bobby Avila	55.00	25.00	7.00
☐ 258 Steve Gromek	50.00	23.00	6.25
☐ 259 Bob Addis	50.00	23.00	6.25
☐ 260 Pete Castiglione	50.00	23.00	6.25
☐ 261 Willie Mays	2600.00	1150.00	325.00
☐ 262 Virgil Trucks	55.00	25.00	7.00
☐ 263 Harry Brecheen	55.00	25.00	7.00
☐ 264 Roy Hartsfield	50.00	23.00	6.25
☐ 265 Chuck Diering	50.00	23.00	6.25
☐ 266 Murry Dickson	50.00	23.00	6.25
☐ 267 Sid Gordon	50.00	23.00	6.25
☐ 268 Bob Lemon	185.00	85.00	23.00
☐ 269 Willard Nixon	50.00	23.00	6.25
☐ 270 Lou Brissie	50.00	23.00	6.25
☐ 271 Jim Delsing	50.00	23.00	6.25
☐ 272 Mike Garcia	55.00	25.00	7.00
☐ 273 Erv Palica	50.00	23.00	6.25
☐ 274 Ralph Branca	85.00	38.00	10.50
☐ 275 Pat Mullin	50.00	23.00	6.25
☐ 276 Jim Wilson	50.00	23.00	6.25
☐ 277 Early Wynn	190.00	85.00	24.00
☐ 278 Allie Clark	50.00	23.00	6.25
☐ 279 Eddie Stewart	50.00	23.00	6.25
☐ 280 Cloyd Boyer	55.00	25.00	7.00
☐ 281 Tommy Brown SP	60.00	27.00	7.50
☐ 282 Birdie Tebbetts SP	65.00	29.00	8.25
☐ 283 Phil Masi SP	60.00	27.00	7.50
☐ 284 Hank Arft SP	60.00	27.00	7.50
☐ 285 Cliff Fannin SP	60.00	27.00	7.50
☐ 286 Joe DeMaestri SP	60.00	27.00	7.50
☐ 287 Steve Bilko SP	60.00	27.00	7.50
☐ 288 Chet Nichols SP	60.00	27.00	7.50
☐ 289 Tommy Holmes SP	65.00	29.00	8.25
☐ 290 Joe Astroth SP	60.00	27.00	7.50
☐ 291 Gil Coan SP	60.00	27.00	7.50
☐ 292 Floyd Baker SP	60.00	27.00	7.50
☐ 293 Sibby Sisti SP	60.00	27.00	7.50
☐ 294 Walker Cooper SP	60.00	27.00	7.50

☐ 295	Phil Cavarretta SP	65.00	29.00	8.25
☐ 296	Red Rolfe SP MG	65.00	29.00	8.25
☐ 297	Andy Seminick SP	60.00	27.00	7.50
☐ 298	Bob Ross SP	60.00	27.00	7.50
☐ 299	Ray Murray SP	60.00	27.00	7.50
☐ 300	Barney McCosky SP	60.00	27.00	7.50
☐ 301	Bob Porterfield	50.00	23.00	6.25
☐ 302	Max Surkont	50.00	23.00	6.25
☐ 303	Harry Dorish	50.00	23.00	6.25
☐ 304	Sam Dente	50.00	23.00	6.25
☐ 305	Paul Richards MG	55.00	25.00	7.00
☐ 306	Lou Sleater	50.00	23.00	6.25
☐ 307	Frank Campos	50.00	23.00	6.25
☐ 308	Luis Aloma	50.00	23.00	6.25
☐ 309	Jim Busby	50.00	23.00	6.25
☐ 310	George Metkovich	60.00	27.00	7.50
☐ 311	Mickey Mantle DP	32000.	9600.	3200.
☐ 312	Jackie Robinson DP	1350.	600.00	170.00
☐ 313	Bobby Thomson DP	250.00	115.00	31.00
☐ 314	Roy Campanella	2100.00	950.00	275.00
☐ 315	Leo Durocher MG	375.00	170.00	47.50
☐ 316	Dave Williams	225.00	100.00	28.00
☐ 317	Conrado Marrero	200.00	90.00	25.00
☐ 318	Harold Gregg	190.00	85.00	24.00
☐ 319	Al Walker	190.00	85.00	24.00
☐ 320	John Rutherford	200.00	90.00	25.00
☐ 321	Joe Black	250.00	115.00	31.00
☐ 322	Randy Jackson	190.00	85.00	24.00
☐ 323	Bubba Church	190.00	85.00	24.00
☐ 324	Warren Hacker	190.00	85.00	24.00
☐ 325	Bill Serena	190.00	85.00	24.00
☐ 326	George Shuba	250.00	115.00	31.00
☐ 327	Al Wilson	190.00	85.00	24.00
☐ 328	Bob Borkowski	190.00	85.00	24.00
☐ 329	Ike Delock	200.00	90.00	25.00
☐ 330	Turk Lown	190.00	85.00	24.00
☐ 331	Tom Morgan	190.00	85.00	24.00
☐ 332	Anthony Bartirome	190.00	85.00	24.00
☐ 333	Pee Wee Reese	1250.00	575.00	160.00
☐ 334	Wilmer Mizell	210.00	95.00	26.00
☐ 335	Ted Lepcio	190.00	85.00	24.00
☐ 336	Dave Koslo	190.00	85.00	24.00
☐ 337	Jim Hearn	190.00	85.00	24.00
☐ 338	Sal Yvars	190.00	85.00	24.00
☐ 339	Russ Meyer	190.00	85.00	24.00
☐ 340	Bob Hooper	190.00	85.00	24.00
☐ 341	Hal Jeffcoat	190.00	85.00	24.00
☐ 342	Clem Labine	225.00	100.00	28.00
☐ 343	Dick Gernert	190.00	85.00	24.00
☐ 344	Ewell Blackwell	225.00	100.00	28.00
☐ 345	Sammy White	190.00	85.00	24.00
☐ 346	George Spencer	190.00	85.00	24.00
☐ 347	Joe Adcock	225.00	100.00	28.00
☐ 348	Robert Kelly	190.00	85.00	24.00
☐ 349	Bob Cain	190.00	85.00	24.00
☐ 350	Cal Abrams	190.00	85.00	24.00
☐ 351	Alvin Dark	225.00	100.00	28.00
☐ 352	Karl Drews	190.00	85.00	24.00
☐ 353	Bobby Del Greco	190.00	85.00	24.00
☐ 354	Fred Hatfield	190.00	85.00	24.00
☐ 355	Bobby Morgan	190.00	85.00	24.00
☐ 356	Toby Atwell	190.00	85.00	24.00
☐ 357	Smoky Burgess	250.00	115.00	31.00
☐ 358	John Kucab	190.00	85.00	24.00
☐ 359	Dee Fondy	190.00	85.00	24.00
☐ 360	George Crowe	200.00	90.00	25.00
☐ 361	William Posedel CO	190.00	85.00	24.00
☐ 362	Ken Heintzelman	190.00	85.00	24.00
☐ 363	Dick Rozek	190.00	85.00	24.00
☐ 364	Clyde Sukeforth CO	190.00	85.00	24.00
☐ 365	Cookie Lavagetto CO	200.00	90.00	25.00
☐ 366	Dave Madison	190.00	85.00	24.00
☐ 367	Ben Thorpe	190.00	85.00	24.00
☐ 368	Ed Wright	190.00	85.00	24.00
☐ 369	Dick Groat	350.00	160.00	45.00
☐ 370	Billy Hoeft	200.00	90.00	25.00
☐ 371	Bobby Hofman	190.00	85.00	24.00
☐ 372	Gil McDougald	350.00	160.00	45.00
☐ 373	Jim Turner CO	200.00	90.00	25.00
☐ 374	John Benton	190.00	85.00	24.00
☐ 375	John Merson	190.00	85.00	24.00
☐ 376	Faye Throneberry	190.00	85.00	24.00
☐ 377	Chuck Dressen MG	200.00	90.00	25.00
☐ 378	Leroy Fusselman	190.00	85.00	24.00
☐ 379	Joe Rossi	190.00	85.00	24.00
☐ 380	Clem Koshorek	190.00	85.00	24.00
☐ 381	Milton Stock CO	190.00	85.00	24.00
☐ 382	Sam Jones	200.00	90.00	25.00
☐ 383	Del Wilber	190.00	85.00	24.00
☐ 384	Frank Crosetti CO	250.00	115.00	31.00
☐ 385	Herman Franks CO	200.00	90.00	25.00
☐ 386	John Yuhas	190.00	85.00	24.00
☐ 387	Billy Meyer MG	190.00	85.00	24.00
☐ 388	Bob Chipman	190.00	85.00	24.00
☐ 389	Ben Wade	190.00	85.00	24.00
☐ 390	Glenn Nelson	190.00	85.00	24.00
☐ 391	Ben Chapman CO	190.00	85.00	24.00
	UER (Photo actually			
	Sam Chapman)			
☐ 392	Hoyt Wilhelm	725.00	325.00	90.00
☐ 393	Ebba St.Claire	190.00	85.00	24.00
☐ 394	Billy Herman CO	300.00	135.00	38.00
☐ 395	Jake Pitler CO	190.00	85.00	24.00
☐ 396	Dick Williams	250.00	115.00	31.00
☐ 397	Forrest Main	190.00	85.00	24.00
☐ 398	Hal Rice	190.00	85.00	24.00
☐ 399	Jim Fridley	190.00	85.00	24.00
☐ 400	Bill Dickey CO	700.00	325.00	90.00
☐ 401	Bob Schultz	190.00	85.00	24.00
☐ 402	Earl Harrist	190.00	85.00	24.00
☐ 403	Bill Miller	190.00	85.00	24.00
☐ 404	Dick Brodowski	190.00	85.00	24.00

			NRMT	VG-E	GOOD
☐	405	Eddie Pellagrini	190.00	85.00	24.00
☐	406	Joe Nuxhall	250.00	115.00	31.00
☐	407	Eddie Mathews	3250.00	800.00	250.00

1953 Topps

The cards in this 274-card set measure 2 5/8" by 3 3/4". Although the last card is numbered 280, there are only 274 cards in the set since numbers 253, 261, 267, 268, 271, and 275 were never issued. The 1953 Topps series contains line drawings of players in full color. The name and team panel at the card base is easily damaged, making it very difficult to complete a mint set. The high number series, 221 to 280, was produced in shorter supply late in the year and hence is more difficult to complete than the lower numbers. The key cards in the set are Mickey Mantle (82) and Willie Mays (244). The key rookies in this set are Roy Face, Jim Gilliam, and Johnny Podres, all from the last series. There are a number of double-printed cards (actually not double but 50 percent more of each of these numbers were printed compared to the other cards in the series) indicated by DP in the checklist below. There were five players (10 Smoky Burgess, 44 Ellis Kinder, 61 Early Wynn, 72 Fred Hutchinson, and 81 Joe Black) held out of the first run of 1-85 (but printed in with numbers 86-165), who are each marked by SP in the checklist below. In addition, there are five numbers which were printed in with the more plentiful series 166-220; these cards (94, 107, 131,

145, and 156) are also indicated by DP in the checklist below. There were some three-card advertising panels produced by Topps; the players include Johnny Mize/Clem Koshorek/Toby Atwell and Mickey Mantle/Johnny Wyrostek/Sal Yvars. When cut apart, these advertising cards are distinguished by the non-standard card back, i.e., part of an advertisement for the 1953 Topps set instead of the typical statistics and biographical information about the player pictured.

		NRMT	VG-E	GOOD
COMPLETE SET (274)		14250.	6400.	1800.
COMMON PLAYER (1-165)		28.00	12.50	3.50
COMMON PLAYER (166-220)		22.00	10.00	2.80
COMMON PLAYER (221-280)		100.00	45.00	12.50

			NRMT	VG-E	GOOD
☐	1	Jackie Robinson DP	600.00	275.00	75.00
☐	2	Luke Easter DP	17.00	7.75	2.10
☐	3	George Crowe	28.00	12.50	3.50
☐	4	Ben Wade	28.00	12.50	3.50
☐	5	Joe Dobson	28.00	12.50	3.50
☐	6	Sam Jones	30.00	13.50	3.80
☐	7	Bob Borkowski DP	16.00	7.25	2.00
☐	8	Clem Koshorek DP	16.00	7.25	2.00
☐	9	Joe Collins	35.00	16.00	4.40
☐	10	Smoky Burgess SP	50.00	23.00	6.25
☐	11	Sal Yvars	28.00	12.50	3.50
☐	12	Howie Judson DP	16.00	7.25	2.00
☐	13	Conrado Marrero DP	16.00	7.25	2.00
☐	14	Clem Labine DP	18.00	8.00	2.30
☐	15	Bobo Newsom DP	25.00	11.50	3.10
☐	16	Peanuts Lowrey DP	16.00	7.25	2.00
☐	17	Billy Hitchcock	28.00	12.50	3.50
☐	18	Ted Lepcio DP	16.00	7.25	2.00
☐	19	Mel Parnell DP	17.00	7.75	2.10
☐	20	Hank Thompson	30.00	13.50	3.80
☐	21	Billy Johnson	28.00	12.50	3.50
☐	22	Howie Fox	28.00	12.50	3.50
☐	23	Toby Atwell DP	16.00	7.25	2.00
☐	24	Ferris Fain	30.00	13.50	3.80
☐	25	Ray Boone	30.00	13.50	3.80
☐	26	Dale Mitchell DP	17.00	7.75	2.10
☐	27	Roy Campanella DP	210.00	95.00	26.00
☐	28	Eddie Pellagrini	28.00	12.50	3.50
☐	29	Hal Jeffcoat	28.00	12.50	3.50
☐	30	Willard Nixon	28.00	12.50	3.50
☐	31	Ewell Blackwell	45.00	20.00	5.75
☐	32	Clyde Vollmer	28.00	12.50	3.50
☐	33	Bob Kennedy DP	17.00	7.75	2.10
☐	34	George Shuba	28.00	12.50	3.50
☐	35	Irv Noren DP	17.00	7.75	2.10
☐	36	Johnny Groth DP	16.00	7.25	2.00
☐	37	Eddie Mathews DP	110.00	50.00	14.00

☐ 38	Jim Hearn DP	16.00	7.25	2.00
☐ 39	Eddie Miksis	28.00	12.50	3.50
☐ 40	John Lipon	28.00	12.50	3.50
☐ 41	Enos Slaughter	90.00	40.00	11.50
☐ 42	Gus Zernial DP	18.00	8.00	2.30
☐ 43	Gil McDougald	50.00	23.00	6.25
☐ 44	Ellis Kinder SP	35.00	16.00	4.40
☐ 45	Grady Hatton DP	16.00	7.25	2.00
☐ 46	Johnny Klippstein DP	16.00	7.25	2.00
☐ 47	Bubba Church DP	16.00	7.25	2.00
☐ 48	Bob Del Greco DP	16.00	7.25	2.00
☐ 49	Faye Throneberry DP	16.00	7.25	2.00
☐ 50	Chuck Dressen MG DP	25.00	11.50	3.10
☐ 51	Frank Campos DP	16.00	7.25	2.00
☐ 52	Ted Gray DP	16.00	7.25	2.00
☐ 53	Sherm Lollar DP	17.00	7.75	2.10
☐ 54	Bob Feller DP	110.00	50.00	14.00
☐ 55	Maurice McDermott DP	16.00	7.25	2.00
☐ 56	Gerry Staley DP	16.00	7.25	2.00
☐ 57	Carl Scheib	28.00	12.50	3.50
☐ 58	George Metkovich	28.00	12.50	3.50
☐ 59	Karl Drews DP	16.00	7.25	2.00
☐ 60	Cloyd Boyer DP	16.00	7.25	2.00
☐ 61	Early Wynn SP	100.00	45.00	12.50
☐ 62	Monte Irvin SP	40.00	18.00	5.00
☐ 63	Gus Niarhos DP	16.00	7.25	2.00
☐ 64	Dave Philley	28.00	12.50	3.50
☐ 65	Earl Harrist	28.00	12.50	3.50
☐ 66	Minnie Minoso	45.00	20.00	5.75
☐ 67	Roy Sievers DP	17.00	7.75	2.10
☐ 68	Del Rice	28.00	12.50	3.50
☐ 69	Dick Brodowski	28.00	12.50	3.50
☐ 70	Ed Yuhas	28.00	12.50	3.50
☐ 71	Tony Bartirome	28.00	12.50	3.50
☐ 72	Fred Hutchinson SP MG	40.00	18.00	5.00
☐ 73	Eddie Robinson	28.00	12.50	3.50
☐ 74	Joe Rossi	28.00	12.50	3.50
☐ 75	Mike Garcia	30.00	13.50	3.80
☐ 76	Pee Wee Reese	165.00	75.00	21.00
☐ 77	Johnny Mize DP	60.00	27.00	7.50
☐ 78	Red Schoendienst	65.00	29.00	8.25
☐ 79	Johnny Wyrostek	28.00	12.50	3.50
☐ 80	Jim Hegan	30.00	13.50	3.80
☐ 81	Joe Black SP	65.00	29.00	8.25
☐ 82	Mickey Mantle	3300.00	1500.00	425.00
☐ 83	Howie Pollet	28.00	12.50	3.50
☐ 84	Bob Hooper DP	16.00	7.25	2.00
☐ 85	Bobby Morgan DP	16.00	7.25	2.00
☐ 86	Billy Martin	150.00	70.00	19.00
☐ 87	Ed Lopat	40.00	18.00	5.00
☐ 88	Willie Jones DP	16.00	7.25	2.00
☐ 89	Chuck Stobbs DP	16.00	7.25	2.00
☐ 90	Hank Edwards DP	16.00	7.25	2.00
☐ 91	Ebba St.Claire DP	16.00	7.25	2.00
☐ 92	Paul Minner DP	16.00	7.25	2.00
☐ 93	Hal Rice DP	16.00	7.25	2.00
☐ 94	Bill Kennedy DP	16.00	7.25	2.00
☐ 95	Willard Marshall DP	16.00	7.25	2.00
☐ 96	Virgil Trucks	30.00	13.50	3.80
☐ 97	Don Kolloway DP	16.00	7.25	2.00
☐ 98	Cal Abrams DP	16.00	7.25	2.00
☐ 99	Dave Madison	28.00	12.50	3.50
☐ 100	Bill Miller	28.00	12.50	3.50
☐ 101	Ted Wilks	28.00	12.50	3.50
☐ 102	Connie Ryan DP	16.00	7.25	2.00
☐ 103	Joe Astroth DP	16.00	7.25	2.00
☐ 104	Yogi Berra	275.00	125.00	34.00
☐ 105	Joe Nuxhall DP	17.00	7.75	2.10
☐ 106	Johnny Antonelli	30.00	13.50	3.80
☐ 107	Danny O'Connell DP	16.00	7.25	2.00
☐ 108	Bob Porterfield DP	16.00	7.25	2.00
☐ 109	Alvin Dark	35.00	16.00	4.40
☐ 110	Herman Wehmeier DP	16.00	7.25	2.00
☐ 111	Hank Sauer DP	17.00	7.75	2.10
☐ 112	Ned Garver DP	16.00	7.25	2.00
☐ 113	Jerry Priddy	28.00	12.50	3.50
☐ 114	Phil Rizzuto	125.00	57.50	15.50
☐ 115	George Spencer	28.00	12.50	3.50
☐ 116	Frank Smith DP	16.00	7.25	2.00
☐ 117	Sid Gordon DP	16.00	7.25	2.00
☐ 118	Gus Bell DP	17.00	7.75	2.10
☐ 119	Johnny Sain SP	45.00	20.00	5.75
☐ 120	Davey Williams	30.00	13.50	3.80
☐ 121	Walt Dropo	30.00	13.50	3.80
☐ 122	Elmer Valo	28.00	12.50	3.50
☐ 123	Tommy Byrne DP	16.00	7.25	2.00
☐ 124	Sibby Sisti DP	16.00	7.25	2.00
☐ 125	Dick Williams DP	20.00	9.00	2.50
☐ 126	Bill Connelly DP	16.00	7.25	2.00
☐ 127	Clint Courtney DP	16.00	7.25	2.00
☐ 128	Wilmer Mizell DP	17.00	7.75	2.10
	(Inconsistent design, logo on front with black birds)			
☐ 129	Keith Thomas	28.00	12.50	3.50
☐ 130	Turk Lown DP	16.00	7.25	2.00
☐ 131	Harry Byrd DP	16.00	7.25	2.00
☐ 132	Tom Morgan	28.00	12.50	3.50
☐ 133	Gil Coan	28.00	12.50	3.50
☐ 134	Rube Walker	30.00	13.50	3.80
☐ 135	Al Rosen DP	35.00	16.00	4.40
☐ 136	Ken Heintzelman DP	16.00	7.25	2.00
☐ 137	John Rutherford DP	16.00	7.25	2.00
☐ 138	George Kell	55.00	25.00	7.00
☐ 139	Sammy White	28.00	12.50	3.50
☐ 140	Tommy Glaviano	28.00	12.50	3.50
☐ 141	Allie Reynolds	35.00	16.00	4.40
☐ 142	Vic Wertz	30.00	13.50	3.80
☐ 143	Billy Pierce	35.00	16.00	4.40
☐ 144	Bob Schultz DP	16.00	7.25	2.00
☐ 145	Harry Dorish DP	16.00	7.25	2.00
☐ 146	Granny Hamner	28.00	12.50	3.50
☐ 147	Warren Spahn	140.00	65.00	17.50
☐ 148	Mickey Grasso	28.00	12.50	3.50

☐	149 Dom DiMaggio DP	35.00	16.00	4.40
☐	150 Harry Simpson DP	16.00	7.25	2.00
☐	151 Hoyt Wilhelm	70.00	32.00	8.75
☐	152 Bob Adams DP	16.00	7.25	2.00
☐	153 Andy Seminick DP	16.00	7.25	2.00
☐	154 Dick Groat	40.00	18.00	5.00
☐	155 Dutch Leonard	28.00	12.50	3.50
☐	156 Jim Rivera DP	17.00	7.75	2.10
☐	157 Bob Addis DP	16.00	7.25	2.00
☐	158 Johnny Logan	35.00	16.00	4.40
☐	159 Wayne Terwilliger DP	16.00	7.25	2.00
☐	160 Bob Young	28.00	12.50	3.50
☐	161 Vern Bickford DP	16.00	7.25	2.00
☐	162 Ted Kluszewski	50.00	23.00	6.25
☐	163 Fred Hatfield DP	16.00	7.25	2.00
☐	164 Frank Shea DP	16.00	7.25	2.00
☐	165 Billy Hoeft	30.00	13.50	3.80
☐	166 Billy Hunter	22.00	10.00	2.80
☐	167 Art Schult	22.00	10.00	2.80
☐	168 Willard Schmidt	22.00	10.00	2.80
☐	169 Dizzy Trout	24.00	11.00	3.00
☐	170 Bill Werle	22.00	10.00	2.80
☐	171 Bill Glynn	22.00	10.00	2.80
☐	172 Rip Repulski	22.00	10.00	2.80
☐	173 Preston Ward	22.00	10.00	2.80
☐	174 Billy Loes	27.00	12.00	3.40
☐	175 Ron Kline	22.00	10.00	2.80
☐	176 Don Hoak	30.00	13.50	3.80
☐	177 Jim Dyck	22.00	10.00	2.80
☐	178 Jim Waugh	22.00	10.00	2.80
☐	179 Gene Hermanski	22.00	10.00	2.80
☐	180 Virgil Stallcup	22.00	10.00	2.80
☐	181 Al Zarilla	22.00	10.00	2.80
☐	182 Bobby Hofman	22.00	10.00	2.80
☐	183 Stu Miller	27.00	12.00	3.40
☐	184 Hal Brown	22.00	10.00	2.80
☐	185 Jim Pendleton	22.00	10.00	2.80
☐	186 Charlie Bishop	22.00	10.00	2.80
☐	187 Jim Fridley	22.00	10.00	2.80
☐	188 Andy Carey	35.00	16.00	4.40
☐	189 Ray Jablonski	22.00	10.00	2.80
☐	190 Dixie Walker CO	24.00	11.00	3.00
☐	191 Ralph Kiner	65.00	29.00	8.25
☐	192 Wally Westlake	22.00	10.00	2.80
☐	193 Mike Clark	22.00	10.00	2.80
☐	194 Eddie Kazak	22.00	10.00	2.80
☐	195 Ed McGhee	22.00	10.00	2.80
☐	196 Bob Keegan	22.00	10.00	2.80
☐	197 Del Crandall	24.00	11.00	3.00
☐	198 Forrest Main	22.00	10.00	2.80
☐	199 Marion Fricano	22.00	10.00	2.80
☐	200 Gordon Goldsberry	22.00	10.00	2.80
☐	201 Paul LaPalme	22.00	10.00	2.80
☐	202 Carl Sawatski	22.00	10.00	2.80
☐	203 Cliff Fannin	22.00	10.00	2.80
☐	204 Dick Bokelman	22.00	10.00	2.80
☐	205 Vern Benson	22.00	10.00	2.80

☐	206 Ed Bailey	27.00	12.00	3.40
☐	207 Whitey Ford	165.00	75.00	21.00
☐	208 Jim Wilson	22.00	10.00	2.80
☐	209 Jim Greengrass	22.00	10.00	2.80
☐	210 Bob Cerv	30.00	13.50	3.80
☐	211 J.W. Porter	22.00	10.00	2.80
☐	212 Jack Dittmer	22.00	10.00	2.80
☐	213 Ray Scarborough	22.00	10.00	2.80
☐	214 Bill Bruton	27.00	12.00	3.40
☐	215 Gene Conley	27.00	12.00	3.40
☐	216 Jim Hughes	22.00	10.00	2.80
☐	217 Murray Wall	22.00	10.00	2.80
☐	218 Les Fusselman	22.00	10.00	2.80
☐	219 Pete Runnels UER	24.00	11.00	3.00
	(Photo actually			
	Don Johnson)			
☐	220 Satchel Paige UER	475.00	210.00	60.00
	(Misspelled Satchell			
	on card front)			
☐	221 Bob Milliken	100.00	45.00	12.50
☐	222 Vic Janowicz DP	55.00	25.00	7.00
☐	223 Johnny O'Brien DP	55.00	25.00	7.00
☐	224 Lou Sleater DP	50.00	23.00	6.25
☐	225 Bobby Shantz	110.00	50.00	14.00
☐	226 Ed Erautt	100.00	45.00	12.50
☐	227 Morrie Martin	100.00	45.00	12.50
☐	228 Hal Newhouser	150.00	70.00	19.00
☐	229 Rocky Krsnich	100.00	45.00	12.50
☐	230 Johnny Lindell DP	50.00	23.00	6.25
☐	231 Solly Hemus DP	50.00	23.00	6.25
☐	232 Dick Kokos	100.00	45.00	12.50
☐	233 Al Aber	100.00	45.00	12.50
☐	234 Ray Murray DP	50.00	23.00	6.25
☐	235 John Hetki DP	50.00	23.00	6.25
☐	236 Harry Perkowski DP	50.00	23.00	6.25
☐	237 Bud Podbielan DP	50.00	23.00	6.25
☐	238 Cal Hogue DP	50.00	23.00	6.25
☐	239 Jim Delsing	100.00	45.00	12.50
☐	240 Fred Marsh	100.00	45.00	12.50
☐	241 Al Sima DP	50.00	23.00	6.25
☐	242 Charlie Silvera	110.00	50.00	14.00
☐	243 Carlos Bernier DP	50.00	23.00	6.25
☐	244 Willie Mays	2500.00	750.00	250.00
☐	245 Bill Norman CO	100.00	45.00	12.50
☐	246 Roy Face DP	90.00	40.00	11.50
☐	247 Mike Sandlock DP	50.00	23.00	6.25
☐	248 Gene Stephens DP	50.00	23.00	6.25
☐	249 Eddie O'Brien	100.00	45.00	12.50
☐	250 Bob Wilson	100.00	45.00	12.50
☐	251 Sid Hudson	100.00	45.00	12.50
☐	252 Hank Foiles	100.00	45.00	12.50
☐	253 Does not exist	.00	.00	.00
☐	254 Preacher Roe DP	90.00	40.00	11.50
☐	255 Dixie Howell	100.00	45.00	12.50
☐	256 Les Peden	100.00	45.00	12.50
☐	257 Bob Boyd	100.00	45.00	12.50
☐	258 Jim Gilliam	275.00	125.00	34.00

			NRMT	VG-E	GOOD
☐	259	Roy McMillan DP 55.00	25.00	7.00
☐	260	Sam Calderone 100.00	45.00	12.50
☐	261	Does not exist..............00	.00	.00
☐	262	Bob Oldis 100.00	45.00	12.50
☐	263	Johnny Podres..........275.00	125.00	34.00
☐	264	Gene Woodling DP 65.00	29.00	8.25
☐	265	Jackie Jensen 115.00	52.50	14.50
☐	266	Bob Cain 100.00	45.00	12.50
☐	267	Does not exist..............00	.00	.00
☐	268	Does not exist..............00	.00	.00
☐	269	Duane Pillette..........100.00	45.00	12.50
☐	270	Vern Stephens 110.00	50.00	14.00
☐	271	Does not exist..............00	.00	.00
☐	272	Bill Antonello 100.00	45.00	12.50
☐	273	Harvey Haddix..........125.00	57.50	15.50
☐	274	John Riddle CO 100.00	45.00	12.50
☐	275	Does not exist..............00	.00	.00
☐	276	Ken Raffensberger 100.00	45.00	12.50
☐	277	Don Lund 100.00	45.00	12.50
☐	278	Willie Miranda..........100.00	45.00	12.50
☐	279	Joe Coleman DP 50.00	23.00	6.25
☐	280	Milt Bolling 325.00	65.00	19.50

1954 Topps

The cards in this 250-card set measure approximately 2 5/8" by 3 3/4". Each of the cards in the 1954 Topps set contains a large "head" shot of the player in color plus a smaller full-length photo in black and white set against a color background. This series contains the rookie cards of Hank Aaron, Ernie Banks, and Al Kaline and two separate cards of Ted Williams (number 1 and number 250). Conspicuous by his absence is Mickey Mantle who apparently was the exclusive property of Bowman during 1954 (and 1955). The first two

issues of *Sports Illustrated* magazine contained "card" inserts on regular paper stock which showed actual cards in the set in color and some created cards in black and white, including Mickey Mantle.

			NRMT	VG-E	GOOD
	COMPLETE SET (250) ....8250.	3700.	1050.
	COMMON PLAYER (1-50) 15.00	6.75	1.90
	COMMON PLAYER (51-75) ...30.00	13.50	3.80
	COMMON PLAYER (76-125) ..15.00	6.75	1.90
	COMMON PLAYER (126-250) .15.00	6.75	1.90

			NRMT	VG-E	GOOD
☐	1	Ted Williams 650.00	200.00	65.00
☐	2	Gus Zernial 16.00	7.25	2.00
☐	3	Monte Irvin 35.00	16.00	4.40
☐	4	Hank Sauer 16.00	7.25	2.00
☐	5	Ed Lopat 22.50	10.00	2.80
☐	6	Pete Runnels...................16.00	7.25	2.00
☐	7	Ted Kluszewski...............30.00	13.50	3.80
☐	8	Bob Young 15.00	6.75	1.90
☐	9	Harvey Haddix.................16.00	7.25	2.00
☐	10	Jackie Robinson.............300.00	135.00	38.00
☐	11	Paul Leslie Smith............15.00	6.75	1.90
☐	12	Del Crandall....................16.00	7.25	2.00
☐	13	Billy Martin 85.00	38.00	10.50
☐	14	Preacher Roe 21.00	9.50	2.60
☐	15	Al Rosen........................25.00	11.50	3.10
☐	16	Vic Janowicz...................18.00	8.00	2.30
☐	17	Phil Rizzuto 75.00	34.00	9.50
☐	18	Walt Dropo......................16.00	7.25	2.00
☐	19	Johnny Lipon 15.00	6.75	1.90
☐	20	Warren Spahn................100.00	45.00	12.50
☐	21	Bobby Shantz..................16.00	7.25	2.00
☐	22	Jim Greengrass...............15.00	6.75	1.90
☐	23	Luke Easter.....................16.00	7.25	2.00
☐	24	Granny Hamner...............15.00	6.75	1.90
☐	25	Harvey Kuenn 40.00	18.00	5.00
☐	26	Ray Jablonski 15.00	6.75	1.90
☐	27	Ferris Fain 16.00	7.25	2.00
☐	28	Paul Minner.....................15.00	6.75	1.90
☐	29	Jim Hegan.......................16.00	7.25	2.00
☐	30	Eddie Mathews 100.00	45.00	12.50
☐	31	Johnny Klippstein 15.00	6.75	1.90
☐	32	Duke Snider 150.00	70.00	19.00
☐	33	Johnny Schmitz...............15.00	6.75	1.90
☐	34	Jim Rivera......................15.00	6.75	1.90
☐	35	Jim Gilliam......................30.00	13.50	3.80
☐	36	Hoyt Wilhelm...................50.00	23.00	6.25
☐	37	Whitey Ford 110.00	50.00	14.00
☐	38	Eddie Stanky MG 16.00	7.25	2.00
☐	39	Sherm Lollar...................16.00	7.25	2.00
☐	40	Mel Parnell.....................16.00	7.25	2.00
☐	41	Willie Jones 15.00	6.75	1.90
☐	42	Don Mueller....................16.00	7.25	2.00
☐	43	Dick Groat......................20.00	9.00	2.50
☐	44	Ned Garver.....................15.00	6.75	1.90

☐	45	Richie Ashburn	45.00	20.00	5.75
☐	46	Ken Raffensberger	15.00	6.75	1.90
☐	47	Ellis Kinder	15.00	6.75	1.90
☐	48	Billy Hunter	15.00	6.75	1.90
☐	49	Ray Murray	15.00	6.75	1.90
☐	50	Yogi Berra	250.00	115.00	31.00
☐	51	Johnny Lindell	32.50	14.50	4.10
☐	52	Vic Power	35.00	16.00	4.40
☐	53	Jack Dittmer	30.00	13.50	3.80
☐	54	Vern Stephens	32.50	14.50	4.10
☐	55	Phil Cavarretta MG	35.00	16.00	4.40
☐	56	Willie Miranda	30.00	13.50	3.80
☐	57	Luis Aloma	30.00	13.50	3.80
☐	58	Bob Wilson	30.00	13.50	3.80
☐	59	Gene Conley	32.50	14.50	4.10
☐	60	Frank Baumholtz	30.00	13.50	3.80
☐	61	Bob Cain	30.00	13.50	3.80
☐	62	Eddie Robinson	30.00	13.50	3.80
☐	63	Johnny Pesky	35.00	16.00	4.40
☐	64	Hank Thompson	35.00	16.00	4.40
☐	65	Bob Swift CO	30.00	13.50	3.80
☐	66	Ted Lepcio	30.00	13.50	3.80
☐	67	Jim Willis	30.00	13.50	3.80
☐	68	Sam Calderone	30.00	13.50	3.80
☐	69	Bud Podbielan	30.00	13.50	3.80
☐	70	Larry Doby	70.00	32.00	8.75
☐	71	Frank Smith	30.00	13.50	3.80
☐	72	Preston Ward	30.00	13.50	3.80
☐	73	Wayne Terwilliger	30.00	13.50	3.80
☐	74	Bill Taylor	30.00	13.50	3.80
☐	75	Fred Haney MG	30.00	13.50	3.80
☐	76	Bob Scheffing CO	15.00	6.75	1.90
☐	77	Ray Boone	16.00	7.25	2.00
☐	78	Ted Kazanski	15.00	6.75	1.90
☐	79	Andy Pafko	16.00	7.25	2.00
☐	80	Jackie Jensen	20.00	9.00	2.50
☐	81	Dave Hoskins	15.00	6.75	1.90
☐	82	Milt Bolling	15.00	6.75	1.90
☐	83	Joe Collins	18.00	8.00	2.30
☐	84	Dick Cole	15.00	6.75	1.90
☐	85	Bob Turley	30.00	13.50	3.80
☐	86	Billy Herman CO	27.00	12.00	3.40
☐	87	Roy Face	17.50	8.00	2.20
☐	88	Matt Batts	15.00	6.75	1.90
☐	89	Howie Pollet	15.00	6.75	1.90
☐	90	Willie Mays	525.00	240.00	65.00
☐	91	Bob Oldis	15.00	6.75	1.90
☐	92	Wally Westlake	15.00	6.75	1.90
☐	93	Sid Hudson	15.00	6.75	1.90
☐	94	Ernie Banks	825.00	375.00	105.00
☐	95	Hal Rice	15.00	6.75	1.90
☐	96	Charlie Silvera	16.00	7.25	2.00
☐	97	Jerald Hal Lane	15.00	6.75	1.90
☐	98	Joe Black	23.00	10.50	2.90
☐	99	Bobby Hofman	15.00	6.75	1.90
☐	100	Bob Keegan	15.00	6.75	1.90
☐	101	Gene Woodling	24.00	11.00	3.00
☐	102	Gil Hodges	85.00	38.00	10.50
☐	103	Jim Lemon	20.00	9.00	2.50
☐	104	Mike Sandlock	15.00	6.75	1.90
☐	105	Andy Carey	20.00	9.00	2.50
☐	106	Dick Kokos	15.00	6.75	1.90
☐	107	Duane Pillette	15.00	6.75	1.90
☐	108	Thornton Kipper	15.00	6.75	1.90
☐	109	Bill Bruton	16.00	7.25	2.00
☐	110	Harry Dorish	15.00	6.75	1.90
☐	111	Jim Delsing	15.00	6.75	1.90
☐	112	Bill Renna	15.00	6.75	1.90
☐	113	Bob Boyd	15.00	6.75	1.90
☐	114	Dean Stone	15.00	6.75	1.90
☐	115	Rip Repulski	15.00	6.75	1.90
☐	116	Steve Bilko	15.00	6.75	1.90
☐	117	Solly Hemus	15.00	6.75	1.90
☐	118	Carl Scheib	15.00	6.75	1.90
☐	119	Johnny Antonelli	16.00	7.25	2.00
☐	120	Roy McMillan	16.00	7.25	2.00
☐	121	Clem Labine	20.00	9.00	2.50
☐	122	Johnny Logan	16.00	7.25	2.00
☐	123	Bobby Adams	15.00	6.75	1.90
☐	124	Marion Fricano	15.00	6.75	1.90
☐	125	Harry Perkowski	15.00	6.75	1.90
☐	126	Ben Wade	15.00	6.75	1.90
☐	127	Steve O'Neill MG	15.00	6.75	1.90
☐	128	Hank Aaron	2100.00	950.00	275.00
☐	129	Forrest Jacobs	15.00	6.75	1.90
☐	130	Hank Bauer	35.00	16.00	4.40
☐	131	Reno Bertoia	15.00	6.75	1.90
☐	132	Tom Lasorda	165.00	75.00	21.00
☐	133	Dave Baker CO	15.00	6.75	1.90
☐	134	Cal Hogue	15.00	6.75	1.90
☐	135	Joe Presko	15.00	6.75	1.90
☐	136	Connie Ryan	15.00	6.75	1.90
☐	137	Wally Moon	30.00	13.50	3.80
☐	138	Bob Borkowski	15.00	6.75	1.90
☐	139	The O'Briens	30.00	13.50	3.80
		Johnny O'Brien			
		Eddie O'Brien			
☐	140	Tom Wright	15.00	6.75	1.90
☐	141	Joey Jay	20.00	9.00	2.50
☐	142	Tom Poholsky	15.00	6.75	1.90
☐	143	Rollie Hemsley CO	15.00	6.75	1.90
☐	144	Bill Werle	15.00	6.75	1.90
☐	145	Elmer Valo	15.00	6.75	1.90
☐	146	Don Johnson	15.00	6.75	1.90
☐	147	Johnny Riddle CO	15.00	6.75	1.90
☐	148	Bob Trice	15.00	6.75	1.90
☐	149	Al Robertson	15.00	6.75	1.90
☐	150	Dick Kryhoski	15.00	6.75	1.90
☐	151	Alex Grammas	15.00	6.75	1.90
☐	152	Michael Blyzka	15.00	6.75	1.90
☐	153	Al Walker	15.00	6.75	1.90
☐	154	Mike Fornieles	15.00	6.75	1.90
☐	155	Bob Kennedy	16.00	7.25	2.00
☐	156	Joe Coleman	15.00	6.75	1.90

☐	157	Don Lenhardt	15.00	6.75	1.90
☐	158	Peanuts Lowrey	15.00	6.75	1.90
☐	159	Dave Philley	15.00	6.75	1.90
☐	160	Ralph Kress CO	15.00	6.75	1.90
☐	161	John Hetki	15.00	6.75	1.90
☐	162	Herman Wehmeier	15.00	6.75	1.90
☐	163	Frank House	15.00	6.75	1.90
☐	164	Stu Miller	16.00	7.25	2.00
☐	165	Jim Pendleton	15.00	6.75	1.90
☐	166	Johnny Podres	30.00	13.50	3.80
☐	167	Don Lund	15.00	6.75	1.90
☐	168	Morrie Martin	15.00	6.75	1.90
☐	169	Jim Hughes	15.00	6.75	1.90
☐	170	James(Dusty) Rhodes	20.00	9.00	2.50
☐	171	Leo Kiely	15.00	6.75	1.90
☐	172	Harold Brown	15.00	6.75	1.90
☐	173	Jack Harshman	15.00	6.75	1.90
☐	174	Tom Qualters	15.00	6.75	1.90
☐	175	Frank Leja	22.00	10.00	2.80
☐	176	Robert Keely CO	15.00	6.75	1.90
☐	177	Bob Milliken	15.00	6.75	1.90
☐	178	Bill Glynn	15.00	6.75	1.90
☐	179	Gair Allie	15.00	6.75	1.90
☐	180	Wes Westrum	16.00	7.25	2.00
☐	181	Mel Roach	15.00	6.75	1.90
☐	182	Chuck Harmon	15.00	6.75	1.90
☐	183	Earle Combs CO	27.00	12.00	3.40
☐	184	Ed Bailey	18.00	8.00	2.30
☐	185	Chuck Stobbs	15.00	6.75	1.90
☐	186	Karl Olson	15.00	6.75	1.90
☐	187	Heinie Manush CO	27.00	12.00	3.40
☐	188	Dave Jolly	15.00	6.75	1.90
☐	189	Bob Ross	15.00	6.75	1.90
☐	190	Ray Herbert	15.00	6.75	1.90
☐	191	John(Dick) Schofield	20.00	9.00	2.50
☐	192	Ellis Deal CO	15.00	6.75	1.90
☐	193	Johnny Hopp CO	16.00	7.25	2.00
☐	194	Bill Sarni	15.00	6.75	1.90
☐	195	Billy Consolo	18.00	8.00	2.30
☐	196	Stan Jok	15.00	6.75	1.90
☐	197	Lynwood Rowe CO ("Schoolboy")	16.00	7.25	2.00
☐	198	Carl Sawatski	15.00	6.75	1.90
☐	199	Glenn(Rocky) Nelson	15.00	6.75	1.90
☐	200	Larry Jansen	16.00	7.25	2.00
☐	201	Al Kaline	900.00	400.00	115.00
☐	202	Bob Purkey	20.00	9.00	2.50
☐	203	Harry Brecheen CO	16.00	7.25	2.00
☐	204	Angel Scull	15.00	6.75	1.90
☐	205	Johnny Sain	30.00	13.50	3.80
☐	206	Ray Crone	15.00	6.75	1.90
☐	207	Tom Oliver CO	15.00	6.75	1.90
☐	208	Grady Hatton	15.00	6.75	1.90
☐	209	Chuck Thompson	15.00	6.75	1.90
☐	210	Bob Buhl	20.00	9.00	2.50
☐	211	Don Hoak	18.00	8.00	2.30
☐	212	Bob Micelotta	15.00	6.75	1.90
☐	213	Johnny Fitzpatrick CO	15.00	6.75	1.90
☐	214	Arnie Portocarrero	15.00	6.75	1.90
☐	215	Ed McGhee	15.00	6.75	1.90
☐	216	Al Sima	15.00	6.75	1.90
☐	217	Paul Schreiber CO	15.00	6.75	1.90
☐	218	Fred Marsh	15.00	6.75	1.90
☐	219	Chuck Kress	15.00	6.75	1.90
☐	220	Ruben Gomez	16.00	7.25	2.00
☐	221	Dick Brodowski	15.00	6.75	1.90
☐	222	Bill Wilson	15.00	6.75	1.90
☐	223	Joe Haynes CO	15.00	6.75	1.90
☐	224	Dick Weik	15.00	6.75	1.90
☐	225	Don Liddle	15.00	6.75	1.90
☐	226	Jehosie Heard	15.00	6.75	1.90
☐	227	Colonel Mills CO	15.00	6.75	1.90
☐	228	Gene Hermanski	15.00	6.75	1.90
☐	229	Bob Talbot	15.00	6.75	1.90
☐	230	Bob Kuzava	16.00	7.25	2.00
☐	231	Roy Smalley	15.00	6.75	1.90
☐	232	Lou Limmer	15.00	6.75	1.90
☐	233	Augie Galan CO	15.00	6.75	1.90
☐	234	Jerry Lynch	20.00	9.00	2.50
☐	235	Vernon Law	16.00	7.25	2.00
☐	236	Paul Penson	15.00	6.75	1.90
☐	237	Mike Ryba CO	15.00	6.75	1.90
☐	238	Al Aber	15.00	6.75	1.90
☐	239	Bill Skowron	85.00	38.00	10.50
☐	240	Sam Mele	15.00	6.75	1.90
☐	241	Robert Miller	15.00	6.75	1.90
☐	242	Curt Roberts	15.00	6.75	1.90
☐	243	Ray Blades CO	15.00	6.75	1.90
☐	244	Leroy Wheat	15.00	6.75	1.90
☐	245	Roy Sievers	18.00	8.00	2.30
☐	246	Howie Fox	15.00	6.75	1.90
☐	247	Ed Mayo CO	15.00	6.75	1.90
☐	248	Al Smith	20.00	9.00	2.50
☐	249	Wilmer Mizell	16.00	7.25	2.00
☐	250	Ted Williams	700.00	210.00	70.00

1955 Topps

The cards in this 206-card set measure approximately 2 5/8" by 3 3/4". Both the large "head" shot and the smaller full-length photos used on each card of the 1955 Topps set are in color. The card fronts were designed horizontally for the first time in Topps's history. The first card features Dusty Rhodes, hitting star for the Giants' 1954 World Series sweep over the Indians. A "high" series, 161 to 210, is more difficult to find than cards 1 to 160.

*Numbers 175, 186, 203, and 209 were
never issued. To fill in for the four cards
not issued in the high number series,
Topps double printed four players, those
appearing on cards 170, 172, 184, and
188. Although rarely seen, there exist
salesman sample panels of three cards
containing the fronts of regular cards with
ad information for the 1955 Topps regular
and the 1955 Topps Doubleheaders on the
back. One such ad panel depicts (from top
to bottom) Danny Schell, Jake Thies, and
Howie Pollet. The key rookies in this set
are Ken Boyer, Roberto Clemente,
Harmon Killebrew, and Sandy Koufax.*

		NRMT	VG-E	GOOD
	COMPLETE SET (206)	7600.	3400.	950.00
	COMMON PLAYER (1-150)	9.00	4.00	1.15
	COMMON PLAYER (151-160)	18.00	8.00	2.30
	COMMON PLAYER (161-210)	28.00	12.50	3.50
☐	1 Dusty Rhodes	45.00	9.00	2.70
☐	2 Ted Williams	425.00	190.00	52.50
☐	3 Art Fowler	10.00	4.50	1.25
☐	4 Al Kaline	250.00	115.00	31.00
☐	5 Jim Gilliam	15.00	6.75	1.90
☐	6 Stan Hack MG	11.00	4.90	1.40
☐	7 Jim Hegan	10.00	4.50	1.25
☐	8 Harold Smith	9.00	4.00	1.15
☐	9 Robert Miller	9.00	4.00	1.15
☐	10 Bob Keegan	9.00	4.00	1.15
☐	11 Ferris Fain	10.00	4.50	1.25
☐	12 Vernon(Jake) Thies	9.00	4.00	1.15
☐	13 Fred Marsh	9.00	4.00	1.15
☐	14 Jim Finigan	9.00	4.00	1.15
☐	15 Jim Pendleton	9.00	4.00	1.15
☐	16 Roy Sievers	10.00	4.50	1.25
☐	17 Bobby Hofman	9.00	4.00	1.15
☐	18 Russ Kemmerer	9.00	4.00	1.15
☐	19 Billy Herman CO	15.00	6.75	1.90
☐	20 Andy Carey	12.00	5.50	1.50
☐	21 Alex Grammas	9.00	4.00	1.15
☐	22 Bill Skowron	20.00	9.00	2.50
☐	23 Jack Parks	9.00	4.00	1.15
☐	24 Hal Newhouser	20.00	9.00	2.50
☐	25 Johnny Podres	20.00	9.00	2.50
☐	26 Dick Groat	12.00	5.50	1.50
☐	27 Billy Gardner	10.00	4.50	1.25
☐	28 Ernie Banks	225.00	100.00	28.00
☐	29 Herman Wehmeier	9.00	4.00	1.15
☐	30 Vic Power	10.00	4.50	1.25
☐	31 Warren Spahn	85.00	38.00	10.50
☐	32 Warren McGhee	9.00	4.00	1.15
☐	33 Tom Qualters	9.00	4.00	1.15
☐	34 Wayne Terwilliger	9.00	4.00	1.15
☐	35 Dave Jolly	9.00	4.00	1.15
☐	36 Leo Kiely	9.00	4.00	1.15
☐	37 Joe Cunningham	12.50	5.75	1.55
☐	38 Bob Turley	15.00	6.75	1.90
☐	39 Bill Glynn	9.00	4.00	1.15
☐	40 Don Hoak	10.00	4.50	1.25
☐	41 Chuck Stobbs	9.00	4.00	1.15
☐	42 John(Windy) McCall	9.00	4.00	1.15
☐	43 Harvey Haddix	10.00	4.50	1.25
☐	44 Harold Valentine	9.00	4.00	1.15
☐	45 Hank Sauer	10.00	4.50	1.25
☐	46 Ted Kazanski	9.00	4.00	1.15
☐	47 Hank Aaron UER	400.00	180.00	50.00
	(Birth incorrectly listed as 2/10)			
☐	48 Bob Kennedy	10.00	4.50	1.25
☐	49 J.W. Porter	9.00	4.00	1.15
☐	50 Jackie Robinson	250.00	115.00	31.00
☐	51 Jim Hughes	9.00	4.00	1.15
☐	52 Bill Tremel	9.00	4.00	1.15
☐	53 Bill Taylor	9.00	4.00	1.15
☐	54 Lou Limmer	9.00	4.00	1.15
☐	55 Rip Repulski	9.00	4.00	1.15
☐	56 Ray Jablonski	9.00	4.00	1.15
☐	57 Billy O'Dell	9.00	4.00	1.15
☐	58 Jim Rivera	9.00	4.00	1.15
☐	59 Gair Allie	9.00	4.00	1.15
☐	60 Dean Stone	9.00	4.00	1.15
☐	61 Forrest Jacobs	9.00	4.00	1.15
☐	62 Thornton Kipper	9.00	4.00	1.15
☐	63 Joe Collins	10.00	4.50	1.25
☐	64 Gus Triandos	12.50	5.75	1.55
☐	65 Ray Boone	10.00	4.50	1.25
☐	66 Ron Jackson	9.00	4.00	1.15
☐	67 Wally Moon	10.00	4.50	1.25
☐	68 Jim Davis	9.00	4.00	1.15
☐	69 Ed Bailey	10.00	4.50	1.25
☐	70 Al Rosen	14.00	6.25	1.75
☐	71 Ruben Gomez	9.00	4.00	1.15
☐	72 Karl Olson	9.00	4.00	1.15
☐	73 Jack Shepard	9.00	4.00	1.15
☐	74 Bob Borkowski	9.00	4.00	1.15
☐	75 Sandy Amoros	25.00	11.50	3.10
☐	76 Howie Pollet	9.00	4.00	1.15

☐ 77 Arnie Portocarrero	9.00	4.00	1.15
☐ 78 Gordon Jones	9.00	4.00	1.15
☐ 79 Clyde(Danny) Schell	9.00	4.00	1.15
☐ 80 Bob Grim	15.00	6.75	1.90
☐ 81 Gene Conley	10.00	4.50	1.25
☐ 82 Chuck Harmon	9.00	4.00	1.15
☐ 83 Tom Brewer	9.00	4.00	1.15
☐ 84 Camilo Pascual	15.00	6.75	1.90
☐ 85 Don Mossi	15.00	6.75	1.90
☐ 86 Bill Wilson	9.00	4.00	1.15
☐ 87 Frank House	9.00	4.00	1.15
☐ 88 Bob Skinner	15.00	6.75	1.90
☐ 89 Joe Frazier	10.00	4.50	1.25
☐ 90 Karl Spooner	15.00	6.75	1.90
☐ 91 Milt Bolling	9.00	4.00	1.15
☐ 92 Don Zimmer	40.00	18.00	5.00
☐ 93 Steve Bilko	9.00	4.00	1.15
☐ 94 Reno Bertoia	9.00	4.00	1.15
☐ 95 Preston Ward	9.00	4.00	1.15
☐ 96 Chuck Bishop	9.00	4.00	1.15
☐ 97 Carlos Paula	9.00	4.00	1.15
☐ 98 John Riddle CO	9.00	4.00	1.15
☐ 99 Frank Leja	11.00	4.90	1.40
☐ 100 Monte Irvin	30.00	13.50	3.80
☐ 101 Johnny Gray	9.00	4.00	1.15
☐ 102 Wally Westlake	9.00	4.00	1.15
☐ 103 Chuck White	9.00	4.00	1.15
☐ 104 Jack Harshman	9.00	4.00	1.15
☐ 105 Chuck Diering	9.00	4.00	1.15
☐ 106 Frank Sullivan	9.00	4.00	1.15
☐ 107 Curt Roberts	9.00	4.00	1.15
☐ 108 Al Walker	9.00	4.00	1.15
☐ 109 Ed Lopat	15.00	6.75	1.90
☐ 110 Gus Zernial	10.00	4.50	1.25
☐ 111 Bob Milliken	9.00	4.00	1.15
☐ 112 Nelson King	9.00	4.00	1.15
☐ 113 Harry Brecheen CO	10.00	4.50	1.25
☐ 114 Louis Ortiz	9.00	4.00	1.15
☐ 115 Ellis Kinder	9.00	4.00	1.15
☐ 116 Tom Hurd	9.00	4.00	1.15
☐ 117 Mel Roach	9.00	4.00	1.15
☐ 118 Bob Purkey	9.00	4.00	1.15
☐ 119 Bob Lennon	9.00	4.00	1.15
☐ 120 Ted Kluszewski	25.00	11.50	3.10
☐ 121 Bill Renna	9.00	4.00	1.15
☐ 122 Carl Sawatski	9.00	4.00	1.15
☐ 123 Sandy Koufax	1300.00	575.00	160.00
☐ 124 Harmon Killebrew	425.00	190.00	52.50
☐ 125 Ken Boyer	75.00	34.00	9.50
☐ 126 Dick Hall	9.00	4.00	1.15
☐ 127 Dale Long	12.50	5.75	1.55
☐ 128 Ted Lepcio	9.00	4.00	1.15
☐ 129 Elvin Tappe	9.00	4.00	1.15
☐ 130 Mayo Smith MG	9.00	4.00	1.15
☐ 131 Grady Hatton	9.00	4.00	1.15
☐ 132 Bob Trice	9.00	4.00	1.15
☐ 133 Dave Hoskins	9.00	4.00	1.15
☐ 134 Joey Jay	10.00	4.50	1.25
☐ 135 Johnny O'Brien	10.00	4.50	1.25
☐ 136 Veston(Bunky) Stewart	9.00	4.00	1.15
☐ 137 Harry Elliott	9.00	4.00	1.15
☐ 138 Ray Herbert	9.00	4.00	1.15
☐ 139 Steve Kraly	9.00	4.00	1.15
☐ 140 Mel Parnell	10.00	4.50	1.25
☐ 141 Tom Wright	9.00	4.00	1.15
☐ 142 Jerry Lynch	10.00	4.50	1.25
☐ 143 John(Dick) Schofield	10.00	4.50	1.25
☐ 144 John(Joe) Amalfitano	12.50	5.75	1.55
☐ 145 Elmer Valo	9.00	4.00	1.15
☐ 146 Dick Donovan	12.50	5.75	1.55
☐ 147 Hugh Pepper	9.00	4.00	1.15
☐ 148 Hector Brown	9.00	4.00	1.15
☐ 149 Ray Crone	9.00	4.00	1.15
☐ 150 Mike Higgins MG	9.00	4.00	1.15
☐ 151 Ralph Kress CO	18.00	8.00	2.30
☐ 152 Harry Agganis	85.00	38.00	10.50
☐ 153 Bud Podbielan	18.00	8.00	2.30
☐ 154 Willie Miranda	18.00	8.00	2.30
☐ 155 Eddie Mathews	130.00	57.50	16.50
☐ 156 Joe Black	35.00	16.00	4.40
☐ 157 Robert Miller	18.00	8.00	2.30
☐ 158 Tommy Carroll	18.00	8.00	2.30
☐ 159 Johnny Schmitz	18.00	8.00	2.30
☐ 160 Ray Narleski	25.00	11.50	3.10
☐ 161 Chuck Tanner	35.00	16.00	4.40
☐ 162 Joe Coleman	28.00	12.50	3.50
☐ 163 Faye Throneberry	28.00	12.50	3.50
☐ 164 Roberto Clemente	1650.00	750.00	210.00
☐ 165 Don Johnson	28.00	12.50	3.50
☐ 166 Hank Bauer	55.00	25.00	7.00
☐ 167 Thomas Casagrande	28.00	12.50	3.50
☐ 168 Duane Pillette	28.00	12.50	3.50
☐ 169 Bob Oldis	28.00	12.50	3.50
☐ 170 Jim Pearce DP	16.00	7.25	2.00
☐ 171 Dick Brodowski	28.00	12.50	3.50
☐ 172 Frank Baumholtz DP	16.00	7.25	2.00
☐ 173 Bob Kline	28.00	12.50	3.50
☐ 174 Rudy Minarcin	28.00	12.50	3.50
☐ 175 Does not exist	.00	.00	.00
☐ 176 Norm Zauchin	28.00	12.50	3.50
☐ 177 Al Robertson	28.00	12.50	3.50
☐ 178 Bobby Adams	28.00	12.50	3.50
☐ 179 Jim Bolger	28.00	12.50	3.50
☐ 180 Clem Labine	35.00	16.00	4.40
☐ 181 Roy McMillan	30.00	13.50	3.80
☐ 182 Humberto Robinson	28.00	12.50	3.50
☐ 183 Anthony Jacobs	28.00	12.50	3.50
☐ 184 Harry Perkowski DP	16.00	7.25	2.00
☐ 185 Don Ferrarese	28.00	12.50	3.50
☐ 186 Does not exist	.00	.00	.00
☐ 187 Gil Hodges	165.00	75.00	21.00
☐ 188 Charlie Silvera DP	16.00	7.25	2.00
☐ 189 Phil Rizzuto	165.00	75.00	21.00
☐ 190 Gene Woodling	35.00	16.00	4.40

		NRMT	VG-E	GOOD
☐	191 Eddie Stanky MG	35.00	16.00	4.40
☐	192 Jim Delsing	28.00	12.50	3.50
☐	193 Johnny Sain	45.00	20.00	5.75
☐	194 Willie Mays	550.00	250.00	70.00
☐	195 Ed Roebuck	35.00	16.00	4.40
☐	196 Gale Wade	28.00	12.50	3.50
☐	197 Al Smith	30.00	13.50	3.80
☐	198 Yogi Berra	250.00	115.00	31.00
☐	199 Odbert Hamric	28.00	12.50	3.50
☐	200 Jackie Jensen	50.00	23.00	6.25
☐	201 Sherm Lollar	33.00	15.00	4.10
☐	202 Jim Owens	28.00	12.50	3.50
☐	203 Does not exist	.00	.00	.00
☐	204 Frank Smith	28.00	12.50	3.50
☐	205 Gene Freese	35.00	16.00	4.40
☐	206 Pete Daley	28.00	12.50	3.50
☐	207 Billy Consolo	28.00	12.50	3.50
☐	208 Ray Moore	28.00	12.50	3.50
☐	209 Does not exist	.00	.00	.00
☐	210 Duke Snider	550.00	140.00	45.00

1956 Topps

The cards in this 340-card set measure approximately 2 5/8" by 3 3/4". Following up with another horizontally oriented card in 1956, Topps improved the format by layering the color "head" shot onto an actual action sequence involving the player. Cards 1 to 180 come with either white or gray backs: in the 1 to 100 sequence, gray backs are less common (worth about 10 percent more) and in the 101 to 180 sequence, white backs are less common (worth 30 percent more). The team cards, used for the first time in a regular set by Topps, are found dated 1955, or undated, with the team name appearing on either side. The dated team cards in the first series were not printed on the gray stock. The two unnumbered checklist cards are highly prized (must be unmarked to qualify as excellent or mint). The complete set price below does not include the unnumbered checklist cards or any of the variations. The key rookies in this set are Walt Alston, Luis Aparicio, and Roger Craig. There are ten double-printed cards in the first series as evidenced by the discovery of an uncut sheet of 110 cards (10 by 11); these DP's are listed below.

	NRMT	VG-E	GOOD
COMPLETE SET (340)	7700.	3500.	950.00
COMMON PLAYER (1-100)	8.50	3.80	1.05
COMMON PLAYER (101-180)	11.50	5.25	1.45
COMMON PLAYER (181-260)	16.00	7.25	2.00
COMMON PLAYER (261-340)	12.50	5.75	1.55

		NRMT	VG-E	GOOD
☐	1 William Harridge (AL President)	125.00	31.00	10.00
☐	2 Warren Giles (NL President)	20.00	9.00	2.50
☐	3 Elmer Valo	8.50	3.80	1.05
☐	4 Carlos Paula	8.50	3.80	1.05
☐	5 Ted Williams	325.00	145.00	40.00
☐	6 Ray Boone	10.00	4.50	1.25
☐	7 Ron Negray	8.50	3.80	1.05
☐	8 Walter Alston MG	42.00	19.00	5.25
☐	9 Ruben Gomez DP	8.50	3.80	1.05
☐	10 Warren Spahn	85.00	38.00	10.50
☐	11A Chicago Cubs (Centered)	30.00	13.50	3.80
☐	11B Cubs Team (Dated 1955)	60.00	27.00	7.50
☐	11C Cubs Team (Name at far left)	30.00	13.50	3.80
☐	12 Andy Carey	10.00	4.50	1.25
☐	13 Roy Face	11.00	4.90	1.40
☐	14 Ken Boyer DP	15.00	6.75	1.90
☐	15 Ernie Banks DP	100.00	45.00	12.50
☐	16 Hector Lopez	12.50	5.75	1.55
☐	17 Gene Conley	10.00	4.50	1.25
☐	18 Dick Donovan	8.50	3.80	1.05
☐	19 Chuck Diering	8.50	3.80	1.05
☐	20 Al Kaline	125.00	57.50	15.50
☐	21 Joe Collins DP	10.00	4.50	1.25
☐	22 Jim Finigan	8.50	3.80	1.05
☐	23 Fred Marsh	8.50	3.80	1.05
☐	24 Dick Groat	12.50	5.75	1.55
☐	25 Ted Kluszewski	25.00	11.50	3.10
☐	26 Grady Hatton	8.50	3.80	1.05
☐	27 Nelson Burbrink	8.50	3.80	1.05
☐	28 Bobby Hofman	8.50	3.80	1.05
☐	29 Jack Harshman	8.50	3.80	1.05

☐ 30	Jackie Robinson DP...165.00	75.00	21.00
☐ 31	Hank Aaron UER 275.00	125.00	34.00
	(Small photo		
	actually W.Mays)		
☐ 32	Frank House.................8.50	3.80	1.05
☐ 33	Roberto Clemente 425.00	190.00	52.50
☐ 34	Tom Brewer..................8.50	3.80	1.05
☐ 35	Al Rosen....................12.50	5.75	1.55
☐ 36	Rudy Minarcin..............8.50	3.80	1.05
☐ 37	Alex Grammas..............8.50	3.80	1.05
☐ 38	Bob Kennedy...............10.00	4.50	1.25
☐ 39	Don Mossi 10.00	4.50	1.25
☐ 40	Bob Turley..................12.50	5.75	1.55
☐ 41	Hank Sauer.................10.00	4.50	1.25
☐ 42	Sandy Amoros 14.00	6.25	1.75
☐ 43	Ray Moore 8.50	3.80	1.05
☐ 44	Windy McCall................8.50	3.80	1.05
☐ 45	Gus Zernial 10.00	4.50	1.25
☐ 46	Gene Freese DP............8.50	3.80	1.05
☐ 47	Art Fowler....................8.50	3.80	1.05
☐ 48	Jim Hegan...................10.00	4.50	1.25
☐ 49	Pedro Ramos 8.50	3.80	1.05
☐ 50	Dusty Rhodes 10.00	4.50	1.25
☐ 51	Ernie Oravetz...............8.50	3.80	1.05
☐ 52	Bob Grim 10.00	4.50	1.25
☐ 53	Arnie Portocarrero.........8.50	3.80	1.05
☐ 54	Bob Keegan..................8.50	3.80	1.05
☐ 55	Wally Moon 10.00	4.50	1.25
☐ 56	Dale Long 10.00	4.50	1.25
☐ 57	Duke Maas 8.50	3.80	1.05
☐ 58	Ed Roebuck.................10.00	4.50	1.25
☐ 59	Jose Santiago...............8.50	3.80	1.05
☐ 60	Mayo Smith MG DP....8.50	3.80	1.05
☐ 61	Bill Skowron 18.00	8.00	2.30
☐ 62	Hal Smith 8.50	3.80	1.05
☐ 63	Roger Craig.................30.00	13.50	3.80
☐ 64	Luis Arroyo 12.50	5.75	1.55
☐ 65	Johnny O'Brien 10.00	4.50	1.25
☐ 66	Bob Speake...................8.50	3.80	1.05
☐ 67	Vic Power 10.00	4.50	1.25
☐ 68	Chuck Stobbs 8.50	3.80	1.05
☐ 69	Chuck Tanner...............12.50	5.75	1.55
☐ 70	Jim Rivera 8.50	3.80	1.05
☐ 71	Frank Sullivan...............8.50	3.80	1.05
☐ 72A	Phillies Team 30.00	13.50	3.80
	(Centered)		
☐ 72B	Phillies Team 60.00	27.00	7.50
	(Dated 1955)		
☐ 72C	Phillies Team 30.00	13.50	3.80
	(Name at far left)		
☐ 73	Wayne Terwilliger 8.50	3.80	1.05
☐ 74	Jim King 8.50	3.80	1.05
☐ 75	Roy Sievers DP...........10.00	4.50	1.25
☐ 76	Ray Crone 8.50	3.80	1.05
☐ 77	Harvey Haddix............10.00	4.50	1.25
☐ 78	Herman Wehmeier.........8.50	3.80	1.05
☐ 79	Sandy Koufax..............425.00	190.00	52.50

☐ 80	Gus Triandos DP..........10.00	4.50	1.25
☐ 81	Wally Westlake 8.50	3.80	1.05
☐ 82	Bill Renna 8.50	3.80	1.05
☐ 83	Karl Spooner................10.00	4.50	1.25
☐ 84	Babe Birrer....................8.50	3.80	1.05
☐ 85A	Cleveland Indians 30.00	13.50	3.80
	(Centered)		
☐ 85B	Indians Team 60.00	27.00	7.50
	(Dated 1955)		
☐ 85C	Indians Team 30.00	13.50	3.80
	(Name at far left)		
☐ 86	Ray Jablonski DP...........8.50	3.80	1.05
☐ 87	Dean Stone 8.50	3.80	1.05
☐ 88	Johnny Kucks..............12.50	5.75	1.55
☐ 89	Norm Zauchin 8.50	3.80	1.05
☐ 90A	Cincinnati Redlegs 30.00	13.50	3.80
	Team (Centered)		
☐ 90B	Reds Team 60.00	27.00	7.50
	(Dated 1955)		
☐ 90C	Reds Team 30.00	13.50	3.80
	(Name at far left)		
☐ 91	Gail Harris 8.50	3.80	1.05
☐ 92	Bob(Red) Wilson 8.50	3.80	1.05
☐ 93	George Susce 8.50	3.80	1.05
☐ 94	Ron Kline 8.50	3.80	1.05
☐ 95A	Milwaukee Braves 35.00	16.00	4.40
	Team (Centered)		
☐ 95B	Braves Team 70.00	32.00	8.75
	(Dated 1955)		
☐ 95C	Braves Team 35.00	16.00	4.40
	(Name at far left)		
☐ 96	Bill Tremel....................8.50	3.80	1.05
☐ 97	Jerry Lynch 10.00	4.50	1.25
☐ 98	Camilo Pascual 10.00	4.50	1.25
☐ 99	Don Zimmer................18.00	8.00	2.30
☐ 100A	Baltimore Orioles 35.00	16.00	4.40
	Team (centered)		
☐ 100B	Orioles Team 70.00	32.00	8.75
	(Dated 1955)		
☐ 100C	Orioles Team 35.00	16.00	4.40
	(Name at far left)		
☐ 101	Roy Campanella.........140.00	65.00	17.50
☐ 102	Jim Davis...................11.50	5.25	1.45
☐ 103	Willie Miranda 11.50	5.25	1.45
☐ 104	Bob Lennon 11.50	5.25	1.45
☐ 105	Al Smith....................11.50	5.25	1.45
☐ 106	Joe Astroth 11.50	5.25	1.45
☐ 107	Eddie Mathews 65.00	29.00	8.25
☐ 108	Laurin Pepper 11.50	5.25	1.45
☐ 109	Enos Slaughter 35.00	16.00	4.40
☐ 110	Yogi Berra 160.00	70.00	20.00
☐ 111	Boston Red Sox..........35.00	16.00	4.40
	Team Card		
☐ 112	Dee Fondy.................11.50	5.25	1.45
☐ 113	Phil Rizzuto...............60.00	27.00	7.50
☐ 114	Jim Owens.................11.50	5.25	1.45
☐ 115	Jackie Jensen 15.00	6.75	1.90

☐	116 Eddie O'Brien	11.50	5.25	1.45
☐	117 Virgil Trucks	13.00	5.75	1.65
☐	118 Nellie Fox	35.00	16.00	4.40
☐	119 Larry Jackson	15.00	6.75	1.90
☐	120 Richie Ashburn	35.00	16.00	4.40
☐	121 Pittsburgh Pirates	35.00	16.00	4.40
	Team Card			
☐	122 Willard Nixon	11.50	5.25	1.45
☐	123 Roy McMillan	13.00	5.75	1.65
☐	124 Don Kaiser	11.50	5.25	1.45
☐	125 Minnie Minoso	25.00	11.50	3.10
☐	126 Jim Brady	11.50	5.25	1.45
☐	127 Willie Jones	11.50	5.25	1.45
☐	128 Eddie Yost	13.00	5.75	1.65
☐	129 Jake Martin	11.50	5.25	1.45
☐	130 Willie Mays	375.00	170.00	47.50
☐	131 Bob Roselli	11.50	5.25	1.45
☐	132 Bobby Avila	11.50	5.25	1.45
☐	133 Ray Narleski	11.50	5.25	1.45
☐	134 St. Louis Cardinals	35.00	16.00	4.40
	Team Card			
☐	135 Mickey Mantle	1150.00	525.00	145.00
☐	136 Johnny Logan	13.00	5.75	1.65
☐	137 Al Silvera	11.50	5.25	1.45
☐	138 Johnny Antonelli	13.00	5.75	1.65
☐	139 Tommy Carroll	11.50	5.25	1.45
☐	140 Herb Score	35.00	16.00	4.40
☐	141 Joe Frazier	11.50	5.25	1.45
☐	142 Gene Baker	11.50	5.25	1.45
☐	143 Jim Piersall	16.00	7.25	2.00
☐	144 Leroy Powell	11.50	5.25	1.45
☐	145 Gil Hodges	55.00	25.00	7.00
☐	146 Washington Nationals	35.00	16.00	4.40
	Team Card			
☐	147 Earl Torgeson	11.50	5.25	1.45
☐	148 Alvin Dark	15.00	6.75	1.90
☐	149 Dixie Howell	11.50	5.25	1.45
☐	150 Duke Snider	150.00	70.00	19.00
☐	151 Spook Jacobs	13.00	5.75	1.65
☐	152 Billy Hoeft	13.00	5.75	1.65
☐	153 Frank Thomas	14.00	6.25	1.75
☐	154 Dave Pope	11.50	5.25	1.45
☐	155 Harvey Kuenn	18.00	8.00	2.30
☐	156 Wes Westrum	13.00	5.75	1.65
☐	157 Dick Brodowski	11.50	5.25	1.45
☐	158 Wally Post	13.00	5.75	1.65
☐	159 Clint Courtney	11.50	5.25	1.45
☐	160 Billy Pierce	15.00	6.75	1.90
☐	161 Joe DeMaestri	11.50	5.25	1.45
☐	162 Dave(Gus) Bell	13.00	5.75	1.65
☐	163 Gene Woodling	15.00	6.75	1.90
☐	164 Harmon Killebrew	175.00	80.00	22.00
☐	165 Red Schoendienst	32.00	14.50	4.00
☐	166 Brooklyn Dodgers	190.00	85.00	24.00
	Team Card			
☐	167 Harry Dorish	11.50	5.25	1.45
☐	168 Sammy White	11.50	5.25	1.45
☐	169 Bob Nelson	11.50	5.25	1.45
☐	170 Bill Virdon	16.00	7.25	2.00
☐	171 Jim Wilson	11.50	5.25	1.45
☐	172 Frank Torre	15.00	6.75	1.90
☐	173 Johnny Podres	18.00	8.00	2.30
☐	174 Glen Gorbous	11.50	5.25	1.45
☐	175 Del Crandall	13.00	5.75	1.65
☐	176 Alex Kellner	11.50	5.25	1.45
☐	177 Hank Bauer	21.00	9.50	2.60
☐	178 Joe Black	16.00	7.25	2.00
☐	179 Harry Chiti	11.50	5.25	1.45
☐	180 Robin Roberts	40.00	18.00	5.00
☐	181 Billy Martin	100.00	45.00	12.50
☐	182 Paul Minner	16.00	7.25	2.00
☐	183 Stan Lopata	16.00	7.25	2.00
☐	184 Don Bessent	16.00	7.25	2.00
☐	185 Bill Bruton	18.00	8.00	2.30
☐	186 Ron Jackson	16.00	7.25	2.00
☐	187 Early Wynn	40.00	18.00	5.00
☐	188 Chicago White Sox	40.00	18.00	5.00
	Team Card			
☐	189 Ned Garver	16.00	7.25	2.00
☐	190 Carl Furillo	30.00	13.50	3.80
☐	191 Frank Lary	20.00	9.00	2.50
☐	192 Smoky Burgess	18.00	8.00	2.30
☐	193 Wilmer Mizell	18.00	8.00	2.30
☐	194 Monte Irvin	35.00	16.00	4.40
☐	195 George Kell	35.00	16.00	4.40
☐	196 Tom Poholsky	16.00	7.25	2.00
☐	197 Granny Hamner	16.00	7.25	2.00
☐	198 Ed Fitzgerald	16.00	7.25	2.00
☐	199 Hank Thompson	18.00	8.00	2.30
☐	200 Bob Feller	150.00	70.00	19.00
☐	201 Rip Repulski	16.00	7.25	2.00
☐	202 Jim Hearn	16.00	7.25	2.00
☐	203 Bill Tuttle	16.00	7.25	2.00
☐	204 Art Swanson	16.00	7.25	2.00
☐	205 Whitey Lockman	18.00	8.00	2.30
☐	206 Erv Palica	16.00	7.25	2.00
☐	207 Jim Small	16.00	7.25	2.00
☐	208 Elston Howard	55.00	25.00	7.00
☐	209 Max Surkont	16.00	7.25	2.00
☐	210 Mike Garcia	18.00	8.00	2.30
☐	211 Murry Dickson	16.00	7.25	2.00
☐	212 Johnny Temple	20.00	9.00	2.50
☐	213 Detroit Tigers	55.00	25.00	7.00
	Team Card			
☐	214 Bob Rush	16.00	7.25	2.00
☐	215 Tommy Byrne	16.00	7.25	2.00
☐	216 Jerry Schoonmaker	16.00	7.25	2.00
☐	217 Billy Klaus	16.00	7.25	2.00
☐	218 Joe Nuxhall UER	18.00	8.00	2.30
	(Misspelled Nuxall)			
☐	219 Lew Burdette	22.00	10.00	2.80
☐	220 Del Ennis	18.00	8.00	2.30
☐	221 Bob Friend	18.00	8.00	2.30
☐	222 Dave Philley	16.00	7.25	2.00

☐ 223	Randy Jackson	16.00	7.25	2.00
☐ 224	Bud Podbielan	16.00	7.25	2.00
☐ 225	Gil McDougald	30.00	13.50	3.80
☐ 226	New York Giants	75.00	34.00	9.50
	Team Card			
☐ 227	Russ Meyer	16.00	7.25	2.00
☐ 228	Mickey Vernon	18.00	8.00	2.30
☐ 229	Harry Brecheen CO	18.00	8.00	2.30
☐ 230	Chico Carrasquel	16.00	7.25	2.00
☐ 231	Bob Hale	16.00	7.25	2.00
☐ 232	Toby Atwell	16.00	7.25	2.00
☐ 233	Carl Erskine	30.00	13.50	3.80
☐ 234	Pete Runnels	18.00	8.00	2.30
☐ 235	Don Newcombe	55.00	25.00	7.00
☐ 236	Kansas City Athletics	35.00	16.00	4.40
	Team Card			
☐ 237	Jose Valdivielso	16.00	7.25	2.00
☐ 238	Walt Dropo	18.00	8.00	2.30
☐ 239	Harry Simpson	16.00	7.25	2.00
☐ 240	Whitey Ford	150.00	70.00	19.00
☐ 241	Don Mueller UER	18.00	8.00	2.30
	(6" tall)			
☐ 242	Hershell Freeman	16.00	7.25	2.00
☐ 243	Sherm Lollar	18.00	8.00	2.30
☐ 244	Bob Buhl	18.00	8.00	2.30
☐ 245	Billy Goodman	18.00	8.00	2.30
☐ 246	Tom Gorman	16.00	7.25	2.00
☐ 247	Bill Sarni	16.00	7.25	2.00
☐ 248	Bob Porterfield	16.00	7.25	2.00
☐ 249	Johnny Klippstein	16.00	7.25	2.00
☐ 250	Larry Doby	25.00	11.50	3.10
☐ 251	New York Yankees	210.00	95.00	26.00
	Team Card UER			
	(Don Larsen misspelled			
	as Larson on front)			
☐ 252	Vern Law	18.00	8.00	2.30
☐ 253	Irv Noren	20.00	9.00	2.50
☐ 254	George Crowe	16.00	7.25	2.00
☐ 255	Bob Lemon	35.00	16.00	4.40
☐ 256	Tom Hurd	16.00	7.25	2.00
☐ 257	Bobby Thomson	25.00	11.50	3.10
☐ 258	Art Ditmar	16.00	7.25	2.00
☐ 259	Sam Jones	18.00	8.00	2.30
☐ 260	Pee Wee Reese	150.00	70.00	19.00
☐ 261	Bobby Shantz	14.00	6.25	1.75
☐ 262	Howie Pollet	12.50	5.75	1.55
☐ 263	Bob Miller	12.50	5.75	1.55
☐ 264	Ray Monzant	12.50	5.75	1.55
☐ 265	Sandy Consuegra	12.50	5.75	1.55
☐ 266	Don Ferrarese	12.50	5.75	1.55
☐ 267	Bob Nieman	12.50	5.75	1.55
☐ 268	Dale Mitchell	18.00	8.00	2.30
☐ 269	Jack Meyer	12.50	5.75	1.55
☐ 270	Billy Loes	14.00	6.25	1.75
☐ 271	Foster Castleman	12.50	5.75	1.55
☐ 272	Danny O'Connell	12.50	5.75	1.55
☐ 273	Walker Cooper	12.50	5.75	1.55

☐ 274	Frank Baumholtz	12.50	5.75	1.55
☐ 275	Jim Greengrass	12.50	5.75	1.55
☐ 276	George Zuverink	12.50	5.75	1.55
☐ 277	Daryl Spencer	12.50	5.75	1.55
☐ 278	Chet Nichols	12.50	5.75	1.55
☐ 279	Johnny Groth	12.50	5.75	1.55
☐ 280	Jim Gilliam	21.00	9.50	2.60
☐ 281	Art Houtteman	12.50	5.75	1.55
☐ 282	Warren Hacker	12.50	5.75	1.55
☐ 283	Hal Smith	12.50	5.75	1.55
☐ 284	Ike Delock	12.50	5.75	1.55
☐ 285	Eddie Miksis	12.50	5.75	1.55
☐ 286	Bill Wight	12.50	5.75	1.55
☐ 287	Bobby Adams	12.50	5.75	1.55
☐ 288	Bob Cerv	30.00	13.50	3.80
☐ 289	Hal Jeffcoat	12.50	5.75	1.55
☐ 290	Curt Simmons	14.00	6.25	1.75
☐ 291	Frank Kellert	12.50	5.75	1.55
☐ 292	Luis Aparicio	150.00	70.00	19.00
☐ 293	Stu Miller	15.00	6.75	1.90
☐ 294	Ernie Johnson	14.00	6.25	1.75
☐ 295	Clem Labine	15.00	6.75	1.90
☐ 296	Andy Seminick	12.50	5.75	1.55
☐ 297	Bob Skinner	14.00	6.25	1.75
☐ 298	Johnny Schmitz	12.50	5.75	1.55
☐ 299	Charlie Neal	30.00	13.50	3.80
☐ 300	Vic Wertz	14.00	6.25	1.75
☐ 301	Marv Grissom	12.50	5.75	1.55
☐ 302	Eddie Robinson	12.50	5.75	1.55
☐ 303	Jim Dyck	12.50	5.75	1.55
☐ 304	Frank Malzone	20.00	9.00	2.50
☐ 305	Brooks Lawrence	12.50	5.75	1.55
☐ 306	Curt Roberts	12.50	5.75	1.55
☐ 307	Hoyt Wilhelm	35.00	16.00	4.40
☐ 308	Chuck Harmon	12.50	5.75	1.55
☐ 309	Don Blasingame	15.00	6.75	1.90
☐ 310	Steve Gromek	12.50	5.75	1.55
☐ 311	Hal Naragon	12.50	5.75	1.55
☐ 312	Andy Pafko	14.00	6.25	1.75
☐ 313	Gene Stephens	12.50	5.75	1.55
☐ 314	Hobie Landrith	12.50	5.75	1.55
☐ 315	Milt Bolling	12.50	5.75	1.55
☐ 316	Jerry Coleman	15.00	6.75	1.90
☐ 317	Al Aber	12.50	5.75	1.55
☐ 318	Fred Hatfield	12.50	5.75	1.55
☐ 319	Jack Crimian	12.50	5.75	1.55
☐ 320	Joe Adcock	15.00	6.75	1.90
☐ 321	Jim Konstanty	15.00	6.75	1.90
☐ 322	Karl Olson	12.50	5.75	1.55
☐ 323	Willard Schmidt	12.50	5.75	1.55
☐ 324	Rocky Bridges	12.50	5.75	1.55
☐ 325	Don Liddle	12.50	5.75	1.55
☐ 326	Connie Johnson	12.50	5.75	1.55
☐ 327	Bob Wiesler	12.50	5.75	1.55
☐ 328	Preston Ward	12.50	5.75	1.55
☐ 329	Lou Berberet	12.50	5.75	1.55
☐ 330	Jim Busby	12.50	5.75	1.55

☐	331 Dick Hall	12.50	5.75	1.55
☐	332 Don Larsen	45.00	20.00	5.75
☐	333 Rube Walker	12.50	5.75	1.55
☐	334 Bob Miller	12.50	5.75	1.55
☐	335 Don Hoak	14.00	6.25	1.75
☐	336 Ellis Kinder	12.50	5.75	1.55
☐	337 Bobby Morgan	12.50	5.75	1.55
☐	338 Jim Delsing	12.50	5.75	1.55
☐	339 Rance Pless	12.50	5.75	1.55
☐	340 Mickey McDermott	50.00	10.00	3.00
☐	NNO Checklist 1/3	300.00	45.00	15.00
☐	NNO Checklist 2/4	300.00	45.00	15.00

1957 Topps

The cards in this 407-card set measure 2 1/2" by 3 1/2". In 1957, Topps returned to the vertical obverse, adopted what we now call the standard card size, and used a large, uncluttered color photo for the first time since 1952. Cards in the series 265 to 352 and the unnumbered checklist cards are scarcer than other cards in the set. However within this scarce series (265-352) there are 22 cards which were printed in double the quantity of the other cards in the series; these 22 double prints are indicated by DP in the checklist below. The first star combination cards, cards 400 and 407, are quite popular with collectors. They feature the big stars of the previous season's World Series teams, the Dodgers (Furillo, Hodges, Campanella, and Snider) and Yankees (Berra and Mantle). The complete set price below does not include the unnumbered checklist cards. The key rookies in this set are Jim Bunning, Rocky Colavito, Don Drysdale, Whitey Herzog,

Tony Kubek, Bobby Richardson, Brooks Robinson, and Frank Robinson.

	NRMT	VG-E	GOOD
COMPLETE SET (407)	7700.	3500.	950.00
COMMON PLAYER (1-88)	8.50	3.80	1.05
COMMON PLAYER (89-176)	7.50	3.40	.95
COMMON PLAYER (177-264)	6.50	2.90	.80
COMMON PLAYER (265-352)	22.00	10.00	2.80
COMMON PLAYER (353-407)	7.00	3.10	.85

☐	1 Ted Williams	450.00	135.00	45.00
☐	2 Yogi Berra	150.00	70.00	19.00
☐	3 Dale Long	9.50	4.30	1.20
☐	4 Johnny Logan	10.00	4.50	1.25
☐	5 Sal Maglie	11.00	4.90	1.40
☐	6 Hector Lopez	9.50	4.30	1.20
☐	7 Luis Aparicio	45.00	20.00	5.75
☐	8 Don Mossi	9.50	4.30	1.20
☐	9 Johnny Temple	9.50	4.30	1.20
☐	10 Willie Mays	250.00	115.00	31.00
☐	11 George Zuverink	8.50	3.80	1.05
☐	12 Dick Groat	11.00	4.90	1.40
☐	13 Wally Burnette	8.50	3.80	1.05
☐	14 Bob Nieman	8.50	3.80	1.05
☐	15 Robin Roberts	27.00	12.00	3.40
☐	16 Walt Moryn	8.50	3.80	1.05
☐	17 Billy Gardner	8.50	3.80	1.05
☐	18 Don Drysdale	225.00	100.00	28.00
☐	19 Bob Wilson	8.50	3.80	1.05
☐	20 Hank Aaron UER	250.00	115.00	31.00
	(Reverse negative photo on front)			
☐	21 Frank Sullivan	8.50	3.80	1.05
☐	22 Jerry Snyder UER	8.50	3.80	1.05
	(Photo actually Ed Fitzgerald)			
☐	23 Sherm Lollar	9.50	4.30	1.20
☐	24 Bill Mazeroski	70.00	32.00	8.75
☐	25 Whitey Ford	65.00	29.00	8.25
☐	26 Bob Boyd	8.50	3.80	1.05
☐	27 Ted Kazanski	8.50	3.80	1.05
☐	28 Gene Conley	9.50	4.30	1.20
☐	29 Whitey Herzog	35.00	16.00	4.40
☐	30 Pee Wee Reese	70.00	32.00	8.75
☐	31 Ron Northey	8.50	3.80	1.05
☐	32 Hershell Freeman	8.50	3.80	1.05
☐	33 Jim Small	8.50	3.80	1.05
☐	34 Tom Sturdivant	8.50	3.80	1.05
☐	35 Frank Robinson	300.00	135.00	38.00
☐	36 Bob Grim	8.50	3.80	1.05
☐	37 Frank Torre	9.50	4.30	1.20
☐	38 Nellie Fox	25.00	11.50	3.10
☐	39 Al Worthington	8.50	3.80	1.05
☐	40 Early Wynn	25.00	11.50	3.10
☐	41 Hal W. Smith	8.50	3.80	1.05
☐	42 Dee Fondy	8.50	3.80	1.05

☐ 43	Connie Johnson	8.50	3.80	1.05
☐ 44	Joe DeMaestri	8.50	3.80	1.05
☐ 45	Carl Furillo	18.00	8.00	2.30
☐ 46	Robert J. Miller	8.50	3.80	1.05
☐ 47	Don Blasingame	8.50	3.80	1.05
☐ 48	Bill Bruton	10.00	4.50	1.25
☐ 49	Daryl Spencer	8.50	3.80	1.05
☐ 50	Herb Score	18.00	8.00	2.30
☐ 51	Clint Courtney	8.50	3.80	1.05
☐ 52	Lee Walls	8.50	3.80	1.05
☐ 53	Clem Labine	11.00	4.90	1.40
☐ 54	Elmer Valo	8.50	3.80	1.05
☐ 55	Ernie Banks	120.00	55.00	15.00
☐ 56	Dave Sisler	8.50	3.80	1.05
☐ 57	Jim Lemon	9.50	4.30	1.20
☐ 58	Ruben Gomez	8.50	3.80	1.05
☐ 59	Dick Williams	10.50	4.70	1.30
☐ 60	Billy Hoeft	9.50	4.30	1.20
☐ 61	James(Dusty) Rhodes	9.50	4.30	1.20
☐ 62	Billy Martin	50.00	23.00	6.25
☐ 63	Ike Delock	8.50	3.80	1.05
☐ 64	Pete Runnels	9.50	4.30	1.20
☐ 65	Wally Moon	9.50	4.30	1.20
☐ 66	Brooks Lawrence	8.50	3.80	1.05
☐ 67	Chico Carrasquel	8.50	3.80	1.05
☐ 68	Ray Crone	8.50	3.80	1.05
☐ 69	Roy McMillan	9.50	4.30	1.20
☐ 70	Richie Ashburn	25.00	11.50	3.10
☐ 71	Murry Dickson	8.50	3.80	1.05
☐ 72	Bill Tuttle	8.50	3.80	1.05
☐ 73	George Crowe	8.50	3.80	1.05
☐ 74	Vito Valentinetti	8.50	3.80	1.05
☐ 75	Jim Piersall	12.50	5.75	1.55
☐ 76	Roberto Clemente	250.00	115.00	31.00
☐ 77	Paul Foytack	8.50	3.80	1.05
☐ 78	Vic Wertz	9.50	4.30	1.20
☐ 79	Lindy McDaniel	12.50	5.75	1.55
☐ 80	Gil Hodges	50.00	23.00	6.25
☐ 81	Herman Wehmeier	8.50	3.80	1.05
☐ 82	Elston Howard	20.00	9.00	2.50
☐ 83	Lou Skizas	8.50	3.80	1.05
☐ 84	Moe Drabowsky	9.50	4.30	1.20
☐ 85	Larry Doby	11.00	4.90	1.40
☐ 86	Bill Sarni	8.50	3.80	1.05
☐ 87	Tom Gorman	8.50	3.80	1.05
☐ 88	Harvey Kuenn	12.00	5.50	1.50
☐ 89	Roy Sievers	8.50	3.80	1.05
☐ 90	Warren Spahn	75.00	34.00	9.50
☐ 91	Mack Burk	7.50	3.40	.95
☐ 92	Mickey Vernon	8.50	3.80	1.05
☐ 93	Hal Jeffcoat	7.50	3.40	.95
☐ 94	Bobby Del Greco	7.50	3.40	.95
☐ 95	Mickey Mantle	1100.00	325.00	110.00
☐ 96	Hank Aguirre	7.50	3.40	.95
☐ 97	New York Yankees	60.00	27.00	7.50
	Team Card			
☐ 98	Alvin Dark	9.00	4.00	1.15
☐ 99	Bob Keegan	7.50	3.40	.95
☐ 100	League Presidents	12.00	5.50	1.50
	Warren Giles			
	Will Harridge			
☐ 101	Chuck Stobbs	7.50	3.40	.95
☐ 102	Ray Boone	8.50	3.80	1.05
☐ 103	Joe Nuxhall	8.50	3.80	1.05
☐ 104	Hank Foiles	7.50	3.40	.95
☐ 105	Johnny Antonelli	8.50	3.80	1.05
☐ 106	Ray Moore	7.50	3.40	.95
☐ 107	Jim Rivera	7.50	3.40	.95
☐ 108	Tommy Byrne	7.50	3.40	.95
☐ 109	Hank Thompson	8.50	3.80	1.05
☐ 110	Bill Virdon	9.00	4.00	1.15
☐ 111	Hal R. Smith	7.50	3.40	.95
☐ 112	Tom Brewer	7.50	3.40	.95
☐ 113	Wilmer Mizell	8.50	3.80	1.05
☐ 114	Milwaukee Braves	20.00	9.00	2.50
	Team Card			
☐ 115	Jim Gilliam	12.50	5.75	1.55
☐ 116	Mike Fornieles	7.50	3.40	.95
☐ 117	Joe Adcock	9.00	4.00	1.15
☐ 118	Bob Porterfield	7.50	3.40	.95
☐ 119	Stan Lopata	7.50	3.40	.95
☐ 120	Bob Lemon	25.00	11.50	3.10
☐ 121	Clete Boyer	25.00	11.50	3.10
☐ 122	Ken Boyer	15.00	6.75	1.90
☐ 123	Steve Ridzik	7.50	3.40	.95
☐ 124	Dave Philley	7.50	3.40	.95
☐ 125	Al Kaline	110.00	50.00	14.00
☐ 126	Bob Wiesler	7.50	3.40	.95
☐ 127	Bob Buhl	8.50	3.80	1.05
☐ 128	Ed Bailey	8.50	3.80	1.05
☐ 129	Saul Rogovin	7.50	3.40	.95
☐ 130	Don Newcombe	15.00	6.75	1.90
☐ 131	Milt Bolling	7.50	3.40	.95
☐ 132	Art Ditmar	8.50	3.80	1.05
☐ 133	Del Crandall	8.50	3.80	1.05
☐ 134	Don Kaiser	7.50	3.40	.95
☐ 135	Bill Skowron	15.00	6.75	1.90
☐ 136	Jim Hegan	8.50	3.80	1.05
☐ 137	Bob Rush	7.50	3.40	.95
☐ 138	Minnie Minoso	15.00	6.75	1.90
☐ 139	Lou Kretlow	7.50	3.40	.95
☐ 140	Frank Thomas	8.50	3.80	1.05
☐ 141	Al Aber	7.50	3.40	.95
☐ 142	Charley Thompson	7.50	3.40	.95
☐ 143	Andy Pafko	8.50	3.80	1.05
☐ 144	Ray Narleski	7.50	3.40	.95
☐ 145	Al Smith	7.50	3.40	.95
☐ 146	Don Ferrarese	7.50	3.40	.95
☐ 147	Al Walker	7.50	3.40	.95
☐ 148	Don Mueller	8.50	3.80	1.05
☐ 149	Bob Kennedy	8.50	3.80	1.05
☐ 150	Bob Friend	8.50	3.80	1.05
☐ 151	Willie Miranda	7.50	3.40	.95
☐ 152	Jack Harshman	7.50	3.40	.95

☐	153	Karl Olson 7.50	3.40	.95
☐	154	Red Schoendienst......25.00	11.50	3.10
☐	155	Jim Brosnan 8.50	3.80	1.05
☐	156	Gus Triandos 8.50	3.80	1.05
☐	157	Wally Post...................8.50	3.80	1.05
☐	158	Curt Simmons 8.50	3.80	1.05
☐	159	Solly Drake 7.50	3.40	.95
☐	160	Billy Pierce 10.00	4.50	1.25
☐	161	Pittsburgh Pirates 15.00	6.75	1.90
		Team Card		
☐	162	Jack Meyer 7.50	3.40	.95
☐	163	Sammy White 7.50	3.40	.95
☐	164	Tommy Carroll 7.50	3.40	.95
☐	165	Ted Kluszewski..........36.00	16.00	4.50
☐	166	Roy Face 9.50	4.30	1.20
☐	167	Vic Power 8.50	3.80	1.05
☐	168	Frank Lary 8.50	3.80	1.05
☐	169	Herb Plews 7.50	3.40	.95
☐	170	Duke Snider 110.00	50.00	14.00
☐	171	Boston Red Sox 15.00	6.75	1.90
		Team Card		
☐	172	Gene Woodling 8.50	3.80	1.05
☐	173	Roger Craig...............15.00	6.75	1.90
☐	174	Willie Jones 7.50	3.40	.95
☐	175	Don Larsen 20.00	9.00	2.50
☐	176A	Gene Baker ERR 350.00	160.00	45.00
		(Misspelled Bakep		
		on card back)		
☐	176B	Gene Baker COR 7.50	3.40	.95
☐	177	Eddie Yost...................7.50	3.40	.95
☐	178	Don Bessent................6.50	2.90	.80
☐	179	Ernie Oravetz..............6.50	2.90	.80
☐	180	Gus Bell 7.50	3.40	.95
☐	181	Dick Donovan 6.50	2.90	.80
☐	182	Hobie Landrith.............6.50	2.90	.80
☐	183	Chicago Cubs.............15.00	6.75	1.90
		Team Card		
☐	184	Tito Francona...............9.00	4.00	1.15
☐	185	Johnny Kucks 6.50	2.90	.80
☐	186	Jim King 6.50	2.90	.80
☐	187	Virgil Trucks 7.50	3.40	.95
☐	188	Felix Mantilla...............8.50	3.80	1.05
☐	189	Willard Nixon 6.50	2.90	.80
☐	190	Randy Jackson.............6.50	2.90	.80
☐	191	Joe Margoneri..............6.50	2.90	.80
☐	192	Jerry Coleman..............7.50	3.40	.95
☐	193	Del Rice 6.50	2.90	.80
☐	194	Hal Brown 6.50	2.90	.80
☐	195	Bobby Avila 6.50	2.90	.80
☐	196	Larry Jackson...............7.50	3.40	.95
☐	197	Hank Sauer 7.50	3.40	.95
☐	198	Detroit Tigers 15.00	6.75	1.90
		Team Card		
☐	199	Vern Law.....................7.50	3.40	.95
☐	200	Gil McDougald 15.00	6.75	1.90
☐	201	Sandy Amoros 8.50	3.80	1.05
☐	202	Dick Gernert................6.50	2.90	.80
☐	203	Hoyt Wilhelm 22.00	10.00	2.80
☐	204	Kansas City Athletics .15.00	6.75	1.90
		Team Card		
☐	205	Charlie Maxwell............7.50	3.40	.95
☐	206	Willard Schmidt 6.50	2.90	.80
☐	207	Gordon(Billy) Hunter....6.50	2.90	.80
☐	208	Lou Burdette 10.00	4.50	1.25
☐	209	Bob Skinner 7.50	3.40	.95
☐	210	Roy Campanella 110.00	50.00	14.00
☐	211	Camilo Pascual 7.50	3.40	.95
☐	212	Rocky Colavito 135.00	60.00	17.00
☐	213	Les Moss 6.50	2.90	.80
☐	214	Philadelphia Phillies ...15.00	6.75	1.90
		Team Card		
☐	215	Enos Slaughter...........27.00	12.00	3.40
☐	216	Marv Grissom 6.50	2.90	.80
☐	217	Gene Stephens.............6.50	2.90	.80
☐	218	Ray Jablonski 6.50	2.90	.80
☐	219	Tom Acker 6.50	2.90	.80
☐	220	Jackie Jensen.............11.00	4.90	1.40
☐	221	Dixie Howell 6.50	2.90	.80
☐	222	Alex Grammas 6.50	2.90	.80
☐	223	Frank House.................6.50	2.90	.80
☐	224	Marv Blaylock 6.50	2.90	.80
☐	225	Harry Simpson 6.50	2.90	.80
☐	226	Preston Ward 6.50	2.90	.80
☐	227	Gerry Staley 6.50	2.90	.80
☐	228	Smoky Burgess UER......8.50	3.80	1.05
		(Misspelled Smokey		
		on card back)		
☐	229	George Susce 6.50	2.90	.80
☐	230	George Kell 22.00	10.00	2.80
☐	231	Solly Hemus 6.50	2.90	.80
☐	232	Whitey Lockman 7.50	3.40	.95
☐	233	Art Fowler 6.50	2.90	.80
☐	234	Dick Cole 6.50	2.90	.80
☐	235	Tom Poholsky...............6.50	2.90	.80
☐	236	Joe Ginsberg...............6.50	2.90	.80
☐	237	Foster Castleman 6.50	2.90	.80
☐	238	Eddie Robinson............6.50	2.90	.80
☐	239	Tom Morgan 6.50	2.90	.80
☐	240	Hank Bauer 15.00	6.75	1.90
☐	241	Joe Lonnett.................6.50	2.90	.80
☐	242	Charlie Neal.................8.50	3.80	1.05
☐	243	St. Louis Cardinals 15.00	6.75	1.90
		Team Card		
☐	244	Billy Loes 7.50	3.40	.95
☐	245	Rip Repulski.................6.50	2.90	.80
☐	246	Jose Valdivielso 6.50	2.90	.80
☐	247	Turk Lown....................6.50	2.90	.80
☐	248	Jim Finigan 6.50	2.90	.80
☐	249	Dave Pope....................6.50	2.90	.80
☐	250	Eddie Mathews 45.00	20.00	5.75
☐	251	Baltimore Orioles 15.00	6.75	1.90
		Team Card		
☐	252	Carl Erskine 12.50	5.75	1.55
☐	253	Gus Zernial 7.50	3.40	.95

☐ 254	Ron Negray	6.50	2.90	.80
☐ 255	Charlie Silvera	7.50	3.40	.95
☐ 256	Ron Kline	6.50	2.90	.80
☐ 257	Walt Dropo	6.50	2.90	.80
☐ 258	Steve Gromek	6.50	2.90	.80
☐ 259	Eddie O'Brien	6.50	2.90	.80
☐ 260	Del Ennis	7.50	3.40	.95
☐ 261	Bob Chakales	6.50	2.90	.80
☐ 262	Bobby Thomson	12.00	5.50	1.50
☐ 263	George Strickland	6.50	2.90	.80
☐ 264	Bob Turley	15.00	6.75	1.90
☐ 265	Harvey Haddix DP	15.00	6.75	1.90
☐ 266	Ken Kuhn DP	13.00	5.75	1.65
☐ 267	Danny Kravitz	22.00	10.00	2.80
☐ 268	Jack Collum	22.00	10.00	2.80
☐ 269	Bob Cerv	24.00	11.00	3.00
☐ 270	Washington Senators Team Card	50.00	23.00	6.25
☐ 271	Danny O'Connell DP	13.00	5.75	1.65
☐ 272	Bobby Shantz	30.00	13.50	3.80
☐ 273	Jim Davis	22.00	10.00	2.80
☐ 274	Don Hoak	24.00	11.00	3.00
☐ 275	Cleveland Indians Team Card	50.00	23.00	6.25
☐ 276	Jim Pyburn	22.00	10.00	2.80
☐ 277	Johnny Podres DP	55.00	25.00	7.00
☐ 278	Fred Hatfield DP	13.00	5.75	1.65
☐ 279	Bob Thurman	22.00	10.00	2.80
☐ 280	Alex Kellner	22.00	10.00	2.80
☐ 281	Gail Harris	22.00	10.00	2.80
☐ 282	Jack Dittmer DP	13.00	5.75	1.65
☐ 283	Wes Covington DP	15.00	6.75	1.90
☐ 284	Don Zimmer	30.00	13.50	3.80
☐ 285	Ned Garver	22.00	10.00	2.80
☐ 286	Bobby Richardson	130.00	57.50	16.50
☐ 287	Sam Jones	24.00	11.00	3.00
☐ 288	Ted Lepcio	22.00	10.00	2.80
☐ 289	Jim Bolger DP	13.00	5.75	1.65
☐ 290	Andy Carey DP	15.00	6.75	1.90
☐ 291	Windy McCall	22.00	10.00	2.80
☐ 292	Billy Klaus	22.00	10.00	2.80
☐ 293	Ted Abernathy	22.00	10.00	2.80
☐ 294	Rocky Bridges DP	13.00	5.75	1.65
☐ 295	Joe Collins DP	15.00	6.75	1.90
☐ 296	Johnny Klippstein	22.00	10.00	2.80
☐ 297	Jack Crimian	22.00	10.00	2.80
☐ 298	Irv Noren DP	13.00	5.75	1.65
☐ 299	Chuck Harmon	22.00	10.00	2.80
☐ 300	Mike Garcia	24.00	11.00	3.00
☐ 301	Sammy Esposito DP	13.00	5.75	1.65
☐ 302	Sandy Koufax DP	360.00	160.00	45.00
☐ 303	Billy Goodman	24.00	11.00	3.00
☐ 304	Joe Cunningham	24.00	11.00	3.00
☐ 305	Chico Fernandez	22.00	10.00	2.80
☐ 306	Darrell Johnson DP	15.00	6.75	1.90
☐ 307	Jack D. Phillips DP	13.00	5.75	1.65
☐ 308	Dick Hall	22.00	10.00	2.80
☐ 309	Jim Busby DP	13.00	5.75	1.65
☐ 310	Max Surkont DP	13.00	5.75	1.65
☐ 311	Al Pilarcik DP	13.00	5.75	1.65
☐ 312	Tony Kubek DP	125.00	57.50	15.50
☐ 313	Mel Parnell	24.00	11.00	3.00
☐ 314	Ed Bouchee DP	13.00	5.75	1.65
☐ 315	Lou Berberet DP	13.00	5.75	1.65
☐ 316	Billy O'Dell	22.00	10.00	2.80
☐ 317	New York Giants Team Card	60.00	27.00	7.50
☐ 318	Mickey McDermott	22.00	10.00	2.80
☐ 319	Gino Cimoli	25.00	11.50	3.10
☐ 320	Neil Chrisley	22.00	10.00	2.80
☐ 321	John(Red) Murff	22.00	10.00	2.80
☐ 322	Cincinnati Reds Team Card	60.00	27.00	7.50
☐ 323	Wes Westrum	24.00	11.00	3.00
☐ 324	Brooklyn Dodgers Team Card	120.00	55.00	15.00
☐ 325	Frank Bolling	22.00	10.00	2.80
☐ 326	Pedro Ramos	22.00	10.00	2.80
☐ 327	Jim Pendleton	22.00	10.00	2.80
☐ 328	Brooks Robinson	425.00	190.00	52.50
☐ 329	Chicago White Sox Team Card	50.00	23.00	6.25
☐ 330	Jim Wilson	22.00	10.00	2.80
☐ 331	Ray Katt	22.00	10.00	2.80
☐ 332	Bob Bowman	22.00	10.00	2.80
☐ 333	Ernie Johnson	24.00	11.00	3.00
☐ 334	Jerry Schoonmaker	22.00	10.00	2.80
☐ 335	Granny Hamner	22.00	10.00	2.80
☐ 336	Haywood Sullivan	25.00	11.50	3.10
☐ 337	Rene Valdes	22.00	10.00	2.80
☐ 338	Jim Bunning	150.00	70.00	19.00
☐ 339	Bob Speake	22.00	10.00	2.80
☐ 340	Bill Wight	22.00	10.00	2.80
☐ 341	Don Gross	22.00	10.00	2.80
☐ 342	Gene Mauch	25.00	11.50	3.10
☐ 343	Taylor Phillips	22.00	10.00	2.80
☐ 344	Paul LaPalme	22.00	10.00	2.80
☐ 345	Paul Smith	22.00	10.00	2.80
☐ 346	Dick Littlefield	22.00	10.00	2.80
☐ 347	Hal Naragon	22.00	10.00	2.80
☐ 348	Jim Hearn	22.00	10.00	2.80
☐ 349	Nellie King	22.00	10.00	2.80
☐ 350	Eddie Miksis	22.00	10.00	2.80
☐ 351	Dave Hillman	22.00	10.00	2.80
☐ 352	Ellis Kinder	22.00	10.00	2.80
☐ 353	Cal Neeman	7.00	3.10	.85
☐ 354	W. (Rip) Coleman	7.00	3.10	.85
☐ 355	Frank Malzone	9.00	4.00	1.15
☐ 356	Faye Throneberry	7.00	3.10	.85
☐ 357	Earl Torgeson	7.00	3.10	.85
☐ 358	Jerry Lynch	8.00	3.60	1.00
☐ 359	Tom Cheney	8.00	3.60	1.00
☐ 360	Johnny Groth	7.00	3.10	.85
☐ 361	Curt Barclay	7.00	3.10	.85

☐ 362	Roman Mejias	8.00	3.60	1.00
☐ 363	Eddie Kasko	7.00	3.10	.85
☐ 364	Cal McLish	8.00	3.60	1.00
☐ 365	Ozzie Virgil	7.00	3.10	.85
☐ 366	Ken Lehman	7.00	3.10	.85
☐ 367	Ed Fitzgerald	7.00	3.10	.85
☐ 368	Bob Purkey	7.00	3.10	.85
☐ 369	Milt Graff	7.00	3.10	.85
☐ 370	Warren Hacker	7.00	3.10	.85
☐ 371	Bob Lennon	7.00	3.10	.85
☐ 372	Norm Zauchin	7.00	3.10	.85
☐ 373	Pete Whisenant	7.00	3.10	.85
☐ 374	Don Cardwell	7.00	3.10	.85
☐ 375	Jim Landis	8.00	3.60	1.00
☐ 376	Don Elston	7.00	3.10	.85
☐ 377	Andre Rodgers	7.00	3.10	.85
☐ 378	Elmer Singleton	7.00	3.10	.85
☐ 379	Don Lee	7.00	3.10	.85
☐ 380	Walker Cooper	7.00	3.10	.85
☐ 381	Dean Stone	7.00	3.10	.85
☐ 382	Jim Brideweser	7.00	3.10	.85
☐ 383	Juan Pizarro	7.00	3.10	.85
☐ 384	Bobby G. Smith	7.00	3.10	.85
☐ 385	Art Houtteman	7.00	3.10	.85
☐ 386	Lyle Luttrell	7.00	3.10	.85
☐ 387	Jack Sanford	9.00	4.00	1.15
☐ 388	Pete Daley	7.00	3.10	.85
☐ 389	Dave Jolly	7.00	3.10	.85
☐ 390	Reno Bertoia	7.00	3.10	.85
☐ 391	Ralph Terry	11.00	4.90	1.40
☐ 392	Chuck Tanner	8.00	3.60	1.00
☐ 393	Raul Sanchez	7.00	3.10	.85
☐ 394	Luis Arroyo	8.00	3.60	1.00
☐ 395	Bubba Phillips	7.00	3.10	.85
☐ 396	Casey Wise	7.00	3.10	.85
☐ 397	Roy Smalley	7.00	3.10	.85
☐ 398	Al Cicotte	8.00	3.60	1.00
☐ 399	Billy Consolo	7.00	3.10	.85
☐ 400	Dodgers' Sluggers	225.00	100.00	28.00
	Carl Furillo			
	Gil Hodges			
	Roy Campanella			
	Duke Snider			
☐ 401	Earl Battey	9.00	4.00	1.15
☐ 402	Jim Pisoni	7.00	3.10	.85
☐ 403	Dick Hyde	7.00	3.10	.85
☐ 404	Harry Anderson	7.00	3.10	.85
☐ 405	Duke Maas	7.00	3.10	.85
☐ 406	Bob Hale	7.00	3.10	.85
☐ 407	Yankee Power Hitters	400.00	180.00	50.00
	Mickey Mantle			
	Yogi Berra			
☐ NNO	Checklist 1/2	250.00	115.00	31.00
☐ NNO	Checklist 2/3	400.00	180.00	50.00
☐ NNO	Checklist 3/4	700.00	325.00	90.00
☐ NNO	Checklist 4/5	900.00	400.00	115.00
☐ NNO	Saturday, May 4th	30.00	13.50	3.80

	Boston Red Sox vs.			
	Cincinnati Redlegs			
	Cleveland Indians vs.			
	New York Giants			
☐ NNO	Saturday, June 22nd	30.00	13.50	3.80
	Brooklyn Dodgers vs.			
	Chicago White Sox			
	St. Louis Cardinals vs.			
	New York Yankees			

1958 Topps

The cards in this 494-card set measure 2 1/2" by 3 1/2". Although the last card is numbered 495, number 145 was not issued, bringing the set total to 494 cards. The 1958 Topps set contains the first Sport Magazine All-Star Selection series (475-495) and expanded use of combination cards. The team cards carried series checklists on back (Milwaukee, Detroit, Baltimore, and Cincinnati are also found with players listed alphabetically). Cards with the scarce yellow name (YL) or team (YT) lettering, as opposed to the common white lettering, are noted in the checklist. In the last series, cards of Stan Musial and Mickey Mantle were triple printed; the cards they replaced (443, 446, 450, and 462) on the printing sheet were hence printed in shorter supply than other cards in the last series and are marked with an SP in the list below. Technically the New York Giants team card (19) is an error as the Giants had already moved to San Francisco. The key rookies in this set are Orlando Cepeda, Curt Flood, Roger Maris, and Vada Pinson.

	NRMT	VG-E	GOOD
COMPLETE SET (494)	5500.00	2500.00	700.00
COMMON PLAYER (1-110)	8.25	3.70	1.05
COMMON PLAYER (111-198) ..	6.00	2.70	.75
COMMON PLAYER (199-352) ..	5.00	2.30	.60
COMMON PLAYER (353-440) ..	4.50	2.00	.55
COMMON PLAYER (441-474) ..	4.25	1.90	.55
COMMON AS (475-495)	4.50	2.00	.55

		NRMT	VG-E	GOOD
☐ 1	Ted Williams	375.00	115.00	38.00
☐ 2A	Bob Lemon	22.00	10.00	2.80
☐ 2B	Bob Lemon YT	45.00	20.00	5.75
☐ 3	Alex Kellner	8.25	3.70	1.05
☐ 4	Hank Foiles	8.25	3.70	1.05
☐ 5	Willie Mays	200.00	90.00	25.00
☐ 6	George Zuverink	8.25	3.70	1.05
☐ 7	Dale Long	9.00	4.00	1.15
☐ 8A	Eddie Kasko	8.25	3.70	1.05
☐ 8B	Eddie Kasko YL	35.00	16.00	4.40
☐ 9	Hank Bauer	13.00	5.75	1.65
☐ 10	Lou Burdette	10.50	4.70	1.30
☐ 11A	Jim Rivera	8.25	3.70	1.05
☐ 11B	Jim Rivera YT	30.00	13.50	3.80
☐ 12	George Crowe	8.25	3.70	1.05
☐ 13A	Billy Hoeft	8.25	3.70	1.05
☐ 13B	Billy Hoeft YL	35.00	16.00	4.40
☐ 14	Rip Repulski	8.25	3.70	1.05
☐ 15	Jim Lemon	9.00	4.00	1.15
☐ 16	Charlie Neal	9.00	4.00	1.15
☐ 17	Felix Mantilla	8.25	3.70	1.05
☐ 18	Frank Sullivan	8.25	3.70	1.05
☐ 19	New York Giants	35.00	16.00	4.40
	Team Card			
	(Checklist on back)			
☐ 20A	Gil McDougald	13.00	5.75	1.65
☐ 20B	Gil McDougald YL	40.00	18.00	5.00
☐ 21	Curt Barclay	8.25	3.70	1.05
☐ 22	Hal Naragon	8.25	3.70	1.05
☐ 23A	Bill Tuttle	8.25	3.70	1.05
☐ 23B	Bill Tuttle YL	35.00	16.00	4.40
☐ 24A	Hobie Landrith	8.25	3.70	1.05
☐ 24B	Hobie Landrith YL	35.00	16.00	4.40
☐ 25	Don Drysdale	80.00	36.00	10.00
☐ 26	Ron Jackson	8.25	3.70	1.05
☐ 27	Bud Freeman	8.25	3.70	1.05
☐ 28	Jim Busby	8.25	3.70	1.05
☐ 29	Ted Lepcio	8.25	3.70	1.05
☐ 30A	Hank Aaron	210.00	95.00	26.00
☐ 30B	Hank Aaron YL	350.00	160.00	45.00
☐ 31	Tex Clevenger	8.25	3.70	1.05
☐ 32A	J.W. Porter	8.25	3.70	1.05
☐ 32B	J.W. Porter YL	35.00	16.00	4.40
☐ 33A	Cal Neeman	8.25	3.70	1.05
☐ 33B	Cal Neeman YT	30.00	13.50	3.80
☐ 34	Bob Thurman	8.25	3.70	1.05
☐ 35A	Don Mossi	9.00	4.00	1.15
☐ 35B	Don Mossi YT	30.00	13.50	3.80
☐ 36	Ted Kazanski	8.25	3.70	1.05
☐ 37	Mike McCormick UER ...	10.00	4.50	1.25
	(Photo actually			
	Ray Monzant)			
☐ 38	Dick Gernert	8.25	3.70	1.05
☐ 39	Bob Martyn	8.25	3.70	1.05
☐ 40	George Kell	16.00	7.25	2.00
☐ 41	Dave Hillman	8.25	3.70	1.05
☐ 42	John Roseboro	16.00	7.25	2.00
☐ 43	Sal Maglie	10.00	4.50	1.25
☐ 44	Washington Senators ...	20.00	9.00	2.50
	Team Card			
	(Checklist on back)			
☐ 45	Dick Groat	10.00	4.50	1.25
☐ 46A	Lou Sleater	8.25	3.70	1.05
☐ 46B	Lou Sleater YL	35.00	16.00	4.40
☐ 47	Roger Maris	450.00	200.00	57.50
☐ 48	Chuck Harmon	8.25	3.70	1.05
☐ 49	Smoky Burgess	9.00	4.00	1.15
☐ 50A	Billy Pierce	10.00	4.50	1.25
☐ 50B	Billy Pierce YT	35.00	16.00	4.40
☐ 51	Del Rice	8.25	3.70	1.05
☐ 52A	Bob Clemente	200.00	90.00	25.00
☐ 52B	Bob Clemente YT	325.00	145.00	40.00
☐ 53A	Morrie Martin	8.25	3.70	1.05
☐ 53B	Morrie Martin YL	35.00	16.00	4.40
☐ 54	Norm Siebern	10.00	4.50	1.25
☐ 55	Chico Carrasquel	8.25	3.70	1.05
☐ 56	Bill Fischer	8.25	3.70	1.05
☐ 57A	Tim Thompson	8.25	3.70	1.05
☐ 57B	Tim Thompson YL	35.00	16.00	4.40
☐ 58A	Art Schult	8.25	3.70	1.05
☐ 58B	Art Schult YT	30.00	13.50	3.80
☐ 59	Dave Sisler	8.25	3.70	1.05
☐ 60A	Del Ennis	9.00	4.00	1.15
☐ 60B	Del Ennis YL	35.00	16.00	4.40
☐ 61A	Darrell Johnson	9.00	4.00	1.15
☐ 61B	Darrell Johnson YL	35.00	16.00	4.40
☐ 62	Joe DeMaestri	8.25	3.70	1.05
☐ 63	Joe Nuxhall	9.00	4.00	1.15
☐ 64	Joe Lonnett	8.25	3.70	1.05
☐ 65A	Von McDaniel	10.00	4.50	1.25
☐ 65B	Von McDaniel YL	36.00	16.00	4.50
☐ 66	Lee Walls	8.25	3.70	1.05
☐ 67	Joe Ginsberg	8.25	3.70	1.05
☐ 68	Daryl Spencer	8.25	3.70	1.05
☐ 69	Wally Burnette	8.25	3.70	1.05
☐ 70A	Al Kaline	90.00	40.00	11.50
☐ 70B	Al Kaline YL	175.00	80.00	22.00
☐ 71	Dodgers Team	45.00	20.00	5.75
	(Checklist on back)			
☐ 72	Bud Byerly	8.25	3.70	1.05
☐ 73	Pete Daley	8.25	3.70	1.05
☐ 74	Roy Face	9.00	4.00	1.15
☐ 75	Gus Bell	9.00	4.00	1.15
☐ 76A	Dick Farrell	9.00	4.00	1.15
☐ 76B	Dick Farrell YT	30.00	13.50	3.80

☐	77A	Don Zimmer	12.50	5.75	1.55
☐	77B	Don Zimmer YT	35.00	16.00	4.40
☐	78A	Ernie Johnson	9.00	4.00	1.15
☐	78B	Ernie Johnson YL	35.00	16.00	4.40
☐	79A	Dick Williams	10.00	4.50	1.25
☐	79B	Dick Williams YT	35.00	16.00	4.40
☐	80	Dick Drott	8.25	3.70	1.05
☐	81A	Steve Boros	10.00	4.50	1.25
☐	81B	Steve Boros YT	35.00	16.00	4.40
☐	82	Ron Kline	8.25	3.70	1.05
☐	83	Bob Hazle	10.00	4.50	1.25
☐	84	Billy O'Dell	8.25	3.70	1.05
☐	85A	Luis Aparicio	26.00	11.50	3.30
☐	85B	Luis Aparicio YT	50.00	23.00	6.25
☐	86	Valmy Thomas	8.25	3.70	1.05
☐	87	Johnny Kucks	8.25	3.70	1.05
☐	88	Duke Snider	75.00	34.00	9.50
☐	89	Billy Klaus	8.25	3.70	1.05
☐	90	Robin Roberts	22.00	10.00	2.80
☐	91	Chuck Tanner	9.00	4.00	1.15
☐	92A	Clint Courtney	8.25	3.70	1.05
☐	92B	Clint Courtney YL	35.00	16.00	4.40
☐	93	Sandy Amoros	9.00	4.00	1.15
☐	94	Bob Skinner	9.00	4.00	1.15
☐	95	Frank Bolling	8.25	3.70	1.05
☐	96	Joe Durham	8.25	3.70	1.05
☐	97A	Larry Jackson	9.00	4.00	1.15
☐	97B	Larry Jackson YL	35.00	16.00	4.40
☐	98A	Billy Hunter	8.25	3.70	1.05
☐	98B	Billy Hunter YL	35.00	16.00	4.40
☐	99	Bobby Adams	8.25	3.70	1.05
☐	100A	Early Wynn	22.00	10.00	2.80
☐	100B	Early Wynn YT	50.00	23.00	6.25
☐	101A	Bobby Richardson	21.00	9.50	2.60
☐	101B	Bobby Richardson YL	45.00	20.00	5.75
☐	102	George Strickland	8.25	3.70	1.05
☐	103	Jerry Lynch	9.00	4.00	1.15
☐	104	Jim Pendleton	8.25	3.70	1.05
☐	105	Billy Gardner	8.25	3.70	1.05
☐	106	Dick Schofield	9.00	4.00	1.15
☐	107	Ossie Virgil	8.25	3.70	1.05
☐	108A	Jim Landis	8.25	3.70	1.05
☐	108B	Jim Landis YT	30.00	13.50	3.80
☐	109	Herb Plews	8.25	3.70	1.05
☐	110	Johnny Logan	9.00	4.00	1.15
☐	111	Stu Miller	8.00	3.60	1.00
☐	112	Gus Zernial	6.50	2.90	.80
☐	113	Jerry Walker	8.00	3.60	1.00
☐	114	Irv Noren	6.50	2.90	.80
☐	115	Jim Bunning	22.00	10.00	2.80
☐	116	Dave Philley	6.00	2.70	.75
☐	117	Frank Torre	6.50	2.90	.80
☐	118	Harvey Haddix	6.50	2.90	.80
☐	119	Harry Chiti	6.00	2.70	.75
☐	120	Johnny Podres	10.00	4.50	1.25
☐	121	Eddie Miksis	6.00	2.70	.75
☐	122	Walt Moryn	6.00	2.70	.75
☐	123	Dick Tomanek	6.00	2.70	.75
☐	124	Bobby Usher	6.00	2.70	.75
☐	125	Alvin Dark	7.50	3.40	.95
☐	126	Stan Palys	6.00	2.70	.75
☐	127	Tom Sturdivant	6.50	2.90	.80
☐	128	Willie Kirkland	6.50	2.90	.80
☐	129	Jim Derrington	6.00	2.70	.75
☐	130	Jackie Jensen	12.00	5.50	1.50
☐	131	Bob Henrich	6.00	2.70	.75
☐	132	Vern Law	6.50	2.90	.80
☐	133	Russ Nixon	7.50	3.40	.95
☐	134	Philadelphia Phillies Team Card (Checklist on back)	14.00	6.25	1.75
☐	135	Mike(Moe) Drabowsky	6.50	2.90	.80
☐	136	Jim Finigan	6.00	2.70	.75
☐	137	Russ Kemmerer	6.00	2.70	.75
☐	138	Earl Torgeson	6.00	2.70	.75
☐	139	George Brunet	6.00	2.70	.75
☐	140	Wes Covington	6.50	2.90	.80
☐	141	Ken Lehman	6.00	2.70	.75
☐	142	Enos Slaughter	25.00	11.50	3.10
☐	143	Billy Muffett	7.50	3.40	.95
☐	144	Bobby Morgan	6.00	2.70	.75
☐	145	Never issued		.00	.00
☐	146	Dick Gray	6.00	2.70	.75
☐	147	Don McMahon	9.00	4.00	1.15
☐	148	Billy Consolo	6.00	2.70	.75
☐	149	Tom Acker	6.00	2.70	.75
☐	150	Mickey Mantle	600.00	275.00	75.00
☐	151	Buddy Pritchard	6.00	2.70	.75
☐	152	Johnny Antonelli	6.50	2.90	.80
☐	153	Les Moss	6.00	2.70	.75
☐	154	Harry Byrd	6.00	2.70	.75
☐	155	Hector Lopez	6.50	2.90	.80
☐	156	Dick Hyde	6.00	2.70	.75
☐	157	Dee Fondy	6.00	2.70	.75
☐	158	Cleveland Indians Team Card (Checklist on back)	14.00	6.25	1.75
☐	159	Taylor Phillips	6.00	2.70	.75
☐	160	Don Hoak	6.50	2.90	.80
☐	161	Don Larsen	12.50	5.75	1.55
☐	162	Gil Hodges	30.00	13.50	3.80
☐	163	Jim Wilson	6.00	2.70	.75
☐	164	Bob Taylor	6.00	2.70	.75
☐	165	Bob Nieman	6.00	2.70	.75
☐	166	Danny O'Connell	6.00	2.70	.75
☐	167	Frank Baumann	6.00	2.70	.75
☐	168	Joe Cunningham	6.50	2.90	.80
☐	169	Ralph Terry	6.50	2.90	.80
☐	170	Vic Wertz	6.50	2.90	.80
☐	171	Harry Anderson	6.00	2.70	.75
☐	172	Don Gross	6.00	2.70	.75
☐	173	Eddie Yost	6.50	2.90	.80
☐	174	Athletics Team (Checklist on back)	14.00	6.25	1.75

☐ 175 Marv Throneberry	12.50	5.75	1.55
☐ 176 Bob Buhl	6.50	2.90	.80
☐ 177 Al Smith	6.00	2.70	.75
☐ 178 Ted Kluszewski	12.50	5.75	1.55
☐ 179 Willie Miranda	6.00	2.70	.75
☐ 180 Lindy McDaniel	6.50	2.90	.80
☐ 181 Willie Jones	6.00	2.70	.75
☐ 182 Joe Caffie	6.00	2.70	.75
☐ 183 Dave Jolly	6.00	2.70	.75
☐ 184 Elvin Tappe	6.00	2.70	.75
☐ 185 Ray Boone	6.50	2.90	.80
☐ 186 Jack Meyer	6.00	2.70	.75
☐ 187 Sandy Koufax	225.00	100.00	28.00
☐ 188 Milt Bolling UER	6.00	2.70	.75
(Photo actually			
Lou Berberet)			
☐ 189 George Susce	6.00	2.70	.75
☐ 190 Red Schoendienst	21.00	9.50	2.60
☐ 191 Art Ceccarelli	6.00	2.70	.75
☐ 192 Milt Graff	6.00	2.70	.75
☐ 193 Jerry Lumpe	7.50	3.40	.95
☐ 194 Roger Craig	10.00	4.50	1.25
☐ 195 Whitey Lockman	6.50	2.90	.80
☐ 196 Mike Garcia	6.50	2.90	.80
☐ 197 Haywood Sullivan	6.50	2.90	.80
☐ 198 Bill Virdon	7.50	3.40	.95
☐ 199 Don Blasingame	5.00	2.30	.60
☐ 200 Bob Keegan	5.00	2.30	.60
☐ 201 Jim Bolger	5.00	2.30	.60
☐ 202 Woody Held	6.50	2.90	.80
☐ 203 Al Walker	5.00	2.30	.60
☐ 204 Leo Kiely	5.00	2.30	.60
☐ 205 Johnny Temple	5.50	2.50	.70
☐ 206 Bob Shaw	6.50	2.90	.80
☐ 207 Solly Hemus	5.00	2.30	.60
☐ 208 Cal McLish	5.00	2.30	.60
☐ 209 Bob Anderson	5.00	2.30	.60
☐ 210 Wally Moon	5.50	2.50	.70
☐ 211 Pete Burnside	5.00	2.30	.60
☐ 212 Bubba Phillips	5.00	2.30	.60
☐ 213 Red Wilson	5.00	2.30	.60
☐ 214 Willard Schmidt	5.00	2.30	.60
☐ 215 Jim Gilliam	10.50	4.70	1.30
☐ 216 St. Louis Cardinals	14.00	6.25	1.75
Team Card			
(Checklist on back)			
☐ 217 Jack Harshman	5.00	2.30	.60
☐ 218 Dick Rand	5.00	2.30	.60
☐ 219 Camilo Pascual	5.50	2.50	.70
☐ 220 Tom Brewer	5.00	2.30	.60
☐ 221 Jerry Kindall	6.50	2.90	.80
☐ 222 Bud Daley	5.00	2.30	.60
☐ 223 Andy Pafko	5.50	2.50	.70
☐ 224 Bob Grim	5.50	2.50	.70
☐ 225 Billy Goodman	5.50	2.50	.70
☐ 226 Bob Smith	5.00	2.30	.60
☐ 227 Gene Stephens	5.00	2.30	.60
☐ 228 Duke Maas	5.00	2.30	.60
☐ 229 Frank Zupo	5.00	2.30	.60
☐ 230 Richie Ashburn	18.00	8.00	2.30
☐ 231 Lloyd Merritt	5.00	2.30	.60
☐ 232 Reno Bertoia	5.00	2.30	.60
☐ 233 Mickey Vernon	5.50	2.50	.70
☐ 234 Carl Sawatski	5.00	2.30	.60
☐ 235 Tom Gorman	5.00	2.30	.60
☐ 236 Ed Fitzgerald	5.00	2.30	.60
☐ 237 Bill Wight	5.00	2.30	.60
☐ 238 Bill Mazeroski	16.00	7.25	2.00
☐ 239 Chuck Stobbs	5.00	2.30	.60
☐ 240 Bill Skowron	13.00	5.75	1.65
☐ 241 Dick Littlefield	5.00	2.30	.60
☐ 242 Johnny Klippstein	5.00	2.30	.60
☐ 243 Larry Raines	5.00	2.30	.60
☐ 244 Don Demeter	5.00	2.30	.60
☐ 245 Frank Lary	5.50	2.50	.70
☐ 246 New York Yankees	50.00	23.00	6.25
Team Card			
(Checklist on back)			
☐ 247 Casey Wise	5.00	2.30	.60
☐ 248 Herman Wehmeier	5.00	2.30	.60
☐ 249 Ray Moore	5.00	2.30	.60
☐ 250 Roy Sievers	5.50	2.50	.70
☐ 251 Warren Hacker	5.00	2.30	.60
☐ 252 Bob Trowbridge	5.00	2.30	.60
☐ 253 Don Mueller	5.50	2.50	.70
☐ 254 Alex Grammas	5.00	2.30	.60
☐ 255 Bob Turley	10.00	4.50	1.25
☐ 256 Chicago White Sox	14.00	6.25	1.75
Team Card			
(Checklist on back)			
☐ 257 Hal Smith	5.00	2.30	.60
☐ 258 Carl Erskine	10.00	4.50	1.25
☐ 259 Al Pilarcik	5.00	2.30	.60
☐ 260 Frank Malzone	5.50	2.50	.70
☐ 261 Turk Lown	5.00	2.30	.60
☐ 262 Johnny Groth	5.00	2.30	.60
☐ 263 Eddie Bressoud	5.50	2.50	.70
☐ 264 Jack Sanford	5.50	2.50	.70
☐ 265 Pete Runnels	5.50	2.50	.70
☐ 266 Connie Johnson	5.00	2.30	.60
☐ 267 Sherm Lollar	5.50	2.50	.70
☐ 268 Granny Hamner	5.00	2.30	.60
☐ 269 Paul Smith	5.00	2.30	.60
☐ 270 Warren Spahn	60.00	27.00	7.50
☐ 271 Billy Martin	21.00	9.50	2.60
☐ 272 Ray Crone	5.00	2.30	.60
☐ 273 Hal Smith	5.00	2.30	.60
☐ 274 Rocky Bridges	5.00	2.30	.60
☐ 275 Elston Howard	15.00	6.75	1.90
☐ 276 Bobby Avila	5.50	2.50	.70
☐ 277 Virgil Trucks	5.50	2.50	.70
☐ 278 Mack Burk	5.00	2.30	.60
☐ 279 Bob Boyd	5.00	2.30	.60
☐ 280 Jim Piersall	7.50	3.40	.95

☐ 281	Sammy Taylor	5.00	2.30	.60
☐ 282	Paul Foytack	5.00	2.30	.60
☐ 283	Ray Shearer	5.00	2.30	.60
☐ 284	Ray Katt	5.00	2.30	.60
☐ 285	Frank Robinson	110.00	50.00	14.00
☐ 286	Gino Cimoli	5.00	2.30	.60
☐ 287	Sam Jones	5.50	2.50	.70
☐ 288	Harmon Killebrew	95.00	42.50	12.00
☐ 289	Series Hurling Rivals	6.50	2.90	.80
	Lou Burdette			
	Bobby Shantz			
☐ 290	Dick Donovan	5.00	2.30	.60
☐ 291	Don Landrum	5.00	2.30	.60
☐ 292	Ned Garver	5.00	2.30	.60
☐ 293	Gene Freese	5.00	2.30	.60
☐ 294	Hal Jeffcoat	5.00	2.30	.60
☐ 295	Minnie Minoso	10.00	4.50	1.25
☐ 296	Ryne Duren	13.50	6.00	1.70
☐ 297	Don Buddin	5.00	2.30	.60
☐ 298	Jim Hearn	5.00	2.30	.60
☐ 299	Harry Simpson	5.00	2.30	.60
☐ 300	League Presidents	8.50	3.80	1.05
	Will Harridge			
	Warren Giles			
☐ 301	Randy Jackson	5.00	2.30	.60
☐ 302	Mike Baxes	5.00	2.30	.60
☐ 303	Neil Chrisley	5.00	2.30	.60
☐ 304	Tigers' Big Bats	17.00	7.75	2.10
	Harvey Kuenn			
	Al Kaline			
☐ 305	Clem Labine	5.50	2.50	.70
☐ 306	Whammy Douglas	5.00	2.30	.60
☐ 307	Brooks Robinson	125.00	57.50	15.50
☐ 308	Paul Giel	5.50	2.50	.70
☐ 309	Gail Harris	5.00	2.30	.60
☐ 310	Ernie Banks	100.00	45.00	12.50
☐ 311	Bob Purkey	5.00	2.30	.60
☐ 312	Boston Red Sox	14.00	6.25	1.75
	Team Card			
	(Checklist on back)			
☐ 313	Bob Rush	5.00	2.30	.60
☐ 314	Dodgers' Boss and	25.00	11.50	3.10
	Power: Duke Snider			
	Walt Alston MG			
☐ 315	Bob Friend	5.50	2.50	.70
☐ 316	Tito Francona	5.50	2.50	.70
☐ 317	Albie Pearson	5.50	2.50	.70
☐ 318	Frank House	5.00	2.30	.60
☐ 319	Lou Skizas	5.00	2.30	.60
☐ 320	Whitey Ford	50.00	23.00	6.25
☐ 321	Sluggers Supreme	45.00	20.00	5.75
	Ted Kluszewski			
	Ted Williams			
☐ 322	Harding Peterson	5.50	2.50	.70
☐ 323	Elmer Valo	5.00	2.30	.60
☐ 324	Hoyt Wilhelm	20.00	9.00	2.50
☐ 325	Joe Adcock	7.00	3.10	.85
☐ 326	Bob Miller	5.00	2.30	.60
☐ 327	Chicago Cubs	14.00	6.25	1.75
	Team Card			
	(Checklist on back)			
☐ 328	Ike Delock	5.00	2.30	.60
☐ 329	Bob Cerv	5.50	2.50	.70
☐ 330	Ed Bailey	5.50	2.50	.70
☐ 331	Pedro Ramos	5.00	2.30	.60
☐ 332	Jim King	5.00	2.30	.60
☐ 333	Andy Carey	5.50	2.50	.70
☐ 334	Mound Aces	5.50	2.50	.70
	Bob Friend			
	Billy Pierce			
☐ 335	Ruben Gomez	5.00	2.30	.60
☐ 336	Bert Hamric	5.00	2.30	.60
☐ 337	Hank Aguirre	5.00	2.30	.60
☐ 338	Walt Dropo	5.50	2.50	.70
☐ 339	Fred Hatfield	5.00	2.30	.60
☐ 340	Don Newcombe	10.00	4.50	1.25
☐ 341	Pittsburgh Pirates	14.00	6.25	1.75
	Team Card			
	(Checklist on back)			
☐ 342	Jim Brosnan	5.50	2.50	.70
☐ 343	Orlando Cepeda	80.00	36.00	10.00
☐ 344	Bob Porterfield	5.00	2.30	.60
☐ 345	Jim Hegan	5.50	2.50	.70
☐ 346	Steve Bilko	5.00	2.30	.60
☐ 347	Don Rudolph	5.00	2.30	.60
☐ 348	Chico Fernandez	5.00	2.30	.60
☐ 349	Murry Dickson	5.00	2.30	.60
☐ 350	Ken Boyer	13.00	5.75	1.65
☐ 351	Braves Fence Busters	30.00	13.50	3.80
	Del Crandall			
	Eddie Mathews			
	Hank Aaron			
	Joe Adcock			
☐ 352	Herb Score	8.50	3.80	1.05
☐ 353	Stan Lopata	4.50	2.00	.55
☐ 354	Art Ditmar	5.00	2.30	.60
☐ 355	Bill Bruton	5.00	2.30	.60
☐ 356	Bob Malkmus	4.50	2.00	.55
☐ 357	Danny McDevitt	4.50	2.00	.55
☐ 358	Gene Baker	4.50	2.00	.55
☐ 359	Billy Loes	5.00	2.30	.60
☐ 360	Roy McMillan	5.00	2.30	.60
☐ 361	Mike Fornieles	4.50	2.00	.55
☐ 362	Ray Jablonski	4.50	2.00	.55
☐ 363	Don Elston	4.50	2.00	.55
☐ 364	Earl Battey	4.50	2.00	.55
☐ 365	Tom Morgan	4.50	2.00	.55
☐ 366	Gene Green	4.50	2.00	.55
☐ 367	Jack Urban	4.50	2.00	.55
☐ 368	Rocky Colavito	35.00	16.00	4.40
☐ 369	Ralph Lumenti	4.50	2.00	.55
☐ 370	Yogi Berra	100.00	45.00	12.50
☐ 371	Marty Keough	4.50	2.00	.55
☐ 372	Don Cardwell	4.50	2.00	.55

☐ 373	Joe Pignatano............4.50	2.00	.55
☐ 374	Brooks Lawrence 4.50	2.00	.55
☐ 375	Pee Wee Reese 55.00	25.00	7.00
☐ 376	Charley Rabe.............4.50	2.00	.55
☐ 377A	Milwaukee Braves....14.00	6.25	1.75
	Team Card		
	(Alphabetical)		
☐ 377B	Milwaukee Team.......85.00	38.00	10.50
	numerical checklist		
☐ 378	Hank Sauer................5.00	2.30	.60
☐ 379	Ray Herbert...............4.50	2.00	.55
☐ 380	Charlie Maxwell.........5.00	2.30	.60
☐ 381	Hal Brown.................4.50	2.00	.55
☐ 382	Al Cicotte.................4.50	2.00	.55
☐ 383	Lou Berberet..............4.50	2.00	.55
☐ 384	John Goryl.................4.50	2.00	.55
☐ 385	Wilmer Mizell.............5.00	2.30	.60
☐ 386	Birdie's Sluggers.......10.00	4.50	1.25
	Ed Bailey		
	Birdie Tebbetts MG		
	Frank Robinson		
☐ 387	Wally Post.................5.00	2.30	.60
☐ 388	Billy Moran................4.50	2.00	.55
☐ 389	Bill Taylor.................4.50	2.00	.55
☐ 390	Del Crandall...............5.00	2.30	.60
☐ 391	Dave Melton..............4.50	2.00	.55
☐ 392	Bennie Daniels...........4.50	2.00	.55
☐ 393	Tony Kubek..............20.00	9.00	2.50
☐ 394	Jim Grant..................7.00	3.10	.85
☐ 395	Willard Nixon.............4.50	2.00	.55
☐ 396	Dutch Dotterer...........4.50	2.00	.55
☐ 397A	Detroit Tigers...........14.00	6.25	1.75
	Team Card		
	(Alphabetical)		
☐ 397B	Detroit Team.............85.00	38.00	10.50
	numerical checklist		
☐ 398	Gene Woodling 5.00	2.30	.60
☐ 399	Marv Grissom.............4.50	2.00	.55
☐ 400	Nellie Fox...............15.00	6.75	1.90
☐ 401	Don Bessent...............4.50	2.00	.55
☐ 402	Bobby Gene Smith......4.50	2.00	.55
☐ 403	Steve Korcheck...........4.50	2.00	.55
☐ 404	Curt Simmons............5.00	2.30	.60
☐ 405	Ken Aspromonte 4.50	2.00	.55
☐ 406	Vic Power..................5.00	2.30	.60
☐ 407	Carlton Willey.............5.00	2.30	.60
☐ 408A	Baltimore Orioles.......14.00	6.25	1.75
	Team Card		
	(Alphabetical)		
☐ 408B	Baltimore Team 85.00	38.00	10.50
	numerical checklist		
☐ 409	Frank Thomas.............5.00	2.30	.60
☐ 410	Murray Wall...............4.50	2.00	.55
☐ 411	Tony Taylor................8.00	3.60	1.00
☐ 412	Gerry Staley...............4.50	2.00	.55
☐ 413	Jim Davenport............7.00	3.10	.85
☐ 414	Sammy White 4.50	2.00	.55
☐ 415	Bob Bowman 4.50	2.00	.55
☐ 416	Foster Castleman 4.50	2.00	.55
☐ 417	Carl Furillo...............10.00	4.50	1.25
☐ 418	World Series Batting..175.00	80.00	22.00
	Foes: Mickey Mantle		
	Hank Aaron		
☐ 419	Bobby Shantz.............5.00	2.30	.60
☐ 420	Vada Pinson..............30.00	13.50	3.80
☐ 421	Dixie Howell..............4.50	2.00	.55
☐ 422	Norm Zauchin.............4.50	2.00	.55
☐ 423	Phil Clark..................4.50	2.00	.55
☐ 424	Larry Doby.................7.00	3.10	.85
☐ 425	Sammy Esposito..........4.50	2.00	.55
☐ 426	Johnny O'Brien 5.00	2.30	.60
☐ 427	Al Worthington............4.50	2.00	.55
☐ 428A	Cincinnati Reds.........14.00	6.25	1.75
	Team Card		
	(Alphabetical)		
☐ 428B	Cincinnati Team.......85.00	38.00	10.50
	numerical checklist		
☐ 429	Gus Triandos..............5.00	2.30	.60
☐ 430	Bobby Thomson..........7.00	3.10	.85
☐ 431	Gene Conley...............5.00	2.30	.60
☐ 432	John Powers...............4.50	2.00	.55
☐ 433A	Pancho Herrer ERR..500.00	230.00	65.00
☐ 433B	Pancho Herrera COR .4.50	2.00	.55
☐ 434	Harvey Kuenn 7.00	3.10	.85
☐ 435	Ed Roebuck................5.00	2.30	.60
☐ 436	Rival Fence Busters ..60.00	27.00	7.50
	Willie Mays		
	Duke Snider		
☐ 437	Bob Speake................4.50	2.00	.55
☐ 438	Whitey Herzog............8.00	3.60	1.00
☐ 439	Ray Narleski..............4.50	2.00	.55
☐ 440	Eddie Mathews..........40.00	18.00	5.00
☐ 441	Jim Marshall..............4.75	2.10	.60
☐ 442	Phil Paine..................4.25	1.90	.55
☐ 443	Billy Harrell SP.........15.00	6.75	1.90
☐ 444	Danny Kravitz.............4.25	1.90	.55
☐ 445	Bob Smith..................4.25	1.90	.55
☐ 446	Carroll Hardy SP.......15.00	6.75	1.90
☐ 447	Ray Monzant...............4.25	1.90	.55
☐ 448	Charlie Lau.................8.00	3.60	1.00
☐ 449	Gene Fodge................4.25	1.90	.55
☐ 450	Preston Ward SP.......15.00	6.75	1.90
☐ 451	Joe Taylor..................4.25	1.90	.55
☐ 452	Roman Mejias.............4.25	1.90	.55
☐ 453	Tom Qualters..............4.25	1.90	.55
☐ 454	Harry Hanebrink..........4.25	1.90	.55
☐ 455	Hal Griggs.................4.25	1.90	.55
☐ 456	Dick Brown................4.25	1.90	.55
☐ 457	Milt Pappas................7.00	3.10	.85
☐ 458	Julio Becquer.............4.25	1.90	.55
☐ 459	Ron Blackburn............4.25	1.90	.55
☐ 460	Chuck Essegian...........4.25	1.90	.55
☐ 461	Ed Mayer...................4.25	1.90	.55
☐ 462	Gary Geiger SP.........15.00	6.75	1.90

		NRMT	VG-E	GOOD
☐	463 Vito Valentinetti	4.25	1.90	.55
☐	464 Curt Flood	26.00	11.50	3.30
☐	465 Arnie Portocarrero	4.25	1.90	.55
☐	466 Pete Whisenant	4.25	1.90	.55
☐	467 Glen Hobbie	4.25	1.90	.55
☐	468 Bob Schmidt	4.25	1.90	.55
☐	469 Don Ferrarese	4.25	1.90	.55
☐	470 R.C. Stevens	4.25	1.90	.55
☐	471 Lenny Green	4.25	1.90	.55
☐	472 Joey Jay	4.75	2.10	.60
☐	473 Bill Renna	4.25	1.90	.55
☐	474 Roman Semproch	4.25	1.90	.55
☐	475 Fred Haney AS MG	20.00	9.00	2.50
	Casey Stengel AS MG			
	(Checklist back)			
☐	476 Stan Musial AS TP	40.00	18.00	5.00
☐	477 Bill Skowron AS	7.50	3.40	.95
☐	478 Johnny Temple AS	4.50	2.00	.55
☐	479 Nellie Fox AS	8.50	3.80	1.05
☐	480 Eddie Mathews AS	16.00	7.25	2.00
☐	481 Frank Malzone AS	4.50	2.00	.55
☐	482 Ernie Banks AS	25.00	11.50	3.10
☐	483 Luis Aparicio AS	15.00	6.75	1.90
☐	484 Frank Robinson AS	25.00	11.50	3.10
☐	485 Ted Williams AS	75.00	34.00	9.50
☐	486 Willie Mays AS	50.00	23.00	6.25
☐	487 Mickey Mantle AS TP	100.00	45.00	12.50
☐	488 Hank Aaron AS	50.00	23.00	6.25
☐	489 Jackie Jensen AS	5.00	2.30	.60
☐	490 Ed Bailey AS	4.50	2.00	.55
☐	491 Sherm Lollar AS	4.50	2.00	.55
☐	492 Bob Friend AS	4.50	2.00	.55
☐	493 Bob Turley AS	5.00	2.30	.60
☐	494 Warren Spahn AS	17.50	8.00	2.20
☐	495 Herb Score AS	16.00	3.20	.95
☐	xx Contest Cards !	20.00	9.00	2.50

1959 Topps

The cards in this 572-card set measure 2 1/2" by 3 1/2". The 1959 Topps set contains bust pictures of the players in a colored circle. Card numbers 551 to 572 are Sporting News All-Star Selections. High numbers 507 to 572 have the card number in a black background on the reverse rather than a green background as in the lower numbers. The high numbers are more difficult to obtain. Several cards in the 300s exist with or without an extra traded or option line on the back of the card. Cards 199 to 286 exist with either white or gray backs. Cards 461 to 470 contain "Highlights" while cards 116 to 146 give an alphabetically ordered listing of "Rookie Prospects." These Rookie Prospects (RP) were Topps' first organized inclusion of untested "Rookie" cards. Card 440 features Lew Burdette erroneously posing as a left-handed pitcher. There were some three-card advertising panels produced by Topps; the players included are from the first series. One advertising panel shows Don McMahon, Red Wilson, and Bob Boyd on the front with Ted Kluszewski's reverse on one of the backs. Another panel shows Joe Pignatano, Sam Jones, and Jack Urban on the front with Ted Kluszewski's reverse on one of the backs. Another panel shows Billy Hunter, Chuck Stobbs, and Carl Sawatski on the front with Nellie Fox's reverse on one of the backs. Another panel shows Vito Valentinetti, Ken Lehman, and Ed Bouchee on the front with Nellie Fox's reverse on one of the backs. When cut apart, these advertising cards are distinguished by the non-standard card back, i.e., part of an advertisement for the 1959 Topps set instead of the typical statistics and biographical information about the player pictured. The key rookies in this set are Sparky Anderson, Bob Gibson, and Bill White.

	NRMT	VG-E	GOOD
COMPLETE SET (572)	5400.	2400.	700.00
COMMON PLAYER (1-110)	6.50	2.90	.80
COMMON PLAYER (111-198)	4.00	1.80	.50
COMMON PLAYER (199-506)	3.75	1.70	.45
COMMON PLAYER (507-550)	17.00	7.75	2.10
COMMON AS (551-572)	18.00	8.00	2.30

		NRMT	VG-E	GOOD
☐	1 Ford Frick COMM	80.00	16.00	4.80
	(Commissioner)			

☐ 2	Eddie Yost	7.00	3.10	.85
☐ 3	Don McMahon	7.00	3.10	.85
☐ 4	Albie Pearson	7.00	3.10	.85
☐ 5	Dick Donovan	6.50	2.90	.80
☐ 6	Alex Grammas	6.50	2.90	.80
☐ 7	Al Pilarcik	6.50	2.90	.80
☐ 8	Phillies Team	40.00	8.00	2.40
	(Checklist on back)			
☐ 9	Paul Giel	7.00	3.10	.85
☐ 10	Mickey Mantle	475.00	210.00	60.00
☐ 11	Billy Hunter	6.50	2.90	.80
☐ 12	Vern Law	7.00	3.10	.85
☐ 13	Dick Gernert	6.50	2.90	.80
☐ 14	Pete Whisenant	6.50	2.90	.80
☐ 15	Dick Drott	6.50	2.90	.80
☐ 16	Joe Pignatano	6.50	2.90	.80
☐ 17	Danny's Stars	7.00	3.10	.85
	Frank Thomas			
	Danny Murtaugh MG			
	Ted Kluszewski			
☐ 18	Jack Urban	6.50	2.90	.80
☐ 19	Eddie Bressoud	6.50	2.90	.80
☐ 20	Duke Snider	65.00	29.00	8.25
☐ 21	Connie Johnson	6.50	2.90	.80
☐ 22	Al Smith	6.50	2.90	.80
☐ 23	Murry Dickson	7.00	3.10	.85
☐ 24	Red Wilson	6.50	2.90	.80
☐ 25	Don Hoak	7.00	3.10	.85
☐ 26	Chuck Stobbs	6.50	2.90	.80
☐ 27	Andy Pafko	7.00	3.10	.85
☐ 28	Al Worthington	6.50	2.90	.80
☐ 29	Jim Bolger	6.50	2.90	.80
☐ 30	Nellie Fox	15.00	6.75	1.90
☐ 31	Ken Lehman	6.50	2.90	.80
☐ 32	Don Buddin	6.50	2.90	.80
☐ 33	Ed Fitzgerald	6.50	2.90	.80
☐ 34	Pitchers Beware	14.00	6.25	1.75
	Al Kaline			
	Charlie Maxwell			
☐ 35	Ted Kluszewski	12.50	5.75	1.55
☐ 36	Hank Aguirre	6.50	2.90	.80
☐ 37	Gene Green	6.50	2.90	.80
☐ 38	Morrie Martin	6.50	2.90	.80
☐ 39	Ed Bouchee	6.50	2.90	.80
☐ 40A	Warren Spahn ERR	90.00	40.00	11.50
	(Born 1931)			
☐ 40B	Warren Spahn ERR	125.00	57.50	15.50
	(Born 1931, but three			
	is partially obscured)			
☐ 40C	Warren Spahn COR	60.00	27.00	7.50
	(Born 1921)			
☐ 41	Bob Martyn	6.50	2.90	.80
☐ 42	Murray Wall	6.50	2.90	.80
☐ 43	Steve Bilko	6.50	2.90	.80
☐ 44	Vito Valentinetti	6.50	2.90	.80
☐ 45	Andy Carey	7.00	3.10	.85
☐ 46	Bill R. Henry	6.50	2.90	.80

☐ 47	Jim Finigan	6.50	2.90	.80
☐ 48	Orioles Team	22.00	4.40	1.30
	(Checklist on back)			
☐ 49	Bill Hall	6.50	2.90	.80
☐ 50	Willie Mays	180.00	80.00	23.00
☐ 51	Rip Coleman	6.50	2.90	.80
☐ 52	Coot Veal	6.50	2.90	.80
☐ 53	Stan Williams	10.00	4.50	1.25
☐ 54	Mel Roach	6.50	2.90	.80
☐ 55	Tom Brewer	6.50	2.90	.80
☐ 56	Carl Sawatski	6.50	2.90	.80
☐ 57	Al Cicotte	6.50	2.90	.80
☐ 58	Eddie Miksis	6.50	2.90	.80
☐ 59	Irv Noren	7.00	3.10	.85
☐ 60	Bob Turley	10.00	4.50	1.25
☐ 61	Dick Brown	6.50	2.90	.80
☐ 62	Tony Taylor	7.00	3.10	.85
☐ 63	Jim Hearn	6.50	2.90	.80
☐ 64	Joe DeMaestri	6.50	2.90	.80
☐ 65	Frank Torre	7.00	3.10	.85
☐ 66	Joe Ginsberg	6.50	2.90	.80
☐ 67	Brooks Lawrence	6.50	2.90	.80
☐ 68	Dick Schofield	7.00	3.10	.85
☐ 69	Giants Team	22.00	4.40	1.30
	(Checklist on back)			
☐ 70	Harvey Kuenn	10.00	4.50	1.25
☐ 71	Don Bessent	6.50	2.90	.80
☐ 72	Bill Renna	6.50	2.90	.80
☐ 73	Ron Jackson	6.50	2.90	.80
☐ 74	Directing Power	7.00	3.10	.85
	Jim Lemon			
	Cookie Lavagetto MG			
	Roy Sievers			
☐ 75	Sam Jones	7.00	3.10	.85
☐ 76	Bobby Richardson	10.00	8.00	2.30
☐ 77	John Goryl	6.50	2.90	.80
☐ 78	Pedro Ramos	6.50	2.90	.80
☐ 79	Harry Chiti	6.50	2.90	.80
☐ 80	Minnie Minoso	10.00	4.50	1.25
☐ 81	Hal Jeffcoat	6.50	2.90	.80
☐ 82	Bob Boyd	6.50	2.90	.80
☐ 83	Bob Smith	6.50	2.90	.80
☐ 84	Reno Bertoia	6.50	2.90	.80
☐ 85	Harry Anderson	6.50	2.90	.80
☐ 86	Bob Keegan	6.50	2.90	.80
☐ 87	Danny O'Connell	6.50	2.90	.80
☐ 88	Herb Score	9.00	4.00	1.15
☐ 89	Billy Gardner	6.50	2.90	.80
☐ 90	Bill Skowron	12.50	5.75	1.55
☐ 91	Herb Moford	6.50	2.90	.80
☐ 92	Dave Philley	6.50	2.90	.80
☐ 93	Julio Becquer	6.50	2.90	.80
☐ 94	White Sox Team	22.00	4.40	1.30
	(Checklist on back)			
☐ 95	Carl Willey	6.50	2.90	.80
☐ 96	Lou Berberet	6.50	2.90	.80
☐ 97	Jerry Lynch	7.00	3.10	.85

☐ 98 Arnie Portocarrero	6.50	2.90	.80
☐ 99 Ted Kazanski	6.50	2.90	.80
☐ 100 Bob Cerv	7.00	3.10	.85
☐ 101 Alex Kellner	6.50	2.90	.80
☐ 102 Felipe Alou	25.00	11.50	3.10
☐ 103 Billy Goodman	7.00	3.10	.85
☐ 104 Del Rice	6.50	2.90	.80
☐ 105 Lee Walls	6.50	2.90	.80
☐ 106 Hal Woodeshick	6.50	2.90	.80
☐ 107 Norm Larker	7.00	3.10	.85
☐ 108 Zack Monroe	7.00	3.10	.85
☐ 109 Bob Schmidt	6.50	2.90	.80
☐ 110 George Witt	7.00	3.10	.85
☐ 111 Redlegs Team	11.00	2.20	.65
(Checklist on back)			
☐ 112 Billy Consolo	4.00	1.80	.50
☐ 113 Taylor Phillips	4.00	1.80	.50
☐ 114 Earl Battey	4.00	1.80	.50
☐ 115 Mickey Vernon	4.50	2.00	.55
☐ 116 Bob Allison RP	8.00	3.60	1.00
☐ 117 John Blanchard RP	7.50	3.40	.95
☐ 118 John Buzhardt RP	4.50	2.00	.55
☐ 119 John Callison RP	8.00	3.60	1.00
☐ 120 Chuck Coles RP	4.50	2.00	.55
☐ 121 Bob Conley RP	4.50	2.00	.55
☐ 122 Bennie Daniels RP	4.50	2.00	.55
☐ 123 Don Dillard RP	4.50	2.00	.55
☐ 124 Dan Dobbek RP	4.50	2.00	.55
☐ 125 Ron Fairly RP	7.50	3.40	.95
☐ 126 Ed Haas RP	5.00	2.30	.60
☐ 127 Kent Hadley RP	4.50	2.00	.55
☐ 128 Bob Hartman RP	4.50	2.00	.55
☐ 129 Frank Herrera RP	4.50	2.00	.55
☐ 130 Lou Jackson RP	5.00	2.30	.60
☐ 131 Deron Johnson RP	7.00	3.10	.85
☐ 132 Don Lee RP	4.50	2.00	.55
☐ 133 Bob Lillis RP	5.00	2.30	.60
☐ 134 Jim McDaniel RP	4.50	2.00	.55
☐ 135 Gene Oliver RP	4.50	2.00	.55
☐ 136 Jim O'Toole RP	5.00	2.30	.60
☐ 137 Dick Ricketts RP	5.00	2.30	.60
☐ 138 John Romano RP	5.00	2.30	.60
☐ 139 Ed Sadowski RP	4.50	2.00	.55
☐ 140 Charlie Secrest RP	4.50	2.00	.55
☐ 141 Joe Shipley RP	4.50	2.00	.55
☐ 142 Dick Stigman RP	4.50	2.00	.55
☐ 143 Willie Tasby RP	5.00	2.30	.60
☐ 144 Jerry Walker RP	5.00	2.30	.60
☐ 145 Dom Zanni RP	4.50	2.00	.55
☐ 146 Jerry Zimmerman RP	4.50	2.00	.55
☐ 147 Cubs Clubbers	12.50	5.75	1.55
Dale Long			
Ernie Banks			
Walt Moryn			
☐ 148 Mike McCormick	4.50	2.00	.55
☐ 149 Jim Bunning	12.00	5.50	1.50
☐ 150 Stan Musial	175.00	80.00	22.00
☐ 151 Bob Malkmus	4.00	1.80	.50
☐ 152 Johnny Klippstein	4.00	1.80	.50
☐ 153 Jim Marshall	4.00	1.80	.50
☐ 154 Ray Herbert	4.00	1.80	.50
☐ 155 Enos Slaughter	20.00	9.00	2.50
☐ 156 Ace Hurlers	7.00	3.10	.85
Billy Pierce			
Robin Roberts			
☐ 157 Felix Mantilla	4.00	1.80	.50
☐ 158 Walt Dropo	4.00	1.80	.50
☐ 159 Bob Shaw	4.00	1.80	.50
☐ 160 Dick Groat	4.50	2.00	.55
☐ 161 Frank Baumann	4.00	1.80	.50
☐ 162 Bobby G. Smith	4.00	1.80	.50
☐ 163 Sandy Koufax	175.00	80.00	22.00
☐ 164 Johnny Groth	4.00	1.80	.50
☐ 165 Bill Bruton	4.00	1.80	.50
☐ 166 Destruction Crew	7.00	3.10	.85
Minnie Minoso			
Rocky Colavito			
(Misspelled Colovito			
on card back)			
Larry Doby			
☐ 167 Duke Maas	4.00	1.80	.50
☐ 168 Carroll Hardy	4.00	1.80	.50
☐ 169 Ted Abernathy	4.00	1.80	.50
☐ 170 Gene Woodling	4.50	2.00	.55
☐ 171 Willard Schmidt	4.00	1.80	.50
☐ 172 Athletics Team	11.00	2.20	.65
(Checklist on back)			
☐ 173 Bill Monbouquette	4.50	2.00	.55
☐ 174 Jim Pendleton	4.00	1.80	.50
☐ 175 Dick Farrell	4.50	2.00	.55
☐ 176 Preston Ward	4.00	1.80	.50
☐ 177 John Briggs	4.00	1.80	.50
☐ 178 Ruben Amaro	6.00	2.70	.75
☐ 179 Don Rudolph	4.00	1.80	.50
☐ 180 Yogi Berra	90.00	40.00	11.50
☐ 181 Bob Porterfield	4.00	1.80	.50
☐ 182 Milt Graff	4.00	1.80	.50
☐ 183 Stu Miller	4.50	2.00	.55
☐ 184 Harvey Haddix	4.50	2.00	.55
☐ 185 Jim Busby	4.00	1.80	.50
☐ 186 Mudcat Grant	4.50	2.00	.55
☐ 187 Bubba Phillips	4.00	1.80	.50
☐ 188 Juan Pizarro	4.00	1.80	.50
☐ 189 Neil Chrisley	4.00	1.80	.50
☐ 190 Bill Virdon	5.50	2.50	.70
☐ 191 Russ Kemmerer	4.00	1.80	.50
☐ 192 Charlie Beamon	4.00	1.80	.50
☐ 193 Sammy Taylor	4.00	1.80	.50
☐ 194 Jim Brosnan	4.50	2.00	.55
☐ 195 Rip Repulski	4.00	1.80	.50
☐ 196 Billy Moran	4.00	1.80	.50
☐ 197 Ray Semproch	4.00	1.80	.50
☐ 198 Jim Davenport	4.50	2.00	.55
☐ 199 Leo Kiely	3.75	1.70	.45

□ 200	Warren Giles	6.00	2.70	.75
	(NL President)			
□ 201	Tom Acker	3.75	1.70	.45
□ 202	Roger Maris	150.00	70.00	19.00
□ 203	Ossie Virgil	3.75	1.70	.45
□ 204	Casey Wise	3.75	1.70	.45
□ 205	Don Larsen	5.50	2.50	.70
□ 206	Carl Furillo	5.50	2.50	.70
□ 207	George Strickland	3.75	1.70	.45
□ 208	Willie Jones	3.75	1.70	.45
□ 209	Lenny Green	3.75	1.70	.45
□ 210	Ed Bailey	3.75	1.70	.45
□ 211	Bob Blaylock	3.75	1.70	.45
□ 212	Fence Busters	45.00	20.00	5.75
	Hank Aaron			
	Eddie Mathews			
□ 213	Jim Rivera	3.75	1.70	.45
□ 214	Marcelino Solis	3.75	1.70	.45
□ 215	Jim Lemon	4.25	1.90	.55
□ 216	Andre Rodgers	3.75	1.70	.45
□ 217	Carl Erskine	5.50	2.50	.70
□ 218	Roman Mejias	3.75	1.70	.45
□ 219	George Zuverink	3.75	1.70	.45
□ 220	Frank Malzone	4.25	1.90	.55
□ 221	Bob Bowman	3.75	1.70	.45
□ 222	Bobby Shantz	5.00	2.30	.60
□ 223	Cardinals Team	11.00	2.20	.65
	(Checklist on back)			
□ 224	Claude Osteen	6.00	2.70	.75
□ 225	Johnny Logan	4.25	1.90	.55
□ 226	Art Ceccarelli	3.75	1.70	.45
□ 227	Hal W. Smith	3.75	1.70	.45
□ 228	Don Gross	3.75	1.70	.45
□ 229	Vic Power	4.25	1.90	.55
□ 230	Bill Fischer	3.75	1.70	.45
□ 231	Ellis Burton	3.75	1.70	.45
□ 232	Eddie Kasko	3.75	1.70	.45
□ 233	Paul Foytack	3.75	1.70	.45
□ 234	Chuck Tanner	4.25	1.90	.55
□ 235	Valmy Thomas	3.75	1.70	.45
□ 236	Ted Bowsfield	3.75	1.70	.45
□ 237	Run Preventers	8.00	3.60	1.00
	Gil McDougald			
	Bob Turley			
	Bobby Richardson			
□ 238	Gene Baker	3.75	1.70	.45
□ 239	Bob Trowbridge	3.75	1.70	.45
□ 240	Hank Bauer	5.50	2.50	.70
□ 241	Billy Muffett	3.75	1.70	.45
□ 242	Ron Samford	3.75	1.70	.45
□ 243	Marv Grissom	3.75	1.70	.45
□ 244	Ted Gray	3.75	1.70	.45
□ 245	Ned Garver	3.75	1.70	.45
□ 246	J.W. Porter	3.75	1.70	.45
□ 247	Don Ferrarese	3.75	1.70	.45
□ 248	Red Sox Team	11.00	2.20	.65
	(Checklist on back)			
□ 249	Bobby Adams	3.75	1.70	.45
□ 250	Billy O'Dell	3.75	1.70	.45
□ 251	Clete Boyer	5.50	2.50	.70
□ 252	Ray Boone	4.25	1.90	.55
□ 253	Seth Morehead	3.75	1.70	.45
□ 254	Zeke Bella	3.75	1.70	.45
□ 255	Del Ennis	4.25	1.90	.55
□ 256	Jerry Davie	3.75	1.70	.45
□ 257	Leon Wagner	5.25	2.40	.65
□ 258	Fred Kipp	3.75	1.70	.45
□ 259	Jim Pisoni	3.75	1.70	.45
□ 260	Early Wynn UER	15.00	6.75	1.90
	(1957 Cleevland)			
□ 261	Gene Stephens	3.75	1.70	.45
□ 262	Hitters' Foes	7.50	3.40	.95
	Johnny Podres			
	Clem Labine			
	Don Drysdale			
□ 263	Bud Daley	3.75	1.70	.45
□ 264	Chico Carrasquel	3.75	1.70	.45
□ 265	Ron Kline	3.75	1.70	.45
□ 266	Woody Held	3.75	1.70	.45
□ 267	John Romonosky	3.75	1.70	.45
□ 268	Tito Francona	4.25	1.90	.55
□ 269	Jack Meyer	3.75	1.70	.45
□ 270	Gil Hodges	21.00	9.50	2.60
□ 271	Orlando Pena	3.75	1.70	.45
□ 272	Jerry Lumpe	3.75	1.70	.45
□ 273	Joey Jay	4.25	1.90	.55
□ 274	Jerry Kindall	4.25	1.90	.55
□ 275	Jack Sanford	4.25	1.90	.55
□ 276	Pete Daley	3.75	1.70	.45
□ 277	Turk Lown	3.75	1.70	.45
□ 278	Chuck Essegian	3.75	1.70	.45
□ 279	Ernie Johnson	4.25	1.90	.55
□ 280	Frank Bolling	3.75	1.70	.45
□ 281	Walt Craddock	3.75	1.70	.45
□ 282	R.C. Stevens	3.75	1.70	.45
□ 283	Russ Heman	3.75	1.70	.45
□ 284	Steve Korcheck	3.75	1.70	.45
□ 285	Joe Cunningham	4.25	1.90	.55
□ 286	Dean Stone	3.75	1.70	.45
□ 287	Don Zimmer	4.25	1.90	.55
□ 288	Dutch Dotterer	3.75	1.70	.45
□ 289	Johnny Kucks	3.75	1.70	.45
□ 290	Wes Covington	4.25	1.90	.55
□ 291	Pitching Partners	4.25	1.90	.55
	Pedro Ramos			
	Camilo Pascual			
□ 292	Dick Williams	4.25	1.90	.55
□ 293	Ray Moore	3.75	1.70	.45
□ 294	Hank Foiles	3.75	1.70	.45
□ 295	Billy Martin	15.00	6.75	1.90
□ 296	Ernie Broglio	5.00	2.30	.60
□ 297	Jackie Brandt	3.75	1.70	.45
□ 298	Tex Clevenger	3.75	1.70	.45
□ 299	Billy Klaus	3.75	1.70	.45

☐	300	Richie Ashburn 12.50	5.75	1.55
☐	301	Earl Averill.................3.75	1.70	.45
☐	302	Don Mossi 4.25	1.90	.55
☐	303	Marty Keough 3.75	1.70	.45
☐	304	Cubs Team 11.00	2.20	.65
		(Checklist on back)		
☐	305	Curt Raydon 3.75	1.70	.45
☐	306	Jim Gilliam..................6.00	2.70	.75
☐	307	Curt Barclay 3.75	1.70	.45
☐	308	Norm Siebern 3.75	1.70	.45
☐	309	Sal Maglie 5.00	2.30	.60
☐	310	Luis Aparicio 20.00	9.00	2.50
☐	311	Norm Zauchin 3.75	1.70	.45
☐	312	Don Newcombe 5.00	2.30	.60
☐	313	Frank House................3.75	1.70	.45
☐	314	Don Cardwell 3.75	1.70	.45
☐	315	Joe Adcock 4.25	1.90	.55
☐	316A	Ralph Lumenti UER ...3.75	1.70	.45
		(Option)		
		(Photo actually		
		Camilo Pascual)		
☐	316B	Ralph Lumenti UER .90.00	40.00	11.50
		(No option)		
		(Photo actually		
		Camilo Pascual)		
☐	317	Hitting Kings 30.00	13.50	3.80
		Willie Mays		
		Richie Ashburn		
☐	318	Rocky Bridges............3.75	1.70	.45
☐	319	Dave Hillman..............3.75	1.70	.45
☐	320	Bob Skinner 4.25	1.90	.55
☐	321A	Bob Giallombardo.....3.75	1.70	.45
		(Option)		
☐	321B	Bob Giallombardo....90.00	40.00	11.50
		(No option)		
☐	322A	Harry Hanebrink 3.75	1.70	.45
		(Traded)		
☐	322B	Harry Hanebrink 90.00	40.00	11.50
		(No trade)		
☐	323	Frank Sullivan............3.75	1.70	.45
☐	324	Don Demeter...............3.75	1.70	.45
☐	325	Ken Boyer 9.00	4.00	1.15
☐	326	Marv Throneberry.......5.00	2.30	.60
☐	327	Gary Bell 3.75	1.70	.45
☐	328	Lou Skizas 3.75	1.70	.45
☐	329	Tigers Team 11.00	2.20	.65
		(Checklist on back)		
☐	330	Gus Triandos 4.25	1.90	.55
☐	331	Steve Boros 3.75	1.70	.45
☐	332	Ray Monzant...............3.75	1.70	.45
☐	333	Harry Simpson............3.75	1.70	.45
☐	334	Glen Hobbie 3.75	1.70	.45
☐	335	Johnny Temple 4.25	1.90	.55
☐	336A	Billy Loes 4.25	1.90	.55
		(With traded line)		
☐	336B	Billy Loes.................90.00	40.00	11.50
		(No trade)		

☐	337	George Crowe.............3.75	1.70	.45
☐	338	Sparky Anderson......45.00	20.00	5.75
☐	339	Roy Face 5.00	2.30	.60
☐	340	Roy Sievers.................4.25	1.90	.55
☐	341	Tom Qualters 3.75	1.70	.45
☐	342	Ray Jablonski 3.75	1.70	.45
☐	343	Billy Hoeft..................3.75	1.70	.45
☐	344	Russ Nixon 3.75	1.70	.45
☐	345	Gil McDougald 7.50	3.40	.95
☐	346	Batter Bafflers.............3.75	1.70	.45
		Dave Sisler		
		Tom Brewer		
☐	347	Bob Buhl 4.25	1.90	.55
☐	348	Ted Lepcio..................3.75	1.70	.45
☐	349	Hoyt Wilhelm 18.00	8.00	2.30
☐	350	Ernie Banks..............75.00	34.00	9.50
☐	351	Earl Torgeson 3.75	1.70	.45
☐	352	Robin Roberts...........18.00	8.00	2.30
☐	353	Curt Flood 5.50	2.50	.70
☐	354	Pete Burnside 3.75	1.70	.45
☐	355	Jim Piersall 5.00	2.30	.60
☐	356	Bob Mabe 3.75	1.70	.45
☐	357	Dick Stuart.................6.00	2.70	.75
☐	358	Ralph Terry 4.25	1.90	.55
☐	359	Bill White 30.00	13.50	3.80
☐	360	Al Kaline..................70.00	32.00	8.75
☐	361	Willard Nixon 3.75	1.70	.45
☐	362A	Dolan Nichols 3.75	1.70	.45
		(With option line)		
☐	362B	Dolan Nichols 90.00	40.00	11.50
		(No option)		
☐	363	Bobby Avila................3.75	1.70	.45
☐	364	Danny McDevitt 3.75	1.70	.45
☐	365	Gus Bell 4.25	1.90	.55
☐	366	Humberto Robinson 3.75	1.70	.45
☐	367	Cal Neeman................3.75	1.70	.45
☐	368	Don Mueller 4.25	1.90	.55
☐	369	Dick Tomanek 3.75	1.70	.45
☐	370	Pete Runnels...............4.25	1.90	.55
☐	371	Dick Brodowski...........3.75	1.70	.45
☐	372	Jim Hegan 4.25	1.90	.55
☐	373	Herb Plews 3.75	1.70	.45
☐	374	Art Ditmar 3.75	1.70	.45
☐	375	Bob Nieman 3.75	1.70	.45
☐	376	Hal Naragon 3.75	1.70	.45
☐	377	John Antonelli.............4.25	1.90	.55
☐	378	Gail Harris..................3.75	1.70	.45
☐	379	Bob Miller 3.75	1.70	.45
☐	380	Hank Aaron 125.00	57.50	15.50
☐	381	Mike Baxes 3.75	1.70	.45
☐	382	Curt Simmons 4.25	1.90	.55
☐	383	Words of Wisdom......9.00	4.00	1.15
		Don Larsen		
		Casey Stengel MG		
☐	384	Dave Sisler.................3.75	1.70	.45
☐	385	Sherm Lollar...............4.25	1.90	.55
☐	386	Jim Delsing 3.75	1.70	.45

☐ 387	Don Drysdale 40.00	18.00	5.00
☐ 388	Bob Will 3.75	1.70	.45
☐ 389	Joe Nuxhall 4.25	1.90	.55
☐ 390	Orlando Cepeda 20.00	9.00	2.50
☐ 391	Milt Pappas 4.25	1.90	.55
☐ 392	Whitey Herzog 6.00	2.70	.75
☐ 393	Frank Lary 4.25	1.90	.55
☐ 394	Randy Jackson 3.75	1.70	.45
☐ 395	Elston Howard 9.00	4.00	1.15
☐ 396	Bob Rush 3.75	1.70	.45
☐ 397	Senators Team 11.00	2.20	.65
	(Checklist on back)		
☐ 398	Wally Post 4.25	1.90	.55
☐ 399	Larry Jackson 3.75	1.70	.45
☐ 400	Jackie Jensen 5.00	2.30	.60
☐ 401	Ron Blackburn 3.75	1.70	.45
☐ 402	Hector Lopez 4.25	1.90	.55
☐ 403	Clem Labine 4.25	1.90	.55
☐ 404	Hank Sauer 4.25	1.90	.55
☐ 405	Roy McMillan 4.25	1.90	.55
☐ 406	Solly Drake 3.75	1.70	.45
☐ 407	Moe Drabowsky 4.25	1.90	.55
☐ 408	Keystone Combo...........9.00	4.00	1.15
	Nellie Fox		
	Luis Aparicio		
☐ 409	Gus Zernial 4.25	1.90	.55
☐ 410	Billy Pierce 4.75	2.10	.60
☐ 411	Whitey Lockman 4.25	1.90	.55
☐ 412	Stan Lopata 3.75	1.70	.45
☐ 413	Camilo Pascual UER 4.25	1.90	.55
	(Listed as Camillo		
	on front and Pasqual		
	on back)		
☐ 414	Dale Long 4.25	1.90	.55
☐ 415	Bill Mazeroski 8.50	3.80	1.05
☐ 416	Haywood Sullivan 4.25	1.90	.55
☐ 417	Virgil Trucks 4.25	1.90	.55
☐ 418	Gino Cimoli 3.75	1.70	.45
☐ 419	Braves Team 11.00	4.90	1.40
	(Checklist on back)		
☐ 420	Rocky Colavito 20.00	9.00	2.50
☐ 421	Herman Wehmeier 3.75	1.70	.45
☐ 422	Hobie Landrith 3.75	1.70	.45
☐ 423	Bob Grim 4.25	1.90	.55
☐ 424	Ken Aspromonte 3.75	1.70	.45
☐ 425	Del Crandall 4.25	1.90	.55
☐ 426	Gerry Staley 3.75	1.70	.45
☐ 427	Charlie Neal 4.25	1.90	.55
☐ 428	Buc Hill Aces...............4.25	1.90	.55
	Ron Kline		
	Bob Friend		
	Vernon Law		
	Roy Face		
☐ 429	Bobby Thomson 5.00	2.30	.60
☐ 430	Whitey Ford 45.00	20.00	5.75
☐ 431	Whammy Douglas 3.75	1.70	.45
☐ 432	Smoky Burgess.............4.25	1.90	.55
☐ 433	Billy Harrell 3.75	1.70	.45
☐ 434	Hal Griggs....................3.75	1.70	.45
☐ 435	Frank Robinson.............55.00	25.00	7.00
☐ 436	Granny Hamner.............3.75	1.70	.45
☐ 437	Ike Delock....................3.75	1.70	.45
☐ 438	Sammy Esposito 3.75	1.70	.45
☐ 439	Brooks Robinson...........65.00	29.00	8.25
☐ 440	Lou Burdette..................7.00	3.10	.85
	(Posing as if		
	lefthanded)		
☐ 441	John Roseboro 4.25	1.90	.55
☐ 442	Ray Narleski.................3.75	1.70	.45
☐ 443	Daryl Spencer 3.75	1.70	.45
☐ 444	Ron Hansen...................5.00	2.30	.60
☐ 445	Cal McLish...................3.75	1.70	.45
☐ 446	Rocky Nelson 3.75	1.70	.45
☐ 447	Bob Anderson................3.75	1.70	.45
☐ 448	Vada Pinson UER...........7.00	3.10	.85
	(Born: 8/8/38,		
	should be 8/11/38)		
☐ 449	Tom Gorman..................3.75	1.70	.45
☐ 450	Eddie Mathews 30.00	13.50	3.80
☐ 451	Jimmy Constable 3.75	1.70	.45
☐ 452	Chico Fernandez 3.75	1.70	.45
☐ 453	Les Moss 3.75	1.70	.45
☐ 454	Phil Clark 3.75	1.70	.45
☐ 455	Larry Doby 5.00	2.30	.60
☐ 456	Jerry Casale 3.75	1.70	.45
☐ 457	Dodgers Team 20.00	4.00	1.20
	(Checklist on back)		
☐ 458	Gordon Jones 3.75	1.70	.45
☐ 459	Bill Tuttle....................3.75	1.70	.45
☐ 460	Bob Friend 4.25	1.90	.55
☐ 461	Mickey Mantle Hits 55.00	25.00	7.00
	Homer		
☐ 462	Rocky Colavito's 10.00	4.50	1.25
	Catch		
☐ 463	Al Kaline Batting..........16.00	7.25	2.00
	Champ		
☐ 464	Willie Mays' Series 25.00	11.50	3.10
	Catch		
☐ 465	Roy Sievers Sets Mark.5.00	2.30	.60
☐ 466	Billy Pierce All-Star 5.00	2.30	.60
☐ 467	Hank Aaron Clubs 25.00	11.50	3.10
	Homer		
☐ 468	Duke Snider's Play........17.00	7.75	2.10
☐ 469	Hustler Ernie Banks 17.00	7.75	2.10
☐ 470	Stan Musial's 3000th.21.00	9.50	2.60
	Hit		
☐ 471	Tom Sturdivant 3.75	1.70	.45
☐ 472	Gene Freese 3.75	1.70	.45
☐ 473	Mike Fornieles..............3.75	1.70	.45
☐ 474	Moe Thacker 3.75	1.70	.45
☐ 475	Jack Harshman..............3.75	1.70	.45
☐ 476	Indians Team 11.00	2.20	.65
	(Checklist on back)		
☐ 477	Barry Latman 3.75	1.70	.45

☐ 478	Bob Clemente 125.00	57.50	15.50
☐ 479	Lindy McDaniel.............4.25	1.90	.55
☐ 480	Red Schoendienst....15.00	6.75	1.90
☐ 481	Charlie Maxwell............4.25	1.90	.55
☐ 482	Russ Meyer....................3.75	1.70	.45
☐ 483	Clint Courtney..............3.75	1.70	.45
☐ 484	Willie Kirkland..............3.75	1.70	.45
☐ 485	Ryne Duren....................6.00	2.70	.75
☐ 486	Sammy White................3.75	1.70	.45
☐ 487	Hal Brown.....................3.75	1.70	.45
☐ 488	Walt Moryn....................3.75	1.70	.45
☐ 489	John Powers..................3.75	1.70	.45
☐ 490	Frank Thomas...............4.25	1.90	.55
☐ 491	Don Blasingame............3.75	1.70	.45
☐ 492	Gene Conley..................4.25	1.90	.55
☐ 493	Jim Landis....................3.75	1.70	.45
☐ 494	Don Pavletich...............3.75	1.70	.45
☐ 495	Johnny Podres...............5.00	2.30	.60
☐ 496	Wayne Terwilliger UER 3.75	1.70	.45
	(Athlftics on front)		
☐ 497	Hal R. Smith.................3.75	1.70	.45
☐ 498	Dick Hyde......................3.75	1.70	.45
☐ 499	Johnny O'Brion 1.20	1.00	.55
☐ 500	Vic Wertz......................4.25	1.90	.55
☐ 501	Bob Tiefenauer.............3.75	1.70	.45
☐ 502	Alvin Dark.....................5.00	2.30	.60
☐ 503	Jim Owens....................3.75	1.70	.45
☐ 504	Ossie Alvarez...............3.75	1.70	.45
☐ 505	Tony Kubek.................12.50	5.75	1.55
☐ 506	Bob Purkey....................3.75	1.70	.45
☐ 507	Bob Hale......................17.00	7.75	2.10
☐ 508	Art Fowler....................17.00	7.75	2.10
☐ 509	Norm Cash...................70.00	32.00	8.75
☐ 510	Yankees Team..............85.00	17.00	5.00
	(Checklist on back)		
☐ 511	George Susce 17.00	7.75	2.10
☐ 512	George Altman.............17.00	7.75	2.10
☐ 513	Tommy Carroll..............17.00	7.75	2.10
☐ 514	Bob Gibson................400.00	180.00	50.00
☐ 515	Harmon Killebrew....150.00	70.00	19.00
☐ 516	Mike Garcia................19.00	8.50	2.40
☐ 517	Joe Koppe...................17.00	7.75	2.10
☐ 518	Mike Cueller UER......25.00	11.50	3.10
	(Sic, Cuellar)		
☐ 519	Infield Power...............19.00	8.50	2.40
	Pete Runnels		
	Dick Gernert		
	Frank Malzone		
☐ 520	Don Elston...................17.00	7.75	2.10
☐ 521	Gary Geiger..................17.00	7.75	2.10
☐ 522	Gene Snyder.................17.00	7.75	2.10
☐ 523	Harry Bright..................17.00	7.75	2.10
☐ 524	Larry Osborne..............17.00	7.75	2.10
☐ 525	Jim Coates...................17.00	7.75	2.10
☐ 526	Bob Speake...................17.00	7.75	2.10
☐ 527	Solly Hemus.................17.00	7.75	2.10
☐ 528	Pirates Team...............50.00	23.00	6.25

	(Checklist on back)		
☐ 529	George Bamberger.....20.00	9.00	2.50
☐ 530	Wally Moon..................19.00	8.50	2.40
☐ 531	Ray Webster 17.00	7.75	2.10
☐ 532	Mark Freeman.............17.00	7.75	2.10
☐ 533	Darrell Johnson...........19.00	8.50	2.40
☐ 534	Faye Throneberry........17.00	7.75	2.10
☐ 535	Ruben Gomez...............17.00	7.75	2.10
☐ 536	Danny Kravitz..............17.00	7.75	2.10
☐ 537	Rudolph Arias..............17.00	7.75	2.10
☐ 538	Chick King...................17.00	7.75	2.10
☐ 539	Gary Blaylock..............17.00	7.75	2.10
☐ 540	Willie Miranda.............17.00	7.75	2.10
☐ 541	Bob Thurman...............17.00	7.75	2.10
☐ 542	Jim Perry.....................25.00	11.50	3.10
☐ 543	Corsair Trio.................70.00	32.00	8.75
	Bob Skinner		
	Bill Virdon		
	Roberto Clemente		
☐ 544	Lee Tate.......................17.00	7.75	2.10
☐ 545	Tom Morgan.................17.00	7.75	2.10
☐ 546	Al Schroll.....................17.00	7.75	2.10
☐ 547	Jim Baxco 17.00	7.75	2.10
☐ 548	Elmer Singleton...........17.00	7.75	2.10
☐ 549	Howie Nunn..................17.00	7.75	2.10
☐ 550	Roy Campanella........175.00	80.00	22.00
	(Symbol of Courage!)		
☐ 551	Fred Haney MG AS......18.00	8.00	2.30
☐ 552	Casey Stengel MG AS 35.00	16.00	4.40
☐ 553	Orlando Cepeda AS....25.00	11.50	3.10
☐ 554	Bill Skowron AS 25.00	11.50	3.10
☐ 555	Bill Mazeroski AS 25.00	11.50	3.10
☐ 556	Nellie Fox AS..............25.00	11.50	3.10
☐ 557	Ken Boyer AS..............25.00	11.50	3.10
☐ 558	Frank Malzone AS.......18.00	8.00	2.30
☐ 559	Ernie Banks AS...........55.00	25.00	7.00
☐ 560	Luis Aparicio AS.........35.00	16.00	4.40
☐ 561	Hank Aaron AS..........130.00	57.50	16.50
☐ 562	Al Kaline AS.................60.00	27.00	7.50
☐ 563	Willie Mays AS..........130.00	57.50	16.50
☐ 564	Mickey Mantle AS 300.00	135.00	38.00
☐ 565	Wes Covington AS.......18.00	8.00	2.30
☐ 566	Roy Sievers AS............18.00	8.00	2.30
☐ 567	Del Crandall AS...........18.00	8.00	2.30
☐ 568	Gus Triandos AS..........18.00	8.00	2.30
☐ 569	Bob Friend AS..............18.00	8.00	2.30
☐ 570	Bob Turley AS..............18.00	8.00	2.30
☐ 571	Warren Spahn AS.........40.00	18.00	5.00
☐ 572	Billy Pierce AS.............35.00	8.75	2.80

1960 Topps

The cards in this 572-card set measure 2 1/2" by 3 1/2". The 1960 Topps set is the only Topps standard size issue to use a horizontally oriented front. World Series cards appeared for the first time (385 to 391), and there is a Rookie Prospect (RP) series (117-148), the most famous of which is Carl Yastrzemski, and a Sport Magazine All-Star Selection (AS) series (553-572). There are 16 manager cards listed alphabetically from 212 through 227. The 1959 Topps All-Rookie team is featured on cards 316-325. The coaching staff of each team was also afforded their own card in a 16-card subset (455-470). Cards 375 to 440 come with either gray or white backs, and the high series (507-572) were printed on a more limited basis than the rest of the set. The team cards have series checklists on the reverse. The key rookies in this set are Willie McCovey and Carl Yastrzemski.

	NRMT	VG-E	GOOD
COMPLETE SET (572)	4000.	1800.	500.00
COMMON PLAYER (1-110)	3.75	1.70	.45
COMMON PLAYER (111-198)	3.00	1.35	.40
COMMON PLAYER (199-286)	3.50	1.55	.45
COMMON PLAYER (287-440)	3.75	1.70	.45
COMMON PLAYER (441-506)	5.00	2.30	.60
COMMON PLAYER (507-552)	12.00	5.50	1.50
COMMON AS (553-572)	15.00	6.75	1.90

			NRMT	VG-E	GOOD
☐	1	Early Wynn	40.00	10.00	3.20
☐	2	Roman Mejias	3.75	1.70	.45
☐	3	Joe Adcock	4.25	1.90	.55
☐	4	Bob Purkey	3.75	1.70	.45
☐	5	Wally Moon	4.25	1.90	.55
☐	6	Lou Berberet	3.75	1.70	.45
☐	7	Master and Mentor	20.00	9.00	2.50
		Willie Mays			
		Bill Rigney MG			
☐	8	Bud Daley	3.75	1.70	.45
☐	9	Faye Throneberry	3.75	1.70	.45
☐	10	Ernie Banks	55.00	25.00	7.00
☐	11	Norm Siebern	3.75	1.70	.45
☐	12	Milt Pappas	4.25	1.90	.55
☐	13	Wally Post	4.25	1.90	.55
☐	14	Jim Grant	4.25	1.90	.55
☐	15	Pete Runnels	4.25	1.90	.55
☐	16	Ernie Broglio	4.25	1.90	.55
☐	17	Johnny Callison	5.00	2.30	.60
☐	18	Dodgers Team	20.00	9.00	2.50
		(Checklist on back)			
☐	19	Felix Mantilla	3.75	1.70	.45
☐	20	Roy Face	5.00	2.30	.60
☐	21	Dutch Dotterer	3.75	1.70	.45
☐	22	Rocky Bridges	3.75	1.70	.45
☐	23	Eddie Fisher	3.75	1.70	.45
☐	24	Dick Gray	3.75	1.70	.45
☐	25	Roy Sievers	4.25	1.90	.55
☐	26	Wayne Terwilliger	3.75	1.70	.45
☐	27	Dick Drott	3.75	1.70	.45
☐	28	Brooks Robinson	55.00	25.00	7.00
☐	29	Clem Labine	4.25	1.90	.55
☐	30	Tito Francona	3.75	1.70	.45
☐	31	Sammy Esposito	3.75	1.70	.45
☐	32	Sophomore Stalwarts	3.75	1.70	.45
		Jim O'Toole			
		Vada Pinson			
☐	33	Tom Morgan	3.75	1.70	.45
☐	34	Sparky Anderson	11.00	4.90	1.40
☐	35	Whitey Ford	45.00	20.00	5.75
☐	36	Russ Nixon	3.75	1.70	.45
☐	37	Bill Bruton	3.75	1.70	.45
☐	38	Jerry Casale	3.75	1.70	.45
☐	39	Earl Averill	3.75	1.70	.45
☐	40	Joe Cunningham	4.25	1.90	.55
☐	41	Barry Latman	3.75	1.70	.45
☐	42	Hobie Landrith	3.75	1.70	.45
☐	43	Senators Team	9.00	4.00	1.15
		(Checklist on back)			
☐	44	Bobby Locke	3.75	1.70	.45
☐	45	Roy McMillan	4.25	1.90	.55
☐	46	Jerry Fisher	3.75	1.70	.45
☐	47	Don Zimmer	4.25	1.90	.55
☐	48	Hal W. Smith	3.75	1.70	.45
☐	49	Curt Raydon	3.75	1.70	.45
☐	50	Al Kaline	55.00	25.00	7.00
☐	51	Jim Coates	3.75	1.70	.45
☐	52	Dave Philley	3.75	1.70	.45
☐	53	Jackie Brandt	3.75	1.70	.45
☐	54	Mike Fornieles	3.75	1.70	.45
☐	55	Bill Mazeroski	7.00	3.10	.85
☐	56	Steve Korcheck	3.75	1.70	.45

☐ 57	Win Savers 3.75	1.70	.45
	Turk Lown		
	Gerry Staley		
☐ 58	Gino Cimoli 3.75	1.70	.45
☐ 59	Juan Pizarro 3.75	1.70	.45
☐ 60	Gus Triandos 4.25	1.90	.55
☐ 61	Eddie Kasko 3.75	1.70	.45
☐ 62	Roger Craig 5.50	2.50	.70
☐ 63	George Strickland 3.75	1.70	.45
☐ 64	Jack Meyer 3.75	1.70	.45
☐ 65	Elston Howard 7.00	3.10	.85
☐ 66	Bob Trowbridge 3.75	1.70	.45
☐ 67	Jose Pagan 3.75	1.70	.45
☐ 68	Dave Hillman 3.75	1.70	.45
☐ 69	Billy Goodman 4.25	1.90	.55
☐ 70	Lew Burdette 6.00	2.70	.75
☐ 71	Marty Keough 3.75	1.70	.45
☐ 72	Tigers Team 9.00	4.00	1.15
	(Checklist on back)		
☐ 73	Bob Gibson 70.00	32.00	8.75
☐ 74	Walt Moryn 3.75	1.70	.45
☐ 75	Vic Power 4.25	1.90	.55
☐ 76	Bill Fischer 3.75	1.70	.45
☐ 77	Hank Foiles 3.75	1.70	.45
☐ 78	Bob Grim 3.75	1.70	.45
☐ 79	Walt Dropo 3.75	1.70	.45
☐ 80	Johnny Antonelli 4.25	1.90	.55
☐ 81	Russ Snyder 3.75	1.70	.45
☐ 82	Ruben Gomez 3.75	1.70	.45
☐ 83	Tony Kubek 7.50	3.40	.95
☐ 84	Hal R. Smith 3.75	1.70	.45
☐ 85	Frank Lary 4.25	1.90	.55
☐ 86	Dick Gernert 3.75	1.70	.45
☐ 87	John Romonosky 3.75	1.70	.45
☐ 88	John Roseboro 4.25	1.90	.55
☐ 89	Hal Brown 3.75	1.70	.45
☐ 90	Bobby Avila 3.75	1.70	.45
☐ 91	Bennie Daniels 3.75	1.70	.45
☐ 92	Whitey Herzog 5.50	2.50	.70
☐ 93	Art Schult 3.75	1.70	.45
☐ 94	Leo Kiely 3.75	1.70	.45
☐ 95	Frank Thomas 4.25	1.90	.55
☐ 96	Ralph Terry 4.25	1.90	.55
☐ 97	Ted Lepcio 3.75	1.70	.45
☐ 98	Gordon Jones 3.75	1.70	.45
☐ 99	Lenny Green 3.75	1.70	.45
☐ 100	Nellie Fox 10.00	4.50	1.25
☐ 101	Bob Miller 3.75	1.70	.45
☐ 102	Kent Hadley 3.75	1.70	.45
☐ 103	Dick Farrell 4.25	1.90	.55
☐ 104	Dick Schofield 4.25	1.90	.55
☐ 105	Larry Sherry 5.50	2.50	.70
☐ 106	Billy Gardner 3.75	1.70	.45
☐ 107	Carlton Willey 3.75	1.70	.45
☐ 108	Pete Daley 3.75	1.70	.45
☐ 109	Clete Boyer 6.50	2.90	.80
☐ 110	Cal McLish 3.75	1.70	.45

☐ 111	Vic Wertz 3.50	1.55	.45
☐ 112	Jack Harshman 3.00	1.35	.40
☐ 113	Bob Skinner 3.50	1.55	.45
☐ 114	Ken Aspromonte 3.00	1.35	.40
☐ 115	Fork and Knuckler 6.00	2.70	.75
	Roy Face		
	Hoyt Wilhelm		
☐ 116	Jim Rivera 3.00	1.35	.40
☐ 117	Tom Borland RP 3.50	1.55	.45
☐ 118	Bob Bruce RP 3.50	1.55	.45
☐ 119	Chico Cardenas RP 4.00	1.80	.50
☐ 120	Duke Carmel RP 3.50	1.55	.45
☐ 121	Camilo Carreon RP 3.50	1.55	.45
☐ 122	Don Dillard RP 3.50	1.55	.45
☐ 123	Dan Dobbek RP 3.50	1.55	.45
☐ 124	Jim Donohue RP 3.50	1.55	.45
☐ 125	Dick Ellsworth RP 5.00	2.30	.60
☐ 126	Chuck Estrada RP 5.00	2.30	.60
☐ 127	Ron Hansen RP 4.00	1.80	.50
☐ 128	Bill Harris RP 3.50	1.55	.45
☐ 129	Bob Hartman RP 3.50	1.55	.45
☐ 130	Frank Herrera RP 3.50	1.55	.45
☐ 131	Ed Hobaugh RP 3.50	1.55	.45
☐ 132	Frank Howard RP 18.00	8.00	2.30
☐ 133	Manuel Javier RP 5.50	2.50	.70
	(Sic, Julian)		
☐ 134	Deron Johnson RP 4.00	1.80	.50
☐ 135	Ken Johnson RP 4.00	1.80	.50
☐ 136	Jim Kaat RP 40.00	18.00	5.00
☐ 137	Lou Klimchock RP 3.50	1.55	.45
☐ 138	Art Mahaffey RP 3.50	1.55	.45
☐ 139	Carl Mathias RP 3.50	1.55	.45
☐ 140	Julio Navarro RP 5.00	2.30	.60
☐ 141	Jim Proctor RP 3.50	1.55	.45
☐ 142	Bill Short RP 3.50	1.55	.45
☐ 143	Al Spangler RP 3.50	1.55	.45
☐ 144	Al Stieglitz RP 3.50	1.55	.45
☐ 145	Jim Umbricht RP 3.50	1.55	.45
☐ 146	Ted Wieand RP 3.50	1.55	.45
☐ 147	Bob Will RP 3.50	1.55	.45
☐ 148	Carl Yastrzemski RP 300.00	135.00	38.00
☐ 149	Bob Nieman 3.00	1.35	.40
☐ 150	Billy Pierce 3.50	1.55	.45
☐ 151	Giants Team 8.00	3.60	1.00
	(Checklist on back)		
☐ 152	Gail Harris 3.00	1.35	.40
☐ 153	Bobby Thomson 3.50	1.55	.45
☐ 154	Jim Davenport 3.50	1.55	.45
☐ 155	Charlie Neal 3.50	1.55	.45
☐ 156	Art Ceccarelli 3.00	1.35	.40
☐ 157	Rocky Nelson 3.50	1.55	.45
☐ 158	Wes Covington 3.50	1.55	.45
☐ 159	Jim Piersall 4.50	2.00	.55
☐ 160	Rival All-Stars 55.00	25.00	7.00
	Mickey Mantle		
	Ken Boyer		
☐ 161	Ray Narleski 3.00	1.35	.40

☐ 162	Sammy Taylor	3.00	1.35	.40
☐ 163	Hector Lopez	3.50	1.55	.45
☐ 164	Reds Team	8.00	3.60	1.00
	(Checklist on back)			
☐ 165	Jack Sanford	3.50	1.55	.45
☐ 166	Chuck Essegian	3.00	1.35	.40
☐ 167	Valmy Thomas	3.00	1.35	.40
☐ 168	Alex Grammas	3.00	1.35	.40
☐ 169	Jake Striker	3.00	1.35	.40
☐ 170	Del Crandall	3.50	1.55	.45
☐ 171	Johnny Groth	3.00	1.35	.40
☐ 172	Willie Kirkland	3.00	1.35	.40
☐ 173	Billy Martin	12.00	5.50	1.50
☐ 174	Indians Team	8.00	3.60	1.00
	(Checklist on back)			
☐ 175	Pedro Ramos	3.00	1.35	.40
☐ 176	Vada Pinson	5.50	2.50	.70
☐ 177	Johnny Kucks	3.00	1.35	.40
☐ 178	Woody Held	3.00	1.35	.40
☐ 179	Rip Coleman	3.00	1.35	.40
☐ 180	Harry Simpson	3.00	1.35	.40
☐ 181	Billy Loes	3.50	1.55	.45
☐ 182	Glen Hobbie	3.00	1.35	.40
☐ 183	Eli Grba	3.00	1.35	.40
☐ 184	Gary Geiger	3.00	1.35	.40
☐ 185	Jim Owens	3.00	1.35	.40
☐ 186	Dave Sisler	3.00	1.35	.40
☐ 187	Jay Hook	3.00	1.35	.40
☐ 188	Dick Williams	3.50	1.55	.45
☐ 189	Don McMahon	3.00	1.35	.40
☐ 190	Gene Woodling	3.50	1.55	.45
☐ 191	Johnny Klippstein	3.00	1.35	.40
☐ 192	Danny O'Connell	3.00	1.35	.40
☐ 193	Dick Hydo	3.00	1.35	.40
☐ 194	Bobby Gene Smith	3.00	1.35	.40
☐ 195	Lindy McDaniel	3.50	1.55	.45
☐ 196	Andy Carey	3.50	1.55	.45
☐ 197	Ron Kline	3.00	1.35	.40
☐ 198	Jerry Lynch	3.50	1.55	.45
☐ 199	Dick Donovan	4.00	1.80	.50
☐ 200	Willie Mays	125.00	57.50	15.50
☐ 201	Larry Osborne	3.50	1.55	.45
☐ 202	Fred Kipp	3.50	1.55	.45
☐ 203	Sammy White	3.50	1.55	.45
☐ 204	Ryne Duren	5.00	2.30	.60
☐ 205	Johnny Logan	4.00	1.80	.50
☐ 206	Claude Osteen	4.00	1.80	.50
☐ 207	Bob Boyd	3.50	1.55	.45
☐ 208	White Sox Team	8.00	3.60	1.00
	(Checklist on back)			
☐ 209	Ron Blackburn	3.50	1.55	.45
☐ 210	Harmon Killebrew	30.00	13.50	3.80
☐ 211	Taylor Phillips	3.50	1.55	.45
☐ 212	Walt Alston MG	12.00	5.50	1.50
☐ 213	Chuck Dressen MG	4.25	1.90	.55
☐ 214	Jimmy Dykes MG	4.25	1.90	.55
☐ 215	Bob Elliott MG	4.25	1.90	.55
☐ 216	Joe Gordon MG	4.25	1.90	.55
☐ 217	Charlie Grimm MG	4.25	1.90	.55
☐ 218	Solly Hemus MG	3.75	1.70	.45
☐ 219	Fred Hutchinson MG	4.25	1.90	.55
☐ 220	Billy Jurges MG	3.75	1.70	.45
☐ 221	Cookie Lavagetto MG	3.75	1.70	.45
☐ 222	Al Lopez MG	6.50	2.90	.80
☐ 223	Danny Murtaugh MG	4.50	2.00	.55
☐ 224	Paul Richards MG	4.25	1.90	.55
☐ 225	Bill Rigney MG	3.75	1.70	.45
☐ 226	Eddie Sawyer MG	3.75	1.70	.45
☐ 227	Casey Stengel MG	20.00	9.00	2.50
☐ 228	Ernie Johnson	4.00	1.80	.50
☐ 229	Joe M. Morgan	4.50	2.00	.55
☐ 230	Mound Magicians	7.00	3.10	.85
	Lou Burdette			
	Warren Spahn			
	Bob Buhl			
☐ 231	Hal Naragon	3.50	1.55	.45
☐ 232	Jim Busby	3.50	1.55	.45
☐ 233	Don Elston	3.50	1.55	.45
☐ 234	Don Demeter	3.50	1.55	.45
☐ 235	Gus Bell	4.00	1.80	.50
☐ 236	Dick Ricketts	3.50	1.55	.45
☐ 237	Elmer Valo	3.50	1.55	.45
☐ 238	Danny Kravitz	3.50	1.55	.45
☐ 239	Joe Shipley	3.50	1.55	.45
☐ 240	Luis Aparicio	15.00	6.75	1.90
☐ 241	Albie Pearson	4.00	1.80	.50
☐ 242	Cardinals Team	8.00	3.60	1.00
	(Checklist on back)			
☐ 243	Bubba Phillips	3.50	1.55	.45
☐ 244	Hal Griggs	3.50	1.55	.45
☐ 245	Eddie Yost	4.00	1.80	.50
☐ 246	Lee Maye	4.00	1.80	.50
☐ 247	Gil McDougald	5.25	2.40	.65
☐ 248	Del Rice	3.50	1.55	.45
☐ 249	Earl Wilson	5.00	2.30	.60
☐ 250	Stan Musial	110.00	50.00	14.00
☐ 251	Bob Malkmus	3.50	1.55	.45
☐ 252	Ray Herbert	3.50	1.55	.45
☐ 253	Eddie Bressoud	3.50	1.55	.45
☐ 254	Arnie Portocarrero	3.50	1.55	.45
☐ 255	Jim Gilliam	5.00	2.30	.60
☐ 256	Dick Brown	3.50	1.55	.45
☐ 257	Gordy Coleman	5.00	2.30	.60
☐ 258	Dick Groat	5.50	2.50	.70
☐ 259	George Altman	3.50	1.55	.45
☐ 260	Power Plus	5.25	2.40	.65
	Rocky Colavito			
	Tito Francona			
☐ 261	Pete Burnside	3.50	1.55	.45
☐ 262	Hank Bauer	4.25	1.90	.55
☐ 263	Darrell Johnson	3.50	1.55	.45
☐ 264	Robin Roberts	14.00	6.25	1.75
☐ 265	Rip Repulski	3.50	1.55	.45
☐ 266	Joey Jay	4.00	1.80	.50

☐	267	Jim Marshall	3.50	1.55	.45	☐ 321 Ron Fairly	5.00	2.30	.60

☐ 267	Jim Marshall	3.50	1.55	.45
☐ 268	Al Worthington	3.50	1.55	.45
☐ 269	Gene Green	3.50	1.55	.45
☐ 270	Bob Turley	5.00	2.30	.60
☐ 271	Julio Becquer	3.50	1.55	.45
☐ 272	Fred Green	3.50	1.55	.45
☐ 273	Neil Chrisley	3.50	1.55	.45
☐ 274	Tom Acker	3.50	1.55	.45
☐ 275	Curt Flood	5.00	2.30	.60
☐ 276	Ken McBride	3.50	1.55	.45
☐ 277	Harry Bright	3.50	1.55	.45
☐ 278	Stan Williams	4.00	1.80	.50
☐ 279	Chuck Tanner	4.00	1.80	.50
☐ 280	Frank Sullivan	3.50	1.55	.45
☐ 281	Ray Boone	4.00	1.80	.50
☐ 282	Joe Nuxhall	4.00	1.80	.50
☐ 283	John Blanchard	4.50	2.00	.55
☐ 284	Don Gross	3.50	1.55	.45
☐ 285	Harry Anderson	3.50	1.55	.45
☐ 286	Ray Semproch	3.50	1.55	.45
☐ 287	Felipe Alou	7.00	3.10	.85
☐ 288	Bob Mabe	3.75	1.70	.45
☐ 289	Willie Jones	3.75	1.70	.45
☐ 290	Jerry Lumpe	3.75	1.70	.45
☐ 291	Bob Keegan	3.75	1.70	.45
☐ 292	Dodger Backstops	4.25	1.90	.55
	Joe Pignatano			
	John Roseboro			
☐ 293	Gene Conley	4.25	1.90	.55
☐ 294	Tony Taylor	4.25	1.90	.55
☐ 295	Gil Hodges	20.00	9.00	2.50
☐ 296	Nelson Chittum	3.75	1.70	.45
☐ 297	Reno Bertoia	3.75	1.70	.45
☐ 298	George Witt	3.75	1.70	.45
☐ 299	Earl Torgeson	3.75	1.70	.45
☐ 300	Hank Aaron	125.00	57.50	15.50
☐ 301	Jerry Davie	3.75	1.70	.45
☐ 302	Phillies Team	8.00	3.60	1.00
	(Checklist on back)			
☐ 303	Billy O'Dell	3.75	1.70	.45
☐ 304	Joe Ginsberg	3.75	1.70	.45
☐ 305	Richie Ashburn	10.00	4.50	1.25
☐ 306	Frank Baumann	3.75	1.70	.45
☐ 307	Gene Oliver	3.75	1.70	.45
☐ 308	Dick Hall	3.75	1.70	.45
☐ 309	Bob Hale	3.75	1.70	.45
☐ 310	Frank Malzone	4.25	1.90	.55
☐ 311	Raul Sanchez	3.75	1.70	.45
☐ 312	Charley Lau	4.25	1.90	.55
☐ 313	Turk Lown	3.75	1.70	.45
☐ 314	Chico Fernandez	3.75	1.70	.45
☐ 315	Bobby Shantz	4.25	1.90	.55
☐ 316	Willie McCovey	250.00	115.00	31.00
☐ 317	Pumpsie Green	4.75	2.10	.60
☐ 318	Jim Baxes	4.25	1.90	.55
☐ 319	Joe Koppe	4.25	1.90	.55
☐ 320	Bob Allison	5.00	2.30	.60

☐ 321	Ron Fairly	5.00	2.30	.60
☐ 322	Willie Tasby	4.25	1.90	.55
☐ 323	John Romano	4.25	1.90	.55
☐ 324	Jim Perry	5.00	2.30	.60
☐ 325	Jim O'Toole	4.75	2.10	.60
☐ 326	Bob Clemente	125.00	57.50	15.50
☐ 327	Ray Sadecki	5.00	2.30	.60
☐ 328	Earl Battey	3.75	1.70	.45
☐ 329	Zack Monroe	3.75	1.70	.45
☐ 330	Harvey Kuenn	5.00	2.30	.60
☐ 331	Henry Mason	3.75	1.70	.45
☐ 332	Yankees Team	30.00	13.50	3.80
	(Checklist on back)			
☐ 333	Danny McDevitt	3.75	1.70	.45
☐ 334	Ted Abernathy	3.75	1.70	.45
☐ 335	Red Schoendienst	12.50	5.75	1.55
☐ 336	Ike Delock	3.75	1.70	.45
☐ 337	Cal Neeman	3.75	1.70	.45
☐ 338	Ray Monzant	3.75	1.70	.45
☐ 339	Harry Chiti	3.75	1.70	.45
☐ 340	Harvey Haddix	4.25	1.90	.55
☐ 341	Carroll Hardy	3.75	1.70	.45
☐ 342	Casey Wise	3.75	1.70	.45
☐ 343	Sandy Koufax	150.00	70.00	19.00
☐ 344	Clint Courtney	3.75	1.70	.45
☐ 345	Don Newcombe	5.00	2.30	.60
☐ 346	J.C. Martin UER	4.25	1.90	.55
	(Face actually			
	Gary Peters)			
☐ 347	Ed Bouchee	3.75	1.70	.45
☐ 348	Barry Shetrone	3.75	1.70	.45
☐ 349	Moe Drabowsky	4.25	1.90	.55
☐ 350	Mickey Mantle	400.00	180.00	50.00
☐ 351	Don Nottebart	3.75	1.70	.45
☐ 352	Cincy Clouters	6.50	2.90	.80
	Gus Bell			
	Frank Robinson			
	Jerry Lynch			
☐ 353	Don Larsen	4.50	2.00	.55
☐ 354	Bob Lillis	3.75	1.70	.45
☐ 355	Bill White	7.50	3.40	.95
☐ 356	Joe Amalfitano	3.75	1.70	.45
☐ 357	Al Schroll	3.75	1.70	.45
☐ 358	Joe DeMaestri	3.75	1.70	.45
☐ 359	Buddy Gilbert	3.75	1.70	.45
☐ 360	Herb Score	5.00	2.30	.60
☐ 361	Bob Oldis	3.75	1.70	.45
☐ 362	Russ Kemmerer	3.75	1.70	.45
☐ 363	Gene Stephens	3.75	1.70	.45
☐ 364	Paul Foytack	3.75	1.70	.45
☐ 365	Minnie Minoso	5.50	2.50	.70
☐ 366	Dallas Green	9.00	4.00	1.15
☐ 367	Bill Tuttle	3.75	1.70	.45
☐ 368	Daryl Spencer	3.75	1.70	.45
☐ 369	Billy Hoeft	3.75	1.70	.45
☐ 370	Bill Skowron	8.00	3.60	1.00
☐ 371	Bud Byerly	3.75	1.70	.45

□	372	Frank House	3.75	1.70	.45
□	373	Don Hoak	4.25	1.90	.55
□	374	Bob Buhl	4.25	1.90	.55
□	375	Dale Long	4.25	1.90	.55
□	376	John Briggs	3.75	1.70	.45
□	377	Roger Maris	120.00	55.00	15.00
□	378	Stu Miller	4.25	1.90	.55
□	379	Red Wilson	3.75	1.70	.45
□	380	Bob Shaw	3.75	1.70	.45
□	381	Braves Team	8.00	3.60	1.00
		(Checklist on back)			
□	382	Ted Bowsfield	3.75	1.70	.45
□	383	Leon Wagner	3.75	1.70	.45
□	384	Don Cardwell	3.75	1.70	.45
□	385	World Series Game 1	6.00	2.70	.75
		Charlie Neal			
		Steals Second			
□	386	World Series Game 2	6.00	2.70	.75
		Charlie Neal			
		Belts Second Homer			
□	387	World Series Game 3	6.00	2.70	.75
		Carl Furillo			
		Breaks Game			
□	388	World Series Game 4	10.00	4.50	1.25
		Gil Hodges' Homer			
□	389	World Series Game 5	10.00	4.50	1.25
		Luis Aparicio			
		Swipes Base			
□	390	World Series Game 6	6.00	2.70	.75
		Scrambling After Ball			
□	391	World Series Summary	6.00	2.70	.75
		The Champs Celebrate			
□	392	Tex Clevenger	3.75	1.70	.45
□	393	Smoky Burgess	4.25	1.90	.55
□	394	Norm Larker	4.25	1.90	.55
□	395	Hoyt Wilhelm	12.50	5.75	1.55
□	396	Steve Bilko	3.75	1.70	.45
□	397	Don Blasingame	3.75	1.70	.45
□	398	Mike Cuellar	4.25	1.90	.55
□	399	Young Hill Stars	4.25	1.90	.55
		Milt Pappas			
		Jack Fisher			
		Jerry Walker			
□	400	Rocky Colavito	12.50	5.75	1.55
□	401	Bob Duliba	3.75	1.70	.45
□	402	Dick Stuart	4.25	1.90	.55
□	403	Ed Sadowski	3.75	1.70	.45
□	404	Bob Rush	3.75	1.70	.45
□	405	Bobby Richardson	8.50	3.80	1.05
□	406	Billy Klaus	3.75	1.70	.45
□	407	Gary Peters UER	5.00	2.30	.60
		(Face actually			
		J.C. Martin)			
□	408	Carl Furillo	6.00	2.70	.75
□	409	Ron Samford	3.75	1.70	.45
□	410	Sam Jones	4.25	1.90	.55
□	411	Ed Bailey	3.75	1.70	.45
□	412	Bob Anderson	3.75	1.70	.45
□	413	Athletics Team	8.00	3.60	1.00
		(Checklist on back)			
□	414	Don Williams	3.75	1.70	.45
□	415	Bob Cerv	3.75	1.70	.45
□	416	Humberto Robinson	3.75	1.70	.45
□	417	Chuck Cottier	5.00	2.30	.60
□	418	Don Mossi	4.25	1.90	.55
□	419	George Crowe	3.75	1.70	.45
□	420	Eddie Mathews	35.00	16.00	4.40
□	421	Duke Maas	3.75	1.70	.45
□	422	John Powers	3.75	1.70	.45
□	423	Ed Fitzgerald	3.75	1.70	.45
□	424	Pete Whisenant	3.75	1.70	.45
□	425	Johnny Podres	5.00	2.30	.60
□	426	Ron Jackson	3.75	1.70	.45
□	427	Al Grunwald	3.75	1.70	.45
□	428	Al Smith	3.75	1.70	.45
□	429	AL Kings	6.00	2.70	.75
		Nellie Fox			
		Harvey Kuenn			
□	430	Art Ditmar	3.75	1.70	.45
□	431	Andre Rodgers	3.75	1.70	.45
□	432	Chuck Stobbs	3.75	1.70	.45
□	433	Irv Noren	3.75	1.70	.45
□	434	Brooks Lawrence	3.75	1.70	.45
□	435	Gene Freese	3.75	1.70	.45
□	436	Marv Throneberry	4.50	2.00	.55
□	437	Bob Friend	4.25	1.90	.55
□	438	Jim Coker	3.75	1.70	.45
□	439	Tom Brewer	3.75	1.70	.45
□	440	Jim Lemon	4.25	1.90	.55
□	441	Gary Bell	5.00	2.30	.60
□	442	Joe Pignatano	5.00	2.30	.60
□	443	Charlie Maxwell	5.50	2.50	.70
□	444	Jerry Kindall	5.50	2.50	.70
□	445	Warren Spahn	55.00	25.00	7.00
□	446	Ellis Burton	5.00	2.30	.60
□	447	Ray Moore	5.00	2.30	.60
□	448	Jim Gentile	12.50	5.75	1.55
□	449	Jim Brosnan	5.50	2.50	.70
□	450	Orlando Cepeda	20.00	9.00	2.50
□	451	Curt Simmons	5.50	2.50	.70
□	452	Ray Webster	5.00	2.30	.60
□	453	Vern Law	7.00	3.10	.85
□	454	Hal Woodshick	5.00	2.30	.60
□	455	Baltimore Coaches	6.00	2.70	.75
		Eddie Robinson			
		Harry Brecheen			
		Luman Harris			
□	456	Red Sox Coaches	7.50	3.40	.95
		Rudy York			
		Billy Herman			
		Sal Maglie			
		Del Baker			
□	457	Cubs Coaches	6.00	2.70	.75
		Charlie Root			

Lou Klein
Elvin Tappe
☐ 458 White Sox Coaches......6.00   2.70   .75
Johnny Cooney
Don Gutteridge
Tony Cuccinello
Ray Berres
☐ 459 Reds Coaches.............6.00   2.70   .75
Reggie Otero
Cot Deal
Wally Moses
☐ 460 Indians Coaches ....7.50   3.40   .95
Mel Harder
Jo-Jo White
Bob Lemon
Ralph(Red) Kress
☐ 461 Tigers Coaches............7.50   3.40   .95
Tom Ferrick
Luke Appling
Billy Hitchcock
☐ 462 Athletics Coaches......6.00   2.70   .75
Fred Fitzsimmons
Don Heffner
Walker Cooper
☐ 463 Dodgers Coaches........6.50   2.90   .80
Bobby Bragan
Pete Reiser
Joe Becker
Greg Mulleavy
☐ 464 Braves Coaches ....6.00   2.70   .75
Bob Scheffing
Whitlow Wyatt
Andy Pafko
George Myatt
☐ 465 Yankees Coaches.......15.00   6.75   1.90
Bill Dickey
Ralph Houk
Frank Crosetti
Ed Lopat
☐ 466 Phillies Coaches..........6.00   2.70   .75
Ken Silvestri
Dick Carter
Andy Cohen
☐ 467 Pirates Coaches..........6.00   2.70   .75
Mickey Vernon
Frank Oceak
Sam Narron
Bill Burwell
☐ 468 Cardinals Coaches ......6.00   2.70   .75
Johnny Keane
Howie Pollet
Ray Katt
Harry Walker
☐ 469 Giants Coaches...........6.00   2.70   .75
Wes Westrum
Salty Parker
Bill Posedel

☐ 470 Senators Coaches.......6.00   2.70   .75
Bob Swift
Ellis Clary
Sam Mele
☐ 471 Ned Garver..................5.00   2.30   .60
☐ 472 Alvin Dark...................5.50   2.50   .70
☐ 473 Al Cicotte....................5.00   2.30   .60
☐ 474 Haywood Sullivan........5.50   2.50   .70
☐ 475 Don Drysdale.............50.00 23.00 6.25
☐ 476 Lou Johnson...............5.00   2.30   .60
☐ 477 Don Ferrarese.............5.00   2.30   .60
☐ 478 Frank Torre.................5.50   2.50   .70
☐ 479 Georges Maranda........5.00   2.30   .60
☐ 480 Yogi Berra.................85.00 38.00 10.50
☐ 481 Wes Stock...................5.50   2.50   .70
☐ 482 Frank Bolling...............5.00   2.30   .60
☐ 483 Camilo Pascual...........5.50   2.50   .70
☐ 484 Pirates Team..............25.00 11.50 3.10
(Checklist on back)
☐ 485 Ken Boyer..................12.50   5.75   1.55
☐ 486 Bobby Del Greco.........5.00   2.30   .60
☐ 487 Tom Sturdivant............5.00   2.30   .60
☐ 488 Norm Cash.................12.50   5.75   1.55
☐ 489 Steve Ridzik................5.00   2.30   .60
☐ 490 Frank Robinson...........65.00 29.00 8.25
☐ 491 Mel Roach...................5.00   2.30   .60
☐ 492 Larry Jackson..............5.00   2.30   .60
☐ 493 Duke Snider...............65.00 29.00 8.25
☐ 494 Orioles Team..............12.50   5.75   1.55
(Checklist on back)
☐ 495 Sherm Lollar...............5.50   2.50   .70
☐ 496 Bill Virdon...................7.00   3.10   .85
☐ 497 John Tsitouris..............5.00   2.30   .60
☐ 498 Al Pilarcik...................5.00   2.30   .60
☐ 499 Johnny James.............5.00   2.30   .60
☐ 500 Johnny Temple.............5.50   2.50   .70
☐ 501 Bob Schmidt................5.00   2.30   .60
☐ 502 Jim Bunning...............12.50   5.75   1.55
☐ 503 Don Lee ....5.00   2.30   .60
☐ 504 Seth Morehead............5.00   2.30   .60
☐ 505 Ted Kluszewski...........12.50   5.75   1.55
☐ 506 Lee Walls....................5.00   2.30   .60
☐ 507 Dick Stigman..............14.50   6.50   1.80
☐ 508 Billy Consolo..............12.00   5.50   1.50
☐ 509 Tommy Davis..............30.00 13.50 3.80
☐ 510 Gerry Staley...............12.00   5.50   1.50
☐ 511 Ken Walters................12.00   5.50   1.50
☐ 512 Joe Gibbon 12.00   5.50   1.50
☐ 513 Chicago Cubs..............36.00 16.00 4.50
Team Card
(Checklist on back)
☐ 514 Steve Barber..............18.00   8.00   2.30
☐ 515 Stan Lopata................12.00   5.50   1.50
☐ 516 Marty Kutyna...............12.00   5.50   1.50
☐ 517 Charlie James 12.00   5.50   1.50
☐ 518 Tony Gonzalez............14.50   6.50   1.80
☐ 519 Ed Roebuck................12.00   5.50   1.50

☐ 520	Don Buddin................12.00	5.50	1.50
☐ 521	Mike Lee 12.00	5.50	1.50
☐ 522	Ken Hunt 12.00	5.50	1.50
☐ 523	Clay Dalrymple 12.00	5.50	1.50
☐ 524	Bill Henry 12.00	5.50	1.50
☐ 525	Marv Breeding 12.00	5.50	1.50
☐ 526	Paul Giel 14.50	6.50	1.80
☐ 527	Jose Valdivielso 12.00	5.50	1.50
☐ 528	Ben Johnson..............12.00	5.50	1.50
☐ 529	Norm Sherry 18.00	8.00	2.30
☐ 530	Mike McCormick........14.50	6.50	1.80
☐ 531	Sandy Amoros 14.50	6.50	1.80
☐ 532	Mike Garcia...............14.50	6.50	1.80
☐ 533	Lu Clinton 12.00	5.50	1.50
☐ 534	Ken MacKenzie 12.00	5.50	1.50
☐ 535	Whitey Lockman.........14.50	6.50	1.80
☐ 536	Wynn Hawkins 12.00	5.50	1.50
☐ 537	Boston Red Sox...........36.00	16.00	4.50
	Team Card		
	(Checklist on back)		
☐ 538	Frank Barnes..............12.00	5.50	1.50
☐ 539	Gene Baker 12.00	5.50	1.50
☐ 540	Jerry Walker 12.00	5.50	1.50
☐ 541	Tony Curry 12.00	5.50	1.50
☐ 542	Ken Hamlin 12.00	5.50	1.50
☐ 543	Elio Chacon...............12.00	5.50	1.50
☐ 544	Bill Monbouquette......12.00	5.50	1.50
☐ 545	Carl Sawatski 12.00	5.50	1.50
☐ 546	Hank Aguirre 12.00	5.50	1.50
☐ 547	Bob Aspromonte..........12.00	5.50	1.50
☐ 548	Don Mincher 14.50	6.50	1.80
☐ 549	John Buzhardt............12.00	5.50	1.50
☐ 550	Jim Landis 12.00	5.50	1.50
☐ 551	Ed Rakow 12.00	5.50	1.50
☐ 552	Walt Bond 12.00	5.50	1.50
☐ 553	Bill Skowron AS..........18.00	8.00	2.30
☐ 554	Willie McCovey AS......70.00	32.00	8.75
☐ 555	Nellie Fox AS.............20.00	9.00	2.50
☐ 556	Charlie Neal AS 15.00	6.75	1.90
☐ 557	Frank Malzone AS 15.00	6.75	1.90
☐ 558	Eddie Mathews AS.......35.00	16.00	4.40
☐ 559	Luis Aparicio AS 25.00	11.50	3.10
☐ 560	Ernie Banks AS 60.00	27.00	7.50
☐ 561	Al Kaline AS...............60.00	27.00	7.50
☐ 562	Joe Cunningham AS 15.00	6.75	1.90
☐ 563	Mickey Mantle AS.....300.00	135.00	38.00
☐ 564	Willie Mays AS 125.00	57.50	15.50
☐ 565	Roger Maris AS 120.00	55.00	15.00
☐ 566	Hank Aaron AS 125.00	57.50	15.50
☐ 567	Sherm Lollar AS..........15.00	6.75	1.90
☐ 568	Del Crandall AS..........15.00	6.75	1.90
☐ 569	Camilo Pascual AS 15.00	6.75	1.90
☐ 570	Don Drysdale AS.........35.00	16.00	4.40
☐ 571	Billy Pierce AS 15.00	6.75	1.90
☐ 572	Johnny Antonelli AS...25.00	7.50	2.50

1961 Topps

The cards in this 587-card set measure 2 1/2" by 3 1/2". In 1961, Topps returned to the vertical obverse format. Introduced for the first time were "League Leaders" (41 to 50) and separate, numbered checklist cards. Two number 463s exist: the Braves team card carrying that number was meant to be card 426. There are three versions of the second series checklist card number 98; the variations are distinguished by the color of the "CHECKLIST" headline on the front of the card, the color of the printing of the card number on the bottom of the reverse, and the presence of the copyright notice running vertically on the card back. There are two groups of managers (131-139 and 219-226) as well as separate series of World Series cards (306-313), Baseball Thrills (401 to 410), previous MVP's (AL 471-478 and NL 479-486) and Sporting News All-Stars (566 to 589). The usual last series scarcity (523 to 589) exists. The set actually totals 587 cards since numbers 587 and 588 were never issued. The key rookies in this set are ex-Cubs Ron Santo and Billy Williams.

	NRMT	VG-E	GOOD
COMPLETE SET (587) ....5850.		2600.	750.00
COMMON PLAYER (1-109) 3.00		1.35	.40
COMMON PLAYER (110-370) ...3.00		1.35	.40
COMMON PLAYER (371-446) ...4.50		2.00	.55
COMMON PLAYER (447-522) ...5.50		2.50	.70
COMMON PLAYER (523-565) .34.00		15.50	4.20
COMMON AS (566-589) 36.00		16.00	4.50

☐ 1	Dick Groat.................20.00	4.00	1.20
☐ 2	Roger Maris................180.00	80.00	23.00

☐ 3	John Buzhardt.............3.00	1.35	.40
☐ 4	Lenny Green...............3.00	1.35	.40
☐ 5	John Romano..............3.00	1.35	.40
☐ 6	Ed Roebuck................3.00	1.35	.40
☐ 7	White Sox Team..........6.50	2.90	.80
☐ 8	Dick Williams.............3.50	1.55	.45
☐ 9	Bob Purkey................3.00	1.35	.40
☐ 10	Brooks Robinson 35.00	16.00	4.40
☐ 11	Curt Simmons............3.50	1.55	.45
☐ 12	Moe Thacker..............3.00	1.35	.40
☐ 13	Chuck Cottier.............3.00	1.35	.40
☐ 14	Don Mossi.................3.50	1.55	.45
☐ 15	Willie Kirkland............3.00	1.35	.40
☐ 16	Billy Muffett...............3.00	1.35	.40
☐ 17	Checklist 1..............10.00	2.00	.60
☐ 18	Jim Grant..................3.50	1.55	.45
☐ 19	Clete Boyer................4.50	2.00	.55
☐ 20	Robin Roberts.............12.50	5.75	1.55
☐ 21	Zorro Versalles UER......4.50	2.00	.55
	(First name should		
	be Zoilo)		
☐ 22	Clem Labine..............3.50	1.55	.45
☐ 23	Don Demeter..............3.00	1.35	.40
☐ 24	Ken Johnson..............3.00	1.35	.40
☐ 25	Reds' Heavy Artillery......7.00	3.10	.85
	Vada Pinson		
	Gus Bell		
	Frank Robinson		
☐ 26	Wes Stock.................3.00	1.35	.40
☐ 27	Jerry Kindall..............3.00	1.35	.40
☐ 28	Hector Lopez..............3.00	1.35	.40
☐ 29	Don Nottebart.............3.00	1.35	.40
☐ 30	Nellie Fox..................7.50	3.40	.95
☐ 31	Bob Schmidt...............3.00	1.35	.40
☐ 32	Ray Sadecki...............3.00	1.35	.40
☐ 33	Gary Geiger...............3.00	1.35	.40
☐ 34	Wynn Hawkins............3.00	1.35	.40
☐ 35	Ron Santo................55.00	25.00	7.00
☐ 36	Jack Kralick...............3.00	1.35	.40
☐ 37	Charlie Maxwell...........3.50	1.55	.45
☐ 38	Bob Lillis..................3.00	1.35	.40
☐ 39	Leo Posada...............3.00	1.35	.40
☐ 40	Bob Turley.................3.50	1.55	.45
☐ 41	NL Batting Leaders 9.00	4.00	1.15
	Dick Groat		
	Norm Larker		
	Willie Mays		
	Roberto Clemente		
☐ 42	AL Batting Leaders.........5.00	2.30	.60
	Pete Runnels		
	Al Smith		
	Minnie Minoso		
	Bill Skowron		
☐ 43	NL Home Run Leaders.12.00	5.50	1.50
	Ernie Banks		
	Hank Aaron		
	Ed Mathews		

	Ken Boyer		
☐ 44	AL Home Run Leaders.35.00	16.00	4.40
	Mickey Mantle		
	Roger Maris		
	Jim Lemon		
	Rocky Colavito		
☐ 45	NL ERA Leaders.............5.00	2.30	.60
	Mike McCormick		
	Ernie Broglio		
	Don Drysdale		
	Bob Friend		
	Stan Williams		
☐ 46	AL ERA Leaders.............5.00	2.30	.60
	Frank Baumann		
	Jim Bunning		
	Art Ditmar		
	Hal Brown		
☐ 47	NL Pitching Leaders........5.00	2.30	.60
	Ernie Broglio		
	Warren Spahn		
	Vern Law		
	Lou Burdette		
☐ 48	AL Pitching Leaders.........5.00	2.30	.60
	Chuck Estrada		
	Jim Perry		
	Bud Daley		
	Art Ditmar		
	Frank Lary		
	Milt Pappas		
☐ 49	NL Strikeout Leaders 7.00	3.10	.85
	Don Drysdale		
	Sandy Koufax		
	Sam Jones		
	Ernie Broglio		
☐ 50	AL Strikeout Leaders.........5.00	2.30	.60
	Jim Bunning		
	Pedro Ramos		
	Early Wynn		
	Frank Lary		
☐ 51	Detroit Tigers.............6.50	2.90	.80
	Team Card		
☐ 52	George Crowe.............3.00	1.35	.40
☐ 53	Russ Nixon 3.00	1.35	.40
☐ 54	Earl Francis...............3.00	1.35	.40
☐ 55	Jim Davenport............3.50	1.55	.45
☐ 56	Russ Kemmerer...........3.00	1.35	.40
☐ 57	Marv Throneberry.........4.00	1.80	.50
☐ 58	Joe Schaffernoth...........3.00	1.35	.40
☐ 59	Jim Woods.................3.00	1.35	.40
☐ 60	Woody Held...............3.00	1.35	.40
☐ 61	Ron Piche.................3.00	1.35	.40
☐ 62	Al Pilarcik................3.00	1.35	.40
☐ 63	Jim Kaat...................8.50	3.80	1.05
☐ 64	Alex Grammas.............3.00	1.35	.40
☐ 65	Ted Kluszewski............6.00	2.70	.75
☐ 66	Bill Henry.................3.00	1.35	.40
☐ 67	Ossie Virgil...............3.00	1.35	.40

☐ 68	Deron Johnson 3.50	1.55	.45
☐ 69	Earl Wilson 3.50	1.55	.45
☐ 70	Bill Virdon 3.50	1.55	.45
☐ 71	Jerry Adair 3.00	1.35	.40
☐ 72	Stu Miller 3.50	1.55	.45
☐ 73	Al Spangler 3.00	1.35	.40
☐ 74	Joe Pignatano 3.00	1.35	.40
☐ 75	Lindy Shows Larry ...3.50	1.55	.45
	Lindy McDaniel		
	Larry Jackson		
☐ 76	Harry Anderson 3.00	1.35	.40
☐ 77	Dick Stigman 3.00	1.35	.40
☐ 78	Lee Walls 3.00	1.35	.40
☐ 79	Joe Ginsberg 3.00	1.35	.40
☐ 80	Harmon Killebrew 25.00	11.50	3.10
☐ 81	Tracy Stallard 3.00	1.35	.40
☐ 82	Joe Christopher 3.00	1.35	.40
☐ 83	Bob Bruce 3.00	1.35	.40
☐ 84	Lee Maye 3.00	1.35	.40
☐ 85	Jerry Walker 3.00	1.35	.40
☐ 86	Los Angeles Dodgers....6.50	2.90	.80
	Team Card		
☐ 87	Joe Amalfitano 3.00	1.35	.40
☐ 88	Richie Ashburn 8.00	3.60	1.00
☐ 89	Billy Martin 8.50	3.80	1.05
☐ 90	Gerry Staley 3.00	1.35	.40
☐ 91	Walt Moryn 3.00	1.35	.40
☐ 92	Hal Naragon 3.00	1.35	.40
☐ 93	Tony Gonzalez 3.00	1.35	.40
☐ 94	Johnny Kucks 3.00	1.35	.40
☐ 95	Norm Cash 6.50	2.90	.80
☐ 96	Billy O'Dell 3.00	1.35	.40
☐ 97	Jerry Lynch 3.50	1.55	.45
☐ 98A	Checklist 2 ....10.00	2.00	.60
	(Red "Checklist", 98 black on white)		
☐ 98B	Checklist 2 ....10.00	2.00	.60
	(Yellow "Checklist", 98 black on white)		
☐ 98C	Checklist 2 ....10.00	2.00	.60
	(Yellow "Checklist", 98 white on black, no copyright)		
☐ 99	Don Buddin UER 3.00	1.35	.40
	(66 HR's)		
☐ 100	Harvey Haddix 3.50	1.55	.45
☐ 101	Bubba Phillips 3.00	1.35	.40
☐ 102	Gene Stephens 3.00	1.35	.40
☐ 103	Ruben Amaro 3.00	1.35	.40
☐ 104	John Blanchard 3.50	1.55	.45
☐ 105	Carl Willey 3.00	1.35	.40
☐ 106	Whitey Herzog 5.00	2.30	.60
☐ 107	Seth Morehead 3.00	1.35	.40
☐ 108	Dan Dobbek 3.00	1.35	.40
☐ 109	Johnny Podres 3.50	1.55	.45
☐ 110	Vada Pinson 4.50	2.00	.55
☐ 111	Jack Meyer 3.00	1.35	.40
☐ 112	Chico Fernandez 3.00	1.35	.40
☐ 113	Mike Fornieles 3.00	1.35	.40
☐ 114	Hobie Landrith 3.00	1.35	.40
☐ 115	Johnny Antonelli 3.50	1.55	.45
☐ 116	Joe DeMaestri 3.00	1.35	.40
☐ 117	Dale Long 3.50	1.55	.45
☐ 118	Chris Cannizzaro 3.00	1.35	.40
☐ 119	A's Big Armor 3.50	1.55	.45
	Norm Siebern		
	Hank Bauer		
	Jerry Lumpe		
☐ 120	Eddie Mathews 30.00	13.50	3.80
☐ 121	Eli Grba 3.00	1.35	.40
☐ 122	Chicago Cubs 6.50	2.90	.80
	Team Card		
☐ 123	Billy Gardner 3.00	1.35	.40
☐ 124	J.C. Martin 3.00	1.35	.40
☐ 125	Steve Barber 3.00	1.35	.40
☐ 126	Dick Stuart 3.50	1.55	.45
☐ 127	Ron Kline 3.00	1.35	.40
☐ 128	Rip Repulski 3.00	1.35	.40
☐ 129	Ed Hobaugh 3.00	1.35	.40
☐ 130	Norm Larker 3.00	1.35	.40
☐ 131	Paul Richards MG 4.00	1.80	.50
☐ 132	Al Lopez MG 4.50	2.00	.55
☐ 133	Ralph Houk MG 5.00	2.30	.60
☐ 134	Mickey Vernon MG 4.00	1.80	.50
☐ 135	Fred Hutchinson MG....4.00	1.80	.50
☐ 136	Walt Alston MG 6.00	2.70	.75
☐ 137	Chuck Dressen MG 4.00	1.80	.50
☐ 138	Danny Murtaugh MG....4.50	2.00	.55
☐ 139	Solly Hemus MG 3.50	1.55	.45
☐ 140	Gus Triandos 3.50	1.55	.45
☐ 141	Billy Williams 110.00	50.00	14.00
☐ 142	Luis Arroyo 3.50	1.55	.45
☐ 143	Russ Snyder 3.00	1.35	.40
☐ 144	Jim Coker 3.00	1.35	.40
☐ 145	Bob Buhl 3.50	1.55	.45
☐ 146	Marty Keough 3.00	1.35	.40
☐ 147	Ed Rakow 3.00	1.35	.40
☐ 148	Julian Javier 3.50	1.55	.45
☐ 149	Bob Oldis 3.00	1.35	.40
☐ 150	Willie Mays 125.00	57.50	15.50
☐ 151	Jim Donohue 3.00	1.35	.40
☐ 152	Earl Torgeson 3.00	1.35	.40
☐ 153	Don Lee 3.00	1.35	.40
☐ 154	Bobby Del Greco 3.00	1.35	.40
☐ 155	Johnny Temple 3.50	1.55	.45
☐ 156	Ken Hunt 3.00	1.35	.40
☐ 157	Cal McLish 3.00	1.35	.40
☐ 158	Pete Daley 3.00	1.35	.40
☐ 159	Orioles Team 6.50	2.90	.80
☐ 160	Whitey Ford UER 40.00	18.00	5.00
	(Incorrectly listed as 5'0" tall)		
☐ 161	Sherman Jones UER....3.00	1.35	.40
	(Photo actually		

Eddie Fisher)

☐ 162	Jay Hook	3.00	1.35	.40
☐ 163	Ed Sadowski	3.00	1.35	.40
☐ 164	Felix Mantilla	3.00	1.35	.40
☐ 165	Gino Cimoli	3.00	1.35	.40
☐ 166	Danny Kravitz	3.00	1.35	.40
☐ 167	San Francisco Giants	6.50	2.90	.80

Team Card

☐ 168	Tommy Davis	6.00	2.70	.75
☐ 169	Don Elston	3.00	1.35	.40
☐ 170	Al Smith	3.00	1.35	.40
☐ 171	Paul Foytack	3.00	1.35	.40
☐ 172	Don Dillard	3.00	1.35	.40
☐ 173	Beantown Bombers	3.50	1.55	.45

Frank Malzone
Vic Wertz
Jackie Jensen

☐ 174	Ray Semproch	3.00	1.35	.40
☐ 175	Gene Freese	3.00	1.35	.40
☐ 176	Ken Aspromonte	3.00	1.35	.40
☐ 177	Don Larsen	4.50	2.00	.55
☐ 178	Bob Nieman	3.00	1.35	.40
☐ 179	Joe Koppe	3.00	1.35	.40
☐ 180	Bobby Richardson	8.00	3.60	1.00
☐ 181	Fred Green	3.00	1.35	.40
☐ 182	Dave Nicholson	3.00	1.35	.40
☐ 183	Andre Rodgers	3.00	1.35	.40
☐ 184	Steve Bilko	3.00	1.35	.40
☐ 185	Herb Score	4.50	2.00	.55
☐ 186	Elmer Valo	3.00	1.35	.40
☐ 187	Billy Klaus	3.00	1.35	.40
☐ 188	Jim Marshall	3.00	1.35	.40
☐ 189A	Checklist 3	10.00	2.00	.60

(Copyright symbol
almost adjacent to
263 Ken Hamlin)

☐ 189B	Checklist 3	10.00	2.00	.60

(Copyright symbol
adjacent to
264 Glen Hobbie)

☐ 190	Stan Williams	3.50	1.55	.45
☐ 191	Mike DeLaHoz	3.00	1.35	.40
☐ 192	Dick Brown	3.00	1.35	.40
☐ 193	Gene Conley	3.50	1.55	.45
☐ 194	Gordy Coleman	3.50	1.55	.45
☐ 195	Jerry Casale	3.00	1.35	.40
☐ 196	Ed Bouchee	3.00	1.35	.40
☐ 197	Dick Hall	3.00	1.35	.40
☐ 198	Carl Sawatski	3.00	1.35	.40
☐ 199	Bob Boyd	3.00	1.35	.40
☐ 200	Warren Spahn	35.00	16.00	4.40
☐ 201	Pete Whisenant	3.00	1.35	.40
☐ 202	Al Neiger	3.00	1.35	.40
☐ 203	Eddie Bressoud	3.00	1.35	.40
☐ 204	Bob Skinner	3.50	1.55	.45
☐ 205	Billy Pierce	3.50	1.55	.45
☐ 206	Gene Green	3.00	1.35	.40

☐ 207	Dodger Southpaws	21.00	9.50	2.60

Sandy Koufax
Johnny Podres

☐ 208	Larry Osborne	3.00	1.35	.40
☐ 209	Ken McBride	3.00	1.35	.40
☐ 210	Pete Runnels	3.50	1.55	.45
☐ 211	Bob Gibson	40.00	18.00	5.00
☐ 212	Haywood Sullivan	3.50	1.55	.45
☐ 213	Bill Stafford	3.00	1.35	.40
☐ 214	Danny Murphy	3.00	1.35	.40
☐ 215	Gus Bell	3.50	1.55	.45
☐ 216	Ted Bowsfield	3.00	1.35	.40
☐ 217	Mel Roach	3.00	1.35	.40
☐ 218	Hal Brown	3.00	1.35	.40
☐ 219	Gene Mauch MG	4.00	1.80	.50
☐ 220	Alvin Dark MG	4.00	1.80	.50
☐ 221	Mike Higgins MG	3.50	1.55	.45
☐ 222	Jimmy Dykes MG	4.50	2.00	.55
☐ 223	Bob Scheffing MG	3.50	1.55	.45
☐ 224	Joe Gordon MG	4.50	2.00	.55
☐ 225	Bill Rigney MG	3.50	1.55	.45
☐ 226	Cookie Lavagetto MG	3.50	1.55	.45
☐ 227	Juan Pizarro	3.00	1.35	.40
☐ 228	New York Yankees	30.00	13.50	3.80

Team Card

☐ 229	Rudy Hernandez	3.00	1.35	.40
☐ 230	Don Hoak	3.50	1.55	.45
☐ 231	Dick Drott	3.00	1.35	.40
☐ 232	Bill White	6.00	2.70	.75
☐ 233	Joey Jay	3.50	1.55	.45
☐ 234	Ted Lepcio	3.00	1.35	.40
☐ 235	Camilo Pascual	3.50	1.55	.45
☐ 236	Don Gile	3.00	1.35	.40
☐ 237	Billy Loes	3.50	1.55	.45
☐ 238	Jim Gilliam	4.50	2.00	.55
☐ 239	Dave Sisler	3.00	1.35	.40
☐ 240	Ron Hansen	3.00	1.35	.40
☐ 241	Al Cicotte	3.00	1.35	.40
☐ 242	Hal Smith	3.00	1.35	.40
☐ 243	Frank Lary	3.50	1.55	.45
☐ 244	Chico Cardenas	3.50	1.55	.45
☐ 245	Joe Adcock	3.50	1.55	.45
☐ 246	Bob Davis	3.00	1.35	.40
☐ 247	Billy Goodman	3.50	1.55	.45
☐ 248	Ed Keegan	3.00	1.35	.40
☐ 249	Cincinnati Reds	6.50	2.90	.80

Team Card

☐ 250	Buc Hill Aces	3.50	1.55	.45

Vern Law
Roy Face

☐ 251	Bill Bruton	3.00	1.35	.40
☐ 252	Bill Short	3.00	1.35	.40
☐ 253	Sammy Taylor	3.00	1.35	.40
☐ 254	Ted Sadowski	3.00	1.35	.40
☐ 255	Vic Power	3.50	1.55	.45
☐ 256	Billy Hoeft	3.00	1.35	.40
☐ 257	Carroll Hardy	3.00	1.35	.40

☐	258 Jack Sanford.............3.50	1.55	.45
☐	259 John Schaive 3.00	1.35	.40
☐	260 Don Drysdale 30.00	13.50	3.80
☐	261 Charlie Lau...............3.50	1.55	.45
☐	262 Tony Curry 3.00	1.35	.40
☐	263 Ken Hamlin 3.00	1.35	.40
☐	264 Glen Hobbie 3.00	1.35	.40
☐	265 Tony Kubek...............9.00	4.00	1.15
☐	266 Lindy McDaniel 3.50	1.55	.45
☐	267 Norm Siebern............3.00	1.35	.40
☐	268 Ike Delock................3.00	1.35	.40
☐	269 Harry Chiti...............3.00	1.35	.40
☐	270 Bob Friend 3.50	1.55	.45
☐	271 Jim Landis................3.00	1.35	.40
☐	272 Tom Morgan.............3.00	1.35	.40
☐	273A Checklist 4...........15.00	3.00	.90
	(Copyright symbol		
	adjacent to		
	336 Don Mincher)		
☐	273B Checklist 4...........10.00	2.00	.60
	(Copyright symbol		
	adjacent to		
	339 Gene Baker)		
☐	274 Gary Bell 3.00	1.35	.40
☐	275 Gene Woodling 3.50	1.55	.45
☐	276 Ray Rippelmeyer........3.00	1.35	.40
☐	277 Hank Foiles 3.00	1.35	.40
☐	278 Don McMahon 3.00	1.35	.40
☐	279 Jose Pagan 3.00	1.35	.40
☐	280 Frank Howard 5.50	2.50	.70
☐	281 Frank Sullivan 3.00	1.35	.40
☐	282 Faye Throneberry........3.00	1.35	.40
☐	283 Bob Anderson 3.00	1.35	.40
☐	284 Dick Gernert 3.00	1.35	.40
☐	285 Sherm Lollar.............3.50	1.55	.45
☐	286 George Witt..............3.00	1.35	.40
☐	287 Carl Yastrzemski 150.00	70.00	19.00
☐	288 Albie Pearson...........3.50	1.55	.45
☐	289 Ray Moore 3.00	1.35	.40
☐	290 Stan Musial............110.00	50.00	14.00
☐	291 Tex Clevenger...........3.00	1.35	.40
☐	292 Jim Baumer..............3.00	1.35	.40
☐	293 Tom Sturdivant..........3.00	1.35	.40
☐	294 Don Blasingame.........3.00	1.35	.40
☐	295 Milt Pappas..............3.50	1.55	.45
☐	296 Wes Covington 3.50	1.55	.45
☐	297 Athletics Team..........6.50	2.90	.80
☐	298 Jim Golden 3.00	1.35	.40
☐	299 Clay Dalrymple..........3.00	1.35	.40
☐	300 Mickey Mantle........425.00	190.00	52.50
☐	301 Chet Nichols 3.00	1.35	.40
☐	302 Al Heist 3.00	1.35	.40
☐	303 Gary Peters..............3.50	1.55	.45
☐	304 Rocky Nelson 3.00	1.35	.40
☐	305 Mike McCormick.........3.50	1.55	.45
☐	306 World Series Game 1 ...7.25	3.30	.90
	Bill Virdon Saves Game		
☐	307 World Series Game 2.40.00	18.00	5.00
	Mickey Mantle		
	Two Homers		
☐	308 World Series Game 3...7.25	3.30	.90
	Bobby Richardson		
	Is Hero		
☐	309 World Series Game 4...7.25	3.30	.90
	Gino Cimoli Safe		
☐	310 World Series Game 5...7.25	3.30	.90
	Roy Face Saves Day		
☐	311 World Series Game 6.11.00	4.90	1.40
	Whitey Ford		
	Second Shutout		
☐	312 World Series Game 7.12.50	5.75	1.55
	Bill Mazeroski's Homer		
☐	313 World Series Summary9.00	4.00	1.15
	Pirates Celebrate		
☐	314 Bob Miller 3.00	1.35	.40
☐	315 Earl Battey...............3.00	1.35	.40
☐	316 Bobby Gene Smith 3.00	1.35	.40
☐	317 Jim Brewer 3.00	1.35	.40
☐	318 Danny O'Connell 3.00	1.35	.40
☐	319 Valmy Thomas...........3.00	1.35	.40
☐	320 Lou Burdette.............3.50	1.55	.45
☐	321 Marv Breeding 3.00	1.35	.40
☐	322 Bill Kunkel...............3.50	1.55	.45
☐	323 Sammy Esposito 3.00	1.35	.40
☐	324 Hank Aguirre.............3.00	1.35	.40
☐	325 Wally Moon 3.50	1.55	.45
☐	326 Dave Hillman 3.00	1.35	.40
☐	327 Matty Alou 7.00	3.10	.85
☐	328 Jim O'Toole..............3.50	1.55	.45
☐	329 Julio Becquer 3.00	1.35	.40
☐	330 Hocky Colavito.........12.00	5.50	1.50
☐	331 Ned Garver...............3.00	1.35	.40
☐	332 Dutch Dotterer UER 3.00	1.35	.40
	(Photo actually		
	Tommy Dotterer,		
	Dutch's brother)		
☐	333 Fritz Brickell 3.00	1.35	.40
☐	334 Walt Bond 3.00	1.35	.40
☐	335 Frank Bolling 3.00	1.35	.40
☐	336 Don Mincher.............3.50	1.55	.45
☐	337 Al's Aces................5.00	2.30	.60
	Early Wynn		
	Al Lopez		
	Herb Score		
☐	338 Don Landrum 3.00	1.35	.40
☐	339 Gene Baker 3.00	1.35	.40
☐	340 Vic Wertz.................3.50	1.55	.45
☐	341 Jim Owens 3.00	1.35	.40
☐	342 Clint Courtney 3.00	1.35	.40
☐	343 Earl Robinson 3.00	1.35	.40
☐	344 Sandy Koufax..........110.00	50.00	14.00
☐	345 Jim Piersall..............4.00	1.80	.50
☐	346 Howie Nunn 3.00	1.35	.40
☐	347 St. Louis Cardinals......6.50	2.90	.80

☐		Team Card		
☐	348	Steve Boros 3.00	1.35	.40
☐	349	Danny McDevitt 3.00	1.35	.40
☐	350	Ernie Banks 40.00	18.00	5.00
☐	351	Jim King 3.00	1.35	.40
☐	352	Bob Shaw 3.00	1.35	.40
☐	353	Howie Bedell 3.00	1.35	.40
☐	354	Billy Harrell 3.00	1.35	.40
☐	355	Bob Allison 3.50	1.55	.45
☐	356	Ryne Duren 4.00	1.80	.50
☐	357	Daryl Spencer 3.00	1.35	.40
☐	358	Earl Averill 3.00	1.35	.40
☐	359	Dallas Green 4.00	1.80	.50
☐	360	Frank Robinson 45.00	20.00	5.75
☐	361A	Checklist 5 ....10.00	2.00	.60
		(No ad on back)		
☐	361B	Checklist 5 ....15.00	3.00	.90
		(Special Feature		
		ad on back)		
☐	362	Frank Funk 3.00	1.35	.40
☐	363	John Roseboro 3.50	1.55	.45
☐	364	Moe Drabowsky 3.50	1.55	.45
☐	365	Jerry Lumpe 3.00	1.35	.40
☐	366	Eddie Fisher 3.00	1.35	.40
☐	367	Jim Rivera 3.00	1.35	.40
☐	368	Bennie Daniels 3.00	1.35	.40
☐	369	Dave Philley 3.00	1.35	.40
☐	370	Roy Face 4.00	1.80	.50
☐	371	Bill Skowron SP 40.00	18.00	5.00
☐	372	Bob Hendley 4.50	2.00	.55
☐	373	Boston Red Sox 9.00	4.00	1.15
		Team Card		
☐	374	Paul Giel 5.00	2.30	.60
☐	375	Ken Boyer 8.00	3.60	1.00
☐	376	Mike Roarke 5.00	2.30	.60
☐	377	Ruben Gomez 4.50	2.00	.55
☐	378	Wally Post 5.00	2.30	.60
☐	379	Bobby Shantz 5.00	2.30	.60
☐	380	Minnie Minoso 5.00	2.30	.60
☐	381	Dave Wickersham 4.50	2.00	.55
☐	382	Frank Thomas 5.50	2.50	.70
☐	383	Frisco First Liners 5.00	2.30	.60
		Mike McCormick		
		Jack Sanford		
		Billy O'Dell		
☐	384	Chuck Essegian 4.50	2.00	.55
☐	385	Jim Perry 5.00	2.30	.60
☐	386	Joe Hicks 4.50	2.00	.55
☐	387	Duke Maas 4.50	2.00	.55
☐	388	Bob Clemente 110.00	50.00	14.00
☐	389	Ralph Terry 5.50	2.50	.70
☐	390	Del Crandall 5.50	2.50	.70
☐	391	Winston Brown 4.50	2.00	.55
☐	392	Reno Bertoia 4.50	2.00	.55
☐	393	Batter Bafflers 4.50	2.00	.55
		Don Cardwell		
		Glen Hobbie		

☐	394	Ken Walters 4.50	2.00	.55
☐	395	Chuck Estrada 5.00	2.30	.60
☐	396	Bob Aspromonte 4.50	2.00	.55
☐	397	Hal Woodeshick 4.50	2.00	.55
☐	398	Hank Bauer 5.00	2.30	.60
☐	399	Cliff Cook 4.50	2.00	.55
☐	400	Vern Law 5.50	2.50	.70
☐	401	Babe Ruth 60th Homer30.00	13.50	3.80
☐	402	Perfect Game 20.00	9.00	2.50
		(Don Larsen)		
☐	403	26 Inning Tie 6.00	2.70	.75
☐	404	Rogers Hornsby .424.10.00	4.50	1.25
		Average		
☐	405	Lou Gehrig's Streak ...25.00	11.50	3.10
☐	406	Mickey Mantle 565 ....55.00	25.00	7.00
		Foot Homer		
☐	407	Jack Chesbro Wins 41 .6.00	2.70	.75
☐	408	Christy Mathewson 10.00	4.50	1.25
		Fans 267		
☐	409	Walter Johnson 10.00	4.50	1.25
		Shutouts		
☐	410	Harvey Haddix 12 ....7.00	3.10	.85
		Perfect Innings		
☐	411	Tony Taylor 5.00	2.30	.60
☐	412	Larry Sherry 5.00	2.30	.60
☐	413	Eddie Yost 5.00	2.30	.60
☐	414	Dick Donovan 4.50	2.00	.55
☐	415	Hank Aaron 135.00	60.00	17.00
☐	416	Dick Howser 9.00	4.00	1.15
☐	417	Juan Marichal 150.00	70.00	19.00
☐	418	Ed Bailey 5.00	2.30	.60
☐	419	Tom Borland 4.50	2.00	.55
☐	420	Ernie Broglio 5.00	2.30	.60
☐	421	Ty Cline 4.50	2.00	.55
☐	422	Bud Daley 4.50	2.00	.55
☐	423	Charlie Neal SP 10.00	4.50	1.25
☐	424	Turk Lown 4.50	2.00	.55
☐	425	Yogi Berra 75.00	34.00	9.50
☐	426	Milwaukee Braves 9.00	4.00	1.15
		Team Card		
		(Back numbered 463)		
☐	427	Dick Ellsworth 5.00	2.30	.60
☐	428	Ray Barker SP 10.00	4.50	1.25
☐	429	Al Kaline 45.00	20.00	5.75
☐	430	Bill Mazeroski SP 40.00	18.00	5.00
☐	431	Chuck Stobbs 4.50	2.00	.55
☐	432	Coot Veal 4.50	2.00	.55
☐	433	Art Mahaffey 4.50	2.00	.55
☐	434	Tom Brewer 4.50	2.00	.55
☐	435	Orlando Cepeda UER .11.00	4.90	1.40
		(San Francis on		
		card front)		
☐	436	Jim Maloney 10.00	4.50	1.25
☐	437A	Checklist 6 ....15.00	3.00	.90
		440 Louis Aparicio		
☐	437B	Checklist 6 ....15.00	3.00	.90
		440 Luis Aparicio		

☐ 438	Curt Flood	5.50	2.50	.70
☐ 439	Phil Regan	5.00	2.30	.60
☐ 440	Luis Aparicio	15.00	6.75	1.90
☐ 441	Dick Bertell	4.50	2.00	.55
☐ 442	Gordon Jones	4.50	2.00	.55
☐ 443	Duke Snider	45.00	20.00	5.75
☐ 444	Joe Nuxhall	5.50	2.50	.70
☐ 445	Frank Malzone	5.00	2.30	.60
☐ 446	Bob Taylor	4.50	2.00	.55
☐ 447	Harry Bright	5.50	2.50	.70
☐ 448	Del Rice	5.50	2.50	.70
☐ 449	Bob Bolin	5.50	2.50	.70
☐ 450	Jim Lemon	6.00	2.70	.75
☐ 451	Power for Ernie	6.50	2.90	.80
	Daryl Spencer			
	Bill White			
	Ernie Broglio			
☐ 452	Bob Allen	5.50	2.50	.70
☐ 453	Dick Schofield	6.00	2.70	.75
☐ 454	Pumpsie Green	6.00	2.70	.75
☐ 455	Early Wynn	14.00	6.25	1.75
☐ 456	Hal Bevan	5.50	2.50	.70
☐ 457	Johnny James	5.50	2.50	.70
	(Listed as Angel,			
	but wearing Yankee			
	uniform and cap)			
☐ 458	Willie Tasby	5.50	2.50	.70
☐ 459	Terry Fox	5.50	2.50	.70
☐ 460	Gil Hodges	16.00	7.25	2.00
☐ 461	Smoky Burgess	6.50	2.90	.80
☐ 462	Lou Klimchock	5.50	2.50	.70
☐ 463	Jack Fisher	6.00	2.70	.75
	(See also 426)			
☐ 464	Lee Thomas	7.00	3.10	.85
	(Pictured with Yankee			
	cap but listed as			
	Los Angeles Angel)			
☐ 465	Roy McMillan	6.00	2.70	.75
☐ 466	Ron Moeller	5.50	2.50	.70
☐ 467	Cleveland Indians	9.00	4.00	1.15
	Team Card			
☐ 468	John Callison	6.50	2.90	.80
☐ 469	Ralph Lumenti	5.50	2.50	.70
☐ 470	Roy Sievers	6.00	2.70	.75
☐ 471	Phil Rizzuto MVP	15.00	6.75	1.90
☐ 472	Yogi Berra MVP	55.00	25.00	7.00
☐ 473	Bob Shantz MVP	6.50	2.90	.80
☐ 474	Al Rosen MVP	6.50	2.90	.80
☐ 475	Mickey Mantle MVP	125.00	57.50	15.50
☐ 476	Jackie Jensen MVP	6.50	2.90	.80
☐ 477	Nellie Fox MVP	8.50	3.80	1.05
☐ 478	Roger Maris MVP	45.00	20.00	5.75
☐ 479	Jim Konstanty MVP	6.50	2.90	.80
☐ 480	Roy Campanella MVP	35.00	16.00	4.40
☐ 481	Hank Sauer MVP	6.50	2.90	.80
☐ 482	Willie Mays MVP	45.00	20.00	5.75
☐ 483	Don Newcombe MVP	6.50	2.90	.80
☐ 484	Hank Aaron MVP	45.00	20.00	5.75
☐ 485	Ernie Banks MVP	30.00	13.50	3.80
☐ 486	Dick Groat MVP	6.50	2.90	.80
☐ 487	Gene Oliver	5.50	2.50	.70
☐ 488	Joe McClain	5.50	2.50	.70
☐ 489	Walt Dropo	5.50	2.50	.70
☐ 490	Jim Bunning	10.00	4.50	1.25
☐ 491	Philadelphia Phillies	9.00	4.00	1.15
	Team Card			
☐ 492	Ron Fairly	6.00	2.70	.75
☐ 493	Don Zimmer UER	7.00	3.10	.85
	(Brooklyn A.L.)			
☐ 494	Tom Cheney	5.50	2.50	.70
☐ 495	Elston Howard	9.50	4.30	1.20
☐ 496	Ken MacKenzie	5.50	2.50	.70
☐ 497	Willie Jones	5.50	2.50	.70
☐ 498	Ray Herbert	5.50	2.50	.70
☐ 499	Chuck Schilling	5.50	2.50	.70
☐ 500	Harvey Kuenn	7.00	3.10	.85
☐ 501	John DeMerit	5.50	2.50	.70
☐ 502	Clarence Coleman	7.00	3.10	.85
☐ 503	Tito Francona	5.50	2.50	.70
☐ 504	Billy Consolo	5.50	2.50	.70
☐ 505	Red Schoendienst	15.00	6.75	1.90
☐ 506	Willie Davis	18.00	8.00	2.30
☐ 507	Pete Burnside	5.50	2.50	.70
☐ 508	Rocky Bridges	5.50	2.50	.70
☐ 509	Camilo Carreon	5.50	2.50	.70
☐ 510	Art Ditmar	5.50	2.50	.70
☐ 511	Joe M. Morgan	6.00	2.70	.75
☐ 512	Bob Will	5.50	2.50	.70
☐ 513	Jim Brosnan	6.50	2.90	.80
☐ 514	Jake Wood	5.50	2.50	.70
☐ 515	Jackie Brandt	5.50	2.50	.70
☐ 516	Checklist 7	15.00	3.00	.90
☐ 517	Willie McCovey	65.00	29.00	8.25
☐ 518	Andy Carey	6.00	2.70	.75
☐ 519	Jim Pagliaroni	6.00	2.70	.75
☐ 520	Joe Cunningham	6.00	2.70	.75
☐ 521	Brother Battery	6.00	2.70	.75
	Norm Sherry			
	Larry Sherry			
☐ 522	Dick Farrell UER	6.00	2.70	.75
	(Phillies cap, but			
	listed on Dodgers)			
☐ 523	Joe Gibbon	34.00	15.50	4.20
☐ 524	Johnny Logan	40.00	18.00	5.00
☐ 525	Ron Perranoski	40.00	18.00	5.00
☐ 526	R.C. Stevens	34.00	15.50	4.20
☐ 527	Gene Leek	34.00	15.50	4.20
☐ 528	Pedro Ramos	34.00	15.50	4.20
☐ 529	Bob Roselli	34.00	15.50	4.20
☐ 530	Bob Malkmus	34.00	15.50	4.20
☐ 531	Jim Coates	34.00	15.50	4.20
☐ 532	Bob Hale	34.00	15.50	4.20
☐ 533	Jack Curtis	34.00	15.50	4.20
☐ 534	Eddie Kasko	34.00	15.50	4.20

☐ 535	Larry Jackson	34.00	15.50 4.20
☐ 536	Bill Tuttle	34.00	15.50 4.20
☐ 537	Bobby Locke	34.00	15.50 4.20
☐ 538	Chuck Hiller	34.00	15.50 4.20
☐ 539	Johnny Klippstein	34.00	15.50 4.20
☐ 540	Jackie Jensen	40.00	18.00 5.00
☐ 541	Roland Sheldon	40.00	18.00 5.00
☐ 542	Minnesota Twins	70.00	32.00 8.75
	Team Card		
☐ 543	Roger Craig	40.00	18.00 5.00
☐ 544	George Thomas	34.00	15.50 4.20
☐ 545	Hoyt Wilhelm	65.00	29.00 8.25
☐ 546	Marty Kutyna	34.00	15.50 4.20
☐ 547	Leon Wagner	34.00	15.50 4.20
☐ 548	Ted Wills	34.00	15.50 4.20
☐ 549	Hal R. Smith	34.00	15.50 4.20
☐ 550	Frank Baumann	34.00	15.50 4.20
☐ 551	George Altman	34.00	15.50 4.20
☐ 552	Jim Archer	34.00	15.50 4.20
☐ 553	Bill Fischer	34.00	15.50 4.20
☐ 554	Pittsburgh Pirates	70.00	32.00 8.75
	Team Card		
☐ 555	Sam Jones	37.50	17.00 4.70
☐ 556	Ken R. Hunt	34.00	15.50 4.20
☐ 557	Jose Valdivielso	34.00	15.50 4.20
☐ 558	Don Ferrarese	34.00	15.50 4.20
☐ 559	Jim Gentile	37.50	17.00 4.70
☐ 560	Barry Latman	34.00	15.50 4.20
☐ 561	Charley James	34.00	15.50 4.20
☐ 562	Bill Monbouquette	34.00	15.50 4.20
☐ 563	Bob Cerv	40.00	18.00 5.00
☐ 564	Don Cardwell	34.00	15.50 4.20
☐ 565	Felipe Alou	45.00	20.00 5.75
☐ 566	Paul Richards MG AS	36.00	16.00 4.50
☐ 567	D. Murtaugh MG AS	36.00	16.00 4.50
☐ 568	Bill Skowron AS	40.00	18.00 5.00
☐ 569	Frank Herrera AS	36.00	16.00 4.50
☐ 570	Nellie Fox AS	45.00	20.00 5.75
☐ 571	Bill Mazeroski AS	40.00	18.00 5.00
☐ 572	Brooks Robinson AS	100.00	45.00 12.50
☐ 573	Ken Boyer AS	40.00	18.00 5.00
☐ 574	Luis Aparicio AS	50.00	23.00 6.25
☐ 575	Ernie Banks AS	100.00	45.00 12.50
☐ 576	Roger Maris AS	165.00	75.00 21.00
☐ 577	Hank Aaron AS	175.00	80.00 22.00
☐ 578	Mickey Mantle AS	400.00	180.00 50.00
☐ 579	Willie Mays AS	175.00	80.00 22.00
☐ 580	Al Kaline AS	100.00	45.00 12.50
☐ 581	Frank Robinson AS	100.00	45.00 12.50
☐ 582	Earl Battey AS	36.00	16.00 4.50
☐ 583	Del Crandall AS	36.00	16.00 4.50
☐ 584	Jim Perry AS	36.00	16.00 4.50
☐ 585	Bob Friend AS	36.00	16.00 4.50
☐ 586	Whitey Ford AS	100.00	45.00 12.50
☐ 587	Does not exist	.00	.00 .00
☐ 588	Does not exist	.00	.00 .00
☐ 589	Warren Spahn AS	160.00	70.00 20.00

1962 Topps

The cards in this 598-card set measure 2 1/2" by 3 1/2". The 1962 Topps set contains a mini-series spotlighting Babe Ruth (135-144). Other subsets in the set include League Leaders (51-60), World Series cards (232-237), In Action cards (311-319), NL All Stars (390-399), AL All Stars (466-475), and Rookie Prospects (591-598). The All-Star selections were again provided by Sport Magazine, as in 1958 and 1960. The second series had two distinct printings which are distinguishable by numerous color and pose variations. Those cards with a distinctive "green tint" are valued at a slight premium as they are basically the result of a flawed printing process occurring early in the second series run. Card number 139 exists as A: Babe Ruth Special card, B: Hal Reniff with arms over head, or C: Hal Reniff in the same pose as card number 159. In addition, two poses exist for players depicted on card numbers 129, 132, 134, 147, 174, 176, and 190. The high number series, 523 to 598, is somewhat more difficult to obtain than other cards in the set. Within the last series (523-598) there are 43 cards which were printed in lesser quantities; these are marked SP in the checklist below. The set price listed does not include the pose variations (see checklist below for individual values). The key rookies in this set are Lou Brock, Tim McCarver, Gaylord Perry, and Bob Uecker.

	NRMT	VG-E	GOOD
COMPLETE SET (598)	5400.	2400.	700.00
COMMON PLAYER (1-109)	2.50	1.15	.30

COMMON PLAYER (110-196)	2.50	1.15	.30
COMMON PLAYER (197-283)	3.00	1.35	.40
COMMON PLAYER (284-370)	3.50	1.55	.45
COMMON PLAYER (371-446)	5.50	2.50	.70
COMMON PLAYER (447-522)	7.00	3.10	.85
COMMON PLAYER (523-590)	15.00	6.75	1.90
COMMON ROOKIES (591-598)	33.00	15.00	4.10

☐ 1	Roger Maris	250.00	115.00	31.00
☐ 2	Jim Brosnan	2.50	1.15	.30
☐ 3	Pete Runnels	3.00	1.35	.40
☐ 4	John DeMerit	2.50	1.15	.30
☐ 5	Sandy Koufax UER	125.00	57.50	15.50
	(Struck ou 18)			
☐ 6	Marv Breeding	2.50	1.15	.30
☐ 7	Frank Thomas	3.50	1.55	.45
☐ 8	Ray Herbert	2.50	1.15	.30
☐ 9	Jim Davenport	3.00	1.35	.40
☐ 10	Bob Clemente	115.00	52.50	14.50
☐ 11	Tom Morgan	2.50	1.15	.30
☐ 12	Harry Craft MG	2.50	1.15	.30
☐ 13	Dick Howser	3.00	1.35	.40
☐ 14	Bill White	4.50	2.00	.55
☐ 15	Dick Donovan	2.50	1.15	.30
☐ 16	Darrell Johnson	2.50	1.15	.30
☐ 17	John Callison	3.00	1.35	.40
☐ 18	Managers' Dream	125.00	57.50	15.50
	Mickey Mantle			
	Willie Mays			
☐ 19	Ray Washburn	2.50	1.15	.30
☐ 20	Rocky Colavito	10.00	4.50	1.25
☐ 21	Jim Kaat	6.00	2.70	.75
☐ 22A	Checklist 1 ERR	10.00	1.50	.50
	(121-176 on back)			
☐ 22B	Checklist 1 COR	10.00	1.50	.50
☐ 23	Norm Larker	2.50	1.15	.30
☐ 24	Tigers Team	6.00	2.70	.75
☐ 25	Ernie Banks	45.00	20.00	5.75
☐ 26	Chris Cannizzaro	2.50	1.15	.30
☐ 27	Chuck Cottier	2.50	1.15	.30
☐ 28	Minnie Minoso	4.50	2.00	.55
☐ 29	Casey Stengel MG	20.00	9.00	2.50
☐ 30	Eddie Mathews	20.00	9.00	2.50
☐ 31	Tom Tresh	18.00	8.00	2.30
☐ 32	John Roseboro	3.00	1.35	.40
☐ 33	Don Larsen	3.00	1.35	.40
☐ 34	Johnny Temple	3.00	1.35	.40
☐ 35	Don Schwall	3.00	1.35	.40
☐ 36	Don Leppert	2.50	1.15	.30
☐ 37	Tribe Hill Trio	3.00	1.35	.40
	Barry Latman			
	Dick Stigman			
	Jim Perry			
☐ 38	Gene Stephens	2.50	1.15	.30
☐ 39	Joe Koppe	2.50	1.15	.30
☐ 40	Orlando Cepeda	9.00	4.00	1.15
☐ 41	Cliff Cook	2.50	1.15	.30

☐ 42	Jim King	2.50	1.15	.30
☐ 43	Los Angeles Dodgers	6.00	2.70	.75
	Team Card			
☐ 44	Don Taussig	2.50	1.15	.30
☐ 45	Brooks Robinson	40.00	18.00	5.00
☐ 46	Jack Baldschun	2.50	1.15	.30
☐ 47	Bob Will	2.50	1.15	.30
☐ 48	Ralph Terry	3.00	1.35	.40
☐ 49	Hal Jones	2.50	1.15	.30
☐ 50	Stan Musial	110.00	50.00	14.00
☐ 51	AL Batting Leaders	5.00	2.30	.60
	Norm Cash			
	Jim Piersall			
	Al Kaline			
	Elston Howard			
☐ 52	NL Batting Leaders	6.50	2.90	.80
	Bob Clemente			
	Vada Pinson			
	Ken Boyer			
	Wally Moon			
☐ 53	AL Home Run Leaders	50.00	23.00	6.25
	Roger Maris			
	Mickey Mantle			
	Jim Gentile			
	Harmon Killebrew			
☐ 54	NL Home Run Leaders	7.00	3.10	.85
	Orlando Cepeda			
	Willie Mays			
	Frank Robinson			
☐ 55	AL ERA Leaders	4.50	2.00	.55
	Dick Donovan			
	Bill Stafford			
	Don Mossi			
	Milt Pappas			
☐ 56	NL ERA Leaders	5.00	2.30	.60
	Warren Spahn			
	Jim O'Toole			
	Curt Simmons			
	Mike McCormick			
☐ 57	AL Wins Leaders	5.00	2.30	.60
	Whitey Ford			
	Frank Lary			
	Steve Barber			
	Jim Bunning			
☐ 58	NL Wins Leaders	5.00	2.30	.60
	Warren Spahn			
	Joe Jay			
	Jim O'Toole			
☐ 59	AL Strikeout Leaders	4.50	2.00	.55
	Camilo Pascual			
	Whitey Ford			
	Jim Bunning			
	Juan Pizarro			
☐ 60	NL Strikeout Leaders	8.00	3.60	1.00
	Sandy Koufax			
	Stan Williams			
	Don Drysdale			

Jim O'Toole

☐ 61	Cardinals Team	6.00	2.70	.75
☐ 62	Steve Boros	2.50	1.15	.30
☐ 63	Tony Cloninger	3.50	1.55	.45
☐ 64	Russ Snyder	2.50	1.15	.30
☐ 65	Bobby Richardson	6.50	2.90	.80
☐ 66	Cuno Barragan	2.50	1.15	.30
☐ 67	Harvey Haddix	3.00	1.35	.40
☐ 68	Ken Hunt	2.50	1.15	.30
☐ 69	Phil Ortega	2.50	1.15	.30
☐ 70	Harmon Killebrew	20.00	9.00	2.50
☐ 71	Dick LeMay	2.50	1.15	.30
☐ 72	Bob's Pupils	2.50	1.15	.30

Steve Boros
Bob Scheffing MG
Jake Wood

☐ 73	Nellie Fox	7.00	3.10	.85
☐ 74	Bob Lillis	2.50	1.15	.30
☐ 75	Milt Pappas	3.00	1.35	.40
☐ 76	Howie Bedell	2.50	1.15	.30
☐ 77	Tony Taylor	3.00	1.35	.40
☐ 78	Gene Green	2.50	1.15	.30
☐ 79	Ed Hobaugh	2.50	1.15	.30
☐ 80	Vada Pinson	4.50	2.00	.55
☐ 81	Jim Pagliaroni	2.50	1.15	.30
☐ 82	Deron Johnson	3.00	1.35	.40
☐ 83	Larry Jackson	2.50	1.15	.30
☐ 84	Lenny Green	2.50	1.15	.30
☐ 85	Gil Hodges	16.00	7.25	2.00
☐ 86	Donn Clendenon	4.00	1.80	.50
☐ 87	Mike Roarke	2.50	1.15	.30
☐ 88	Ralph Houk MG	3.50	1.55	.45

(Berra in background)

☐ 89	Barney Schultz	2.50	1.15	.30
☐ 90	Jim Piersall	3.00	1.35	.40
☐ 91	J.C. Martin	2.50	1.15	.30
☐ 92	Sam Jones	2.50	1.15	.30
☐ 93	John Blanchard	3.00	1.35	.40
☐ 94	Jay Hook	2.50	1.15	.30
☐ 95	Don Hoak	3.00	1.35	.40
☐ 96	Eli Grba	2.50	1.15	.30
☐ 97	Tito Francona	2.50	1.15	.30
☐ 98	Checklist 2	10.00	1.50	.50
☐ 99	John (Boog) Powell	21.00	9.50	2.60
☐ 100	Warren Spahn	32.00	14.50	4.00
☐ 101	Carroll Hardy	2.50	1.15	.30
☐ 102	Al Schroll	2.50	1.15	.30
☐ 103	Don Blasingame	2.50	1.15	.30
☐ 104	Ted Savage	2.50	1.15	.30
☐ 105	Don Mossi	3.00	1.35	.40
☐ 106	Carl Sawatski	2.50	1.15	.30
☐ 107	Mike McCormick	3.00	1.35	.40
☐ 108	Willie Davis	4.00	1.80	.50
☐ 109	Bob Shaw	2.50	1.15	.30
☐ 110	Bill Skowron	5.00	2.30	.60
☐ 111	Dallas Green	3.00	1.35	.40
☐ 112	Hank Foiles	2.50	1.15	.30

☐ 113	Chicago White Sox	6.00	2.70	.75
	Team Card			
☐ 114	Howie Koplitz	2.50	1.15	.30
☐ 115	Bob Skinner	3.00	1.35	.40
☐ 116	Herb Score	4.00	1.80	.50
☐ 117	Gary Geiger	2.50	1.15	.30
☐ 118	Julian Javier	3.00	1.35	.40
☐ 119	Danny Murphy	2.50	1.15	.30
☐ 120	Bob Purkey	2.50	1.15	.30
☐ 121	Billy Hitchcock MG	2.50	1.15	.30
☐ 122	Norm Bass	2.50	1.15	.30
☐ 123	Mike De La Hoz	2.50	1.15	.30
☐ 124	Bill Pleis	2.50	1.15	.30
☐ 125	Gene Woodling	3.00	1.35	.40
☐ 126	Al Cicotte	2.50	1.15	.30
☐ 127	Pride of A's	3.00	1.35	.40

Norm Siebern
Hank Bauer MG
Jerry Lumpe

☐ 128	Art Fowler	2.50	1.15	.30
☐ 129A	Lee Walls	2.50	1.15	.30
	(Facing right)			
☐ 129B	Lee Walls	26.00	11.50	3.30
	(Facing left)			
☐ 130	Frank Bolling	2.50	1.15	.30
☐ 131	Pete Richert	2.50	1.15	.30
☐ 132A	Angels Team	6.00	2.70	.75
	(Without photo)			
☐ 132B	Angels Team	26.00	11.50	3.30
	(With photo)			
☐ 133	Felipe Alou	5.00	2.30	.60
☐ 134A	Billy Hoeft	2.50	1.15	.30
	(Facing right)			
☐ 134B	Billy Hoeft	26.00	11.50	3.30
	(Facing straight)			
☐ 135	Babe Ruth Special 1	18.00	8.00	2.30
	Babe as a Boy			
☐ 136	Babe Ruth Special 2	18.00	8.00	2.30
	Babe Joins Yanks			
☐ 137	Babe Ruth Special 3	18.00	8.00	2.30
	Babe with Huggins			
☐ 138	Babe Ruth Special 4	18.00	8.00	2.30
	Famous Slugger			
☐ 139A	Babe Ruth Special 5	25.00	11.50	3.10
	Babe Hits 60			
☐ 139B	Hal Reniff PORT	13.00	5.75	1.65
☐ 139C	Hal Reniff	55.00	25.00	7.00
	(Pitching)			
☐ 140	Babe Ruth Special 6	25.00	11.50	3.10
	Gehrig and Ruth			
☐ 141	Babe Ruth Special 7	18.00	8.00	2.30
	Twilight Years			
☐ 142	Babe Ruth Special 8	18.00	8.00	2.30
	Coaching Dodgers			
☐ 143	Babe Ruth Special 9	18.00	8.00	2.30
	Greatest Sports Hero			
☐ 144	Babe Ruth Special 10	18.00	8.00	2.30

	Farewell Speech		
☐ 145	Barry Latman 2.50	1.15	.30
☐ 146	Don Demeter...............2.50	1.15	.30
☐ 147A	Bill Kunkel PORT 2.50	1.15	.30
☐ 147B	Bill Kunkel.................26.00	11.50	3.30
	(Pitching pose)		
☐ 148	Wally Post..................3.00	1.35	.40
☐ 149	Bob Duliba 3.00	1.15	.30
☐ 150	Al Kaline..................35.00	16.00	4.40
☐ 151	Johnny Klippstein 2.50	1.15	.30
☐ 152	Mickey Vernon MG ...3.00	1.35	.40
☐ 153	Pumpsie Green 3.00	1.35	.40
☐ 154	Lee Thomas 3.00	1.35	.40
☐ 155	Stu Miller 3.00	1.35	.40
☐ 156	Merritt Ranew 2.50	1.15	.30
☐ 157	Wes Covington 3.00	1.35	.40
☐ 158	Braves Team...............6.00	2.70	.75
☐ 159	Hal Reniff 4.00	1.80	.50
☐ 160	Dick Stuart.................3.00	1.35	.40
☐ 161	Frank Baumann 2.50	1.15	.30
☐ 162	Sammy Drake 2.50	1.15	.30
☐ 163	Hot Corner Guard.......3.00	1.35	.40
	Billy Gardner		
	Cletis Boyer		
☐ 164	Hal Naragon...............2.50	1.15	.30
☐ 165	Jackie Brandt.............2.50	1.15	.30
☐ 166	Don Lee 2.50	1.15	.30
☐ 167	Tim McCarver 35.00	16.00	4.40
☐ 168	Leo Posada 2.50	1.15	.30
☐ 169	Bob Cerv 3.00	1.35	.40
☐ 170	Ron Santo 12.00	5.50	1.50
☐ 171	Dave Sisler 2.50	1.15	.30
☐ 172	Fred Hutchinson MG....3.00	1.35	.40
☐ 173	Chico Fernandez 2.50	1.15	.30
☐ 174A	Carl Willey 2.50	1.15	.30
	(Capless)		
☐ 174B	Carl Willey 26.00	11.50	3.30
	(With cap)		
☐ 175	Frank Howard 5.00	2.30	.60
☐ 176A	Eddie Yost PORT 3.00	1.35	.40
☐ 176B	Eddie Yost BATTING26.00	11.50	3.30
☐ 177	Bobby Shantz..............3.00	1.35	.40
☐ 178	Camilo Carreon 2.50	1.15	.30
☐ 179	Tom Sturdivant 2.50	1.15	.30
☐ 180	Bob Allison 3.00	1.35	.40
☐ 181	Paul Brown 2.50	1.15	.30
☐ 182	Bob Nieman................2.50	1.15	.30
☐ 183	Roger Craig 4.00	1.80	.50
☐ 184	Haywood Sullivan 3.00	1.35	.40
☐ 185	Roland Sheldon 2.50	1.15	.30
☐ 186	Mack Jones.................2.50	1.15	.30
☐ 187	Gene Conley 3.00	1.35	.40
☐ 188	Chuck Hiller 2.50	1.15	.30
☐ 189	Dick Hall 2.50	1.15	.30
☐ 190A	Wally Moon PORT 3.00	1.35	.40
☐ 190B	Wally Moon BATTING26.00	11.50	3.30
☐ 191	Jim Brewer 2.50	1.15	.30

☐ 192A	Checklist 3 ....10.00	1.50	.50
	(Without comma)		
☐ 192B	Checklist 3 ....10.00	1.50	.50
	(Comma after		
	Checklist)		
☐ 193	Eddie Kasko...............2.50	1.15	.30
☐ 194	Dean Chance..............4.00	1.80	.50
☐ 195	Joe Cunningham 3.00	1.35	.40
☐ 196	Terry Fox...................2.50	1.15	.30
☐ 197	Daryl Spencer 3.00	1.35	.40
☐ 198	Johnny Keane MG.......3.50	1.55	.45
☐ 199	Gaylord Perry 180.00	80.00	23.00
☐ 200	Mickey Mantle.........500.00	230.00	65.00
☐ 201	Ike Delock 3.00	1.35	.40
☐ 202	Carl Warwick...............3.00	1.35	.40
☐ 203	Jack Fisher 3.00	1.35	.40
☐ 204	Johnny Weekly 3.00	1.35	.40
☐ 205	Gene Freese 3.00	1.35	.40
☐ 206	Senators Team............6.00	2.70	.75
☐ 207	Pete Burnside 3.00	1.35	.40
☐ 208	Billy Martin 8.00	3.60	1.00
☐ 209	Jim Fregosi 9.50	4.30	1.20
☐ 210	Roy Face 4.00	1.80	.50
☐ 211	Midway Masters 3.50	1.55	.45
	Frank Bolling		
	Roy McMillan		
☐ 212	Jim Owens 3.00	1.35	.40
☐ 213	Richie Ashburn 10.00	4.50	1.25
☐ 214	Dom Zanni 3.00	1.35	.40
☐ 215	Woody Held 3.00	1.35	.40
☐ 216	Ron Kline 3.00	1.35	.40
☐ 217	Walt Alston MG 5.00	2.30	.60
☐ 218	Joe Torre 25.00	11.50	3.10
☐ 219	Al Downing 5.00	2.30	.60
☐ 220	Roy Sievers 3.50	1.55	.45
☐ 221	Bill Short 3.00	1.35	.40
☐ 222	Jerry Zimmerman 3.00	1.35	.40
☐ 223	Alex Grammas 3.00	1.35	.40
☐ 224	Don Rudolph................3.00	1.35	.40
☐ 225	Frank Malzone............3.50	1.55	.45
☐ 226	San Francisco Giants ..6.00	2.70	.75
	Team Card		
☐ 227	Bob Tiefenauer...........3.00	1.35	.40
☐ 228	Dale Long 3.50	1.55	.45
☐ 229	Jesus McFarlane 3.00	1.35	.40
☐ 230	Camilo Pascual 3.50	1.55	.45
☐ 231	Ernie Bowman 3.00	1.35	.40
☐ 232	World Series Game 1 ...5.50	2.50	.70
	Yanks win opener		
☐ 233	World Series Game 2 ...5.50	2.50	.70
	Joey Jay ties it up		
☐ 234	World Series Game 3.20.00	9.00	2.50
	Roger Maris wins		
	in 9th		
☐ 235	World Series Game 4 ...8.50	3.80	1.05
	Whitey Ford sets		
	new mark		

☐ 236	World Series Game 5...5.50	2.50	.70
	Yanks crush Reds		
☐ 237	World Series Summary5.50	2.50	.70
	Yanks celebrate		
☐ 238	Norm Sherry 3.50	1.55	.45
☐ 239	Cecil Butler 3.00	1.35	.40
☐ 240	George Altman 3.00	1.35	.40
☐ 241	Johnny Kucks 3.00	1.35	.40
☐ 242	Mel McGaha MG 3.00	1.35	.40
☐ 243	Robin Roberts 12.50	5.75	1.55
☐ 244	Don Gile 3.00	1.35	.40
☐ 245	Ron Hansen 3.00	1.35	.40
☐ 246	Art Ditmar 3.00	1.35	.40
☐ 247	Joe Pignatano 3.00	1.35	.40
☐ 248	Bob Aspromonte 3.00	1.35	.40
☐ 249	Ed Keegan 3.00	1.35	.40
☐ 250	Norm Cash 7.00	3.10	.85
☐ 251	New York Yankees ...24.00	11.00	3.00
	Team Card		
☐ 252	Earl Francis 3.00	1.35	.40
☐ 253	Harry Chiti MG 3.00	1.35	.40
☐ 254	Gordon Windhorn 3.00	1.35	.40
☐ 255	Juan Pizarro 3.00	1.35	.40
☐ 256	Elio Chacon 3.00	1.35	.40
☐ 257	Jack Spring 3.00	1.35	.40
☐ 258	Marty Keough 3.00	1.35	.40
☐ 259	Lou Klimchock 3.00	1.35	.40
☐ 260	Billy Pierce 3.50	1.55	.45
☐ 261	George Alusik 3.00	1.35	.40
☐ 262	Bob Schmidt 3.00	1.35	.40
☐ 263	The Right Pitch 3.50	1.55	.45
	Bob Purkey		
	Jim Turner CO		
	Joe Jay		
☐ 264	Dick Ellsworth 3.50	1.55	.45
☐ 265	Joe Adcock 3.50	1.55	.45
☐ 266	John Anderson 3.00	1.35	.40
☐ 267	Dan Dobbek 3.00	1.35	.40
☐ 268	Ken McBride 3.00	1.35	.40
☐ 269	Bob Oldis 3.00	1.35	.40
☐ 270	Dick Groat 4.00	1.80	.50
☐ 271	Ray Rippelmeyer 3.00	1.35	.40
☐ 272	Earl Robinson 3.00	1.35	.40
☐ 273	Gary Bell 3.00	1.35	.40
☐ 274	Sammy Taylor 3.00	1.35	.40
☐ 275	Norm Siebern 3.00	1.35	.40
☐ 276	Hal Kolstad 3.00	1.35	.40
☐ 277	Checklist 4 ....10.00	1.50	.50
☐ 278	Ken Johnson 3.00	1.35	.40
☐ 279	Hobie Landrith UER 3.00	1.35	.40
	(Wrong birthdate)		
☐ 280	Johnny Podres 3.50	1.55	.45
☐ 281	Jake Gibbs 3.50	1.55	.45
☐ 282	Dave Hillman 3.00	1.35	.40
☐ 283	Charlie Smith 3.00	1.35	.40
☐ 284	Ruben Amaro 3.50	1.55	.45
☐ 285	Curt Simmons 4.00	1.80	.50

☐ 286	Al Lopez MG 5.00	2.30	.60
☐ 287	George Witt 3.50	1.55	.45
☐ 288	Billy Williams 45.00	20.00	5.75
☐ 289	Mike Krsnich 3.50	1.55	.45
☐ 290	Jim Gentile 5.50	2.50	.70
☐ 291	Hal Stowe 3.50	1.55	.45
☐ 292	Jerry Kindall 3.50	1.55	.45
☐ 293	Bob Miller 3.50	1.55	.45
☐ 294	Phillies Team 7.00	3.10	.85
☐ 295	Vern Law 4.00	1.80	.50
☐ 296	Ken Hamlin 3.50	1.55	.45
☐ 297	Ron Perranoski 4.00	1.80	.50
☐ 298	Bill Tuttle 3.50	1.55	.45
☐ 299	Don Wert 3.50	1.55	.45
☐ 300	Willie Mays 150.00	70.00	19.00
☐ 301	Galen Cisco 5.00	2.30	.60
☐ 302	Johnny Edwards 3.50	1.55	.45
☐ 303	Frank Torre 4.00	1.80	.50
☐ 304	Dick Farrell 3.50	1.55	.45
☐ 305	Jerry Lumpe 3.50	1.55	.45
☐ 306	Redbird Rippers 4.00	1.80	.50
	Lindy McDaniel		
	Larry Jackson		
☐ 307	Jim Grant 4.00	1.80	.50
☐ 308	Neil Chrisley 3.50	1.55	.45
☐ 309	Moe Morhardt 3.50	1.55	.45
☐ 310	Whitey Ford 40.00	18.00	5.00
☐ 311	Tony Kubek IA 6.50	2.90	.80
☐ 312	Warren Spahn IA 10.00	4.50	1.25
☐ 313	Roger Maris IA 24.00	11.00	3.00
☐ 314	Rocky Colavito IA.......6.00	2.70	.75
☐ 315	Whitey Ford IA 10.00	4.50	1.25
☐ 316	Harmon Killebrew IA..10.00	4.50	1.25
☐ 317	Stan Musial IA 20.00	9.00	2.50
☐ 318	Mickey Mantle IA 65.00	29.00	8.25
☐ 319	Mike McCormick IA 4.00	1.80	.50
☐ 320	Hank Aaron 150.00	70.00	19.00
☐ 321	Lee Stange 3.50	1.55	.45
☐ 322	Alvin Dark MG 4.00	1.80	.50
☐ 323	Don Landrum 3.50	1.55	.45
☐ 324	Joe McClain 3.50	1.55	.45
☐ 325	Luis Aparicio 15.00	6.75	1.90
☐ 326	Tom Parsons 3.50	1.55	.45
☐ 327	Ozzie Virgil 3.50	1.55	.45
☐ 328	Ken Walters 3.50	1.55	.45
☐ 329	Bob Bolin 3.50	1.55	.45
☐ 330	John Romano 3.50	1.55	.45
☐ 331	Moe Drabowsky 4.00	1.80	.50
☐ 332	Don Buddin 3.50	1.55	.45
☐ 333	Frank Cipriani 3.50	1.55	.45
☐ 334	Boston Red Sox 7.00	3.10	.85
	Team Card		
☐ 335	Bill Bruton 3.50	1.55	.45
☐ 336	Billy Muffett 3.50	1.55	.45
☐ 337	Jim Marshall 3.50	1.55	.45
☐ 338	Billy Gardner 3.50	1.55	.45
☐ 339	Jose Valdivielso 3.50	1.55	.45

☐ 340 Don Drysdale	40.00	18.00	5.00
☐ 341 Mike Hershberger	3.50	1.55	.45
☐ 342 Ed Rakow	3.50	1.55	.45
☐ 343 Albie Pearson	4.00	1.80	.50
☐ 344 Ed Bauta	3.50	1.55	.45
☐ 345 Chuck Schilling	3.50	1.55	.45
☐ 346 Jack Kralick	3.50	1.55	.45
☐ 347 Chuck Hinton	3.50	1.55	.45
☐ 348 Larry Burright	3.50	1.55	.45
☐ 349 Paul Foytack	3.50	1.55	.45
☐ 350 Frank Robinson	50.00	23.00	6.25
☐ 351 Braves' Backstops	6.00	2.70	.75
Joe Torre			
Del Crandall			
☐ 352 Frank Sullivan	3.50	1.55	.45
☐ 353 Bill Mazeroski	7.50	3.40	.95
☐ 354 Roman Mejias	3.50	1.55	.45
☐ 355 Steve Barber	3.50	1.55	.45
☐ 356 Tom Haller	5.00	2.30	.60
☐ 357 Jerry Walker	3.50	1.55	.45
☐ 358 Tommy Davis	6.50	2.90	.80
☐ 359 Bobby Locke	3.50	1.55	.45
☐ 360 Yogi Berra	80.00	36.00	10.00
☐ 361 Bob Hendley	3.50	1.55	.45
☐ 362 Ty Cline	3.50	1.55	.45
☐ 363 Bob Roselli	3.50	1.55	.45
☐ 364 Ken Hunt	3.50	1.55	.45
☐ 365 Charlie Neal	5.00	2.30	.60
☐ 366 Phil Regan	4.00	1.80	.50
☐ 367 Checklist 5	10.00	1.50	.50
☐ 368 Bob Tillman	3.50	1.55	.45
☐ 369 Ted Bowsfield	3.50	1.55	.45
☐ 370 Ken Boyer	7.00	3.10	.85
☐ 3/1 Earl Battey	5.50	2.50	.70
☐ 372 Jack Curtis	5.50	2.50	.70
☐ 373 Al Heist	5.50	2.50	.70
☐ 374 Gene Mauch MG	6.00	2.70	.75
☐ 375 Ron Fairly	6.00	2.70	.75
☐ 376 Bud Daley	5.50	2.50	.70
☐ 377 John Orsino	5.50	2.50	.70
☐ 378 Bennie Daniels	5.50	2.50	.70
☐ 379 Chuck Essegian	5.50	2.50	.70
☐ 380 Lou Burdette	6.50	2.90	.80
☐ 381 Chico Cardenas	6.00	2.70	.75
☐ 382 Dick Williams	6.00	2.70	.75
☐ 383 Ray Sadecki	5.50	2.50	.70
☐ 384 K.C. Athletics	10.00	4.50	1.25
Team Card			
☐ 385 Early Wynn	20.00	9.00	2.50
☐ 386 Don Mincher	6.00	2.70	.75
☐ 387 Lou Brock	250.00	115.00	31.00
☐ 388 Ryne Duren	7.00	3.10	.85
☐ 389 Smoky Burgess	6.00	2.70	.75
☐ 390 Orlando Cepeda AS	8.00	3.60	1.00
☐ 391 Bill Mazeroski AS	8.00	3.60	1.00
☐ 392 Ken Boyer AS	8.00	3.60	1.00
☐ 393 Roy McMillan AS	6.00	2.70	.75

☐ 394 Hank Aaron AS	45.00	20.00	5.75
☐ 395 Willie Mays AS	45.00	20.00	5.75
☐ 396 Frank Robinson AS	15.00	6.75	1.90
☐ 397 John Roseboro AS	6.00	2.70	.75
☐ 398 Don Drysdale AS	15.00	6.75	1.90
☐ 399 Warren Spahn AS	15.00	6.75	1.90
☐ 400 Elston Howard	10.00	4.50	1.25
☐ 401 AL/NL Homer Kings	40.00	18.00	5.00
Roger Maris			
Orlando Cepeda			
☐ 402 Gino Cimoli	5.50	2.50	.70
☐ 403 Chet Nichols	5.50	2.50	.70
☐ 404 Tim Harkness	5.50	2.50	.70
☐ 405 Jim Perry	7.00	3.10	.85
☐ 406 Bob Taylor	5.50	2.50	.70
☐ 407 Hank Aguirre	5.50	2.50	.70
☐ 408 Gus Bell	6.00	2.70	.75
☐ 409 Pittsburgh Pirates	10.00	4.50	1.25
Team Card			
☐ 410 Al Smith	5.50	2.50	.70
☐ 411 Danny O'Connell	5.50	2.50	.70
☐ 412 Charlie James	5.50	2.50	.70
☐ 413 Matty Alou	6.50	2.90	.80
☐ 414 Joe Gaines	5.50	2.50	.70
☐ 415 Bill Virdon	6.00	2.70	.75
☐ 416 Bob Scheffing MG	5.50	2.50	.70
☐ 417 Joe Azcue	5.50	2.50	.70
☐ 418 Andy Carey	5.50	2.50	.70
☐ 419 Bob Bruce	5.50	2.50	.70
☐ 420 Gus Triandos	6.00	2.70	.75
☐ 421 Ken MacKenzie	5.50	2.50	.70
☐ 422 Steve Bilko	5.50	2.50	.70
☐ 423 Rival League	7.00	3.10	.85
Relief Aces:			
Roy Face			
Hoyt Wilhelm			
☐ 424 Al McBean	6.00	2.70	.75
☐ 425 Carl Yastrzemski	225.00	100.00	28.00
☐ 426 Bob Farley	5.50	2.50	.70
☐ 427 Jake Wood	5.50	2.50	.70
☐ 428 Joe Hicks	5.50	2.50	.70
☐ 429 Billy O'Dell	5.50	2.50	.70
☐ 430 Tony Kubek	10.00	4.50	1.25
☐ 431 Bob Rodgers	8.00	3.60	1.00
☐ 432 Jim Pendleton	5.50	2.50	.70
☐ 433 Jim Archer	5.50	2.50	.70
☐ 434 Clay Dalrymple	5.50	2.50	.70
☐ 435 Larry Sherry	6.00	2.70	.75
☐ 436 Felix Mantilla	5.50	2.50	.70
☐ 437 Ray Moore	5.50	2.50	.70
☐ 438 Dick Brown	5.50	2.50	.70
☐ 439 Jerry Buchek	5.50	2.50	.70
☐ 440 Joey Jay	5.50	2.50	.70
☐ 441 Checklist 6	15.00	2.30	.75
☐ 442 Wes Stock	5.50	2.50	.70
☐ 443 Del Crandall	6.00	2.70	.75
☐ 444 Ted Wills	5.50	2.50	.70

☐	445	Vic Power	6.00	2.70	.75		
☐	446	Don Elston	5.50	2.50	.70		
☐	447	Willie Kirkland	7.00	3.10	.85		
☐	448	Joe Gibbon	7.00	3.10	.85		
☐	449	Jerry Adair	7.00	3.10	.85		
☐	450	Jim O'Toole	8.00	3.60	1.00		
☐	451	Jose Tartabull	8.50	3.80	1.05		
☐	452	Earl Averill Jr.	7.00	3.10	.85		
☐	453	Cal McLish	7.00	3.10	.85		
☐	454	Floyd Robinson	7.00	3.10	.85		
☐	455	Luis Arroyo	8.00	3.60	1.00		
☐	456	Joe Amalfitano	7.00	3.10	.85		
☐	457	Lou Clinton	7.00	3.10	.85		
☐	458A	Bob Buhl	8.00	3.60	1.00		
		(Braves emblem on cap)					
☐	458B	Bob Buhl	50.00	23.00	6.25		
		(No emblem on cap)					
☐	459	Ed Bailey	7.00	3.10	.85		
☐	460	Jim Bunning	11.00	4.90	1.40		
☐	461	Ken Hubbs	25.00	11.50	3.10		
☐	462A	Willie Tasby	7.00	3.10	.85		
		(Senators emblem on cap)					
☐	462B	Willie Tasby	50.00	23.00	6.25		
		(No emblem on cap)					
☐	463	Hank Bauer MG	8.00	3.60	1.00		
☐	464	Al Jackson	9.00	4.00	1.15		
☐	465	Reds Team	14.00	6.25	1.75		
☐	466	Norm Cash AS	9.00	4.00	1.15		
☐	467	Chuck Schilling AS	7.50	3.40	.95		
☐	468	Brooks Robinson AS	18.00	8.00	2.30		
☐	469	Luis Aparicio AS	11.00	4.90	1.40		
☐	470	Al Kaline AS	20.00	9.00	2.50		
☐	471	Mickey Mantle AS	150.00	70.00	19.00		
☐	472	Rocky Colavito AS	10.00	4.50	1.25		
☐	473	Elston Howard AS	9.00	4.00	1.15		
☐	474	Frank Lary AS	7.50	3.40	.95		
☐	475	Whitey Ford AS	15.00	6.75	1.90		
☐	476	Orioles Team	14.00	6.25	1.75		
☐	477	Andre Rodgers	7.00	3.10	.85		
☐	478	Don Zimmer	8.50	3.80	1.05		
		(Shown with Mets cap, but listed as with Cincinnati)					
☐	479	Joel Horlen	9.00	4.00	1.15		
☐	480	Harvey Kuenn	8.50	3.80	1.05		
☐	481	Vic Wertz	8.00	3.60	1.00		
☐	482	Sam Mele MG	7.00	3.10	.85		
☐	483	Don McMahon	7.00	3.10	.85		
☐	484	Dick Schofield	7.00	3.10	.85		
☐	485	Pedro Ramos	7.00	3.10	.85		
☐	486	Jim Gilliam	9.00	4.00	1.15		
☐	487	Jerry Lynch	7.00	3.10	.85		
☐	488	Hal Brown	7.00	3.10	.85		
☐	489	Julio Gotay	7.00	3.10	.85		
☐	490	Clete Boyer	9.00	4.00	1.15		
☐	491	Leon Wagner	7.00	3.10	.85		
☐	492	Hal W. Smith	7.00	3.10	.85		
☐	493	Danny McDevitt	7.00	3.10	.85		
☐	494	Sammy White	7.00	3.10	.85		
☐	495	Don Cardwell	7.00	3.10	.85		
☐	496	Wayne Causey	7.00	3.10	.85		
☐	497	Ed Bouchee	7.00	3.10	.85		
☐	498	Jim Donohue	7.00	3.10	.85		
☐	499	Zoilo Versalles	7.50	3.40	.95		
☐	500	Duke Snider	55.00	25.00	7.00		
☐	501	Claude Osteen	7.50	3.40	.95		
☐	502	Hector Lopez	7.50	3.40	.95		
☐	503	Danny Murtaugh MG	7.50	3.40	.95		
☐	504	Eddie Bressoud	7.00	3.10	.85		
☐	505	Juan Marichal	45.00	20.00	5.75		
☐	506	Charlie Maxwell	7.50	3.40	.95		
☐	507	Ernie Broglio	7.50	3.40	.95		
☐	508	Gordy Coleman	7.50	3.40	.95		
☐	509	Dave Giusti	9.00	4.00	1.15		
☐	510	Jim Lemon	7.00	3.10	.85		
☐	511	Bubba Phillips	7.00	3.10	.85		
☐	512	Mike Fornieles	7.00	3.10	.85		
☐	513	Whitey Herzog	8.50	3.80	1.05		
☐	514	Sherm Lollar	7.50	3.40	.95		
☐	515	Stan Williams	7.50	3.40	.95		
☐	516	Checklist 7	15.00	2.30	.75		
☐	517	Dave Wickersham	7.00	3.10	.85		
☐	518	Lee Maye	7.00	3.10	.85		
☐	519	Bob Johnson	7.00	3.10	.85		
☐	520	Bob Friend	8.00	3.60	1.00		
☐	521	Jacke Davis UER	7.00	3.10	.85		
		(Listed as OF on front and P on back)					
☐	522	Lindy McDaniel	8.00	3.60	1.00		
☐	523	Russ Nixon SP	26.00	11.50	3.30		
☐	524	Howie Nunn SP	26.00	11.50	3.30		
☐	525	George Thomas	15.00	6.75	1.90		
☐	526	Hal Woodeshick SP	26.00	11.50	3.30		
☐	527	Dick McAuliffe	20.00	9.00	2.50		
☐	528	Turk Lown	15.00	6.75	1.90		
☐	529	John Schaive SP	26.00	11.50	3.30		
☐	530	Bob Gibson SP	175.00	80.00	22.00		
☐	531	Bobby G. Smith	15.00	6.75	1.90		
☐	532	Dick Stigman	15.00	6.75	1.90		
☐	533	Charley Lau SP	27.00	12.00	3.40		
☐	534	Tony Gonzalez SP	26.00	11.50	3.30		
☐	535	Ed Roebuck	15.00	6.75	1.90		
☐	536	Dick Gernert	15.00	6.75	1.90		
☐	537	Cleveland Indians	42.50	19.00	5.25		
		Team Card					
☐	538	Jack Sanford	16.00	7.25	2.00		
☐	539	Billy Moran	15.00	6.75	1.90		
☐	540	Jim Landis SP	26.00	11.50	3.30		
☐	541	Don Nottebart SP	26.00	11.50	3.30		
☐	542	Dave Philley	15.00	6.75	1.90		
☐	543	Bob Allen SP	26.00	11.50	3.30		
☐	544	Willie McCovey SP	175.00	80.00	22.00		

☐ 545	Hoyt Wilhelm SP	55.00	25.00	7.00
☐ 546	Moe Thacker SP	26.00	11.50	3.30
☐ 547	Don Ferrarese	15.00	6.75	1.90
☐ 548	Bobby Del Greco SP	15.00	6.75	1.90
☐ 549	Bill Rigney MG SP	26.00	11.50	3.30
☐ 550	Art Mahaffey SP	26.00	11.50	3.30
☐ 551	Harry Bright	15.00	6.75	1.90
☐ 552	Chicago Cubs SP Team Card	50.00	23.00	6.25
☐ 553	Jim Coates	15.00	6.75	1.90
☐ 554	Bubba Morton SP	26.00	11.50	3.30
☐ 555	John Buzhardt SP	26.00	11.50	3.30
☐ 556	Al Spangler	15.00	6.75	1.90
☐ 557	Bob Anderson SP	26.00	11.50	3.30
☐ 558	John Goryl	15.00	6.75	1.90
☐ 559	Mike Higgins MG	15.00	6.75	1.90
☐ 560	Chuck Estrada SP	26.00	11.50	3.30
☐ 561	Gene Oliver SP	26.00	11.50	3.30
☐ 562	Bill Henry	15.00	6.75	1.90
☐ 563	Ken Aspromonte	15.00	6.75	1.90
☐ 564	Bob Grim	15.00	6.75	1.90
☐ 565	Jose Pagan	15.00	6.75	1.90
☐ 566	Marty Kutyna SP	26.00	11.50	3.30
☐ 567	Tracy Stallard SP	26.00	11.50	3.30
☐ 568	Jim Golden	15.00	6.75	1.90
☐ 569	Ed Sadowski SP	26.00	11.50	3.30
☐ 570	Bill Stafford SP	30.00	13.50	3.80
☐ 571	Billy Klaus SP	26.00	11.50	3.30
☐ 572	Bob G. Miller SP	30.00	13.50	3.80
☐ 573	Johnny Logan	16.00	7.25	2.00
☐ 574	Dean Stone	15.00	6.75	1.90
☐ 575	Red Schoendienst SP	50.00	23.00	6.25
☐ 576	Russ Kemmerer SP	26.00	11.50	3.30
☐ 577	Dave Nicholson SP	26.00	11.50	3.30
☐ 578	Jim Duffalo	15.00	6.75	1.90
☐ 579	Jim Schaffer SP	26.00	11.50	3.30
☐ 580	Bill Monbouquette	15.00	6.75	1.90
☐ 581	Mel Roach	15.00	6.75	1.90
☐ 582	Ron Piche	15.00	6.75	1.90
☐ 583	Larry Osborne	15.00	6.75	1.90
☐ 584	Minnesota Twins SP Team Card	50.00	23.00	6.25
☐ 585	Glen Hobbie SP	26.00	11.50	3.30
☐ 586	Sammy Esposito SP	26.00	11.50	3.30
☐ 587	Frank Funk SP	26.00	11.50	3.30
☐ 588	Birdie Tebbetts MG	17.50	8.00	2.20
☐ 589	Bob Turley	16.00	7.25	2.00
☐ 590	Curt Flood	20.00	9.00	2.50
☐ 591	Rookie Pitchers SP	60.00	27.00	7.50

Sam McDowell
Ron Taylor
Ron Nischwitz
Art Quirk
Dick Radatz

☐ 592	Rookie Pitchers SP	75.00	34.00	9.50

Dan Pfister
Bo Belinsky
Dave Stenhouse
Jim Bouton
Joe Bonikowski

☐ 593	Rookie Pitchers SP	33.00	15.00	4.10

Jack Lamabe
Craig Anderson
Jack Hamilton
Bob Moorhead
Bob Veale

☐ 594	Rookie Catchers SP	100.00	45.00	12.50

Doc Edwards
Ken Retzer
Bob Uecker
Doug Camilli
Don Pavletich

☐ 595	Rookie Infielders SP	33.00	15.00	4.10

Bob Sadowski
Felix Torres
Marlan Coughtry
Ed Charles

☐ 596	Rookie Infielders SP	65.00	29.00	8.25

Bernie Allen
Joe Pepitone
Phil Linz
Rich Rollins

☐ 597	Rookie Infielders SP	40.00	18.00	5.00

Jim McKnight
Rod Kanehl
Amado Samuel
Denis Menke

☐ 598	Rookie Outfielders SP	75.00	34.00	9.50

Al Luplow
Manny Jimenez
Howie Goss
Jim Hickman
Ed Olivares

1963 Topps

The cards in this 576-card set measure 2 1/2" by 3 1/2". The sharp color photographs of the 1963 set are a vivid contrast to the drab pictures of 1962. In addition to the "League Leaders" series (1-10) and World Series cards (142-148), the seventh and last series of cards (523-576) contains seven rookie cards (each depicting four players). There were some three-card advertising panels produced by Topps; the players included are from the first series; one panel shows Hoyt Wilhelm, Don Lock, and Bob Duliba on the front with a Stan Musial ad/endorsement on one of the backs. This set has gained special prominence in recent years since it contains the Rookie Card of Pete Rose (537). Other key rookies in this set are Tony Oliva, Willie Stargell, and Rusty Staub.

	NRMT	VG-E	GOOD
COMPLETE SET (576)	5300.00	2400.00	650.00
COMMON PLAYER (1-109)	2.00	.90	.25
COMMON PLAYER (110-196)	2.25	1.00	.30
COMMON PLAYER (197-283)	3.00	1.35	.40
COMMON PLAYER (284-370)	4.00	1.80	.50
COMMON PLAYER (371-446)	4.50	2.00	.55
COMMON PLAYER (447-522)	14.00	6.25	1.75
COMMON PLAYER (523-576)	10.00	4.50	1.25

		NRMT	VG-E	GOOD
☐ 1	NL Batting Leaders	36.00	7.25	2.20
	Tommy Davis			
	Frank Robinson			
	Stan Musial			
	Hank Aaron			
	Bill White			
☐ 2	AL Batting Leaders	20.00	9.00	2.50
	Pete Runnels			
	Mickey Mantle			
	Floyd Robinson			
	Norm Siebern			
	Chuck Hinton			
☐ 3	NL Home Run Leaders	20.00	9.00	2.50
	Willie Mays			
	Hank Aaron			
	Frank Robinson			
	Orlando Cepeda			
	Ernie Banks			
☐ 4	AL Home Run Leaders	7.50	3.40	.95
	Harmon Killebrew			
	Norm Cash			
	Rocky Colavito			
	Roger Maris			
	Jim Gentile			
	Leon Wagner			
☐ 5	NL ERA Leaders	8.00	3.60	1.00
	Sandy Koufax			
	Bob Shaw			
	Bob Purkey			
	Bob Gibson			
	Don Drysdale			
☐ 6	AL ERA Leaders	5.00	2.30	.60
	Hank Aguirre			
	Robin Roberts			
	Whitey Ford			
	Eddie Fisher			
	Dean Chance			
☐ 7	NL Pitching Leaders	5.00	2.30	.60
	Don Drysdale			
	Jack Sanford			
	Bob Purkey			
	Billy O'Dell			
	Art Mahaffey			
	Joe Jay			
☐ 8	AL Pitching Leaders	4.50	2.00	.55
	Ralph Terry			
	Dick Donovan			
	Ray Herbert			
	Jim Bunning			
	Camilo Pascual			
☐ 9	NL Strikeout Leaders	8.00	3.60	1.00
	Don Drysdale			
	Sandy Koufax			
	Bob Gibson			
	Billy O'Dell			
	Dick Farrell			
☐ 10	AL Strikeout Leaders	4.50	2.00	.55
	Camilo Pascual			
	Jim Bunning			
	Ralph Terry			
	Juan Pizarro			
	Jim Kaat			
☐ 11	Lee Walls	2.00	.90	.25
☐ 12	Steve Barber	2.00	.90	.25
☐ 13	Philadelphia Phillies	4.50	2.00	.55
	Team Card			
☐ 14	Pedro Ramos	2.00	.90	.25
☐ 15	Ken Hubbs UER	3.50	1.55	.45
	(No position listed			
	on front of card)			
☐ 16	Al Smith	2.00	.90	.25
☐ 17	Ryne Duren	2.50	1.15	.30
☐ 18	Buc Blasters	15.00	6.75	1.90
	Smoky Burgess			
	Dick Stuart			
	Bob Clemente			
	Bob Skinner			
☐ 19	Pete Burnside	2.00	.90	.25
☐ 20	Tony Kubek	4.50	2.00	.55
☐ 21	Marty Keough	2.00	.90	.25
☐ 22	Curt Simmons	2.50	1.15	.30
☐ 23	Ed Lopat MG	2.50	1.15	.30
☐ 24	Bob Bruce	2.00	.90	.25
☐ 25	Al Kaline	35.00	16.00	4.40

☐ 26	Ray Moore	2.00	.90	.25
☐ 27	Choo Choo Coleman	2.00	.90	.25
☐ 28	Mike Fornieles	2.00	.90	.25
☐ 29A	1962 Rookie Stars	5.50	2.50	.70
	Sammy Ellis			
	Ray Culp			
	John Boozer			
	Jesse Gonder			
☐ 29B	1963 Rookie Stars	3.25	1.45	.40
	Sammy Ellis			
	Ray Culp			
	John Boozer			
	Jesse Gonder			
☐ 30	Harvey Kuenn	2.50	1.15	.30
☐ 31	Cal Koonce	2.00	.90	.25
☐ 32	Tony Gonzalez	2.00	.90	.25
☐ 33	Bo Belinsky	2.50	1.15	.30
☐ 34	Dick Schofield	2.00	.90	.25
☐ 35	John Buzhardt	2.00	.90	.25
☐ 36	Jerry Kindall	2.00	.90	.25
☐ 37	Jerry Lynch	2.00	.90	.25
☐ 38	Bud Daley	2.00	.90	.25
☐ 39	Angels Team	4.50	2.00	.55
☐ 40	Vic Power	2.50	1.15	.30
☐ 41	Charley Lau	2.50	1.15	.30
☐ 42	Stan Williams	2.50	1.15	.30
	(Listed as Yankee on card but LA cap)			
☐ 43	Veteran Masters	4.00	1.80	.50
	Casey Stengel MG			
	Gene Woodling			
☐ 44	Terry Fox	2.00	.90	.25
☐ 45	Bob Aspromonte	2.00	.90	.25
☐ 46	Tommie Aaron	3.25	1.45	.40
☐ 47	Don Lock	2.00	.90	.25
☐ 48	Birdie Tebbetts MG	2.50	1.15	.30
☐ 49	Dal Maxvill	3.25	1.45	.40
☐ 50	Billy Pierce	2.50	1.15	.30
☐ 51	George Alusik	2.00	.90	.25
☐ 52	Chuck Schilling	2.00	.90	.25
☐ 53	Joe Moeller	2.00	.90	.25
☐ 54A	1962 Rookie Stars	14.00	6.25	1.75
	Nelson Mathews			
	Harry Fanok			
	Jack Cullen			
	Dave DeBusschere			
☐ 54B	1963 Rookie Stars	6.00	2.70	.75
	Nelson Mathews			
	Harry Fanok			
	Jack Cullen			
	Dave DeBusschere			
☐ 55	Bill Virdon	2.50	1.15	.30
☐ 56	Dennis Bennett	2.00	.90	.25
☐ 57	Billy Moran	2.00	.90	.25
☐ 58	Bob Will	2.00	.90	.25
☐ 59	Craig Anderson	2.00	.90	.25
☐ 60	Elston Howard	6.00	2.70	.75
☐ 61	Ernie Bowman	2.00	.90	.25
☐ 62	Bob Hendley	2.00	.90	.25
☐ 63	Reds Team	4.50	2.00	.55
☐ 64	Dick McAuliffe	2.50	1.15	.30
☐ 65	Jackie Brandt	2.00	.90	.25
☐ 66	Mike Joyce	2.00	.90	.25
☐ 67	Ed Charles	2.00	.90	.25
☐ 68	Friendly Foes	11.00	4.90	1.40
	Duke Snider			
	Gil Hodges			
☐ 69	Bud Zipfel	2.00	.90	.25
☐ 70	Jim O'Toole	2.50	1.15	.30
☐ 71	Bobby Wine	2.50	1.15	.30
☐ 72	Johnny Romano	2.00	.90	.25
☐ 73	Bobby Bragan MG	3.00	1.35	.40
☐ 74	Denny Lemaster	2.00	.90	.25
☐ 75	Bob Allison	2.50	1.15	.30
☐ 76	Earl Wilson	2.50	1.15	.30
☐ 77	Al Spangler	2.00	.90	.25
☐ 78	Marv Throneberry	3.00	1.35	.40
☐ 79	Checklist 1	10.00	1.50	.50
☐ 80	Jim Gilliam	3.50	1.55	.45
☐ 81	Jim Schaffer	2.00	.90	.25
☐ 82	Ed Rakow	2.00	.90	.25
☐ 83	Charley James	2.00	.90	.25
☐ 84	Ron Kline	2.00	.90	.25
☐ 85	Tom Haller	2.50	1.15	.30
☐ 86	Charley Maxwell	2.50	1.15	.30
☐ 87	Bob Veale	2.50	1.15	.30
☐ 88	Ron Hansen	2.00	.90	.25
☐ 89	Dick Stigman	2.00	.90	.25
☐ 90	Gordy Coleman	2.50	1.15	.30
☐ 91	Dallas Green	2.50	1.15	.30
☐ 92	Hector Lopez	2.50	1.15	.30
☐ 93	Galen Cisco	2.00	.90	.25
☐ 94	Bob Schmidt	2.00	.90	.25
☐ 95	Larry Jackson	2.00	.90	.25
☐ 96	Lou Clinton	2.00	.90	.25
☐ 97	Bob Duliba	2.00	.90	.25
☐ 98	George Thomas	2.00	.90	.25
☐ 99	Jim Umbricht	2.00	.90	.25
☐ 100	Joe Cunningham	2.00	.90	.25
☐ 101	Joe Gibbon	2.00	.90	.25
☐ 102A	Checklist 2	10.00	1.50	.50
	(Red on yellow)			
☐ 102B	Checklist 2	10.00	1.50	.50
	(White on red)			
☐ 103	Chuck Essegian	2.00	.90	.25
☐ 104	Lew Krausse	2.00	.90	.25
☐ 105	Ron Fairly	2.50	1.15	.30
☐ 106	Bobby Bolin	2.00	.90	.25
☐ 107	Jim Hickman	2.50	1.15	.30
☐ 108	Hoyt Wilhelm	10.50	4.70	1.30
☐ 109	Lee Maye	2.00	.90	.25
☐ 110	Rich Rollins	2.75	1.25	.35
☐ 111	Al Jackson	2.25	1.00	.30
☐ 112	Dick Brown	2.25	1.00	.30

☐ 113	Don Landrum UER.......2.25	1.00	.30
	(Photo actually		
	Ron Santo)		
☐ 114	Dan Osinski...............2.25	1.00	.30
☐ 115	Carl Yastrzemski........65.00	29.00	8.25
☐ 116	Jim Brosnan..............2.75	1.25	.35
☐ 117	Jacke Davis...............2.25	1.00	.30
☐ 118	Sherm Lollar..............2.25	1.00	.30
☐ 119	Bob Lillis..................2.25	1.00	.30
☐ 120	Roger Maris...............65.00	29.00	8.25
☐ 121	Jim Hannan...............2.25	1.00	.30
☐ 122	Julio Gotay.................2.25	1.00	.30
☐ 123	Frank Howard.............3.50	1.55	.45
☐ 124	Dick Howser..............2.75	1.25	.35
☐ 125	Robin Roberts............11.00	4.90	1.40
☐ 126	Bob Uecker...............25.00	11.50	3.10
☐ 127	Bill Tuttle.................2.25	1.00	.30
☐ 128	Matty Alou 2.75	1.25	.35
☐ 129	Gary Bell..................2.25	1.00	.30
☐ 130	Dick Groat................3.25	1.45	.40
☐ 131	Washington Senators ..4.50	2.00	.55
	Team Card		
☐ 132	Jack Hamilton............2.25	1.00	.30
☐ 133	Gene Freese..............2.25	1.00	.30
☐ 134	Bob Scheffing MG.......2.25	1.00	.30
☐ 135	Richie Ashburn..........9.50	4.30	1.20
☐ 136	Ike Delock................2.25	1.00	.30
☐ 137	Mack Jones...............2.25	1.00	.30
☐ 138	Pride of NL...............36.00	16.00	4.50
	Willie Mays		
	Stan Musial		
☐ 139	Earl Averill................2.25	1.00	.30
☐ 140	Frank Lary................2.75	1.25	.35
☐ 141	Manny Mota..............6.50	2.90	.80
☐ 142	World Series Game 1...7.00	3.10	.85
	Whitey Ford wins		
	series opener		
☐ 143	World Series Game 2...5.00	2.30	.60
	Jack Sanford flashes		
	shutout magic		
☐ 144	World Series Game 3.11.00	4.90	1.40
	Roger Maris sparks		
	Yankee rally		
☐ 145	World Series Game 4...5.00	2.30	.60
	Chuck Hiller blasts		
	grand slammer		
☐ 146	World Series Game 5...5.00	2.30	.60
	Tom Tresh's homer		
	defeats Giants		
☐ 147	World Series Game 6...5.00	2.30	.60
	Billy Pierce stars in		
	3 hit victory		
☐ 148	World Series Game 7...5.00	2.30	.60
	Yanks celebrate		
	as Ralph Terry wins		
☐ 149	Marv Breeding 2.25	1.00	.30
☐ 150	Johnny Podres............2.75	1.25	.35

☐ 151	Pirates Team..............4.50	2.00	.55
☐ 152	Ron Nischwitz............2.25	1.00	.30
☐ 153	Hal Smith.................2.25	1.00	.30
☐ 154	Walt Alston MG...........4.50	2.00	.55
☐ 155	Bill Stafford...............2.25	1.00	.30
☐ 156	Roy McMillan.............2.75	1.25	.35
☐ 157	Diego Segui...............2.25	1.00	.30
☐ 158	Rookie Stars..............4.00	1.80	.50
	Rogelio Alvares		
	Dave Roberts		
	Tommy Harper		
	Bob Saverine		
☐ 159	Jim Pagliaroni............2.25	1.00	.30
☐ 160	Juan Pizarro..............2.25	1.00	.30
☐ 161	Frank Torre...............2.75	1.25	.35
☐ 162	Twins Team...............4.50	2.00	.55
☐ 163	Don Larsen................2.75	1.25	.35
☐ 164	Bubba Morton............2.25	1.00	.30
☐ 165	Jim Kaat...................5.25	2.40	.65
☐ 166	Johnny Keane MG........2.25	1.00	.30
☐ 167	Jim Fregosi...............4.00	1.80	.50
☐ 168	Russ Nixon................2.25	1.00	.30
☐ 169	Rookie Stars..............35.00	16.00	4.40
	Dick Egan		
	Julio Navarro		
	Tommie Sisk		
	Gaylord Perry		
☐ 170	Joe Adcock 3.50	1.55	.45
☐ 171	Steve Hamilton..........2.25	1.00	.30
☐ 172	Gene Oliver...............2.25	1.00	.30
☐ 173	Bombers' Best 80.00	36.00	10.00
	Tom Tresh		
	Mickey Mantle		
	Bobby Richardson		
☐ 174	Larry Burright 2.25	1.00	.30
☐ 175	Bob Buhl..................2.75	1.25	.35
☐ 176	Jim King..................2.25	1.00	.30
☐ 177	Bubba Phillips............2.25	1.00	.30
☐ 178	Johnny Edwards..........2.25	1.00	.30
☐ 179	Ron Piche.................2.25	1.00	.30
☐ 180	Bill Skowron..............4.00	1.80	.50
☐ 181	Sammy Esposito..........2.25	1.00	.30
☐ 182	Albie Pearson............2.75	1.25	.35
☐ 183	Joe Pepitone.............4.00	1.80	.50
☐ 184	Vern Law.................2.75	1.25	.35
☐ 185	Chuck Hiller..............2.25	1.00	.30
☐ 186	Jerry Zimmerman.........2.25	1.00	.30
☐ 187	Willie Kirkland............2.25	1.00	.30
☐ 188	Eddie Bressoud..........2.25	1.00	.30
☐ 189	Dave Giusti...............2.75	1.25	.35
☐ 190	Minnie Minoso............4.00	1.80	.50
☐ 191	Checklist 3...............10.00	1.50	.50
☐ 192	Clay Dalrymple...........2.25	1.00	.30
☐ 193	Andre Rodgers...........2.25	1.00	.30
☐ 194	Joe Nuxhall...............2.75	1.25	.35
☐ 195	Manny Jimenez...........2.25	1.00	.30
☐ 196	Doug Camilli..............2.25	1.00	.30

☐ 197	Roger Craig	4.00	1.80	.50
☐ 198	Lenny Green	3.00	1.35	.40
☐ 199	Joe Amalfitano	3.00	1.35	.40
☐ 200	Mickey Mantle	450.00	200.00	57.50
☐ 201	Cecil Butler	3.00	1.35	.40
☐ 202	Boston Red Sox	6.00	2.70	.75
	Team Card			
☐ 203	Chico Cardenas	3.50	1.55	.45
☐ 204	Don Nottebart	3.00	1.35	.40
☐ 205	Luis Aparicio	15.00	6.75	1.90
☐ 206	Ray Washburn	3.00	1.35	.40
☐ 207	Ken Hunt	3.00	1.35	.40
☐ 208	Rookie Stars	3.00	1.35	.40
	Ron Herbel			
	John Miller			
	Wally Wolf			
	Ron Taylor			
☐ 209	Hobie Landrith	3.00	1.35	.40
☐ 210	Sandy Koufax	175.00	80.00	22.00
☐ 211	Fred Whitfield	3.00	1.35	.40
☐ 212	Glen Hobbie	3.00	1.35	.40
☐ 213	Billy Hitchcock MG	3.00	1.35	.40
☐ 214	Orlando Pena	3.00	1.35	.40
☐ 215	Bob Skinner	3.50	1.55	.45
☐ 216	Gene Conley	3.50	1.55	.45
☐ 217	Joe Christopher	3.00	1.35	.40
☐ 218	Tiger Twirlers	3.50	1.55	.45
	Frank Lary			
	Don Mossi			
	Jim Bunning			
☐ 219	Chuck Cottier	3.00	1.35	.40
☐ 220	Camilo Pascual	3.50	1.55	.45
☐ 221	Cookie Rojas	4.50	2.00	.55
☐ 222	Cubs Team	6.00	2.70	.75
☐ 223	Eddie Fisher	3.00	1.35	.40
☐ 224	Mike Roarke	3.00	1.35	.40
☐ 225	Joey Jay	3.00	1.35	.40
☐ 226	Julian Javier	3.50	1.55	.45
☐ 227	Jim Grant	3.50	1.55	.45
☐ 228	Rookie Stars	55.00	25.00	7.00
	Max Alvis			
	Bob Bailey			
	Tony Oliva			
	(Listed as Pedro)			
	Ed Kranepool			
☐ 229	Willie Davis	3.50	1.55	.45
☐ 230	Pete Runnels	3.50	1.55	.45
☐ 231	Eli Grba UER	3.00	1.35	.40
	(Large photo is			
	Ryne Duren)			
☐ 232	Frank Malzone	3.50	1.55	.45
☐ 233	Casey Stengel MG	17.00	7.75	2.10
☐ 234	Dave Nicholson	3.00	1.35	.40
☐ 235	Billy O'Dell	3.00	1.35	.40
☐ 236	Bill Bryan	3.00	1.35	.40
☐ 237	Jim Coates	3.00	1.35	.40
☐ 238	Lou Johnson	3.50	1.55	.45

☐ 239	Harvey Haddix	3.50	1.55	.45
☐ 240	Rocky Colavito	10.00	4.50	1.25
☐ 241	Bob Smith	3.00	1.35	.40
☐ 242	Power Plus	35.00	16.00	4.40
	Ernie Banks			
	Hank Aaron			
☐ 243	Don Leppert	3.00	1.35	.40
☐ 244	John Tsitouris	3.00	1.35	.40
☐ 245	Gil Hodges	20.00	9.00	2.50
☐ 246	Lee Stange	3.00	1.35	.40
☐ 247	Yankees Team	20.00	9.00	2.50
☐ 248	Tito Francona	3.00	1.35	.40
☐ 249	Leo Burke	3.00	1.35	.40
☐ 250	Stan Musial	125.00	57.50	15.50
☐ 251	Jack Lamabe	3.00	1.35	.40
☐ 252	Ron Santo	7.50	3.40	.95
☐ 253	Rookie Stars	3.50	1.55	.45
	Len Gabrielson			
	Pete Jernigan			
	John Wojcik			
	Deacon Jones			
☐ 254	Mike Hershberger	3.00	1.35	.40
☐ 255	Bob Shaw	3.00	1.35	.40
☐ 256	Jerry Lumpe	3.00	1.35	.40
☐ 257	Hank Aguirre	3.00	1.35	.40
☐ 258	Alvin Dark MG	3.50	1.55	.45
☐ 259	Johnny Logan	3.50	1.55	.45
☐ 260	Jim Gentile	3.50	1.55	.45
☐ 261	Bob Miller	3.00	1.35	.40
☐ 262	Ellis Burton	3.00	1.35	.40
☐ 263	Dave Stenhouse	3.00	1.35	.40
☐ 264	Phil Linz	3.50	1.55	.45
☐ 265	Vada Pinson	5.00	2.30	.60
☐ 266	Bob Allen	3.00	1.35	.40
☐ 267	Carl Sawatski	3.00	1.35	.40
☐ 268	Don Demeter	3.00	1.35	.40
☐ 269	Don Mincher	3.00	1.35	.40
☐ 270	Felipe Alou	5.00	2.30	.60
☐ 271	Dean Stone	3.00	1.35	.40
☐ 272	Danny Murphy	3.00	1.35	.40
☐ 273	Sammy Taylor	3.00	1.35	.40
☐ 274	Checklist 4	10.00	1.50	.50
☐ 275	Eddie Mathews	20.00	9.00	2.50
☐ 276	Barry Shetrone	3.00	1.35	.40
☐ 277	Dick Farrell	3.00	1.35	.40
☐ 278	Chico Fernandez	3.00	1.35	.40
☐ 279	Wally Moon	3.50	1.55	.45
☐ 280	Bob Rodgers	5.00	2.30	.60
☐ 281	Tom Sturdivant	3.00	1.35	.40
☐ 282	Bobby Del Greco	3.00	1.35	.40
☐ 283	Roy Sievers	3.50	1.55	.45
☐ 284	Dave Sisler	4.00	1.80	.50
☐ 285	Dick Stuart	4.50	2.00	.55
☐ 286	Stu Miller	4.50	2.00	.55
☐ 287	Dick Bertell	4.00	1.80	.50
☐ 288	Chicago White Sox	9.00	4.00	1.15
	Team Card			

☐ 289 Hal Brown	4.00	1.80	.50
☐ 290 Bill White	6.50	2.90	.80
☐ 291 Don Rudolph	4.00	1.80	.50
☐ 292 Pumpsie Green	4.50	2.00	.55
☐ 293 Bill Pleis	4.00	1.80	.50
☐ 294 Bill Rigney MG	4.00	1.80	.50
☐ 295 Ed Roebuck	4.00	1.80	.50
☐ 296 Doc Edwards	4.00	1.80	.50
☐ 297 Jim Golden	4.00	1.80	.50
☐ 298 Don Dillard	4.00	1.80	.50
☐ 299 Rookie Stars	4.50	2.00	.55
Dave Morehead			
Bob Dustal			
Tom Butters			
Dan Schneider			
☐ 300 Willie Mays	180.00	80.00	23.00
☐ 301 Bill Fischer	4.00	1.80	.50
☐ 302 Whitey Herzog	6.50	2.90	.80
☐ 303 Earl Francis	4.00	1.80	.50
☐ 304 Harry Bright	4.00	1.80	.50
☐ 305 Don Hoak	4.50	2.00	.55
☐ 306 Star Receivers	5.00	2.30	.60
Earl Battey			
Elston Howard			
☐ 307 Chet Nichols	4.00	1.80	.50
☐ 308 Camilo Carreon	4.00	1.80	.50
☐ 309 Jim Brewer	4.00	1.80	.50
☐ 310 Tommy Davis	6.00	2.70	.75
☐ 311 Joe McClain	4.00	1.80	.50
☐ 312 Houston Colts	15.00	6.75	1.90
Team Card			
☐ 313 Ernie Broglio	4.50	2.00	.55
☐ 314 John Goryl	4.00	1.80	.50
☐ 315 Ralph Terry	4.50	2.00	.55
☐ 316 Norm Sherry	4.50	2.00	.55
☐ 317 Sam McDowell	5.00	2.30	.60
☐ 318 Gene Mauch MG	4.50	2.00	.55
☐ 319 Joe Gaines	4.00	1.80	.50
☐ 320 Warren Spahn	40.00	18.00	5.00
☐ 321 Gino Cimoli	4.00	1.80	.50
☐ 322 Bob Turley	4.50	2.00	.55
☐ 323 Bill Mazeroski	6.50	2.90	.80
☐ 324 Rookie Stars	5.00	2.30	.60
George Williams			
Pete Ward			
Phil Roof			
Vic Davalillo			
☐ 325 Jack Sanford	4.00	1.80	.50
☐ 326 Hank Foiles	4.00	1.80	.50
☐ 327 Paul Foytack	4.00	1.80	.50
☐ 328 Dick Williams	4.50	2.00	.55
☐ 329 Lindy McDaniel	4.50	2.00	.55
☐ 330 Chuck Hinton	4.00	1.80	.50
☐ 331 Series Foes	4.50	2.00	.55
Bill Stafford			
Bill Pierce			
☐ 332 Joel Horlen	4.50	2.00	.55

☐ 333 Carl Warwick	4.00	1.80	.50
☐ 334 Wynn Hawkins	4.00	1.80	.50
☐ 335 Leon Wagner	4.00	1.80	.50
☐ 336 Ed Bauta	4.00	1.80	.50
☐ 337 Dodgers Team	12.50	5.75	1.55
☐ 338 Russ Kemmerer	4.00	1.80	.50
☐ 339 Ted Bowsfield	4.00	1.80	.50
☐ 340 Yogi Berra	75.00	34.00	9.50
(Player/coach)			
☐ 341 Jack Baldschun	4.00	1.80	.50
☐ 342 Gene Woodling	4.50	2.00	.55
☐ 343 Johnny Pesky MG	4.50	2.00	.55
☐ 344 Don Schwall	4.50	2.00	.55
☐ 345 Brooks Robinson	55.00	25.00	7.00
☐ 346 Billy Hoeft	4.00	1.80	.50
☐ 347 Joe Torre	8.50	3.80	1.05
☐ 348 Vic Wertz	4.50	2.00	.55
☐ 349 Zoilo Versalles	4.50	2.00	.55
☐ 350 Bob Purkey	4.00	1.80	.50
☐ 351 Al Luplow	4.00	1.80	.50
☐ 352 Ken Johnson	4.00	1.80	.50
☐ 353 Billy Williams	25.00	11.50	3.10
☐ 354 Dom Zanni	4.00	1.80	.50
☐ 355 Dean Chance	5.00	2.30	.60
☐ 356 John Schaive	4.00	1.80	.50
☐ 357 George Altman	4.00	1.80	.50
☐ 358 Milt Pappas	4.50	2.00	.55
☐ 359 Haywood Sullivan	4.50	2.00	.55
☐ 360 Don Drysdale	40.00	18.00	5.00
☐ 361 Clete Boyer	6.50	2.90	.80
☐ 362 Checklist 5	10.00	1.50	.50
☐ 363 Dick Radatz	5.00	2.30	.60
☐ 364 Howie Goss	4.00	1.80	.50
☐ 365 Jim Bunning	10.00	4.50	1.25
☐ 366 Tony Taylor	4.50	2.00	.55
☐ 367 Tony Cloninger	4.00	1.80	.50
☐ 368 Ed Bailey	4.00	1.80	.50
☐ 369 Jim Lemon	4.00	1.80	.50
☐ 370 Dick Donovan	4.00	1.80	.50
☐ 371 Rod Kanehl	4.50	2.00	.55
☐ 372 Don Lee	4.50	2.00	.55
☐ 373 Jim Campbell	4.50	2.00	.55
☐ 374 Claude Osteen	5.00	2.30	.60
☐ 375 Ken Boyer	9.00	4.00	1.15
☐ 376 John Wyatt	4.50	2.00	.55
☐ 377 Baltimore Orioles	9.00	4.00	1.15
Team Card			
☐ 378 Bill Henry	4.50	2.00	.55
☐ 379 Bob Anderson	4.50	2.00	.55
☐ 380 Ernie Banks	70.00	32.00	8.75
☐ 381 Frank Baumann	4.50	2.00	.55
☐ 382 Ralph Houk MG	6.50	2.90	.80
☐ 383 Pete Richert	4.50	2.00	.55
☐ 384 Bob Tillman	4.50	2.00	.55
☐ 385 Art Mahaffey	4.50	2.00	.55
☐ 386 Rookie Stars	5.00	2.30	.60
Ed Kirkpatrick			

John Bateman
Larry Bearnarth
Garry Roggenburk

☐ 387	Al McBean	4.50	2.00	.55
☐ 388	Jim Davenport	5.00	2.30	.60
☐ 389	Frank Sullivan	4.50	2.00	.55
☐ 390	Hank Aaron	150.00	70.00	19.00
☐ 391	Bill Dailey	4.50	2.00	.55
☐ 392	Tribe Thumpers	4.50	2.00	.55

Johnny Romano
Tito Francona

☐ 393	Ken MacKenzie	4.50	2.00	.55
☐ 394	Tim McCarver	15.00	6.75	1.90
☐ 395	Don McMahon	4.50	2.00	.55
☐ 396	Joe Koppe	4.50	2.00	.55
☐ 397	Kansas City Athletics	9.00	4.00	1.15

Team Card

☐ 398	Boog Powell	25.00	11.50	3.10
☐ 399	Dick Ellsworth	5.00	2.30	.60
☐ 400	Frank Robinson	50.00	23.00	6.25
☐ 401	Jim Bouton	9.50	4.30	1.20
☐ 402	Mickey Vernon MG	4.50	2.30	.60
☐ 403	Ron Perranoski	5.00	2.30	.60
☐ 404	Bob Oldis	4.50	2.00	.55
☐ 405	Floyd Robinson	4.50	2.00	.55
☐ 406	Howie Koplitz	4.50	2.00	.55
☐ 407	Rookie Stars	4.50	2.00	.55

Frank Kostro
Chico Ruiz
Larry Elliot
Dick Simpson

☐ 408	Billy Gardner	4.50	2.00	.55
☐ 409	Roy Face	5.50	2.50	.70
☐ 410	Earl Battey	4.50	2.00	.55
☐ 411	Jim Constable	4.50	2.00	.55
☐ 412	Dodger Big Three	35.00	16.00	4.40

Johnny Podres
Don Drysdale
Sandy Koufax

☐ 413	Jerry Walker	4.50	2.00	.55
☐ 414	Ty Cline	4.50	2.00	.55
☐ 415	Bob Gibson	50.00	23.00	6.25
☐ 416	Alex Grammas	4.50	2.00	.55
☐ 417	Giants Team	9.00	4.00	1.15
☐ 418	John Orsino	4.50	2.00	.55
☐ 419	Tracy Stallard	4.50	2.00	.55
☐ 420	Bobby Richardson	11.00	4.90	1.40
☐ 421	Tom Morgan	4.50	2.00	.55
☐ 422	Fred Hutchinson MG	5.00	2.30	.60
☐ 423	Ed Hobaugh	4.50	2.00	.55
☐ 424	Charlie Smith	4.50	2.00	.55
☐ 425	Smoky Burgess	5.00	2.30	.60
☐ 426	Barry Latman	4.50	2.00	.55
☐ 427	Bernie Allen	4.50	2.00	.55
☐ 428	Carl Boles	4.50	2.00	.55
☐ 429	Lou Burdette	6.00	2.70	.75
☐ 430	Norm Siebern	4.50	2.00	.55

☐ 431A	Checklist 6	10.00	1.50	.50
	(White on red)			
☐ 431B	Checklist 6	22.00	3.30	1.10
	(Black on orange)			
☐ 432	Roman Mejias	4.50	2.00	.55
☐ 433	Denis Menke	4.50	2.00	.55
☐ 434	John Callison	5.00	2.30	.60
☐ 435	Woody Held	4.50	2.00	.55
☐ 436	Tim Harkness	4.50	2.00	.55
☐ 437	Bill Bruton	4.50	2.00	.55
☐ 438	Wes Stock	4.50	2.00	.55
☐ 439	Don Zimmer	6.50	2.90	.80
☐ 440	Juan Marichal	30.00	13.50	3.80
☐ 441	Lee Thomas	5.00	2.30	.60
☐ 442	J.C. Hartman	4.50	2.00	.55
☐ 443	Jim Piersall	5.50	2.50	.70
☐ 444	Jim Maloney	6.50	2.90	.80
☐ 445	Norm Cash	6.50	2.90	.80
☐ 446	Whitey Ford	40.00	18.00	5.00
☐ 447	Felix Mantilla	14.00	6.25	1.75
☐ 448	Jack Kralick	14.00	6.25	1.75
☐ 449	Jose Tartabull	14.00	6.25	1.75
☐ 450	Bob Friend	16.00	7.25	2.00
☐ 451	Indians Team	35.00	16.00	4.40
☐ 452	Barney Schultz	14.00	6.25	1.75
☐ 453	Jake Wood	14.00	6.25	1.75
☐ 454A	Art Fowler	14.00	6.25	1.75
	(Card number on			
	white background)			
☐ 454B	Art Fowler	28.00	12.50	3.50
	(Card number on			
	orange background)			
☐ 455	Ruben Amaro	14.00	6.25	1.75
☐ 456	Jim Coker	14.00	6.25	1.75
☐ 457	Tex Clevenger	14.00	6.25	1.75
☐ 458	Al Lopez MG	20.00	9.00	2.50
☐ 459	Dick LeMay	14.00	6.25	1.75
☐ 460	Del Crandall	16.00	7.25	2.00
☐ 461	Norm Bass	14.00	6.25	1.75
☐ 462	Wally Post	16.00	7.25	2.00
☐ 463	Joe Schaffernoth	14.00	6.25	1.75
☐ 464	Ken Aspromonte	14.00	6.25	1.75
☐ 465	Chuck Estrada	14.00	6.25	1.75
☐ 466	Rookie Stars SP	55.00	25.00	7.00

Nate Oliver
Tony Martinez
Bill Freehan
Jerry Robinson

☐ 467	Phil Ortega	14.00	6.25	1.75
☐ 468	Carroll Hardy	14.00	6.25	1.75
☐ 469	Jay Hook	14.00	6.25	1.75
☐ 470	Tom Tresh SP	50.00	23.00	6.25
☐ 471	Ken Retzer	14.00	6.25	1.75
☐ 472	Lou Brock	150.00	70.00	19.00
☐ 473	New York Mets	120.00	55.00	15.00

Team Card

☐ 474	Jack Fisher	14.00	6.25	1.75

☐ 475	Gus Triandos 16.00	7.25	2.00
☐ 476	Frank Funk 14.00	6.25	1.75
☐ 477	Donn Clendenon 16.00	7.25	2.00
☐ 478	Paul Brown 14.00	6.25	1.75
☐ 479	Ed Brinkman 14.00	6.25	1.75
☐ 480	Bill Monbouquette......14.00	6.25	1.75
☐ 481	Bob Taylor.................14.00	6.25	1.75
☐ 482	Felix Torres 14.00	6.25	1.75
☐ 483	Jim Owens 14.00	6.25	1.75
☐ 484	Dale Long SP 22.00	10.00	2.80
☐ 485	Jim Landis 14.00	6.25	1.75
☐ 486	Ray Sadecki 14.00	6.25	1.75
☐ 487	John Roseboro 16.00	7.25	2.00
☐ 488	Jerry Adair.................14.00	6.25	1.75
☐ 489	Paul Toth 14.00	6.25	1.75
☐ 490	Willie McCovey 150.00	70.00	19.00
☐ 491	Harry Craft MG..........14.00	6.25	1.75
☐ 492	Dave Wickersham 14.00	6.25	1.75
☐ 493	Walt Bond 14.00	6.25	1.75
☐ 494	Phil Regan 16.00	7.26	2.00
☐ 495	Frank Thomas SP 25.00	11.50	3.10
☐ 496	Rookie Stars 14.00	6.25	1.75
	Steve Dalkowski		
	Fred Newman		
	Jack Smith		
	Carl Bouldin		
☐ 497	Bennie Daniels 14.00	6.25	1.75
☐ 498	Eddie Kasko 14.00	6.25	1.75
☐ 499	J.C. Martin.................14.00	6.25	1.75
☐ 500	Harmon Killebrew SP150.00	70.00	19.00
☐ 501	Joe Azcue 14.00	6.25	1.75
☐ 502	Daryl Spencer 14.00	6.25	1.75
☐ 503	Braves Team...............35.00	16.00	4.40
☐ 504	Bob Johnson...............14.00	6.25	1.75
☐ 505	Curt Flood 20.00	9.00	2.50
☐ 506	Gene Green 14.00	6.25	1.75
☐ 507	Roland Sheldon 14.00	6.25	1.75
☐ 508	Ted Savage 14.00	6.25	1.75
☐ 509A	Checklist 7 ....22.00	3.30	1.10
	(Copyright centered)		
☐ 509B	Checklist 7 ....22.00	3.30	1.10
	(Copyright to right)		
☐ 510	Ken McBride...............14.00	6.25	1.75
☐ 511	Charlie Neal...............16.00	7.25	2.00
☐ 512	Cal McLish.................14.00	6.25	1.75
☐ 513	Gary Geiger................14.00	6.25	1.75
☐ 514	Larry Osborne 14.00	6.25	1.75
☐ 515	Don Elston 14.00	6.25	1.75
☐ 516	Purnell Goldy 14.00	6.25	1.75
☐ 517	Hal Woodeshick..........14.00	6.25	1.75
☐ 518	Don Blasingame..........14.00	6.25	1.75
☐ 519	Claude Raymond.........18.00	8.00	2.30
☐ 520	Orlando Cepeda 25.00	11.50	3.10
☐ 521	Dan Pfister 14.00	6.25	1.75
☐ 522	Rookie Stars 16.00	7.25	2.00
	Mel Nelson		
	Gary Peters		

	Jim Roland		
	Art Quirk		
☐ 523	Bill Kunkel................10.00	4.50	1.25
☐ 524	Cardinals Team 25.00	11.50	3.10
☐ 525	Nellie Fox 20.00	9.00	2.50
☐ 526	Dick Hall 10.00	4.50	1.25
☐ 527	Ed Sadowski 10.00	4.50	1.25
☐ 528	Carl Willey................10.00	4.50	1.25
☐ 529	Wes Covington 11.00	4.90	1.40
☐ 530	Don Mossi 11.00	4.90	1.40
☐ 531	Sam Mele MG 10.00	4.50	1.25
☐ 532	Steve Boros 10.00	4.50	1.25
☐ 533	Bobby Shantz.............12.50	5.75	1.55
☐ 534	Ken Walters 10.00	4.50	1.25
☐ 535	Jim Perry 12.50	5.75	1.55
☐ 536	Norm Larker...............10.00	4.50	1.25
☐ 537	Rookie Stars 925.00	425.00	115.00
	Pedro Gonzalez		
	Ken McMullen		
	Al Weis		
	Pete Rose		
☐ 538	George Brunet............10.00	4.50	1.25
☐ 539	Wayne Causey 10.00	4.50	1.25
☐ 540	Bob Clemente 225.00	100.00	28.00
☐ 541	Ron Moeller...............10.00	4.50	1.25
☐ 542	Lou Klimchock 10.00	4.50	1.25
☐ 543	Russ Snyder 10.00	4.50	1.25
☐ 544	Rookie Stars 42.00	19.00	5.25
	Duke Carmel		
	Bill Haas		
	Rusty Staub		
	Dick Phillips		
☐ 545	Jose Pagan 10.00	4.50	1.25
☐ 546	Hal Reniff 10.00	4.50	1.25
☐ 547	Gus Bell 11.00	4.90	1.40
☐ 548	Tom Satriano 10.00	4.50	1.25
☐ 549	Rookie Stars 10.00	4.50	1.25
	Marcelino Lopez		
	Pete Lovrich		
	Paul Ratliff		
	Elmo Plaskett		
☐ 550	Duke Snider...............85.00	38.00	10.50
☐ 551	Billy Klaus 10.00	4.50	1.25
☐ 552	Detroit Tigers.............32.00	14.50	4.00
	Team Card		
☐ 553	Rookie Stars 275.00	125.00	34.00
	Brock Davis		
	Jim Gosger		
	Willie Stargell		
	John Herrnstein		
☐ 554	Hank Fischer 10.00	4.50	1.25
☐ 555	John Blanchard...........11.00	4.90	1.40
☐ 556	Al Worthington 10.00	4.50	1.25
☐ 557	Cuno Barragan 10.00	4.50	1.25
☐ 558	Rookie Stars 15.00	6.75	1.90
	Bill Faul		
	Ron Hunt		

Al Moran
Bob Lipski

☐	559	Danny Murtaugh MG .11.00	4.90	1.40
☐	560	Ray Herbert................10.00	4.50	1.25
☐	561	Mike De La Hoz.......10.00	4.50	1.25
☐	562	Rookie Stars 20.00	9.00	2.50

Randy Cardinal
Dave McNally
Ken Rowe
Don Rowe

☐	563	Mike McCormick.......11.00	4.90	1.40
☐	564	George Banks 10.00	4.50	1.25
☐	565	Larry Sherry.............11.00	4.90	1.40
☐	566	Cliff Cook.................10.00	4.50	1.25
☐	567	Jim Duffalo...............10.00	4.50	1.25
☐	568	Bob Sadowski............10.00	4.50	1.25
☐	569	Luis Arroyo 11.00	4.90	1.40
☐	570	Frank Bolling.............10.00	4.50	1.25
☐	571	Johnny Klippstein 10.00	4.50	1.25
☐	572	Jack Spring...............10.00	4.50	1.25
☐	573	Coot Veal.................10.00	4.50	1.25
☐	574	Hal Kolstad..............10.00	4.50	1.25
☐	575	Don Cardwell............10.00	4.50	1.25
☐	576	Johnny Temple 15.00	6.75	1.90

1964 Topps

The cards in this 587-card set measure 2 1/2" by 3 1/2". Players in the 1964 Topps baseball series were easy to sort by team due to the giant block lettering found at the top of each card. The name and position of the player are found underneath the picture, and the card is numbered in a ball design on the orange-colored back. The usual last series scarcity holds for this set (523 to 587). Subsets within this set include League Leaders (1-12) and World

Series cards (136-140). There were some three-card advertising panels produced by Topps; the players included are from the first series; one panel shows Walt Alston, Bill Henry, and Vada Pinson on the front with a Mickey Mantle card back on one of the backs. Another panel shows Carl Willey, White Sox Rookies, and Bob Friend on the front with a Mickey Mantle card back on one of the backs. The key rookie cards in this set are Richie Allen, Tommy John, Tony LaRussa, Lou Piniella, and Phil Niekro.

		NRMT	VG-E	GOOD
	COMPLETE SET (587) ....3400.	1500.	425.00
	COMMON PLAYER (1-196) ...2.00	.90	.25
	COMMON PLAYER (197-370) ..3.00	1.35	.40
	COMMON PLAYER (371-522) ...5.00	2.30	.60
	COMMON PLAYER (523-587) .10.00	4.50	1.25

☐	1	NL ERA Leaders............20.00	5.00	1.60

Sandy Koufax
Dick Ellsworth
Bob Friend

☐	2	AL ERA Leaders..............3.50	1.55	.45

Gary Peters
Juan Pizarro
Camilo Pascual

☐	3	NL Pitching Leaders.......11.00	4.90	1.40

Sandy Koufax
Juan Marichal
Warren Spahn
Jim Maloney

☐	4	AL Pitching Leaders.........4.00	1.80	.50

Whitey Ford
Camilo Pascual
Jim Bouton

☐	5	NL Strikeout Leaders 9.00	4.00	1.15

Sandy Koufax
Jim Maloney
Don Drysdale

☐	6	AL Strikeout Leaders 3.50	1.55	.45

Camilo Pascual
Jim Bunning
Dick Stigman

☐	7	NL Batting Leaders 8.00	3.60	1.00

Tommy Davis
Bob Clemente
Dick Groat
Hank Aaron

☐	8	AL Batting Leaders...........8.00	3.60	1.00

Carl Yastrzemski
Al Kaline
Rich Rollins

☐	9	NL Home Run Leaders...15.00	6.75	1.90

Hank Aaron

Willie McCovey
Willie Mays
Orlando Cepeda

☐ 10	AL Home Run Leaders...4.50	2.00	.55
	Harmon Killebrew		
	Dick Stuart		
	Bob Allison		
☐ 11	NL RBI Leaders.............8.00	3.60	1.00
	Hank Aaron		
	Ken Boyer		
	Bill White		
☐ 12	AL RBI Leaders.............6.00	2.70	.75
	Dick Stuart		
	Al Kaline		
	Harmon Killebrew		
☐ 13	Hoyt Wilhelm 9.00	4.00	1.15
☐ 14	Dodgers Rookies 2.00	.90	.25
	Dick Nen		
	Nick Willhite		
☐ 15	Zoilo Versalles.............2.50	1.15	.30
☐ 16	John Boozer..................2.00	.90	.25
☐ 17	Willie Kirkland..............2.00	.90	.25
☐ 18	Billy O'Dell...................2.00	.90	.25
☐ 19	Don Wert......................2.00	.90	.25
☐ 20	Bob Friend 2.50	1.15	.30
☐ 21	Yogi Berra MG.............40.00	18.00	5.00
☐ 22	Jerry Adair...................2.00	.90	.25
☐ 23	Chris Zachary...............2.00	.90	.25
☐ 24	Carl Sawatski...............2.00	.90	.25
☐ 25	Bill Monbouquette.........2.00	.90	.25
☐ 26	Gino Cimoli..................2.00	.90	.25
☐ 27	New York Mets.............7.00	3.10	.85
	Team Card		
☐ 28	Claude Osteen.............2.50	1.15	.30
☐ 29	Lou Brock...................40.00	18.00	5.00
☐ 30	Ron Perranoski............2.50	1.15	.30
☐ 31	Dave Nicholson............2.00	.90	.25
☐ 32	Dean Chance................3.00	1.35	.40
☐ 33	Reds Rookies................2.50	1.15	.30
	Sammy Ellis		
	Mel Queen		
☐ 34	Jim Perry.....................2.50	1.15	.30
☐ 35	Eddie Mathews............20.00	9.00	2.50
☐ 36	Hal Reniff....................2.00	.90	.25
☐ 37	Smoky Burgess.............2.50	1.15	.30
☐ 38	Jim Wynn.....................6.50	2.90	.80
☐ 39	Hank Aguirre................2.00	.90	.25
☐ 40	Dick Groat....................2.50	1.15	.30
☐ 41	Friendly Foes...............5.00	2.30	.60
	Willie McCovey		
	Leon Wagner		
☐ 42	Moe Drabowsky............2.50	1.15	.30
☐ 43	Roy Sievers..................2.50	1.15	.30
☐ 44	Duke Carmel.................2.00	.90	.25
☐ 45	Milt Pappas...................2.50	1.15	.30
☐ 46	Ed Brinkman.................2.00	.90	.25
☐ 47	Giants Rookies..............3.50	1.55	.45

Jesus Alou
Ron Herbel

☐ 48	Bob Perry.....................2.00	.90	.25
☐ 49	Bill Henry.....................2.00	.90	.25
☐ 50	Mickey Mantle.............250.00	115.00	31.00
☐ 51	Pete Richert..................2.00	.90	.25
☐ 52	Chuck Hinton................2.00	.90	.25
☐ 53	Denis Menke.................2.00	.90	.25
☐ 54	Sam Mele MG................2.00	.90	.25
☐ 55	Ernie Banks.................30.00	13.50	3.80
☐ 56	Hal Brown.....................2.00	.90	.25
☐ 57	Tim Harkness................2.00	.90	.25
☐ 58	Don Demeter.................2.00	.90	.25
☐ 59	Ernie Broglio.................2.00	.90	.25
☐ 60	Frank Malzone...............2.50	1.15	.30
☐ 61	Angel Backstops...........2.50	1.15	.30
	Bob Rodgers		
	Ed Sadowski		
☐ 62	Ted Savage...................2.00	.90	.25
☐ 63	John Orsino..................2.00	.90	.25
☐ 64	Ted Abernathy...............2.00	.90	.25
☐ 65	Felipe Alou...................3.50	1.55	.45
☐ 66	Eddie Fisher..................2.00	.90	.25
☐ 67	Tigers Team..................4.00	1.80	.50
☐ 68	Willie Davis..................2.50	1.15	.30
☐ 69	Clete Boyer...................3.00	1.35	.40
☐ 70	Joe Torre......................4.50	2.00	.55
☐ 71	Jack Spring...................2.00	.90	.25
☐ 72	Chico Cardenas.............2.50	1.15	.30
☐ 73	Jimmie Hall...................2.50	1.15	.30
☐ 74	Pirates Rookies.............2.00	.90	.25
	Bob Priddy		
	Tom Butters		
☐ 75	Wayne Causey...............2.00	.90	.25
☐ 76	Checklist 1...................9.00	1.35	.45
☐ 77	Jerry Walker..................2.00	.90	.25
☐ 78	Merritt Ranew................2.00	.90	.25
☐ 79	Bob Heffner...................2.00	.90	.25
☐ 80	Vada Pinson..................3.50	1.55	.45
☐ 81	All-Star Vets.................7.00	3.10	.85
	Nellie Fox		
	Harmon Killebrew		
☐ 82	Jim Davenport...............2.50	1.15	.30
☐ 83	Gus Triandos 2.50	1.15	.30
☐ 84	Carl Willey....................2.00	.90	.25
☐ 85	Pete Ward.....................2.00	.90	.25
☐ 86	Al Downing....................3.00	1.35	.40
☐ 87	St. Louis Cardinals.........5.00	2.30	.60
	Team Card		
☐ 88	John Roseboro...............2.50	1.15	.30
☐ 89	Boog Powell..................5.00	2.30	.60
☐ 90	Earl Battey....................2.00	.90	.25
☐ 91	Bob Bailey.....................2.50	1.15	.30
☐ 92	Steve Ridzik..................2.00	.90	.25
☐ 93	Gary Geiger...................2.00	.90	.25
☐ 94	Braves Rookies..............2.00	.90	.25
	Jim Britton		

	Larry Maxie			
☐ 95	George Altman	2.00	.90	.25
☐ 96	Bob Buhl	2.50	1.15	.30
☐ 97	Jim Fregosi	2.50	1.15	.30
☐ 98	Bill Bruton	2.00	.90	.25
☐ 99	Al Stanek	2.00	.90	.25
☐ 100	Elston Howard	5.00	2.30	.60
☐ 101	Walt Alston MG	4.00	1.80	.50
☐ 102	Checklist 2	9.00	1.35	.45
☐ 103	Curt Flood	3.00	1.35	.40
☐ 104	Art Mahaffey	2.00	.90	.25
☐ 105	Woody Held	2.00	.90	.25
☐ 106	Joe Nuxhall	2.50	1.15	.30
☐ 107	White Sox Rookies	2.00	.90	.25
	Bruce Howard			
	Frank Kreutzer			
☐ 108	John Wyatt	2.00	.90	.25
☐ 109	Rusty Staub	7.50	3.40	.95
☐ 110	Albie Pearson	2.50	1.15	.30
☐ 111	Don Elston	2.00	.90	.25
☐ 112	Bob Tillman	2.00	.90	.25
☐ 113	Grover Powell	2.00	.90	.25
☐ 114	Don Lock	2.00	.90	.25
☐ 115	Frank Bolling	2.00	.90	.25
☐ 116	Twins Rookies	15.00	6.75	1.90
	Jay Ward			
	Tony Oliva			
☐ 117	Earl Francis	2.00	.90	.25
☐ 118	John Blanchard	2.50	1.15	.30
☐ 119	Gary Kolb	2.00	.90	.25
☐ 120	Don Drysdale	20.00	9.00	2.50
☐ 121	Pete Runnels	2.50	1.15	.30
☐ 122	Don McMahon	2.00	.90	.25
☐ 123	Jose Pagan	2.00	.90	.25
☐ 124	Orlando Pena	2.00	.90	.25
☐ 125	Pete Rose	175.00	80.00	22.00
☐ 126	Russ Snyder	2.00	.90	.25
☐ 127	Angels Rookies	2.00	.90	.25
	Aubrey Gatewood			
	Dick Simpson			
☐ 128	Mickey Lolich	18.00	8.00	2.30
☐ 129	Amado Samuel	2.00	.90	.25
☐ 130	Gary Peters	2.50	1.15	.30
☐ 131	Steve Boros	2.00	.90	.25
☐ 132	Braves Team	4.00	1.80	.50
☐ 133	Jim Grant	2.50	1.15	.30
☐ 134	Don Zimmer	2.50	1.15	.30
☐ 135	Johnny Callison	2.50	1.15	.30
☐ 136	World Series Game 1	14.00	6.25	1.75
	Sandy Koufax			
	strikes out 15			
☐ 137	World Series Game 2	4.00	1.80	.50
	Tommy Davis			
	sparks rally			
☐ 138	World Series Game 3	4.00	1.80	.50
	LA Three Straight			
	(Ron Fairly)			

☐ 139	World Series Game 4	4.00	1.80	.50
	Sealing Yanks doom			
	(Frank Howard)			
☐ 140	World Series Summary	4.00	1.80	.50
	Dodgers celebrate			
☐ 141	Danny Murtaugh MG	2.50	1.15	.30
☐ 142	John Bateman	2.00	.90	.25
☐ 143	Bubba Phillips	2.00	.90	.25
☐ 144	Al Worthington	2.00	.90	.25
☐ 145	Norm Siebern	2.00	.90	.25
☐ 146	Indians Rookies	70.00	32.00	8.75
	Tommy John			
	Bob Chance			
☐ 147	Ray Sadecki	2.00	.90	.25
☐ 148	J.C. Martin	2.00	.90	.25
☐ 149	Paul Foytack	2.00	.90	.25
☐ 150	Willie Mays	110.00	50.00	14.00
☐ 151	Athletics Team	4.00	1.80	.50
☐ 152	Denny Lemaster	2.00	.90	.25
☐ 153	Dick Williams	2.50	1.15	.30
☐ 154	Dick Tracewski	3.00	1.35	.40
☐ 155	Duke Snider	33.00	15.00	4.10
☐ 156	Bill Dailey	2.00	.90	.25
☐ 157	Gene Mauch MG	2.50	1.15	.30
☐ 158	Ken Johnson	2.00	.90	.25
☐ 159	Charlie Dees	2.00	.90	.25
☐ 160	Ken Boyer	5.50	2.50	.70
☐ 161	Dave McNally	3.50	1.55	.45
☐ 162	Hitting Area	2.50	1.15	.30
	Dick Sisler CO			
	Vada Pinson			
☐ 163	Donn Clendenon	2.50	1.15	.30
☐ 164	Bud Daley	2.00	.90	.25
☐ 165	Jerry Lumpe	2.00	.90	.25
☐ 166	Marty Keough	2.00	.90	.25
☐ 167	Senators Rookies	32.00	14.50	4.00
	Mike Brumley			
	Lou Piniella			
☐ 168	Al Weis	2.00	.90	.25
☐ 169	Del Crandall	2.50	1.15	.30
☐ 170	Dick Radatz	2.50	1.15	.30
☐ 171	Ty Cline	2.00	.90	.25
☐ 172	Indians Team	4.00	1.80	.50
☐ 173	Ryne Duren	2.50	1.15	.30
☐ 174	Doc Edwards	2.00	.90	.25
☐ 175	Billy Williams	20.00	9.00	2.50
☐ 176	Tracy Stallard	2.00	.90	.25
☐ 177	Harmon Killebrew	20.00	9.00	2.50
☐ 178	Hank Bauer MG	2.50	1.15	.30
☐ 179	Carl Warwick	2.00	.90	.25
☐ 180	Tommy Davis	3.50	1.55	.45
☐ 181	Dave Wickersham	2.00	.90	.25
☐ 182	Sox Sockers	12.50	5.75	1.55
	Carl Yastrzemski			
	Chuck Schilling			
☐ 183	Ron Taylor	2.00	.90	.25
☐ 184	Al Luplow	2.00	.90	.25

☐ 185	Jim O'Toole	2.50	1.15	.30
☐ 186	Roman Mejias	2.00	.90	.25
☐ 187	Ed Roebuck	2.00	.90	.25
☐ 188	Checklist 3	9.00	1.35	.45
☐ 189	Bob Hendley	2.00	.90	.25
☐ 190	Bobby Richardson	6.50	2.90	.80
☐ 191	Clay Dalrymple	2.00	.90	.25
☐ 192	Cubs Rookies	2.00	.90	.25
	John Boccabella			
	Billy Cowan			
☐ 193	Jerry Lynch	2.00	.90	.25
☐ 194	John Goryl	2.00	.90	.25
☐ 195	Floyd Robinson	2.00	.90	.25
☐ 196	Jim Gentile	3.50	1.55	.45
☐ 197	Frank Lary	3.50	1.55	.45
☐ 198	Len Gabrielson	3.00	1.35	.40
☐ 199	Joe Azcue	3.00	1.35	.40
☐ 200	Sandy Koufax	110.00	50.00	14.00
☐ 201	Orioles Rookies	3.50	1.55	.45
	Sam Bowens			
	Wally Bunker			
☐ 202	Galen Cisco	3.50	1.55	.45
☐ 203	John Kennedy	3.50	1.55	.45
☐ 204	Matty Alou	4.00	1.80	.50
☐ 205	Nellie Fox	6.00	2.70	.75
☐ 206	Steve Hamilton	3.00	1.35	.40
☐ 207	Fred Hutchinson MG	3.50	1.55	.45
☐ 208	Wes Covington	3.50	1.55	.45
☐ 209	Bob Allen	3.00	1.35	.40
☐ 210	Carl Yastrzemski	65.00	29.00	8.25
☐ 211	Jim Coker	3.00	1.35	.40
☐ 212	Pete Lovrich	3.00	1.35	.40
☐ 213	Angels Team	6.00	2.70	.75
☐ 214	Ken McMullen	3.50	1.55	.45
☐ 215	Ray Herbert	3.00	1.35	.40
☐ 216	Mike DeLaHoz	3.00	1.35	.40
☐ 217	Jim King	3.00	1.35	.40
☐ 218	Hank Fischer	3.00	1.35	.40
☐ 219	Young Aces	4.50	2.00	.55
	Al Downing			
	Jim Bouton			
☐ 220	Dick Ellsworth	3.50	1.55	.45
☐ 221	Bob Saverine	3.00	1.35	.40
☐ 222	Billy Pierce	3.50	1.55	.45
☐ 223	George Banks	3.00	1.35	.40
☐ 224	Tommie Sisk	3.00	1.35	.40
☐ 225	Roger Maris	65.00	29.00	8.25
☐ 226	Colts Rookies	5.00	2.30	.60
	Jerry Grote			
	Larry Yellen			
☐ 227	Barry Latman	3.00	1.35	.40
☐ 228	Felix Mantilla	3.00	1.35	.40
☐ 229	Charley Lau	3.50	1.55	.45
☐ 230	Brooks Robinson	35.00	16.00	4.40
☐ 231	Dick Calmus	3.00	1.35	.40
☐ 232	Al Lopez MG	5.00	2.30	.60
☐ 233	Hal Smith	3.00	1.35	.40
☐ 234	Gary Bell	3.00	1.35	.40
☐ 235	Ron Hunt	3.00	1.35	.40
☐ 236	Bill Faul	3.00	1.35	.40
☐ 237	Cubs Team	6.00	2.70	.75
☐ 238	Roy McMillan	3.50	1.55	.45
☐ 239	Herm Starrette	3.00	1.35	.40
☐ 240	Bill White	4.50	2.00	.55
☐ 241	Jim Owens	3.00	1.35	.40
☐ 242	Harvey Kuenn	3.50	1.55	.45
☐ 243	Phillies Rookies	25.00	11.50	3.10
	Richie Allen			
	John Herrnstein			
☐ 244	Tony LaRussa	25.00	11.50	3.10
☐ 245	Dick Stigman	3.00	1.35	.40
☐ 246	Manny Mota	4.00	1.80	.50
☐ 247	Dave DeBusschere	4.00	1.80	.50
☐ 248	Johnny Romano MG	3.50	1.55	.45
☐ 249	Doug Camilli	3.00	1.35	.40
☐ 250	Al Kaline	35.00	16.00	4.40
☐ 251	Choo Choo Coleman	3.00	1.35	.40
☐ 252	Ken Aspromonte	3.00	1.35	.40
☐ 253	Wally Post	3.50	1.55	.45
☐ 254	Don Hoak	3.50	1.55	.45
☐ 255	Lee Thomas	3.50	1.55	.45
☐ 256	Johnny Weekly	3.00	1.35	.40
☐ 257	San Francisco Giants	6.00	2.70	.75
	Team Card			
☐ 258	Garry Roggenburk	3.00	1.35	.40
☐ 259	Harry Bright	3.00	1.35	.40
☐ 260	Frank Robinson	27.00	12.00	3.40
☐ 261	Jim Hannan	3.00	1.35	.40
☐ 262	Cards Rookies	6.00	2.70	.75
	Mike Shannon			
	Harry Fanok			
☐ 263	Chuck Estrada	3.00	1.35	.40
☐ 264	Jim Landis	3.00	1.35	.40
☐ 265	Jim Bunning	6.00	2.70	.75
☐ 266	Gene Freese	3.00	1.35	.40
☐ 267	Wilbur Wood	6.00	2.70	.75
☐ 268	Bill's Got It	3.50	1.55	.45
	Danny Murtaugh MG			
	Bill Virdon			
☐ 269	Ellis Burton	3.00	1.35	.40
☐ 270	Rich Rollins	3.50	1.55	.45
☐ 271	Bob Sadowski	3.00	1.35	.40
☐ 272	Jake Wood	3.00	1.35	.40
☐ 273	Mel Nelson	3.00	1.35	.40
☐ 274	Checklist 4	9.00	1.35	.45
☐ 275	John Tsitouris	3.00	1.35	.40
☐ 276	Jose Tartabull	3.50	1.55	.45
☐ 277	Ken Retzer	3.00	1.35	.40
☐ 278	Bobby Shantz	3.50	1.55	.45
☐ 279	Joe Koppe UER	3.50	1.55	.45
	(Glove on wrong hand)			
☐ 280	Juan Marichal	12.50	5.75	1.55
☐ 281	Yankees Rookies	3.50	1.55	.45
	Jake Gibbs			

	Tom Metcalf			
☐ 282	Bob Bruce	3.00	1.35	.40
☐ 283	Tom McCraw	4.00	1.80	.50
☐ 284	Dick Schofield	3.00	1.35	.40
☐ 285	Robin Roberts	10.00	4.50	1.25
☐ 286	Don Landrum	3.00	1.35	.40
☐ 287	Red Sox Rookies	35.00	16.00	4.40
	Tony Conigliaro			
	Bill Spanswick			
☐ 288	Al Moran	3.00	1.35	.40
☐ 289	Frank Funk	3.00	1.35	.40
☐ 290	Bob Allison	3.50	1.55	.45
☐ 291	Phil Ortega	3.00	1.35	.40
☐ 292	Mike Roarke	3.00	1.35	.40
☐ 293	Phillies Team	6.00	2.70	.75
☐ 294	Ken L. Hunt	3.00	1.35	.40
☐ 295	Roger Craig	3.50	1.55	.45
☐ 296	Ed Kirkpatrick	3.00	1.35	.40
☐ 297	Ken MacKenzie	3.00	1.35	.40
☐ 298	Harry Craft MG	3.00	1.35	.40
☐ 299	Bill Stafford	3.00	1.35	.40
☐ 300	Hank Aaron	125.00	57.50	15.50
☐ 301	Larry Brown	3.00	1.35	.40
☐ 302	Dan Pfister	3.00	1.35	.40
☐ 303	Jim Campbell	3.00	1.35	.40
☐ 304	Bob Johnson	3.00	1.35	.40
☐ 305	Jack Lamabe	3.00	1.35	.40
☐ 306	Giant Gunners	25.00	11.50	3.10
	Willie Mays			
	Orlando Cepeda			
☐ 307	Joe Gibbon	3.00	1.35	.40
☐ 308	Gene Stephens	3.00	1.35	.40
☐ 309	Paul Toth	3.00	1.35	.40
☐ 310	Jim Gilliam	4.50	2.00	.55
☐ 311	Tom Brown	3.00	1.35	.40
☐ 312	Tigers Rookies	3.00	1.35	.40
	Fritz Fisher			
	Fred Gladding			
☐ 313	Chuck Hiller	3.00	1.35	.40
☐ 314	Jerry Buchek	3.00	1.35	.40
☐ 315	Bo Belinsky	3.50	1.55	.45
☐ 316	Gene Oliver	3.00	1.35	.40
☐ 317	Al Smith	3.00	1.35	.40
☐ 318	Minnesota Twins	6.00	2.70	.75
	Team Card			
☐ 319	Paul Brown	3.00	1.35	.40
☐ 320	Rocky Colavito	8.00	3.60	1.00
☐ 321	Bob Lillis	3.00	1.35	.40
☐ 322	George Brunet	3.00	1.35	.40
☐ 323	John Buzhardt	3.00	1.35	.40
☐ 324	Casey Stengel MG	17.00	7.75	2.10
☐ 325	Hector Lopez	3.50	1.55	.45
☐ 326	Ron Brand	3.00	1.35	.40
☐ 327	Don Blasingame	3.00	1.35	.40
☐ 328	Bob Shaw	3.00	1.35	.40
☐ 329	Russ Nixon	3.00	1.35	.40
☐ 330	Tommy Harper	3.50	1.55	.45

☐ 331	AL Bombers	125.00	57.50	15.50
	Roger Maris			
	Norm Cash			
	Mickey Mantle			
	Al Kaline			
☐ 332	Ray Washburn	3.00	1.35	.40
☐ 333	Billy Moran	3.00	1.35	.40
☐ 334	Lew Krausse	3.00	1.35	.40
☐ 335	Don Mossi	3.50	1.55	.45
☐ 336	Andre Rodgers	3.00	1.35	.40
☐ 337	Dodgers Rookies	8.50	3.80	1.05
	Al Ferrara			
	Jeff Torborg			
☐ 338	Jack Kralick	3.00	1.35	.40
☐ 339	Walt Bond	3.00	1.35	.40
☐ 340	Joe Cunningham	3.00	1.35	.40
☐ 341	Jim Roland	3.00	1.35	.40
☐ 342	Willie Stargell	45.00	20.00	5.75
☐ 343	Senators Team	6.00	2.70	.75
☐ 344	Phil Linz	3.50	1.55	.45
☐ 345	Frank Thomas	3.50	1.55	.45
☐ 346	Joey Jay	3.00	1.35	.40
☐ 347	Bobby Wine	3.00	1.35	.40
☐ 348	Ed Lopat MG	3.50	1.55	.45
☐ 349	Art Fowler	3.00	1.35	.40
☐ 350	Willie McCovey	30.00	13.50	3.80
☐ 351	Dan Schneider	3.00	1.35	.40
☐ 352	Eddie Bressoud	3.00	1.35	.40
☐ 353	Wally Moon	3.50	1.55	.45
☐ 354	Dave Giusti	3.00	1.35	.40
☐ 355	Vic Power	3.50	1.55	.45
☐ 356	Reds Rookies	3.50	1.55	.45
	Bill McCool			
	Chico Ruiz			
☐ 357	Charley James	3.00	1.35	.40
☐ 358	Ron Kline	3.00	1.35	.40
☐ 359	Jim Schaffer	3.00	1.35	.40
☐ 360	Joe Pepitone	4.50	2.00	.55
☐ 361	Jay Hook	3.00	1.35	.40
☐ 362	Checklist 5	9.00	1.35	.45
☐ 363	Dick McAuliffe	3.50	1.55	.45
☐ 364	Joe Gaines	3.00	1.35	.40
☐ 365	Cal McLish	3.00	1.35	.40
☐ 366	Nelson Mathews	3.00	1.35	.40
☐ 367	Fred Whitfield	3.00	1.35	.40
☐ 368	White Sox Rookies	3.50	1.55	.45
	Fritz Ackley			
	Don Buford			
☐ 369	Jerry Zimmerman	3.00	1.35	.40
☐ 370	Hal Woodeshick	3.00	1.35	.40
☐ 371	Frank Howard	6.50	2.90	.80
☐ 372	Howie Koplitz	5.00	2.30	.60
☐ 373	Pirates Team	10.00	4.50	1.25
☐ 374	Bobby Bolin	5.00	2.30	.60
☐ 375	Ron Santo	7.00	3.10	.85
☐ 376	Dave Morehead	5.00	2.30	.60
☐ 377	Bob Skinner	5.50	2.50	.70

☐ 378	Braves Rookies............6.00	2.70	.75	
	Woody Woodward			
	Jack Smith			
☐ 379	Tony Gonzalez............5.00	2.30	.60	
☐ 380	Whitey Ford...............30.00	13.50	3.80	
☐ 381	Bob Taylor..................5.00	2.30	.60	
☐ 382	Wes Stock....................5.00	2.30	.60	
☐ 383	Bill Rigney MG............5.00	2.30	.60	
☐ 384	Ron Hansen.................5.00	2.30	.60	
☐ 385	Curt Simmons............5.50	2.50	.70	
☐ 386	Lenny Green...............5.00	2.30	.60	
☐ 387	Terry Fox....................5.00	2.30	.60	
☐ 388	A's Rookies.................5.50	2.50	.70	
	John O'Donoghue			
	George Williams			
☐ 389	Jim Umbricht...............5.50	2.50	.70	
	(Card back mentions			
	his death)			
☐ 390	Orlando Cepeda..........8.50	3.80	1.05	
☐ 391	Sam McDowell............5.50	2.50	.70	
☐ 392	Jim Pagliaroni............5.00	2.30	.60	
☐ 393	Casey Teaches............6.50	2.90	.80	
	Casey Stengel MG			
	Ed Kranepool			
☐ 394	Bob Miller..................5.00	2.30	.60	
☐ 395	Tom Tresh..................7.00	3.10	.85	
☐ 396	Dennis Bennett 5.00	2.30	.60	
☐ 397	Chuck Cottier.............5.00	2.30	.60	
☐ 398	Mets Rookies.............5.00	2.30	.60	
	Bill Haas			
	Dick Smith			
☐ 399	Jackie Brandt.............5.00	2.30	.60	
☐ 400	Warren Spahn............36.00	16.00	4.50	
☐ 401	Charlie Maxwell..........5.50	2.50	.70	
☐ 402	Tom Sturdivant...........5.00	2.30	.60	
☐ 403	Reds Team................10.00	4.50	1.25	
☐ 404	Tony Martinez............5.00	2.30	.60	
☐ 405	Ken McBride...............5.00	2.30	.60	
☐ 406	Al Spangler................5.00	2.30	.60	
☐ 407	Bill Freehan...............6.50	2.90	.80	
☐ 408	Cubs Rookies.............5.00	2.30	.60	
	Jim Stewart			
	Fred Burdette			
☐ 409	Bill Fischer 5.00	2.30	.60	
☐ 410	Dick Stuart.................5.50	2.50	.70	
☐ 411	Lee Walls...................5.00	2.30	.60	
☐ 412	Ray Culp....................5.00	2.30	.60	
☐ 413	Johnny Keane MG........5.00	2.30	.60	
☐ 414	Jack Sanford..............5.00	2.30	.60	
☐ 415	Tony Kubek................8.00	3.60	1.00	
☐ 416	Lee Maye...................5.00	2.30	.60	
☐ 417	Don Cardwell..............5.00	2.30	.60	
☐ 418	Orioles Rookies...........5.50	2.50	.70	
	Darold Knowles			
	Les Narum			
☐ 419	Ken Harrelson............8.50	3.80	1.05	
☐ 420	Jim Maloney...............5.50	2.50	.70	
☐ 421	Camilo Carreon..........5.00	2.30	.60	
☐ 422	Jack Fisher................5.00	2.30	.60	
☐ 423	Tops in NL................110.00	50.00	14.00	
	Hank Aaron			
	Willie Mays			
☐ 424	Dick Bertell................5.00	2.30	.60	
☐ 425	Norm Cash.................6.50	2.90	.80	
☐ 426	Bob Rodgers..............5.50	2.50	.70	
☐ 427	Don Rudolph...............5.00	2.30	.60	
☐ 428	Red Sox Rookies 5.00	2.30	.60	
	Archie Skeen			
	Pete Smith			
	(Back states Archie			
	has retired)			
☐ 429	Tim McCarver 9.00	4.00	1.15	
☐ 430	Juan Pizarro...............5.00	2.30	.60	
☐ 431	George Alusik 5.00	2.30	.60	
☐ 432	Ruben Amaro..............5.00	2.30	.60	
☐ 433	Yankees Team...........15.00	6.75	1.90	
☐ 434	Don Nottebart............5.00	2.30	.60	
☐ 435	Vic Davalillo..............5.00	2.30	.60	
☐ 436	Charlie Neal..............5.50	2.50	.70	
☐ 437	Ed Bailey..................5.00	2.30	.60	
☐ 438	Checklist 6 ....15.00	2.30	.75	
☐ 439	Harvey Haddix............5.50	2.50	.70	
☐ 440	Bob Clemente UER...150.00	70.00	19.00	
	(1960 Pittsburfh)			
☐ 441	Bob Duliba..................5.00	2.30	.60	
☐ 442	Pumpsie Green...........5.50	2.50	.70	
☐ 443	Chuck Dressen MG 5.50	2.50	.70	
☐ 444	Larry Jackson.............5.00	2.30	.60	
☐ 445	Bill Skowron..............6.00	2.70	.75	
☐ 446	Julian Javier..............5.50	2.50	.70	
☐ 447	Ted Bowsfield 5.00	2.30	.60	
☐ 448	Cookie Rojas...............5.50	2.50	.70	
☐ 449	Deron Johnson............5.50	2.50	.70	
☐ 450	Steve Barber..............5.00	2.30	.60	
☐ 451	Joe Amalfitano............5.00	2.30	.60	
☐ 452	Giants Rookies............7.00	3.10	.85	
	Gil Garrido			
	Jim Ray Hart			
☐ 453	Frank Baumann..........5.00	2.30	.60	
☐ 454	Tommie Aaron............5.50	2.50	.70	
☐ 455	Bernie Allen...............5.00	2.30	.60	
☐ 456	Dodgers Rookies.........7.50	3.40	.95	
	Wes Parker			
	John Werhas			
☐ 457	Jesse Gonder.............5.00	2.30	.60	
☐ 458	Ralph Terry................5.50	2.50	.70	
☐ 459	Red Sox Rookies 5.00	2.30	.60	
	Pete Charton			
	Dalton Jones			
☐ 460	Bob Gibson...............40.00	18.00	5.00	
☐ 461	George Thomas 5.00	2.30	.60	
☐ 462	Birdie Tebbetts MG 5.50	2.50	.70	
☐ 463	Don Leppert...............5.00	2.30	.60	
☐ 464	Dallas Green..............5.50	2.50	.70	

☐ 465	Mike Hershberger 5.00	2.30	.60
☐ 466	A's Rookies................5.50	2.50	.70
	Dick Green		
	Aurelio Monteagudo		
☐ 467	Bob Aspromonte 5.00	2.30	.60
☐ 468	Gaylord Perry 45.00	20.00	5.75
☐ 469	Cubs Rookies..............5.50	2.50	.70
	Fred Norman		
	Sterling Slaughter		
☐ 470	Jim Bouton 7.00	3.10	.85
☐ 471	Gates Brown 8.00	3.60	1.00
☐ 472	Vern Law..................5.50	2.50	.70
☐ 473	Baltimore Orioles 10.00	4.50	1.25
	Team Card		
☐ 474	Larry Sherry 5.50	2.50	.70
☐ 475	Ed Charles.................5.00	2.30	.60
☐ 476	Braves Rookies 10.00	4.50	1.25
	Rico Carty		
	Dick Kelley		
☐ 477	Mike Joyce.................5.00	2.30	.60
☐ 478	Dick Howser 5.50	2.50	.70
☐ 479	Cardinals Rookies.........5.00	2.30	.60
	Dave Bakenhaster		
	Johnny Lewis		
☐ 480	Bob Purkey 5.00	2.30	.60
☐ 481	Chuck Schilling............5.00	2.30	.60
☐ 482	Phillies Rookies...........5.50	2.50	.70
	John Briggs		
	Danny Cater		
☐ 483	Fred Valentine 5.00	2.30	.60
☐ 484	Bill Pleis..................5.00	2.30	.60
☐ 485	Tom Haller 5.50	2.50	.70
☐ 486	Bob Kennedy MG..........5.50	2.50	.70
☐ 487	Mike McCormick...........5.50	2.50	.70
☐ 488	Yankees Rookies..........5.50	2.50	.70
	Pete Mikkelsen		
	Bob Meyer		
☐ 489	Julio Navarro 5.00	2.30	.60
☐ 490	Ron Fairly 5.50	2.50	.70
☐ 491	Ed Rakow..................5.00	2.30	.60
☐ 492	Colts Rookies..............6.00	2.70	.75
	Jim Beauchamp		
	Mike White		
☐ 493	Don Lee 5.00	2.30	.60
☐ 494	Al Jackson 5.00	2.30	.60
☐ 495	Bill Virdon 5.50	2.50	.70
☐ 496	White Sox Team...........10.00	4.50	1.25
☐ 497	Jeoff Long 5.00	2.30	.60
☐ 498	Dave Stenhouse............5.00	2.30	.60
☐ 499	Indians Rookies 5.50	2.50	.70
	Chico Salmon		
	Gordon Seyfried		
☐ 500	Camilo Pascual 5.50	2.50	.70
☐ 501	Bob Veale..................5.50	2.50	.70
☐ 502	Angels Rookies............6.00	2.70	.75
	Bobby Knoop		
	Bob Lee		

☐ 503	Earl Wilson 5.50	2.50	.70
☐ 504	Claude Raymond...........5.50	2.50	.70
☐ 505	Stan Williams...............5.50	2.50	.70
☐ 506	Bobby Bragan MG..........5.00	2.30	.60
☐ 507	Johnny Edwards............5.00	2.30	.60
☐ 508	Diego Segui 5.00	2.30	.60
☐ 509	Pirates Rookies 10.00	4.50	1.25
	Gene Alley		
	Orlando McFarlane		
☐ 510	Lindy McDaniel 5.50	2.50	.70
☐ 511	Lou Jackson 5.50	2.50	.70
☐ 512	Tigers Rookies...........14.00	6.25	1.75
	Willie Horton		
	Joe Sparma		
☐ 513	Don Larsen 6.50	2.90	.80
☐ 514	Jim Hickman 5.50	2.50	.70
☐ 515	Johnny Romano 5.00	2.30	.60
☐ 516	Twins Rookies 5.00	2.30	.60
	Jerry Arrigo		
	Dwight Siebler		
☐ 517A	Checklist 7 ERR 25.00	3.80	1.25
	(Incorrect numbering		
	sequence on back)		
☐ 517B	Checklist 7 COR 15.00	2.30	.75
	(Correct numbering		
	on back)		
☐ 518	Carl Bouldin 5.00	2.30	.60
☐ 519	Charlie Smith 5.00	2.30	.60
☐ 520	Jack Baldschun 5.00	2.30	.60
☐ 521	Tom Satriano 5.00	2.30	.60
☐ 522	Bob Tiefenauer 5.00	2.30	.60
☐ 523	Lou Burdette UER 10.00	4.50	1.25
	(Pitching lefty)		
☐ 524	Reds Rookies.............10.00	4.50	1.25
	Jim Dickson		
	Bobby Klaus		
☐ 525	Al McBean.................10.00	4.50	1.25
☐ 526	Lou Clinton 10.00	4.50	1.25
☐ 527	Larry Bearnarth...........10.00	4.50	1.25
☐ 528	A's Rookies...............15.00	6.75	1.90
	Dave Duncan		
	Tommie Reynolds		
☐ 529	Alvin Dark MG............12.00	5.50	1.50
☐ 530	Leon Wagner 10.00	4.50	1.25
☐ 531	Los Angeles Dodgers..24.00	11.00	3.00
	Team Card		
☐ 532	Twins Rookies 12.00	5.50	1.50
	Bud Bloomfield		
	(Bloomfield photo		
	actually Jay Ward)		
	Joe Nossek		
☐ 533	Johnny Klippstein 10.00	4.50	1.25
☐ 534	Gus Bell 12.00	5.50	1.50
☐ 535	Phil Regan 12.00	5.50	1.50
☐ 536	Mets Rookies 10.00	4.50	1.25
	Larry Elliot		
	John Stephenson		

☐ 537	Dan Osinski	10.00	4.50	1.25
☐ 538	Minnie Minoso	12.50	5.75	1.55
☐ 539	Roy Face	12.00	5.50	1.50
☐ 540	Luis Aparicio	21.00	9.50	2.60
☐ 541	Braves Rookies	210.00	95.00	26.00
	Phil Roof			
	Phil Niekro			
☐ 542	Don Mincher	10.00	4.50	1.25
☐ 543	Bob Uecker	50.00	23.00	6.25
☐ 544	Colts Rookies	12.00	5.50	1.50
	Steve Hertz			
	Joe Hoerner			
☐ 545	Max Alvis	10.00	4.50	1.25
☐ 546	Joe Christopher	10.00	4.50	1.25
☐ 547	Gil Hodges MG	15.00	6.75	1.90
☐ 548	NL Rookies	10.00	4.50	1.25
	Wayne Schurr			
	Paul Speckenbach			
☐ 549	Joe Moeller	10.00	4.50	1.25
☐ 550	Ken Hubbs MEM	25.00	11.50	3.10
	(In memoriam)			
☐ 551	Billy Hoeft	10.00	4.50	1.25
☐ 552	Indians Rookies	12.00	5.50	1.50
	Tom Kelley			
	Sonny Siebert			
☐ 553	Jim Brewer	10.00	4.50	1.25
☐ 554	Hank Foiles	10.00	4.50	1.25
☐ 555	Lee Stange	19.00	4.50	1.25
☐ 556	Mets Rookies	10.00	4.50	1.25
	Steve Dillon			
	Ron Locke			
☐ 557	Leo Burke	10.00	4.50	1.25
☐ 558	Don Schwall	10.00	4.50	1.25
☐ 559	Dick Phillips	10.00	4.50	1.25
☐ 560	Dick Farrell	10.00	4.50	1.25
☐ 561	Phillies Rookies UER	12.50	5.75	1.55
	Dave Bennett			
	(19 ... is 18)			
	Rick Wise			
☐ 562	Pedro Ramos	10.00	4.50	1.25
☐ 563	Dal Maxvill	12.00	5.50	1.50
☐ 564	AL Rookies	10.00	4.50	1.25
	Joe McCabe			
	Jerry McNertney			
☐ 565	Stu Miller	12.00	5.50	1.50
☐ 566	Ed Kranepool	14.00	6.25	1.75
☐ 567	Jim Kaat	15.00	6.75	1.90
☐ 568	NL Rookies	10.00	4.50	1.25
	Phil Gagliano			
	Cap Peterson			
☐ 569	Fred Newman	10.00	4.50	1.25
☐ 570	Bill Mazeroski	15.00	6.75	1.90
☐ 571	Gene Conley	12.00	5.50	1.50
☐ 572	AL Rookies	10.00	4.50	1.25
	Dave Gray			
	Dick Egan			
☐ 573	Jim Duffalo	10.00	4.50	1.25

☐ 574	Manny Jimenez	10.00	4.50	1.25
☐ 575	Tony Cloninger	10.00	4.50	1.25
☐ 576	Mets Rookies	10.00	4.50	1.25
	Jerry Hinsley			
	Bill Wakefield			
☐ 577	Gordy Coleman	12.00	5.50	1.50
☐ 578	Glen Hobbie	10.00	4.50	1.25
☐ 579	Red Sox Team	20.00	9.00	2.50
☐ 580	Johnny Podres	12.00	5.50	1.50
☐ 581	Yankees Rookies	10.00	4.50	1.25
	Pedro Gonzalez			
	Archie Moore			
☐ 582	Rod Kanehl	10.00	4.50	1.25
☐ 583	Tito Francona	10.00	4.50	1.25
☐ 584	Joel Horlen	12.00	5.50	1.50
☐ 585	Tony Taylor	12.00	5.50	1.50
☐ 586	Jim Piersall	12.50	5.75	1.55
☐ 587	Bennie Daniels	14.00	6.25	1.75

1965 Topps

The cards in this 598-card set measure 2 1/2" by 3 1/2". The cards comprising the 1965 Topps set have team names located within a distinctive pennant design below the picture. The cards have blue borders on the reverse and were issued by series. Cards 523 to 598 are more difficult to obtain than all other series. Within this last series there are 44 cards that were printed in lesser quantities than the other cards in that series; these shorter-printed cards are marked by SP in the checklist below. In addition, the sixth series (447-522) is more difficult to obtain than series one through five. Featured subsets within this set include League Leaders (1-12) and World Series cards (132-139). Key cards in this

set include Steve Carlton's rookie, Mickey Mantle, and Pete Rose. Other key rookies in this set are Jim Hunter, Joe Morgan, and Tony Perez.

	NRMT	VG-E	GOOD
COMPLETE SET (598)	3750.	1700.	475.00
COMMON PLAYER (1-196)	1.50	.65	.19
COMMON PLAYER (197-283) ..	2.00	.90	.25
COMMON PLAYER (284-370) ..	3.50	1.55	.45
COMMON PLAYER (371-446) ..	5.00	2.30	.60
COMMON PLAYER (447-522) ..	6.00	2.70	.75
COMMON PLAYER (523-598) ..	6.00	2.70	.75

☐ 1	AL Batting Leaders.........	15.00	4.50	1.50
	Tony Oliva			
	Elston Howard			
	Brooks Robinson			
☐ 2	NL Batting Leaders	9.00	4.00	1.15
	Bob Clemente			
	Hank Aaron			
	Rico Carty			
☐ 3	AL Home Run Leaders...	20.00	9.00	2.50
	Harmon Killebrew			
	Mickey Mantle			
	Boog Powell			
☐ 4	NL Home Run Leaders.....	7.50	3.40	.95
	Willie Mays			
	Billy Williams			
	Jim Ray Hart			
	Orlando Cepeda			
	Johnny Callison			
☐ 5	AL RBI Leaders...............	20.00	9.00	2.50
	Brooks Robinson			
	Harmon Killebrew			
	Mickey Mantle			
	Dick Stuart			
☐ 6	NL RBI Leaders...............	5.00	2.30	.60
	Ken Boyer			
	Willie Mays			
	Ron Santo			
☐ 7	AL ERA Leaders	3.00	1.35	.40
	Dean Chance			
	Joel Horlen			
☐ 8	NL ERA Leaders.............	9.50	4.30	1.20
	Sandy Koufax			
	Don Drysdale			
☐ 9	AL Pitching Leaders.........	3.00	1.35	.40
	Dean Chance			
	Gary Peters			
	Dave Wickersham			
	Juan Pizarro			
	Wally Bunker			
☐ 10	NL Pitching Leaders.......	3.00	1.35	.40
	Larry Jackson			
	Ray Sadecki			
	Juan Marichal			
☐ 11	AL Strikeout Leaders	3.00	1.35	.40
	Al Downing			
	Dean Chance			
	Camilo Pascual			
☐ 12	NL Strikeout Leaders	4.50	2.00	.55
	Bob Veale			
	Don Drysdale			
	Bob Gibson			
☐ 13	Pedro Ramos...............	1.50	.65	.19
☐ 14	Len Gabrielson..............	1.50	.65	.19
☐ 15	Robin Roberts...............	8.00	3.60	1.00
☐ 16	Houston Rookies.......	175.00	80.00	22.00
	Joe Morgan			
	Sonny Jackson			
☐ 17	Johnny Romano	1.50	.65	.19
☐ 18	Bill McCool	1.50	.65	.19
☐ 19	Gates Brown	2.00	.90	.25
☐ 20	Jim Bunning	4.50	2.00	.55
☐ 21	Don Blasingame...........	1.50	.65	.19
☐ 22	Charlie Smith	1.50	.65	.19
☐ 23	Bob Tiefenauer.............	1.50	.65	.19
☐ 24	Minnesota Twins...........	3.00	1.35	.40
	Team Card			
☐ 25	Al McBean...................	1.50	.65	.19
☐ 26	Bobby Knoop	1.50	.65	.19
☐ 27	Dick Bertell	1.50	.65	.19
☐ 28	Barney Schultz	1.50	.65	.19
☐ 29	Felix Mantilla	1.50	.65	.19
☐ 30	Jim Bouton	3.00	1.35	.40
☐ 31	Mike White	1.50	.65	.19
☐ 32	Herman Franks MG	1.50	.65	.19
☐ 33	Jackie Brandt	1.50	.65	.19
☐ 34	Cal Koonce	1.50	.65	.19
☐ 35	Ed Charles...................	1.50	.65	.19
☐ 36	Bobby Wine	1.50	.65	.19
☐ 37	Fred Gladding	1.50	.65	.19
☐ 38	Jim King	1.50	.65	.19
☐ 39	Gerry Arrigo	1.50	.65	.19
☐ 40	Frank Howard	3.00	1.35	.40
☐ 41	White Sox Rookies........	1.50	.65	.19
	Bruce Howard			
	Marv Staehle			
☐ 42	Earl Wilson	2.00	.90	.25
☐ 43	Mike Shannon..............	2.00	.90	.25
	(Name in red, other			
	Cardinals in yellow)			
☐ 44	Wade Blasingame.........	1.50	.65	.19
☐ 45	Roy McMillan...............	2.00	.90	.25
☐ 46	Bob Lee......................	1.50	.65	.19
☐ 47	Tommy Harper..............	2.00	.90	.25
☐ 48	Claude Raymond..........	2.00	.90	.25
☐ 49	Orioles Rookies............	2.50	1.15	.30
	Curt Blefary			
	John Miller			
☐ 50	Juan Marichal	11.00	4.90	1.40
☐ 51	Bill Bryan	1.50	.65	.19
☐ 52	Ed Roebuck..................	1.50	.65	.19

☐ 53 Dick McAuliffe	2.00	.90	.25
☐ 54 Joe Gibbon	1.50	.65	.19
☐ 55 Tony Conigliaro	9.00	4.00	1.15
☐ 56 Ron Kline	1.50	.65	.19
☐ 57 Cardinals Team	3.00	1.35	.40
☐ 58 Fred Talbot	1.50	.65	.19
☐ 59 Nate Oliver	1.50	.65	.19
☐ 60 Jim O'Toole	2.00	.90	.25
☐ 61 Chris Cannizzaro	1.50	.65	.19
☐ 62 Jim Katt UER	4.50	2.00	.55
(Sic, Kaat)			
☐ 63 Ty Cline	1.50	.65	.19
☐ 64 Lou Burdette	2.00	.90	.25
☐ 65 Tony Kubek	4.00	1.80	.50
☐ 66 Bill Rigney MG	1.50	.65	.19
☐ 67 Harvey Haddix	2.00	.90	.25
☐ 68 Del Crandall	2.00	.90	.25
☐ 69 Bill Virdon	2.00	.90	.25
☐ 70 Bill Skowron	2.00	.90	.25
☐ 71 John O'Donoghue	1.50	.65	.19
☐ 72 Tony Gonzalez	1.50	.65	.19
☐ 73 Dennis Ribant	1.50	.65	.19
☐ 74 Red Sox Rookies	7.00	3.10	.85
Rico Petrocelli			
Jerry Stephenson			
☐ 75 Deron Johnson	2.00	.90	.25
☐ 76 Sam McDowell	2.00	.90	.25
☐ 77 Doug Camilli	1.50	.65	.19
☐ 78 Dal Maxvill	1.50	.65	.19
☐ 79A Checklist 1	9.00	1.35	.45
(61 Cannizzaro)			
☐ 79B Checklist 1	9.00	1.35	.45
(61 C.Cannizzaro)			
☐ 80 Turk Farrell	1.50	.65	.19
☐ 81 Don Buford	2.00	.90	.25
☐ 82 Braves Rookies	4.00	1.80	.50
Santos Alomar			
John Braun			
☐ 83 George Thomas	1.50	.65	.19
☐ 84 Ron Herbel	1.50	.65	.19
☐ 85 Willie Smith	1.50	.65	.19
☐ 86 Les Narum	1.50	.65	.19
☐ 87 Nelson Mathews	1.50	.65	.19
☐ 88 Jack Lamabe	1.50	.65	.19
☐ 89 Mike Hershberger	1.50	.65	.19
☐ 90 Rich Rollins	2.00	.90	.25
☐ 91 Cubs Team	3.00	1.35	.40
☐ 92 Dick Howser	2.00	.90	.25
☐ 93 Jack Fisher	1.50	.65	.19
☐ 94 Charlie Lau	2.00	.90	.25
☐ 95 Bill Mazeroski	3.50	1.55	.45
☐ 96 Sonny Siebert	2.00	.90	.25
☐ 97 Pedro Gonzalez	1.50	.65	.19
☐ 98 Bob Miller	1.50	.65	.19
☐ 99 Gil Hodges MG	6.00	2.70	.75
☐ 100 Ken Boyer	3.50	1.55	.45
☐ 101 Fred Newman	1.50	.65	.19

☐ 102 Steve Boros	1.50	.65	.19
☐ 103 Harvey Kuenn	2.00	.90	.25
☐ 104 Checklist 2	9.00	1.35	.45
☐ 105 Chico Salmon	1.50	.65	.19
☐ 106 Gene Oliver	1.50	.65	.19
☐ 107 Phillies Rookies	2.50	1.15	.30
Pat Corrales			
Costen Shockley			
☐ 108 Don Mincher	1.50	.65	.19
☐ 109 Walt Bond	1.50	.65	.19
☐ 110 Ron Santo	4.00	1.80	.50
☐ 111 Lee Thomas	2.00	.90	.25
☐ 112 Derrell Griffith	1.50	.65	.19
☐ 113 Steve Barber	1.50	.65	.19
☐ 114 Jim Hickman	2.00	.90	.25
☐ 115 Bobby Richardson	4.00	1.80	.50
☐ 116 Cardinals Rookies	2.50	1.15	.30
Dave Dowling			
Bob Tolan			
☐ 117 Wes Stock	1.50	.65	.19
☐ 118 Hal Lanier	2.50	1.15	.30
☐ 119 John Kennedy	1.50	.65	.19
☐ 120 Frank Robinson	30.00	13.50	3.80
☐ 121 Gene Alley	2.00	.90	.25
☐ 122 Bill Pleis	1.50	.65	.19
☐ 123 Frank Thomas	2.00	.90	.25
☐ 124 Tom Satriano	1.50	.65	.19
☐ 125 Juan Pizarro	1.50	.65	.19
☐ 126 Dodgers Team	4.00	1.80	.50
☐ 127 Frank Lary	1.50	.65	.19
☐ 128 Vic Davalillo	1.50	.65	.19
☐ 129 Bennie Daniels	1.50	.65	.19
☐ 130 Al Kaline	30.00	13.50	3.80
☐ 131 Johnny Keane MG	1.50	.65	.19
☐ 132 World Series Game 1	4.00	1.80	.50
Cards take opener			
(Mike Shannon)			
☐ 133 World Series Game 2	4.00	1.80	.50
Mel Stottlemyre wins			
☐ 134 World Series Game 3	45.00	20.00	5.75
Mickey Mantle's homer			
☐ 135 World Series Game 4	4.00	1.80	.50
Ken Boyer's grand-slam			
☐ 136 World Series Game 5	4.00	1.80	.50
10th inning triumph			
(Tim McCarver being			
greeted at home)			
☐ 137 World Series Game 6	4.00	1.80	.50
Jim Bouton wins again			
☐ 138 World Series Game 7	10.00	4.50	1.25
Bob Gibson wins finale			
☐ 139 World Series Summary	4.00	1.80	.50
Cards celebrate			
☐ 140 Dean Chance	2.00	.90	.25
☐ 141 Charlie James	1.50	.65	.19
☐ 142 Bill Monbouquette	1.50	.65	.19
☐ 143 Pirates Rookies	1.50	.65	.19

	John Gelnar			
	Jerry May			
☐ 144	Ed Kranepool	2.00	.90	.25
☐ 145	Luis Tiant	15.00	6.75	1.90
☐ 146	Ron Hansen	1.50	.65	.19
☐ 147	Dennis Bennett	1.50	.65	.19
☐ 148	Willie Kirkland	1.50	.65	.19
☐ 149	Wayne Schurr	1.50	.65	.19
☐ 150	Brooks Robinson	30.00	13.50	3.80
☐ 151	Athletics Team	3.00	1.35	.40
☐ 152	Phil Ortega	1.50	.65	.19
☐ 153	Norm Cash	4.00	1.80	.50
☐ 154	Bob Humphreys	1.50	.65	.19
☐ 155	Roger Maris	65.00	29.00	8.25
☐ 156	Bob Sadowski	1.50	.65	.19
☐ 157	Zoilo Versalles	2.50	1.15	.30
☐ 158	Dick Sisler	1.50	.65	.19
☐ 159	Jim Duffalo	1.50	.65	.19
☐ 160	Bob Clemente UER	80.00	36.00	10.00
	(1960 Pittsburfh)			
☐ 161	Frank Baumann	1.50	.65	.19
☐ 162	Russ Nixon	1.50	.65	.19
☐ 163	Johnny Briggs	1.50	.65	.19
☐ 164	Al Spangler	1.50	.65	.19
☐ 165	Dick Ellsworth	1.50	.65	.19
☐ 166	Indians Rookies	3.50	1.55	.45
	George Culver			
	Tommie Agee			
☐ 167	Bill Wakefield	1.50	.65	.19
☐ 168	Dick Green	1.50	.65	.19
☐ 169	Dave Vineyard	1.50	.65	.19
☐ 170	Hank Aaron	100.00	45.00	12.50
☐ 171	Jim Roland	1.50	.65	.19
☐ 172	Jim Piersall	2.00	.90	.25
☐ 173	Detroit Tigers	3.00	1.35	.40
	Team Card			
☐ 174	Joey Jay	1.50	.65	.19
☐ 175	Bob Aspromonte	1.50	.65	.19
☐ 176	Willie McCovey	20.00	9.00	2.50
☐ 177	Pete Mikkelsen	1.50	.65	.19
☐ 178	Dalton Jones	1.50	.65	.19
☐ 179	Hal Woodeshick	1.50	.65	.19
☐ 180	Bob Allison	2.00	.90	.25
☐ 181	Senators Rookies	1.50	.65	.19
	Don Loun			
	Joe McCabe			
☐ 182	Mike DeLaHoz	1.50	.65	.19
☐ 183	Dave Nicholson	1.50	.65	.19
☐ 184	John Boozer	1.50	.65	.19
☐ 185	Max Alvis	1.50	.65	.19
☐ 186	Billy Cowan	1.50	.65	.19
☐ 187	Casey Stengel MG	15.00	6.75	1.90
☐ 188	Sam Bowens	1.50	.65	.19
☐ 189	Checklist 3	9.00	1.35	.45
☐ 190	Bill White	3.50	1.55	.45
☐ 191	Phil Regan	2.00	.90	.25
☐ 192	Jim Coker	1.50	.65	.19

☐ 193	Gaylord Perry	20.00	9.00	2.50
☐ 194	Rookie Stars	1.50	.65	.19
	Bill Kelso			
	Rick Reichardt			
☐ 195	Bob Veale	2.00	.90	.25
☐ 196	Ron Fairly	1.50	.65	.19
☐ 197	Diego Segui	2.00	.90	.25
☐ 198	Smoky Burgess	2.50	1.15	.30
☐ 199	Bob Heffner	2.00	.90	.25
☐ 200	Joe Torre	4.50	2.00	.55
☐ 201	Twins Rookies	3.00	1.35	.40
	Sandy Valdespino			
	Cesar Tovar			
☐ 202	Leo Burke	2.00	.90	.25
☐ 203	Dallas Green	2.50	1.15	.30
☐ 204	Russ Snyder	2.00	.90	.25
☐ 205	Warren Spahn	27.00	12.00	3.40
☐ 206	Willie Horton	3.50	1.55	.45
☐ 207	Pete Rose	175.00	80.00	22.00
☐ 208	Tommy John	15.00	6.75	1.90
☐ 209	Pirates Team	4.00	1.80	.50
☐ 210	Jim Fregosi	2.50	1.15	.30
☐ 211	Steve Ridzik	2.00	.90	.25
☐ 212	Ron Brand	2.00	.90	.25
☐ 213	Jim Davenport	2.00	.90	.25
☐ 214	Bob Purkey	2.00	.90	.25
☐ 215	Pete Ward	2.00	.90	.25
☐ 216	Al Worthington	2.00	.90	.25
☐ 217	Walt Alston MG	4.00	1.80	.50
☐ 218	Dick Schofield	2.00	.90	.25
☐ 219	Bob Meyer	2.00	.90	.25
☐ 220	Billy Williams	15.00	6.75	1.90
☐ 221	John Tsitouris	2.00	.90	.25
☐ 222	Bob Tillman	2.00	.90	.25
☐ 223	Dan Osinski	2.00	.90	.25
☐ 224	Bob Chance	2.00	.90	.25
☐ 225	Bo Belinsky	2.50	1.15	.30
☐ 226	Yankees Rookies	2.00	.90	.25
	Elvio Jimenez			
	Jake Gibbs			
☐ 227	Bobby Klaus	2.00	.90	.25
☐ 228	Jack Sanford	2.00	.90	.25
☐ 229	Lou Clinton	2.00	.90	.25
☐ 230	Ray Sadecki	2.00	.90	.25
☐ 231	Jerry Adair	2.00	.90	.25
☐ 232	Steve Blass	3.50	1.55	.45
☐ 233	Don Zimmer	2.50	1.15	.30
☐ 234	White Sox Team	4.00	1.80	.50
☐ 235	Chuck Hinton	2.00	.90	.25
☐ 236	Denny McLain	25.00	11.50	3.10
☐ 237	Bernie Allen	2.00	.90	.25
☐ 238	Joe Moeller	2.00	.90	.25
☐ 239	Doc Edwards	2.00	.90	.25
☐ 240	Bob Bruce	2.00	.90	.25
☐ 241	Mack Jones	2.00	.90	.25
☐ 242	George Brunet	2.00	.90	.25
☐ 243	Reds Rookies	3.00	1.35	.40

	Ted Davidson			
	Tommy Helms			
244	Lindy McDaniel	2.50	1.15	.30
245	Joe Pepitone	2.50	1.15	.30
246	Tom Butters	2.00	.90	.25
247	Wally Moon	2.50	1.15	.30
248	Gus Triandos	2.50	1.15	.30
249	Dave McNally	3.00	1.35	.40
250	Willie Mays	100.00	45.00	12.50
251	Billy Herman MG	2.50	1.15	.30
252	Pete Richert	2.00	.90	.25
253	Danny Cater	2.00	.90	.25
254	Roland Sheldon	2.00	.90	.25
255	Camilo Pascual	2.50	1.15	.30
256	Tito Francona	2.00	.90	.25
257	Jim Wynn	3.00	1.35	.40
258	Larry Bearnarth	2.00	.90	.25
259	Tigers Rookies	4.50	2.00	.55
	Jim Northrup			
	Ray Oyler			
260	Don Drysdale	20.00	9.00	2.50
261	Duke Carmel	2.00	.90	.25
262	Bud Daley	2.00	.90	.25
263	Marty Keough	2.00	.90	.25
264	Bob Buhl	2.50	1.15	.30
265	Jim Pagliaroni	2.00	.90	.25
266	Bert Campaneris	8.00	3.60	1.00
267	Senators Team	4.00	1.80	.50
268	Ken McBride	2.00	.90	.25
269	Frank Bolling	2.00	.90	.25
270	Milt Pappas	2.50	1.15	.30
271	Don Wert	2.00	.90	.25
272	Chuck Schilling	2.00	.90	.25
273	Checklist 4	9.00	1.35	.45
274	Lum Harris MG	2.00	.90	.25
275	Dick Groat	3.00	1.35	.40
276	Hoyt Wilhelm	8.00	3.60	1.00
277	Johnny Lewis	2.00	.90	.25
278	Ken Retzer	2.00	.90	.25
279	Dick Tracewski	2.00	.90	.25
280	Dick Stuart	2.50	1.15	.30
281	Bill Stafford	2.00	.90	.25
282	Giants Rookies	5.00	2.30	.60
	Dick Estelle			
	Masanori Murakami			
283	Fred Whitfield	2.00	.90	.25
284	Nick Willhite	3.50	1.55	.45
285	Ron Hunt	3.50	1.55	.45
286	Athletics Rookies	3.50	1.55	.45
	Jim Dickson			
	Aurelio Monteagudo			
287	Gary Kolb	3.50	1.55	.45
288	Jack Hamilton	3.50	1.55	.45
289	Gordy Coleman	4.00	1.80	.50
290	Wally Bunker	4.00	1.80	.50
291	Jerry Lynch	3.50	1.55	.45
292	Larry Yellen	3.50	1.55	.45
293	Angels Team	6.50	2.90	.80
294	Tim McCarver	6.00	2.70	.75
295	Dick Radatz	4.00	1.80	.50
296	Tony Taylor	3.50	1.55	.45
297	Dave DeBusschere	4.00	1.80	.50
298	Jim Stewart	3.50	1.55	.45
299	Jerry Zimmerman	3.50	1.55	.45
300	Sandy Koufax	125.00	57.50	15.50
301	Birdie Tebbetts MG	4.00	1.80	.50
302	Al Stanek	3.50	1.55	.45
303	John Orsino	3.50	1.55	.45
304	Dave Stenhouse	3.50	1.55	.45
305	Rico Carty	4.50	2.00	.55
306	Bubba Phillips	3.50	1.55	.45
307	Barry Latman	3.50	1.55	.45
308	Mets Rookies	7.50	3.40	.95
	Cleon Jones			
	Tom Parsons			
309	Steve Hamilton	3.50	1.55	.45
310	Johnny Callison	4.00	1.80	.50
311	Orlando Pena	3.50	1.55	.45
312	Joe Nuxhall	4.00	1.80	.50
313	Jim Schaffer	0.00	1.55	.45
314	Sterling Slaughter	3.50	1.55	.45
315	Frank Malzone	4.00	1.80	.50
316	Reds Team	6.50	2.90	.80
317	Don McMahon	3.50	1.55	.45
318	Matty Alou	4.00	1.80	.50
319	Ken McMullen	3.50	1.55	.45
320	Bob Gibson	35.00	16.00	4.40
321	Rusty Staub	6.00	2.70	.75
322	Rick Wise	4.00	1.80	.50
323	Hank Bauer MG	4.00	1.80	.50
324	Bobby Locke	3.50	1.55	.45
325	Donn Clendenon	4.00	1.80	.50
326	Dwight Siebler	3.50	1.55	.45
327	Denis Menke	3.50	1.55	.45
328	Eddie Fisher	3.50	1.55	.45
329	Hawk Taylor	3.50	1.55	.45
330	Whitey Ford	35.00	16.00	4.40
331	Dodgers Rookies	4.00	1.80	.50
	Al Ferrara			
	John Purdin			
332	Ted Abernathy	3.50	1.55	.45
333	Tom Reynolds	3.50	1.55	.45
334	Vic Roznovsky	3.50	1.55	.45
335	Mickey Lolich	6.00	2.70	.75
336	Woody Held	3.50	1.55	.45
337	Mike Cuellar	4.00	1.80	.50
338	Philadelphia Phillies	6.50	2.90	.80
	Team Card			
339	Ryne Duren	4.00	1.80	.50
340	Tony Oliva	12.50	5.75	1.55
341	Bob Bolin	3.50	1.55	.45
342	Bob Rodgers	4.00	1.80	.50
343	Mike McCormick	4.00	1.80	.50
344	Wes Parker	4.00	1.80	.50

☐ 345	Floyd Robinson	3.50	1.55	.45
☐ 346	Bobby Bragan MG	3.50	1.55	.45
☐ 347	Roy Face	4.50	2.00	.55
☐ 348	George Banks	3.50	1.55	.45
☐ 349	Larry Miller	3.50	1.55	.45
☐ 350	Mickey Mantle	500.00	230.00	65.00
☐ 351	Jim Perry	4.00	1.80	.50
☐ 352	Alex Johnson	4.50	2.00	.55
☐ 353	Jerry Lumpe	3.50	1.55	.45
☐ 354	Cubs Rookies	3.50	1.55	.45
	Billy Ott			
	Jack Warner			
☐ 355	Vada Pinson	4.00	1.80	.50
☐ 356	Bill Spanswick	3.50	1.55	.45
☐ 357	Carl Warwick	3.50	1.55	.45
☐ 358	Albie Pearson	4.00	1.80	.50
☐ 359	Ken Johnson	3.50	1.55	.45
☐ 360	Orlando Cepeda	8.00	3.60	1.00
☐ 361	Checklist 5	3.50	.55	.18
☐ 362	Don Schwall	3.50	1.55	.45
☐ 363	Bob Johnson	3.50	1.55	.45
☐ 364	Galen Cisco	3.50	1.55	.45
☐ 365	Jim Gentile	4.00	1.80	.50
☐ 366	Dan Schneider	3.50	1.55	.45
☐ 367	Leon Wagner	3.50	1.55	.45
☐ 368	White Sox Rookies	4.00	1.80	.50
	Ken Berry			
	Joel Gibson			
☐ 369	Phil Linz	4.00	1.80	.50
☐ 370	Tommy Davis	4.00	1.80	.50
☐ 371	Frank Kreutzer	5.00	2.30	.60
☐ 372	Clay Dalrymple	5.00	2.30	.60
☐ 373	Curt Simmons	5.50	2.50	.70
☐ 374	Angels Rookies	7.00	3.10	.85
	Jose Cardenal			
	Dick Simpson			
☐ 375	Dave Wickersham	5.00	2.30	.60
☐ 376	Jim Landis	5.00	2.30	.60
☐ 377	Willie Stargell	32.00	14.50	4.00
☐ 378	Chuck Estrada	5.00	2.30	.60
☐ 379	Giants Team	9.00	4.00	1.15
☐ 380	Rocky Colavito	9.00	4.00	1.15
☐ 381	Al Jackson	5.00	2.30	.60
☐ 382	J.C. Martin	5.00	2.30	.60
☐ 383	Felipe Alou	6.50	2.90	.80
☐ 384	Johnny Klippstein	5.00	2.30	.60
☐ 385	Carl Yastrzemski	85.00	38.00	10.50
☐ 386	Cubs Rookies	5.00	2.30	.60
	Paul Jaeckel			
	Fred Norman			
☐ 387	Johnny Podres	5.50	2.50	.70
☐ 388	John Blanchard	5.00	2.30	.60
☐ 389	Don Larsen	5.50	2.50	.70
☐ 390	Bill Freehan	6.50	2.90	.80
☐ 391	Mel McGaha MG	5.00	2.30	.60
☐ 392	Bob Friend	5.50	2.50	.70
☐ 393	Ed Kirkpatrick	5.00	2.30	.60

☐ 394	Jim Hannan	5.00	2.30	.60
☐ 395	Jim Ray Hart	5.50	2.50	.70
☐ 396	Frank Bertaina	5.00	2.30	.60
☐ 397	Jerry Buchek	5.00	2.30	.60
☐ 398	Reds Rookies	5.50	2.50	.70
	Dan Neville			
	Art Shamsky			
☐ 399	Ray Herbert	5.00	2.30	.60
☐ 400	Harmon Killebrew	35.00	16.00	4.40
☐ 401	Carl Willey	5.00	2.30	.60
☐ 402	Joe Amalfitano	5.00	2.30	.60
☐ 403	Boston Red Sox	9.00	4.00	1.15
	Team Card			
☐ 404	Stan Williams	5.50	2.50	.70
	(Listed as Indian			
	but Yankee cap)			
☐ 405	John Roseboro	5.50	2.50	.70
☐ 406	Ralph Terry	5.50	2.50	.70
☐ 407	Lee Maye	5.00	2.30	.60
☐ 408	Larry Sherry	5.50	2.50	.70
☐ 409	Astros Rookies	6.50	2.90	.80
	Jim Beauchamp			
	Larry Dierker			
☐ 410	Luis Aparicio	10.00	4.50	1.25
☐ 411	Roger Craig	5.50	2.50	.70
☐ 412	Bob Bailey	5.50	2.50	.70
☐ 413	Hal Reniff	5.00	2.30	.60
☐ 414	Al Lopez MG	6.50	2.90	.80
☐ 415	Curt Flood	7.50	3.40	.95
☐ 416	Jim Brewer	5.00	2.30	.60
☐ 417	Ed Brinkman	5.00	2.30	.60
☐ 418	Johnny Edwards	5.00	2.30	.60
☐ 419	Ruben Amaro	5.00	2.30	.60
☐ 420	Larry Jackson	5.00	2.30	.60
☐ 421	Twins Rookies	5.00	2.30	.60
	Gary Dotter			
	Jay Ward			
☐ 422	Aubrey Gatewood	5.00	2.30	.60
☐ 423	Jesse Gonder	5.00	2.30	.60
☐ 424	Gary Bell	5.00	2.30	.60
☐ 425	Wayne Causey	5.00	2.30	.60
☐ 426	Braves Team	9.00	4.00	1.15
☐ 427	Bob Saverine	5.00	2.30	.60
☐ 428	Bob Shaw	5.00	2.30	.60
☐ 429	Don Demeter	5.00	2.30	.60
☐ 430	Gary Peters	5.00	2.30	.60
☐ 431	Cards Rookies	6.50	2.90	.80
	Nelson Briles			
	Wayne Spiezio			
☐ 432	Jim Grant	5.50	2.50	.70
☐ 433	John Bateman	5.00	2.30	.60
☐ 434	Dave Morehead	5.00	2.30	.60
☐ 435	Willie Davis	5.50	2.50	.70
☐ 436	Don Elston	5.00	2.30	.60
☐ 437	Chico Cardenas	5.50	2.50	.70
☐ 438	Harry Walker MG	5.00	2.30	.60
☐ 439	Moe Drabowsky	5.50	2.50	.70

☐ 440 Tom Tresh	6.00	2.70	.75
☐ 441 Denny Lemaster	5.00	2.30	.60
☐ 442 Vic Power	5.50	2.50	.70
☐ 443 Checklist 6	12.00	1.80	.60
☐ 444 Bob Hendley	5.00	2.30	.60
☐ 445 Don Lock	5.00	2.30	.60
☐ 446 Art Mahaffey	5.00	2.30	.60
☐ 447 Julian Javier	6.50	2.90	.80
☐ 448 Lee Stange	6.00	2.70	.75
☐ 449 Mets Rookies	6.00	2.70	.75
Jerry Hinsley			
Gary Kroll			
☐ 450 Elston Howard	8.00	3.60	1.00
☐ 451 Jim Owens	6.00	2.70	.75
☐ 452 Gary Geiger	6.00	2.70	.75
☐ 453 Dodgers Rookies	6.50	2.90	.80
Willie Crawford			
John Werhas			
☐ 454 Ed Rakow	6.00	2.70	.75
☐ 455 Norm Siebern	6.00	2.70	.75
☐ 456 Bill Henry	6.00	2.70	.75
☐ 457 Bob Kennedy MG	6.50	2.90	.80
☐ 458 John Buzhardt	6.00	2.70	.75
☐ 459 Frank Kostro	6.00	2.70	.75
☐ 460 Richie Allen	27.00	12.00	3.40
☐ 461 Braves Rookies	60.00	27.00	7.50
Clay Carroll			
Phil Niekro			
☐ 462 Lew Krausse UER	6.50	2.90	.80
(Photo actually			
Pete Lovrich)			
☐ 463 Manny Mota	7.00	3.10	.85
☐ 464 Ron Piche	6.00	2.70	.75
☐ 465 Tom Haller	7.00	3.10	.85
☐ 466 Senators Rookies	6.00	2.70	.75
Pete Craig			
Dick Nen			
☐ 467 Ray Washburn	6.00	2.70	.75
☐ 468 Larry Brown	6.00	2.70	.75
☐ 469 Don Nottebart	6.00	2.70	.75
☐ 470 Yogi Berra P/CO	60.00	27.00	7.50
☐ 471 Billy Hoeft	6.00	2.70	.75
☐ 472 Don Pavletich	6.00	2.70	.75
☐ 473 Orioles Rookies	12.50	5.75	1.55
Paul Blair			
Dave Johnson			
☐ 474 Cookie Rojas	7.00	3.10	.85
☐ 475 Clete Boyer	7.50	3.40	.95
☐ 476 Billy O'Dell	6.00	2.70	.75
☐ 477 Cards Rookies	575.00	250.00	70.00
Fritz Ackley			
Steve Carlton			
☐ 478 Wilbur Wood	7.00	3.10	.85
☐ 479 Ken Harrelson	7.50	3.40	.95
☐ 480 Joel Horlen	6.00	2.70	.75
☐ 481 Cleveland Indians	12.00	5.50	1.50
Team Card			
☐ 482 Bob Priddy	6.00	2.70	.75
☐ 483 George Smith	6.00	2.70	.75
☐ 484 Ron Perranoski	7.00	3.10	.85
☐ 485 Nellie Fox P/CO	12.00	5.50	1.50
☐ 486 Angels Rookies	6.00	2.70	.75
Tom Egan			
Pat Rogan			
☐ 487 Woody Woodward	6.50	2.90	.80
☐ 488 Ted Wills	6.00	2.70	.75
☐ 489 Gene Mauch MG	6.50	2.90	.80
☐ 490 Earl Battey	6.00	2.70	.75
☐ 491 Tracy Stallard	6.00	2.70	.75
☐ 492 Gene Freese	6.00	2.70	.75
☐ 493 Tigers Rookies	6.00	2.70	.75
Bill Roman			
Bruce Brubaker			
☐ 494 Jay Ritchie	6.00	2.70	.75
☐ 495 Joe Christopher	6.00	2.70	.75
☐ 496 Joe Cunningham	6.00	2.70	.75
☐ 497 Giants Rookies	6.50	2.90	.80
Ken Henderson			
Jack Hiatt			
☐ 498 Gene Stephens	6.00	2.70	.75
☐ 499 Stu Miller	6.50	2.90	.80
☐ 500 Eddie Mathews	36.00	16.00	4.50
☐ 501 Indians Rookies	6.00	2.70	.75
Ralph Gagliano			
Jim Rittwage			
☐ 502 Don Cardwell	6.00	2.70	.75
☐ 503 Phil Gagliano	6.00	2.70	.75
☐ 504 Jerry Grote	6.00	2.70	.75
☐ 505 Ray Culp	6.00	2.70	.75
☐ 506 Sam Mele MG	6.00	2.70	.75
☐ 507 Sammy Ellis	6.00	2.70	.75
☐ 508 Checklist 7	12.00	1.80	.60
☐ 509 Red Sox Rookies	6.00	2.70	.75
Bob Guindon			
Gerry Vezendy			
☐ 510 Ernie Banks	80.00	36.00	10.00
☐ 511 Ron Locke	6.00	2.70	.75
☐ 512 Cap Peterson	6.00	2.70	.75
☐ 513 New York Yankees	16.00	7.25	2.00
Team Card			
☐ 514 Joe Azcue	6.00	2.70	.75
☐ 515 Vern Law	7.00	3.10	.85
☐ 516 Al Weis	6.00	2.70	.75
☐ 517 Angels Rookies	6.50	2.90	.80
Paul Schaal			
Jack Warner			
☐ 518 Ken Rowe	6.00	2.70	.75
☐ 519 Bob Uecker UER	35.00	16.00	4.40
(Posing as a left-			
handed batter)			
☐ 520 Tony Cloninger	6.00	2.70	.75
☐ 521 Phillies Rookies	6.00	2.70	.75
Dave Bennett			
Morrie Stevens			

☐ 522	Hank Aguirre................6.00	2.70	.75
☐ 523	Mike Brumley SP 11.00	4.90	1.40
☐ 524	Dave Giusti SP 11.00	4.90	1.40
☐ 525	Eddie Bressoud 6.00	2.70	.75
☐ 526	Athletics Rookies SP150.00	70.00	19.00
	Rene Lachemann		
	Johnny Odom		
	Jim Hunter ERR		
	("Tim" on back)		
	Skip Lockwood		
☐ 527	Jeff Torborg SP 15.00	6.75	1.90
☐ 528	George Altman 6.00	2.70	.75
☐ 529	Jerry Fosnow SP 11.00	4.90	1.40
☐ 530	Jim Maloney 7.00	3.10	.85
☐ 531	Chuck Hiller 6.00	2.70	.75
☐ 532	Hector Lopez 6.50	2.90	.80
☐ 533	Mets Rookies SP 32.00	14.50	4.00
	Dan Napoleon		
	Ron Swoboda		
	Tug McGraw		
	Jim Bethke		
☐ 534	John Herrnstein 6.00	2.70	.75
☐ 535	Jack Kralick SP 11.00	4.90	1.40
☐ 536	Andre Rodgers SP 11.00	4.90	1.40
☐ 537	Angels Rookies 7.50	3.40	.95
	Marcelino Lopez		
	Phil Roof		
	Rudy May		
☐ 538	Chuck Dressen MG SP12.00	5.50	1.50
☐ 539	Herm Starrette 6.00	2.70	.75
☐ 540	Lou Brock SP 50.00	23.00	6.25
☐ 541	White Sox Rookies........6.00	2.70	.75
	Greg Bollo		
	Bob Locker		
☐ 542	Lou Klimchock...............6.00	2.70	.75
☐ 543	Ed Connolly SP 11.00	4.90	1.40
☐ 544	Howie Reed....................6.00	2.70	.75
☐ 545	Jesus Alou SP 11.00	4.90	1.40
☐ 546	Indians Rookies 6.00	2.70	.75
	Bill Davis		
	Mike Hedlund		
	Ray Barker		
	Floyd Weaver		
☐ 547	Jake Wood SP 11.00	4.90	1.40
☐ 548	Dick Stigman 6.00	2.70	.75
☐ 549	Cubs Rookies SP 17.00	7.75	2.10
	Roberto Pena		
	Glenn Beckert		
☐ 550	Mel Stottlemyre SP 35.00	16.00	4.40
☐ 551	New York Mets SP 35.00	16.00	4.40
	Team Card		
☐ 552	Julio Gotay 6.00	2.70	.75
☐ 553	Astros Rookies 6.00	2.70	.75
	Dan Coombs		
	Gene Ratliff		
	Jack McClure		
☐ 554	Chico Ruiz SP 11.00	4.90	1.40
☐ 555	Jack Baldschun SP 11.00	4.90	1.40
☐ 556	Red Schoendienst ...20.00	9.00	2.50
	MG SP		
☐ 557	Jose Santiago 6.00	2.70	.75
☐ 558	Tommie Sisk..................6.00	2.70	.75
☐ 559	Ed Bailey SP 11.00	4.90	1.40
☐ 560	Boog Powell SP 20.00	9.00	2.50
☐ 561	Dodgers Rookies 12.50	5.75	1.55
	Dennis Daboll		
	Mike Kekich		
	Hector Valle		
	Jim Lefebvre		
☐ 562	Billy Moran 6.00	2.70	.75
☐ 563	Julio Navarro 6.00	2.70	.75
☐ 564	Mel Nelson....................6.00	2.70	.75
☐ 565	Ernie Broglio SP 11.00	4.90	1.40
☐ 566	Yankees Rookies SP ...11.00	4.90	1.40
	Gil Blanco		
	Ross Moschitto		
	Art Lopez		
☐ 567	Tommie Aaron 7.00	3.10	.85
☐ 568	Ron Taylor SP 11.00	4.90	1.40
☐ 569	Gino Cimoli SP.............11.00	4.90	1.40
☐ 570	Claude Osteen SP 11.00	4.90	1.40
☐ 571	Ossie Virgil SP 11.00	4.90	1.40
☐ 572	Baltimore Orioles SP .30.00	13.50	3.80
	Team Card		
☐ 573	Red Sox Rookies SP .25.00	11.50	3.10
	Jim Lonborg		
	Gerry Moses		
	Bill Schlesinger		
	Mike Ryan		
☐ 574	Roy Sievers...................7.00	3.10	.85
☐ 575	Jose Pagan 6.00	2.70	.75
☐ 576	Terry Fox SP 11.00	4.90	1.40
☐ 577	AL Rookie Stars SP 12.00	5.50	1.50
	Darold Knowles		
	Don Buschhorn		
	Richie Scheinblum		
☐ 578	Camilo Carreon SP.......11.00	4.90	1.40
☐ 579	Dick Smith SP 11.00	4.90	1.40
☐ 580	Jimmie Hall SP 11.00	4.90	1.40
☐ 581	NL Rookie Stars SP .165.00	75.00	21.00
	Tony Perez		
	Dave Ricketts		
	Kevin Collins		
☐ 582	Bob Schmidt SP 11.00	4.90	1.40
☐ 583	Wes Covington SP 11.00	4.90	1.40
☐ 584	Harry Bright 6.00	2.70	.75
☐ 585	Hank Fischer 6.00	2.70	.75
☐ 586	Tom McCraw SP 11.00	4.90	1.40
☐ 587	Joe Sparma 6.00	2.70	.75
☐ 588	Lenny Green 6.00	2.70	.75
☐ 589	Giants Rookies SP 11.00	4.90	1.40
	Frank Linzy		
	Bob Schroder		
☐ 590	John Wyatt 6.00	2.70	.75

		NRMT	VG-E	GOOD
☐ 591	Bob Skinner SP	12.00	5.50	1.50
☐ 592	Frank Bork SP	11.00	4.90	1.40
☐ 593	Tigers Rookies SP	15.00	6.75	1.90
	Jackie Moore			
	John Sullivan			
☐ 594	Joe Gaines	6.00	2.70	.75
☐ 595	Don Lee	6.00	2.70	.75
☐ 596	Don Landrum SP	11.00	4.90	1.40
☐ 597	Twins Rookies	6.00	2.70	.75
	Joe Nossek			
	John Sevcik			
	Dick Reese			
☐ 598	Al Downing SP	20.00	9.00	2.50

1966 Topps

The cards in this 598-card set measure 2 1/2" by 3 1/2". There are the same number of cards as in the 1965 set. Once again, the seventh series cards (523 to 598) are considered more difficult to obtain than the cards of any other series in the set. Within this last series there are 43 cards that were printed in lesser quantities than the other cards in that series; these shorter-printed cards are marked by SP in the checklist below. The only featured subset within this set is League Leaders (215-226). Noteworthy rookie cards in the set include Jim Palmer (126), Ferguson Jenkins (254), and Don Sutton (288). Palmer is described in the bio (on his card back) as a left-hander.

	NRMT	VG-E	GOOD
COMPLETE SET (598)	4400.	2000.	550.00
COMMON PLAYER (1-109)	1.50	.65	.19
COMMON PLAYER (110-196)	2.00	.90	.25

	NRMT	VG-E	GOOD
COMMON PLAYER (197-283)	2.50	1.15	.30
COMMON PLAYER (284-370)	3.00	1.35	.40
COMMON PLAYER (371-446)	4.50	2.00	.55
COMMON PLAYER (447-522)	7.50	3.40	.95
COMMON PLAYER (523-598)	15.00	6.75	1.90

			NRMT	VG-E	GOOD
☐ 1	Willie Mays		150.00	45.00	15.00
☐ 2	Ted Abernathy		1.50	.65	.19
☐ 3	Sam Mele MG		1.50	.65	.19
☐ 4	Ray Culp		1.50	.65	.19
☐ 5	Jim Fregosi		2.00	.90	.25
☐ 6	Chuck Schilling		1.50	.65	.19
☐ 7	Tracy Stallard		1.50	.65	.19
☐ 8	Floyd Robinson		1.50	.65	.19
☐ 9	Clete Boyer		2.00	.90	.25
☐ 10	Tony Cloninger		1.50	.65	.19
☐ 11	Senators Rookies		1.50	.65	.19
	Brant Alyea				
	Pete Craig				
☐ 12	John Tsitouris		1.50	.65	.19
☐ 13	Lou Johnson		2.00	.90	.25
☐ 14	Norm Siebern		1.50	.65	.19
☐ 15	Vern Law		2.00	.90	.25
☐ 16	Larry Brown		1.50	.65	.19
☐ 17	John Stephenson		1.50	.65	.19
☐ 18	Roland Sheldon		1.50	.65	.19
☐ 19	San Francisco Giants		3.00	1.35	.40
	Team Card				
☐ 20	Willie Horton		2.00	.90	.25
☐ 21	Don Nottebart		1.50	.65	.19
☐ 22	Joe Nossek		1.50	.65	.19
☐ 23	Jack Sanford		1.50	.65	.19
☐ 24	Don Kessinger		4.00	1.80	.50
☐ 25	Pete Ward		1.50	.65	.19
☐ 26	Ray Sadecki		1.50	.65	.19
☐ 27	Orioles Rookies		1.50	.65	.19
	Darold Knowles				
	Andy Etchebarren				
☐ 28	Phil Niekro		20.00	9.00	2.50
☐ 29	Mike Brumley		1.50	.65	.19
☐ 30	Pete Rose DP		50.00	23.00	6.25
☐ 31	Jack Cullen		1.50	.65	.19
☐ 32	Adolfo Phillips		1.50	.65	.19
☐ 33	Jim Pagliaroni		1.50	.65	.19
☐ 34	Checklist 1		8.00	1.20	.40
☐ 35	Ron Swoboda		2.50	1.15	.30
☐ 36	Jim Hunter UER		30.00	13.50	3.80
	(Stats say 1963 and				
	1964, should be				
	1963 and 1964)				
☐ 37	Billy Herman MG		2.00	.90	.25
☐ 38	Ron Nischwitz		1.50	.65	.19
☐ 39	Ken Henderson		1.50	.65	.19
☐ 40	Jim Grant		1.50	.65	.19
☐ 41	Don LeJohn		1.50	.65	.19
☐ 42	Aubrey Gatewood		1.50	.65	.19
☐ 43A	Don Landrum		2.00	.90	.25

(Dark button on pants showing)
- [ ] 43B Don Landrum ....2.00 .90 .25
(Button on pants partially airbrushed)
- [ ] 43C Don Landrum ....2.00 .90 .25
(Button on pants not showing)
- [ ] 44 Indians Rookies ....1.50 .65 .19
  Bill Davis
  Tom Kelley
- [ ] 45 Jim Gentile...................2.00 .90 .25
- [ ] 46 Howie Koplitz ....1.50 .65 .19
- [ ] 47 J.C. Martin ....1.50 .65 .19
- [ ] 48 Paul Blair ....2.00 .90 .25
- [ ] 49 Woody Woodward ....2.00 .90 .25
- [ ] 50 Mickey Mantle DP 200.00 90.00 25.00
- [ ] 51 Gordon Richardson......1.50 .65 .19
- [ ] 52 Power Plus ....2.00 .90 .25
  Wes Covington
  Johnny Callison
- [ ] 53 Bob Duliba ....1.50 .65 .19
- [ ] 54 Jose Pagan ....1.50 .65 .19
- [ ] 55 Ken Harrelson ....2.00 .90 .25
- [ ] 56 Sandy Valdespino ....1.50 .65 .19
- [ ] 57 Jim Lefebvre ....2.00 .90 .25
- [ ] 58 Dave Wickersham.........1.50 .65 .19
- [ ] 59 Reds Team...................3.00 1.35 .40
- [ ] 60 Curt Flood ....2.00 .90 .25
- [ ] 61 Bob Bolin ....1.50 .65 .19
- [ ] 62A Merritt Ranew...............1.50 .65 .19
  (With sold line)
- [ ] 62B Merritt Ranew.............32.00 14.50 4.00
  (Without sold line)
- [ ] 63 Jim Stewart...................1.50 .65 .19
- [ ] 64 Bob Bruce ....1.50 .65 .19
- [ ] 65 Leon Wagner ....1.50 .65 .19
- [ ] 66 Al Weis ....1.50 .65 .19
- [ ] 67 Mets Rookies.................2.00 .90 .25
  Cleon Jones
  Dick Selma
- [ ] 68 Hal Reniff ....1.50 .65 .19
- [ ] 69 Ken Hamlin ....1.50 .65 .19
- [ ] 70 Carl Yastrzemski..........40.00 18.00 5.00
- [ ] 71 Frank Carpin ....1.50 .65 .19
- [ ] 72 Tony Perez...................35.00 16.00 4.40
- [ ] 73 Jerry Zimmerman ....1.50 .65 .19
- [ ] 74 Don Mossi ....2.00 .90 .25
- [ ] 75 Tommy Davis ....2.00 .90 .25
- [ ] 76 Red Schoendienst MG ..4.00 1.80 .50
- [ ] 77 John Orsino ....1.50 .65 .19
- [ ] 78 Frank Linzy ....1.50 .65 .19
- [ ] 79 Joe Pepitone ....2.00 .90 .25
- [ ] 80 Richie Allen ....4.50 2.00 .55
- [ ] 81 Ray Oyler ....1.50 .65 .19
- [ ] 82 Bob Hendley..................1.50 .65 .19
- [ ] 83 Albie Pearson................2.00 .90 .25

- [ ] 84 Braves Rookies.............1.50 .65 .19
  Jim Beauchamp
  Dick Kelley
- [ ] 85 Eddie Fisher ....1.50 .65 .19
- [ ] 86 John Bateman ....1.50 .65 .19
- [ ] 87 Dan Napoleon ....1.50 .65 .19
- [ ] 88 Fred Whitfield ....1.50 .65 .19
- [ ] 89 Ted Davidson.................1.50 .65 .19
- [ ] 90 Luis Aparicio ....7.00 3.10 .85
- [ ] 91A Bob Uecker TR............16.00 7.25 2.00
- [ ] 91B Bob Uecker NTR..........55.00 25.00 7.00
- [ ] 92 Yankees Team...............4.00 1.80 .50
- [ ] 93 Jim Lonborg ....3.00 1.35 .40
- [ ] 94 Matty Alou ....2.00 .90 .25
- [ ] 95 Pete Richert ....1.50 .65 .19
- [ ] 96 Felipe Alou ....2.00 .90 .25
- [ ] 97 Jim Merritt......................1.50 .65 .19
- [ ] 98 Don Demeter...................1.50 .65 .19
- [ ] 99 Buc Belters ....4.00 1.80 .50
  Willie Stargell
  Donn Clendenon
- [ ] 100 Sandy Koufax...........110.00 50.00 14.00
- [ ] 101A Checklist 2...............16.00 2.40 .80
  (115 W. Spahn) ERR
- [ ] 101B Checklist 2...............10.00 1.50 .50
  (115 Bill Henry) COR
- [ ] 102 Ed Kirkpatrick..............1.50 .65 .19
- [ ] 103A Dick Groat TR ....2.00 .90 .25
- [ ] 103B Dick Groat NTR.........32.00 14.50 4.00
- [ ] 104A Alex Johnson TR ....2.00 .90 .25
- [ ] 104B Alex Johnson NTR....32.00 14.50 4.00
- [ ] 105 Milt Pappas ....2.00 .90 .25
- [ ] 106 Rusty Staub ....3.50 1.55 .45
- [ ] 107 A's Rookies...................1.50 .65 .19
  Larry Stahl
  Ron Tompkins
- [ ] 108 Bobby Klaus..................1.50 .65 .19
- [ ] 109 Ralph Terry ....2.00 .90 .25
- [ ] 110 Ernie Banks................25.00 11.50 3.10
- [ ] 111 Gary Peters ....2.00 .90 .25
- [ ] 112 Manny Mota..................2.50 1.15 .30
- [ ] 113 Hank Aguirre ....2.00 .90 .25
- [ ] 114 Jim Gosger ....2.00 .90 .25
- [ ] 115 Bill Henry ....2.00 .90 .25
- [ ] 116 Walt Alston MG.............4.00 1.80 .50
- [ ] 117 Jake Gibbs ....2.50 1.15 .30
- [ ] 118 Mike McCormick...........2.50 1.15 .30
- [ ] 119 Art Shamsky ....2.00 .90 .25
- [ ] 120 Harmon Killebrew.......20.00 9.00 2.50
- [ ] 121 Ray Herbert..................2.00 .90 .25
- [ ] 122 Joe Gaines ....2.00 .90 .25
- [ ] 123 Pirates Rookies.............2.00 .90 .25
  Frank Bork
  Jerry May
- [ ] 124 Tug McGraw..................5.00 2.30 .60
- [ ] 125 Lou Brock 25.00 11.50 3.10
- [ ] 126 Jim Palmer UER.........225.00 100.00 28.00

(Described as a
lefthander on
card back)

☐ 127 Ken Berry	2.00	.90	.25
☐ 128 Jim Landis	2.00	.90	.25
☐ 129 Jack Kralick	2.00	.90	.25
☐ 130 Joe Torre	4.00	1.80	.50
☐ 131 Angels Team	4.00	1.80	.50
☐ 132 Orlando Cepeda	6.00	2.70	.75
☐ 133 Don McMahon	2.00	.90	.25
☐ 134 Wes Parker	2.50	1.15	.30
☐ 135 Dave Morehead	2.00	.90	.25
☐ 136 Woody Held	2.00	.90	.25
☐ 137 Pat Corrales	2.50	1.15	.30
☐ 138 Roger Repoz	2.00	.90	.25
☐ 139 Cubs Rookies	2.00	.90	.25

Byron Browne
Don Young

☐ 140 Jim Maloney	2.50	1.15	.30
☐ 141 Tom McCraw	2.00	.90	.25
☐ 142 Don Dennis	2.00	.90	.25
☐ 143 Jose Tartabull	2.50	1.15	.30
☐ 144 Don Schwall	2.00	.90	.25
☐ 145 Bill Freehan	3.00	1.35	.40
☐ 146 George Altman	2.00	.90	.25
☐ 147 Lum Harris MG	2.00	.90	.25
☐ 148 Bob Johnson	2.00	.90	.25
☐ 149 Dick Nen	2.00	.90	.25
☐ 150 Rocky Colavito	5.00	2.30	.60
☐ 151 Gary Wagner	2.00	.90	.25
☐ 152 Frank Malzone	2.50	1.15	.30
☐ 153 Rico Carty	2.50	1.15	.30
☐ 154 Chuck Hiller	2.00	.90	.25
☐ 155 Marcelino Lopez	2.00	.90	.25
☐ 156 Double Play Combo	2.00	.90	.25

Dick Schofield
Hal Lanier

☐ 157 Rene Lachemann	2.50	1.15	.30
☐ 158 Jim Brewer	2.00	.90	.25
☐ 159 Chico Ruiz	2.00	.90	.25
☐ 160 Whitey Ford	25.00	11.50	3.10
☐ 161 Jerry Lumpe	2.00	.90	.25
☐ 162 Lee Maye	2.00	.90	.25
☐ 163 Tito Francona	2.00	.90	.25
☐ 164 White Sox Rookies	2.50	1.15	.30

Tommie Agee
Marv Staehle

☐ 165 Don Lock	2.00	.90	.25
☐ 166 Chris Krug	2.00	.90	.25
☐ 167 Boog Powell	4.50	2.00	.55
☐ 168 Dan Osinski	2.00	.90	.25
☐ 169 Duke Sims	2.00	.90	.25
☐ 170 Cookie Rojas	2.50	1.15	.30
☐ 171 Nick Willhite	2.00	.90	.25
☐ 172 Mets Team	4.00	1.80	.50
☐ 173 Al Spangler	2.00	.90	.25
☐ 174 Ron Taylor	2.00	.90	.25
☐ 175 Bert Campaneris	2.50	1.15	.30
☐ 176 Jim Davenport	2.00	.90	.25
☐ 177 Hector Lopez	2.00	.90	.25
☐ 178 Bob Tillman	2.00	.90	.25
☐ 179 Cards Rookies	2.50	1.15	.30

Dennis Aust
Bob Tolan

☐ 180 Vada Pinson	2.50	1.15	.30
☐ 181 Al Worthington	2.00	.90	.25
☐ 182 Jerry Lynch	2.00	.90	.25
☐ 183A Checklist 3	8.00	1.20	.40

(Large print
on front)

☐ 183B Checklist 3	8.00	1.20	.40

(Small print
on front)

☐ 184 Denis Menke	2.00	.90	.25
☐ 185 Bob Buhl	2.50	1.15	.30
☐ 186 Ruben Amaro	2.00	.90	.25
☐ 187 Chuck Dressen MG	2.50	1.15	.30
☐ 188 Al Luplow	2.00	.90	.25
☐ 189 John Roseboro	2.50	1.15	.30
☐ 190 Jimmie Hall	2.00	.90	.25
☐ 191 Darrell Sutherland	2.00	.90	.25
☐ 192 Vic Power	2.50	1.15	.30
☐ 193 Dave McNally	2.50	1.15	.30
☐ 194 Senators Team	4.00	1.80	.50
☐ 195 Joe Morgan	45.00	20.00	5.75
☐ 196 Don Pavletich	2.00	.90	.25
☐ 197 Sonny Siebert	2.50	1.15	.30
☐ 198 Mickey Stanley	3.50	1.55	.45
☐ 199 Chisox Clubbers	3.00	1.35	.40

Bill Skowron
Johnny Romano
Floyd Robinson

☐ 200 Eddie Mathews	12.50	5.75	1.55
☐ 201 Jim Dickson	2.50	1.15	.30
☐ 202 Clay Dalrymple	2.50	1.15	.30
☐ 203 Jose Santiago	2.50	1.15	.30
☐ 204 Cubs Team	4.50	2.00	.55
☐ 205 Tom Tresh	3.00	1.35	.40
☐ 206 Al Jackson	2.50	1.15	.30
☐ 207 Frank Quilici	2.50	1.15	.30
☐ 208 Bob Miller	2.50	1.15	.30
☐ 209 Tigers Rookies	3.50	1.55	.45

Fritz Fisher
John Hiller

☐ 210 Bill Mazeroski	3.75	1.70	.45
☐ 211 Frank Kreutzer	2.50	1.15	.30
☐ 212 Ed Kranepool	3.00	1.35	.40
☐ 213 Fred Newman	2.50	1.15	.30
☐ 214 Tommy Harper	3.00	1.35	.40
☐ 215 NL Batting Leaders	25.00	11.50	3.10

Bob Clemente
Hank Aaron
Willie Mays

☐ 216 AL Batting Leaders	5.50	2.50	.70

Tony Oliva
Carl Yastrzemski
Vic Davalillo
- [ ] 217 NL Home Run Leaders 15.00 6.75 1.90
Willie Mays
Willie McCovey
Billy Williams
- [ ] 218 AL Home Run Leaders .3.75 1.70 .45
Tony Conigliaro
Norm Cash
Willie Horton
- [ ] 219 NL RBI Leaders............7.00 3.10 .85
Deron Johnson
Frank Robinson
Willie Mays
- [ ] 220 AL RBI Leaders...........3.75 1.70 .45
Rocky Colavito
Willie Horton
Tony Oliva
- [ ] 221 NL ERA Leaders...........7.00 3.10 .85
Sandy Koufax
Juan Marichal
Vern Law
- [ ] 222 AL ERA Leaders...........3.75 1.70 .45
Sam McDowell
Eddie Fisher
Sonny Siebert
- [ ] 223 NL Pitching Leaders.....7.00 3.10 .85
Sandy Koufax
Tony Cloninger
Don Drysdale
- [ ] 224 AL Pitching Leaders .3.75 1.70 .45
Jim Grant
Mel Stottlemyre
Jim Kaat
- [ ] 225 NL Strikeout Leaders ...7.00 3.10 .85
Sandy Koufax
Bob Veale
Bob Gibson
- [ ] 226 AL Strikeout Leaders ...3.75 1.70 .45
Sam McDowell
Mickey Lolich
Dennis McLain
Sonny Siebert
- [ ] 227 Russ Nixon ....2.50 1.15 .30
- [ ] 228 Larry Dierker ....2.50 1.15 .30
- [ ] 229 Hank Bauer MG ....3.00 1.35 .40
- [ ] 230 Johnny Callison ....3.00 1.35 .40
- [ ] 231 Floyd Weaver ....2.50 1.15 .30
- [ ] 232 Glenn Beckert ....3.00 1.35 .40
- [ ] 233 Dom Zanni ....2.50 1.15 .30
- [ ] 234 Yankees Rookies..........7.00 3.10 .85
Rich Beck
Roy White
- [ ] 235 Don Cardwell ....2.50 1.15 .30
- [ ] 236 Mike Hershberger ......2.50 1.15 .30
- [ ] 237 Billy O'Dell ....2.50 1.15 .30

- [ ] 238 Dodgers Team ....4.50 2.00 .55
- [ ] 239 Orlando Pena ....2.50 1.15 .30
- [ ] 240 Earl Battey.................2.50 1.15 .30
- [ ] 241 Dennis Ribant.............2.50 1.15 .30
- [ ] 242 Jesus Alou.................2.50 1.15 .30
- [ ] 243 Nelson Briles.............3.00 1.35 .40
- [ ] 244 Astros Rookies............2.50 1.15 .30
Chuck Harrison
Sonny Jackson
- [ ] 245 John Buzhardt............2.50 1.15 .30
- [ ] 246 Ed Bailey..................2.50 1.15 .30
- [ ] 247 Carl Warwick..............2.50 1.15 .30
- [ ] 248 Pete Mikkelsen..........2.50 1.15 .30
- [ ] 249 Bill Rigney MG ....2.50 1.15 .30
- [ ] 250 Sammy Ellis ....2.50 1.15 .30
- [ ] 251 Ed Brinkman ....2.50 1.15 .30
- [ ] 252 Denny Lemaster ....2.50 1.15 .30
- [ ] 253 Don Wert ....2.50 1.15 .30
- [ ] 254 Phillies Rookies 135.00 60.00 17.00
Ferguson Jenkins
Bill Sorrell
- [ ] 255 Willie Stargell...........20.00 9.00 2.50
- [ ] 256 Lew Krausse..............2.50 1.15 .30
- [ ] 257 Jeff Torborg...............3.00 1.35 .40
- [ ] 258 Dave Giusti................2.50 1.15 .30
- [ ] 259 Boston Red Sox..........4.50 2.00 .55
Team Card
- [ ] 260 Bob Shaw ....2.50 1.15 .30
- [ ] 261 Ron Hansen ....2.50 1.15 .30
- [ ] 262 Jack Hamilton ....2.50 1.15 .30
- [ ] 263 Tom Egan ....2.50 1.15 .30
- [ ] 264 Twins Rookies.............2.50 1.15 .30
Andy Kosco
Ted Uhlaender
- [ ] 265 Stu Miller...................3.00 1.35 .40
- [ ] 266 Pedro Gonzalez UER ....2.50 1.15 .30
(Misspelled Gonzales
on card back)
- [ ] 267 Joe Sparma................2.50 1.15 .30
- [ ] 268 John Blanchard............2.50 1.15 .30
- [ ] 269 Don Heffner MG...........2.50 1.15 .30
- [ ] 270 Claude Osteen.............3.00 1.35 .40
- [ ] 271 Hal Lanier ....2.50 1.15 .30
- [ ] 272 Jack Baldschun............2.50 1.15 .30
- [ ] 273 Astro Aces ....3.00 1.35 .40
Bob Aspromonte
Rusty Staub
- [ ] 274 Buster Narum ....2.50 1.15 .30
- [ ] 275 Tim McCarver...............5.00 2.30 .60
- [ ] 276 Jim Bouton ....3.50 1.55 .45
- [ ] 277 George Thomas ....2.50 1.15 .30
- [ ] 278 Cal Koonce..................2.50 1.15 .30
- [ ] 279 Checklist 4 ....8.00 1.20 .40
- [ ] 280 Bobby Knoop ....2.50 1.15 .30
- [ ] 281 Bruce Howard ....2.50 1.15 .30
- [ ] 282 Johnny Lewis...............2.50 1.15 .30
- [ ] 283 Jim Perry ....3.00 1.35 .40

☐ 284	Bobby Wine	3.50	1.55	.45
☐ 285	Luis Tiant	4.50	2.00	.55
☐ 286	Gary Geiger	3.00	1.35	.40
☐ 287	Jack Aker	3.00	1.35	.40
☐ 288	Dodgers Rookies	150.00	70.00	19.00
	Bill Singer			
	Don Sutton			
☐ 289	Larry Sherry	3.50	1.55	.45
☐ 290	Ron Santo	4.50	2.00	.55
☐ 291	Moe Drabowsky	3.50	1.55	.45
☐ 292	Jim Coker	3.00	1.35	.40
☐ 293	Mike Shannon	3.50	1.55	.45
☐ 294	Steve Ridzik	3.00	1.35	.40
☐ 295	Jim Ray Hart	3.50	1.55	.45
☐ 296	Johnny Keane MG	3.00	1.35	.40
☐ 297	Jim Owens	3.00	1.35	.40
☐ 298	Rico Petrocelli	4.00	1.80	.50
☐ 299	Lou Burdette	3.50	1.55	.45
☐ 300	Bob Clemente	100.00	45.00	12.50
☐ 301	Greg Bollo	3.00	1.35	.40
☐ 302	Ernie Bowman	3.00	1.35	.40
☐ 303	Cleveland Indians	5.00	2.30	.60
	Team Card			
☐ 304	John Herrnstein	3.00	1.35	.40
☐ 305	Camilo Pascual	3.50	1.55	.45
☐ 306	Ty Cline	3.00	1.35	.40
☐ 307	Clay Carroll	3.50	1.55	.45
☐ 308	Tom Haller	3.50	1.55	.45
☐ 309	Diego Segui	3.00	1.35	.40
☐ 310	Frank Robinson	40.00	18.00	5.00
☐ 311	Reds Rookies	3.50	1.55	.45
	Tommy Helms			
	Dick Simpson			
☐ 312	Bob Saverine	3.00	1.35	.40
☐ 313	Chris Zachary	3.00	1.35	.40
☐ 314	Hector Valle	3.00	1.35	.40
☐ 315	Norm Cash	4.00	1.80	.50
☐ 316	Jack Fisher	3.00	1.35	.40
☐ 317	Dalton Jones	3.00	1.35	.40
☐ 318	Harry Walker MG	3.00	1.35	.40
☐ 319	Gene Freese	3.00	1.35	.40
☐ 320	Bob Gibson	30.00	13.50	3.80
☐ 321	Rick Reichardt	3.00	1.35	.40
☐ 322	Bill Faul	3.00	1.35	.40
☐ 323	Ray Barker	3.00	1.35	.40
☐ 324	John Boozer	3.00	1.35	.40
☐ 325	Vic Davalillo	3.00	1.35	.40
☐ 326	Braves Team	5.00	2.30	.60
☐ 327	Bernie Allen	3.00	1.35	.40
☐ 328	Jerry Grote	3.00	1.35	.40
☐ 329	Pete Charton	3.00	1.35	.40
☐ 330	Ron Fairly	3.50	1.55	.45
☐ 331	Ron Herbel	3.00	1.35	.40
☐ 332	Bill Bryan	3.00	1.35	.40
☐ 333	Senators Rookies	3.50	1.55	.45
	Joe Coleman			
	Jim French			
☐ 334	Marty Keough	3.00	1.35	.40
☐ 335	Juan Pizarro	3.00	1.35	.40
☐ 336	Gene Alley	3.50	1.55	.45
☐ 337	Fred Gladding	3.00	1.35	.40
☐ 338	Dal Maxvill	3.00	1.35	.40
☐ 339	Del Crandall	3.50	1.55	.45
☐ 340	Dean Chance	3.50	1.55	.45
☐ 341	Wes Westrum MG	3.50	1.55	.45
☐ 342	Bob Humphreys	3.00	1.35	.40
☐ 343	Joe Christopher	3.00	1.35	.40
☐ 344	Steve Blass	3.50	1.55	.45
☐ 345	Bob Allison	3.50	1.55	.45
☐ 346	Mike DeLaHoz	3.00	1.35	.40
☐ 347	Phil Regan	3.50	1.55	.45
☐ 348	Orioles Team	5.00	2.30	.60
☐ 349	Cap Peterson	3.00	1.35	.40
☐ 350	Mel Stottlemyre	4.50	2.00	.55
☐ 351	Fred Valentine	3.00	1.35	.40
☐ 352	Bob Aspromonte	3.00	1.35	.40
☐ 353	Al McBean	3.00	1.35	.40
☐ 354	Smoky Burgess	3.50	1.55	.45
☐ 355	Wade Blasingame	3.00	1.35	.40
☐ 356	Red Sox Rookies	3.00	1.35	.40
	Owen Johnson			
	Ken Sanders			
☐ 357	Gerry Arrigo	3.00	1.35	.40
☐ 358	Charlie Smith	3.00	1.35	.40
☐ 359	Johnny Briggs	3.00	1.35	.40
☐ 360	Ron Hunt	3.00	1.35	.40
☐ 361	Tom Satriano	3.00	1.35	.40
☐ 362	Gates Brown	3.50	1.55	.45
☐ 363	Checklist 5	10.00	1.50	.50
☐ 364	Nate Oliver	3.00	1.35	.40
☐ 365	Roger Maris	60.00	27.00	7.50
☐ 366	Wayne Causey	3.00	1.35	.40
☐ 367	Mel Nelson	3.00	1.35	.40
☐ 368	Charlie Lau	3.50	1.55	.45
☐ 369	Jim King	3.00	1.35	.40
☐ 370	Chico Cardenas	3.00	1.35	.40
☐ 371	Lee Stange	4.50	2.00	.55
☐ 372	Harvey Kuenn	5.00	2.30	.60
☐ 373	Giants Rookies	5.00	2.30	.60
	Jack Hiatt			
	Dick Estelle			
☐ 374	Bob Locker	4.50	2.00	.55
☐ 375	Donn Clendenon	5.00	2.30	.60
☐ 376	Paul Schaal	4.50	2.00	.55
☐ 377	Turk Farrell	4.50	2.00	.55
☐ 378	Dick Tracewski	4.50	2.00	.55
☐ 379	Cardinal Team	8.00	3.60	1.00
☐ 380	Tony Conigliaro	8.50	3.80	1.05
☐ 381	Hank Fischer	4.50	2.00	.55
☐ 382	Phil Roof	4.50	2.00	.55
☐ 383	Jackie Brandt	4.50	2.00	.55
☐ 384	Al Downing	5.00	2.30	.60
☐ 385	Ken Boyer	5.50	2.50	.70
☐ 386	Gil Hodges MG	7.00	3.10	.85

☐ 387	Howie Reed	4.50	2.00	.55
☐ 388	Don Mincher	4.50	2.00	.55
☐ 389	Jim O'Toole	5.00	2.30	.60
☐ 390	Brooks Robinson	35.00	16.00	4.40
☐ 391	Chuck Hinton	4.50	2.00	.55
☐ 392	Cubs Rookies	5.00	2.30	.60
	Bill Hands			
	Randy Hundley			
☐ 393	George Brunet	4.50	2.00	.55
☐ 394	Ron Brand	4.50	2.00	.55
☐ 395	Len Gabrielson	4.50	2.00	.55
☐ 396	Jerry Stephenson	4.50	2.00	.55
☐ 397	Bill White	5.50	2.50	.70
☐ 398	Danny Cater	4.50	2.00	.55
☐ 399	Ray Washburn	4.50	2.00	.55
☐ 400	Zoilo Versalles	4.50	2.00	.55
☐ 401	Ken McMullen	4.50	2.00	.55
☐ 402	Jim Hickman	4.50	2.00	.55
☐ 403	Fred Talbot	4.50	2.00	.55
☐ 404	Pittsburgh Pirates	8.00	3.60	1.00
	Team Card			
☐ 405	Elston Howard	6.00	2.70	.75
☐ 406	Joey Jay	4.50	2.00	.55
☐ 407	John Kennedy	4.50	2.00	.55
☐ 408	Lee Thomas	5.00	2.30	.60
☐ 409	Billy Hoeft	4.50	2.00	.55
☐ 410	Al Kaline	33.00	15.00	4.10
☐ 411	Gene Mauch MG	5.00	2.30	.60
☐ 412	Sam Bowens	4.50	2.00	.55
☐ 413	Johnny Romano	4.50	2.00	.55
☐ 414	Dan Coombs	4.50	2.00	.55
☐ 415	Max Alvis	4.50	2.00	.55
☐ 416	Phil Ortega	4.50	2.00	.55
☐ 417	Angels Rookies	5.00	2.30	.60
	Jim McGlothlin			
	Ed Sukla			
☐ 418	Phil Gagliano	4.50	2.00	.55
☐ 419	Mike Ryan	4.50	2.00	.55
☐ 420	Juan Marichal	12.50	5.75	1.55
☐ 421	Roy McMillan	5.00	2.30	.60
☐ 422	Ed Charles	4.50	2.00	.55
☐ 423	Ernie Broglio	4.50	2.00	.55
☐ 424	Reds Rookies	7.50	3.40	.95
	Lee May			
	Darrell Osteen			
☐ 425	Bob Veale	5.00	2.30	.60
☐ 426	White Sox Team	8.00	3.60	1.00
☐ 427	John Miller	4.50	2.00	.55
☐ 428	Sandy Alomar	5.00	2.30	.60
☐ 429	Bill Monbouquette	4.50	2.00	.55
☐ 430	Don Drysdale	20.00	9.00	2.50
☐ 431	Walt Bond	4.50	2.00	.55
☐ 432	Bob Heffner	4.50	2.00	.55
☐ 433	Alvin Dark MG	5.00	2.30	.60
☐ 434	Willie Kirkland	4.50	2.00	.55
☐ 435	Jim Bunning	7.50	3.40	.95
☐ 436	Julian Javier	5.00	2.30	.60
☐ 437	Al Stanek	4.50	2.00	.55
☐ 438	Willie Smith	4.50	2.00	.55
☐ 439	Pedro Ramos	4.50	2.00	.55
☐ 440	Deron Johnson	5.00	2.30	.60
☐ 441	Tommie Sisk	4.50	2.00	.55
☐ 442	Orioles Rookies	4.50	2.00	.55
	Ed Barnowski			
	Eddie Watt			
☐ 443	Bill Wakefield	4.50	2.00	.55
☐ 444	Checklist 6	10.00	1.50	.50
☐ 445	Jim Kaat	7.50	3.40	.95
☐ 446	Mack Jones	4.50	2.00	.55
☐ 447	Dick Ellsworth UER	9.00	4.00	1.15
	(Photo actually			
	Ken Hubbs)			
☐ 448	Eddie Stanky MG	8.50	3.80	1.05
☐ 449	Joe Moeller	7.50	3.40	.95
☐ 450	Tony Oliva	11.00	4.90	1.40
☐ 451	Barry Latman	7.50	3.40	.95
☐ 452	Joe Azcue	7.50	3.40	.95
☐ 453	Ron Kline	7.50	3.40	.95
☐ 454	Jerry Buchek	7.50	3.40	.95
☐ 455	Mickey Lolich	10.00	4.50	1.25
☐ 456	Red Sox Rookies	7.50	3.40	.95
	Darrell Brandon			
	Joe Foy			
☐ 457	Joe Gibbon	7.50	3.40	.95
☐ 458	Manny Jiminez	7.50	3.40	.95
☐ 459	Bill McCool	7.50	3.40	.95
☐ 460	Curt Blefary	7.50	3.40	.95
☐ 461	Roy Face	8.50	3.80	1.05
☐ 462	Bob Rodgers	8.50	3.80	1.05
☐ 463	Philadelphia Phillies	12.00	5.50	1.50
	Team Card			
☐ 464	Larry Bearnarth	7.50	3.40	.95
☐ 465	Don Buford	8.50	3.80	1.05
☐ 466	Ken Johnson	7.50	3.40	.95
☐ 467	Vic Roznovsky	7.50	3.40	.95
☐ 468	Johnny Podres	8.50	3.80	1.05
☐ 469	Yankees Rookies	27.00	12.00	3.40
	Bobby Murcer			
	Dooley Womack			
☐ 470	Sam McDowell	8.50	3.80	1.05
☐ 471	Bob Skinner	8.50	3.80	1.05
☐ 472	Terry Fox	7.50	3.40	.95
☐ 473	Rich Rollins	7.50	3.40	.95
☐ 474	Dick Schofield	7.50	3.40	.95
☐ 475	Dick Radatz	8.50	3.80	1.05
☐ 476	Bobby Bragan MG	7.50	3.40	.95
☐ 477	Steve Barber	7.50	3.40	.95
☐ 478	Tony Gonzalez	7.50	3.40	.95
☐ 479	Jim Hannan	7.50	3.40	.95
☐ 480	Dick Stuart	8.50	3.80	1.05
☐ 481	Bob Lee	7.50	3.40	.95
☐ 482	Cubs Rookies	7.50	3.40	.95
	John Boccabella			
	Dave Dowling			

☐ 483	Joe Nuxhall	8.50	3.80	1.05
☐ 484	Wes Covington	7.50	3.40	.95
☐ 485	Bob Bailey	8.00	3.60	1.00
☐ 486	Tommy John	15.00	6.75	1.90
☐ 487	Al Ferrara	7.50	3.40	.95
☐ 488	George Banks	7.50	3.40	.95
☐ 489	Curt Simmons	8.50	3.80	1.05
☐ 490	Bobby Richardson	12.50	5.75	1.55
☐ 491	Dennis Bennett	7.50	3.40	.95
☐ 492	Athletics Team	12.00	5.50	1.50
☐ 493	Johnny Klippstein	7.50	3.40	.95
☐ 494	Gordy Coleman	8.50	3.80	1.05
☐ 495	Dick McAuliffe	8.50	3.80	1.05
☐ 496	Lindy McDaniel	8.50	3.80	1.05
☐ 497	Chris Cannizzaro	7.50	3.40	.95
☐ 498	Pirates Rookies	8.50	3.80	1.05
	Luke Walker			
	Woody Fryman			
☐ 499	Wally Bunker	7.50	3.40	.95
☐ 500	Hank Aaron	125.00	57.50	15.50
☐ 501	John O'Donoghue	7.50	3.40	.95
☐ 502	Lenny Green UER	7.50	3.40	.95
	(Born: aJn. 6, 1933)			
☐ 503	Steve Hamilton	7.50	3.40	.95
☐ 504	Grady Hatton MG	7.50	3.40	.95
☐ 505	Jose Cardenal	8.50	3.80	1.05
☐ 506	Bo Belinsky	8.50	3.80	1.05
☐ 507	Johnny Edwards	7.50	3.40	.95
☐ 508	Steve Hargan	9.00	4.00	1.15
☐ 509	Jake Wood	7.50	3.40	.95
☐ 510	Hoyt Wilhelm	14.00	6.25	1.75
☐ 511	Giants Rookies	9.00	4.00	1.15
	Bob Barton			
	Tito Fuentes			
☐ 512	Dick Stigman	7.50	3.40	.95
☐ 513	Camilo Carreon	7.50	3.40	.95
☐ 514	Hal Woodeshick	7.50	3.40	.95
☐ 515	Frank Howard	10.00	4.50	1.25
☐ 516	Eddie Bressoud	7.50	3.40	.95
☐ 517A	Checklist 7	16.00	2.40	.80
	529 White Sox Rookies			
	544 Cardinals Rookies			
☐ 517B	Checklist 7	16.00	2.40	.80
	529 W. Sox Rookies			
	544 Cards Rookies			
☐ 518	Braves Rookies	7.50	3.40	.95
	Herb Hippauf			
	Arnie Umbach			
☐ 519	Bob Friend	9.00	4.00	1.15
☐ 520	Jim Wynn	8.50	3.80	1.05
☐ 521	John Wyatt	7.50	3.40	.95
☐ 522	Phil Linz	8.50	3.80	1.05
☐ 523	Bob Sadowski	17.50	8.00	2.20
☐ 524	Giants Rookies SP	30.00	13.50	3.80
	Ollie Brown			
	Don Mason			
☐ 525	Gary Bell SP	30.00	13.50	3.80
☐ 526	Twins Team SP	75.00	34.00	9.50
☐ 527	Julio Navarro	15.00	6.75	1.90
☐ 528	Jesse Gonder SP	30.00	13.50	3.80
☐ 529	White Sox Rookies	17.50	8.00	2.20
	Lee Elia			
	Dennis Higgins			
	Bill Voss			
☐ 530	Robin Roberts	50.00	23.00	6.25
☐ 531	Joe Cunningham	15.00	6.75	1.90
☐ 532	Aurelio Monteagudo SP	30.00	13.50	3.80
☐ 533	Jerry Adair SP	30.00	13.50	3.80
☐ 534	Mets Rookies	15.00	6.75	1.90
	Dave Eilers			
	Rob Gardner			
☐ 535	Willie Davis SP	50.00	23.00	6.25
☐ 536	Dick Egan	15.00	6.75	1.90
☐ 537	Herman Franks MG	15.00	6.75	1.90
☐ 538	Bob Allen SP	30.00	13.50	3.80
☐ 539	Astros Rookies	15.00	6.75	1.90
	Bill Heath			
	Carroll Sembera			
☐ 540	Denny McLain SP	75.00	34.00	9.50
☐ 541	Gene Oliver SP	30.00	13.50	3.80
☐ 542	George Smith	15.00	6.75	1.90
☐ 543	Roger Craig SP	40.00	18.00	5.00
☐ 544	Cardinals Rookies SP	35.00	16.00	4.40
	Joe Hoerner			
	George Kernek			
	Jimy Williams UER			
	(Misspelled Jimmy			
	on card)			
☐ 545	Dick Green SP	30.00	13.50	3.80
☐ 546	Dwight Siebler	15.00	6.75	1.90
☐ 547	Horace Clarke SP	50.00	23.00	6.25
☐ 548	Gary Kroll SP	30.00	13.50	3.80
☐ 549	Senators Rookies	15.00	6.75	1.90
	Al Closter			
	Casey Cox			
☐ 550	Willie McCovey SP	125.00	57.50	15.50
☐ 551	Bob Purkey SP	30.00	13.50	3.80
☐ 552	Birdie Tebbetts	30.00	13.50	3.80
	MG SP			
☐ 553	Rookie Stars	15.00	6.75	1.90
	Pat Garrett			
	Jackie Warner			
☐ 554	Jim Northrup SP	30.00	13.50	3.80
☐ 555	Ron Perranoski SP	30.00	13.50	3.80
☐ 556	Mel Queen SP	30.00	13.50	3.80
☐ 557	Felix Mantilla SP	30.00	13.50	3.80
☐ 558	Red Sox Rookies	27.00	12.00	3.40
	Guido Grilli			
	Pete Magrini			
	George Scott			
☐ 559	Roberto Pena SP	30.00	13.50	3.80
☐ 560	Joel Horlen	15.00	6.75	1.90
☐ 561	ChooChoo Coleman SP	50.00	23.00	6.25
☐ 562	Russ Snyder	15.00	6.75	1.90

☐ 563	Twins Rookies	15.00	6.75	1.90
	Pete Cimino			
	Cesar Tovar			
☐ 564	Bob Chance SP	30.00	13.50	3.80
☐ 565	Jim Piersall SP	40.00	18.00	5.00
☐ 566	Mike Cuellar SP	35.00	16.00	4.40
☐ 567	Dick Howser SP	35.00	16.00	4.40
☐ 568	Athletics Rookies	17.50	8.00	2.20
	Paul Lindblad			
	Ron Stone			
☐ 569	Orlando McFarlane SP	30.00	13.50	3.80
☐ 570	Art Mahaffey SP	30.00	13.50	3.80
☐ 571	Dave Roberts SP	30.00	13.50	3.80
☐ 572	Bob Priddy	15.00	6.75	1.90
☐ 573	Derrell Griffith	15.00	6.75	1.90
☐ 574	Mets Rookies	15.00	6.75	1.90
	Bill Hepler			
	Bill Murphy			
☐ 575	Earl Wilson	17.50	8.00	2.20
☐ 576	Dave Nicholson SP	30.00	13.50	3.80
☐ 577	Jack Lamabe SP	30.00	13.50	3.80
☐ 578	Chi Chi Olivo SP	30.00	13.50	3.80
☐ 579	Orioles Rookies	18.00	8.00	2.30
	Frank Bertaina			
	Gene Brabender			
	Dave Johnson			
☐ 580	Billy Williams SP	100.00	45.00	12.50
☐ 581	Tony Martinez	15.00	6.75	1.90
☐ 582	Garry Roggenburk ...	15.00	6.75	1.90
☐ 583	Tigers Team SP	140.00	65.00	17.50
☐ 584	Yankees Rookies	15.00	6.75	1.90
	Frank Fernandez			
	Fritz Peterson			
☐ 585	Tony Taylor	15.00	6.75	1.90
☐ 586	Claude Raymond SP ..	30.00	13.50	3.80
☐ 587	Dick Bertell	15.00	6.75	1.90
☐ 588	Athletics Rookies	15.00	6.75	1.90
	Chuck Dobson			
	Ken Suarez			
☐ 589	Lou Klimchock SP	35.00	16.00	4.40
☐ 590	Bill Skowron SP	45.00	20.00	5.75
☐ 591	NL Rookies SP	50.00	23.00	6.25
	Bart Shirley			
	Grant Jackson			
☐ 592	Andre Rodgers	15.00	6.75	1.90
☐ 593	Doug Camilli SP	30.00	13.50	3.80
☐ 594	Chico Salmon	15.00	6.75	1.90
☐ 595	Larry Jackson	15.00	6.75	1.90
☐ 596	Astros Rookies SP ...	18.00	8.00	2.30
	Nate Colbert			
	Greg Sims			
☐ 597	John Sullivan	15.00	6.75	1.90
☐ 598	Gaylord Perry SP	300.00	135.00	38.00

1967 Topps

The cards in this 609-card set measure
2 1/2" by 3 1/2". The 1967 Topps series is
considered by some collectors to be one of
the company's finest accomplishments in
baseball card production. Excellent color
photographs are combined with easy-to-
read backs. Cards 458 to 533 are slightly
harder to find than numbers 1 to 457, and
the inevitable (difficult to find) high series
(534 to 609) exists. Each checklist card
features a small circular picture of a popular player included in that series. Printing
discrepancies resulted in some high series
cards being in shorter supply. The checklist below identifies (by DP) 22 double-
printed high numbers; of the 76 cards in
the last series, 54 cards were short printed
and the other 22 cards are much more
plentiful. Featured subsets within this set
include World Series cards (151-155) and
League Leaders (233-244). Although there
are several relatively expensive cards in
this popular set, the key cards in the set
are undoubtedly the Tom Seaver Rookie
Card (581) and the Rod Carew Rookie
Card (569). Although rarely seen, there
exists a salesman's sample panel of three
cards, that pictures Earl Battey, Manny
Mota, and Gene Brabender with ad information on the back about the "new" Topps
cards.

	NRMT	VG-E	GOOD
COMPLETE SET (609)	5250.	2400.	650.00
COMMON PLAYER (1-109) ...	1.50	.65	.19
COMMON PLAYER (110-196) ...	2.00	.90	.25
COMMON PLAYER (197-283) ...	2.50	1.15	.30
COMMON PLAYER (284-370) ...	3.00	1.35	.40

COMMON PLAYER (371-457)	4.00	1.80	.50
COMMON PLAYER (458-533)	7.00	3.10	.85
COMMON PLAYER (534-609)	18.00	8.00	2.30

☐ 1	The Champs DP	18.00	5.50	1.80
	Frank Robinson			
	Hank Bauer MG			
	Brooks Robinson			
☐ 2	Jack Hamilton	1.50	.65	.19
☐ 3	Duke Sims	1.50	.65	.19
☐ 4	Hal Lanier	1.50	.65	.19
☐ 5	Whitey Ford UER	20.00	9.00	2.50
	(1953 listed as			
	1933 in stats on back)			
☐ 6	Dick Simpson	1.50	.65	.19
☐ 7	Don McMahon	1.50	.65	.19
☐ 8	Chuck Harrison	1.50	.65	.19
☐ 9	Ron Hansen	1.50	.65	.19
☐ 10	Matty Alou	2.00	.90	.25
☐ 11	Barry Moore	1.50	.65	.19
☐ 12	Dodgers Rookies	2.00	.90	.25
	Jim Campanis			
	Bill Singer			
☐ 13	Joe Sparma	1.50	.65	.19
☐ 14	Phil Linz	2.00	.90	.25
☐ 15	Earl Battey	1.50	.65	.19
☐ 16	Bill Hands	1.50	.65	.19
☐ 17	Jim Gosger	1.50	.65	.19
☐ 18	Gene Oliver	1.50	.65	.19
☐ 19	Jim McGlothlin	1.50	.65	.19
☐ 20	Orlando Cepeda	7.50	3.40	.95
☐ 21	Dave Bristol MG	1.50	.65	.19
☐ 22	Gene Brabender	1.50	.65	.19
☐ 23	Larry Elliot	1.50	.65	.19
☐ 24	Bob Allen	1.50	.65	.19
☐ 25	Elston Howard	4.00	1.80	.50
☐ 26A	Bob Priddy NTR	30.00	13.50	3.80
☐ 26B	Bob Priddy TR	1.50	.65	.19
☐ 27	Bob Saverine	1.50	.65	.19
☐ 28	Barry Latman	1.50	.65	.19
☐ 29	Tom McCraw	1.50	.65	.19
☐ 30	Al Kaline DP	16.00	7.25	2.00
☐ 31	Jim Brewer	1.50	.65	.19
☐ 32	Bob Bailey	2.00	.90	.25
☐ 33	Athletic Rookies	4.50	2.00	.55
	Sal Bando			
	Randy Schwartz			
☐ 34	Pete Cimino	1.50	.65	.19
☐ 35	Rico Carty	2.00	.90	.25
☐ 36	Bob Tillman	1.50	.65	.19
☐ 37	Rick Wise	2.00	.90	.25
☐ 38	Bob Johnson	1.50	.65	.19
☐ 39	Curt Simmons	2.00	.90	.25
☐ 40	Rick Reichardt	1.50	.65	.19
☐ 41	Joe Hoerner	1.50	.65	.19
☐ 42	Mets Team	3.00	1.35	.40
☐ 43	Chico Salmon	1.50	.65	.19
☐ 44	Joe Nuxhall	2.00	.90	.25
☐ 45	Roger Maris	50.00	23.00	6.25
☐ 46	Lindy McDaniel	2.00	.90	.25
☐ 47	Ken McMullen	1.50	.65	.19
☐ 48	Bill Freehan	2.00	.90	.25
☐ 49	Roy Face	2.00	.90	.25
☐ 50	Tony Oliva	5.00	2.30	.60
☐ 51	Astros Rookies	1.50	.65	.19
	Dave Adlesh			
	Wes Bales			
☐ 52	Dennis Higgins	1.50	.65	.19
☐ 53	Clay Dalrymple	1.50	.65	.19
☐ 54	Dick Green	1.50	.65	.19
☐ 55	Don Drysdale	15.00	6.75	1.90
☐ 56	Jose Tartabull	2.00	.90	.25
☐ 57	Pat Jarvis	1.50	.65	.19
☐ 58	Paul Schaal	1.50	.65	.19
☐ 59	Ralph Terry	2.00	.90	.25
☐ 60	Luis Aparicio	6.50	2.90	.80
☐ 61	Gordy Coleman	2.00	.90	.25
☐ 62	Checklist 1	6.50	1.95	.65
	Frank Robinson			
☐ 63	Cards' Clubbers	7.50	3.40	.95
	Lou Brock			
	Curt Flood			
☐ 64	Fred Valentine	1.50	.65	.19
☐ 65	Tom Haller	2.00	.90	.25
☐ 66	Manny Mota	2.00	.90	.25
☐ 67	Ken Berry	1.50	.65	.19
☐ 68	Bob Buhl	2.00	.90	.25
☐ 69	Vic Davalillo	1.50	.65	.19
☐ 70	Ron Santo	3.50	1.55	.45
☐ 71	Camilo Pascual	2.00	.90	.25
☐ 72	Tigers Rookies	1.50	.65	.19
	George Korince			
	(Photo actually			
	James Murray Brown)			
	John (Tom) Matchick			
☐ 73	Rusty Staub	3.50	1.55	.45
☐ 74	Wes Stock	1.50	.65	.19
☐ 75	George Scott	2.50	1.15	.30
☐ 76	Jim Barbieri	1.50	.65	.19
☐ 77	Dooley Womack	1.50	.65	.19
☐ 78	Pat Corrales	2.00	.90	.25
☐ 79	Bubba Morton	1.50	.65	.19
☐ 80	Jim Maloney	2.00	.90	.25
☐ 81	Eddie Stanky MG	2.00	.90	.25
☐ 82	Steve Barber	1.50	.65	.19
☐ 83	Ollie Brown	1.50	.65	.19
☐ 84	Tommie Sisk	1.50	.65	.19
☐ 85	Johnny Callison	2.00	.90	.25
☐ 86A	Mike McCormick NTR	30.00	13.50	3.80
	(Senators on front			
	and Senators on back)			
☐ 86B	Mike McCormick TR	2.00	.90	.25
	(Traded line			
	at end of bio;			

Senators on front,
but Giants on back)

☐ 87	George Altman	1.50	.65	.19
☐ 88	Mickey Lolich	4.00	1.80	.50
☐ 89	Felix Millan	2.00	.90	.25
☐ 90	Jim Nash	1.50	.65	.19
☐ 91	Johnny Lewis	1.50	.65	.19
☐ 92	Ray Washburn	1.50	.65	.19
☐ 93	Yankees Rookies	3.50	1.55	.45

Stan Bahnsen
Bobby Murcer

☐ 94	Ron Fairly	2.00	.90	.25
☐ 95	Sonny Siebert	1.50	.65	.19
☐ 96	Art Shamsky	1.50	.65	.19
☐ 97	Mike Cuellar	2.00	.90	.25
☐ 98	Rich Rollins	1.50	.65	.19
☐ 99	Lee Stange	1.50	.65	.19
☐ 100	Frank Robinson DP	18.00	8.00	2.30
☐ 101	Ken Johnson	1.50	.65	.19
☐ 102	Philadelphia Phillies	3.00	1.35	.40

Team Card

☐ 103	Checklist 2	9.00	2.70	.90

Mickey Mantle

☐ 104	Minnie Rojas	1.50	.65	.19
☐ 105	Ken Boyer	3.00	1.35	.40
☐ 106	Randy Hundley	2.00	.90	.25
☐ 107	Joel Horlen	1.50	.65	.19
☐ 108	Alex Johnson	2.00	.90	.25
☐ 109	Tribe Thumpers	2.50	1.15	.30

Rocky Colavito
Leon Wagner

☐ 110	Jack Aker	2.50	1.15	.30
☐ 111	John Kennedy	2.00	.90	.25
☐ 112	Dave Wickersham	2.00	.90	.25
☐ 113	Dave Nicholson	2.00	.90	.25
☐ 114	Jack Baldschun	2.00	.90	.25
☐ 115	Paul Casanova	2.00	.90	.25
☐ 116	Herman Franks MG	2.00	.90	.25
☐ 117	Darrell Brandon	2.00	.90	.25
☐ 118	Bernie Allen	2.00	.90	.25
☐ 119	Wade Blasingame	2.00	.90	.25
☐ 120	Floyd Robinson	2.00	.90	.25
☐ 121	Eddie Bressoud	2.00	.90	.25
☐ 122	George Brunet	2.00	.90	.25
☐ 123	Pirates Rookies	2.00	.90	.25

Jim Price
Luke Walker

☐ 124	Jim Stewart	2.00	.90	.25
☐ 125	Moe Drabowsky	2.50	1.15	.30
☐ 126	Tony Taylor	2.00	.90	.25
☐ 127	John O'Donoghue	2.00	.90	.25
☐ 128	Ed Spiezio	2.00	.90	.25
☐ 129	Phil Roof	2.00	.90	.25
☐ 130	Phil Regan	2.50	1.15	.30
☐ 131	Yankees Team	5.00	2.30	.60
☐ 132	Ozzie Virgil	2.00	.90	.25
☐ 133	Ron Kline	2.00	.90	.25

☐ 134	Gates Brown	2.50	1.15	.30
☐ 135	Deron Johnson	2.50	1.15	.30
☐ 136	Carroll Sembera	2.00	.90	.25
☐ 137	Twins Rookies	2.50	1.15	.30

Ron Clark
Jim Ollum

☐ 138	Dick Kelley	2.00	.90	.25
☐ 139	Dalton Jones	2.00	.90	.25
☐ 140	Willie Stargell	20.00	9.00	2.50
☐ 141	John Miller	2.00	.90	.25
☐ 142	Jackie Brandt	2.00	.90	.25
☐ 143	Sox Sockers	2.00	.90	.25

Pete Ward
Don Buford

☐ 144	Bill Hepler	2.00	.90	.25
☐ 145	Larry Brown	2.00	.90	.25
☐ 146	Steve Carlton	125.00	57.50	15.50
☐ 147	Tom Egan	2.00	.90	.25
☐ 148	Adolfo Phillips	2.00	.90	.25
☐ 149	Joe Moeller	2.00	.90	.25
☐ 150	Mickey Mantle	250.00	115.00	31.00
☐ 151	World Series Game 1	3.75	1.70	.45

Moe mows down 11
(Moe Drabowsky)

☐ 152	World Series Game 2	7.00	3.10	.85

Jim Palmer blanks
Dodgers

☐ 153	World Series Game 3	3.75	1.70	.45

Paul Blair's homer
defeats L.A.

☐ 154	World Series Game 4	3.75	1.70	.45

Orioles 4 straight
(Brooks Robinson
and Dave McNally)

☐ 155	World Series Summary	3.75	1.70	.45

Winners celebrate

☐ 156	Ron Herbel	2.00	.90	.25
☐ 157	Danny Cater	2.00	.90	.25
☐ 158	Jimmie Coker	2.00	.90	.25
☐ 159	Bruce Howard	2.00	.90	.25
☐ 160	Willie Davis	2.50	1.15	.30
☐ 161	Dick Williams MG	2.50	1.15	.30
☐ 162	Billy O'Dell	2.00	.90	.25
☐ 163	Vic Roznovsky	2.00	.90	.25
☐ 164	Dwight Siebler UER	2.00	.90	.25

(Last line of stats
shows 1960 Minnesota)

☐ 165	Cleon Jones	2.50	1.15	.30
☐ 166	Eddie Mathews	13.00	5.75	1.65
☐ 167	Senators Rookies	2.00	.90	.25

Joe Coleman
Tim Cullen

☐ 168	Ray Culp	2.00	.90	.25
☐ 169	Horace Clarke	2.00	.90	.25
☐ 170	Dick McAuliffe	2.50	1.15	.30
☐ 171	Cal Koonce	2.00	.90	.25
☐ 172	Bill Heath	2.00	.90	.25

☐ 173	St. Louis Cardinals.......4.00	1.80	.50
	Team Card		
☐ 174	Dick Radatz...............2.50	1.15	.30
☐ 175	Bobby Knoop 2.00	.90	.25
☐ 176	Sammy Ellis..............2.00	.90	.25
☐ 177	Tito Fuentes 2.00	.90	.25
☐ 178	John Buzhardt...........2.00	.90	.25
☐ 179	Braves Rookies.........2.00	.90	.25
	Charles Vaughan		
	Cecil Upshaw		
☐ 180	Curt Blefary..............2.00	.90	.25
☐ 181	Terry Fox..................2.00	.90	.25
☐ 182	Ed Charles................2.00	.90	.25
☐ 183	Jim Pagliaroni...........2.00	.90	.25
☐ 184	George Thomas 2.00	.90	.25
☐ 185	Ken Holtzman 4.50	2.00	.55
☐ 186	Mets Maulers............2.50	1.15	.30
	Ed Kranepool		
	Ron Swoboda		
☐ 187	Pedro Ramos 2.00	.90	.25
☐ 188	Ken Harrelson 2.50	1.15	.30
☐ 189	Chuck Hinton 2.00	.90	.25
☐ 190	Turk Farrell 2.00	.90	.25
☐ 191A	Checklist 3 ....7.50	2.30	.75
	(214 Tom Kelley)		
	(Willie Mays)		
☐ 191B	Checklist 3 ....12.50	3.80	1.25
	(214 Dick Kelley)		
	(Willie Mays)		
☐ 192	Fred Gladding 2.00	.90	.25
☐ 193	Jose Cardenal 2.50	1.15	.30
☐ 194	Bob Allison 2.50	1.15	.30
☐ 195	Al Jackson 2.00	.90	.25
☐ 196	Johnny Romano 2.00	.90	.25
☐ 197	Ron Perranoski 3.00	1.35	.40
☐ 198	Chuck Hiller 2.50	1.15	.30
☐ 199	Billy Hitchcock MG......2.50	1.15	.30
☐ 200	Willie Mays UER 100.00	45.00	12.50
	('63 Sna Francisco		
	on card back stats)		
☐ 201	Hal Reniff 2.50	1.15	.30
☐ 202	Johnny Edwards..........2.50	1.15	.30
☐ 203	Al McBean.................2.50	1.15	.30
☐ 204	Orioles Rookies..........3.00	1.35	.40
	Mike Epstein		
	Tom Phoebus		
☐ 205	Dick Groat.................3.00	1.35	.40
☐ 206	Dennis Bennett 2.50	1.15	.30
☐ 207	John Orsino 2.50	1.15	.30
☐ 208	Jack Lamabe..............2.50	1.15	.30
☐ 209	Joe Nossek 2.50	1.15	.30
☐ 210	Bob Gibson 20.00	9.00	2.50
☐ 211	Twins Team 4.00	1.80	.50
☐ 212	Chris Zachary 2.50	1.15	.30
☐ 213	Jay Johnstone............3.50	1.55	.45
☐ 214	Dick Kelley 2.50	1.15	.30
☐ 215	Ernie Banks..............20.00	9.00	2.50
☐ 216	Bengal Belters............8.50	3.80	1.05
	Norm Cash		
	Al Kaline		
☐ 217	Rob Gardner 2.50	1.15	.30
☐ 218	Wes Parker 3.00	1.35	.40
☐ 219	Clay Carroll 3.00	1.35	.40
☐ 220	Jim Ray Hart..............3.00	1.35	.40
☐ 221	Woody Fryman 3.00	1.35	.40
☐ 222	Reds Rookies..............3.00	1.35	.40
	Darrell Osteen		
	Lee May		
☐ 223	Mike Ryan 2.50	1.15	.30
☐ 224	Walt Bond 2.50	1.15	.30
☐ 225	Mel Stottlemyre 3.50	1.55	.45
☐ 226	Julian Javier 3.00	1.35	.40
☐ 227	Paul Lindblad 2.50	1.15	.30
☐ 228	Gil Hodges MG 5.00	2.30	.60
☐ 229	Larry Jackson 2.50	1.15	.30
☐ 230	Boog Powell 4.00	1.80	.50
☐ 231	John Bateman 2.50	1.15	.30
☐ 232	Don Buford 2.50	1.15	.30
☐ 233	AL ERA Leaders 3.50	1.55	.45
	Gary Peters		
	Joel Horlen		
	Steve Hargan		
☐ 234	NL ERA Leaders...........8.00	3.60	1.00
	Sandy Koufax		
	Mike Cuellar		
	Juan Marichal		
☐ 235	AL Pitching Leaders......3.50	1.55	.45
	Jim Kaat		
	Denny McLain		
	Earl Wilson		
☐ 236	NL Pitching Leaders...15.00	6.75	1.90
	Sandy Koufax		
	Juan Marichal		
	Bob Gibson		
	Gaylord Perry		
☐ 237	AL Strikeout Leaders ...3.50	1.55	.45
	Sam McDowell		
	Jim Kaat		
	Earl Wilson		
☐ 238	NL Strikeout Leaders ...6.50	2.90	.80
	Sandy Koufax		
	Jim Bunning		
	Bob Veale		
☐ 239	AL Batting Leaders......6.00	2.70	.75
	Frank Robinson		
	Tony Oliva		
	Al Kaline		
☐ 240	NL Batting Leaders 3.50	1.55	.45
	Matty Alou		
	Felipe Alou		
	Rico Carty		
☐ 241	AL RBI Leaders...........6.00	2.70	.75
	Frank Robinson		
	Harmon Killebrew		

	Boog Powell			
☐ 242	NL RBI Leaders..........10.00	4.50	1.25	
	Hank Aaron			
	Bob Clemente			
	Richie Allen			
☐ 243	AL Home Run Leaders.6.00	2.70	.75	
	Frank Robinson			
	Harmon Killebrew			
	Boog Powell			
☐ 244	NL Home Run Leaders10.00	4.50	1.25	
	Hank Aaron			
	Richie Allen			
	Willie Mays			
☐ 245	Curt Flood 3.50	1.55	.45	
☐ 246	Jim Perry 3.00	1.35	.40	
☐ 247	Jerry Lumpe 2.50	1.15	.30	
☐ 248	Gene Mauch MG 3.00	1.35	.40	
☐ 249	Nick Willhite 2.50	1.15	.30	
☐ 250	Hank Aaron UER 100.00	45.00	12.50	
	(Second 1961 in stats			
	should be 1962)			
☐ 251	Woody Held 2.50	1.15	.30	
☐ 252	Bob Bolin 2.50	1.15	.30	
☐ 253	Indians Rookies 2.50	1.15	.30	
	Bill Davis			
	Gus Gil			
☐ 254	Milt Pappas 3.00	1.35	.40	
	(No facsimile auto-			
	graph on card front)			
☐ 255	Frank Howard 3.50	1.55	.45	
☐ 256	Bob Hendley 2.50	1.15	.30	
☐ 257	Charlie Smith 2.50	1.15	.30	
☐ 258	Lee Maye 2.50	1.15	.30	
☐ 259	Don Dennis 2.50	1.15	.30	
☐ 260	Jim Lefebvre 3.00	1.35	.40	
☐ 261	John Wyatt 2.50	1.15	.30	
☐ 262	Athletics Team 4.00	1.80	.50	
☐ 263	Hank Aguirre 2.50	1.15	.30	
☐ 264	Ron Swoboda 3.00	1.35	.40	
☐ 265	Lou Burdette 3.00	1.35	.40	
☐ 266	Pitt Power 4.00	1.80	.50	
	Willie Stargell			
	Donn Clendenon			
☐ 267	Don Schwall 2.50	1.15	.30	
☐ 268	Johnny Briggs 2.50	1.15	.30	
☐ 269	Don Nottebart 2.50	1.15	.30	
☐ 270	Zoilo Versalles 2.50	1.15	.30	
☐ 271	Eddie Watt 2.50	1.15	.30	
☐ 272	Cubs Rookies 3.50	1.55	.45	
	Bill Connors			
	Dave Dowling			
☐ 273	Dick Lines 2.50	1.15	.30	
☐ 274	Bob Aspromonte 2.50	1.15	.30	
☐ 275	Fred Whitfield 2.50	1.15	.30	
☐ 276	Bruce Brubaker 2.50	1.15	.30	
☐ 277	Steve Whitaker 2.50	1.15	.30	
☐ 278	Checklist 4 ....6.50	1.95	.65	

	Jim Kaat			
☐ 279	Frank Linzy 2.50	1.15	.30	
☐ 280	Tony Conigliaro...........7.50	3.40	.95	
☐ 281	Bob Rodgers 3.00	1.35	.40	
☐ 282	John Odom 2.50	1.15	.30	
☐ 283	Gene Alley 3.00	1.35	.40	
☐ 284	Johnny Podres 3.50	1.55	.45	
☐ 285	Lou Brock 25.00	11.50	3.10	
☐ 286	Wayne Causey 3.00	1.35	.40	
☐ 287	Mets Rookies 3.00	1.35	.40	
	Greg Goossen			
	Bart Shirley			
☐ 288	Denny Lemaster...........3.00	1.35	.40	
☐ 289	Tom Tresh 4.00	1.80	.50	
☐ 290	Bill White 4.00	1.80	.50	
☐ 291	Jim Hannan 3.00	1.35	.40	
☐ 292	Don Pavletich 3.00	1.35	.40	
☐ 293	Ed Kirkpatrick 3.00	1.35	.40	
☐ 294	Walt Alston MG 4.00	1.80	.50	
☐ 295	Sam McDowell 3.50	1.55	.45	
☐ 296	Glenn Beckert 3.50	1.55	.45	
☐ 297	Dave Morehead 3.00	1.35	.40	
☐ 298	Ron Davis 3.00	1.35	.40	
☐ 299	Norm Siebern 3.00	1.35	.40	
☐ 300	Jim Kaat 4.50	2.00	.55	
☐ 301	Jesse Gonder 3.00	1.35	.40	
☐ 302	Orioles Team 6.00	2.70	.75	
☐ 303	Gil Blanco 3.00	1.35	.40	
☐ 304	Phil Gagliano 3.00	1.35	.40	
☐ 305	Earl Wilson 3.50	1.55	.45	
☐ 306	Bud Harrelson 4.50	2.00	.55	
☐ 307	Jim Beauchamp 3.00	1.35	.40	
☐ 308	Al Downing 3.50	1.55	.45	
☐ 309	Hurlers Beware 3.50	1.55	.45	
	Johnny Callison			
	Richie Allen			
☐ 310	Gary Peters 3.00	1.35	.40	
☐ 311	Ed Brinkman 3.00	1.35	.40	
☐ 312	Don Mincher 3.00	1.35	.40	
☐ 313	Bob Lee 3.00	1.35	.40	
☐ 314	Red Sox Rookies 8.00	3.60	1.00	
	Mike Andrews			
	Reggie Smith			
☐ 315	Billy Williams 12.50	5.75	1.55	
☐ 316	Jack Kralick 3.00	1.35	.40	
☐ 317	Cesar Tovar 3.50	1.55	.45	
☐ 318	Dave Giusti 3.00	1.35	.40	
☐ 319	Paul Blair 3.50	1.55	.45	
☐ 320	Gaylord Perry 15.00	6.75	1.90	
☐ 321	Mayo Smith MG 3.00	1.35	.40	
☐ 322	Jose Pagan 3.00	1.35	.40	
☐ 323	Mike Hershberger 3.00	1.35	.40	
☐ 324	Hal Woodeshick 3.00	1.35	.40	
☐ 325	Chico Cardenas 3.50	1.55	.45	
☐ 326	Bob Uecker 20.00	9.00	2.50	
☐ 327	California Angels 6.00	2.70	.75	
	Team Card			

☐ 328	Clete Boyer UER..........3.50 (Stats only go up through 1965)	1.55	.45		
☐ 329	Charlie Lau.................3.50	1.55	.45		
☐ 330	Claude Osteen............3.50	1.55	.45		
☐ 331	Joe Foy 3.00	1.35	.40		
☐ 332	Jesus Alou 3.00	1.35	.40		
☐ 333	Fergie Jenkins...........35.00	16.00	4.40		
☐ 334	Twin Terrors ....4.50 Bob Allison Harmon Killebrew	2.00	.55		
☐ 335	Bob Veale...................3.50	1.55	.45		
☐ 336	Joe Azcue 3.00	1.35	.40		
☐ 337	Joe Morgan................25.00	11.50	3.10		
☐ 338	Bob Locker 3.00	1.35	.40		
☐ 339	Chico Ruiz..................3.00	1.35	.40		
☐ 340	Joe Pepitone...............3.50	1.55	.45		
☐ 341	Giants Rookies............3.00 Dick Dietz Bill Sorrell	1.35	.40		
☐ 342	Hank Fischer...............3.00	1.35	.40		
☐ 343	Tom Satriano 3.00	1.35	.40		
☐ 344	Ossie Chavarria..........3.00	1.35	.40		
☐ 345	Stu Miller...................3.50	1.55	.45		
☐ 346	Jim Hickman...............3.00	1.35	.40		
☐ 347	Grady Hatton MG.........3.00	1.35	.40		
☐ 348	Tug McGraw................4.50	2.00	.55		
☐ 349	Bob Chance.................3.00	1.35	.40		
☐ 350	Joe Torre 4.50	2.00	.55		
☐ 351	Vern Law 3.50	1.55	.45		
☐ 352	Ray Oyler...................3.00	1.35	.40		
☐ 353	Bill McCool 3.00	1.35	.40		
☐ 354	Cubs Team..................6.00	2.70	.75		
☐ 355	Carl Yastrzemski.........80.00	36.00	10.00		
☐ 356	Larry Jaster................3.00	1.35	.40		
☐ 357	Bill Skowron...............3.50	1.55	.45		
☐ 358	Ruben Amaro...............3.00	1.35	.40		
☐ 359	Dick Ellsworth.............3.00	1.35	.40		
☐ 360	Leon Wagner...............3.00	1.35	.40		
☐ 361	Checklist 5.................7.50 Roberto Clemente	2.30	.75		
☐ 362	Darold Knowles...........3.00	1.35	.40		
☐ 363	Dave Johnson.............3.50	1.55	.45		
☐ 364	Claude Raymond..........3.00	1.35	.40		
☐ 365	John Roseboro.............3.50	1.55	.45		
☐ 366	Andy Kosco.................3.00	1.35	.40		
☐ 367	Angels Rookies............3.00 Bill Kelso Don Wallace	1.35	.40		
☐ 368	Jack Hiatt 3.00	1.35	.40		
☐ 369	Jim Hunter................20.00	9.00	2.50		
☐ 370	Tommy Davis...............3.50	1.55	.45		
☐ 371	Jim Lonborg................5.00	2.30	.60		
☐ 372	Mike DeLaHoz.............4.00	1.80	.50		
☐ 373	White Sox Rookies DP .4.00 Duane Josephson Fred Klages	1.80	.50		

☐ 374A	Mel Queen ERR DP....4.00 (Incomplete stat line on back)	1.80	.50
☐ 374B	Mel Queen COR DP....4.00 (Complete stat line on back)	1.80	.50
☐ 375	Jake Gibbs 4.00	1.80	.50
☐ 376	Don Lock DP...............4.00	1.80	.50
☐ 377	Luis Tiant..................5.00	2.30	.60
☐ 378	Detroit Tigers.............8.00 Team Card UER (Willie Horton with 262 RBI's in 1966)	3.60	1.00
☐ 379	Jerry May DP 4.00	1.80	.50
☐ 380	Dean Chance DP..........4.00	1.80	.50
☐ 381	Dick Schofield DP 4.00	1.80	.50
☐ 382	Dave McNally..............4.50	2.00	.55
☐ 383	Ken Henderson DP........4.00	1.80	.50
☐ 384	Cardinals Rookies........4.00 Jim Cosman Dick Hughes	1.80	.50
☐ 385	Jim Fregosi................4.50 (Batting wrong)	2.00	.55
☐ 386	Dick Selma DP............4.00	1.80	.50
☐ 387	Cap Peterson DP 4.00	1.80	.50
☐ 388	Arnold Earley DP..........4.00	1.80	.50
☐ 389	Alvin Dark MG DP 4.50	2.00	.55
☐ 390	Jim Wynn DP 4.50	2.00	.55
☐ 391	Wilbur Wood DP...........4.50	2.00	.55
☐ 392	Tommy Harper DP 4.50	2.00	.55
☐ 393	Jim Bouton DP 4.50	2.00	.55
☐ 394	Jake Wood DP 4.00	1.80	.50
☐ 395	Chris Short 4.50	2.00	.55
☐ 396	Atlanta Aces...............4.00 Denis Menke Tony Cloninger	1.80	.50
☐ 397	Willie Smith DP 4.00	1.80	.50
☐ 398	Jeff Torborg...............4.50	2.00	.55
☐ 399	Al Worthington DP........4.00	1.80	.50
☐ 400	Bob Clemente DP........75.00	34.00	9.50
☐ 401	Jim Coates.................4.00	1.80	.50
☐ 402	Phillies Rookies DP......4.50 Grant Jackson Billy Wilson	2.00	.55
☐ 403	Dick Nen...................4.00	1.80	.50
☐ 404	Nelson Briles.............4.50	2.00	.55
☐ 405	Russ Snyder...............4.00	1.80	.50
☐ 406	Lee Elia DP 4.00	1.80	.50
☐ 407	Reds Team.................8.00	3.60	1.00
☐ 408	Jim Northrup DP..........4.50	2.00	.55
☐ 409	Ray Sadecki...............4.00	1.80	.50
☐ 410	Lou Johnson DP...........4.00	1.80	.50
☐ 411	Dick Howser DP...........4.50	2.00	.55
☐ 412	Astros Rookies............4.50 Norm Miller Doug Rader	2.00	.55
☐ 413	Jerry Grote.................4.00	1.80	.50

☐ 414 Casey Cox	4.00	1.80	.50
☐ 415 Sonny Jackson	4.00	1.80	.50
☐ 416 Roger Repoz	4.00	1.80	.50
☐ 417A Bob Bruce ERR DP	30.00	13.50	3.80
(RBAVES on back)			
☐ 417B Bob Bruce COR DP	4.00	1.80	.50
☐ 418 Sam Mele MG	4.00	1.80	.50
☐ 419 Don Kessinger DP	4.50	2.00	.55
☐ 420 Denny McLain	7.50	3.40	.95
☐ 421 Dal Maxvill DP	4.00	1.80	.50
☐ 422 Hoyt Wilhelm	9.00	4.00	1.15
☐ 423 Fence Busters DP	25.00	11.50	3.10
Willie Mays			
Willie McCovey			
☐ 424 Pedro Gonzalez	4.00	1.80	.50
☐ 425 Pete Mikkelsen	4.00	1.80	.50
☐ 426 Lou Clinton	4.00	1.80	.50
☐ 427A Ruben Gomez ERR DP	4.00	1.80	.50
(Incomplete stat line on back)			
☐ 427B Ruben Gomez COR DP	4.00	1.80	.50
(Complete stat line on back)			
☐ 428 Dodgers Rookies DP	4.50	2.00	.55
Tom Hutton			
Gene Michael			
☐ 429 Garry Roggenburk DP	4.00	1.80	.50
☐ 430 Pete Rose	80.00	36.00	10.00
☐ 431 Ted Uhlaender	4.00	1.80	.50
☐ 432 Jimmie Hall DP	4.00	1.80	.50
☐ 433 Al Luplow DP	4.00	1.80	.50
☐ 434 Eddie Fisher DP	4.00	1.80	.50
☐ 435 Mack Jones DP	4.00	1.80	.50
☐ 436 Pete Ward	4.00	1.80	.50
☐ 437 Senators Team	8.00	3.60	1.00
☐ 438 Chuck Dobson	4.00	1.80	.50
☐ 439 Byron Browne	4.00	1.80	.50
☐ 440 Steve Hargan	4.00	1.80	.50
☐ 441 Jim Davenport	4.00	1.80	.50
☐ 442 Yankees Rookies DP	4.50	2.00	.55
Bill Robinson			
Joe Verbanic			
☐ 443 Tito Francona DP	4.00	1.80	.50
☐ 444 George Smith	4.00	1.80	.50
☐ 445 Don Sutton	36.00	16.00	4.50
☐ 446 Russ Nixon DP	4.00	1.80	.50
☐ 447A Bo Belinsky ERR DP	4.50	2.00	.55
(Incomplete stat line on back)			
☐ 447B Bo Belinsky COR DP	4.50	2.00	.55
(Complete stat line on back)			
☐ 448 Harry Walker MG DP	4.00	1.80	.50
☐ 449 Orlando Pena	4.00	1.80	.50
☐ 450 Richie Allen	7.50	3.40	.95
☐ 451 Fred Newman DP	4.00	1.80	.50
☐ 452 Ed Kranepool	4.50	2.00	.55
☐ 453 Aurelio Monteagudo DP	4.00	1.80	.50
☐ 454A Checklist 6 DP	7.50	2.30	.75
Juan Marichal			
(Missing left ear)			
☐ 454B Checklist 6 DP	7.50	2.30	.75
Juan Marichal			
(left ear showing)			
☐ 455 Tommie Agee	4.50	2.00	.55
☐ 456 Phil Niekro	18.00	8.00	2.30
☐ 457 Andy Etchebarren DP	4.50	2.00	.55
☐ 458 Lee Thomas	8.00	3.60	1.00
☐ 459 Senators Rookies	8.00	3.60	1.00
Dick Bosman			
Pete Craig			
☐ 460 Harmon Killebrew	55.00	25.00	7.00
☐ 461 Bob Miller	7.00	3.10	.85
☐ 462 Bob Barton	7.00	3.10	.85
☐ 463 Hill Aces	8.00	3.60	1.00
Sam McDowell			
Sonny Siebert			
☐ 464 Dan Coombs	7.00	3.10	.85
☐ 465 Willie Horton	8.00	3.60	1.00
☐ 466 Bobby Wine	7.00	3.10	.85
☐ 467 Jim O'Toole	8.00	3.60	1.00
☐ 468 Ralph Houk MG	8.00	3.60	1.00
☐ 469 Len Gabrielson	7.00	3.10	.85
☐ 470 Bob Shaw	7.00	3.10	.85
☐ 471 Rene Lachemann	8.00	3.60	1.00
☐ 472 Rookies Pirates	7.00	3.10	.85
John Gelnar			
George Spriggs			
☐ 473 Jose Santiago	7.00	3.10	.85
☐ 474 Bob Tolan	8.00	3.60	1.00
☐ 475 Jim Palmer	110.00	50.00	14.00
☐ 476 Tony Perez SP	100.00	45.00	12.50
☐ 477 Braves Team	14.00	6.25	1.75
☐ 478 Bob Humphreys	7.00	3.10	.85
☐ 479 Gary Bell	7.00	3.10	.85
☐ 480 Willie McCovey	40.00	18.00	5.00
☐ 481 Leo Durocher MG	13.00	5.75	1.65
☐ 482 Bill Monbouquette	7.00	3.10	.85
☐ 483 Jim Landis	7.00	3.10	.85
☐ 484 Jerry Adair	7.00	3.10	.85
☐ 485 Tim McCarver	25.00	11.50	3.10
☐ 486 Twins Rookies	7.00	3.10	.85
Rich Reese			
Bill Whitby			
☐ 487 Tommie Reynolds	7.00	3.10	.85
☐ 488 Gerry Arrigo	7.00	3.10	.85
☐ 489 Doug Clemens	7.00	3.10	.85
☐ 490 Tony Cloninger	7.00	3.10	.85
☐ 491 Sam Bowens	7.00	3.10	.85
☐ 492 Pittsburgh Pirates	14.00	6.25	1.75
Team Card			
☐ 493 Phil Ortega	7.00	3.10	.85
☐ 494 Bill Rigney MG	7.00	3.10	.85
☐ 495 Fritz Peterson	7.00	3.10	.85

□ 496	Orlando McFarlane......7.00	3.10	.85
□ 497	Ron Campbell 7.00	3.10	.85
□ 498	Larry Dierker..............7.00	3.10	.85
□ 499	Indians Rookies 7.00	3.10	.85
	George Culver		
	Jose Vidal		
□ 500	Juan Marichal 25.00	11.50	3.10
□ 501	Jerry Zimmerman 7.00	3.10	.85
□ 502	Derrell Griffith 7.00	3.10	.85
□ 503	Los Angeles Dodgers.14.00	6.25	1.75
	Team Card		
□ 504	Orlando Martinez........7.00	3.10	.85
□ 505	Tommy Helms 8.00	3.60	1.00
□ 506	Smoky Burgess.........8.00	3.60	1.00
□ 507	Orioles Rookies..........7.00	3.10	.85
	Ed Barnowski		
	Larry Haney		
□ 508	Dick Hall 7.00	3.10	.85
□ 509	Jim King 7.00	3.10	.85
□ 510	Bill Mazeroski 12.50	5.75	1.55
□ 511	Don Wert 7.00	3.10	.85
□ 512	Red Schoendienst MG12.50	5.75	1.55
□ 513	Marcelino Lopez 7.00	3.10	.85
□ 514	John Werhas..............7.00	3.10	.85
□ 515	Bert Campaneris 8.00	3.60	1.00
□ 516	Giants Team 14.00	6.25	1.75
□ 517	Fred Talbot...............7.00	3.10	.85
□ 518	Denis Menke 7.00	3.10	.85
□ 519	Ted Davidson.............7.00	3.10	.85
□ 520	Max Alvis..................7.00	3.10	.85
□ 521	Bird Bombers.............8.00	3.60	1.00
	Boog Powell		
	Curt Blefary		
□ 522	John Stephenson........7.00	3.10	.85
□ 523	Jim Merritt.................7.00	3.10	.85
□ 524	Felix Mantilla 7.00	3.10	.85
□ 525	Ron Hunt 7.00	3.10	.85
□ 526	Tigers Rookies...........9.00	4.00	1.15
	Pat Dobson		
	George Korince		
	(See 67T-72)		
□ 527	Dennis Ribant 7.00	3.10	.85
□ 528	Rico Petrocelli..........11.00	4.90	1.40
□ 529	Gary Wagner 7.00	3.10	.85
□ 530	Felipe Alou 11.00	4.90	1.40
□ 531	Checklist 7 ....12.50	3.80	1.15
	Brooks Robinson		
□ 532	Jim Hicks...................7.00	3.10	.85
□ 533	Jack Fisher................7.00	3.10	.85
□ 534	Hank Bauer MG DP 10.00	4.50	1.25
□ 535	Donn Clendenon 20.50	9.25	2.60
□ 536	Cubs Rookies...........40.00	18.00	5.00
	Joe Niekro		
	Paul Popovich		
□ 537	Chuck Estrada DP 10.00	4.50	1.25
□ 538	J.C. Martin................18.00	8.00	2.30
□ 539	Dick Egan DP 10.00	4.50	1.25
□ 540	Norm Cash...............50.00	23.00	6.25
□ 541	Joe Gibbon 18.00	8.00	2.30
□ 542	Athletics Rookies DP .12.50	5.75	1.55
	Rick Monday		
	Tony Pierce		
□ 543	Dan Schneider 18.00	8.00	2.30
□ 544	Cleveland Indians......30.00	13.50	3.80
	Team Card		
□ 545	Jim Grant.................18.00	8.00	2.30
□ 546	Woody Woodward 20.50	9.25	2.60
□ 547	Red Sox Rookies DP ..10.00	4.50	1.25
	Russ Gibson		
	Bill Rohr		
□ 548	Tony Gonzalez DP 10.00	4.50	1.25
□ 549	Jack Sanford............18.00	8.00	2.30
□ 550	Vada Pinson DP 12.50	5.75	1.55
□ 551	Doug Camilli DP 10.00	4.50	1.25
□ 552	Ted Savage 18.00	8.00	2.30
□ 553	Yankees Rookies........35.00	16.00	4.40
	Mike Hegan		
	Thad Tillotson		
□ 554	Andre Rodgers DP 10.00	4.50	1.25
□ 555	Don Cardwell............18.00	8.00	2.30
□ 556	Al Weis DP................10.00	4.50	1.25
□ 557	Al Ferrara 18.00	8.00	2.30
□ 558	Orioles Rookies.........60.00	27.00	7.50
	Mark Belanger		
	Bill Dillman		
□ 559	Dick Tracewski DP 10.00	4.50	1.25
□ 560	Jim Bunning 60.00	27.00	7.50
□ 561	Sandy Alomar 20.50	9.25	2.60
□ 562	Steve Blass DP 11.00	4.90	1.40
□ 563	Joe Adcock 25.00	11.50	3.10
□ 564	Astros Rookies DP 11.00	4.90	1.40
	Alonzo Harris		
	Aaron Pointer		
□ 565	Lew Krausse 18.00	8.00	2.30
□ 566	Gary Geiger DP 10.00	4.50	1.25
□ 567	Steve Hamilton 18.00	8.00	2.30
□ 568	John Sullivan 18.00	8.00	2.30
□ 569	AL Rookies DP 550.00	250.00	70.00
	Rod Carew		
	Hank Allen		
□ 570	Maury Wills 100.00	45.00	12.50
□ 571	Larry Sherry.............18.00	8.00	2.30
□ 572	Don Demeter.............25.00	11.50	3.10
□ 573	Chicago White Sox....30.00	13.50	3.80
	Team Card UER		
	(Indians team		
	stats on back)		
□ 574	Jerry Buchek.............18.00	8.00	2.30
□ 575	Dave Boswell 18.00	8.00	2.30
□ 576	NL Rookies 25.00	11.50	3.10
	Ramon Hernandez		
	Norm Gigon		
□ 577	Bill Short 18.00	8.00	2.30
□ 578	John Boccabella........18.00	8.00	2.30

		NRMT-MT	EXC	G-VG
☐	579 Bill Henry	18.00	8.00	2.30
☐	580 Rocky Colavito	80.00	36.00	10.00
☐	581 Mets Rookies	1400.00	650.00	180.00
	Bill Denehy			
	Tom Seaver			
☐	582 Jim Owens DP	10.00	4.50	1.25
☐	583 Ray Barker	18.00	8.00	2.30
☐	584 Jim Piersall	30.00	13.50	3.80
☐	585 Wally Bunker	18.00	8.00	2.30
☐	586 Manny Jimenez	18.00	8.00	2.30
☐	587 NL Rookies	30.00	13.50	3.80
	Don Shaw			
	Gary Sutherland			
☐	588 Johnny Klippstein DP	10.00	4.50	1.25
☐	589 Dave Ricketts DP	10.00	4.50	1.25
☐	590 Pete Richert	18.00	8.00	2.30
☐	591 Ty Cline	18.00	8.00	2.30
☐	592 NL Rookies	25.00	11.50	3.10
	Jim Shellenback			
	Ron Willis			
☐	593 Wes Westrum MG	20.50	9.25	2.60
☐	594 Dan Osinski	25.00	11.50	3.10
☐	595 Cookie Rojas	20.50	9.25	2.60
☐	596 Galen Cisco DP	10.00	4.50	1.25
☐	597 Ted Abernathy	18.00	8.00	2.30
☐	598 White Sox Rookies	20.50	9.25	2.60
	Walt Williams			
	Ed Stroud			
☐	599 Bob Duliba DP	10.00	4.50	1.25
☐	600 Brooks Robinson	250.00	115.00	31.00
☐	601 Bill Bryan DP	10.00	4.50	1.25
☐	602 Juan Pizarro	18.00	8.00	2.30
☐	603 Athletics Rookies	18.00	8.00	2.30
	Tim Talton			
	Ramon Webster			
☐	604 Red Sox Team	125.00	57.50	15.50
☐	605 Mike Shannon	50.00	23.00	6.25
☐	606 Ron Taylor	18.00	8.00	2.30
☐	607 Mickey Stanley	40.00	18.00	5.00
☐	608 Cubs Rookies DP	10.00	4.50	1.25
	Rich Nye			
	John Upham			
☐	609 Tommy John	125.00	31.00	10.00

1968 Topps

The cards in this 598-card set measure 2 1/2" by 3 1/2". The 1968 Topps set includes Sporting News All-Star Selections as card numbers 361 to 380. Other subsets in the set include League Leaders (1-12) and World Series cards (151-158). The

front of each checklist card features a picture of a popular player inside a circle. High numbers 534 to 598 are slightly more difficult to obtain. The first series looks different from the other series, as it has a lighter, wider mesh background on the card front. The later series all had a much darker, finer mesh pattern. Key cards in the set are the rookie cards of Johnny Bench (247) and Nolan Ryan (177).

	NRMT-MT	EXC	G-VG
COMPLETE SET (598)	3300.	1500.	425.00
COMMON PLAYER (1-109)	1.50	.65	.19
COMMON PLAYER (110-196)	1.50	.65	.19
COMMON PLAYER (197-283)	1.50	.65	.19
COMMON PLAYER (284-370)	1.50	.65	.19
COMMON PLAYER (371-457)	1.50	.65	.19
COMMON PLAYER (458-533)	3.00	1.35	.40
COMMON PLAYER (534-598)	3.75	1.70	.45

		NRMT-MT	EXC	G-VG
☐	1 NL Batting Leaders	16.00	4.80	1.60
	Bob Clemente			
	Tony Gonzalez			
	Matty Alou			
☐	2 AL Batting Leaders	10.00	4.50	1.25
	Carl Yastrzemski			
	Frank Robinson			
	Al Kaline			
☐	3 NL RBI Leaders	7.00	3.10	.85
	Orlando Cepeda			
	Bob Clemente			
	Hank Aaron			
☐	4 AL RBI Leaders	10.00	4.50	1.25
	Carl Yastrzemski			
	Harmon Killebrew			
	Frank Robinson			
☐	5 NL Home Run Leaders	6.00	2.70	.75
	Hank Aaron			
	Jim Wynn			
	Ron Santo			
	Willie McCovey			
☐	6 AL Home Run Leaders	7.50	3.40	.95

Carl Yastrzemski
Harmon Killebrew
Frank Howard

☐ 7	NL ERA Leaders	3.00	1.35	.40
	Phil Niekro			
	Jim Bunning			
	Chris Short			
☐ 8	AL ERA Leaders	3.00	1.35	.40
	Joel Horlen			
	Gary Peters			
	Sonny Siebert			
☐ 9	NL Pitching Leaders	3.50	1.55	.45
	Mike McCormick			
	Ferguson Jenkins			
	Jim Bunning			
	Claude Osteen			
☐ 10A	AL Pitching Leaders	3.50	1.55	.45
	Jim Lonborg ERR			
	(Misspelled Lonberg			
	on card back)			
	Earl Wilson			
	Dean Chance			
☐ 10B	AL Pitching Leaders	3.50	1.55	.45
	Jim Lonborg COR			
	Earl Wilson			
	Dean Chance			
☐ 11	NL Strikeout Leaders	4.00	1.80	.50
	Jim Bunning			
	Ferguson Jenkins			
	Gaylord Perry			
☐ 12	AL Strikeout Leaders	3.00	1.35	.40
	Jim Lonborg UER			
	(Misspelled Longberg			
	on card back)			
	Sam McDowell			
	Dean Chance			
☐ 13	Chuck Hartenstein	1.50	.65	.19
☐ 14	Jerry McNertney	1.50	.65	.19
☐ 15	Ron Hunt	1.50	.65	.19
☐ 16	Indians Rookies	4.50	2.00	.55
	Lou Piniella			
	Richie Scheinblum			
☐ 17	Dick Hall	1.50	.65	.19
☐ 18	Mike Hershberger	1.50	.65	.19
☐ 19	Juan Pizarro	1.50	.65	.19
☐ 20	Brooks Robinson	25.00	11.50	3.10
☐ 21	Ron Davis	1.50	.65	.19
☐ 22	Pat Dobson	2.00	.90	.25
☐ 23	Chico Cardenas	2.00	.90	.25
☐ 24	Bobby Locke	1.50	.65	.19
☐ 25	Julian Javier	2.00	.90	.25
☐ 26	Darrell Brandon	1.50	.65	.19
☐ 27	Gil Hodges MG	7.50	3.40	.95
☐ 28	Ted Uhlaender	1.50	.65	.19
☐ 29	Joe Verbanic	1.50	.65	.19
☐ 30	Joe Torre	3.00	1.35	.40
☐ 31	Ed Stroud	1.50	.65	.19

☐ 32	Joe Gibbon	1.50	.65	.19
☐ 33	Pete Ward	1.50	.65	.19
☐ 34	Al Ferrara	1.50	.65	.19
☐ 35	Steve Hargan	1.50	.65	.19
☐ 36	Pirates Rookies	2.00	.90	.25
	Bob Moose			
	Bob Robertson			
☐ 37	Billy Williams	10.00	4.50	1.25
☐ 38	Tony Pierce	1.50	.65	.19
☐ 39	Cookie Rojas	2.00	.90	.25
☐ 40	Denny McLain	12.50	5.75	1.55
☐ 41	Julio Gotay	1.50	.65	.19
☐ 42	Larry Haney	1.50	.65	.19
☐ 43	Gary Bell	1.50	.65	.19
☐ 44	Frank Kostro	1.50	.65	.19
☐ 45	Tom Seaver	250.00	115.00	31.00
☐ 46	Dave Ricketts	1.50	.65	.19
☐ 47	Ralph Houk MG	2.00	.90	.25
☐ 48	Ted Davidson	1.50	.65	.19
☐ 49A	Eddie Brinkman	1.50	.65	.19
	(White team name)			
☐ 49B	Eddie Brinkman	40.00	18.00	5.00
	(Yellow team name)			
☐ 50	Willie Mays	70.00	32.00	8.75
☐ 51	Bob Locker	1.50	.65	.19
☐ 52	Hawk Taylor	1.50	.65	.19
☐ 53	Gene Alley	2.00	.90	.25
☐ 54	Stan Williams	2.00	.90	.25
☐ 55	Felipe Alou	2.00	.90	.25
☐ 56	Orioles Rookies	1.50	.65	.19
	Dave Leonhard			
	Dave May			
☐ 57	Dan Schneider	1.50	.65	.19
☐ 58	Eddie Mathews	12.50	5.75	1.55
☐ 59	Don Lock	1.50	.65	.19
☐ 60	Ken Holtzman	2.00	.90	.25
☐ 61	Reggie Smith	2.50	1.15	.30
☐ 62	Chuck Dobson	1.50	.65	.19
☐ 63	Dick Kenworthy	1.50	.65	.19
☐ 64	Jim Merritt	1.50	.65	.19
☐ 65	John Roseboro	2.00	.90	.25
☐ 66A	Casey Cox	1.50	.65	.19
	(White team name)			
☐ 66B	Casey Cox	100.00	45.00	12.50
	(Yellow team name)			
☐ 67	Checklist 1	6.00	1.50	.50
	Jim Kaat			
☐ 68	Ron Willis	1.50	.65	.19
☐ 69	Tom Tresh	2.00	.90	.25
☐ 70	Bob Veale	2.00	.90	.25
☐ 71	Vern Fuller	1.50	.65	.19
☐ 72	Tommy John	5.00	2.30	.60
☐ 73	Jim Ray Hart	2.00	.90	.25
☐ 74	Milt Pappas	2.00	.90	.25
☐ 75	Don Mincher	1.50	.65	.19
☐ 76	Braves Rookies	2.00	.90	.25
	Jim Britton			

☐		Ron Reed		
☐	77	Don Wilson 2.00	.90	.25
☐	78	Jim Northrup 2.00	.90	.25
☐	79	Ted Kubiak 1.50	.65	.19
☐	80	Rod Carew 150.00	70.00	19.00
☐	81	Larry Jackson 1.50	.65	.19
☐	82	Sam Bowens 1.50	.65	.19
☐	83	John Stephenson 1.50	.65	.19
☐	84	Bob Tolan 2.00	.90	.25
☐	85	Gaylord Perry 11.00	4.90	1.40
☐	86	Willie Stargell 12.50	5.75	1.55
☐	87	Dick Williams MG 2.00	.90	.25
☐	88	Phil Regan 2.00	.90	.25
☐	89	Jake Gibbs 1.50	.65	.19
☐	90	Vada Pinson 2.50	1.15	.30
☐	91	Jim Ollom 1.50	.65	.19
☐	92	Ed Kranepool 2.00	.90	.25
☐	93	Tony Cloninger 1.50	.65	.19
☐	94	Lee Maye 1.50	.65	.19
☐	95	Bob Aspromonte 1.50	.65	.19
☐	96	Senator Rookies 1.50	.65	.19
☐		Frank Coggins		
☐		Dick Nold		
☐	97	Tom Phoebus 1.50	.65	.19
☐	98	Gary Sutherland 1.50	.65	.19
☐	99	Rocky Colavito 4.00	1.80	.50
☐	100	Bob Gibson 25.00	11.50	3.10
☐	101	Glenn Beckert 2.00	.90	.25
☐	102	Jose Cardenal 2.00	.90	.25
☐	103	Don Sutton 12.50	5.75	1.55
☐	104	Dick Dietz 1.50	.65	.19
☐	105	Al Downing 2.00	.90	.25
☐	106	Dalton Jones 1.50	.65	.19
☐	107A	Checklist 2 ....6.00	1.50	.50
☐		Juan Marichal		
☐		(Tan wide mesh)		
☐	107B	Checklist 2 ....6.00	1.50	.50
☐		Juan Marichal		
☐		(Brown fine mesh)		
☐	108	Don Pavletich 1.50	.65	.19
☐	109	Bert Campaneris 2.00	.90	.25
☐	110	Hank Aaron 75.00	34.00	9.50
☐	111	Rich Reese 1.50	.65	.19
☐	112	Woody Fryman 1.50	.65	.19
☐	113	Tigers Rookies 1.50	.65	.19
☐		Tom Matchick		
☐		Daryl Patterson		
☐	114	Ron Swoboda 2.00	.90	.25
☐	115	Sam McDowell 2.00	.90	.25
☐	116	Ken McMullen 1.50	.65	.19
☐	117	Larry Jaster 1.50	.65	.19
☐	118	Mark Belanger 2.00	.90	.25
☐	119	Ted Savage 1.50	.65	.19
☐	120	Mel Stottlemyre 2.50	1.15	.30
☐	121	Jimmie Hall 1.50	.65	.19
☐	122	Gene Mauch MG 2.00	.90	.25
☐	123	Jose Santiago 1.50	.65	.19

☐	124	Nate Oliver 1.50	.65	.19
☐	125	Joel Horlen 1.50	.65	.19
☐	126	Bobby Etheridge 1.50	.65	.19
☐	127	Paul Lindblad 1.50	.65	.19
☐	128	Astros Rookies 1.50	.65	.19
☐		Tom Dukes		
☐		Alonzo Harris		
☐	129	Mickey Stanley 2.50	1.15	.30
☐	130	Tony Perez 15.00	6.75	1.90
☐	131	Frank Bertaina 1.50	.65	.19
☐	132	Bud Harrelson 2.00	.90	.25
☐	133	Fred Whitfield 1.50	.65	.19
☐	134	Pat Jarvis 1.50	.65	.19
☐	135	Paul Blair 2.00	.90	.25
☐	136	Randy Hundley 2.00	.90	.25
☐	137	Twins Team 3.00	1.35	.40
☐	138	Ruben Amaro 1.50	.65	.19
☐	139	Chris Short 1.50	.65	.19
☐	140	Tony Conigliaro 5.00	2.30	.60
☐	141	Dal Maxvill 1.50	.65	.19
☐	142	White Sox Rookies 1.50	.65	.19
☐		Buddy Bradford		
☐		Bill Voss		
☐	143	Pete Cimino 1.50	.65	.19
☐	144	Joe Morgan 20.00	9.00	2.50
☐	145	Don Drysdale 11.00	4.90	1.40
☐	146	Sal Bando 2.00	.90	.25
☐	147	Frank Linzy 1.50	.65	.19
☐	148	Dave Bristol MG 1.50	.65	.19
☐	149	Bob Saverine 1.50	.65	.19
☐	150	Bob Clemente 55.00	25.00	7.00
☐	151	World Series Game 1 ...8.00	3.60	1.00
☐		Lou Brock socks 4		
☐		hits in opener		
☐	152	World Series Game 2 .10.00	4.50	1.25
☐		Carl Yastrzemski		
☐		smashes 2 homers		
☐	153	World Series Game 3 ...4.00	1.80	.50
☐		Nellie Briles		
☐		cools Boston		
☐	154	World Series Game 4 ...8.00	3.60	1.00
☐		Bob Gibson hurls		
☐		shutout		
☐	155	World Series Game 5 ...4.00	1.80	.50
☐		Jim Lonborg wins		
☐		again		
☐	156	World Series Game 6 ...4.00	1.80	.50
☐		Rico Petrocelli		
☐		two homers		
☐	157	World Series Game 7 ...4.00	1.80	.50
☐		St. Louis wins it		
☐	158	World Series Summary 4.00	1.80	.50
☐		Cardinals celebrate		
☐	159	Don Kessinger 2.00	.90	.25
☐	160	Earl Wilson 2.00	.90	.25
☐	161	Norm Miller 1.50	.65	.19
☐	162	Cards Rookies 2.00	.90	.25

Hal Gilson
Mike Torrez

☐	163 Gene Brabender	1.50	.65	.19
☐	164 Ramon Webster	1.50	.65	.19
☐	165 Tony Oliva	4.00	1.80	.50
☐	166 Claude Raymond	1.50	.65	.19
☐	167 Elston Howard	3.00	1.35	.40
☐	168 Dodgers Team	3.00	1.35	.40
☐	169 Bob Bolin	1.50	.65	.19
☐	170 Jim Fregosi	2.00	.90	.25
☐	171 Don Nottebart	1.50	.65	.19
☐	172 Walt Williams	1.50	.65	.19
☐	173 John Boozer	1.50	.65	.19
☐	174 Bob Tillman	1.50	.65	.19
☐	175 Maury Wills	4.50	2.00	.55
☐	176 Bob Allen	1.50	.65	.19
☐	177 Mets Rookies	1650.00	750.00	210.00

Jerry Koosman
Nolan Ryan

☐	178 Don Wert	1.50	.65	.19
☐	179 Bill Stoneman	1.50	.65	.19
☐	180 Curt Flood	2.00	.90	.25
☐	181 Jerry Zimmerman	1.50	.65	.19
☐	182 Dave Giusti	1.50	.65	.19
☐	183 Bob Kennedy MG	2.00	.90	.25
☐	184 Lou Johnson	2.00	.90	.25
☐	185 Tom Haller	1.50	.65	.19
☐	186 Eddie Watt	1.50	.65	.19
☐	187 Sonny Jackson	1.50	.65	.19
☐	188 Cap Peterson	1.50	.65	.19
☐	189 Bill Landis	1.50	.65	.19
☐	190 Bill White	2.50	1.15	.30
☐	191 Dan Frisella	1.50	.65	.19
☐	192A Checklist 3	7.50	1.90	.60

Carl Yastrzemski
(Special Baseball
Playing Card)

☐	192B Checklist 3	7.50	1.90	.60

Carl Yastrzemski
(Special Baseball
Playing Card Game)

☐	193 Jack Hamilton	1.50	.65	.19
☐	194 Don Buford	1.50	.65	.19
☐	195 Joe Pepitone	2.00	.90	.25
☐	196 Gary Nolan	2.00	.90	.25
☐	197 Larry Brown	1.50	.65	.19
☐	198 Roy Face	2.00	.90	.25
☐	199 A's Rookies	1.50	.65	.19

Roberto Rodriquez
Darrell Osteen

☐	200 Orlando Cepeda	5.00	2.30	.60
☐	201 Mike Marshall	3.00	1.35	.40
☐	202 Adolfo Phillips	1.50	.65	.19
☐	203 Dick Kelley	1.50	.65	.19
☐	204 Andy Etchebarren	1.50	.65	.19
☐	205 Juan Marichal	10.00	4.50	1.25
☐	206 Cal Ermer MG	1.50	.65	.19

☐	207 Carroll Sembera	1.50	.65	.19
☐	208 Willie Davis	2.00	.90	.25
☐	209 Tim Cullen	1.50	.65	.19
☐	210 Gary Peters	1.50	.65	.19
☐	211 J.C. Martin	1.50	.65	.19
☐	212 Dave Morehead	1.50	.65	.19
☐	213 Chico Ruiz	1.50	.65	.19
☐	214 Yankees Rookies	2.00	.90	.25

Stan Bahnsen
Frank Fernandez

☐	215 Jim Bunning	4.50	2.00	.55
☐	216 Bubba Morton	1.50	.65	.19
☐	217 Dick Farrell	1.50	.65	.19
☐	218 Ken Suarez	1.50	.65	.19
☐	219 Rob Gardner	1.50	.65	.19
☐	220 Harmon Killebrew	15.00	6.75	1.90
☐	221 Braves Team	3.00	1.35	.40
☐	222 Jim Hardin	1.50	.65	.19
☐	223 Ollie Brown	1.50	.65	.19
☐	224 Jack Aker	1.50	.65	.19
☐	225 Richie Allen	4.50	2.00	.55
☐	226 Jimmie Price	1.50	.65	.19
☐	227 Joe Hoerner	1.50	.65	.19
☐	228 Dodgers Rookies	2.00	.90	.25

Jack Billingham
Jim Fairey

☐	229 Fred Klages	1.50	.65	.19
☐	230 Pete Rose	40.00	18.00	5.00
☐	231 Dave Baldwin	1.50	.65	.19
☐	232 Denis Menke	1.50	.65	.19
☐	233 George Scott	2.00	.90	.25
☐	234 Bill Monbouquette	1.50	.65	.19
☐	235 Ron Santo	4.00	1.80	.50
☐	236 Tug McGraw	3.00	1.35	.40
☐	237 Alvin Dark MG	2.00	.90	.25
☐	238 Tom Satriano	1.50	.65	.19
☐	239 Bill Henry	1.50	.65	.19
☐	240 Al Kaline	25.00	11.50	3.10
☐	241 Felix Millan	1.50	.65	.19
☐	242 Moe Drabowsky	2.00	.90	.25
☐	243 Rich Rollins	1.50	.65	.19
☐	244 John Donaldson	1.50	.65	.19
☐	245 Tony Gonzalez	1.50	.65	.19
☐	246 Fritz Peterson	1.50	.65	.19
☐	247 Reds Rookies	275.00	125.00	34.00

Johnny Bench
Ron Tompkins

☐	248 Fred Valentine	1.50	.65	.19
☐	249 Bill Singer	1.50	.65	.19
☐	250 Carl Yastrzemski	40.00	18.00	5.00
☐	251 Manny Sanguillen	5.00	2.30	.60
☐	252 Angels Team	3.00	1.35	.40
☐	253 Dick Hughes	1.50	.65	.19
☐	254 Cleon Jones	2.00	.90	.25
☐	255 Dean Chance	2.00	.90	.25
☐	256 Norm Cash	6.00	2.70	.75
☐	257 Phil Niekro	8.00	3.60	1.00

☐ 258	Cubs Rookies................1.50	.65	.19
	Jose Arcia		
	Bill Schlesinger		
☐ 259	Ken Boyer 2.50	1.15	.30
☐ 260	Jim Wynn 2.00	.90	.25
☐ 261	Dave Duncan 2.00	.90	.25
☐ 262	Rick Wise 2.00	.90	.25
☐ 263	Horace Clarke 1.50	.65	.19
☐ 264	Ted Abernathy 1.50	.65	.19
☐ 265	Tommy Davis 2.00	.90	.25
☐ 266	Paul Popovich 1.50	.65	.19
☐ 267	Herman Franks MG 1.50	.65	.19
☐ 268	Bob Humphreys 1.50	.65	.19
☐ 269	Bob Tiefenauer 1.50	.65	.19
☐ 270	Matty Alou 2.00	.90	.25
☐ 271	Bobby Knoop 1.50	.65	.19
☐ 272	Ray Culp 1.50	.65	.19
☐ 273	Dave Johnson 2.00	.90	.25
☐ 274	Mike Cuellar 2.00	.90	.25
☐ 275	Tim McCarver 4.00	1.80	.50
☐ 276	Jim Roland 1.50	.65	.19
☐ 277	Jerry Buchek 1.50	.65	.19
☐ 278	Checklist 4 ....6.00	1.50	.50
	Orlando Cepeda		
☐ 279	Bill Hands 1.50	.65	.19
☐ 280	Mickey Mantle.........240.00	110.00	30.00
☐ 281	Jim Campanis 1.50	.65	.19
☐ 282	Rick Monday 2.00	.90	.25
☐ 283	Mel Queen 1.50	.65	.19
☐ 284	Johnny Briggs 1.50	.65	.19
☐ 285	Dick McAuliffe..............2.00	.90	.25
☐ 286	Cecil Upshaw 1.50	.65	.19
☐ 287	White Sox Rookies......1.50	.65	.19
	Mickey Abarbanel		
	Cisco Carlos		
☐ 288	Dave Wickersham 1.50	.65	.19
☐ 289	Woody Held 1.50	.65	.19
☐ 290	Willie McCovey 12.50	5.75	1.55
☐ 291	Dick Lines 1.50	.65	.19
☐ 292	Art Shamsky 1.50	.65	.19
☐ 293	Bruce Howard 1.50	.65	.19
☐ 294	Red Schoendienst MG .4.00	1.80	.50
☐ 295	Sonny Siebert 1.50	.65	.19
☐ 296	Byron Browne 1.50	.65	.19
☐ 297	Russ Gibson 1.50	.65	.19
☐ 298	Jim Brewer 1.50	.65	.19
☐ 299	Gene Michael 2.00	.90	.25
☐ 300	Rusty Staub 3.50	1.55	.45
☐ 301	Twins Rookies 1.50	.65	.19
	George Mitterwald		
	Rick Renick		
☐ 302	Gerry Arrigo 1.50	.65	.19
☐ 303	Dick Green 1.50	.65	.19
☐ 304	Sandy Valdespino 1.50	.65	.19
☐ 305	Minnie Rojas 1.50	.65	.19
☐ 306	Mike Ryan 1.50	.65	.19
☐ 307	John Hiller 2.00	.90	.25

☐ 308	Pirates Team................3.00	1.35	.40
☐ 309	Ken Henderson 1.50	.65	.19
☐ 310	Luis Aparicio 6.00	2.70	.75
☐ 311	Jack Lamabe 1.50	.65	.19
☐ 312	Curt Blefary 1.50	.65	.19
☐ 313	Al Weis 1.50	.65	.19
☐ 314	Red Sox Rookies..........1.50	.65	.19
	Bill Rohr		
	George Spriggs		
☐ 315	Zoilo Versalles 1.50	.65	.19
☐ 316	Steve Barber 1.50	.65	.19
☐ 317	Ron Brand 1.50	.65	.19
☐ 318	Chico Salmon 1.50	.65	.19
☐ 319	George Culver 1.50	.65	.19
☐ 320	Frank Howard 3.00	1.35	.40
☐ 321	Leo Durocher MG 3.00	1.35	.40
☐ 322	Dave Boswell 1.50	.65	.19
☐ 323	Deron Johnson 2.00	.90	.25
☐ 324	Jim Nash 1.50	.65	.19
☐ 325	Manny Mota 2.00	.90	.25
☐ 326	Dennis Ribant 1.50	.65	.19
☐ 327	Tony Taylor 1.50	.65	.19
☐ 328	Angels Rookies 1.50	.65	.19
	Chuck Vinson		
	Jim Weaver		
☐ 329	Duane Josephson 1.50	.65	.19
☐ 330	Roger Maris 40.00	18.00	5.00
☐ 331	Dan Osinski 1.50	.65	.19
☐ 332	Doug Rader 2.00	.90	.25
☐ 333	Ron Herbel 1.50	.65	.19
☐ 334	Orioles Team 3.00	1.35	.40
☐ 335	Bob Allison 2.00	.90	.25
☐ 336	John Purdin 1.50	.65	.19
☐ 337	Bill Robinson 2.00	.90	.25
☐ 338	Bob Johnson 1.50	.65	.19
☐ 339	Rich Nye 1.50	.65	.19
☐ 340	Max Alvis 1.50	.65	.19
☐ 341	Jim Lemon MG 1.50	.65	.19
☐ 342	Ken Johnson 1.50	.65	.19
☐ 343	Jim Gosger 1.50	.65	.19
☐ 344	Donn Clendenon 2.00	.90	.25
☐ 345	Bob Hendley 1.50	.65	.19
☐ 346	Jerry Adair 1.50	.65	.19
☐ 347	George Brunet 1.50	.65	.19
☐ 348	Phillies Rookies 1.50	.65	.19
	Larry Colton		
	Dick Thoenen		
☐ 349	Ed Spiezio 1.50	.65	.19
☐ 350	Hoyt Wilhelm 7.00	3.10	.85
☐ 351	Bob Barton 1.50	.65	.19
☐ 352	Jackie Hernandez 1.50	.65	.19
☐ 353	Mack Jones 1.50	.65	.19
☐ 354	Pete Richert 1.50	.65	.19
☐ 355	Ernie Banks 25.00	11.50	3.10
☐ 356A	Checklist 5..................6.00	1.50	.50
	Ken Holtzman		
	(Head centered		

	within circle)		
☐ 356B	Checklist 5....................6.00	1.50	.50
	Ken Holtzman		
	(Head shifted right		
	within circle)		
☐ 357	Len Gabrielson...........1.50	.65	.19
☐ 358	Mike Epstein 1.50	.65	.19
☐ 359	Joe Moeller..................1.50	.65	.19
☐ 360	Willie Horton.................2.50	1.15	.30
☐ 361	Harmon Killebrew AS...8.00	3.60	1.00
☐ 362	Orlando Cepeda AS......3.00	1.35	.40
☐ 363	Rod Carew AS.............14.00	6.25	1.75
☐ 364	Joe Morgan AS 10.00	4.50	1.25
☐ 365	Brooks Robinson AS..10.00	4.50	1.25
☐ 366	Ron Santo AS...............3.00	1.35	.40
☐ 367	Jim Fregosi AS............2.25	1.00	.30
☐ 368	Gene Alley AS..............2.25	1.00	.30
☐ 369	Carl Yastrzemski AS..12.50	5.75	1.55
☐ 370	Hank Aaron AS...........15.00	6.75	1.90
☐ 371	Tony Oliva AS...............3.00	1.35	.40
☐ 372	Lou Brock AS..............10.00	4.50	1.25
☐ 373	Frank Robinson AS ...10.00	4.50	1.25
☐ 374	Bob Clemente AS........15.00	6.75	1.90
☐ 375	Bill Freehan AS............2.25	1.00	.30
☐ 376	Tim McCarver AS..........3.00	1.35	.40
☐ 377	Joel Horlen AS.............2.25	1.00	.30
☐ 378	Bob Gibson AS............10.00	4.50	1.25
☐ 379	Gary Peters AS............2.25	1.00	.30
☐ 380	Ken Holtzman AS..........2.25	1.00	.30
☐ 381	Boog Powell..................3.00	1.35	.40
☐ 382	Ramon Hernandez 1.50	.65	.19
☐ 383	Steve Whitaker............1.50	.65	.19
☐ 384	Reds Rookies.............12.50	5.75	1.55
	Bill Henry		
	Hal McRae		
☐ 385	Jim Hunter..................15.00	6.75	1.90
☐ 386	Greg Goossen..............1.50	.65	.19
☐ 387	Joe Foy........................1.50	.65	.19
☐ 388	Ray Washburn..............1.50	.65	.19
☐ 389	Jay Johnstone.............2.00	.90	.25
☐ 390	Bill Mazeroski.............3.50	1.55	.45
☐ 391	Bob Priddy...................1.50	.65	.19
☐ 392	Grady Hatton MG.........1.50	.65	.19
☐ 393	Jim Perry 2.00	.90	.25
☐ 394	Tommie Aaron..............2.00	.90	.25
☐ 395	Camilo Pascual............2.00	.90	.25
☐ 396	Bobby Wine 1.50	.65	.19
☐ 397	Vic Davalillo................1.50	.65	.19
☐ 398	Jim Grant.....................1.50	.65	.19
☐ 399	Ray Oyler.....................1.50	.65	.19
☐ 400A	Mike McCormick........2.00	.90	.25
	(Yellow letters)		
☐ 400B	Mike McCormick......100.00	45.00	12.50
	(Team name in		
	white letters)		
☐ 401	Mets Team...................3.00	1.35	.40
☐ 402	Mike Hegan..................1.50	.65	.19
☐ 403	John Buzhardt..............1.50	.65	.19
☐ 404	Floyd Robinson............1.50	.65	.19
☐ 405	Tommy Helms...............2.00	.90	.25
☐ 406	Dick Ellsworth.............1.50	.65	.19
☐ 407	Gary Kolb.....................1.50	.65	.19
☐ 408	Steve Carlton............60.00	27.00	7.50
☐ 409	Orioles Rookies...........1.50	.65	.19
	Frank Peters		
	Ron Stone		
☐ 410	Fergie Jenkins...........20.00	9.00	2.50
☐ 411	Ron Hansen.................1.50	.65	.19
☐ 412	Clay Carroll.................2.00	.90	.25
☐ 413	Tom McCraw 1.50	.65	.19
☐ 414	Mickey Lolich..............5.00	2.30	.60
☐ 415	Johnny Callison 2.00	.90	.25
☐ 416	Bill Rigney MG.............1.50	.65	.19
☐ 417	Willie Crawford............1.50	.65	.19
☐ 418	Eddie Fisher................1.50	.65	.19
☐ 419	Jack Hiatt....................1.50	.65	.19
☐ 420	Cesar Tovar.................1.50	.65	.19
☐ 421	Ron Taylor...................1.50	.65	.19
☐ 422	Rene Lachemann 2.00	.90	.25
☐ 423	Fred Gladding 1.50	.65	.19
☐ 424	Chicago White Sox.....3.00	1.35	.40
	Team Card		
☐ 425	Jim Maloney................2.00	.90	.25
☐ 426	Hank Allen...................1.50	.65	.19
☐ 427	Dick Calmus................1.50	.65	.19
☐ 428	Vic Roznovsky 1.50	.65	.19
☐ 429	Tommie Sisk................1.50	.65	.19
☐ 430	Rico Petrocelli.............2.00	.90	.25
☐ 431	Dooley Womack............1.50	.65	.19
☐ 432	Indians Rookies...........1.50	.65	.19
	Bill Davis		
	Jose Vidal		
☐ 433	Bob Rodgers................2.00	.90	.25
☐ 434	Ricardo Joseph............1.50	.65	.19
☐ 435	Ron Perranoski............2.00	.90	.25
☐ 436	Hal Lanier....................1.50	.65	.19
☐ 437	Don Cardwell...............1.50	.65	.19
☐ 438	Lee Thomas.................2.00	.90	.25
☐ 439	Lum Harris MG 1.50	.65	.19
☐ 440	Claude Osteen.............2.00	.90	.25
☐ 441	Alex Johnson...............2.00	.90	.25
☐ 442	Dick Bosman...............1.50	.65	.19
☐ 443	Joe Azcue....................1.50	.65	.19
☐ 444	Jack Fisher..................1.50	.65	.19
☐ 445	Mike Shannon..............2.00	.90	.25
☐ 446	Ron Kline.....................1.50	.65	.19
☐ 447	Tigers Rookies............1.50	.65	.19
	George Korince		
	Fred Lasher		
☐ 448	Gary Wagner................1.50	.65	.19
☐ 449	Gene Oliver.................1.50	.65	.19
☐ 450	Jim Kaat......................4.50	2.00	.55
☐ 451	Al Spangler.................1.50	.65	.19
☐ 452	Jesus Alou 1.50	.65	.19

☐ 453	Sammy Ellis	1.50	.65	.19	☐ 496	Steve Hamilton	3.00	1.35	.40
☐ 454A	Checklist 6	7.50	1.90	.60	☐ 497	Cardinals Team	6.00	2.70	.75
	Frank Robinson				☐ 498	Bill Bryan	3.00	1.35	.40
	(Cap complete				☐ 499	Steve Blass	3.50	1.55	.45
	within circle)				☐ 500	Frank Robinson	30.00	13.50	3.80
☐ 454B	Checklist 6	7.50	1.90	.60	☐ 501	John Odom	3.00	1.35	.40
	Frank Robinson				☐ 502	Mike Andrews	3.00	1.35	.40
	(Cap partially				☐ 503	Al Jackson	3.00	1.35	.40
	within circle)				☐ 504	Russ Snyder	3.00	1.35	.40
☐ 455	Rico Carty	2.00	.90	.25	☐ 505	Joe Sparma	6.00	2.70	.75
☐ 456	John O'Donoghue	1.50	.65	.19	☐ 506	Clarence Jones	5.00	2.30	.60
☐ 457	Jim Lefebvre	2.00	.90	.25	☐ 507	Wade Blasingame	3.00	1.35	.40
☐ 458	Lew Krausse	3.50	1.55	.45	☐ 508	Duke Sims	3.00	1.35	.40
☐ 459	Dick Simpson	3.00	1.35	.40	☐ 509	Dennis Higgins	3.00	1.35	.40
☐ 460	Jim Lonborg	5.00	2.30	.60	☐ 510	Ron Fairly	3.50	1.55	.45
☐ 461	Chuck Hiller	3.00	1.35	.40	☐ 511	Bill Kelso	3.00	1.35	.40
☐ 462	Barry Moore	3.00	1.35	.40	☐ 512	Grant Jackson	3.00	1.35	.40
☐ 463	Jim Schaffer	3.00	1.35	.40	☐ 513	Hank Bauer MG	3.50	1.55	.45
☐ 464	Don McMahon	3.00	1.35	.40	☐ 514	Al McBean	3.00	1.35	.40
☐ 465	Tommie Agee	3.50	1.55	.45	☐ 515	Russ Nixon	3.00	1.35	.40
☐ 466	Bill Dillman	3.00	1.35	.40	☐ 516	Pete Mikkelsen	3.00	1.35	.40
☐ 467	Dick Howser	3.50	1.55	.45	☐ 517	Diego Segui	3.00	1.35	.40
☐ 468	Larry Sherry	3.00	1.35	.40	☐ 518A	Checklist 7 ERR	8.00	2.00	.65
☐ 469	Ty Cline	3.00	1.35	.40		(539 AL Rookies)			
☐ 470	Bill Freehan	5.00	2.30	.60		(Clete Boyer)			
☐ 471	Orlando Pena	3.00	1.35	.40	☐ 518B	Checklist 7 COR	12.00	3.00	.95
☐ 472	Walt Alston MG	4.50	2.00	.55		(539 ML Rookies)			
☐ 473	Al Worthington	3.00	1.35	.40		(Clete Boyer)			
☐ 474	Paul Schaal	3.00	1.35	.40	☐ 519	Jerry Stephenson	3.00	1.35	.40
☐ 475	Joe Niekro	4.50	2.00	.55	☐ 520	Lou Brock	25.00	11.50	3.10
☐ 476	Woody Woodward	3.50	1.55	.45	☐ 521	Don Shaw	3.00	1.35	.40
☐ 477	Philadelphia Phillies	6.00	2.70	.75	☐ 522	Wayne Causey	3.00	1.35	.40
	Team Card				☐ 523	John Tsitouris	3.00	1.35	.40
☐ 478	Dave McNally	3.50	1.55	.45	☐ 524	Andy Kosco	3.00	1.35	.40
☐ 479	Phil Gagliano	3.00	1.35	.40	☐ 525	Jim Davenport	3.00	1.35	•40
☐ 480	Manager's Dream	35.00	16.00	4.40	☐ 526	Bill Denehy	3.00	1.35	.40
	Tony Oliva				☐ 527	Tito Francona	3.00	1.35	.40
	Chico Cardenas				☐ 528	Tigers Team	70.00	32.00	8.75
	Bob Clemente				☐ 529	Bruce Von Hoff	3.00	1.35	.40
☐ 481	John Wyatt	3.00	1.35	.40	☐ 530	Bird Belters	15.00	6.75	1.90
☐ 482	Jose Pagan	3.00	1.35	.40		Brooks Robinson			
☐ 483	Darold Knowles	3.00	1.35	.40		Frank Robinson			
☐ 484	Phil Roof	3.00	1.35	.40	☐ 531	Chuck Hinton	3.00	1.35	.40
☐ 485	Ken Berry	3.00	1.35	.40	☐ 532	Luis Tiant	5.00	2.30	.60
☐ 486	Cal Koonce	3.00	1.35	.40	☐ 533	Wes Parker	3.50	1.55	.45
☐ 487	Lee May	5.00	2.30	.60	☐ 534	Bob Miller	3.75	1.70	.45
☐ 488	Dick Tracewski	3.00	1.35	.40	☐ 535	Danny Cater	3.75	1.70	.45
☐ 489	Wally Bunker	3.00	1.35	.40	☐ 536	Bill Short	3.75	1.70	.45
☐ 490	Super Stars	125.00	57.50	15.50	☐ 537	Norm Siebern	3.75	1.70	.45
	Harmon Killebrew				☐ 538	Manny Jimenez	3.75	1.70	.45
	Willie Mays				☐ 539	Major League Rookies	3.75	1.70	.45
	Mickey Mantle					Jim Ray			
☐ 491	Denny Lemaster	3.00	1.35	.40		Mike Ferraro			
☐ 492	Jeff Torborg	3.50	1.55	.45	☐ 540	Nelson Briles	4.50	2.00	.55
☐ 493	Jim McGlothlin	3.00	1.35	.40	☐ 541	Sandy Alomar	4.50	2.00	.55
☐ 494	Ray Sadecki	3.00	1.35	.40	☐ 542	John Boccabella	3.75	1.70	.45
☐ 495	Leon Wagner	3.00	1.35	.40	☐ 543	Bob Lee	3.75	1.70	.45

☐ 544	Mayo Smith MG	5.00	2.30	.60
☐ 545	Lindy McDaniel	4.50	2.00	.55
☐ 546	Roy White	4.50	2.00	.55
☐ 547	Dan Coombs	3.75	1.70	.45
☐ 548	Bernie Allen	3.75	1.70	.45
☐ 549	Orioles Rookies	3.75	1.70	.45
	Curt Motton			
	Roger Nelson			
☐ 550	Clete Boyer	4.50	2.00	.55
☐ 551	Darrell Sutherland	3.75	1.70	.45
☐ 552	Ed Kirkpatrick	3.75	1.70	.45
☐ 553	Hank Aguirre	3.75	1.70	.45
☐ 554	A's Team	7.50	3.40	.95
☐ 555	Jose Tartabull	4.50	2.00	.55
☐ 556	Dick Selma	3.75	1.70	.45
☐ 557	Frank Quilici	3.75	1.70	.45
☐ 558	Johnny Edwards	3.75	1.70	.45
☐ 559	Pirates Rookies	3.75	1.70	.45
	Carl Taylor			
	Luke Walker			
☐ 560	Paul Casanova	3.75	1.70	.45
☐ 561	Lee Elia	4.25	1.90	.55
☐ 562	Jim Bouton	6.00	2.70	.75
☐ 563	Ed Charles	3.75	1.70	.45
☐ 564	Eddie Stanky MG	4.50	2.00	.55
☐ 565	Larry Dierker	4.25	1.90	.55
☐ 566	Ken Harrelson	4.50	2.00	.55
☐ 567	Clay Dalrymple	3.75	1.70	.45
☐ 568	Willie Smith	3.75	1.70	.45
☐ 569	NL Rookies	3.75	1.70	.45
	Ivan Murrell			
	Les Rohr			
☐ 570	Rick Reichardt	3.75	1.70	.45
☐ 571	Tony LaRussa	8.00	3.60	1.00
☐ 572	Don Bosch	3.75	1.70	.45
☐ 573	Joe Coleman	3.75	1.70	.45
☐ 574	Cincinnati Reds	7.50	3.40	.95
	Team Card			
☐ 575	Jim Palmer	65.00	29.00	8.25
☐ 576	Dave Adlesh	3.75	1.70	.45
☐ 577	Fred Talbot	3.75	1.70	.45
☐ 578	Orlando Martinez	3.75	1.70	.45
☐ 579	NL Rookies	5.50	2.50	.70
	Larry Hisle			
	Mike Lum			
☐ 580	Bob Bailey	3.75	1.70	.45
☐ 581	Garry Roggenburk	3.75	1.70	.45
☐ 582	Jerry Grote	3.75	1.70	.45
☐ 583	Gates Brown	6.00	2.70	.75
☐ 584	Larry Shepard MG	3.75	1.70	.45
☐ 585	Wilbur Wood	4.50	2.00	.55
☐ 586	Jim Pagliaroni	3.75	1.70	.45
☐ 587	Roger Repoz	3.75	1.70	.45
☐ 588	Dick Schofield	3.75	1.70	.45
☐ 589	Twins Rookies	3.75	1.70	.45
	Ron Clark			
	Moe Ogier			

☐ 590	Tommy Harper	4.50	2.00	.55
☐ 591	Dick Nen	3.75	1.70	.45
☐ 592	John Bateman	3.75	1.70	.45
☐ 593	Lee Stange	3.75	1.70	.45
☐ 594	Phil Linz	4.50	2.00	.55
☐ 595	Phil Ortega	3.75	1.70	.45
☐ 596	Charlie Smith	3.75	1.70	.45
☐ 597	Bill McCool	3.75	1.70	.45
☐ 598	Jerry May	5.00	2.30	.60

1969 Topps

The cards in this 664-card set measure
2 1/2" by 3 1/2". The 1969 Topps set
includes Sporting News All-Star Selections
as card numbers 416 to 435. Other popular subsets within this set include League
Leaders (1-12) and World Series cards
(162-169). The fifth series contains several
variations; the more difficult variety consists of cards with the player's first name,
last name, and/or position in white letters
instead of lettering in some other color.
These are designated in the checklist
below by WL (white letters). Each checklist
card features a different popular player's
picture inside a circle on the front of the
checklist card. Two different poses of Clay
Dalrymple and Donn Clendenon exist, as
indicated in the checklist. The key Rookie
Cards in this set are Rollie Fingers, Reggie
Jackson, and Graig Nettles. This was the
last year that Topps issued multi-player
special star cards, ending a 13-year tradition, which they had begun in 1957. There
were cropping differences in checklist
cards 57, 214, and 412, due to their each
being printed with two different series. The

differences are difficult to explain and have not been greatly sought by collectors; hence they are not listed explicitly in the list below. The All-Star cards 426-435, when turned over and placed together, form a puzzle back of Pete Rose.

	NRMT-MT	EXC	G-VG
COMPLETE SET (664)	2650.00	1200.00	325.00
COMMON PLAYER (1-109)	1.50	.65	.19
COMMON PLAYER (110-218)	1.50	.65	.19
COMMON PLAYER (219-327)	2.50	1.15	.30
COMMON PLAYER (328-425)	1.50	.65	.19
COMMON PLAYER (426-512)	1.50	.65	.19
COMMON PLAYER (513-588)	2.00	.90	.25
COMMON PLAYER (589-664)	2.25	1.00	.30

☐ 1 AL Batting Leaders	12.00	3.60	1.20
Carl Yastrzemski			
Danny Cater			
Tony Oliva			
☐ 2 NL Batting Leaders	5.50	2.50	.70
Pete Rose			
Matty Alou			
Felipe Alou			
☐ 3 AL RBI Leaders	3.00	1.35	.40
Ken Harrelson			
Frank Howard			
Jim Northrup			
☐ 4 NL RBI Leaders	4.50	2.00	.55
Willie McCovey			
Ron Santo			
Billy Williams			
☐ 5 AL Home Run Leaders	3.00	1.35	.40
Frank Howard			
Willie Horton			
Ken Harrelson			
☐ 6 NL Home Run Leaders	4.50	2.00	.55
Willie McCovey			
Richie Allen			
Ernie Banks			
☐ 7 AL ERA Leaders	3.00	1.35	.40
Luis Tiant			
Sam McDowell			
Dave McNally			
☐ 8 NL ERA Leaders	3.00	1.35	.40
Bob Gibson			
Bobby Bolin			
Bob Veale			
☐ 9 AL Pitching Leaders	3.00	1.35	.40
Denny McLain			
Dave McNally			
Luis Tiant			
Mel Stottlemyre			
☐ 10 NL Pitching Leaders	5.00	2.30	.60
Juan Marichal			
Bob Gibson			
Fergie Jenkins			
☐ 11 AL Strikeout Leaders	3.00	1.35	.40
Sam McDowell			
Denny McLain			
Luis Tiant			
☐ 12 NL Strikeout Leaders	3.50	1.55	.45
Bob Gibson			
Fergie Jenkins			
Bill Singer			
☐ 13 Mickey Stanley	2.00	.90	.25
☐ 14 Al McBean	1.50	.65	.19
☐ 15 Boog Powell	3.00	1.35	.40
☐ 16 Giants Rookies	1.50	.65	.19
Cesar Gutierrez			
Rich Robertson			
☐ 17 Mike Marshall	2.00	.90	.25
☐ 18 Dick Schofield	1.50	.65	.19
☐ 19 Ken Suarez	1.50	.65	.19
☐ 20 Ernie Banks	20.00	9.00	2.50
☐ 21 Jose Santiago	1.50	.65	.19
☐ 22 Jesus Alou	1.50	.65	.19
☐ 23 Lew Krausse	1.50	.65	.19
☐ 24 Walt Alston MG	2.50	1.15	.30
☐ 25 Roy White	2.00	.90	.25
☐ 26 Clay Carroll	2.00	.90	.25
☐ 27 Bernie Allen	1.50	.65	.19
☐ 28 Mike Ryan	1.50	.65	.19
☐ 29 Dave Morehead	1.50	.65	.19
☐ 30 Bob Allison	2.00	.90	.25
☐ 31 Mets Rookies	3.00	1.35	.40
Gary Gentry			
Amos Otis			
☐ 32 Sammy Ellis	1.50	.65	.19
☐ 33 Wayne Causey	1.50	.65	.19
☐ 34 Gary Peters	1.50	.65	.19
☐ 35 Joe Morgan	12.50	5.75	1.55
☐ 36 Luke Walker	1.50	.65	.19
☐ 37 Curt Motton	1.50	.65	.19
☐ 38 Zoilo Versalles	1.50	.65	.19
☐ 39 Dick Hughes	1.50	.65	.19
☐ 40 Mayo Smith MG	1.50	.65	.19
☐ 41 Bob Barton	1.50	.65	.19
☐ 42 Tommy Harper	2.00	.90	.25
☐ 43 Joe Niekro	2.00	.90	.25
☐ 44 Danny Cater	1.50	.65	.19
☐ 45 Maury Wills	3.00	1.35	.40
☐ 46 Fritz Peterson	1.50	.65	.19
☐ 47A Paul Popovich	1.50	.65	.19
(No helmet emblem)			
☐ 47B Paul Popovich	25.00	11.50	3.10
(C emblem on helmet)			
☐ 48 Brant Alyea	1.50	.65	.19
☐ 49A Royals Rookies ERR	1.50	.65	.19
Steve Jones			
E. Rodriguez "q"			
☐ 49B Royals Rookies COR	25.00	11.50	3.10
Steve Jones			

E. Rodriguez "g"
- [ ] 50 Bob Clemente UER.......50.00 . 23.00 . 6.25
  (Bats Right listed twice)
- [ ] 51 Woody Fryman ....1.50 . .65 . .19
- [ ] 52 Mike Andrews ....1.50 . .65 . .19
- [ ] 53 Sonny Jackson ....1.50 . .65 . .19
- [ ] 54 Cisco Carlos..................1.50 . .65 . .19
- [ ] 55 Jerry Grote....................1.50 . .65 . .19
- [ ] 56 Rich Reese...................1.50 . .65 . .19
- [ ] 57 Checklist 1 ....5.50 . 1.40 . .45
  Denny McLain
- [ ] 58 Fred Gladding ....1.50 . .65 . .19
- [ ] 59 Jay Johnstone..............2.00 . .90 . .25
- [ ] 60 Nelson Briles................2.00 . .90 . .25
- [ ] 61 Jimmie Hall ....1.50 . .65 . .19
- [ ] 62 Chico Salmon ....1.50 . .65 . .19
- [ ] 63 Jim Hickman.................2.00 . .90 . .25
- [ ] 64 Bill Monbouquette........1.50 . .65 . .19
- [ ] 65 Willie Davis ....2.00 . .90 . .25
- [ ] 66 Orioles Rookies.............2.00 . .90 . .25
  Mike Adamson
  Merv Rettenmund
- [ ] 67 Bill Stoneman ....1.50 . .65 . .19
- [ ] 68 Dave Duncan.................2.00 . .90 . .25
- [ ] 69 Steve Hamilton ....1.50 . .65 . .19
- [ ] 70 Tommy Helms................2.00 . .90 . .25
- [ ] 71 Steve Whitaker..............1.50 . .65 . .19
- [ ] 72 Ron Taylor ....1.50 . .65 . .19
- [ ] 73 Johnny Briggs................1.50 . .65 . .19
- [ ] 74 Preston Gomez MG........1.50 . .65 . .19
- [ ] 75 Luis Aparicio.................5.50 . 2.50 . .70
- [ ] 76 Norm Miller....................1.50 . .65 . .19
- [ ] 77A Ron Perranoski...........2.00 . .90 . .25
  (No emblem on cap)
- [ ] 77B Ron Perranoski.........25.00 . 11.50 . 3.10
  (LA on cap)
- [ ] 78 Tom Satriano ....1.50 . .65 . .19
- [ ] 79 Milt Pappas ....2.00 . .90 . .25
- [ ] 80 Norm Cash....................3.00 . 1.35 . .40
- [ ] 81 Mel Queen.....................1.50 . .65 . .19
- [ ] 82 Pirates Rookies............11.00 . 4.90 . 1.40
  Rich Hebner
  Al Oliver
- [ ] 83 Mike Ferraro ....2.00 . .90 . .25
- [ ] 84 Bob Humphreys.............1.50 . .65 . .19
- [ ] 85 Lou Brock.....................25.00 . 11.50 . 3.10
- [ ] 86 Pete Richert ....1.50 . .65 . .19
- [ ] 87 Horace Clarke................1.50 . .65 . .19
- [ ] 88 Rich Nye ....1.50 . .65 . .19
- [ ] 89 Russ Gibson ....1.50 . .65 . .19
- [ ] 90 Jerry Koosman...............6.00 . 2.70 . .75
- [ ] 91 Alvin Dark MG...............2.00 . .90 . .25
- [ ] 92 Jack Billingham..............1.50 . .65 . .19
- [ ] 93 Joe Foy ....1.50 . .65 . .19
- [ ] 94 Hank Aguirre..................1.50 . .65 . .19
- [ ] 95 Johnny Bench ....140.00 . 65.00 . 17.50

- [ ] 96 Denny Lemaster............1.50 . .65 . .19
- [ ] 97 Buddy Bradford..............1.50 . .65 . .19
- [ ] 98 Dave Giusti ....1.50 . .65 . .19
- [ ] 99A Twins Rookies ....20.00 . 9.00 . 2.50
  Danny Morris
  Graig Nettles
  (No loop)
- [ ] 99B Twins Rookies ....24.00 . 11.00 . 3.00
  Danny Morris
  Graig Nettles
  (Errant loop in
  upper left corner
  of obverse)
- [ ] 100 Hank Aaron................60.00 . 27.00 . 7.50
- [ ] 101 Daryl Patterson............1.50 . .65 . .19
- [ ] 102 Jim Davenport.............1.50 . .65 . .19
- [ ] 103 Roger Repoz................1.50 . .65 . .19
- [ ] 104 Steve Blass ....2.00 . .90 . .25
- [ ] 105 Rick Monday.................2.00 . .90 . .25
- [ ] 106 Jim Hannan..................1.50 . .65 . .19
- [ ] 107A Checklist 2 ERR.........5.50 . 1.40 . .45
  (161 Jim Purdin)
  (Bob Gibson)
- [ ] 107B Checklist 2 COR.........7.50 . 1.90 . .60
  (161 John Purdin)
  (Bob Gibson)
- [ ] 108 Tony Taylor..................1.50 . .65 . .19
- [ ] 109 Jim Lonborg ....2.00 . .90 . .25
- [ ] 110 Mike Shannon..............2.00 . .90 . .25
- [ ] 111 Johnny Morris ....1.50 . .65 . .19
- [ ] 112 J.C. Martin...................1.50 . .65 . .19
- [ ] 113 Dave May.....................1.50 . .65 . .19
- [ ] 114 Yankees Rookies..........1.50 . .65 . .19
  Alan Closter
  John Cumberland
- [ ] 115 Bill Hands....................1.50 . .65 . .19
- [ ] 116 Chuck Harrison............1.50 . .65 . .19
- [ ] 117 Jim Fairey....................1.50 . .65 . .19
- [ ] 118 Stan Williams...............1.50 . .65 . .19
- [ ] 119 Doug Rader..................2.00 . .90 . .25
- [ ] 120 Pete Rose..................35.00 . 16.00 . 4.40
- [ ] 121 Joe Grzenda................1.50 . .65 . .19
- [ ] 122 Ron Fairly....................2.00 . .90 . .25
- [ ] 123 Wilbur Wood................2.00 . .90 . .25
- [ ] 124 Hank Bauer MG............2.00 . .90 . .25
- [ ] 125 Ray Sadecki.................1.50 . .65 . .19
- [ ] 126 Dick Tracewski.............1.50 . .65 . .19
- [ ] 127 Kevin Collins................2.00 . .90 . .25
- [ ] 128 Tommie Aaron...............2.00 . .90 . .25
- [ ] 129 Bill McCool...................1.50 . .65 . .19
- [ ] 130 Carl Yastrzemski.......30.00 . 13.50 . 3.80
- [ ] 131 Chris Cannizzaro..........1.50 . .65 . .19
- [ ] 132 Dave Baldwin...............1.50 . .65 . .19
- [ ] 133 Johnny Callison............2.00 . .90 . .25
- [ ] 134 Jim Weaver..................1.50 . .65 . .19
- [ ] 135 Tommy Davis................2.00 . .90 . .25
- [ ] 136 Cards Rookies..............1.50 . .65 . .19

	Steve Huntz			
	Mike Torrez			
☐ 137	Wally Bunker	1.50	.65	.19
☐ 138	John Bateman	1.50	.65	.19
☐ 139	Andy Kosco	1.50	.65	.19
☐ 140	Jim Lefebvre	2.00	.90	.25
☐ 141	Bill Dillman	1.50	.65	.19
☐ 142	Woody Woodward	2.00	.90	.25
☐ 143	Joe Nossek	1.50	.65	.19
☐ 144	Bob Hendley	1.50	.65	.19
☐ 145	Max Alvis	1.50	.65	.19
☐ 146	Jim Perry	2.00	.90	.25
☐ 147	Leo Durocher MG	3.00	1.35	.40
☐ 148	Lee Stange	1.50	.65	.19
☐ 149	Ollie Brown	1.50	.65	.19
☐ 150	Denny McLain	5.00	2.30	.60
☐ 151A	Clay Dalrymple	1.50	.65	.19
	(Portrait, Orioles)			
☐ 151B	Clay Dalrymple	15.00	6.75	1.90
	(Catching, Phillies)			
☐ 152	Tommie Sisk	1.50	.65	.19
☐ 153	Ed Brinkman	1.50	.65	.19
☐ 154	Jim Britton	1.50	.65	.19
☐ 155	Pete Ward	1.50	.65	.19
☐ 156	Houston Rookies	1.50	.65	.19
	Hal Gilson			
	Leon McFadden			
☐ 157	Bob Rodgers	2.00	.90	.25
☐ 158	Joe Gibbon	1.50	.65	.19
☐ 159	Jerry Adair	1.50	.65	.19
☐ 160	Vada Pinson	2.00	.90	.25
☐ 161	John Purdin	1.50	.65	.19
☐ 162	World Series Game 1	6.00	2.70	.75
	Bob Gibson fans 17			
☐ 163	World Series Game 2	3.50	1.55	.45
	Tiger homers			
	deck the Cards			
	(Willie Horton)			
☐ 164	World Series Game 3	6.00	2.70	.75
	Tim McCarver's homer			
☐ 165	World Series Game 4	6.00	2.70	.75
	Lou Brock lead-off			
	homer			
☐ 166	World Series Game 5	7.50	3.40	.95
	Al Kaline's key hit			
☐ 167	World Series Game 6	3.50	1.55	.45
	Jim Northrup grandslam			
☐ 168	World Series Game 7	6.00	2.70	.75
	Mickey Lolich outduels			
	Bob Gibson			
☐ 169	World Series Summary	3.50	1.55	.45
	Tigers celebrate			
	(Dick McAuliffe,			
	Denny McLain, and			
	Willie Horton)			
☐ 170	Frank Howard	2.50	1.15	.30
☐ 171	Glenn Beckert	2.00	.90	.25
☐ 172	Jerry Stephenson	1.50	.65	.19
☐ 173	White Sox Rookies	1.50	.65	.19
	Bob Christian			
	Gerry Nyman			
☐ 174	Grant Jackson	1.50	.65	.19
☐ 175	Jim Bunning	3.50	1.55	.45
☐ 176	Joe Azcue	1.50	.65	.19
☐ 177	Ron Reed	1.50	.65	.19
☐ 178	Ray Oyler	1.50	.65	.19
☐ 179	Don Pavletich	1.50	.65	.19
☐ 180	Willie Horton	2.00	.90	.25
☐ 181	Mel Nelson	1.50	.65	.19
☐ 182	Bill Rigney MG	1.50	.65	.19
☐ 183	Don Shaw	1.50	.65	.19
☐ 184	Roberto Pena	1.50	.65	.19
☐ 185	Tom Phoebus	1.50	.65	.19
☐ 186	Johnny Edwards	1.50	.65	.19
☐ 187	Leon Wagner	1.50	.65	.19
☐ 188	Rick Wise	2.00	.90	.25
☐ 189	Red Sox Rookies	1.50	.65	.19
	Joe Lahoud			
	John Thibodeau			
☐ 190	Willie Mays	65.00	29.00	8.25
☐ 191	Lindy McDaniel	2.00	.90	.25
☐ 192	Jose Pagan	1.50	.65	.19
☐ 193	Don Cardwell	1.50	.65	.19
☐ 194	Ted Uhlaender	1.50	.65	.19
☐ 195	John Odom	1.50	.65	.19
☐ 196	Lum Harris MG	1.50	.65	.19
☐ 197	Dick Selma	1.50	.65	.19
☐ 198	Willie Smith	1.50	.65	.19
☐ 199	Jim French	1.50	.65	.19
☐ 200	Bob Gibson	15.00	6.75	1.90
☐ 201	Russ Snyder	1.50	.65	.19
☐ 202	Don Wilson	2.00	.90	.25
☐ 203	Dave Johnson	2.00	.90	.25
☐ 204	Jack Hiatt	1.50	.65	.19
☐ 205	Rick Reichardt	1.50	.65	.19
☐ 206	Phillies Rookies	2.00	.90	.25
	Larry Hisle			
	Barry Lersch			
☐ 207	Roy Face	2.00	.90	.25
☐ 208A	Donn Clendenon	2.00	.90	.25
	(Houston)			
☐ 208B	Donn Clendenon	15.00	6.75	1.90
	(Expos)			
☐ 209	Larry Haney UER	1.50	.65	.19
	(Reverse negative)			
☐ 210	Felix Millan	1.50	.65	.19
☐ 211	Galen Cisco	1.50	.65	.19
☐ 212	Tom Tresh	2.00	.90	.25
☐ 213	Gerry Arrigo	1.50	.65	.19
☐ 214	Checklist 3	5.50	1.40	.45
	With 69T deckle CL			
	on back (no player)			
☐ 215	Rico Petrocelli	2.00	.90	.25
☐ 216	Don Sutton	9.00	4.00	1.15

☐ 217 John Donaldson	1.50	.65	.19
☐ 218 John Roseboro	2.00	.90	.25
☐ 219 Freddie Patek	4.00	1.80	.50
☐ 220 Sam McDowell	3.00	1.35	.40
☐ 221 Art Shamsky	2.50	1.15	.30
☐ 222 Duane Josephson	2.50	1.15	.30
☐ 223 Tom Dukes	2.50	1.15	.30
☐ 224 Angels Rookies	2.50	1.15	.30
Bill Harrelson			
Steve Kealey			
☐ 225 Don Kessinger	3.00	1.35	.40
☐ 226 Bruce Howard	2.50	1.15	.30
☐ 227 Frank Johnson	2.50	1.15	.30
☐ 228 Dave Leonhard	2.50	1.15	.30
☐ 229 Don Lock	2.50	1.15	.30
☐ 230 Rusty Staub	4.00	1.80	.50
☐ 231 Pat Dobson	3.00	1.35	.40
☐ 232 Dave Ricketts	2.50	1.15	.30
☐ 233 Steve Barber	2.50	1.15	.30
☐ 234 Dave Bristol MG	2.50	1.15	.30
☐ 235 Jim Hunter	15.00	6.75	1.90
☐ 236 Manny Mota	3.00	1.35	.40
☐ 237 Bobby Cox	5.00	2.30	.60
☐ 238 Ken Johnson	2.50	1.15	.00
☐ 239 Bob Taylor	2.50	1.15	.30
☐ 240 Ken Harrelson	3.00	1.35	.40
☐ 241 Jim Brewer	2.50	1.15	.30
☐ 242 Frank Kostro	2.50	1.15	.30
☐ 243 Ron Kline	2.50	1.15	.30
☐ 244 Indians Rookies	3.50	1.55	.45
Ray Fosse			
George Woodson			
☐ 245 Ed Charles	2.50	1.15	.30
☐ 246 Joe Coleman	2.50	1.15	.30
☐ 247 Gene Oliver	2.50	1.15	.30
☐ 248 Bob Priddy	2.50	1.15	.30
☐ 249 Ed Spiezio	2.50	1.15	.30
☐ 250 Frank Robinson	30.00	13.50	3.80
☐ 251 Ron Herbel	2.50	1.15	.30
☐ 252 Chuck Cottier	2.50	1.15	.30
☐ 253 Jerry Johnson	2.50	1.15	.30
☐ 254 Joe Schultz MG	2.50	1.15	.30
☐ 255 Steve Carlton	55.00	25.00	7.00
☐ 256 Gates Brown	3.00	1.35	.40
☐ 257 Jim Ray	2.50	1.15	.30
☐ 258 Jackie Hernandez	2.50	1.15	.30
☐ 259 Bill Short	2.50	1.15	.30
☐ 260 Reggie Jackson	725.00	325.00	90.00
☐ 261 Bob Johnson	2.50	1.15	.30
☐ 262 Mike Kekich	2.50	1.15	.30
☐ 263 Jerry May	2.50	1.15	.30
☐ 264 Bill Landis	2.50	1.15	.30
☐ 265 Chico Cardenas	3.00	1.35	.40
☐ 266 Dodger Rookies	2.50	1.15	.30
Tom Hutton			
Alan Foster			
☐ 267 Vicente Romo	2.50	1.15	.30
☐ 268 Al Spangler	2.50	1.15	.30
☐ 269 Al Weis	2.50	1.15	.30
☐ 270 Mickey Lolich	4.50	2.00	.55
☐ 271 Larry Stahl	2.50	1.15	.30
☐ 272 Ed Stroud	2.50	1.15	.30
☐ 273 Ron Willis	2.50	1.15	.30
☐ 274 Clyde King MG	2.50	1.15	.30
☐ 275 Vic Davalillo	2.50	1.15	.30
☐ 276 Gary Wagner	2.50	1.15	.30
☐ 277 Elrod Hendricks	4.00	1.80	.50
☐ 278 Gary Geiger UER	2.50	1.15	.30
(Batting wrong)			
☐ 279 Roger Nelson	2.50	1.15	.30
☐ 280 Alex Johnson	3.00	1.35	.40
☐ 281 Ted Kubiak	2.50	1.15	.30
☐ 282 Pat Jarvis	2.50	1.15	.30
☐ 283 Sandy Alomar	3.00	1.35	.40
☐ 284 Expos Rookies	2.50	1.15	.30
Jerry Robertson			
Mike Wegener			
☐ 285 Don Mincher	2.50	1.15	.30
☐ 286 Dock Ellis	3.00	1.35	.40
☐ 287 Jose Tartabull	3.00	1.35	.40
☐ 288 Ken Holtzman	3.00	1.35	.40
☐ 289 Bart Shirley	2.50	1.15	.30
☐ 290 Jim Kaat	4.50	2.00	.55
☐ 291 Vern Fuller	2.50	1.15	.30
☐ 292 Al Downing	3.00	1.35	.40
☐ 293 Dick Dietz	2.50	1.15	.30
☐ 294 Jim Lemon MG	2.50	1.15	.30
☐ 295 Tony Perez	15.00	6.75	1.90
☐ 296 Andy Messersmith	4.00	1.80	.50
☐ 297 Deron Johnson	2.50	1.15	.30
☐ 298 Dave Nicholson	2.50	1.15	.30
☐ 299 Mark Belanger	3.00	1.35	.40
☐ 300 Felipe Alou	4.00	1.80	.50
☐ 301 Darrell Brandon	2.50	1.15	.30
☐ 302 Jim Pagliaroni	2.50	1.15	.30
☐ 303 Cal Koonce	2.50	1.15	.30
☐ 304 Padres Rookies	7.50	3.40	.95
Bill Davis			
Clarence Gaston			
☐ 305 Dick McAuliffe	3.00	1.35	.40
☐ 306 Jim Grant	2.50	1.15	.30
☐ 307 Gary Kolb	2.50	1.15	.30
☐ 308 Wade Blasingame	2.50	1.15	.30
☐ 309 Walt Williams	2.50	1.15	.30
☐ 310 Tom Haller	2.50	1.15	.30
☐ 311 Sparky Lyle	15.00	6.75	1.90
☐ 312 Lee Elia	3.00	1.35	.40
☐ 313 Bill Robinson	3.00	1.35	.40
☐ 314 Checklist 4	5.50	1.40	.45
Don Drysdale			
☐ 315 Eddie Fisher	2.50	1.15	.30
☐ 316 Hal Lanier	2.50	1.15	.30
☐ 317 Bruce Look	2.50	1.15	.30
☐ 318 Jack Fisher	2.50	1.15	.30

☐ 319	Ken McMullen UER 2.50	1.15	.30
	(Headings on back		
	are for a pitcher)		
☐ 320	Dal Maxvill 2.50	1.15	.30
☐ 321	Jim McAndrew 2.50	1.15	.30
☐ 322	Jose Vidal 2.50	1.15	.30
☐ 323	Larry Miller 2.50	1.15	.30
☐ 324	Tiger Rookies 2.50	1.15	.30
	Les Cain		
	Dave Campbell		
☐ 325	Jose Cardenal 3.00	1.35	.40
☐ 326	Gary Sutherland 2.50	1.15	.30
☐ 327	Willie Crawford 2.50	1.15	.30
☐ 328	Joel Horlen 1.50	.65	.19
☐ 329	Rick Joseph 1.50	.65	.19
☐ 330	Tony Conigliaro 4.00	1.80	.50
☐ 331	Braves Rookies 2.50	1.15	.30
	Gil Garrido		
	Tom House		
☐ 332	Fred Talbot.............1.50	.65	.19
☐ 333	Ivan Murrell 1.50	.65	.19
☐ 334	Phil Roof...............1.50	.65	.19
☐ 335	Bill Mazeroski 3.00	1.35	.40
☐ 336	Jim Roland 1.50	.65	.19
☐ 337	Marty Martinez 1.50	.65	.19
☐ 338	Del Unser 1.50	.65	.19
☐ 339	Reds Rookies...........1.50	.65	.19
	Steve Mingori		
	Jose Pena		
☐ 340	Dave McNally 2.00	.90	.25
☐ 341	Dave Adlesh 1.50	.65	.19
☐ 342	Bubba Morton 1.50	.65	.19
☐ 343	Dan Frisella 1.50	.65	.19
☐ 344	Tom Matchick 1.50	.65	.19
☐ 345	Frank Linzy 1.50	.65	.19
☐ 346	Wayne Comer 1.50	.65	.19
☐ 347	Randy Hundley 1.50	.65	.19
☐ 348	Steve Hargan 1.50	.65	.19
☐ 349	Dick Williams MG 2.00	.90	.25
☐ 350	Richie Allen 4.00	1.80	.50
☐ 351	Carroll Sembera 1.50	.65	.19
☐ 352	Paul Schaal 1.50	.65	.19
☐ 353	Jeff Torborg 2.00	.90	.25
☐ 354	Nate Oliver 1.50	.65	.19
☐ 355	Phil Niekro 6.50	2.90	.80
☐ 356	Frank Quilici 1.50	.65	.19
☐ 357	Carl Taylor 1.50	.65	.19
☐ 358	Athletics Rookies.......1.50	.65	.19
	George Lauzerique		
	Roberto Rodriquez		
☐ 359	Dick Kelley.............1.50	.65	.19
☐ 360	Jim Wynn 2.00	.90	.25
☐ 361	Gary Holman 1.50	.65	.19
☐ 362	Jim Maloney 2.00	.90	.25
☐ 363	Russ Nixon 1.50	.65	.19
☐ 364	Tommie Agee............2.00	.90	.25
☐ 365	Jim Fregosi.............2.00	.90	.25

☐ 366	Bo Belinsky 2.00	.90	.25
☐ 367	Lou Johnson 2.00	.90	.25
☐ 368	Vic Roznovsky 1.50	.65	.19
☐ 369	Bob Skinner 2.00	.90	.25
☐ 370	Juan Marichal 7.50	3.40	.95
☐ 371	Sal Bando 2.00	.90	.25
☐ 372	Adolfo Phillips 1.50	.65	.19
☐ 373	Fred Lasher 1.50	.65	.19
☐ 374	Bob Tillman................1.50	.65	.19
☐ 375	Harmon Killebrew 20.00	9.00	2.50
☐ 376	Royals Rookies 2.50	1.15	.30
	Mike Fiore		
	Jim Rooker		
☐ 377	Gary Bell 1.50	.65	.19
☐ 378	Jose Herrera 1.50	.65	.19
☐ 379	Ken Boyer 2.50	1.15	.30
☐ 380	Stan Bahnsen 1.50	.65	.19
☐ 381	Ed Kranepool 2.00	.90	.25
☐ 382	Pat Corrales 2.00	.90	.25
☐ 383	Casey Cox 1.50	.65	.19
☐ 384	Larry Shepard MG 1.50	.65	.19
☐ 385	Orlando Cepeda 3.50	1.55	.45
☐ 386	Jim McGlothlin 1.50	.65	.19
☐ 387	Bobby Klaus 1.50	.65	.19
☐ 388	Tom McCraw 1.50	.65	.19
☐ 389	Dan Coombs 1.50	.65	.19
☐ 390	Bill Freehan 2.50	1.15	.30
☐ 391	Ray Culp 1.50	.65	.19
☐ 392	Bob Burda 1.50	.65	.19
☐ 393	Gene Brabender 1.50	.65	.19
☐ 394	Pilots Rookies 4.50	2.00	.55
	Lou Piniella		
	Marv Staehle		
☐ 395	Chris Short 1.50	.65	.19
☐ 396	Jim Campanis 1.50	.65	.19
☐ 397	Chuck Dobson 1.50	.65	.19
☐ 398	Tito Francona.............1.50	.65	.19
☐ 399	Bob Bailey 1.50	.65	.19
☐ 400	Don Drysdale 11.00	4.90	1.40
☐ 401	Jake Gibbs 1.50	.65	.19
☐ 402	Ken Boswell 1.50	.65	.19
☐ 403	Bob Miller 1.50	.65	.19
☐ 404	Cubs Rookies 1.50	.65	.19
	Vic LaRose		
	Gary Ross		
☐ 405	Lee May 2.00	.90	.25
☐ 406	Phil Ortega 1.50	.65	.19
☐ 407	Tom Egan 1.50	.65	.19
☐ 408	Nate Colbert..............1.50	.65	.19
☐ 409	Bob Moose 1.50	.65	.19
☐ 410	Al Kaline.................20.00	9.00	2.50
☐ 411	Larry Dierker 1.50	.65	.19
☐ 412	Checklist 5 DP 8.00	2.00	.65
	Mickey Mantle		
☐ 413	Roland Sheldon 1.50	.65	.19
☐ 414	Duke Sims 1.50	.65	.19
☐ 415	Ray Washburn 1.50	.65	.19

☐ 416	Willie McCovey AS......6.50	2.90	.80
☐ 417	Ken Harrelson AS.........2.25	1.00	.30
☐ 418	Tommy Helms AS..........2.25	1.00	.30
☐ 419	Rod Carew AS............10.00	4.50	1.25
☐ 420	Ron Santo AS.............2.50	1.15	.30
☐ 421	Brooks Robinson AS...7.50	3.40	.95
☐ 422	Don Kessinger AS........2.25	1.00	.30
☐ 423	Bert Campaneris AS ...2.25	1.00	.30
☐ 424	Pete Rose AS...........12.50	5.75	1.55
☐ 425	Carl Yastrzemski AS..12.00	5.50	1.50
☐ 426	Curt Flood AS............2.25	1.00	.30
☐ 427	Tony Oliva AS.............2.50	1.15	.30
☐ 428	Lou Brock AS..............6.00	2.70	.75
☐ 429	Willie Horton AS..........2.25	1.00	.30
☐ 430	Johnny Bench AS.......15.00	6.75	1.90
☐ 431	Bill Freehan AS............2.25	1.00	.30
☐ 432	Bob Gibson AS...........5.00	2.30	.60
☐ 433	Denny McLain AS........2.25	1.00	.30
☐ 434	Jerry Koosman AS.......2.25	1.00	.30
☐ 435	Sam McDowell AS.......2.25	1.00	.30
☐ 436	Gene Alley................2.00	.90	.25
☐ 437	Luis Alcaraz...........1.50	.65	.19
☐ 438	Gary Waslewski 1:50	.65	.19
☐ 439	White Sox Rookies....1.50	.65	.19
	Ed Herrmann		
	Dan Lazar		
☐ 440A	Willie McCovey 15.00	6.75	1.90
☐ 440B	Willie McCovey WL 100.00	45.00	12.50
	(McCovey white)		
☐ 441A	Dennis Higgins 1.50	.65	.19
☐ 441B	Dennis Higgins 21.00	9.50	2.60
	(Higgins white)		
☐ 442	Ty Cline.................1.50	.65	.19
☐ 443	Don Wert.................1.50	.65	.19
☐ 444A	Joe Moeller............1.50	.65	.19
☐ 444B	Joe Moeller WL 21.00	9.50	2.60
	(Moeller white)		
☐ 445	Bobby Knoop............1.50	.65	.19
☐ 446	Claude Raymond.........1.50	.65	.19
☐ 447A	Ralph Houk MG........2.00	.90	.25
☐ 447B	Ralph Houk WL 21.00	9.50	2.60
	MG (Houk white)		
☐ 448	Bob Tolan...............2.00	.90	.25
☐ 449	Paul Lindblad...........1.50	.65	.19
☐ 450	Billy Williams..........6.50	2.90	.80
☐ 451A	Rich Rollins 1.50	.65	.19
☐ 451B	Rich Rollins WL 21.00	9.50	2.60
	(Rich and 3B white)		
☐ 452A	Al Ferrara...........1.50	.65	.19
☐ 452B	Al Ferrara WL 21.00	9.50	2.60
	(Al and OF white)		
☐ 453	Mike Cuellar...........2.50	1.15	.30
☐ 454A	Phillies Rookies 2.00	.90	.25
	Larry Colton		
	Don Money		
☐ 454B	Phillies Rookies WL.21.00	9.50	2.60
	Larry Colton		
	Don Money		
	(Names in white)		
☐ 455	Sonny Siebert.........1.50	.65	.19
☐ 456	Bud Harrelson..........2.00	.90	.25
☐ 457	Dalton Jones............1.50	.65	.19
☐ 458	Curt Blefary.............1.50	.65	.19
☐ 459	Dave Boswell..........1.50	.65	.19
☐ 460	Joe Torre...............3.00	1.35	.40
☐ 461A	Mike Epstein 1.50	.65	.19
☐ 461B	Mike Epstein WL....21.00	9.50	2.60
	(Epstein white)		
☐ 462	Red Schoendienst...2.50	1.15	.30
	MG		
☐ 463	Dennis Ribant..........1.50	.65	.19
☐ 464A	Dave Marshall...........1.50	.65	.19
☐ 464B	Dave Marshall WL ...21.00	9.50	2.60
	(Marshall white)		
☐ 465	Tommy John............4.00	1.80	.50
☐ 466	John Boccabella........1.50	.65	.19
☐ 467	Tommie Reynolds......1.50	.65	.19
☐ 468A	Pirates Rookies.......1.50	.65	.19
	Bruce Dal Canton		
	Bob Robertson		
☐ 468B	Pirates Rookies WL .21.00	9.50	2.60
	Bruce Dal Canton		
	Bob Robertson		
	(Names in white)		
☐ 469	Chico Ruiz..............1.50	.65	.19
☐ 470A	Mel Stottlemyre 2.50	1.15	.30
☐ 470B	Mel Stottlemyre WL.25.00	11.50	3.10
	(Stottlemyre white)		
☐ 471A	Ted Savage 1.50	.65	.19
☐ 471B	Ted Savage WL.......21.00	9.50	2.60
	(Savage white)		
☐ 472	Jim Price...............1.50	.65	.19
☐ 473A	Jose Arcia 1.50	.65	.19
☐ 473B	Jose Arcia WL 21.00	9.50	2.60
	(Jose and 2B white)		
☐ 474	Tom Murphy............1.50	.65	.19
☐ 475	Tim McCarver..........3.00	1.35	.40
☐ 476A	Boston Rookies 2.50	1.15	.30
	Ken Brett		
	Gerry Moses		
☐ 476B	Boston Rookies WL.22.50	10.00	2.80
	Ken Brett		
	Gerry Moses		
	(Names in white)		
☐ 477	Jeff James 1.50	.65	.19
☐ 478	Don Buford 1.50	.65	.19
☐ 479	Richie Scheinblum.....1.50	.65	.19
☐ 480	Tom Seaver..........135.00	60.00	17.00
☐ 481	Bill Melton...............2.00	.90	.25
☐ 482A	Jim Gosger 1.50	.65	.19
☐ 482B	Jim Gosger WL......21.00	9.50	2.60
	(Jim and OF white)		
☐ 483	Ted Abernathy...........1.50	.65	.19
☐ 484	Joe Gordon MG.........2.00	.90	.25

☐ 485A	Gaylord Perry 10.00	4.50	1.25
☐ 485B	Gaylord Perry WL ...75.00	34.00	9.50
	(Perry white)		
☐ 486A	Paul Casanova 1.50	.65	.19
☐ 486B	Paul Casanova WL...21.00	9.50	2.60
	(Casanova white)		
☐ 487	Denis Menke 1.50	.65	.19
☐ 488	Joe Sparma.................1.50	.65	.19
☐ 489	Clete Boyer 2.00	.90	.25
☐ 490	Matty Alou 2.00	.90	.25
☐ 491A	Twins Rookies 1.50	.65	.19
	Jerry Crider		
	George Mitterwald		
☐ 491B	Twins Rookies WL...21.00	9.50	2.60
	Jerry Crider		
	George Mitterwald		
	(Names in white)		
☐ 492	Tony Cloninger 1.50	.65	.19
☐ 493A	Wes Parker 2.00	.90	.25
☐ 493B	Wes Parker WL.........21.00	9.50	2.60
	(Parker white)		
☐ 494	Ken Berry 1.50	.65	.19
☐ 495	Bert Campaneris 2.00	.90	.25
☐ 496	Larry Jaster 1.50	.65	.19
☐ 497	Julian Javier...............2.00	.90	.25
☐ 498	Juan Pizarro...............2.00	.90	.25
☐ 499	Astro Rookies 1.50	.65	.19
	Don Bryant		
	Steve Shea.		
☐ 500A	Mickey Mantle UER250.00	115.00	31.00
	(No Topps copy-		
	right on card back)		
☐ 500B	Mickey Mantle WL.650.00	300.00	80.00
	(Mantle in white;		
	no Topps copyright		
	on card back) UER		
☐ 501A	Tony Gonzalez 1.50	.65	.19
☐ 501B	Tony Gonzalez WL...21.00	9.50	2.60
	(Tony and OF white)		
☐ 502	Minnie Rojas...............1.50	.65	.19
☐ 503	Larry Brown 1.50	.65	.19
☐ 504	Checklist 6 ....7.00	1.75	.55
	Brooks Robinson		
☐ 505A	Bobby Bolin 1.50	.65	.19
☐ 505B	Bobby Bolin WL.......21.00	9.50	2.60
	(Bolin white)		
☐ 506	Paul Blair 2.00	.90	.25
☐ 507	Cookie Rojas...............2.00	.90	.25
☐ 508	Moe Drabowsky 1.50	.65	.19
☐ 509	Manny Sanguillen 2.00	.90	.25
☐ 510	Rod Carew.................80.00	36.00	10.00
☐ 511A	Diego Segui 1.50	.65	.19
☐ 511B	Diego Segui WL.......21.00	9.50	2.60
	(Diego and P white)		
☐ 512	Cleon Jones 2.00	.90	.25
☐ 513	Camilo Pascual 2.50	1.15	.30
☐ 514	Mike Lum....................2.00	.90	.25

☐ 515	Dick Green..................2.00	.90	.25
☐ 516	Earl Weaver MG.......12.50	5.75	1.55
☐ 517	Mike McCormick.........2.50	1.15	.30
☐ 518	Fred Whitfield 2.00	.90	.25
☐ 519	Yankees Rookies........2.00	.90	.25
	Jerry Kenney		
	Len Boehmer		
☐ 520	Bob Veale...................2.50	1.15	.30
☐ 521	George Thomas 2.00	.90	.25
☐ 522	Joe Hoerner................2.00	.90	.25
☐ 523	Bob Chance.................2.00	.90	.25
☐ 524	Expos Rookies............2.00	.90	.25
	Jose Laboy		
	Floyd Wicker		
☐ 525	Earl Wilson 2.50	1.15	.30
☐ 526	Hector Torres..............2.00	.90	.25
☐ 527	Al Lopez MG 3.00	1.35	.40
☐ 528	Claude Osteen............2.50	1.15	.30
☐ 529	Ed Kirkpatrick.............2.00	.90	.25
☐ 530	Cesar Tovar................2.00	.90	.25
☐ 531	Dick Farrell.................2.00	.90	.25
☐ 532	Bird Hill Aces.............2.50	1.15	.30
	Tom Phoebus		
	Jim Hardin		
	Dave McNally		
	Mike Cuellar		
☐ 533	Nolan Ryan 550.00	250.00	70.00
☐ 534	Jerry McNertney 2.00	.90	.25
☐ 535	Phil Regan 2.50	1.15	.30
☐ 536	Padres Rookies...........2.00	.90	.25
	Danny Breeden		
	Dave Roberts		
☐ 537	Mike Paul....................2.00	.90	.25
☐ 538	Charlie Smith..............2.00	.90	.25
☐ 539	Ted Shows How 7.00	3.10	.85
	Mike Epstein		
	Ted Williams MG		
☐ 540	Curt Flood 3.00	1.35	.40
☐ 541	Joe Verbanic..............2.00	.90	.25
☐ 542	Bob Aspromonte..........2.00	.90	.25
☐ 543	Fred Newman..............2.00	.90	.25
☐ 544	Tigers Rookies............2.00	.90	.25
	Mike Kilkenny		
	Ron Woods		
☐ 545	Willie Stargell...........16.00	7.25	2.00
☐ 546	Jim Nash....................2.00	.90	.25
☐ 547	Billy Martin MG...........6.00	2.70	.75
☐ 548	Bob Locker..................2.00	.90	.25
☐ 549	Ron Brand...................2.00	.90	.25
☐ 550	Brooks Robinson.......25.00	11.50	3.10
☐ 551	Wayne Granger...........2.00	.90	.25
☐ 552	Dodgers Rookies.........3.00	1.35	.40
	Ted Sizemore		
	Bill Sudakis		
☐ 553	Ron Davis 2.00	.90	.25
☐ 554	Frank Bertaina............2.00	.90	.25
☐ 555	Jim Ray Hart...............2.50	1.15	.30

☐ 556	A's Stars 2.50	1.15	.30
	Sal Bando		
	Bert Campaneris		
	Danny Cater		
☐ 557	Frank Fernandez..........2.00	.90	.25
☐ 558	Tom Burgmeier..........2.50	1.15	.30
☐ 559	Cardinals Rookies........2.00	.90	.25
	Joe Hague		
	Jim Hicks		
☐ 560	Luis Tiant..............3.00	1.35	.40
☐ 561	Ron Clark..............2.00	.90	.25
☐ 562	Bob Watson............4.00	1.80	.50
☐ 563	Marty Pattin...........2.00	.90	.25
☐ 564	Gil Hodges MG........10.00	4.50	1.25
☐ 565	Hoyt Wilhelm..........7.00	3.10	.85
☐ 566	Ron Hansen............2.00	.90	.25
☐ 567	Pirates Rookies..........2.00	.90	.25
	Elvio Jimenez		
	Jim Shellenback		
☐ 568	Cecil Upshaw...........2.00	.90	.25
☐ 569	Billy Harris............2.00	.90	.25
☐ 570	Ron Santo..............5.50	2.50	.70
☐ 571	Cap Peterson..........2.00	.90	.25
☐ 572	Giants Heroes 12.50	5.75	1.55
	Willie McCovey		
	Juan Marichal		
☐ 573	Jim Palmer..........45.00	20.00	5.75
☐ 574	George Scott..........2.50	1.15	.30
☐ 575	Bill Singer............2.50	1.15	.30
☐ 576	Phillies Rookies 2.00	.90	.25
	Ron Stone		
	Bill Wilson		
☐ 577	Mike Hegan...........2.00	.90	.25
☐ 578	Don Bosch............2.00	.90	.25
☐ 579	Dave Nelson..........2.50	1.15	.30
☐ 580	Jim Northrup..........2.50	1.15	.30
☐ 581	Gary Nolan............2.50	1.15	.30
☐ 582A	Checklist 7............5.50	1.40	.45
	(White circle on back)		
	(Tony Oliva)		
☐ 582B	Checklist 7............7.50	1.90	.60
	(Red circle on back)		
	(Tony Oliva)		
☐ 583	Clyde Wright..........2.00	.90	.25
☐ 584	Don Mason............2.00	.90	.25
☐ 585	Ron Swoboda..........2.50	1.15	.30
☐ 586	Tim Cullen............2.00	.90	.25
☐ 587	Joe Rudi..............5.00	2.30	.60
☐ 588	Bill White.............3.00	1.35	.40
☐ 589	Joe Pepitone..........2.75	1.25	.35
☐ 590	Rico Carty............2.75	1.25	.35
☐ 591	Mike Hedlund..........2.25	1.00	.30
☐ 592	Padres Rookies..........2.25	1.00	.30
	Rafael Robles		
	Al Santorini		
☐ 593	Don Nottebart.........2.25	1.00	.30
☐ 594	Dooley Womack.........2.25	1.00	.30
☐ 595	Lee Maye 2.25	1.00	.30
☐ 596	Chuck Hartenstein....2.25	1.00	.30
☐ 597	A.L. Rookies 150.00	70.00	19.00
	Bob Floyd		
	Larry Burchart		
	Rollie Fingers		
☐ 598	Ruben Amaro..........2.25	1.00	.30
☐ 599	John Boozer...........2.25	1.00	.30
☐ 600	Tony Oliva............6.50	2.90	.80
☐ 601	Tug McGraw 4.50	2.00	.55
☐ 602	Cubs Rookies..........2.25	1.00	.30
	Alec Distaso		
	Don Young		
	Jim Qualls		
☐ 603	Joe Keough...........2.25	1.00	.30
☐ 604	Bobby Etheridge......2.25	1.00	.30
☐ 605	Dick Ellsworth........2.25	1.00	.30
☐ 606	Gene Mauch MG.......2.75	1.25	.35
☐ 607	Dick Bosman..........2.25	1.00	.30
☐ 608	Dick Simpson.........2.25	1.00	.30
☐ 609	Phil Gagliano.........2.25	1.00	.30
☐ 610	Jim Hardin............2.25	1.00	.30
☐ 611	Braves Rookies........3.50	1.55	.45
	Bob Didier		
	Walt Hriniak		
	Gary Neibauer		
☐ 612	Jack Aker.............2.25	1.00	.30
☐ 613	Jim Beauchamp......2.25	1.00	.30
☐ 614	Houston Rookies......2.25	1.00	.30
	Tom Griffin		
	Skip Guinn		
☐ 615	Len Gabrielson........2.25	1.00	.30
☐ 616	Don McMahon.........2.25	1.00	.30
☐ 617	Jesse Gonder.........2.25	1.00	.30
☐ 618	Ramon Webster.......2.25	1.00	.30
☐ 619	Royals Rookies........2.25	1.00	.30
	Bill Butler		
	Pat Kelly		
	Juan Rios		
☐ 620	Dean Chance..........2.75	1.25	.35
☐ 621	Bill Voss.............2.25	1.00	.30
☐ 622	Dan Osinski..........2.25	1.00	.30
☐ 623	Hank Allen............2.25	1.00	.30
☐ 624	NL Rookies............3.50	1.55	.45
	Darrel Chaney		
	Duffy Dyer		
	Terry Harmon		
☐ 625	Mack Jones UER.......2.25	1.00	.30
	(Batting wrong)		
☐ 626	Gene Michael 2.75	1.25	.35
☐ 627	George Stone.........2.25	1.00	.30
☐ 628	Red Sox Rookies......4.00	1.80	.50
	Bill Conigliaro		
	Syd O'Brien		
	Fred Wenz		
☐ 629	Jack Hamilton........2.25	1.00	.30
☐ 630	Bobby Bonds 40.00	18.00	5.00

☐ 631	John Kennedy	2.25	1.00	.30
☐ 632	Jon Warden	2.25	1.00	.30
☐ 633	Harry Walker MG	2.25	1.00	.30
☐ 634	Andy Etchebarren	2.25	1.00	.30
☐ 635	George Culver	2.25	1.00	.30
☐ 636	Woody Held	2.25	1.00	.30
☐ 637	Padres Rookies	2.25	1.00	.30
	Jerry DaVanon			
	Frank Reberger			
	Clay Kirby			
☐ 638	Ed Sprague	2.25	1.00	.30
☐ 639	Barry Moore	2.25	1.00	.30
☐ 640	Fergie Jenkins	22.00	10.00	2.80
☐ 641	NL Rookies	2.25	1.00	.30
	Bobby Darwin			
	John Miller			
	Tommy Dean			
☐ 642	John Hiller	2.25	1.00	.30
☐ 643	Billy Cowan	2.25	1.00	.30
☐ 644	Chuck Hinton	2.25	1.00	.30
☐ 645	George Brunet	2.25	1.00	.30
☐ 646	Expos Rookies	2.75	1.25	.35
	Dan McGinn			
	Carl Morton			
☐ 647	Dave Wickersham	2.25	1.00	.30
☐ 648	Bobby Wine	2.25	1.00	.30
☐ 649	Al Jackson	2.25	1.00	.30
☐ 650	Ted Williams MG	12.50	5.75	1.55
☐ 651	Gus Gil	2.25	1.00	.30
☐ 652	Eddie Watt	2.25	1.00	.30
☐ 653	Aurelio Rodriguez UER	3.00	1.35	.40
	(Photo actually			
	Angels' batboy)			
☐ 654	White Sox Rookies	4.00	1.80	.50
	Carlos May			
	Don Secrist			
	Rich Morales			
☐ 655	Mike Hershberger	2.25	1.00	.30
☐ 656	Dan Schneider	2.25	1.00	.30
☐ 657	Bobby Murcer	5.00	2.30	.60
☐ 658	AL Rookies	2.75	1.25	.35
	Tom Hall			
	Bill Burbach			
	Jim Miles			
☐ 659	Johnny Podres	3.00	1.35	.40
☐ 660	Reggie Smith	4.50	2.00	.55
☐ 661	Jim Merritt	2.25	1.00	.30
☐ 662	Royals Rookies	2.75	1.25	.35
	Dick Drago			
	George Spriggs			
	Bob Oliver			
☐ 663	Dick Radatz	2.75	1.25	.35
☐ 664	Ron Hunt	4.00	1.80	.50

1970 Topps

The cards in this 720-card set measure 2 1/2" by 3 1/2". The Topps set for 1970 has color photos surrounded by white frame lines and gray borders. The backs have a blue biographical section and a yellow record section. All-Star selections are featured on cards 450 to 469. Other topical subsets within this set include League Leaders (61-72), Playoffs cards (195-202), and World Series cards (305-310). There are graduations of scarcity, terminating in the high series (634-720), which are outlined in the value summary. The key Rookie Cardin this set is Thurman Munson.

	NRMT-MT	EXC	G-VG
COMPLETE SET (720)	2250.	1000.	275.00
COMMON PLAYER (1-132)	.70	.30	.09
COMMON PLAYER (133-263)	.80	.35	.10
COMMON PLAYER (264-372)	1.00	.45	.13
COMMON PLAYER (373-459)	1.25	.55	.16
COMMON PLAYER (460-546)	1.50	.65	.19
COMMON PLAYER (547-633)	3.00	1.35	.40
COMMON PLAYER (634-720)	6.00	2.70	.75

☐ 1	New York Mets	12.50	2.50	.75
	Team Card			
☐ 2	Diego Segui	.70	.30	.09
☐ 3	Darrel Chaney	.70	.30	.09
☐ 4	Tom Egan	.70	.30	.09
☐ 5	Wes Parker	1.00	.45	.13
☐ 6	Grant Jackson	.70	.30	.09
☐ 7	Indians Rookies	.70	.30	.09
	Gary Boyd			
	Russ Nagelson			
☐ 8	Jose Martinez	1.00	.45	.13
☐ 9	Checklist 1	5.00	.50	.15

☐ 10	Carl Yastrzemski	25.00	11.50	3.10
☐ 11	Nate Colbert	.70	.30	.09
☐ 12	John Hiller	1.00	.45	.13
☐ 13	Jack Hiatt	.70	.30	.09
☐ 14	Hank Allen	.70	.30	.09
☐ 15	Larry Dierker	.70	.30	.09
☐ 16	Charlie Metro MG	.70	.30	.09
☐ 17	Hoyt Wilhelm	4.00	1.80	.50
☐ 18	Carlos May	1.00	.45	.13
☐ 19	John Boccabella	.70	.30	.09
☐ 20	Dave McNally	1.00	.45	.13
☐ 21	A's Rookies	7.00	3.10	.85
	Vida Blue			
	Gene Tenace			
☐ 22	Ray Washburn	.70	.30	.09
☐ 23	Bill Robinson	1.00	.45	.13
☐ 24	Dick Selma	.70	.30	.09
☐ 25	Cesar Tovar	.70	.30	.09
☐ 26	Tug McGraw	1.50	.65	.19
☐ 27	Chuck Hinton	.70	.30	.09
☐ 28	Billy Wilson	.70	.30	.09
☐ 29	Sandy Alomar	1.00	.45	.13
☐ 30	Matty Alou	1.00	.45	.13
☐ 31	Marty Pattin	.70	.30	.09
☐ 32	Harry Walker MG	.70	.30	.09
☐ 33	Don Wert	.70	.30	.09
☐ 34	Willie Crawford	.70	.30	.09
☐ 35	Joel Horlen	.70	.30	.09
☐ 36	Red Rookies	1.00	.45	.13
	Danny Breeden			
	Bernie Carbo			
☐ 37	Dick Drago	.70	.30	.09
☐ 38	Mack Jones	.70	.30	.09
☐ 39	Mike Nagy	.70	.30	.09
☐ 40	Rich Allen	2.00	.90	.25
☐ 41	George Lauzerique	.70	.30	.09
☐ 42	Tito Fuentes	.70	.30	.09
☐ 43	Jack Aker	.70	.30	.09
☐ 44	Roberto Pena	.70	.30	.09
☐ 45	Dave Johnson	1.00	.45	.13
☐ 46	Ken Rudolph	.70	.30	.09
☐ 47	Bob Miller	.70	.30	.09
☐ 48	Gil Garrido	.70	.30	.09
☐ 49	Tim Cullen	.70	.30	.09
☐ 50	Tommie Agee	1.00	.45	.13
☐ 51	Bob Christian	.70	.30	.09
☐ 52	Bruce Dal Canton	.70	.30	.09
☐ 53	John Kennedy	.70	.30	.09
☐ 54	Jeff Torborg	1.00	.45	.13
☐ 55	John Odom	.70	.30	.09
☐ 56	Phillies Rookies	.70	.30	.09
	Joe Lis			
	Scott Reid			
☐ 57	Pat Kelly	.70	.30	.09
☐ 58	Dave Marshall	.70	.30	.09
☐ 59	Dick Ellsworth	.70	.30	.09
☐ 60	Jim Wynn	1.00	.45	.13
☐ 61	NL Batting Leaders	5.00	2.30	.60
	Pete Rose			
	Bob Clemente			
	Cleon Jones			
☐ 62	AL Batting Leaders	3.00	1.35	.40
	Rod Carew			
	Reggie Smith			
	Tony Oliva			
☐ 63	NL RBI Leaders	3.00	1.35	.40
	Willie McCovey			
	Ron Santo			
	Tony Perez			
☐ 64	AL RBI Leaders	4.50	2.00	.55
	Harmon Killebrew			
	Boog Powell			
	Reggie Jackson			
☐ 65	NL Home Run Leaders	4.00	1.80	.50
	Willie McCovey			
	Hank Aaron			
	Lee May			
☐ 66	AL Home Run Leaders	4.50	2.00	.55
	Harmon Killebrew			
	Frank Howard			
	Reggie Jackson			
☐ 67	NL ERA Leaders	5.00	2.30	.60
	Juan Marichal			
	Steve Carlton			
	Bob Gibson			
☐ 68	AL ERA Leaders	2.00	.90	.25
	Dick Bosman			
	Jim Palmer			
	Mike Cuellar			
☐ 69	NL Pitching Leaders	5.00	2.30	.60
	Tom Seaver			
	Phil Niekro			
	Fergie Jenkins			
	Juan Marichal			
☐ 70	AL Pitching Leaders	2.00	.90	.25
	Dennis McLain			
	Mike Cuellar			
	Dave Boswell			
	Dave McNally			
	Jim Perry			
	Mel Stottlemyre			
☐ 71	NL Strikeout Leaders	3.00	1.35	.40
	Fergie Jenkins			
	Bob Gibson			
	Bill Singer			
☐ 72	AL Strikeout Leaders	2.00	.90	.25
	Sam McDowell			
	Mickey Lolich			
	Andy Messersmith			
☐ 73	Wayne Granger	.70	.30	.09
☐ 74	Angels Rookies	.70	.30	.09
	Greg Washburn			
	Wally Wolf			
☐ 75	Jim Kaat	2.00	.90	.25

☐ 76	Carl Taylor	.70	.30	.09
☐ 77	Frank Linzy	.70	.30	.09
☐ 78	Joe Lahoud	.70	.30	.09
☐ 79	Clay Kirby	.70	.30	.09
☐ 80	Don Kessinger	1.00	.45	.13
☐ 81	Dave May	.70	.30	.09
☐ 82	Frank Fernandez	.70	.30	.09
☐ 83	Don Cardwell	.70	.30	.09
☐ 84	Paul Casanova	.70	.30	.09
☐ 85	Max Alvis	.70	.30	.09
☐ 86	Lum Harris MG	.70	.30	.09
☐ 87	Steve Renko	.70	.30	.09
☐ 88	Pilots Rookies	.70	.30	.09
	Miguel Fuentes			
	Dick Baney			
☐ 89	Juan Rios	.70	.30	.09
☐ 90	Tim McCarver	1.50	.65	.19
☐ 91	Rich Morales	.70	.30	.09
☐ 92	George Culver	.70	.30	.09
☐ 93	Rick Renick	.70	.30	.09
☐ 94	Freddie Patek	1.00	.45	.13
☐ 95	Earl Wilson	1.00	.45	.13
☐ 96	Cardinals Rookies	3.00	1.35	.40
	Leron Lee			
	Jerry Reuss			
☐ 97	Joe Moeller	.70	.30	.09
☐ 98	Gates Brown	1.00	.45	.13
☐ 99	Bobby Pfeil	.70	.30	.09
☐ 100	Mel Stottlemyre	1.50	.65	.19
☐ 101	Bobby Floyd	.70	.30	.09
☐ 102	Joe Rudi	1.00	.45	.13
☐ 103	Frank Reberger	.70	.30	.09
☐ 104	Gerry Moses	.70	.30	.09
☐ 105	Tony Gonzalez	.70	.30	.09
☐ 106	Darold Knowles	.70	.30	.09
☐ 107	Bobby Etheridge	.70	.30	.09
☐ 108	Tom Burgmeier	.70	.30	.09
☐ 109	Expos Rookies	.70	.30	.09
	Garry Jestadt			
	Carl Morton			
☐ 110	Bob Moose	.70	.30	.09
☐ 111	Mike Hegan	.70	.30	.09
☐ 112	Dave Nelson	.70	.30	.09
☐ 113	Jim Ray	.70	.30	.09
☐ 114	Gene Michael	1.00	.45	.13
☐ 115	Alex Johnson	1.00	.45	.13
☐ 116	Sparky Lyle	1.50	.65	.19
☐ 117	Don Young	.70	.30	.09
☐ 118	George Mitterwald	.70	.30	.09
☐ 119	Chuck Taylor	.70	.30	.09
☐ 120	Sal Bando	1.00	.45	.13
☐ 121	Orioles Rookies	1.00	.45	.13
	Fred Beene			
	Terry Crowley			
☐ 122	George Stone	.70	.30	.09
☐ 123	Don Gutteridge MG	.70	.30	.09
☐ 124	Larry Jaster	.70	.30	.09
☐ 125	Deron Johnson	.70	.30	.09
☐ 126	Marty Martinez	.70	.30	.09
☐ 127	Joe Coleman	.70	.30	.09
☐ 128A	Checklist 2 ERR	5.00	.50	.15
	(226 R Perranoski)			
☐ 128B	Checklist 2 COR	5.00	.50	.15
	(226 R. Perranoski)			
☐ 129	Jimmie Price	.70	.30	.09
☐ 130	Ollie Brown	.70	.30	.09
☐ 131	Dodgers Rookies	.70	.30	.09
	Ray Lamb			
	Bob Stinson			
☐ 132	Jim McGlothlin	.70	.30	.09
☐ 133	Clay Carroll	.80	.35	.10
☐ 134	Danny Walton	.80	.35	.10
☐ 135	Dick Dietz	.80	.35	.10
☐ 136	Steve Hargan	.80	.35	.10
☐ 137	Art Shamsky	.80	.35	.10
☐ 138	Joe Foy	.80	.35	.10
☐ 139	Rich Nye	.80	.35	.10
☐ 140	Reggie Jackson	200.00	90.00	25.00
☐ 141	Pirates Rookies	1.00	.45	.13
	Dave Cash			
	Johnny Jeter			
☐ 142	Fritz Peterson	.80	.35	.10
☐ 143	Phil Gagliano	.80	.35	.10
☐ 144	Ray Culp	.80	.35	.10
☐ 145	Rico Carty	1.00	.45	.13
☐ 146	Danny Murphy	.80	.35	.10
☐ 147	Angel Hermoso	.80	.35	.10
☐ 148	Earl Weaver MG	2.50	1.15	.30
☐ 149	Billy Champion	.80	.35	.10
☐ 150	Harmon Killebrew	8.50	3.80	1.05
☐ 151	Dave Roberts	.80	.35	.10
☐ 152	Ike Brown	.80	.35	.10
☐ 153	Gary Gentry	.80	.35	.10
☐ 154	Senators Rookies	.80	.35	.10
	Jim Miles			
	Jan Dukes			
☐ 155	Denis Menke	.80	.35	.10
☐ 156	Eddie Fisher	.80	.35	.10
☐ 157	Manny Mota	1.00	.45	.13
☐ 158	Jerry McNertney	.80	.35	.10
☐ 159	Tommy Helms	1.00	.45	.13
☐ 160	Phil Niekro	5.00	2.30	.60
☐ 161	Richie Scheinblum	.80	.35	.10
☐ 162	Jerry Johnson	.80	.35	.10
☐ 163	Syd O'Brien	.80	.35	.10
☐ 164	Ty Cline	.80	.35	.10
☐ 165	Ed Kirkpatrick	.80	.35	.10
☐ 166	Al Oliver	2.50	1.15	.30
☐ 167	Bill Burbach	.80	.35	.10
☐ 168	Dave Watkins	.80	.35	.10
☐ 169	Tom Hall	.80	.35	.10
☐ 170	Billy Williams	7.50	3.40	.95
☐ 171	Jim Nash	.80	.35	.10
☐ 172	Braves Rookies	2.50	1.15	.30

Garry Hill
Ralph Garr

☐ 173 Jim Hicks	.80	.35	.10
☐ 174 Ted Sizemore	1.00	.45	.13
☐ 175 Dick Bosman	.80	.35	.10
☐ 176 Jim Ray Hart	1.00	.45	.13
☐ 177 Jim Northrup	1.00	.45	.13
☐ 178 Denny Lemaster	.80	.35	.10
☐ 179 Ivan Murrell	.80	.35	.10
☐ 180 Tommy John	3.00	1.35	.40
☐ 181 Sparky Anderson MG	2.50	1.15	.30
☐ 182 Dick Hall	.80	.35	.10
☐ 183 Jerry Grote	.80	.35	.10
☐ 184 Ray Fosse	.80	.35	.10
☐ 185 Don Mincher	.80	.35	.10
☐ 186 Rick Joseph	.80	.35	.10
☐ 187 Mike Hedlund	.80	.35	.10
☐ 188 Manny Sanguillen	1.00	.45	.13
☐ 189 Yankees Rookies	100.00	45.00	12.50

Thurman Munson
Dave McDonald

☐ 190 Joe Torre	2.50	1.15	.30
☐ 191 Vicente Romo	.80	.35	.10
☐ 192 Jim Qualls	.80	.35	.10
☐ 193 Mike Wegener	.80	.35	.10
☐ 194 Chuck Manuel	.80	.35	.10
☐ 195 NL Playoff Game 1	12.00	5.50	1.50

Tom Seaver wins opener

☐ 196 NL Playoff Game 2	2.25	1.00	.30

Mets show muscle
(Ken Boswell)

☐ 197 NL Playoff Game 3	20.00	9.00	2.50

Nolan Ryan saves
the day

☐ 198 NL Playoff Summary	8.00	3.60	1.00

Mets celebrate
(Nolan Ryan)

☐ 199 AL Playoff Game 1	2.25	1.00	.30

Orioles win squeaker
(Mike Cuellar)

☐ 200 AL Playoff Game 2	2.25	1.00	.30

Boog Powell scores
winning run

☐ 201 AL Playoff Game 3	2.25	1.00	.30

Birds wrap it up
(Boog Powell and
Andy Etchebarren)

☐ 202 AL Playoff Summary	2.25	1.00	.30

Orioles celebrate

☐ 203 Rudy May	.80	.35	.10
☐ 204 Len Gabrielson	.80	.35	.10
☐ 205 Bert Campaneris	1.00	.45	.13
☐ 206 Clete Boyer	1.00	.45	.13
☐ 207 Tigers Rookies	.80	.35	.10

Norman McRae
Bob Reed

☐ 208 Fred Gladding	.80	.35	.10
☐ 209 Ken Suarez	.80	.35	.10
☐ 210 Juan Marichal	6.00	2.70	.75
☐ 211 Ted Williams MG	9.00	4.00	1.15
☐ 212 Al Santorini	.80	.35	.10
☐ 213 Andy Etchebarren	.80	.35	.10
☐ 214 Ken Boswell	.80	.35	.10
☐ 215 Reggie Smith	2.00	.90	.25
☐ 216 Chuck Hartenstein	.80	.35	.10
☐ 217 Ron Hansen	.80	.35	.10
☐ 218 Ron Stone	.80	.35	.10
☐ 219 Jerry Kenney	.80	.35	.10
☐ 220 Steve Carlton	35.00	16.00	4.40
☐ 221 Ron Brand	.80	.35	.10
☐ 222 Jim Rooker	1.00	.45	.13
☐ 223 Nate Oliver	.80	.35	.10
☐ 224 Steve Barber	.80	.35	.10
☐ 225 Lee May	1.00	.45	.13
☐ 226 Ron Perranoski	1.00	.45	.13
☐ 227 Astros Rookies	1.50	.65	.19

John Mayberry
Bob Watkins

☐ 228 Aurelio Rodriguez	1.00	.45	.13
☐ 229 Rich Robertson	.80	.35	.10
☐ 230 Brooks Robinson	12.50	5.75	1.55
☐ 231 Luis Tiant	2.00	.90	.25
☐ 232 Bob Didier	.80	.35	.10
☐ 233 Lew Krausse	.80	.35	.10
☐ 234 Tommy Dean	.80	.35	.10
☐ 235 Mike Epstein	.80	.35	.10
☐ 236 Bob Veale	1.00	.45	.13
☐ 237 Russ Gibson	.80	.35	.10
☐ 238 Jose Laboy	.80	.35	.10
☐ 239 Ken Berry	.80	.35	.10
☐ 240 Fergie Jenkins	10.00	4.50	1.25
☐ 241 Royals Rookies	.80	.35	.10

Al Fitzmorris
Scott Northey

☐ 242 Walter Alston MG	2.00	.90	.25
☐ 243 Joe Sparma	.80	.35	.10
☐ 244A Checklist 3	5.00	.50	.15

(Red bat on front)

☐ 244B Checklist 3	5.00	.50	.15

(Brown bat on front)

☐ 245 Leo Cardenas	.80	.35	.10
☐ 246 Jim McAndrew	.80	.35	.10
☐ 247 Lou Klimchock	.80	.35	.10
☐ 248 Jesus Alou	.80	.35	.10
☐ 249 Bob Locker	.80	.35	.10
☐ 250 Willie McCovey UER	10.00	4.50	1.25

(1963 San Francisci)

☐ 251 Dick Schofield	.80	.35	.10
☐ 252 Lowell Palmer	.80	.35	.10
☐ 253 Ron Woods	.80	.35	.10
☐ 254 Camilo Pascual	1.00	.45	.13
☐ 255 Jim Spencer	.80	.35	.10
☐ 256 Vic Davalillo	.80	.35	.10
☐ 257 Dennis Higgins	.80	.35	.10

☐	258 Paul Popovich...............80	.35	.10
☐	259 Tommie Reynolds........80	.35	.10
☐	260 Claude Osteen............1.00	.45	.13
☐	261 Curt Motton 80	.35	.10
☐	262 Padres Rookies 80	.35	.10
	Jerry Morales		
	Jim Williams		
☐	263 Duane Josephson 1.00	.45	.13
☐	264 Rich Hebner 1.25	.55	.16
☐	265 Randy Hundley 1.00	.45	.13
☐	266 Wally Bunker 1.00	.45	.13
☐	267 Twins Rookies 1.00	.45	.13
	Herman Hill		
	Paul Ratliff		
☐	268 Claude Raymond........1.00	.45	.13
☐	269 Cesar Gutierrez 1.00	.45	.13
☐	270 Chris Short 1.00	.45	.13
☐	271 Greg Goossen 1.00	.45	.13
☐	272 Hector Torres 1.00	.45	.13
☐	273 Ralph Houk MG 1.25	.55	.16
☐	274 Gerry Arrigo 1.00	.45	.13
☐	275 Duke Sims 1.00	.45	.13
☐	276 Ron Hunt 1.00	.45	.13
☐	277 Paul Doyle.................1.00	.45	.13
☐	278 Tommie Aaron............1.25	.55	.16
☐	279 Bill Lee ....•...........2.00	.90	.25
☐	280 Donn Clendenon 1.25	.55	.16
☐	281 Casey Cox 1.00	.45	.13
☐	282 Steve Huntz...............1.00	.45	.13
☐	283 Angel Bravo 1.00	.45	.13
☐	284 Jack Baldschun..........1.00	.45	.13
☐	285 Paul Blair 1.25	.55	.16
☐	286 Dodgers Rookies 9.00	4.00	1.15
	Jack Jenkins		
	Bill Buckner		
☐	287 Fred Talbot 1.00	.45	.13
☐	288 Larry Hisle 1.25	.55	.16
☐	289 Gene Brabender 1.00	.45	.13
☐	290 Rod Carew 50.00	23.00	6.25
☐	291 Leo Durocher MG 2.00	.90	.25
☐	292 Eddie Leon 1.00	.45	.13
☐	293 Bob Bailey 1.00	.45	.13
☐	294 Jose Azcue 1.00	.45	.13
☐	295 Cecil Upshaw 1.00	.45	.13
☐	296 Woody Woodward 1.25	.55	.16
☐	297 Curt Blefary...............1.00	.45	.13
☐	298 Ken Henderson 1.00	.45	.13
☐	299 Buddy Bradford..........1.00	.45	.13
☐	300 Tom Seaver 110.00	50.00	14.00
☐	301 Chico Salmon 1.00	.45	.13
☐	302 Jeff James 1.00	.45	.13
☐	303 Brant Alyea 1.00	.45	.13
☐	304 Bill Russell 3.50	1.55	.45
☐	305 World Series Game 1....2.50	1.15	.30
	Don Buford leadoff		
	homer		
☐	306 World Series Game 2....2.50	1.15	.30

	Donn Clendenon's		
	homer breaks ice		
☐	307 World Series Game 3...2.50	1.15	.30
	Tommie Agee's catch		
	saves the day		
☐	308 World Series Game 4...2.50	1.15	.30
	J.C. Martin's bunt		
	ends deadlock		
☐	309 World Series Game 5...2.50	1.15	.30
	Jerry Koosman		
	shuts door		
☐	310 World Series Summary4.00	1.80	.50
	Mets whoop it up		
☐	311 Dick Green 1.00	.45	.13
☐	312 Mike Torrez 1.25	.55	.16
☐	313 Mayo Smith MG 1.00	.45	.13
☐	314 Bill McCool 1.00	.45	.13
☐	315 Luis Aparicio 4.50	2.00	.55
☐	316 Skip Guinn 1.00	.45	.13
☐	317 Red Sox Rookies 1.25	.55	.16
	Billy Conigliaro		
	Luis Alvarado		
☐	318 Willie Smith 1.00	.45	.13
☐	319 Clay Dalrymple...........1.00	.45	.13
☐	320 Jim Maloney 1.25	.55	.16
☐	321 Lou Piniella 2.50	1.15	.30
☐	322 Luke Walker 1.00	.45	.13
☐	323 Wayne Comer 1.00	.45	.13
☐	324 Tony Taylor 1.00	.45	.13
☐	325 Dave Boswell 1.00	.45	.13
☐	326 Bill Voss 1.00	.45	.13
☐	327 Hal King 1.00	.45	.13
☐	328 George Brunet............1.00	.45	.13
☐	329 Chris Cannizzaro 1.00	.45	.13
☐	330 Lou Brock 10.00	4.50	1.25
☐	331 Chuck Dobson 1.00	.45	.13
☐	332 Bobby Wine 1.00	.45	.13
☐	333 Bobby Murcer............2.00	.90	.25
☐	334 Phil Regan 1.25	.55	.16
☐	335 Bill Freehan 1.25	.55	.16
☐	336 Del Unser 1.00	.45	.13
☐	337 Mike McCormick 1.25	.55	.16
☐	338 Paul Schaal 1.00	.45	.13
☐	339 Johnny Edwards 1.00	.45	.13
☐	340 Tony Conigliaro 2.00	.90	.25
☐	341 Bill Sudakis 1.00	.45	.13
☐	342 Wilbur Wood 1.25	.55	.16
☐	343A Checklist 4 ....5.00	.50	.15
	(Red bat on front)		
☐	343B Checklist 4 ....5.00	.50	.15
	(Brown bat on front)		
☐	344 Marcelino Lopez 1.00	.45	.13
☐	345 Al Ferrara 1.00	.45	.13
☐	346 Red Schoendienst MG .2.00	.90	.25
☐	347 Russ Snyder 1.00	.45	.13
☐	348 Mets Rookies 1.25	.55	.16
	Mike Jorgensen		

	Jesse Hudson		
☐ 349	Steve Hamilton 1.00	.45	.13
☐ 350	Roberto Clemente 50.00	23.00	6.25
☐ 351	Tom Murphy 1.00	.45	.13
☐ 352	Bob Barton..................1.00	.45	.13
☐ 353	Stan Williams..............1.00	.45	.13
☐ 354	Amos Otis 1.25	.55	.16
☐ 355	Doug Rader..................1.25	.55	.16
☐ 356	Fred Lasher.................1.00	.45	.13
☐ 357	Bob Burda....................1.00	.45	.13
☐ 358	Pedro Borbon 1.00	.45	.13
☐ 359	Phil Roof.....................1.00	.45	.13
☐ 360	Curt Flood 1.75	.80	.22
☐ 361	Ray Jarvis...................1.00	.45	.13
☐ 362	Joe Hague 1.00	.45	.13
☐ 363	Tom Shopay 1.00	.45	.13
☐ 364	Dan McGinn..................1.00	.45	.13
☐ 365	Zoilo Versalles..............1.00	.45	.13
☐ 366	Barry Moore..................1.00	.45	.13
☐ 367	Mike Lum.....................1.00	.45	.13
☐ 368	Ed Herrmann................1.00	.45	.13
☐ 369	Alan Foster..................1.00	.45	.13
☐ 370	Tommy Harper...............1.25	.55	.16
☐ 371	Rod Gaspar..................1.00	.45	.13
☐ 372	Dave Giusti..................1.25	.55	.16
☐ 373	Roy White....................1.50	.65	.19
☐ 374	Tommie Sisk.................1.25	.55	.16
☐ 375	Johnny Callison 1.50	.65	.19
☐ 376	Lefty Phillips MG 1.25	.55	.16
☐ 377	Bill Butler....................1.25	.55	.16
☐ 378	Jim Davenport..............1.25	.55	.16
☐ 379	Tom Tischinski.............1.25	.55	.16
☐ 380	Tony Perez...................9.00	4.00	1.15
☐ 381	Athletics Rookies.........1.25	.55	.16
	Bobby Brooks		
	Mike Olivo		
☐ 382	Jack DiLauro................1.25	.55	.16
☐ 383	Mickey Stanley.............1.50	.65	.19
☐ 384	Gary Neibauer..............1.25	.55	.16
☐ 385	George Scott................1.50	.65	.19
☐ 386	Bill Dillman.................1.25	.55	.16
☐ 387	Baltimore Orioles.........2.50	1.15	.30
	Team Card		
☐ 388	Byron Browne 1.25	.55	.16
☐ 389	Jim Shellenback...........1.25	.55	.16
☐ 390	Willie Davis 1.50	.65	.19
☐ 391	Larry Brown.................1.25	.55	.16
☐ 392	Walt Hriniak.................1.25	.55	.16
☐ 393	John Gelnar..................1.25	.55	.16
☐ 394	Gil Hodges MG.............4.50	2.00	.55
☐ 395	Walt Williams...............1.25	.55	.16
☐ 396	Steve Blass 1.50	.65	.19
☐ 397	Roger Repoz.................1.25	.55	.16
☐ 398	Bill Stoneman...............1.25	.55	.16
☐ 399	New York Yankees........2.50	1.15	.30
	Team Card		
☐ 400	Denny McLain...............2.00	.90	.25

☐ 401	Giants Rookies.............1.25	.55	.16
	John Harrell		
	Bernie Williams		
☐ 402	Ellie Rodriguez.............1.25	.55	.16
☐ 403	Jim Bunning.................3.00	1.35	.40
☐ 404	Rich Reese...................1.25	.55	.16
☐ 405	Bill Hands....................1.25	.55	.16
☐ 406	Mike Andrews...............1.25	.55	.16
☐ 407	Bob Watson..................1.50	.65	.19
☐ 408	Paul Lindblad...............1.25	.55	.16
☐ 409	Bob Tolan....................1.50	.65	.19
☐ 410	Boog Powell.................3.50	1.55	.45
☐ 411	Los Angeles Dodgers....2.50	1.15	.30
	Team Card		
☐ 412	Larry Burchart..............1.25	.55	.16
☐ 413	Sonny Jackson.............1.25	.55	.16
☐ 414	Paul Edmondson..........1.25	.55	.16
☐ 415	Julian Javier................1.50	.65	.19
☐ 416	Joe Verbanic................1.25	.55	.16
☐ 417	John Bateman...............1.25	.55	.16
☐ 418	John Donaldson............1.25	.55	.16
☐ 419	Ron Taylor 1.25	.55	.16
☐ 420	Ken McMullen..............1.50	.65	.19
☐ 421	Pat Dobson..................1.25	.55	.16
☐ 422	Royals Team................2.50	1.15	.30
☐ 423	Jerry May....................1.25	.55	.16
☐ 424	Mike Kilkenny 1.25	.55	.16
	(Inconsistent design,		
	card number in		
	white circle)		
☐ 425	Bobby Bonds 7.50	3.40	.95
☐ 426	Bill Rigney MG 1.25	.55	.16
☐ 427	Fred Norman.................1.25	.55	.16
☐ 428	Don Buford...................1.25	.55	.16
☐ 429	Cubs Rookies...............1.25	.55	.16
	Randy Bobb		
	Jim Cosman		
☐ 430	Andy Messersmith........1.50	.65	.19
☐ 431	Ron Swoboda.............1.50	.65	.19
☐ 432A	Checklist 5.................5.00	.50	.15
	("Baseball" in		
	yellow letters)		
☐ 432B	Checklist 5.................5.00	.50	.15
	("Baseball" in		
	white letters)		
☐ 433	Ron Bryant...................1.25	.55	.16
☐ 434	Felipe Alou...................1.75	.80	.22
☐ 435	Nelson Briles...............1.50	.65	.19
☐ 436	Philadelphia Phillies......2.50	1.15	.30
	Team Card		
☐ 437	Danny Cater.................1.25	.55	.16
☐ 438	Pat Jarvis....................1.25	.55	.16
☐ 439	Lee Maye.....................1.25	.55	.16
☐ 440	Bill Mazeroski..............2.50	1.15	.30
☐ 441	John O'Donoghue 1.25	.55	.16
☐ 442	Gene Mauch MG 1.50	.65	.19
☐ 443	Al Jackson...................1.25	.55	.16

☐ 444	White Sox Rookies.......1.25	.55	.16
	Billy Farmer		
	John Matias		
☐ 445	Vada Pinson..................2.00	.90	.25
☐ 446	Billy Grabarkewitz 1.25	.55	.16
☐ 447	Lee Stange..................1.25	.55	.16
☐ 448	Houston Astros.............2.50	1.15	.30
	Team Card		
☐ 449	Jim Palmer 25.00	11.50	3.10
☐ 450	Willie McCovey AS....5.50	2.50	.70
☐ 451	Boog Powell AS 1.50	.65	.19
☐ 452	Felix Millan AS...........1.50	.65	.19
☐ 453	Rod Carew AS.............7.50	3.40	.95
☐ 454	Ron Santo AS...............2.50	1.15	.30
☐ 455	Brooks Robinson AS....5.50	2.50	.70
☐ 456	Don Kessinger AS........1.50	.65	.19
☐ 457	Rico Petrocelli AS 1.50	.65	.19
☐ 458	Pete Rose AS.............14.00	6.25	1.75
☐ 459	Reggie Jackson AS ..27.00	12.00	3.40
☐ 460	Matty Alou AS.............2.25	1.00	.30
☐ 461	Carl Yastrzemski AS..12.00	5.50	1.50
☐ 462	Hank Aaron AS..........15.00	6.75	1.90
☐ 463	Frank Robinson AS......7.50	3.40	.95
☐ 464	Johnny Bench AS.......15.00	6.75	1.90
☐ 465	Bill Freehan AS...........2.25	1.00	.30
☐ 466	Juan Marichal AS........4.50	2.00	.55
☐ 467	Denny McLain AS.........2.25	1.00	.30
☐ 468	Jerry Koosman AS........2.25	1.00	.30
☐ 469	Sam McDowell AS........2.25	1.00	.30
☐ 470	Willie Stargell............11.00	4.90	1.40
☐ 471	Chris Zachary.............1.50	.65	.19
☐ 472	Braves Team................3.00	1.35	.40
☐ 473	Don Bryant..................1.50	.65	.19
☐ 474	Dick Kelley..................1.50	.65	.19
☐ 475	Dick McAuliffe.............2.00	.90	.25
☐ 476	Don Shaw....................1.50	.65	.19
☐ 477	Orioles Rookies...........1.50	.65	.19
	Al Severinsen		
	Roger Freed		
☐ 478	Bobby Heise................1.50	.65	.19
☐ 479	Dick Woodson 1.50	.65	.19
☐ 480	Glenn Beckert 2.00	.90	.25
☐ 481	Jose Tartabull 2.00	.90	.25
☐ 482	Tom Hilgendorf...........1.50	.65	.19
☐ 483	Gail Hopkins................1.50	.65	.19
☐ 484	Gary Nolan..................2.00	.90	.25
☐ 485	Jay Johnstone..............2.00	.90	.25
☐ 486	Terry Harmon..............1.50	.65	.19
☐ 487	Cisco Carlos................1.50	.65	.19
☐ 488	J.C. Martin..................1.50	.65	.19
☐ 489	Eddie Kasko MG..........1.50	.65	.19
☐ 490	Bill Singer 2.00	.90	.25
☐ 491	Graig Nettles...............6.00	2.70	.75
☐ 492	Astros Rookies 1.50	.65	.19
	Keith Lampard		
	Scipio Spinks		
☐ 493	Lindy McDaniel............2.00	.90	.25
☐ 494	Larry Stahl..................1.50	.65	.19
☐ 495	Dave Morehead............1.50	.65	.19
☐ 496	Steve Whitaker............1.50	.65	.19
☐ 497	Eddie Watt...................1.50	.65	.19
☐ 498	Al Weis 1.50	.65	.19
☐ 499	Skip Lockwood.............1.50	.65	.19
☐ 500	Hank Aaron................60.00	27.00	7.50
☐ 501	Chicago White Sox......3.00	1.35	.40
	Team Card		
☐ 502	Rollie Fingers............40.00	18.00	5.00
☐ 503	Dal Maxvill..................1.50	.65	.19
☐ 504	Don Pavletich..............1.50	.65	.19
☐ 505	Ken Holtzman...............2.00	.90	.25
☐ 506	Ed Stroud....................1.50	.65	.19
☐ 507	Pat Corrales................2.00	.90	.25
☐ 508	Joe Niekro..................2.00	.90	.25
☐ 509	Montreal Expos............3.00	1.35	.40
	Team Card		
☐ 510	Tony Oliva..................3.00	1.35	.40
☐ 511	Joe Hoerner................1.50	.65	.19
☐ 512	Billy Harris 1.50	.65	.19
☐ 513	Preston Gomez MG.......1.50	.65	.19
☐ 514	Steve Hovley 1.50	.65	.19
☐ 515	Don Wilson..................2.00	.90	.25
☐ 516	Yankees Rookies..........1.50	.65	.19
	John Ellis		
	Jim Lyttle		
☐ 517	Joe Gibbon..................1.50	.65	.19
☐ 518	Bill Melton 1.50	.65	.19
☐ 519	Don McMahon..............1.50	.65	.19
☐ 520	Willie Horton................2.00	.90	.25
☐ 521	Cal Koonce..................1.50	.65	.19
☐ 522	Angels Team................3.00	1.35	.40
☐ 523	Jose Pena...................1.50	.65	.19
☐ 524	Alvin Dark MG.............2.00	.90	.25
☐ 525	Jerry Adair..................1.50	.65	.19
☐ 526	Ron Herbel..................1.50	.65	.19
☐ 527	Don Bosch...................1.50	.65	.19
☐ 528	Elrod Hendricks 1.50	.65	.19
☐ 529	Bob Aspromonte 1.50	.65	.19
☐ 530	Bob Gibson................15.00	6.75	1.90
☐ 531	Ron Clark....................1.50	.65	.19
☐ 532	Danny Murtaugh MG 2.00	.90	.25
☐ 533	Buzz Stephen 1.50	.65	.19
☐ 534	Minnesota Twins...........3.00	1.35	.40
	Team Card		
☐ 535	Andy Kosco.................1.50	.65	.19
☐ 536	Mike Kekich.................1.50	.65	.19
☐ 537	Joe Morgan................15.00	6.75	1.90
☐ 538	Bob Humphreys............1.50	.65	.19
☐ 539	Phillies Rookies...........5.00	2.30	.60
	Denny Doyle		
	Larry Bowa		
☐ 540	Gary Peters..................1.50	.65	.19
☐ 541	Bill Heath 1.50	.65	.19
☐ 542	Checklist 6..................5.00	.50	.15
☐ 543	Clyde Wright................1.50	.65	.19

☐ 544	Cincinnati Reds............3.00	1.35	.40
	Team Card		
☐ 545	Ken Harrelson..............2.00	.90	.25
☐ 546	Ron Reed......................1.50	.65	.19
☐ 547	Rick Monday.................3.50	1.55	.45
☐ 548	Howie Reed...................3.00	1.35	.40
☐ 549	St. Louis Cardinals........6.00	2.70	.75
	Team Card		
☐ 550	Frank Howard................5.00	2.30	.60
☐ 551	Dock Ellis.....................3.50	1.55	.45
☐ 552	Royals Rookies...............3.00	1.35	.40
	Don O'Riley		
	Dennis Paepke		
	Fred Rico		
☐ 553	Jim Lefebvre.................3.50	1.55	.45
☐ 554	Tom Timmermann.........3.00	1.35	.40
☐ 555	Orlando Cepeda.............5.50	2.50	.70
☐ 556	Dave Bristol MG............3.00	1.35	.40
☐ 557	Ed Kranepool................3.50	1.55	.45
☐ 558	Vern Fuller 3.00	1.35	.40
☐ 559	Tommy Davis.................3.50	1.55	.45
☐ 560	Gaylord Perry..............15.00	6.75	1.90
☐ 561	Tom McCraw..................3.00	1.35	.40
☐ 562	Ted Abernathy...............3.00	1.35	.40
☐ 563	Boston Red Sox.............6.00	2.70	.75
	Team Card		
☐ 564	Johnny Briggs...............3.00	1.35	.40
☐ 565	Jim Hunter..................15.00	6.75	1.90
☐ 566	Gene Alley....................3.50	1.55	.45
☐ 567	Bob Oliver....................3.00	1.35	.40
☐ 568	Stan Bahnsen................3.50	1.55	.45
☐ 569	Cookie Rojas.................3.50	1.55	.45
☐ 570	Jim Fregosi...................3.50	1.55	.45
☐ 571	Jim Brewer...................3.00	1.35	.40
☐ 572	Frank Quilici MG 3.00	1.35	.40
☐ 573	Padres Rookies..............3.00	1.35	.40
	Jim Corkins		
	Rafael Robles		
	Ron Slocum		
☐ 574	Bobby Bolin..................3.00	1.35	.40
☐ 575	Cleon Jones..................3.50	1.55	.45
☐ 576	Milt Pappas..................3.50	1.55	.45
☐ 577	Bernie Allen.................3.00	1.35	.40
☐ 578	Tom Griffin...................3.00	1.35	.40
☐ 579	Detroit Tigers...............6.00	2.70	.75
	Team Card		
☐ 580	Pete Rose....................65.00	29.00	8.25
☐ 581	Tom Satriano................3.00	1.35	.40
☐ 582	Mike Paul.....................3.00	1.35	.40
☐ 583	Hal Lanier....................3.00	1.35	.40
☐ 584	Al Downing...................3.50	1.55	.45
☐ 585	Rusty Staub..................5.00	2.30	.60
☐ 586	Rickey Clark.................3.00	1.35	.40
☐ 587	Jose Arcia....................3.00	1.35	.40
☐ 588A	Checklist 7 ERR.........8.00	.80	.24
	(666 Adolfo)		
☐ 588B	Checklist 7 COR.........5.00	.50	.15

	(666 Adolpho)		
☐ 589	Joe Keough...................3.00	1.35	.40
☐ 590	Mike Cuellar.................3.50	1.55	.45
☐ 591	Mike Ryan UER.............3.00	1.35	.40
	(Pitching Record		
	header on card back)		
☐ 592	Daryl Patterson.............3.00	1.35	.40
☐ 593	Chicago Cubs................6.00	2.70	.75
	Team Card		
☐ 594	Jake Gibbs...................3.00	1.35	.40
☐ 595	Maury Wills..................4.50	2.00	.55
☐ 596	Mike Hershberger..........3.00	1.35	.40
☐ 597	Sonny Siebert...............3.00	1.35	.40
☐ 598	Joe Pepitone.................3.50	1.55	.45
☐ 599	Senators Rookies...........3.50	1.55	.45
	Dick Stelmaszek		
	Gene Martin		
	Dick Such		
☐ 600	Willie Mays.................85.00	38.00	10.50
☐ 601	Pete Richert.................3.00	1.35	.40
☐ 602	Ted Savage...................3.00	1.35	.40
☐ 603	Ray Oyler.....................3.00	1.35	.40
☐ 604	Clarence Gaston............4.00	1.80	.50
☐ 605	Rick Wise.....................3.50	1.55	.45
☐ 606	Chico Ruiz....................3.00	1.35	.40
☐ 607	Gary Waslewski.............3.00	1.35	.40
☐ 608	Pittsburgh Pirates.........6.00	2.70	.75
	Team Card		
☐ 609	Buck Martinez..............4.00	1.80	.50
	(Inconsistent design,		
	card number in		
	white circle)		
☐ 610	Jerry Koosman..............5.00	2.30	.60
☐ 611	Norm Cash...................5.00	2.30	.60
☐ 612	Jim Hickman.................3.50	1.55	.45
☐ 613	Dave Baldwin................3.00	1.35	.40
☐ 614	Mike Shannon...............3.50	1.55	.45
☐ 615	Mark Belanger...............3.50	1.55	.45
☐ 616	Jim Merritt...................3.00	1.35	.40
☐ 617	Jim French...................3.00	1.35	.40
☐ 618	Billy Wynne..................3.00	1.35	.40
☐ 619	Norm Miller..................3.00	1.35	.40
☐ 620	Jim Perry.....................5.00	2.30	.60
☐ 621	Braves Rookies............30.00	13.50	3.80
	Mike McQueen		
	Darrell Evans		
	Rick Kester		
☐ 622	Don Sutton..................15.00	6.75	1.90
☐ 623	Horace Clarke................3.00	1.35	.40
☐ 624	Clyde King MG...............3.00	1.35	.40
☐ 625	Dean Chance.................3.00	1.35	.40
☐ 626	Dave Ricketts................3.00	1.35	.40
☐ 627	Gary Wagner.................3.00	1.35	.40
☐ 628	Wayne Garrett...............3.00	1.35	.40
☐ 629	Merv Rettenmund...........3.00	1.35	.40
☐ 630	Ernie Banks................40.00	18.00	5.00
☐ 631	Oakland Athletics..........6.00	2.70	.75

	Team Card			
☐ 632	Gary Sutherland 3.00	1.35	.40
☐ 633	Roger Nelson 3.00	1.35	.40
☐ 634	Bud Harrelson 6.50	2.90	.80
☐ 635	Bob Allison 6.50	2.90	.80
☐ 636	Jim Stewart 6.00	2.70	.75
☐ 637	Cleveland Indians.......12.00	5.50	1.50
	Team Card			
☐ 638	Frank Bertaina 6.00	2.70	.75
☐ 639	Dave Campbell 6.00	2.70	.75
☐ 640	Al Kaline.......................50.00	23.00	6.25
☐ 641	Al McBean 6.00	2.70	.75
☐ 642	Angels Rookies 6.00	2.70	.75
	Greg Garrett			
	Gordon Lund			
	Jarvis Tatum			
☐ 643	Jose Pagan 6.00	2.70	.75
☐ 644	Gerry Nyman 6.00	2.70	.75
☐ 645	Don Money 7.00	3.10	.85
☐ 646	Jim Britton 6.00	2.70	.75
☐ 647	Tom Matchick 6.00	2.70	.75
☐ 648	Larry Haney 6.00	2.70	.75
☐ 649	Jimmie Hall 6.00	2.70	.75
☐ 650	Sam McDowell 7.00	3.10	.85
☐ 651	Jim Gosger 6.00	2.70	.75
☐ 652	Rich Rollins 6.00	2.70	.75
☐ 653	Moe Drabowsky 6.00	2.70	.75
☐ 654	NL Rookies 7.00	3.10	.85
	Oscar Gamble			
	Boots Day			
	Angel Mangual			
☐ 655	John Roseboro 7.00	3.10	.85
☐ 656	Jim Hardin 6.00	2.70	.75
☐ 657	San Diego Padres 12.00	5.50	1.50
	Team Card			
☐ 658	Ken Tatum 6.00	2.70	.75
☐ 659	Pete Ward 6.00	2.70	.75
☐ 660	Johnny Bench 180.00	80.00	23.00
☐ 661	Jerry Robertson 6.00	2.70	.75
☐ 662	Frank Lucchesi MG 6.00	2.70	.75
☐ 663	Tito Francona 6.00	2.70	.75
☐ 664	Bob Robertson 6.00	2.70	.75
☐ 665	Jim Lonborg 7.00	3.10	.85
☐ 666	Adolpho Phillips 6.00	2.70	.75
☐ 667	Bob Meyer 6.00	2.70	.75
☐ 668	Bob Tillman 6.00	2.70	.75
☐ 669	White Sox Rookies 6.50	2.90	.80
	Bart Johnson			
	Dan Lazar			
	Mickey Scott			
☐ 670	Ron Santo 8.50	3.80	1.05
☐ 671	Jim Campanis 6.00	2.70	.75
☐ 672	Leon McFadden 6.00	2.70	.75
☐ 673	Ted Uhlaender 6.00	2.70	.75
☐ 674	Dave Leonhard 6.00	2.70	.75
☐ 675	Jose Cardenal 7.00	3.10	.85

☐ 676	Washington Senators 12.00	5.50	1.50
	Team Card			
☐ 677	Woodie Fryman...............6.00	2.70	.75
☐ 678	Dave Duncan..................6.50	2.90	.80
☐ 679	Ray Sadecki 6.00	2.70	.75
☐ 680	Rico Petrocelli................7.00	3.10	.85
☐ 681	Bob Garibaldi 6.00	2.70	.75
☐ 682	Dalton Jones 6.00	2.70	.75
☐ 683	Reds Rookies 8.50	3.80	1.05
	Vern Geishert			
	Hal McRae			
	Wayne Simpson			
☐ 684	Jack Fisher 6.00	2.70	.75
☐ 685	Tom Haller 6.00	2.70	.75
☐ 686	Jackie Hernandez 6.00	2.70	.75
☐ 687	Bob Priddy 6.00	2.70	.75
☐ 688	Ted Kubiak 6.00	2.70	.75
☐ 689	Frank Tepedino 6.00	2.70	.75
☐ 690	Ron Fairly 7.00	3.10	.85
☐ 691	Joe Grzenda 6.00	2.70	.75
☐ 692	Duffy Dyer 6.00	2.70	.75
☐ 693	Bob Johnson 6.00	2.70	.75
☐ 694	Gary Ross 6.00	2.70	.75
☐ 695	Bobby Knoop 6.00	2.70	.75
☐ 696	San Francisco Giants .12.00	5.50	1.50
	Team Card			
☐ 697	Jim Hannan 6.00	2.70	.75
☐ 698	Tom Tresh 8.00	3.60	1.00
☐ 699	Hank Aguirre 6.00	2.70	.75
☐ 700	Frank Robinson.............45.00	20.00	5.75
☐ 701	Jack Billingham 6.00	2.70	.75
☐ 702	AL Rookies 6.00	2.70	.75
	Bob Johnson			
	Ron Klimkowski			
	Bill Zepp			
☐ 703	Lou Marone 6.00	2.70	.75
☐ 704	Frank Baker 6.00	2.70	.75
☐ 705	Tony Cloninger UER.......6.00	2.70	.75
	(Batter headings			
	on card back)			
☐ 706	John McNamara MG.......6.00	2.70	.75
☐ 707	Kevin Collins 7.00	3.10	.85
☐ 708	Jose Santiago 6.00	2.70	.75
☐ 709	Mike Fiore 6.00	2.70	.75
☐ 710	Felix Millan 6.00	2.70	.75
☐ 711	Ed Brinkman 6.00	2.70	.75
☐ 712	Nolan Ryan 550.00	250.00	70.00
☐ 713	Seattle Pilots................25.00	11.50	3.10
	Team Card			
☐ 714	Al Spangler 6.00	2.70	.75
☐ 715	Mickey Lolich 7.50	3.40	.95
☐ 716	Cardinals Rookies..........7.00	3.10	.85
	Sal Campisi			
	Reggie Cleveland			
	Santiago Guzman			
☐ 717	Tom Phoebus 6.00	2.70	.75

☐ 718 Ed Spiezio	6.00	2.70	.75
☐ 719 Jim Roland	6.00	2.70	.75
☐ 720 Rick Reichardt	7.50	3.40	.95

1971 Topps

The cards in this 752-card set measure 2 1/2" by 3 1/2". The 1971 Topps set is a challenge to complete in strict mint condition because the black obverse border is easily scratched and damaged. An unusual feature of this set is that the player is also pictured in black and white on the back of the card. Featured subsets within this set include League Leaders (61-72), Playoffs cards (195-202), and World Series cards (327-332). Cards 524-643 and the last series (644-752) are somewhat scarce. The last series was printed in two sheets of 132. On the printing sheets 44 cards were printed in 50 percent greater quantity than the other 66 cards. These 66 (slightly) shorter-printed numbers are identified in the checklist below by SP. The key rookie cards in this set are the multi-player Rookie Card of Dusty Baker and Don Baylor and the individual cards of Bert Blyleven, Dave Concepcion, Steve Garvey, and Ted Simmons.

	NRMT-MT	EXC	G-VG
COMPLETE SET (752)	2200.	1000.	275.00
COMMON PLAYER (1-132)	.90	.40	.11
COMMON PLAYER (133-263)	1.00	.45	.13
COMMON PLAYER (264-393)	1.25	.55	.16
COMMON PLAYER (394-523)	2.00	.90	.25
COMMON PLAYER (524-643)	4.00	1.80	.50

COMMON PLAYER (644-752)	5.00	2.30	.60
☐ 1 Baltimore Orioles Team Card	12.50	2.50	.75
☐ 2 Dock Ellis	1.00	.45	.13
☐ 3 Dick McAuliffe	1.00	.45	.13
☐ 4 Vic Davalillo	.90	.40	.11
☐ 5 Thurman Munson	40.00	18.00	5.00
☐ 6 Ed Spiezio	.90	.40	.11
☐ 7 Jim Holt	.90	.40	.11
☐ 8 Mike McQueen	.90	.40	.11
☐ 9 George Scott	1.00	.45	.13
☐ 10 Claude Osteen	1.00	.45	.13
☐ 11 Elliott Maddox	1.00	.45	.13
☐ 12 Johnny Callison	1.00	.45	.13
☐ 13 White Sox Rookies Charlie Brinkman Dick Moloney	.90	.40	.11
☐ 14 Dave Concepcion	24.00	11.00	3.00
☐ 15 Andy Messersmith	1.00	.45	.13
☐ 16 Ken Singleton	3.50	1.55	.45
☐ 17 Billy Sorrell	.90	.40	.11
☐ 18 Norm Miller	.90	.40	.11
☐ 19 Skip Pitlock	.90	.40	.11
☐ 20 Reggie Jackson	135.00	60.00	17.00
☐ 21 Dan McGinn	.90	.40	.11
☐ 22 Phil Roof	.90	.40	.11
☐ 23 Oscar Gamble	1.00	.45	.13
☐ 24 Rich Hand	.90	.40	.11
☐ 25 Clarence Gaston	2.00	.90	.25
☐ 26 Bert Blyleven	65.00	29.00	8.25
☐ 27 Pirates Rookies Fred Cambria Gene Clines	1.25	.55	.16
☐ 28 Ron Klimkowski	.90	.40	.11
☐ 29 Don Buford	.90	.40	.11
☐ 30 Phil Niekro	5.00	2.30	.60
☐ 31 Eddie Kasko MG	.90	.40	.11
☐ 32 Jerry DaVanon	.90	.40	.11
☐ 33 Del Unser	.90	.40	.11
☐ 34 Sandy Vance	.90	.40	.11
☐ 35 Lou Piniella	2.00	.90	.25
☐ 36 Dean Chance	.90	.40	.11
☐ 37 Rich McKinney	.90	.40	.11
☐ 38 Jim Colborn	.90	.40	.11
☐ 39 Tiger Rookies Lerrin LaGrow Gene Lamont	1.50	.65	.19
☐ 40 Lee May	1.00	.45	.13
☐ 41 Rick Austin	.90	.40	.11
☐ 42 Boots Day	.90	.40	.11
☐ 43 Steve Kealey	.90	.40	.11
☐ 44 Johnny Edwards	.90	.40	.11
☐ 45 Jim Hunter	7.00	3.10	.85
☐ 46 Dave Campbell	.90	.40	.11
☐ 47 Johnny Jeter	.90	.40	.11

☐ 48 Dave Baldwin	.90	.40	.11
☐ 49 Don Money	.90	.40	.11
☐ 50 Willie McCovey	10.00	4.50	1.25
☐ 51 Steve Kline	.90	.40	.11
☐ 52 Braves Rookies	1.25	.55	.16
Oscar Brown			
Earl Williams			
☐ 53 Paul Blair	1.00	.45	.13
☐ 54 Checklist 1	5.00	2.30	.60
☐ 55 Steve Carlton	33.00	15.00	4.10
☐ 56 Duane Josephson	.90	.40	.11
☐ 57 Von Joshua	.90	.40	.11
☐ 58 Bill Lee	1.00	.45	.13
☐ 59 Gene Mauch MG	1.00	.45	.13
☐ 60 Dick Bosman	.90	.40	.11
☐ 61 AL Batting Leaders	3.50	1.55	.45
Alex Johnson			
Carl Yastrzemski			
Tony Oliva			
☐ 62 NL Batting Leaders	2.50	1.15	.30
Rico Carty			
Joe Torre			
Manny Sanguillen			
☐ 63 AL RBI Leaders	2.50	1.15	.30
Frank Howard			
Tony Conigliaro			
Boog Powell			
☐ 64 NL RBI Leaders	4.00	1.80	.50
Johnny Bench			
Tony Perez			
Billy Williams			
☐ 65 AL HR Leaders	3.50	1.55	.45
Frank Howard			
Harmon Killebrew			
Carl Yastrzemski			
☐ 66 NL HR Leaders	4.25	1.90	.55
Johnny Bench			
Billy Williams			
Tony Perez			
☐ 67 AL ERA Leaders	3.00	1.35	.40
Diego Segui			
Jim Palmer			
Clyde Wright			
☐ 68 NL ERA Leaders	3.00	1.35	.40
Tom Seaver			
Wayne Simpson			
Luke Walker			
☐ 69 AL Pitching Leaders	2.50	1.15	.30
Mike Cuellar			
Dave McNally			
Jim Perry			
☐ 70 NL Pitching Leaders	4.25	1.90	.55
Bob Gibson			
Gaylord Perry			
Fergie Jenkins			
☐ 71 AL Strikeout Leaders	2.50	1.15	.30
Sam McDowell			
Mickey Lolich			
Bob Johnson			
☐ 72 NL Strikeout Leaders	5.00	2.30	.60
Tom Seaver			
Bob Gibson			
Fergie Jenkins			
☐ 73 George Brunet	.90	.40	.11
☐ 74 Twins Rookies	.90	.40	.11
Pete Hamm			
Jim Nettles			
☐ 75 Gary Nolan	1.00	.45	.13
☐ 76 Ted Savage	.90	.40	.11
☐ 77 Mike Compton	.90	.40	.11
☐ 78 Jim Spencer	.90	.40	.11
☐ 79 Wade Blasingame	.90	.40	.11
☐ 80 Bill Melton	.90	.40	.11
☐ 81 Felix Millan	.90	.40	.11
☐ 82 Casey Cox	.90	.40	.11
☐ 83 Met Rookies	1.25	.55	.16
Tim Foli			
Randy Bobb			
☐ 84 Marcel Lachemann	1.50	.65	.19
☐ 85 Billy Grabarkewitz	.90	.40	.11
☐ 86 Mike Kilkenny	.90	.40	.11
☐ 87 Jack Heidemann	.90	.40	.11
☐ 88 Hal King	.90	.40	.11
☐ 89 Ken Brett	.90	.40	.11
☐ 90 Joe Pepitone	1.00	.45	.13
☐ 91 Bob Lemon MG	1.75	.80	.22
☐ 92 Fred Wenz	.90	.40	.11
☐ 93 Senators Rookies	.90	.40	.11
Norm McRae			
Denny Riddleberger			
☐ 94 Don Hahn	.90	.40	.11
☐ 95 Luis Tiant	2.00	.90	.25
☐ 96 Joe Hague	.90	.40	.11
☐ 97 Floyd Wicker	.90	.40	.11
☐ 98 Joe Decker	.90	.40	.11
☐ 99 Mark Belanger	1.00	.45	.13
☐ 100 Pete Rose	45.00	20.00	5.75
☐ 101 Les Cain	.90	.40	.11
☐ 102 Astros Rookies	1.00	.45	.13
Ken Forsch			
Larry Howard			
☐ 103 Rich Severson	.90	.40	.11
☐ 104 Dan Frisella	.90	.40	.11
☐ 105 Tony Conigliaro	1.75	.80	.22
☐ 106 Tom Dukes	.90	.40	.11
☐ 107 Roy Foster	.90	.40	.11
☐ 108 John Cumberland	.90	.40	.11
☐ 109 Steve Hovley	.90	.40	.11
☐ 110 Bill Mazeroski	2.00	.90	.25
☐ 111 Yankee Rookies	.90	.40	.11
Loyd Colson			
Bobby Mitchell			
☐ 112 Manny Mota	1.00	.45	.13
☐ 113 Jerry Crider	.90	.40	.11

☐ 114	Billy Conigliaro	1.00	.45	.13
☐ 115	Donn Clendenon	1.00	.45	.13
☐ 116	Ken Sanders	.90	.40	.11
☐ 117	Ted Simmons	24.00	11.00	3.00
☐ 118	Cookie Rojas	1.00	.45	.13
☐ 119	Frank Lucchesi MG	.90	.40	.11
☐ 120	Willie Horton	1.00	.45	.13
☐ 121	Cubs Rookies	.90	.40	.11
	Jim Dunegan			
	Roe Skidmore			
☐ 122	Eddie Watt	.90	.40	.11
☐ 123A	Checklist 2	5.00	2.30	.60
	(Card number			
	at bottom right)			
☐ 123B	Checklist 2	5.00	2.30	.60
	(Card number			
	centered)			
☐ 124	Don Gullett	1.50	.65	.19
☐ 125	Ray Fosse	1.00	.45	.13
☐ 126	Danny Coombs	.90	.40	.11
☐ 127	Danny Thompson	1.00	.45	.13
☐ 128	Frank Johnson	.90	.40	.11
☐ 129	Aurelio Monteagudo	.90	.40	.11
☐ 130	Denis Menke	.90	.40	.11
☐ 131	Curt Blefary	.90	.40	.11
☐ 132	Jose Laboy	.90	.40	.11
☐ 133	Mickey Lolich	2.00	.90	.25
☐ 134	Jose Arcia	1.00	.45	.13
☐ 135	Rick Monday	1.25	.55	.16
☐ 136	Duffy Dyer	1.00	.45	.13
☐ 137	Marcelino Lopez	1.00	.45	.13
☐ 138	Phillies Rookies	1.25	.55	.16
	Joe Lis			
	Willie Montanez			
☐ 139	Paul Casanova	1.00	.45	.13
☐ 140	Gaylord Perry	8.50	3.80	1.05
☐ 141	Frank Quilici	1.00	.45	.13
☐ 142	Mack Jones	1.00	.45	.13
☐ 143	Steve Blass	1.25	.55	.16
☐ 144	Jackie Hernandez	1.00	.45	.13
☐ 145	Bill Singer	1.25	.55	.16
☐ 146	Ralph Houk MG	1.25	.55	.16
☐ 147	Bob Priddy	1.00	.45	.13
☐ 148	John Mayberry	1.25	.55	.16
☐ 149	Mike Hershberger	1.00	.45	.13
☐ 150	Sam McDowell	1.25	.55	.16
☐ 151	Tommy Davis	1.25	.55	.16
☐ 152	Angels Rookies	1.00	.45	.13
	Lloyd Allen			
	Winston Llenas			
☐ 153	Gary Ross	1.00	.45	.13
☐ 154	Cesar Gutierrez	1.00	.45	.13
☐ 155	Ken Henderson	1.00	.45	.13
☐ 156	Bart Johnson	1.00	.45	.13
☐ 157	Bob Bailey	1.00	.45	.13
☐ 158	Jerry Reuss	2.00	.90	.25
☐ 159	Jarvis Tatum	1.00	.45	.13
☐ 160	Tom Seaver	65.00	29.00	8.25
☐ 161	Coin Checklist	5.00	2.30	.60
☐ 162	Jack Billingham	1.00	.45	.13
☐ 163	Buck Martinez	1.00	.45	.13
☐ 164	Reds Rookies	1.25	.55	.16
	Frank Duffy			
	Milt Wilcox			
☐ 165	Cesar Tovar	1.00	.45	.13
☐ 166	Joe Hoerner	1.00	.45	.13
☐ 167	Tom Grieve	2.00	.90	.25
☐ 168	Bruce Dal Canton	1.00	.45	.13
☐ 169	Ed Herrmann	1.00	.45	.13
☐ 170	Mike Cuellar	1.25	.55	.16
☐ 171	Bobby Wine	1.00	.45	.13
☐ 172	Duke Sims	1.00	.45	.13
☐ 173	Gil Garrido	1.00	.45	.13
☐ 174	Dave LaRoche	1.50	.65	.19
☐ 175	Jim Hickman	1.00	.45	.13
☐ 176	Red Sox Rookies	1.50	.65	.19
	Bob Montgomery			
	Doug Griffin			
☐ 177	Hal McRae	2.50	1.15	.30
☐ 178	Dave Duncan	1.00	.45	.13
☐ 179	Mike Corkins	1.00	.45	.13
☐ 180	Al Kaline UER	20.00	9.00	2.50
	(Home instead			
	of Birth)			
☐ 181	Hal Lanier	1.00	.45	.13
☐ 182	Al Downing	1.25	.55	.16
☐ 183	Gil Hodges MG	5.00	2.30	.60
☐ 184	Stan Bahnsen	1.00	.45	.13
☐ 185	Julian Javier	1.25	.55	.16
☐ 186	Bob Spence	1.00	.45	.13
☐ 187	Ted Abernathy	1.00	.45	.13
☐ 188	Dodgers Rookies	4.00	1.80	.50
	Bob Valentine			
	Mike Strahler			
☐ 189	George Mitterwald	1.00	.45	.13
☐ 190	Bob Tolan	1.25	.55	.16
☐ 191	Mike Andrews	1.00	.45	.13
☐ 192	Billy Wilson	1.00	.45	.13
☐ 193	Bob Grich	5.00	2.30	.60
☐ 194	Mike Lum	1.00	.45	.13
☐ 195	AL Playoff Game 1	2.50	1.15	.30
	Boog Powell muscles			
	Twins			
☐ 196	AL Playoff Game 2	2.50	1.15	.30
	Dave McNally makes			
	it two straight			
☐ 197	AL Playoff Game 3	4.00	1.80	.50
	Jim Palmer mows'em down			
☐ 198	AL Playoff Summary	2.50	1.15	.30
	Orioles celebrate			
☐ 199	NL Playoff Game 1	2.50	1.15	.30
	Ty Cline pinch-triple			
	decides it			
☐ 200	NL Playoff Game 2	2.50	1.15	.30

	Bobby Tolan scores		
	for third time		
☐ 201	NL Playoff Game 3......2.50	1.15	.30
	Ty Cline scores		
	winning run		
☐ 202	NL Playoff Summary...2.50	1.15	.30
	Reds celebrate		
☐ 203	Larry Gura.................1.50	.65	.19
☐ 204	Brewers Rookies..........1.00	.45	.13
	Bernie Smith		
	George Kopacz		
☐ 205	Gerry Moses................1.00	.45	.13
☐ 206	Checklist 3...................5.00	2.30	.60
☐ 207	Alan Foster..................1.00	.45	.13
☐ 208	Billy Martin MG..........3.50	1.55	.45
☐ 209	Steve Renko.................1.00	.45	.13
☐ 210	Rod Carew.................48.00	22.00	6.00
☐ 211	Phil Hennigan............1.00	.45	.13
☐ 212	Rich Hebner...............1.25	.55	.16
☐ 213	Frank Baker................1.00	.45	.13
☐ 214	Al Ferrara...................1.00	.45	.13
☐ 215	Diego Segui.................1.00	.45	.13
☐ 216	Cards Rookies..............1.00	.45	.13
	Reggie Cleveland		
	Luis Melendez		
☐ 217	Ed Stroud....................1.00	.45	.13
☐ 218	Tony Cloninger............1.00	.45	.13
☐ 219	Elrod Hendricks...........1.00	.45	.13
☐ 220	Ron Santo....................2.50	1.15	.30
☐ 221	Dave Morehead...........1.00	.45	.13
☐ 222	Bob Watson.................1.25	.55	.16
☐ 223	Cecil Upshaw...............1.00	.45	.13
☐ 224	Alan Gallagher............1.00	.45	.13
☐ 225	Gary Peters.................1.00	.45	.13
☐ 226	Bill Russell..................2.00	.90	.25
☐ 227	Floyd Weaver..............1.00	.45	.13
☐ 228	Wayne Garrett.............1.00	.45	.13
☐ 229	Jim Hannan.................1.00	.45	.13
☐ 230	Willie Stargell............10.00	4.50	1.25
☐ 231	Indians Rookies..........1.50	.65	.19
	Vince Colbert		
	John Lowenstein		
☐ 232	John Strohmayer........1.00	.45	.13
☐ 233	Larry Bowa.................2.00	.90	.25
☐ 234	Jim Lyttle...................1.00	.45	.13
☐ 235	Nate Colbert................1.00	.45	.13
☐ 236	Bob Humphreys...........1.00	.45	.13
☐ 237	Cesar Cedeno.............3.50	1.55	.45
☐ 238	Chuck Dobson..............1.00	.45	.13
☐ 239	Red Schoendienst MG .2.00	.90	.25
☐ 240	Clyde Wright...............1.00	.45	.13
☐ 241	Dave Nelson................1.00	.45	.13
☐ 242	Jim Ray......................1.00	.45	.13
☐ 243	Carlos May..................1.25	.55	.16
☐ 244	Bob Tillman.................1.00	.45	.13
☐ 245	Jim Kaat.....................3.00	1.35	.40
☐ 246	Tony Taylor.................1.00	.45	.13

☐ 247	Royals Rookies.............1.75	.80	.22
	Jerry Cram		
	Paul Splittorff		
☐ 248	Hoyt Wilhelm..............4.25	1.90	.55
☐ 249	Chico Salmon..............1.00	.45	.13
☐ 250	Johnny Bench............55.00	25.00	7.00
☐ 251	Frank Reberger...........1.00	.45	.13
☐ 252	Eddie Leon..................1.00	.45	.13
☐ 253	Bill Sudakis.................1.00	.45	.13
☐ 254	Cal Koonce..................1.00	.45	.13
☐ 255	Bob Robertson............1.25	.55	.16
☐ 256	Tony Gonzalez.............1.00	.45	.13
☐ 257	Nelson Briles...............1.00	.45	.13
☐ 258	Dick Green...................1.00	.45	.13
☐ 259	Dave Marshall..............1.00	.45	.13
☐ 260	Tommy Harper.............1.25	.55	.16
☐ 261	Darold Knowles............1.00	.45	.13
☐ 262	Padres Rookies.............1.00	.45	.13
	Jim Williams		
	Dave Robinson		
☐ 263	John Ellis....................1.25	.55	.16
☐ 264	Joe Morgan................10.00	4.50	1.25
☐ 265	Jim Northrup...............1.50	.65	.19
☐ 266	Bill Stoneman..............1.25	.55	.16
☐ 267	Rich Morales................1.25	.55	.16
☐ 268	Philadelphia Phillies....2.50	1.15	.30
	Team Card		
☐ 269	Gail Hopkins...............1.25	.55	.16
☐ 270	Rico Carty...................1.50	.65	.19
☐ 271	Bill Zepp.....................1.25	.55	.16
☐ 272	Tommy Helms..............1.50	.65	.19
☐ 273	Pete Richert.................1.25	.55	.16
☐ 274	Ron Slocum.................1.25	.55	.16
☐ 275	Vada Pinson................2.00	.90	.25
☐ 276	Giants Rookies.............9.00	4.00	1.15
	Mike Davison		
	George Foster		
☐ 277	Gary Waslewski..........1.25	.55	.16
☐ 278	Jerry Grote.................1.25	.55	.16
☐ 279	Lefty Phillips MG.........1.25	.55	.16
☐ 280	Fergie Jenkins...........12.00	5.50	1.50
☐ 281	Danny Walton..............1.25	.55	.16
☐ 282	Jose Pagan..................1.25	.55	.16
☐ 283	Dick Such....................1.25	.55	.16
☐ 284	Jim Gosger..................1.25	.55	.16
☐ 285	Sal Bando....................1.50	.65	.19
☐ 286	Jerry McNertney..........1.25	.55	.16
☐ 287	Mike Fiore...................1.25	.55	.16
☐ 288	Joe Moeller..................1.25	.55	.16
☐ 289	Chicago White Sox.......2.50	1.15	.30
	Team Card		
☐ 290	Tony Oliva...................3.50	1.55	.45
☐ 291	George Culver..............1.25	.55	.16
☐ 292	Jay Johnstone..............1.50	.65	.19
☐ 293	Pat Corrales.................1.50	.65	.19
☐ 294	Steve Dunning.............1.25	.55	.16
☐ 295	Bobby Bonds...............4.50	2.00	.55

☐ 296	Tom Timmermann 1.25	.55	.16
☐ 297	Johnny Briggs.............1.25	.55	.16
☐ 298	Jim Nelson..................1.25	.55	.16
☐ 299	Ed Kirkpatrick 1.25	.55	.16
☐ 300	Brooks Robinson 20.00	9.00	2.50
☐ 301	Earl Wilson 1.35	.60	.17
☐ 302	Phil Gagliano...............1.25	.55	.16
☐ 303	Lindy McDaniel 1.50	.65	.19
☐ 304	Ron Brand...................1.25	.55	.16
☐ 305	Reggie Smith...............2.00	.90	.25
☐ 306	Jim Nash.....................1.25	.55	.16
☐ 307	Don Wert 1.25	.55	.16
☐ 308	St. Louis Cardinals....2.50	1.15	.30
	Team Card		
☐ 309	Dick Ellsworth 1.25	.55	.16
☐ 310	Tommie Agee...............1.50	.65	.19
☐ 311	Lee Stange 1.25	.55	.16
☐ 312	Harry Walker MG 1.25	.55	.16
☐ 313	Tom Hall 1.25	.55	.16
☐ 314	Jeff Torborg................1.50	.65	.19
☐ 315	Ron Fairly 1.50	.65	.19
☐ 316	Fred Scherman 1.25	.55	.16
☐ 317	Athletic Rookies...........1.25	.55	.16
	Jim Driscoll		
	Angel Mangual		
☐ 318	Rudy May 1.25	.55	.16
☐ 319	Ty Cline......................1.25	.55	.16
☐ 320	Dave McNally 1.50	.65	.19
☐ 321	Tom Matchick 1.25	.55	.16
☐ 322	Jim Beauchamp 1.25	.55	.16
☐ 323	Billy Champion 1.25	.55	.16
☐ 324	Graig Nettles 3.50	1.55	.45
☐ 325	Juan Marichal..............6.00	2.70	.75
☐ 326	Richie Scheinblum........1.25	.55	.16
☐ 327	World Series Game 1...2.50	1.15	.30
	Boog Powell homers		
	to opposite field		
☐ 328	World Series Game 2...2.50	1.15	.30
	(Don Buford)		
☐ 329	World Series Game 3...4.00	1.80	.50
	Frank Robinson		
	shows muscle		
☐ 330	World Series Game 4...2.50	1.15	.30
	Reds stay alive		
☐ 331	World Series Game 5...4.50	2.00	.55
	Brooks Robinson		
	commits robbery		
☐ 332	World Series Summary2.50	1.15	.30
	Orioles celebrate		
☐ 333	Clay Kirby 1.25	.55	.16
☐ 334	Roberto Pena...............1.25	.55	.16
☐ 335	Jerry Koosman 2.50	1.15	.30
☐ 336	Detroit Tigers...............2.50	1.15	.30
	Team Card		
☐ 337	Jesus Alou 1.25	.55	.16
☐ 338	Gene Tenace 2.00	.90	.25
☐ 339	Wayne Simpson...........1.25	.55	.16
☐ 340	Rico Petrocelli.............1.50	.65	.19
☐ 341	Steve Garvey..............70.00	32.00	8.75
☐ 342	Frank Tepedino............1.25	.55	.16
☐ 343	Pirates Rookies............1.75	.80	.22
	Ed Acosta		
	Milt May		
☐ 344	Ellie Rodriguez............1.25	.55	.16
☐ 345	Joel Horlen 1.25	.55	.16
☐ 346	Lum Harris MG.............1.25	.55	.16
☐ 347	Ted Uhlaender.............1.25	.55	.16
☐ 348	Fred Norman................1.25	.55	.16
☐ 349	Rich Reese..................1.25	.55	.16
☐ 350	Billy Williams 6.50	2.90	.80
☐ 351	Jim Shellenback..........1.25	.55	.16
☐ 352	Denny Doyle 1.25	.55	.16
☐ 353	Carl Taylor 1.25	.55	.16
☐ 354	Don McMahon 1.25	.55	.16
☐ 355	Bud Harrelson.............1.50	.65	.19
☐ 356	Bob Locker 1.25	.55	.16
☐ 357	Cincinnati Reds...........2.50	1.15	.30
	Team Card		
☐ 358	Danny Cater 1.25	.55	.16
☐ 359	Ron Reed 1.25	.55	.16
☐ 360	Jim Fregosi.................1.50	.65	.19
☐ 361	Don Sutton 8.00	3.60	1.00
☐ 362	Orioles Rookies...........1.25	.55	.16
	Mike Adamson		
	Roger Freed		
☐ 363	Mike Nagy 1.25	.55	.16
☐ 364	Tommy Dean 1.25	.55	.16
☐ 365	Bob Johnson................1.25	.55	.16
☐ 366	Ron Stone...................1.25	.55	.16
☐ 367	Dalton Jones...............1.25	.55	.16
☐ 368	Bob Veale....................1.50	.65	.19
☐ 369	Checklist 4 ....5.00	.50	.15
☐ 370	Joe Torre 3.50	1.55	.45
☐ 371	Jack Hiatt 1.25	.55	.16
☐ 372	Lew Krausse 1.25	.55	.16
☐ 373	Tom McCraw 1.25	.55	.16
☐ 374	Clete Boyer 1.50	.65	.19
☐ 375	Steve Hargan 1.25	.55	.16
☐ 376	Expos Rookies.............1.25	.55	.16
	Clyde Mashore		
	Ernie McAnally		
☐ 377	Greg Garrett................1.25	.55	.16
☐ 378	Tito Fuentes 1.25	.55	.16
☐ 379	Wayne Granger............1.25	.55	.16
☐ 380	Ted Williams MG 8.00	3.60	1.00
☐ 381	Fred Gladding 1.25	.55	.16
☐ 382	Jake Gibbs 1.25	.55	.16
☐ 383	Rod Gaspar 1.25	.55	.16
☐ 384	Rollie Fingers............17.50	8.00	2.20
☐ 385	Maury Wills.................2.50	1.15	.30
☐ 386	Boston Red Sox...........2.50	1.15	.30
	Team Card		
☐ 387	Ron Herbel 1.25	.55	.16
☐ 388	Al Oliver......................3.00	1.35	.40

☐ 389 Ed Brinkman	1.25	.55	.16
☐ 390 Glenn Beckert	1.50	.65	.19
☐ 391 Twins Rookies	1.25	.55	.16
Steve Brye			
Cotton Nash			
☐ 392 Grant Jackson	1.25	.55	.16
☐ 393 Merv Rettenmund	1.50	.65	.19
☐ 394 Clay Carroll	2.50	1.15	.30
☐ 395 Roy White	2.50	1.15	.30
☐ 396 Dick Schofield	2.00	.90	.25
☐ 397 Alvin Dark MG	2.50	1.15	.30
☐ 398 Howie Reed	2.00	.90	.25
☐ 399 Jim French	2.00	.90	.25
☐ 400 Hank Aaron	60.00	27.00	7.50
☐ 401 Tom Murphy	2.00	.90	.25
☐ 402 Los Angeles Dodgers	4.00	1.80	.50
Team Card			
☐ 403 Joe Coleman	2.00	.90	.25
☐ 404 Astros Rookies	2.00	.90	.25
Buddy Harris			
Roger Metzger			
☐ 405 Leo Cardenas	2.00	.90	.25
☐ 406 Ray Sadecki	2.00	.90	.25
☐ 407 Joe Rudi	2.50	1.15	.30
☐ 408 Rafael Robles	2.00	.90	.25
☐ 409 Don Pavletich	2.00	.90	.25
☐ 410 Ken Holtzman	2.50	1.15	.30
☐ 411 George Spriggs	2.00	.90	.25
☐ 412 Jerry Johnson	2.00	.90	.25
☐ 413 Pat Kelly	2.50	1.15	.30
☐ 414 Woodie Fryman	2.50	1.15	.30
☐ 415 Mike Hegan	2.00	.90	.25
☐ 416 Gene Alley	2.00	.90	.25
☐ 417 Dick Hall	2.00	.90	.25
☐ 418 Adolfo Phillips	2.00	.90	.25
☐ 419 Ron Hansen	2.00	.90	.25
☐ 420 Jim Merritt	2.00	.90	.25
☐ 421 John Stephenson	2.00	.90	.25
☐ 422 Frank Bertaina	2.00	.90	.25
☐ 423 Tigers Rookies	2.00	.90	.25
Dennis Saunders			
Tim Marting			
☐ 424 Roberto Rodriquez	2.00	.90	.25
☐ 425 Doug Rader	2.50	1.15	.30
☐ 426 Chris Cannizzaro	2.00	.90	.25
☐ 427 Bernie Allen	2.00	.90	.25
☐ 428 Jim McAndrew	2.00	.90	.25
☐ 429 Chuck Hinton	2.00	.90	.25
☐ 430 Wes Parker	2.50	1.15	.30
☐ 431 Tom Burgmeier	2.00	.90	.25
☐ 432 Bob Didier	2.00	.90	.25
☐ 433 Skip Lockwood	2.00	.90	.25
☐ 434 Gary Sutherland	2.00	.90	.25
☐ 435 Jose Cardenal	2.50	1.15	.30
☐ 436 Wilbur Wood	2.50	1.15	.30
☐ 437 Danny Murtaugh MG	2.50	1.15	.30
☐ 438 Mike McCormick	2.50	1.15	.30

☐ 439 Phillies Rookies	5.00	2.30	.60
Greg Luzinski			
Scott Reid			
☐ 440 Bert Campaneris	2.50	1.15	.30
☐ 441 Milt Pappas	2.50	1.15	.30
☐ 442 California Angels	4.00	1.80	.50
Team Card			
☐ 443 Rich Robertson	2.00	.90	.25
☐ 444 Jimmie Price	2.00	.90	.25
☐ 445 Art Shamsky	2.00	.90	.25
☐ 446 Bobby Bolin	2.00	.90	.25
☐ 447 Cesar Geronimo	2.50	1.15	.30
☐ 448 Dave Roberts	2.00	.90	.25
☐ 449 Brant Alyea	2.00	.90	.25
☐ 450 Bob Gibson	16.00	7.25	2.00
☐ 451 Joe Keough	2.00	.90	.25
☐ 452 John Boccabella	2.00	.90	.25
☐ 453 Terry Crowley	2.00	.90	.25
☐ 454 Mike Paul	2.00	.90	.25
☐ 455 Don Kessinger	2.50	1.15	.30
☐ 456 Bob Meyer	2.00	.90	.25
☐ 457 Willie Smith	2.00	.90	.25
☐ 458 White Sox Rookies	2.00	.90	.25
Ron Lolich			
Dave Lemonds			
☐ 459 Jim Lefebvre	2.00	.90	.25
☐ 460 Fritz Peterson	2.00	.90	.25
☐ 461 Jim Ray Hart	2.50	1.15	.30
☐ 462 Washington Senators	4.00	1.80	.50
Team Card			
☐ 463 Tom Kelley	2.00	.90	.25
☐ 464 Aurelio Rodriguez	2.00	.90	.25
☐ 465 Tim McCarver	2.50	1.15	.30
☐ 466 Ken Berry	2.00	.90	.25
☐ 467 Al Santorini	2.00	.90	.25
☐ 468 Frank Fernandez	2.00	.90	.25
☐ 469 Bob Aspromonte	2.00	.90	.25
☐ 470 Bob Oliver	2.00	.90	.25
☐ 471 Tom Griffin	2.00	.90	.25
☐ 472 Ken Rudolph	2.00	.90	.25
☐ 473 Gary Wagner	2.00	.90	.25
☐ 474 Jim Fairey	2.00	.90	.25
☐ 475 Ron Perranoski	2.50	1.15	.30
☐ 476 Dal Maxvill	2.00	.90	.25
☐ 477 Earl Weaver MG	3.50	1.55	.45
☐ 478 Bernie Carbo	2.00	.90	.25
☐ 479 Dennis Higgins	2.00	.90	.25
☐ 480 Manny Sanguillen	2.50	1.15	.30
☐ 481 Daryl Patterson	2.00	.90	.25
☐ 482 San Diego Padres	4.00	1.80	.50
Team Card			
☐ 483 Gene Michael	2.50	1.15	.30
☐ 484 Don Wilson	2.50	1.15	.30
☐ 485 Ken McMullen	2.00	.90	.25
☐ 486 Steve Huntz	2.00	.90	.25
☐ 487 Paul Schaal	2.00	.90	.25
☐ 488 Jerry Stephenson	2.00	.90	.25

□	489	Luis Alvarado	2.00	.90	.25
□	490	Deron Johnson	2.00	.90	.25
□	491	Jim Hardin	2.00	.90	.25
□	492	Ken Boswell	2.00	.90	.25
□	493	Dave May	2.00	.90	.25
□	494	Braves Rookies	2.50	1.15	.30
		Ralph Garr			
		Rick Kester			
□	495	Felipe Alou	3.00	1.35	.40
□	496	Woody Woodward	2.50	1.15	.30
□	497	Horacio Pina	2.00	.90	.25
□	498	John Kennedy	2.00	.90	.25
□	499	Checklist 5	5.00	.50	.15
□	500	Jim Perry	2.50	1.15	.30
□	501	Andy Etchebarren	2.00	.90	.25
□	502	Chicago Cubs	4.00	1.80	.50
		Team Card			
□	503	Gates Brown	2.50	1.15	.30
□	504	Ken Wright	2.00	.90	.25
□	505	Ollie Brown	2.00	.90	.25
□	506	Bobby Knoop	2.00	.90	.25
□	507	George Stone	2.00	.90	.25
□	508	Roger Repoz	2.00	.90	.25
□	509	Jim Grant	2.00	.90	.25
□	510	Ken Harrelson	2.50	1.15	.30
□	511	Chris Short	2.00	.90	.25
□	512	Red Sox Rookies	2.00	.90	.25
		Dick Mills			
		Mike Garman			
□	513	Nolan Ryan	250.00	115.00	31.00
□	514	Ron Woods	2.00	.90	.25
□	515	Carl Morton	2.00	.90	.25
□	516	Ted Kubiak	2.00	.90	.25
□	517	Charlie Fox MG	2.00	.90	.25
□	518	Joe Grzenda	2.00	.90	.25
□	519	Willie Crawford	2.00	.90	.25
□	520	Tommy John	5.00	2.30	.60
□	521	Leron Lee	2.00	.90	.25
□	522	Minnesota Twins	4.00	1.80	.50
		Team Card			
□	523	John Odom	2.00	.90	.25
□	524	Mickey Stanley	4.50	2.00	.55
□	525	Ernie Banks	45.00	20.00	5.75
□	526	Ray Jarvis	4.00	1.80	.50
□	527	Cleon Jones	4.50	2.00	.55
□	528	Wally Bunker	4.00	1.80	.50
□	529	NL Rookie Infielders	6.00	2.70	.75
		Enzo Hernandez			
		Bill Buckner			
		Marty Perez			
□	530	Carl Yastrzemski	40.00	18.00	5.00
□	531	Mike Torrez	4.50	2.00	.55
□	532	Bill Rigney MG	4.00	1.80	.50
□	533	Mike Ryan	4.00	1.80	.50
□	534	Luke Walker	4.00	1.80	.50
□	535	Curt Flood	5.00	2.30	.60
□	536	Claude Raymond	4.00	1.80	.50
□	537	Tom Egan	4.00	1.80	.50
□	538	Angel Bravo	4.00	1.80	.50
□	539	Larry Brown	4.00	1.80	.50
□	540	Larry Dierker	4.00	1.80	.50
□	541	Bob Burda	4.00	1.80	.50
□	542	Bob Miller	4.00	1.80	.50
□	543	New York Yankees	8.00	3.60	1.00
		Team Card			
□	544	Vida Blue	6.00	2.70	.75
□	545	Dick Dietz	4.00	1.80	.50
□	546	John Matias	4.00	1.80	.50
□	547	Pat Dobson	4.50	2.00	.55
□	548	Don Mason	4.00	1.80	.50
□	549	Jim Brewer	4.00	1.80	.50
□	550	Harmon Killebrew	25.00	11.50	3.10
□	551	Frank Linzy	4.00	1.80	.50
□	552	Buddy Bradford	4.00	1.80	.50
□	553	Kevin Collins	4.50	2.00	.55
□	554	Lowell Palmer	4.00	1.80	.50
□	555	Walt Williams	4.00	1.80	.50
□	556	Jim McGlothlin	4.00	1.80	.50
□	557	Tom Satriano	4.00	1.80	.50
□	558	Hector Torres	4.00	1.80	.50
□	559	AL Rookie Pitchers	4.00	1.80	.50
		Terry Cox			
		Bill Gogolewski			
		Gary Jones			
□	560	Rusty Staub	5.00	2.30	.60
□	561	Syd O'Brien	4.00	1.80	.50
□	562	Dave Giusti	4.00	1.80	.50
□	563	San Francisco Giants	8.00	3.60	1.00
		Team Card			
□	564	Al Fitzmorris	4.00	1.80	.50
□	565	Jim Wynn	4.50	2.00	.55
□	566	Tim Cullen	4.00	1.80	.50
□	567	Walt Alston MG	5.00	2.30	.60
□	568	Sal Campisi	4.00	1.80	.50
□	569	Ivan Murrell	4.00	1.80	.50
□	570	Jim Palmer	40.00	18.00	5.00
□	571	Ted Sizemore	4.00	1.80	.50
□	572	Jerry Kenney	4.00	1.80	.50
□	573	Ed Kranepool	4.50	2.00	.55
□	574	Jim Bunning	6.00	2.70	.75
□	575	Bill Freehan	4.50	2.00	.55
□	576	Cubs Rookies	4.00	1.80	.50
		Adrian Garrett			
		Brock Davis			
		Garry Jestadt			
□	577	Jim Lonborg	4.50	2.00	.55
□	578	Ron Hunt	4.00	1.80	.50
□	579	Marty Pattin	4.00	1.80	.50
□	580	Tony Perez	13.00	5.75	1.65
□	581	Roger Nelson	4.00	1.80	.50
□	582	Dave Cash	5.00	2.30	.60
□	583	Ron Cook	4.00	1.80	.50
□	584	Cleveland Indians	8.00	3.60	1.00
		Team Card			

☐	585	Willie Davis	4.50	2.00	.55
☐	586	Dick Woodson	4.00	1.80	.50
☐	587	Sonny Jackson	4.00	1.80	.50
☐	588	Tom Bradley	4.00	1.80	.50
☐	589	Bob Barton	4.00	1.80	.50
☐	590	Alex Johnson	4.50	2.00	.55
☐	591	Jackie Brown	4.50	2.00	.55
☐	592	Randy Hundley	4.00	1.80	.50
☐	593	Jack Aker	4.00	1.80	.50
☐	594	Cards Rookies	6.00	2.70	.75
		Bob Chlupsa			
		Bob Stinson			
		Al Hrabosky			
☐	595	Dave Johnson	4.50	2.00	.55
☐	596	Mike Jorgensen	4.00	1.80	.50
☐	597	Ken Suarez	4.00	1.80	.50
☐	598	Rick Wise	4.50	2.00	.55
☐	599	Norm Cash	6.00	2.70	.75
☐	600	Willie Mays	90.00	40.00	11.50
☐	601	Ken Tatum	4.00	1.80	.50
☐	602	Marty Martinez	4.00	1.80	.50
☐	603	Pittsburgh Pirates	8.00	3.60	1.00
		Team Card			
☐	604	John Gelnar	4.00	1.80	.50
☐	605	Orlando Cepeda	6.00	2.70	.75
☐	606	Chuck Taylor	4.00	1.80	.50
☐	607	Paul Ratliff	4.00	1.80	.50
☐	608	Mike Wegener	4.00	1.80	.50
☐	609	Leo Durocher MG	6.00	2.70	.75
☐	610	Amos Otis	4.50	2.00	.55
☐	611	Tom Phoebus	4.00	1.80	.50
☐	612	Indians Rookies	4.00	1.80	.50
		Lou Camilli			
		Ted Ford			
		Steve Mingori			
☐	613	Pedro Borbon	4.00	1.80	.50
☐	614	Billy Cowan	4.00	1.80	.50
☐	615	Mel Stottlemyre	6.00	2.70	.75
☐	616	Larry Hisle	4.50	2.00	.55
☐	617	Clay Dalrymple	4.00	1.80	.50
☐	618	Tug McGraw	5.50	2.50	.70
☐	619A	Checklist 6 ERR	5.00	.50	.15
		(No copyright)			
☐	619B	Checklist 6 COR	10.00	1.00	.30
		(Copyright on back)			
☐	620	Frank Howard	5.50	2.50	.70
☐	621	Ron Bryant	4.00	1.80	.50
☐	622	Joe Lahoud	4.00	1.80	.50
☐	623	Pat Jarvis	4.00	1.80	.50
☐	624	Oakland Athletics	8.00	3.60	1.00
		Team Card			
☐	625	Lou Brock	30.00	13.50	3.80
☐	626	Freddie Patek	4.50	2.00	.55
☐	627	Steve Hamilton	4.00	1.80	.50
☐	628	John Bateman	4.00	1.80	.50
☐	629	John Hiller	4.50	2.00	.55
☐	630	Roberto Clemente	65.00	29.00	8.25

☐	631	Eddie Fisher	4.00	1.80	.50
☐	632	Darrel Chaney	4.00	1.80	.50
☐	633	AL Rookie Outfielders	4.00	1.80	.50
		Bobby Brooks			
		Pete Koegel			
		Scott Northey			
☐	634	Phil Regan	4.50	2.00	.55
☐	635	Bobby Murcer	7.00	3.10	.85
☐	636	Denny Lemaster	4.00	1.80	.50
☐	637	Dave Bristol MG	4.00	1.80	.50
☐	638	Stan Williams	4.00	1.80	.50
☐	639	Tom Haller	4.00	1.80	.50
☐	640	Frank Robinson	40.00	18.00	5.00
☐	641	New York Mets	10.00	4.50	1.25
		Team Card			
☐	642	Jim Roland	4.00	1.80	.50
☐	643	Rick Reichardt	5.00	2.30	.60
☐	644	Jim Stewart SP	9.00	4.00	1.15
☐	645	Jim Maloney SP	10.00	4.50	1.25
☐	646	Bobby Floyd SP	9.00	4.00	1.15
☐	647	Juan Pizarro	5.00	2.30	.60
☐	648	Mets Rookies SP	15.00	6.75	1.90
		Rich Folkers			
		Ted Martinez			
		Jon Matlack			
☐	649	Sparky Lyle SP	15.00	6.75	1.90
☐	650	Rich Allen SP	27.00	12.00	3.40
☐	651	Jerry Robertson SP	9.00	4.00	1.15
☐	652	Atlanta Braves	12.00	5.50	1.50
		Team Card			
☐	653	Russ Snyder SP	9.00	4.00	1.15
☐	654	Don Shaw SP	9.00	4.00	1.15
☐	655	Mike Epstein SP	9.00	4.00	1.15
☐	656	Gerry Nyman SP	9.00	4.00	1.15
☐	657	Jose Azcue	5.00	2.30	.60
☐	658	Paul Lindblad SP	9.00	4.00	1.15
☐	659	Byron Browne SP	9.00	4.00	1.15
☐	660	Ray Culp	5.00	2.30	.60
☐	661	Chuck Tanner MG SP	9.00	4.00	1.15
☐	662	Mike Hedlund SP	9.00	4.00	1.15
☐	663	Marv Staehle	5.00	2.30	.60
☐	664	Rookie Pitchers SP	9.00	4.00	1.15
		Archie Reynolds			
		Bob Reynolds			
		Ken Reynolds			
☐	665	Ron Swoboda SP	12.00	5.50	1.50
☐	666	Gene Brabender SP	9.00	4.00	1.15
☐	667	Pete Ward	5.00	2.30	.60
☐	668	Gary Neibauer	5.00	2.30	.60
☐	669	Ike Brown SP	9.00	4.00	1.15
☐	670	Bill Hands	5.00	2.30	.60
☐	671	Bill Voss SP	9.00	4.00	1.15
☐	672	Ed Crosby SP	9.00	4.00	1.15
☐	673	Gerry Janeski SP	9.00	4.00	1.15
☐	674	Montreal Expos	12.00	5.50	1.50
		Team Card			
☐	675	Dave Boswell	5.00	2.30	.60

☐ 676	Tommie Reynolds........5.00	2.30	.60
☐ 677	Jack DiLauro SP........9.00	4.00	1.15
☐ 678	George Thomas 5.00	2.30	.60
☐ 679	Don O'Riley.................5.00	2.30	.60
☐ 680	Don Mincher SP..........9.00	4.00	1.15
☐ 681	Bill Butler 5.00	2.30	.60
☐ 682	Terry Harmon 5.00	2.30	.60
☐ 683	Bill Burbach SP 9.00	4.00	1.15
☐ 684	Curt Motton 5.00	2.30	.60
☐ 685	Moe Drabowsky 5.00	2.30	.60
☐ 686	Chico Ruiz SP 9.00	4.00	1.15
☐ 687	Ron Taylor SP 9.00	4.00	1.15
☐ 688	Sparky Anderson MG SP21.00	9.50	2.60
☐ 689	Frank Baker 5.00	2.30	.60
☐ 690	Bob Moose 5.00	2.30	.60
☐ 691	Bobby Heise................5.00	2.30	.60
☐ 692	AL Rookie Pitchers SP.9.00	4.00	1.15
	Hal Haydel		
	Rogelio Moret		
	Wayne Twitchell		
☐ 693	Jose Pena SP 9.00	4.00	1.15
☐ 694	Rick Renick SP 9.00	4.00	1.15
☐ 695	Joe Niekro..................5.50	2.50	.70
☐ 696	Jerry Morales...............5.00	2.30	.60
☐ 697	Rickey Clark SP 9.00	4.00	1.15
☐ 698	Milwaukee Brewers SP18.00	8.00	2.30
	Team Card		
☐ 699	Jim Britton 5.00	2.30	.60
☐ 700	Boog Powell SP 20.00	9.00	2.50
☐ 701	Bob Garibaldi 5.00	2.30	.60
☐ 702	Milt Ramirez 5.00	2.30	.60
☐ 703	Mike Kekich 5.00	2.30	.60
☐ 704	J.C. Martin SP............9.00	4.00	1.15
☐ 705	Dick Selma SP 9.00	4.00	1.15
☐ 706	Joe Foy SP 9.00	4.00	1.15
☐ 707	Fred Lasher 5.00	2.30	.60
☐ 708	Russ Nagelson SP 9.00	4.00	1.15
☐ 709	Rookie Outfielders SP60.00	27.00	7.50
	Dusty Baker		
	Don Baylor		
	Tom Paciorek		
☐ 710	Sonny Siebert..............5.00	2.30	.60
☐ 711	Larry Stahl SP 9.00	4.00	1.15
☐ 712	Jose Martinez 5.00	2.30	.60
☐ 713	Mike Marshall SP.........9.00	4.00	1.15
☐ 714	Dick Williams MG SP...9.00	4.00	1.15
☐ 715	Horace Clarke SP 9.00	4.00	1.15
☐ 716	Dave Leonhard.............5.00	2.30	.60
☐ 717	Tommie Aaron SP........9.00	4.00	1.15
☐ 718	Billy Wynne.................5.00	2.30	.60
☐ 719	Jerry May SP 9.00	4.00	1.15
☐ 720	Matty Alou 5.50	2.50	.70
☐ 721	John Morris 5.00	2.30	.60
☐ 722	Houston Astros SP ...18.00	8.00	2.30
	Team Card		
☐ 723	Vicente Romo SP.........9.00	4.00	1.15
☐ 724	Tom Tischinski SP 9.00	4.00	1.15

☐ 725	Gary Gentry SP 9.00	4.00	1.15
☐ 726	Paul Popovich..............5.00	2.30	.60
☐ 727	Ray Lamb SP 9.00	4.00	1.15
☐ 728	NL Rookie Outfielders ...5.00	2.30	.60
	Wayne Redmond		
	Keith Lampard		
	Bernie Williams		
☐ 729	Dick Billings...............5.00	2.30	.60
☐ 730	Jim Rooker 5.00	2.30	.60
☐ 731	Jim Qualls SP 9.00	4.00	1.15
☐ 732	Bob Reed 5.00	2.30	.60
☐ 733	Lee Maye SP 9.00	4.00	1.15
☐ 734	Rob Gardner SP...........9.00	4.00	1.15
☐ 735	Mike Shannon SP 9.00	4.00	1.15
☐ 736	Mel Queen SP 9.00	4.00	1.15
☐ 737	Preston Gomez MG SP 9.00	4.00	1.15
☐ 738	Russ Gibson SP...........9.00	4.00	1.15
☐ 739	Barry Lersch SP 9.00	4.00	1.15
☐ 740	Luis Aparicio SP UER 21.00	9.50	2.60
	(Led AL in steals		
	from 1965 to 1964,		
	should be 1956 to 1964)		
☐ 741	Skip Guinn 5.00	2.30	.60
☐ 742	Kansas City Royals 12.00	5.50	1.50
	Team Card		
☐ 743	John O'Donoghue SP ..9.00	4.00	1.15
☐ 744	Chuck Manuel SP........9.00	4.00	1.15
☐ 745	Sandy Alomar SP.........9.00	4.00	1.15
☐ 746	Andy Kosco.................5.00	2.30	.60
☐ 747	NL Rookie Pitchers 5.00	2.30	.60
	Al Severinsen		
	Scipio Spinks		
	Balor Moore		
☐ 748	John Purdin SP............9.00	4.00	1.15
☐ 749	Ken Szotkiewicz 5.00	2.30	.60
☐ 750	Denny McLain SP 18.00	8.00	2.30
☐ 751	Al Weis SP 15.00	6.75	1.90
☐ 752	Dick Drago..................9.00	4.00	1.15

1972 Topps

The cards in this 787-card set measure 2 1/2" by 3 1/2". The 1972 Topps set contained the most cards ever for a Topps set to that point in time. Features appearing for the first time were "Boyhood Photos" (KP: 341-348 and 491-498), Awards and Trophy cards (621-626), "In Action" (distributed throughout the set), and "Traded Cards" (TR: 751-757). Other subsets included League Leaders (85-96), Playoffs cards (221-222), and World Series cards

(223-230). The curved lines of the color picture are a departure from the rectangular designs of other years. There is a series of intermediate scarcity (526-656) and the usual high numbers (657-787). The key Rookie Card in this set is Carlton Fisk.

	NRMT-MT	EXC	G-VG
COMPLETE SET (787)	2000.	900.00	250.00
COMMON PLAYER (1-132)	.60	.25	.08
COMMON PLAYER (133-263)	.75	.35	.09
COMMON PLAYER (264-394)	1.00	.45	.13
COMMON PLAYER (395-525)	1.50	.65	.19
COMMON PLAYER (526-656)	3.00	1.35	.40
COMMON PLAYER (657-787)	6.50	2.90	.80

☐ 1	Pittsburgh Pirates	7.00	1.40	.40
	Team Card			
☐ 2	Ray Culp	.60	.25	.08
☐ 3	Bob Tolan	.60	.25	.08
☐ 4	Checklist 1	4.00	.40	.12
☐ 5	John Bateman	.60	.25	.08
☐ 6	Fred Scherman	.60	.25	.08
☐ 7	Enzo Hernandez	.60	.25	.08
☐ 8	Ron Swoboda	.85	.40	.11
☐ 9	Stan Williams	.60	.25	.08
☐ 10	Amos Otis	.85	.40	.11
☐ 11	Bobby Valentine	1.00	.45	.13
☐ 12	Jose Cardenal	.60	.25	.08
☐ 13	Joe Grzenda	.60	.25	.08
☐ 14	Phillies Rookies	.60	.25	.08
	Pete Koegel			
	Mike Anderson			
	Wayne Twitchell			
☐ 15	Walt Williams	.60	.25	.08
☐ 16	Mike Jorgensen	.60	.25	.08
☐ 17	Dave Duncan	.60	.25	.08
☐ 18A	Juan Pizarro	.60	.25	.08
	(Yellow underline			
	C and S of Cubs)			
☐ 18B	Juan Pizarro	5.00	2.30	.60
	(Green underline			
	C and S of Cubs)			
☐ 19	Billy Cowan	.60	.25	.08
☐ 20	Don Wilson	.60	.25	.08
☐ 21	Atlanta Braves	1.50	.65	.19
	Team Card			
☐ 22	Rob Gardner	.60	.25	.08
☐ 23	Ted Kubiak	.60	.25	.08
☐ 24	Ted Ford	.60	.25	.08
☐ 25	Bill Singer	.60	.25	.08
☐ 26	Andy Etchebarren	.60	.25	.08
☐ 27	Bob Johnson	.60	.25	.08
☐ 28	Twins Rookies	.60	.25	.08
	Bob Gebhard			
	Steve Brye			
	Hal Haydel			
☐ 29A	Bill Bonham	.60	.25	.08
	(Yellow underline			
	C and S of Cubs)			
☐ 29B	Bill Bonham	5.00	2.30	.60
	(Green underline			
	C and S of Cubs)			
☐ 30	Rico Petrocelli	.85	.40	.11
☐ 31	Cleon Jones	.85	.40	.11
☐ 32	Jones In Action	.60	.25	.08
☐ 33	Billy Martin MG	3.50	1.55	.45
☐ 34	Martin In Action	1.75	.80	.22
☐ 35	Jerry Johnson	.60	.25	.08
☐ 36	Johnson In Action	.60	.25	.08
☐ 37	Carl Yastrzemski	15.00	6.75	1.90
☐ 38	Yastrzemski In Action	7.50	3.40	.95
☐ 39	Bob Barton	.60	.25	.08
☐ 40	Barton In Action	.60	.25	.08
☐ 41	Tommy Davis	.85	.40	.11
☐ 42	Davis In Action	.60	.25	.08
☐ 43	Rick Wise	.85	.40	.11
☐ 44	Wise In Action	.60	.25	.08
☐ 45A	Glenn Beckert	.85	.40	.11
	(Yellow underline			
	C and S of Cubs)			
☐ 45B	Glenn Beckert	5.00	2.30	.60
	(Green underline			
	C and S of Cubs)			
☐ 46	Beckert In Action	.60	.25	.08
☐ 47	John Ellis	.60	.25	.08
☐ 48	Ellis In Action	.60	.25	.08
☐ 49	Willie Mays	27.00	12.00	3.40
☐ 50	Mays In Action	13.50	6.00	1.70
☐ 51	Harmon Killebrew	6.00	2.70	.75
☐ 52	Killebrew In Action	3.00	1.35	.40
☐ 53	Bud Harrelson	.85	.40	.11
☐ 54	Harrelson In Action	.60	.25	.08
☐ 55	Clyde Wright	.60	.25	.08
☐ 56	Rich Chiles	.60	.25	.08
☐ 57	Bob Oliver	.60	.25	.08
☐ 58	Ernie McAnally	.60	.25	.08
☐ 59	Fred Stanley	.60	.25	.08
☐ 60	Manny Sanguillen	.85	.40	.11

☐ 61	Cubs Rookies.................1.50	.65	.19
	Burt Hooton		
	Gene Hiser		
	Earl Stephenson		
☐ 62	Angel Mangual.................60	.25	.08
☐ 63	Duke Sims........................60	.25	.08
☐ 64	Pete Broberg....................60	.25	.08
☐ 65	Cesar Cedeno.................1.25	.55	.16
☐ 66	Ray Corbin........................60	.25	.08
☐ 67	Red Schoendienst MG ...1.25	.55	.16
☐ 68	Jim York...........................60	.25	.08
☐ 69	Roger Freed 60	.25	.08
☐ 70	Mike Cuellar.....................85	.40	.11
☐ 71	California Angels.............1.50	.65	.19
	Team Card		
☐ 72	Bruce Kison 1.00	.45	.13
☐ 73	Steve Huntz......................60	.25	.08
☐ 74	Cecil Upshaw....................60	.25	.08
☐ 75	Bert Campaneris...............85	.40	.11
☐ 76	Don Carrithers..................60	.25	.08
☐ 77	Ron Theobald....................60	.25	.08
☐ 78	Steve Arlin 60	.25	.08
☐ 79	Red Sox Rookies 120.00	55.00	15.00
	Mike Garman		
	Cecil Cooper		
	Carlton Fisk		
☐ 80	Tony Perez......................4.50	2.00	.55
☐ 81	Mike Hedlund....................60	.25	.08
☐ 82	Ron Woods 60	.25	.08
☐ 83	Dalton Jones.....................60	.25	.08
☐ 84	Vince Colbert....................60	.25	.08
☐ 85	NL Batting Leaders 1.50	.65	.19
	Joe Torre		
	Ralph Garr		
	Glenn Beckert		
☐ 86	AL Batting Leaders.........1.50	.65	.19
	Tony Oliva		
	Bobby Murcer		
	Merv Rettenmund		
☐ 87	NL RBI Leaders..............3.00	1.35	.40
	Joe Torre		
	Willie Stargell		
	Hank Aaron		
☐ 88	AL RBI Leaders..............3.00	1.35	.40
	Harmon Killebrew		
	Frank Robinson		
	Reggie Smith		
☐ 89	NL Home Run Leaders...2.50	1.15	.30
	Willie Stargell		
	Hank Aaron		
	Lee May		
☐ 90	AL Home Run Leaders...1.50	.65	.19
	Bill Melton		
	Norm Cash		
	Reggie Jackson		
☐ 91	NL ERA Leaders..............2.00	.90	.25
	Tom Seaver		
	Dave Roberts UER		
	(Photo actually		
	Danny Coombs)		
	Don Wilson		
☐ 92	AL ERA Leaders.............1.50	.65	.19
	Vida Blue		
	Wilbur Wood		
	Jim Palmer		
☐ 93	NL Pitching Leaders.......3.00	1.35	.40
	Fergie Jenkins		
	Steve Carlton		
	Al Downing		
	Tom Seaver		
☐ 94	AL Pitching Leaders.......1.50	.65	.19
	Mickey Lolich		
	Vida Blue		
	Wilbur Wood		
☐ 95	NL Strikeout Leaders 3.00	1.35	.40
	Tom Seaver		
	Fergie Jenkins		
	Bill Stoneman		
☐ 96	AL Strikeout Leaders 1.50	.65	.19
	Mickey Lolich		
	Vida Blue		
	Joe Coleman		
☐ 97	Tom Kelley........................60	.25	.08
☐ 98	Chuck Tanner MG..............85	.40	.11
☐ 99	Ross Grimsley...................60	.25	.08
☐ 100	Frank Robinson...............6.00	2.70	.75
☐ 101	Astros Rookies 2.00	.90	.25
	Bill Greif		
	J.R. Richard		
	Ray Busse		
☐ 102	Lloyd Allen.......................60	.25	.08
☐ 103	Checklist 2.......................4.00	.40	.12
☐ 104	Toby Harrah.....................2.00	.90	.25
☐ 105	Gary Gentry......................60	.25	.08
☐ 106	Milwaukee Brewers........1.50	.65	.19
	Team Card		
☐ 107	Jose Cruz........................2.50	1.15	.30
☐ 108	Gary Waslewski................60	.25	.08
☐ 109	Jerry May.........................60	.25	.08
☐ 110	Ron Hunt 60	.25	.08
☐ 111	Jim Grant.........................60	.25	.08
☐ 112	Greg Luzinski.................1.50	.65	.19
☐ 113	Rogelio Moret...................60	.25	.08
☐ 114	Bill Buckner....................2.00	.90	.25
☐ 115	Jim Fregosi.......................85	.40	.11
☐ 116	Ed Farmer 1.00	.45	.13
☐ 117A	Cleo James.......................60	.25	.08
	(Yellow underline		
	C and S of Cubs)		
☐ 117B	Cleo James.....................5.00	2.30	.60
	(Green underline		
	C and S of Cubs)		
☐ 118	Skip Lockwood..................60	.25	.08
☐ 119	Marty Perez......................60	.25	.08

☐	120	Bill Freehan	.85	.40	.11	☐	165	Chris Speier	1.25	.55	.16
☐	121	Ed Sprague	.60	.25	.08	☐	166	Speier In Action	1.00	.45	.13
☐	122	Larry Biittner	.60	.25	.08	☐	167	Deron Johnson	.75	.35	.09
☐	123	Ed Acosta	.60	.25	.08	☐	168	Johnson In Action	.75	.35	.09
☐	124	Yankees Rookies	.60	.25	.08	☐	169	Vida Blue	1.50	.65	.19
		Alan Closter				☐	170	Blue In Action	1.00	.45	.13
		Rusty Torres				☐	171	Darrell Evans	2.00	.90	.25
		Roger Hambright				☐	172	Evans In Action	1.00	.45	.13
☐	125	Dave Cash	.85	.40	.11	☐	173	Clay Kirby	.75	.35	.09
☐	126	Bart Johnson	.60	.25	.08	☐	174	Kirby In Action	.75	.35	.09
☐	127	Duffy Dyer	.60	.25	.08	☐	175	Tom Haller	.75	.35	.09
☐	128	Eddie Watt	.60	.25	.08	☐	176	Haller In Action	.75	.35	.09
☐	129	Charlie Fox MG	.60	.25	.08	☐	177	Paul Schaal	.75	.35	.09
☐	130	Bob Gibson	6.50	2.90	.80	☐	178	Schaal In Action	.75	.35	.09
☐	131	Jim Nettles	.60	.25	.08	☐	179	Dock Ellis	.75	.35	.09
☐	132	Joe Morgan	6.00	2.70	.75	☐	180	Ellis In Action	.75	.35	.09
☐	133	Joe Keough	.75	.35	.09	☐	181	Ed Kranepool	.75	.35	.09
☐	134	Carl Morton	.75	.35	.09	☐	182	Kranepool In Action	.75	.35	.09
☐	135	Vada Pinson	1.25	.55	.16	☐	183	Bill Melton	.75	.35	.09
☐	136	Darrel Chaney	.75	.35	.09	☐	184	Melton In Action	.75	.35	.09
☐	137	Dick Williams MG	1.00	.45	.13	☐	185	Ron Bryant	.75	.35	.09
☐	138	Mike Kekich	.75	.35	.09	☐	186	Bryant In Action	.75	.35	.09
☐	139	Tim McCarver	1.25	.55	.16	☐	187	Gates Brown	1.00	.45	.13
☐	140	Pat Dobson	1.00	.45	.13	☐	188	Frank Lucchesi MG	.75	.35	.09
☐	141	Mets Rookies	1.00	.45	.13	☐	189	Gene Tenace	1.00	.45	.13
		Buzz Capra				☐	190	Dave Giusti	.75	.35	.09
		Lee Stanton				☐	191	Jeff Burroughs	1.25	.55	.16
		Jon Matlack				☐	192	Chicago Cubs	1.50	.65	.19
☐	142	Chris Chambliss	3.50	1.55	.45			Team Card			
☐	143	Garry Jestadt	.75	.35	.09	☐	193	Kurt Bevacqua	.75	.35	.09
☐	144	Marty Pattin	.75	.35	.09	☐	194	Fred Norman	.75	.35	.09
☐	145	Don Kessinger	1.00	.45	.13	☐	195	Orlando Cepeda	3.00	1.35	.40
☐	146	Steve Kealey	.75	.35	.09	☐	196	Mel Queen	.75	.35	.09
☐	147	Dave Kingman	7.00	3.10	.85	☐	197	Johnny Briggs	.75	.35	.09
☐	148	Dick Billings	.75	.35	.09	☐	198	Dodgers Rookies	5.00	2.30	.60
☐	149	Gary Neibauer	.75	.35	.09			Charlie Hough			
☐	150	Norm Cash	1.00	.45	.13			Bob O'Brien			
☐	151	Jim Brewer	.75	.35	.09			Mike Strahler			
☐	152	Gene Clines	.75	.35	.09	☐	199	Mike Fiore	.75	.35	.09
☐	153	Rick Auerbach	.75	.35	.09	☐	200	Lou Brock	6.50	2.90	.80
☐	154	Ted Simmons	3.50	1.55	.45	☐	201	Phil Roof	.75	.35	.09
☐	155	Larry Dierker	.75	.35	.09	☐	202	Scipio Spinks	.75	.35	.09
☐	156	Minnesota Twins	1.50	.65	.19	☐	203	Ron Blomberg	.75	.35	.09
		Team Card				☐	204	Tommy Helms	.75	.35	.09
☐	157	Don Gullett	1.00	.45	.13	☐	205	Dick Drago	.75	.35	.09
☐	158	Jerry Kenney	.75	.35	.09	☐	206	Dal Maxvill	.75	.35	.09
☐	159	John Boccabella	.75	.35	.09	☐	207	Tom Egan	.75	.35	.09
☐	160	Andy Messersmith	1.00	.45	.13	☐	208	Milt Pappas	1.00	.45	.13
☐	161	Brock Davis	.75	.35	.09	☐	209	Joe Rudi	1.00	.45	.13
☐	162	Brewers Rookies UER	1.00	.45	.13	☐	210	Denny McLain	1.50	.65	.19
		Jerry Bell				☐	211	Gary Sutherland	.75	.35	.09
		Darrell Porter				☐	212	Grant Jackson	.75	.35	.09
		Bob Reynolds				☐	213	Angels Rookies	1.00	.45	.13
		(Porter and Bell						Billy Parker			
		photos switched)						Art Kusnyer			
☐	163	Tug McGraw	1.50	.65	.19			Tom Silverio			
☐	164	McGraw In Action	1.00	.45	.13	☐	214	Mike McQueen	.75	.35	.09

☐	215	Alex Johnson	1.00	.45	.13			
☐	216	Joe Niekro	1.00	.45	.13			
☐	217	Roger Metzger	.75	.35	.09			
☐	218	Eddie Kasko MG	.75	.35	.09			
☐	219	Rennie Stennett	1.00	.45	.13			
☐	220	Jim Perry	1.00	.45	.13			
☐	221	NL Playoffs	1.50	.65	.19			
		Bucs champs						
☐	222	AL Playoffs	2.00	.90	.25			
		Orioles champs						
		(Brooks Robinson)						
☐	223	World Series Game 1	1.50	.65	.19			
		(Dave McNally pitching)						
☐	224	World Series Game 2	1.50	.65	.19			
		(Dave Johnson and						
		Mark Belanger)						
☐	225	World Series Game 3	1.50	.65	.19			
		(Manny Sanguillen						
		scoring)						
☐	226	World Series Game 4	3.50	1.55	.45			
		(Roberto Clemente						
		on second)						
☐	227	World Series Game 5	1.50	.65	.19			
		(Nellie Briles						
		pitching)						
☐	228	World Series Game 6	1.50	.65	.19			
		(Frank Robinson and						
		Manny Sanguillen)						
☐	229	World Series Game 7	1.50	.65	.19			
		(Steve Blass pitching)						
☐	230	World Series Summary	1.50	.65	.19			
		(Pirates celebrate)						
☐	231	Casey Cox	.75	.35	.09			
☐	232	Giants Rookies	.75	.35	.09			
		Chris Arnold						
		Jim Barr						
		Dave Rader						
☐	233	Jay Johnstone	1.00	.45	.13			
☐	234	Ron Taylor	.75	.35	.09			
☐	235	Merv Rettenmund	.75	.35	.09			
☐	236	Jim McGlothlin	.75	.35	.09			
☐	237	New York Yankees	1.50	.65	.19			
		Team Card						
☐	238	Leron Lee	.75	.35	.09			
☐	239	Tom Timmermann	.75	.35	.09			
☐	240	Rich Allen	3.00	1.35	.40			
☐	241	Rollie Fingers	8.00	3.60	1.00			
☐	242	Don Mincher	.75	.35	.09			
☐	243	Frank Linzy	.75	.35	.09			
☐	244	Steve Braun	.75	.35	.09			
☐	245	Tommie Agee	1.00	.45	.13			
☐	246	Tom Burgmeier	.75	.35	.09			
☐	247	Milt May	.75	.35	.09			
☐	248	Tom Bradley	.75	.35	.09			
☐	249	Harry Walker MG	.75	.35	.09			
☐	250	Boog Powell	1.50	.65	.19			
☐	251	Checklist 3	4.00	.40	.12			
☐	252	Ken Reynolds	.75	.35	.09			
☐	253	Sandy Alomar	1.00	.45	.13			
☐	254	Boots Day	.75	.35	.09			
☐	255	Jim Lonborg	1.00	.45	.13			
☐	256	George Foster	2.25	1.00	.30			
☐	257	Tigers Rookies	.75	.35	.09			
		Jim Foor						
		Tim Hosley						
		Paul Jata						
☐	258	Randy Hundley	.75	.35	.09			
☐	259	Sparky Lyle	1.25	.55	.16			
☐	260	Ralph Garr	1.00	.45	.13			
☐	261	Steve Mingori	.75	.35	.09			
☐	262	San Diego Padres	1.50	.65	.19			
		Team Card						
☐	263	Felipe Alou	1.25	.55	.16			
☐	264	Tommy John	2.50	1.15	.30			
☐	265	Wes Parker	1.25	.55	.16			
☐	266	Bobby Bolin	1.00	.45	.13			
☐	267	Dave Concepcion	3.50	1.55	.45			
☐	268	A's Rookies	1.00	.45	.13			
		Dwain Anderson						
		Chris Floethe						
☐	269	Don Hahn	1.00	.45	.13			
☐	270	Jim Palmer	15.00	6.75	1.90			
☐	271	Ken Rudolph	1.00	.45	.13			
☐	272	Mickey Rivers	1.50	.65	.19			
☐	273	Bobby Floyd	1.00	.45	.13			
☐	274	Al Severinsen	1.00	.45	.13			
☐	275	Cesar Tovar	1.00	.45	.13			
☐	276	Gene Mauch MG	1.25	.55	.16			
☐	277	Elliott Maddox	1.00	.45	.13			
☐	278	Dennis Higgins	1.00	.45	.13			
☐	279	Larry Brown	1.00	.45	.13			
☐	280	Willie McCovey	6.50	2.90	.80			
☐	281	Bill Parsons	1.00	.45	.13			
☐	282	Houston Astros	2.00	.90	.25			
		Team Card						
☐	283	Darrell Brandon	1.00	.45	.13			
☐	284	Ike Brown	1.00	.45	.13			
☐	285	Gaylord Perry	7.00	3.10	.85			
☐	286	Gene Alley	1.25	.55	.16			
☐	287	Jim Hardin	1.00	.45	.13			
☐	288	Johnny Jeter	1.00	.45	.13			
☐	289	Syd O'Brien	1.00	.45	.13			
☐	290	Sonny Siebert	1.00	.45	.13			
☐	291	Hal McRae	2.00	.90	.25			
☐	292	McRae In Action	1.25	.55	.16			
☐	293	Dan Frisella	1.00	.45	.13			
☐	294	Frisella In Action	1.00	.45	.13			
☐	295	Dick Dietz	1.00	.45	.13			
☐	296	Dietz In Action	1.00	.45	.13			
☐	297	Claude Osteen	1.25	.55	.16			
☐	298	Osteen In Action	1.00	.45	.13			
☐	299	Hank Aaron	35.00	16.00	4.40			
☐	300	Aaron in Action	17.50	8.00	2.20			
☐	301	George Mitterwald	1.00	.45	.13			

☐ 302	Mitterwald In Action.....1.00	.45	.13		
☐ 303	Joe Pepitone 1.25	.55	.16		
☐ 304	Pepitone In Action 1.00	.45	.13		
☐ 305	Ken Boswell 1.00	.45	.13		
☐ 306	Boswell In Action 1.00	.45	.13		
☐ 307	Steve Renko 1.00	.45	.13		
☐ 308	Renko In Action 1.00	.45	.13		
☐ 309	Roberto Clemente 35.00	16.00	4.40		
☐ 310	Clemente In Action....17.50	8.00	2.20		
☐ 311	Clay Carroll 1.00	.45	.13		
☐ 312	Carroll In Action..........1.00	.45	.13		
☐ 313	Luis Aparicio................3.00	1.35	.40		
☐ 314	Aparicio In Action 1.50	.65	.19		
☐ 315	Paul Splittorff.............1.00	.45	.13		
☐ 316	Cardinals Rookies 1.25	.55	.16		
	Jim Bibby				
	Jorge Roque				
	Santiago Guzman				
☐ 317	Rich Hand 1.00	.45	.13		
☐ 318	Sonny Jackson 1.00	.45	.13		
☐ 319	Aurelio Rodriguez 1.00	.45	.13		
☐ 320	Steve Blass 1.25	.55	.16		
☐ 321	Joe Lahoud 1.00	.45	.13		
☐ 322	Jose Pena 1.00	.45	.13		
☐ 323	Earl Weaver MG 2.00	.90	.25		
☐ 324	Mike Ryan 1.00	.45	.13		
☐ 325	Mel Stottlemyre 1.25	.55	.16		
☐ 326	Pat Kelly 1.00	.45	.13		
☐ 327	Steve Stone 1.75	.80	.22		
☐ 328	Boston Red Sox............2.00	.90	.25		
	Team Card				
☐ 329	Roy Foster 1.00	.45	.13		
☐ 330	Jim Hunter 5.00	2.30	.60		
☐ 331	Stan Swanson 1.00	.45	.13		
☐ 332	Buck Martinez 1.00	.45	.13		
☐ 333	Steve Barber 1.00	.45	.13		
☐ 334	Rangers Rookies..........1.00	.45	.13		
	Bill Fahey				
	Jim Mason				
	Tom Ragland				
☐ 335	Bill Hands 1.00	.45	.13		
☐ 336	Marty Martinez 1.00	.45	.13		
☐ 337	Mike Kilkenny 1.00	.45	.13		
☐ 338	Bob Grich 1.50	.65	.19		
☐ 339	Ron Cook 1.00	.45	.13		
☐ 340	Roy White 1.25	.55	.16		
☐ 341	KP: Joe Torre 1.25	.55	.16		
☐ 342	KP: Wilbur Wood 1.25	.55	.16		
☐ 343	KP: Willie Stargell 1.50	.65	.19		
☐ 344	KP: Dave McNally 1.25	.55	.16		
☐ 345	KP: Rick Wise 1.25	.55	.16		
☐ 346	KP: Jim Fregosi...........1.25	.55	.16		
☐ 347	KP: Tom Seaver 4.00	1.80	.50		
☐ 348	KP: Sal Bando 1.25	.55	.16		
☐ 349	Al Fitzmorris 1.00	.45	.13		
☐ 350	Frank Howard 1.50	.65	.19		
☐ 351	Braves Rookies............1.25	.55	.16		
	Tom House				
	Rick Kester				
	Jimmy Britton				
☐ 352	Dave LaRoche.............1.00	.45	.13		
☐ 353	Art Shamsky 1.00	.45	.13		
☐ 354	Tom Murphy 1.00	.45	.13		
☐ 355	Bob Watson 1.25	.55	.16		
☐ 356	Gerry Moses 1.00	.45	.13		
☐ 357	Woody Fryman 1.00	.45	.13		
☐ 358	Sparky Anderson MG....2.00	.90	.25		
☐ 359	Don Pavletich 1.00	.45	.13		
☐ 360	Dave Roberts 1.00	.45	.13		
☐ 361	Mike Andrews 1.00	.45	.13		
☐ 362	New York Mets 2.00	.90	.25		
	Team Card				
☐ 363	Ron Klimkowski...........1.00	.45	.13		
☐ 364	Johnny Callison...........1.25	.55	.16		
☐ 365	Dick Bosman...............1.00	.45	.13		
☐ 366	Jimmy Rosario 1.00	.45	.13		
☐ 367	Ron Perranoski 1.25	.55	.16		
☐ 368	Danny Thompson 1.00	.45	.13		
☐ 369	Jim Lefebvre 1.25	.55	.16		
☐ 370	Don Buford 1.00	.45	.13		
☐ 371	Denny Lemaster...........1.00	.45	.13		
☐ 372	Royals Rookies............1.00	.45	.13		
	Lance Clemons				
	Monty Montgomery				
☐ 373	John Mayberry 1.25	.55	.16		
☐ 374	Jack Heidemann 1.00	.45	.13		
☐ 375	Reggie Cleveland 1.00	.45	.13		
☐ 376	Andy Kosco 1.00	.45	.13		
☐ 377	Terry Harmon 1.00	.45	.13		
☐ 378	Checklist 4 ....4.00	.40	.12		
☐ 379	Ken Berry 1.00	.45	.13		
☐ 380	Earl Williams 1.00	.45	.13		
☐ 381	Chicago White Sox.......2.00	.90	.25		
	Team Card				
☐ 382	Joe Gibbon 1.00	.45	.13		
☐ 383	Brant Alyea 1.00	.45	.13		
☐ 384	Dave Campbell 1.00	.45	.13		
☐ 385	Mickey Stanley 1.25	.55	.16		
☐ 386	Jim Colborn 1.00	.45	.13		
☐ 387	Horace Clarke 1.00	.45	.13		
☐ 388	Charlie Williams 1.00	.45	.13		
☐ 389	Bill Rigney MG 1.00	.45	.13		
☐ 390	Willie Davis 1.25	.55	.16		
☐ 391	Ken Sanders 1.00	.45	.13		
☐ 392	Pirates Rookies............1.50	.65	.19		
	Fred Cambria				
	Richie Zisk				
☐ 393	Curt Motton 1.00	.45	.13		
☐ 394	Ken Forsch...................1.25	.55	.16		
☐ 395	Matty Alou 1.75	.80	.22		
☐ 396	Paul Lindblad 1.50	.65	.19		
☐ 397	Philadelphia Phillies....3.00	1.35	.40		
	Team Card				
☐ 398	Larry Hisle 1.75	.80	.22		

☐ 399	Milt Wilcox	1.50	.65	.19
☐ 400	Tony Oliva	2.50	1.15	.30
☐ 401	Jim Nash	1.50	.65	.19
☐ 402	Bobby Heise	1.50	.65	.19
☐ 403	John Cumberland	1.50	.65	.19
☐ 404	Jeff Torborg	1.75	.80	.22
☐ 405	Ron Fairly	1.75	.80	.22
☐ 406	George Hendrick	2.00	.90	.25
☐ 407	Chuck Taylor	1.50	.65	.19
☐ 408	Jim Northrup	1.75	.80	.22
☐ 409	Frank Baker	1.50	.65	.19
☐ 410	Fergie Jenkins	7.50	3.40	.95
☐ 411	Bob Montgomery	1.50	.65	.19
☐ 412	Dick Kelley	1.50	.65	.19
☐ 413	White Sox Rookies	1.50	.65	.19
	Don Eddy			
	Dave Lemonds			
☐ 414	Bob Miller	1.50	.65	.19
☐ 415	Cookie Rojas	1.75	.80	.22
☐ 416	Johnny Edwards	1.50	.65	.19
☐ 417	Tom Hall	1.50	.65	.19
☐ 418	Tom Shopay	1.50	.65	.19
☐ 419	Jim Spencer	1.50	.65	.19
☐ 420	Steve Carlton	25.00	11.50	3.10
☐ 421	Ellie Rodriguez	1.50	.65	.19
☐ 422	Ray Lamb	1.50	.65	.19
☐ 423	Oscar Gamble	1.75	.80	.22
☐ 424	Bill Gogolewski	1.50	.65	.19
☐ 425	Ken Singleton	2.50	1.15	.30
☐ 426	Singleton In Action	1.75	.80	.22
☐ 427	Tito Fuentes	1.50	.65	.19
☐ 428	Fuentes In Action	1.50	.65	.19
☐ 429	Bob Robertson	1.50	.65	.19
☐ 430	Robertson In Action	1.50	.65	.19
☐ 431	Clarence Gaston	2.50	1.15	.30
☐ 432	Gaston In Action	1.75	.80	.22
☐ 433	Johnny Bench	45.00	20.00	5.75
☐ 434	Bench In Action	22.50	10.00	2.80
☐ 435	Reggie Jackson	55.00	25.00	7.00
☐ 436	Jackson In Action	27.50	12.50	3.40
☐ 437	Maury Wills	2.50	1.15	.30
☐ 438	Wills In Action	2.00	.90	.25
☐ 439	Billy Williams	5.00	2.30	.60
☐ 440	Williams In Action	2.50	1.15	.30
☐ 441	Thurman Munson	20.00	9.00	2.50
☐ 442	Munson In Action	10.00	4.50	1.25
☐ 443	Ken Henderson	1.50	.65	.19
☐ 444	Henderson In Action	1.50	.65	.19
☐ 445	Tom Seaver	40.00	18.00	5.00
☐ 446	Seaver In Action	20.00	9.00	2.50
☐ 447	Willie Stargell	6.00	2.70	.75
☐ 448	Stargell In Action	3.00	1.35	.40
☐ 449	Bob Lemon MG	1.75	.80	.22
☐ 450	Mickey Lolich	2.50	1.15	.30
☐ 451	Tony LaRussa	3.00	1.35	.40
☐ 452	Ed Herrmann	1.50	.65	.19
☐ 453	Barry Lersch	1.50	.65	.19
☐ 454	Oakland A's	3.00	1.35	.40
	Team Card			
☐ 455	Tommy Harper	1.75	.80	.22
☐ 456	Mark Belanger	1.75	.80	.22
☐ 457	Padres Rookies	1.50	.65	.19
	Darcy Fast			
	Derrel Thomas			
	Mike Ivie			
☐ 458	Aurelio Monteagudo	1.50	.65	.19
☐ 459	Rick Renick	1.50	.65	.19
☐ 460	Al Downing	1.50	.65	.19
☐ 461	Tim Cullen	1.50	.65	.19
☐ 462	Rickey Clark	1.50	.65	.19
☐ 463	Bernie Carbo	1.50	.65	.19
☐ 464	Jim Roland	1.50	.65	.19
☐ 465	Gil Hodges MG	4.50	2.00	.55
☐ 466	Norm Miller	1.50	.65	.19
☐ 467	Steve Kline	1.50	.65	.19
☐ 468	Richie Scheinblum	1.50	.65	.19
☐ 469	Ron Herbel	1.50	.65	.19
☐ 470	Ray Fosse	1.50	.65	.19
☐ 471	Luke Walker	1.50	.65	.19
☐ 472	Phil Gagliano	1.50	.65	.19
☐ 473	Dan McGinn	1.50	.65	.19
☐ 474	Orioles Rookies	7.00	3.10	.85
	Don Baylor			
	Roric Harrison			
	Johnny Oates			
☐ 475	Gary Nolan	1.75	.80	.22
☐ 476	Lee Richard	1.50	.65	.19
☐ 477	Tom Phoebus	1.50	.65	.19
☐ 478	Checklist 5	4.00	.40	.12
☐ 479	Don Shaw	1.50	.65	.19
☐ 480	Lee May	1.75	.80	.22
☐ 481	Billy Conigliaro	1.75	.80	.22
☐ 482	Joe Hoerner	1.50	.65	.19
☐ 483	Ken Suarez	1.50	.65	.19
☐ 484	Lum Harris MG	1.50	.65	.19
☐ 485	Phil Regan	1.75	.80	.22
☐ 486	John Lowenstein	1.50	.65	.19
☐ 487	Detroit Tigers	3.00	1.35	.40
	Team Card			
☐ 488	Mike Nagy	1.50	.65	.19
☐ 489	Expos Rookies	1.50	.65	.19
	Terry Humphrey			
	Keith Lampard			
☐ 490	Dave McNally	1.75	.80	.22
☐ 491	KP: Lou Piniella	2.00	.90	.25
☐ 492	KP: Mel Stottlemyre	1.75	.80	.22
☐ 493	KP: Bob Bailey	1.75	.80	.22
☐ 494	KP: Willie Horton	1.75	.80	.22
☐ 495	KP: Bill Melton	1.75	.80	.22
☐ 496	KP: Bud Harrelson	1.75	.80	.22
☐ 497	KP: Jim Perry	1.75	.80	.22
☐ 498	KP: Brooks Robinson	2.50	1.15	.30
☐ 499	Vicente Romo	1.50	.65	.19
☐ 500	Joe Torre	2.50	1.15	.30

☐ 501	Pete Hamm	1.50	.65	.19
☐ 502	Jackie Hernandez	1.50	.65	.19
☐ 503	Gary Peters	1.50	.65	.19
☐ 504	Ed Spiezio	1.50	.65	.19
☐ 505	Mike Marshall	1.75	.80	.22
☐ 506	Indians Rookies	1.50	.65	.19
	Terry Ley			
	Jim Moyer			
	Dick Tidrow			
☐ 507	Fred Gladding	1.50	.65	.19
☐ 508	Elrod Hendricks	1.50	.65	.19
☐ 509	Don McMahon	1.50	.65	.19
☐ 510	Ted Williams MG	7.50	3.40	.95
☐ 511	Tony Taylor	1.50	.65	.19
☐ 512	Paul Popovich	1.50	.65	.19
☐ 513	Lindy McDaniel	1.75	.80	.22
☐ 514	Ted Sizemore	1.50	.65	.19
☐ 515	Bert Blyleven	12.50	5.75	1.55
☐ 516	Oscar Brown	1.50	.65	.19
☐ 517	Ken Brett	1.50	.65	.19
☐ 518	Wayne Garrett	1.50	.65	.19
☐ 519	Ted Abernathy	1.50	.65	.19
☐ 520	Larry Bowa	2.00	.90	.25
☐ 521	Alan Foster	1.50	.65	.19
☐ 522	Los Angeles Dodgers	3.00	1.35	.40
	Team Card			
☐ 523	Chuck Dobson	1.50	.65	.19
☐ 524	Reds Rookies	1.50	.65	.19
	Ed Armbrister			
	Mel Behney			
☐ 525	Carlos May	1.75	.80	.22
☐ 526	Bob Bailey	3.50	1.55	.45
☐ 527	Dave Leonhard	3.00	1.35	.40
☐ 528	Ron Stone	3.00	1.35	.40
☐ 529	Dave Nelson	3.00	1.35	.40
☐ 530	Don Sutton	6.50	2.90	.80
☐ 531	Freddie Patek	3.50	1.55	.45
☐ 532	Fred Kendall	3.00	1.35	.40
☐ 533	Ralph Houk MG	3.50	1.55	.45
☐ 534	Jim Hickman	3.50	1.55	.45
☐ 535	Ed Brinkman	3.00	1.35	.40
☐ 536	Doug Rader	3.50	1.55	.45
☐ 537	Bob Locker	3.00	1.35	.40
☐ 538	Charlie Sands	3.00	1.35	.40
☐ 539	Terry Forster	4.00	1.80	.50
☐ 540	Felix Millan	3.00	1.35	.40
☐ 541	Roger Repoz	3.00	1.35	.40
☐ 542	Jack Billingham	3.00	1.35	.40
☐ 543	Duane Josephson	3.00	1.35	.40
☐ 544	Ted Martinez	3.00	1.35	.40
☐ 545	Wayne Granger	3.00	1.35	.40
☐ 546	Joe Hague	3.00	1.35	.40
☐ 547	Cleveland Indians	6.00	2.70	.75
	Team Card			
☐ 548	Frank Reberger	3.00	1.35	.40
☐ 549	Dave May	3.00	1.35	.40
☐ 550	Brooks Robinson	25.00	11.50	3.10
☐ 551	Ollie Brown	3.00	1.35	.40
☐ 552	Brown In Action	3.00	1.35	.40
☐ 553	Wilbur Wood	3.50	1.55	.45
☐ 554	Wood In Action	3.00	1.35	.40
☐ 555	Ron Santo	4.50	2.00	.55
☐ 556	Santo In Action	4.00	1.80	.50
☐ 557	John Odom	3.00	1.35	.40
☐ 558	Odom In Action	3.00	1.35	.40
☐ 559	Pete Rose	50.00	23.00	6.25
☐ 560	Rose In Action	25.00	11.50	3.10
☐ 561	Leo Cardenas	3.00	1.35	.40
☐ 562	Cardenas In Action	3.00	1.35	.40
☐ 563	Ray Sadecki	3.00	1.35	.40
☐ 564	Sadecki In Action	3.00	1.35	.40
☐ 565	Reggie Smith	3.50	1.55	.45
☐ 566	Smith In Action	3.00	1.35	.40
☐ 567	Juan Marichal	7.00	3.10	.85
☐ 568	Marichal In Action	3.50	1.55	.45
☐ 569	Ed Kirkpatrick	3.00	1.35	.40
☐ 570	Kirkpatrick In Action	3.00	1.35	.40
☐ 571	Nate Colbert	3.00	1.35	.40
☐ 572	Colbert In Action	3.00	1.35	.40
☐ 573	Fritz Peterson	3.00	1.35	.40
☐ 574	Peterson In Action	3.00	1.35	.40
☐ 575	Al Oliver	4.00	1.80	.50
☐ 576	Leo Durocher MG	4.00	1.80	.50
☐ 577	Mike Paul	3.00	1.35	.40
☐ 578	Billy Grabarkewitz	3.00	1.35	.40
☐ 579	Doyle Alexander	3.50	1.55	.45
☐ 580	Lou Piniella	5.00	2.30	.60
☐ 581	Wade Blasingame	3.00	1.35	.40
☐ 582	Montreal Expos	6.00	2.70	.75
	Team Card			
☐ 583	Darold Knowles	3.00	1.35	.40
☐ 584	Jerry McNertney	3.00	1.35	.40
☐ 585	George Scott	3.50	1.55	.45
☐ 586	Denis Menke	3.00	1.35	.40
☐ 587	Billy Wilson	3.00	1.35	.40
☐ 588	Jim Holt	3.00	1.35	.40
☐ 589	Hal Lanier	3.00	1.35	.40
☐ 590	Graig Nettles	5.00	2.30	.60
☐ 591	Paul Casanova	3.00	1.35	.40
☐ 592	Lew Krausse	3.00	1.35	.40
☐ 593	Rich Morales	3.00	1.35	.40
☐ 594	Jim Beauchamp	3.00	1.35	.40
☐ 595	Nolan Ryan	260.00	115.00	33.00
☐ 596	Manny Mota	3.50	1.55	.45
☐ 597	Jim Magnuson	3.00	1.35	.40
☐ 598	Hal King	3.00	1.35	.40
☐ 599	Billy Champion	3.00	1.35	.40
☐ 600	Al Kaline	25.00	11.50	3.10
☐ 601	George Stone	3.00	1.35	.40
☐ 602	Dave Bristol MG	3.00	1.35	.40
☐ 603	Jim Ray	3.00	1.35	.40
☐ 604A	Checklist 6	9.00	.90	.27
	(Copyright on back			
	bottom right)			

☐ 604B	Checklist 6	9.00	.90	.27	☐ 657	Bobby Wine	6.50	2.90	.80

☐ 604B	Checklist 6	9.00	.90	.27	☐ 657	Bobby Wine	6.50	2.90	.80
	(Copyright on back				☐ 658	Steve Dunning	6.50	2.90	.80
	bottom left)				☐ 659	Bob Aspromonte	6.50	2.90	.80
☐ 605	Nelson Briles	3.50	1.55	.45	☐ 660	Paul Blair	7.50	3.40	.95
☐ 606	Luis Melendez	3.00	1.35	.40	☐ 661	Bill Virdon MG	7.50	3.40	.95
☐ 607	Frank Duffy	3.00	1.35	.40	☐ 662	Stan Bahnsen	6.50	2.90	.80
☐ 608	Mike Corkins	3.00	1.35	.40	☐ 663	Fran Healy	7.50	3.40	.95
☐ 609	Tom Grieve	3.50	1.55	.45	☐ 664	Bobby Knoop	6.50	2.90	.80
☐ 610	Bill Stoneman	3.00	1.35	.40	☐ 665	Chris Short	6.50	2.90	.80
☐ 611	Rich Reese	3.00	1.35	.40	☐ 666	Hector Torres	6.50	2.90	.80
☐ 612	Joe Decker	3.00	1.35	.40	☐ 667	Ray Newman	6.50	2.90	.80
☐ 613	Mike Ferraro	3.00	1.35	.40	☐ 668	Texas Rangers	15.00	6.75	1.90
☐ 614	Ted Uhlaender	3.00	1.35	.40		Team Card			
☐ 615	Steve Hargan	3.00	1.35	.40	☐ 669	Willie Crawford	6.50	2.90	.80
☐ 616	Joe Ferguson	3.50	1.55	.45	☐ 670	Ken Holtzman	7.50	3.40	.95
☐ 617	Kansas City Royals	6.00	2.70	.75	☐ 671	Donn Clendenon	7.50	3.40	.95
	Team Card				☐ 672	Archie Reynolds	6.50	2.90	.80
☐ 618	Rich Robertson	3.00	1.35	.40	☐ 673	Dave Marshall	6.50	2.90	.80
☐ 619	Rich McKinney	3.00	1.35	.40	☐ 674	John Kennedy	6.50	2.90	.80
☐ 620	Phil Niekro	7.00	3.10	.85	☐ 675	Pat Jarvis	6.50	2.90	.80
☐ 621	Commissioners Award	4.00	1.80	.50	☐ 676	Danny Cater	6.50	2.90	.80
☐ 622	MVP Award	4.00	1.80	.50	☐ 677	Ivan Murrell	6.50	2.90	.80
☐ 623	Cy Young Award	4.00	1.80	.50	☐ 678	Steve Luebber	6.50	2.90	.80
☐ 624	Minor League Player	4.00	1.80	.50	☐ 679	Astros Rookies	6.50	2.90	.80
☐ 625	Rookie of the Year	4.00	1.80	.50		Bob Fenwick			
☐ 626	Babe Ruth Award	4.00	1.80	.50		Bob Stinson			
☐ 627	Moe Drabowsky	3.00	1.35	.40	☐ 680	Dave Johnson	7.50	3.40	.95
☐ 628	Terry Crowley	3.00	1.35	.40	☐ 681	Bobby Pfeil	6.50	2.90	.80
☐ 629	Paul Doyle	3.00	1.35	.40	☐ 682	Mike McCormick	7.50	3.40	.95
☐ 630	Rich Hebner	3.50	1.55	.45	☐ 683	Steve Hovley	6.50	2.90	.80
☐ 631	John Strohmayer	3.00	1.35	.40	☐ 684	Hal Breeden	7.50	3.40	.95
☐ 632	Mike Hegan	3.00	1.35	.40	☐ 685	Joel Horlen	6.50	2.90	.80
☐ 633	Jack Hiatt	3.00	1.35	.40	☐ 686	Steve Garvey	70.00	32.00	8.75
☐ 634	Dick Woodson	3.00	1.35	.40	☐ 687	Del Unser	6.50	2.90	.80
☐ 635	Don Money	3.50	1.55	.45	☐ 688	St. Louis Cardinals	12.00	5.50	1.50
☐ 636	Bill Lee	3.50	1.55	.45		Team Card			
☐ 637	Preston Gomez MG	3.00	1.35	.40	☐ 689	Eddie Fisher	6.50	2.90	.80
☐ 638	Ken Wright	3.00	1.35	.40	☐ 690	Willie Montanez	7.50	3.40	.95
☐ 639	J.C. Martin	3.00	1.35	.40	☐ 691	Curt Blefary	6.50	2.90	.80
☐ 640	Joe Coleman	3.00	1.35	.40	☐ 692	Blefary In Action	6.50	2.90	.80
☐ 641	Mike Lum	3.00	1.35	.40	☐ 693	Alan Gallagher	6.50	2.90	.80
☐ 642	Dennis Riddleberger	3.00	1.35	.40	☐ 694	Gallagher In Action	6.50	2.90	.80
☐ 643	Russ Gibson	3.00	1.35	.40	☐ 695	Rod Carew	90.00	40.00	11.50
☐ 644	Bernie Allen	3.00	1.35	.40	☐ 696	Carew In Action	45.00	20.00	5.75
☐ 645	Jim Maloney	3.50	1.55	.45	☐ 697	Jerry Koosman	15.00	6.75	1.90
☐ 646	Chico Salmon	3.00	1.35	.40	☐ 698	Koosman In Action	10.00	4.50	1.25
☐ 647	Bob Moose	3.00	1.35	.40	☐ 699	Bobby Murcer	15.00	6.75	1.90
☐ 648	Jim Lyttle	3.00	1.35	.40	☐ 700	Murcer In Action	10.00	4.50	1.25
☐ 649	Pete Richert	3.00	1.35	.40	☐ 701	Jose Pagan	6.50	2.90	.80
☐ 650	Sal Bando	3.50	1.55	.45	☐ 702	Pagan In Action	6.50	2.90	.80
☐ 651	Cincinnati Reds	6.00	2.70	.75	☐ 703	Doug Griffin	6.50	2.90	.80
	Team Card				☐ 704	Griffin In Action	6.50	2.90	.80
☐ 652	Marcelino Lopez	3.00	1.35	.40	☐ 705	Pat Corrales	7.50	3.40	.95
☐ 653	Jim Fairey	3.00	1.35	.40	☐ 706	Corrales In Action	6.50	2.90	.80
☐ 654	Horacio Pina	3.00	1.35	.40	☐ 707	Tim Foli	6.50	2.90	.80
☐ 655	Jerry Grote	3.00	1.35	.40	☐ 708	Foli In Action	6.50	2.90	.80
☐ 656	Rudy May	3.00	1.35	.40	☐ 709	Jim Kaat	15.00	6.75	1.90

☐ 710	Kaat In Action 10.00	4.50	1.25
☐ 711	Bobby Bonds 18.00	8.00	2.30
☐ 712	Bonds In Action 11.50	5.25	1.45
☐ 713	Gene Michael 7.50	3.40	.95
☐ 714	Michael In Action 7.50	3.40	.95
☐ 715	Mike Epstein 6.50	2.90	.80
☐ 716	Jesus Alou 6.50	2.90	.80
☐ 717	Bruce Dal Canton 6.50	2.90	.80
☐ 718	Del Rice MG...............6.50	2.90	.80
☐ 719	Cesar Geronimo 6.50	2.90	.80
☐ 720	Sam McDowell 7.50	3.40	.95
☐ 721	Eddie Leon 6.50	2.90	.80
☐ 722	Bill Sudakis 6.50	2.90	.80
☐ 723	Al Santorini 6.50	2.90	.80
☐ 724	AL Rookie Pitchers 6.50	2.90	.80
	John Curtis		
	Rich Hinton		
	Mickey Scott		
☐ 725	Dick McAuliffe 7.50	3.40	.95
☐ 726	Dick Selma.................6.50	2.90	.80
☐ 727	Jose Laboy 6.50	2.90	.80
☐ 728	Gail Hopkins 6.50	2.90	.80
☐ 729	Bob Veale 7.50	3.40	.95
☐ 730	Rick Monday 7.50	3.40	.95
☐ 731	Baltimore Orioles 12.00	5.50	1.50
	Team Card		
☐ 732	George Culver 6.50	2.90	.80
☐ 733	Jim Ray Hart 7.50	3.40	.95
☐ 734	Bob Burda 6.50	2.90	.80
☐ 735	Diego Segui 6.50	2.90	.80
☐ 736	Bill Russell 8.50	3.80	1.05
☐ 737	Len Randle 6.50	2.90	.80
☐ 738	Jim Merritt 6.50	2.90	.80
☐ 739	Don Mason 6.50	2.90	.80
☐ 740	Rico Carty 7.50	3.40	.95
☐ 741	Rookie First Basemen 10.00	4.50	1.25
	Tom Hutton		
	John Milner		
	Rick Miller		
☐ 742	Jim Rooker 6.50	2.90	.80
☐ 743	Cesar Gutierrez 6.50	2.90	.80
☐ 744	Jim Slaton 6.50	2.90	.80
☐ 745	Julian Javier 7.50	3.40	.95
☐ 746	Lowell Palmer 6.50	2.90	.80
☐ 747	Jim Stewart.................6.50	2.90	.80
☐ 748	Phil Hennigan 6.50	2.90	.80
☐ 749	Walter Alston MG 10.00	4.50	1.25
☐ 750	Willie Horton 7.50	3.40	.95
☐ 751	Steve Carlton TR........60.00	27.00	7.50
☐ 752	Joe Morgan TR 45.00	20.00	5.75
☐ 753	Denny McLain TR 13.00	5.75	1.65
☐ 754	Frank Robinson TR 35.00	16.00	4.40
☐ 755	Jim Fregosi TR 7.00	3.10	.85
☐ 756	Rick Wise TR 7.00	3.10	.85
☐ 757	Jose Cardenal TR........7.00	3.10	.85
☐ 758	Gil Garrido 6.50	2.90	.80
☐ 759	Chris Cannizzaro 6.50	2.90	.80

☐ 760	Bill Mazeroski 9.00	4.00	1.15
☐ 761	Rookie Outfielders 28.00	12.50	3.50
	Ben Oglivie		
	Ron Cey		
	Bernie Williams		
☐ 762	Wayne Simpson...........6.50	2.90	.80
☐ 763	Ron Hansen 6.50	2.90	.80
☐ 764	Dusty Baker 12.00	5.50	1.50
☐ 765	Ken McMullen 6.50	2.90	.80
☐ 766	Steve Hamilton 6.50	2.90	.80
☐ 767	Tom McCraw 6.50	2.90	.80
☐ 768	Denny Doyle 6.50	2.90	.80
☐ 769	Jack Aker 6.50	2.90	.80
☐ 770	Jim Wynn 7.50	3.40	.95
☐ 771	San Francisco Giants .12.00	5.50	1.50
	Team Card		
☐ 772	Ken Tatum 6.50	2.90	.80
☐ 773	Ron Brand 6.50	2.90	.80
☐ 774	Luis Alvarado 6.50	2.90	.80
☐ 775	Jerry Reuss 7.50	3.40	.95
☐ 776	Bill Voss 6.50	2.90	.80
☐ 777	Hoyt Wilhelm 20.00	9.00	2.50
☐ 778	Twins Rookies 15.00	6.75	1.90
	Vic Albury		
	Rick Dempsey		
	Jim Strickland		
☐ 779	Tony Cloninger 6.50	2.90	.80
☐ 780	Dick Green 6.50	2.90	.80
☐ 781	Jim McAndrew.............6.50	2.90	.80
☐ 782	Larry Stahl 6.50	2.90	.80
☐ 783	Les Cain 6.50	2.90	.80
☐ 784	Ken Aspromonte 6.50	2.90	.80
☐ 785	Vic Davalillo 6.50	2.90	.80
☐ 786	Chuck Brinkman 6.50	2.90	.80
☐ 787	Ron Reed 8.00	3.60	1.00

1973 Topps

The cards in this 660-card set measure 2 1/2" by 3 1/2". The 1973 Topps set marked the last year in which Topps marketed baseball cards in consecutive series. The last series (529-660) is more difficult to obtain. Beginning in 1974, all Topps cards were printed at the same time, thus eliminating the "high number" factor. The set features team leader cards with small individual pictures of the coaching staff members and a larger picture of the manager. The "background" variations below with respect to these leader cards are subtle and are best understood after a side-

*by-side comparison of the two varieties. An
"All-Time Leaders" series (471-478)
appeared for the first time in this set. Kid
Pictures appeared again for the second
year in a row (341-346). Other topical sub-
sets within the set included League
Leaders (61-68), Playoffs cards (201-202),
World Series cards (203-210), and Rookie
Prospects (601-616). The key rookie cards
in this set are all in the Rookie Prospect
series: Bob Boone, Dwight Evans, and
Mike Schmidt.*

	NRMT-MT	EXC	G-VG
COMPLETE SET (660)	1200.	550.00	150.00
COMMON PLAYER (1-132)	.50	.23	.06
COMMON PLAYER (133-264)	.50	.23	.06
COMMON PLAYER (265-396)	.65	.30	.08
COMMON PLAYER (397-528)	1.25	.55	.16
COMMON PLAYER (529-660)	3.00	1.35	.40

☐ 1 All-Time HR Leaders	30.00	7.50	2.40
Babe Ruth 714			
Hank Aaron 673			
Willie Mays 654			
☐ 2 Rich Hebner	.75	.35	.09
☐ 3 Jim Lonborg	.75	.35	.09
☐ 4 John Milner	.50	.23	.06
☐ 5 Ed Brinkman	.50	.23	.06
☐ 6 Mac Scarce	.50	.23	.06
☐ 7 Texas Rangers	1.00	.45	.13
Team Card			
☐ 8 Tom Hall	.50	.23	.06
☐ 9 Johnny Oates	.80	.35	.10
☐ 10 Don Sutton	3.50	1.55	.45
☐ 11 Chris Chambliss	1.00	.45	.13
☐ 12A Padres Leaders	.80	.35	.10
Don Zimmer MG			
Dave Garcia CO			
Johnny Podres CO			
Bob Skinner CO			
Whitey Wietelmann CO			
(Podres no right ear)			
☐ 12B Padres Leaders	1.50	.65	.19
(Podres has right ear)			
☐ 13 George Hendrick	.75	.35	.09
☐ 14 Sonny Siebert	.50	.23	.06
☐ 15 Ralph Garr	.75	.35	.09
☐ 16 Steve Braun	.50	.23	.06
☐ 17 Fred Gladding	.50	.23	.06
☐ 18 Leroy Stanton	.50	.23	.06
☐ 19 Tim Foli	.50	.23	.06
☐ 20 Stan Bahnsen	.50	.23	.06
☐ 21 Randy Hundley	.50	.23	.06
☐ 22 Ted Abernathy	.50	.23	.06
☐ 23 Dave Kingman	1.50	.65	.19
☐ 24 Al Santorini	.50	.23	.06
☐ 25 Roy White	.75	.35	.09
☐ 26 Pittsburgh Pirates	1.00	.45	.13
Team Card			
☐ 27 Bill Gogolewski	.50	.23	.06
☐ 28 Hal McRae	1.25	.55	.16
☐ 29 Tony Taylor	.50	.23	.06
☐ 30 Tug McGraw	1.00	.45	.13
☐ 31 Buddy Bell	3.50	1.55	.45
☐ 32 Fred Norman	.50	.23	.06
☐ 33 Jim Breazeale	.50	.23	.06
☐ 34 Pat Dobson	.50	.23	.06
☐ 35 Willie Davis	.75	.35	.09
☐ 36 Steve Barber	.50	.23	.06
☐ 37 Bill Robinson	.75	.35	.09
☐ 38 Mike Epstein	.50	.23	.06
☐ 39 Dave Roberts	.50	.23	.06
☐ 40 Reggie Smith	.90	.40	.11
☐ 41 Tom Walker	.50	.23	.06
☐ 42 Mike Andrews	.50	.23	.06
☐ 43 Randy Moffitt	.50	.23	.06
☐ 44 Rick Monday	.75	.35	.09
☐ 45 Ellie Rodriguez UER	.50	.23	.06
(Photo actually			
John Felske)			
☐ 46 Lindy McDaniel	.75	.35	.09
☐ 47 Luis Melendez	.50	.23	.06
☐ 48 Paul Splittorff	.50	.23	.06
☐ 49A Twins Leaders	.80	.35	.10
Frank Quilici MG			
Vern Morgan CO			
Bob Rodgers CO			
Ralph Rowe CO			
Al Worthington CO			
(Solid backgrounds)			
☐ 49B Twins Leaders	1.50	.65	.19
(Natural backgrounds)			
☐ 50 Roberto Clemente	35.00	16.00	4.40
☐ 51 Chuck Seelbach	.50	.23	.06
☐ 52 Denis Menke	.50	.23	.06
☐ 53 Steve Dunning	.50	.23	.06
☐ 54 Checklist 1	3.00	.30	.09
☐ 55 Jon Matlack	.75	.35	.09
☐ 56 Merv Rettenmund	.50	.23	.06

☐ 57	Derrel Thomas	.50	.23	.06
☐ 58	Mike Paul	.50	.23	.06
☐ 59	Steve Yeager	1.00	.45	.13
☐ 60	Ken Holtzman	.75	.35	.09
☐ 61	Batting Leaders	2.50	1.15	.30
	Billy Williams			
	Rod Carew			
☐ 62	Home Run Leaders	2.50	1.15	.30
	Johnny Bench			
	Dick Allen			
☐ 63	RBI Leaders	2.50	1.15	.30
	Johnny Bench			
	Dick Allen			
☐ 64	Stolen Base Leaders	1.75	.80	.22
	Lou Brock			
	Bert Campaneris			
☐ 65	ERA Leaders	1.75	.80	.22
	Steve Carlton			
	Luis Tiant			
☐ 66	Victory Leaders	1.75	.80	.22
	Steve Carlton			
	Gaylord Perry			
	Wilbur Wood			
☐ 67	Strikeout Leaders	10.00	4.50	1.25
	Steve Carlton			
	Nolan Ryan			
☐ 68	Leading Firemen	1.00	.45	.13
	Clay Carroll			
	Sparky Lyle			
☐ 69	Phil Gagliano	.50	.23	.06
☐ 70	Milt Pappas	.75	.35	.09
☐ 71	Johnny Briggs	.50	.23	.06
☐ 72	Ron Reed	.50	.23	.06
☐ 73	Ed Herrmann	.50	.23	.06
☐ 74	Billy Champion	.50	.23	.06
☐ 75	Vada Pinson	1.00	.45	.13
☐ 76	Doug Rader	.50	.23	.06
☐ 77	Mike Torrez	.75	.35	.09
☐ 78	Richie Scheinblum	.50	.23	.06
☐ 79	Jim Willoughby	.50	.23	.06
☐ 80	Tony Oliva UER	1.50	.65	.19
	(Minnseota on front)			
☐ 81A	Cubs Leaders	1.00	.45	.13
	Whitey Lockman MG			
	Hank Aguirre CO			
	Ernie Banks CO			
	Larry Jansen CO			
	Pete Reiser CO			
	(Solid backgrounds)			
☐ 81B	Cubs Leaders	2.00	.90	.25
	(Natural backgrounds)			
☐ 82	Fritz Peterson	.50	.23	.06
☐ 83	Leron Lee	.50	.23	.06
☐ 84	Rollie Fingers	7.00	3.10	.85
☐ 85	Ted Simmons	2.50	1.15	.30
☐ 86	Tom McCraw	.50	.23	.06
☐ 87	Ken Boswell	.50	.23	.06

☐ 88	Mickey Stanley	.75	.35	.09
☐ 89	Jack Billingham	.50	.23	.06
☐ 90	Brooks Robinson	7.00	3.10	.85
☐ 91	Los Angeles Dodgers	1.00	.45	.13
	Team Card			
☐ 92	Jerry Bell	.50	.23	.06
☐ 93	Jesus Alou	.50	.23	.06
☐ 94	Dick Billings	.50	.23	.06
☐ 95	Steve Blass	.75	.35	.09
☐ 96	Doug Griffin	.50	.23	.06
☐ 97	Willie Montanez	.75	.35	.09
☐ 98	Dick Woodson	.50	.23	.06
☐ 99	Carl Taylor	.50	.23	.06
☐ 100	Hank Aaron	25.00	11.50	3.10
☐ 101	Ken Henderson	.50	.23	.06
☐ 102	Rudy May	.50	.23	.06
☐ 103	Celerino Sanchez	.50	.23	.06
☐ 104	Reggie Cleveland	.50	.23	.06
☐ 105	Carlos May	.50	.23	.06
☐ 106	Terry Humphrey	.50	.23	.06
☐ 107	Phil Hennigan	.50	.23	.06
☐ 108	Bill Russell	.75	.35	.09
☐ 109	Doyle Alexander	.75	.35	.09
☐ 110	Bob Watson	.75	.35	.09
☐ 111	Dave Nelson	.50	.23	.06
☐ 112	Gary Ross	.50	.23	.06
☐ 113	Jerry Grote	.50	.23	.06
☐ 114	Lynn McGlothen	.50	.23	.06
☐ 115	Ron Santo	1.00	.45	.13
☐ 116A	Yankees Leaders	.80	.35	.10
	Ralph Houk MG			
	Jim Hegan CO			
	Elston Howard CO			
	Dick Howser CO			
	Jim Turner CO			
	(Solid backgrounds)			
☐ 116B	Yankees Leaders	1.50	.65	.19
	(Natural backgrounds)			
☐ 117	Ramon Hernandez	.50	.23	.06
☐ 118	John Mayberry	.75	.35	.09
☐ 119	Larry Bowa	1.00	.45	.13
☐ 120	Joe Coleman	.50	.23	.06
☐ 121	Dave Rader	.50	.23	.06
☐ 122	Jim Strickland	.50	.23	.06
☐ 123	Sandy Alomar	.75	.35	.09
☐ 124	Jim Hardin	.50	.23	.06
☐ 125	Ron Fairly	.50	.23	.06
☐ 126	Jim Brewer	.50	.23	.06
☐ 127	Milwaukee Brewers	1.00	.45	.13
	Team Card			
☐ 128	Ted Sizemore	.50	.23	.06
☐ 129	Terry Forster	.75	.35	.09
☐ 130	Pete Rose	18.00	8.00	2.30
☐ 131A	Red Sox Leaders	.80	.35	.10
	Eddie Kasko MG			
	Doug Camilli CO			
	Don Lenhardt CO			

Eddie Popowski CO
(No right ear)
Lee Stange CO

☐ 131B	Red Sox Leaders 1.50	.65	.19
	(Popowski has right ear showing)		
☐ 132	Matty Alou 75	.35	.09
☐ 133	Dave Roberts 50	.23	.06
☐ 134	Milt Wilcox....................50	.23	.06
☐ 135	Lee May UER 75	.35	.09
	(Career average .000)		
☐ 136A	Orioles Leaders..........1.00	.45	.13

Earl Weaver MG
George Bamberger CO
Jim Frey CO
Billy Hunter CO
George Staller CO
(Orange backgrounds)

☐ 136B	Orioles Leaders..........2.00	.90	.25
	(Dark pale backgrounds)		
☐ 137	Jim Beauchamp 50	.23	.06
☐ 138	Horacio Pina 50	.23	.06
☐ 139	Carmen Fanzone 50	.23	.06
☐ 140	Lou Piniella 1.00	.45	.13
☐ 141	Bruce Kison 50	.23	.06
☐ 142	Thurman Munson 10.00	4.50	1.25
☐ 143	John Curtis 50	.23	.06
☐ 144	Marty Perez 50	.23	.06
☐ 145	Bobby Bonds 2.00	.90	.25
☐ 146	Woodie Fryman 50	.23	.06
☐ 147	Mike Anderson 50	.23	.06
☐ 148	Dave Goltz....................50	.23	.06
☐ 149	Ron Hunt 50	.23	.06
☐ 150	Wilbur Wood 75	.35	.09
☐ 151	Wes Parker 75	.35	.09
☐ 152	Dave May 50	.23	.06
☐ 153	Al Hrabosky 75	.35	.09
☐ 154	Jeff Torborg 75	.35	.09
☐ 155	Sal Bando 75	.35	.09
☐ 156	Cesar Geronimo 50	.23	.06
☐ 157	Denny Riddleberger 50	.23	.06
☐ 158	Houston Astros 1.00	.45	.13
	Team Card		
☐ 159	Clarence Gaston...........1.00	.45	.13
☐ 160	Jim Palmer 12.50	5.75	1.55
☐ 161	Ted Martinez 50	.23	.06
☐ 162	Pete Broberg.................50	.23	.06
☐ 163	Vic Davalillo 50	.23	.06
☐ 164	Monty Montgomery 50	.23	.06
☐ 165	Luis Aparicio 2.75	1.25	.35
☐ 166	Terry Harmon 50	.23	.06
☐ 167	Steve Stone 75	.35	.09
☐ 168	Jim Northrup 75	.35	.09
☐ 169	Ron Schueler 75	.35	.09
☐ 170	Harmon Killebrew 5.00	2.30	.60
☐ 171	Bernie Carbo 50	.23	.06

☐ 172	Steve Kline....................50	.23	.06
☐ 173	Hal Breeden 50	.23	.06
☐ 174	Rich Gossage............20.00	9.00	2.50
☐ 175	Frank Robinson...........6.00	2.70	.75
☐ 176	Chuck Taylor..................50	.23	.06
☐ 177	Bill Plummer 50	.23	.06
☐ 178	Don Rose.......................50	.23	.06
☐ 179A	A's Leaders....................80	.35	.10

Dick Williams MG
Jerry Adair CO
Vern Hoscheit CO
Irv Noren CO
Wes Stock CO
(Hoscheit left ear showing)

☐ 179B	A's Leaders...............1.50	.65	.19
	(Hoscheit left ear not showing)		
☐ 180	Fergie Jenkins.............5.00	2.30	.60
☐ 181	Jack Brohamer...............50	.23	.06
☐ 182	Mike Caldwell.................50	.23	.06
☐ 183	Don Buford 50	.23	.06
☐ 184	Jerry Koosman 75	.35	.09
☐ 185	Jim Wynn 75	.35	.09
☐ 186	Bill Fahey 50	.23	.06
☐ 187	Luke Walker...................50	.23	.06
☐ 188	Cookie Rojas 75	.35	.09
☐ 189	Greg Luzinski 1.00	.45	.13
☐ 190	Bob Gibson 6.00	2.70	.75
☐ 191	Detroit Tigers 1.00	.45	.13
	Team Card		
☐ 192	Pat Jarvis......................50	.23	.06
☐ 193	Carlton Fisk...............45.00	20.00	5.75
☐ 194	Jorge Orta.....................50	.23	.06
☐ 195	Clay Carroll 50	.23	.06
☐ 196	Ken McMullen 50	.23	.06
☐ 197	Ed Goodson 50	.23	.06
☐ 198	Horace Clarke 50	.23	.06
☐ 199	Bert Blyleven 5.00	2.30	.60
☐ 200	Billy Williams 4.00	1.80	.50
☐ 201	A.L. Playoffs...............1.00	.45	.13
	A's over Tigers; George Hendrick scores winning run		
☐ 202	N.L. Playoffs...............1.00	.45	.13
	Reds over Pirates George Foster's run decides		
☐ 203	World Series Game 1 ...1.00	.45	.13
	Gene Tenace the Menace		
☐ 204	World Series Game 2 ...1.00	.45	.13
	A's two straight		
☐ 205	World Series Game 3 ...1.00	.45	.13
	Reds win squeeker (Tony Perez)		
☐ 206	World Series Game 4 ...1.00	.45	.13
	Gene Tenace singles		

in ninth
☐ 207	World Series Game 5 ...1.00	.45	.13
	Blue Moon Odom out		
	at plate		
☐ 208	World Series Game 6...1.00	.45	.13
	Reds' slugging		
	ties series		
	(Johnny Bench)		
☐ 209	World Series Game 7...1.00	.45	.13
	Bert Campaneris starts		
	winning rally		
☐ 210	World Series Summary1.00	.45	.13
	World champions:		
	A's Win		
☐ 211	Balor Moore 50	.23	.06
☐ 212	Joe Lahoud 50	.23	.06
☐ 213	Steve Garvey 12.50	5.75	1.55
☐ 214	Steve Hamilton 50	.23	.06
☐ 215	Dusty Baker 1.00	.45	.13
☐ 216	Toby Harrah 80	.35	.10
☐ 217	Don Wilson 50	.23	.06
☐ 218	Aurelio Rodriguez 50	.23	.06
☐ 219	St. Louis Cardinals......1.00	.45	.13
	Team Card		
☐ 220	Nolan Ryan 90.00	40.00	11.50
☐ 221	Fred Kendall 50	.23	.06
☐ 222	Rob Gardner 50	.23	.06
☐ 223	Bud Harrelson 75	.35	.09
☐ 224	Bill Lee 75	.35	.09
☐ 225	Al Oliver 1.25	.55	.16
☐ 226	Ray Fosse 50	.23	.06
☐ 227	Wayne Twitchell.............50	.23	.06
☐ 228	Bobby Darwin 50	.23	.06
☐ 229	Roric Harrison 50	.23	.06
☐ 230	Joe Morgan 6.50	2.90	.80
☐ 231	Bill Parsons 50	.23	.06
☐ 232	Ken Singleton 75	.35	.09
☐ 233	Ed Kirkpatrick 50	.23	.06
☐ 234	Bill North 50	.23	.06
☐ 235	Jim Hunter 4.00	1.80	.50
☐ 236	Tito Fuentes 50	.23	.06
☐ 237A	Braves Leaders 1.50	.65	.19
	Eddie Mathews MG		
	Lew Burdette CO		
	Jim Busby CO		
	Roy Hartsfield CO		
	Ken Silvestri CO		
	(Burdette right ear		
	showing)		
☐ 237B	Braves Leaders 3.00	1.35	.40
	(Burdette right ear		
	not showing)		
☐ 238	Tony Muser.....................50	.23	.06
☐ 239	Pete Richert 50	.23	.06
☐ 240	Bobby Murcer 80	.35	.10
☐ 241	Dwain Anderson 50	.23	.06
☐ 242	George Culver 50	.23	.06

☐ 243	California Angels..........1.00	.45	.13
	Team Card		
☐ 244	Ed Acosta 50	.23	.06
☐ 245	Carl Yastrzemski 15.00	6.75	1.90
☐ 246	Ken Sanders 50	.23	.06
☐ 247	Del Unser 50	.23	.06
☐ 248	Jerry Johnson................50	.23	.06
☐ 249	Larry Biittner 50	.23	.06
☐ 250	Manny Sanguillen 75	.35	.09
☐ 251	Roger Nelson 50	.23	.06
☐ 252A	Giants Leaders 80	.35	.10
	Charlie Fox MG		
	Joe Amalfitano CO		
	Andy Gilbert CO		
	Don McMahon CO		
	John McNamara CO		
	(Orange backgrounds)		
☐ 252B	Giants Leaders 1.50	.65	.19
	(Dark pale		
	backgrounds)		
☐ 253	Mark Belanger................75	.35	.09
☐ 254	Bill Stoneman 50	.23	.06
☐ 255	Reggie Jackson.........33.00	15.00	4.10
☐ 256	Chris Zachary 50	.23	.06
☐ 257A	Mets Leaders 2.50	1.15	.30
	Yogi Berra MG		
	Roy McMillan CO		
	Joe Pignatano CO		
	Rube Walker CO		
	Eddie Yost CO		
	(Orange backgrounds)		
☐ 257B	Mets Leaders 5.00	2.30	.60
	(Dark pale		
	backgrounds)		
☐ 258	Tommy John................1.75	.80	.22
☐ 259	Jim Holt 50	.23	.06
☐ 260	Gary Nolan 75	.35	.09
☐ 261	Pat Kelly 50	.23	.06
☐ 262	Jack Aker 50	.23	.06
☐ 263	George Scott..................75	.35	.09
☐ 264	Checklist 2 ....3.00	.30	.09
☐ 265	Gene Michael 90	.40	.11
☐ 266	Mike Lum 65	.30	.08
☐ 267	Lloyd Allen 65	.30	.08
☐ 268	Jerry Morales.................65	.30	.08
☐ 269	Tim McCarver 1.00	.45	.13
☐ 270	Luis Tiant 90	.40	.11
☐ 271	Tom Hutton 65	.30	.08
☐ 272	Ed Farmer 65	.30	.08
☐ 273	Chris Speier 65	.30	.08
☐ 274	Darold Knowles 65	.30	.08
☐ 275	Tony Perez 4.00	1.80	.50
☐ 276	Joe Lovitto 65	.30	.08
☐ 277	Bob Miller 65	.30	.08
☐ 278	Baltimore Orioles.........1.25	.55	.16
	Team Card		
☐ 279	Mike Strahler 65	.30	.08

☐	280	Al Kaline.................6.00	2.70	.75
☐	281	Mike Jorgensen.............65	.30	.08
☐	282	Steve Hovley................65	.30	.08
☐	283	Ray Sadecki.................65	.30	.08
☐	284	Glenn Borgmann............65	.30	.08
☐	285	Don Kessinger...............90	.40	.11
☐	286	Frank Linzy..................65	.30	.08
☐	287	Eddie Leon...................65	.30	.08
☐	288	Gary Gentry..................65	.30	.08
☐	289	Bob Oliver...................65	.30	.08
☐	290	Cesar Cedeno................90	.40	.11
☐	291	Rogelio Moret................65	.30	.08
☐	292	Jose Cruz.................1.25	.55	.16
☐	293	Bernie Allen.................65	.30	.08
☐	294	Steve Arlin..................65	.30	.08
☐	295	Bert Campaneris.............90	.40	.11
☐	296	Reds Leaders............1.50	.65	.19
		Sparky Anderson MG		
		Alex Grammas CO		
		Ted Kluszewski CO		
		George Scherger CO		
		Larry Shepard CO		
☐	297	Walt Williams...............65	.30	.08
☐	298	Ron Bryant...................65	.30	.08
☐	299	Ted Ford.....................65	.30	.08
☐	300	Steve Carlton.............15.00	6.75	1.90
☐	301	Billy Grabarkewitz...........65	.30	.08
☐	302	Terry Crowley................65	.30	.08
☐	303	Nelson Briles................90	.40	.11
☐	304	Duke Sims...................65	.30	.08
☐	305	Willie Mays...............40.00	18.00	5.00
☐	306	Tom Burgmeier...............65	.30	.08
☐	307	Boots Day...................65	.30	.08
☐	308	Skip Lockwood...............65	.30	.08
☐	309	Paul Popovich...............65	.30	.08
☐	310	Dick Allen.................1.75	.80	.22
☐	311	Joe Decker...................65	.30	.08
☐	312	Oscar Brown.................65	.30	.08
☐	313	Jim Ray......................65	.30	.08
☐	314	Ron Swoboda.................90	.40	.11
☐	315	John Odom...................65	.30	.08
☐	316	San Diego Padres........1.25	.55	.16
		Team Card		
☐	317	Danny Cater..................65	.30	.08
☐	318	Jim McGlothlin...............65	.30	.08
☐	319	Jim Spencer.................65	.30	.08
☐	320	Lou Brock..................6.50	2.90	.80
☐	321	Rich Hinton..................65	.30	.08
☐	322	Garry Maddox..............1.50	.65	.19
☐	323	Tigers Leaders............1.00	.45	.13
		Billy Martin MG		
		Art Fowler CO		
		Charlie Silvera CO		
		Dick Tracewski CO		
☐	324	Al Downing...................65	.30	.08
☐	325	Boog Powell................1.00	.45	.13
☐	326	Darrell Brandon.............65	.30	.08
☐	327	John Lowenstein.............65	.30	.08
☐	328	Bill Bonham.................65	.30	.08
☐	329	Ed Kranepool................65	.30	.08
☐	330	Rod Carew................18.00	8.00	2.30
☐	331	Carl Morton.................65	.30	.08
☐	332	John Felske.................65	.30	.08
☐	333	Gene Clines.................65	.30	.08
☐	334	Freddie Patek...............90	.40	.11
☐	335	Bob Tolan...................65	.30	.08
☐	336	Tom Bradley.................65	.30	.08
☐	337	Dave Duncan.................65	.30	.08
☐	338	Checklist 3...............3.00	.30	.09
☐	339	Dick Tidrow.................65	.30	.08
☐	340	Nate Colbert................65	.30	.08
☐	341	KP: Jim Palmer...........1.75	.80	.22
☐	342	KP: Sam McDowell...........80	.35	.10
☐	343	KP: Bobby Murcer...........80	.35	.10
☐	344	KP: Jim Hunter...........1.50	.65	.19
☐	345	KP: Chris Speier............80	.35	.10
☐	346	KP: Gaylord Perry........1.50	.65	.19
☐	347	Kansas City Royals......1.25	.55	.16
		Team Card		
☐	348	Rennie Stennett.............65	.30	.08
☐	349	Dick McAuliffe...............90	.40	.11
☐	350	Tom Seaver...............30.00	13.50	3.80
☐	351	Jimmy Stewart...............65	.30	.08
☐	352	Don Stanhouse..............65	.30	.08
☐	353	Steve Brye..................65	.30	.08
☐	354	Billy Parker.................65	.30	.08
☐	355	Mike Marshall...............90	.40	.11
☐	356	White Sox Leaders..........80	.35	.10
		Chuck Tanner MG		
		Joe Lonnett CO		
		Jim Mahoney CO		
		Al Monchak CO		
		Johnny Sain CO		
☐	357	Ross Grimsley...............65	.30	.08
☐	358	Jim Nettles.................65	.30	.08
☐	359	Cecil Upshaw................65	.30	.08
☐	360	Joe Rudi UER................90	.40	.11
		(Photo actually		
		Gene Tenace)		
☐	361	Fran Healy..................65	.30	.08
☐	362	Eddie Watt..................65	.30	.08
☐	363	Jackie Hernandez............65	.30	.08
☐	364	Rick Wise...................65	.30	.08
☐	365	Rico Petrocelli.............90	.40	.11
☐	366	Brock Davis.................65	.30	.08
☐	367	Burt Hooton.................90	.40	.11
☐	368	Bill Buckner..............1.00	.45	.13
☐	369	Lerrin LaGrow...............65	.30	.08
☐	370	Willie Stargell...........5.00	2.30	.60
☐	371	Mike Kekich.................65	.30	.08
☐	372	Oscar Gamble................90	.40	.11
☐	373	Clyde Wright................65	.30	.08
☐	374	Darrell Evans.............1.00	.45	.13
☐	375	Larry Dierker...............65	.30	.08

☐ 376	Frank Duffy	65	.30	.08
☐ 377	Expos Leaders	80	.35	.10
	Gene Mauch MG			
	Dave Bristol CO			
	Larry Doby CO			
	Cal McLish CO			
	Jerry Zimmerman CO			
☐ 378	Len Randle	65	.30	.08
☐ 379	Cy Acosta	65	.30	.08
☐ 380	Johnny Bench	25.00	11.50	3.10
☐ 381	Vicente Romo	65	.30	.08
☐ 382	Mike Hegan	65	.30	.08
☐ 383	Diego Segui	65	.30	.08
☐ 384	Don Baylor	3.00	1.35	.40
☐ 385	Jim Perry	90	.40	.11
☐ 386	Don Money	90	.40	.11
☐ 387	Jim Barr	65	.30	.08
☐ 388	Ben Oglivie	90	.40	.11
☐ 389	New York Mets	3.00	1.35	.40
	Team Card			
☐ 390	Mickey Lolich	90	.40	.11
☐ 391	Lee Lacy	1.00	.45	.13
☐ 392	Dick Drago	65	.30	.08
☐ 393	Jose Cardenal	65	.30	.08
☐ 394	Sparky Lyle	1.00	.45	.13
☐ 395	Roger Metzger	65	.30	.08
☐ 396	Grant Jackson	90	.40	.11
☐ 397	Dave Cash	1.50	.65	.19
☐ 398	Rich Hand	1.25	.55	.16
☐ 399	George Foster	2.00	.90	.25
☐ 400	Gaylord Perry	5.00	2.30	.60
☐ 401	Clyde Mashore	1.25	.55	.16
☐ 402	Jack Hiatt	1.25	.55	.16
☐ 403	Sonny Jackson	1.25	.55	.16
☐ 404	Chuck Brinkman	1.25	.55	.16
☐ 405	Cesar Tovar	1.25	.55	.16
☐ 406	Paul Lindblad	1.25	.55	.16
☐ 407	Felix Millan	1.25	.55	.16
☐ 408	Jim Colborn	1.25	.55	.16
☐ 409	Ivan Murrell	1.25	.55	.16
☐ 410	Willie McCovey	6.00	2.70	.75
	(Bench behind plate)			
☐ 411	Ray Corbin	1.25	.55	.16
☐ 412	Manny Mota	1.75	.80	.22
☐ 413	Tom Timmermann	1.25	.55	.16
☐ 414	Ken Rudolph	1.25	.55	.16
☐ 415	Marty Pattin	1.25	.55	.16
☐ 416	Paul Schaal	1.25	.55	.16
☐ 417	Scipio Spinks	1.25	.55	.16
☐ 418	Bob Grich	1.75	.80	.22
☐ 419	Casey Cox	1.25	.55	.16
☐ 420	Tommie Agee	1.50	.65	.19
☐ 421A	Angels Leaders	1.50	.65	.19
	Bobby Winkles MG			
	Tom Morgan CO			
	Salty Parker CO			
	Jimmie Reese CO			

	John Roseboro CO			
	(Orange backgrounds)			
☐ 421B	Angels Leaders	3.00	1.35	.40
	(Dark pale			
	backgrounds)			
☐ 422	Bob Robertson	1.25	.55	.16
☐ 423	Johnny Jeter	1.25	.55	.16
☐ 424	Denny Doyle	1.25	.55	.16
☐ 425	Alex Johnson	1.50	.65	.19
☐ 426	Dave LaRoche	1.25	.55	.16
☐ 427	Rick Auerbach	1.25	.55	.16
☐ 428	Wayne Simpson	1.25	.55	.16
☐ 429	Jim Fairey	1.25	.55	.16
☐ 430	Vida Blue	1.75	.80	.22
☐ 431	Gerry Moses	1.25	.55	.16
☐ 432	Dan Frisella	1.25	.55	.16
☐ 433	Willie Horton	1.75	.80	.22
☐ 434	San Francisco Giants	2.50	1.15	.30
	Team Card			
☐ 435	Rico Carty	1.75	.80	.22
☐ 436	Jim McAndrew	1.25	.55	.16
☐ 437	John Kennedy	1.25	.55	.16
☐ 438	Enzo Hernandez	1.25	.55	.16
☐ 439	Eddie Fisher	1.25	.55	.16
☐ 440	Glenn Beckert	1.50	.65	.19
☐ 441	Gail Hopkins	1.25	.55	.16
☐ 442	Dick Dietz	1.25	.55	.16
☐ 443	Danny Thompson	1.25	.55	.16
☐ 444	Ken Brett	1.25	.55	.16
☐ 445	Ken Berry	1.25	.55	.16
☐ 446	Jerry Reuss	1.50	.65	.19
☐ 447	Joe Hague	1.25	.55	.16
☐ 448	John Hiller	1.50	.65	.19
☐ 449A	Indians Leaders	2.00	.90	.25
	Ken Aspromonte MG			
	Rocky Colavito CO			
	Joe Lutz CO			
	Warren Spahn CO			
	(Spahn's right			
	ear pointed)			
☐ 449B	Indians Leaders	4.00	1.80	.50
	(Spahn's right			
	ear round)			
☐ 450	Joe Torre	2.00	.90	.25
☐ 451	John Vukovich	1.50	.65	.19
☐ 452	Paul Casanova	1.25	.55	.16
☐ 453	Checklist 4	3.00	.30	.09
☐ 454	Tom Haller	1.25	.55	.16
☐ 455	Bill Melton	1.25	.55	.16
☐ 456	Dick Green	1.25	.55	.16
☐ 457	John Strohmayer	1.25	.55	.16
☐ 458	Jim Mason	1.25	.55	.16
☐ 459	Jimmy Howarth	1.25	.55	.16
☐ 460	Bill Freehan	1.75	.80	.22
☐ 461	Mike Corkins	1.25	.55	.16
☐ 462	Ron Blomberg	1.25	.55	.16
☐ 463	Ken Tatum	1.25	.55	.16

☐ 464	Chicago Cubs............2.50	1.15	.30
	Team Card		
☐ 465	Dave Giusti 1.25	.55	.16
☐ 466	Jose Arcia................1.25	.55	.16
☐ 467	Mike Ryan 1.25	.55	.16
☐ 468	Tom Griffin 1.25	.55	.16
☐ 469	Dan Monzon 1.25	.55	.16
☐ 470	Mike Cuellar..............1.50	.65	.19
☐ 471	Hits Leaders.............5.00	2.30	.60
	Ty Cobb 4191		
☐ 472	Grand Slam Leaders 6.00	2.70	.75
	Lou Gehrig 23		
☐ 473	Total Bases Leaders....5.00	2.30	.60
	Hank Aaron 6172		
☐ 474	RBI Leaders 10.00	4.50	1.25
	Babe Ruth 2209		
☐ 475	Batting Leaders..........5.00	2.30	.60
	Ty Cobb .367		
☐ 476	Shutout Leaders 2.25	1.00	.30
	Walter Johnson 113		
☐ 477	Victory Leaders..........2.25	1.00	.30
	Cy Young 511		
☐ 478	Strikeout Leaders........2.25	1.00	.30
	Walter Johnson 3508		
☐ 479	Hal Lanier.................1.25	.55	.16
☐ 480	Juan Marichal............5.00	2.30	.60
☐ 481	Chicago White Sox.......2.50	1.15	.30
	Team Card		
☐ 482	Rick Reuschel............4.00	1.80	.50
☐ 483	Dal Maxvill...............1.25	.55	.16
☐ 484	Ernie McAnally...........1.25	.55	.16
☐ 485	Norm Cash................1.75	.80	.22
☐ 486A	Phillies Leaders 1.50	.65	.19
	Danny Ozark MG		
	Carroll Beringer CO		
	Billy DeMars CO		
	Ray Rippelmeyer CO		
	Bobby Wine CO		
	(Orange backgrounds)		
☐ 486B	Phillies Leaders 3.00	1.35	.40
	(Dark pale		
	backgrounds)		
☐ 487	Bruce Dal Canton 1.25	.55	.16
☐ 488	Dave Campbell............1.25	.55	.16
☐ 489	Jeff Burroughs...........1.50	.65	.19
☐ 490	Claude Osteen............1.50	.65	.19
☐ 491	Bob Montgomery 1.25	.55	.16
☐ 492	Pedro Borbon.............1.25	.55	.16
☐ 493	Duffy Dyer................1.25	.55	.16
☐ 494	Rich Morales.............1.25	.55	.16
☐ 495	Tommy Helms 1.25	.55	.16
☐ 496	Ray Lamb 1.25	.55	.16
☐ 497A	Cardinals Leaders 2.00	.90	.25
	Red Schoendienst MG		
	Vern Benson CO		
	George Kissell CO		
	Barney Schultz CO		

	(Orange backgrounds)		
☐ 497B	Cardinals Leaders......4.00	1.80	.50
	(Dark pale		
	backgrounds)		
☐ 498	Graig Nettles 3.00	1.35	.40
☐ 499	Bob Moose 1.25	.55	.16
☐ 500	Oakland A's...............2.50	1.15	.30
	Team Card		
☐ 501	Larry Gura 1.50	.65	.19
☐ 502	Bobby Valentine..........1.50	.65	.19
☐ 503	Phil Niekro 5.00	2.30	.60
☐ 504	Earl Williams 1.25	.55	.16
☐ 505	Bob Bailey................1.25	.55	.16
☐ 506	Bart Johnson 1.25	.55	.16
☐ 507	Darrel Chaney 1.25	.55	.16
☐ 508	Gates Brown 1.25	.55	.16
☐ 509	Jim Nash..................1.25	.55	.16
☐ 510	Amos Otis.................1.75	.80	.22
☐ 511	Sam McDowell............1.50	.65	.19
☐ 512	Dalton Jones 1.25	.55	.16
☐ 513	Dave Marshall............1.25	.55	.16
☐ 514	Jerry Kenney.............1.25	.55	.16
☐ 515	Andy Messersmith........1.50	.65	.19
☐ 516	Danny Walton.............1.25	.55	.16
☐ 517A	Pirates Leaders..........1.50	.65	.19
	Bill Virdon MG		
	Don Leppert CO		
	Bill Mazeroski CO		
	Dave Ricketts CO		
	Mel Wright CO		
	(Mazeroski has		
	no right ear)		
☐ 517B	Pirates Leaders 3.00	1.35	.40
	(Mazeroski has		
	right ear)		
☐ 518	Bob Veale.................1.50	.65	.19
☐ 519	Johnny Edwards...........1.25	.55	.16
☐ 520	Mel Stottlemyre 1.75	.80	.22
☐ 521	Atlanta Braves............2.50	1.15	.30
	Team Card		
☐ 522	Leo Cardenas 1.25	.55	.16
☐ 523	Wayne Granger 1.25	.55	.16
☐ 524	Gene Tenace 1.50	.65	.19
☐ 525	Jim Fregosi 1.75	.80	.22
☐ 526	Ollie Brown 1.25	.55	.16
☐ 527	Dan McGinn 1.25	.55	.16
☐ 528	Paul Blair 1.50	.65	.19
☐ 529	Milt May 3.50	1.55	.45
☐ 530	Jim Kaat..................5.00	2.30	.60
☐ 531	Ron Woods 3.00	1.35	.40
☐ 532	Steve Mingori 3.00	1.35	.40
☐ 533	Larry Stahl...............3.00	1.35	.40
☐ 534	Dave Lemonds.............3.00	1.35	.40
☐ 535	Johnny Callison...........3.50	1.55	.45
☐ 536	Philadelphia Phillies 6.00	2.70	.75
	Team Card		
☐ 537	Bill Slayback 3.00	1.35	.40

☐ 538 Jim Ray Hart	3.50	1.55	.45
☐ 539 Tom Murphy	3.00	1.35	.40
☐ 540 Cleon Jones	3.50	1.55	.45
☐ 541 Bob Bolin	3.00	1.35	.40
☐ 542 Pat Corrales	3.50	1.55	.45
☐ 543 Alan Foster	3.00	1.35	.40
☐ 544 Von Joshua	3.00	1.35	.40
☐ 545 Orlando Cepeda	4.50	2.00	.55
☐ 546 Jim York	3.00	1.35	.40
☐ 547 Bobby Heise	3.00	1.35	.40
☐ 548 Don Durham	3.00	1.35	.40
☐ 549 Rangers Leaders	5.00	2.30	.60

Whitey Herzog MG
Chuck Estrada CO
Chuck Hiller CO
Jackie Moore CO

☐ 550 Dave Johnson	3.50	1.55	.45
☐ 551 Mike Kilkenny	3.00	1.35	.40
☐ 552 J.C. Martin	3.00	1.35	.40
☐ 553 Mickey Scott	3.00	1.35	.40
☐ 554 Dave Concepcion	5.00	2.30	.60
☐ 555 Bill Hands	3.00	1.35	.40
☐ 556 New York Yankees	7.50	3.40	.95

Team Card

☐ 557 Bernie Williams	3.00	1.35	.40
☐ 558 Jerry May	3.00	1.35	.40
☐ 559 Barry Lersch	3.00	1.35	.40
☐ 560 Frank Howard	4.50	2.00	.55
☐ 561 Jim Geddes	3.00	1.35	.40
☐ 562 Wayne Garrett	3.00	1.35	.40
☐ 563 Larry Haney	3.00	1.35	.40
☐ 564 Mike Thompson	3.00	1.35	.40
☐ 565 Jim Hickman	3.00	1.35	.40
☐ 566 Lew Krausse	3.00	1.35	.40
☐ 567 Bob Fenwick	3.00	1.35	.40
☐ 568 Ray Newman	3.00	1.35	.40
☐ 569 Dodgers Leaders	4.50	2.00	.55

Walt Alston MG
Red Adams CO
Monty Basgall CO
Jim Gilliam CO
Tom Lasorda CO

☐ 570 Bill Singer	3.50	1.55	.45
☐ 571 Rusty Torres	3.00	1.35	.40
☐ 572 Gary Sutherland	3.00	1.35	.40
☐ 573 Fred Beene	3.00	1.35	.40
☐ 574 Bob Didier	3.00	1.35	.40
☐ 575 Dock Ellis	3.00	1.35	.40
☐ 576 Montreal Expos	6.00	2.70	.75

Team Card

☐ 577 Eric Soderholm	3.00	1.35	.40
☐ 578 Ken Wright	3.00	1.35	.40
☐ 579 Tom Grieve	3.50	1.55	.45
☐ 580 Joe Pepitone	3.50	1.55	.45
☐ 581 Steve Kealey	3.00	1.35	.40
☐ 582 Darrell Porter	3.50	1.55	.45
☐ 583 Bill Grief	3.00	1.35	.40

☐ 584 Chris Arnold	3.00	1.35	.40
☐ 585 Joe Niekro	3.50	1.55	.45
☐ 586 Bill Sudakis	3.00	1.35	.40
☐ 587 Rich McKinney	3.00	1.35	.40
☐ 588 Checklist 5	20.00	2.00	.60
☐ 589 Ken Forsch	3.00	1.35	.40
☐ 590 Deron Johnson	3.00	1.35	.40
☐ 591 Mike Hedlund	3.00	1.35	.40
☐ 592 John Boccabella	3.00	1.35	.40
☐ 593 Royals Leaders	3.50	1.55	.45

Jack McKeon MG
Galen Cisco CO
Harry Dunlop CO
Charlie Lau CO

☐ 594 Vic Harris	3.00	1.35	.40
☐ 595 Don Gullett	3.50	1.55	.45
☐ 596 Boston Red Sox	6.00	2.70	.75

Team Card

☐ 597 Mickey Rivers	3.50	1.55	.45
☐ 598 Phil Roof	3.00	1.35	.40
☐ 599 Ed Crosby	3.00	1.35	.40
☐ 600 Dave McNally	3.50	1.55	.45
☐ 601 Rookie Catchers	3.25	1.45	.40

Sergio Robles
George Pena
Rick Stelmaszek

☐ 602 Rookie Pitchers	3.25	1.45	.40

Mel Behney
Ralph Garcia
Doug Rau

☐ 603 Rookie 3rd Basemen	3.25	1.45	.40

Terry Hughes
Bill McNulty
Ken Reitz

☐ 604 Rookie Pitchers	3.25	1.45	.40

Jesse Jefferson
Dennis O'Toole
Bob Strampe

☐ 605 Rookie 1st Basemen	4.00	1.80	.50

Enos Cabell
Pat Bourque
Gonzalo Marquez

☐ 606 Rookie Outfielders	5.00	2.30	.60

Gary Matthews
Tom Paciorek
Jorge Roque

☐ 607 Rookie Shortstops	3.25	1.45	.40

Pepe Frias
Ray Busse
Mario Guerrero

☐ 608 Rookie Pitchers	4.00	1.80	.50

Steve Busby
Dick Colpaert
George Medich

☐ 609 Rookie 2nd Basemen	5.00	2.30	.60

Larvell Blanks
Pedro Garcia

Dave Lopes
- ☐ 610 Rookie Pitchers............5.00   2.30   .60
  Jimmy Freeman
  Charlie Hough
  Hank Webb
- ☐ 611 Rookie Outfielders ....3.25   1.45   .40
  Rich Coggins
  Jim Wohlford
  Richie Zisk
- ☐ 612 Rookie Pitchers............3.25   1.45   .40
  Steve Lawson
  Bob Reynolds
  Brent Strom
- ☐ 613 Rookie Catchers........50.00   23.00   6.25
  Bob Boone
  Skip Jutze
  Mike Ivie
- ☐ 614 Rookie Outfielders 60.00   27.00   7.50
  Al Bumbry
  Dwight Evans
  Charlie Spikes
- ☐ 615 Rookie 3rd Basemen 500.00   230.00   65.00
  Ron Cey
  John Hilton
  Mike Schmidt
- ☐ 616 Rookie Pitchers............3.25   1.45   .40
  Norm Angelini
  Steve Blateric
  Mike Garman
- ☐ 617 Rich Chiles ....3.00   1.35   .40
- ☐ 618 Andy Etchebarren ....3.00   1.35   .40
- ☐ 619 Billy Wilson ....3.00   1.35   .40
- ☐ 620 Tommy Harper ....3.50   1.55   .45
- ☐ 621 Joe Ferguson ....3.50   1.55   .45
- ☐ 622 Larry Hisle ....3.50   1.55   .45
- ☐ 623 Steve Renko ....3.00   1.35   .40
- ☐ 624 Astros Leaders ....4.50   2.00   .55
  Leo Durocher MG
  Preston Gomez CO
  Grady Hatton CO
  Hub Kittle CO
  Jim Owens CO
- ☐ 625 Angel Mangual ....3.00   1.35   .40
- ☐ 626 Bob Barton ....3.00   1.35   .40
- ☐ 627 Luis Alvarado ....3.00   1.35   .40
- ☐ 628 Jim Slaton ....3.00   1.35   .40
- ☐ 629 Cleveland Indians........6.00   2.70   .75
  Team Card
- ☐ 630 Denny McLain ....4.50   2.00   .55
- ☐ 631 Tom Matchick ....3.00   1.35   .40
- ☐ 632 Dick Selma ....3.00   1.35   .40
- ☐ 633 Ike Brown ....3.00   1.35   .40
- ☐ 634 Alan Closter ....3.00   1.35   .40
- ☐ 635 Gene Alley ....3.50   1.55   .40
- ☐ 636 Rickey Clark ....3.00   1.35   .40
- ☐ 637 Norm Miller ....3.00   1.35   .40
- ☐ 638 Ken Reynolds ....3.00   1.35   .40

- ☐ 639 Willie Crawford ....3.00   1.35   .40
- ☐ 640 Dick Bosman................3.00   1.35   .40
- ☐ 641 Cincinnati Reds...........6.00   2.70   .75
  Team Card
- ☐ 642 Jose Laboy ....3.00   1.35   .40
- ☐ 643 Al Fitzmorris ....3.00   1.35   .40
- ☐ 644 Jack Heidemann ....3.00   1.35   .40
- ☐ 645 Bob Locker ....3.00   1.35   .40
- ☐ 646 Brewers Leaders ....3.50   1.55   .45
  Del Crandall MG
  Harvey Kuenn CO
  Joe Nossek CO
  Bob Shaw CO
  Jim Walton CO
- ☐ 647 George Stone ....3.00   1.35   .40
- ☐ 648 Tom Egan ....3.00   1.35   .40
- ☐ 649 Rich Folkers ....3.00   1.35   .40
- ☐ 650 Felipe Alou ....3.50   1.55   .45
- ☐ 651 Don Carrithers ....3.00   1.35   .40
- ☐ 652 Ted Kubiak ....3.00   1.35   .40
- ☐ 653 Joe Hoerner ....3.00   1.35   .40
- ☐ 654 Minnesota Twins..........6.00   2.70   .75
  Team Card
- ☐ 655 Clay Kirby ....3.00   1.35   .40
- ☐ 656 John Ellis ....3.00   1.35   .40
- ☐ 657 Bob Johnson ....3.00   1.35   .40
- ☐ 658 Elliott Maddox ....3.00   1.35   .40
- ☐ 659 Jose Pagan ....3.00   1.35   .40
- ☐ 660 Fred Scherman ....4.00   1.80   .50

1974 Topps

The cards in this 660-card set measure 2 1/2" by 3 1/2". This year marked the first time Topps issued all the cards of its baseball set at the same time rather than in series. Some interesting variations were created by the rumored move of the San

Diego Padres to Washington. Fifteen cards (13 players, the team card, and the Rookie Card(599) of the Padres were printed either as "San Diego" (SD) or "Washington." The latter are the scarcer variety and are denoted in the checklist below by WAS. Each team's manager and his coaches again have a combined card with small pictures of each coach below the larger photo of the team's manager. The first six cards in the set (1-6) feature Hank Aaron and his illustrious career. Other topical subsets included in the set are League Leaders (201-208), All-Star selections (331-339), Playoffs cards (470-471), World Series cards (472-479), and Rookie Prospects (596-608). The card backs for the All-Stars (331-339) have no statistics, but form a picture puzzle of Bobby Bonds, the 1973 All-Star Game MVP. The key rookies in this set are Ken Griffey Sr., Dave Parker, and Dave Winfield.

	NRMT-MT	EXC	G-VG
COMPLETE SET (660)	650.00	300.00	80.00
COMMON PLAYER (1-660)	.50	.23	.06
☐ 1 Hank Aaron	30.00	7.50	2.40
All-Time Home Run King			
(Complete ML record)			
☐ 2 Aaron Special 54-57	6.00	2.70	.75
(Records on back)			
☐ 3 Aaron Special 58-61	6.00	2.70	.75
(Memorable homers)			
☐ 4 Aaron Special 62-65	6.00	2.70	.75
(Life in ML's 1954-63)			
☐ 5 Aaron Special 66-69	6.00	2.70	.75
(Life in ML's 1964-73)			
☐ 6 Aaron Special 70-73	6.00	2.70	.75
(Milestone homers)			
☐ 7 Jim Hunter	5.00	2.30	.60
☐ 8 George Theodore	.50	.23	.06
☐ 9 Mickey Lolich	.75	.35	.09
☐ 10 Johnny Bench	17.00	7.75	2.10
☐ 11 Jim Bibby	.50	.23	.06
☐ 12 Dave May	.50	.23	.06
☐ 13 Tom Hilgendorf	.50	.23	.06
☐ 14 Paul Popovich	.50	.23	.06
☐ 15 Joe Torre	1.00	.45	.13
☐ 16 Baltimore Orioles	1.00	.45	.13
Team Card			
☐ 17 Doug Bird	.50	.23	.06
☐ 18 Gary Thomasson	.50	.23	.06
☐ 19 Gerry Moses	.50	.23	.06
☐ 20 Nolan Ryan	75.00	34.00	9.50
☐ 21 Bob Gallagher	.50	.23	.06

☐ 22 Cy Acosta	.50	.23	.06
☐ 23 Craig Robinson	.50	.23	.06
☐ 24 John Hiller	.60	.25	.08
☐ 25 Ken Singleton	.60	.25	.08
☐ 26 Bill Campbell	.50	.23	.06
☐ 27 George Scott	.60	.25	.08
☐ 28 Manny Sanguillen	.60	.25	.08
☐ 29 Phil Niekro	4.00	1.80	.50
☐ 30 Bobby Bonds	1.75	.80	.22
☐ 31 Astros Leaders	.60	.25	.08
Preston Gomez MG			
Roger Craig CO			
Hub Kittle CO			
Grady Hatton CO			
Bob Lillis CO			
☐ 32A Johnny Grubb SD	.50	.23	.06
☐ 32B Johnny Grubb WAS	6.00	2.70	.75
☐ 33 Don Newhauser	.50	.23	.06
☐ 34 Andy Kosco	.50	.23	.06
☐ 35 Gaylord Perry	4.00	1.80	.50
☐ 36 St. Louis Cardinals	1.00	.45	.13
Team Card			
☐ 37 Dave Sells	.50	.23	.06
☐ 38 Don Kessinger	.60	.25	.08
☐ 39 Ken Suarez	.50	.23	.06
☐ 40 Jim Palmer	10.00	4.50	1.25
☐ 41 Bobby Floyd	.50	.23	.06
☐ 42 Claude Osteen	.60	.25	.08
☐ 43 Jim Wynn	.60	.25	.08
☐ 44 Mel Stottlemyre	.60	.25	.08
☐ 45 Dave Johnson	.60	.25	.08
☐ 46 Pat Kelly	.50	.23	.06
☐ 47 Dick Ruthven	.50	.23	.06
☐ 48 Dick Sharon	.50	.23	.06
☐ 49 Steve Renko	.50	.23	.06
☐ 50 Rod Carew	12.50	5.75	1.55
☐ 51 Bobby Heise	.50	.23	.06
☐ 52 Al Oliver	1.00	.45	.13
☐ 53A Fred Kendall SD	.50	.23	.06
☐ 53B Fred Kendall WAS	6.00	2.70	.75
☐ 54 Elias Sosa	.50	.23	.06
☐ 55 Frank Robinson	6.00	2.70	.75
☐ 56 New York Mets	1.00	.45	.13
Team Card			
☐ 57 Darold Knowles	.50	.23	.06
☐ 58 Charlie Spikes	.50	.23	.06
☐ 59 Ross Grimsley	.50	.23	.06
☐ 60 Lou Brock	6.00	2.70	.75
☐ 61 Luis Aparicio	2.50	1.15	.30
☐ 62 Bob Locker	.50	.23	.06
☐ 63 Bill Sudakis	.50	.23	.06
☐ 64 Doug Rau	.50	.23	.06
☐ 65 Amos Otis	.60	.25	.08
☐ 66 Sparky Lyle	.75	.35	.09
☐ 67 Tommy Helms	.50	.23	.06
☐ 68 Grant Jackson	.50	.23	.06
☐ 69 Del Unser	.50	.23	.06

☐ 70	Dick Allen....................1.00	.45	.13
☐ 71	Dan Frisella....................50	.23	.06
☐ 72	Aurelio Rodriguez 50	.23	.06
☐ 73	Mike Marshall..................60	.25	.08
☐ 74	Minnesota Twins............1.00	.45	.13
	Team Card		
☐ 75	Jim Colborn 50	.23	.06
☐ 76	Mickey Rivers 60	.25	.08
☐ 77A	Rich Troedson SD 50	.23	.06
☐ 77B	Rich Troedson WAS 6.00	2.70	.75
☐ 78	Giants Leaders..............60	.25	.08
	Charlie Fox MG		
	John McNamara CO		
	Joe Amalfitano CO		
	Andy Gilbert CO		
	Don McMahon CO		
☐ 79	Gene Tenace 60	.25	.08
☐ 80	Tom Seaver..................21.00	9.50	2.60
☐ 81	Frank Duffy 50	.23	.06
☐ 82	Dave Giusti 50	.23	.06
☐ 83	Orlando Cepeda 1.50	.65	.19
☐ 84	Rick Wise 50	.23	.06
☐ 85	Joe Morgan....................6.00	2.70	.75
☐ 86	Joe Ferguson 60	.25	.08
☐ 87	Fergie Jenkins 4.50	2.00	.55
☐ 88	Freddie Patek 60	.25	.08
☐ 89	Jackie Brown 50	.23	.06
☐ 90	Bobby Murcer 75	.35	.09
☐ 91	Ken Forsch......................50	.23	.06
☐ 92	Paul Blair 60	.25	.08
☐ 93	Rod Gilbreath 50	.23	.06
☐ 94	Detroit Tigers..................1.00	.45	.13
	Team Card		
☐ 95	Steve Carlton 12.50	5.75	1.55
☐ 96	Jerry Hairston 50	.23	.06
☐ 97	Bob Bailey 50	.23	.06
☐ 98	Bert Blyleven................4.00	1.80	.50
☐ 99	Brewers Leaders............60	.25	.08
	Del Crandall MG		
	Harvey Kuenn CO		
	Joe Nossek CO		
	Jim Walton CO		
	Al Widmar CO		
☐ 100	Willie Stargell................4.50	2.00	.55
☐ 101	Bobby Valentine 60	.25	.08
☐ 102A	Bill Greif SD 50	.23	.06
☐ 102B	Bill Greif WAS 6.00	2.70	.75
☐ 103	Sal Bando........................60	.25	.08
☐ 104	Ron Bryant......................50	.23	.06
☐ 105	Carlton Fisk.................25.00	11.50	3.10
☐ 106	Harry Parker 50	.23	.06
☐ 107	Alex Johnson 50	.23	.06
☐ 108	Al Hrabosky 60	.25	.08
☐ 109	Bob Grich........................75	.35	.09
☐ 110	Billy Williams................4.00	1.80	.50
☐ 111	Clay Carroll 50	.23	.06
☐ 112	Dave Lopes....................1.00	.45	.13
☐ 113	Dick Drago 50	.23	.06
☐ 114	Angels Team 1.00	.45	.13
☐ 115	Willie Horton 60	.25	.08
☐ 116	Jerry Reuss 60	.25	.08
☐ 117	Ron Blomberg 50	.23	.06
☐ 118	Bill Lee 60	.25	.08
☐ 119	Phillies Leaders..............60	.25	.08
	Danny Ozark MG		
	Ray Ripplemeyer CO		
	Bobby Wine CO		
	Carroll Beringer CO		
	Billy DeMars CO		
☐ 120	Wilbur Wood..................50	.23	.06
☐ 121	Larry Lintz......................50	.23	.06
☐ 122	Jim Holt 50	.23	.06
☐ 123	Nelson Briles 60	.25	.08
☐ 124	Bobby Coluccio................50	.23	.06
☐ 125A	Nate Colbert SD 60	.25	.08
☐ 125B	Nate Colbert WAS 6.00	2.70	.75
☐ 126	Checklist 1 ....2.50	.25	.07
☐ 127	Tom Paciorek..................60	.25	.08
☐ 128	John Ellis 50	.23	.06
☐ 129	Chris Speier 50	.23	.06
☐ 130	Reggie Jackson............33.00	15.00	4.10
☐ 131	Bob Boone 5.00	2.30	.60
☐ 132	Felix Millan 50	.23	.06
☐ 133	David Clyde......................60	.25	.08
☐ 134	Denis Menke 50	.23	.06
☐ 135	Roy White 60	.25	.08
☐ 136	Rick Reuschel................75	.35	.09
☐ 137	Al Bumbry 50	.23	.06
☐ 138	Eddie Brinkman 50	.23	.06
☐ 139	Aurelio Monteagudo 50	.23	.06
☐ 140	Darrell Evans..................75	.35	.09
☐ 141	Pat Bourque 50	.23	.06
☐ 142	Pedro Garcia 50	.23	.06
☐ 143	Dick Woodson 50	.23	.06
☐ 144	Dodgers Leaders............1.50	.65	.19
	Walter Alston MG		
	Tom Lasorda CO		
	Jim Gilliam CO		
	Red Adams CO		
	Monty Basgall CO		
☐ 145	Dock Ellis 50	.23	.06
☐ 146	Ron Fairly 50	.23	.06
☐ 147	Bart Johnson 50	.23	.06
☐ 148A	Dave Hilton SD 50	.23	.06
☐ 148B	Dave Hilton WAS 6.00	2.70	.75
☐ 149	Mac Scarce 50	.23	.06
☐ 150	John Mayberry................60	.25	.08
☐ 151	Diego Segui 50	.23	.06
☐ 152	Oscar Gamble 60	.25	.08
☐ 153	Jon Matlack 60	.25	.08
☐ 154	Houston Astros..............1.00	.45	.13
	Team Card		
☐ 155	Bert Campaneris 60	.25	.08
☐ 156	Randy Moffitt 50	.23	.06

☐ 157	Vic Harris	.50	.23	.06
☐ 158	Jack Billingham	.50	.23	.06
☐ 159	Jim Ray Hart	.60	.25	.08
☐ 160	Brooks Robinson	6.00	2.70	.75
☐ 161	Ray Burris UER	.60	.25	.08
	(Card number is			
	printed sideways)			
☐ 162	Bill Freehan	.60	.25	.08
☐ 163	Ken Berry	.50	.23	.06
☐ 164	Tom House	.50	.23	.06
☐ 165	Willie Davis	.60	.25	.08
☐ 166	Royals Leaders	.60	.25	.08
	Jack McKeon MG			
	Charlie Lau CO			
	Harry Dunlop CO			
	Galen Cisco CO			
☐ 167	Luis Tiant	.75	.35	.09
☐ 168	Danny Thompson	.50	.23	.06
☐ 169	Steve Rogers	.60	.25	.08
☐ 170	Bill Melton	.50	.23	.06
☐ 171	Eduardo Rodriguez	.50	.23	.06
☐ 172	Gene Clines	.50	.23	.06
☐ 173A	Randy Jones SD	.80	.35	.10
☐ 173B	Randy Jones WAS	8.00	3.60	1.00
☐ 174	Bill Robinson	.60	.25	.08
☐ 175	Reggie Cleveland	.50	.23	.06
☐ 176	John Lowenstein	.50	.23	.06
☐ 177	Dave Roberts	.50	.23	.06
☐ 178	Garry Maddox	.60	.25	.08
☐ 179	Mets Leaders	2.00	.90	.25
	Yogi Berra MG			
	Rube Walker CO			
	Eddie Yost CO			
	Roy McMillan CO			
	Joe Pignatano CO			
☐ 180	Ken Holtzman	.60	.25	.08
☐ 181	Cesar Geronimo	.50	.23	.06
☐ 182	Lindy McDaniel	.60	.25	.08
☐ 183	Johnny Oates	.60	.25	.08
☐ 184	Texas Rangers	1.00	.45	.13
	Team Card			
☐ 185	Jose Cardenal	.50	.23	.06
☐ 186	Fred Scherman	.50	.23	.06
☐ 187	Don Baylor	2.75	1.25	.35
☐ 188	Rudy Meoli	.50	.23	.06
☐ 189	Jim Brewer	.50	.23	.06
☐ 190	Tony Oliva	1.50	.65	.19
☐ 191	Al Fitzmorris	.50	.23	.06
☐ 192	Mario Guerrero	.50	.23	.06
☐ 193	Tom Walker	.50	.23	.06
☐ 194	Darrell Porter	.60	.25	.08
☐ 195	Carlos May	.50	.23	.06
☐ 196	Jim Fregosi	.60	.25	.08
☐ 197A	Vicente Romo SD	.50	.23	.06
☐ 197B	Vicente Romo WAS	6.00	2.70	.75
☐ 198	Dave Cash	.50	.23	.06
☐ 199	Mike Kekich	.50	.23	.06

☐ 200	Cesar Cedeno	.60	.25	.08
☐ 201	Batting Leaders	5.00	2.30	.60
	Rod Carew			
	Pete Rose			
☐ 202	Home Run Leaders	4.50	2.00	.55
	Reggie Jackson			
	Willie Stargell			
☐ 203	RBI Leaders	4.50	2.00	.55
	Reggie Jackson			
	Willie Stargell			
☐ 204	Stolen Base Leaders	1.25	.55	.16
	Tommy Harper			
	Lou Brock			
☐ 205	Victory Leaders	1.00	.45	.13
	Wilbur Wood			
	Ron Bryant			
☐ 206	ERA Leaders	5.00	2.30	.60
	Jim Palmer			
	Tom Seaver			
☐ 207	Strikeout Leaders	12.00	5.50	1.50
	Nolan Ryan			
	Tom Seaver			
☐ 208	Leading Firemen	1.00	.45	.13
	John Hiller			
	Mike Marshall			
☐ 209	Ted Sizemore	.50	.23	.06
☐ 210	Bill Singer	.50	.23	.06
☐ 211	Chicago Cubs Team	1.00	.45	.13
☐ 212	Rollie Fingers	6.00	2.70	.75
☐ 213	Dave Rader	.50	.23	.06
☐ 214	Billy Grabarkewitz	.50	.23	.06
☐ 215	Al Kaline UER	6.00	2.70	.75
	(No copyright on back)			
☐ 216	Ray Sadecki	.50	.23	.06
☐ 217	Tim Foli	.50	.23	.06
☐ 218	Johnny Briggs	.50	.23	.06
☐ 219	Doug Griffin	.50	.23	.06
☐ 220	Don Sutton	4.00	1.80	.50
☐ 221	White Sox Leaders	.60	.25	.08
	Chuck Tanner MG			
	Jim Mahoney CO			
	Alex Monchak CO			
	Johnny Sain CO			
	Joe Lonnett CO			
☐ 222	Ramon Hernandez	.50	.23	.06
☐ 223	Jeff Burroughs	.75	.35	.09
☐ 224	Roger Metzger	.50	.23	.06
☐ 225	Paul Splittorff	.50	.23	.06
☐ 226A	Padres Team SD	1.00	.45	.13
☐ 226B	Padres Team WAS	8.00	3.60	1.00
☐ 227	Mike Lum	.50	.23	.06
☐ 228	Ted Kubiak	.50	.23	.06
☐ 229	Fritz Peterson	.50	.23	.06
☐ 230	Tony Perez	4.00	1.80	.50
☐ 231	Dick Tidrow	.50	.23	.06
☐ 232	Steve Brye	.50	.23	.06
☐ 233	Jim Barr	.50	.23	.06

☐ 234	John Milner	.50	.23	.06
☐ 235	Dave McNally	.60	.25	.08
☐ 236	Cardinals Leaders	.80	.35	.10
	Red Schoendienst MG			
	Barney Schultz CO			
	George Kissell CO			
	Johnny Lewis CO			
	Vern Benson CO			
☐ 237	Ken Brett	.50	.23	.06
☐ 238	Fran Healy HOR	.60	.25	.08
	(Munson sliding			
	in background)			
☐ 239	Bill Russell	.60	.25	.08
☐ 240	Joe Coleman	.50	.23	.06
☐ 241A	Glenn Beckert SD	.60	.25	.08
☐ 241B	Glenn Beckert WAS	6.00	2.70	.75
☐ 242	Bill Gogolewski	.50	.23	.06
☐ 243	Bob Oliver	.50	.23	.06
☐ 244	Carl Morton	.50	.23	.06
☐ 245	Cleon Jones	.60	.25	.08
☐ 246	Oakland Athletics	1.00	.45	.13
	Team Card			
☐ 247	Rick Miller	.50	.23	.06
☐ 248	Tom Hall	.50	.23	.06
☐ 249	George Mitterwald	.50	.23	.06
☐ 250A	Willie McCovey SD	6.00	2.70	.75
☐ 250B	Willie McCovey WAS	30.00	13.50	3.80
☐ 251	Graig Nettles	2.00	.90	.25
☐ 252	Dave Parker	30.00	13.50	3.80
☐ 253	John Boccabella	.50	.23	.06
☐ 254	Stan Bahnsen	.50	.23	.06
☐ 255	Larry Bowa	.75	.35	.09
☐ 256	Tom Griffin	.50	.23	.06
☐ 257	Buddy Bell	.90	.40	.11
☐ 258	Jerry Morales	.50	.23	.06
☐ 259	Bob Reynolds	.50	.23	.06
☐ 260	Ted Simmons	2.50	1.15	.30
☐ 261	Jerry Bell	.50	.23	.06
☐ 262	Ed Kirkpatrick	.50	.23	.06
☐ 263	Checklist 2	2.50	.25	.07
☐ 264	Joe Rudi	.60	.25	.08
☐ 265	Tug McGraw	1.00	.45	.13
☐ 266	Jim Northrup	.60	.25	.08
☐ 267	Andy Messersmith	.60	.25	.08
☐ 268	Tom Grieve	.60	.25	.08
☐ 269	Bob Johnson	.50	.23	.06
☐ 270	Ron Santo	1.00	.45	.13
☐ 271	Bill Hands	.50	.23	.06
☐ 272	Paul Casanova	.50	.23	.06
☐ 273	Checklist 3	2.50	.25	.07
☐ 274	Fred Beene	.50	.23	.06
☐ 275	Ron Hunt	.50	.23	.06
☐ 276	Angels Leaders	.60	.25	.08
	Bobby Winkles MG			
	John Roseboro CO			
	Tom Morgan CO			
	Jimmie Reese CO			

	Salty Parker CO			
☐ 277	Gary Nolan	.60	.25	.08
☐ 278	Cookie Rojas	.60	.25	.08
☐ 279	Jim Crawford	.50	.23	.06
☐ 280	Carl Yastrzemski	12.50	5.75	1.55
☐ 281	San Francisco Giants	1.00	.45	.13
	Team Card			
☐ 282	Doyle Alexander	.60	.25	.08
☐ 283	Mike Schmidt	100.00	45.00	12.50
☐ 284	Dave Duncan	.50	.23	.06
☐ 285	Reggie Smith	.60	.25	.08
☐ 286	Tony Muser	.50	.23	.06
☐ 287	Clay Kirby	.50	.23	.06
☐ 288	Gorman Thomas	1.75	.80	.22
☐ 289	Rick Auerbach	.50	.23	.06
☐ 290	Vida Blue	.75	.35	.09
☐ 291	Don Hahn	.50	.23	.06
☐ 292	Chuck Seelbach	.50	.23	.06
☐ 293	Milt May	.50	.23	.06
☐ 294	Steve Foucault	.50	.23	.06
☐ 295	Rick Monday	.60	.25	.08
☐ 296	Ray Corbin	.50	.23	.06
☐ 297	Hal Breeden	.50	.23	.06
☐ 298	Roric Harrison	.50	.23	.06
☐ 299	Gene Michael	.60	.25	.08
☐ 300	Pete Rose	12.50	5.75	1.55
☐ 301	Bob Montgomery	.50	.23	.06
☐ 302	Rudy May	.50	.23	.06
☐ 303	George Hendrick	.60	.25	.08
☐ 304	Don Wilson	.50	.23	.06
☐ 305	Tito Fuentes	.50	.23	.06
☐ 306	Orioles Leaders	1.00	.45	.13
	Earl Weaver MG			
	Jim Frey CO			
	George Bamberger CO			
	Billy Hunter CO			
	George Staller CO			
☐ 307	Luis Melendez	.50	.23	.06
☐ 308	Bruce Dal Canton	.50	.23	.06
☐ 309A	Dave Roberts SD	.50	.23	.06
☐ 309B	Dave Roberts WAS	8.00	3.60	1.00
☐ 310	Terry Forster	.60	.25	.08
☐ 311	Jerry Grote	.50	.23	.06
☐ 312	Deron Johnson	.50	.23	.06
☐ 313	Barry Lersch	.50	.23	.06
☐ 314	Milwaukee Brewers	1.00	.45	.13
	Team Card			
☐ 315	Ron Cey	1.00	.45	.13
☐ 316	Jim Perry	.60	.25	.08
☐ 317	Richie Zisk	.60	.25	.08
☐ 318	Jim Merritt	.50	.23	.06
☐ 319	Randy Hundley	.50	.23	.06
☐ 320	Dusty Baker	.80	.35	.10
☐ 321	Steve Braun	.50	.23	.06
☐ 322	Ernie McAnally	.50	.23	.06
☐ 323	Richie Scheinblum	.50	.23	.06
☐ 324	Steve Kline	.50	.23	.06

☐ 325	Tommy Harper	.60	.25	.08
☐ 326	Reds Leaders	.80	.35	.10
	Sparky Anderson MG			
	Larry Shepard CO			
	George Scherger CO			
	Alex Grammas CO			
	Ted Kluszewski CO			
☐ 327	Tom Timmermann	.50	.23	.06
☐ 328	Skip Jutze	.50	.23	.06
☐ 329	Mark Belanger	.60	.25	.08
☐ 330	Juan Marichal	3.00	1.35	.40
☐ 331	All-Star Catchers	6.50	2.90	.80
	Carlton Fisk			
	Johnny Bench			
☐ 332	All-Star 1B	3.50	1.55	.45
	Dick Allen			
	Hank Aaron			
☐ 333	All-Star 2B	3.00	1.35	.40
	Rod Carew			
	Joe Morgan			
☐ 334	All-Star 3B	2.00	.90	.25
	Brooks Robinson			
	Ron Santo			
☐ 335	All-Star SS	.75	.35	.09
	Bert Campaneris			
	Chris Speier			
☐ 336	All-Star LF	3.00	1.35	.40
	Bobby Murcer			
	Pete Rose			
☐ 337	All-Star CF	.75	.35	.09
	Amos Otis			
	Cesar Cedeno			
☐ 338	All-Star RF	4.50	2.00	.55
	Reggie Jackson			
	Billy Williams			
☐ 339	All-Star Pitchers	1.25	.55	.16
	Jim Hunter			
	Rick Wise			
☐ 340	Thurman Munson	10.00	4.50	1.25
☐ 341	Dan Driessen	.80	.35	.10
☐ 342	Jim Lonborg	.60	.25	.08
☐ 343	Royals Team	1.00	.45	.13
☐ 344	Mike Caldwell	.50	.23	.06
☐ 345	Bill North	.50	.23	.06
☐ 346	Ron Reed	.50	.23	.06
☐ 347	Sandy Alomar	.60	.25	.08
☐ 348	Pete Richert	.50	.23	.06
☐ 349	John Vukovich	.50	.23	.06
☐ 350	Bob Gibson	6.00	2.70	.75
☐ 351	Dwight Evans	12.50	5.75	1.55
☐ 352	Bill Stoneman	.50	.23	.06
☐ 353	Rich Coggins	.50	.23	.06
☐ 354	Cubs Leaders	.60	.25	.08
	Whitey Lockman MG			
	J.C. Martin CO			
	Hank Aguirre CO			
	Al Spangler CO			
	Jim Marshall CO			
☐ 355	Dave Nelson	.50	.23	.06
☐ 356	Jerry Koosman	.75	.35	.09
☐ 357	Buddy Bradford	.50	.23	.06
☐ 358	Dal Maxvill	.50	.23	.06
☐ 359	Brent Strom	.50	.23	.06
☐ 360	Greg Luzinski	.75	.35	.09
☐ 361	Don Carrithers	.50	.23	.06
☐ 362	Hal King	.50	.23	.06
☐ 363	New York Yankees	1.00	.45	.13
	Team Card			
☐ 364A	Cito Gaston SD	.75	.35	.09
☐ 364B	Cito Gaston WAS	10.00	4.50	1.25
☐ 365	Steve Busby	.60	.25	.08
☐ 366	Larry Hisle	.60	.25	.08
☐ 367	Norm Cash	.75	.35	.09
☐ 368	Manny Mota	.60	.25	.08
☐ 369	Paul Lindblad	.50	.23	.06
☐ 370	Bob Watson	.60	.25	.08
☐ 371	Jim Slaton	.50	.23	.06
☐ 372	Ken Reitz	.50	.23	.06
☐ 373	John Curtis	.50	.23	.06
☐ 374	Marty Perez	.50	.23	.06
☐ 375	Earl Williams	.50	.23	.06
☐ 376	Jorge Orta	.50	.23	.06
☐ 377	Ron Woods	.50	.23	.06
☐ 378	Burt Hooton	.60	.25	.08
☐ 379	Rangers Leaders	1.00	.45	.13
	Billy Martin MG			
	Frank Lucchesi CO			
	Art Fowler CO			
	Charlie Silvera CO			
	Jackie Moore CO			
☐ 380	Bud Harrelson	.60	.25	.08
☐ 381	Charlie Sands	.50	.23	.06
☐ 382	Bob Moose	.50	.23	.06
☐ 383	Philadelphia Phillies	1.00	.45	.13
	Team Card			
☐ 384	Chris Chambliss	.60	.25	.08
☐ 385	Don Gullett	.60	.25	.08
☐ 386	Gary Matthews	.60	.25	.08
☐ 387A	Rich Morales SD	.50	.23	.06
☐ 387B	Rich Morales WAS	8.00	3.60	1.00
☐ 388	Phil Roof	.50	.23	.06
☐ 389	Gates Brown	.50	.23	.06
☐ 390	Lou Piniella	1.00	.45	.13
☐ 391	Billy Champion	.50	.23	.06
☐ 392	Dick Green	.50	.23	.06
☐ 393	Orlando Pena	.50	.23	.06
☐ 394	Ken Henderson	.50	.23	.06
☐ 395	Doug Rader	.50	.23	.06
☐ 396	Tommy Davis	.60	.25	.08
☐ 397	George Stone	.50	.23	.06
☐ 398	Duke Sims	.50	.23	.06
☐ 399	Mike Paul	.50	.23	.06
☐ 400	Harmon Killebrew	5.00	2.30	.60
☐ 401	Elliott Maddox	.50	.23	.06

402	Jim Rooker	.50	.23	.06
403	Red Sox Leaders	.60	.25	.08
	Darrell Johnson MG			
	Eddie Popowski CO			
	Lee Stange CO			
	Don Zimmer CO			
	Don Bryant CO			
404	Jim Howarth	.50	.23	.06
405	Ellie Rodriguez	.50	.23	.06
406	Steve Arlin	.50	.23	.06
407	Jim Wohlford	.50	.23	.06
408	Charlie Hough	.60	.25	.08
409	Ike Brown	.50	.23	.06
410	Pedro Borbon	.50	.23	.06
411	Frank Baker	.50	.23	.06
412	Chuck Taylor	.50	.23	.06
413	Don Money	.60	.25	.08
414	Checklist 4	2.50	.25	.07
415	Gary Gentry	.50	.23	.06
416	Chicago White Sox	1.00	.45	.13
	Team Card			
417	Rich Folkers	.50	.23	.06
418	Walt Williams	.50	.23	.06
419	Wayne Twitchell	.60	.00	.00
420	Ray Fosse	.50	.23	.06
421	Dan Fife	.50	.23	.06
422	Gonzalo Marquez	.50	.23	.06
423	Fred Stanley	.50	.23	.06
424	Jim Beauchamp	.50	.23	.06
425	Pete Broberg	.50	.23	.06
426	Rennie Stennett	.50	.23	.06
427	Bobby Bolin	.50	.23	.06
428	Gary Sutherland	.50	.23	.06
429	Dick Lange	.50	.23	.06
430	Matty Alou	.60	.25	.08
431	Gene Garber	.75	.35	.09
432	Chris Arnold	.50	.23	.06
433	Lerrin LaGrow	.50	.23	.06
434	Ken McMullen	.50	.23	.06
435	Dave Concepcion	2.50	1.15	.30
436	Don Hood	.50	.23	.06
437	Jim Lyttle	.50	.23	.06
438	Ed Herrmann	.50	.23	.06
439	Norm Miller	.50	.23	.06
440	Jim Kaat	1.50	.65	.19
441	Tom Ragland	.50	.23	.06
442	Alan Foster	.50	.23	.06
443	Tom Hutton	.50	.23	.06
444	Vic Davalillo	.50	.23	.06
445	George Medich	.50	.23	.06
446	Len Randle	.50	.23	.06
447	Twins Leaders	.60	.25	.08
	Frank Quilici MG			
	Ralph Rowe CO			
	Bob Rodgers CO			
	Vern Morgan CO			
448	Ron Hodges	.50	.23	.06
449	Tom McCraw	.50	.23	.06
450	Rich Hebner	.60	.25	.08
451	Tommy John	2.00	.90	.25
452	Gene Hiser	.50	.23	.06
453	Balor Moore	.50	.23	.06
454	Kurt Bevacqua	.50	.23	.06
455	Tom Bradley	.50	.23	.06
456	Dave Winfield	160.00	70.00	20.00
457	Chuck Goggin	.50	.23	.06
458	Jim Ray	.50	.23	.06
459	Cincinnati Reds	1.00	.45	.13
	Team Card			
460	Boog Powell	1.00	.45	.13
461	John Odom	.50	.23	.06
462	Luis Alvarado	.50	.23	.06
463	Pat Dobson	.50	.23	.06
464	Jose Cruz	.60	.25	.08
465	Dick Bosman	.50	.23	.06
466	Dick Billings	.50	.23	.06
467	Winston Llenas	.50	.23	.06
468	Pepe Frias	.50	.23	.06
469	Joe Decker	.50	.23	.06
470	AL Playoffs	6.00	2.70	.75
	A's over Orioles			
	(Reggie Jackson)			
471	NL Playoffs	1.00	.45	.13
	Mets over Reds			
	(Jon Matlack pitching)			
472	World Series Game 1	1.00	.45	.13
	(Darold Knowles pitching)			
473	World Series Game 2	5.00	2.30	.60
	(Willie Mays batting)			
474	World Series Game 3	1.00	.45	.13
	(Bert Campaneris stealing)			
475	World Series Game 4	1.00	.45	.13
	(Rusty Staub batting)			
476	World Series Game 5	1.00	.45	.13
	(Cleon Jones scoring)			
477	World Series Game 6	6.00	2.70	.75
	(Reggie Jackson)			
478	World Series Game 7	1.00	.45	.13
	(Bert Campaneris batting)			
479	World Series Summary	1.00	.45	.13
	A's celebrate; win 2nd consecutive championship			
480	Willie Crawford	.50	.23	.06
481	Jerry Terrell	.50	.23	.06
482	Bob Didier	.50	.23	.06
483	Atlanta Braves	1.00	.45	.13
	Team Card			
484	Carmen Fanzone	.50	.23	.06
485	Felipe Alou	.80	.35	.10
486	Steve Stone	.60	.25	.08

☐ 487	Ted Martinez	.50	.23	.06
☐ 488	Andy Etchebarren	.50	.23	.06
☐ 489	Pirates Leaders	.60	.25	.08

Danny Murtaugh MG
Don Osborn CO
Don Leppert CO
Bill Mazeroski CO
Bob Skinner CO

☐ 490	Vada Pinson	.80	.35	.10
☐ 491	Roger Nelson	.50	.23	.06
☐ 492	Mike Rogodzinski	.50	.23	.06
☐ 493	Joe Hoerner	.50	.23	.06
☐ 494	Ed Goodson	.50	.23	.06
☐ 495	Dick McAuliffe	.60	.25	.08
☐ 496	Tom Murphy	.50	.23	.06
☐ 497	Bobby Mitchell	.50	.23	.06
☐ 498	Pat Corrales	.60	.25	.08
☐ 499	Rusty Torres	.50	.23	.06
☐ 500	Lee May	.60	.25	.08
☐ 501	Eddie Leon	.50	.23	.06
☐ 502	Dave LaRoche	.50	.23	.06
☐ 503	Eric Soderholm	.50	.23	.06
☐ 504	Joe Niekro	.60	.25	.08
☐ 505	Bill Buckner	1.00	.45	.13
☐ 506	Ed Farmer	.50	.23	.06
☐ 507	Larry Stahl	.50	.23	.06
☐ 508	Montreal Expos	1.00	.45	.13

Team Card

☐ 509	Jesse Jefferson	.50	.23	.06
☐ 510	Wayne Garrett	.50	.23	.06
☐ 511	Toby Harrah	.60	.25	.08
☐ 512	Joe Lahoud	.50	.23	.06
☐ 513	Jim Campanis	.50	.23	.06
☐ 514	Paul Schaal	.50	.23	.06
☐ 515	Willie Montanez	.50	.23	.06
☐ 516	Horacio Pina	.50	.23	.06
☐ 517	Mike Hegan	.50	.23	.06
☐ 518	Derrel Thomas	.50	.23	.06
☐ 519	Bill Sharp	.50	.23	.06
☐ 520	Tim McCarver	.80	.35	.10
☐ 521	Indians Leaders	.60	.25	.08

Ken Aspromonte MG
Clay Bryant CO
Tony Pacheco CO

☐ 522	J.R. Richard	.60	.25	.08
☐ 523	Cecil Cooper	1.75	.80	.22
☐ 524	Bill Plummer	.50	.23	.06
☐ 525	Clyde Wright	.50	.23	.06
☐ 526	Frank Tepedino	.50	.23	.06
☐ 527	Bobby Darwin	.50	.23	.06
☐ 528	Bill Bonham	.50	.23	.06
☐ 529	Horace Clarke	.50	.23	.06
☐ 530	Mickey Stanley	.60	.25	.08
☐ 531	Expos Leaders	.60	.25	.08

Gene Mauch MG
Dave Bristol CO
Cal McLish CO

Larry Doby CO
Jerry Zimmerman CO

☐ 532	Skip Lockwood	.50	.23	.06
☐ 533	Mike Phillips	.50	.23	.06
☐ 534	Eddie Watt	.50	.23	.06
☐ 535	Bob Tolan	.50	.23	.06
☐ 536	Duffy Dyer	.50	.23	.06
☐ 537	Steve Mingori	.50	.23	.06
☐ 538	Cesar Tovar	.50	.23	.06
☐ 539	Lloyd Allen	.50	.23	.06
☐ 540	Bob Robertson	.50	.23	.06
☐ 541	Cleveland Indians	1.00	.45	.13

Team Card

☐ 542	Rich Gossage	5.00	2.30	.60
☐ 543	Danny Cater	.50	.23	.06
☐ 544	Ron Schueler	.50	.23	.06
☐ 545	Billy Conigliaro	.60	.25	.08
☐ 546	Mike Corkins	.50	.23	.06
☐ 547	Glenn Borgmann	.50	.23	.06
☐ 548	Sonny Siebert	.50	.23	.06
☐ 549	Mike Jorgensen	.50	.23	.06
☐ 550	Sam McDowell	.60	.25	.08
☐ 551	Von Joshua	.50	.23	.06
☐ 552	Denny Doyle	.50	.23	.06
☐ 553	Jim Willoughby	.50	.23	.06
☐ 554	Tim Johnson	.50	.23	.06
☐ 555	Woodie Fryman	.50	.23	.06
☐ 556	Dave Campbell	.50	.23	.06
☐ 557	Jim McGlothlin	.50	.23	.06
☐ 558	Bill Fahey	.50	.23	.06
☐ 559	Darrel Chaney	.50	.23	.06
☐ 560	Mike Cuellar	.60	.25	.08
☐ 561	Ed Kranepool	.50	.23	.06
☐ 562	Jack Aker	.50	.23	.06
☐ 563	Hal McRae	1.00	.45	.13
☐ 564	Mike Ryan	.50	.23	.06
☐ 565	Milt Wilcox	.50	.23	.06
☐ 566	Jackie Hernandez	.50	.23	.06
☐ 567	Boston Red Sox	1.00	.45	.13

Team Card

☐ 568	Mike Torrez	.60	.25	.08
☐ 569	Rick Dempsey	.75	.35	.09
☐ 570	Ralph Garr	.60	.25	.08
☐ 571	Rich Hand	.50	.23	.06
☐ 572	Enzo Hernandez	.50	.23	.06
☐ 573	Mike Adams	.50	.23	.06
☐ 574	Bill Parsons	.50	.23	.06
☐ 575	Steve Garvey	10.00	4.50	1.25
☐ 576	Scipio Spinks	.50	.23	.06
☐ 577	Mike Sadek	.50	.23	.06
☐ 578	Ralph Houk MG	.60	.25	.08
☐ 579	Cecil Upshaw	.50	.23	.06
☐ 580	Jim Spencer	.50	.23	.06
☐ 581	Fred Norman	.50	.23	.06
☐ 582	Bucky Dent	2.00	.90	.25
☐ 583	Marty Pattin	.50	.23	.06
☐ 584	Ken Rudolph	.50	.23	.06

☐ 585	Merv Rettenmund 50	.23	.06
☐ 586	Jack Brohamer 50	.23	.06
☐ 587	Larry Christenson 50	.23	.06
☐ 588	Hal Lanier 50	.23	.06
☐ 589	Boots Day 50	.23	.06
☐ 590	Roger Moret 50	.23	.06
☐ 591	Sonny Jackson 50	.23	.06
☐ 592	Ed Bane 50	.23	.06
☐ 593	Steve Yeager 60	.25	.08
☐ 594	Leroy Stanton 50	.23	.06
☐ 595	Steve Blass 60	.25	.08
☐ 596	Rookie Pitchers...........60	.25	.08
	Wayne Garland		
	Fred Holdsworth		
	Mark Littell		
	Dick Pole		
☐ 597	Rookie Shortstops 75	.35	.09
	Dave Chalk		
	John Gamble		
	Pete MacKanin		
	Manny Trillo		
☐ 598	Rookie Outfielders 25.00	11.50	3.10
	Dave Augustine		
	Ken Griffey		
	Steve Ontiveros		
	Jim Tyrone		
☐ 599A	Rookie Pitchers WAS.1.00	.45	.13
	Ron Diorio		
	Dave Freisleben		
	Frank Riccelli		
	Greg Shanahan		
☐ 599B	Rookie Pitchers SD....4.00	1.80	.50
	(SD in large print)		
☐ 599C	Rookie Pitchers SD....7.50	3.40	.95
	(SD in small print)		
☐ 600	Rookie Infielders..........5.00	2.30	.60
	Ron Cash		
	Jim Cox		
	Bill Madlock		
	Reggie Sanders		
☐ 601	Rookie Outfielders 6.00	2.70	.75
	Ed Armbrister		
	Rich Bladt		
	Brian Downing		
	Bake McBride		
☐ 602	Rookie Pitchers..............70	.30	.09
	Glen Abbott		
	Rick Henninger		
	Craig Swan		
	Dan Vossler		
☐ 603	Rookie Catchers.............60	.25	.08
	Barry Foote		
	Tom Lundstedt		
	Charlie Moore		
	Sergio Robles		
☐ 604	Rookie Infielders..........5.00	2.30	.60
	Terry Hughes		

	John Knox		
	Andre Thornton		
	Frank White		
☐ 605	Rookie Pitchers...........5.00	2.30	.60
	Vic Albury		
	Ken Frailing		
	Kevin Kobel		
	Frank Tanana		
☐ 606	Rookie Outfielders 60	.25	.08
	Jim Fuller		
	Wilbur Howard		
	Tommy Smith		
	Otto Velez		
☐ 607	Rookie Shortstops 60	.25	.08
	Leo Foster		
	Tom Heintzelman		
	Dave Rosello		
	Frank Taveras		
☐ 608A	Rookie Pitchers: ERR 2.00	.90	.25
	Bob Apodaco (sic)		
	Dick Baney		
	John D'Acquisto		
	Mike Wallace		
☐ 608B	Rookie Pitchers: COR ...75	.35	.09
	Bob Apodaca		
	Dick Baney		
	John D'Acquisto		
	Mike Wallace		
☐ 609	Rico Petrocelli................60	.25	.08
☐ 610	Dave Kingman 1.25	.55	.16
☐ 611	Rich Stelmaszek 50	.23	.06
☐ 612	Luke Walker 50	.23	.06
☐ 613	Dan Monzon 50	.23	.06
☐ 614	Adrian Devine 50	.23	.06
☐ 615	Johnny Jeter UER 50	.23	.06
	(Misspelled Johnnie		
	on card back)		
☐ 616	Larry Gura 50	.23	.06
☐ 617	Ted Ford 50	.23	.06
☐ 618	Jim Mason 50	.23	.06
☐ 619	Mike Anderson 50	.23	.06
☐ 620	Al Downing 50	.23	.06
☐ 621	Bernie Carbo 50	.23	.06
☐ 622	Phil Gagliano 50	.23	.06
☐ 623	Celerino Sanchez 50	.23	.06
☐ 624	Bob Miller 50	.23	.06
☐ 625	Ollie Brown 50	.23	.06
☐ 626	Pittsburgh Pirates 1.00	.45	.13
	Team Card		
☐ 627	Carl Taylor 50	.23	.06
☐ 628	Ivan Murrell 50	.23	.06
☐ 629	Rusty Staub 1.00	.45	.13
☐ 630	Tommie Agee...............60	.25	.08
☐ 631	Steve Barber 50	.23	.06
☐ 632	George Culver 50	.23	.06
☐ 633	Dave Hamilton 50	.23	.06
☐ 634	Braves Leaders 1.25	.55	.16

Eddie Mathews MG
Herm Starrette CO
Connie Ryan CO
Jim Busby CO
Ken Silvestri CO

☐	635 Johnny Edwards	.50	.23	.06
☐	636 Dave Goltz	.50	.23	.06
☐	637 Checklist 5	2.50	.25	.07
☐	638 Ken Sanders	.50	.23	.06
☐	639 Joe Lovitto	.50	.23	.06
☐	640 Milt Pappas	.60	.25	.08
☐	641 Chuck Brinkman	.50	.23	.06
☐	642 Terry Harmon	.50	.23	.06
☐	643 Dodgers Team	1.00	.45	.13
☐	644 Wayne Granger	.50	.23	.06
☐	645 Ken Boswell	.50	.23	.06
☐	646 George Foster	2.00	.90	.25
☐	647 Juan Beniquez	.60	.25	.08
☐	648 Terry Crowley	.50	.23	.06
☐	649 Fernando Gonzalez	.50	.23	.06
☐	650 Mike Epstein	.50	.23	.06
☐	651 Leron Lee	.50	.23	.06
☐	652 Gail Hopkins	.50	.23	.06
☐	653 Bob Stinson	.50	.23	.06
☐	654A Jesus Alou ERR	.60	.25	.08
	(No position)			
☐	654B Jesus Alou COR	7.00	3.10	.85
	(Outfield)			
☐	655 Mike Tyson	.50	.23	.06
☐	656 Adrian Garrett	.50	.23	.06
☐	657 Jim Shellenback	.50	.23	.06
☐	658 Lee Lacy	.50	.23	.06
☐	659 Joe Lis	.50	.23	.06
☐	660 Larry Dierker	.75	.35	.09

1974 Topps Traded

*The cards in this 44-card set measure
2 1/2" by 3 1/2". The 1974 Topps Traded
set contains 43 player cards and one
unnumbered checklist card. The obverses
have the word "traded" in block letters and
the backs are designed in newspaper
style. Card numbers are the same as in
the regular set except they are followed by
a "T." No known scarcities exist for this set.
The cards were issued heavily mixed in
with regular wax packs of the 1974 Topps
cards toward the end of the distribution
cycle; they were produced in large enough
quantity that they are no scarcer than the
regular Topps cards.*

			NRMT-MT	EXC	G-VG
	COMPLETE SET (44)		13.00	5.75	1.65
	COMMON PLAYER		.35	.16	.04
☐	23T Craig Robinson	.35	.16	.04
☐	42T Claude Osteen	.45	.20	.06
☐	43T Jim Wynn	.45	.20	.06
☐	51T Bobby Heise	.35	.16	.04
☐	59T Ross Grimsley	.35	.16	.04
☐	62T Bob Locker	.35	.16	.04
☐	63T Bill Sudakis	.35	.16	.04
☐	73T Mike Marshall	.65	.30	.08
☐	123T Nelson Briles	.45	.20	.06
☐	139T Aurelio Monteagudo	.35	.16	.04
☐	151T Diego Segui	.35	.16	.04
☐	165T Willie Davis	.45	.20	.06
☐	175T Reggie Cleveland	.35	.16	.04
☐	182T Lindy McDaniel	.45	.20	.06
☐	186T Fred Scherman	.35	.16	.04
☐	249T George Mitterwald	.35	.16	.04
☐	262T Ed Kirkpatrick	.35	.16	.04
☐	269T Bob Johnson	.35	.16	.04
☐	270T Ron Santo	.65	.30	.08
☐	313T Barry Lersch	.35	.16	.04
☐	319T Randy Hundley	.35	.16	.04
☐	330T Juan Marichal	2.50	1.15	.30
☐	348T Pete Richert	.35	.16	.04
☐	373T John Curtis	.35	.16	.04
☐	390T Lou Piniella	.65	.30	.08
☐	428T Gary Sutherland	.35	.16	.04
☐	454T Kurt Bevacqua	.35	.16	.04
☐	458T Jim Ray	.35	.16	.04
☐	485T Felipe Alou	.65	.30	.08
☐	486T Steve Stone	.65	.30	.08
☐	496T Tom Murphy	.35	.16	.04
☐	516T Horacio Pina	.35	.16	.04
☐	534T Eddie Watt	.35	.16	.04
☐	538T Cesar Tovar	.35	.16	.04
☐	544T Ron Schueler	.35	.16	.04
☐	579T Cecil Upshaw	.35	.16	.04
☐	585T Merv Rettenmund	.35	.16	.04

☐ 612T	Luke Walker	35	.16	.04
☐ 616T	Larry Gura	45	.20	.06
☐ 618T	Jim Mason	35	.16	.04
☐ 630T	Tommie Agee	45	.20	.06
☐ 648T	Terry Crowley	35	.16	.04
☐ 649T	Fernando Gonzalez	35	.16	.04
☐ NNO	Traded Checklist	1.00	.10	.03

1975 Topps

The cards in the 1975 Topps set were
issued in two different sizes: a regular
standard size (2 1/2" by 3 1/2") and a mini
size (2 1/2" by 3 1/8") which was issued as
a test in certain areas of the country. The
660-card Topps baseball set for 1975 was
radically different in appearance from sets
of the preceding years. The most prominent change was the use of a two-color
frame surrounding the picture area rather
than a single, subdued color. A facsimile
autograph appears on the picture, and the
backs are printed in red and green on gray.
Cards 189-212 depict the MVP's of both
leagues from 1951 through 1974. The first
seven cards (1-7) feature players (listed in
alphabetical order) breaking records or
achieving milestones during the previous
season. Cards 306-313 picture league
leaders in various statistical categories.
Cards 459-466 depict the results of post-
season action. Team cards feature a
checklist back for players on that team and
show a small inset photo of the manager
on the front. The Phillies Team card number 46 erroneously lists Terry Harmon as
number 339 instead of number 399. The
following players' regular issue cards are

explicitly denoted as All-Stars, 1, 50, 80,
140, 170, 180, 260, 320, 350, 390, 400,
420, 440, 470, 530, 570, and 600. This set
is quite popular with collectors, at least in
part due to the fact that the rookie cards of
Robin Yount, George Brett, Gary Carter,
Jim Rice, Fred Lynn, and Keith Hernandez
are all in the set. Topps minis have the
same checklist and are valued from
approximately 1.25 times to double the
prices listed below.

	NRMT-MT	EXC	G-VG
COMPLETE SET (660)	900.00	400.00	115.00
COMMON PLAYER (1-132)	.50	.23	.06
COMMON PLAYER (133-264)	.50	.23	.06
COMMON PLAYER (265-660)	.50	.23	.06
☐ 1 RB: Hank Aaron	30.00	7.50	2.40
Sets Homer Mark			
☐ 2 RB: Lou Brock	3.50	1.55	.45
118 Stolen Bases			
☐ 3 RB: Bob Gibson	3.50	1.55	.45
3000th Strikeout			
☐ 4 RB: Al Kaline	4.00	1.80	.50
3000 Hit Club			
☐ 5 RB: Nolan Ryan	20.00	9.00	2.50
Fans 300 for			
3rd Year in a Row			
☐ 6 RB: Mike Marshall	.75	.35	.09
Hurls 106 Games			
☐ 7 No Hitters	5.00	2.30	.60
Steve Busby			
Dick Bosman			
Nolan Ryan			
☐ 8 Rogelio Moret	.50	.23	.06
☐ 9 Frank Tepedino	.50	.23	.06
☐ 10 Willie Davis	.60	.25	.08
☐ 11 Bill Melton	.50	.23	.06
☐ 12 David Clyde	.50	.23	.06
☐ 13 Gene Locklear	.50	.23	.06
☐ 14 Milt Wilcox	.50	.23	.06
☐ 15 Jose Cardenal	.50	.23	.06
☐ 16 Frank Tanana	2.00	.90	.25
☐ 17 Dave Concepcion	2.50	1.15	.30
☐ 18 Tigers: Team/Mgr.	1.50	.65	.19
Ralph Houk			
(Checklist back)			
☐ 19 Jerry Koosman	.75	.35	.09
☐ 20 Thurman Munson	9.00	4.00	1.15
☐ 21 Rollie Fingers	5.00	2.30	.60
☐ 22 Dave Cash	.50	.23	.06
☐ 23 Bill Russell	.60	.25	.08
☐ 24 Al Fitzmorris	.50	.23	.06
☐ 25 Lee May	.60	.25	.08
☐ 26 Dave McNally	.60	.25	.08
☐ 27 Ken Reitz	.50	.23	.06

☐ 28	Tom Murphy	.50	.23	.06
☐ 29	Dave Parker	8.00	3.60	1.00
☐ 30	Bert Blyleven	3.00	1.35	.40
☐ 31	Dave Rader	.50	.23	.06
☐ 32	Reggie Cleveland	.50	.23	.06
☐ 33	Dusty Baker	.75	.35	.09
☐ 34	Steve Renko	.50	.23	.06
☐ 35	Ron Santo	1.00	.45	.13
☐ 36	Joe Lovitto	.50	.23	.06
☐ 37	Dave Freisleben	.50	.23	.06
☐ 38	Buddy Bell	.75	.35	.09
☐ 39	Andre Thornton	.60	.25	.08
☐ 40	Bill Singer	.50	.23	.06
☐ 41	Cesar Geronimo	.50	.23	.06
☐ 42	Joe Coleman	.50	.23	.06
☐ 43	Cleon Jones	.60	.25	.08
☐ 44	Pat Dobson	.50	.23	.06
☐ 45	Joe Rudi	.60	.25	.08
☐ 46	Phillies: Team/Mgr.	1.50	.65	.19
	Danny Ozark UER			
	(Checklist back)			
☐ 47	Tommy John	2.00	.90	.25
☐ 48	Freddie Patek	.60	.25	.08
☐ 49	Larry Dierker	.50	.23	.06
☐ 50	Brooks Robinson	6.00	2.70	.75
☐ 51	Bob Forsch	.90	.40	.11
☐ 52	Darrell Porter	.60	.25	.08
☐ 53	Dave Giusti	.50	.23	.06
☐ 54	Eric Soderholm	.50	.23	.06
☐ 55	Bobby Bonds	1.50	.65	.19
☐ 56	Rick Wise	.60	.25	.08
☐ 57	Dave Johnson	.60	.25	.08
☐ 58	Chuck Taylor	.50	.23	.06
☐ 59	Ken Henderson	.50	.23	.06
☐ 60	Fergie Jenkins	4.50	2.00	.55
☐ 61	Dave Winfield	55.00	25.00	7.00
☐ 62	Fritz Peterson	.50	.23	.06
☐ 63	Steve Swisher	.50	.23	.06
☐ 64	Dave Chalk	.50	.23	.06
☐ 65	Don Gullett	.60	.25	.08
☐ 66	Willie Horton	.60	.25	.08
☐ 67	Tug McGraw	1.00	.45	.13
☐ 68	Ron Blomberg	.50	.23	.06
☐ 69	John Odom	.50	.23	.06
☐ 70	Mike Schmidt	65.00	29.00	8.25
☐ 71	Charlie Hough	.60	.25	.08
☐ 72	Royals: Team/Mgr.	1.50	.65	.19
	Jack McKeon			
	(Checklist back)			
☐ 73	J.R. Richard	.60	.25	.08
☐ 74	Mark Belanger	.60	.25	.08
☐ 75	Ted Simmons	2.00	.90	.25
☐ 76	Ed Sprague	.50	.23	.06
☐ 77	Richie Zisk	.60	.25	.08
☐ 78	Ray Corbin	.50	.23	.06
☐ 79	Gary Matthews	.60	.25	.08
☐ 80	Carlton Fisk	24.00	11.00	3.00

☐ 81	Ron Reed	.50	.23	.06
☐ 82	Pat Kelly	.50	.23	.06
☐ 83	Jim Merritt	.50	.23	.06
☐ 84	Enzo Hernandez	.50	.23	.06
☐ 85	Bill Bonham	.50	.23	.06
☐ 86	Joe Lis	.50	.23	.06
☐ 87	George Foster	2.00	.90	.25
☐ 88	Tom Egan	.50	.23	.06
☐ 89	Jim Ray	.50	.23	.06
☐ 90	Rusty Staub	1.00	.45	.13
☐ 91	Dick Green	.50	.23	.06
☐ 92	Cecil Upshaw	.50	.23	.06
☐ 93	Dave Lopes	1.00	.45	.13
☐ 94	Jim Lonborg	.60	.25	.08
☐ 95	John Mayberry	.60	.25	.08
☐ 96	Mike Cosgrove	.50	.23	.06
☐ 97	Earl Williams	.50	.23	.06
☐ 98	Rich Folkers	.50	.23	.06
☐ 99	Mike Hegan	.50	.23	.06
☐ 100	Willie Stargell	4.00	1.80	.50
☐ 101	Expos: Team/Mgr.	1.50	.65	.19
	Gene Mauch			
	(Checklist back)			
☐ 102	Joe Decker	.50	.23	.06
☐ 103	Rick Miller	.50	.23	.06
☐ 104	Bill Madlock	1.25	.55	.16
☐ 105	Buzz Capra	.50	.23	.06
☐ 106	Mike Hargrove	.80	.35	.10
☐ 107	Jim Barr	.50	.23	.06
☐ 108	Tom Hall	.50	.23	.06
☐ 109	George Hendrick	.60	.25	.08
☐ 110	Wilbur Wood	.50	.23	.06
☐ 111	Wayne Garrett	.50	.23	.06
☐ 112	Larry Hardy	.50	.23	.06
☐ 113	Elliott Maddox	.50	.23	.06
☐ 114	Dick Lange	.50	.23	.06
☐ 115	Joe Ferguson	.50	.23	.06
☐ 116	Lerrin LaGrow	.50	.23	.06
☐ 117	Orioles: Team/Mgr.	1.50	.65	.19
	Earl Weaver			
	(Checklist back)			
☐ 118	Mike Anderson	.50	.23	.06
☐ 119	Tommy Helms	.50	.23	.06
☐ 120	Steve Busby UER	.60	.25	.08
	(Photo actually			
	Fran Healy)			
☐ 121	Bill North	.50	.23	.06
☐ 122	Al Hrabosky	.60	.25	.08
☐ 123	Johnny Briggs	.50	.23	.06
☐ 124	Jerry Reuss	.60	.25	.08
☐ 125	Ken Singleton	.60	.25	.08
☐ 126	Checklist 1-132	2.00	.20	.06
☐ 127	Glenn Borgmann	.50	.23	.06
☐ 128	Bill Lee	.60	.25	.08
☐ 129	Rick Monday	.50	.23	.06
☐ 130	Phil Niekro	4.00	1.80	.50
☐ 131	Toby Harrah	.60	.25	.08

□ 132	Randy Moffitt	.50	.23	.06
□ 133	Dan Driessen	.60	.25	.08
□ 134	Ron Hodges	.50	.23	.06
□ 135	Charlie Spikes	.50	.23	.06
□ 136	Jim Mason	.50	.23	.06
□ 137	Terry Forster	.60	.25	.08
□ 138	Del Unser	.50	.23	.06
□ 139	Horacio Pina	.50	.23	.06
□ 140	Steve Garvey	7.00	3.10	.85
□ 141	Mickey Stanley	.60	.25	.08
□ 142	Bob Reynolds	.50	.23	.06
□ 143	Cliff Johnson	.60	.25	.08
□ 144	Jim Wohlford	.50	.23	.06
□ 145	Ken Holtzman	.60	.25	.08
□ 146	Padres: Team/Mgr.	1.50	.65	.19
	John McNamara			
	(Checklist back)			
□ 147	Pedro Garcia	.50	.23	.06
□ 148	Jim Rooker	.50	.23	.06
□ 149	Tim Foli	.50	.23	.06
□ 150	Bob Gibson	6.00	2.70	.75
□ 151	Steve Brye	.50	.23	.06
□ 152	Mario Guerrero	.50	.23	.06
□ 153	Rick Reuschel	.60	.25	.08
□ 154	Mike Lum	.50	.23	.06
□ 155	Jim Bibby	.50	.23	.06
□ 156	Dave Kingman	1.00	.45	.13
□ 157	Pedro Borbon	.50	.23	.06
□ 158	Jerry Grote	.50	.23	.06
□ 159	Steve Arlin	.50	.23	.06
□ 160	Graig Nettles	1.50	.65	.19
□ 161	Stan Bahnsen	.50	.23	.06
□ 162	Willie Montanez	.50	.23	.06
□ 163	Jim Brewer	.50	.23	.06
□ 164	Mickey Rivers	.60	.25	.08
□ 165	Doug Rader	.60	.25	.08
□ 166	Woodie Fryman	.50	.23	.06
□ 167	Rich Coggins	.50	.23	.06
□ 168	Bill Greif	.50	.23	.06
□ 169	Cookie Rojas	.60	.25	.08
□ 170	Bert Campaneris	.60	.25	.08
□ 171	Ed Kirkpatrick	.50	.23	.06
□ 172	Red Sox: Team/Mgr.	1.50	.65	.19
	Darrell Johnson			
	(Checklist back)			
□ 173	Steve Rogers	.60	.25	.08
□ 174	Bake McBride	.60	.25	.08
□ 175	Don Money	.60	.25	.08
□ 176	Burt Hooton	.60	.25	.08
□ 177	Vic Correll	.50	.23	.06
□ 178	Cesar Tovar	.50	.23	.06
□ 179	Tom Bradley	.50	.23	.06
□ 180	Joe Morgan	7.50	3.40	.95
□ 181	Fred Beene	.50	.23	.06
□ 182	Don Hahn	.50	.23	.06
□ 183	Mel Stottlemyre	.60	.25	.08
□ 184	Jorge Orta	.50	.23	.06

□ 185	Steve Carlton	10.00	4.50	1.25
□ 186	Willie Crawford	.50	.23	.06
□ 187	Denny Doyle	.50	.23	.06
□ 188	Tom Griffin	.50	.23	.06
□ 189	1951 MVP's	2.50	1.15	.30
	Larry (Yogi) Berra			
	Roy Campanella			
	(Campy never issued)			
□ 190	1952 MVP's	1.00	.45	.13
	Bobby Shantz			
	Hank Sauer			
□ 191	1953 MVP's	1.25	.55	.16
	Al Rosen			
	Roy Campanella			
□ 192	1954 MVP's	2.50	1.15	.30
	Yogi Berra			
	Willie Mays			
□ 193	1955 MVP's	2.50	1.15	.30
	Yogi Berra			
	Roy Campanella			
	(Campy card never			
	issued, pictured			
	with LA cap, sic)			
□ 194	1956 MVP's	7.00	3.10	.85
	Mickey Mantle			
	Don Newcombe			
□ 195	1957 MVP's	11.00	4.90	1.40
	Mickey Mantle			
	Hank Aaron			
□ 196	1958 MVP's	1.00	.45	.13
	Jackie Jensen			
	Ernie Banks			
□ 197	1959 MVP's	1.25	.55	.16
	Nellie Fox			
	Ernie Banks			
□ 198	1960 MVP's	1.00	.45	.13
	Roger Maris			
	Dick Groat			
□ 199	1961 MVP's	1.25	.55	.30
	Roger Maris			
	Frank Robinson			
□ 200	1962 MVP's	7.00	3.10	.85
	Mickey Mantle			
	Maury Wills			
	(Wills never issued)			
□ 201	1963 MVP's	1.25	.55	.16
	Elston Howard			
	Sandy Koufax			
□ 202	1964 MVP's	1.25	.55	.16
	Brooks Robinson			
	Ken Boyer			
□ 203	1965 MVP's	1.25	.55	.16
	Zoilo Versalles			
	Willie Mays			
□ 204	1966 MVP's	2.50	1.15	.30
	Frank Robinson			
	Bob Clemente			

☐ 205	1967 MVP's..............1.50	.65	.19
	Carl Yastrzemski		
	Orlando Cepeda		
☐ 206	1968 MVP's..............1.50	.65	.19
	Denny McLain		
	Bob Gibson		
☐ 207	1969 MVP's..............1.50	.65	.19
	Harmon Killebrew		
	Willie McCovey		
☐ 208	1970 MVP's..............1.25	.55	.16
	Boog Powell		
	Johnny Bench		
☐ 209	1971 MVP's..............1.00	.45	.13
	Vida Blue		
	Joe Torre		
☐ 210	1972 MVP's..............1.25	.55	.16
	Rich Allen		
	Johnny Bench		
☐ 211	1973 MVP's..............6.00	2.70	.75
	Reggie Jackson		
	Pete Rose		
☐ 212	1974 MVP's..............1.00	.45	.13
	Jeff Burroughs		
	Steve Garvey		
☐ 213	Oscar Gamble 60	.25	.08
☐ 214	Harry Parker 50	.23	.06
☐ 215	Bobby Valentine 60	.25	.08
☐ 216	Giants: Team/Mgr...1.50	.65	.19
	Wes Westrum		
	(Checklist back)		
☐ 217	Lou Piniella 1.00	.45	.13
☐ 218	Jerry Johnson 50	.23	.06
☐ 219	Ed Herrmann 50	.23	.06
☐ 220	Don Sutton 4.00	1.80	.50
☐ 221	Aurelio Rodriguez 50	.23	.06
☐ 222	Dan Spillner 50	.23	.06
☐ 223	Robin Yount 225.00	100.00	28.00
☐ 224	Ramon Hernandez 50	.23	.06
☐ 225	Bob Grich 75	.35	.09
☐ 226	Bill Campbell 50	.23	.06
☐ 227	Bob Watson 60	.25	.08
☐ 228	George Brett 225.00	100.00	28.00
☐ 229	Barry Foote 50	.23	.06
☐ 230	Jim Hunter 4.00	1.80	.50
☐ 231	Mike Tyson 50	.23	.06
☐ 232	Diego Segui 50	.23	.06
☐ 233	Billy Grabarkewitz 50	.23	.06
☐ 234	Tom Grieve 60	.25	.08
☐ 235	Jack Billingham 50	.23	.06
☐ 236	Angels: Team/Mgr...1.50	.65	.19
	Dick Williams		
	(Checklist back)		
☐ 237	Carl Morton 50	.23	.06
☐ 238	Dave Duncan 50	.23	.06
☐ 239	George Stone 50	.23	.06
☐ 240	Garry Maddox 60	.25	.08
☐ 241	Dick Tidrow 50	.23	.06

☐ 242	Jay Johnstone 60	.25	.08
☐ 243	Jim Kaat 1.25	.55	.16
☐ 244	Bill Buckner 1.00	.45	.13
☐ 245	Mickey Lolich 75	.35	.09
☐ 246	Cardinals: Team/Mgr...1.50	.65	.19
	Red Schoendienst		
	(Checklist back)		
☐ 247	Enos Cabell 50	.23	.06
☐ 248	Randy Jones 60	.25	.08
☐ 249	Danny Thompson 50	.23	.06
☐ 250	Ken Brett 50	.23	.06
☐ 251	Fran Healy 50	.23	.06
☐ 252	Fred Scherman 50	.23	.06
☐ 253	Jesus Alou 50	.23	.06
☐ 254	Mike Torrez 60	.25	.08
☐ 255	Dwight Evans 6.50	2.90	.80
☐ 256	Billy Champion 50	.23	.06
☐ 257	Checklist: 133-264 ....2.00	.20	.06
☐ 258	Dave LaRoche 50	.23	.06
☐ 259	Len Randle 50	.23	.06
☐ 260	Johnny Bench 15.00	6.75	1.90
☐ 261	Andy Hassler 50	.23	.06
☐ 262	Rowland Office 50	.23	.06
☐ 263	Jim Perry 60	.25	.08
☐ 264	John Milner 50	.23	.06
☐ 265	Ron Bryant 50	.23	.06
☐ 266	Sandy Alomar 60	.25	.08
☐ 267	Dick Ruthven 50	.23	.06
☐ 268	Hal McRae 75	.35	.09
☐ 269	Doug Rau 50	.23	.06
☐ 270	Ron Fairly 50	.23	.06
☐ 271	Gerry Moses 50	.23	.06
☐ 272	Lynn McGlothen 50	.23	.06
☐ 273	Steve Braun 50	.23	.06
☐ 274	Vicente Romo 50	.23	.06
☐ 275	Paul Blair 60	.25	.08
☐ 276	White Sox Team/Mgr...1.50	.65	.19
	Chuck Tanner		
	(Checklist back)		
☐ 277	Frank Taveras 50	.23	.06
☐ 278	Paul Lindblad 50	.23	.06
☐ 279	Milt May 50	.23	.06
☐ 280	Carl Yastrzemski 10.00	4.50	1.25
☐ 281	Jim Slaton 50	.23	.06
☐ 282	Jerry Morales 50	.23	.06
☐ 283	Steve Foucault 50	.23	.06
☐ 284	Ken Griffey 4.00	1.80	.50
☐ 285	Ellie Rodriguez 50	.23	.06
☐ 286	Mike Jorgensen 50	.23	.06
☐ 287	Roric Harrison 50	.23	.06
☐ 288	Bruce Ellingsen 50	.23	.06
☐ 289	Ken Rudolph 50	.23	.06
☐ 290	Jon Matlack 50	.23	.06
☐ 291	Bill Sudakis 50	.23	.06
☐ 292	Ron Schueler 50	.23	.06
☐ 293	Dick Sharon 50	.23	.06
☐ 294	Geoff Zahn 50	.23	.06

☐	295	Vada Pinson	.75	.35 .09
☐	296	Alan Foster	.50	.23 .06
☐	297	Craig Kusick	.50	.23 .06
☐	298	Johnny Grubb	.50	.23 .06
☐	299	Bucky Dent	.75	.35 .09
☐	300	Reggie Jackson	28.00	12.50 3.50
☐	301	Dave Roberts	.50	.23 .06
☐	302	Rick Burleson	.75	.35 .09
☐	303	Grant Jackson	.50	.23 .06
☐	304	Pirates: Team/Mgr.	1.50	.65 .19
		Danny Murtaugh		
		(Checklist back)		
☐	305	Jim Colborn	.50	.23 .06
☐	306	Batting Leaders	1.25	.55 .16
		Rod Carew		
		Ralph Garr		
☐	307	Home Run Leaders	3.00	1.35 .40
		Dick Allen		
		Mike Schmidt		
☐	308	RBI Leaders	1.50	.65 .19
		Jeff Burroughs		
		Johnny Bench		
☐	309	Stolen Base Leaders	1.50	.65 .19
		Bill North		
		Lou Brock		
☐	310	Victory Leaders	1.25	.55 .16
		Jim Hunter		
		Fergie Jenkins		
		Andy Messersmith		
		Phil Niekro		
☐	311	ERA Leaders	1.25	.55 .16
		Jim Hunter		
		Buzz Capra		
☐	312	Strikeout Leaders	12.00	5.50 1.50
		Nolan Ryan		
		Steve Carlton		
☐	313	Leading Firemen	1.00	.45 .13
		Terry Forster		
		Mike Marshall		
☐	314	Buck Martinez	.50	.23 .06
☐	315	Don Kessinger	.60	.25 .08
☐	316	Jackie Brown	.50	.23 .06
☐	317	Joe Lahoud	.50	.23 .06
☐	318	Ernie McAnally	.50	.23 .06
☐	319	Johnny Oates	.60	.25 .08
☐	320	Pete Rose	15.00	6.75 1.90
☐	321	Rudy May	.50	.23 .06
☐	322	Ed Goodson	.50	.23 .06
☐	323	Fred Holdsworth	.50	.23 .06
☐	324	Ed Kranepool	.50	.23 .06
☐	325	Tony Oliva	1.25	.55 .16
☐	326	Wayne Twitchell	.50	.23 .06
☐	327	Jerry Hairston	.50	.23 .06
☐	328	Sonny Siebert	.50	.23 .06
☐	329	Ted Kubiak	.50	.23 .06
☐	330	Mike Marshall	.60	.25 .08
☐	331	Indians: Team/Mgr.	1.50	.65 .19
		Frank Robinson		
		(Checklist back)		
☐	332	Fred Kendall	.50	.23 .06
☐	333	Dick Drago	.50	.23 .06
☐	334	Greg Gross	.50	.23 .06
☐	335	Jim Palmer	10.00	4.50 1.25
☐	336	Rennie Stennett	.50	.23 .06
☐	337	Kevin Kobel	.50	.23 .06
☐	338	Rich Stelmaszek	.50	.23 .06
☐	339	Jim Fregosi	.60	.25 .08
☐	340	Paul Splittorff	.50	.23 .06
☐	341	Hal Breeden	.50	.23 .06
☐	342	Leroy Stanton	.50	.23 .06
☐	343	Danny Frisella	.50	.23 .06
☐	344	Ben Oglivie	.60	.25 .08
☐	345	Clay Carroll	.50	.23 .06
☐	346	Bobby Darwin	.50	.23 .06
☐	347	Mike Caldwell	.50	.23 .06
☐	348	Tony Muser	.50	.23 .06
☐	349	Ray Sadecki	.50	.23 .06
☐	350	Bobby Murcer	.75	.35 .09
☐	351	Bob Boone	1.50	.65 .19
☐	352	Darold Knowles	.50	.23 .06
☐	353	Luis Melendez	.50	.23 .06
☐	354	Dick Bosman	.50	.23 .06
☐	355	Chris Cannizzaro	.50	.23 .06
☐	356	Rico Petrocelli	.60	.25 .08
☐	357	Ken Forsch	.50	.23 .06
☐	358	Al Bumbry	.50	.23 .06
☐	359	Paul Popovich	.50	.23 .06
☐	360	George Scott	.60	.25 .08
☐	361	Dodgers: Team/Mgr.	1.50	.65 .19
		Walter Alston		
		(Checklist back)		
☐	362	Steve Hargan	.50	.23 .06
☐	363	Carmen Fanzone	.50	.23 .06
☐	364	Doug Bird	.50	.23 .06
☐	365	Bob Bailey	.50	.23 .06
☐	366	Ken Sanders	.50	.23 .06
☐	367	Craig Robinson	.50	.23 .06
☐	368	Vic Albury	.50	.23 .06
☐	369	Merv Rettenmund	.50	.23 .06
☐	370	Tom Seaver	20.00	9.00 2.50
☐	371	Gates Brown	.50	.23 .06
☐	372	John D'Acquisto	.50	.23 .06
☐	373	Bill Sharp	.50	.23 .06
☐	374	Eddie Watt	.50	.23 .06
☐	375	Roy White	.60	.25 .08
☐	376	Steve Yeager	.60	.25 .08
☐	377	Tom Hilgendorf	.50	.23 .06
☐	378	Derrel Thomas	.50	.23 .06
☐	379	Bernie Carbo	.50	.23 .06
☐	380	Sal Bando	.60	.25 .08
☐	381	John Curtis	.50	.23 .06
☐	382	Don Baylor	2.00	.90 .25
☐	383	Jim York	.50	.23 .06
☐	384	Brewers: Team/Mgr.	1.50	.65 .19

Del Crandall
(Checklist back)

☐ 385	Dock Ellis	.50	.23	.06
☐ 386	Checklist: 265-396	2.00	.20	.06
☐ 387	Jim Spencer	.50	.23	.06
☐ 388	Steve Stone	.60	.25	.08
☐ 389	Tony Solaita	.50	.23	.06
☐ 390	Ron Cey	1.00	.45	.13
☐ 391	Don DeMola	.50	.23	.06
☐ 392	Bruce Bochte	.50	.23	.06
☐ 393	Gary Gentry	.50	.23	.06
☐ 394	Larvell Blanks	.50	.23	.06
☐ 395	Bud Harrelson	.60	.25	.08
☐ 396	Fred Norman	.50	.23	.06
☐ 397	Bill Freehan	.60	.25	.08
☐ 398	Elias Sosa	.50	.23	.06
☐ 399	Terry Harmon	.50	.23	.06
☐ 400	Dick Allen	1.00	.45	.13
☐ 401	Mike Wallace	.50	.23	.06
☐ 402	Bob Tolan	.50	.23	.06
☐ 403	Tom Buskey	.50	.23	.06
☐ 404	Ted Sizemore	.50	.23	.06
☐ 405	John Montague	.50	.23	.06
☐ 406	Bob Gallagher	.50	.23	.06
☐ 407	Herb Washington	.50	.23	.06
☐ 408	Clyde Wright	.50	.23	.06
☐ 409	Bob Robertson	.50	.23	.06
☐ 410	Mike Cueller UER	.60	.25	.08
	(Sic, Cuellar)			
☐ 411	George Mitterwald	.50	.23	.06
☐ 412	Bill Hands	.50	.23	.06
☐ 413	Marty Pattin	.50	.23	.06
☐ 414	Manny Mota	.60	.25	.08
☐ 415	John Hiller	.60	.25	.08
☐ 416	Larry Lintz	.50	.23	.06
☐ 417	Skip Lockwood	.50	.23	.06
☐ 418	Leo Foster	.50	.23	.06
☐ 419	Dave Goltz	.50	.23	.06
☐ 420	Larry Bowa	.75	.35	.09
☐ 421	Mets: Team/Mgr.	1.50	.65	.19
	Yogi Berra			
	(Checklist back)			
☐ 422	Brian Downing	1.50	.65	.19
☐ 423	Clay Kirby	.50	.23	.06
☐ 424	John Lowenstein	.50	.23	.06
☐ 425	Tito Fuentes	.50	.23	.06
☐ 426	George Medich	.50	.23	.06
☐ 427	Clarence Gaston	.60	.25	.08
☐ 428	Dave Hamilton	.50	.23	.06
☐ 429	Jim Dwyer	.50	.23	.06
☐ 430	Luis Tiant	.75	.35	.09
☐ 431	Rod Gilbreath	.50	.23	.06
☐ 432	Ken Berry	.50	.23	.06
☐ 433	Larry Demery	.50	.23	.06
☐ 434	Bob Locker	.50	.23	.06
☐ 435	Dave Nelson	.50	.23	.06
☐ 436	Ken Frailing	.50	.23	.06
☐ 437	Al Cowens	.60	.25	.08
☐ 438	Don Carrithers	.50	.23	.06
☐ 439	Ed Brinkman	.50	.23	.06
☐ 440	Andy Messersmith	.60	.25	.08
☐ 441	Bobby Heise	.50	.23	.06
☐ 442	Maximino Leon	.50	.23	.06
☐ 443	Twins: Team/Mgr.	1.50	.65	.19
	Frank Quilici			
	(Checklist back)			
☐ 444	Gene Garber	.60	.25	.08
☐ 445	Felix Millan	.50	.23	.06
☐ 446	Bart Johnson	.50	.23	.06
☐ 447	Terry Crowley	.50	.23	.06
☐ 448	Frank Duffy	.50	.23	.06
☐ 449	Charlie Williams	.50	.23	.06
☐ 450	Willie McCovey	5.00	2.30	.60
☐ 451	Rick Dempsey	.75	.35	.09
☐ 452	Angel Mangual	.50	.23	.06
☐ 453	Claude Osteen	.60	.25	.08
☐ 454	Doug Griffin	.50	.23	.06
☐ 455	Don Wilson	.50	.23	.06
☐ 456	Bob Coluccio	.50	.23	.06
☐ 457	Mario Mendoza	.50	.23	.06
☐ 458	Ross Grimsley	.50	.23	.06
☐ 459	1974 AL Champs	1.00	.45	.13
	A's over Orioles			
	(Second base action			
	pictured)			
☐ 460	1974 NL Champs	1.25	.55	.16
	Dodgers over Pirates			
	(Frank Taveras and			
	Steve Garvey at second)			
☐ 461	World Series Game 1	3.50	1.55	.45
	(Reggie Jackson)			
☐ 462	World Series Game 2	1.00	.45	.13
	(Dodger dugout)			
☐ 463	World Series Game 3	1.25	.55	.16
	(Rollie Fingers			
	pitching)			
☐ 464	World Series Game 4	1.00	.45	.13
	(A's batter)			
☐ 465	World Series Game 5	1.00	.45	.13
	(Joe Rudi rounding			
	third)			
☐ 466	World Series Summary	1.25	.55	.16
	A's do it again;			
	win third straight			
	(A's group picture)			
☐ 467	Ed Halicki	.50	.23	.06
☐ 468	Bobby Mitchell	.50	.23	.06
☐ 469	Tom Dettore	.50	.23	.06
☐ 470	Jeff Burroughs	.60	.25	.08
☐ 471	Bob Stinson	.50	.23	.06
☐ 472	Bruce Dal Canton	.50	.23	.06
☐ 473	Ken McMullen	.50	.23	.06
☐ 474	Luke Walker	.50	.23	.06
☐ 475	Darrell Evans	.75	.35	.09

☐ 476	Ed Figueroa	.50	.23	.06
☐ 477	Tom Hutton	.50	.23	.06
☐ 478	Tom Burgmeier	.50	.23	.06
☐ 479	Ken Boswell	.50	.23	.06
☐ 480	Carlos May	.50	.23	.06
☐ 481	Will McEnaney	.50	.23	.06
☐ 482	Tom McCraw	.50	.23	.06
☐ 483	Steve Ontiveros	.50	.23	.06
☐ 484	Glenn Beckert	.60	.25	.08
☐ 485	Sparky Lyle	.75	.35	.09
☐ 486	Ray Fosse	.50	.23	.06
☐ 487	Astros: Team/Mgr.	1.50	.65	.19
	Preston Gomez			
	(Checklist back)			
☐ 488	Bill Travers	.50	.23	.06
☐ 489	Cecil Cooper	1.25	.55	.16
☐ 490	Reggie Smith	.75	.35	.09
☐ 491	Doyle Alexander	.60	.25	.08
☐ 492	Rich Hebner	.60	.25	.08
☐ 493	Don Stanhouse	.50	.23	.06
☐ 494	Pete LaCock	.50	.23	.06
☐ 495	Nelson Briles	.60	.25	.08
☐ 496	Pepe Frias	.50	.23	.06
☐ 497	Jim Nettles	.50	.23	.06
☐ 498	Al Downing	.50	.23	.06
☐ 499	Marty Perez	.50	.23	.06
☐ 500	Nolan Ryan	75.00	34.00	9.50
☐ 501	Bill Robinson	.60	.25	.08
☐ 502	Pat Bourque	.50	.23	.06
☐ 503	Fred Stanley	.50	.23	.06
☐ 504	Buddy Bradford	.50	.23	.06
☐ 505	Chris Speier	.50	.23	.06
☐ 506	Leron Lee	.50	.23	.06
☐ 507	Tom Carroll	.50	.23	.06
☐ 508	Bob Hansen	.50	.23	.06
☐ 509	Dave Hilton	.50	.23	.06
☐ 510	Vida Blue	.75	.35	.09
☐ 511	Rangers: Team/Mgr.	1.50	.65	.19
	Billy Martin			
	(Checklist back)			
☐ 512	Larry Milbourne	.50	.23	.06
☐ 513	Dick Pole	.50	.23	.06
☐ 514	Jose Cruz	.75	.35	.09
☐ 515	Manny Sanguillen	.60	.25	.08
☐ 516	Don Hood	.50	.23	.06
☐ 517	Checklist: 397-528	2.00	.20	.06
☐ 518	Leo Cardenas	.50	.23	.06
☐ 519	Jim Todd	.50	.23	.06
☐ 520	Amos Otis	.60	.25	.08
☐ 521	Dennis Blair	.50	.23	.06
☐ 522	Gary Sutherland	.50	.23	.06
☐ 523	Tom Paciorek	.60	.25	.08
☐ 524	John Doherty	.50	.23	.06
☐ 525	Tom House	.50	.23	.06
☐ 526	Larry Hisle	.60	.25	.08
☐ 527	Mac Scarce	.50	.23	.06
☐ 528	Eddie Leon	.50	.23	.06
☐ 529	Gary Thomasson	.50	.23	.06
☐ 530	Gaylord Perry	4.00	1.80	.50
☐ 531	Reds: Team/Mgr.	2.50	1.15	.30
	Sparky Anderson			
	(Checklist back)			
☐ 532	Gorman Thomas	.75	.35	.09
☐ 533	Rudy Meoli	.50	.23	.06
☐ 534	Alex Johnson	.50	.23	.06
☐ 535	Gene Tenace	.60	.25	.08
☐ 536	Bob Moose	.50	.23	.06
☐ 537	Tommy Harper	.60	.25	.08
☐ 538	Duffy Dyer	.50	.23	.06
☐ 539	Jesse Jefferson	.50	.23	.06
☐ 540	Lou Brock	5.00	2.30	.60
☐ 541	Roger Metzger	.50	.23	.06
☐ 542	Pete Broberg	.50	.23	.06
☐ 543	Larry Biittner	.50	.23	.06
☐ 544	Steve Mingori	.50	.23	.06
☐ 545	Billy Williams	4.00	1.80	.50
☐ 546	John Knox	.50	.23	.06
☐ 547	Von Joshua	.50	.23	.06
☐ 548	Charlie Sands	.50	.23	.06
☐ 549	Bill Butler	.50	.23	.06
☐ 550	Ralph Garr	.60	.25	.08
☐ 551	Larry Christenson	.50	.23	.06
☐ 552	Jack Brohamer	.50	.23	.06
☐ 553	John Boccabella	.50	.23	.06
☐ 554	Rich Gossage	3.00	1.35	.40
☐ 555	Al Oliver	1.00	.45	.13
☐ 556	Tim Johnson	.50	.23	.06
☐ 557	Larry Gura	.50	.23	.06
☐ 558	Dave Roberts	.50	.23	.06
☐ 559	Bob Montgomery	.50	.23	.06
☐ 560	Tony Perez	4.00	1.80	.50
☐ 561	A's: Team/Mgr.	1.50	.65	.19
	Alvin Dark			
	(Checklist back)			
☐ 562	Gary Nolan	.60	.25	.08
☐ 563	Wilbur Howard	.50	.23	.06
☐ 564	Tommy Davis	.60	.25	.08
☐ 565	Joe Torre	1.00	.45	.13
☐ 566	Ray Burris	.50	.23	.06
☐ 567	Jim Sundberg	1.00	.45	.13
☐ 568	Dale Murray	.50	.23	.06
☐ 569	Frank White	1.00	.45	.13
☐ 570	Jim Wynn	.60	.25	.08
☐ 571	Dave Lemanczyk	.50	.23	.06
☐ 572	Roger Nelson	.50	.23	.06
☐ 573	Orlando Pena	.50	.23	.06
☐ 574	Tony Taylor	.50	.23	.06
☐ 575	Gene Clines	.50	.23	.06
☐ 576	Phil Roof	.50	.23	.06
☐ 577	John Morris	.50	.23	.06
☐ 578	Dave Tomlin	.50	.23	.06
☐ 579	Skip Pitlock	.50	.23	.06
☐ 580	Frank Robinson	5.00	2.30	.60
☐ 581	Darrel Chaney	.50	.23	.06

☐ 582	Eduardo Rodriguez 50	.23	.06
☐ 583	Andy Etchebarren 50	.23	.06
☐ 584	Mike Garman 50	.23	.06
☐ 585	Chris Chambliss 60	.25	.08
☐ 586	Tim McCarver 80	.35	.10
☐ 587	Chris Ward 50	.23	.06
☐ 588	Rick Auerbach 50	.23	.06
☐ 589	Braves: Team/Mgr. 1.50	.65	.19
	Clyde King		
	(Checklist back)		
☐ 590	Cesar Cedeno 60	.25	.08
☐ 591	Glenn Abbott 50	.23	.06
☐ 592	Balor Moore 50	.23	.06
☐ 593	Gene Lamont 50	.23	.06
☐ 594	Jim Fuller 50	.23	.06
☐ 595	Joe Niekro 60	.25	.08
☐ 596	Ollie Brown 50	.23	.06
☐ 597	Winston Llenas 50	.23	.06
☐ 598	Bruce Kison 50	.23	.06
☐ 599	Nate Colbert 50	.23	.06
☐ 600	Rod Carew 12.00	5.50	1.50
☐ 601	Juan Beniquez 50	.23	.06
☐ 602	John Vukovich 50	.23	.06
☐ 603	Lew Krausse 50	.23	.06
☐ 604	Oscar Zamora 50	.23	.06
☐ 605	John Ellis 50	.23	.06
☐ 606	Bruce Miller 50	.23	.06
☐ 607	Jim Holt 50	.23	.06
☐ 608	Gene Michael 60	.25	.08
☐ 609	Elrod Hendricks 50	.23	.06
☐ 610	Ron Hunt 50	.23	.06
☐ 611	Yankees: Team/Mgr. 1.50	.65	.19
	Bill Virdon		
	(Checklist back)		
☐ 612	Terry Hughes 50	.23	.06
☐ 613	Bill Parsons 50	.23	.06
☐ 614	Rookie Pitchers 65	.30	.08
	Jack Kucek		
	Dyar Miller		
	Vern Ruhle		
	Paul Siebert		
☐ 615	Rookie Pitchers 1.00	.45	.13
	Pat Darcy		
	Dennis Leonard		
	Tom Underwood		
	Hank Webb		
☐ 616	Rookie Outfielders 24.00	11.00	3.00
	Dave Augustine		
	Pepe Mangual		
	Jim Rice		
	John Scott		
☐ 617	Rookie Infielders 2.50	1.15	.30
	Mike Cubbage		
	Doug DeCinces		
	Reggie Sanders		
	Manny Trillo		
☐ 618	Rookie Pitchers 1.25	.55	.16

	Jamie Easterly		
	Tom Johnson		
	Scott McGregor		
	Rick Rhoden		
☐ 619	Rookie Outfielders 65	.30	.08
	Benny Ayala		
	Nyls Nyman		
	Tommy Smith		
	Jerry Turner		
☐ 620	Rookie Catcher/OF 50.00	23.00	6.25
	Gary Carter		
	Marc Hill		
	Danny Meyer		
	Leon Roberts		
☐ 621	Rookie Pitchers 1.00	.45	.13
	John Denny		
	Rawly Eastwick		
	Jim Kern		
	Juan Veintidos		
☐ 622	Rookie Outfielders 12.00	5.50	1.50
	Ed Armbrister		
	Fred Lynn		
	Tom Poquette		
	Terry Whitfield UER		
	(Listed as Ney York)		
☐ 623	Rookie Infielders 20.00	9.00	2.50
	Phil Garner		
	Keith Hernandez UER		
	(Sic, bats right)		
	Bob Sheldon		
	Tom Veryzer		
☐ 624	Rookie Pitchers 65	.30	.08
	Doug Konieczny		
	Gary Lavelle		
	Jim Otten		
	Eddie Solomon		
☐ 625	Boog Powell 1.00	.45	.13
☐ 626	Larry Haney UER 50	.23	.06
	(Photo actually		
	Dave Duncan)		
☐ 627	Tom Walker 50	.23	.06
☐ 628	Ron LeFlore 75	.35	.09
☐ 629	Joe Hoerner 50	.23	.06
☐ 630	Greg Luzinski 75	.35	.09
☐ 631	Lee Lacy 50	.23	.06
☐ 632	Morris Nettles 50	.23	.06
☐ 633	Paul Casanova 50	.23	.06
☐ 634	Cy Acosta 50	.23	.06
☐ 635	Chuck Dobson 50	.23	.06
☐ 636	Charlie Moore 50	.23	.06
☐ 637	Ted Martinez 50	.23	.06
☐ 638	Cubs: Team/Mgr. 1.50	.65	.19
	Jim Marshall		
	(Checklist back)		
☐ 639	Steve Kline 50	.23	.06
☐ 640	Harmon Killebrew 5.00	2.30	.60
☐ 641	Jim Northrup 50	.23	.06

☐	642 Mike Phillips 50	.23	.06
☐	643 Brent Strom 50	.23	.06
☐	644 Bill Fahey 50	.23	.06
☐	645 Danny Cater 50	.23	.06
☐	646 Checklist: 529-660 .....2.00	.20	.06
☐	647 Claudell Washington 90	.40	.11
☐	648 Dave Pagan 50	.23	.06
☐	649 Jack Heidemann 50	.23	.06
☐	650 Dave May 50	.23	.06
☐	651 John Morlan 50	.23	.06
☐	652 Lindy McDaniel 60	.25	.08
☐	653 Lee Richard UER 50	.23	.06
	(Listed as Richards		
	on card front)		
☐	654 Jerry Terrell 50	.23	.06
☐	655 Rico Carty 60	.25	.08
☐	656 Bill Plummer 50	.23	.06
☐	657 Bob Oliver 50	.23	.06
☐	658 Vic Harris 50	.23	.06
☐	659 Bob Apodaca 50	.23	.06
☐	660 Hank Aaron 30.00	7.50	2.40

1976 Topps

The 1976 Topps set of 660 cards (measuring 2 1/2" by 3 1/2") is known for its sharp color photographs and interesting presentation of subjects. Team cards feature a checklist back for players on that team and show a small inset photo of the manager on the front. A "Father and Son" series (66-70) spotlights five Major Leaguers whose fathers also made the "Big Show." Other subseries include "All Time All Stars" (341-350), "Record Breakers" from the previous season (1-6), League Leaders (191-205), Post-season cards (461-462), and Rookie Prospects (589-599). The fol-

lowing players' regular issue cards are explicitly denoted as All-Stars, 10, 48, 60, 140, 150, 165, 169, 240, 300, 370, 380, 395, 400, 420, 475, 500, 580, and 650. The key rookies in this set are Dennis Eckersley, Ron Guidry, and Willie Randolph.

	NRMT-MT	EXC	G-VG
COMPLETE SET (660) 475.00		210.00	60.00
COMMON PLAYER (1-660) 30		.14	.04
☐ 1 RB: Hank Aaron 15.00		6.75	1.90
Most RBI's, 2262			
☐ 2 RB: Bobby Bonds 75		.35	.09
Most leadoff HR's 32;			
plus three seasons			
30 homers/30 steals			
☐ 3 RB: Mickey Lolich 50		.23	.06
Lefthander, Most			
Strikeouts, 2679			
☐ 4 RB: Dave Lopes 50		.23	.06
Most Consecutive			
SB attempts, 38			
☐ 5 RB: Tom Seaver 3.50		1.55	.45
Most Cons. seasons			
with 200 SO's, 8			
☐ 6 RB: Rennie Stennett 50		.23	.06
Most Hits in a 9			
inning game, 7			
☐ 7 Jim Umbarger 30		.14	.04
☐ 8 Tito Fuentes 30		.14	.04
☐ 9 Paul Lindblad 30		.14	.04
☐ 10 Lou Brock 5.00		2.30	.60
☐ 11 Jim Hughes 30		.14	.04
☐ 12 Richie Zisk 40		.18	.05
☐ 13 John Wockenfuss 30		.14	.04
☐ 14 Gene Garber 30		.14	.04
☐ 15 George Scott 40		.18	.05
☐ 16 Bob Apodaca 30		.14	.04
☐ 17 New York Yankees ...1.25		.55	.16
Team Card;			
Billy Martin MG			
(Checklist back)			
☐ 18 Dale Murray 30		.14	.04
☐ 19 George Brett 60.00		27.00	7.50
☐ 20 Bob Watson 40		.18	.05
☐ 21 Dave LaRoche 30		.14	.04
☐ 22 Bill Russell 40		.18	.05
☐ 23 Brian Downing 1.00		.45	.13
☐ 24 Cesar Geronimo 30		.14	.04
☐ 25 Mike Torrez 40		.18	.05
☐ 26 Andre Thornton 40		.18	.05
☐ 27 Ed Figueroa 30		.14	.04
☐ 28 Dusty Baker 60		.25	.08
☐ 29 Rick Burleson 40		.18	.05
☐ 30 John Montefusco 40		.18	.05

☐ 31 Len Randle	.30	.14	.04
☐ 32 Danny Frisella	.30	.14	.04
☐ 33 Bill North	.30	.14	.04
☐ 34 Mike Garman	.30	.14	.04
☐ 35 Tony Oliva	1.00	.45	.13
☐ 36 Frank Taveras	.30	.14	.04
☐ 37 John Hiller	.40	.18	.05
☐ 38 Garry Maddox	.40	.18	.05
☐ 39 Pete Broberg	.30	.14	.04
☐ 40 Dave Kingman	1.00	.45	.13
☐ 41 Tippy Martinez	.40	.18	.05
☐ 42 Barry Foote	.30	.14	.04
☐ 43 Paul Splittorff	.30	.14	.04
☐ 44 Doug Rader	.40	.18	.05
☐ 45 Boog Powell	.75	.35	.09
☐ 46 Los Angeles Dodgers	1.25	.55	.16
Team Card;			
Walter Alston MG			
(Checklist back)			
☐ 47 Jesse Jefferson	.30	.14	.04
☐ 48 Dave Concepcion	1.50	.65	.19
☐ 49 Dave Duncan	.30	.14	.04
☐ 50 Fred Lynn	1.50	.65	.19
☐ 51 Ray Burris	.30	.14	.04
☐ 52 Dave Chalk	.30	.14	.04
☐ 53 Mike Beard	.30	.14	.04
☐ 54 Dave Rader	.30	.14	.04
☐ 55 Gaylord Perry	3.50	1.55	.45
☐ 56 Bob Tolan	.30	.14	.04
☐ 57 Phil Garner	1.00	.45	.13
☐ 58 Ron Reed	.30	.14	.04
☐ 59 Larry Hisle	.40	.18	.05
☐ 60 Jerry Reuss	.40	.18	.05
☐ 61 Ron LeFlore	.40	.18	.05
☐ 62 Johnny Oates	.40	.18	.05
☐ 63 Bobby Darwin	.30	.14	.04
☐ 64 Jerry Koosman	.50	.23	.06
☐ 65 Chris Chambliss	.40	.18	.05
☐ 66 Father and Son	.50	.23	.06
Gus Bell			
Buddy Bell			
☐ 67 Father and Son	.75	.35	.09
Ray Boone			
Bob Boone			
☐ 68 Father and Son	.50	.23	.06
Joe Coleman			
Joe Coleman Jr.			
☐ 69 Father and Son	.50	.23	.06
Jim Hegan			
Mike Hegan			
☐ 70 Father and Son	.50	.23	.06
Roy Smalley			
Roy Smalley Jr.			
☐ 71 Steve Rogers	.40	.18	.05
☐ 72 Hal McRae	.75	.35	.09
☐ 73 Baltimore Orioles	1.25	.55	.16
Team Card;			

Earl Weaver MG			
(Checklist back)			
☐ 74 Oscar Gamble	.40	.18	.05
☐ 75 Larry Dierker	.30	.14	.04
☐ 76 Willie Crawford	.30	.14	.04
☐ 77 Pedro Borbon	.30	.14	.04
☐ 78 Cecil Cooper	.75	.35	.09
☐ 79 Jerry Morales	.30	.14	.04
☐ 80 Jim Kaat	1.25	.55	.16
☐ 81 Darrell Evans	.50	.23	.06
☐ 82 Von Joshua	.30	.14	.04
☐ 83 Jim Spencer	.30	.14	.04
☐ 84 Brent Strom	.30	.14	.04
☐ 85 Mickey Rivers	.40	.18	.05
☐ 86 Mike Tyson	.30	.14	.04
☐ 87 Tom Burgmeier	.30	.14	.04
☐ 88 Duffy Dyer	.30	.14	.04
☐ 89 Vern Ruhle	.30	.14	.04
☐ 90 Sal Bando	.40	.18	.05
☐ 91 Tom Hutton	.30	.14	.04
☐ 92 Eduardo Rodriguez	.30	.14	.04
☐ 93 Mike Phillips	.30	.14	.04
☐ 94 Jim Dwyer	.30	.14	.04
☐ 95 Brooks Robinson	6.00	2.70	.75
☐ 96 Doug Bird	.30	.14	.04
☐ 97 Wilbur Howard	.30	.14	.04
☐ 98 Dennis Eckersley	65.00	29.00	8.25
☐ 99 Lee Lacy	.30	.14	.04
☐ 100 Jim Hunter	3.50	1.55	.45
☐ 101 Pete LaCock	.30	.14	.04
☐ 102 Jim Willoughby	.30	.14	.04
☐ 103 Biff Pocoroba	.30	.14	.04
☐ 104 Cincinnati Reds	2.00	.90	.25
Team Card;			
Sparky Anderson MG			
(Checklist back)			
☐ 105 Gary Lavelle	.30	.14	.04
☐ 106 Tom Grieve	.40	.18	.05
☐ 107 Dave Roberts	.30	.14	.04
☐ 108 Don Kirkwood	.30	.14	.04
☐ 109 Larry Lintz	.30	.14	.04
☐ 110 Carlos May	.30	.14	.04
☐ 111 Danny Thompson	.30	.14	.04
☐ 112 Kent Tekulve	1.50	.65	.19
☐ 113 Gary Sutherland	.30	.14	.04
☐ 114 Jay Johnstone	.40	.18	.05
☐ 115 Ken Holtzman	.40	.18	.05
☐ 116 Charlie Moore	.30	.14	.04
☐ 117 Mike Jorgensen	.30	.14	.04
☐ 118 Boston Red Sox	1.25	.55	.16
Team Card;			
Darrell Johnson MG			
(Checklist back)			
☐ 119 Checklist 1-132	1.50	.15	.05
☐ 120 Rusty Staub	.75	.35	.09
☐ 121 Tony Solaita	.30	.14	.04
☐ 122 Mike Cosgrove	.30	.14	.04

☐ 123	Walt Williams	30	.14	.04
☐ 124	Doug Rau	30	.14	.04
☐ 125	Don Baylor	1.50	.65	.19
☐ 126	Tom Dettore	30	.14	.04
☐ 127	Larvell Blanks	30	.14	.04
☐ 128	Ken Griffey	2.50	1.15	.30
☐ 129	Andy Etchebarren	30	.14	.04
☐ 130	Luis Tiant	50	.23	.06
☐ 131	Bill Stein	30	.14	.04
☐ 132	Don Hood	30	.14	.04
☐ 133	Gary Matthews	40	.18	.05
☐ 134	Mike Ivie	30	.14	.04
☐ 135	Bake McBride	40	.18	.05
☐ 136	Dave Goltz	30	.14	.04
☐ 137	Bill Robinson	40	.18	.05
☐ 138	Lerrin LaGrow	30	.14	.04
☐ 139	Gorman Thomas	50	.23	.06
☐ 140	Vida Blue	50	.23	.06
☐ 141	Larry Parrish	1.25	.55	.16
☐ 142	Dick Drago	30	.14	.04
☐ 143	Jerry Grote	30	.14	.04
☐ 144	Al Fitzmorris	30	.14	.04
☐ 145	Larry Bowa	75	.35	.09
☐ 146	George Medich	30	.14	.04
☐ 147	Houston Astros	1.25	.55	.16
	Team Card;			
	Bill Virdon MG			
	(Checklist back)			
☐ 148	Stan Thomas	30	.14	.04
☐ 149	Tommy Davis	40	.18	.05
☐ 150	Steve Garvey	5.00	2.30	.60
☐ 151	Bill Bonham	30	.14	.04
☐ 152	Leroy Stanton	30	.14	.04
☐ 153	Buzz Capra	30	.14	.04
☐ 154	Bucky Dent	75	.35	.09
☐ 155	Jack Billingham	30	.14	.04
☐ 156	Rico Carty	40	.18	.05
☐ 157	Mike Caldwell	30	.14	.04
☐ 158	Ken Reitz	30	.14	.04
☐ 159	Jerry Terrell	30	.14	.04
☐ 160	Dave Winfield	27.00	12.00	3.40
☐ 161	Bruce Kison	30	.14	.04
☐ 162	Jack Pierce	30	.14	.04
☐ 163	Jim Slaton	30	.14	.04
☐ 164	Pepe Mangual	30	.14	.04
☐ 165	Gene Tenace	40	.18	.05
☐ 166	Skip Lockwood	30	.14	.04
☐ 167	Freddie Patek	40	.18	.05
☐ 168	Tom Hilgendorf	30	.14	.04
☐ 169	Graig Nettles	1.50	.65	.19
☐ 170	Rick Wise	30	.14	.04
☐ 171	Greg Gross	30	.14	.04
☐ 172	Texas Rangers	1.25	.55	.16
	Team Card;			
	Frank Lucchesi MG			
	(Checklist back)			
☐ 173	Steve Swisher	30	.14	.04
☐ 174	Charlie Hough	40	.18	.05
☐ 175	Ken Singleton	40	.18	.05
☐ 176	Dick Lange	30	.14	.04
☐ 177	Marty Perez	30	.14	.04
☐ 178	Tom Buskey	30	.14	.04
☐ 179	George Foster	1.00	.45	.13
☐ 180	Rich Gossage	2.50	1.15	.30
☐ 181	Willie Montanez	30	.14	.04
☐ 182	Harry Rasmussen	30	.14	.04
☐ 183	Steve Braun	30	.14	.04
☐ 184	Bill Greif	30	.14	.04
☐ 185	Dave Parker	4.00	1.80	.50
☐ 186	Tom Walker	30	.14	.04
☐ 187	Pedro Garcia	30	.14	.04
☐ 188	Fred Scherman	30	.14	.04
☐ 189	Claudell Washington	40	.18	.05
☐ 190	Jon Matlack	30	.14	.04
☐ 191	NL Batting Leaders	75	.35	.09
	Bill Madlock			
	Ted Simmons			
	Manny Sanguillen			
☐ 192	AL Batting Leaders	2.50	1.15	.30
	Rod Carew			
	Fred Lynn			
	Thurman Munson			
☐ 193	NL Home Run Leaders	2.25	1.00	.30
	Mike Schmidt			
	Dave Kingman			
	Greg Luzinski			
☐ 194	AL Home Run Leaders	2.50	1.15	.30
	Reggie Jackson			
	George Scott			
	John Mayberry			
☐ 195	NL RBI Leaders	1.50	.65	.19
	Greg Luzinski			
	Johnny Bench			
	Tony Perez			
☐ 196	AL RBI Leaders	75	.35	.09
	George Scott			
	John Mayberry			
	Fred Lynn			
☐ 197	NL Steals Leaders	1.50	.65	.19
	Dave Lopes			
	Joe Morgan			
	Lou Brock			
☐ 198	AL Steals Leaders	75	.35	.09
	Mickey Rivers			
	Claudell Washington			
	Amos Otis			
☐ 199	NL Victory Leaders	1.25	.55	.16
	Tom Seaver			
	Randy Jones			
	Andy Messersmith			
☐ 200	AL Victory Leaders	1.50	.65	.19
	Jim Hunter			
	Jim Palmer			
	Vida Blue			

☐ 201 NL ERA Leaders............1.25	.55	.16
Randy Jones		
Andy Messersmith		
Tom Seaver		
☐ 202 AL ERA Leaders............4.00	1.80	.50
Jim Palmer		
Jim Hunter		
Dennis Eckersley		
☐ 203 NL Strikeout Leaders ...1.25	.55	.16
Tom Seaver		
John Montefusco		
Andy Messersmith		
☐ 204 AL Strikeout Leaders ...1.00	.45	.13
Frank Tanana		
Bert Blyleven		
Gaylord Perry		
☐ 205 Leading Firemen 75	.35	.09
Al Hrabosky		
Rich Gossage		
☐ 206 Manny Trillo..................30	.14	.04
☐ 207 Andy Hassler................30	.14	.04
☐ 208 Mike Lum.....................30	.14	.04
☐ 209 Alan Ashby..................40	.18	.05
☐ 210 Lee May........................40	.18	.05
☐ 211 Clay Carroll..................30	.14	.04
☐ 212 Pat Kelly.......................30	.14	.04
☐ 213 Dave Heaverlo...............30	.14	.04
☐ 214 Eric Soderholm.............30	.14	.04
☐ 215 Reggie Smith...............50	.23	.06
☐ 216 Montreal Expos............1.25	.55	.16
Team Card;		
Karl Kuehl MG		
(Checklist back)		
☐ 217 Dave Freisleben............30	.14	.04
☐ 218 John Knox....................30	.14	.04
☐ 219 Tom Murphy..................30	.14	.04
☐ 220 Manny Sanguillen..........40	.18	.05
☐ 221 Jim Todd.......................30	.14	.04
☐ 222 Wayne Garrett...............30	.14	.04
☐ 223 Ollie Brown...................30	.14	.04
☐ 224 Jim York.......................30	.14	.04
☐ 225 Roy White.....................40	.18	.05
☐ 226 Jim Sundberg...............40	.18	.05
☐ 227 Oscar Zamora...............30	.14	.04
☐ 228 John Hale......................30	.14	.04
☐ 229 Jerry Remy....................60	.25	.08
☐ 230 Carl Yastrzemski..........8.00	3.60	1.00
☐ 231 Tom House....................30	.14	.04
☐ 232 Frank Duffy...................30	.14	.04
☐ 233 Grant Jackson...............30	.14	.04
☐ 234 Mike Sadek...................30	.14	.04
☐ 235 Bert Blyleven...............2.50	1.15	.30
☐ 236 Kansas City Royals.......1.25	.55	.16
Team Card;		
Whitey Herzog MG		
(Checklist back)		
☐ 237 Dave Hamilton...............30	.14	.04

☐ 238 Larry Biittner................30	.14	.04
☐ 239 John Curtis...................30	.14	.04
☐ 240 Pete Rose 12.50	5.75	1.55
☐ 241 Hector Torres................30	.14	.04
☐ 242 Dan Meyer....................30	.14	.04
☐ 243 Jim Rooker....................30	.14	.04
☐ 244 Bill Sharp......................30	.14	.04
☐ 245 Felix Millan....................30	.14	.04
☐ 246 Cesar Tovar...................30	.14	.04
☐ 247 Terry Harmon................30	.14	.04
☐ 248 Dick Tidrow...................30	.14	.04
☐ 249 Cliff Johnson.................40	.18	.05
☐ 250 Fergie Jenkins.............3.50	1.55	.45
☐ 251 Rick Monday..................40	.18	.05
☐ 252 Tim Nordbrook..............30	.14	.04
☐ 253 Bill Buckner..................75	.35	.09
☐ 254 Rudy Meoli....................30	.14	.04
☐ 255 Fritz Peterson................30	.14	.04
☐ 256 Rowland Office..............30	.14	.04
☐ 257 Ross Grimsley...............30	.14	.04
☐ 258 Nyls Nyman...................30	.14	.04
☐ 259 Darrel Chaney...............30	.14	.04
☐ 260 Steve Busby..................30	.14	.04
☐ 261 Gary Thomasson...........30	.14	.04
☐ 262 Checklist 133-264.........1.50	.15	.05
☐ 263 Lyman Bostock.............50	.23	.06
☐ 264 Steve Renko..................30	.14	.04
☐ 265 Willie Davis...................40	.18	.05
☐ 266 Alan Foster...................30	.14	.04
☐ 267 Aurelio Rodriguez..........30	.14	.04
☐ 268 Del Unser.....................30	.14	.04
☐ 269 Rick Austin...................30	.14	.04
☐ 270 Willie Stargell..............3.50	1.55	.45
☐ 271 Jim Lonborg..................40	.18	.05
☐ 272 Rick Dempsey...............40	.18	.05
☐ 273 Joe Niekro....................40	.18	.05
☐ 274 Tommy Harper...............40	.18	.05
☐ 275 Rick Manning................60	.25	.08
☐ 276 Mickey Scott.................30	.14	.04
☐ 277 Chicago Cubs...............1.25	.55	.16
Team Card;		
Jim Marshall MG		
(Checklist back)		
☐ 278 Bernie Carbo.................30	.14	.04
☐ 279 Roy Howell...................30	.14	.04
☐ 280 Burt Hooton..................40	.18	.05
☐ 281 Dave May......................30	.14	.04
☐ 282 Dan Osborn...................30	.14	.04
☐ 283 Merv Rettenmund..........30	.14	.04
☐ 284 Steve Ontiveros.............30	.14	.04
☐ 285 Mike Cuellar..................40	.18	.05
☐ 286 Jim Wohlford.................30	.14	.04
☐ 287 Pete Mackanin..............30	.14	.04
☐ 288 Bill Campbell.................30	.14	.04
☐ 289 Enzo Hernandez............30	.14	.04
☐ 290 Ted Simmons...............1.50	.65	.19
☐ 291 Ken Sanders..................30	.14	.04

☐ 292	Leon Roberts	.30	.14	.04
☐ 293	Bill Castro	.50	.23	.06
☐ 294	Ed Kirkpatrick	.30	.14	.04
☐ 295	Dave Cash	.30	.14	.04
☐ 296	Pat Dobson	.30	.14	.04
☐ 297	Roger Metzger	.30	.14	.04
☐ 298	Dick Bosman	.30	.14	.04
☐ 299	Champ Summers	.30	.14	.04
☐ 300	Johnny Bench	12.50	5.75	1.55
☐ 301	Jackie Brown	.30	.14	.04
☐ 302	Rick Miller	.30	.14	.04
☐ 303	Steve Foucault	.30	.14	.04
☐ 304	California Angels	1.25	.55	.16
	Team Card;			
	Dick Williams MG			
	(Checklist back)			
☐ 305	Andy Messersmith	.40	.18	.05
☐ 306	Rod Gilbreath	.30	.14	.04
☐ 307	Al Bumbry	.30	.14	.04
☐ 308	Jim Barr	.30	.14	.04
☐ 309	Bill Melton	.30	.14	.04
☐ 310	Randy Jones	.50	.23	.06
☐ 311	Cookie Rojas	.40	.18	.05
☐ 312	Don Carrithers	.30	.14	.04
☐ 313	Dan Ford	.30	.14	.04
☐ 314	Ed Kranepool	.30	.14	.04
☐ 315	Al Hrabosky	.40	.18	.05
☐ 316	Robin Yount	60.00	27.00	7.50
☐ 317	John Candelaria	3.50	1.55	.45
☐ 318	Bob Boone	1.00	.45	.13
☐ 319	Larry Gura	.30	.14	.04
☐ 320	Willie Horton	.40	.18	.05
☐ 321	Jose Cruz	.50	.23	.06
☐ 322	Glenn Abbott	.30	.14	.04
☐ 323	Rob Sperring	.30	.14	.04
☐ 324	Jim Bibby	.30	.14	.04
☐ 325	Tony Perez	2.50	1.15	.30
☐ 326	Dick Pole	.30	.14	.04
☐ 327	Dave Moates	.30	.14	.04
☐ 328	Carl Morton	.30	.14	.04
☐ 329	Joe Ferguson	.30	.14	.04
☐ 330	Nolan Ryan	60.00	27.00	7.50
☐ 331	San Diego Padres	1.25	.55	.16
	Team Card;			
	John McNamara MG			
	(Checklist back)			
☐ 332	Charlie Williams	.30	.14	.04
☐ 333	Bob Coluccio	.30	.14	.04
☐ 334	Dennis Leonard	.40	.18	.05
☐ 335	Bob Grich	.50	.23	.06
☐ 336	Vic Albury	.30	.14	.04
☐ 337	Bud Harrelson	.40	.18	.05
☐ 338	Bob Bailey	.30	.14	.04
☐ 339	John Denny	.40	.18	.05
☐ 340	Jim Rice	6.50	2.90	.80
☐ 341	All-Time 1B	6.50	2.90	.80
	Lou Gehrig			

☐ 342	All-Time 2B	3.00	1.35	.40
	Rogers Hornsby			
☐ 343	All-Time 3B	1.00	.45	.13
	Pie Traynor			
☐ 344	All-Time SS	3.50	1.55	.45
	Honus Wagner			
☐ 345	All-Time OF	10.00	4.50	1.25
	Babe Ruth			
☐ 346	All-Time OF	6.50	2.90	.80
	Ty Cobb			
☐ 347	All-Time OF	6.50	2.90	.80
	Ted Williams			
☐ 348	All-Time C	1.00	.45	.13
	Mickey Cochrane			
☐ 349	All-Time RHP	2.50	1.15	.30
	Walter Johnson			
☐ 350	All-Time LHP	1.00	.45	.13
	Lefty Grove			
☐ 351	Randy Hundley	.30	.14	.04
☐ 352	Dave Giusti	.30	.14	.04
☐ 353	Sixto Lezcano	.40	.18	.05
☐ 354	Ron Blomberg	.30	.14	.04
☐ 355	Steve Carlton	8.50	3.80	1.05
☐ 356	Ted Martinez	.30	.14	.04
☐ 357	Ken Forsch	.30	.14	.04
☐ 358	Buddy Bell	.50	.23	.06
☐ 359	Rick Reuschel	.40	.18	.05
☐ 360	Jeff Burroughs	.40	.18	.05
☐ 361	Detroit Tigers	1.25	.55	.16
	Team Card;			
	Ralph Houk MG			
	(Checklist back)			
☐ 362	Will McEnaney	.30	.14	.04
☐ 363	Dave Collins	.75	.35	.09
☐ 364	Elias Sosa	.30	.14	.04
☐ 365	Carlton Fisk	11.00	4.90	1.40
☐ 366	Bobby Valentine	.40	.18	.05
☐ 367	Bruce Miller	.30	.14	.04
☐ 368	Wilbur Wood	.30	.14	.04
☐ 369	Frank White	.50	.23	.06
☐ 370	Ron Cey	1.00	.45	.13
☐ 371	Elrod Hendricks	.30	.14	.04
☐ 372	Rick Baldwin	.30	.14	.04
☐ 373	Johnny Briggs	.30	.14	.04
☐ 374	Dan Warthen	.50	.23	.06
☐ 375	Ron Fairly	.30	.14	.04
☐ 376	Rich Hebner	.40	.18	.05
☐ 377	Mike Hegan	.30	.14	.04
☐ 378	Steve Stone	.40	.18	.05
☐ 379	Ken Boswell	.30	.14	.04
☐ 380	Bobby Bonds	1.25	.55	.16
☐ 381	Denny Doyle	.30	.14	.04
☐ 382	Matt Alexander	.30	.14	.04
☐ 383	John Ellis	.30	.14	.04
☐ 384	Philadelphia Phillies	1.25	.55	.16
	Team Card;			
	Danny Ozark MG			

(Checklist back)

☐	385 Mickey Lolich	.50	.23	.06
☐	386 Ed Goodson	.30	.14	.04
☐	387 Mike Miley	.30	.14	.04
☐	388 Stan Perzanowski	.30	.14	.04
☐	389 Glenn Adams	.30	.14	.04
☐	390 Don Gullett	.40	.18	.05
☐	391 Jerry Hairston	.30	.14	.04
☐	392 Checklist 265-396	1.50	.15	.05
☐	393 Paul Mitchell	.30	.14	.04
☐	394 Fran Healy	.30	.14	.04
☐	395 Jim Wynn	.40	.18	.05
☐	396 Bill Lee	.30	.14	.04
☐	397 Tim Foli	.30	.14	.04
☐	398 Dave Tomlin	.30	.14	.04
☐	399 Luis Melendez	.30	.14	.04
☐	400 Rod Carew	9.00	4.00	1.15
☐	401 Ken Brett	.30	.14	.04
☐	402 Don Money	.40	.18	.05
☐	403 Geoff Zahn	.30	.14	.04
☐	404 Enos Cabell	.30	.14	.04
☐	405 Rollie Fingers	4.00	1.80	.50
☐	406 Ed Herrmann	.30	.14	.04
☐	407 Tom Underwood	.30	.14	.04
☐	408 Charlie Spikes	.30	.14	.04
☐	409 Dave Lemanczyk	.30	.14	.04
☐	410 Ralph Garr	.40	.18	.05
☐	411 Bill Singer	.30	.14	.04
☐	412 Toby Harrah	.40	.18	.05
☐	413 Pete Varney	.30	.14	.04
☐	414 Wayne Garland	.30	.14	.04
☐	415 Vada Pinson	.50	.23	.06
☐	416 Tommy John	1.50	.65	.19
☐	417 Gene Clines	.30	.14	.04
☐	418 Jose Morales	.50	.23	.06
☐	419 Reggie Cleveland	.30	.14	.04
☐	420 Joe Morgan	6.50	2.90	.80
☐	421 Oakland A's	1.25	.55	.16
	Team Card;			
	(No MG on front;			
	checklist back)			
☐	422 Johnny Grubb	.30	.14	.04
☐	423 Ed Halicki	.30	.14	.04
☐	424 Phil Roof	.30	.14	.04
☐	425 Rennie Stennett	.30	.14	.04
☐	426 Bob Forsch	.30	.14	.04
☐	427 Kurt Bevacqua	.30	.14	.04
☐	428 Jim Crawford	.30	.14	.04
☐	429 Fred Stanley	.30	.14	.04
☐	430 Jose Cardenal	.30	.14	.04
☐	431 Dick Ruthven	.30	.14	.04
☐	432 Tom Veryzer	.30	.14	.04
☐	433 Rick Waits	.30	.14	.04
☐	434 Morris Nettles	.30	.14	.04
☐	435 Phil Niekro	2.50	1.15	.30
☐	436 Bill Fahey	.30	.14	.04
☐	437 Terry Forster	.30	.14	.04

☐	438 Doug DeCinces	.60	.25	.08
☐	439 Rick Rhoden	.40	.18	.05
☐	440 John Mayberry	.40	.18	.05
☐	441 Gary Carter	12.50	5.75	1.55
☐	442 Hank Webb	.30	.14	.04
☐	443 San Francisco Giants	1.25	.55	.16
	Team Card;			
	(No MG on front;			
	checklist back)			
☐	444 Gary Nolan	.30	.14	.04
☐	445 Rico Petrocelli	.40	.18	.05
☐	446 Larry Haney	.30	.14	.04
☐	447 Gene Locklear	.30	.14	.04
☐	448 Tom Johnson	.30	.14	.04
☐	449 Bob Robertson	.30	.14	.04
☐	450 Jim Palmer	8.00	3.60	1.00
☐	451 Buddy Bradford	.30	.14	.04
☐	452 Tom Hausman	.30	.14	.04
☐	453 Lou Piniella	.75	.35	.09
☐	454 Tom Griffin	.30	.14	.04
☐	455 Dick Allen	.80	.35	.10
☐	456 Joe Coleman	.30	.14	.04
☐	457 Ed Crosby	.30	.14	.04
☐	458 Earl Williams	.30	.14	.04
☐	459 Jim Brewer	.30	.14	.04
☐	460 Cesar Cedeno	.40	.18	.05
☐	461 NL and AL Champs	.60	.25	.08
	Reds sweep Bucs,			
	Bosox surprise A's			
☐	462 '75 World Series	.60	.25	.08
	Reds Champs			
☐	463 Steve Hargan	.30	.14	.04
☐	464 Ken Henderson	.30	.14	.04
☐	465 Mike Marshall	.40	.18	.05
☐	466 Bob Stinson	.30	.14	.04
☐	467 Woodie Fryman	.30	.14	.04
☐	468 Jesus Alou	.30	.14	.04
☐	469 Rawly Eastwick	.30	.14	.04
☐	470 Bobby Murcer	.75	.35	.09
☐	471 Jim Burton	.30	.14	.04
☐	472 Bob Davis	.30	.14	.04
☐	473 Paul Blair	.40	.18	.05
☐	474 Ray Corbin	.30	.14	.04
☐	475 Joe Rudi	.40	.18	.05
☐	476 Bob Moose	.30	.14	.04
☐	477 Cleveland Indians	1.25	.55	.16
	Team Card;			
	Frank Robinson MG			
	(Checklist Back)			
☐	478 Lynn McGlothen	.30	.14	.04
☐	479 Bobby Mitchell	.30	.14	.04
☐	480 Mike Schmidt	35.00	16.00	4.40
☐	481 Rudy May	.30	.14	.04
☐	482 Tim Hosley	.30	.14	.04
☐	483 Mickey Stanley	.30	.14	.04
☐	484 Eric Raich	.30	.14	.04
☐	485 Mike Hargrove	.40	.18	.05

□ 486	Bruce Dal Canton	.30	.14	.04
□ 487	Leron Lee	.30	.14	.04
□ 488	Claude Osteen	.40	.18	.05
□ 489	Skip Jutze	.30	.14	.04
□ 490	Frank Tanana	1.00	.45	.13
□ 491	Terry Crowley	.30	.14	.04
□ 492	Marty Pattin	.30	.14	.04
□ 493	Derrel Thomas	.30	.14	.04
□ 494	Craig Swan	.40	.18	.05
□ 495	Nate Colbert	.30	.14	.04
□ 496	Juan Beniquez	.30	.14	.04
□ 497	Joe McIntosh	.30	.14	.04
□ 498	Glenn Borgmann	.30	.14	.04
□ 499	Mario Guerrero	.30	.14	.04
□ 500	Reggie Jackson	21.00	9.50	2.60
□ 501	Billy Champion	.30	.14	.04
□ 502	Tim McCarver	.75	.35	.09
□ 503	Elliott Maddox	.30	.14	.04
□ 504	Pittsburgh Pirates	1.25	.55	.16
	Team Card; Danny Murtaugh MG (Checklist back)			
□ 505	Mark Belanger	.40	.18	.05
□ 506	George Mitterwald	.30	.14	.04
□ 507	Ray Bare	.30	.14	.04
□ 508	Duane Kuiper	.50	.23	.06
□ 509	Bill Hands	.30	.14	.04
□ 510	Amos Otis	.40	.18	.05
□ 511	Jamie Easterley	.30	.14	.04
□ 512	Ellie Rodriguez	.30	.14	.04
□ 513	Bart Johnson	.30	.14	.04
□ 514	Dan Driessen	.40	.18	.05
□ 515	Steve Yeager	.40	.18	.05
□ 516	Wayne Granger	.30	.14	.04
□ 517	John Milner	.30	.14	.04
□ 518	Doug Flynn	.30	.14	.04
□ 519	Steve Brye	.30	.14	.04
□ 520	Willie McCovey	4.00	1.80	.50
□ 521	Jim Colborn	.30	.14	.04
□ 522	Ted Sizemore	.30	.14	.04
□ 523	Bob Montgomery	.30	.14	.04
□ 524	Pete Falcone	.30	.14	.04
□ 525	Billy Williams	3.50	1.55	.45
□ 526	Checklist 397-528	1.50	.15	.05
□ 527	Mike Anderson	.30	.14	.04
□ 528	Dock Ellis	.30	.14	.04
□ 529	Deron Johnson	.30	.14	.04
□ 530	Don Sutton	3.00	1.35	.40
□ 531	New York Mets	1.25	.55	.16
	Team Card; Joe Frazier MG (Checklist back)			
□ 532	Milt May	.30	.14	.04
□ 533	Lee Richard	.30	.14	.04
□ 534	Stan Bahnsen	.30	.14	.04
□ 535	Dave Nelson	.30	.14	.04
□ 536	Mike Thompson	.30	.14	.04
□ 537	Tony Muser	.30	.14	.04
□ 538	Pat Darcy	.30	.14	.04
□ 539	John Balaz	.30	.14	.04
□ 540	Bill Freehan	.40	.18	.05
□ 541	Steve Mingori	.30	.14	.04
□ 542	Keith Hernandez	4.00	1.80	.50
□ 543	Wayne Twitchell	.30	.14	.04
□ 544	Pepe Frias	.30	.14	.04
□ 545	Sparky Lyle	.60	.25	.08
□ 546	Dave Rosello	.30	.14	.04
□ 547	Roric Harrison	.30	.14	.04
□ 548	Manny Mota	.40	.18	.05
□ 549	Randy Tate	.30	.14	.04
□ 550	Hank Aaron	25.00	11.50	3.10
□ 551	Jerry DaVanon	.30	.14	.04
□ 552	Terry Humphrey	.30	.14	.04
□ 553	Randy Moffitt	.30	.14	.04
□ 554	Ray Fosse	.30	.14	.04
□ 555	Dyar Miller	.30	.14	.04
□ 556	Minnesota Twins	1.25	.55	.16
	Team Card; Gene Mauch MG (Checklist back)			
□ 557	Dan Spillner	.30	.14	.04
□ 558	Clarence Gaston	.40	.18	.05
□ 559	Clyde Wright	.30	.14	.04
□ 560	Jorge Orta	.30	.14	.04
□ 561	Tom Carroll	.30	.14	.04
□ 562	Adrian Garrett	.30	.14	.04
□ 563	Larry Demery	.30	.14	.04
□ 564	Bubble Gum Champ	.50	.23	.06
	Kurt Bevacqua			
□ 565	Tug McGraw	.50	.23	.06
□ 566	Ken McMullen	.30	.14	.04
□ 567	George Stone	.30	.14	.04
□ 568	Rob Andrews	.30	.14	.04
□ 569	Nelson Briles	.40	.18	.05
□ 570	George Hendrick	.40	.18	.05
□ 571	Don DeMola	.30	.14	.04
□ 572	Rich Coggins	.30	.14	.04
□ 573	Bill Travers	.30	.14	.04
□ 574	Don Kessinger	.40	.18	.05
□ 575	Dwight Evans	3.00	1.35	.40
□ 576	Maximino Leon	.30	.14	.04
□ 577	Marc Hill	.30	.14	.04
□ 578	Ted Kubiak	.30	.14	.04
□ 579	Clay Kirby	.30	.14	.04
□ 580	Bert Campaneris	.40	.18	.05
□ 581	St. Louis Cardinals	1.25	.55	.16
	Team Card; Red Schoendienst MG (Checklist back)			
□ 582	Mike Kekich	.30	.14	.04
□ 583	Tommy Helms	.30	.14	.04
□ 584	Stan Wall	.30	.14	.04
□ 585	Joe Torre	.60	.25	.08
□ 586	Ron Schueler	.30	.14	.04

☐ 587	Leo Cardenas	.30	.14	.04
☐ 588	Kevin Kobel	.30	.14	.04
☐ 589	Rookie Pitchers	2.00	.90	.25
	Santo Alcala			
	Mike Flanagan			
	Joe Pactwa			
	Pablo Torrealba			
☐ 590	Rookie Outfielders	.75	.35	.09
	Henry Cruz			
	Chet Lemon			
	Ellis Valentine			
	Terry Whitfield			
☐ 591	Rookie Pitchers	.50	.23	.06
	Steve Grilli			
	Craig Mitchell			
	Jose Sosa			
	George Throop			
☐ 592	Rookie Infielders	9.00	4.00	1.15
	Willie Randolph			
	Dave McKay			
	Jerry Royster			
	Roy Staiger			
☐ 593	Rookie Pitchers	.50	.23	.06
	Larry Anderson			
	Ken Crosby			
	Mark Littell			
	Butch Metzger			
☐ 594	Rookie Catchers/OF	.50	.23	.06
	Andy Merchant			
	Ed Ott			
	Royle Stillman			
	Jerry White			
☐ 595	Rookie Pitchers	.50	.23	.06
	Art DeFilippis			
	Randy Lerch			
	Sid Monge			
	Steve Barr			
☐ 596	Rookie Infielders	.50	.23	.06
	Craig Reynolds			
	Lamar Johnson			
	Johnnie LeMaster			
	Jerry Manuel			
☐ 597	Rookie Pitchers	.50	.23	.06
	Don Aase			
	Jack Kucek			
	Frank LaCorte			
	Mike Pazik			
☐ 598	Rookie Outfielders	.50	.23	.06
	Hector Cruz			
	Jamie Quirk			
	Jerry Turner			
	Joe Wallis			
☐ 599	Rookie Pitchers	8.00	3.60	1.00
	Rob Dressler			
	Ron Guidry			
	Bob McClure			
	Pat Zachry			

☐ 600	Tom Seaver	15.00	6.75	1.90
☐ 601	Ken Rudolph	.30	.14	.04
☐ 602	Doug Konieczny	.30	.14	.04
☐ 603	Jim Holt	.30	.14	.04
☐ 604	Joe Lovitto	.30	.14	.04
☐ 605	Al Downing	.30	.14	.04
☐ 606	Milwaukee Brewers	1.25	.55	.16
	Team Card;			
	Alex Grammas MG			
	(Checklist back)			
☐ 607	Rich Hinton	.30	.14	.04
☐ 608	Vic Correll	.30	.14	.04
☐ 609	Fred Norman	.30	.14	.04
☐ 610	Greg Luzinski	.50	.23	.06
☐ 611	Rich Folkers	.30	.14	.04
☐ 612	Joe Lahoud	.30	.14	.04
☐ 613	Tim Johnson	.30	.14	.04
☐ 614	Fernando Arroyo	.30	.14	.04
☐ 615	Mike Cubbage	.30	.14	.04
☐ 616	Buck Martinez	.30	.14	.04
☐ 617	Darold Knowles	.30	.14	.04
☐ 618	Jack Brohamer	.30	.14	.04
☐ 619	Bill Butler	.30	.14	.04
☐ 620	Al Oliver	.75	.35	.09
☐ 621	Tom Hall	.30	.14	.04
☐ 622	Rick Auerbach	.30	.14	.04
☐ 623	Bob Allietta	.30	.14	.04
☐ 624	Tony Taylor	.30	.14	.04
☐ 625	J.R. Richard	.40	.18	.05
☐ 626	Bob Sheldon	.30	.14	.04
☐ 627	Bill Plummer	.30	.14	.04
☐ 628	John D'Acquisto	.30	.14	.04
☐ 629	Sandy Alomar	.40	.18	.05
☐ 630	Chris Speier	.30	.14	.04
☐ 631	Atlanta Braves	1.25	.55	.16
	Team Card;			
	Dave Bristol MG			
	(Checklist back)			
☐ 632	Rogelio Moret	.30	.14	.04
☐ 633	John Stearns	.50	.23	.06
☐ 634	Larry Christenson	.30	.14	.04
☐ 635	Jim Fregosi	.40	.18	.05
☐ 636	Joe Decker	.30	.14	.04
☐ 637	Bruce Bochte	.30	.14	.04
☐ 638	Doyle Alexander	.40	.18	.05
☐ 639	Fred Kendall	.30	.14	.04
☐ 640	Bill Madlock	1.00	.45	.13
☐ 641	Tom Paciorek	.40	.18	.05
☐ 642	Dennis Blair	.30	.14	.04
☐ 643	Checklist 529-660	1.50	.15	.05
☐ 644	Tom Bradley	.30	.14	.04
☐ 645	Darrell Porter	.40	.18	.05
☐ 646	John Lowenstein	.30	.14	.04
☐ 647	Ramon Hernandez	.30	.14	.04
☐ 648	Al Cowens	.30	.14	.04
☐ 649	Dave Roberts	.30	.14	.04
☐ 650	Thurman Munson	8.00	3.60	1.00

☐ 651	John Odom	.30	.14	.04
☐ 652	Ed Armbrister	.30	.14	.04
☐ 653	Mike Norris	.30	.14	.04
☐ 654	Doug Griffin	.30	.14	.04
☐ 655	Mike Vail	.30	.14	.04
☐ 656	Chicago White Sox	1.25	.55	.16
	Team Card;			
	Chuck Tanner MG			
	(Checklist back)			
☐ 657	Roy Smalley	.50	.23	.06
☐ 658	Jerry Johnson	.30	.14	.04
☐ 659	Ben Oglivie	.40	.18	.05
☐ 660	Dave Lopes	1.00	.45	.13

1976 Topps Traded

The cards in this 44-card set measure 2 1/2" by 3 1/2". The 1976 Topps Traded set contains 43 players and one unnumbered checklist card. The individuals pictured were traded after the Topps regular set was printed. A "Sports Extra" heading design is found on each picture and is also used to introduce the biographical section of the reverse. Each card is numbered according to the player's regular 1976 card with the addition of "T" to indicate his new status.

		NRMT-MT	EXC	G-VG
COMPLETE SET (44)		12.00	5.50	1.50
COMMON PLAYER		.30	.14	.04
☐ 27T	Ed Figueroa	.30	.14	.04
☐ 28T	Dusty Baker	.50	.23	.06
☐ 44T	Doug Rader	.40	.18	.05
☐ 58T	Ron Reed	.30	.14	.04
☐ 74T	Oscar Gamble	.50	.23	.06

☐ 80T	Jim Kaat	1.00	.45	.13
☐ 83T	Jim Spencer	.30	.14	.04
☐ 85T	Mickey Rivers	.40	.18	.05
☐ 99T	Lee Lacy	.30	.14	.04
☐ 120T	Rusty Staub	.50	.23	.06
☐ 127T	Larvell Blanks	.30	.14	.04
☐ 146T	George Medich	.30	.14	.04
☐ 158T	Ken Reitz	.30	.14	.04
☐ 208T	Mike Lum	.30	.14	.04
☐ 211T	Clay Carroll	.30	.14	.04
☐ 231T	Tom House	.30	.14	.04
☐ 250T	Fergie Jenkins	2.50	1.15	.30
☐ 259T	Darrel Chaney	.30	.14	.04
☐ 292T	Leon Roberts	.30	.14	.04
☐ 296T	Pat Dobson	.30	.14	.04
☐ 309T	Bill Melton	.30	.14	.04
☐ 338T	Bob Bailey	.30	.14	.04
☐ 380T	Bobby Bonds	.75	.35	.09
☐ 383T	John Ellis	.30	.14	.04
☐ 385T	Mickey Lolich	.50	.23	.06
☐ 401T	Ken Brett	.30	.14	.04
☐ 410T	Ralph Garr	.40	.18	.05
☐ 411T	Bill Singer	.30	.14	.04
☐ 428T	Jim Crawford	.30	.14	.04
☐ 434T	Morris Nettles	.30	.14	.04
☐ 464T	Ken Henderson	.30	.14	.04
☐ 497T	Joe McIntosh	.30	.14	.04
☐ 524T	Pete Falcone	.30	.14	.04
☐ 527T	Mike Anderson	.30	.14	.04
☐ 528T	Dock Ellis	.30	.14	.04
☐ 532T	Milt May	.30	.14	.04
☐ 554T	Ray Fosse	.30	.14	.04
☐ 579T	Clay Kirby	.30	.14	.04
☐ 583T	Tommy Helms	.30	.14	.04
☐ 592T	Willie Randolph	4.50	2.00	.55
☐ 618T	Jack Brohamer	.30	.14	.04
☐ 632T	Rogelio Moret	.30	.14	.04
☐ 649T	Dave Roberts	.30	.14	.04
☐ NNO	Traded Checklist	1.00	.10	.03

1977 Topps

The cards in this 660-card set measure 2 1/2" by 3 1/2". In 1977 for the fifth consecutive year, Topps produced a 660-card baseball set. The player's name, team affiliation, and his position is compactly arranged over the picture area and a facsimile autograph appears on the photo. Team cards feature a checklist of that team's players in the set and a small picture of the manager on the front of the card. Appearing for the first time are the series "Brothers" (631-634) and "Turn Back the Clock" (433-437). Other sub-series in the set are League Leaders (1-8), Record Breakers (231-234), Playoffs cards (276-277), World Series cards (411-413), and Rookie Prospects (472-479 and 487-494). The following players' regular issue cards are explicitly denoted as All-Stars, 30, 70, 100, 120, 170, 210, 240, 265, 301, 347, 400, 420, 450, 500, 521, 550, 560, and 580. The key cards in the set are the rookie cards of Dale Murphy (476) and Andre Dawson (473). Other notable rookie cards in the set include Jack Clark, Dennis Martinez, and Bruce Sutter. Cards numbered 23 or lower, that feature Yankees and do not follow the numbering checklisted below, are not necessarily error cards. They are undoubtedly Burger King cards, a separate set with its own pricing and mass distribution. Burger King cards are indistinguishable from the corresponding Topps cards except for the card numbering difference and the fact that Burger King cards do not have a printing sheet designation (such as A through F like the regular Topps) anywhere on the card back in very small print. There was an aluminum version of the Dale Murphy Rookie Cardnumber 476 produced (legally) in the early '80s; proceeds from the sales (originally priced at 10.00) of this "card" went to the Huntington's Disease Foundation.

	NRMT-MT	EXC	G-VG
COMPLETE SET (660)	440.00	200.00	55.00
COMMON PLAYER (1-660)	.25	.11	.03

☐ 1	Batting Leaders	5.00	1.25	.40
	George Brett			
	Bill Madlock			
☐ 2	Home Run Leaders	1.50	.65	.19
	Graig Nettles			
	Mike Schmidt			
☐ 3	RBI Leaders	.50	.23	.06
	Lee May			
	George Foster			
☐ 4	Stolen Base Leaders	.50	.23	.06
	Bill North			
	Dave Lopes			
☐ 5	Victory Leaders	.75	.35	.09
	Jim Palmer			
	Randy Jones			
☐ 6	Strikeout Leaders	10.00	4.50	1.25
	Nolan Ryan			
	Tom Seaver			
☐ 7	ERA Leaders	.50	.23	.06
	Mark Fidrych			
	John Denny			
☐ 8	Leading Firemen	.50	.23	.06
	Bill Campbell			
	Rawly Eastwick			
☐ 9	Doug Rader	.25	.11	.03
☐ 10	Reggie Jackson	16.00	7.25	2.00
☐ 11	Rob Dressler	.25	.11	.03
☐ 12	Larry Haney	.25	.11	.03
☐ 13	Luis Gomez	.25	.11	.03
☐ 14	Tommy Smith	.25	.11	.03
☐ 15	Don Gullett	.35	.16	.04
☐ 16	Bob Jones	.25	.11	.03
☐ 17	Steve Stone	.35	.16	.04
☐ 18	Indians Team/Mgr.	1.00	.45	.13
	Frank Robinson			
	(Checklist back)			
☐ 19	John D'Acquisto	.25	.11	.03
☐ 20	Graig Nettles	1.00	.45	.13
☐ 21	Ken Forsch	.25	.11	.03
☐ 22	Bill Freehan	.35	.16	.04
☐ 23	Dan Driessen	.25	.11	.03
☐ 24	Carl Morton	.25	.11	.03
☐ 25	Dwight Evans	3.00	1.35	.40
☐ 26	Ray Sadecki	.25	.11	.03
☐ 27	Bill Buckner	.50	.23	.06
☐ 28	Woodie Fryman	.25	.11	.03
☐ 29	Bucky Dent	.60	.25	.08
☐ 30	Greg Luzinski	.45	.20	.06
☐ 31	Jim Todd	.25	.11	.03
☐ 32	Checklist 1	1.25	.13	.04
☐ 33	Wayne Garland	.25	.11	.03
☐ 34	Angels Team/Mgr.	1.00	.45	.13
	Norm Sherry			
	(Checklist back)			
☐ 35	Rennie Stennett	.25	.11	.03
☐ 36	John Ellis	.25	.11	.03
☐ 37	Steve Hargan	.25	.11	.03
☐ 38	Craig Kusick	.25	.11	.03
☐ 39	Tom Griffin	.25	.11	.03
☐ 40	Bobby Murcer	.50	.23	.06
☐ 41	Jim Kern	.25	.11	.03

☐ 42	Jose Cruz	.35	.16	.04
☐ 43	Ray Bare	.25	.11	.03
☐ 44	Bud Harrelson	.35	.16	.04
☐ 45	Rawly Eastwick	.25	.11	.03
☐ 46	Buck Martinez	.25	.11	.03
☐ 47	Lynn McGlothen	.25	.11	.03
☐ 48	Tom Paciorek	.35	.16	.04
☐ 49	Grant Jackson	.25	.11	.03
☐ 50	Ron Cey	.50	.23	.06
☐ 51	Brewers Team/Mgr.	1.00	.45	.13
	Alex Grammas			
	(Checklist back)			
☐ 52	Ellis Valentine	.25	.11	.03
☐ 53	Paul Mitchell	.25	.11	.03
☐ 54	Sandy Alomar	.35	.16	.04
☐ 55	Jeff Burroughs	.35	.16	.04
☐ 56	Rudy May	.25	.11	.03
☐ 57	Marc Hill	.25	.11	.03
☐ 58	Chet Lemon	.35	.16	.04
☐ 59	Larry Christenson	.25	.11	.03
☐ 60	Jim Rice	4.00	1.80	.50
☐ 61	Manny Sanguillen	.35	.16	.04
☐ 62	Eric Raich	.25	.11	.03
☐ 63	Tito Fuentes	.25	.11	.03
☐ 64	Larry Biittner	.25	.11	.03
☐ 65	Skip Lockwood	.25	.11	.03
☐ 66	Roy Smalley	.35	.16	.04
☐ 67	Joaquin Andujar	.60	.25	.08
☐ 68	Bruce Bochte	.25	.11	.03
☐ 69	Jim Crawford	.25	.11	.03
☐ 70	Johnny Bench	10.00	4.50	1.25
☐ 71	Dock Ellis	.25	.11	.03
☐ 72	Mike Anderson	.25	.11	.03
☐ 73	Charlie Williams	.25	.11	.03
☐ 74	A's Team/Mgr.	1.00	.45	.13
	Jack McKeon			
	(Checklist back)			
☐ 75	Dennis Leonard	.35	.16	.04
☐ 76	Tim Foli	.25	.11	.03
☐ 77	Dyar Miller	.25	.11	.03
☐ 78	Bob Davis	.25	.11	.03
☐ 79	Don Money	.35	.16	.04
☐ 80	Andy Messersmith	.35	.16	.04
☐ 81	Juan Beniquez	.25	.11	.03
☐ 82	Jim Rooker	.25	.11	.03
☐ 83	Kevin Bell	.25	.11	.03
☐ 84	Ollie Brown	.25	.11	.03
☐ 85	Duane Kuiper	.25	.11	.03
☐ 86	Pat Zachry	.25	.11	.03
☐ 87	Glenn Borgmann	.25	.11	.03
☐ 88	Stan Wall	.25	.11	.03
☐ 89	Butch Hobson	.80	.35	.10
☐ 90	Cesar Cedeno	.35	.16	.04
☐ 91	John Verhoeven	.25	.11	.03
☐ 92	Dave Rosello	.25	.11	.03
☐ 93	Tom Poquette	.25	.11	.03
☐ 94	Craig Swan	.25	.11	.03
☐ 95	Keith Hernandez	2.00	.90	.25
☐ 96	Lou Piniella	.50	.23	.06
☐ 97	Dave Heaverlo	.25	.11	.03
☐ 98	Milt May	.25	.11	.03
☐ 99	Tom Hausman	.25	.11	.03
☐ 100	Joe Morgan	5.00	2.30	.60
☐ 101	Dick Bosman	.25	.11	.03
☐ 102	Jose Morales	.25	.11	.03
☐ 103	Mike Bacsik	.25	.11	.03
☐ 104	Omar Moreno	.35	.16	.04
☐ 105	Steve Yeager	.35	.16	.04
☐ 106	Mike Flanagan	.50	.23	.06
☐ 107	Bill Melton	.25	.11	.03
☐ 108	Alan Foster	.25	.11	.03
☐ 109	Jorge Orta	.25	.11	.03
☐ 110	Steve Carlton	8.00	3.60	1.00
☐ 111	Rico Petrocelli	.35	.16	.04
☐ 112	Bill Greif	.25	.11	.03
☐ 113	Blue Jays Leaders	1.00	.45	.13
	Roy Hartsfield MG			
	Don Leppert CO			
	Bob Miller CO			
	Jackie Moore CO			
	Harry Warner CO			
	(Checklist back)			
☐ 114	Bruce Dal Canton	.25	.11	.03
☐ 115	Rick Manning	.25	.11	.03
☐ 116	Joe Niekro	.35	.16	.04
☐ 117	Frank White	.35	.16	.04
☐ 118	Rick Jones	.25	.11	.03
☐ 119	John Stearns	.25	.11	.03
☐ 120	Rod Carew	8.00	3.60	1.00
☐ 121	Gary Nolan	.25	.11	.03
☐ 122	Ben Oglivie	.35	.16	.04
☐ 123	Fred Stanley	.25	.11	.03
☐ 124	George Mitterwald	.25	.11	.03
☐ 125	Bill Travers	.25	.11	.03
☐ 126	Rod Gilbreath	.25	.11	.03
☐ 127	Ron Fairly	.25	.11	.03
☐ 128	Tommy John	1.00	.45	.13
☐ 129	Mike Sadek	.25	.11	.03
☐ 130	Al Oliver	.60	.25	.08
☐ 131	Orlando Ramirez	.25	.11	.03
☐ 132	Chip Lang	.25	.11	.03
☐ 133	Ralph Garr	.35	.16	.04
☐ 134	Padres Team/Mgr.	1.00	.45	.13
	John McNamara			
	(Checklist back)			
☐ 135	Mark Belanger	.35	.16	.04
☐ 136	Jerry Mumphrey	.25	.11	.03
☐ 137	Jeff Terpko	.25	.11	.03
☐ 138	Bob Stinson	.25	.11	.03
☐ 139	Fred Norman	.25	.11	.03
☐ 140	Mike Schmidt	25.00	11.50	3.10
☐ 141	Mark Littell	.25	.11	.03
☐ 142	Steve Dillard	.25	.11	.03
☐ 143	Ed Herrmann	.25	.11	.03

☐ 144	Bruce Sutter.................5.00	2.30	.60
☐ 145	Tom Veryzer 25	.11	.03
☐ 146	Dusty Baker...................45	.20	.06
☐ 147	Jackie Brown 25	.11	.03
☐ 148	Fran Healy.....................25	.11	.03
☐ 149	Mike Cubbage 25	.11	.03
☐ 150	Tom Seaver..............12.50	5.75	1.55
☐ 151	Johnny LeMaster 25	.11	.03
☐ 152	Gaylord Perry 2.50	1.15	.30
☐ 153	Ron Jackson 25	.11	.03
☐ 154	Dave Giusti...................25	.11	.03
☐ 155	Joe Rudi 35	.16	.04
☐ 156	Pete Mackanin..............25	.11	.03
☐ 157	Ken Brett.......................25	.11	.03
☐ 158	Ted Kubiak 25	.11	.03
☐ 159	Bernie Carbo 25	.11	.03
☐ 160	Will McEnaney 25	.11	.03
☐ 161	Garry Templeton 1.25	.55	.16
☐ 162	Mike Cuellar.................35	.16	.04
☐ 163	Dave Hilton 25	.11	.03
☐ 164	Tug McGraw 45	.20	.06
☐ 165	Jim Wynn 35	.16	.04
☐ 166	Bill Campbell 25	.11	.03
☐ 167	Rich Hebner 35	.16	.04
☐ 168	Charlie Spikes 25	.11	.03
☐ 169	Darold Knowles 25	.11	.03
☐ 170	Thurman Munson 6.00	2.70	.75
☐ 171	Ken Sanders 25	.11	.03
☐ 172	John Milner...................25	.11	.03
☐ 173	Chuck Scrivener 25	.11	.03
☐ 174	Nelson Briles 35	.16	.04
☐ 175	Butch Wynegar 25	.11	.03
☐ 176	Bob Robertson 25	.11	.03
☐ 177	Bart Johnson 25	.11	.03
☐ 178	Bombo Rivera 25	.11	.03
☐ 179	Paul Hartzell.................25	.11	.03
☐ 180	Dave Lopes 45	.20	.06
☐ 181	Ken McMullen...............25	.11	.03
☐ 182	Dan Spillner 25	.11	.03
☐ 183	Cardinals Team/Mgr. ...1.00	.45	.13
	Vern Rapp		
	(Checklist back)		
☐ 184	Bo McLaughlin...............25	.11	.03
☐ 185	Sixto Lezcano 25	.11	.03
☐ 186	Doug Flynn 25	.11	.03
☐ 187	Dick Pole......................25	.11	.03
☐ 188	Bob Tolan 25	.11	.03
☐ 189	Rick Dempsey 35	.16	.04
☐ 190	Ray Burris 25	.11	.03
☐ 191	Doug Griffin 25	.11	.03
☐ 192	Clarence Gaston 35	.16	.04
☐ 193	Larry Gura 25	.11	.03
☐ 194	Gary Matthews 35	.16	.04
☐ 195	Ed Figueroa..................25	.11	.03
☐ 196	Len Randle....................25	.11	.03
☐ 197	Ed Ott..........................25	.11	.03
☐ 198	Wilbur Wood..................25	.11	.03
☐ 199	Pepe Frias.....................25	.11	.03
☐ 200	Frank Tanana 75	.35	.09
☐ 201	Ed Kranepool.................25	.11	.03
☐ 202	Tom Johnson..................25	.11	.03
☐ 203	Ed Armbrister................25	.11	.03
☐ 204	Jeff Newman 40	.18	.05
☐ 205	Pete Falcone 25	.11	.03
☐ 206	Boog Powell..................60	.25	.08
☐ 207	Glenn Abbott.................25	.11	.03
☐ 208	Checklist 2 ....1.25	.13	.04
☐ 209	Rob Andrews 25	.11	.03
☐ 210	Fred Lynn...................1.00	.45	.13
☐ 211	Giants Team/Mgr. 1.00	.45	.13
	Joe Altobelli		
	(Checklist back)		
☐ 212	Jim Mason.....................25	.11	.03
☐ 213	Maximino Leon 25	.11	.03
☐ 214	Darrell Porter 35	.16	.04
☐ 215	Butch Metzger...............25	.11	.03
☐ 216	Doug DeCinces 35	.16	.04
☐ 217	Tom Underwood 25	.11	.03
☐ 218	John Wathan 75	.35	.09
☐ 219	Joe Coleman 25	.11	.03
☐ 220	Chris Chambliss 35	.16	.04
☐ 221	Bob Bailey 25	.11	.03
☐ 222	Francisco Barrios 25	.11	.03
☐ 223	Earl Williams 25	.11	.03
☐ 224	Rusty Torres 25	.11	.03
☐ 225	Bob Apodaca..................25	.11	.03
☐ 226	Leroy Stanton 25	.11	.03
☐ 227	Joe Sambito..................25	.11	.03
☐ 228	Twins Team/Mgr. 1.00	.45	.13
	Gene Mauch		
	(Checklist back)		
☐ 229	Don Kessinger 35	.16	.04
☐ 230	Vida Blue......................45	.20	.06
☐ 231	RB: George Brett..........9.00	4.00	1.15
	Most cons. games		
	with 3 or more hits		
☐ 232	RB: Minnie Minoso......60	.25	.08
	Oldest to hit safely		
☐ 233	RB: Jose Morales, Most..35	.16	.04
	pinch-hits, season		
☐ 234	RB: Nolan Ryan.........13.50	6.00	1.70
	Most seasons, 300		
	or more strikeouts		
☐ 235	Cecil Cooper 60	.25	.08
☐ 236	Tom Buskey...................25	.11	.03
☐ 237	Gene Clines...................25	.11	.03
☐ 238	Tippy Martinez 35	.16	.04
☐ 239	Bill Plummer 25	.11	.03
☐ 240	Ron LeFlore 35	.16	.04
☐ 241	Dave Tomlin 25	.11	.03
☐ 242	Ken Henderson 25	.11	.03
☐ 243	Ron Reed 25	.11	.03
☐ 244	John Mayberry 45	.20	.06
	(Cartoon mentions		

T206 Wagner)

☐ 245	Rick Rhoden	.35	.16	.04
☐ 246	Mike Vail	.25	.11	.03
☐ 247	Chris Knapp	.25	.11	.03
☐ 248	Wilbur Howard	.25	.11	.03
☐ 249	Pete Redfern	.25	.11	.03
☐ 250	Bill Madlock	.60	.25	.08
☐ 251	Tony Muser	.25	.11	.03
☐ 252	Dale Murray	.25	.11	.03
☐ 253	John Hale	.25	.11	.03
☐ 254	Doyle Alexander	.25	.11	.03
☐ 255	George Scott	.35	.16	.04
☐ 256	Joe Hoerner	.25	.11	.03
☐ 257	Mike Miley	.25	.11	.03
☐ 258	Luis Tiant	.45	.20	.06
☐ 259	Mets Team/Mgr.	1.00	.45	.13

Joe Frazier
(Checklist back)

☐ 260	J.R. Richard	.35	.16	.04
☐ 261	Phil Garner	.45	.20	.06
☐ 262	Al Cowens	.25	.11	.03
☐ 263	Mike Marshall	.35	.16	.04
☐ 264	Tom Hutton	.25	.11	.03
☐ 265	Mark Fidrych	1.75	.80	.22
☐ 266	Derrel Thomas	.25	.11	.03
☐ 267	Ray Fosse	.25	.11	.03
☐ 268	Rick Sawyer	.25	.11	.03
☐ 269	Joe Lis	.25	.11	.03
☐ 270	Dave Parker	3.00	1.35	.40
☐ 271	Terry Forster	.25	.11	.03
☐ 272	Lee Lacy	.25	.11	.03
☐ 273	Eric Soderholm	.25	.11	.03
☐ 274	Don Stanhouse	.25	.11	.03
☐ 275	Mike Hargrove	.35	.16	.04
☐ 276	AL Champs	.50	.23	.06

Chris Chambliss'
homer decides it

☐ 277	NL Champs	1.25	.55	.16

Reds sweep Phillies

☐ 278	Danny Frisella	.25	.11	.03
☐ 279	Joe Wallis	.25	.11	.03
☐ 280	Jim Hunter	2.50	1.15	.30
☐ 281	Roy Staiger	.25	.11	.03
☐ 282	Sid Monge	.25	.11	.03
☐ 283	Jerry DaVanon	.25	.11	.03
☐ 284	Mike Norris	.25	.11	.03
☐ 285	Brooks Robinson	4.50	2.00	.55
☐ 286	Johnny Grubb	.25	.11	.03
☐ 287	Reds Team/Mgr.	1.00	.45	.13

Sparky Anderson
(Checklist back)

☐ 288	Bob Montgomery	.25	.11	.03
☐ 289	Gene Garber	.25	.11	.03
☐ 290	Amos Otis	.35	.16	.04
☐ 291	Jason Thompson	.45	.20	.06
☐ 292	Rogelio Moret	.25	.11	.03
☐ 293	Jack Brohamer	.25	.11	.03

☐ 294	George Medich	.25	.11	.03
☐ 295	Gary Carter	7.50	3.40	.95
☐ 296	Don Hood	.25	.11	.03
☐ 297	Ken Reitz	.25	.11	.03
☐ 298	Charlie Hough	.35	.16	.04
☐ 299	Otto Velez	.25	.11	.03
☐ 300	Jerry Koosman	.45	.20	.06
☐ 301	Toby Harrah	.35	.16	.04
☐ 302	Mike Garman	.25	.11	.03
☐ 303	Gene Tenace	.35	.16	.04
☐ 304	Jim Hughes	.25	.11	.03
☐ 305	Mickey Rivers	.35	.16	.04
☐ 306	Rick Waits	.25	.11	.03
☐ 307	Gary Sutherland	.25	.11	.03
☐ 308	Gene Pentz	.25	.11	.03
☐ 309	Red Sox Team/Mgr.	1.00	.45	.13

Don Zimmer
(Checklist back)

☐ 310	Larry Bowa	.45	.20	.06
☐ 311	Vern Ruhle	.25	.11	.03
☐ 312	Rob Belloir	.25	.11	.03
☐ 313	Paul Blair	.35	.16	.04
☐ 314	Steve Mingori	.25	.11	.03
☐ 315	Dave Chalk	.25	.11	.03
☐ 316	Steve Rogers	.25	.11	.03
☐ 317	Kurt Bevacqua	.25	.11	.03
☐ 318	Duffy Dyer	.25	.11	.03
☐ 319	Rich Gossage	1.25	.55	.16
☐ 320	Ken Griffey	1.50	.65	.19
☐ 321	Dave Goltz	.25	.11	.03
☐ 322	Bill Russell	.35	.16	.04
☐ 323	Larry Lintz	.25	.11	.03
☐ 324	John Curtis	.25	.11	.03
☐ 325	Mike Ivie	.25	.11	.03
☐ 326	Jesse Jefferson	.25	.11	.03
☐ 327	Astros Team/Mgr.	1.00	.45	.13

Bill Virdon
(Checklist back)

☐ 328	Tommy Boggs	.25	.11	.03
☐ 329	Ron Hodges	.25	.11	.03
☐ 330	George Hendrick	.35	.16	.04
☐ 331	Jim Colborn	.25	.11	.03
☐ 332	Elliott Maddox	.25	.11	.03
☐ 333	Paul Reuschel	.25	.11	.03
☐ 334	Bill Stein	.25	.11	.03
☐ 335	Bill Robinson	.35	.16	.04
☐ 336	Denny Doyle	.25	.11	.03
☐ 337	Ron Schueler	.25	.11	.03
☐ 338	Dave Duncan	.25	.11	.03
☐ 339	Adrian Devine	.25	.11	.03
☐ 340	Hal McRae	.45	.20	.06
☐ 341	Joe Kerrigan	.40	.18	.05
☐ 342	Jerry Remy	.25	.11	.03
☐ 343	Ed Halicki	.25	.11	.03
☐ 344	Brian Downing	.60	.25	.08
☐ 345	Reggie Smith	.45	.20	.06
☐ 346	Bill Singer	.25	.11	.03

☐ 347	George Foster 1.25	.55	.16
☐ 348	Brent Strom 25	.11	.03
☐ 349	Jim Holt 25	.11	.03
☐ 350	Larry Dierker 25	.11	.03
☐ 351	Jim Sundberg 35	.16	.04
☐ 352	Mike Phillips 25	.11	.03
☐ 353	Stan Thomas 25	.11	.03
☐ 354	Pirates Team/Mgr. 1.00	.45	.13
	Chuck Tanner		
	(Checklist back)		
☐ 355	Lou Brock 4.00	1.80	.50
☐ 356	Checklist 3 ....1.25	.13	.04
☐ 357	Tim McCarver 50	.23	.06
☐ 358	Tom House 25	.11	.03
☐ 359	Willie Randolph 2.50	1.15	.30
☐ 360	Rick Monday 35	.16	.04
☐ 361	Eduardo Rodriguez 25	.11	.03
☐ 362	Tommy Davis 35	.16	.04
☐ 363	Dave Roberts 25	.11	.03
☐ 364	Vic Correll 25	.11	.03
☐ 365	Mike Torrez 35	.16	.04
☐ 366	Ted Sizemore 25	.11	.03
☐ 367	Dave Hamilton 25	.11	.03
☐ 368	Mike Jorgensen 25	.11	.03
☐ 369	Terry Humphrey 25	.11	.03
☐ 370	John Montefusco 35	.16	.04
☐ 371	Royals Team/Mgr. 1.00	.45	.13
	Whitey Herzog		
	(Checklist back)		
☐ 372	Rich Folkers 25	.11	.03
☐ 373	Bert Campaneris 35	.16	.04
☐ 374	Kent Tekulve 45	.20	.06
☐ 375	Larry Hisle 35	.16	.04
☐ 376	Nino Espinosa 25	.11	.03
☐ 377	Dave McKay 25	.11	.03
☐ 378	Jim Umbarger 25	.11	.03
☐ 379	Larry Cox 25	.11	.03
☐ 380	Lee May 35	.16	.04
☐ 381	Bob Forsch 25	.11	.03
☐ 382	Charlie Moore 25	.11	.03
☐ 383	Stan Bahnsen 25	.11	.03
☐ 384	Darrel Chaney 25	.11	.03
☐ 385	Dave LaRoche 25	.11	.03
☐ 386	Manny Mota 35	.16	.04
☐ 387	Yankees Team 1.50	.65	.19
	(Checklist back)		
☐ 388	Terry Harmon 25	.11	.03
☐ 389	Ken Kravec 25	.11	.03
☐ 390	Dave Winfield 20.00	9.00	2.50
☐ 391	Dan Warthen 25	.11	.03
☐ 392	Phil Roof 25	.11	.03
☐ 393	John Lowenstein 25	.11	.03
☐ 394	Bill Laxton 25	.11	.03
☐ 395	Manny Trillo 25	.11	.03
☐ 396	Tom Murphy 25	.11	.03
☐ 397	Larry Herndon 50	.23	.06
☐ 398	Tom Burgmeier 25	.11	.03

☐ 399	Bruce Boisclair 25	.11	.03
☐ 400	Steve Garvey 4.00	1.80	.50
☐ 401	Mickey Scott 25	.11	.03
☐ 402	Tommy Helms 25	.11	.03
☐ 403	Tom Grieve 35	.16	.04
☐ 404	Eric Rasmussen 25	.11	.03
☐ 405	Claudell Washington 35	.16	.04
☐ 406	Tim Johnson 25	.11	.03
☐ 407	Dave Freisleben 25	.11	.03
☐ 408	Cesar Tovar 25	.11	.03
☐ 409	Pete Broberg 25	.11	.03
☐ 410	Willie Montanez 25	.11	.03
☐ 411	W.S. Games 1 and 2 ......1.50	.65	.19
	Joe Morgan homers		
	in opener;		
	Johnny Bench stars as		
	Reds take 2nd game		
☐ 412	W.S. Games 3 and 4 ......1.25	.55	.16
	Reds stop Yankees;		
	Johnny Bench's two		
	homers wrap it up		
☐ 413	World Series Summary 60	.25	.08
	Cincy wins 2nd		
	straight series		
☐ 414	Tommy Harper 35	.16	.04
☐ 415	Jay Johnstone 35	.16	.04
☐ 416	Chuck Hartenstein 25	.11	.03
☐ 417	Wayne Garrett 25	.11	.03
☐ 418	White Sox Team/Mgr. ...1.00	.45	.13
	Bob Lemon		
	(Checklist back)		
☐ 419	Steve Swisher 25	.11	.03
☐ 420	Rusty Staub 45	.20	.06
☐ 421	Doug Rau 25	.11	.03
☐ 422	Freddie Patek 35	.16	.04
☐ 423	Gary Lavelle 25	.11	.03
☐ 424	Steve Brye 25	.11	.03
☐ 425	Joe Torre 50	.23	.06
☐ 426	Dick Drago 25	.11	.03
☐ 427	Dave Rader 25	.11	.03
☐ 428	Rangers Team/Mgr. 1.00	.45	.13
	Frank Lucchesi		
	(Checklist back)		
☐ 429	Ken Boswell 25	.11	.03
☐ 430	Fergie Jenkins 3.00	1.35	.40
☐ 431	Dave Collins UER 35	.16	.04
	(Photo actually		
	Bobby Jones)		
☐ 432	Buzz Capra 25	.11	.03
☐ 433	Turn back clock 1972 35	.16	.04
	Nate Colbert		
☐ 434	Turn back clock 1967 ..1.50	.65	.19
	Carl Yastrzemski		
	Triple Crown		
☐ 435	Turn back clock 1962 35	.16	.04
	Maury Wills 104 steals		
☐ 436	Turn back clock 1957 35	.16	.04

	Bob Keegan hurls			
	Majors' only no-hitter			
☐ 437	Turn back clock 1952 50	.23	.06	
	Ralph Kiner leads NL in			
	HR's 7th straight year			
☐ 438	Marty Perez....................25	.11	.03	
☐ 439	Gorman Thomas 35	.16	.04	
☐ 440	Jon Matlack 25	.11	.03	
☐ 441	Larvell Blanks 25	.11	.03	
☐ 442	Braves Team/Mgr. 1.00	.45	.13	
	Dave Bristol			
	(Checklist back)			
☐ 443	Lamar Johnson 25	.11	.03	
☐ 444	Wayne Twitchell.............25	.11	.03	
☐ 445	Ken Singleton 35	.16	.04	
☐ 446	Bill Bonham 25	.11	.03	
☐ 447	Jerry Turner 25	.11	.03	
☐ 448	Ellie Rodriguez 25	.11	.03	
☐ 449	Al Fitzmorris.................25	.11	.03	
☐ 450	Pete Rose 9.00	4.00	1.15	
☐ 451	Checklist 4 ....1.25	.13	.04	
☐ 452	Mike Caldwell................25	.11	.03	
☐ 453	Pedro Garcia 25	.11	.03	
☐ 454	Andy Etchebarren..........25	.11	.03	
☐ 455	Rick Wise......................25	.11	.03	
☐ 456	Leon Roberts 25	.11	.03	
☐ 457	Steve Luebber...............25	.11	.03	
☐ 458	Leo Foster.....................25	.11	.03	
☐ 459	Steve Foucault 25	.11	.03	
☐ 460	Willie Stargell...............3.00	1.35	.40	
☐ 461	Dick Tidrow....................25	.11	.03	
☐ 462	Don Baylor 1.25	.55	.16	
☐ 463	Jamie Quirk 25	.11	.03	
☐ 464	Randy Moffitt.................25	.11	.03	
☐ 465	Rico Carty.....................35	.16	.04	
☐ 466	Fred Holdsworth 25	.11	.03	
☐ 467	Phillies Team/Mgr.........1.00	.45	.13	
	Danny Ozark			
	(Checklist back)			
☐ 468	Ramon Hernandez 25	.11	.03	
☐ 469	Pat Kelly.......................25	.11	.03	
☐ 470	Ted Simmons 1.00	.45	.13	
☐ 471	Del Unser......................25	.11	.03	
☐ 472	Rookie Pitchers...............35	.16	.04	
	Don Aase			
	Bob McClure			
	Gil Patterson			
	Dave Wehrmeister			
☐ 473	Rookie Outfielders 75.00	34.00	9.50	
	Andre Dawson			
	Gene Richards			
	John Scott			
	Denny Walling			
☐ 474	Rookie Shortstops 50	.23	.06	
	Bob Bailor			
	Kiko Garcia			
	Craig Reynolds			

	Alex Taveras			
☐ 475	Rookie Pitchers..............50	.23	.06	
	Chris Batton			
	Rick Camp			
	Scott McGregor			
	Manny Sarmiento			
☐ 476	Rookie Catchers........30.00	13.50	3.80	
	Gary Alexander			
	Rick Cerone			
	Dale Murphy			
	Kevin Pasley			
☐ 477	Rookie Infielders.............35	.16	.04	
	Doug Ault			
	Rich Dauer			
	Orlando Gonzalez			
	Phil Mankowski			
☐ 478	Rookie Pitchers...............35	.16	.04	
	Jim Gideon			
	Leon Hooten			
	Dave Johnson			
	Mark Lemongello			
☐ 479	Rookie Outfielders 35	.16	.04	
	Brian Asselstine			
	Wayne Gross			
	Sam Mejias			
	Alvis Woods			
☐ 480	Carl Yastrzemski 6.00	2.70	.75	
☐ 481	Roger Metzger...............25	.11	.03	
☐ 482	Tony Solaita...................25	.11	.03	
☐ 483	Richie Zisk....................25	.11	.03	
☐ 484	Burt Hooton 35	.16	.04	
☐ 485	Roy White 35	.16	.04	
☐ 486	Ed Bane........................25	.11	.03	
☐ 487	Rookie Pitchers...............35	.16	.04	
	Larry Anderson			
	Ed Glynn			
	Joe Henderson			
	Greg Terlecky			
☐ 488	Rookie Outfielders 10.00	4.50	1.25	
	Jack Clark			
	Ruppert Jones			
	Lee Mazzilli			
	Dan Thomas			
☐ 489	Rookie Pitchers...............35	.16	.04	
	Len Barker			
	Randy Lerch			
	Greg Minton			
	Mike Overy			
☐ 490	Rookie Shortstops...........35	.16	.04	
	Billy Almon			
	Mickey Klutts			
	Tommy McMillan			
	Mark Wagner			
☐ 491	Rookie Pitchers............8.00	3.60	1.00	
	Mike Dupree			
	Dennis Martinez			
	Craig Mitchell			

	Bob Sykes		
☐ 492	Rookie Outfielders 75	.35	.09
	Tony Armas		
	Steve Kemp		
	Carlos Lopez		
	Gary Woods		
☐ 493	Rookie Pitchers...............40	.18	.05
	Mike Krukow		
	Jim Otten		
	Gary Wheelock		
	Mike Willis		
☐ 494	Rookie Infielders..........2.00	.90	.25
	Juan Bernhardt		
	Mike Champion		
	Jim Gantner		
	Bump Wills		
☐ 495	Al Hrabosky 25	.11	.03
☐ 496	Gary Thomasson...........25	.11	.03
☐ 497	Clay Carroll 25	.11	.03
☐ 498	Sal Bando 35	.16	.04
☐ 499	Pablo Torrealba...........25	.11	.03
☐ 500	Dave Kingman...............60	.25	.08
☐ 501	Jim Bibby 25	.11	.03
☐ 502	Randy Hundley 25	.11	.03
☐ 503	Bill Lee 25	.11	.03
☐ 504	Dodgers Team/Mgr. ..1.00	.45	.13
	Tom Lasorda		
	(Checklist back)		
☐ 505	Oscar Gamble 35	.16	.04
☐ 506	Steve Grilli 25	.11	.03
☐ 507	Mike Hegan 25	.11	.03
☐ 508	Dave Pagan...............25	.11	.03
☐ 509	Cookie Rojas...............35	.16	.04
☐ 510	John Candelaria............65	.30	.08
☐ 511	Bill Fahey 25	.11	.03
☐ 512	Jack Billingham............25	.11	.03
☐ 513	Jerry Terrell 25	.11	.03
☐ 514	Cliff Johnson...............25	.11	.03
☐ 515	Chris Speier 25	.11	.03
☐ 516	Bake McBride...............35	.16	.04
☐ 517	Pete Vuckovich............40	.18	.05
☐ 518	Cubs Team/Mgr. 1.00	.45	.13
	Herman Franks		
	(Checklist back)		
☐ 519	Don Kirkwood 25	.11	.03
☐ 520	Garry Maddox...............25	.11	.03
☐ 521	Bob Grich...............45	.20	.06
☐ 522	Enzo Hernandez 25	.11	.03
☐ 523	Rollie Fingers............4.00	1.80	.50
☐ 524	Rowland Office 25	.11	.03
☐ 525	Dennis Eckersley......20.00	9.00	2.50
☐ 526	Larry Parrish...............35	.16	.04
☐ 527	Dan Meyer 25	.11	.03
☐ 528	Bill Castro 25	.11	.03
☐ 529	Jim Essian 50	.23	.06
☐ 530	Rick Reuschel...............35	.16	.04
☐ 531	Lyman Bostock...............35	.16	.04

☐ 532	Jim Willoughby...............25	.11	.03
☐ 533	Mickey Stanley...............25	.11	.03
☐ 534	Paul Splittorff...............25	.11	.03
☐ 535	Cesar Geronimo 25	.11	.03
☐ 536	Vic Albury 25	.11	.03
☐ 537	Dave Roberts 25	.11	.03
☐ 538	Frank Taveras 25	.11	.03
☐ 539	Mike Wallace...............25	.11	.03
☐ 540	Bob Watson 35	.16	.04
☐ 541	John Denny 35	.16	.04
☐ 542	Frank Duffy 25	.11	.03
☐ 543	Ron Blomberg...............25	.11	.03
☐ 544	Gary Ross 25	.11	.03
☐ 545	Bob Boone 75	.35	.09
☐ 546	Orioles Team/Mgr. 1.00	.45	.13
	Earl Weaver		
	(Checklist back)		
☐ 547	Willie McCovey 4.00	1.80	.50
☐ 548	Joel Youngblood............25	.11	.03
☐ 549	Jerry Royster 25	.11	.03
☐ 550	Randy Jones 35	.16	.04
☐ 551	Bill North...............25	.11	.03
☐ 552	Pepe Mangual...............25	.11	.03
☐ 553	Jack Heidemann 25	.11	.03
☐ 554	Bruce Kimm 25	.11	.03
☐ 555	Dan Ford 25	.11	.03
☐ 556	Doug Bird 25	.11	.03
☐ 557	Jerry White 25	.11	.03
☐ 558	Elias Sosa 25	.11	.03
☐ 559	Alan Bannister 25	.11	.03
☐ 560	Dave Concepcion 1.00	.45	.13
☐ 561	Pete LaCock 25	.11	.03
☐ 562	Checklist 5 ....1.25	.13	.04
☐ 563	Bruce Kison 25	.11	.03
☐ 564	Alan Ashby 25	.11	.03
☐ 565	Mickey Lolich...............45	.20	.06
☐ 566	Rick Miller 25	.11	.03
☐ 567	Enos Cabell 25	.11	.03
☐ 568	Carlos May 25	.11	.03
☐ 569	Jim Lonborg 35	.16	.04
☐ 570	Bobby Bonds 75	.35	.09
☐ 571	Darrell Evans 35	.16	.04
☐ 572	Ross Grimsley...............25	.11	.03
☐ 573	Joe Ferguson 25	.11	.03
☐ 574	Aurelio Rodriguez 25	.11	.03
☐ 575	Dick Ruthven 25	.11	.03
☐ 576	Fred Kendall...............25	.11	.03
☐ 577	Jerry Augustine...............25	.11	.03
☐ 578	Bob Randall 25	.11	.03
☐ 579	Don Carrithers 25	.11	.03
☐ 580	George Brett 35.00	16.00	4.40
☐ 581	Pedro Borbon 25	.11	.03
☐ 582	Ed Kirkpatrick 25	.11	.03
☐ 583	Paul Lindblad 25	.11	.03
☐ 584	Ed Goodson 25	.11	.03
☐ 585	Rick Burleson 35	.16	.04
☐ 586	Steve Renko 25	.11	.03

☐ 587	Rick Baldwin	.25	.11	.03
☐ 588	Dave Moates	.25	.11	.03
☐ 589	Mike Cosgrove	.25	.11	.03
☐ 590	Buddy Bell	.40	.18	.05
☐ 591	Chris Arnold	.25	.11	.03
☐ 592	Dan Briggs	.25	.11	.03
☐ 593	Dennis Blair	.25	.11	.03
☐ 594	Biff Pocoroba	.25	.11	.03
☐ 595	John Hiller	.25	.11	.03
☐ 596	Jerry Martin	.25	.11	.03
☐ 597	Mariners Leaders	1.00	.45	.13
	Darrell Johnson MG			
	Don Bryant CO			
	Jim Busby CO			
	Vada Pinson CO			
	Wes Stock CO			
	(Checklist back)			
☐ 598	Sparky Lyle	.60	.25	.08
☐ 599	Mike Tyson	.25	.11	.03
☐ 600	Jim Palmer	7.50	3.40	.95
☐ 601	Mike Lum	.25	.11	.03
☐ 602	Andy Hassler	.25	.11	.03
☐ 603	Willie Davis	.35	.16	.04
☐ 604	Jim Slaton	.25	.11	.03
☐ 605	Felix Millan	.25	.11	.03
☐ 606	Steve Braun	.25	.11	.03
☐ 607	Larry Demery	.25	.11	.03
☐ 608	Roy Howell	.25	.11	.03
☐ 609	Jim Barr	.25	.11	.03
☐ 610	Jose Cardenal	.25	.11	.03
☐ 611	Dave Lemanczyk	.25	.11	.03
☐ 612	Barry Foote	.25	.11	.03
☐ 613	Reggie Cleveland	.25	.11	.03
☐ 614	Greg Gross	.25	.11	.03
☐ 615	Phil Niekro	2.50	1.15	.30
☐ 616	Tommy Sandt	.40	.18	.05
☐ 617	Bobby Darwin	.25	.11	.03
☐ 618	Pat Dobson	.25	.11	.03
☐ 619	Johnny Oates	.25	.11	.03
☐ 620	Don Sutton	2.50	1.15	.30
☐ 621	Tigers Team/Mgr.	1.00	.45	.13
	Ralph Houk			
	(Checklist back)			
☐ 622	Jim Wohlford	.25	.11	.03
☐ 623	Jack Kucek	.25	.11	.03
☐ 624	Hector Cruz	.25	.11	.03
☐ 625	Ken Holtzman	.35	.16	.04
☐ 626	Al Bumbry	.25	.11	.03
☐ 627	Bob Myrick	.25	.11	.03
☐ 628	Mario Guerrero	.25	.11	.03
☐ 629	Bobby Valentine	.35	.16	.04
☐ 630	Bert Blyleven	2.00	.90	.25
☐ 631	Big League Brothers	5.00	2.30	.60
	George Brett			
	Ken Brett			
☐ 632	Big League Brothers	.35	.16	.04
	Bob Forsch			

	Ken Forsch			
☐ 633	Big League Brothers	.35	.16	.04
	Lee May			
	Carlos May			
☐ 634	Big League Brothers	.35	.16	.04
	Paul Reuschel			
	Rick Reuschel UER			
	(Photos switched)			
☐ 635	Robin Yount	35.00	16.00	4.40
☐ 636	Santo Alcala	.25	.11	.03
☐ 637	Alex Johnson	.25	.11	.03
☐ 638	Jim Kaat	1.00	.45	.13
☐ 639	Jerry Morales	.25	.11	.03
☐ 640	Carlton Fisk	10.00	4.50	1.25
☐ 641	Dan Larson	.25	.11	.03
☐ 642	Willie Crawford	.25	.11	.03
☐ 643	Mike Pazik	.25	.11	.03
☐ 644	Matt Alexander	.25	.11	.03
☐ 645	Jerry Reuss	.35	.16	.04
☐ 646	Andres Mora	.25	.11	.03
☐ 647	Expos Team/Mgr.	1.00	.45	.13
	Dick Williams			
	(Checklist back)			
☐ 648	Jim Spencer	.25	.11	.03
☐ 649	Dave Cash	.25	.11	.03
☐ 650	Nolan Ryan	40.00	18.00	5.00
☐ 651	Von Joshua	.25	.11	.03
☐ 652	Tom Walker	.25	.11	.03
☐ 653	Diego Segui	.25	.11	.03
☐ 654	Ron Pruitt	.25	.11	.03
☐ 655	Tony Perez	2.00	.90	.25
☐ 656	Ron Guidry	2.00	.90	.25
☐ 657	Mick Kelleher	.25	.11	.03
☐ 658	Marty Pattin	.25	.11	.03
☐ 659	Merv Rettenmund	.25	.11	.03
☐ 660	Willie Horton	.50	.23	.06

1978 Topps

The cards in this 726-card set measure 2 1/2" by 3 1/2". The 1978 Topps set experienced an increase in number of cards from the previous five regular issue sets of 660. Card numbers 1 through 7 feature Record Breakers (RB) of the 1977 season. Other subsets within this set include League Leaders (201-208), Post-season cards (411-413), and Rookie Prospects (701-711). The key Rookie Cards in this set are the multi-player Rookie Card of Paul Molitor and Alan Trammell, Jack Morris, Eddie Murray, Lance Parrish, and Lou Whitaker. The manager cards in the

set feature a "then and now" format on the card front showing the manager as he looked many years before, e.g., during his playing days. While no scarcities exist, 66 of the cards are more abundant in supply, as they were "double printed." These 66 double-printed cards are noted in the checklist by DP. Team cards again feature a checklist of that team's players in the set on the back. Cards numbered 23 or lower, that feature Astros, Rangers, Tigers, or Yankees and do not follow the numbering checklisted below, are not necessarily error cards. They are undoubtedly Burger King cards, a separate set with its own pricing and mass distribution. Burger King cards are indistinguishable from the corresponding Topps cards except for the card numbering difference and the fact that Burger King cards do not have a printing sheet designation (such as A through F like the regular Topps) anywhere on the card back in very small print.

	NRMT-MT	EXC	G-VG
COMPLETE SET (726)	325.00	145.00	40.00
COMMON PLAYER (1-726)	.20	.09	.03
COMMON PLAYER DP	.10	.05	.01

☐ 1	RB: Lou Brock	3.00	.75	.24
	Most steals, lifetime			
☐ 2	RB: Sparky Lyle	.35	.16	.04
	Most games, pure			
	relief, lifetime			
☐ 3	RB: Willie McCovey	1.25	.55	.16
	Most times, 2 HR's			
	in inning, lifetime			
☐ 4	RB: Brooks Robinson	1.50	.65	.19
	Most consecutive			
	seasons with one club			
☐ 5	RB: Pete Rose	3.00	1.35	.40
	Most hits, switch			
	hitter, lifetime			
☐ 6	RB: Nolan Ryan	8.00	3.60	1.00
	Most games with			
	10 or more			
	strikeouts, lifetime			
☐ 7	RB: Reggie Jackson	4.00	1.80	.50
	Most homers,			
	one World Series			
☐ 8	Mike Sadek	.10	.05	.01
☐ 9	Doug DeCinces	.20	.09	.03
☐ 10	Phil Niekro	2.00	.90	.25
☐ 11	Rick Manning	.10	.05	.01
☐ 12	Don Aase	.10	.05	.01
☐ 13	Art Howe	.75	.35	.09
☐ 14	Lerrin LaGrow	.10	.05	.01
☐ 15	Tony Perez DP	.75	.35	.09
☐ 16	Roy White	.20	.09	.03
☐ 17	Mike Krukow	.10	.05	.01
☐ 18	Bob Grich	.30	.14	.04
☐ 19	Darrell Porter	.20	.09	.03
☐ 20	Pete Rose DP	4.00	1.80	.50
☐ 21	Steve Kemp	.10	.05	.01
☐ 22	Charlie Hough	.20	.09	.03
☐ 23	Bump Wills	.10	.05	.01
☐ 24	Don Money DP	.10	.05	.01
☐ 25	Jon Matlack	.10	.05	.01
☐ 26	Rich Hebner	.10	.05	.01
☐ 27	Geoff Zahn	.10	.05	.01
☐ 28	Ed Ott	.10	.05	.01
☐ 29	Bob Lacey	.10	.05	.01
☐ 30	George Hendrick	.20	.09	.03
☐ 31	Glenn Abbott	.10	.05	.01
☐ 32	Garry Templeton	.30	.14	.04
☐ 33	Dave Lemanczyk	.10	.05	.01
☐ 34	Willie McCovey	3.00	1.35	.40
☐ 35	Sparky Lyle	.30	.14	.04
☐ 36	Eddie Murray	75.00	34.00	9.50
☐ 37	Rick Waits	.10	.05	.01
☐ 38	Willie Montanez	.10	.05	.01
☐ 39	Floyd Bannister	.60	.25	.08
☐ 40	Carl Yastrzemski	4.50	2.00	.55
☐ 41	Burt Hooton	.20	.09	.03
☐ 42	Jorge Orta	.10	.05	.01
☐ 43	Bill Atkinson	.10	.05	.01
☐ 44	Toby Harrah	.20	.09	.03
☐ 45	Mark Fidrych	.50	.23	.06
☐ 46	Al Cowens	.10	.05	.01
☐ 47	Jack Billingham	.10	.05	.01
☐ 48	Don Baylor	1.00	.45	.13
☐ 49	Ed Kranepool	.10	.05	.01
☐ 50	Rick Reuschel	.20	.09	.03
☐ 51	Charlie Moore DP	.10	.05	.01
☐ 52	Jim Lonborg	.10	.05	.01
☐ 53	Phil Garner DP	.10	.05	.01
☐ 54	Tom Johnson	.10	.05	.01
☐ 55	Mitchell Page	.10	.05	.01
☐ 56	Randy Jones	.10	.05	.01
☐ 57	Dan Meyer	.10	.05	.01

☐ 58	Bob Forsch	.10	.05	.01
☐ 59	Otto Velez	.10	.05	.01
☐ 60	Thurman Munson	5.00	2.30	.60
☐ 61	Larvell Blanks	.10	.05	.01
☐ 62	Jim Barr	.10	.05	.01
☐ 63	Don Zimmer MG	.20	.09	.03
☐ 64	Gene Pentz	.10	.05	.01
☐ 65	Ken Singleton	.20	.09	.03
☐ 66	Chicago White Sox	.75	.35	.09
	Team Card			
	(Checklist back)			
☐ 67	Claudell Washington	.20	.09	.03
☐ 68	Steve Foucault DP	.10	.05	.01
☐ 69	Mike Vail	.10	.05	.01
☐ 70	Rich Gossage	1.00	.45	.13
☐ 71	Terry Humphrey	.10	.05	.01
☐ 72	Andre Dawson	25.00	11.50	3.10
☐ 73	Andy Hassler	.10	.05	.01
☐ 74	Checklist 1	1.00	.45	.13
☐ 75	Dick Ruthven	.10	.05	.01
☐ 76	Steve Ontiveros	.10	.05	.01
☐ 77	Ed Kirkpatrick	.10	.05	.01
☐ 78	Pablo Torrealba	.10	.05	.01
☐ 79	Darrell Johnson DP MG	.10	.05	.01
☐ 80	Ken Griffey	1.00	.45	.13
☐ 81	Pete Redfern	.10	.05	.01
☐ 82	San Francisco Giants	.75	.35	.09
	Team Card			
	(Checklist back)			
☐ 83	Bob Montgomery	.10	.05	.01
☐ 84	Kent Tekulve	.20	.09	.03
☐ 85	Ron Fairly	.10	.05	.01
☐ 86	Dave Tomlin	.10	.05	.01
☐ 87	John Lowenstein	.10	.05	.01
☐ 88	Mike Phillips	.10	.05	.01
☐ 89	Ken Clay	.10	.05	.01
☐ 90	Larry Bowa	.30	.14	.04
☐ 91	Oscar Zamora	.10	.05	.01
☐ 92	Adrian Devine	.10	.05	.01
☐ 93	Bobby Cox DP	.10	.05	.01
☐ 94	Chuck Scrivener	.10	.05	.01
☐ 95	Jamie Quirk	.10	.05	.01
☐ 96	Baltimore Orioles	.75	.35	.09
	Team Card			
	(Checklist back)			
☐ 97	Stan Bahnsen	.10	.05	.01
☐ 98	Jim Essian	.20	.09	.03
☐ 99	Willie Hernandez	.60	.25	.08
☐ 100	George Brett	25.00	11.50	3.10
☐ 101	Sid Monge	.10	.05	.01
☐ 102	Matt Alexander	.10	.05	.01
☐ 103	Tom Murphy	.10	.05	.01
☐ 104	Lee Lacy	.10	.05	.01
☐ 105	Reggie Cleveland	.10	.05	.01
☐ 106	Bill Plummer	.10	.05	.01
☐ 107	Ed Halicki	.10	.05	.01
☐ 108	Von Joshua	.10	.05	.01
☐ 109	Joe Torre MG	.50	.23	.06
☐ 110	Richie Zisk	.10	.05	.01
☐ 111	Mike Tyson	.10	.05	.01
☐ 112	Houston Astros	.75	.35	.09
	Team Card			
	(Checklist back)			
☐ 113	Don Carrithers	.10	.05	.01
☐ 114	Paul Blair	.20	.09	.03
☐ 115	Gary Nolan	.10	.05	.01
☐ 116	Tucker Ashford	.10	.05	.01
☐ 117	John Montague	.10	.05	.01
☐ 118	Terry Harmon	.10	.05	.01
☐ 119	Dennis Martinez	2.50	1.15	.30
☐ 120	Gary Carter	4.50	2.00	.55
☐ 121	Alvis Woods	.10	.05	.01
☐ 122	Dennis Eckersley	9.00	4.00	1.15
☐ 123	Manny Trillo	.10	.05	.01
☐ 124	Dave Rozema	.10	.05	.01
☐ 125	George Scott	.20	.09	.03
☐ 126	Paul Moskau	.10	.05	.01
☐ 127	Chet Lemon	.20	.09	.03
☐ 128	Bill Russell	.20	.09	.03
☐ 129	Jim Colborn	.10	.05	.01
☐ 130	Jeff Burroughs	.20	.09	.03
☐ 131	Bert Blyleven	1.00	.45	.13
☐ 132	Enos Cabell	.10	.05	.01
☐ 133	Jerry Augustine	.10	.05	.01
☐ 134	Steve Henderson	.10	.05	.01
☐ 135	Ron Guidry DP	.75	.35	.09
☐ 136	Ted Sizemore	.10	.05	.01
☐ 137	Craig Kusick	.10	.05	.01
☐ 138	Larry Demery	.10	.05	.01
☐ 139	Wayne Gross	.10	.05	.01
☐ 140	Rollie Fingers	3.50	1.55	.45
☐ 141	Ruppert Jones	.10	.05	.01
☐ 142	John Montefusco	.20	.09	.03
☐ 143	Keith Hernandez	1.75	.80	.22
☐ 144	Jesse Jefferson	.10	.05	.01
☐ 145	Rick Monday	.20	.09	.03
☐ 146	Doyle Alexander	.10	.05	.01
☐ 147	Lee Mazzilli	.10	.05	.01
☐ 148	Andre Thornton	.20	.09	.03
☐ 149	Dale Murray	.10	.05	.01
☐ 150	Bobby Bonds	.40	.18	.05
☐ 151	Milt Wilcox	.10	.05	.01
☐ 152	Ivan DeJesus	.10	.05	.01
☐ 153	Steve Stone	.20	.09	.03
☐ 154	Cecil Cooper DP	.25	.11	.03
☐ 155	Butch Hobson	.30	.14	.04
☐ 156	Andy Messersmith	.20	.09	.03
☐ 157	Pete LaCock DP	.10	.05	.01
☐ 158	Joaquin Andujar	.20	.09	.03
☐ 159	Lou Piniella	.40	.18	.05
☐ 160	Jim Palmer	5.00	2.30	.60
☐ 161	Bob Boone	.75	.35	.09
☐ 162	Paul Thormodsgard	.10	.05	.01
☐ 163	Bill North	.10	.05	.01

☐ 164	Bob Owchinko	.10	.05	.01
☐ 165	Rennie Stennett	.10	.05	.01
☐ 166	Carlos Lopez	.10	.05	.01
☐ 167	Tim Foli	.10	.05	.01
☐ 168	Reggie Smith	.20	.09	.03
☐ 169	Jerry Johnson	.10	.05	.01
☐ 170	Lou Brock	3.50	1.55	.45
☐ 171	Pat Zachry	.10	.05	.01
☐ 172	Mike Hargrove	.20	.09	.03
☐ 173	Robin Yount UER	25.00	11.50	3.10
	(Played for Newark			
	in 1973, not 1971)			
☐ 174	Wayne Garland	.10	.05	.01
☐ 175	Jerry Morales	.10	.05	.01
☐ 176	Milt May	.10	.05	.01
☐ 177	Gene Garber DP	.10	.05	.01
☐ 178	Dave Chalk	.10	.05	.01
☐ 179	Dick Tidrow	.10	.05	.01
☐ 180	Dave Concepcion	1.00	.45	.13
☐ 181	Ken Forsch	.10	.05	.01
☐ 182	Jim Spencer	.10	.05	.01
☐ 183	Doug Bird	.10	.05	.01
☐ 184	Checklist 2	1.00	.45	.13
☐ 185	Ellis Valentine	.10	.05	.01
☐ 186	Bob Stanley DP	.10	.05	.01
☐ 187	Jerry Royster DP	.10	.05	.01
☐ 188	Al Bumbry	.10	.05	.01
☐ 189	Tom Lasorda MG	.30	.14	.04
☐ 190	John Candelaria	.20	.09	.03
☐ 191	Rodney Scott	.10	.05	.01
☐ 192	San Diego Padres	.75	.35	.09
	Team Card			
	(Checklist back)			
☐ 193	Rich Chiles	.10	.05	.01
☐ 194	Derrel Thomas	.10	.05	.01
☐ 195	Larry Dierker	.10	.05	.01
☐ 196	Bob Bailor	.10	.05	.01
☐ 197	Nino Espinosa	.10	.05	.01
☐ 198	Ron Pruitt	.10	.05	.01
☐ 199	Craig Reynolds	.10	.05	.01
☐ 200	Reggie Jackson	14.00	6.25	1.75
☐ 201	Batting Leaders	1.25	.55	.16
	Dave Parker			
	Rod Carew			
☐ 202	Home Run Leaders DP	.20	.09	.03
	George Foster			
	Jim Rice			
☐ 203	RBI Leaders	.40	.18	.05
	George Foster			
	Larry Hisle			
☐ 204	Steals Leaders DP	.20	.09	.03
	Frank Taveras			
	Freddie Patek			
☐ 205	Victory Leaders	1.50	.65	.19
	Steve Carlton			
	Dave Goltz			
	Dennis Leonard			

	Jim Palmer			
☐ 206	Strikeout Leaders DP	2.00	.90	.25
	Phil Niekro			
	Nolan Ryan			
☐ 207	ERA Leaders DP	.20	.09	.03
	John Candelaria			
	Frank Tanana			
☐ 208	Top Firemen	.75	.35	.09
	Rollie Fingers			
	Bill Campbell			
☐ 209	Dock Ellis	.10	.05	.01
☐ 210	Jose Cardenal	.10	.05	.01
☐ 211	Earl Weaver MG DP	.25	.11	.03
☐ 212	Mike Caldwell	.10	.05	.01
☐ 213	Alan Bannister	.10	.05	.01
☐ 214	California Angels	.75	.35	.09
	Team Card			
	(Checklist back)			
☐ 215	Darrell Evans	.30	.14	.04
☐ 216	Mike Paxton	.10	.05	.01
☐ 217	Rod Gilbreath	.10	.05	.01
☐ 218	Marty Pattin	.10	.05	.01
☐ 219	Mike Cubbage	.10	.05	.01
☐ 220	Pedro Borbon	.10	.05	.01
☐ 221	Chris Speier	.10	.05	.01
☐ 222	Jerry Martin	.10	.05	.01
☐ 223	Bruce Kison	.10	.05	.01
☐ 224	Jerry Tabb	.10	.05	.01
☐ 225	Don Gullett DP	.10	.05	.01
☐ 226	Joe Ferguson	.10	.05	.01
☐ 227	Al Fitzmorris	.10	.05	.01
☐ 228	Manny Mota DP	.10	.05	.01
☐ 229	Leo Foster	.10	.05	.01
☐ 230	Al Hrabosky	.10	.05	.01
☐ 231	Wayne Nordhagen	.10	.05	.01
☐ 232	Mickey Stanley	.10	.05	.01
☐ 233	Dick Pole	.10	.05	.01
☐ 234	Herman Franks MG	.10	.05	.01
☐ 235	Tim McCarver	.20	.09	.03
☐ 236	Terry Whitfield	.10	.05	.01
☐ 237	Rich Dauer	.10	.05	.01
☐ 238	Juan Beniquez	.10	.05	.01
☐ 239	Dyar Miller	.10	.05	.01
☐ 240	Gene Tenace	.20	.09	.03
☐ 241	Pete Vuckovich	.20	.09	.03
☐ 242	Barry Bonnell DP	.10	.05	.01
☐ 243	Bob McClure	.10	.05	.01
☐ 244	Montreal Expos	.40	.18	.05
	Team Card DP			
	(Checklist back)			
☐ 245	Rick Burleson	.20	.09	.03
☐ 246	Dan Driessen	.10	.05	.01
☐ 247	Larry Christenson	.10	.05	.01
☐ 248	Frank White DP	.10	.05	.01
☐ 249	Dave Goltz DP	.10	.05	.01
☐ 250	Graig Nettles DP	.30	.14	.04
☐ 251	Don Kirkwood	.10	.05	.01

☐	252	Steve Swisher DP	.10	.05	.01	☐	303	Sam Hinds	.10	.05	.01

☐ 252 Steve Swisher DP .10 .05 .01	☐ 303 Sam Hinds .10 .05 .01
☐ 253 Jim Kern .10 .05 .01	☐ 304 John Milner .10 .05 .01
☐ 254 Dave Collins .20 .09 .03	☐ 305 Rico Carty .20 .09 .03
☐ 255 Jerry Reuss .20 .09 .03	☐ 306 Joe Niekro .20 .09 .03
☐ 256 Joe Altobelli MG .10 .05 .01	☐ 307 Glenn Borgmann .10 .05 .01
☐ 257 Hector Cruz .10 .05 .01	☐ 308 Jim Rooker .10 .05 .01
☐ 258 John Hiller .10 .05 .01	☐ 309 Cliff Johnson .10 .05 .01
☐ 259 Los Angeles Dodgers .75 .35 .09	☐ 310 Don Sutton 2.50 1.15 .30
Team Card	☐ 311 Jose Baez DP .10 .05 .01
(Checklist back)	☐ 312 Greg Minton .10 .05 .01
☐ 260 Bert Campaneris .20 .09 .03	☐ 313 Andy Etchebarren .10 .05 .01
☐ 261 Tim Hosley .10 .05 .01	☐ 314 Paul Lindblad .10 .05 .01
☐ 262 Rudy May .10 .05 .01	☐ 315 Mark Belanger .20 .09 .03
☐ 263 Danny Walton .10 .05 .01	☐ 316 Henry Cruz DP .10 .05 .01
☐ 264 Jamie Easterly .10 .05 .01	☐ 317 Dave Johnson .10 .05 .01
☐ 265 Sal Bando DP .10 .05 .01	☐ 318 Tom Griffin .10 .05 .01
☐ 266 Bob Shirley .10 .05 .01	☐ 319 Alan Ashby .10 .05 .01
☐ 267 Doug Ault .10 .05 .01	☐ 320 Fred Lynn 1.00 .45 .13
☐ 268 Gil Flores .10 .05 .01	☐ 321 Santo Alcala .10 .05 .01
☐ 269 Wayne Twitchell .10 .05 .01	☐ 322 Tom Paciorek .20 .09 .03
☐ 270 Carlton Fisk 7.50 3.40 .95	☐ 323 Jim Fregosi DP .10 .05 .01
☐ 271 Randy Lerch DP .10 .05 .01	☐ 324 Vern Rapp MG .10 .05 .01
☐ 272 Royle Stillman .10 .05 .01	☐ 325 Bruce Sutter 1.25 .55 .16
☐ 273 Fred Norman .10 .05 .01	☐ 326 Mike Lum DP .10 .05 .01
☐ 274 Freddie Patek .20 .09 .03	☐ 327 Rick Langford DP .10 .05 .01
☐ 275 Dan Ford .10 .05 .01	☐ 328 Milwaukee Brewers .75 .35 .09
☐ 276 Bill Bonham DP .10 .05 .01	Team Card
☐ 277 Bruce Boisclair .10 .05 .01	(Checklist back)
☐ 278 Enrique Romo .10 .05 .01	☐ 329 John Verhoeven .10 .05 .01
☐ 279 Bill Virdon MG .10 .05 .01	☐ 330 Bob Watson .20 .09 .03
☐ 280 Buddy Bell .20 .09 .03	☐ 331 Mark Littell .10 .05 .01
☐ 281 Eric Rasmussen DP .10 .05 .01	☐ 332 Duane Kuiper .10 .05 .01
☐ 282 New York Yankees 1.25 .55 .16	☐ 333 Jim Todd .10 .05 .01
Team Card	☐ 334 John Stearns .10 .05 .01
(Checklist back)	☐ 335 Bucky Dent .60 .25 .08
☐ 283 Omar Moreno .10 .05 .01	☐ 336 Steve Busby .10 .05 .01
☐ 284 Randy Moffitt .10 .05 .01	☐ 337 Tom Grieve .20 .09 .03
☐ 285 Steve Yeager DP .10 .05 .01	☐ 338 Dave Heaverlo .10 .05 .01
☐ 286 Ben Oglivie .20 .09 .03	☐ 339 Mario Guerrero .10 .05 .01
☐ 287 Kiko Garcia .10 .05 .01	☐ 340 Bake McBride .20 .09 .03
☐ 288 Dave Hamilton .10 .05 .01	☐ 341 Mike Flanagan .40 .18 .05
☐ 289 Checklist 3 1.00 .45 .13	☐ 342 Aurelio Rodriguez .10 .05 .01
☐ 290 Willie Horton .20 .09 .03	☐ 343 John Wathan DP .10 .05 .01
☐ 291 Gary Ross .10 .05 .01	☐ 344 Sam Ewing .10 .05 .01
☐ 292 Gene Richards .10 .05 .01	☐ 345 Luis Tiant .30 .14 .04
☐ 293 Mike Willis .10 .05 .01	☐ 346 Larry Biittner .10 .05 .01
☐ 294 Larry Parrish .20 .09 .03	☐ 347 Terry Forster .10 .05 .01
☐ 295 Bill Lee .10 .05 .01	☐ 348 Del Unser .10 .05 .01
☐ 296 Biff Pocoroba .10 .05 .01	☐ 349 Rick Camp DP .10 .05 .01
☐ 297 Warren Brusstar DP .10 .05 .01	☐ 350 Steve Garvey 3.00 1.35 .40
☐ 298 Tony Armas .20 .09 .03	☐ 351 Jeff Torborg .20 .09 .03
☐ 299 Whitey Herzog MG .20 .09 .03	☐ 352 Tony Scott .10 .05 .01
☐ 300 Joe Morgan 3.50 1.55 .45	☐ 353 Doug Bair .10 .05 .01
☐ 301 Buddy Schultz .10 .05 .01	☐ 354 Cesar Geronimo .10 .05 .01
☐ 302 Chicago Cubs .75 .35 .09	☐ 355 Bill Travers .10 .05 .01
Team Card	☐ 356 New York Mets .75 .35 .09
(Checklist back)	Team Card

(Checklist back)

☐	357	Tom Poquette 10	.05	.01
☐	358	Mark Lemongello 10	.05	.01
☐	359	Marc Hill 10	.05	.01
☐	360	Mike Schmidt 18.00	8.00	2.30
☐	361	Chris Knapp 10	.05	.01
☐	362	Dave May 10	.05	.01
☐	363	Bob Randall 10	.05	.01
☐	364	Jerry Turner 10	.05	.01
☐	365	Ed Figueroa 10	.05	.01
☐	366	Larry Milbourne DP 10	.05	.01
☐	367	Rick Dempsey 20	.09	.03
☐	368	Balor Moore 10	.05	.01
☐	369	Tim Nordbrook 10	.05	.01
☐	370	Rusty Staub 30	.14	.04
☐	371	Ray Burris 10	.05	.01
☐	372	Brian Asselstine 10	.05	.01
☐	373	Jim Willoughby 10	.05	.01
☐	374	Jose Morales 10	.05	.01
☐	375	Tommy John 1.00	.45	.13
☐	376	Jim Wohlford 10	.05	.01
☐	377	Manny Sarmiento 10	.05	.01
☐	378	Bobby Winkles MG 10	.05	.01
☐	379	Skip Lockwood 10	.05	.01
☐	380	Ted Simmons 1.00	.45	.13
☐	381	Philadelphia Phillies 75	.35	.09
		Team Card		
		(Checklist back)		
☐	382	Joe Lahoud 10	.05	.01
☐	383	Mario Mendoza 10	.05	.01
☐	384	Jack Clark 2.00	.90	.25
☐	385	Tito Fuentes 10	.05	.01
☐	386	Bob Gorinski 10	.05	.01
☐	387	Ken Holtzman 10	.05	.01
☐	388	Bill Fahey DP 10	.05	.01
☐	389	Julio Gonzalez 10	.05	.01
☐	390	Oscar Gamble 20	.09	.03
☐	391	Larry Haney 10	.05	.01
☐	392	Billy Almon 10	.05	.01
☐	393	Tippy Martinez 20	.09	.03
☐	394	Roy Howell DP 10	.05	.01
☐	395	Jim Hughes 10	.05	.01
☐	396	Bob Stinson DP 10	.05	.01
☐	397	Greg Gross 10	.05	.01
☐	398	Don Hood 10	.05	.01
☐	399	Pete Mackanin 10	.05	.01
☐	400	Nolan Ryan 30.00	13.50	3.80
☐	401	Sparky Anderson MG 20	.09	.03
☐	402	Dave Campbell 10	.05	.01
☐	403	Bud Harrelson 10	.05	.01
☐	404	Detroit Tigers 75	.35	.09
		Team Card		
		(Checklist back)		
☐	405	Rawly Eastwick 10	.05	.01
☐	406	Mike Jorgensen 10	.05	.01
☐	407	Odell Jones 10	.05	.01
☐	408	Joe Zdeb 10	.05	.01

☐	409	Ron Schueler 10	.05	.01
☐	410	Bill Madlock 50	.23	.06
☐	411	AL Champs 50	.23	.06
		Yankees rally to		
		defeat Royals		
☐	412	NL Champs 50	.23	.06
		Dodgers overpower		
		Phillies in four		
☐	413	World Series 4.00	1.80	.50
		Reggie and Yankees		
		reign supreme		
☐	414	Darold Knowles DP 10	.05	.01
☐	415	Ray Fosse 10	.05	.01
☐	416	Jack Brohamer 10	.05	.01
☐	417	Mike Garman DP 10	.05	.01
☐	418	Tony Muser 10	.05	.01
☐	419	Jerry Garvin 10	.05	.01
☐	420	Greg Luzinski 30	.14	.04
☐	421	Junior Moore 10	.05	.01
☐	422	Steve Braun 10	.05	.01
☐	423	Dave Rosello 10	.05	.01
☐	424	Boston Red Sox 75	.35	.09
		Team Card		
		(Checklist back)		
☐	425	Steve Rogers DP 10	.05	.01
☐	426	Fred Kendall 10	.05	.01
☐	427	Mario Soto 40	.18	.05
☐	428	Joel Youngblood 10	.05	.01
☐	429	Mike Barlow 10	.05	.01
☐	430	Al Oliver 50	.23	.06
☐	431	Butch Metzger 10	.05	.01
☐	432	Terry Bulling 10	.05	.01
☐	433	Fernando Gonzalez 10	.05	.01
☐	434	Mike Norris 10	.05	.01
☐	435	Checklist 4 ....1.00	.45	.13
☐	436	Vic Harris DP 10	.05	.01
☐	437	Bo McLaughlin 10	.05	.01
☐	438	John Ellis 10	.05	.01
☐	439	Ken Kravec 10	.05	.01
☐	440	Dave Lopes 30	.14	.04
☐	441	Larry Gura 10	.05	.01
☐	442	Elliott Maddox 10	.05	.01
☐	443	Darrel Chaney 10	.05	.01
☐	444	Roy Hartsfield MG 10	.05	.01
☐	445	Mike Ivie 10	.05	.01
☐	446	Tug McGraw 30	.14	.04
☐	447	Leroy Stanton 10	.05	.01
☐	448	Bill Castro 10	.05	.01
☐	449	Tim Blackwell DP 10	.05	.01
☐	450	Tom Seaver 8.00	3.60	1.00
☐	451	Minnesota Twins 75	.35	.09
		Team Card		
		(Checklist back)		
☐	452	Jerry Mumphrey 10	.05	.01
☐	453	Doug Flynn 10	.05	.01
☐	454	Dave LaRoche 10	.05	.01
☐	455	Bill Robinson 20	.09	.03

☐ 456 Vern Ruhle	10	.05	.01
☐ 457 Bob Bailey	10	.05	.01
☐ 458 Jeff Newman	10	.05	.01
☐ 459 Charlie Spikes	10	.05	.01
☐ 460 Jim Hunter	2.50	1.15	.30
☐ 461 Rob Andrews DP	10	.05	.01
☐ 462 Rogelio Moret	10	.05	.01
☐ 463 Kevin Bell	10	.05	.01
☐ 464 Jerry Grote	10	.05	.01
☐ 465 Hal McRae	30	.14	.04
☐ 466 Dennis Blair	10	.05	.01
☐ 467 Alvin Dark MG	20	.09	.03
☐ 468 Warren Cromartie	40	.18	.05
☐ 469 Rick Cerone	20	.09	.03
☐ 470 J.R. Richard	20	.09	.03
☐ 471 Roy Smalley	20	.09	.03
☐ 472 Ron Reed	10	.05	.01
☐ 473 Bill Buckner	40	.18	.05
☐ 474 Jim Slaton	10	.05	.01
☐ 475 Gary Matthews	20	.09	.03
☐ 476 Bill Stein	10	.05	.01
☐ 477 Doug Capilla	10	.05	.01
☐ 478 Jerry Remy	10	.05	.01
☐ 479 St. Louis Cardinals	75	.35	.09
Team Card			
(Checklist back)			
☐ 480 Ron LeFlore	20	.09	.03
☐ 481 Jackson Todd	10	.05	.01
☐ 482 Rick Miller	10	.05	.01
☐ 483 Ken Macha	10	.05	.01
☐ 484 Jim Norris	10	.05	.01
☐ 485 Chris Chambliss	20	.09	.03
☐ 486 John Curtis	10	.05	.01
☐ 487 Jim Tyrone	10	.05	.01
☐ 488 Dan Spillner	10	.05	.01
☐ 489 Rudy Meoli	10	.05	.01
☐ 490 Amos Otis	20	.09	.03
☐ 491 Scott McGregor	20	.09	.03
☐ 492 Jim Sundberg	20	.09	.03
☐ 493 Steve Renko	10	.05	.01
☐ 494 Chuck Tanner MG	20	.09	.03
☐ 495 Dave Cash	10	.05	.01
☐ 496 Jim Clancy DP	20	.09	.03
☐ 497 Glenn Adams	10	.05	.01
☐ 498 Joe Sambito	10	.05	.01
☐ 499 Seattle Mariners	75	.35	.09
Team Card			
(Checklist back)			
☐ 500 George Foster	90	.40	.11
☐ 501 Dave Roberts	10	.05	.01
☐ 502 Pat Rockett	10	.05	.01
☐ 503 Ike Hampton	10	.05	.01
☐ 504 Roger Freed	10	.05	.01
☐ 505 Felix Millan	10	.05	.01
☐ 506 Ron Blomberg	10	.05	.01
☐ 507 Willie Crawford	10	.05	.01
☐ 508 Johnny Oates	10	.05	.01
☐ 509 Brent Strom	10	.05	.01
☐ 510 Willie Stargell	3.00	1.35	.40
☐ 511 Frank Duffy	10	.05	.01
☐ 512 Larry Herndon	10	.05	.01
☐ 513 Barry Foote	10	.05	.01
☐ 514 Rob Sperring	10	.05	.01
☐ 515 Tim Corcoran	10	.05	.01
☐ 516 Gary Beare	10	.05	.01
☐ 517 Andres Mora	10	.05	.01
☐ 518 Tommy Boggs DP	10	.05	.01
☐ 519 Brian Downing	60	.25	.08
☐ 520 Larry Hisle	10	.05	.01
☐ 521 Steve Staggs	10	.05	.01
☐ 522 Dick Williams MG	20	.09	.03
☐ 523 Donnie Moore	10	.05	.01
☐ 524 Bernie Carbo	10	.05	.01
☐ 525 Jerry Terrell	10	.05	.01
☐ 526 Cincinnati Reds	75	.35	.09
Team Card			
(Checklist back)			
☐ 527 Vic Correll	10	.05	.01
☐ 528 Rob Picciolo	10	.05	.01
☐ 529 Paul Hartzell	10	.05	.01
☐ 530 Dave Winfield	14.00	6.25	1.75
☐ 531 Tom Underwood	10	.05	.01
☐ 532 Skip Jutze	10	.05	.01
☐ 533 Sandy Alomar	20	.09	.03
☐ 534 Wilbur Howard	10	.05	.01
☐ 535 Checklist 5	1.00	.45	.13
☐ 536 Roric Harrison	10	.05	.01
☐ 537 Bruce Bochte	10	.05	.01
☐ 538 Johnny LeMaster	10	.05	.01
☐ 539 Vic Davalillo DP	10	.05	.01
☐ 540 Steve Carlton	6.00	2.70	.75
☐ 541 Larry Cox	10	.05	.01
☐ 542 Tim Johnson	10	.05	.01
☐ 543 Larry Harlow DP	10	.05	.01
☐ 544 Len Randle DP	10	.05	.01
☐ 545 Bill Campbell	10	.05	.01
☐ 546 Ted Martinez	10	.05	.01
☐ 547 John Scott	10	.05	.01
☐ 548 Billy Hunter MG DP	10	.05	.01
☐ 549 Joe Kerrigan	10	.05	.01
☐ 550 John Mayberry	20	.09	.03
☐ 551 Atlanta Braves	75	.35	.09
Team Card			
(Checklist back)			
☐ 552 Francisco Barrios	10	.05	.01
☐ 553 Terry Puhl	40	.18	.05
☐ 554 Joe Coleman	10	.05	.01
☐ 555 Butch Wynegar	10	.05	.01
☐ 556 Ed Armbrister	10	.05	.01
☐ 557 Tony Solaita	10	.05	.01
☐ 558 Paul Mitchell	10	.05	.01
☐ 559 Phil Mankowski	10	.05	.01
☐ 560 Dave Parker	3.00	1.35	.40
☐ 561 Charlie Williams	10	.05	.01

☐ 562	Glenn Burke 10	.05	.01
☐ 563	Dave Rader 10	.05	.01
☐ 564	Mick Kelleher 10	.05	.01
☐ 565	Jerry Koosman 30	.14	.04
☐ 566	Merv Rettenmund 10	.05	.01
☐ 567	Dick Drago 10	.05	.01
☐ 568	Tom Hutton 10	.05	.01
☐ 569	Lary Sorensen 10	.05	.01
☐ 570	Dave Kingman 50	.23	.06
☐ 571	Buck Martinez 10	.05	.01
☐ 572	Rick Wise 10	.05	.01
☐ 573	Luis Gomez 10	.05	.01
☐ 574	Bob Lemon MG 40	.18	.05
☐ 575	Pat Dobson 10	.05	.01
☐ 576	Sam Mejias 10	.05	.01
☐ 577	Oakland A's....................75	.35	.09
	Team Card		
	(Checklist back)		
☐ 578	Buzz Capra 10	.05	.01
☐ 579	Rance Mulliniks 10	.05	.01
☐ 580	Rod Carew 6.00	2.70	.75
☐ 581	Lynn McGlothen 10	.05	.01
☐ 582	Fran Healy 10	.05	.01
☐ 583	George Medich 10	.05	.01
☐ 584	John Hale 10	.05	.01
☐ 585	Woodie Fryman DP 10	.05	.01
☐ 586	Ed Goodson 10	.05	.01
☐ 587	John Urrea 10	.05	.01
☐ 588	Jim Mason 10	.05	.01
☐ 589	Bob Knepper 50	.23	.06
☐ 590	Bobby Murcer 30	.14	.04
☐ 591	George Zeber 10	.05	.01
☐ 592	Bob Apodaca 10	.05	.01
☐ 593	Dave Skaggs 10	.05	.01
☐ 594	Dave Freisleben 10	.05	.01
☐ 595	Sixto Lezcano 10	.05	.01
☐ 596	Gary Wheelock 10	.05	.01
☐ 597	Steve Dillard 10	.05	.01
☐ 598	Eddie Solomon 10	.05	.01
☐ 599	Gary Woods 10	.05	.01
☐ 600	Frank Tanana 40	.18	.05
☐ 601	Gene Mauch MG 20	.09	.03
☐ 602	Eric Soderholm 10	.05	.01
☐ 603	Will McEnaney 10	.05	.01
☐ 604	Earl Williams 10	.05	.01
☐ 605	Rick Rhoden 20	.09	.03
☐ 606	Pittsburgh Pirates...........75	.35	.09
	Team Card		
	(Checklist back)		
☐ 607	Fernando Arroyo 10	.05	.01
☐ 608	Johnny Grubb 10	.05	.01
☐ 609	John Denny 10	.05	.01
☐ 610	Garry Maddox 20	.09	.03
☐ 611	Pat Scanlon 10	.05	.01
☐ 612	Ken Henderson 10	.05	.01
☐ 613	Marty Perez 10	.05	.01
☐ 614	Joe Wallis 10	.05	.01

☐ 615	Clay Carroll 10	.05	.01
☐ 616	Pat Kelly 10	.05	.01
☐ 617	Joe Nolan 10	.05	.01
☐ 618	Tommy Helms 10	.05	.01
☐ 619	Thad Bosley DP 10	.05	.01
☐ 620	Willie Randolph 1.00	.45	.13
☐ 621	Craig Swan DP 10	.05	.01
☐ 622	Champ Summers 10	.05	.01
☐ 623	Eduardo Rodriguez 10	.05	.01
☐ 624	Gary Alexander DP 10	.05	.01
☐ 625	Jose Cruz 20	.09	.03
☐ 626	Toronto Blue Jays...........40	.18	.05
	Team Card DP		
	(Checklist back)		
☐ 627	David Johnson 10	.05	.01
☐ 628	Ralph Garr 10	.05	.01
☐ 629	Don Stanhouse 10	.05	.01
☐ 630	Ron Cey 40	.18	.05
☐ 631	Danny Ozark MG 10	.05	.01
☐ 632	Rowland Office 10	.05	.01
☐ 633	Tom Veryzer 10	.05	.01
☐ 634	Len Barker 10	.05	.01
☐ 635	Joe Rudi 20	.09	.03
☐ 636	Jim Bibby 10	.05	.01
☐ 637	Duffy Dyer 10	.05	.01
☐ 638	Paul Splittorff..............10	.05	.01
☐ 639	Gene Clines 10	.05	.01
☐ 640	Lee May DP 10	.05	.01
☐ 641	Doug Rau 10	.05	.01
☐ 642	Denny Doyle 10	.05	.01
☐ 643	Tom House 10	.05	.01
☐ 644	Jim Dwyer 10	.05	.01
☐ 645	Mike Torrez 20	.09	.03
☐ 646	Rick Auerbach DP 10	.05	.01
☐ 647	Steve Dunning 10	.05	.01
☐ 648	Gary Thomasson 10	.05	.01
☐ 649	Moose Haas 10	.05	.01
☐ 650	Cesar Cedeno 20	.09	.03
☐ 651	Doug Rader 10	.05	.01
☐ 652	Checklist 6 ....1.00	.45	.13
☐ 653	Ron Hodges DP 10	.05	.01
☐ 654	Pepe Frias 10	.05	.01
☐ 655	Lyman Bostock 20	.09	.03
☐ 656	Dave Garcia MG 10	.05	.01
☐ 657	Bombo Rivera 10	.05	.01
☐ 658	Manny Sanguillen 20	.09	.03
☐ 659	Texas Rangers................75	.35	.09
	Team Card		
	(Checklist back)		
☐ 660	Jason Thompson 20	.09	.03
☐ 661	Grant Jackson 10	.05	.01
☐ 662	Paul Dade 10	.05	.01
☐ 663	Paul Reuschel 10	.05	.01
☐ 664	Fred Stanley 10	.05	.01
☐ 665	Dennis Leonard 20	.09	.03
☐ 666	Billy Smith 10	.05	.01
☐ 667	Jeff Byrd 10	.05	.01

☐ 668	Dusty Baker	.30	.14	.04
☐ 669	Pete Falcone	.10	.05	.01
☐ 670	Jim Rice	3.00	1.35	.40
☐ 671	Gary Lavelle	.10	.05	.01
☐ 672	Don Kessinger	.20	.09	.03
☐ 673	Steve Brye	.10	.05	.01
☐ 674	Ray Knight	2.00	.90	.25
☐ 675	Jay Johnstone	.30	.14	.04
☐ 676	Bob Myrick	.10	.05	.01
☐ 677	Ed Herrmann	.10	.05	.01
☐ 678	Tom Burgmeier	.10	.05	.01
☐ 679	Wayne Garrett	.10	.05	.01
☐ 680	Vida Blue	.30	.14	.04
☐ 681	Rob Belloir	.10	.05	.01
☐ 682	Ken Brett	.10	.05	.01
☐ 683	Mike Champion	.10	.05	.01
☐ 684	Ralph Houk MG	.20	.09	.03
☐ 685	Frank Taveras	.10	.05	.01
☐ 686	Gaylord Perry	2.50	1.15	.30
☐ 687	Julio Cruz	.10	.05	.01
☐ 688	George Mitterwald	.10	.05	.01
☐ 689	Cleveland Indians	.75	.35	.09
	Team Card			
	(Checklist back)			
☐ 690	Mickey Rivers	.20	.09	.03
☐ 691	Ross Grimsley	.10	.05	.01
☐ 692	Ken Reitz	.10	.05	.01
☐ 693	Lamar Johnson	.10	.05	.01
☐ 694	Elias Sosa	.10	.05	.01
☐ 695	Dwight Evans	2.00	.90	.25
☐ 696	Steve Mingori	.10	.05	.01
☐ 697	Roger Metzger	.10	.05	.01
☐ 698	Juan Bernhardt	.10	.05	.01
☐ 699	Jackie Brown	.10	.05	.01
☐ 700	Johnny Bench	5.00	2.30	.60
☐ 701	Rookie Pitchers	.30	.14	.04
	Tom Hume			
	Larry Landreth			
	Steve McCatty			
	Bruce Taylor			
☐ 702	Rookie Catchers	.30	.14	.04
	Bill Nahorodny			
	Kevin Pasley			
	Rick Sweet			
	Don Werner			
☐ 703	Rookie Pitchers DP	18.00	8.00	2.30
	Larry Andersen			
	Tim Jones			
	Mickey Mahler			
	Jack Morris			
☐ 704	Rookie 2nd Basemen	20.00	9.00	2.50
	Garth Iorg			
	Dave Oliver			
	Sam Perlozzo			
	Lou Whitaker			
☐ 705	Rookie Outfielders	.50	.23	.06
	Dave Bergman			
	Miguel Dilone			
	Clint Hurdle			
	Willie Norwood			
☐ 706	Rookie 1st Basemen	.30	.14	.04
	Wayne Cage			
	Ted Cox			
	Pat Putnam			
	Dave Revering			
☐ 707	Rookie Shortstops	50.00	23.00	6.25
	Mickey Klutts			
	Paul Molitor			
	Alan Trammell			
	U.L. Washington			
☐ 708	Rookie Catchers	16.00	7.25	2.00
	Bo Diaz			
	Dale Murphy			
	Lance Parrish			
	Ernie Whitt			
☐ 709	Rookie Pitchers	.30	.14	.04
	Steve Burke			
	Matt Keough			
	Lance Rautzhan			
	Dan Schatzeder			
☐ 710	Rookie Outfielders	.60	.25	.08
	Dell Alston			
	Rick Bosetti			
	Mike Easler			
	Keith Smith			
☐ 711	Rookie Pitchers DP	.30	.14	.04
	Cardell Camper			
	Dennis Lamp			
	Craig Mitchell			
	Roy Thomas			
☐ 712	Bobby Valentine	.20	.09	.03
☐ 713	Bob Davis	.10	.05	.01
☐ 714	Mike Anderson	.10	.05	.01
☐ 715	Jim Kaat	.75	.35	.09
☐ 716	Clarence Gaston	.20	.09	.03
☐ 717	Nelson Briles	.10	.05	.01
☐ 718	Ron Jackson	.10	.05	.01
☐ 719	Randy Elliott	.10	.05	.01
☐ 720	Fergie Jenkins	2.50	1.15	.30
☐ 721	Billy Martin MG	.60	.25	.08
☐ 722	Pete Broberg	.10	.05	.01
☐ 723	John Wockenfuss	.10	.05	.01
☐ 724	Kansas City Royals	.75	.35	.09
	Team Card			
	(Checklist back)			
☐ 725	Kurt Bevacqua	.10	.05	.01
☐ 726	Wilbur Wood	.30	.14	.04

1979 Topps

	NRMT-MT	EXC	G-VG
COMPLETE SET (726)	250.00	115.00	31.00
COMMON PLAYER (1-726)	.15	.07	.02
COMMON PLAYER DP	.08	.04	.01

The cards in this 726-card set measure 2 1/2" by 3 1/2". Topps continued with the same number of cards as in 1978. Various series spotlight League Leaders (1-8), "Season and Career Record Holders" (411-418), "Record Breakers of 1978" (201-206), and one "Prospects" card for each team (701-726). Team cards feature a checklist on back of that team's players in the set and a small picture of the manager on the front of the card. There are 66 cards that were double printed and these are noted in the checklist by the abbreviation DP. Bump Wills (369) was initially depicted in a Ranger uniform but with a Blue Jays affiliation; later printings correctly labeled him with Texas. The set price listed does not include the scarcer Wills (Rangers) card. The key rookie cards in this set are Pedro Guerrero, Carney Lansford, Ozzie Smith, and Bob Welch. Cards numbered 23 or lower, which feature Phillies or Yankees and do not follow the numbering checklisted below, are not necessarily error cards. They are undoubtedly Burger King cards, separate sets for each team each with its own pricing and mass distribution. Burger King cards are indistinguishable from the corresponding Topps cards except for the card numbering difference and the fact that Burger King cards do not have a printing sheet designation (such as A through F like the regular Topps) anywhere on the card back in very small print.

		NRMT-MT	EXC	G-VG
☐ 1	Batting Leaders	3.00	.60	.18
	Rod Carew			
	Dave Parker			
☐ 2	Home Run Leaders	.35	.16	.04
	Jim Rice			
	George Foster			
☐ 3	RBI Leaders	.35	.16	.04
	Jim Rice			
	George Foster			
☐ 4	Stolen Base Leaders	.35	.16	.04
	Ron LeFlore			
	Omar Moreno			
☐ 5	Victory Leaders	.35	.16	.04
	Ron Guidry			
	Gaylord Perry			
☐ 6	Strikeout Leaders	4.00	1.80	.50
	Nolan Ryan			
	J.R. Richard			
☐ 7	ERA Leaders	.35	.16	.04
	Ron Guidry			
	Craig Swan			
☐ 8	Leading Firemen	.50	.23	.06
	Rich Gossage			
	Rollie Fingers			
☐ 9	Dave Campbell	.08	.04	.01
☐ 10	Lee May	.18	.08	.02
☐ 11	Marc Hill	.08	.04	.01
☐ 12	Dick Drago	.08	.04	.01
☐ 13	Paul Dade	.08	.04	.01
☐ 14	Rafael Landestoy	.08	.04	.01
☐ 15	Ross Grimsley	.08	.04	.01
☐ 16	Fred Stanley	.08	.04	.01
☐ 17	Donnie Moore	.08	.04	.01
☐ 18	Tony Solaita	.08	.04	.01
☐ 19	Larry Gura DP	.08	.04	.01
☐ 20	Joe Morgan DP	1.25	.55	.16
☐ 21	Kevin Kobel	.08	.04	.01
☐ 22	Mike Jorgensen	.08	.04	.01
☐ 23	Terry Forster	.08	.04	.01
☐ 24	Paul Molitor	14.00	6.25	1.75
☐ 25	Steve Carlton	4.00	1.80	.50
☐ 26	Jamie Quirk	.08	.04	.01
☐ 27	Dave Goltz	.08	.04	.01
☐ 28	Steve Brye	.08	.04	.01
☐ 29	Rick Langford	.08	.04	.01
☐ 30	Dave Winfield	10.00	4.50	1.25
☐ 31	Tom House DP	.08	.04	.01
☐ 32	Jerry Mumphrey	.08	.04	.01
☐ 33	Dave Rozema	.08	.04	.01
☐ 34	Rob Andrews	.08	.04	.01
☐ 35	Ed Figueroa	.08	.04	.01
☐ 36	Alan Ashby	.08	.04	.01

☐ 37 Joe Kerrigan DP	.08	.04	.01
☐ 38 Bernie Carbo	.08	.04	.01
☐ 39 Dale Murphy	7.50	3.40	.95
☐ 40 Dennis Eckersley	7.50	3.40	.95
☐ 41 Twins Team/Mgr.	.60	.25	.08
Gene Mauch			
(Checklist back)			
☐ 42 Ron Blomberg	.08	.04	.01
☐ 43 Wayne Twitchell	.08	.04	.01
☐ 44 Kurt Bevacqua	.08	.04	.01
☐ 45 Al Hrabosky	.08	.04	.01
☐ 46 Ron Hodges	.08	.04	.01
☐ 47 Fred Norman	.08	.04	.01
☐ 48 Merv Rettenmund	.08	.04	.01
☐ 49 Vern Ruhle	.08	.04	.01
☐ 50 Steve Garvey DP	1.50	.65	.19
☐ 51 Ray Fosse DP	.08	.04	.01
☐ 52 Randy Lerch	.08	.04	.01
☐ 53 Mick Kelleher	.08	.04	.01
☐ 54 Dell Alston DP	.08	.04	.01
☐ 55 Willie Stargell	2.50	1.15	.30
☐ 56 John Hale	.08	.04	.01
☐ 57 Eric Rasmussen	.08	.04	.01
☐ 58 Bob Randall DP	.08	.04	.01
☐ 59 John Denny DP	.08	.04	.01
☐ 60 Mickey Rivers	.18	.08	.02
☐ 61 Bo Diaz	.08	.04	.01
☐ 62 Randy Moffitt	.08	.04	.01
☐ 63 Jack Brohamer	.08	.04	.01
☐ 64 Tom Underwood	.08	.04	.01
☐ 65 Mark Belanger	.18	.08	.02
☐ 66 Tigers Team/Mgr.	.60	.25	.08
Les Moss			
(Checklist back)			
☐ 67 Jim Mason DP	.08	.04	.01
☐ 68 Joe Niekro DP	.08	.04	.01
☐ 69 Elliott Maddox	.08	.04	.01
☐ 70 John Candelaria	.18	.08	.02
☐ 71 Brian Downing	.50	.23	.06
☐ 72 Steve Mingori	.08	.04	.01
☐ 73 Ken Henderson	.08	.04	.01
☐ 74 Shane Rawley	.35	.16	.04
☐ 75 Steve Yeager	.18	.08	.02
☐ 76 Warren Cromartie	.18	.08	.02
☐ 77 Dan Briggs DP	.08	.04	.01
☐ 78 Elias Sosa	.08	.04	.01
☐ 79 Ted Cox	.08	.04	.01
☐ 80 Jason Thompson	.18	.08	.02
☐ 81 Roger Erickson	.08	.04	.01
☐ 82 Mets Team/Mgr.	.60	.25	.08
Joe Torre			
(Checklist back)			
☐ 83 Fred Kendall	.08	.04	.01
☐ 84 Greg Minton	.08	.04	.01
☐ 85 Gary Matthews	.18	.08	.02
☐ 86 Rodney Scott	.08	.04	.01
☐ 87 Pete Falcone	.08	.04	.01
☐ 88 Bob Molinaro	.08	.04	.01
☐ 89 Dick Tidrow	.08	.04	.01
☐ 90 Bob Boone	.50	.23	.06
☐ 91 Terry Crowley	.08	.04	.01
☐ 92 Jim Bibby	.08	.04	.01
☐ 93 Phil Mankowski	.08	.04	.01
☐ 94 Len Barker	.08	.04	.01
☐ 95 Robin Yount	15.00	6.75	1.90
☐ 96 Indians Team/Mgr.	.60	.25	.08
Jeff Torborg			
(Checklist back)			
☐ 97 Sam Mejias	.08	.04	.01
☐ 98 Ray Burris	.08	.04	.01
☐ 99 John Wathan	.18	.08	.02
☐ 100 Tom Seaver DP	3.75	1.70	.45
☐ 101 Roy Howell	.08	.04	.01
☐ 102 Mike Anderson	.08	.04	.01
☐ 103 Jim Todd	.08	.04	.01
☐ 104 Johnny Oates DP	.08	.04	.01
☐ 105 Rick Camp DP	.08	.04	.01
☐ 106 Frank Duffy	.08	.04	.01
☐ 107 Jesus Alou DP	.08	.04	.01
☐ 108 Eduardo Rodriguez	.08	.04	.01
☐ 109 Joel Youngblood	.08	.04	.01
☐ 110 Vida Blue	.18	.08	.02
☐ 111 Roger Freed	.08	.04	.01
☐ 112 Phillies Team/Mgr.	.60	.25	.08
Danny Ozark			
(Checklist back)			
☐ 113 Pete Redfern	.08	.04	.01
☐ 114 Cliff Johnson	.08	.04	.01
☐ 115 Nolan Ryan	27.00	12.00	3.40
☐ 116 Ozzie Smith	75.00	34.00	9.50
☐ 117 Grant Jackson	.08	.04	.01
☐ 118 Bud Harrelson	.08	.04	.01
☐ 119 Don Stanhouse	.08	.04	.01
☐ 120 Jim Sundberg	.18	.08	.02
☐ 121 Checklist 1 DP	.30	.03	.01
☐ 122 Mike Paxton	.08	.04	.01
☐ 123 Lou Whitaker	8.00	3.60	1.00
☐ 124 Dan Schatzeder	.08	.04	.01
☐ 125 Rick Burleson	.08	.04	.01
☐ 126 Doug Bair	.08	.04	.01
☐ 127 Thad Bosley	.08	.04	.01
☐ 128 Ted Martinez	.08	.04	.01
☐ 129 Marty Pattin DP	.08	.04	.01
☐ 130 Bob Watson DP	.08	.04	.01
☐ 131 Jim Clancy	.08	.04	.01
☐ 132 Rowland Office	.08	.04	.01
☐ 133 Bill Castro	.08	.04	.01
☐ 134 Alan Bannister	.08	.04	.01
☐ 135 Bobby Murcer	.18	.08	.02
☐ 136 Jim Kaat	.75	.35	.09
☐ 137 Larry Wolfe DP	.08	.04	.01
☐ 138 Mark Lee	.08	.04	.01
☐ 139 Luis Pujols	.08	.04	.01
☐ 140 Don Gullett	.18	.08	.02

☐ 141 Tom Paciorek	.18	.08	.02
☐ 142 Charlie Williams	.08	.04	.01
☐ 143 Tony Scott	.08	.04	.01
☐ 144 Sandy Alomar	.18	.08	.02
☐ 145 Rick Rhoden	.08	.04	.01
☐ 146 Duane Kuiper	.08	.04	.01
☐ 147 Dave Hamilton	.08	.04	.01
☐ 148 Bruce Boisclair	.08	.04	.01
☐ 149 Manny Sarmiento	.08	.04	.01
☐ 150 Wayne Cage	.08	.04	.01
☐ 151 John Hiller	.08	.04	.01
☐ 152 Rick Cerone	.08	.04	.01
☐ 153 Dennis Lamp	.08	.04	.01
☐ 154 Jim Gantner DP	.30	.14	.04
☐ 155 Dwight Evans	1.50	.65	.19
☐ 156 Buddy Solomon	.08	.04	.01
☐ 157 U.L. Washington UER	.08	.04	.01
(Sic, bats left, should be right)			
☐ 158 Joe Sambito	.08	.04	.01
☐ 159 Roy White	.18	.08	.02
☐ 160 Mike Flanagan	.30	.14	.04
☐ 161 Barry Foote	.08	.04	.01
☐ 162 Tom Johnson	.08	.04	.01
☐ 163 Glenn Burke	.08	.04	.01
☐ 164 Mickey Lolich	.18	.08	.02
☐ 165 Frank Taveras	.08	.04	.01
☐ 166 Leon Roberts	.08	.04	.01
☐ 167 Roger Metzger DP	.08	.04	.01
☐ 168 Dave Freisleben	.08	.04	.01
☐ 169 Bill Nahorodny	.08	.04	.01
☐ 170 Don Sutton	1.50	.65	.19
☐ 171 Gene Clines	.08	.04	.01
☐ 172 Mike Bruhert	.08	.04	.01
☐ 173 John Lowenstein	.08	.04	.01
☐ 174 Rick Auerbach	.08	.04	.01
☐ 175 George Hendrick	.18	.08	.02
☐ 176 Aurelio Rodriguez	.08	.04	.01
☐ 177 Ron Reed	.08	.04	.01
☐ 178 Alvis Woods	.08	.04	.01
☐ 179 Jim Beattie DP	.08	.04	.01
☐ 180 Larry Hisle	.08	.04	.01
☐ 181 Mike Garman	.08	.04	.01
☐ 182 Tim Johnson	.08	.04	.01
☐ 183 Paul Splittorff	.08	.04	.01
☐ 184 Darrel Chaney	.08	.04	.01
☐ 185 Mike Torrez	.18	.08	.02
☐ 186 Eric Soderholm	.08	.04	.01
☐ 187 Mark Lemongello	.08	.04	.01
☐ 188 Pat Kelly	.08	.04	.01
☐ 189 Eddie Whitson	.75	.35	.09
☐ 190 Ron Cey	.40	.18	.05
☐ 191 Mike Norris	.08	.04	.01
☐ 192 Cardinals Team/Mgr.	.60	.25	.08
Ken Boyer (Checklist back)			
☐ 193 Glenn Adams	.08	.04	.01

☐ 194 Randy Jones	.08	.04	.01
☐ 195 Bill Madlock	.40	.18	.05
☐ 196 Steve Kemp DP	.08	.04	.01
☐ 197 Bob Apodaca	.08	.04	.01
☐ 198 Johnny Grubb	.08	.04	.01
☐ 199 Larry Milbourne	.08	.04	.01
☐ 200 Johnny Bench DP	3.00	1.35	.40
☐ 201 RB: Mike Edwards	.20	.09	.03
Most unassisted DP's, second basemen			
☐ 202 RB: Ron Guidry, Most	.30	.14	.04
strikeouts, lefthander, nine inning game			
☐ 203 RB: J.R. Richard	.20	.09	.03
Most strikeouts, season, righthander			
☐ 204 RB: Pete Rose	1.75	.80	.22
Most consecutive games batting safely			
☐ 205 RB: John Stearns	.20	.09	.03
Most SB's by catcher, season			
☐ 206 RB: Sammy Stewart	.20	.09	.03
7 straight SO's, first ML game			
☐ 207 Dave Lemanczyk	.08	.04	.01
☐ 208 Clarence Gaston	.18	.08	.02
☐ 209 Reggie Cleveland	.08	.04	.01
☐ 210 Larry Bowa	.18	.08	.02
☐ 211 Denny Martinez	1.50	.65	.19
☐ 212 Carney Lansford	5.00	2.30	.60
☐ 213 Bill Travers	.08	.04	.01
☐ 214 Red Sox Team/Mgr.	.60	.25	.08
Don Zimmer (Checklist back)			
☐ 215 Willie McCovey	2.50	1.15	.30
☐ 216 Wilbur Wood	.08	.04	.01
☐ 217 Steve Dillard	.08	.04	.01
☐ 218 Dennis Leonard	.18	.08	.02
☐ 219 Roy Smalley	.18	.08	.02
☐ 220 Cesar Geronimo	.08	.04	.01
☐ 221 Jesse Jefferson	.08	.04	.01
☐ 222 Bob Beall	.08	.04	.01
☐ 223 Kent Tekulve	.18	.08	.02
☐ 224 Dave Revering	.08	.04	.01
☐ 225 Rich Gossage	1.00	.45	.13
☐ 226 Ron Pruitt	.08	.04	.01
☐ 227 Steve Stone	.18	.08	.02
☐ 228 Vic Davalillo	.08	.04	.01
☐ 229 Doug Flynn	.08	.04	.01
☐ 230 Bob Forsch	.08	.04	.01
☐ 231 John Wockenfuss	.08	.04	.01
☐ 232 Jimmy Sexton	.08	.04	.01
☐ 233 Paul Mitchell	.08	.04	.01
☐ 234 Toby Harrah	.18	.08	.02
☐ 235 Steve Rogers	.08	.04	.01
☐ 236 Jim Dwyer	.08	.04	.01

☐ 237	Billy Smith	.08	.04	.01
☐ 238	Balor Moore	.08	.04	.01
☐ 239	Willie Horton	.18	.08	.02
☐ 240	Rick Reuschel	.18	.08	.02
☐ 241	Checklist 2 DP	.30	.03	.01
☐ 242	Pablo Torrealba	.08	.04	.01
☐ 243	Buck Martinez DP	.08	.04	.01
☐ 244	Pirates Team/Mgr.	.60	.25	.08
	Chuck Tanner			
	(Checklist back)			
☐ 245	Jeff Burroughs	.08	.04	.01
☐ 246	Darrell Jackson	.08	.04	.01
☐ 247	Tucker Ashford DP	.08	.04	.01
☐ 248	Pete LaCock	.08	.04	.01
☐ 249	Paul Thormodsgard	.08	.04	.01
☐ 250	Willie Randolph	.75	.35	.09
☐ 251	Jack Morris	8.00	3.60	1.00
☐ 252	Bob Stinson	.08	.04	.01
☐ 253	Rick Wise	.08	.04	.01
☐ 254	Luis Gomez	.08	.04	.01
☐ 255	Tommy John	1.00	.45	.13
☐ 256	Mike Sadek	.08	.04	.01
☐ 257	Adrian Devine	.08	.04	.01
☐ 258	Mike Phillips	.08	.04	.01
☐ 259	Reds Team/Mgr.	.60	.25	.08
	Sparky Anderson			
	(Checklist back)			
☐ 260	Richie Zisk	.08	.04	.01
☐ 261	Mario Guerrero	.08	.04	.01
☐ 262	Nelson Briles	.08	.04	.01
☐ 263	Oscar Gamble	.18	.08	.02
☐ 264	Don Robinson	.60	.25	.08
☐ 265	Don Money	.08	.04	.01
☐ 266	Jim Willoughby	.08	.04	.01
☐ 267	Joe Rudi	.18	.08	.02
☐ 268	Julio Gonzalez	.08	.04	.01
☐ 269	Woodie Fryman	.08	.04	.01
☐ 270	Butch Hobson	.18	.08	.02
☐ 271	Rawly Eastwick	.08	.04	.01
☐ 272	Tim Corcoran	.08	.04	.01
☐ 273	Jerry Terrell	.08	.04	.01
☐ 274	Willie Norwood	.08	.04	.01
☐ 275	Junior Moore	.08	.04	.01
☐ 276	Jim Colborn	.08	.04	.01
☐ 277	Tom Grieve	.18	.08	.02
☐ 278	Andy Messersmith	.18	.08	.02
☐ 279	Jerry Grote DP	.08	.04	.01
☐ 280	Andre Thornton	.18	.08	.02
☐ 281	Vic Correll DP	.08	.04	.01
☐ 282	Blue Jays Team/Mgr.	.60	.25	.08
	Roy Hartsfield			
	(Checklist back)			
☐ 283	Ken Kravec	.08	.04	.01
☐ 284	Johnnie LeMaster	.08	.04	.01
☐ 285	Bobby Bonds	.40	.18	.05
☐ 286	Duffy Dyer	.08	.04	.01
☐ 287	Andres Mora	.08	.04	.01

☐ 288	Milt Wilcox	.08	.04	.01
☐ 289	Jose Cruz	.18	.08	.02
☐ 290	Dave Lopes	.18	.08	.02
☐ 291	Tom Griffin	.08	.04	.01
☐ 292	Don Reynolds	.08	.04	.01
☐ 293	Jerry Garvin	.08	.04	.01
☐ 294	Pepe Frias	.08	.04	.01
☐ 295	Mitchell Page	.08	.04	.01
☐ 296	Preston Hanna	.08	.04	.01
☐ 297	Ted Sizemore	.08	.04	.01
☐ 298	Rich Gale	.08	.04	.01
☐ 299	Steve Ontiveros	.08	.04	.01
☐ 300	Rod Carew	4.00	1.80	.50
☐ 301	Tom Hume	.08	.04	.01
☐ 302	Braves Team/Mgr.	.60	.25	.08
	Bobby Cox			
	(Checklist back)			
☐ 303	Lary Sorensen DP	.08	.04	.01
☐ 304	Steve Swisher	.08	.04	.01
☐ 305	Willie Montanez	.08	.04	.01
☐ 306	Floyd Bannister	.08	.04	.01
☐ 307	Larvell Blanks	.08	.04	.01
☐ 308	Bert Blyleven	1.00	.45	.13
☐ 309	Ralph Garr	.08	.04	.01
☐ 310	Thurman Munson	3.50	1.55	.45
☐ 311	Gary Lavelle	.08	.04	.01
☐ 312	Bob Robertson	.08	.04	.01
☐ 313	Dyar Miller	.08	.04	.01
☐ 314	Larry Harlow	.08	.04	.01
☐ 315	Jon Matlack	.08	.04	.01
☐ 316	Milt May	.08	.04	.01
☐ 317	Jese Cardenal	.08	.04	.01
☐ 318	Bob Welch	6.00	2.70	.75
☐ 319	Wayne Garrett	.08	.04	.01
☐ 320	Carl Yastrzemski	3.50	1.55	.45
☐ 321	Gaylord Perry	2.50	1.15	.30
☐ 322	Danny Goodwin	.08	.04	.01
☐ 323	Lynn McGlothen	.08	.04	.01
☐ 324	Mike Tyson	.08	.04	.01
☐ 325	Cecil Cooper	.35	.16	.04
☐ 326	Pedro Borbon	.08	.04	.01
☐ 327	Art Howe DP	.08	.04	.01
☐ 328	Oakland A's Team/Mgr.	.60	.25	.08
	Jack McKeon			
	(Checklist back)			
☐ 329	Joe Coleman	.08	.04	.01
☐ 330	George Brett	15.00	6.75	1.90
☐ 331	Mickey Mahler	.08	.04	.01
☐ 332	Gary Alexander	.08	.04	.01
☐ 333	Chet Lemon	.18	.08	.02
☐ 334	Craig Swan	.08	.04	.01
☐ 335	Chris Chambliss	.18	.08	.02
☐ 336	Bobby Thompson	.08	.04	.01
☐ 337	John Montague	.08	.04	.01
☐ 338	Vic Harris	.08	.04	.01
☐ 339	Ron Jackson	.08	.04	.01
☐ 340	Jim Palmer	3.50	1.55	.45

☐	341	Willie Upshaw............18	.08	.02
☐	342	Dave Roberts............08	.04	.01
☐	343	Ed Glynn............08	.04	.01
☐	344	Jerry Royster............08	.04	.01
☐	345	Tug McGraw............28	.13	.04
☐	346	Bill Buckner............28	.13	.04
☐	347	Doug Rau............08	.04	.01
☐	348	Andre Dawson............15.00	6.75	1.90
☐	349	Jim Wright............08	.04	.01
☐	350	Garry Templeton............18	.08	.02
☐	351	Wayne Nordhagen DP............08	.04	.01
☐	352	Steve Renko............08	.04	.01
☐	353	Checklist 3............75	.08	.02
☐	354	Bill Bonham............08	.04	.01
☐	355	Lee Mazzilli............08	.04	.01
☐	356	Giants Team/Mgr.............60	.25	.08
		Joe Altobelli		
		(Checklist back)		
☐	357	Jerry Augustine............08	.04	.01
☐	358	Alan Trammell............9.00	4.00	1.15
☐	359	Dan Spillner DP............08	.04	.01
☐	360	Amos Otis............18	.08	.02
☐	361	Tom Dixon............08	.04	.01
☐	362	Mike Cubbage............08	.04	.01
☐	363	Craig Skok............08	.04	.01
☐	364	Gene Richards............08	.04	.01
☐	365	Sparky Lyle............28	.13	.04
☐	366	Juan Bernhardt............08	.04	.01
☐	367	Dave Skaggs............08	.04	.01
☐	368	Don Aase............08	.04	.01
☐	369A	Bump Wills ERR............3.00	1.35	.40
		(Blue Jays)		
☐	369B	Bump Wills COR............3.00	1.35	.40
		(Rangers)		
☐	370	Dave Kingman............40	.18	.05
☐	371	Jeff Holly............08	.04	.01
☐	372	Lamar Johnson............08	.04	.01
☐	373	Lance Rautzhan............08	.04	.01
☐	374	Ed Herrmann............08	.04	.01
☐	375	Bill Campbell............08	.04	.01
☐	376	Gorman Thomas............18	.08	.02
☐	377	Paul Moskau............08	.04	.01
☐	378	Rob Picciolo DP............08	.04	.01
☐	379	Dale Murray............08	.04	.01
☐	380	John Mayberry............18	.08	.02
☐	381	Astros Team/Mgr.............60	.25	.08
		Bill Virdon		
		(Checklist back)		
☐	382	Jerry Martin............08	.04	.01
☐	383	Phil Garner............18	.08	.02
☐	384	Tommy Boggs............08	.04	.01
☐	385	Dan Ford............08	.04	.01
☐	386	Francisco Barrios............08	.04	.01
☐	387	Gary Thomasson............08	.04	.01
☐	388	Jack Billingham............08	.04	.01
☐	389	Joe Zdeb............08	.04	.01
☐	390	Rollie Fingers............2.00	.90	.25

☐	391	Al Oliver............35	.16	.04
☐	892	Doug Ault............08	.04	.01
☐	393	Scott McGregor............18	.08	.02
☐	394	Randy Stein............08	.04	.01
☐	395	Dave Cash............08	.04	.01
☐	396	Bill Plummer............08	.04	.01
☐	397	Sergio Ferrer............08	.04	.01
☐	398	Ivan DeJesus............08	.04	.01
☐	399	David Clyde............08	.04	.01
☐	400	Jim Rice............2.00	.90	.25
☐	401	Ray Knight............50	.23	.06
☐	402	Paul Hartzell............08	.04	.01
☐	403	Tim Foli............08	.04	.01
☐	404	White Sox Team/Mgr.............60	.25	.08
		Don Kessinger		
		(Checklist back)		
☐	405	Butch Wynegar DP............08	.04	.01
☐	406	Joe Wallis DP............08	.04	.01
☐	407	Pete Vuckovich............18	.08	.02
☐	408	Charlie Moore DP............08	.04	.01
☐	409	Willie Wilson............2.75	1.25	.35
☐	410	Darrell Evans............28	.13	.04
☐	411	Hits Record............50	.23	.06
		Season: George Sisler		
		Career: Ty Cobb		
☐	412	RBI Record............50	.23	.06
		Season: Hack Wilson		
		Career: Hank Aaron		
☐	413	Home Run Record............1.00	.45	.13
		Season: Roger Maris		
		Career: Hank Aaron		
☐	414	Batting Record............50	.23	.06
		Season: Rogers Hornsby		
		Career: Ty Cobb		
☐	415	Steals Record............50	.23	.06
		Season: Lou Brock		
		Career: Lou Brock		
☐	416	Wins Record............25	.11	.03
		Season: Jack Chesbro		
		Career: Cy Young		
☐	417	Strikeout Record DP............1.50	.65	.19
		Season: Nolan Ryan		
		Career: Walter Johnson		
☐	418	ERA Record DP............12	.05	.02
		Season: Dutch Leonard		
		Career: Walter Johnson		
☐	419	Dick Ruthven............08	.04	.01
☐	420	Ken Griffey............1.00	.45	.13
☐	421	Doug DeCinces............18	.08	.02
☐	422	Ruppert Jones............08	.04	.01
☐	423	Bob Montgomery............08	.04	.01
☐	424	Angels Team/Mgr.............60	.25	.08
		Jim Fregosi		
		(Checklist back)		
☐	425	Rick Manning............08	.04	.01
☐	426	Chris Speier............08	.04	.01
☐	427	Andy Replogle............08	.04	.01

☐ 428	Bobby Valentine	18	.08	.02
☐ 429	John Urrea DP	08	.04	.01
☐ 430	Dave Parker	2.00	.90	.25
☐ 431	Glenn Borgmann	08	.04	.01
☐ 432	Dave Heaverlo	08	.04	.01
☐ 433	Larry Biittner	08	.04	.01
☐ 434	Ken Clay	08	.04	.01
☐ 435	Gene Tenace	18	.08	.02
☐ 436	Hector Cruz	08	.04	.01
☐ 437	Rick Williams	08	.04	.01
☐ 438	Horace Speed	08	.04	.01
☐ 439	Frank White	18	.08	.02
☐ 440	Rusty Staub	28	.13	.04
☐ 441	Lee Lacy	08	.04	.01
☐ 442	Doyle Alexander	08	.04	.01
☐ 443	Bruce Bochte	08	.04	.01
☐ 444	Aurelio Lopez	08	.04	.01
☐ 445	Steve Henderson	08	.04	.01
☐ 446	Jim Lonborg	08	.04	.01
☐ 447	Manny Sanguillen	18	.08	.02
☐ 448	Moose Haas	08	.04	.01
☐ 449	Bombo Rivera	08	.04	.01
☐ 450	Dave Concepcion	75	.35	.09
☐ 451	Royals Team/Mgr.	60	.25	.08
	Whitey Herzog			
	(Checklist back)			
☐ 452	Jerry Morales	08	.04	.01
☐ 453	Chris Knapp	08	.04	.01
☐ 454	Len Randle	08	.04	.01
☐ 455	Bill Lee DP	08	.04	.01
☐ 456	Chuck Baker	08	.04	.01
☐ 457	Bruce Sutter	1.25	.55	.16
☐ 458	Jim Essian	08	.04	.01
☐ 459	Sid Monge	08	.04	.01
☐ 460	Graig Nettles	50	.23	.06
☐ 461	Jim Barr DP	08	.04	.01
☐ 462	Otto Velez	08	.04	.01
☐ 463	Steve Comer	08	.04	.01
☐ 464	Joe Nolan	08	.04	.01
☐ 465	Reggie Smith	18	.08	.02
☐ 466	Mark Littell	08	.04	.01
☐ 467	Don Kessinger DP	08	.04	.01
☐ 468	Stan Bahnsen DP	08	.04	.01
☐ 469	Lance Parrish	2.50	1.15	.30
☐ 470	Garry Maddox DP	08	.04	.01
☐ 471	Joaquin Andujar	18	.08	.02
☐ 472	Craig Kusick	08	.04	.01
☐ 473	Dave Roberts	08	.04	.01
☐ 474	Dick Davis	08	.04	.01
☐ 475	Dan Driessen	08	.04	.01
☐ 476	Tom Poquette	08	.04	.01
☐ 477	Bob Grich	18	.08	.02
☐ 478	Juan Beniquez	08	.04	.01
☐ 479	Padres Team/Mgr.	60	.25	.08
	Roger Craig			
	(Checklist back)			
☐ 480	Fred Lynn	75	.35	.09
☐ 481	Skip Lockwood	08	.04	.01
☐ 482	Craig Reynolds	08	.04	.01
☐ 483	Checklist 4 DP	30	.03	.01
☐ 484	Rick Waits	08	.04	.01
☐ 485	Bucky Dent	18	.08	.02
☐ 486	Bob Knepper	08	.04	.01
☐ 487	Miguel Dilone	08	.04	.01
☐ 488	Bob Owchinko	08	.04	.01
☐ 489	Larry Cox UER	08	.04	.01
	(Photo actually			
	Dave Rader)			
☐ 490	Al Cowens	08	.04	.01
☐ 491	Tippy Martinez	18	.08	.02
☐ 492	Bob Bailor	08	.04	.01
☐ 493	Larry Christenson	08	.04	.01
☐ 494	Jerry White	08	.04	.01
☐ 495	Tony Perez	1.00	.45	.13
☐ 496	Barry Bonnell DP	08	.04	.01
☐ 497	Glenn Abbott	08	.04	.01
☐ 498	Rich Chiles	08	.04	.01
☐ 499	Rangers Team/Mgr.	60	.25	.08
	Pat Corrales			
	(Checklist back)			
☐ 500	Ron Guidry	75	.35	.09
☐ 501	Junior Kennedy	08	.04	.01
☐ 502	Steve Braun	08	.04	.01
☐ 503	Terry Humphrey	08	.04	.01
☐ 504	Larry McWilliams	08	.04	.01
☐ 505	Ed Kranepool	08	.04	.01
☐ 506	John D'Acquisto	08	.04	.01
☐ 507	Tony Armas	08	.04	.01
☐ 508	Charlie Hough	18	.08	.02
☐ 509	Mario Mendoza UER	08	.04	.01
	(Career BA .278,			
	should say .204)			
☐ 510	Ted Simmons	75	.35	.09
☐ 511	Paul Reuschel DP	08	.04	.01
☐ 512	Jack Clark	1.25	.55	.16
☐ 513	Dave Johnson	08	.04	.01
☐ 514	Mike Proly	08	.04	.01
☐ 515	Enos Cabell	08	.04	.01
☐ 516	Champ Summers DP	08	.04	.01
☐ 517	Al Bumbry	08	.04	.01
☐ 518	Jim Umbarger	08	.04	.01
☐ 519	Ben Oglivie	18	.08	.02
☐ 520	Gary Carter	4.00	1.80	.50
☐ 521	Sam Ewing	08	.04	.01
☐ 522	Ken Holtzman	08	.04	.01
☐ 523	John Milner	08	.04	.01
☐ 524	Tom Burgmeier	08	.04	.01
☐ 525	Freddie Patek	08	.04	.01
☐ 526	Dodgers Team/Mgr.	60	.25	.08
	Tom Lasorda			
	(Checklist back)			
☐ 527	Lerrin LaGrow	08	.04	.01
☐ 528	Wayne Gross DP	08	.04	.01
☐ 529	Brian Asselstine	08	.04	.01

☐ 530	Frank Tanana	.40	.18	.05
☐ 531	Fernando Gonzalez	.08	.04	.01
☐ 532	Buddy Schultz	.08	.04	.01
☐ 533	Leroy Stanton	.08	.04	.01
☐ 534	Ken Forsch	.08	.04	.01
☐ 535	Ellis Valentine	.08	.04	.01
☐ 536	Jerry Reuss	.18	.08	.02
☐ 537	Tom Veryzer	.08	.04	.01
☐ 538	Mike Ivie DP	.08	.04	.01
☐ 539	John Ellis	.08	.04	.01
☐ 540	Greg Luzinski	.28	.13	.04
☐ 541	Jim Slaton	.08	.04	.01
☐ 542	Rick Bosetti	.08	.04	.01
☐ 543	Kiko Garcia	.08	.04	.01
☐ 544	Fergie Jenkins	1.50	.65	.19
☐ 545	John Stearns	.08	.04	.01
☐ 546	Bill Russell	.18	.08	.02
☐ 547	Clint Hurdle	.08	.04	.01
☐ 548	Enrique Romo	.08	.04	.01
☐ 549	Bob Bailey	.08	.04	.01
☐ 550	Sal Bando	.18	.08	.02
☐ 551	Cubs Team/Mgr.	.60	.25	.08
	Herman Franks			
	(Checklist back)			
☐ 552	Jose Morales	.08	.04	.01
☐ 553	Denny Walling	.08	.04	.01
☐ 554	Matt Keough	.08	.04	.01
☐ 555	Biff Pocoroba	.08	.04	.01
☐ 556	Mike Lum	.08	.04	.01
☐ 557	Ken Brett	.08	.04	.01
☐ 558	Jay Johnstone	.18	.08	.02
☐ 559	Greg Pryor	.08	.04	.01
☐ 560	John Montefusco	.08	.04	.01
☐ 561	Ed Ott	.08	.04	.01
☐ 562	Dusty Baker	.28	.13	.04
☐ 563	Roy Thomas	.08	.04	.01
☐ 564	Jerry Turner	.08	.04	.01
☐ 565	Rico Carty	.18	.08	.02
☐ 566	Nino Espinosa	.08	.04	.01
☐ 567	Richie Hebner	.08	.04	.01
☐ 568	Carlos Lopez	.08	.04	.01
☐ 569	Bob Sykes	.08	.04	.01
☐ 570	Cesar Cedeno	.18	.08	.02
☐ 571	Darrell Porter	.08	.04	.01
☐ 572	Rod Gilbreath	.08	.04	.01
☐ 573	Jim Kern	.08	.04	.01
☐ 574	Claudell Washington	.18	.08	.02
☐ 575	Luis Tiant	.18	.08	.02
☐ 576	Mike Parrott	.08	.04	.01
☐ 577	Brewers Team/Mgr.	.60	.25	.08
	George Bamberger			
	(Checklist back)			
☐ 578	Pete Broberg	.08	.04	.01
☐ 579	Greg Gross	.08	.04	.01
☐ 580	Ron Fairly	.08	.04	.01
☐ 581	Darold Knowles	.08	.04	.01
☐ 582	Paul Blair	.18	.08	.02
☐ 583	Julio Cruz	.08	.04	.01
☐ 584	Jim Rooker	.08	.04	.01
☐ 585	Hal McRae	.18	.08	.02
☐ 586	Bob Horner	1.00	.45	.13
☐ 587	Ken Reitz	.08	.04	.01
☐ 588	Tom Murphy	.08	.04	.01
☐ 589	Terry Whitfield	.08	.04	.01
☐ 590	J.R. Richard	.18	.08	.02
☐ 591	Mike Hargrove	.18	.08	.02
☐ 592	Mike Krukow	.08	.04	.01
☐ 593	Rick Dempsey	.18	.08	.02
☐ 594	Bob Shirley	.08	.04	.01
☐ 595	Phil Niekro	1.50	.65	.19
☐ 596	Jim Wohlford	.08	.04	.01
☐ 597	Bob Stanley	.08	.04	.01
☐ 598	Mark Wagner	.08	.04	.01
☐ 599	Jim Spencer	.08	.04	.01
☐ 600	George Foster	.60	.25	.08
☐ 601	Dave LaRoche	.08	.04	.01
☐ 602	Checklist 5	.75	.08	.02
☐ 603	Rudy May	.08	.04	.01
☐ 604	Jeff Newman	.08	.04	.01
☐ 605	Rick Monday DP	.08	.04	.01
☐ 606	Expos Team/Mgr.	.60	.25	.08
	Dick Williams			
	(Checklist back)			
☐ 607	Omar Moreno	.18	.08	.02
☐ 608	Dave McKay	.08	.04	.01
☐ 609	Silvio Martinez	.08	.04	.01
☐ 610	Mike Schmidt	10.00	4.50	1.25
☐ 611	Jim Norris	.08	.04	.01
☐ 612	Rick Honeycutt	.60	.25	.08
☐ 613	Mike Edwards	.08	.04	.01
☐ 614	Willie Hernandez	.18	.08	.02
☐ 615	Ken Singleton	.18	.08	.02
☐ 616	Billy Almon	.08	.04	.01
☐ 617	Terry Puhl	.18	.08	.02
☐ 618	Jerry Remy	.08	.04	.01
☐ 619	Ken Landreaux	.18	.08	.02
☐ 620	Bert Campaneris	.18	.08	.02
☐ 621	Pat Zachry	.08	.04	.01
☐ 622	Dave Collins	.18	.08	.02
☐ 623	Bob McClure	.08	.04	.01
☐ 624	Larry Herndon	.08	.04	.01
☐ 625	Mark Fidrych	.30	.14	.04
☐ 626	Yankees Team/Mgr.	.60	.25	.08
	Bob Lemon			
	(Checklist back)			
☐ 627	Gary Serum	.08	.04	.01
☐ 628	Del Unser	.08	.04	.01
☐ 629	Gene Garber	.08	.04	.01
☐ 630	Bake McBride	.18	.08	.02
☐ 631	Jorge Orta	.08	.04	.01
☐ 632	Don Kirkwood	.08	.04	.01
☐ 633	Rob Wilfong DP	.08	.04	.01
☐ 634	Paul Lindblad	.08	.04	.01
☐ 635	Don Baylor	1.00	.45	.13

☐ 636 Wayne Garland	.08	.04	.01
☐ 637 Bill Robinson	.18	.08	.02
☐ 638 Al Fitzmorris	.08	.04	.01
☐ 639 Manny Trillo	.08	.04	.01
☐ 640 Eddie Murray	25.00	11.50	3.10
☐ 641 Bobby Castillo	.08	.04	.01
☐ 642 Wilbur Howard DP	.08	.04	.01
☐ 643 Tom Hausman	.08	.04	.01
☐ 644 Manny Mota	.18	.08	.02
☐ 645 George Scott DP	.08	.04	.01
☐ 646 Rick Sweet	.08	.04	.01
☐ 647 Bob Lacey	.08	.04	.01
☐ 648 Lou Piniella	.35	.16	.04
☐ 649 John Curtis	.08	.04	.01
☐ 650 Pete Rose	5.00	2.30	.60
☐ 651 Mike Caldwell	.08	.04	.01
☐ 652 Stan Papi	.08	.04	.01
☐ 653 Warren Brusstar DP	.08	.04	.01
☐ 654 Rick Miller	.08	.04	.01
☐ 655 Jerry Koosman	.18	.08	.02
☐ 656 Hosken Powell	.08	.04	.01
☐ 657 George Medich	.08	.04	.01
☐ 658 Taylor Duncan	.08	.04	.01
☐ 659 Mariners Team/Mgr.	.60	.25	.08
Darrell Johnson			
(Checklist back)			
☐ 660 Ron LeFlore DP	.08	.04	.01
☐ 661 Bruce Kison	.08	.04	.01
☐ 662 Kevin Bell	.08	.04	.01
☐ 663 Mike Vail	.08	.04	.01
☐ 664 Doug Bird	.08	.04	.01
☐ 665 Lou Brock	3.00	1.35	.40
☐ 666 Rich Dauer	.08	.04	.01
☐ 667 Don Hood	.08	.04	.01
☐ 668 Bill North	.08	.04	.01
☐ 669 Checklist 6	.75	.08	.02
☐ 670 Jim Hunter DP	.75	.35	.09
☐ 671 Joe Ferguson DP	.08	.04	.01
☐ 672 Ed Halicki	.08	.04	.01
☐ 673 Tom Hutton	.08	.04	.01
☐ 674 Dave Tomlin	.08	.04	.01
☐ 675 Tim McCarver	.35	.16	.04
☐ 676 Johnny Sutton	.08	.04	.01
☐ 677 Larry Parrish	.18	.08	.02
☐ 678 Geoff Zahn	.08	.04	.01
☐ 679 Derrel Thomas	.08	.04	.01
☐ 680 Carlton Fisk	6.00	2.70	.75
☐ 681 John Henry Johnson	.08	.04	.01
☐ 682 Dave Chalk	.08	.04	.01
☐ 683 Dan Meyer DP	.08	.04	.01
☐ 684 Jamie Easterly DP	.08	.04	.01
☐ 685 Sixto Lezcano	.08	.04	.01
☐ 686 Ron Schueler DP	.08	.04	.01
☐ 687 Rennie Stennett	.08	.04	.01
☐ 688 Mike Willis	.08	.04	.01
☐ 689 Orioles Team/Mgr.	.60	.25	.08
Earl Weaver			

(Checklist back)			
☐ 690 Buddy Bell DP	.08	.04	.01
☐ 691 Dock Ellis DP	.08	.04	.01
☐ 692 Mickey Stanley	.08	.04	.01
☐ 693 Dave Rader	.08	.04	.01
☐ 694 Burt Hooton	.18	.08	.02
☐ 695 Keith Hernandez	1.50	.65	.19
☐ 696 Andy Hassler	.08	.04	.01
☐ 697 Dave Bergman	.08	.04	.01
☐ 698 Bill Stein	.08	.04	.01
☐ 699 Hal Dues	.08	.04	.01
☐ 700 Reggie Jackson DP	3.75	1.70	.45
☐ 701 Orioles Prospects	.20	.09	.03
Mark Corey			
John Flinn			
Sammy Stewart			
☐ 702 Red Sox Prospects	.20	.09	.03
Joel Finch			
Garry Hancock			
Allen Ripley			
☐ 703 Angels Prospects	.20	.09	.03
Jim Anderson			
Dave Frost			
Bob Slater			
☐ 704 White Sox Prospects	.20	.09	.03
Ross Baumgarten			
Mike Colbern			
Mike Squires			
☐ 705 Indians Prospects	.60	.25	.08
Alfredo Griffin			
Tim Norrid			
Dave Oliver			
☐ 706 Tigers Prospects	.20	.09	.03
Dave Stegman			
Dave Tobik			
Kip Young			
☐ 707 Royals Prospects	.20	.09	.03
Randy Bass			
Jim Gaudet			
Randy McGilberry			
☐ 708 Brewers Prospects	1.00	.45	.13
Kevin Bass			
Eddie Romero			
Ned Yost			
☐ 709 Twins Prospects	.20	.09	.03
Sam Perlozzo			
Rick Sofield			
Kevin Stanfield			
☐ 710 Yankees Prospects	.30	.14	.04
Brian Doyle			
Mike Heath			
Dave Rajsich			
☐ 711 A's Prospects	.30	.14	.04
Dwayne Murphy			
Bruce Robinson			
Alan Wirth			
☐ 712 Mariners Prospects	.20	.09	.03

Bud Anderson
Greg Biercevicz
Byron McLaughlin

☐ 713 Rangers Prospects 60   .25   .08
Danny Darwin
Pat Putnam
Billy Sample

☐ 714 Blue Jays Prospects........20   .09   .03
Victor Cruz
Pat Kelly
Ernie Whitt

☐ 715 Braves Prospects............20   .09   .03
Bruce Benedict
Glenn Hubbard
Larry Whisenton

☐ 716 Cubs Prospects...............20   .09   .03
Dave Geisel
Karl Pagel
Scot Thompson

☐ 717 Reds Prospects................35   .16   .04
Mike LaCoss
Ron Oester
Harry Spilman

☐ 718 Astros Prospects 20   .09   .03
Bruce Bochy
Mike Fischlin
Don Pisker

☐ 719 Dodgers Prospects ......6.00   2.70   .75
Pedro Guerrero
Rudy Law
Joe Simpson

☐ 720 Expos Prospects...........1.50   .65   .19
Jerry Fry
Jerry Pirtle
Scott Sanderson

☐ 721 Mets Prospects...............30   .14   .04
Juan Berenguer
Dwight Bernard
Dan Norman

☐ 722 Phillies Prospects.........1.25   .55   .16
Jim Morrison
Lonnie Smith
Jim Wright

☐ 723 Pirates Prospects............20   .09   .03
Dale Berra
Eugenio Cotes
Ben Wiltbank

☐ 724 Cardinals Prospects........60   .25   .08
Tom Bruno
George Frazier
Terry Kennedy

☐ 725 Padres Prospects............20   .09   .03
Jim Beswick
Steve Mura
Broderick Perkins

☐ 726 Giants Prospects.............30   .14   .04
Greg Johnston

Joe Strain
John Tamargo

1980 Topps

*The cards in this 726-card set measure
2 1/2" by 3 1/2". In 1980 Topps released
another set of the same size and number
of cards as the previous two years. As with
those sets, Topps again has produced 66
double-printed cards in the set; they are
noted by DP in the checklist below. The
player's name appears over the picture
and his position and team are found in
pennant design. Every card carries a facsimile autograph. Team cards feature a
team checklist of players in the set on the
back and the manager's name on the front.
Cards 1-6 show Highlights (HL) of the
1979 season, cards 201-207 are League
Leaders, and cards 661-686 feature
American and National League rookie
"Future Stars," one card for each team
showing three young prospects. The key
Rookie Card in this set is Rickey
Henderson; other noteworthy rookies
included are Dave Stieb and Rick Sutcliffe.*

	NRMT-MT	EXC	G-VG
COMPLETE SET (726)	275.00	125.00	34.00
COMMON PLAYER (1-726)	.15	.07	.02
COMMON PLAYER DP	.08	.04	.01

☐ 1 HL: Lou Brock and..........2.50   .50   .15
Carl Yastrzemski
Enter 3000 hit circle

☐ 2 HL: Willie McCovey,........1.00   .45   .13
512th homer sets new
mark for NL lefties

☐ 3 HL: Manny Mota, All-time pinch-hits, 145	.25	.11	.03
☐ 4 HL: Pete Rose, Career Record 10th season with 200 or more hits	2.00	.90	.25
☐ 5 HL: Garry Templeton, First with 100 hits from each side of plate	.25	.11	.03
☐ 6 HL: Del Unser, 3rd cons. pinch homer sets new ML standard	.25	.11	.03
☐ 7 Mike Lum	.08	.04	.01
☐ 8 Craig Swan	.08	.04	.01
☐ 9 Steve Braun	.08	.04	.01
☐ 10 Dennis Martinez	.75	.35	.09
☐ 11 Jimmy Sexton	.08	.04	.01
☐ 12 John Curtis DP	.08	.04	.01
☐ 13 Ron Pruitt	.08	.04	.01
☐ 14 Dave Cash	.08	.04	.01
☐ 15 Bill Campbell	.08	.04	.01
☐ 16 Jerry Narron	.08	.04	.01
☐ 17 Bruce Sutter	.75	.35	.09
☐ 18 Ron Jackson	.08	.04	.01
☐ 19 Balor Moore	.08	.04	.01
☐ 20 Dan Ford	.08	.04	.01
☐ 21 Manny Sarmiento	.08	.04	.01
☐ 22 Pat Putnam	.08	.04	.01
☐ 23 Derrel Thomas	.08	.04	.01
☐ 24 Jim Slaton	.08	.04	.01
☐ 25 Lee Mazzilli	.08	.04	.01
☐ 26 Marty Pattin	.08	.04	.01
☐ 27 Del Unser	.08	.04	.01
☐ 28 Bruce Kison	.08	.04	.01
☐ 29 Mark Wagner	.08	.04	.01
☐ 30 Vida Blue	.18	.08	.02
☐ 31 Jay Johnstone	.18	.08	.02
☐ 32 Julio Cruz DP	.08	.04	.01
☐ 33 Tony Scott	.08	.04	.01
☐ 34 Jeff Newman DP	.08	.04	.01
☐ 35 Luis Tiant	.18	.08	.02
☐ 36 Rusty Torres	.08	.04	.01
☐ 37 Kiko Garcia	.08	.04	.01
☐ 38 Dan Spillner DP	.08	.04	.01
☐ 39 Rowland Office	.08	.04	.01
☐ 40 Carlton Fisk	5.00	2.30	.60
☐ 41 Rangers Team/Mgr. Pat Corrales (Checklist back)	.50	.23	.06
☐ 42 David Palmer	.18	.08	.02
☐ 43 Bombo Rivera	.08	.04	.01
☐ 44 Bill Fahey	.08	.04	.01
☐ 45 Frank White	.18	.08	.02
☐ 46 Rico Carty	.18	.08	.02
☐ 47 Bill Bonham DP	.08	.04	.01
☐ 48 Rick Miller	.08	.04	.01
☐ 49 Mario Guerrero	.08	.04	.01
☐ 50 J.R. Richard	.18	.08	.02
☐ 51 Joe Ferguson DP	.08	.04	.01
☐ 52 Warren Brusstar	.08	.04	.01
☐ 53 Ben Oglivie	.18	.08	.02
☐ 54 Dennis Lamp	.08	.04	.01
☐ 55 Bill Madlock	.40	.18	.05
☐ 56 Bobby Valentine	.18	.08	.02
☐ 57 Pete Vuckovich	.18	.08	.02
☐ 58 Doug Flynn	.08	.04	.01
☐ 59 Eddy Putman	.08	.04	.01
☐ 60 Bucky Dent	.18	.08	.02
☐ 61 Gary Serum	.08	.04	.01
☐ 62 Mike Ivie	.08	.04	.01
☐ 63 Bob Stanley	.08	.04	.01
☐ 64 Joe Nolan	.08	.04	.01
☐ 65 Al Bumbry	.08	.04	.01
☐ 66 Royals Team/Mgr. Jim Frey (Checklist back)	.50	.23	.06
☐ 67 Doyle Alexander	.08	.04	.01
☐ 68 Larry Harlow	.08	.04	.01
☐ 69 Rick Williams	.08	.04	.01
☐ 70 Gary Carter	3.00	1.35	.40
☐ 71 John Milner DP	.08	.04	.01
☐ 72 Fred Howard DP	.08	.04	.01
☐ 73 Dave Collins	.08	.04	.01
☐ 74 Sid Monge	.08	.04	.01
☐ 75 Bill Russell	.18	.08	.02
☐ 76 John Stearns	.08	.04	.01
☐ 77 Dave Stieb	3.50	1.55	.45
☐ 78 Ruppert Jones	.08	.04	.01
☐ 79 Bob Owchinko	.08	.04	.01
☐ 80 Ron LeFlore	.18	.08	.02
☐ 81 Ted Sizemore	.08	.04	.01
☐ 82 Astros Team/Mgr. Bill Virdon (Checklist back)	.50	.23	.06
☐ 83 Steve Trout	.08	.04	.01
☐ 84 Gary Lavelle	.08	.04	.01
☐ 85 Ted Simmons	.60	.25	.08
☐ 86 Dave Hamilton	.08	.04	.01
☐ 87 Pepe Frias	.08	.04	.01
☐ 88 Ken Landreaux	.08	.04	.01
☐ 89 Don Hood	.08	.04	.01
☐ 90 Manny Trillo	.08	.04	.01
☐ 91 Rick Dempsey	.18	.08	.02
☐ 92 Rick Rhoden	.08	.04	.01
☐ 93 Dave Roberts DP	.08	.04	.01
☐ 94 Neil Allen	.20	.09	.03
☐ 95 Cecil Cooper	.20	.09	.03
☐ 96 A's Team/Mgr. Jim Marshall (Checklist back)	.50	.23	.06
☐ 97 Bill Lee	.08	.04	.01
☐ 98 Jerry Terrell	.08	.04	.01
☐ 99 Victor Cruz	.08	.04	.01
☐ 100 Johnny Bench	4.50	2.00	.55
☐ 101 Aurelio Lopez	.08	.04	.01

☐ 102	Rich Dauer	.08	.04	.01
☐ 103	Bill Caudill	.08	.04	.01
☐ 104	Manny Mota	.18	.08	.02
☐ 105	Frank Tanana	.25	.11	.03
☐ 106	Jeff Leonard	.40	.18	.05
☐ 107	Francisco Barrios	.08	.04	.01
☐ 108	Bob Horner	.18	.08	.02
☐ 109	Bill Travers	.08	.04	.01
☐ 110	Fred Lynn DP	.25	.11	.03
☐ 111	Bob Knepper	.08	.04	.01
☐ 112	White Sox Team/Mgr.	.50	.23	.06
	Tony LaRussa			
	(Checklist back)			
☐ 113	Geoff Zahn	.08	.04	.01
☐ 114	Juan Beniquez	.08	.04	.01
☐ 115	Sparky Lyle	.18	.08	.02
☐ 116	Larry Cox	.08	.04	.01
☐ 117	Dock Ellis	.08	.04	.01
☐ 118	Phil Garner	.18	.08	.02
☐ 119	Sammy Stewart	.08	.04	.01
☐ 120	Greg Luzinski	.28	.13	.04
☐ 121	Checklist 1	.60	.25	.08
☐ 122	Dave Rosello DP	.08	.04	.01
☐ 123	Lynn Jones	.08	.04	.01
☐ 124	Dave Lemanczyk	.08	.04	.01
☐ 125	Tony Perez	1.00	.45	.13
☐ 126	Dave Tomlin	.08	.04	.01
☐ 127	Gary Thomasson	.08	.04	.01
☐ 128	Tom Burgmeier	.08	.04	.01
☐ 129	Craig Reynolds	.08	.04	.01
☐ 130	Amos Otis	.18	.08	.02
☐ 131	Paul Mitchell	.08	.04	.01
☐ 132	Biff Pocoroba	.08	.04	.01
☐ 133	Jerry Turner	.08	.04	.01
☐ 134	Matt Keough	.08	.04	.01
☐ 135	Bill Buckner	.18	.08	.02
☐ 136	Dick Ruthven	.08	.04	.01
☐ 137	John Castino	.08	.04	.01
☐ 138	Ross Baumgarten	.08	.04	.01
☐ 139	Dane Iorg	.08	.04	.01
☐ 140	Rich Gossage	.75	.35	.09
☐ 141	Gary Alexander	.08	.04	.01
☐ 142	Phil Huffman	.08	.04	.01
☐ 143	Bruce Bochte DP	.08	.04	.01
☐ 144	Steve Comer	.08	.04	.01
☐ 145	Darrell Evans	.18	.08	.02
☐ 146	Bob Welch	.75	.35	.09
☐ 147	Terry Puhl	.08	.04	.01
☐ 148	Manny Sanguillen	.18	.08	.02
☐ 149	Tom Hume	.08	.04	.01
☐ 150	Jason Thompson	.18	.08	.02
☐ 151	Tom Hausman DP	.08	.04	.01
☐ 152	John Fulgham	.08	.04	.01
☐ 153	Tim Blackwell	.08	.04	.01
☐ 154	Lary Sorensen	.08	.04	.01
☐ 155	Jerry Remy	.08	.04	.01
☐ 156	Tony Brizzolara	.08	.04	.01
☐ 157	Willie Wilson DP	.35	.16	.04
☐ 158	Rob Picciolo DP	.08	.04	.01
☐ 159	Ken Clay	.08	.04	.01
☐ 160	Eddie Murray	12.50	5.75	1.55
☐ 161	Larry Christenson	.08	.04	.01
☐ 162	Bob Randall	.08	.04	.01
☐ 163	Steve Swisher	.08	.04	.01
☐ 164	Greg Pryor	.08	.04	.01
☐ 165	Omar Moreno	.08	.04	.01
☐ 166	Glenn Abbott	.08	.04	.01
☐ 167	Jack Clark	1.00	.45	.13
☐ 168	Rick Waits	.08	.04	.01
☐ 169	Luis Gomez	.08	.04	.01
☐ 170	Burt Hooton	.18	.08	.02
☐ 171	Fernando Gonzalez	.08	.04	.01
☐ 172	Ron Hodges	.08	.04	.01
☐ 173	John Henry Johnson	.08	.04	.01
☐ 174	Ray Knight	.18	.08	.02
☐ 175	Rick Reuschel	.18	.08	.02
☐ 176	Champ Summers	.08	.04	.01
☐ 177	Dave Heaverlo	.08	.04	.01
☐ 178	Tim McCarver	.30	.14	.04
☐ 179	Ron Davis	.08	.04	.01
☐ 180	Warren Cromartie	.08	.04	.01
☐ 181	Moose Haas	.08	.04	.01
☐ 182	Ken Reitz	.08	.04	.01
☐ 183	Jim Anderson DP	.08	.04	.01
☐ 184	Steve Renko DP	.08	.04	.01
☐ 185	Hal McRae	.18	.08	.02
☐ 186	Junior Moore	.08	.04	.01
☐ 187	Alan Ashby	.08	.04	.01
☐ 188	Terry Crowley	.08	.04	.01
☐ 189	Kevin Kobel	.08	.04	.01
☐ 190	Buddy Bell	.18	.08	.02
☐ 191	Ted Martinez	.08	.04	.01
☐ 192	Braves Team/Mgr.	.50	.23	.06
	Bobby Cox			
	(Checklist back)			
☐ 193	Dave Goltz	.08	.04	.01
☐ 194	Mike Easler	.08	.04	.01
☐ 195	John Montefusco	.08	.04	.01
☐ 196	Lance Parrish	.90	.40	.11
☐ 197	Byron McLaughlin	.08	.04	.01
☐ 198	Dell Alston DP	.08	.04	.01
☐ 199	Mike LaCoss	.08	.04	.01
☐ 200	Jim Rice	1.00	.45	.13
☐ 201	Batting Leaders	.30	.14	.04
	Keith Hernandez			
	Fred Lynn			
☐ 202	Home Run Leaders	.30	.14	.04
	Dave Kingman			
	Gorman Thomas			
☐ 203	RBI Leaders	1.00	.45	.13
	Dave Winfield			
	Don Baylor			
☐ 204	Stolen Base Leaders	.30	.14	.04
	Omar Moreno			

☐ 205	Willie Wilson Victory Leaders	.30	.14	.04
	Joe Niekro Phil Niekro Mike Flanagan			
☐ 206	Strikeout Leaders	3.00	1.35	.40
	J.R. Richard Nolan Ryan			
☐ 207	ERA Leaders	.30	.14	.04
	J.R. Richard Ron Guidry			
☐ 208	Wayne Cage	.08	.04	.01
☐ 209	Von Joshua	.08	.04	.01
☐ 210	Steve Carlton	4.25	1.90	.55
☐ 211	Dave Skaggs DP	.08	.04	.01
☐ 212	Dave Roberts	.08	.04	.01
☐ 213	Mike Jorgensen DP	.08	.04	.01
☐ 214	Angels Team/Mgr.	.50	.23	.06
	Jim Fregosi (Checklist back)			
☐ 215	Sixto Lezcano	.08	.04	.01
☐ 216	Phil Mankowski	.08	.04	.01
☐ 217	Ed Halicki	.08	.04	.01
☐ 218	Jose Morales	.08	.04	.01
☐ 219	Steve Mingori	.08	.04	.01
☐ 220	Dave Concepcion	.60	.25	.08
☐ 221	Joe Cannon	.08	.04	.01
☐ 222	Ron Hassey	.40	.18	.05
☐ 223	Bob Sykes	.08	.04	.01
☐ 224	Willie Montanez	.08	.04	.01
☐ 225	Lou Piniella	.25	.11	.03
☐ 226	Bill Stein	.08	.04	.01
☐ 227	Len Barker	.08	.04	.01
☐ 228	Johnny Oates	.08	.04	.01
☐ 229	Jim Bibby	.08	.04	.01
☐ 230	Dave Winfield	7.50	3.40	.95
☐ 231	Steve McCatty	.08	.04	.01
☐ 232	Alan Trammell	4.00	1.80	.50
☐ 233	LaRue Washington	.08	.04	.01
☐ 234	Vern Ruhle	.08	.04	.01
☐ 235	Andre Dawson	10.00	4.50	1.25
☐ 236	Marc Hill	.08	.04	.01
☐ 237	Scott McGregor	.18	.08	.02
☐ 238	Rob Wilfong	.08	.04	.01
☐ 239	Don Aase	.08	.04	.01
☐ 240	Dave Kingman	.35	.16	.04
☐ 241	Checklist 2	.60	.25	.08
☐ 242	Lamar Johnson	.08	.04	.01
☐ 243	Jerry Augustine	.08	.04	.01
☐ 244	Cardinals Team/Mgr.	.50	.23	.06
	Ken Boyer (Checklist back)			
☐ 245	Phil Niekro	1.50	.65	.19
☐ 246	Tim Foli DP	.08	.04	.01
☐ 247	Frank Riccelli	.08	.04	.01
☐ 248	Jamie Quirk	.08	.04	.01
☐ 249	Jim Clancy	.08	.04	.01
☐ 250	Jim Kaat	.40	.18	.05
☐ 251	Kip Young	.08	.04	.01
☐ 252	Ted Cox	.08	.04	.01
☐ 253	John Montague	.08	.04	.01
☐ 254	Paul Dade DP	.08	.04	.01
☐ 255	Dusty Baker DP	.08	.04	.01
☐ 256	Roger Erickson	.08	.04	.01
☐ 257	Larry Herndon	.08	.04	.01
☐ 258	Paul Moskau	.08	.04	.01
☐ 259	Mets Team/Mgr.	.50	.23	.06
	Joe Torre (Checklist back)			
☐ 260	Al Oliver	.35	.16	.04
☐ 261	Dave Chalk	.08	.04	.01
☐ 262	Benny Ayala	.08	.04	.01
☐ 263	Dave LaRoche DP	.08	.04	.01
☐ 264	Bill Robinson	.18	.08	.02
☐ 265	Robin Yount	12.50	5.75	1.55
☐ 266	Bernie Carbo	.08	.04	.01
☐ 267	Dan Schatzeder	.08	.04	.01
☐ 268	Rafael Landestoy	.08	.04	.01
☐ 269	Dave Tobik	.08	.04	.01
☐ 270	Mike Schmidt DP	4.50	2.00	.55
☐ 271	Dick Drago DP	.08	.04	.01
☐ 272	Ralph Garr	.08	.04	.01
☐ 273	Eduardo Rodriguez	.08	.04	.01
☐ 274	Dale Murphy	4.00	1.80	.50
☐ 275	Jerry Koosman	.18	.08	.02
☐ 276	Tom Veryzer	.08	.04	.01
☐ 277	Rick Bosetti	.08	.04	.01
☐ 278	Jim Spencer	.08	.04	.01
☐ 279	Rob Andrews	.08	.04	.01
☐ 280	Gaylord Perry	1.50	.65	.19
☐ 281	Paul Blair	.18	.08	.02
☐ 282	Mariners Team/Mgr.	.50	.23	.06
	Darrell Johnson (Checklist back)			
☐ 283	John Ellis	.08	.04	.01
☐ 284	Larry Murray DP	.08	.04	.01
☐ 285	Don Baylor	.60	.25	.08
☐ 286	Darold Knowles DP	.08	.04	.01
☐ 287	John Lowenstein	.08	.04	.01
☐ 288	Dave Rozema	.08	.04	.01
☐ 289	Bruce Bochy	.08	.04	.01
☐ 290	Steve Garvey	1.50	.65	.19
☐ 291	Randy Scarberry	.08	.04	.01
☐ 292	Dale Berra	.08	.04	.01
☐ 293	Elias Sosa	.08	.04	.01
☐ 294	Charlie Spikes	.08	.04	.01
☐ 295	Larry Gura	.08	.04	.01
☐ 296	Dave Rader	.08	.04	.01
☐ 297	Tim Johnson	.08	.04	.01
☐ 298	Ken Holtzman	.08	.04	.01
☐ 299	Steve Henderson	.08	.04	.01
☐ 300	Ron Guidry	.60	.25	.08
☐ 301	Mike Edwards	.08	.04	.01
☐ 302	Dodgers Team/Mgr.	.50	.23	.06

Tom Lasorda
(Checklist back)

☐	303	Bill Castro	.08	.04	.01
☐	304	Butch Wynegar	.08	.04	.01
☐	305	Randy Jones	.08	.04	.01
☐	306	Denny Walling	.08	.04	.01
☐	307	Rick Honeycutt	.18	.08	.02
☐	308	Mike Hargrove	.18	.08	.02
☐	309	Larry McWilliams	.08	.04	.01
☐	310	Dave Parker	1.50	.65	.19
☐	311	Roger Metzger	.08	.04	.01
☐	312	Mike Barlow	.08	.04	.01
☐	313	Johnny Grubb	.08	.04	.01
☐	314	Tim Stoddard	.08	.04	.01
☐	315	Steve Kemp	.08	.04	.01
☐	316	Bob Lacey	.08	.04	.01
☐	317	Mike Anderson DP	.08	.04	.01
☐	318	Jerry Reuss	.18	.08	.02
☐	319	Chris Speier	.08	.04	.01
☐	320	Dennis Eckersley	4.00	1.80	.50
☐	321	Keith Hernandez	1.00	.45	.13
☐	322	Claudell Washington	.18	.08	.02
☐	323	Mick Kelleher	.08	.04	.01
☐	324	Tom Underwood	.08	.04	.01
☐	325	Dan Driessen	.08	.04	.01
☐	326	Bo McLaughlin	.08	.04	.01
☐	327	Ray Fosse DP	.08	.04	.01
☐	328	Twins Team/Mgr.	.50	.23	.06

Gene Mauch
(Checklist back)

☐	329	Bert Roberge	.08	.04	.01
☐	330	Al Cowens	.08	.04	.01
☐	331	Richie Hebner	.08	.04	.01
☐	332	Enrique Romo	.08	.04	.01
☐	333	Jim Norris DP	.08	.04	.01
☐	334	Jim Beattie	.08	.04	.01
☐	335	Willie McCovey	2.00	.90	.25
☐	336	George Medich	.08	.04	.01
☐	337	Carney Lansford	1.00	.45	.13
☐	338	John Wockenfuss	.08	.04	.01
☐	339	John D'Acquisto	.08	.04	.01
☐	340	Ken Singleton	.18	.08	.02
☐	341	Jim Essian	.08	.04	.01
☐	342	Odell Jones	.08	.04	.01
☐	343	Mike Vail	.08	.04	.01
☐	344	Randy Lerch	.08	.04	.01
☐	345	Larry Parrish	.18	.08	.02
☐	346	Buddy Solomon	.08	.04	.01
☐	347	Harry Chappas	.08	.04	.01
☐	348	Checklist 3	.60	.25	.08
☐	349	Jack Brohamer	.08	.04	.01
☐	350	George Hendrick	.18	.08	.02
☐	351	Bob Davis	.08	.04	.01
☐	352	Dan Briggs	.08	.04	.01
☐	353	Andy Hassler	.08	.04	.01
☐	354	Rick Auerbach	.08	.04	.01
☐	355	Gary Matthews	.18	.08	.02

☐	356	Padres Team/Mgr.	.50	.23	.06

Jerry Coleman
(Checklist back)

☐	357	Bob McClure	.08	.04	.01
☐	358	Lou Whitaker	4.00	1.80	.50
☐	359	Randy Moffitt	.08	.04	.01
☐	360	Darrell Porter DP	.08	.04	.01
☐	361	Wayne Garland	.08	.04	.01
☐	362	Danny Goodwin	.08	.04	.01
☐	363	Wayne Gross	.08	.04	.01
☐	364	Ray Burris	.08	.04	.01
☐	365	Bobby Murcer	.18	.08	.02
☐	366	Rob Dressler	.08	.04	.01
☐	367	Billy Smith	.08	.04	.01
☐	368	Willie Aikens	.18	.08	.02
☐	369	Jim Kern	.08	.04	.01
☐	370	Cesar Cedeno	.18	.08	.02
☐	371	Jack Morris	5.00	2.30	.60
☐	372	Joel Youngblood	.08	.04	.01
☐	373	Dan Petry DP	.25	.11	.03
☐	374	Jim Gantner	.18	.08	.02
☐	375	Ross Grimsley	.08	.04	.01
☐	376	Gary Allenson	.25	.11	.03
☐	377	Junior Kennedy	.08	.04	.01
☐	378	Jerry Mumphrey	.08	.04	.01
☐	379	Kevin Bell	.08	.04	.01
☐	380	Garry Maddox	.08	.04	.01
☐	381	Cubs Team/Mgr.	.50	.23	.06

Preston Gomez
(Checklist back)

☐	382	Dave Freisleben	.08	.04	.01
☐	383	Ed Ott	.08	.04	.01
☐	384	Joey McLaughlin	.08	.04	.01
☐	385	Enos Cabell	.08	.04	.01
☐	386	Darrell Jackson	.08	.04	.01
☑	387A	Fred Stanley	1.00	.45	.13

(Yellow name on front)

☐	387B	Fred Stanley	.08	.04	.01

(Red name on front)

☐	388	Mike Paxton	.08	.04	.01
☐	389	Pete LaCock	.08	.04	.01
☐	390	Fergie Jenkins	1.50	.65	.19
☐	391	Tony Armas DP	.08	.04	.01
☐	392	Milt Wilcox	.08	.04	.01
☐	393	Ozzie Smith	18.00	8.00	2.30
☐	394	Reggie Cleveland	.08	.04	.01
☐	395	Ellis Valentine	.08	.04	.01
☐	396	Dan Meyer	.08	.04	.01
☐	397	Roy Thomas DP	.08	.04	.01
☐	398	Barry Foote	.08	.04	.01
☐	399	Mike Proly DP	.08	.04	.01
☐	400	George Foster	.50	.23	.06
☐	401	Pete Falcone	.08	.04	.01
☐	402	Merv Rettenmund	.08	.04	.01
☐	403	Pete Redfern DP	.08	.04	.01
☐	404	Orioles Team/Mgr.	.50	.23	.06

Earl Weaver

(Checklist back)

☐ 405 Dwight Evans	1.25	.55	.16
☐ 406 Paul Molitor	6.50	2.90	.80
☐ 407 Tony Solaita	.08	.04	.01
☐ 408 Bill North	.08	.04	.01
☐ 409 Paul Splittorff	.08	.04	.01
☐ 410 Bobby Bonds	.28	.13	.04
☐ 411 Frank LaCorte	.08	.04	.01
☐ 412 Thad Bosley	.08	.04	.01
☐ 413 Allen Ripley	.08	.04	.01
☐ 414 George Scott	.18	.08	.02
☐ 415 Bill Atkinson	.08	.04	.01
☐ 416 Tom Brookens	.08	.04	.01
☐ 417 Craig Chamberlain DP	.08	.04	.01
☐ 418 Roger Freed DP	.08	.04	.01
☐ 419 Vic Correll	.08	.04	.01
☐ 420 Butch Hobson	.18	.08	.02
☐ 421 Doug Bird	.08	.04	.01
☐ 422 Larry Milbourne	.08	.04	.01
☐ 423 Dave Frost	.08	.04	.01
☐ 424 Yankees Team/Mgr.	.50	.23	.06

Dick Howser
(Checklist back)

☐ 425 Mark Belanger	.18	.08	.02
☐ 426 Grant Jackson	.08	.04	.01
☐ 427 Tom Hutton DP	.08	.04	.01
☐ 428 Pat Zachry	.08	.04	.01
☐ 429 Duane Kuiper	.08	.04	.01
☐ 430 Larry Hisle DP	.08	.04	.01
☐ 431 Mike Krukow	.08	.04	.01
☐ 432 Willie Norwood	.08	.04	.01
☐ 433 Rich Gale	.08	.04	.01
☐ 434 Johnnie LeMaster	.08	.04	.01
☐ 435 Don Gullett	.18	.08	.02
☐ 436 Billy Almon	.08	.04	.01
☐ 437 Joe Niekro	.18	.08	.02
☐ 438 Dave Revering	.08	.04	.01
☐ 439 Mike Phillips	.08	.04	.01
☐ 440 Don Sutton	1.50	.65	.19
☐ 441 Eric Soderholm	.08	.04	.01
☐ 442 Jorge Orta	.08	.04	.01
☐ 443 Mike Parrott	.08	.04	.01
☐ 444 Alvis Woods	.08	.04	.01
☐ 445 Mark Fidrych	.18	.08	.02
☐ 446 Duffy Dyer	.08	.04	.01
☐ 447 Nino Espinosa	.08	.04	.01
☐ 448 Jim Wohlford	.08	.04	.01
☐ 449 Doug Bair	.08	.04	.01
☐ 450 George Brett	12.50	5.75	1.55
☐ 451 Indians Team/Mgr.	.50	.23	.06

Dave Garcia
(Checklist back)

☐ 452 Steve Dillard	.08	.04	.01
☐ 453 Mike Bacsik	.08	.04	.01
☐ 454 Tom Donohue	.08	.04	.01
☐ 455 Mike Torrez	.08	.04	.01
☐ 456 Frank Taveras	.08	.04	.01
☐ 457 Bert Blyleven	.75	.35	.09
☐ 458 Billy Sample	.08	.04	.01
☐ 459 Mickey Lolich DP	.08	.04	.01
☐ 460 Willie Randolph	.75	.35	.09
☐ 461 Dwayne Murphy	.08	.04	.01
☐ 462 Mike Sadek DP	.08	.04	.01
☐ 463 Jerry Royster	.08	.04	.01
☐ 464 John Denny	.08	.04	.01
☐ 465 Rick Monday	.18	.08	.02
☐ 466 Mike Squires	.08	.04	.01
☐ 467 Jesse Jefferson	.08	.04	.01
☐ 468 Aurelio Rodriguez	.08	.04	.01
☐ 469 Randy Niemann DP	.08	.04	.01
☐ 470 Bob Boone	.50	.23	.06
☐ 471 Hosken Powell DP	.08	.04	.01
☐ 472 Willie Hernandez	.18	.08	.02
☐ 473 Bump Wills	.08	.04	.01
☐ 474 Steve Busby	.08	.04	.01
☐ 475 Cesar Geronimo	.08	.04	.01
☐ 476 Bob Shirley	.08	.04	.01
☐ 477 Buck Martinez	.08	.04	.01
☐ 478 Gil Flores	.08	.04	.01
☐ 479 Expos Team/Mgr.	.50	.23	.06

Dick Williams
(Checklist back)

☐ 480 Bob Watson	.18	.08	.02
☐ 481 Tom Paciorek	.18	.08	.02
☐ 482 Rickey Henderson	120.00	55.00	15.00

UER (7 steals at Modesto,
should be at Fresno)

☐ 483 Bo Diaz	.08	.04	.01
☐ 484 Checklist 4	.60	.25	.08
☐ 485 Mickey Rivers	.18	.08	.02
☐ 486 Mike Tyson DP	.08	.04	.01
☐ 487 Wayne Nordhagen	.08	.04	.01
☐ 488 Roy Howell	.08	.04	.01
☐ 489 Preston Hanna DP	.08	.04	.01
☐ 490 Lee May	.18	.08	.02
☐ 491 Steve Mura DP	.08	.04	.01
☐ 492 Todd Cruz	.08	.04	.01
☐ 493 Jerry Martin	.08	.04	.01
☐ 494 Craig Minetto	.08	.04	.01
☐ 495 Bake McBride	.18	.08	.02
☐ 496 Silvio Martinez	.08	.04	.01
☐ 497 Jim Mason	.08	.04	.01
☐ 498 Danny Darwin	.08	.04	.01
☐ 499 Giants Team/Mgr.	.50	.23	.06

Dave Bristol
(Checklist back)

☐ 500 Tom Seaver	4.50	2.00	.55
☐ 501 Rennie Stennett	.08	.04	.01
☐ 502 Rich Wortham DP	.08	.04	.01
☐ 503 Mike Cubbage	.08	.04	.01
☐ 504 Gene Garber	.08	.04	.01
☐ 505 Bert Campaneris	.18	.08	.02
☐ 506 Tom Buskey	.08	.04	.01
☐ 507 Leon Roberts	.08	.04	.01

☐	508 U.L. Washington	.08	.04	.01
☐	509 Ed Glynn	.08	.04	.01
☐	510 Ron Cey	.35	.16	.04
☐	511 Eric Wilkins	.08	.04	.01
☐	512 Jose Cardenal	.08	.04	.01
☐	513 Tom Dixon DP	.08	.04	.01
☐	514 Steve Ontiveros	.08	.04	.01
☐	515 Mike Caldwell	.08	.04	.01
☐	516 Hector Cruz	.08	.04	.01
☐	517 Don Stanhouse	.08	.04	.01
☐	518 Nelson Norman	.08	.04	.01
☐	519 Steve Nicosia	.08	.04	.01
☐	520 Steve Rogers	.08	.04	.01
☐	521 Ken Brett	.08	.04	.01
☐	522 Jim Morrison	.08	.04	.01
☐	523 Ken Henderson	.08	.04	.01
☐	524 Jim Wright DP	.08	.04	.01
☐	525 Clint Hurdle	.08	.04	.01
☐	526 Phillies Team/Mgr.	.50	.23	.06
	Dallas Green			
	(Checklist back)			
☐	527 Doug Rau DP	.08	.04	.01
☐	528 Adrian Devine	.08	.04	.01
☐	529 Jim Barr	.08	.04	.01
☐	530 Jim Sundberg DP	.08	.04	.01
☐	531 Eric Rasmussen	.08	.04	.01
☐	532 Willie Horton	.18	.08	.02
☐	533 Checklist 5	.60	.25	.08
☐	534 Andre Thornton	.18	.08	.02
☐	535 Bob Forsch	.08	.04	.01
☐	536 Lee Lacy	.08	.04	.01
☐	537 Alex Trevino	.08	.04	.01
☐	538 Joe Strain	.08	.04	.01
☐	539 Rudy May	.08	.04	.01
☐	540 Pete Rose	4.50	2.00	.55
☐	541 Miguel Dilone	.08	.04	.01
☐	542 Joe Coleman	.08	.04	.01
☐	543 Pat Kelly	.08	.04	.01
☐	544 Rick Sutcliffe	4.00	1.80	.50
☐	545 Jeff Burroughs	.08	.04	.01
☐	546 Rick Langford	.08	.04	.01
☐	547 John Wathan	.08	.04	.01
☐	548 Dave Rajsich	.08	.04	.01
☐	549 Larry Wolfe	.08	.04	.01
☐	550 Ken Griffey	.60	.25	.08
☐	551 Pirates Team/Mgr.	.50	.23	.06
	Chuck Tanner			
	(Checklist back)			
☐	552 Bill Nahorodny	.08	.04	.01
☐	553 Dick Davis	.08	.04	.01
☐	554 Art Howe	.18	.08	.02
☐	555 Ed Figueroa	.08	.04	.01
☐	556 Joe Rudi	.18	.08	.02
☐	557 Mark Lee	.08	.04	.01
☐	558 Alfredo Griffin	.18	.04	.01
☐	559 Dale Murray	.08	.04	.01
☐	560 Dave Lopes	.18	.08	.02
☐	561 Eddie Whitson	.18	.08	.02
☐	562 Joe Wallis	.08	.04	.01
☐	563 Will McEnaney	.08	.04	.01
☐	564 Rick Manning	.08	.04	.01
☐	565 Dennis Leonard	.18	.08	.02
☐	566 Bud Harrelson	.08	.04	.01
☐	567 Skip Lockwood	.08	.04	.01
☐	568 Gary Roenicke	.18	.08	.02
☐	569 Terry Kennedy	.18	.08	.02
☐	570 Roy Smalley	.18	.08	.02
☐	571 Joe Sambito	.08	.04	.01
☐	572 Jerry Morales DP	.08	.04	.01
☐	573 Kent Tekulve	.18	.08	.02
☐	574 Scot Thompson	.08	.04	.01
☐	575 Ken Kravec	.08	.04	.01
☐	576 Jim Dwyer	.08	.04	.01
☐	577 Blue Jays Team/Mgr.	.50	.23	.06
	Bobby Mattick			
	(Checklist back)			
☐	578 Scott Sanderson	.40	.18	.05
☐	579 Charlie Moore	.08	.04	.01
☐	580 Nolan Ryan	21.00	9.50	2.60
☐	581 Bob Bailor	.08	.04	.01
☐	582 Brian Doyle	.08	.04	.01
☐	583 Bob Stinson	.08	.04	.01
☐	584 Kurt Bevacqua	.08	.04	.01
☐	585 Al Hrabosky	.08	.04	.01
☐	586 Mitchell Page	.08	.04	.01
☐	587 Garry Templeton	.18	.08	.02
☐	588 Greg Minton	.08	.04	.01
☐	589 Chet Lemon	.18	.08	.02
☐	590 Jim Palmer	3.50	1.55	.45
☐	591 Rick Cerone	.08	.04	.01
☐	592 Jon Matlack	.08	.04	.01
☐	593 Jesus Alou	.08	.04	.01
☐	594 Dick Tidrow	.08	.04	.01
☐	595 Don Money	.08	.04	.01
☐	596 Rick Matula	.08	.04	.01
☐	597 Tom Poquette	.08	.04	.01
☐	598 Fred Kendall DP	.08	.04	.01
☐	599 Mike Norris	.08	.04	.01
☐	600 Reggie Jackson	8.50	3.80	1.05
☐	601 Buddy Schultz	.08	.04	.01
☐	602 Brian Downing	.25	.11	.03
☐	603 Jack Billingham DP	.08	.04	.01
☐	604 Glenn Adams	.08	.04	.01
☐	605 Terry Forster	.08	.04	.01
☐	606 Reds Team/Mgr.	.50	.23	.06
	John McNamara			
	(Checklist back)			
☐	607 Woodie Fryman	.08	.04	.01
☐	608 Alan Bannister	.08	.04	.01
☐	609 Ron Reed	.08	.04	.01
☐	610 Willie Stargell	2.00	.90	.25
☐	611 Jerry Garvin DP	.08	.04	.01
☐	612 Cliff Johnson	.08	.04	.01
☐	613 Randy Stein	.08	.04	.01

☐	614 John Hiller	.08	.04	.01
☐	615 Doug DeCinces	.18	.08	.02
☐	616 Gene Richards	.08	.04	.01
☐	617 Joaquin Andujar	.18	.08	.02
☐	618 Bob Montgomery DP	.08	.04	.01
☐	619 Sergio Ferrer	.08	.04	.01
☐	620 Richie Zisk	.08	.04	.01
☐	621 Bob Grich	.18	.08	.02
☐	622 Mario Soto	.08	.04	.01
☐	623 Gorman Thomas	.18	.08	.02
☐	624 Lerrin LaGrow	.08	.04	.01
☐	625 Chris Chambliss	.18	.08	.02
☐	626 Tigers Team/Mgr.	.50	.23	.06
	Sparky Anderson			
	(Checklist back)			
☐	627 Pedro Borbon	.08	.04	.01
☐	628 Doug Capilla	.08	.04	.01
☐	629 Jim Todd	.08	.04	.01
☐	630 Larry Bowa	.18	.08	.02
☐	631 Mark Littell	.08	.04	.01
☐	632 Barry Bonnell	.08	.04	.01
☐	633 Bob Apodaca	.08	.04	.01
☐	634 Glenn Borgmann DP	.08	.04	.01
☐	635 John Candelaria	.18	.08	.02
☐	636 Toby Harrah	.18	.08	.02
☐	637 Joe Simpson	.08	.04	.01
☐	638 Mark Clear	.08	.04	.01
☐	639 Larry Biittner	.08	.04	.01
☐	640 Mike Flanagan	.18	.08	.02
☐	641 Ed Kranepool	.08	.04	.01
☐	642 Ken Forsch DP	.08	.04	.01
☐	643 John Mayberry	.08	.04	.01
☐	644 Charlie Hough	.18	.08	.02
☐	645 Rick Burleson	.08	.04	.01
☐	646 Checklist 6	.60	.25	.08
☐	647 Milt May	.08	.04	.01
☐	648 Roy White	.18	.08	.02
☐	649 Tom Griffin	.08	.04	.01
☐	650 Joe Morgan	2.00	.90	.25
☐	651 Rollie Fingers	2.00	.90	.25
☐	652 Mario Mendoza	.08	.04	.01
☐	653 Stan Bahnsen	.08	.04	.01
☐	654 Bruce Boisclair DP	.08	.04	.01
☐	655 Tug McGraw	.18	.08	.02
☐	656 Larvell Blanks	.08	.04	.01
☐	657 Dave Edwards	.08	.04	.01
☐	658 Chris Knapp	.08	.04	.01
☐	659 Brewers Team/Mgr.	.50	.23	.06
	George Bamberger			
	(Checklist back)			
☐	660 Rusty Staub	.18	.08	.02
☐	661 Orioles Rookies	.20	.09	.03
	Mark Corey			
	Dave Ford			
	Wayne Krenchicki			
☐	662 Red Sox Rookies	.20	.09	.03
	Joel Finch			
	Mike O'Berry			
	Chuck Rainey			
☐	663 Angels Rookies	1.00	.45	.13
	Ralph Botting			
	Bob Clark			
	Dickie Thon			
☐	664 White Sox Rookies	.20	.09	.03
	Mike Colbern			
	Guy Hoffman			
	Dewey Robinson			
☐	665 Indians Rookies	.30	.14	.04
	Larry Andersen			
	Bobby Cuellar			
	Sandy Wihtol			
☐	666 Tigers Rookies	.20	.09	.03
	Mike Chris			
	Al Greene			
	Bruce Robbins			
☐	667 Royals Rookies	2.50	1.15	.30
	Renie Martin			
	Bill Paschall			
	Dan Quisenberry			
☐	668 Brewers Rookies	.20	.09	.03
	Danny Boitano			
	Willie Mueller			
	Lenn Sakata			
☐	669 Twins Rookies	.20	.09	.03
	Dan Graham			
	Rick Sofield			
	Gary Ward			
☐	670 Yankees Rookies	.20	.09	.03
	Bobby Brown			
	Brad Gulden			
	Darryl Jones			
☐	671 A's Rookies	2.50	1.15	.30
	Derek Bryant			
	Brian Kingman			
	Mike Morgan			
☐	672 Mariners Rookies	.20	.09	.03
	Charlie Beamon			
	Rodney Craig			
	Rafael Vasquez			
☐	673 Rangers Rookies	.20	.09	.03
	Brian Allard			
	Jerry Don Gleaton			
	Greg Mahlberg			
☐	674 Blue Jays Rookies	.20	.09	.03
	Butch Edge			
	Pat Kelly			
	Ted Wilborn			
☐	675 Braves Rookies	.20	.09	.03
	Bruce Benedict			
	Larry Bradford			
	Eddie Miller			
☐	676 Cubs Rookies	.20	.09	.03
	Dave Geisel			
	Steve Macko			

☐ 677	Karl Pagel Reds Rookies	20	.09	.03
	Art DeFreites			
	Frank Pastore			
	Harry Spilman			
☐ 678	Astros Rookies	20	.09	.03
	Reggie Baldwin			
	Alan Knicely			
	Pete Ladd			
☐ 679	Dodgers Rookies	30	.14	.04
	Joe Beckwith			
	Mickey Hatcher			
	Dave Patterson			
☐ 680	Expos Rookies	30	.14	.04
	Tony Bernazard			
	Randy Miller			
	John Tamargo			
☐ 681	Mets Rookies	3.00	1.35	.40
	Dan Norman			
	Jesse Orosco			
	Mike Scott			
☐ 682	Phillies Rookies	20	.09	.03
	Ramon Aviles			
	Dickie Noles			
	Kevin Saucier			
☐ 683	Pirates Rookies	20	.09	.03
	Dorian Boyland			
	Alberto Lois			
	Harry Saferight			
☐ 684	Cardinals Rookies	60	.25	.08
	George Frazier			
	Tom Herr			
	Dan O'Brien			
☐ 685	Padres Rookies	20	.09	.03
	Tim Flannery			
	Brian Greer			
	Jim Wilhelm			
☐ 686	Giants Rookies	20	.09	.03
	Greg Johnston			
	Dennis Littlejohn			
	Phil Nastu			
☐ 687	Mike Heath DP	08	.04	.01
☐ 688	Steve Stone	25	.11	.03
☐ 689	Red Sox Team/Mgr.	50	.23	.06
	Don Zimmer			
	(Checklist back)			
☐ 690	Tommy John	50	.23	.06
☐ 691	Ivan DeJesus	08	.04	.01
☐ 692	Rawly Eastwick DP	08	.04	.01
☐ 693	Craig Kusick	08	.04	.01
☐ 694	Jim Rooker	08	.04	.01
☐ 695	Reggie Smith	18	.08	.02
☐ 696	Julio Gonzalez	08	.04	.01
☐ 697	David Clyde	08	.04	.01
☐ 698	Oscar Gamble	18	.08	.02
☐ 699	Floyd Bannister	08	.04	.01
☐ 700	Rod Carew DP	1.75	.80	.22

☐ 701	Ken Oberkfell	35	.16	.04
☐ 702	Ed Farmer	08	.04	.01
☐ 703	Otto Velez	08	.04	.01
☐ 704	Gene Tenace	18	.08	.02
☐ 705	Freddie Patek	08	.04	.01
☐ 706	Tippy Martinez	18	.08	.02
☐ 707	Elliott Maddox	08	.04	.01
☐ 708	Bob Tolan	08	.04	.01
☐ 709	Pat Underwood	08	.04	.01
☐ 710	Graig Nettles	30	.14	.04
☐ 711	Bob Galasso	08	.04	.01
☐ 712	Rodney Scott	08	.04	.01
☐ 713	Terry Whitfield	08	.04	.01
☐ 714	Fred Norman	08	.04	.01
☐ 715	Sal Bando	18	.08	.02
☐ 716	Lynn McGlothen	08	.04	.01
☐ 717	Mickey Klutts DP	08	.04	.01
☐ 718	Greg Gross	08	.04	.01
☐ 719	Don Robinson	18	.08	.02
☐ 720	Carl Yastrzemski DP	1.75	.80	.22
☐ 721	Paul Hartzell	08	.04	.01
☐ 722	Jose Cruz	18	.08	.02
☐ 723	Shane Rawley	08	.04	.01
☐ 724	Jerry White	08	.04	.01
☐ 725	Rick Wise	08	.04	.01
☐ 726	Steve Yeager	25	.11	.03

1981 Topps

The cards in this 726-card set measure 2 1/2" by 3 1/2". League Leaders (1-8), Record Breakers (201-208), and Post-season cards (401-404) are topical subsets found in this set marketed by Topps in 1981. The team cards are all grouped together (661-686) and feature team checklist backs and a very small photo of the team's manager in the upper right cor-

ner of the obverse. The obverses carry the player's position and team in a baseball cap design, and the company name is printed in a small baseball. The backs are red and gray. The 66 double-printed cards are noted in the checklist by DP. The key Rookie Cards in the set include Harold Baines, Kirk Gibson, Bruce Hurst, Tim Raines, Jeff Reardon, and Fernando Valenzuela. Other Rookie Cards in the set are Mike Boddicker, Hubie Brooks, Bill Gullickson, Charlie Leibrandt, Lloyd Moseby, Tony Pena, and John Tudor.

	NRMT-MT	EXC	G-VG
COMPLETE SET (726)	90.00	40.00	11.50
COMMON PLAYER (1-726)	.10	.05	.01
COMMON PLAYER DP	.05	.02	.01
☐ 1 Batting Leaders	2.50	.50	.15
George Brett			
Bill Buckner			
☐ 2 Home Run Leaders	.60	.25	.08
Reggie Jackson			
Ben Oglivie			
Mike Schmidt			
☐ 3 RBI Leaders	.50	.23	.06
Cecil Cooper			
Mike Schmidt			
☐ 4 Stolen Base Leaders	1.75	.80	.22
Rickey Henderson			
Ron LeFlore			
☐ 5 Victory Leaders	.30	.14	.04
Steve Stone			
Steve Carlton			
☐ 6 Strikeout Leaders	.30	.14	.04
Len Barker			
Steve Carlton			
☐ 7 ERA Leaders	.20	.09	.03
Rudy May			
Don Sutton			
☐ 8 Leading Firemen	.35	.16	.04
Dan Quisenberry			
Rollie Fingers			
Tom Hume			
☐ 9 Pete LaCock DP	.05	.02	.01
☐ 10 Mike Flanagan	.10	.05	.01
☐ 11 Jim Wohlford DP	.05	.02	.01
☐ 12 Mark Clear	.05	.02	.01
☐ 13 Joe Charboneau	.10	.05	.01
☐ 14 John Tudor	.50	.23	.06
☐ 15 Larry Parrish	.05	.02	.01
☐ 16 Ron Davis	.05	.02	.01
☐ 17 Cliff Johnson	.05	.02	.01
☐ 18 Glenn Adams	.05	.02	.01
☐ 19 Jim Clancy	.05	.02	.01
☐ 20 Jeff Burroughs	.05	.02	.01
☐ 21 Ron Oester	.05	.02	.01
☐ 22 Danny Darwin	.05	.02	.01
☐ 23 Alex Trevino	.05	.02	.01
☐ 24 Don Stanhouse	.05	.02	.01
☐ 25 Sixto Lezcano	.05	.02	.01
☐ 26 U.L. Washington	.05	.02	.01
☐ 27 Champ Summers DP	.05	.02	.01
☐ 28 Enrique Romo	.05	.02	.01
☐ 29 Gene Tenace	.05	.02	.01
☐ 30 Jack Clark	.40	.18	.05
☐ 31 Checklist 1-121 DP	.15	.02	.00
☐ 32 Ken Oberkfell	.05	.02	.01
☐ 33 Rick Honeycutt	.05	.02	.01
☐ 34 Aurelio Rodriguez	.05	.02	.01
☐ 35 Mitchell Page	.05	.02	.01
☐ 36 Ed Farmer	.05	.02	.01
☐ 37 Gary Roenicke	.05	.02	.01
☐ 38 Win Remmerswaal	.05	.02	.01
☐ 39 Tom Veryzer	.05	.02	.01
☐ 40 Tug McGraw	.10	.05	.01
☐ 41 Ranger Rookies	.12	.05	.02
Bob Babcock			
John Butcher			
Jerry Don Gleaton			
☐ 42 Jerry White DP	.05	.02	.01
☐ 43 Jose Morales	.05	.02	.01
☐ 44 Larry McWilliams	.05	.02	.01
☐ 45 Enos Cabell	.05	.02	.01
☐ 46 Rick Bosetti	.05	.02	.01
☐ 47 Ken Brett	.05	.02	.01
☐ 48 Dave Skaggs	.05	.02	.01
☐ 49 Bob Shirley	.05	.02	.01
☐ 50 Dave Lopes	.10	.05	.01
☐ 51 Bill Robinson DP	.05	.02	.01
☐ 52 Hector Cruz	.05	.02	.01
☐ 53 Kevin Saucier	.05	.02	.01
☐ 54 Ivan DeJesus	.05	.02	.01
☐ 55 Mike Norris	.05	.02	.01
☐ 56 Buck Martinez	.05	.02	.01
☐ 57 Dave Roberts	.05	.02	.01
☐ 58 Joel Youngblood	.05	.02	.01
☐ 59 Dan Petry	.10	.05	.01
☐ 60 Willie Randolph	.10	.05	.01
☐ 61 Butch Wynegar	.05	.02	.01
☐ 62 Joe Pettini	.05	.02	.01
☐ 63 Steve Renko DP	.05	.02	.01
☐ 64 Brian Asselstine	.05	.02	.01
☐ 65 Scott McGregor	.05	.02	.01
☐ 66 Royals Rookies	.12	.05	.02
Manny Castillo			
Tim Ireland			
Mike Jones			
☐ 67 Ken Kravec	.05	.02	.01
☐ 68 Matt Alexander DP	.05	.02	.01
☐ 69 Ed Halicki	.05	.02	.01
☐ 70 Al Oliver DP	.05	.02	.01
☐ 71 Hal Dues	.05	.02	.01

☐ 72	Barry Evans DP	.05	.02	.01
☐ 73	Doug Bair	.05	.02	.01
☐ 74	Mike Hargrove	.10	.05	.01
☐ 75	Reggie Smith	.10	.05	.01
☐ 76	Mario Mendoza	.05	.02	.01
☐ 77	Mike Barlow	.05	.02	.01
☐ 78	Steve Dillard	.05	.02	.01
☐ 79	Bruce Robbins	.05	.02	.01
☐ 80	Rusty Staub	.10	.05	.01
☐ 81	Dave Stapleton	.05	.02	.01
☐ 82	Astros Rookies DP	.12	.05	.02
	Danny Heep			
	Alan Knicely			
	Bobby Sprowl			
☐ 83	Mike Proly	.05	.02	.01
☐ 84	Johnnie LeMaster	.05	.02	.01
☐ 85	Mike Caldwell	.05	.02	.01
☐ 86	Wayne Gross	.05	.02	.01
☐ 87	Rick Camp	.05	.02	.01
☐ 88	Joe Lefebvre	.05	.02	.01
☐ 89	Darrell Jackson	.05	.02	.01
☐ 90	Bake McBride	.05	.02	.01
☐ 91	Tim Stoddard DP	.05	.02	.01
☐ 92	Mike Easler	.05	.02	.01
☐ 93	Ed Glynn DP	.05	.02	.01
☐ 94	Harry Spilman DP	.05	.02	.01
☐ 95	Jim Sundberg	.10	.05	.01
☐ 96	A's Rookies	.12	.05	.02
	Dave Beard			
	Ernie Camacho			
	Pat Dempsey			
☐ 97	Chris Speier	.05	.02	.01
☐ 98	Clint Hurdle	.05	.02	.01
☐ 99	Eric Wilkins	.05	.02	.01
☐ 100	Rod Carew	3.00	1.35	.40
☐ 101	Benny Ayala	.05	.02	.01
☐ 102	Dave Tobik	.05	.02	.01
☐ 103	Jerry Martin	.05	.02	.01
☐ 104	Terry Forster	.05	.02	.01
☐ 105	Jose Cruz	.10	.05	.01
☐ 106	Don Money	.05	.02	.01
☐ 107	Rich Wortham	.05	.02	.01
☐ 108	Bruce Benedict	.05	.02	.01
☐ 109	Mike Scott	.35	.16	.04
☐ 110	Carl Yastrzemski	3.00	1.35	.40
☐ 111	Greg Minton	.05	.02	.01
☐ 112	White Sox Rookies	.12	.05	.02
	Rusty Kuntz			
	Fran Mullin			
	Leo Sutherland			
☐ 113	Mike Phillips	.05	.02	.01
☐ 114	Tom Underwood	.05	.02	.01
☐ 115	Roy Smalley	.05	.02	.01
☐ 116	Joe Simpson	.05	.02	.01
☐ 117	Pete Falcone	.05	.02	.01
☐ 118	Kurt Bevacqua	.05	.02	.01
☐ 119	Tippy Martinez	.10	.05	.01

☐ 120	Larry Bowa	.10	.05	.01
☐ 121	Larry Harlow	.05	.02	.01
☐ 122	John Denny	.05	.02	.01
☐ 123	Al Cowens	.05	.02	.01
☐ 124	Jerry Garvin	.05	.02	.01
☐ 125	Andre Dawson	3.50	1.55	.45
☐ 126	Charlie Leibrandt	1.25	.55	.16
☐ 127	Rudy Law	.05	.02	.01
☐ 128	Gary Allenson DP	.05	.02	.01
☐ 129	Art Howe	.10	.05	.01
☐ 130	Larry Gura	.05	.02	.01
☐ 131	Keith Moreland	.10	.05	.01
☐ 132	Tommy Boggs	.05	.02	.01
☐ 133	Jeff Cox	.05	.02	.01
☐ 134	Steve Mura	.05	.02	.01
☐ 135	Gorman Thomas	.10	.05	.01
☐ 136	Doug Capilla	.05	.02	.01
☐ 137	Hosken Powell	.05	.02	.01
☐ 138	Rich Dotson DP	.05	.02	.01
☐ 139	Oscar Gamble	.05	.02	.01
☐ 140	Bob Forsch	.05	.02	.01
☐ 141	Miguel Dilone	.05	.02	.01
☐ 142	Jackson Todd	.05	.02	.01
☐ 143	Dan Meyer	.05	.02	.01
☐ 144	Allen Ripley	.05	.02	.01
☐ 145	Mickey Rivers	.10	.05	.01
☐ 146	Bobby Castillo	.05	.02	.01
☐ 147	Dale Berra	.05	.02	.01
☐ 148	Randy Niemann	.05	.02	.01
☐ 149	Joe Nolan	.05	.02	.01
☐ 150	Mark Fidrych	.10	.05	.01
☐ 151	Claudell Washington	.05	.02	.01
☐ 152	John Urrea	.05	.02	.01
☐ 153	Tom Poquette	.05	.02	.01
☐ 154	Rick Langford	.05	.02	.01
☐ 155	Chris Chambliss	.10	.05	.01
☐ 156	Bob McClure	.05	.02	.01
☐ 157	John Wathan	.05	.02	.01
☐ 158	Fergie Jenkins	1.00	.45	.13
☐ 159	Brian Doyle	.05	.02	.01
☐ 160	Garry Maddox	.05	.02	.01
☐ 161	Dan Graham	.05	.02	.01
☐ 162	Doug Corbett	.05	.02	.01
☐ 163	Bill Almon	.05	.02	.01
☐ 164	LaMarr Hoyt	.10	.05	.01
☐ 165	Tony Scott	.05	.02	.01
☐ 166	Floyd Bannister	.05	.02	.01
☐ 167	Terry Whitfield	.05	.02	.01
☐ 168	Don Robinson DP	.05	.02	.01
☐ 169	John Mayberry	.05	.02	.01
☐ 170	Ross Grimsley	.05	.02	.01
☐ 171	Gene Richards	.05	.02	.01
☐ 172	Gary Woods	.05	.02	.01
☐ 173	Bump Wills	.05	.02	.01
☐ 174	Doug Rau	.05	.02	.01
☐ 175	Dave Collins	.05	.02	.01
☐ 176	Mike Krukow	.05	.02	.01

☐	177	Rick Peters	.05	.02	.01
☐	178	Jim Essian DP	.05	.02	.01
☐	179	Rudy May	.05	.02	.01
☐	180	Pete Rose	3.50	1.55	.45
☐	181	Elias Sosa	.05	.02	.01
☐	182	Bob Grich	.10	.05	.01
☐	183	Dick Davis DP	.05	.02	.01
☐	184	Jim Dwyer	.05	.02	.01
☐	185	Dennis Leonard	.05	.02	.01
☐	186	Wayne Nordhagen	.05	.02	.01
☐	187	Mike Parrott	.05	.02	.01
☐	188	Doug DeCinces	.10	.05	.01
☐	189	Craig Swan	.05	.02	.01
☐	190	Cesar Cedeno	.10	.05	.01
☐	191	Rick Sutcliffe	.50	.23	.06
☐	192	Braves Rookies	.25	.11	.03
		Terry Harper			
		Ed Miller			
		Rafael Ramirez			
☐	193	Pete Vuckovich	.10	.05	.01
☐	194	Rod Scurry	.05	.02	.01
☐	195	Rich Murray	.05	.02	.01
☐	196	Duffy Dyer	.05	.02	.01
☐	197	Jim Kern	.05	.02	.01
☐	198	Jerry Dybzinski	.05	.02	.01
☐	199	Chuck Rainey	.05	.02	.01
☐	200	George Foster	.25	.11	.03
☐	201	RB: Johnny Bench	.75	.35	.09
		Most homers,			
		lifetime, catcher			
☐	202	RB: Steve Carlton	.75	.35	.09
		Most strikeouts,			
		lefthander, lifetime			
☐	203	RB: Bill Gullickson	.35	.16	.04
		Most strikeouts,			
		game, rookie			
☐	204	RB: Ron LeFlore and	.20	.09	.03
		Rodney Scott			
		Most stolen bases,			
		teammates, season			
☐	205	RB: Pete Rose	.90	.40	.11
		Most cons. seasons			
		600 or more at-bats			
☐	206	RB: Mike Schmidt	1.25	.55	.16
		Most homers, third			
		baseman, season			
☐	207	RB: Ozzie Smith	1.25	.55	.16
		Most assists,			
		season, shortstop			
☐	208	RB: Willie Wilson	.20	.09	.03
		Most at-bats, season			
☐	209	Dickie Thon DP	.05	.02	.01
☐	210	Jim Palmer	2.50	1.15	.30
☐	211	Derrel Thomas	.05	.02	.01
☐	212	Steve Nicosia	.05	.02	.01
☐	213	Al Holland	.05	.02	.01
☐	214	Angels Rookies	.12	.05	.02
		Ralph Botting			
		Jim Dorsey			
		John Harris			
☐	215	Larry Hisle	.05	.02	.01
☐	216	John Henry Johnson	.05	.02	.01
☐	217	Rich Hebner	.05	.02	.01
☐	218	Paul Splittorff	.05	.02	.01
☐	219	Ken Landreaux	.05	.02	.01
☐	220	Tom Seaver	3.00	1.35	.40
☐	221	Bob Davis	.05	.02	.01
☐	222	Jorge Orta	.05	.02	.01
☐	223	Roy Lee Jackson	.05	.02	.01
☐	224	Pat Zachry	.05	.02	.01
☐	225	Ruppert Jones	.05	.02	.01
☐	226	Manny Sanguillen DP	.05	.02	.01
☐	227	Fred Martinez	.05	.02	.01
☐	228	Tom Paciorek	.10	.05	.01
☐	229	Rollie Fingers	2.00	.90	.25
☐	230	George Hendrick	.10	.05	.01
☐	231	Joe Beckwith	.05	.02	.01
☐	232	Mickey Klutts	.05	.02	.01
☐	233	Skip Lockwood	.05	.02	.01
☐	234	Lou Whitaker	1.25	.55	.16
☐	235	Scott Sanderson	.10	.05	.01
☐	236	Mike Ivie	.05	.02	.01
☐	237	Charlie Moore	.05	.02	.01
☐	238	Willie Hernandez	.10	.05	.01
☐	239	Rick Miller DP	.05	.02	.01
☐	240	Nolan Ryan	12.00	5.50	1.50
☐	241	Checklist 122-242 DP	.15	.02	.00
☐	242	Chet Lemon	.05	.02	.01
☐	243	Sal Butera	.05	.02	.01
☐	244	Cardinals Rookies	.05	.02	.01
		Tito Landrum			
		Al Olmsted			
		Andy Rincon			
☐	245	Ed Figueroa	.05	.02	.01
☐	246	Ed Ott DP	.05	.02	.01
☐	247	Glenn Hubbard DP	.05	.02	.01
☐	248	Joey McLaughlin	.05	.02	.01
☐	249	Larry Cox	.05	.02	.01
☐	250	Ron Guidry	.40	.18	.05
☐	251	Tom Brookens	.05	.02	.01
☐	252	Victor Cruz	.05	.02	.01
☐	253	Dave Bergman	.05	.02	.01
☐	254	Ozzie Smith	5.00	2.30	.60
☐	255	Mark Littell	.05	.02	.01
☐	256	Bombo Rivera	.05	.02	.01
☐	257	Rennie Stennett	.05	.02	.01
☐	258	Joe Price	.05	.02	.01
☐	259	Mets Rookies	1.50	.65	.19
		Juan Berenguer			
		Hubie Brooks			
		Mookie Wilson			
☐	260	Ron Cey	.10	.05	.01
☐	261	Rickey Henderson	16.00	7.25	2.00
☐	262	Sammy Stewart	.05	.02	.01

☐ 263 Brian Downing	10	.05	.01
☐ 264 Jim Norris	05	.02	.01
☐ 265 John Candelaria	10	.05	.01
☐ 266 Tom Herr	10	.05	.01
☐ 267 Stan Bahnsen	05	.02	.01
☐ 268 Jerry Royster	05	.02	.01
☐ 269 Ken Forsch	05	.02	.01
☐ 270 Greg Luzinski	10	.05	.01
☐ 271 Bill Castro	05	.02	.01
☐ 272 Bruce Kimm	05	.02	.01
☐ 273 Stan Papi	05	.02	.01
☐ 274 Craig Chamberlain	05	.02	.01
☐ 275 Dwight Evans	50	.23	.06
☐ 276 Dan Spillner	05	.02	.01
☐ 277 Alfredo Griffin	05	.02	.01
☐ 278 Rick Sofield	05	.02	.01
☐ 279 Bob Knepper	05	.02	.01
☐ 280 Ken Griffey	50	.23	.06
☐ 281 Fred Stanley	05	.02	.01
☐ 282 Mariners Rookies	12	.05	.02
Rick Anderson			
Greg Biercevicz			
Rodney Craig			
☐ 283 Billy Sample	05	.02	.01
☐ 284 Brian Kingman	05	.02	.01
☐ 285 Jerry Turner	05	.02	.01
☐ 286 Dave Frost	05	.02	.01
☐ 287 Lenn Sakata	05	.02	.01
☐ 288 Bob Clark	05	.02	.01
☐ 289 Mickey Hatcher	05	.02	.01
☐ 290 Bob Boone DP	05	.02	.01
☐ 291 Aurelio Lopez	05	.02	.01
☐ 292 Mike Squires	05	.02	.01
☐ 293 Charlie Lea	05	.02	.01
☐ 294 Mike Tyson DP	05	.02	.01
☐ 295 Hal McRae	10	.05	.01
☐ 296 Bill Nahorodny DP	05	.02	.01
☐ 297 Bob Bailor	05	.02	.01
☐ 298 Buddy Solomon	05	.02	.01
☐ 299 Elliott Maddox	05	.02	.01
☐ 300 Paul Molitor	2.00	.90	.25
☐ 301 Matt Keough	05	.02	.01
☐ 302 Dodgers Rookies	3.00	1.35	.40
Jack Perconte			
Mike Scioscia			
Fernando Valenzuela			
☐ 303 Johnny Oates	05	.02	.01
☐ 304 John Castino	05	.02	.01
☐ 305 Ken Clay	05	.02	.01
☐ 306 Juan Beniquez DP	05	.02	.01
☐ 307 Gene Garber	05	.02	.01
☐ 308 Rick Manning	05	.02	.01
☐ 309 Luis Salazar	25	.11	.03
☐ 310 Vida Blue DP	05	.02	.01
☐ 311 Freddie Patek	05	.02	.01
☐ 312 Rick Rhoden	05	.02	.01
☐ 313 Luis Pujols	05	.02	.01
☐ 314 Rich Dauer	05	.02	.01
☐ 315 Kirk Gibson	3.00	1.35	.40
☐ 316 Craig Minetto	05	.02	.01
☐ 317 Lonnie Smith	25	.11	.03
☐ 318 Steve Yeager	05	.02	.01
☐ 319 Rowland Office	05	.02	.01
☐ 320 Tom Burgmeier	05	.02	.01
☐ 321 Leon Durham	10	.05	.01
☐ 322 Neil Allen	05	.02	.01
☐ 323 Jim Morrison DP	05	.02	.01
☐ 324 Mike Willis	05	.02	.01
☐ 325 Ray Knight	10	.05	.01
☐ 326 Biff Pocoroba	05	.02	.01
☐ 327 Moose Haas	05	.02	.01
☐ 328 Twins Rookies	12	.05	.02
Dave Engle			
Greg Johnston			
Gary Ward			
☐ 329 Joaquin Andujar	10	.05	.01
☐ 330 Frank White	10	.05	.01
☐ 331 Dennis Lamp	05	.02	.01
☐ 332 Lee Lacy DP	05	.02	.01
☐ 333 Sid Monge	05	.02	.01
☐ 334 Dane Iorg	05	.02	.01
☐ 335 Rick Cerone	05	.02	.01
☐ 336 Eddie Whitson	05	.02	.01
☐ 337 Lynn Jones	05	.02	.01
☐ 338 Checklist 243-363	30	.03	.01
☐ 339 John Ellis	05	.02	.01
☐ 340 Bruce Kison	05	.02	.01
☐ 341 Dwayne Murphy	05	.02	.01
☐ 342 Eric Rasmussen DP	05	.02	.01
☐ 343 Frank Taveras	05	.02	.01
☐ 344 Byron McLaughlin	05	.02	.01
☐ 345 Warren Cromartie	05	.02	.01
☐ 346 Larry Christenson DP	05	.02	.01
☐ 347 Harold Baines	4.00	1.80	.50
☐ 348 Bob Sykes	05	.02	.01
☐ 349 Glenn Hoffman	05	.02	.01
☐ 350 J.R. Richard	10	.05	.01
☐ 351 Otto Velez	05	.02	.01
☐ 352 Dick Tidrow DP	05	.02	.01
☐ 353 Terry Kennedy	10	.05	.01
☐ 354 Mario Soto	05	.02	.01
☐ 355 Bob Horner	10	.05	.01
☐ 356 Padres Rookies	12	.05	.02
George Stablein			
Craig Stimac			
Tom Tellmann			
☐ 357 Jim Slaton	05	.02	.01
☐ 358 Mark Wagner	05	.02	.01
☐ 359 Tom Hausman	05	.02	.01
☐ 360 Willie Wilson	30	.14	.04
☐ 361 Joe Strain	05	.02	.01
☐ 362 Bo Diaz	05	.02	.01
☐ 363 Geoff Zahn	05	.02	.01
☐ 364 Mike Davis	10	.05	.01

☐ 365	Graig Nettles DP	.05	.02	.01
☐ 366	Mike Ramsey	.05	.02	.01
☐ 367	Dennis Martinez	.50	.23	.06
☐ 368	Leon Roberts	.05	.02	.01
☐ 369	Frank Tanana	.10	.05	.01
☐ 370	Dave Winfield	4.50	2.00	.55
☐ 371	Charlie Hough	.10	.05	.01
☐ 372	Jay Johnstone	.10	.05	.01
☐ 373	Pat Underwood	.05	.02	.01
☐ 374	Tommy Hutton	.05	.02	.01
☐ 375	Dave Concepcion	.25	.11	.03
☐ 376	Ron Reed	.05	.02	.01
☐ 377	Jerry Morales	.05	.02	.01
☐ 378	Dave Rader	.05	.02	.01
☐ 379	Lary Sorensen	.05	.02	.01
☐ 380	Willie Stargell	1.50	.65	.19
☐ 381	Cubs Rookies	.12	.05	.02
	Carlos Lezcano			
	Steve Macko			
	Randy Martz			
☐ 382	Paul Mirabella	.05	.02	.01
☐ 383	Eric Soderholm DP	.05	.02	.01
☐ 384	Mike Sadek	.05	.02	.01
☐ 385	Joe Sambito	.05	.02	.01
☐ 386	Dave Edwards	.05	.02	.01
☐ 387	Phil Niekro	1.00	.45	.13
☐ 388	Andre Thornton	.10	.05	.01
☐ 389	Marty Pattin	.05	.02	.01
☐ 390	Cesar Geronimo	.05	.02	.01
☐ 391	Dave Lemanczyk DP	.05	.02	.01
☐ 392	Lance Parrish	.40	.18	.05
☐ 393	Broderick Perkins	.05	.02	.01
☐ 394	Woodie Fryman	.05	.02	.01
☐ 395	Scot Thompson	.05	.02	.01
☐ 396	Bill Campbell	.05	.02	.01
☐ 397	Julio Cruz	.05	.02	.01
☐ 398	Ross Baumgarten	.05	.02	.01
☐ 399	Orioles Rookies	.75	.35	.09
	Mike Boddicker			
	Mark Corey			
	Floyd Rayford			
☐ 400	Reggie Jackson	4.00	1.80	.50
☐ 401	AL Champs	1.25	.55	.16
	Royals sweep Yanks			
	(George Brett swinging)			
☐ 402	NL Champs	.20	.09	.03
	Phillies squeak			
	past Astros			
☐ 403	1980 World Series	.20	.09	.03
	Phillies beat			
	Royals in six			
☐ 404	1980 World Series	.20	.09	.03
	Phillies win first			
	World Series			
☐ 405	Nino Espinosa	.05	.02	.01
☐ 406	Dickie Noles	.05	.02	.01
☐ 407	Ernie Whitt	.05	.02	.01
☐ 408	Fernando Arroyo	.05	.02	.01
☐ 409	Larry Herndon	.05	.02	.01
☐ 410	Bert Campaneris	.10	.05	.01
☐ 411	Terry Puhl	.05	.02	.01
☐ 412	Britt Burns	.10	.05	.01
☐ 413	Tony Bernazard	.05	.02	.01
☐ 414	John Pacella DP	.05	.02	.01
☐ 415	Ben Oglivie	.10	.05	.01
☐ 416	Gary Alexander	.05	.02	.01
☐ 417	Dan Schatzeder	.05	.02	.01
☐ 418	Bobby Brown	.05	.02	.01
☐ 419	Tom Hume	.05	.02	.01
☐ 420	Keith Hernandez	.50	.23	.06
☐ 421	Bob Stanley	.05	.02	.01
☐ 422	Dan Ford	.05	.02	.01
☐ 423	Shane Rawley	.05	.02	.01
☐ 424	Yankees Rookies	.12	.05	.02
	Tim Lollar			
	Bruce Robinson			
	Dennis Werth			
☐ 425	Al Bumbry	.05	.02	.01
☐ 426	Warren Brusstar	.05	.02	.01
☐ 427	John D'Acquisto	.05	.02	.01
☐ 428	John Stearns	.05	.02	.01
☐ 429	Mick Kelleher	.05	.02	.01
☐ 430	Jim Bibby	.05	.02	.01
☐ 431	Dave Roberts	.05	.02	.01
☐ 432	Len Barker	.05	.02	.01
☐ 433	Rance Mulliniks	.05	.02	.01
☐ 434	Roger Erickson	.05	.02	.01
☐ 435	Jim Spencer	.05	.02	.01
☐ 436	Gary Lucas	.05	.02	.01
☐ 437	Mike Heath DP	.05	.02	.01
☐ 438	John Montefusco	.05	.02	.01
☐ 439	Denny Walling	.05	.02	.01
☐ 440	Jerry Reuss	.10	.05	.01
☐ 441	Ken Reitz	.05	.02	.01
☐ 442	Ron Pruitt	.05	.02	.01
☐ 443	Jim Beattie DP	.05	.02	.01
☐ 444	Garth Iorg	.05	.02	.01
☐ 445	Ellis Valentine	.05	.02	.01
☐ 446	Checklist 364-484	.30	.03	.01
☐ 447	Junior Kennedy DP	.05	.02	.01
☐ 448	Tim Corcoran	.05	.02	.01
☐ 449	Paul Mitchell	.05	.02	.01
☐ 450	Dave Kingman DP	.05	.02	.01
☐ 451	Indians Rookies	.12	.05	.02
	Chris Bando			
	Tom Brennan			
	Sandy Wihtol			
☐ 452	Renie Martin	.05	.02	.01
☐ 453	Rob Wilfong DP	.05	.02	.01
☐ 454	Andy Hassler	.05	.02	.01
☐ 455	Rick Burleson	.05	.02	.01
☐ 456	Jeff Reardon	10.00	4.50	1.25
☐ 457	Mike Lum	.05	.02	.01
☐ 458	Randy Jones	.05	.02	.01

☐ 459	Greg Gross	.05	.02	.01
☐ 460	Rich Gossage	.30	.14	.04
☐ 461	Dave McKay	.05	.02	.01
☐ 462	Jack Brohamer	.05	.02	.01
☐ 463	Milt May	.05	.02	.01
☐ 464	Adrian Devine	.05	.02	.01
☐ 465	Bill Russell	.10	.05	.01
☐ 466	Bob Molinaro	.05	.02	.01
☐ 467	Dave Stieb	.50	.23	.06
☐ 468	John Wockenfuss	.05	.02	.01
☐ 469	Jeff Leonard	.10	.05	.01
☐ 470	Manny Trillo	.05	.02	.01
☐ 471	Mike Vail	.05	.02	.01
☐ 472	Dyar Miller DP	.05	.02	.01
☐ 473	Jose Cardenal	.05	.02	.01
☐ 474	Mike LaCoss	.05	.02	.01
☐ 475	Buddy Bell	.10	.05	.01
☐ 476	Jerry Koosman	.10	.05	.01
☐ 477	Luis Gomez	.05	.02	.01
☐ 478	Juan Eichelberger	.05	.02	.01
☐ 479	Expos Rookies	7.50	3.40	.95
	Tim Raines			
	Roberto Ramos			
	Bobby Pate			
☐ 480	Carlton Fisk	3.00	1.35	.40
☐ 481	Bob Lacey DP	.05	.02	.01
☐ 482	Jim Gantner	.10	.05	.01
☐ 483	Mike Griffin	.05	.02	.01
☐ 484	Max Venable DP	.05	.02	.01
☐ 485	Garry Templeton	.10	.05	.01
☐ 486	Marc Hill	.05	.02	.01
☐ 487	Dewey Robinson	.05	.02	.01
☐ 488	Damaso Garcia	.10	.05	.01
☐ 489	John Littlefield	.05	.02	.01
☐ 490	Eddie Murray	4.00	1.80	.50
☐ 491	Gordy Pladson	.05	.02	.01
☐ 492	Barry Foote	.05	.02	.01
☐ 493	Dan Quisenberry	.40	.18	.05
☐ 494	Bob Walk	.50	.23	.06
☐ 495	Dusty Baker	.10	.05	.01
☐ 496	Paul Dade	.05	.02	.01
☐ 497	Fred Norman	.05	.02	.01
☐ 498	Pat Putnam	.05	.02	.01
☐ 499	Frank Pastore	.05	.02	.01
☐ 500	Jim Rice	.50	.23	.06
☐ 501	Tim Foli DP	.05	.02	.01
☐ 502	Giants Rookies	.12	.05	.02
	Chris Bourjos			
	Al Hargesheimer			
	Mike Rowland			
☐ 503	Steve McCatty	.05	.02	.01
☐ 504	Dale Murphy	1.50	.65	.19
☐ 505	Jason Thompson	.05	.02	.01
☐ 506	Phil Huffman	.05	.02	.01
☐ 507	Jamie Quirk	.05	.02	.01
☐ 508	Rob Dressler	.05	.02	.01
☐ 509	Pete Mackanin	.05	.02	.01
☐ 510	Lee Mazzilli	.05	.02	.01
☐ 511	Wayne Garland	.05	.02	.01
☐ 512	Gary Thomasson	.05	.02	.01
☐ 513	Frank LaCorte	.05	.02	.01
☐ 514	George Riley	.05	.02	.01
☐ 515	Robin Yount	6.00	2.70	.75
☐ 516	Doug Bird	.05	.02	.01
☐ 517	Richie Zisk	.05	.02	.01
☐ 518	Grant Jackson	.05	.02	.01
☐ 519	John Tamargo DP	.05	.02	.01
☐ 520	Steve Stone	.10	.05	.01
☐ 521	Sam Mejias	.05	.02	.01
☐ 522	Mike Colbern	.05	.02	.01
☐ 523	John Fulgham	.05	.02	.01
☐ 524	Willie Aikens	.05	.02	.01
☐ 525	Mike Torrez	.05	.02	.01
☐ 526	Phillies Rookies	.12	.05	.02
	Marty Bystrom			
	Jay Loviglio			
	Jim Wright			
☐ 527	Danny Goodwin	.05	.02	.01
☐ 528	Gary Matthews	.10	.05	.01
☐ 529	Dave LaRoche	.05	.02	.01
☐ 530	Steve Garvey	1.00	.45	.13
☐ 531	John Curtis	.05	.02	.01
☐ 532	Bill Stein	.05	.02	.01
☐ 533	Jesus Figueroa	.05	.02	.01
☐ 534	Dave Smith	.35	.16	.04
☐ 535	Omar Moreno	.05	.02	.01
☐ 536	Bob Owchinko DP	.05	.02	.01
☐ 537	Ron Hodges	.05	.02	.01
☐ 538	Tom Griffin	.05	.02	.01
☐ 539	Rodney Scott	.05	.02	.01
☐ 540	Mike Schmidt DP	3.00	1.35	.40
☐ 541	Steve Swisher	.05	.02	.01
☐ 542	Larry Bradford DP	.05	.02	.01
☐ 543	Terry Crowley	.05	.02	.01
☐ 544	Rich Gale	.05	.02	.01
☐ 545	Johnny Grubb	.05	.02	.01
☐ 546	Paul Moskau	.05	.02	.01
☐ 547	Mario Guerrero	.05	.02	.01
☐ 548	Dave Goltz	.05	.02	.01
☐ 549	Jerry Remy	.05	.02	.01
☐ 550	Tommy John	.30	.14	.04
☐ 551	Pirates Rookies	1.00	.45	.13
	Vance Law			
	Tony Pena			
	Pascual Perez			
☐ 552	Steve Trout	.05	.02	.01
☐ 553	Tim Blackwell	.05	.02	.01
☐ 554	Bert Blyleven UER	.75	.35	.09
	(1 is missing from			
	1980 on card back)			
☐ 555	Cecil Cooper	.10	.05	.01
☐ 556	Jerry Mumphrey	.05	.02	.01
☐ 557	Chris Knapp	.05	.02	.01
☐ 558	Barry Bonnell	.05	.02	.01

☐ 559	Willie Montanez	.05	.02	.01
☐ 560	Joe Morgan	1.25	.55	.16
☐ 561	Dennis Littlejohn	.05	.02	.01
☐ 562	Checklist 485-605	.30	.03	.01
☐ 563	Jim Kaat	.30	.14	.04
☐ 564	Ron Hassey DP	.05	.02	.01
☐ 565	Burt Hooton	.05	.02	.01
☐ 566	Del Unser	.05	.02	.01
☐ 567	Mark Bomback	.05	.02	.01
☐ 568	Dave Revering	.05	.02	.01
☐ 569	Al Williams DP	.05	.02	.01
☐ 570	Ken Singleton	.10	.05	.01
☐ 571	Todd Cruz	.05	.02	.01
☐ 572	Jack Morris	3.00	1.35	.40
☐ 573	Phil Garner	.10	.05	.01
☐ 574	Bill Caudill	.05	.02	.01
☐ 575	Tony Perez	.60	.25	.08
☐ 576	Reggie Cleveland	.05	.02	.01
☐ 577	Blue Jays Rookies	.12	.05	.02
	Luis Leal			
	Brian Milner			
	Ken Schrom			
☐ 578	Bill Gullickson	1.50	.65	.19
☐ 579	Tim Flannery	.05	.02	.01
☐ 580	Don Baylor	.10	.05	.01
☐ 581	Roy Howell	.05	.02	.01
☐ 582	Gaylord Perry	1.00	.45	.13
☐ 583	Larry Milbourne	.05	.02	.01
☐ 584	Randy Lerch	.05	.02	.01
☐ 585	Amos Otis	.10	.05	.01
☐ 586	Silvio Martinez	.05	.02	.01
☐ 587	Jeff Newman	.05	.02	.01
☐ 588	Gary Lavelle	.05	.02	.01
☐ 589	Lamar Johnson	.05	.02	.01
☐ 590	Bruce Sutter	.30	.14	.04
☐ 591	John Lowenstein	.05	.02	.01
☐ 592	Steve Comer	.05	.02	.01
☐ 593	Steve Kemp	.05	.02	.01
☐ 594	Preston Hanna DP	.05	.02	.01
☐ 595	Butch Hobson	.10	.05	.01
☐ 596	Jerry Augustine	.05	.02	.01
☐ 597	Rafael Landestoy	.05	.02	.01
☐ 598	George Vukovich DP	.05	.02	.01
☐ 599	Dennis Kinney	.05	.02	.01
☐ 600	Johnny Bench	3.00	1.35	.40
☐ 601	Don Aase	.05	.02	.01
☐ 602	Bobby Murcer	.10	.05	.01
☐ 603	John Verhoeven	.05	.02	.01
☐ 604	Rob Picciolo	.05	.02	.01
☐ 605	Don Sutton	1.00	.45	.13
☐ 606	Reds Rookies DP	.12	.05	.02
	Bruce Berenyi			
	Geoff Combe			
	Paul Householder			
☐ 607	David Palmer	.05	.02	.01
☐ 608	Greg Pryor	.05	.02	.01
☐ 609	Lynn McGlothen	.05	.02	.01
☐ 610	Darrell Porter	.05	.02	.01
☐ 611	Rick Matula DP	.05	.02	.01
☐ 612	Duane Kuiper	.05	.02	.01
☐ 613	Jim Anderson	.05	.02	.01
☐ 614	Dave Rozema	.05	.02	.01
☐ 615	Rick Dempsey	.10	.05	.01
☐ 616	Rick Wise	.05	.02	.01
☐ 617	Craig Reynolds	.05	.02	.01
☐ 618	John Milner	.05	.02	.01
☐ 619	Steve Henderson	.05	.02	.01
☐ 620	Dennis Eckersley	2.50	1.15	.30
☐ 621	Tom Donohue	.05	.02	.01
☐ 622	Randy Moffitt	.05	.02	.01
☐ 623	Sal Bando	.10	.05	.01
☐ 624	Bob Welch	.50	.23	.06
☐ 625	Bill Buckner	.10	.05	.01
☐ 626	Tigers Rookies	.12	.05	.02
	Dave Steffen			
	Jerry Ujdur			
	Roger Weaver			
☐ 627	Luis Tiant	.10	.05	.01
☐ 628	Vic Correll	.05	.02	.01
☐ 629	Tony Armas	.10	.05	.01
☐ 630	Steve Carlton	3.00	1.35	.40
☐ 631	Ron Jackson	.05	.02	.01
☐ 632	Alan Bannister	.05	.02	.01
☐ 633	Bill Lee	.05	.02	.01
☐ 634	Doug Flynn	.05	.02	.01
☐ 635	Bobby Bonds	.10	.05	.01
☐ 636	Al Hrabosky	.05	.02	.01
☐ 637	Jerry Narron	.05	.02	.01
☐ 638	Checklist 606-726	.30	.03	.01
☐ 639	Carney Lansford	.40	.18	.05
☐ 640	Dave Parker	.60	.25	.08
☐ 641	Mark Belanger	.10	.05	.01
☐ 642	Vern Ruhle	.05	.02	.01
☐ 643	Lloyd Moseby	.25	.11	.03
☐ 644	Ramon Aviles DP	.05	.02	.01
☐ 645	Rick Reuschel	.10	.05	.01
☐ 646	Marvis Foley	.05	.02	.01
☐ 647	Dick Drago	.05	.02	.01
☐ 648	Darrell Evans	.10	.05	.01
☐ 649	Manny Sarmiento	.05	.02	.01
☐ 650	Bucky Dent	.10	.05	.01
☐ 651	Pedro Guerrero	.60	.25	.08
☐ 652	John Montague	.05	.02	.01
☐ 653	Bill Fahey	.05	.02	.01
☐ 654	Ray Burris	.05	.02	.01
☐ 655	Dan Driessen	.05	.02	.01
☐ 656	Jon Matlack	.05	.02	.01
☐ 657	Mike Cubbage DP	.05	.02	.01
☐ 658	Milt Wilcox	.05	.02	.01
☐ 659	Brewers Rookies	.12	.05	.02
	John Flinn			
	Ed Romero			
	Ned Yost			
☐ 660	Gary Carter	1.50	.65	.19

□ 661	Orioles Team/Mgr...........25 Earl Weaver (Checklist back)	.11	.03
□ 662	Red Sox Team/Mgr........25 Ralph Houk (Checklist back)	.11	.03
□ 663	Angels Team/Mgr. ....25 Jim Fregosi (Checklist back)	.11	.03
□ 664	White Sox Team/Mgr. ......25 Tony LaRussa (Checklist back)	.11	.03
□ 665	Indians Team/Mgr...........25 Dave Garcia (Checklist back)	.11	.03
□ 666	Tigers Team/Mgr. ....25 Sparky Anderson (Checklist back)	.11	.03
□ 667	Royals Team/Mgr............25 Jim Frey (Checklist back)	.11	.03
□ 668	Brewers Team/Mgr..........25 Bob Rodgers (Checklist back)	.11	.03
□ 669	Twins Team/Mgr.............25 John Goryl (Checklist back)	.11	.03
□ 670	Yankees Team/Mgr.........25 Gene Michael (Checklist back)	.11	.03
□ 671	A's Team/Mgr................25 Billy Martin (Checklist back)	.11	.03
□ 672	Mariners Team/Mgr.........25 Maury Wills (Checklist back)	.11	.03
□ 673	Rangers Team/Mgr..........25 Don Zimmer (Checklist back)	.11	.03
□ 674	Blue Jays Team/Mgr. ......25 Bobby Mattick (Checklist back)	.11	.03
□ 675	Braves Team/Mgr. ....25 Bobby Cox (Checklist back)	.11	.03
□ 676	Cubs Team/Mgr..............25 Joe Amalfitano (Checklist back)	.11	.03
□ 677	Reds Team/Mgr. ....25 John McNamara (Checklist back)	.11	.03
□ 678	Astros Team/Mgr............25 Bill Virdon (Checklist back)	.11	.03
□ 679	Dodgers Team/Mgr..........25 Tom Lasorda (Checklist back)	.11	.03
□ 680	Expos Team/Mgr.............25 Dick Williams (Checklist back)	.11	.03
□ 681	Mets Team/Mgr. ....25 Joe Torre (Checklist back)	.11	.03
□ 682	Phillies Team/Mgr............25 Dallas Green (Checklist back)	.11	.03
□ 683	Pirates Team/Mgr. ....25 Chuck Tanner (Checklist back)	.11	.03
□ 684	Cardinals Team/Mgr. ......25 Whitey Herzog (Checklist back)	.11	.03
□ 685	Padres Team/Mgr............25 Frank Howard (Checklist back)	.11	.03
□ 686	Giants Team/Mgr. ....25 Dave Bristol (Checklist back)	.11	.03
□ 687	Jeff Jones 05	.02	.01
□ 688	Kiko Garcia 05	.02	.01
□ 689	Red Sox Rookies ....2.00 Bruce Hurst Keith MacWhorter Reid Nichols	.90	.25
□ 690	Bob Watson 10	.05	.01
□ 691	Dick Ruthven..................05	.02	.01
□ 692	Lenny Randle 05	.02	.01
□ 693	Steve Howe....................10	.05	.01
□ 694	Bud Harrelson DP 05	.02	.01
□ 695	Kent Tekulve 10	.05	.01
□ 696	Alan Ashby 05	.02	.01
□ 697	Rick Waits......................05	.02	.01
□ 698	Mike Jorgensen 05	.02	.01
□ 699	Glenn Abbott..................05	.02	.01
□ 700	George Brett 6.00	2.70	.75
□ 701	Joe Rudi 10	.05	.01
□ 702	George Medich 05	.02	.01
□ 703	Alvis Woods....................05	.02	.01
□ 704	Bill Travers DP 05	.02	.01
□ 705	Ted Simmons 30	.14	.04
□ 706	Dave Ford 05	.02	.01
□ 707	Dave Cash......................05	.02	.01
□ 708	Doyle Alexander..............05	.02	.01
□ 709	Alan Trammell DP 1.00	.45	.13
□ 710	Ron LeFlore DP...............05	.02	.01
□ 711	Joe Ferguson 05	.02	.01
□ 712	Bill Bonham 05	.02	.01
□ 713	Bill North.......................05	.02	.01
□ 714	Pete Redfern 05	.02	.01
□ 715	Bill Madlock 10	.05	.01
□ 716	Glenn Borgmann..............05	.02	.01
□ 717	Jim Barr DP 05	.02	.01
□ 718	Larry Biittner..................05	.02	.01
□ 719	Sparky Lyle 10	.05	.01

		NRMT-MT	EXC	G-VG
☐	720 Fred Lynn	10	.05	.01
☐	721 Toby Harrah	10	.05	.01
☐	722 Joe Niekro	10	.05	.01
☐	723 Bruce Bochte	05	.02	.01
☐	724 Lou Piniella	10	.05	.01
☐	725 Steve Rogers	05	.02	.01
☐	726 Rick Monday	25	.11	.03

1981 Topps Traded

*The cards in this 132-card set measure
2 1/2" by 3 1/2". For the first time since
1976, Topps issued a "traded" set in 1981.
Unlike the small traded sets of 1974 and
1976, this set contains a larger number of
cards and was sequentially numbered,
alphabetically, from 727 to 858. Thus, this
set gives the impression it is a continuation
of their regular issue of this year. The sets
were issued only through hobby card dealers and were boxed in complete sets of
132 cards. There are no key Rookie Cards
in this set although Tim Raines, Jeff
Reardon, and Fernando Valenzuela are
depicted in their rookie year for cards.*

	NRMT-MT	EXC	G-VG
COMPLETE SET (132)	50.00	23.00	6.25
COMMON PLAYER (727-858)	15	.07	.02

		NRMT-MT	EXC	G-VG
☐	727 Danny Ainge	4.50	2.00	.55
☐	728 Doyle Alexander	15	.07	.02
☐	729 Gary Alexander	15	.07	.02
☐	730 Bill Almon	15	.07	.02
☐	731 Joaquin Andujar	25	.11	.03
☐	732 Bob Bailor	15	.07	.02
☐	733 Juan Beniquez	15	.07	.02
☐	734 Dave Bergman	15	.07	.02
☐	735 Tony Bernazard	15	.07	.02
☐	736 Larry Biittner	15	.07	.02
☐	737 Doug Bird	15	.07	.02
☐	738 Bert Blyleven	1.50	.65	.19
☐	739 Mark Bomback	15	.07	.02
☐	740 Bobby Bonds	25	.11	.03
☐	741 Rick Bosetti	15	.07	.02
☐	742 Hubie Brooks	90	.40	.11
☐	743 Rick Burleson	15	.07	.02
☐	744 Ray Burris	15	.07	.02
☐	745 Jeff Burroughs	15	.07	.02
☐	746 Enos Cabell	15	.07	.02
☐	747 Ken Clay	15	.07	.02
☐	748 Mark Clear	15	.07	.02
☐	749 Larry Cox	15	.07	.02
☐	750 Hector Cruz	15	.07	.02
☐	751 Victor Cruz	15	.07	.02
☐	752 Mike Cubbage	25	.11	.03
☐	753 Dick Davis	15	.07	.02
☐	754 Brian Doyle	15	.07	.02
☐	755 Dick Drago	15	.07	.02
☐	756 Leon Durham	25	.11	.03
☐	757 Jim Dwyer	15	.07	.02
☐	758 Dave Edwards	15	.07	.02
☐	759 Jim Essian	15	.07	.02
☐	760 Bill Fahey	15	.07	.02
☐	761 Rollie Fingers	3.50	1.55	.45
☐	762 Carlton Fisk	7.00	3.10	.85
☐	763 Barry Foote	15	.07	.02
☐	764 Ken Forsch	15	.07	.02
☐	765 Kiko Garcia	15	.07	.02
☐	766 Cesar Geronimo	15	.07	.02
☐	767 Gary Gray	15	.07	.02
☐	768 Mickey Hatcher	15	.07	.02
☐	769 Steve Henderson	15	.07	.02
☐	770 Marc Hill	15	.07	.02
☐	771 Butch Hobson	25	.11	.03
☐	772 Rick Honeycutt	15	.07	.02
☐	773 Roy Howell	15	.07	.02
☐	774 Mike Ivie	15	.07	.02
☐	775 Roy Lee Jackson	15	.07	.02
☐	776 Cliff Johnson	15	.07	.02
☐	777 Randy Jones	15	.07	.02
☐	778 Ruppert Jones	15	.07	.02
☐	779 Mick Kelleher	15	.07	.02
☐	780 Terry Kennedy	25	.11	.03
☐	781 Dave Kingman	25	.11	.03
☐	782 Bob Knepper	15	.07	.02
☐	783 Ken Kravec	15	.07	.02
☐	784 Bob Lacey	15	.07	.02
☐	785 Dennis Lamp	15	.07	.02
☐	786 Rafael Landestoy	15	.07	.02
☐	787 Ken Landreaux	15	.07	.02
☐	788 Carney Lansford	75	.35	.09
☐	789 Dave LaRoche	15	.07	.02
☐	790 Joe Lefebvre	15	.07	.02
☐	791 Ron LeFlore	25	.11	.03

☐ 792	Randy Lerch	15	.07	.02
☐ 793	Sixto Lezcano	15	.07	.02
☐ 794	John Littlefield	15	.07	.02
☐ 795	Mike Lum	15	.07	.02
☐ 796	Greg Luzinski	25	.11	.03
☐ 797	Fred Lynn	25	.11	.03
☐ 798	Jerry Martin	15	.07	.02
☐ 799	Buck Martinez	15	.07	.02
☐ 800	Gary Matthews	25	.11	.03
☐ 801	Mario Mendoza	15	.07	.02
☐ 802	Larry Milbourne	15	.07	.02
☐ 803	Rick Miller	15	.07	.02
☐ 804	John Montefusco	15	.07	.02
☐ 805	Jerry Morales	15	.07	.02
☐ 806	Jose Morales	15	.07	.02
☐ 807	Joe Morgan	3.00	1.35	.40
☐ 808	Jerry Mumphrey	15	.07	.02
☐ 809	Gene Nelson	25	.11	.03
☐ 810	Ed Ott	15	.07	.02
☐ 811	Bob Owchinko	15	.07	.02
☐ 812	Gaylord Perry	2.50	1.15	.30
☐ 813	Mike Phillips	15	.07	.02
☐ 814	Darrell Porter	15	.07	.02
☐ 815	Mike Proly	15	.07	.02
☐ 816	Tim Raines	12.00	5.50	1.50
☐ 817	Lenny Randle	15	.07	.02
☐ 818	Doug Rau	15	.07	.02
☐ 819	Jeff Reardon	18.00	8.00	2.30
☐ 820	Ken Reitz	15	.07	.02
☐ 821	Steve Renko	15	.07	.02
☐ 822	Rick Reuschel	25	.11	.03
☐ 823	Dave Revering	15	.07	.02
☐ 824	Dave Roberts	15	.07	.02
☐ 825	Leon Roberts	15	.07	.02
☐ 826	Joe Rudi	25	.11	.03
☐ 827	Kevin Saucier	15	.07	.02
☐ 828	Tony Scott	15	.07	.02
☐ 829	Bob Shirley	15	.07	.02
☐ 830	Ted Simmons	50	.23	.06
☐ 831	Lary Sorensen	15	.07	.02
☐ 832	Jim Spencer	15	.07	.02
☐ 833	Harry Spilman	15	.07	.02
☐ 834	Fred Stanley	15	.07	.02
☐ 835	Rusty Staub	25	.11	.03
☐ 836	Bill Stein	15	.07	.02
☐ 837	Joe Strain	15	.07	.02
☐ 838	Bruce Sutter	50	.23	.06
☐ 839	Don Sutton	2.50	1.15	.30
☐ 840	Steve Swisher	15	.07	.02
☐ 841	Frank Tanana	25	.11	.03
☐ 842	Gene Tenace	15	.07	.02
☐ 843	Jason Thompson	25	.11	.03
☐ 844	Dickie Thon	25	.11	.03
☐ 845	Bill Travers	15	.07	.02
☐ 846	Tom Underwood	15	.07	.02
☐ 847	John Urrea	15	.07	.02
☐ 848	Mike Vail	15	.07	.02

☐ 849	Ellis Valentine	15	.07	.02
☐ 850	Fernando Valenzuela	2.50	1.15	.30
☐ 851	Pete Vuckovich	25	.11	.03
☐ 852	Mark Wagner	15	.07	.02
☐ 853	Bob Walk	60	.25	.08
☐ 854	Claudell Washington	15	.07	.02
☐ 855	Dave Winfield	10.00	4.50	1.25
☐ 856	Geoff Zahn	15	.07	.02
☐ 857	Richie Zisk	15	.07	.02
☐ 858	Checklist 727-858	15	.02	.00

1982 Topps

The cards in this 792-card set measure 2 1/2" by 3 1/2". The 1982 baseball series was the first of the largest sets Topps issued at one printing. The 66-card increase from the previous year's total eliminated the "double print" practice, that had occurred in every regular issue since 1978. Cards 1-6 depict Highlights (HL) of the 1981 season, cards 161-168 picture League Leaders, and there are mini-series of AL (547-557) and NL (337-347) All-Stars (AS). The abbreviation "SA" in the checklist is given for the 40 "Super Action" cards introduced in this set. The team cards are actually Team Leader (TL) cards picturing the batting (BA: batting average) and pitching leader for that team with a checklist back. The key Rookie Cards in this set are George Bell, Cal Ripken, Steve Sax, Lee Smith, and Dave Stewart.

	NRMT-MT	EXC	G-VG
COMPLETE SET (792)	150.00	70.00	19.00
COMMON PLAYER (1-792)	.10	.05	.01

☐ 1	HL: Steve Carlton.........75 Sets new NL strikeout record	.19	.06
☐ 2	HL: Ron Davis.........15 Fans 8 straight in relief	.07	.02
☐ 3	HL: Tim Raines.........35 Swipes 71 bases as rookie	.16	.04
☐ 4	HL: Pete Rose.........75 Sets NL career hits mark	.35	.09
☐ 5	HL: Nolan Ryan.........3.00 Pitches fifth career no-hitter	1.35	.40
☐ 6	HL: Fern. Valenzuela.........15 8 shutouts as rookie	.07	.02
☐ 7	Scott Sanderson.........15	.07	.02
☐ 8	Rich Dauer.........10	.05	.01
☐ 9	Ron Guidry.........30	.14	.04
☐ 10	SA: Ron Guidry.........15	.07	.02
☐ 11	Gary Alexander.........10	.05	.01
☐ 12	Moose Haas.........10	.05	.01
☐ 13	Lamar Johnson.........10	.05	.01
☐ 14	Steve Howe.........10	.05	.01
☐ 15	Ellis Valentine.........10	.05	.01
☐ 16	Steve Comer.........10	.05	.01
☐ 17	Darrell Evans.........15	.07	.02
☐ 18	Fernando Arroyo.........10	.05	.01
☐ 19	Ernie Whitt.........10	.05	.01
☐ 20	Garry Maddox.........10	.05	.01
☐ 21	Orioles Rookies.........75.00 Bob Bonner Cal Ripken Jeff Schneider	34.00	9.50
☐ 22	Jim Beattie.........10	.05	.01
☐ 23	Willie Hernandez.........15	.07	.02
☐ 24	Dave Frost.........10	.05	.01
☐ 25	Jerry Remy.........10	.05	.01
☐ 26	Jorge Orta.........10	.05	.01
☐ 27	Tom Herr.........15	.07	.02
☐ 28	John Urrea.........10	.05	.01
☐ 29	Dwayne Murphy.........10	.05	.01
☐ 30	Tom Seaver.........2.00	.90	.25
☐ 31	SA: Tom Seaver.........1.00	.45	.13
☐ 32	Gene Garber.........10	.05	.01
☐ 33	Jerry Morales.........10	.05	.01
☐ 34	Joe Sambito.........10	.05	.01
☐ 35	Willie Aikens.........10	.05	.01
☐ 36	Rangers TL.........20 BA: Al Oliver Pitching: Doc Medich	.09	.03
☐ 37	Dan Graham.........10	.05	.01
☐ 38	Charlie Lea.........10	.05	.01
☐ 39	Lou Whitaker.........75	.35	.09
☐ 40	Dave Parker.........50	.23	.06
☐ 41	SA: Dave Parker.........25	.11	.03

☐ 42	Rick Sofield.........10	.05	.01
☐ 43	Mike Cubbage.........10	.05	.01
☐ 44	Britt Burns.........10	.05	.01
☐ 45	Rick Cerone.........10	.05	.01
☐ 46	Jerry Augustine.........10	.05	.01
☐ 47	Jeff Leonard.........10	.05	.01
☐ 48	Bobby Castillo.........10	.05	.01
☐ 49	Alvis Woods.........10	.05	.01
☐ 50	Buddy Bell.........15	.07	.02
☐ 51	Cubs Rookies.........40 Jay Howell Carlos Lezcano Ty Waller	.18	.05
☐ 52	Larry Andersen.........10	.05	.01
☐ 53	Greg Gross.........10	.05	.01
☐ 54	Ron Hassey.........10	.05	.01
☐ 55	Rick Burleson.........10	.05	.01
☐ 56	Mark Littell.........10	.05	.01
☐ 57	Craig Reynolds.........10	.05	.01
☐ 58	John D'Acquisto.........10	.05	.01
☐ 59	Rich Gedman.........20	.09	.03
☐ 60	Tony Armas.........10	.05	.01
☐ 61	Tommy Boggs.........10	.05	.01
☐ 62	Mike Tyson.........10	.05	.01
☐ 63	Mario Soto.........10	.05	.01
☐ 64	Lynn Jones.........10	.05	.01
☐ 65	Terry Kennedy.........10	.05	.01
☐ 66	Astros TL.........1.00 BA: Art Howe Pitching: Nolan Ryan	.45	.13
☐ 67	Rich Gale.........10	.05	.01
☐ 68	Roy Howell.........10	.05	.01
☐ 69	Al Williams.........10	.05	.01
☐ 70	Tim Raines.........1.75	.80	.22
☐ 71	Roy Lee Jackson.........10	.05	.01
☐ 72	Rick Auerbach.........10	.05	.01
☐ 73	Buddy Solomon.........10	.05	.01
☐ 74	Bob Clark.........10	.05	.01
☐ 75	Tommy John.........30	.14	.04
☐ 76	Greg Pryor.........10	.05	.01
☐ 77	Miguel Dilone.........10	.05	.01
☐ 78	George Medich.........10	.05	.01
☐ 79	Bob Bailor.........10	.05	.01
☐ 80	Jim Palmer.........1.75	.80	.22
☐ 81	SA: Jim Palmer.........75	.35	.09
☐ 82	Bob Welch.........40	.18	.05
☐ 83	Yankees Rookies.........15 Steve Balboni Andy McGaffigan Andre Robertson	.07	.02
☐ 84	Rennie Stennett.........10	.05	.01
☐ 85	Lynn McGlothen.........10	.05	.01
☐ 86	Dane Iorg.........10	.05	.01
☐ 87	Matt Keough.........10	.05	.01
☐ 88	Biff Pocoroba.........10	.05	.01
☐ 89	Steve Henderson.........10	.05	.01
☐ 90	Nolan Ryan.........11.00	4.90	1.40

☐ 91	Carney Lansford 15	.07	.02
☐ 92	Brad Havens 10	.05	.01
☐ 93	Larry Hisle 10	.05	.01
☐ 94	Andy Hassler 10	.05	.01
☐ 95	Ozzie Smith..................3.00	1.35	.40
☐ 96	Royals TL........................50	.23	.06
	BA: George Brett		
	Pitching: Larry Gura		
☐ 97	Paul Moskau 10	.05	.01
☐ 98	Terry Bulling 10	.05	.01
☐ 99	Barry Bonnell 10	.05	.01
☐ 100	Mike Schmidt...............3.50	1.55	.45
☐ 101	SA: Mike Schmidt 1.50	.65	.19
☐ 102	Dan Briggs 10	.05	.01
☐ 103	Bob Lacey 10	.05	.01
☐ 104	Rance Mulliniks 10	.05	.01
☐ 105	Kirk Gibson 75	.35	.09
☐ 106	Enrique Romo 10	.05	.01
☐ 107	Wayne Krenchicki 10	.05	.01
☐ 108	Bob Sykes 10	.05	.01
☐ 109	Dave Revering..................10	.05	.01
☐ 110	Carlton Fisk..................2.00	.90	.25
☐ 111	SA: Carlton Fisk 1.00	.45	.13
☐ 112	Billy Sample.....................10	.05	.01
☐ 113	Steve McCatty 10	.05	.01
☐ 114	Ken Landreaux 10	.05	.01
☐ 115	Gaylord Perry 75	.35	.09
☐ 116	Jim Wohlford 10	.05	.01
☐ 117	Rawly Eastwick 10	.05	.01
☐ 118	Expos Rookies 35	.16	.04
	Terry Francona		
	Brad Mills		
	Bryn Smith		
☐ 119	Joe Pittman.....................10	.05	.01
☐ 120	Gary Lucas 10	.05	.01
☐ 121	Ed Lynch 10	.05	.01
☐ 122	Jamie Easterly UER 10	.05	.01
	(Photo actually		
	Reggie Cleveland)		
☐ 123	Danny Goodwin 10	.05	.01
☐ 124	Reid Nichols 10	.05	.01
☐ 125	Danny Ainge 1.25	.55	.16
☐ 126	Braves TL........................20	.09	.03
	BA: Claudell Washington		
	Pitching: Rick Mahler		
☐ 127	Lonnie Smith 15	.07	.02
☐ 128	Frank Pastore 10	.05	.01
☐ 129	Checklist 1-132 15	.02	.00
☐ 130	Julio Cruz 10	.05	.01
☐ 131	Stan Bahnsen...................10	.05	.01
☐ 132	Lee May 10	.05	.01
☐ 133	Pat Underwood 10	.05	.01
☐ 134	Dan Ford 10	.05	.01
☐ 135	Andy Rincon 10	.05	.01
☐ 136	Lenn Sakata 10	.05	.01
☐ 137	George Cappuzzello 10	.05	.01
☐ 138	Tony Pena........................25	.11	.03

☐ 139	Jeff Jones 10	.05	.01
☐ 140	Ron LeFlore 15	.07	.02
☐ 141	Indians Rookies 40	.18	.05
	Chris Bando		
	Tom Brennan		
	Von Hayes		
☐ 142	Dave LaRoche 10	.05	.01
☐ 143	Mookie Wilson 15	.07	.02
☐ 144	Fred Breining 10	.05	.01
☐ 145	Bob Horner 15	.07	.02
☐ 146	Mike Griffin 10	.05	.01
☐ 147	Denny Walling 10	.05	.01
☐ 148	Mickey Klutts 10	.05	.01
☐ 149	Pat Putnam 10	.05	.01
☐ 150	Ted Simmons 15	.07	.02
☐ 151	Dave Edwards 10	.05	.01
☐ 152	Ramon Aviles 10	.05	.01
☐ 153	Roger Erickson 10	.05	.01
☐ 154	Dennis Werth 10	.05	.01
☐ 155	Otto Velez 10	.05	.01
☐ 156	Oakland A's TL 75	.35	.09
	BA: Rickey Henderson		
	Pitching: Steve McCatty		
☐ 157	Steve Crawford 10	.05	.01
☐ 158	Brian Downing 15	.07	.02
☐ 159	Larry Biittner 10	.05	.01
☐ 160	Luis Tiant 15	.07	.02
☐ 161	Batting Leaders 20	.09	.03
	Bill Madlock		
	Carney Lansford		
☐ 162	Home Run Leaders 50	.23	.06
	Mike Schmidt		
	Tony Armas		
	Dwight Evans		
	Bobby Grich		
	Eddie Murray		
☐ 163	RBI Leaders 75	.35	.09
	Mike Schmidt		
	Eddie Murray		
☐ 164	Stolen Base Leaders 1.50	.65	.19
	Tim Raines		
	Rickey Henderson		
☐ 165	Victory Leaders 20	.09	.03
	Tom Seaver		
	Denny Martinez		
	Steve McCatty		
	Jack Morris		
	Pete Vuckovich		
☐ 166	Strikeout Leaders.............20	.09	.03
	Fernando Valenzuela		
	Len Barker		
☐ 167	ERA Leaders 1.50	.65	.19
	Nolan Ryan		
	Steve McCatty		
☐ 168	Leading Firemen 25	.11	.03
	Bruce Sutter		
	Rollie Fingers		

☐ 169	Charlie Leibrandt	.15	.07	.02
☐ 170	Jim Bibby	.10	.05	.01
☐ 171	Giants Rookies	1.50	.65	.19
	Bob Brenly			
	Chili Davis			
	Bob Tufts			
☐ 172	Bill Gullickson	.35	.16	.04
☐ 173	Jamie Quirk	.10	.05	.01
☐ 174	Dave Ford	.10	.05	.01
☐ 175	Jerry Mumphrey	.10	.05	.01
☐ 176	Dewey Robinson	.10	.05	.01
☐ 177	John Ellis	.10	.05	.01
☐ 178	Dyar Miller	.10	.05	.01
☐ 179	Steve Garvey	.75	.35	.09
☐ 180	SA: Steve Garvey	.35	.16	.04
☐ 181	Silvio Martinez	.10	.05	.01
☐ 182	Larry Herndon	.10	.05	.01
☐ 183	Mike Proly	.10	.05	.01
☐ 184	Mick Kelleher	.10	.05	.01
☐ 185	Phil Niekro	.75	.35	.09
☐ 186	Cardinals TL	.20	.09	.03
	BA: Keith Hernandez			
	Pitching: Bob Forsch			
☐ 187	Jeff Newman	.10	.05	.01
☐ 188	Randy Martz	.10	.05	.01
☐ 189	Glenn Hoffman	.10	.05	.01
☐ 190	J.R. Richard	.15	.07	.02
☐ 191	Tim Wallach	1.50	.65	.19
☐ 192	Broderick Perkins	.10	.05	.01
☐ 193	Darrell Jackson	.10	.05	.01
☐ 194	Mike Vail	.10	.05	.01
☐ 195	Paul Molitor	1.50	.65	.19
☐ 196	Willie Upshaw	.10	.05	.01
☐ 197	Shane Rawley	.10	.05	.01
☐ 198	Chris Speier	.10	.05	.01
☐ 199	Don Aase	.10	.05	.01
☐ 200	George Brett	4.00	1.80	.50
☐ 201	SA: George Brett	2.00	.90	.25
☐ 202	Rick Manning	.10	.05	.01
☐ 203	Blue Jays Rookies	.90	.40	.11
	Jesse Barfield			
	Brian Milner			
	Boomer Wells			
☐ 204	Gary Roenicke	.10	.05	.01
☐ 205	Neil Allen	.10	.05	.01
☐ 206	Tony Bernazard	.10	.05	.01
☐ 207	Rod Scurry	.10	.05	.01
☐ 208	Bobby Murcer	.15	.07	.02
☐ 209	Gary Lavelle	.10	.05	.01
☐ 210	Keith Hernandez	.35	.16	.04
☐ 211	Dan Petry	.10	.05	.01
☐ 212	Mario Mendoza	.10	.05	.01
☐ 213	Dave Stewart	4.50	2.00	.55
☐ 214	Brian Asselstine	.10	.05	.01
☐ 215	Mike Krukow	.10	.05	.01
☐ 216	White Sox TL	.20	.09	.03
	BA: Chet Lemon			
	Pitching: Dennis Lamp			
☐ 217	Bo McLaughlin	.10	.05	.01
☐ 218	Dave Roberts	.10	.05	.01
☐ 219	John Curtis	.10	.05	.01
☐ 220	Manny Trillo	.10	.05	.01
☐ 221	Jim Slaton	.10	.05	.01
☐ 222	Butch Wynegar	.10	.05	.01
☐ 223	Lloyd Moseby	.10	.05	.01
☐ 224	Bruce Bochte	.10	.05	.01
☐ 225	Mike Torrez	.10	.05	.01
☐ 226	Checklist 133-264	.15	.02	.00
☐ 227	Ray Burris	.10	.05	.01
☐ 228	Sam Mejias	.10	.05	.01
☐ 229	Geoff Zahn	.10	.05	.01
☐ 230	Willie Wilson	.15	.07	.02
☐ 231	Phillies Rookies	.30	.14	.04
	Mark Davis			
	Bob Dernier			
	Ozzie Virgil			
☐ 232	Terry Crowley	.10	.05	.01
☐ 233	Duane Kuiper	.10	.05	.01
☐ 234	Ron Hodges	.10	.05	.01
☐ 235	Mike Easler	.10	.05	.01
☐ 236	John Martin	.10	.05	.01
☐ 237	Rusty Kuntz	.10	.05	.01
☐ 238	Kevin Saucier	.10	.05	.01
☐ 239	Jon Matlack	.10	.05	.01
☐ 240	Bucky Dent	.15	.07	.02
☐ 241	SA: Bucky Dent	.10	.05	.01
☐ 242	Milt May	.10	.05	.01
☐ 243	Bob Owchinko	.10	.05	.01
☐ 244	Rufino Linares	.10	.05	.01
☐ 245	Ken Reitz	.10	.05	.01
☐ 246	New York Mets TL	.20	.09	.03
	BA: Hubie Brooks			
	Pitching: Mike Scott			
☐ 247	Pedro Guerrero	.40	.18	.05
☐ 248	Frank LaCorte	.10	.05	.01
☐ 249	Tim Flannery	.10	.05	.01
☐ 250	Tug McGraw	.15	.07	.02
☐ 251	Fred Lynn	.15	.07	.02
☐ 252	SA: Fred Lynn	.10	.05	.01
☐ 253	Chuck Baker	.10	.05	.01
☐ 254	Jorge Bell	8.00	3.60	1.00
☐ 255	Tony Perez	.50	.23	.06
☐ 256	SA: Tony Perez	.25	.11	.03
☐ 257	Larry Harlow	.10	.05	.01
☐ 258	Bo Diaz	.10	.05	.01
☐ 259	Rodney Scott	.10	.05	.01
☐ 260	Bruce Sutter	.25	.11	.03
☐ 261	Tigers Rookies UER	.12	.05	.02
	Howard Bailey			
	Marty Castillo			
	Dave Rucker			
	(Rucker photo act-			
	ually Roger Weaver)			
☐ 262	Doug Bair	.10	.05	.01

☐	263 Victor Cruz	10	.05	.01
☐	264 Dan Quisenberry	15	.07	.02
☐	265 Al Bumbry	10	.05	.01
☐	266 Rick Leach	10	.05	.01
☐	267 Kurt Bevacqua	10	.05	.01
☐	268 Rickey Keeton	10	.05	.01
☐	269 Jim Essian	10	.05	.01
☐	270 Rusty Staub	15	.07	.02
☐	271 Larry Bradford	10	.05	.01
☐	272 Bump Wills	10	.05	.01
☐	273 Doug Bird	10	.05	.01
☐	274 Bob Ojeda	60	.25	.08
☐	275 Bob Watson	15	.07	.02
☐	276 Angels TL	25	.11	.03
	BA: Rod Carew			
	Pitching: Ken Forsch			
☐	277 Terry Puhl	10	.05	.01
☐	278 John Littlefield	10	.05	.01
☐	279 Bill Russell	15	.07	.02
☐	280 Ben Oglivie	15	.07	.02
☐	281 John Verhoeven	10	.05	.01
☐	282 Ken Macha	10	.05	.01
☐	283 Brian Allard	10	.05	.01
☐	284 Bob Grich	15	.07	.02
☐	285 Sparky Lyle	15	.07	.02
☐	286 Bill Fahey	10	.05	.01
☐	287 Alan Bannister	10	.05	.01
☐	288 Garry Templeton	15	.07	.02
☐	289 Bob Stanley	10	.05	.01
☐	290 Ken Singleton	15	.07	.02
☐	291 Pirates Rookies	20	.09	.03
	Vance Law			
	Bob Long			
	Johnny Ray			
☐	292 David Palmer	10	.05	.01
☐	293 Rob Picciolo	10	.05	.01
☐	294 Mike LaCoss	10	.05	.01
☐	295 Jason Thompson	10	.05	.01
☐	296 Bob Walk	10	.05	.01
☐	297 Clint Hurdle	10	.05	.01
☐	298 Danny Darwin	10	.05	.01
☐	299 Steve Trout	10	.05	.01
☐	300 Reggie Jackson	3.00	1.35	.40
☐	301 SA: Reggie Jackson	1.50	.65	.19
☐	302 Doug Flynn	10	.05	.01
☐	303 Bill Caudill	10	.05	.01
☐	304 Johnnie LeMaster	10	.05	.01
☐	305 Don Sutton	75	.35	.09
☐	306 SA: Don Sutton	35	.16	.04
☐	307 Randy Bass	10	.05	.01
☐	308 Charlie Moore	10	.05	.01
☐	309 Pete Redfern	10	.05	.01
☐	310 Mike Hargrove	15	.07	.02
☐	311 Dodgers TL	20	.09	.03
	BA: Dusty Baker			
	Pitching: Burt Hooton			
☐	312 Lenny Randle	10	.05	.01
☐	313 John Harris	10	.05	.01
☐	314 Buck Martinez	10	.05	.01
☐	315 Burt Hooton	10	.05	.01
☐	316 Steve Braun	10	.05	.01
☐	317 Dick Ruthven	10	.05	.01
☐	318 Mike Heath	10	.05	.01
☐	319 Dave Rozema	10	.05	.01
☐	320 Chris Chambliss	15	.07	.02
☐	321 SA: Chris Chambliss	10	.05	.01
☐	322 Garry Hancock	10	.05	.01
☐	323 Bill Lee	10	.05	.01
☐	324 Steve Dillard	10	.05	.01
☐	325 Jose Cruz	15	.07	.02
☐	326 Pete Falcone	10	.05	.01
☐	327 Joe Nolan	10	.05	.01
☐	328 Ed Farmer	10	.05	.01
☐	329 U.L. Washington	10	.05	.01
☐	330 Rick Wise	10	.05	.01
☐	331 Benny Ayala	10	.05	.01
☐	332 Don Robinson	10	.05	.01
☐	333 Brewers Rookies	12	.05	.02
	Frank DiPino			
	Marshall Edwards			
	Chuck Porter			
☐	334 Aurelio Rodriguez	10	.05	.01
☐	335 Jim Sundberg	15	.07	.02
☐	336 Mariners TL	20	.09	.03
	BA: Tom Paciorek			
	Pitching: Glenn Abbott			
☐	337 Pete Rose AS	90	.40	.11
☐	338 Dave Lopes AS	15	.07	.02
☐	339 Mike Schmidt AS	1.25	.55	.16
☐	340 Dave Concepcion AS	15	.07	.02
☐	341 Andre Dawson AS	1.00	.45	.13
☐	342A George Foster AS	15	.07	.02
	(With autograph)			
☐	342B George Foster AS	1.00	.45	.13
	(W/o autograph)			
☐	343 Dave Parker AS	20	.09	.03
☐	344 Gary Carter AS	50	.23	.06
☐	345 Fernando Valenzuela AS	.15	.07	.02
☐	346A Tom Seaver AS ERR	1.25	.55	.16
	("ted")			
☐	346B Tom Seaver AS COR	75	.35	.09
	("tied")			
☐	347 Bruce Sutter AS	15	.07	.02
☐	348 Derrel Thomas	10	.05	.01
☐	349 George Frazier	10	.05	.01
☐	350 Thad Bosley	10	.05	.01
☐	351 Reds Rookies	12	.05	.02
	Scott Brown			
	Geoff Combe			
	Paul Householder			
☐	352 Dick Davis	10	.05	.01
☐	353 Jack O'Connor	10	.05	.01
☐	354 Roberto Ramos	10	.05	.01
☐	355 Dwight Evans	35	.16	.04

☐ 356 Denny Lewallyn	.10	.05	.01
☐ 357 Butch Hobson	.15	.07	.02
☐ 358 Mike Parrott	.10	.05	.01
☐ 359 Jim Dwyer	.10	.05	.01
☐ 360 Len Barker	.10	.05	.01
☐ 361 Rafael Landestoy	.10	.05	.01
☐ 362 Jim Wright UER	.10	.05	.01
(Wrong Jim Wright pictured)			
☐ 363 Bob Molinaro	.10	.05	.01
☐ 364 Doyle Alexander	.10	.05	.01
☐ 365 Bill Madlock	.15	.07	.02
☐ 366 Padres TL	.20	.09	.03
BA: Luis Salazar Pitching: Juan Eichelberger			
☐ 367 Jim Kaat	.20	.09	.03
☐ 368 Alex Trevino	.10	.05	.01
☐ 369 Champ Summers	.10	.05	.01
☐ 370 Mike Norris	.10	.05	.01
☐ 371 Jerry Don Gleaton	.10	.05	.01
☐ 372 Luis Gomez	.10	.05	.01
☐ 373 Gene Nelson	.10	.05	.01
☐ 374 Tim Blackwell	.10	.05	.01
☐ 375 Dusty Baker	.15	.07	.02
☐ 376 Chris Welsh	.10	.05	.01
☐ 377 Kiko Garcia	.10	.05	.01
☐ 378 Mike Caldwell	.10	.05	.01
☐ 379 Rob Wilfong	.10	.05	.01
☐ 380 Dave Stieb	.30	.14	.04
☐ 381 Red Sox Rookies	.50	.23	.06
Bruce Hurst Dave Schmidt Julio Valdez			
☐ 382 Joe Simpson	.10	.05	.01
☐ 383A Pascual Perez ERR	.20.00	9.00	2.50
(No position on front)			
☐ 383B Pascual Perez COR	.15	.07	.02
☐ 384 Keith Moreland	.10	.05	.01
☐ 385 Ken Forsch	.10	.05	.01
☐ 386 Jerry White	.10	.05	.01
☐ 387 Tom Veryzer	.10	.05	.01
☐ 388 Joe Rudi	.10	.05	.01
☐ 389 George Vukovich	.10	.05	.01
☐ 390 Eddie Murray	3.00	1.35	.40
☐ 391 Dave Tobik	.10	.05	.01
☐ 392 Rick Bosetti	.10	.05	.01
☐ 393 Al Hrabosky	.10	.05	.01
☐ 394 Checklist 265-396	.15	.02	.00
☐ 395 Omar Moreno	.10	.05	.01
☐ 396 Twins TL	.20	.09	.03
BA: John Castino Pitching: Fernando Arroyo			
☐ 397 Ken Brett	.10	.05	.01
☐ 398 Mike Squires	.10	.05	.01

☐ 399 Pat Zachry	.10	.05	.01
☐ 400 Johnny Bench	2.00	.90	.25
☐ 401 SA: Johnny Bench	1.00	.45	.13
☐ 402 Bill Stein	.10	.05	.01
☐ 403 Jim Tracy	.10	.05	.01
☐ 404 Dickie Thon	.10	.05	.01
☐ 405 Rick Reuschel	.15	.07	.02
☐ 406 Al Holland	.10	.05	.01
☐ 407 Danny Boone	.10	.05	.01
☐ 408 Ed Romero	.10	.05	.01
☐ 409 Don Cooper	.10	.05	.01
☐ 410 Ron Cey	.15	.07	.02
☐ 411 SA: Ron Cey	.10	.05	.01
☐ 412 Luis Leal	.10	.05	.01
☐ 413 Dan Meyer	.10	.05	.01
☐ 414 Elias Sosa	.10	.05	.01
☐ 415 Don Baylor	.15	.07	.02
☐ 416 Marty Bystrom	.10	.05	.01
☐ 417 Pat Kelly	.10	.05-	.01
☐ 418 Rangers Rookies	.12	.05	.02
John Butcher Bobby Johnson Dave Schmidt			
☐ 419 Steve Stone	.15	.07	.02
☐ 420 George Hendrick	.15	.07	.02
☐ 421 Mark Clear	.10	.05	.01
☐ 422 Cliff Johnson	.10	.05	.01
☐ 423 Stan Papi	.10	.05	.01
☐ 424 Bruce Benedict	.10	.05	.01
☐ 425 John Candelaria	.10	.05	.01
☐ 426 Orioles TL	.35	.16	.04
BA: Eddie Murray Pitching: Sammy Stewart			
☐ 427 Ron Oester	.10	.05	.01
☐ 428 LaMarr Hoyt	.10	.05	.01
☐ 429 John Wathan	.10	.05	.01
☐ 430 Vida Blue	.15	.07	.02
☐ 431 SA: Vida Blue	.10	.05	.01
☐ 432 Mike Scott	.15	.07	.02
☐ 433 Alan Ashby	.10	.05	.01
☐ 434 Joe Lefebvre	.10	.05	.01
☐ 435 Robin Yount	4.00	1.80	.50
☐ 436 Joe Strain	.10	.05	.01
☐ 437 Juan Berenguer	.10	.05	.01
☐ 438 Pete Mackanin	.10	.05	.01
☐ 439 Dave Righetti	.75	.35	.09
☐ 440 Jeff Burroughs	.10	.05	.01
☐ 441 Astros Rookies	.12	.05	.02
Danny Heep Billy Smith Bobby Sprowl			
☐ 442 Bruce Kison	.10	.05	.01
☐ 443 Mark Wagner	.10	.05	.01
☐ 444 Terry Forster	.10	.05	.01
☐ 445 Larry Parrish	.10	.05	.01
☐ 446 Wayne Garland	.10	.05	.01
☐ 447 Darrell Porter	.10	.05	.01

☐ 448 SA: Darrell Porter	10	.05	.01
☐ 449 Luis Aguayo	10	.05	.01
☐ 450 Jack Morris	2.50	1.15	.30
☐ 451 Ed Miller	10	.05	.01
☐ 452 Lee Smith	10.00	4.50	1.25
☐ 453 Art Howe	10	.05	.01
☐ 454 Rick Langford	10	.05	.01
☐ 455 Tom Burgmeier	10	.05	.01
☐ 456 Chicago Cubs TL	20	.09	.03
BA: Bill Buckner			
Pitching: Randy Martz			
☐ 457 Tim Stoddard	10	.05	.01
☐ 458 Willie Montanez	10	.05	.01
☐ 459 Bruce Berenyi	10	.05	.01
☐ 460 Jack Clark	30	.14	.04
☐ 461 Rich Dotson	10	.05	.01
☐ 462 Dave Chalk	10	.05	.01
☐ 463 Jim Kern	10	.05	.01
☐ 464 Juan Bonilla	10	.05	.01
☐ 465 Lee Mazzilli	10	.05	.01
☐ 466 Randy Lerch	10	.05	.01
☐ 467 Mickey Hatcher	10	.05	.01
☐ 468 Floyd Bannister	10	.05	.01
☐ 469 Ed Ott	10	.05	.01
☐ 470 John Mayberry	10	.05	.01
☐ 471 Royals Rookies	12	.05	.02
Atlee Hammaker			
Mike Jones			
Darryl Motley			
☐ 472 Oscar Gamble	10	.05	.01
☐ 473 Mike Stanton	10	.05	.01
☐ 474 Ken Oberkfell	10	.05	.01
☐ 475 Alan Trammell	90	.40	.11
☐ 476 Brian Kingman	10	.05	.01
☐ 477 Steve Yeager	10	.05	.01
☐ 478 Ray Searage	10	.05	.01
☐ 479 Rowland Office	10	.05	.01
☐ 480 Steve Carlton	2.00	.90	.25
☐ 481 SA: Steve Carlton	1.00	.45	.13
☐ 482 Glenn Hubbard	10	.05	.01
☐ 483 Gary Woods	10	.05	.01
☐ 484 Ivan DeJesus	10	.05	.01
☐ 485 Kent Tekulve	15	.07	.02
☐ 486 Yankees TL	20	.09	.03
BA: Jerry Mumphrey			
Pitching: Tommy John			
☐ 487 Bob McClure	10	.05	.01
☐ 488 Ron Jackson	10	.05	.01
☐ 489 Rick Dempsey	15	.07	.02
☐ 490 Dennis Eckersley	2.50	1.15	.30
☐ 491 Checklist 397-528	15	.02	.00
☐ 492 Joe Price	10	.05	.01
☐ 493 Chet Lemon	10	.05	.01
☐ 494 Hubie Brooks	35	.16	.04
☐ 495 Dennis Leonard	10	.05	.01
☐ 496 Johnny Grubb	10	.05	.01
☐ 497 Jim Anderson	10	.05	.01
☐ 498 Dave Bergman	10	.05	.01
☐ 499 Paul Mirabella	10	.05	.01
☐ 500 Rod Carew	2.00	.90	.25
☐ 501 SA: Rod Carew	1.00	.45	.13
☐ 502 Braves Rookies	3.00	1.35	.40
Steve Bedrosian UER			
(Photo actually			
Larry Owen)			
Brett Butler			
Larry Owen			
☐ 503 Julio Gonzalez	10	.05	.01
☐ 504 Rick Peters	10	.05	.01
☐ 505 Graig Nettles	15	.07	.02
☐ 506 SA: Graig Nettles	10	.05	.01
☐ 507 Terry Harper	10	.05	.01
☐ 508 Jody Davis	15	.07	.02
☐ 509 Harry Spilman	10	.05	.01
☐ 510 Fernando Valenzuela	35	.16	.04
☐ 511 Ruppert Jones	10	.05	.01
☐ 512 Jerry Dybzinski	10	.05	.01
☐ 513 Rick Rhoden	10	.05	.01
☐ 514 Joe Ferguson	10	.05	.01
☐ 515 Larry Bowa	15	.07	.02
☐ 516 SA: Larry Bowa	10	.05	.01
☐ 517 Mark Brouhard	10	.05	.01
☐ 518 Garth Iorg	10	.05	.01
☐ 519 Glenn Adams	10	.05	.01
☐ 520 Mike Flanagan	15	.07	.02
☐ 521 Bill Almon	10	.05	.01
☐ 522 Chuck Rainey	10	.05	.01
☐ 523 Gary Gray	10	.05	.01
☐ 524 Tom Hausman	10	.05	.01
☐ 525 Ray Knight	15	.07	.02
☐ 526 Expos TL	20	.09	.03
BA: Warren Cromartie			
Pitching: Bill Gullickson			
☐ 527 John Henry Johnson	10	.05	.01
☐ 528 Matt Alexander	10	.05	.01
☐ 529 Allen Ripley	10	.05	.01
☐ 530 Dickie Noles	10	.05	.01
☐ 531 A's Rookies	12	.05	.02
Rich Bordi			
Mark Budaska			
Kelvin Moore			
☐ 532 Toby Harrah	15	.07	.02
☐ 533 Joaquin Andujar	15	.07	.02
☐ 534 Dave McKay	10	.05	.01
☐ 535 Lance Parrish	35	.16	.04
☐ 536 Rafael Ramirez	10	.05	.01
☐ 537 Doug Capilla	10	.05	.01
☐ 538 Lou Piniella	15	.07	.02
☐ 539 Vern Ruhle	10	.05	.01
☐ 540 Andre Dawson	3.00	1.35	.40
☐ 541 Barry Evans	10	.05	.01
☐ 542 Ned Yost	10	.05	.01
☐ 543 Bill Robinson	15	.07	.02
☐ 544 Larry Christenson	10	.05	.01

□	545	Reggie Smith	15	.07	.02
□	546	SA: Reggie Smith	10	.05	.01
□	547	Rod Carew AS	90	.40	.11
□	548	Willie Randolph AS	15	.07	.02
□	549	George Brett AS	1.75	.80	.22
□	550	Bucky Dent AS	15	.07	.02
□	551	Reggie Jackson AS	1.50	.65	.19
□	552	Ken Singleton AS	15	.07	.02
□	553	Dave Winfield AS	1.50	.65	.19
□	554	Carlton Fisk AS	75	.35	.09
□	555	Scott McGregor AS	15	.07	.02
□	556	Jack Morris AS	60	.25	.08
□	557	Rich Gossage AS	15	.07	.02
□	558	John Tudor	15	.07	.02
□	559	Indians TL	20	.09	.03
		BA: Mike Hargrove			
		Pitching: Bert Blyleven			
□	560	Doug Corbett	10	.05	.01
□	561	Cardinals Rookies	12	.05	.02
		Glenn Brummer			
		Luis DeLeon			
		Gene Roof			
□	562	Mike O'Berry	10	.05	.01
□	563	Ross Baumgarten	10	.05	.01
□	564	Doug DeCinces	15	.07	.02
□	565	Jackson Todd	10	.05	.01
□	566	Mike Jorgensen	10	.05	.01
□	567	Bob Babcock	10	.05	.01
□	568	Joe Pettini	10	.05	.01
□	569	Willie Randolph	15	.07	.02
□	570	SA: Willie Randolph	10	.05	.01
□	571	Glenn Abbott	10	.05	.01
□	572	Juan Beniquez	10	.05	.01
□	573	Rick Waits	10	.05	.01
□	574	Mike Ramsey	10	.05	.01
□	575	Al Cowens	10	.05	.01
□	576	Giants TL	20	.09	.03
		BA: Milt May			
		Pitching: Vida Blue			
□	577	Rick Monday	10	.05	.01
□	578	Shooty Babitt	10	.05	.01
□	579	Rick Mahler	10	.05	.01
□	580	Bobby Bonds	15	.07	.02
□	581	Ron Reed	15	.07	.02
□	582	Luis Pujols	10	.05	.01
□	583	Tippy Martinez	10	.05	.01
□	584	Hosken Powell	10	.05	.01
□	585	Rollie Fingers	1.00	.45	.13
□	586	SA: Rollie Fingers	50	.23	.06
□	587	Tim Lollar	10	.05	.01
□	588	Dale Berra	10	.05	.01
□	589	Dave Stapleton	10	.05	.01
□	590	Al Oliver	15	.07	.02
□	591	SA: Al Oliver	10	.05	.01
□	592	Craig Swan	10	.05	.01
□	593	Billy Smith	10	.05	.01
□	594	Renie Martin	10	.05	.01
□	595	Dave Collins	10	.05	.01
□	596	Damaso Garcia	10	.05	.01
□	597	Wayne Nordhagen	10	.05	.01
□	598	Bob Galasso	10	.05	.01
□	599	White Sox Rookies	12	.05	.02
		Jay Loviglio			
		Reggie Patterson			
		Leo Sutherland			
□	600	Dave Winfield	4.00	1.80	.50
□	601	Sid Monge	10	.05	.01
□	602	Freddie Patek	10	.05	.01
□	603	Rich Hebner	10	.05	.01
□	604	Orlando Sanchez	10	.05	.01
□	605	Steve Rogers	10	.05	.01
□	606	Blue Jays TL	20	.09	.03
		BA: John Mayberry			
		Pitching: Dave Stieb			
□	607	Leon Durham	10	.05	.01
□	608	Jerry Royster	10	.05	.01
□	609	Rick Sutcliffe	40	.18	.05
□	610	Rickey Henderson	7.00	3.10	.85
□	611	Joe Niekro	15	.07	.02
□	612	Gary Ward	10	.05	.01
□	613	Jim Gantner	15	.07	.02
□	614	Juan Eichelberger	10	.05	.01
□	615	Bob Boone	15	.07	.02
□	616	SA: Bob Boone	10	.05	.01
□	617	Scott McGregor	10	.05	.01
□	618	Tim Foli	10	.05	.01
□	619	Bill Campbell	10	.05	.01
□	620	Ken Griffey	40	.18	.05
□	621	SA: Ken Griffey	20	.09	.03
□	622	Dennis Lamp	10	.05	.01
□	623	Mets Rookies	35	.16	.04
		Ron Gardenhire			
		Terry Leach			
		Tim Leary			
□	624	Fergie Jenkins	75	.35	.09
□	625	Hal McRae	15	.07	.02
□	626	Randy Jones	10	.05	.01
□	627	Enos Cabell	10	.05	.01
□	628	Bill Travers	10	.05	.01
□	629	John Wockenfuss	10	.05	.01
□	630	Joe Charboneau	10	.05	.01
□	631	Gene Tenace	10	.05	.01
□	632	Bryan Clark	10	.05	.01
□	633	Mitchell Page	10	.05	.01
□	634	Checklist 529-660	15	.02	.00
□	635	Ron Davis	10	.05	.01
□	636	Phillies TL	40	.18	.05
		BA: Pete Rose			
		Pitching: Steve Carlton			
□	637	Rick Camp	10	.05	.01
□	638	John Milner	10	.05	.01
□	639	Ken Kravec	10	.05	.01
□	640	Cesar Cedeno	15	.07	.02
□	641	Steve Mura	10	.05	.01

☐ 642	Mike Scioscia	.25	.11	.03
☐ 643	Pete Vuckovich	.15	.07	.02
☐ 644	John Castino	.10	.05	.01
☐ 645	Frank White	.15	.07	.02
☐ 646	SA: Frank White	.10	.05	.01
☐ 647	Warren Brusstar	.10	.05	.01
☐ 648	Jose Morales	.10	.05	.01
☐ 649	Ken Clay	.10	.05	.01
☐ 650	Carl Yastrzemski	2.00	.90	.25
☐ 651	SA: Carl Yastrzemski	1.00	.45	.13
☐ 652	Steve Nicosia	.10	.05	.01
☐ 653	Angels Rookies	1.25	.55	.16
	Tom Brunansky			
	Luis Sanchez			
	Daryl Sconiers			
☐ 654	Jim Morrison	.10	.05	.01
☐ 655	Joel Youngblood	.10	.05	.01
☐ 656	Eddie Whitson	.10	.05	.01
☐ 657	Tom Poquette	.10	.05	.01
☐ 658	Tito Landrum	.10	.05	.01
☐ 659	Fred Martinez	.10	.05	.01
☐ 660	Dave Concepcion	.15	.07	.02
☐ 661	SA: Dave Concepcion	.10	.05	.01
☐ 662	Luis Salazar	.10	.05	.01
☐ 663	Hector Cruz	.10	.05	.01
☐ 664	Dan Spillner	.10	.05	.01
☐ 665	Jim Clancy	.10	.05	.01
☐ 666	Tigers TL	.20	.09	.03
	BA: Steve Kemp			
	Pitching: Dan Petry			
☐ 667	Jeff Reardon	3.00	1.35	.40
☐ 668	Dale Murphy	1.50	.65	.19
☐ 669	Larry Milbourne	.10	.05	.01
☐ 670	Steve Kemp	.10	.05	.01
☐ 671	Mike Davis	.10	.05	.01
☐ 672	Bob Knepper	.10	.05	.01
☐ 673	Keith Drumwright	.10	.05	.01
☐ 674	Dave Goltz	.10	.05	.01
☐ 675	Cecil Cooper	.15	.07	.02
☐ 676	Sal Butera	.10	.05	.01
☐ 677	Alfredo Griffin	.10	.05	.01
☐ 678	Tom Paciorek	.15	.07	.02
☐ 679	Sammy Stewart	.10	.05	.01
☐ 680	Gary Matthews	.15	.07	.02
☐ 681	Dodgers Rookies	5.00	2.30	.60
	Mike Marshall			
	Ron Roenicke			
	Steve Sax			
☐ 682	Jesse Jefferson	.10	.05	.01
☐ 683	Phil Garner	.15	.07	.02
☐ 684	Harold Baines	1.25	.55	.16
☐ 685	Bert Blyleven	.50	.23	.06
☐ 686	Gary Allenson	.10	.05	.01
☐ 687	Greg Minton	.10	.05	.01
☐ 688	Leon Roberts	.10	.05	.01
☐ 689	Lary Sorensen	.10	.05	.01
☐ 690	Dave Kingman	.15	.07	.02
☐ 691	Dan Schatzeder	.10	.05	.01
☐ 692	Wayne Gross	.10	.05	.01
☐ 693	Cesar Geronimo	.10	.05	.01
☐ 694	Dave Wehrmeister	.10	.05	.01
☐ 695	Warren Cromartie	.10	.05	.01
☐ 696	Pirates TL	.20	.09	.03
	BA: Bill Madlock			
	Pitching: Eddie Solomon			
☐ 697	John Montefusco	.10	.05	.01
☐ 698	Tony Scott	.10	.05	.01
☐ 699	Dick Tidrow	.10	.05	.01
☐ 700	George Foster	.15	.07	.02
☐ 701	SA: George Foster	.10	.05	.01
☐ 702	Steve Renko	.10	.05	.01
☐ 703	Brewers TL	.20	.09	.03
	BA: Cecil Cooper			
	Pitching: Pete Vuckovich			
☐ 704	Mickey Rivers	.10	.05	.01
☐ 705	SA: Mickey Rivers	.10	.05	.01
☐ 706	Barry Foote	.10	.05	.01
☐ 707	Mark Bomback	.10	.05	.01
☐ 708	Gene Richards	.10	.05	.01
☐ 709	Don Money	.10	.05	.01
☐ 710	Jerry Reuss	.10	.05	.01
☐ 711	Mariners Rookies	1.50	.65	.19
	Dave Edler			
	Dave Henderson			
	Reggie Walton			
☐ 712	Dennis Martinez	.40	.18	.05
☐ 713	Del Unser	.10	.05	.01
☐ 714	Jerry Koosman	.15	.07	.02
☐ 715	Willie Stargell	1.00	.45	.13
☐ 716	SA: Willie Stargell	.50	.23	.06
☐ 717	Rick Miller	.10	.05	.01
☐ 718	Charlie Hough	.15	.07	.02
☐ 719	Jerry Narron	.10	.05	.01
☐ 720	Greg Luzinski	.15	.07	.02
☐ 721	SA: Greg Luzinski	.10	.05	.01
☐ 722	Jerry Martin	.10	.05	.01
☐ 723	Junior Kennedy	.10	.05	.01
☐ 724	Dave Rosello	.10	.05	.01
☐ 725	Amos Otis	.15	.07	.02
☐ 726	SA: Amos Otis	.10	.05	.01
☐ 727	Sixto Lezcano	.10	.05	.01
☐ 728	Aurelio Lopez	.10	.05	.01
☐ 729	Jim Spencer	.10	.05	.01
☐ 730	Gary Carter	1.25	.55	.16
☐ 731	Padres Rookies	.12	.05	.02
	Mike Armstrong			
	Doug Gwosdz			
	Fred Kuhaulua			
☐ 732	Mike Lum	.10	.05	.01
☐ 733	Larry McWilliams	.10	.05	.01
☐ 734	Mike Ivie	.10	.05	.01
☐ 735	Rudy May	.10	.05	.01
☐ 736	Jerry Turner	.10	.05	.01
☐ 737	Reggie Cleveland	.10	.05	.01

☐	738	Dave Engle.................10	.05	.01
☐	739	Joey McLaughlin..........10	.05	.01
☐	740	Dave Lopes.................15	.07	.02
☐	741	SA: Dave Lopes..........10	.05	.01
☐	742	Dick Drago.................10	.05	.01
☐	743	John Stearns................10	.05	.01
☐	744	Mike Witt...................20	.09	.03
☐	745	Bake McBride..............10	.05	.01
☐	746	Andre Thornton............15	.07	.02
☐	747	John Lowenstein...........10	.05	.01
☐	748	Marc Hill....................10	.05	.01
☐	749	Bob Shirley.................10	.05	.01
☐	750	Jim Rice....................40	.18	.05
☐	751	Rick Honeycutt............10	.05	.01
☐	752	Lee Lacy...................10	.05	.01
☐	753	Tom Brookens..............10	.05	.01
☐	754	Joe Morgan...............1.00	.45	.13
☐	755	SA: Joe Morgan 50	.23	.06
☐	756	Reds TL.....................35	.16	.04
		BA: Ken Griffey		
		Pitching: Tom Seaver		
☐	757	Tom Underwood 10	.05	.01
☐	758	Claudell Washington 10	.05	.01
☐	759	Paul Splittorff.............10	.05	.01
☐	760	Bill Buckner................15	.07	.02
☐	761	Dave Smith.................10	.05	.01
☐	762	Mike Phillips................10	.05	.01
☐	763	Tom Hume....................10	.05	.01
☐	764	Steve Swisher..............10	.05	.01
☐	765	Gorman Thomas 15	.07	.02
☐	766	Twins Rookies 3.00	1.35	.40
		Lenny Faedo		
		Kent Hrbek		
		Tim Laudner		
☐	767	Roy Smalley................10	.05	.01
☐	768	Jerry Garvin.................10	.05	.01
☐	769	Richie Zisk.................10	.05	.01
☐	770	Rich Gossage...............30	.14	.04
☐	771	SA: Rich Gossage.........15	.07	.02
☐	772	Bert Campaneris............15	.07	.02
☐	773	John Denny..................10	.05	.01
☐	774	Jay Johnstone..............15	.07	.02
☐	775	Bob Forsch..................10	.05	.01
☐	776	Mark Belanger..............15	.07	.02
☐	777	Tom Griffin..................10	.05	.01
☐	778	Kevin Hickey................10	.05	.01
☐	779	Grant Jackson...............10	.05	.01
☐	780	Pete Rose................2.00	.90	.25
☐	781	SA: Pete Rose...........1.00	.45	.13
☐	782	Frank Taveras..............10	.05	.01
☐	783	Greg Harris.................30	.14	.04
☐	784	Milt Wilcox.................10	.05	.01
☐	785	Dan Driessen...............10	.05	.01
☐	786	Red Sox TL.................20	.09	.03
		BA: Carney Lansford		
		Pitching: Mike Torrez		
☐	787	Fred Stanley.................10	.05	.01

☐	788	Woodie Fryman..............10	.05	.01
☐	789	Checklist 661-792..........15	.02	.00
☐	790	Larry Gura...................10	.05	.01
☐	791	Bobby Brown 10	.05	.01
☐	792	Frank Tanana 20	.09	.03

1982 Topps Traded

*The cards in this 132-card set measure
2 1/2" by 3 1/2". The 1982 Topps Traded
or extended series is distinguished by a
"T" printed after the number (located on
the reverse). This was the first time Topps
began a tradition of newly numbering (and
alphabetizing) their traded series from 1T
to 132T. Of the total cards, 70 players represent the American League and 61 represent the National League, with the remaining card a numbered checklist (132T). The
Cubs lead the pack with 12 changes, while
the Red Sox are the only team in either
league to have no new additions. All 131
player photos used in the set are completely new. Of this total, 112 individuals
are seen in the uniform of their new team,
11 others have been elevated to single
card status from "Future Stars" cards, and
eight more are entirely new to the 1982
Topps lineup. The backs are almost completely red in color with black print. There
are no key Rookie Cards in this set.
Although the Cal Ripken card is this set's
most valuable card, it is not his Rookie
Card since he had already been included
in the 1982 regular set, albeit on a multi-
player card.*

		NRMT-MT	EXC	G-VG
	COMPLETE SET (132)	300.00	135.00	38.00
	COMMON PLAYER (1T-132T)	.40	.18	.05
☐ 1T	Doyle Alexander	.40	.18	.05
☐ 2T	Jesse Barfield	1.00	.45	.13
☐ 3T	Ross Baumgarten	.40	.18	.05
☐ 4T	Steve Bedrosian	.50	.23	.06
☐ 5T	Mark Belanger	.50	.23	.06
☐ 6T	Kurt Bevacqua	.40	.18	.05
☐ 7T	Tim Blackwell	.40	.18	.05
☐ 8T	Vida Blue	.50	.23	.06
☐ 9T	Bob Boone	.50	.23	.06
☐ 10T	Larry Bowa	.50	.23	.06
☐ 11T	Dan Briggs	.40	.18	.05
☐ 12T	Bobby Brown	.40	.18	.05
☐ 13T	Tom Brunansky	2.00	.90	.25
☐ 14T	Jeff Burroughs	.40	.18	.05
☐ 15T	Enos Cabell	.40	.18	.05
☐ 16T	Bill Campbell	.40	.18	.05
☐ 17T	Bobby Castillo	.40	.18	.05
☐ 18T	Bill Caudill	.40	.18	.05
☐ 19T	Cesar Cedeno	.50	.23	.06
☐ 20T	Dave Collins	.40	.18	.05
☐ 21T	Doug Corbett	.40	.18	.05
☐ 22T	Al Cowens	.40	.18	.05
☐ 23T	Chili Davis	2.00	.90	.25
☐ 24T	Dick Davis	.40	.18	.05
☐ 25T	Ron Davis	.40	.18	.05
☐ 26T	Doug DeCinces	.50	.23	.06
☐ 27T	Ivan DeJesus	.40	.18	.05
☐ 28T	Bob Dernier	.40	.18	.05
☐ 29T	Bo Diaz	.40	.18	.05
☐ 30T	Roger Erickson	.40	.18	.05
☐ 31T	Jim Essian	.40	.18	.05
☐ 32T	Ed Farmer	.40	.18	.05
☐ 33T	Doug Flynn	.40	.18	.05
☐ 34T	Tim Foli	.40	.18	.05
☐ 35T	Dan Ford	.40	.18	.05
☐ 36T	George Foster	.50	.23	.06
☐ 37T	Dave Frost	.40	.18	.05
☐ 38T	Rich Gale	.40	.18	.05
☐ 39T	Ron Gardenhire	.40	.18	.05
☐ 40T	Ken Griffey	.75	.35	.09
☐ 41T	Greg Harris	.50	.23	.06
☐ 42T	Von Hayes	.60	.25	.08
☐ 43T	Larry Herndon	.40	.18	.05
☐ 44T	Kent Hrbek	6.00	2.70	.75
☐ 45T	Mike Ivie	.40	.18	.05
☐ 46T	Grant Jackson	.40	.18	.05
☐ 47T	Reggie Jackson	10.00	4.50	1.25
☐ 48T	Ron Jackson	.40	.18	.05
☐ 49T	Fergie Jenkins	2.50	1.15	.30
☐ 50T	Lamar Johnson	.40	.18	.05
☐ 51T	Randy Johnson	.40	.18	.05
☐ 52T	Jay Johnstone	.50	.23	.06
☐ 53T	Mick Kelleher	.40	.18	.05
☐ 54T	Steve Kemp	.40	.18	.05
☐ 55T	Junior Kennedy	.40	.18	.05
☐ 56T	Jim Kern	.40	.18	.05
☐ 57T	Ray Knight	.50	.23	.06
☐ 58T	Wayne Krenchicki	.40	.18	.05
☐ 59T	Mike Krukow	.40	.18	.05
☐ 60T	Duane Kuiper	.40	.18	.05
☐ 61T	Mike LaCoss	.40	.18	.05
☐ 62T	Chet Lemon	.40	.18	.05
☐ 63T	Sixto Lezcano	.40	.18	.05
☐ 64T	Dave Lopes	.50	.23	.06
☐ 65T	Jerry Martin	.40	.18	.05
☐ 66T	Renie Martin	.40	.18	.05
☐ 67T	John Mayberry	.40	.18	.05
☐ 68T	Lee Mazzilli	.40	.18	.05
☐ 69T	Bake McBride	.40	.18	.05
☐ 70T	Dan Meyer	.40	.18	.05
☐ 71T	Larry Milbourne	.40	.18	.05
☐ 72T	Eddie Milner	.40	.18	.05
☐ 73T	Sid Monge	.40	.18	.05
☐ 74T	John Montefusco	.40	.18	.05
☐ 75T	Jose Morales	.40	.18	.05
☐ 76T	Keith Moreland	.40	.18	.05
☐ 77T	Jim Morrison	.40	.18	.05
☐ 78T	Rance Mulliniks	.40	.18	.05
☐ 79T	Steve Mura	.40	.18	.05
☐ 80T	Gene Nelson	.40	.18	.05
☐ 81T	Joe Nolan	.40	.18	.05
☐ 82T	Dickie Noles	.40	.18	.05
☐ 83T	Al Oliver	.50	.23	.06
☐ 84T	Jorge Orta	.40	.18	.05
☐ 85T	Tom Paciorek	.50	.23	.06
☐ 86T	Larry Parrish	.40	.18	.05
☐ 87T	Jack Perconte	.40	.18	.05
☐ 88T	Gaylord Perry	2.50	1.15	.30
☐ 89T	Rob Picciolo	.40	.18	.05
☐ 90T	Joe Pittman	.40	.18	.05
☐ 91T	Hosken Powell	.40	.18	.05
☐ 92T	Mike Proly	.40	.18	.05
☐ 93T	Greg Pryor	.40	.18	.05
☐ 94T	Charlie Puleo	.40	.18	.05
☐ 95T	Shane Rawley	.40	.18	.05
☐ 96T	Johnny Ray	.50	.23	.06
☐ 97T	Dave Revering	.40	.18	.05
☐ 98T	Cal Ripken	275.00	125.00	34.00
☐ 99T	Allen Ripley	.40	.18	.05
☐ 100T	Bill Robinson	.50	.23	.06
☐ 101T	Aurelio Rodriguez	.40	.18	.05
☐ 102T	Joe Rudi	.40	.18	.05
☐ 103T	Steve Sax	8.00	3.60	1.00
☐ 104T	Dan Schatzeder	.40	.18	.05
☐ 105T	Bob Shirley	.40	.18	.05
☐ 106T	Eric Show	.50	.23	.06
☐ 107T	Roy Smalley	.50	.23	.06
☐ 108T	Lonnie Smith	.50	.23	.06
☐ 109T	Ozzie Smith	20.00	9.00	2.50
☐ 110T	Reggie Smith	.50	.23	.06

☐ 111T Lary Sorensen	.40	.18	.05
☐ 112T Elias Sosa	.40	.18	.05
☐ 113T Mike Stanton	.40	.18	.05
☐ 114T Steve Stroughter	.40	.18	.05
☐ 115T Champ Summers	.40	.18	.05
☐ 116T Rick Sutcliffe	1.00	.45	.13
☐ 117T Frank Tanana	.50	.23	.06
☐ 118T Frank Taveras	.40	.18	.05
☐ 119T Garry Templeton	.50	.23	.06
☐ 120T Alex Trevino	.40	.18	.05
☐ 121T Jerry Turner	.40	.18	.05
☐ 122T Ed VandeBerg	.40	.18	.05
☐ 123T Tom Veryzer	.40	.18	.05
☐ 124T Ron Washington	.40	.18	.05
☐ 125T Bob Watson	.50	.23	.06
☐ 126T Dennis Werth	.40	.18	.05
☐ 127T Eddie Whitson	.40	.18	.05
☐ 128T Rob Wilfong	.40	.18	.05
☐ 129T Bump Wills	.40	.18	.05
☐ 130T Gary Woods	.40	.18	.05
☐ 131T Butch Wynegar	.40	.18	.05
☐ 132T Checklist: 1-132	.40	.04	.01

1983 Topps

The cards in this 792-card set measure 2 1/2" by 3 1/2". Each regular card of the Topps set for 1983 features a large action shot of a player with a small cameo portrait at bottom right. There are special series for AL and NL All Stars (386-407), League Leaders (701-708), and Record Breakers (1-6). In addition, there are 34 "Super Veteran" (SV) cards and six numbered checklist cards. The Super Veteran cards are oriented horizontally and show two pictures of the featured player, a recent picture and a picture showing the player as a

rookie when he broke in. The cards are numbered on the reverse at the upper left corner. The team cards are actually Team Leader (TL) cards picturing the batting (BA: batting average) and pitching leader for that team with a checklist back. The key Rookie Cards in this set are Wade Boggs, Tony Gwynn, Willie McGee, Ryne Sandberg, and Frank Viola.

	NRMT-MT	EXC	G-VG
COMPLETE SET (792)	180.00	80.00	23.00
COMMON PLAYER (1-792)	.10	.05	.01
☐ 1 RB: Tony Armas	.20	.09	.03
11 putouts by rightfielder			
☐ 2 RB: Rickey Henderson	1.75	.80	.22
Sets modern record for steals, season			
☐ 3 RB: Greg Minton	.15	.07	.02
269 1/3 homerless innings streak			
☐ 4 RB: Lance Parrish	.15	.07	.02
Threw out three baserunners in All-Star game			
☐ 5 RB: Manny Trillo	.15	.07	.02
479 consecutive errorless chances, second baseman			
☐ 6 RB: John Wathan	.15	.07	.02
ML steals record for catchers, 31			
☐ 7 Gene Richards	.10	.05	.01
☐ 8 Steve Balboni	.10	.05	.01
☐ 9 Joey McLaughlin	.10	.05	.01
☐ 10 Gorman Thomas	.10	.05	.01
☐ 11 Billy Gardner MG	.10	.05	.01
☐ 12 Paul Mirabella	.10	.05	.01
☐ 13 Larry Herndon	.10	.05	.01
☐ 14 Frank LaCorte	.10	.05	.01
☐ 15 Ron Cey	.15	.07	.02
☐ 16 George Vukovich	.10	.05	.01
☐ 17 Kent Tekulve	.15	.07	.02
☐ 18 SV: Kent Tekulve	.10	.05	.01
☐ 19 Oscar Gamble	.10	.05	.01
☐ 20 Carlton Fisk	2.00	.90	.25
☐ 21 Baltimore Orioles TL	.40	.18	.05
BA: Eddie Murray ERA: Jim Palmer			
☐ 22 Randy Martz	.10	.05	.01
☐ 23 Mike Heath	.10	.05	.01
☐ 24 Steve Mura	.10	.05	.01
☐ 25 Hal McRae	.10	.07	.02
☐ 26 Jerry Royster	.10	.05	.01
☐ 27 Doug Corbett	.10	.05	.01

☐ 28	Bruce Bochte	.10	.05	.01
☐ 29	Randy Jones	.10	.05	.01
☐ 30	Jim Rice	.30	.14	.04
☐ 31	Bill Gullickson	.25	.11	.03
☐ 32	Dave Bergman	.10	.05	.01
☐ 33	Jack O'Connor	.10	.05	.01
☐ 34	Paul Householder	.10	.05	.01
☐ 35	Rollie Fingers	1.00	.45	.13
☐ 36	SV: Rollie Fingers	.40	.18	.05
☐ 37	Darrell Johnson MG	.10	.05	.01
☐ 38	Tim Flannery	.10	.05	.01
☐ 39	Terry Puhl	.10	.05	.01
☐ 40	Fernando Valenzuela	.25	.11	.03
☐ 41	Jerry Turner	.10	.05	.01
☐ 42	Dale Murray	.10	.05	.01
☐ 43	Bob Dernier	.10	.05	.01
☐ 44	Don Robinson	.10	.05	.01
☐ 45	John Mayberry	.10	.05	.01
☐ 46	Richard Dotson	.10	.05	.01
☐ 47	Dave McKay	.10	.05	.01
☐ 48	Lary Sorensen	.10	.05	.01
☐ 49	Willie McGee	4.00	1.80	.50
☐ 50	Bob Horner UER	.15	.07	.02
	('82 RBI total 7)			
☐ 51	Chicago Cubs TL	.20	.09	.03
	BA: Leon Durham			
	ERA: Fergie Jenkins			
☐ 52	Onix Concepcion	.10	.05	.01
☐ 53	Mike Witt	.10	.05	.01
☐ 54	Jim Maler	.10	.05	.01
☐ 55	Mookie Wilson	.15	.07	.02
☐ 56	Chuck Rainey	.10	.05	.01
☐ 57	Tim Blackwell	.10	.05	.01
☐ 58	Al Holland	.10	.05	.01
☐ 59	Benny Ayala	.10	.05	.01
☐ 60	Johnny Bench	2.00	.90	.25
☐ 61	SV: Johnny Bench	1.00	.45	.13
☐ 62	Bob McClure	.10	.05	.01
☐ 63	Rick Monday	.10	.05	.01
☐ 64	Bill Stein	.10	.05	.01
☐ 65	Jack Morris	1.75	.80	.22
☐ 66	Bob Lillis MG	.10	.05	.01
☐ 67	Sal Butera	.10	.05	.01
☐ 68	Eric Show	.10	.05	.01
☐ 69	Lee Lacy	.10	.05	.01
☐ 70	Steve Carlton	2.00	.90	.25
☐ 71	SV: Steve Carlton	1.00	.45	.13
☐ 72	Tom Paciorek	.15	.07	.02
☐ 73	Allen Ripley	.10	.05	.01
☐ 74	Julio Gonzalez	.10	.05	.01
☐ 75	Amos Otis	.10	.05	.01
☐ 76	Rick Mahler	.10	.05	.01
☐ 77	Hosken Powell	.10	.05	.01
☐ 78	Bill Caudill	.10	.05	.01
☐ 79	Mick Kelleher	.10	.05	.01
☐ 80	George Foster	.15	.07	.02
☐ 81	Yankees TL	.15	.07	.02

	BA: Jerry Mumphrey			
	ERA: Dave Righetti			
☐ 82	Bruce Hurst	.15	.07	.02
☐ 83	Ryne Sandberg	60.00	27.00	7.50
☐ 84	Milt May	.10	.05	.01
☐ 85	Ken Singleton	.15	.07	.02
☐ 86	Tom Hume	.10	.05	.01
☐ 87	Joe Rudi	.10	.05	.01
☐ 88	Jim Gantner	.15	.07	.02
☐ 89	Leon Roberts	.10	.05	.01
☐ 90	Jerry Reuss	.10	.05	.01
☐ 91	Larry Milbourne	.10	.05	.01
☐ 92	Mike LaCoss	.10	.05	.01
☐ 93	John Castino	.10	.05	.01
☐ 94	Dave Edwards	.10	.05	.01
☐ 95	Alan Trammell	.90	.40	.11
☐ 96	Dick Howser MG	.10	.05	.01
☐ 97	Ross Baumgarten	.10	.05	.01
☐ 98	Vance Law	.10	.05	.01
☐ 99	Dickie Noles	.10	.05	.01
☐ 100	Pete Rose	2.00	.90	.25
☐ 101	SV: Pete Rose	1.00	.45	.13
☐ 102	Dave Beard	.10	.05	.01
☐ 103	Darrell Porter	.10	.05	.01
☐ 104	Bob Walk	.10	.05	.01
☐ 105	Don Baylor	.15	.07	.02
☐ 106	Gene Nelson	.10	.05	.01
☐ 107	Mike Jorgensen	.10	.05	.01
☐ 108	Glenn Hoffman	.10	.05	.01
☐ 109	Luis Leal	.10	.05	.01
☐ 110	Ken Griffey	.35	.16	.04
☐ 111	Montreal Expos TL	.15	.07	.02
	BA: Al Oliver			
	ERA: Steve Rogers			
☐ 112	Bob Shirley	.10	.05	.01
☐ 113	Ron Roenicke	.10	.05	.01
☐ 114	Jim Slaton	.10	.05	.01
☐ 115	Chili Davis	.50	.23	.06
☐ 116	Dave Schmidt	.10	.05	.01
☐ 117	Alan Knicely	.10	.05	.01
☐ 118	Chris Welsh	.10	.05	.01
☐ 119	Tom Brookens	.10	.05	.01
☐ 120	Len Barker	.10	.05	.01
☐ 121	Mickey Hatcher	.10	.05	.01
☐ 122	Jimmy Smith	.10	.05	.01
☐ 123	George Frazier	.10	.05	.01
☐ 124	Marc Hill	.10	.05	.01
☐ 125	Leon Durham	.10	.05	.01
☐ 126	Joe Torre MG	.15	.07	.02
☐ 127	Preston Hanna	.10	.05	.01
☐ 128	Mike Ramsey	.10	.05	.01
☐ 129	Checklist: 1-132	.15	.02	.00
☐ 130	Dave Stieb	.25	.11	.03
☐ 131	Ed Ott	.10	.05	.01
☐ 132	Todd Cruz	.10	.05	.01
☐ 133	Jim Barr	.10	.05	.01
☐ 134	Hubie Brooks	.20	.09	.03

☐ 135	Dwight Evans	.35	.16	.04
☐ 136	Willie Aikens	.10	.05	.01
☐ 137	Woodie Fryman	.10	.05	.01
☐ 138	Rick Dempsey	.15	.07	.02
☐ 139	Bruce Berenyi	.10	.05	.01
☐ 140	Willie Randolph	.15	.07	.02
☐ 141	Indians TL	.15	.07	.02
	BA: Toby Harrah			
	ERA: Rick Sutcliffe			
☐ 142	Mike Caldwell	.10	.05	.01
☐ 143	Joe Pettini	.10	.05	.01
☐ 144	Mark Wagner	.10	.05	.01
☐ 145	Don Sutton	.50	.23	.06
☐ 146	SV: Don Sutton	.25	.11	.03
☐ 147	Rick Leach	.10	.05	.01
☐ 148	Dave Roberts	.10	.05	.01
☐ 149	Johnny Ray	.10	.05	.01
☐ 150	Bruce Sutter	.25	.11	.03
☐ 151	SV: Bruce Sutter	.10	.05	.01
☐ 152	Jay Johnstone	.15	.07	.02
☐ 153	Jerry Koosman	.15	.07	.02
☐ 154	Johnnie LeMaster	.10	.05	.01
☐ 155	Dan Quisenberry	.15	.07	.02
☐ 156	Billy Martin MG	.20	.09	.03
☐ 157	Steve Bedrosian	.10	.05	.01
☐ 158	Rob Wilfong	.10	.05	.01
☐ 159	Mike Stanton	.10	.05	.01
☐ 160	Dave Kingman	.15	.07	.02
☐ 161	SV: Dave Kingman	.10	.05	.01
☐ 162	Mark Clear	.10	.05	.01
☐ 163	Cal Ripken	25.00	11.50	3.10
☐ 164	David Palmer	.10	.05	.01
☐ 165	Dan Driessen	.10	.05	.01
☐ 166	John Pacella	.10	.05	.01
☐ 167	Mark Brouhard	.10	.05	.01
☐ 168	Juan Eichelberger	.10	.05	.01
☐ 169	Doug Flynn	.10	.05	.01
☐ 170	Steve Howe	.10	.05	.01
☐ 171	Giants TL	.20	.09	.03
	BA: Joe Morgan			
	ERA: Bill Laskey			
☐ 172	Vern Ruhle	.10	.05	.01
☐ 173	Jim Morrison	.10	.05	.01
☐ 174	Jerry Ujdur	.10	.05	.01
☐ 175	Bo Diaz	.10	.05	.01
☐ 176	Dave Righetti	.20	.09	.03
☐ 177	Harold Baines	.75	.35	.09
☐ 178	Luis Tiant	.15	.07	.02
☐ 179	SV: Luis Tiant	.10	.05	.01
☐ 180	Rickey Henderson	5.50	2.50	.70
☐ 181	Terry Felton	.10	.05	.01
☐ 182	Mike Fischlin	.10	.05	.01
☐ 183	Ed VandeBerg	.10	.05	.01
☐ 184	Bob Clark	.10	.05	.01
☐ 185	Tim Lollar	.10	.05	.01
☐ 186	Whitey Herzog MG	.10	.05	.01
☐ 187	Terry Leach	.15	.07	.02
☐ 188	Rick Miller	.10	.05	.01
☐ 189	Dan Schatzeder	.10	.05	.01
☐ 190	Cecil Cooper	.15	.07	.02
☐ 191	Joe Price	.10	.05	.01
☐ 192	Floyd Rayford	.10	.05	.01
☐ 193	Harry Spilman	.10	.05	.01
☐ 194	Cesar Geronimo	.10	.05	.01
☐ 195	Bob Stoddard	.10	.05	.01
☐ 196	Bill Fahey	.10	.05	.01
☐ 197	Jim Eisenreich	.40	.18	.05
☐ 198	Kiko Garcia	.10	.05	.01
☐ 199	Marty Bystrom	.10	.05	.01
☐ 200	Rod Carew	2.00	.90	.25
☐ 201	SV: Rod Carew	1.00	.45	.13
☐ 202	Blue Jays TL	.15	.07	.02
	BA: Damaso Garcia			
	ERA: Dave Stieb			
☐ 203	Mike Morgan	.50	.23	.06
☐ 204	Junior Kennedy	.10	.05	.01
☐ 205	Dave Parker	.50	.23	.06
☐ 206	Ken Oberkfell	.10	.05	.01
☐ 207	Rick Camp	.10	.05	.01
☐ 208	Dan Meyer	.10	.05	.01
☐ 209	Mike Moore	1.75	.80	.22
☐ 210	Jack Clark	.20	.09	.03
☐ 211	John Denny	.10	.05	.01
☐ 212	John Stearns	.10	.05	.01
☐ 213	Tom Burgmeier	.10	.05	.01
☐ 214	Jerry White	.10	.05	.01
☐ 215	Mario Soto	.10	.05	.01
☐ 216	Tony LaRussa MG	.15	.07	.02
☐ 217	Tim Stoddard	.10	.05	.01
☐ 218	Roy Howell	.10	.05	.01
☐ 219	Mike Armstrong	.10	.05	.01
☐ 220	Dusty Baker	.15	.07	.02
☐ 221	Joe Niekro	.15	.07	.02
☐ 222	Damaso Garcia	.10	.05	.01
☐ 223	John Montefusco	.10	.05	.01
☐ 224	Mickey Rivers	.10	.05	.01
☐ 225	Enos Cabell	.10	.05	.01
☐ 226	Enrique Romo	.10	.05	.01
☐ 227	Chris Bando	.10	.05	.01
☐ 228	Joaquin Andujar	.10	.05	.01
☐ 229	Phillies TL	.20	.09	.03
	BA: Bo Diaz			
	ERA: Steve Carlton			
☐ 230	Fergie Jenkins	.50	.23	.06
☐ 231	SV: Fergie Jenkins	.25	.11	.03
☐ 232	Tom Brunansky	.30	.14	.04
☐ 233	Wayne Gross	.10	.05	.01
☐ 234	Larry Andersen	.10	.05	.01
☐ 235	Claudell Washington	.10	.05	.01
☐ 236	Steve Renko	.10	.05	.01
☐ 237	Dan Norman	.10	.05	.01
☐ 238	Bud Black	.50	.23	.06
☐ 239	Dave Stapleton	.10	.05	.01
☐ 240	Rich Gossage	.25	.11	.03

☐ 241 SV: Rich Gossage 10	.05	.01
☐ 242 Joe Nolan.......................10	.05	.01
☐ 243 Duane Walker 10	.05	.01
☐ 244 Dwight Bernard..............10	.05	.01
☐ 245 Steve Sax.....................1.00	.45	.13
☐ 246 George Bamberger MG ...10	.05	.01
☐ 247 Dave Smith 10	.05	.01
☐ 248 Bake McBride.................10	.05	.01
☐ 249 Checklist: 133-264.........15	.02	.00
☐ 250 Bill Buckner...................15	.07	.02
☐ 251 Alan Wiggins.................10	.05	.01
☐ 252 Luis Aguayo 10	.05	.01
☐ 253 Larry McWilliams...........10	.05	.01
☐ 254 Rick Cerone 10	.05	.01
☐ 255 Gene Garber..................10	.05	.01
☐ 256 SV: Gene Garber 10	.05	.01
☐ 257 Jesse Barfield 20	.09	.03
☐ 258 Manny Castillo 10	.05	.01
☐ 259 Jeff Jones 10	.05	.01
☐ 260 Steve Kemp 10	.05	.01
☐ 261 Tigers TL 15	.07	.02
BA: Larry Herndon		
ERA: Dan Petry		
☐ 262 Ron Jackson 10	.05	.01
☐ 263 Renie Martin 10	.05	.01
☐ 264 Jamie Quirk 10	.05	.01
☐ 265 Joel Youngblood 10	.05	.01
☐ 266 Paul Boris 10	.05	.01
☐ 267 Terry Francona 10	.05	.01
☐ 268 Storm Davis 25	.11	.03
☐ 269 Ron Oester 10	.05	.01
☐ 270 Dennis Eckersley...........1.75	.80	.22
☐ 271 Ed Romero 10	.05	.01
☐ 272 Frank Tanana 15	.07	.02
☐ 273 Mark Belanger 10	.05	.01
☐ 274 Terry Kennedy 10	.05	.01
☐ 275 Ray Knight 15	.07	.02
☐ 276 Gene Mauch MG 10	.05	.01
☐ 277 Rance Mulliniks 10	.05	.01
☐ 278 Kevin Hickey 10	.05	.01
☐ 279 Greg Gross 10	.05	.01
☐ 280 Bert Blyleven 40	.18	.05
☐ 281 Andre Robertson............10	.05	.01
☐ 282 Reggie Smith 50	.23	.06
(Ryne Sandberg		
ducking back)		
☐ 283 SV: Reggie Smith...........10	.05	.01
☐ 284 Jeff Lahti.......................10	.05	.01
☐ 285 Lance Parrish 20	.09	.03
☐ 286 Rick Langford 10	.05	.01
☐ 287 Bobby Brown 10	.05	.01
☐ 288 Joe Cowley 10	.05	.01
☐ 289 Jerry Dybzinski 10	.05	.01
☐ 290 Jeff Reardon 2.00	.90	.25
☐ 291 Pirates TL 15	.07	.02
BA: Bill Madlock		
ERA: John Candelaria		
☐ 292 Craig Swan 10	.05	.01
☐ 293 Glenn Gulliver 10	.05	.01
☐ 294 Dave Engle 10	.05	.01
☐ 295 Jerry Remy 10	.05	.01
☐ 296 Greg Harris 10	.05	.01
☐ 297 Ned Yost 10	.05	.01
☐ 298 Floyd Chiffer 10	.05	.01
☐ 299 George Wright 10	.05	.01
☐ 300 Mike Schmidt 3.00	1.35	.40
☐ 301 SV: Mike Schmidt 1.50	.65	.19
☐ 302 Ernie Whitt 10	.05	.01
☐ 303 Miguel Dilone 10	.05	.01
☐ 304 Dave Rucker 10	.05	.01
☐ 305 Larry Bowa 15	.07	.02
☐ 306 Tom Lasorda MG 15	.07	.02
☐ 307 Lou Piniella 15	.07	.02
☐ 308 Jesus Vega 10	.05	.01
☐ 309 Jeff Leonard 10	.05	.01
☐ 310 Greg Luzinski 15	.07	.02
☐ 311 Glenn Brummer 10	.05	.01
☐ 312 Brian Kingman 10	.05	.01
☐ 313 Gary Gray......................10	.05	.01
☐ 314 Ken Dayley 10	.05	.01
☐ 315 Rick Burleson 10	.05	.01
☐ 316 Paul Splittorff................10	.05	.01
☐ 317 Gary Rajsich 10	.05	.01
☐ 318 John Tudor 15	.07	.02
☐ 319 Lenn Sakata 10	.05	.01
☐ 320 Steve Rogers 10	.05	.01
☐ 321 Brewers TL 35	.16	.04
BA: Robin Yount		
ERA: Pete Vuckovich		
☐ 322 Dave Van Gorder............10	.05	.01
☐ 323 Luis DeLeon...................10	.05	.01
☐ 324 Mike Marshall 15	.07	.02
☐ 325 Von Hayes.....................15	.07	.02
☐ 326 Garth Iorg 10	.05	.01
☐ 327 Bobby Castillo 10	.05	.01
☐ 328 Craig Reynolds 10	.05	.01
☐ 329 Randy Niemann 10	.05	.01
☐ 330 Buddy Bell 15	.07	.02
☐ 331 Mike Krukow 10	.05	.01
☐ 332 Glenn Wilson 15	.07	.02
☐ 333 Dave LaRoche 10	.05	.01
☐ 334 SV: Dave LaRoche 10	.05	.01
☐ 335 Steve Henderson............10	.05	.01
☐ 336 Rene Lachemann MG........10	.05	.01
☐ 337 Tito Landrum 10	.05	.01
☐ 338 Bob Owchinko 10	.05	.01
☐ 339 Terry Harper 10	.05	.01
☐ 340 Larry Gura 10	.05	.01
☐ 341 Doug DeCinces 15	.07	.02
☐ 342 Atlee Hammaker 10	.05	.01
☐ 343 Bob Bailor 10	.05	.01
☐ 344 Roger LaFrancois............10	.05	.01
☐ 345 Jim Clancy 10	.05	.01
☐ 346 Joe Pittman....................10	.05	.01

☐	347	Sammy Stewart	.10	.05	.01	☐	400	Dave Concepcion AS	.12	.05	.02
☐	348	Alan Bannister	.10	.05	.01	☐	401	Dale Murphy AS	.40	.18	.05
☐	349	Checklist: 265-396	.15	.02	.00	☐	402	Andre Dawson AS	.90	.40	.11
☐	350	Robin Yount	3.50	1.55	.45	☐	403	Tim Raines AS	.35	.16	.04
☐	351	Reds TL	.15	.07	.02	☐	404	Gary Carter AS	.40	.18	.05
		BA: Cesar Cedeno				☐	405	Steve Rogers AS	.12	.05	.02
		ERA: Mario Soto				☐	406	Steve Carlton AS	.75	.35	.09
☐	352	Mike Scioscia	.15	.07	.02	☐	407	Bruce Sutter AS	.12	.05	.02
☐	353	Steve Comer	.10	.05	.01	☐	408	Rudy May	.10	.05	.01
☐	354	Randy Johnson	.10	.05	.01	☐	409	Marvis Foley	.10	.05	.01
☐	355	Jim Bibby	.10	.05	.01	☐	410	Phil Niekro	.60	.25	.08
☐	356	Gary Woods	.10	.05	.01	☐	411	SV: Phil Niekro	.30	.14	.04
☐	357	Len Matuszek	.10	.05	.01	☐	412	Rangers TL	.15	.07	.02
☐	358	Jerry Garvin	.10	.05	.01			BA: Buddy Bell			
☐	359	Dave Collins	.10	.05	.01			ERA: Charlie Hough			
☐	360	Nolan Ryan	9.00	4.00	1.15	☐	413	Matt Keough	.10	.05	.01
☐	361	SV: Nolan Ryan	4.50	2.00	.55	☐	414	Julio Cruz	.10	.05	.01
☐	362	Bill Almon	.10	.05	.01	☐	415	Bob Forsch	.10	.05	.01
☐	363	John Stuper	.10	.05	.01	☐	416	Joe Ferguson	.10	.05	.01
☐	364	Brett Butler	.75	.35	.09	☐	417	Tom Hausman	.10	.05	.01
☐	365	Dave Lopes	.15	.07	.02	☐	418	Greg Pryor	.10	.05	.01
☐	366	Dick Williams MG	.10	.05	.01	☐	419	Steve Crawford	.10	.05	.01
☐	367	Bud Anderson	.10	.05	.01	☐	420	Al Oliver	.15	.07	.02
☐	368	Richie Zisk	.10	.05	.01	☐	421	SV: Al Oliver	.10	.05	.01
☐	369	Jesse Orosco	.10	.05	.01	☐	422	George Cappuzzello	.10	.05	.01
☐	370	Gary Carter	1.00	.45	.13	☐	423	Tom Lawless	.10	.05	.01
☐	371	Mike Richardt	.10	.05	.01	☐	424	Jerry Augustine	.10	.05	.01
☐	372	Terry Crowley	.10	.05	.01	☐	425	Pedro Guerrero	.35	.16	.04
☐	373	Kevin Saucier	.10	.05	.01	☐	426	Earl Weaver MG	.15	.07	.02
☐	374	Wayne Krenchicki	.10	.05	.01	☐	427	Roy Lee Jackson	.10	.05	.01
☐	375	Pete Vuckovich	.10	.05	.01	☐	428	Champ Summers	.10	.05	.01
☐	376	Ken Landreaux	.10	.05	.01	☐	429	Eddie Whitson	.10	.05	.01
☐	377	Lee May	.10	.05	.01	☐	430	Kirk Gibson	.60	.25	.08
☐	378	SV: Lee May	.10	.05	.01	☐	431	Gary Gaetti	.60	.25	.08
☐	379	Guy Sularz	.10	.05	.01	☐	432	Porfirio Altamirano	.10	.05	.01
☐	380	Ron Davis	.10	.05	.01	☐	433	Dale Berra	.10	.05	.01
☐	381	Red Sox TL	.15	.07	.02	☐	434	Dennis Lamp	.10	.05	.01
		BA: Jim Rice				☐	435	Tony Armas	.10	.05	.01
		ERA: Bob Stanley				☐	436	Bill Campbell	.10	.05	.01
☐	382	Bob Knepper	.10	.05	.01	☐	437	Rick Sweet	.10	.05	.01
☐	383	Ozzie Virgil	.10	.05	.01	☐	438	Dave LaPoint	.15	.07	.02
☐	384	Dave Dravecky	.75	.35	.09	☐	439	Rafael Ramirez	.10	.05	.01
☐	385	Mike Easler	.10	.05	.01	☐	440	Ron Guidry	.25	.11	.03
☐	386	Rod Carew AS	.75	.35	.09	☐	441	Astros TL	.15	.07	.02
☐	387	Bob Grich AS	.12	.05	.02			BA: Ray Knight			
☐	388	George Brett AS	1.25	.55	.16			ERA: Joe Niekro			
☐	389	Robin Yount AS	1.25	.55	.16	☐	442	Brian Downing	.15	.07	.02
☐	390	Reggie Jackson AS	.90	.40	.11	☐	443	Don Hood	.10	.05	.01
☐	391	Rickey Henderson AS	2.00	.90	.25	☐	444	Wally Backman	.15	.07	.02
☐	392	Fred Lynn AS	.12	.05	.02	☐	445	Mike Flanagan	.15	.07	.02
☐	393	Carlton Fisk AS	.75	.35	.09	☐	446	Reid Nichols	.10	.05	.01
☐	394	Pete Vuckovich AS	.12	.05	.02	☐	447	Bryn Smith	.10	.05	.01
☐	395	Larry Gura AS	.12	.05	.02	☐	448	Darrell Evans	.15	.07	.02
☐	396	Dan Quisenberry AS	.12	.05	.02	☐	449	Eddie Milner	.10	.05	.01
☐	397	Pete Rose AS	.75	.35	.09	☐	450	Ted Simmons	.15	.07	.02
☐	398	Manny Trillo AS	.12	.05	.02	☐	451	SV: Ted Simmons	.10	.05	.01
☐	399	Mike Schmidt AS	1.25	.55	.16	☐	452	Lloyd Moseby	.10	.05	.01

☐ 453 Lamar Johnson	.10	.05	.01
☐ 454 Bob Welch	.35	.16	.04
☐ 455 Sixto Lezcano	.10	.05	.01
☐ 456 Lee Elia MG	.10	.05	.01
☐ 457 Milt Wilcox	.10	.05	.01
☐ 458 Ron Washington	.10	.05	.01
☐ 459 Ed Farmer	.10	.05	.01
☐ 460 Roy Smalley	.10	.05	.01
☐ 461 Steve Trout	.10	.05	.01
☐ 462 Steve Nicosia	.10	.05	.01
☐ 463 Gaylord Perry	.60	.25	.08
☐ 464 SV: Gaylord Perry	.30	.14	.04
☐ 465 Lonnie Smith	.15	.07	.02
☐ 466 Tom Underwood	.10	.05	.01
☐ 467 Rufino Linares	.10	.05	.01
☐ 468 Dave Goltz	.10	.05	.01
☐ 469 Ron Gardenhire	.10	.05	.01
☐ 470 Greg Minton	.10	.05	.01
☐ 471 K.C. Royals TL	.15	.07	.02
BA: Willie Wilson			
ERA: Vida Blue			
☐ 472 Gary Allenson	.10	.05	.01
☐ 473 John Lowenstein	.10	.05	.01
☐ 474 Ray Burris	.10	.05	.01
☐ 475 Cesar Cedeno	.15	.07	.02
☐ 476 Rob Picciolo	.10	.05	.01
☐ 477 Tom Niedenfuer	.10	.05	.01
☐ 478 Phil Garner	.15	.07	.02
☐ 479 Charlie Hough	.15	.07	.02
☐ 480 Toby Harrah	.10	.05	.01
☐ 481 Scot Thompson	.10	.05	.01
☐ 482 Tony Gwynn UER	40.00	18.00	5.00
(No Topps logo under			
card number on back)			
☐ 483 Lynn Jones	.10	.05	.01
☐ 484 Dick Ruthven	.10	.05	.01
☐ 485 Omar Moreno	.10	.05	.01
☐ 486 Clyde King MG	.10	.05	.01
☐ 487 Jerry Hairston	.10	.05	.01
☐ 488 Alfredo Griffin	.10	.05	.01
☐ 489 Tom Herr	.15	.07	.02
☐ 490 Jim Palmer	1.50	.65	.19
☐ 491 SV: Jim Palmer	.75	.35	.09
☐ 492 Paul Serna	.10	.05	.01
☐ 493 Steve McCatty	.10	.05	.01
☐ 494 Bob Brenly	.10	.05	.01
☐ 495 Warren Cromartie	.10	.05	.01
☐ 496 Tom Veryzer	.10	.05	.01
☐ 497 Rick Sutcliffe	.30	.14	.04
☐ 498 Wade Boggs	35.00	16.00	4.40
☐ 499 Jeff Little	.10	.05	.01
☐ 500 Reggie Jackson	2.00	.90	.25
☐ 501 SV: Reggie Jackson	1.00	.45	.13
☐ 502 Atlanta Braves TL	.25	.11	.03
BA: Dale Murphy			
ERA: Phil Niekro			
☐ 503 Moose Haas	.10	.05	.01

☐ 504 Don Werner	.10	.05	.01
☐ 505 Garry Templeton	.15	.07	.02
☐ 506 Jim Gott	.20	.09	.03
☐ 507 Tony Scott	.10	.05	.01
☐ 508 Tom Filer	.10	.05	.01
☐ 509 Lou Whitaker	.75	.35	.09
☐ 510 Tug McGraw	.15	.07	.02
☐ 511 SV: Tug McGraw	.10	.05	.01
☐ 512 Doyle Alexander	.10	.05	.01
☐ 513 Fred Stanley	.10	.05	.01
☐ 514 Rudy Law	.10	.05	.01
☐ 515 Gene Tenace	.10	.05	.01
☐ 516 Bill Virdon MG	.10	.05	.01
☐ 517 Gary Ward	.10	.05	.01
☐ 518 Bill Laskey	.10	.05	.01
☐ 519 Terry Bulling	.10	.05	.01
☐ 520 Fred Lynn	.15	.07	.02
☐ 521 Bruce Benedict	.10	.05	.01
☐ 522 Pat Zachry	.10	.05	.01
☐ 523 Carney Lansford	.15	.07	.02
☐ 524 Tom Brennan	.10	.05	.01
☐ 525 Frank White	.15	.07	.02
☐ 526 Checklist: 397-528	.15	.02	.00
☐ 527 Larry Biittner	.10	.05	.01
☐ 528 Jamie Easterly	.10	.05	.01
☐ 529 Tim Laudner	.10	.05	.01
☐ 530 Eddie Murray	2.50	1.15	.30
☐ 531 Oakland A's TL	.50	.23	.06
BA: Rickey Henderson			
ERA: Rick Langford			
☐ 532 Dave Stewart	1.00	.45	.13
☐ 533 Luis Salazar	.10	.05	.01
☐ 534 John Butcher	.10	.05	.01
☐ 535 Manny Trillo	.10	.05	.01
☐ 536 John Wockenfuss	.10	.05	.01
☐ 537 Rod Scurry	.10	.05	.01
☐ 538 Danny Heep	.10	.05	.01
☐ 539 Roger Erickson	.10	.05	.01
☐ 540 Ozzie Smith	2.50	1.15	.30
☐ 541 Britt Burns	.10	.05	.01
☐ 542 Jody Davis	.10	.05	.01
☐ 543 Alan Fowlkes	.10	.05	.01
☐ 544 Larry Whisenton	.10	.05	.01
☐ 545 Floyd Bannister	.10	.05	.01
☐ 546 Dave Garcia MG	.10	.05	.01
☐ 547 Geoff Zahn	.10	.05	.01
☐ 548 Brian Giles	.10	.05	.01
☐ 549 Charlie Puleo	.10	.05	.01
☐ 550 Carl Yastrzemski	2.00	.90	.25
☐ 551 SV: Carl Yastrzemski	1.00	.45	.13
☐ 552 Tim Wallach	.30	.14	.04
☐ 553 Dennis Martinez	.15	.07	.02
☐ 554 Mike Vail	.10	.05	.01
☐ 555 Steve Yeager	.10	.05	.01
☐ 556 Willie Upshaw	.10	.05	.01
☐ 557 Rick Honeycutt	.10	.05	.01
☐ 558 Dickie Thon	.10	.05	.01

☐ 559 Pete Redfern	10	.05	.01
☐ 560 Ron LeFlore	15	.07	.02
☐ 561 Cardinals TL	15	.07	.02
BA: Lonnie Smith			
ERA: Joaquin Andujar			
☐ 562 Dave Rozema	10	.05	.01
☐ 563 Juan Bonilla	10	.05	.01
☐ 564 Sid Monge	10	.05	.01
☐ 565 Bucky Dent	15	.07	.02
☐ 566 Manny Sarmiento	10	.05	.01
☐ 567 Joe Simpson	10	.05	.01
☐ 568 Willie Hernandez	15	.07	.02
☐ 569 Jack Perconte	10	.05	.01
☐ 570 Vida Blue	15	.07	.02
☐ 571 Mickey Klutts	10	.05	.01
☐ 572 Bob Watson	15	.07	.02
☐ 573 Andy Hassler	10	.05	.01
☐ 574 Glenn Adams	10	.05	.01
☐ 575 Neil Allen	10	.05	.01
☐ 576 Frank Robinson MG	35	.16	.04
☐ 577 Luis Aponte	10	.05	.01
☐ 578 David Green	10	.05	.01
☐ 579 Rich Dauer	10	.05	.01
☐ 580 Tom Seaver	2.00	.90	.25
☐ 581 SV: Tom Seaver	1.00	.45	.13
☐ 582 Marshall Edwards	10	.05	.01
☐ 583 Terry Forster	10	.05	.01
☐ 584 Dave Hostetler	10	.05	.01
☐ 585 Jose Cruz	15	.07	.02
☐ 586 Frank Viola	5.00	2.30	.60
☐ 587 Ivan DeJesus	10	.05	.01
☐ 588 Pat Underwood	10	.05	.01
☐ 589 Alvis Woods	10	.05	.01
☐ 590 Tony Pena	15	.07	.02
☐ 591 White Sox TL	15	.07	.02
BA: Greg Luzinski			
ERA: LaMarr Hoyt			
☐ 592 Shane Rawley	10	.05	.01
☐ 593 Broderick Perkins	10	.05	.01
☐ 594 Eric Rasmussen	10	.05	.01
☐ 595 Tim Raines	1.00	.45	.13
☐ 596 Randy Johnson	10	.05	.01
☐ 597 Mike Proly	10	.05	.01
☐ 598 Dwayne Murphy	10	.05	.01
☐ 599 Don Aase	10	.05	.01
☐ 600 George Brett	3.50	1.55	.45
☐ 601 Ed Lynch	10	.05	.01
☐ 602 Rich Gedman	10	.05	.01
☐ 603 Joe Morgan	1.00	.45	.13
☐ 604 SV: Joe Morgan	50	.23	.06
☐ 605 Gary Roenicke	10	.05	.01
☐ 606 Bobby Cox MG	10	.05	.01
☐ 607 Charlie Leibrandt	15	.07	.02
☐ 608 Don Money	10	.05	.01
☐ 609 Danny Darwin	10	.05	.01
☐ 610 Steve Garvey	60	.25	.08
☐ 611 Bert Roberge	10	.05	.01
☐ 612 Steve Swisher	10	.05	.01
☐ 613 Mike Ivie	10	.05	.01
☐ 614 Ed Glynn	10	.05	.01
☐ 615 Garry Maddox	10	.05	.01
☐ 616 Bill Nahorodny	10	.05	.01
☐ 617 Butch Wynegar	10	.05	.01
☐ 618 LaMarr Hoyt	10	.05	.01
☐ 619 Keith Moreland	10	.05	.01
☐ 620 Mike Norris	10	.05	.01
☐ 621 New York Mets TL	15	.07	.02
BA: Mookie Wilson			
ERA: Craig Swan			
☐ 622 Dave Edler	10	.05	.01
☐ 623 Luis Sanchez	10	.05	.01
☐ 624 Glenn Hubbard	10	.05	.01
☐ 625 Ken Forsch	10	.05	.01
☐ 626 Jerry Martin	10	.05	.01
☐ 627 Doug Bair	10	.05	.01
☐ 628 Julio Valdez	10	.05	.01
☐ 629 Charlie Lea	10	.05	.01
☐ 630 Paul Molitor	1.25	.55	.16
☐ 631 Tippy Martinez	10	.05	.01
☐ 632 Alex Trevino	10	.05	.01
☐ 633 Vicente Romo	10	.05	.01
☐ 634 Max Venable	10	.05	.01
☐ 635 Graig Nettles	15	.07	.02
☐ 636 SV: Graig Nettles	10	.05	.01
☐ 637 Pat Corrales MG	10	.05	.01
☐ 638 Dan Petry	10	.05	.01
☐ 639 Art Howe	10	.05	.01
☐ 640 Andre Thornton	10	.05	.01
☐ 641 Billy Sample	10	.05	.01
☐ 642 Checklist: 529-660	15	.02	.00
☐ 643 Bump Wills	10	.05	.01
☐ 644 Joe Lefebvre	10	.05	.01
☐ 645 Bill Madlock	15	.07	.02
☐ 646 Jim Essian	10	.05	.01
☐ 647 Bobby Mitchell	10	.05	.01
☐ 648 Jeff Burroughs	10	.05	.01
☐ 649 Tommy Boggs	10	.05	.01
☐ 650 George Hendrick	10	.05	.01
☐ 651 Angels TL	20	.09	.03
BA: Rod Carew			
ERA: Mike Witt			
☐ 652 Butch Hobson	15	.07	.02
☐ 653 Ellis Valentine	10	.05	.01
☐ 654 Bob Ojeda	15	.07	.02
☐ 655 Al Bumbry	10	.05	.01
☐ 656 Dave Frost	10	.05	.01
☐ 657 Mike Gates	10	.05	.01
☐ 658 Frank Pastore	10	.05	.01
☐ 659 Charlie Moore	10	.05	.01
☐ 660 Mike Hargrove	15	.07	.02
☐ 661 Bill Russell	15	.07	.02
☐ 662 Joe Sambito	10	.05	.01
☐ 663 Tom O'Malley	10	.05	.01
☐ 664 Bob Molinaro	10	.05	.01

☐ 665	Jim Sundberg	15	.07	.02
☐ 666	Sparky Anderson MG	15	.07	.02
☐ 667	Dick Davis	10	.05	.01
☐ 668	Larry Christenson	10	.05	.01
☐ 669	Mike Squires	10	.05	.01
☐ 670	Jerry Mumphrey	10	.05	.01
☐ 671	Lenny Faedo	10	.05	.01
☐ 672	Jim Kaat	20	.09	.03
☐ 673	SV: Jim Kaat	10	.05	.01
☐ 674	Kurt Bevacqua	10	.05	.01
☐ 675	Jim Beattie	10	.05	.01
☐ 676	Biff Pocoroba	10	.05	.01
☐ 677	Dave Revering	10	.05	.01
☐ 678	Juan Beniquez	10	.05	.01
☐ 679	Mike Scott	15	.07	.02
☐ 680	Andre Dawson	2.50	1.15	.30
☐ 681	Dodgers Leaders	15	.07	.02
	BA: Pedro Guerrero			
	ERA: Fernando Valenzuela			
☐ 682	Bob Stanley	10	.05	.01
☐ 683	Dan Ford	10	.05	.01
☐ 684	Rafael Landestoy	10	.05	.01
☐ 685	Lee Mazzilli	10	.05	.01
☐ 686	Randy Lerch	10	.05	.01
☐ 687	U.L. Washington	10	.05	.01
☐ 688	Jim Wohlford	10	.05	.01
☐ 689	Ron Hassey	10	.05	.01
☐ 690	Kent Hrbek	75	.35	.09
☐ 691	Dave Tobik	10	.05	.01
☐ 692	Denny Walling	10	.05	.01
☐ 693	Sparky Lyle	15	.07	.02
☐ 694	SV: Sparky Lyle	10	.05	.01
☐ 695	Ruppert Jones	10	.05	.01
☐ 696	Chuck Tanner MG	10	.05	.01
☐ 697	Barry Foote	10	.05	.01
☐ 698	Tony Bernazard	10	.05	.01
☐ 699	Lee Smith	3.00	1.35	.40
☐ 700	Keith Hernandez	30	.14	.04
☐ 701	Batting Leaders	20	.09	.03
	AL: Willie Wilson			
	NL: Al Oliver			
☐ 702	Home Run Leaders	30	.14	.04
	AL: Reggie Jackson			
	AL: Gorman Thomas			
	NL: Dave Kingman			
☐ 703	RBI Leaders	20	.09	.03
	AL: Hal McRae			
	NL: Dale Murphy			
	NL: Al Oliver			
☐ 704	SB Leaders	1.00	.45	.13
	AL: Rickey Henderson			
	NL: Tim Raines			
☐ 705	Victory Leaders	25	.11	.03
	AL: LaMarr Hoyt			
	NL: Steve Carlton			
☐ 706	Strikeout Leaders	20	.09	.03
	AL: Floyd Bannister			

	NL: Steve Carlton			
☐ 707	ERA Leaders	20	.09	.03
	AL: Rick Sutcliffe			
	NL: Steve Rogers			
☐ 708	Leading Firemen	20	.09	.03
	AL: Dan Quisenberry			
	NL: Bruce Sutter			
☐ 709	Jimmy Sexton	10	.05	.01
☐ 710	Willie Wilson	15	.07	.02
☐ 711	Mariners TL	15	.07	.02
	BA: Bruce Bochte			
	ERA: Jim Beattie			
☐ 712	Bruce Kison	10	.05	.01
☐ 713	Ron Hodges	10	.05	.01
☐ 714	Wayne Nordhagen	10	.05	.01
☐ 715	Tony Perez	40	.18	.05
☐ 716	SV: Tony Perez	20	.09	.03
☐ 717	Scott Sanderson	10	.05	.01
☐ 718	Jim Dwyer	10	.05	.01
☐ 719	Rich Gale	10	.05	.01
☐ 720	Dave Concepcion	15	.07	.02
☐ 721	John Martin	10	.05	.01
☐ 722	Jorge Orta	10	.05	.01
☐ 723	Randy Moffitt	10	.05	.01
☐ 724	Johnny Grubb	10	.05	.01
☐ 725	Dan Spillner	10	.05	.01
☐ 726	Harvey Kuenn MG	15	.07	.02
☐ 727	Chet Lemon	10	.05	.01
☐ 728	Ron Reed	10	.05	.01
☐ 729	Jerry Morales	10	.05	.01
☐ 730	Jason Thompson	10	.05	.01
☐ 731	Al Williams	10	.05	.01
☐ 732	Dave Henderson	40	.18	.05
☐ 733	Buck Martinez	10	.05	.01
☐ 734	Steve Braun	10	.05	.01
☐ 735	Tommy John	20	.09	.03
☐ 736	SV: Tommy John	15	.07	.02
☐ 737	Mitchell Page	10	.05	.01
☐ 738	Tim Foli	10	.05	.01
☐ 739	Rick Ownbey	10	.05	.01
☐ 740	Rusty Staub	15	.07	.02
☐ 741	SV: Rusty Staub	10	.05	.01
☐ 742	Padres TL	15	.07	.02
	BA: Terry Kennedy			
	ERA: Tim Lollar			
☐ 743	Mike Torrez	10	.05	.01
☐ 744	Brad Mills	10	.05	.01
☐ 745	Scott McGregor	10	.05	.01
☐ 746	John Wathan	10	.05	.01
☐ 747	Fred Breining	10	.05	.01
☐ 748	Derrel Thomas	10	.05	.01
☐ 749	Jon Matlack	10	.05	.01
☐ 750	Ben Oglivie	10	.05	.01
☐ 751	Brad Havens	10	.05	.01
☐ 752	Luis Pujols	10	.05	.01
☐ 753	Elias Sosa	10	.05	.01
☐ 754	Bill Robinson	15	.07	.02

☐ 755 John Candelaria	.10	.05	.01
☐ 756 Russ Nixon MG	.10	.05	.01
☐ 757 Rick Manning	.10	.05	.01
☐ 758 Aurelio Rodriguez	.10	.05	.01
☐ 759 Doug Bird	.10	.05	.01
☐ 760 Dale Murphy	1.25	.55	.16
☐ 761 Gary Lucas	.10	.05	.01
☐ 762 Cliff Johnson	.10	.05	.01
☐ 763 Al Cowens	.10	.05	.01
☐ 764 Pete Falcone	.10	.05	.01
☐ 765 Bob Boone	.15	.07	.02
☐ 766 Barry Bonnell	.10	.05	.01
☐ 767 Duane Kuiper	.10	.05	.01
☐ 768 Chris Speier	.10	.05	.01
☐ 769 Checklist: 661-792	.15	.02	.00
☐ 770 Dave Winfield	3.00	1.35	.40
☐ 771 Twins TL	.15	.07	.02
BA: Kent Hrbek			
ERA: Bobby Castillo			
☐ 772 Jim Kern	.10	.05	.01
☐ 773 Larry Hisle	.10	.05	.01
☐ 774 Alan Ashby	.10	.05	.01
☐ 775 Burt Hooton	.10	.05	.01
☐ 776 Larry Parrish	.10	.05	.01
☐ 777 John Curtis	.10	.05	.01
☐ 778 Rich Hebner	.10	.05	.01
☐ 779 Rick Waits	.10	.05	.01
☐ 780 Gary Matthews	.15	.07	.02
☐ 781 Rick Rhoden	.10	.05	.01
☐ 782 Bobby Murcer	.15	.07	.02
☐ 783 SV: Bobby Murcer	.10	.05	.01
☐ 784 Jeff Newman	.10	.05	.01
☐ 785 Dennis Leonard	.10	.05	.01
☐ 786 Ralph Houk MG	.10	.05	.01
☐ 787 Dick Tidrow	.10	.05	.01
☐ 788 Dane Iorg	.10	.05	.01
☐ 789 Bryan Clark	.10	.05	.01
☐ 790 Bob Grich	.15	.07	.02
☐ 791 Gary Lavelle	.10	.05	.01
☐ 792 Chris Chambliss	.20	.09	.03

1983 Topps Traded

The cards in this 132-card set measure 2 1/2" by 3 1/2". For the third year in a row, Topps issued a 132-card Traded (or extended) set featuring some of the year's top rookies and players who had changed teams during the year, but were featured with their old team in the Topps regular issue of 1983. The cards were available through hobby dealers only and were print-

ed in Ireland by the Topps affiliate in that country. The set is numbered alphabetically by the last name of the player of the card. The Darryl Strawberry card number 108 can be found with either one or two asterisks (in the lower left corner of the reverse). The key (extended) Rookie Card in this set is obviously Darryl Strawberry. Also noteworthy is Julio Franco's first Topps (extended) card.

	NRMT-MT	EXC	G-VG
COMPLETE SET (132)	110.00	50.00	14.00
COMMON PLAYER (1T-132T)	.15	.07	.02

☐ 1T Neil Allen	.15	.07	.02
☐ 2T Bill Almon	.15	.07	.02
☐ 3T Joe Altobelli MG	.15	.07	.02
☐ 4T Tony Armas	.15	.07	.02
☐ 5T Doug Bair	.15	.07	.02
☐ 6T Steve Baker	.15	.07	.02
☐ 7T Floyd Bannister	.15	.07	.02
☐ 8T Don Baylor	.25	.11	.03
☐ 9T Tony Bernazard	.15	.07	.02
☐ 10T Larry Biittner	.15	.07	.02
☐ 11T Dann Bilardello	.15	.07	.02
☐ 12T Doug Bird	.15	.07	.02
☐ 13T Steve Boros MG	.15	.07	.02
☐ 14T Greg Brock	.25	.11	.03
☐ 15T Mike C. Brown	.15	.07	.02
(Red Sox pitcher)			
☐ 16T Tom Burgmeier	.15	.07	.02
☐ 17T Randy Bush	.25	.11	.03
☐ 18T Bert Campaneris	.25	.11	.03
☐ 19T Ron Cey	.25	.11	.03
☐ 20T Chris Codiroli	.15	.07	.02
☐ 21T Dave Collins	.15	.07	.02
☐ 22T Terry Crowley	.15	.07	.02
☐ 23T Julio Cruz	.15	.07	.02
☐ 24T Mike Davis	.15	.07	.02
☐ 25T Frank DiPino	.15	.07	.02
☐ 26T Bill Doran	.90	.40	.11
☐ 27T Jerry Dybzinski	.15	.07	.02

☐ 28T Jamie Easterly	.15	.07	.02
☐ 29T Juan Eichelberger	.15	.07	.02
☐ 30T Jim Essian	.15	.07	.02
☐ 31T Pete Falcone	.15	.07	.02
☐ 32T Mike Ferraro MG	.15	.07	.02
☐ 33T Terry Forster	.15	.07	.02
☐ 34T Julio Franco	9.00	4.00	1.15
☐ 35T Rich Gale	.15	.07	.02
☐ 36T Kiko Garcia	.15	.07	.02
☐ 37T Steve Garvey	1.50	.65	.19
☐ 38T Johnny Grubb	.15	.07	.02
☐ 39T Mel Hall	3.00	1.35	.40
☐ 40T Von Hayes	.25	.11	.03
☐ 41T Danny Heep	.15	.07	.02
☐ 42T Steve Henderson	.15	.07	.02
☐ 43T Keith Hernandez	.50	.23	.06
☐ 44T Leo Hernandez	.15	.07	.02
☐ 45T Willie Hernandez	.25	.11	.03
☐ 46T Al Holland	.15	.07	.02
☐ 47T Frank Howard MG	.25	.11	.03
☐ 48T Bobby Johnson	.15	.07	.02
☐ 49T Cliff Johnson	.15	.07	.02
☐ 50T Odell Jones	.15	.07	.02
☐ 51T Mike Jorgensen	.15	.07	.02
☐ 52T Bob Kearney	.15	.07	.02
☐ 53T Steve Kemp	.15	.07	.02
☐ 54T Matt Keough	.15	.07	.02
☐ 55T Ron Kittle	.25	.11	.03
☐ 56T Mickey Klutts	.15	.07	.02
☐ 57T Alan Knicely	.15	.07	.02
☐ 58T Mike Krukow	.15	.07	.02
☐ 59T Rafael Landestoy	.15	.07	.02
☐ 60T Carney Lansford	.25	.11	.03
☐ 61T Joe Lefebvre	.15	.07	.02
☐ 62T Bryan Little	.15	.07	.02
☐ 63T Aurelio Lopez	.15	.07	.02
☐ 64T Mike Madden	.15	.07	.02
☐ 65T Rick Manning	.15	.07	.02
☐ 66T Billy Martin MG	.25	.11	.03
☐ 67T Lee Mazzilli	.15	.07	.02
☐ 68T Andy McGaffigan	.15	.07	.02
☐ 69T Craig McMurtry	.15	.07	.02
☐ 70T John McNamara MG	.15	.07	.02
☐ 71T Orlando Mercado	.15	.07	.02
☐ 72T Larry Milbourne	.15	.07	.02
☐ 73T Randy Moffitt	.15	.07	.02
☐ 74T Sid Monge	.15	.07	.02
☐ 75T Jose Morales	.15	.07	.02
☐ 76T Omar Moreno	.15	.07	.02
☐ 77T Joe Morgan	2.50	1.15	.30
☐ 78T Mike Morgan	.75	.35	.09
☐ 79T Dale Murray	.15	.07	.02
☐ 80T Jeff Newman	.15	.07	.02
☐ 81T Pete O'Brien	.90	.40	.11
☐ 82T Jorge Orta	.15	.07	.02
☐ 83T Alejandro Pena	.75	.35	.09
☐ 84T Pascual Perez	.15	.07	.02
☐ 85T Tony Perez	1.50	.65	.19
☐ 86T Broderick Perkins	.15	.07	.02
☐ 87T Tony Phillips	3.00	1.35	.40
☐ 88T Charlie Puleo	.15	.07	.02
☐ 89T Pat Putnam	.15	.07	.02
☐ 90T Jamie Quirk	.15	.07	.02
☐ 91T Doug Rader MG	.15	.07	.02
☐ 92T Chuck Rainey	.15	.07	.02
☐ 93T Bobby Ramos	.15	.07	.02
☐ 94T Gary Redus	.60	.25	.08
☐ 95T Steve Renko	.15	.07	.02
☐ 96T Leon Roberts	.15	.07	.02
☐ 97T Aurelio Rodriguez	.15	.07	.02
☐ 98T Dick Ruthven	.15	.07	.02
☐ 99T Daryl Sconiers	.15	.07	.02
☐ 100T Mike Scott	.25	.11	.03
☐ 101T Tom Seaver	9.00	4.00	1.15
☐ 102T John Shelby	.25	.11	.03
☐ 103T Bob Shirley	.15	.07	.02
☐ 104T Joe Simpson	.15	.07	.02
☐ 105T Doug Sisk	.15	.07	.02
☐ 106T Mike Smithson	.25	.11	.03
☐ 107T Elias Sosa	.15	.07	.02
☐ 108T Darryl Strawberry	75.00	34.00	9.50
☐ 109T Tom Tellmann	.15	.07	.02
☐ 110T Gene Tenace	.15	.07	.02
☐ 111T Gorman Thomas	.25	.11	.03
☐ 112T Dick Tidrow	.15	.07	.02
☐ 113T Dave Tobik	.15	.07	.02
☐ 114T Wayne Tolleson	.15	.07	.02
☐ 115T Mike Torrez	.15	.07	.02
☐ 116T Manny Trillo	.15	.07	.02
☐ 117T Steve Trout	.15	.07	.02
☐ 118T Lee Tunnell	.15	.07	.02
☐ 119T Mike Vail	.15	.07	.02
☐ 120T Ellis Valentine	.15	.07	.02
☐ 121T Tom Veryzer	.15	.07	.02
☐ 122T George Vukovich	.15	.07	.02
☐ 123T Rick Waits	.15	.07	.02
☐ 124T Greg Walker	.25	.11	.03
☐ 125T Chris Welsh	.15	.07	.02
☐ 126T Len Whitehouse	.15	.07	.02
☐ 127T Eddie Whitson	.15	.07	.02
☐ 128T Jim Wohlford	.15	.07	.02
☐ 129T Matt Young	.25	.11	.03
☐ 130T Joel Youngblood	.15	.07	.02
☐ 131T Pat Zachry	.15	.07	.02
☐ 132T Checklist 1T-132T	.25	.03	.01

1984 Topps

The cards in this 792-card set measure 2 1/2" by 3 1/2". For the second year in a row, Topps utilized a dual picture on the front of the card. A portrait is shown in a square insert and an action shot is featured in the main photo. Card numbers 1-6 feature 1983 Highlights (HL), cards 131-138 depict League Leaders, card numbers 386-407 feature All-Stars, and card numbers 701-718 feature active Major League career leaders in various statistical categories. Each team leader (TL) card features the team's leading hitter and pitcher pictured on the front with a team checklist back. There are six numerical checklist cards in the set. The player cards feature team logos in the upper right corner of the reverse. The key Rookie Cards in this set are Don Mattingly, Darryl Strawberry, and Andy Van Slyke. Topps also produced a specially boxed "glossy" edition, frequently referred to as the Topps Tiffany set. There were supposedly only 10,000 sets of the Tiffany cards produced; they were marketed to hobby dealers. The checklist of cards (792 regular and 132 Traded) is identical to that of the normal non-glossy cards. There are two primary distinguishing features of the Tiffany cards, white card stock reverses and high gloss obverses. These Tiffany cards are valued approximately from five to ten times the values listed below. Topps tested a special send-in offer in Michigan and a few other states whereby collectors could obtain direct from Topps ten cards of their choice. Needless to say most people ordered the key (most valuable) players necessitating the printing

of a special sheet to keep up with the demand. The special sheet had five cards of Darryl Strawberry, three cards of Don Mattingly, etc. The test was apparently a failure in Topps' eyes as they have never tried it again.

	NRMT-MT	EXC	G-VG
COMPLETE SET (792)	85.00	38.00	10.50
COMMON PLAYER (1-792)	.08	.04	.01
☐ 1 HL: Steve Carlton 300th win and all-time SO king	.50	.10	.03
☐ 2 HL: Rickey Henderson 100 stolen bases, three times	1.00	.45	.13
☐ 3 HL: Dan Quisenberry Sets save record	.12	.05	.02
☐ 4 HL: Nolan Ryan, Steve Carlton, and Gaylord Perry (All surpass Johnson)	.60	.25	.08
☐ 5 HL: Dave Righetti, Bob Forsch, and Mike Warren (All pitch no-hitters)	.12	.05	.02
☐ 6 HL: Johnny Bench, Gaylord Perry, and Carl Yastrzemski (Superstars retire)	.40	.18	.05
☐ 7 Gary Lucas	.08	.04	.01
☐ 8 Don Mattingly	12.00	5.50	1.50
☐ 9 Jim Gott	.08	.04	.01
☐ 10 Robin Yount	2.00	.90	.25
☐ 11 Minnesota Twins TL Kent Hrbek Ken Schrom	.12	.05	.02
☐ 12 Billy Sample	.08	.04	.01
☐ 13 Scott Holman	.08	.04	.01
☐ 14 Tom Brookens	.08	.04	.01
☐ 15 Burt Hooton	.08	.04	.01
☐ 16 Omar Moreno	.08	.04	.01
☐ 17 John Denny	.08	.04	.01
☐ 18 Dale Berra	.08	.04	.01
☐ 19 Ray Fontenot	.08	.04	.01
☐ 20 Greg Luzinski	.12	.05	.02
☐ 21 Joe Altobelli MG	.08	.04	.01
☐ 22 Bryan Clark	.08	.04	.01
☐ 23 Keith Moreland	.08	.04	.01
☐ 24 John Martin	.08	.04	.01
☐ 25 Glenn Hubbard	.08	.04	.01
☐ 26 Bud Black	.08	.04	.01
☐ 27 Daryl Sconiers	.08	.04	.01
☐ 28 Frank Viola	.50	.23	.06
☐ 29 Danny Heep	.08	.04	.01
☐ 30 Wade Boggs	4.00	1.80	.50

☐ 31	Andy McGaffigan	.08	.04	.01
☐ 32	Bobby Ramos	.08	.04	.01
☐ 33	Tom Burgmeier	.08	.04	.01
☐ 34	Eddie Milner	.08	.04	.01
☐ 35	Don Sutton	.35	.16	.04
☐ 36	Denny Walling	.08	.04	.01
☐ 37	Texas Rangers TL	.12	.05	.02
	Buddy Bell			
	Rick Honeycutt			
☐ 38	Luis DeLeon	.08	.04	.01
☐ 39	Garth Iorg	.08	.04	.01
☐ 40	Dusty Baker	.12	.05	.02
☐ 41	Tony Bernazard	.08	.04	.01
☐ 42	Johnny Grubb	.08	.04	.01
☐ 43	Ron Reed	.08	.04	.01
☐ 44	Jim Morrison	.08	.04	.01
☐ 45	Jerry Mumphrey	.08	.04	.01
☐ 46	Ray Smith	.08	.04	.01
☐ 47	Rudy Law	.08	.04	.01
☐ 48	Julio Franco	1.00	.45	.13
☐ 49	John Stuper	.08	.04	.01
☐ 50	Chris Chambliss	.12	.05	.02
☐ 51	Jim Frey MG	.08	.04	.01
☐ 52	Paul Splittorff	.08	.04	.01
☐ 53	Juan Beniquez	.08	.04	.01
☐ 54	Jesse Orosco	.08	.04	.01
☐ 55	Dave Concepcion	.12	.05	.02
☐ 56	Gary Allenson	.08	.04	.01
☐ 57	Dan Schatzeder	.08	.04	.01
☐ 58	Max Venable	.08	.04	.01
☐ 59	Sammy Stewart	.08	.04	.01
☐ 60	Paul Molitor UER	.60	.25	.08
	('83 stats .272, 613,			
	167; should be .270,			
	608, 164)			
☐ 61	Chris Codiroli	.08	.04	.01
☐ 62	Dave Hostetler	.08	.04	.01
☐ 63	Ed VandeBerg	.08	.04	.01
☐ 64	Mike Scioscia	.12	.05	.02
☐ 65	Kirk Gibson	.25	.11	.03
☐ 66	Houston Astros TL	.40	.18	.05
	Jose Cruz			
	Nolan Ryan			
☐ 67	Gary Ward	.08	.04	.01
☐ 68	Luis Salazar	.08	.04	.01
☐ 69	Rod Scurry	.08	.04	.01
☐ 70	Gary Matthews	.12	.05	.02
☐ 71	Leo Hernandez	.08	.04	.01
☐ 72	Mike Squires	.08	.04	.01
☐ 73	Jody Davis	.08	.04	.01
☐ 74	Jerry Martin	.08	.04	.01
☐ 75	Bob Forsch	.08	.04	.01
☐ 76	Alfredo Griffin	.08	.04	.01
☐ 77	Brett Butler	.25	.11	.03
☐ 78	Mike Torrez	.08	.04	.01
☐ 79	Rob Wilfong	.08	.04	.01
☐ 80	Steve Rogers	.08	.04	.01
☐ 81	Billy Martin MG	.15	.07	.02
☐ 82	Doug Bird	.08	.04	.01
☐ 83	Richie Zisk	.08	.04	.01
☐ 84	Lenny Faedo	.08	.04	.01
☐ 85	Atlee Hammaker	.08	.04	.01
☐ 86	John Shelby	.08	.04	.01
☐ 87	Frank Pastore	.08	.04	.01
☐ 88	Rob Picciolo	.08	.04	.01
☐ 89	Mike Smithson	.08	.04	.01
☐ 90	Pedro Guerrero	.12	.05	.02
☐ 91	Dan Spillner	.08	.04	.01
☐ 92	Lloyd Moseby	.08	.04	.01
☐ 93	Bob Knepper	.08	.04	.01
☐ 94	Mario Ramirez	.08	.04	.01
☐ 95	Aurelio Lopez	.08	.04	.01
☐ 96	K.C. Royals TL	.12	.05	.02
	Hal McRae			
	Larry Gura			
☐ 97	LaMarr Hoyt	.08	.04	.01
☐ 98	Steve Nicosia	.08	.04	.01
☐ 99	Craig Lefferts	.25	.11	.03
☐ 100	Reggie Jackson	1.25	.55	.16
☐ 101	Porfirio Altamirano	.08	.04	.01
☐ 102	Ken Oberkfell	.08	.04	.01
☐ 103	Dwayne Murphy	.08	.04	.01
☐ 104	Ken Dayley	.08	.04	.01
☐ 105	Tony Armas	.08	.04	.01
☐ 106	Tim Stoddard	.08	.04	.01
☐ 107	Ned Yost	.08	.04	.01
☐ 108	Randy Moffitt	.08	.04	.01
☐ 109	Brad Wellman	.08	.04	.01
☐ 110	Ron Guidry	.12	.05	.02
☐ 111	Bill Virdon MG	.08	.04	.01
☐ 112	Tom Niedenfuer	.08	.04	.01
☐ 113	Kelly Paris	.08	.04	.01
☐ 114	Checklist 1-132	.12	.01	.00
☐ 115	Andre Thornton	.08	.04	.01
☐ 116	George Bjorkman	.08	.04	.01
☐ 117	Tom Veryzer	.08	.04	.01
☐ 118	Charlie Hough	.12	.05	.02
☐ 119	John Wockenfuss	.08	.04	.01
☐ 120	Keith Hernandez	.12	.05	.02
☐ 121	Pat Sheridan	.08	.04	.01
☐ 122	Cecilio Guante	.08	.04	.01
☐ 123	Butch Wynegar	.08	.04	.01
☐ 124	Damaso Garcia	.08	.04	.01
☐ 125	Britt Burns	.08	.04	.01
☐ 126	Atlanta Braves TL	.15	.07	.02
	Dale Murphy			
	Craig McMurtry			
☐ 127	Mike Madden	.08	.04	.01
☐ 128	Rick Manning	.08	.04	.01
☐ 129	Bill Laskey	.08	.04	.01
☐ 130	Ozzie Smith	1.25	.55	.16
☐ 131	Batting Leaders	.60	.25	.08
	Bill Madlock			
	Wade Boggs			

☐ 132	Home Run Leaders 30	.14	.04
	Mike Schmidt		
	Jim Rice		
☐ 133	RBI Leaders 20	.09	.03
	Dale Murphy		
	Cecil Cooper		
	Jim Rice		
☐ 134	Stolen Base Leaders 75	.35	.09
	Tim Raines		
	Rickey Henderson		
☐ 135	Victory Leaders 12	.05	.02
	John Denny		
	LaMarr Hoyt		
☐ 136	Strikeout Leaders............30	.14	.04
	Steve Carlton		
	Jack Morris		
☐ 137	ERA Leaders 12	.05	.02
	Atlee Hammaker		
	Rick Honeycutt		
☐ 138	Leading Firemen 12	.05	.02
	Al Holland		
	Dan Quisenberry		
☐ 139	Bert Campaneris 12	.05	.02
☐ 140	Storm Davis 08	.04	.01
☐ 141	Pat Corrales MG.............08	.04	.01
☐ 142	Rich Gale 08	.04	.01
☐ 143	Jose Morales 08	.04	.01
☐ 144	Brian Harper 75	.35	.09
☐ 145	Gary Lavelle 08	.04	.01
☐ 146	Ed Romero 08	.04	.01
☐ 147	Dan Petry 08	.04	.01
☐ 148	Joe Lefebvre 08	.04	.01
☐ 149	Jon Matlack 08	.04	.01
☐ 150	Dale Murphy 75	.35	.09
☐ 151	Steve Trout 08	.04	.01
☐ 152	Glenn Brummer 08	.04	.01
☐ 153	Dick Tidrow....................08	.04	.01
☐ 154	Dave Henderson 12	.05	.02
☐ 155	Frank White....................12	.05	.02
☐ 156	Oakland A's TL................25	.11	.03
	Rickey Henderson		
	Tim Conroy		
☐ 157	Gary Gaetti.....................12	.05	.02
☐ 158	John Curtis.....................08	.04	.01
☐ 159	Darryl Cias.....................08	.04	.01
☐ 160	Mario Soto 08	.04	.01
☐ 161	Junior Ortiz....................08	.04	.01
☐ 162	Bob Ojeda 08	.04	.01
☐ 163	Lorenzo Gray 08	.04	.01
☐ 164	Scott Sanderson 08	.04	.01
☐ 165	Ken Singleton 12	.05	.02
☐ 166	Jamie Nelson 08	.04	.01
☐ 167	Marshall Edwards 08	.04	.01
☐ 168	Juan Bonilla 08	.04	.01
☐ 169	Larry Parrish..................08	.04	.01
☐ 170	Jerry Reuss....................08	.04	.01
☐ 171	Frank Robinson MG........15	.07	.02

☐ 172	Frank DiPino 08	.04	.01
☐ 173	Marvell Wynne 08	.04	.01
☐ 174	Juan Berenguer..............08	.04	.01
☐ 175	Graig Nettles..................12	.05	.02
☐ 176	Lee Smith 75	.35	.09
☐ 177	Jerry Hairston................08	.04	.01
☐ 178	Bill Krueger 15	.07	.02
☐ 179	Buck Martinez 08	.04	.01
☐ 180	Manny Trillo 08	.04	.01
☐ 181	Roy Thomas 08	.04	.01
☐ 182	Darryl Strawberry 12.00	5.50	1.50
☐ 183	Al Williams.....................08	.04	.01
☐ 184	Mike O'Berry 08	.04	.01
☐ 185	Sixto Lezcano 08	.04	.01
☐ 186	Cardinal TL 12	.05	.02
	Lonnie Smith		
	John Stuper		
☐ 187	Luis Aponte 08	.04	.01
☐ 188	Bryan Little 08	.04	.01
☐ 189	Tim Conroy 08	.04	.01
☐ 190	Ben Oglivie....................08	.04	.01
☐ 191	Mike Boddicker...............08	.04	.01
☐ 192	Nick Esasky 12	.05	.02
☐ 193	Darrell Brown 08	.04	.01
☐ 194	Domingo Ramos..............08	.04	.01
☐ 195	Jack Morris....................1.00	.45	.13
☐ 196	Don Slaught 15	.07	.02
☐ 197	Garry Hancock 08	.04	.01
☐ 198	Bill Doran 20	.09	.03
☐ 199	Willie Hernandez 12	.05	.02
☐ 200	Andre Dawson 1.25	.55	.16
☐ 201	Bruce Kison 08	.04	.01
☐ 202	Bobby Cox MG................08	.04	.01
☐ 203	Matt Keough 08	.04	.01
☐ 204	Bobby Meacham..............08	.04	.01
☐ 205	Greg Minton 08	.04	.01
☐ 206	Andy Van Slyke 3.00	1.35	.40
☐ 207	Donnie Moore 08	.04	.01
☐ 208	Jose Oquendo 15	.07	.02
☐ 209	Manny Sarmiento............08	.04	.01
☐ 210	Joe Morgan 40	.18	.05
☐ 211	Rick Sweet.....................08	.04	.01
☐ 212	Broderick Perkins 08	.04	.01
☐ 213	Bruce Hurst....................12	.05	.02
☐ 214	Paul Householder............08	.04	.01
☐ 215	Tippy Martinez 08	.04	.01
☐ 216	White Sox TL..................15	.07	.02
	Carlton Fisk		
	Richard Dotson		
☐ 217	Alan Ashby 08	.04	.01
☐ 218	Rick Waits......................08	.04	.01
☐ 219	Joe Simpson 08	.04	.01
☐ 220	Fernando Valenzuela 12	.05	.02
☐ 221	Cliff Johnson..................08	.04	.01
☐ 222	Rick Honeycutt 08	.04	.01
☐ 223	Wayne Krenchicki............08	.04	.01
☐ 224	Sid Monge 08	.04	.01

☐ 225	Lee Mazzilli	.08	.04	.01
☐ 226	Juan Eichelberger	.08	.04	.01
☐ 227	Steve Braun	.08	.04	.01
☐ 228	John Rabb	.08	.04	.01
☐ 229	Paul Owens MG	.08	.04	.01
☐ 230	Rickey Henderson	4.00	1.80	.50
☐ 231	Gary Woods	.08	.04	.01
☐ 232	Tim Wallach	.12	.05	.02
☐ 233	Checklist 133-264	.12	.01	.00
☐ 234	Rafael Ramirez	.08	.04	.01
☐ 235	Matt Young	.08	.04	.01
☐ 236	Ellis Valentine	.08	.04	.01
☐ 237	John Castino	.08	.04	.01
☐ 238	Reid Nichols	.08	.04	.01
☐ 239	Jay Howell	.12	.05	.02
☐ 240	Eddie Murray	1.50	.65	.19
☐ 241	Bill Almon	.08	.04	.01
☐ 242	Alex Trevino	.08	.04	.01
☐ 243	Pete Ladd	.08	.04	.01
☐ 244	Candy Maldonado	.25	.11	.03
☐ 245	Rick Sutcliffe	.12	.05	.02
☐ 246	New York Mets TL	.20	.09	.03
	Mookie Wilson			
	Tom Seaver			
☐ 247	Onix Concepcion	.08	.04	.01
☐ 248	Bill Dawley	.08	.04	.01
☐ 249	Jay Johnstone	.12	.05	.02
☐ 250	Bill Madlock	.12	.05	.02
☐ 251	Tony Gwynn	5.00	2.30	.60
☐ 252	Larry Christenson	.08	.04	.01
☐ 253	Jim Wohlford	.08	.04	.01
☐ 254	Shane Rawley	.08	.04	.01
☐ 255	Bruce Benedict	.08	.04	.01
☐ 256	Dave Geisel	.08	.04	.01
☐ 257	Julio Cruz	.08	.04	.01
☐ 258	Luis Sanchez	.08	.04	.01
☐ 259	Sparky Anderson MG	.12	.05	.02
☐ 260	Scott McGregor	.08	.04	.01
☐ 261	Bobby Brown	.08	.04	.01
☐ 262	Tom Candiotti	.50	.23	.06
☐ 263	Jack Fimple	.08	.04	.01
☐ 264	Doug Frobel	.08	.04	.01
☐ 265	Donnie Hill	.08	.04	.01
☐ 266	Steve Lubratich	.08	.04	.01
☐ 267	Carmelo Martinez	.12	.05	.02
☐ 268	Jack O'Connor	.08	.04	.01
☐ 269	Aurelio Rodriguez	.08	.04	.01
☐ 270	Jeff Russell	.30	.14	.04
☐ 271	Moose Haas	.08	.04	.01
☐ 272	Rick Dempsey	.12	.05	.02
☐ 273	Charlie Puleo	.08	.04	.01
☐ 274	Rick Monday	.08	.04	.01
☐ 275	Len Matuszek	.08	.04	.01
☐ 276	Angels TL	.15	.07	.02
	Rod Carew			
	Geoff Zahn			
☐ 277	Eddie Whitson	.08	.04	.01
☐ 278	Jorge Bell	.75	.35	.09
☐ 279	Ivan DeJesus	.08	.04	.01
☐ 280	Floyd Bannister	.08	.04	.01
☐ 281	Larry Milbourne	.08	.04	.01
☐ 282	Jim Barr	.08	.04	.01
☐ 283	Larry Biittner	.08	.04	.01
☐ 284	Howard Bailey	.08	.04	.01
☐ 285	Darrell Porter	.08	.04	.01
☐ 286	Lary Sorensen	.08	.04	.01
☐ 287	Warren Cromartie	.08	.04	.01
☐ 288	Jim Beattie	.08	.04	.01
☐ 289	Randy Johnson	.08	.04	.01
☐ 290	Dave Dravecky	.08	.01	.00
☐ 291	Chuck Tanner MG	.08	.04	.01
☐ 292	Tony Scott	.08	.04	.01
☐ 293	Ed Lynch	.08	.04	.01
☐ 294	U.L. Washington	.08	.04	.01
☐ 295	Mike Flanagan	.08	.04	.01
☐ 296	Jeff Newman	.08	.04	.01
☐ 297	Bruce Berenyi	.08	.04	.01
☐ 298	Jim Gantner	.12	.05	.02
☐ 299	John Butcher	.08	.04	.01
☐ 300	Pete Rose	1.25	.55	.16
☐ 301	Frank LaCorte	.08	.04	.01
☐ 302	Barry Bonnell	.08	.04	.01
☐ 303	Marty Castillo	.08	.04	.01
☐ 304	Warren Brusstar	.08	.04	.01
☐ 305	Roy Smalley	.08	.04	.01
☐ 306	Dodgers TL	.12	.05	.02
	Pedro Guerrero			
	Bob Welch			
☐ 307	Bobby Mitchell	.08	.04	.01
☐ 308	Ron Hassey	.08	.04	.01
☐ 309	Tony Phillips	.60	.25	.08
☐ 310	Willie McGee	.30	.14	.04
☐ 311	Jerry Koosman	.12	.05	.02
☐ 312	Jorge Orta	.08	.04	.01
☐ 313	Mike Jorgensen	.08	.04	.01
☐ 314	Orlando Mercado	.08	.04	.01
☐ 315	Bob Grich	.12	.05	.02
☐ 316	Mark Bradley	.08	.04	.01
☐ 317	Greg Pryor	.08	.04	.01
☐ 318	Bill Gullickson	.12	.05	.02
☐ 319	Al Bumbry	.08	.04	.01
☐ 320	Bob Stanley	.08	.04	.01
☐ 321	Harvey Kuenn MG	.08	.01	.00
☐ 322	Ken Schrom	.08	.04	.01
☐ 323	Alan Knicely	.08	.04	.01
☐ 324	Alejandro Pena	.20	.09	.03
☐ 325	Darrell Evans	.12	.05	.02
☐ 326	Bob Kearney	.08	.04	.01
☐ 327	Ruppert Jones	.08	.04	.01
☐ 328	Vern Ruhle	.08	.04	.01
☐ 329	Pat Tabler	.08	.04	.01
☐ 330	John Candelaria	.08	.04	.01
☐ 331	Bucky Dent	.12	.05	.02
☐ 332	Kevin Gross	.15	.07	.02

☐ 333 Larry Herndon	.08	.04	.01
☐ 334 Chuck Rainey	.08	.04	.01
☐ 335 Don Baylor	.12	.05	.02
☐ 336 Seattle Mariners TL	.12	.05	.02
Pat Putnam			
Matt Young			
☐ 337 Kevin Hagen	.08	.04	.01
☐ 338 Mike Warren	.08	.04	.01
☐ 339 Roy Lee Jackson	.08	.04	.01
☐ 340 Hal McRae	.12	.05	.02
☐ 341 Dave Tobik	.08	.04	.01
☐ 342 Tim Foli	.08	.04	.01
☐ 343 Mark Davis	.12	.05	.02
☐ 344 Rick Miller	.08	.04	.01
☐ 345 Kent Hrbek	.30	.14	.04
☐ 346 Kurt Bevacqua	.08	.04	.01
☐ 347 Allan Ramirez	.08	.04	.01
☐ 348 Toby Harrah	.08	.04	.01
☐ 349 Bob L. Gibson	.08	.04	.01
(Brewers Pitcher)			
☐ 350 George Foster	.12	.05	.02
☐ 351 Russ Nixon MG	.08	.04	.01
☐ 352 Dave Stewart	.30	.14	.04
☐ 353 Jim Anderson	.08	.04	.01
☐ 354 Jeff Burroughs	.08	.04	.01
☐ 355 Jason Thompson	.08	.04	.01
☐ 356 Glenn Abbott	.08	.04	.01
☐ 357 Ron Cey	.12	.05	.02
☐ 358 Bob Dernier	.08	.04	.01
☐ 359 Jim Acker	.08	.04	.01
☐ 360 Willie Randolph	.12	.05	.02
☐ 361 Dave Smith	.08	.04	.01
☐ 362 David Green	.08	.04	.01
☐ 363 Tim Laudner	.08	.04	.01
☐ 364 Scott Fletcher	.08	.04	.01
☐ 365 Steve Bedrosian	.12	.05	.02
☐ 366 Padres TL	.12	.05	.02
Terry Kennedy			
Dave Dravecky			
☐ 367 Jamie Easterly	.08	.04	.01
☐ 368 Hubie Brooks	.12	.05	.02
☐ 369 Steve McCatty	.08	.04	.01
☐ 370 Tim Raines	.40	.18	.05
☐ 371 Dave Gumpert	.08	.04	.01
☐ 372 Gary Roenicke	.08	.04	.01
☐ 373 Bill Scherrer	.08	.04	.01
☐ 374 Don Money	.08	.04	.01
☐ 375 Dennis Leonard	.08	.04	.01
☐ 376 Dave Anderson	.12	.05	.02
☐ 377 Danny Darwin	.08	.04	.01
☐ 378 Bob Brenly	.08	.04	.01
☐ 379 Checklist 265-396	.12	.01	.00
☐ 380 Steve Garvey	.40	.18	.05
☐ 381 Ralph Houk MG	.12	.05	.02
☐ 382 Chris Nyman	.08	.04	.01
☐ 383 Terry Puhl	.08	.04	.01
☐ 384 Lee Tunnell	.08	.04	.01
☐ 385 Tony Perez	.25	.11	.03
☐ 386 George Hendrick AS	.12	.05	.02
☐ 387 Johnny Ray AS	.12	.05	.02
☐ 388 Mike Schmidt AS	.75	.35	.09
☐ 389 Ozzie Smith AS	.40	.18	.05
☐ 390 Tim Raines AS	.15	.07	.02
☐ 391 Dale Murphy AS	.25	.11	.03
☐ 392 Andre Dawson AS	.40	.18	.05
☐ 393 Gary Carter AS	.20	.09	.03
☐ 394 Steve Rogers AS	.12	.05	.02
☐ 395 Steve Carlton AS	.35	.16	.04
☐ 396 Jesse Orosco AS	.12	.05	.02
☐ 397 Eddie Murray AS	.40	.18	.05
☐ 398 Lou Whitaker AS	.15	.07	.02
☐ 399 George Brett AS	.65	.30	.08
☐ 400 Cal Ripken AS	2.00	.90	.25
☐ 401 Jim Rice AS	.12	.05	.02
☐ 402 Dave Winfield AS	.60	.25	.08
☐ 403 Lloyd Moseby AS	.12	.05	.02
☐ 404 Ted Simmons AS	.12	.05	.02
☐ 405 LaMarr Hoyt AS	.12	.05	.02
☐ 406 Ron Guidry AS	.12	.05	.02
☐ 407 Dan Quisenberry AS	.12	.05	.02
☐ 408 Lou Piniella	.12	.05	.02
☐ 409 Juan Agosto	.08	.04	.01
☐ 410 Claudell Washington	.08	.04	.01
☐ 411 Houston Jimenez	.08	.04	.01
☐ 412 Doug Rader MG	.08	.04	.01
☐ 413 Spike Owen	.15	.07	.02
☐ 414 Mitchell Page	.08	.04	.01
☐ 415 Tommy John	.12	.05	.02
☐ 416 Dane Iorg	.08	.04	.01
☐ 417 Mike Armstrong	.08	.04	.01
☐ 418 Ron Hodges	.08	.04	.01
☐ 419 John Henry Johnson	.08	.04	.01
☐ 420 Cecil Cooper	.12	.05	.02
☐ 421 Charlie Lea	.08	.04	.01
☐ 422 Jose Cruz	.12	.05	.02
☐ 423 Mike Morgan	.12	.05	.02
☐ 424 Dann Bilardello	.08	.04	.01
☐ 425 Steve Howe	.08	.04	.01
☐ 426 Orioles TL	1.00	.45	.13
Cal Ripken			
Mike Boddicker			
☐ 427 Rick Leach	.08	.04	.01
☐ 428 Fred Breining	.08	.04	.01
☐ 429 Randy Bush	.12	.05	.02
☐ 430 Rusty Staub	.12	.05	.02
☐ 431 Chris Bando	.08	.04	.01
☐ 432 Charles Hudson	.08	.04	.01
☐ 433 Rich Hebner	.08	.04	.01
☐ 434 Harold Baines	.25	.11	.03
☐ 435 Neil Allen	.08	.04	.01
☐ 436 Rick Peters	.08	.04	.01
☐ 437 Mike Proly	.08	.04	.01
☐ 438 Biff Pocoroba	.08	.04	.01
☐ 439 Bob Stoddard	.08	.04	.01

☐	440	Steve Kemp	.08	.04	.01			
☐	441	Bob Lillis MG	.08	.04	.01			
☐	442	Byron McLaughlin	.08	.04	.01			
☐	443	Benny Ayala	.08	.04	.01			
☐	444	Steve Renko	.08	.04	.01			
☐	445	Jerry Remy	.08	.04	.01			
☐	446	Luis Pujols	.08	.04	.01			
☐	447	Tom Brunansky	.12	.05	.02			
☐	448	Ben Hayes	.08	.04	.01			
☐	449	Joe Pettini	.08	.04	.01			
☐	450	Gary Carter	.60	.25	.08			
☐	451	Bob Jones	.08	.04	.01			
☐	452	Chuck Porter	.08	.04	.01			
☐	453	Willie Upshaw	.08	.04	.01			
☐	454	Joe Beckwith	.08	.04	.01			
☐	455	Terry Kennedy	.08	.04	.01			
☐	456	Chicago Cubs TL	.12	.05	.02			
		Keith Moreland						
		Fergie Jenkins						
☐	457	Dave Rozema	.08	.04	.01			
☐	458	Kiko Garcia	.08	.04	.01			
☐	459	Kevin Hickey	.08	.04	.01			
☐	460	Dave Winfield	1.75	.80	.22			
☐	461	Jim Maler	.08	.04	.01			
☐	462	Lee Lacy	.08	.04	.01			
☐	463	Dave Engle	.08	.04	.01			
☐	464	Jeff A. Jones	.08	.04	.01			
		(A's Pitcher)						
☐	465	Mookie Wilson	.12	.05	.02			
☐	466	Gene Garber	.08	.04	.01			
☐	467	Mike Ramsey	.08	.04	.01			
☐	468	Geoff Zahn	.08	.04	.01			
☐	469	Tom O'Malley	.08	.04	.01			
☐	470	Nolan Ryan	6.00	2.70	.75			
☐	471	Dick Howser MG	.08	.04	.01			
☐	472	Mike G. Brown	.08	.04	.01			
		(Red Sox Pitcher)						
☐	473	Jim Dwyer	.08	.04	.01			
☐	474	Greg Bargar	.08	.04	.01			
☐	475	Gary Redus	.15	.07	.02			
☐	476	Tom Tellmann	.08	.04	.01			
☐	477	Rafael Landestoy	.08	.04	.01			
☐	478	Alan Bannister	.08	.04	.01			
☐	479	Frank Tanana	.12	.05	.02			
☐	480	Ron Kittle	.12	.05	.02			
☐	481	Mark Thurmond	.08	.04	.01			
☐	482	Enos Cabell	.08	.04	.01			
☐	483	Fergie Jenkins	.35	.16	.04			
☐	484	Ozzie Virgil	.08	.04	.01			
☐	485	Rick Rhoden	.08	.04	.01			
☐	486	N.Y. Yankees TL	.12	.05	.02			
		Don Baylor						
		Ron Guidry						
☐	487	Ricky Adams	.08	.04	.01			
☐	488	Jesse Barfield	.12	.05	.02			
☐	489	Dave Von Ohlen	.08	.04	.01			
☐	490	Cal Ripken	8.00	3.60	1.00			
☐	491	Bobby Castillo	.08	.04	.01			
☐	492	Tucker Ashford	.08	.04	.01			
☐	493	Mike Norris	.08	.04	.01			
☐	494	Chili Davis	.12	.05	.02			
☐	495	Rollie Fingers	.40	.18	.05			
☐	496	Terry Francona	.08	.04	.01			
☐	497	Bud Anderson	.08	.04	.01			
☐	498	Rich Gedman	.08	.04	.01			
☐	499	Mike Witt	.08	.04	.01			
☐	500	George Brett	2.00	.90	.25			
☐	501	Steve Henderson	.08	.04	.01			
☐	502	Joe Torre MG	.12	.05	.02			
☐	503	Elias Sosa	.08	.04	.01			
☐	504	Mickey Rivers	.08	.04	.01			
☐	505	Pete Vuckovich	.08	.04	.01			
☐	506	Ernie Whitt	.08	.04	.01			
☐	507	Mike LaCoss	.08	.04	.01			
☐	508	Mel Hall	.40	.18	.05			
☐	509	Brad Havens	.08	.04	.01			
☐	510	Alan Trammell	.40	.18	.05			
☐	511	Marty Bystrom	.08	.04	.01			
☐	512	Oscar Gamble	.08	.04	.01			
☐	513	Dave Beard	.08	.04	.01			
☐	514	Floyd Rayford	.08	.04	.01			
☐	515	Gorman Thomas	.08	.04	.01			
☐	516	Montreal Expos TL	.12	.05	.02			
		Al Oliver						
		Charlie Lea						
☐	517	John Moses	.08	.04	.01			
☐	518	Greg Walker	.12	.05	.02			
☐	519	Ron Davis	.08	.04	.01			
☐	520	Bob Boone	.12	.05	.02			
☐	521	Pete Falcone	.08	.04	.01			
☐	522	Dave Bergman	.08	.04	.01			
☐	523	Glenn Hoffman	.08	.04	.01			
☐	524	Carlos Diaz	.08	.04	.01			
☐	525	Willie Wilson	.12	.05	.02			
☐	526	Ron Oester	.08	.04	.01			
☐	527	Checklist 397-528	.12	.01	.00			
☐	528	Mark Brouhard	.08	.04	.01			
☐	529	Keith Atherton	.08	.04	.01			
☐	530	Dan Ford	.08	.04	.01			
☐	531	Steve Boros MG	.08	.04	.01			
☐	532	Eric Show	.08	.04	.01			
☐	533	Ken Landreaux	.08	.04	.01			
☐	534	Pete O'Brien	.20	.09	.03			
☐	535	Bo Diaz	.08	.04	.01			
☐	536	Doug Bair	.08	.04	.01			
☐	537	Johnny Ray	.08	.04	.01			
☐	538	Kevin Bass	.08	.04	.01			
☐	539	George Frazier	.08	.04	.01			
☐	540	George Hendrick	.08	.04	.01			
☐	541	Dennis Lamp	.08	.04	.01			
☐	542	Duane Kuiper	.08	.04	.01			
☐	543	Craig McMurtry	.08	.04	.01			
☐	544	Cesar Geronimo	.08	.04	.01			
☐	545	Bill Buckner	.12	.05	.02			

☐ 546	Indians TL 12	.05	.02
	Mike Hargrove		
	Lary Sorensen		
☐ 547	Mike Moore 15	.07	.02
☐ 548	Ron Jackson 08	.04	.01
☐ 549	Walt Terrell 12	.05	.02
☐ 550	Jim Rice 15	.07	.02
☐ 551	Scott Ullger 08	.04	.01
☐ 552	Ray Burris 08	.04	.01
☐ 553	Joe Nolan 08	.04	.01
☐ 554	Ted Power 08	.04	.01
☐ 555	Greg Brock 08	.04	.01
☐ 556	Joey McLaughlin 08	.04	.01
☐ 557	Wayne Tolleson 08	.04	.01
☐ 558	Mike Davis 08	.04	.01
☐ 559	Mike Scott 12	.05	.02
☐ 560	Carlton Fisk 1.25	.55	.16
☐ 561	Whitey Herzog MG 08	.04	.01
☐ 562	Manny Castillo 08	.04	.01
☐ 563	Glenn Wilson 08	.04	.01
☐ 564	Al Holland 08	.04	.01
☐ 565	Leon Durham 08	.04	.01
☐ 566	Jim Bibby 08	.04	.01
☐ 567	Mike Heath 08	.04	.01
☐ 568	Pete Filson 08	.04	.01
☐ 569	Bake McBride 08	.04	.01
☐ 570	Dan Quisenberry 12	.05	.02
☐ 571	Bruce Bochy 08	.04	.01
☐ 572	Jerry Royster 08	.04	.01
☐ 573	Dave Kingman 12	.05	.02
☐ 574	Brian Downing 12	.05	.02
☐ 575	Jim Clancy 08	.04	.01
☐ 576	Giants TL 12	.05	.02
	Jeff Leonard		
	Atlee Hammaker		
☐ 577	Mark Clear 08	.04	.01
☐ 578	Lenn Sakata 08	.04	.01
☐ 579	Bob James 08	.04	.01
☐ 580	Lonnie Smith 12	.05	.02
☐ 581	Jose DeLeon 12	.05	.02
☐ 582	Bob McClure 08	.04	.01
☐ 583	Derrel Thomas 08	.04	.01
☐ 584	Dave Schmidt 08	.04	.01
☐ 585	Dan Driessen 08	.04	.01
☐ 586	Joe Niekro 12	.05	.02
☐ 587	Von Hayes 12	.05	.02
☐ 588	Milt Wilcox 08	.04	.01
☐ 589	Mike Easler 08	.04	.01
☐ 590	Dave Stieb 12	.05	.02
☐ 591	Tony LaRussa MG 12	.05	.02
☐ 592	Andre Robertson 08	.04	.01
☐ 593	Jeff Lahti 08	.04	.01
☐ 594	Gene Richards 08	.04	.01
☐ 595	Jeff Reardon 75	.35	.09
☐ 596	Ryne Sandberg 8.00	3.60	1.00
☐ 597	Rick Camp 08	.04	.01
☐ 598	Rusty Kuntz 08	.04	.01

☐ 599	Doug Sisk 08	.04	.01
☐ 600	Rod Carew 1.25	.55	.16
☐ 601	John Tudor 12	.05	.02
☐ 602	John Wathan 08	.04	.01
☐ 603	Renie Martin 08	.04	.01
☐ 604	John Lowenstein 08	.04	.01
☐ 605	Mike Caldwell 08	.04	.01
☐ 606	Blue Jays TL 12	.05	.02
	Lloyd Moseby		
	Dave Stieb		
☐ 607	Tom Hume 08	.04	.01
☐ 608	Bobby Johnson 08	.04	.01
☐ 609	Dan Meyer 08	.04	.01
☐ 610	Steve Sax 30	.14	.04
☐ 611	Chet Lemon 08	.04	.01
☐ 612	Harry Spilman 08	.04	.01
☐ 613	Greg Gross 08	.04	.01
☐ 614	Len Barker 08	.04	.01
☐ 615	Garry Templeton 12	.05	.02
☐ 616	Don Robinson 08	.04	.01
☐ 617	Rick Cerone 08	.04	.01
☐ 618	Dickie Noles 08	.04	.01
☐ 619	Jerry Dybzinski 08	.04	.01
☐ 620	Al Oliver 12	.05	.02
☐ 621	Frank Howard MG 08	.04	.01
☐ 622	Al Cowens 08	.04	.01
☐ 623	Ron Washington 08	.04	.01
☐ 624	Terry Harper 08	.04	.01
☐ 625	Larry Gura 08	.04	.01
☐ 626	Bob Clark 08	.04	.01
☐ 627	Dave LaPoint 12	.05	.02
☐ 628	Ed Jurak 08	.04	.01
☐ 629	Rick Langford 08	.04	.01
☐ 630	Ted Simmons 12	.05	.02
☐ 631	Dennis Martinez 12	.05	.02
☐ 632	Tom Foley 08	.04	.01
☐ 633	Mike Krukow 08	.04	.01
☐ 634	Mike Marshall 12	.05	.02
☐ 635	Dave Righetti 12	.05	.02
☐ 636	Pat Putnam 08	.04	.01
☐ 637	Phillies TL 12	.05	.02
	Gary Matthews		
	John Denny		
☐ 638	George Vukovich 08	.04	.01
☐ 639	Rick Lysander 08	.04	.01
☐ 640	Lance Parrish 15	.07	.02
☐ 641	Mike Richardt 08	.04	.01
☐ 642	Tom Underwood 08	.04	.01
☐ 643	Mike C. Brown 08	.04	.01
	(Angels OF)		
☐ 644	Tim Lollar 08	.04	.01
☐ 645	Tony Pena 12	.05	.02
☐ 646	Checklist 529-660 12	.01	.00
☐ 647	Ron Roenicke 08	.04	.01
☐ 648	Len Whitehouse 08	.04	.01
☐ 649	Tom Herr 12	.05	.02
☐ 650	Phil Niekro 35	.16	.04

☐ 651	John McNamara MG.......08	.04	.01
☐ 652	Rudy May 08	.04	.01
☐ 653	Dave Stapleton..............08	.04	.01
☐ 654	Bob Bailor.....................08	.04	.01
☐ 655	Amos Otis 08	.04	.01
☐ 656	Bryn Smith....................08	.04	.01
☐ 657	Thad Bosley 08	.04	.01
☐ 658	Jerry Augustine.............08	.04	.01
☐ 659	Duane Walker 08	.04	.01
☐ 660	Ray Knight 12	.05	.02
☐ 661	Steve Yeager.................08	.04	.01
☐ 662	Tom Brennan 08	.04	.01
☐ 663	Johnnie LeMaster..........08	.04	.01
☐ 664	Dave Stegman................08	.04	.01
☐ 665	Buddy Bell.....................12	.05	.02
☐ 666	Detroit Tigers TL 20	.09	.03
	Lou Whitaker		
	Jack Morris		
☐ 667	Vance Law.....................08	.04	.01
☐ 668	Larry McWilliams...........08	.04	.01
☐ 669	Dave Lopes 12	.05	.02
☐ 670	Rich Gossage.................15	.07	.02
☐ 671	Jamie Quirk...................08	.04	.01
☐ 672	Ricky Nelson 08	.04	.01
☐ 673	Mike Walters..................08	.04	.01
☐ 674	Tim Flannery 08	.04	.01
☐ 675	Pascual Perez 08	.04	.01
☐ 676	Brian Giles 08	.04	.01
☐ 677	Doyle Alexander.............08	.04	.01
☐ 678	Chris Speier 08	.04	.01
☐ 679	Art Howe.......................08	.04	.01
☐ 680	Fred Lynn......................12	.05	.02
☐ 681	Tom Lasorda MG 12	.05	.02
☐ 682	Dan Morogiello...............08	.04	.01
☐ 683	Marty Barrett.................12	.05	.02
☐ 684	Bob Shirley 08	.04	.01
☐ 685	Willie Aikens 08	.04	.01
☐ 686	Joe Price.......................08	.04	.01
☐ 687	Roy Howell 08	.04	.01
☐ 688	George Wright 08	.04	.01
☐ 689	Mike Fischlin.................08	.04	.01
☐ 690	Jack Clark 12	.05	.02
☐ 691	Steve Lake 08	.04	.01
☐ 692	Dickie Thon...................08	.04	.01
☐ 693	Alan Wiggins.................08	.04	.01
☐ 694	Mike Stanton.................08	.04	.01
☐ 695	Lou Whitaker 40	.18	.05
☐ 696	Pirates TL 12	.05	.02
	Bill Madlock		
	Rick Rhoden		
☐ 697	Dale Murray 08	.04	.01
☐ 698	Marc Hill.......................08	.04	.01
☐ 699	Dave Rucker 08	.04	.01
☐ 700	Mike Schmidt...........2.50	1.15	.30
☐ 701	NL Active Batting 15	.07	.02
	Bill Madlock		
	Pete Rose		

	Dave Parker		
☐ 702	NL Active Hits................15	.07	.02
	Pete Rose		
	Rusty Staub		
	Tony Perez		
☐ 703	NL Active Home Run......15	.07	.02
	Mike Schmidt		
	Tony Perez		
	Dave Kingman		
☐ 704	NL Active RBI................12	.05	.02
	Tony Perez		
	Rusty Staub		
	Al Oliver		
☐ 705	NL Active Steals............12	.05	.02
	Joe Morgan		
	Cesar Cedeno		
	Larry Bowa		
☐ 706	NL Active Victory 25	.11	.03
	Steve Carlton		
	Fergie Jenkins		
	Tom Seaver		
☐ 707	NL Active Strikeout.........75	.35	.09
	Steve Carlton		
	Nolan Ryan		
	Tom Seaver		
☐ 708	NL Active ERA...............20	.09	.03
	Tom Seaver		
	Steve Carlton		
	Steve Rogers		
☐ 709	NL Active Save..............12	.05	.02
	Bruce Sutter		
	Tug McGraw		
	Gene Garber		
☐ 710	AL Active Batting 20	.09	.03
	Rod Carew		
	George Brett		
	Cecil Cooper		
☐ 711	AL Active Hits 20	.09	.03
	Rod Carew		
	Bert Campaneris		
	Reggie Jackson		
☐ 712	AL Active Home Run.......20	.09	.03
	Reggie Jackson		
	Graig Nettles		
	Greg Luzinski		
☐ 713	AL Active RBI................20	.09	.03
	Reggie Jackson		
	Ted Simmons		
	Graig Nettles		
☐ 714	AL Active Steals.............12	.05	.02
	Bert Campaneris		
	Dave Lopes		
	Omar Moreno		
☐ 715	AL Active Victory 15	.07	.02
	Jim Palmer		
	Don Sutton		
	Tommy John		

☐	716	AL Active Strikeout 12	.05	.02
		Don Sutton		
		Bert Blyleven		
		Jerry Koosman		
☐	717	AL Active ERA 15	.07	.02
		Jim Palmer		
		Rollie Fingers		
		Ron Guidry		
☐	718	AL Active Save 15	.07	.02
		Rollie Fingers		
		Rich Gossage		
		Dan Quisenberry		
☐	719	Andy Hassler 08	.04	.01
☐	720	Dwight Evans 20	.09	.03
☐	721	Del Crandall MG 08	.04	.01
☐	722	Bob Welch 15	.07	.02
☐	723	Rich Dauer 08	.04	.01
☐	724	Eric Rasmussen 08	.04	.01
☐	725	Cesar Cedeno 12	.05	.02
☐	726	Brewers TL 12	.05	.02
		Ted Simmons		
		Moose Haas		
☐	727	Joel Youngblood 08	.04	.01
☐	728	Tug McGraw ,.................12	.05	.02
☐	729	Gene Tenace 08	.04	.01
☐	730	Bruce Sutter 12	.05	.02
☐	731	Lynn Jones 08	.04	.01
☐	732	Terry Crowley 08	.04	.01
☐	733	Dave Collins 08	.04	.01
☐	734	Odell Jones 08	.04	.01
☐	735	Rick Burleson 08	.04	.01
☐	736	Dick Ruthven 08	.04	.01
☐	737	Jim Essian 08	.04	.01
☐	738	Bill Schroeder 08	.04	.01
☐	739	Bob Watson 12	.05	.02
☐	740	Tom Seaver 1.25	.55	.16
☐	741	Wayne Gross 08	.04	.01
☐	742	Dick Williams MG 08	.04	.01
☐	743	Don Hood 08	.04	.01
☐	744	Jamie Allen 08	.04	.01
☐	745	Dennis Eckersley 1.00	.45	.13
☐	746	Mickey Hatcher 08	.04	.01
☐	747	Pat Zachry 08	.04	.01
☐	748	Jeff Leonard 08	.04	.01
☐	749	Doug Flynn 08	.04	.01
☐	750	Jim Palmer 1.25	.55	.16
☐	751	Charlie Moore 08	.04	.01
☐	752	Phil Garner 12	.05	.02
☐	753	Doug Gwosdz 08	.04	.01
☐	754	Kent Tekulve 12	.05	.02
☐	755	Garry Maddox 08	.04	.01
☐	756	Reds TL 12	.05	.02
		Ron Oester		
		Mario Soto		
☐	757	Larry Bowa 12	.05	.02
☐	758	Bill Stein 08	.04	.01
☐	759	Richard Dotson 08	.04	.01

☐	760	Bob Horner 12	.05	.02
☐	761	John Montefusco 08	.04	.01
☐	762	Rance Mulliniks 08	.04	.01
☐	763	Craig Swan 08	.04	.01
☐	764	Mike Hargrove 12	.05	.02
☐	765	Ken Forsch 08	.04	.01
☐	766	Mike Vail 08	.04	.01
☐	767	Carney Lansford 12	.05	.02
☐	768	Champ Summers 08	.04	.01
☐	769	Bill Caudill 08	.04	.01
☐	770	Ken Griffey 12	.05	.02
☐	771	Billy Gardner MG 08	.04	.01
☐	772	Jim Slaton 08	.04	.01
☐	773	Todd Cruz 08	.04	.01
☐	774	Tom Gorman 08	.04	.01
☐	775	Dave Parker 25	.11	.03
☐	776	Craig Reynolds 08	.04	.01
☐	777	Tom Paciorek 12	.05	.02
☐	778	Andy Hawkins 12	.05	.02
☐	779	Jim Sundberg 12	.05	.02
☐	780	Steve Carlton 1.25	.55	.16
☐	781	Checklist 661-792 12	.01	.00
☐	782	Steve Balboni 08	.04	.01
☐	783	Luis Leal 08	.04	.01
☐	784	Leon Roberts 08	.04	.01
☐	785	Joaquin Andujar 08	.04	.01
☐	786	Red Sox TL 50	.23	.06
		Wade Boggs		
		Bob Ojeda		
☐	787	Bill Campbell 08	.04	.01
☐	788	Milt May 08	.04	.01
☐	789	Bert Blyleven 20	.09	.03
☐	790	Doug DeCinces 08	.04	.01
☐	791	Terry Forster 08	.04	.01
☐	792	Bill Russell 12	.05	.02

1984 Topps Traded

The cards in this 132-card set measure 2 1/2" by 3 1/2". In its now standard procedure, Topps issued its Traded (or extended) set for the fourth year in a row. Because all photos and statistics of its regular set for the year were developed during the fall and winter months of the preceding year, players who changed teams during the fall, winter, and spring months are portrayed with the teams they were with in 1983. The Traded set updates the shortcomings of the regular set by presenting the players with their proper teams for the current year. Several of 1984's top rookies

not contained in the regular set are pictured in the Traded set. The key (extended) Rookie Cards in this set are Alvin Davis, Dwight Gooden, Mark Langston, Jose Rijo, and Bret Saberhagen. Again this year, the Topps affiliate in Ireland printed the cards, and the cards were available through hobby channels only. Topps also produced a specially boxed "glossy" edition, frequently referred to as the Topps Traded Tiffany set. There were supposedly only 10,000 sets of the Tiffany cards produced; they were marketed to hobby dealers. The checklist of cards is identical to that of the normal non-glossy cards. There are two primary distinguishing features of the Tiffany cards, white card stock reverses and high gloss obverses. These Tiffany cards are valued approximately from five to ten times the values listed below. The set numbering is in alphabetical order by player's name.

	NRMT-MT	EXC	G-VG
COMPLETE SET (132)	90.00	40.00	11.50
COMMON PLAYER (1T-132T)	.20	.09	.03

		NRMT-MT	EXC	G-VG
☐ 1T	Willie Aikens	.20	.09	.03
☐ 2T	Luis Aponte	.20	.09	.03
☐ 3T	Mike Armstrong	.20	.09	.03
☐ 4T	Bob Bailor	.20	.09	.03
☐ 5T	Dusty Baker	.30	.14	.04
☐ 6T	Steve Balboni	.20	.09	.03
☐ 7T	Alan Bannister	.20	.09	.03
☐ 8T	Dave Beard	.20	.09	.03
☐ 9T	Joe Beckwith	.20	.09	.03
☐ 10T	Bruce Berenyi	.20	.09	.03
☐ 11T	Dave Bergman	.20	.09	.03
☐ 12T	Tony Bernazard	.20	.09	.03
☐ 13T	Yogi Berra MG	1.00	.45	.13
☐ 14T	Barry Bonnell	.20	.09	.03
☐ 15T	Phil Bradley	.30	.14	.04
☐ 16T	Fred Breining	.20	.09	.03
☐ 17T	Bill Buckner	.30	.14	.04
☐ 18T	Ray Burris	.20	.09	.03
☐ 19T	John Butcher	.20	.09	.03
☐ 20T	Brett Butler	1.00	.45	.13
☐ 21T	Enos Cabell	.20	.09	.03
☐ 22T	Bill Campbell	.20	.09	.03
☐ 23T	Bill Caudill	.20	.09	.03
☐ 24T	Bob Clark	.20	.09	.03
☐ 25T	Bryan Clark	.20	.09	.03
☐ 26T	Jaime Cocanower	.20	.09	.03
☐ 27T	Ron Darling	3.50	1.55	.45
☐ 28T	Alvin Davis	.75	.35	.09
☐ 29T	Ken Dayley	.20	.09	.03
☐ 30T	Jeff Dedmon	.20	.09	.03
☐ 31T	Bob Dernier	.20	.09	.03
☐ 32T	Carlos Diaz	.20	.09	.03
☐ 33T	Mike Easler	.20	.09	.03
☐ 34T	Dennis Eckersley	7.00	3.10	.85
☐ 35T	Jim Essian	.20	.09	.03
☐ 36T	Darrell Evans	.30	.14	.04
☐ 37T	Mike Fitzgerald	.20	.09	.03
☐ 38T	Tim Foli	.20	.09	.03
☐ 39T	George Frazier	.20	.09	.03
☐ 40T	Rich Gale	.20	.09	.03
☐ 41T	Barbaro Garbey	.20	.09	.03
☐ 42T	Dwight Gooden	27.00	12.00	3.40
☐ 43T	Rich Gossage	.50	.23	.06
☐ 44T	Wayne Gross	.20	.09	.03
☐ 45T	Mark Gubicza	1.75	.80	.22
☐ 46T	Jackie Gutierrez	.20	.09	.03
☐ 47T	Mel Hall	.75	.35	.09
☐ 48T	Toby Harrah	.20	.09	.03
☐ 49T	Ron Hassey	.20	.09	.03
☐ 50T	Rich Hebner	.20	.09	.03
☐ 51T	Willie Hernandez	.30	.14	.04
☐ 52T	Ricky Horton	.20	.09	.03
☐ 53T	Art Howe	.20	.09	.03
☐ 54T	Dane Iorg	.20	.09	.03
☐ 55T	Brook Jacoby	.50	.23	.06
☐ 56T	Mike Jeffcoat	.20	.09	.03
☐ 57T	Dave Johnson MG	.30	.14	.04
☐ 58T	Lynn Jones	.20	.09	.03
☐ 59T	Ruppert Jones	.20	.09	.03
☐ 60T	Mike Jorgensen	.20	.09	.03
☐ 61T	Bob Kearney	.20	.09	.03
☐ 62T	Jimmy Key	5.00	2.30	.60
☐ 63T	Dave Kingman	.30	.14	.04
☐ 64T	Jerry Koosman	.30	.14	.04
☐ 65T	Wayne Krenchicki	.20	.09	.03
☐ 66T	Rusty Kuntz	.20	.09	.03
☐ 67T	Rene Lachemann MG	.20	.09	.03
☐ 68T	Frank LaCorte	.20	.09	.03
☐ 69T	Dennis Lamp	.20	.09	.03
☐ 70T	Mark Langston	9.00	4.00	1.15
☐ 71T	Rick Leach	.20	.09	.03
☐ 72T	Craig Lefferts	.50	.23	.06
☐ 73T	Gary Lucas	.20	.09	.03

☐	74T Jerry Martin 20	.09	.03
☐	75T Carmelo Martinez.........30	.14	.04
☐	76T Mike Mason 20	.09	.03
☐	77T Gary Matthews............30	.14	.04
☐	78T Andy McGaffigan 20	.09	.03
☐	79T Larry Milbourne 20	.09	.03
☐	80T Sid Monge 20	.09	.03
☐	81T Jackie Moore MG.........20	.09	.03
☐	82T Joe Morgan............3.50	1.55	.45
☐	83T Graig Nettles.............30	.14	.04
☐	84T Phil Niekro 3.00	1.35	.40
☐	85T Ken Oberkfell 20	.09	.03
☐	86T Mike O'Berry..............20	.09	.03
☐	87T Al Oliver 30	.14	.04
☐	88T Jorge Orta 20	.09	.03
☐	89T Amos Otis 30	.14	.04
☐	90T Dave Parker...........1.75	.80	.22
☐	91T Tony Perez 3.00	1.35	.40
☐	92T Gerald Perry 30	.14	.04
☐	93T Gary Pettis 30	.14	.04
☐	94T Rob Picciolo 20	.09	.03
☐	95T Vern Rapp MG 20	.09	.03
☐	96T Floyd Rayford 20	.09	.03
☐	97T Randy Ready..............30	.14	.04
☐	98T Ron Reed 20	.09	.03
☐	99T Gene Richards 20	.09	.03
☐	100T Jose Rijo...............10.00	4.50	1.25
☐	101T Jeff D. Robinson.........30	.14	.04
	(Giants pitcher)		
☐	102T Ron Romanick............20	.09	.03
☐	103T Pete Rose............9.00	4.00	1.15
☐	104T Bret Saberhagen 14.00	6.25	1.75
☐	105T Juan Samuel...........1.00	.45	.13
☐	106T Scott Sanderson.........20	.09	.03
☐	107T Dick Schofield 50	.23	.06
☐	108T Tom Seaver...........9.00	4.00	1.15
☐	109T Jim Slaton 20	.09	.03
☐	110T Mike Smithson...........20	.09	.03
☐	111T Lary Sorensen............20	.09	.03
☐	112T Tim Stoddard 20	.09	.03
☐	113T Champ Summers..........20	.09	.03
☐	114T Jim Sundberg............30	.14	.04
☐	115T Rick Sutcliffe............50	.23	.06
☐	116T Craig Swan 20	.09	.03
☐	117T Tim Teufel 50	.23	.06
☐	118T Derrel Thomas...........20	.09	.03
☐	119T Gorman Thomas..........20	.09	.03
☐	120T Alex Trevino 20	.09	.03
☐	121T Manny Trillo 20	.09	.03
☐	122T John Tudor...............30	.14	.04
☐	123T Tom Underwood..........20	.09	.03
☐	124T Mike Vail 20	.09	.03
☐	125T Tom Waddell.............20	.09	.03
☐	126T Gary Ward 20	.09	.03
☐	127T Curt Wilkerson 20	.09	.03
☐	128T Frank Williams...........20	.09	.03
☐	129T Glenn Wilson 20	.09	.03

☐	130T John Wockenfuss 20	.09	.03
☐	131T Ned Yost 20	.09	.03
☐	132T Checklist 1-132...........30	.03	.01

1985 Topps

The cards in this 792-card set measure 2 1/2" by 3 1/2". The 1985 Topps set contains full color cards. The fronts feature both the Topps and team logos along with the team name, player's name, and his position. The backs feature player statistics with ink colors of light green and maroon on a gray stock. A trivia quiz is included on the lower portion of the backs. The first ten cards (1-10) are Record Breakers (RB), cards 131-143 are Father and Son (FS) cards, and cards 701 to 722 portray All-Star selections (AS). Cards 271 to 282 represent "First Draft Picks" still active in professional baseball and cards 389-404 feature the coach and eligible (not returning to college) players on the 1984 U.S. Olympic Baseball Team. The manager cards in the set are important in that they contain the checklist of that team's players on the back. The key Rookie Cards in this set are Roger Clemens, Eric Davis, Shawon Dunston, Dwight Gooden, Orel Hershiser, Mark Langston, Shane Mack, Mark McGwire, Terry Pendleton, Kirby Puckett, Jose Rijo, and Bret Saberhagen. Topps also produced a specially boxed "glossy" edition, frequently referred to as the Topps Tiffany set. There were supposedly only 8,000 sets of the Tiffany cards produced; they were marketed to hobby dealers. The checklist of cards (792 regu-

lar and 132 Traded) is identical to that of the normal non-glossy cards. There are two primary distinguishing features of the Tiffany cards, white card stock reverses and high gloss obverses. These Tiffany cards are valued approximately from five to ten times the values listed below.

		NRMT-MT	EXC	G-VG
	COMPLETE SET (792)	100.00	45.00	12.50
	COMMON PLAYER (1-792)	.07	.03	.01
☐ 1	Carlton Fisk RB	.40	.10	.03
	Longest game by catcher			
☐ 2	Steve Garvey RB	.15	.07	.02
	Consecutive error-less games, 1B			
☐ 3	Dwight Gooden RB	.90	.40	.11
	Most strikeouts, rookie, season			
☐ 4	Cliff Johnson RB	.12	.05	.02
	Most pinch homers, lifetime			
☐ 5	Joe Morgan RB	.15	.07	.02
	Most homers, 2B, lifetime			
☐ 6	Pete Rose RB	.40	.18	.05
	Most singles, lifetime			
☐ 7	Nolan Ryan RB	1.25	.55	.16
	Most strikeouts, lifetime			
☐ 8	Juan Samuel RB	.12	.05	.02
	Most stolen bases, rookie, season			
☐ 9	Bruce Sutter RB	.12	.05	.02
	Most saves, season, NL			
☐ 10	Don Sutton RB	.15	.07	.02
	Most seasons, 100 or more K's			
☐ 11	Ralph Houk MG	.10		.01
	(Checklist back)			
☐ 12	Dave Lopes	.10	.05	.01
	(Now with Cubs on card front)			
☐ 13	Tim Lollar	.07	.03	.01
☐ 14	Chris Bando	.07	.03	.01
☐ 15	Jerry Koosman	.10	.05	.01
☐ 16	Bobby Meacham	.07	.03	.01
☐ 17	Mike Scott	.10	.05	.01
☐ 18	Mickey Hatcher	.07	.03	.01
☐ 19	George Frazier	.07	.03	.01
☐ 20	Chet Lemon	.07	.03	.01
☐ 21	Lee Tunnell	.07	.03	.01
☐ 22	Duane Kuiper	.07	.03	.01
☐ 23	Bret Saberhagen	2.00	.90	.25
☐ 24	Jesse Barfield	.10	.05	.01
☐ 25	Steve Bedrosian	.10	.05	.01
☐ 26	Roy Smalley	.07	.03	.01
☐ 27	Bruce Berenyi	.07	.03	.01
☐ 28	Dann Bilardello	.07	.03	.01
☐ 29	Odell Jones	.07	.03	.01
☐ 30	Cal Ripken	4.00	1.80	.50
☐ 31	Terry Whitfield	.07	.03	.01
☐ 32	Chuck Porter	.07	.03	.01
☐ 33	Tito Landrum	.07	.03	.01
☐ 34	Ed Nunez	.07	.03	.01
☐ 35	Graig Nettles	.10	.05	.01
☐ 36	Fred Breining	.07	.03	.01
☐ 37	Reid Nichols	.07	.03	.01
☐ 38	Jackie Moore MG	.10	.05	.01
	(Checklist back)			
☐ 39	John Wockenfuss	.07	.03	.01
☐ 40	Phil Niekro	.20	.09	.03
☐ 41	Mike Fischlin	.07	.03	.01
☐ 42	Luis Sanchez	.07	.03	.01
☐ 43	Andre David	.07	.03	.01
☐ 44	Dickie Thon	.07	.03	.01
☐ 45	Greg Minton	.07	.03	.01
☐ 46	Gary Woods	.07	.03	.01
☐ 47	Dave Rozema	.07	.03	.01
☐ 48	Tony Fernandez	.50	.23	.06
☐ 49	Butch Davis	.07	.03	.01
☐ 50	John Candelaria	.10	.05	.01
☐ 51	Bob Watson	.10	.05	.01
☐ 52	Jerry Dybzinski	.07	.03	.01
☐ 53	Tom Gorman	.07	.03	.01
☐ 54	Cesar Cedeno	.10	.05	.01
☐ 55	Frank Tanana	.10	.05	.01
☐ 56	Jim Dwyer	.07	.03	.01
☐ 57	Pat Zachry	.07	.03	.01
☐ 58	Orlando Mercado	.07	.03	.01
☐ 59	Rick Waits	.07	.03	.01
☐ 60	George Hendrick	.07	.03	.01
☐ 61	Curt Kaufman	.07	.03	.01
☐ 62	Mike Ramsey	.07	.03	.01
☐ 63	Steve McCatty	.07	.03	.01
☐ 64	Mark Bailey	.07	.03	.01
☐ 65	Bill Buckner	.10	.05	.01
☐ 66	Dick Williams MG	.10	.05	.01
	(Checklist back)			
☐ 67	Rafael Santana	.07	.03	.01
☐ 68	Von Hayes	.07	.03	.01
☐ 69	Jim Winn	.07	.03	.01
☐ 70	Don Baylor	.10	.05	.01
☐ 71	Tim Laudner	.07	.03	.01
☐ 72	Rick Sutcliffe	.10	.05	.01
☐ 73	Rusty Kuntz	.07	.03	.01
☐ 74	Mike Krukow	.07	.03	.01
☐ 75	Willie Upshaw	.07	.03	.01
☐ 76	Alan Bannister	.07	.03	.01
☐ 77	Joe Beckwith	.07	.03	.01

☐ 78 Scott Fletcher	07	.03	.01
☐ 79 Rick Mahler	07	.03	.01
☐ 80 Keith Hernandez	10	.05	.01
☐ 81 Lenn Sakata	07	.03	.01
☐ 82 Joe Price	07	.03	.01
☐ 83 Charlie Moore	07	.03	.01
☐ 84 Spike Owen	07	.03	.01
☐ 85 Mike Marshall	07	.03	.01
☐ 86 Don Aase	07	.03	.01
☐ 87 David Green	07	.03	.01
☐ 88 Bryn Smith	07	.03	.01
☐ 89 Jackie Gutierrez	07	.03	.01
☐ 90 Rich Gossage	10	.05	.01
☐ 91 Jeff Burroughs	07	.03	.01
☐ 92 Paul Owens MG	10	.05	.01
(Checklist back)			
☐ 93 Don Schulze	07	.03	.01
☐ 94 Toby Harrah	07	.03	.01
☐ 95 Jose Cruz	10	.05	.01
☐ 96 Johnny Ray	07	.03	.01
☐ 97 Pete Filson	07	.03	.01
☐ 98 Steve Lake	07	.03	.01
☐ 99 Milt Wilcox	07	.03	.01
☐ 100 George Brett	1.25	.55	.16
☐ 101 Jim Acker	07	.03	.01
☐ 102 Tommy Dunbar	07	.03	.01
☐ 103 Randy Lerch	07	.03	.01
☐ 104 Mike Fitzgerald	07	.03	.01
☐ 105 Ron Kittle	10	.05	.01
☐ 106 Pascual Perez	07	.03	.01
☐ 107 Tom Foley	07	.03	.01
☐ 108 Darnell Coles	10	.05	.01
☐ 109 Gary Roenicke	07	.03	.01
☐ 110 Alejandro Pena	07	.03	.01
☐ 111 Doug DeCinces	07	.03	.01
☐ 112 Tom Tellmann	07	.03	.01
☐ 113 Tom Herr	10	.05	.01
☐ 114 Bob James	07	.03	.01
☐ 115 Rickey Henderson	2.00	.90	.25
☐ 116 Dennis Boyd	07	.03	.01
☐ 117 Greg Gross	07	.03	.01
☐ 118 Eric Show	07	.03	.01
☐ 119 Pat Corrales MG	10	.05	.01
(Checklist back)			
☐ 120 Steve Kemp	07	.03	.01
☐ 121 Checklist: 1-132	12	.01	.00
☐ 122 Tom Brunansky	10	.05	.01
☐ 123 Dave Smith	07	.03	.01
☐ 124 Rich Hebner	07	.03	.01
☐ 125 Kent Tekulve	07	.03	.01
☐ 126 Ruppert Jones	07	.03	.01
☐ 127 Mark Gubicza	35	.16	.04
☐ 128 Ernie Whitt	07	.03	.01
☐ 129 Gene Garber	07	.03	.01
☐ 130 Al Oliver	10	.05	.01
☐ 131 Buddy/Gus Bell FS	10	.05	.01
☐ 132 Dale/Yogi Berra FS	15	.07	.02

☐ 133 Bob/Ray Boone FS	10	.05	.01
☐ 134 Terry/Tito Francona FS	10	.05	.01
☐ 135 Terry/Bob Kennedy FS	10	.05	.01
☐ 136 Jeff/Bill Kunkel FS	10	.05	.01
☐ 137 Vance/Vern Law FS	10	.05	.01
☐ 138 Dick/Dick Schofield FS	10	.05	.01
☐ 139 Joel/Bob Skinner FS	10	.05	.01
☐ 140 Roy/Roy Smalley FS	10	.05	.01
☐ 141 Mike/Dave Stenhouse FS	10	.05	.01
☐ 142 Steve/Dizzy Trout FS	10	.05	.01
☐ 143 Ozzie/Ossie Virgil FS	10	.05	.01
☐ 144 Ron Gardenhire	07	.03	.01
☐ 145 Alvin Davis	12	.05	.02
☐ 146 Gary Redus	07	.03	.01
☐ 147 Bill Swaggerty	07	.03	.01
☐ 148 Steve Yeager	07	.03	.01
☐ 149 Dickie Noles	07	.03	.01
☐ 150 Jim Rice	10	.05	.01
☐ 151 Moose Haas	07	.03	.01
☐ 152 Steve Braun	07	.03	.01
☐ 153 Frank LaCorte	07	.03	.01
☐ 154 Argenis Salazar	07	.03	.01
☐ 155 Yogi Berra MG	20	.09	.03
(Checklist back)			
☐ 156 Craig Reynolds	07	.03	.01
☐ 157 Tug McGraw	10	.05	.01
☐ 158 Pat Tabler	07	.03	.01
☐ 159 Carlos Diaz	07	.03	.01
☐ 160 Lance Parrish	10	.05	.01
☐ 161 Ken Schrom	07	.03	.01
☐ 162 Benny Distefano	07	.03	.01
☐ 163 Dennis Eckersley	50	.23	.06
☐ 164 Jorge Orta	07	.03	.01
☐ 165 Dusty Baker	10	.05	.01
☐ 166 Keith Atherton	07	.03	.01
☐ 167 Rufino Linares	07	.03	.01
☐ 168 Garth Iorg	07	.03	.01
☐ 169 Dan Spillner	07	.03	.01
☐ 170 George Foster	10	.05	.01
☐ 171 Bill Stein	07	.03	.01
☐ 172 Jack Perconte	07	.03	.01
☐ 173 Mike Young	07	.03	.01
☐ 174 Rick Honeycutt	07	.03	.01
☐ 175 Dave Parker	20	.09	.03
☐ 176 Bill Schroeder	07	.03	.01
☐ 177 Dave Von Ohlen	07	.03	.01
☐ 178 Miguel Dilone	07	.03	.01
☐ 179 Tommy John	10	.05	.01
☐ 180 Dave Winfield	1.25	.55	.16
☐ 181 Roger Clemens	25.00	11.50	3.10
☐ 182 Tim Flannery	07	.03	.01
☐ 183 Larry McWilliams	07	.03	.01
☐ 184 Carmen Castillo	07	.03	.01
☐ 185 Al Holland	07	.03	.01
☐ 186 Bob Lillis MG	10	.05	.01
(Checklist back)			
☐ 187 Mike Walters	07	.03	.01

☐ 188 Greg Pryor	.07	.03	.01
☐ 189 Warren Brusstar	.07	.03	.01
☐ 190 Rusty Staub	.10	.05	.01
☐ 191 Steve Nicosia	.07	.03	.01
☐ 192 Howard Johnson	1.50	.65	.19
☐ 193 Jimmy Key	.75	.35	.09
☐ 194 Dave Stegman	.07	.03	.01
☐ 195 Glenn Hubbard	.07	.03	.01
☐ 196 Pete O'Brien	.10	.05	.01
☐ 197 Mike Warren	.07	.03	.01
☐ 198 Eddie Milner	.07	.03	.01
☐ 199 Dennis Martinez	.10	.05	.01
☐ 200 Reggie Jackson	.75	.35	.09
☐ 201 Burt Hooton	.07	.03	.01
☐ 202 Gorman Thomas	.07	.03	.01
☐ 203 Bob McClure	.07	.03	.01
☐ 204 Art Howe	.07	.03	.01
☐ 205 Steve Rogers	.07	.03	.01
☐ 206 Phil Garner	.10	.05	.01
☐ 207 Mark Clear	.07	.03	.01
☐ 208 Champ Summers	.07	.03	.01
☐ 209 Bill Campbell	.07	.03	.01
☐ 210 Gary Matthews	.07	.03	.01
☐ 211 Clay Christiansen	.07	.03	.01
☐ 212 George Vukovich	.07	.03	.01
☐ 213 Billy Gardner MG	.10	.05	.01
(Checklist back)			
☐ 214 John Tudor	.10	.05	.01
☐ 215 Bob Brenly	.07	.03	.01
☐ 216 Jerry Don Gleaton	.07	.03	.01
☐ 217 Leon Roberts	.07	.03	.01
☐ 218 Doyle Alexander	.07	.03	.01
☐ 219 Gerald Perry	.07	.03	.01
☐ 220 Fred Lynn	.10	.05	.01
☐ 221 Ron Reed	.07	.03	.01
☐ 222 Hubie Brooks	.10	.05	.01
☐ 223 Tom Hume	.07	.03	.01
☐ 224 Al Cowens	.07	.03	.01
☐ 225 Mike Boddicker	.07	.03	.01
☐ 226 Juan Beniquez	.07	.03	.01
☐ 227 Danny Darwin	.07	.03	.01
☐ 228 Dion James	.07	.03	.01
☐ 229 Dave LaPoint	.07	.03	.01
☐ 230 Gary Carter	.35	.16	.04
☐ 231 Dwayne Murphy	.07	.03	.01
☐ 232 Dave Beard	.07	.03	.01
☐ 233 Ed Jurak	.07	.03	.01
☐ 234 Jerry Narron	.07	.03	.01
☐ 235 Garry Maddox	.07	.03	.01
☐ 236 Mark Thurmond	.07	.03	.01
☐ 237 Julio Franco	.35	.16	.04
☐ 238 Jose Rijo	1.50	.65	.19
☐ 239 Tim Teufel	.12	.05	.02
☐ 240 Dave Stieb	.10	.05	.01
☐ 241 Jim Frey MG	.10	.05	.01
(Checklist back)			
☐ 242 Greg Harris	.07	.03	.01

☐ 243 Barbaro Garbey	.07	.03	.01
☐ 244 Mike Jones	.07	.03	.01
☐ 245 Chili Davis	.10	.05	.01
☐ 246 Mike Norris	.07	.03	.01
☐ 247 Wayne Tolleson	.07	.03	.01
☐ 248 Terry Forster	.07	.03	.01
☐ 249 Harold Baines	.20	.09	.03
☐ 250 Jesse Orosco	.07	.03	.01
☐ 251 Brad Gulden	.07	.03	.01
☐ 252 Dan Ford	.07	.03	.01
☐ 253 Sid Bream	.40	.18	.05
☐ 254 Pete Vuckovich	.07	.03	.01
☐ 255 Lonnie Smith	.07	.03	.01
☐ 256 Mike Stanton	.07	.03	.01
☐ 257 Bryan Little	.07	.03	.01
☐ 258 Mike C. Brown	.07	.03	.01
(Angels Outfielder)			
☐ 259 Gary Allenson	.07	.03	.01
☐ 260 Dave Righetti	.10	.05	.01
☐ 261 Checklist: 133-264	.12	.01	.00
☐ 262 Greg Booker	.07	.03	.01
☐ 263 Mel Hall	.12	.05	.02
☐ 264 Joe Sambito	.07	.03	.01
☐ 265 Juan Samuel	.12	.05	.02
☐ 266 Frank Viola	.20	.09	.03
☐ 267 Henry Cotto	.07	.03	.01
☐ 268 Chuck Tanner MG	.10	.05	.01
(Checklist back)			
☐ 269 Doug Baker	.07	.03	.01
☐ 270 Dan Quisenberry	.10	.05	.01
☐ 271 Tim Foli FDP68	.10	.05	.01
☐ 272 Jeff Burroughs FDP69	.10	.05	.01
☐ 273 Bill Almon FDP74	.10	.05	.01
☐ 274 Floyd Bannister FDP76	.10	.05	.01
☐ 275 Harold Baines FDP77	.15	.07	.02
☐ 276 Bob Horner FDP78	.10	.05	.01
☐ 277 Al Chambers FDP79	.10	.05	.01
☐ 278 Darryl Strawberry	1.50	.65	.19
FDP80			
☐ 279 Mike Moore FDP81	.12	.05	.02
☐ 280 Shawon Dunston FDP82	.90	.40	.11
☐ 281 Tim Belcher FDP83	1.00	.45	.13
☐ 282 Shawn Abner FDP84	.15	.07	.02
☐ 283 Fran Mullins	.07	.03	.01
☐ 284 Marty Bystrom	.07	.03	.01
☐ 285 Dan Driessen	.07	.03	.01
☐ 286 Rudy Law	.07	.03	.01
☐ 287 Walt Terrell	.07	.03	.01
☐ 288 Jeff Kunkel	.07	.03	.01
☐ 289 Tom Underwood	.07	.03	.01
☐ 290 Cecil Cooper	.10	.05	.01
☐ 291 Bob Welch	.12	.05	.02
☐ 292 Brad Komminsk	.07	.03	.01
☐ 293 Curt Young	.07	.03	.01
☐ 294 Tom Nieto	.07	.03	.01
☐ 295 Joe Niekro	.10	.05	.01
☐ 296 Ricky Nelson	.07	.03	.01

☐ 297	Gary Lucas	.07	.03	.01
☐ 298	Marty Barrett	.07	.03	.01
☐ 299	Andy Hawkins	.07	.03	.01
☐ 300	Rod Carew	.60	.25	.08
☐ 301	John Montefusco	.07	.03	.01
☐ 302	Tim Corcoran	.07	.03	.01
☐ 303	Mike Jeffcoat	.07	.03	.01
☐ 304	Gary Gaetti	.10	.05	.01
☐ 305	Dale Berra	.07	.03	.01
☐ 306	Rick Reuschel	.10	.05	.01
☐ 307	Sparky Anderson MG	.10	.05	.01
	(Checklist back)			
☐ 308	John Wathan	.07	.03	.01
☐ 309	Mike Witt	.07	.03	.01
☐ 310	Manny Trillo	.07	.03	.01
☐ 311	Jim Gott	.07	.03	.01
☐ 312	Marc Hill	.07	.03	.01
☐ 313	Dave Schmidt	.07	.03	.01
☐ 314	Ron Oester	.07	.03	.01
☐ 315	Doug Sisk	.07	.03	.01
☐ 316	John Lowenstein	.07	.03	.01
☐ 317	Jack Lazorko	.07	.03	.01
☐ 318	Ted Simmons	.10	.05	.01
☐ 319	Jeff Jones	.07	.03	.01
☐ 320	Dale Murphy	.40	.18	.05
☐ 321	Ricky Horton	.07	.03	.01
☐ 322	Dave Stapleton	.07	.03	.01
☐ 323	Andy McGaffigan	.07	.03	.01
☐ 324	Bruce Bochy	.07	.03	.01
☐ 325	John Denny	.07	.03	.01
☐ 326	Kevin Bass	.07	.03	.01
☐ 327	Brook Jacoby	.12	.05	.02
☐ 328	Bob Shirley	.07	.03	.01
☐ 329	Ron Washington	.07	.03	.01
☐ 330	Leon Durham	.07	.03	.01
☐ 331	Bill Laskey	.07	.03	.01
☐ 332	Brian Harper	.20	.09	.03
☐ 333	Willie Hernandez	.07	.03	.01
☐ 334	Dick Howser MG	.10	.05	.01
	(Checklist back)			
☐ 335	Bruce Benedict	.07	.03	.01
☐ 336	Rance Mulliniks	.07	.03	.01
☐ 337	Billy Sample	.07	.03	.01
☐ 338	Britt Burns	.07	.03	.01
☐ 339	Danny Heep	.07	.03	.01
☐ 340	Robin Yount	1.25	.55	.16
☐ 341	Floyd Rayford	.07	.03	.01
☐ 342	Ted Power	.07	.03	.01
☐ 343	Bill Russell	.10	.05	.01
☐ 344	Dave Henderson	.10	.05	.01
☐ 345	Charlie Lea	.07	.03	.01
☐ 346	Terry Pendleton	4.00	1.80	.50
☐ 347	Rick Langford	.07	.03	.01
☐ 348	Bob Boone	.10	.05	.01
☐ 349	Domingo Ramos	.07	.03	.01
☐ 350	Wade Boggs	2.00	.90	.25
☐ 351	Juan Agosto	.07	.03	.01
☐ 352	Joe Morgan	.25	.11	.03
☐ 353	Julio Solano	.07	.03	.01
☐ 354	Andre Robertson	.07	.03	.01
☐ 355	Bert Blyleven	.15	.07	.02
☐ 356	Dave Meier	.07	.03	.01
☐ 357	Rich Bordi	.07	.03	.01
☐ 358	Tony Pena	.10	.05	.01
☐ 359	Pat Sheridan	.07	.03	.01
☐ 360	Steve Carlton	.50	.23	.06
☐ 361	Alfredo Griffin	.07	.03	.01
☐ 362	Craig McMurtry	.07	.03	.01
☐ 363	Ron Hodges	.07	.03	.01
☐ 364	Richard Dotson	.07	.03	.01
☐ 365	Danny Ozark MG	.10	.05	.01
	(Checklist back)			
☐ 366	Todd Cruz	.07	.03	.01
☐ 367	Keefe Cato	.07	.03	.01
☐ 368	Dave Bergman	.07	.03	.01
☐ 369	R.J. Reynolds	.07	.03	.01
☐ 370	Bruce Sutter	.10	.05	.01
☐ 371	Mickey Rivers	.07	.03	.01
☐ 372	Roy Howell	.07	.03	.01
☐ 373	Mike Moore	.10	.05	.02
☐ 374	Brian Downing	.10	.05	.01
☐ 375	Jeff Reardon	.40	.18	.05
☐ 376	Jeff Newman	.07	.03	.01
☐ 377	Checklist: 265-396	.12	.01	.00
☐ 378	Alan Wiggins	.07	.03	.01
☐ 379	Charles Hudson	.07	.03	.01
☐ 380	Ken Griffey	.10	.05	.01
☐ 381	Roy Smith	.07	.03	.01
☐ 382	Denny Walling	.07	.03	.01
☐ 383	Rick Lysander	.07	.03	.01
☐ 384	Jody Davis	.07	.03	.01
☐ 385	Jose DeLeon	.07	.03	.01
☐ 386	Dan Gladden	.20	.09	.03
☐ 387	Buddy Biancalana	.07	.03	.01
☐ 388	Bert Roberge	.07	.03	.01
☐ 389	Rod Dedeaux OLY CO	.12	.05	.02
☐ 390	Sid Akins OLY	.12	.05	.02
☐ 391	Flavio Alfaro OLY	.12	.05	.02
☐ 392	Don August OLY	.15	.07	.02
☐ 393	Scott Bankhead OLY	.40	.18	.05
☐ 394	Bob Caffrey OLY	.12	.05	.02
☐ 395	Mike Dunne OLY	.12	.05	.02
☐ 396	Gary Green OLY	.12	.05	.02
☐ 397	John Hoover OLY	.12	.05	.02
☐ 398	Shane Mack OLY	3.00	1.35	.40
☐ 399	John Marzano OLY	.12	.05	.02
☐ 400	Oddibe McDowell OLY	.15	.07	.02
☐ 401	Mark McGwire OLY	30.00	13.50	3.80
☐ 402	Pat Pacillo OLY	.12	.05	.02
☐ 403	Cory Snyder OLY	1.25	.55	.16
☐ 404	Billy Swift OLY	1.00	.45	.13
☐ 405	Tom Veryzer	.07	.03	.01
☐ 406	Len Whitehouse	.07	.03	.01
☐ 407	Bobby Ramos	.07	.03	.01

☐	408	Sid Monge	.07	.03	.01	☐	462	Gary Lavelle	.07	.03	.01
☐	409	Brad Wellman	.07	.03	.01	☐	463	Dave Collins	.07	.03	.01
☐	410	Bob Horner	.10	.05	.01	☐	464	Mike Mason	.07	.03	.01
☐	411	Bobby Cox MG	.10	.05	.01	☐	465	Bob Grich	.10	.05	.01
		(Checklist back)				☐	466	Tony LaRussa MG	.10	.05	.01
☐	412	Bud Black	.07	.03	.01			(Checklist back)			
☐	413	Vance Law	.07	.03	.01	☐	467	Ed Lynch	.07	.03	.01
☐	414	Gary Ward	.07	.03	.01	☐	468	Wayne Krenchicki	.07	.03	.01
☐	415	Ron Darling UER	.20	.09	.03	☐	469	Sammy Stewart	.07	.03	.01
		(No trivia answer)				☐	470	Steve Sax	.20	.09	.03
☐	416	Wayne Gross	.07	.03	.01	☐	471	Pete Ladd	.07	.03	.01
☐	417	John Franco	.50	.23	.06	☐	472	Jim Essian	.07	.03	.01
☐	418	Ken Landreaux	.07	.03	.01	☐	473	Tim Wallach	.10	.05	.01
☐	419	Mike Caldwell	.07	.03	.01	☐	474	Kurt Kepshire	.07	.03	.01
☐	420	Andre Dawson	.75	.35	.09	☐	475	Andre Thornton	.07	.03	.01
☐	421	Dave Rucker	.07	.03	.01	☐	476	Jeff Stone	.07	.03	.01
☐	422	Carney Lansford	.10	.05	.01	☐	477	Bob Ojeda	.07	.03	.01
☐	423	Barry Bonnell	.07	.03	.01	☐	478	Kurt Bevacqua	.07	.03	.01
☐	424	Al Nipper	.07	.03	.01	☐	479	Mike Madden	.07	.03	.01
☐	425	Mike Hargrove	.10	.05	.01	☐	480	Lou Whitaker	.25	.11	.03
☐	426	Vern Ruhle	.07	.03	.01	☐	481	Dale Murray	.07	.03	.01
☐	427	Mario Ramirez	.07	.03	.01	☐	482	Harry Spilman	.07	.03	.01
☐	428	Larry Andersen	.07	.03	.01	☐	483	Mike Smithson	.07	.03	.01
☐	429	Rick Cerone	.07	.03	.01	☐	484	Larry Bowa	.10	.05	.01
☐	430	Ron Davis	.07	.03	.01	☐	485	Matt Young	.07	.03	.01
☐	431	U.L. Washington	.07	.03	.01	☐	486	Steve Balboni	.07	.03	.01
☐	432	Thad Bosley	.07	.03	.01	☐	487	Frank Williams	.07	.03	.01
☐	433	Jim Morrison	.07	.03	.01	☐	488	Joel Skinner	.07	.03	.01
☐	434	Gene Richards	.07	.03	.01	☐	489	Bryan Clark	.07	.03	.01
☐	435	Dan Petry	.07	.03	.01	☐	490	Jason Thompson	.07	.03	.01
☐	436	Willie Aikens	.07	.03	.01	☐	491	Rick Camp	.07	.03	.01
☐	437	Al Jones	.07	.03	.01	☐	492	Dave Johnson MG	.10	.05	.01
☐	438	Joe Torre MG	.10	.05	.01			(Checklist back)			
		(Checklist back)				☐	493	Orel Hershiser	1.50	.65	.19
☐	439	Junior Ortiz	.07	.03	.01	☐	494	Rich Dauer	.07	.03	.01
☐	440	Fernando Valenzuela	.10	.05	.01	☐	495	Mario Soto	.07	.03	.01
☐	441	Duane Walker	.07	.03	.01	☐	496	Donnie Scott	.07	.03	.01
☐	442	Ken Forsch	.07	.03	.01	☐	497	Gary Pettis UER	.10	.05	.01
☐	443	George Wright	.07	.03	.01			(Photo actually			
☐	444	Tony Phillips	.10	.05	.01			Gary's little			
☐	445	Tippy Martinez	.07	.03	.01			brother, Lynn)			
☐	446	Jim Sundberg	.10	.05	.01	☐	498	Ed Romero	.07	.03	.01
☐	447	Jeff Lahti	.07	.03	.01	☐	499	Danny Cox	.07	.03	.01
☐	448	Derrel Thomas	.07	.03	.01	☐	500	Mike Schmidt	2.00	.90	.25
☐	449	Phil Bradley	.10	.05	.01	☐	501	Dan Schatzeder	.07	.03	.01
☐	450	Steve Garvey	.25	.11	.03	☐	502	Rick Miller	.07	.03	.01
☐	451	Bruce Hurst	.10	.05	.01	☐	503	Tim Conroy	.07	.03	.01
☐	452	John Castino	.07	.03	.01	☐	504	Jerry Willard	.07	.03	.01
☐	453	Tom Waddell	.07	.03	.01	☐	505	Jim Beattie	.07	.03	.01
☐	454	Glenn Wilson	.07	.03	.01	☐	506	Franklin Stubbs	.10	.05	.01
☐	455	Bob Knepper	.07	.03	.01	☐	507	Ray Fontenot	.07	.03	.01
☐	456	Tim Foli	.07	.03	.01	☐	508	John Shelby	.07	.03	.01
☐	457	Cecilio Guante	.07	.03	.01	☐	509	Milt May	.07	.03	.01
☐	458	Randy Johnson	.07	.03	.01	☐	510	Kent Hrbek	.20	.09	.03
☐	459	Charlie Leibrandt	.10	.05	.01	☐	511	Lee Smith	.40	.18	.05
☐	460	Ryne Sandberg	4.00	1.80	.50	☐	512	Tom Brookens	.07	.03	.01
☐	461	Marty Castillo	.07	.03	.01	☐	513	Lynn Jones	.07	.03	.01

☐ 514 Jeff Cornell	.07	.03	.01		
☐ 515 Dave Concepcion	.10	.05	.01		
☐ 516 Roy Lee Jackson	.07	.03	.01		
☐ 517 Jerry Martin	.07	.03	.01		
☐ 518 Chris Chambliss	.10	.05	.01		
☐ 519 Doug Rader MG	.10	.05	.01		
(Checklist back)					
☐ 520 LaMarr Hoyt	.07	.03	.01		
☐ 521 Rick Dempsey	.07	.03	.01		
☐ 522 Paul Molitor	.35	.16	.04		
☐ 523 Candy Maldonado	.10	.05	.01		
☐ 524 Rob Wilfong	.07	.03	.01		
☐ 525 Darrell Porter	.07	.03	.01		
☐ 526 David Palmer	.07	.03	.01		
☐ 527 Checklist: 397-528	.12	.01	.00		
☐ 528 Bill Krueger	.10	.05	.01		
☐ 529 Rich Gedman	.07	.03	.01		
☐ 530 Dave Dravecky	.10	.05	.01		
☐ 531 Joe Lefebvre	.07	.03	.01		
☐ 532 Frank DiPino	.07	.03	.01		
☐ 533 Tony Bernazard	.07	.03	.01		
☐ 534 Brian Dayett	.07	.03	.01		
☐ 535 Pat Putnam	.07	.03	.01		
☐ 536 Kirby Puckett	22.00	10.00	2.80		
☐ 537 Don Robinson	.07	.03	.01		
☐ 538 Keith Moreland	.07	.03	.01		
☐ 539 Aurelio Lopez	.07	.03	.01		
☐ 540 Claudell Washington	.07	.03	.01		
☐ 541 Mark Davis	.10	.05	.01		
☐ 542 Don Slaught	.07	.03	.01		
☐ 543 Mike Squires	.07	.03	.01		
☐ 544 Bruce Kison	.07	.03	.01		
☐ 545 Lloyd Moseby	.07	.03	.01		
☐ 546 Brent Gaff	.07	.03	.01		
☐ 547 Pete Rose MG	.40	.18	.05		
(Checklist back)					
☐ 548 Larry Parrish	.07	.03	.01		
☐ 549 Mike Scioscia	.10	.05	.01		
☐ 550 Scott McGregor	.07	.03	.01		
☐ 551 Andy Van Slyke	.75	.35	.09		
☐ 552 Chris Codiroli	.07	.03	.01		
☐ 553 Bob Clark	.07	.03	.01		
☐ 554 Doug Flynn	.07	.03	.01		
☐ 555 Bob Stanley	.07	.03	.01		
☐ 556 Sixto Lezcano	.07	.03	.01		
☐ 557 Len Barker	.07	.03	.01		
☐ 558 Carmelo Martinez	.07	.03	.01		
☐ 559 Jay Howell	.10	.05	.01		
☐ 560 Bill Madlock	.10	.05	.01		
☐ 561 Darryl Motley	.07	.03	.01		
☐ 562 Houston Jimenez	.07	.03	.01		
☐ 563 Dick Ruthven	.07	.03	.01		
☐ 564 Alan Ashby	.07	.03	.01		
☐ 565 Kirk Gibson	.15	.07	.02		
☐ 566 Ed VandeBerg	.07	.03	.01		
☐ 567 Joel Youngblood	.07	.03	.01		
☐ 568 Cliff Johnson	.07	.03	.01		
☐ 569 Ken Oberkfell	.07	.03	.01		
☐ 570 Darryl Strawberry	3.00	1.35	.40		
☐ 571 Charlie Hough	.10	.05	.01		
☐ 572 Tom Paciorek	.10	.05	.01		
☐ 573 Jay Tibbs	.07	.03	.01		
☐ 574 Joe Altobelli MG	.10	.05	.01		
(Checklist back)					
☐ 575 Pedro Guerrero	.10	.05	.01		
☐ 576 Jaime Cocanower	.07	.03	.01		
☐ 577 Chris Speier	.07	.03	.01		
☐ 578 Terry Francona	.07	.03	.01		
☐ 579 Ron Romanick	.07	.03	.01		
☐ 580 Dwight Evans	.12	.05	.02		
☐ 581 Mark Wagner	.07	.03	.01		
☐ 582 Ken Phelps	.07	.03	.01		
☐ 583 Bobby Brown	.07	.03	.01		
☐ 584 Kevin Gross	.07	.03	.01		
☐ 585 Butch Wynegar	.07	.03	.01		
☐ 586 Bill Scherrer	.07	.03	.01		
☐ 587 Doug Frobel	.07	.03	.01		
☐ 588 Bobby Castillo	.07	.03	.01		
☐ 589 Bob Dernier	.07	.03	.01		
☐ 590 Ray Knight	.10	.05	.01		
☐ 591 Larry Herndon	.07	.03	.01		
☐ 592 Jeff D. Robinson	.10	.05	.01		
(Giants pitcher)					
☐ 593 Rick Leach	.07	.03	.01		
☐ 594 Curt Wilkerson	.07	.03	.01		
☐ 595 Larry Gura	.07	.03	.01		
☐ 596 Jerry Hairston	.07	.03	.01		
☐ 597 Brad Lesley	.07	.03	.01		
☐ 598 Jose Oquendo	.10	.05	.01		
☐ 599 Storm Davis	.07	.03	.01		
☐ 600 Pete Rose	.60	.25	.08		
☐ 601 Tom Lasorda MG	.10	.05	.01		
(Checklist back)					
☐ 602 Jeff Dedmon	.07	.03	.01		
☐ 603 Rick Manning	.07	.03	.01		
☐ 604 Daryl Sconiers	.07	.03	.01		
☐ 605 Ozzie Smith	.90	.40	.11		
☐ 606 Rich Gale	.07	.03	.01		
☐ 607 Bill Almon	.07	.03	.01		
☐ 608 Craig Lefferts	.10	.05	.01		
☐ 609 Broderick Perkins	.07	.03	.01		
☐ 610 Jack Morris	.50	.23	.06		
☐ 611 Ozzie Virgil	.07	.03	.01		
☐ 612 Mike Armstrong	.07	.03	.01		
☐ 613 Terry Puhl	.07	.03	.01		
☐ 614 Al Williams	.07	.03	.01		
☐ 615 Marvell Wynne	.07	.03	.01		
☐ 616 Scott Sanderson	.07	.03	.01		
☐ 617 Willie Wilson	.10	.05	.01		
☐ 618 Pete Falcone	.07	.03	.01		
☐ 619 Jeff Leonard	.07	.03	.01		
☐ 620 Dwight Gooden	3.50	1.55	.45		
☐ 621 Marvis Foley	.07	.03	.01		
☐ 622 Luis Leal	.07	.03	.01		

☐ 623 Greg Walker	07	.03	.01
☐ 624 Benny Ayala	07	.03	.01
☐ 625 Mark Langston	1.25	.55	.16
☐ 626 German Rivera	07	.03	.01
☐ 627 Eric Davis	3.50	1.55	.45
☐ 628 Rene Lachemann MG	10	.05	.01
(Checklist back)			
☐ 629 Dick Schofield	07	.03	.01
☐ 630 Tim Raines	20	.09	.03
☐ 631 Bob Forsch	07	.03	.01
☐ 632 Bruce Bochte	07	.03	.01
☐ 633 Glenn Hoffman	07	.03	.01
☐ 634 Bill Dawley	07	.03	.01
☐ 635 Terry Kennedy	07	.03	.01
☐ 636 Shane Rawley	07	.03	.01
☐ 637 Brett Butler	20	.09	.03
☐ 638 Mike Pagliarulo	10	.05	.01
☐ 639 Ed Hodge	07	.03	.01
☐ 640 Steve Henderson	07	.03	.01
☐ 641 Rod Scurry	07	.03	.01
☐ 642 Dave Owen	07	.03	.01
☐ 643 Johnny Grubb	07	.03	.01
☐ 644 Mark Huismann	07	.03	.01
☐ 645 Damaso Garcia	07	.03	.01
☐ 646 Scot Thompson	07	.03	.01
☐ 647 Rafael Ramirez	07	.03	.01
☐ 648 Bob Jones	07	.03	.01
☐ 649 Sid Fernandez	35	.16	.04
☐ 650 Greg Luzinski	10	.05	.01
☐ 651 Jeff Russell	12	.05	.02
☐ 652 Joe Nolan	07	.03	.01
☐ 653 Mark Brouhard	07	.03	.01
☐ 654 Dave Anderson	07	.03	.01
☐ 655 Joaquin Andujar	07	.03	.01
☐ 656 Chuck Cottier MG	10	.05	.01
(Checklist back)			
☐ 657 Jim Slaton	07	.03	.01
☐ 658 Mike Stenhouse	07	.03	.01
☐ 659 Checklist: 529-660	12	.01	.00
☐ 660 Tony Gwynn	2.50	1.15	.30
☐ 661 Steve Crawford	07	.03	.01
☐ 662 Mike Heath	07	.03	.01
☐ 663 Luis Aguayo	07	.03	.01
☐ 664 Steve Farr	30	.14	.04
☐ 665 Don Mattingly	3.00	1.35	.40
☐ 666 Mike LaCoss	07	.03	.01
☐ 667 Dave Engle	07	.03	.01
☐ 668 Steve Trout	07	.03	.01
☐ 669 Lee Lacy	07	.03	.01
☐ 670 Tom Seaver	60	.25	.08
☐ 671 Dane Iorg	07	.03	.01
☐ 672 Juan Berenguer	07	.03	.01
☐ 673 Buck Martinez	07	.03	.01
☐ 674 Atlee Hammaker	07	.03	.01
☐ 675 Tony Perez	15	.07	.02
☐ 676 Albert Hall	07	.03	.01
☐ 677 Wally Backman	07	.03	.01

☐ 678 Joey McLaughlin	07	.03	.01
☐ 679 Bob Kearney	07	.03	.01
☐ 680 Jerry Reuss	07	.03	.01
☐ 681 Ben Oglivie	07	.03	.01
☐ 682 Doug Corbett	07	.03	.01
☐ 683 Whitey Herzog MG	10	.05	.01
(Checklist back)			
☐ 684 Bill Doran	10	.05	.01
☐ 685 Bill Caudill	07	.03	.01
☐ 686 Mike Easler	07	.03	.01
☐ 687 Bill Gullickson	10	.05	.01
☐ 688 Len Matuszek	07	.03	.01
☑ 689 Luis DeLeon	07	.03	.01
☐ 690 Alan Trammell	25	.11	.03
☐ 691 Dennis Rasmussen	07	.03	.01
☐ 692 Randy Bush	07	.03	.01
☐ 693 Tim Stoddard	07	.03	.01
☐ 694 Joe Carter	4.00	1.80	.50
☐ 695 Rick Rhoden	07	.03	.01
☐ 696 John Rabb	07	.03	.01
☐ 697 Onix Concepcion	07	.03	.01
☐ 698 Jorge Bell	40	.18	.05
☐ 699 Donnie Moore	07	.03	.01
☐ 700 Eddie Murray	90	.40	.11
☐ 701 Eddie Murray AS	35	.16	.04
☐ 702 Damaso Garcia AS	10	.05	.01
☐ 703 George Brett AS	60	.25	.08
☐ 704 Cal Ripken AS	1.25	.55	.16
☐ 705 Dave Winfield AS	50	.23	.06
☐ 706 Rickey Henderson AS	60	.25	.08
☐ 707 Tony Armas AS	10	.05	.01
☐ 708 Lance Parrish AS	10	.05	.01
☐ 709 Mike Boddicker AS	10	.05	.01
☐ 710 Frank Viola AS	15	.07	.02
☐ 711 Dan Quisenberry AS	10	.05	.01
☐ 712 Keith Hernandez AS	10	.05	.01
☐ 713 Ryne Sandberg AS	1.50	.65	.19
☐ 714 Mike Schmidt AS	65	.30	.08
☐ 715 Ozzie Smith AS	35	.16	.04
☐ 716 Dale Murphy AS	20	.09	.03
☐ 717 Tony Gwynn AS	75	.35	.09
☐ 718 Jeff Leonard AS	10	.05	.01
☐ 719 Gary Carter AS	15	.07	.02
☐ 720 Rick Sutcliffe AS	10	.05	.01
☐ 721 Bob Knepper AS	10	.05	.01
☐ 722 Bruce Sutter AS	10	.05	.01
☐ 723 Dave Stewart	20	.09	.03
☐ 724 Oscar Gamble	07	.03	.01
☐ 725 Floyd Bannister	07	.03	.01
☐ 726 Al Bumbry	07	.03	.01
☐ 727 Frank Pastore	07	.03	.01
☐ 728 Bob Bailor	07	.03	.01
☐ 729 Don Sutton	20	.09	.03
☐ 730 Dave Kingman	10	.05	.01
☐ 731 Neil Allen	07	.03	.01
☐ 732 John McNamara MG	10	.05	.01
(Checklist back)			

☐	733 Tony Scott	.07	.03	.01
☐	734 John Henry Johnson	.07	.03	.01
☐	735 Garry Templeton	.07	.03	.01
☐	736 Jerry Mumphrey	.07	.03	.01
☐	737 Bo Diaz	.07	.03	.01
☐	738 Omar Moreno	.07	.03	.01
☐	739 Ernie Camacho	.07	.03	.01
☐	740 Jack Clark	.10	.05	.01
☐	741 John Butcher	.07	.03	.01
☐	742 Ron Hassey	.07	.03	.01
☐	743 Frank White	.10	.05	.01
☐	744 Doug Bair	.07	.03	.01
☐	745 Buddy Bell	.10	.05	.01
☐	746 Jim Clancy	.07	.03	.01
☐	747 Alex Trevino	.07	.03	.01
☐	748 Lee Mazzilli	.07	.03	.01
☐	749 Julio Cruz	.07	.03	.01
☐	750 Rollie Fingers	.20	.09	.03
☐	751 Kelvin Chapman	.07	.03	.01
☐	752 Bob Owchinko	.07	.03	.01
☐	753 Greg Brock	.07	.03	.01
☐	754 Larry Milbourne	.07	.03	.01
☐	755 Ken Singleton	.10	.05	.01
☐	756 Rob Picciolo	.07	.03	.01
☐	757 Willie McGee	.20	.09	.03
☐	758 Ray Burris	.07	.03	.01
☐	759 Jim Fanning MG	.10	.05	.01
	(Checklist back)			
☐	760 Nolan Ryan	4.50	2.00	.55
☐	761 Jerry Remy	.07	.03	.01
☐	762 Eddie Whitson	.07	.03	.01
☐	763 Kiko Garcia	.07	.03	.01
☐	764 Jamie Easterly	.07	.03	.01
☐	765 Willie Randolph	.10	.05	.01
☐	766 Paul Mirabella	.07	.03	.01
☐	767 Darrell Brown	.07	.03	.01
☐	768 Ron Cey	.10	.05	.01
☐	769 Joe Cowley	.07	.03	.01
☐	770 Carlton Fisk	.75	.35	.09
☐	771 Geoff Zahn	.07	.03	.01
☐	772 Johnnie LeMaster	.07	.03	.01
☐	773 Hal McRae	.10	.05	.01
☐	774 Dennis Lamp	.07	.03	.01
☐	775 Mookie Wilson	.10	.05	.01
☐	776 Jerry Royster	.07	.03	.01
☐	777 Ned Yost	.07	.03	.01
☐	778 Mike Davis	.07	.03	.01
☐	779 Nick Esasky	.07	.03	.01
☐	780 Mike Flanagan	.07	.03	.01
☐	781 Jim Gantner	.10	.05	.01
☐	782 Tom Niedenfuer	.07	.03	.01
☐	783 Mike Jorgensen	.07	.03	.01
☐	784 Checklist: 661-792	.12	.01	.00
☐	785 Tony Armas	.10	.05	.01
☐	786 Enos Cabell	.07	.03	.01
☐	787 Jim Wohlford	.07	.03	.01
☐	788 Steve Comer	.07	.03	.01

☐	789 Luis Salazar	.07	.03	.01
☐	790 Ron Guidry	.10	.05	.01
☐	791 Ivan DeJesus	.07	.03	.01
☐	792 Darrell Evans	.12	.05	.02

1985 Topps Traded

The cards in this 132-card set measure 2 1/2" by 3 1/2". In its now standard procedure, Topps issued its Traded (or extended) set for the fifth year in a row. Topps did however test on a limited basis the issuance of these Traded cards in wax packs. Because all photos and statistics of its regular set for the year were developed during the fall and winter months of the preceding year, players who changed teams during the fall, winter, and spring months are portrayed in the 1985 regular issue set with the teams they were with in 1984. The Traded set updates the shortcomings of the regular set by presenting the players with their proper teams for the current year. Most of 1985's top rookies not contained in the regular set are picked up in the Traded set. The key (extended) Rookie Cards in this set are Vince Coleman, Ozzie Guillen, and Mickey Tettleton. Again this year, the Topps affiliate in Ireland printed the cards, and the cards were available through hobby channels only. Topps also produced a specially boxed "glossy" edition, frequently referred to as the Topps Traded Tiffany set. There were supposedly only 8,000 sets of the Tiffany cards produced; they were marketed to hobby dealers. The checklist of cards is identical to that of the normal non-glossy cards. There are two primary distinguishing features of the Tiffany cards, white card stock reverses and high gloss obverses. These Tiffany cards are valued from approximately five to ten times the values listed below. The set numbering is in alphabetical order by player's name.

	NRMT-MT	EXC	G-VG
COMPLETE SET (132)	30.00	13.50	3.80
COMMON PLAYER (1T-132T)	.15	.07	.02

☐ 1T Don Aase	.15	.07	.02
☐ 2T Bill Almon	.15	.07	.02
☐ 3T Benny Ayala	.15	.07	.02
☐ 4T Dusty Baker	.20	.09	.03
☐ 5T Geo.Bamberger MG	.15	.07	.02
☐ 6T Dale Berra	.15	.07	.02
☐ 7T Rich Bordi	.15	.07	.02
☐ 8T Daryl Boston	.25	.11	.03
☐ 9T Hubie Brooks	.20	.09	.03
☐ 10T Chris Brown	.15	.07	.02
☐ 11T Tom Browning	1.00	.45	.13
☐ 12T Al Bumbry	.15	.07	.02
☐ 13T Ray Burris	.15	.07	.02
☐ 14T Jeff Burroughs	.15	.07	.02
☐ 15T Bill Campbell	.15	.07	.02
☐ 16T Don Carman	.15	.07	.02
☐ 17T Gary Carter	1.00	.45	.13
☐ 18T Bobby Castillo	.15	.07	.02
☐ 19T Bill Caudill	.15	.07	.02
☐ 20T Rick Cerone	.15	.07	.02
☐ 21T Bryan Clark	.15	.07	.02
☐ 22T Jack Clark	.20	.09	.03
☐ 23T Pat Clements	.15	.07	.02
☐ 24T Vince Coleman	4.00	1.80	.50
☐ 25T Dave Collins	.15	.07	.02
☐ 26T Danny Darwin	.15	.07	.02
☐ 27T Jim Davenport MG	.15	.07	.02
☐ 28T Jerry Davis	.15	.07	.02
☐ 29T Brian Dayett	.15	.07	.02
☐ 30T Ivan DeJesus	.15	.07	.02
☐ 31T Ken Dixon	.15	.07	.02
☐ 32T Mariano Duncan	1.25	.55	.16
☐ 33T John Felske MG	.15	.07	.02
☐ 34T Mike Fitzgerald	.15	.07	.02
☐ 35T Ray Fontenot	.15	.07	.02
☐ 36T Greg Gagne	.40	.18	.05
☐ 37T Oscar Gamble	.15	.07	.02
☐ 38T Scott Garrelts	.15	.07	.02
☐ 39T Bob L. Gibson	.15	.07	.02
☐ 40T Jim Gott	.15	.07	.02
☐ 41T David Green	.15	.07	.02
☐ 42T Alfredo Griffin	.15	.07	.02
☐ 43T Ozzie Guillen	1.25	.55	.16
☐ 44T Eddie Haas MG	.15	.07	.02
☐ 45T Terry Harper	.15	.07	.02
☐ 46T Toby Harrah	.15	.07	.02
☐ 47T Greg Harris	.15	.07	.02
☐ 48T Ron Hassey	.15	.07	.02
☐ 49T Rickey Henderson	5.00	2.30	.60
☐ 50T Steve Henderson	.15	.07	.02
☐ 51T George Hendrick	.15	.07	.02
☐ 52T Joe Hesketh	.25	.11	.03
☐ 53T Teddy Higuera	.25	.11	.03
☐ 54T Donnie Hill	.15	.07	.02
☐ 55T Al Holland	.15	.07	.02
☐ 56T Burt Hooton	.15	.07	.02
☐ 57T Jay Howell	.20	.09	.03
☐ 58T Ken Howell	.15	.07	.02
☐ 59T LaMarr Hoyt	.15	.07	.02
☐ 60T Tim Hulett	.15	.07	.02
☐ 61T Bob James	.15	.07	.02
☐ 62T Steve Jeltz	.15	.07	.02
☐ 63T Cliff Johnson	.15	.07	.02
☐ 64T Howard Johnson	2.00	.90	.25
☐ 65T Ruppert Jones	.15	.07	.02
☐ 66T Steve Kemp	.15	.07	.02
☐ 67T Bruce Kison	.15	.07	.02
☐ 68T Alan Knicely	.15	.07	.02
☐ 69T Mike LaCoss	.15	.07	.02
☐ 70T Lee Lacy	.15	.07	.02
☐ 71T Dave LaPoint	.15	.07	.02
☐ 72T Gary Lavelle	.15	.07	.02
☐ 73T Vance Law	.15	.07	.02
☐ 74T Johnnie LeMaster	.15	.07	.02
☐ 75T Sixto Lezcano	.15	.07	.02
☐ 76T Tim Lollar	.15	.07	.02
☐ 77T Fred Lynn	.20	.09	.03
☐ 78T Billy Martin MG	.25	.11	.03
☐ 79T Ron Mathis	.15	.07	.02
☐ 80T Len Matuszek	.15	.07	.02
☐ 81T Gene Mauch MG	.15	.07	.02
☐ 82T Oddibe McDowell	.20	.09	.03
☐ 83T Roger McDowell	.40	.18	.05
☐ 84T John McNamara MG	.15	.07	.02
☐ 85T Donnie Moore	.15	.07	.02
☐ 86T Gene Nelson	.15	.07	.02
☐ 87T Steve Nicosia	.15	.07	.02
☐ 88T Al Oliver	.20	.09	.03
☐ 89T Joe Orsulak	.60	.25	.08
☐ 90T Rob Picciolo	.15	.07	.02
☐ 91T Chris Pittaro	.15	.07	.02
☐ 92T Jim Presley	.15	.07	.02
☐ 93T Rick Reuschel	.20	.09	.03
☐ 94T Bert Roberge	.15	.07	.02
☐ 95T Bob Rodgers MG	.15	.07	.02
☐ 96T Jerry Royster	.15	.07	.02
☐ 97T Dave Rozema	.15	.07	.02
☐ 98T Dave Rucker	.15	.07	.02
☐ 99T Vern Ruhle	.15	.07	.02
☐ 100T Paul Runge	.15	.07	.02
☐ 101T Mark Salas	.15	.07	.02
☐ 102T Luis Salazar	.15	.07	.02

☐	103T	Joe Sambito	15	.07	.02
☐	104T	Rick Schu	15	.07	.02
☐	105T	Donnie Scott	15	.07	.02
☐	106T	Larry Sheets	15	.07	.02
☐	107T	Don Slaught	15	.07	.02
☐	108T	Roy Smalley	15	.07	.02
☐	109T	Lonnie Smith	20	.09	.03
☐	110T	Nate Snell UER	15	.07	.02
		(Headings on back			
		for a batter)			
☐	111T	Chris Speier	15	.07	.02
☐	112T	Mike Stenhouse	15	.07	.02
☐	113T	Tim Stoddard	15	.07	.02
☐	114T	Jim Sundberg	20	.09	.03
☐	115T	Bruce Sutter	20	.09	.03
☐	116T	Don Sutton	75	.35	.09
☐	117T	Kent Tekulve	15	.07	.02
☐	118T	Tom Tellmann	15	.07	.02
☐	119T	Walt Terrell	15	.07	.02
☐	120T	Mickey Tettleton	5.00	2.30	.60
☐	121T	Derrel Thomas	15	.07	.02
☐	122T	Rich Thompson	15	.07	.02
☐	123T	Alex Trevino	15	.07	.02
☐	124T	John Tudor	20	.09	.03
☐	125T	Jose Uribe	25	.11	.03
☐	126T	Bobby Valentine MG	20	.09	.03
☐	127T	Dave Von Ohlen	15	.07	.02
☐	128T	U.L. Washington	15	.07	.02
☐	129T	Earl Weaver MG	20	.09	.03
☐	130T	Eddie Whitson	15	.07	.02
☐	131T	Herm Winningham	30	.14	.04
☐	132T	Checklist 1-132	20	.02	.01

1986 Topps

The cards in this 792-card set are stand-dard-size (2 1/2" by 3 1/2"). The first seven cards are a tribute to Pete Rose and his

career. Card numbers 2-7 show small photos of Pete's Topps cards of the given years on the front with biographical information pertaining to those years on the back. The team leader cards were done differently with a simple player action shot on a white background; the player pictured is dubbed the "Dean" of that team, i.e., the player with the longest continuous service with that team. Topps again features a "Turn Back the Clock" series (401-405). Record breakers of the previous year are acknowledged on card numbers 201 to 207. Card numbers 701-722 feature All-Star selections from each league. Manager cards feature the team checklist on the reverse. Ryne Sandberg (690) is the only player card in the set without a Topps logo on the front of the card; this omission was never corrected by Topps. There are two other uncorrected errors involving misnumbered cards; see card numbers 51, 57, 141, and 171 in the checklist below. The backs of all the cards have a distinctive red background. The key Rookie Cards in this set are Vince Coleman, Len Dykstra, Cecil Fielder, and Mickey Tettleton. Topps also produced a specially boxed "glossy" edition, frequently referred to as the Topps Tiffany set. There were supposedly only 5,000 sets of the Tiffany cards produced; they were marketed to hobby dealers. The checklist of cards (792 regular and 132 Traded) is identical to that of the normal non-glossy cards. There are two primary distinguishing features of the Tiffany cards, white card stock reverses and high gloss obverses. These Tiffany cards are valued approximately from five to ten times the values listed below.

		MT	EX-MT	VG
COMPLETE SET (792)	40.00	18.00	5.00
COMPLETE FACT.SET (792)	40.00	18.00	5.00
COMMON PLAYER (1-792)	.05	.02	.01
☐ 1	Pete Rose	1.00	.25	.08
☐ 2	Rose Special: '63-'66	.30	.14	.04
☐ 3	Rose Special: '67-'70	.30	.14	.04
☐ 4	Rose Special: '71-'74	.30	.14	.04
☐ 5	Rose Special: '75-'78	.30	.14	.04
☐ 6	Rose Special: '79-'82	.30	.14	.04
☐ 7	Rose Special: '83-'85	.30	.14	.04
☐ 8	Dwayne Murphy	.05	.02	.01
☐ 9	Roy Smith	.05	.02	.01
☐ 10	Tony Gwynn	1.25	.55	.16

☐ 11 Bob Ojeda	.05	.02	.01
☐ 12 Jose Uribe	.10	.05	.01
☐ 13 Bob Kearney	.05	.02	.01
☐ 14 Julio Cruz	.05	.02	.01
☐ 15 Eddie Whitson	.05	.02	.01
☐ 16 Rick Schu	.05	.02	.01
☐ 17 Mike Stenhouse	.05	.02	.01
☐ 18 Brent Gaff	.05	.02	.01
☐ 19 Rich Hebner	.05	.02	.01
☐ 20 Lou Whitaker	.12	.05	.02
☐ 21 George Bamberger MG	.08	.04	.01
(Checklist back)			
☐ 22 Duane Walker	.05	.02	.01
☐ 23 Manny Lee	.25	.11	.03
☐ 24 Len Barker	.05	.02	.01
☐ 25 Willie Wilson	.05	.02	.01
☐ 26 Frank DiPino	.05	.02	.01
☐ 27 Ray Knight	.08	.04	.01
☐ 28 Eric Davis	.50	.23	.06
☐ 29 Tony Phillips	.08	.04	.01
☐ 30 Eddie Murray	.45	.20	.06
☐ 31 Jamie Easterly	.05	.02	.01
☐ 32 Steve Yeager	.05	.02	.01
☐ 33 Jeff Lahti	.05	.02	.01
☐ 34 Ken Phelps	.05	.02	.01
☐ 35 Jeff Reardon	.25	.11	.03
☐ 36 Tigers Leaders	.08	.04	.01
Lance Parrish			
☐ 37 Mark Thurmond	.05	.02	.01
☐ 38 Glenn Hoffman	.05	.02	.01
☐ 39 Dave Rucker	.05	.02	.01
☐ 40 Ken Griffey	.08	.04	.01
☐ 41 Brad Wellman	.05	.02	.01
☐ 42 Geoff Zahn	.05	.02	.01
☐ 43 Dave Engle	.05	.02	.01
☐ 44 Lance McCullers	.05	.02	.01
☐ 45 Damaso Garcia	.05	.02	.01
☐ 46 Billy Hatcher	.08	.04	.01
☐ 47 Juan Berenguer	.05	.02	.01
☐ 48 Bill Almon	.05	.02	.01
☐ 49 Rick Manning	.05	.02	.01
☐ 50 Dan Quisenberry	.08	.04	.01
☐ 51 Bobby Wine MG ERR	.08	.04	.01
(Checklist back)			
(Number of card on			
back is actually 57)			
☐ 52 Chris Welsh	.05	.02	.01
☐ 53 Len Dykstra	.75	.35	.09
☐ 54 John Franco	.10	.05	.01
☐ 55 Fred Lynn	.08	.04	.01
☐ 56 Tom Niedenfuer	.05	.02	.01
☐ 57 Bill Doran	.05	.02	.01
(See also 51)			
☐ 58 Bill Krueger	.05	.02	.01
☐ 59 Andre Thornton	.05	.02	.01
☐ 60 Dwight Evans	.10	.05	.01
☐ 61 Karl Best	.05	.02	.01

☐ 62 Bob Boone	.08	.04	.01
☐ 63 Ron Roenicke	.05	.02	.01
☐ 64 Floyd Bannister	.05	.02	.01
☐ 65 Dan Driessen	.05	.02	.01
☐ 66 Cardinals Leaders	.08	.04	.01
Bob Forsch			
☐ 67 Carmelo Martinez	.05	.02	.01
☐ 68 Ed Lynch	.05	.02	.01
☐ 69 Luis Aguayo	.05	.02	.01
☐ 70 Dave Winfield	.60	.25	.08
☐ 71 Ken Schrom	.05	.02	.01
☐ 72 Shawon Dunston	.12	.05	.02
☐ 73 Randy O'Neal	.05	.02	.01
☐ 74 Rance Mulliniks	.05	.02	.01
☐ 75 Jose DeLeon	.05	.02	.01
☐ 76 Dion James	.05	.02	.01
☐ 77 Charlie Leibrandt	.08	.04	.01
☐ 78 Bruce Benedict	.05	.02	.01
☐ 79 Dave Schmidt	.05	.02	.01
☐ 80 Darryl Strawberry	1.00	.45	.13
☐ 81 Gene Mauch MG	.08	.04	.01
(Checklist back)			
☐ 82 Tippy Martinez	.05	.02	.01
☐ 83 Phil Garner	.08	.04	.01
☐ 84 Curt Young	.05	.02	.01
☐ 85 Tony Perez	.12	.05	.02
(Eric Davis also			
shown on card)			
☐ 86 Tom Waddell	.05	.02	.01
☐ 87 Candy Maldonado	.08	.04	.01
☐ 88 Tom Nieto	.05	.02	.01
☐ 89 Randy St.Claire	.05	.02	.01
☐ 90 Garry Templeton	.05	.02	.01
☐ 91 Steve Crawford	.05	.02	.01
☐ 92 Al Cowens	.05	.02	.01
☐ 93 Scot Thompson	.05	.02	.01
☐ 94 Rich Bordi	.05	.02	.01
☐ 95 Ozzie Virgil	.05	.02	.01
☐ 96 Blue Jays Leaders	.08	.04	.01
Jim Clancy			
☐ 97 Gary Gaetti	.08	.04	.01
☐ 98 Dick Ruthven	.05	.02	.01
☐ 99 Buddy Biancalana	.05	.02	.01
☐ 100 Nolan Ryan	3.00	1.35	.40
☐ 101 Dave Bergman	.05	.02	.01
☐ 102 Joe Orsulak	.15	.07	.02
☐ 103 Luis Salazar	.05	.02	.01
☐ 104 Sid Fernandez	.12	.05	.02
☐ 105 Gary Ward	.05	.02	.01
☐ 106 Ray Burris	.05	.02	.01
☐ 107 Rafael Ramirez	.05	.02	.01
☐ 108 Ted Power	.05	.02	.01
☐ 109 Len Matuszek	.05	.02	.01
☐ 110 Scott McGregor	.05	.02	.01
☐ 111 Roger Craig MG	.08	.04	.01
(Checklist back)			
☐ 112 Bill Campbell	.05	.02	.01

☐ 113	U.L. Washington	.05	.02	.01		
☐ 114	Mike C. Brown (Pirates Outfielder)	.05	.02	.01		
☐ 115	Jay Howell	.08	.04	.01		
☐ 116	Brook Jacoby	.05	.02	.01		
☐ 117	Bruce Kison	.05	.02	.01		
☐ 118	Jerry Royster	.05	.02	.01		
☐ 119	Barry Bonnell	.05	.02	.01		
☐ 120	Steve Carlton	.40	.18	.05		
☐ 121	Nelson Simmons	.05	.02	.01		
☐ 122	Pete Filson	.05	.02	.01		
☐ 123	Greg Walker	.05	.02	.01		
☐ 124	Luis Sanchez	.05	.02	.01		
☐ 125	Dave Lopes	.08	.04	.01		
☐ 126	Mets Leaders Mookie Wilson	.08	.04	.01		
☐ 127	Jack Howell	.05	.02	.01		
☐ 128	John Wathan	.05	.02	.01		
☐ 129	Jeff Dedmon	.05	.02	.01		
☐ 130	Alan Trammell	.15	.07	.02		
☐ 131	Checklist: 1-132	.10	.01	.00		
☐ 132	Razor Shines	.05	.02	.01		
☐ 133	Andy McGaffigan	.05	.02	.01		
☐ 134	Carney Lansford	.08	.04	.01		
☐ 135	Joe Niekro	.08	.04	.01		
☐ 136	Mike Hargrove	.08	.04	.01		
☐ 137	Charlie Moore	.05	.02	.01		
☐ 138	Mark Davis	.08	.04	.01		
☐ 139	Daryl Boston	.05	.02	.01		
☐ 140	John Candelaria	.05	.02	.01		
☐ 141	Chuck Cottier MG (Checklist back) (See also 171)	.08	.04	.01		
☐ 142	Bob Jones	.05	.02	.01		
☐ 143	Dave Van Gorder	.05	.02	.01		
☐ 144	Doug Sisk	.05	.02	.01		
☐ 145	Pedro Guerrero	.10	.05	.01		
☐ 146	Jack Perconte	.05	.02	.01		
☐ 147	Larry Sheets	.05	.02	.01		
☐ 148	Mike Heath	.05	.02	.01		
☐ 149	Brett Butler	.10	.05	.01		
☐ 150	Joaquin Andujar	.05	.02	.01		
☐ 151	Dave Stapleton	.05	.02	.01		
☐ 152	Mike Morgan	.08	.04	.01		
☐ 153	Ricky Adams	.05	.02	.01		
☐ 154	Bert Roberge	.05	.02	.01		
☐ 155	Bob Grich	.08	.04	.01		
☐ 156	White Sox Leaders Richard Dotson	.08	.04	.01		
☐ 157	Ron Hassey	.05	.02	.01		
☐ 158	Derrel Thomas	.05	.02	.01		
☐ 159	Orel Hershiser UER (82 Alburquerque)	.25	.11	.03		
☐ 160	Chet Lemon	.05	.02	.01		
☐ 161	Lee Tunnell	.05	.02	.01		
☐ 162	Greg Gagne	.08	.04	.01		
☐ 163	Pete Ladd	.05	.02	.01		
☐ 164	Steve Balboni	.05	.02	.01
☐ 165	Mike Davis	.05	.02	.01
☐ 166	Dickie Thon	.05	.02	.01
☐ 167	Zane Smith	.15	.07	.02
☐ 168	Jeff Burroughs	.05	.02	.01
☐ 169	George Wright	.05	.02	.01
☐ 170	Gary Carter	.20	.09	.03
☐ 171	Bob Rodgers MG ERR (Checklist back) (Number of card on back actually 141)	.08	.04	.01
☐ 172	Jerry Reed	.05	.02	.01
☐ 173	Wayne Gross	.05	.02	.01
☐ 174	Brian Snyder	.05	.02	.01
☐ 175	Steve Sax	.10	.05	.01
☐ 176	Jay Tibbs	.05	.02	.01
☐ 177	Joel Youngblood	.05	.02	.01
☐ 178	Ivan DeJesus	.05	.02	.01
☐ 179	Stu Cliburn	.05	.02	.01
☐ 180	Don Mattingly	1.00	.45	.13
☐ 181	Al Nipper	.05	.02	.01
☐ 182	Bobby Brown	.05	.02	.01
☐ 183	Larry Andersen	.05	.02	.01
☐ 184	Tim Laudner	.05	.02	.01
☐ 185	Rollie Fingers	.15	.07	.02
☐ 186	Astros Leaders Jose Cruz	.08	.04	.01
☐ 187	Scott Fletcher	.05	.02	.01
☐ 188	Bob Dernier	.05	.02	.01
☐ 189	Mike Mason	.05	.02	.01
☐ 190	George Hendrick	.05	.02	.01
☐ 191	Wally Backman	.05	.02	.01
☐ 192	Milt Wilcox	.05	.02	.01
☐ 193	Daryl Sconiers	.05	.02	.01
☐ 194	Craig McMurtry	.05	.02	.01
☐ 195	Dave Concepcion	.08	.04	.01
☐ 196	Doyle Alexander	.05	.02	.01
☐ 197	Enos Cabell	.05	.02	.01
☐ 198	Ken Dixon	.05	.02	.01
☐ 199	Dick Howser MG (Checklist back)	.08	.04	.01
☐ 200	Mike Schmidt	1.00	.45	.13
☐ 201	RB: Vince Coleman Most stolen bases, season, rookie	.20	.09	.03
☐ 202	RB: Dwight Gooden Youngest 20 game winner	.20	.09	.03
☐ 203	RB: Keith Hernandez Most game-winning RBI's	.10	.05	.01
☐ 204	RB: Phil Niekro Oldest shutout pitcher	.10	.05	.01
☐ 205	RB: Tony Perez Oldest grand slammer	.10	.05	.01
☐ 206	RB: Pete Rose	.30	.14	.04

☐ 207	RB:Fernando Valenzuela		
	Most hits, lifetime .10	.05	.01
	Most cons. innings, start of season, no earned runs		
☐ 208	Ramon Romero .05	.02	.01
☐ 209	Randy Ready .05	.02	.01
☐ 210	Calvin Schiraldi .05	.02	.01
☐ 211	Ed Wojna .05	.02	.01
☐ 212	Chris Speier .05	.02	.01
☐ 213	Bob Shirley .05	.02	.01
☐ 214	Randy Bush .05	.02	.01
☐ 215	Frank White .08	.04	.01
☐ 216	A's Leaders .08	.04	.01
	Dwayne Murphy		
☐ 217	Bill Scherrer .05	.02	.01
☐ 218	Randy Hunt .05	.02	.01
☐ 219	Dennis Lamp .05	.02	.01
☐ 220	Bob Horner .08	.04	.01
☐ 221	Dave Henderson .10	.05	.01
☐ 222	Craig Gerber .05	.02	.01
☐ 223	Atlee Hammaker .05	.02	.01
☐ 224	Cesar Cedeno .08	.04	.01
☐ 225	Ron Darling .10	.05	.01
☐ 226	Lee Lacy .05	.02	.01
☐ 227	Al Jones .05	.02	.01
☐ 228	Tom Lawless .05	.02	.01
☐ 229	Bill Gullickson .08	.04	.01
☐ 230	Terry Kennedy .05	.02	.01
☐ 231	Jim Frey MG .08	.04	.01
	(Checklist back)		
☐ 232	Rick Rhoden .05	.02	.01
☐ 233	Steve Lyons .05	.02	.01
☐ 234	Doug Corbett .05	.02	.01
☐ 235	Butch Wynegar .05	.02	.01
☐ 236	Frank Eufemia .05	.02	.01
☐ 237	Ted Simmons .08	.04	.01
☐ 238	Larry Parrish .05	.02	.01
☐ 239	Joel Skinner .05	.02	.01
☐ 240	Tommy John .10	.05	.01
☐ 241	Tony Fernandez .12	.05	.02
☐ 242	Rich Thompson .05	.02	.01
☐ 243	Johnny Grubb .05	.02	.01
☐ 244	Craig Lefferts .08	.04	.01
☐ 245	Jim Sundberg .08	.04	.01
☐ 246	Phillies Leaders .15	.07	.02
	Steve Carlton		
☐ 247	Terry Harper .05	.02	.01
☐ 248	Spike Owen .05	.02	.01
☐ 249	Rob Deer .30	.14	.04
☐ 250	Dwight Gooden .50	.23	.06
☐ 251	Rich Dauer .05	.02	.01
☐ 252	Bobby Castillo .05	.02	.01
☐ 253	Dann Bilardello .05	.02	.01
☐ 254	Ozzie Guillen .25	.11	.03
☐ 255	Tony Armas .05	.02	.01
☐ 256	Kurt Kepshire .05	.02	.01
☐ 257	Doug DeCinces .05	.02	.01
☐ 258	Tim Burke .10	.05	.01
☐ 259	Dan Pasqua .08	.04	.01
☐ 260	Tony Pena .08	.04	.01
☐ 261	Bobby Valentine MG .08	.04	.01
	(Checklist back)		
☐ 262	Mario Ramirez .05	.02	.01
☐ 263	Checklist: 133-264 .10	.01	.00
☐ 264	Darren Daulton 1.00	.45	.13
☐ 265	Ron Davis .05	.02	.01
☐ 266	Keith Moreland .05	.02	.01
☐ 267	Paul Molitor .20	.09	.03
☐ 268	Mike Scott .08	.04	.01
☐ 269	Dane Iorg .05	.02	.01
☐ 270	Jack Morris .35	.16	.04
☐ 271	Dave Collins .05	.02	.01
☐ 272	Tim Tolman .05	.02	.01
☐ 273	Jerry Willard .05	.02	.01
☐ 274	Ron Gardenhire .05	.02	.01
☐ 275	Charlie Hough .05	.02	.01
☐ 276	Yankees Leaders .08	.04	.01
	Willie Randolph		
☐ 277	Jaime Cocanower .05	.02	.01
☐ 278	Sixto Lezcano .05	.02	.01
☐ 279	Al Pardo .05	.02	.01
☐ 280	Tim Raines .15	.07	.02
☐ 281	Steve Mura .05	.02	.01
☐ 282	Jerry Mumphrey .05	.02	.01
☐ 283	Mike Fischlin .05	.02	.01
☐ 284	Brian Dayett .05	.02	.01
☐ 285	Buddy Bell .08	.04	.01
☐ 286	Luis DeLeon .05	.02	.01
☐ 287	John Christensen .05	.02	.01
☐ 288	Don Aase .05	.02	.01
☐ 289	Johnnie LeMaster .05	.02	.01
☐ 290	Carlton Fisk .40	.18	.05
☐ 291	Tom Lasorda MG .08	.04	.01
	(Checklist back)		
☐ 292	Chuck Porter .05	.02	.01
☐ 293	Chris Chambliss .08	.04	.01
☐ 294	Danny Cox .05	.02	.01
☐ 295	Kirk Gibson .10	.05	.01
☐ 296	Geno Petralli .05	.02	.01
☐ 297	Tim Lollar .05	.02	.01
☐ 298	Craig Reynolds .05	.02	.01
☐ 299	Bryn Smith .05	.02	.01
☐ 300	George Brett .75	.35	.09
☐ 301	Dennis Rasmussen .05	.02	.01
☐ 302	Greg Gross .05	.02	.01
☐ 303	Curt Wardle .05	.02	.01
☐ 304	Mike Gallego .10	.05	.01
☐ 305	Phil Bradley .05	.02	.01
☐ 306	Padres Leaders .08	.04	.01
	Terry Kennedy		
☐ 307	Dave Sax .05	.02	.01
☐ 308	Ray Fontenot .05	.02	.01
☐ 309	John Shelby .05	.02	.01

☐ 310	Greg Minton	.05	.02	.01
☐ 311	Dick Schofield	.05	.02	.01
☐ 312	Tom Filer	.05	.02	.01
☐ 313	Joe DeSa	.05	.02	.01
☐ 314	Frank Pastore	.05	.02	.01
☐ 315	Mookie Wilson	.08	.04	.01
☐ 316	Sammy Khalifa	.05	.02	.01
☐ 317	Ed Romero	.05	.02	.01
☐ 318	Terry Whitfield	.05	.02	.01
☐ 319	Rick Camp	.05	.02	.01
☐ 320	Jim Rice	.10	.05	.01
☐ 321	Earl Weaver MG	.08	.04	.01
	(Checklist back)			
☐ 322	Bob Forsch	.05	.02	.01
☐ 323	Jerry Davis	.05	.02	.01
☐ 324	Dan Schatzeder	.05	.02	.01
☐ 325	Juan Beniquez	.05	.02	.01
☐ 326	Kent Tekulve	.05	.02	.01
☐ 327	Mike Pagliarulo	.05	.02	.01
☐ 328	Pete O'Brien	.05	.02	.01
☐ 329	Kirby Puckett	4.00	1.80	.50
☐ 330	Rick Sutcliffe	.08	.04	.01
☐ 331	Alan Ashby	.05	.02	.01
☐ 332	Darryl Motley	.05	.02	.01
☐ 333	Tom Henke	.35	.16	.04
☐ 334	Ken Oberkfell	.05	.02	.01
☐ 335	Don Sutton	.12	.05	.02
☐ 336	Indians Leaders	.08	.04	.01
	Andre Thornton			
☐ 337	Darnell Coles	.08	.04	.01
☐ 338	Jorge Bell	.25	.11	.03
☐ 339	Bruce Berenyi	.05	.02	.01
☐ 340	Cal Ripken	2.50	1.15	.30
☐ 341	Frank Williams	.05	.02	.01
☐ 342	Gary Redus	.05	.02	.01
☐ 343	Carlos Diaz	.05	.02	.01
☐ 344	Jim Wohlford	.05	.02	.01
☐ 345	Donnie Moore	.05	.02	.01
☐ 346	Bryan Little	.05	.02	.01
☐ 347	Teddy Higuera	.10	.05	.01
☐ 348	Cliff Johnson	.05	.02	.01
☐ 349	Mark Clear	.05	.02	.01
☐ 350	Jack Clark	.08	.04	.01
☐ 351	Chuck Tanner MG	.08	.04	.01
	(Checklist back)			
☐ 352	Harry Spilman	.05	.02	.01
☐ 353	Keith Atherton	.05	.02	.01
☐ 354	Tony Bernazard	.05	.02	.01
☐ 355	Lee Smith	.25	.11	.03
☐ 356	Mickey Hatcher	.05	.02	.01
☐ 357	Ed VandeBerg	.05	.02	.01
☐ 358	Rick Dempsey	.05	.02	.01
☐ 359	Mike LaCoss	.05	.02	.01
☐ 360	Lloyd Moseby	.05	.02	.01
☐ 361	Shane Rawley	.05	.02	.01
☐ 362	Tom Paciorek	.08	.04	.01
☐ 363	Terry Forster	.05	.02	.01
☐ 364	Reid Nichols	.05	.02	.01
☐ 365	Mike Flanagan	.05	.02	.01
☐ 366	Reds Leaders	.08	.04	.01
	Dave Concepcion			
☐ 367	Aurelio Lopez	.05	.02	.01
☐ 368	Greg Brock	.05	.02	.01
☐ 369	Al Holland	.05	.02	.01
☐ 370	Vince Coleman	.90	.40	.11
☐ 371	Bill Stein	.05	.02	.01
☐ 372	Ben Oglivie	.05	.02	.01
☐ 373	Urbano Lugo	.05	.02	.01
☐ 374	Terry Francona	.05	.02	.01
☐ 375	Rich Gedman	.05	.02	.01
☐ 376	Bill Dawley	.05	.02	.01
☐ 377	Joe Carter	1.00	.45	.13
☐ 378	Bruce Bochte	.05	.02	.01
☐ 379	Bobby Meacham	.05	.02	.01
· ☐ 380	LaMarr Hoyt	.05	.02	.01
☐ 381	Ray Miller MG	.08	.04	.01
	(Checklist back)			
☐ 382	Ivan Calderon	.50	.23	.06
☐ 383	Chris Brown	.05	.02	.01
☐ 384	Steve Trout	.05	.02	.01
☐ 385	Cecil Cooper	.08	.04	.01
☐ 386	Cecil Fielder	6.50	2.90	.80
☐ 387	Steve Kemp	.05	.02	.01
☐ 388	Dickie Noles	.05	.02	.01
☐ 389	Glenn Davis	.40	.18	.05
☐ 390	Tom Seaver	.40	.18	.05
☐ 391	Julio Franco	.15	.07	.02
☐ 392	John Russell	.05	.02	.01
☐ 393	Chris Pittaro	.05	.02	.01
☐ 394	Checklist: 265-396	.10	.01	.00
☐ 395	Scott Garrelts	.05	.02	.01
☐ 396	Red Sox Leaders	.08	.04	.01
	Dwight Evans			
☐ 397	Steve Buechele	.40	.18	.05
☐ 398	Earnie Riles	.05	.02	.01
☐ 399	Bill Swift	.15	.07	.02
☐ 400	Rod Carew	.45	.20	.06
☐ 401	Turn Back 5 Years	.10	.05	.01
	Fernando Valenzuela '81			
☐ 402	Turn Back 10 Years	.20	.09	.03
	Tom Seaver '76			
☐ 403	Turn Back 15 Years	.15	.07	.02
	Willie Mays '71			
☐ 404	Turn Back 20 Years	.12	.05	.02
	Frank Robinson '66			
☐ 405	Turn Back 25 Years	.15	.07	.02
	Roger Maris '61			
☐ 406	Scott Sanderson	.05	.02	.01
☐ 407	Sal Butera	.05	.02	.01
☐ 408	Dave Smith	.05	.02	.01
☐ 409	Paul Runge	.05	.02	.01
☐ 410	Dave Kingman	.08	.04	.01
☐ 411	Sparky Anderson MG	.08	.04	.01
	(Checklist back)			

☐ 412	Jim Clancy	.05	.02	.01
☐ 413	Tim Flannery	.05	.02	.01
☐ 414	Tom Gorman	.05	.02	.01
☐ 415	Hal McRae	.08	.04	.01
☐ 416	Dennis Martinez	.08	.04	.01
☐ 417	R.J. Reynolds	.05	.02	.01
☐ 418	Alan Knicely	.05	.02	.01
☐ 419	Frank Wills	.05	.02	.01
☐ 420	Von Hayes	.05	.02	.01
☐ 421	David Palmer	.05	.02	.01
☐ 422	Mike Jorgensen	.05	.02	.01
☐ 423	Dan Spillner	.05	.02	.01
☐ 424	Rick Miller	.05	.02	.01
☐ 425	Larry McWilliams	.05	.02	.01
☐ 426	Brewers Leaders	.08	.04	.01
	Charlie Moore			
☐ 427	Joe Cowley	.05	.02	.01
☐ 428	Max Venable	.05	.02	.01
☐ 429	Greg Booker	.05	.02	.01
☐ 430	Kent Hrbek	.12	.05	.02
☐ 431	George Frazier	.05	.02	.01
☐ 432	Mark Bailey	.05	.02	.01
☐ 433	Chris Codiroli	.05	.02	.01
☐ 434	Curt Wilkerson	.05	.02	.01
☐ 435	Bill Caudill	.05	.02	.01
☐ 436	Doug Flynn	.05	.02	.01
☐ 437	Rick Mahler	.05	.02	.01
☐ 438	Clint Hurdle	.05	.02	.01
☐ 439	Rick Honeycutt	.05	.02	.01
☐ 440	Alvin Davis	.05	.02	.01
☐ 441	Whitey Herzog MG	.08	.04	.01
	(Checklist back)			
☐ 442	Ron Robinson	.05	.02	.01
☐ 443	Bill Buckner	.08	.04	.01
☐ 444	Alex Trevino	.05	.02	.01
☐ 445	Bert Blyleven	.10	.05	.01
☐ 446	Lenn Sakata	.05	.02	.01
☐ 447	Jerry Don Gleaton	.05	.02	.01
☐ 448	Herm Winningham	.10	.05	.01
☐ 449	Rod Scurry	.05	.02	.01
☐ 450	Graig Nettles	.08	.04	.01
☐ 451	Mark Brown	.05	.02	.01
☐ 452	Bob Clark	.05	.02	.01
☐ 453	Steve Jeltz	.05	.02	.01
☐ 454	Burt Hooton	.05	.02	.01
☐ 455	Willie Randolph	.08	.04	.01
☐ 456	Braves Leaders	.10	.05	.01
	Dale Murphy			
☐ 457	Mickey Tettleton	1.00	.45	.13
☐ 458	Kevin Bass	.05	.02	.01
☐ 459	Luis Leal	.05	.02	.01
☐ 460	Leon Durham	.05	.02	.01
☐ 461	Walt Terrell	.05	.02	.01
☐ 462	Domingo Ramos	.05	.02	.01
☐ 463	Jim Gott	.05	.02	.01
☐ 464	Ruppert Jones	.05	.02	.01
☐ 465	Jesse Orosco	.05	.02	.01
☐ 466	Tom Foley	.05	.02	.01
☐ 467	Bob James	.05	.02	.01
☐ 468	Mike Scioscia	.05	.02	.01
☐ 469	Storm Davis	.05	.02	.01
☐ 470	Bill Madlock	.08	.04	.01
☐ 471	Bobby Cox MG	.08	.04	.01
	(Checklist back)			
☐ 472	Joe Hesketh	.08	.04	.01
☐ 473	Mark Brouhard	.08	.04	.01
☐ 474	John Tudor	.08	.04	.01
☐ 475	Juan Samuel	.08	.04	.01
☐ 476	Ron Mathis	.05	.02	.01
☐ 477	Mike Easler	.05	.02	.01
☐ 478	Andy Hawkins	.05	.02	.01
☐ 479	Bob Melvin	.05	.02	.01
☐ 480	Oddibe McDowell	.05	.02	.01
☐ 481	Scott Bradley	.05	.02	.01
☐ 482	Rick Lysander	.05	.02	.01
☐ 483	George Vukovich	.05	.02	.01
☐ 484	Donnie Hill	.05	.02	.01
☐ 485	Gary Matthews	.05	.02	.01
☐ 486	Angels Leaders	.05	.02	.01
	Bobby Grich			
☐ 487	Bret Saberhagen	.40	.18	.05
☐ 488	Lou Thornton	.05	.02	.01
☐ 489	Jim Winn	.05	.02	.01
☐ 490	Jeff Leonard	.05	.02	.01
☐ 491	Pascual Perez	.05	.02	.01
☐ 492	Kelvin Chapman	.05	.02	.01
☐ 493	Gene Nelson	.05	.02	.01
☐ 494	Gary Roenicke	.05	.02	.01
☐ 495	Mark Langston	.20	.09	.03
☐ 496	Jay Johnstone	.08	.04	.01
☐ 497	John Stuper	.05	.02	.01
☐ 498	Tito Landrum	.05	.02	.01
☐ 499	Bob L. Gibson	.05	.02	.01
☐ 500	Rickey Henderson	1.00	.45	.13
☐ 501	Dave Johnson MG	.08	.04	.01
	(Checklist back)			
☐ 502	Glen Cook	.05	.02	.01
☐ 503	Mike Fitzgerald	.05	.02	.01
☐ 504	Denny Walling	.05	.02	.01
☐ 505	Jerry Koosman	.08	.04	.01
☐ 506	Bill Russell	.08	.04	.01
☐ 507	Steve Ontiveros	.05	.02	.01
☐ 508	Alan Wiggins	.05	.02	.01
☐ 509	Ernie Camacho	.05	.02	.01
☐ 510	Wade Boggs	1.00	.45	.13
☐ 511	Ed Nunez	.05	.02	.01
☐ 512	Thad Bosley	.05	.02	.01
☐ 513	Ron Washington	.05	.02	.01
☐ 514	Mike Jones	.05	.02	.01
☐ 515	Darrell Evans	.08	.04	.01
☐ 516	Giants Leaders	.08	.04	.01
	Greg Minton			
☐ 517	Milt Thompson	.10	.05	.01
☐ 518	Buck Martinez	.05	.02	.01

□	519	Danny Darwin	.05	.02	.01
□	520	Keith Hernandez	.10	.05	.01
□	521	Nate Snell	.05	.02	.01
□	522	Bob Bailor	.05	.02	.01
□	523	Joe Price	.05	.02	.01
□	524	Darrell Miller	.05	.02	.01
□	525	Marvell Wynne	.05	.02	.01
□	526	Charlie Lea	.05	.02	.01
□	527	Checklist: 397-528	.10	.01	.00
□	528	Terry Pendleton	.60	.25	.08
□	529	Marc Sullivan	.05	.02	.01
□	530	Rich Gossage	.10	.05	.01
□	531	Tony LaRussa MG	.08	.04	.01
		(Checklist back)			
□	532	Don Carman	.05	.02	.01
□	533	Billy Sample	.05	.02	.01
□	534	Jeff Calhoun	.05	.02	.01
□	535	Toby Harrah	.05	.02	.01
□	536	Jose Rijo	.25	.11	.03
□	537	Mark Salas	.05	.02	.01
□	538	Dennis Eckersley	.30	.14	.04
□	539	Glenn Hubbard	.05	.02	.01
□	540	Dan Petry	.05	.02	.01
□	541	Jorge Orta	.05	.02	.01
□	542	Don Schulze	.05	.02	.01
□	543	Jerry Narron	.05	.02	.01
□	544	Eddie Milner	.05	.02	.01
□	545	Jimmy Key	.20	.09	.03
□	546	Mariners Leaders	.08	.04	.01
		Dave Henderson			
□	547	Roger McDowell	.12	.05	.02
□	548	Mike Young	.05	.02	.01
□	549	Bob Welch	.10	.05	.01
□	550	Tom Herr	.05	.02	.01
□	551	Dave LaPoint	.05	.02	.01
□	552	Marc Hill	.05	.02	.01
□	553	Jim Morrison	.05	.02	.01
□	554	Paul Householder	.05	.02	.01
□	555	Hubie Brooks	.05	.02	.01
□	556	John Denny	.05	.02	.01
□	557	Gerald Perry	.05	.02	.01
□	558	Tim Stoddard	.05	.02	.01
□	559	Tommy Dunbar	.05	.02	.01
□	560	Dave Righetti	.08	.04	.01
□	561	Bob Lillis MG	.08	.04	.01
		(Checklist back)			
□	562	Joe Beckwith	.05	.02	.01
□	563	Alejandro Sanchez	.05	.02	.01
□	564	Warren Brusstar	.05	.02	.01
□	565	Tom Brunansky	.08	.04	.01
□	566	Alfredo Griffin	.05	.02	.01
□	567	Jeff Barkley	.05	.02	.01
□	568	Donnie Scott	.05	.02	.01
□	569	Jim Acker	.05	.02	.01
□	570	Rusty Staub	.08	.04	.01
□	571	Mike Jeffcoat	.05	.02	.01
□	572	Paul Zuvella	.05	.02	.01

□	573	Tom Hume	.05	.02	.01
□	574	Ron Kittle	.05	.02	.01
□	575	Mike Boddicker	.05	.02	.01
□	576	Expos Leaders	.15	.07	.02
		Andre Dawson			
□	577	Jerry Reuss	.05	.02	.01
□	578	Lee Mazzilli	.05	.02	.01
□	579	Jim Slaton	.05	.02	.01
□	580	Willie McGee	.10	.05	.01
□	581	Bruce Hurst	.08	.04	.01
□	582	Jim Gantner	.05	.02	.01
□	583	Al Bumbry	.05	.02	.01
□	584	Brian Fisher	.05	.02	.01
□	585	Garry Maddox	.05	.02	.01
□	586	Greg Harris	.05	.02	.01
□	587	Rafael Santana	.05	.02	.01
□	588	Steve Lake	.05	.02	.01
□	589	Sid Bream	.08	.04	.01
□	590	Bob Knepper	.05	.02	.01
□	591	Jackie Moore MG	.08	.04	.01
		(Checklist back)			
□	592	Frank Tanana	.08	.04	.01
□	593	Jesse Barfield	.08	.04	.01
□	594	Chris Bando	.05	.02	.01
□	595	Dave Parker	.12	.05	.02
□	596	Onix Concepcion	.05	.02	.01
□	597	Sammy Stewart	.05	.02	.01
□	598	Jim Presley	.05	.02	.01
□	599	Rick Aguilera	.75	.35	.09
□	600	Dale Murphy	.25	.11	.03
□	601	Gary Lucas	.05	.02	.01
□	602	Mariano Duncan	.25	.11	.03
□	603	Bill Laskey	.05	.02	.01
□	604	Gary Pettis	.05	.02	.01
□	605	Dennis Boyd	.05	.02	.01
□	606	Royals Leaders	.08	.04	.01
		Hal McRae			
□	607	Ken Dayley	.05	.02	.01
□	608	Bruce Bochy	.05	.02	.01
□	609	Barbaro Garbey	.05	.02	.01
□	610	Ron Guidry	.08	.04	.01
□	611	Gary Woods	.05	.02	.01
□	612	Richard Dotson	.05	.02	.01
□	613	Roy Smalley	.05	.02	.01
□	614	Rick Waits	.05	.02	.01
□	615	Johnny Ray	.05	.02	.01
□	616	Glenn Brummer	.05	.02	.01
□	617	Lonnie Smith	.05	.02	.01
□	618	Jim Pankovits	.05	.02	.01
□	619	Danny Heep	.05	.02	.01
□	620	Bruce Sutter	.08	.04	.01
□	621	John Felske MG	.08	.04	.01
		(Checklist back)			
□	622	Gary Lavelle	.05	.02	.01
□	623	Floyd Rayford	.05	.02	.01
□	624	Steve McCatty	.05	.02	.01
□	625	Bob Brenly	.05	.02	.01

☐ 626	Roy Thomas 05	.02	.01
☐ 627	Ron Oester 05	.02	.01
☐ 628	Kirk McCaskill 15	.07	.02
☐ 629	Mitch Webster 05	.02	.01
☐ 630	Fernando Valenzuela ...08	.04	.01
☐ 631	Steve Braun 05	.02	.01
☐ 632	Dave Von Ohlen 05	.02	.01
☐ 633	Jackie Gutierrez 05	.02	.01
☐ 634	Roy Lee Jackson 05	.02	.01
☐ 635	Jason Thompson 05	.02	.01
☐ 636	Cubs Leaders 15	.07	.02
	Lee Smith		
☐ 637	Rudy Law 05	.02	.01
☐ 638	John Butcher 05	.02	.01
☐ 639	Bo Diaz 05	.02	.01
☐ 640	Jose Cruz 05	.02	.01
☐ 641	Wayne Tolleson 05	.02	.01
☐ 642	Ray Searage 05	.02	.01
☐ 643	Tom Brookens 05	.02	.01
☐ 644	Mark Gubicza 08	.04	.01
☐ 645	Dusty Baker 08	.04	.01
☐ 646	Mike Moore 10	.05	.01
☐ 647	Mel Hall 10	.05	.01
☐ 648	Steve Bedrosian 05	.02	.01
☐ 649	Ronn Reynolds 05	.02	.01
☐ 650	Dave Stieb 08	.04	.01
☐ 651	Billy Martin MG 10	.05	.01
	(Checklist back)		
☐ 652	Tom Browning 12	.05	.02
☐ 653	Jim Dwyer 05	.02	.01
☐ 654	Ken Howell 05	.02	.01
☐ 655	Manny Trillo 05	.02	.01
☐ 656	Brian Harper 12	.05	.02
☐ 657	Juan Agosto 05	.02	.01
☐ 658	Rob Wilfong 05	.02	.01
☐ 659	Checklist: 529-660 10	.01	.00
☐ 660	Steve Garvey 15	.07	.02
☐ 661	Roger Clemens 4.50	2.00	.55
☐ 662	Bill Schroeder 05	.02	.01
☐ 663	Neil Allen 05	.02	.01
☐ 664	Tim Corcoran 05	.02	.01
☐ 665	Alejandro Pena 05	.02	.01
☐ 666	Rangers Leaders 08	.04	.01
	Charlie Hough		
☐ 667	Tim Teufel 05	.02	.01
☐ 668	Cecilio Guante 05	.02	.01
☐ 669	Ron Cey 08	.04	.01
☐ 670	Willie Hernandez 05	.02	.01
☐ 671	Lynn Jones 05	.02	.01
☐ 672	Rob Picciolo 05	.02	.01
☐ 673	Ernie Whitt 05	.02	.01
☐ 674	Pat Tabler 05	.02	.01
☐ 675	Claudell Washington 05	.02	.01
☐ 676	Matt Young 05	.02	.01
☐ 677	Nick Esasky 05	.02	.01
☐ 678	Dan Gladden 05	.02	.01
☐ 679	Britt Burns 05	.02	.01

☐ 680	George Foster 05	.02	.01
☐ 681	Dick Williams MG 08	.04	.01
	(Checklist back)		
☐ 682	Junior Ortiz 05	.02	.01
☐ 683	Andy Van Slyke 30	.14	.04
☐ 684	Bob McClure 05	.02	.01
☐ 685	Tim Wallach 08	.04	.01
☐ 686	Jeff Stone 05	.02	.01
☐ 687	Mike Trujillo 05	.02	.01
☐ 688	Larry Herndon 05	.02	.01
☐ 689	Dave Stewart 12	.05	.02
☐ 690	Ryne Sandberg UER 2.00	.90	.25
	(No Topps logo		
	on front)		
☐ 691	Mike Madden 05	.02	.01
☐ 692	Dale Berra 05	.02	.01
☐ 693	Tom Tellmann 05	.02	.01
☐ 694	Garth Iorg 05	.02	.01
☐ 695	Mike Smithson 05	.02	.01
☐ 696	Dodgers Leaders 08	.04	.01
	Bill Russell		
☐ 697	Bud Black 05	.02	.01
☐ 698	Brad Komminsk 05	.02	.01
☐ 699	Pat Corrales MG 08	.04	.01
	(Checklist back)		
☐ 700	Reggie Jackson 40	.18	.05
☐ 701	Keith Hernandez AS 08	.04	.01
☐ 702	Tom Herr AS 08	.04	.01
☐ 703	Tim Wallach AS 08	.04	.01
☐ 704	Ozzie Smith AS 20	.09	.03
☐ 705	Dale Murphy AS 12	.05	.02
☐ 706	Pedro Guerrero AS 08	.04	.01
☐ 707	Willie McGee AS 08	.04	.01
☐ 708	Gary Carter AS 10	.05	.01
☐ 709	Dwight Gooden AS 20	.09	.03
☐ 710	John Tudor AS 08	.04	.01
☐ 711	Jeff Reardon AS 15	.07	.02
☐ 712	Don Mattingly AS 40	.18	.05
☐ 713	Damaso Garcia AS 08	.04	.01
☐ 714	George Brett AS 35	.16	.04
☐ 715	Cal Ripken AS 1.00	.45	.13
☐ 716	Rickey Henderson AS 40	.18	.05
☐ 717	Dave Winfield AS 30	.14	.04
☐ 718	George Bell AS 15	.07	.02
☐ 719	Carlton Fisk AS 20	.09	.03
☐ 720	Bret Saberhagen AS 15	.07	.02
☐ 721	Ron Guidry AS 08	.04	.01
☐ 722	Dan Quisenberry AS 08	.04	.01
☐ 723	Marty Bystrom 05	.02	.01
☐ 724	Tim Hulett 05	.02	.01
☐ 725	Mario Soto 05	.02	.01
☐ 726	Orioles Leaders 08	.04	.01
	Rick Dempsey		
☐ 727	David Green 05	.02	.01
☐ 728	Mike Marshall 05	.02	.01
☐ 729	Jim Beattie 05	.02	.01
☐ 730	Ozzie Smith 45	.20	.06

□	731	Don Robinson	05	.02	.01
□	732	Floyd Youmans	05	.02	.01
□	733	Ron Romanick	05	.02	.01
□	734	Marty Barrett	05	.02	.01
□	735	Dave Dravecky	08	.04	.01
□	736	Glenn Wilson	05	.02	.01
□	737	Pete Vuckovich	05	.02	.01
□	738	Andre Robertson	05	.02	.01
□	739	Dave Rozema	05	.02	.01
□	740	Lance Parrish	08	.04	.01
□	741	Pete Rose MG	40	.18	.05
		(Checklist back)			
□	742	Frank Viola	15	.07	.02
□	743	Pat Sheridan	05	.02	.01
□	744	Lary Sorensen	05	.02	.01
□	745	Willie Upshaw	05	.02	.01
□	746	Denny Gonzalez	05	.02	.01
□	747	Rick Cerone	05	.02	.01
□	748	Steve Henderson	05	.02	.01
□	749	Ed Jurak	05	.02	.01
□	750	Gorman Thomas	05	.02	.01
□	751	Howard Johnson	35	.16	.04
□	752	Mike Krukow	05	.02	.01
□	753	Dan Ford	05	.02	.01
□	754	Pat Clements	05	.02	.01
□	755	Harold Baines	12	.05	.02
□	756	Pirates Leaders	08	.04	.01
		Rick Rhoden			
□	757	Darrell Porter	05	.02	.01
□	758	Dave Anderson	05	.02	.01
□	759	Moose Haas	05	.02	.01
□	760	Andre Dawson	50	.23	.06
□	761	Don Slaught	05	.02	.01
□	762	Eric Show	05	.02	.01
□	763	Terry Puhl	05	.02	.01
□	764	Kevin Gross	05	.02	.01
□	765	Don Baylor	08	.04	.01
□	766	Rick Langford	05	.02	.01
□	767	Jody Davis	05	.02	.01
□	768	Vern Ruhle	05	.02	.01
□	769	Harold Reynolds	25	.11	.03
□	770	Vida Blue	08	.04	.01
□	771	John McNamara MG	08	.04	.01
		(Checklist back)			
□	772	Brian Downing	08	.04	.01
□	773	Greg Pryor	05	.02	.01
□	774	Terry Leach	05	.02	.01
□	775	Al Oliver	08	.04	.01
□	776	Gene Garber	05	.02	.01
□	777	Wayne Krenchicki	05	.02	.01
□	778	Jerry Hairston	05	.02	.01
□	779	Rick Reuschel	08	.04	.01
□	780	Robin Yount	75	.35	.09
□	781	Joe Nolan	05	.02	.01
□	782	Ken Landreaux	05	.02	.01
□	783	Ricky Horton	05	.02	.01
□	784	Alan Bannister	05	.02	.01

□	785	Bob Stanley	05	.02	.01
□	786	Twins Leaders	08	.04	.01
		Mickey Hatcher			
□	787	Vance Law	05	.02	.01
□	788	Marty Castillo	05	.02	.01
□	789	Kurt Bevacqua	05	.02	.01
□	790	Phil Niekro	12	.05	.02
□	791	Checklist: 661-792	10	.01	.00
□	792	Charles Hudson	08	.02	.01

1986 Topps Traded

This 132-card Traded or extended set was distributed by Topps to dealers in a special red and white box as a complete set. The card fronts are identical in style to the Topps regular issue and are also 2 1/2" by 3 1/2". The backs are printed in red and black on white card stock. Cards are numbered (with a T suffix) alphabetically according to the name of the player. The key (extended) Rookie Cards in this set are Barry Bonds, Bobby Bonilla, Jose Canseco, Will Clark, Bo Jackson, and Kevin Mitchell. Topps also produced a specially boxed "glossy" edition frequently referred to as the Topps Traded Tiffany set. There were supposedly only 5,000 sets of the Tiffany set produced; they were marketed to hobby dealers. The checklist of cards is identical to that of the normal non-glossy cards. There are two primary distinguishing features of the Tiffany cards, white card stock reverses and high gloss obverses. These Tiffany cards are valued approximately from five to ten times the values listed below.

		MT	EX-MT	VG
	COMPLETE SET (132)	24.00	11.00	3.00
	COMMON PLAYER (1T-132T)	.06	.03	.01
☐ 1T	Andy Allanson	.06	.03	.01
☐ 2T	Neil Allen	.06	.03	.01
☐ 3T	Joaquin Andujar	.06	.03	.01
☐ 4T	Paul Assenmacher	.06	.03	.01
☐ 5T	Scott Bailes	.06	.03	.01
☐ 6T	Don Baylor	.10	.04	.01
☐ 7T	Steve Bedrosian	.06	.03	.01
☐ 8T	Juan Beniquez	.06	.03	.01
☐ 9T	Juan Berenguer	.06	.03	.01
☐ 10T	Mike Bielecki	.15	.07	.02
☐ 11T	Barry Bonds	6.00	2.70	.75
☐ 12T	Bobby Bonilla	2.50	1.15	.30
☐ 13T	Juan Bonilla	.06	.03	.01
☐ 14T	Rich Bordi	.06	.03	.01
☐ 15T	Steve Boros MG	.06	.03	.01
☐ 16T	Rick Burleson	.06	.03	.01
☐ 17T	Bill Campbell	.06	.03	.01
☐ 18T	Tom Candiotti	.15	.07	.02
☐ 19T	John Cangelosi	.06	.03	.01
☐ 20T	Jose Canseco	6.00	2.70	.75
☐ 21T	Carmen Castillo	.06	.03	.01
☐ 22T	Rick Cerone	.06	.03	.01
☐ 23T	John Cerutti	.06	.03	.01
☐ 24T	Will Clark	6.00	2.70	.75
☐ 25T	Mark Clear	.06	.03	.01
☐ 26T	Darnell Coles	.06	.03	.01
☐ 27T	Dave Collins	.06	.03	.01
☐ 28T	Tim Conroy	.06	.03	.01
☐ 29T	Joe Cowley	.06	.03	.01
☐ 30T	Joel Davis	.06	.03	.01
☐ 31T	Rob Deer	.20	.09	.03
☐ 32T	John Denny	.06	.03	.01
☐ 33T	Mike Easler	.06	.03	.01
☐ 34T	Mark Eichhorn	.10	.04	.01
☐ 35T	Steve Farr	.10	.04	.01
☐ 36T	Scott Fletcher	.06	.03	.01
☐ 37T	Terry Forster	.06	.03	.01
☐ 38T	Terry Francona	.06	.03	.01
☐ 39T	Jim Fregosi MG	.06	.03	.01
☐ 40T	Andres Galarraga	.25	.11	.03
☐ 41T	Ken Griffey	.10	.04	.01
☐ 42T	Bill Gullickson	.10	.04	.01
☐ 43T	Jose Guzman	.30	.14	.04
☐ 44T	Moose Haas	.06	.03	.01
☐ 45T	Billy Hatcher	.10	.04	.01
☐ 46T	Mike Heath	.06	.03	.01
☐ 47T	Tom Hume	.06	.03	.01
☐ 48T	Pete Incaviglia	.25	.11	.03
☐ 49T	Dane Iorg	.06	.03	.01
☐ 50T	Bo Jackson	2.50	1.15	.30
☐ 51T	Wally Joyner	1.00	.45	.13
☐ 52T	Charlie Kerfeld	.10	.04	.01
☐ 53T	Eric King	.06	.03	.01
☐ 54T	Bob Kipper	.06	.03	.01
☐ 55T	Wayne Krenchicki	.06	.03	.01
☐ 56T	John Kruk	.90	.40	.11
☐ 57T	Mike LaCoss	.06	.03	.01
☐ 58T	Pete Ladd	.06	.03	.01
☐ 59T	Mike Laga	.06	.03	.01
☐ 60T	Hal Lanier MG	.06	.03	.01
☐ 61T	Dave LaPoint	.06	.03	.01
☐ 62T	Rudy Law	.06	.03	.01
☐ 63T	Rick Leach	.06	.03	.01
☐ 64T	Tim Leary	.06	.03	.01
☐ 65T	Dennis Leonard	.06	.03	.01
☐ 66T	Jim Leyland MG	.25	.11	.03
☐ 67T	Steve Lyons	.06	.03	.01
☐ 68T	Mickey Mahler	.06	.03	.01
☐ 69T	Candy Maldonado	.10	.04	.01
☐ 70T	Roger Mason	.10	.05	.01
☐ 71T	Bob McClure	.06	.03	.01
☐ 72T	Andy McGaffigan	.06	.03	.01
☐ 73T	Gene Michael MG	.06	.03	.01
☐ 74T	Kevin Mitchell	1.25	.55	.16
☐ 75T	Omar Moreno	.06	.03	.01
☐ 76T	Jerry Mumphrey	.06	.03	.01
☐ 77T	Phil Niekro	.25	.11	.03
☐ 78T	Randy Niemann	.06	.03	.01
☐ 79T	Juan Nieves	.06	.03	.01
☐ 80T	Otis Nixon	.60	.25	.08
☐ 81T	Bob Ojeda	.06	.03	.01
☐ 82T	Jose Oquendo	.06	.03	.01
☐ 83T	Tom Paciorek	.10	.04	.01
☐ 84T	David Palmer	.06	.03	.01
☐ 85T	Frank Pastore	.06	.03	.01
☐ 86T	Lou Piniella MG	.10	.04	.01
☐ 87T	Dan Plesac	.15	.07	.02
☐ 88T	Darrell Porter	.06	.03	.01
☐ 89T	Rey Quinones	.06	.03	.01
☐ 90T	Gary Redus	.06	.03	.01
☐ 91T	Bip Roberts	.60	.25	.08
☐ 92T	Billy Joe Robidoux	.06	.03	.01
☐ 93T	Jeff D. Robinson	.10	.04	.01
☐ 94T	Gary Roenicke	.06	.03	.01
☐ 95T	Ed Romero	.06	.03	.01
☐ 96T	Argenis Salazar	.06	.03	.01
☐ 97T	Joe Sambito	.06	.03	.01
☐ 98T	Billy Sample	.06	.03	.01
☐ 99T	Dave Schmidt	.06	.03	.01
☐ 100T	Ken Schrom	.06	.03	.01
☐ 101T	Tom Seaver	.50	.23	.06
☐ 102T	Ted Simmons	.10	.04	.01
☐ 103T	Sammy Stewart	.06	.03	.01
☐ 104T	Kurt Stillwell	.15	.07	.02
☐ 105T	Franklin Stubbs	.06	.03	.01
☐ 106T	Dale Sveum	.06	.03	.01
☐ 107T	Chuck Tanner MG	.06	.03	.01
☐ 108T	Danny Tartabull	.90	.40	.11
☐ 109T	Tim Teufel	.06	.03	.01
☐ 110T	Bob Tewksbury	.40	.18	.05

			MT	EX-MT	VG

☐ 111T Andres Thomas.............06 .03 .01
☐ 112T Milt Thompson ....10 .04 .01
☐ 113T Robby Thompson ....25 .11 .03
☐ 114T Jay Tibbs ....06 .03 .01
☐ 115T Wayne Tolleson ....06 .03 .01
☐ 116T Alex Trevino.................06 .03 .01
☐ 117T Manny Trillo.................06 .03 .01
☐ 118T Ed VandeBerg.............06 .03 .01
☐ 119T Ozzie Virgil.................06 .03 .01
☐ 120T Bob Walk....................06 .03 .01
☐ 121T Gene Walter................06 .03 .01
☐ 122T Claudell Washington ...06 .03 .01
☐ 123T Bill Wegman ....25 .11 .03
☐ 124T Dick Williams MG ....06 .03 .01
☐ 125T Mitch Williams...........20 .09 .03
☐ 126T Bobby Witt..................25 .11 .03
☐ 127T Todd Worrell ....20 .09 .03
☐ 128T George Wright ....06 .03 .01
☐ 129T Ricky Wright ....06 .03 .01
☐ 130T Steve Yeager ....06 .03 .01
☐ 131T Paul Zuvella ....06 .03 .01
☐ 132T Checklist 1-132...........10 .01 .00

1987 Topps

This 792-card set is reminiscent of the 1962 Topps baseball cards with their simulated wood grain borders. The cards measure the standard size (2 1/2" by 3 1/2"). The backs are printed in yellow and blue on gray card stock. The manager cards contain a checklist of the respective team's players on the back. Subsets in the set include Record Breakers (1-7), Turn Back the Clock (311-315), and All-Star selections (595-616). The Team Leader cards typically show players conferring on the mound inside a white cloud. The wax pack

wrapper gives details of "Spring Fever Baseball" where a lucky collector can win a trip for four to Spring Training. The key Rookie Cards in this set are Barry Bonds, Bobby Bonilla, Will Clark, Mike Greenwell, Bo Jackson, Barry Larkin, Dave Magadan, Kevin Mitchell, Rafael Palmiero, and Ruben Sierra. Topps also produced a specially boxed "glossy" edition, frequently referred to as the Topps Tiffany set. This year Topps did not disclose the number of sets they produced or sold. It is apparent from the availability that there were many more sets produced this year compared to the 1984-86 Tiffany sets, perhaps 30,000 sets, more than three times as many. The checklist of cards (792 regular and 132 Traded) is identical to that of the normal non-glossy cards. There are two primary distinguishing features of the Tiffany cards, white card stock reverses and high gloss obverses. These Tiffany cards are valued approximately from three to five times the values listed below.

	MT	EX-MT	VG
COMPLETE SET (792) 25.00		11.50	3.10
COMPLETE FACT.SET (792) 30.00		13.50	3.80
COMMON PLAYER (1-792) 04		.02	.01

☐ 1 RB: Roger Clemens...........40 .10 .03
    Most strikeouts, nine inning game
☐ 2 RB: Jim Deshaies...............05 .02 .01
    Most cons. K's, start of game
☐ 3 RB: Dwight Evans ....05 .02 .01
    Earliest home run, season
☐ 4 RB: Davey Lopes...............05 .02 .01
    Most steals, season, 40-year-old
☐ 5 RB: Dave Righetti...............05 .02 .01
    Most saves, season
☐ 6 RB: Ruben Sierra.............35 .16 .04
    Youngest player to switch hit homers in game
☐ 7 RB: Todd Worrell................05 .02 .01
    Most saves, season, rookie
☐ 8 Terry Pendleton ....25 .11 .03
☐ 9 Jay Tibbs ....04 .02 .01
☐ 10 Cecil Cooper ....07 .03 .01
☐ 11 Indians Team ....04 .02 .01
    (Mound conference)
☐ 12 Jeff Sellers......................04 .02 .01

☐ 13 Nick Esasky	.04	.02	.01
☐ 14 Dave Stewart	.10	.05	.01
☐ 15 Claudell Washington	.04	.02	.01
☐ 16 Pat Clements	.04	.02	.01
☐ 17 Pete O'Brien	.04	.02	.01
☐ 18 Dick Howser MG	.06	.03	.01
(Checklist back)			
☐ 19 Matt Young	.04	.02	.01
☐ 20 Gary Carter	.12	.05	.02
☐ 21 Mark Davis	.04	.02	.01
☐ 22 Doug DeCinces	.04	.02	.01
☐ 23 Lee Smith	.15	.07	.02
☐ 24 Tony Walker	.04	.02	.01
☐ 25 Bert Blyleven	.10	.05	.01
☐ 26 Greg Brock	.04	.02	.01
☐ 27 Joe Cowley	.04	.02	.01
☐ 28 Rick Dempsey	.04	.02	.01
☐ 29 Jimmy Key	.07	.03	.01
☐ 30 Tim Raines	.10	.05	.01
☐ 31 Braves Team	.05	.02	.01
(Glenn Hubbard and			
Rafael Ramirez)			
☐ 32 Tim Leary	.04	.02	.01
☐ 33 Andy Van Slyke	.20	.09	.03
☐ 34 Jose Rijo	.12	.05	.02
☐ 35 Sid Bream	.07	.03	.01
☐ 36 Eric King	.04	.02	.01
☐ 37 Marvell Wynne	.04	.02	.01
☐ 38 Dennis Leonard	.04	.02	.01
☐ 39 Marty Barrett	.04	.02	.01
☐ 40 Dave Righetti	.07	.03	.01
☐ 41 Bo Diaz	.04	.02	.01
☐ 42 Gary Redus	.04	.02	.01
☐ 43 Gene Michael MG	.06	.03	.01
(Checklist back)			
☐ 44 Greg Harris	.04	.02	.01
☐ 45 Jim Presley	.04	.02	.01
☐ 46 Dan Gladden	.04	.02	.01
☐ 47 Dennis Powell	.04	.02	.01
☐ 48 Wally Backman	.04	.02	.01
☐ 49 Terry Harper	.04	.02	.01
☐ 50 Dave Smith	.04	.02	.01
☐ 51 Mel Hall	.07	.03	.01
☐ 52 Keith Atherton	.04	.02	.01
☐ 53 Ruppert Jones	.04	.02	.01
☐ 54 Bill Dawley	.04	.02	.01
☐ 55 Tim Wallach	.07	.03	.01
☐ 56 Brewers Team	.05	.02	.01
(Mound conference)			
☐ 57 Scott Nielsen	.04	.02	.01
☐ 58 Thad Bosley	.04	.02	.01
☐ 59 Ken Dayley	.04	.02	.01
☐ 60 Tony Pena	.04	.02	.01
☐ 61 Bobby Thigpen	.25	.11	.03
☐ 62 Bobby Meacham	.04	.02	.01
☐ 63 Fred Toliver	.04	.02	.01
☐ 64 Harry Spilman	.04	.02	.01
☐ 65 Tom Browning	.07	.03	.01
☐ 66 Marc Sullivan	.04	.02	.01
☐ 67 Bill Swift	.10	.05	.01
☐ 68 Tony LaRussa MG	.06	.03	.01
(Checklist back)			
☐ 69 Lonnie Smith	.04	.02	.01
☐ 70 Charlie Hough	.04	.02	.01
☐ 71 Mike Aldrete	.04	.02	.01
☐ 72 Walt Terrell	.04	.02	.01
☐ 73 Dave Anderson	.04	.02	.01
☐ 74 Dan Pasqua	.07	.03	.01
☐ 75 Ron Darling	.07	.03	.01
☐ 76 Rafael Ramirez	.04	.02	.01
☐ 77 Bryan Oelkers	.04	.02	.01
☐ 78 Tom Foley	.04	.02	.01
☐ 79 Juan Nieves	.04	.02	.01
☐ 80 Wally Joyner	.50	.23	.06
☐ 81 Padres Team	.05	.02	.01
(Andy Hawkins and			
Terry Kennedy)			
☐ 82 Rob Murphy	.04	.02	.01
☐ 83 Mike Davis	.04	.02	.01
☐ 84 Steve Lake	.04	.02	.01
☐ 85 Kevin Bass	.04	.02	.01
☐ 86 Nate Snell	.04	.02	.01
☐ 87 Mark Salas	.04	.02	.01
☐ 88 Ed Wojna	.04	.02	.01
☐ 89 Ozzie Guillen	.07	.03	.01
☐ 90 Dave Stieb	.07	.03	.01
☐ 91 Harold Reynolds	.04	.02	.01
☐ 92A Urbano Lugo	.30	.14	.04
ERR (no trademark)			
☐ 92B Urbano Lugo COR	.04	.02	.01
☐ 93 Jim Leyland MG	.12	.05	.02
(Checklist back)			
☐ 94 Calvin Schiraldi	.04	.02	.01
☐ 95 Oddibe McDowell	.04	.02	.01
☐ 96 Frank Williams	.04	.02	.01
☐ 97 Glenn Wilson	.04	.02	.01
☐ 98 Bill Scherrer	.04	.02	.01
☐ 99 Darryl Motley	.04	.02	.01
(Now with Braves			
on card front)			
☐ 100 Steve Garvey	.12	.05	.02
☐ 101 Carl Willis	.10	.05	.01
☐ 102 Paul Zuvella	.04	.02	.01
☐ 103 Rick Aguilera	.12	.05	.02
☐ 104 Billy Sample	.04	.02	.01
☐ 105 Floyd Youmans	.04	.02	.01
☐ 106 Blue Jays Team	.04	.02	.01
(George Bell and			
Jesse Barfield)			
☐ 107 John Butcher	.04	.02	.01
☐ 108 Jim Gantner UER	.04	.02	.01
(Brewers logo			
reversed)			
☐ 109 R.J. Reynolds	.04	.02	.01

☐ 110	John Tudor	07	.03	.01
☐ 111	Alfredo Griffin	04	.02	.01
☐ 112	Alan Ashby	04	.02	.01
☐ 113	Neil Allen	04	.02	.01
☐ 114	Billy Beane	04	.02	.01
☐ 115	Donnie Moore	04	.02	.01
☐ 116	Bill Russell	07	.03	.01
☐ 117	Jim Beattie	04	.02	.01
☐ 118	Bobby Valentine MG	06	.03	.01
	(Checklist back)			
☐ 119	Ron Robinson	04	.02	.01
☐ 120	Eddie Murray	25	.11	.03
☐ 121	Kevin Romine	04	.02	.01
☐ 122	Jim Clancy	04	.02	.01
☐ 123	John Kruk	60	.25	.08
☐ 124	Ray Fontenot	04	.02	.01
☐ 125	Bob Brenly	04	.02	.01
☐ 126	Mike Loynd	04	.02	.01
☐ 127	Vance Law	04	.02	.01
☐ 128	Checklist 1-132	06	.01	.00
☐ 129	Rick Cerone	04	.02	.01
☐ 130	Dwight Gooden	20	.09	.03
☐ 131	Pirates Team	05	.02	.01
	(Sid Bream and			
	Tony Pena)			
☐ 132	Paul Assenmacher	04	.02	.01
☐ 133	Jose Oquendo	04	.02	.01
☐ 134	Rich Yett	04	.02	.01
☐ 135	Mike Easler	04	.02	.01
☐ 136	Ron Romanick	04	.02	.01
☐ 137	Jerry Willard	04	.02	.01
☐ 138	Roy Lee Jackson	04	.02	.01
☐ 139	Devon White	40	.18	.05
☐ 140	Bret Saberhagen	15	.07	.02
☐ 141	Herm Winningham	04	.02	.01
☐ 142	Rick Sutcliffe	07	.03	.01
☐ 143	Steve Boros MG	06	.03	.01
	(Checklist back)			
☐ 144	Mike Scioscia	04	.02	.01
☐ 145	Charlie Kerfeld	04	.02	.01
☐ 146	Tracy Jones	04	.02	.01
☐ 147	Randy Niemann	04	.02	.01
☐ 148	Dave Collins	04	.02	.01
☐ 149	Ray Searage	04	.02	.01
☐ 150	Wade Boggs	40	.18	.05
☐ 151	Mike LaCoss	04	.02	.01
☐ 152	Toby Harrah	04	.02	.01
☐ 153	Duane Ward	30	.14	.04
☐ 154	Tom O'Malley	04	.02	.01
☐ 155	Eddie Whitson	04	.02	.01
☐ 156	Mariners Team	05	.02	.01
	(Mound conference)			
☐ 157	Danny Darwin	04	.02	.01
☐ 158	Tim Teufel	04	.02	.01
☐ 159	Ed Olwine	04	.02	.01
☐ 160	Julio Franco	15	.07	.02
☐ 161	Steve Ontiveros	04	.02	.01
☐ 162	Mike LaValliere	15	.07	.02
☐ 163	Kevin Gross	04	.02	.01
☐ 164	Sammy Khalifa	04	.02	.01
☐ 165	Jeff Reardon	15	.07	.02
☐ 166	Bob Boone	07	.03	.01
☐ 167	Jim Deshaies	10	.05	.01
☐ 168	Lou Piniella MG	06	.03	.01
	(Checklist back)			
☐ 169	Ron Washington	04	.02	.01
☐ 170	Bo Jackson	90	.40	.11
☐ 171	Chuck Cary	04	.02	.01
☐ 172	Ron Oester	04	.02	.01
☐ 173	Alex Trevino	04	.02	.01
☐ 174	Henry Cotto	04	.02	.01
☐ 175	Bob Stanley	04	.02	.01
☐ 176	Steve Buechele	07	.03	.01
☐ 177	Keith Moreland	04	.02	.01
☐ 178	Cecil Fielder	90	.40	.11
☐ 179	Bill Wegman	04	.02	.01
☐ 180	Chris Brown	04	.02	.01
☐ 181	Cardinals Team	05	.02	.01
	(Mound conference)			
☐ 182	Lee Lacy	04	.02	.01
☐ 183	Andy Hawkins	04	.02	.01
☐ 184	Bobby Bonilla	90	.40	.11
☐ 185	Roger McDowell	04	.02	.01
☐ 186	Bruce Benedict	04	.02	.01
☐ 187	Mark Huismann	04	.02	.01
☐ 188	Tony Phillips	07	.03	.01
☐ 189	Joe Hesketh	04	.02	.01
☐ 190	Jim Sundberg	04	.02	.01
☐ 191	Charles Hudson	04	.02	.01
☐ 192	Cory Snyder	10	.05	.01
☐ 193	Roger Craig MG	06	.03	.01
	(Checklist back)			
☐ 194	Kirk McCaskill	04	.02	.01
☐ 195	Mike Pagliarulo	04	.02	.01
☐ 196	Randy O'Neal UER	04	.02	.01
	(Wrong ML career			
	W-L totals)			
☐ 197	Mark Bailey	04	.02	.01
☐ 198	Lee Mazzilli	04	.02	.01
☐ 199	Mariano Duncan	04	.02	.01
☐ 200	Pete Rose	30	.14	.04
☐ 201	John Cangelosi	04	.02	.01
☐ 202	Ricky Wright	04	.02	.01
☐ 203	Mike Kingery	04	.02	.01
☐ 204	Sammy Stewart	04	.02	.01
☐ 205	Graig Nettles	07	.03	.01
☐ 206	Twins Team	05	.02	.01
	(Frank Viola and			
	Tim Laudner)			
☐ 207	George Frazier	04	.02	.01
☐ 208	John Shelby	04	.02	.01
☐ 209	Rick Schu	04	.02	.01
☐ 210	Lloyd Moseby	04	.02	.01
☐ 211	John Morris	04	.02	.01

☐ 212	Mike Fitzgerald	.04	.02	.01
☐ 213	Randy Myers	.15	.07	.02
☐ 214	Omar Moreno	.04	.02	.01
☐ 215	Mark Langston	.12	.05	.02
☐ 216	B.J. Surhoff	.12	.05	.02
☐ 217	Chris Codiroli	.04	.02	.01
☐ 218	Sparky Anderson MG	.06	.03	.01
	(Checklist back)			
☐ 219	Cecilio Guante	.04	.02	.01
☐ 220	Joe Carter	.40	.18	.05
☐ 221	Vern Ruhle	.04	.02	.01
☐ 222	Denny Walling	.04	.02	.01
☐ 223	Charlie Leibrandt	.07	.03	.01
☐ 224	Wayne Tolleson	.04	.02	.01
☐ 225	Mike Smithson	.04	.02	.01
☐ 226	Max Venable	.04	.02	.01
☐ 227	Jamie Moyer	.04	.02	.01
☐ 228	Curt Wilkerson	.04	.02	.01
☐ 229	Mike Birkbeck	.04	.02	.01
☐ 230	Don Baylor	.07	.03	.01
☐ 231	Giants Team	.05	.02	.01
	(Bob Brenly and			
	Jim Gott)			
☐ 232	Reggie Williams	.04	.02	.01
☐ 233	Russ Morman	.04	.02	.01
☐ 234	Pat Sheridan	.04	.02	.01
☐ 235	Alvin Davis	.04	.02	.01
☐ 236	Tommy John	.07	.03	.01
☐ 237	Jim Morrison	.04	.02	.01
☐ 238	Bill Krueger	.04	.02	.01
☐ 239	Juan Espino	.04	.02	.01
☐ 240	Steve Balboni	.04	.02	.01
☐ 241	Danny Heep	.04	.02	.01
☐ 242	Rick Mahler	.04	.02	.01
☐ 243	Whitey Herzog MG	.06	.03	.01
	(Checklist back)			
☐ 244	Dickie Noles	.04	.02	.01
☐ 245	Willie Upshaw	.04	.02	.01
☐ 246	Jim Dwyer	.04	.02	.01
☐ 247	Jeff Reed	.04	.02	.01
☐ 248	Gene Walter	.04	.02	.01
☐ 249	Jim Pankovits	.04	.02	.01
☐ 250	Teddy Higuera	.04	.02	.01
☐ 251	Rob Wilfong	.04	.02	.01
☐ 252	Dennis Martinez	.07	.03	.01
☐ 253	Eddie Milner	.04	.02	.01
☐ 254	Bob Tewksbury	.25	.11	.03
☐ 255	Juan Samuel	.04	.02	.01
☐ 256	Royals Team	.10	.05	.01
	(George Brett and			
	Frank White)			
☐ 257	Bob Forsch	.04	.02	.01
☐ 258	Steve Yeager	.04	.02	.01
☐ 259	Mike Greenwell	.40	.18	.05
☐ 260	Vida Blue	.07	.03	.01
☐ 261	Ruben Sierra	1.75	.80	.22
☐ 262	Jim Winn	.04	.02	.01

☐ 263	Stan Javier	.04	.02	.01
☐ 264	Checklist 133-264	.06	.01	.00
☐ 265	Darrell Evans	.07	.03	.01
☐ 266	Jeff Hamilton	.04	.02	.01
☐ 267	Howard Johnson	.20	.09	.03
☐ 268	Pat Corrales MG	.06	.03	.01
	(Checklist back)			
☐ 269	Cliff Speck	.04	.02	.01
☐ 270	Jody Davis	.04	.02	.01
☐ 271	Mike G. Brown	.04	.02	.01
	(Mariners pitcher)			
☐ 272	Andres Galarraga	.12	.05	.02
☐ 273	Gene Nelson	.04	.02	.01
☐ 274	Jeff Hearron UER	.04	.02	.01
	(Duplicate 1986			
	stat line on back)			
☐ 275	LaMarr Hoyt	.04	.02	.01
☐ 276	Jackie Gutierrez	.04	.02	.01
☐ 277	Juan Agosto	.04	.02	.01
☐ 278	Gary Pettis	.04	.02	.01
☐ 279	Dan Plesac	.10	.05	.01
☐ 280	Jeff Leonard	.04	.02	.01
☐ 281	Reds Team	.10	.05	.01
	(Pete Rose, Bo Diaz,			
	and Bill Gullickson)			
☐ 282	Jeff Calhoun	.04	.02	.01
☐ 283	Doug Drabek	.60	.25	.08
☐ 284	John Moses	.04	.02	.01
☐ 285	Dennis Boyd	.04	.02	.01
☐ 286	Mike Woodard	.04	.02	.01
☐ 287	Dave Von Ohlen	.04	.02	.01
☐ 288	Tito Landrum	.04	.02	.01
☐ 289	Bob Kipper	.04	.02	.01
☐ 290	Leon Durham	.04	.02	.01
☐ 291	Mitch Williams	.15	.07	.02
☐ 292	Franklin Stubbs	.04	.02	.01
☐ 293	Bob Rodgers MG	.06	.03	.01
	(Checklist back,			
	inconsistent design			
	on card back)			
☐ 294	Steve Jeltz	.04	.02	.01
☐ 295	Len Dykstra	.12	.05	.02
☐ 296	Andres Thomas	.04	.02	.01
☐ 297	Don Schulze	.04	.02	.01
☐ 298	Larry Herndon	.04	.02	.01
☐ 299	Joel Davis	.04	.02	.01
☐ 300	Reggie Jackson	.30	.14	.04
☐ 301	Luis Aquino UER	.04	.02	.01
	(No trademark,			
	never corrected)			
☐ 302	Bill Schroeder	.04	.02	.01
☐ 303	Juan Berenguer	.04	.02	.01
☐ 304	Phil Garner	.07	.03	.01
☐ 305	John Franco	.10	.05	.01
☐ 306	Red Sox Team	.10	.05	.01
	(Tom Seaver,			
	John McNamara MG,			

and Rich Gedman)			
☐ 307 Lee Guetterman	.04	.02	.01
☐ 308 Don Slaught	.04	.02	.01
☐ 309 Mike Young	.04	.02	.01
☐ 310 Frank Viola	.12	.05	.02
☐ 311 Turn Back 1982	.20	.09	.03
Rickey Henderson			
☐ 312 Turn Back 1977	.10	.05	.01
Reggie Jackson			
☐ 313 Turn Back 1972	.10	.05	.01
Roberto Clemente			
☐ 314 Turn Back 1967 UER	.10	.05	.01
Carl Yastrzemski			
(Sic, 112 RBI's			
on back)			
☐ 315 Turn Back 1962	.05	.02	.01
Maury Wills			
☐ 316 Brian Fisher	.04	.02	.01
☐ 317 Clint Hurdle	.04	.02	.01
☐ 318 Jim Fregosi MG	.06	.03	.01
(Checklist back)			
☐ 319 Greg Swindell	.60	.25	.08
☐ 320 Barry Bonds	2.25	1.00	.30
☐ 321 Mike Laga	.04	.02	.01
☐ 322 Chris Bando	.04	.02	.01
☐ 323 Al Newman	.04	.02	.01
☐ 324 David Palmer	.04	.02	.01
☐ 325 Garry Templeton	.04	.02	.01
☐ 326 Mark Gubicza	.04	.02	.01
☐ 327 Dale Sveum	.04	.02	.01
☐ 328 Bob Welch	.07	.03	.01
☐ 329 Ron Roenicke	.04	.02	.01
☐ 330 Mike Scott	.07	.03	.01
☐ 331 Mets Team	.15	.07	.02
(Gary Carter and			
Darryl Strawberry)			
☐ 332 Joe Price	.04	.02	.01
☐ 333 Ken Phelps	.04	.02	.01
☐ 334 Ed Correa	.04	.02	.01
☐ 335 Candy Maldonado	.07	.03	.01
☐ 336 Allan Anderson	.04	.02	.01
☐ 337 Darrell Miller	.04	.02	.01
☐ 338 Tim Conroy	.04	.02	.01
☐ 339 Donnie Hill	.04	.02	.01
☐ 340 Roger Clemens	1.25	.55	.16
☐ 341 Mike C. Brown	.04	.02	.01
(Pirates Outfielder)			
☐ 342 Bob James	.04	.02	.01
☐ 343 Hal Lanier MG	.06	.03	.01
(Checklist back)			
☐ 344A Joe Niekro	.07	.03	.01
(Copyright inside			
righthand border)			
☐ 344B Joe Niekro	.30	.14	.04
(Copyright outside			
righthand border)			
☐ 345 Andre Dawson	.25	.11	.03

☐ 346 Shawon Dunston	.07	.03	.01
☐ 347 Mickey Brantley	.04	.02	.01
☐ 348 Carmelo Martinez	.04	.02	.01
☐ 349 Storm Davis	.04	.02	.01
☐ 350 Keith Hernandez	.07	.03	.01
☐ 351 Gene Garber	.04	.02	.01
☐ 352 Mike Felder	.04	.02	.01
☐ 353 Ernie Camacho	.04	.02	.01
☐ 354 Jamie Quirk	.04	.02	.01
☐ 355 Don Carman	.04	.02	.01
☐ 356 White Sox Team	.05	.02	.01
(Mound conference)			
☐ 357 Steve Fireovid	.04	.02	.01
☐ 358 Sal Butera	.04	.02	.01
☐ 359 Doug Corbett	.04	.02	.01
☐ 360 Pedro Guerrero	.07	.03	.01
☐ 361 Mark Thurmond	.04	.02	.01
☐ 362 Luis Quinones	.04	.02	.01
☐ 363 Jose Guzman	.07	.03	.01
☐ 364 Randy Bush	.04	.02	.01
☐ 365 Rick Rhoden	.04	.02	.01
☐ 366 Mark McGwire	2.00	.90	.25
☐ 367 Jeff Lahti	.04	.02	.01
☐ 368 John McNamara MG	.06	.03	.01
(Checklist back)			
☐ 369 Brian Dayett	.04	.02	.01
☐ 370 Fred Lynn	.07	.03	.01
☐ 371 Mark Eichhorn	.07	.03	.01
☐ 372 Jerry Mumphrey	.04	.02	.01
☐ 373 Jeff Dedmon	.04	.02	.01
☐ 374 Glenn Hoffman	.04	.02	.01
☐ 375 Ron Guidry	.07	.03	.01
☐ 376 Scott Bradley	.04	.02	.01
☐ 377 John Henry Johnson	.04	.02	.01
☐ 378 Rafael Santana	.04	.02	.01
☐ 379 John Russell	.04	.02	.01
☐ 380 Rich Gossage	.08	.04	.01
☐ 381 Expos Team	.05	.02	.01
(Mound conference)			
☐ 382 Rudy Law	.04	.02	.01
☐ 383 Ron Davis	.04	.02	.01
☐ 384 Johnny Grubb	.04	.02	.01
☐ 385 Orel Hershiser	.12	.05	.02
☐ 386 Dickie Thon	.04	.02	.01
☐ 387 T.R. Bryden	.04	.02	.01
☐ 388 Geno Petralli	.04	.02	.01
☐ 389 Jeff D. Robinson	.04	.02	.01
☐ 390 Gary Matthews	.07	.03	.01
☐ 391 Jay Howell	.07	.03	.01
☐ 392 Checklist 265-396	.06	.01	.00
☐ 393 Pete Rose MG	.20	.09	.03
(Checklist back)			
☐ 394 Mike Bielecki	.04	.02	.01
☐ 395 Damaso Garcia	.04	.02	.01
☐ 396 Tim Lollar	.04	.02	.01
☐ 397 Greg Walker	.04	.02	.01
☐ 398 Brad Havens	.04	.02	.01

☐ 399 Curt Ford	.04	.02	.01
☐ 400 George Brett	.35	.16	.04
☐ 401 Billy Joe Robidoux	.04	.02	.01
☐ 402 Mike Trujillo	.04	.02	.01
☐ 403 Jerry Royster	.04	.02	.01
☐ 404 Doug Sisk	.04	.02	.01
☐ 405 Brook Jacoby	.04	.02	.01
☐ 406 Yankees Team	.20	.09	.03
(Rickey Henderson and			
Don Mattingly)			
☐ 407 Jim Acker	.04	.02	.01
☐ 408 John Mizerock	.04	.02	.01
☐ 409 Milt Thompson	.07	.03	.01
☐ 410 Fernando Valenzuela	.07	.03	.01
☐ 411 Darnell Coles	.04	.02	.01
☐ 412 Eric Davis	.20	.09	.03
☐ 413 Moose Haas	.04	.02	.01
☐ 414 Joe Orsulak	.04	.02	.01
☐ 415 Bobby Witt	.15	.07	.02
☐ 416 Tom Nieto	.04	.02	.01
☐ 417 Pat Perry	.04	.02	.01
☐ 418 Dick Williams MG	.06	.03	.01
(Checklist back)			
☐ 419 Mark Portugal	.12	.05	.02
☐ 420 Will Clark	2.25	1.00	.30
☐ 421 Jose DeLeon	.04	.02	.01
☐ 422 Jack Howell	.04	.02	.01
☐ 423 Jaime Cocanower	.04	.02	.01
☐ 424 Chris Speier	.04	.02	.01
☐ 425 Tom Seaver	.25	.11	.03
☐ 426 Floyd Rayford	.04	.02	.01
☐ 427 Edwin Nunez	.04	.02	.01
☐ 428 Bruce Bochy	.04	.02	.01
☐ 429 Tim Pyznarski	.04	.02	.01
☐ 430 Mike Schmidt	.50	.23	.06
☐ 431 Dodgers Team	.05	.02	.01
(Mound conference)			
☐ 432 Jim Slaton	.04	.02	.01
☐ 433 Ed Hearn	.04	.02	.01
☐ 434 Mike Fischlin	.04	.02	.01
☐ 435 Bruce Sutter	.07	.03	.01
☐ 436 Andy Allanson	.04	.02	.01
☐ 437 Ted Power	.04	.02	.01
☐ 438 Kelly Downs	.10	.05	.01
☐ 439 Karl Best	.04	.02	.01
☐ 440 Willie McGee	.07	.03	.01
☐ 441 Dave Leiper	.04	.02	.01
☐ 442 Mitch Webster	.04	.02	.01
☐ 443 John Felske MG	.06	.03	.01
(Checklist back)			
☐ 444 Jeff Russell	.07	.03	.01
☐ 445 Dave Lopes	.07	.03	.01
☐ 446 Chuck Finley	.20	.09	.03
☐ 447 Bill Almon	.04	.02	.01
☐ 448 Chris Bosio	.20	.09	.03
☐ 449 Pat Dodson	.04	.02	.01
☐ 450 Kirby Puckett	1.00	.45	.13

☐ 451 Joe Sambito	.04	.02	.01
☐ 452 Dave Henderson	.07	.03	.01
☐ 453 Scott Terry	.04	.02	.01
☐ 454 Luis Salazar	.04	.02	.01
☐ 455 Mike Boddicker	.04	.02	.01
☐ 456 A's Team	.05	.02	.01
(Mound conference)			
☐ 457 Len Matuszek	.04	.02	.01
☐ 458 Kelly Gruber	.25	.11	.03
☐ 459 Dennis Eckersley	.20	.09	.03
☐ 460 Darryl Strawberry	.40	.18	.05
☐ 461 Craig McMurtry	.04	.02	.01
☐ 462 Scott Fletcher	.04	.02	.01
☐ 463 Tom Candiotti	.07	.03	.01
☐ 464 Butch Wynegar	.04	.02	.01
☐ 465 Todd Worrell	.07	.03	.01
☐ 466 Kal Daniels	.10	.05	.01
☐ 467 Randy St.Claire	.04	.02	.01
☐ 468 George Bamberger MG	.06	.03	.01
(Checklist back)			
☐ 469 Mike Diaz	.04	.02	.01
☐ 470 Dave Dravecky	.07	.03	.01
☐ 471 Ronn Reynolds	.04	.02	.01
☐ 472 Bill Doran	.04	.02	.01
☐ 473 Steve Farr	.07	.03	.01
☐ 474 Jerry Narron	.04	.02	.01
☐ 475 Scott Garrelts	.04	.02	.01
☐ 476 Danny Tartabull	.40	.18	.05
☐ 477 Ken Howell	.04	.02	.01
☐ 478 Tim Laudner	.04	.02	.01
☐ 479 Bob Sebra	.04	.02	.01
☐ 480 Jim Rice	.10	.05	.01
☐ 481 Phillies Team	.05	.02	.01
(Glenn Wilson,			
Juan Samuel, and			
Von Hayes)			
☐ 482 Daryl Boston	.04	.02	.01
☐ 483 Dwight Lowry	.04	.02	.01
☐ 484 Jim Traber	.04	.02	.01
☐ 485 Tony Fernandez	.10	.05	.01
☐ 486 Otis Nixon	.25	.11	.03
☐ 487 Dave Gumpert	.04	.02	.01
☐ 488 Ray Knight	.07	.03	.01
☐ 489 Bill Gullickson	.07	.03	.01
☐ 490 Dale Murphy	.15	.07	.02
☐ 491 Ron Karkovice	.07	.03	.01
☐ 492 Mike Heath	.04	.02	.01
☐ 493 Tom Lasorda MG	.06	.03	.01
(Checklist back)			
☐ 494 Barry Jones	.04	.02	.01
☐ 495 Gorman Thomas	.04	.02	.01
☐ 496 Bruce Bochte	.04	.02	.01
☐ 497 Dale Mohorcic	.04	.02	.01
☐ 498 Bob Kearney	.04	.02	.01
☐ 499 Bruce Ruffin	.04	.02	.01
☐ 500 Don Mattingly	.40	.18	.05
☐ 501 Craig Lefferts	.07	.03	.01

☐ 502 Dick Schofield	.04	.02	.01
☐ 503 Larry Andersen	.04	.02	.01
☐ 504 Mickey Hatcher	.04	.02	.01
☐ 505 Bryn Smith	.04	.02	.01
☐ 506 Orioles Team	.05	.02	.01
(Mound conference)			
☐ 507 Dave L. Stapleton	.04	.02	.01
(Infielder)			
☐ 508 Scott Bankhead	.04	.02	.01
☐ 509 Enos Cabell	.04	.02	.01
☐ 510 Tom Henke	.07	.03	.01
☐ 511 Steve Lyons	.04	.02	.01
☐ 512 Dave Magadan	.15	.07	.02
☐ 513 Carmen Castillo	.04	.02	.01
☐ 514 Orlando Mercado	.04	.02	.01
☐ 515 Willie Hernandez	.04	.02	.01
☐ 516 Ted Simmons	.07	.03	.01
☐ 517 Mario Soto	.04	.02	.01
☐ 518 Gene Mauch MG	.06	.03	.01
(Checklist back)			
☐ 519 Curt Young	.04	.02	.01
☐ 520 Jack Clark	.07	.03	.01
☐ 521 Rick Reuschel	.04	.02	.01
☐ 522 Checklist 397-528	.06	.01	.00
☐ 523 Earnie Riles	.04	.02	.01
☐ 524 Bob Shirley	.04	.02	.01
☐ 525 Phil Bradley	.04	.02	.01
☐ 526 Roger Mason	.07	.03	.01
☐ 527 Jim Wohlford	.04	.02	.01
☐ 528 Ken Dixon	.04	.02	.01
☐ 529 Alvaro Espinoza	.10	.05	.01
☐ 530 Tony Gwynn	.50	.23	.06
☐ 531 Astros Team	.10	.05	.01
(Yogi Berra conference)			
☐ 532 Jeff Stone	.04	.02	.01
☐ 533 Argenis Salazar	.04	.02	.01
☐ 534 Scott Sanderson	.04	.02	.01
☐ 535 Tony Armas	.04	.02	.01
☐ 536 Terry Mulholland	.30	.14	.04
☐ 537 Rance Mulliniks	.04	.02	.01
☐ 538 Tom Niedenfuer	.04	.02	.01
☐ 539 Reid Nichols	.04	.02	.01
☐ 540 Terry Kennedy	.04	.02	.01
☐ 541 Rafael Belliard	.12	.05	.02
☐ 542 Ricky Horton	.04	.02	.01
☐ 543 Dave Johnson MG	.06	.03	.01
(Checklist back)			
☐ 544 Zane Smith	.04	.02	.01
☐ 545 Buddy Bell	.07	.03	.01
☐ 546 Mike Morgan	.07	.03	.01
☐ 547 Rob Deer	.12	.05	.02
☐ 548 Bill Mooneyham	.04	.02	.01
☐ 549 Bob Melvin	.04	.02	.01
☐ 550 Pete Incaviglia	.15	.07	.02
☐ 551 Frank Wills	.04	.02	.01
☐ 552 Larry Sheets	.04	.02	.01
☐ 553 Mike Maddux	.04	.02	.01
☐ 554 Buddy Biancalana	.04	.02	.01
☐ 555 Dennis Rasmussen	.04	.02	.01
☐ 556 Angels Team	.05	.02	.01
(Rene Lachemann CO,			
Mike Witt, and			
Bob Boone)			
☐ 557 John Cerutti	.04	.02	.01
☐ 558 Greg Gagne	.07	.03	.01
☐ 559 Lance McCullers	.04	.02	.01
☐ 560 Glenn Davis	.12	.05	.02
☐ 561 Rey Quinones	.04	.02	.01
☐ 562 Bryan Clutterbuck	.04	.02	.01
☐ 563 John Stefero	.04	.02	.01
☐ 564 Larry McWilliams	.04	.02	.01
☐ 565 Dusty Baker	.07	.03	.01
☐ 566 Tim Hulett	.04	.02	.01
☐ 567 Greg Mathews	.04	.02	.01
☐ 568 Earl Weaver MG	.06	.03	.01
(Checklist back)			
☐ 569 Wade Rowdon	.04	.02	.01
☐ 570 Sid Fernandez	.07	.03	.01
☐ 571 Ozzie Virgil	.04	.02	.01
☐ 572 Pete Ladd	.04	.02	.01
☐ 573 Hal McRae	.07	.03	.01
☐ 574 Manny Lee	.07	.03	.01
☐ 575 Pat Tabler	.04	.02	.01
☐ 576 Frank Pastore	.04	.02	.01
☐ 577 Dann Bilardello	.04	.02	.01
☐ 578 Billy Hatcher	.07	.03	.01
☐ 579 Rick Burleson	.04	.02	.01
☐ 580 Mike Krukow	.04	.02	.01
☐ 581 Cubs Team	.05	.02	.01
(Ron Cey and			
Steve Trout)			
☐ 582 Bruce Berenyi	.04	.02	.01
☐ 583 Junior Ortiz	.04	.02	.01
☐ 584 Ron Kittle	.04	.02	.01
☐ 585 Scott Bailes	.04	.02	.01
☐ 586 Ben Oglivie	.04	.02	.01
☐ 587 Eric Plunk	.04	.02	.01
☐ 588 Wallace Johnson	.04	.02	.01
☐ 589 Steve Crawford	.04	.02	.01
☐ 590 Vince Coleman	.12	.05	.02
☐ 591 Spike Owen	.04	.02	.01
☐ 592 Chris Welsh	.04	.02	.01
☐ 593 Chuck Tanner MG	.06	.03	.01
(Checklist back)			
☐ 594 Rick Anderson	.04	.02	.01
☐ 595 Keith Hernandez AS	.05	.02	.01
☐ 596 Steve Sax AS	.05	.02	.01
☐ 597 Mike Schmidt AS	.25	.11	.03
☐ 598 Ozzie Smith AS	.12	.05	.02
☐ 599 Tony Gwynn AS	.25	.11	.03
☐ 600 Dave Parker AS	.05	.02	.01
☐ 601 Darryl Strawberry AS	.25	.11	.03
☐ 602 Gary Carter AS	.08	.04	.01
☐ 603A Dwight Gooden AS	.40	.18	.05

	ERR (no trademark)			
☐ 603B	Dwight Gooden AS COR.12	.05	.02
☐ 604	Fernando Valenzuela AS..05	.02	.01
☐ 605	Todd Worrell AS 05	.02	.01
☐ 606A	Don Mattingly AS.........75	.35	.09
	ERR (no trademark)			
☐ 606B	Don Mattingly AS COR .25	.11	.03
☐ 607	Tony Bernazard AS 05	.02	.01
☐ 608	Wade Boggs AS 20	.09	.03
☐ 609	Cal Ripken AS 50	.23	.06
☐ 610	Jim Rice AS 05	.02	.01
☐ 611	Kirby Puckett AS 50	.23	.06
☐ 612	George Bell AS...........05	.02	.01
☐ 613	Lance Parrish AS UER 05	.02	.01
	(Pitcher heading			
	on back)			
☐ 614	Roger Clemens AS 50	.23	.06
☐ 615	Teddy Higuera AS 05	.02	.01
☐ 616	Dave Righetti AS 05	.02	.01
☐ 617	Al Nipper 04	.02	.01
☐ 618	Tom Kelly MG 06	.03	.01
	(Checklist back)			
☐ 619	Jerry Reed 04	.02	.01
☐ 620	Jose Canseco............2.00	.90	.25
☐ 621	Danny Cox 04	.02	.01
☐ 622	Glenn Braggs 10	.05	.01
☐ 623	Kurt Stillwell 10	.05	.01
☐ 624	Tim Burke 04	.02	.01
☐ 625	Mookie Wilson 07	.03	.01
☐ 626	Joel Skinner 04	.02	.01
☐ 627	Ken Oberkfell 04	.02	.01
☐ 628	Bob Walk 04	.02	.01
☐ 629	Larry Parrish 04	.02	.01
☐ 630	John Candelaria 04	.02	.01
☐ 631	Tigers Team 05	.02	.01
	(Mound conference)			
☐ 632	Rob Woodward 04	.02	.01
☐ 633	Jose Uribe..............04	.02	.01
☐ 634	Rafael Palmeiro.........1.25	.55	.16
☐ 635	Ken Schrom 04	.02	.01
☐ 636	Darren Daulton 15	.07	.02
☐ 637	Bip Roberts 35	.16	.04
☐ 638	Rich Bordi..............04	.02	.01
☐ 639	Gerald Perry 04	.02	.01
☐ 640	Mark Clear 04	.02	.01
☐ 641	Domingo Ramos 04	.02	.01
☐ 642	Al Pulido 04	.02	.01
☐ 643	Ron Shepherd 04	.02	.01
☐ 644	John Denny 04	.02	.01
☐ 645	Dwight Evans 08	.04	.01
☐ 646	Mike Mason 04	.02	.01
☐ 647	Tom Lawless 04	.02	.01
☐ 648	Barry Larkin 1.00	.45	.13
☐ 649	Mickey Tettleton 15	.07	.02
☐ 650	Hubie Brooks 04	.02	.01
☐ 651	Benny Distefano 04	.02	.01
☐ 652	Terry Forster 04	.02	.01

☐ 653	Kevin Mitchell 75	.35	.09
☐ 654	Checklist 529-660.........06	.01	.00
☐ 655	Jesse Barfield 07	.03	.01
☐ 656	Rangers Team 05	.02	.01
	(Bobby Valentine MG			
	and Ricky Wright)			
☐ 657	Tom Waddell.............04	.02	.01
☐ 658	Robby Thompson 15	.07	.02
☐ 659	Aurelio Lopez 04	.02	.01
☐ 660	Bob Horner 07	.03	.01
☐ 661	Lou Whitaker 10	.05	.01
☐ 662	Frank DiPino 04	.02	.01
☐ 663	Cliff Johnson 04	.02	.01
☐ 664	Mike Marshall 04	.02	.01
☐ 665	Rod Scurry 04	.02	.01
☐ 666	Von Hayes 04	.02	.01
☐ 667	Ron Hassey 04	.02	.01
☐ 668	Juan Bonilla 04	.02	.01
☐ 669	Bud Black 04	.02	.01
☐ 670	Jose Cruz 04	.02	.01
☐ 671A	Ray Soff ERR 04	.02	.01
	(No D* before			
	copyright line)			
☐ 671B	Ray Soff COR...........04	.02	.01
	(D* before			
	copyright line)			
☐ 672	Chili Davis 07	.03	.01
☐ 673	Don Sutton 10	.05	.01
☐ 674	Bill Campbell 04	.02	.01
☐ 675	Ed Romero 04	.02	.01
☐ 676	Charlie Moore 04	.02	.01
☐ 677	Bob Grich 07	.03	.01
☐ 678	Carney Lansford 07	.03	.01
☐ 679	Kent Hrbek 10	.05	.01
☐ 680	Ryne Sandberg 75	.35	.09
☐ 681	George Bell 15	.07	.02
☐ 682	Jerry Reuss.............04	.02	.01
☐ 683	Gary Roenicke 04	.02	.01
☐ 684	Kent Tekulve 04	.02	.01
☐ 685	Jerry Hairston 04	.02	.01
☐ 686	Doyle Alexander 04	.02	.01
☐ 687	Alan Trammell 12	.05	.02
☐ 688	Juan Beniquez 04	.02	.01
☐ 689	Darrell Porter 04	.02	.01
☐ 690	Dane Iorg...............04	.02	.01
☐ 691	Dave Parker 10	.05	.01
☐ 692	Frank White 04	.02	.01
☐ 693	Terry Puhl 04	.02	.01
☐ 694	Phil Niekro 10	.05	.01
☐ 695	Chico Walker 07	.03	.01
☐ 696	Gary Lucas 04	.02	.01
☐ 697	Ed Lynch 04	.02	.01
☐ 698	Ernie Whitt 04	.02	.01
☐ 699	Ken Landreaux 04	.02	.01
☐ 700	Dave Bergman 04	.02	.01
☐ 701	Willie Randolph..........07	.03	.01
☐ 702	Greg Gross 04	.02	.01

☐ 703	Dave Schmidt	.04	.02	.01
☐ 704	Jesse Orosco	.04	.02	.01
☐ 705	Bruce Hurst	.07	.03	.01
☐ 706	Rick Manning	.04	.02	.01
☐ 707	Bob McClure	.04	.02	.01
☐ 708	Scott McGregor	.04	.02	.01
☐ 709	Dave Kingman	.07	.03	.01
☐ 710	Gary Gaetti	.04	.02	.01
☐ 711	Ken Griffey	.07	.03	.01
☐ 712	Don Robinson	.04	.02	.01
☐ 713	Tom Brookens	.04	.02	.01
☐ 714	Dan Quisenberry	.07	.03	.01
☐ 715	Bob Dernier	.04	.02	.01
☐ 716	Rick Leach	.04	.02	.01
☐ 717	Ed VandeBerg	.04	.02	.01
☐ 718	Steve Carlton	.25	.11	.03
☐ 719	Tom Hume	.04	.02	.01
☐ 720	Richard Dotson	.04	.02	.01
☐ 721	Tom Herr	.04	.02	.01
☐ 722	Bob Knepper	.04	.02	.01
☐ 723	Brett Butler	.10	.05	.01
☐ 724	Greg Minton	.04	.02	.01
☐ 725	George Hendrick	.04	.02	.01
☐ 726	Frank Tanana	.04	.02	.01
☐ 727	Mike Moore	.04	.02	.01
☐ 728	Tippy Martinez	.04	.02	.01
☐ 729	Tom Paciorek	.07	.03	.01
☐ 730	Eric Show	.04	.02	.01
☐ 731	Dave Concepcion	.07	.03	.01
☐ 732	Manny Trillo	.04	.02	.01
☐ 733	Bill Caudill	.04	.02	.01
☐ 734	Bill Madlock	.07	.03	.01
☐ 735	Rickey Henderson	.40	.18	.05
☐ 736	Steve Bedrosian	.04	.02	.01
☐ 737	Floyd Bannister	.04	.02	.01
☐ 738	Jorge Orta	.04	.02	.01
☐ 739	Chet Lemon	.04	.02	.01
☐ 740	Rich Gedman	.04	.02	.01
☐ 741	Paul Molitor	.15	.07	.02
☐ 742	Andy McGaffigan	.04	.02	.01
☐ 743	Dwayne Murphy	.04	.02	.01
☐ 744	Roy Smalley	.04	.02	.01
☐ 745	Glenn Hubbard	.04	.02	.01
☐ 746	Bob Ojeda	.04	.02	.01
☐ 747	Johnny Ray	.04	.02	.01
☐ 748	Mike Flanagan	.04	.02	.01
☐ 749	Ozzie Smith	.25	.11	.03
☐ 750	Steve Trout	.04	.02	.01
☐ 751	Garth Iorg	.04	.02	.01
☐ 752	Dan Petry	.04	.02	.01
☐ 753	Rick Honeycutt	.04	.02	.01
☐ 754	Dave LaPoint	.04	.02	.01
☐ 755	Luis Aguayo	.04	.02	.01
☐ 756	Carlton Fisk	.25	.11	.03
☐ 757	Nolan Ryan	1.00	.45	.13
☐ 758	Tony Bernazard	.04	.02	.01
☐ 759	Joel Youngblood	.04	.02	.01

☐ 760	Mike Witt	.04	.02	.01
☐ 761	Greg Pryor	.04	.02	.01
☐ 762	Gary Ward	.04	.02	.01
☐ 763	Tim Flannery	.04	.02	.01
☐ 764	Bill Buckner	.07	.03	.01
☐ 765	Kirk Gibson	.08	.04	.01
☐ 766	Don Aase	.04	.02	.01
☐ 767	Ron Cey	.07	.03	.01
☐ 768	Dennis Lamp	.04	.02	.01
☐ 769	Steve Sax	.10	.05	.01
☐ 770	Dave Winfield	.30	.14	.04
☐ 771	Shane Rawley	.04	.02	.01
☐ 772	Harold Baines	.10	.05	.01
☐ 773	Robin Yount	.35	.16	.04
☐ 774	Wayne Krenchicki	.04	.02	.01
☐ 775	Joaquin Andujar	.04	.02	.01
☐ 776	Tom Brunansky	.07	.03	.01
☐ 777	Chris Chambliss	.07	.03	.01
☐ 778	Jack Morris	.20	.09	.03
☐ 779	Craig Reynolds	.04	.02	.01
☐ 780	Andre Thornton	.04	.02	.01
☐ 781	Atlee Hammaker	.04	.02	.01
☐ 782	Brian Downing	.04	.02	.01
☐ 783	Willie Wilson	.04	.02	.01
☐ 784	Cal Ripken	1.00	.45	.13
☐ 785	Terry Francona	.04	.02	.01
☐ 786	Jimy Williams MG	.06	.03	.01
	(Checklist back)			
☐ 787	Alejandro Pena	.04	.02	.01
☐ 788	Tim Stoddard	.04	.02	.01
☐ 789	Dan Schatzeder	.04	.02	.01
☐ 790	Julio Cruz	.04	.02	.01
☐ 791	Lance Parrish UER	.07	.03	.01
	(No trademark,			
	never corrected)			
☐ 792	Checklist 661-792	.06	.01	.00

1987 Topps Traded

This 132-card Traded or extended set was distributed by Topps to dealers in a special green and white box as a complete set. The card fronts are identical in style to the Topps regular issue and are also 2 1/2" by 3 1/2". The backs are printed in yellow and blue on white card stock. Cards are numbered (with a T suffix) alphabetically according to the name of the player. The key (extended) rookies in this set (without any prior cards) are Ellis Burks and Matt Williams. Extended rookies in this set (with prior cards but not from Topps) are David

Cone, Greg Maddux, and Fred McGriff. Topps also produced a specially boxed "glossy" edition, frequently referred to as the Topps Traded Tiffany set. This year Topps did not disclose the number of sets they produced or sold. It is apparent from the availability that there were many more sets produced this year compared to the 1984-86 Tiffany sets, perhaps 30,000 sets, more than three times as many. The checklist of cards is identical to that of the normal non-glossy cards. There are two primary distinguishing features of the Tiffany cards, white card stock reverses and high gloss obverses. These Tiffany cards are valued approximately from three to five times the values listed below.

		MT	EX-MT	VG
	COMPLETE SET (132)	10.00	4.50	1.25
	COMMON PLAYER (1T-132T)	.05	.02	.01

		MT	EX-MT	VG
☐	1T Bill Almon	.05	.02	.01
☐	2T Scott Bankhead	.05	.02	.01
☐	3T Eric Bell	.05	.02	.01
☐	4T Juan Beniquez	.05	.02	.01
☐	5T Juan Berenguer	.05	.02	.01
☐	6T Greg Booker	.05	.02	.01
☐	7T Thad Bosley	.05	.02	.01
☐	8T Larry Bowa MG	.08	.04	.01
☐	9T Greg Brock	.05	.02	.01
☐	10T Bob Brower	.05	.02	.01
☐	11T Jerry Browne	.08	.04	.01
☐	12T Ralph Bryant	.08	.04	.01
☐	13T DeWayne Buice	.05	.02	.01
☐	14T Ellis Burks	.50	.23	.06
☐	15T Ivan Calderon	.12	.05	.02
☐	16T Jeff Calhoun	.05	.02	.01
☐	17T Casey Candaele	.05	.02	.01
☐	18T John Cangelosi	.05	.02	.01
☐	19T Steve Carlton	.25	.11	.03
☐	20T Juan Castillo	.05	.02	.01
☐	21T Rick Cerone	.05	.02	.01
☐	22T Ron Cey	.08	.04	.01
☐	23T John Christensen	.05	.02	.01
☐	24T David Cone	2.00	.90	.25
☐	25T Chuck Crim	.05	.02	.01
☐	26T Storm Davis	.05	.02	.01
☐	27T Andre Dawson	.30	.14	.04
☐	28T Rick Dempsey	.05	.02	.01
☐	29T Doug Drabek	.40	.18	.05
☐	30T Mike Dunne	.05	.02	.01
☐	31T Dennis Eckersley	.35	.16	.04
☐	32T Lee Elia MG	.05	.02	.01
☐	33T Brian Fisher	.05	.02	.01
☐	34T Terry Francona	.05	.02	.01
☐	35T Willie Fraser	.05	.02	.01
☐	36T Billy Gardner MG	.05	.02	.01
☐	37T Ken Gerhart	.05	.02	.01
☐	38T Dan Gladden	.05	.02	.01
☐	39T Jim Gott	.05	.02	.01
☐	40T Cecilio Guante	.05	.02	.01
☐	41T Albert Hall	.05	.02	.01
☐	42T Terry Harper	.05	.02	.01
☐	43T Mickey Hatcher	.05	.02	.01
☐	44T Brad Havens	.05	.02	.01
☐	45T Neal Heaton	.05	.02	.01
☐	46T Mike Henneman	.25	.11	.03
☐	47T Donnie Hill	.05	.02	.01
☐	48T Guy Hoffman	.05	.02	.01
☐	49T Brian Holton	.05	.02	.01
☐	50T Charles Hudson	.05	.02	.01
☐	51T Danny Jackson	.05	.02	.01
☐	52T Reggie Jackson	.35	.16	.04
☐	53T Chris James	.10	.05	.01
☐	54T Dion James	.05	.02	.01
☐	55T Stan Jefferson	.05	.02	.01
☐	56T Joe Johnson	.05	.02	.01
☐	57T Terry Kennedy	.05	.02	.01
☐	58T Mike Kingery	.05	.02	.01
☐	59T Ray Knight	.08	.04	.01
☐	60T Gene Larkin	.15	.07	.02
☐	61T Mike LaValliere	.08	.04	.01
☐	62T Jack Lazorko	.05	.02	.01
☐	63T Terry Leach	.05	.02	.01
☐	64T Tim Leary	.05	.02	.01
☐	65T Jim Lindeman	.05	.02	.01
☐	66T Steve Lombardozzi	.05	.02	.01
☐	67T Bill Long	.05	.02	.01
☐	68T Barry Lyons	.05	.02	.01
☐	69T Shane Mack	.60	.25	.08
☐	70T Greg Maddux	3.00	1.35	.40
☐	71T Bill Madlock	.08	.04	.01
☐	72T Joe Magrane	.10	.05	.01
☐	73T Dave Martinez	.15	.07	.02
☐	74T Fred McGriff	2.25	1.00	.30
☐	75T Mark McLemore	.12	.05	.02
☐	76T Kevin McReynolds	.08	.04	.01
☐	77T Dave Meads	.05	.02	.01
☐	78T Eddie Milner	.05	.02	.01

☐	79T	Greg Minton	.05	.02	.01
☐	80T	John Mitchell	.05	.02	.01
☐	81T	Kevin Mitchell	.50	.23	.06
☐	82T	Charlie Moore	.05	.02	.01
☐	83T	Jeff Musselman	.05	.02	.01
☐	84T	Gene Nelson	.05	.02	.01
☐	85T	Graig Nettles	.08	.04	.01
☐	86T	Al Newman	.05	.02	.01
☐	87T	Reid Nichols	.05	.02	.01
☐	88T	Tom Niedenfuer	.05	.02	.01
☐	89T	Joe Niekro	.08	.04	.01
☐	90T	Tom Nieto	.05	.02	.01
☐	91T	Matt Nokes	.25	.11	.03
☐	92T	Dickie Noles	.05	.02	.01
☐	93T	Pat Pacillo	.05	.02	.01
☐	94T	Lance Parrish	.08	.04	.01
☐	95T	Tony Pena	.05	.02	.01
☐	96T	Luis Polonia	.40	.18	.05
☐	97T	Randy Ready	.05	.02	.01
☐	98T	Jeff Reardon	.20	.09	.03
☐	99T	Gary Redus	.05	.02	.01
☐	100T	Jeff Reed	.05	.02	.01
☐	101T	Rick Rhoden	.05	.02	.01
☐	102T	Cal Ripken Sr. MG	.08	.04	.01
☐	103T	Wally Ritchie	.05	.02	.01
☐	104T	Jeff M. Robinson	.08	.04	.01
☐	105T	Gary Roenicke	.05	.02	.01
☐	106T	Jerry Royster	.05	.02	.01
☐	107T	Mark Salas	.05	.02	.01
☐	108T	Luis Salazar	.05	.02	.01
☐	109T	Benny Santiago	.35	.16	.04
☐	110T	Dave Schmidt	.05	.02	.01
☐	111T	Kevin Seitzer	.25	.11	.03
☐	112T	John Shelby	.05	.02	.01
☐	113T	Steve Shields	.05	.02	.01
☐	114T	John Smiley	.75	.35	.09
☐	115T	Chris Speier	.05	.02	.01
☐	116T	Mike Stanley	.05	.02	.01
☐	117T	Terry Steinbach	.30	.14	.04
☐	118T	Les Straker	.05	.02	.01
☐	119T	Jim Sundberg	.05	.02	.01
☐	120T	Danny Tartabull	.25	.11	.03
☐	121T	Tom Trebelhorn MG	.05	.02	.01
☐	122T	Dave Valle	.05	.02	.01
☐	123T	Ed VandeBerg	.05	.02	.01
☐	124T	Andy Van Slyke	.20	.09	.03
☐	125T	Gary Ward	.05	.02	.01
☐	126T	Alan Wiggins	.05	.02	.01
☐	127T	Bill Wilkinson	.05	.02	.01
☐	128T	Frank Williams	.05	.02	.01
☐	129T	Matt Williams	1.50	.65	.19
☐	130T	Jim Winn	.05	.02	.01
☐	131T	Matt Young	.05	.02	.01
☐	132T	Checklist 1T-132T	.05	.01	.00

1988 Topps

This 792-card set features backs that are printed in orange and black on light gray card stock. The manager cards contain a checklist of the respective team's players on the back. Subsets in the set include Record Breakers (1-7), Turn Back the Clock (661-665), and All-Star selections (386-407). The Team Leader cards typically show two players together inside a white cloud. The key Rookie Cards in this set are Ellis Burks, Tom Glavine, and Matt Williams. Topps also produced a specially boxed "glossy" edition, frequently referred to as the Topps Tiffany set. This year, again, Topps did not disclose the number of Tiffany sets they produced or sold. It is apparent from the availability that there were many more sets produced this year compared to the 1984-86 Tiffany sets, perhaps 25,000 sets. The checklist of cards (792 regular and 132 Traded) is identical to that of the normal non-glossy cards. There are two primary distinguishing features of the Tiffany cards, white card stock reverses and high gloss obverses. These Tiffany cards are valued approximately from three to five times the values listed below.

	MT	EX-MT	VG
COMPLETE SET (792)	20.00	9.00	2.50
COMPLETE FACT.SET (792)	20.00	9.00	2.50
COMMON PLAYER (1-792)	.04	.02	.01

☐ 1	Vince Coleman RB	.10	.03	.01
	100 Steals for Third Cons. Season			
☐ 2	Don Mattingly RB	.12	.05	.02

Six Grand Slams

☐ 3A Mark McGwire RB 40	.18	.05
Rookie Homer Record		
(White spot behind		
left foot)		
☐ 3B Mark McGwire RB 25	.11	.03
Rookie Homer Record		
(No white spot)		
☐ 4A Eddie Murray RB 40	.18	.05
Switch Home Runs,		
Two Straight Games		
(Caption in box		
on card front)		
☐ 4B Eddie Murray RB 10	.05	.01
Switch Home Runs,		
Two Straight Games		
(No caption on front)		
☐ 5 Phil/Joe Niekro RB........05	.02	.01
Brothers Win Record		
☐ 6 Nolan Ryan RB................40	.18	.05
11th Season with		
200 Strikeouts		
☐ 7 Benito Santiago RB.........05	.02	.01
34-Game Hitting Streak,		
Rookie Record		
☐ 8 Kevin Elster...................04	.02	.01
☐ 9 Andy Hawkins 04	.02	.01
☐ 10 Ryne Sandberg 50	.23	.06
☐ 11 Mike Young 04	.02	.01
☐ 12 Bill Schroeder 04	.02	.01
☐ 13 Andres Thomas.............04	.02	.01
☐ 14 Sparky Anderson MG.....06	.03	.01
(Checklist back)		
☐ 15 Chili Davis 07	.03	.01
☐ 16 Kirk McCaskill 04	.02	.01
☐ 17 Ron Oester 04	.02	.01
☐ 18A Al Leiter ERR 15	.07	.02
(Photo actually		
Steve George,		
right ear visible)		
☐ 18B Al Leiter COR 04	.02	.01
(Left ear visible)		
☐ 19 Mark Davidson..............04	.02	.01
☐ 20 Kevin Gross 04	.02	.01
☐ 21 Red Sox TL 08	.04	.01
Wade Boggs and		
Spike Owen		
☐ 22 Greg Swindell 15	.07	.02
☐ 23 Ken Landreaux 04	.02	.01
☐ 24 Jim Deshaies................04	.02	.01
☐ 25 Andres Galarraga 04	.02	.01
☐ 26 Mitch Williams 07	.03	.01
☐ 27 R.J. Reynolds...............04	.02	.01
☐ 28 Jose Nunez..................04	.02	.01
☐ 29 Argenis Salazar 04	.02	.01
☐ 30 Sid Fernandez 07	.03	.01
☐ 31 Bruce Bochy 04	.02	.01

☐ 32 Mike Morgan.................07	.03	.01
☐ 33 Rob Deer.....................07	.03	.01
☐ 34 Ricky Horton 04	.02	.01
☐ 35 Harold Baines...............07	.03	.01
☐ 36 Jamie Moyer 04	.02	.01
☐ 37 Ed Romero 04	.02	.01
☐ 38 Jeff Calhoun.................04	.02	.01
☐ 39 Gerald Perry 04	.02	.01
☐ 40 Orel Hershiser 07	.03	.01
☐ 41 Bob Melvin 04	.02	.01
☐ 42 Bill Landrum 07	.03	.01
☐ 43 Dick Schofield 04	.02	.01
☐ 44 Lou Piniella MG.............06	.03	.01
(Checklist back)		
☐ 45 Kent Hrbek...................07	.03	.01
☐ 46 Darnell Coles 04	.02	.01
☐ 47 Joaquin Andujar............04	.02	.01
☐ 48 Alan Ashby 04	.02	.01
☐ 49 Dave Clark...................04	.02	.01
☐ 50 Hubie Brooks 04	.02	.01
☐ 51 Orioles TL 25	.11	.03
Eddie Murray and		
Cal Ripken		
☐ 52 Don Robinson 04	.02	.01
☐ 53 Curt Wilkerson 04	.02	.01
☐ 54 Jim Clancy 04	.02	.01
☐ 55 Phil Bradley..................04	.02	.01
☐ 56 Ed Hearn 04	.02	.01
☐ 57 Tim Crews 04	.02	.01
☐ 58 Dave Magadan 07	.03	.01
☐ 59 Danny Cox 04	.02	.01
☐ 60 Rickey Henderson 30	.14	.04
☐ 61 Mark Knudson 04	.02	.01
☐ 62 Jeff Hamilton 04	.02	.01
☐ 63 Jimmy Jones 04	.02	.01
☐ 64 Ken Caminiti 30	.14	.04
☐ 65 Leon Durham 04	.02	.01
☐ 66 Shane Rawley 04	.02	.01
☐ 67 Ken Oberkfell 04	.02	.01
☐ 68 Dave Dravecky 07	.03	.01
☐ 69 Mike Hart 04	.02	.01
☐ 70 Roger Clemens 50	.23	.06
☐ 71 Gary Pettis 04	.02	.01
☐ 72 Dennis Eckersley...........15	.07	.02
☐ 73 Randy Bush 04	.02	.01
☐ 74 Tom Lasorda MG 06	.03	.01
(Checklist back)		
☐ 75 Joe Carter....................25	.11	.03
☐ 76 Dennis Martinez 07	.03	.01
☐ 77 Tom O'Malley................04	.02	.01
☐ 78 Dan Petry 04	.02	.01
☐ 79 Ernie Whitt 04	.02	.01
☐ 80 Mark Langston 07	.03	.01
☐ 81 Reds TL 05	.02	.01
Ron Robinson		
and John Franco		
☐ 82 Darrel Akerfelds 04	.02	.01

☐ 83 Jose Oquendo	.04	.02	.01
☐ 84 Cecilio Guante	.04	.02	.01
☐ 85 Howard Johnson	.10	.05	.01
☐ 86 Ron Karkovice	.04	.02	.01
☐ 87 Mike Mason	.04	.02	.01
☐ 88 Earnie Riles	.04	.02	.01
☐ 89 Gary Thurman	.04	.02	.01
☐ 90 Dale Murphy	.10	.05	.01
☐ 91 Joey Cora	.07	.03	.01
☐ 92 Len Matuszek	.04	.02	.01
☐ 93 Bob Sebra	.04	.02	.01
☐ 94 Chuck Jackson	.04	.02	.01
☐ 95 Lance Parrish	.07	.03	.01
☐ 96 Todd Benzinger	.10	.05	.01
☐ 97 Scott Garrelts	.04	.02	.01
☐ 98 Rene Gonzales	.12	.05	.02
☐ 99 Chuck Finley	.07	.03	.01
☐ 100 Jack Clark	.07	.03	.01
☐ 101 Allan Anderson	.04	.02	.01
☐ 102 Barry Larkin	.25	.11	.03
☐ 103 Curt Young	.04	.02	.01
☐ 104 Dick Williams MG	.06	.03	.01
(Checklist back)			
☐ 105 Jesse Orosco	.04	.02	.01
☐ 106 Jim Walewander	.04	.02	.01
☐ 107 Scott Bailes	.04	.02	.01
☐ 108 Steve Lyons	.04	.02	.01
☐ 109 Joel Skinner	.04	.02	.01
☐ 110 Teddy Higuera	.04	.02	.01
☐ 111 Expos TL	.05	.02	.01
Hubie Brooks and			
Vance Law			
☐ 112 Les Lancaster	.04	.02	.01
☐ 113 Kelly Gruber	.07	.03	.01
☐ 114 Jeff Russell	.04	.02	.01
☐ 115 Johnny Ray	.04	.02	.01
☐ 116 Jerry Don Gleaton	.04	.02	.01
☐ 117 James Steels	.04	.02	.01
☐ 118 Bob Welch	.07	.03	.01
☐ 119 Robbie Wine	.04	.02	.01
☐ 120 Kirby Puckett	.40	.18	.05
☐ 121 Checklist 1-132	.06	.01	.00
☐ 122 Tony Bernazard	.04	.02	.01
☐ 123 Tom Candiotti	.04	.02	.01
☐ 124 Ray Knight	.07	.03	.01
☐ 125 Bruce Hurst	.07	.03	.01
☐ 126 Steve Jeltz	.04	.02	.01
☐ 127 Jim Gott	.04	.02	.01
☐ 128 Johnny Grubb	.04	.02	.01
☐ 129 Greg Minton	.04	.02	.01
☐ 130 Buddy Bell	.07	.03	.01
☐ 131 Don Schulze	.04	.02	.01
☐ 132 Donnie Hill	.04	.02	.01
☐ 133 Greg Mathews	.04	.02	.01
☐ 134 Chuck Tanner MG	.06	.03	.01
(Checklist back)			
☐ 135 Dennis Rasmussen	.04	.02	.01
☐ 136 Brian Dayett	.04	.02	.01
☐ 137 Chris Bosio	.07	.03	.01
☐ 138 Mitch Webster	.04	.02	.01
☐ 139 Jerry Browne	.04	.02	.01
☐ 140 Jesse Barfield	.04	.02	.01
☐ 141 Royals TL	.10	.05	.01
George Brett and			
Bret Saberhagen			
☐ 142 Andy Van Slyke	.10	.05	.01
☐ 143 Mickey Tettleton	.12	.05	.02
☐ 144 Don Gordon	.04	.02	.01
☐ 145 Bill Madlock	.07	.03	.01
☐ 146 Donell Nixon	.04	.02	.01
☐ 147 Bill Buckner	.07	.03	.01
☐ 148 Carmelo Martinez	.04	.02	.01
☐ 149 Ken Howell	.04	.02	.01
☐ 150 Eric Davis	.10	.05	.01
☐ 151 Bob Knepper	.04	.02	.01
☐ 152 Jody Reed	.25	.11	.03
☐ 153 John Habyan	.04	.02	.01
☐ 154 Jeff Stone	.04	.02	.01
☐ 155 Bruce Sutter	.07	.03	.01
☐ 156 Gary Matthews	.04	.02	.01
☐ 157 Atlee Hammaker	.04	.02	.01
☐ 158 Tim Hulett	.04	.02	.01
☐ 159 Brad Arnsberg	.04	.02	.01
☐ 160 Willie McGee	.07	.03	.01
☐ 161 Bryn Smith	.04	.02	.01
☐ 162 Mark McLemore	.04	.02	.01
☐ 163 Dale Mohorcic	.04	.02	.01
☐ 164 Dave Johnson MG	.06	.03	.01
(Checklist back)			
☐ 165 Robin Yount	.25	.11	.03
☐ 166 Rick Rodriguez	.04	.02	.01
☐ 167 Rance Mulliniks	.04	.02	.01
☐ 168 Barry Jones	.04	.02	.01
☐ 169 Ross Jones	.04	.02	.01
☐ 170 Rich Gossage	.07	.03	.01
☐ 171 Cubs TL	.05	.02	.01
Shawon Dunston			
and Manny Trillo			
☐ 172 Lloyd McClendon	.04	.02	.01
☐ 173 Eric Plunk	.04	.02	.01
☐ 174 Phil Garner	.07	.03	.01
☐ 175 Kevin Bass	.04	.02	.01
☐ 176 Jeff Reed	.04	.02	.01
☐ 177 Frank Tanana	.04	.02	.01
☐ 178 Dwayne Henry	.04	.02	.01
☐ 179 Charlie Puleo	.04	.02	.01
☐ 180 Terry Kennedy	.04	.02	.01
☐ 181 David Cone	.50	.23	.06
☐ 182 Ken Phelps	.04	.02	.01
☐ 183 Tom Lawless	.04	.02	.01
☐ 184 Ivan Calderon	.07	.03	.01
☐ 185 Rick Rhoden	.04	.02	.01
☐ 186 Rafael Palmeiro	.30	.14	.04
☐ 187 Steve Kiefer	.04	.02	.01

☐ 188	John Russell	04	.02	.01
☐ 189	Wes Gardner	04	.02	.01
☐ 190	Candy Maldonado	04	.02	.01
☐ 191	John Cerutti	04	.02	.01
☐ 192	Devon White	10	.05	.01
☐ 193	Brian Fisher	04	.02	.01
☐ 194	Tom Kelly MG	06	.03	.01
	(Checklist back)			
☐ 195	Dan Quisenberry	07	.03	.01
☐ 196	Dave Engle	04	.02	.01
☐ 197	Lance McCullers	04	.02	.01
☐ 198	Franklin Stubbs	04	.02	.01
☐ 199	Dave Meads	04	.02	.01
☐ 200	Wade Boggs	30	.14	.04
☐ 201	Rangers TL	05	.02	.01
	Bobby Valentine MG,			
	Pete O'Brien,			
	Pete Incaviglia, and			
	Steve Buechele			
☐ 202	Glenn Hoffman	04	.02	.01
☐ 203	Fred Toliver	04	.02	.01
☐ 204	Paul O'Neill	12	.05	.02
☐ 205	Nelson Liriano	04	.02	.01
☐ 206	Domingo Ramos	04	.02	.01
☐ 207	John Mitchell	04	.02	.01
☐ 208	Steve Lake	04	.02	.01
☐ 209	Richard Dotson	04	.02	.01
☐ 210	Willie Randolph	07	.03	.01
☐ 211	Frank DiPino	04	.02	.01
☐ 212	Greg Brock	04	.02	.01
☐ 213	Albert Hall	04	.02	.01
☐ 214	Dave Schmidt	04	.02	.01
☐ 215	Von Hayes	04	.02	.01
☐ 216	Jerry Reuss	04	.02	.01
☐ 217	Harry Spilman	04	.02	.01
☐ 218	Dan Schatzeder	04	.02	.01
☐ 219	Mike Stanley	04	.02	.01
☐ 220	Tom Henke	07	.03	.01
☐ 221	Rafael Belliard	04	.02	.01
☐ 222	Steve Farr	04	.02	.01
☐ 223	Stan Jefferson	04	.02	.01
☐ 224	Tom Trebelhorn MG	06	.03	.01
	(Checklist back)			
☐ 225	Mike Scioscia	04	.02	.01
☐ 226	Dave Lopes	07	.03	.01
☐ 227	Ed Correa	04	.02	.01
☐ 228	Wallace Johnson	04	.02	.01
☐ 229	Jeff Musselman	04	.02	.01
☐ 230	Pat Tabler	04	.02	.01
☐ 231	Pirates TL	12	.05	.02
	Barry Bonds and			
	Bobby Bonilla			
☐ 232	Bob James	04	.02	.01
☐ 233	Rafael Santana	04	.02	.01
☐ 234	Ken Dayley	04	.02	.01
☐ 235	Gary Ward	04	.02	.01
☐ 236	Ted Power	04	.02	.01
☐ 237	Mike Heath	04	.02	.01
☐ 238	Luis Polonia	25	.11	.03
☐ 239	Roy Smalley	04	.02	.01
☐ 240	Lee Smith	15	.07	.02
☐ 241	Damaso Garcia	04	.02	.01
☐ 242	Tom Niedenfuer	04	.02	.01
☐ 243	Mark Ryal	04	.02	.01
☐ 244	Jeff D. Robinson	04	.02	.01
☐ 245	Rich Gedman	04	.02	.01
☐ 246	Mike Campbell	04	.02	.01
☐ 247	Thad Bosley	04	.02	.01
☐ 248	Storm Davis	04	.02	.01
☐ 249	Mike Marshall	04	.02	.01
☐ 250	Nolan Ryan	75	.35	.09
☐ 251	Tom Foley	04	.02	.01
☐ 252	Bob Brower	04	.02	.01
☐ 253	Checklist 133-264	06	.01	.00
☐ 254	Lee Elia MG	06	.03	.01
	(Checklist back)			
☐ 255	Mookie Wilson	07	.03	.01
☐ 256	Ken Schrom	04	.02	.01
☐ 257	Jerry Royster	04	.02	.01
☐ 258	Ed Nunez	04	.02	.01
☐ 259	Ron Kittle	04	.02	.01
☐ 260	Vince Coleman	07	.03	.01
☐ 261	Giants TL	05	.02	.01
	(Five players)			
☐ 262	Drew Hall	04	.02	.01
☐ 263	Glenn Braggs	04	.02	.01
☐ 264	Les Straker	04	.02	.01
☐ 265	Bo Diaz	04	.02	.01
☐ 266	Paul Assenmacher	04	.02	.01
☐ 267	Billy Bean	04	.02	.01
☐ 268	Bruce Ruffin	04	.02	.01
☐ 269	Ellis Burks	25	.11	.03
☐ 270	Mike Witt	04	.02	.01
☐ 271	Ken Gerhart	04	.02	.01
☐ 272	Steve Ontiveros	04	.02	.01
☐ 273	Garth Iorg	04	.02	.01
☐ 274	Junior Ortiz	04	.02	.01
☐ 275	Kevin Seitzer	07	.03	.01
☐ 276	Luis Salazar	04	.02	.01
☐ 277	Alejandro Pena	04	.02	.01
☐ 278	Jose Cruz	04	.02	.01
☐ 279	Randy St.Claire	04	.02	.01
☐ 280	Pete Incaviglia	07	.03	.01
☐ 281	Jerry Hairston	04	.02	.01
☐ 282	Pat Perry	04	.02	.01
☐ 283	Phil Lombardi	04	.02	.01
☐ 284	Larry Bowa MG	06	.03	.01
	(Checklist back)			
☐ 285	Jim Presley	04	.02	.01
☐ 286	Chuck Crim	04	.02	.01
☐ 287	Manny Trillo	04	.02	.01
☐ 288	Pat Pacillo	04	.02	.01
	(Chris Sabo in			
	background of photo)			

☐ 289	Dave Bergman	.04	.02	.01
☐ 290	Tony Fernandez	.07	.03	.01
☐ 291	Astros TL	.05	.02	.01
	Billy Hatcher			
	and Kevin Bass			
☐ 292	Carney Lansford	.07	.03	.01
☐ 293	Doug Jones	.25	.11	.03
☐ 294	Al Pedrique	.04	.02	.01
☐ 295	Bert Blyleven	.07	.03	.01
☐ 296	Floyd Rayford	.04	.02	.01
☐ 297	Zane Smith	.04	.02	.01
☐ 298	Milt Thompson	.04	.02	.01
☐ 299	Steve Crawford	.04	.02	.01
☐ 300	Don Mattingly	.30	.14	.04
☐ 301	Bud Black	.04	.02	.01
☐ 302	Jose Uribe	.04	.02	.01
☐ 303	Eric Show	.04	.02	.01
☐ 304	George Hendrick	.04	.02	.01
☐ 305	Steve Sax	.07	.03	.01
☐ 306	Billy Hatcher	.04	.02	.01
☐ 307	Mike Trujillo	.04	.02	.01
☐ 308	Lee Mazzilli	.04	.02	.01
☐ 309	Bill Long	.04	.02	.01
☐ 310	Tom Herr	.04	.02	.01
☐ 311	Scott Sanderson	.04	.02	.01
☐ 312	Joey Meyer	.04	.02	.01
☐ 313	Bob McClure	.04	.02	.01
☐ 314	Jimy Williams MG	.06	.03	.01
	(Checklist back)			
☐ 315	Dave Parker	.07	.03	.01
☐ 316	Jose Rijo	.10	.05	.01
☐ 317	Tom Nieto	.04	.02	.01
☐ 318	Mel Hall	.04	.02	.01
☐ 319	Mike Loynd	.04	.02	.01
☐ 320	Alan Trammell	.07	.03	.01
☐ 321	White Sox TL	.05	.02	.01
	Harold Baines and			
	Carlton Fisk			
☐ 322	Vicente Palacios	.10	.05	.01
☐ 323	Rick Leach	.04	.02	.01
☐ 324	Danny Jackson	.04	.02	.01
☐ 325	Glenn Hubbard	.04	.02	.01
☐ 326	Al Nipper	.04	.02	.01
☐ 327	Larry Sheets	.04	.02	.01
☐ 328	Greg Cadaret	.04	.02	.01
☐ 329	Chris Speier	.04	.02	.01
☐ 330	Eddie Whitson	.04	.02	.01
☐ 331	Brian Downing	.04	.02	.01
☐ 332	Jerry Reed	.04	.02	.01
☐ 333	Wally Backman	.04	.02	.01
☐ 334	Dave LaPoint	.04	.02	.01
☐ 335	Claudell Washington	.04	.02	.01
☐ 336	Ed Lynch	.04	.02	.01
☐ 337	Jim Gantner	.04	.02	.01
☐ 338	Brian Holton UER	.04	.02	.01
	(1987 ERA .389,			
	should be 3.89)			
☐ 339	Kurt Stillwell	.04	.02	.01
☐ 340	Jack Morris	.12	.05	.02
☐ 341	Carmen Castillo	.04	.02	.01
☐ 342	Larry Andersen	.04	.02	.01
☐ 343	Greg Gagne	.04	.02	.01
☐ 344	Tony LaRussa MG	.06	.03	.01
	(Checklist back)			
☐ 345	Scott Fletcher	.04	.02	.01
☐ 346	Vance Law	.04	.02	.01
☐ 347	Joe Johnson	.04	.02	.01
☐ 348	Jim Eisenreich	.04	.02	.01
☐ 349	Bob Walk	.04	.02	.01
☐ 350	Will Clark	.60	.25	.08
☐ 351	Cardinals TL	.05	.02	.01
	Red Schoendienst CO			
	and Tony Pena			
☐ 352	Billy Ripken	.10	.05	.01
☐ 353	Ed Olwine	.04	.02	.01
☐ 354	Marc Sullivan	.04	.02	.01
☐ 355	Roger McDowell	.04	.02	.01
☐ 356	Luis Aguayo	.04	.02	.01
☐ 357	Floyd Bannister	.04	.02	.01
☐ 358	Rey Quinones	.04	.02	.01
☐ 359	Tim Stoddard	.04	.02	.01
☐ 360	Tony Gwynn	.30	.14	.04
☐ 361	Greg Maddux	.75	.35	.09
☐ 362	Juan Castillo	.04	.02	.01
☐ 363	Willie Fraser	.04	.02	.01
☐ 364	Nick Esasky	.04	.02	.01
☐ 365	Floyd Youmans	.04	.02	.01
☐ 366	Chet Lemon	.04	.02	.01
☐ 367	Tim Leary	.04	.02	.01
☐ 368	Gerald Young	.04	.02	.01
☐ 369	Greg Harris	.04	.02	.01
☐ 370	Jose Canseco	.60	.25	.08
☐ 371	Joe Hesketh	.04	.02	.01
☐ 372	Matt Williams	.90	.40	.11
☐ 373	Checklist 265-396	.06	.01	.00
☐ 374	Doc Edwards MG	.06	.03	.01
	(Checklist back)			
☐ 375	Tom Brunansky	.07	.03	.01
☐ 376	Bill Wilkinson	.04	.02	.01
☐ 377	Sam Horn	.12	.05	.02
☐ 378	Todd Frohwirth	.04	.02	.01
☐ 379	Rafael Ramirez	.04	.02	.01
☐ 380	Joe Magrane	.10	.05	.01
☐ 381	Angels TL	.05	.02	.01
	Wally Joyner and			
	Jack Howell			
☐ 382	Keith A. Miller	.20	.09	.03
	(New York Mets)			
☐ 383	Eric Bell	.04	.02	.01
☐ 384	Neil Allen	.04	.02	.01
☐ 385	Carlton Fisk	.20	.09	.03
☐ 386	Don Mattingly AS	.15	.07	.02
☐ 387	Willie Randolph AS	.05	.02	.01
☐ 388	Wade Boggs AS	.15	.07	.02

☐ 389 Alan Trammell AS	.05	.02	.01
☐ 390 George Bell AS	.05	.02	.01
☐ 391 Kirby Puckett AS	.20	.09	.03
☐ 392 Dave Winfield AS	.15	.07	.02
☐ 393 Matt Nokes AS	.05	.02	.01
☐ 394 Roger Clemens AS	.25	.11	.03
☐ 395 Jimmy Key AS	.05	.02	.01
☐ 396 Tom Henke AS	.05	.02	.01
☐ 397 Jack Clark AS	.05	.02	.01
☐ 398 Juan Samuel AS	.05	.02	.01
☐ 399 Tim Wallach AS	.05	.02	.01
☐ 400 Ozzie Smith AS	.12	.05	.02
☐ 401 Andre Dawson AS	.12	.05	.02
☐ 402 Tony Gwynn AS	.15	.07	.02
☐ 403 Tim Raines AS	.05	.02	.01
☐ 404 Benny Santiago AS	.05	.02	.01
☐ 405 Dwight Gooden AS	.10	.05	.01
☐ 406 Shane Rawley AS	.05	.02	.01
☐ 407 Steve Bedrosian AS	.05	.02	.01
☐ 408 Dion James	.04	.02	.01
☐ 409 Joel McKeon	.04	.02	.01
☐ 410 Tony Pena	.04	.02	.01
☐ 411 Wayne Tolleson	.04	.02	.01
☐ 412 Randy Myers	.07	.03	.01
☐ 413 John Christensen	.04	.02	.01
☐ 414 John McNamara MG	.06	.03	.01
(Checklist back)			
☐ 415 Don Carman	.04	.02	.01
☐ 416 Keith Moreland	.04	.02	.01
☐ 417 Mark Ciardi	.04	.02	.01
☐ 418 Joel Youngblood	.04	.02	.01
☐ 419 Scott McGregor	.04	.02	.01
☐ 420 Wally Joyner	.12	.05	.02
☐ 421 Ed VandeBerg	.04	.02	.01
☐ 422 Dave Concepcion	.07	.03	.01
☐ 423 John Smiley	.40	.18	.05
☐ 424 Dwayne Murphy	.04	.02	.01
☐ 425 Jeff Reardon	.12	.05	.02
☐ 426 Randy Ready	.04	.02	.01
☐ 427 Paul Kilgus	.04	.02	.01
☐ 428 John Shelby	.04	.02	.01
☐ 429 Tigers TL	.05	.02	.01
Alan Trammell and			
Kirk Gibson			
☐ 430 Glenn Davis	.07	.03	.01
☐ 431 Casey Candaele	.04	.02	.01
☐ 432 Mike Moore	.04	.02	.01
☐ 433 Bill Pecota	.10	.05	.01
☐ 434 Rick Aguilera	.07	.03	.01
☐ 435 Mike Pagliarulo	.04	.02	.01
☐ 436 Mike Bielecki	.04	.02	.01
☐ 437 Fred Manrique	.04	.02	.01
☐ 438 Rob Ducey	.04	.02	.01
☐ 439 Dave Martinez	.08	.04	.01
☐ 440 Steve Bedrosian	.04	.02	.01
☐ 441 Rick Manning	.04	.02	.01
☐ 442 Tom Bolton	.04	.02	.01

☐ 443 Ken Griffey	.07	.03	.01
☐ 444 Cal Ripken, Sr. MG	.06	.03	.01
(Checklist back)			
UER (two copyrights)			
☐ 445 Mike Krukow	.04	.02	.01
☐ 446 Doug DeCinces	.04	.02	.01
(Now with Cardinals			
on card front)			
☐ 447 Jeff Montgomery	.35	.16	.04
☐ 448 Mike Davis	.04	.02	.01
☐ 449 Jeff M. Robinson	.07	.03	.01
☐ 450 Barry Bonds	.60	.25	.08
☐ 451 Keith Atherton	.04	.02	.01
☐ 452 Willie Wilson	.04	.02	.01
☐ 453 Dennis Powell	.04	.02	.01
☐ 454 Marvell Wynne	.04	.02	.01
☐ 455 Shawn Hillegas	.04	.02	.01
☐ 456 Dave Anderson	.04	.02	.01
☐ 457 Terry Leach	.04	.02	.01
☐ 458 Ron Hassey	.04	.02	.01
☐ 459 Yankees TL	.05	.02	.01
Dave Winfield and			
Willie Randolph			
☐ 460 Ozzie Smith	.20	.09	.03
☐ 461 Danny Darwin	.04	.02	.01
☐ 462 Don Slaught	.04	.02	.01
☐ 463 Fred McGriff	.75	.35	.09
☐ 464 Jay Tibbs	.04	.02	.01
☐ 465 Paul Molitor	.12	.05	.02
☐ 466 Jerry Mumphrey	.04	.02	.01
☐ 467 Don Aase	.04	.02	.01
☐ 468 Darren Daulton	.07	.03	.01
☐ 469 Jeff Dedmon	.04	.02	.01
☐ 470 Dwight Evans	.07	.03	.01
☐ 471 Donnie Moore	.04	.02	.01
☐ 472 Robby Thompson	.07	.03	.01
☐ 473 Joe Niekro	.07	.03	.01
☐ 474 Tom Brookens	.04	.02	.01
☐ 475 Pete Rose MG	.20	.09	.03
(Checklist back)			
☐ 476 Dave Stewart	.07	.03	.01
☐ 477 Jamie Quirk	.04	.02	.01
☐ 478 Sid Bream	.07	.03	.01
☐ 479 Brett Butler	.10	.05	.01
☐ 480 Dwight Gooden	.12	.05	.02
☐ 481 Mariano Duncan	.04	.02	.01
☐ 482 Mark Davis	.04	.02	.01
☐ 483 Rod Booker	.04	.02	.01
☐ 484 Pat Clements	.04	.02	.01
☐ 485 Harold Reynolds	.04	.02	.01
☐ 486 Pat Keedy	.04	.02	.01
☐ 487 Jim Pankovits	.04	.02	.01
☐ 488 Andy McGaffigan	.04	.02	.01
☐ 489 Dodgers TL	.05	.02	.01
Pedro Guerrero and			
Fernando Valenzuela			
☐ 490 Larry Parrish	.04	.02	.01

☐ 491 B.J. Surhoff	.07	.03	.01
☐ 492 Doyle Alexander	.04	.02	.01
☐ 493 Mike Greenwell	.10	.05	.01
☐ 494 Wally Ritchie	.04	.02	.01
☐ 495 Eddie Murray	.20	.09	.03
☐ 496 Guy Hoffman	.04	.02	.01
☐ 497 Kevin Mitchell	.15	.07	.02
☐ 498 Bob Boone	.07	.03	.01
☐ 499 Eric King	.04	.02	.01
☐ 500 Andre Dawson	.20	.09	.03
☐ 501 Tim Birtsas	.04	.02	.01
☐ 502 Dan Gladden	.04	.02	.01
☐ 503 Junior Noboa	.04	.02	.01
☐ 504 Bob Rodgers MG	.06	.03	.01
(Checklist back)			
☐ 505 Willie Upshaw	.04	.02	.01
☐ 506 John Cangelosi	.04	.02	.01
☐ 507 Mark Gubicza	.04	.02	.01
☐ 508 Tim Teufel	.04	.02	.01
☐ 509 Bill Dawley	.04	.02	.01
☐ 510 Dave Winfield	.20	.09	.03
☐ 511 Joel Davis	.04	.02	.01
☐ 512 Alex Trevino	.04	.02	.01
☐ 513 Tim Flannery	.04	.02	.01
☐ 514 Pat Sheridan	.04	.02	.01
☐ 515 Juan Nieves	.04	.02	.01
☐ 516 Jim Sundberg	.04	.02	.01
☐ 517 Ron Robinson	.04	.02	.01
☐ 518 Greg Gross	.04	.02	.01
☐ 519 Mariners TL	.05	.02	.01
Harold Reynolds and			
Phil Bradley			
☐ 520 Dave Smith	.04	.02	.01
☐ 521 Jim Dwyer	.04	.02	.01
☐ 522 Bob Patterson	.04	.02	.01
☐ 523 Gary Roenicke	.04	.02	.01
☐ 524 Gary Lucas	.04	.02	.01
☐ 525 Marty Barrett	.04	.02	.01
☐ 526 Juan Berenguer	.04	.02	.01
☐ 527 Steve Henderson	.04	.02	.01
☐ 528A Checklist 397-528	.30	.03	.01
ERR (455 S. Carlton)			
☐ 528B Checklist 397-528	.06	.01	.00
COR (455 S. Hillegas)			
☐ 529 Tim Burke	.04	.02	.01
☐ 530 Gary Carter	.10	.05	.01
☐ 531 Rich Yett	.04	.02	.01
☐ 532 Mike Kingery	.04	.02	.01
☐ 533 John Farrell	.04	.02	.01
☐ 534 John Wathan MG	.06	.03	.01
(Checklist back)			
☐ 535 Ron Guidry	.07	.03	.01
☐ 536 John Morris	.04	.02	.01
☐ 537 Steve Buechele	.04	.02	.01
☐ 538 Bill Wegman	.04	.02	.01
☐ 539 Mike LaValliere	.04	.02	.01
☐ 540 Bret Saberhagen	.10	.05	.01

☐ 541 Juan Beniquez	.04	.02	.01
☐ 542 Paul Noce	.04	.02	.01
☐ 543 Kent Tekulve	.04	.02	.01
☐ 544 Jim Traber	.04	.02	.01
☐ 545 Don Baylor	.07	.03	.01
☐ 546 John Candelaria	.04	.02	.01
☐ 547 Felix Fermin	.04	.02	.01
☐ 548 Shane Mack	.25	.11	.03
☐ 549 Braves TL	.05	.02	.01
Albert Hall,			
Dale Murphy,			
Ken Griffey,			
and Dion James			
☐ 550 Pedro Guerrero	.07	.03	.01
☐ 551 Terry Steinbach	.07	.03	.01
☐ 552 Mark Thurmond	.04	.02	.01
☐ 553 Tracy Jones	.04	.02	.01
☐ 554 Mike Smithson	.04	.02	.01
☐ 555 Brook Jacoby	.04	.02	.01
☐ 556 Stan Clarke	.04	.02	.01
☐ 557 Craig Reynolds	.04	.02	.01
☐ 558 Bob Ojeda	.04	.02	.01
☐ 559 Ken Williams	.04	.02	.01
☐ 560 Tim Wallach	.07	.03	.01
☐ 561 Rick Cerone	.04	.02	.01
☐ 562 Jim Lindeman	.04	.02	.01
☐ 563 Jose Guzman	.07	.03	.01
☐ 564 Frank Lucchesi MG	.06	.03	.01
(Checklist back)			
☐ 565 Lloyd Moseby	.04	.02	.01
☐ 566 Charlie O'Brien	.04	.02	.01
☐ 567 Mike Diaz	.04	.02	.01
☐ 568 Chris Brown	.04	.02	.01
☐ 569 Charlie Leibrandt	.04	.02	.01
☐ 570 Jeffrey Leonard	.04	.02	.01
☐ 571 Mark Williamson	.04	.02	.01
☐ 572 Chris James	.04	.02	.01
☐ 573 Bob Stanley	.04	.02	.01
☐ 574 Graig Nettles	.07	.03	.01
☐ 575 Don Sutton	.10	.05	.01
☐ 576 Tommy Hinzo	.04	.02	.01
☐ 577 Tom Browning	.04	.02	.01
☐ 578 Gary Gaetti	.04	.02	.01
☐ 579 Mets TL	.05	.02	.01
Gary Carter and			
Kevin McReynolds			
☐ 580 Mark McGwire	.50	.23	.06
☐ 581 Tito Landrum	.04	.02	.01
☐ 582 Mike Henneman	.15	.07	.02
☐ 583 Dave Valle	.04	.02	.01
☐ 584 Steve Trout	.04	.02	.01
☐ 585 Ozzie Guillen	.07	.03	.01
☐ 586 Bob Forsch	.04	.02	.01
☐ 587 Terry Puhl	.04	.02	.01
☐ 588 Jeff Parrett	.04	.02	.01
☐ 589 Geno Petralli	.04	.02	.01
☐ 590 George Bell	.10	.05	.01

☐ 591	Doug Drabek	.10	.05	.01
☐ 592	Dale Sveum	.04	.02	.01
☐ 593	Bob Tewksbury	.07	.03	.01
☐ 594	Bobby Valentine MG	.06	.03	.01
	(Checklist back)			
☐ 595	Frank White	.04	.02	.01
☐ 596	John Kruk	.15	.07	.02
☐ 597	Gene Garber	.04	.02	.01
☐ 598	Lee Lacy	.04	.02	.01
☐ 599	Calvin Schiraldi	.04	.02	.01
☐ 600	Mike Schmidt	.40	.18	.05
☐ 601	Jack Lazorko	.04	.02	.01
☐ 602	Mike Aldrete	.04	.02	.01
☐ 603	Rob Murphy	.04	.02	.01
☐ 604	Chris Bando	.04	.02	.01
☐ 605	Kirk Gibson	.07	.03	.01
☐ 606	Moose Haas	.04	.02	.01
☐ 607	Mickey Hatcher	.04	.02	.01
☐ 608	Charlie Kerfeld	.04	.02	.01
☐ 609	Twins TL	.05	.02	.01
	Gary Gaetti and			
	Kent Hrbek			
☐ 610	Keith Hernandez	.07	.03	.01
☐ 611	Tommy John	.07	.03	.01
☐ 612	Curt Ford	.04	.02	.01
☐ 613	Bobby Thigpen	.07	.03	.01
☐ 614	Herm Winningham	.04	.02	.01
☐ 615	Jody Davis	.04	.02	.01
☐ 616	Jay Aldrich	.04	.02	.01
☐ 617	Oddibe McDowell	.04	.02	.01
☐ 618	Cecil Fielder	.30	.14	.04
☐ 619	Mike Dunne	.04	.02	.01
	(Inconsistent design,			
	black name on front)			
☐ 620	Cory Snyder	.07	.03	.01
☐ 621	Gene Nelson	.04	.02	.01
☐ 622	Kal Daniels	.07	.03	.01
☐ 623	Mike Flanagan	.04	.02	.01
☐ 624	Jim Leyland MG	.06	.03	.01
	(Checklist back)			
☐ 625	Frank Viola	.07	.03	.01
☐ 626	Glenn Wilson	.04	.02	.01
☐ 627	Joe Boever	.04	.02	.01
☐ 628	Dave Henderson	.07	.03	.01
☐ 629	Kelly Downs	.04	.02	.01
☐ 630	Darrell Evans	.07	.03	.01
☐ 631	Jack Howell	.04	.02	.01
☐ 632	Steve Shields	.04	.02	.01
☐ 633	Barry Lyons	.04	.02	.01
☐ 634	Jose DeLeon	.04	.02	.01
☐ 635	Terry Pendleton	.15	.07	.02
☐ 636	Charles Hudson	.04	.02	.01
☐ 637	Jay Bell	.30	.14	.04
☐ 638	Steve Balboni	.04	.02	.01
☐ 639	Brewers TL	.05	.02	.01
	Glenn Braggs			
	and Tony Muser CO			

☐ 640	Garry Templeton	.04	.02	.01
	(Inconsistent design,			
	green border)			
☐ 641	Rick Honeycutt	.04	.02	.01
☐ 642	Bob Dernier	.04	.02	.01
☐ 643	Rocky Childress	.04	.02	.01
☐ 644	Terry McGriff	.04	.02	.01
☐ 645	Matt Nokes	.20	.09	.03
☐ 646	Checklist 529-660	.06	.01	.00
☐ 647	Pascual Perez	.04	.02	.01
☐ 648	Al Newman	.04	.02	.01
☐ 649	DeWayne Buice	.04	.02	.01
☐ 650	Cal Ripken	.60	.25	.08
☐ 651	Mike Jackson	.10	.05	.01
☐ 652	Bruce Benedict	.04	.02	.01
☐ 653	Jeff Sellers	.04	.02	.01
☐ 654	Roger Craig MG	.06	.03	.01
	(Checklist back)			
☐ 655	Len Dykstra	.07	.03	.01
☐ 656	Lee Guetterman	.04	.02	.01
☐ 657	Gary Redus	.04	.02	.01
☐ 658	Tim Conroy	.04	.02	.01
	(Inconsistent design,			
	name in white)			
☐ 659	Bobby Meacham	.04	.02	.01
☐ 660	Rick Reuschel	.04	.02	.01
☐ 661	Turn Back Clock 1983	.35	.16	.04
	Nolan Ryan			
☐ 662	Turn Back Clock 1978	.05	.02	.01
	Jim Rice			
☐ 663	Turn Back Clock 1973	.05	.02	.01
	Ron Blomberg			
☐ 664	Turn Back Clock 1968	.10	.05	.01
	Bob Gibson			
☐ 665	Turn Back Clock 1963	.10	.05	.01
	Stan Musial			
☐ 666	Mario Soto	.04	.02	.01
☐ 667	Luis Quinones	.04	.02	.01
☐ 668	Walt Terrell	.04	.02	.01
☐ 669	Phillies TL	.05	.02	.01
	Lance Parrish			
	and Mike Ryan CO			
☐ 670	Dan Plesac	.04	.02	.01
☐ 671	Tim Laudner	.04	.02	.01
☐ 672	John Davis	.04	.02	.01
☐ 673	Tony Phillips	.04	.02	.01
☐ 674	Mike Fitzgerald	.04	.02	.01
☐ 675	Jim Rice	.07	.03	.01
☐ 676	Ken Dixon	.04	.02	.01
☐ 677	Eddie Milner	.04	.02	.01
☐ 678	Jim Acker	.04	.02	.01
☐ 679	Darrell Miller	.04	.02	.01
☐ 680	Charlie Hough	.04	.02	.01
☐ 681	Bobby Bonilla	.25	.11	.03
☐ 682	Jimmy Key	.07	.03	.01
☐ 683	Julio Franco	.10	.05	.01
☐ 684	Hal Lanier MG	.06	.03	.01

(Checklist back)

☐ 685	Ron Darling	.07	.03	.01
☐ 686	Terry Francona	.04	.02	.01
☐ 687	Mickey Brantley	.04	.02	.01
☐ 688	Jim Winn	.04	.02	.01
☐ 689	Tom Pagnozzi	.25	.11	.03
☐ 690	Jay Howell	.04	.02	.01
☐ 691	Dan Pasqua	.04	.02	.01
☐ 692	Mike Birkbeck	.04	.02	.01
☐ 693	Benito Santiago	.10	.05	.01
☐ 694	Eric Nolte	.04	.02	.01
☐ 695	Shawon Dunston	.07	.03	.01
☐ 696	Duane Ward	.07	.03	.01
☐ 697	Steve Lombardozzi	.04	.02	.01
☐ 698	Brad Havens	.04	.02	.01
☐ 699	Padres TL	.10	.05	.01
	Benito Santiago			
	and Tony Gwynn			
☐ 700	George Brett	.25	.11	.03
☐ 701	Sammy Stewart	.04	.02	.01
☐ 702	Mike Gallego	.04	.02	.01
☐ 703	Bob Brenly	.04	.02	.01
☐ 704	Dennis Boyd	.04	.02	.01
☐ 705	Juan Samuel	.04	.02	.01
☐ 706	Rick Mahler	.04	.02	.01
☐ 707	Fred Lynn	.07	.03	.01
☐ 708	Gus Polidor	.04	.02	.01
☐ 709	George Frazier	.04	.02	.01
☐ 710	Darryl Strawberry	.30	.14	.04
☐ 711	Bill Gullickson	.04	.02	.01
☐ 712	John Moses	.04	.02	.01
☐ 713	Willie Hernandez	.04	.02	.01
☐ 714	Jim Fregosi MG	.06	.03	.01
	(Checklist back)			
☐ 715	Todd Worrell	.07	.03	.01
☐ 716	Lenn Sakata	.04	.02	.01
☐ 717	Jay Baller	.04	.02	.01
☐ 718	Mike Felder	.04	.02	.01
☐ 719	Denny Walling	.04	.02	.01
☐ 720	Tim Raines	.07	.03	.01
☐ 721	Pete O'Brien	.04	.02	.01
☐ 722	Manny Lee	.04	.02	.01
☐ 723	Bob Kipper	.04	.02	.01
☐ 724	Danny Tartabull	.15	.07	.02
☐ 725	Mike Boddicker	.04	.02	.01
☐ 726	Alfredo Griffin	.04	.02	.01
☐ 727	Greg Booker	.04	.02	.01
☐ 728	Andy Allanson	.04	.02	.01
☐ 729	Blue Jays TL	.05	.02	.01
	George Bell and			
	Fred McGriff			
☐ 730	John Franco	.07	.03	.01
☐ 731	Rick Schu	.04	.02	.01
☐ 732	David Palmer	.04	.02	.01
☐ 733	Spike Owen	.04	.02	.01
☐ 734	Craig Lefferts	.04	.02	.01
☐ 735	Kevin McReynolds	.07	.03	.01

☐ 736	Matt Young	.04	.02	.01
☐ 737	Butch Wynegar	.04	.02	.01
☐ 738	Scott Bankhead	.04	.02	.01
☐ 739	Daryl Boston	.04	.02	.01
☐ 740	Rick Sutcliffe	.07	.03	.01
☐ 741	Mike Easler	.04	.02	.01
☐ 742	Mark Clear	.04	.02	.01
☐ 743	Larry Herndon	.04	.02	.01
☐ 744	Whitey Herzog MG	.06	.03	.01
	(Checklist back)			
☐ 745	Bill Doran	.04	.02	.01
☐ 746	Gene Larkin	.10	.05	.01
☐ 747	Bobby Witt	.07	.03	.01
☐ 748	Reid Nichols	.04	.02	.01
☐ 749	Mark Eichhorn	.04	.02	.01
☐ 750	Bo Jackson	.30	.14	.04
☐ 751	Jim Morrison	.04	.02	.01
☐ 752	Mark Grant	.04	.02	.01
☐ 753	Danny Heep	.04	.02	.01
☐ 754	Mike LaCoss	.04	.02	.01
☐ 755	Ozzie Virgil	.04	.02	.01
☐ 756	Mike Maddux	.04	.02	.01
☐ 757	John Marzano	.04	.02	.01
☐ 758	Eddie Williams	.04	.02	.01
☐ 759	A's TL UER	.25	.11	.03
	Mark McGwire			
	and Jose Canseco			
	(two copyrights)			
☐ 760	Mike Scott	.07	.03	.01
☐ 761	Tony Armas	.04	.02	.01
☐ 762	Scott Bradley	.04	.02	.01
☐ 763	Doug Sisk	.04	.02	.01
☐ 764	Greg Walker	.04	.02	.01
☐ 765	Neal Heaton	.04	.02	.01
☐ 766	Henry Cotto	.04	.02	.01
☐ 767	Jose Lind	.15	.07	.02
☐ 768	Dickie Noles	.04	.02	.01
	(Now with Tigers			
	on card front)			
☐ 769	Cecil Cooper	.07	.03	.01
☐ 770	Lou Whitaker	.07	.03	.01
☐ 771	Ruben Sierra	.40	.18	.05
☐ 772	Sal Butera	.04	.02	.01
☐ 773	Frank Williams	.04	.02	.01
☐ 774	Gene Mauch MG	.06	.03	.01
	(Checklist back)			
☐ 775	Dave Stieb	.07	.03	.01
☐ 776	Checklist 661-792	.06	.01	.00
☐ 777	Lonnie Smith	.04	.02	.01
☐ 778A	Keith Comstock ERR	2.50	1.15	.30
	(White "Padres")			
☐ 778B	Keith Comstock COR	.04	.02	.01
	(Blue "Padres")			
☐ 779	Tom Glavine	2.25	1.00	.30
☐ 780	Fernando Valenzuela	.07	.03	.01
☐ 781	Keith Hughes	.04	.02	.01
☐ 782	Jeff Ballard	.04	.02	.01

☐	783	Ron Roenicke	.04	.02	.01
☐	784	Joe Sambito	.04	.02	.01
☐	785	Alvin Davis	.04	.02	.01
☐	786	Joe Price	.04	.02	.01
		(Inconsistent design, orange team name)			
☐	787	Bill Almon	.04	.02	.01
☐	788	Ray Searage	.04	.02	.01
☐	789	Indians' TL	.10	.05	.01
		Joe Carter and Cory Snyder			
☐	790	Dave Righetti	.04	.02	.01
☐	791	Ted Simmons	.07	.03	.01
☐	792	John Tudor	.04	.02	.01

1988 Topps Traded

This 132-card Traded or extended set was distributed by Topps to dealers in a special blue and white box as a complete set. The card fronts are identical in style to the Topps regular issue and are also 2 1/2" by 3 1/2". The backs are printed in orange and black on white card stock. Cards are numbered (with a T suffix) alphabetically according to the name of the player. This set has generated additional interest due to the inclusion of the 1988 U.S. Olympic baseball team members. These Olympians are indicated in the checklist below by OLY. The key (extended) Rookie Cards in this set are Jim Abbott, Roberto Alomar, Brady Anderson, Andy Benes, Ron Gant, Mark Grace, Roberto Kelly, Tino Martinez, Jack McDowell, Charles Nagy, Chris Sabo, Robin Ventura, and Walt Weiss. Topps also produced a specially boxed "glossy" edition, frequently referred to as the Topps

Traded Tiffany set. This year, again, Topps did not disclose the number of Tiffany sets they produced or sold. It is apparent from the availability that there were many more sets produced this year compared to the 1984-86 Tiffany sets, perhaps 25,000 sets. The checklist of cards is identical to that of the normal non-glossy cards. There are two primary distinguishing features of the Tiffany cards, white card stock reverses and high gloss obverses. These Tiffany cards are valued approximately from three to five times the values listed below.

		MT	EX-MT	VG
COMPLETE SET (132)		30.00	13.50	3.80
COMMON PLAYER (1T-132T)		.05	.02	.01

			MT	EX-MT	VG
☐	1T	Jim Abbott OLY	6.50	2.90	.80
☐	2T	Juan Agosto	.05	.02	.01
☐	3T	Luis Alicea	.15	.07	.02
☐	4T	Roberto Alomar	9.00	4.00	1.15
☐	5T	Brady Anderson	1.50	.65	.19
☐	6T	Jack Armstrong	.20	.09	.03
☐	7T	Don August	.05	.02	.01
☐	8T	Floyd Bannister	.05	.02	.01
☐	9T	Bret Barberie OLY	.50	.23	.06
☐	10T	Jose Bautista	.05	.02	.01
☐	11T	Don Baylor	.08	.04	.01
☐	12T	Tim Belcher	.15	.07	.02
☐	13T	Buddy Bell	.08	.04	.01
☐	14T	Andy Benes OLY	3.00	1.35	.40
☐	15T	Damon Berryhill	.20	.09	.03
☐	16T	Bud Black	.05	.02	.01
☐	17T	Pat Borders	.60	.25	.08
☐	18T	Phil Bradley	.05	.02	.01
☐	19T	Jeff Branson OLY	.30	.14	.04
☐	20T	Tom Brunansky	.08	.04	.01
☐	21T	Jay Buhner	.60	.25	.08
☐	22T	Brett Butler	.12	.05	.02
☐	23T	Jim Campanis OLY	.20	.09	.03
☐	24T	Sil Campusano	.05	.02	.01
☐	25T	John Candelaria	.05	.02	.01
☐	26T	Jose Cecena	.05	.02	.01
☐	27T	Rick Cerone	.05	.02	.01
☐	28T	Jack Clark	.08	.04	.01
☐	29T	Kevin Coffman	.05	.02	.01
☐	30T	Pat Combs OLY	.15	.07	.02
☐	31T	Henry Cotto	.05	.02	.01
☐	32T	Chili Davis	.08	.04	.01
☐	33T	Mike Davis	.05	.02	.01
☐	34T	Jose DeLeon	.05	.02	.01
☐	35T	Richard Dotson	.05	.02	.01
☐	36T	Cecil Espy	.10	.05	.01
☐	37T	Tom Filer	.05	.02	.01
☐	38T	Mike Fiore OLY	.05	.02	.01
☐	39T	Ron Gant	2.25	1.00	.30

☐ 40T	Kirk Gibson	.08	.04	.01
☐ 41T	Rich Gossage	.08	.04	.01
☐ 42T	Mark Grace	2.25	1.00	.30
☐ 43T	Alfredo Griffin	.05	.02	.01
☐ 44T	Ty Griffin OLY	.12	.05	.02
☐ 45T	Bryan Harvey	.60	.25	.08
☐ 46T	Ron Hassey	.05	.02	.01
☐ 47T	Ray Hayward	.05	.02	.01
☐ 48T	Dave Henderson	.08	.04	.01
☐ 49T	Tom Herr	.05	.02	.01
☐ 50T	Bob Horner	.08	.04	.01
☐ 51T	Ricky Horton	.05	.02	.01
☐ 52T	Jay Howell	.05	.02	.01
☐ 53T	Glenn Hubbard	.05	.02	.01
☐ 54T	Jeff Innis	.05	.02	.01
☐ 55T	Danny Jackson	.05	.02	.01
☐ 56T	Darrin Jackson	.50	.23	.06
☐ 57T	Roberto Kelly	1.00	.45	.13
☐ 58T	Ron Kittle	.05	.02	.01
☐ 59T	Ray Knight	.08	.04	.01
☐ 60T	Vance Law	.05	.02	.01
☐ 61T	Jeffrey Leonard	.05	.02	.01
☐ 62T	Mike Macfarlane	.40	.18	.05
☐ 63T	Scotti Madison	.05	.02	.01
☐ 64T	Kirt Manwaring	.05	.02	.01
☐ 65T	Mark Marquess OLY CO	.05	.02	.01
☐ 66T	Tino Martinez OLY	1.25	.55	.16
☐ 67T	Billy Masse OLY	.12	.05	.02
☐ 68T	Jack McDowell	2.25	1.00	.30
☐ 69T	Jack McKeon MG	.05	.02	.01
☐ 70T	Larry McWilliams	.05	.02	.01
☐ 71T	Mickey Morandini OLY	.75	.35	.09
☐ 72T	Keith Moreland	.05	.02	.01
☐ 73T	Mike Morgan	.05	.02	.01
☐ 74T	Charles Nagy OLY	3.00	1.35	.40
☐ 75T	Al Nipper	.05	.02	.01
☐ 76T	Russ Nixon MG	.05	.02	.01
☐ 77T	Jesse Orosco	.05	.02	.01
☐ 78T	Joe Orsulak	.05	.02	.01
☐ 79T	Dave Palmer	.05	.02	.01
☐ 80T	Mark Parent	.05	.02	.01
☐ 81T	Dave Parker	.08	.04	.01
☐ 82T	Dan Pasqua	.05	.02	.01
☐ 83T	Melido Perez	.60	.25	.08
☐ 84T	Steve Peters	.05	.02	.01
☐ 85T	Dan Petry	.05	.02	.01
☐ 86T	Gary Pettis	.05	.02	.01
☐ 87T	Jeff Pico	.05	.02	.01
☐ 88T	Jim Poole OLY	.12	.05	.02
☐ 89T	Ted Power	.05	.02	.01
☐ 90T	Rafael Ramirez	.05	.02	.01
☐ 91T	Dennis Rasmussen	.05	.02	.01
☐ 92T	Jose Rijo	.15	.07	.02
☐ 93T	Ernie Riles	.05	.02	.01
☐ 94T	Luis Rivera	.05	.02	.01
☐ 95T	Doug Robbins OLY	.15	.07	.02
☐ 96T	Frank Robinson MG	.15	.07	.02

☐ 97T	Cookie Rojas MG	.05	.02	.01
☐ 98T	Chris Sabo	.75	.35	.09
☐ 99T	Mark Salas	.05	.02	.01
☐ 100T	Luis Salazar	.05	.02	.01
☐ 101T	Rafael Santana	.05	.02	.01
☐ 102T	Nelson Santovenia	.05	.02	.01
☐ 103T	Mackey Sasser	.10	.05	.01
☐ 104T	Calvin Schiraldi	.05	.02	.01
☐ 105T	Mike Schooler	.15	.07	.02
☐ 106T	Scott Servais OLY	.20	.09	.03
☐ 107T	Dave Silvestri OLY	.40	.18	.05
☐ 108T	Don Slaught	.05	.02	.01
☐ 109T	Joe Slusarski OLY	.30	.14	.04
☐ 110T	Lee Smith	.20	.09	.03
☐ 111T	Pete Smith	.50	.23	.06
☐ 112T	Jim Snyder MG	.05	.02	.01
☐ 113T	Ed Sprague OLY	1.00	.45	.13
☐ 114T	Pete Stanicek	.05	.02	.01
☐ 115T	Kurt Stillwell	.05	.02	.01
☐ 116T	Todd Stottlemyre	.50	.23	.06
☐ 117T	Bill Swift	.12	.05	.02
☐ 118T	Pat Tabler	.05	.02	.01
☐ 119T	Scott Terry	.05	.02	.01
☐ 120T	Mickey Tettleton	.20	.09	.03
☐ 121T	Dickie Thon	.05	.02	.01
☐ 122T	Jeff Treadway	.12	.05	.02
☐ 123T	Willie Upshaw	.05	.02	.01
☐ 124T	Robin Ventura OLY	10.00	4.50	1.25
☐ 125T	Ron Washington	.05	.02	.01
☐ 126T	Walt Weiss	.25	.11	.03
☐ 127T	Bob Welch	.08	.04	.01
☐ 128T	David Wells	.20	.09	.03
☐ 129T	Glenn Wilson	.05	.02	.01
☐ 130T	Ted Wood OLY	.25	.11	.03
☐ 131T	Don Zimmer MG	.08	.04	.01
☐ 132T	Checklist 1T-132T	.08	.01	.00

1989 Topps

This 792-card set features backs that are printed in pink and black on gray card stock. The cards measure the standard size (2 1/2" by 3 1/2"). The manager cards contain a checklist of the respective team's players on the back. Subsets in the set include Record Breakers (1-7), Turn Back the Clock (661-665), and All-Star selections (386-407). The bonus cards distributed throughout the set, which are indicated on the Topps checklist cards, are actually Team Leader (TL) cards. Also sprinkled throughout the set are Future Stars

(FS) and First Draft Picks (FDP). There are subtle variations found in the Future Stars cards with respect to the placement of photo and type on the card; in fact, each card has at least two varieties but they are difficult to detect (requiring precise measurement) as well as difficult to explain. The key rookies in this set are Jim Abbott, Sandy Alomar Jr., Brady Anderson, Steve Avery, Andy Benes, Ramon Martinez, Gary Sheffield, John Smoltz, and Robin Ventura. Topps also produced a specially boxed "glossy" edition, frequently referred to as the Topps Tiffany set. This year, again, Topps did not disclose the number of Tiffany sets they produced or sold but it seems that production quantities were roughly similar (or slightly smaller, approximately 15,000 sets) to the previous two years. The checklist of cards (792 regular and 132 Traded) is identical to that of the normal non-glossy cards. There are two primary distinguishing features of the Tiffany cards, white card stock reverses and high gloss obverses. These Tiffany cards are valued approximately from three to five times the values listed below.

	MT	EX-MT	VG
COMPLETE SET (792)	20.00	9.00	2.50
COMPLETE FACT.SET (792)	20.00	9.00	2.50
COMMON PLAYER (1-792)	.04	.02	.01
☐ 1 George Bell RB	.10	.05	.01
Slams 3 HR on Opening Day			
☐ 2 Wade Boggs RB	.12	.05	.02
Gets 200 Hits 6th Straight Season			
☐ 3 Gary Carter RB	.05	.02	.01
Sets Record for Career Putouts			
☐ 4 Andre Dawson RB	.08	.04	.01
Logs Double Figures in HR and SB			
☐ 5 Orel Hershiser RB	.05	.02	.01
Pitches 59 Scoreless Innings			
☐ 6 Doug Jones RB UER	.05	.02	.01
Earns His 15th Straight Save (Photo actually Chris Codiroli)			
☐ 7 Kevin McReynolds RB	.05	.02	.01
Steals 21 Without Being Caught			
☐ 8 Dave Eiland	.04	.02	.01
☐ 9 Tim Teufel	.04	.02	.01
☐ 10 Andre Dawson	.15	.07	.02
☐ 11 Bruce Sutter	.07	.03	.01
☐ 12 Dale Sveum	.04	.02	.01
☐ 13 Doug Sisk	.04	.02	.01
☐ 14 Tom Kelly MG	.06	.03	.01
(Team checklist back)			
☐ 15 Robby Thompson	.04	.02	.01
☐ 16 Ron Robinson	.04	.02	.01
☐ 17 Brian Downing	.04	.02	.01
☐ 18 Rick Rhoden	.04	.02	.01
☐ 19 Greg Gagne	.04	.02	.01
☐ 20 Steve Bedrosian	.04	.02	.01
☐ 21 Chicago White Sox TL	.05	.02	.01
Greg Walker			
☐ 22 Tim Crews	.04	.02	.01
☐ 23 Mike R. Fitzgerald	.04	.02	.01
Montreal Expos			
☐ 24 Larry Andersen	.04	.02	.01
☐ 25 Frank White	.04	.02	.01
☐ 26 Dale Mohorcic	.04	.02	.01
☐ 27A Orestes Destrade	.20	.09	.03
(F* next to copyright)			
☐ 27B Orestes Destrade	.20	.09	.03
(E*F* next to copyright)			
☐ 28 Mike Moore	.04	.02	.01
☐ 29 Kelly Gruber	.07	.03	.01
☐ 30 Dwight Gooden	.12	.05	.02
☐ 31 Terry Francona	.04	.02	.01
☐ 32 Dennis Rasmussen	.04	.02	.01
☐ 33 B.J. Surhoff	.04	.02	.01
☐ 34 Ken Williams	.04	.02	.01
☐ 35 John Tudor UER	.04	.02	.01
('84 Pirates record, should be Red Sox)			
☐ 36 Mitch Webster	.04	.02	.01
☐ 37 Bob Stanley	.04	.02	.01
☐ 38 Paul Runge	.04	.02	.01
☐ 39 Mike Maddux	.04	.02	.01
☐ 40 Steve Sax	.07	.03	.01
☐ 41 Terry Mulholland	.07	.03	.01
☐ 42 Jim Eppard	.04	.02	.01

☐ 43	Guillermo Hernandez	.04	.02	.01
☐ 44	Jim Snyder MG	.06	.03	.01
	(Team checklist back)			
☐ 45	Kal Daniels	.07	.03	.01
☐ 46	Mark Portugal	.04	.02	.01
☐ 47	Carney Lansford	.07	.03	.01
☐ 48	Tim Burke	.04	.02	.01
☐ 49	Craig Biggio	.40	.18	.05
☐ 50	George Bell	.10	.05	.01
☐ 51	California Angels TL	.05	.02	.01
	Mark McLemore			
☐ 52	Bob Brenly	.04	.02	.01
☐ 53	Ruben Sierra	.30	.14	.04
☐ 54	Steve Trout	.04	.02	.01
☐ 55	Julio Franco	.07	.03	.01
☐ 56	Pat Tabler	.04	.02	.01
☐ 57	Alejandro Pena	.04	.02	.01
☐ 58	Lee Mazzilli	.04	.02	.01
☐ 59	Mark Davis	.04	.02	.01
☐ 60	Tom Brunansky	.07	.03	.01
☐ 61	Neil Allen	.04	.02	.01
☐ 62	Alfredo Griffin	.04	.02	.01
☐ 63	Mark Clear	.04	.02	.01
☐ 64	Alex Trevino	.04	.02	.01
☐ 65	Rick Reuschel	.04	.02	.01
☐ 66	Manny Trillo	.04	.02	.01
☐ 67	Dave Palmer	.04	.02	.01
☐ 68	Darrell Miller	.04	.02	.01
☐ 69	Jeff Ballard	.04	.02	.01
☐ 70	Mark McGwire	.40	.18	.05
☐ 71	Mike Boddicker	.04	.02	.01
☐ 72	John Moses	.04	.02	.01
☐ 73	Pascual Perez	.04	.02	.01
☐ 74	Nick Leyva MG	.06	.03	.01
	(Team checklist back)			
☐ 75	Tom Henke	.07	.03	.01
☐ 76	Terry Blocker	.04	.02	.01
☐ 77	Doyle Alexander	.04	.02	.01
☐ 78	Jim Sundberg	.04	.02	.01
☐ 79	Scott Bankhead	.04	.02	.01
☐ 80	Cory Snyder	.04	.02	.01
☐ 81	Montreal Expos TL	.05	.02	.01
	Tim Raines			
☐ 82	Dave Leiper	.04	.02	.01
☐ 83	Jeff Blauser	.07	.03	.01
☐ 84	Bill Bene FDP	.04	.02	.01
☐ 85	Kevin McReynolds	.07	.03	.01
☐ 86	Al Nipper	.04	.02	.01
☐ 87	Larry Owen	.04	.02	.01
☐ 88	Darryl Hamilton	.20	.09	.03
☐ 89	Dave LaPoint	.04	.02	.01
☐ 90	Vince Coleman UER	.07	.03	.01
	(Wrong birth year)			
☐ 91	Floyd Youmans	.04	.02	.01
☐ 92	Jeff Kunkel	.04	.02	.01
☐ 93	Ken Howell	.04	.02	.01
☐ 94	Chris Speier	.04	.02	.01
☐ 95	Gerald Young	.04	.02	.01
☐ 96	Rick Cerone	.04	.02	.01
	(Ellis Burks in			
	background of photo)			
☐ 97	Greg Mathews	.04	.02	.01
☐ 98	Larry Sheets	.04	.02	.01
☐ 99	Sherman Corbett	.04	.02	.01
☐ 100	Mike Schmidt	.40	.18	.05
☐ 101	Les Straker	.04	.02	.01
☐ 102	Mike Gallego	.04	.02	.01
☐ 103	Tim Birtsas	.04	.02	.01
☐ 104	Dallas Green MG	.06	.03	.01
	(Team checklist back)			
☐ 105	Ron Darling	.07	.03	.01
☐ 106	Willie Upshaw	.04	.02	.01
☐ 107	Jose DeLeon	.04	.02	.01
☐ 108	Fred Manrique	.04	.02	.01
☐ 109	Hipolito Pena	.04	.02	.01
☐ 110	Paul Molitor	.10	.05	.01
☐ 111	Cincinnati Reds TL	.05	.02	.01
	Eric Davis			
	(Swinging bat)			
☐ 112	Jim Presley	.04	.02	.01
☐ 113	Lloyd Moseby	.04	.02	.01
☐ 114	Bob Kipper	.04	.02	.01
☐ 115	Jody Davis	.04	.02	.01
☐ 116	Jeff Montgomery	.07	.03	.01
☐ 117	Dave Anderson	.04	.02	.01
☐ 118	Checklist 1-132	.05	.01	.00
☐ 119	Terry Puhl	.04	.02	.01
☐ 120	Frank Viola	.07	.03	.01
☐ 121	Garry Templeton	.04	.02	.01
☐ 122	Lance Johnson	.07	.03	.01
☐ 123	Spike Owen	.04	.02	.01
☐ 124	Jim Traber	.04	.02	.01
☐ 125	Mike Krukow	.04	.02	.01
☐ 126	Sid Bream	.04	.02	.01
☐ 127	Walt Terrell	.04	.02	.01
☐ 128	Milt Thompson	.04	.02	.01
☐ 129	Terry Clark	.04	.02	.01
☐ 130	Gerald Perry	.04	.02	.01
☐ 131	Dave Otto	.04	.02	.01
☐ 132	Curt Ford	.04	.02	.01
☐ 133	Bill Long	.04	.02	.01
☐ 134	Don Zimmer MG	.06	.03	.01
	(Team checklist back)			
☐ 135	Jose Rijo	.07	.03	.01
☐ 136	Joey Meyer	.04	.02	.01
☐ 137	Geno Petralli	.04	.02	.01
☐ 138	Wallace Johnson	.04	.02	.01
☐ 139	Mike Flanagan	.04	.02	.01
☐ 140	Shawon Dunston	.07	.03	.01
☐ 141	Cleveland Indians TL	.05	.02	.01
	Brook Jacoby			
☐ 142	Mike Diaz	.04	.02	.01
☐ 143	Mike Campbell	.04	.02	.01
☐ 144	Jay Bell	.07	.03	.01

☐ 145	Dave Stewart	.07	.03	.01
☐ 146	Gary Pettis	.04	.02	.01
☐ 147	DeWayne Buice	.04	.02	.01
☐ 148	Bill Pecota	.04	.02	.01
☐ 149	Doug Dascenzo	.04	.02	.01
☐ 150	Fernando Valenzuela	.07	.03	.01
☐ 151	Terry McGriff	.04	.02	.01
☐ 152	Mark Thurmond	.04	.02	.01
☐ 153	Jim Pankovits	.04	.02	.01
☐ 154	Don Carman	.04	.02	.01
☐ 155	Marty Barrett	.04	.02	.01
☐ 156	Dave Gallagher	.04	.02	.01
☐ 157	Tom Glavine	.50	.23	.06
☐ 158	Mike Aldrete	.04	.02	.01
☐ 159	Pat Clements	.04	.02	.01
☐ 160	Jeffrey Leonard	.04	.02	.01
☐ 161	Gregg Olson FDP UER	.40	.18	.05
	(Born Scribner, NE, should be Omaha, NE)			
☐ 162	John Davis	.04	.02	.01
☐ 163	Bob Forsch	.04	.02	.01
☐ 164	Hal Lanier MG	.06	.03	.01
	(Team checklist back)			
☐ 165	Mike Dunne	.04	.02	.01
☐ 166	Doug Jennings	.04	.02	.01
☐ 167	Steve Searcy FS	.04	.02	.01
☐ 168	Willie Wilson	.04	.02	.01
☐ 169	Mike Jackson	.04	.02	.01
☐ 170	Tony Fernandez	.07	.03	.01
☐ 171	Atlanta Braves TL	.05	.02	.01
	Andres Thomas			
☐ 172	Frank Williams	.04	.02	.01
☐ 173	Mel Hall	.04	.02	.01
☐ 174	Todd Burns	.04	.02	.01
☐ 175	John Shelby	.04	.02	.01
☐ 176	Jeff Parrett	.04	.02	.01
☐ 177	Monty Fariss FDP	.30	.14	.04
☐ 178	Mark Grant	.04	.02	.01
☐ 179	Ozzie Virgil	.04	.02	.01
☐ 180	Mike Scott	.04	.02	.01
☐ 181	Craig Worthington	.04	.02	.01
☐ 182	Bob McClure	.04	.02	.01
☐ 183	Oddibe McDowell	.04	.02	.01
☐ 184	John Costello	.04	.02	.01
☐ 185	Claudell Washington	.04	.02	.01
☐ 186	Pat Perry	.04	.02	.01
☐ 187	Darren Daulton	.07	.03	.01
☐ 188	Dennis Lamp	.04	.02	.01
☐ 189	Kevin Mitchell	.10	.05	.01
☐ 190	Mike Witt	.04	.02	.01
☐ 191	Sil Campusano	.04	.02	.01
☐ 192	Paul Mirabella	.04	.02	.01
☐ 193	Sparky Anderson MG	.06	.03	.01
	(Team checklist back) UER (553 Salazer)			
☐ 194	Greg W. Harris	.10	.05	.01
	San Diego Padres			
☐ 195	Ozzie Guillen	.04	.02	.01
☐ 196	Denny Walling	.04	.02	.01
☐ 197	Neal Heaton	.04	.02	.01
☐ 198	Danny Heep	.04	.02	.01
☐ 199	Mike Schooler	.10	.05	.01
☐ 200	George Brett	.20	.09	.03
☐ 201	Blue Jays TL	.05	.02	.01
	Kelly Gruber			
☐ 202	Brad Moore	.04	.02	.01
☐ 203	Rob Ducey	.04	.02	.01
☐ 204	Brad Havens	.04	.02	.01
☐ 205	Dwight Evans	.07	.03	.01
☐ 206	Roberto Alomar	.75	.35	.09
☐ 207	Terry Leach	.04	.02	.01
☐ 208	Tom Pagnozzi	.04	.02	.01
☐ 209	Jeff Bittiger	.04	.02	.01
☐ 210	Dale Murphy	.10	.05	.01
☐ 211	Mike Pagliarulo	.04	.02	.01
☐ 212	Scott Sanderson	.04	.02	.01
☐ 213	Rene Gonzales	.04	.02	.01
☐ 214	Charlie O'Brien	.04	.02	.01
☐ 215	Kevin Gross	.04	.02	.01
☐ 216	Jack Howell	.04	.02	.01
☐ 217	Joe Price	.04	.02	.01
☐ 218	Mike LaValliere	.04	.02	.01
☐ 219	Jim Clancy	.04	.02	.01
☐ 220	Gary Gaetti	.04	.02	.01
☐ 221	Cecil Espy	.04	.02	.01
☐ 222	Mark Lewis FDP	.30	.14	.04
☐ 223	Jay Buhner	.12	.05	.02
☐ 224	Tony LaRussa MG	.06	.03	.01
	(Team checklist back)			
☐ 225	Ramon Martinez	.50	.23	.06
☐ 226	Bill Doran	.04	.02	.01
☐ 227	John Farrell	.04	.02	.01
☐ 228	Nelson Santovenia	.04	.02	.01
☐ 229	Jimmy Key	.07	.03	.01
☐ 230	Ozzie Smith	.15	.07	.02
☐ 231	San Diego Padres TL	.12	.05	.02
	Roberto Alomar (Gary Carter at plate)			
☐ 232	Ricky Horton	.04	.02	.01
☐ 233	Gregg Jefferies FS	.25	.11	.03
☐ 234	Tom Browning	.07	.03	.01
☐ 235	John Kruk	.07	.03	.01
☐ 236	Charles Hudson	.04	.02	.01
☐ 237	Glenn Hubbard	.04	.02	.01
☐ 238	Eric King	.04	.02	.01
☐ 239	Tim Laudner	.04	.02	.01
☐ 240	Greg Maddux	.30	.14	.04
☐ 241	Brett Butler	.07	.03	.01
☐ 242	Ed VandeBerg	.04	.02	.01
☐ 243	Bob Boone	.07	.03	.01
☐ 244	Jim Acker	.04	.02	.01
☐ 245	Jim Rice	.07	.03	.01
☐ 246	Rey Quinones	.04	.02	.01
☐ 247	Shawn Hillegas	.04	.02	.01

☐ 248 Tony Phillips	.04	.02	.01
☐ 249 Tim Leary	.04	.02	.01
☐ 250 Cal Ripken	.50	.23	.06
☐ 251 John Dopson	.04	.02	.01
☐ 252 Billy Hatcher	.04	.02	.01
☐ 253 Jose Alvarez	.04	.02	.01
☐ 254 Tom Lasorda MG	.06	.03	.01
(Team checklist back)			
☐ 255 Ron Guidry	.07	.03	.01
☐ 256 Benny Santiago	.07	.03	.01
☐ 257 Rick Aguilera	.07	.03	.01
☐ 258 Checklist 133-264	.05	.01	.00
☐ 259 Larry McWilliams	.04	.02	.01
☐ 260 Dave Winfield	.20	.09	.03
☐ 261 St.Louis Cardinals TL	.05	.02	.01
Tom Brunansky			
(With Luis Alicea)			
☐ 262 Jeff Pico	.04	.02	.01
☐ 263 Mike Felder	.04	.02	.01
☐ 264 Rob Dibble	.20	.09	.03
☐ 265 Kent Hrbek	.07	.03	.01
☐ 266 Luis Aquino	.04	.02	.01
☐ 267 Jeff M. Robinson	.04	.02	.01
Detroit Tigers			
☐ 268 N. Keith Miller	.04	.02	.01
Philadelphia Phillies			
☐ 269 Tom Bolton	.04	.02	.01
☐ 270 Wally Joyner	.08	.04	.01
☐ 271 Jay Tibbs	.04	.02	.01
☐ 272 Ron Hassey	.04	.02	.01
☐ 273 Jose Lind	.04	.02	.01
☐ 274 Mark Eichhorn	.04	.02	.01
☐ 275 Danny Tartabull UER	.12	.05	.02
(Born San Juan, PR			
should be Miami, FL)			
☐ 276 Paul Kilgus	.04	.02	.01
☐ 277 Mike Davis	.04	.02	.01
☐ 278 Andy McGaffigan	.04	.02	.01
☐ 279 Scott Bradley	.04	.02	.01
☐ 280 Bob Knepper	.04	.02	.01
☐ 281 Gary Redus	.04	.02	.01
☐ 282 Cris Carpenter	.10	.05	.01
☐ 283 Andy Allanson	.04	.02	.01
☐ 284 Jim Leyland MG	.06	.03	.01
(Team checklist back)			
☐ 285 John Candelaria	.04	.02	.01
☐ 286 Darrin Jackson	.15	.07	.02
☐ 287 Juan Nieves	.04	.02	.01
☐ 288 Pat Sheridan	.04	.02	.01
☐ 289 Ernie Whitt	.04	.02	.01
☐ 290 John Franco	.07	.03	.01
☐ 291 New York Mets TL	.08	.04	.01
Darryl Strawberry			
(With Keith Hernandez			
and Kevin McReynolds)			
☐ 292 Jim Corsi	.10	.05	.01
☐ 293 Glenn Wilson	.04	.02	.01
☐ 294 Juan Berenguer	.04	.02	.01
☐ 295 Scott Fletcher	.04	.02	.01
☐ 296 Ron Gant	.50	.23	.06
☐ 297 Oswald Peraza	.04	.02	.01
☐ 298 Chris James	.04	.02	.01
☐ 299 Steve Ellsworth	.04	.02	.01
☐ 300 Darryl Strawberry	.25	.11	.03
☐ 301 Charlie Leibrandt	.04	.02	.01
☐ 302 Gary Ward	.04	.02	.01
☐ 303 Felix Fermin	.04	.02	.01
☐ 304 Joel Youngblood	.04	.02	.01
☐ 305 Dave Smith	.04	.02	.01
☐ 306 Tracy Woodson	.04	.02	.01
☐ 307 Lance McCullers	.04	.02	.01
☐ 308 Ron Karkovice	.04	.02	.01
☐ 309 Mario Diaz	.04	.02	.01
☐ 310 Rafael Palmeiro	.20	.09	.03
☐ 311 Chris Bosio	.04	.02	.01
☐ 312 Tom Lawless	.04	.02	.01
☐ 313 Dennis Martinez	.07	.03	.01
☐ 314 Bobby Valentine MG	.06	.03	.01
(Team checklist back)			
☐ 315 Greg Swindell	.07	.03	.01
☐ 316 Walt Weiss	.07	.03	.01
☐ 317 Jack Armstrong	.12	.05	.02
☐ 318 Gene Larkin	.04	.02	.01
☐ 319 Greg Booker	.04	.02	.01
☐ 320 Lou Whitaker	.07	.03	.01
☐ 321 Boston Red Sox TL	.05	.02	.01
Jody Reed			
☐ 322 John Smiley	.07	.03	.01
☐ 323 Gary Thurman	.04	.02	.01
☐ 324 Bob Milacki	.10	.05	.01
☐ 325 Jesse Barfield	.04	.02	.01
☐ 326 Dennis Boyd	.04	.02	.01
☐ 327 Mark Lemke	.15	.07	.02
☐ 328 Rick Honeycutt	.04	.02	.01
☐ 329 Bob Melvin	.04	.02	.01
☐ 330 Eric Davis	.12	.05	.02
☐ 331 Curt Wilkerson	.04	.02	.01
☐ 332 Tony Armas	.04	.02	.01
☐ 333 Bob Ojeda	.04	.02	.01
☐ 334 Steve Lyons	.04	.02	.01
☐ 335 Dave Righetti	.04	.02	.01
☐ 336 Steve Balboni	.04	.02	.01
☐ 337 Calvin Schiraldi	.04	.02	.01
☐ 338 Jim Adduci	.04	.02	.01
☐ 339 Scott Bailes	.04	.02	.01
☐ 340 Kirk Gibson	.07	.03	.01
☐ 341 Jim Deshaies	.04	.02	.01
☐ 342 Tom Brookens	.04	.02	.01
☐ 343 Gary Sheffield FS	2.00	.90	.25
☐ 344 Tom Trebelhorn MG	.06	.03	.01
(Team checklist back)			
☐ 345 Charlie Hough	.04	.02	.01
☐ 346 Rex Hudler	.04	.02	.01
☐ 347 John Cerutti	.04	.02	.01

☐ 348	Ed Hearn	.04	.02	.01
☐ 349	Ron Jones	.04	.02	.01
☐ 350	Andy Van Slyke	.10	.05	.01
☐ 351	San Fran. Giants TL	.05	.02	.01
	Bob Melvin			
	(With Bill Fahey CO)			
☐ 352	Rick Schu	.04	.02	.01
☐ 353	Marvell Wynne	.04	.02	.01
☐ 354	Larry Parrish	.04	.02	.01
☐ 355	Mark Langston	.07	.03	.01
☐ 356	Kevin Elster	.04	.02	.01
☐ 357	Jerry Reuss	.04	.02	.01
☐ 358	Ricky Jordan	.10	.05	.01
☐ 359	Tommy John	.07	.03	.01
☐ 360	Ryne Sandberg	.40	.18	.05
☐ 361	Kelly Downs	.04	.02	.01
☐ 362	Jack Lazorko	.04	.02	.01
☐ 363	Rich Yett	.04	.02	.01
☐ 364	Rob Deer	.07	.03	.01
☐ 365	Mike Henneman	.07	.03	.01
☐ 366	Herm Winningham	.04	.02	.01
☐ 367	Johnny Paredes	.04	.02	.01
☐ 368	Brian Holton	.04	.02	.01
☐ 369	Ken Caminiti	.07	.03	.01
☐ 370	Dennis Eckersley	.12	.05	.02
☐ 371	Manny Lee	.04	.02	.01
☐ 372	Craig Lefferts	.04	.02	.01
☐ 373	Tracy Jones	.04	.02	.01
☐ 374	John Wathan MG	.06	.03	.01
	(Team checklist back)			
☐ 375	Terry Pendleton	.12	.05	.02
☐ 376	Steve Lombardozzi	.04	.02	.01
☐ 377	Mike Smithson	.04	.02	.01
☐ 378	Checklist 265-396	.05	.01	.00
☐ 379	Tim Flannery	.04	.02	.01
☐ 380	Rickey Henderson	.25	.11	.03
☐ 381	Baltimore Orioles TL	.05	.02	.01
	Larry Sheets			
☐ 382	John Smoltz	.60	.25	.08
☐ 383	Howard Johnson	.07	.03	.01
☐ 384	Mark Salas	.04	.02	.01
☐ 385	Von Hayes	.04	.02	.01
☐ 386	Andres Galarraga AS	.05	.02	.01
☐ 387	Ryne Sandberg AS	.20	.09	.03
☐ 388	Bobby Bonilla AS	.10	.05	.01
☐ 389	Ozzie Smith AS	.10	.05	.01
☐ 390	Darryl Strawberry AS	.12	.05	.02
☐ 391	Andre Dawson AS	.10	.05	.01
☐ 392	Andy Van Slyke AS	.08	.04	.01
☐ 393	Gary Carter AS	.05	.02	.01
☐ 394	Orel Hershiser AS	.05	.02	.01
☐ 395	Danny Jackson AS	.05	.02	.01
☐ 396	Kirk Gibson AS	.05	.02	.01
☐ 397	Don Mattingly AS	.12	.05	.02
☐ 398	Julio Franco AS	.05	.02	.01
☐ 399	Wade Boggs AS	.12	.05	.02
☐ 400	Alan Trammell AS	.08	.04	.01
☐ 401	Jose Canseco AS	.20	.09	.03
☐ 402	Mike Greenwell AS	.08	.04	.01
☐ 403	Kirby Puckett AS	.20	.09	.03
☐ 404	Bob Boone AS	.05	.02	.01
☐ 405	Roger Clemens AS	.20	.09	.03
☐ 406	Frank Viola AS	.05	.02	.01
☐ 407	Dave Winfield AS	.10	.05	.01
☐ 408	Greg Walker	.04	.02	.01
☐ 409	Ken Dayley	.04	.02	.01
☐ 410	Jack Clark	.07	.03	.01
☐ 411	Mitch Williams	.07	.03	.01
☐ 412	Barry Lyons	.04	.02	.01
☐ 413	Mike Kingery	.04	.02	.01
☐ 414	Jim Fregosi MG	.06	.03	.01
	(Team checklist back)			
☐ 415	Rich Gossage	.07	.03	.01
☐ 416	Fred Lynn	.07	.03	.01
☐ 417	Mike LaCoss	.04	.02	.01
☐ 418	Bob Dernier	.04	.02	.01
☐ 419	Tom Filer	.04	.02	.01
☐ 420	Joe Carter	.25	.11	.03
☐ 421	Kirk McCaskill	.04	.02	.01
☐ 422	Bo Diaz	.04	.02	.01
☐ 423	Brian Fisher	.04	.02	.01
☐ 424	Luis Polonia UER	.07	.03	.01
	(Wrong birthdate)			
☐ 425	Jay Howell	.04	.02	.01
☐ 426	Dan Gladden	.04	.02	.01
☐ 427	Eric Show	.04	.02	.01
☐ 428	Craig Reynolds	.04	.02	.01
☐ 429	Minnesota Twins TL	.05	.02	.01
	Greg Gagne			
	(Taking throw at 2nd)			
☐ 430	Mark Gubicza	.04	.02	.01
☐ 431	Luis Rivera	.04	.02	.01
☐ 432	Chad Kreuter	.04	.02	.01
☐ 433	Albert Hall	.04	.02	.01
☐ 434	Ken Patterson	.04	.02	.01
☐ 435	Len Dykstra	.07	.03	.01
☐ 436	Bobby Meacham	.04	.02	.01
☐ 437	Andy Benes FDP	.60	.25	.08
☐ 438	Greg Gross	.04	.02	.01
☐ 439	Frank DiPino	.04	.02	.01
☐ 440	Bobby Bonilla	.20	.09	.03
☐ 441	Jerry Reed	.04	.02	.01
☐ 442	Jose Oquendo	.04	.02	.01
☐ 443	Rod Nichols	.04	.02	.01
☐ 444	Moose Stubing MG	.06	.03	.01
	(Team checklist back)			
☐ 445	Matt Nokes	.07	.03	.01
☐ 446	Rob Murphy	.04	.02	.01
☐ 447	Donell Nixon	.04	.02	.01
☐ 448	Eric Plunk	.04	.02	.01
☐ 449	Carmelo Martinez	.04	.02	.01
☐ 450	Roger Clemens	.40	.18	.05
☐ 451	Mark Davidson	.04	.02	.01
☐ 452	Israel Sanchez	.04	.02	.01

☐	453 Tom Prince	.04	.02	.01
☐	454 Paul Assenmacher	.04	.02	.01
☐	455 Johnny Ray	.04	.02	.01
☐	456 Tim Belcher	.07	.03	.01
☐	457 Mackey Sasser	.04	.02	.01
☐	458 Donn Pall	.04	.02	.01
☐	459 Seattle Mariners TL	.05	.02	.01
	Dave Valle			
☐	460 Dave Stieb	.07	.03	.01
☐	461 Buddy Bell	.07	.03	.01
☐	462 Jose Guzman	.07	.03	.01
☐	463 Steve Lake	.04	.02	.01
☐	464 Bryn Smith	.04	.02	.01
☐	465 Mark Grace	.40	.18	.05
☐	466 Chuck Crim	.04	.02	.01
☐	467 Jim Walewander	.04	.02	.01
☐	468 Henry Cotto	.04	.02	.01
☐	469 Jose Bautista	.04	.02	.01
☐	470 Lance Parrish	.07	.03	.01
☐	471 Steve Curry	.04	.02	.01
☐	472 Brian Harper	.07	.03	.01
☐	473 Don Robinson	.04	.02	.01
☐	474 Bob Rodgers MG	.06	.03	.01
	(Team checklist back)			
☐	475 Dave Parker	.07	.03	.01
☐	476 Jon Perlman	.04	.02	.01
☐	477 Dick Schofield	.04	.02	.01
☐	478 Doug Drabek	.07	.03	.01
☐	479 Mike Macfarlane	.15	.07	.02
☐	480 Keith Hernandez	.07	.03	.01
☐	481 Chris Brown	.04	.02	.01
☐	482 Steve Peters	.04	.02	.01
☐	483 Mickey Hatcher	.04	.02	.01
☐	484 Steve Shields	.04	.02	.01
☐	485 Hubie Brooks	.04	.02	.01
☐	486 Jack McDowell	.40	.18	.05
☐	487 Scott Lusader	.04	.02	.01
☐	488 Kevin Coffman	.04	.02	.01
	("Now with Cubs")			
☐	489 Phila. Phillies TL	.10	.05	.01
	Mike Schmidt			
☐	490 Chris Sabo	.25	.11	.03
☐	491 Mike Birkbeck	.04	.02	.01
☐	492 Alan Ashby	.04	.02	.01
☐	493 Todd Benzinger	.04	.02	.01
☐	494 Shane Rawley	.04	.02	.01
☐	495 Candy Maldonado	.04	.02	.01
☐	496 Dwayne Henry	.04	.02	.01
☐	497 Pete Stanicek	.04	.02	.01
☐	498 Dave Valle	.04	.02	.01
☐	499 Don Heinkel	.04	.02	.01
☐	500 Jose Canseco	.40	.18	.05
☐	501 Vance Law	.04	.02	.01
☐	502 Duane Ward	.07	.03	.01
☐	503 Al Newman	.04	.02	.01
☐	504 Bob Walk	.04	.02	.01
☐	505 Pete Rose MG	.15	.07	.02

	(Team checklist back)			
☐	506 Kirt Manwaring	.04	.02	.01
☐	507 Steve Farr	.04	.02	.01
☐	508 Wally Backman	.04	.02	.01
☐	509 Bud Black	.04	.02	.01
☐	510 Bob Horner	.04	.02	.01
☐	511 Richard Dotson	.04	.02	.01
☐	512 Donnie Hill	.04	.02	.01
☐	513 Jesse Orosco	.04	.02	.01
☐	514 Chet Lemon	.04	.02	.01
☐	515 Barry Larkin	.15	.07	.02
☐	516 Eddie Whitson	.04	.02	.01
☐	517 Greg Brock	.04	.02	.01
☐	518 Bruce Ruffin	.04	.02	.01
☐	519 New York Yankees TL	.05	.02	.01
	Willie Randolph			
☐	520 Rick Sutcliffe	.07	.03	.01
☐	521 Mickey Tettleton	.07	.03	.01
☐	522 Randy Kramer	.04	.02	.01
☐	523 Andres Thomas	.04	.02	.01
☐	524 Checklist 397-528	.05	.01	.00
☐	525 Chili Davis	.07	.03	.01
☐	526 Wes Gardner	.04	.02	.01
☐	527 Dave Henderson	.07	.03	.01
☐	528 Luis Medina	.04	.02	.01
	(Lower left front			
	has white triangle)			
☐	529 Tom Foley	.04	.02	.01
☐	530 Nolan Ryan	.60	.25	.08
☐	531 Dave Hengel	.04	.02	.01
☐	532 Jerry Browne	.04	.02	.01
☐	533 Andy Hawkins	.04	.02	.01
☐	534 Doc Edwards MG	.06	.03	.01
	(Team checklist back)			
☐	535 Todd Worrell UER	.07	.03	.01
	(4 wins in '88,			
	should be 5)			
☐	536 Joel Skinner	.04	.02	.01
☐	537 Pete Smith	.07	.03	.01
☐	538 Juan Castillo	.04	.02	.01
☐	539 Barry Jones	.04	.02	.01
☐	540 Bo Jackson	.20	.09	.03
☐	541 Cecil Fielder	.25	.11	.03
☐	542 Todd Frohwirth	.04	.02	.01
☐	543 Damon Berryhill	.04	.02	.01
☐	544 Jeff Sellers	.04	.02	.01
☐	545 Mookie Wilson	.07	.03	.01
☐	546 Mark Williamson	.04	.02	.01
☐	547 Mark McLemore	.04	.02	.01
☐	548 Bobby Witt	.07	.03	.01
☐	549 Chicago Cubs TL	.05	.02	.01
	Jamie Moyer			
	(Pitching)			
☐	550 Orel Hershiser	.07	.03	.01
☐	551 Randy Ready	.04	.02	.01
☐	552 Greg Cadaret	.04	.02	.01
☐	553 Luis Salazar	.04	.02	.01

☐ 554 Nick Esasky	.04	.02	.01		
☐ 555 Bert Blyleven	.07	.03	.01		
☐ 556 Bruce Fields	.04	.02	.01		
☐ 557 Keith A. Miller	.04	.02	.01		
New York Mets					
☐ 558 Dan Pasqua	.04	.02	.01		
☐ 559 Juan Agosto	.04	.02	.01		
☐ 560 Tim Raines	.07	.03	.01		
☐ 561 Luis Aguayo	.04	.02	.01		
☐ 562 Danny Cox	.04	.02	.01		
☐ 563 Bill Schroeder	.04	.02	.01		
☐ 564 Russ Nixon MG	.06	.03	.01		
(Team checklist back)					
☐ 565 Jeff Russell	.04	.02	.01		
☐ 566 Al Pedrique	.04	.02	.01		
☐ 567 David Wells UER	.10	.05	.01		
(Complete Pitching					
Recor)					
☐ 568 Mickey Brantley	.04	.02	.01		
☐ 569 German Jimenez	.04	.02	.01		
☐ 570 Tony Gwynn UER	.25	.11	.03		
('88 average should					
be italicized as					
league leader)					
☐ 571 Billy Ripken	.04	.02	.01		
☐ 572 Atlee Hammaker	.04	.02	.01		
☐ 573 Jim Abbott FDP	1.00	.45	.13		
☐ 574 Dave Clark	.04	.02	.01		
☐ 575 Juan Samuel	.04	.02	.01		
☐ 576 Greg Minton	.04	.02	.01		
☐ 577 Randy Bush	.04	.02	.01		
☐ 578 John Morris	.04	.02	.01		
☐ 579 Houston Astros TL	.05	.02	.01		
Glenn Davis					
(Batting stance)					
☐ 580 Harold Reynolds	.04	.02	.01		
☐ 581 Gene Nelson	.04	.02	.01		
☐ 582 Mike Marshall	.04	.02	.01		
☐ 583 Paul Gibson	.04	.02	.01		
☐ 584 Randy Velarde UER	.04	.02	.01		
(Signed 1935,					
should be 1985)					
☐ 585 Harold Baines	.07	.03	.01		
☐ 586 Joe Boever	.04	.02	.01		
☐ 587 Mike Stanley	.04	.02	.01		
☐ 588 Luis Alicea	.10	.05	.01		
☐ 589 Dave Meads	.04	.02	.01		
☐ 590 Andres Galarraga	.04	.02	.01		
☐ 591 Jeff Musselman	.04	.02	.01		
☐ 592 John Cangelosi	.04	.02	.01		
☐ 593 Drew Hall	.04	.02	.01		
☐ 594 Jimy Williams MG	.06	.03	.01		
(Team checklist back)					
☐ 595 Teddy Higuera	.04	.02	.01		
☐ 596 Kurt Stillwell	.04	.02	.01		
☐ 597 Terry Taylor	.04	.02	.01		
☐ 598 Ken Gerhart	.04	.02	.01		

☐ 599 Tom Candiotti	.04	.02	.01		
☐ 600 Wade Boggs	.25	.11	.03		
☐ 601 Dave Dravecky	.07	.03	.01		
☐ 602 Devon White	.07	.03	.01		
☐ 603 Frank Tanana	.04	.02	.01		
☐ 604 Paul O'Neill	.07	.03	.01		
☐ 605A Bob Welch ERR	2.25	1.00	.30		
(Missing line on back,					
"Complete M.L.					
Pitching Record")					
☐ 605B Bob Welch COR	.07	.03	.01		
☐ 606 Rick Dempsey	.04	.02	.01		
☐ 607 Willie Ansley FDP	.12	.05	.02		
☐ 608 Phil Bradley	.04	.02	.01		
☐ 609 Detroit Tigers TL	.05	.02	.01		
Frank Tanana					
(With Alan Trammell					
and Mike Heath)					
☐ 610 Randy Myers	.07	.03	.01		
☐ 611 Don Slaught	.04	.02	.01		
☐ 612 Dan Quisenberry	.07	.03	.01		
☐ 613 Gary Varsho	.04	.02	.01		
☐ 614 Joe Hesketh	.04	.02	.01		
☐ 615 Robin Yount	.20	.09	.03		
☐ 616 Steve Rosenberg	.04	.02	.01		
☐ 617 Mark Parent	.04	.02	.01		
☐ 618 Rance Mulliniks	.04	.02	.01		
☐ 619 Checklist 529-660	.05	.01	.00		
☐ 620 Barry Bonds	.40	.18	.05		
☐ 621 Rick Mahler	.04	.02	.01		
☐ 622 Stan Javier	.04	.02	.01		
☐ 623 Fred Toliver	.04	.02	.01		
☐ 624 Jack McKeon MG	.06	.03	.01		
(Team checklist back)					
☐ 625 Eddie Murray	.15	.07	.02		
☐ 626 Jeff Reed	.04	.02	.01		
☐ 627 Greg A. Harris	.04	.02	.01		
Philadelphia Phillies					
☐ 628 Matt Williams	.15	.07	.02		
☐ 629 Pete O'Brien	.04	.02	.01		
☐ 630 Mike Greenwell	.07	.03	.01		
☐ 631 Dave Bergman	.04	.02	.01		
☐ 632 Bryan Harvey	.25	.11	.03		
☐ 633 Daryl Boston	.04	.02	.01		
☐ 634 Marvin Freeman	.04	.02	.01		
☐ 635 Willie Randolph	.07	.03	.01		
☐ 636 Bill Wilkinson	.04	.02	.01		
☐ 637 Carmen Castillo	.04	.02	.01		
☐ 638 Floyd Bannister	.04	.02	.01		
☐ 639 Oakland A's TL	.05	.02	.01		
Walt Weiss					
☐ 640 Willie McGee	.07	.03	.01		
☐ 641 Curt Young	.04	.02	.01		
☐ 642 Argenis Salazar	.04	.02	.01		
☐ 643 Louie Meadows	.04	.02	.01		
☐ 644 Lloyd McClendon	.04	.02	.01		
☐ 645 Jack Morris	.12	.05	.02		

☐ 646	Kevin Bass	.04	.02	.01
☐ 647	Randy Johnson	.35	.16	.04
☐ 648	Sandy Alomar FS	.25	.11	.03
☐ 649	Stewart Cliburn	.04	.02	.01
☐ 650	Kirby Puckett	.40	.18	.05
☐ 651	Tom Niedenfuer	.04	.02	.01
☐ 652	Rich Gedman	.04	.02	.01
☐ 653	Tommy Barrett	.04	.02	.01
☐ 654	Whitey Herzog MG	.06	.03	.01
	(Team checklist back)			
☐ 655	Dave Magadan	.07	.03	.01
☐ 656	Ivan Calderon	.04	.02	.01
☐ 657	Joe Magrane	.04	.02	.01
☐ 658	R.J. Reynolds	.04	.02	.01
☐ 659	Al Leiter	.04	.02	.01
☐ 660	Will Clark	.40	.18	.05
☐ 661	Dwight Gooden TBC84	.10	.05	.01
☐ 662	Lou Brock TBC79	.08	.04	.01
☐ 663	Hank Aaron TBC74	.10	.05	.01
☐ 664	Gil Hodges TBC69	.05	.02	.01
☐ 665A	Tony Oliva TBC64	2.00	.90	.25
	ERR (fabricated card is enlarged version of Oliva's 64T card; Topps copyright missing)			
☐ 665B	Tony Oliva TBC64	.05	.02	.01
	COR (fabricated card)			
☐ 666	Randy St.Claire	.04	.02	.01
☐ 667	Dwayne Murphy	.04	.02	.01
☐ 668	Mike Bielecki	.04	.02	.01
☐ 669	L.A. Dodgers TL	.05	.02	.01
	Orel Hershiser (Mound conference with Mike Scioscia)			
☐ 670	Kevin Seitzer	.07	.03	.01
☐ 671	Jim Gantner	.04	.02	.01
☐ 672	Allan Anderson	.04	.02	.01
☐ 673	Don Baylor	.07	.03	.01
☐ 674	Otis Nixon	.07	.03	.01
☐ 675	Bruce Hurst	.07	.03	.01
☐ 676	Ernie Riles	.04	.02	.01
☐ 677	Dave Schmidt	.04	.02	.01
☐ 678	Dion James	.04	.02	.01
☐ 679	Willie Fraser	.04	.02	.01
☐ 680	Gary Carter	.07	.03	.01
☐ 681	Jeff D. Robinson	.04	.02	.01
	Pittsburgh Pirates			
☐ 682	Rick Leach	.04	.02	.01
☐ 683	Jose Cecena	.04	.02	.01
☐ 684	Dave Johnson MG	.06	.03	.01
	(Team checklist back)			
☐ 685	Jeff Treadway	.04	.02	.01
☐ 686	Scott Terry	.04	.02	.01
☐ 687	Alvin Davis	.04	.02	.01
☐ 688	Zane Smith	.04	.02	.01

☐ 689A	Stan Jefferson	.04	.02	.01
	(Pink triangle on front bottom left)			
☐ 689B	Stan Jefferson	.04	.02	.01
	(Violet triangle on front bottom left)			
☐ 690	Doug Jones	.07	.03	.01
☐ 691	Roberto Kelly UER	.20	.09	.03
	(83 Oneonta)			
☐ 692	Steve Ontiveros	.04	.02	.01
☐ 693	Pat Borders	.30	.14	.04
☐ 694	Les Lancaster	.04	.02	.01
☐ 695	Carlton Fisk	.15	.07	.02
☐ 696	Don August	.04	.02	.01
☐ 697A	Franklin Stubbs	.04	.02	.01
	(Team name on front in white)			
☐ 697B	Franklin Stubbs	.04	.02	.01
	(Team name on front in gray)			
☐ 698	Keith Atherton	.04	.02	.01
☐ 699	Pittsburgh Pirates TL	.05	.02	.01
	Al Pedrique (Tony Gwynn sliding)			
☐ 700	Don Mattingly	.25	.11	.03
☐ 701	Storm Davis	.04	.02	.01
☐ 702	Jamie Quirk	.04	.02	.01
☐ 703	Scott Garrelts	.04	.02	.01
☐ 704	Carlos Quintana	.10	.05	.01
☐ 705	Terry Kennedy	.04	.02	.01
☐ 706	Pete Incaviglia	.04	.02	.01
☐ 707	Steve Jeltz	.04	.02	.01
☐ 708	Chuck Finley	.07	.03	.01
☐ 709	Tom Herr	.04	.02	.01
☐ 710	David Cone	.15	.07	.02
☐ 711	Candy Sierra	.04	.02	.01
☐ 712	Bill Swift	.07	.03	.01
☐ 713	Ty Griffin FDP	.08	.04	.01
☐ 714	Joe Morgan MG	.06	.03	.01
	(Team checklist back)			
☐ 715	Tony Pena	.04	.02	.01
☐ 716	Wayne Tolleson	.04	.02	.01
☐ 717	Jamie Moyer	.04	.02	.01
☐ 718	Glenn Braggs	.04	.02	.01
☐ 719	Danny Darwin	.04	.02	.01
☐ 720	Tim Wallach	.07	.03	.01
☐ 721	Ron Tingley	.04	.02	.01
☐ 722	Todd Stottlemyre	.10	.05	.01
☐ 723	Rafael Belliard	.04	.02	.01
☐ 724	Jerry Don Gleaton	.04	.02	.01
☐ 725	Terry Steinbach	.07	.03	.01
☐ 726	Dickie Thon	.04	.02	.01
☐ 727	Joe Orsulak	.04	.02	.01
☐ 728	Charlie Puleo	.04	.02	.01
☐ 729	Texas Rangers TL	.05	.02	.01
	Steve Buechele (Inconsistent design,			

team name on front
surrounded by black,
should be white)

☐ 730	Danny Jackson	.04	.02	.01
☐ 731	Mike Young	.04	.02	.01
☐ 732	Steve Buechele	.04	.02	.01
☐ 733	Randy Bockus	.04	.02	.01
☐ 734	Jody Reed	.04	.02	.01
☐ 735	Roger McDowell	.04	.02	.01
☐ 736	Jeff Hamilton	.04	.02	.01
☐ 737	Norm Charlton	.20	.09	.03
☐ 738	Darnell Coles	.04	.02	.01
☐ 739	Brook Jacoby	.04	.02	.01
☐ 740	Dan Plesac	.04	.02	.01
☐ 741	Ken Phelps	.04	.02	.01
☐ 742	Mike Harkey FS	.12	.05	.02
☐ 743	Mike Heath	.04	.02	.01
☐ 744	Roger Craig MG	.06	.03	.01
	(Team checklist back)			
☐ 745	Fred McGriff	.25	.11	.03
☐ 746	German Gonzalez UER	.04	.02	.01
	(Wrong birthdate)			
☐ 747	Wil Tejada	.04	.02	.01
☐ 748	Jimmy Jones	.04	.02	.01
☐ 749	Rafael Ramirez	.04	.02	.01
☐ 750	Bret Saberhagen	.07	.03	.01
☐ 751	Ken Oberkfell	.04	.02	.01
☐ 752	Jim Gott	.04	.02	.01
☐ 753	Jose Uribe	.04	.02	.01
☐ 754	Bob Brower	.04	.02	.01
☐ 755	Mike Scioscia	.04	.02	.01
☐ 756	Scott Medvin	.04	.02	.01
☐ 757	Brady Anderson	.60	.25	.08
☐ 758	Gene Walter	.04	.02	.01
☐ 759	Milwaukee Brewers TL	.05	.02	.01
	Rob Deer			
☐ 760	Lee Smith	.07	.03	.01
☐ 761	Dante Bichette	.25	.11	.03
☐ 762	Bobby Thigpen	.04	.02	.01
☐ 763	Dave Martinez	.07	.03	.01
☐ 764	Robin Ventura FDP	1.25	.55	.16
☐ 765	Glenn Davis	.07	.03	.01
☐ 766	Cecilio Guante	.04	.02	.01
☐ 767	Mike Capel	.04	.02	.01
☐ 768	Bill Wegman	.04	.02	.01
☐ 769	Junior Ortiz	.04	.02	.01
☐ 770	Alan Trammell	.07	.03	.01
☐ 771	Ron Kittle	.04	.02	.01
☐ 772	Ron Oester	.04	.02	.01
☐ 773	Keith Moreland	.04	.02	.01
☐ 774	Frank Robinson MG	.10	.05	.01
	(Team checklist back)			
☐ 775	Jeff Reardon	.07	.03	.01
☐ 776	Nelson Liriano	.04	.02	.01
☐ 777	Ted Power	.04	.02	.01
☐ 778	Bruce Benedict	.04	.02	.01
☐ 779	Craig McMurtry	.04	.02	.01
☐ 780	Pedro Guerrero	.07	.03	.01
☐ 781	Greg Briley	.10	.05	.01
☐ 782	Checklist 661-792	.05	.01	.00
☐ 783	Trevor Wilson	.12	.05	.02
☐ 784	Steve Avery FDP	1.25	1.25	1.25
☐ 785	Ellis Burks	.07	.03	.01
☐ 786	Melido Perez	.15	.07	.02
☐ 787	Dave West	.10	.05	.01
☐ 788	Mike Morgan	.07	.03	.01
☐ 789	Kansas City Royals TL	.10	.05	.01
	Bo Jackson			
	(Throwing)			
☐ 790	Sid Fernandez	.07	.03	.01
☐ 791	Jim Lindeman	.04	.02	.01
☐ 792	Rafael Santana	.04	.02	.01

1989 Topps Traded

The 1989 Topps Traded set contains 132
standard-size (2 1/2" by 3 1/2") cards. The
fronts have white borders; the horizontally
oriented backs are red and pink. From the
front the cards' style is indistinguishable
from the 1989 Topps regular issue. The
cards were distributed as a boxed set. The
key rookies in this set are Ken Griffey Jr.,
Deion Sanders, and Jerome Walton.
Topps also produced a specially boxed
"glossy" edition frequently referred to as
the Topps Traded Tiffany set. This year,
again, Topps did not disclose the number
of Tiffany sets they produced or sold but it
seems that production quantities were
roughly similar (or slightly smaller, 15,000
sets) to the previous two years. The
checklist of cards is identical to that of the
normal non-glossy cards. There are two
primary distinguishing features of the

Tiffany cards, white card stock reverses and high gloss obverses. These Tiffany cards are valued approximately from three to five times the values listed below.

	MT	EX-MT	VG
COMPLETE SET (132)	7.50	3.40	.95
COMMON PLAYER (1T-132T)	.05	.02	.01

	Player	MT	EX-MT	VG
☐ 1T	Don Aase	.05	.02	.01
☐ 2T	Jim Abbott	1.00	.45	.13
☐ 3T	Kent Anderson	.05	.02	.01
☐ 4T	Keith Atherton	.05	.02	.01
☐ 5T	Wally Backman	.05	.02	.01
☐ 6T	Steve Balboni	.05	.02	.01
☐ 7T	Jesse Barfield	.05	.02	.01
☐ 8T	Steve Bedrosian	.05	.02	.01
☐ 9T	Todd Benzinger	.05	.02	.01
☐ 10T	Geronimo Berroa	.05	.02	.01
☐ 11T	Bert Blyleven	.08	.04	.01
☐ 12T	Bob Boone	.08	.04	.01
☐ 13T	Phil Bradley	.05	.02	.01
☐ 14T	Jeff Brantley	.10	.05	.01
☐ 15T	Kevin Brown	.30	.14	.04
☐ 16T	Jerry Browne	.05	.02	.01
☐ 17T	Chuck Cary	.05	.02	.01
☐ 18T	Carmen Castillo	.05	.02	.01
☐ 19T	Jim Clancy	.05	.02	.01
☐ 20T	Jack Clark	.08	.04	.01
☐ 21T	Bryan Clutterbuck	.05	.02	.01
☐ 22T	Jody Davis	.05	.02	.01
☐ 23T	Mike Devereaux	.35	.16	.04
☐ 24T	Frank DiPino	.05	.02	.01
☐ 25T	Benny Distefano	.05	.02	.01
☐ 26T	John Dopson	.05	.02	.01
☐ 27T	Len Dykstra	.08	.04	.01
☐ 28T	Jim Eisenreich	.05	.02	.01
☐ 29T	Nick Esasky	.05	.02	.01
☐ 30T	Alvaro Espinoza	.05	.02	.01
☐ 31T	Darrell Evans UER	.08	.04	.01
	(Stat headings on back are for a pitcher)			
☐ 32T	Junior Felix	.25	.11	.03
☐ 33T	Felix Fermin	.05	.02	.01
☐ 34T	Julio Franco	.08	.04	.01
☐ 35T	Terry Francona	.05	.02	.01
☐ 36T	Cito Gaston MG	.08	.04	.01
☐ 37T	Bob Geren UER	.05	.02	.01
	(Photo actually Mike Fennell)			
☐ 38T	Tom Gordon	.10	.05	.01
☐ 39T	Tommy Gregg	.05	.02	.01
☐ 40T	Ken Griffey Sr.	.08	.04	.01
☐ 41T	Ken Griffey Jr.	4.00	1.80	.50
☐ 42T	Kevin Gross	.05	.02	.01
☐ 43T	Lee Guetterman	.05	.02	.01
☐ 44T	Mel Hall	.05	.02	.01
☐ 45T	Erik Hanson	.20	.09	.03
☐ 46T	Gene Harris	.10	.05	.01
☐ 47T	Andy Hawkins	.05	.02	.01
☐ 48T	Rickey Henderson	.25	.11	.03
☐ 49T	Tom Herr	.05	.02	.01
☐ 50T	Ken Hill	.40	.18	.05
☐ 51T	Brian Holman	.10	.05	.01
☐ 52T	Brian Holton	.05	.02	.01
☐ 53T	Art Howe MG	.05	.02	.01
☐ 54T	Ken Howell	.05	.02	.01
☐ 55T	Bruce Hurst	.08	.04	.01
☐ 56T	Chris James	.05	.02	.01
☐ 57T	Randy Johnson	.15	.07	.02
☐ 58T	Jimmy Jones	.05	.02	.01
☐ 59T	Terry Kennedy	.05	.02	.01
☐ 60T	Paul Kilgus	.05	.02	.01
☐ 61T	Eric King	.05	.02	.01
☐ 62T	Ron Kittle	.05	.02	.01
☐ 63T	John Kruk	.08	.04	.01
☐ 64T	Randy Kutcher	.05	.02	.01
☐ 65T	Steve Lake	.05	.02	.01
☐ 66T	Mark Langston	.08	.04	.01
☐ 67T	Dave LaPoint	.05	.02	.01
☐ 68T	Rick Leach	.05	.02	.01
☐ 69T	Terry Leach	.05	.02	.01
☐ 70T	Jim Lefebvre MG	.05	.02	.01
☐ 71T	Al Leiter	.05	.02	.01
☐ 72T	Jeffrey Leonard	.05	.02	.01
☐ 73T	Derek Lilliquist	.10	.05	.01
☐ 74T	Rick Mahler	.05	.02	.01
☐ 75T	Tom McCarthy	.05	.02	.01
☐ 76T	Lloyd McClendon	.05	.02	.01
☐ 77T	Lance McCullers	.05	.02	.01
☐ 78T	Oddibe McDowell	.05	.02	.01
☐ 79T	Roger McDowell	.05	.02	.01
☐ 80T	Larry McWilliams	.05	.02	.01
☐ 81T	Randy Milligan	.05	.02	.01
☐ 82T	Mike Moore	.05	.02	.01
☐ 83T	Keith Moreland	.05	.02	.01
☐ 84T	Mike Morgan	.08	.04	.01
☐ 85T	Jamie Moyer	.05	.02	.01
☐ 86T	Rob Murphy	.05	.02	.01
☐ 87T	Eddie Murray	.15	.07	.02
☐ 88T	Pete O'Brien	.05	.02	.01
☐ 89T	Gregg Olson	.40	.18	.05
☐ 90T	Steve Ontiveros	.05	.02	.01
☐ 91T	Jesse Orosco	.05	.02	.01
☐ 92T	Spike Owen	.05	.02	.01
☐ 93T	Rafael Palmeiro	.20	.09	.03
☐ 94T	Clay Parker	.05	.02	.01
☐ 95T	Jeff Parrett	.05	.02	.01
☐ 96T	Lance Parrish	.08	.04	.01
☐ 97T	Dennis Powell	.05	.02	.01
☐ 98T	Rey Quinones	.05	.02	.01
☐ 99T	Doug Rader MG	.05	.02	.01
☐ 100T	Willie Randolph	.08	.04	.01
☐ 101T	Shane Rawley	.05	.02	.01

☐	102T	Randy Ready	.05	.02	.01
☐	103T	Bip Roberts	.08	.04	.01
☐	104T	Kenny Rogers	.08	.04	.01
☐	105T	Ed Romero	.05	.02	.01
☐	106T	Nolan Ryan	1.25	.55	.16
☐	107T	Luis Salazar	.05	.02	.01
☐	108T	Juan Samuel	.05	.02	.01
☐	109T	Alex Sanchez	.05	.02	.01
☐	110T	Deion Sanders	2.00	.90	.25
☐	111T	Steve Sax	.08	.04	.01
☐	112T	Rick Schu	.05	.02	.01
☐	113T	Dwight Smith	.10	.05	.01
☐	114T	Lonnie Smith	.05	.02	.01
☐	115T	Billy Spiers	.10	.05	.01
☐	116T	Kent Tekulve	.05	.02	.01
☐	117T	Walt Terrell	.05	.02	.01
☐	118T	Milt Thompson	.05	.02	.01
☐	119T	Dickie Thon	.05	.02	.01
☐	120T	Jeff Torborg MG	.05	.02	.01
☐	121T	Jeff Treadway	.08	.04	.01
☐	122T	Omar Vizquel	.15	.07	.02
☐	123T	Jerome Walton	.10	.05	.01
☐	124T	Gary Ward	.05	.02	.01
☐	125T	Claudell Washington	.05	.02	.01
☐	126T	Curt Wilkerson	.05	.02	.01
☐	127T	Eddie Williams	.05	.02	.01
☐	128T	Frank Williams	.05	.02	.01
☐	129T	Ken Williams	.05	.02	.01
☐	130T	Mitch Williams	.08	.04	.01
☐	131T	Steve Wilson	.05	.02	.01
☐	132T	Checklist 1T-132T	.08	.01	.00

1990 Topps

The 1990 Topps set contains 792 standard-size (2 1/2" by 3 1/2") cards. The front borders are various colors. The horizontally oriented backs are yellowish

green. Cards 385-407 contain the All-Stars. Cards 661-665 contain the Turn Back the Clock cards. The manager cards this year contain information that had been on the backs of the Team Leader cards in the past few years; the Team Leader cards were discontinued, apparently in order to allow better individual player card selection. Topps really concentrated on individual player cards in this set with 725, the most ever in a baseball card set. The checklist cards are oriented alphabetically by team name and player name. The key Rookie Cards in this set are Delino DeShields, Juan Gonzalez, Marquis Grissom, Ben McDonald, Frank Thomas, and Larry Walker. There exists a printing variation on the Jeff King (454) card where the card number, Topps logo, name, and personal information block on the card back is erroneously shaded in yellow as the rest of the back. Topps also produced a specially boxed "glossy" edition frequently referred to as the Topps Tiffany set. This year, again, Topps did not disclose the number of Tiffany sets they produced or sold but it seems that production quantities were roughly similar (approximately 15,000 sets) to the previous year. The checklist of cards is identical to that of the normal non-glossy cards. There are two primary distinguishing features of the Tiffany cards, white card stock reverses and high gloss obverses. These Tiffany cards are valued approximately from three to five times the values listed below.

		MT	EX-MT	VG
	COMPLETE SET (792)	20.00	9.00	2.50
	COMPLETE FACT.SET (792)	25.00	11.50	3.10
	COMMON PLAYER (1-792)	.04	.02	.01
☐ 1	Nolan Ryan	.60	.25	.08
☐ 2	Nolan Ryan Salute New York Mets	.25	.11	.03
☐ 3	Nolan Ryan Salute California Angels	.25	.11	.03
☐ 4	Nolan Ryan Salute Houston Astros	.25	.11	.03
☐ 5	Nolan Ryan Salute Texas Rangers UER (Says Texas Stadium rather than Arlington Stadium)	.25	.11	.03
☐ 6	Vince Coleman RB (50 consecutive stolen bases)	.05	.02	.01

☐ 7	Rickey Henderson RB 10	.05	.01	
	(40 career leadoff			
	home runs)			
☐ 8	Cal Ripken RB 20	.09	.03	
	(20 or more homers for			
	8 consecutive years,			
	record for shortstops)			
☐ 9	Eric Plunk 04	.02	.01	
☐ 10	Barry Larkin 12	.05	.02	
☐ 11	Paul Gibson 04	.02	.01	
☐ 12	Joe Girardi 04	.02	.01	
☐ 13	Mark Williamson 04	.02	.01	
☐ 14	Mike Fetters 10	.05	.01	
☐ 15	Teddy Higuera...................04	.02	.01	
☐ 16	Kent Anderson 04	.02	.01	
☐ 17	Kelly Downs 04	.02	.01	
☐ 18	Carlos Quintana 07	.03	.01	
☐ 19	Al Newman 04	.02	.01	
☐ 20	Mark Gubicza 04	.02	.01	
☐ 21	Jeff Torborg MG 04	.02	.01	
☐ 22	Bruce Ruffin 04	.02	.01	
☐ 23	Randy Velarde 04	.02	.01	
☐ 24	Joe Hesketh 04	.02	.01	
☐ 25	Willie Randolph.................07	.03	.01	
☐ 26	Don Slaught 04	.02	.01	
☐ 27	Rick Leach 04	.02	.01	
☐ 28	Duane Ward 04	.02	.01	
☐ 29	John Cangelosi 04	.02	.01	
☐ 30	David Cone 12	.05	.02	
☐ 31	Henry Cotto 04	.02	.01	
☐ 32	John Farrell 04	.02	.01	
☐ 33	Greg Walker 04	.02	.01	
☐ 34	Tony Fossas 04	.02	.01	
☐ 35	Benito Santiago.................07	.03	.01	
☐ 36	John Costello.....................04	.02	.01	
☐ 37	Domingo Ramos.................04	.02	.01	
☐ 38	Wes Gardner......................04	.02	.01	
☐ 39	Curt Ford 04	.02	.01	
☐ 40	Jay Howell 04	.02	.01	
☐ 41	Matt Williams 10	.05	.01	
☐ 42	Jeff M. Robinson 04	.02	.01	
☐ 43	Dante Bichette...................07	.03	.01	
☐ 44	Roger Salkeld FDP 25	.11	.03	
☐ 45	Dave Parker UER 07	.03	.01	
	(Born in Jackson,			
	not Calhoun)			
☐ 46	Rob Dibble 07	.03	.01	
☐ 47	Brian Harper 07	.03	.01	
☐ 48	Zane Smith 04	.02	.01	
☐ 49	Tom Lawless 04	.02	.01	
☐ 50	Glenn Davis 07	.03	.01	
☐ 51	Doug Rader MG 04	.02	.01	
☐ 52	Jack Daugherty..................04	.02	.01	
☐ 53	Mike LaCoss 04	.02	.01	
☐ 54	Joel Skinner 04	.02	.01	
☐ 55	Darrell Evans UER.............07	.03	.01	
	(HR total should be			
	414, not 424)			
☐ 56	Franklin Stubbs.................04	.02	.01	
☐ 57	Greg Vaughn......................15	.07	.02	
☐ 58	Keith Miller 04	.02	.01	
☐ 59	Ted Power 04	.02	.01	
☐ 60	George Brett 15	.07	.02	
☐ 61	Deion Sanders 40	.18	.05	
☐ 62	Ramon Martinez 15	.07	.02	
☐ 63	Mike Pagliarulo 04	.02	.01	
☐ 64	Danny Darwin 04	.02	.01	
☐ 65	Devon White 07	.03	.01	
☐ 66	Greg Litton 04	.02	.01	
☐ 67	Scott Sanderson 04	.02	.01	
☐ 68	Dave Henderson 04	.02	.01	
☐ 69	Todd Frohwirth 04	.02	.01	
☐ 70	Mike Greenwell 07	.03	.01	
☐ 71	Allan Anderson 04	.02	.01	
☐ 72	Jeff Huson 10	.05	.01	
☐ 73	Bob Milacki 04	.02	.01	
☐ 74	Jeff Jackson FDP 10	.05	.01	
☐ 75	Doug Jones 07	.03	.01	
☐ 76	Dave Valle 04	.02	.01	
☐ 77	Dave Bergman 04	.02	.01	
☐ 78	Mike Flanagan 04	.02	.01	
☐ 79	Ron Kittle 04	.02	.01	
☐ 80	Jeff Russell 04	.02	.01	
☐ 81	Bob Rodgers MG 04	.02	.01	
☐ 82	Scott Terry 04	.02	.01	
☐ 83	Hensley Meulens................07	.03	.01	
☐ 84	Ray Searage.......................04	.02	.01	
☐ 85	Juan Samuel 04	.02	.01	
☐ 86	Paul Kilgus 04	.02	.01	
☐ 87	Rick Luecken 04	.02	.01	
☐ 88	Glenn Braggs 04	.02	.01	
☐ 89	Clint Zavaras 04	.02	.01	
☐ 90	Jack Clark 07	.03	.01	
☐ 91	Steve Frey 10	.05	.01	
☐ 92	Mike Stanley 04	.02	.01	
☐ 93	Shawn Hillegas 04	.02	.01	
☐ 94	Herm Winningham...............04	.02	.01	
☐ 95	Todd Worrell......................04	.02	.01	
☐ 96	Jody Reed 04	.02	.01	
☐ 97	Curt Schilling 15	.07	.02	
☐ 98	Jose Gonzalez 04	.02	.01	
☐ 99	Rich Monteleone 04	.02	.01	
☐ 100	Will Clark 30	.14	.04	
☐ 101	Shane Rawley 04	.02	.01	
☐ 102	Stan Javier 04	.02	.01	
☐ 103	Marvin Freeman.................04	.02	.01	
☐ 104	Bob Knepper 04	.02	.01	
☐ 105	Randy Myers 07	.03	.01	
☐ 106	Charlie O'Brien 04	.02	.01	
☐ 107	Fred Lynn 07	.03	.01	
☐ 108	Rod Nichols 04	.02	.01	
☐ 109	Roberto Kelly 10	.05	.01	
☐ 110	Tommy Helms MG 04	.02	.01	
☐ 111	Ed Whited 04	.02	.01	

☐ 112	Glenn Wilson	.04	.02	.01
☐ 113	Manny Lee	.04	.02	.01
☐ 114	Mike Bielecki	.04	.02	.01
☐ 115	Tony Pena	.04	.02	.01
☐ 116	Floyd Bannister	.04	.02	.01
☐ 117	Mike Sharperson	.04	.02	.01
☐ 118	Erik Hanson	.07	.03	.01
☐ 119	Billy Hatcher	.04	.02	.01
☐ 120	John Franco	.07	.03	.01
☐ 121	Robin Ventura	.60	.25	.08
☐ 122	Shawn Abner	.04	.02	.01
☐ 123	Rich Gedman	.04	.02	.01
☐ 124	Dave Dravecky	.07	.03	.01
☐ 125	Kent Hrbek	.07	.03	.01
☐ 126	Randy Kramer	.04	.02	.01
☐ 127	Mike Devereaux	.07	.03	.01
☐ 128	Checklist 1	.05	.01	.00
☐ 129	Ron Jones	.04	.02	.01
☐ 130	Bert Blyleven	.07	.03	.01
☐ 131	Matt Nokes	.04	.02	.01
☐ 132	Lance Blankenship	.04	.02	.01
☐ 133	Ricky Horton	.04	.02	.01
☐ 134	Earl Cunningham FDP	.12	.05	.02
☐ 135	Dave Magadan	.07	.03	.01
☐ 136	Kevin Brown	.10	.05	.01
☐ 137	Marty Pevey	.04	.02	.01
☐ 138	Al Leiter	.04	.02	.01
☐ 139	Greg Brock	.04	.02	.01
☐ 140	Andre Dawson	.12	.05	.02
☐ 141	John Hart MG	.04	.02	.01
☐ 142	Jeff Wetherby	.04	.02	.01
☐ 143	Rafael Belliard	.04	.02	.01
☐ 144	Bud Black	.04	.02	.01
☐ 145	Terry Steinbach	.07	.03	.01
☐ 146	Rob Richie	.04	.02	.01
☐ 147	Chuck Finley	.07	.03	.01
☐ 148	Edgar Martinez	.25	.11	.03
☐ 149	Steve Farr	.04	.02	.01
☐ 150	Kirk Gibson	.07	.03	.01
☐ 151	Rick Mahler	.04	.02	.01
☐ 152	Lonnie Smith	.04	.02	.01
☐ 153	Randy Milligan	.04	.02	.01
☐ 154	Mike Maddux	.04	.02	.01
☐ 155	Ellis Burks	.07	.03	.01
☐ 156	Ken Patterson	.04	.02	.01
☐ 157	Craig Biggio	.10	.05	.01
☐ 158	Craig Lefferts	.04	.02	.01
☐ 159	Mike Felder	.04	.02	.01
☐ 160	Dave Righetti	.04	.02	.01
☐ 161	Harold Reynolds	.04	.02	.01
☐ 162	Todd Zeile	.15	.07	.02
☐ 163	Phil Bradley	.04	.02	.01
☐ 164	Jeff Juden FDP	.20	.09	.03
☐ 165	Walt Weiss	.04	.02	.01
☐ 166	Bobby Witt	.07	.03	.01
☐ 167	Kevin Appier	.25	.11	.03
☐ 168	Jose Lind	.04	.02	.01
☐ 169	Richard Dotson	.04	.02	.01
☐ 170	George Bell	.07	.03	.01
☐ 171	Russ Nixon MG	.04	.02	.01
☐ 172	Tom Lampkin	.04	.02	.01
☐ 173	Tim Belcher	.07	.03	.01
☐ 174	Jeff Kunkel	.04	.02	.01
☐ 175	Mike Moore	.04	.02	.01
☐ 176	Luis Quinones	.04	.02	.01
☐ 177	Mike Henneman	.04	.02	.01
☐ 178	Chris James	.04	.02	.01
☐ 179	Brian Holton	.04	.02	.01
☐ 180	Tim Raines	.07	.03	.01
☐ 181	Juan Agosto	.04	.02	.01
☐ 182	Mookie Wilson	.04	.02	.01
☐ 183	Steve Lake	.04	.02	.01
☐ 184	Danny Cox	.04	.02	.01
☐ 185	Ruben Sierra	.20	.09	.03
☐ 186	Dave LaPoint	.04	.02	.01
☐ 187	Rick Wrona	.04	.02	.01
☐ 188	Mike Smithson	.04	.02	.01
☐ 189	Dick Schofield	.04	.02	.01
☐ 190	Rick Reuschel	.04	.02	.01
☐ 191	Pat Borders	.07	.03	.01
☐ 192	Don August	.04	.02	.01
☐ 193	Andy Benes	.15	.07	.02
☐ 194	Glenallen Hill	.07	.03	.01
☐ 195	Tim Burke	.04	.02	.01
☐ 196	Gerald Young	.04	.02	.01
☐ 197	Doug Drabek	.07	.03	.01
☐ 198	Mike Marshall	.04	.02	.01
☐ 199	Sergio Valdez	.04	.02	.01
☐ 200	Don Mattingly	.20	.09	.03
☐ 201	Cito Gaston MG	.07	.03	.01
☐ 202	Mike Macfarlane	.04	.02	.01
☐ 203	Mike Roesler	.04	.02	.01
☐ 204	Bob Dernier	.04	.02	.01
☐ 205	Mark Davis	.04	.02	.01
☐ 206	Nick Esasky	.04	.02	.01
☐ 207	Bob Ojeda	.04	.02	.01
☐ 208	Brook Jacoby	.04	.02	.01
☐ 209	Greg Mathews	.04	.02	.01
☐ 210	Ryne Sandberg	.35	.16	.04
☐ 211	John Cerutti	.04	.02	.01
☐ 212	Joe Orsulak	.04	.02	.01
☐ 213	Scott Bankhead	.04	.02	.01
☐ 214	Terry Francona	.04	.02	.01
☐ 215	Kirk McCaskill	.04	.02	.01
☐ 216	Ricky Jordan	.04	.02	.01
☐ 217	Don Robinson	.04	.02	.01
☐ 218	Wally Backman	.04	.02	.01
☐ 219	Donn Pall	.04	.02	.01
☐ 220	Barry Bonds	.30	.14	.04
☐ 221	Gary Mielke	.04	.02	.01
☐ 222	Kurt Stillwell UER	.04	.02	.01
	(Graduate misspelled			
	as gradute)			
☐ 223	Tommy Gregg	.04	.02	.01

☐	224	Delino DeShields	.60	.25	.08
☐	225	Jim Deshaies	.04	.02	.01
☐	226	Mickey Hatcher	.04	.02	.01
☐	227	Kevin Tapani	.35	.16	.04
☐	228	Dave Martinez	.07	.03	.01
☐	229	David Wells	.07	.03	.01
☐	230	Keith Hernandez	.07	.03	.01
☐	231	Jack McKeon MG	.04	.02	.01
☐	232	Darnell Coles	.04	.02	.01
☐	233	Ken Hill	.15	.07	.02
☐	234	Mariano Duncan	.04	.02	.01
☐	235	Jeff Reardon	.07	.03	.01
☐	236	Hal Morris	.15	.07	.02
☐	237	Kevin Ritz	.10	.05	.01
☐	238	Felix Jose	.20	.09	.03
☐	239	Eric Show	.04	.02	.01
☐	240	Mark Grace	.20	.09	.03
☐	241	Mike Krukow	.04	.02	.01
☐	242	Fred Manrique	.04	.02	.01
☐	243	Barry Jones	.04	.02	.01
☐	244	Bill Schroeder	.04	.02	.01
☐	245	Roger Clemens	.35	.16	.04
☐	246	Jim Eisenreich	.04	.02	.01
☐	247	Jerry Reed	.04	.02	.01
☐	248	Dave Anderson	.04	.02	.01
☐	249	Mike(Texas) Smith	.04	.02	.01
☐	250	Jose Canseco	.30	.14	.04
☐	251	Jeff Blauser	.07	.03	.01
☐	252	Otis Nixon	.07	.03	.01
☐	253	Mark Portugal	.04	.02	.01
☐	254	Francisco Cabrera	.10	.05	.01
☐	255	Bobby Thigpen	.04	.02	.01
☐	256	Marvell Wynne	.04	.02	.01
☐	257	Jose DeLeon	.04	.02	.01
☐	258	Barry Lyons	.04	.02	.01
☐	259	Lance McCullers	.04	.02	.01
☐	260	Eric Davis	.10	.05	.01
☐	261	Whitey Herzog MG	.07	.03	.01
☐	262	Checklist 2	.05	.01	.00
☐	263	Mel Stottlemyre Jr.	.04	.02	.01
☐	264	Bryan Clutterbuck	.04	.02	.01
☐	265	Pete O'Brien	.04	.02	.01
☐	266	German Gonzalez	.04	.02	.01
☐	267	Mark Davidson	.04	.02	.01
☐	268	Rob Murphy	.04	.02	.01
☐	269	Dickie Thon	.04	.02	.01
☐	270	Dave Stewart	.07	.03	.01
☐	271	Chet Lemon	.04	.02	.01
☐	272	Bryan Harvey	.07	.03	.01
☐	273	Bobby Bonilla	.12	.05	.02
☐	274	Mauro Gozzo	.04	.02	.01
☐	275	Mickey Tettleton	.07	.03	.01
☐	276	Gary Thurman	.04	.02	.01
☐	277	Lenny Harris	.04	.02	.01
☐	278	Pascual Perez	.04	.02	.01
☐	279	Steve Buechele	.04	.02	.01
☐	280	Lou Whitaker	.07	.03	.01
☐	281	Kevin Bass	.04	.02	.01
☐	282	Derek Lilliquist	.04	.02	.01
☐	283	Joey Belle	.50	.23	.06
☐	284	Mark Gardner	.12	.05	.02
☐	285	Willie McGee	.07	.03	.01
☐	286	Lee Guetterman	.04	.02	.01
☐	287	Vance Law	.04	.02	.01
☐	288	Greg Briley	.04	.02	.01
☐	289	Norm Charlton	.07	.03	.01
☐	290	Robin Yount	.15	.07	.02
☐	291	Dave Johnson MG	.07	.03	.01
☐	292	Jim Gott	.04	.02	.01
☐	293	Mike Gallego	.04	.02	.01
☐	294	Craig McMurtry	.04	.02	.01
☐	295	Fred McGriff	.20	.09	.03
☐	296	Jeff Ballard	.04	.02	.01
☐	297	Tommy Herr	.04	.02	.01
☐	298	Dan Gladden	.04	.02	.01
☐	299	Adam Peterson	.04	.02	.01
☐	300	Bo Jackson	.15	.07	.02
☐	301	Don Aase	.04	.02	.01
☐	302	Marcus Lawton	.04	.02	.01
☐	303	Rick Cerone	.04	.02	.01
☐	304	Marty Clary	.04	.02	.01
☐	305	Eddie Murray	.10	.05	.01
☐	306	Tom Niedenfuer	.04	.02	.01
☐	307	Bip Roberts	.07	.03	.01
☐	308	Jose Guzman	.04	.02	.01
☐	309	Eric Yelding	.04	.02	.01
☐	310	Steve Bedrosian	.04	.02	.01
☐	311	Dwight Smith	.04	.02	.01
☐	312	Dan Quisenberry	.07	.03	.01
☐	313	Gus Polidor	.04	.02	.01
☐	314	Donald Harris FDP	.10	.05	.01
☐	315	Bruce Hurst	.07	.03	.01
☐	316	Carney Lansford	.07	.03	.01
☐	317	Mark Guthrie	.04	.02	.01
☐	318	Wallace Johnson	.04	.02	.01
☐	319	Dion James	.04	.02	.01
☐	320	Dave Stieb	.07	.03	.01
☐	321	Joe Morgan MG	.04	.02	.01
☐	322	Junior Ortiz	.04	.02	.01
☐	323	Willie Wilson	.04	.02	.01
☐	324	Pete Harnisch	.10	.05	.01
☐	325	Robby Thompson	.04	.02	.01
☐	326	Tom McCarthy	.04	.02	.01
☐	327	Ken Williams	.04	.02	.01
☐	328	Curt Young	.04	.02	.01
☐	329	Oddibe McDowell	.04	.02	.01
☐	330	Ron Darling	.07	.03	.01
☐	331	Juan Gonzalez	2.00	.90	.25
☐	332	Paul O'Neill	.07	.03	.01
☐	333	Bill Wegman	.04	.02	.01
☐	334	Johnny Ray	.04	.02	.01
☐	335	Andy Hawkins	.04	.02	.01
☐	336	Ken Griffey Jr.	1.25	.55	.16
☐	337	Lloyd McClendon	.04	.02	.01

☐ 338	Dennis Lamp	.04	.02	.01
☐ 339	Dave Clark	.04	.02	.01
☐ 340	Fernando Valenzuela	.07	.03	.01
☐ 341	Tom Foley	.04	.02	.01
☐ 342	Alex Trevino	.04	.02	.01
☐ 343	Frank Tanana	.04	.02	.01
☐ 344	George Canale	.04	.02	.01
☐ 345	Harold Baines	.07	.03	.01
☐ 346	Jim Presley	.04	.02	.01
☐ 347	Junior Felix	.07	.03	.01
☐ 348	Gary Wayne	.04	.02	.01
☐ 349	Steve Finley	.10	.05	.01
☐ 350	Bret Saberhagen	.07	.03	.01
☐ 351	Roger Craig MG	.04	.02	.01
☐ 352	Bryn Smith	.04	.02	.01
☐ 353	Sandy Alomar Jr.	.10	.05	.01
	(Not listed as Jr.			
	on card front)			
☐ 354	Stan Belinda	.15	.07	.02
☐ 355	Marty Barrett	.04	.02	.01
☐ 356	Randy Ready	.04	.02	.01
☐ 357	Dave West	.04	.02	.01
☐ 358	Andres Thomas	.04	.02	.01
☐ 359	Jimmy Jones	.04	.02	.01
☐ 360	Paul Molitor	.10	.05	.01
☐ 361	Randy McCament	.04	.02	.01
☐ 362	Damon Berryhill	.04	.02	.01
☐ 363	Dan Petry	.04	.02	.01
☐ 364	Rolando Roomes	.04	.02	.01
☐ 365	Ozzie Guillen	.04	.02	.01
☐ 366	Mike Heath	.04	.02	.01
☐ 367	Mike Morgan	.04	.02	.01
☐ 368	Bill Doran	.04	.02	.01
☐ 369	Todd Burns	.04	.02	.01
☐ 370	Tim Wallach	.07	.03	.01
☐ 371	Jimmy Key	.07	.03	.01
☐ 372	Terry Kennedy	.04	.02	.01
☐ 373	Alvin Davis	.04	.02	.01
☐ 374	Steve Cummings	.04	.02	.01
☐ 375	Dwight Evans	.07	.03	.01
☐ 376	Checklist 3 UER	.05	.01	.00
	(Higuera misalphabet-			
	ized in Brewer list)			
☐ 377	Mickey Weston	.04	.02	.01
☐ 378	Luis Salazar	.04	.02	.01
☐ 379	Steve Rosenberg	.04	.02	.01
☐ 380	Dave Winfield	.15	.07	.02
☐ 381	Frank Robinson MG	.07	.03	.01
☐ 382	Jeff Musselman	.04	.02	.01
☐ 383	John Morris	.04	.02	.01
☐ 384	Pat Combs	.07	.03	.01
☐ 385	Fred McGriff AS	.10	.05	.01
☐ 386	Julio Franco AS	.05	.02	.01
☐ 387	Wade Boggs AS	.10	.05	.01
☐ 388	Cal Ripken AS	.20	.09	.03
☐ 389	Robin Yount AS	.10	.05	.01
☐ 390	Ruben Sierra AS	.12	.05	.02
☐ 391	Kirby Puckett AS	.12	.05	.02
☐ 392	Carlton Fisk AS	.08	.04	.01
☐ 393	Bret Saberhagen AS	.05	.02	.01
☐ 394	Jeff Ballard AS	.05	.02	.01
☐ 395	Jeff Russell AS	.05	.02	.01
☐ 396	A.Bartlett Giamatti	.20	.09	.03
	COMM MEM			
☐ 397	Will Clark AS	.15	.07	.02
☐ 398	Ryne Sandberg AS	.20	.09	.03
☐ 399	Howard Johnson AS	.05	.02	.01
☐ 400	Ozzie Smith AS	.08	.04	.01
☐ 401	Kevin Mitchell AS	.05	.02	.01
☐ 402	Eric Davis AS	.08	.04	.01
☐ 403	Tony Gwynn AS	.12	.05	.02
☐ 404	Craig Biggio AS	.05	.02	.01
☐ 405	Mike Scott AS	.05	.02	.01
☐ 406	Joe Magrane AS	.05	.02	.01
☐ 407	Mark Davis AS	.05	.02	.01
☐ 408	Trevor Wilson	.04	.02	.01
☐ 409	Tom Brunansky	.07	.03	.01
☐ 410	Joe Boever	.04	.02	.01
☐ 411	Ken Phelps	.04	.02	.01
☐ 412	Jamie Moyer	.04	.02	.01
☐ 413	Brian DuBois	.04	.02	.01
☐ 414A	Frank Thomas FDP	.6.00	2.70	.75
	ERR (Name missing			
	on card front)			
☐ 414B	Frank Thomas FDP COR	4.00	1.80	.50
☐ 415	Shawon Dunston	.07	.03	.01
☐ 416	Dave Johnson (P)	.04	.02	.01
☐ 417	Jim Gantner	.04	.02	.01
☐ 418	Tom Browning	.04	.02	.01
☐ 419	Beau Allred	.04	.02	.01
☐ 420	Carlton Fisk	.10	.05	.01
☐ 421	Greg Minton	.04	.02	.01
☐ 422	Pat Sheridan	.04	.02	.01
☐ 423	Fred Toliver	.04	.02	.01
☐ 424	Jerry Reuss	.04	.02	.01
☐ 425	Bill Landrum	.04	.02	.01
☐ 426	Jeff Hamilton	.04	.02	.01
☐ 427	Carmen Castillo	.04	.02	.01
☐ 428	Steve Davis	.04	.02	.01
☐ 429	Tom Kelly MG	.04	.02	.01
☐ 430	Pete Incaviglia	.04	.02	.01
☐ 431	Randy Johnson	.07	.03	.01
☐ 432	Damaso Garcia	.04	.02	.01
☐ 433	Steve Olin	.20	.09	.03
☐ 434	Mark Carreon	.04	.02	.01
☐ 435	Kevin Seitzer	.07	.03	.01
☐ 436	Mel Hall	.04	.02	.01
☐ 437	Les Lancaster	.04	.02	.01
☐ 438	Greg Myers	.04	.02	.01
☐ 439	Jeff Parrett	.04	.02	.01
☐ 440	Alan Trammell	.07	.03	.01
☐ 441	Bob Kipper	.04	.02	.01
☐ 442	Jerry Browne	.04	.02	.01
☐ 443	Cris Carpenter	.04	.02	.01

☐ 444 Kyle Abbott FDP	20	.09	.03
☐ 445 Danny Jackson	04	.02	.01
☐ 446 Dan Pasqua	04	.02	.01
☐ 447 Atlee Hammaker	04	.02	.01
☐ 448 Greg Gagne	04	.02	.01
☐ 449 Dennis Rasmussen	04	.02	.01
☐ 450 Rickey Henderson	20	.09	.03
☐ 451 Mark Lemke	07	.03	.01
☐ 452 Luis De Los Santos	04	.02	.01
☐ 453 Jody Davis	04	.02	.01
☐ 454 Jeff King	07	.03	.01
☐ 455 Jeffrey Leonard	04	.02	.01
☐ 456 Chris Gwynn	04	.02	.01
☐ 457 Gregg Jefferies	12	.05	.02
☐ 458 Bob McClure	04	.02	.01
☐ 459 Jim Lefebvre MG	04	.02	.01
☐ 460 Mike Scott	04	.02	.01
☐ 461 Carlos Martinez	04	.02	.01
☐ 462 Denny Walling	04	.02	.01
☐ 463 Drew Hall	04	.02	.01
☐ 464 Jerome Walton	07	.03	.01
☐ 465 Kevin Gross	04	.02	.01
☐ 466 Rance Mulliniks	04	.02	.01
☐ 467 Juan Nieves	04	.02	.01
☐ 468 Bill Ripken	04	.02	.01
☐ 469 John Kruk	07	.03	.01
☐ 470 Frank Viola	07	.03	.01
☐ 471 Mike Brumley	04	.02	.01
☐ 472 Jose Uribe	04	.02	.01
☐ 473 Joe Price	04	.02	.01
☐ 474 Rich Thompson	04	.02	.01
☐ 475 Bob Welch	07	.03	.01
☐ 476 Brad Komminsk	04	.02	.01
☐ 477 Willie Fraser	04	.02	.01
☐ 478 Mike LaValliere	04	.02	.01
☐ 479 Frank White	04	.02	.01
☐ 480 Sid Fernandez	07	.03	.01
☐ 481 Garry Templeton	04	.02	.01
☐ 482 Steve Carter	04	.02	.01
☐ 483 Alejandro Pena	04	.02	.01
☐ 484 Mike Fitzgerald	04	.02	.01
☐ 485 John Candelaria	04	.02	.01
☐ 486 Jeff Treadway	04	.02	.01
☐ 487 Steve Searcy	04	.02	.01
☐ 488 Ken Oberkfell	04	.02	.01
☐ 489 Nick Leyva MG	04	.02	.01
☐ 490 Dan Plesac	04	.02	.01
☐ 491 Dave Cochrane	10	.05	.01
☐ 492 Ron Oester	04	.02	.01
☐ 493 Jason Grimsley	10	.05	.01
☐ 494 Terry Puhl	04	.02	.01
☐ 495 Lee Smith	07	.03	.01
☐ 496 Cecil Espy UER	04	.02	.01
('88 stats have 3			
SB's, should be 33)			
☐ 497 Dave Schmidt	04	.02	.01
☐ 498 Rick Schu	04	.02	.01
☐ 499 Bill Long	04	.02	.01
☐ 500 Kevin Mitchell	10	.05	.01
☐ 501 Matt Young	04	.02	.01
☐ 502 Mitch Webster	04	.02	.01
☐ 503 Randy St.Claire	04	.02	.01
☐ 504 Tom O'Malley	04	.02	.01
☐ 505 Kelly Gruber	07	.03	.01
☐ 506 Tom Glavine	25	.11	.03
☐ 507 Gary Redus	04	.02	.01
☐ 508 Terry Leach	04	.02	.01
☐ 509 Tom Pagnozzi	04	.02	.01
☐ 510 Dwight Gooden	10	.05	.01
☐ 511 Clay Parker	04	.02	.01
☐ 512 Gary Pettis	04	.02	.01
☐ 513 Mark Eichhorn	04	.02	.01
☐ 514 Andy Allanson	04	.02	.01
☐ 515 Len Dykstra	07	.03	.01
☐ 516 Tim Leary	04	.02	.01
☐ 517 Roberto Alomar	40	.18	.05
☐ 518 Bill Krueger	04	.02	.01
☐ 519 Bucky Dent MG	04	.02	.01
☐ 520 Mitch Williams	07	.03	.01
☐ 521 Craig Worthington	04	.02	.01
☐ 522 Mike Dunne	04	.02	.01
☐ 523 Jay Bell	07	.03	.01
☐ 524 Daryl Boston	04	.02	.01
☐ 525 Wally Joyner	07	.03	.01
☐ 526 Checklist 4	05	.01	.00
☐ 527 Ron Hassey	04	.02	.01
☐ 528 Kevin Wickander	04	.02	.01
☐ 529 Greg Harris	04	.02	.01
☐ 530 Mark Langston	07	.03	.01
☐ 531 Ken Caminiti	07	.03	.01
☐ 532 Cecilio Guante	04	.02	.01
☐ 533 Tim Jones	04	.02	.01
☐ 534 Louie Meadows	04	.02	.01
☐ 535 John Smoltz	25	.11	.03
☐ 536 Bob Geren	04	.02	.01
☐ 537 Mark Grant	04	.02	.01
☐ 538 Bill Spiers UER	04	.02	.01
(Photo actually			
George Canale)			
☐ 539 Neal Heaton	04	.02	.01
☐ 540 Danny Tartabull	10	.05	.01
☐ 541 Pat Perry	04	.02	.01
☐ 542 Darren Daulton	07	.03	.01
☐ 543 Nelson Liriano	04	.02	.01
☐ 544 Dennis Boyd	04	.02	.01
☐ 545 Kevin McReynolds	07	.03	.01
☐ 546 Kevin Hickey	04	.02	.01
☐ 547 Jack Howell	04	.02	.01
☐ 548 Pat Clements	04	.02	.01
☐ 549 Don Zimmer MG	04	.02	.01
☐ 550 Julio Franco	07	.03	.01
☐ 551 Tim Crews	04	.02	.01
☐ 552 Mike(Miss.) Smith	04	.02	.01
☐ 553 Scott Scudder UER	04	.02	.01

(Cedar Rap1ds)

☐ 554	Jay Buhner	.07	.03	.01
☐ 555	Jack Morris	.10	.05	.01
☐ 556	Gene Larkin	.04	.02	.01
☐ 557	Jeff Innis	.04	.02	.01
☐ 558	Rafael Ramirez	.04	.02	.01
☐ 559	Andy McGaffigan	.04	.02	.01
☐ 560	Steve Sax	.07	.03	.01
☐ 561	Ken Dayley	.04	.02	.01
☐ 562	Chad Kreuter	.04	.02	.01
☐ 563	Alex Sanchez	.04	.02	.01
☐ 564	Tyler Houston FDP	.10	.05	.01
☐ 565	Scott Fletcher	.04	.02	.01
☐ 566	Mark Knudson	.04	.02	.01
☐ 567	Ron Gant	.25	.11	.03
☐ 568	John Smiley	.07	.03	.01
☐ 569	Ivan Calderon	.04	.02	.01
☐ 570	Cal Ripken	.40	.18	.05
☐ 571	Brett Butler	.07	.03	.01
☐ 572	Greg A. Harris	.04	.02	.01
☐ 573	Danny Heep	.04	.02	.01
☐ 574	Bill Swift	.07	.03	.01
☐ 575	Lance Parrish	.07	.03	.01
☐ 576	Mike Dyer	.04	.02	.01
☐ 577	Charlie Hayes	.12	.05	.02
☐ 578	Joe Magrane	.04	.02	.01
☐ 579	Art Howe MG	.04	.02	.01
☐ 580	Joe Carter	.20	.09	.03
☐ 581	Ken Griffey Sr.	.07	.03	.01
☐ 582	Rick Honeycutt	.04	.02	.01
☐ 583	Bruce Benedict	.04	.02	.01
☐ 584	Phil Stephenson	.04	.02	.01
☐ 585	Kal Daniels	.04	.02	.01
☐ 586	Edwin Nunez	.04	.02	.01
☐ 587	Lance Johnson	.07	.03	.01
☐ 588	Rick Rhoden	.04	.02	.01
☐ 589	Mike Aldrete	.04	.02	.01
☐ 590	Ozzie Smith	.12	.05	.02
☐ 591	Todd Stottlemyre	.04	.02	.01
☐ 592	R.J. Reynolds	.04	.02	.01
☐ 593	Scott Bradley	.04	.02	.01
☐ 594	Luis Sojo	.15	.07	.02
☐ 595	Greg Swindell	.07	.03	.01
☐ 596	Jose DeJesus	.04	.02	.01
☐ 597	Chris Bosio	.04	.02	.01
☐ 598	Brady Anderson	.12	.05	.02
☐ 599	Frank Williams	.04	.02	.01
☐ 600	Darryl Strawberry	.20	.09	.03
☐ 601	Luis Rivera	.04	.02	.01
☐ 602	Scott Garrelts	.04	.02	.01
☐ 603	Tony Armas	.04	.02	.01
☐ 604	Ron Robinson	.04	.02	.01
☐ 605	Mike Scioscia	.04	.02	.01
☐ 606	Storm Davis	.04	.02	.01
☐ 607	Steve Jeltz	.04	.02	.01
☐ 608	Eric Anthony	.30	.14	.04
☐ 609	Sparky Anderson MG	.04	.02	.01
☐ 610	Pedro Guerrero	.07	.03	.01
☐ 611	Walt Terrell	.04	.02	.01
☐ 612	Dave Gallagher	.04	.02	.01
☐ 613	Jeff Pico	.04	.02	.01
☐ 614	Nelson Santovenia	.04	.02	.01
☐ 615	Rob Deer	.07	.03	.01
☐ 616	Brian Holman	.04	.02	.01
☐ 617	Geronimo Berroa	.04	.02	.01
☐ 618	Ed Whitson	.04	.02	.01
☐ 619	Rob Ducey	.04	.02	.01
☐ 620	Tony Castillo	.04	.02	.01
☐ 621	Melido Perez	.07	.03	.01
☐ 622	Sid Bream	.04	.02	.01
☐ 623	Jim Corsi	.04	.02	.01
☐ 624	Darrin Jackson	.07	.03	.01
☐ 625	Roger McDowell	.04	.02	.01
☐ 626	Bob Melvin	.04	.02	.01
☐ 627	Jose Rijo	.07	.03	.01
☐ 628	Candy Maldonado	.04	.02	.01
☐ 629	Eric Hetzel	.04	.02	.01
☐ 630	Gary Gaetti	.04	.02	.01
☐ 631	John Wetteland	.15	.07	.02
☐ 632	Scott Lusader	.04	.02	.01
☐ 633	Dennis Cook	.04	.02	.01
☐ 634	Luis Polonia	.07	.03	.01
☐ 635	Brian Downing	.04	.02	.01
☐ 636	Jesse Orosco	.04	.02	.01
☐ 637	Craig Reynolds	.04	.02	.01
☐ 638	Jeff Montgomery	.07	.03	.01
☐ 639	Tony LaRussa MG	.07	.03	.01
☐ 640	Rick Sutcliffe	.07	.03	.01
☐ 641	Doug Strange	.10	.05	.01
☐ 642	Jack Armstrong	.07	.03	.01
☐ 643	Alfredo Griffin	.04	.02	.01
☐ 644	Paul Assenmacher	.04	.02	.01
☐ 645	Jose Oquendo	.04	.02	.01
☐ 646	Checklist 5	.05	.01	.00
☐ 647	Rex Hudler	.04	.02	.01
☐ 648	Jim Clancy	.04	.02	.01
☐ 649	Dan Murphy	.10	.05	.01
☐ 650	Mike Witt	.04	.02	.01
☐ 651	Rafael Santana	.04	.02	.01
☐ 652	Mike Boddicker	.04	.02	.01
☐ 653	John Moses	.04	.02	.01
☐ 654	Paul Coleman FDP	.12	.05	.02
☐ 655	Gregg Olson	.10	.05	.01
☐ 656	Mackey Sasser	.04	.02	.01
☐ 657	Terry Mulholland	.07	.03	.01
☐ 658	Donell Nixon	.04	.02	.01
☐ 659	Greg Cadaret	.04	.02	.01
☐ 660	Vince Coleman	.07	.03	.01
☐ 661	Dick Howser TBC'85	.05	.02	.01
	UER (Seaver's 300th on 7/11/85, should be 8/4/85)			
☐ 662	Mike Schmidt TBC'80	.10	.05	.01
☐ 663	Fred Lynn TBC'75	.05	.02	.01

☐ 664 Johnny Bench TBC'70	.08	.04	.01
☐ 665 Sandy Koufax TBC'65	.08	.04	.01
☐ 666 Brian Fisher	.04	.02	.01
☐ 667 Curt Wilkerson	.04	.02	.01
☐ 668 Joe Oliver	.10	.05	.01
☐ 669 Tom Lasorda MG	.07	.03	.01
☐ 670 Dennis Eckersley	.12	.05	.02
☐ 671 Bob Boone	.07	.03	.01
☐ 672 Roy Smith	.04	.02	.01
☐ 673 Joey Meyer	.04	.02	.01
☐ 674 Spike Owen	.04	.02	.01
☐ 675 Jim Abbott	.20	.09	.03
☐ 676 Randy Kutcher	.04	.02	.01
☐ 677 Jay Tibbs	.04	.02	.01
☐ 678 Kirt Manwaring UER	.04	.02	.01
('88 Phoenix stats			
repeated)			
☐ 679 Gary Ward	.04	.02	.01
☐ 680 Howard Johnson	.07	.03	.01
☐ 681 Mike Schooler	.04	.02	.01
☐ 682 Dann Bilardello	.04	.02	.01
☐ 683 Kenny Rogers	.04	.02	.01
☐ 684 Julio Machado	.04	.02	.01
☐ 685 Tony Fernandez	.07	.03	.01
☐ 686 Carmelo Martinez	.04	.02	.01
☐ 687 Tim Birtsas	.04	.02	.01
☐ 688 Milt Thompson	.04	.02	.01
☐ 689 Rich Yett	.04	.02	.01
☐ 690 Mark McGwire	.30	.14	.04
☐ 691 Chuck Cary	.04	.02	.01
☐ 692 Sammy Sosa	.15	.07	.02
☐ 693 Calvin Schiraldi	.04	.02	.01
☐ 694 Mike Stanton	.15	.07	.02
☐ 695 Tom Henke	.07	.03	.01
☐ 696 B.J. Surhoff	.04	.02	.01
☐ 697 Mike Davis	.04	.02	.01
☐ 698 Omar Vizquel	.07	.03	.01
☐ 699 Jim Leyland MG	.04	.02	.01
☐ 700 Kirby Puckett	.30	.14	.04
☐ 701 Bernie Williams	.30	.14	.04
☐ 702 Tony Phillips	.04	.02	.01
☐ 703 Jeff Brantley	.04	.02	.01
☐ 704 Chip Hale	.04	.02	.01
☐ 705 Claudell Washington	.04	.02	.01
☐ 706 Geno Petralli	.04	.02	.01
☐ 707 Luis Aquino	.04	.02	.01
☐ 708 Larry Sheets	.04	.02	.01
☐ 709 Juan Berenguer	.04	.02	.01
☐ 710 Von Hayes	.04	.02	.01
☐ 711 Rick Aguilera	.07	.03	.01
☐ 712 Todd Benzinger	.04	.02	.01
☐ 713 Tim Drummond	.04	.02	.01
☐ 714 Marquis Grissom	.60	.25	.08
☐ 715 Greg Maddux	.20	.09	.03
☐ 716 Steve Balboni	.04	.02	.01
☐ 717 Ron Karkovice	.04	.02	.01
☐ 718 Gary Sheffield	.50	.23	.06
☐ 719 Wally Whitehurst	.04	.02	.01
☐ 720 Andres Galarraga	.04	.02	.01
☐ 721 Lee Mazzilli	.04	.02	.01
☐ 722 Felix Fermin	.04	.02	.01
☐ 723 Jeff D. Robinson	.04	.02	.01
☐ 724 Juan Bell	.04	.02	.01
☐ 725 Terry Pendleton	.10	.05	.01
☐ 726 Gene Nelson	.04	.02	.01
☐ 727 Pat Tabler	.04	.02	.01
☐ 728 Jim Acker	.04	.02	.01
☐ 729 Bobby Valentine MG	.04	.02	.01
☐ 730 Tony Gwynn	.20	.09	.03
☐ 731 Don Carman	.04	.02	.01
☐ 732 Ernest Riles	.04	.02	.01
☐ 733 John Dopson	.04	.02	.01
☐ 734 Kevin Elster	.04	.02	.01
☐ 735 Charlie Hough	.04	.02	.01
☐ 736 Rick Dempsey	.04	.02	.01
☐ 737 Chris Sabo	.07	.03	.01
☐ 738 Gene Harris	.04	.02	.01
☐ 739 Dale Sveum	.04	.02	.01
☐ 740 Jesse Barfield	.04	.02	.01
☐ 741 Steve Wilson	.04	.02	.01
☐ 742 Ernie Whitt	.04	.02	.01
☐ 743 Tom Candiotti	.04	.02	.01
☐ 744 Kelly Mann	.04	.02	.01
☐ 745 Hubie Brooks	.04	.02	.01
☐ 746 Dave Smith	.04	.02	.01
☐ 747 Randy Bush	.04	.02	.01
☐ 748 Doyle Alexander	.04	.02	.01
☐ 749 Mark Parent UER	.04	.02	.01
('87 BA .80,			
should be .080)			
☐ 750 Dale Murphy	.10	.05	.01
☐ 751 Steve Lyons	.04	.02	.01
☐ 752 Tom Gordon	.07	.03	.01
☐ 753 Chris Speier	.04	.02	.01
☐ 754 Bob Walk	.04	.02	.01
☐ 755 Rafael Palmeiro	.10	.05	.01
☐ 756 Ken Howell	.04	.02	.01
☐ 757 Larry Walker	.90	.40	.11
☐ 758 Mark Thurmond	.04	.02	.01
☐ 759 Tom Trebelhorn MG	.04	.02	.01
☐ 760 Wade Boggs	.20	.09	.03
☐ 761 Mike Jackson	.04	.02	.01
☐ 762 Doug Dascenzo	.04	.02	.01
☐ 763 Dennis Martinez	.07	.03	.01
☐ 764 Tim Teufel	.04	.02	.01
☐ 765 Chili Davis	.07	.03	.01
☐ 766 Brian Meyer	.04	.02	.01
☐ 767 Tracy Jones	.04	.02	.01
☐ 768 Chuck Crim	.04	.02	.01
☐ 769 Greg Hibbard	.20	.09	.03
☐ 770 Cory Snyder	.04	.02	.01
☐ 771 Pete Smith	.07	.03	.01
☐ 772 Jeff Reed	.04	.02	.01
☐ 773 Dave Leiper	.04	.02	.01

☐ 774	Ben McDonald	.50	.23	.06
☐ 775	Andy Van Slyke	.10	.05	.01
☐ 776	Charlie Leibrandt	.04	.02	.01
☐ 777	Tim Laudner	.04	.02	.01
☐ 778	Mike Jeffcoat	.04	.02	.01
☐ 779	Lloyd Moseby	.04	.02	.01
☐ 780	Orel Hershiser	.07	.03	.01
☐ 781	Mario Diaz	.04	.02	.01
☐ 782	Jose Alvarez	.04	.02	.01
☐ 783	Checklist 6	.05	.01	.00
☐ 784	Scott Bailes	.04	.02	.01
☐ 785	Jim Rice	.07	.03	.01
☐ 786	Eric King	.04	.02	.01
☐ 787	Rene Gonzales	.04	.02	.01
☐ 788	Frank DiPino	.04	.02	.01
☐ 789	John Wathan MG	.04	.02	.01
☐ 790	Gary Carter	.07	.03	.01
☐ 791	Alvaro Espinoza	.04	.02	.01
☐ 792	Gerald Perry	.04	.02	.01

1990 Topps Traded

The 1990 Topps Traded Set was the tenth consecutive year Topps issued a set at the end of the year. This 132-card standard size (2 1/2" by 3 1/2") set was arranged alphabetically by player and includes a mix of traded players and rookies for whom Topps did not include a card in the regular set. The key Rookie Cards in this set are Carlos Baerga, Scott Erickson, Travis Fryman, Dave Hollins, Dave Justice, Kevin Maas, and John Olerud. Also for the first time, Topps not only issued the set in a special collector boxes (made in Ireland) but distributed (on a significant basis) the set via their own wax packs. The wax pack cards were produced Topps' Duryea,

Pennsylvania plant. There were sever cards in the packs and the wrapper high lighted the set as containing promising rookies, players who changed teams, and new managers. The cards differ in that the Irish-made cards have the whiter-type backs typical of the cards made in Ireland while the American cards have the typica Topps gray-type card stock on the back Topps also produced a specially boxed "glossy" edition frequently referred to as the Topps Traded Tiffany set. This year again, Topps did not disclose the number of Tiffany sets they produced or sold but i seems that production quantities were roughly similar (approximately 15,000 sets to the previous year. The checklist of cards is identical to that of the normal non-glossy cards. There are two primary distinguish ing features of the Tiffany cards, white card stock reverses and high gloss observ es. These Tiffany cards are valued approx imately from three to five times the values listed below.

	MT	EX-MT	VG
COMPLETE SET (132)	6.00	2.70	.75
COMMON PLAYER (1T-132T)	.05	.02	.01

☐ 1T	Darrel Akerfelds	.05	.02	.01
☐ 2T	Sandy Alomar Jr.	.10	.05	.01
☐ 3T	Brad Arnsberg	.05	.02	.01
☐ 4T	Steve Avery	.60	.25	.08
☐ 5T	Wally Backman	.05	.02	.01
☐ 6T	Carlos Baerga	1.25	.55	.16
☐ 7T	Kevin Bass	.05	.02	.01
☐ 8T	Willie Blair	.10	.05	.01
☐ 9T	Mike Blowers	.05	.02	.01
☐ 10T	Shawn Boskie	.10	.05	.01
☐ 11T	Daryl Boston	.05	.02	.01
☐ 12T	Dennis Boyd	.05	.02	.01
☐ 13T	Glenn Braggs	.05	.02	.01
☐ 14T	Hubie Brooks	.05	.02	.01
☐ 15T	Tom Brunansky	.08	.04	.01
☐ 16T	John Burkett	.10	.05	.01
☐ 17T	Casey Candaele	.05	.02	.01
☐ 18T	John Candelaria	.05	.02	.01
☐ 19T	Gary Carter	.08	.04	.01
☐ 20T	Joe Carter	.20	.09	.03
☐ 21T	Rick Cerone	.05	.02	.01
☐ 22T	Scott Coolbaugh	.05	.02	.01
☐ 23T	Bobby Cox MG	.05	.02	.01
☐ 24T	Mark Davis	.05	.02	.01
☐ 25T	Storm Davis	.05	.02	.01
☐ 26T	Edgar Diaz	.05	.02	.01
☐ 27T	Wayne Edwards	.05	.02	.01
☐ 28T	Mark Eichhorn	.05	.02	.01

☐ 29T	Scott Erickson	.75	.35	.09
☐ 30T	Nick Esasky	.05	.02	.01
☐ 31T	Cecil Fielder	.20	.09	.03
☐ 32T	John Franco	.08	.04	.01
☐ 33T	Travis Fryman	1.50	.65	.19
☐ 34T	Bill Gullickson	.05	.02	.01
☐ 35T	Darryl Hamilton	.08	.04	.01
☐ 36T	Mike Harkey	.08	.04	.01
☐ 37T	Bud Harrelson MG	.05	.02	.01
☐ 38T	Billy Hatcher	.05	.02	.01
☐ 39T	Keith Hernandez	.08	.04	.01
☐ 40T	Joe Hesketh	.05	.02	.01
☐ 41T	Dave Hollins	.60	.25	.08
☐ 42T	Sam Horn	.05	.02	.01
☐ 43T	Steve Howard	.08	.04	.01
☐ 44T	Todd Hundley	.15	.07	.02
☐ 45T	Jeff Huson	.05	.02	.01
☐ 46T	Chris James	.05	.02	.01
☐ 47T	Stan Javier	.05	.02	.01
☐ 48T	Dave Justice	1.25	.55	.16
☐ 49T	Jeff Kaiser	.05	.02	.01
☐ 50T	Dana Kiecker	.05	.02	.01
☐ 51T	Joe Klink	.05	.02	.01
☐ 52T	Brent Knackert	.10	.05	.01
☐ 53T	Brad Komminsk	.05	.02	.01
☐ 54T	Mark Langston	.08	.04	.01
☐ 55T	Tim Layana	.05	.02	.01
☐ 56T	Rick Leach	.05	.02	.01
☐ 57T	Terry Leach	.05	.02	.01
☐ 58T	Tim Leary	.05	.02	.01
☐ 59T	Craig Lefferts	.05	.02	.01
☐ 60T	Charlie Leibrandt	.05	.02	.01
☐ 61T	Jim Leyritz	.10	.05	.01
☐ 62T	Fred Lynn	.08	.04	.01
☐ 63T	Kevin Maas	.25	.11	.03
☐ 64T	Shane Mack	.08	.04	.01
☐ 65T	Candy Maldonado	.05	.02	.01
☐ 66T	Fred Manrique	.05	.02	.01
☐ 67T	Mike Marshall	.05	.02	.01
☐ 68T	Carmelo Martinez	.05	.02	.01
☐ 69T	John Marzano	.05	.02	.01
☐ 70T	Ben McDonald	.50	.23	.06
☐ 71T	Jack McDowell	.20	.09	.03
☐ 72T	John McNamara MG	.05	.02	.01
☐ 73T	Orlando Mercado	.05	.02	.01
☐ 74T	Stump Merrill MG	.05	.02	.01
☐ 75T	Alan Mills	.12	.05	.02
☐ 76T	Hal Morris	.15	.07	.02
☐ 77T	Lloyd Moseby	.05	.02	.01
☐ 78T	Randy Myers	.08	.04	.01
☐ 79T	Tim Naehring	.15	.07	.02
☐ 80T	Junior Noboa	.05	.02	.01
☐ 81T	Matt Nokes	.05	.02	.01
☐ 82T	Pete O'Brien	.05	.02	.01
☐ 83T	John Olerud	.60	.25	.08
☐ 84T	Greg Olson	.10	.05	.01
☐ 85T	Junior Ortiz	.05	.02	.01
☐ 86T	Dave Parker	.08	.04	.01
☐ 87T	Rick Parker	.05	.02	.01
☐ 88T	Bob Patterson	.05	.02	.01
☐ 89T	Alejandro Pena	.05	.02	.01
☐ 90T	Tony Pena	.05	.02	.01
☐ 91T	Pascual Perez	.05	.02	.01
☐ 92T	Gerald Perry	.05	.02	.01
☐ 93T	Dan Petry	.05	.02	.01
☐ 94T	Gary Pettis	.05	.02	.01
☐ 95T	Tony Phillips	.05	.02	.01
☐ 96T	Lou Piniella MG	.08	.04	.01
☐ 97T	Luis Polonia	.08	.04	.01
☐ 98T	Jim Presley	.05	.02	.01
☐ 99T	Scott Radinsky	.15	.07	.02
☐ 100T	Willie Randolph	.08	.04	.01
☐ 101T	Jeff Reardon	.08	.04	.01
☐ 102T	Greg Riddoch MG	.05	.02	.01
☐ 103T	Jeff Robinson	.05	.02	.01
☐ 104T	Ron Robinson	.05	.02	.01
☐ 105T	Kevin Romine	.05	.02	.01
☐ 106T	Scott Ruskin	.05	.02	.01
☐ 107T	John Russell	.05	.02	.01
☐ 108T	Bill Sampen	.05	.02	.01
☐ 109T	Juan Samuel	.05	.02	.01
☐ 110T	Scott Sanderson	.05	.02	.01
☐ 111T	Jack Savage	.05	.02	.01
☐ 112T	Dave Schmidt	.05	.02	.01
☐ 113T	Red Schoendienst MG	.08	.04	.01
☐ 114T	Terry Shumpert	.05	.02	.01
☐ 115T	Matt Sinatro	.05	.02	.01
☐ 116T	Don Slaught	.05	.02	.01
☐ 117T	Bryn Smith	.05	.02	.01
☐ 118T	Lee Smith	.08	.04	.01
☐ 119T	Paul Sorrento	.25	.11	.03
☐ 120T	Franklin Stubbs UER	.05	.02	.01
	('84 says '99 and has			
	the same stats as '89,			
	'83 stats are missing)			
☐ 121T	Russ Swan	.10	.05	.01
☐ 122T	Bob Tewksbury	.08	.04	.01
☐ 123T	Wayne Tolleson	.05	.02	.01
☐ 124T	John Tudor	.05	.02	.01
☐ 125T	Randy Veres	.05	.02	.01
☐ 126T	Hector Villanueva	.10	.05	.01
☐ 127T	Mitch Webster	.05	.02	.01
☐ 128T	Ernie Whitt	.05	.02	.01
☐ 129T	Frank Wills	.05	.02	.01
☐ 130T	Dave Winfield	.15	.07	.02
☐ 131T	Matt Young	.05	.02	.01
☐ 132T	Checklist Card	.08	.01	.00

1991 Topps

The 1991 Topps Set consists of 792 cards in the now standard size of 2 1/2" by 3 1/2". This set marks Topps tenth consecutive year of issuing a 792-card set. Topps also commemorated their fortieth anniversary by including a "Topps 40" logo on the front and back of each card. Virtually all of the cards have been discovered without the 40th logo on the back. As a special promotion Topps inserted (randomly) into their wax packs one of every previous card they ever issued. Topps again issued their checklists in team order (and alphabetically within team) and included a special 22-card All-Star set (386-407). There are five players listed as Future Stars, 114 Lance Dickson, 211 Brian Barnes, 561 Tim McIntosh, 587 Jose Offerman, and 594 Rich Garces. There are nine players listed as First Draft Picks, 74 Shane Andrews, 103 Tim Costo, 113 Carl Everett, 278 Alex Fernandez, 471 Mike Lieberthal, 491 Kurt Miller, 529 Marc Newfield, 596 Ronnie Walden, and 767 Dan Wilson. The key Rookie Cards in this set are Wes Chamberlain, Brian McRae, Marc Newfield, and Phil Plantier. The complete 1991 Topps set was also issued as a factory set of micro baseball cards with cards measuring approximately one-fourth the size of the regular size cards but identical in other respects. The micro set and its cards are valued at approximately half the values listed below for the regular size cards. The set was also issued with a gold "Operation Desert Shield" emblem stamped on the cards. It has been reported that Topps sent wax cases (equivalent

to 6,313 sets) as gifts to U.S. troops stationed in the Persian Gulf. These Desert Shield cards are quite valuable in comparison to the regular issue of Topps; but one must be careful as counterfeits of these cards are known. These counterfeit Desert Shield cards can typically be detected by the shape of the gold shield stamped on the card. The bottom of the shield on the original is rounded, almost flat; the known forgeries come to a point. Due to the scarcity of these Desert Shield cards, they are usually sold at one hundred times the value of the corresponding regular card. Topps also produced a specially boxed "glossy" edition frequently referred to as the Topps Tiffany set. This year, again, Topps did not disclose the number of Tiffany sets they produced or sold. The checklist of cards is identical to that of the normal non-glossy cards. There are two primary distinguishing features of the Tiffany cards, white card stock reverses and high gloss obverses. These Tiffany cards are valued approximately from three to five times the values listed below.

	MT	EX-MT	VG
COMPLETE SET (792)	20.00	9.00	2.50
COMPLETE FACT.SET (792)	25.00	11.50	3.10
COMMON PLAYER (1-792)	.04	.02	.01

		MT	EX-MT	VG
☐ 1	Nolan Ryan	.50	.23	.06
☐ 2	George Brett RB	.10	.05	.01
☐ 3	Carlton Fisk RB	.10	.05	.01
☐ 4	Kevin Maas RB	.05	.02	.01
☐ 5	Cal Ripken RB	.15	.07	.02
☐ 6	Nolan Ryan RB	.25	.11	.03
☐ 7	Ryne Sandberg RB	.12	.05	.02
☐ 8	Bobby Thigpen RB	.05	.02	.01
☐ 9	Darrin Fletcher	.04	.02	.01
☐ 10	Gregg Olson	.07	.03	.01
☐ 11	Roberto Kelly	.07	.03	.01
☐ 12	Paul Assenmacher	.04	.02	.01
☐ 13	Mariano Duncan	.04	.02	.01
☐ 14	Dennis Lamp	.04	.02	.01
☐ 15	Von Hayes	.04	.02	.01
☐ 16	Mike Heath	.04	.02	.01
☐ 17	Jeff Brantley	.04	.02	.01
☐ 18	Nelson Liriano	.04	.02	.01
☐ 19	Jeff Robinson	.04	.02	.01
	New York Yankees			
☐ 20	Pedro Guerrero	.07	.03	.01
☐ 21	Joe Morgan MG	.04	.02	.01
☐ 22	Storm Davis	.04	.02	.01
☐ 23	Jim Gantner	.04	.02	.01
☐ 24	Dave Martinez	.04	.02	.01

☐ 25	Tim Belcher	.07	.03	.01
☐ 26	Luis Sojo UER	.04	.02	.01
	(Born in Barquisimento, not Carquis)			
☐ 27	Bobby Witt	.04	.02	.01
☐ 28	Alvaro Espinoza	.04	.02	.01
☐ 29	Bob Walk	.04	.02	.01
☐ 30	Gregg Jefferies	.07	.03	.01
☐ 31	Colby Ward	.04	.02	.01
☐ 32	Mike Simms	.10	.05	.01
☐ 33	Barry Jones	.04	.02	.01
☐ 34	Atlee Hammaker	.04	.02	.01
☐ 35	Greg Maddux	.10	.05	.01
☐ 36	Donnie Hill	.04	.02	.01
☐ 37	Tom Bolton	.04	.02	.01
☐ 38	Scott Bradley	.04	.02	.01
☐ 39	Jim Neidlinger	.04	.02	.01
☐ 40	Kevin Mitchell	.07	.03	.01
☐ 41	Ken Dayley	.04	.02	.01
☐ 42	Chris Hoiles	.15	.07	.02
☐ 43	Roger McDowell	.04	.02	.01
☐ 44	Mike Felder	.04	.02	.01
☐ 45	Chris Sabo	.07	.03	.01
☐ 46	Tim Drummond	.04	.02	.01
☐ 47	Brook Jacoby	.04	.02	.01
☐ 48	Dennis Boyd	.04	.02	.01
☐ 49A	Pat Borders ERR	.25	.11	.03
	(40 steals at Kinston in '86)			
☐ 49B	Pat Borders COR	.04	.02	.01
	(0 steals at Kinston in '86)			
☐ 50	Bob Welch	.04	.02	.01
☐ 51	Art Howe MG	.04	.02	.01
☐ 52	Francisco Oliveras	.04	.02	.01
☐ 53	Mike Sharperson UER	.04	.02	.01
	(Born in 1961, not 1960)			
☐ 54	Gary Mielke	.04	.02	.01
☐ 55	Jeffrey Leonard	.04	.02	.01
☐ 56	Jeff Parrett	.04	.02	.01
☐ 57	Jack Howell	.04	.02	.01
☐ 58	Mel Stottlemyre Jr.	.04	.02	.01
☐ 59	Eric Yelding	.04	.02	.01
☐ 60	Frank Viola	.07	.03	.01
☐ 61	Stan Javier	.04	.02	.01
☐ 62	Lee Guetterman	.04	.02	.01
☐ 63	Milt Thompson	.04	.02	.01
☐ 64	Tom Herr	.04	.02	.01
☐ 65	Bruce Hurst	.07	.03	.01
☐ 66	Terry Kennedy	.04	.02	.01
☐ 67	Rick Honeycutt	.04	.02	.01
☐ 68	Gary Sheffield	.25	.11	.03
☐ 69	Steve Wilson	.04	.02	.01
☐ 70	Ellis Burks	.07	.03	.01
☐ 71	Jim Acker	.04	.02	.01
☐ 72	Junior Ortiz	.04	.02	.01
☐ 73	Craig Worthington	.04	.02	.01
☐ 74	Shane Andrews	.20	.09	.03
☐ 75	Jack Morris	.10	.05	.01
☐ 76	Jerry Browne	.04	.02	.01
☐ 77	Drew Hall	.04	.02	.01
☐ 78	Geno Petralli	.04	.02	.01
☐ 79	Frank Thomas	1.25	.55	.16
☐ 80A	Fernando Valenzuela	.25	.11	.03
	ERR (104 earned runs in '90 tied for league lead)			
☐ 80B	Fernando Valenzuela	.07	.03	.01
	COR (104 earned runs in '90 led league, 20 CG's in 1986 now italicized)			
☐ 81	Cito Gaston MG	.04	.02	.01
☐ 82	Tom Glavine	.20	.09	.03
☐ 83	Daryl Boston	.04	.02	.01
☐ 84	Bob McClure	.04	.02	.01
☐ 85	Jesse Barfield	.04	.02	.01
☐ 86	Les Lancaster	.04	.02	.01
☐ 87	Tracy Jones	.04	.02	.01
☐ 88	Bob Tewksbury	.07	.03	.01
☐ 89	Darren Daulton	.07	.03	.01
☐ 90	Danny Tartabull	.07	.03	.01
☐ 91	Greg Colbrunn	.25	.11	.03
☐ 92	Danny Jackson	.04	.02	.01
☐ 93	Ivan Calderon	.04	.02	.01
☐ 94	John Dopson	.04	.02	.01
☐ 95	Paul Molitor	.10	.05	.01
☐ 96	Trevor Wilson	.04	.02	.01
☐ 97A	Brady Anderson ERR	.25	.11	.03
	(September, 2 RBI and 3 hits, should be 3 RBI and 14 hits			
☐ 97B	Brady Anderson COR	.07	.03	.01
☐ 98	Sergio Valdez	.04	.02	.01
☐ 99	Chris Gwynn	.04	.02	.01
☐ 100A	Don Mattingly ERR	.50	.23	.06
	(10 hits in 1990)			
☐ 100B	Don Mattingly COR	.15	.07	.02
	(101 hits in 1990)			
☐ 101	Rob Ducey	.04	.02	.01
☐ 102	Gene Larkin	.04	.02	.01
☐ 103	Tim Costo	.20	.09	.03
☐ 104	Don Robinson	.04	.02	.01
☐ 105	Kevin McReynolds	.07	.03	.01
☐ 106	Ed Nunez	.04	.02	.01
☐ 107	Luis Polonia	.07	.03	.01
☐ 108	Matt Young	.04	.02	.01
☐ 109	Greg Riddoch MG	.04	.02	.01
☐ 110	Tom Henke	.07	.03	.01
☐ 111	Andres Thomas	.04	.02	.01
☐ 112	Frank DiPino	.04	.02	.01
☐ 113	Carl Everett	.25	.11	.03
☐ 114	Lance Dickson	.10	.05	.01
☐ 115	Hubie Brooks	.04	.02	.01

☐ 116	Mark Davis	.04	.02	.01
☐ 117	Dion James	.04	.02	.01
☐ 118	Tom Edens	.10	.05	.01
☐ 119	Carl Nichols	.04	.02	.01
☐ 120	Joe Carter	.12	.05	.02
☐ 121	Eric King	.04	.02	.01
☐ 122	Paul O'Neill	.07	.03	.01
☐ 123	Greg A. Harris	.04	.02	.01
☐ 124	Randy Bush	.04	.02	.01
☐ 125	Steve Bedrosian	.04	.02	.01
☐ 126	Bernard Gilkey	.15	.07	.02
☐ 127	Joe Price	.04	.02	.01
☐ 128	Travis Fryman UER	.40	.18	.05

(Front has SS,
back has SS-3B)

☐ 129	Mark Eichhorn	.04	.02	.01
☐ 130	Ozzie Smith	.10	.05	.01
☐ 131A	Checklist 1 ERR	.15	.02	.00

727 Phil Bradley

☐ 131B	Checklist 1 COR	.06	.01	.00

717 Phil Bradley

☐ 132	Jamie Quirk	.04	.02	.01
☐ 133	Greg Briley	.04	.02	.01
☐ 134	Kevin Elster	.04	.02	.01
☐ 135	Jerome Walton	.04	.02	.01
☐ 136	Dave Schmidt	.04	.02	.01
☐ 137	Randy Ready	.04	.02	.01
☐ 138	Jamie Moyer	.04	.02	.01
☐ 139	Jeff Treadway	.04	.02	.01
☐ 140	Fred McGriff	.12	.05	.02
☐ 141	Nick Leyva MG	.04	.02	.01
☐ 142	Curt Wilkerson	.04	.02	.01
☐ 143	John Smiley	.07	.03	.01
☐ 144	Dave Henderson	.04	.02	.01
☐ 145	Lou Whitaker	.07	.03	.01
☐ 146	Dan Plesac	.04	.02	.01
☐ 147	Carlos Baerga	.20	.09	.03
☐ 148	Rey Palacios	.04	.02	.01
☐ 149	Al Osuna UER	.10	.05	.01

(Shown throwing right,
but bio says lefty)

☐ 150	Cal Ripken	.30	.14	.04
☐ 151	Tom Browning	.04	.02	.01
☐ 152	Mickey Hatcher	.04	.02	.01
☐ 153	Bryan Harvey	.04	.02	.01
☐ 154	Jay Buhner	.07	.03	.01
☐ 155A	Dwight Evans ERR	.25	.11	.03

(Led league with
162 games in '82)

☐ 155B	Dwight Evans COR	.07	.03	.01

(Tied for lead with
162 games in '82)

☐ 156	Carlos Martinez	.04	.02	.01
☐ 157	John Smoltz	.10	.05	.01
☐ 158	Jose Uribe	.04	.02	.01
☐ 159	Joe Boever	.04	.02	.01
☐ 160	Vince Coleman UER	.07	.03	.01

(Wrong birth year,
born 9/22/60)

☐ 161	Tim Leary	.04	.02	.01
☐ 162	Ozzie Canseco	.08	.04	.01
☐ 163	Dave Johnson	.04	.02	.01
☐ 164	Edgar Diaz	.04	.02	.01
☐ 165	Sandy Alomar Jr.	.07	.03	.01
☐ 166	Harold Baines	.07	.03	.01
☐ 167A	Randy Tomlin ERR	.50	.23	.06

(Harrisburg)

☐ 167B	Randy Tomlin COR	.20	.09	.03

(Harrisburg)

☐ 168	John Olerud	.15	.07	.02
☐ 169	Luis Aquino	.04	.02	.01
☐ 170	Carlton Fisk	.10	.05	.01
☐ 171	Tony LaRussa MG	.04	.02	.01
☐ 172	Pete Incaviglia	.04	.02	.01
☐ 173	Jason Grimsley	.04	.02	.01
☐ 174	Ken Caminiti	.07	.03	.01
☐ 175	Jack Armstrong	.04	.02	.01
☐ 176	John Orton	.04	.02	.01
☐ 177	Reggie Harris	.10	.05	.01
☐ 178	Dave Valle	.04	.02	.01
☐ 179	Pete Harnisch	.07	.03	.01
☐ 180	Tony Gwynn	.12	.05	.02
☐ 181	Duane Ward	.04	.02	.01
☐ 182	Junior Noboa	.04	.02	.01
☐ 183	Clay Parker	.04	.02	.01
☐ 184	Gary Green	.04	.02	.01
☐ 185	Joe Magrane	.04	.02	.01
☐ 186	Rod Booker	.04	.02	.01
☐ 187	Greg Cadaret	.04	.02	.01
☐ 188	Damon Berryhill	.04	.02	.01
☐ 189	Daryl Irvine	.04	.02	.01
☐ 190	Matt Williams	.07	.03	.01
☐ 191	Willie Blair	.04	.02	.01
☐ 192	Rob Deer	.07	.03	.01
☐ 193	Felix Fermin	.04	.02	.01
☐ 194	Xavier Hernandez	.04	.02	.01
☐ 195	Wally Joyner	.07	.03	.01
☐ 196	Jim Vatcher	.04	.02	.01
☐ 197	Chris Nabholz	.10	.05	.01
☐ 198	R.J. Reynolds	.04	.02	.01
☐ 199	Mike Hartley	.04	.02	.01
☐ 200	Darryl Strawberry	.12	.05	.02
☐ 201	Tom Kelly MG	.04	.02	.01
☐ 202	Jim Leyritz	.04	.02	.01
☐ 203	Gene Harris	.04	.02	.01
☐ 204	Herm Winningham	.04	.02	.01
☐ 205	Mike Perez	.15	.07	.02
☐ 206	Carlos Quintana	.04	.02	.01
☐ 207	Gary Wayne	.04	.02	.01
☐ 208	Willie Wilson	.04	.02	.01
☐ 209	Ken Howell	.04	.02	.01
☐ 210	Lance Parrish	.07	.03	.01
☐ 211	Brian Barnes	.12	.05	.02
☐ 212	Steve Finley	.07	.03	.01

☐ 213	Frank Wills	.04	.02	.01
☐ 214	Joe Girardi	.04	.02	.01
☐ 215	Dave Smith	.04	.02	.01
☐ 216	Greg Gagne	.04	.02	.01
☐ 217	Chris Bosio	.04	.02	.01
☐ 218	Rick Parker	.04	.02	.01
☐ 219	Jack McDowell	.10	.05	.01
☐ 220	Tim Wallach	.07	.03	.01
☐ 221	Don Slaught	.04	.02	.01
☐ 222	Brian McRae	.20	.09	.03
☐ 223	Allan Anderson	.04	.02	.01
☐ 224	Juan Gonzalez	.35	.16	.04
☐ 225	Randy Johnson	.07	.03	.01
☐ 226	Alfredo Griffin	.04	.02	.01
☐ 227	Steve Avery UER	.20	.09	.03
	(Pitched 13 games for			
	Durham in 1989, not 2)			
☐ 228	Rex Hudler	.04	.02	.01
☐ 229	Rance Mulliniks	.04	.02	.01
☐ 230	Sid Fernandez	.07	.03	.01
☐ 231	Doug Rader MG	.04	.02	.01
☐ 232	Jose DeJesus	.04	.02	.01
☐ 233	Al Leiter	.04	.02	.01
☐ 234	Scott Erickson	.15	.07	.02
☐ 235	Dave Parker	.07	.03	.01
☐ 236A	Frank Tanana ERR	.25	.11	.03
	(Tied for lead with			
	269 K's in '75)			
☐ 236B	Frank Tanana COR	.04	.02	.01
	(Led league with			
	269 K's in '75)			
☐ 237	Rick Cerone	.04	.02	.01
☐ 238	Mike Dunne	.04	.02	.01
☐ 239	Darren Lewis	.10	.05	.01
☐ 240	Mike Scott	.04	.02	.01
☐ 241	Dave Clark UER	.04	.02	.01
	(Career totals 19 HR			
	and 5 3B, should			
	be 22 and 3)			
☐ 242	Mike LaCoss	.04	.02	.01
☐ 243	Lance Johnson	.04	.02	.01
☐ 244	Mike Jeffcoat	.04	.02	.01
☐ 245	Kal Daniels	.04	.02	.01
☐ 246	Kevin Wickander	.04	.02	.01
☐ 247	Jody Reed	.04	.02	.01
☐ 248	Tom Gordon	.07	.03	.01
☐ 249	Bob Melvin	.04	.02	.01
☐ 250	Dennis Eckersley	.10	.05	.01
☐ 251	Mark Lemke	.04	.02	.01
☐ 252	Mel Rojas	.10	.05	.01
☐ 253	Garry Templeton	.04	.02	.01
☐ 254	Shawn Boskie	.04	.02	.01
☐ 255	Brian Downing	.04	.02	.01
☐ 256	Greg Hibbard	.04	.02	.01
☐ 257	Tom O'Malley	.04	.02	.01
☐ 258	Chris Hammond	.10	.05	.01
☐ 259	Hensley Meulens	.07	.03	.01

☐ 260	Harold Reynolds	.04	.02	.01
☐ 261	Bud Harrelson MG	.04	.02	.01
☐ 262	Tim Jones	.04	.02	.01
☐ 263	Checklist 2	.06	.01	.00
☐ 264	Dave Hollins	.12	.05	.02
☐ 265	Mark Gubicza	.04	.02	.01
☐ 266	Carmelo Castillo	.04	.02	.01
☐ 267	Mark Knudson	.04	.02	.01
☐ 268	Tom Brookens	.04	.02	.01
☐ 269	Joe Hesketh	.04	.02	.01
☐ 270A	Mark McGwire ERR	.20	.09	.03
	(1987 Slugging Pctg.			
	listed as 618)			
☐ 270B	Mark McGwire COR	.20	.09	.03
	(1987 Slugging Pctg.			
	listed as .618)			
☐ 271	Omar Olivares	.12	.05	.02
☐ 272	Jeff King	.04	.02	.01
☐ 273	Johnny Ray	.04	.02	.01
☐ 274	Ken Williams	.04	.02	.01
☐ 275	Alan Trammell	.07	.03	.01
☐ 276	Bill Swift	.04	.02	.01
☐ 277	Scott Coolbaugh	.04	.02	.01
☐ 278	Alex Fernandez UER	.15	.07	.02
	(No '90 White Sox stats)			
☐ 279A	Jose Gonzalez ERR	.25	.11	.03
	(Photo actually			
	Billy Bean)			
☐ 279B	Jose Gonzalez COR	.04	.02	.01
☐ 280	Bret Saberhagen	.07	.03	.01
☐ 281	Larry Sheets	.04	.02	.01
☐ 282	Don Carman	.04	.02	.01
☐ 283	Marquis Grissom	.15	.07	.02
☐ 284	Billy Spiers	.04	.02	.01
☐ 285	Jim Abbott	.12	.05	.02
☐ 286	Ken Oberkfell	.04	.02	.01
☐ 287	Mark Grant	.04	.02	.01
☐ 288	Derrick May	.07	.03	.01
☐ 289	Tim Birtsas	.04	.02	.01
☐ 290	Steve Sax	.07	.03	.01
☐ 291	John Wathan MG	.04	.02	.01
☐ 292	Bud Black	.04	.02	.01
☐ 293	Jay Bell	.07	.03	.01
☐ 294	Mike Moore	.04	.02	.01
☐ 295	Rafael Palmeiro	.10	.05	.01
☐ 296	Mark Williamson	.04	.02	.01
☐ 297	Manny Lee	.04	.02	.01
☐ 298	Omar Vizquel	.04	.02	.01
☐ 299	Scott Radinsky	.04	.02	.01
☐ 300	Kirby Puckett	.20	.09	.03
☐ 301	Steve Farr	.04	.02	.01
☐ 302	Tim Teufel	.04	.02	.01
☐ 303	Mike Boddicker	.04	.02	.01
☐ 304	Kevin Reimer	.10	.05	.01
☐ 305	Mike Scioscia	.04	.02	.01
☐ 306A	Lonnie Smith ERR	.25	.11	.03
	(136 games in '90)			

☐ 306B Lonnie Smith COR	.07	.03	.01
(135 games in '90)			
☐ 307 Andy Benes	.10	.05	.01
☐ 308 Tom Pagnozzi	.04	.02	.01
☐ 309 Norm Charlton	.07	.03	.01
☐ 310 Gary Carter	.07	.03	.01
☐ 311 Jeff Pico	.04	.02	.01
☐ 312 Charlie Hayes	.04	.02	.01
☐ 313 Ron Robinson	.04	.02	.01
☐ 314 Gary Pettis	.04	.02	.01
☐ 315 Roberto Alomar	.20	.09	.03
☐ 316 Gene Nelson	.04	.02	.01
☐ 317 Mike Fitzgerald	.04	.02	.01
☐ 318 Rick Aguilera	.07	.03	.01
☐ 319 Jeff McKnight	.04	.02	.01
☐ 320 Tony Fernandez	.07	.03	.01
☐ 321 Bob Rodgers MG	.04	.02	.01
☐ 322 Terry Shumpert	.04	.02	.01
☐ 323 Cory Snyder	.04	.02	.01
☐ 324A Ron Kittle ERR	.25	.11	.03
(Set another			
standard ...)			
☐ 324B Ron Kittle COR	.04	.02	.01
(Tied another			
standard ...)			
☐ 325 Brett Butler	.07	.03	.01
☐ 326 Ken Patterson	.04	.02	.01
☐ 327 Ron Hassey	.04	.02	.01
☐ 328 Walt Terrell	.04	.02	.01
☐ 329 Dave Justice UER	.30	.14	.04
(Drafted third round			
on card, should say			
fourth pick)			
☐ 330 Dwight Gooden	.07	.03	.01
☐ 331 Eric Anthony	.07	.03	.01
☐ 332 Kenny Rogers	.04	.02	.01
☐ 333 Chipper Jones FDP	.75	.35	.09
☐ 334 Todd Benzinger	.04	.02	.01
☐ 335 Mitch Williams	.04	.02	.01
☐ 336 Matt Nokes	.04	.02	.01
☐ 337A Keith Comstock ERR	.25	.11	.03
(Cubs logo on front)			
☐ 337B Keith Comstock COR	.04	.02	.01
(Mariners logo on front)			
☐ 338 Luis Rivera	.04	.02	.01
☐ 339 Larry Walker	.20	.09	.03
☐ 340 Ramon Martinez	.08	.04	.01
☐ 341 John Moses	.04	.02	.01
☐ 342 Mickey Morandini	.12	.05	.02
☐ 343 Jose Oquendo	.04	.02	.01
☐ 344 Jeff Russell	.04	.02	.01
☐ 345 Len Dykstra	.07	.03	.01
☐ 346 Jesse Orosco	.04	.02	.01
☐ 347 Greg Vaughn	.08	.04	.01
☐ 348 Todd Stottlemyre	.07	.03	.01
☐ 349 Dave Gallagher	.04	.02	.01
☐ 350 Glenn Davis	.07	.03	.01

☐ 351 Joe Torre MG	.07	.03	.01
☐ 352 Frank White	.04	.02	.01
☐ 353 Tony Castillo	.04	.02	.01
☐ 354 Sid Bream	.04	.02	.01
☐ 355 Chili Davis	.07	.03	.01
☐ 356 Mike Marshall	.04	.02	.01
☐ 357 Jack Savage	.04	.02	.01
☐ 358 Mark Parent	.04	.02	.01
☐ 359 Chuck Cary	.04	.02	.01
☐ 360 Tim Raines	.07	.03	.01
☐ 361 Scott Garrelts	.04	.02	.01
☐ 362 Hector Villenueva	.04	.02	.01
☐ 363 Rick Mahler	.04	.02	.01
☐ 364 Dan Pasqua	.04	.02	.01
☐ 365 Mike Schooler	.04	.02	.01
☐ 366A Checklist 3 ERR	.15	.02	.00
19 Carl Nichols			
☐ 366B Checklist 3 COR	.06	.01	.00
119 Carl Nichols			
☐ 367 Dave Walsh	.10	.05	.01
☐ 368 Felix Jose	.07	.03	.01
☐ 369 Steve Searcy	.04	.02	.01
☐ 370 Kelly Gruber	.07	.03	.01
☐ 371 Jeff Montgomery	.04	.02	.01
☐ 372 Spike Owen	.04	.02	.01
☐ 373 Darrin Jackson	.07	.03	.01
☐ 374 Larry Casian	.04	.02	.01
☐ 375 Tony Pena	.04	.02	.01
☐ 376 Mike Harkey	.07	.03	.01
☐ 377 Rene Gonzales	.04	.02	.01
☐ 378A Wilson Alvarez ERR	.40	.18	.05
('89 Port Charlotte			
and '90 Birmingham			
stat lines omitted)			
☐ 378B Wilson Alvarez COR	.10	.05	.01
(Text still says 143			
K's in 1988, whereas			
stats say 134)			
☐ 379 Randy Velarde	.04	.02	.01
☐ 380 Willie McGee	.07	.03	.01
☐ 381 Jim Leyland MG	.04	.02	.01
☐ 382 Mackey Sasser	.04	.02	.01
☐ 383 Pete Smith	.07	.03	.01
☐ 384 Gerald Perry	.04	.02	.01
☐ 385 Mickey Tettleton	.07	.03	.01
☐ 386 Cecil Fielder AS	.10	.05	.01
☐ 387 Julio Franco AS	.05	.02	.01
☐ 388 Kelly Gruber AS	.05	.02	.01
☐ 389 Alan Trammell AS	.05	.02	.01
☐ 390 Jose Canseco AS	.12	.05	.02
☐ 391 Rickey Henderson AS	.10	.05	.01
☐ 392 Ken Griffey Jr. AS	.25	.11	.03
☐ 393 Carlton Fisk AS	.10	.05	.01
☐ 394 Bob Welch AS	.05	.02	.01
☐ 395 Chuck Finley AS	.05	.02	.01
☐ 396 Bobby Thigpen AS	.05	.02	.01
☐ 397 Eddie Murray AS	.10	.05	.01

☐ 398 Ryne Sandberg AS	.12	.05	.02
☐ 399 Matt Williams AS	.05	.02	.01
☐ 400 Barry Larkin AS	.08	.04	.01
☐ 401 Barry Bonds AS	.10	.05	.01
☐ 402 Darryl Strawberry AS	.10	.05	.01
☐ 403 Bobby Bonilla AS	.08	.04	.01
☐ 404 Mike Scioscia AS	.05	.02	.01
☐ 405 Doug Drabek AS	.05	.02	.01
☐ 406 Frank Viola AS	.05	.02	.01
☐ 407 John Franco AS	.05	.02	.01
☐ 408 Earnie Riles	.04	.02	.01
☐ 409 Mike Stanley	.04	.02	.01
☐ 410 Dave Righetti	.04	.02	.01
☐ 411 Lance Blankenship	.04	.02	.01
☐ 412 Dave Bergman	.04	.02	.01
☐ 413 Terry Mulholland	.04	.02	.01
☐ 414 Sammy Sosa	.07	.03	.01
☐ 415 Rick Sutcliffe	.07	.03	.01
☐ 416 Randy Milligan	.04	.02	.01
☐ 417 Bill Krueger	.04	.02	.01
☐ 418 Nick Esasky	.04	.02	.01
☐ 419 Jeff Reed	.04	.02	.01
☐ 420 Bobby Thigpen	.04	.02	.01
☐ 421 Alex Cole	.04	.02	.01
☐ 422 Rick Reuschel	.04	.02	.01
☐ 423 Rafael Ramirez UER	.04	.02	.01
(Born 1959, not 1958)			
☐ 424 Calvin Schiraldi	.04	.02	.01
☐ 425 Andy Van Slyke	.10	.05	.01
☐ 426 Joe Grahe	.15	.07	.02
☐ 427 Rick Dempsey	.04	.02	.01
☐ 428 John Barfield	.04	.02	.01
☐ 429 Stump Merrill MG	.04	.02	.01
☐ 430 Gary Gaetti	.04	.02	.01
☐ 431 Paul Gibson	.04	.02	.01
☐ 432 Delino DeShields	.15	.07	.02
☐ 433 Pat Tabler	.04	.02	.01
☐ 434 Julio Machado	.04	.02	.01
☐ 435 Kevin Maas	.08	.04	.01
☐ 436 Scott Bankhead	.04	.02	.01
☐ 437 Doug Dascenzo	.04	.02	.01
☐ 438 Vicente Palacios	.04	.02	.01
☐ 439 Dickie Thon	.04	.02	.01
☐ 440 George Bell	.07	.03	.01
☐ 441 Zane Smith	.04	.02	.01
☐ 442 Charlie O'Brien	.04	.02	.01
☐ 443 Jeff Innis	.04	.02	.01
☐ 444 Glenn Braggs	.04	.02	.01
☐ 445 Greg Swindell	.07	.03	.01
☐ 446 Craig Grebeck	.04	.02	.01
☐ 447 John Burkett	.04	.02	.01
☐ 448 Craig Lefferts	.04	.02	.01
☐ 449 Juan Berenguer	.04	.02	.01
☐ 450 Wade Boggs	.12	.05	.02
☐ 451 Neal Heaton	.04	.02	.01
☐ 452 Bill Schroeder	.04	.02	.01
☐ 453 Lenny Harris	.04	.02	.01
☐ 454A Kevin Appier ERR	.25	.11	.03
('90 Omaha stat line omitted)			
☐ 454B Kevin Appier COR	.07	.03	.01
☐ 455 Walt Weiss	.04	.02	.01
☐ 456 Charlie Leibrandt	.04	.02	.01
☐ 457 Todd Hundley	.04	.02	.01
☐ 458 Brian Holman	.04	.02	.01
☐ 459 Tom Trebelhorn MG UER	.04	.02	.01
(Pitching and batting columns switched)			
☐ 460 Dave Stieb	.04	.02	.01
☐ 461 Robin Ventura	.20	.09	.03
☐ 462 Steve Frey	.04	.02	.01
☐ 463 Dwight Smith	.04	.02	.01
☐ 464 Steve Buechele	.04	.02	.01
☐ 465 Ken Griffey Sr.	.07	.03	.01
☐ 466 Charles Nagy	.40	.18	.05
☐ 467 Dennis Cook	.04	.02	.01
☐ 468 Tim Hulett	.04	.02	.01
☐ 469 Chet Lemon	.04	.02	.01
☐ 470 Howard Johnson	.07	.03	.01
☐ 471 Mike Lieberthal	.20	.09	.03
☐ 472 Kirt Manwaring	.04	.02	.01
☐ 473 Curt Young	.04	.02	.01
☐ 474 Phil Plantier	.50	.23	.06
☐ 475 Teddy Higuera	.04	.02	.01
☐ 476 Glenn Wilson	.04	.02	.01
☐ 477 Mike Fetters	.04	.02	.01
☐ 478 Kurt Stillwell	.04	.02	.01
☐ 479 Bob Patterson UER	.04	.02	.01
(Has a decimal point between 7 and 9)			
☐ 480 Dave Magadan	.07	.03	.01
☐ 481 Eddie Whitson	.04	.02	.01
☐ 482 Tino Martinez	.10	.05	.01
☐ 483 Mike Aldrete	.04	.02	.01
☐ 484 Dave LaPoint	.04	.02	.01
☐ 485 Terry Pendleton	.10	.05	.01
☐ 486 Tommy Greene	.04	.02	.01
☐ 487 Rafael Belliard	.04	.02	.01
☐ 488 Jeff Manto	.04	.02	.01
☐ 489 Bobby Valentine MG	.04	.02	.01
☐ 490 Kirk Gibson	.07	.03	.01
☐ 491 Kurt Miller	.25	.11	.03
☐ 492 Ernie Whitt	.04	.02	.01
☐ 493 Jose Rijo	.07	.03	.01
☐ 494 Chris James	.04	.02	.01
☐ 495 Charlie Hough	.04	.02	.01
☐ 496 Marty Barrett	.04	.02	.01
☐ 497 Ben McDonald	.10	.05	.01
☐ 498 Mark Salas	.04	.02	.01
☐ 499 Melido Perez	.07	.03	.01
☐ 500 Will Clark	.20	.09	.03
☐ 501 Mike Bielecki	.04	.02	.01
☐ 502 Carney Lansford	.07	.03	.01
☐ 503 Roy Smith	.04	.02	.01

☐ 504 Julio Valera	.15	.07	.02
☐ 505 Chuck Finley	.07	.03	.01
☐ 506 Darnell Coles	.04	.02	.01
☐ 507 Steve Jeltz	.04	.02	.01
☐ 508 Mike York	.04	.02	.01
☐ 509 Glenallen Hill	.04	.02	.01
☐ 510 John Franco	.07	.03	.01
☐ 511 Steve Balboni	.04	.02	.01
☐ 512 Jose Mesa	.04	.02	.01
☐ 513 Jerald Clark	.04	.02	.01
☐ 514 Mike Stanton	.04	.02	.01
☐ 515 Alvin Davis	.04	.02	.01
☐ 516 Karl Rhodes	.04	.02	.01
☐ 517 Joe Oliver	.04	.02	.01
☐ 518 Cris Carpenter	.04	.02	.01
☐ 519 Sparky Anderson MG	.04	.02	.01
☐ 520 Mark Grace	.10	.05	.01
☐ 521 Joe Orsulak	.04	.02	.01
☐ 522 Stan Belinda	.04	.02	.01
☐ 523 Rodney McCray	.04	.02	.01
☐ 524 Darrel Akerfelds	.04	.02	.01
☐ 525 Willie Randolph	.07	.03	.01
☐ 526A Moises Alou ERR	.50	.23	.06
(37 runs in 2 games for '90 Pirates)			
☐ 526B Moises Alou COR	.25	.11	.03
(0 runs in 2 games for '90 Pirates)			
☐ 527A Checklist 4 ERR	.15	.02	.00
105 Keith Miller 719 Kevin McReynolds			
☐ 527B Checklist 4 COR	.06	.01	.00
105 Kevin McReynolds 719 Keith Miller			
☐ 528 Denny Martinez	.07	.03	.01
☐ 529 Marc Newfield	.40	.18	.05
☐ 530 Roger Clemens	.25	.11	.03
☐ 531 Dave Rohde	.04	.02	.01
☐ 532 Kirk McCaskill	.04	.02	.01
☐ 533 Oddibe McDowell	.04	.02	.01
☐ 534 Mike Jackson	.04	.02	.01
☐ 535 Ruben Sierra UER	.15	.07	.02
(Back reads 100 Runs amd 100 RBI's)			
☐ 536 Mike Witt	.04	.02	.01
☐ 537 Jose Lind	.04	.02	.01
☐ 538 Bip Roberts	.07	.03	.01
☐ 539 Scott Terry	.04	.02	.01
☐ 540 George Brett	.10	.05	.01
☐ 541 Domingo Ramos	.04	.02	.01
☐ 542 Rob Murphy	.04	.02	.01
☐ 543 Junior Felix	.04	.02	.01
☐ 544 Alejandro Pena	.04	.02	.01
☐ 545 Dale Murphy	.07	.03	.01
☐ 546 Jeff Ballard	.04	.02	.01
☐ 547 Mike Pagliarulo	.04	.02	.01
☐ 548 Jaime Navarro	.07	.03	.01

☐ 549 John McNamara MG	.04	.02	.01
☐ 550 Eric Davis	.07	.03	.01
☐ 551 Bob Kipper	.04	.02	.01
☐ 552 Jeff Hamilton	.04	.02	.01
☐ 553 Joe Klink	.04	.02	.01
☐ 554 Brian Harper	.04	.02	.01
☐ 555 Turner Ward	.10	.05	.01
☐ 556 Gary Ward	.04	.02	.01
☐ 557 Wally Whitehurst	.04	.02	.01
☐ 558 Otis Nixon	.07	.03	.01
☐ 559 Adam Peterson	.04	.02	.01
☐ 560 Greg Smith	.04	.02	.01
☐ 561 Tim McIntosh	.04	.02	.01
☐ 562 Jeff Kunkel	.04	.02	.01
☐ 563 Brent Knackert	.04	.02	.01
☐ 564 Dante Bichette	.04	.02	.01
☐ 565 Craig Biggio	.07	.03	.01
☐ 566 Craig Wilson	.10	.05	.01
☐ 567 Dwayne Henry	.04	.02	.01
☐ 568 Ron Karkovice	.04	.02	.01
☐ 569 Curt Schilling	.07	.03	.01
☐ 570 Barry Bonds	.20	.09	.03
☐ 571 Pat Combs	.04	.02	.01
☐ 572 Dave Anderson	.04	.02	.01
☐ 573 Rich Rodriguez UER	.10	.05	.01
(Stats say drafted 4th, but bio says 9th round)			
☐ 574 John Marzano	.04	.02	.01
☐ 575 Robin Yount	.10	.05	.01
☐ 576 Jeff Kaiser	.04	.02	.01
☐ 577 Bill Doran	.04	.02	.01
☐ 578 Dave West	.04	.02	.01
☐ 579 Roger Craig MG	.04	.02	.01
☐ 580 Dave Stewart	.07	.03	.01
☐ 581 Luis Quinones	.04	.02	.01
☐ 582 Marty Clary	.04	.02	.01
☐ 583 Tony Phillips	.04	.02	.01
☐ 584 Kevin Brown	.07	.03	.01
☐ 585 Pete O'Brien	.04	.02	.01
☐ 586 Fred Lynn	.07	.03	.01
☐ 587 Jose Offerman UER	.10	.05	.01
(Text says he signed 7/24/86, but bio says 1988)			
☐ 588 Mark Whiten	.12	.05	.02
☐ 589 Scott Ruskin	.04	.02	.01
☐ 590 Eddie Murray	.10	.05	.01
☐ 591 Ken Hill	.07	.03	.01
☐ 592 B.J. Surhoff	.04	.02	.01
☐ 593A Mike Walker ERR	.25	.11	.03
('90 Canton-Akron stat line omitted)			
☐ 593B Mike Walker COR	.04	.02	.01
☐ 594 Rich Garces	.10	.05	.01
☐ 595 Bill Landrum	.04	.02	.01
☐ 596 Ronnie Walden	.10	.05	.01
☐ 597 Jerry Don Gleaton	.04	.02	.01

☐ 598	Sam Horn	.04	.02	.01
☐ 599A	Greg Myers ERR	.25	.11	.03
	('90 Syracuse			
	stat line omitted)			
☐ 599B	Greg Myers COR	.04	.02	.01
☐ 600	Bo Jackson	.12	.05	.02
☐ 601	Bob Ojeda	.04	.02	.01
☐ 602	Casey Candaele	.04	.02	.01
☐ 603A	Wes Chamberlain ERR	.60	.25	.08
	(Photo actually			
	Louie Meadows)			
☐ 603B	Wes Chamberlain COR	.20	.09	.03
☐ 604	Billy Hatcher	.04	.02	.01
☐ 605	Jeff Reardon	.07	.03	.01
☐ 606	Jim Gott	.04	.02	.01
☐ 607	Edgar Martinez	.07	.03	.01
☐ 608	Todd Burns	.04	.02	.01
☐ 609	Jeff Torborg MG	.04	.02	.01
☐ 610	Andres Galarraga	.04	.02	.01
☐ 611	Dave Eiland	.04	.02	.01
☐ 612	Steve Lyons	.04	.02	.01
☐ 613	Eric Show	.04	.02	.01
☐ 614	Luis Salazar	.04	.02	.01
☐ 615	Bert Blyleven	.07	.03	.01
☐ 616	Todd Zeile	.07	.03	.01
☐ 617	Bill Wegman	.04	.02	.01
☐ 618	Sil Campusano	.04	.02	.01
☐ 619	David Wells	.04	.02	.01
☐ 620	Ozzie Guillen	.04	.02	.01
☐ 621	Ted Power	.04	.02	.01
☐ 622	Jack Daugherty	.04	.02	.01
☐ 623	Jeff Blauser	.04	.02	.01
☐ 624	Tom Candiotti	.04	.02	.01
☐ 625	Terry Steinbach	.07	.03	.01
☐ 626	Gerald Young	.04	.02	.01
☐ 627	Tim Layana	.04	.02	.01
☐ 628	Greg Litton	.04	.02	.01
☐ 629	Wes Gardner	.04	.02	.01
☐ 630	Dave Winfield	.10	.05	.01
☐ 631	Mike Morgan	.04	.02	.01
☐ 632	Lloyd Moseby	.04	.02	.01
☐ 633	Kevin Tapani	.07	.03	.01
☐ 634	Henry Cotto	.04	.02	.01
☐ 635	Andy Hawkins	.04	.02	.01
☐ 636	Geronimo Pena	.10	.05	.01
☐ 637	Bruce Ruffin	.04	.02	.01
☐ 638	Mike Macfarlane	.04	.02	.01
☐ 639	Frank Robinson MG	.10	.05	.01
☐ 640	Andre Dawson	.10	.05	.01
☐ 641	Mike Henneman	.04	.02	.01
☐ 642	Hal Morris	.07	.03	.01
☐ 643	Jim Presley	.04	.02	.01
☐ 644	Chuck Crim	.04	.02	.01
☐ 645	Juan Samuel	.04	.02	.01
☐ 646	Andujar Cedeno	.12	.05	.02
☐ 647	Mark Portugal	.04	.02	.01
☐ 648	Lee Stevens	.04	.02	.01
☐ 649	Bill Sampen	.04	.02	.01
☐ 650	Jack Clark	.07	.03	.01
☐ 651	Alan Mills	.04	.02	.01
☐ 652	Kevin Romine	.04	.02	.01
☐ 653	Anthony Telford	.04	.02	.01
☐ 654	Paul Sorrento	.07	.03	.01
☐ 655	Erik Hanson	.04	.02	.01
☐ 656A	Checklist 5 ERR	.15	.02	.00
	348 Vicente Palacios			
	381 Jose Lind			
	537 Mike LaValliere			
	665 Jim Leyland			
☐ 656B	Checklist 5 ERR	.15	.02	.00
	433 Vicente Palacios			
	(Palacios should be 438)			
	537 Jose Lind			
	665 Mike LaValliere			
	381 Jim Leyland			
☐ 656C	Checklist 5 COR	.15	.02	.00
	438 Vicente Palacios			
	537 Jose Lind			
	665 Mike LaValliere			
	381 Jim Leyland			
☐ 657	Mike Kingery	.04	.02	.01
☐ 658	Scott Aldred	.10	.05	.01
☐ 659	Oscar Azocar	.04	.02	.01
☐ 660	Lee Smith	.07	.03	.01
☐ 661	Steve Lake	.04	.02	.01
☐ 662	Ron Dibble	.07	.03	.01
☐ 663	Greg Brock	.04	.02	.01
☐ 664	John Farrell	.04	.02	.01
☐ 665	Mike LaValliere	.04	.02	.01
☐ 666	Danny Darwin	.04	.02	.01
☐ 667	Kent Anderson	.04	.02	.01
☐ 668	Bill Long	.04	.02	.01
☐ 669	Lou Piniella MG	.04	.02	.01
☐ 670	Rickey Henderson	.12	.05	.02
☐ 671	Andy McGaffigan	.04	.02	.01
☐ 672	Shane Mack	.07	.03	.01
☐ 673	Greg Olson UER	.04	.02	.01
	(6 RBI in '88 at Tide-			
	water and 2 RBI in '87,			
	should be 48 and 15)			
☐ 674A	Kevin Gross ERR	.25	.11	.03
	(89 BB with Phillies			
	in '88 tied for			
	league lead)			
☐ 674B	Kevin Gross COR	.04	.02	.01
	(89 BB with Phillies			
	in '88 led league)			
☐ 675	Tom Brunansky	.07	.03	.01
☐ 676	Scott Chiamparino	.07	.03	.01
☐ 677	Billy Ripken	.04	.02	.01
☐ 678	Mark Davidson	.04	.02	.01
☐ 679	Bill Bathe	.04	.02	.01
☐ 680	David Cone	.10	.05	.01
☐ 681	Jeff Schaefer	.04	.02	.01

☐ 682 Ray Lankford	.40	.18	.05
☐ 683 Derek Lilliquist	.04	.02	.01
☐ 684 Milt Cuyler	.10	.05	.01
☐ 685 Doug Drabek	.07	.03	.01
☐ 686 Mike Gallego	.04	.02	.01
☐ 687A John Cerutti ERR	.25	.11	.03
(4.46 ERA in '90)			
☐ 687B John Cerutti COR	.04	.02	.01
(4.76 ERA in '90)			
☐ 688 Rosario Rodriguez	.10	.05	.01
☐ 689 John Kruk	.07	.03	.01
☐ 690 Orel Hershiser	.07	.03	.01
☐ 691 Mike Blowers	.04	.02	.01
☐ 692A Efrain Valdez ERR	.25	.11	.03
(Born 6/11/66)			
☐ 692B Efrain Valdez COR	.04	.02	.01
(Born 7/11/66 and two			
lines of text added)			
☐ 693 Francisco Cabrera	.04	.02	.01
☐ 694 Randy Veres	.04	.02	.01
☐ 695 Kevin Seitzer	.07	.03	.01
☐ 696 Steve Olin	.07	.03	.01
☐ 697 Shawn Abner	.04	.02	.01
☐ 698 Mark Guthrie	.04	.02	.01
☐ 699 Jim Lefebvre MG	.04	.02	.01
☐ 700 Jose Canseco	.20	.09	.03
☐ 701 Pascual Perez	.04	.02	.01
☐ 702 Tim Naehring	.07	.03	.01
☐ 703 Juan Agosto	.04	.02	.01
☐ 704 Devon White	.07	.03	.01
☐ 705 Robby Thompson	.04	.02	.01
☐ 706A Brad Arnsberg ERR	.25	.11	.03
(68.2 IP in '90)			
☐ 706B Brad Arnsberg COR	.04	.02	.01
(62.2 IP in '90)			
☐ 707 Jim Eisenreich	.04	.02	.01
☐ 708 John Mitchell	.04	.02	.01
☐ 709 Matt Sinatro	.04	.02	.01
☐ 710 Kent Hrbek	.07	.03	.01
☐ 711 Jose DeLeon	.04	.02	.01
☐ 712 Ricky Jordan	.04	.02	.01
☐ 713 Scott Scudder	.04	.02	.01
☐ 714 Marvell Wynne	.04	.02	.01
☐ 715 Tim Burke	.04	.02	.01
☐ 716 Bob Geren	.04	.02	.01
☐ 717 Phil Bradley	.04	.02	.01
☐ 718 Steve Crawford	.04	.02	.01
☐ 719 Keith Miller	.04	.02	.01
☐ 720 Cecil Fielder	.12	.05	.02
☐ 721 Mark Lee	.10	.05	.01
☐ 722 Wally Backman	.04	.02	.01
☐ 723 Candy Maldonado	.04	.02	.01
☐ 724 David Segui	.04	.02	.01
☐ 725 Ron Gant	.12	.05	.02
☐ 726 Phil Stephenson	.04	.02	.01
☐ 727 Mookie Wilson	.04	.02	.01
☐ 728 Scott Sanderson	.04	.02	.01
☐ 729 Don Zimmer MG	.04	.02	.01
☐ 730 Barry Larkin	.10	.05	.01
☐ 731 Jeff Gray	.04	.02	.01
☐ 732 Franklin Stubbs	.04	.02	.01
☐ 733 Kelly Downs	.04	.02	.01
☐ 734 John Russell	.04	.02	.01
☐ 735 Ron Darling	.07	.03	.01
☐ 736 Dick Schofield	.04	.02	.01
☐ 737 Tim Crews	.04	.02	.01
☐ 738 Mel Hall	.04	.02	.01
☐ 739 Russ Swan	.04	.02	.01
☐ 740 Ryne Sandberg	.25	.11	.03
☐ 741 Jimmy Key	.04	.02	.01
☐ 742 Tommy Gregg	.04	.02	.01
☐ 743 Bryn Smith	.04	.02	.01
☐ 744 Nelson Santovenia	.04	.02	.01
☐ 745 Doug Jones	.04	.02	.01
☐ 746 John Shelby	.04	.02	.01
☐ 747 Tony Fossas	.04	.02	.01
☐ 748 Al Newman	.04	.02	.01
☐ 749 Greg W. Harris	.04	.02	.01
☐ 750 Bobby Bonilla	.10	.05	.01
☐ 751 Wayne Edwards	.04	.02	.01
☐ 752 Kevin Bass	.04	.02	.01
☐ 753 Paul Marak UER	.04	.02	.01
(Stats say drafted in			
Jan., but bio says May)			
☐ 754 Bill Pecota	.04	.02	.01
☐ 755 Mark Langston	.07	.03	.01
☐ 756 Jeff Huson	.04	.02	.01
☐ 757 Mark Gardner	.04	.02	.01
☐ 758 Mike Devereaux	.07	.03	.01
☐ 759 Bobby Cox MG	.04	.02	.01
☐ 760 Benny Santiago	.07	.03	.01
☐ 761 Larry Andersen	.04	.02	.01
☐ 762 Mitch Webster	.04	.02	.01
☐ 763 Dana Kiecker	.04	.02	.01
☐ 764 Mark Carreon	.04	.02	.01
☐ 765 Shawon Dunston	.07	.03	.01
☐ 766 Jeff Robinson	.04	.02	.01
☐ 767 Dan Wilson	.15	.07	.02
☐ 768 Don Pall	.04	.02	.01
☐ 769 Tim Sherrill	.10	.05	.01
☐ 770 Jay Howell	.04	.02	.01
☐ 771 Gary Redus UER	.04	.02	.01
(Born in Tanner,			
should say Athens)			
☐ 772 Kent Mercker UER	.07	.03	.01
(Born in Indianapolis,			
should say Dublin, Ohio)			
☐ 773 Tom Foley	.04	.02	.01
☐ 774 Dennis Rasmussen	.04	.02	.01
☐ 775 Julio Franco	.07	.03	.01
☐ 776 Brent Mayne	.04	.02	.01
☐ 777 John Candelaria	.04	.02	.01
☐ 778 Dan Gladden	.04	.02	.01
☐ 779 Carmelo Martinez	.04	.02	.01

☐	780A	Randy Myers ERR (15 career losses)	.25	.11	.03
☐	780B	Randy Myers COR (19 career losses)	.07	.03	.01
☐	781	Darryl Hamilton	.07	.03	.01
☐	782	Jim Deshaies	.04	.02	.01
☐	783	Joel Skinner	.04	.02	.01
☐	784	Willie Fraser	.04	.02	.01
☐	785	Scott Fletcher	.04	.02	.01
☐	786	Eric Plunk	.04	.02	.01
☐	787	Checklist 6	.06	.01	.00
☐	788	Bob Milacki	.04	.02	.01
☐	789	Tom Lasorda MG	.04	.02	.01
☐	790	Ken Griffey Jr.	.50	.23	.06
☐	791	Mike Benjamin	.04	.02	.01
☐	792	Mike Greenwell	.07	.03	.01

1991 Topps Traded

The 1991 Topps Traded set contains 132 cards measuring the standard size (2 1/2" by 3 1/2"). The set includes a Team U.S.A. subset, featuring 25 of America's top collegiate players; these players are indicated in the checklist below by USA. The cards were sold in wax packs as well as factory sets. The cards in the wax packs (gray backs) and collated factory sets (white backs) are from different card stock. The fronts have color action player photos, with two different color borders on a white card face. The player's position and name are given in the thicker border below the picture. In blue print on a pink and gray background, the horizontally oriented backs have biographical information and statistics. The cards are numbered on the back in the upper left corner; the set numbering

corresponds to alphabetical order. The key Rookie Cards in this set are Jeff Bagwell, Jeffrey Hammonds, Charles Johnson, Phil Nevin, and Ivan Rodriguez.

			MT	EX-MT	VG
	COMPLETE SET (132)		12.00	5.50	1.50
	COMMON PLAYER (1T-132T)		.05	.02	.01
☐	1T	Juan Agosto	.05	.02	.01
☐	2T	Roberto Alomar	.20	.09	.03
☐	3T	Wally Backman	.05	.02	.01
☐	4T	Jeff Bagwell	1.25	.55	.16
☐	5T	Skeeter Barnes	.05	.02	.01
☐	6T	Steve Bedrosian	.05	.02	.01
☐	7T	Derek Bell	.30	.14	.04
☐	8T	George Bell	.08	.04	.01
☐	9T	Rafael Belliard	.05	.02	.01
☐	10T	Dante Bichette	.05	.02	.01
☐	11T	Bud Black	.05	.02	.01
☐	12T	Mike Boddicker	.05	.02	.01
☐	13T	Sid Bream	.05	.02	.01
☐	14T	Hubie Brooks	.05	.02	.01
☐	15T	Brett Butler	.08	.04	.01
☐	16T	Ivan Calderon	.05	.02	.01
☐	17T	John Candelaria	.05	.02	.01
☐	18T	Tom Candiotti	.05	.02	.01
☐	19T	Gary Carter	.08	.04	.01
☐	20T	Joe Carter	.12	.05	.02
☐	21T	Rick Cerone	.05	.02	.01
☐	22T	Jack Clark	.08	.04	.01
☐	23T	Vince Coleman	.08	.04	.01
☐	24T	Scott Coolbaugh	.05	.02	.01
☐	25T	Danny Cox	.05	.02	.01
☐	26T	Danny Darwin	.05	.02	.01
☐	27T	Chili Davis	.08	.04	.01
☐	28T	Glenn Davis	.08	.04	.01
☐	29T	Steve Decker	.15	.07	.02
☐	30T	Rob Deer	.05	.02	.01
☐	31T	Rich DeLucia	.05	.02	.01
☐	32T	John Dettmer USA	.20	.09	.03
☐	33T	Brian Downing	.05	.02	.01
☐	34T	Darren Dreifort USA	.35	.16	.04
☐	35T	Kirk Dressendorfer	.10	.05	.01
☐	36T	Jim Essian MG	.05	.02	.01
☐	37T	Dwight Evans	.08	.04	.01
☐	38T	Steve Farr	.05	.02	.01
☐	39T	Jeff Fassero	.10	.05	.01
☐	40T	Junior Felix	.05	.02	.01
☐	41T	Tony Fernandez	.08	.04	.01
☐	42T	Steve Finley	.08	.04	.01
☐	43T	Jim Fregosi MG	.05	.02	.01
☐	44T	Gary Gaetti	.05	.02	.01
☐	45T	Jason Giambi USA	.40	.18	.05
☐	46T	Kirk Gibson	.08	.04	.01
☐	47T	Leo Gomez	.25	.11	.03
☐	48T	Luis Gonzalez	.20	.09	.03

☐ 49T	Jeff Granger USA	.30	.14	.04
☐ 50T	Todd Greene USA	.25	.11	.03
☐ 51T	Jeffrey Hammonds USA	1.50	.65	.19
☐ 52T	Mike Hargrove MG	.05	.02	.01
☐ 53T	Pete Harnisch	.08	.04	.01
☐ 54T	Rick Helling USA UER	.40	.18	.05
	(Misspelled Hellings on card back)			
☐ 55T	Glenallen Hill	.05	.02	.01
☐ 56T	Charlie Hough	.05	.02	.01
☐ 57T	Pete Incaviglia	.05	.02	.01
☐ 58T	Bo Jackson	.12	.05	.02
☐ 59T	Danny Jackson	.05	.02	.01
☐ 60T	Reggie Jefferson	.15	.07	.02
☐ 61T	Charles Johnson USA	1.25	.55	.16
☐ 62T	Jeff Johnson	.10	.05	.01
☐ 63T	Todd Johnson USA	.25	.11	.03
☐ 64T	Barry Jones	.05	.02	.01
☐ 65T	Chris Jones	.05	.02	.01
☐ 66T	Scott Kamieniecki	.10	.05	.01
☐ 67T	Pat Kelly	.15	.07	.02
☐ 68T	Darryl Kile	.10	.05	.01
☐ 69T	Chuck Knoblauch	.40	.18	.05
☐ 70T	Bill Krueger	.05	.02	.01
☐ 71T	Scott Leius	.10	.05	.01
☐ 72T	Donnie Leshnock USA	.25	.11	.03
☐ 73T	Mark Lewis	.10	.05	.01
☐ 74T	Candy Maldonado	.05	.02	.01
☐ 75T	Jason McDonald USA	.20	.09	.03
☐ 76T	Willie McGee	.08	.04	.01
☐ 77T	Fred McGriff	.12	.05	.02
☐ 78T	Billy McMillon USA	.20	.09	.03
☐ 79T	Hal McRae MG	.05	.02	.01
☐ 80T	Dan Melendez USA	.25	.11	.03
☐ 81T	Orlando Merced	.20	.09	.03
☐ 82T	Jack Morris	.10	.05	.01
☐ 83T	Phil Nevin USA	2.00	.90	.25
☐ 84T	Otis Nixon	.08	.04	.01
☐ 85T	Johnny Oates MG	.05	.02	.01
☐ 86T	Bob Ojeda	.05	.02	.01
☐ 87T	Mike Pagliarulo	.05	.02	.01
☐ 88T	Dean Palmer	.20	.09	.03
☐ 89T	Dave Parker	.08	.04	.01
☐ 90T	Terry Pendleton	.10	.05	.01
☐ 91T	Tony Phillips (P) USA	.15	.07	.02
☐ 92T	Doug Piatt	.10	.05	.01
☐ 93T	Ron Polk USA CO	.05	.02	.01
☐ 94T	Tim Raines	.08	.04	.01
☐ 95T	Willie Randolph	.08	.04	.01
☐ 96T	Dave Righetti	.05	.02	.01
☐ 97T	Ernie Riles	.05	.02	.01
☐ 98T	Chris Roberts USA	.60	.25	.08
☐ 99T	Jeff D. Robinson	.05	.02	.01
☐ 100T	Jeff M. Robinson	.05	.02	.01
☐ 101T	Ivan Rodriguez	1.25	.55	.16
☐ 102T	Steve Rodriguez USA	.20	.09	.03
☐ 103T	Tom Runnells MG	.05	.02	.01

☐ 104T	Scott Sanderson	.05	.02	.01
☐ 105T	Bob Scanlan	.10	.05	.01
☐ 106T	Pete Schourek	.12	.05	.02
☐ 107T	Gary Scott	.15	.07	.02
☐ 108T	Paul Shuey USA	.50	.23	.06
☐ 109T	Doug Simons	.05	.02	.01
☐ 110T	Dave Smith	.05	.02	.01
☐ 111T	Cory Snyder	.05	.02	.01
☐ 112T	Luis Sojo	.05	.02	.01
☐ 113T	Kennie Steenstra USA	.20	.09	.03
☐ 114T	Darryl Strawberry	.12	.05	.02
☐ 115T	Franklin Stubbs	.05	.02	.01
☐ 116T	Todd Taylor USA	.20	.09	.03
☐ 117T	Wade Taylor	.05	.02	.01
☐ 118T	Garry Templeton	.05	.02	.01
☐ 119T	Mickey Tettleton	.08	.04	.01
☐ 120T	Tim Teufel	.05	.02	.01
☐ 121T	Mike Timlin	.10	.05	.01
☐ 122T	David Tuttle USA	.20	.09	.03
☐ 123T	Mo Vaughn	.20	.09	.03
☐ 124T	Jeff Ware USA	.25	.11	.03
☐ 125T	Devon White	.08	.04	.01
☐ 126T	Mark Whiten	.10	.05	.01
☐ 127T	Mitch Williams	.05	.02	.01
☐ 128T	Craig Wilson USA	.20	.09	.03
☐ 129T	Willie Wilson	.05	.02	.01
☐ 130T	Chris Wimmer	.30	.14	.04
☐ 131T	Ivan Zweig USA	.20	.09	.03
☐ 132T	Checklist Card	.08	.01	.00

1992 Topps

The 1992 Topps set contains 792 cards measuring the standard size (2 1/2" by 3 1/2"). The fronts have either posed or action color player photos on a white card face. Different color stripes frame the pictures, and the player's name and team *name appear in two short color stripes respectively at the bottom. In a horizontal format, the backs have biography and complete career batting or pitching record. In addition, some of the cards have a picture of a baseball field and stadium on the back. Special subsets included are Record Breakers (2-5), Prospects (58, 126, 179, 473, 551, 591, 618, 656, 676), and All-Stars (386-407). The cards are numbered on the back. These cards were not issued with bubble gum and feature white card stock. The key Rookie Cards in this set are Cliff Floyd, Tyler Green, Manny Ramirez, and Brien Taylor.*

	MT	EX-MT	VG
COMPLETE SET (792)	20.00	9.00	2.50
COMPLETE FACT.SET (802)	30.00	13.50	3.80
COMPLETE HOLIDAY SET (811)	33.00	15.00	4.10
COMMON PLAYER (1-792)	.04	.02	.01

☐ 1	Nolan Ryan	.40	.18	.05
☐ 2A	Ricky Henderson RB	.25	.11	.03
	(print marks on front show year as 1.991)			
☐ 2B	Ricky Henderson RB	.15	.07	.02
	(year on front is 1991)			
☐ 3	Jeff Reardon RB	.04	.02	.01
☐ 4	Nolan Ryan RB	.25	.11	.03
☐ 5	Dave Winfield RB	.10	.05	.01
☐ 6	Brien Taylor	2.50	1.15	.30
☐ 7	Jim Olander	.10	.05	.01
☐ 8	Bryan Hickerson	.10	.05	.01
☐ 9	Jon Farrell	.10	.05	.01
☐ 10	Wade Boggs	.12	.05	.02
☐ 11	Jack McDowell	.07	.03	.01
☐ 12	Luis Gonzalez	.07	.03	.01
☐ 13	Mike Scioscia	.04	.02	.01
☐ 14	Wes Chamberlain	.07	.03	.01
☐ 15	Dennis Martinez	.07	.03	.01
☐ 16	Jeff Montgomery	.04	.02	.01
☐ 17	Randy Milligan	.04	.02	.01
☐ 18	Greg Cadaret	.04	.02	.01
☐ 19	Jamie Quirk	.04	.02	.01
☐ 20	Bip Roberts	.07	.03	.01
☐ 21	Buck Rogers MG	.04	.02	.01
☐ 22	Bill Wegman	.04	.02	.01
☐ 23	Chuck Knoblauch	.20	.09	.03
☐ 24	Randy Myers	.07	.03	.01
☐ 25	Ron Gant	.10	.05	.01
☐ 26	Mike Bielecki	.04	.02	.01
☐ 27	Juan Gonzalez	.35	.16	.04
☐ 28	Mike Schooler	.04	.02	.01
☐ 29	Mickey Tettleton	.07	.03	.01
☐ 30	John Kruk	.07	.03	.01
☐ 31	Bryn Smith	.04	.02	.01

☐ 32	Chris Nabholz	.07	.03	.01
☐ 33	Carlos Baerga	.15	.07	.02
☐ 34	Jeff Juden	.08	.04	.01
☐ 35	Dave Righetti	.04	.02	.01
☐ 36	Scott Ruffcorn	.25	.11	.03
☐ 37	Luis Polonia	.07	.03	.01
☐ 38	Tom Candiotti	.04	.02	.01
☐ 39	Greg Olson	.04	.02	.01
☐ 40	Cal Ripken	.25	.11	.03
☐ 41	Craig Lefferts	.04	.02	.01
☐ 42	Mike Macfarlane	.04	.02	.01
☐ 43	Jose Lind	.04	.02	.01
☐ 44	Rick Aguilera	.07	.03	.01
☐ 45	Gary Carter	.07	.03	.01
☐ 46	Steve Farr	.04	.02	.01
☐ 47	Rex Hudler	.04	.02	.01
☐ 48	Scott Scudder	.04	.02	.01
☐ 49	Damon Berryhill	.04	.02	.01
☐ 50	Ken Griffey Jr.	.50	.23	.06
☐ 51	Tom Runnells MG	.04	.02	.01
☐ 52	Juan Bell	.04	.02	.01
☐ 53	Tommy Gregg	.04	.02	.01
☐ 54	David Wells	.04	.02	.01
☐ 55	Rafael Palmeiro	.07	.03	.01
☐ 56	Charlie O'Brien	.04	.02	.01
☐ 57	Donn Pall	.04	.02	.01
☐ 58	1992 Prospects C	.35	.16	.04
	Brad Ausmus			
	Jim Campanis Jr.			
	Dave Nilsson			
	Doug Robbins			
☐ 59	Mo Vaughn	.07	.03	.01
☐ 60	Tony Fernandez	.07	.03	.01
☐ 61	Paul O'Neill	.07	.03	.01
☐ 62	Gene Nelson	.04	.02	.01
☐ 63	Randy Ready	.04	.02	.01
☐ 64	Bob Kipper	.04	.02	.01
☐ 65	Willie McGee	.07	.03	.01
☐ 66	Scott Stahoviak	.20	.09	.03
☐ 67	Luis Salazar	.04	.02	.01
☐ 68	Marvin Freeman	.04	.02	.01
☐ 69	Kenny Lofton	.40	.18	.05
☐ 70	Gary Gaetti	.04	.02	.01
☐ 71	Erik Hanson	.04	.02	.01
☐ 72	Eddie Zosky	.07	.03	.01
☐ 73	Brian Barnes	.04	.02	.01
☐ 74	Scott Leius	.04	.02	.01
☐ 75	Bret Saberhagen	.07	.03	.01
☐ 76	Mike Gallego	.04	.02	.01
☐ 77	Jack Armstrong	.04	.02	.01
☐ 78	Ivan Rodriguez	.30	.14	.04
☐ 79	Jesse Orosco	.04	.02	.01
☐ 80	David Justice	.20	.09	.03
☐ 81	Ced Landrum	.04	.02	.01
☐ 82	Doug Simons	.04	.02	.01
☐ 83	Tommy Greene	.04	.02	.01
☐ 84	Leo Gomez	.10	.05	.01

☐ 85 Jose DeLeon	.04	.02	.01
☐ 86 Steve Finley	.07	.03	.01
☐ 87 Bob MacDonald	.04	.02	.01
☐ 88 Darrin Jackson	.07	.03	.01
☐ 89 Neal Heaton	.04	.02	.01
☐ 90 Robin Yount	.10	.05	.01
☐ 91 Jeff Reed	.04	.02	.01
☐ 92 Lenny Harris	.04	.02	.01
☐ 93 Reggie Jefferson	.07	.03	.01
☐ 94 Sammy Sosa	.04	.02	.01
☐ 95 Scott Bailes	.04	.02	.01
☐ 96 Tom McKinnon	.10	.05	.01
☐ 97 Luis Rivera	.04	.02	.01
☐ 98 Mike Harkey	.07	.03	.01
☐ 99 Jeff Treadway	.04	.02	.01
☐ 100 Jose Canseco	.20	.09	.03
☐ 101 Omar Vizquel	.04	.02	.01
☐ 102 Scott Kamienieckí	.04	.02	.01
☐ 103 Ricky Jordan	.04	.02	.01
☐ 104 Jeff Ballard	.04	.02	.01
☐ 105 Felix Jose	.07	.03	.01
☐ 106 Mike Boddicker	.04	.02	.01
☐ 107 Dan Pasqua	.04	.02	.01
☐ 108 Mike Timlin	.04	.02	.01
☐ 109 Roger Craig MG	.04	.02	.01
☐ 110 Ryne Sandberg	.25	.11	.03
☐ 111 Mark Carreon	.04	.02	.01
☐ 112 Oscar Azocar	.04	.02	.01
☐ 113 Mike Greenwell	.07	.03	.01
☐ 114 Mark Portugal	.04	.02	.01
☐ 115 Terry Pendleton	.10	.05	.01
☐ 116 Willie Randolph	.07	.03	.01
☐ 117 Scott Terry	.04	.02	.01
☐ 118 Chili Davis	.07	.03	.01
☐ 119 Mark Gardner	.04	.02	.01
☐ 120 Alan Trammell	.07	.03	.01
☐ 121 Derek Bell	.10	.05	.01
☐ 122 Gary Varsho	.04	.02	.01
☐ 123 Bob Ojeda	.04	.02	.01
☐ 124 Shawn Livsey	.10	.05	.01
☐ 125 Chris Hoiles	.07	.03	.01
☐ 126 1992 Prospects 1B	.90	.40	.11
Ryan Klesko			
John Jaha			
Rico Brogna			
Dave Staton			
☐ 127 Carlos Quintana	.04	.02	.01
☐ 128 Kurt Stillwell	.04	.02	.01
☐ 129 Melido Perez	.07	.03	.01
☐ 130 Alvin Davis	.04	.02	.01
☐ 131 Checklist 1-132	.05	.01	.00
☐ 132 Eric Show	.04	.02	.01
☐ 133 Rance Mulliniks	.04	.02	.01
☐ 134 Darryl Kile	.04	.02	.01
☐ 135 Von Hayes	.04	.02	.01
☐ 136 Bill Doran	.04	.02	.01
☐ 137 Jeff Robinson	.04	.02	.01
☐ 138 Monty Fariss	.04	.02	.01
☐ 139 Jeff Innis	.04	.02	.01
☐ 140 Mark Grace UER	.07	.03	.01
(Home Calie., should			
be Calif.)			
☐ 141 Jim Leyland MG UER	.04	.02	.01
(No closed parenthesis			
after East in 1991)			
☐ 142 Todd Van Poppel	.20	.09	.03
☐ 143 Paul Gibson	.04	.02	.01
☐ 144 Bill Swift	.04	.02	.01
☐ 145 Danny Tartabull	.07	.03	.01
☐ 146 Al Newman	.04	.02	.01
☐ 147 Cris Carpenter	.04	.02	.01
☐ 148 Anthony Young	.07	.03	.01
☐ 149 Brian Bohanon	.04	.02	.01
☐ 150 Roger Clemens UER	.25	.11	.03
(League leading ERA in			
1990 not italicized)			
☐ 151 Jeff Hamilton	.04	.02	.01
☐ 152 Charlie Leibrandt	.04	.02	.01
☐ 153 Ron Karkovice	.04	.02	.01
☐ 154 Hensley Meulens	.04	.02	.01
☐ 155 Scott Bankhead	.04	.02	.01
☐ 156 Manny Ramjrez	.60	.25	.08
☐ 157 Keith Miller	.04	.02	.01
☐ 158 Todd Frohwirth	.04	.02	.01
☐ 159 Darrin Fletcher	.04	.02	.01
☐ 160 Bobby Bonilla	.10	.05	.01
☐ 161 Casey Candaele	.04	.02	.01
☐ 162 Paul Faries	.04	.02	.01
☐ 163 Dana Kiecker	.04	.02	.01
☐ 164 Shane Mack	.07	.03	.01
☐ 165 Mark Langston	.07	.03	.01
☐ 166 Geronimo Pena	.04	.02	.01
☐ 167 Andy Allanson	.04	.02	.01
☐ 168 Dwight Smith	.04	.02	.01
☐ 169 Chuck Crim	.04	.02	.01
☐ 170 Alex Cole	.04	.02	.01
☐ 171 Bill Plummer MG	.04	.02	.01
☐ 172 Juan Berenguer	.04	.02	.01
☐ 173 Brian Downing	.04	.02	.01
☐ 174 Steve Frey	.04	.02	.01
☐ 175 Orel Hershiser	.07	.03	.01
☐ 176 Ramon Garcia	.04	.02	.01
☐ 177 Dan Gladden	.04	.02	.01
☐ 178 Jim Acker	.04	.02	.01
☐ 179 1992 Prospects 2B	.25	.11	.03
Bobby DeJardin			
Cesar Bernhardt			
Armando Moreno			
Andy Stankiewicz			
☐ 180 Kevin Mitchell	.07	.03	.01
☐ 181 Hector Villanueva	.04	.02	.01
☐ 182 Jeff Reardon	.07	.03	.01
☐ 183 Brent Mayne	.04	.02	.01
☐ 184 Jimmy Jones	.04	.02	.01

☐ 185	Benito Santiago	.07	.03	.01
☐ 186	Cliff Floyd	.75	.35	.09
☐ 187	Ernie Riles	.04	.02	.01
☐ 188	Jose Guzman	.04	.02	.01
☐ 189	Junior Felix	.04	.02	.01
☐ 190	Glenn Davis	.07	.03	.01
☐ 191	Charlie Hough	.04	.02	.01
☐ 192	Dave Fleming	.50	.23	.06
☐ 193	Omar Olivares	.04	.02	.01
☐ 194	Eric Karros	.50	.23	.06
☐ 195	David Cone	.07	.03	.01
☐ 196	Frank Castillo	.08	.04	.01
☐ 197	Glenn Braggs	.04	.02	.01
☐ 198	Scott Aldred	.04	.02	.01
☐ 199	Jeff Blauser	.04	.02	.01
☐ 200	Len Dykstra	.07	.03	.01
☐ 201	Buck Showalter MG	.10	.05	.01
☐ 202	Rick Honeycutt	.04	.02	.01
☐ 203	Greg Myers	.04	.02	.01
☐ 204	Trevor Wilson	.04	.02	.01
☐ 205	Jay Howell	.04	.02	.01
☐ 206	Luis Sojo	.04	.02	.01
☐ 207	Jack Clark	.07	.03	.01
☐ 208	Julio Machado	.04	.02	.01
☐ 209	Lloyd McClendon	.04	.02	.01
☐ 210	Ozzie Guillen	.04	.02	.01
☐ 211	Jeremy Hernandez	.10	.05	.01
☐ 212	Randy Velarde	.04	.02	.01
☐ 213	Les Lancaster	.04	.02	.01
☐ 214	Andy Mota	.04	.02	.01
☐ 215	Rich Gossage	.07	.03	.01
☐ 216	Brent Gates	.50	.23	.06
☐ 217	Brian Harper	.04	.02	.01
☐ 218	Mike Flanagan	.04	.02	.01
☐ 219	Jerry Browne	.04	.02	.01
☐ 220	Jose Rijo	.07	.03	.01
☐ 221	Skeeter Barnes	.04	.02	.01
☐ 222	Jaime Navarro	.07	.03	.01
☐ 223	Mel Hall	.04	.02	.01
☐ 224	Bret Barberie	.04	.02	.01
☐ 225	Roberto Alomar	.20	.09	.03
☐ 226	Pete Smith	.07	.03	.01
☐ 227	Daryl Boston	.04	.02	.01
☐ 228	Eddie Whitson	.04	.02	.01
☐ 229	Shawn Boskie	.04	.02	.01
☐ 230	Dick Schofield	.04	.02	.01
☐ 231	Brian Drahman	.04	.02	.01
☐ 232	John Smiley	.07	.03	.01
☐ 233	Mitch Webster	.04	.02	.01
☐ 234	Terry Steinbach	.07	.03	.01
☐ 235	Jack Morris	.10	.05	.01
☐ 236	Bill Pecota	.04	.02	.01
☐ 237	Jose Hernandez	.10	.05	.01
☐ 238	Greg Litton	.04	.02	.01
☐ 239	Brian Holman	.04	.02	.01
☐ 240	Andres Galarraga	.04	.02	.01
☐ 241	Gerald Young	.04	.02	.01
☐ 242	Mike Mussina	.50	.23	.06
☐ 243	Alvaro Espinoza	.04	.02	.01
☐ 244	Darren Daulton	.07	.03	.01
☐ 245	John Smoltz	.10	.05	.01
☐ 246	Jason Pruitt	.10	.05	.01
☐ 247	Chuck Finley	.04	.02	.01
☐ 248	Jim Gantner	.04	.02	.01
☐ 249	Tony Fossas	.04	.02	.01
☐ 250	Ken Griffey Sr.	.07	.03	.01
☐ 251	Kevin Elster	.04	.02	.01
☐ 252	Dennis Rasmussen	.04	.02	.01
☐ 253	Terry Kennedy	.04	.02	.01
☐ 254	Ryan Bowen	.07	.03	.01
☐ 255	Robin Ventura	.15	.07	.02
☐ 256	Mike Aldrete	.04	.02	.01
☐ 257	Jeff Russell	.04	.02	.01
☐ 258	Jim Lindeman	.04	.02	.01
☐ 259	Ron Darling	.07	.03	.01
☐ 260	Devon White	.07	.03	.01
☐ 261	Tom Lasorda MG	.04	.02	.01
☐ 262	Terry Lee	.04	.02	.01
☐ 263	Bob Patterson	.04	.02	.01
☐ 264	Checklist 133-264	.05	.01	.00
☐ 265	Teddy Higuera	.04	.02	.01
☐ 266	Roberto Kelly	.07	.03	.01
☐ 267	Steve Bedrosian	.04	.02	.01
☐ 268	Brady Anderson	.07	.03	.01
☐ 269	Ruben Amaro Jr.	.04	.02	.01
☐ 270	Tony Gwynn	.12	.05	.02
☐ 271	Tracy Jones	.04	.02	.01
☐ 272	Jerry Don Gleaton	.04	.02	.01
☐ 273	Craig Grebeck	.04	.02	.01
☐ 274	Bob Scanlan	.04	.02	.01
☐ 275	Todd Zeile	.04	.02	.01
☐ 276	Shawn Green	.25	.11	.03
☐ 277	Scott Chiamparino	.04	.02	.01
☐ 278	Darryl Hamilton	.07	.03	.01
☐ 279	Jim Clancy	.04	.02	.01
☐ 280	Carlos Martinez	.04	.02	.01
☐ 281	Kevin Appier	.07	.03	.01
☐ 282	John Wehner	.04	.02	.01
☐ 283	Reggie Sanders	.25	.11	.03
☐ 284	Gene Larkin	.04	.02	.01
☐ 285	Bob Welch	.04	.02	.01
☐ 286	Gilberto Reyes	.04	.02	.01
☐ 287	Pete Schourek	.07	.03	.01
☐ 288	Andujar Cedeno	.07	.03	.01
☐ 289	Mike Morgan	.04	.02	.01
☐ 290	Bo Jackson	.12	.05	.02
☐ 291	Phil Garner MG	.04	.02	.01
☐ 292	Ray Lankford	.15	.07	.02
☐ 293	Mike Henneman	.04	.02	.01
☐ 294	Dave Valle	.04	.02	.01
☐ 295	Alonzo Powell	.04	.02	.01
☐ 296	Tom Brunansky	.07	.03	.01
☐ 297	Kevin Brown	.07	.03	.01
☐ 298	Kelly Gruber	.07	.03	.01

☐ 299	Charles Nagy	10	.05	.01
☐ 300	Don Mattingly	12	.05	.02
☐ 301	Kirk McCaskill	04	.02	.01
☐ 302	Joey Cora	04	.02	.01
☐ 303	Dan Plesac	04	.02	.01
☐ 304	Joe Oliver	04	.02	.01
☐ 305	Tom Glavine	12	.05	.02
☐ 306	Al Shirley	20	.09	.03
☐ 307	Bruce Ruffin	04	.02	.01
☐ 308	Craig Shipley	10	.05	.01
☐ 309	Dave Martinez	04	.02	.01
☐ 310	Jose Mesa	04	.02	.01
☐ 311	Henry Cotto	04	.02	.01
☐ 312	Mike LaValliere	04	.02	.01
☐ 313	Kevin Tapani	07	.03	.01
☐ 314	Jeff Huson	04	.02	.01
	(Shows Jose Canseco			
	sliding into second)			
☐ 315	Juan Samuel	04	.02	.01
☐ 316	Curt Schilling	07	.03	.01
☐ 317	Mike Bordick	08	.04	.01
☐ 318	Steve Howe	04	.02	.01
☐ 319	Tony Phillips	04	.02	.01
☐ 320	George Bell	07	.03	.01
☐ 321	Lou Piniella MG	04	.02	.01
☐ 322	Tim Burke	04	.02	.01
☐ 323	Milt Thompson	04	.02	.01
☐ 324	Danny Darwin	04	.02	.01
☐ 325	Joe Orsulak	04	.02	.01
☐ 326	Eric King	04	.02	.01
☐ 327	Jay Buhner	07	.03	.01
☐ 328	Joel Johnston	04	.02	.01
☐ 329	Franklin Stubbs	04	.02	.01
☐ 330	Will Clark	20	.09	.03
☐ 331	Steve Lake	04	.02	.01
☐ 332	Chris Jones	04	.02	.01
☐ 333	Pat Tabler	04	.02	.01
☐ 334	Kevin Gross	04	.02	.01
☐ 335	Dave Henderson	04	.02	.01
☐ 336	Greg Anthony	15	.07	.02
☐ 337	Alejandro Pena	04	.02	.01
☐ 338	Shawn Abner	04	.02	.01
☐ 339	Tom Browning	04	.02	.01
☐ 340	Otis Nixon	07	.03	.01
☐ 341	Bob Geren	04	.02	.01
☐ 342	Tim Spehr	04	.02	.01
☐ 343	John Vander Wal	15	.07	.02
☐ 344	Jack Daugherty	04	.02	.01
☐ 345	Zane Smith	04	.02	.01
☐ 346	Rheal Cormier	04	.02	.01
☐ 347	Kent Hrbek	07	.03	.01
☐ 348	Rick Wilkins	04	.02	.01
☐ 349	Steve Lyons	04	.02	.01
☐ 350	Gregg Olson	07	.03	.01
☐ 351	Greg Riddoch MG	04	.02	.01
☐ 352	Ed Nunez	04	.02	.01
☐ 353	Braulio Castillo	15	.07	.02
☐ 354	Dave Bergman	04	.02	.01
☐ 355	Warren Newson	04	.02	.01
☐ 356	Luis Quinones	04	.02	.01
☐ 357	Mike Witt	04	.02	.01
☐ 358	Ted Wood	10	.05	.01
☐ 359	Mike Moore	04	.02	.01
☐ 360	Lance Parrish	07	.03	.01
☐ 361	Barry Jones	04	.02	.01
☐ 362	Javier Ortiz	04	.02	.01
☐ 363	John Candelaria	04	.02	.01
☐ 364	Glenallen Hill	04	.02	.01
☐ 365	Duane Ward	04	.02	.01
☐ 366	Checklist 265-396	05	.01	.00
☐ 367	Rafael Belliard	04	.02	.01
☐ 368	Bill Krueger	04	.02	.01
☐ 369	Steve Whitaker	10	.05	.01
☐ 370	Shawon Dunston	07	.03	.01
☐ 371	Dante Bichette	04	.02	.01
☐ 372	Kip Gross	10	.05	.01
☐ 373	Don Robinson	04	.02	.01
☐ 374	Bernie Williams	08	.04	.01
☐ 375	Bert Blyleven	07	.03	.01
☐ 376	Chris Donnels	04	.02	.01
☐ 377	Bob Zupcic	25	.11	.03
☐ 378	Joel Skinner	04	.02	.01
☐ 379	Steve Chitren	04	.02	.01
☐ 380	Barry Bonds	15	.07	.02
☐ 381	Sparky Anderson MG	04	.02	.01
☐ 382	Sid Fernandez	07	.03	.01
☐ 383	Dave Hollins	07	.03	.01
☐ 384	Mark Lee	04	.02	.01
☐ 385	Tim Wallach	07	.03	.01
☐ 386	Will Clark AS	10	.05	.01
☐ 387	Ryne Sandberg AS	10	.05	.01
☐ 388	Howard Johnson AS	05	.02	.01
☐ 389	Barry Larkin AS	08	.04	.01
☐ 390	Barry Bonds AS	10	.05	.01
☐ 391	Ron Gant AS	10	.05	.01
☐ 392	Bobby Bonilla AS	08	.04	.01
☐ 393	Craig Biggio AS	05	.02	.01
☐ 394	Dennis Martinez AS	05	.02	.01
☐ 395	Tom Glavine AS	10	.05	.01
☐ 396	Lee Smith AS	05	.02	.01
☐ 397	Cecil Fielder AS	10	.05	.01
☐ 398	Julio Franco AS	05	.02	.01
☐ 399	Wade Boggs AS	10	.05	.01
☐ 400	Cal Ripken AS	15	.07	.02
☐ 401	Jose Canseco AS	10	.05	.01
☐ 402	Joe Carter AS	10	.05	.01
☐ 403	Ruben Sierra AS	10	.05	.01
☐ 404	Matt Nokes AS	05	.02	.01
☐ 405	Roger Clemens AS	12	.05	.02
☐ 406	Jim Abbott AS	10	.05	.01
☐ 407	Bryan Harvey AS	05	.02	.01
☐ 408	Bob Milacki	04	.02	.01
☐ 409	Geno Petralli	04	.02	.01
☐ 410	Dave Stewart	07	.03	.01

☐	411	Mike Jackson	.04	.02	.01	☐	468	Greg Harris	.04	.02	.01
☐	412	Luis Aquino	.04	.02	.01	☐	469	Jim Eisenreich	.04	.02	.01
☐	413	Tim Teufel	.04	.02	.01	☐	470	Pedro Guerrero	.07	.03	.01
☐	414	Jeff Ware	.12	.05	.02	☐	471	Jose DeJesus	.04	.02	.01
☐	415	Jim Deshaies	.04	.02	.01	☐	472	Rich Rowland	.12	.05	.02
☐	416	Ellis Burks	.07	.03	.01	☐	473	1992 Prospects 3B UER	.25	.11	.03
☐	417	Allan Anderson	.04	.02	.01			Frank Bolick			
☐	418	Alfredo Griffin	.04	.02	.01			Craig Paquette			
☐	419	Wally Whitehurst	.04	.02	.01			Tom Redington			
☐	420	Sandy Alomar Jr.	.07	.03	.01			Paul Russo			
☐	421	Juan Agosto	.04	.02	.01			(Line around top border)			
☐	422	Sam Horn	.04	.02	.01	☐	474	Mike Rossiter	.10	.05	.01
☐	423	Jeff Fassero	.04	.02	.01	☐	475	Robby Thompson	.04	.02	.01
☐	424	Paul McClellan	.04	.02	.01	☐	476	Randy Bush	.04	.02	.01
☐	425	Cecil Fielder	.12	.05	.02	☐	477	Greg Hibbard	.04	.02	.01
☐	426	Tim Raines	.07	.03	.01	☐	478	Dale Sveum	.04	.02	.01
☐	427	Eddie Taubensee	.12	.05	.02	☐	479	Chito Martinez	.04	.02	.01
☐	428	Dennis Boyd	.04	.02	.01	☐	480	Scott Sanderson	.04	.02	.01
☐	429	Tony LaRussa MG	.04	.02	.01	☐	481	Tino Martinez	.07	.03	.01
☐	430	Steve Sax	.07	.03	.01	☐	482	Jimmy Key	.04	.02	.01
☐	431	Tom Gordon	.04	.02	.01	☐	483	Terry Shumpert	.04	.02	.01
☐	432	Billy Hatcher	.04	.02	.01	☐	484	Mike Hartley	.04	.02	.01
☐	433	Cal Eldred	.35	.16	.04	☐	485	Chris Sabo	.07	.03	.01
☐	434	Wally Backman	.04	.02	.01	☐	486	Bob Walk	.04	.02	.01
☐	435	Mark Eichhorn	.04	.02	.01	☐	487	John Cerutti	.04	.02	.01
☐	436	Mookie Wilson	.04	.02	.01	☐	488	Scott Cooper	.07	.03	.01
☐	437	Scott Servais	.04	.02	.01	☐	489	Bobby Cox MG	.04	.02	.01
☐	438	Mike Maddux	.04	.02	.01	☐	490	Julio Franco	.07	.03	.01
☐	439	Chico Walker	.04	.02	.01	☐	491	Jeff Brantley	.04	.02	.01
☐	440	Doug Drabek	.07	.03	.01	☐	492	Mike Devereaux	.07	.03	.01
☐	441	Rob Deer	.07	.03	.01	☐	493	Jose Offerman	.07	.03	.01
☐	442	Dave West	.04	.02	.01	☐	494	Gary Thurman	.04	.02	.01
☐	443	Spike Owen	.04	.02	.01	☐	495	Carney Lansford	.07	.03	.01
☐	444	Tyrone Hill	.35	.16	.04	☐	496	Joe Grahe	.04	.02	.01
☐	445	Matt Williams	.07	.03	.01	☐	497	Andy Ashby	.04	.02	.01
☐	446	Mark Lewis	.07	.03	.01	☐	498	Gerald Perry	.04	.02	.01
☐	447	David Segui	.04	.02	.01	☐	499	Dave Otto	.04	.02	.01
☐	448	Tom Pagnozzi	.04	.02	.01	☐	500	Vince Coleman	.07	.03	.01
☐	449	Jeff Johnson	.04	.02	.01	☐	501	Rob Mallicoat	.04	.02	.01
☐	450	Mark McGwire	.20	.09	.03	☐	502	Greg Briley	.04	.02	.01
☐	451	Tom Henke	.07	.03	.01	☐	503	Pascual Perez	.04	.02	.01
☐	452	Wilson Alvarez	.04	.02	.01	☐	504	Aaron Sele	.40	.18	.05
☐	453	Gary Redus	.04	.02	.01	☐	505	Bobby Thigpen	.04	.02	.01
☐	454	Darren Holmes	.04	.02	.01	☐	506	Todd Benzinger	.04	.02	.01
☐	455	Pete O'Brien	.04	.02	.01	☐	507	Candy Maldonado	.04	.02	.01
☐	456	Pat Combs	.04	.02	.01	☐	508	Bill Gullickson	.04	.02	.01
☐	457	Hubie Brooks	.04	.02	.01	☐	509	Doug Dascenzo	.04	.02	.01
☐	458	Frank Tanana	.04	.02	.01	☐	510	Frank Viola	.07	.03	.01
☐	459	Tom Kelly MG	.04	.02	.01	☐	511	Kenny Rogers	.04	.02	.01
☐	460	Andre Dawson	.10	.05	.01	☐	512	Mike Heath	.04	.02	.01
☐	461	Doug Jones	.04	.02	.01	☐	513	Kevin Bass	.04	.02	.01
☐	462	Rich Rodriguez	.04	.02	.01	☐	514	Kim Batiste	.04	.02	.01
☐	463	Mike Simms	.04	.02	.01	☐	515	Delino DeShields	.10	.05	.01
☐	464	Mike Jeffcoat	.04	.02	.01	☐	516	Ed Sprague Jr.	.07	.03	.01
☐	465	Barry Larkin	.10	.05	.01	☐	517	Jim Gott	.04	.02	.01
☐	466	Stan Belinda	.04	.02	.01	☐	518	Jose Melendez	.04	.02	.01
☐	467	Lonnie Smith	.04	.02	.01	☐	519	Hal McRae MG	.04	.02	.01

☐ 520	Jeff Bagwell	.25	.11	.03
☐ 521	Joe Hesketh	.04	.02	.01
☐ 522	Milt Cuyler	.04	.02	.01
☐ 523	Shawn Hillegas	.04	.02	.01
☐ 524	Don Slaught	.04	.02	.01
☐ 525	Randy Johnson	.07	.03	.01
☐ 526	Doug Piatt	.04	.02	.01
☐ 527	Checklist 397-528	.05	.01	.00
☐ 528	Steve Foster	.10	.05	.01
☐ 529	Joe Girardi	.04	.02	.01
☐ 530	Jim Abbott	.12	.05	.02
☐ 531	Larry Walker	.15	.07	.02
☐ 532	Mike Huff	.04	.02	.01
☐ 533	Mackey Sasser	.04	.02	.01
☐ 534	Benji Gil	.20	.09	.03
☐ 535	Dave Stieb	.04	.02	.01
☐ 536	Willie Wilson	.04	.02	.01
☐ 537	Mark Leiter	.04	.02	.01
☐ 538	Jose Uribe	.04	.02	.01
☐ 539	Thomas Howard	.04	.02	.01
☐ 540	Ben McDonald	.10	.05	.01
☐ 541	Jose Tolentino	.10	.05	.01
☐ 542	Keith Mitchell	.07	.03	.01
☐ 543	Jerome Walton	.04	.02	.01
☐ 544	Cliff Brantley	.10	.05	.01
☐ 545	Andy Van Slyke	.07	.03	.01
☐ 546	Paul Sorrento	.07	.03	.01
☐ 547	Herm Winningham	.04	.02	.01
☐ 548	Mark Guthrie	.04	.02	.01
☐ 549	Joe Torre MG	.04	.02	.01
☐ 550	Darryl Strawberry	.12	.05	.02
☐ 551	1992 Prospects SS UER	.60	.25	.08
	Wilfredo Cordero			
	Chipper Jones			
	Manny Alexander			
	Alex Arias			
	(No line around			
	top border)			
☐ 552	Dave Gallagher	.04	.02	.01
☐ 553	Edgar Martinez	.07	.03	.01
☐ 554	Donald Harris	.04	.02	.01
☐ 555	Frank Thomas	.75	.35	.09
☐ 556	Storm Davis	.04	.02	.01
☐ 557	Dickie Thon	.04	.02	.01
☐ 558	Scott Garrelts	.04	.02	.01
☐ 559	Steve Olin	.04	.02	.01
☐ 560	Rickey Henderson	.12	.05	.02
☐ 561	Jose Vizcaino	.04	.02	.01
☐ 562	Wade Taylor	.04	.02	.01
☐ 563	Pat Borders	.04	.02	.01
☐ 564	Jimmy Gonzalez	.10	.05	.01
☐ 565	Lee Smith	.07	.03	.01
☐ 566	Bill Sampen	.04	.02	.01
☐ 567	Dean Palmer	.10	.05	.01
☐ 568	Bryan Harvey	.04	.02	.01
☐ 569	Tony Pena	.04	.02	.01
☐ 570	Lou Whitaker	.07	.03	.01

☐ 571	Randy Tomlin	.04	.02	.01
☐ 572	Greg Vaughn	.07	.03	.01
☐ 573	Kelly Downs	.04	.02	.01
☐ 574	Steve Avery UER	.15	.07	.02
	(Should be 13 games			
	for Durham in 1989)			
☐ 575	Kirby Puckett	.20	.09	.03
☐ 576	Heathcliff Slocumb	.04	.02	.01
☐ 577	Kevin Seitzer	.07	.03	.01
☐ 578	Lee Guetterman	.04	.02	.01
☐ 579	Johnny Oates MG	.04	.02	.01
☐ 580	Greg Maddux	.07	.03	.01
☐ 581	Stan Javier	.04	.02	.01
☐ 582	Vicente Palacios	.04	.02	.01
☐ 583	Mel Rojas	.04	.02	.01
☐ 584	Wayne Rosenthal	.10	.05	.01
☐ 585	Lenny Webster	.04	.02	.01
☐ 586	Rod Nichols	.04	.02	.01
☐ 587	Mickey Morandini	.07	.03	.01
☐ 588	Russ Swan	.04	.02	.01
☐ 589	Mariano Duncan	.04	.02	.01
☐ 590	Howard Johnson	.07	.03	.01
☐ 591	1992 Prospects OF	.35	.16	.04
	Jeromy Burnitz			
	Jacob Brumfield			
	Alan Cockrell			
	D.J. Dozier			
☐ 592	Denny Neagle	.04	.02	.01
☐ 593	Steve Decker	.04	.02	.01
☐ 594	Brian Barber	.20	.09	.03
☐ 595	Bruce Hurst	.07	.03	.01
☐ 596	Kent Mercker	.04	.02	.01
☐ 597	Mike Magnante	.12	.05	.02
☐ 598	Jody Reed	.04	.02	.01
☐ 599	Steve Searcy	.04	.02	.01
☐ 600	Paul Molitor	.07	.03	.01
☐ 601	Dave Smith	.04	.02	.01
☐ 602	Mike Fetters	.04	.02	.01
☐ 603	Luis Mercedes	.07	.03	.01
☐ 604	Chris Gwynn	.04	.02	.01
☐ 605	Scott Erickson	.08	.04	.01
☐ 606	Brook Jacoby	.04	.02	.01
☐ 607	Todd Stottlemyre	.07	.03	.01
☐ 608	Scott Bradley	.04	.02	.01
☐ 609	Mike Hargrove MG	.04	.02	.01
☐ 610	Eric Davis	.07	.03	.01
☐ 611	Brian Hunter	.10	.05	.01
☐ 612	Pat Kelly	.07	.03	.01
☐ 613	Pedro Munoz	.07	.03	.01
☐ 614	Al Osuna	.04	.02	.01
☐ 615	Matt Merullo	.04	.02	.01
☐ 616	Larry Andersen	.04	.02	.01
☐ 617	Junior Ortiz	.04	.02	.01
☐ 618	1992 Prospects OF	.40	.18	.05
	Cesar Hernandez			
	Steve Hosey			
	Jeff McNeely			

Dan Peltier

☐ 619	Danny Jackson	.04	.02	.01
☐ 620	George Brett	.10	.05	.01
☐ 621	Dan Gakeler	.04	.02	.01
☐ 622	Steve Buechele	.04	.02	.01
☐ 623	Bob Tewksbury	.07	.03	.01
☐ 624	Shawn Estes	.15	.07	.02
☐ 625	Kevin McReynolds	.07	.03	.01
☐ 626	Chris Haney	.04	.02	.01
☐ 627	Mike Sharperson	.04	.02	.01
☐ 628	Mark Williamson	.04	.02	.01
☐ 629	Wally Joyner	.07	.03	.01
☐ 630	Carlton Fisk	.10	.05	.01
☐ 631	Armando Reynoso	.10	.05	.01
☐ 632	Felix Fermin	.04	.02	.01
☐ 633	Mitch Williams	.04	.02	.01
☐ 634	Manuel Lee	.04	.02	.01
☐ 635	Harold Baines	.07	.03	.01
☐ 636	Greg Harris	.04	.02	.01
☐ 637	Orlando Merced	.07	.03	.01
☐ 638	Chris Bosio	.04	.02	.01
☐ 639	Wayne Housie	.10	.05	.01
☐ 640	Xavier Hernandez	.04	.02	.01
☐ 641	David Howard	.04	.02	.01
☐ 642	Tim Crews	.04	.02	.01
☐ 643	Rick Cerone	.04	.02	.01
☐ 644	Terry Leach	.04	.02	.01
☐ 645	Deion Sanders	.15	.07	.02
☐ 646	Craig Wilson	.04	.02	.01
☐ 647	Marquis Grissom	.10	.05	.01
☐ 648	Scott Fletcher	.04	.02	.01
☐ 649	Norm Charlton	.07	.03	.01
☐ 650	Jesse Barfield	.04	.02	.01
☐ 651	Joe Slusarski	.04	.02	.01
☐ 652	Bobby Rose	.04	.02	.01
☐ 653	Dennis Lamp	.04	.02	.01
☐ 654	Allen Watson	.25	.11	.03
☐ 655	Brett Butler	.07	.03	.01
☐ 656	1992 Prospects OF	.35	.16	.04

Rudy Pemberton
Henry Rodriguez
Lee Tinsley
Gerald Williams

☐ 657	Dave Johnson	.04	.02	.01
☐ 658	Checklist 529-660	.05	.01	.00
☐ 659	Brian McRae	.07	.03	.01
☐ 660	Fred McGriff	.12	.05	.02
☐ 661	Bill Landrum	.04	.02	.01
☐ 662	Juan Guzman	.75	.35	.09
☐ 663	Greg Gagne	.04	.02	.01
☐ 664	Ken Hill	.04	.02	.01
☐ 665	Dave Haas	.04	.02	.01
☐ 666	Tom Foley	.04	.02	.01
☐ 667	Roberto Hernandez	.12	.05	.02
☐ 668	Dwayne Henry	.04	.02	.01
☐ 669	Jim Fregosi MG	.04	.02	.01
☐ 670	Harold Reynolds	.04	.02	.01

☐ 671	Mark Whiten	.04	.02	.01
☐ 672	Eric Plunk	.04	.02	.01
☐ 673	Todd Hundley	.04	.02	.01
☐ 674	Mo Sanford	.04	.02	.01
☐ 675	Bobby Witt	.04	.02	.01
☐ 676	1992 Prospects P	.60	.25	.08

Sam Militello
Pat Mahomes
Turk Wendell
Roger Salkeld

☐ 677	John Marzano	.04	.02	.01
☐ 678	Joe Klink	.04	.02	.01
☐ 679	Pete Incaviglia	.04	.02	.01
☐ 680	Dale Murphy	.07	.03	.01
☐ 681	Rene Gonzales	.04	.02	.01
☐ 682	Andy Benes	.07	.03	.01
☐ 683	Jim Poole	.04	.02	.01
☐ 684	Trever Miller	.10	.05	.01
☐ 685	Scott Livingstone	.10	.05	.01
☐ 686	Rich DeLucia	.04	.02	.01
☐ 687	Harvey Pulliam	.08	.04	.01
☐ 688	Tim Belcher	.07	.03	.01
☐ 689	Mark Lemke	.04	.02	.01
☐ 690	John Franco	.07	.03	.01
☐ 691	Walt Weiss	.04	.02	.01
☐ 692	Scott Ruskin	.04	.02	.01
☐ 693	Jeff King	.04	.02	.01
☐ 694	Mike Gardiner	.04	.02	.01
☐ 695	Gary Sheffield	.20	.09	.03
☐ 696	Joe Boever	.04	.02	.01
☐ 697	Mike Felder	.04	.02	.01
☐ 698	John Habyan	.04	.02	.01
☐ 699	Cito Gaston MG	.04	.02	.01
☐ 700	Ruben Sierra	.15	.07	.02
☐ 701	Scott Radinsky	.04	.02	.01
☐ 702	Lee Stevens	.04	.02	.01
☐ 703	Mark Wohlers	.08	.04	.01
☐ 704	Curt Young	.04	.02	.01
☐ 705	Dwight Evans	.07	.03	.01
☐ 706	Rob Murphy	.04	.02	.01
☐ 707	Gregg Jefferies	.07	.03	.01
☐ 708	Tom Bolton	.04	.02	.01
☐ 709	Chris James	.04	.02	.01
☐ 710	Kevin Maas	.07	.03	.01
☐ 711	Ricky Bones	.08	.04	.01
☐ 712	Curt Wilkerson	.04	.02	.01
☐ 713	Roger McDowell	.04	.02	.01
☐ 714	Calvin Reese	.15	.07	.02
☐ 715	Craig Biggio	.07	.03	.01
☐ 716	Kirk Dressendorfer	.04	.02	.01
☐ 717	Ken Dayley	.04	.02	.01
☐ 718	B.J. Surhoff	.04	.02	.01
☐ 719	Terry Mulholland	.04	.02	.01
☐ 720	Kirk Gibson	.07	.03	.01
☐ 721	Mike Pagliarulo	.04	.02	.01
☐ 722	Walt Terrell	.04	.02	.01
☐ 723	Jose Oquendo	.04	.02	.01

☐ 724	Kevin Morton	.04	.02	.01
☐ 725	Dwight Gooden	.07	.03	.01
☐ 726	Kirt Manwaring	.04	.02	.01
☐ 727	Chuck McElroy	.04	.02	.01
☐ 728	Dave Burba	.04	.02	.01
☐ 729	Art Howe	.04	.02	.01
☐ 730	Ramon Martinez	.07	.03	.01
☐ 731	Donnie Hill	.04	.02	.01
☐ 732	Nelson Santovenia	.04	.02	.01
☐ 733	Bob Melvin	.04	.02	.01
☐ 734	Scott Hatteberg	.10	.05	.01
☐ 735	Greg Swindell	.07	.03	.01
☐ 736	Lance Johnson	.04	.02	.01
☐ 737	Kevin Reimer	.04	.02	.01
☐ 738	Dennis Eckersley	.10	.05	.01
☐ 739	Rob Ducey	.04	.02	.01
☐ 740	Ken Caminiti	.07	.03	.01
☐ 741	Mark Gubicza	.04	.02	.01
☐ 742	Billy Spiers	.04	.02	.01
☐ 743	Darren Lewis	.07	.03	.01
☐ 744	Chris Hammond	.04	.02	.01
☐ 745	Dave Magadan	.07	.03	.01
☐ 746	Bernard Gilkey	.07	.03	.01
☐ 747	Willie Banks	.04	.02	.01
☐ 748	Matt Nokes	.04	.02	.01
☐ 749	Jerald Clark	.04	.02	.01
☐ 750	Travis Fryman	.30	.14	.04
☐ 751	Steve Wilson	.04	.02	.01
☐ 752	Billy Ripken	.04	.02	.01
☐ 753	Paul Assenmacher	.04	.02	.01
☐ 754	Charlie Hayes	.04	.02	.01
☐ 755	Alex Fernandez	.07	.03	.01
☐ 756	Gary Pettis	.04	.02	.01
☐ 757	Rob Dibble	.07	.03	.01
☐ 758	Tim Naehring	.07	.03	.01
☐ 759	Jeff Torborg MG	.04	.02	.01
☐ 760	Ozzie Smith	.10	.05	.01
☐ 761	Mike Fitzgerald	.04	.02	.01
☐ 762	John Burkett	.04	.02	.01
☐ 763	Kyle Abbott	.07	.03	.01
☐ 764	Tyler Green	.25	.11	.03
☐ 765	Pete Harnisch	.04	.02	.01
☐ 766	Mark Davis	.04	.02	.01
☐ 767	Kal Daniels	.04	.02	.01
☐ 768	Jim Thome	.12	.05	.02
☐ 769	Jack Howell	.04	.02	.01
☐ 770	Sid Bream	.04	.02	.01
☐ 771	Arthur Rhodes	.15	.07	.02
☐ 772	Garry Templeton	.04	.02	.01
☐ 773	Hal Morris	.07	.03	.01
☐ 774	Bud Black	.04	.02	.01
☐ 775	Ivan Calderon	.04	.02	.01
☐ 776	Doug Henry	.15	.07	.02
☐ 777	John Olerud	.10	.05	.01
☐ 778	Tim Leary	.04	.02	.01
☐ 779	Jay Bell	.04	.02	.01
☐ 780	Eddie Murray	.10	.05	.01

☐ 781	Paul Abbott	.04	.02	.01
☐ 782	Phil Plantier	.15	.07	.02
☐ 783	Joe Magrane	.04	.02	.01
☐ 784	Ken Patterson	.04	.02	.01
☐ 785	Albert Belle	.12	.05	.02
☐ 786	Royce Clayton	.15	.07	.02
☐ 787	Checklist 661-792	.05	.01	.00
☐ 788	Mike Stanton	.04	.02	.01
☐ 789	Bobby Valentine MG	.04	.02	.01
☐ 790	Joe Carter	.12	.05	.02
☐ 791	Danny Cox	.04	.02	.01
☐ 792	Dave Winfield	.10	.05	.01

1992 Topps Gold

Topps produced a 792-card Topps Gold factory set packaged in a foil display box. Only this set contained an additional card of Brien Taylor, numbered 793 and hand signed by him. The production run was 12,000 sets. The Topps Gold cards were also available in regular series packs. According to Topps, on average collectors would find one Topps Gold card in every 36 wax packs, one in every 18 cello packs, one in every 12 rak packs, five per vending box, one in every six jumbo packs, and ten per regular set. The packs also featured "Match-the-Stats" game cards in which the consumer could score "Runs." For 2.00 and every 100 Runs saved in this game, the consumer could receive through a mail-in offer ten Topps Gold cards. These particular Topps Gold cards carry the word "Winner" in gold foil on the card front. The checklist cards in the regular set were replaced with six individual rookie player cards (131, 264, 366, 527, 658, 787) in the gold set. There were a number of uncorrected errors in the Gold set. Chuck Finley (86) has gold band indicating he is Mark Davidson of the Astros. Andujar Cedeno (288) is listed as a member of the New York Yankees. Mike Huff (532) is listed as a member of the Boston Red Sox. Barry Larkin (465) is listed as a member of the Houston Astros but is correctly listed as a member of the Cincinnati Reds on his Gold Winners cards. Typically the individual cards are sold at a multiple of the player's respective value in the regular set.

	MT	EX-MT	VG
COMPLETE SET (792)	400.00	180.00	50.00
COMPLETE FACT.SET (793)	500.00	230.00	65.00
COM GOLD CARDS (1G-792G)	.75	.35	.09
COMP WINNERS SET (792)	125.00	57.50	15.50
COM WINNERS (1GW-792GW)	.25	.11	.03

☐ 86G Chuck Finley UER	1.50	.65	.19
(Gold band has			
Mark Davidson, Astros)			
☐ 131G Terry Mathews	1.50	.65	.19
(Replaces Checklist 1)			
☐ 131GW Terry Mathews	.50	.23	.06
(Replaces Checklist 1)			
☐ 264G Rod Beck	3.00	1.35	.40
(Replaces Checklist 2)			
☐ 264GW Rod Beck	1.00	.45	.13
(Replaces Checklist 2)			
☐ 288G Andujar Cedeno UER	1.50	.65	.19
(Listed on Yankees)			
☐ 366G Tony Perezchica	1.50	.65	.19
(Replaces Checklist 3)			
☐ 366GW Tony Perezchica	.50	.23	.06
(Replaces Checklist 3)			
☐ 465G Barry Larkin UER	4.50	2.00	.55
(Listed on Astros)			
☐ 465GA Barry Larkin ERR	3.00	1.35	.40
(Listed on Astros)			
☐ 465GWB Barry Larkin COR	3.00	1.35	.40
(Listed on Reds)			
☐ 527G Terry McDaniel	1.50	.65	.19
(Replaces Checklist 4)			
☐ 527GW Terry McDaniel	.50	.23	.06
(Replaces Checklist 4)			
☐ 532G Mike Huff UER	1.50	.65	.19
(Listed on Red Sox)			
☐ 658G John Ramos	1.50	.65	.19
(Replaces Checklist 5)			
☐ 658GW John Ramos	.50	.23	.06
(Replaces Checklist 5)			
☐ 787G Brian Williams	7.50	3.40	.95
(Replaces Checklist 6)			
☐ 787GW Brian Williams	2.50	1.15	.30
(Replaces Checklist 6)			
☐ 793G Brien Taylor SP AU	135.00	60.00	17.00

1992 Topps Traded

The 1992 Topps Traded set comprises 132 cards, each measuring the standard size (2 1/2" by 3 1/2"). As in past editions, the set focuses on promising rookies, new managers, and players who changed teams. The set also includes a Team U.S.A. subset, featuring 25 of America's top college players and the Team U.S.A. coach. Inside a white outer border, the fronts display color action photos that have two-color (white and another color) picture frames. The player's name appears in a short color bar at the lower left corner while the team name is given in a different color bar at the lower right corner. In a horizontal format, the backs carry biography, statistics, player summary, or a small color picture of the team's stadium. The cards are arranged in alphabetical order by player's last name and numbered on the back. The key Rookie Cards in this set are Pat Listach, Calvin Murray, Michael Tucker, and B.J. Wallace.

	MT	EX-MT	VG
COMPLETE SET (132)	14.00	6.25	1.75
COMMON PLAYER (1T-132T)	.05	.02	.01

☐ 1T Willie Adams USA	.20	.09	.03
☐ 2T Jeff Alkire USA	.30	.14	.04
☐ 3T Felipe Alou MG	.05	.02	.01
☐ 4T Moises Alou	.10	.05	.01

☐	5T	Ruben Amaro	.05	.02	.01			
☐	6T	Jack Armstrong	.05	.02	.01			
☐	7T	Scott Bankhead	.05	.02	.01			
☐	8T	Tim Belcher	.08	.04	.01			
☐	9T	George Bell	.08	.04	.01			
☐	10T	Freddie Benavides	.05	.02	.01			
☐	11T	Todd Benzinger	.05	.02	.01			
☐	12T	Joe Boever	.05	.02	.01			
☐	13T	Ricky Bones	.08	.04	.01			
☐	14T	Bobby Bonilla	.10	.05	.01			
☐	15T	Hubie Brooks	.05	.02	.01			
☐	16T	Jerry Browne	.05	.02	.01			
☐	17T	Jim Bullinger	.10	.05	.01			
☐	18T	Dave Burba	.05	.02	.01			
☐	19T	Kevin Campbell	.10	.05	.01			
☐	20T	Tom Candiotti	.05	.02	.01			
☐	21T	Mark Carreon	.05	.02	.01			
☐	22T	Gary Carter	.08	.04	.01			
☐	23T	Archi Cianfrocco	.15	.07	.02			
☐	24T	Phil Clark	.05	.02	.01			
☐	25T	Chad Curtis	.25	.11	.03			
☐	26T	Eric Davis	.08	.04	.01			
☐	27T	Tim Davis USA	.20	.09	.03			
☐	28T	Gary DiSarcina	.05	.02	.01			
☐	29T	Darren Dreifort USA	.15	.07	.02			
☐	30T	Mariano Duncan	.05	.02	.01			
☐	31T	Mike Fitzgerald	.05	.02	.01			
☐	32T	John Flaherty	.10	.05	.01			
☐	33T	Darrin Fletcher	.05	.02	.01			
☐	34T	Scott Fletcher	.05	.02	.01			
☐	35T	Ron Fraser CO USA	.12	.05	.02			
☐	36T	Andres Galarraga	.05	.02	.01			
☐	37T	Dave Gallagher	.05	.02	.01			
☐	38T	Mike Gallego	.05	.02	.01			
☐	39T	Nomar Garciaparra USA	.30	.14	.04			
☐	40T	Jason Giambi USA	.15	.07	.02			
☐	41T	Danny Gladden	.05	.02	.01			
☐	42T	Rene Gonzales	.05	.02	.01			
☐	43T	Jeff Granger USA	.12	.05	.02			
☐	44T	Rick Greene USA	.25	.11	.03			
☐	45T	Jeffrey Hammonds USA	.75	.35	.09			
☐	46T	Charlie Hayes	.05	.02	.01			
☐	47T	Von Hayes	.05	.02	.01			
☐	48T	Rick Helling USA	.15	.07	.02			
☐	49T	Butch Henry	.12	.05	.02			
☐	50T	Carlos Hernandez	.05	.02	.01			
☐	51T	Ken Hill	.08	.04	.01			
☐	52T	Butch Hobson	.05	.02	.01			
☐	53T	Vince Horsman	.10	.05	.01			
☐	54T	Pete Incaviglia	.05	.02	.01			
☐	55T	Gregg Johnson	.10	.05	.01			
☑	56T	Charles Johnson USA	.50	.23	.06			
☐	57T	Doug Jones	.05	.02	.01			
☐	58T	Brian Jordan	.25	.11	.03			
☐	59T	Wally Joyner	.08	.04	.01			
☐	60T	Daron Kirkreit USA	.35	.16	.04			
☐	61T	Bill Krueger	.05	.02	.01			

☐	62T	Gene Lamont MG	.05	.02	.01
☐	63T	Jim Lefebvre MG	.05	.02	.01
☐	64T	Danny Leon	.10	.05	.01
☐	65T	Pat Listach	1.50	.65	.19
☐	66T	Kenny Lofton	.40	.18	.05
☐	67T	Dave Martinez	.05	.02	.01
☐	68T	Derrick May	.08	.04	.01
☐	69T	Kirk McCaskill	.05	.02	.01
☐	70T	Chad McConnell USA	.30	.14	.04
☐	71T	Kevin McReynolds	.08	.04	.01
☐	72T	Rusty Meacham	.05	.02	.01
☐	73T	Keith Miller	.05	.02	.01
☐	74T	Kevin Mitchell	.08	.04	.01
☐	75T	Jason Moler USA	.20	.09	.03
☐	76T	Mike Morgan	.05	.02	.01
☐	77T	Jack Morris	.10	.05	.01
☐	78T	Calvin Murray USA	.75	.35	.09
☐	79T	Eddie Murray	.10	.05	.01
☐	80T	Randy Myers	.08	.04	.01
☐	81T	Denny Neagle	.05	.02	.01
☐	82T	Phil Nevin USA	1.00	.45	.13
☐	83T	Dave Nilsson	.15	.07	.02
☐	84T	Junior Ortiz	.05	.02	.01
☐	85T	Donovan Osborne	.30	.14	.04
☐	86T	Bill Pecota	.05	.02	.01
☐	87T	Melido Perez	.08	.04	.01
☐	88T	Mike Perez	.05	.02	.01
☐	89T	Hipolito Pichardo	.10	.05	.01
☐	90T	Willie Randolph	.08	.04	.01
☐	91T	Darren Reed	.05	.02	.01
☐	92T	Bip Roberts	.08	.04	.01
☐	93T	Chris Roberts USA	.25	.11	.03
☐	94T	Steve Rodriguez USA	.10	.05	.01
☐	95T	Bruce Ruffin	.05	.02	.01
☐	96T	Scott Ruskin	.05	.02	.01
☐	97T	Bret Saberhagen	.08	.04	.01
☐	98T	Rey Sanchez	.12	.05	.02
☐	99T	Steve Sax	.08	.04	.01
☐	100T	Curt Schilling	.08	.04	.01
☐	101T	Dick Schofield	.05	.02	.01
☐	102T	Gary Scott	.08	.04	.01
☐	103T	Kevin Seitzer	.08	.04	.01
☐	104T	Frank Seminara	.20	.09	.03
☐	105T	Gary Sheffield	.25	.11	.03
☐	106T	John Smiley	.08	.04	.01
☐	107T	Cory Snyder	.05	.02	.01
☐	108T	Paul Sorrento	.08	.04	.01
☐	109T	Sammy Sosa	.05	.02	.01
☐	110T	Matt Stairs	.15	.07	.02
☐	111T	Andy Stankiewicz	.15	.07	.02
☐	112T	Kurt Stillwell	.05	.02	.01
☐	113T	Rick Sutcliffe	.08	.04	.01
☐	114T	Bill Swift	.05	.02	.01
☐	115T	Jeff Tackett	.08	.04	.01
☐	116T	Danny Tartabull	.08	.04	.01
☐	117T	Eddie Taubensee	.10	.05	.01
☐	118T	Dickie Thon	.05	.02	.01

		MT	EX-MT	VG
☐ 119T	Michael Tucker USA	1.25	.55	.16
☐ 120T	Scooter Tucker	.10	.05	.01
☐ 121T	Marc Valdes USA	.20	.09	.03
☐ 122T	Julio Valera	.08	.04	.01
☐ 123T	Jason Varitek USA	.30	.14	.04
☐ 124T	Ron Villone USA	.25	.11	.03
☐ 125T	Frank Viola	.08	.04	.01
☐ 126T	B.J. Wallace USA	1.00	.45	.13
☐ 127T	Dan Walters	.15	.07	.02
☐ 128T	Craig Wilson USA	.12	.05	.02
☐ 129T	Chris Wimmer USA	.10	.05	.01
☐ 130T	Dave Winfield	.12	.05	.02
☐ 131T	Herm Winningham	.05	.02	.01
☐ 132T	Checklist Card	.08	.01	.00

1993 Topps

The 1993 Topps baseball set (first series) consists of 396 cards measuring the standard size (2 1/2" by 3 1/2"). A Topps Gold card was inserted in every 15-card pack, and Topps Black Gold cards were randomly inserted throughout the packs. The fronts feature color action player photos with white borders. The player's name appears in a stripe at the bottom of the picture, and this stripe and two short diagonal stripes at the bottom corners of the picture are team color-coded. The backs are colorful and carry a color head shot, biography, complete statistical information, with a career highlight if space permitted. The cards are numbered on the back.

	MT	EX-MT	VG
COMPLETE SET (396)	15.00	6.75	1.90
COMMON PLAYER (1-396)	.04	.02	.01

		MT	EX-MT	VG
GOLD COMPLETE SET (396)		150.00	70.00	19.00
GOLD COMMON (1-396)		.25	.11	.03
☐ 1	Robin Yount	.10	.05	.01
☐ 2	Barry Bonds	.15	.07	.02
☐ 3	Ryne Sandberg	.20	.09	.03
☐ 4	Roger Clemens	.25	.11	.03
☐ 5	Tony Gwynn	.12	.05	.02
☐ 6	Jeff Tackett	.25	.11	.03
☐ 7	Pete Incaviglia	.25	.11	.03
☐ 8	Mark Wohlers	.28	.13	.04
☐ 9	Kent Hrbek	.28	.13	.04
☐ 10	Will Clark	.15	.07	.02
☐ 11	Eric Karros	.35	.16	.04
☐ 12	Lee Smith	.25	.11	.03
☐ 13	Esteban Beltre	.25	.11	.03
☐ 14	Greg Briley	.25	.11	.03
☐ 15	Marquis Grissom	.10	.05	.01
☐ 16	Dan Plesac	.25	.11	.03
☐ 17	Dave Hollins	.28	.13	.04
☐ 18	Terry Steinbach	.28	.13	.04
☐ 19	Ed Nunez	.25	.11	.03
☐ 20	Tim Salmon	.25	.11	.03
☐ 21	Luis Salazar	.25	.11	.03
☐ 22	Jim Eisenreich	.25	.11	.03
☐ 23	Todd Stottlemyre	.25	.11	.03
☐ 24	Tim Naehring	.25	.11	.03
☐ 25	John Franco	.25	.11	.03
☐ 26	Skeeter Barnes	.25	.11	.03
☐ 27	Carlos Garcia	.25	.11	.03
☐ 28	Joe Orsulak	.25	.11	.03
☐ 29	Dwayne Henry	.25	.11	.03
☐ 30	Fred McGriff	.12	.05	.02
☐ 31	Derek Lilliquist	.25	.11	.03
☐ 32	Don Mattingly	.12	.05	.02
☐ 33	B.J. Wallace	.40	.18	.05
☐ 34	Juan Gonzalez	.30	.14	.04
☐ 35	John Smoltz	.10	.05	.01
☐ 36	Scott Servais	.25	.11	.03
☐ 37	Lenny Webster	.25	.11	.03
☐ 38	Chris James	.25	.11	.03
☐ 39	Roger McDowell	.25	.11	.03
☐ 40	Ozzie Smith	.10	.05	.01
☐ 41	Alex Fernandez	.28	.13	.04
☐ 42	Spike Owen	.25	.11	.03
☐ 43	Ruben Amaro	.25	.11	.03
☐ 44	Kevin Seitzer	.28	.13	.04
☐ 45	Dave Fleming	.20	.09	.03
☐ 46	Eric Fox	.25	.11	.03
☐ 47	Bob Scanlan	.25	.11	.03
☐ 48	Bert Blyleven	.28	.13	.04
☐ 49	Brian McRae	.25	.11	.03
☐ 50	Roberto Alomar	.20	.09	.03
☐ 51	Mo Vaughn	.28	.13	.04
☐ 52	Bobby Bonilla	.10	.05	.01
☐ 53	Frank Tanana	.25	.11	.03
☐ 54	Mike LaValliere	.25	.11	.03

☐	55 Mark McLemore	.25	.11	.03			
☐	56 Chad Mottola	.75	.35	.09			
☐	57 Norm Charlton	.28	.13	.04			
☐	58 José Melendez	.25	.11	.03			
☐	59 Carlos Martinez	.25	.11	.03			
☐	60 Roberto Kelly	.28	.13	.04			
☐	61 Gene Larkin	.25	.11	.03			
☐	62 Rafael Belliard	.25	.11	.03			
☐	63 Al Osuna	.25	.11	.03			
☐	64 Scott Chiamparino	.25	.11	.03			
☐	65 Brett Butler	.28	.13	.04			
☐	66 John Burkett	.25	.11	.03			
☐	67 Felix Jose	.28	.13	.04			
☐	68 Omar Vizquel	.25	.11	.03			
☐	69 John Vander Wal	.25	.11	.03			
☐	70 Roberto Hernandez	.25	.11	.03			
☐	71 Ricky Bones	.25	.11	.03			
☐	72 Jeff Grotewold	.25	.11	.03			
☐	73 Mike Moore	.25	.11	.03			
☐	74 Steve Buechele	.25	.11	.03			
☐	75 Juan Guzman	.30	.14	.04			
☐	76 Kevin Appier	.28	.13	.04			
☐	77 Junior Felix	.25	.11	.03			
☐	78 Greg W. Harris	.25	.11	.03			
☐	79 Dick Schofield	.25	.11	.03			
☐	80 Cecil Fielder	.12	.05	.02			
☐	81 Lloyd McClendon	.25	.11	.03			
☐	82 David Segui	.25	.11	.03			
☐	83 Reggie Sanders	.12	.05	.02			
☐	84 Kurt Stillwell	.25	.11	.03			
☐	85 Sandy Alomar	.28	.13	.04			
☐	86 John Habyan	.25	.11	.03			
☐	87 Kevin Reimer	.25	.11	.03			
☐	88 Mike Stanton	.25	.11	.03			
☐	89 Eric Anthony	.28	.13	.04			
☐	90 Scott Erickson	.28	.13	.04			
☐	91 Craig Colbert	.25	.11	.03			
☐	92 Tom Pagnozzi	.25	.11	.03			
☐	93 Pedro Astacio	.20	.09	.03			
☐	94 Lance Johnson	.25	.11	.03			
☐	95 Larry Walker	.12	.05	.02			
☐	96 Russ Swan	.25	.11	.03			
☐	97 Scott Fletcher	.25	.11	.03			
☐	98 Derek Jeter	.30	.14	.04			
☐	99 Mike Williams	.10	.05	.01			
☐	100 Mark McGwire	.15	.07	.02			
☐	101 Jim Bullinger	.25	.11	.03			
☐	102 Brian Hunter	.28	.13	.04			
☐	103 Jody Reed	.25	.11	.03			
☐	104 Mike Butcher	.25	.11	.03			
☐	105 Gregg Jefferies	.28	.13	.04			
☐	106 Howard Johnson	.28	.13	.04			
☐	107 John Kiely	.25	.11	.03			
☐	108 Jose Lind	.25	.11	.03			
☐	109 Sam Horn	.25	.11	.03			
☐	110 Barry Larkin	.10	.05	.01			
☐	111 Bruce Hurst	.28	.13	.04			
☐	112 Brian Barnes	.25	.11	.03			
☐	113 Thomas Howard	.25	.11	.03			
☐	114 Mel Hall	.25	.11	.03			
☐	115 Robby Thompson	.25	.11	.03			
☐	116 Mark Lemke	.25	.11	.03			
☐	117 Eddie Taubensee	.25	.11	.03			
☐	118 David Hulse	.12	.05	.02			
☐	119 Pedro Munoz	.28	.13	.04			
☐	120 Ramon Martinez	.28	.13	.04			
☐	121 Todd Worrell	.25	.11	.03			
☐	122 Joey Cora	.25	.11	.03			
☐	123 Moises Alou	.28	.13	.04			
☐	124 Franklin Stubbs	.25	.11	.03			
☐	125 Pete O'Brien	.25	.11	.03			
☐	126 Bob Ayrault	.08	.04	.01			
☐	127 Carney Lansford	.28	.13	.04			
☐	128 Kal Daniels	.25	.11	.03			
☐	129 Joe Grahe	.25	.11	.03			
☐	130 Jeff Montgomery	.25	.11	.03			
☐	131 Dave Winfield	.10	.05	.01			
☐	132 Preston Wilson	.40	.18	.05			
☐	133 Steve Wilson	.25	.11	.03			
☐	134 Lee Guetterman	.25	.11	.03			
☐	135 Mickey Tettleton	.28	.13	.04			
☐	136 Jeff King	.25	.11	.03			
☐	137 Alan Mills	.25	.11	.03			
☐	138 Joe Oliver	.25	.11	.03			
☐	139 Gary Gaetti	.25	.11	.03			
☐	140 Gary Sheffield	.15	.07	.02			
☐	141 Dennis Cook	.25	.11	.03			
☐	142 Charlie Hayes	.25	.11	.03			
☐	143 Jeff Huson	.25	.11	.03			
☐	144 Kent Mercker	.25	.11	.03			
☐	145 Eric Young	.12	.05	.02			
☐	146 Scott Leius	.25	.11	.03			
☐	147 Bryan Hickerson	.25	.11	.03			
☐	148 Steve Finley	.25	.11	.03			
☐	149 Rheal Cormier	.25	.11	.03			
☐	150 Frank Thomas	.75	.35	.09			
☐	151 Archi Cianfrocco	.25	.11	.03			
☐	152 Rich DeLucia	.25	.11	.03			
☐	153 Greg Vaughn	.28	.13	.04			
☐	154 Wes Chamberlain	.25	.11	.03			
☐	155 Dennis Eckersley	.10	.05	.01			
☐	156 Sammy Sosa	.25	.11	.03			
☐	157 Gary DiSarcina	.25	.11	.03			
☐	158 Kevin Koslofski	.25	.11	.03			
☐	159 Doug Linton	.10	.05	.01			
☐	160 Lou Whitaker	.28	.13	.04			
☐	161 Chad McConnell	.20	.09	.03			
☐	162 Joe Hesketh	.25	.11	.03			
☐	163 Tim Wakefield	.60	.25	.08			
☐	164 Leo Gomez	.28	.13	.04			
☐	165 Jose Rijo	.28	.13	.04			
☐	166 Tim Scott	.25	.11	.03			
☐	167 Steve Olin	.25	.11	.03			
☐	168 Kevin Maas	.28	.13	.04			

☐ 169	Kenny Rogers	.25	.11	.03
☐ 170	David Justice	.15	.07	.02
☐ 171	Doug Jones	.25	.11	.03
☐ 172	Jeff Reboulet	.08	.04	.01
☐ 173	Andres Galarraga	.25	.11	.03
☐ 174	Randy Velarde	.25	.11	.03
☐ 175	Kirk McCaskill	.25	.11	.03
☐ 176	Darren Lewis	.25	.11	.03
☐ 177	Lenny Harris	.25	.11	.03
☐ 178	Jeff Fassero	.25	.11	.03
☐ 179	Ken Griffey Jr.	.50	.23	.06
☐ 180	Darren Daulton	.28	.13	.04
☐ 181	John Jaha	.10	.05	.01
☐ 182	Ron Darling	.28	.13	.04
☐ 183	Greg Maddux	.10	.05	.01
☐ 184	Damion Easley	.15	.07	.02
☐ 185	Jack Morris	.10	.05	.01
☐ 186	Mike Magnante	.25	.11	.03
☐ 187	John Dopson	.25	.11	.03
☐ 188	Sid Fernandez	.28	.13	.04
☐ 189	Tony Phillips	.25	.11	.03
☐ 190	Doug Drabek	.28	.13	.04
☐ 191	Sean Lowe	.20	.09	.03
☐ 192	Bob Milacki	.25	.11	.03
☐ 193	Steve Foster	.25	.11	.03
☐ 194	Jerald Clark	.25	.11	.03
☐ 195	Pete Harnisch	.25	.11	.03
☐ 196	Pat Kelly	.28	.13	.04
☐ 197	Jeff Frye	.25	.11	.03
☐ 198	Alejandro Pena	.25	.11	.03
☐ 199	Junior Ortiz	.25	.11	.03
☐ 200	Kirby Puckett	.20	.09	.03
☐ 201	Jose Uribe	.25	.11	.03
☐ 202	Mike Scioscia	.25	.11	.03
☐ 203	Bernard Gilkey	.28	.13	.04
☐ 204	Dan Pasqua	.25	.11	.03
☐ 205	Gary Carter	.28	.13	.04
☐ 206	Henry Cotto	.25	.11	.03
☐ 207	Paul Molitor	.28	.13	.04
☐ 208	Mike Hartley	.25	.11	.03
☐ 209	Jeff Parrett	.25	.11	.03
☐ 210	Mark Langston	.28	.13	.04
☐ 211	Doug Dascenzo	.25	.11	.03
☐ 212	Rick Reed	.25	.11	.03
☐ 213	Candy Maldonado	.25	.11	.03
☐ 214	Danny Darwin	.25	.11	.03
☐ 215	Pat Howell	.10	.05	.01
☐ 216	Mark Leiter	.25	.11	.03
☐ 217	Kevin Mitchell	.28	.13	.04
☐ 218	Ben McDonald	.28	.13	.04
☐ 219	Bip Roberts	.28	.13	.04
☐ 220	Benny Santiago	.28	.13	.04
☐ 221	Carlos Baerga	.15	.07	.02
☐ 222	Bernie Williams	.28	.13	.04
☐ 223	Roger Pavlik	.10	.05	.01
☐ 224	Sid Bream	.25	.11	.03
☐ 225	Matt Williams	.28	.13	.04
☐ 226	Willie Banks	.28	.13	.04
☐ 227	Jeff Bagwell	.20	.09	.03
☐ 228	Tom Goodwin	.25	.11	.03
☐ 229	Mike Perez	.25	.11	.03
☐ 230	Carlton Fisk	.10	.05	.01
☐ 231	John Wetteland	.25	.11	.03
☐ 232	Tino Martinez	.28	.13	.04
☐ 233	Rick Greene	.15	.07	.02
☐ 234	Tim McIntosh	.25	.11	.03
☐ 235	Mitch Williams	.25	.11	.03
☐ 236	Kevin Campbell	.25	.11	.03
☐ 237	Jose Vizcaino	.25	.11	.03
☐ 238	Chris Donnels	.25	.11	.03
☐ 239	Mike Boddicker	.25	.11	.03
☐ 240	John Olerud	.10	.05	.01
☐ 241	Mike Gardiner	.25	.11	.03
☐ 242	Charlie O'Brien	.25	.11	.03
☐ 243	Rob Deer	.25	.11	.03
☐ 244	Denny Neagle	.25	.11	.03
☐ 245	Chris Sabo	.28	.13	.04
☐ 246	Gregg Olson	.28	.13	.04
☐ 247	Frank Seminara	.25	.11	.03
☐ 248	Scott Scudder	.25	.11	.03
☐ 249	Tim Burke	.25	.11	.03
☐ 250	Chuck Knoblauch	.15	.07	.02
☐ 251	Mike Bielecki	.25	.11	.03
☐ 252	Xavier Hernandez	.25	.11	.03
☐ 253	Jose Guzman	.25	.11	.03
☐ 254	Cory Snyder	.25	.11	.03
☐ 255	Orel Hershiser	.28	.13	.04
☐ 256	Wilfredo Cordero	.10	.05	.01
☐ 257	Luis Alicea	.25	.11	.03
☐ 258	Mike Schooler	.25	.11	.03
☐ 259	Craig Grebeck	.25	.11	.03
☐ 260	Duane Ward	.25	.11	.03
☐ 261	Bill Wegman	.25	.11	.03
☐ 262	Mickey Morandini	.25	.11	.03
☐ 263	Vince Horsman	.25	.11	.03
☐ 264	Paul Sorrento	.25	.11	.03
☐ 265	Andre Dawson	.10	.05	.01
☐ 266	Rene Gonzales	.25	.11	.03
☐ 267	Keith Miller	.25	.11	.03
☐ 268	Derek Bell	.28	.13	.04
☐ 269	Todd Steverson	.20	.09	.03
☐ 270	Frank Viola	.28	.13	.04
☐ 271	Wally Whitehurst	.25	.11	.03
☐ 272	Kurt Knudsen	.08	.04	.01
☐ 273	Dan Walters	.25	.11	.03
☐ 274	Rick Sutcliffe	.28	.13	.04
☐ 275	Andy Van Slyke	.28	.13	.04
☐ 276	Paul O'Neill	.28	.13	.04
☐ 277	Mark Whiten	.25	.11	.03
☐ 278	Chris Nabholz	.25	.11	.03
☐ 279	Todd Burns	.25	.11	.03
☐ 280	Tom Glavine	.12	.05	.02
☐ 281	Butch Henry	.25	.11	.03
☐ 282	Shane Mack	.28	.13	.04

☐ 283 Mike Jackson	.25	.11	.03
☐ 284 Henry Rodriguez	.28	.13	.04
☐ 285 Bob Tewksbury	.25	.11	.03
☐ 286 Ron Karkovice	.25	.11	.03
☐ 287 Mike Gallego	.25	.11	.03
☐ 288 Dave Cochrane	.25	.11	.03
☐ 289 Jesse Orosco	.25	.11	.03
☐ 290 Dave Stewart	.28	.13	.04
☐ 291 Tommy Greene	.25	.11	.03
☐ 292 Rey Sanchez	.25	.11	.03
☐ 293 Rob Ducey	.25	.11	.03
☐ 294 Brent Mayne	.25	.11	.03
☐ 295 Dave Stieb	.25	.11	.03
☐ 296 Luis Rivera	.25	.11	.03
☐ 297 Jeff Innis	.25	.11	.03
☐ 298 Scott Livingstone	.25	.11	.03
☐ 299 Bob Patterson	.25	.11	.03
☐ 300 Cal Ripken	.25	.11	.03
☐ 301 Cesar Hernandez	.08	.04	.01
☐ 302 Randy Myers	.25	.11	.03
☐ 303 Brook Jacoby	.25	.11	.03
☐ 304 Melido Perez	.25	.11	.03
☐ 305 Rafael Palmeiro	.28	.13	.04
☐ 306 Damon Berryhill	.25	.11	.03
☐ 307 Dan Serafini	.30	.14	.04
☐ 308 Darryl Kile	.25	.11	.03
☐ 309 J.T. Bruett	.10	.05	.01
☐ 310 Dave Righetti	.25	.11	.03
☐ 311 Jay Howell	.25	.11	.03
☐ 312 Geronimo Pena	.25	.11	.03
☐ 313 Greg Hibbard	.25	.11	.03
☐ 314 Mark Gardner	.25	.11	.03
☐ 315 Edgar Martinez	.28	.13	.04
☐ 316 Dave Nilsson	.10	.05	.01
☐ 317 Kyle Abbott	.25	.11	.03
☐ 318 Willie Wilson	.25	.11	.03
☐ 319 Paul Assenmacher	.25	.11	.03
☐ 320 Tim Fortugno	.25	.11	.03
☐ 321 Rusty Meacham	.25	.11	.03
☐ 322 Pat Borders	.25	.11	.03
☐ 323 Mike Greenwell	.28	.13	.04
☐ 324 Willie Randolph	.28	.13	.04
☐ 325 Bill Gullickson	.25	.11	.03
☐ 326 Gary Varsho	.25	.11	.03
☐ 327 Tim Hulett	.25	.11	.03
☐ 328 Scott Ruskin	.25	.11	.03
☐ 329 Mike Maddux	.25	.11	.03
☐ 330 Danny Tartabull	.28	.13	.04
☐ 331 Kenny Lofton	.20	.09	.03
☐ 332 Geno Petralli	.25	.11	.03
☐ 333 Otis Nixon	.25	.11	.03
☐ 334 Jason Kendall	.25	.11	.03
☐ 335 Mark Portugal	.25	.11	.03
☐ 336 Mike Pagliarulo	.25	.11	.03
☐ 337 Kirt Manwaring	.25	.11	.03
☐ 338 Bob Ojeda	.25	.11	.03
☐ 339 Mark Clark	.25	.11	.03
☐ 340 John Kruk	.28	.13	.04
☐ 341 Mel Rojas	.25	.11	.03
☐ 342 Erik Hanson	.25	.11	.03
☐ 343 Doug Henry	.25	.11	.03
☐ 344 Jack McDowell	.28	.13	.04
☐ 345 Harold Baines	.28	.13	.04
☐ 346 Chuck McElroy	.25	.11	.03
☐ 347 Luis Sojo	.25	.11	.03
☐ 348 Andy Stankiewicz	.28	.13	.04
☐ 349 Hipolito Pichardo	.25	.11	.03
☐ 350 Joe Carter	.12	.05	.02
☐ 351 Ellis Burks	.28	.13	.04
☐ 352 Pete Schourek	.28	.13	.04
☐ 353 Bubby Groom	.08	.04	.01
☐ 354 Jay Bell	.25	.11	.03
☐ 355 Brady Anderson	.28	.13	.04
☐ 356 Freddie Benavides	.25	.11	.03
☐ 357 Phil Stephenson	.25	.11	.03
☐ 358 Kevin Wickander	.25	.11	.03
☐ 359 Mike Stanley	.25	.11	.03
☐ 360 Ivan Rodriguez	.20	.09	.03
☐ 361 Scott Bankhead	.25	.11	.03
☐ 362 Luis Gonzalez	.28	.13	.04
☐ 363 John Smiley	.28	.13	.04
☐ 364 Trevor Wilson	.25	.11	.03
☐ 365 Tom Candiotti	.25	.11	.03
☐ 366 Craig Wilson	.25	.11	.03
☐ 367 Steve Sax	.28	.13	.04
☐ 368 Delino DeShields	.10	.05	.01
☐ 369 Jaime Navarro	.28	.13	.04
☐ 370 Dave Valle	.25	.11	.03
☐ 371 Mariano Duncan	.25	.11	.03
☐ 372 Rod Nichols	.25	.11	.03
☐ 373 Mike Morgan	.25	.11	.03
☐ 374 Julio Valera	.25	.11	.03
☐ 375 Wally Joyner	.28	.13	.04
☐ 376 Tom Henke	.28	.13	.04
☐ 377 Herm Winningham	.25	.11	.03
☐ 378 Orlando Merced	.25	.11	.03
☐ 379 Mike Munoz	.25	.11	.03
☐ 380 Todd Hundley	.25	.11	.03
☐ 381 Mike Flanagan	.25	.11	.03
☐ 382 Tim Belcher	.28	.13	.04
☐ 383 Jerry Browne	.25	.11	.03
☐ 384 Mike Benjamin	.25	.11	.03
☐ 385 Jim Leyritz	.25	.11	.03
☐ 386 Ray Lankford	.10	.05	.01
☐ 387 Devon White	.28	.13	.04
☐ 388 Jeremy Hernandez	.25	.11	.03
☐ 389 Brian Harper	.25	.11	.03
☐ 390 Wade Boggs	.12	.05	.02
☐ 391 Derrick May	.28	.13	.04
☐ 392 Travis Fryman	.20	.09	.03
☐ 393 Ron Gant	.08	.04	.01
☐ 394 Checklist 1-132	.25	.03	.01
☐ 395 Checklist 133-264	.25	.03	.01
☐ 396 Checklist 265-396	.25	.03	.01

1993 Topps Black Gold

Topps Black Gold cards 1-22 were randomly inserted in series I wax packs while card numbers 23-44 were featured in series II packs. Hobbyists could obtain the set by collecting individual random insert cards or receive 11, 22, or 44 Black Gold cards by mail when they sent in special "You've Just Won" cards, which were randomly inserted in packs. Series I packs featured three different "You've Just Won" cards, entitling the holder to receive Group A (cards 1-11), Group B (cards 12-22), or Groups A and B (Cards 1-22). In a similar fashion, four "You've Just Won" cards were inserted in series II packs and entitled the holder to receive Group C (23-33), Group D (34-44), Groups C and D (23-44), or Groups A-D (1-44). By returning the "You've Just Won" card with 1.50 for postage and handling, the collector received not only the Black Gold cards won but also a special "You've Just Won" card and a congratulatory letter informing the collector that his/her name had been entered into a drawing for one of 500 uncut sheets of all 44 Topps Black Gold cards in a leatherette frame. These standard-size (2 1/2" by 3 1/2") cards feature different color player photos than either the 1993 Topps regular issue or the Topps Gold issue. The player pictures are cut out and superimposed on a black gloss background. Inside white borders, gold refractory foil edges the top and bottom of the card face. On a black-and-gray pinstripe pattern inside white borders, the horizontal backs

have a a second cut out player photo and a player profile on a blue panel. The player's name appears in gold foil lettering on a blue-and-gray geometric shape. The cards are numbered on the back in the upper left corner.

	MT	EX-MT	VG
COMPLETE SET (22)	75.00	34.00	9.50
COMMON PLAYER (1-22)	3.00	1.35	.40
☐ 1 Barry Bonds	7.50	3.40	.95
☐ 2 Will Clark	7.50	3.40	.95
☐ 3 Darren Daulton	3.00	1.35	.40
☐ 4 Andre Dawson	4.50	2.00	.55
☐ 5 Delino DeShields	4.50	2.00	.55
☐ 6 Tom Glavine	6.00	2.70	.75
☐ 7 Marquis Grissom	4.50	2.00	.55
☐ 8 Tony Gwynn	6.00	2.70	.75
☐ 9 Eric Karros	10.00	4.50	1.25
☐ 10 Ray Lankford	4.50	2.00	.55
☐ 11 Barry Larkin	4.50	2.00	.55
☐ 12 Greg Maddux	4.50	2.00	.55
☐ 13 Fred McGriff	6.00	2.70	.75
☐ 14 Joe Oliver	3.00	1.35	.40
☐ 15 Terry Pendleton	4.00	1.80	.50
☐ 16 Bip Roberts	3.00	1.35	.40
☐ 17 Ryne Sandberg	10.00	4.50	1.25
☐ 18 Gary Sheffield	7.00	3.10	.85
☐ 19 Lee Smith	3.50	1.55	.45
☐ 20 Ozzie Smith	5.00	2.30	.60
☐ 21 Andy Van Slyke	4.00	1.80	.50
☐ 22 Larry Walker	5.00	2.30	.60
☐ A Winner A 1-11	35.00	16.00	4.40
☐ AB Winner A/B 1-22	70.00	32.00	8.75
☐ B Winner B 11-22	35.00	16.00	4.40

1991 Ultra

This 400-card standard size (2 1/2" by 3 1/2") set marked Fleer's first entry into the high-end premium card market. The set was released in wax packs and features the best players in the majors along with a good mix of young prospects. The cards feature full color action photography on the fronts and three full-color photos on the backs along with 1990 and career statistics. Fleer claimed in their original press release that there would only be 15 percent of Ultra issued as there was of the regular issue. Fleer also issued the sets in *their now traditional alphabetical order as well as the teams in alphabetical order. The card numbering is as follows, Atlanta Braves (1-13), Baltimore Orioles (14-26), Boston Red Sox (27-42), California Angels (43-54), Chicago Cubs (55-71), Chicago White Sox (72-86), Cincinnati Reds (87-103), Cleveland Indians (104-119), Detroit Tigers (120-130), Houston Astros (131-142), Kansas City Royals (143-158), Los Angeles Dodgers (159-171), Milwaukee Brewers (172-184), Minnesota Twins (185-196), Montreal Expos (197-210), New York Mets (211-227), New York Yankees (228-242), Oakland Athletics (243-257), Philadelphia Phillies (258-272), Pittsburgh Pirates (273-287), St. Louis Cardinals (288-299), San Diego Padres (300-313), San Francisco Giants (314-331), Seattle Mariners (332-345), Texas Rangers (346-357), Toronto Blue Jays (358-372), Major League Prospects (373-390), Elite Performance (391-396), and Checklists (397-400). The key Rookie Cards in this set are Wes Chamberlain, Eric Karros, Brian McRae, Pedro Munoz, and Phil Plantier.*

	MT	EX-MT	VG
COMPLETE SET (400)	25.00	11.50	3.10
COMMON PLAYER (1-400)	.07	.03	.01

		MT	EX-MT	VG
☐ 1	Steve Avery	.75	.35	.09
☐ 2	Jeff Blauser	.07	.03	.01
☐ 3	Francisco Cabrera	.07	.03	.01
☐ 4	Ron Gant	.30	.14	.04
☐ 5	Tom Glavine	.50	.23	.06
☐ 6	Tommy Gregg	.07	.03	.01
☐ 7	Dave Justice	1.50	.65	.19
☐ 8	Oddibe McDowell	.07	.03	.01
☐ 9	Greg Olson	.07	.03	.01
☐ 10	Terry Pendleton	.12	.05	.02
☐ 11	Lonnie Smith	.07	.03	.01

		MT	EX-MT	VG
☐ 12	John Smoltz	.30	.14	.04
☐ 13	Jeff Treadway	.07	.03	.01
☐ 14	Glenn Davis	.10	.05	.01
☐ 15	Mike Devereaux	.10	.05	.01
☐ 16	Leo Gomez	.60	.25	.08
☐ 17	Chris Hoiles	.25	.11	.03
☐ 18	Dave Johnson	.07	.03	.01
☐ 19	Ben McDonald	.20	.09	.03
☐ 20	Randy Milligan	.07	.03	.01
☐ 21	Gregg Olson	.10	.05	.01
☐ 22	Joe Orsulak	.07	.03	.01
☐ 23	Bill Ripken	.07	.03	.01
☐ 24	Cal Ripken	.75	.35	.09
☐ 25	David Segui	.07	.03	.01
☐ 26	Craig Worthington	.07	.03	.01
☐ 27	Wade Boggs	.30	.14	.04
☐ 28	Tom Bolton	.07	.03	.01
☐ 29	Tom Brunansky	.10	.05	.01
☐ 30	Ellis Burks	.10	.05	.01
☐ 31	Roger Clemens	.60	.25	.08
☐ 32	Mike Greenwell	.12	.05	.02
☐ 33	Greg A. Harris	.07	.03	.01
☐ 34	Daryl Irvine	.07	.03	.01
☐ 35	Mike Marshall UER	.07	.03	.01
	(1990 in stats is shown as 990)			
☐ 36	Tim Naehring	.12	.05	.02
☐ 37	Tony Pena	.07	.03	.01
☐ 38	Phil Plantier	1.25	.55	.16
☐ 39	Carlos Quintana	.07	.03	.01
☐ 40	Jeff Reardon	.12	.05	.02
☐ 41	Jody Reed	.07	.03	.01
☐ 42	Luis Rivera	.07	.03	.01
☐ 43	Jim Abbott	.30	.14	.04
☐ 44	Chuck Finley	.10	.05	.01
☐ 45	Bryan Harvey	.07	.03	.01
☐ 46	Donnie Hill	.07	.03	.01
☐ 47	Jack Howell	.07	.03	.01
☐ 48	Wally Joyner	.10	.05	.01
☐ 49	Mark Langston	.10	.05	.01
☐ 50	Kirk McCaskill	.07	.03	.01
☐ 51	Lance Parrish	.07	.03	.01
☐ 52	Dick Schofield	.07	.03	.01
☐ 53	Lee Stevens	.07	.03	.01
☐ 54	Dave Winfield	.20	.09	.03
☐ 55	George Bell	.10	.05	.01
☐ 56	Damon Berryhill	.07	.03	.01
☐ 57	Mike Bielecki	.07	.03	.01
☐ 58	Andre Dawson	.20	.09	.03
☐ 59	Shawon Dunston	.10	.05	.01
☐ 60	Joe Girardi UER	.07	.03	.01
	(Bats right, LH hitter shown is Doug Dascenzo)			
☐ 61	Mark Grace	.25	.11	.03
☐ 62	Mike Harkey	.10	.05	.01
☐ 63	Les Lancaster	.07	.03	.01
☐ 64	Greg Maddux	.25	.11	.03

	(See also 114)			
☐ 65	Derrick May	.10	.05	.01
☐ 66	Ryne Sandberg	.60	.25	.08
☐ 67	Luis Salazar	.07	.03	.01
☐ 68	Dwight Smith	.07	.03	.01
☐ 69	Hector Villanueva	.07	.03	.01
☐ 70	Jerome Walton	.07	.03	.01
☐ 71	Mitch Williams	.07	.03	.01
☐ 72	Carlton Fisk	.20	.09	.03
☐ 73	Scott Fletcher	.07	.03	.01
☐ 74	Ozzie Guillen	.07	.03	.01
☐ 75	Greg Hibbard	.07	.03	.01
☐ 76	Lance Johnson	.07	.03	.01
☐ 77	Steve Lyons	.07	.03	.01
☐ 78	Jack McDowell	.25	.11	.03
☐ 79	Dan Pasqua	.07	.03	.01
☐ 80	Melido Perez	.10	.05	.01
☐ 81	Tim Raines	.12	.05	.02
☐ 82	Sammy Sosa	.10	.05	.01
☐ 83	Cory Snyder	.07	.03	.01
☐ 84	Bobby Thigpen	.07	.03	.01
☐ 85	Frank Thomas	5.00	2.30	.60
	(Card says he is			
	an outfielder)			
☐ 86	Robin Ventura	.75	.35	.09
☐ 87	Todd Benzinger	.07	.03	.01
☐ 88	Glenn Braggs	.07	.03	.01
☐ 89	Tom Browning UER	.07	.03	.01
	(Front photo actually			
	Norm Charlton)			
☐ 90	Norm Charlton	.10	.05	.01
☐ 91	Eric Davis	.12	.05	.02
☐ 92	Rob Dibble	.10	.05	.01
☐ 93	Bill Doran	.07	.03	.01
☐ 94	Mariano Duncan UER	.07	.03	.01
	(Right back photo			
	is Billy Hatcher)			
☐ 95	Billy Hatcher	.07	.03	.01
☐ 96	Barry Larkin	.20	.09	.03
☐ 97	Randy Myers	.10	.05	.01
☐ 98	Hal Morris	.10	.05	.01
☐ 99	Joe Oliver	.07	.03	.01
☐ 100	Paul O'Neill	.10	.05	.01
☐ 101	Jeff Reed	.07	.03	.01
	(See also 104)			
☐ 102	Jose Rijo	.10	.05	.01
☐ 103	Chris Sabo	.10	.05	.01
	(See also 106)			
☐ 104	Beau Allred UER	.07	.03	.01
	(Card number is 101)			
☐ 105	Sandy Alomar Jr.	.10	.05	.01
☐ 106	Carlos Baerga UER	.50	.23	.06
	(Card number is 103)			
☐ 107	Albert Belle	.40	.18	.05
☐ 108	Jerry Browne	.07	.03	.01
☐ 109	Tom Candiotti	.07	.03	.01
☐ 110	Alex Cole	.07	.03	.01
☐ 111	John Farrell	.07	.03	.01
	(See also 114)			
☐ 112	Felix Fermin	.07	.03	.01
☐ 113	Brook Jacoby	.07	.03	.01
☐ 114	Chris James UER	.07	.03	.01
	(Card number is 111)			
☐ 115	Doug Jones	.07	.03	.01
☐ 116	Steve Olin	.10	.05	.01
	(See also 119)			
☐ 117	Greg Swindell	.10	.05	.01
☐ 118	Turner Ward	.12	.05	.02
☐ 119	Mitch Webster UER	.07	.03	.01
	(Card number is 116)			
☐ 120	Dave Bergman	.07	.03	.01
☐ 121	Cecil Fielder	.30	.14	.04
☐ 122	Travis Fryman	3.00	1.35	.40
☐ 123	Mike Henneman	.07	.03	.01
☐ 124	Lloyd Moseby	.07	.03	.01
☐ 125	Dan Petry	.07	.03	.01
☐ 126	Tony Phillips	.07	.03	.01
☐ 127	Mark Salas	.07	.03	.01
☐ 128	Frank Tanana	.07	.03	.01
☐ 129	Alan Trammell	.12	.05	.02
☐ 130	Lou Whitaker	.12	.05	.02
☐ 131	Eric Anthony	.12	.05	.02
☐ 132	Craig Biggio	.12	.05	.02
☐ 133	Ken Caminiti	.10	.05	.01
☐ 134	Casey Candaele	.07	.03	.01
☐ 135	Andujar Cedeno	.30	.14	.04
☐ 136	Mark Davidson	.07	.03	.01
☐ 137	Jim Deshaies	.07	.03	.01
☐ 138	Mark Portugal	.07	.03	.01
☐ 139	Rafael Ramirez	.07	.03	.01
☐ 140	Mike Scott	.07	.03	.01
☐ 141	Eric Yelding	.07	.03	.01
☐ 142	Gerald Young	.07	.03	.01
☐ 143	Kevin Appier	.10	.05	.01
☐ 144	George Brett	.20	.09	.03
☐ 145	Jeff Conine	.50	.23	.06
☐ 146	Jim Eisenreich	.07	.03	.01
☐ 147	Tom Gordon	.10	.05	.01
☐ 148	Mark Gubicza	.07	.03	.01
☐ 149	Bo Jackson	.25	.11	.03
☐ 150	Brent Mayne	.07	.03	.01
☐ 151	Mike Macfarlane	.07	.03	.01
☐ 152	Brian McRae	.50	.23	.06
☐ 153	Jeff Montgomery	.07	.03	.01
☐ 154	Bret Saberhagen	.10	.05	.01
☐ 155	Kevin Seitzer	.10	.05	.01
☐ 156	Terry Shumpert	.07	.03	.01
☐ 157	Kurt Stillwell	.07	.03	.01
☐ 158	Danny Tartabull	.12	.05	.02
☐ 159	Tim Belcher	.10	.05	.01
☐ 160	Kal Daniels	.07	.03	.01
☐ 161	Alfredo Griffin	.07	.03	.01
☐ 162	Lenny Harris	.07	.03	.01
☐ 163	Jay Howell	.07	.03	.01
☐ 164	Ramon Martinez	.12	.05	.02

☐	165	Mike Morgan	.07	.03	.01			
☐	166	Eddie Murray	.20	.09	.03			
☐	167	Jose Offerman	.12	.05	.02			
☐	168	Juan Samuel	.07	.03	.01			
☐	169	Mike Scioscia	.07	.03	.01			
☐	170	Mike Sharperson	.07	.03	.01			
☐	171	Darryl Strawberry	.30	.14	.04			
☐	172	Greg Brock	.07	.03	.01			
☐	173	Chuck Crim	.07	.03	.01			
☐	174	Jim Gantner	.07	.03	.01			
☐	175	Ted Higuera	.07	.03	.01			
☐	176	Mark Knudson	.07	.03	.01			
☐	177	Tim McIntosh	.07	.03	.01			
☐	178	Paul Molitor	.12	.05	.02			
☐	179	Dan Plesac	.07	.03	.01			
☐	180	Gary Sheffield	.90	.40	.11			
☐	181	Bill Spiers	.07	.03	.01			
☐	182	B.J. Surhoff	.07	.03	.01			
☐	183	Greg Vaughn	.12	.05	.02			
☐	184	Robin Yount	.25	.11	.03			
☐	185	Rick Aguilera	.10	.05	.01			
☐	186	Greg Gagne	.07	.03	.01			
☐	187	Dan Gladden	.07	.03	.01			
☐	188	Brian Harper	.07	.03	.01			
☐	189	Kent Hrbek	.10	.05	.01			
☐	190	Gene Larkin	.07	.03	.01			
☐	191	Shane Mack	.10	.05	.01			
☐	192	Pedro Munoz	.60	.25	.08			
☐	193	Al Newman	.07	.03	.01			
☐	194	Junior Ortiz	.07	.03	.01			
☐	195	Kirby Puckett	.60	.25	.08			
☐	196	Kevin Tapani	.10	.05	.01			
☐	197	Dennis Boyd	.07	.03	.01			
☐	198	Tim Burke	.07	.03	.01			
☐	199	Ivan Calderon	.07	.03	.01			
☐	200	Delino DeShields	.40	.18	.05			
☐	201	Mike Fitzgerald	.07	.03	.01			
☐	202	Steve Frey	.07	.03	.01			
☐	203	Andres Galarraga	.07	.03	.01			
☐	204	Marquis Grissom	.40	.18	.05			
☐	205	Dave Martinez	.07	.03	.01			
☐	206	Dennis Martinez	.10	.05	.01			
☐	207	Junior Noboa	.07	.03	.01			
☐	208	Spike Owen	.07	.03	.01			
☐	209	Scott Ruskin	.07	.03	.01			
☐	210	Tim Wallach	.10	.05	.01			
☐	211	Daryl Boston	.07	.03	.01			
☐	212	Vince Coleman	.10	.05	.01			
☐	213	David Cone	.15	.07	.02			
☐	214	Ron Darling	.10	.05	.01			
☐	215	Kevin Elster	.07	.03	.01			
☐	216	Sid Fernandez	.10	.05	.01			
☐	217	John Franco	.10	.05	.01			
☐	218	Dwight Gooden	.12	.05	.02			
☐	219	Tom Herr	.07	.03	.01			
☐	220	Todd Hundley	.07	.03	.01			
☐	221	Gregg Jefferies	.15	.07	.02			
☐	222	Howard Johnson	.10	.05	.01			
☐	223	Dave Magadan	.10	.05	.01			
☐	224	Kevin McReynolds	.10	.05	.01			
☐	225	Keith Miller	.07	.03	.01			
☐	226	Mackey Sasser	.07	.03	.01			
☐	227	Frank Viola	.10	.05	.01			
☐	228	Jesse Barfield	.07	.03	.01			
☐	229	Greg Cadaret	.07	.03	.01			
☐	230	Alvaro Espinoza	.07	.03	.01			
☐	231	Bob Geren	.07	.03	.01			
☐	232	Lee Guetterman	.07	.03	.01			
☐	233	Mel Hall	.07	.03	.01			
☐	234	Andy Hawkins UER (Back center photo is not him)	.07	.03	.01			
☐	235	Roberto Kelly	.12	.05	.02			
☐	236	Tim Leary	.07	.03	.01			
☐	237	Jim Leyritz	.07	.03	.01			
☐	238	Kevin Maas	.12	.05	.02			
☐	239	Don Mattingly	.30	.14	.04			
☐	240	Hensley Meulens	.10	.05	.01			
☐	241	Eric Plunk	.07	.03	.01			
☐	242	Steve Sax	.10	.05	.01			
☐	243	Todd Burns	.07	.03	.01			
☐	244	Jose Canseco	.50	.23	.06			
☐	245	Dennis Eckersley	.15	.07	.02			
☐	246	Mike Gallego	.07	.03	.01			
☐	247	Dave Henderson	.07	.03	.01			
☐	248	Rickey Henderson	.30	.14	.04			
☐	249	Rick Honeycutt	.07	.03	.01			
☐	250	Carney Lansford	.10	.05	.01			
☐	251	Mark McGwire	.50	.23	.06			
☐	252	Mike Moore	.07	.03	.01			
☐	253	Terry Steinbach	.10	.05	.01			
☐	254	Dave Stewart	.10	.05	.01			
☐	255	Walt Weiss	.07	.03	.01			
☐	256	Bob Welch	.07	.03	.01			
☐	257	Curt Young	.07	.03	.01			
☐	258	Wes Chamberlain	.50	.23	.06			
☐	259	Pat Combs	.07	.03	.01			
☐	260	Darren Daulton	.10	.05	.01			
☐	261	Jose DeJesus	.07	.03	.01			
☐	262	Len Dykstra	.10	.05	.01			
☐	263	Charlie Hayes	.07	.03	.01			
☐	264	Von Hayes	.07	.03	.01			
☐	265	Ken Howell	.07	.03	.01			
☐	266	John Kruk	.10	.05	.01			
☐	267	Roger McDowell	.07	.03	.01			
☐	268	Mickey Morandini	.20	.09	.03			
☐	269	Terry Mulholland	.07	.03	.01			
☐	270	Dale Murphy	.10	.05	.01			
☐	271	Randy Ready	.07	.03	.01			
☐	272	Dickie Thon	.07	.03	.01			
☐	273	Stan Belinda	.07	.03	.01			
☐	274	Jay Bell	.10	.05	.01			
☐	275	Barry Bonds	.50	.23	.06			
☐	276	Bobby Bonilla	.20	.09	.03			

☐ 277	Doug Drabek	.10	.05	.01
☐ 278	Carlos Garcia	.40	.18	.05
☐ 279	Neal Heaton	.07	.03	.01
☐ 280	Jeff King	.07	.03	.01
☐ 281	Bill Landrum	.07	.03	.01
☐ 282	Mike LaValliere	.07	.03	.01
☐ 283	Jose Lind	.07	.03	.01
☐ 284	Orlando Merced	.40	.18	.05
☐ 285	Gary Redus	.07	.03	.01
☐ 286	Don Slaught	.07	.03	.01
☐ 287	Andy Van Slyke	.15	.07	.02
☐ 288	Jose DeLeon	.07	.03	.01
☐ 289	Pedro Guerrero	.10	.05	.01
☐ 290	Ray Lankford	.75	.35	.09
☐ 291	Joe Magrane	.07	.03	.01
☐ 292	Jose Oquendo	.07	.03	.01
☐ 293	Tom Pagnozzi	.07	.03	.01
☐ 294	Bryn Smith	.07	.03	.01
☐ 295	Lee Smith	.10	.05	.01
☐ 296	Ozzie Smith UER	.20	.09	.03
	(Born 12-26, 54,			
	should have hyphen)			
☐ 297	Milt Thompson	.07	.03	.01
☐ 298	Craig Wilson	.12	.05	.02
☐ 299	Todd Zeile	.12	.05	.02
☐ 300	Shawn Abner	.07	.03	.01
☐ 301	Andy Benes	.15	.07	.02
☐ 302	Paul Faries	.07	.03	.01
☐ 303	Tony Gwynn	.30	.14	.04
☐ 304	Greg W. Harris	.07	.03	.01
☐ 305	Thomas Howard	.07	.03	.01
☐ 306	Bruce Hurst	.10	.05	.01
☐ 307	Craig Lefferts	.07	.03	.01
☐ 308	Fred McGriff	.30	.14	.04
☐ 309	Dennis Rasmussen	.07	.03	.01
☐ 310	Bip Roberts	.10	.05	.01
☐ 311	Benito Santiago	.10	.05	.01
☐ 312	Garry Templeton	.07	.03	.01
☐ 313	Ed Whitson	.07	.03	.01
☐ 314	Dave Anderson	.07	.03	.01
☐ 315	Kevin Bass	.07	.03	.01
☐ 316	Jeff Brantley	.07	.03	.01
☐ 317	John Burkett	.07	.03	.01
☐ 318	Will Clark	.50	.23	.06
☐ 319	Steve Decker	.30	.14	.04
☐ 320	Scott Garrelts	.07	.03	.01
☐ 321	Terry Kennedy	.07	.03	.01
☐ 322	Mark Leonard	.15	.07	.02
☐ 323	Darren Lewis	.20	.09	.03
☐ 324	Greg Litton	.07	.03	.01
☐ 325	Willie McGee	.10	.05	.01
☐ 326	Kevin Mitchell	.10	.05	.01
☐ 327	Don Robinson	.07	.03	.01
☐ 328	Andres Santana	.15	.07	.02
☐ 329	Robby Thompson	.07	.03	.01
☐ 330	Jose Uribe	.07	.03	.01
☐ 331	Matt Williams	.10	.05	.01

☐ 332	Scott Bradley	.07	.03	.01
☐ 333	Henry Cotto	.07	.03	.01
☐ 334	Alvin Davis	.07	.03	.01
☐ 335	Ken Griffey Sr.	.10	.05	.01
☐ 336	Ken Griffey Jr.	1.50	.65	.19
☐ 337	Erik Hanson	.07	.03	.01
☐ 338	Brian Holman	.07	.03	.01
☐ 339	Randy Johnson	.10	.05	.01
☐ 340	Edgar Martinez UER	.15	.07	.02
	(Listed as playing SS)			
☐ 341	Tino Martinez	.20	.09	.03
☐ 342	Pete O'Brien	.07	.03	.01
☐ 343	Harold Reynolds	.07	.03	.01
☐ 344	Dave Valle	.07	.03	.01
☐ 345	Omar Vizquel	.07	.03	.01
☐ 346	Brad Arnsberg	.07	.03	.01
☐ 347	Kevin Brown	.10	.05	.01
☐ 348	Julio Franco	.10	.05	.01
☐ 349	Jeff Huson	.07	.03	.01
☐ 350	Rafael Palmeiro	.15	.07	.02
☐ 351	Geno Petralli	.07	.03	.01
☐ 352	Gary Pettis	.07	.03	.01
☐ 353	Kenny Rogers	.07	.03	.01
☐ 354	Jeff Russell	.07	.03	.01
☐ 355	Nolan Ryan	1.25	.55	.16
☐ 356	Ruben Sierra	.40	.18	.05
☐ 357	Bobby Witt	.07	.03	.01
☐ 358	Roberto Alomar	.75	.35	.09
☐ 359	Pat Borders	.07	.03	.01
☐ 360	Joe Carter UER	.30	.14	.04
	(Reverse negative			
	on back photo)			
☐ 361	Kelly Gruber	.10	.05	.01
☐ 362	Tom Henke	.10	.05	.01
☐ 363	Glenallen Hill	.07	.03	.01
☐ 364	Jimmy Key	.07	.03	.01
☐ 365	Manny Lee	.07	.03	.01
☐ 366	Rance Mulliniks	.07	.03	.01
☐ 367	John Olerud UER	.40	.18	.05
	(Throwing left on card;			
	back has throws right)			
☐ 368	Dave Stieb	.07	.03	.01
☐ 369	Duane Ward	.07	.03	.01
☐ 370	David Wells	.07	.03	.01
☐ 371	Mark Whiten	.15	.07	.02
☐ 372	Mookie Wilson	.07	.03	.01
☐ 373	Willie Banks MLP	.50	.23	.06
☐ 374	Steve Carter MLP	.10	.05	.01
☐ 375	Scott Chiamparino MLP	.10	.05	.01
☐ 376	Steve Chitren MLP	.10	.05	.01
☐ 377	Darrin Fletcher MLP	.10	.05	.01
☐ 378	Rich Garces MLP	.15	.07	.02
☐ 379	Reggie Jefferson MLP	.35	.16	.04
☐ 380	Eric Karros MLP	4.00	1.80	.50
☐ 381	Pat Kelly MLP	.30	.14	.04
☐ 382	Chuck Knoblauch MLP	1.25	.55	.16
☐ 383	Denny Neagle MLP	.30	.14	.04

☐ 384 Dan Opperman MLP	.15	.07	.02
☐ 385 John Ramos MLP	.12	.05	.02
☐ 386 Henry Rodriguez MLP	.50	.23	.06
☐ 387 Maurice Vaughn MLP	.50	.23	.06
☐ 388 Gerald Williams MLP	.50	.23	.06
☐ 389 Mike York MLP	.10	.05	.01
☐ 390 Eddie Zosky MLP	.15	.07	.02
☐ 391 Barry Bonds EP	.15	.07	.02
☐ 392 Cecil Fielder EP	.15	.07	.02
☐ 393 Rickey Henderson EP	.15	.07	.02
☐ 394 Dave Justice EP	.35	.16	.04
☐ 395 Nolan Ryan EP	.50	.23	.06
☐ 396 Bobby Thigpen EP	.07	.03	.01
☐ 397 Checklist Card	.07	.01	.00
Gregg Jefferies			
☐ 398 Checklist Card	.07	.01	.00
Von Hayes			
☐ 399 Checklist Card	.07	.01	.00
Terry Kennedy			
☐ 400 Checklist Card	.15	.02	.00
Nolan Ryan			

1991 Ultra Update

The 1991 Fleer Ultra Baseball Update set contains 120 cards and 20 team logo stickers. The set includes the year's hottest rookies and important veteran players traded after the original Ultra series was produced. The cards measure the standard size (2 1/2" by 3 1/2"). The front has a color action shot, while the back has a portrait photo and two full-figure action shots. The cards are numbered (with a U prefix) and checklisted below alphabetically within and according to teams for each league as follow: Baltimore Orioles (1-4), Boston Red Sox (5-7), California Angels (8-12),

Chicago White Sox (13-18), Cleveland Indians (19-21), Detroit Tigers (22-24), Kansas City Royals (25-29), Milwaukee Brewers (30-33), Minnesota Twins (34-39), New York Yankees (40-44), Oakland Athletics (45-48), Seattle Mariners (49-53), Texas Rangers (54-58), Toronto Blue Jays (59-64), Atlanta Braves (65-69), Chicago Cubs (70-75), Cincinnati Reds (76-78), Houston Astros (79-84), Los Angeles Dodgers (85-89), Montreal Expos (90-93), New York Mets (94-97), Philadelphia Phillies (98-101), Pittsburgh Pirates (102-104), St. Louis Cardinals (105-109), San Diego Padres (110-114), and San Francisco Giants (115-119). The key Rookie Cards in this set are Jeff Bagwell, Juan Guzman, Mike Mussina, and Ivan Rodriguez.

	MT	EX-MT	VG
COMPLETE SET (120)	36.00	16.00	4.50
COMMON PLAYER (1-120)	.10	.05	.01

☐ 1 Dwight Evans	.15	.07	.02
☐ 2 Chito Martinez	.30	.14	.04
☐ 3 Bob Melvin	.10	.05	.01
☐ 4 Mike Mussina	10.00	4.50	1.25
☐ 5 Jack Clark	.15	.07	.02
☐ 6 Dana Kiecker	.10	.05	.01
☐ 7 Steve Lyons	.10	.05	.01
☐ 8 Gary Gaetti	.10	.05	.01
☐ 9 Dave Gallagher	.10	.05	.01
☐ 10 Dave Parker	.15	.07	.02
☐ 11 Luis Polonia	.15	.07	.02
☐ 12 Luis Sojo	.10	.05	.01
☐ 13 Wilson Alvarez	.40	.18	.05
☐ 14 Alex Fernandez	.40	.18	.05
☐ 15 Craig Grebeck	.10	.05	.01
☐ 16 Ron Karkovice	.10	.05	.01
☐ 17 Warren Newson	.20	.09	.03
☐ 18 Scott Radinsky	.10	.05	.01
☐ 19 Glenallen Hill	.10	.05	.01
☐ 20 Charles Nagy	1.50	.65	.19
☐ 21 Mark Whiten	.30	.14	.04
☐ 22 Milt Cuyler	.20	.09	.03
☐ 23 Paul Gibson	.10	.05	.01
☐ 24 Mickey Tettleton	.15	.07	.02
☐ 25 Todd Benzinger	.10	.05	.01
☐ 26 Storm Davis	.10	.05	.01
☐ 27 Kirk Gibson	.15	.07	.02
☐ 28 Bill Pecota	.10	.05	.01
☐ 29 Gary Thurman	.10	.05	.01
☐ 30 Darryl Hamilton	.15	.07	.02
☐ 31 Jaime Navarro	.60	.25	.08
☐ 32 Willie Randolph	.15	.07	.02
☐ 33 Bill Wegman	.10	.05	.01

☐ 34	Randy Bush	.10	.05	.01
☐ 35	Chili Davis	.15	.07	.02
☐ 36	Scott Erickson	.75	.35	.09
☐ 37	Chuck Knoblauch	3.00	1.35	.40
☐ 38	Scott Leius	.25	.11	.03
☐ 39	Jack Morris	.15	.07	.02
☐ 40	John Habyan	.10	.05	.01
☐ 41	Pat Kelly	.40	.18	.05
☐ 42	Matt Nokes	.10	.05	.01
☐ 43	Scott Sanderson	.10	.05	.01
☐ 44	Bernie Williams	1.00	.45	.13
☐ 45	Harold Baines	.15	.07	.02
☐ 46	Brook Jacoby	.10	.05	.01
☐ 47	Earnest Riles	.10	.05	.01
☐ 48	Willie Wilson	.10	.05	.01
☐ 49	Jay Buhner	.15	.07	.02
☐ 50	Rich DeLucia	.10	.05	.01
☐ 51	Mike Jackson	.10	.05	.01
☐ 52	Bill Krueger	.10	.05	.01
☐ 53	Bill Swift	.10	.05	.01
☐ 54	Brian Downing	.10	.05	.01
☐ 55	Juan Gonzalez	10.00	4.50	1.25
☐ 56	Dean Palmer	2.50	1.15	.30
☐ 57	Kevin Reimer	.35	.16	.04
☐ 58	Ivan Rodriguez	5.00	2.30	.60
☐ 59	Tom Candiotti	.10	.05	.01
☐ 60	Juan Guzman	11.00	4.90	1.40
☐ 61	Bob MacDonald	.15	.07	.02
☐ 62	Greg Myers	.10	.05	.01
☐ 63	Ed Sprague	.50	.23	.06
☐ 64	Devon White	.15	.07	.02
☐ 65	Rafael Belliard	.10	.05	.01
☐ 66	Juan Berenguer	.10	.05	.01
☐ 67	Brian Hunter	.90	.40	.11
☐ 68	Kent Mercker	.15	.07	.02
☐ 69	Otis Nixon	.15	.07	.02
☐ 70	Danny Jackson	.10	.05	.01
☐ 71	Chuck McElroy	.15	.07	.02
☐ 72	Gary Scott	.40	.18	.05
☐ 73	Heathcliff Slocumb	.10	.05	.01
☐ 74	Chico Walker	.10	.05	.01
☐ 75	Rick Wilkins	.20	.09	.03
☐ 76	Chris Hammond	.20	.09	.03
☐ 77	Luis Quinones	.10	.05	.01
☐ 78	Herm Winningham	.10	.05	.01
☐ 79	Jeff Bagwell	5.00	2.30	.60
☐ 80	Jim Corsi	.10	.05	.01
☐ 81	Steve Finley	.15	.07	.02
☐ 82	Luis Gonzalez	.75	.35	.09
☐ 83	Pete Harnisch	.15	.07	.02
☐ 84	Darryl Kile	.40	.18	.05
☐ 85	Brett Butler	.15	.07	.02
☐ 86	Gary Carter	.15	.07	.02
☐ 87	Tim Crews	.10	.05	.01
☐ 88	Orel Hershiser	.15	.07	.02
☐ 89	Bob Ojeda	.10	.05	.01
☐ 90	Bret Barberie	.50	.23	.06

☐ 91	Barry Jones	.10	.05	.01
☐ 92	Gilberto Reyes	.10	.05	.01
☐ 93	Larry Walker	1.75	.80	.22
☐ 94	Hubie Brooks	.10	.05	.01
☐ 95	Tim Burke	.10	.05	.01
☐ 96	Rick Cerone	.10	.05	.01
☐ 97	Jeff Innis	.10	.05	.01
☐ 98	Wally Backman	.10	.05	.01
☐ 99	Tommy Greene	.10	.05	.01
☐ 100	Ricky Jordan	.10	.05	.01
☐ 101	Mitch Williams	.10	.05	.01
☐ 102	John Smiley	.15	.07	.02
☐ 103	Randy Tomlin	.60	.25	.08
☐ 104	Gary Varsho	.10	.05	.01
☐ 105	Cris Carpenter	.10	.05	.01
☐ 106	Ken Hill	.15	.07	.02
☐ 107	Felix Jose	.25	.11	.03
☐ 108	Omar Olivares	.40	.18	.05
☐ 109	Gerald Perry	.10	.05	.01
☐ 110	Jerald Clark	.10	.05	.01
☐ 111	Tony Fernandez	.15	.07	.02
☐ 112	Darrin Jackson	.15	.07	.02
☐ 113	Mike Maddux	.10	.05	.01
☐ 114	Tim Teufel	.10	.05	.01
☐ 115	Bud Black	.10	.05	.01
☐ 116	Kelly Downs	.10	.05	.01
☐ 117	Mike Felder	.10	.05	.01
☐ 118	Willie McGee	.15	.07	.02
☐ 119	Trevor Wilson	.10	.05	.01
☐ 120	Checklist 1-120	.15	.02	.00

1992 Ultra

The 1992 Fleer Ultra set consists of two series each with 300 cards. The 1992 Fleer Ultra first series contained 300 cards, including a 21-card Ultra Rookies set. Randomly inserted into the packs were a

25-card Ultra Award Winners subset and a ten-card Tony Gwynn subset (Gwynn autographed more than 2,000 of his cards). The cards measure the standard size (2 1/2" by 3 1/2"). The glossy color action player photos on the fronts are full-bleed except at the bottom where a diagonal gold-foil stripe edges a green marbleized border. The player's name and team appear on the marble-colored area in bars that are color-coded by team. The horizontally oriented backs display an action and close-up cut-out player photo against a grid shaded with a gradated team color. The grid, team-colored bars containing stats and the player's name, biographical information, and the team logo all rest on a green marbleized background. The cards are numbered on the back and checklisted below alphabetically within and according to teams for each league as follows: Baltimore Orioles (1-11), Boston Red Sox (12-23), California Angels (24-31), Chicago White Sox (32-44), Cleveland Indians (45-55), Detroit Tigers (56-65), Kansas City Royals (66-77), Milwaukee Brewers (78-87), Minnesota Twins (88-98), New York Yankees (99-108), Oakland Athletics (109-119), Seattle Mariners (120-130), Texas Rangers (131-142), Toronto Blue Jays (143-156), Atlanta Braves (157-171), Chicago Cubs (172-184), Cincinnati Reds (185-197), Houston Astros (198-208), Los Angeles Dodgers (209-219), Montreal Expos (220-226), New York Mets (227-238), Philadelphia Phillies (239-249), Pittsburgh Pirates (250-262), St. Louis Cardinals (263-273), San Diego Padres (274-283), and San Francisco Giants (284-297). The most noteworthy Rookie Card in the first series is Rey Sanchez. The second series of the 1992 Fleer Ultra baseball set contains 300 cards, including traded players, free agents, and more than 50 Ultra Rookies. The foil packs featured two randomly inserted subsets: a ten-card "Ultra All-Rookie Team" and a 20-card "Ultra All-Star Team". The design is identical to that of the first series, with full-bleed color action player photos on the fronts bordered in marble at the bottom and horizontally oriented backs displaying an action and close-up cut-out player photo against a grid shaded with a gradated team color. The Ultra Rookie cards are identified by a Ultra Rookie gold-foil stamped logo. The cards are checklisted

below alphabetically within and according to teams for each league as follows: Baltimore Orioles (301-310), Boston Red Sox (311-320), California Angels (321-331), Chicago White Sox (332-343), Cleveland Indians (344-357), Detroit Tigers (358-368), Kansas City Royals (369-377), Milwaukee Brewers (378-392), Minnesota Twins (393-403), New York Yankees (404-417), Oakland Athletics (418-429), Seattle Mariners (430-436), Texas Rangers (437-447), Toronto Blue Jays (438-454), Atlanta Braves (455-465), Chicago Cubs (466-477), Cincinnati Reds (478-487), Houston Astros (488-498), Los Angeles Dodgers (499-510), Montreal Expos (511-526), New York Mets (527-539), Philadelphia Phillies (540-549), Pittsburgh Pirates (550-561), St. Louis Cardinals (562-574), San Diego Padres (575-585), and San Francisco Giants (586-597). Key Rookie Cards in the second series are Chad Curtis, Pat Listach, and Brian Williams. Some cards have been found without the word Fleer on the front.

		MT	EX-MT	VG
COMPLETE SET (600)		70.00	32.00	8.75
COMPLETE SERIES 1 (300)		40.00	18.00	5.00
COMPLETE SERIES 2 (300)		30.00	13.50	3.80
COMMON PLAYER (1-300)		.15	.07	.02
COMMON PLAYER (301-600)		.15	.07	.02
☐ 1 Glenn Davis	.20	.09	.03
☐ 2 Mike Devereaux	.20	.09	.03
☐ 3 Dwight Evans	.20	.09	.03
☐ 4 Leo Gomez	.50	.23	.06
☐ 5 Chris Hoiles	.25	.11	.03
☐ 6 Sam Horn	.15	.07	.02
☐ 7 Chito Martinez	.15	.07	.02
☐ 8 Randy Milligan	.15	.07	.02
☐ 9 Mike Mussina	3.50	1.55	.45
☐ 10 Billy Ripken	.15	.07	.02
☐ 11 Cal Ripken	1.50	.65	.19
☐ 12 Tom Brunansky	.20	.09	.03
☐ 13 Ellis Burks	.20	.09	.03
☐ 14 Jack Clark	.20	.09	.03
☐ 15 Roger Clemens	1.25	.55	.16
☐ 16 Mike Greenwell	.20	.09	.03
☐ 17 Joe Hesketh	.15	.07	.02
☐ 18 Tony Pena	.15	.07	.02
☐ 19 Carlos Quintana	.15	.07	.02
☐ 20 Jeff Reardon	.20	.09	.03
☐ 21 Jody Reed	.15	.07	.02
☐ 22 Luis Rivera	.15	.07	.02
☐ 23 Mo Vaughn	.25	.11	.03
☐ 24 Gary DiSarcina	.15	.07	.02

☐ 25	Chuck Finley	.15	.07	.02
☐ 26	Gary Gaetti	.15	.07	.02
☐ 27	Bryan Harvey	.15	.07	.02
☐ 28	Lance Parrish	.20	.09	.03
☐ 29	Luis Polonia	.20	.09	.03
☐ 30	Dick Schofield	.15	.07	.02
☐ 31	Luis Sojo	.15	.07	.02
☐ 32	Wilson Alvarez	.15	.07	.02
☐ 33	Carlton Fisk	.40	.18	.05
☐ 34	Craig Grebeck	.15	.07	.02
☐ 35	Ozzie Guillen	.15	.07	.02
☐ 36	Greg Hibbard	.15	.07	.02
☐ 37	Charlie Hough	.15	.07	.02
☐ 38	Lance Johnson	.15	.07	.02
☐ 39	Ron Karkovice	.15	.07	.02
☐ 40	Jack McDowell	.25	.11	.03
☐ 41	Donn Pall	.15	.07	.02
☐ 42	Melido Perez	.20	.09	.03
☐ 43	Tim Raines	.20	.09	.03
☐ 44	Frank Thomas	6.00	2.70	.75
☐ 45	Sandy Alomar Jr.	.20	.09	.03
☐ 46	Carlos Baerga	1.00	.45	.13
☐ 47	Albert Belle	.60	.25	.08
☐ 48	Jerry Browne UER	.15	.07	.02
	(Reversed negative on card back)			
☐ 49	Felix Fermin	.15	.07	.02
☐ 50	Reggie Jefferson UER	.40	.18	.05
	(Born 1968, not 1966)			
☐ 51	Mark Lewis	.20	.09	.03
☐ 52	Carlos Martinez	.15	.07	.02
☐ 53	Steve Olin	.15	.07	.02
☐ 54	Jim Thome	.50	.23	.06
☐ 55	Mark Whiten	.15	.07	.02
☐ 56	Dave Bergman	.15	.07	.02
☐ 57	Milt Cuyler	.15	.07	.02
☐ 58	Rob Deer	.20	.09	.03
☐ 59	Cecil Fielder	.60	.25	.08
☐ 60	Travis Fryman	2.00	.90	.25
☐ 61	Scott Livingstone	.40	.18	.05
☐ 62	Tony Phillips	.15	.07	.02
☐ 63	Mickey Tettleton	.20	.09	.03
☐ 64	Alan Trammell	.25	.11	.03
☐ 65	Lou Whitaker	.25	.11	.03
☐ 66	Kevin Appier	.20	.09	.03
☐ 67	Mike Boddicker	.15	.07	.02
☐ 68	George Brett	.50	.23	.06
☐ 69	Jim Eisenreich	.15	.07	.02
☐ 70	Mark Gubicza	.15	.07	.02
☐ 71	David Howard	.15	.07	.02
☐ 72	Joel Johnson	.15	.07	.02
☐ 73	Mike Macfarlane	.15	.07	.02
☐ 74	Brent Mayne	.15	.07	.02
☐ 75	Brian McRae	.20	.09	.03
☐ 76	Jeff Montgomery	.15	.07	.02
☐ 77	Danny Tartabull	.20	.09	.03
☐ 78	Don August	.15	.07	.02
☐ 79	Dante Bichette	.15	.07	.02
☐ 80	Ted Higuera	.15	.07	.02
☐ 81	Paul Molitor	.25	.11	.03
☐ 82	Jaime Navarro	.20	.09	.03
☐ 83	Gary Sheffield	1.50	.65	.19
☐ 84	Bill Spiers	.15	.07	.02
☐ 85	B.J. Surhoff	.15	.07	.02
☐ 86	Greg Vaughn	.20	.09	.03
☐ 87	Robin Yount	.50	.23	.06
☐ 88	Rick Aguilera	.20	.09	.03
☐ 89	Chili Davis	.20	.09	.03
☐ 90	Scott Erickson	.25	.11	.03
☐ 91	Brian Harper	.15	.07	.02
☐ 92	Kent Hrbek	.20	.09	.03
☐ 93	Chuck Knoblauch	1.00	.45	.13
☐ 94	Scott Leius	.15	.07	.02
☐ 95	Shane Mack	.20	.09	.03
☐ 96	Mike Pagliarulo	.15	.07	.02
☐ 97	Kirby Puckett	1.00	.45	.13
☐ 98	Kevin Tapani	.20	.09	.03
☐ 99	Jesse Barfield	.15	.07	.02
☐ 100	Alvaro Espinoza	.15	.07	.02
☐ 101	Mel Hall	.15	.07	.02
☐ 102	Pat Kelly	.20	.09	.03
☐ 103	Roberto Kelly	.20	.09	.03
☐ 104	Kevin Maas	.20	.09	.03
☐ 105	Don Mattingly	.60	.25	.08
☐ 106	Hensley Meulens	.15	.07	.02
☐ 107	Matt Nokes	.15	.07	.02
☐ 108	Steve Sax	.20	.09	.03
☐ 109	Harold Baines	.20	.09	.03
☐ 110	Jose Canseco	1.00	.45	.13
☐ 111	Ron Darling	.20	.09	.03
☐ 112	Mike Gallego	.15	.07	.02
☐ 113	Dave Henderson	.15	.07	.02
☐ 114	Rickey Henderson	.50	.23	.06
☐ 115	Mark McGwire	1.00	.45	.13
☐ 116	Terry Steinbach	.20	.09	.03
☐ 117	Dave Stewart	.20	.09	.03
☐ 118	Todd Van Poppel	.90	.40	.11
☐ 119	Bob Welch	.15	.07	.02
☐ 120	Greg Briley	.15	.07	.02
☐ 121	Jay Buhner	.20	.09	.03
☐ 122	Rick DeLucia	.15	.07	.02
☐ 123	Ken Griffey Jr.	4.00	1.80	.50
☐ 124	Erik Hanson	.15	.07	.02
☐ 125	Randy Johnson	.20	.09	.03
☐ 126	Edgar Martinez	.20	.09	.03
☐ 127	Tino Martinez	.20	.09	.03
☐ 128	Pete O'Brien	.15	.07	.02
☐ 129	Harold Reynolds	.15	.07	.02
☐ 130	Dave Valle	.15	.07	.02
☐ 131	Julio Franco	.20	.09	.03
☐ 132	Juan Gonzalez	2.50	1.15	.30
☐ 133	Jeff Huson	.15	.07	.02
	(Shows Jose Canseco sliding into second)			

☐ 134	Mike Jeffcoat	.15	.07	.02
☐ 135	Terry Mathews	.20	.09	.03
☐ 136	Rafael Palmeiro	.25	.11	.03
☐ 137	Dean Palmer	1.00	.45	.13
☐ 138	Geno Petralli	.15	.07	.02
☐ 139	Ivan Rodriguez	2.00	.90	.25
☐ 140	Jeff Russell	.15	.07	.02
☐ 141	Nolan Ryan	3.00	1.35	.40
☐ 142	Ruben Sierra	.75	.35	.09
☐ 143	Roberto Alomar	1.00	.45	.13
☐ 144	Pat Borders	.15	.07	.02
☐ 145	Joe Carter	.60	.25	.08
☐ 146	Kelly Gruber	.20	.09	.03
☐ 147	Jimmy Key	.15	.07	.02
☐ 148	Manny Lee	.15	.07	.02
☐ 149	Rance Mulliniks	.15	.07	.02
☐ 150	Greg Myers	.15	.07	.02
☐ 151	John Olerud	.50	.23	.06
☐ 152	Dave Stieb	.15	.07	.02
☐ 153	Todd Stottlemyre	.20	.09	.03
☐ 154	Duane Ward	.15	.07	.02
☐ 155	Devon White	.20	.09	.03
☐ 156	Eddie Zosky	.20	.09	.03
☐ 157	Steve Avery	.90	.40	.11
☐ 158	Rafael Belliard	.15	.07	.02
☐ 159	Jeff Blauser	.15	.07	.02
☐ 160	Sid Bream	.15	.07	.02
☐ 161	Ron Gant	.35	.16	.04
☐ 162	Tom Glavine	.60	.25	.08
☐ 163	Brian Hunter	.40	.18	.05
☐ 164	Dave Justice	1.50	.65	.19
☐ 165	Mark Lemke	.15	.07	.02
☐ 166	Greg Olson	.15	.07	.02
☐ 167	Terry Pendleton	.30	.14	.04
☐ 168	Lonnie Smith	.15	.07	.02
☐ 169	John Smoltz	.35	.16	.04
☐ 170	Mike Stanton	.15	.07	.02
☐ 171	Jeff Treadway	.15	.07	.02
☐ 172	Paul Assenmacher	.15	.07	.02
☐ 173	George Bell	.20	.09	.03
☐ 174	Shawon Dunston	.20	.09	.03
☐ 175	Mark Grace	.30	.14	.04
☐ 176	Danny Jackson	.15	.07	.02
☐ 177	Les Lancaster	.15	.07	.02
☐ 178	Greg Maddux	.30	.14	.04
☐ 179	Luis Salazar	.15	.07	.02
☐ 180	Rey Sanchez	.35	.16	.04
☐ 181	Ryne Sandberg	1.25	.55	.16
☐ 182	Jose Vizcaino	.15	.07	.02
☐ 183	Chico Walker	.15	.07	.02
☐ 184	Jerome Walton	.15	.07	.02
☐ 185	Glenn Braggs	.15	.07	.02
☐ 186	Tom Browning	.15	.07	.02
☐ 187	Rob Dibble	.20	.09	.03
☐ 188	Bill Doran	.15	.07	.02
☐ 189	Chris Hammond	.15	.07	.02
☐ 190	Billy Hatcher	.15	.07	.02
☐ 191	Barry Larkin	.35	.16	.04
☐ 192	Hal Morris	.20	.09	.03
☐ 193	Joe Oliver	.15	.07	.02
☐ 194	Paul O'Neill	.20	.09	.03
☐ 195	Jeff Reed	.15	.07	.02
☐ 196	Jose Rijo	.20	.09	.03
☐ 197	Chris Sabo	.20	.09	.03
☐ 198	Jeff Bagwell	1.50	.65	.19
☐ 199	Craig Biggio	.20	.09	.03
☐ 200	Ken Caminiti	.20	.09	.03
☐ 201	Andujar Cedeno	.20	.09	.03
☐ 202	Steve Finley	.20	.09	.03
☐ 203	Luis Gonzalez	.25	.11	.03
☐ 204	Pete Harnisch	.15	.07	.02
☐ 205	Xavier Hernandez	.15	.07	.02
☐ 206	Darryl Kile	.30	.14	.04
☐ 207	Al Osuna	.15	.07	.02
☐ 208	Curt Schilling	.20	.09	.03
☐ 209	Brett Butler	.20	.09	.03
☐ 210	Kal Daniels	.15	.07	.02
☐ 211	Lenny Harris	.15	.07	.02
☐ 212	Stan Javier	.15	.07	.02
☐ 213	Ramon Martinez	.25	.11	.03
☐ 214	Roger McDowell	.15	.07	.02
☐ 215	Jose Offerman	.20	.09	.03
☐ 216	Juan Samuel	.15	.07	.02
☐ 217	Mike Scioscia	.15	.07	.02
☐ 218	Mike Sharperson	.15	.07	.02
☐ 219	Darryl Strawberry	.60	.25	.08
☐ 220	Delino DeShields	.50	.23	.06
☐ 221	Tom Foley	.15	.07	.02
☐ 222	Steve Frey	.15	.07	.02
☐ 223	Dennis Martinez	.20	.09	.03
☐ 224	Spike Owen	.15	.07	.02
☐ 225	Gilberto Reyes	.15	.07	.02
☐ 226	Tim Wallach	.20	.09	.03
☐ 227	Daryl Boston	.15	.07	.02
☐ 228	Tim Burke	.15	.07	.02
☐ 229	Vince Coleman	.20	.09	.03
☐ 230	David Cone	.20	.09	.03
☐ 231	Kevin Elster	.15	.07	.02
☐ 232	Dwight Gooden	.20	.09	.03
☐ 233	Todd Hundley	.15	.07	.02
☐ 234	Jeff Innis	.15	.07	.02
☐ 235	Howard Johnson	.20	.09	.03
☐ 236	Dave Magadan	.20	.09	.03
☐ 237	Mackey Sasser	.15	.07	.02
☐ 238	Anthony Young	.30	.14	.04
☐ 239	Wes Chamberlain	.20	.09	.03
☐ 240	Darren Daulton	.20	.09	.03
☐ 241	Len Dykstra	.20	.09	.03
☐ 242	Tommy Greene	.15	.07	.02
☐ 243	Charlie Hayes	.15	.07	.02
☐ 244	Dave Hollins	.50	.23	.06
☐ 245	Ricky Jordan	.15	.07	.02
☐ 246	John Kruk	.20	.09	.03
☐ 247	Mickey Morandini	.20	.09	.03

☐ 248	Terry Mulholland	.15	.07	.02
☐ 249	Dale Murphy	.20	.09	.03
☐ 250	Jay Bell	.15	.07	.02
☐ 251	Barry Bonds	1.00	.45	.13
☐ 252	Steve Buechele	.15	.07	.02
☐ 253	Doug Drabek	.20	.09	.03
☐ 254	Mike LaValliere	.15	.07	.02
☐ 255	Jose Lind	.15	.07	.02
☐ 256	Lloyd McClendon	.15	.07	.02
☐ 257	Orlando Merced	.35	.16	.04
☐ 258	Don Slaught	.15	.07	.02
☐ 259	John Smiley	.20	.09	.03
☐ 260	Zane Smith	.15	.07	.02
☐ 261	Randy Tomlin	.25	.11	.03
☐ 262	Andy Van Slyke	.25	.11	.03
☐ 263	Pedro Guerrero	.20	.09	.03
☐ 264	Felix Jose	.20	.09	.03
☐ 265	Ray Lankford	.75	.35	.09
☐ 266	Omar Olivares	.15	.07	.02
☐ 267	Jose Oquendo	.15	.07	.02
☐ 268	Tom Pagnozzi	.15	.07	.02
☐ 269	Bryn Smith	.15	.07	.02
☐ 270	Lee Smith UER	.20	.09	.03
	(1991 record listed as 61-61)			
☐ 271	Ozzie Smith UER	.40	.18	.05
	(Comma before year of birth on card back)			
☐ 272	Milt Thompson	.15	.07	.02
☐ 273	Todd Zeile	.15	.07	.02
☐ 274	Andy Benes	.20	.09	.03
☐ 275	Jerald Clark	.15	.07	.02
☐ 276	Tony Fernandez	.20	.09	.03
☐ 277	Tony Gwynn	.60	.25	.08
☐ 278	Greg W. Harris	.15	.07	.02
☐ 279	Thomas Howard	.15	.07	.02
☐ 280	Bruce Hurst	.20	.09	.03
☐ 281	Mike Maddux	.15	.07	.02
☐ 282	Fred McGriff	.60	.25	.08
☐ 283	Benito Santiago	.20	.09	.03
☐ 284	Kevin Bass	.15	.07	.02
☐ 285	Jeff Brantley	.15	.07	.02
☐ 286	John Burkett	.15	.07	.02
☐ 287	Will Clark	1.00	.45	.13
☐ 288	Royce Clayton	.75	.35	.09
☐ 289	Steve Decker	.15	.07	.02
☐ 290	Kelly Downs	.15	.07	.02
☐ 291	Mike Felder	.15	.07	.02
☐ 292	Darren Lewis	.20	.09	.03
☐ 293	Kirt Manwaring	.15	.07	.02
☐ 294	Willie McGee	.20	.09	.03
☐ 295	Robby Thompson	.15	.07	.02
☐ 296	Matt Williams	.20	.09	.03
☐ 297	Trevor Wilson	.15	.07	.02
☐ 298	Checklist 1-100	.15	.02	.00
☐ 299	Checklist 101-200	.15	.02	.00
☐ 300	Checklist 201-300	.15	.02	.00
☐ 301	Brady Anderson	.20	.09	.03
☐ 302	Todd Frohwirth	.15	.07	.02
☐ 303	Ben McDonald	.30	.14	.04
☐ 304	Mark McLemore	.15	.07	.02
☐ 305	Jose Mesa	.15	.07	.02
☐ 306	Bob Milacki	.15	.07	.02
☐ 307	Gregg Olson	.20	.09	.03
☐ 308	David Segui	.15	.07	.02
☐ 309	Rick Sutcliffe	.20	.09	.03
☐ 310	Jeff Tackett	.20	.09	.03
☐ 311	Wade Boggs	.60	.25	.08
☐ 312	Scott Cooper	.50	.23	.06
☐ 313	John Flaherty	.25	.11	.03
☐ 314	Wayne Housie	.25	.11	.03
☐ 315	Peter Hoy	.25	.11	.03
☐ 316	John Marzano	.15	.07	.02
☐ 317	Tim Naehring	.20	.09	.03
☐ 318	Phil Plantier	.60	.25	.08
☐ 319	Frank Viola	.20	.09	.03
☐ 320	Matt Young	.15	.07	.02
☐ 321	Jim Abbott	.40	.18	.05
☐ 322	Hubie Brooks	.15	.07	.02
☐ 323	Chad Curtis	1.00	.45	.13
☐ 324	Alvin Davis	.15	.07	.02
☐ 325	Junior Felix	.15	.07	.02
☐ 326	Von Hayes	.15	.07	.02
☐ 327	Mark Langston	.20	.09	.03
☐ 328	Scott Lewis	.15	.07	.02
☐ 329	Don Robinson	.15	.07	.02
☐ 330	Bobby Rose	.15	.07	.02
☐ 331	Lee Stevens	.15	.07	.02
☐ 332	George Bell	.20	.09	.03
☐ 333	Esteban Beltre	.30	.14	.04
☐ 334	Joey Cora	.15	.07	.02
☐ 335	Alex Fernandez	.20	.09	.03
☐ 336	Roberto Hernandez	.40	.18	.05
☐ 337	Mike Huff	.15	.07	.02
☐ 338	Kirk McCaskill	.15	.07	.02
☐ 339	Dan Pasqua	.15	.07	.02
☐ 340	Scott Radinsky	.15	.07	.02
☐ 341	Steve Sax	.20	.09	.03
☐ 342	Bobby Thigpen	.15	.07	.02
☐ 343	Robin Ventura	1.00	.45	.13
☐ 344	Jack Armstrong	.15	.07	.02
☐ 345	Alex Cole	.15	.07	.02
☐ 346	Dennis Cook	.15	.07	.02
☐ 347	Glenallen Hill	.15	.07	.02
☐ 348	Thomas Howard	.15	.07	.02
☐ 349	Brook Jacoby	.15	.07	.02
☐ 350	Kenny Lofton	2.50	1.15	.30
☐ 351	Charles Nagy	.50	.23	.06
☐ 352	Rod Nichols	.15	.07	.02
☐ 353	Junior Ortiz	.15	.07	.02
☐ 354	Dave Otto	.15	.07	.02
☐ 355	Tony Perezchica	.15	.07	.02
☐ 356	Scott Scudder	.15	.07	.02
☐ 357	Paul Sorrento	.20	.09	.03

☐	358	Skeeter Barnes	15	.07	.02			
☐	359	Mark Carreon	15	.07	.02			
☐	360	John Doherty	40	.18	.05			
☐	361	Dan Gladden	15	.07	.02			
☐	362	Bill Gullickson	15	.07	.02			
☐	363	Shawn Hare	25	.11	.03			
☐	364	Mike Henneman	15	.07	.02			
☐	365	Chad Kreuter	15	.07	.02			
☐	366	Mark Leiter	15	.07	.02			
☐	367	Mike Munoz	15	.07	.02			
☐	368	Kevin Ritz	15	.07	.02			
☐	369	Mark Davis	15	.07	.02			
☐	370	Tom Gordon	15	.07	.02			
☐	371	Chris Gwynn	15	.07	.02			
☐	372	Gregg Jefferies	20	.09	.03			
☐	373	Wally Joyner	20	.09	.03			
☐	374	Kevin McReynolds	20	.09	.03			
☐	375	Keith Miller	15	.07	.02			
☐	376	Rico Rossy	20	.09	.03			
☐	377	Curtis Wilkerson	15	.07	.02			
☐	378	Ricky Bones	30	.14	.04			
☐	379	Chris Bosio	15	.07	.02			
☐	380	Cal Eldred	2.00	.90	.25			
☐	381	Scott Fletcher	15	.07	.02			
☐	382	Jim Gantner	15	.07	.02			
☐	383	Darryl Hamilton	20	.09	.03			
☐	384	Doug Henry	60	.25	.08			
☐	385	Pat Listach	4.00	1.80	.50			
☐	386	Tim McIntosh	15	.07	.02			
☐	387	Edwin Nunez	15	.07	.02			
☐	388	Dan Plesac	15	.07	.02			
☐	389	Kevin Seitzer	20	.09	.03			
☐	390	Franklin Stubbs	15	.07	.02			
☐	391	William Suero	20	.09	.03			
☐	392	Bill Wegman	15	.07	.02			
☐	393	Willie Banks	50	.23	.06			
☐	394	Jarvis Brown	20	.09	.03			
☐	395	Greg Gagne	15	.07	.02			
☐	396	Mark Guthrie	15	.07	.02			
☐	397	Bill Krueger	15	.07	.02			
☐	398	Pat Mahomes	75	.35	.09			
☐	399	Pedro Munoz	25	.11	.03			
☐	400	John Smiley	20	.09	.03			
☐	401	Gary Wayne	15	.07	.02			
☐	402	Lenny Webster	15	.07	.02			
☐	403	Carl Willis	15	.07	.02			
☐	404	Greg Cadaret	15	.07	.02			
☐	405	Steve Farr	15	.07	.02			
☐	406	Mike Gallego	15	.07	.02			
☐	407	Charlie Hayes	15	.07	.02			
☐	408	Steve Howe	15	.07	.02			
☐	409	Dion James	15	.07	.02			
☐	410	Jeff Johnson	15	.07	.02			
☐	411	Tim Leary	15	.07	.02			
☐	412	Jim Leyritz	15	.07	.02			
☐	413	Melido Perez	20	.09	.03			
☐	414	Scott Sanderson	15	.07	.02			
☐	415	Andy Stankiewicz	40	.18	.05			
☐	416	Mike Stanley	15	.07	.02			
☐	417	Danny Tartabull	25	.11	.03			
☐	418	Lance Blankenship	15	.07	.02			
☐	419	Mike Bordick	30	.14	.04			
☐	420	Scott Brosius	20	.09	.03			
☐	421	Dennis Eckersley	30	.14	.04			
☐	422	Scott Hemond	15	.07	.02			
☐	423	Carney Lansford	20	.09	.03			
☐	424	Henry Mercedes	30	.14	.04			
☐	425	Mike Moore	15	.07	.02			
☐	426	Gene Nelson	15	.07	.02			
☐	427	Randy Ready	15	.07	.02			
☐	428	Bruce Walton	15	.07	.02			
☐	429	Willie Wilson	15	.07	.02			
☐	430	Rich Amaral	20	.09	.03			
☐	431	Dave Cochrane	15	.07	.02			
☐	432	Henry Cotto	15	.07	.02			
☐	433	Calvin Jones	25	.11	.03			
☐	434	Kevin Mitchell	25	.11	.03			
☐	435	Clay Parker	15	.07	.02			
☐	436	Omar Vizquel	15	.07	.02			
☐	437	Floyd Bannister	15	.07	.02			
☐	438	Kevin Brown	20	.09	.03			
☐	439	John Cangelosi	15	.07	.02			
☐	440	Brian Downing	15	.07	.02			
☐	441	Monty Fariss	30	.14	.04			
☐	442	Jose Guzman	15	.07	.02			
☐	443	Donald Harris	15	.07	.02			
☐	444	Kevin Reimer	25	.11	.03			
☐	445	Kenny Rogers	15	.07	.02			
☐	446	Wayne Rosenthal	20	.09	.03			
☐	447	Dickie Thon	15	.07	.02			
☐	448	Derek Bell	60	.25	.08			
☐	449	Juan Guzman	3.50	1.55	.45			
☐	450	Tom Henke	20	.09	.03			
☐	451	Candy Maldonado	15	.07	.02			
☐	452	Jack Morris	25	.11	.03			
☐	453	David Wells	15	.07	.02			
☐	454	Dave Winfield	40	.18	.05			
☐	455	Juan Berenguer	15	.07	.02			
☐	456	Damon Berryhill	15	.07	.02			
☐	457	Mike Bielecki	15	.07	.02			
☐	458	Marvin Freeman	15	.07	.02			
☐	459	Charlie Leibrandt	15	.07	.02			
☐	460	Kent Mercker	15	.07	.02			
☐	461	Otis Nixon	20	.09	.03			
☐	462	Alejandro Pena	15	.07	.02			
☐	463	Ben Rivera	25	.11	.03			
☐	464	Deion Sanders	75	.35	.09			
☐	465	Mark Wohlers	40	.18	.05			
☐	466	Shawn Boskie	15	.07	.02			
☐	467	Frank Castillo	30	.14	.04			
☐	468	Andre Dawson	40	.18	.05			
☐	469	Joe Girardi	15	.07	.02			
☐	470	Chuck McElroy	15	.07	.02			
☐	471	Mike Morgan	15	.07	.02			

☐	472	Ken Patterson	.15	.07	.02			
☐	473	Bob Scanlan	.15	.07	.02			
☐	474	Gary Scott	.20	.09	.03			
☐	475	Dave Smith	.15	.07	.02			
☐	476	Sammy Sosa	.15	.07	.02			
☐	477	Hector Villanueva	.15	.07	.02			
☐	478	Scott Bankhead	.15	.07	.02			
☐	479	Tim Belcher	.20	.09	.03			
☐	480	Freddie Benavides	.15	.07	.02			
☐	481	Jacob Brumfield	.20	.09	.03			
☐	482	Norm Charlton	.20	.09	.03			
☐	483	Dwayne Henry	.15	.07	.02			
☐	484	Dave Martinez	.15	.07	.02			
☐	485	Bip Roberts	.20	.09	.03			
☐	486	Reggie Sanders	1.50	.65	.19			
☐	487	Greg Swindell	.20	.09	.03			
☐	488	Ryan Bowen	.30	.14	.04			
☐	489	Casey Candaele	.15	.07	.02			
☐	490	Juan Guerrero	.40	.18	.05			
☐	491	Pete Incaviglia	.15	.07	.02			
☐	492	Jeff Juden	.30	.14	.04			
☐	493	Rob Murphy	.15	.07	.02			
☐	494	Mark Portugal	.15	.07	.02			
☐	495	Rafael Ramirez	.15	.07	.02			
☐	496	Scott Servais	.15	.07	.02			
☐	497	Ed Taubensee	.40	.18	.05			
☐	498	Brian Williams	.75	.35	.09			
☐	499	Todd Benzinger	.15	.07	.02			
☐	500	John Candelaria	.15	.07	.02			
☐	501	Tom Candiotti	.15	.07	.02			
☐	502	Tim Crews	.15	.07	.02			
☐	503	Eric Davis	.25	.11	.03			
☐	504	Jim Gott	.15	.07	.02			
☐	505	Dave Hansen	.20	.09	.03			
☐	506	Carlos Hernandez	.15	.07	.02			
☐	507	Orel Hershiser	.25	.11	.03			
☐	508	Eric Karros	3.50	1.55	.45			
☐	509	Bob Ojeda	.15	.07	.02			
☐	510	Steve Wilson	.15	.07	.02			
☐	511	Moises Alou	.40	.18	.05			
☐	512	Bret Barberie	.20	.09	.03			
☐	513	Ivan Calderon	.15	.07	.02			
☐	514	Gary Carter	.20	.09	.03			
☐	515	Archi Cianfrocco	.50	.23	.06			
☐	516	Jeff Fassero	.15	.07	.02			
☐	517	Darrin Fletcher	.15	.07	.02			
☐	518	Marquis Grissom	.50	.23	.06			
☐	519	Chris Haney	.20	.09	.03			
☐	520	Ken Hill	.20	.09	.03			
☐	521	Chris Nabholz	.15	.07	.02			
☐	522	Bill Sampen	.15	.07	.02			
☐	523	John Vander Wal	.40	.18	.05			
☐	524	Dave Wainhouse	.15	.07	.02			
☐	525	Larry Walker	.75	.35	.09			
☐	526	John Wetteland	.15	.07	.02			
☐	527	Bobby Bonilla	.35	.16	.04			
☐	528	Sid Fernandez	.20	.09	.03			
☐	529	John Franco	.20	.09	.03			
☐	530	Dave Gallagher	.15	.07	.02			
☐	531	Paul Gibson	.15	.07	.02			
☐	532	Eddie Murray	.40	.18	.05			
☐	533	Junior Noboa	.15	.07	.02			
☐	534	Charlie O'Brien	.15	.07	.02			
☐	535	Bill Pecota	.15	.07	.02			
☐	536	Willie Randolph	.20	.09	.03			
☐	537	Bret Saberhagen	.25	.11	.03			
☐	538	Dick Schofield	.15	.07	.02			
☐	539	Pete Schourek	.20	.09	.03			
☐	540	Ruben Amaro	.20	.09	.03			
☐	541	Andy Ashby	.25	.11	.03			
☐	542	Kim Batiste	.30	.14	.04			
☐	543	Cliff Brantley	.20	.09	.03			
☐	544	Mariano Duncan	.15	.07	.02			
☐	545	Jeff Grotewold	.20	.09	.03			
☐	546	Barry Jones	.15	.07	.02			
☐	547	Julio Peguero	.20	.09	.03			
☐	548	Curt Schilling	.20	.09	.03			
☐	549	Mitch Williams	.15	.07	.02			
☐	550	Stan Belinda	.15	.07	.02			
☐	551	Scott Bullett	.30	.14	.04			
☐	552	Cecil Espy	.15	.07	.02			
☐	553	Jeff King	.15	.07	.02			
☐	554	Roger Mason	.15	.07	.02			
☐	555	Paul Miller	.30	.14	.04			
☐	556	Denny Neagle	.25	.11	.03			
☐	557	Vicente Palacios	.15	.07	.02			
☐	558	Bob Patterson	.15	.07	.02			
☐	559	Tom Prince	.15	.07	.02			
☐	560	Gary Redus	.15	.07	.02			
☐	561	Gary Varsho	.15	.07	.02			
☐	562	Juan Agosto	.15	.07	.02			
☐	563	Cris Carpenter	.15	.07	.02			
☐	564	Mark Clark	.30	.14	.04			
☐	565	Jose DeLeon	.15	.07	.02			
☐	566	Rich Gedman	.15	.07	.02			
☐	567	Bernard Gilkey	.20	.09	.03			
☐	568	Rex Hudler	.15	.07	.02			
☐	569	Tim Jones	.15	.07	.02			
☐	570	Donovan Osborne	1.25	.55	.16			
☐	571	Mike Perez	.20	.09	.03			
☐	572	Gerald Perry	.15	.07	.02			
☐	573	Bob Tewksbury	.20	.09	.03			
☐	574	Todd Worrell	.15	.07	.02			
☐	575	Dave Eiland	.15	.07	.02			
☐	576	Jeremy Hernandez	.25	.11	.03			
☐	577	Craig Lefferts	.15	.07	.02			
☐	578	Jose Melendez	.20	.09	.03			
☐	579	Randy Myers	.20	.09	.03			
☐	580	Gary Pettis	.15	.07	.02			
☐	581	Rich Rodriguez	.15	.07	.02			
☐	582	Gary Sheffield	1.50	.65	.19			
☐	583	Craig Shipley	.20	.09	.03			
☐	584	Kurt Stillwell	.15	.07	.02			
☐	585	Tim Teufel	.15	.07	.02			

☐ 586	Rod Beck	.40	.18	.05
☐ 587	Dave Burba	.15	.07	.02
☐ 588	Craig Colbert	.20	.09	.03
☐ 589	Bryan Hickerson	.20	.09	.03
☐ 590	Mike Jackson	.15	.07	.02
☐ 591	Mark Leonard	.15	.07	.02
☐ 592	Jim McNamara	.25	.11	.03
☐ 593	John Patterson	.40	.18	.05
☐ 594	Dave Righetti	.15	.07	.02
☐ 595	Cory Snyder	.15	.07	.02
☐ 596	Bill Swift	.15	.07	.02
☐ 597	Ted Wood	.30	.14	.04
☐ 598	Checklist 301-400	.15	.02	.00
☐ 599	Checklist 401-500	.15	.02	.00
☐ 600	Checklist 501-600	.15	.02	.00

	MT	EX-MT	VG
COMPLETE SET (10)	40.00	18.00	5.00
COMMON PLAYER (1-10)	2.00	.90	.25

☐ 1	Eric Karros	13.00	5.75	1.65
☐ 2	Andy Stankiewicz	2.50	1.15	.30
☐ 3	Gary DiSarcina	2.00	.90	.25
☐ 4	Archi Cianfrocco	3.00	1.35	.40
☐ 5	Jim McNamara	2.00	.90	.25
☐ 6	Chad Curtis	5.00	2.30	.60
☐ 7	Kenny Lofton	9.00	4.00	1.15
☐ 8	Reggie Sanders	6.00	2.70	.75
☐ 9	Pat Mahomes	4.00	1.80	.50
☐ 10	Donovan Osborne	5.00	2.30	.60

1992 Ultra All-Stars

1992 Ultra All-Rookies

This ten-card standard-size (2 1/2" by 3 1/2") set was randomly inserted in 1992 Fleer Ultra II foil packs. The fronts feature borderless color action player photos except at the bottom where they are edged by a marbleized black wedge. The words "All-Rookie Team" in gold foil lettering appear in a black marbleized inverted triangle at the lower right corner, with the player's name on a color banner. On a black marbleized background, the backs present a color headshot inside an inverted triangle and career summary on a gray marbleized panel. The cards are numbered on the back.

Featuring many of the season's current mega-stars, this 20-card standard-size (2 1/2" by 3 1/2") set was randomly inserted in 1992 Fleer Ultra II foil packs. The front design displays color action player photos enclosed by black marbleized borders. The word "All-Star" and the player's name are printed in gold foil lettering in the bottom border. On a gray marbleized background, the backs carry a color headshot (in a circular format) and a summary of the player's recent performance in on a pastel yellow panel. The cards are numbered on the back.

	MT	EX-MT	VG
COMPLETE SET (20)	75.00	34.00	9.50
COMMON PLAYER (1-20)	2.00	.90	.25

☐ 1	Mark McGwire	6.00	2.70	.75
☐ 2	Roberto Alomar	7.00	3.10	.85

		MT	EX-MT	VG
☐ 3	Cal Ripken Jr. 8.00		3.60	1.00
☐ 4	Wade Boggs 4.00		1.80	.50
☐ 5	Mickey Tettleton 2.00		.90	.25
☐ 6	Ken Griffey Jr. 10.00		4.50	1.25
☐ 7	Roberto Kelly 2.00		.90	.25
☐ 8	Kirby Puckett 6.00		2.70	.75
☐ 9	Frank Thomas 15.00		6.75	1.90
☐ 10	Jack McDowell 3.00		1.35	.40
☐ 11	Will Clark 6.00		2.70	.75
☐ 12	Ryne Sandberg 7.00		3.10	.85
☐ 13	Barry Larkin 3.00		1.35	.40
☐ 14	Gary Sheffield 6.00		2.70	.75
☐ 15	Tom Pagnozzi 2.00		.90	.25
☐ 16	Barry Bonds 6.00		2.70	.75
☐ 17	Deion Sanders 5.00		2.30	.60
☐ 18	Darryl Strawberry 4.00		1.80	.50
☐ 19	David Cone 2.50		1.15	.30
☐ 20	Tom Glavine................5.00		2.30	.60

1992 Ultra
Award Winners

This 25-card set features 18 Gold Glove winners, both Cy Young Award winners, both Rookies of the Year, both league MVP's, and the World Series MVP. The cards measure the standard size (2 1/2" by 3 1/2") and were randomly inserted in 1992 Fleer Ultra I packs. The fronts carry full-bleed color player photos that have a diagonal blue marbleized border at the bottom. The player's name appears in this bottom border, and a diamond-shaped gold foil seal signifying the award the player won is superimposed at the lower right corner. The backs also have blue marbleized borders and carry player profile on

a tan marbleized panel. A head shot of the player appears in a diamond at the upper right corner, with the words "Award Winners" on orange ribbons extending below the diamond. The cards are numbered on the back.

		MT	EX-MT	VG
COMPLETE SET (25) 100.00			45.00	12.50
COMMON PLAYER (1-25) 2.50			1.15	.30
☐ 1	Jack Morris 3.00		1.35	.40
☐ 2	Chuck Knoblauch 5.00		2.30	.60
☐ 3	Jeff Bagwell 7.00		3.10	.85
☐ 4	Terry Pendleton 3.50		1.55	.45
☐ 5	Cal Ripken.................10.00		4.50	1.25
☐ 6	Roger Clemens 8.00		3.60	1.00
☐ 7	Tom Glavine................6.00		2.70	.75
☐ 8	Tom Pagnozzi 2.50		1.15	.30
☐ 9	Ozzie Smith 4.00		1.80	.50
☐ 10	Andy Van Slyke 3.00		1.35	.40
☐ 11	Barry Bonds 7.00		3.10	.85
☐ 12	Tony Gwynn 5.00		2.30	.60
☐ 13	Matt Williams 3.00		1.35	.40
☐ 14	Will Clark 7.00		3.10	.85
☐ 15	Robin Ventura 7.00		3.10	.85
☐ 16	Mark Langston 2.50		1.15	.30
☐ 17	Tony Pena 2.50		1.15	.30
☐ 18	Devon White 2.50		1.15	.30
☐ 19	Don Mattingly 5.00		2.30	.60
☐ 20	Roberto Alomar 8.00		3.60	1.00
☐ 21A	Cal Ripken ERR 12.00		5.50	1.50
	(Reversed negative			
	on card back)			
☐ 21B	Cal Ripken COR 12.00		5.50	1.50
☐ 22	Ken Griffey Jr. 12.00		5.50	1.50
☐ 23	Kirby Puckett 7.00		3.10	.85
☐ 24	Greg Maddux 5.00		2.30	.60
☐ 25	Ryne Sandberg 8.00		3.60	1.00

1989 Upper Deck

This attractive 800-card set was introduced in 1989 as an additional fully licensed major card set. The cards feature full color on both the front and the back and are distinguished by the fact that each card has a hologram on the reverse, thus making the cards essentially copy proof. The cards measure standard size, 2 1/2" by 3 1/2". Cards 668-693 feature a

Orel Hershiser

Hayes, Gregg Olson, Jerome Walton, and Todd Zeile.

	MT	EX-MT	VG
COMPLETE SET (800)	140.00	65.00	17.50
COMPLETE FACT.SET (800)	150.00	70.00	19.00
COMPLETE LO SET (700)	130.00	57.50	16.50
COMPLETE HI SET (100)	13.00	5.75	1.65
COMPLETE HI FACT.SET (100)	13.00	5.75	1.65
COMMON PLAYER (1-700)	.10	.05	.01
COMMON PLAYER (701-800)	.10	.05	.01

"Collector's Choice" (CC) colorful drawing of a player (by artist Vernon Wells) on the card front and a checklist of that team on the card back. Cards 1-26 are designated "Rookie Stars" by Upper Deck. On many cards "Rookie" and team logos can be found with either a "TM" or (R). Cards with missing or duplicate holograms appear to be relatively common and hence there is little, if any, premium value on these "variations". The more significant variations involving changed photos or changed type are listed below. According to the company, the Murphy and Sheridan cards were corrected very early, after only two percent of the cards had been produced. This means, for example, that out of 1,000,000 Dale Murphy '89 Upper Deck cards produced, there are only 20,000 Murphy error cards. Similarly, the Sheffield was corrected after 15 percent had been printed; Varsho, Gallego, and Schroeder were corrected after 20 percent; and Holton, Manrique, and Winningham were corrected 30 percent of the way through. Collectors should also note that many dealers consider that Upper Deck's "planned" production of 1,000,000 of each player was increased (perhaps even doubled) later in the year due to the explosion in popularity of the Upper Deck cards. The key Rookie Cards in the low number series are Sandy Alomar Jr., Ken Griffey Jr., Felix Jose, Ramon Martinez, Gary Sheffield, and John Smoltz. The high number cards (701-800) were made available three different ways: as part of the 800-card factory set, as a separate boxed set of 100 cards in a custom blue box, and in special high number foil packs. The key Rookie Cards in the high number series are Jim Abbott, Norm Charlton, Junior Felix, Steve Finley, Erik Hanson, Pete Harnisch, Charlie

		MT	EX-MT	VG
☐	1 Ken Griffey Jr.	55.00	25.00	7.00
☐	2 Luis Medina	.12	.05	.02
☐	3 Tony Chance	.12	.05	.02
☐	4 Dave Otto	.12	.05	.02
☐	5 Sandy Alomar Jr. UER (Born 6/16/66, should be 6/18/66)	.60	.25	.08
☐	6 Rolando Roomes	.12	.05	.02
☐	7 Dave West	.15	.07	.02
☐	8 Cris Carpenter	.20	.09	.03
☐	9 Gregg Jefferies	.75	.35	.09
☐	10 Doug Dascenzo	.12	.05	.02
☐	11 Ron Jones	.12	.05	.02
☐	12 Luis De Los Santos	.12	.05	.02
☐	13A Gary Sheffield ERR (SS upside down on card front)	12.00	5.50	1.50
☐	13B Gary Sheffield COR	12.00	5.50	1.50
☐	14 Mike Harkey	.25	.11	.03
☐	15 Lance Blankenship	.20	.09	.03
☐	16 William Brennan	.12	.05	.02
☐	17 John Smoltz	4.00	1.80	.50
☐	18 Ramon Martinez	2.00	.90	.25
☐	19 Mark Lemke	.30	.14	.04
☐	20 Juan Bell	.15	.07	.02
☐	21 Rey Palacios	.12	.05	.02
☐	22 Felix Jose	2.00	.90	.25
☐	23 Van Snider	.12	.05	.02
☐	24 Dante Bichette	.50	.23	.06
☐	25 Randy Johnson	1.25	.55	.16
☐	26 Carlos Quintana	.20	.09	.03
☐	27 Star Rookie CL	.10	.01	.00
☐	28 Mike Schooler	.20	.09	.03
☐	29 Randy St.Claire	.10	.05	.01
☐	30 Jerald Clark	.35	.16	.04
☐	31 Kevin Gross	.10	.05	.01
☐	32 Dan Firova	.10	.05	.01
☐	33 Jeff Calhoun	.10	.05	.01
☐	34 Tommy Hinzo	.10	.05	.01
☐	35 Ricky Jordan	.20	.09	.03
☐	36 Larry Parrish	.10	.05	.01
☐	37 Bret Saberhagen UER (Hit total 931, should be 1031)	.12	.05	.02
☐	38 Mike Smithson	.10	.05	.01

☐ 39	Dave Dravecky................12	.05	.02
☐ 40	Ed Romero.....................10	.05	.01
☐ 41	Jeff Musselman...............10	.05	.01
☐ 42	Ed Hearn.......................10	.05	.01
☐ 43	Rance Mulliniks..............10	.05	.01
☐ 44	Jim Eisenreich................10	.05	.01
☐ 45	Sil Campusano...............10	.05	.01
☐ 46	Mike Krukow...................10	.05	.01
☐ 47	Paul Gibson....................10	.05	.01
☐ 48	Mike LaCoss...................10	.05	.01
☐ 49	Larry Herndon..................10	.05	.01
☐ 50	Scott Garrelts..................10	.05	.01
☐ 51	Dwayne Henry.................10	.05	.01
☐ 52	Jim Acker.......................10	.05	.01
☐ 53	Steve Sax......................12	.05	.02
☐ 54	Pete O'Brien...................10	.05	.01
☐ 55	Paul Runge.....................10	.05	.01
☐ 56	Rick Rhoden....................10	.05	.01
☐ 57	John Dopson...................10	.05	.01
☐ 58	Casey Candaele UER......10	.05	.01
	(No stats for Astros		
	for '88 season)		
☐ 59	Dave Righetti 10	.05	.01
☐ 60	Joe Hesketh...................10	.05	.01
☐ 61	Frank DiPino...................10	.05	.01
☐ 62	Tim Laudner...................10	.05	.01
☐ 63	Jamie Moyer...................10	.05	.01
☐ 64	Fred Toliver....................10	.05	.01
☐ 65	Mitch Webster.................10	.05	.01
☐ 66	John Tudor.....................10	.05	.01
☐ 67	John Cangelosi................10	.05	.01
☐ 68	Mike Devereaux...............60	.25	.08
☐ 69	Brian Fisher....................10	.05	.01
☐ 70	Mike Marshall..................10	.05	.01
☐ 71	Zane Smith 10	.05	.01
☐ 72A	Brian Holton ERR.........1.25	.55	.16
	(Photo actually		
	Shawn Hillegas)		
☐ 72B	Brian Holton COR 25	.11	.03
☐ 73	Jose Guzman 12	.05	.02
☐ 74	Rick Mahler....................10	.05	.01
☐ 75	John Shelby....................10	.05	.01
☐ 76	Jim Deshaies...................10	.05	.01
☐ 77	Bobby Meacham...............10	.05	.01
☐ 78	Bryn Smith.....................10	.05	.01
☐ 79	Joaquin Andujar...............10	.05	.01
☐ 80	Richard Dotson................10	.05	.01
☐ 81	Charlie Lea.....................10	.05	.01
☐ 82	Calvin Schiraldi...............10	.05	.01
☐ 83	Les Straker.....................10	.05	.01
☐ 84	Les Lancaster.................10	.05	.01
☐ 85	Allan Anderson................10	.05	.01
☐ 86	Junior Ortiz....................10	.05	.01
☐ 87	Jesse Orosco...................10	.05	.01
☐ 88	Felix Fermin...................10	.05	.01
☐ 89	Dave Anderson................10	.05	.01
☐ 90	Rafael Belliard UER..........10	.05	.01

	(Born '61, not '51)		
☐ 91	Franklin Stubbs...............10	.05	.01
☐ 92	Cecil Espy 10	.05	.01
☐ 93	Albert Hall.....................10	.05	.01
☐ 94	Tim Leary......................10	.05	.01
☐ 95	Mitch Williams.................12	.05	.02
☐ 96	Tracy Jones....................10	.05	.01
☐ 97	Danny Darwin..................10	.05	.01
☐ 98	Gary Ward......................10	.05	.01
☐ 99	Neal Heaton....................10	.05	.01
☐ 100	Jim Pankovits..................10	.05	.01
☐ 101	Bill Doran......................10	.05	.01
☐ 102	Tim Wallach...................12	.05	.02
☐ 103	Joe Magrane...................10	.05	.01
☐ 104	Ozzie Virgil....................10	.05	.01
☐ 105	Alvin Davis 10	.05	.01
☐ 106	Tom Brookens.................10	.05	.01
☐ 107	Shawon Dunston............12	.05	.02
☐ 108	Tracy Woodson...............10	.05	.01
☐ 109	Nelson Liriano.................10	.05	.01
☐ 110	Devon White UER...........12	.05	.02
	(Doubles total 46,		
	should be 56)		
☐ 111	Steve Balboni..................10	.05	.01
☐ 112	Buddy Bell.....................12	.05	.02
☐ 113	German Jimenez..............10	.05	.01
☐ 114	Ken Dayley.....................10	.05	.01
☐ 115	Andres Galarraga.............10	.05	.01
☐ 116	Mike Scioscia..................10	.05	.01
☐ 117	Gary Pettis.....................10	.05	.01
☐ 118	Ernie Whitt.....................10	.05	.01
☐ 119	Bob Boone.....................12	.05	.02
☐ 120	Ryne Sandberg...........1.50	.65	.19
☐ 121	Bruce Benedict................10	.05	.01
☐ 122	Hubie Brooks..................10	.05	.01
☐ 123	Mike Moore.....................10	.05	.01
☐ 124	Wallace Johnson..............10	.05	.01
☐ 125	Bob Horner.....................10	.05	.01
☐ 126	Chili Davis......................12	.05	.02
☐ 127	Manny Trillo...................10	.05	.01
☐ 128	Chet Lemon....................10	.05	.01
☐ 129	John Cerutti...................10	.05	.01
☐ 130	Orel Hershiser................12	.05	.02
☐ 131	Terry Pendleton..............40	.18	.05
☐ 132	Jeff Blauser....................12	.05	.02
☐ 133	Mike Fitzgerald................10	.05	.01
☐ 134	Henry Cotto....................10	.05	.01
☐ 135	Gerald Young..................10	.05	.01
☐ 136	Luis Salazar....................10	.05	.01
☐ 137	Alejandro Pena................10	.05	.01
☐ 138	Jack Howell....................10	.05	.01
☐ 139	Tony Fernandez...............10	.05	.02
☐ 140	Mark Grace.................1.50	.65	.19
☐ 141	Ken Caminiti...................12	.05	.02
☐ 142	Mike Jackson..................10	.05	.01
☐ 143	Larry McWilliams..............10	.05	.01
☐ 144	Andres Thomas................10	.05	.01

□	145	Nolan Ryan	4.00	1.80	.50
		(Triple exposure)			
□	146	Mike Davis	.10	.05	.01
□	147	DeWayne Buice	.10	.05	.01
□	148	Jody Davis	.10	.05	.01
□	149	Jesse Barfield	.10	.05	.01
□	150	Matt Nokes	.12	.05	.02
□	151	Jerry Reuss	.10	.05	.01
□	152	Rick Cerone	.10	.05	.01
□	153	Storm Davis	.10	.05	.01
□	154	Marvell Wynne	.10	.05	.01
□	155	Will Clark	1.50	.65	.19
□	156	Luis Aguayo	.10	.05	.01
□	157	Willie Upshaw	.10	.05	.01
□	158	Randy Bush	.10	.05	.01
□	159	Ron Darling	.12	.05	.02
□	160	Kal Daniels	.12	.05	.02
□	161	Spike Owen	.10	.05	.01
□	162	Luis Polonia	.12	.05	.02
□	163	Kevin Mitchell UER	.30	.14	.04
		('88/total HR's 18/52,			
		should be 19/53)			
□	164	Dave Gallagher	.10	.05	.01
□	165	Benito Santiago	.12	.05	.02
□	166	Greg Gagne	.10	.05	.01
□	167	Ken Phelps	.10	.05	.01
□	168	Sid Fernandez	.12	.05	.02
□	169	Bo Diaz	.10	.05	.01
□	170	Cory Snyder	.10	.05	.01
□	171	Eric Show	.10	.05	.01
□	172	Robby Thompson	.10	.05	.01
□	173	Marty Barrett	.10	.05	.01
□	174	Dave Henderson	.12	.05	.02
□	175	Ozzie Guillen	.10	.05	.01
□	176	Barry Lyons	.10	.05	.01
□	177	Kelvin Torve	.10	.05	.01
□	178	Don Slaught	.10	.05	.01
□	179	Steve Lombardozzi	.10	.05	.01
□	180	Chris Sabo	.60	.25	.08
□	181	Jose Uribe	.10	.05	.01
□	182	Shane Mack	.12	.05	.02
□	183	Ron Karkovice	.10	.05	.01
□	184	Todd Benzinger	.10	.05	.01
□	185	Dave Stewart	.12	.05	.02
□	186	Julio Franco	.12	.05	.02
□	187	Ron Robinson	.10	.05	.01
□	188	Wally Backman	.10	.05	.01
□	189	Randy Velarde	.10	.05	.01
□	190	Joe Carter	.90	.40	.11
□	191	Bob Welch	.12	.05	.02
□	192	Kelly Paris	.10	.05	.01
□	193	Chris Brown	.10	.05	.01
□	194	Rick Reuschel	.10	.05	.01
□	195	Roger Clemens	1.50	.65	.19
□	196	Dave Concepcion	.12	.05	.02
□	197	Al Newman	.10	.05	.01
□	198	Brook Jacoby	.10	.05	.01

□	199	Mookie Wilson	.12	.05	.02
□	200	Don Mattingly	.90	.40	.11
□	201	Dick Schofield	.10	.05	.01
□	202	Mark Gubicza	.10	.05	.01
□	203	Gary Gaetti	.10	.05	.01
□	204	Dan Pasqua	.10	.05	.01
□	205	Andre Dawson	.50	.23	.06
□	206	Chris Speier	.10	.05	.01
□	207	Kent Tekulve	.10	.05	.01
□	208	Rod Scurry	.10	.05	.01
□	209	Scott Bailes	.10	.05	.01
□	210	Rickey Henderson UER	.90	.40	.11
		(Throws Right)			
□	211	Harold Baines	.12	.05	.02
□	212	Tony Armas	.10	.05	.01
□	213	Kent Hrbek	.12	.05	.02
□	214	Darrin Jackson	.30	.14	.04
□	215	George Brett	.75	.35	.09
□	216	Rafael Santana	.10	.05	.01
□	217	Andy Allanson	.10	.05	.01
□	218	Brett Butler	.12	.05	.02
□	219	Steve Jeltz	.10	.05	.01
□	220	Jay Buhner	.35	.16	.04
□	221	Bo Jackson	.60	.25	.08
□	222	Angel Salazar	.10	.05	.01
□	223	Kirk McCaskill	.10	.05	.01
□	224	Steve Lyons	.10	.05	.01
□	225	Bert Blyleven	.12	.05	.02
□	226	Scott Bradley	.10	.05	.01
□	227	Bob Melvin	.10	.05	.01
□	228	Ron Kittle	.10	.05	.01
□	229	Phil Bradley	.10	.05	.01
□	230	Tommy John	.12	.05	.02
□	231	Greg Walker	.10	.05	.01
□	232	Juan Berenguer	.10	.05	.01
□	233	Pat Tabler	.10	.05	.01
□	234	Terry Clark	.10	.05	.01
□	235	Rafael Palmeiro	.75	.35	.09
□	236	Paul Zuvella	.10	.05	.01
□	237	Willie Randolph	.12	.05	.02
□	238	Bruce Fields	.10	.05	.01
□	239	Mike Aldrete	.10	.05	.01
□	240	Lance Parrish	.12	.05	.02
□	241	Greg Maddux	1.00	.45	.13
□	242	John Moses	.10	.05	.01
□	243	Melido Perez	.35	.16	.04
□	244	Willie Wilson	.10	.05	.01
□	245	Mark McLemore	.10	.05	.01
□	246	Von Hayes	.10	.05	.01
□	247	Matt Williams	.60	.25	.08
□	248	John Candelaria UER	.10	.05	.01
		(Listed as Yankee for			
		part of '87,			
		should be Mets)			
□	249	Harold Reynolds	.10	.05	.01
□	250	Greg Swindell	.12	.05	.02
□	251	Juan Agosto	.10	.05	.01

☐ 252	Mike Felder	10	.05	.01
☐ 253	Vince Coleman	12	.05	.02
☐ 254	Larry Sheets	10	.05	.01
☐ 255	George Bell	40	.18	.05
☐ 256	Terry Steinbach	12	.05	.02
☐ 257	Jack Armstrong	30	.14	.04
☐ 258	Dickie Thon	10	.05	.01
☐ 259	Ray Knight	12	.05	.02
☐ 260	Darryl Strawberry	90	.40	.11
☐ 261	Doug Sisk	10	.05	.01
☐ 262	Alex Trevino	10	.05	.01
☐ 263	Jeffrey Leonard	10	.05	.01
☐ 264	Tom Henke	12	.05	.02
☐ 265	Ozzie Smith	50	.23	.06
☐ 266	Dave Bergman	10	.05	.01
☐ 267	Tony Phillips	10	.05	.01
☐ 268	Mark Davis	10	.05	.01
☐ 269	Kevin Elster	10	.05	.01
☐ 270	Barry Larkin	60	.25	.08
☐ 271	Manny Lee	10	.05	.01
☐ 272	Tom Brunansky	12	.05	.02
☐ 273	Craig Biggio	1.25	.55	.16
☐ 274	Jim Gantner	10	.05	.01
☐ 275	Eddie Murray	50	.23	.06
☐ 276	Jeff Reed	10	.05	.01
☐ 277	Tim Teufel	10	.05	.01
☐ 278	Rick Honeycutt	10	.05	.01
☐ 279	Guillermo Hernandez	10	.05	.01
☐ 280	John Kruk	15	.07	.02
☐ 281	Luis Alicea	15	.07	.02
☐ 282	Jim Clancy	10	.05	.01
☐ 283	Billy Ripken	10	.05	.01
☐ 284	Craig Reynolds	10	.05	.01
☐ 285	Robin Yount	75	.35	.09
☐ 286	Jimmy Jones	10	.05	.01
☐ 287	Ron Oester	10	.05	.01
☐ 288	Terry Leach	10	.05	.01
☐ 289	Dennis Eckersley	35	.16	.04
☐ 290	Alan Trammell	12	.05	.02
☐ 291	Jimmy Key	12	.05	.02
☐ 292	Chris Bosio	10	.05	.01
☐ 293	Jose DeLeon	10	.05	.01
☐ 294	Jim Traber	10	.05	.01
☐ 295	Mike Scott	10	.05	.01
☐ 296	Roger McDowell	10	.05	.01
☐ 297	Garry Templeton	10	.05	.01
☐ 298	Doyle Alexander	10	.05	.01
☐ 299	Nick Esasky	10	.05	.01
☐ 300	Mark McGwire UER	1.50	.65	.19
	(Doubles total 52,			
	should be 51)			
☐ 301	Darryl Hamilton	40	.18	.05
☐ 302	Dave Smith	10	.05	.01
☐ 303	Rick Sutcliffe	12	.05	.02
☐ 304	Dave Stapleton	10	.05	.01
☐ 305	Alan Ashby	10	.05	.01
☐ 306	Pedro Guerrero	12	.05	.02
☐ 307	Ron Guidry	12	.05	.02
☐ 308	Steve Farr	10	.05	.01
☐ 309	Curt Ford	10	.05	.01
☐ 310	Claudell Washington	10	.05	.01
☐ 311	Tom Prince	10	.05	.01
☐ 312	Chad Kreuter	10	.05	.01
☐ 313	Ken Oberkfell	10	.05	.01
☐ 314	Jerry Browne	10	.05	.01
☐ 315	R.J. Reynolds	10	.05	.01
☐ 316	Scott Bankhead	10	.05	.01
☐ 317	Milt Thompson	10	.05	.01
☐ 318	Mario Diaz	10	.05	.01
☐ 319	Bruce Ruffin	10	.05	.01
☐ 320	Dave Valle	10	.05	.01
☐ 321A	Gary Varsho ERR	2.00	.90	.25
	(Back photo actually			
	Mike Bielecki bunting)			
☐ 321B	Gary Varsho COR	10	.05	.01
	(In road uniform)			
☐ 322	Paul Mirabella	10	.05	.01
☐ 323	Chuck Jackson	10	.05	.01
☐ 324	Drew Hall	10	.05	.01
☐ 325	Don August	10	.05	.01
☐ 326	Israel Sanchez	10	.05	.01
☐ 327	Denny Walling	10	.05	.01
☐ 328	Joel Skinner	10	.05	.01
☐ 329	Danny Tartabull	40	.18	.05
☐ 330	Tony Pena	10	.05	.01
☐ 331	Jim Sundberg	10	.05	.01
☐ 332	Jeff D. Robinson	10	.05	.01
☐ 333	Oddibe McDowell	10	.05	.01
☐ 334	Jose Lind	10	.05	.01
☐ 335	Paul Kilgus	10	.05	.01
☐ 336	Juan Samuel	10	.05	.01
☐ 337	Mike Campbell	10	.05	.01
☐ 338	Mike Maddux	10	.05	.01
☐ 339	Darnell Coles	10	.05	.01
☐ 340	Bob Dernier	10	.05	.01
☐ 341	Rafael Ramirez	10	.05	.01
☐ 342	Scott Sanderson	10	.05	.01
☐ 343	B.J. Surhoff	10	.05	.01
☐ 344	Billy Hatcher	10	.05	.01
☐ 345	Pat Perry	10	.05	.01
☐ 346	Jack Clark	12	.05	.02
☐ 347	Gary Thurman	10	.05	.01
☐ 348	Tim Jones	10	.05	.01
☐ 349	Dave Winfield	75	.35	.09
☐ 350	Frank White	10	.05	.01
☐ 351	Dave Collins	10	.05	.01
☐ 352	Jack Morris	40	.18	.05
☐ 353	Eric Plunk	10	.05	.01
☐ 354	Leon Durham	10	.05	.01
☐ 355	Ivan DeJesus	10	.05	.01
☐ 356	Brian Holman	25	.11	.03
☐ 357A	Dale Murphy ERR	50.00	23.00	6.25
	(Front has			
	reverse negative)			

☐ 357B Dale Murphy COR	.40	.18	.05
☐ 358 Mark Portugal	.10	.05	.01
☐ 359 Andy McGaffigan	.10	.05	.01
☐ 360 Tom Glavine	2.00	.90	.25
☐ 361 Keith Moreland	.10	.05	.01
☐ 362 Todd Stottlemyre	.30	.14	.04
☐ 363 Dave Leiper	.10	.05	.01
☐ 364 Cecil Fielder	.90	.40	.11
☐ 365 Carmelo Martinez	.10	.05	.01
☐ 366 Dwight Evans	.12	.05	.02
☐ 367 Kevin McReynolds	.12	.05	.02
☐ 368 Rich Gedman	.10	.05	.01
☐ 369 Len Dykstra	.12	.05	.02
☐ 370 Jody Reed	.10	.05	.01
☐ 371 Jose Canseco UER	1.50	.65	.19
(Strikeout total 391, should be 491)			
☐ 372 Rob Murphy	.10	.05	.01
☐ 373 Mike Henneman	.12	.05	.02
☐ 374 Walt Weiss	.12	.05	.02
☐ 375 Rob Dibble	.50	.23	.06
☐ 376 Kirby Puckett	1.50	.65	.19
(Mark McGwire in background)			
☐ 377 Dennis Martinez	.12	.05	.02
☐ 378 Ron Gant	1.75	.80	.22
☐ 379 Brian Harper	.12	.05	.02
☐ 380 Nelson Santovenia	.10	.05	.01
☐ 381 Lloyd Moseby	.10	.05	.01
☐ 382 Lance McCullers	.10	.05	.01
☐ 383 Dave Stieb	.12	.05	.02
☐ 384 Tony Gwynn	.90	.40	.11
☐ 385 Mike Flanagan	.10	.05	.01
☐ 386 Bob Ojeda	.10	.05	.01
☐ 387 Bruce Hurst	.12	.05	.02
☐ 388 Dave Magadan	.12	.05	.02
☐ 389 Wade Boggs	.75	.35	.09
☐ 390 Gary Carter	.12	.05	.02
☐ 391 Frank Tanana	.10	.05	.01
☐ 392 Curt Young	.10	.05	.01
☐ 393 Jeff Treadway	.10	.05	.01
☐ 394 Darrell Evans	.12	.05	.02
☐ 395 Glenn Hubbard	.10	.05	.01
☐ 396 Chuck Cary	.10	.05	.01
☐ 397 Frank Viola	.12	.05	.02
☐ 398 Jeff Parrett	.10	.05	.01
☐ 399 Terry Blocker	.10	.05	.01
☐ 400 Dan Gladden	.10	.05	.01
☐ 401 Louie Meadows	.10	.05	.01
☐ 402 Tim Raines	.12	.05	.02
☐ 403 Joey Meyer	.10	.05	.01
☐ 404 Larry Andersen	.10	.05	.01
☐ 405 Rex Hudler	.10	.05	.01
☐ 406 Mike Schmidt	1.50	.65	.19
☐ 407 John Franco	.12	.05	.02
☐ 408 Brady Anderson	1.75	.80	.22
☐ 409 Don Carman	.10	.05	.01
☐ 410 Eric Davis	.35	.16	.04
☐ 411 Bob Stanley	.10	.05	.01
☐ 412 Pete Smith	.35	.16	.04
☐ 413 Jim Rice	.12	.05	.02
☐ 414 Bruce Sutter	.12	.05	.02
☐ 415 Oil Can Boyd	.10	.05	.01
☐ 416 Ruben Sierra	1.00	.45	.13
☐ 417 Mike LaValliere	.10	.05	.01
☐ 418 Steve Buechele	.10	.05	.01
☐ 419 Gary Redus	.10	.05	.01
☐ 420 Scott Fletcher	.10	.05	.01
☐ 421 Dale Sveum	.10	.05	.01
☐ 422 Bob Knepper	.10	.05	.01
☐ 423 Luis Rivera	.10	.05	.01
☐ 424 Ted Higuera	.10	.05	.01
☐ 425 Kevin Bass	.10	.05	.01
☐ 426 Ken Gerhart	.10	.05	.01
☐ 427 Shane Rawley	.10	.05	.01
☐ 428 Paul O'Neill	.12	.05	.02
☐ 429 Joe Orsulak	.10	.05	.01
☐ 430 Jackie Gutierrez	.10	.05	.01
☐ 431 Gerald Perry	.10	.05	.01
☐ 432 Mike Greenwell	.12	.05	.02
☐ 433 Jerry Royster	.10	.05	.01
☐ 434 Ellis Burks	.12	.05	.02
☐ 435 Ed Olwine	.10	.05	.01
☐ 436 Dave Rucker	.10	.05	.01
☐ 437 Charlie Hough	.10	.05	.01
☐ 438 Bob Walk	.10	.05	.01
☐ 439 Bob Brower	.10	.05	.01
☐ 440 Barry Bonds	1.50	.65	.19
☐ 441 Tom Foley	.10	.05	.01
☐ 442 Rob Deer	.12	.05	.02
☐ 443 Glenn Davis	.12	.05	.02
☐ 444 Dave Martinez	.12	.05	.02
☐ 445 Bill Wegman	.10	.05	.01
☐ 446 Lloyd McClendon	.10	.05	.01
☐ 447 Dave Schmidt	.10	.05	.01
☐ 448 Darren Daulton	.12	.05	.02
☐ 449 Frank Williams	.10	.05	.01
☐ 450 Don Aase	.10	.05	.01
☐ 451 Lou Whitaker	.12	.05	.02
☐ 452 Goose Gossage	.12	.05	.02
☐ 453 Ed Whitson	.10	.05	.01
☐ 454 Jim Walewander	.10	.05	.01
☐ 455 Damon Berryhill	.10	.05	.01
☐ 456 Tim Burke	.10	.05	.01
☐ 457 Barry Jones	.10	.05	.01
☐ 458 Joel Youngblood	.10	.05	.01
☐ 459 Floyd Youmans	.10	.05	.01
☐ 460 Mark Salas	.10	.05	.01
☐ 461 Jeff Russell	.10	.05	.01
☐ 462 Darrell Miller	.10	.05	.01
☐ 463 Jeff Kunkel	.10	.05	.01
☐ 464 Sherman Corbett	.10	.05	.01
☐ 465 Curtis Wilkerson	.10	.05	.01
☐ 466 Bud Black	.10	.05	.01

☐	467	Cal Ripken	2.00	.90	.25	☐	520	Bob Kipper	.10	.05	.01
☐	468	John Farrell	.10	.05	.01	☐	521	Lee Smith	.12	.05	.02
☐	469	Terry Kennedy	.10	.05	.01	☐	522	Juan Castillo	.10	.05	.01
☐	470	Tom Candiotti	.10	.05	.01	☐	523	Don Robinson	.10	.05	.01
☐	471	Roberto Alomar	5.00	2.30	.60	☐	524	Kevin Romine	.10	.05	.01
☐	472	Jeff M. Robinson	.10	.05	.01	☐	525	Paul Molitor	.35	.16	.04
☐	473	Vance Law	.10	.05	.01	☐	526	Mark Langston	.12	.05	.02
☐	474	Randy Ready UER	.10	.05	.01	☐	527	Donnie Hill	.10	.05	.01
		(Strikeout total 136,				☐	528	Larry Owen	.10	.05	.01
		should be 115)				☐	529	Jerry Reed	.10	.05	.01
☐	475	Walt Terrell	.10	.05	.01	☐	530	Jack McDowell	1.50	.65	.19
☐	476	Kelly Downs	.10	.05	.01	☐	531	Greg Mathews	.10	.05	.01
☐	477	Johnny Paredes	.10	.05	.01	☐	532	John Russell	.10	.05	.01
☐	478	Shawn Hillegas	.10	.05	.01	☐	533	Dan Quisenberry	.12	.05	.02
☐	479	Bob Brenly	.10	.05	.01	☐	534	Greg Gross	.10	.05	.01
☐	480	Otis Nixon	.12	.05	.02	☐	535	Danny Cox	.10	.05	.01
☐	481	Johnny Ray	.10	.05	.01	☐	536	Terry Francona	.10	.05	.01
☐	482	Geno Petralli	.10	.05	.01	☐	537	Andy Van Slyke	.30	.14	.04
☐	483	Stu Cliburn	.10	.05	.01	☐	538	Mel Hall	.10	.05	.01
☐	484	Pete Incaviglia	.10	.05	.01	☐	539	Jim Gott	.10	.05	.01
☐	485	Brian Downing	.10	.05	.01	☐	540	Doug Jones	.12	.05	.02
☐	486	Jeff Stone	.10	.05	.01	☐	541	Craig Lefferts	.10	.05	.01
☐	487	Carmen Castillo	.10	.05	.01	☐	542	Mike Boddicker	.10	.05	.01
☐	488	Tom Niedenfuer	.10	.05	.01	☐	543	Greg Brock	.10	.05	.01
☐	489	Jay Bell	.12	.05	.02	☐	544	Atlee Hammaker	.10	.05	.01
☐	490	Rick Schu	.10	.05	.01	☐	545	Tom Bolton	.10	.05	.01
☐	491	Jeff Pico	.10	.05	.01	☐	546	Mike Macfarlane	.40	.18	.05
☐	492	Mark Parent	.10	.05	.01	☐	547	Rich Renteria	.10	.05	.01
☐	493	Eric King	.10	.05	.01	☐	548	John Davis	.10	.05	.01
☐	494	Al Nipper	.10	.05	.01	☐	549	Floyd Bannister	.10	.05	.01
☐	495	Andy Hawkins	.10	.05	.01	☐	550	Mickey Brantley	.10	.05	.01
☐	496	Daryl Boston	.10	.05	.01	☐	551	Duane Ward	.12	.05	.02
☐	497	Ernie Riles	.10	.05	.01	☐	552	Dan Petry	.10	.05	.01
☐	498	Pascual Perez	.10	.05	.01	☐	553	Mickey Tettleton UER	.12	.05	.02
☐	499	Bill Long UER	.10	.05	.01			(Walks total 175,			
		(Games started total						should be 136)			
		70, should be 44)				☐	554	Rick Leach	.10	.05	.01
☐	500	Kirt Manwaring	.10	.05	.01	☐	555	Mike Witt	.10	.05	.01
☐	501	Chuck Crim	.10	.05	.01	☐	556	Sid Bream	.10	.05	.01
☐	502	Candy Maldonado	.10	.05	.01	☐	557	Bobby Witt	.12	.05	.02
☐	503	Dennis Lamp	.10	.05	.01	☐	558	Tommy Herr	.10	.05	.01
☐	504	Glenn Braggs	.10	.05	.01	☐	559	Randy Milligan	.10	.05	.01
☐	505	Joe Price	.10	.05	.01	☐	560	Jose Cecena	.10	.05	.01
☐	506	Ken Williams	.10	.05	.01	☐	561	Mackey Sasser	.10	.05	.01
☐	507	Bill Pecota	.10	.05	.01	☐	562	Carney Lansford	.12	.05	.02
☐	508	Rey Quinones	.10	.05	.01	☐	563	Rick Aguilera	.12	.05	.02
☐	509	Jeff Bittiger	.10	.05	.01	☐	564	Ron Hassey	.10	.05	.01
☐	510	Kevin Seitzer	.12	.05	.02	☐	565	Dwight Gooden	.35	.16	.04
☐	511	Steve Bedrosian	.10	.05	.01	☐	566	Paul Assenmacher	.10	.05	.01
☐	512	Todd Worrell	.12	.05	.02	☐	567	Neil Allen	.10	.05	.01
☐	513	Chris James	.10	.05	.01	☐	568	Jim Morrison	.10	.05	.01
☐	514	Jose Oquendo	.10	.05	.01	☐	569	Mike Pagliarulo	.10	.05	.01
☐	515	David Palmer	.10	.05	.01	☐	570	Ted Simmons	.12	.05	.02
☐	516	John Smiley	.12	.05	.02	☐	571	Mark Thurmond	.10	.05	.01
☐	517	Dave Clark	.10	.05	.01	☐	572	Fred McGriff	.90	.40	.11
☐	518	Mike Dunne	.10	.05	.01	☐	573	Wally Joyner	.15	.07	.02
☐	519	Ron Washington	.10	.05	.01	☐	574	Jose Bautista	.10	.05	.01

☐ 575 Kelly Gruber	.12	.05	.02
☐ 576 Cecilio Guante	.10	.05	.01
☐ 577 Mark Davidson	.10	.05	.01
☐ 578 Bobby Bonilla UER	.60	.25	.08
(Total steals 2 in '87, should be 3)			
☐ 579 Mike Stanley	.10	.05	.01
☐ 580 Gene Larkin	.10	.05	.01
☐ 581 Stan Javier	.10	.05	.01
☐ 582 Howard Johnson	.12	.05	.02
☐ 583A Mike Gallego ERR	1.25	.55	.16
(Front reversed negative)			
☐ 583B Mike Gallego COR	.25	.11	.03
☐ 584 David Cone	.60	.25	.08
☐ 585 Doug Jennings	.10	.05	.01
☐ 586 Charles Hudson	.10	.05	.01
☐ 587 Dion James	.10	.05	.01
☐ 588 Al Leiter	.10	.05	.01
☐ 589 Charlie Puleo	.10	.05	.01
☐ 590 Roberto Kelly	.60	.25	.08
☐ 591 Thad Bosley	.10	.05	.01
☐ 592 Pete Stanicek	.10	.05	.01
☐ 593 Pat Borders	.25	.08	
☐ 594 Bryan Harvey	.60	.25	.08
☐ 595 Jeff Ballard	.10	.05	.01
☐ 596 Jeff Reardon	.12	.05	.02
☐ 597 Doug Drabek	.12	.05	.02
☐ 598 Edwin Correa	.10	.05	.01
☐ 599 Keith Atherton	.10	.05	.01
☐ 600 Dave LaPoint	.10	.05	.01
☐ 601 Don Baylor	.12	.05	.02
☐ 602 Tom Pagnozzi	.10	.05	.01
☐ 603 Tim Flannery	.10	.05	.01
☐ 604 Gene Walter	.10	.05	.01
☐ 605 Dave Parker	.12	.05	.02
☐ 606 Mike Diaz	.10	.05	.01
☐ 607 Chris Gwynn	.10	.05	.01
☐ 608 Odell Jones	.10	.05	.01
☐ 609 Carlton Fisk	.50	.23	.06
☐ 610 Jay Howell	.10	.05	.01
☐ 611 Tim Crews	.10	.05	.01
☐ 612 Keith Hernandez	.12	.05	.02
☐ 613 Willie Fraser	.10	.05	.01
☐ 614 Jim Eppard	.10	.05	.01
☐ 615 Jeff Hamilton	.10	.05	.01
☐ 616 Kurt Stillwell	.10	.05	.01
☐ 617 Tom Browning	.10	.05	.01
☐ 618 Jeff Montgomery	.12	.05	.02
☐ 619 Jose Rijo	.12	.05	.02
☐ 620 Jamie Quirk	.10	.05	.01
☐ 621 Willie McGee	.12	.05	.02
☐ 622 Mark Grant UER	.10	.05	.01
(Glove on wrong hand)			
☐ 623 Bill Swift	.12	.05	.02
☐ 624 Orlando Mercado	.10	.05	.01
☐ 625 John Costello	.10	.05	.01

☐ 626 Jose Gonzalez	.10	.05	.01
☐ 627A Bill Schroeder ERR	1.25	.55	.16
(Back photo actually Ronn Reynolds buckling shin guards)			
☐ 627B Bill Schroeder COR	.25	.11	.03
☐ 628A Fred Manrique ERR	.35	.16	.04
(Back photo actually Ozzie Guillen throwing)			
☐ 628B Fred Manrique COR	.10	.05	.01
(Swinging bat on back)			
☐ 629 Ricky Horton	.10	.05	.01
☐ 630 Dan Plesac	.10	.05	.01
☐ 631 Alfredo Griffin	.10	.05	.01
☐ 632 Chuck Finley	.12	.05	.02
☐ 633 Kirk Gibson	.12	.05	.02
☐ 634 Randy Myers	.12	.05	.02
☐ 635 Greg Minton	.10	.05	.01
☐ 636A Herm Winningham	.35	.16	.04
ERR (W1nningham- on back)			
☐ 636B Herm Winningham COR	.10	.05	.01
☐ 637 Charlie Leibrandt	.10	.05	.01
☐ 638 Tim Birtsas	.10	.05	.01
☐ 639 Bill Buckner	.12	.05	.02
☐ 640 Danny Jackson	.10	.05	.01
☐ 641 Greg Booker	.10	.05	.01
☐ 642 Jim Presley	.10	.05	.01
☐ 643 Gene Nelson	.10	.05	.01
☐ 644 Rod Booker	.10	.05	.01
☐ 645 Dennis Rasmussen	.10	.05	.01
☐ 646 Juan Nieves	.10	.05	.01
☐ 647 Bobby Thigpen	.10	.05	.01
☐ 648 Tim Belcher	.12	.05	.02
☐ 649 Mike Young	.10	.05	.01
☐ 650 Ivan Calderon	.10	.05	.01
☐ 651 Oswaldo Peraza	.10	.05	.01
☐ 652A Pat Sheridan ERR	15.00	6.75	1.90
(No position on front)			
☐ 652B Pat Sheridan COR	.10	.05	.01
☐ 653 Mike Morgan	.10	.05	.01
☐ 654 Mike Heath	.10	.05	.01
☐ 655 Jay Tibbs	.10	.05	.01
☐ 656 Fernando Valenzuela	.12	.05	.02
☐ 657 Lee Mazzilli	.10	.05	.01
☐ 658 AL CY:Frank Viola	.12	.05	.02
☐ 659A AL MVP:Jose Canseco	.50	.23	.06
(Eagle logo in black)			
☐ 659B AL MVP:Jose Canseco	.50	.23	.06
(Eagle logo in blue)			
☐ 660 AL ROY:Walt Weiss	.12	.05	.02
☐ 661 NL CY:Orel Hershiser	.12	.05	.02
☐ 662 NL MVP:Kirk Gibson	.12	.05	.02
☐ 663 NL ROY:Chris Sabo	.20	.09	.03
☐ 664 ALCS MVP:D.Eckersley	.15	.07	.02
☐ 665 NLCS MVP:O.Hershiser	.12	.05	.02
☐ 666 Great WS Moment	.12	.05	.02

	(Kirk Gibson's homer)		
☐ 667	WS MVP:Orel Hershiser..12	.05	.02
☐ 668	Angels Checklist 10	.05	.01
	Wally Joyner		
☐ 669	Astros Checklist...............90	.40	.11
	Nolan Ryan		
☐ 670	Athletics Checklist............40	.18	.05
	Jose Canseco		
☐ 671	Blue Jays Checklist.....25	.11	.03
	Fred McGriff		
☐ 672	Braves Checklist 15	.07	.02
	Dale Murphy		
☐ 673	Brewers Checklist 12	.05	.02
	Paul Molitor		
☐ 674	Cardinals Checklist 20	.09	.03
	Ozzie Smith		
☐ 675	Cubs Checklist 40	.18	.05
	Ryne Sandberg		
☐ 676	Dodgers Checklist.............10	.05	.01
	Kirk Gibson		
☐ 677	Expos Checklist.................10	.05	.01
	Andres Galarraga		
☐ 678	Giants Checklist 40	.18	.05
	Will Clark		
☐ 679	Indians Checklist...............10	.05	.01
	Cory Snyder		
☐ 680	Mariners Checklist 10	.05	.01
	Alvin Davis		
☐ 681	Mets Checklist 25	.11	.03
	Darryl Strawberry		
☐ 682	Orioles Checklist...............50	.23	.06
	Cal Ripken		
☐ 683	Padres Checklist 25	.11	.03
	Tony Gwynn		
☐ 684	Phillies Checklist...............50	.23	.06
	Mike Schmidt		
☐ 685	Pirates Checklist 12	.05	.02
	Andy Van Slyke		
	UER (96 Junior Ortiz)		
☐ 686	Rangers Checklist..........25	.11	.03
	Ruben Sierra		
☐ 687	Red Sox Checklist 25	.11	.03
	Wade Boggs		
☐ 688	Reds Checklist 15	.07	.02
	Eric Davis		
☐ 689	Royals Checklist 20	.09	.03
	George Brett		
☐ 690	Tigers Checklist 12	.05	.02
	Alan Trammell		
☐ 691	Twins Checklist 10	.05	.01
	Frank Viola		
☐ 692	White Sox Checklist 10	.05	.01
	Harold Baines		
☐ 693	Yankees Checklist 25	.11	.03
	Don Mattingly		
☐ 694	Checklist 1-100 10	.01	.00
☐ 695	Checklist 101-200............10	.01	.00

☐ 696	Checklist 201-300............10	.01	.00
☐ 697	Checklist 301-400............10	.01	.00
☐ 698	Checklist 401-500 UER...10	.01	.00
	(467 Cal Ripkin Jr.)		
☐ 699	Checklist 501-600 UER...10	.01	.00
	(543 Greg Booker)		
☐ 700	Checklist 601-700............10	.01	.00
☐ 701	Checklist 701-800............10	.01	.00
☐ 702	Jesse Barfield 10	.05	.01
☐ 703	Walt Terrell 10	.05	.01
☐ 704	Dickie Thon.....................10	.05	.01
☐ 705	Al Leiter 10	.05	.01
☐ 706	Dave LaPoint...................10	.05	.01
☐ 707	Charlie Hayes.................50	.23	.06
☐ 708	Andy Hawkins 10	.05	.01
☐ 709	Mickey Hatcher 10	.05	.01
☐ 710	Lance McCullers 10	.05	.01
☐ 711	Ron Kittle 10	.05	.01
☐ 712	Bert Blyleven 12	.05	.02
☐ 713	Rick Dempsey 10	.05	.01
☐ 714	Ken Williams 10	•.05	.01
☐ 715	Steve Rosenberg.............10	.05	.01
☐ 716	Joe Skalski.....................10	.05	.01
☐ 717	Spike Owen 10	.05	.01
☐ 718	Todd Burns.....................10	.05	.01
☐ 719	Kevin Gross 10	.05	.01
☐ 720	Tommy Herr 10	.05	.01
☐ 721	Rob Ducey 10	.05	.01
☐ 722	Gary Green......................10	.05	.01
☐ 723	Gregg Olson 1.50	.65	.19
☐ 724	Greg W. Harris................25	.11	.03
☐ 725	Craig Worthington...........10	.05	.01
☐ 726	Tom Howard 40	.18	.05
☐ 727	Dale Mohorcic..................10	.05	.01
☐ 728	Rich Yett.........................10	.05	.01
☐ 729	Mel Hall..........................10	.05	.01
☐ 730	Floyd Youmans 10	.05	.01
☐ 731	Lonnie Smith 10	.05	.01
☐ 732	Wally Backman 10	.05	.01
☐ 733	Trevor Wilson 30	.14	.04
☐ 734	Jose Alvarez....................10	.05	.01
☐ 735	Bob Milacki.....................20	.09	.03
☐ 736	Tom Gordon....................25	.11	.03
☐ 737	Wally Whitehurst 12	.05	.02
☐ 738	Mike Aldrete....................10	.05	.01
☐ 739	Keith Miller 10	.05	.01
☐ 740	Randy Milligan.................10	.05	.01
☐ 741	Jeff Parrett.....................10	.05	.01
☐ 742	Steve Finley....................90	.40	.11
☐ 743	Junior Felix 50	.23	.06
☐ 744	Pete Harnisch 50	.23	.06
☐ 745	Bill Spiers 15	.07	.02
☐ 746	Hensley Meulens............25	.11	.03
☐ 747	Juan Bell 15	.07	.02
☐ 748	Steve Sax 12	.05	.02
☐ 749	Phil Bradley 10	.05	.01
☐ 750	Rey Quinones 10	.05	.01

☐ 751	Tommy Gregg	.10	.05	.01
☐ 752	Kevin Brown	.50	.23	.06
☐ 753	Derek Lilliquist	.15	.07	.02
☐ 754	Todd Zeile	1.25	.55	.16
☐ 755	Jim Abbott	4.00	1.80	.50
	(Triple exposure)			
☐ 756	Ozzie Canseco	.35	.16	.04
☐ 757	Nick Esasky	.10	.05	.01
☐ 758	Mike Moore	.10	.05	.01
☐ 759	Rob Murphy	.10	.05	.01
☐ 760	Rick Mahler	.10	.05	.01
☐ 761	Fred Lynn	.12	.05	.02
☐ 762	Kevin Blankenship	.10	.05	.01
☐ 763	Eddie Murray	.50	.23	.06
☐ 764	Steve Searcy	.10	.05	.01
☐ 765	Jerome Walton	.20	.09	.03
☐ 766	Erik Hanson	.50	.23	.06
☐ 767	Bob Boone	.12	.05	.02
☐ 768	Edgar Martinez	1.50	.65	.19
☐ 769	Jose DeJesus	.10	.05	.01
☐ 770	Greg Briley	.15	.07	.02
☐ 771	Steve Peters	.10	.05	.01
☐ 772	Rafael Palmeiro	.75	.35	.09
☐ 773	Jack Clark	.05	.02	
☐ 774	Nolan Ryan	4.00	1.80	.50
	(Throwing football)			
☐ 775	Lance Parrish	.12	.05	.02
☐ 776	Joe Girardi	.20	.09	.03
☐ 777	Willie Randolph	.12	.05	.02
☐ 778	Mitch Williams	.12	.05	.02
☐ 779	Dennis Cook	.12	.05	.02
☐ 780	Dwight Smith	.20	.09	.03
☐ 781	Lenny Harris	.30	.14	.04
☐ 782	Torey Lovullo	.10	.05	.01
☐ 783	Norm Charlton	.50	.23	.06
☐ 784	Chris Brown	.10	.05	.01
☐ 785	Todd Benzinger	.10	.05	.01
☐ 786	Shane Rawley	.10	.05	.01
☐ 787	Omar Vizquel	.35	.16	.04
☐ 788	LaVel Freeman	.10	.05	.01
☐ 789	Jeffrey Leonard	.10	.05	.01
☐ 790	Eddie Williams	.10	.05	.01
☐ 791	Jamie Moyer	.10	.05	.01
☐ 792	Bruce Hurst UER	.12	.05	.02
	(World Series)			
☐ 793	Julio Franco	.12	.05	.02
☐ 794	Claudell Washington	.10	.05	.01
☐ 795	Jody Davis	.10	.05	.01
☐ 796	Oddibe McDowell	.10	.05	.01
☐ 797	Paul Kilgus	.10	.05	.01
☐ 798	Tracy Jones	.10	.05	.01
☐ 799	Steve Wilson	.10	.05	.01
☐ 800	Pete O'Brien	.12	.05	.02

1990 Upper Deck

The 1990 Upper Deck set contains 800 standard-size (2 1/2" by 3 1/2") cards issued in two series, low numbers (1-700) and high numbers (701-800). The front and back borders are white, and both sides feature full-color photos. The horizontally oriented backs have recent stats and anti-counterfeiting holograms. Unlike the 1989 Upper Deck set, the team checklist cards are not grouped numerically at the end of the set, but are mixed in with the first 100 cards. The key Rookie Cards in the first series are Juan Gonzalez, Marquis Grissom, Kevin Maas, Ben McDonald, John Olerud, Dean Palmer, and Larry Walker. Cards 101 through 199 have two minor varieties in that the cards either show or omit "Copyright" 1990 Upper Deck Co. Printed in USA below the two licensing logos. Those without are considered minor errors; they were found in the High Number foil packs. The 1990 Upper Deck Extended Set (of high numbers) was issued in July 1990. The cards were in the same style as the first 700 cards of the 1990 Upper Deck set and were issued either as a separate set in its own collectors box, as part of the complete 1-800 factory set, as well as mixed in with the earlier numbered Upper Deck cards in late-season wax packs. The series also contains a Nolan Ryan variation; all cards produced before August 12th only discuss Ryan's sixth no-hitter while the later-issue cards include a stripe honoring Ryan's 300th victory. The key Rookie Cards in the extended or high-number series are Carlos Baerga, Alex Cole, Delino DeShields,

Dave Hollins, Dave Justice, and Ray Lankford. Card 702 was originally scheduled to be Mike Witt. A few 702 Witt cards and checklist cards showing 702 Witt escaped into early packs; they are characterized by a black rectangle covering much of the card's back.

	MT	EX-MT	VG
COMPLETE SET (800)	45.00	20.00	5.75
COMPLETE FACT.SET (800)	50.00	23.00	6.25
COMPLETE LO SET (700)	35.00	16.00	4.40
COMPLETE HI SET (100)	10.00	4.50	1.25
COMPLETE HI FACT.SET (100)	10.00	4.50	1.25
COMMON PLAYER (1-700)	.05	.02	.01
COMMON PLAYER (701-800)	.05	.02	.01

☐ 1	Star Rookie Checklist	.06	.01	.00
☐ 2	Randy Nosek	.05	.02	.01
☐ 3	Tom Drees UER	.05	.02	.01
	(11th line, hulred, should be hurled)			
☐ 4	Curt Young	.05	.02	.01
☐ 5	Devon White TC	.06	.03	.01
	California Angels			
☐ 6	Luis Salazar	.05	.02	.01
☐ 7	Von Hayes TC	.06	.03	.01
	Philadelphia Phillies			
☐ 8	Jose Bautista	.05	.02	.01
☐ 9	Marquis Grissom	2.00	.90	.25
☐ 10	Orel Hershiser TC	.06	.03	.01
	Los Angeles Dodgers			
☐ 11	Rick Aguilera	.08	.04	.01
☐ 12	Benito Santiago TC	.06	.03	.01
	San Diego Padres			
☐ 13	Deion Sanders	1.50	.65	.19
☐ 14	Marvell Wynne	.05	.02	.01
☐ 15	Dave West	.05	.02	.01
☐ 16	Bobby Bonilla TC	.10	.05	.01
	Pittsburgh Pirates			
☐ 17	Sammy Sosa	.30	.14	.04
☐ 18	Steve Sax TC	.06	.03	.01
	New York Yankees			
☐ 19	Jack Howell	.05	.02	.01
☐ 20	Mike Schmidt Special	.50	.23	.06
	UER (Suprising, should be surprising)			
☐ 21	Robin Ventura UER	2.50	1.15	.30
	(Samta Maria)			
☐ 22	Brian Meyer	.05	.02	.01
☐ 23	Blaine Beatty	.05	.02	.01
☐ 24	Ken Griffey Jr. TC	.50	.23	.06
	Seattle Mariners			
☐ 25	Greg Vaughn UER	.50	.23	.06
	(Association misspelled as assiocation)			
☐ 26	Xavier Hernandez	.15	.07	.02
☐ 27	Jason Grimsley	.15	.07	.02
☐ 28	Eric Anthony UER	.60	.25	.08
	(Ashville, should be Asheville)			
☐ 29	Tim Raines TC	.06	.03	.01
	Montreal Expos UER (Wallach listed before Walker)			
☐ 30	David Wells	.08	.04	.01
☐ 31	Hal Morris	.50	.23	.06
☐ 32	Bo Jackson TC	.20	.09	.03
	Kansas City Royals			
☐ 33	Kelly Mann	.05	.02	.01
☐ 34	Nolan Ryan Special	1.00	.45	.13
☐ 35	Scott Service UER	.05	.02	.01
	(Born Cincinatti on 7/27/67, should be Cincinnati 2/27)			
☐ 36	Mark McGwire TC	.20	.09	.03
	Oakland A's			
☐ 37	Tino Martinez	.40	.18	.05
☐ 38	Chili Davis	.08	.04	.01
☐ 39	Scott Sanderson	.05	.02	.01
☐ 40	Kevin Mitchell TC	.10	.05	.01
	San Francisco Giants			
☐ 41	Lou Whitaker TC	.06	.03	.01
	Detroit Tigers			
☐ 42	Scott Coolbaugh UER	.05	.02	.01
	(Definately)			
☐ 43	Jose Cano UER	.05	.02	.01
	(Born 9/7/62, should be 3/7/62)			
☐ 44	Jose Vizcaino	.15	.07	.02
☐ 45	Bob Hamelin	.15	.07	.02
☐ 46	Jose Offerman UER	.40	.18	.05
	(Posesses)			
☐ 47	Kevin Blankenship	.05	.02	.01
☐ 48	Kirby Puckett TC	.20	.09	.03
	Minnesota Twins			
☐ 49	Tommy Greene UER	.25	.11	.03
	(Livest, should be liveliest)			
☐ 50	Will Clark Special	.30	.14	.04
	UER (Perenial, should be perennial)			
☐ 51	Rob Nelson	.05	.02	.01
☐ 52	Chris Hammond UER	.40	.18	.05
	(Chatanooga)			
☐ 53	Joe Carter TC	.15	.07	.02
	Cleveland Indians			
☐ 54A	Ben McDonald ERR	20.00	9.00	2.50
	(No Rookie designation on card front)			
☐ 54B	Ben McDonald COR	1.50	.65	.19
☐ 55	Andy Benes UER	.75	.35	.09
	(Whichita)			
☐ 56	John Olerud	2.00	.90	.25

☐ 57	Roger Clemens TC 30	.14	.04	
	Boston Red Sox			
☐ 58	Tony Armas 05	.02	.01	
☐ 59	George Canale.................05	.02	.01	
☐ 60A	Mickey Tettleton TC ERR 2.50	1.15	.30	
	Baltimore Orioles			
	(683 Jamie Weston)			
☐ 60B	Mickey Tettleton TC UER .08	.04	.01	
	Baltimore Orioles			
	(683 Mickey Weston)			
☐ 61	Mike Stanton 30	.14	.04	
☐ 62	Dwight Gooden TC............10	.05	.01	
	New York Mets			
☐ 63	Kent Mercker UER 25	.11	.03	
	(Albuquerque)			
☐ 64	Francisco Cabrera 20	.09	.03	
☐ 65	Steve Avery UER............2.50	1.15	.30	
	(Born NJ, should be MI,			
	Merker should be Mercker)			
☐ 66	Jose Canseco..................60	.25	.08	
☐ 67	Matt Merullo 05	.02	.01	
☐ 68	Vince Coleman TC.............06	.03	.01	
	St. Louis Cardinals			
	UER (Guerrero)			
☐ 69	Ron Karkovice..................05	.02	.01	
☐ 70	Kevin Maas 60	.25	.08	
☐ 71	Dennis Cook UER.............05	.02	.01	
	(Shown with righty			
	glove on card back)			
☐ 72	Juan Gonzalez UER.......8.00	3.60	1.00	
	(135 games for Tulsa			
	in '89, should be 133)			
☐ 73	Andre Dawson TC 10	.05	.01	
	Chicago Cubs			
☐ 74	Dean Palmer UER..........1.75	.80	.22	
	(Permanent misspelled			
	as perminant)			
☐ 75	Bo Jackson Special...........25	.11	.03	
	UER (Monsterous,			
	should be monstrous)			
☐ 76	Rob Richie 05	.02	.01	
☐ 77	Bobby Rose UER 08	.04	.01	
	(Pickin, should			
	be pick in)			
☐ 78	Brian DuBois UER............05	.02	.01	
	(Commiting)			
☐ 79	Ozzie Guillen TC..............06	.03	.01	
	Chicago White Sox			
☐ 80	Gene Nelson 05	.02	.01	
☐ 81	Bob McClure 05	.02	.01	
☐ 82	Julio Franco TC 06	.03	.01	
	Texas Rangers			
☐ 83	Greg Minton.....................05	.02	.01	
☐ 84	John Smoltz TC UER.........12	.05	.02	
	Atlanta Braves			
	(Oddibe not Odibbe)			
☐ 85	Willie Fraser 05	.02	.01	
☐ 86	Neal Heaton 05	.02	.01	
☐ 87	Kevin Tapani....................90	.40	.11	
☐ 88	Mike Scott TC 06	.03	.01	
	Houston Astros			
☐ 89A	Jim Gott ERR..............6.00	2.70	.75	
	(Photo actually			
	Rick Reed)			
☐ 89B	Jim Gott COR 08	.04	.01	
☐ 90	Lance Johnson 08	.04	.01	
☐ 91	Robin Yount TC UER.........10	.05	.01	
	Milwaukee Brewers			
	(Checklist on back has			
	178 Rob Deer and			
	176 Mike Felder)			
☐ 92	Jeff Parrett......................05	.02	.01	
☐ 93	Julio Machado UER 05	.02	.01	
	(Valenzuelan, should			
	be Venezuelan)			
☐ 94	Ron Jones 05	.02	.01	
☐ 95	George Bell TC 05	.02	.01	
	Toronto Blue Jays			
☐ 96	Jerry Reuss 05	.02	.01	
☐ 97	Brian Fisher.....................05	.02	.01	
☐ 98	Kevin Ritz UER 12	.05	.02	
	(Amercian)			
☐ 99	Barry Larkin TC 10	.05	.01	
	Cincinnati Reds			
☐ 100	Checklist 1-100................06	.01	.00	
☐ 101	Gerald Perry 05	.02	.01	
☐ 102	Kevin Appier....................90	.40	.11	
☐ 103	Julio Franco 08	.04	.01	
☐ 104	Craig Biggio.....................15	.07	.02	
☐ 105	Bo Jackson UER 30	.14	.04	
	('89 BA wrong,			
	should be .256)			
☐ 106	Junior Felix 08	.04	.01	
☐ 107	Mike Harkey.....................08	.04	.01	
☐ 108	Fred McGriff.....................40	.18	.05	
☐ 109	Rick Sutcliffe...................08	.04	.01	
☐ 110	Pete O'Brien....................05	.02	.01	
☐ 111	Kelly Gruber 08	.04	.01	
☐ 112	Dwight Evans...................08	.04	.01	
☐ 113	Pat Borders.....................08	.04	.01	
☐ 114	Dwight Gooden 12	.05	.02	
☐ 115	Kevin Batiste...................20	.09	.03	
☐ 116	Eric Davis 12	.05	.02	
☐ 117	Kevin Mitchell UER 15	.07	.02	
	(Career HR total 99,			
	should be 100)			
☐ 118	Ron Oester 05	.02	.01	
☐ 119	Brett Butler 08	.04	.01	
☐ 120	Danny Jackson 05	.02	.01	
☐ 121	Tommy Gregg....................05	.02	.01	
☐ 122	Ken Caminiti 08	.04	.01	
☐ 123	Kevin Brown 25	.11	.03	
☐ 124	George Brett UER............30	.14	.04	
	(133 runs, should			

be 1300)

☐ 125	Mike Scott	.05	.02	.01
☐ 126	Cory Snyder	.05	.02	.01
☐ 127	George Bell	.08	.04	.01
☐ 128	Mark Grace	.35	.16	.04
☐ 129	Devon White	.08	.04	.01
☐ 130	Tony Fernandez	.08	.04	.01
☐ 131	Don Aase	.05	.02	.01
☐ 132	Rance Mulliniks	.05	.02	.01
☐ 133	Marty Barrett	.05	.02	.01
☐ 134	Nelson Liriano	.05	.02	.01
☐ 135	Mark Carreon	.05	.02	.01
☐ 136	Candy Maldonado	.05	.02	.01
☐ 137	Tim Birtsas	.05	.02	.01
☐ 138	Tom Brookens	.05	.02	.01
☐ 139	John Franco	.08	.04	.01
☐ 140	Mike LaCoss	.05	.02	.01
☐ 141	Jeff Treadway	.05	.02	.01
☐ 142	Pat Tabler	.05	.02	.01
☐ 143	Darrell Evans	.08	.04	.01
☐ 144	Rafael Ramirez	.05	.02	.01
☐ 145	Oddibe McDowell UER	.05	.02	.01
	(Misspelled Odibbe)			
☐ 146	Brian Downing	.05	.02	.01
☐ 147	Curt Wilkerson	.05	.02	.01
☐ 148	Ernie Whitt	.05	.02	.01
☐ 149	Bill Schroeder	.05	.02	.01
☐ 150	Domingo Ramos UER	.05	.02	.01
	(Says throws right, but shows him throwing lefty)			
☐ 151	Rick Honeycutt	.05	.02	.01
☐ 152	Don Slaught	.05	.02	.01
☐ 153	Mitch Webster	.05	.02	.01
☐ 154	Tony Phillips	.05	.02	.01
☐ 155	Paul Kilgus	.05	.02	.01
☐ 156	Ken Griffey Jr. UER	4.00	1.80	.50
	(Simultaniously)			
☐ 157	Gary Sheffield	1.00	.45	.13
☐ 158	Wally Backman	.05	.02	.01
☐ 159	B.J. Surhoff	.05	.02	.01
☐ 160	Louie Meadows	.05	.02	.01
☐ 161	Paul O'Neill	.08	.04	.01
☐ 162	Jeff McKnight	.05	.02	.01
☐ 163	Alvaro Espinoza	.05	.02	.01
☐ 164	Scott Scudder	.05	.02	.01
☐ 165	Jeff Reed	.05	.02	.01
☐ 166	Gregg Jefferies	.25	.11	.03
☐ 167	Barry Larkin	.25	.11	.03
☐ 168	Gary Carter	.08	.04	.01
☐ 169	Robby Thompson	.05	.02	.01
☐ 170	Rolando Roomes	.05	.02	.01
☐ 171	Mark McGwire UER	.60	.25	.08
	(Total games 427 and hits 479, should be 467 and 427)			
☐ 172	Steve Sax	.08	.04	.01
☐ 173	Mark Williamson	.05	.02	.01
☐ 174	Mitch Williams	.08	.04	.01
☐ 175	Brian Holton	.05	.02	.01
☐ 176	Rob Deer	.08	.04	.01
☐ 177	Tim Raines	.08	.04	.01
☐ 178	Mike Felder	.05	.02	.01
☐ 179	Harold Reynolds	.05	.02	.01
☐ 180	Terry Francona	.05	.02	.01
☐ 181	Chris Sabo	.08	.04	.01
☐ 182	Darryl Strawberry	.40	.18	.05
☐ 183	Willie Randolph	.08	.04	.01
☐ 184	Bill Ripken	.05	.02	.01
☐ 185	Mackey Sasser	.05	.02	.01
☐ 186	Todd Benzinger	.05	.02	.01
☐ 187	Kevin Elster	.05	.02	.01
☐ 188	Jose Uribe	.05	.02	.01
☐ 189	Tom Browning	.05	.02	.01
☐ 190	Keith Miller	.05	.02	.01
☐ 191	Don Mattingly	.40	.18	.05
☐ 192	Dave Parker	.08	.04	.01
☐ 193	Roberto Kelly UER	.25	.11	.03
	(96 RBI, should be 62)			
☐ 194	Phil Bradley	.05	.02	.01
☐ 195	Ron Hassey	.05	.02	.01
☐ 196	Gerald Young	.05	.02	.01
☐ 197	Hubie Brooks	.05	.02	.01
☐ 198	Bill Doran	.05	.02	.01
☐ 199	Al Newman	.05	.02	.01
☐ 200	Checklist 101-200	.06	.01	.00
☐ 201	Terry Puhl	.05	.02	.01
☐ 202	Frank DiPino	.05	.02	.01
☐ 203	Jim Clancy	.05	.02	.01
☐ 204	Bob Ojeda	.05	.02	.01
☐ 205	Alex Trevino	.05	.02	.01
☐ 206	Dave Henderson	.05	.02	.01
☐ 207	Henry Cotto	.05	.02	.01
☐ 208	Rafael Belliard UER	.05	.02	.01
	(Born 1961, not 1951)			
☐ 209	Stan Javier	.05	.02	.01
☐ 210	Jerry Reed	.05	.02	.01
☐ 211	Doug Dascenzo	.05	.02	.01
☐ 212	Andres Thomas	.05	.02	.01
☐ 213	Greg Maddux	.40	.18	.05
☐ 214	Mike Schooler	.05	.02	.01
☐ 215	Lonnie Smith	.05	.02	.01
☐ 216	Jose Rijo	.08	.04	.01
☐ 217	Greg Gagne	.05	.02	.01
☐ 218	Jim Gantner	.05	.02	.01
☐ 219	Allan Anderson	.05	.02	.01
☐ 220	Rick Mahler	.05	.02	.01
☐ 221	Jim Deshaies	.05	.02	.01
☐ 222	Keith Hernandez	.08	.04	.01
☐ 223	Vince Coleman	.08	.04	.01
☐ 224	David Cone	.30	.14	.04
☐ 225	Ozzie Smith	.20	.09	.03
☐ 226	Matt Nokes	.05	.02	.01
☐ 227	Barry Bonds	.60	.25	.08

☐	228 Felix Jose	.35	.16	.04
☐	229 Dennis Powell	.05	.02	.01
☐	230 Mike Gallego	.05	.02	.01
☐	231 Shawon Dunston UER	.08	.04	.01
	('89 stats are			
	Andre Dawson's)			
☐	232 Ron Gant	.60	.25	.08
☐	233 Omar Vizquel	.08	.04	.01
☐	234 Derek Lilliquist	.05	.02	.01
☐	235 Erik Hanson	.08	.04	.01
☐	236 Kirby Puckett UER	.60	.25	.08
	(824 games, should			
	be 924)			
☐	237 Bill Spiers	.05	.02	.01
☐	238 Dan Gladden	.05	.02	.01
☐	239 Bryan Clutterbuck	.05	.02	.01
☐	240 John Moses	.05	.02	.01
☐	241 Ron Darling	.08	.04	.01
☐	242 Joe Magrane	.05	.02	.01
☐	243 Dave Magadan	.08	.04	.01
☐	244 Pedro Guerrero UER	.08	.04	.01
	(Misspelled Guerrero)			
☐	245 Glenn Davis	.08	.04	.01
☐	246 Terry Steinbach	.08	.04	.01
☐	247 Fred Lynn	.08	.04	.01
☐	248 Gary Redus	.05	.02	.01
☐	249 Ken Williams	.05	.02	.01
☐	250 Sid Bream	.05	.02	.01
☐	251 Bob Welch UER	.08	.04	.01
	(2587 career strike-			
	outs, should be 1587)			
☐	252 Bill Buckner	.08	.04	.01
☐	253 Carney Lansford	.08	.04	.01
☐	254 Paul Molitor	.15	.07	.02
☐	255 Jose DeJesus	.05	.02	.01
☐	256 Orel Hershiser	.08	.04	.01
☐	257 Tom Brunansky	.08	.04	.01
☐	258 Mike Davis	.05	.02	.01
☐	259 Jeff Ballard	.05	.02	.01
☐	260 Scott Terry	.05	.02	.01
☐	261 Sid Fernandez	.08	.04	.01
☐	262 Mike Marshall	.05	.02	.01
☐	263 Howard Johnson UER	.08	.04	.01
	(192 SO, should be 592)			
☐	264 Kirk Gibson UER	.08	.04	.01
	(659 runs, should			
	be 669)			
☐	265 Kevin McReynolds	.08	.04	.01
☐	266 Cal Ripken	1.00	.45	.13
☐	267 Ozzie Guillen UER	.05	.02	.01
	(Career triples 27,			
	should be 29)			
☐	268 Jim Traber	.05	.02	.01
☐	269 Bobby Thigpen	.05	.02	.01
☐	270 Joe Orsulak	.05	.02	.01
☐	271 Bob Boone	.08	.04	.01
☐	272 Dave Stewart UER	.08	.04	.01

	(Totals wrong due to			
	omission of '86 stats)			
☐	273 Tim Wallach	.08	.04	.01
☐	274 Luis Aquino UER	.05	.02	.01
	(Says throws lefty,			
	but shows him			
	throwing righty)			
☐	275 Mike Moore	.05	.02	.01
☐	276 Tony Pena	.05	.02	.01
☐	277 Eddie Murray UER	.15	.07	.02
	(Several typos in			
	career total stats)			
☐	278 Milt Thompson	.05	.02	.01
☐	279 Alejandro Pena	.05	.02	.01
☐	280 Ken Dayley	.05	.02	.01
☐	281 Carmen Castillo	.05	.02	.01
☐	282 Tom Henke	.08	.04	.01
☐	283 Mickey Hatcher	.05	.02	.01
☐	284 Roy Smith	.05	.02	.01
☐	285 Manny Lee	.05	.02	.01
☐	286 Dan Pasqua	.05	.02	.01
☐	287 Larry Sheets	.05	.02	.01
☐	288 Garry Templeton	.05	.02	.01
☐	289 Eddie Williams	.05	.02	.01
☐	290 Brady Anderson	.20	.09	.03
☐	291 Spike Owen	.05	.02	.01
☐	292 Storm Davis	.05	.02	.01
☐	293 Chris Bosio	.05	.02	.01
☐	294 Jim Eisenreich	.05	.02	.01
☐	295 Don August	.05	.02	.01
☐	296 Jeff Hamilton	.05	.02	.01
☐	297 Mickey Tettleton	.08	.04	.01
☐	298 Mike Scioscia	.05	.02	.01
☐	299 Kevin Hickey	.05	.02	.01
☐	300 Checklist 201-300	.06	.01	.00
☐	301 Shawn Abner	.05	.02	.01
☐	302 Kevin Bass	.05	.02	.01
☐	303 Bip Roberts	.08	.04	.01
☐	304 Joe Girardi	.05	.02	.01
☐	305 Danny Darwin	.05	.02	.01
☐	306 Mike Heath	.05	.02	.01
☐	307 Mike Macfarlane	.05	.02	.01
☐	308 Ed Whitson	.05	.02	.01
☐	309 Tracy Jones	.05	.02	.01
☐	310 Scott Fletcher	.05	.02	.01
☐	311 Darnell Coles	.05	.02	.01
☐	312 Mike Brumley	.05	.02	.01
☐	313 Bill Swift	.08	.04	.01
☐	314 Charlie Hough	.05	.02	.01
☐	315 Jim Presley	.05	.02	.01
☐	316 Luis Polonia	.08	.04	.01
☐	317 Mike Morgan	.05	.02	.01
☐	318 Lee Guetterman	.05	.02	.01
☐	319 Jose Oquendo	.05	.02	.01
☐	320 Wayne Tolleson	.05	.02	.01
☐	321 Jody Reed	.05	.02	.01
☐	322 Damon Berryhill	.05	.02	.01

☐	323	Roger Clemens	.75	.35	.09
☐	324	Ryne Sandberg	.75	.35	.09
☐	325	Benito Santiago UER (Misspelled Santago on card back)	.08	.04	.01
☐	326	Bret Saberhagen UER (1140 hits, should be 1240; 56 CG, should be 52)	.08	.04	.01
☐	327	Lou Whitaker	.08	.04	.01
☐	328	Dave Gallagher	.05	.02	.01
☐	329	Mike Pagliarulo	.05	.02	.01
☐	330	Doyle Alexander	.05	.02	.01
☐	331	Jeffrey Leonard	.05	.02	.01
☐	332	Torey Lovullo	.05	.02	.01
☐	333	Pete Incaviglia	.05	.02	.01
☐	334	Rickey Henderson	.40	.18	.05
☐	335	Rafael Palmeiro	.20	.09	.03
☐	336	Ken Hill	.40	.18	.05
☐	337	Dave Winfield UER (1418 RBI, should be 1438)	.30	.14	.04
☐	338	Alfredo Griffin	.05	.02	.01
☐	339	Andy Hawkins	.05	.02	.01
☐	340	Ted Power	.05	.02	.01
☐	341	Steve Wilson	.05	.02	.01
☐	342	Jack Clark UER (916 BB, should be 1006; 1142 SO, should be 1130)	.08	.04	.01
☐	343	Ellis Burks	.08	.04	.01
☐	344	Tony Gwynn UER (Doubles stats on card back are wrong)	.40	.18	.05
☐	345	Jerome Walton UER (Total At Bats 476, should be 475)	.08	.04	.01
☐	346	Roberto Alomar UER (61 doubles, should be 51)	1.25	.55	.16
☐	347	Carlos Martinez UER (Born 8/11/64, should be 8/11/65)	.05	.02	.01
☐	348	Chet Lemon	.05	.02	.01
☐	349	Willie Wilson	.05	.02	.01
☐	350	Greg Walker	.05	.02	.01
☐	351	Tom Bolton	.05	.02	.01
☐	352	German Gonzalez	.05	.02	.01
☐	353	Harold Baines	.08	.04	.01
☐	354	Mike Greenwell	.08	.04	.01
☐	355	Ruben Sierra	.40	.18	.05
☐	356	Andres Galarraga	.05	.02	.01
☐	357	Andre Dawson	.20	.09	.03
☐	358	Jeff Brantley	.05	.02	.01
☐	359	Mike Bielecki	.05	.02	.01
☐	360	Ken Oberkfell	.05	.02	.01
☐	361	Kurt Stillwell	.05	.02	.01
☐	362	Brian Holman	.05	.02	.01
☐	363	Kevin Seitzer	.08	.04	.01
☐	364	Alvin Davis	.05	.02	.01
☐	365	Tom Gordon	.08	.04	.01
☐	366	Bobby Bonilla	.25	.11	.03
☐	367	Carlton Fisk	.15	.07	.02
☐	368	Steve Carter UER (Charlotesville)	.05	.02	.01
☐	369	Joel Skinner	.05	.02	.01
☐	370	John Cangelosi	.05	.02	.01
☐	371	Cecil Espy	.05	.02	.01
☐	372	Gary Wayne	.05	.02	.01
☐	373	Jim Rice	.08	.04	.01
☐	374	Mike Dyer	.05	.02	.01
☐	375	Joe Carter	.40	.18	.05
☐	376	Dwight Smith	.05	.02	.01
☐	377	John Wetteland	.40	.18	.05
☐	378	Earnie Riles	.05	.02	.01
☐	379	Otis Nixon	.08	.04	.01
☐	380	Vance Law	.05	.02	.01
☐	381	Dave Bergman	.05	.02	.01
☐	382	Frank White	.05	.02	.01
☐	383	Scott Bradley	.05	.02	.01
☐	384	Israel Sanchez UER (Totals don't include '89 stats)	.05	.02	.01
☐	385	Gary Pettis	.05	.02	.01
☐	386	Donn Pall	.05	.02	.01
☐	387	John Smiley	.08	.04	.01
☐	388	Tom Candiotti	.05	.02	.01
☐	389	Junior Ortiz	.05	.02	.01
☐	390	Steve Lyons	.05	.02	.01
☐	391	Brian Harper	.08	.04	.01
☐	392	Fred Manrique	.05	.02	.01
☐	393	Lee Smith	.08	.04	.01
☐	394	Jeff Kunkel	.05	.02	.01
☐	395	Claudell Washington	.05	.02	.01
☐	396	John Tudor	.05	.02	.01
☐	397	Terry Kennedy UER (Career totals all wrong)	.05	.02	.01
☐	398	Lloyd McClendon	.05	.02	.01
☐	399	Craig Lefferts	.05	.02	.01
☐	400	Checklist 301-400	.06	.01	.00
☐	401	Keith Moreland	.05	.02	.01
☐	402	Rich Gedman	.05	.02	.01
☐	403	Jeff D. Robinson	.05	.02	.01
☐	404	Randy Ready	.05	.02	.01
☐	405	Rick Cerone	.05	.02	.01
☐	406	Jeff Blauser	.08	.04	.01
☐	407	Larry Andersen	.05	.02	.01
☐	408	Joe Boever	.05	.02	.01
☐	409	Felix Fermin	.05	.02	.01
☐	410	Glenn Wilson	.05	.02	.01
☐	411	Rex Hudler	.05	.02	.01
☐	412	Mark Grant	.05	.02	.01
☐	413	Dennis Martinez	.08	.04	.01

☐ 414 Darrin Jackson	.08	.04	.01
☐ 415 Mike Aldrete	.05	.02	.01
☐ 416 Roger McDowell	.05	.02	.01
☐ 417 Jeff Reardon	.08	.04	.01
☐ 418 Darren Daulton	.08	.04	.01
☐ 419 Tim Laudner	.05	.02	.01
☐ 420 Don Carman	.05	.02	.01
☐ 421 Lloyd Moseby	.05	.02	.01
☐ 422 Doug Drabek	.08	.04	.01
☐ 423 Lenny Harris UER	.08	.04	.01
(Walks 2 in '89,			
should be 20)			
☐ 424 Jose Lind	.05	.02	.01
☐ 425 Dave Johnson (P)	.05	.02	.01
☐ 426 Jerry Browne	.05	.02	.01
☐ 427 Eric Yelding	.05	.02	.01
☐ 428 Brad Komminsk	.05	.02	.01
☐ 429 Jody Davis	.05	.02	.01
☐ 430 Mariano Duncan	.05	.02	.01
☐ 431 Mark Davis	.05	.02	.01
☐ 432 Nelson Santovenia	.05	.02	.01
☐ 433 Bruce Hurst	.08	.04	.01
☐ 434 Jeff Huson	.12	.05	.02
☐ 435 Chris James	.05	.02	.01
☐ 436 Mark Guthrie	.05	.02	.01
☐ 437 Charlie Hayes	.08	.04	.01
☐ 438 Shane Rawley	.05	.02	.01
☐ 439 Dickie Thon	.05	.02	.01
☐ 440 Juan Berenguer	.05	.02	.01
☐ 441 Kevin Romine	.05	.02	.01
☐ 442 Bill Landrum	.05	.02	.01
☐ 443 Todd Frohwirth	.05	.02	.01
☐ 444 Craig Worthington	.05	.02	.01
☐ 445 Fernando Valenzuela	.08	.04	.01
☐ 446 Joey Belle	1.50	.65	.19
☐ 447 Ed Whited UER	.05	.02	.01
(Ashville, should			
be Asheville)			
☐ 448 Dave Smith	.05	.02	.01
☐ 449 Dave Clark	.05	.02	.01
☐ 450 Juan Agosto	.05	.02	.01
☐ 451 Dave Valle	.05	.02	.01
☐ 452 Kent Hrbek	.08	.04	.01
☐ 453 Von Hayes	.05	.02	.01
☐ 454 Gary Gaetti	.05	.02	.01
☐ 455 Greg Briley	.05	.02	.01
☐ 456 Glenn Braggs	.05	.02	.01
☐ 457 Kirt Manwaring	.05	.02	.01
☐ 458 Mel Hall	.05	.02	.01
☐ 459 Brook Jacoby	.05	.02	.01
☐ 460 Pat Sheridan	.05	.02	.01
☐ 461 Rob Murphy	.05	.02	.01
☐ 462 Jimmy Key	.08	.04	.01
☐ 463 Nick Esasky	.05	.02	.01
☐ 464 Rob Ducey	.05	.02	.01
☐ 465 Carlos Quintana UER	.08	.04	.01
(Internatinoal)			
☐ 466 Larry Walker	2.50	1.15	.30
☐ 467 Todd Worrell	.05	.02	.01
☐ 468 Kevin Gross	.05	.02	.01
☐ 469 Terry Pendleton	.15	.07	.02
☐ 470 Dave Martinez	.08	.04	.01
☐ 471 Gene Larkin	.05	.02	.01
☐ 472 Len Dykstra UER	.08	.04	.01
('89 and total runs			
understated by 10)			
☐ 473 Barry Lyons	.05	.02	.01
☐ 474 Terry Mulholland	.08	.04	.01
☐ 475 Chip Hale	.05	.02	.01
☐ 476 Jesse Barfield	.05	.02	.01
☐ 477 Dan Plesac	.05	.02	.01
☐ 478A Scott Garrelts ERR	3.50	1.55	.45
(Photo actually			
Bill Bathe)			
☐ 478B Scott Garrelts COR	.08	.04	.01
☐ 479 Dave Righetti	.05	.02	.01
☐ 480 Gus Polidor UER	.05	.02	.01
(Wearing 14 on front,			
but 10 on back)			
☐ 481 Mookie Wilson	.05	.02	.01
☐ 482 Luis Rivera	.05	.02	.01
☐ 483 Mike Flanagan	.05	.02	.01
☐ 484 Dennis Boyd	.05	.02	.01
☐ 485 John Cerutti	.05	.02	.01
☐ 486 John Costello	.05	.02	.01
☐ 487 Pascual Perez	.05	.02	.01
☐ 488 Tommy Herr	.05	.02	.01
☐ 489 Tom Foley	.05	.02	.01
☐ 490 Curt Ford	.05	.02	.01
☐ 491 Steve Lake	.05	.02	.01
☐ 492 Tim Teufel	.05	.02	.01
☐ 493 Randy Bush	.05	.02	.01
☐ 494 Mike Jackson	.05	.02	.01
☐ 495 Steve Jeltz	.05	.02	.01
☐ 496 Paul Gibson	.05	.02	.01
☐ 497 Steve Balboni	.05	.02	.01
☐ 498 Bud Black	.05	.02	.01
☐ 499 Dale Sveum	.05	.02	.01
☐ 500 Checklist 401-500	.06	.01	.00
☐ 501 Tim Jones	.05	.02	.01
☐ 502 Mark Portugal	.05	.02	.01
☐ 503 Ivan Calderon	.05	.02	.01
☐ 504 Rick Rhoden	.05	.02	.01
☐ 505 Willie McGee	.08	.04	.01
☐ 506 Kirk McCaskill	.05	.02	.01
☐ 507 Dave LaPoint	.05	.02	.01
☐ 508 Jay Howell	.05	.02	.01
☐ 509 Johnny Ray	.05	.02	.01
☐ 510 Dave Anderson	.05	.02	.01
☐ 511 Chuck Crim	.05	.02	.01
☐ 512 Joe Hesketh	.05	.02	.01
☐ 513 Dennis Eckersley	.20	.09	.03
☐ 514 Greg Brock	.05	.02	.01
☐ 515 Tim Burke	.05	.02	.01

☐ 516	Frank Tanana	.05	.02	.01
☐ 517	Jay Bell	.08	.04	.01
☐ 518	Guillermo Hernandez	.05	.02	.01
☐ 519	Randy Kramer UER	.05	.02	.01
	(Codiroli misspelled			
	as Codoroli)			
☐ 520	Charles Hudson	.05	.02	.01
☐ 521	Jim Corsi	.05	.02	.01
	(Word "originally" is			
	misspelled on back)			
☐ 522	Steve Rosenberg	.05	.02	.01
☐ 523	Cris Carpenter	.05	.02	.01
☐ 524	Matt Winters	.05	.02	.01
☐ 525	Melido Perez	.08	.04	.01
☐ 526	Chris Gwynn UER	.05	.02	.01
	(Albeguerque)			
☐ 527	Bert Blyleven UER	.08	.04	.01
	(Games career total is			
	wrong, should be 644)			
☐ 528	Chuck Cary	.05	.02	.01
☐ 529	Daryl Boston	.05	.02	.01
☐ 530	Dale Mohorcic	.05	.02	.01
☐ 531	Geronimo Berroa	.05	.02	.01
☐ 532	Edgar Martinez	.40	.18	.05
☐ 533	Dale Murphy	.15	.07	.02
☐ 534	Jay Buhner	.08	.04	.01
☐ 535	John Smoltz UER	.50	.23	.06
	(HEA Stadium)			
☐ 536	Andy Van Slyke	.15	.07	.02
☐ 537	Mike Henneman	.05	.02	.01
☐ 538	Miguel Garcia	.05	.02	.01
☐ 539	Frank Williams	.05	.02	.01
☐ 540	R.J. Reynolds	.05	.02	.01
☐ 541	Shawn Hillegas	.05	.02	.01
☐ 542	Walt Weiss	.05	.02	.01
☐ 543	Greg Hibbard	.30	.14	.04
☐ 544	Nolan Ryan	1.25	.55	.16
☐ 545	Todd Zeile	.30	.14	.04
☐ 546	Hensley Meulens	.08	.04	.01
☐ 547	Tim Belcher	.08	.04	.01
☐ 548	Mike Witt	.05	.02	.01
☐ 549	Greg Cadaret UER	.05	.02	.01
	(Aquiring, should			
	be Acquiring)			
☐ 550	Franklin Stubbs	.05	.02	.01
☐ 551	Tony Castillo	.05	.02	.01
☐ 552	Jeff M. Robinson	.05	.02	.01
☐ 553	Steve Olin	.40	.18	.05
☐ 554	Alan Trammell	.08	.04	.01
☐ 555	Wade Boggs 4X	.40	.18	.05
	(Bo Jackson			
	in background)			
☐ 556	Will Clark	.60	.25	.08
☐ 557	Jeff King	.08	.04	.01
☐ 558	Mike Fitzgerald	.05	.02	.01
☐ 559	Ken Howell	.05	.02	.01
☐ 560	Bob Kipper	.05	.02	.01
☐ 561	Scott Bankhead	.05	.02	.01
☐ 562A	Jeff Innis ERR	2.50	1.15	.30
	(Photo actually			
	David West)			
☐ 562B	Jeff Innis COR	.08	.04	.01
☐ 563	Randy Johnson	.08	.04	.01
☐ 564	Wally Whitehurst	.05	.02	.01
☐ 565	Gene Harris	.05	.02	.01
☐ 566	Norm Charlton	.08	.04	.01
☐ 567	Robin Yount UER	.30	.14	.04
	(7602 career hits,			
	should be 2606)			
☐ 568	Joe Oliver UER	.12	.05	.02
	(Fl.orida)			
☐ 569	Mark Parent	.05	.02	.01
☐ 570	John Farrell UER	.05	.02	.01
	(Loss total added wrong)			
☐ 571	Tom Glavine	.50	.23	.06
☐ 572	Rod Nichols	.05	.02	.01
☐ 573	Jack Morris	.15	.07	.02
☐ 574	Greg Swindell	.08	.04	.01
☐ 575	Steve Searcy	.05	.02	.01
☐ 576	Ricky Jordan	.05	.02	.01
☐ 577	Matt Williams	.15	.07	.02
☐ 578	Mike LaValliere	.05	.02	.01
☐ 579	Bryn Smith	.05	.02	.01
☐ 580	Bruce Ruffin	.05	.02	.01
☐ 581	Randy Myers	.08	.04	.01
☐ 582	Rick Wrona	.05	.02	.01
☐ 583	Juan Samuel	.05	.02	.01
☐ 584	Les Lancaster	.05	.02	.01
☐ 585	Jeff Musselman	.05	.02	.01
☐ 586	Rob Dibble	.08	.04	.01
☐ 587	Eric Show	.05	.02	.01
☐ 588	Jesse Orosco	.05	.02	.01
☐ 589	Herm Winningham	.05	.02	.01
☐ 590	Andy Allanson	.05	.02	.01
☐ 591	Dion James	.05	.02	.01
☐ 592	Carmelo Martinez	.05	.02	.01
☐ 593	Luis Quinones	.05	.02	.01
☐ 594	Dennis Rasmussen	.05	.02	.01
☐ 595	Rich Yott	.05	.02	.01
☐ 596	Bob Walk	.05	.02	.01
☐ 597A	Andy McGaffigan ERR	.35	.16	.04
	(Photo actually			
	Rich Thompson)			
☐ 597B	Andy McGaffigan COR	.08	.04	.01
☐ 598	Billy Hatcher	.05	.02	.01
☐ 599	Bob Knepper	.05	.02	.01
☐ 600	Checklist 501-600 UER	.06	.01	.00
	(599 Bob Kneppers)			
☐ 601	Joey Cora	.05	.02	.01
☐ 602	Steve Finley	.12	.05	.02
☐ 603	Kal Daniels UER	.05	.02	.01
	(12 hits in '87, should			
	be 123; 335 runs,			
	should be 235)			

☐ 604 Gregg Olson	.15	.07	.02
☐ 605 Dave Stieb	.08	.04	.01
☐ 606 Kenny Rogers	.05	.02	.01
(Shown catching football)			
☐ 607 Zane Smith	.05	.02	.01
☐ 608 Bob Geren UER	.05	.02	.01
(Originally)			
☐ 609 Chad Kreuter	.05	.02	.01
☐ 610 Mike Smithson	.05	.02	.01
☐ 611 Jeff Wetherby	.05	.02	.01
☐ 612 Gary Mielke	.05	.02	.01
☐ 613 Pete Smith	.08	.04	.01
☐ 614 Jack Daugherty UER	.05	.02	.01
(Born 7/30/60, should be 7/3/60; origionally)			
☐ 615 Lance McCullers	.05	.02	.01
☐ 616 Don Robinson	.05	.02	.01
☐ 617 Jose Guzman	.05	.02	.01
☐ 618 Steve Bedrosian	.05	.02	.01
☐ 619 Jamie Moyer	.05	.02	.01
☐ 620 Atlee Hammaker	.05	.02	.01
☐ 621 Rick Luecken UER	.05	.02	.01
(Innings pitched wrong)			
☐ 622 Greg W. Harris	.05	.02	.01
☐ 623 Pete Harnisch	.08	.04	.01
☐ 624 Jerald Clark	.08	.04	.01
☐ 625 Jack McDowell	.40	.18	.05
☐ 626 Frank Viola	.08	.04	.01
☐ 627 Teddy Higuera	.05	.02	.01
☐ 628 Marty Pevey	.05	.02	.01
☐ 629 Bill Wegman	.05	.02	.01
☐ 630 Eric Plunk	.05	.02	.01
☐ 631 Drew Hall	.05	.02	.01
☐ 632 Doug Jones	.08	.04	.01
☐ 633 Geno Petralli	.05	.02	.01
☐ 634 Jose Alvarez	.05	.02	.01
☐ 635 Bob Milacki	.05	.02	.01
☐ 636 Bobby Witt	.08	.04	.01
☐ 637 Trevor Wilson	.05	.02	.01
☐ 638 Jeff Russell UER	.05	.02	.01
(Shutout stats wrong)			
☐ 639 Mike Krukow	.05	.02	.01
☐ 640 Rick Leach	.05	.02	.01
☐ 641 Dave Schmidt	.05	.02	.01
☐ 642 Terry Leach	.05	.02	.01
☐ 643 Calvin Schiraldi	.05	.02	.01
☐ 644 Bob Melvin	.05	.02	.01
☐ 645 Jim Abbott	.40	.18	.05
☐ 646 Jaime Navarro	.60	.25	.08
☐ 647 Mark Langston UER	.08	.04	.01
(Several errors in stats totals)			
☐ 648 Juan Nieves	.05	.02	.01
☐ 649 Damaso Garcia	.05	.02	.01
☐ 650 Charlie O'Brien	.05	.02	.01
☐ 651 Eric King	.05	.02	.01
☐ 652 Mike Boddicker	.05	.02	.01
☐ 653 Duane Ward	.05	.02	.01
☐ 654 Bob Stanley	.05	.02	.01
☐ 655 Sandy Alomar Jr.	.15	.07	.02
☐ 656 Danny Tartabull UER	.20	.09	.03
(395 BB, should be 295)			
☐ 657 Randy McCament	.05	.02	.01
☐ 658 Charlie Leibrandt	.05	.02	.01
☐ 659 Dan Quisenberry	.08	.04	.01
☐ 660 Paul Assenmacher	.05	.02	.01
☐ 661 Walt Terrell	.05	.02	.01
☐ 662 Tim Leary	.05	.02	.01
☐ 663 Randy Milligan	.05	.02	.01
☐ 664 Bo Diaz	.05	.02	.01
☐ 665 Mark Lemke UER	.08	.04	.01
(Richmond misspelled as Richomond)			
☐ 666 Jose Gonzalez	.05	.02	.01
☐ 667 Chuck Finley UER	.08	.04	.01
(Born 11/16/62, should be 11/26/62)			
☐ 668 John Kruk	.08	.04	.01
☐ 669 Dick Schofield	.05	.02	.01
☐ 670 Tim Crews	.05	.02	.01
☐ 671 John Dopson	.05	.02	.01
☐ 672 John Orton	.12	.05	.02
☐ 673 Eric Hetzel	.05	.02	.01
☐ 674 Lance Parrish	.08	.04	.01
☐ 675 Ramon Martinez	.25	.11	.03
☐ 676 Mark Gubicza	.05	.02	.01
☐ 677 Greg Litton	.05	.02	.01
☐ 678 Greg Mathews	.05	.02	.01
☐ 679 Dave Dravecky	.08	.04	.01
☐ 680 Steve Farr	.05	.02	.01
☐ 681 Mike Devereaux	.08	.04	.01
☐ 682 Ken Griffey Sr.	.08	.04	.01
☐ 683A Mickey Weston ERR	2.50	1.15	.30
(Listed as Jamie on card)			
☐ 683B Mickey Weston COR	.08	.04	.01
(Technically still an error as birthdate is listed as 3/26/81)			
☐ 684 Jack Armstrong	.08	.04	.01
☐ 685 Steve Buechele	.05	.02	.01
☐ 686 Bryan Harvey	.08	.04	.01
☐ 687 Lance Blankenship	.05	.02	.01
☐ 688 Dante Bichette	.08	.04	.01
☐ 689 Todd Burns	.05	.02	.01
☐ 690 Dan Petry	.05	.02	.01
☐ 691 Kent Anderson	.05	.02	.01
☐ 692 Todd Stottlemyre	.08	.04	.01
☐ 693 Wally Joyner UER	.08	.04	.01
(Several stats errors)			
☐ 694 Mike Rochford	.05	.02	.01
☐ 695 Floyd Bannister	.05	.02	.01
☐ 696 Rick Reuschel	.05	.02	.01

☐ 697 Jose DeLeon	.05	.02	.01
☐ 698 Jeff Montgomery	.08	.04	.01
☐ 699 Kelly Downs	.05	.02	.01
☐ 700A Checklist 601-700	2.50	.25	.07
ERR (683 Jamie Weston)			
☐ 700B Checklist 601-700 UER	.06	.01	.00
(683 Mickey Weston)			
☐ 701 Jim Gott	.05	.02	.01
☐ 702 Rookie Threats	1.00	.45	.13
Delino DeShields			
Marquis Grissom			
Larry Walker			
☐ 703 Alejandro Pena	.05	.02	.01
☐ 704 Willie Randolph	.08	.04	.01
☐ 705 Tim Leary	.05	.02	.01
☐ 706 Chuck McElroy	.25	.11	.03
☐ 707 Gerald Perry	.05	.02	.01
☐ 708 Tom Brunansky	.08	.04	.01
☐ 709 John Franco	.08	.04	.01
☐ 710 Mark Davis	.05	.02	.01
☐ 711 Dave Justice	4.00	1.80	.50
☐ 712 Storm Davis	.05	.02	.01
☐ 713 Scott Ruskin	.05	.02	.01
☐ 714 Glenn Braggs	.05	.02	.01
☐ 715 Kevin Bearse	.05	.02	.01
☐ 716 Jose Nunez	.05	.02	.01
☐ 717 Tim Layana	.05	.02	.01
☐ 718 Greg Myers	.05	.02	.01
☐ 719 Pete O'Brien	.05	.02	.01
☐ 720 John Candelaria	.05	.02	.01
☐ 721 Craig Grebeck	.30	.14	.04
☐ 722 Shawn Boskie	.15	.07	.02
☐ 723 Jim Leyritz	.12	.05	.02
☐ 724 Bill Sampen	.05	.02	.01
☐ 725 Scott Radinsky	.30	.14	.04
☐ 726 Todd Hundley	.30	.14	.04
☐ 727 Scott Hemond	.12	.05	.02
☐ 728 Lenny Webster	.12	.05	.02
☐ 729 Jeff Reardon	.08	.04	.01
☐ 730 Mitch Webster	.05	.02	.01
☐ 731 Brian Bohanon	.12	.05	.02
☐ 732 Rick Parker	.05	.02	.01
☐ 733 Terry Shumpert	.05	.02	.01
☐ 734A Ryan's 6th No-Hitter	6.00	2.70	.75
(No stripe on front)			
☐ 734B Ryan's 6th No-Hitter	1.00	.45	.13
(stripe added on card			
front for 300th win)			
☐ 735 John Burkett	.10	.05	.01
☐ 736 Derrick May	.75	.35	.09
☐ 737 Carlos Baerga	3.00	1.35	.40
☐ 738 Greg Smith	.05	.02	.01
☐ 739 Scott Sanderson	.05	.02	.01
☐ 740 Joe Kraemer	.05	.02	.01
☐ 741 Hector Villanueva	.10	.05	.01
☐ 742 Mike Fetters	.15	.07	.02
☐ 743 Mark Gardner	.20	.09	.03
☐ 744 Matt Nokes	.05	.02	.01
☐ 745 Dave Winfield	.30	.14	.04
☐ 746 Delino DeShields	2.00	.90	.25
☐ 747 Dann Howitt	.05	.02	.01
☐ 748 Tony Pena	.05	.02	.01
☐ 749 Oil Can Boyd	.05	.02	.01
☐ 750 Mike Benjamin	.10	.05	.01
☐ 751 Alex Cole	.35	.16	.04
☐ 752 Eric Gunderson	.12	.05	.02
☐ 753 Howard Farmer	.05	.02	.01
☐ 754 Joe Carter	.40	.18	.05
☐ 755 Ray Lankford	2.50	1.15	.30
☐ 756 Sandy Alomar Jr.	.15	.07	.02
☐ 757 Alex Sanchez	.05	.02	.01
☐ 758 Nick Esasky	.05	.02	.01
☐ 759 Stan Belinda	.30	.14	.04
☐ 760 Jim Presley	.05	.02	.01
☐ 761 Gary DiSarcina	.40	.18	.05
☐ 762 Wayne Edwards	.05	.02	.01
☐ 763 Pat Combs	.05	.02	.01
☐ 764 Mickey Pina	.05	.02	.01
☐ 765 Wilson Alvarez	.50	.23	.06
☐ 766 Dave Parker	.08	.04	.01
☐ 767 Mike Blowers	.05	.02	.01
☐ 768 Tony Phillips	.05	.02	.01
☐ 769 Pascual Perez	.05	.02	.01
☐ 770 Gary Pettis	.05	.02	.01
☐ 771 Fred Lynn	.08	.04	.01
☐ 772 Mel Rojas	.20	.09	.03
☐ 773 David Segui	.15	.07	.02
☐ 774 Gary Carter	.08	.04	.01
☐ 775 Rafael Valdez	.12	.05	.02
☐ 776 Glenallen Hill	.08	.04	.01
☐ 777 Keith Hernandez	.08	.04	.01
☐ 778 Billy Hatcher	.05	.02	.01
☐ 779 Marty Clary	.05	.02	.01
☐ 780 Candy Maldonado	.05	.02	.01
☐ 781 Mike Marshall	.05	.02	.01
☐ 782 Billy Joe Robidoux	.05	.02	.01
☐ 783 Mark Langston	.08	.04	.01
☐ 784 Paul Sorrento	.50	.23	.06
☐ 785 Dave Hollins	1.75	.80	.22
☐ 786 Cecil Fielder	.40	.18	.05
☐ 787 Matt Young	.05	.02	.01
☐ 788 Jeff Huson	.05	.02	.01
☐ 789 Lloyd Moseby	.05	.02	.01
☐ 790 Ron Kittle	.05	.02	.01
☐ 791 Hubie Brooks	.05	.02	.01
☐ 792 Craig Lefferts	.05	.02	.01
☐ 793 Kevin Bass	.05	.02	.01
☐ 794 Bryn Smith	.05	.02	.01
☐ 795 Juan Samuel	.05	.02	.01
☐ 796 Sam Horn	.05	.02	.01
☐ 797 Randy Myers	.08	.04	.01
☐ 798 Chris James	.05	.02	.01
☐ 799 Bill Gullickson	.05	.02	.01
☐ 800 Checklist 701-800	.08	.01	.00

1991 Upper Deck

This set marked the third year Upper Deck has issued a 700-card set in January. The cards measure 2 1/2" by 3 1/2". The set features 26 star rookies to lead off the set as well as other special cards featuring multi-players. The set is made on the typical Upper Deck card stock and features full-color photos on both the front and the back. The team checklist (TC) cards in the set feature an attractive Vernon Wells drawing of a featured player for that particular team. A special Michael Jordan card (numbered SP1) was randomly included in packs on a somewhat limited basis; this Jordan card is not included in the set price below. The Hank Aaron hologram card was randomly inserted in the 1991 Upper Deck high number foil packs. The key Rookie Cards in this set include Wes Chamberlain, Wilfredo Cordero, Luis Gonzalez, Chipper Jones, Eric Karros, Brian McRae, Pedro Munoz, Mike Mussina, Phil Plantier, Reggie Sanders, and Todd Van Poppel. This 100-card extended or high-number series was issued by Upper Deck several months after the release of their first series. The extended series features rookie players as well as players who switched teams between seasons. In the extended wax packs were low number cards, special cards featuring Hank Aaron as the next featured player in their baseball heroes series, and a special card honoring the May 1st exploits of Rickey Henderson and Nolan Ryan. For the first time in Upper Deck's three-year history, they did not issue a factory Extended set. The only

noteworthy Rookie Card in the high-number series is Jeff Bagwell.

	MT	EX-MT	VG
COMPLETE SET (800) 30.00		13.50	3.80
COMPLETE FACT.SET (800) 33.00		15.00	4.10
COMPLETE LO SET (700) 24.00		11.00	3.00
COMPLETE HI SET (100) 6.00		2.70	.75
COMMON PLAYER (1-700) 05		.02	.01
COMMON PLAYER (701-800) 05		.02	.01

		MT	EX-MT	VG
☐	1 Star Rookie Checklist.......06		.01	.00
☐	2 Phil Plantier 90		.40	.11
☐	3 D.J. Dozier 15		.07	.02
☐	4 Dave Hansen.................15		.07	.02
☐	5 Maurice Vaughn.............35		.16	.04
☐	6 Leo Gomez...................50		.23	.06
☐	7 Scott Aldred.................15		.07	.02
☐	8 Scott Chiamparino.........08		.04	.01
☐	9 Lance Dickson..............15		.07	.02
☐	10 Sean Berry...................20		.09	.03
☐	11 Bernie Williams.............40		.18	.05
☐	12 Brian Barnes UER..........15		.07	.02
	(Photo either not him			
	or in wrong jersey)			
☐	13 Narciso Elvira...............10		.05	.01
☐	14 Mike Gardiner...............15		.07	.02
☐	15 Greg Colbrunn 40		.18	.05
☐	16 Bernard Gilkey 25		.11	.03
☐	17 Mark Lewis 20		.09	.03
☐	18 Mickey Morandini..........20		.09	.03
☐	19 Charles Nagy................60		.25	.08
☐	20 Geronimo Pena..............15		.07	.02
☐	21 Henry Rodriguez............35		.16	.04
☐	22 Scott Cooper.................40		.18	.05
☐	23 Anduj ar Cedeno UER......25		.11	.03
	(Shown batting left,			
	back says right)			
☐	24 Eric Karros.................2.50		1.15	.30
☐	25 Steve Decker UER..........25		.11	.03
	(Lewis-Clark State			
	College, not Lewis			
	and Clark)			
☐	26 Kevin Belcher................10		.05	.01
☐	27 Jeff Conine...................40		.18	.05
☐	28 Oakland Athletics TC.......06		.03	.01
	Dave Stewart			
☐	29 Chicago White Sox TC.....10		.05	.01
	Carlton Fisk			
☐	30 Texas Rangers TC...........06		.03	.01
	Rafael Palmeiro			
☐	31 California Angels TC.........06		.03	.01
	Chuck Finley			
☐	32 Seattle Mariners TC.........06		.03	.01
	Harold Reynolds			
☐	33 Kansas City Royals TC......06		.03	.01
	Bret Saberhagen			

☐ 34	Minnesota Twins TC 06	.03	.01
	Gary Gaetti		
☐ 35	Scott Leius.....................15	.07	.02
☐ 36	Neal Heaton 05	.02	.01
☐ 37	Terry Lee........................08	.04	.01
☐ 38	Gary Redus 05	.02	.01
☐ 39	Barry Jones.....................05	.02	.01
☐ 40	Chuck Knoblauch 1.00	.45	.13
☐ 41	Larry Andersen 05	.02	.01
☐ 42	Darryl Hamilton...............08	.04	.01
☐ 43	Boston Red Sox TC 06	.03	.01
	Mike Greenwell		
☐ 44	Toronto Blue Jays TC........06	.03	.01
	Kelly Gruber		
☐ 45	Detroit Tigers TC.............06	.03	.01
	Jack Morris		
☐ 46	Cleveland Indians TC 06	.03	.01
	Sandy Alomar Jr.		
☐ 47	Baltimore Orioles TC........06	.03	.01
	Gregg Olson		
☐ 48	Milwaukee Brewers TC......06	.03	.01
	Dave Parker		
☐ 49	New York Yankees TC.......06	.03	.01
	Roberto Kelly		
☐ 50	Top Prospect Checklist 06	.01	.00
☐ 51	Kyle Abbott 20	.09	.03
☐ 52	Jeff Juden......................20	.09	.03
☐ 53	Todd Van Poppel UER 1.00	.45	.13
	(Born Arlington and		
	attended John Martin HS,		
	should say Hinsdale and		
	James Martin HS)		
☐ 54	Steve Karsay 40	.18	.05
☐ 55	Chipper Jones 1.50	.65	.19
☐ 56	Chris Johnson UER..........10	.05	.01
	(Called Tim on back)		
☐ 57	John Ericks 08	.04	.01
☐ 58	Gary Scott.......................30	.14	.04
☐ 59	Kiki Jones 05	.02	.01
☐ 60	Wilfredo Cordero 1.00	.45	.13
☐ 61	Royce Clayton 60	.25	.08
☐ 62	Tim Costo.......................40	.18	.05
☐ 63	Roger Salkeld 30	.14	.04
☐ 64	Brook Fordyce 15	.07	.02
☐ 65	Mike Mussina 2.50	1.15	.30
☐ 66	Dave Staton 40	.18	.05
☐ 67	Mike Lieberthal 35	.16	.04
☐ 68	Kurt Miller 40	.18	.05
☐ 69	Dan Peltier 20	.09	.03
☐ 70	Greg Blosser 30	.14	.04
☐ 71	Reggie Sanders.............1.25	.55	.16
☐ 72	Brent Mayne 05	.02	.01
☐ 73	Rico Brogna 25	.11	.03
☐ 74	Willie Banks 40	.18	.05
☐ 75	Len Brutcher 10	.05	.01
☐ 76	Pat Kelly 25	.11	.03
☐ 77	Cincinnati Reds TC...........06	.03	.01
	Chris Sabo		
☐ 78	Los Angeles Dodgers TC...06	.03	.01
	Ramon Martinez		
☐ 79	San Fran. Giants TC 06	.03	.01
	Matt Williams		
☐ 80	San Diego Padres TC........12	.05	.02
	Roberto Alomar		
☐ 81	Houston Astros TC............06	.03	.01
	Glenn Davis		
☐ 82	Atlanta Braves TC.............10	.05	.01
	Ron Gant		
☐ 83	Fielder's Feat...................15	.07	.02
	Cecil Fielder		
☐ 84	Orlando Merced 35	.16	.04
☐ 85	Domingo Ramos...............05	.02	.01
☐ 86	Tom Bolton 05	.02	.01
☐ 87	Andres Santana 10	.05	.01
☐ 88	John Dopson 05	.02	.01
☐ 89	Kenny Williams 05	.02	.01
☐ 90	Marty Barrett....................05	.02	.01
☐ 91	Tom Pagnozzi 05	.02	.01
☐ 92	Carmelo Martinez.............05	.02	.01
☐ 93	Save Master 05	.02	.01
	(Bobby Thigpen)		
☐ 94	Pittsburgh Pirates TC 10	.05	.01
	Barry Bonds		
☐ 95	New York Mets TC............06	.03	.01
	Gregg Jefferies		
☐ 96	Montreal Expos TC............06	.03	.01
	Tim Wallach		
☐ 97	Phila. Phillies TC.............06	.03	.01
	Len Dykstra		
☐ 98	St.Louis Cardinals TC 06	.03	.01
	Pedro Guerrero		
☐ 99	Chicago Cubs TC 09	.04	.01
	Mark Grace		
☐ 100	Checklist 1-100................06	.01	.00
☐ 101	Kevin Elster 05	.02	.01
☐ 102	Tom Brookens 05	.02	.01
☐ 103	Mackey Sasser.................05	.02	.01
☐ 104	Felix Fermin 05	.02	.01
☐ 105	Kevin McReynolds............08	.04	.01
☐ 106	Dave Stieb 05	.02	.01
☐ 107	Jeffrey Leonard 05	.02	.01
☐ 108	Dave Henderson 05	.02	.01
☐ 109	Sid Bream 05	.02	.01
☐ 110	Henry Cotto.....................05	.02	.01
☐ 111	Shawon Dunston 08	.04	.01
☐ 112	Mariano Duncan 05	.02	.01
☐ 113	Joe Girardi 05	.02	.01
☐ 114	Billy Hatcher 05	.02	.01
☐ 115	Greg Maddux 15	.07	.02
☐ 116	Jerry Browne 05	.02	.01
☐ 117	Juan Samuel 05	.02	.01
☐ 118	Steve Olin 08	.04	.01
☐ 119	Alfredo Griffin 05	.02	.01
☐ 120	Mitch Webster..................05	.02	.01

☐	121	Joel Skinner	.05	.02	.01	☐	177	Dave Magadan	.08	.04	.01

☐ 121	Joel Skinner	.05	.02	.01
☐ 122	Frank Viola	.08	.04	.01
☐ 123	Cory Snyder	.05	.02	.01
☐ 124	Howard Johnson	.08	.04	.01
☐ 125	Carlos Baerga	.35	.16	.04
☐ 126	Tony Fernandez	.08	.04	.01
☐ 127	Dave Stewart	.08	.04	.01
☐ 128	Jay Buhner	.08	.04	.01
☐ 129	Mike LaValliere	.05	.02	.01
☐ 130	Scott Bradley	.05	.02	.01
☐ 131	Tony Phillips	.05	.02	.01
☐ 132	Ryne Sandberg	.40	.18	.05
☐ 133	Paul O'Neill	.08	.04	.01
☐ 134	Mark Grace	.15	.07	.02
☐ 135	Chris Sabo	.08	.04	.01
☐ 136	Ramon Martinez	.10	.05	.01
☐ 137	Brook Jacoby	.05	.02	.01
☐ 138	Candy Maldonado	.05	.02	.01
☐ 139	Mike Scioscia	.05	.02	.01
☐ 140	Chris James	.05	.02	.01
☐ 141	Craig Worthington	.05	.02	.01
☐ 142	Manny Lee	.05	.02	.01
☐ 143	Tim Raines	.08	.04	.01
☐ 144	Sandy Alomar Jr.	.08	.04	.01
☐ 145	John Olerud	.25	.11	.03
☐ 146	Ozzie Canseco (With Jose)	.10	.05	.01
☐ 147	Pat Borders	.05	.02	.01
☐ 148	Harold Reynolds	.05	.02	.01
☐ 149	Tom Henke	.08	.04	.01
☐ 150	R.J. Reynolds	.05	.02	.01
☐ 151	Mike Gallego	.05	.02	.01
☐ 152	Bobby Bonilla	.15	.07	.02
☐ 153	Terry Steinbach	.08	.04	.01
☐ 154	Barry Bonds	.30	.14	.04
☐ 155	Jose Canseco	.35	.16	.04
☐ 156	Gregg Jefferies	.08	.04	.01
☐ 157	Matt Williams	.08	.04	.01
☐ 158	Craig Biggio	.08	.04	.01
☐ 159	Daryl Boston	.05	.02	.01
☐ 160	Ricky Jordan	.05	.02	.01
☐ 161	Stan Belinda	.05	.02	.01
☐ 162	Ozzie Smith	.15	.07	.02
☐ 163	Tom Brunansky	.08	.04	.01
☐ 164	Todd Zeile	.08	.04	.01
☐ 165	Mike Greenwell	.08	.04	.01
☐ 166	Kal Daniels	.05	.02	.01
☐ 167	Kent Hrbek	.08	.04	.01
☐ 168	Franklin Stubbs	.05	.02	.01
☐ 169	Dick Schofield	.05	.02	.01
☐ 170	Junior Ortiz	.05	.02	.01
☐ 171	Hector Villanueva	.05	.02	.01
☐ 172	Dennis Eckersley	.12	.05	.02
☐ 173	Mitch Williams	.05	.02	.01
☐ 174	Mark McGwire	.35	.16	.04
☐ 175	Fernando Valenzuela 3X	.08	.04	.01
☐ 176	Gary Carter	.08	.04	.01
☐ 177	Dave Magadan	.08	.04	.01
☐ 178	Robby Thompson	.05	.02	.01
☐ 179	Bob Ojeda	.05	.02	.01
☐ 180	Ken Caminiti	.08	.04	.01
☐ 181	Don Slaught	.05	.02	.01
☐ 182	Luis Rivera	.05	.02	.01
☐ 183	Jay Bell	.08	.04	.01
☐ 184	Jody Reed	.05	.02	.01
☐ 185	Wally Backman	.05	.02	.01
☐ 186	Dave Martinez	.05	.02	.01
☐ 187	Luis Polonia	.08	.04	.01
☐ 188	Shane Mack	.08	.04	.01
☐ 189	Spike Owen	.05	.02	.01
☐ 190	Scott Bailes	.05	.02	.01
☐ 191	John Russell	.05	.02	.01
☐ 192	Walt Weiss	.05	.02	.01
☐ 193	Jose Oquendo	.05	.02	.01
☐ 194	Carney Lansford	.08	.04	.01
☐ 195	Jeff Huson	.05	.02	.01
☐ 196	Keith Miller	.05	.02	.01
☐ 197	Eric Yelding	.05	.02	.01
☐ 198	Ron Darling	.08	.04	.01
☐ 199	John Kruk	.08	.04	.01
☐ 200	Checklist 101-200	.06	.01	.00
☐ 201	John Shelby	.05	.02	.01
☐ 202	Bob Geren	.05	.02	.01
☐ 203	Lance McCullers	.05	.02	.01
☐ 204	Alvaro Espinoza	.05	.02	.01
☐ 205	Mark Salas	.05	.02	.01
☐ 206	Mike Pagliarulo	.05	.02	.01
☐ 207	Jose Uribe	.05	.02	.01
☐ 208	Jim Deshaies	.05	.02	.01
☐ 209	Ron Karkovice	.05	.02	.01
☐ 210	Rafael Ramirez	.05	.02	.01
☐ 211	Donnie Hill	.05	.02	.01
☐ 212	Brian Harper	.05	.02	.01
☐ 213	Jack Howell	.05	.02	.01
☐ 214	Wes Gardner	.05	.02	.01
☐ 215	Tim Burke	.05	.02	.01
☐ 216	Doug Jones	.05	.02	.01
☐ 217	Hubie Brooks	.05	.02	.01
☐ 218	Tom Candiotti	.05	.02	.01
☐ 219	Gerald Perry	.05	.02	.01
☐ 220	Jose DeLeon	.05	.02	.01
☐ 221	Wally Whitehurst	.05	.02	.01
☐ 222	Alan Mills	.15	.07	.02
☐ 223	Alan Trammell	.08	.04	.01
☐ 224	Dwight Gooden	.08	.04	.01
☐ 225	Travis Fryman	2.00	.90	.25
☐ 226	Joe Carter	.20	.09	.03
☐ 227	Julio Franco	.08	.04	.01
☐ 228	Craig Lefferts	.05	.02	.01
☐ 229	Gary Pettis	.05	.02	.01
☐ 230	Dennis Rasmussen	.05	.02	.01
☐ 231A	Brian Downing ERR (No position on front)	.25	.11	.03
☐ 231B	Brian Downing COR	.40	.18	.05

(DH on front)

☐	232 Carlos Quintana	.05	.02	.01
☐	233 Gary Gaetti	.05	.02	.01
☐	234 Mark Langston	.08	.04	.01
☐	235 Tim Wallach	.08	.04	.01
☐	236 Greg Swindell	.08	.04	.01
☐	237 Eddie Murray	.15	.07	.02
☐	238 Jeff Manto	.05	.02	.01
☐	239 Lenny Harris	.05	.02	.01
☐	240 Jesse Orosco	.05	.02	.01
☐	241 Scott Lusader	.05	.02	.01
☐	242 Sid Fernandez	.08	.04	.01
☐	243 Jim Leyritz	.05	.02	.01
☐	244 Cecil Fielder	.20	.09	.03
☐	245 Darryl Strawberry	.20	.09	.03
☐	246 Frank Thomas UER	4.00	1.80	.50
	(Comiskey Park			
	misspelled Comisky)			
☐	247 Kevin Mitchell	.08	.04	.01
☐	248 Lance Johnson	.05	.02	.01
☐	249 Rick Reuschel	.05	.02	.01
☐	250 Mark Portugal	.05	.02	.01
☐	251 Derek Lilliquist	.05	.02	.01
☐	252 Brian Holman	.05	.02	.01
☐	253 Rafael Valdez UER	.05	.02	.01
	(Born 4/17/68,			
	should be 12/17/67)			
☐	254 B.J. Surhoff	.05	.02	.01
☐	255 Tony Gwynn	.20	.09	.03
☐	256 Andy Van Slyke	.10	.05	.01
☐	257 Todd Stottlemyre	.08	.04	.01
☐	258 Jose Lind	.05	.02	.01
☐	259 Greg Myers	.05	.02	.01
☐	260 Jeff Ballard	.05	.02	.01
☐	261 Bobby Thigpen	.05	.02	.01
☐	262 Jimmy Kremers	.05	.02	.01
☐	263 Robin Ventura	.40	.18	.05
☐	264 John Smoltz	.20	.09	.03
☐	265 Sammy Sosa	.08	.04	.01
☐	266 Gary Sheffield	.40	.18	.05
☐	267 Len Dykstra	.08	.04	.01
☐	268 Bill Spiers	.05	.02	.01
☐	269 Charlie Hayes	.05	.02	.01
☐	270 Brett Butler	.08	.04	.01
☐	271 Bip Roberts	.08	.04	.01
☐	272 Rob Deer	.08	.04	.01
☐	273 Fred Lynn	.08	.04	.01
☐	274 Dave Parker	.08	.04	.01
☐	275 Andy Benes	.12	.05	.02
☐	276 Glenallen Hill	.05	.02	.01
☐	277 Steve Howard	.10	.05	.01
☐	278 Doug Drabek	.08	.04	.01
☐	279 Joe Oliver	.05	.02	.01
☐	280 Todd Benzinger	.05	.02	.01
☐	281 Eric King	.05	.02	.01
☐	282 Jim Presley	.05	.02	.01
☐	283 Ken Patterson	.05	.02	.01

☐	284 Jack Daugherty	.05	.02	.01
☐	285 Ivan Calderon	.05	.02	.01
☐	286 Edgar Diaz	.05	.02	.01
☐	287 Kevin Bass	.05	.02	.01
☐	288 Don Carman	.05	.02	.01
☐	289 Greg Brock	.05	.02	.01
☐	290 John Franco	.08	.04	.01
☐	291 Joey Cora	.05	.02	.01
☐	292 Bill Wegman	.05	.02	.01
☐	293 Eric Show	.05	.02	.01
☐	294 Scott Bankhead	.05	.02	.01
☐	295 Garry Templeton	.05	.02	.01
☐	296 Mickey Tettleton	.08	.04	.01
☐	297 Luis Sojo	.05	.02	.01
☐	298 Jose Rijo	.08	.04	.01
☐	299 Dave Johnson	.05	.02	.01
☐	300 Checklist 201-300	.06	.01	.00
☐	301 Mark Grant	.05	.02	.01
☐	302 Pete Harnisch	.08	.04	.01
☐	303 Greg Olson	.05	.02	.01
☐	304 Anthony Telford	.05	.02	.01
☐	305 Lonnie Smith	.05	.02	.01
☐	306 Chris Hoiles	.25	.11	.03
☐	307 Bryn Smith	.05	.02	.01
☐	308 Mike Devereaux	.08	.04	.01
☐	309A Milt Thompson ERR	.25	.11	.03
	(Under yr information			
	has print dot)			
☐	309B Milt Thompson COR	.05	.02	.01
	(Under yr information			
	says 86)			
☐	310 Bob Melvin	.05	.02	.01
☐	311 Luis Salazar	.05	.02	.01
☐	312 Ed Whitson	.05	.02	.01
☐	313 Charlie Hough	.05	.02	.01
☐	314 Dave Clark	.05	.02	.01
☐	315 Eric Gunderson	.05	.02	.01
☐	316 Dan Petry	.05	.02	.01
☐	317 Dante Bichette UER	.05	.02	.01
	(Assists misspelled			
	as assissts)			
☐	318 Mike Heath	.05	.02	.01
☐	319 Damon Berryhill	.05	.02	.01
☐	320 Walt Terrell	.05	.02	.01
☐	321 Scott Fletcher	.05	.02	.01
☐	322 Dan Plesac	.05	.02	.01
☐	323 Jack McDowell	.15	.07	.02
☐	324 Paul Molitor	.10	.05	.01
☐	325 Ozzie Guillen	.05	.02	.01
☐	326 Gregg Olson	.08	.04	.01
☐	327 Pedro Guerrero	.08	.04	.01
☐	328 Bob Milacki	.05	.02	.01
☐	329 John Tudor UER	.05	.02	.01
	('90 Cardinals,			
	should be '90 Dodgers)			
☐	330 Steve Finley UER	.08	.04	.01
	(Born 3/12/65,			

should be 5/12)

☐ 331	Jack Clark	.08	.04	.01
☐ 332	Jerome Walton	.05	.02	.01
☐ 333	Andy Hawkins	.05	.02	.01
☐ 334	Derrick May	.08	.04	.01
☐ 335	Roberto Alomar	.50	.23	.06
☐ 336	Jack Morris	.10	.05	.01
☐ 337	Dave Winfield	.15	.07	.02
☐ 338	Steve Searcy	.05	.02	.01
☐ 339	Chili Davis	.08	.04	.01
☐ 340	Larry Sheets	.05	.02	.01
☐ 341	Ted Higuera	.05	.02	.01
☐ 342	David Segui	.05	.02	.01
☐ 343	Greg Cadaret	.05	.02	.01
☐ 344	Robin Yount	.15	.07	.02
☐ 345	Nolan Ryan	.75	.35	.09
☐ 346	Ray Lankford	.35	.16	.04
☐ 347	Cal Ripken	.50	.23	.06
☐ 348	Lee Smith	.08	.04	.01
☐ 349	Brady Anderson	.08	.04	.01
☐ 350	Frank DiPino	.05	.02	.01
☐ 351	Hal Morris	.08	.04	.01
☐ 352	Deion Sanders	.30	.14	.04
☐ 353	Barry Larkin	.15	.07	.02
☐ 354	Don Mattingly	.20	.09	.03
☐ 355	Eric Davis	.08	.04	.01
☐ 356	Jose Offerman	.08	.04	.01
☐ 357	Mel Rojas	.05	.02	.01
☐ 358	Rudy Seanez	.15	.07	.02
☐ 359	Oil Can Boyd	.05	.02	.01
☐ 360	Nelson Liriano	.05	.02	.01
☐ 361	Ron Gant	.20	.09	.03
☐ 362	Howard Farmer	.05	.02	.01
☐ 363	David Justice	.60	.25	.08
☐ 364	Delino DeShields	.25	.11	.03
☐ 365	Steve Avery	.40	.18	.05
☐ 366	David Cone	.12	.05	.02
☐ 367	Lou Whitaker	.08	.04	.01
☐ 368	Von Hayes	.05	.02	.01
☐ 369	Frank Tanana	.05	.02	.01
☐ 370	Tim Teufel	.05	.02	.01
☐ 371	Randy Myers	.08	.04	.01
☐ 372	Roberto Kelly	.08	.04	.01
☐ 373	Jack Armstrong	.05	.02	.01
☐ 374	Kelly Gruber	.08	.04	.01
☐ 375	Kevin Maas	.10	.05	.01
☐ 376	Randy Johnson	.08	.04	.01
☐ 377	David West	.05	.02	.01
☐ 378	Brent Knackert	.05	.02	.01
☐ 379	Rick Honeycutt	.05	.02	.01
☐ 380	Kevin Gross	.05	.02	.01
☐ 381	Tom Foley	.05	.02	.01
☐ 382	Jeff Blauser	.05	.02	.01
☐ 383	Scott Ruskin	.05	.02	.01
☐ 384	Andres Thomas	.05	.02	.01
☐ 385	Dennis Martinez	.08	.04	.01
☐ 386	Mike Henneman	.05	.02	.01
☐ 387	Felix Jose	.08	.04	.01
☐ 388	Alejandro Pena	.05	.02	.01
☐ 389	Chet Lemon	.05	.02	.01
☐ 390	Craig Wilson	.10	.05	.01
☐ 391	Chuck Crim	.05	.02	.01
☐ 392	Mel Hall	.05	.02	.01
☐ 393	Mark Knudson	.05	.02	.01
☐ 394	Norm Charlton	.08	.04	.01
☐ 395	Mike Felder	.05	.02	.01
☐ 396	Tim Layana	.05	.02	.01
☐ 397	Steve Frey	.05	.02	.01
☐ 398	Bill Doran	.05	.02	.01
☐ 399	Dion James	.05	.02	.01
☐ 400	Checklist 301-400	.06	.01	.00
☐ 401	Ron Hassey	.05	.02	.01
☐ 402	Don Robinson	.05	.02	.01
☐ 403	Gene Nelson	.05	.02	.01
☐ 404	Terry Kennedy	.05	.02	.01
☐ 405	Todd Burns	.05	.02	.01
☐ 406	Roger McDowell	.05	.02	.01
☐ 407	Bob Kipper	.05	.02	.01
☐ 408	Darren Daulton	.08	.04	.01
☐ 409	Chuck Cary	.05	.02	.01
☐ 410	Bruce Ruffin	.05	.02	.01
☐ 411	Juan Berenguer	.05	.02	.01
☐ 412	Gary Ward	.05	.02	.01
☐ 413	Al Newman	.05	.02	.01
☐ 414	Danny Jackson	.05	.02	.01
☐ 415	Greg Gagne	.05	.02	.01
☐ 416	Tom Herr	.05	.02	.01
☐ 417	Jeff Parrett	.05	.02	.01
☐ 418	Jeff Reardon	.08	.04	.01
☐ 419	Mark Lemke	.05	.02	.01
☐ 420	Charlie O'Brien	.05	.02	.01
☐ 421	Willie Randolph	.08	.04	.01
☐ 422	Steve Bedrosian	.05	.02	.01
☐ 423	Mike Moore	.05	.02	.01
☐ 424	Jeff Brantley	.05	.02	.01
☐ 425	Bob Welch	.05	.02	.01
☐ 426	Terry Mulholland	.05	.02	.01
☐ 427	Willie Blair	.05	.02	.01
☐ 428	Darrin Fletcher	.05	.02	.01
☐ 429	Mike Witt	.05	.02	.01
☐ 430	Joe Boever	.05	.02	.01
☐ 431	Tom Gordon	.08	.04	.01
☐ 432	Pedro Munoz	.50	.23	.06
☐ 433	Kevin Seitzer	.08	.04	.01
☐ 434	Kevin Tapani	.08	.04	.01
☐ 435	Bret Saberhagen	.08	.04	.01
☐ 436	Ellis Burks	.08	.04	.01
☐ 437	Chuck Finley	.08	.04	.01
☐ 438	Mike Boddicker	.05	.02	.01
☐ 439	Francisco Cabrera	.05	.02	.01
☐ 440	Todd Hundley	.05	.02	.01
☐ 441	Kelly Downs	.05	.02	.01
☐ 442	Dann Howitt	.05	.02	.01
☐ 443	Scott Garrelts	.05	.02	.01

☐	444	Rickey Henderson 3X	.20	.09	.03	☐	497	Oddibe McDowell	.05	.02	.01
☐	445	Will Clark	.30	.14	.04	☐	498	Bill Swift	.05	.02	.01
☐	446	Ben McDonald	.15	.07	.02	☐	499	Jeff Treadway	.05	.02	.01
☐	447	Dale Murphy	.08	.04	.01	☐	500	Checklist 401-500	.06	.01	.00
☐	448	Dave Righetti	.05	.02	.01	☐	501	Gene Larkin	.05	.02	.01
☐	449	Dickie Thon	.05	.02	.01	☐	502	Bob Boone	.08	.04	.01
☐	450	Ted Power	.05	.02	.01	☐	503	Allan Anderson	.05	.02	.01
☐	451	Scott Coolbaugh	.05	.02	.01	☐	504	Luis Aquino	.05	.02	.01
☐	452	Dwight Smith	.05	.02	.01	☐	505	Mark Guthrie	.05	.02	.01
☐	453	Pete Incaviglia	.05	.02	.01	☐	506	Joe Orsulak	.05	.02	.01
☐	454	Andre Dawson	.15	.07	.02	☐	507	Dana Kiecker	.05	.02	.01
☐	455	Ruben Sierra	.25	.11	.03	☐	508	Dave Gallagher	.05	.02	.01
☐	456	Andres Galarraga	.05	.02	.01	☐	509	Greg A. Harris	.05	.02	.01
☐	457	Alvin Davis	.05	.02	.01	☐	510	Mark Williamson	.05	.02	.01
☐	458	Tony Castillo	.05	.02	.01	☐	511	Casey Candaele	.05	.02	.01
☐	459	Pete O'Brien	.05	.02	.01	☐	512	Mookie Wilson	.05	.02	.01
☐	460	Charlie Leibrandt	.05	.02	.01	☐	513	Dave Smith	.05	.02	.01
☐	461	Vince Coleman	.08	.04	.01	☐	514	Chuck Carr	.05	.02	.01
☐	462	Steve Sax	.08	.04	.01	☐	515	Glenn Wilson	.05	.02	.01
☐	463	Omar Olivares	.20	.09	.03	☐	516	Mike Fitzgerald	.05	.02	.01
☐	464	Oscar Azocar	.05	.02	.01	☐	517	Devon White	.08	.04	.01
☐	465	Joe Magrane	.05	.02	.01	☐	518	Dave Hollins	.20	.09	.03
☐	466	Karl Rhodes	.05	.02	.01	☐	519	Mark Eichhorn	.05	.02	.01
☐	467	Benito Santiago	.08	.04	.01	☐	520	Otis Nixon	.08	.04	.01
☐	468	Joe Klink	.05	.02	.01	☐	521	Terry Shumpert	.05	.02	.01
☐	469	Sil Campusano	.05	.02	.01	☐	522	Scott Erickson	.35	.16	.04
☐	470	Mark Parent	.05	.02	.01	☐	523	Danny Tartabull	.08	.04	.01
☐	471	Shawn Boskie UER	.05	.02	.01	☐	524	Orel Hershiser	.08	.04	.01
		(Depleted misspelled				☐	525	George Brett	.15	.07	.02
		as depleated)				☐	526	Greg Vaughn	.10	.05	.01
☐	472	Kevin Brown	.08	.04	.01	☐	527	Tim Naehring	.12	.05	.02
☐	473	Rick Sutcliffe	.08	.04	.01	☐	528	Curt Schilling	.08	.04	.01
☐	474	Rafael Palmeiro	.12	.05	.02	☐	529	Chris Bosio	.05	.02	.01
☐	475	Mike Harkey	.08	.04	.01	☐	530	Sam Horn	.05	.02	.01
☐	476	Jaime Navarro	.08	.04	.01	☐	531	Mike Scott	.05	.02	.01
☐	477	Marquis Grissom UER	.25	.11	.03	☐	532	George Bell	.08	.04	.01
		(DeShields misspelled				☐	533	Eric Anthony	.08	.04	.01
		as DeSheilds)				☐	534	Julio Valera	.25	.11	.03
☐	478	Marty Clary	.05	.02	.01	☐	535	Glenn Davis	.08	.04	.01
☐	479	Greg Briley	.05	.02	.01	☐	536	Larry Walker UER	.30	.14	.04
☐	480	Tom Glavine	.35	.16	.04			(Should have comma			
☐	481	Lee Guetterman	.05	.02	.01			after Expos in text)			
☐	482	Rex Hudler	.05	.02	.01	☐	537	Pat Combs	.05	.02	.01
☐	483	Dave LaPoint	.05	.02	.01	☐	538	Chris Nabholz	.15	.07	.02
☐	484	Terry Pendleton	.10	.05	.01	☐	539	Kirk McCaskill	.05	.02	.01
☐	485	Jesse Barfield	.05	.02	.01	☐	540	Randy Ready	.05	.02	.01
☐	486	Jose DeJesus	.05	.02	.01	☐	541	Mark Gubicza	.05	.02	.01
☐	487	Paul Abbott	.10	.05	.01	☐	542	Rick Aguilera	.08	.04	.01
☐	488	Ken Howell	.05	.02	.01	☐	543	Brian McRae	.35	.16	.04
☐	489	Greg W. Harris	.05	.02	.01	☐	544	Kirby Puckett	.35	.16	.04
☐	490	Roy Smith	.05	.02	.01	☐	545	Bo Jackson	.20	.09	.03
☐	491	Paul Assenmacher	.05	.02	.01	☐	546	Wade Boggs	.20	.09	.03
☐	492	Geno Petralli	.05	.02	.01	☐	547	Tim McIntosh	.05	.02	.01
☐	493	Steve Wilson	.05	.02	.01	☐	548	Randy Milligan	.05	.02	.01
☐	494	Kevin Reimer	.12	.05	.02	☐	549	Dwight Evans	.08	.04	.01
☐	495	Bill Long	.05	.02	.01	☐	550	Billy Ripken	.05	.02	.01
☐	496	Mike Jackson	.05	.02	.01	☐	551	Erik Hanson	.05	.02	.01

☐ 552	Lance Parrish	.08	.04	.01
☐ 553	Tino Martinez	.10	.05	.01
☐ 554	Jim Abbott	.20	.09	.03
☐ 555	Ken Griffey Jr. UER	1.00	.45	.13
	(Second most votes for			
	1991 All-Star Game)			
☐ 556	Milt Cuyler	.15	.07	.02
☐ 557	Mark Leonard	.10	.05	.01
☐ 558	Jay Howell	.05	.02	.01
☐ 559	Lloyd Moseby	.05	.02	.01
☐ 560	Chris Gwynn	.05	.02	.01
☐ 561	Mark Whiten	.20	.09	.03
☐ 562	Harold Baines	.08	.04	.01
☐ 563	Junior Felix	.05	.02	.01
☐ 564	Darren Lewis	.15	.07	.02
☐ 565	Fred McGriff	.20	.09	.03
☐ 566	Kevin Appier	.08	.04	.01
☐ 567	Luis Gonzalez	.40	.18	.05
☐ 568	Frank White	.05	.02	.01
☐ 569	Juan Agosto	.05	.02	.01
☐ 570	Mike Macfarlane	.05	.02	.01
☐ 571	Bert Blyleven	.08	.04	.01
☐ 572	Ken Griffey Sr.	.25	.11	.03
☐ 573	Lee Stevens	.05	.02	.01
☐ 574	Edgar Martinez	.08	.04	.01
☐ 575	Wally Joyner	.08	.04	.01
☐ 576	Tim Belcher	.08	.04	.01
☐ 577	John Burkett	.05	.02	.01
☐ 578	Mike Morgan	.05	.02	.01
☐ 579	Paul Gibson	.05	.02	.01
☐ 580	Jose Vizcaino	.05	.02	.01
☐ 581	Duane Ward	.05	.02	.01
☐ 582	Scott Sanderson	.05	.02	.01
☐ 583	David Wells	.05	.02	.01
☐ 584	Willie McGee	.08	.04	.01
☐ 585	John Cerutti	.05	.02	.01
☐ 586	Danny Darwin	.05	.02	.01
☐ 587	Kurt Stillwell	.05	.02	.01
☐ 588	Rich Gedman	.05	.02	.01
☐ 589	Mark Davis	.05	.02	.01
☐ 590	Bill Gullickson	.05	.02	.01
☐ 591	Matt Young	.05	.02	.01
☐ 592	Bryan Harvey	.05	.02	.01
☐ 593	Omar Vizquel	.05	.02	.01
☐ 594	Scott Lewis	.15	.07	.02
☐ 595	Dave Valle	.05	.02	.01
☐ 596	Tim Crews	.05	.02	.01
☐ 597	Mike Bielecki	.05	.02	.01
☐ 598	Mike Sharperson	.05	.02	.01
☐ 599	Dave Bergman	.05	.02	.01
☐ 600	Checklist 501-600	.06	.01	.00
☐ 601	Steve Lyons	.05	.02	.01
☐ 602	Bruce Hurst	.08	.04	.01
☐ 603	Donn Pall	.05	.02	.01
☐ 604	Jim Vatcher	.05	.02	.01
☐ 605	Dan Pasqua	.05	.02	.01
☐ 606	Kenny Rogers	.05	.02	.01
☐ 607	Jeff Schulz	.05	.02	.01
☐ 608	Brad Arnsberg	.05	.02	.01
☐ 609	Willie Wilson	.05	.02	.01
☐ 610	Jamie Moyer	.05	.02	.01
☐ 611	Ron Oester	.05	.02	.01
☐ 612	Dennis Cook	.05	.02	.01
☐ 613	Rick Mahler	.05	.02	.01
☐ 614	Bill Landrum	.05	.02	.01
☐ 615	Scott Scudder	.05	.02	.01
☐ 616	Tom Edens	.10	.05	.01
☐ 617	1917 Revisited	.10	.05	.01
	(White Sox in vin-			
	tage uniforms)			
☐ 618	Jim Gantner	.05	.02	.01
☐ 619	Darrel Akerfelds	.05	.02	.01
☐ 620	Ron Robinson	.05	.02	.01
☐ 621	Scott Radinsky	.05	.02	.01
☐ 622	Pete Smith	.08	.04	.01
☐ 623	Melido Perez	.08	.04	.01
☐ 624	Jerald Clark	.05	.02	.01
☐ 625	Carlos Martinez	.05	.02	.01
☐ 626	Wes Chamberlain	.40	.18	.05
☐ 627	Bobby Witt	.08	.04	.01
☐ 628	Ken Dayley	.05	.02	.01
☐ 629	John Barfield	.05	.02	.01
☐ 630	Bob Tewksbury	.08	.04	.01
☐ 631	Glenn Braggs	.05	.02	.01
☐ 632	Jim Neidlinger	.05	.02	.01
☐ 633	Tom Browning	.05	.02	.01
☐ 634	Kirk Gibson	.08	.04	.01
☐ 635	Rob Dibble	.08	.04	.01
☐ 636A	Stolen Base Leaders	.25	.11	.03
	(Rickey Henderson and			
	Lou Brock in tuxedos			
	and no date on card)			
☐ 636B	Stolen Base Leaders	.50	.23	.06
	(Dated May 1, 1991			
	on card front)			
☐ 637	Jeff Montgomery	.05	.02	.01
☐ 638	Mike Schooler	.05	.02	.01
☐ 639	Storm Davis	.05	.02	.01
☐ 640	Rich Rodriguez	.10	.05	.01
☐ 641	Phil Bradley	.05	.02	.01
☐ 642	Kent Mercker	.08	.04	.01
☐ 643	Carlton Fisk	.15	.07	.02
☐ 644	Mike Bell	.10	.05	.01
☐ 645	Alex Fernandez	.25	.11	.03
☐ 646	Juan Gonzalez	.90	.40	.11
☐ 647	Ken Hill	.08	.04	.01
☐ 648	Jeff Russell	.05	.02	.01
☐ 649	Chuck Malone	.05	.02	.01
☐ 650	Steve Buechele	.05	.02	.01
☐ 651	Mike Benjamin	.05	.02	.01
☐ 652	Tony Pena	.05	.02	.01
☐ 653	Trevor Wilson	.05	.02	.01
☐ 654	Alex Cole	.05	.02	.01
☐ 655	Roger Clemens	.40	.18	.05

☐ 656	The Bashing Years..........15	.07	.02	
	(Mark McGwire)			
☐ 657	Joe Grahe.....................30	.14	.04	
☐ 658	Jim Eisenreich..............05	.02	.01	
☐ 659	Dan Gladden.................05	.02	.01	
☐ 660	Steve Farr....................05	.02	.01	
☐ 661	Bill Sampen..................05	.02	.01	
☐ 662	Dave Rohde...................05	.02	.01	
☐ 663	Mark Gardner................05	.02	.01	
☐ 664	Mike Simms...................12	.05	.02	
☐ 665	Moises Alou..................50	.23	.06	
☐ 666	Mickey Hatcher..............05	.02	.01	
☐ 667	Jimmy Key.....................05	.02	.01	
☐ 668	John Wetteland..............08	.04	.01	
☐ 669	John Smiley..................08	.04	.01	
☐ 670	Jim Acker.....................05	.02	.01	
☐ 671	Pascual Perez...............05	.02	.01	
☐ 672	Reggie Harris UER.........12	.05	.02	
	(Opportunity misspelled			
	as oppurtint)			
☐ 673	Matt Nokes...................05	.02	.01	
☐ 674	Rafael Novoa.................10	.05	.01	
☐ 675	Hensley Meulens.............08	.04	.01	
☐ 676	Jeff M. Robinson...........05	.02	.01	
☐ 677	Ground Breaking.............20	.09	.03	
	(New Comiskey Park;			
	Carlton Fisk and			
	Robin Ventura)			
☐ 678	Johnny Ray....................05	.02	.01	
☐ 679	Greg Hibbard.................05	.02	.01	
☐ 680	Paul Sorrento...............08	.04	.01	
☐ 681	Mike Marshall................05	.02	.01	
☐ 682	Jim Clancy....................05	.02	.01	
☐ 683	Rob Murphy....................05	.02	.01	
☐ 684	Dave Schmidt.................05	.02	.01	
☐ 685	Jeff Gray.....................05	.02	.01	
☐ 686	Mike Hartley.................05	.02	.01	
☐ 687	Jeff King....................05	.02	.01	
☐ 688	Stan Javier..................05	.02	.01	
☐ 689	Bob Walk......................05	.02	.01	
☐ 690	Jim Gott......................05	.02	.01	
☐ 691	Mike LaCoss..................05	.02	.01	
☐ 692	John Farrell.................05	.02	.01	
☐ 693	Tim Leary.....................05	.02	.01	
☐ 694	Mike Walker...................05	.02	.01	
☐ 695	Eric Plunk....................05	.02	.01	
☐ 696	Mike Fetters.................05	.02	.01	
☐ 697	Wayne Edwards.................05	.02	.01	
☐ 698	Tim Drummond.................05	.02	.01	
☐ 699	Willie Fraser...............05	.02	.01	
☐ 700	Checklist 601-700...........06	.01	.00	
☐ 701	Mike Heath....................05	.02	.01	
☐ 702	Rookie Threats...............50	.23	.06	
	Luis Gonzalez			
	Karl Rhodes			
	Jeff Bagwell			
☐ 703	Jose Mesa.....................05	.02	.01	

☐ 704	Dave Smith....................05	.02	.01	
☐ 705	Danny Darwin..................05	.02	.01	
☐ 706	Rafael Belliard.............05	.02	.01	
☐ 707	Rob Murphy....................05	.02	.01	
☐ 708	Terry Pendleton.............10	.05	.01	
☐ 709	Mike Pagliarulo.............05	.02	.01	
☐ 710	Sid Bream.....................05	.02	.01	
☐ 711	Junior Felix.................05	.02	.01	
☐ 712	Dante Bichette...............05	.02	.01	
☐ 713	Kevin Gross...................05	.02	.01	
☐ 714	Luis Sojo.....................05	.02	.01	
☐ 715	Bob Ojeda.....................05	.02	.01	
☐ 716	Julio Machado................05	.02	.01	
☐ 717	Steve Farr....................05	.02	.01	
☐ 718	Franklin Stubbs.............05	.02	.01	
☐ 719	Mike Boddicker...............05	.02	.01	
☐ 720	Willie Randolph.............08	.04	.01	
☐ 721	Willie McGee.................08	.04	.01	
☐ 722	Chili Davis...................08	.04	.01	
☐ 723	Danny Jackson................05	.02	.01	
☐ 724	Cory Snyder...................05	.02	.01	
☐ 725	MVP Lineup....................15	.07	.02	
	Andre Dawson			
	George Bell			
	Ryne Sandberg			
☐ 726	Rob Deer......................08	.04	.01	
☐ 727	Rich DeLucia.................05	.02	.01	
☐ 728	Mike Perez....................20	.09	.03	
☐ 729	Mickey Tettleton............08	.04	.01	
☐ 730	Mike Blowers.................05	.02	.01	
☐ 731	Gary Gaetti...................05	.02	.01	
☐ 732	Brett Butler.................08	.04	.01	
☐ 733	Dave Parker...................08	.04	.01	
☐ 734	Eddie Zosky...................15	.07	.02	
☐ 735	Jack Clark....................08	.04	.01	
☐ 736	Jack Morris...................10	.05	.01	
☐ 737	Kirk Gibson...................08	.04	.01	
☐ 738	Steve Bedrosian.............05	.02	.01	
☐ 739	Candy Maldonado.............05	.02	.01	
☐ 740	Matt Young....................05	.02	.01	
☐ 741	Rich Garces...................12	.05	.02	
☐ 742	George Bell...................08	.04	.01	
☐ 743	Deion Sanders................30	.14	.04	
☐ 744	Bo Jackson....................20	.09	.03	
☐ 745	Luis Mercedes................40	.18	.05	
☐ 746	Reggie Jefferson UER.......30	.14	.04	
	(Throwing left on card;			
	back has throws right)			
☐ 747	Pete Incaviglia.............05	.02	.01	
☐ 748	Chris Hammond................10	.05	.01	
☐ 749	Mike Stanton..................05	.02	.01	
☐ 750	Scott Sanderson.............05	.02	.01	
☐ 751	Paul Faries...................05	.02	.01	
☐ 752	Al Osuna......................10	.05	.01	
☐ 753	Steve Chitren................10	.05	.01	
☐ 754	Tony Fernandez...............08	.04	.01	
☐ 755	Jeff Bagwell UER............2.00	.90	.25	

(Strikeout and walk
totals reversed)

			MT	EX-MT	VG
☐	756	Kirk Dressendorfer..........10	.05	.01
☐	757	Glenn Davis...................08	.04	.01
☐	758	Gary Carter...................08	.04	.01
☐	759	Zane Smith...................05	.02	.01
☐	760	Vance Law....................05	.02	.01
☐	761	Denis Boucher 20	.09	.03
☐	762	Turner Ward 10	.05	.01
☐	763	Roberto Alomar............50	.23	.06
☐	764	Albert Belle..................30	.14	.04
☐	765	Joe Carter....................20	.09	.03
☐	766	Pete Schourek...............20	.09	.03
☐	767	Heathcliff Slocumb.......05	.02	.01
☐	768	Vince Coleman..............08	.04	.01
☐	769	Mitch Williams..............05	.02	.01
☐	770	Brian Downing 05	.02	.01
☐	771	Dana Allison.................12	.05	.02
☐	772	Pete Harnisch...............08	.04	.01
☐	773	Tim Raines...................08	.04	.01
☐	774	Darryl Kile...................20	.09	.03
☐	775	Fred McGriff.................20	.09	.03
☐	776	Dwight Evans................08	.04	.01
☐	777	Joe Slusarski................15	.07	.02
☐	778	Dave Righetti................05	.02	.01
☐	779	Jeff Hamilton 05	.02	.01
☐	780	Ernest Riles.................05	.02	.01
☐	781	Ken Dayley...................05	.02	.01
☐	782	Eric King.....................05	.02	.01
☐	783	Devon White.................08	.04	.01
☐	784	Beau Allred..................05	.02	.01
☐	785	Mike Timlin..................15	.07	.02
☐	786	Ivan Calderon...............05	.02	.01
☐	787	Hubie Brooks 05	.02	.01
☐	788	Juan Agosto..................05	.02	.01
☐	789	Barry Jones..................05	.02	.01
☐	790	Wally Backman..............05	.02	.01
☐	791	Jim Presley..................05	.02	.01
☐	792	Charlie Hough...............05	.02	.01
☐	793	Larry Andersen.............05	.02	.01
☐	794	Steve Finley.................08	.04	.01
☐	795	Shawn Abner................05	.02	.01
☐	796	Jeff M. Robinson 05	.02	.01
☐	797	Joe Bitker....................05	.02	.01
☐	798	Eric Show.....................05	.02	.01
☐	799	Bud Black.....................05	.02	.01
☐	800	Checklist 701-800.........06	.01	.00
☐	HH1	Hank Aaron Hologram.2.50	1.15	.30
☐	SP1	Michael Jordan SP 10.00	4.50	1.25

(Shown batting in
White Sox uniform)

☐	SP2	Henderson/Ryan..........4.00	1.80	.50

(Rickey and Nolan)
(Commemorating 5/1/91
record breaking)

1991 Upper Deck Final Edition

*The 1991 Upper Deck Final Edition boxed
set contains 100 cards and showcases
players who made major contributions during their team's late-season pennant drive.
In addition to the late season traded and
impact Rookie Cards (22-78), the set
includes two special subsets: Diamond
Skills cards (1-21), depicting the best
Minor League prospects, and All-Star
cards (80-99). Six assorted hologram
cards were issued with each set. The
cards measure the standard size (2 1/2" by
3 1/2"). The fronts feature posed or action
color player photos on a white card face,
with the upper left corner of the picture cut
out to provide space for the Upper Deck
logo. The pictures are bordered in green
on the left, with the player's name in a tan
border below the picture. Two-thirds of the
back are occupied by another color action
photo, with biography, statistics, and
career highlights in a horizontally oriented
red rectangle to the left of the picture. The
cards are numbered on the back with an F
suffix. Among the outstanding Rookie
Cards in this set are Ryan Klesko, Pedro
Martinez, Marc Newfield, Frankie
Rodriguez, Ivan Rodriguez, and Dmitri
Young.*

	MT	EX-MT	VG
COMPLETE SET (100) 14.00	6.25	1.75
COMMON PLAYER (1F-100F).......05	.02	.01

☐ 1F Diamond Skills.................40	.12	.04

Checklist Card

(Ryan Klesko and
Reggie Sanders)

☐	2F	Pedro Martinez	.90	.40	.11
☐	3F	Lance Dickson	.10	.05	.01
☐	4F	Royce Clayton	.30	.14	.04
☐	5F	Scott Bryant	.15	.07	.02
☐	6F	Dan Wilson	.30	.14	.04
☐	7F	Dmitri Young	1.50	.65	.19
☐	8F	Ryan Klesko	1.50	.65	.19
☐	9F	Tom Goodwin	.15	.07	.02
☐	10F	Rondell White	1.00	.45	.13
☐	11F	Reggie Sanders	.40	.18	.05
☐	12F	Todd Van Poppel	.35	.16	.04
☐	13F	Arthur Rhodes	.75	.35	.09
☐	14F	Eddie Zosky	.08	.04	.01
☐	15F	Gerald Williams	.40	.18	.05
☐	16F	Robert Eenhoorn	.15	.07	.02
☐	17F	Jim Thome	.40	.18	.05
☐	18F	Marc Newfield	.75	.35	.09
☐	19F	Kerwin Moore	.20	.09	.03
☐	20F	Jeff McNeely	.30	.14	.04
☐	21F	Frankie Rodriguez	.75	.35	.09
☐	22F	Andy Mota	.12	.05	.02
☐	23F	Chris Haney	.20	.09	.03
☐	24F	Kenny Lofton	1.75	.80	.22
☐	25F	Dave Nilsson	.60	.25	.08
☐	26F	Derek Bell	.50	.23	.06
☐	27F	Frank Castillo	.25	.11	.03
☐	28F	Candy Maldonado	.05	.02	.01
☐	29F	Chuck McElroy	.05	.02	.01
☐	30F	Chito Martinez	.15	.07	.02
☐	31F	Steve Howe	.05	.02	.01
☐	32F	Freddie Benavides	.05	.02	.01
☐	33F	Scott Kamieniecki	.12	.05	.02
☐	34F	Denny Neagle	.20	.09	.03
☐	35F	Mike Humphreys	.20	.09	.03
☐	36F	Mike Remlinger	.05	.02	.01
☐	37F	Scott Coolbaugh	.05	.02	.01
☐	38F	Darren Lewis	.10	.05	.01
☐	39F	Thomas Howard	.05	.02	.01
☐	40F	John Candelaria	.05	.02	.01
☐	41F	Todd Benzinger	.05	.02	.01
☐	42F	Wilson Alvarez	.10	.05	.01
☐	43F	Patrick Lennon	.20	.09	.03
☐	44F	Rusty Meacham	.15	.07	.02
☐	45F	Ryan Bowen	.20	.09	.03
☐	46F	Rick Wilkins	.12	.05	.02
☐	47F	Ed Sprague	.30	.14	.04
☐	48F	Bob Scanlan	.12	.05	.02
☐	49F	Tom Candiotti	.05	.02	.01
☐	50F	Perfecto	.08	.04	.01

(Dennis Martinez)

☐	51F	Oil Can Boyd	.05	.02	.01
☐	52F	Glenallen Hill	.05	.02	.01
☐	53F	Scott Livingstone	.35	.16	.04
☐	54F	Brian Hunter	.40	.18	.05
☐	55F	Ivan Rodriguez	2.00	.90	.25

☐	56F	Keith Mitchell	.30	.14	.04
☐	57F	Roger McDowell	.05	.02	.01
☐	58F	Otis Nixon	.08	.04	.01
☐	59F	Juan Bell	.05	.02	.01
☐	60F	Bill Krueger	.05	.02	.01
☐	61F	Chris Donnels	.15	.07	.02
☐	62F	Tommy Greene	.05	.02	.01
☐	63F	Doug Simons	.05	.02	.01
☐	64F	Andy Ashby	.20	.09	.03
☐	65F	Anthony Young	.25	.11	.03
☐	66F	Kevin Morton	.15	.07	.02
☐	67F	Bret Barberie	.20	.09	.03
☐	68F	Scott Servais	.10	.05	.01
☐	69F	Ron Darling	.08	.04	.01
☐	70F	Tim Burke	.05	.02	.01
☐	71F	Vicente Palacios	.05	.02	.01
☐	72F	Gerald Alexander	.10	.05	.01
☐	73F	Reggie Jefferson	.15	.07	.02
☐	74F	Dean Palmer	.30	.14	.04
☐	75F	Mark Whiten	.12	.05	.02
☐	76F	Randy Tomlin	.40	.18	.05
☐	77F	Mark Wohlers	.35	.16	.04
☐	78F	Brook Jacoby	.05	.02	.01
☐	79F	All-Star Checklist	.30	.09	.03

(Ken Griffey Jr. and
Ryne Sandberg)

☐	80F	Jack Morris AS	.08	.04	.01
☐	81F	Sandy Alomar Jr. AS	.05	.02	.01
☐	82F	Cecil Fielder AS	.15	.07	.02
☐	83F	Roberto Alomar AS	.25	.11	.03
☐	84F	Wade Boggs AS	.15	.07	.02
☐	85F	Cal Ripken AS	.50	.23	.06
☐	86F	Rickey Henderson AS	.15	.07	.02
☐	87F	Ken Griffey Jr. AS	.50	.23	.06
☐	88F	Dave Henderson AS	.05	.02	.01
☐	89F	Danny Tartabull AS	.08	.04	.01
☐	90F	Tom Glavine AS	.15	.07	.02
☐	91F	Benito Santiago AS	.05	.02	.01
☐	92F	Will Clark AS	.20	.09	.03
☐	93F	Ryne Sandberg AS	.25	.11	.03
☐	94F	Chris Sabo AS	.05	.02	.01
☐	95F	Ozzie Smith AS	.10	.05	.01
☐	96F	Ivan Calderon AS	.05	.02	.01
☐	97F	Tony Gwynn AS	.15	.07	.02
☐	98F	Andre Dawson AS	.10	.05	.01
☐	99F	Bobby Bonilla AS	.08	.04	.01
☐	100F	Checklist 1-100	.08	.01	.00

1991 Upper Deck Silver Sluggers

The Upper Deck Silver Slugger set features nine players from each league, representing the nine batting positions on the team. The cards measure the standard size (2 1/2" by 3 1/2"). The fronts have glossy color action player photos, with white borders on three sides and a "Silver Slugger" bat serving as the border on the left side. The player's name appears in a tan stripe below the picture, with the team logo superimposed at the lower right corner. The card back is dominated by another color action photo with career highlights in a horizontally oriented rectangle to the left of the picture. The cards are numbered on the back with an SS prefix.

	MT	EX-MT	VG
COMPLETE SET (18)	20.00	9.00	2.50
COMMON PLAYER (SS1-SS18)	.75	.35	.09
☐ SS1 Julio Franco	.75	.35	.09
☐ SS2 Alan Trammell	.75	.35	.09
☐ SS3 Rickey Henderson	2.50	1.15	.30
☐ SS4 Jose Canseco	3.50	1.55	.45
☐ SS5 Barry Bonds	3.50	1.55	.45
☐ SS6 Eddie Murray	1.25	.55	.16
☐ SS7 Kelly Gruber	.75	.35	.09
☐ SS8 Ryne Sandberg	4.00	1.80	.50
☐ SS9 Darryl Strawberry	2.50	1.15	.30
☐ SS10 Ellis Burks	.75	.35	.09
☐ SS11 Lance Parrish	.75	.35	.09
☐ SS12 Cecil Fielder	2.50	1.15	.30
☐ SS13 Matt Williams	1.00	.45	.13
☐ SS14 Dave Parker	.75	.35	.09
☐ SS15 Bobby Bonilla	1.50	.65	.19
☐ SS16 Don Robinson	.75	.35	.09
☐ SS17 Benito Santiago	.75	.35	.09
☐ SS18 Barry Larkin	1.50	.65	.19

1992 Upper Deck

The 1992 Upper Deck set contains 800 standard-size (2 1/2" by 3 1/2") cards. The set was produced in two series: a low-number series of 700 cards and a high-number series of 100 cards later in the season. Special subsets included in the set are Star Rookies (1-27; SR), Team Checklists (29-40, 86-99; TC), with player portraits by Vernon Wells; Top Prospects (52-77; TP); Bloodlines (79-85), and Diamond Skills (640-650; DS). Moreover, a nine-card Baseball Heroes subset (randomly inserted in packs) focuses on the career of Ted Williams. He autographed and numbered 2,500 cards, which were randomly inserted in low series foil packs. The cards are numbered on the back. The key Rookie Cards in the low-number series are Shawn Green, Tyler Green, Joey Hamilton, David McCarty, Eduardo Perez, Manny Ramirez, Mark Smith, Joe Vitiello, and Brian Williams. By mailing in 15 low number foil wrappers, a completed order form, and a handling fee, the collector could receive an 8 1/2" by 11" numbered, black and white lithograph picturing Ted Williams in his batting swing. A standard-size Ted Williams hologram card was randomly inserted in 1992 low number foil packs. The front design of the Williams hologram is horizontally oriented and features the artwork of Vernon Wells showing

Williams in three different poses. The horizontally oriented back has a full-bleed sepia-tone photo of Williams and career highlights printed in black over the photo. Factory sets feature a unique gold-foil hologram on the card backs (in contrast to the silver hologram on foil pack cards). In addition to traded players and called-up rookies, the extended series features a National League Diamond Skills subset (711-721), a Diamond Debuts subset (771-780), two expansion-team player cards (701 Clemente Nunez and 710 Ryan Turner), and two commemorative cards highlighting Eddie Murray's 400th home run (728) and Rickey Henderson's 1,000th stolen base (782). Randomly inserted into high number foil packs were a 20-card Ted Williams' Best Hitters subset, a three-card hologram subset featuring College Player of the Year winners for 1989 through 1991, a ten-card Baseball Heroes subset highlighting the careers of Joe Morgan and Johnny Bench and featuring 2,500 dual autographed checklist cards. and a special card picturing Tom Selleck and Frank Thomas and commemorating the movie "Mr. Baseball." The fronts features shadow-bordered action color player photos on a white card face. The player's name appears above the photo, with the team name superimposed at the lower right corner. The backs include color action player photos, biography, and statistics. The cards are numbered on the back. Key Rookie Cards in the extended include Chad Curtis, Mike Kelly, Pat Listach, Clemente Nunez, and Ryan Turner.

	MT	EX-MT	VG
COMPLETE SET (800)	30.00	13.50	3.80
COMPLETE FACT.SET (800)	48.00	22.00	6.00
COMPLETE LO SET (700)	24.00	11.00	3.00
COMPLETE HI SET (100)	7.00	3.10	.85
COMMON PLAYER (1-700)	.05	.02	.01
COMMON PLAYER (701-800)	.05	.02	.01

		MT	EX-MT	VG
☐ 1	Star Rookie Checklist	.25	.08	.03
	Ryan Klesko			
	Jim Thome			
☐ 2	Royce Clayton SR	.20	.09	.03
☐ 3	Brian Jordan SR	.30	.14	.04
☐ 4	Dave Fleming SR	.75	.35	.09
☐ 5	Jim Thome SR	.15	.07	.02
☐ 6	Jeff Juden SR	.08	.04	.01
☐ 7	Roberto Hernandez SR	.15	.07	.02
☐ 8	Kyle Abbott SR	.09	.04	.01

		MT	EX-MT	VG
☐ 9	Chris George SR	.06	.03	.01
☐ 10	Rob Maurer SR	.15	.07	.02
☐ 11	Donald Harris SR	.06	.03	.01
☐ 12	Ted Wood SR	.12	.05	.02
☐ 13	Patrick Lennon SR	.06	.03	.01
☐ 14	Willie Banks SR	.09	.04	.01
☐ 15	Roger Salkeld SR UER	.10	.05	.01
	(Bill was his grandfather, not his father)			
☐ 16	Wilfredo Cordero SR	.20	.09	.03
☐ 17	Arthur Rhodes SR	.20	.09	.03
☐ 18	Pedro Martinez SR	.25	.11	.03
☐ 19	Andy Ashby SR	.06	.03	.01
☐ 20	Tom Goodwin SR	.10	.05	.01
☐ 21	Braulio Castillo SR	.20	.09	.03
☐ 22	Todd Van Poppel SR	.25	.11	.03
☐ 23	Brian Williams SR	.35	.16	.04
☐ 24	Ryan Klesko SR	.75	.35	.09
☐ 25	Kenny Lofton SR	.50	.23	.06
☐ 26	Derek Bell SR	.12	.05	.02
☐ 27	Reggie Sanders SR	.30	.14	.04
☐ 28	Dave Winfield's 400th	.10	.05	.01
☐ 29	Atlanta TC	.12	.05	.02
	Dave Justice			
☐ 30	Cincinnati TC	.06	.03	.01
	Rob Dibble			
☐ 31	Houston TC	.06	.03	.01
	Craig Biggio			
☐ 32	Los Angeles TC	.10	.05	.01
	Eddie Murray			
☐ 33	San Diego TC	.10	.05	.01
	Fred McGriff			
☐ 34	San Francisco TC	.06	.03	.01
	Willie McGee			
☐ 35	Chicago Cubs TC	.06	.03	.01
	Shawon Dunston			
☐ 36	Montreal TC	.09	.04	.01
	Delino DeShields			
☐ 37	New York Mets TC	.06	.03	.01
	Howard Johnson			
☐ 38	Philadelphia TC	.06	.03	.01
	John Kruk			
☐ 39	Pittsburgh TC	.06	.03	.01
	Doug Drabek			
☐ 40	St. Louis TC	.06	.03	.01
	Todd Zeile			
☐ 41	Playoff Perfection	.15	.07	.02
	Steve Avery			
☐ 42	Jeremy Hernandez	.12	.05	.02
☐ 43	Doug Henry	.20	.09	.03
☐ 44	Chris Donnels	.05	.02	.01
☐ 45	Mo Sanford	.05	.02	.01
☐ 46	Scott Kamieniecki	.05	.02	.01
☐ 47	Mark Lemke	.05	.02	.01
☐ 48	Steve Farr	.05	.02	.01
☐ 49	Francisco Oliveras	.05	.02	.01
☐ 50	Ced Landrum	.05	.02	.01

☐ 140	Pat Borders	.05	.02	.01
☐ 141	Bip Roberts	.08	.04	.01
☐ 142	Rob Dibble	.08	.04	.01
☐ 143	Mark Grace	.08	.04	.01
☐ 144	Barry Larkin	.12	.05	.02
☐ 145	Ryne Sandberg	.30	.14	.04
☐ 146	Scott Erickson	.10	.05	.01
☐ 147	Luis Polonia	.08	.04	.01
☐ 148	John Burkett	.05	.02	.01
☐ 149	Luis Sojo	.05	.02	.01
☐ 150	Dickie Thon	.05	.02	.01
☐ 151	Walt Weiss	.05	.02	.01
☐ 152	Mike Scioscia	.05	.02	.01
☐ 153	Mark McGwire	.25	.11	.03
☐ 154	Matt Williams	.08	.04	.01
☐ 155	Rickey Henderson	.15	.07	.02
☐ 156	Sandy Alomar Jr.	.08	.04	.01
☐ 157	Brian McRae	.08	.04	.01
☐ 158	Harold Baines	.08	.04	.01
☐ 159	Kevin Appier	.08	.04	.01
☐ 160	Felix Fermin	.05	.02	.01
☐ 161	Leo Gomez	.12	.05	.02
☐ 162	Craig Biggio	.08	.04	.01
☐ 163	Ben McDonald	.10	.05	.01
☐ 164	Randy Johnson	.08	.04	.01
☐ 165	Cal Ripken	.35	.16	.04
☐ 166	Frank Thomas	1.00	.45	.13
☐ 167	Delino DeShields	.12	.05	.02
☐ 168	Greg Gagne	.05	.02	.01
☐ 169	Ron Karkovice	.05	.02	.01
☐ 170	Charlie Leibrandt	.05	.02	.01
☐ 171	Dave Righetti	.05	.02	.01
☐ 172	Dave Henderson	.05	.02	.01
☐ 173	Steve Decker	.05	.02	.01
☐ 174	Darryl Strawberry	.15	.07	.02
☐ 175	Will Clark	.25	.11	.03
☐ 176	Ruben Sierra	.20	.09	.03
☐ 177	Ozzie Smith	.12	.05	.02
☐ 178	Charles Nagy	.12	.05	.02
☐ 179	Gary Pettis	.05	.02	.01
☐ 180	Kirk Gibson	.08	.04	.01
☐ 181	Randy Milligan	.05	.02	.01
☐ 182	Dave Valle	.05	.02	.01
☐ 183	Chris Hoiles	.08	.04	.01
☐ 184	Tony Phillips	.05	.02	.01
☐ 185	Brady Anderson	.08	.04	.01
☐ 186	Scott Fletcher	.05	.02	.01
☐ 187	Gene Larkin	.05	.02	.01
☐ 188	Lance Johnson	.05	.02	.01
☐ 189	Greg Olson	.05	.02	.01
☐ 190	Melido Perez	.08	.04	.01
☐ 191	Lenny Harris	.05	.02	.01
☐ 192	Terry Kennedy	.05	.02	.01
☐ 193	Mike Gallego	.05	.02	.01
☐ 194	Willie McGee	.08	.04	.01
☐ 195	Juan Samuel	.05	.02	.01
☐ 196	Jeff Huson	.05	.02	.01

(Shows Jose Canseco
sliding into second)

☐ 197	Alex Cole	.05	.02	.01
☐ 198	Ron Robinson	.05	.02	.01
☐ 199	Joel Skinner	.05	.02	.01
☐ 200	Checklist 101-200	.05	.01	.00
☐ 201	Kevin Reimer	.08	.04	.01
☐ 202	Stan Belinda	.05	.02	.01
☐ 203	Pat Tabler	.05	.02	.01
☐ 204	Jose Guzman	.05	.02	.01
☐ 205	Jose Lind	.05	.02	.01
☐ 206	Spike Owen	.05	.02	.01
☐ 207	Joe Orsulak	.05	.02	.01
☐ 208	Charlie Hayes	.05	.02	.01
☐ 209	Mike Devereaux	.08	.04	.01
☐ 210	Mike Fitzgerald	.05	.02	.01
☐ 211	Willie Randolph	.08	.04	.01
☐ 212	Rod Nichols	.05	.02	.01
☐ 213	Mike Boddicker	.05	.02	.01
☐ 214	Bill Spiers	.05	.02	.01
☐ 215	Steve Olin	.05	.02	.01
☐ 216	David Howard	.05	.02	.01
☐ 217	Gary Varsho	.05	.02	.01
☐ 218	Mike Harkey	.08	.04	.01
☐ 219	Luis Aquino	.05	.02	.01
☐ 220	Chuck McElroy	.05	.02	.01
☐ 221	Doug Drabek	.08	.04	.01
☐ 222	Dave Winfield	.12	.05	.02
☐ 223	Rafael Palmeiro	.08	.04	.01
☐ 224	Joe Carter	.15	.07	.02
☐ 225	Bobby Bonilla	.12	.05	.02
☐ 226	Ivan Calderon	.05	.02	.01
☐ 227	Gregg Olson	.08	.04	.01
☐ 228	Tim Wallach	.08	.04	.01
☐ 229	Terry Pendleton	.10	.05	.01
☐ 230	Gilberto Reyes	.05	.02	.01
☐ 231	Carlos Baerga	.25	.11	.03
☐ 232	Greg Vaughn	.08	.04	.01
☐ 233	Bret Saberhagen	.08	.04	.01
☐ 234	Gary Sheffield	.35	.16	.04
☐ 235	Mark Lewis	.08	.04	.01
☐ 236	George Bell	.08	.04	.01
☐ 237	Danny Tartabull	.08	.04	.01
☐ 238	Willie Wilson	.05	.02	.01
☐ 239	Doug Dascenzo	.05	.02	.01
☐ 240	Bill Pecota	.05	.02	.01
☐ 241	Julio Franco	.08	.04	.01
☐ 242	Ed Sprague	.08	.04	.01
☐ 243	Juan Gonzalez	.50	.23	.06
☐ 244	Chuck Finley	.05	.02	.01
☐ 245	Ivan Rodriguez	.50	.23	.06
☐ 246	Len Dykstra	.08	.04	.01
☐ 247	Deion Sanders	.20	.09	.03
☐ 248	Dwight Evans	.08	.04	.01
☐ 249	Larry Walker	.20	.09	.03
☐ 250	Billy Ripken	.05	.02	.01
☐ 251	Mickey Tettleton	.08	.04	.01

☐	252	Tony Pena	.05	.02	.01				
☐	253	Benito Santiago	.08	.04	.01				
☐	254	Kirby Puckett	.25	.11	.03				
☐	255	Cecil Fielder	.15	.07	.02				
☐	256	Howard Johnson	.08	.04	.01				
☐	257	Andujar Cedeno	.08	.04	.01				
☐	258	Jose Rijo	.08	.04	.01				
☐	259	Al Osuna	.05	.02	.01				
☐	260	Todd Hundley	.05	.02	.01				
☐	261	Orel Hershiser	.08	.04	.01				
☐	262	Ray Lankford	.20	.09	.03				
☐	263	Robin Ventura	.20	.09	.03				
☐	264	Felix Jose	.08	.04	.01				
☐	265	Eddie Murray	.12	.05	.02				
☐	266	Kevin Mitchell	.08	.04	.01				
☐	267	Gary Carter	.08	.04	.01				
☐	268	Mike Benjamin	.05	.02	.01				
☐	269	Dick Schofield	.05	.02	.01				
☐	270	Jose Uribe	.05	.02	.01				
☐	271	Pete Incaviglia	.05	.02	.01				
☐	272	Tony Fernandez	.08	.04	.01				
☐	273	Alan Trammell	.08	.04	.01				
☐	274	Tony Gwynn	.15	.07	.02				
☐	275	Mike Greenwell	.08	.04	.01				
☐	276	Jeff Bagwell	.40	.18	.05				
☐	277	Frank Viola	.08	.04	.01				
☐	278	Randy Myers	.08	.04	.01				
☐	279	Ken Caminiti	.08	.04	.01				
☐	280	Bill Doran	.05	.02	.01				
☐	281	Dan Pasqua	.05	.02	.01				
☐	282	Alfredo Griffin	.05	.02	.01				
☐	283	Jose Oquendo	.05	.02	.01				
☐	284	Kal Daniels	.05	.02	.01				
☐	285	Bobby Thigpen	.05	.02	.01				
☐	286	Robby Thompson	.05	.02	.01				
☐	287	Mark Eichhorn	.05	.02	.01				
☐	288	Mike Felder	.05	.02	.01				
☐	289	Dave Gallagher	.05	.02	.01				
☐	290	Dave Anderson	.05	.02	.01				
☐	291	Mel Hall	.05	.02	.01				
☐	292	Jerald Clark	.05	.02	.01				
☐	293	Al Newman	.05	.02	.01				
☐	294	Rob Deer	.08	.04	.01				
☐	295	Matt Nokes	.05	.02	.01				
☐	296	Jack Armstrong	.05	.02	.01				
☐	297	Jim Deshaies	.05	.02	.01				
☐	298	Jeff Innis	.05	.02	.01				
☐	299	Jeff Reed	.05	.02	.01				
☐	300	Checklist 201-300	.05	.01	.00				
☐	301	Lonnie Smith	.05	.02	.01				
☐	302	Jimmy Key	.05	.02	.01				
☐	303	Junior Felix	.05	.02	.01				
☐	304	Mike Heath	.05	.02	.01				
☐	305	Mark Langston	.08	.04	.01				
☐	306	Greg W. Harris	.05	.02	.01				
☐	307	Brett Butler	.08	.04	.01				
☐	308	Luis Rivera	.05	.02	.01				
☐	309	Bruce Ruffin	.05	.02	.01
☐	310	Paul Faries	.05	.02	.01
☐	311	Terry Leach	.05	.02	.01
☐	312	Scott Brosius	.10	.05	.01
☐	313	Scott Leius	.05	.02	.01
☐	314	Harold Reynolds	.05	.02	.01
☐	315	Jack Morris	.12	.05	.02
☐	316	David Segui	.05	.02	.01
☐	317	Bill Gullickson	.05	.02	.01
☐	318	Todd Frohwirth	.05	.02	.01
☐	319	Mark Leiter	.05	.02	.01
☐	320	Jeff M. Robinson	.05	.02	.01
☐	321	Gary Gaetti	.05	.02	.01
☐	322	John Smoltz	.12	.05	.02
☐	323	Andy Benes	.08	.04	.01
☐	324	Kelly Gruber	.08	.04	.01
☐	325	Jim Abbott	.12	.05	.02
☐	326	John Kruk	.08	.04	.01
☐	327	Kevin Seitzer	.08	.04	.01
☐	328	Darrin Jackson	.05	.02	.01
☐	329	Kurt Stillwell	.05	.02	.01
☐	330	Mike Maddux	.05	.02	.01
☐	331	Dennis Eckersley	.12	.05	.02
☐	332	Dan Gladden	.05	.02	.01
☐	333	Jose Canseco	.25	.11	.03
☐	334	Kent Hrbek	.08	.04	.01
☐	335	Ken Griffey Sr.	.08	.04	.01
☐	336	Greg Swindell	.08	.04	.01
☐	337	Trevor Wilson	.05	.02	.01
☐	338	Sam Horn	.05	.02	.01
☐	339	Mike Henneman	.05	.02	.01
☐	340	Jerry Browne	.05	.02	.01
☐	341	Glenn Braggs	.05	.02	.01
☐	342	Tom Glavine	.15	.07	.02
☐	343	Wally Joyner	.08	.04	.01
☐	344	Fred McGriff	.15	.07	.02
☐	345	Ron Gant	.12	.05	.02
☐	346	Ramon Martinez	.08	.04	.01
☐	347	Wes Chamberlain	.08	.04	.01
☐	348	Terry Shumpert	.05	.02	.01
☐	349	Tim Teufel	.05	.02	.01
☐	350	Wally Backman	.05	.02	.01
☐	351	Joe Girardi	.05	.02	.01
☐	352	Devon White	.08	.04	.01
☐	353	Greg Maddux	.12	.05	.02
☐	354	Ryan Bowen	.08	.04	.01
☐	355	Roberto Alomar	.30	.14	.04
☐	356	Don Mattingly	.15	.07	.02
☐	357	Pedro Guerrero	.08	.04	.01
☐	358	Steve Sax	.08	.04	.01
☐	359	Joey Cora	.05	.02	.01
☐	360	Jim Gantner	.05	.02	.01
☐	361	Brian Barnes	.05	.02	.01
☐	362	Kevin McReynolds	.08	.04	.01
☐	363	Bret Barberie	.05	.02	.01
☐	364	David Cone	.08	.04	.01
☐	365	Dennis Martinez	.08	.04	.01

☐ 366	Brian Hunter	.10	.05	.01	☐ 423	Paul Molitor	.08	.04	.01
☐ 367	Edgar Martinez	.08	.04	.01	☐ 424	Ken Griffey Jr.	.75	.35	.09
☐ 368	Steve Finley	.08	.04	.01	☐ 425	Phil Plantier	.20	.09	.03
☐ 369	Greg Briley	.05	.02	.01	☐ 426	Denny Neagle	.05	.02	.01
☐ 370	Jeff Blauser	.05	.02	.01	☐ 427	Von Hayes	.05	.02	.01
☐ 371	Todd Stottlemyre	.08	.04	.01	☐ 428	Shane Mack	.08	.04	.01
☐ 372	Luis Gonzalez	.08	.04	.01	☐ 429	Darren Daulton	.08	.04	.01
☐ 373	Rick Wilkins	.05	.02	.01	☐ 430	Dwayne Henry	.05	.02	.01
☐ 374	Darryl Kile	.08	.04	.01	☐ 431	Lance Parrish	.08	.04	.01
☐ 375	John Olerud	.12	.05	.02	☐ 432	Mike Humphreys	.08	.04	.01
☐ 376	Lee Smith	.08	.04	.01	☐ 433	Tim Burke	.05	.02	.01
☐ 377	Kevin Maas	.08	.04	.01	☐ 434	Bryan Harvey	.05	.02	.01
☐ 378	Dante Bichette	.05	.02	.01	☐ 435	Pat Kelly	.08	.04	.01
☐ 379	Tom Pagnozzi	.05	.02	.01	☐ 436	Ozzie Guillen	.05	.02	.01
☐ 380	Mike Flanagan	.05	.02	.01	☐ 437	Bruce Hurst	.08	.04	.01
☐ 381	Charlie O'Brien	.05	.02	.01	☐ 438	Sammy Sosa	.05	.02	.01
☐ 382	Dave Martinez	.05	.02	.01	☐ 439	Dennis Rasmussen	.05	.02	.01
☐ 383	Keith Miller	.05	.02	.01	☐ 440	Ken Patterson	.05	.02	.01
☐ 384	Scott Ruskin	.05	.02	.01	☐ 441	Jay Buhner	.08	.04	.01
☐ 385	Kevin Elster	.05	.02	.01	☐ 442	Pat Combs	.05	.02	.01
☐ 386	Alvin Davis	.05	.02	.01	☐ 443	Wade Boggs	.15	.07	.02
☐ 387	Casey Candaele	.05	.02	.01	☐ 444	George Brett	.12	.05	.02
☐ 388	Pete O'Brien	.05	.02	.01	☐ 445	Mo Vaughn	.08	.04	.01
☐ 389	Jeff Treadway	.05	.02	.01	☐ 446	Chuck Knoblauch	.25	.11	.03
☐ 390	Scott Bradley	.05	.02	.01	☐ 447	Tom Candiotti	.05	.02	.01
☐ 391	Mookie Wilson	.05	.02	.01	☐ 448	Mark Portugal	.05	.02	.01
☐ 392	Jimmy Jones	.05	.02	.01	☐ 449	Mickey Morandini	.08	.04	.01
☐ 393	Candy Maldonado	.05	.02	.01	☐ 450	Duane Ward	.05	.02	.01
☐ 394	Eric Yelding	.05	.02	.01	☐ 451	Otis Nixon	.08	.04	.01
☐ 395	Tom Henke	.08	.04	.01	☐ 452	Bob Welch	.05	.02	.01
☐ 396	Franklin Stubbs	.05	.02	.01	☐ 453	Rusty Meacham	.05	.02	.01
☐ 397	Milt Thompson	.05	.02	.01	☐ 454	Keith Mitchell	.08	.04	.01
☐ 398	Mark Carreon	.05	.02	.01	☐ 455	Marquis Grissom	.12	.05	.02
☐ 399	Randy Velarde	.05	.02	.01	☐ 456	Robin Yount	.12	.05	.02
☐ 400	Checklist 301-400	.05	.01	.00	☐ 457	Harvey Pulliam	.10	.05	.01
☐ 401	Omar Vizquel	.05	.02	.01	☐ 458	Jose DeLeon	.05	.02	.01
☐ 402	Joe Boever	.05	.02	.01	☐ 459	Mark Gubicza	.05	.02	.01
☐ 403	Bill Krueger	.05	.02	.01	☐ 460	Darryl Hamilton	.08	.04	.01
☐ 404	Jody Reed	.05	.02	.01	☐ 461	Tom Browning	.05	.02	.01
☐ 405	Mike Schooler	.05	.02	.01	☐ 462	Monty Fariss	.10	.05	.01
☐ 406	Jason Grimsley	.05	.02	.01	☐ 463	Jerome Walton	.05	.02	.01
☐ 407	Greg Myers	.05	.02	.01	☐ 464	Paul O'Neill	.08	.04	.01
☐ 408	Randy Ready	.05	.02	.01	☐ 465	Dean Palmer	.12	.05	.02
☐ 409	Mike Timlin	.05	.02	.01	☐ 466	Travis Fryman	.50	.23	.06
☐ 410	Mitch Williams	.05	.02	.01	☐ 467	John Smiley	.08	.04	.01
☐ 411	Garry Templeton	.05	.02	.01	☐ 468	Lloyd Moseby	.05	.02	.01
☐ 412	Greg Cadaret	.05	.02	.01	☐ 469	John Wehner	.05	.02	.01
☐ 413	Donnie Hill	.05	.02	.01	☐ 470	Skeeter Barnes	.05	.02	.01
☐ 414	Wally Whitehurst	.05	.02	.01	☐ 471	Steve Chitren	.05	.02	.01
☐ 415	Scott Sanderson	.05	.02	.01	☐ 472	Kent Mercker	.05	.02	.01
☐ 416	Thomas Howard	.05	.02	.01	☐ 473	Terry Steinbach	.08	.04	.01
☐ 417	Neal Heaton	.05	.02	.01	☐ 474	Andres Galarraga	.05	.02	.01
☐ 418	Charlie Hough	.05	.02	.01	☐ 475	Steve Avery	.20	.09	.03
☐ 419	Jack Howell	.05	.02	.01	☐ 476	Tom Gordon	.05	.02	.01
☐ 420	Greg Hibbard	.05	.02	.01	☐ 477	Cal Eldred	.60	.25	.08
☐ 421	Carlos Quintana	.05	.02	.01	☐ 478	Omar Olivares	.05	.02	.01
☐ 422	Kim Batiste	.05	.02	.01	☐ 479	Julio Machado	.05	.02	.01

☐	480	Bob Milacki	.05	.02	.01			
☐	481	Les Lancaster	.05	.02	.01			
☐	482	John Candelaria	.05	.02	.01			
☐	483	Brian Downing	.05	.02	.01			
☐	484	Roger McDowell	.05	.02	.01			
☐	485	Scott Scudder	.05	.02	.01			
☐	486	Zane Smith	.05	.02	.01			
☐	487	John Cerutti	.05	.02	.01			
☐	488	Steve Buechele	.05	.02	.01			
☐	489	Paul Gibson	.05	.02	.01			
☐	490	Curtis Wilkerson	.05	.02	.01			
☐	491	Marvin Freeman	.05	.02	.01			
☐	492	Tom Foley	.05	.02	.01			
☐	493	Juan Berenguer	.05	.02	.01			
☐	494	Ernest Riles	.05	.02	.01			
☐	495	Sid Bream	.05	.02	.01			
☐	496	Chuck Crim	.05	.02	.01			
☐	497	Mike Macfarlane	.05	.02	.01			
☐	498	Dale Sveum	.05	.02	.01			
☐	499	Storm Davis	.05	.02	.01			
☐	500	Checklist 401-500	.05	.01	.00			
☐	501	Jeff Reardon	.08	.04	.01			
☐	502	Shawn Abner	.05	.02	.01			
☐	503	Tony Fossas	.05	.02	.01			
☐	504	Cory Snyder	.05	.02	.01			
☐	505	Matt Young	.05	.02	.01			
☐	506	Allan Anderson	.05	.02	.01			
☐	507	Mark Lee	.05	.02	.01			
☐	508	Gene Nelson	.05	.02	.01			
☐	509	Mike Pagliarulo	.05	.02	.01			
☐	510	Rafael Belliard	.05	.02	.01			
☐	511	Jay Howell	.05	.02	.01			
☐	512	Bob Tewksbury	.08	.04	.01			
☐	513	Mike Morgan	.05	.02	.01			
☐	514	John Franco	.08	.04	.01			
☐	515	Kevin Gross	.05	.02	.01			
☐	516	Lou Whitaker	.08	.04	.01			
☐	517	Orlando Merced	.08	.04	.01			
☐	518	Todd Benzinger	.05	.02	.01			
☐	519	Gary Redus	.05	.02	.01			
☐	520	Walt Terrell	.05	.02	.01			
☐	521	Jack Clark	.08	.04	.01			
☐	522	Dave Parker	.08	.04	.01			
☐	523	Tim Naehring	.08	.04	.01			
☐	524	Mark Whiten	.05	.02	.01			
☐	525	Ellis Burks	.08	.04	.01			
☐	526	Frank Castillo	.10	.05	.01			
☐	527	Brian Harper	.05	.02	.01			
☐	528	Brook Jacoby	.05	.02	.01			
☐	529	Rick Sutcliffe	.08	.04	.01			
☐	530	Joe Klink	.05	.02	.01			
☐	531	Terry Bross	.05	.02	.01			
☐	532	Jose Offerman	.08	.04	.01			
☐	533	Todd Zeile	.05	.02	.01			
☐	534	Eric Karros	.75	.35	.09			
☐	535	Anthony Young	.10	.05	.01			
☐	536	Milt Cuyler	.05	.02	.01			

☐	537	Randy Tomlin	.05	.02	.01
☐	538	Scott Livingstone	.12	.05	.02
☐	539	Jim Eisenreich	.05	.02	.01
☐	540	Don Slaught	.05	.02	.01
☐	541	Scott Cooper	.08	.04	.01
☐	542	Joe Grahe	.05	.02	.01
☐	543	Tom Brunansky	.08	.04	.01
☐	544	Eddie Zosky	.08	.04	.01
☐	545	Roger Clemens	.30	.14	.04
☐	546	David Justice	.30	.14	.04
☐	547	Dave Stewart	.08	.04	.01
☐	548	David West	.05	.02	.01
☐	549	Dave Smith	.05	.02	.01
☐	550	Dan Plesac	.05	.02	.01
☐	551	Alex Fernandez	.08	.04	.01
☐	552	Bernard Gilkey	.08	.04	.01
☐	553	Jack McDowell	.08	.04	.01
☐	554	Tino Martinez	.08	.04	.01
☐	555	Bo Jackson	.15	.07	.02
☐	556	Bernie Williams	.10	.05	.01
☐	557	Mark Gardner	.05	.02	.01
☐	558	Glenallen Hill	.05	.02	.01
☐	559	Oil Can Boyd	.05	.02	.01
☐	560	Chris James	.05	.02	.01
☐	561	Scott Servais	.05	.02	.01
☐	562	Rey Sanchez	.15	.07	.02
☐	563	Paul McClellan	.05	.02	.01
☐	564	Andy Mota	.05	.02	.01
☐	565	Darren Lewis	.08	.04	.01
☐	566	Jose Melendez	.05	.02	.01
☐	567	Tommy Greene	.05	.02	.01
☐	568	Rich Rodriguez	.05	.02	.01
☐	569	Heathcliff Slocumb	.05	.02	.01
☐	570	Joe Hesketh	.05	.02	.01
☐	571	Carlton Fisk	.12	.05	.02
☐	572	Erik Hanson	.05	.02	.01
☐	573	Wilson Alvarez	.05	.02	.01
☐	574	Rheal Cormier	.05	.02	.01
☐	575	Tim Raines	.08	.04	.01
☐	576	Bobby Witt	.05	.02	.01
☐	577	Roberto Kelly	.08	.04	.01
☐	578	Kevin Brown	.08	.04	.01
☐	579	Chris Nabholz	.08	.04	.01
☐	580	Jesse Orosco	.05	.02	.01
☐	581	Jeff Brantley	.05	.02	.01
☐	582	Rafael Ramirez	.05	.02	.01
☐	583	Kelly Downs	.05	.02	.01
☐	584	Mike Simms	.05	.02	.01
☐	585	Mike Remlinger	.05	.02	.01
☐	586	Dave Hollins	.08	.04	.01
☐	587	Larry Andersen	.05	.02	.01
☐	588	Mike Gardiner	.05	.02	.01
☐	589	Craig Lefferts	.05	.02	.01
☐	590	Paul Assenmacher	.05	.02	.01
☐	591	Bryn Smith	.05	.02	.01
☐	592	Donn Pall	.05	.02	.01
☐	593	Mike Jackson	.05	.02	.01

☐	594	Scott Radinsky	.05	.02	.01			
☐	595	Brian Holman	.05	.02	.01			
☐	596	Geronimo Pena	.05	.02	.01			
☐	597	Mike Jeffcoat	.05	.02	.01			
☐	598	Carlos Martinez	.05	.02	.01			
☐	599	Geno Petralli	.05	.02	.01			
☐	600	Checklist 501-600	.05	.01	.00			
☐	601	Jerry Don Gleaton	.05	.02	.01			
☐	602	Adam Peterson	.05	.02	.01			
☐	603	Craig Grebeck	.05	.02	.01			
☐	604	Mark Guthrie	.05	.02	.01			
☐	605	Frank Tanana	.05	.02	.01			
☐	606	Hensley Meulens	.05	.02	.01			
☐	607	Mark Davis	.05	.02	.01			
☐	608	Eric Plunk	.05	.02	.01			
☐	609	Mark Williamson	.05	.02	.01			
☐	610	Lee Guetterman	.05	.02	.01			
☐	611	Bobby Rose	.05	.02	.01			
☐	612	Bill Wegman	.05	.02	.01			
☐	613	Mike Hartley	.05	.02	.01			
☐	614	Chris Beasley	.12	.05	.02			
☐	615	Chris Bosio	.05	.02	.01			
☐	616	Henry Cotto	.05	.02	.01			
☐	617	Chico Walker	.05	.02	.01			
☐	618	Russ Swan	.05	.02	.01			
☐	619	Bob Walk	.05	.02	.01			
☐	620	Billy Swift	.05	.02	.01			
☐	621	Warren Newson	.05	.02	.01			
☐	622	Steve Bedrosian	.05	.02	.01			
☐	623	Ricky Bones	.10	.05	.01			
☐	624	Kevin Tapani	.08	.04	.01			
☐	625	Juan Guzman	1.00	.45	.13			
☐	626	Jeff Johnson	.05	.02	.01			
☐	627	Jeff Montgomery	.05	.02	.01			
☐	628	Ken Hill	.08	.04	.01			
☐	629	Gary Thurman	.05	.02	.01			
☐	630	Steve Howe	.05	.02	.01			
☐	631	Jose DeJesus	.05	.02	.01			
☐	632	Kirk Dressendorfer	.05	.02	.01			
☐	633	Jaime Navarro	.08	.04	.01			
☐	634	Lee Stevens	.05	.02	.01			
☐	635	Pete Harnisch	.05	.02	.01			
☐	636	Bill Landrum	.05	.02	.01			
☐	637	Rich DeLucia	.05	.02	.01			
☐	638	Luis Salazar	.05	.02	.01			
☐	639	Rob Murphy	.05	.02	.01			
☐	640	Diamond Skills	.20	.06	.02			
		Checklist						
		Jose Canseco						
		Rickey Henderson						
☐	641	Roger Clemens DS	.15	.07	.02			
☐	642	Jim Abbott DS	.10	.05	.01			
☐	643	Travis Fryman DS	.30	.14	.04			
☐	644	Jesse Barfield DS	.05	.02	.01			
☐	645	Cal Ripken DS	.20	.09	.03			
☐	646	Wade Boggs DS	.12	.05	.02			
☐	647	Cecil Fielder DS	.12	.05	.02			

☐	648	Rickey Henderson DS	.12	.05	.02
☐	649	Jose Canseco DS	.15	.07	.02
☐	650	Ken Griffey Jr. DS	.40	.18	.05
☐	651	Kenny Rogers	.05	.02	.01
☐	652	Luis Mercedes	.08	.04	.01
☐	653	Mike Stanton	.05	.02	.01
☐	654	Glenn Davis	.08	.04	.01
☐	655	Nolan Ryan	.50	.23	.06
☐	656	Reggie Jefferson	.15	.07	.02
☐	657	Javier Ortiz	.05	.02	.01
☐	658	Greg A. Harris	.05	.02	.01
☐	659	Mariano Duncan	.05	.02	.01
☐	660	Jeff Shaw	.05	.02	.01
☐	661	Mike Moore	.05	.02	.01
☐	662	Chris Haney	.05	.02	.01
☐	663	Joe Slusarski	.05	.02	.01
☐	664	Wayne Housie	.12	.05	.02
☐	665	Carlos Garcia	.15	.07	.02
☐	666	Bob Ojeda	.05	.02	.01
☐	667	Bryan Hickerson	.12	.05	.02
☐	668	Tim Belcher	.08	.04	.01
☐	669	Ron Darling	.08	.04	.01
☐	670	Rex Hudler	.05	.02	.01
☐	671	Sid Fernandez	.08	.04	.01
☐	672	Chito Martinez	.05	.02	.01
☐	673	Pete Schourek	.05	.02	.01
☐	674	Armando Reynoso	.12	.05	.02
☐	675	Mike Mussina	.75	.35	.09
☐	676	Kevin Morton	.05	.02	.01
☐	677	Norm Charlton	.08	.04	.01
☐	678	Danny Darwin	.05	.02	.01
☐	679	Eric King	.05	.02	.01
☐	680	Ted Power	.05	.02	.01
☐	681	Barry Jones	.05	.02	.01
☐	682	Carney Lansford	.08	.04	.01
☐	683	Mel Rojas	.05	.02	.01
☐	684	Rick Honeycutt	.05	.02	.01
☐	685	Jeff Fassero	.05	.02	.01
☐	686	Cris Carpenter	.05	.02	.01
☐	687	Tim Crews	.05	.02	.01
☐	688	Scott Terry	.05	.02	.01
☐	689	Chris Gwynn	.05	.02	.01
☐	690	Gerald Perry	.05	.02	.01
☐	691	John Barfield	.05	.02	.01
☐	692	Bob Melvin	.05	.02	.01
☐	693	Juan Agosto	.05	.02	.01
☐	694	Alejandro Pena	.05	.02	.01
☐	695	Jeff Russell	.05	.02	.01
☐	696	Carmelo Martinez	.05	.02	.01
☐	697	Bud Black	.05	.02	.01
☐	698	Dave Otto	.05	.02	.01
☐	699	Billy Hatcher	.05	.02	.01
☐	700	Checklist 601-700	.07	.01	.00
☐	701	Clemente Nunez	.40	.18	.05
☐	702	Rookie Threats	.30	.14	.04
☐	703	Mike Morgan	.05	.02	.01
☐	704	Keith Miller	.05	.02	.01

☐ 705 Kurt Stillwell	.05	.02	.01
☐ 706 Damon Berryhill	.05	.02	.01
☐ 707 Von Hayes	.05	.02	.01
☐ 708 Rick Sutcliffe	.08	.04	.01
☐ 709 Hubie Brooks	.05	.02	.01
☐ 710 Ryan Turner	.50	.23	.06
☐ 711 Diamond Skills Checklist	.15	.07	.02
Barry Bonds			
Andy Van Slyke			
☐ 712 Jose Rijo DS	.06	.03	.01
☐ 713 Tom Glavine DS	.12	.05	.02
☐ 714 Shawon Dunston DS	.06	.03	.01
☐ 715 Andy Van Slyke DS	.09	.04	.01
☐ 716 Ozzie Smith DS	.12	.05	.02
☐ 717 Tony Gwynn DS	.12	.05	.02
☐ 718 Will Clark DS	.20	.09	.03
☐ 719 Marquis Grissom DS	.10	.05	.01
☐ 720 Howard Johnson DS	.06	.03	.01
☐ 721 Barry Bonds DS	.20	.09	.03
☐ 722 Kirk McCaskill	.05	.02	.01
☐ 723 Sammy Sosa	.05	.02	.01
☐ 724 George Bell	.08	.04	.01
☐ 725 Gregg Jefferies	.08	.04	.01
☐ 726 Gary DiSarcina	.05	.02	.01
☐ 727 Mike Bordick	.10	.05	.01
☐ 728 Eddie Murray	.15	.07	.02
400 Home Run Club			
☐ 729 Rene Gonzales	.05	.02	.01
☐ 730 Mike Bielecki	.05	.02	.01
☐ 731 Calvin Jones	.12	.05	.02
☐ 732 Jack Morris	.08	.04	.01
☐ 733 Frank Viola	.08	.04	.01
☐ 734 Dave Winfield	.12	.05	.02
☐ 735 Kevin Mitchell	.08	.04	.01
☐ 736 Bill Swift	.05	.02	.01
☐ 737 Dan Gladden	.05	.02	.01
☐ 738 Mike Jackson	.05	.02	.01
☐ 739 Mark Carreon	.05	.02	.01
☐ 740 Kirt Manwaring	.05	.02	.01
☐ 741 Randy Myers	.08	.04	.01
☐ 742 Kevin McReynolds	.08	.04	.01
☐ 743 Steve Sax	.08	.04	.01
☐ 744 Wally Joyner	.08	.04	.01
☐ 745 Gary Sheffield	.35	.16	.04
☐ 746 Danny Tartabull	.08	.04	.01
☐ 747 Julio Valera	.08	.04	.01
☐ 748 Denny Neagle	.05	.02	.01
☐ 749 Lance Blankenship	.05	.02	.01
☐ 750 Mike Gallego	.05	.02	.01
☐ 751 Bret Saberhagen	.08	.04	.01
☐ 752 Ruben Amaro	.05	.02	.01
☐ 753 Eddie Murray	.12	.05	.02
☐ 754 Kyle Abbott	.08	.04	.01
☐ 755 Bobby Bonilla	.12	.05	.02
☐ 756 Eric Davis	.08	.04	.01
☐ 757 Eddie Taubensee	.15	.07	.02
☐ 758 Andres Galarraga	.05	.02	.01

☐ 759 Pete Incaviglia	.05	.02	.01
☐ 760 Tom Candiotti	.05	.02	.01
☐ 761 Tim Belcher	.08	.04	.01
☐ 762 Ricky Bones	.10	.05	.01
☐ 763 Bip Roberts	.08	.04	.01
☐ 764 Pedro Munoz	.08	.04	.01
☐ 765 Greg Swindell	.08	.04	.01
☐ 766 Kenny Lofton	.40	.18	.05
☐ 767 Gary Carter	.08	.04	.01
☐ 768 Charlie Hayes	.05	.02	.01
☐ 769 Dickie Thon	.05	.02	.01
☐ 770 Diamond Debut	.20	.06	.02
Checklist			
☐ 771 Bret Boone DD	.75	.35	.09
☐ 772 Archi Cianfrocco DD	.20	.09	.03
☐ 773 Mark Clark DD	.12	.05	.02
☐ 774 Chad Curtis DD	.35	.16	.04
☐ 775 Pat Listach DD	1.75	.80	.22
☐ 776 Pat Mahomes DD	.25	.11	.03
☐ 777 Donovan Osborne DD	.40	.18	.05
☐ 778 John Patterson DD	.15	.07	.02
☐ 779 Andy Stankiewicz DD	.20	.09	.03
☐ 780 Turk Wendell DD	.15	.07	.02
☐ 781 Bill Krueger	.05	.02	.01
☐ 782 Rickey Henderson	.15	.07	.02
Grand Theft			
☐ 783 Kevin Seitzer	.08	.04	.01
☐ 784 Dave Martinez	.05	.02	.01
☐ 785 John Smiley	.08	.04	.01
☐ 786 Matt Stairs	.20	.09	.03
☐ 787 Scott Scudder	.05	.02	.01
☐ 788 John Wetteland	.05	.02	.01
☐ 789 Jack Armstrong	.05	.02	.01
☐ 790 Ken Hill	.08	.04	.01
☐ 791 Dick Schofield	.05	.02	.01
☐ 792 Mariano Duncan	.05	.02	.01
☐ 793 Bill Pecota	.05	.02	.01
☐ 794 Mike Kelly	1.00	.45	.13
☐ 795 Willie Randolph	.08	.04	.01
☐ 796 Butch Henry	.05	.02	.01
☐ 797 Carlos Hernandez	.05	.02	.01
☐ 798 Doug Jones	.05	.02	.01
☐ 799 Melido Perez	.08	.04	.01
☐ 800 Checklist 701-800	.07	.01	.00
☐ CP1 David McCarty holo	1.00	.45	.13
☐ CP2 Mike Kelly Holo	1.00	.45	.13
☐ CP3 Ben McDonald Holo	.50	.23	.06
☐ HH2 Ted Williams Holo	6.00	2.70	.75
(Top left corner says,			
91 Upper Deck 92)			
☐ SP3 Deion Sanders SP	10.00	4.50	1.25
(Two-sport card)			
☐ SP4 Tom Selleck and	10.00	4.50	1.25
Frank Thomas SP			
(Mr. Baseball)			

1992 Upper Deck Home Run Heroes

		MT	EX-MT	VG
☐ 14	Jack Clark	.50	.23	.06
☐ 15	Paul O'Neill	.50	.23	.06
☐ 16	Darryl Strawberry	1.25	.55	.16
☐ 17	Dave Winfield	.75	.35	.09
☐ 18	Jay Buhner	.50	.23	.06
☐ 19	Juan Gonzalez	3.00	1.35	.40
☐ 20	Greg Vaughan	.50	.23	.06
☐ 21	Barry Bonds	1.50	.65	.19
☐ 22	Matt Nokes	.50	.23	.06
☐ 23	John Kruk	.50	.23	.06
☐ 24	Ivan Calderon	.50	.23	.06
☐ 25	Jeff Bagwell	2.00	.90	.25
☐ 26	Todd Zeile	.50	.23	.06

This 26-card subset measures the standard size (2 1/2" by 3 1/2") and was randomly inserted into 1992 Upper Deck baseball jumbo foil packs. The set spotlights the 1991 home run leaders from each of the 26 Major League teams. The fronts display color action player photos with a shadow strip around the picture for a three-dimensional effect. A gold bat icon runs vertically down the left side and contains the words "Homerun Heroes" printed in white. The backs have action photos in color and career highlights on a white background. AL players have their name printed in a red bar while NL players' names are printed in a green bar. The cards are numbered on the back with an HR prefix.

1992 Upper Deck Scouting Report

	MT	EX-MT	VG
COMPLETE SET (26)	24.00	11.00	3.00
COMMON PLAYER (1-26)	.50	.23	.06

		MT	EX-MT	VG
☐ 1	Jose Canseco	2.00	.90	.25
☐ 2	Cecil Fielder	1.25	.55	.16
☐ 3	Howard Johnson	.50	.23	.06
☐ 4	Cal Ripken	3.00	1.35	.40
☐ 5	Matt Williams	.50	.23	.06
☐ 6	Joe Carter	1.25	.55	.16
☐ 7	Ron Gant	.75	.35	.09
☐ 8	Frank Thomas	5.00	2.30	.60
☐ 9	Andre Dawson	.75	.35	.09
☐ 10	Fred McGriff	1.25	.55	.16
☐ 11	Danny Tartabull	.50	.23	.06
☐ 12	Chili Davis	.50	.23	.06
☐ 13	Albert Belle	1.00	.45	.13

Randomly inserted one per high series jumbo pack, this 25-card set features outstanding prospects in baseball. The cards measure the standard size (2 1/2" by 3 1/2"). The fronts carry color action player photos that are full-bleed on the top and right, bordered below by a black stripe with the player's name, and by a black jagged left border that resembles torn paper. The words "Scouting Report" are printed vertically in silver lettering in the left border. The back design features a clipboard with three items held fast by the clamp: 1) a color player photo; 2) a 4" by 6" index card with major league rating in five categories (average, power, speed, fielding, and arm), and an 8 1/2" by 11" piece of paper typed with a player profile. The cards are num-

bered on the back with an SR prefix. The card numbering follows alphabetical order by player's name.

	MT	EX-MT	VG
COMPLETE SET (25)	27.00	12.00	3.40
COMMON PLAYER (1-25)	.50	.23	.06
☐ 1 Andy Ashby	.50	.23	.06
☐ 2 Willie Banks	1.00	.45	.13
☐ 3 Kim Batiste	.50	.23	.06
☐ 4 Derek Bell	1.00	.45	.13
☐ 5 Archi Cianfrocco	.60	.25	.08
☐ 6 Royce Clayton	1.00	.45	.13
☐ 7 Gary DiSarcina	.50	.23	.06
☐ 8 Dave Fleming	3.00	1.35	.40
☐ 9 Butch Henry	.50	.23	.06
☐ 10 Todd Hundley	.50	.23	.06
☐ 11 Brian Jordan	1.00	.45	.13
☐ 12 Eric Karros	7.00	3.10	.85
☐ 13 Pat Listach	7.00	3.10	.85
☐ 14 Scott Livingstone	.50	.23	.06
☐ 15 Kenny Lofton	4.00	1.80	.50
☐ 16 Pat Mahomes	1.50	.65	.19
☐ 17 Denny Neagle	.50	.23	.06
☐ 18 Dave Nilsson	1.25	.55	.16
☐ 19 Donovan Osborne	2.00	.90	.25
☐ 20 Reggie Sanders	2.50	1.15	.30
☐ 21 Andy Stankiewicz	.60	.25	.08
☐ 22 Jim Thome	1.00	.45	.13
☐ 23 Julio Valera	.50	.23	.06
☐ 24 Mark Wohlers	.75	.35	.09
☐ 25 Anthony Young	.50	.23	.06

1992 Upper Deck Ted Williams Best

This 20-card set contains Ted Williams' choices of best current and future hitters in the game. The standard size cards (2 1/2" by 3 1/2") were randomly inserted in Upper Deck high number foil packs. The fronts feature full-bleed color action photos with the player's name in a black field separated from the picture by Ted Williams' gold-stamped signature. The back design displays a color close-up of the player in a purple and gold bordered oval on a gray cement-textured background. The upper right corner appears peeled back to reveal the Upper Deck hologram. A Ted Williams'

quote about the player is included below the photo. Player's statistics in a purple and gold bordered box round out the card back. The cards are numbered on the back with a T prefix.

	MT	EX-MT	VG
COMPLETE SET (20)	60.00	27.00	7.50
COMMON PLAYER (1-20)	1.50	.65	.19
☐ 1 Wade Boggs	2.50	1.15	.30
☐ 2 Barry Bonds	4.00	1.80	.50
☐ 3 Jose Canseco	4.00	1.80	.50
☐ 4 Will Clark	4.00	1.80	.50
☐ 5 Cecil Fielder	3.00	1.35	.40
☐ 6 Tony Gwynn	3.00	1.35	.40
☐ 7 Rickey Henderson	3.00	1.35	.40
☐ 8 Fred McGriff	3.00	1.35	.40
☐ 9 Kirby Puckett	4.00	1.80	.50
☐ 10 Ruben Sierra	3.00	1.35	.40
☐ 11 Roberto Alomar	4.50	2.00	.55
☐ 12 Jeff Bagwell	4.00	1.80	.50
☐ 13 Albert Belle	2.50	1.15	.30
☐ 14 Juan Gonzalez	6.00	2.70	.75
☐ 15 Ken Griffey Jr	9.00	4.00	1.15
☐ 16 Chris Hoiles	1.50	.65	.19
☐ 17 David Justice	3.50	1.55	.45
☐ 18 Phil Plantier	2.00	.90	.25
☐ 19 Frank Thomas	12.00	5.50	1.50
☐ 20 Robin Ventura	3.00	1.35	.40

1993 Upper Deck

The first series of the 1993 Upper Deck baseball set consists of 420 cards measuring the standard size (2 1/2" by 3 1/2"). A ten-card hobby-only insert set featured Triple Crown Contenders while a 26-card Walter Iooss Collection was found in retail

foil packs only. A ten-card Baseball Heroes insert set pays tribute to Willie Mays. Also a nine-card "Then and Now" hologram set was randomly inserted in foil packs and one card of a 28-card insert set was featured exclusively in each jumbo foil pack. Finally a special card (SP5) was randomly inserted in packs to commemorate the 3,000th hit of Brett and Yount. The front designs features color action player photos bordered in white. The company name is printed along the photo surface of the card top. The player's name appears in script in a color stripe cutting across the bottom of the picture while the team name and his position appear in another color stripe immediately below. The backs have a color close-up photo on the upper portion and biography, statistics, and career highlights on the lower portion. Special subsets featured include Star Rookies (1-29), Community Heroes (30-40), and American League Teammates (41-55). The cards are numbered on the back.

	MT	EX-MT	VG
COMPLETE SET (420)	30.00	13.50	3.80
COMMON PLAYER (1-420)	.06	.03	.01

		MT	EX-MT	VG
☐ 1	Star Rookie CL	.25	.08	.03
	Tim Salmon			
☐ 2	Mike Piazza SR	.50	.23	.06
☐ 3	Rene Arocha SR	.50	.23	.06
☐ 4	Willie Greene SR	.25	.11	.03
☐ 5	Manny Alexander SR	.15	.07	.02
☐ 6	Dan Wilson SR	.10	.05	.01
☐ 7	Dan Smith SR	.15	.07	.02
☐ 8	Kevin Rogers SR	.15	.07	.02
☐ 9	Kurt Miller SR	2.00	.90	.25
☐ 10	Joe Vitko SR	.30	.14	.04
☐ 11	Tim Costo SR	.15	.07	.02
☐ 12	Alan Embree SR	.40	.18	.05
☐ 13	Jim Tatum SR	.30	.14	.04
☐ 14	Cris Colon SR	.15	.07	.02
☐ 15	Steve Hosey SR	.25	.11	.03
☐ 16	Sterling Hitchcock SR	.50	.23	.06
☐ 17	Dave Mlicki SR	.25	.11	.03
☐ 18	Jessie Hollins SR	.30	.14	.04
☐ 19	Bobby Jones SR	.50	.23	.06
☐ 20	Kurt Miller SR	.10	.05	.01
☐ 21	Melvin Nieves SR	.50	.23	.06
☐ 22	Billy Ashley SR	.40	.18	.05
☐ 23	J.T. Snow SR	.75	.35	.09
☐ 24	Chipper Jones SR	.40	.18	.05
☐ 25	Tim Salmon SR	.40	.18	.05
☐ 26	Tim Pugh SR	.35	.16	.04
☐ 27	David Nied SR	2.00	.90	.25
☐ 28	Mike Trombley SR	.20	.09	.03
☐ 29	Javy Lopez SR	.50	.23	.06
☐ 30	Community Heroes CL	.12	.04	.01
	Jim Abbott			
☐ 31	Jim Abbott CH	.12	.05	.02
☐ 32	Dale Murphy CH	.09	.04	.01
☐ 33	Tony Pena CH	.07	.03	.01
☐ 34	Kirby Puckett CH	.20	.09	.03
☐ 35	Harold Reynolds CH	.07	.03	.01
☐ 36	Cal Ripken CH	.25	.11	.03
☐ 37	Nolan Ryan CH	.30	.14	.04
☐ 38	Ryne Sandberg CH	.20	.09	.03
☐ 39	Dave Stewart CH	.09	.04	.01
☐ 40	Dave Winfield CH	.10	.05	.01
☐ 41	Teammates CL	.15	.05	.02
	Joe Carter			
	Mark McGwire			
☐ 42	Blockbuster Trade	.15	.07	.02
	Joe Carter			
	Roberto Alomar			
☐ 43	Brew Crew	.25	.11	.03
	Paul Molitor			
	Pat Listach			
	Robin Yount			
☐ 44	Iron and Steel	.20	.09	.03
	Cal Ripken			
	Brady Anderson			
☐ 45	Youthful Tribe	.15	.07	.02
	Albert Belle			
	Sandy Alomar Jr.			
	Jim Thome			
	Carlos Baerga			
	Kenny Lofton			
☐ 46	Motown Mashers	.12	.05	.02
	Cecil Fielder			
	Mickey Tettleton			
☐ 47	Yankee Pride	.12	.05	.02
	Roberto Kelly			
	Don Mattingly			
☐ 48	Boston Cy Sox	.12	.05	.02
	Frank Viola			
	Roger Clemens			
☐ 49	Bash Brothers	.15	.07	.02

	Ruben Sierra		
	Mark McGwire		
☐ 50	Twin Titles 12	.05	.02
	Kent Hrbek		
	Kirby Puckett		
☐ 51	Southside Sluggers...........40	.18	.05
	Robin Ventura		
	Frank Thomas		
☐ 52	Latin Stars 35	.16	.04
	Juan Gonzalez		
	Jose Canseco		
	Ivan Rodriguez		
	Rafael Palmeiro		
☐ 53	Lethal Lefties 07	.03	.01
	Mark Langston		
	Jim Abbott		
	Chuck Finley		
☐ 54	Royal Family 12	.05	.02
	Wally Joyner		
	Gregg Jefferies		
	George Brett		
☐ 55	Pacific Sock Exchange......25	.11	.03
	Kevin Mitchell		
	Ken Griffey Jr.		
	Jay Buhner		
☐ 56	George Brett 15	.07	.02
☐ 57	Scott Cooper 08	.04	.01
☐ 58	Mike Maddux 06	.03	.01
☐ 59	Rusty Meacham 06	.03	.01
☐ 60	Wilfredo Cordero 15	.07	.02
☐ 61	Tim Teufel 06	.03	.01
☐ 62	Jeff Montgomery 06	.03	.01
☐ 63	Scott Livingstone 08	.04	.01
☐ 64	Doug Dascenzo 20	.09	.03
☐ 65	Bret Boone 40	.18	.05
☐ 66	Tim Wakefield 90	.40	.11
☐ 67	Curt Schilling 06	.03	.01
☐ 68	Frank Tanana 06	.03	.01
☐ 69	Len Dykstra.....................08	.04	.01
☐ 70	Derek Lilliquist 06	.03	.01
☐ 71	Anthony Young 08	.04	.01
☐ 72	Hipolito Pichardo 06	.03	.01
☐ 73	Rod Beck 08	.04	.01
☐ 74	Kent Hrbek 08	.04	.01
☐ 75	Tom Glavine 20	.09	.03
☐ 76	Kevin Brown 08	.04	.01
☐ 77	Chuck Finley 06	.03	.01
☐ 78	Bob Walk 06	.03	.01
☐ 79	Rheal Cormier 06	.03	.01
☐ 80	Rick Sutcliffe 08	.04	.01
☐ 81	Harold Baines 08	.04	.01
☐ 82	Lee Smith 08	.04	.01
☐ 83	Geno Petralli 06	.03	.01
☐ 84	Jose Oquendo 06	.03	.01
☐ 85	Mark Gubicza 06	.03	.01
☐ 86	Mickey Tettleton 08	.04	.01
☐ 87	Bobby Witt 06	.03	.01

☐ 88	Mark Lewis 08	.04	.01
☐ 89	Kevin Appier 08	.04	.01
☐ 90	Mike Stanton 06	.03	.01
☐ 91	Rafael Belliard 06	.03	.01
☐ 92	Kenny Rogers 06	.03	.01
☐ 93	Randy Velarde 06	.03	.01
☐ 94	Luis Sojo 06	.03	.01
☐ 95	Mark Leiter 06	.03	.01
☐ 96	Jody Reed 06	.03	.01
☐ 97	Pete Harnisch 06	.03	.01
☐ 98	Tom Candiotti 06	.03	.01
☐ 99	Mark Portugal 06	.03	.01
☐ 100	Dave Valle 06	.03	.01
☐ 101	Shawon Dunston 08	.04	.01
☐ 102	B.J. Surhoff 06	.03	.01
☐ 103	Jay Bell 06	.03	.01
☐ 104	Sid Bream 06	.03	.01
☐ 105	Checklist 1-105................11	.03	.01
	Frank Thomas		
☐ 106	Mike Morgan....................06	.03	.01
☐ 107	Bill Doran 06	.03	.01
☐ 108	Lance Blankenship 06	.03	.01
☐ 109	Mark Lemke.....................06	.03	.01
☐ 110	Brian Harper 06	.03	.01
☐ 111	Brady Anderson 08	.04	.01
☐ 112	Bip Roberts 08	.04	.01
☐ 113	Mitch Williams 06	.03	.01
☐ 114	Craig Biggio 08	.04	.01
☐ 115	Eddie Murray 15	.07	.02
☐ 116	Matt Nokes 06	.03	.01
☐ 117	Lance Parrish 08	.04	.01
☐ 118	Bill Swift 06	.03	.01
☐ 119	Jeff Innis 06	.03	.01
☐ 120	Mike LaValliere 06	.03	.01
☐ 121	Hal Morris 08	.04	.01
☐ 122	Walt Weiss 06	.03	.01
☐ 123	Ivan Rodriguez.................30	.14	.04
☐ 124	Andy Van Slyke 08	.04	.01
☐ 125	Roberto Alomar 35	.16	.04
☐ 126	Robby Thompson 06	.03	.01
☐ 127	Sammy Sosa 08	.04	.01
☐ 128	Mark Langston 08	.04	.01
☐ 129	Jerry Browne 06	.03	.01
☐ 130	Chuck McElroy 06	.03	.01
☐ 131	Frank Viola 08	.04	.01
☐ 132	Leo Gomez......................08	.04	.01
☐ 133	Ramon Martinez 08	.04	.01
☐ 134	Don Mattingly 20	.09	.03
☐ 135	Roger Clemens 35	.16	.04
☐ 136	Rickey Henderson 20	.09	.03
☐ 137	Darren Daulton 08	.04	.01
☐ 138	Ken Hill 08	.04	.01
☐ 139	Ozzie Guillen 06	.03	.01
☐ 140	Jerald Clark 06	.03	.01
☐ 141	Dave Fleming 30	.14	.04
☐ 142	Delino DeShields 15	.07	.02
☐ 143	Matt Williams 08	.04	.01

☐ 144 Larry Walker	.20	.09	.03	
☐ 145 Ruben Sierra	.25	.11	.03	
☐ 146 Ozzie Smith	.15	.07	.02	
☐ 147 Chris Sabo	.08	.04	.01	
☐ 148 Carlos Hernandez	.08	.04	.01	
☐ 149 Pat Borders	.06	.03	.01	
☐ 150 Orlando Merced	.08	.04	.01	
☐ 151 Royce Clayton	.08	.04	.01	
☐ 152 Kurt Stillwell	.06	.03	.01	
☐ 153 Dave Hollins	.08	.04	.01	
☐ 154 Mike Greenwell	.08	.04	.01	
☐ 155 Nolan Ryan	.60	.25	.08	
☐ 156 Felix Jose	.08	.04	.01	
☐ 157 Junior Felix	.06	.03	.01	
☐ 158 Derek Bell	.08	.04	.01	
☐ 159 Steve Buechele	.06	.03	.01	
☐ 160 John Burkett	.06	.03	.01	
☐ 161 Pat Howell	.15	.07	.02	
☐ 162 Milt Cuyler	.06	.03	.01	
☐ 163 Terry Pendleton	.08	.04	.01	
☐ 164 Jack Morris	.10	.05	.01	
☐ 165 Tony Gwynn	.20	.09	.03	
☐ 166 Deion Sanders	.20	.09	.03	
☐ 167 Mike Devereaux	.08	.04	.01	
☐ 168 Ron Darling	.08	.04	.01	
☐ 169 Orel Hershiser	.08	.04	.01	
☐ 170 Mike Jackson	.06	.03	.01	
☐ 171 Doug Jones	.06	.03	.01	
☐ 172 Dan Walters	.06	.03	.01	
☐ 173 Darren Lewis	.06	.03	.01	
☐ 174 Carlos Baerga	.25	.11	.03	
☐ 175 Ryne Sandberg	.35	.16	.04	
☐ 176 Gregg Jefferies	.08	.04	.01	
☐ 177 John Jaha	.08	.04	.01	
☐ 178 Luis Polonia	.06	.03	.01	
☐ 179 Kirt Manwaring	.06	.03	.01	
☐ 180 Mike Magnante	.06	.03	.01	
☐ 181 Billy Ripken	.06	.03	.01	
☐ 182 Mike Moore	.06	.03	.01	
☐ 183 Eric Anthony	.08	.04	.01	
☐ 184 Lenny Harris	.06	.03	.01	
☐ 185 Tony Pena	.06	.03	.01	
☐ 186 Mike Felder	.06	.03	.01	
☐ 187 Greg Olson	.06	.03	.01	
☐ 188 Rene Gonzales	.06	.03	.01	
☐ 189 Mike Bordick	.08	.04	.01	
☐ 190 Mel Rojas	.06	.03	.01	
☐ 191 Todd Frohwirth	.06	.03	.01	
☐ 192 Darryl Hamilton	.08	.04	.01	
☐ 193 Mike Fetters	.06	.03	.01	
☐ 194 Omar Olivares	.06	.03	.01	
☐ 195 Tony Phillips	.06	.03	.01	
☐ 196 Paul Sorrento	.06	.03	.01	
☐ 197 Trevor Wilson	.06	.03	.01	
☐ 198 Kevin Gross	.06	.03	.01	
☐ 199 Ron Karkovice	.06	.03	.01	
☐ 200 Brook Jacoby	.06	.03	.01	
☐ 201 Mariano Duncan	.06	.03	.01	
☐ 202 Dennis Cook	.06	.03	.01	
☐ 203 Daryl Boston	.06	.03	.01	
☐ 204 Mike Perez	.08	.04	.01	
☐ 205 Manuel Lee	.06	.03	.01	
☐ 206 Steve Olin	.06	.03	.01	
☐ 207 Charlie Hough	.06	.03	.01	
☐ 208 Scott Scudder	.06	.03	.01	
☐ 209 Charlie O'Brien	.06	.03	.01	
☐ 210 Checklist 106-210	.09	.02	.01	
Barry Bonds				
☐ 211 Jose Vizcaino	.06	.03	.01	
☐ 212 Scott Leius	.06	.03	.01	
☐ 213 Kevin Mitchell	.08	.04	.01	
☐ 214 Brian Barnes	.06	.03	.01	
☐ 215 Pat Kelly	.08	.04	.01	
☐ 216 Chris Hammond	.06	.03	.01	
☐ 217 Rob Deer	.08	.04	.01	
☐ 218 Cory Snyder	.06	.03	.01	
☐ 219 Gary Carter	.08	.04	.01	
☐ 220 Danny Darwin	.06	.03	.01	
☐ 221 Tom Gordon	.06	.03	.01	
☐ 222 Gary Sheffield	.30	.14	.04	
☐ 223 Joe Carter	.20	.09	.03	
☐ 224 Jay Buhner	.08	.04	.01	
☐ 225 Jose Offerman	.08	.04	.01	
☐ 226 Jose Rijo	.08	.04	.01	
☐ 227 Mark Whiten	.08	.04	.01	
☐ 228 Randy Milligan	.06	.03	.01	
☐ 229 Bud Black	.06	.03	.01	
☐ 230 Gary DiSarcina	.08	.04	.01	
☐ 231 Steve Finley	.06	.03	.01	
☐ 232 Dennis Martinez	.08	.04	.01	
☐ 233 Mike Mussina	.50	.23	.06	
☐ 234 Joe Oliver	.06	.03	.01	
☐ 235 Chad Curtis	.20	.09	.03	
☐ 236 Shane Mack	.08	.04	.01	
☐ 237 Jaime Navarro	.08	.04	.01	
☐ 238 Brian McRae	.08	.04	.01	
☐ 239 Chili Davis	.08	.04	.01	
☐ 240 Jeff King	.06	.03	.01	
☐ 241 Dean Palmer	.08	.04	.01	
☐ 242 Danny Tartabull	.08	.04	.01	
☐ 243 Charles Nagy	.08	.04	.01	
☐ 244 Ray Lankford	.15	.07	.02	
☐ 245 Barry Larkin	.15	.07	.02	
☐ 246 Steve Avery	.25	.11	.03	
☐ 247 John Kruk	.08	.04	.01	
☐ 248 Derrick May	.08	.04	.01	
☐ 249 Stan Javier	.06	.03	.01	
☐ 250 Roger McDowell	.06	.03	.01	
☐ 251 Dan Gladden	.06	.03	.01	
☐ 252 Wally Joyner	.08	.04	.01	
☐ 253 Pat Listach	.60	.25	.08	
☐ 254 Chuck Knoblauch	.25	.11	.03	
☐ 255 Sandy Alomar Jr.	.06	.03	.01	
☐ 256 Jeff Bagwell	.30	.14	.04	

□	257	Andy Stankiewicz	.08	.04	.01
□	258	Darrin Jackson	.06	.03	.01
□	259	Brett Butler	.08	.04	.01
□	260	Joe Orsulak	.06	.03	.01
□	261	Andy Benes	.08	.04	.01
□	262	Kenny Lofton	.30	.14	.04
□	263	Robin Ventura	.25	.11	.03
□	264	Ron Gant	.08	.04	.01
□	265	Ellis Burks	.06	.03	.01
□	266	Juan Guzman	.50	.23	.06
□	267	Wes Chamberlain	.06	.03	.01
□	268	John Smiley	.08	.04	.01
□	269	Franklin Stubbs	.06	.03	.01
□	270	Tom Browning	.06	.03	.01
□	271	Dennis Eckersley	.10	.05	.01
□	272	Carlton Fisk	.15	.07	.02
□	273	Lou Whitaker	.08	.04	.01
□	274	Phil Plantier	.15	.07	.02
□	275	Bobby Bonilla	.15	.07	.02
□	276	Ben McDonald	.08	.04	.01
□	277	Bob Zupcic	.08	.04	.01
□	278	Terry Steinbach	.08	.04	.01
□	279	Terry Mulholland	.06	.03	.01
□	280	Lance Johnson	.06	.03	.01
□	281	Willie McGee	.08	.04	.01
□	282	Bret Saberhagen	.08	.04	.01
□	283	Randy Myers	.06	.03	.01
□	284	Randy Tomlin	.06	.03	.01
□	285	Mickey Morandini	.08	.04	.01
□	286	Brian Williams	.08	.04	.01
□	287	Tino Martinez	.08	.04	.01
□	288	Jose Melendez	.06	.03	.01
□	289	Jeff Huson	.06	.03	.01
□	290	Joe Grahe	.06	.03	.01
□	291	Mel Hall	.06	.03	.01
□	292	Otis Nixon	.06	.03	.01
□	293	Todd Hundley	.06	.03	.01
□	294	Casey Candaele	.06	.03	.01
□	295	Kevin Seitzer	.08	.04	.01
□	296	Eddie Taubensee	.06	.03	.01
□	297	Moises Alou	.08	.04	.01
□	298	Scott Radinsky	.06	.03	.01
□	299	Thomas Howard	.06	.03	.01
□	300	Kyle Abbott	.06	.03	.01
□	301	Omar Vizquel	.06	.03	.01
□	302	Keith Miller	.06	.03	.01
□	303	Rick Aguilera	.08	.04	.01
□	304	Bruce Hurst	.08	.04	.01
□	305	Ken Caminiti	.08	.04	.01
□	306	Mike Pagliarulo	.06	.03	.01
□	307	Frank Seminara	.06	.03	.01
□	308	Andre Dawson	.15	.07	.02
□	309	Jose Lind	.06	.03	.01
□	310	Joe Boever	.06	.03	.01
□	311	Jeff Parrett	.06	.03	.01
□	312	Alan Mills	.06	.03	.01
□	313	Kevin Tapani	.08	.04	.01
□	314	Darryl Kile	.06	.03	.01
□	315	Checklist 211-315	.09	.02	.01
		Will Clark			
□	316	Mike Sharperson	.06	.03	.01
□	317	John Orton	.06	.03	.01
□	318	Bob Tewksbury	.08	.04	.01
□	319	Xavier Hernandez	.06	.03	.01
⊟	320	Paul Assenmacher	.06	.03	.01
□	321	John Franco	.06	.03	.01
□	322	Mike Timlin	.06	.03	.01
□	323	Jose Guzman	.06	.03	.01
□	324	Pedro Martinez	.10	.04	.01
□	325	Bill Spiers	.06	.03	.01
□	326	Melido Perez	.06	.03	.01
□	327	Mike Macfarlane	.06	.03	.01
□	328	Ricky Bones	.06	.03	.01
□	329	Scott Bankhead	.06	.03	.01
□	330	Rich Rodriguez	.06	.03	.01
□	331	Geronimo Pena	.06	.03	.01
□	332	Bernie Williams	.08	.04	.01
□	333	Paul Molitor	.08	.04	.01
□	334	Carlos Garcia	.08	.04	.01
□	335	David Cone	.08	.04	.01
□	336	Randy Johnson	.08	.04	.01
□	337	Pat Mahomes	.08	.04	.01
□	338	Erik Hanson	.06	.03	.01
□	339	Duane Ward	.06	.03	.01
□	340	Al Martin	.10	.04	.01
□	341	Pedro Munoz	.08	.04	.01
□	342	Greg Colbrunn	.06	.03	.01
□	343	Julio Valera	.08	.04	.01
□	344	John Olerud	.15	.07	.02
□	345	George Bell	.08	.04	.01
□	346	Devon White	.08	.04	.01
□	347	Donovan Osborne	.20	.09	.03
□	348	Mark Gardner	.06	.03	.01
□	349	Zane Smith	.06	.03	.01
□	350	Wilson Alvarez	.06	.03	.01
□	351	Kevin Koslofski	.06	.03	.01
□	352	Roberto Hernandez	.06	.03	.01
□	353	Glenn Davis	.08	.04	.01
□	354	Reggie Sanders	.20	.09	.03
□	355	Ken Griffey Jr.	.75	.35	.09
□	356	Marquis Grissom	.15	.07	.02
□	357	Jack McDowell	.08	.04	.01
□	358	Jimmy Key	.06	.03	.01
□	359	Stan Belinda	.06	.03	.01
□	360	Gerald Williams	.08	.04	.01
□	361	Sid Fernandez	.08	.04	.01
□	362	Alex Fernandez	.08	.04	.01
□	363	John Smoltz	.15	.07	.02
□	364	Travis Fryman	.30	.14	.04
□	365	Jose Canseco	.30	.14	.04
□	366	David Justice	.30	.14	.04
□	367	Pedro Astacio	.30	.14	.04
□	368	Tim Belcher	.08	.04	.01
□	369	Steve Sax	.08	.04	.01

☐	370	Gary Gaetti	.06	.03	.01
☐	371	Jeff Frye	.06	.03	.01
☐	372	Bob Wickman	.15	.07	.02
☐	373	Ryan Thompson	.30	.14	.04
☐	374	David Hulse	.15	.07	.02
☐	375	Cal Eldred	.30	.14	.04
☐	376	Ryan Klesko	.40	.18	.05
☐	377	Damion Easley	.20	.09	.03
☐	378	John Kiely	.06	.03	.01
☐	379	Jim Bullinger	.08	.04	.01
☐	380	Brian Bohanon	.06	.03	.01
☐	381	Rod Brewer	.20	.09	.03
☐	382	Fernando Ramsey	.15	.07	.02
☐	383	Sam Militello	.25	.11	.03
☐	384	Arthur Rhodes	.15	.07	.02
☐	385	Eric Karros	.50	.23	.06
☐	386	Rico Brogna	.08	.04	.01
☐	387	John Valentin	.20	.09	.03
☐	388	Kerry Woodson	.06	.03	.01
☐	389	Ben Rivera	.08	.04	.01
☐	390	Matt Whiteside	.15	.07	.02
☐	391	Henry Rodriguez	.08	.04	.01
☐	392	John Wetteland	.06	.03	.01
☐	393	Kent Mercker	.06	.03	.01
☐	394	Bernard Gilkey	.08	.04	.01
☐	395	Doug Henry	.06	.03	.01
☐	396	Mo Vaughn	.08	.04	.01
☐	397	Scott Erickson	.08	.04	.01
☐	398	Bill Gullickson	.06	.03	.01
☐	399	Mark Guthrie	.06	.03	.01
☐	400	Dave Martinez	.06	.03	.01
☐	401	Jeff Kent	.12	.05	.02
☐	402	Chris Hoiles	.08	.04	.01
☐	403	Mike Henneman	.06	.03	.01
☐	404	Chris Nabholz	.08	.04	.01
☐	405	Tom Pagnozzi	.06	.03	.01
☐	406	Kelly Gruber	.08	.04	.01
☐	407	Bob Welch	.06	.03	.01
☐	408	Frank Castillo	.06	.03	.01
☐	409	John Dopson	.06	.03	.01
☐	410	Steve Farr	.06	.03	.01
☐	411	Henry Cotto	.06	.03	.01
☐	412	Bob Patterson	.06	.03	.01
☐	413	Todd Stottlemyre	.08	.04	.01
☐	414	Greg A. Harris	.06	.03	.01
☐	415	Denny Neagle	.06	.03	.01
☐	416	Bill Wegman	.06	.03	.01
☐	417	Willie Wilson	.06	.03	.01
☐	418	Terry Leach	.06	.03	.01
☐	419	Willie Randolph	.08	.04	.01
☐	420	Checklist 316-420 Mark McGwire	.09	.02	.01
☐	SP5	George Brett and Robin Yount (Commemorating 3,000th Hit)	10.00	4.50	1.25

1993 Upper Deck Then And Now

This nine-card, standard-size (2 1/2" by 3 1/2") hologram set highlights nine veteran stars in their rookie year and today, reflecting on how they and the game have changed. The cards were randomly inserted in series I foil packs. The horizontal fronts have a color close-up photo cutout and superimposed at the left corner of a full-bleed hologram portraying the player in an action scene. The skyline of the player's city serves as the background for the holograms. The player's name and the manufacturer's name form a right angle at the upper right corner. At the upper left corner, a "Then and Now" logo which includes the length of the player's career in years rounds out the front. On a sand-colored panel that resembles a postage stamp, the backs present career summary. The cards are numbered on the back with a TN prefix and arranged alphabetically according to player's last name.

		MT	EX-MT	VG
	COMPLETE SET (9)	40.00	18.00	5.00
	COMMON PLAYER (1-9)	4.00	1.80	.50
☐ 1	Wade Boggs	4.00	1.80	.50
☐ 2	George Brett	5.00	2.30	.60
☐ 3	Rickey Henderson	5.00	2.30	.60
☐ 4	Cal Ripken	8.00	3.60	1.00
☐ 5	Nolan Ryan	10.00	4.50	1.25
☐ 6	Ryne Sandberg	7.00	3.10	.85
☐ 7	Ozzie Smith	4.00	1.80	.50
☐ 8	Darryl Strawberry	4.00	1.80	.50
☐ 9	Dave Winfield	4.00	1.80	.50

1993 Upper Deck Triple Crown

This ten-card, standard-size (2 1/2" by 3 1/2") subset highlights ten players who were selected by Upper Deck as having the best shot at winning Major League Baseball's Triple Crown. The cards were randomly inserted in series I foil packs sold by hobby dealers only. The fronts display glossy full-bleed color player photos.

At the bottom, a purple ribbon edged in gold foil carries the words "Triple Crown Contenders," while the player's name appears in gold foil lettering immediately below on a gradated black background. A crown overlays the ribbon at the lower left corner and rounds out the front. On a gradated black background, the backs summarize the player's performance in home runs, RBIs, and batting average. The cards are numbered on the back with a TC prefix and arranged alphabetically by player's last name.

	MT	EX-MT	VG
COMPLETE SET (10)	60.00	27.00	7.50
COMMON PLAYER (1-10)	5.00	2.30	.60
☐ 1 Barry Bonds	8.00	3.60	1.00
☐ 2 Jose Canseco	8.00	3.60	1.00
☐ 3 Will Clark	8.00	3.60	1.00
☐ 4 Ken Griffey Jr.	12.00	5.50	1.50
☐ 5 Fred McGriff	7.00	3.10	.85
☐ 6 Kirby Puckett	8.00	3.60	1.00
☐ 7 Cal Ripken Jr.	10.00	4.50	1.25
☐ 8 Gary Sheffield	7.00	3.10	.85
☐ 9 Frank Thomas	15.00	6.75	1.90
☐ 10 Larry Walker	5.00	2.30	.60

Acknowledgments

Each year we refine the process of developing the most accurate and up-to-date information for this book. I believe this year's Price Guide is our best yet. For that, you can thank all of the contributors nationwide (listed below) as well as our staff here in Dallas.

Part of this refining process involves an ever larger number of people and types of expertise on our home team.

For example, our company now boasts a substantial Technical Services team which has made (and is continuing to make) direct and important contributions to this work. Technical Services capably handled numerous technical details and provided able assistance in pricing for this edition of the annual guide. It is very difficult to be "accurate" — one can only do one's best. But this job is especially difficult since we're shooting at a moving target: Prices are fluctuating all the time. Having a several full-time pricing experts has definitely proven to be better than just one, and I thank all of them for working together to provide you, our readers, with the most accurate prices possible.

That effort was directed by Technical Services manager Pepper Hastings.

He was assisted by Technical Services assistant manager Marry Gregory, coordinator Grant Sandground, Price Guide analysts Theo Chen, Mike Hersh, Dan Hitt, Mary Huston, Rich Klein, Allan Muir, Bob Smith, Dave Sliepka, and Steve Smith. Analyst Tom Layberger played a major part in this year's book, working closely with our computer software development team to streamline the pricing process, allowing us to provide even more timely prices. Also contributing to our Technical Services functions were Peter Tepp and Todd Davis.

The price gathering and analytical talents of this fine group of hobbyists has helped make our Beckett team stronger, while making this guide and its companion monthly Price Guides more widely recognized as the hobby's most reliable and relied upon sources of pricing information.

Granted, the production of any book is a total staff effort. However, I owe special thanks to the members of our Book Team who demonstrated extraordinary contributions to this baseball book.

Scott Layton, assistant manager of Special Projects, served as point man in the demanding area of new set entry and was a key person in the organization of both technological and people resources for the book. He was ably assisted by Jana Threatt and Maria Neubauer, who ensured the proper administration of our contributor price guide surveys and performed various other tasks. Pricing analysts Theo Chen, Rich Klein, Mary Huston, Tom Layberger and Grant Sandground track the baseball card market year round, and their baseline analysis and careful proofreading were key contributions to the accuracy of this annual.

Our computer services team — technological experts Sammy Cantrell, Rich Olivieri and Dan Ferguson — spent months programming, testing and implementing new software to simplify the handling of thousands of prices that must be checked and updated for each edition of this book.

Therese Bellar and Lisa O'Neill contributed new designs and artwork to enhance readability. Airey Baringer spent many late-night hours testing new software, then paginating and typesetting the text layout. Mary Gonzalez-Davis was responsible for many of the card photos you see throughout the book, as well as overseeing paste-up. Production Manager Reed Poole offered his usual fine direction in providing resources and production talent. Tracy Hinton spent tireless hours on the phone attending to the wishes of our dealer advertisers under the direction of advertising manager Jeff Anthony. Once the ad specifications were delivered to our offices, John Marshall used his computer skills to turn raw copy into attractive display advertisements that were carefully proofed by Bruce Felps.

And overseeing it all, Managing Editor of Special Projects, Susan K. Elliott, set up initial schedules and ensured that all deadlines were met, while looking for all the fine points to improve our process and presentation throughout the cycle.

This year's volume is the result of a great deal of diligence, hard work, and dedicated effort. It would not have been possible without the expert input and generous amount of time given by our many contributors. Our sincere thanks are extended to each and every one of you.

Those who have worked closely with us on this and many other books have again proven themselves invaluable — Johnny and Sandy Adams, Frank and Vivian Barning (Baseball Hobby News), Chris Benjamin, Sy Berger (Topps), Levi Bleam, Peter Brennan, Card Collectors Co., Cartophilium (Andrew Pywowarczuk), Ira Cetron, Ric Chandgie, Barry Colla, Mike Cramer (Pacific Trading Cards), Bill and Diane Dodge, Doubleheaders (Wayne Varner, Mike Wheat, and Bill Zimpleman), Fleer Corporation (Paul Mullen, Vincent Murray, and Jeff Massien), Steve Freedman, Gervise Ford, Larry and Jeff Fritsch, Tony Galovich (American Card Exchange), Georgia Music and Sports (Dick DeCourcey), Dick Gilkeson, Steve Gold (AU Sports), Bill Goodwin (St. Louis Baseball Cards), Mike and Howard Gordon, George Grauer, John Greenwald, Wayne Grove, Bill Haber, Bill Henderson, Jerry and Etta Hersh, Jay and Mary Kasper, Allan Kaye, David Kohler (SportsCards Plus), Paul Lewicki, Neil Lewis (Leaf), Lew Lipset, Mike Livingston (University Trading Cards), Mark Macrae, Bill Madden, Major League Marketing, Michael McDonald (The Sports Page), Mid-Atlantic Sports Cards (Bill Bossert), Brian Morris, B.A. Murry, Ralph Nozaki, Mike O'Brien, Oldies and Goodies (Nigel Spill),

Optigraphics/Score Group, Jack Pollard, Jeff Prillaman, Gavin Riley, Alan Rosen (Mr. Mint), Clifton Rouse, John Rumierz, San Diego Sport Collectibles (Bill Goepner and Nacho Arredondo), Kevin Savage (Sports Gallery), Mike Schechter, Barry Sloate, John E. Spalding, Phil Spector (Scoreboard, Inc.), Sports Collectors Store, Rick Starks (Megacards), Frank Steele, Murvin Sterling, Lee Temanson, Treat (Harold Anderson), Ed Twombly (New England Bullpen), Bill Vizas, Gary Walter, Bill Wesslund (Portland Sports Card Co.), Craig Williamson, Kit Young, and Ted Zanidakis. Of special help on this edition was B.A. Murry, who in early 1991 laid the groundwork for our Technical Services department before becoming our Senior Pricing Consultant.

Many people have provided price input, illustrative material, checklist verifications, errata, and/or background information. We should like to individually thank AbD Cards (Dale Wesolewski), Jerry Adamic, Ben Agave, Michael Albert, Will Allison, David S. Anderson, Dennis Anderson, Ed Anderson, Glenn Anderson, Shane Anderson, Bruce W. Andrews, Tom Antonowicz, Scott Apple, Ric Apter, Jason Arasate, Burl Armstrong, Neil Armstrong (World Series Cards), Bill Aubin (Field of Dreams), Robert August, Chris Austin, Shawn Bailey, Darryl B. Baker, Jeremy Baldwin, Ball Four Cards (Frank and Steve Pemper), Tim Bamford, John Barbier, Joe Barney, Daniel Barry, David M. Bartlett, Bob Bartosz (Baseball Card Shop), Nathan Basford, Ron Beatty, Robert Beaumont, Elvis Begley, Ken Behr, Jeff Belding, Eddie Benton, Carl Berg, Raymond P. Berg, C.D. Bergstrom, Dave Berman, Mark Besser, Beulah Sports (Jeff Blatt), Seth Bienstock, Brian Bigelow, John R. Bigus, Randy Binns, Josh Bird, George Birsic, Benjamin Blake, David Blanchard, Ron Bloede, James L. Boak, Robert Bodis, Bob Boffa, Steve Bohnenblust, Tim Bond (Tim's Cards & Comics), Matt Bosse, Brian W. Bottles, Bottom of the 9th, Michael Bow, Jeff Breitenfield, John Brenner, Bob Bresnahan, John Brigandi, Dan Britton, Philip Bronikowski, Chuck Brooks, D. Bruce Brown, Jenny Brown, Jody Brown, Garry M. Brownfield, David Brundage, Dan Bruner, Celeste Buckhalt, Ed Burkey Jr., Bubba Burnett, Raleigh Burns, Virgil Burns, Ned Busby, Grant Calhoun, California Card Co., Luis Canino, Danny Cariseo, Jim Carr, Patrick Carroll, Sam Carter, Pedro Cartes, Carves Cards, Ed Caston, Ira Cetron, Sandy Chan, Dwight Chapin, Ray Cherry, Bigg Wayne Christian, Richard Cianciotta, Cincinnati Baseball Cards, Chris Clark, Dave Clark, Derrick F. Clark, Marvin C. Clark, James Claugherty, Coin Corner & Hobbie, Collection de Sport AZ (Ronald Villaneuve), G. Collett, Andrew T. Collier, Les Colvin, Charles A. Coon, Curt Cooter, Kimberly Cooter, Steven Cooter, Lou Costanzo (Champion Sports), Tina Cox, Coyne Cards, Taylor Crane (Cranes Cards), James Craven, Chad Cripe, James

Critzer, Tom Crook, Brian Cunningham, Paul Curran, Allen Custer, W.F. Cyrus Jr., Jim Dahl, Larry Daigneault, Phillip D'Amato, Dave Dame, Brett Daniel, Roy Datema, Jeffrey J. Daub, Brad Davis, Travis Deaton, Dee's Baseball Cards, Eric Delgadillo, Jonathan Delmas, Tim DelVecchio, Steve Dempski, Drew Dennington, John Derossett, Gilberto Diaz, David Dickens, Joel Dilley, Ken Dinerman (California Cruizers), Joe Dinglasan, Walter D. Dinkfelt, Discount Dorothy, Walter J. Dodds Sr., Richard Dolloff (Dolloff Coin Center), Dan Domino, Mike Donatelli, Peter E. D'Onofrio, Ron Dorsey, Thomas Drye, Richard Duglin (Baseball Cards-n-More), B.M. Dungan, Mike Dunn, Gerald Dupire, Heather A. Eades, Ron Edge, Ken Edick (Home Plate of Utah), John Ehm, Marc Ely, William Ension Jr., Richard Eudaley, Doak Ewing, Matt Fagerlind, Gail Fairbrother, R.J. Faletti, James Feathersmith, John Fedak, Daniel Fellows, Adam Felsenthal, David Festberg, Sam P. Figaro, Anthony Fillizola, Louis Fineberg, Jay Finglass, Anthony Fisher, Michael G. Fisher, Aaron Fong, Fremont Fong, Perry Fong, Craig Frank, Mark Franke, Watter Franklin, Gary Frazier, Guy Frodl, Timothy Fuller, Gary Fullerton, Richard Galasso, R. Gallagher, Stephen Gamblin, David Garza, Gerald R. Gatlin, David Gaumer, Ricky Gelboim, Willie George, Tim Gerdes, Raymond Gillen, Herbert Gladhill, Pat Gobble, Dick Goddard, Steve Gold, Alvin Goldblum, Brian Goldner, Greg Goldstein (Dragon's Den), Jeff Goldstein, Ron Gomez, Aaron A. Goodwin, Bryan Greaves, David D. Gresham, Dayton Griffith, Kraig Gross, Terry Gutberiet, Travis Ryan Habey, Shawn Hagene, Evan Hahn, Iran Hall Jr., Hall's Nostalgia, Hershell Hanks, Josh Hanman, Joel Hansen, Gregg Hara, Zac Hargis, Jed Hart, Walter Y. Hashimoto, Alex Haugh, Trevor Hawkins, Michael Head, Rick Heckler, Kevin Heimbigner, Joel Hellman, Arthur W. Henkel, Scott Heuer, Matt Hibbett, Austin Hill, Eric Hitchcock, Greg Hlavka, Adam Hochfeld, Irwin Hoffman, Gary L. Holcomb, Bob Hooper, Craig Huckaby, Travis Hummel, Aaron Hunt, Tom Imboden, Chris Imbriaco, Corey Inskip, Vern Isenberg, Robert A. Ivanjack (Kit Young Cards), Paul S. Jastrzembski, Paul Jennen, Donn Jennings Cards, Michael Jessap, Doug Jodts, L.D. Johansen, Don Johnson, Fred Johnson, Justin Johnson, Rob Johnson, Anthony Johnston, Richard A. Jones, Stewart W. Jones, Joe Juhasz, A.A. Julian III, Charles Juliana, Loyd Jungling, Dave Jurgensmeier, John Just, Kurt Kalafsky, Nick Kasemeotes, Frank J. Katen, Jerry I. Katz, Andrew F. Kazmierski, Don Kelemer, Marty Kenton, Rick Keplinger, Kevin's Kards, Michael Keyton, Gene Kieffer, John Kilian, Larry Killian, Jamie King, L. Kirkwood, Steve Klein, Steven Koenigsberg, Kenneth Krieger, Jeff Kroll, K & S Companies, Scott Ku, Thomas Kunnecke, Arthur A. Kusserou, Michael Landolina, Howard

Landrum, Jason Lassic, Allan Latawiec, Rocco Lattanzi, Gerald A. Lavelle, Dan Lavin, William Lawrence, Joshua Lawson, Jerry Leahy, Cory Leader, Jonathan Lee, Morley Leeking, Ronald Lenhardt, Carmen Leon, Don Lepore, Irv Lerner, Shawn Leubner, Dr. Ernest J. Lewis, Tim Licitra, David Lloyd, Sue Longaker, Allan H. Lowenberg, Robert Luce, Lummus, Corinne Lyon, Dan Mabey, David Macaray, Jim Macie, Mike MacRoberts, Richard Maddigan, Robert F. Maerten Jr., Joe Magnani, Paul Marchant, Steve Markovic, Bob Marquette, Saul Martinez, Pat Massa, Bill Mastro, Duane Matthes, Dr. William McAvoy, McDag Productions Inc., Jessica L. McDaniel, Branson H. McKay, Christopher McKay, Scott McKevitt, Tony McLaughlin, Dan McPartland, Mendal Mearkle, Timothy Meggers, Ken Melanson, Ari Melber, William Mendel, Mendy's Sports Cards, Eric Meredith, Eric Merrill, Dallin Merrill, Blake Meyer (Lone Star Sportscards), Charles L. Meyers, Joe Michalowicz, Lee Milazzo, Jimmy Milburn, D. Allan Miles (D.A.M. Cards of Richmond), Cary Miller, David (Otis) Miller, George Miller, Harold M. Miller, Jason Miller, Wayne Miller, Dick Millerd, Mitchell's Baseball Cards, Craig T. Miyamoto, Perry Miyashita, Jeff Moerssen, Peter Molick, Frank Monzo, Rick Moore, Bob Mosher, Mike Mosier, Matt Mozingo, Joe Mullins, William Munn, Jim Munter, Tony Murello, Mark Murphy, John R. Musacchio, Joseph Nardini, Eduardo Navarro, New York Card Company (David Greenhill), Eric Newport, Jim Newsom (Jim's Cards), Devin Nielsen, Sharon Niemi, David B. Niethamer, William R. Norris Jr., Eugene Nunes, Andy Nunnally, Bud Obermeyer (Baseball Cards, etc.), Mark Obert, Francisco Ochoa, John O'Hara, Keith Olbermann, William Oldfather, Ryan Ollila, Danny Orear, Dick Ornstein, John Ortega, Ron Oser, Luther Owen, Stephen Padwe, Travers Paine, Dave Pappenheim, Robert Parramore, Past Times, Clay Pasternack, James Paul, Rhett Paul, John Pawleska, Mickey Payne, Gary Pecherkiewicz, Michael Perrotta, Jon Peterson (Hit and Run Cards), Tom Pfirrmann, Larry D. Philbrick, Robert Pirro, Steve Pittard, David Pollack, George Pollitt, Seth Poppel, Coy Priest, Bob Ragonese, Janice P. Rahm, Randy Ramuglia, Richard H. Ranck, Rick Rapa, Robert Ray, Phil Regli, Tom Reid, Fred Reis, H. Glenn Renick, Lonny Renick, John Revell, Dave Ring, Randy Rioux, Vincent Roberto, Jason Roberts, Dee Robinson, Tyler Rodin, Bill Rodman, Steven Rondorf, Michael H. Rosen, Martin Rotunno, Clifton Rouse, R.W. Roy, Jeremy Royels, Ernesto Ruiz, Joseph Rushlow, George Rusnak, Mark Russell, Tom Rutlin, Terry Sack, Joe Sak, Jennifer Salems, Barry Sanders, Everett Sands, Jon Sands, Gary Sawatzki, Fred Scade Jr., Michael Scarborough, Dave Schau (Baseball Cards), Kurt Schell, Joe Schenone, A.J. Schmidt, Sam Schmidt, W. Schoolcraft, Aron Schor, Joseph J. Schuld, Bruce M. Schwartz, Richard

Searing, Charlie Seaver, Chris Sebelius, John Selsam, Tom Shanyfelt, Richard Sheldon, Geoff Shmidt, Don Shoaff, Jeff Shoemaker, Mark Shreve, Jerry Simmons, Art Smith, Eric Smith, John E. Smith, Michael Smith, David Snover, Fred M. Snyder, Joe Soldano, Mike Solis, John Spadora, John Spadora Jr., Carl Specht, Dave Spencer, D. Spurgeon, Dennis Srnel, John G. Stanek, Star City Cards, John Starkman, Chris Starks, Scott Steinbruegge, Lenny Steren, Bob Stern, Jim Stiern, Mark Stillwell, Brett Stiltner, Chad Stockwell, William A. Stone, Tim Strandberg (East Texas Sports Cards), Edward Strauss, Richard Strobino, Mark Sumlin, Superior Sport Card, Brad Sutton, Dr. Richard Swales, Ian Taylor, Lyle Telfer, L.E. Temanson, Sam Tessier, Ron Tetrault, Larry Tharp, Chris Thiemann, The Thirdhand Shoppe, James Thomas, Jim Thompson, Paul B. Thornton, Eric Thorson, Carl Thrower, Jim Thurtell, Tom Tillotson (Highland Sports Cards), Reece Todd, Al Tom, Patrick Tomberlin, Bud Tompkins (Minnesota Connection), Fred Tremiti, Harvey Trevino, Dr. Ralph Triplette, Mike Trotta, Umpire's Choice Inc., Eric Unglaub, Paul Valecce, Valley Cards, Jeff Vanover, Alan Vickroy, Steven Wagman, Brian Wagner, Frank Walls, Rob Walton, Jerry Wasilko, Jay Weaver, John Weaver, Mark Weber, Jordan Weinstein, John and Joe Weisenburger, Richard West, What-A-Card, Justin White, Mike White, Richard Wiercinski, Christopher M. Wiley, Ed Willett, Jeff Williams, Terry Williams, Scott Williard, Mark Willis, Darrell Winfield, Opry Winston, Chris Wohlfarth, D. Woldin, John Wolf Jr., Jay Wolt (Cavalcade of Sports), Carl Womack, John Wood, William L. Wood, Pete Wooten, Paul Yarnold, Ray Yeary, Yesterday's Heroes, Mark Yin, Kevin Yoho, Wes Young, Barry Zabell, Robert Zanze, Dean Zindler, Tom Zmuda (Koinz & Kardz), and Tim Zwick.

Every year we make active solicitations for expert input. We are particularly appreciative of help (however extensive or cursory) provided for this volume. We receive many inquiries, comments and questions regarding material within this book. In fact, each and every one is read and digested. Time constraints, however, prevent us from personally replying. But keep sharing your knowledge. Your letters and input are part of the "big picture" of hobby information we can pass along to readers in our books and magazines. Even though we cannot respond to each letter, you are making significant contributions to the hobby through your interest and comments.

In the years since this guide debuted, Beckett Publications has grown beyond any rational expectation. A great many talented and hard working individuals have been instrumental in this growth and success. Our whole team is to be congratulated for what we together have accomplished. Our Beckett Publications team is lead by Associate Publisher

Claire B. Backus, Vice Presidents Joe Galindo and Fred Reed III, and Director of Marketing Jeff Amano. They are ably assisted by Theresa Anderson, Therese Bellar, Dianne Boudreaux, Patrick Cunningham, Mary Gregory, Jeff Greer, Tracy Hinton, Teri McGahey, Kirk McKinney, Jeff Anthony, Kaye Ball, Marvin Bang, Wayne Bangs, Airey Baringer, Barbara Barry, Nancy Bassi, Kimberly Bauer, James R. Beane, Louise Bird, Cathryn Black, Terry Bloom, Lisa Borden, Lisa Boyer, Amy Brougher, Anthony Brown, Michael Brunelli, Chris Calandro, Randy Calvert, Emily Camp, Renata Campos, Mary Campana, Sammy Cantrell, Susan Catka, Jud Chappell, Albert Chavez, Theo Chen, Lynne Chinn, Tommy Collins, Belinda Cross, Randy Cummings, Shannon Cunningham, Todd Davis, Gail Docekal, Alejandro Egusquiza, Carrie Ehrhardt, Susan K. Elliott, Danny Evans, Bruce Felps, George Field, Sara Field, Gean Paul Figari, Jeany Finch, Kim Ford, Gayle Gasperin, Loretta Gibbs, Maria L. Gonzalez-Davis, Rosanna Gonzalez-Oleachea, Anita Gonzalez, Jenifer Grellhesl, Julie Grove, Patti Harris, Vivian Harmon, Beth Harwell, Jenny Harwell, Mark Harwell, Pepper Hastings, Joanna Hayden, Chris Hellem, Mike Hersh, Barbara Hinkle, Dan Hitt, E.J. Hradek, Rex Hudson, Mary Huston, Don James, Sara Jenks, Julia Jernigan, Jay Johnson, David Johnson, Fran Keng, Monte King, Sheri Kirk, Amy Kirk, Wendy Kizer, Rudy J. Klancnik, Rich Klein, Frances Knight, Tamera Krause, Tom Layberger, Jane Ann Layton, Scott Layton, Lori Lindsey, Cheryl Lingenfelter, Robert Luke, Louis Marroquin, John Marshall, Kaki Matheson, Lisa McQuilkin Monaghan, Omar Mediano, Edras Mendez, Theresa Merola, Sherry Monday, Robert Montenegro, Glen Morante, Mila Morante, Mike Moss, Randy Mosty, Daniel Moscoso Jr., Allan Muir, Hugh Murphy, Shawn Murphy, Maria Neubauer, Wendy Neumann, Brad Newton, Lisa O'Neill, Rich Olivieri, Stacy Olivieri, Abraham Pacheco, Laura Patterson, Mike Payne, Ronda Pearson, Robert Piekenbrock, Tim Polzer, Julie Polomis, Reed Poole, Roger Randall, Patrick Richard, Yamile Romero, Gary Santaniello, Grant Sandground, Walter Santos, Maggie Seward, Elaine Simmons, Dave Sliepka, Judi Smalling, Bob Smith, Steve Smith, Lynn Smith, Lisa Spaight, Margaret Steele, Cindy Struble, Dan Swanson, Doree Tate, Diane Taylor, Peter Tepp, Jim Tereschuk, Jana Threatt, Valerie Voigt, Steve Wilson, Carol Ann Wurster, and Robert Yearby.

The whole Beckett Publications team has my thanks for jobs well done. Thank you, everyone.

I also thank my family, especially my wife, Patti, and daughters, Christina, Rebecca, and Melissa, for putting up with me again.

America's 1st Full Time Dealer - Serving Collectors Since 1948

4 CARD SETS FOR 1993

Topps Factory (792) $40.95 ppd.
Fleer (720) $46.50 ppd.
Donruss (796) $59.50 ppd.
Score (660) $36.00 ppd.

All four 1993 baseball sets (shipped together)

$167.95 ppd.

PARTIAL LIST OF SETS AVAILABLE

(All sets are in EM to NrMT condition) See shipping and insurance table.
NOTE: All prices subject to change without notice.

BASEBALL SETS

1992 Topps (792) Factory	$31.75	1988 Donruss Best	24.95
1992 Fleer (720) Factory	39.95	1988 Score Glossy (660)	44.95
1992 Donruss (792) Factory	52.50	1988 Topps Glossy (792)	135.00
1992 Score (900) Factory	29.00	1988 Fleer Glossy (660)	53.50
1992 Upper Deck Factory	47.50	1988 Fleer Factory	135.00
1992 Conlon Collection	27.95	1987 Fleer Glossy (660 in collectors tin)	
1992 Conlon Babe Ruth	19.95		89.95
1991 Topps (792) Factory	29.75	1987 Topps Glossy (792)	125.00
1991 Fleer (720) Factory	24.50	1987 Topps Glossy (132)	17.50
1991 Score (900) Factory	34.50	1987 Fleer Update (132)	17.50
1991 Upper Deck Factory	44.50	1987 Donruss Rookies (56)	24.00
1991 Bowman (660) Factory	28.95	1986 Topps (792)	50.00
1991 Topps Traded (132)	14.50	1986 Topps Traded (132)	30.00
1991 Fleer Update (132)	13.95	1986 Fleer (660)	140.00
1991 Score Traded (110)	13.75	1986 Fleer Update (132)	35.00
1990 Upper Deck Factory	49.75	1986 Donruss (660)	225.00
1990 Topps Traded (132)	13.75	1986 Sportflics (200)	48.00
1990 Fleer Update (132)	13.95	1985 Topps (792)	110.00
1990 Score Traded (110)	22.00	1985 Topps Traded (132)	30.00
1990 Bowman (528)	10.95	1985 Fleer (660)	200.00
1990 Topps (792) Factory	24.75	1985 Fleer Update (132)	35.00
1990 Fleer (660) Factory	24.75	1984 Topps (792) lacking Mattingly	90.00
1990 Score Factory (714)	42.75	1984 Topps Traded (132)	125.00
1989 Topps (792) Factory	27.50	1984 Fleer Update (132)	995.00
1989 Topps (792)	26.50	1984 Donruss (660)	500.00
1989 Fleer (660)	31.50	1983 Topps (792)	190.00
1989 Score (660)	27.50	1983 Fleer (660)	160.00
1989 Donruss (660) Factory	37.50	1983 Topps Traded (132)	315.00
1989 Bowman (484) Factory	32.95	1983 Donruss (660)	130.00
1989 Topps Traded (132)	15.00	1982 Topps (792)	160.00
1989 Fleer Update (132)	12.95	1982 Donruss (660)	110.00
1989 Score Traded (110)	14.00	1981 Topps (726)	120.00
1989 Donruss Rookies (56)	21.95	1981 Donruss (605)	50.00
1989 Topps Glossy (792)	195.00	1981 Fleer (660)	62.50
1989 Bowman Wax (468)	12.00	1980 Topps (726)	65.00
1988 Topps (792)	35.00	1980 Topps (726)	300.00
1988 Fleer (660) Factory	50.00	1979 Topps (726)	225.00
1988 Score Factory (660)	27.50	1978 Topps (726)	225.00
1988 Donruss (660) Factory	32.50	1977 Topps (660)	425.00
1988 Topps Traded (132)	37.50	1976 Topps (660) (Lacking #599)	450.00
1988 Fleer Update (132)	17.50	1975 Topps (660)	795.00
1988 Score Traded (110)	15.00	1974 Topps (660)	625.00
1988 Donruss Rookies (56)	20.00	1973 Topps (660)	1,125.00

WE ARE BUYING! All cards and collectibles issued prior to 1969!

Before you sell...SEE US!! With over 46 years in card collecting and buying by anyone; our reputation is beyond repute. We do NOT make wild, unrealistic listed claims...we BUY CARDS AT A HIGHER PRICE THAN ANYONE All purchases made are strictly confidential, so don't keep that about our "Buys" we are private individuals. Try us.

Our experience and knowledge, give us the edge...with a mailing list of over 110,000 active collectors, we have more exposure, we can pay higher prices. We will pay shipping (both ways if we do not buy your collection) on cards or coins, we lend each purchase alike.

We also take items on consignment. Call for details. (715) 344-8687

128-PAGE CATALOG! A must for the novice as well as the serious collector!

Send $1.00 per issue for shipping for our catalog.

Subscribe today and receive the largest catalog we've ever put together! This 128 page issue is jam packed with baseball, football, basketball and hockey cards from the 1960's to 1992 sets and singles. Also included are magazines and hobby supplies... plus much more! If you need single cards from 1880 to 1980 / any sport / browse through our 76 page "One of a kind" section or use the "New Concept" form in which there are over 8 million cards available to you.

Canada residents send $3.00 (shipped 1st class)

BASEBALL CARDS BY SERIES SALE (1968-1974)

NOW IS THE TIME TO COMPLETE YOUR SETS! During the golden era of baseball cards (1952-1974), Topps issued their sets by series. The 1st series came out in the spring and the last series came out in the fall, with the others in between. Certain areas would not receive all the series, therefore making it difficult to complete a set. We have some of these complete series available from 1968-1974. These are cards that were purchased from Topps in the given year and have been in our warehouse since. The numbers in parenthesis indicate the card numbers in the particular series. These cards have been virtually untouched by human hands, although pressing and cutting flaws do exist. We grade the series in at least excellent-mint to near-mint condition.

1968 Series #4 (284-370) includes Banks, Marris, McCovey	$195.00
Series #5 (458-533) lacking 7 commons	210.00
Series #7 (534-598) includes Hisle, Palmer, Bouton (scarce)	170.00
1969 Series #1 (1-109) includes Brock, Clemente, Bench	180.00
Series #5 (426-512) includes Mantle, Carew, Seaver	435.00
Series #5 (426-512) same as above except lacking #500 Mantle	265.00
1970 Series #4 (264-372) includes Clemente, Seaver, Brock	235.00
Series #4 (373-459) includes Powell, Bonds	180.00
Series #5 (460-546) includes Aaron, Gibson	180.00
Series #5 (547-633) includes Mays, Rose, Hunter, Banks	270.00
Series #7 (634-720) includes Jenkins, Bench, F. Robinson, Ryan	850.00
1971 Series #1 (1-132) includes Munson, R. Jackson, Rose	230.00
Series #2 (133-263) includes Bench, Carew, Seaver, Kaline, Stargell	180.00
Series #3 (264-393) lacking #341 Garvey	70.00
Series #4 (394-523) includes Aaron, Gibson, Ryan, John	285.00
1973 Series #1 (1-132) includes Aaron, Rose, Clemente	150.00
Series #2 (133-264) includes Yaz, Jackson, Garvey, Fisk	165.00
Series #3 (265-396) includes Mays, Seaver, Bench	140.00
Series #4 (397-528) includes Schmidt	340.00
1974 Series #4 (397-528) includes Winfield, Killebrew	265.00
Series #5 (529-660) includes Madlock, Griffey, Garvey, Gossage	75.00

NEED SINGLE CARDS?

If you need single cards from 1880 to 1980 any sport, please write (send SASE for call or a "New Concept" form in which there are over 8 million single cards available to you. Reduce the history of sports with a single purchase. CALL OR WRITE TODAY!

SHIPPING AND INSURANCE TABLE

$.01 to $25.00 ...add $4.95
$25.01 to $50.00 ...add $5.95
$50.01 and over ...add $6.95

All prices subject to change. Call to verify prices.

CHECK POLICY:
All personal checks will be held 15 working days for clearance. For fast service, please send postal money order.

CANADA CUSTOMERS:
Please send postal money order in U.S. Funds only and an additional $7.00 per set for sets over 250 cards, $3.50 per set for sets under 250 cards for shipping your sets.

LARRY FRITSCH CARDS, INC.

735 Old Wausau Rd.
P.O. Box 863, Dept. 517
Stevens Point, WI 54481

(715) 344-8687
FAX
(715) 344-1778

ALASKA, HAWAII, PUERTO RICO, & P.O. CUSTOMERS:
Add an additional $5.00 per set for sets over 250 cards and $3.00 per set for sets under 250 cards for shipping your set (if you have a P.O. Box and want your order shipped via UPS, please include your UPS shipping address.)

WITH OVER 50 MILLION CARDS IN STOCK...WE HAVE AMERICA'S MOST COMPLETE STOCK OF SPORTS TRADING CARDS. Full money back guarantee if you are not completely satisfied with our service and products. YOU, the customer are always NO. 1 to us!

To receive Super Service it is necessary to send a POSTAL MONEY ORDER with your order. (All personal checks are held 15 days for clearance.) (Charge orders add 5% to total.) Minimum charge order $20.00. WI residents add 5.5% sales tax.

BILL HENDERSON'S CARDS
"King of the Commons"

FOUNDING MEMBER

"ALWAYS BUYING"
Call or Write for Quote

2320 Ruger Ave. PG 15
Janesville, WI 53545

"ALWAYS BUYING"
Call or Write for Quote

1(608) 755-0922 • Fax 1(608) 755-0802

Set	EX/MT to MINT CONDITION PRICE R — HI # OR SEMI HI SCARCE SERIES	COMMON CARD	EX/MT to MINT — COMMON EACH	OTHER SERIES	COMMON CARD	50 Diff.	100 Diff.	200 Asst.	300 Asst.	500 Asst	VG+ 50	VG+ 100	VG+ 200 Different
1948 BOWMAN (37-48)	30.00	25.00											
1949 BOWMAN (145-240)	90.00	18.00	18.00	(37-72)	20.00	850.					540.		
50-51 BOWMAN 50(1-72) 51(253-324)	60.00	18.00	18.00	51 (2-36)	25.00	900.					600.		
1952 TOPPS (251-310)	60.00	30.00		(2-80)	60.00	1350.					900.		
1952 BOWMAN (37-72) 20.00	(217-252) 35.00	18.00		(2-36)	22.00	850.					540.		
1953 TOPPS (220-280)	100.00	30.00		(166-219)	20.00	900.					600.		
1953 BOWMAN (129-160)	45.00	35.00		(113-128)	55.00	1575.					950.		
1954 TOPPS				(51-75)	30.00	675.					450.		
1954 BOWMAN		10.00		(129-224)	15.00	450.	850.				270.	510.	
1955 TOPPS (161-210)	30.00	10.00		(151-160)	20.00	450.					270.		
1955 BOWMAN (225-320) 18.-30.Umps.		8.00		(2-96)	8.50	360.	700.				210.	400.	
1956 TOPPS (101-180) 12.00 (261-340) 14.00		10.00		(181-260)	18.00	450.	850.				270.	510.	
1957 TOPPS (265-352)	25.00	7.50		(1-88)	8.50	350.	680.				225.	430.	
1958 TOPPS (111-198)	6.00	5.00		(1-110)	8.50	230.	450.	880.	1275.		140.	260.	
1959 TOPPS (507-572)	17.50	4.00		(1-110)	7.00	190.	370.	720.	1000.		115.	220.	430.
1960 TOPPS (441-506) 5.00	(507-572) 15.00	4.00		(27-110)	4.50	190.	370.	620.	900.		115.	220.	430.
1961 TOPPS (447-522) 6.00	(523-589) 35.00	3.50		(371-446)	5.00	165.	320.	530.	765.		100.	190.	370.
1962 TOPPS (371-522) 6.00	(523-590) 15.00	4.00		(284-370)	4.00	140.	270.				85.	160.	310.
1963 TOPPS (447-522) 15.00	(523-573) 10.00	3.00		(284-446)	4.50	140.	270.				85.	160.	
1964 TOPPS (371-522) 5.00	(523-587) 10.00	2.50		(197-370)	3.50	115.	220.	*430.			70.	130.	250.
1965 TOPPS (447-522) 6.50	(523-598) 6.50	2.50		(284-446)	5.00	115.	220.				70.	130.	
1966 TOPPS (447-522) 7.50	(523-598) 15.00	2.50		(371-446)	5.00	115.	220.	*340.			70.	130.	250.
1967 TOPPS (458-533) 7.50	(534-609) 20.00	2.00		(284-457)	4.00	90.	175.	*340.			60.	110.	210.
1968 TOPPS (534-598)	4.00	1.50		(458-533)	3.50	65.	125.	*240.			37.	70.	130.
1969 TOPPS (513-664) 2.00	(589-664) 2.50	1.50		(219-327)	2.50	65.	125.	*240.			37.	70.	150.
1970 TOPPS (547-633) 3.50	(634-720) 7.00	1.00		(460-546)	2.00	45.	88.	*170.	250.	400.	27.	52.	100.
1971 TOPPS (524-643) 4.00	(644-752) 7.00	1.00		(394-523)	2.00	45.	88.	*170.	250.	400.	27.	52.	100.
1972 TOPPS (526-656) 3.50	(657-787) 7.00	.75		(395-525)	1.50	35.	68.	*130.	*190.	300.	21.	40.	78.
1973 TOPPS (529-660)	3.00	.60		(397-528)	1.50	28.	54.	*105.	*150.	215.	18.	34.	65.
1974 TOPPS		.50				23.	45.	*85.	*125.	*170.	27.	50.	
1975 TOPPS		.50				23.	45.	*85.	*125.		27.	50.	
1976-77 TOPPS & 84 DONRUSS		.30				28.	*54.	*80.	*125.		16.	30.	
1978-1980 TOPPS		.15				13.	*25.	*38.	*65.		8.	15.	
1981 thru 1993 Topps, 1981-1989 Fleer .10 & Donruss except those listed below (specify year)						9.	*17	*26	*40.				
						Per Yr.	Per Yr.	Per Yr.	Per Yr.				
1985-86 DONRUSS, 1984-86 FLEER .15						8.	*25.	*38.	*65.				

SPECIAL IN VG+ to EX CONDITION-POSTPAID

Equal Distribution of Each Year

250	58-62	450.00
500	58-62	850.00
250	60-69	350.00
500	60-69	650.00
1000	60-69	1250.00
250	70-79	70.00
500	70-79	130.00
1000	70-79	250.00
250	80-84	15.00
500	80-84	28.00
1000	80-84	55.00

Special 1 Different from each year 1949-80 EX/MT $160.00 VG-EX $110.00
Special 100 Different from each year 1956-80 EX/MT $4600.00 VG-EX $3000.00
Special 10 Different from each year 1956-80 EX/MT $470.00 VG-EX $300.00

All lot groups are my choice only.

All assorted lots will contain as many different as possible.
Please list alternates whenever possible.
Send your want list and I will fill them at the above price for commons. High numbers, specials, scarce series, and stars are priced at current Beckett®.
You can use your MasterCard or Visa to charge your purchases.
Minumum order $7.50 - Postage and handling 50¢ per 100 cards (minimum $2.50)

ANY CARD NOT LISTED ON PRICE SHEET IS PRICED AT CURRENT BECKETT® MONTHLY HIGH COLUMN.

SETS AVAILABLE

Topps 1988, 1989, 1990, 1991, 1992

22.95 ea. + 2.50 UPS
6 for 22.95 ea. +9.00 UPS
18 for 22.35 ea. + 20.00 UPS
MIX OR MATCH

If you're vacationing in New York or if you're just escaping the city, then **THE DRAGON'S DEN** is the place to visit. Located in the heart of Westchester's finest shopping area, **THE DRAGON'S DEN** is only thirty minutes from midtown Manhattan and easily accessible to all major New York roadways. Check out our enormous inventory of collectibles, including:

- Baseball, football, basketball & hockey stars, sets & unopened material from 1909 to present
- Plastic sheets, binders, lucites, cases & boxes
- Over 1,000,000 back issue Marvel, D.C. & alternate comics
- All New comic releases
- Comic bags, boxes and mylars
- Fantasy role playing games and figures

Along with our impressive inventory, we have a veteran staff that will be happy to assist you in your selection. We accept all major credit cards and we're even open every day. What more could you ask for? Convenient parking? We have that too!

NOW TWO GREAT LOCATIONS!

THE DRAGON'S DEN

2614 Central Park Ave.
Yonkers, NY 10710
(914) 793-4630
Fax (914) 793-5303

43 Greenwich Avenue
Greenwich, CT 06830
(203) 622-1171

NEW!

Only **$8.95** *Monthly*

SportsNet STADIUM™

The Electronic Card Show™
&
Computer Trading Network

Buy, sell & trade with hundreds of dealers and collectors 24-Hours-A-Day. Use your computer to get cards and comics at today's prices.

Plus SportsNet TODAY, the electronic magazine, is another great reason to join the network. Get instant news on the hobby every day! It's FREE for members.

SportsNet STADIUM is a collector/dealer network and a division of SportsNet - the world's FIRST and LARGEST collectibles network. Join today!

#1-800-821-9275
SportsNet STADIUM, Dept. B
108 Main St., Norwalk, CT 06851
Call or Write For a <u>FREE</u> Brochure!

Take Control of Your Card Collection...

Put the Power of Your Computer to Work for You.

The Card Collector, from AbleSoft, is the Leader in sportscard inventory software. With sales of over 50,000 copies, it is the most successful sportscard software ever! Use your computer to track just which cards you have, how much they're worth, and which you need to complete sets.

The Card Collector features:
- Quick & Easy Inventory Entry
- Available Monthly Price & Data Updates
- Create and Print Detailed Reports & Lists
- Add your own Custom Sets

THE Card Collector™

Able Soft™

INCLUDED FREE

Baseball Card Data (including prices!) for 1948-Present, over 75,000 cards!
- Bowman
- Donruss
- Fleer
- Leaf
- O-Pee-Chee
- Pinnacle
- Score
- Select
- Studio
- Stadium Club
- Topps
- Ultra
- Upper Deck

Also Includes Insert Sets!

Create reports based on any criteria...
- Inventory Reports
- Rookie Cards
- First Cards
- All cards for a single player
- Cards to complete a set
- Premium Cards
- Want Lists
- Special Cards

Look for The Card Collector discounted at:
- ☑ Electronics Boutique
- ☑ Egghead Software
- ☑ WaldenSoftware
- ☑ Software, Etc.
- ☑ Pace Warehouse
- ☑ Circuit City
- ☑ Babbage's
- ☑ CompUSA
- ☑ Price Club
- ☑ Wal-Mart
- ☑ Sam's Club
- ☑ MicroCenter

Sugg. Retail Price: **$49.95**

For info or to order, call:
1-800-545-9009

MARK R. JORDAN, INC.

Autographs and Memorabilia

Mark Jordan is an autograph and memorabilia dealer/collector with 25 years of experience. His memorabilia company specializes in baseball Hall of Fame autographs, uniforms, bats, rings, and one of a kind significant pieces from all sports, as well as those from history, politics, and Hollywood. In addition, Mark is the president of Professional Sports Appraisers, Inc., a company which authenticates and appraises autographs and memorabilia. He is a nationally recognized authentication expert, having appeared on The Today Show, ESPN, CBS, plus numerous publications and radio broadcasts.

Mark Jordan's knowledge and reputation have served as a great benefit to the sports collectibles industry. He has been a consultant to four prominent auction houses, and he has contributed to several autograph reference guides. Currently, he serves as a Director and Founding Member of SCAI, the ethics organization of the industry.

WE OFFER THE FOLLOWING SERVICES:

Appraisals/Authentication

Given the dramatic rapid growth of the sports collectibles business, this service is vital to insurance coverage, sound investments and estate planning. We will evaluate one piece or an entire collection. Our fees are very reasonable and the return time is ordinarily one week.

Buying

As leaders in he autograph and memorabilia field we aggressively purchase signatures of deceased Hall of Famers (before 1980) on letters, photos, 3x5 cards and balls – both single signed and team balls. In addition, we buy uniforms, bats, rings and trophies. We are interested in autographs and personal items from all sports.

We solicit wants from prominent collectors nationwide who pay top dollar for quality pieces. We offer courteous, confidential, no-nonsense dealings with immediate payment. Call us today.

Selling

Why not buy with confidence from a nationally recognized expert? Every item we sell comes with a lifetime guarantee of authenticity. We have a vast inventory with quality pieces to fit every budget. Our bi-monthly catalog offers something for everyone, from the beginning collector to the serious investor. Call for your copy.

We strongly encourage want lists because most significant pieces are sold before they are advertised.

Our integrity and courteous service have consistently built our business. We value our reputation.

MARK R. JORDAN, INC.

FIRST INTERNATIONAL BANK BLDG.
1600 AIRPORT FWY., #508
(800) 888-3784 TOLL FREE
(817) 267-0400 • (817) 685-9555 FAX

Unopened Boxes • Guaranteed Unopened

Baseball

Wax or Foil Boxes

1993 Topps Series 1 (540 Cards)	$24.00
1993 Topps Series 2 (540 Cards)	24.00
1992 Topps (540)	18.00
1991 Topps (540)	16.00
1990 Topps (576)	16.00
1989 Topps (540)	16.00
1988 Topps (540)	16.00
1987 Topps (612)	32.00
1986 Topps (540)	45.00
1991 '53 Topps Archives (432)	90.00
1992 Stadium Club 1 (540)	45.00
1992 Stadium Club 2 (540)	45.00
1992 Stadium Club 3 (540)	45.00
1991 Stadium Club 1 (432)	200.00
1991 Stadium Club 2 (432)	135.00
1993 Action Packed (216)	50.00
1991 Bowman (504)	17.00
1990 Bowman (504)	17.00
1989 Bowman (432)	17.00
1992 Classic Best Minor League (432)	25.00
1993 Donruss Series 1 (540)	35.00
1993 Donruss Series 2 (540)	35.00
1992 Donruss Series 1 (540)	35.00
1992 Donruss Series 2 (540)	30.00
1991 Donruss Series 1 (576)	16.00
1991 Donruss Series 2 (576)	16.00
1990 Donruss (576)	14.00
1989 Donruss (540)	16.00
1988 Donruss (540)	14.00
1987 Donruss (540)	55.00
1985 Donruss (540)	350.00
1982 Donruss (540)	300.00
1992 Donruss Triple Play (540)	20.00
1993 Fleer Series 1 (540)	35.00
1993 Fleer Series 2 (540)	35.00
1992 Fleer (612)	33.00
1991 Fleer (540)	16.00
1989 Fleer (540)	27.00
1987 Fleer (612)	150.00
1992 Fleer Ultra 1 (504)	90.00
1992 Fleer Ultra 2 (504)	50.00
1991 Fleer Ultra (504)	25.00
1992 Leaf Studio (480)	45.00
1991 Leaf Studio (480)	40.00
1992 Leaf Series 1 (540)	40.00
1992 Leaf Series 2 (540)	40.00
1991 Leaf Series 1 (540)	40.00
1991 Leaf Series 2 (540)	40.00
1990 Leaf Series 1 (540)	325.00
1990 Leaf Series 2 (540)	325.00
1991 O-Pee-Chee Premier (252)	30.00
1993 Score (576)	24.00
1992 Score Series 1 (576)	18.00
1992 Score Series 2 (576)	18.00
1991 Score Series 1 (576)	16.00
1991 Score Series 2 (576)	19.00
1990 Score (576)	25.00
1989 Score (612)	16.00
1988 Score (612)	16.00
1993 Score Select (540)	45.00
1993 Score Pinnacle 1 (576)	55.00
1993 Upper Deck LO# (540)	40.00
1992 Upper Deck LO# (540)	30.00
1992 Upper Deck HI# (540)	30.00
1991 Upper Deck LO# (540)	30.00
1991 Upper Deck HI# (540)	30.00
1990 Upper Deck LO# (540)	40.00
1990 Upper Deck HI# (540)	50.00
1989 Upper Deck LO# (540)	160.00
1989 Upper Deck HI# (540)	140.00

Rack-Pack Boxes

1991 Topps (1,080 cards)	28.00
1990 Topps (1,104)	28.00
1989 Topps (1,032)	28.00
1988 Topps (1,032)	28.00
1987 Topps (1,080)	45.00
1986 Topps (1,176)	60.00
1988 Score (1,320)	30.00
1989 Bowman (936)	30.00

Cello Boxes

1989 Donruss (864 cards)	18.00
1988 Donruss (864)	15.00

Topps 500 Count Vending Boxes

1991	15.00
1990	16.00
1989	16.00
1988	16.00
1987	25.00
1986	28.00

Arena Hologram

Frank Thomas (1)	4.00
Ken Griffey Jr. (1)	4.00

Silver Star Hologram

Rickey Henderson (1)	7.00
Nolan Ryan (1)	7.00

Call for prices & availability on any 1993 products that are not listed.
We also carry football, basketball, hockey &
non-sports cards. Call for prices.
All prices include shipping
Same day service with VISA or MasterCard
Please provide adequate street address for U.P.S. delivery
U.S. funds only
Alaska and Hawaii add 15% postage • Foreign add 25% postage
All prices subject to change

BILL DODGE
P.O. BOX 40154
Bay Village, OH 44140
Phone: (216) 899-9901

Fifteen years of quality mail order service

Complete Baseball Card Sets

Regular Issues

1993 Topps (792 Cards)	$28.00
1992 Topps (792)	25.00
1991 Topps (792)	25.00
1990 Topps (792)	25.00
1989 Topps (792)	25.00
1988 Topps (792)	25.00
Topps Sets 88-93	145.00
1987 Topps (792)	35.00
1986 Topps (792)	45.00
Topps Sets 86-93	220.00
1985 Topps (792)	110.00
1984 Topps (792)	100.00
1991 Topps '53 Archives (330)	95.00
1992 Stadium Club 1 (300)	38.00
1992 Stadium Club 2 (300)	38.00
1992 Stadium Club 3 (300)	38.00
1991 Stadium Club 1 (300)	160.00
1991 Stadium Club 2 (300)	110.00
1992 Stadium Club Skydome (200)	50.00
1993 Action Packed (84)	35.00
1991 Bowman (704)	20.00
1990 Bowman (528)	20.00
1989 Bowman (484)	20.00
All 3 Above Bowman Sets	57.00
1993 Donruss Series 1 (396)	20.00
1993 Donruss Series 2 (396)	20.00
1992 Donruss (784)	30.00
1991 Donruss W/Leaf Promo	30.00
1990 Donruss (716)	17.00
1989 Donruss (660)	22.00
1988 Donruss (660)	24.00
All 7 above Donruss Sets	155.00
1987 Donruss (660)	65.00
1993 Fleer Series 1 (360)	20.00
1993 Fleer Series 2 (360)	20.00
1992 Fleer (720)	45.00
1991 Fleer (720)	20.00
1990 Fleer (660)	17.00
1989 Fleer (660)	23.00
All 6 above Fleer Sets	135.00
1988 Fleer (660)	40.00
1987 Fleer (660)	100.00
1986 Fleer (660)	135.00
1992 Fleer Ultra 1 (300)	50.00
1992 Fleer Ultra 2 (300)	35.00
1991 Fleer Ultra (400)	30.00
1992 Leaf Studio (264)	30.00
1991 Leaf Studio (264)	40.00
1992 Leaf (528)	50.00
1991 Leaf (528)	55.00
1992 Leaf (528)	290.00
1992 O-Pee-Chee Premier (198)	25.00
1991 O-Pee-Chee Premier (132)	25.00
1990 O-Pee-Chee (792)	30.00
1989 O-Pee-Chee (396)	16.00
1988 O-Pee-Chee (396)	25.00
1993 Score (660)	25.00
1992 Score (900)	35.00
1991 Score (900)	25.00
1990 Score (704)	25.00
All 4 Above Score Sets	100.00
1990 Score (714)	35.00
1989 Score (660)	20.00
1988 Score (660)	20.00
1993 Score Select (405)	35.00
1993 Score Pinnacle 1 (310)	40.00
1993 Score Pinnacle 1 (310)	40.00
1992 Score Pinnacle 1 (310)	40.00
1992 Score Pinnacle 2 (310)	30.00
1990 Sportflics (225)	38.00
1989 Sportflics (225)	42.00
1987 Sportflics (200)	32.00
1993 Upper Deck Series 1 (420)	30.00
1993 Upper Deck Series 2 (420)	30.00
1992 Upper Deck (800)	52.00
1991 Upper Deck (800)	40.00
1990 Upper Deck (800)	55.00
1989 Upper Deck (800)	160.00

Traded or Update Issues

1992 Topps (132)	20.00
1991 Topps (132)	15.00
1990 Topps (132)	9.00
1989 Topps (132)	11.00
1988 Topps (132)	36.00
1987 Topps (132)	14.00
1986 Topps (132)	30.00
1985 Topps (132)	35.00
'85 to '92 Topps Traded	160.00
1992 Classic Best Minor League Update (50)	20.00
1991 Donruss Rookies (56)	8.00
1990 Donruss Rookies (56)	9.00
1989 Donruss Rookies (56)	20.00
1988 Donruss Rookies (56)	23.00
1987 Donruss Rookies (56)	25.00
All 5 Above Donruss Sets	80.00
1992 Fleer (132)	Call for Price
1991 Fleer (132)	10.00
1990 Fleer (132)	10.00
1989 Fleer (132)	14.00
1988 Fleer (132)	21.00
1987 Fleer (132)	18.00
1986 Fleer (132)	35.00
1985 Fleer (132)	40.00
All 7 Above Fleer Sets	140.00
1992 Fleer Ultra (120)	40.00
1992 Score (110)	20.00
1991 Score (110)	10.00
1990 Score (110)	22.00
1989 Score (110)	14.00
All 4 Above Score Sets '89-'92	60.00
1988 Score (110)	105.00
1992 Score Pinnacle Rookies (30)	15.00
1986 Sportflics Rookies (50)	20.00
1992 Upper Deck (100)	20.00
1991 Upper Deck, Final Edition (100)	20.00
1991 Upper Deck (100)	12.00
1990 Upper Deck (100)	15.00
1989 Upper Deck (100)	17.00

Specialty Sets

1991 Classic Draft Pick (51)	15.00
1987 Donruss Opening Day (272)	20.00
1987 Donruss Highlights (56)	5.00
1992 Fleer Ultra Award Winners (25)	135.00
1987 Fleer Minis (120)	10.00
1986 Fleer Minis (120)	12.00
1991 Leaf Gold Bonus (26)	110.00
1991 Leaf Promo Cards (26)	200.00
1992 Score Pinnacle Team 2000 (80)	55.00
1989 Score Masters (42)	12.00
1991 Topps Micro (792)	15.00
1991 Topps '90 Debut (171)	40.00
1990 Topps '89 Debut (152)	17.00
1990 Topps Bigs (330)	30.00
1989 Topps Bigs (264)	30.00
1989 Topps Sr. League (132)	9.00
1990 Topps Glossy All Stars (22)	6.00
1988 Topps Glossy All Stars (22)	6.00
1986 Topps Supers (60)	8.00
1991 Upper Deck Silver Sluggers (18)	45.00
1992 Upper Deck Home Run Heroes (26)	50.00
1992 Upper Deck All-Star Fan Fest (54)	25.00
1992 Upper Deck Hologram (54)	30.00

BILL DODGE
P.O. BOX 40154
Bay Village, OH 44140
Phone: (216) 899-9901

Fifteen years of quality mail order service

FREE ILLUSTRATED CATALOGUE

We are one of the first full-time dealers in the country. Mr. Young has been featured in dozens of articles, including ones in the **Wall Street Journal**, **USA Today**, **LA Times**, **NY Daily News**, **Forbes**, **Sporting News**, **Parade Magazine**, **Sport Magazine**, and dozens of other newspapers nationwide. He has appeared on dozens of television features, including **NBC Nightly News With Tom Brokaw**.

He is a founding member of the dealer trade association SCAI, and is one of 29 dealers nationally to receive the "10 Year Customer Service Award" from Krause Publications for his "exemplary service."

Our catalogue is the hobby's leading catalogue, offering more individual cards and sets than any other. These 88-page catalogues are sent monthly to over 25,000 collectors. Each sale features Star Cards, Rookie Cards, Complete Sets, 1950s, '60s & '70s Cards, Investors Specials, Unopened Cases and Gum Packs, Pre-War Cards, Card Lots, Football and Basketball Cards, and much more. No catalogue offers as many premium collectibles! **To receive our current catalogue (plus future ones), please send five (5) 29¢ stamps.**

KIT YOUNG

DEPT. Z
11535 SORRENTO VALLEY ROAD, #403
SAN DIEGO, CA 92121
(619) 259-1300

"SERVING COLLECTORS SINCE 1976"

BUYING CARDS

We have been buying cards through the mail (or at conventions) since 1976, and make hundreds of purchases each year.

We will buy the following:

A) **Complete Collections** - including accumulations of all sizes
B) **Complete Sets** - from 1983 and older, including partial sets
C) **Star Cards** - Hall of Famers and Rookies, 1983 and older
D) **Older Cards** - All cards (Baseball & Football) before 1970, including Pre-War cards

If you have cards to sell, please call or write us (see address above). We will handle all transactions professionally and confidentially.

Beckett® Baseball Card Monthly

Name *(please print)* _____ Age _____

Address _____

City _____ State _____ ZIP _____

Payment enclosed via:
❏ Check or Money Order *(US funds only)*   ❏ Visa/MasterCard   *(please do not send cash)*

Card No. _____ Exp. _____

Cardholder's Signature _____

Cardholder's Name *(please print)* _____

Check One Please: ❏ 1 year (12 issues) $19.95
                     ❏ 2 years (24 issues) $35.95

Satisfaction guaranteed! All foreign addresses add $12 per year per title for postage (includes G.S.T.).
For subscription Customer Service please call (614) 383-5772. Please allow 6 to 8 weeks for delivery of first issue.

Mail to: *Beckett® Baseball Card Monthly*, P.O. Box 2048, Marion, OH 43305-2048   DBH94-9

Beckett® Football Card Monthly

Name *(please print)* _____ Age _____

Address _____

City _____ State _____ ZIP _____

Payment enclosed via:
❏ Check or Money Order *(US funds only)*   ❏ Visa/MasterCard   *(please do not send cash)*

Card No. _____ Exp. _____

Cardholder's Signature _____

Cardholder's Name *(please print)* _____

Check One Please: ❏ 1 year (12 issues) $19.95
                     ❏ 2 years (24 issues) $35.95

Satisfaction guaranteed! All foreign addresses add $12 per year per title for postage (includes G.S.T.).
For subscription Customer Service please call (614) 383-5772. Please allow 6 to 8 weeks for delivery of first issue.

Mail to: *Beckett® Football Card Monthly*, P.O. Box 1915, Marion, OH 43305-1915   DBH94-9

Beckett® Basketball Monthly

Name *(please print)* _____ Age _____

Address _____

City _____ State _____ ZIP _____

Payment enclosed via:
❏ Check or Money Order *(US funds only)* ❏ Visa/MasterCard *(please do not send cash)*

Card No. _____ Exp. _____

Cardholder's Signature _____

Cardholder's Name *(please print)* _____

Check One Please: ❏ 1 year (12 issues) $19.95 ❏ 2 years (24 issues) $35.95

Satisfaction guaranteed! All foreign addresses add $12 per year per title for postage (includes G.S.T.).
For subscription Customer Service please call (614) 383-5772. Please allow 6 to 8 weeks for delivery of first issue.

Mail to: *Beckett® Basketball Monthly*, P.O. Box 1915, Marion, OH 43305-1915   DBH94-9

Beckett® Hockey Monthly

Name *(please print)* _____ Age _____

Address _____

City _____ State _____ ZIP _____

Payment enclosed via:
❏ Check or Money Order *(US funds only)* ❏ Visa/MasterCard *(please do not send cash)*

Card No. _____ Exp. _____

Cardholder's Signature _____

Cardholder's Name *(please print)* _____

Check One Please: ❏ 1 year (12 issues) $19.95 ❏ 2 years (24 issues) $35.95

Satisfaction guaranteed! All foreign addresses add $12 per year per title for postage (includes G.S.T.).
For subscription Customer Service please call (614) 383-5772. Please allow 6 to 8 weeks for delivery of first issue.

Mail to: *Beckett® Hockey Monthly*, P.O. Box 1915, Marion, OH 43305-1915   DBH94-9

Beckett Focus on Future Stars®

Name *(please print)* _____ Age _____

Address _____

City _____ State _____ ZIP _____

Payment enclosed via:
❏ Check or Money Order *(US funds only)* ❏ Visa/MasterCard *(please do not send cash)*

Card No. _____ Exp. _____

Cardholder's Signature _____

Cardholder's Name *(please print)* _____

Check One Please: ❏ 1 year (12 issues) $19.95 ❏ 2 years (24 issues) $35.95

Satisfaction guaranteed! All foreign addresses add $12 per year per title for postage (includes G.S.T.).
For subscription Customer Service please call (614) 383-5772. Please allow 6 to 8 weeks for delivery of first issue.

Mail to: *Beckett Focus on Future Stars®*, P.O. Box 1915, Marion, OH 43305-1915   DBH94-9